MORNINGSTAR®
Stocks500™

Annual Sourcebook
2007 Edition

Introduction by
James Levin,
Managing Editor

Editor
Pat Dorsey

Managing Editor
James Levin

Chief of Securities Analysis
Haywood Kelly

Director of Stock Analysis
Pat Dorsey

Stock Analysts
Karen Andersen
Rod Bare
Rachel Barnard
Ryan Batchelor
Joseph Beaulieu
Bill Bergman
Jaime Black
Joel Bloomer
Heather Brilliant
Scott Burns
Ben Butwin
Larry Cao
Michelle Chang
Eric Chenoweth
Anthony Chukumba
Elizabeth Collins
Michael Corty
Mitchell Corwin
Michael Cumming
Tom D'Amore
Akash Dave
Sumit Desai
Lauren DeSanto
Dafina Dunmore
Patrick Elgrably
Adam Fleck
Mike Ford-Taggart
Justin Fuller
Jeremy Glaser
Andrew Golomb
Michael Hodel
Brett Horn
Ben Johnson
Paul Justice
John Kearney
Jill Kiersky
Michael Kon
Parvathy Krishnan
Brian Laegeler
Eric Landry
Brady Lemos
Ryan Lentell
Irina Logovinsky
Chris Lozier
Ryan McLean
Catharina Milostan
Matt Moran
Alex Morozov
Matt Nellans
Brian Nelson
Andy Ng
Allan Nichols
John Novak
Patrick O'Shaughnessy
Arthur Oduma
John Owens
Justin Perucki

Kimberly Picciola
Ramesh Poola
Jeffrey Ptak
Ganesh Rathnam
Matthew Reilly
Kristan Rowland
Jim Ryan
Jonathan Schrader
John Slack
Heather Smith
Peter Smith
Jason Stevens
Julie Stralow
Rick Summer
Erin Swanson
Marisa Thompson
Michael Tian
Toan Tran
Brandon Troegle
Jeff Viksjo
James Walden
Kevin Walkush
Debbie Wang
Greggory Warren
Matthew Warren
Larry Witt
Bill Yan
Norman Young

Copy Editors
Sylvia Hauser
Ryun Patterson
Jason Stipp

Director of Technology
Fred Wong

Programmers
Eider Deleoz
Rebekah Lai
Dongsheng Wu

Data Analysts
Alvin Calalang
Desiree DeLeoz
Jeffrey Manczko
Katherine Nasser
Neelm Pradhan

Director of Design
David Williams

Designers
Christopher Cantore
Lisa Lindsay

Project Manager
Stavroula Pawlicki

Product Manager
Carolyn Messitte

President, Securities Research
Catherine Gillis Odelbo

Chairman and CEO
Joe Mansueto

Copyright © 2007 by Morningstar, Inc. All rights reserved

Published by John Wiley & Sons, Inc., Hoboken, New Jersey
Published simultaneously in Canada

No part of this publication may be reproduced, stored in a retrieval system, or transmitted in any form or by any means, electronic, mechanical, photocopying, recording, scanning, or otherwise, except as permitted under Section 107 or 108 of the 1976 United States Copyright Act, without either the prior written permission of the Publisher, or authorization through payment of the appropriate per-copy fee to the Copyright Clearance Center, Inc., 222 Rosewood Drive, Danvers, MA 01923, (978) 750-8400, fax (978) 750-4470, or on the web at www.copyright.com. Requests to the Publisher for permission should be addressed to the Permissions Department, John Wiley & Sons, Inc., 111 River Street, Hoboken, NJ 07030, (201) 748-6011, fax (201) 748-6008, or online at http://www.wiley.com/go/permissions.

Limit of Liability/Disclaimer of Warranty: While the publisher and author have used their best efforts in preparing this book, they make no representations or warranties with respect to the accuracy or completeness of the contents of this book and specifically disclaim any implied warranties of merchantability or fitness for a particular purpose. No warranty may be created or extended by sales representatives or written sales materials. The advice and strategies contained herein may not be suitable for your situation. You should consult with a professional where appropriate. Neither the publisher nor author shall be liable for any loss of profit or any other commercial damages, including but not limited to special, incidental, consequential, or other damages.

Morningstar, Inc. does not have a selling agreement of any kind with the stocks listed herein.

For general information on our other products and services or for technical support, please contact our Customer Care Department within the United States at (800) 762-2974, outside the United States at (317) 572-3993 or fax (317) 572-4002.

For general information about Morningstar's other products and services, please contact Morningstar's product sales line at 866-608-9570 or visit www.morningstar.com.

Wiley also publishes its books in a variety of electronic formats. Some content that appears in print may not be available in electronic books. For more information about Wiley products, visit our web site at www.wiley.com.

Library of Congress Cataloging-in-Publication Data:

ISBN-13 978-0-471-78665-8
ISBN-10 0-471-78665-9

Printed in the United States of America

10 9 8 7 6 5 4 3 2 1

Table of Contents

2	The Year in Review
5	How to Use the Morningstar Stocks 500
8	Our Approach to Equity Research
9	Why Popular Stocks Are a Sucker's Bet
11	Avoid Being Mr. Market
13	The Predictable Returns of Dividends
15	Digging an Economic Moat
17	Six Reasons to Not Take Returns at Face Value
20	How We Selected This Year's Stocks

Index and Tables

23	Morningstar Stocks 500—Company Index
32	Morningstar Stocks 500—Industry Index
38	Benchmark Performance—Market Index
40	Industry Performance
42	Industry Averages
44	Top- and Bottom-Performing Stocks
46	Most Attractive Stocks
47	Least Attractive Stocks
48	Stocks with Below Average Risk Measure
49	Largest Market Capitalization and Highest Sales
50	Highest Return on Equity and Return on Assets
51	Highest Dividend Yield and Cash Return
52	Lowest & Highest Price Multiples
54	Companies with Wide Economic Moats
55	Companies with Narrow Economic Moats
56	Companies with No Economic Moat

Report Pages

59	Stock Reports

Glossary

561	Glossary

Welcome to the 2007 Edition of *Morningstar Stocks 500*.

Just as they did in 2005, the markets closed out 2006 with a bang. The Morningstar US Market Index returned 16% for the year through Dec. 20, with approximately half of that gain coming in the last quarter. This marks the fourth straight year of gains for equities after the brutal bear market of 2000 through 2002.

A flurry of merger and acquisition activity has contributed to the surge, as companies and private equity funds have scrambled to deploy cash, paying premiums to purchase other businesses. Among the more notable acquisitions have been mining company Freeport-McMoRan (FCX) swallowing Phelps Dodge (PD), Bank of New York (BK) taking over Mellon Financial (MEL), Bank of America (BAC) scooping up asset management unit U.S. Trust from Charles Schwab (SCHW), Wachovia (WB) merging with Golden West Financial (GDW) (a former recipient of the Morningstar CEO of the Year Award), AT&T (T) combining with BellSouth Corporation (BLS), and CVS (CVS) and Express Scripts (ESRX) both placing bids for Caremark (CMX).

Other moves of big financiers and investors included Kirk Kerkorian abruptly and sourly eliminating his interest in embattled automaker General Motors (GM) and Carl Icahn selling his stake in media giant Time Warner (TWX). Private-equity played its part in 2006 by taking a number of notable companies private. A group led by Thomas H. Lee Partners and Bain Capital took over Clear Channel Communications (CCU), the Blackstone Group purchased Equity Office Properties (EOP) as well as Motorola's (MOT) 2004 semiconductor division spin-off Freescale Semiconductor (FSL), Harrah's Entertainment (HET) accepted a takeover from firms Texas Pacific Group and Apollo Management, and in one of the largest leveraged buyout deals ever, HCA (HCA) was taken private by founder Thomas Frist Jr. in conjunction with Bain Capital, Merrill Lynch (MER), and Kohlberg Kravis Roberts & Co. In another hefty leveraged buyout, Kinder Morgan (KMI), former recipient of the Morningstar CEO of the Year Award, accepted a bid from a takeover consortium composed of co-founder Bill Morgan, private equity firms Carlyle Group and Riverstone Holdings LLC, and insurance giant American International Group (AIG).

If merger and acquisition activity was frenzied, Ben Bernanke and the Federal Reserve were sedate. The Fed left short-term rates alone as neither inflation nor a dramatic slowdown seemed threatening. Oil prices stabilized in the low $60s, easing the pressure on Bernanke (high oil prices can potentially spur both inflation and a slowdown, rendering a Fed banker hamstrung), and natural-gas prices recovered after a late summer swoon.

The bond market continued betting that Bernanke would lower rates, evinced by investors' seemingly strange willingness to accept lower yield payments on longer-term bonds than on shorter-term bonds. This "inverted" yield curve (the plot of yields based on bonds' maturities) has kept mortgage rates low. Observers debate whether the housing slump has reached its nadir or is in the early stages. Homebuilding stocks appear to have stabilized from their struggles in late summer 2006.

At the sector level, telecommunications led its peers with a 33% gain for the year through Dec. 20. Foreign service providers such as Telekomunikasi Indonesia (TLK) surged 88%. BT Group (BT) jumped 66%, taking it out of 5-star territory, where it began the year. Utilities also did well, continuing their multiyear run with a 32% surge. After posting a loss in 2005, the media sector came alive with a 24% gain. Cable TV businesses DirecTV (DTV) and Comcast (CMCSA) posted 78% and 65% gains, respectively. DirecTV was in 5-star territory early in the year.

Health care brought up the rear with an 8% gain. Biopharmaceutical company Celgene (CELG) rocketed up 82% on the success of Revlimid, its immunomodulatory drug. Merck (MRK) also surged nearly 42%, despite lingering litigation over Vioxx and the specter of drugs coming off patents in the next five years. The laggards in health care include many medical device makers, and here we find some stocks currently trading well below our fair value estimates. Boston Scientific (BSX) dropped 31% through Dec. 20 for a second year, as it struggled with product recalls and to digest acquisitions for which it paid dearly. Nevertheless, we remain upbeat about Boston's longer-term prospects because of its increased product diversification and history of innovation. Boston's competitor Medtronic (MDT) has also been hit hard by the implantable cardioverter defibrillator (ICD) recall, falling 6% for the year. It has bounced hard off of its lows, however, and we anticipate the market for its products stabilizing and its ability to create new products positioning it well for the future.

At the industry level, steel/iron returned 61% for the year through Dec. 20. Chaparral Steel (CHAP) added a whopping 194%. The newly combined Arcelor Mittal (MT) is now the world's largest steel producer, uniquely positioned to respond to market demands. Shares of Mittal jumped 61% for the year. Gambling/hotel casinos also did well, adding 54% for the year through Dec. 20. Las Vegas Sands (LVS) surged 131%, and Wynn Resorts (WYNN) rose 80%. Education stumbled, dropping 14% for the year through Dec. 21. Apollo Group (APOL) shed 36% amid fears of slowing growth, earnings restatements, and an investigation into stock-option backdating. Despite these recent troubles, we believe that demographics serve Apollo well, given the number of working adults seeking to improve their careers through higher education. Homebuilders finished last, dropping 18% for the year through Dec. 20. Many of them, such as Centex (CTX), Pulte (PHM), and Toll Brother (TOL), have bounced off their lows from the late summer when they sat on the 5-star list, to approach our analysts' fair value estimates.

Whether the stock market will be up or down in 2007 is anyone's guess. Fortunately, though, attractively priced stocks can exist in almost any market environment. Instead of worrying about the market, investors can best utilize their time with the careful analysis of individual securities: It is this analysis that truly separates the good investors from the bad. We hope that you'll find *Morningstar Stocks 500* to be a valuable asset in your endeavor to build and maintain a strong portfolio and generate wealth.

James Levin, Managing Editor *Morningstar Stocks 500*

How to Use the Morningstar Stocks 500

by Joe Beaulieu

Company Profile
A short description of what the company does.

Management
At Morningstar, we pay a lot of attention to whether management and the board are acting in shareholders' best interests. Our Stewardship Grade factors in management compensation, the transparency and trustworthiness of the company's financial statements, the ability of outside shareholders to influence the direction of the company, and many other nuggets of information we get from poring through the company's regulatory filings. Just like in school, an A is much better than a D.

Thesis
Here we explain what makes the company tick and what we think of its competitive position. You'll learn what we think of the business, whether the company operates in an attractive or unattractive industry, and what we think of the company's long-term prospects.

Rating
The Morningstar Rating for stocks tells you how attractive we think the stock is at its current price. This rating is calculated using three factors: the analyst's fair value estimate, the most recent closing price, and our business risk rating. The lower the price and risk, all else equal, the higher the star rating. And since we prefer a larger margin of safety before we recommend riskier stocks, it takes a larger discount to our fair value estimate for a riskier stock to achieve our highest ratings.

Fair Value Estimate
This is what we think the company's shares are worth. Since we view shares as pieces of a business, rather than mere pieces of paper, we dig into the company's financial statements, project cash flows into the future, and discount those flows back to present value to try to discern the intrinsic value of the stock.

Consider Buy
This is the price at which we believe investors could purchase the shares with a reasonable margin of safety should something unexpected happen to the firm. This margin of safety is directly tied to our business risk rating, and the riskier the business the larger of a margin of safety we think investors should demand.

Consider Sell
This is the price at which we think the shares might be worth selling. As always, investors should consider tax implications and the availability of more attractive investment opportunities.

Last Close
This is the stock price as of the publication date. It is used to calculate the Morningstar Rating for stocks.

Yield
Yield is the current dividend rate (such as the most recent quarterly payment times four) divided by the current stock price. Yield provides instant gratification in the form of regular income payments. A high yield could be a sign that the company doesn't have a lot of growth opportunities, and is therefore returning cash to investors. However, a high yield could also be a result of a plummeting stock price.

Moat Size
We use the term "economic moat" to describe a firm's long-term competitive advantage. In the same way that a moat kept invaders of medieval castles at bay, an economic moat keeps competitors from attacking a firm's revenue and profits. We rate moats as "Wide," "Narrow," or "None." The most common factors contributing to an economic moat are real or perceived product differentiation (which can lead to pricing power); the ability to offer products or services at a lower price than competitors due to structural or managerial factors (which can help increase market share); the ability to lock in customers by creating high switching costs (which creates pricing power); and the existence of barriers to entry due either to high regulatory or economic hurdles (which help maintain market share and pricing power).

Business Risk
A company's business risk is the primary determinant of the margin of safety below our fair value estimate that we'd require before recommending the stock. We consider factors such as the company's size, profitability, free cash flow generation, long-term competitive advantages over the competition (or lack thereof), and the strength of its balance sheet.

Investment Style
The Morningstar style box for stocks shows you whether we consider a stock to be a "growth" or "value" stock (or somewhere in between) and whether it is a large-cap, mid-cap or small-cap stock. This is one way to look at how a stock might fit into a diversified portfolio.

Industry and Sector
We divide our coverage universe into three sectors (information, service, and manufacturing). Each sector contains four subsectors: software, hardware, media, and telecommunications within the information sector; health care, consumer services, business services, and financial services within the service sector; and consumer goods, industrial materials, energy, and utilities within the manufacturing sector.

Price Volatility
This shows up to six years of monthly price history, with annual highs and lows.

Historical Financial Data
Use this table to spot trends over the past six years.

Annual Total Return %
The total return an investor would have realized, including both changes in the share price and dividends during the period in question.

Revenue, Net Income, Earnings Per Share, Shares Outstanding
While these measures are just starting points, they can give you a sense of where the company is headed. For example, look for trends in revenue and net income (preferably both are increasing). If only revenue is growing (or if revenue is growing much more quickly than net income), it could signal that the company is in a weak competitive position. If revenue is falling, the company could be losing business or pricing power. If the number of shares outstanding is growing, that means that the company is giving away shares either as employee compensation or to make acquisitions.

Return on Equity
Return on equity (net income divided by shareholders' equity) is the percentage of shareholder investment in a company generated as profit each year. The higher the better.

The three components of return on equity are as follows:

Net Margin %
Net margin (net income divided by total sales) is the percentage of every dollar of revenue that is left over after a company pays its bills, its lenders, and the tax man. We prefer companies that have stable or improving margins. Declining margins might suggest increased competition.

Asset Turnover
We typically like firms with higher asset turnover (revenue divided by total assets), because this means that they are generating a lot of revenue with a small asset base.

Financial Leverage
The higher a firm's financial leverage (total assets divided by shareholders' equity), the more debt and other liabilities a firm has. Nearly all firms have some liabilities, such as money owed to suppliers, but typically the closer this ratio is to one, the stronger the balance sheet.

Valuation Ratios
This section shows how the stock price stacks up on four of the most commonly used valuation ratios. Since these figures are only marginally useful on their own, we also show how each ratio compares with that of the company's industry, as well as that of the S&P 500. We believe these ratios are most useful when used in conjunction with a more fundamental metric, such as intrinsic value.

Major Fund Holders
Here you'll see which mutual funds are making the biggest bets on the stock.

Operations
This tells you where to write the company's investor relations department to request annual reports and important SEC filings like the 10-K, the 10-Q, and the proxy. Most firms also provide these forms on their Web sites.

Competition
These are some of the company's major rivals. Market cap and sales will give you a good idea as to how the company stacks up to the competition on size, while the other fields provide a thumbnail sketch of how the company compares on valuation, profitability, and financial health.

Growth
When available, this shows how quickly revenues have grown over the past four years, and whether earnings, book value, and dividend growth have lagged or surpassed revenue growth. A big difference between revenue growth and earnings growth could signal a change in the company's competitive position or in the industry's outlook.

Profitability
This section contains some of the most important information on the page. High returns on assets suggest high margins, a low fixed asset base, or both. We also like companies with operating cash flows that are positive and growing. Finally, we love companies that have free cash flows that are positive and growing, as free cash flows are a key component to our fair value estimates.

Financial Health
Debt isn't always a bad thing, but too much of it can lead to financial distress or the inability to capitalize on growth opportunities. A stable (or declining) debt/equity ratio is a good first check of a company's overall financial health. M

Our Approach to Equity Research

by Pat Dorsey, CFA,
Editor, Morningstar Stocks 500

We evaluate stocks for what they truly are—pieces of a business. Instead of prognosticating short-term price movements or momentum, our analysts focus on determining the value of a business, its risks, and whether the stock price accurately reflects both the value and risk.

Simply put, we look for superior businesses that trade at discounts to their fair values. The market, of course, doesn't always agree with us, so sometimes our recommendations are out of step with consensus thinking. But we believe this approach is the most sensible way to create wealth over the long term.

Determining Fair Value

This philosophy of fundamental research is the foundation for our valuation model. We believe that:

- How much capital a company invests and what it earns on that capital drive shareholder value.

- Free cash flow—not reported earnings—is what counts.

- As Warren Buffett has said, "Growth is always a component in the calculation of value—sometimes a positive, often a negative." If a company can't earn its cost of capital, growth destroys value instead of creating it.

- Competitive advantages disappear over time.

- It's dangerous to assume that the future will be better than the past.

- Some companies—but not all—are able to create durable competitive advantages that protect high returns on capital.

These core beliefs guide our stock analysts as they estimate future cash flow, using their in-depth knowledge of each company and its competitive position within its industry. Our analysts forecast revenue growth, profit margins, and capital investment (and all of the numbers that go into them) for each firm they cover.

Their forecasts for each company populate our discounted cash-flow model, which calculates the present value of the company's future discretionary cash flow based on its cost of capital, as determined by our analysts.

A Margin of Safety

Estimating fair values is no easy process, and we don't presume we'll always be right. So we look for stocks with a deep enough discount to our fair value to offer a reasonable margin of safety—something recommended long ago by Benjamin Graham. Even if we're wrong about our fair value estimate, there is a cushion for investors.

The discount required to earn our highest rating depends on the quality of the company. We believe investors are better served paying a fair price for a firm with great long-term prospects—one that creates economic value—than a "cheap" price for a wealth-destroying company.

One thing we look for is an "economic moat," an ability to keep competitors at bay via factors such as high switching costs for customers, patents or copyrights, or being a low-cost producer. In general, the wider the economic moat and the lower the risk of the business, the smaller the discount we demand before recommending a stock as a sound investment. M

Why Popular Stocks Are a Sucker's Bet

by Haywood Kelly, CFA

A recent study points out, yet again, how fickle we humans are.

Any student of the market is by necessity a student of human psychology and the behavior of crowds. With that in mind, consider a study published in the Feb. 10, 2006 issue of *Science* magazine. The authors, Matthew J. Salganik and Peter Sheridan Dodds of Columbia University, and Duncan J. Watts of the Santa Fe Institute, studied how people judged music when left to their own devices, versus how they judged music when they knew how popular the music was among their peers. It offers a nice demonstration of people's suggestibility and dovetails with our own thoughts about market behavior and the behavior of crowds.

Can you guess the results?

First, the Study

The paper's authors created an artificial music market on the Internet, recruiting more than 14,000 participants. They invited each participant to listen to a set of songs by various obscure bands, and offered them the option of downloading any song they liked.

The authors divided these 14,000 individuals randomly into nine groups. One group—called the "independent" group—simply saw a list of 48 songs in random order. They then sampled this music and downloaded the songs they liked. As you would expect, this resulted in a wide dispersion in the number of downloads. A few songs got downloaded a lot, and a few songs were hardly downloaded at all.

The other eight groups—the "social influence" groups—had the same list of songs to choose from, but also saw the number of times each song had been downloaded by other members of their respective groups. Within each of these eight groups, two factors therefore contributed to whether a song was downloaded: the quality of the song, and the influence of the popularity of the song on each participant.

Why eight different social-influence groups? This way, the authors could essentially create eight different worlds in order to see whether each world evolved along similar lines, or if their paths diverged. In many real-life situations—like the stock market—we only have one history to study, and we don't know if that one history was the way things had to be, or whether it was the result of blind, stupid chance.

The Results

The study's key results are threefold, and have some rather obvious parallels with investor behavior.

The addition of peer influence widens the gap between the winners and losers.
In other words, peer influence makes the most popular songs even more popular, and the least popular songs less popular. The authors used the Gini coefficient to measure this. Economists use the Gini coefficient to measure things like the income inequality across different countries (the United States versus France, for example) or within the same country over time (the U.S. of 1900 versus the U.S. of 2000). Based on this measure, the gulf between the most-popular and least-popular songs widened in each of the eight "peer influence" groups versus the independent group.

Does this remind you of the stock market? A given industry or asset class—Japan in 1989, emerging markets in 1994, Internet stocks in 1999, or (dare we say) commodity stocks right now—soars far beyond what the fundamentals justify and then comes crashing back to earth. As Benjamin Graham told us many years ago, in the short term markets are voting machines. And as this study and others like it suggest, the very fact that something is popular makes it even more so, for a while at least.

When you introduce peer influence, you increase the unpredictability of the results.
Not only does the difference between winners and losers widen, but it gets tougher to predict who the winners and losers will be. The authors calculated the differences in "market share" for each song in the eight different social-influence worlds and compared this to differences in market share in various random samplings of the "independent" group. The unpre-

dictability between different social-influence worlds was dramatically larger than in the independent worlds.

This is further confirmation, if any were needed, that our knowledge of the future is severely limited. What stocks will go up this year? Where will interest rates head? Where will the Dow finish? Easy questions to ask, but impossible ones to answer. (This doesn't stop the answers from coming, unfortunately.) As the authors put it: "We conjecture...that experts fail to predict success not because they are incompetent judges or misinformed about the preferences of others, but because when individual decisions are subject to social influence, markets do not simply aggregate pre-existing individual preferences. In such a world, there are inherent limits on the predictability of outcomes, irrespective of how much skill or information one has."

The greater the peer influence, the stronger are the first two results.
The researchers repeated the experiment twice. The second time, the social-influence groups saw the songs ranked in descending order of downloads, whereas in the previous experiment they had appeared in random order. This made it easier for participants to see which songs were most popular. In this case, the first two results—a more extreme dispersion between the most- and least-popular songs, and an increase in unpredictability—were even more pronounced. The authors' conclusion: "Increasing the strength of social influence increased both inequality and unpredictability of success."

Profiting from the Crowd's Madness
In any given year, it's impossible to predict which stocks (or bonds, or mutual funds, etc.) will be popular or unpopular, but the great thing about investing for the long term is that it doesn't matter. We don't have to predict what will be popular next year. We just have to wait for great companies to become unpopular. In fact, the more bipolar the market is, the more profitable a disciplined long-term investment strategy will be. Ultimately, stock prices depend on the cash a company generates. And if you keep your eyes focused on that, and not the best-performers' list, you'll do just fine.

Profiting from the ebbs and flows of popularity is what the Morningstar Rating for stocks is designed to do. The stocks you see rated 5 stars are those that we think the market is substantially undervaluing, and those rated 1 star are those we think the market is way too optimistic about. By allocating capital to 5-star stocks and avoiding the 1 stars, we think you can turn the fickleness of the crowd to your advantage. M

The article is "Experimental Study of Inequality and Unpredictability in an Artificial Cultural Market," by Matthew J. Salganik, Peter Sheridan Dodds, and Duncan J. Watts, Science 10 February 2006 311: 854–856.

Avoid Being Mr. Market

by Josh Peters, CFA
Editor, Morningstar
DividendInvestor

When you push that "Place Order" button or get that confirmation in the mail, do you ever wonder who is on the other end of that trade? Who sold you those shares? What does that guy know about the company that you don't?

Or could it be "Mr. Market" who's selling his shares to you? Mr. Market, Ben Graham's mythical investor with bipolar disorder, acts out his mania and depression with buy and sell tickets. He'll sell to you when he's desperate for an out, often at ridiculously low prices. And he'll want to buy shares from you at correspondingly high prices when momentum and "news flow" render valuation meaningless. And he trades much too frequently, donating heavily to Wall Street's daily charity drive of commissions and fees.

These awful psychological characteristics make Mr. Market a terrible investor, but a great person to trade with. The question every investor should ask themselves—before every trade, in fact—is this: am I being Mr. Market?

The Market Personality Test
There's a Mr. Market in all of us, and every once in a while, I still succumb to his way of doing business. But too much Mr. Market in your investment style will almost certainly prevent you from earning a decent return from stocks.

Do any of these statements fit your approach?

When a stock I own drops 20%, I sell.
Plenty of investors employ a rule like this. Some even dump at declines of 5% or 10%. But stocks are volatile. Mr. Market whips the price up and down, putting share prices far from what a knowledgeable, well-heeled buyer would pay for the entire business. Show me a portfolio with sell stops at 5%, and I'll show you a portfolio that will lose 5% a year like clockwork.

Think back to the thwackings 3M MMM and United Parcel Service UPS took in July 2006. Were either of these businesses really suddenly worth 15% or 20% less than they were at the beginning of that month? Had the stream of future cash flows and dividends diminished that greatly? Were customers fleeing to competitors, or simply expiring from the planet? Were these companies' assets materially impaired? Hardly. The actual value of the business is at the whip's handle—moving to and fro ever so slightly. The market price is the end of the whip—and that whip has stung the short-term crowd badly.

Never forget that the market price of a stock at any given moment is where the weakest current owners and the most indifferent group of buyers meet. I was not the least bit concerned that 3M was down from $84 to $69 in July. Mr. Market couldn't have my shares for less than $110.

The good long-term investors don't sell at a 20% loss, but they do go back and aggressively review their investment case. If the fundamentals are unchanged, they hold or buy more. If the business is not as strong as they expected—that is, if they made a mistake analyzing the business in the first place—then, and only then, will they sell.

When a stock I own rises 5%, I lock in my gains.
"Nobody goes broke taking a gain," or so goes the old Wall Street saw. Nobody ever got rich taking gains in 5% increments, either. Peter Lynch calls this tendency by amateur investors to harvest small gains while taking larger losses on the downside "watering the weeds."

To benefit from holding stocks, you've got to be willing to hang on for a long time—a horizon measured in years, not days. The events that drive share prices up in big increments (a surprise improvement in earnings, a big dividend increase, improving sales growth) can't be pinpointed to a particular day or week. The best approach is "don't just do something, sit there!"

If the fact that a stock is "going nowhere" bothers you, why not consider higher-yielding names that will pay you handsomely—in cash—to wait? The model Dividend Portfolio in our monthly *Morningstar DividendInvestor* newsletter provides a yield of 4.6% with annual dividend growth of more than 6%.

I only look for stocks that have been going up.
"The trend is your friend" is another Wall Street adage whose timelessness is matched only by its uselessness. Stocks are just about the only items that consumers buy that seem to become more desirable as they get more expensive. All else being equal, as the price you pay for a stock rises, its future return potential falls. It's not just that "past performance is not a promise of future results," as mutual fund advertisements declare in the fine print, but quite the opposite—yesterday's performance is just as likely to set the stage for opposite results tomorrow.

Grab Your Wallet
One of the amazing things about Mr. Market is how much he pays in fees. Make no mistake, these contributions to Wall Street's annual bonuses are purely voluntary, and they come straight out of his total returns. A $50,000 brokerage account that makes just two trades a week at $10 apiece stands to shell out 2% of its value annually just in commissions. And while that 2% may not sound like much as a percent of assets, it's a whopping 20% of the market's historic return before fees.

Wall Street has no shortage of cheerleaders, lauding the billions of shares worth of "liquidity" it provides investors and the steady decline in per-transaction commissions. But is a $10 or $20 trade "cheap"? Wall Street is not dumb—it's more than made up for this with volume. It's simple economics: Slash the price of something, and you'll sell a lot more of it.

I'm grateful for all this liquidity, but not for the same reason Mr. Market is. The ease with which Mr. Market can make bad decisions creates opportunity for longer-term investors.

Make Mr. Market Work for You
Even though I think an investor can do well owning individual stocks, it's not for everyone. If you're in the game as a Mr. Market impersonator, odds are you'll be better off with an index fund. And if you just can't stand short-term fluctuations in paper value, a savings account or a shoebox under the bed is the place for you.

I spend a lot of time thinking about my competitive advantages (or disadvantages) as an investor and as manager of the Dividend Portfolio. The way I see it, there are only two ways to play.

One way is to pursue superior information. If you know much more about the business than the average holder of its shares, you're in a better place to judge whether the current price is too high or too low and can act accordingly. But this is very tough to do, even with tiny firms. Wall Street pays its analyst ranks millions of dollars to cover large-cap firms like Dell DELL and Amazon AMZN, yet they're usually caught off guard on short-term problems like the rest of us.

The other way—which I try to employ through the Dividend Portfolio—is to pursue a superior point of view. I can't tell you whether Wells Fargo WFC or Sysco SYY is going to meet, beat, or miss on its next quarterly earnings report. I guess I was late for class on the day they handed out clairvoyance.

My point of view holds that a stock's total return over time will equal the dividend yield I get on day one plus the subsequent growth rate of dividends per share. I say nuts to beating the market and instead rely on dividends to provide my return. For Wells and Sysco, I can judge that their yields are attractive and the dividends themselves will continue to grow at very healthy rates. What's more, by evaluating the businesses from the standpoint of competitive advantage, they should both be able to maintain high rates of dividend growth for very long periods of time. If I hold the stock long enough, my total return will converge to this combination of yield and growth—and I won't have to donate to Wall Street's charity drive to earn it. M

To learn more about Morningstar DividendInvestor, visit:
http://www.morningstar.com/Products/Store_StocksMDI.html

The Predictable Returns of Dividends

by Josh Peters, CFA
Editor, Morningstar
DividendInvestor

Despite the low returns, I can see why some investors like bonds. They're a lot less work. Bonds spell out the exact terms of future cash payments. As long as the issuer is solvent, the yield you see (if you hold to maturity) is the return you get. All the potential buyer needs to judge is creditworthiness (Is it safe?) and the attractiveness of the yield (What's the return?).

Common stocks have no such contractual terms. Moreover, with current dividend yields far lower than what most of us would consider an acceptable long-term total return, most of the value of the average stock is contained in future, uncertain dividend increases (Can it grow?).

Can we find almost bond-like consistency from stocks? Some of the 1,800-plus stocks Morningstar covers are far more predictable than others. Narrowing our field to these blue chips is a low-stress strategy that can still offer attractive, even market-beating returns.

Buy-to-Sell Versus Buy-to-Hold
Your average amateur stock-pickers—and an overwhelming number of professionals—think in terms of buy low, sell high. Sounds simple enough, but this is quite difficult in practice. For starters, have you ever pondered what "low" means? Is it buying companies in trouble, whose depressed share prices could rebound when challenges abate? Or does it mean looking for catalysts—change factors that will lead to materially higher earnings that the market doesn't yet appreciate? Either way, the investor is forced to speculate on a change in current earnings, cash generation, or even news flow.

Worse yet, what is "high"? I'm no great fan of selling stocks—even at a gain—since it poses not one but two significant problems. A "high" sale implies that the price discounts any and all future gains in dividend-paying ability, leaving only an inferior future return. (Again, we find ourselves speculating on the future.) And having sold one investment, we're obliged to replace that stream of total returns with one at least as attractive—and after paying transaction costs and taxes, we have less capital to put at work.

I'm not afraid to sell when the underlying economics of a business are deteriorating, or when we might find a truly compelling opportunity. But the hurdle for such moves is necessarily high.

What I'm really after are annuitylike streams of predictable, growing income that I can hold indefinitely. Warren Buffett describes his preferred holding period as forever. My term, indefinite, simply means that I don't care to buy stocks with a purpose to sell them later. To benefit from dividends and dividend growth, you've got to participate—and that takes time.

In Praise of Consistency
Just consider the benefits of a consistent stream of dividend increases:

More-predictable returns.
Over long stretches of time, the return from a stock will tend to correlate to the initial dividend yield plus subsequent dividend growth. In any given year, many other factors—swings in earnings, stock market fads, economic booms and busts—can overwhelm this formula. Over a lengthy time horizon (three to five years or more) these cyclical variations start to get smoothed out. But we can also increase the predictability of our returns by seeking consistent dividend-raisers. The more predictable a dividend seems, the more likely our returns will stay in a range that reflects that.

Less volatility.
Hedge funds and other hot-money investors overwhelmingly prefer volatility, since it gives them plenty of opportunities to buy low and sell high. But when the bulk of a stock's total return is built with steady dividends, there's less reason for investors to obsess about quarterly earnings estimates, management soap operas, merger rumors, and the like. The company acquires a long-term, low-turnover base of owners who have reasonable expectations—and little reason to dump at every short-term bump in the road.

Easily appraised management 'will.'
Projecting dividends—as opposed to earnings—adds the question of where the cash will go, rather than just how much there will be. A steady record signals that management will indeed share earnings growth through dividends.

Enforcement.
This is probably my favorite side effect of a long, lustrous dividend record. Having attracted owners that expect regular, consistent payouts, management dares not risk alienating these holders with a halt in growth, much less a dividend cut. The best dividend-growers thus manage their enterprises in a way that supports sustainable dividend expansion—a conservative balance sheet, efficient generation of cash, a focus on core operations, and appropriate investment for growth in earnings and dividends.

In Search of Consistency
When you've got a consistent record—such as Johnson & Johnson JNJ and Coca-Cola KO—the question shifts from "What will growth be?" to the much simpler "Can it continue?" It's easier to confirm an admirable record than it is to speculate on the future. Moreover, the all-important will to raise the dividend (as opposed to the theoretical way) is much clearer.

But while achievement gets us started, the record alone isn't enough. Fulton Financial FULT, for example, stands out with arguably the most consistent dividend record in Morningstar's coverage. Since 1995, it has raised its annual payout by an average of 10.4%—never more than 11.6%, never less than 9.1%. But Fulton hasn't achieved this with earnings alone, which have risen at only a 6.5% annual clip. Instead, the payout ratio has crept from 38% to 54%. At a 54% payout and a 13% return on equity, future increases should fall to about 6%.

Fulton may go on raising the dividend faster than earnings for a while longer—sending the payout ratio higher and higher—but unless ROE improves, doing so only erodes growth potential while possibly placing the payment itself at risk.

The best achievers for investment are those with sustainable financial metrics—the kind our Dividend Drill used in *DividendInvestor* easily reveals—and those that have indicated total returns within our 10%–12% target range.

What's It Worth?
One question remains: Is the implied total return (current yield plus our growth estimate) enough to make the investment worthwhile? Take Consolidated Edison ED, whose dividend has risen in each year for three decades now. That's nice to know, but in the last 10 years, that dividend has grown at a piddling 1.2% per annum. Over this same stretch, the consumer price index has climbed at a 2.5% annual clip, more than twice as fast. The $2.04 dividend Con Ed was paying in early 1996 was actually worth more than the $2.30 it's paying now, adjusted for inflation. With a 1.2% growth rate and a yield of 5.3%, our prospective total return doesn't stand to be much more than 6.5%. I'd much rather go with a stock like Sysco SYY, whose yield (2.2%) is less than half of Con Ed's, but whose dividend is rising some 10 times faster.

And we shouldn't limit ourselves to past achievers only. There are plenty of meritorious stocks that haven't paid dividends for a full 10 years yet; others—like Kinder Morgan Energy Partners KMP—may be in a temporary payout-growth lull. Yet with all stocks, no matter how long or short, good or bad their records, we want to be forward-looking in our analyses. If we correctly pick future achievers, then all the benefits of a consistent, lengthening record will accrue to us as shareholders. ∎

To learn more about Morningstar DividendInvestor, visit:
http://www.morningstar.com/Products/Store_StocksMDI.html

Digging an Ecomonic Moat

by Pat Dorsey, CFA, Editor,
Morningstar Stocks 500

A special feature of Morningstar's stock analyses is our rating of each company's "economic moat." The concept of economic moats is so important to the way we think about stocks that we wanted to explicitly break it out for our subscribers so they can see at a glance exactly what our thinking is on the stocks that we cover.

Basically, the idea of an economic moat refers to how likely companies are to keep competitors at bay for an extended period. All businesses that earn excess economic profits attract competition, and the bigger those profits are, the more capital will pour into those areas of the economy to compete with existing firms. That's the basic nature of any (reasonably) free market. One of the keys to finding superior long-term investments is buying companies that will be able to stay one step ahead of their competitors, and it's this characteristic—think of it as the strength and sustainability of a firm's competitive advantage—that we're trying to capture with the economic moat rating.

Obviously, assigning moats is a complicated process, and relies heavily on our analysts' knowledge of their companies and industries. One of the first things we do when we're thinking about the size of a firm's economic moat is look at the company's historical financial performance. Companies that have generated returns on capital higher than their cost of capital for many years running are usually doing something right, especially if their returns on capital have been rising or are fairly stable—Wrigley WWY or Microsoft MSFT are good examples.

Of course, the past is a highly imperfect predictor of the future, so we look carefully at the source of a company's excess economic profits before assigning a moat rating. For example, a competitive advantage created by a hot new technology usually isn't very sustainable, because it won't be too long until someone comes along and invents a better widget. Tech companies with wide economic moats—like Microsoft, Intel INTC, or Adobe ADBE—usually have some kind of strength other than technological prowess. Microsoft and Adobe have the network effect on their side and Intel has economies of scale relative to smaller competitors. These competitive advantages are all much harder to duplicate than a piece of hardware or software that just has more features than everyone else's.

So, what are some attributes that can give companies economic moats? There are quite a few, but here are some of the big ones:

1. Low-Cost Producer

You can have the lowest costs without being the biggest. For example, Dell DELL and Southwest Airlines LUV haven't always dwarfed their competitors, but they've been able to make PCs and fly planes cheaper than any of their competitors. This advantage is especially potent in commodity industries.

2. Patents, Copyrights, or Governmental Approvals and Licenses

This is a sticky one. Drug companies, for example, generate enormous profits when their drugs are patent-protected, but patent extensions are often successfully challenged by generic competitors. Similarly, the value of governmental licenses—such as the approvals granted to local television stations or wireless carriers—can be quite high or quite low depending on the situation and the ease with which other licenses can be obtained.

3. High Customer-Switching Costs

This can create a gigantic economic moat. If you can make it tough for your customers to use a competitor, it's usually easy to keep ratcheting prices up just a bit year after year—which can lead to big profits. Most data-processing firms—like First Data FDC—have this characteristic, as do most banks. Oracle ORCL is another good example.

4. The Network Effect

This is a relatively rare, but potentially quite potent, source of competitive advantage, and often accrues by the first mover in an emerging technology. Since a network's value increases as more people use it, the company that creates the network can dig a massive economic moat. The classic example is eBay EBAY—more buyers attract more sellers, which attract more buyers, and so forth—but companies that sell industry-standard software (like Adobe Systems ADBE and Autodesk ADSK) also fall into this group. Western Union WU, which went public in 2006, is another good example—its agent network is three times larger than its nearest competitor.

5. Strong Brands

Having a strong brand can enable a company to charge a premium for its products relative to competitors selling similar goods or services. The key is to make sure that this premium does not erode over time. Take Sony SNE, for example—how much extra would you really pay for a Sony CD player relative to one made by Panasonic? On the other hand, there's Tiffany TIF, which can charge a huge premium for a virtually identical diamond.

Six Reasons to Not Take Returns at Face Value

by Haywood Kelly, CFA

We all know that past returns are not indicative of future results. But past returns may not be indicative of true past results, either.

Come again? Surely nothing's more straightforward than a return calculation. Well, the more time you spend analyzing returns, the more wrinkles you find. There are dozens of reasons that a stock or fund return might be misleading or not reflect true changes in investor wealth. Some of these effects are small—small enough that you can live a long and peaceful investing life and never think twice about them. Some can be quite large, however.

In the spirit that the informed investor is a better investor, let's walk through six oddities.

1. A stock begins the year at $20 per share. It ends the year at $25. The annual return of the stock is therefore 25%. Would I really have earned a 25% return on the stock if I had bought at the start of the year and sold at the end?

That's what the math says, but the 25% is a hypothetical return—there's no guarantee you could have earned it. If you're trading a small number of shares, meaning your trade represents only a small fraction of the shares traded on any given day, yes, your return would probably have been 25%. You could have bought at $20 and sold at $25. If, however, you're a big-time money manager, or if few shares of the stock change hands on a daily basis, you may not have been able to buy at $20 or sell at $25.

To see why, let's begin with the $20 price quote. This means that at the beginning of the year, two parties exchanged the stock at $20. A price quote is simply a record of a historical transaction—it's the price at which the last transaction occurred. There's no guarantee that the next transaction will occur at $20. If you place a small buy order—100 shares, say, for a stock that trades 100,000 shares in a typical day—chances are, some seller will be willing to part with the stock at or very near the last transaction price.

But let's say the order was for 100,000 shares. Perhaps one seller is willing to sell you 10,000 shares for $20.05. Another seller will part with 5,000 shares at $20.10. Another will sell 7,000 at $20.20. And so on. Your ultimate price may be well above $20, and it will depend on how quickly you want to buy (the less patient you are, the costlier the trade) and how much depth there is to the market. The same analysis applies when you go to sell the shares at year-end.

It's akin to Heisenberg's uncertainty principles in physics. If you touch the stock, you change what the return would have been. Such transaction costs are very real, and they are a key reason why investors should always question the results of paper portfolios or back-testing, particularly if the proposed investment strategy involves buying illiquid stocks. For a good discussion of these issues, I'd recommend David Leinweber's paper "Using Information from Trading and Portfolio Management: Ten Years Later."

2. A mutual fund has a five-year annualized return of 30%. Are the fund's shareholders, as a group, a lot richer today?

Maybe, maybe not. When you look at the published return of a stock or mutual fund, you see the time-weighted return, which is the return investors would have received had they bought and held over the entire time period. Few investors actually do this. Instead, many buy in when the price is high and sell when the price is low. If you measure the returns that mutual fund investors actually earned in a fund—using so-called dollar-weighted returns—they're almost always lower than the time-weighted returns.

There's also a difference between time- and dollar-weighted returns when it comes to stocks, although there's an important difference. For any single stock investor, the dollar-weighted return will depend on the timing of purchases and sales, just as with a mutual fund. For investors in the aggregate, though, one person's well-timed trade is someone else's poorly timed trade, so the winners cancel out the losers.

What drives a wedge between aggregate dollar-weighted returns and published returns are stock issuances and other changes to firms' capital accounts, and the academic evidence suggests that companies (and their investment banks) are good at selling high. In a 2004 paper, Ilia Dichev finds dollar-weighted returns to be 1.3% lower than time-weighted returns for stocks on the New York Stock Exchange and more than 5% lower for Nasdaq stocks.

3. The market was down 5% today, but my stock was flat. Why is that?

Chances are, your stock bucked the trend for a good reason related to the fundamentals of the company. But there's also a chance the price of your stock is stale. Remember that price quotes are records of historical transactions. If your stock didn't trade toward the close of the day, the last quoted transaction could be old. Academics call this nonsynchronous trading. The price quotes of some stocks reflect up-to-date market information, but some may not.

Nonsynchronous trading is behind the stale-price arbitrage that hedge funds have used to milk mutual fund investors out of money. Let's say an investor buys mutual fund shares on Tuesday at that day's ending net asset value (NAV) for the fund, which might be $10. If the fund holds a lot of stocks that haven't traded in a while—like Asian stocks, for which the markets closed much earlier, or illiquid stocks in the U.S. market—the NAV could be based partly on stale prices. If the U.S. market rose sharply on Tuesday, it's a good bet that Asian markets and illiquid U.S. stocks will rise on Wednesday. Buy the mutual fund, short an index to reduce market risk, and you've got yourself a good chance of a small positive return.

Do it enough times in any given year and the compound returns can become quite large. Academics actually calculated how much an investor could earn by following this strategy before Eliot Spitzer's mutual fund probe made stale-price arbitrage (or "market-timing") front-page news. The paper is "Predictable Changes in NAV: The wildcard option in transacting mutual fund shares" by Chalmers, Edelen, and Kadlec.

4. I own a stock that dropped 5% today. Am I 5% poorer?

Not necessarily. Over short time periods like a day or a week, there's evidence of return reversals. A stock that drops 5% tends, on the average, to get some of that return back.

There are two likely reasons. First, there's the bid-ask bounce. Even if there's no news for a stock, the price quote can bounce around between the bid and the ask price. Or consider a stock that falls on a given day. Chances are that the last trade of the day occurred at or near the bid price; a seller came to the market with a sell order and sold the stock at the best available price a buyer was willing to pay, which is the bid. The following day, however, there's an equal chance of the first trade occurring at either the bid or the ask price. If the first trade is at the asking price, the price of the stock will go up, when in fact we're simply seeing transactions move between the bid and the ask.

Second, there are liquidity-driven price moves. Maybe the price dropped because a trader with no new information—a so-called noise trader—sold off a big position. If other traders come to believe the seller really had no fundamental reason to sell, the stock price will quickly gravitate back to its presale price.

The academic literature on return reversals is rich. One of the more recent papers is "Liquidity and Autocorrelations in Individual Stock Returns" by Adramov, Chordia, and Goyal.

5. My mutual fund had a great day—up 5%. Am I 5% richer?

Not necessarily. The 5% reflects the one-day change in the fund's reported net asset value. There are at least three reasons reported NAVs may not correspond to the fund's true net asset value. The first is nonsynchronous trading, which we explained in Part One of this article. The second is that the fund company mis-estimated the value of a holding for which a market price wasn't readily available. The third is the focus of a recent academic paper, "Live Prices and Stale Quantities: T+1 Accounting and Mutual Fund Mispricing" by Tufano, Quinn, and Taliaferro. By a quirk of fund-company accounting, the prices used to calculate NAV at the end of each trading day are current, but the quantities are a day old.

For example, if a fund owns 10,000 shares of Microsoft MSFT on Tuesday and buys an additional 1,000 shares on Wednesday, the NAV at the end of the day Wednesday is calculated using 10,000 shares of Microsoft, not the 11,000 actually in the portfolio. If Microsoft's stock moved sharply late on Wednesday after the trade, the fund's NAV will be inaccurate. Fortunately, this is one of the return oddities that's small enough for most investors to ignore.

6. My fund was up 5% in the last week of the quarter, while the market was flat.

The fund may have been juicing returns near quarter-end. In a 2002 paper called "Leaning for the Tape: Evidence of Gaming Behavior in Equity Mutual Funds" by Carhart, Kaniel, Musto, and Reed, the authors claim to "present strong evidence that some mutual fund managers mark up their holdings at quarter end through aggressive trading of stocks they already hold."

It works like this. Say I'm a fund manager who owns 500,000 shares of an illiquid stock that's been flat. As the quarter-end approaches, I place aggressive buy orders for an additional 50,000 shares, moving the stock up 20% in the last week of the quarter. Suddenly my return on the stock goes to 20%. If the stock were 2% of my portfolio, I've just boosted my fund's quarterly return by 40 basis points. And because my trading had nothing to do with the fundamentals of the company, the share price is likely to drift back down after the quarter closes. By that time, though, I've managed to post a slightly better quarterly return, which might get me a few more dollars in inflows in the upcoming months.

Conclusion
Of these six return oddities, the first two are the ones most of us should focus on. The other four teach us much about how markets work, but the impact on our pocketbooks is minimal.

How much does the first oddity—trades moving prices—cost us? Even if my own trades aren't big enough to move prices, the funds I outsource my investing to might face this problem. The bigger such funds become, or the more rapid their managers trade, the bigger the bite such transaction costs take out of my wealth. Various studies suggest that such transaction costs can be in the ballpark of 100 basis points per year for some investing styles.

As for dollar-weighted returns, my colleague Russel Kinnel ran a study in *Morningstar FundInvestor* in July 2005. He found that bad timing in large-growth funds cost investors 3.4 percentage points in annualized return over the past 10 years. And that was wonderful compared with investors in technology funds, who posted dollar-weighted returns that were 14 percentage points behind the official time-weighted returns. M

How We Selected This Year's Stocks

by Pat Dorsey, CFA,
Editor, Morningstar Stocks 500

We're often asked how we select the 500 stocks in this book from the nearly 1,900 that we cover at Morningstar. In the past, the book has been a mix of stocks we thought would make excellent long-term holdings at the right price, as well as stocks in companies facing serious competitive threats too big to ignore, such as General Motors GM, Ford F, Sun Microsystems SUNW, Eastman Kodak EK, or Kroger KR.

This year, we're taking a different approach, and we think you'll like it. We've added more great businesses with economic moats, and to make room for them, we've dropped the behemoths with bad economics. As a result, you're holding a book with more potential long-term investment ideas than ever before, from niche manufacturers like Actuant ATU, to hugely profitable foreign firms like Bank of Nova Scotia BNS, to fast-growing technology firms like F5 Networks FFIV.

Rest assured that we haven't dropped coverage of household names like GM or Kodak; you can still read our up-to-date opinions on these companies on Morningstar.com as part of our Premium Service. But if they're not in the running when it comes to picking our favorite businesses, they're not in this book. These cigar-butt investments (potentially worth an opportunistic purchase at a very cheap valuation) are not businesses likely to create value over the long haul.

Economic Moats

So what makes a business good or bad, in our view? The biggest factor is whether that business has, or is building, what we call an economic moat. You can read more about economic moats on Page 15, but the basic notion is that all successful firms face competitive threats, and only firms with some kind of competitive advantage, or economic moat, are able to fend off the competition for a long time.

Moats matter to us because we think one of the most efficient ways to build wealth in the stock market is to let strong businesses with high returns on capital compound your investments over the long term. If a business can earn sustainable returns on its capital base of 20% or more, your money is better off staying in that investment than trading in and out of various opportunities, with all of the attendant tax and transaction costs that can be incurred.

Wide, Narrow, and None

In this year's *Stocks 500*, there are almost 160 companies with wide economic moats, ranging from giants like ExxonMobil XOM at more than $400 billion in market capitalization, to niche asset managers like Calamos CLMS at a little more than $500 million in market value. Wide-moat stocks are topnotch in our coverage universe. They are the companies we think are likely to earn high returns on capital for many years to come, and 5-star, wide-moat stocks are a great place to start when you're looking for core portfolio holdings.

Narrow-moat companies may not have the staying power of wide-moat ones, but they are high-quality businesses just the same. They tend to be smaller than wide-moat firms; the median market cap of the narrow-moat companies in this book is about $10 billion, which is half the median market cap of our wide-moat companies, so they also tend to have more high-growth years yet to come. Don't count a company out just because it has only a narrow moat, since many of these businesses have excellent returns on capital and solid growth prospects.

Finally, we do have a small number of no-moat companies in this year's edition. We've included them because we think they're running their businesses well and are good candidates for becoming narrow-moat companies in the near future. One key component of successful investing is to invest in businesses that perform better than the market expects them to, and we think this small group of companies has the potential to do just that. M

Index and Tables

This section serves as an overview of the companies included in the Morningstar Stocks 500. Data as of December 29, 2006 unless otherwise noted.

Morningstar Stocks 500
Company Index

Pg	Company	Industry	Star Rating	Fair Value Estimate ($)	Business Risk	Stewardship Grade	Market Cap ($Mil)	Revenue ($Mil)	Price/ Earnings	Dividend Yield %
59	3M Company	Diversified	★★★★	89.00	-Avg	B	57,385	22,466	16.8	2.4
60	Abbott Laboratories	Drugs	★★★	51.00	-Avg	B	74,763	22,306	23.7	2.4
61	Abercrombie & Fitch A	Clothing Stores	★★	60.00	Avg	C	6,145	3,141	19.0	1.0
62	Accenture	Consultants	★★★	41.00	Avg	C	28,867	18,852	23.2	0.9
63	ACE	Insurance (Property)	★★★	58.00	+Avg	B	19,755	13,047	10.8	1.6
64	Actuant A	Electric Equipment	★★★	52.00	Avg	A	1,301	1,201	15.8	0.2
65	Adobe Systems	Development Tools	★★★	38.00	Avg	C	23,987	2,404	49.0	0.0
66	Advanced Medical Optics	Medical Equipment	★★★	36.00	Avg	B	2,085	1,007	17.3	0.0
67	Aetna	Managed Care	★★	35.00	Avg	D	22,540	24,654	14.6	0.1
68	Aflac	Insurance (Life)	★★★★	52.00	Avg	B	22,747	14,496	15.3	1.2
69	Air Products and Chemicals	Chemicals	★★★	65.00	Avg	C	15,246	8,850	21.4	1.9
70	AirTran Holdings	Air Transport	★★★	13.00	+Avg	B	1,069	1,841	90.3	0.0
71	Alberto-Culver	Household & Personal Prod	★★★	20.00	Avg	B	2,010	3,772	9.8	1.7
72	Alcatel Lucent ADR	Wireline Equipment	★★★★	18.00	Avg	—	20,314	16,448	16.5	1.4
73	Alcoa	Aluminum	★★★★★	40.00	Avg	B	26,022	29,666	12.6	2.0
74	Alcon	Drugs	★★	102.00	-Avg	C	34,256	4,369	37.5	1.2
75	Alleghany	Insurance (Property)	★★★★	450.00	Avg	A	2,892	1,192	12.6	0.0
76	Allergan	Drugs	★★★	114.00	Avg	C	18,143	2,817	—	0.3
77	Alliancebernstein Holding LP	Money Management	★	58.00	Avg	C	6,812	3,712	20.4	4.4
78	Alliant Techsystems	Aerospace & Defense	★★★	87.00	Avg	B	2,575	3,343	19.0	0.0
79	Allied Capital	Finance	★★★	29.00	+Avg	C	4,763	433	8.5	7.4
80	Allied Irish Banks ADR	International Banks	★★★	66.00	Avg	—	27,911	4,567	16.8	2.7
81	Allied Waste Industries	Waste Management	★★★★	15.00	+Avg	D	4,523	6,003	25.1	0.0
82	Allstate	Insurance (Property)	★★	57.00	Avg	A	40,690	35,639	8.7	2.2
83	Alltel	Wireless Service	★★★	56.00	Avg	C	22,597	10,548	17.6	1.7
84	Altera	Semiconductors	★★★	19.00	Avg	C	7,121	1,250	24.6	0.0
85	Altria Group	Tobacco	★★★	90.00	+Avg	C	179,868	100,499	15.9	3.9
86	Amazon.com	Online Retail	★★	32.00	Avg	A	16,254	9,702	58.0	0.0
87	AmBev ADR	Alcoholic Drinks	★★★	48.00	+Avg	—	32,148	6,491	50.6	2.8
88	America Movil SA ADR	Telecom Services	★★★	44.00	+Avg	—	81,952	16,897	28.0	0.5
89	American Express	Finance	★★★★	70.00	-Avg	A	73,094	26,507	21.2	0.9
90	American International Group	Insurance (Property)	★★★	80.00	Avg	B	186,296	110,593	17.1	0.9
91	American Power Conversion	Electric Equipment	★★★	31.00	Avg	B	5,810	2,239	58.8	1.3
92	AmeriCredit	Finance	★★★	29.00	+Avg	B	2,907	—	12.1	0.0
93	AmeriGas Partners	Oil/Gas Products	★★★	36.00	Avg	C	1,848	2,119	20.5	7.1
94	Ameriprise Financial	Finance	★★★	51.00	Avg	C	13,187	7,848	—	0.8
95	Amgen	Biotechnology	★★★★★	91.00	Avg	C	79,685	13,704	28.0	0.0
96	Anadarko Petroleum	Oil & Gas	★★★★	55.00	Avg	C	20,008	9,838	5.5	0.8
97	Analog Devices	Semiconductors	★★★★★	48.00	Avg	B	11,242	2,573	22.2	1.8
98	Anheuser-Busch Companies	Alcoholic Drinks	★★★★	57.00	-Avg	A	37,826	15,691	19.0	2.3
99	Ann Taylor Stores	Clothing Stores	★★★	33.00	Avg	B	2,358	2,306	29.1	0.0
100	Apache	Oil & Gas	★★★★	86.00	Avg	C	21,909	8,424	7.9	0.7
101	Apollo Group A	Education	★★★★★	65.00	Avg	C	6,733	2,409	15.3	0.0
102	Apple Computer	Computer Equipment	★	66.00	Avg	C	72,901	19,315	37.4	0.0
103	Applebee's International	Restaurants	★★★★★	33.00	Avg	B	1,831	1,296	22.2	0.9
104	Applied Materials	Semiconductor Equipment	★★★	20.00	Avg	B	25,696	9,167	19.0	1.0
105	Arthur J. Gallagher & Co.	Insurance (General)	★★★★	35.00	Avg	B	2,899	1,495	25.9	4.1
106	Associated Banc-Corp	Regional Banks	★★★	36.00	-Avg	B	4,545	981	14.2	3.3
107	AstraZeneca PLC ADR	Drugs	★★★	51.00	Avg	—	84,438	23,950	18.4	2.6
108	AT&T	Telecom Services	★	28.00	Avg	D	137,384	60,171	19.2	2.8
109	Autodesk	Business Applications	★★★	43.00	Avg	A	9,375	1,604	30.4	0.0
110	Automatic Data Processing	Data Processing	★★★★	54.00	-Avg	B	27,117	9,177	26.6	1.6
111	AutoNation	Auto Retail	★★★	23.00	Avg	B	4,429	19,384	15.3	0.0
112	AutoZone	Auto Retail	★★★	115.00	-Avg	A	8,167	6,003	15.4	0.0
113	AvalonBay Communities	REITS	★	64.00	Avg	B	9,702	716	67.7	2.4
114	Avid Technology	Business Applications	★★★★	47.00	Avg	C	1,527	917	55.6	0.0
115	Avon Products	Household & Personal Prod	★★★★	41.00	Avg	A	14,688	8,540	31.2	2.1
116	Axcan Pharma	Drugs	★★★	15.00	Avg	—	651	251	25.4	0.0
117	Baker Hughes	Oil & Gas Services	★	59.00	Avg	C	23,946	8,564	10.8	0.7
118	Bank of America	International Banks	★★★★	67.00	Avg	B	239,758	68,368	12.4	4.0

Morningstar Stocks 500
Company Index

Pg	Company	Industry	Star Rating	Fair Value Estimate ($)	Business Risk	Stewardship Grade	Market Cap ($Mil)	Revenue ($Mil)	Price/ Earnings	Dividend Yield %
119	Bank of Montreal	International Banks	★★★	67.00	Avg	—	29,638	8,753	13.1	3.4
120	Bank of New York Company	International Banks	★★★★	48.00	Avg	B	41,334	7,308	18.8	2.2
121	Bank of Nova Scotia	International Banks	★★★	43.00	Avg	—	44,330	10,211	14.4	3.1
122	BankAtlantic Bancorp A	Regional Banks	★★★★	16.00	Avg	C	844	544	57.5	1.1
123	Barclays PLC ADR	International Banks	★★★	62.00	Avg	—	94,325	31,638	15.1	3.5
124	Barr Pharmaceuticals	Drugs	★★★★	62.00	Avg	A	5,332	1,336	16.1	0.0
125	Baxter International	Medical Equipment	★★	40.00	Avg	B	30,360	10,106	24.0	1.3
126	BB&T	Super Regional Banks	★★★	49.00	Avg	B	23,763	6,190	14.0	3.6
127	Bear Stearns Companies	Securities	★	126.00	Avg	B	19,096	8,701	12.4	0.7
128	Becton, Dickinson and Company	Medical Equipment	★★★	74.00	-Avg	C	17,302	5,835	23.8	1.3
129	Bed Bath & Beyond	Furniture Retail	★★★	43.00	Avg	D	10,770	6,137	19.8	0.0
130	Bemis	Packaging	★★★	35.00	Avg	B	3,562	3,631	20.2	2.2
131	Berkshire Hathaway B	Insurance (General)	★★★★★	4550.00	-Avg	A	169,636	97,676	13.5	0.0
132	Best Buy Co.	Electronics Stores	★★★★	58.00	Avg	B	23,624	32,590	21.7	0.7
133	BG Group PLC ADR	Oil & Gas	★★	57.00	Avg	—	48,575	9,900	17.4	0.9
134	Biogen Idec	Biotechnology	★★★	51.00	Avg	B	16,583	2,608	106.9	0.0
135	Biomarin Pharmaceutical	Biotechnology	★★★	18.00	+Avg	B	1,497	72	—	0.0
136	Blackrock	Money Management	★	117.00	Avg	C	17,686	1,449	44.9	1.1
137	Blue Nile	Jewelry/Accessories	★★★★	42.00	Avg	B	591	234	52.0	0.0
138	Boeing	Aerospace & Defense	★★★	95.00	Avg	B	70,249	59,114	41.1	1.4
139	Boston Beer Company A	Alcoholic Drinks	★★★	33.00	Avg	C	506	277	28.6	0.0
140	Boston Scientific	Medical Equipment	★★★★★	25.00	Avg	C	25,323	7,296	—	0.0
141	BP PLC ADR	Oil & Gas	★★★	72.00	Avg	—	231,015	239,792	10.9	3.4
142	Bristol-Myers Squibb	Drugs	★★★	26.00	+Avg	C	51,764	18,720	23.3	4.3
143	British American Tobacco PLC ADR	Tobacco	★★★	60.00	+Avg	—	59,384	43,778	18.5	3.1
144	Broadcom	Semiconductors	★★★★	40.00	+Avg	D	17,619	3,021	39.3	0.0
145	Brookfield Asset Management	Finance	★★★	48.00	Avg	B	41,886	5,256	26.6	1.4
146	Brown & Brown	Insurance (General)	★★★	30.00	Avg	A	3,948	860	23.1	0.7
147	Brown-Forman B	Alcoholic Drinks	★★★	68.00	-Avg	C	8,153	2,606	20.7	1.7
148	Brunswick	Recreation	★★★★	37.00	Avg	B	2,929	5,993	9.7	1.9
149	BT Group PLC ADR	Telecom Services	★★★	59.00	Avg	B	51,717	35,025	18.4	4.0
150	Buckeye Partners LP	Pipelines	★★★	51.00	-Avg	C	1,833	442	17.8	6.5
151	Burlington Northern Santa Fe	Land Transport	★★★	82.00	Avg	B	26,513	14,653	15.4	1.2
152	Cadbury Schweppes PLC ADR	Food Mfg.	★★★★	49.00	-Avg	—	22,367	11,879	17.6	2.2
153	Calamos Asset Management A	Money Management	★★★	26.00	Avg	D	621	477	18.9	1.3
154	Campbell Soup	Food Mfg.	★★★	37.00	-Avg	B	15,125	7,494	21.4	2.0
155	Canadian Imperial Bank of Commerce	International Banks	★★★	79.00	Avg	—	28,319	9,934	12.9	2.9
156	Canadian National Railway	Land Transport	★★★	45.00	Avg	A	23,096	5,983	18.8	1.3
157	Canadian Natural Resources	Oil & Gas	★★★	53.00	Avg	B	28,550	7,224	33.0	0.5
158	Capital One Financial	Finance	★★★	87.00	+Avg	B	23,411	11,731	10.3	0.1
159	Cardinal Health	Medical Goods & Services	★★★	78.00	Avg	C	26,095	83,483	22.2	0.5
160	CarMax	Auto Retail	★★★★	63.00	Avg	B	5,729	6,862	38.6	0.0
161	Carnival	Recreation	★★★★	58.00	Avg	B	40,975	11,595	18.4	2.1
162	Caterpillar	Construction Machinery	★★★	66.00	Avg	B	39,897	40,177	12.0	1.8
163	CBOT Holdings	Securities	★★★★	193.00	Avg	B	8,004	582	—	0.0
164	CBS B	Media Conglomerates	★★★★	36.00	Avg	C	24,368	14,650	—	2.4
165	CDW	Distributors	★★★	76.00	Avg	B	5,512	6,569	20.2	0.7
166	Celgene	Biotechnology	★	42.00	+Avg	B	20,276	773	—	0.0
167	Cemex SAB de CV ADR	Building Materials	★★★★★	45.00	Avg	—	26,008	15,094	11.3	0.0
168	Centex	Home Building	★★★★	64.00	Avg	A	6,679	14,672	6.1	0.3
169	Centurytel	Telecom Services	★★	37.00	Avg	C	5,012	2,461	14.4	0.6
170	CH Robinson Worldwide	Transportation - Misc	★★★	45.00	Avg	B	7,121	6,497	28.4	1.4
171	Charles River Laboratories International	Research Services	★★★★	51.00	Avg	B	2,893	1,174	—	0.0
172	Checkfree	Systems & Security	★★★★★	55.00	Avg	D	3,555	894	31.1	0.0
173	Chevron	Oil & Gas	★★★	77.00	Avg	B	160,294	216,166	9.3	2.7
174	Chicago Mercantile Exchange	Securities	★★★★	627.00	Avg	B	17,747	1,062	46.9	0.5
175	Chico's FAS	Clothing Stores	★★★★	27.00	Avg	B	3,636	1,576	19.5	0.0
176	Chipotle Mexican Grill A	Restaurants	★★★	51.00	Avg	B	1,860	777	—	0.7
177	Cimarex Energy	Oil & Gas	★★★★★	59.00	Avg	B	3,024	1,401	6.4	0.4
178	Cintas	Business Support	★★★	45.00	Avg	A	6,376	3,494	20.5	0.9

24   Index and Tables

Morningstar Stocks 500
Company Index

Pg	Company	Industry	Star Rating	Fair Value Estimate ($)	Business Risk	Stewardship Grade	Market Cap ($Mil)	Revenue ($Mil)	Price/ Earnings	Dividend Yield %
179	Cisco Systems	Data Networking	★★★	30.00	Avg	B	165,967	30,118	30.7	0.0
180	CIT Group	Finance	★★★	60.00	Avg	B	11,059	3,953	11.3	1.4
181	Citigroup	International Banks	★★★	60.00	Avg	B	273,691	86,566	13.3	3.5
182	Citizens Communications	Telecom Services	★★★	13.00	Avg	C	4,626	2,184	17.1	7.0
183	City National	Regional Banks	★★★	74.00	Avg	B	3,612	846	15.2	2.3
184	Clear Channel Outdoor Holdings	Advertising	★	20.00	Avg	C	9,894	2,802	—	0.4
185	Clorox	Household & Personal Prod	★★★	61.00	-Avg	B	9,739	4,701	22.2	1.8
186	CNOOC ADR	Oil & Gas	★★	79.00	+Avg	—	38,850	8,462	12.7	3.0
187	Coach	Jewelry/Accessories	★★	38.00	Avg	B	15,787	2,216	33.8	0.0
188	Coca-Cola	Beverage Mfg.	★★★★	55.00	Avg	C	113,088	23,707	21.5	2.6
189	Colgate-Palmolive	Household & Personal Prod	★★★	63.00	-Avg	B	33,554	11,933	27.4	1.9
190	Comcast A	Cable TV	★★★	38.00	Avg	C	88,095	24,531	45.0	0.0
191	Comerica	Regional Banks	★★★	66.00	Avg	B	9,322	2,904	11.8	4.0
192	Commerce Bancorp NJ	Regional Banks	★★★	36.00	Avg	D	6,614	1,771	23.8	1.4
193	Companhia Vale Do Rio Doce	Steel/Iron	★	21.00	+Avg	—	68,492	12,792	14.2	1.8
194	Compass Minerals International	Mining	★★★★★	41.00	Avg	B	1,012	733	27.0	3.9
195	ConocoPhillips	Oil & Gas	★★★	73.00	Avg	C	118,413	198,161	6.9	2.0
196	Consolidated Edison	Electric Utilities	★★★	49.00	-Avg	B	12,344	12,481	17.5	4.8
197	Costco Wholesale	Discount Stores	★★★	51.00	Avg	A	24,229	60,151	23.0	1.0
198	Countrywide Financial	Savings & Loans	★★★	46.00	Avg	C	26,365	11,251	9.8	1.4
199	Covance	Research Services	★★★	60.00	Avg	B	3,769	1,390	27.8	0.0
200	CVS	Specialty Retail	★★★	32.00	Avg	C	25,456	41,480	19.4	0.5
201	Danaher	Electric Equipment	★★★	78.00	Avg	B	22,297	9,200	22.2	0.1
202	Darden Restaurants	Restaurants	★★★	44.00	-Avg	B	5,898	5,767	18.6	1.1
203	DCP Midstream Partners LP	Pipelines	★★★	33.00	Avg	D	365	591	—	3.6
204	Deere & Company	Agricultural Machinery	★★★	90.00	Avg	A	21,631	22,148	15.4	1.7
205	Dell	Computer Equipment	★★★★★	34.00	Avg	D	56,995	56,738	17.2	0.0
206	Devon Energy	Oil & Gas	★★★★★	93.00	Avg	C	29,649	11,274	9.4	0.7
207	DeVry	Education	★★★	30.00	Avg	C	1,983	867	45.9	0.2
208	Diageo PLC ADR	Alcoholic Drinks	★★★	86.00	-Avg	—	60,493	12,931	16.6	2.9
209	DirecTV	Cable TV	★★	20.00	Avg	C	30,516	14,168	27.1	0.0
210	Discovery Holding Company A	Media Conglomerates	★★★	16.00	Avg	F	4,508	664	—	0.0
211	Dominion Resources	Electric Utilities	★★★	85.00	Avg	B	29,656	17,641	18.3	3.3
212	Donaldson	Environmental Control	★★	29.00	Avg	B	2,801	1,737	22.4	1.0
213	Dover	Diversified	★★★	53.00	Avg	B	10,008	6,969	16.9	1.4
214	Dow Jones & Company	Media Conglomerates	★★★	35.00	Avg	D	3,170	1,853	21.2	2.6
215	DR Horton	Home Building	★★★	29.00	Avg	C	8,306	15,051	6.8	1.9
216	Dun & Bradstreet	Business/Online Services	★★	64.00	-Avg	C	5,084	1,503	23.1	0.0
217	Eaton	Electric Equipment	★★★	75.00	Avg	C	11,196	12,181	13.0	2.0
218	Eaton Vance	Money Management	★★★	33.00	Avg	B	4,194	832	25.6	1.3
219	eBay	Online Retail	★★★★★	45.00	-Avg	B	41,921	5,579	40.6	0.0
220	EchoStar Communications	Cable TV	★★	33.00	Avg	B	16,923	9,398	28.8	0.0
221	Ecolab	Chemicals	★★★★	50.00	-Avg	C	11,352	4,766	33.2	0.9
222	Educate	Education	★★★	8.00	Avg	C	306	353	—	0.0
223	Electronic Arts	Entertain./Education Media	★★★★	61.00	Avg	B	15,536	3,107	67.2	0.0
224	Eli Lilly & Company	Drugs	★★★★	61.00	Avg	B	58,956	15,325	17.4	3.1
225	Embarq	Telecom Services	★★★	58.00	Avg	C	7,857	6,349	—	1.9
226	EMC	Computer Equipment	★★★★★	19.00	Avg	D	29,072	10,651	30.7	0.0
227	Emerson Electric	Electric Equipment	★★★	43.00	-Avg	B	35,376	20,133	19.7	2.1
228	Empresa Brasileira ADR	Aerospace & Defense	★★★	44.00	+Avg	—	7,440	—	19.7	2.0
229	Energy Transfer Equity LP	Oil & Gas Services	★★★★★	39.00	-Avg	D	6,595	7,859	—	0.9
230	Energy Transfer Partners	Oil & Gas	★★★★★	69.00	-Avg	C	5,999	7,859	17.2	4.7
231	Enersis ADR	Electric Utilities	★★★	15.00	+Avg	—	10,448	5,710	—	1.2
232	ENI SpA ADR	Oil & Gas	★★★	67.00	Avg	—	53,896	93,324	4.6	4.7
233	Enterprise GP Holdings LP	Natural Gas Utilities	★★★★	43.00	Avg	B	3,286	14,421	—	3.3
234	EOG Resources	Oil & Gas	★★★★	77.00	Avg	B	15,205	4,186	10.1	0.4
235	Equifax	Business Support	★★★	37.00	Avg	C	5,080	1,518	19.4	0.4
236	Equity Residential	REITS	★	35.00	-Avg	A	14,826	2,187	115.3	3.5
237	Estee Lauder A	Household & Personal Prod	★★★	41.00	Avg	C	8,522	6,560	27.4	1.2
238	Expedia	Online Retail	★★★★★	30.00	Avg	—	6,947	2,201	—	0.0

Morningstar Stocks 500
Company Index

Pg	Company	Industry	Star Rating	Fair Value Estimate ($)	Business Risk	Stewardship Grade	Market Cap ($Mil)	Revenue ($Mil)	Price/ Earnings	Dividend Yield %
239	Expeditors International	Transportation - Misc	★★★★★	56.00	-Avg	A	8,633	4,486	32.9	0.5
240	ExxonMobil	Oil & Gas	★★★	79.00	-Avg	B	446,944	386,951	11.7	1.7
241	F5 Networks	Data Networking	★★★	72.00	+Avg	B	3,050	394	46.7	0.0
242	Fair Isaac	Data Processing	★★★	44.00	Avg	B	2,349	825	25.6	0.2
243	Fairfax Financial Holdings	Insurance (General)	★★★	275.00	Spec	C	3,705	5,878	—	0.0
244	Fastenal	Distributors	★★★★★	53.00	-Avg	A	5,416	1,745	28.0	1.1
245	Federated Investors B	Money Management	★★★★★	46.00	Avg	C	3,548	971	18.9	2.0
246	FedEx	Transportation - Misc	★★★	122.00	Avg	C	33,307	33,132	18.6	0.3
247	FEMSA ADR	Beverage Mfg.	★★★	123.00	Avg	—	10,475	9,794	29.0	0.7
248	Fidelity National Financial	Insurance (Title)	★★★	25.00	Avg	C	4,163	6,048	—	4.9
249	Fifth Third Bancorp	Super Regional Banks	★★★	44.00	Avg	B	22,842	5,431	15.7	3.9
250	First American	Insurance (Title)	★★★★★	61.00	Avg	A	3,932	8,360	8.4	1.8
251	First Data	Data Processing	★★★	23.00	Avg	D	19,543	10,806	12.3	0.8
252	First Horizon National	Regional Banks	★★★★	52.00	Avg	B	5,200	2,275	17.4	4.3
253	FirstEnergy	Electric Utilities	★★★	59.00	Avg	C	19,248	11,923	16.6	3.0
254	Fiserv	Data Processing	★★★	49.00	Avg	C	9,078	4,425	19.5	0.0
255	Forest Laboratories	Drugs	★★	42.00	Avg	B	16,026	2,965	24.3	0.0
256	Forward Air	Land Transport	★★★★★	40.00	Avg	B	881	349	18.7	1.0
257	France Telecom SA ADR	Telecom Services	★★★★	34.00	Avg	—	72,105	61,407	10.1	4.5
258	Franklin Resources	Money Management	★	77.00	Avg	A	27,932	5,051	22.7	0.5
259	Gamco Investors	Money Management	★★★★	44.00	Avg	D	1,086	250	17.6	0.3
260	Gannett	Media Conglomerates	★★★	65.00	Avg	D	14,167	7,880	12.5	2.0
261	Gap	Clothing Stores	★★★★	23.00	+Avg	A	15,807	15,834	15.7	1.9
262	Genentech	Biotechnology	★★★	86.00	Avg	C	85,511	8,462	47.2	0.0
263	General Dynamics	Aerospace & Defense	★★★	70.00	Avg	A	30,085	23,582	18.2	1.2
264	General Electric	Electric Equipment	★★★	38.00	Avg	B	383,564	161,022	19.8	2.8
265	General Mills	Food Mfg.	★★★	57.00	-Avg	C	19,761	11,821	19.9	2.4
266	Gen-Probe	Research Services	★★★	53.00	Avg	C	2,727	352	45.9	0.0
267	Genuine Parts	Auto Retail	★★★	48.00	-Avg	B	8,082	10,325	17.6	2.8
268	Genzyme	Biotechnology	★★★★	71.00	Avg	B	16,187	3,061	46.7	0.0
269	Gerdau SA ADR PN	Steel/Iron	★★★★	20.00	+Avg	—	10,681	8,894	9.5	3.7
270	Getty Images	Business Support	★★★★★	69.00	Avg	C	2,559	790	19.1	0.0
271	Gilead Sciences	Biotechnology	★★★	57.00	+Avg	C	29,857	2,736	41.1	0.0
272	Given Imaging	Medical Equipment	★★★★	25.00	Avg	—	541	87	92.1	0.0
273	GlaxoSmithKline PLC ADR	Drugs	★★★★	63.00	Avg	—	157,300	39,536	17.6	3.3
274	Global Cash Access Holdings	Data Processing	★★★★	20.00	+Avg	B	1,336	522	—	0.0
275	Goldman Sachs Group	Securities	★★	161.00	Avg	B	84,890	34,181	12.1	0.7
276	Google	Business/Online Services	★	315.00	Avg	C	140,519	9,319	58.6	0.0
277	Graco	Machinery	★★★	43.00	Avg	B	2,664	799	18.8	1.5
278	Groupe Danone ADR	Food Mfg.	★★★	33.00	Avg	—	43,070	16,309	22.2	1.2
279	H & R Block	Personal Services	★★★	25.00	+Avg	C	7,426	4,757	15.7	2.3
280	H.J. Heinz	Food Mfg.	★★	40.00	Avg	C	14,830	8,878	34.9	3.0
281	Halliburton	Oil & Gas Services	★	23.00	Avg	C	31,221	22,886	12.0	1.0
282	Hansen Natural	Beverage Mfg.	★★★★	46.00	+Avg	A	3,060	479	37.5	0.0
283	Harley-Davidson	Recreation	★★★	64.00	Avg	B	18,261	6,008	18.6	1.1
284	Harrah's Entertainment	Gambling/Hotel Casinos	★★★	82.00	Avg	B	15,388	9,439	43.5	1.8
285	Hawaiian Electric Industries	Electric Utilities	★★★	28.00	-Avg	B	2,556	—	17.3	4.6
286	Heartland Payment Systems	Data Processing	★★★	31.00	+Avg	C	1,050	1,036	—	0.2
287	Hershey Company	Food Mfg.	★★★	55.00	-Avg	C	11,546	4,951	20.9	2.1
288	Hewlett-Packard	Computer Equipment	★	30.00	Avg	B	112,070	91,658	18.9	0.8
289	Hilton Hotels	Hotels	★	26.00	Avg	C	13,493	7,013	30.4	0.5
290	Home Depot	Home Supply	★★★★	44.00	-Avg	D	81,961	90,061	14.8	1.7
291	Honeywell International	Diversified	★★	37.00	Avg	C	36,939	30,367	18.7	2.0
292	Hospira	Drugs	★★★★	43.00	Avg	B	5,232	2,628	25.1	0.0
293	HSBC Holdings PLC ADR	International Banks	★★★	97.00	Avg	—	204,784	49,836	13.6	4.1
294	IAC/InterActiveCorp	Online Retail	★★★★	42.00	Avg	C	11,864	6,568	40.4	0.0
295	IBM	Computer Equipment	★★★	94.00	-Avg	B	146,342	89,593	16.8	1.1
296	Idexx Laboratories	Drugs	★★★	73.00	-Avg	B	2,482	714	29.5	0.0
297	Illinois Tool Works	Machinery	★★★	50.00	Avg	B	26,184	13,798	15.7	1.6
298	Imperial Oil	Oil & Gas	★★★	38.00	Avg	B	35,457	23,051	37.4	0.8

Index and Tables

Morningstar Stocks 500
Company Index

Pg	Company	Industry	Star Rating	Fair Value Estimate ($)	Business Risk	Stewardship Grade	Market Cap ($Mil)	Revenue ($Mil)	Price/ Earnings	Dividend Yield %
299	Imperial Tobacco Group PLC ADR	Tobacco	★★★	70.00	+Avg	—	28,814	20,706	27.3	2.7
300	Infosys Technologies ADR	Business Applications	★★	48.00	Avg	—	29,525	2,152	54.6	0.9
301	Ingersoll-Rand A	Machinery	★★★★	44.00	Avg	B	11,997	11,232	11.6	1.7
302	Intel	Semiconductors	★★★	21.00	Avg	B	116,762	35,889	20.3	2.0
303	IntercontinentalExchange	Securities	★★★	110.00	+Avg	B	6,198	260	—	0.0
304	International Game Tech	Gambling/Hotel Casinos	★★★	44.00	Avg	B	15,492	2,512	34.5	1.1
305	International Speedway A	Recreation	★★★★	63.00	Avg	C	2,724	782	16.6	0.2
306	Intuit	Business Applications	★★★	33.00	Avg	B	10,637	2,400	29.1	0.0
307	Iowa Telecommunications Services	Telecom Services	★★★	18.00	+Avg	B	625	232	15.1	8.2
308	Iron Mountain	Business Support	★★★★	30.67	-Avg	A	5,474	2,279	45.5	0.0
309	J.P. Morgan Chase & Co.	International Banks	★★★★	61.00	Avg	A	167,551	59,650	13.7	2.8
310	Jack Henry & Associates	Data Processing	★★★★	25.00	-Avg	B	1,941	606	22.3	1.0
311	Jacobs Engineering Group	Engineering & Construction	★★	68.00	Avg	B	4,816	7,421	24.9	0.0
312	Janus Capital Group	Money Management	★★★	21.00	+Avg	D	4,279	1,008	42.3	0.2
313	JB Hunt Transport Services	Transportation - Misc	★★★★	24.00	Avg	B	2,997	3,335	14.2	1.5
314	JetBlue Airways	Air Transport	★	6.00	+Avg	A	2,495	2,176	—	0.0
315	John Wiley & Sons A	Publishing	★★★	39.00	-Avg	B	1,811	1,093	20.8	1.0
316	Johnson & Johnson	Drugs	★★★★	76.00	-Avg	B	191,415	52,252	17.4	2.2
317	Johnson Controls	Auto Parts	★★★	80.00	Avg	B	16,822	32,235	16.4	1.4
318	Jones Apparel Group	Apparel Makers	★★★	34.00	Avg	C	3,686	4,751	21.3	1.5
319	Jones Lang LaSalle	Real Estate	★	66.00	Avg	B	3,366	1,808	18.9	0.7
320	Juniper Networks	Data Networking	★★★★	22.00	Avg	B	10,715	2,182	32.1	0.0
321	Kellogg	Food Mfg.	★★★	50.00	-Avg	B	19,941	10,717	19.8	2.3
322	KeyCorp	Super Regional Banks	★★★	34.00	Avg	C	15,272	5,038	13.0	4.5
323	Kimberly-Clark	Household & Personal Prod	★★★	67.00	-Avg	B	31,142	16,449	22.4	2.9
324	Kinder Morgan Energy Partners	Pipelines	★★★	52.00	-Avg	A	7,797	9,919	33.7	6.7
325	Kinetic Concepts	Medical Equipment	★★★	37.00	+Avg	C	2,760	1,322	15.2	0.0
326	KLA-Tencor	Semiconductor Equipment	★★★	48.00	Avg	C	9,905	1,982	28.4	1.0
327	Kohl's	Discount Stores	★	53.00	Avg	C	22,378	14,765	28.2	0.0
328	Kraft Foods	Food Mfg.	★★★	35.00	-Avg	C	58,683	34,648	18.4	2.7
329	Laboratory Corp of America	Diagnostics	★★	64.00	Avg	B	9,213	3,515	23.9	0.0
330	Lee Enterprises	Publishing	★★★	29.00	Avg	C	1,430	1,129	19.9	2.3
331	Legg Mason	Money Management	★★★★	114.00	Avg	C	12,491	3,810	28.4	0.8
332	Lehman Brothers Holdings	Securities	★	61.00	Avg	B	41,408	16,740	12.2	0.6
333	Lennar	Home Building	★★★★	60.00	Avg	D	8,313	17,031	6.2	1.2
334	Leucadia National	Diversified	★★★	26.00	Avg	B	6,100	1,259	57.0	0.9
335	Lexmark International	Computer Equipment	★	53.00	Avg	C	7,168	5,104	23.8	0.0
336	Linear Technology	Semiconductors	★★★★★	45.00	Avg	B	9,064	1,129	22.1	2.0
337	Liz Claiborne	Apparel Makers	★★★★	50.00	Avg	B	4,454	4,865	17.5	0.5
338	Lloyds TSB Group PLC ADR	International Banks	★★★	49.00	Avg	—	63,492	41,482	14.1	5.4
339	Lockheed Martin	Aerospace & Defense	★★★	92.00	Avg	B	39,028	39,009	17.0	1.4
340	Lowe's Companies	Home Supply	★★★	33.00	-Avg	B	47,435	47,330	18.0	0.5
341	M & T Bank	Regional Banks	★★★	113.00	Avg	A	13,519	2,838	16.8	1.8
342	Macrovision	Business Applications	★★	23.00	Avg	C	1,448	234	70.7	0.0
343	Magellan Midstream Holdings LP	Pipelines	★★★★	25.00	-Avg	C	1,397	1,217	—	2.5
344	Manulife Financial	Insurance (General)	★★	29.00	Avg	—	53,527	26,485	20.1	1.9
345	Markel	Insurance (Property)	★★★	525.00	Avg	A	4,639	2,448	12.2	0.0
346	Marriott International A	Hotels	★	37.00	Avg	B	18,868	11,720	28.9	0.5
347	Marsh & McLennan Companies	Insurance (General)	★★★★★	43.00	Avg	B	16,897	11,715	28.7	2.2
348	Martin Marietta Materials	Mining	★★★	98.00	Avg	B	4,691	2,185	21.1	1.0
349	MasterCard	Data Processing	★★★	105.00	Avg	C	13,293	3,203	—	0.1
350	Maxim Integrated Products	Semiconductors	★★★★★	52.00	Avg	B	9,820	1,749	22.4	1.8
351	MBIA	Insurance (General)	★★★	76.00	+Avg	B	9,849	2,617	12.2	1.7
352	McCormick & Company	Food Mfg.	★★	35.00	-Avg	B	5,067	2,650	25.2	1.9
353	McDonald's	Restaurants	★★★	43.00	-Avg	A	54,825	21,790	19.2	2.3
354	McGraw-Hill Companies	Publishing	★★	58.00	-Avg	B	24,093	6,202	29.1	1.1
355	Medtronic	Medical Equipment	★★★★★	64.00	-Avg	A	61,597	11,808	25.6	0.8
356	Mellon Financial	International Banks	★★★★	50.00	Avg	C	17,360	5,092	20.3	2.0
357	Merck	Drugs	★★★	38.00	+Avg	B	94,656	22,358	18.8	3.5
358	Merrill Lynch & Company	Securities	★	71.00	Avg	B	82,298	32,796	14.1	1.1

Morningstar Stocks 500
Company Index

Pg	Company	Industry	Star Rating	Fair Value Estimate ($)	Business Risk	Stewardship Grade	Market Cap ($Mil)	Revenue ($Mil)	Price/ Earnings	Dividend Yield %
359	Metropolitan Life Insurance	Insurance (Life)	★★★	59.00	Avg	B	44,861	47,120	15.8	1.0
360	MGIC Investment	Insurance (Property)	★★★★	76.00	Avg	A	5,192	1,473	9.5	1.6
361	MGM Mirage	Gambling/Hotel Casinos	★★★	54.00	Avg	C	16,125	7,451	30.7	0.0
362	Microsoft	Business Applications	★★★★	34.00	-Avg	A	293,538	45,352	24.9	1.2
363	Millennium Pharmaceuticals	Biotechnology	★★★	11.00	+Avg	D	3,445	469	—	0.0
364	Mittal Steel Co NV	Steel/Iron	★★★	45.00	Avg	—	29,697	28,132	8.6	1.2
365	Mohawk Industries	Textiles	★★★★	95.00	Avg	B	5,070	7,812	12.8	0.0
366	Molson Coors Brewing Company	Alcoholic Drinks	★★★	76.00	Avg	C	6,595	5,698	22.6	1.7
367	Monsanto Company	Agrochemical	★★★	52.00	Avg	B	28,540	7,344	41.4	0.8
368	Monster Worldwide	Advertising	★	35.00	Avg	D	5,987	1,050	45.7	0.0
369	Moody's	Business Support	★★	57.00	-Avg	B	19,323	1,920	32.7	0.4
370	Morgan Stanley	Securities	★★★	83.00	Avg	B	86,198	32,195	12.3	1.3
371	Motorola	Wireless Equipment	★★★★	25.00	Avg	C	49,703	42,707	13.0	0.9
372	MSC Industrial Direct Co.	Distributors	★★★★★	60.00	Avg	B	2,622	1,318	19.6	1.4
373	Municipal Mortgage & Equity LLC	Finance	★★★	31.00	Avg	C	1,240	302	17.4	6.2
374	Nalco Holding	Chemicals	★★★	21.00	+Avg	B	2,927	3,519	34.1	0.0
375	Nasdaq Stock Market	Securities	★★★★★	52.00	+Avg	B	3,450	1,470	46.7	0.0
376	National City	Super Regional Banks	★★★★	43.00	Avg	B	22,015	7,757	12.2	4.2
377	Network Appliance	Computer Equipment	★	31.00	Avg	C	14,684	2,409	56.9	0.0
378	New Jersey Resources	Natural Gas Utilities	★★★★	56.00	-Avg	B	1,345	3,300	17.4	3.0
379	New York Times A	Media Conglomerates	★★★	22.00	Avg	C	3,503	3,392	19.7	2.8
380	News Corporation	Media Conglomerates	★★★	21.00	-Avg	C	70,411	25,559	24.2	0.4
381	Nike B	Shoes	★★★	105.00	Avg	B	24,827	15,287	18.8	1.3
382	Nokia ADR	Wireless Equipment	★★★	21.00	Avg	A	90,097	42,815	19.6	2.2
383	Norfolk Southern	Land Transport	★★★★	60.00	Avg	B	19,960	9,345	14.4	1.4
384	Nortel Networks	Wireline Equipment	★★★	30.00	+Avg	—	11,591	11,078	—	0.0
385	Northern Trust	International Banks	★★★	59.00	Avg	B	13,230	2,913	20.9	1.5
386	Northrop Grumman	Aerospace & Defense	★★★	64.00	Avg	B	23,384	30,448	16.7	1.7
387	Novartis AG ADR	Drugs	★★★★★	73.00	-Avg	—	134,175	32,526	21.9	1.6
388	Novo Nordisk ADR	Drugs	★★	69.00	Avg	—	27,072	5,671	27.9	1.2
389	Nucor	Steel/Iron	★★★	49.00	Avg	A	16,514	14,490	10.1	0.7
390	Nuveen Investments	Money Management	★★★	53.00	-Avg	B	4,085	671	23.7	1.8
391	NYSE Group	Securities	★★★★	128.00	+Avg	B	15,183	1,633	—	0.0
392	Occidental Petroleum	Oil & Gas	★★★	52.00	Avg	C	41,070	17,548	8.6	1.6
393	Odyssey Re Holdings	Reinsurance	★★★	36.00	+Avg	B	2,654	2,866	7.9	0.3
394	Omnicom Group	Advertising	★★★	95.00	Avg	B	17,866	11,100	21.8	1.0
395	ONEOK Partners LP	Pipelines	★★★	58.00	-Avg	C	2,939	3,730	12.8	5.7
396	Oracle	Business Applications	★★★★	22.00	Avg	B	89,050	15,203	26.8	0.0
397	Oshkosh Truck	Truck Makers	★★★	48.00	Avg	B	3,572	3,427	17.5	0.8
398	PACCAR	Truck Makers	★★★	61.00	Avg	C	16,116	15,860	11.5	1.2
399	Panera Bread	Restaurants	★★★★	66.00	Avg	C	1,768	769	31.8	0.0
400	Parker Hannifin	Machinery	★★★	82.00	Avg	B	9,066	9,824	14.6	1.3
401	Patterson Companies	Medical Goods & Services	★★★	36.00	Avg	C	4,941	2,727	24.8	0.0
402	Paychex	Data Processing	★★★	43.00	-Avg	A	15,069	1,785	32.4	1.7
403	PepsiCo	Beverage Mfg.	★★★★	74.00	-Avg	B	102,712	34,850	21.4	1.9
404	PetroChina Company ADR	Oil & Gas	★	104.00	+Avg	—	252,026	67,281	15.4	3.4
405	Petroleo Brasileiro ADR	Oil & Gas	★	78.00	+Avg	—	112,932	56,324	11.1	3.7
406	PetSmart	Specialty Retail	★★★★	34.00	Avg	B	3,917	4,118	23.1	0.4
407	Pfizer	Drugs	★★★	29.00	Avg	C	186,751	52,208	15.1	3.7
408	Pharmaceutical Product Development	Research Services	★★★	32.00	Avg	B	3,777	1,196	24.2	0.2
409	Philadelphia Consolidated Holding	Insurance (Property)	★	31.00	Avg	A	3,139	1,197	13.4	0.0
410	Pitney Bowes	Office Equipment	★★★	46.00	-Avg	C	10,249	5,737	19.4	2.8
411	Plains All American Pipeline LP	Pipelines	★★★★	61.00	Avg	B	4,147	26,767	17.1	5.6
412	PNC Financial Services Group	Super Regional Banks	★★★	76.00	Avg	B	21,754	8,735	8.6	2.9
413	Posco ADR	Steel/Iron	★★★	75.00	Avg	—	26,486	25,544	6.7	0.0
414	Potash Corp of Saskatchewan	Mining	★	115.00	Avg	A	14,951	3,674	27.0	0.4
415	Praxair	Chemicals	★★★	54.00	Avg	B	19,158	8,221	20.8	1.7
416	Precision Castparts	Metal Products	★★★	82.00	Avg	B	10,623	4,258	30.5	0.2
417	Procter & Gamble	Household & Personal Prod	★★★	67.00	-Avg	B	203,656	72,214	24.4	1.9
418	Progressive	Insurance (Property)	★★★	26.00	Avg	A	18,448	14,692	12.5	0.1

Morningstar Stocks 500
Company Index

Pg	Company	Industry	Star Rating	Fair Value Estimate ($)	Business Risk	Stewardship Grade	Market Cap ($Mil)	Revenue ($Mil)	Price/ Earnings	Dividend Yield %
419	ProLogis Trust	REITS	★	46.00	Avg	B	15,037	2,288	34.3	2.6
420	Pulte Homes	Home Building	★★★	37.00	Avg	B	8,432	15,017	7.0	0.5
421	Qualcomm	Wireless Equipment	★★★★	46.00	Avg	A	62,450	7,526	26.2	1.2
422	Quest Diagnostics	Diagnostics	★★★	57.00	Avg	B	10,338	6,194	17.9	0.7
423	Raytheon	Aerospace & Defense	★★★	50.00	Avg	B	23,476	22,766	19.7	1.8
424	Regency Energy Partners LP	Natural Gas Utilities	★★★	28.00	Avg	D	1,269	931	—	3.5
425	Reliance Steel and Aluminum	Metal Products	★★★★	45.00	Avg	A	2,974	5,042	8.3	0.6
426	Renaissance Re Holdings	Reinsurance	★★★★	75.00	+Avg	B	4,328	1,854	12.5	1.4
427	Republic Services A	Waste Management	★★★★	46.00	-Avg	B	5,307	3,043	20.4	1.5
428	Research in Motion	Computer Equipment	★★	110.00	+Avg	B	23,767	2,066	65.2	0.0
429	ResMed	Medical Equipment	★★	41.00	Avg	B	3,743	643	42.4	0.0
430	Resources Global Professionals	Employment	★	23.00	Avg	C	1,530	649	27.2	0.0
431	Respironics	Medical Equipment	★★★	39.00	Avg	C	3,019	1,073	27.8	0.0
432	Reynolds American	Tobacco	★★★	63.00	+Avg	C	19,353	8,488	16.2	4.2
433	Robert Half International	Employment	★★	32.00	-Avg	A	6,220	3,838	23.6	0.9
434	Rockwell Automation	Electric Equipment	★★★	64.00	Avg	B	10,394	5,561	17.5	1.6
435	Rockwell Collins	Aerospace & Defense	★★★	58.00	Avg	B	10,582	3,863	23.2	0.9
436	Ross Stores	Clothing Stores	★★	26.00	Avg	C	4,095	5,373	21.5	0.8
437	Royal Bank of Canada	International Banks	★★	41.00	Avg	B	61,039	20,637	13.2	2.7
438	Royal Caribbean Cruises	Recreation	★★★★★	55.00	Avg	B	8,775	5,106	15.1	1.5
439	Royal Dutch Shell PLC ADR A	Oil & Gas	★★★	73.00	-Avg	—	230,956	306,731	9.2	3.5
440	Ryanair Holdings PLC ADR	Air Transport	★	54.00	Avg	—	12,568	2,073	33.5	0.0
441	Salesforce.com	Business Applications	★★★	34.00	Avg	C	4,137	444	—	0.0
442	SanDisk	Semiconductors	★★★★	57.00	+Avg	B	8,464	2,844	23.5	0.0
443	Sanofi-Aventis ADR	Drugs	★★★	48.00	Avg	—	129,397	35,705	43.9	2.1
444	Sara Lee	Food Mfg.	★★★	15.00	Avg	D	12,719	16,072	32.1	3.5
445	Sasol ADR	Chemicals	★★★	32.00	+Avg	—	22,984	9,525	10.7	2.7
446	Schering-Plough	Drugs	★★★	27.00	+Avg	C	35,048	10,268	36.9	0.9
447	Schlumberger	Oil & Gas Services	★	30.00	Avg	C	74,416	17,904	24.0	0.8
448	Sealed Air	Packaging	★★★	68.00	Avg	A	5,234	4,258	23.1	0.9
449	SEI Investments	Business Support	★	44.00	-Avg	B	5,891	1,064	26.8	0.4
450	Siemens AG ADR	Wireline Equipment	★★	80.00	Avg	—	87,817	107,241	24.2	1.6
451	Sigma-Aldrich	Chemicals	★★★★	45.00	Avg	B	5,125	1,744	20.0	1.1
452	SLM	Finance	★★★★	57.00	-Avg	A	19,935	4,063	13.9	2.0
453	Smith & Nephew ADR	Medical Equipment	★★★	51.00	Avg	—	9,845	2,568	29.0	1.0
454	Smithfield Foods	Food Mfg.	★★★★	31.00	+Avg	B	2,870	11,183	15.9	0.0
455	Sony ADR	Audio/Video Equipment	★★★★	50.00	Avg	—	42,870	66,335	41.3	0.5
456	Southern	Electric Utilities	★★★	38.00	-Avg	B	28,133	14,494	17.8	4.2
457	Southwest Airlines	Air Transport	★★★	16.00	Avg	A	12,131	8,798	22.5	0.1
458	Sprint Nextel	Wireless Service	★★★★★	28.00	Avg	B	53,177	46,267	29.1	0.5
459	St. Jude Medical	Medical Equipment	★★★	41.00	Avg	C	12,923	3,229	34.5	0.0
460	Starbucks	Restaurants	★★★	35.00	Avg	C	26,737	7,787	49.9	0.0
461	Starwood Hotels & Resorts	Hotels	★★★	57.00	Avg	C	13,250	5,923	13.1	1.3
462	State Street	International Banks	★★	57.00	Avg	B	22,395	6,105	21.8	1.2
463	Steel Dynamics	Steel/Iron	★★★	32.00	Avg	A	2,981	2,969	9.6	1.1
464	Stericycle	Waste Management	★★	66.00	Avg	B	3,351	748	45.5	0.0
465	Strayer Education	Education	★★★	117.00	Avg	B	1,523	251	30.0	1.0
466	Stryker	Medical Equipment	★★★	51.00	-Avg	C	22,439	5,221	29.8	0.4
467	Student Loan	Finance	★★★★	235.00	-Avg	B	4,146	—	13.6	2.4
468	Suburban Propane Partners	Oil/Gas Products	★★★	38.00	Avg	C	1,152	1,662	13.4	6.6
469	Suncor Energy	Oil & Gas	★	62.00	Avg	A	36,114	9,162	35.8	0.3
470	SunTrust Banks	Super Regional Banks	★★★	83.00	-Avg	B	29,907	8,070	14.4	2.9
471	Synchronoss Technologies	Business Support	★★★★	18.00	+Avg	B	439	67	—	0.0
472	Synovus Financial	Regional Banks	★★★	31.00	Avg	B	10,019	3,138	17.0	2.5
473	Sysco	Food Wholesale	★★★	38.00	-Avg	B	22,722	33,290	27.2	1.9
474	T Rowe Price Group	Money Management	★★	36.00	Avg	A	11,539	1,729	24.4	1.3
475	Taiwan Semiconductor ADR	Semiconductors	★★★	9.50	+Avg	—	55,682	8,264	19.2	3.5
476	Target	Discount Stores	★★★★	65.00	-Avg	A	49,000	56,727	21.1	0.8
477	TCF Financial	Regional Banks	★★★	29.00	Avg	A	3,590	1,027	13.9	3.4
478	Telecom Corp of New Zealand	Telecom Services	★★★	30.00	Avg	—	6,599	3,879	—	6.5

Morningstar Stocks 500
Company Index

Pg	Company	Industry	Star Rating	Fair Value Estimate ($)	Business Risk	Stewardship Grade	Market Cap ($Mil)	Revenue ($Mil)	Price/ Earnings	Dividend Yield %
479	Telefonica SA ADR	Telecom Services	★★★★	78.00	Avg	—	104,574	49,213	18.6	3.2
480	Telefonos de Mexico SA de CV ADR	Telecom Services	★★★	30.00	Avg	—	31,150	15,116	12.4	2.6
481	Tellabs	Wireline Equipment	★★★★	12.00	Avg	C	4,533	2,108	18.0	0.0
482	TEPPCO Partners	Pipelines	★★★	43.00	-Avg	B	3,052	10,039	23.3	6.7
483	Ternium SA ADR	Steel/Iron	★★★★	35.00	+Avg	—	5,922	4,448	—	0.0
484	Tessera Technologies	Semiconductor Equipment	★★	33.00	Avg	B	1,894	183	35.7	0.0
485	Teva Pharmaceutical Industries ADR	Drugs	★★★	34.00	Avg	A	20,098	5,250	19.6	0.8
486	Texas Instruments	Semiconductors	★★★★	34.00	Avg	A	42,736	15,173	16.8	0.5
487	Textron	Aerospace & Defense	★★★	90.00	Avg	B	11,763	10,990	18.2	1.7
488	THQ	Entertain./Education Media	★★★	36.00	Avg	C	2,092	787	62.5	0.0
489	Tiffany	Jewelry/Accessories	★★★	36.00	Avg	C	5,311	2,520	22.4	1.0
490	Tim Hortons	Restaurants	★	22.00	Avg	—	5,581	1,597	—	0.4
491	Timberland	Shoes	★★★	35.00	Avg	C	1,971	1,545	17.8	0.0
492	Time Warner	Media Conglomerates	★★★	20.00	-Avg	C	86,932	44,532	19.1	1.0
493	TJX Companies	Clothing Stores	★★★	27.00	Avg	B	12,979	17,102	20.2	0.9
494	Toll Brothers	Home Building	★★★	32.00	Avg	C	4,947	6,335	6.5	0.0
495	Torchmark	Insurance (Life)	★★★	63.00	Avg	B	6,253	3,333	13.0	0.8
496	Toronto-Dominion Bank	International Banks	★★★	58.00	Avg	—	43,027	11,488	10.8	1.4
497	Total SA ADR	Oil & Gas	★★★	70.00	Avg	—	176,957	153,547	11.1	3.0
498	Total System Services	Data Processing	★★★	24.00	Avg	C	5,197	1,704	24.4	1.0
499	Toyota Motor ADR	Auto Makers	★★	108.00	Avg	—	217,700	186,677	18.0	0.0
500	Transatlantic Holdings	Reinsurance	★★★★	85.00	+Avg	B	4,097	3,929	12.6	0.8
501	TransCanada	Pipelines	★★★	33.00	-Avg	A	17,029	5,061	17.1	3.2
502	Tribune	Media Conglomerates	★★★	35.00	Avg	D	7,353	5,527	16.0	2.3
503	Tyco International	Diversified	★★★★	36.00	Avg	B	60,461	40,960	15.4	1.3
504	UAP Holding	Chemicals	★★	22.00	Avg	B	1,284	2,779	19.8	3.0
505	UBS AG	International Banks	★★★	60.00	Avg	—	118,774	7,706	—	2.1
506	Ultra Petroleum	Oil & Gas	★★★★	63.00	+Avg	C	7,254	609	30.6	0.0
507	Unilever NV	Food Mfg.	★★★	27.00	-Avg	—	46,726	49,679	17.4	3.1
508	United Parcel Service B	Transportation - Misc	★★★★★	88.00	-Avg	B	80,494	46,873	19.9	2.0
509	United Technologies	Diversified	★★★	60.00	-Avg	A	62,748	46,303	17.6	1.6
510	UnitedHealth Group	Managed Care	★★★	58.00	Avg	D	72,374	51,787	21.0	0.1
511	US Bancorp	Super Regional Banks	★★★	38.00	Avg	A	63,617	13,499	14.1	3.8
512	UST	Tobacco	★	44.00	Avg	C	9,364	1,840	18.6	3.9
513	UTi Worldwide	Transportation - Misc	★★★★	38.00	Avg	C	2,885	3,338	33.2	0.2
514	Valassis Communications	Publishing	★★★	14.00	Avg	B	693	1,066	10.7	0.0
515	Valero GP Holdings	Pipelines	★★★	26.00	Avg	—	1,055	—	—	1.0
516	Varian Medical Systems	Medical Equipment	★★★	47.00	Avg	B	6,140	1,598	26.4	0.0
517	VCA Antech	Medical Goods & Services	★★★	33.00	Avg	C	2,688	958	26.4	0.0
518	Ventana Medical Systems	Medical Equipment	★★★	47.00	Avg	B	1,593	226	51.2	0.0
519	Verizon Communications	Telecom Services	★★★	39.00	Avg	C	108,723	88,881	16.1	4.4
520	Viacom B	Media Conglomerates	★★★	40.00	Avg	C	28,691	10,598	—	0.0
521	Vodafone Group PLC ADR	Wireless Service	★★★	30.00	Avg	B	127,867	52,679	—	4.5
522	Vornado Realty Trust	REITS	★★	103.00	-Avg	C	17,259	2,696	38.2	2.7
523	Vulcan Materials	Mining	★★★	80.00	Avg	B	8,486	3,281	20.0	1.6
524	W.P. Stewart & Company	Money Management	★★★★	18.00	Avg	F	742	148	18.2	7.1
525	W.W. Grainger	Distributors	★★★	67.00	-Avg	B	6,017	5,812	16.5	1.6
526	Wachovia	Super Regional Banks	★★★	58.00	Avg	A	90,049	27,749	13.0	3.8
527	Walgreen	Specialty Retail	★★★	51.00	Avg	B	46,048	47,409	26.7	0.6
528	Wal-Mart Stores	Discount Stores	★★★★★	58.00	-Avg	A	192,479	339,150	17.2	1.5
529	Walt Disney	Media Conglomerates	★★	31.00	-Avg	B	70,886	34,285	20.9	0.9
530	Warner Music Group	Media Conglomerates	★★★	26.00	+Avg	C	3,423	3,516	57.4	1.7
531	Washington Mutual	Savings & Loans	★★★★	52.00	Avg	B	42,998	14,984	13.5	4.5
532	Washington Post Co	Media Conglomerates	★★★★	850.00	-Avg	B	7,167	3,813	21.4	1.0
533	Waste Management	Waste Management	★★★★	45.00	Avg	B	19,672	13,452	17.0	2.4
534	Waters	Medical Equipment	★★★	50.00	-Avg	B	4,970	1,226	24.1	0.0
535	Weight Watchers International	Personal Services	★★★	54.00	Avg	B	5,115	1,199	25.9	1.3
536	WellPoint	Managed Care	★★★★	88.00	Avg	C	48,789	54,285	17.2	0.0
537	Wells Fargo	Super Regional Banks	★★★★	41.00	Avg	B	120,049	34,770	14.7	3.0
538	Wendy's International	Restaurants	★★★	33.00	Avg	B	3,905	3,777	20.3	1.8

Morningstar Stocks 500
Company Index

Pg	Company	Industry	Star Rating	Fair Value Estimate ($)	Business Risk	Stewardship Grade	Market Cap ($Mil)	Revenue ($Mil)	Price/ Earnings	Dividend Yield %
539	Wesco Financial	Insurance (General)	★★★★	515.00	-Avg	A	3,275	914	10.6	0.3
540	Westamerica Bancorporation	Regional Banks	★★★	54.00	-Avg	B	1,558	244	15.7	2.6
541	White Mountains Insurance Group	Insurance (Property)	★★★★★	795.00	Avg	A	6,246	4,503	15.5	1.4
542	Whole Foods Market	Groceries	★★★★★	72.00	Avg	A	6,708	5,607	33.3	1.3
543	Williams Companies	Pipelines	★★★	24.00	Avg	B	15,576	12,719	65.3	1.3
544	Williams Partners LP	Pipelines	★★★	43.00	Avg	C	836	60	—	4.1
545	Williams-Sonoma	Furniture Retail	★★★★	39.00	Avg	B	3,526	3,687	17.4	1.0
546	Windstream	Telecom Services	★★★	13.00	Avg	C	6,780	558	—	8.7
547	Wipro ADR	Business Applications	★★	14.00	Avg	—	23,026	2,397	50.2	0.7
548	Wisconsin Energy	Electric Utilities	★★	43.00	-Avg	B	5,552	4,036	17.3	1.9
549	Wm. Wrigley Jr.	Food Mfg.	★★★★	59.00	-Avg	C	14,371	4,568	36.8	1.9
550	Wyeth	Drugs	★★★	45.00	Avg	C	68,574	19,877	17.0	2.0
551	Wyndham Worldwide	Hotels	★★★★	42.00	Avg	C	6,344	3,733	—	0.0
552	Xerox	Office Equipment	★★★	18.00	Avg	B	16,361	15,766	13.4	0.0
553	Xilinx	Semiconductors	★★★★	28.00	Avg	B	8,006	1,870	23.8	1.4
554	XTO Energy	Oil & Gas	★★★	53.00	Avg	D	17,217	4,554	9.2	0.7
555	Yahoo	Media Conglomerates	★★★★★	34.00	Avg	C	34,740	6,224	32.3	0.0
556	Yum Brands	Restaurants	★★★	61.00	Avg	C	15,586	9,444	20.6	0.9
557	Zebra Technologies	Computer Equipment	★★★★	45.00	Avg	C	2,451	729	30.8	0.0
558	Zimmer Holdings	Medical Equipment	★★★	79.00	-Avg	B	18,705	3,410	24.6	0.0

Morningstar Stocks 500
Industry Index

Pg	Industry/Company	Morningstar Rating	Moat
Software Sector			
	Business Applications		
109	Autodesk	★★★	Wide
114	Avid Technology	★★★★	Narrow
300	Infosys Technologies ADR	★★	Narrow
306	Intuit	★★★	Wide
342	Macrovision	★★	Narrow
362	Microsoft	★★★★	Wide
396	Oracle	★★★★	Wide
441	Salesforce.com	★★★	Narrow
547	Wipro ADR	★★	Narrow
Hardware Sector			
	Computer Equipment		
102	Apple Computer	★	Narrow
205	Dell	★★★★★	Wide
226	EMC	★★★★★	Narrow
288	Hewlett-Packard	★	Narrow
295	IBM	★★★	Wide
335	Lexmark International	★	Narrow
377	Network Appliance	★	Narrow
428	Research in Motion	★★	Narrow
557	Zebra Technologies	★★★★	Narrow
	Data Networking		
179	Cisco Systems	★★★	Wide
241	F5 Networks	★★★	Narrow
320	Juniper Networks	★★★★	Narrow
	Wireless Equipment		
371	Motorola	★★★★	Narrow
382	Nokia ADR	★★★	Narrow
421	Qualcomm	★★★★	Wide
Media Sector			
	Cable TV		
190	Comcast A	★★★	Wide
209	DirecTV	★★	Narrow
220	EchoStar Communications	★★	Narrow
	Media Conglomerates		
164	CBS B	★★★★	Narrow
210	Discovery Holding Company A	★★★	Narrow
214	Dow Jones & Company	★★★	Wide
260	Gannett	★★★	Narrow
379	New York Times A	★★★	Narrow
380	News Corporation	★★★	Narrow
492	Time Warner	★★★	Narrow
Telecom Sector			
	Telecom Services		
108	AT&T	★	Narrow
88	America Movil SA ADR	★★★	Narrow
149	BT Group PLC ADR	★★★	Narrow
169	Centurytel	★★	Narrow
182	Citizens Communications	★★★	Narrow
225	Embarq	★★★	Narrow
257	France Telecom SA ADR	★★★★	Narrow
307	Iowa Telecommunications Services	★★★	Narrow
478	Telecom Corp of New Zealand	★★★	Narrow

Pg	Industry/Company	Morningstar Rating	Moat
	Development Tools		
65	Adobe Systems	★★★	Wide
	Entertain./Education Media		
223	Electronic Arts	★★★★	Wide
488	THQ	★★★	None
	Systems & Security		
172	Checkfree	★★★★★	Wide
	Wireline Equipment		
72	Alcatel Lucent ADR	★★★★	Narrow
384	Nortel Networks	★★★	Narrow
450	Siemens AG ADR	★★	Narrow
481	Tellabs	★★★★	Narrow
	Semiconductor Equipment		
104	Applied Materials	★★★	Wide
326	KLA-Tencor	★★★	Wide
484	Tessera Technologies	★★	Narrow
	Semiconductors		
84	Altera	★★★	Narrow
97	Analog Devices	★★★★★	Narrow
144	Broadcom	★★★★	Narrow
302	Intel	★★★	Wide
336	Linear Technology	★★★★★	Wide
350	Maxim Integrated Products	★★★★★	Wide
442	SanDisk	★★★★	Narrow
475	Taiwan Semiconductor ADR	★★★	Narrow
486	Texas Instruments	★★★★	Narrow
553	Xilinx	★★★★	Narrow
502	Tribune	★★★	Narrow
520	Viacom B	★★★	Narrow
529	Walt Disney	★★	Narrow
530	Warner Music Group	★★★	Narrow
532	Washington Post Co	★★★★	Wide
555	Yahoo	★★★★★	Narrow
	Publishing		
315	John Wiley & Sons A	★★★	Wide
330	Lee Enterprises	★★★	Narrow
354	McGraw-Hill Companies	★★	Wide
514	Valassis Communications	★★★	Narrow
479	Telefonica SA ADR	★★★★	Narrow
480	Telefonos de Mexico SA de CV ADR	★★★	Narrow
519	Verizon Communications	★★★	Narrow
546	Windstream	★★★	Narrow
	Wireless Service		
83	Alltel	★★★	Narrow
458	Sprint Nextel	★★★★★	Narrow
521	Vodafone Group PLC ADR	★★★	Narrow

Morningstar Stocks 500
Industry Index

Pg	Industry/Company	Morningstar Rating	Moat
Healthcare Sector			
	Biotechnology		
95	Amgen	★★★★★	Wide
134	Biogen Idec	★★★	Wide
135	Biomarin Pharmaceutical	★★★	Narrow
166	Celgene	★	Narrow
262	Genentech	★★★	Wide
268	Genzyme	★★★★	Wide
271	Gilead Sciences	★★★	Narrow
363	Millennium Pharmaceuticals	★★★	Narrow
	Drugs		
60	Abbott Laboratories	★★★	Wide
74	Alcon	★★	Wide
76	Allergan	★★★	Wide
107	AstraZeneca PLC ADR	★★★	Wide
116	Axcan Pharma	★★★	Narrow
124	Barr Pharmaceuticals	★★★★	Narrow
142	Bristol-Myers Squibb	★★★	Wide
224	Eli Lilly & Company	★★★★	Wide
255	Forest Laboratories	★★	Narrow
273	GlaxoSmithKline PLC ADR	★★★★	Wide
292	Hospira	★★★★	Narrow
296	Idexx Laboratories	★★★	Narrow
316	Johnson & Johnson	★★★★	Wide
357	Merck	★★★	Wide
387	Novartis AG ADR	★★★★★	Wide
388	Novo Nordisk ADR	★★	Wide
407	Pfizer	★★★	Wide
443	Sanofi-Aventis ADR	★★★	Wide
446	Schering-Plough	★★★	Wide
485	Teva Pharmaceutical Industries ADR	★★★	Narrow
550	Wyeth	★★★	Wide
	Research Services		
171	Charles River Laboratories Internation	★★★★	Narrow
199	Covance	★★★	Narrow
266	Gen-Probe	★★★	Narrow
408	Pharmaceutical Product Development	★★★	Narrow
	Managed Care		
67	Aetna	★★	None
510	UnitedHealth Group	★★★	Narrow
536	WellPoint	★★★★	Narrow
	Diagnostics		
329	Laboratory Corp of America	★★	Narrow
422	Quest Diagnostics	★★★	Narrow
	Medical Equipment		
66	Advanced Medical Optics	★★★	Narrow
125	Baxter International	★★	Narrow
128	Becton, Dickinson and Company	★★★	Narrow
140	Boston Scientific	★★★★★	Wide
272	Given Imaging	★★★★	Narrow
325	Kinetic Concepts	★★★	Narrow
355	Medtronic	★★★★★	Wide
429	ResMed	★★	Narrow
431	Respironics	★★★	Narrow
453	Smith & Nephew ADR	★★★	Narrow
459	St. Jude Medical	★★★	Narrow
466	Stryker	★★★	Wide
516	Varian Medical Systems	★★★	Narrow
518	Ventana Medical Systems	★★★	Narrow
534	Waters	★★★	Wide
558	Zimmer Holdings	★★★	Wide
	Medical Goods & Services		
159	Cardinal Health	★★★★	Narrow
401	Patterson Companies	★★★	Narrow
517	VCA Antech	★★★	Narrow
Consumer Services			
	Education		
101	Apollo Group A	★★★★★	Wide
207	DeVry	★★★	Wide
222	Educate	★★★	Narrow
465	Strayer Education	★★★	Wide
	Personal Services		
279	H & R Block	★★★	Wide
535	Weight Watchers International	★★★	Wide
	Home Building		
168	Centex	★★★★	Narrow
215	DR Horton	★★★	Narrow
333	Lennar	★★★★	Narrow
420	Pulte Homes	★★★	Narrow
494	Toll Brothers	★★★	Narrow
	Home Supply		
290	Home Depot	★★★★	Wide
340	Lowe's Companies	★★★	Wide
	Auto Retail		
111	AutoNation	★★★	Narrow
112	AutoZone	★★★	Narrow
160	CarMax	★★★★	Narrow
267	Genuine Parts	★★★	Narrow
	Clothing Stores		
61	Abercrombie & Fitch A	★★	Narrow
99	Ann Taylor Stores	★★★	Narrow
175	Chico's FAS	★★★★	Narrow
261	Gap	★★★★	Narrow
436	Ross Stores	★★	Narrow
493	TJX Companies	★★★	Narrow
	Discount Stores		
197	Costco Wholesale	★★★	Narrow
327	Kohl's	★	Narrow
476	Target	★★★★	Narrow
528	Wal-Mart Stores	★★★★★	Wide
	Electronics Stores		
132	Best Buy Co.	★★★★	Narrow

Morningstar Stocks 500
Industry Index

Pg	Industry/Company	Morningstar Rating	Moat	Pg	Industry/Company	Morningstar Rating	Moat
Consumer Services (cont.)							
	Groceries				**Gambling/Hotel Casinos**		
542	Whole Foods Market	★★★★★	Narrow	284	Harrah's Entertainment	★★★	Narrow
	Food Wholesale			304	International Game Tech	★★★	Wide
473	Sysco	★★★	Wide	361	MGM Mirage	★★★	Narrow
	Furniture Retail				**Hotels**		
129	Bed Bath & Beyond	★★★	None	289	Hilton Hotels	★	Narrow
545	Williams-Sonoma	★★★★	Narrow	346	Marriott International A	★	Narrow
	Online Retail			461	Starwood Hotels & Resorts	★★★	Narrow
86	Amazon.com	★★	Wide	551	Wyndham Worldwide	★★★★	Narrow
238	Expedia	★★★★★	Narrow		**Restaurants**		
294	IAC/InterActiveCorp	★★★★	Narrow	103	Applebee's International	★★★★★	Narrow
219	eBay	★★★★★	Wide	176	Chipotle Mexican Grill A	★★★	None
	Specialty Retail			202	Darden Restaurants	★★★	Narrow
200	CVS	★★★	Narrow	353	McDonald's	★★★	Narrow
406	PetSmart	★★★★	Narrow	399	Panera Bread	★★★★	None
527	Walgreen	★★★	Wide	460	Starbucks	★★★	Narrow
				490	Tim Hortons	★	Narrow
				538	Wendy's International	★★★	Narrow
				556	Yum Brands	★★★	Narrow
Business Services							
	Advertising			251	First Data	★★★	Wide
184	Clear Channel Outdoor Holdings	★	Narrow	254	Fiserv	★★★	Wide
368	Monster Worldwide	★	Narrow	274	Global Cash Access Holdings	★★★★	Narrow
394	Omnicom Group	★★★	Narrow	286	Heartland Payment Systems	★★★	Narrow
	Business Support			310	Jack Henry & Associates	★★★★	Wide
178	Cintas	★★★	Wide	349	MasterCard	★★★	Wide
235	Equifax	★★★	Wide	402	Paychex	★★★	Wide
270	Getty Images	★★★★★	Wide	498	Total System Services	★★★	Wide
308	Iron Mountain	★★★★	Wide		**Distributors**		
369	Moody's	★★	Wide	165	CDW	★★★	Narrow
449	SEI Investments	★	Wide	244	Fastenal	★★★★★	Wide
471	Synchronoss Technologies	★★★★	Narrow	372	MSC Industrial Direct Co.	★★★★★	Narrow
	Consultants			525	W.W. Grainger	★★★	Narrow
62	Accenture	★★★	Narrow		**Air Transport**		
	Employment			70	AirTran Holdings	★★★	Narrow
430	Resources Global Professionals	★	Narrow	314	JetBlue Airways	★	Narrow
433	Robert Half International	★★	Narrow	440	Ryanair Holdings PLC ADR	★	Narrow
				457	Southwest Airlines	★★★	Narrow
	Engineering & Construction				**Land Transport**		
311	Jacobs Engineering Group	★★	Narrow	151	Burlington Northern Santa Fe	★★★	None
	Environmental Control			156	Canadian National Railway	★★★	Narrow
212	Donaldson	★★	Narrow	256	Forward Air	★★★★★	Wide
	Waste Management			383	Norfolk Southern	★★★★	None
81	Allied Waste Industries	★★★★	Narrow		**Transportation - Misc**		
427	Republic Services A	★★★★	Narrow	170	CH Robinson Worldwide	★★★	Wide
464	Stericycle	★★	Wide	239	Expeditors International	★★★★★	Wide
533	Waste Management	★★★★	Narrow	246	FedEx	★★★	Narrow
	Business/Online Services			313	JB Hunt Transport Services	★★★★	Narrow
216	Dun & Bradstreet	★★	Wide	513	UTi Worldwide	★★★★	Narrow
276	Google	★	Narrow	508	United Parcel Service B	★★★★★	Wide
	Data Processing						
110	Automatic Data Processing	★★★★	Wide				
242	Fair Isaac	★★★	Narrow				

Morningstar Stocks 500
Industry Index

Pg	Industry/Company	Morningstar Rating	Moat
Financial Services			
	International Banks		
80	Allied Irish Banks ADR	★★★	Wide
118	Bank of America	★★★★	Wide
119	Bank of Montreal	★★★	Wide
120	Bank of New York Company	★★★★	Wide
121	Bank of Nova Scotia	★★★	Wide
123	Barclays PLC ADR	★★★	Wide
155	Canadian Imperial Bank of Commerce	★★★	Wide
181	Citigroup	★★★	Wide
293	HSBC Holdings PLC ADR	★★★	Wide
309	J.P. Morgan Chase & Co.	★★★★	Wide
338	Lloyds TSB Group PLC ADR	★★★	Wide
356	Mellon Financial	★★★★	Wide
385	Northern Trust	★★★	Wide
437	Royal Bank of Canada	★★	Wide
462	State Street	★★	Wide
496	Toronto-Dominion Bank	★★★	Wide
505	UBS AG	★★★	Wide
	Regional Banks		
106	Associated Banc-Corp	★★★	Narrow
122	BankAtlantic Bancorp A	★★★★	Narrow
183	City National	★★★	Narrow
191	Comerica	★★★	Narrow
192	Commerce Bancorp NJ	★★★	Narrow
252	First Horizon National	★★★★	Narrow
341	M & T Bank	★★★	Narrow
472	Synovus Financial	★★★	Wide
477	TCF Financial	★★★	Narrow
540	Westamerica Bancorporation	★★★	Narrow
	Super Regional Banks		
126	BB&T	★★★	Narrow
249	Fifth Third Bancorp	★★★	Narrow
322	KeyCorp	★★★	Narrow
376	National City	★★★★	Narrow
412	PNC Financial Services Group	★★★	Narrow
470	SunTrust Banks	★★★	Narrow
511	US Bancorp	★★★	Wide
526	Wachovia	★★★	Narrow
537	Wells Fargo	★★★★	Wide
	Finance		
79	Allied Capital	★★★	Narrow
92	AmeriCredit	★★★	Narrow
89	American Express	★★★★	Wide
94	Ameriprise Financial	★★★	None
145	Brookfield Asset Management	★★★	Narrow
180	CIT Group	★★★	Narrow
158	Capital One Financial	★★★	Wide
373	Municipal Mortgage & Equity LLC	★★★	Narrow
452	SLM	★★★★	Wide
467	Student Loan	★★★★	Narrow
	Money Management		
77	Alliancebernstein Holding LP	★	Wide
136	Blackrock	★	Wide
153	Calamos Asset Management A	★★★	Wide
218	Eaton Vance	★★★	Wide
245	Federated Investors B	★★★★★	Wide
258	Franklin Resources	★	Wide
259	Gamco Investors	★★★★	Wide
312	Janus Capital Group	★★★	Narrow
331	Legg Mason	★★★★	Wide
390	Nuveen Investments	★★★	Wide
474	T Rowe Price Group	★★	Wide
524	W.P. Stewart & Company	★★★★	Wide
	Savings & Loans		
198	Countrywide Financial	★★★	Narrow
531	Washington Mutual	★★★★	Narrow
	Securities		
127	Bear Stearns Companies	★	Narrow
163	CBOT Holdings	★★★★	Wide
174	Chicago Mercantile Exchange	★★★★	Wide
275	Goldman Sachs Group	★★	Wide
303	IntercontinentalExchange	★★★	Wide
332	Lehman Brothers Holdings	★	Narrow
358	Merrill Lynch & Company	★	Wide
370	Morgan Stanley	★★★	Wide
391	NYSE Group	★★★★	Narrow
375	Nasdaq Stock Market	★★★★★	Narrow
	Insurance (General)		
105	Arthur J. Gallagher & Co.	★★★★	Narrow
131	Berkshire Hathaway B	★★★★★	Wide
146	Brown & Brown	★★★	Wide
243	Fairfax Financial Holdings	★★★	Narrow
351	MBIA	★★★	Narrow
344	Manulife Financial	★★	Narrow
347	Marsh & McLennan Companies	★★★★★	Wide
539	Wesco Financial	★★★★	Narrow
	Insurance (Life)		
68	Aflac	★★★★	Wide
359	Metropolitan Life Insurance	★★★	Narrow
495	Torchmark	★★★	Narrow
	Insurance (Property)		
63	ACE	★★★	Narrow
75	Alleghany	★★★★	Narrow
82	Allstate	★★	Narrow
90	American International Group	★★★	Narrow
360	MGIC Investment	★★★★	Narrow
345	Markel	★★★	Narrow
409	Philadelphia Consolidated Holding	★	Narrow
418	Progressive	★★★	Wide
541	White Mountains Insurance Group	★★★★★	Narrow
	Insurance (Title)		
248	Fidelity National Financial	★★★	Narrow
250	First American	★★★★★	Narrow
	Reinsurance		
393	Odyssey Re Holdings	★★★	Narrow
426	Renaissance Re Holdings	★★★★	Wide
500	Transatlantic Holdings	★★★★	Narrow
	Real Estate		
319	Jones Lang LaSalle	★	Narrow
	REITS		
113	AvalonBay Communities	★	Narrow
236	Equity Residential	★	Narrow
419	ProLogis Trust	★	Narrow
522	Vornado Realty Trust	★★	Narrow

Morningstar Stocks 500
Industry Index

Pg	Industry/Company	Morningstar Rating	Moat

Consumer Goods

Apparel Makers
318	Jones Apparel Group	★★★	Narrow
337	Liz Claiborne	★★★★	Narrow

Shoes
381	Nike B	★★★	Narrow
491	Timberland	★★★	Narrow

Textiles
365	Mohawk Industries	★★★★	Narrow

Auto Makers
499	Toyota Motor ADR	★★	Narrow

Audio/Video Equipment
455	Sony ADR	★★★★	Narrow

Jewelry/Accessories
137	Blue Nile	★★★★	Narrow
187	Coach	★★	Narrow
489	Tiffany	★★★	Narrow

Recreation
148	Brunswick	★★★★	Narrow
161	Carnival	★★★★	Narrow
283	Harley-Davidson	★★★	Wide
305	International Speedway A	★★★★	Wide
438	Royal Caribbean Cruises	★★★★★	Narrow

Alcoholic Drinks
87	AmBev ADR	★★★	Wide
98	Anheuser-Busch Companies	★★★★	Wide
139	Boston Beer Company A	★★★	Narrow
147	Brown-Forman B	★★★	Narrow
208	Diageo PLC ADR	★★★	Wide
366	Molson Coors Brewing Company	★★★	Narrow

Beverage Mfg.
188	Coca-Cola	★★★★	Wide
247	FEMSA ADR	★★★	Narrow
282	Hansen Natural	★★★★	Narrow
403	PepsiCo	★★★★	Wide

Food Mfg.
152	Cadbury Schweppes PLC ADR	★★★★	Wide
154	Campbell Soup	★★★	Wide
265	General Mills	★★★	Narrow
278	Groupe Danone ADR	★★★	Narrow
280	H.J. Heinz	★★	Narrow
287	Hershey Company	★★★	Wide
321	Kellogg	★★★	Narrow
328	Kraft Foods	★★★	Narrow
352	McCormick & Company	★★	Wide
444	Sara Lee	★★★	None
454	Smithfield Foods	★★★★	Narrow
507	Unilever NV	★★★	Narrow
549	Wm. Wrigley Jr.	★★★★	Wide

Household & Personal Prod
71	Alberto-Culver	★★★	None
115	Avon Products	★★★★	Wide
185	Clorox	★★★	Narrow
189	Colgate-Palmolive	★★★	Wide
237	Estee Lauder A	★★★	Narrow
323	Kimberly-Clark	★★★	Narrow
417	Procter & Gamble	★★★	Wide

Packaging
130	Bemis	★★★	Narrow
448	Sealed Air	★★★	Narrow

Tobacco
85	Altria Group	★★★	Wide
143	British American Tobacco PLC ADR	★★★	Wide
299	Imperial Tobacco Group PLC ADR	★★★	Wide
432	Reynolds American	★★★	Narrow
512	UST	★	Wide

Industrial Materials

Aerospace & Defense
78	Alliant Techsystems	★★★	Narrow
138	Boeing	★★★	Narrow
228	Empresa Brasileira ADR	★★★	Narrow
263	General Dynamics	★★★	Wide
339	Lockheed Martin	★★★	Wide
386	Northrop Grumman	★★★	Narrow
423	Raytheon	★★★	Narrow
435	Rockwell Collins	★★★	Narrow
487	Textron	★★★	Narrow

Agrochemical
367	Monsanto Company	★★★	Narrow

Chemicals
69	Air Products and Chemicals	★★★	Narrow
221	Ecolab	★★★★	Narrow
374	Nalco Holding	★★★	Narrow
415	Praxair	★★★	Narrow
445	Sasol ADR	★★★	Narrow
451	Sigma-Aldrich	★★★★	Narrow
504	UAP Holding	★★	Narrow

Agricultural Machinery
204	Deere & Company	★★★	Narrow

Construction Machinery
162	Caterpillar	★★★	Wide

Electric Equipment
64	Actuant A	★★★	Narrow
91	American Power Conversion	★★★	Narrow
201	Danaher	★★★	Narrow
217	Eaton	★★★	Narrow
227	Emerson Electric	★★★	Narrow
264	General Electric	★★★	Wide
434	Rockwell Automation	★★★	Narrow

Machinery
277	Graco	★★★	Narrow
297	Illinois Tool Works	★★★	Narrow
301	Ingersoll-Rand A	★★★★	None
400	Parker Hannifin	★★★	Narrow

Morningstar Stocks 500
Industry Index

Pg	Industry/Company	Morningstar Rating	Moat
Industrial Materials (cont.)			
	Office Equipment		
410	Pitney Bowes	★★★	Wide
552	Xerox	★★★	Narrow
	Truck Makers		
397	Oshkosh Truck	★★★	Narrow
398	PACCAR	★★★	Narrow
	Auto Parts		
317	Johnson Controls	★★★	Narrow
	Building Materials		
167	Cemex SAB de CV ADR	★★★★★	Narrow
	Diversified		
59	3M Company	★★★★	Wide
213	Dover	★★★	Narrow
291	Honeywell International	★★	Narrow
334	Leucadia National	★★★	Narrow
503	Tyco International	★★★★	Narrow
509	United Technologies	★★★	Wide
	Aluminum		
73	Alcoa	★★★★★	Narrow
	Metal Products		
416	Precision Castparts	★★★	Narrow
425	Reliance Steel and Aluminum	★★★★	Narrow
	Mining		
194	Compass Minerals International	★★★★★	Narrow
348	Martin Marietta Materials	★★★	Narrow
414	Potash Corp of Saskatchewan	★	Narrow
523	Vulcan Materials	★★★	Narrow
	Steel/Iron		
193	Companhia Vale Do Rio Doce	★	Narrow
269	Gerdau SA ADR PN	★★★★	Narrow
364	Mittal Steel Co NV	★★★	Narrow
389	Nucor	★★★	Narrow
413	Posco ADR	★★★	Narrow
463	Steel Dynamics	★★★	Narrow
483	Ternium SA ADR	★★★★	Narrow
Energy			
	Oil & Gas		
96	Anadarko Petroleum	★★★★	Narrow
100	Apache	★★★★	Narrow
133	BG Group PLC ADR	★★	Narrow
141	BP PLC ADR	★★★	Narrow
186	CNOOC ADR	★★	Narrow
157	Canadian Natural Resources	★★★	Narrow
173	Chevron	★★★	Narrow
177	Cimarex Energy	★★★★★	Narrow
195	ConocoPhillips	★★★	Narrow
206	Devon Energy	★★★★★	Narrow
232	ENI SpA ADR	★★★	Narrow
234	EOG Resources	★★★★	Narrow
230	Energy Transfer Partners	★★★★★	Narrow
240	ExxonMobil	★★★	Wide
298	Imperial Oil	★★★	Narrow
392	Occidental Petroleum	★★★	Narrow
404	PetroChina Company ADR	★	Narrow
405	Petroleo Brasileiro ADR	★	Narrow
439	Royal Dutch Shell PLC ADR A	★★★	Narrow
469	Suncor Energy	★	Narrow
497	Total SA ADR	★★★	Narrow
506	Ultra Petroleum	★★★★	Narrow
554	XTO Energy	★★★	Narrow
	Oil/Gas Products		
93	AmeriGas Partners	★★★	Narrow
468	Suburban Propane Partners	★★★	Narrow
	Oil & Gas Services		
117	Baker Hughes	★	Narrow
229	Energy Transfer Equity LP	★★★★★	Narrow
281	Halliburton	★	Narrow
447	Schlumberger	★	Narrow
	Pipelines		
150	Buckeye Partners LP	★★★	Wide
203	DCP Midstream Partners LP	★★★	Narrow
324	Kinder Morgan Energy Partners	★★★	Wide
343	Magellan Midstream Holdings LP	★★★★	Wide
395	ONEOK Partners LP	★★★	Wide
411	Plains All American Pipeline LP	★★★★	Narrow
482	TEPPCO Partners	★★★	Wide
501	TransCanada	★★★	Narrow
515	Valero GP Holdings	★★★	Narrow
543	Williams Companies	★★★	Narrow
544	Williams Partners LP	★★★	Narrow
Utilities			
	Electric Utilities		
196	Consolidated Edison	★★★	Narrow
211	Dominion Resources	★★★	Narrow
231	Enersis ADR	★★★	Narrow
253	FirstEnergy	★★★	Narrow
285	Hawaiian Electric Industries	★★★	Narrow
456	Southern	★★★	Narrow
548	Wisconsin Energy	★★	Narrow
	Natural Gas Utilities		
233	Enterprise GP Holdings LP	★★★★	Narrow
378	New Jersey Resources	★★★★	Narrow
424	Regency Energy Partners LP	★★★	Narrow

Benchmark Performance
Market Index

Category	Annual Total Return %					Annualized Total Return%		
	2006	2005	2004	2003	2002	3-Year	5-Year	10-Year
Index Benchmarks								
Morningstar Indexes								
Morningstar US Market	15.70	6.52	12.35	30.73	−22.17	11.46	7.10	8.48
Morningstar US Growth	6.83	6.41	4.37	34.12	−33.20	5.87	1.23	—
Morningstar US Core	15.76	5.19	15.62	28.63	−21.18	12.08	7.38	—
Morningstar US Value	24.10	7.82	16.85	29.75	−13.68	16.06	11.86	—
Morningstar Large Cap	15.91	4.87	9.54	27.04	−23.47	10.02	5.30	7.59
Morningstar Large Growth	5.68	3.43	0.19	30.65	−33.15	3.08	−0.89	—
Morningstar Large Core	15.54	3.82	13.99	24.71	−23.82	11.00	5.37	—
Morningstar Large Value	25.78	7.05	14.05	26.26	−15.05	15.37	10.50	—
Morningstar Mid Cap	14.32	12.70	19.66	38.38	−18.06	15.52	11.82	10.44
Morningstar Mid Growth	9.63	16.27	15.45	40.02	−32.54	13.75	6.81	—
Morningstar Mid Core	14.72	10.05	19.05	38.68	−12.42	14.55	12.79	—
Morningstar Mid Value	18.81	11.54	24.30	35.94	−10.00	18.10	15.04	—
Morningstar Small Cap	17.05	5.76	20.44	47.70	−20.36	14.24	11.89	10.25
Morningstar Small Growth	10.04	5.77	13.48	52.65	−36.87	9.72	4.94	—
Morningstar Small Core	21.16	6.30	23.61	42.59	−14.16	16.77	14.28	—
Morningstar Small Value	20.03	5.12	24.03	48.87	−8.24	16.10	16.41	—
Domestic Stock								
Dow Jones Industrial Average	19.05	1.72	5.31	28.28	−15.01	8.44	6.81	8.91
Dow Jones Utilities Average	16.63	25.14	30.24	29.39	−23.38	23.87	13.51	11.15
Dow Jones Transportation Average	9.81	11.65	27.73	31.84	−11.48	16.13	12.82	8.66
NASDAQ Composite	9.52	1.37	8.59	50.01	−31.53	6.43	4.37	6.46
Standard & Poor's 500 PR	13.62	3.00	8.99	26.38	−23.37	8.45	4.32	6.71
Russell Top 200 Value	22.99	4.60	13.34	26.75	−18.02	13.39	8.66	9.93
Russell Top 200 Growth	8.56	2.88	3.74	26.63	−27.98	5.03	1.11	4.78
Standard & Poor's Midcap 400 PR	8.99	11.27	15.16	34.02	−15.45	11.77	9.61	12.15
Russell Midcap Value	20.22	12.65	23.71	38.07	−9.64	18.77	15.88	13.65
Russell Midcap Growth	10.66	12.10	15.48	42.71	−27.41	12.73	8.22	8.62
DJ Wilshire 4500	16.07	10.27	18.57	43.72	−17.81	14.92	12.38	9.74
DJ Wilshire 5000	15.97	6.24	12.62	31.64	−20.86	11.54	7.65	8.67
Russell 2000	18.37	4.55	18.33	47.25	−20.48	13.56	11.39	9.44
Russell 2000 Value	23.48	4.71	22.25	46.03	−11.43	16.48	15.37	13.27
Russell 2000 Growth	13.35	4.15	14.31	48.54	−30.26	10.51	6.93	4.88
DJ Wilshire REIT	36.13	14.00	33.14	36.06	3.60	27.37	23.84	15.29
International Stock								
MSCI EAFE ID	23.47	10.86	17.59	35.28	−17.52	17.20	12.43	5.75
MSCI World ID	17.95	7.56	12.84	30.81	−21.06	12.70	8.13	6.11
MSCI Europe ID	30.22	6.54	17.85	34.79	−20.11	17.81	11.98	8.20
MSCI Pacific IL	9.58	35.39	12.32	19.74	−18.27	18.56	10.28	1.81
MSCI EM Latin America ID	39.34	44.92	34.77	67.06	−24.79	39.61	27.87	12.69
MSCI EM ID	29.18	30.31	22.45	51.59	−7.97	27.26	23.52	6.73
Bonds								
Lehman Brothers Aggregate Bond	4.33	2.43	4.34	4.10	10.25	3.70	5.06	6.24
Lehman Brothers Credit Bond	4.26	1.96	5.24	7.70	10.52	3.81	5.90	6.56
Credit Suisse High Yield	11.93	2.26	11.96	27.93	3.11	8.62	11.07	7.09
Miscellaneous								
3 Month T-Bill	5.06	3.34	1.43	1.05	1.68	3.27	2.50	3.76
Consumer Price Index(non-seasonallyadj)	3.42	3.26	1.88	2.38	1.55	3.30	2.61	2.60
JSE Gold (USD)	5.54	43.34	−27.75	11.47	130.33	3.01	22.92	2.68

Benchmark Performance
Market Index

Category	Annual Total Return %					Annualized Total Return%		
	2006	2005	2004	2003	2002	3-Year	5-Year	10-Year
Mutual Fund Benchmarks								
Domestic Stock								
Large Value	18.18	5.87	13.25	28.73	−18.00	12.27	8.38	8.80
Large Blend	14.15	6.00	10.40	27.90	−21.45	10.05	5.92	7.79
Large Growth	6.93	6.61	8.16	29.18	−26.82	7.15	2.88	5.88
Mid-Cap Value	15.89	8.25	18.76	36.14	−12.99	14.01	11.55	10.86
Mid-Cap Blend	13.92	9.19	16.34	37.86	−16.44	12.87	10.51	10.99
Mid-Cap Growth	9.01	10.03	13.87	36.19	−25.86	10.85	6.48	8.31
Small Value	16.26	5.81	20.93	42.73	−9.42	14.04	13.85	12.39
Small Blend	15.06	6.97	18.83	43.59	−16.44	13.49	11.72	11.24
Small Growth	10.49	5.91	11.87	46.15	−28.33	9.22	6.12	8.02
Stock Benchmarks								
Sectors								
Information Economy								
Software	16.43	−0.62	12.69	27.94	−29.93	7.99	2.04	8.75
Hardware	9.99	3.64	−1.53	65.45	−44.66	1.87	−0.10	6.26
Media	23.44	−8.42	5.10	31.50	−30.06	5.23	1.58	5.16
Telecommunications	34.97	−3.52	14.21	21.70	−22.68	12.20	7.86	4.95
Service Economy								
Health Care	7.73	10.23	4.17	24.66	−21.20	7.56	4.67	8.98
Consumer Services	11.27	1.83	19.92	33.98	−19.17	10.97	8.09	13.47
Business Services	15.95	12.55	15.21	32.93	−19.47	14.89	10.40	6.43
Financial Services	23.72	9.43	14.44	36.34	−12.98	15.22	13.10	13.60
Manufacturing Economy								
Consumer Goods	24.09	5.16	12.26	23.99	−3.91	13.55	12.11	8.49
Industrial Materials	22.99	9.70	20.92	39.93	−17.94	16.45	13.31	9.09
Energy	23.98	31.97	27.08	36.27	−5.86	25.54	21.04	14.39
Utilities	33.00	14.51	28.18	30.58	−18.56	24.92	15.73	10.64

Industry Performance
129 Industries, 7100 Stocks

Industry	Annual Total Return %					Annualized Total Return%		
	2006	2005	2004	2003	2002	3-Year	5-Year	10-Year
Advertising	24.58	-0.65	6.07	30.64	-36.56	9.44	1.61	11.18
Aerospace & Defense	28.35	17.67	21.89	16.68	-0.21	22.82	16.00	7.69
Agricultural Machinery	27.73	9.80	19.80	41.60	6.11	19.08	19.76	8.47
Agriculture	30.92	7.15	40.84	31.85	-6.55	25.46	20.56	6.97
Agrochemical	32.69	34.96	72.23	46.11	-30.99	45.53	26.55	9.02
Air Transport	33.92	12.50	-5.78	36.95	-30.38	12.17	4.87	6.52
Alcoholic Drinks	34.54	9.92	9.27	18.87	1.68	17.05	14.32	14.20
Aluminum	14.70	-0.08	-7.82	67.38	-29.48	1.87	3.52	7.79
Apparel Makers	28.48	8.15	24.39	24.21	3.49	20.31	16.21	10.44
Appliance & Furniture Makers	-0.26	7.29	3.24	35.75	-9.70	3.49	5.46	6.94
Assisted Living	28.05	20.18	13.96	80.87	-18.77	20.79	21.21	8.17
Audio/Video Equipment	10.98	2.40	3.65	31.92	-30.06	5.16	0.46	6.37
Auto Makers	34.77	8.39	6.71	41.81	-10.68	15.66	13.60	8.65
Auto Parts	19.72	-13.63	9.44	52.04	-11.74	4.18	8.03	3.93
Auto Retail	15.83	9.96	9.46	39.01	-10.68	12.08	12.68	7.62
Beverage Mfg.	18.11	7.39	-3.04	14.85	-6.68	7.33	5.87	4.53
Biotechnology	-3.76	22.66	8.46	54.50	-41.10	8.32	3.56	12.51
Broadcast TV	31.92	-6.55	-12.00	48.41	-45.36	2.77	-2.99	6.60
Building Materials	24.16	23.09	43.77	43.20	-12.80	29.88	21.73	11.66
Business Applications	19.80	0.14	10.06	20.63	-25.66	9.55	2.29	11.66
Business Support	4.72	6.52	19.12	38.25	-18.48	10.06	8.33	6.70
Business/Online Services	14.30	56.89	-0.42	71.17	-24.71	20.85	17.11	-5.45
Cable TV	53.13	-14.51	0.84	42.67	-34.87	9.66	3.23	4.60
Chemicals	20.68	4.97	25.90	35.74	-1.39	16.73	15.58	7.68
Clothing Stores	12.19	9.77	19.20	39.68	-2.43	14.32	13.46	15.24
Coal	-11.11	47.14	57.33	77.38	-14.87	26.42	25.25	13.43
Components	23.86	-2.20	-1.22	42.04	-29.74	6.08	2.22	4.05
Computer Equipment	15.67	-1.73	13.72	36.23	-34.37	8.74	1.48	7.65
Construction Machinery	15.62	25.78	24.60	90.21	-10.93	22.01	24.40	15.96
Consultants	21.60	2.96	10.47	40.18	-51.94	11.43	-1.55	0.16
Contract Manufacturers	-11.90	-11.71	-14.35	77.69	-59.99	-13.04	-15.26	3.65
Data Networking	47.50	-12.25	-16.96	88.98	-30.10	2.27	4.34	8.69
Data Processing	12.12	4.60	6.07	23.57	-23.43	7.59	3.28	9.69
Department Stores	29.33	27.72	33.25	45.70	-13.99	31.08	22.36	8.80
Development Tools	8.54	12.96	5.52	55.38	-41.65	8.84	1.65	2.27
Diagnostics	15.81	12.38	31.77	45.48	-27.39	19.59	13.37	20.29
Discount Stores	10.63	-2.83	17.76	9.46	-15.54	8.84	3.17	18.41
Distributors	3.00	7.82	20.54	35.05	-23.95	10.11	5.61	6.03
Diversified	11.16	-3.32	13.10	47.42	-38.88	6.77	2.07	6.59
Drugs	13.54	5.37	-2.00	18.45	-20.30	5.23	2.45	8.12
Education	-13.75	-14.05	3.12	61.48	7.46	-9.15	5.81	9.17
Electric Equipment	10.97	2.03	20.17	34.37	-32.59	10.71	3.74	10.05
Electric Utilities	33.87	14.62	28.97	31.14	-19.10	25.41	15.99	10.63
Electronics Stores	4.84	8.01	14.96	93.51	-49.72	10.08	4.83	20.05
Employment	25.80	6.02	-1.01	54.70	-28.81	9.25	6.31	4.35
Engineering & Construction	21.58	28.25	20.96	43.66	-21.67	23.71	16.17	4.03
Entertainment/Education Media	0.55	-6.43	31.91	82.14	-32.07	7.30	7.75	8.41
Environmental Control	43.97	-2.97	25.97	42.51	-1.42	20.94	20.37	14.72
Film & TV Production	20.01	-27.89	7.63	101.94	-39.50	-2.41	2.33	-9.82
Finance	15.00	-2.92	20.97	27.90	-9.92	10.74	9.11	12.66
Food Mfg.	20.70	1.10	14.60	10.64	5.10	12.00	11.15	9.11
Food Wholesale	18.89	-14.58	6.79	31.18	7.45	3.07	9.08	16.00
Forestry/Wood	11.59	0.30	20.80	51.50	-7.59	10.46	13.26	8.50
Furniture Retail	-0.90	-12.40	-4.06	26.24	6.39	-5.32	2.12	14.02
Gambling/Hotel Casinos	53.29	-5.07	44.90	53.69	10.11	28.41	28.65	23.21
Gold & Silver	13.72	25.27	-7.71	41.11	60.29	9.32	23.87	5.48
Groceries	13.46	14.05	7.58	6.59	-40.43	11.86	-2.09	1.41
Home Building	-16.81	14.76	37.42	100.72	1.18	10.66	22.14	23.43
Home Health	-1.51	-1.73	18.10	19.79	-5.45	4.41	5.84	6.17
Home Supply	-1.62	2.55	15.59	48.93	-44.94	5.87	-0.61	16.47
Hospitals	-0.85	0.45	-7.36	17.76	-36.67	-2.76	-7.34	4.28
Hotels	41.20	9.20	45.47	43.68	-12.34	31.10	22.33	11.79
Household & Personal Products	18.92	1.53	12.94	18.30	3.56	11.22	11.08	10.65
Insurance (General)	21.86	9.32	10.84	22.60	-13.64	13.90	9.64	12.54
Insurance (Life)	37.65	23.95	16.42	31.21	-23.16	25.42	14.91	13.40

Index and Tables

Industry Performance
129 Industries, 7100 Stocks

Industry	Annual Total Return %					Annualized Total Return%		
	2006	2005	2004	2003	2002	3-Year	5-Year	10-Year
Insurance (Property)	13.04	12.72	8.25	24.90	-25.02	11.17	5.60	8.92
Insurance (Title)	-2.37	26.20	13.56	47.54	19.40	11.42	19.88	16.83
International Banks	26.47	10.70	14.27	46.90	-14.67	16.80	14.32	14.55
Jewelry/Accessories	20.01	9.00	15.42	88.65	-2.96	15.43	22.06	19.79
Land Transport	13.19	25.14	31.00	29.12	-1.34	22.71	17.53	14.18
Machinery	14.38	5.71	18.31	40.22	-2.18	12.84	13.92	10.64
Managed Care	-3.48	42.21	49.09	46.43	-0.03	26.72	25.08	19.41
Manufacturing - Misc.	49.99	20.15	24.68	42.44	-30.41	30.83	16.22	12.07
Media Conglomerates	17.82	-7.38	7.87	31.78	-32.17	5.31	0.42	5.65
Medical Equipment	4.76	2.73	14.13	33.24	-12.44	7.23	8.12	10.81
Medical Goods & Services	-2.05	24.50	3.77	17.10	-9.52	8.92	6.51	8.55
Metal Products	48.51	42.53	25.61	50.93	-14.35	38.42	27.85	11.78
Mining (Nonferrous & Nonmetals)	30.94	43.14	21.53	66.63	2.70	31.12	30.28	14.29
Money Management	19.29	29.66	26.58	37.44	-23.65	24.72	14.74	19.20
Natural Gas Utilities	23.18	12.39	18.30	28.81	-19.67	17.59	11.05	10.46
Office Equipment	15.24	-10.38	18.02	48.67	-16.35	7.10	8.27	0.21
Oil & Gas	26.68	29.15	25.68	37.76	-2.85	26.81	22.45	16.04
Oil & Gas Services	14.74	51.84	36.00	15.17	-8.95	33.39	21.05	9.70
Oil/Gas Products	7.73	64.49	49.66	52.53	5.24	38.14	33.16	16.68
Online Retail	-17.33	-17.15	30.43	89.57	-7.95	-3.01	8.60	18.43
Optical Equipment	4.15	30.74	-8.87	91.11	-57.50	7.47	-2.43	-2.68
Packaging	22.88	-1.11	17.56	22.62	11.33	13.01	13.66	4.23
Paints/Coatings	30.63	-3.72	28.85	19.49	7.83	17.22	15.06	9.56
Paper	21.12	-10.63	9.00	23.03	-6.07	5.62	5.72	4.68
Personal Services	10.02	-0.18	8.95	21.40	-3.40	5.93	7.36	3.69
Photography & Imaging	36.41	-0.03	14.48	19.38	1.21	16.00	12.92	6.59
Physicians	0.18	13.26	10.13	29.91	-38.46	7.15	0.53	-1.76
Pipelines	21.78	17.86	22.49	49.48	-48.66	20.68	6.22	8.91
Plastics	37.80	-2.08	24.64	48.34	-30.10	19.45	11.89	8.68
Printing	12.23	0.55	15.04	23.82	-6.88	8.94	8.00	6.71
Publishing	18.70	-0.45	15.96	13.64	-15.82	10.96	5.13	4.80
REITS	33.29	11.94	31.15	36.08	4.89	25.12	22.65	14.80
Radio	-14.57	-13.11	-11.73	25.92	-21.92	-14.04	-9.11	5.04
Real Estate	25.95	8.42	31.70	38.67	5.61	21.31	21.25	13.43
Recreation	-0.18	-7.28	39.83	39.10	-10.09	8.97	9.74	7.69
Regional Banks	11.04	-1.93	18.29	35.96	3.61	8.94	12.46	13.00
Reinsurance	10.17	-1.43	4.92	18.22	-13.79	4.31	3.51	11.54
Rental & Repair Services	24.83	-1.85	9.07	61.81	-30.30	10.11	9.01	7.55
Research Services	11.80	11.77	32.11	28.15	-8.86	18.16	15.20	9.58
Restaurants	23.21	6.56	28.23	41.78	-18.11	19.24	13.49	12.20
Rubber Products	16.18	1.83	26.98	30.17	-33.30	14.43	4.94	-1.32
Savings & Loans	13.20	-2.70	13.86	46.06	14.56	8.19	15.53	14.01
Securities	38.62	19.41	8.91	47.01	-25.97	22.01	12.85	20.59
Security Services	24.25	20.24	55.52	24.46	-17.18	31.60	18.91	-1.34
Semiconductor Equipment	13.27	5.82	-22.86	77.72	-40.18	-2.28	-2.57	9.95
Semiconductors	-2.41	11.52	-18.44	89.91	-51.55	-4.08	-6.17	4.84
Shoes	18.06	-0.64	33.40	55.32	-16.33	16.32	14.86	7.80
Specialty Retail	13.09	11.98	14.52	40.24	-13.72	13.78	11.79	11.05
Steel/Iron	61.43	29.17	67.79	56.91	-12.56	50.98	35.96	14.02
Super Regional Banks	16.96	1.20	8.83	27.62	4.93	9.18	11.23	11.72
Systems & Security	6.89	-12.24	33.09	69.88	-52.98	7.54	-1.42	-2.40
Telecommunication Services	35.26	-4.15	18.04	17.38	-20.41	14.74	6.38	5.16
Textiles	-4.38	-7.54	27.26	26.26	-2.75	3.61	6.09	3.90
Tobacco	26.86	24.91	25.06	39.75	1.04	25.45	22.89	15.83
Toys/Hobbies	83.55	-7.01	17.88	11.98	-28.77	26.16	9.68	9.70
Transport Equipment	27.25	8.31	15.34	37.43	-11.40	16.55	13.90	6.83
Transportation - Misc	7.38	-1.46	25.47	24.21	10.18	10.14	11.87	9.94
Truck Makers	37.89	3.66	32.26	83.38	1.47	23.77	27.57	15.95
Waste Management	24.14	8.52	7.19	28.52	-20.60	12.69	8.77	4.38
Water Transport	19.78	2.98	64.02	49.92	1.59	26.20	24.93	16.49
Water Utilities	33.07	18.63	30.00	15.41	11.89	26.85	21.46	15.61
Wireless Equipment	4.96	12.12	27.34	44.15	-42.44	14.01	3.37	11.24
Wireless Service	34.32	-1.97	6.62	30.90	-28.62	11.40	5.06	8.98
Wireline Equipment	11.48	-4.91	5.05	113.56	-61.53	3.23	-3.52	1.68

Industry Averages

129 Industries, 7100 Stocks

Industry	% of US Economy (Revenue)	Industry Averages Market Cap ($Mil)	Revenue ($Mil)	Price/ Book	Price/ Sales	Price/ Earnings	Dividend Yield %
Advertising	0.22	10,918	5,865	4.20	2.63	25.79	0.7
Aerospace & Defense	1.25	32,613	29,837	4.40	1.24	24.98	1.2
Agricultural Machinery	0.29	14,400	14,831	2.67	1.04	18.19	1.2
Agriculture	0.29	13,824	24,426	3.09	1.91	20.53	1.4
Agrochemical	0.07	22,515	6,203	4.24	3.50	36.22	0.8
Air Transport	1.34	7,686	13,108	3.20	1.58	18.57	0.3
Alcoholic Drinks	0.41	34,748	10,050	13.30	7.84	25.60	2.0
Aluminum	0.37	18,691	20,496	2.18	1.14	18.08	2.3
Apparel Makers	0.24	4,408	3,089	3.32	1.62	25.49	0.8
Appliance & Furniture Makers	0.31	3,563	8,395	4.37	0.88	23.19	2.3
Assisted Living	0.06	3,171	1,855	5.49	0.87	24.18	1.6
Audio/Video Equipment	0.88	33,763	40,121	2.24	1.06	27.82	0.9
Auto Makers	5.48	119,174	150,983	2.27	0.86	18.19	1.2
Auto Parts	1.11	7,341	14,799	2.45	0.98	16.26	1.3
Auto Retail	0.48	5,086	7,618	5.91	0.95	19.54	0.8
Beverage Mfg.	0.65	81,292	24,735	5.87	3.50	22.21	2.0
Biotechnology	0.26	43,224	5,692	8.22	11.36	43.21	0.0
Broadcast TV	0.09	7,271	2,706	3.31	3.34	31.91	0.3
Building Materials	0.85	16,428	13,216	3.69	1.42	15.92	1.6
Business Applications	0.57	163,871	25,488	8.11	6.97	30.79	0.8
Business Support	0.32	6,932	2,123	4.39	5.09	27.27	0.4
Business/Online Services	0.24	83,545	6,478	11.24	14.04	55.43	0.0
Cable TV	0.45	47,117	14,685	11.85	2.95	34.34	0.3
Chemicals	2.06	24,340	21,138	3.24	1.52	18.26	2.1
Clothing Stores	0.55	6,992	6,839	4.76	1.53	21.55	0.9
Coal	0.12	5,492	2,930	4.25	2.13	17.00	2.6
Components	0.13	10,261	6,110	2.08	1.81	26.50	0.7
Computer Equipment	2.47	72,760	51,353	5.58	2.43	27.30	0.5
Construction Machinery	0.30	28,960	28,897	4.82	1.24	13.71	1.3
Consultants	0.42	13,644	10,804	7.05	2.42	30.97	0.5
Contract Manufacturers	0.35	3,642	9,181	1.62	0.61	34.12	0.5
Data Networking	0.21	142,315	25,852	6.49	5.79	31.09	0.0
Data Processing	0.29	13,774	4,682	4.88	3.42	23.97	0.7
Department Stores	0.48	14,636	17,308	3.21	0.98	25.98	1.4
Development Tools	0.10	9,604	1,350	4.57	6.42	41.59	0.2
Diagnostics	0.07	6,489	3,140	5.56	4.06	24.94	0.3
Discount Stores	3.07	115,206	194,412	3.91	0.91	22.32	1.0
Distributors	0.56	4,307	9,916	3.08	1.07	23.27	0.7
Diversified	0.81	51,722	32,847	3.32	1.81	18.18	1.8
Drugs	2.34	113,179	29,201	5.45	4.35	24.03	2.2
Education	0.06	3,453	1,097	10.96	2.75	24.98	0.1
Electric Equipment	1.95	246,907	108,798	3.42	2.16	21.55	2.1
Electric Utilities	3.66	33,513	21,368	3.92	1.81	18.17	3.5
Electronics Stores	0.29	18,788	26,897	4.20	0.71	23.86	0.8
Employment	0.36	6,659	11,666	4.35	0.92	24.63	0.8
Engineering & Construction	0.40	3,113	5,429	3.68	0.88	33.70	0.4
Entertainment/Education Media	0.04	9,623	2,089	4.56	5.02	78.06	0.0
Environmental Control	0.31	19,625	20,417	7.58	1.23	31.39	1.3
Film & TV Production	0.02	1,887	450	3.58	5.02	29.54	1.0
Finance	0.51	36,182	9,516	4.61	5.40	17.81	2.0
Food Mfg.	2.36	56,152	34,939	5.22	1.86	22.02	2.0
Food Wholesale	0.38	17,203	27,373	5.87	0.58	26.80	1.7
Forestry/Wood	0.21	9,871	11,568	2.33	1.70	19.84	3.2
Furniture Retail	0.09	7,068	4,456	4.98	1.64	18.82	0.4
Gambling/Hotel Casinos	0.21	15,672	3,399	8.32	6.90	46.52	0.6
Gold & Silver	0.09	9,100	1,915	4.49	8.81	43.32	0.5
Groceries	1.29	11,139	35,310	3.13	0.43	21.99	0.8
Home Building	0.67	5,377	10,106	1.89	0.79	8.24	0.8
Home Health	0.05	1,711	959	2.93	1.78	23.03	0.1
Home Supply	0.75	68,341	73,376	3.29	1.09	16.01	1.2
Hospitals	0.19	3,200	4,191	2.40	1.03	20.69	0.3
Hotels	0.20	11,510	5,901	5.91	3.10	24.51	0.7
Household & Personal Products	0.94	118,496	42,302	6.27	2.79	24.65	1.7
Insurance (General)	1.63	95,620	62,649	2.02	1.73	15.37	1.4
Insurance (Life)	2.36	47,118	42,321	3.29	2.35	28.04	1.8

Industry Averages
129 Industries, 7100 Stocks

Industry	% of US Economy (Revenue)	Market Cap ($Mil)	Revenue ($Mil)	Price/ Book	Price/ Sales	Price/ Earnings	Dividend Yield %
Insurance (Property)	2.59	79,731	59,393	1.77	1.44	14.44	1.2
Insurance (Title)	0.11	3,270	6,043	1.18	0.44	9.93	2.8
International Banks	3.99	124,167	36,141	2.63	3.55	18.45	2.8
Jewelry/Accessories	0.08	9,883	2,222	9.01	4.97	28.80	0.7
Land Transport	0.49	18,133	9,155	2.52	2.31	17.16	1.1
Machinery	0.44	10,863	7,182	3.14	1.58	20.42	1.4
Managed Care	1.55	38,867	37,750	3.58	1.21	20.27	0.1
Manufacturing - Misc.	0.22	23,918	14,685	8.52	2.02	37.33	1.4
Media Conglomerates	0.93	52,007	23,090	3.52	3.17	25.66	0.8
Medical Equipment	0.55	20,165	4,963	5.30	4.51	29.78	0.5
Medical Goods & Services	1.41	14,059	54,987	3.07	0.62	23.75	0.4
Metal Products	0.38	17,407	5,462	3.56	1.90	18.98	1.3
Mining (Nonferrous & Nonmetals)	1.01	51,466	20,886	4.58	3.74	17.67	2.1
Money Management	0.13	14,084	2,634	4.55	5.72	30.90	1.3
Natural Gas Utilities	0.69	11,183	11,026	3.12	1.04	16.18	2.1
Office Equipment	0.26	10,626	9,749	5.67	1.39	18.00	0.9
Oil & Gas	12.21	182,118	163,455	3.45	1.93	12.68	2.4
Oil & Gas Services	1.10	30,137	15,954	5.00	3.16	18.27	0.9
Oil/Gas Products	1.17	16,826	34,086	3.25	2.54	14.41	3.0
Online Retail	0.17	25,641	5,736	20.42	5.09	43.32	0.1
Optical Equipment	0.09	17,908	3,901	3.76	4.66	22.82	0.1
Packaging	0.29	4,044	4,587	3.71	1.08	24.70	1.8
Paints/Coatings	0.08	5,821	5,438	4.27	1.06	17.99	2.0
Paper	0.65	7,992	10,096	3.05	1.17	32.74	2.7
Personal Services	0.11	3,972	2,359	3.53	2.22	23.62	1.8
Photography & Imaging	0.43	53,953	27,879	2.90	1.79	30.40	1.2
Physicians	0.13	2,796	4,446	2.96	1.54	36.33	0.1
Pipelines	0.66	9,703	8,002	2.58	1.81	28.66	3.9
Plastics	0.10	3,066	6,091	1.71	0.70	7.77	1.2
Printing	0.10	3,767	4,273	2.35	0.90	35.16	2.1
Publishing	0.29	15,497	4,947	6.30	2.86	27.03	1.8
REITS	0.38	8,338	1,293	3.95	7.62	48.73	3.5
Radio	0.07	10,282	3,766	8.72	3.78	25.82	1.6
Real Estate	0.15	17,080	2,179	9.28	8.95	25.94	1.9
Recreation	0.35	27,702	8,310	5.56	3.01	19.58	1.8
Regional Banks	0.42	4,707	1,217	2.98	5.65	18.06	2.4
Reinsurance	0.23	6,074	4,512	1.24	1.50	12.50	1.3
Rental & Repair Services	0.13	1,396	1,800	2.60	1.26	18.21	0.4
Research Services	0.03	2,758	961	3.74	3.52	35.18	0.1
Restaurants	0.64	24,646	10,985	6.18	2.09	27.62	1.1
Rubber Products	0.14	2,494	9,719	9.07	0.56	20.38	1.1
Savings & Loans	0.27	17,231	5,990	1.78	4.81	18.29	2.8
Securities	0.88	54,674	20,788	3.73	3.50	17.35	0.7
Security Services	0.03	2,190	1,535	3.75	1.79	33.12	0.1
Semiconductor Equipment	0.19	10,267	3,313	3.94	3.51	27.52	0.6
Semiconductors	0.87	40,780	11,768	3.79	4.27	28.45	1.1
Shoes	0.14	15,656	9,653	3.89	2.05	19.10	0.9
Specialty Retail	1.10	23,167	26,971	3.99	1.04	24.10	0.5
Steel/Iron	1.04	30,374	13,118	5.01	2.71	12.96	1.5
Super Regional Banks	0.77	76,205	21,943	2.25	3.64	13.50	3.4
Systems & Security	0.13	8,733	2,209	4.24	6.41	70.04	0.1
Telecommunication Services	4.48	59,584	36,254	4.46	2.16	17.95	3.1
Textiles	0.07	3,599	5,570	1.72	0.60	12.97	0.5
Tobacco	1.07	117,209	67,979	20.61	1.78	17.86	3.6
Toys/Hobbies	0.08	23,617	4,157	4.19	5.62	32.30	1.4
Transport Equipment	0.05	1,508	1,649	3.59	1.30	18.17	0.5
Transportation - Misc	0.76	45,699	30,067	4.60	1.52	20.89	1.5
Truck Makers	0.36	18,027	20,978	3.06	0.91	16.09	1.8
Waste Management	0.17	10,733	7,419	3.43	1.93	23.43	1.4
Water Transport	0.11	1,537	808	2.05	2.64	11.22	5.5
Water Utilities	0.05	8,208	2,522	2.63	3.63	23.22	3.3
Wireless Equipment	0.77	59,471	25,195	4.86	3.66	21.60	1.3
Wireless Service	1.24	96,428	31,451	2.96	3.65	23.88	2.0
Wireline Equipment	0.80	54,206	64,294	3.09	1.33	25.04	1.1

Top- and Bottom-Performing Stocks
Morningstar Stocks 500 Universe

Last 12 Months

Pg	Company	Industry	Annualized Return (%)
	Top Performers		
303	IntercontinentalExchange	Securities	196.84
391	NYSE Group	Securities	94.40
160	CarMax	Auto Retail	93.75
428	Research in Motion	Computer Equipment	93.58
463	Steel Dynamics	Steel/Iron	85.97
319	Jones Lang LaSalle	Real Estate	84.32
414	Potash Corp of Saskatchewan	Mining	80.04
404	PetroChina Company ADR	Oil & Gas	79.05
166	Celgene	Biotechnology	77.56
209	DirecTV	Cable TV	76.63
282	Hansen Natural	Beverage Mfg.	70.94
389	Nucor	Steel/Iron	70.67
342	Macrovision	Business Applications	68.92
413	Posco ADR	Steel/Iron	66.98
230	Energy Transfer Partners	Oil & Gas	65.52
149	BT Group PLC ADR	Telecom Services	63.56
190	Comcast A	Cable TV	63.31
335	Lexmark International	Computer Equipment	63.28
364	Mittal Steel Co NV	Steel/Iron	62.46
395	ONEOK Partners LP	Pipelines	61.79
449	SEI Investments	Business Support	61.73
163	CBOT Holdings	Securities	61.55
247	FEMSA ADR	Beverage Mfg.	61.25
179	Cisco Systems	Data Networking	59.64
275	Goldman Sachs Group	Securities	57.41
	Bottom Performers		
175	Chico's FAS	Clothing Stores	-52.90
270	Getty Images	Business Support	-52.03
514	Valassis Communications	Publishing	-50.12
222	Educate	Education	-39.66
542	Whole Foods Market	Groceries	-37.19
101	Apollo Group A	Education	-35.54
555	Yahoo	Media Conglomerates	-34.81
114	Avid Technology	Business Applications	-31.96
442	SanDisk	Semiconductors	-31.50
219	eBay	Online Retail	-30.43
140	Boston Scientific	Medical Equipment	-29.85
524	W.P. Stewart & Company	Money Management	-28.09
485	Teva Pharmaceutical Industries ADR	Drugs	-27.22
459	St. Jude Medical	Medical Equipment	-27.17
70	AirTran Holdings	Air Transport	-26.76
545	Williams-Sonoma	Furniture Retail	-26.53
272	Given Imaging	Medical Equipment	-25.86
215	DR Horton	Home Building	-24.41
292	Hospira	Drugs	-21.51
168	Centex	Home Building	-21.05
256	Forward Air	Land Transport	-20.42
148	Brunswick	Recreation	-20.12
331	Legg Mason	Money Management	-19.99
124	Barr Pharmaceuticals	Drugs	-19.54
557	Zebra Technologies	Computer Equipment	-18.81

Last 3 Years

Pg	Company	Industry	Annualized Return (%)
	Top Performers		
282	Hansen Natural	Beverage Mfg.	217.43
102	Apple Computer	Computer Equipment	99.50
174	Chicago Mercantile Exchange	Securities	93.01
166	Celgene	Biotechnology	72.44
88	America Movil SA ADR	Telecom Services	70.93
364	Mittal Steel Co NV	Steel/Iron	69.58
319	Jones Lang LaSalle	Real Estate	65.09
157	Canadian Natural Resources	Oil & Gas	62.69
389	Nucor	Steel/Iron	61.94
269	Gerdau SA ADR PN	Steel/Iron	61.18
405	Petroleo Brasileiro ADR	Oil & Gas	58.46
506	Ultra Petroleum	Oil & Gas	57.11
428	Research in Motion	Computer Equipment	56.38
367	Monsanto Company	Agrochemical	55.88
145	Brookfield Asset Management	Finance	55.29
193	Companhia Vale Do Rio Doce	Steel/Iron	51.79
416	Precision Castparts	Metal Products	51.38
414	Potash Corp of Saskatchewan	Mining	50.37
109	Autodesk	Business Applications	48.92
375	Nasdaq Stock Market	Securities	48.25
247	FEMSA ADR	Beverage Mfg.	48.00
469	Suncor Energy	Oil & Gas	47.25
230	Energy Transfer Partners	Oil & Gas	46.15
361	MGM Mirage	Gambling/Hotel Casinos	45.02
113	AvalonBay Communities	REITS	44.77
	Bottom Performers		
140	Boston Scientific	Medical Equipment	-22.40
514	Valassis Communications	Publishing	-20.95
379	New York Times A	Media Conglomerates	-18.45
101	Apollo Group A	Education	-16.86
363	Millennium Pharmaceuticals	Biotechnology	-16.39
502	Tribune	Media Conglomerates	-14.30
384	Nortel Networks	Wireline Equipment	-14.19
553	Xilinx	Semiconductors	-14.10
350	Maxim Integrated Products	Semiconductors	-13.83
302	Intel	Semiconductors	-13.04
347	Marsh & McLennan Companies	Insurance (General)	-11.83
260	Gannett	Media Conglomerates	-10.70
205	Dell	Computer Equipment	-9.62
97	Analog Devices	Semiconductors	-9.35
336	Linear Technology	Semiconductors	-9.24
86	Amazon.com	Online Retail	-9.15
330	Lee Enterprises	Publishing	-9.00
249	Fifth Third Bancorp	Super Regional Banks	-8.44
114	Avid Technology	Business Applications	-8.10
557	Zebra Technologies	Computer Equipment	-7.70
407	Pfizer	Drugs	-7.16
224	Eli Lilly & Company	Drugs	-7.10
314	JetBlue Airways	Air Transport	-7.05
178	Cintas	Business Support	-6.78
255	Forest Laboratories	Drugs	-6.45

Top- and Bottom-Performing Stocks
Morningstar Stocks 500 Universe

Last 5 Years

Pg	Company	Industry	Annualized Return (%)
	Top Performers		
282	Hansen Natural	Beverage Mfg.	129.85
364	Mittal Steel Co NV	Steel/Iron	89.93
506	Ultra Petroleum	Oil & Gas	73.40
269	Gerdau SA ADR PN	Steel/Iron	66.59
428	Research in Motion	Computer Equipment	60.87
404	PetroChina Company ADR	Oil & Gas	59.70
157	Canadian Natural Resources	Oil & Gas	55.50
187	Coach	Jewelry/Accessories	54.54
102	Apple Computer	Computer Equipment	50.60
166	Celgene	Biotechnology	48.45
88	America Movil SA ADR	Telecom Services	47.61
145	Brookfield Asset Management	Finance	46.44
554	XTO Energy	Oil & Gas	44.92
442	SanDisk	Semiconductors	42.98
186	CNOOC ADR	Oil & Gas	42.41
463	Steel Dynamics	Steel/Iron	42.13
405	Petroleo Brasileiro ADR	Oil & Gas	41.88
416	Precision Castparts	Metal Products	41.25
469	Suncor Energy	Oil & Gas	40.47
517	VCA Antech	Medical Goods & Services	39.65
67	Aetna	Managed Care	39.34
281	Halliburton	Oil & Gas Services	38.89
319	Jones Lang LaSalle	Real Estate	38.89
230	Energy Transfer Partners	Oil & Gas	38.76
445	Sasol ADR	Chemicals	37.95
	Bottom Performers		
384	Nortel Networks	Wireline Equipment	-18.64
514	Valassis Communications	Publishing	-16.45
363	Millennium Pharmaceuticals	Biotechnology	-14.96
503	Tyco International	Diversified	-11.74
350	Maxim Integrated Products	Semiconductors	-9.49
379	New York Times A	Media Conglomerates	-9.30
553	Xilinx	Semiconductors	-8.91
142	Bristol-Myers Squibb	Drugs	-8.50
347	Marsh & McLennan Companies	Insurance (General)	-8.41
302	Intel	Semiconductors	-7.55
481	Tellabs	Wireline Equipment	-7.27
492	Time Warner	Media Conglomerates	-7.14
134	Biogen Idec	Biotechnology	-6.53
446	Schering-Plough	Drugs	-6.27
407	Pfizer	Drugs	-6.01
224	Eli Lilly & Company	Drugs	-5.65
249	Fifth Third Bancorp	Super Regional Banks	-5.26
97	Analog Devices	Semiconductors	-5.17
214	Dow Jones & Company	Media Conglomerates	-4.72
257	France Telecom SA ADR	Telecom Services	-4.64
92	AmeriCredit	Finance	-4.42
342	Macrovision	Business Applications	-4.31
312	Janus Capital Group	Money Management	-4.29
524	W.P. Stewart & Company	Money Management	-4.24
336	Linear Technology	Semiconductors	-3.99

Last 10 Years

Pg	Company	Industry	Annualized Return (%)
	Top Performers		
282	Hansen Natural	Beverage Mfg.	73.92
175	Chico's FAS	Clothing Stores	56.35
166	Celgene	Biotechnology	51.11
506	Ultra Petroleum	Oil & Gas	46.48
132	Best Buy Co.	Electronics Stores	45.62
555	Yahoo	Media Conglomerates	43.11
397	Oshkosh Truck	Truck Makers	40.92
554	XTO Energy	Oil & Gas	37.02
271	Gilead Sciences	Biotechnology	35.44
469	Suncor Energy	Oil & Gas	33.90
116	Axcan Pharma	Drugs	33.70
429	ResMed	Medical Equipment	33.44
442	SanDisk	Semiconductors	33.25
488	THQ	Entertain./Education Media	33.18
399	Panera Bread	Restaurants	32.91
449	SEI Investments	Business Support	32.64
102	Apple Computer	Computer Equipment	32.16
421	Qualcomm	Wireless Equipment	31.95
64	Actuant A	Electric Equipment	31.15
239	Expeditors International	Transportation - Misc	30.79
422	Quest Diagnostics	Diagnostics	30.49
220	EchoStar Communications	Cable TV	30.44
146	Brown & Brown	Insurance (General)	30.25
324	Kinder Morgan Energy Partners	Pipelines	29.63
256	Forward Air	Land Transport	29.46
	Bottom Performers		
384	Nortel Networks	Wireline Equipment	-9.90
481	Tellabs	Wireline Equipment	-5.88
231	Enersis ADR	Electric Utilities	-4.35
552	Xerox	Office Equipment	-3.39
111	AutoNation	Auto Retail	-2.74
72	Alcatel Lucent ADR	Wireline Equipment	-0.40
514	Valassis Communications	Publishing	0.29
188	Coca-Cola	Beverage Mfg.	0.82
140	Boston Scientific	Medical Equipment	1.37
478	Telecom Corp of New Zealand	Telecom Services	1.74
371	Motorola	Wireless Equipment	2.22
533	Waste Management	Waste Management	2.26
154	Campbell Soup	Food Mfg.	2.51
458	Sprint Nextel	Wireless Service	2.61
302	Intel	Semiconductors	2.72
81	Allied Waste Industries	Waste Management	2.88
406	PetSmart	Specialty Retail	2.95
455	Sony ADR	Audio/Video Equipment	3.18
142	Bristol-Myers Squibb	Drugs	3.20
423	Raytheon	Aerospace & Defense	3.25
214	Dow Jones & Company	Media Conglomerates	3.39
379	New York Times A	Media Conglomerates	4.01
444	Sara Lee	Food Mfg.	4.14
357	Merck	Drugs	4.30
498	Total System Services	Data Processing	4.43

Most Attractive Stocks
Based on Morningstar Rating

Pg	Company	Industry	Morningstar Ratings Star Rating	Business Risk	Economic Moat	Valuation Fair Value Estimate ($)	Consider Buying ($)	Consider Selling ($)
73	Alcoa	Aluminum	★★★★★	Avg	Narrow	40.00	30.80	50.10
95	Amgen	Biotechnology	★★★★★	Avg	Wide	91.00	70.20	114.00
97	Analog Devices	Semiconductors	★★★★★	Avg	Narrow	48.00	37.00	60.10
101	Apollo Group A	Education	★★★★★	Avg	Wide	65.00	50.10	81.40
103	Applebee's International	Restaurants	★★★★★	Avg	Narrow	33.00	25.40	41.30
131	Berkshire Hathaway B	Insurance (General)	★★★★★	-Avg	Wide	4550.00	3877.10	5973.70
140	Boston Scientific	Medical Equipment	★★★★★	Avg	Wide	25.00	19.30	31.30
167	Cemex SAB de CV ADR	Building Materials	★★★★★	Avg	Narrow	45.00	34.70	56.40
172	Checkfree	Systems & Security	★★★★★	Avg	Wide	55.00	42.40	68.90
177	Cimarex Energy	Oil & Gas	★★★★★	Avg	Narrow	59.00	45.50	73.90
194	Compass Minerals International	Mining	★★★★★	Avg	Narrow	41.00	31.60	51.40
205	Dell	Computer Equipment	★★★★★	Avg	Wide	34.00	26.20	42.60
206	Devon Energy	Oil & Gas	★★★★★	Avg	Narrow	93.00	71.70	116.50
226	EMC	Computer Equipment	★★★★★	Avg	Narrow	19.00	14.70	23.80
229	Energy Transfer Equity LP	Oil & Gas Services	★★★★★	-Avg	Narrow	39.00	33.20	51.20
230	Energy Transfer Partners	Oil & Gas	★★★★★	-Avg	Narrow	69.00	58.80	90.60
238	Expedia	Online Retail	★★★★★	Avg	Narrow	30.00	23.10	37.60
239	Expeditors International	Transportation - Misc	★★★★★	-Avg	Wide	56.00	47.70	73.50
244	Fastenal	Distributors	★★★★★	-Avg	Wide	53.00	45.20	69.60
245	Federated Investors B	Money Management	★★★★★	Avg	Wide	46.00	35.50	57.60
250	First American	Insurance (Title)	★★★★★	Avg	Narrow	61.00	47.00	76.40
256	Forward Air	Land Transport	★★★★★	Avg	Wide	40.00	30.80	50.10
270	Getty Images	Business Support	★★★★★	Avg	Wide	69.00	53.20	86.50
336	Linear Technology	Semiconductors	★★★★★	Avg	Wide	45.00	34.70	56.40
372	MSC Industrial Direct Co.	Distributors	★★★★★	Avg	Narrow	60.00	46.30	75.20
347	Marsh & McLennan Companies	Insurance (General)	★★★★★	Avg	Wide	43.00	33.20	53.90
350	Maxim Integrated Products	Semiconductors	★★★★★	Avg	Wide	52.00	40.10	65.20
355	Medtronic	Medical Equipment	★★★★★	-Avg	Wide	64.00	54.50	84.00
375	Nasdaq Stock Market	Securities	★★★★★	+Avg	Narrow	52.00	33.10	62.70
387	Novartis AG ADR	Drugs	★★★★★	-Avg	Wide	73.00	62.20	95.80
438	Royal Caribbean Cruises	Recreation	★★★★★	Avg	Narrow	55.00	42.40	68.90
458	Sprint Nextel	Wireless Service	★★★★★	Avg	Narrow	28.00	21.60	35.10
508	United Parcel Service B	Transportation - Misc	★★★★★	-Avg	Wide	88.00	75.00	115.50
528	Wal-Mart Stores	Discount Stores	★★★★★	-Avg	Wide	58.00	49.40	76.10
541	White Mountains Insurance Group	Insurance (Property)	★★★★★	Avg	Narrow	795.00	613.00	996.10
542	Whole Foods Market	Groceries	★★★★★	Avg	Narrow	72.00	55.50	90.20
555	Yahoo	Media Conglomerates	★★★★★	Avg	Narrow	34.00	26.20	42.60
219	eBay	Online Retail	★★★★★	-Avg	Wide	45.00	38.30	59.10
471	Synchronoss Technologies	Business Support	★★★★	+Avg	Narrow	18.00	11.50	21.70
476	Target	Discount Stores	★★★★	-Avg	Narrow	65.00	55.40	85.30
479	Telefonica SA ADR	Telecom Services	★★★★	Avg	Narrow	78.00	60.10	97.70
481	Tellabs	Wireline Equipment	★★★★	Avg	Narrow	12.00	9.30	15.00
483	Ternium SA ADR	Steel/Iron	★★★★	+Avg	Narrow	35.00	22.30	42.20
486	Texas Instruments	Semiconductors	★★★★	Avg	Narrow	34.00	26.20	42.60
500	Transatlantic Holdings	Reinsurance	★★★★	+Avg	Narrow	85.00	54.20	102.50
503	Tyco International	Diversified	★★★★	Avg	Narrow	36.00	27.80	45.10
513	UTi Worldwide	Transportation - Misc	★★★★	Avg	Narrow	38.00	29.30	47.60
506	Ultra Petroleum	Oil & Gas	★★★★	+Avg	Narrow	63.00	40.10	76.00
524	W.P. Stewart & Company	Money Management	★★★★	Avg	Wide	18.00	13.90	22.60
531	Washington Mutual	Savings & Loans	★★★★	Avg	Narrow	52.00	40.10	65.20
532	Washington Post Co	Media Conglomerates	★★★★	-Avg	Wide	850.00	724.30	1116.00
533	Waste Management	Waste Management	★★★★	Avg	Narrow	45.00	34.70	56.40
536	WellPoint	Managed Care	★★★★	Avg	Narrow	88.00	67.90	110.30
537	Wells Fargo	Super Regional Banks	★★★★	Avg	Wide	41.00	31.60	51.40
539	Wesco Financial	Insurance (General)	★★★★	-Avg	Narrow	515.00	438.80	676.10
545	Williams-Sonoma	Furniture Retail	★★★★	Avg	Narrow	39.00	30.10	48.90
549	Wm. Wrigley Jr.	Food Mfg.	★★★★	-Avg	Wide	59.00	50.30	77.50
551	Wyndham Worldwide	Hotels	★★★★	Avg	Narrow	42.00	32.40	52.60
553	Xilinx	Semiconductors	★★★★	Avg	Narrow	28.00	21.60	35.10
557	Zebra Technologies	Computer Equipment	★★★★	Avg	Narrow	45.00	34.70	56.40

Least Attractive Stocks
Based on Morningstar Rating

Pg	Company	Industry	Morningstar Ratings Star Rating	Business Risk	Economic Moat	Valuation Fair Value Estimate ($)	Consider Buying ($)	Consider Selling ($)
108	AT&T	Telecom Services	★	Avg	Narrow	28.00	21.60	35.10
77	Alliancebernstein Holding LP	Money Management	★	Avg	Wide	58.00	44.70	72.70
102	Apple Computer	Computer Equipment	★	Avg	Narrow	66.00	50.90	82.70
113	AvalonBay Communities	REITS	★	Avg	Narrow	64.00	49.40	80.20
117	Baker Hughes	Oil & Gas Services	★	Avg	Narrow	59.00	45.50	73.90
127	Bear Stearns Companies	Securities	★	Avg	Narrow	126.00	97.20	157.90
136	Blackrock	Money Management	★	Avg	Wide	117.00	90.20	146.60
166	Celgene	Biotechnology	★	+Avg	Narrow	42.00	26.80	50.70
184	Clear Channel Outdoor Holdings	Advertising	★	Avg	Narrow	20.00	15.40	25.10
193	Companhia Vale Do Rio Doce	Steel/Iron	★	+Avg	Narrow	21.00	13.40	25.30
236	Equity Residential	REITS	★	-Avg	Narrow	35.00	29.80	46.00
258	Franklin Resources	Money Management	★	Avg	Wide	77.00	59.40	96.50
276	Google	Business/Online Services	★	Avg	Narrow	315.00	242.90	394.70
281	Halliburton	Oil & Gas Services	★	Avg	Narrow	23.00	17.70	28.80
288	Hewlett-Packard	Computer Equipment	★	Avg	Narrow	30.00	23.10	37.60
289	Hilton Hotels	Hotels	★	Avg	Narrow	26.00	20.00	32.60
314	JetBlue Airways	Air Transport	★	+Avg	Narrow	6.00	3.80	7.20
319	Jones Lang LaSalle	Real Estate	★	Avg	Narrow	66.00	50.90	82.70
327	Kohl's	Discount Stores	★	Avg	Narrow	53.00	40.90	66.40
332	Lehman Brothers Holdings	Securities	★	Avg	Narrow	61.00	47.00	76.40
335	Lexmark International	Computer Equipment	★	Avg	Narrow	53.00	40.90	66.40
346	Marriott International A	Hotels	★	Avg	Narrow	37.00	28.50	46.40
358	Merrill Lynch & Company	Securities	★	Avg	Wide	71.00	54.70	89.00
368	Monster Worldwide	Advertising	★	Avg	Narrow	35.00	27.00	43.90
377	Network Appliance	Computer Equipment	★	Avg	Narrow	31.00	23.90	38.80
404	PetroChina Company ADR	Oil & Gas	★	+Avg	Narrow	104.00	66.30	125.40
405	Petroleo Brasileiro ADR	Oil & Gas	★	+Avg	Narrow	78.00	49.70	94.10
409	Philadelphia Consolidated Holding	Insurance (Property)	★	Avg	Narrow	31.00	23.90	38.80
414	Potash Corp of Saskatchewan	Mining	★	Avg	Narrow	115.00	88.70	144.10
419	ProLogis Trust	REITS	★	Avg	Narrow	46.00	35.50	57.60
430	Resources Global Professionals	Employment	★	Avg	Narrow	23.00	17.70	28.80
440	Ryanair Holdings PLC ADR	Air Transport	★	Avg	Narrow	54.00	41.60	67.70
449	SEI Investments	Business Support	★	-Avg	Wide	44.00	37.50	57.80
447	Schlumberger	Oil & Gas Services	★	Avg	Narrow	30.00	23.10	37.60
469	Suncor Energy	Oil & Gas	★	Avg	Narrow	62.00	47.80	77.70
490	Tim Hortons	Restaurants	★	Avg	Narrow	22.00	17.00	27.60
512	UST	Tobacco	★	Avg	Wide	44.00	33.90	55.10
61	Abercrombie & Fitch A	Clothing Stores	★★	Avg	Narrow	60.00	46.30	75.20
67	Aetna	Managed Care	★★	Avg	None	35.00	27.00	43.90
74	Alcon	Drugs	★★	-Avg	Wide	102.00	86.90	133.90
82	Allstate	Insurance (Property)	★★	Avg	Narrow	57.00	44.00	71.40
86	Amazon.com	Online Retail	★★	Avg	Wide	32.00	24.70	40.10
133	BG Group PLC ADR	Oil & Gas	★★	Avg	Narrow	57.00	44.00	71.40
125	Baxter International	Medical Equipment	★★	Avg	Narrow	40.00	30.80	50.10
186	CNOOC ADR	Oil & Gas	★★	+Avg	Narrow	79.00	50.30	95.30
169	Centurytel	Telecom Services	★★	Avg	Narrow	37.00	28.50	46.40
187	Coach	Jewelry/Accessories	★★	Avg	Narrow	38.00	29.30	47.60
209	DirecTV	Cable TV	★★	Avg	Narrow	20.00	15.40	25.10
212	Donaldson	Environmental Control	★★	Avg	Narrow	29.00	22.40	36.30
216	Dun & Bradstreet	Business/Online Services	★★	-Avg	Wide	64.00	54.50	84.00
220	EchoStar Communications	Cable TV	★★	Avg	Narrow	33.00	25.40	41.30
255	Forest Laboratories	Drugs	★★	Avg	Narrow	42.00	32.40	52.60
275	Goldman Sachs Group	Securities	★★	Avg	Wide	161.00	124.10	201.70
280	H.J. Heinz	Food Mfg.	★★	Avg	Narrow	40.00	30.80	50.10
291	Honeywell International	Diversified	★★	Avg	Narrow	37.00	28.50	46.40
300	Infosys Technologies ADR	Business Applications	★★	Avg	Narrow	48.00	37.00	60.10
311	Jacobs Engineering Group	Engineering & Construction	★★	Avg	Narrow	68.00	52.40	85.20
329	Laboratory Corp of America	Diagnostics	★★	Avg	Narrow	64.00	49.40	80.20
342	Macrovision	Business Applications	★★	Avg	Narrow	23.00	17.70	28.80
344	Manulife Financial	Insurance (General)	★★	Avg	Narrow	29.00	22.40	36.30

Stocks with Below Average Risk Measure
Morningstar Stocks 500 Universe

Pg	Company	Industry	Morningstar Rating
131	Berkshire Hathaway B	Insurance (General)	★★★★★
219	eBay	Online Retail	★★★★★
229	Energy Transfer Equity LP	Oil & Gas Services	★★★★★
230	Energy Transfer Partners	Oil & Gas	★★★★★
239	Expeditors International	Transportation - Misc	★★★★★
244	Fastenal	Distributors	★★★★★
355	Medtronic	Medical Equipment	★★★★★
387	Novartis AG ADR	Drugs	★★★★★
508	United Parcel Service B	Transportation - Misc	★★★★★
528	Wal-Mart Stores	Discount Stores	★★★★★
59	3M Company	Diversified	★★★★
89	American Express	Finance	★★★★
98	Anheuser-Busch Companies	Alcoholic Drinks	★★★★
110	Automatic Data Processing	Data Processing	★★★★
152	Cadbury Schweppes PLC ADR	Food Mfg.	★★★★
188	Coca-Cola	Beverage Mfg.	★★★★
221	Ecolab	Chemicals	★★★★
290	Home Depot	Home Supply	★★★★
308	Iron Mountain	Business Support	★★★★
310	Jack Henry & Associates	Data Processing	★★★★
316	Johnson & Johnson	Drugs	★★★★
343	Magellan Midstream Holdings LP	Pipelines	★★★★
362	Microsoft	Business Applications	★★★★
378	New Jersey Resources	Natural Gas Utilities	★★★★
403	PepsiCo	Beverage Mfg.	★★★★
427	Republic Services A	Waste Management	★★★★
452	SLM	Finance	★★★★
467	Student Loan	Finance	★★★★
476	Target	Discount Stores	★★★★
532	Washington Post Co	Media Conglomerates	★★★★
539	Wesco Financial	Insurance (General)	★★★★
549	Wm. Wrigley Jr.	Food Mfg.	★★★★
60	Abbott Laboratories	Drugs	★★★
106	Associated Banc-Corp	Regional Banks	★★★
112	AutoZone	Auto Retail	★★★
128	Becton, Dickinson and Company	Medical Equipment	★★★
147	Brown-Forman B	Alcoholic Drinks	★★★
150	Buckeye Partners LP	Pipelines	★★★
154	Campbell Soup	Food Mfg.	★★★
185	Clorox	Household & Personal Prod	★★★
189	Colgate-Palmolive	Household & Personal Prod	★★★
196	Consolidated Edison	Electric Utilities	★★★
202	Darden Restaurants	Restaurants	★★★
208	Diageo PLC ADR	Alcoholic Drinks	★★★
227	Emerson Electric	Electric Equipment	★★★
240	ExxonMobil	Oil & Gas	★★★
265	General Mills	Food Mfg.	★★★
267	Genuine Parts	Auto Retail	★★★
285	Hawaiian Electric Industries	Electric Utilities	★★★
287	Hershey Company	Food Mfg.	★★★
295	IBM	Computer Equipment	★★★
296	Idexx Laboratories	Drugs	★★★
315	John Wiley & Sons A	Publishing	★★★
321	Kellogg	Food Mfg.	★★★
323	Kimberly-Clark	Household & Personal Prod	★★★
324	Kinder Morgan Energy Partners	Pipelines	★★★
328	Kraft Foods	Food Mfg.	★★★
340	Lowe's Companies	Home Supply	★★★
353	McDonald's	Restaurants	★★★
380	News Corporation	Media Conglomerates	★★★
390	Nuveen Investments	Money Management	★★★
395	ONEOK Partners LP	Pipelines	★★★
402	Paychex	Data Processing	★★★
410	Pitney Bowes	Office Equipment	★★★
417	Procter & Gamble	Household & Personal Prod	★★★
439	Royal Dutch Shell PLC ADR A	Oil & Gas	★★★
456	Southern	Electric Utilities	★★★
466	Stryker	Medical Equipment	★★★
470	SunTrust Banks	Super Regional Banks	★★★
473	Sysco	Food Wholesale	★★★
482	TEPPCO Partners	Pipelines	★★★
492	Time Warner	Media Conglomerates	★★★
501	TransCanada	Pipelines	★★★
507	Unilever NV	Food Mfg.	★★★
509	United Technologies	Diversified	★★★
525	W.W. Grainger	Distributors	★★★
534	Waters	Medical Equipment	★★★
540	Westamerica Bancorporation	Regional Banks	★★★
558	Zimmer Holdings	Medical Equipment	★★★
74	Alcon	Drugs	★★
216	Dun & Bradstreet	Business/Online Services	★★
352	McCormick & Company	Food Mfg.	★★
354	McGraw-Hill Companies	Publishing	★★
369	Moody's	Business Support	★★
433	Robert Half International	Employment	★★
522	Vornado Realty Trust	REITS	★★
529	Walt Disney	Media Conglomerates	★★
548	Wisconsin Energy	Electric Utilities	★★
236	Equity Residential	REITS	★
449	SEI Investments	Business Support	★

Largest Market Capitalization and Highest Sales
Morningstar Stocks 500 Universe

Market Capitalization

Pg	Company	Industry	$Mil
240	ExxonMobil	Oil & Gas	446,944
264	General Electric	Electric Equipment	383,564
362	Microsoft	Business Applications	293,538
181	Citigroup	International Banks	273,691
404	PetroChina Company ADR	Oil & Gas	252,026
118	Bank of America	International Banks	239,758
141	BP PLC ADR	Oil & Gas	231,015
439	Royal Dutch Shell PLC ADR A	Oil & Gas	230,956
499	Toyota Motor ADR	Auto Makers	217,700
293	HSBC Holdings PLC ADR	International Banks	204,784
417	Procter & Gamble	Household & Personal Prod	203,656
528	Wal-Mart Stores	Discount Stores	192,479
316	Johnson & Johnson	Drugs	191,415
407	Pfizer	Drugs	186,751
90	American International Group	Insurance (Property)	186,296
85	Altria Group	Tobacco	179,868
497	Total SA ADR	Oil & Gas	176,957
131	Berkshire Hathaway B	Insurance (General)	169,636
309	J.P. Morgan Chase & Co.	International Banks	167,551
179	Cisco Systems	Data Networking	165,967
173	Chevron	Oil & Gas	160,294
273	GlaxoSmithKline PLC ADR	Drugs	157,300
295	IBM	Computer Equipment	146,342
276	Google	Business/Online Services	140,979
108	AT&T	Telecom Services	137,384
387	Novartis AG ADR	Drugs	134,175
443	Sanofi-Aventis ADR	Drugs	129,397
521	Vodafone Group PLC ADR	Wireless Service	127,867
537	Wells Fargo	Super Regional Banks	120,049
505	UBS AG	International Banks	118,774
195	ConocoPhillips	Oil & Gas	118,413
302	Intel	Semiconductors	116,762
188	Coca-Cola	Beverage Mfg.	113,088
405	Petroleo Brasileiro ADR	Oil & Gas	112,932
288	Hewlett-Packard	Computer Equipment	112,070
519	Verizon Communications	Telecom Services	108,723
479	Telefonica SA ADR	Telecom Services	104,574
403	PepsiCo	Beverage Mfg.	102,712
357	Merck	Drugs	94,656
123	Barclays PLC ADR	International Banks	94,325
382	Nokia ADR	Wireless Equipment	90,097
526	Wachovia	Super Regional Banks	90,049
396	Oracle	Business Applications	89,050
190	Comcast A	Cable TV	88,095
450	Siemens AG ADR	Wireline Equipment	87,817
492	Time Warner	Media Conglomerates	86,932
370	Morgan Stanley	Securities	86,198
262	Genentech	Biotechnology	85,511
275	Goldman Sachs Group	Securities	84,890
107	AstraZeneca PLC ADR	Drugs	84,438

Median Market Capitalization ($Mil)   13,393

Sales

Pg	Company	Industry	$Mil
240	ExxonMobil	Oil & Gas	386,951
528	Wal-Mart Stores	Discount Stores	339,150
439	Royal Dutch Shell PLC ADR A	Oil & Gas	306,731
141	BP PLC ADR	Oil & Gas	239,792
173	Chevron	Oil & Gas	216,166
195	ConocoPhillips	Oil & Gas	198,161
499	Toyota Motor ADR	Auto Makers	186,677
264	General Electric	Electric Equipment	161,022
497	Total SA ADR	Oil & Gas	153,547
90	American International Group	Insurance (Property)	110,593
450	Siemens AG ADR	Wireline Equipment	107,241
85	Altria Group	Tobacco	100,499
131	Berkshire Hathaway B	Insurance (General)	97,676
232	ENI SpA ADR	Oil & Gas	93,324
288	Hewlett-Packard	Computer Equipment	91,658
290	Home Depot	Home Supply	90,061
295	IBM	Computer Equipment	89,593
519	Verizon Communications	Telecom Services	88,881
181	Citigroup	International Banks	86,566
159	Cardinal Health	Medical Goods & Services	83,483
417	Procter & Gamble	Household & Personal Prod	72,214
118	Bank of America	International Banks	68,368
404	PetroChina Company ADR	Oil & Gas	67,281
455	Sony ADR	Audio/Video Equipment	66,335
257	France Telecom SA ADR	Telecom Services	61,407
108	AT&T	Telecom Services	60,171
197	Costco Wholesale	Discount Stores	60,151
309	J.P. Morgan Chase & Co.	International Banks	59,650
138	Boeing	Aerospace & Defense	59,114
205	Dell	Computer Equipment	56,738
476	Target	Discount Stores	56,727
405	Petroleo Brasileiro ADR	Oil & Gas	56,324
536	WellPoint	Managed Care	54,285
521	Vodafone Group PLC ADR	Wireless Service	52,679
316	Johnson & Johnson	Drugs	52,252
407	Pfizer	Drugs	52,208
510	UnitedHealth Group	Managed Care	51,787
293	HSBC Holdings PLC ADR	International Banks	49,836
507	Unilever NV	Food Mfg.	49,679
479	Telefonica SA ADR	Telecom Services	49,213
527	Walgreen	Specialty Retail	47,409
340	Lowe's Companies	Home Supply	47,330
359	Metropolitan Life Insurance	Insurance (Life)	47,120
508	United Parcel Service B	Transportation - Misc	46,873
509	United Technologies	Diversified	46,303
458	Sprint Nextel	Wireless Service	46,267
362	Microsoft	Business Applications	45,352
492	Time Warner	Media Conglomerates	44,532
143	British American Tobacco PLC ADR	Tobacco	43,778
382	Nokia ADR	Wireless Equipment	42,815

Median Sales ($Mil)   5,901

Highest Return on Equity and Return on Assets
Morningstar Stocks 500 Universe

Return on Equity (Trailing 12 Months)

Pg	Company	Industry	%
229	Energy Transfer Equity LP	Oil & Gas Services	**232.50**
86	Amazon.com	Online Retail	**148.98**
112	AutoZone	Auto Retail	**107.61**
101	Apollo Group A	Education	**104.10**
530	Warner Music Group	Media Conglomerates	**103.45**
149	BT Group PLC ADR	Telecom Services	**101.85**
205	Dell	Computer Equipment	**100.77**
189	Colgate-Palmolive	Household & Personal Prod	**93.58**
468	Suburban Propane Partners	Oil/Gas Products	**85.82**
534	Waters	Medical Equipment	**83.36**
214	Dow Jones & Company	Media Conglomerates	**82.01**
273	GlaxoSmithKline PLC ADR	Drugs	**69.74**
287	Hershey Company	Food Mfg.	**69.36**
390	Nuveen Investments	Money Management	**69.02**
325	Kinetic Concepts	Medical Equipment	**64.33**
556	Yum Brands	Restaurants	**60.92**
62	Accenture	Consultants	**60.48**
154	Campbell Soup	Food Mfg.	**59.54**
269	Gerdau SA ADR PN	Steel/Iron	**53.54**
507	Unilever NV	Food Mfg.	**50.01**
193	Companhia Vale Do Rio Doce	Steel/Iron	**49.26**
115	Avon Products	Household & Personal Prod	**48.50**
98	Anheuser-Busch Companies	Alcoholic Drinks	**46.38**
117	Baker Hughes	Oil & Gas Services	**45.26**
277	Graco	Machinery	**45.02**
282	Hansen Natural	Beverage Mfg.	**44.46**
187	Coach	Jewelry/Accessories	**44.15**
298	Imperial Oil	Oil & Gas	**43.33**
506	Ultra Petroleum	Oil & Gas	**43.03**
514	Valassis Communications	Publishing	**41.23**
93	AmeriGas Partners	Oil/Gas Products	**41.21**
208	Diageo PLC ADR	Alcoholic Drinks	**41.12**
321	Kellogg	Food Mfg.	**41.11**
479	Telefonica SA ADR	Telecom Services	**39.88**
435	Rockwell Collins	Aerospace & Defense	**39.55**
281	Halliburton	Oil & Gas Services	**39.39**
449	SEI Investments	Business Support	**39.06**
452	SLM	Finance	**39.00**
162	Caterpillar	Construction Machinery	**38.78**
493	TJX Companies	Clothing Stores	**37.78**
88	America Movil SA ADR	Telecom Services	**36.94**
145	Brookfield Asset Management	Finance	**36.82**
405	Petroleo Brasileiro ADR	Oil & Gas	**36.75**
245	Federated Investors B	Money Management	**36.72**
74	Alcon	Drugs	**36.42**
182	Citizens Communications	Telecom Services	**36.35**
461	Starwood Hotels & Resorts	Hotels	**36.33**
000	Nucor	Steel/Iron	**36.24**
218	Eaton Vance	Money Management	**36.14**
486	Texas Instruments	Semiconductors	**35.99**
	Average Return on Equity (%)		**21.15**

Return on Assets (Trailing 12 Months)

Pg	Company	Industry	%
369	Moody's	Business Support	**54.14**
101	Apollo Group A	Education	**43.55**
512	UST	Tobacco	**38.20**
282	Hansen Natural	Beverage Mfg.	**33.05**
187	Coach	Jewelry/Accessories	**31.39**
486	Texas Instruments	Semiconductors	**29.27**
277	Graco	Machinery	**28.79**
300	Infosys Technologies ADR	Business Applications	**26.86**
117	Baker Hughes	Oil & Gas Services	**26.78**
524	W.P. Stewart & Company	Money Management	**26.25**
218	Eaton Vance	Money Management	**24.91**
325	Kinetic Concepts	Medical Equipment	**24.23**
245	Federated Investors B	Money Management	**24.05**
256	Forward Air	Land Transport	**23.63**
449	SEI Investments	Business Support	**22.97**
506	Ultra Petroleum	Oil & Gas	**22.58**
535	Weight Watchers International	Personal Services	**21.86**
255	Forest Laboratories	Drugs	**21.84**
186	CNOOC ADR	Oil & Gas	**21.70**
389	Nucor	Steel/Iron	**21.41**
193	Companhia Vale Do Rio Doce	Steel/Iron	**21.38**
109	Autodesk	Business Applications	**20.93**
547	Wipro ADR	Business Applications	**20.36**
283	Harley-Davidson	Recreation	**20.28**
362	Microsoft	Business Applications	**19.79**
298	Imperial Oil	Oil & Gas	**19.75**
465	Strayer Education	Education	**19.56**
244	Fastenal	Distributors	**19.32**
433	Robert Half International	Employment	**19.02**
107	AstraZeneca PLC ADR	Drugs	**19.02**
61	Abercrombie & Fitch A	Clothing Stores	**18.81**
474	T Rowe Price Group	Money Management	**18.76**
273	GlaxoSmithKline PLC ADR	Drugs	**18.75**
163	CBOT Holdings	Securities	**18.59**
175	Chico's FAS	Clothing Stores	**18.59**
316	Johnson & Johnson	Drugs	**18.50**
336	Linear Technology	Semiconductors	**18.42**
475	Taiwan Semiconductor ADR	Semiconductors	**18.41**
484	Tessera Technologies	Semiconductor Equipment	**18.23**
240	ExxonMobil	Oil & Gas	**17.84**
74	Alcon	Drugs	**17.81**
404	PetroChina Company ADR	Oil & Gas	**17.65**
281	Halliburton	Oil & Gas Services	**17.47**
382	Nokia ADR	Wireless Equipment	**17.06**
296	Idexx Laboratories	Drugs	**16.96**
188	Coca-Cola	Beverage Mfg.	**16.82**
137	Blue Nile	Jewelry/Accessories	**16.73**
216	Dun & Bradstreet	Business/Online Services	**16.53**
428	Research in Motion	Computer Equipment	**16.53**
234	EOG Resources	Oil & Gas	**16.51**
	Average Return on Assets (%)		**8.25**

Highest Dividend Yield and Cash Return
Morningstar Stocks 500 Universe

Dividend Yield

Pg	Company	Industry	%
546	Windstream	Telecom Services	8.70
307	Iowa Telecommunications Services	Telecom Services	8.20
79	Allied Capital	Finance	7.40
524	W.P. Stewart & Company	Money Management	7.10
93	AmeriGas Partners	Oil/Gas Products	7.10
182	Citizens Communications	Telecom Services	7.00
482	TEPPCO Partners	Pipelines	6.70
324	Kinder Morgan Energy Partners	Pipelines	6.70
468	Suburban Propane Partners	Oil/Gas Products	6.60
150	Buckeye Partners LP	Pipelines	6.50
478	Telecom Corp of New Zealand	Telecom Services	6.50
373	Municipal Mortgage & Equity LLC	Finance	6.20
395	ONEOK Partners LP	Pipelines	5.70
411	Plains All American Pipeline LP	Pipelines	5.60
338	Lloyds TSB Group PLC ADR	International Banks	5.40
248	Fidelity National Financial	Insurance (Title)	4.90
196	Consolidated Edison	Electric Utilities	4.80
230	Energy Transfer Partners	Oil & Gas	4.70
232	ENI SpA ADR	Oil & Gas	4.70
285	Hawaiian Electric Industries	Electric Utilities	4.60
322	KeyCorp	Super Regional Banks	4.50
531	Washington Mutual	Savings & Loans	4.50
257	France Telecom SA ADR	Telecom Services	4.50
521	Vodafone Group PLC ADR	Wireless Service	4.50
77	Alliancebernstein Holding LP	Money Management	4.40
519	Verizon Communications	Telecom Services	4.40
252	First Horizon National	Regional Banks	4.30
142	Bristol-Myers Squibb	Drugs	4.30
456	Southern	Electric Utilities	4.20
432	Reynolds American	Tobacco	4.20
376	National City	Super Regional Banks	4.20
544	Williams Partners LP	Pipelines	4.10
105	Arthur J. Gallagher & Co.	Insurance (General)	4.10
293	HSBC Holdings PLC ADR	International Banks	4.10
191	Comerica	Regional Banks	4.00
118	Bank of America	International Banks	4.00
149	BT Group PLC ADR	Telecom Services	4.00
249	Fifth Third Bancorp	Super Regional Banks	3.90
85	Altria Group	Tobacco	3.90
512	UST	Tobacco	3.90
194	Compass Minerals International	Mining	3.90
526	Wachovia	Super Regional Banks	3.80
511	US Bancorp	Super Regional Banks	3.80
407	Pfizer	Drugs	3.70
405	Petroleo Brasileiro ADR	Oil & Gas	3.70
269	Gerdau SA ADR PN	Steel/Iron	3.70
126	BB&T	Super Regional Banks	3.60
203	DCP Midstream Partners LP	Pipelines	3.60
424	Regency Energy Partners LP	Natural Gas Utilities	3.50
357	Merck	Drugs	3.50

Average Dividend Yield (%)   1.10

Cash Return (Free Cash Flow/Market Cap)

Pg	Company	Industry	%
69	Air Products and Chemicals	Chemicals	68.39
232	ENI SpA ADR	Oil & Gas	17.55
483	Ternium SA ADR	Steel/Iron	13.48
203	DCP Midstream Partners LP	Pipelines	13.39
389	Nucor	Steel/Iron	11.51
251	First Data	Data Processing	10.29
315	John Wiley & Sons A	Publishing	9.94
99	Ann Taylor Stores	Clothing Stores	9.70
71	Alberto-Culver	Household & Personal Prod	9.68
281	Halliburton	Oil & Gas Services	9.52
514	Valassis Communications	Publishing	9.51
116	Axcan Pharma	Drugs	9.04
261	Gap	Clothing Stores	9.02
468	Suburban Propane Partners	Oil/Gas Products	8.99
288	Hewlett-Packard	Computer Equipment	8.98
478	Telecom Corp of New Zealand	Telecom Services	8.94
217	Eaton	Electric Equipment	8.85
238	Expedia	Online Retail	8.83
407	Pfizer	Drugs	8.82
521	Vodafone Group PLC ADR	Wireless Service	8.67
371	Motorola	Wireless Equipment	8.55
124	Barr Pharmaceuticals	Drugs	8.55
463	Steel Dynamics	Steel/Iron	8.53
240	ExxonMobil	Oil & Gas	8.47
327	Kohl's	Discount Stores	8.45
413	Posco ADR	Steel/Iron	8.40
392	Occidental Petroleum	Oil & Gas	8.36
62	Accenture	Consultants	8.30
335	Lexmark International	Computer Equipment	8.25
507	Unilever NV	Food Mfg.	8.19
423	Raytheon	Aerospace & Defense	8.13
138	Boeing	Aerospace & Defense	8.03
205	Dell	Computer Equipment	7.96
225	Embarq	Telecom Services	7.96
242	Fair Isaac	Data Processing	7.90
510	UnitedHealth Group	Managed Care	7.82
101	Apollo Group A	Education	7.77
318	Jones Apparel Group	Apparel Makers	7.76
270	Getty Images	Business Support	7.69
257	France Telecom SA ADR	Telecom Services	7.68
306	Intuit	Business Applications	7.61
167	Cemex SAB de CV ADR	Building Materials	7.59
364	Mittal Steel Co NV	Steel/Iron	7.55
365	Mohawk Industries	Textiles	7.52
84	Altera	Semiconductors	7.52
107	AstraZeneca PLC ADR	Drugs	7.52
394	Omnicom Group	Advertising	7.50
173	Chevron	Oil & Gas	7.45
295	IBM	Computer Equipment	7.44
395	ONEOK Partners LP	Pipelines	7.41

Average Cash Return   2.90

Lowest & Highest Price Multiples
Morningstar Stocks 500 Universe

Price/Earnings Ratio (Trailing 12 Months)*

Pg	Company	Industry	Ratio
	Lowest		
232	ENI SpA ADR	Oil & Gas	4.59
96	Anadarko Petroleum	Oil & Gas	5.51
168	Centex	Home Building	6.12
333	Lennar	Home Building	6.24
177	Cimarex Energy	Oil & Gas	6.43
494	Toll Brothers	Home Building	6.52
413	Posco ADR	Steel/Iron	6.72
215	DR Horton	Home Building	6.79
195	ConocoPhillips	Oil & Gas	6.87
420	Pulte Homes	Home Building	7.00
393	Odyssey Re Holdings	Reinsurance	7.85
100	Apache	Oil & Gas	7.89
425	Reliance Steel and Aluminum	Metal Products	8.30
250	First American	Insurance (Title)	8.39
79	Allied Capital	Finance	8.51
412	PNC Financial Services Group	Super Regional Banks	8.55
392	Occidental Petroleum	Oil & Gas	8.57
364	Mittal Steel Co NV	Steel/Iron	8.61
82	Allstate	Insurance (Property)	8.72
554	XTO Energy	Oil & Gas	9.23
439	Royal Dutch Shell PLC ADR A	Oil & Gas	9.24
173	Chevron	Oil & Gas	9.28
206	Devon Energy	Oil & Gas	9.37
360	MGIC Investment	Insurance (Property)	9.45
269	Gerdau SA ADR PN	Steel/Iron	9.52
	Highest		
272	Given Imaging	Medical Equipment	92.14
70	AirTran Holdings	Air Transport	90.31
342	Macrovision	Business Applications	70.65
113	AvalonBay Communities	REITS	67.73
223	Electronic Arts	Entertain./Education Media	67.15
543	Williams Companies	Pipelines	65.30
428	Research in Motion	Computer Equipment	65.19
488	THQ	Entertain./Education Media	62.54
91	American Power Conversion	Electric Equipment	58.83
276	Google	Business/Online Services	58.59
86	Amazon.com	Online Retail	58.03
122	BankAtlantic Bancorp A	Regional Banks	57.54
530	Warner Music Group	Media Conglomerates	57.38
334	Leucadia National	Diversified	56.97
377	Network Appliance	Computer Equipment	56.93
114	Avid Technology	Business Applications	55.61
300	Infosys Technologies ADR	Business Applications	54.56
137	Blue Nile	Jewelry/Accessories	51.96
518	Ventana Medical Systems	Medical Equipment	51.23
87	AmBev ADR	Alcoholic Drinks	50.62
547	Wipro ADR	Business Applications	50.16
460	Starbucks	Restaurants	49.89
65	Adobe Systems	Development Tools	48.95
262	Genentech	Biotechnology	47.17
174	Chicago Mercantile Exchange	Securities	46.94
	Average Price/Earnings Ratio		**23.34**

Price/Book Ratio

Pg	Company	Industry	Ratio
	Lowest		
521	Vodafone Group PLC ADR	Wireless Service	0.89
136	Blackrock	Money Management	0.96
177	Cimarex Energy	Oil & Gas	1.01
164	CBS B	Media Conglomerates	1.07
366	Molson Coors Brewing Company	Alcoholic Drinks	1.13
232	ENI SpA ADR	Oil & Gas	1.14
71	Alberto-Culver	Household & Personal Prod	1.16
243	Fairfax Financial Holdings	Insurance (General)	1.16
360	MGIC Investment	Insurance (Property)	1.28
215	DR Horton	Home Building	1.30
250	First American	Insurance (Title)	1.31
420	Pulte Homes	Home Building	1.31
222	Educate	Education	1.33
413	Posco ADR	Steel/Iron	1.35
393	Odyssey Re Holdings	Reinsurance	1.36
195	ConocoPhillips	Oil & Gas	1.38
386	Northrop Grumman	Aerospace & Defense	1.38
294	IAC/InterActiveCorp	Online Retail	1.40
539	Wesco Financial	Insurance (General)	1.40
111	AutoNation	Auto Retail	1.41
351	MBIA	Insurance (General)	1.41
81	Allied Waste Industries	Waste Management	1.42
330	Lee Enterprises	Publishing	1.42
454	Smithfield Foods	Food Mfg.	1.42
458	Sprint Nextel	Wireless Service	1.42
	Highest		
299	Imperial Tobacco Group PLC ADR	Tobacco	116.67
512	UST	Tobacco	108.40
86	Amazon.com	Online Retail	86.45
216	Dun & Bradstreet	Business/Online Services	71.26
530	Warner Music Group	Media Conglomerates	59.30
189	Colgate-Palmolive	Household & Personal Prod	25.65
166	Celgene	Biotechnology	24.51
441	Salesforce.com	Business Applications	22.02
534	Waters	Medical Equipment	20.11
149	BT Group PLC ADR	Telecom Services	18.77
112	AutoZone	Auto Retail	18.68
282	Hansen Natural	Beverage Mfg.	16.68
300	Infosys Technologies ADR	Business Applications	16.48
390	Nuveen Investments	Money Management	16.35
298	Imperial Oil	Oil & Gas	16.22
137	Blue Nile	Jewelry/Accessories	16.12
101	Apollo Group A	Education	15.97
115	Avon Products	Household & Personal Prod	15.12
205	Dell	Computer Equipment	14.86
287	Hershey Company	Food Mfg	14.51
187	Coach	Jewelry/Accessories	14.07
74	Alcon	Drugs	13.66
506	Ultra Petroleum	Oil & Gas	13.17
547	Wipro ADR	Business Applications	13.01
109	Autodesk	Business Applications	12.64
	Average Price/Book Ratio		**5.50**

* Excludes companies with P/E ratios above 100.

Lowest & Highest Price Multiples
Morningstar Stocks 500 Universe

Price/Cash Flow Ratio (Trailing 12 Months)

Pg	Company	Industry	Ratio
	Lowest		
69	Air Products and Chemicals	Chemicals	1.21
232	ENI SpA ADR	Oil & Gas	2.84
177	Cimarex Energy	Oil & Gas	3.03
96	Anadarko Petroleum	Oil & Gas	3.94
519	Verizon Communications	Telecom Services	4.31
206	Devon Energy	Oil & Gas	4.42
257	France Telecom SA ADR	Telecom Services	4.78
100	Apache	Oil & Gas	4.86
413	Posco ADR	Steel/Iron	4.94
149	BT Group PLC ADR	Telecom Services	5.30
234	EOG Resources	Oil & Gas	5.39
195	ConocoPhillips	Oil & Gas	5.40
478	Telecom Corp of New Zealand	Telecom Services	5.47
182	Citizens Communications	Telecom Services	5.65
454	Smithfield Foods	Food Mfg.	5.73
81	Allied Waste Industries	Waste Management	5.99
458	Sprint Nextel	Wireless Service	6.06
554	XTO Energy	Oil & Gas	6.15
521	Vodafone Group PLC ADR	Wireless Service	6.24
169	Centurytel	Telecom Services	6.36
365	Mohawk Industries	Textiles	6.53
392	Occidental Petroleum	Oil & Gas	6.53
482	TEPPCO Partners	Pipelines	6.54
307	Iowa Telecommunications Services	Telecom Services	6.62
173	Chevron	Oil & Gas	6.63
	Highest		
222	Educate	Education	130.83
461	Starwood Hotels & Resorts	Hotels	61.68
300	Infosys Technologies ADR	Business Applications	50.55
547	Wipro ADR	Business Applications	50.35
488	THQ	Entertain./Education Media	50.09
282	Hansen Natural	Beverage Mfg.	49.57
114	Avid Technology	Business Applications	47.03
160	CarMax	Auto Retail	46.71
416	Precision Castparts	Metal Products	46.09
289	Hilton Hotels	Hotels	45.28
441	Salesforce.com	Business Applications	45.10
272	Given Imaging	Medical Equipment	43.33
262	Genentech	Biotechnology	43.15
244	Fastenal	Distributors	42.85
276	Google	Business/Online Services	42.58
117	Baker Hughes	Oil & Gas Services	41.80
453	Smith & Nephew ADR	Medical Equipment	40.52
557	Zebra Technologies	Computer Equipment	40.26
429	ResMed	Medical Equipment	37.80
518	Ventana Medical Systems	Medical Equipment	36.01
144	Broadcom	Semiconductors	35.57
414	Potash Corp of Saskatchewan	Mining	34.24
102	Apple Computer	Computer Equipment	33.49
298	Imperial Oil	Oil & Gas	32.00
516	Varian Medical Systems	Medical Equipment	31.93
	Average Price/Cash Flow Ratio		**16.98**

Price/Sales Ratio (Trailing 12 Months)

Pg	Company	Industry	Ratio
	Lowest		
411	Plains All American Pipeline LP	Pipelines	0.16
454	Smithfield Foods	Food Mfg.	0.25
111	AutoNation	Auto Retail	0.27
482	TEPPCO Partners	Pipelines	0.29
159	Cardinal Health	Medical Goods & Services	0.34
378	New Jersey Resources	Natural Gas Utilities	0.41
197	Costco Wholesale	Discount Stores	0.42
250	First American	Insurance (Title)	0.48
504	UAP Holding	Chemicals	0.48
333	Lennar	Home Building	0.50
148	Brunswick	Recreation	0.51
168	Centex	Home Building	0.52
317	Johnson Controls	Auto Parts	0.52
71	Alberto-Culver	Household & Personal Prod	0.53
243	Fairfax Financial Holdings	Insurance (General)	0.55
195	ConocoPhillips	Oil & Gas	0.56
215	DR Horton	Home Building	0.56
425	Reliance Steel and Aluminum	Metal Products	0.56
232	ENI SpA ADR	Oil & Gas	0.57
420	Pulte Homes	Home Building	0.57
528	Wal-Mart Stores	Discount Stores	0.62
70	AirTran Holdings	Air Transport	0.63
200	CVS	Specialty Retail	0.63
365	Mohawk Industries	Textiles	0.65
514	Valassis Communications	Publishing	0.65
	Highest		
166	Celgene	Biotechnology	26.57
135	Biomarin Pharmaceutical	Biotechnology	18.05
174	Chicago Mercantile Exchange	Securities	16.84
276	Google	Business/Online Services	15.21
300	Infosys Technologies ADR	Business Applications	14.07
441	Salesforce.com	Business Applications	13.96
113	AvalonBay Communities	REITS	13.68
506	Ultra Petroleum	Oil & Gas	12.71
428	Research in Motion	Computer Equipment	12.06
271	Gilead Sciences	Biotechnology	11.37
369	Moody's	Business Support	10.66
79	Allied Capital	Finance	10.60
484	Tessera Technologies	Semiconductor Equipment	10.58
262	Genentech	Biotechnology	10.36
65	Adobe Systems	Development Tools	9.75
547	Wipro ADR	Business Applications	9.58
402	Paychex	Data Processing	9.00
336	Linear Technology	Semiconductors	8.68
421	Qualcomm	Wireless Equipment	8.61
145	Brookfield Asset Management	Finance	8.40
74	Alcon	Drugs	7.99
187	Coach	Jewelry/Accessories	7.92
266	Gen-Probe	Research Services	7.84
241	F5 Networks	Data Networking	7.82
219	eBay	Online Retail	7.71
	Average Price/Sales Ratio		**3.14**

Companies with Wide Economic Moats
Largest Companies in Morningstar Stocks 500 Universe

Pg	Company	Industry	Morningstar Rating
95	Amgen	Biotechnology	★★★★★
101	Apollo Group A	Education	★★★★★
131	Berkshire Hathaway B	Insurance (General)	★★★★★
140	Boston Scientific	Medical Equipment	★★★★★
172	Checkfree	Systems & Security	★★★★★
205	Dell	Computer Equipment	★★★★★
219	eBay	Online Retail	★★★★★
239	Expeditors International	Transportation - Misc	★★★★★
244	Fastenal	Distributors	★★★★★
245	Federated Investors B	Money Management	★★★★★
256	Forward Air	Land Transport	★★★★★
270	Getty Images	Business Support	★★★★★
336	Linear Technology	Semiconductors	★★★★★
347	Marsh & McLennan Companies	Insurance (General)	★★★★★
350	Maxim Integrated Products	Semiconductors	★★★★★
355	Medtronic	Medical Equipment	★★★★★
387	Novartis AG ADR	Drugs	★★★★★
508	United Parcel Service B	Transportation - Misc	★★★★★
528	Wal-Mart Stores	Discount Stores	★★★★★
59	3M Company	Diversified	★★★★
68	Aflac	Insurance (Life)	★★★★
89	American Express	Finance	★★★★
98	Anheuser-Busch Companies	Alcoholic Drinks	★★★★
110	Automatic Data Processing	Data Processing	★★★★
115	Avon Products	Household & Personal Prod	★★★★
118	Bank of America	International Banks	★★★★
120	Bank of New York Company	International Banks	★★★★
152	Cadbury Schweppes PLC ADR	Food Mfg.	★★★★
163	CBOT Holdings	Securities	★★★★
174	Chicago Mercantile Exchange	Securities	★★★★
188	Coca-Cola	Beverage Mfg.	★★★★
223	Electronic Arts	Entertain./Education Media	★★★★
224	Eli Lilly & Company	Drugs	★★★★
259	Gamco Investors	Money Management	★★★★
268	Genzyme	Biotechnology	★★★★
273	GlaxoSmithKline PLC ADR	Drugs	★★★★
290	Home Depot	Home Supply	★★★★
305	International Speedway A	Recreation	★★★★
308	Iron Mountain	Business Support	★★★★
309	J.P. Morgan Chase & Co.	International Banks	★★★★
310	Jack Henry & Associates	Data Processing	★★★★
316	Johnson & Johnson	Drugs	★★★★
331	Legg Mason	Money Management	★★★★
343	Magellan Midstream Holdings LP	Pipelines	★★★★
356	Mellon Financial	International Banks	★★★★
362	Microsoft	Business Applications	★★★★
396	Oracle	Business Applications	★★★★
403	PepsiCo	Beverage Mfg.	★★★★
421	Qualcomm	Wireless Equipment	★★★★
426	Renaissance Re Holdings	Reinsurance	★★★★
452	SLM	Finance	★★★★
524	W.P. Stewart & Company	Money Management	★★★★
532	Washington Post Co	Media Conglomerates	★★★★
537	Wells Fargo	Super Regional Banks	★★★★
549	Wm. Wrigley Jr.	Food Mfg.	★★★★
60	Abbott Laboratories	Drugs	★★★
65	Adobe Systems	Development Tools	★★★
76	Allergan	Drugs	★★★
80	Allied Irish Banks ADR	International Banks	★★★
85	Altria Group	Tobacco	★★★
87	AmBev ADR	Alcoholic Drinks	★★★
104	Applied Materials	Semiconductor Equipment	★★★
107	AstraZeneca PLC ADR	Drugs	★★★
109	Autodesk	Business Applications	★★★
119	Bank of Montreal	International Banks	★★★
121	Bank of Nova Scotia	International Banks	★★★
123	Barclays PLC ADR	International Banks	★★★
134	Biogen Idec	Biotechnology	★★★
142	Bristol-Myers Squibb	Drugs	★★★
143	British American Tobacco PLC ADR	Tobacco	★★★
146	Brown & Brown	Insurance (General)	★★★
150	Buckeye Partners LP	Pipelines	★★★
153	Calamos Asset Management A	Money Management	★★★
154	Campbell Soup	Food Mfg.	★★★
158	Capital One Financial	Finance	★★★
162	Caterpillar	Construction Machinery	★★★
170	CH Robinson Worldwide	Transportation - Misc	★★★
178	Cintas	Business Support	★★★
179	Cisco Systems	Data Networking	★★★
181	Citigroup	International Banks	★★★
189	Colgate-Palmolive	Household & Personal Prod	★★★
190	Comcast A	Cable TV	★★★
207	DeVry	Education	★★★
208	Diageo PLC ADR	Alcoholic Drinks	★★★
214	Dow Jones & Company	Media Conglomerates	★★★
218	Eaton Vance	Money Management	★★★
235	Equifax	Business Support	★★★
240	ExxonMobil	Oil & Gas	★★★
251	First Data	Data Processing	★★★
254	Fiserv	Data Processing	★★★
262	Genentech	Biotechnology	★★★
263	General Dynamics	Aerospace & Defense	★★★
264	General Electric	Electric Equipment	★★★
279	H & R Block	Personal Services	★★★
283	Harley-Davidson	Recreation	★★★
287	Hershey Company	Food Mfg.	★★★
293	HSBC Holdings PLC ADR	International Banks	★★★
295	IBM	Computer Equipment	★★★
299	Imperial Tobacco Group PLC ADR	Tobacco	★★★
302	Intel	Semiconductors	★★★
303	IntercontinentalExchange	Securities	★★★
304	International Game Tech	Gambling/Hotel Casinos	★★★
306	Intuit	Business Applications	★★★
315	John Wiley & Sons A	Publishing	★★★
324	Kinder Morgan Energy Partners	Pipelines	★★★
326	KLA-Tencor	Semiconductor Equipment	★★★
338	Lloyds TSB Group PLC ADR	International Banks	★★★
339	Lockheed Martin	Aerospace & Defense	★★★
340	Lowe's Companies	Home Supply	★★★
349	MasterCard	Data Processing	★★★
357	Merck	Drugs	★★★
370	Morgan Stanley	Securities	★★★
385	Northern Trust	International Banks	★★★
390	Nuveen Investments	Money Management	★★★
395	ONEOK Partners LP	Pipelines	★★★
402	Paychex	Data Processing	★★★
407	Pfizer	Drugs	★★★
410	Pitney Bowes	Office Equipment	★★★
417	Procter & Gamble	Household & Personal Prod	★★★
418	Progressive	Insurance (Property)	★★★
443	Sanofi-Aventis ADR	Drugs	★★★
446	Schering-Plough	Drugs	★★★
465	Strayer Education	Education	★★★
466	Stryker	Medical Equipment	★★★
472	Synovus Financial	Regional Banks	★★★
473	Sysco	Food Wholesale	★★★
482	TEPPCO Partners	Pipelines	★★★
496	Toronto-Dominion Bank	International Banks	★★★
498	Total System Services	Data Processing	★★★
505	UBS AG	International Banks	★★★

Companies with Narrow Economic Moats
Largest Companies in Morningstar Stocks 500 Universe

Pg	Company	Industry	Morningstar Rating	Pg	Company	Industry	Morningstar Rating
73	Alcoa	Aluminum	★★★★★	367	Monsanto Company	Agrochemical	★★★
167	Cemex SAB de CV ADR	Building Materials	★★★★★	380	News Corporation	Media Conglomerates	★★★
206	Devon Energy	Oil & Gas	★★★★★	381	Nike B	Shoes	★★★
226	EMC	Computer Equipment	★★★★★	382	Nokia ADR	Wireless Equipment	★★★
458	Sprint Nextel	Wireless Service	★★★★★	386	Northrop Grumman	Aerospace & Defense	★★★
555	Yahoo	Media Conglomerates	★★★★★	389	Nucor	Steel/Iron	★★★
72	Alcatel Lucent ADR	Wireline Equipment	★★★★	392	Occidental Petroleum	Oil & Gas	★★★
96	Anadarko Petroleum	Oil & Gas	★★★★	394	Omnicom Group	Advertising	★★★
100	Apache	Oil & Gas	★★★★	398	PACCAR	Truck Makers	★★★
132	Best Buy Co.	Electronics Stores	★★★★	412	PNC Financial Services Group	Super Regional Banks	★★★
144	Broadcom	Semiconductors	★★★★	413	Posco ADR	Steel/Iron	★★★
159	Cardinal Health	Medical Goods & Services	★★★★	415	Praxair	Chemicals	★★★
161	Carnival	Recreation	★★★★	423	Raytheon	Aerospace & Defense	★★★
164	CBS B	Media Conglomerates	★★★★	432	Reynolds American	Tobacco	★★★
257	France Telecom SA ADR	Telecom Services	★★★★	439	Royal Dutch Shell PLC ADR A	Oil & Gas	★★★
261	Gap	Clothing Stores	★★★★	445	Sasol ADR	Chemicals	★★★
371	Motorola	Wireless Equipment	★★★★	456	Southern	Electric Utilities	★★★
376	National City	Super Regional Banks	★★★★	460	Starbucks	Restaurants	★★★
455	Sony ADR	Audio/Video Equipment	★★★★	470	SunTrust Banks	Super Regional Banks	★★★
476	Target	Discount Stores	★★★★	475	Taiwan Semiconductor ADR	Semiconductors	★★★
479	Telefonica SA ADR	Telecom Services	★★★★	480	Telefonos de Mexico SA de CV ADR	Telecom Services	★★★
486	Texas Instruments	Semiconductors	★★★★	485	Teva Pharmaceutical Industries ADR	Drugs	★★★
503	Tyco International	Diversified	★★★★	492	Time Warner	Media Conglomerates	★★★
531	Washington Mutual	Savings & Loans	★★★★	497	Total SA ADR	Oil & Gas	★★★
533	Waste Management	Waste Management	★★★★	501	TransCanada	Pipelines	★★★
536	WellPoint	Managed Care	★★★★	507	Unilever NV	Food Mfg.	★★★
62	Accenture	Consultants	★★★	510	UnitedHealth Group	Managed Care	★★★
63	ACE	Insurance (Property)	★★★	519	Verizon Communications	Telecom Services	★★★
83	Alltel	Wireless Service	★★★	520	Viacom B	Media Conglomerates	★★★
88	America Movil SA ADR	Telecom Services	★★★	521	Vodafone Group PLC ADR	Wireless Service	★★★
90	American International Group	Insurance (Property)	★★★	526	Wachovia	Super Regional Banks	★★★
126	BB&T	Super Regional Banks	★★★	552	Xerox	Office Equipment	★★★
128	Becton, Dickinson and Company	Medical Equipment	★★★	554	XTO Energy	Oil & Gas	★★★
138	Boeing	Aerospace & Defense	★★★	82	Allstate	Insurance (Property)	★★
141	BP PLC ADR	Oil & Gas	★★★	125	Baxter International	Medical Equipment	★★
145	Brookfield Asset Management	Finance	★★★	133	BG Group PLC ADR	Oil & Gas	★★
149	BT Group PLC ADR	Telecom Services	★★★	186	CNOOC ADR	Oil & Gas	★★
156	Canadian National Railway	Land Transport	★★★	209	DirecTV	Cable TV	★★
157	Canadian Natural Resources	Oil & Gas	★★★	220	EchoStar Communications	Cable TV	★★
173	Chevron	Oil & Gas	★★★	255	Forest Laboratories	Drugs	★★
195	ConocoPhillips	Oil & Gas	★★★	291	Honeywell International	Diversified	★★
197	Costco Wholesale	Discount Stores	★★★	300	Infosys Technologies ADR	Business Applications	★★
198	Countrywide Financial	Savings & Loans	★★★	344	Manulife Financial	Insurance (General)	★★
200	CVS	Specialty Retail	★★★	428	Research in Motion	Computer Equipment	★★
201	Danaher	Electric Equipment	★★★	450	Siemens AG ADR	Wireline Equipment	★★
204	Deere & Company	Agricultural Machinery	★★★	499	Toyota Motor ADR	Auto Makers	★★
211	Dominion Resources	Electric Utilities	★★★	522	Vornado Realty Trust	REITS	★★
227	Emerson Electric	Electric Equipment	★★★	529	Walt Disney	Media Conglomerates	★★
232	ENI SpA ADR	Oil & Gas	★★★	547	Wipro ADR	Business Applications	★★
246	FedEx	Transportation - Misc	★★★	102	Apple Computer	Computer Equipment	★
249	Fifth Third Bancorp	Super Regional Banks	★★★	108	AT&T	Telecom Services	★
253	FirstEnergy	Electric Utilities	★★★	117	Baker Hughes	Oil & Gas Services	★
265	General Mills	Food Mfg.	★★★	127	Bear Stearns Companies	Securities	★
271	Gilead Sciences	Biotechnology	★★★	166	Celgene	Biotechnology	★
278	Groupe Danone ADR	Food Mfg.	★★★	193	Companhia Vale Do Rio Doce	Steel/Iron	★
297	Illinois Tool Works	Machinery	★★★	276	Google	Business/Online Services	★
298	Imperial Oil	Oil & Gas	★★★	281	Halliburton	Oil & Gas Services	★
317	Johnson Controls	Auto Parts	★★★	288	Hewlett-Packard	Computer Equipment	★
321	Kellogg	Food Mfg.	★★★	327	Kohl's	Discount Stores	★
323	Kimberly-Clark	Household & Personal Prod	★★★	332	Lehman Brothers Holdings	Securities	★
328	Kraft Foods	Food Mfg.	★★★	346	Marriott International A	Hotels	★
353	McDonald's	Restaurants	★★★	404	PetroChina Company ADR	Oil & Gas	★
359	Metropolitan Life Insurance	Insurance (Life)	★★★	405	Petroleo Brasileiro ADR	Oil & Gas	★
361	MGM Mirage	Gambling/Hotel Casinos	★★★	447	Schlumberger	Oil & Gas Services	★
364	Mittal Steel Co NV	Steel/Iron	★★★	469	Suncor Energy	Oil & Gas	★

Companies with No Economic Moat
Morningstar Stocks 500 Universe

Pg	Company	Industry	Morningstar Rating
301	Ingersoll-Rand A	Machinery	★★★★
383	Norfolk Southern	Land Transport	★★★★
399	Panera Bread	Restaurants	★★★★
71	Alberto-Culver	Household & Personal Prod	★★★
94	Ameriprise Financial	Finance	★★★
129	Bed Bath & Beyond	Furniture Retail	★★★
151	Burlington Northern Santa Fe	Land Transport	★★★
176	Chipotle Mexican Grill A	Restaurants	★★★
444	Sara Lee	Food Mfg.	★★★
488	THQ	Entertain./Education Media	★★★
67	Aetna	Managed Care	★★

Report Pages

This section offers a full-page report on each of the 500 stocks.

Morningstar analysts do not own shares of the companies they cover.

3M Company MMM

Data as of 12-29-06

Rating	Fair Value	Last Close	Consider Buy	Consider Sell	Yield %
★★★★	$89.00	$77.93	$75.80	$116.80	2.36

Company Profile

3M manufactures adhesive, coating, electronic, and health-care products. The firm operates in more than 200 countries (more than half of its sales come from outside the United States) and makes more than 55,000 products. Best known for its Post-it and Scotch brands, 3M offers a diverse array of items, ranging from dental products to brightness-enhancement films for electronic displays to reflective sheeting used on highway signs.

Management — Stewardship Grade [B]

In December 2005, 3M selected Brunswick CEO and chairman George Buckley as its new CEO and chairman. Buckley succeeded the highly regarded James McNerney, who departed to take the top job at Boeing in June 2005. McNerney left some big shoes to fill, but we think Buckley is up to the challenge. Under Buckley's leadership, Brunswick completed a transformation and turnaround similar to the one accomplished at 3M under McNerney's watch. If McNerney had any weaknesses, we believe that they were in consumer marketing and brand development. Buckley will bring ample experience in these areas to 3M, and he may actually be a better fit for 3M's growth strategies. The biggest challenge for Buckley will be handling a company that is 5 times the size of Brunswick and even more diversified. Luckily for Buckley, McNerney left behind a company that is hitting on all cylinders and has a deep bench of experienced managers. Buckley has had a rough start so far, but we believe part of that is cleaning up any messes that McNerney might have left behind.

3M Center
St. Paul, MN 55144-1000
www.3m.com

Growth [C]

	2002	2003	2004	2005
Revenue %	1.7	11.6	9.8	5.8
Earnings/Share %	39.7	20.8	24.2	9.9
Book Value/Share %	-0.4	30.6	31.3	-0.1
Dividends/Share %	3.3	6.5	9.1	16.7

Profitability [A+]

	2003	2004	2005	TTM
Return on Assets %	13.7	14.4	15.6	15.5
Oper Cash Flow $Mil	3,773	4,282	4,258	3,737
- Cap Spending $Mil	677	937	943	1,046
= Free Cash Flow $Mil	3,096	3,345	3,315	2,691

Financial Health [A+]

	2003	2004	2005	06-30-06
Long-term Debt $Mil	1,735	727	1,309	1,230
Total Equity $Mil	7,885	10,378	10,100	10,983
Debt/Equity Ratio	0.2	0.1	0.1	0.1

Industry	Business Risk	Moat Size	Investment Style	Sector
Diversified	Below Avg	Wide	Large Core	Industrial Materials

Competition

	Market Cap $Mil	12 Mo Trailing Sales $Mil	Price/Cash Flow	Return On Assets%	Debt/Equity	Total Return% 1 Yr	3 Yr
3M Company	57,385	22,466	15.4	15.5	0.1	3.0	-0.1
Johnson & Johnson	191,415	52,252	14.5	18.5	0.0	12.4	10.8
Imperial Chemical Industr	10,555	10,609	16.1	8.6	NMF	59.1	38.8

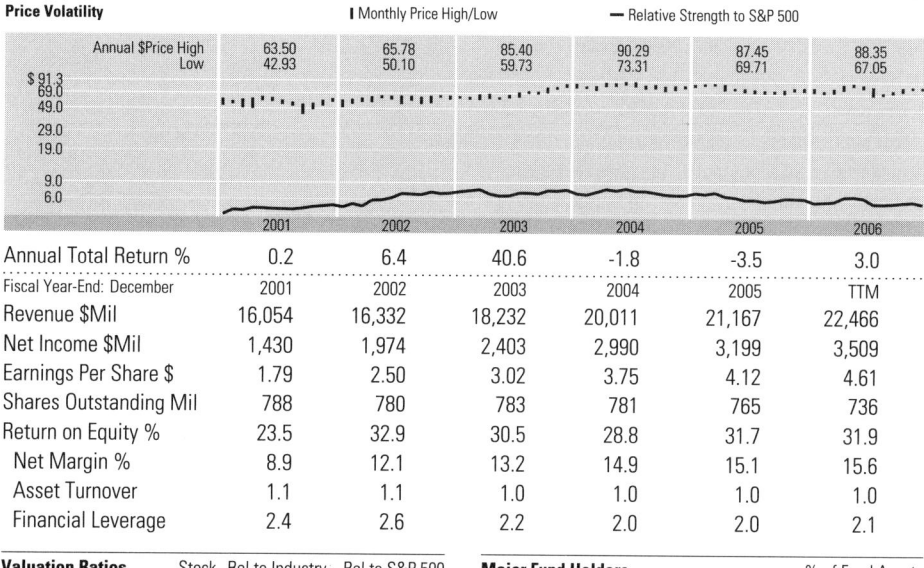

Price Volatility — Monthly Price High/Low — Relative Strength to S&P 500

Annual $ Price High/Low	63.50 / 42.93	65.78 / 50.10	85.40 / 59.73	90.29 / 73.31	87.45 / 69.71	88.35 / 67.05

$91.3 / 69.0

	2001	2002	2003	2004	2005	2006
Annual Total Return %	0.2	6.4	40.6	-1.8	-3.5	3.0
Fiscal Year-End: December	2001	2002	2003	2004	2005	TTM
Revenue $Mil	16,054	16,332	18,232	20,011	21,167	22,466
Net Income $Mil	1,430	1,974	2,403	2,990	3,199	3,509
Earnings Per Share $	1.79	2.50	3.02	3.75	4.12	4.61
Shares Outstanding Mil	788	780	783	781	765	736
Return on Equity %	23.5	32.9	30.5	28.8	31.7	31.9
Net Margin %	8.9	12.1	13.2	14.9	15.1	15.6
Asset Turnover	1.1	1.1	1.0	1.0	1.0	1.0
Financial Leverage	2.4	2.6	2.2	2.0	2.0	2.1

Valuation Ratios

	Stock	Rel to Industry	Rel to S&P 500
Price/Earnings	16.8	0.9	0.8
Price/Book	5.2	1.6	1.3
Price/Sales	2.6	1.4	0.9
Price/Cash Flow	15.4	1.2	1.1

Major Fund Holders

	% of Fund Assets
Ashport Large Cap C	6.16
Fidelity Select Chemicals	6.08
Holland Balanced	4.50
Archer Balanced	4.37

Thesis By Scott Burns, 12-14-06 Stock Price as of Analysis: $78.77

Innovation and strong manufacturing capabilities have long been the trademarks of 3M. After a period of stagnation in the 1990s, a reinvigorated 3M has returned to its accustomed leadership position in the industrial world.

3M is synonymous with research and development and a corporate culture that breeds innovation. The firm has historically pumped more than 6.5% of its revenue back into R&D and has always been able to attract top-tier scientists and engineers to staff its labs.

Another 3M advantage is its ability to leverage technologies across different businesses and continuously find new uses for basic technologies. For example the film technology that makes LCD screens clearer and brighter evolved from microreplication technology originally used to make road signs more visible.

3M's history of innovation often overshadows the company's ability to generate strong profits on mundane products. Although many of 3M's products are high-margin branded or patented products, the company has made things such as sandpaper, adhesives, Post-it notes, and Scotch tape for decades. 3M fiercely protects its patents and uses its protected period to perfect its production processes.

Combining this production expertise with the company's global manufacturing base makes it cost-prohibitive for rivals to undercut its prices once items fall off patent. As a result of its patents, brands, and low-cost production, 3M has averaged 18% operating margins over the past five years.

Although 3M's operating margins are the envy of the industrial world, growth stalled at the firm during the 1990s. In 2001, the company hired General Electric star James McNerney to helm the turnaround. Under his leadership, the company slashed indirect costs and funneled research money to higher-growth businesses. As a result of this new focus, margins increased from 14% in 2001 to 24% in 2005.

In December 2005, 3M hired Brunswick CEO George Buckley as its new CEO and chairman after McNerney left to run Boeing. Buckley led a successful turnaround at Brunswick, but his tenure at 3M so far has been mixed. We expect him to spend some time cleaning out any skeletons that McNerney may have left behind, and he has been actively selling some of the more tangential businesses in 3M's portfolio. We think that Buckley is up to the task and that 3M's management bench strength is strong enough to support him.

Data as of 12-29-06

Abbott Laboratories ABT

	Rating	Fair Value	Last Close	Consider Buy	Consider Sell	Yield %
	★★★	$51.00	$48.71	$43.50	$67.00	2.38

Company Profile
Abbott Laboratories manufactures and markets pharmaceuticals, medical devices, diagnostic kits, and nutritional health-care products. Products include prescription drugs, imaging products, blood-screening tests, coronary and carotid stents, and nutritional liquids for infants and adults. The company generates just over 50% of revenue from pharmaceuticals, about 20% from nutritional products, and 18% from diagnostics, with the vascular business constituting the remainder.

Management Stewardship Grade [B]
Abbott gets solid marks for stewardship. We give management credit for repositioning the company toward higher-growth businesses and successfully spinning off the hospital-supply unit. Chairman and CEO Miles White has put setbacks--like the Food and Drug Administration consent decree levied against the company's Lake County manufacturing facility--behind it. We like the policy of cumulative voting rights in the election of directors, as this gives more clout to minority shareholders. The audit and compensation committees are composed entirely of independent directors. Compensation for top executives is well balanced between cash and equity and in line with industry practices. We'd like to see Abbott follow the lead of former subsidiary Hospira and separate the positions of CEO and chairman.

100 Abbott Park Road www.abbott.com
Abbott Park, IL 60064-6400

Growth [C+]	2002	2003	2004	2005
Revenue %	9.8	13.1	13.9	13.5
Earnings/Share %	79.8	-1.7	17.7	4.9
Book Value/Share %	17.5	22.3	9.0	1.2
Dividends/Share %	11.6	6.0	5.7	5.9

Profitability [A+]	2003	2004	2005	TTM
Return on Assets %	10.6	11.2	11.6	9.5
Oper Cash Flow $Mil	3,385	4,306	5,047	5,334
- Cap Spending $Mil	1,050	1,292	1,207	1,335
= Free Cash Flow $Mil	2,335	3,014	3,840	3,998

Financial Health [A-]	2003	2004	2005	09-30-06
Long-term Debt $Mil	3,452	4,788	4,572	7,508
Total Equity $Mil	13,072	14,326	14,415	15,633
Debt/Equity Ratio	0.3	0.3	0.3	0.5

Industry	Business Risk	Moat Size	Investment Style	Sector
Drugs	Below Avg	Wide	Large Core	Healthcare

Competition	Market Cap $Mil	12 Mo Trailing Sales $Mil	Price/Cash Flow	Return On Assets%	Debt/Equity	Total Return% 1 Yr	Total Return% 3 Yr
Abbott Laboratories	74,763	22,306	14.0	9.5	0.5	26.9	3.9
Johnson & Johnson	191,415	52,252	14.5	18.5	0.0	12.4	10.8
Pfizer	186,751	52,208	10.5	11.6	0.1	15.2	-7.4

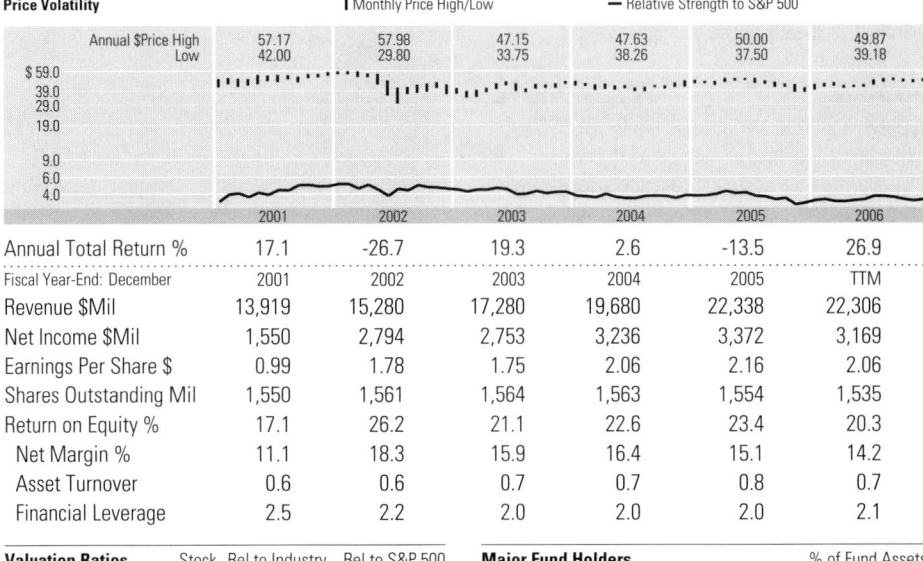

	2001	2002	2003	2004	2005	2006
Annual $Price High	57.17	57.98	47.15	47.63	50.00	49.87
Low	42.00	29.80	33.75	38.26	37.50	39.18
Annual Total Return %	17.1	-26.7	19.3	2.6	-13.5	26.9

Fiscal Year-End: December	2001	2002	2003	2004	2005	TTM
Revenue $Mil	13,919	15,280	17,280	19,680	22,338	22,306
Net Income $Mil	1,550	2,794	2,753	3,236	3,372	3,169
Earnings Per Share $	0.99	1.78	1.75	2.06	2.16	2.06
Shares Outstanding Mil	1,550	1,561	1,564	1,563	1,554	1,535
Return on Equity %	17.1	26.2	21.1	22.6	23.4	20.3
Net Margin %	11.1	18.3	15.9	16.4	15.1	14.2
Asset Turnover	0.6	0.6	0.7	0.7	0.8	0.7
Financial Leverage	2.5	2.2	2.0	2.0	2.0	2.1

Valuation Ratios	Stock	Rel to Industry	Rel to S&P 500
Price/Earnings	23.6	1.0	1.1
Price/Book	4.8	0.9	1.2
Price/Sales	3.4	0.8	1.2
Price/Cash Flow	14.0	0.9	1.0

Major Fund Holders	% of Fund Assets
BlackRock Healthcare I	7.02
ProFunds Pharmaceuticals UltraSector Inv	6.53
Hartford Global Health HLS IA	5.73
Hartford Global Health A	5.48

Thesis By Heather Brilliant, CFA, 12-11-06 Stock Price as of Analysis: $47.82

Abbott Labs has built itself into a diversified health-care giant, and we think it is well positioned to generate growth for years to come. In addition to its solid pharmaceutical business, the firm is a leader in diagnostics and is quickly emerging as a formidable competitor in the vascular stent market. While recent acquisitions have put a damper on Abbott's returns on invested capital in the near term, we think these assets will help the firm continue to generate strong returns in the long run.

Abbott's pharmaceutical division struck gold a few years ago with Humira, the firm's monoclonal antibody for rheumatoid arthritis. This drug competes with Amgen's Enbrel and Johnson & Johnson's Remicade in a market that is fast approaching $10 billion, and as the newest drug in its class, Humira has been growing faster than its competitors. We think this trend will continue, as Abbott has been focusing its research spending on developing additional indications for Humira. The drug is currently approved for a handful of smaller indications in addition to rheumatoid arthritis, and Abbott expects to receive Food and Drug Administration approval for Humira to treat Crohn's disease and psoriasis, among other diseases, within the next few years.

Outside of Humira, Abbott's pipeline did not hold much to speak of in late-stage development until it decided to acquire Kos Pharmaceuticals in late 2006. Kos brings Niaspan, a drug that raises HDL (or good cholesterol), as well as a handful of additional products to boost Abbott's pipeline in treating cardiovascular and respiratory diseases. While we're pleased to see the benefits Kos will bring, we think Abbott is paying full price for the business. However, with Abbott's superior sales and marketing abilities, it should be able to generate value from Niaspan and the rest of Kos' pipeline.

Abbott is not just a pharmaceutical story, however. With almost half of its sales coming from medical devices and nutritionals, Abbott is insulated from some of the pipeline volatility its big pharma competitors face. It also holds several product lines that are well-positioned to take advantage of positive industry trends, such as international nutritionals, a business that will expand as income levels improve in developing countries.

We're enthusiastic about the firm's prospects in vascular products as well. We expect Abbott's Xience drug-coated stent will compete favorably with the likes of Boston Scientific and J&J in this concentrated market.

Data as of 12-29-06

Abercrombie & Fitch A ANF

Rating ★★	Fair Value $60.00	Last Close $69.63	Consider Buy $46.30	Consider Sell $75.20	Yield % 1.01

Industry	Business Risk	Moat Size	Investment Style	Sector
Clothing Stores	Average	Narrow	Mid Growth	Consumer Services

Company Profile

Abercrombie & Fitch is a specialty retailer of casual apparel and accessories for young women and men that has roughly 950 stores in the U.S. and Canada. The company's namesake chain markets preppy, East Coast-lifestyle clothing to college students, while abercrombie focuses on 7- to 14-year-olds. Hollister offers surfing-inspired, West Coast-lifestyle merchandise to high school students. Ruehl targets post-college women and men with trendy sportswear and fashion items.

Management   Stewardship Grade [C]

Michael Jeffries led the major shift in Abercrombie's image that started in 1992, when he became CEO. Under Jeffries' leadership, the company has grown into a dominant youth apparel retailer. Executive compensation seems a bit excessive, in our opinion. In 2005, each of the five highest-paid employees was given over $2 million in total compensation. Jeffries was paid a salary of $1.2 million and an annual bonus of $2.9 million. The firm also provides personal use of the corporate jet and helicopter and generous retirement contributions; Jeffries is slated to receive 50% of his final compensation for life. Jeffries' total package, worth over $5 million in 2005, was roughly equivalent to his haul in 2004. Abercrombie's compensation policy is tied to unclear company financial goals, although we believe Jeffries' interests are aligned with those of long-term shareholders. Jeffries owns about 7% of the shares outstanding. We believe the board is sufficiently independent, yet we think staggered three-year terms for directors limit the influence of outside investors. Corporate governance would be improved if the entire board were up for re-election annually and if Jeffries' chairman and CEO roles were split between two individuals.

6301 Fitch Path   www.abercrombie.com
New Albany, OH 43054

Growth [A+]	2003	2004	2005	2006
Revenue %	16.9	7.0	18.4	37.8
Earnings/Share %	19.8	6.2	10.7	60.5
Book Value/Share %	29.5	17.6	-18.2	54.6
Dividends/Share %	NMF	NMF	NMF	20.0

Profitability [A+]	2004	2005	2006	TTM
Return on Assets %	14.6	15.6	18.7	18.8
Oper Cash Flow $Mil	341	424	454	532
- Cap Spending $Mil	160	185	256	373
= Free Cash Flow $Mil	181	239	197	159

Financial Health [A+]	2004	2005	2006	10-31-06
Long-term Debt $Mil	—	—	—	—
Total Equity $Mil	858	669	995	1,212
Debt/Equity Ratio	—	—	—	—

Competition

	Market Cap $Mil	12 Mo Trailing Sales $Mil	Price/Cash Flow	Return On Assets %	Debt/ Equity	Total Return % 1 Yr	3 Yr
Abercrombie & Fitch A	6,145	3,141	11.5	18.8	—	8.0	44.0
Gap	15,807	15,834	8.6	9.7	0.0	12.5	-3.7
American Eagle Outfitters	6,959	2,578	10.0	18.7	—	105.5	80.5

Price Volatility | Monthly Price High/Low   — Relative Strength to S&P 500

	2001	2002	2003	2004	2005	2006
Annual $Price High	47.50	33.85	33.65	47.45	74.10	79.42
Low	16.21	15.00	20.46	23.07	44.17	49.98
Annual Total Return %	32.7	-22.9	20.8	92.7	40.3	8.0

Fiscal Year-End: January	2002	2003	2004	2005	2006	TTM
Revenue $Mil	1,365	1,596	1,708	2,021	2,785	3,141
Net Income $Mil	167	195	205	216	334	389
Earnings Per Share $	1.62	1.94	2.06	2.28	3.66	4.23
Shares Outstanding Mil	99	98	97	93	87	88
Return on Equity %	28.6	26.5	23.9	32.3	33.6	32.1
Net Margin %	12.2	12.2	12.0	10.7	12.0	12.4
Asset Turnover	1.5	1.3	1.2	1.5	1.6	1.5
Financial Leverage	1.6	1.6	1.6	2.1	1.8	1.7

Valuation Ratios	Stock	Rel to Industry	Rel to S&P 500
Price/Earnings	16.5	0.8	0.8
Price/Book	5.1	1.2	1.2
Price/Sales	2.0	1.4	0.7
Price/Cash Flow	11.5	0.9	0.8

Major Fund Holders	% of Fund Assets
Columbia Acorn Select Z	5.14
Prasad Growth	4.63
JHancock Mid Cap Growth A	3.75
PF Van Kampen Mid-Cap Growth A	3.32

Thesis By Brady Lemos, 12-14-06 Stock Price as of Analysis: $69.25

Abercrombie & Fitch has distinguished itself as the fashion leader among teen apparel retailers. Considering the notoriously fickle buying habits of teenagers, we are impressed the retailer has maintained brand cachet and high returns on invested capital since it was spun off from Limited Brands in 1998. For these reasons, we think A&F is one of the few specialty retailers to own a narrow economic moat.

A&F's brand-building strategy is based on a premium pricing strategy that gives its merchandise aspirational appeal to brand-conscious youth. To this end, the company shuns seasonal clearance events and refuses to use the term "sale" in any of its stores. Running a high-end retail store isn't cheap, however, and A&F must invest in regular store remodels and high staffing levels. The retailer is also opening flagship stores in high-rent areas like New York's Fifth Avenue. Due to these expenses, operating profit margins are comparable with those of top competitors like American Eagle Outfitters.

A&F leveraged its merchandising expertise to develop a portfolio of successful apparel retailing concepts. Young consumers tend to outgrow brands, so we like that A&F targets specific market segments rather than trying to cater to an overly broad demographic, an issue Gap has struggled with.

Hollister, in particular, has been an exceptional success story for the company. In 2006 the West Coast lifestyle brand outproduced A&F on a sales-per-square foot basis while exceeding $1 billion in revenue. With approximately 400 stores, Hollister is now the largest concept in A&F's portfolio.

Other concepts including abercrombie, its kids business, and Ruehl, its postcollege market entry, offer further portfolio diversification. A store aimed at older consumers makes sense to us, since it allows the company to target customers who have outgrown A&F's styles and have deeper pockets. With only about 15 stores, Ruehl has been cautiously rolled out while merchandising is fine-tuned. A&F has even more expansion opportunity internationally in markets like Canada and the U.K., where the firm plans to enter in 2007.

Even with plenty of growth opportunities and an impressive record of navigating ever-changing teen tastes, A&F is not immune to the competitive and fashion risks inherent to the industry. We anticipate sales and profitability will continue to fluctuate over the next five years and would invest in the stock only at a reasonable discount to our fair value estimate.

Data as of 12-29-06

Accenture ACN

	Rating	Fair Value	Last Close	Consider Buy	Consider Sell	Yield %
	★★★	$41.00	$36.93	$31.60	$51.40	0.95

Company Profile

With 140,000 employees in 150 cities worldwide, Accenture is a leading provider of IT consulting and outsourcing to commercial enterprises and government agencies around the globe. A little less than half of revenue comes from North America (39% from the United States). Consulting contributes 60% of total revenue. The firm's business is broadly divided into five operating groups: communications and high-tech, financial services, products, resources, and government.

Industry	Business Risk	Moat Size	Investment Style	Sector
Business Appl.	Average	Narrow	Large Growth	Business Services

Competition	Market Cap $Mil	12 Mo Trailing Sales $Mil	Price/Cash Flow	Return On Assets%	Debt/Equity	Total Return% 1 Yr	3 Yr
Accenture	28,867	18,852	11.7	11.3	0.0	29.3	13.4
IBM	146,342	89,593	9.8	8.8	0.4	19.8	3.0
Infosys Technologies ADR	29,525	2,152	49.3	26.9	—	36.8	31.5

Management   Stewardship Grade [C]

William Green, a 28-year Accenture veteran, assumed the CEO mantle in September 2004 and two years later took on the chairman role as well when longtime leader Joe Forehand retired. Green earned $2.3 million in total compensation in fiscal 2005, and his fiscal 2006 base salary was $2.4 million. Given the continual outperformance of Accenture relative to peers, that is money well paid, especially considering that Green travels nonstop around the globe (Accenture has no formal operational headquarters and Green has no official office). At the beginning of November 2006, Pamela Craig took over as chief financial officer after 24 years at the firm. Former CFO Michael McGrath has moved on to another executive position within Accenture. Overall, we believe that the executive officers and board of directors do a good job of corporate stewardship. The compensation committee has done well at explaining executive compensation criteria. Executives and directors own large stock positions, aligning their interests with outside shareholders. However, high issuance of stock options and restricted-stock units, along with the combined CEO and chairmanship roles, lowers Accenture's stewardship grade to a C.

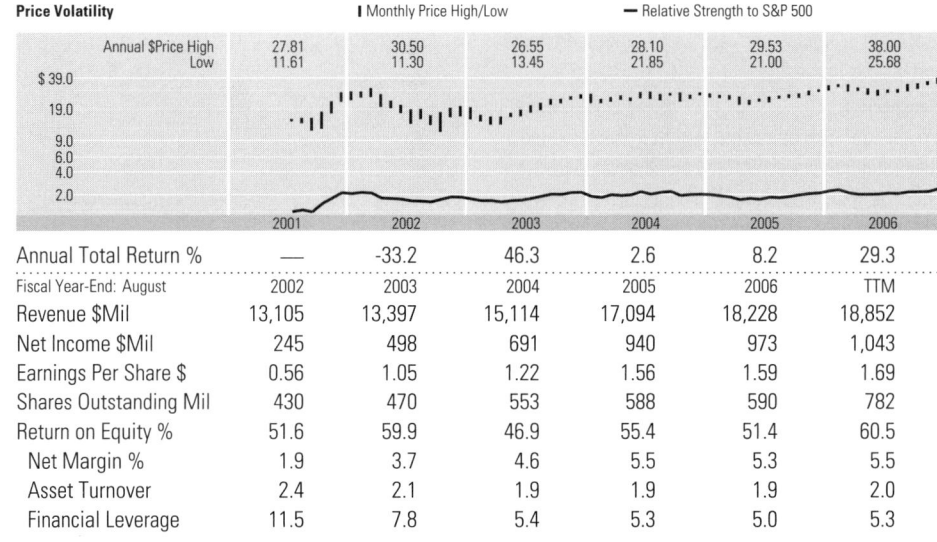

Price Volatility — Monthly Price High/Low — Relative Strength to S&P 500

| | 27.81 | 30.50 | 26.55 | 28.10 | 29.53 | 38.00 |
| Annual $Price High Low | 11.61 | 11.30 | 13.45 | 21.85 | 21.00 | 25.68 |

		2001	2002	2003	2004	2005	2006
Annual Total Return %		—	-33.2	46.3	2.6	8.2	29.3
Fiscal Year-End: August		2002	2003	2004	2005	2006	TTM
Revenue $Mil		13,105	13,397	15,114	17,094	18,228	18,852
Net Income $Mil		245	498	691	940	973	1,043
Earnings Per Share $		0.56	1.05	1.22	1.56	1.59	1.69
Shares Outstanding Mil		430	470	553	588	590	782
Return on Equity %		51.6	59.9	46.9	55.4	51.4	60.5
Net Margin %		1.9	3.7	4.6	5.5	5.3	5.5
Asset Turnover		2.4	2.1	1.9	1.9	1.9	2.0
Financial Leverage		11.5	7.8	5.4	5.3	5.0	5.3

Valuation Ratios	Stock	Rel to Industry	Rel to S&P 500
Price/Earnings	21.9	0.7	1.1
Price/Book	16.7	2.0	4.1
Price/Sales	1.5	0.6	0.5
Price/Cash Flow	11.7	0.7	0.8

Major Fund Holders	% of Fund Assets
Ariel Appreciation	5.79
FMI Large Cap	5.45
Van Kampen American Franchise A	4.95
Ariel Focus	4.80

Thesis By Mike Ford-Taggart, CFA, 11-17-06 Stock Price as of Analysis: $35.15

If all information technology services stocks were trading below our Consider Buying price and we could buy only one, we'd take a full position in Accenture. The firm's broad service portfolio, truly global operations, and established presence in low-cost areas will enable continued strong revenue growth and industry-leading operating efficiency, in our opinion.

The breadth of Accenture's domain expertise sets it apart from rivals. The firm offers clients a panoply of services, ranging from strategy and customer relationship business consultants to systems integration and enterprise architecture software engineers to call center representatives and data processors. The scope of its industry knowledge (covering 17 groups, including auto, media, chemicals, and capital markets) also protects Accenture competitively, as few rivals can compete directly across all categories.

Whereas offshore operations and global delivery networks seem to have been an afterthought for many rivals, they are seemingly the essence of Accenture. The company was created out of 40 partnerships across 47 countries. While most employees work on-site at client locations or in one of Accenture's near-shore or offshore facilities, managers and executives are constantly traveling the globe to check on projects and employees. It is estimated that 1,000 Accenture employees travel through London's Heathrow airport daily. This nomadic, dispersed nature of the firm shows up in results: Almost two thirds of revenue is generated outside the United States, and with less overhead, Accenture carries the highest margins and returns on invested capital among its rivals.

Like its competitors, Accenture is busy opening new facilities in India and Eastern Europe. The difference is that Accenture has about a dozen separate facilities across India, has hired 19,000 people in India and China (with plans to almost triple that number in three years), and has near-shore facilities in every major Eastern European country. Unlike many of its rivals, Accenture's management team is not attempting to catch up with delivery and technological standards; it is setting the standards.

On top of this stellar positioning is one last treat: The firm has converted more than 10% of its revenue to free cash flow since 2000, by our estimates, using that cash to develop new technology solutions, acquire other firms, and buy back shares.

22 Victoria Street Canon's Court   www.accenture.com
Hamilton, Bermuda HM12

Growth [C+]	2002	2003	2004	2005
Revenue %	2.2	12.8	13.1	6.6
Earnings/Share %	87.5	16.2	27.9	1.9
Book Value/Share %	61.4	48.3	8.3	9.9
Dividends/Share %	NMF	NMF	NMF	NMF

Profitability [A]	2003	2004	2005	TTM
Return on Assets %	8.6	10.5	10.3	11.3
Oper Cash Flow $Mil	1,756	1,887	2,668	2,465
- Cap Spending $Mil	282	318	306	295
= Free Cash Flow $Mil	1,474	1,569	2,362	2,170

Financial Health [A]	2003	2004	2005	05-31-06
Long-term Debt $Mil	32	44	27	5
Total Equity $Mil	1,472	1,697	1,894	1,724
Debt/Equity Ratio	0.0	0.0	0.0	0.0

Data as of 12-29-06

ACE ACE

	Rating	Fair Value	Last Close	Consider Buy	Consider Sell	Yield %
	★★★	$58.00	$60.57	$37.00	$70.00	1.62

Industry	Business Risk	Moat Size	Investment Style	Sector
Insurance (Property)	Above Avg	Narrow	Large Value	Financial Services

Company Profile
Bermuda-domiciled insurer ACE Limited offers a diverse range of insurance, reinsurance, and financial services to a client base spanning more than 50 countries. Its insurance products include excess liability, property, casualty, and marine, and constitute more than 90% of sales. Select products are offered via the Lloyd's market. ACE Re reinsures life insurance contracts and owns 35% of Assured Guaranty.

Competition

	Market Cap $Mil	12 Mo Trailing Sales $Mil	Price/Cash Flow	Return On Assets %	Debt/ Equity	Total Return % 1 Yr	3 Yr
ACE	19,755	13,047	—	2.8	—	15.4	15.9
American International Gr	186,296	110,593	—	1.2	—	6.1	3.2
Berkshire Hathaway B	169,636	97,676	—	5.2	—	24.9	9.4

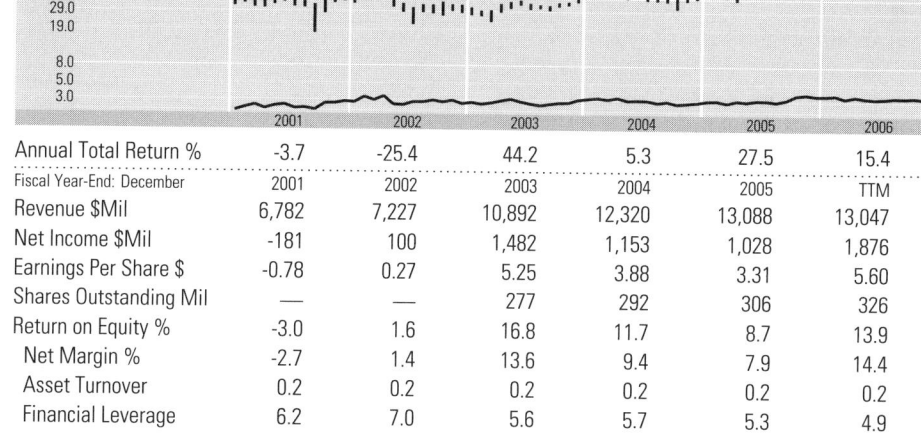

	2001	2002	2003	2004	2005	2006
Annual $Price High	43.19	44.98	41.98	52.20	56.85	61.90
Low	18.10	22.01	23.59	31.80	38.36	47.81
Annual Total Return %	-3.7	-25.4	44.2	5.3	27.5	15.4

Fiscal Year-End: December

	2001	2002	2003	2004	2005	TTM
Revenue $Mil	6,782	7,227	10,892	12,320	13,088	13,047
Net Income $Mil	-181	100	1,482	1,153	1,028	1,876
Earnings Per Share $	-0.78	0.27	5.25	3.88	3.31	5.60
Shares Outstanding Mil	—	—	277	292	306	326
Return on Equity %	-3.0	1.6	16.8	11.7	8.7	13.9
Net Margin %	-2.7	1.4	13.6	9.4	7.9	14.4
Asset Turnover	0.2	0.2	0.2	0.2	0.2	0.2
Financial Leverage	6.2	7.0	5.6	5.7	5.3	4.9

Management — Stewardship Grade [B]
We admire ACE's managers. Since current chairman Brian Duperreault arrived in 1994, book value per share has increased close to 14% annually. However, we would prefer that management took a larger stake in the firm's long-term results. ACE's results are volatile, and many policies require future payments based on uncertain events. In addition, it can take several years for current claims to develop, and current loss estimates are necessarily imprecise, providing an incentive to push losses into the future. CEO Evan Greenberg owns about $18 million of ACE stock, while Duperreault boasts a $42 million investment. Greenberg was paid $4.6 million in 2005, plus $4.5 million in restricted stock and $3.8 million in options. Duperreault also received a substantial salary relative to his investment. We think the managers' stake in the firm minimally exceeds the importance of their annual salary, at best. We prefer to invest in insurance firms where managers succeed or fail along with shareholders.

Valuation Ratios

	Stock	Rel to Industry	Rel to S&P 500
Price/Earnings	10.8	0.8	0.5
Price/Book	1.5	0.9	0.4
Price/Sales	1.5	1.1	0.5
Price/Cash Flow	—	—	—

Major Fund Holders

	% of Fund Assets
Fidelity Select Insurance	6.32
BlackRock Global Financial Svcs B	4.17
Fidelity Focused Stock	4.12
Hartford Global Financial Svcs HLS IA	4.03

Thesis By Matt Nellans, 11-15-06 Stock Price as of Analysis: $57.16

Facing a liability insurance shortage in 1985, several Fortune 500 firms formed ACE to accept risks other insurers refused. ACE maintains this appetite for risk, which endows a narrow economic moat. Our fair value estimate is $58 per share.

In addition to meeting the needs of large multinationals, ACE is widely known and respected by insurance brokers for its breadth and consistency, which helps build a virtuous sales cycle. Brokers prefer insurers that predictably accept sales. ACE has evolved into a sought-after provider of large risk policies for companies with specialized risk-management needs. In turn, ACE gains a naturally diversified client base, which spans financial, energy, retail, and transportation firms. This helps limit the impact of losses in any segment of the overall business.

ACE's returns on capital are boosted by the large volume of float the insurance businesses generate. In 2005, ACE incurred $8.6 billion of losses, but paid only $5.4 billion in claims. The difference will be paid in the future, but in the meantime the cash is invested to benefit shareholders. Even better, since 1994 ACE's average underwriting profit margin is 1.4%, which means ACE's float has been the economic equivalent of a negative 1.4% interest rate on a loan. Currently, ACE sports $2.62 of investments for every $1 of shareholder capital, so it earns leveraged investment returns. ACE's investment earnings alone produced a 10% return on equity in 2005. This provides a useful base for shareholders and reduces managerial incentives to sell mispriced insurance in pursuit of illusory growth.

Insuring large, specialized risks that generate massive float volume is not entirely pleasant. The ultimate cost of current insurance will not be known for several years, and the adequacy of ACE's claim reserves is uncertain. If ACE underestimates its 2005 claims by only 1 percentage point, it will lose more than $85 million. The recent hard market--high insurance prices--has masked some of ACE's negative reserve development. For example, reserves at the end of 2004 were increased by $86 million in 2005. Of course, if ACE overestimates its claim costs, each percentage point will free more than $85 million. However, ACE has had only one such favorable year over the past decade.

17 Woodbourne Avenue www.acelimited.com
Hamilton, Bermuda HM 08

Growth [B-]

	2002	2003	2004	2005
Revenue %	6.6	50.7	13.1	6.2
Earnings/Share %	NMF	EUB	-26.1	-14.7
Book Value/Share %	-34.6	84.6	6.0	14.8
Dividends/Share %	13.8	12.1	10.8	9.8

Profitability [B-]

	2003	2004	2005	TTM
Return on Assets %	3.0	2.1	1.6	2.8
Oper Cash Flow $Mil	4,285	4,939	4,308	—
- Cap Spending $Mil	—	—	—	—
= Free Cash Flow $Mil	—	—	—	—

Financial Health [NA]

	2003	2004	2005	09-30-06
Long-term Debt $Mil	—	—	—	—
Total Equity $Mil	8,823	9,843	11,810	13,509
Debt/Equity Ratio	—	—	—	—

© 2007 Morningstar, Inc. All rights reserved. Intended for United States residents only, this report is for information purposes and should not be considered a solicitation to buy or sell any security. Download your free reports at http://www.morningstar.com/goto/2007Stocks500

Actuant A ATU

Data as of 12-29-06

	Rating	Fair Value	Last Close	Consider Buy	Consider Sell	Yield %
	★★★	$52.00	$47.65	$40.10	$65.20	0.17

Industry	Business Risk	Moat Size	Investment Style	Sector
Electric Equip.	Average	Narrow	Small Core	Industrial Materials

Company Profile
Actuant is a diversified manufacturing firm that provides a wide range of industrial products and engineered solutions. Its tools and supplies segment (63% of sales in 2006) sells specialized electrical and industrial tools and supplies to hydraulic, electrical, and specialty wholesale distributors and OEMs, and through various retail distribution channels. The engineered solutions segment manufactures customized motion control systems primarily for OEMs in various niche markets.

Management   Stewardship Grade [A]
Robert Arzbaecher has been the chairman of the board, CEO, and president of Actuant since the company spun off from Applied Power in 2000. Before assuming these lead positions, Arzbaecher had held a number of senior finance roles at Applied Power after joining the firm as a corporate controller in 1992. We applaud Arzbaecher and his team for their turnaround efforts at Actuant: transforming a debt-laden, spin-off into a more profitable, fast-growing company. We believe that management has been following a disciplined acquisition strategy for growth by paying low multiples for businesses and steadily reducing debt. Overall corporate governance is sound. Six out of eight board members are independent, and the board is not staggered. Management compensation appears to be reasonable. Arzbaecher earned about $1.1 million in 2005, excluding options, meeting 81% of his bonus target. Executive compensation includes cash bonus and stock options and is based on meeting an adjusted net earnings target. We think management's variable compensation plan, which is tied to pretax ROIC, promotes alignment with shareholder interests.

6100 North Baker Road
Milwaukee, WI 53209
www.actuant.com

Growth [A]	2003	2004	2005	2006
Revenue %	26.4	24.2	34.3	23.1
Earnings/Share %	NMF	11.9	83.3	24.4
Book Value/Share %	NMF	NMF	600.1	11.8
Dividends/Share %	NMF	NMF	NMF	NMF

Profitability [B+]	2004	2005	2006	TTM
Return on Assets %	8.2	7.2	7.6	7.6
Oper Cash Flow $Mil	48	97	122	122
- Cap Spending $Mil	11	15	20	20
= Free Cash Flow $Mil	37	82	102	102

Financial Health [B]	2004	2005	2006	08-31-06
Long-term Debt $Mil	189	443	461	461
Total Equity $Mil	32	245	363	363
Debt/Equity Ratio	6.0	1.8	1.3	1.3

Competition	Market Cap $Mil	12 Mo Trailing Sales $Mil	Price/Cash Flow	Return On Assets%	Debt/ Equity	Total Return% 1 Yr	3 Yr
Actuant A	1,301	1,201	10.6	7.6	1.3	-14.5	8.7
SPX	3,510	4,570	19.4	2.5	0.4	36.1	4.1
Thomas & Betts	2,832	1,826	15.3	8.2	0.4	12.7	27.1

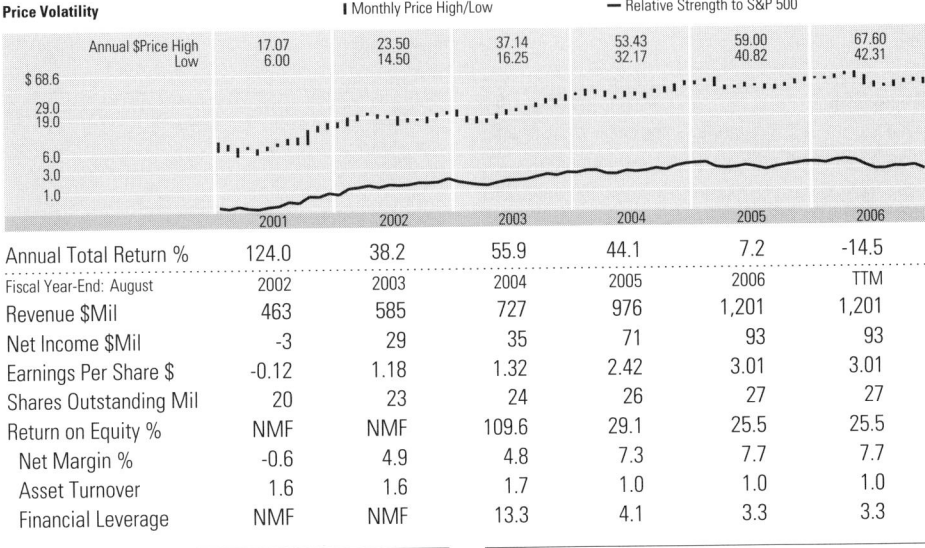

Price Volatility — Monthly Price High/Low — Relative Strength to S&P 500

	2001	2002	2003	2004	2005	2006	TTM
Annual $Price High	17.07	23.50	37.14	53.43	59.00	67.60	
Low	6.00	14.50	16.25	32.17	40.82	42.31	
Annual Total Return %	124.0	38.2	55.9	44.1	7.2	-14.5	
Fiscal Year-End: August		2002	2003	2004	2005	2006	TTM
Revenue $Mil		463	585	727	976	1,201	1,201
Net Income $Mil		-3	29	35	71	93	93
Earnings Per Share $		-0.12	1.18	1.32	2.42	3.01	3.01
Shares Outstanding Mil		20	23	24	26	27	27
Return on Equity %		NMF	NMF	109.6	29.1	25.5	25.5
Net Margin %		-0.6	4.9	4.8	7.3	7.7	7.7
Asset Turnover		1.6	1.6	1.7	1.0	1.0	1.0
Financial Leverage		NMF	NMF	13.3	4.1	3.3	3.3

Valuation Ratios	Stock	Rel to Industry	Rel to S&P 500
Price/Earnings	15.8	0.7	0.8
Price/Book	3.6	1.0	0.9
Price/Sales	1.1	0.5	0.4
Price/Cash Flow	10.6	0.8	0.7

Major Fund Holders	% of Fund Assets
Needham Small Cap Growth	3.98
Lord Abbett Small-Cap Blend A	2.69
PF NB Fasciano Small Equity A	2.18
Harbor Small Cap Growth Instl	2.06

Thesis By Ramesh Poola, Ph.D., 10-27-06   Stock Price as of Analysis: $50.75

Actuant uses its strong brands in specialty tools and supplies and dominant share in niche markets to earn above-average returns. Combined with its strong distribution network, Actuant has secured a narrow economic moat rating.

We think that branded tools and patented actuation solutions are at the core of Actuant's competitive advantages. Actuant boasts a stable of globally recognized brands of hydraulic tools and bolting products built upon proprietary designs. In actuation systems, Actuant is one of two global players that dominate the markets for convertible car retractable hardtops and hydraulic cab tilt systems for trucks. Additionally, the firm's Gardner-Bender-branded, new circuit alert tools consistently win innovation awards from retailers and electrical contractors. All of these product lines fetch high premium prices and continue to gain market share in the fiercely competitive retail market. Each of these competitive positions is reinforced by Actuant's strong relationship with distributors and OEMs. This superior position has helped Actuant deliver impressive results. Returns on invested capital, averaging over 20%, have surpassed the firm's cost of capital since it was spun off from Applied Power in 2000.

Actuant's focus on acquisitions is crucial for its growth, as newly acquired businesses help to further strengthen its leadership position in industrial tools. Since 2001, Actuant has completed 13 acquisitions that now account for 45% of sales. These acquisitions are also creating cross-selling opportunities and facilitating Actuant's expansion into fast-growing markets. For instance, by acquiring bolting businesses Hydratight Sweeney and Hedley Purvis, Actuant not only leveraged the leadership position of its Enerpac business in industrial tools, but also expanded its presence into the oil, gas, and power generation markets. We think Actuant's bolt on acquisitions are strategic, disciplined, and vital to expand its customer base and maintain its competitive position at the same time.

Despite many of its advantages, top-line growth could suffer as the company faces cyclical demand for its RV, truck, and auto products. The firm's organic growth is limited due to its scale and market presence, which has seen low-single-digit revenue growth over the last three years including a 2% decline in 2005. Returns could also suffer as the company faces increasing competition in tools and electrical supplies, particularly in the retail market.

Data as of 12-29-06

Adobe Systems ADBE

	Rating	Fair Value	Last Close	Consider Buy	Consider Sell	Yield %
	★★★	$38.00	$41.12	$29.30	$47.60	0.00

Industry	Business Risk	Moat Size	Investment Style	Sector
Development Tools	Average	Wide	Large Growth	Software

Company Profile

Adobe Systems has long been a pioneering firm in software. Today, Adobe is best known for its Photoshop, Illustrator, Acrobat, and Flash products, which are used to create much of the content we see in print, television, and the Internet. The firm targets corporations with its LiveCycle server products, which manage electronic documents. Adobe also sells a complete line of digital photography and video editing software to consumers and professionals.

Management   Stewardship Grade [C]

Adobe relies on the marketing savvy of CEO Bruce Chizen, who joined the firm in 1994 as part of the Aldus acquisition. COO Shantanu Narayen complements Chizen nicely on the product strategy side. There has been significant turnover among top management. Bryan Lamkin, head of the Creative Solutions group (which includes Photoshop), retired in early 2006. Ivan Koon, a high-profile hire a few years ago tapped to build Adobe's enterprise business, resigned in late 2005. Stephen Elop, who had been Macromedia's CEO, is running worldwide sales. Adobe recently named Randy Furr, formerly president and COO of Sanmina-SCI, as CFO. Adobe's corporate governance has been lackluster over the years. In the past, the firm has issued a plethora of employee stock options, repriced options, and even ignored a majority of shareholders voting in favor of expensing stock options. Nevertheless, the company has made several improvements; it has decreased option grants in recent years, and it now has minimum ownership requirements for executives. We think there is room for further gains, as Adobe still has several antitakeover provisions on its books. We evaluated Adobe's historical option grants and did not find evidence of backdating.

345 Park Avenue
San Jose, CA 95110-2704
www.adobe.com

Growth [A]	2002	2003	2004	2005
Revenue %	-5.3	11.2	28.7	18.0
Earnings/Share %	-4.8	39.2	65.5	30.8
Book Value/Share %	11.8	63.3	26.5	28.0
Dividends/Share %	0.0	0.0	0.0	-50.0

Profitability [A+]	2003	2004	2005	TTM
Return on Assets %	17.1	23.0	24.7	8.5
Oper Cash Flow $Mil	433	684	730	822
- Cap Spending $Mil	39	63	49	61
= Free Cash Flow $Mil	394	621	681	761

Financial Health [A+]	2003	2004	2005	08-31-06
Long-term Debt $Mil	—	—	—	—
Total Equity $Mil	1,101	1,423	1,864	4,914
Debt/Equity Ratio	—	—	—	—

Competition	Market Cap $Mil	12 Mo Trailing Sales $Mil	Price/Cash Flow	Return On Assets %	Debt/Equity	Total Return % 1 Yr	Total Return % 3 Yr
Adobe Systems	23,987	2,403	29.2	8.5	—	11.3	28.2
Microsoft	293,538	45,352	20.8	19.8	—	15.8	7.6
Quark							

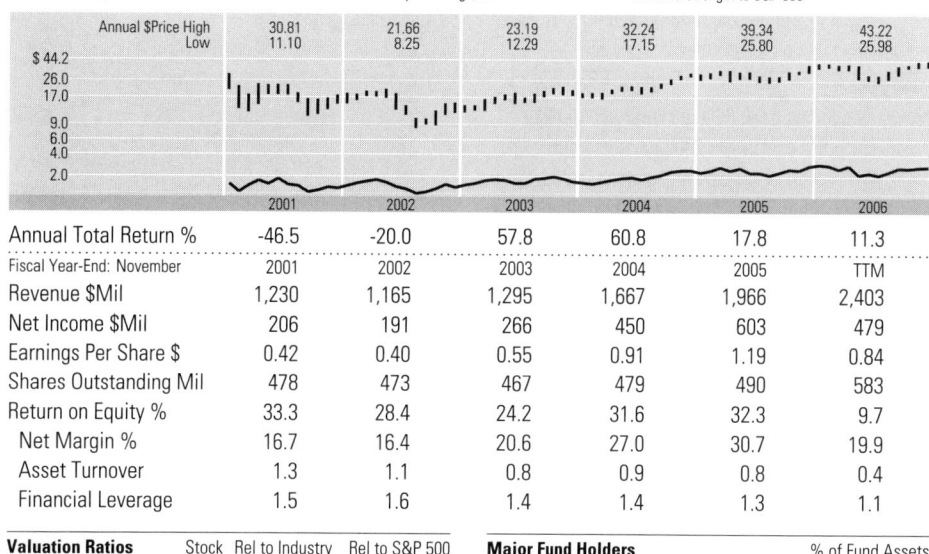

Price Volatility — Monthly Price High/Low — Relative Strength to S&P 500

	2001	2002	2003	2004	2005	2006
Annual $Price High	30.81	21.66	23.19	32.24	39.34	43.22
Low	11.10	8.25	12.29	17.15	25.80	25.98
Annual Total Return %	-46.5	-20.0	57.8	60.8	17.8	11.3

Fiscal Year-End: November	2001	2002	2003	2004	2005	TTM
Revenue $Mil	1,230	1,165	1,295	1,667	1,966	2,403
Net Income $Mil	206	191	266	450	603	479
Earnings Per Share $	0.42	0.40	0.55	0.91	1.19	0.84
Shares Outstanding Mil	478	473	467	479	490	583
Return on Equity %	33.3	28.4	24.2	31.6	32.3	9.7
Net Margin %	16.7	16.4	20.6	27.0	30.7	19.9
Asset Turnover	1.3	1.1	0.8	0.9	0.8	0.4
Financial Leverage	1.5	1.6	1.4	1.4	1.3	1.1

Valuation Ratios	Stock	Rel to Industry	Rel to S&P 500
Price/Earnings	49.0	1.2	2.4
Price/Book	4.9	1.1	1.2
Price/Sales	10.0	1.6	3.4
Price/Cash Flow	29.2	1.3	2.0

Major Fund Holders	% of Fund Assets
Firsthand Technology Leaders	5.21
Victory Focused Growth A	5.13
Jennison Technology A	4.74
DWS Technology A	4.25

Thesis By Toan Tran, 11-21-06 Stock Price as of Analysis: $42.55

Although there are competitive threats on the horizon, Adobe is well positioned to benefit from several powerful growth trends.

We think Adobe has two wide-moat businesses in its Creative Suite and Acrobat products. Almost all creative professionals are trained to use Photoshop and Illustrator, and high switching costs make it difficult for rivals to gain market acceptance. The ubiquitous Acrobat PDF format is the standard for portable documents, and Adobe benefits from a strong network effect. We also like Adobe's Flash business, which was acquired with Macromedia, but other technologies are viable threats.

Adobe is situated at the epicenter of several strong growth trends. The emergence of next-generation Web applications (collectively referred to as Web 2.0) bodes well for Flash and Acrobat as tools to create and share media-rich content. Flash Player and Acrobat Reader have been installed on more than 600 million PCs and other devices, providing developers a near-universal platform for Web applications. In addition, the growing popularity of digital photography and video should drive sales of products like Photoshop and Premiere. Adobe also has agreements with the top six cell phone manufacturers to install Flash Lite on handsets. Thus, the firm has an opportunity to establish its products as the standard for mobile content.

In our opinion, the two largest threats to Adobe come from Microsoft and industry-standard technologies like Ajax. With the release of Windows Vista and Office 2007, Microsoft will introduce XPS, a competing format to Acrobat and PostScript. To some extent, the success of XPS will depend on its adoption by non-Windows users, as one of Acrobat's key advantages is its portability across all platforms (i.e., Mac, Linux, mobile). Adobe increases this lead with each installation of Acrobat Reader, but we cannot ignore the challenge posed by Microsoft's dominance of the desktop.

Flash is currently the most polished platform for rich Web applications, but we think Ajax and other technologies will continue to be refined and may eventually supplant Flash. Ajax is a programming technique based on standard tools embedded in every Web browser. Therefore, unlike Flash, Web sites that use Ajax do not have to spend money on Adobe development tools or require the user to download a separate player.

Advanced Medical Optics EYE

Data as of 12-29-06

Rating	Fair Value	Last Close	Consider Buy	Consider Sell	Yield %
★★★	$36.00	$35.20	$27.80	$45.10	0.00

Company Profile
A 2002 spin-off from Allergan, Advanced Medical Optics develops and manufactures medical devices for the eye. The company's cataract segment includes products such as Tecnis IOLs and Sovereign lens-removal systems. The company is the leader in LASIK, where its VISX Star system has a 60% share of the market in the United States. The consumer eye-care segment is led by sales of its Complete multi-purpose solution. AMO generated 65% of sales outside the U.S. in 2005.

Management   Stewardship Grade [B]
James Mazzo has been CEO of Advanced Medical Optics since the company's 2002 spin-off from Allergan. Previously, Mazzo served in numerous positions at Allergan dating back to 1980. We believe management deserves credit for transitioning AMO through the last four years. The company's acquisitions of Pfizer's ophthalmic surgical business in 2004 and VISX in 2005 make strategic sense and should increase shareholder value over the long run. We are pleased with several of AMO's shareholder-friendly policies. Directors are paid half in stock and encouraged to own shares of the company worth at least 5 times their annual cash pay. We believe this aligns the interests of the board with those of shareholders. However, we would like to see a few changes. AMO has several anti-takeover measures, including a poison pill and staggered director elections. Also, Mazzo was named chairman of the board in May 2006. We prefer the roles of chairman and CEO to be separate in order to encourage board independence.

1700 E. St. Andrew Place
Santa Ana, CA 92705   www.amo-inc.com

Growth [B]	2002	2003	2004	2005
Revenue %	-0.9	11.8	23.4	24.1
Earnings/Share %	NMF	NMF	NMF	NMF
Book Value/Share %	—	NMF	103.0	122.1
Dividends/Share %	NMF	NMF	NMF	NMF

Profitability [C+]	2003	2004	2005	TTM
Return on Assets %	2.2	-12.0	-22.9	4.5
Oper Cash Flow $Mil	48	40	21	217
- Cap Spending $Mil	13	17	23	30
= Free Cash Flow $Mil	35	22	-2	187

Financial Health [D-]	2003	2004	2005	09-30-06
Long-term Debt $Mil	234	551	500	851
Total Equity $Mil	93	276	1,010	689
Debt/Equity Ratio	2.5	2.0	0.5	1.2

Industry	Business Risk	Moat Size	Investment Style	Sector
Medical Equip.	Average	Narrow	Mid Growth	Healthcare

Competition	Market Cap $Mil	12 Mo Trailing Sales $Mil	Price/Cash Flow	Return On Assets%	Debt/ Equity	Total Return% 1 Yr	3 Yr
Advanced Medical Optics	2,085	1,007	9.6	4.5	1.2	-15.8	19.9
Alcon	34,256	4,369	27.7	17.8	0.0	-12.6	24.3
Bausch & Lomb	2,799	—	—	—	—	-22.6	1.1

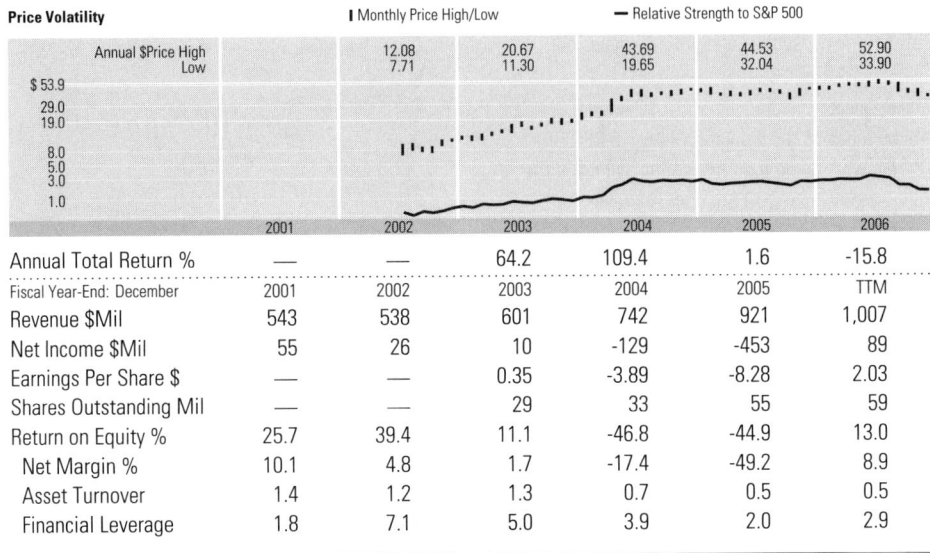

	2001	2002	2003	2004	2005	TTM
Annual Total Return %	—	—	64.2	109.4	1.6	-15.8
Fiscal Year-End: December	2001	2002	2003	2004	2005	TTM
Revenue $Mil	543	538	601	742	921	1,007
Net Income $Mil	55	26	10	-129	-453	89
Earnings Per Share $	—	—	0.35	-3.89	-8.28	2.03
Shares Outstanding Mil	—	—	29	33	55	59
Return on Equity %	25.7	39.4	11.1	-46.8	-44.9	13.0
Net Margin %	10.1	4.8	1.7	-17.4	-49.2	8.9
Asset Turnover	1.4	1.2	1.3	0.7	0.5	0.5
Financial Leverage	1.8	7.1	5.0	3.9	2.0	2.9

Valuation Ratios	Stock	Rel to Industry	Rel to S&P 500
Price/Earnings	17.3	0.6	0.8
Price/Book	3.0	0.5	0.7
Price/Sales	2.1	0.4	0.7
Price/Cash Flow	9.6	0.4	0.7

Major Fund Holders	% of Fund Assets
Villere Balanced	3.49
Legg Mason Special Investment Prim	2.52
Rice Hall James Mid-Cap Inv	2.19
Ivy Science & Technology C	2.07

Thesis By Jeff Viksjo, 12-13-06 Stock Price as of Analysis: $35.73

Advanced Medical Optics' (AMO) acquisition of VISX creates a defendable niche for the company in higher-end eye-care services and secures its narrow moat.

VISX brought a market-leading LASIK business to AMO, which we believe increases the combined firm's ability to sell its refractive intra-ocular lenses (IOLs). These lenses give cataract patients an unprecedented full range of vision and represent the highest technology available. Surgeons who perform both cataract and LASIK procedures are best-positioned to sell refractive IOLs to patients, because these doctors have financing options available and the experience necessary to effectively sell products not eligible for insurance reimbursement. We think AMO's refractive IOLs will gain market share against competitors as the strength of its LASIK business provides a great cross-selling opportunity and marketing niche.

Furthermore, profitability should improve as eye-care markets transition into higher-end technologies. AMO sells its LASIK equipment to surgeons and then receives a licensing fee for each standard or custom surgery performed. Custom LASIK uses a computer to diagnose the errors in a patient's eyes, in contrast to standard LASIK, which uses a traditional eye exam. AMO receives $110 for the standard procedure and $245 for the custom procedure, yet the expense to the firm remains the same, so profitability should expand as custom surgeries gain market share. A similar situation exists in the cataract segment, where AMO receives $895 for its refractive IOL and just $150 for its monofocal IOL, despite similar manufacturing costs.

However, because LASIK surgery and refractive IOLs are usually not covered by Medicare or private health insurance, price is a considerable obstacle in getting patients to switch to higher-end products. In addition, demand tends to be cyclical as patients are less likely to pay for elective procedures during an economic downturn. Also, AMO will continue to lag rival Alcon on several fronts: Alcon benefits from large R&D and marketing budgets and a diverse product base, which would be difficult for AMO to replicate. As a result, AMO has less operating leverage and faces an uphill battle in marketing and innovation.

Despite this, we think AMO will prosper in its higher-end services niche. In addition, we believe the company's cataract products that are typically covered by Medicare, such as monofocal IOLs, will provide stability in times of economic decline.

Data as of 12-29-06

Aetna AET

Rating	Fair Value	Last Close	Consider Buy	Consider Sell	Yield %
★★	$35.00	$43.18	$27.00	$43.90	0.09

Company Profile
Aetna is one of the largest health-care and related benefit organizations, providing a full spectrum of products including health care, dental, vision, pharmacy, group life, disability, and long-term care coverage. The company also manages a variety of retirement products. Aetna provides products and services to about 15.4 million medical members, two thirds of which are fee-based. Aetna also serves 13.4 million dental members, and 15.3 million group insurance customers.

Management
Stewardship Grade [D]

This is a year of transition for Aetna's management. In February, CEO duties were passed from Jack Rowe to Ron Williams. Williams has also assumed the chairman's role. In addition, CFO Alan Bennett will retire in early 2007. Management transitions can cause disruptions, but we are not concerned in this case, as Williams is an experienced industry executive who we believe was instrumental in Aetna's turnaround. However, we would prefer to see the chairman and CEO roles split, providing more checks and balances in the executive suite.

This management team is highly paid, with the top five executives all receiving multimillion-dollar pay packages. There have already been sizable grants in 2006, so we expect to see executive compensation continue to climb this year. Aetna targets pay based upon performance, with the median pay of its peer group targeted for median performance. We believe in pay for performance, but this plan still poses some problems, as managed care executives are among the highest paid executives, and many are rewarded based on performance that can be more related to favorable industry conditions than to actual value-added. We will closely monitor the company's follow-through on this policy in what we anticipate will be a tougher climate ahead for insurers.

151 Farmington Avenue
Hartford, CT 06156
www.aetna.com

Growth [C]	2002	2003	2004	2005
Revenue %	-21.1	-9.6	10.7	13.0
Earnings/Share %	NMF	NMF	142.3	-24.6
Book Value/Share %	-33.8	9.9	15.5	15.3
Dividends/Share %	0.0	0.0	0.0	100.0

Profitability [B-]	2003	2004	2005	TTM
Return on Assets %	2.3	5.3	3.7	3.7
Oper Cash Flow $Mil	371	1,437	1,893	—
- Cap Spending $Mil	211	190	272	—
= Free Cash Flow $Mil	—	—	—	—

Financial Health [NA]	2003	2004	2005	09-30-06
Long-term Debt $Mil	—	—	—	—
Total Equity $Mil	7,924	9,081	10,105	9,650
Debt/Equity Ratio	—	—	—	—

Industry	Business Risk	Moat Size	Investment Style	Sector
Managed Care	Average	None	Large Core	Healthcare

Competition

	Market Cap $Mil	12 Mo Trailing Sales $Mil	Price/Cash Flow	Return On Assets%	Debt/Equity	Total Return% 1 Yr	3 Yr
Aetna	22,540	24,654	—	3.7	—	-8.3	36.7
UnitedHealth Group	72,374	51,787	11.9	7.7	0.4	-13.5	22.2
WellPoint	48,789	54,285	—	5.7	—	-1.4	27.3

Price Volatility

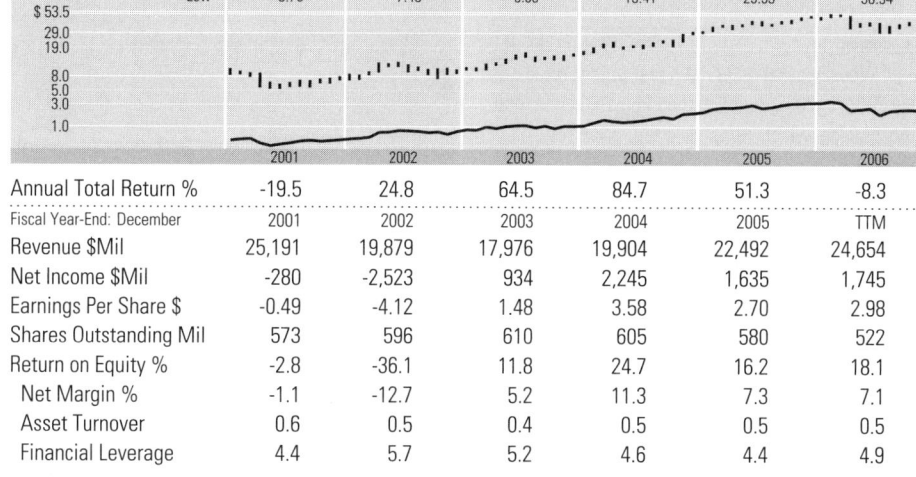

| Annual $Price High | 10.67 | 12.98 | 17.50 | 31.89 | 49.68 | 52.48 |
| Low | 5.75 | 7.48 | 9.98 | 16.41 | 29.93 | 30.94 |

	2001	2002	2003	2004	2005	2006
Annual Total Return %	-19.5	24.8	64.5	84.7	51.3	-8.3

Fiscal Year-End: December

	2001	2002	2003	2004	2005	TTM
Revenue $Mil	25,191	19,879	17,976	19,904	22,492	24,654
Net Income $Mil	-280	-2,523	934	2,245	1,635	1,745
Earnings Per Share $	-0.49	-4.12	1.48	3.58	2.70	2.98
Shares Outstanding Mil	573	596	610	605	580	522
Return on Equity %	-2.8	-36.1	11.8	24.7	16.2	18.1
Net Margin %	-1.1	-12.7	5.2	11.3	7.3	7.1
Asset Turnover	0.6	0.5	0.4	0.5	0.5	0.5
Financial Leverage	4.4	5.7	5.2	4.6	4.4	4.9

Valuation Ratios	Stock	Rel to Industry	Rel to S&P 500
Price/Earnings	14.6	0.7	0.7
Price/Book	2.3	0.7	0.6
Price/Sales	0.9	0.8	0.3
Price/Cash Flow	—	—	—

Major Fund Holders	% of Fund Assets
Allianz OCC Core Equity Instl	4.89
Hillman Focused Advantage	4.74
JHancock Large Cap Equity A	4.15
Legg Mason Growth Trust Primary	4.11

Thesis
By Brandon Troegle, 12-13-06   Stock Price as of Analysis: $42.69

Aetna faces a difficult road ahead as it attempts to improve profitability with premium increases in an industry with lackluster organic growth opportunities. It's only been a couple of years since Aetna re-emerged as a true competitor in the managed care industry after several years of disappointing results.

Aetna underwent a corporate makeover beginning in 2000, selling its financial services and international business, and withdrawing from unprofitable commercial health-maintenance organization and Medicare products. In an attempt to control its medical loss ratio (MLR), which is defined as medical costs paid divided by premiums, the company pushed through aggressive price increases and severed ties with its most expensive members, shedding 6 million members in the process. After posting losses in 2001 and 2002, Aetna returned to profitability in 2003. In 2004 and 2005, the company modestly grew enrollment, and experienced rising profits.

We think execution will be challenging going forward, as the company operates in many different markets where it will need to accurately address the profitability of members and adjust rates accordingly. Medical membership is lower this year than originally anticipated, and we expect commercial enrollment growth to be difficult in 2007. Aetna had to get more aggressive on premium pricing this year to combat rising MLRs, seeking margin improvement even at the expense of higher membership and revenue growth. We prefer to see margin growth to revenue growth and like the strides the company recently made, but we recognize Aetna faces a potentially sustained period of difficult organic growth due to challenging industry conditions.

The news isn't all bad, as Aetna has some products with potential. Self-funded fee-based membership has experienced moderate increases in 2005 and 2006, though some of this is attributable to a migration from risk-based plans. The company's consumer-driven health plan is experiencing very strong growth, but with a small base that's just 3% of total medical membership, this plan is a long way from being a meaningful part of the company's revenue base.

Aflac AFL

Data as of 12-29-06

	Rating	Fair Value	Last Close	Consider Buy	Consider Sell	Yield %
	★★★★	$52.00	$46.00	$40.10	$65.20	1.20

Company Profile

Aflac sells supplemental health insurance and some life insurance in Japan and the U.S. It made a name selling cancer policies but now writes a variety of supplemental insurance policies for things like accident and disability and long-term care. Aflac doesn't employ its own salesforce; most policies are sold at company work sites through independent agents, and the consumer--not the employer--pays the premiums. Aflac has no plans to expand beyond the U.S. and Japan.

Management   Stewardship Grade [B]

Daniel Amos has been chairman and CEO of Aflac since 2001. In 2005, Amos earned $6.5 million in total compensation, which we think is fair, given his contribution to the stock's total return. Amos owns about $506 million in company stock, which aligns his interests with shareholders', in our opinion. Aflac's management has consistently demonstrated a propensity to make long-term investments to build the firm's value, even if this comes at a cost to shorter-term earnings and sales growth. Directors and officers collectively own 4% of the firm, which is why we think they consistently act to accumulate long-term value. As an example, management has consistently repurchased large quantities of Aflac stock over the years at prices we think were sensible, adding significantly to investor returns.

1932 Wynnton Road
Columbus, GA 31999
www.aflac.com

Growth [B]	2002	2003	2004	2005
Revenue %	6.9	11.6	16.0	8.1
Earnings/Share %	21.6	-3.3	66.7	19.2
Book Value/Share %	10.4	2.7	15.2	6.6
Dividends/Share %	19.5	30.4	26.7	15.8

Profitability [A]	2003	2004	2005	TTM
Return on Assets %	1.5	2.1	2.6	2.6
Oper Cash Flow $Mil	3,389	4,486	4,433	—
- Cap Spending $Mil	21	21	16	—
= Free Cash Flow $Mil	—	—	—	—

Financial Health [NA]	2003	2004	2005	09-30-06
Long-term Debt $Mil	—	—	—	—
Total Equity $Mil	6,648	7,576	7,927	8,027
Debt/Equity Ratio	—	—	—	—

Industry	Business Risk	Moat Size	Investment Style	Sector
Insurance (Life)	Average	Wide	Large Core	Financial Services

Competition	Market Cap $Mil	12 Mo Trailing Sales $Mil	Price/Cash Flow	Return On Assets%	Debt/Equity	Total Return% 1 Yr	3 Yr
Aflac	22,747	14,496	—	2.6	—	0.3	9.6
American International Gr	186,296	110,593	—	1.2	—	6.1	3.2
Metropolitan Life Insuran	44,861	47,120	—	0.6	—	21.7	22.0

Price Volatility
| Monthly Price High/Low — Relative Strength to S&P 500

Annual $Price High/Low	36.09/23.00	33.45/23.10	36.91/28.00	42.60/33.85	49.65/35.50	49.40/41.63
	2001	2002	2003	2004	2005	2006
Annual Total Return %	-31.5	23.6	21.2	11.2	17.7	0.3
Fiscal Year-End: December	2001	2002	2003	2004	2005	TTM
Revenue $Mil	9,598	10,257	11,447	13,281	14,363	14,496
Net Income $Mil	654	785	768	1,266	1,483	1,514
Earnings Per Share $	1.25	1.52	1.47	2.45	2.92	3.01
Shares Outstanding Mil	523	516	512	508	501	495
Return on Equity %	12.1	12.3	11.6	16.7	18.7	18.9
Net Margin %	6.8	7.7	6.7	9.5	10.3	10.4
Asset Turnover	0.3	0.2	0.2	0.2	0.3	0.2
Financial Leverage	7.0	7.0	7.7	7.8	7.1	7.3

Valuation Ratios	Stock	Rel to Industry	Rel to S&P 500
Price/Earnings	15.3	0.5	0.7
Price/Book	2.8	0.8	0.7
Price/Sales	1.6	0.7	0.6
Price/Cash Flow	—	—	—

Major Fund Holders	% of Fund Assets
Oak Value	5.47
Blue Chip Investor	4.71
Fidelity Select Insurance	4.31
Parnassus Workplace	4.28

Thesis By Dafina Dunmore, 12-01-06 Stock Price as of Analysis: $43.75

Aflac is one of the few gems in the commodified insurance industry. The insurer boasts tremendous brand recognition, a low-cost structure, and industry-leading client retention, which we think earns it a wide economic moat. Our fair value estimate is $52 per share.

Aging populations, rising health-care costs, and hefty government debt are squeezing publicly funded social insurance programs in Japan and the United States. This trend increases demand for private supplemental insurance, which plays right into Aflac's hands. Aflac is one of the most recognized brands in Japan and is the clear market leader for third-sector products, like supplemental health insurance. The industry's product mix has been shifting away from cancer policies to higher-margin medical insurance products, though, where Aflac faces tougher competition.

Industry sales of medical products have recently languished because of continued uncertainty regarding previously imposed regulatory sanctions on a number of competitors. We expect this to pressure industry sales through the first half of 2007. Although no sanctions were imposed on Aflac, it will probably experience the greatest impact as the market leader. An increasing number of competitors are offering medical products, which also makes consumer decisions difficult. However, product innovation and low operating costs allow Aflac to offer attractive value relative to its rivals, which we think consumers will eventually flush out.

Despite poor sales results, the Japan operation continues to deliver solid earnings and respectable premium growth. We attribute this to Aflac's market-leading client retention. Keeping current customers is more profitable than writing new business because of the steep cost to acquire a customer.

Rising health-care costs should boost demand for Aflac's products in the underpenetrated U.S. market as well. Employers seek to offer more extensive health-care options to employees, but mounting health-care prices make it cost-prohibitive. Aflac is a market leader in supplemental insurance, where employees pay a portion or the entire premium. Aflac consumes 6% of the U.S. small-business market, leaving plenty of room for growth. We expect that Aflac's U.S. growth will exceed its growth in Japan over the longer term. As in Japan, Aflac has a well-recognized brand in the United States, and recent advertising spending aimed at better defining its brand appears to be paying off.

Data as of 12-29-06

Air Products and Chemicals APD

	Rating	Fair Value	Last Close	Consider Buy	Consider Sell	Yield %
	★★★	$65.00	$70.28	$50.10	$81.40	1.94

Industry	Business Risk	Moat Size	Investment Style	Sector
Chemicals	Average	Narrow	Large Core	Industrial Materials

Company Profile

Air Products is an industrial gas company with a shrinking chemical operation on the side, thanks to recently completed and planned acquisitions. The firm supplies products ranging from medical oxygen to the flavor-preserving nitrogen found in potato chip bags. The firm's remaining chemical unit will focus on performance materials. Air Products also supplies highly efficient liquefied natural gas equipment.

Competition

	Market Cap $Mil	12 Mo Trailing Sales $Mil	Price/Cash Flow	Return On Assets%	Debt/Equity	Total Return% 1 Yr	3 Yr
Air Products and Chemicals	15,246	8,850	1.2	6.5	0.5	21.2	12.4
Praxair	19,158	8,221	12.2	8.5	1.0	14.0	18.2
AIQUY							

Management Stewardship Grade [C]

John Jones, a 32-year company veteran, has been CEO since December 2000. He is part of an industrywide movement to bolster pricing power and returns on capital. We do have some concerns about the company investing in new gas plants that serve only the merchant gas market, as the profitability of these plants can vary significantly along with volume and pricing power in a regional market. Also, soaring raw-material costs have dented returns in the company's chemical segment. While recent price increases have improved results, the bottom line is that most of the firm's chemical products are global commodities, with pricing and profits determined by customer demand and the collective actions of all industry players. The economics of this unit simply don't measure up to those of its more attractive industrial gas franchise. We are encouraged by management's recently announced decision to sell the less attractive portions of this business. Management pay is in line with industry practices, and incentive compensation is tied to meeting returns on operating assets, which should help management maintain the proper focus.

Price Volatility

Annual $Price High Low	49.00 32.10	53.51 40.20	53.07 36.97	59.18 46.71	65.81 53.00	72.45 58.01
Annual Total Return %	16.6	-7.2	26.1	12.0	4.3	21.2

Fiscal Year-End: September	2002	2003	2004	2005	2006	TTM
Revenue $Mil	5,401	6,297	7,032	7,768	8,850	8,850
Net Income $Mil	525	397	604	712	723	723
Earnings Per Share $	2.36	1.78	2.64	3.08	3.18	3.18
Shares Outstanding Mil	217	220	224	226	222	217
Return on Equity %	15.2	10.5	13.6	15.6	14.7	14.7
Net Margin %	9.7	6.3	8.6	9.2	8.2	8.2
Asset Turnover	0.6	0.7	0.7	0.7	0.8	0.8
Financial Leverage	2.5	2.5	2.3	2.3	2.3	2.3

Valuation Ratios	Stock	Rel to Industry	Rel to S&P 500
Price/Earnings	21.4	1.2	1.0
Price/Book	3.1	0.9	0.8
Price/Sales	1.7	1.0	0.6
Price/Cash Flow	1.2	0.1	0.1

Major Fund Holders	% of Fund Assets
Van Kampen Exchange	7.23
Fidelity Select Chemicals	6.18
ICON Materials	4.23
Allianz RCM Global Resources Instl	3.44

Thesis By Matthew Warren, 12-18-06 Stock Price as of Analysis: $72.13

Air Products continues to jettison the struggling portions of its chemical business, leaving investors with an industrial gas portfolio that has concentrated exposure to the fast-growing energy and electronics markets.

Air Products sells products ranging from specialty gases used in electronics production to hydrogen used in oil refineries. Although industrial gases of similar purity are essentially commodities, prohibitive transport costs make this a regional game. In fact, Air Products' gas business is similar to that of its competitor, Praxair. A notable difference is Air Products' concentrated exposure to the electronics, medical oxygen, and energy markets.

Air Products' most reliable sales are to customers that opt to have gas production facilities built adjacent to their own factories. This is a win-win arrangement for several reasons. With transport costs eliminated, Air Products offers discounted pricing and a highly reliable supply. Despite significant up-front costs, Air Products' "on-site" plants are attractive because they offer steady sales--contracts usually include a take-or-pay clause mandating minimum purchases--and margins that are protected by the ability to pass along higher electricity or natural-gas costs. When contracts are up for renewal, Air Products can outbid competitors that have to factor in the cost of a new plant. This virtually ensures a steady relationship over the life of a customer's facility.

On-site plants also engage in piggybacking, which involves the sale of excess gas--such as oxygen and argon byproducts from an air separation plant built to supply a customer with nitrogen--to supply the merchant market by truck. Largely tied to regional industrial activity, these shorter-duration contracts are characterized by more variable demand. While piggybacking helps spread fixed costs across additional sales, Air Products has been fairly aggressive (especially in Asia) building stand-alone merchant plants, which increases its risk profile compared with some peers.

Air Products continues to sell off the worst-performing portions of its historically volatile chemical business. The firm's argument for retaining the performance material unit is that it shares some customers with its electronics gas business and that application development drives volume growth, a characteristic shared with the industrial gas portfolio. While we have our doubts about this decision, we are pleased that management continues to offload the majority of this commoditylike business.

7201 Hamilton Boulevard www.airproducts.com
Allentown, PA 18195-1501

Growth [B]	2002	2003	2004	2005
Revenue %	16.6	11.7	10.5	13.9
Earnings/Share %	-24.6	48.3	16.7	3.2
Book Value/Share %	9.0	14.6	2.0	9.3
Dividends/Share %	7.3	18.2	20.2	7.2

Profitability [A-]	2003	2004	2005	TTM
Return on Assets %	6.0	6.8	6.5	6.5
Oper Cash Flow $Mil	1,088	1,331	13,223	13,223
- Cap Spending $Mil	687	923	1,261	1,261
= Free Cash Flow $Mil	401	408	11,962	11,962

Financial Health [A]	2003	2004	2005	06-30-06
Long-term Debt $Mil	2,114	2,053	2,280	2,280
Total Equity $Mil	4,444	4,576	4,924	4,924
Debt/Equity Ratio	0.5	0.4	0.5	0.5

Data as of 12-29-06

AirTran Holdings AAI

	Rating	Fair Value	Last Close	Consider Buy	Consider Sell	Yield %
	★★★	$13.00	$11.74	$8.30	$15.70	0.00

Company Profile

AirTran Holdings provides low-cost air transportation targeting both leisure and business passengers. The firm operates a fleet of 127 Boeing jets, comprising mostly 717s and a growing number of new 737-700s. With about 7,000 employees, AirTran serves more than 40 airports across the nation from its Atlanta hub. AirTran is the second-largest carrier at Atlanta's Hartsfield International Airport.

Management Stewardship Grade [B]

AirTran's top six executives each average more than 20 years of airline industry experience, led by chairman and CEO Joseph Leonard's 30 years. Leonard is an airline veteran with stints at American and Northwest Airlines as well as Boeing. Leonard joined AirTran in 1999, the same year that Robert Fornaro was hired to lead the operating subsidiary. Fornaro also has extensive experience, serving in operations roles at US Airways and in other roles at Northwest and TWA. Executive compensation is above the industry average, which management arguably has earned because it has achieved one of the industry's lowest cost structures. All officers and directors combined own about 5.0% of outstanding shares, with Leonard owning about half of those. Management's incentives are aligned with shareholders' as long-term compensation is based on profitability and cost controls. We appreciate management's forthright disclosure, and the company has even taken the unusual step of setting out corporate governance guidelines on its Web site. However, Leonard occupies both the CEO and chairman positions, and the board has staggered elections, which could make it difficult for outsiders to enact changes within the airline.

9955 AirTran Boulevard www.airtran.com
Orlando, FL 32827

Growth [A]	2002	2003	2004	2005
Revenue %	10.3	25.2	13.4	39.3
Earnings/Share %	NMF	706.7	-88.4	-85.7
Book Value/Share %	49.4	402.3	4.9	7.1
Dividends/Share %	NMF	NMF	NMF	NMF

Profitability [B-]	2003	2004	2005	TTM
Return on Assets %	12.4	1.4	0.1	0.9
Oper Cash Flow $Mil	133	38	65	91
- Cap Spending $Mil	21	26	35	75
= Free Cash Flow $Mil	112	12	29	16

Financial Health [B-]	2003	2004	2005	09-30-06
Long-term Debt $Mil	242	300	401	576
Total Equity $Mil	302	334	352	390
Debt/Equity Ratio	0.8	0.9	1.1	1.5

Industry	Business Risk	Moat Size	Investment Style	Sector
Air Transport	Above Avg	Narrow	Small Growth	Business Services

Competition	Market Cap $Mil	12 Mo Trailing Sales $Mil	Price/Cash Flow	Return On Assets %	Debt/ Equity	Total Return% 1 Yr	3 Yr
AirTran Holdings	1,069	1,841	11.8	0.9	1.5	-26.8	-1.4
Southwest Airlines	12,131	8,798	8.6	4.1	0.2	-6.7	-1.2
AMR	6,482	22,334	3.8	-1.3	NMF	36.0	32.5

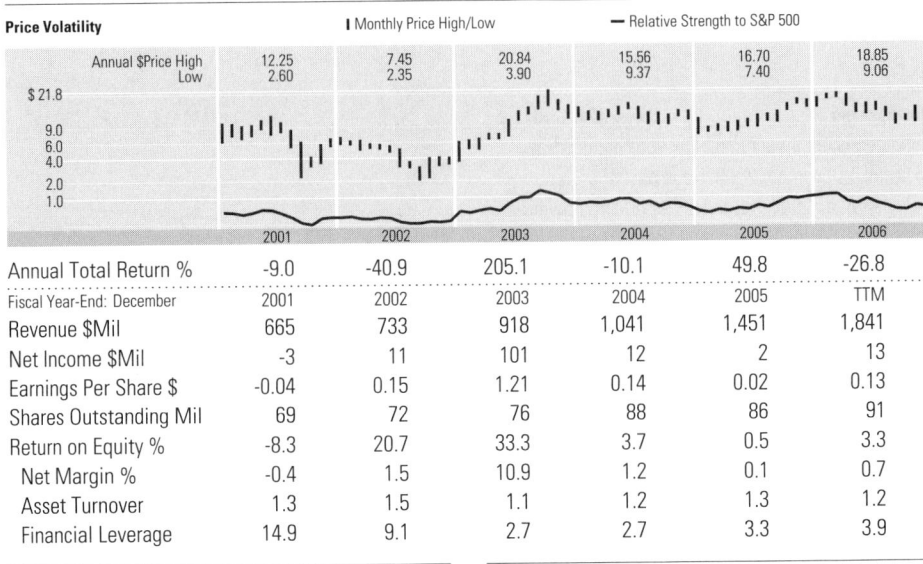

Price Volatility — Monthly Price High/Low — Relative Strength to S&P 500

Annual $Price High / Low	12.25 / 2.60	7.45 / 2.35	20.84 / 3.90	15.56 / 9.37	16.70 / 7.40	18.85 / 9.06
Annual Total Return %	-9.0	-40.9	205.1	-10.1	49.8	-26.8

Fiscal Year-End: December	2001	2002	2003	2004	2005	TTM
Revenue $Mil	665	733	918	1,041	1,451	1,841
Net Income $Mil	-3	11	101	12	2	13
Earnings Per Share $	-0.04	0.15	1.21	0.14	0.02	0.13
Shares Outstanding Mil	69	72	76	88	86	91
Return on Equity %	-8.3	20.7	33.3	3.7	0.5	3.3
Net Margin %	-0.4	1.5	10.9	1.2	0.1	0.7
Asset Turnover	1.3	1.5	1.1	1.2	1.3	1.2
Financial Leverage	14.9	9.1	2.7	2.7	3.3	3.9

Valuation Ratios	Stock	Rel to Industry	Rel to S&P 500
Price/Earnings	90.3	4.9	4.4
Price/Book	2.7	0.7	0.7
Price/Sales	0.6	0.4	0.2
Price/Cash Flow	11.8	1.2	0.8

Major Fund Holders	% of Fund Assets
Aston/Veredus Aggressive Growth N	2.78
Diamond Hill Small Cap A	2.73
Fidelity Select Air Transportation	2.54
Diamond Hill Small-Mid Cap I	2.40

Thesis By Marisa E. Thompson, 12-28-06 Stock Price as of Analysis: $11.97

AirTran is one of the first low-cost carriers to dip its toe into the rising tide of airline consolidation.

In the highly commodified airline business, low unit operating costs are synonymous with profitability. AirTran's entire business model is built on the tenets of operating efficiently. After adjusting for length of haul and excluding fuel, AirTran operates with the second-lowest unit cost in the industry, just behind perennial leader Southwest. AirTran operates just two kinds of airplanes, the Boeing 717 and the 737, which allows for both maintenance and training cost savings. While largely unionized, AirTran's relatively young workforce works longer hours and receives incentives to purchase stock monthly at a discount to market prices. As a result, unit labor costs are higher only than those of JetBlue, whose longer flight lengths tend to skew this figure downward. AirTran also contains costs by distributing tickets primarily over the Internet, and the airline recently negotiated lower commissions for the 25% of fares booked through third parties.

AirTran is hoping to transfer its low-cost might and gain scale in a consolidating airline industry by combining with Milwaukee-based Midwest Airlines, a carrier that flies complementary routes using Boeing 717s. With little route overlap and the network effect of a larger airline enjoying more city pairs and stronger passenger traffic, management's goal of $20 million in revenue synergies is readily achievable, in our opinion. Plus, some of the targeted cost synergies will be relatively straightforward. Eliminating redundant overhead, replacing inefficient MD-80s with new 737s already on order at AirTran, combining maintenance operations, and shifting many of the Signature Service flights to a mix of coach and business class will go a long way toward meeting management's $40 million goal.

However, the integration process will involve some more tricky maneuvers. Merging unionized workforces with disparate work rules, folding in Midwest's regional carrier (which operates small planes with lower unit costs), and melding cultures that operate at dissimilar productivity levels will all be challenging. Though management might be successful at implementing some of its best practices at Midwest, the end result may be that AirTran's non-fuel unit costs never return to its premerger level.

In the end, though, we still think Midwest represents a compelling fit. This and the fact that both airlines are limited in their abilities to grow and connect new city pairs separately make us supporters of the merger.

Alberto-Culver ACV

Data as of 12-29-06

Rating	Fair Value	Last Close	Consider Buy	Consider Sell	Yield %
★★★	$20.00	$21.45	$15.40	$25.10	1.75

Company Profile
Alberto manufactures and markets leading personal-care products--including Alberto VO5, TRESemme, Nexxus, and St. Ives Swiss Formula--in the United States and internationally.

Industry	Business Risk	Moat Size	Investment Style	Sector
Household Products	Average	None	Mid Value	Consumer Goods

Competition

	Market Cap $Mil	12 Mo Trailing Sales $Mil	Price/Cash Flow	Return On Assets%	Debt/Equity	Total Return% 1 Yr	3 Yr
Alberto-Culver	2,010	3,772	7.8	8.0	0.1	19.2	10.2
Procter & Gamble	203,656	72,214	16.8	6.8	0.6	13.4	11.3
Johnson & Johnson	191,415	52,252	14.5	18.5	0.0	12.4	10.8

Price Volatility

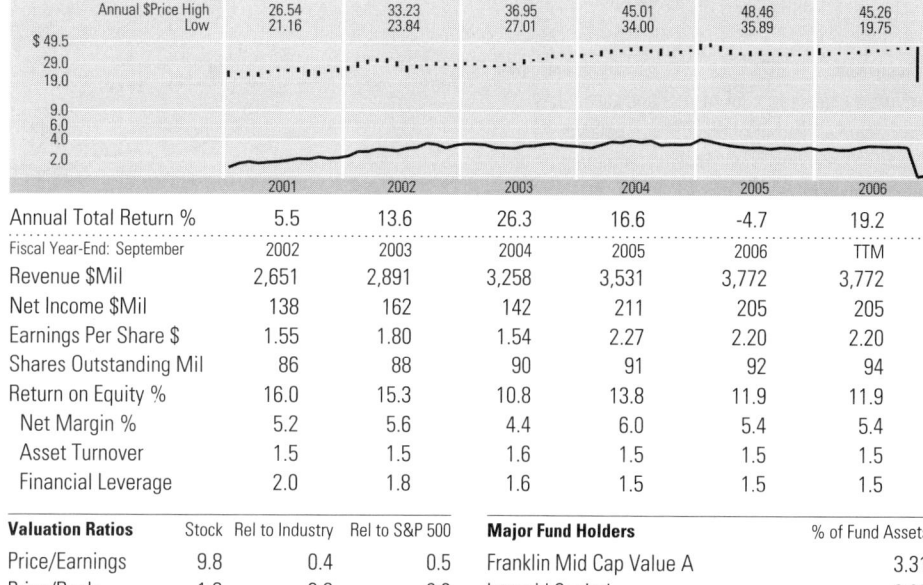

Monthly Price High/Low — Relative Strength to S&P 500

	2001	2002	2003	2004	2005	2006
Annual $Price High	26.54	33.23	36.95	45.01	48.46	45.26
Low	21.16	23.84	27.01	34.00	35.89	19.75
Annual Total Return %	5.5	13.6	26.3	16.6	-4.7	19.2

Fiscal Year-End: September	2002	2003	2004	2005	2006	TTM
Revenue $Mil	2,651	2,891	3,258	3,531	3,772	3,772
Net Income $Mil	138	162	142	211	205	205
Earnings Per Share $	1.55	1.80	1.54	2.27	2.20	2.20
Shares Outstanding Mil	86	88	90	91	92	94
Return on Equity %	16.0	15.3	10.8	13.8	11.9	11.9
Net Margin %	5.2	5.6	4.4	6.0	5.4	5.4
Asset Turnover	1.5	1.5	1.6	1.5	1.5	1.5
Financial Leverage	2.0	1.8	1.6	1.5	1.5	1.5

Valuation Ratios

	Stock	Rel to Industry	Rel to S&P 500
Price/Earnings	9.8	0.4	0.5
Price/Book	1.2	0.2	0.3
Price/Sales	0.5	0.2	0.2
Price/Cash Flow	7.8	0.4	0.5

Major Fund Holders

	% of Fund Assets
Franklin Mid Cap Value A	3.31
Intrepid Capital	2.96
Touchstone Family Heritage(R) A	2.85
Gabelli Woodland Sm Cp Value AAA	2.76

Management Stewardship Grade [B]

Leonard Lavin and his wife, Bernice Lavin, founded Alberto-Culver in 1955. In the fall of 2006, Sally Beauty Holdings was spun off, and longtime CEO Howard Bernick, the Lavins' son-in-law, retired. Their daughter and Bernick's wife, Carol Bernick, was chairman of the old Alberto-Culver, and she continues in the role at the stand-alone company. James Marino, former president of the consumer products division at Alberto-Culver, is now CEO of the company. The firm has a record of paying very moderate salary and bonus compensation, and Marino received 3.2% of all options granted to employees during the year, which is fairly reasonable. For the most part, we view Alberto-Culver as essentially a family-run enterprise, but we have yet to see any evidence that shareholder interests take a backseat, given the family's influence. Management put in a solid performance over the past year as it explored its options to spin off Sally and executed the transaction. We had hoped management would take the separation with Sally as an opportunity to declassify its board structure but that hasn't happened, and we're also not big fans of the firm's other anti-takeover defenses. All officers and directors hold 15.4% of shares outstanding.

2525 Armitage Avenue www.alberto.com
Melrose Park, IL 60160

Growth [B-]	2002	2003	2004	2005
Revenue %	9.1	12.7	8.4	6.8
Earnings/Share %	16.4	-14.4	47.4	-3.1
Book Value/Share %	21.7	21.0	15.5	12.4
Dividends/Share %	14.9	24.8	32.0	10.1

Profitability [A-]	2003	2004	2005	TTM
Return on Assets %	6.9	9.2	8.0	8.0
Oper Cash Flow $Mil	250	209	257	257
- Cap Spending $Mil	75	91	80	80
= Free Cash Flow $Mil	175	118	177	177

Financial Health [A+]	2003	2004	2005	06-30-06
Long-term Debt $Mil	121	124	122	122
Total Equity $Mil	1,314	1,532	1,730	1,730
Debt/Equity Ratio	0.1	0.1	0.1	0.1

Thesis By Lauren DeSanto, 11-22-06 Stock Price as of Analysis: $20.79

Alberto-Culver's distribution business has always nicely balanced the consumer product side, but with the recent split of the company, Alberto's consumer business is now a small stand-alone player in the beauty-care aisle.

Historically, Alberto's consumer product division has manufactured value-price personal-care products, including Alberto VO5 shampoo and St. Ives lotion. Rivals Procter & Gamble and L'Oreal dwarf its roughly $1.3 billion in annual sales, but smart investments, incremental product improvements, and Alberto's nimble size have helped the firm maintain its products on store shelves. More recently, as competition in the value segment of hair care has heated up (with deep-discount brands driving down profitability), Alberto has moved upscale by purchasing neglected premium salon brands like TRESemme and Nexxus and relaunching them at mass retail.

While this strategy has served Alberto well, we don't think it can be replicated indefinitely. Many consumer product firms have moved away from value-positioned products, realizing that even at mass retail, consumers are willing to trade up to premium-priced brands. P&G, for example, has pruned its hair-care brands over the years, most recently selling off Pert, in order to focus on its higher-priced offerings. Alberto's management has said it would like to add another skin-care brand to its portfolio. It clearly needs to move beyond the hair-care category with its next acquisition, if only to avoid competing with itself, and yet hair care is also where the firm has the greatest expertise.

We don't doubt Alberto's ability to identify lagging brands that can be turned around successfully, much less its disciplined approach to paying for and integrating them. Given that it is so reliant on finding these targets, however, we're not convinced that Alberto has a moat. Based on pro forma data, its returns on invested capital exceed our estimate of Alberto's cost of capital, but it may take some time before we have a solid grasp of the firm's overhead expenses and the opportunity for margin expansion.

In the meantime, Alberto is doing a solid job with the brands that it has, scoring a big win by sponsoring the hit show Project Runway, which showcases TRESemme, and the company remains a sound operator. Alberto has a solid leader in CEO James Marino, in our opinion, but we'd wait to see more of a track record for the firm as a stand-alone entity before we'd be interested in the shares.

Data as of 12-29-06

Alcatel Lucent ADR ALU

	Rating	Fair Value	Last Close	Consider Buy	Consider Sell	Yield %
	★★★★	$18.00	$14.22	$13.90	$22.60	1.43

Company Profile

The combined Alcatel-Lucent is the world's largest vendor of telecom equipment, with about $25 billion in annual revenue. It produces a wide range of network equipment including broadband-access systems, data-networking gear, optical systems, and wireless systems. The combined company will have a more balanced geographic footprint than its former parents, with post-merger sales being divided roughly in equal thirds among Europe, North America, and the rest of the world.

Management   Stewardship Grade [NA]

While the combination of Alcatel and Lucent has been called a "merger of equals," we believe Alcatel's management will make a larger imprint on the combined company. Serge Tchuruk, Alcatel's former CEO, will remain as the chairman, and Lucent's former CEO Pat Russo will be CEO of the combined company. Given what we view as Russo's spotty record at Lucent, we would much rather have seen Tchuruk's heir apparent, Alcatel's COO Mike Quigley, assume the head of the combined company. Quigley has been at the front of the turnaround in Alcatel's wireline business, and we believe he has a stronger strategic vision and greater operational expertise than Russo. Instead, Quigley will serve as president of science, technology and strategy in the combined company. The bulk of the remaining senior management positions that have been announced thus far have been Alcatel executives. Former Alcatel shareholders now control about 60% of the company, while former Lucent shareholders control about 40%. Post-merger, Alcatel-Lucent is incorporated in France and headquartered in Paris. Its board is made up of 14 directors, with six members each nominated by Alcatel and Lucent, and will also include two new independent directors from Europe.

54, rue La Boetie www.alcatel.com
Paris Cedex 08, France 75008

Growth [NA]	2002	2003	2004	2005
Revenue %	-34.7	-24.4	-2.2	7.3
Earnings/Share %	NMF	NMF	NMF	61.9
Book Value/Share %	NMF	-46.0	51.5	30.4
Dividends/Share %	—	—	—	—

Profitability [NA]	2003	2004	2005	TTM
Return on Assets %	-8.2	2.8	4.8	4.8
Oper Cash Flow $Mil	497	72	1,063	1,063
- Cap Spending $Mil	283	719	799	799
= Free Cash Flow $Mil	214	-647	264	264

Financial Health [NA]	2003	2004	2005	12-31-05
Long-term Debt $Mil	—	551	427	427
Total Equity $Mil	3,788	7,251	7,989	7,989
Debt/Equity Ratio	—	0.1	0.1	0.1

	Industry	Business Risk	Moat Size	Investment Style	Sector
	Wireline Equip.	Average	Narrow	Large Growth	Hardware

Competition	Market Cap $Mil	12 Mo Trailing Sales $Mil	Price/Cash Flow	Return On Assets%	Debt/Equity	Total Return% 1 Yr	3 Yr
Alcatel Lucent ADR	20,314	16,448	19.1	4.8	0.1	16.6	3.4
Cisco Systems	165,967	30,118	18.9	13.2	0.3	59.6	4.1
Corning	29,268	5,005	16.0	9.2	0.2	-4.8	22.1

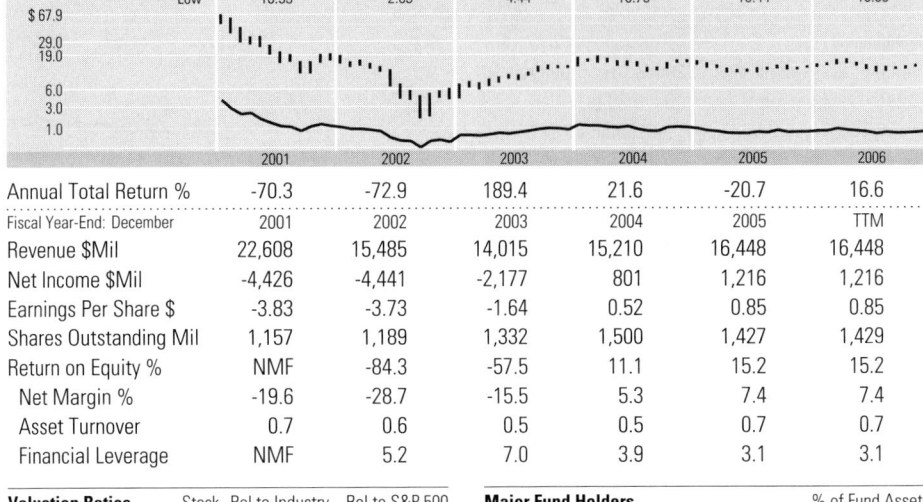

Price Volatility — Monthly Price High/Low — Relative Strength to S&P 500

	2001	2002	2003	2004	2005	2006
Annual $Price High	66.94	19.15	13.68	18.32	15.75	16.51
Low	10.53	2.03	4.44	10.76	10.44	10.63
Annual Total Return %	-70.3	-72.9	189.4	21.6	-20.7	16.6

Fiscal Year-End: December	2001	2002	2003	2004	2005	TTM
Revenue $Mil	22,608	15,485	14,015	15,210	16,448	16,448
Net Income $Mil	-4,426	-4,441	-2,177	801	1,216	1,216
Earnings Per Share $	-3.83	-3.73	-1.64	0.52	0.85	0.85
Shares Outstanding Mil	1,157	1,189	1,332	1,500	1,427	1,429
Return on Equity %	NMF	-84.3	-57.5	11.1	15.2	15.2
Net Margin %	-19.6	-28.7	-15.5	5.3	7.4	7.4
Asset Turnover	0.7	0.6	0.5	0.5	0.7	0.7
Financial Leverage	NMF	5.2	7.0	3.9	3.1	3.1

Valuation Ratios	Stock	Rel to Industry	Rel to S&P 500
Price/Earnings	16.5	0.7	0.8
Price/Book	2.5	0.5	0.6
Price/Sales	1.2	0.2	0.4
Price/Cash Flow	19.1	1.2	1.3

Major Fund Holders	% of Fund Assets
Constellation JSAM Large Cap Value	5.22
Touchstone Large Cap Value A	4.58
Rydex Telecommunications Inv	2.39
TCW Diversified Value N	1.85

Thesis By John Slack, 12-01-06 Stock Price as of Analysis: $13.36

With the closing of one of the largest cross-border technology mergers ever, Alcatel-Lucent's broad product portfolio and geographic diversification should better position the combined company in the communications equipment industry. We believe the combined firm will reap considerable cost savings that should improve returns to investors, but it will likely take the company several years to realize these improvements.

The merger of Alcatel and Lucent brings together two of the most storied names in telecom and should give the combined company better scope and scale to compete against niche vendors and Asian upstarts. The combined company will have a more balanced geographic footprint with post-merger sales being divided roughly in thirds between Europe, North America, and the rest of the world. The combined company will also have relationships with nearly every major carrier in the world, which should better insulate the firm from individual carriers' spending patterns.

This combination was motivated primarily by cost savings more than anything, and Alcatel-Lucent expects annual cost savings of $1.8 billion, a number we view as plausible given the considerable overlap in administrative and research-and-development expenses. As part of the cost savings plans, the combined company expects to lay off 10% of its 88,000-member workforce. Management anticipates that the job cuts will be divided evenly between the companies. These cost savings should drive operating margins for the combined company from the high single digits to the midteens over the next few years.

From a strategic perspective, the companies' product portfolios are relatively complementary. Alcatel brings arguably the best-positioned wireline access equipment business in the industry, which plugs a number of product gaps in Lucent's wireline equipment portfolio, and the combination of both companies' wireless businesses should give them scale when going head-to-head against industry leader Ericsson.

Although we view this deal as generally favorable, our main concern about the combination relates to execution risk. This is clearly a complex transaction. Mega-mergers in technology are always difficult, and the cross-border nature of this deal further complicates the picture. Both companies have worked through difficult restructurings over the past several years, and the prospect of yet another major restructuring and integration could weigh on employee morale.

Data as of 12-29-06

Alcoa AA

	Rating	Fair Value	Last Close	Consider Buy	Consider Sell	Yield %
	★★★★★	$40.00	$30.01	$30.80	$50.10	2.00

Company Profile
Alcoa is the world's largest aluminum producer, controlling more than 13% of the world's smelting. The company comprises five segments in two categories. Upstream segments involve bauxite mining, alumina refining, and primary aluminum production. Downstream businesses produce beverage cans, aerospace components, industrial gas turbines, automotive and building products, plastic packaging, and telecommunications parts.

Management
Stewardship Grade [B]

Alain Belda became CEO in 1999 and chairman in 2001. His management tenure at the company dates back to 1979, when he was president of Alcoa Aluminio SA. Results to date of Belda's tenure can be best described as mixed. The company has struggled with events beyond its control such as the curtailment of aerospace spending post-9/11 and the emergence of strong and low-cost competitors. To management's credit, the company responded to the downturn with an impressive set of cost-cutting initiatives and managed to even expand its presence in developing regions. Management compensation is roughly in line with what we expect for a company of Alcoa's size. A significant portion of the compensation comes in the form of stock options, and we feel that these options are structured and priced in such a way to reward management for creating shareholder value. We feel that Alcoa practices acceptable corporate governance. Nine of the 10 board members are independent, with Belda sitting only on the executive committee. There were no reported related-party transactions. We are encouraged by the company's decision to use a return on capital measure in determining incentive awards.

201 Isabella Street
Pittsburgh, PA 15212-5858
www.alcoa.com

Growth [B]	2002	2003	2004	2005
Revenue %	-9.3	5.8	11.3	12.6
Earnings/Share %	-53.3	120.4	38.0	-6.0
Book Value/Share %	-5.6	20.0	8.4	0.4
Dividends/Share %	0.0	0.0	0.0	0.0

Profitability [B]	2003	2004	2005	TTM
Return on Assets %	3.0	4.0	3.7	5.8
Oper Cash Flow $Mil	2,434	2,199	1,676	2,273
- Cap Spending $Mil	870	1,143	2,138	2,820
= Free Cash Flow $Mil	1,564	1,056	-462	-547

Financial Health [B-]	2003	2004	2005	09-30-06
Long-term Debt $Mil	—	5,345	5,279	4,446
Total Equity $Mil	12,075	13,245	13,318	14,650
Debt/Equity Ratio	—	0.4	0.4	0.3

Industry	Business Risk	Moat Size	Investment Style	Sector
Aluminum	Average	Narrow	Large Value	Industrial Materials

Competition	Market Cap $Mil	12 Mo Trailing Sales $Mil	Price/Cash Flow	Return On Assets%	Debt/ Equity	Total Return% 1 Yr	3 Yr
Alcoa	26,022	29,666	11.4	5.8	0.3	3.5	-5.3
Alcan	18,330	21,589	6.9	2.2	0.5	20.8	6.2
Aluminum Corp of China AD	10,387	4,536	9.9	12.1	0.3	30.6	9.8

Price Volatility
Monthly Price High/Low — Relative Strength to S&P 500

Annual $Price High	45.71	39.75	38.92	39.44	32.29	36.96
Low	27.36	17.62	18.45	28.51	22.28	26.39
	2001	2002	2003	2004	2005	2006
Annual Total Return %	7.9	-34.6	70.9	-15.7	-3.9	3.5

Fiscal Year-End: December	2001	2002	2003	2004	2005	TTM
Revenue $Mil	21,750	19,728	20,871	23,236	26,159	29,666
Net Income $Mil	908	420	938	1,310	1,233	2,113
Earnings Per Share $	1.05	0.49	1.08	1.49	1.40	2.41
Shares Outstanding Mil	857	857	861	873	874	867
Return on Equity %	8.6	4.2	7.8	9.9	9.3	14.4
Net Margin %	4.2	2.1	4.5	5.6	4.7	7.1
Asset Turnover	0.8	0.7	0.7	0.7	0.8	0.8
Financial Leverage	2.7	3.0	2.6	2.5	2.5	2.5

Valuation Ratios	Stock	Rel to Industry	Rel to S&P 500
Price/Earnings	12.6	0.7	0.6
Price/Book	1.8	0.8	0.4
Price/Sales	0.9	0.8	0.3
Price/Cash Flow	11.4	1.1	0.8

Major Fund Holders	% of Fund Assets
Fidelity Select Materials	4.72
ProFunds Basic Materials UltraSector Inv	4.72
Snow Capital Opportunity A	3.44
Hotchkis and Wiley Large Cap Value I	3.42

Thesis
By Scott Burns, 12-14-06 Stock Price as of Analysis: $30.76

Although Alcoa is facing challenges to its dominance of the aluminum market, positive trends in aluminum consumption and the company's commendable cost-cutting efforts are boosting profits.

Alcoa is the king of the aluminum industry, and its sheer size affords it economies of scale and a low-cost position. Alcoa controls an estimated 24% of the world's bauxite reserves and produces aluminum on every continent. The company has significant relationships with large aluminum consumers such as Boeing and General Motors and generally ranks as one of their largest suppliers.

In addition to being the world's largest primary aluminum producer, Alcoa has expanded up the value chain and rolls sheet for aluminum cans, casts engine blocks for cars, and even makes the Reynolds foil that you find in the grocery store. The combined scale and integration allows Alcoa to capture economic profit throughout the aluminum spectrum and helps insulate the company to some degree from movements in the price of aluminum.

Despite its size and integration, Alcoa has struggled to maintain its cost leadership in recent years. The company has met headwinds in the form of rising energy, transportation, and raw-material costs. Historically, these costs have been highly correlated to aluminum prices, but a sizable disconnect occurred in 2005, and profits lagged as a result. The firm is reworking its contracts to encompass more of these cost variables, but it remains to be seen if customers will accept these new terms.

In addition to these cost headwinds, Alcoa is also facing stiffer competition from new and old names in the aluminum sector. The "new" Alcan, formed from the merger of Alcan with Pechiney, is a behemoth in its own right, and the emergence of several Russian companies threatens Alcoa's dominance. Alcoa has responded by cutting costs, jettisoning underperforming assets, and moving production to locations with cost advantages, such as the Caribbean, Iceland, and Brazil.

Counterbalancing these negatives is the fact that aluminum prices are relatively healthy. Fueled by economic expansion in developing regions, demand for aluminum has outstripped global production for the past two years. These regions' auto and aerospace industries are still nascent, and we expect consumption to grow exponentially. Alcoa is in a good position to exploit this demand, given that its costs are nearly 25% lower than most of the domestic producers in these regions.

Data as of 12-29-06

Alcon ACL

	Rating	Fair Value	Last Close	Consider Buy	Consider Sell	Yield %
	★★	$102.00	$111.77	$86.90	$133.90	1.21

Company Profile

Alcon is a leader in eye care. AcrySof intraocular lenses and Infiniti lens-removal systems lead the cataract surgical business, while glaucoma drug Travatan, anti-infective Vigamox, and eye-allergy medication Patanol make up about a third of a broad-based pharmaceutical offering. The company generates about 15% of sales from its consumer eye-care division. Alcon is based in Switzerland but generates about half of its $4.3 billion in sales in the United States.

Management   Stewardship Grade [C]

Cary Rayment has been with the company for 17 years and has been CEO since 2004. Rayment previously served as vice president of both Alcon U.S. and Alcon Japan, as well as general manager of the surgical unit. We are impressed by Rayment's hands-on knowledge of the company's operations. Despite this, we don't consider Alcon particularly shareholder-friendly. The company has several antitakeover measures in place, including a poison pill and staggered elections of directors. We believe Alcon should separate the positions of chairman and CEO in order to promote a more independent board, and we would also encourage more disclosure of performance targets. In addition, Nestle's 75% ownership in the company leaves minority shareholders with little or no power.

Bosch 69 P.O. Box 62   www.alconlabs.com
Hunenberg, Switzerland

Growth [C+]	2002	2003	2004	2005
Revenue %	9.5	13.2	14.9	11.6
Earnings/Share %	NMF	NMF	45.8	6.4
Book Value/Share %	—	NMF	36.9	16.4
Dividends/Share %	NMF	NMF	NMF	171.4

Profitability [A+]	2003	2004	2005	TTM
Return on Assets %	14.1	19.5	17.8	17.8
Oper Cash Flow $Mil	915	1,048	1,235	1,235
- Cap Spending $Mil	158	146	162	162
= Free Cash Flow $Mil	758	902	1,073	1,073

Financial Health [A+]	2003	2004	2005	12-31-05
Long-term Debt $Mil	75	72	56	56
Total Equity $Mil	1,592	2,188	2,556	2,556
Debt/Equity Ratio	0.0	0.0	0.0	0.0

Industry	Business Risk	Moat Size	Investment Style	Sector
Drugs	Below Avg	Wide	Large Growth	Healthcare

Competition	Market Cap $Mil	12 Mo Trailing Sales $Mil	Price/Cash Flow	Return On Assets%	Debt/Equity	Total Return% 1 Yr	3 Yr
Alcon	34,256	4,369	27.7	17.8	0.0	-12.6	24.3
Allergan	18,143	2,817	28.8	-2.2	0.5	11.3	16.4
Bausch & Lomb	2,799	—	—	—	—	-22.6	1.1

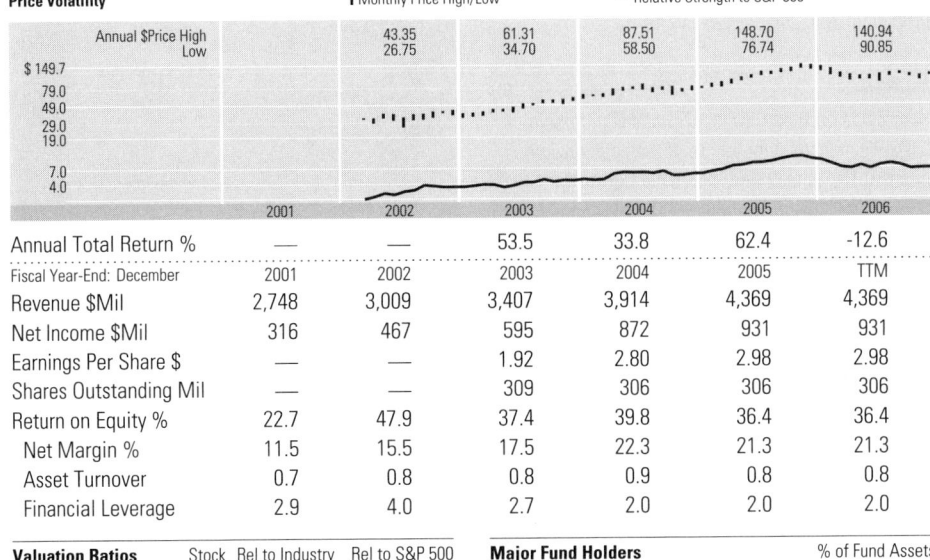

	2001	2002	2003	2004	2005	2006
Annual Total Return %	—	—	53.5	33.8	62.4	-12.6
Fiscal Year-End: December	2001	2002	2003	2004	2005	TTM
Revenue $Mil	2,748	3,009	3,407	3,914	4,369	4,369
Net Income $Mil	316	467	595	872	931	931
Earnings Per Share $	—	—	1.92	2.80	2.98	2.98
Shares Outstanding Mil	—	—	309	306	306	306
Return on Equity %	22.7	47.9	37.4	39.8	36.4	36.4
Net Margin %	11.5	15.5	17.5	22.3	21.3	21.3
Asset Turnover	0.7	0.8	0.8	0.9	0.8	0.8
Financial Leverage	2.9	4.0	2.7	2.0	2.0	2.0

Valuation Ratios	Stock	Rel to Industry	Rel to S&P 500	Major Fund Holders	% of Fund Assets
Price/Earnings	37.5	1.6	1.8	Fidelity Select Medical Equip/Systems	5.61
Price/Book	13.4	2.5	3.3	AllianceBernstein Global Health Care B	4.70
Price/Sales	7.8	1.8	2.7	MassMutual Select Large Cap Growth S	3.21
Price/Cash Flow	27.7	1.7	1.9	AllianceBernstein Large Cap Growth A	3.13

Thesis   By Jeff Viksjo, 11-16-06   Stock Price as of Analysis: $103.05

Alcon is a leader in eye care and generates substantial cash flow by investing in businesses where it has a dominant position. We think its size advantage and diverse product offering secure Alcon's wide moat.

High switching costs should preserve Alcon's leadership in the cataract market. The firm's Infiniti vision system--used to remove the lens during surgery--represents a large up-front investment and requires extensive initial training. Surgeons are reluctant to switch to a competing system once they become familiar with Infiniti's specific technology. The firm's intraocular lens business has similar advantages. Alcon bundles its intraocular lenses with its complete surgical product offering, increasing surgeons' reliance on its products.

Alcon's diverse product offering and large salesforce enable significant cross-selling opportunities. The firm has the largest portfolio of ophthalmic drugs in the world, but retains a targeted client focus. This allows it to market its drugs to a smaller group of doctors. The cost savings are significant, and new drugs can be sold by the existing salesforce. This efficiency carries over into the cataract surgical segment, where the Infiniti vision system requires accessories for each surgery performed, guaranteeing Alcon a steady stream of consumables sales over the life of the machine. Cross-selling opportunities also exist between business segments. For example, Alcon's drug Nevanac is comarketed by the pharmaceutical and surgical salesforces to prevent and treat inflammation for patients undergoing cataract surgery.

Recent pipeline failures may hurt Alcon's pharmaceutical business in the next two to three years. The company's once-promising drug Retaane for macular degeneration was recently withdrawn from consideration for European approval. Also, Alcon is facing patent expirations on key drugs, including Patanol for allergies. Initiatives to launch existing drugs outside the United States may pressure operating margins as the company faces expensive marketing battles. For instance, Alcon will sell anti-infective drug Vigamox in the Japanese market, where Japanese rival Santen holds an 80% share.

Ultimately, though, Alcon's innovation prowess should lead to long-term success. Alcon's size and profitability allow for large investments in research and development and a salesforce of more than 2,700 people worldwide. This presents barriers to entry for smaller firms and should give Alcon time to reinvigorate its pharmaceutical offering.

Data as of 12-29-06

Alleghany Y

	Rating	Fair Value	Last Close	Consider Buy	Consider Sell	Yield %
	★★★★	$450.00	$363.60	$347.00	$563.80	0.00

Company Profile
Alleghany is an investment holding company that uses a value-oriented philosophy to acquire interests in attractive businesses. Alleghany purchases fractional and outright stakes and generally holds investments for long periods. Alleghany's three insurance subsidiaries--RSUI Holdings, Capitol Transamerica, and Darwin Underwriters--supply a broad range of specialty, property, and casualty protection. Subsidiary Alleghany Properties is a Sacramento, Calif., landlord.

Management
Stewardship Grade [A]

We heartily approve of Alleghany's stewardship. Longtime chairman Fred Kirby and his family own about 35% of the stock, and they acquired it the old-fashioned way--they bought it. Thanks in part to the Kirbys' large stake, directors and officers collectively own about 24% of the shares, which embeds a huge incentive to maximize returns, in our view. Excluding the Kirby family, directors and officers own about 4%. CEO Weston Hicks took home about $1.6 million in 2005, which we think is reasonable. Incentives reflect Alleghany's conservative bent. Management payouts vest if book value growth exceeds 7% over at least five years. This relatively low goal reflects the firm's limited leverage and the board's desire to avoid incentives that necessitate excessive risk taking. Incentives vest more rapidly if book value growth exceeds 10%, and we note that Hicks is aiming to expand book value faster than the S&P 500. Our only gripe is that we'd like to see directors elected annually--but as long as Alleghany continues striving to enrich its shareholders over the long run, this is small potatoes.

375 Park Avenue www.alleghanyfunds.com
New York, NY 10152

Growth [A-]	2002	2003	2004	2005
Revenue %	528.3	48.3	49.6	14.7
Earnings/Share %	-75.3	189.5	-28.1	-55.8
Book Value/Share %	0.0	10.9	11.8	4.8
Dividends/Share %	NMF	NMF	NMF	NMF

Profitability [B+]	2003	2004	2005	TTM
Return on Assets %	4.6	2.7	0.9	3.8
Oper Cash Flow $Mil	431	402	380	—
- Cap Spending $Mil	5	7	10	—
= Free Cash Flow $Mil	—	—	—	—

Financial Health [NA]	2003	2004	2005	09-30-06
Long-term Debt $Mil	—	—	—	—
Total Equity $Mil	1,574	1,773	1,868	2,045
Debt/Equity Ratio	—	—	—	—

Industry	Business Risk	Moat Size	Investment Style	Sector
Insurance (Property)	Average	Narrow	Mid Core	Financial Services

Competition	Market Cap $Mil	12 Mo Trailing Sales $Mil	Price/Cash Flow	Return On Assets%	Debt/ Equity	Total Return% 1 Yr	3 Yr
Alleghany	2,892	1,192	—	3.8	—	30.6	20.6
St. Paul Travelers Compan	37,047	24,802	—	2.8	—	22.9	13.7
Chubb	21,780	14,104	—	5.1	—	10.5	18.3

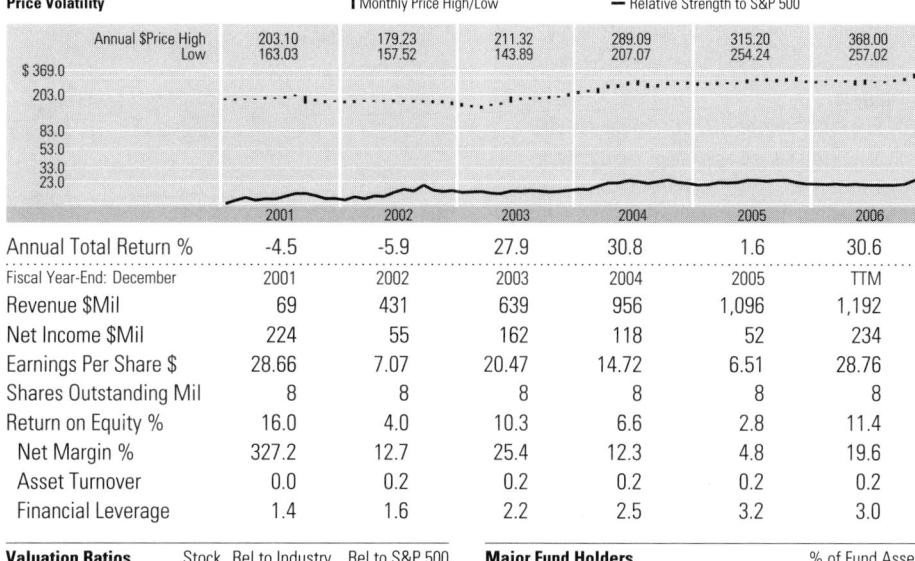

	2001	2002	2003	2004	2005	TTM
Annual Total Return %	-4.5	-5.9	27.9	30.8	1.6	30.6
Fiscal Year-End: December	2001	2002	2003	2004	2005	TTM
Revenue $Mil	69	431	639	956	1,096	1,192
Net Income $Mil	224	55	162	118	52	234
Earnings Per Share $	28.66	7.07	20.47	14.72	6.51	28.76
Shares Outstanding Mil	8	8	8	8	8	8
Return on Equity %	16.0	4.0	10.3	6.6	2.8	11.4
Net Margin %	327.2	12.7	25.4	12.3	4.8	19.6
Asset Turnover	0.0	0.2	0.2	0.2	0.2	0.2
Financial Leverage	1.4	1.6	2.2	2.5	3.2	3.0

Valuation Ratios	Stock	Rel to Industry	Rel to S&P 500
Price/Earnings	12.6	0.9	0.6
Price/Book	1.4	0.8	0.3
Price/Sales	2.4	1.7	0.8
Price/Cash Flow	—	—	—

Major Fund Holders	% of Fund Assets
CNI Charter RCB Sm Cap Val R	5.08
Artisan Mid Cap Value	3.48
Robeco Boston Partners All Cap Val Instl	2.59
Champlain Small Company Adv	2.43

Thesis By Justin Fuller, CFA, 12-14-06 Stock Price as of Analysis: $349.00

Alleghany's shrewd value-investing philosophy, coupled with a talented management team and information advantages at its insurance subsidiaries, endows favorable prospects. However, we think Alleghany's economic moat is only narrow, as returns depend on sustained managerial skill and rationality.

Alleghany's long-term, value-oriented investment structure provides a useful advantage. By sharply focusing on buying businesses it expects to own for long periods, Alleghany's team can pursue opportunities that competing investors with shorter horizons shun. A longer horizon also offers more time for intensive research and knowledge accumulation, reduces transaction expenses, and defers capital gains. Management looks to invest at a 50% discount to fair value and balances risk by looking for opportunities with $3 of upside for every $1 of downside, which we consider a sensible approach to boost returns.

Importantly, Alleghany's team demonstrates a strong preference for investing in businesses it understands. Alleghany already has rich experience investing in financial-services firms and asset-intensive industries--the firm began life as a railroad holding company--and has historically earned attractive gains, including a return approaching 500% on its largest current holding, Burlington Northern Santa Fe. In addition, the firm has recently branched out to begin making investments in other industries where it has an expertise, and next to Burlington Northern, it now has a hefty investment in the energy industry. Management has also indicated that longer term, it expects to begin making private equity investments, somewhat akin to the way Berkshire Hathaway has gravitated toward private investments, which we think is great.

We're also impressed by Alleghany's wholly owned insurance subsidiaries, as the holding company can also pledge its equity investments as insurance capital, effectively using that capital twice. The largest of these firms, RSUI, seeks to develop an expertise in lines of insurance for specialty or hard-to-place risks. This information advantage helps RSUI earn small price premiums on the policies it writes. What's more, since RSUI's underwriters are compensated only for underwriting profitability, they are encouraged to refuse business that doesn't meet the firm's underwriting criteria. As such, we expect RSUI--and thus Alleghany's--underwriting profitability to remain strong, which we expect will boost growth in book value per share over the long haul.

Data as of 12-29-06

Allergan AGN

	Rating	Fair Value	Last Close	Consider Buy	Consider Sell	Yield %
	★★★	$114.00	$119.74	$87.90	$142.80	0.33

Company Profile
Allergan is one of the largest specialty pharmaceutical firms in the world and the maker of Botox, which constituted 36% of sales in 2005. Through its acquisition of Inamed in early 2006, the company increased its proportion of the cosmetic surgical market and now sells breast implants, dermal fillers, and products to treat obesity. Roughly half of the company's sales come from its eye care pharmaceutical division, led by Alphagan P and Lumigan for glaucoma and dry-eye drug Restasis.

Management
Stewardship Grade [C]

David E. I. Pyott became CEO of Allergan in 1998. Previously, Pyott served as head of the nutritional division at Novartis. We believe he deserves a good deal of credit for Allergan's recent successes. The company's sales have climbed from $1.2 billion in 1998 to $2.3 billion in 2005, and the Botox franchise has been well managed. Allergan's board of directors is composed of industry heavyweights, including Herbert W. Boyer, Ph.D, a founder of Genentech, and Robert A. Ingram, the former COO of pharmaceuticals at GlaxoSmithKline. However, we see a need for change in some of the company's corporate governance policies. Allergan has an extensive list of anti-takeover measures in place, including staggered director elections, a poison-pill, and golden parachutes for more than 70 executives. Furthermore, we prefer to see executive bonuses linked to returns on capital, instead of earnings per share and other more easily manipulated measures. Also, Pyott serves as both CEO and chairman, roles we prefer to be separated.

2525 Dupont Drive P.O. Box 19534 www.allergan.com
Irvine, CA 92612

Growth [B]	2002	2003	2004	2005
Revenue %	21.3	27.9	15.5	13.4
Earnings/Share %	-66.3	NMF	NMF	6.7
Book Value/Share %	-16.6	-10.6	52.5	39.9
Dividends/Share %	0.0	0.0	0.0	11.1

Profitability [B+]	2003	2004	2005	TTM
Return on Assets %	-3.0	16.7	14.2	-2.2
Oper Cash Flow $Mil	435	549	425	631
- Cap Spending $Mil	110	96	79	116
= Free Cash Flow $Mil	326	452	346	515

Financial Health [A]	2003	2004	2005	09-30-06
Long-term Debt $Mil	573	570	58	1,606
Total Equity $Mil	719	1,116	1,567	3,025
Debt/Equity Ratio	0.8	0.5	0.0	0.5

Industry	Business Risk	Moat Size	Investment Style	Sector
Drugs	Average	Wide	Large Growth	Healthcare

Competition	Market Cap $Mil	12 Mo Trailing Sales $Mil	Price/Cash Flow	Return On Assets%	Debt/Equity	Total Return% 1 Yr	3 Yr
Allergan	18,143	2,817	28.8	-2.2	0.5	11.3	16.4
Pfizer	186,751	52,208	10.5	11.6	0.1	15.2	-7.4
Alcon	34,256	4,369	27.7	17.8	0.0	-12.6	24.3

Price Volatility
| Monthly Price High/Low   — Relative Strength to S&P 500

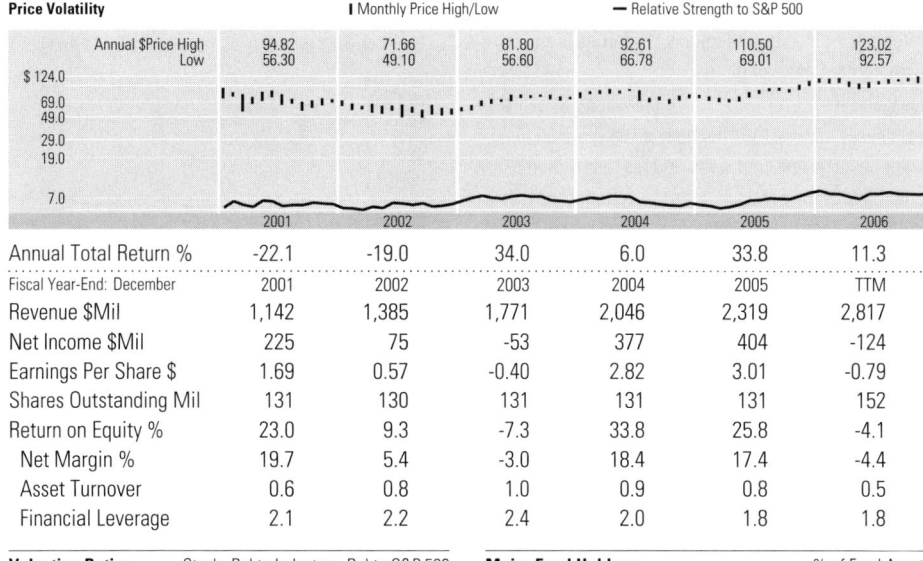

| Annual $Price High | 94.82 | 71.66 | 81.80 | 92.61 | 110.50 | 123.02 |
| Low | 56.30 | 49.10 | 56.60 | 66.78 | 69.01 | 92.57 |

	2001	2002	2003	2004	2005	2006
Annual Total Return %	-22.1	-19.0	34.0	6.0	33.8	11.3
Fiscal Year-End: December	2001	2002	2003	2004	2005	TTM
Revenue $Mil	1,142	1,385	1,771	2,046	2,319	2,817
Net Income $Mil	225	75	-53	377	404	-124
Earnings Per Share $	1.69	0.57	-0.40	2.82	3.01	-0.79
Shares Outstanding Mil	131	130	131	131	131	152
Return on Equity %	23.0	9.3	-7.3	33.8	25.8	-4.1
Net Margin %	19.7	5.4	-3.0	18.4	17.4	-4.4
Asset Turnover	0.6	0.8	1.0	0.9	0.8	0.5
Financial Leverage	2.1	2.2	2.4	2.0	1.8	1.8

Valuation Ratios	Stock	Rel to Industry	Rel to S&P 500
Price/Earnings	NMF	—	—
Price/Book	6.0	1.1	1.5
Price/Sales	6.4	1.5	2.2
Price/Cash Flow	28.8	1.8	2.0

Major Fund Holders	% of Fund Assets
Fidelity Select Medical Equip/Systems	10.27
Transamerica Premier Focus Inv	6.44
MassMutual Select Aggressive Growth S	5.03
Constellation Sands Capital Inst Growth	4.97

Thesis By Jeff Viksjo, 12-12-06 Stock Price as of Analysis: $121.56

Allergan's wide moat in specialty pharmaceuticals is bolstered by its commitment to research and development and its leadership position across several niche markets. We think Allergan will continue to ride the Botox wave and yield additional successes throughout its solid pipeline of products.

Allergan owes much of its success to Botox, which now generates more than one third of the firm's revenue. While Botox is approved to treat a long list of medical conditions, the product is most widely known for its use in cosmetic surgery, where it enjoys very high market share and strong brand recognition. Botox benefits from high barriers to entry. Allergan's large investments in marketing and sales are unlikely to be matched by most outside firms. In addition, the product's manufacturing process is complex and would be very difficult to replicate.

Allergan's scale and product selection have enabled the firm to be successful across several other specialty niche markets. In cosmetic surgery, the company paves the way for its less established products, such as dermal fillers and breast implants, by cross-selling them with Botox. As a result, the company saves on marketing costs and achieves greater market penetration for most of its products. Allergan's competitors typically offer just one or two products, and cannot replicate the company's scale advantages or match its product diversification. Allergan has built similar advantages in eye care, where the company markets drugs to treat everything from glaucoma to dry-eye.

Allergan spent $390 million on research and development in 2005, more than 4 times the combined total for cosmetic surgery competitors Mentor and Medicis Pharmaceuticals, and twice that of eye care rival Bausch & Lomb. Not surprisingly, its pipeline pulses with promise. Eye implant drug Posurdex is the first of its kind and has been proven to effectively treat macular edema, or swelling, in early clinical trials. Further, the company recently received Food and Drug Administration approval for dermal filler Juvederm and its silicone breast implants.

In addition, Allergan's existing products have good long-term viability. The Lap-Band--a minimally invasive alternative to gastric bypass surgery--is the only product of its kind in the U.S. and should see increased demand as obesity continues to become more pervasive. Also, the company's cosmetic procedures and eye care drugs target a demographic that is expected to grow substantially larger as the baby boomers age.

Alliancebernstein Holding LP AB

Data as of 12-29-06

Rating	Fair Value	Last Close	Consider Buy	Consider Sell	Yield %
★	$58.00	$80.40	$44.70	$72.70	4.43

Company Profile
AllianceBernstein Holding offers investment management services to institutional and retail investors through various investment vehicles, including a broad line of mutual funds. Its Sanford C. Bernstein business sells independent investment research and brokerage services. The holding company is structured as a master limited partnership: It typically pays out around 100% of its net operating earnings to unitholders and pays minimal corporate taxes.

Management
Stewardship Grade [C]

CEO Lewis Sanders took the helm of Alliance in June 2003. The previous slate of executives were fired or resigned following the firm's involvement in the mutual fund market-timing scandal. The new management team is drawn primarily from Sanford C. Bernstein, where Sanders spent the majority of his career working his way up the ladder. French insurer AXA Financial owns 61% of the outstanding AllianceBernstein units and effectively controls the firm. Management members have very small stakes. Though base salaries are relatively modest at Alliance, management is extremely well paid overall. The company shelled out more for executive perks (like personal use of the company jet) than it did in salary during 2005. Also, incentive compensation is high by industry standards. Sanders negotiated a lucrative employment agreement that netted him more than $15.3 million in 2005. The other four executives made more than $6 million apiece.

1345 Avenue of The Americas www.alliancecapital.com
New York, NY 10105

Growth [C]	2002	2003	2004	2005
Revenue %	-8.1	-0.5	10.5	6.4
Earnings/Share %	-0.4	-46.0	112.4	22.3
Book Value/Share %	-0.4	-4.7	8.9	2.1
Dividends/Share %	-19.0	-14.3	-39.6	135.3

Profitability [NA]	2003	2004	2005	TTM
Return on Assets %	4.0	8.0	9.1	10.4
Oper Cash Flow $Mil	758	968	460	—
- Cap Spending $Mil	29	57	73	—
= Free Cash Flow $Mil	—	—	—	—

Financial Health [NA]	2003	2004	2005	09-30-06
Long-term Debt $Mil	—	—	—	—
Total Equity $Mil	3,778	4,141	4,259	4,404
Debt/Equity Ratio	—	—	—	—

Industry	Business Risk	Moat Size	Investment Style	Sector
Money Mgmt.	Average	Wide	Mid Core	Financial Services

Competition

	Market Cap $Mil	12 Mo Trailing Sales $Mil	Price/Cash Flow	Return On Assets%	Debt/ Equity	Total Return% 1 Yr	3 Yr
Alliancebernstein Holding LP	6,812	3,712	—	10.4	—	50.2	39.2
Franklin Resources	27,932	5,051	—	13.3	—	17.8	30.3
Marsh & McLennan Companie	16,897	11,715	—	4.5	—	-1.2	-11.9

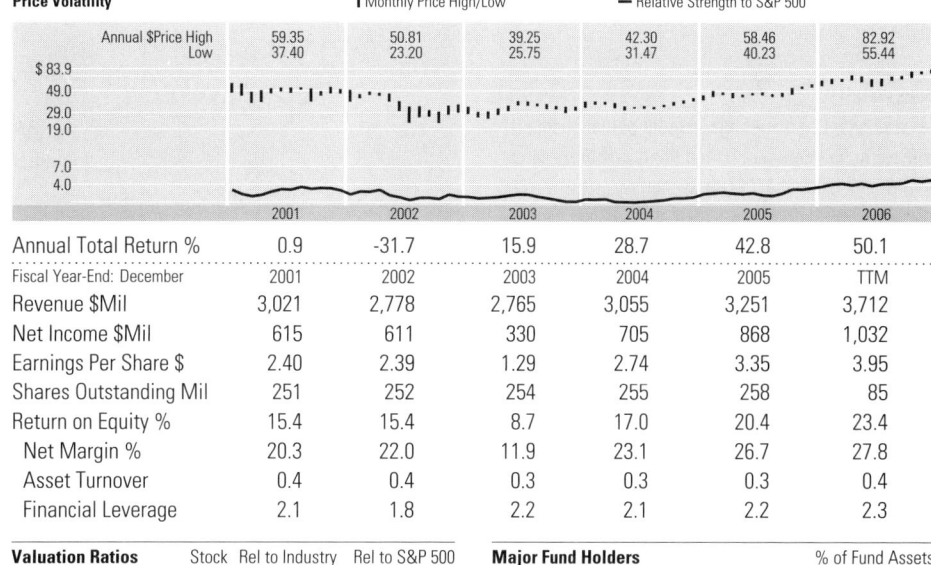

Price Volatility — Monthly Price High/Low — Relative Strength to S&P 500

	2001	2002	2003	2004	2005	2006
Annual $Price High	59.35	50.81	39.25	42.30	58.46	82.92
Low	37.40	23.20	25.75	31.47	40.23	55.44
Annual Total Return %	0.9	-31.7	15.9	28.7	42.8	50.1
Fiscal Year-End: December	2001	2002	2003	2004	2005	TTM
Revenue $Mil	3,021	2,778	2,765	3,055	3,251	3,712
Net Income $Mil	615	611	330	705	868	1,032
Earnings Per Share $	2.40	2.39	1.29	2.74	3.35	3.95
Shares Outstanding Mil	251	252	254	255	258	85
Return on Equity %	15.4	15.4	8.7	17.0	20.4	23.4
Net Margin %	20.3	22.0	11.9	23.1	26.7	27.8
Asset Turnover	0.4	0.4	0.3	0.3	0.3	0.4
Financial Leverage	2.1	1.8	2.2	2.1	2.2	2.3

Valuation Ratios	Stock	Rel to Industry	Rel to S&P 500
Price/Earnings	20.4	0.7	1.0
Price/Book	1.5	0.3	0.4
Price/Sales	1.8	0.3	0.6
Price/Cash Flow	—	—	—

Major Fund Holders	% of Fund Assets
Royce Select I Inv	5.73
Royce Heritage Service	5.05
Boyle Marathon	4.98
TA IDEX Transamerica Value Balanced A	4.90

Thesis By Jeffrey Ptak, CPA, CFA, 12-14-06 Stock Price as of Analysis: $79.15

AllianceBernstein's manifold strengths are becoming increasingly evident as the firm puts scandal and poor performance behind it.

For a while, it seemed easy to consign AllianceBernstein to the dustbin of the asset-management business. The company was mired in controversy a few years ago, thanks to its role in the mutual fund trading scandal. The firm's transgressions, which ultimately cost it $250 million in fines plus fee reductions, came atop dreadful bear-market performance at many of Alliance's flagship growth mutual funds. Taken together, this drove many investors away and cast a pall over Alliance's mutual fund business.

Alliance has bounced back under the watch of CEO Lew Sanders, who took the helm in the wake of the scandal. Sanders promptly cleaned house, appointed a number of his fellow alumni from Sanford C. Bernstein (which Alliance bought in 2000) to fill key management slots, and instituted a sweeping set of reforms aimed at removing the taint from the Alliance brand. Those efforts came as part of a larger "Bernsteinization" of Alliance, whereby the firm lessened its emphasis on marketing glitz in favor of a renewed focus on client service, diversification, and robust investment research.

Sanders' push has succeeded in taking the focus off Alliance's missteps and putting the firm's core strengths--namely, its global footprint and faculty in value and foreign investing--on fuller display. Indeed, unlike most other pure-play asset managers, Alliance boasts a substantial overseas presence, which helps it to court increasingly affluent investors abroad while also supporting a wide array of foreign strategies. What's more, Sanders has made great strides in putting Bernstein's respected and successful value-investing teams front and center. These efforts have spurred impressive growth recently, as investors have pumped billions of dollars into the firm's blend and global strategies amid strong performance in those areas.

Yet, we think that Alliance's advantages run deeper than its ability to exploit potentially fleeting short-term trends such as the boom in emerging markets. For instance, Alliance boasts an unusually stable book of business since a large chunk of its assets under management is attributable to stickier institutional accounts. In addition, Alliance's scale and diversification--its strategies span virtually every asset class and style and are offered in numerous locales--position it well to support one-stop shopping.

Data as of 12-29-06

Alliant Techsystems ATK

	Rating	Fair Value	Last Close	Consider Buy	Consider Sell	Yield %
	★★★	$87.00	$78.19	$67.10	$109.00	0.00

Company Profile
Based in Edina, Minn., Alliant Techsystems manufactures weapons, ammunition, and space systems for the U.S. government and allies. It operates in three divisions: mission systems, ammunition systems, and launch systems. The company employs 15,000 people in 22 states. Alliant is the leading supplier of bullets to the U.S. military and the producer of the rockets found on NASA's space shuttles.

Management   Stewardship Grade [B]
Alliant has a very experienced team of management with military, engineering, and financial backgrounds guiding the company. CEO Dan Murphy joined in 2000 and is the primary "flag officer," or ex-military officer, of the team. Since contract wins in the industry are largely political, he is key to relationship management. Murphy's total compensation in 2006 was reseasonable--slightly under $2 million--with over half in bonus. We also like that management pay is strongly based on long-term performance, and that the team has made several key acquisitions that have created shareholder value. The board is compensated with cash and restricted stock units, tying board members' interests to those of shareholders. However, Murphy is both CEO and chairman of the board of directors. (We prefer these roles to be separated.) Alliant further misses the mark in management ownership, as management together owns less than 1% of outstanding shares, and the board doesn't require much more of the team. Gains here would certainly better align management's focus with that of shareholders.

5050 Lincoln Drive   www.atk.com
Edina, MN 55436

Growth [B]	2003	2004	2005	2006
Revenue %	20.6	8.9	18.4	14.8
Earnings/Share %	60.4	31.0	-2.7	2.0
Book Value/Share %	-23.2	18.4	25.2	6.0
Dividends/Share %	NMF	NMF	NMF	NMF

Profitability [B+]	2004	2005	2006	TTM
Return on Assets %	5.8	5.1	5.3	5.3
Oper Cash Flow $Mil	181	196	217	105
- Cap Spending $Mil	59	63	65	80
= Free Cash Flow $Mil	122	133	151	25

Financial Health [C]	2004	2005	2006	06-30-06
Long-term Debt $Mil	1,080	1,131	1,096	1,383
Total Equity $Mil	564	686	628	507
Debt/Equity Ratio	1.9	1.6	1.7	2.7

Industry	Business Risk	Moat Size	Investment Style	Sector
Aerospace/Defense	Average	Narrow	Mid Core	Industrial Materials

Competition	Market Cap $Mil	12 Mo Trailing Sales $Mil	Price/Cash Flow	Return On Assets%	Debt/ Equity	Total Return% 1 Yr	3 Yr
Alliant Techsystems	2,575	3,343	24.5	5.3	2.7	2.7	11.3
Boeing	70,249	59,114	9.4	2.7	0.8	28.4	30.4
United Technologies	62,748	46,303	14.6	7.0	0.4	13.7	11.6

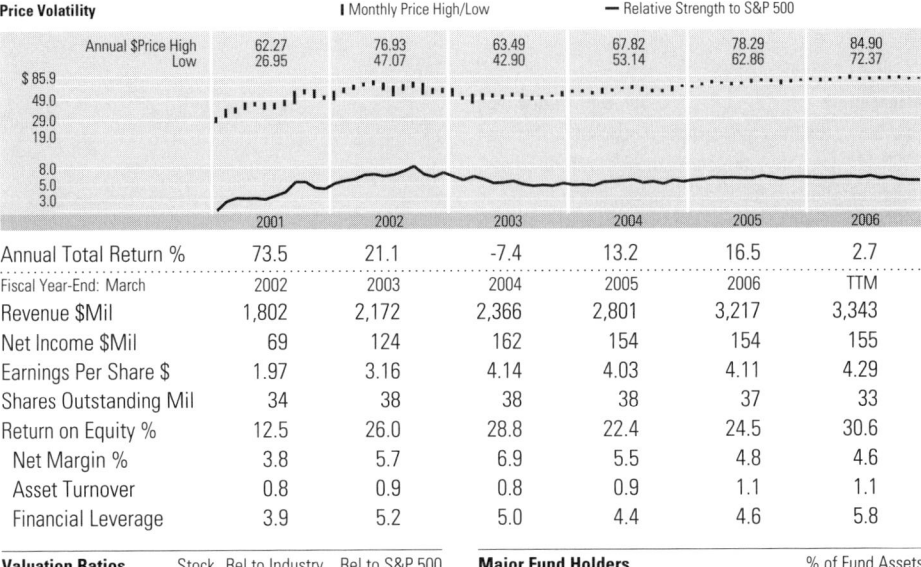

Price Volatility — Monthly Price High/Low — Relative Strength to S&P 500

Annual $Price High Low	62.27 26.95	76.93 47.07	63.49 42.90	67.82 53.14	78.29 62.86	84.90 72.37
Annual Total Return %	73.5	21.1	-7.4	13.2	16.5	2.7

Fiscal Year-End: March	2002	2003	2004	2005	2006	TTM
Revenue $Mil	1,802	2,172	2,366	2,801	3,217	3,343
Net Income $Mil	69	124	162	154	154	155
Earnings Per Share $	1.97	3.16	4.14	4.03	4.11	4.29
Shares Outstanding Mil	34	38	38	38	37	33
Return on Equity %	12.5	26.0	28.8	22.4	24.5	30.6
Net Margin %	3.8	5.7	6.9	5.5	4.8	4.6
Asset Turnover	0.8	0.9	0.8	0.9	1.1	1.1
Financial Leverage	3.9	5.2	5.0	4.4	4.6	5.8

Valuation Ratios	Stock	Rel to Industry	Rel to S&P 500
Price/Earnings	18.2	0.7	0.9
Price/Book	5.1	1.2	1.2
Price/Sales	0.8	0.6	0.3
Price/Cash Flow	24.5	1.8	1.7

Major Fund Holders	% of Fund Assets
Granum Value	6.69
Fidelity Select Defense & Aerospace	5.25
Ashport Small/Mid Cap C	3.09
Gabelli Woodland Sm Cp Value AAA	2.74

Thesis By Adam Fleck, 11-06-06 Stock Price as of Analysis: $77.37

Alliant Techsystems' low-cost production, coupled with high barriers to industry entry, carves a narrow moat that should continue to generate impressive profitability and robust free cash flow, in our opinion.

Rocket production for NASA and bullet manufacturing--in which participants are stringently regulated--account for a quarter of Alliant's total revenue. The company supplies the U.S. military with more than 75% of its small-caliber ammunition and 50% of its medium- and large-caliber needs, and is the sole provider of rocket motors for NASA's space shuttle program. Diversified precision weapons manufacturing constitutes the remaining 75% of sales. In this area, Alliant is able to secure contracts against larger players because of its proven ability to control costs and deliver on time, critical factors in winning government contracts.

Alliant's results reflect these advantages. Its operating margins are around 11%, better than the industry average of 5%-6%. Alliant is able to keep margins high by focusing primarily on "fixed-price" contracts, under which it is not reimbursed for costs but is instead paid a set price, rewarding cost-cutting efforts. Further indicating solid cost control, research-and-development spending as a percentage of sales is much lower than the comparable measure at Boeing, Alliant's largest competitor.

Future growth is likely to stem from continued contract wins, as well as increased production of civil ammunition (used by hunters and police forces). In the second quarter of 2007, Alliant's sporting ammunition sales growth outpaced all other products. If demand for the company's military bullets declines, Alliant can shift production to sports ammunition from military products.

Since nearly 80% of the company's contracts are with the U.S. government, domestic defense spending is critical for Alliant. In the event that this spending slows (which we view as inevitable), Alliant is not likely to lose its largest contracts--small-caliber ammunition and space shuttle rockets. However, we believe that the firm's high-growth, fixed-price product line would suffer. Alliant is somewhat prepared for this scenario with "platform independent" products that work with both current and future technology--reducing development costs--but a drastic cut could nevertheless hinder cash flows in the long run.

Still, we believe that Alliant will continue to be the leading bullet manufacturer over the next five years and will leverage its strong reputation to win future weapons contracts.

Data as of 12-29-06

Allied Capital ALD

Rating	Fair Value	Last Close	Consider Buy	Consider Sell	Yield %
★★★	$29.00	$32.68	$18.50	$35.00	7.41

Company Profile
Allied Capital is a business-development company that raises capital through debt and equity offerings, which it then uses to invest in small and midsize private companies. Allied typically pays substantially all of its interest income and capital gains to shareholders through dividends.

Industry	Business Risk	Moat Size	Investment Style	Sector
Finance	Above Avg	Narrow	Mid Core	Financial Services

Competition

	Market Cap $Mil	12 Mo Trailing Sales $Mil	Price/Cash Flow	Return On Assets %	Debt/ Equity	Total Return% 1 Yr	3 Yr
Allied Capital	4,763	433	—	11.8	—	20.6	14.9
American Capital Strategi	6,578	620	—	8.5	—	39.3	27.2
Apollo Investment	1,837	186	—	8.4	—	37.3	—

Management Stewardship Grade [C]
William L. Walton has been chairman and CEO since 1997 and a board member since 1986. Previously a managing director at Butler Capital, Walton has extensive experience in private equity. Top management is paid handsomely but not lavishly, although the firm consistently provides large numbers of stock options to management. For example, Allied gave away options representing about 5% of its outstanding shares in 2005, and almost 6% the year before, a significant dilution to shareholders. We are happy to see that management owns almost 9% of the company, putting it in the same boat with shareholders. We're also pleased that Allied has taken steps to improve its disclosures, including providing more details in its annual report about the operations and valuation of specific large holdings. Additionally, the firm provides excellent supporting disclosures outside of its regulatory filings, which help explain the firm's business and its strategy.

Price Volatility
Monthly Price High/Low — Relative Strength to S&P 500

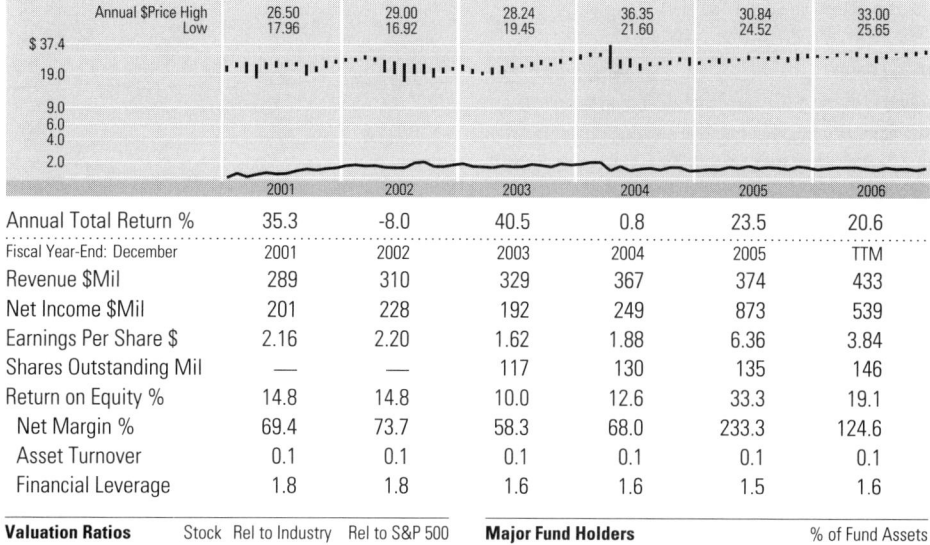

	2001	2002	2003	2004	2005	2006
Annual $Price High	26.50	29.00	28.24	36.35	30.84	33.00
Low	17.96	16.92	19.45	21.60	24.52	25.65
Annual Total Return %	35.3	-8.0	40.5	0.8	23.5	20.6
Fiscal Year-End: December	2001	2002	2003	2004	2005	TTM
Revenue $Mil	289	310	329	367	374	433
Net Income $Mil	201	228	192	249	873	539
Earnings Per Share $	2.16	2.20	1.62	1.88	6.36	3.84
Shares Outstanding Mil	—	—	117	130	135	146
Return on Equity %	14.8	14.8	10.0	12.6	33.3	19.1
Net Margin %	69.4	73.7	58.3	68.0	233.3	124.6
Asset Turnover	0.1	0.1	0.1	0.1	0.1	0.1
Financial Leverage	1.8	1.8	1.6	1.6	1.5	1.6

Valuation Ratios

	Stock	Rel to Industry	Rel to S&P 500
Price/Earnings	8.5	0.4	0.4
Price/Book	1.7	0.4	0.4
Price/Sales	11.0	2.0	3.8
Price/Cash Flow	—	—	—

Major Fund Holders

	% of Fund Assets
Hillman Focused Advantage	4.77
Hillman Advantage Equity	2.57
FAM Value Inv	2.19
Cullen High Dividend Equity A	2.19

1919 Pennsylvania Avenue N.W. www.alliedcapital.com
Washington, DC 20006

Growth [C]	2002	2003	2004	2005
Revenue %	7.2	6.2	11.5	1.9
Earnings/Share %	1.9	-26.4	16.0	238.3
Book Value/Share %	2.4	8.4	-7.6	28.0
Dividends/Share %	10.9	2.2	0.9	1.3

Profitability [A+]	2003	2004	2005	TTM
Return on Assets %	6.4	7.7	21.7	11.8
Oper Cash Flow $Mil	80	-179	116	—
- Cap Spending $Mil	—	—	—	—
= Free Cash Flow $Mil	—	—	—	—

Financial Health [NA]	2003	2004	2005	09-30-06
Long-term Debt $Mil	—	—	—	—
Total Equity $Mil	1,915	1,980	2,621	2,824
Debt/Equity Ratio	—	—	—	—

Thesis By Ryan Batchelor, CPA, 12-01-06 Stock Price as of Analysis: $30.86

Allied Capital has a consistent record and a healthy dividend that it is dedicated to maintaining and increasing. Despite the risks in the firm's portfolio of private debt and equity, we think the shares could be attractive to income-seeking investors.

Allied invests its capital primarily in private businesses in the middle market. Although investments in these firms are illiquid and inherently risky because there is generally no collateral, Allied has proved to be a disciplined and selective investor. Its target investments are companies in less cyclical industries that have high returns on invested capital, management teams with meaningful equity stakes, strong balance sheets, and the ability to generate free cash flow. These investment criteria are very similar to what we at Morningstar look for in potential investments. We appreciate Allied Capital's discipline, which we believe will allow the firm to continue its run of more than 40 years of highly profitable operations.

The firm is committed to paying basically all of the investment income and capital gains from its investments to shareholders as dividends. As a result, most of investors' total return comes from dividend income. However, because there is little reinvestment of profits in the business, and strict limits on the amount of debt it can use, Allied must raise additional equity to expand its business and raise its dividend payout. If Allied were unable to sell new shares for a sustained period, its business--and its dividend--would not be able to expand very much.

Recently, an enormous quantity of private-equity capital has been raised in the United States. More than $170 billion was raised in 2005 alone, not far from the total of the previous five years combined. We think this does not bode well for the private-equity industry as a whole, because huge capital inflows tend to be followed by higher deal prices and, consequently, lower returns.

We also worry about lenders demanding inadequate compensation for the risks they are taking in such a boom environment. Our fears are tempered somewhat by Allied's management team's focus on investing in higher-quality assets that provide more downside protection in case times get tough, but these assets also provide lower interest income. Thus, we expect the average yield on investments to continue its recent declining trend as the firm moves up the quality ladder. Because of some large gains that the firm has carried forward from prior asset sales, however, we have no concerns about the near-term safety of Allied's dividend.

Data as of 12-29-06

Allied Irish Banks ADR AIB

	Rating	Fair Value	Last Close	Consider Buy	Consider Sell	Yield %
	★★★	$66.00	$60.78	$50.90	$82.70	2.71

Company Profile

Allied Irish Banks is one of the top three banks in Ireland and has more than 20% market share. It provides deposit and loan, custodial, insurance, and stock brokerage services. The firm runs a specialty banking operation in Great Britain focused on providing financial services to high-income professionals. Allied Irish holds a controlling stake in Poland's fifth-largest bank, and in the United States, it has a 22.5% stake in M&T Bank.

Management
Stewardship Grade [NA]

Allied Irish has solid corporate-governance practices. The company requires the CEO and chairman offices to be split, a substantial majority of the board must be independent, and options issued over any 10-year period may sum to no more than 10% of total equity capital. Additionally, the senior independent director serves as a shareholder ombudsman, and any concerned investors are able to air issues with him. Chairman Dermot Gleeson, a lawyer by training, has served on the board since 2000. Eugene Sheehy replaced Michael Buckley as CEO in July 2005. Sheehy has been with Allied Irish since 1971. Before becoming CEO, the 51-year-old Sheehy was CEO of M&T Bank's Mid-Atlantic region. Compensation at Allied Irish is moderate by U.S. standards, amounting to 18.7 million euros for all directors and executive officers in 2005. Though insider ownership of shares is negligible, option grants are very nominal. Compensation is based on performance metrics such as earnings growth and the generation of economic profits.

Bankcentre, Ballsbridge PO Box 452 www.aibgroup.com
Dublin, Ireland 4

Growth [NA]	2002	2003	2004	2005
Revenue %	NMF	-18.4	3.2	12.6
Earnings/Share %	37.5	-34.5	76.5	11.8
Book Value/Share %	-8.3	18.5	27.3	1.9
Dividends/Share %	—	—	—	—

Profitability [NA]	2003	2004	2005	TTM
Return on Assets %	0.7	1.0	1.1	1.1
Oper Cash Flow $Mil	1,454	4,210	5,651	—
- Cap Spending $Mil	1,175	84	125	—
= Free Cash Flow $Mil	—	—	—	—

Financial Health [NA]	2003	2004	2005	12-31-05
Long-term Debt $Mil	—	—	—	—
Total Equity $Mil	6,396	8,866	8,535	8,535
Debt/Equity Ratio	—	—	—	—

Industry	Business Risk	Moat Size	Investment Style	Sector
International Banks	Average	Wide	Large Value	Financial Services

Competition	Market Cap $Mil	12 Mo Trailing Sales $Mil	Price/Cash Flow	Return On Assets%	Debt/Equity	Total Return% 1 Yr	3 Yr
Allied Irish Banks ADR	27,911	4,567	—	1.1	—	46.3	28.9
National Australia Bank A	49,915	15,732	—	1.1	—	40.3	18.1
Governor and Company of t	21,842	6,544	—	0.8	—	50.4	23.1

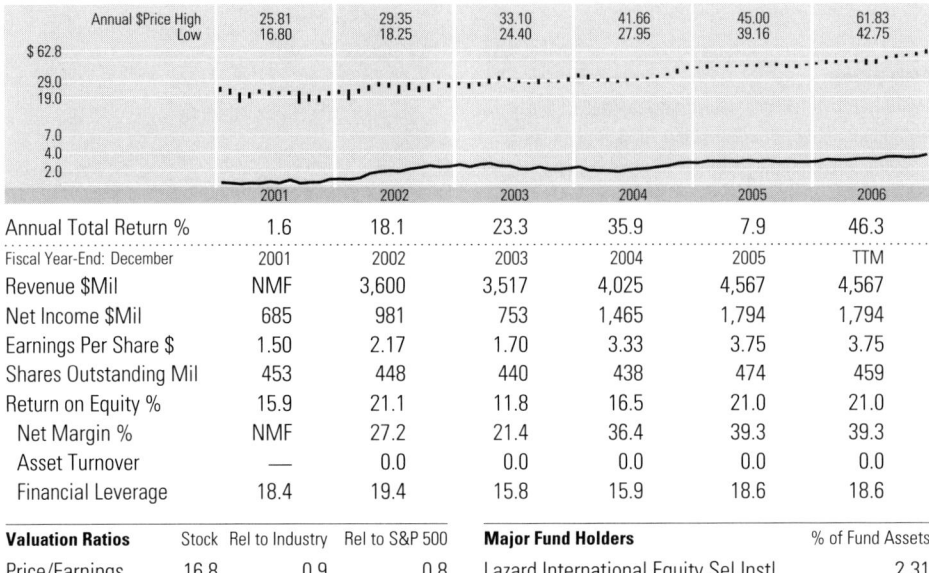

Annual Total Return %	1.6	18.1	23.3	35.9	7.9	46.3
Fiscal Year-End: December	2001	2002	2003	2004	2005	TTM
Revenue $Mil	NMF	3,600	3,517	4,025	4,567	4,567
Net Income $Mil	685	981	753	1,465	1,794	1,794
Earnings Per Share $	1.50	2.17	1.70	3.33	3.75	3.75
Shares Outstanding Mil	453	448	440	438	474	459
Return on Equity %	15.9	21.1	11.8	16.5	21.0	21.0
Net Margin %	NMF	27.2	21.4	36.4	39.3	39.3
Asset Turnover	—	0.0	0.0	0.0	0.0	0.0
Financial Leverage	18.4	19.4	15.8	15.9	18.6	18.6

Valuation Ratios	Stock	Rel to Industry	Rel to S&P 500
Price/Earnings	16.8	0.9	0.8
Price/Book	3.3	1.3	0.8
Price/Sales	6.1	1.5	2.1
Price/Cash Flow	—	—	—

Major Fund Holders	% of Fund Assets
Lazard International Equity Sel Instl	2.31
Sparrow Growth A	2.27
Aston/River Road Dynamic Equity Income N	1.99
Eaton Vance Dividend Income A	1.45

Thesis By Ganesh Rathnam, 11-07-06 Stock Price as of Analysis: $55.79

Allied Irish Banks is the dominant bank in fast-growing Ireland. We expect Allied Irish to benefit from significant tailwinds provided by continued job growth, worker migration into Ireland, economic prosperity, and the country's overall good credit quality.

Allied Irish, with other Irish banks, is the primary beneficiary of the favorable demographics sweeping Ireland. Hitherto an exporter of labor, Ireland has been experiencing rapid population growth and job growth since its economic revival. In 2005, an estimated 70,000 migrants into Ireland spurred job growth by 5%. In addition, most migrants are in the 25-44 age group, a demographic ripe for consuming a variety of financial services. They have immediate need for checking accounts, mortgages, and investment services, which Allied Irish happily provides.

Allied Irish's success is also explained by several other initiatives. Most banking in Ireland is relationship-oriented, and Allied Irish has done a splendid job on this front. It has an army of about 1,600 relationship managers, each with either 500 individual clients or 200 corporate clients. Compensation is tied to the profitability of portfolios rather than raw sales. The bank invested in a customer-relationship management system that assists these managers in making appropriate product pitches to clients on the basis of their profiles.

Allied Irish adopts a very different business strategy in the United Kingdom: It specializes in niche banking categories like legal services and private education. Law firms carry significant client funds in liquid instruments such as deposits, whereas private education institutions borrow heavily to invest in schools and infrastructure. We think this sound strategy has spurred double-digit deposit and loan growth in a consolidated, oligopolistic market.

Operational excellence and credit discipline buttress Allied Irish's business model. The bank does not sacrifice underwriting standards in its pursuit of loan growth. For example, despite a hot real estate market, the firm does not provide 100% financing in housing purchases. Moreover, first-time buyers account for only 10% of the bank's mortgage book. Consequently, charge-offs are minuscule. Further, Allied Irish is committed to cost control, striving to limit cost growth to 300 basis points less than revenue growth each year. We think the deck is stacked in Allied Irish's favor, and we'd happily recommend the shares in 5-star territory.

Data as of 12-29-06

Allied Waste Industries AW

	Rating	Fair Value	Last Close	Consider Buy	Consider Sell	Yield %
	★★★★	$15.00	$12.29	$9.60	$18.10	0.00

Company Profile

Allied Waste is the second-largest waste-services company in the United States. It offers nonhazardous-waste collection, transfer, recycling, and disposal services to about 10 million customers. Allied generates about 30% of its collection revenue from residential customers, 50% from commercial customers, and 20% from industrial and construction customers. It owns and operates 169 solid-waste landfills, 166 transfer stations, and 57 recycling facilities.

Management   Stewardship Grade [D]

Allied's senior management team has only recently begun to solidify after undergoing a series of changes punctuated by the departure of 12-year veteran Thomas Van Weelden from the CEO post in October 2004. The most recent change has been the permanent replacement of interim CEO Charles Cotros (who remains on Allied's board) with John Zillmer, who now holds the chairmanship as well. Zillmer's expertise derives primarily from his career at the food-services firm Aramark, where he held various management positions over a period of 18 years. He also previously served on the board of Casella Waste Systems. Other members of Allied's top brass have been with the firm for 10 or more years and bring industry experience from various firms acquired by Allied. Our Stewardship Grade for Allied is suppressed most heavily by a number of related-party transactions between the firm and former executives. Among these is Allied's continuing obligation to make royalty payments to Van Weelden and his family's trust as part of a landfill sale made by Van Weelden to Environmental Development Corp., which was later acquired by Allied.

15880 North Greenway-Hayden Loop Suite 100
Scottsdale, AZ 85260   www.alliedwaste.com

Growth [C-]	2002	2003	2004	2005
Revenue %	-0.1	1.4	2.4	4.0
Earnings/Share %	—	NMF	NMF	411.1
Book Value/Share %	—	NMF	-40.1	3.7
Dividends/Share %	NMF	NMF	NMF	NMF

Profitability [C]	2003	2004	2005	TTM
Return on Assets %	-3.3	0.2	1.1	1.2
Oper Cash Flow $Mil	784	650	713	710
- Cap Spending $Mil	492	583	696	714
= Free Cash Flow $Mil	292	67	17	-5

Financial Health [D-]	2003	2004	2005	09-30-06
Long-term Debt $Mil	—	8,086	7,508	7,468
Total Equity $Mil	2,518	2,272	2,526	2,999
Debt/Equity Ratio	—	3.6	3.0	2.5

Industry	Business Risk	Moat Size	Investment Style	Sector
Waste Management	Above Avg	Narrow	Mid Core	Business Services

Competition

	Market Cap $Mil	12 Mo Trailing Sales $Mil	Price/Cash Flow	Return On Assets%	Debt/Equity	Total Return% 1 Yr	3 Yr
Allied Waste Industries	4,523	6,003	6.4	1.2	2.5	40.6	-4.0
Waste Management	19,672	13,452	7.8	5.7	1.3	24.2	10.1
Republic Services A	5,307	3,043	9.2	6.1	1.2	9.9	17.6

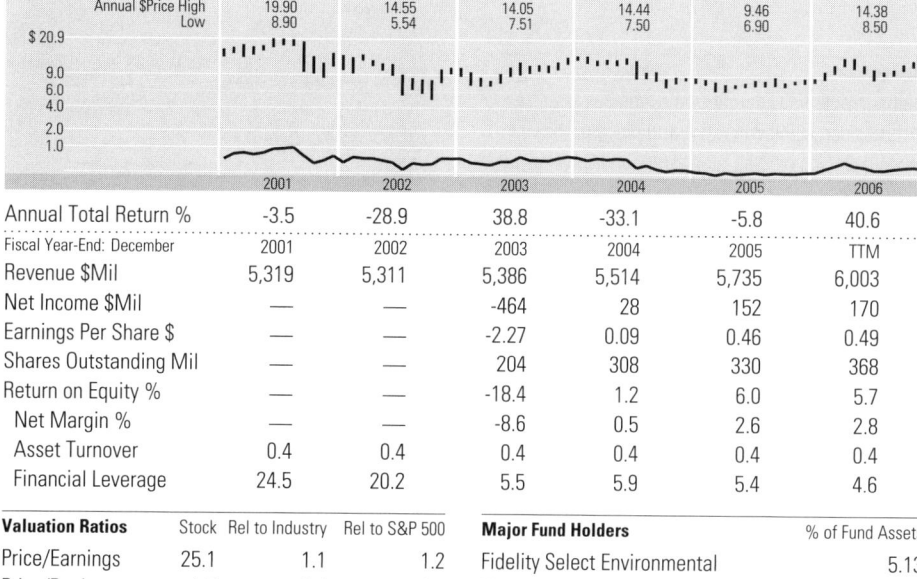

	2001	2002	2003	2004	2005	TTM
Annual Total Return %	-3.5	-28.9	38.8	-33.1	-5.8	40.6
Fiscal Year-End: December	2001	2002	2003	2004	2005	TTM
Revenue $Mil	5,319	5,311	5,386	5,514	5,735	6,003
Net Income $Mil	—	—	-464	28	152	170
Earnings Per Share $	—	—	-2.27	0.09	0.46	0.49
Shares Outstanding Mil	—	—	204	308	330	368
Return on Equity %	—	—	-18.4	1.2	6.0	5.7
Net Margin %	—	—	-8.6	0.5	2.6	2.8
Asset Turnover	0.4	0.4	0.4	0.4	0.4	0.4
Financial Leverage	24.5	20.2	5.5	5.9	5.4	4.6

Valuation Ratios	Stock	Rel to Industry	Rel to S&P 500
Price/Earnings	25.1	1.1	1.2
Price/Book	1.5	0.4	0.4
Price/Sales	0.8	0.4	0.3
Price/Cash Flow	6.4	0.6	0.4

Major Fund Holders	% of Fund Assets
Fidelity Select Environmental	5.13
Phoenix Mid-Cap Value A	3.63
Meridian Value	2.62
Rice Hall James Mid-Cap Inv	2.62

Thesis By Brian Nelson, 11-02-06 Stock Price as of Analysis: $12.43

Masked by its debt-laden balance sheet, Allied Waste's turnaround efforts continue to gain traction, bolstered by cost-cutting efforts, a strategic shift in corporate culture, and an improving industry pricing environment.

Allied owns the second-largest (after Waste Management) domestic network of landfill operations--a long-term competitive advantage that's nearly impossible to duplicate due to substantial regulatory and political barriers to entry. With this vast network, Allied often controls landfill pricing, and in some isolated markets, charges elevated dumping fees (tipping fees) to local waste collectors lacking viable disposal alternatives. As landfill space dwindles and tipping fees escalate, Allied's lasting disposal capacity should drive increased profitability, further separating its economics from those of smaller competitors.

But enduring landfill capacity is not all that separates Allied from its waste-hauling brethren. Its 73% internalization rate (the percentage of company-collected waste that is dumped in company-owned landfills) is the highest of the trash firms we cover: Waste Management (66%), Republic Services (57%), and Waste Connections (69%). Garbage haulers with high internalization rates generally boast high margins since they avoid paying expensive tipping fees to dump waste at a competitor's landfill. Allied's operating margins (16% in 2005) are a testament to its highly integrated network and remain strong relative to national competitors, despite falling in recent years due to increased subcontractor and truck-maintenance costs.

What's more, we view Allied's current margin weakness as more of an opportunity than a concern, particularly considering its shift to centralized (from regional) pricing decisions and new CEO John Zillmer's fresh focus on return-on-capital metrics. Prior to Zillmer taking the reins, Allied entrusted decision-making to regional field managers who often priced local business at razor-thin margins to capture market share. But with its new centralized approach to pricing, Allied is now better-positioned to pass over lower-margin business or demand price hikes from existing customers. This change should boost return on capital and, due to Allied's sheer size, improve the economics of the entire solid-waste industry. With other industry participants now adopting return on capital as a key focus, we expect Allied's revamped pricing strategy should augment the firm's cost-cutting efforts to drive improving returns on capital for many years to come.

Data as of 12-29-06

Allstate ALL

Rating ★★	Fair Value $57.00	Last Close $65.11	Consider Buy $44.00	Consider Sell $71.40	Yield % 2.15

Industry	Business Risk	Moat Size	Investment Style	Sector
Insurance (Property)	Average	Narrow	Large Value	Financial Services

Company Profile
On the basis of premium sales, Allstate is the second-largest U.S. personal-lines property-casualty insurer. Personal auto and homeowner insurance accounts for more than 75% of Allstate's sales. Allstate Financial's life insurance, mutual funds, and annuities contribute 10% of sales. In addition to 13,000 company agents, Allstate products are sold in North America by independent agents, banks, and brokers.

Management
Stewardship Grade [A]

Chairman and CEO Edward Liddy, who has led Allstate since 1999, will retire at the end of the year. Tom Wilson has worked for Allstate and Liddy for 12 years and is a suitable replacement. Directors and officers collectively own about 0.9% of outstanding shares, which is less than we'd like to see, but understandable given Allstate's large market cap. Annual manager compensation measures include combined ratio, policy count growth, and operating earnings. The long-term incentive structure, determined by performance compared with peer group return on equity, is based on a three-year cycle, which we think makes sense for an insurance company. However, the minimum ROE to gain eligibility is about 7%, which we think is aiming extremely low. With the retirement of Liddy, who will stay on as chairman, Allstate will now have separate occupants of the CEO and chairman positions. We are raising our Stewardship Grade to an A.

2775 Sanders Road
Northbrook, IL 60062-6127
www.allstate.com

Growth [C]	2002	2003	2004	2005
Revenue %	2.5	8.7	5.6	4.3
Earnings/Share %	0.0	139.4	18.5	-41.9
Book Value/Share %	3.6	18.3	7.0	-3.1
Dividends/Share %	10.5	9.5	21.7	14.3

Profitability [B+]	2003	2004	2005	TTM
Return on Assets %	2.0	2.1	1.1	3.0
Oper Cash Flow $Mil	5,691	5,468	5,605	—
- Cap Spending $Mil	169	200	196	—
= Free Cash Flow $Mil	—	—	—	—

Financial Health [NA]	2003	2004	2005	09-30-06
Long-term Debt $Mil	—	—	—	—
Total Equity $Mil	20,565	21,823	20,186	22,200
Debt/Equity Ratio	—	—	—	—

Competition	Market Cap $Mil	12 Mo Trailing Sales $Mil	Price/Cash Flow	Return On Assets%	Debt/ Equity	Total Return% 1 Yr	3 Yr
Allstate	40,690	35,639	—	3.0	—	23.4	17.2
Berkshire Hathaway B	169,636	97,676	—	5.2	—	24.9	9.4
Progressive	18,448	14,692	—	7.7	—	-16.9	5.7

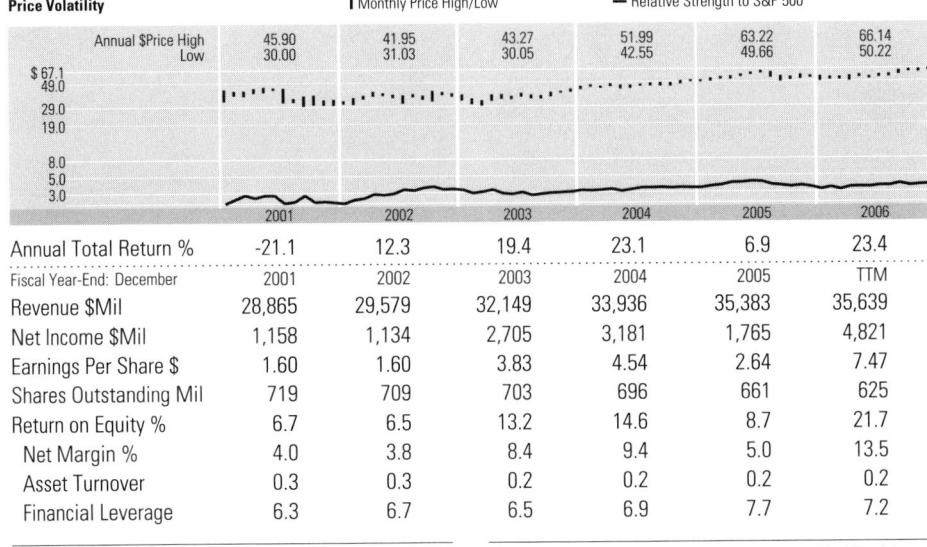

Price Volatility — Monthly Price High/Low — Relative Strength to S&P 500

	2001	2002	2003	2004	2005	2006
Annual $Price High	45.90	41.95	43.27	51.99	63.22	66.14
Low	30.00	31.03	30.05	42.55	49.66	50.22
Annual Total Return %	-21.1	12.3	19.4	23.1	6.9	23.4

Fiscal Year-End: December	2001	2002	2003	2004	2005	TTM
Revenue $Mil	28,865	29,579	32,149	33,936	35,383	35,639
Net Income $Mil	1,158	1,134	2,705	3,181	1,765	4,821
Earnings Per Share $	1.60	1.60	3.83	4.54	2.64	7.47
Shares Outstanding Mil	719	709	703	696	661	625
Return on Equity %	6.7	6.5	13.2	14.6	8.7	21.7
Net Margin %	4.0	3.8	8.4	9.4	5.0	13.5
Asset Turnover	0.3	0.3	0.2	0.2	0.2	0.2
Financial Leverage	6.3	6.7	6.5	6.9	7.7	7.2

Valuation Ratios	Stock	Rel to Industry	Rel to S&P 500
Price/Earnings	8.7	0.6	0.4
Price/Book	1.8	1.1	0.4
Price/Sales	1.1	0.8	0.4
Price/Cash Flow	—	—	—

Major Fund Holders	% of Fund Assets
New River Core Equity	5.28
Pioneer Value A	5.23
Muhlenkamp	4.81
Federated MDT Tax Aware/All Cap Core I	4.54

Thesis By Jim Ryan, 11-02-06 Stock Price as of Analysis: $61.15

Allstate leverages its customer base and widespread agent network with solid risk selection to carve a narrow economic moat. Our fair value estimate is $57 per share.

As America's third-largest property-casualty insurer, Allstate sports formidable advantages. It has a prominent brand and relationships with more than 16 million households--a large audience to sell additional products to. Allstate's distribution network includes nearly 25,000 agents, yielding massive selling power. And the firm's scale yields considerable economies; Allstate's administrative expenses are several percentage points lower than those of most insurers we follow.

Allstate's size would be nugatory without decent underwriting to control the firm's largest and most uncertain cost: claims. We think the firm's strategic underwriting initiative targets the two critical profitability drivers: underwriting profits and customer longevity. Allstate is striving to segment its market more finely, helping it to offer more attractive pricing to lower-risk drivers. In our opinion, this will boost underwriting profits and reduce customer acquisition costs, which can prove substantial for customers who switch insurers frequently. While we doubt that Allstate can match Progressive's industry-leading pricing sophistication, we do think it can generate a sustainable improvement and outpace many rivals that have less capacity to invest in such underwriting systems.

Allstate's underwriting discipline is enough to protect the firm's profits in the near term, but we think the economics of personal lines insurance prevent the firm from digging a wide moat. Even though Allstate is the third-largest property-casualty insurer, it accounts for only 6% of industry premiums, resulting in scant pricing power. The barriers to enter Allstate's business are minimal, and policyholders can switch insurers at no cost and receive largely the same policy. Over time, these factors will hinder Allstate's returns.

Allstate's lack of control over its property business is our biggest concern. The firm is precluded by regulation from pricing policies commensurate with risk. Even worse, regulation often prohibits the firm from canceling policies and leaving horribly unprofitable markets. Therefore, Allstate will periodically incur a massive loss without being able to raise prices to compensate.

Data as of 12-29-06

Alltel AT

	Rating	Fair Value	Last Close	Consider Buy	Consider Sell	Yield %
	★★★	$56.00	$60.48	$43.20	$70.20	1.69

Company Profile

Alltel serves more than 11.2 million subscribers, making it the fifth-largest carrier in the nation. The firm spun off its fixed-line phone unit in July 2006 and merged this business with Valor Communications, so wireless services now constitute the vast majority of revenue. Alltel's wireless territory covers about 77 million people and more than half the landmass of the continental U.S.

Industry	Business Risk	Moat Size	Investment Style	Sector
Wireless Svcs.	Average	Narrow	Large Value	Telecommunication

Competition

	Market Cap $Mil	12 Mo Trailing Sales $Mil	Price/Cash Flow	Return On Assets%	Debt/ Equity	Total Return% 1 Yr	3 Yr
Alltel	22,597	10,548	8.4	6.0	0.2	19.5	19.5
AT&T	137,384	60,171	9.0	4.9	0.5	51.6	16.3
Verizon Communications	108,723	88,881	4.4	3.7	0.7	34.9	8.0

Price Volatility

| Monthly Price High/Low — Relative Strength to S&P 500

Annual $Price High	56.21	51.76	46.01	49.61	55.80	62.66
Low	40.45	28.91	33.30	38.12	44.35	48.12
	2001	2002	2003	2004	2005	2006
Annual Total Return %	1.7	-14.1	-5.1	30.5	10.7	19.5

Fiscal Year-End: December	2001	2002	2003	2004	2005	TTM
Revenue $Mil	6,616	7,112	7,980	8,246	9,487	10,548
Net Income $Mil	1,067	924	1,330	1,046	1,331	1,169
Earnings Per Share $	3.40	2.96	4.25	3.39	3.87	2.95
Shares Outstanding Mil	312	311	311	308	340	374
Return on Equity %	19.2	15.4	18.9	14.7	10.2	8.7
Net Margin %	16.1	13.0	16.7	12.7	14.0	11.1
Asset Turnover	0.5	0.4	0.5	0.5	0.4	0.5
Financial Leverage	2.2	2.7	2.4	2.3	1.8	1.4

Management Stewardship Grade [C]

Chairman Joe Ford, who has been with Alltel since 1959 and is largely responsible for the firm's expansion strategy, relinquished the CEO post to his son Scott in July 2002. Scott Ford has been president since 1997 and also sits on the company's 11-member board. The Fords own less than 1% of shares outstanding. While we generally think Alltel is well run, our biggest concern with the firm's stewardship is its compensation practices. While compensation isn't as outrageous as at the large phone companies, the Fords have been very handsomely paid. Scott received nearly $4.5 million in cash, $1.6 million of restricted stock, and 120,000 options during 2005. Joe continues to draw a $250,000 annual salary and other benefits, including country club memberships and use of the corporate jet. The firm's short- and long-term incentive plans have been based entirely on earnings per share, which can be more easily manipulated from year to year than many other financial measures. The firm is establishing a new incentive structure, but the new plan gives the board extremely broad discretion in setting objectives. A shareholder rights plan would also probably make it difficult, if not impossible, for a suitor to acquire Alltel without the board's blessing.

One Allied Drive www.alltel.com
Little Rock, AR 72202

Valuation Ratios	Stock	Rel to Industry	Rel to S&P 500
Price/Earnings	17.6	0.7	0.9
Price/Book	1.7	0.5	0.4
Price/Sales	2.1	0.6	0.7
Price/Cash Flow	8.4	1.0	0.6

Major Fund Holders	% of Fund Assets
Profunds UltraSector Mobile Telecomm Inv	23.23
Fidelity Select Wireless	10.00
Fidelity Select Utilities Growth	4.61
Fidelity Select Telecommunications	4.32

Growth [B+]	2002	2003	2004	2005
Revenue %	7.5	12.2	3.3	15.0
Earnings/Share %	-12.9	43.6	-20.2	14.2
Book Value/Share %	8.3	16.8	3.0	63.8
Dividends/Share %	19.8	-10.9	4.9	2.3

Profitability [A]	2003	2004	2005	TTM
Return on Assets %	8.0	6.3	5.5	6.0
Oper Cash Flow $Mil	2,475	2,467	2,697	2,686
- Cap Spending $Mil	1,298	1,311	2,440	2,018
= Free Cash Flow $Mil	1,176	1,156	257	668

Financial Health [NA]	2003	2004	2005	09-30-06
Long-term Debt $Mil	5,581	5,352	5,783	2,712
Total Equity $Mil	7,022	7,128	13,015	13,357
Debt/Equity Ratio	0.8	0.8	0.4	0.2

Thesis By Michael Hodel, CFA, 12-15-06 Stock Price as of Analysis: $58.01

We believe Alltel has a unique position in the wireless industry that gives it a competitive advantage. With the spin-off of its fixed-line business complete, the firm also enjoys a fantastic financial position from which to attack the wireless market.

Generally, we think size conveys significant advantages in the wireless industry. The nation's two largest carriers, Verizon Wireless and Cingular, have dominated recently, taking an increasingly large share of industrywide customer growth. Verizon, in particular, has been able to market aggressively and invest heavily in its networks while maintaining very strong margins. Cingular has also dramatically improved margins since making a major acquisition.

Even the smallest of the four nationwide wireless carriers in the U.S., Deutsche Telekom's T-Mobile, is more than twice Alltel's size. However, we think Alltel's concentration in smaller markets and its broad geographic coverage make up for its smaller stature. About two thirds of the firm's customers reside in smaller markets and rural areas, which might contain two or three competitors, rather than the four or more seen in urban markets. The appeal of rural relative to urban markets is likely to grow over time. Several smaller competitors, like Leap and MetroPCS, are attacking large markets, and additional wireless spectrum recently auctioned by the government is better suited to urban areas.

Serving rural markets has also made Alltel an important partner to all of the industry's giants. The firm's networks cover more than half of the continental U.S., including vast areas rivals don't reach. Alltel uses wireless spectrum that is superior to that of many other carriers in its ability to cover large, sparsely populated areas. Alltel can offer service to others at lower rates than they could obtain by building networks while still generating nice margins. Also, Alltel's ability to offer roaming services to other carriers gives it leverage in negotiating rates for access to those carriers' networks so that it can profitably offer its customers nationwide calling, which should ensure that the firm's narrower coverage isn't an impediment to its ability to compete for customers over the long term.

We do expect that the scale benefits larger carriers enjoy will pressure Alltel's ability to grow and expand margins. The firm still has to face the industry's giants in many of its markets. For example, in addition to being a partner, Verizon Wireless is a tough competitor, one that covers around 40% of Alltel's wireless territory. Wireless service is largely a commodity, and competition is often based on price.

Data as of 12-29-06

Altera ALTR

	Rating	Fair Value	Last Close	Consider Buy	Consider Sell	Yield %
	★★★	$19.00	$19.68	$14.70	$23.80	0.00

Company Profile
Altera designs and produces programmable-logic semiconductor devices. The firm's standard programmable-logic chips are offered in varying levels of logic integration and performance. Customers in the communications, computer and storage, industrial, and consumer markets use the company's software to configure and program these chips for a wide variety of end uses.

Industry	Business Risk	Moat Size	Investment Style	Sector
Semiconductor	Average	Narrow	Mid Growth	Hardware

Competition

	Market Cap $Mil	12 Mo Trailing Sales $Mil	Price/Cash Flow	Return On Assets%	Debt/ Equity	Total Return% 1 Yr	3 Yr
Altera	7,121	1,250	15.1	13.1	0.0	6.2	-4.6
Xilinx	8,006	1,870	14.6	11.7	—	-4.3	-14.0
Lattice Semiconductor	742	238	36.2	-3.0	0.2	50.0	-13.3

Management
Stewardship Grade [C]

President and CEO John Daane has held the top spot at Altera since 2000 and was appointed as chairman of the board in 2003. Daane has solid experience in the semiconductor industry, having spent 15 years in various executive roles at LSI Logic. After CFO Nathan Sarkisian retired in 2006, the company is still looking for a replacement. Executive cash compensation is roughly in line with competitors, and insiders own about 3% of the firm. In 2003, Altera allowed employees to exchange stock options that were far out of the money for ones at a lower strike price, a practice we frown upon. Altera completed its internal review of options granting practices in October 2006 and is current in its financial filings with regulatory bodies.

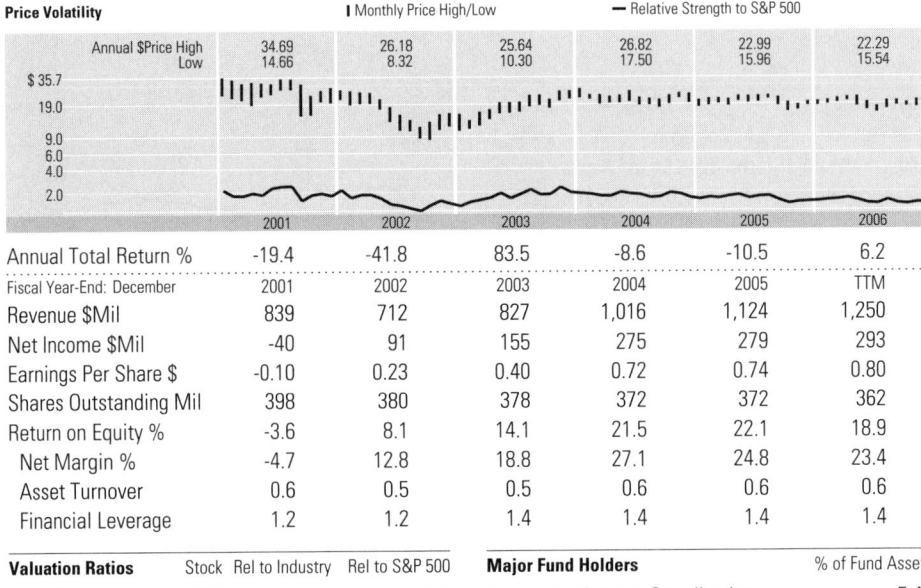

Price Volatility

	2001	2002	2003	2004	2005	2006
Annual $Price High	34.69	26.18	25.64	26.82	22.99	22.29
Low	14.66	8.32	10.30	17.50	15.96	15.54
Annual Total Return %	-19.4	-41.8	83.5	-8.6	-10.5	6.2

Fiscal Year-End: December	2001	2002	2003	2004	2005	TTM
Revenue $Mil	839	712	827	1,016	1,124	1,250
Net Income $Mil	-40	91	155	275	279	293
Earnings Per Share $	-0.10	0.23	0.40	0.72	0.74	0.80
Shares Outstanding Mil	398	380	378	372	372	362
Return on Equity %	-3.6	8.1	14.1	21.5	22.1	18.9
Net Margin %	-4.7	12.8	18.8	27.1	24.8	23.4
Asset Turnover	0.6	0.5	0.5	0.6	0.6	0.6
Financial Leverage	1.2	1.2	1.4	1.4	1.4	1.4

Valuation Ratios	Stock	Rel to Industry	Rel to S&P 500
Price/Earnings	24.6	0.9	1.2
Price/Book	4.6	1.3	1.1
Price/Sales	5.7	1.4	2.0
Price/Cash Flow	15.1	0.9	1.0

Major Fund Holders	% of Fund Assets
Neuberger Berman Guardian Inv	5.48
Neuberger Berman Socially Resp Inv	5.30
Principal Inv Ptr SmCp Gr III Inst	4.23
Fidelity Advisor Electronics T	4.18

101 Innovation Dr.
San Jose, CA 95134
www.altera.com

Growth [B-]	2002	2003	2004	2005
Revenue %	-15.2	16.2	22.9	10.6
Earnings/Share %	NMF	73.9	80.0	2.8
Book Value/Share %	1.8	-0.3	17.7	0.3
Dividends/Share %	NMF	NMF	NMF	NMF

Profitability [A]	2003	2004	2005	TTM
Return on Assets %	10.2	15.6	15.3	13.1
Oper Cash Flow $Mil	326	314	415	471
- Cap Spending $Mil	14	25	26	33
= Free Cash Flow $Mil	312	289	389	437

Financial Health [A]	2003	2004	2005	09-30-06
Long-term Debt $Mil	0	0	4	1
Total Equity $Mil	1,102	1,279	1,264	1,553
Debt/Equity Ratio	0.0	0.0	0.0	0.0

Thesis
By Larry Cao, CFA, 11-21-06 Stock Price as of Analysis: $20.47

After some costly missteps in product transitions in the late 1990s, Altera has started to show signs of promise since the successful launch of its current generation products in 2002.

As a leading producer of programmable logic devices (PLDs), Altera has benefited from the rapid growth of the industry, which outpaced the overall semiconductor industry. PLDs are logic devices that are programmed after production. The design flexibility allows users to reduce a product's time-to-market and avoid the high up-front cost of developing custom chips known as application-specific integrated circuits (ASICs). However, the redundant logic and routing make the PLD architecture inherently more costly and, for many years, limited its application to mostly prototypes for new products.

Advances in manufacturing technology are tilting the cost-benefit calculations more in favor of PLDs. At each new process node, pricing comes down more for PLDs, and up-front design cost goes up more for ASICs. These favorable dynamics have driven more widespread adoption of PLDs, often at the expense of ASICs. As the ASIC market is several times the size of PLDs, we believe Altera's growth rate will continue to outpace the overall chip industry.

We think switching costs are the source of Altera's moat. Altera and competitor Xilinx combined have 80% share of the PLD market, each having a few standard platforms. It takes time for designers to get comfortable with the proprietary chip architectures and software. Consequently, designers tend not to switch unless a competitive product has a clear advantage. Long product cycles in communications equipment and industrial sectors make the incumbents nearly impossible to replace.

Switching costs prevented Altera from losing share in the previous product cycle when Altera's design software was introduced prematurely; however, this also makes it a slow process for Altera's current generation of products to gain share from Xilinx. Altera launched its current core products ahead of Xilinx in 2002. The low-cost field-programmable gate array (FPGA) platform Cyclone and structured ASIC product HardCopy have successfully extended Altera's reach into new applications. We estimate Altera's market share increased by about a few percentage points in the last four years. We believe the success of Altera's latest product families introduced in 2005 bodes well for the company as they become mainstream products in the next few years.

Data as of 12-29-06

Altria Group MO

Rating	Fair Value	Last Close	Consider Buy	Consider Sell	Yield %
★★★	$90.00	$85.82	$57.30	$108.50	3.87

Company Profile
Altria is one of the largest producers of consumer packaged goods in the world. Wholly owned subsidiaries Philip Morris USA and Philip Morris International manufacture and sell tobacco products worldwide. The company holds a majority interest (87%) in Kraft Foods, the second-largest packaged food company in the world, and an equity interest (29%) in SABMiller, the world's second-largest brewer. Altria also invests in finance leases through Philip Morris Capital.

Management Stewardship Grade [C]
Louis Camilleri has been chairman and CEO of Altria Group since 2002, having previously served as the company's CFO from 1996 to 2002. Camilleri is also the chairman of Kraft Foods, a subsidiary of Altria. Following the sale of 15% of Kraft's outstanding shares through an initial public offering in 2001, Altria retained an 87% economic interest in the firm and holds 98% of the voting rights. Its ownership of the packaged food company has done little to quell the controversy associated with its tobacco divisions, Philip Morris USA and Philip Morris International. Altria's domestic tobacco arm has been the target of countless lawsuits over the years and currently pays out close to $5 billion in annual settlement costs and legal fees. While the international litigation environment has been benign, the firm has had to contend with extremely high excise taxes, which foreign governments use to recapture health-care costs and help curb smoking. Despite the current moratorium on share repurchases and special dividends, the firm has traditionally returned free cash flow to shareholders. While we believe that management has reported honestly and straightforwardly to shareholders, we do question the nearly 33% increase in Louis Camilleri's compensation in 2005.

120 Park Avenue www.altria.com
New York, NY 10017

Growth [C+]	2002	2003	2004	2005
Revenue %	-0.6	1.7	10.2	9.2
Earnings/Share %	34.6	-13.2	0.9	9.4
Book Value/Share %	3.0	34.7	20.8	14.8
Dividends/Share %	9.9	8.2	6.8	8.5

Profitability [A]	2003	2004	2005	TTM
Return on Assets %	9.6	9.3	9.7	10.5
Oper Cash Flow $Mil	10,816	10,890	11,060	14,249
- Cap Spending $Mil	1,974	1,913	2,206	2,218
= Free Cash Flow $Mil	8,842	8,977	8,854	12,031

Financial Health [A]	2003	2004	2005	09-30-06
Long-term Debt $Mil	21,163	16,462	15,653	13,221
Total Equity $Mil	25,077	30,714	35,707	41,190
Debt/Equity Ratio	0.8	0.5	0.4	0.3

Industry	Business Risk	Moat Size	Investment Style	Sector
Tobacco	Above Avg	Wide	Large Value	Consumer Goods

Competition	Market Cap $Mil	12 Mo Trailing Sales $Mil	Price/Cash Flow	Return On Assets %	Debt/Equity	Total Return% 1 Yr	3 Yr
Altria Group	179,868	100,499	12.6	10.5	0.3	19.9	21.8
British American Tobacco	59,384	43,778	14.0	10.5	0.8	30.1	32.1
Reynolds American	19,353	8,488	13.3	7.5	0.6	43.9	38.3

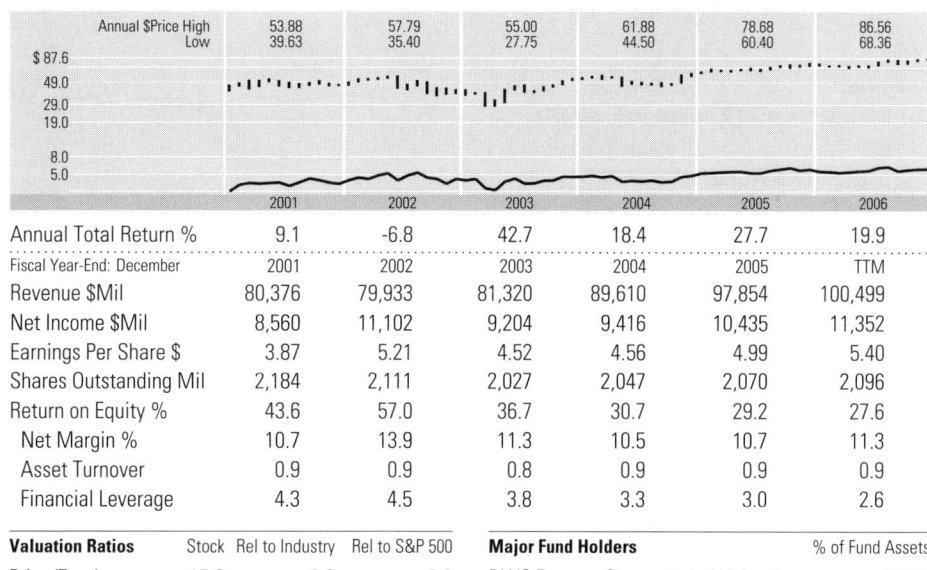

Annual Total Return %	9.1	-6.8	42.7	18.4	27.7	19.9
Fiscal Year-End: December	2001	2002	2003	2004	2005	TTM
Revenue $Mil	80,376	79,933	81,320	89,610	97,854	100,499
Net Income $Mil	8,560	11,102	9,204	9,416	10,435	11,352
Earnings Per Share $	3.87	5.21	4.52	4.56	4.99	5.40
Shares Outstanding Mil	2,184	2,111	2,027	2,047	2,070	2,096
Return on Equity %	43.6	57.0	36.7	30.7	29.2	27.6
Net Margin %	10.7	13.9	11.3	10.5	10.7	11.3
Asset Turnover	0.9	0.9	0.8	0.9	0.9	0.9
Financial Leverage	4.3	4.5	3.8	3.3	3.0	2.6

Valuation Ratios	Stock	Rel to Industry	Rel to S&P 500
Price/Earnings	15.9	0.9	0.8
Price/Book	4.4	0.2	1.1
Price/Sales	1.8	1.0	0.6
Price/Cash Flow	12.6	0.9	0.9

Major Fund Holders	% of Fund Assets
DWS Dreman Concentrated Value A	13.15
ProFunds Consumer Goods UltraSector Inv	10.48
Dreman Contrarian Large Cap Value	8.46
Van Kampen American Franchise A	7.58

Thesis By Greggory Warren, CFA, 12-11-06 Stock Price as of Analysis: $85.02

It's beginning to look like the only thing that can bring Altria to its knees is kryptonite. Despite years spent battling tobacco litigation and fending off deep-discount cigarette manufacturers, the company remains one of the most profitable in the world. With the domestic litigation environment improving and the firm regaining solid command of its tobacco markets worldwide, it looks like investors might finally see a breakup of the company. We believe this could help unlock some of the value that has been suppressed by market fears over tobacco lawsuits and costly settlements and bring Altria's shares more in line with our own fair value estimate.

Altria's leading position in the global cigarette market and its ever-increasing importance to government coffers has cemented its wide-moat status. With 18% share globally, Philip Morris is the second-largest seller of cigarettes in the world (behind China National Tobacco, which is owned and operated by the Chinese government). Philip Morris sells six of the top 20 brands in the world, with Marlboro being the premier franchise in its portfolio. A higher mix of popular premium brands allows the company to charge much higher prices for its cigarettes.

Altria's tobacco profits are further secured by the dependency that governments around the world have on the cash flows that cigarette sales generate for them. Of the $63 billion Philip Morris collected in 2005 from the sale of tobacco products worldwide, roughly $29 billion (or 46%) went toward excise taxes. Another $5 billion went to cover legal fees and settlement costs. On top of that, governments tack their own sales taxes on the company's products at retail, which produces even more tax revenues for their coffers. Despite the steep price tag, these payments actually help solidify the cartel-like grip that the major tobacco manufacturers have on their markets and provides governments with a vested interest in keeping the tobacco industry viable.

With the litigation environment improving, management is now serious about breaking up the company. The company plans to give out more detailed information about the planned spin-off of its Kraft Foods subsidiary in early 2007, setting the stage for a possible separation of Philip Morris USA and Philip Morris International longer term. While we view this as positive news for investors, given the uncertainty that remains on the litigation front and the fact that the stock trades primarily on litigation-related news, we'd still require a significant margin of safety before purchasing the shares.

Data as of 12-29-06

Amazon.com AMZN

	Rating	Fair Value	Last Close	Consider Buy	Consider Sell	Yield %
	★★	$32.00	$39.46	$24.70	$40.10	0.00

Company Profile
Amazon.com markets books, music, videos, tools, small appliances, electronics, apparel, toys, groceries, and numerous other products over the Internet. It sells products from third parties including large businesses, small businesses, and individuals. Amazon operates separate sites for consumers in Canada, the United Kingdom, Germany, France, and Japan. The company also owns The Internet Movie Database (imdb.com).

Management
Stewardship Grade [A]

CEO Jeff Bezos founded Amazon.com in 1994. Tom Szkutak became chief financial officer in September 2002 after 20 years at General Electric, most recently as CFO of GE Lighting. We think that the quality of management and corporate governance is very good in terms of management incentives, shareholder friendliness, and transparency. Management compensation is very reasonable, and we were especially pleased to see the company take the lead in expensing stock-based compensation. Additionally, not even the most senior managers have golden parachutes. Bezos owns about 25% of the shares, takes no equity compensation or bonus pay, and collects a paltry salary. While the board is small, it is elected every year, receives no cash compensation, avoids insider relationships, and hasn't implemented antitakeover provisions. Finally, the company's financial statements are very transparent, and management provides a great deal of supplementary financial data in its quarterly releases.

1200 12th Avenue South Suite 1200
Seattle, WA 98144-2734
www.amazon.com

Growth [A]	2002	2003	2004	2005
Revenue %	26.0	33.8	31.5	22.7
Earnings/Share %	NMF	NMF	EUB	-39.6
Book Value/Share %	NMF	NMF	NMF	NMF
Dividends/Share %	NMF	NMF	NMF	NMF

Profitability [D+]	2003	2004	2005	TTM
Return on Assets %	1.6	18.1	9.7	8.9
Oper Cash Flow $Mil	393	566	733	588
- Cap Spending $Mil	46	89	204	221
= Free Cash Flow $Mil	347	477	529	367

Financial Health [B+]	2003	2004	2005	09-30-06
Long-term Debt $Mil	1,945	1,855	1,521	1,304
Total Equity $Mil	-1,036	-227	246	196
Debt/Equity Ratio	ELB	ELB	6.2	6.7

Industry	Business Risk	Moat Size	Investment Style	Sector
Online Retail	Average	Wide	Large Growth	Consumer Services

Competition	Market Cap $Mil	12 Mo Trailing Sales $Mil	Price/Cash Flow	Return On Assets %	Debt/ Equity	Total Return % 1 Yr	3 Yr
Amazon.com	16,254	9,702	27.6	8.9	6.7	-16.3	-8.7
eBay	41,921	5,579	19.5	7.9	—	-30.4	-1.5
Best Buy Co.	23,624	32,590	12.7	10.0	0.0	13.9	14.1

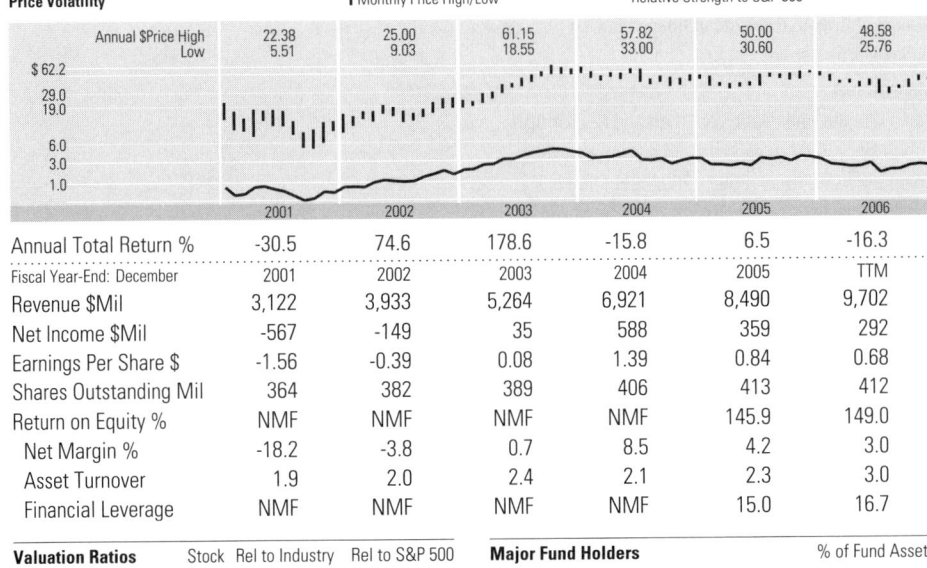

	2001	2002	2003	2004	2005	TTM
Annual Total Return %	-30.5	74.6	178.6	-15.8	6.5	-16.3
Fiscal Year-End: December	2001	2002	2003	2004	2005	TTM
Revenue $Mil	3,122	3,933	5,264	6,921	8,490	9,702
Net Income $Mil	-567	-149	35	588	359	292
Earnings Per Share $	-1.56	-0.39	0.08	1.39	0.84	0.68
Shares Outstanding Mil	364	382	389	406	413	412
Return on Equity %	NMF	NMF	NMF	NMF	145.9	149.0
Net Margin %	-18.2	-3.8	0.7	8.5	4.2	3.0
Asset Turnover	1.9	2.0	2.4	2.1	2.3	3.0
Financial Leverage	NMF	NMF	NMF	NMF	15.0	16.7

Valuation Ratios	Stock	Rel to Industry	Rel to S&P 500
Price/Earnings	58.0	1.3	2.8
Price/Book	82.9	4.6	20.2
Price/Sales	1.7	0.4	0.6
Price/Cash Flow	27.6	1.4	1.9

Major Fund Holders	% of Fund Assets
Legg Mason Growth Trust Primary	6.15
ProFunds Internet UltraSector Inv	5.55
Legg Mason Special Investment Prim	5.35
TCW Select Equities I	5.12

Thesis By Joseph Beaulieu, 12-14-06 Stock Price as of Analysis: $39.02

Through 2006, Amazon has continued to use rock-bottom pricing and generous shipping deals to drive impressive revenue growth. However, low gross margins on merchandise, combined with money-losing shipping deals and aggressive spending on new technology, have eaten into the company's operating margins. We think that Amazon's business model has the potential for substantial operating leverage, but we're not building much margin expansion into our model until we see evidence that the company's spending is more under control.

Even though we think that Amazon's spending on peripheral projects has been excessive, we're still fans of the company's core businesses. We still think that Amazon's massive and loyal customer base, along with its ability to substantially increase sales with limited capital expenditures, is the foundation of a wide economic moat. Newer product categories (while perhaps less profitable than the core books/music/movies business) deliver incremental revenue while leveraging its fixed costs.

We're not convinced that Amazon will become a major grocery destination, or that selling toys or auto parts directly to customers will be more profitable than providing services to another toy seller, but we still think it is worthwhile for the firm to add new product categories. Amazon's low-price strategy and free-shipping offers should help the firm gain market share in all of its product lines, and the company's largely fixed cost structure allows new product categories to generate positive returns on capital.

At this point, there aren't a lot of product categories that the firm can add, so it is investing more in developing IT services. We're pleased that the company is looking for new ways to leverage its fixed assets and drive incremental growth. However, we aren't as upbeat about the company's expenditures on things like the A9 search engine and the related storefront photograph database.

Assuming that management eventually slows spending growth, operating margins should benefit from the firm's considerable operating leverage. This ought to drive improvements to the firm's already-impressive returns on invested capital and would provide further evidence of Amazon's wide economic moat. We don't want the firm to stop looking for new growth engines, as it makes sense to leverage its fixed assets, but we think that investors would be better served if Amazon kept a closer eye on spending.

Com de Bebidas das Americas ADR ABV

Data as of 12-29-06

Rating	Fair Value	Last Close	Consider Buy	Consider Sell	Yield %
★★★	$48.00	$48.80	$30.60	$57.90	2.79

Company Profile

AmBev was formed in 2000 through the combination of Brazil's two largest beverage companies, Brahma and Antarctica. AmBev produces, distributes, and sells beer and PepsiCo products in Brazil and several Latin American countries. Its also owns nearly 100% of Argentina's largest brewer, Quinsa, which has operations in a number of Latin American countries. In 2004, AmBev merged with Canadian brewer Labatt, and Interbrew (now InBev) gained a controlling interest in AmBev.

Management   Stewardship Grade [NA]

Co-CEOs Luiz Edmond (Latin America) and Miguel Patricio (North America) report to the Brazil-based AmBev board. The AmBev board, in turn, reports to the InBev board. Carlos Brito, former co-CEO of AmBev, now serves as CEO of InBev. Minority shareholders in AmBev have very few rights and no voting power. AmBev is controlled by InBev, now the world's largest brewer by volume, but AmBev shareholders have no stake in InBev. AmBev and InBev each continue to exist as separately traded public companies. AmBev has several layers of holding companies and incorporations that seem aimed at minimizing taxes. This makes it very difficult to get a clear read on corporate governance and adds to the risk of an investment. The company has two classes of shares, common and preferred. Preferred-class shares pay a dividend 10% higher than common shares but sacrifice voting rights. Because minority shareholders are essentially disenfranchised anyway (because of InBev's majority), there is little advantage to holding voting rights. Corporate taxes seem to be a constant area of contention with Brazilian companies, and the government has claimed that AmBev owes upward of 4 billion reais, none of which has been recorded as a liability, increasing AmBev's risk.

Rua Renato Paes de Barros, 1017 3 andar   www.ambev.com.br
Sao Paulo, Brazil 04530-001

Growth [NA]	2002	2003	2004	2005
Revenue %	12.3	18.5	38.3	32.9
Earnings/Share %	117.2	1.4	-42.7	11.3
Book Value/Share %	38.5	15.1	169.8	-2.3
Dividends/Share %	—	—	—	—

Profitability [NA]	2003	2004	2005	TTM
Return on Assets %	8.7	3.2	4.4	4.4
Oper Cash Flow $Mil	798	1,171	1,688	1,688
- Cap Spending $Mil	272	436	557	557
= Free Cash Flow $Mil	526	734	1,131	1,131

Financial Health [NA]	2003	2004	2005	12-31-05
Long-term Debt $Mil	—	2,565	3,563	3,563
Total Equity $Mil	1,511	6,389	8,527	8,527
Debt/Equity Ratio	—	0.4	0.4	0.4

Industry	Business Risk	Moat Size	Investment Style	Sector
Alcoholic Beverages	Above Avg	Wide	Large Growth	Consumer Goods

Competition

	Market Cap $Mil	12 Mo Trailing Sales $Mil	Price/Cash Flow	Return On Assets %	Debt/ Equity	Total Return% 1 Yr	3 Yr
Companhia de Bebidas das Americas ADR	32,148	6,491	19.0	4.4	0.4	32.2	43.3
Fomento Economico Mexican	10,475	9,794	8.2	6.5	0.4	61.3	47.8
Grupo Empresarial Bavaria							

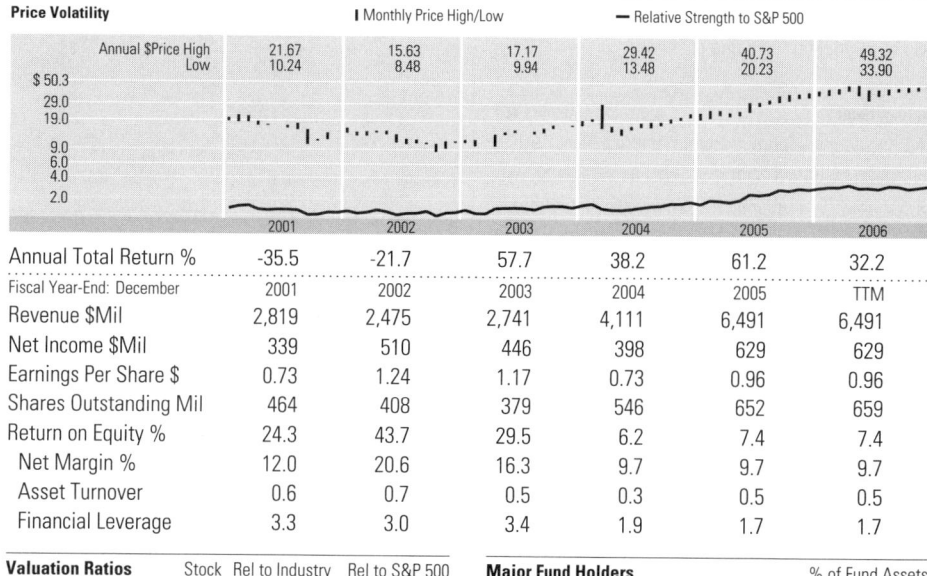

Price Volatility — Monthly Price High/Low — Relative Strength to S&P 500

	2001	2002	2003	2004	2005	2006
Annual $Price High	21.67	15.63	17.17	29.42	40.73	49.32
Low	10.24	8.48	9.94	13.48	20.23	33.90
Annual Total Return %	-35.5	-21.7	57.7	38.2	61.2	32.2

Fiscal Year-End: December	2001	2002	2003	2004	2005	TTM
Revenue $Mil	2,819	2,475	2,741	4,111	6,491	6,491
Net Income $Mil	339	510	446	398	629	629
Earnings Per Share $	0.73	1.24	1.17	0.73	0.96	0.96
Shares Outstanding Mil	464	408	379	546	652	659
Return on Equity %	24.3	43.7	29.5	6.2	7.4	7.4
Net Margin %	12.0	20.6	16.3	9.7	9.7	9.7
Asset Turnover	0.6	0.7	0.5	0.3	0.5	0.5
Financial Leverage	3.3	3.0	3.4	1.9	1.7	1.7

Valuation Ratios	Stock	Rel to Industry	Rel to S&P 500
Price/Earnings	50.6	2.0	2.5
Price/Book	3.8	0.4	0.9
Price/Sales	5.0	0.9	1.7
Price/Cash Flow	19.0	0.8	1.3

Major Fund Holders	% of Fund Assets
BlackRock Latin America A	3.40
Vice Fund	1.84
DWS Latin America Equity S	1.82
Lazard Emerging Markets Instl	1.53

Thesis By Matthew Reilly, 12-11-06 Stock Price as of Analysis: $48.19

AmBev is an extremely well-run, highly profitable brewer. It has dominant market shares in most of the markets where it operates and extremely strong brands. This forms a solid foundation for the company's wide moat. AmBev also has significantly better growth prospects in its core markets, save Canada, than the vast majority of major international brewers.

AmBev absolutely dominates the Brazilian beer market, with a market share of close to 70% and operating margins over 40%. The company has also has developed strong market positions in several Latin American beer markets, largely through its now almost 100% ownership in Quinsa. AmBev complements most of its brewing operations with carbonated soft drink bottlers that fabricate and distribute PepsiCo products as well as AmBev-owned brands. The two classes of beverage products allow the company to better leverage its infrastructure in several markets.

AmBev was acquired by then Interbrew (now InBev) in 2004, and since AmBev's management has taken over much of InBev, making the deal seem like a reverse acquisition. As the result of this somewhat complicated transaction, InBev, now the world's largest brewer by volume, took a controlling stake in AmBev. AmBev ended up with ownership of Labatt, a participant in the Canadian beer duopoly that has significantly lower growth potential than the rest of AmBev's operations.

AmBev's management has increased profitability in the Canadian operations by aggressively cutting costs, the calling card of this extremely efficient organization. We think that there are a few more efficiencies to be squeezed out of this operation, but cost cutting will only go so far in a no-growth environment. However, given the duopoly in the market and a rational competitor, we think cash flow will remain robust.

While we feel that AmBev makes an excellent long-term holding, it will likely take a hiccup in the Brazilian economy accompanied by significant weakness in the real in order to create an attractive valuation given our requirement for a large margin of safety necessitated by the high economic and political risk in several AmBev markets. Other than this risk, the only issue surrounding AmBev that gives us some pause is the uncertainty surrounding the company's tax liability. Various Brazilian government agencies claim that AmBev owes back taxes that run well into billions of reais, and it is very difficult to gauge the validity of these claims.

Data as of 12-29-06

America Movil SA ADR AMX

	Rating	Fair Value	Last Close	Consider Buy	Consider Sell	Yield %
	★★★	$44.00	$45.22	$28.00	$53.10	0.48

Company Profile
America Movil was originally the wireless side of Telmex, the incumbent telephone operator in Mexico. America Movil was spun off in 2000 and has since expanded into the rest of Latin America. It is the largest wireless operator in Latin America, with 114 million wireless subscribers, including 40.7 million, or more than 70% of the wireless market, in Mexico and 7.2 million wireless customers in the United States. It also has 2 million fixed-line customers in Central America

Management
Stewardship Grade [NA]

Like its sister company, Telmex, America Movil is controlled by Carlos Slim Helu. He has stepped down as chairman, but remains honorary chairman for life and is still very much involved. His son Patrick Slim Domit is chairman and his son-in-law Daniel Hajj Aboumrad is CEO. Patrick Slim is also CEO of Grupo Carso, which is a holding company for many of Carlos Slim's businesses. Hajj was CEO of Telcel, the Mexican wireless division of Telmex before America Movil was formed and has been America Movil's CEO since its spin-off. Before that he was CEO of Slim's tire business, which was subsequently sold to Continental. Carlos Garcia Moreno Elizondo has been CFO since America Movil's creation. Before that he was director of public credit in the Mexican Ministry of Finance under Ernesto Zedillo. The firm has two classes of stock, with 66% of the voting shares owned by America Telecom, which is controlled by Slim, and 25% of the voting shares by AT&T. America Telecom also owns 28% of the nonvoting shares, providing it with 40% total ownership. We generally don't like dual classes of stock, but Slim has done a great job for all shareholders. He has also begun to use his financial muscle to affect politics, particularly if it will help his companies.

Lago Alberto 366 Colonia Anahuac   www.americamovil.com
Mexico, D.F., Mexico 11320

Growth [NA]	2002	2003	2004	2005
Revenue %	31.4	43.9	49.1	30.8
Earnings/Share %	NMF	223.1	7.1	93.3
Book Value/Share %	NMF	39.1	9.3	11.4
Dividends/Share %	—	—	—	—

Profitability [NA]	2003	2004	2005	TTM
Return on Assets %	10.5	8.8	13.8	13.8
Oper Cash Flow $Mil	3,000	3,628	5,616	5,616
- Cap Spending $Mil	2,254	2,035	4,349	4,349
= Free Cash Flow $Mil	745	1,594	1,267	1,267

Financial Health [NA]	2003	2004	2005	12-31-05
Long-term Debt $Mil	3,598	5,154	4,780	4,780
Total Equity $Mil	6,693	7,131	7,946	7,946
Debt/Equity Ratio	0.5	0.7	0.6	0.6

Industry	Business Risk	Moat Size	Investment Style	Sector
Telecom Svcs.	Above Avg	Narrow	Large Growth	Telecommunication

Competition	Market Cap $Mil	12 Mo Trailing Sales $Mil	Price/Cash Flow	Return On Assets%	Debt/Equity	Total Return% 1 Yr	3 Yr
America Movil SA ADR	81,952	16,897	14.6	13.8	0.6	55.5	68.9
Telefonica SA ADR	104,574	49,213	7.5	6.9	2.0	47.1	17.7
Telecom Italia SPA ADR	39,906	37,466	3.2	4.0	1.6	9.2	3.9

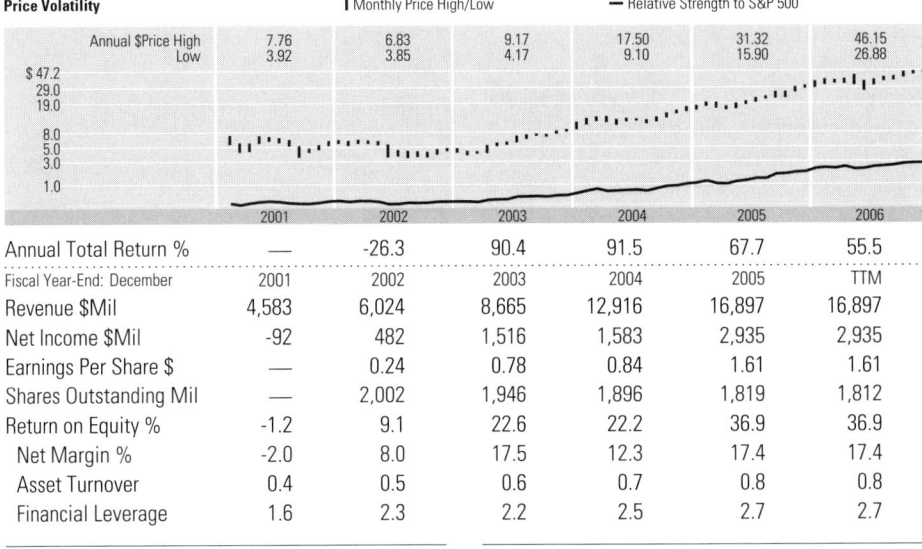

	2001	2002	2003	2004	2005	TTM
Annual Total Return %	—	-26.3	90.4	91.5	67.7	55.5
Fiscal Year-End: December	2001	2002	2003	2004	2005	TTM
Revenue $Mil	4,583	6,024	8,665	12,916	16,897	16,897
Net Income $Mil	-92	482	1,516	1,583	2,935	2,935
Earnings Per Share $	—	0.24	0.78	0.84	1.61	1.61
Shares Outstanding Mil	—	2,002	1,946	1,896	1,819	1,812
Return on Equity %	-1.2	9.1	22.6	22.2	36.9	36.9
Net Margin %	-2.0	8.0	17.5	12.3	17.4	17.4
Asset Turnover	0.4	0.5	0.6	0.7	0.8	0.8
Financial Leverage	1.6	2.3	2.2	2.5	2.7	2.7

Valuation Ratios	Stock	Rel to Industry	Rel to S&P 500
Price/Earnings	28.0	1.5	1.4
Price/Book	10.3	2.4	2.5
Price/Sales	4.9	2.1	1.7
Price/Cash Flow	14.6	1.6	1.0

Major Fund Holders	% of Fund Assets
DWS Latin America Equity S	12.92
T. Rowe Price Latin America	11.33
Fidelity Latin America	10.02
Fidelity Advisor Latin America A	9.86

Thesis By Allan C. Nichols, CFA, 11-06-06 Stock Price as of Analysis: $43.35

We continue to be impressed by America Movil's subscriber and revenue growth and are more confident in its ability to increase profitability outside Mexico, which should allow this trend to continue.

America Movil dominates Mexico. Despite increased competition, the firm still has 70% wireless telephony share by revenue and an even greater share of total customers. This size disparity between it and its competitors provides a huge cost advantage, which shows up in its operating margins of about 44%, some of the highest in the industry worldwide. However, we do expect competition to slowly lower America Movil's margins in Mexico as the firm increases spending on marketing and retention efforts.

America Movil is using the huge cash flow it generates in Mexico to build out a Latin American network. It now has 114 million wireless subscribers across the region, making it the fifth-largest wireless operator in the world. While other markets don't have the margins Mexico does, the firm's scale provides advantages throughout its geographies, allowing high returns on capital and providing it with a narrow moat, in our opinion. For example, in Colombia in 2006, after two huge quarters of subscriber growth, America Movil scaled back its marketing and saw margins shoot up. We think as growth slows, margins will expand across the firm's developing markets.

Consolidation continues throughout Latin America, and more wireless markets are coming down to America Movil and Telefonica, lowering competition and helping margin expansion. Most markets do have one or two other operators, but they are generally small and don't have a larger network to draw on to gain scale advantages. We don't see any other firm being able to enter the Latin markets and reach the scale of America Movil and Telefonica.

The one big exception continues to be Brazil. Here Telecom Italia has a strong presence and has the backing of its Italian network. The country also has some local operators, particularly Telemar, that have done well. Telemar is the incumbent fixed-line operator in the north and eastern states, and within this area it has done very well, thanks to its name recognition and bundling of services. However, even in Brazil, where competition has been very intense and profits in most cases very low or negative, there are signs the various operators are realizing that pricing has gotten out of hand, and margins are starting to come back. We expect this trend to continue.

Data as of 12-29-06

American Express AXP

Rating	Fair Value	Last Close	Consider Buy	Consider Sell	Yield %
★★★★	$70.00	$60.67	$59.60	$91.90	0.89

Company Profile
American Express, best known for its flagship green charge card, is segmented into three main businesses: U.S. Card Services, International Card & Global Commercial Services, and Global Network & Merchant Services. Its former financial advisor segment, American Express Financial Advisors, was spun off to shareholders on Sept. 30, 2005, and is now known as Ameriprise.

Management Stewardship Grade [A]
CEO Ken Chenault has managed admirably through some difficult times. After recovering from the 9/11 attacks and heavy losses in non-investment-grade debt in the financial advisor segment, Chenault pursued a companywide process-improvement program that has produced cost benefits of more than $1 billion annually since 2001. Top brass compensation has been commensurate with the company's strong recent performance, but total pay levels do not make us queasy. Amex is a shareholder-friendly firm and has an explicit goal of returning 65% of its free cash flows to shareholders through dividends and share repurchases, and it has lived up to this promise over the past several years. To this end, the firm increased its dividend by 25% in May 2006 and simultaneously announced a share repurchase program of up to 200 million shares, or about 16% of its total shares outstanding. We also admire management for maintaining a good balance between managing for immediate results and investing in the future. For example, instead of using its re-engineering cost benefits to boost short-term earnings, it has invested heavily in marketing, promotions, and other business-building expenses, which we believe will benefit the firm for years to come.

World Financial Center 200 Vesey Street
New York, NY 10285 www.americanexpress.com

Growth [B]	2002	2003	2004	2005
Revenue %	2.1	8.1	12.4	10.5
Earnings/Share %	105.1	14.4	16.5	10.8
Book Value/Share %	15.9	13.1	5.6	-32.7
Dividends/Share %	25.0	-5.0	-15.8	50.0

Profitability [A]	2003	2004	2005	TTM
Return on Assets %	1.7	1.8	3.3	2.9
Oper Cash Flow $Mil	2,538	9,143	8,045	—
- Cap Spending $Mil	888	616	608	—
= Free Cash Flow $Mil	—	—	—	—

Financial Health [NA]	2003	2004	2005	09-30-06
Long-term Debt $Mil	—	—	—	—
Total Equity $Mil	15,323	16,020	10,549	10,756
Debt/Equity Ratio	—	—	—	—

Industry	Business Risk	Moat Size	Investment Style	Sector
Finance	Below Avg	Wide	Large Growth	Financial Services

Competition	Market Cap $Mil	12 Mo Trailing Sales $Mil	Price/Cash Flow	Return On Assets%	Debt/ Equity	Total Return% 1 Yr	3 Yr
American Express	73,094	26,507	—	2.9	—	19.1	14.2
Citigroup	273,691	86,566	—	1.3	—	19.6	8.4
Bank of America	239,758	68,368	—	1.3	—	20.7	15.2

Price Volatility | Monthly Price High/Low — Relative Strength to S&P 500

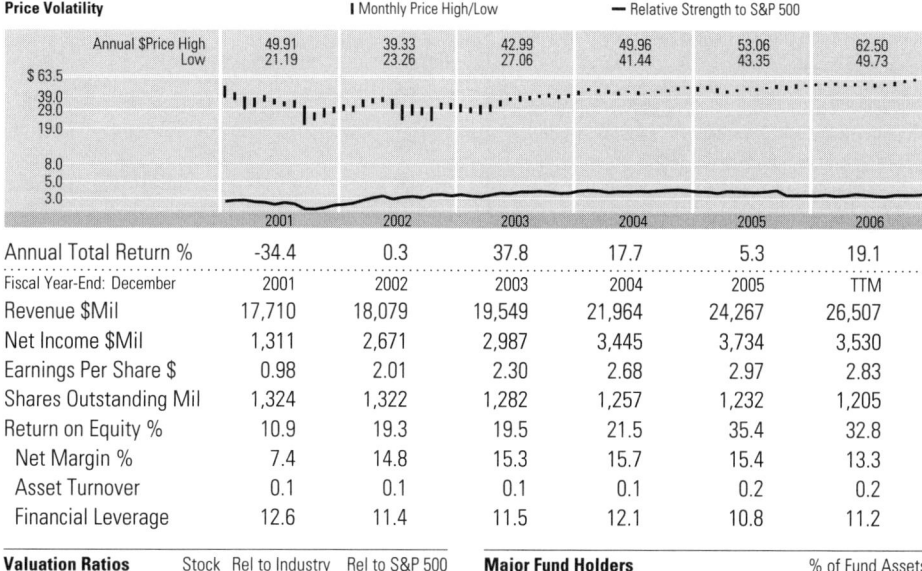

Annual $Price High/Low	49.91/21.19	39.33/23.26	42.99/27.06	49.96/41.44	53.06/43.35	62.50/49.73
	2001	2002	2003	2004	2005	2006
Annual Total Return %	-34.4	0.3	37.8	17.7	5.3	19.1

Fiscal Year-End: December	2001	2002	2003	2004	2005	TTM
Revenue $Mil	17,710	18,079	19,549	21,964	24,267	26,507
Net Income $Mil	1,311	2,671	2,987	3,445	3,734	3,530
Earnings Per Share $	0.98	2.01	2.30	2.68	2.97	2.83
Shares Outstanding Mil	1,324	1,322	1,282	1,257	1,232	1,205
Return on Equity %	10.9	19.3	19.5	21.5	35.4	32.8
Net Margin %	7.4	14.8	15.3	15.7	15.4	13.3
Asset Turnover	0.1	0.1	0.1	0.1	0.2	0.2
Financial Leverage	12.6	11.4	11.5	12.1	10.8	11.2

Valuation Ratios	Stock	Rel to Industry	Rel to S&P 500
Price/Earnings	21.2	1.1	1.0
Price/Book	6.8	1.6	1.7
Price/Sales	2.8	0.5	1.0
Price/Cash Flow	—	—	—

Major Fund Holders	% of Fund Assets
Davis Financial A	11.87
JHT Financial Services Trust Ser I	10.50
Clipper	8.52
Wisdom Inv	7.50

Thesis By Ryan Batchelor, CPA, 12-15-06 Stock Price as of Analysis: $61.64

American Express has a fantastic business model and is poised for continued success. We think the firm's late 2005 spin-off of its advisory unit, Ameriprise Financial, has allowed Amex's flagship card-related business to really shine in 2006, and we expect a very bright future.

Amex's core business model is based on the fact that Amex cardholders spend more than an average customer, which allows the firm to charge a high per-transaction fee to merchants. For example, in 2005, the average cardholder spent about $10,400 with Amex cards, and through the first nine months of 2006, spending has been about 7% higher than 2005. This amount is several times larger than the average annual spending of a typical Visa or MasterCard customer. These dynamics allow Amex to charge merchants a discount fee that averaged 2.57% of every purchase in the third quarter of 2006, which is much higher than the average fee charged by Visa and MasterCard. Because high spending is so critical to the firm, Amex's CEO, Ken Chenault, has a laser focus on ensuring that the firm does all it can to entice cardmembers to use their cards even more.

In addition to higher customer spending, Amex has another key competitive advantage. Unlike its card-issuing rivals, Amex uses its own network to process transactions made with its cards. This "closed loop" allows Amex access to both the cardholder and the merchant side of any transaction. Through this closed loop, Amex retains the entire value chain in a card purchase: It issues the card and maintains the customer relationship; it keeps the entire discount fee; it owns the associated credit card receivable and earns interest income from it; and it also has access to detailed spending data, which allows it to target its products to specific types of consumers and merchants.

Amex has also recently begun partnering with other card companies to issue cobranded American Express cards, which are processed on the Amex network. Early results from its first few partnerships have been promising, and although it's a miniscule part of Amex's current business, we believe these arrangements will provide earnings growth with little invested capital--a dream scenario, in our view.

Reward programs have also helped boost spending and increase credit quality. The company typically sees a 25%-30% increase in consumer spending after reward program enrollment. In addition, attrition is 75% lower and credit performance is better because customers won't risk losing their rewards by not paying Amex.

Data as of 12-29-06

American International Group AIG

	Rating	Fair Value	Last Close	Consider Buy	Consider Sell	Yield %
	★★★	$80.00	$71.66	$61.70	$100.20	0.88

Industry	Business Risk	Moat Size	Investment Style	Sector
Insurance (Property)	Average	Narrow	Large Value	Financial Services

Company Profile
American International Group is a diversified financial-services firm that offers property-casualty insurance, life insurance, asset management, retirement income, private banking, aircraft leasing, mortgages, credit cards, and derivative products to a global client base of individuals and institutions. Insurance makes up more than 60% of AIG's sales. The majority of AIG's life insurance sales originate in Asia, where the firm has important operations in China and Japan.

Management   Stewardship Grade [B]
AIG's internal control weaknesses and financial reporting restatements result in a B Stewardship Grade. When the firm remedies the control weaknesses we will review our stewardship grade, probably raising it to an A. AIG's managers are focused on widening the firm's moat, which isn't surprising, considering directors' and officers' $316 million stake in AIG stock. The managers' annual compensation will roughly track the performance of the firm, in our view. AIG's managers are compensated based on two-year cumulative earnings per share and book value per share increases measured over a three-year period. Measuring performance over periods greater than one year makes sense, but we'd like to see return on capital targets. On the whole, we think AIG's managers are working to make money with, not from, shareholders.

Competition

	Market Cap $Mil	12 Mo Trailing Sales $Mil	Price/Cash Flow	Return On Assets%	Debt/Equity	Total Return% 1 Yr	Total Return% 3 Yr
American International Group	186,296	110,593	—	1.2	—	6.1	3.2
ING Groep NV ADR	97,390	89,085	—	0.7	—	31.7	29.3
China Life Insurance Comp	90,126	11,966	—	1.6	—	283.2	57.6

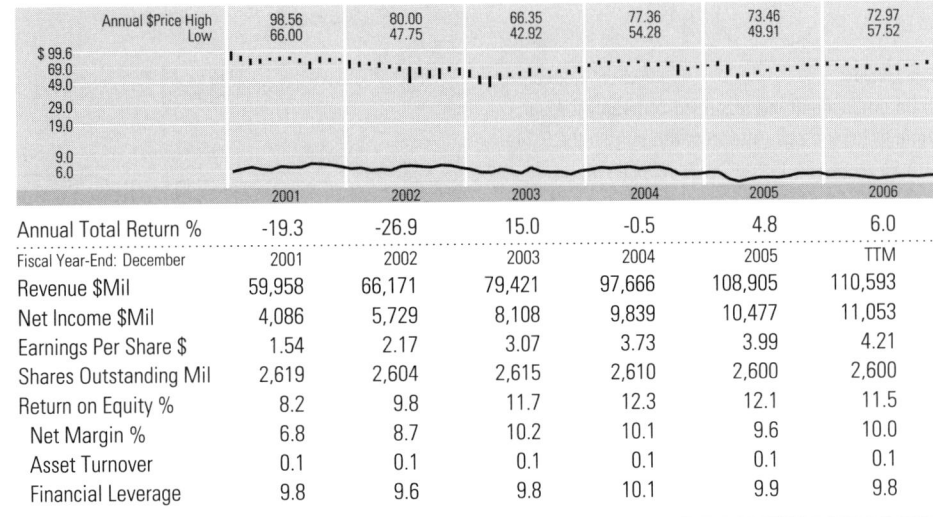

	2001	2002	2003	2004	2005	TTM
Annual Total Return %	-19.3	-26.9	15.0	-0.5	4.8	6.0
Fiscal Year-End: December	2001	2002	2003	2004	2005	TTM
Revenue $Mil	59,958	66,171	79,421	97,666	108,905	110,593
Net Income $Mil	4,086	5,729	8,108	9,839	10,477	11,053
Earnings Per Share $	1.54	2.17	3.07	3.73	3.99	4.21
Shares Outstanding Mil	2,619	2,604	2,615	2,610	2,600	2,600
Return on Equity %	8.2	9.8	11.7	12.3	12.1	11.5
Net Margin %	6.8	8.7	10.2	10.1	9.6	10.0
Asset Turnover	0.1	0.1	0.1	0.1	0.1	0.1
Financial Leverage	9.8	9.6	9.8	10.1	9.9	9.8

Valuation Ratios	Stock	Rel to Industry	Rel to S&P 500
Price/Earnings	17.1	1.2	0.8
Price/Book	1.9	1.1	0.5
Price/Sales	1.7	1.2	0.6
Price/Cash Flow	—	—	—

Major Fund Holders	% of Fund Assets
Allianz RCM Financial Services Instl	9.57
Clipper	9.17
Fidelity Select Financial Services	9.00
Fidelity Select Insurance	8.58

Thesis By Matt Nellans, 11-21-06 Stock Price as of Analysis: $71.84

American International Group's share price has increased about 80-fold since 1971, and we think it is likely to sustain its record as one of the market's great wealth-compounding machines. The insurance conglomerate's narrow moat, rapidly growing marketplace, and freedom from obsolescence risk endow some competitive insulation and abundant opportunity to grow. We think AIG shares are worth $80 apiece.

AIG's multifaceted moat originates in a series of long-ago decisions that established a powerful distribution foundation and the sustained execution that built one of the insurance world's strongest balance sheets. A long history in many global markets endows AIG with valuable relationships that yield an edge in winning--and keeping--insurance licenses, as well as a familiar brand name in some often-unfamiliar markets. And as AIG's brand becomes a useful selling point for one type of insurance, its renowned innovation gradually adds new products. The resultant geographic and product distribution reinforces AIG's balance sheet by insulating it from shocks, which in turn helps its investment portfolio continue compounding, creating a virtuous cycle of sustainable strength and wealth generation.

An often underappreciated attribute AIG's products enjoy is low obsolescence risk. The risk of loss is an ever-present phenomenon, as is the desire of businesses and consumers to mitigate it--even at the price of an insurance policy. So unlike the manufacturers of buggy whips and black-and-white televisions, AIG needs almost never fear newer technologies. This is why many insurance firms are centuries old. What's more, as people get richer, they have more money to purchase insurance and other savings products, and they buy more insurance as the consequences of the risks they bear expand.

Here's where AIG's moat can really juice its prospects. The large emerging-market distribution networks that AIG's ancestors established can power decades of growth. These markets account for about 10% of global premiums--but they have much larger populations. Better still, insurance accounted for around 1%-2% of GDP in these nations, compared with 4%-8% in developed markets. And because emerging-market GDP is only around 10% of the developed markets, AIG is positioned to "double-dip" on growth as its products gain an increasing share of an expanding market.

---

70 Pine Street
New York, NY 10270
www.aig.com

Growth [B+]	2002	2003	2004	2005
Revenue %	10.4	20.0	23.0	11.5
Earnings/Share %	40.9	41.5	21.5	7.0
Book Value/Share %	17.5	10.7	15.2	8.8
Dividends/Share %	12.7	25.8	25.0	96.4

Profitability [B-]	2003	2004	2005	TTM
Return on Assets %	1.2	1.2	1.2	1.2
Oper Cash Flow $Mil	33,241	30,716	25,138	—
- Cap Spending $Mil	6,591	5,810	8,211	—
= Free Cash Flow $Mil	—	—	—	—

Financial Health [NA]	2003	2004	2005	09-30-06
Long-term Debt $Mil	—	—	—	—
Total Equity $Mil	69,230	79,673	86,317	96,154
Debt/Equity Ratio	—	—	—	—

American Power Conversion APCC

Data as of 12-29-06

	Rating	Fair Value	Last Close	Consider Buy	Consider Sell	Yield %
	★★★	$31.00	$30.59	$23.90	$38.80	1.31

Company Profile
American Power Conversion manufactures power-conditioning devices used to protect microprocessor-based hardware such as computers, servers, data-storage and telecom gear, and electronic entertainment devices. Products include surge protectors, uninterruptible power supplies, racking systems, precision air conditioners, and infrastructure consulting services. The company operates in three business segments: small systems, large systems, and other.

Management   Stewardship Grade [B]
Former MIT scientists Emanuel Landsman, Neil Rasmussen, and Ervin Lyon founded APC in 1981. The last two remain on the seven-member board, while Landsman is a director emeritus. Longtime chairman and CEO Rodger Dowdell stepped down in 2006. While the board conducts a formal search for a replacement, another longtime manager, Rob Johnson, will be the interim CEO. Recent turnover in other top management slots doesn't thrill us. Don Muir, CFO since 1995, resigned in May 2005 and was replaced by Richard Thompson, most recently of Artesyn Technologies. Tom Goldman, who arrived with the acquisition of NetBotz in late 2005 and was inserted as the head of global sales, recently left the company. APC is one of the few companies that does not provide guidance on short-term financial results. Annual incentive compensation is based on sales growth and customer satisfaction. For long-term incentives, restricted-stock units have been used since 2004. Dowdell hadn't received options or restricted stock since 2000.

132 Fairgrounds Road   www.apc.com
West Kingston, RI 02892

Growth [B]	2002	2003	2004	2005
Revenue %	-7.5	12.7	16.0	16.5
Earnings/Share %	-27.6	109.5	2.3	-20.0
Book Value/Share %	7.5	11.8	-0.8	10.0
Dividends/Share %	NMF	NMF	125.0	11.1

Profitability [A]	2003	2004	2005	TTM
Return on Assets %	9.8	9.8	6.9	5.1
Oper Cash Flow $Mil	120	141	159	36
- Cap Spending $Mil	22	29	49	84
= Free Cash Flow $Mil	98	112	109	-49

Financial Health [A+]	2003	2004	2005	09-30-06
Long-term Debt $Mil	—	—	—	—
Total Equity $Mil	1,511	1,502	1,640	1,550
Debt/Equity Ratio	—	—	—	—

Industry	Business Risk	Moat Size	Investment Style	Sector
Electric Equip.	Average	Narrow	Mid Growth	Industrial Materials

Competition	Market Cap $Mil	12 Mo Trailing Sales $Mil	Price/Cash Flow	Return On Assets%	Debt/Equity	Total Return% 1 Yr	3 Yr
American Power Conversion	5,810	2,239	EUB	5.1	—	41.8	9.9
Emerson Electric	35,376	20,133	14.1	9.9	0.4	20.7	13.5
Eaton	11,196	12,181	7.8	8.2	0.4	14.4	14.3

Price Volatility | Monthly Price High/Low   — Relative Strength to S&P 500

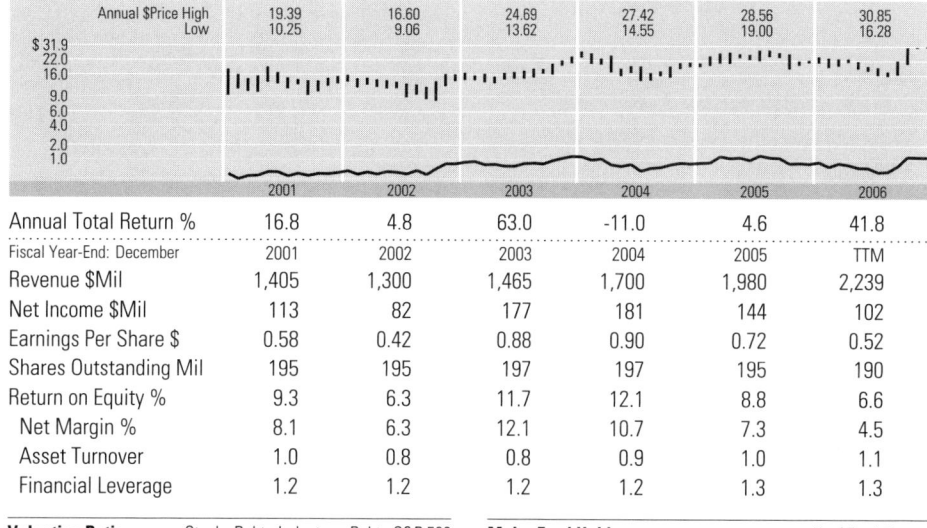

	2001	2002	2003	2004	2005	2006
Annual Total Return %	16.8	4.8	63.0	-11.0	4.6	41.8
Fiscal Year-End: December	2001	2002	2003	2004	2005	TTM
Revenue $Mil	1,405	1,300	1,465	1,700	1,980	2,239
Net Income $Mil	113	82	177	181	144	102
Earnings Per Share $	0.58	0.42	0.88	0.90	0.72	0.52
Shares Outstanding Mil	195	195	197	197	195	190
Return on Equity %	9.3	6.3	11.7	12.1	8.8	6.6
Net Margin %	8.1	6.3	12.1	10.7	7.3	4.5
Asset Turnover	1.0	0.8	0.8	0.9	1.0	1.1
Financial Leverage	1.2	1.2	1.2	1.2	1.3	1.3

Valuation Ratios	Stock	Rel to Industry	Rel to S&P 500
Price/Earnings	58.8	2.7	2.9
Price/Book	3.8	1.1	0.9
Price/Sales	2.6	1.1	0.9
Price/Cash Flow	EUB	—	—

Major Fund Holders	% of Fund Assets
Wells Fargo Advantage C&B Mid Cap Val D	4.98
Wells Fargo Advantage Growth and Inc Inv	3.97
MassMutual Select Mid-Cap Value S	3.94
Wells Fargo Advantage Large Co Core A	3.69

Thesis By Tom D'Amore, CFA, 10-30-06 Stock Price as of Analysis: $30.02

American Power Conversion boasts a highly respected brand-name franchise serving the attractive and fast-growing network power market. However, profit margins have been slipping over the past several years because of the costs of the company's aggressive campaign to rapidly expand its large-systems business. With a new CEO at the helm, we expect APC to downshift from a maximum-growth strategy to one of more moderate growth and to restore operating profitability to double-digit levels.

APC enjoys a dominant market position supplying power-management products to small and midsize companies. The small-systems business has been growing at a double-digit rate for the past three years, the result of customers' high spending for mission-critical IT applications. APC boasts the broadest product line in the marketplace and has established efficient low-cost manufacturing facilities for most of its products, giving it a crucial edge against competitors. However, rapidly rising raw-material prices and supply-chain restructuring have taken a bite out of its historically high margins.

APC also sells larger power-management and cooling systems to bigger customers operating complex data centers. The business operates under a different channel to market that involves more direct customer contact and a more extended decision process for customers. APC has made excellent headway in the market with its innovative InfraStruXure (ISX) design, which offers scalable expansion capabilities and compelling life cycle cost advantages to customers. Large-systems sales have responded to APC's significant investments to build the business, growing a whopping 33% in 2005.

The large-systems segment has struggled in terms of profitability, however. We estimate it has negative operating margins of about 10%. Combined with slipping profits at small systems, APC's overall operating margin declined to just 3.9% in the first half of 2006, compared with 12% in 2004. In September, Rodger Dowdell, the CEO who championed the maximum-growth strategy, stepped down under pressure from the board. We expect his interim successor, Rob Johnson, to concentrate on more moderate growth goals while stepping up the focus on increasing profit margins.

We think APC is on the right track with its new strategy. We expect the company to throttle back on aggressive sales and marketing practices and cut costs where possible. We think profit margins will recover to about 12% by 2010. We expect returns on capital to follow suit, increasing from a projected

Data as of 12-29-06

AmeriCredit ACF

Rating ★★★	Fair Value $29.00	Last Close $25.17	Consider Buy $18.50	Consider Sell $35.00	Yield % 0.00

Industry	Business Risk	Moat Size	Investment Style	Sector
Finance	Above Avg	Narrow	Mid Value	Financial Services

Company Profile
AmeriCredit is a specialty-finance company focusing on auto financing for subprime individuals. It is an indirect lender, receiving referrals from thousands of auto dealers, almost all of which are franchised dealerships of big-name auto manufacturers. About two thirds of the firm's originations are used to finance used vehicles. The firm reports its results using a fiscal year calendar that begins on July 1.

Management
Stewardship Grade [B]

We think that AmeriCredit has a very capable management team. The team made some critical changes that saved AmeriCredit from bankruptcy, such as reducing origination volume, cutting operating expenses to match volume, and regaining access to the secondary market for securitization. We were impressed with management's candor throughout the difficult times, and we think CEO Daniel Berce has proved his mettle, which should serve shareholders well in the future. As the firm has been recovering, we've been particularly impressed with management's shareholder-friendliness. The company began expensing options in 2003, and it has repurchased about $1.25 billion in stock from April 2004 to October 2006, with authorizations to repurchase substantial additional amounts. Because of share repurchases, earnings per share have been growing much faster than net income, and existing shareholders essentially own proportionally more of the firm without doing anything, which are both positive developments. Although we're fond of management, the company remains largely dependent on the economy and other factors beyond its control. So we reiterate our above-average risk rating for the firm.

801 Cherry Street Suite 3900
Fort Worth, TX 76102
www.americredit.com

Growth [NA]	2003	2004	2005	2006
Revenue %	—	—	—	—
Earnings/Share %	-95.7	813.3	26.3	20.2
Book Value/Share %	-16.3	-3.6	0.1	6.3
Dividends/Share %	NMF	NMF	NMF	NMF

Profitability [A]	2004	2005	2006	TTM
Return on Assets %	2.6	2.6	2.3	2.2
Oper Cash Flow $Mil	505	614	961	—
- Cap Spending $Mil	5	8	6	—
= Free Cash Flow $Mil	—	—	—	—

Financial Health [NA]	2004	2005	2006	09-30-06
Long-term Debt $Mil	—	—	—	—
Total Equity $Mil	2,125	2,122	2,009	1,723
Debt/Equity Ratio	—	—	—	—

Competition	Market Cap $Mil	12 Mo Trailing Sales $Mil	Price/Cash Flow	Return On Assets %	Debt/Equity	Total Return % 1 Yr	3 Yr
AmeriCredit	2,907	NMF	—	2.2	—	-1.8	16.6
Wells Fargo	120,049	34,770	—	1.7	—	16.8	10.4
Capital One Financial	23,411	11,731	—	2.4	—	-11.0	8.6

Price Volatility | Monthly Price High/Low — Relative Strength to S&P 500

	2001	2002	2003	2004	2005	2006
Annual $Price High	64.90	46.93	15.98	24.98	27.59	31.70
Low	14.00	5.92	1.55	15.68	21.31	21.68
Annual Total Return %	15.8	-75.5	105.8	53.5	4.8	-1.8

Fiscal Year-End: June	2002	2003	2004	2005	2006	TTM
Revenue $Mil	NMF	NMF	NMF	NMF	NMF	NMF
Net Income $Mil	315	21	227	286	306	326
Earnings Per Share $	3.50	0.15	1.37	1.73	2.08	2.27
Shares Outstanding Mil	85	141	157	152	134	116
Return on Equity %	22.0	1.1	10.7	13.5	15.2	18.9
Net Margin %	NMF	NMF	NMF	NMF	NMF	NMF
Asset Turnover	—	—	—	—	—	—
Financial Leverage	3.0	4.3	4.2	5.2	6.5	8.6

Valuation Ratios	Stock	Rel to Industry	Rel to S&P 500
Price/Earnings	11.1	0.6	0.5
Price/Book	1.7	0.4	0.4
Price/Sales	—	—	—
Price/Cash Flow	—	—	—

Major Fund Holders	% of Fund Assets
Yacktman Focused	5.07
Yacktman	3.73
Wasatch Core Growth	3.38
Nuveen NWQ Multi-Cap Value R	3.15

Thesis By Ryan Batchelor, CPA, 11-21-06 Stock Price as of Analysis: $25.44

We think AmeriCredit has good long-term prospects, and management has learned valuable lessons from overcoming a very large crisis. However, we think the firm's fate depends on the strength of the economy, so we believe things may get a little tougher for the company than they've been recently.

AmeriCredit purchases loans made by auto dealerships for primarily subprime borrowers (individuals with poor credit histories) who meet the firm's criteria. We think its relationships with auto dealers provide AmeriCredit with a competitive advantage. The company maintains a network of regional offices that market AmeriCredit's services to new dealers and nurture existing relationships. The branch offices are also responsible for the underwriting and purchasing of individual loans, using the firm's proprietary credit scoring system. Because of its experience and technology, AmeriCredit can typically make quick decisions and provide swift funding to auto dealers, which makes the firm a valuable partner, in our opinion. This, combined with the fact that the firm provides financing for a vital consumer good in a massive market, makes us believers in AmeriCredit's future.

The firm's performance at the beginning of this century illustrates some of the potential risks. From 1998 through 2001, AmeriCredit's business--and stock price--soared. But as the economy hiccuped in 2001, defaults began to rise. In addition, the auto-resale market experienced a severe decline. Because AmeriCredit is a secured lender, it expects to offset a portion of loan losses with cash proceeds from the vehicles it repossesses and sells. But as used-auto values plunged, credit losses spiked, a liquidity crisis ensued, and AmeriCredit's stock lost 97% of its value by March 2003.

AmeriCredit has come back strongly, thanks to an improved economy and a more seasoned (and humbled) management team. Management righted the ship by downsizing its workforce, reducing originations, consolidating its operations, and--perhaps most important--raising capital through a stock offering. It also improved the transparency of the firm by discontinuing off-balance-sheet financing. Only recently--after the firm's performance has significantly stabilized--has management begun to increase the size of the portfolio. Additionally, management plans to curb its asset growth and quickly cut expenses if industry conditions do not look favorable. We approve of this strategy, given that the firm is subject to the ebbs and flows of the economy and other conditions that management can't control.

Stocks 500

AmeriGas Partners APU

Data as of 12-29-06

Rating	Fair Value	Last Close	Consider Buy	Consider Sell	Yield %
★★★	$36.00	$32.53	$27.80	$45.10	7.07

Industry	Business Risk	Moat Size	Investment Style	Sector
Oil/Gas Products	Average	Narrow	Small Value	Energy

Company Profile

AmeriGas Partners is the largest retail propane marketer in the United States. The company sells about 1 billion gallons of propane annually to 1.3 million customers from 650 locations in 46 states. AmeriGas also sells, installs, and services propane appliances, including heating systems. The general partner is AmeriGas Inc., which is a wholly owned subsidiary of UGI.

Competition

	Market Cap $Mil	12 Mo Trailing Sales $Mil	Price/Cash Flow	Return On Assets%	Debt/Equity	Total Return% 1 Yr	Total Return% 3 Yr
AmeriGas Partners	1,848	2,119	10.4	5.6	4.3	24.0	13.3
Energy Transfer Partners	5,999	7,859	11.0	7.3	1.6	65.5	47.7
Ferrellgas Partners LP	1,344	1,886	14.1	1.3	3.3	13.4	5.1

Price Volatility

Annual $Price High/Low	25.35 / 16.63	24.70 / 17.15	28.37 / 22.50	30.56 / 25.09	35.00 / 27.10	33.10 / 28.22
	2001	2002	2003	2004	2005	2006
Annual Total Return %	48.5	17.4	28.0	14.1	2.7	24.0

Fiscal Year-End: September	2002	2003	2004	2005	2006	TTM
Revenue $Mil	1,308	1,628	1,776	1,963	2,119	2,119
Net Income $Mil	55	71	91	60	90	90
Earnings Per Share $	1.12	1.42	1.71	1.10	1.59	1.59
Shares Outstanding Mil	49	50	53	55	57	57
Return on Equity %	24.0	28.1	31.8	18.0	41.2	41.2
Net Margin %	4.2	4.4	5.1	3.1	4.3	4.3
Asset Turnover	0.9	1.1	1.1	1.2	1.3	1.3
Financial Leverage	6.5	5.9	5.4	5.0	7.4	7.4

Valuation Ratios	Stock	Rel to Industry	Rel to S&P 500
Price/Earnings	20.5	1.4	1.0
Price/Book	8.4	3.0	2.0
Price/Sales	0.9	0.5	0.3
Price/Cash Flow	10.4	1.3	0.7

Major Fund Holders	% of Fund Assets

Management — Stewardship Grade [C]

AmeriGas' general partner (responsible for managing the limited partnership) is owned by utility company UGI. UGI also owns 44% of the limited partner. Eugene Bissell has been CEO of the general partner since July 2000. Before becoming CEO, Bissell served as senior vice president of sales and marketing, as well as vice president of sales and operations. In fiscal 2006, Bissell received a salary of $409,625, a bonus of $188,805, and other compensation of $62,074. Chairman Lon Greenberg took home $920,000 in salary and a $997,234 bonus; his compensation is tied to his position as chairman, president, and CEO of UGI. We believe compensation is generous, but reasonable. We are slightly more concerned that management is compensated with UGI rather than AmeriGas stock. Further, because of its structure as a master limited partnership and UGI's stake, unitholders will not have much influence in the future of the company. But, overall, AmeriGas' stewardship to shareholders is similar to that of the other master limited partnerships in our coverage universe. The firm could boost its Stewardship Grade by providing a balance sheet or cash-flow statement with its quarterly press releases, which would improve the transparency of financial reporting.

460 North Gulph Road
King of Prussia, PA 19406
www.amerigas.com

Growth [D]	2003	2004	2005	2006
Revenue %	24.5	9.1	10.6	7.9
Earnings/Share %	26.8	20.4	-35.7	44.5
Book Value/Share %	8.4	6.4	13.5	-36.8
Dividends/Share %	0.0	0.0	0.9	2.7

Profitability [B-]	2004	2005	2006	TTM
Return on Assets %	5.9	3.6	5.6	5.6
Oper Cash Flow $Mil	178	184	178	178
- Cap Spending $Mil	62	63	71	71
= Free Cash Flow $Mil	116	122	107	107

Financial Health [C+]	2004	2005	2006	09-30-06
Long-term Debt $Mil	841	795	932	932
Total Equity $Mil	286	334	219	219
Debt/Equity Ratio	2.9	2.4	4.3	4.3

Thesis By Michael Tian, 12-13-06 Stock Price as of Analysis: $33.03

AmeriGas has a lucrative business with high customer switching costs, and its units would yield 6.4% in distributions at our fair value estimate. We're big fans of AmeriGas' propane business, and we think management's target of 3% annual distribution increases makes the firm's units attractive for income-oriented investors.

Most propane users don't own the tanks on their properties; instead, they lease tanks from propane providers. Switching providers is a pain because the customer must arrange for the new company to swap tanks with the existing provider. Only a sizable price difference would motivate AmeriGas' clients to switch. Customers are also unlikely to switch fuels. Electricity is generally more expensive than propane for heating. Fuel oil is comparable, but appliances are built for one or the other, so switching would mean expensive new appliances. As a result, propane providers generally earn attractive returns on invested capital, and AmeriGas is no exception.

While AmeriGas' customers aren't likely to defect, they are sensitive to prices and weather. They'll turn down their thermostats in response to high propane prices. And with colossal heating bills, more customers may be unable to make payments. Further, warm weather means less need for fuel. When these events occur, AmeriGas' sales volume and profits suffer. But even then, AmeriGas's economic moat aids in preserving margins.

Propane is a mature industry with minimal internal growth opportunities. AmeriGas rose to the top by scooping up smaller distributors. Many of these mom-and-pop shops are cashing in before retirement; others are finding it difficult to stay afloat because of escalating insurance costs. Serial acquisitors usually make us nervous, but we think AmeriGas can generate value in acquiring these smaller players by eliminating duplicate costs. As the industry continues to consolidate, we think competition among large distributors to acquire small ones might drive average prices upward.

Besides distributing propane to customers' homes, AmeriGas sells and exchanges prefilled portable propane tanks. We don't like the economics of this business as much as traditional propane distribution. First, there are no customer switching costs. And the big-box retailers--Wal-Mart and Home Depot, where AmeriGas sells its prefilled tanks--have incredible bargaining power and are sure to extract the value from this relationship. Still, this business offers more growth opportunities than home heating.

Ameriprise Financial AMP

Data as of 12-29-06

Rating	Fair Value	Last Close	Consider Buy	Consider Sell	Yield %
★★★	$51.00	$54.50	$39.30	$63.90	0.81

Industry	Business Risk	Moat Size	Investment Style	Sector
Finance	Average	None	Large Core	Financial Services

Company Profile
Ameriprise Financial was spun off from American Express in September 2005. The firm has one of the largest branded advisor networks in the country, with about 10,500 branded advisors and 1,700 independent agents. Ameriprise offers financial planning, brokerage, banking, and retirement products along with life and disability insurance. The firm also offers auto and home insurance to consumers on a direct basis. Ameriprise has about 11,900 employees.

Management
Stewardship Grade [C]

James Cracchiolo, 47, has been chairman and CEO of Ameriprise Financial since its separation from American Express in September 2005. He has held various executive positions, including chairman and CEO of American Express Financial Corporation since 2001. Cracchiolo received $15 million in total compensation for 2005, which we think is excessive, given Ameriprise's mediocre operating performance during that period. Cracchiolo owns about $10 million in company stock, which doesn't appear to be as important as his cash compensation. However, we expect his ownership to increase in the future, which will further align his interests with shareholders. Board members receive $150,000 in compensation, which is higher than at the firm's peers and could compromise objectivity.

707 2nd Avenue South
Minneapolis, MN 55474
www.ameriprise.com

Growth [B-]	2002	2003	2004	2005
Revenue %	17.5	10.4	14.2	6.5
Earnings/Share %	NMF	NMF	NMF	NMF
Book Value/Share %	—	—	—	—
Dividends/Share %	NMF	NMF	NMF	NMF

Profitability [D]	2003	2004	2005	TTM
Return on Assets %	0.8	0.9	0.6	0.6
Oper Cash Flow $Mil	-370	683	945	—
- Cap Spending $Mil	133	125	141	—
= Free Cash Flow $Mil	—	—	—	—

Financial Health [NA]	2003	2004	2005	09-30-06
Long-term Debt $Mil	—	—	—	—
Total Equity $Mil	7,288	6,702	7,687	7,753
Debt/Equity Ratio	—	—	—	—

Competition

	Market Cap $Mil	12 Mo Trailing Sales $Mil	Price/Cash Flow	Return On Assets%	Debt/ Equity	Total Return% 1 Yr	3 Yr
Ameriprise Financial	13,187	7,848	—	0.6	—	34.2	—
Wachovia	90,049	27,749	—	1.3	—	12.0	11.3
Morgan Stanley	86,198	32,195	—	0.8	—	45.9	14.8

Price Volatility
Monthly Price High/Low — Relative Strength to S&P 500

Annual $Price High/Low: 2005: 44.78/32.00; 2006: 55.79/40.30

	2001	2002	2003	2004	2005	TTM
Annual Total Return %	—	—	—	—	—	34.2
Revenue $Mil	4,744	5,575	6,155	7,027	7,484	7,848
Net Income $Mil	87	674	725	794	574	571
Earnings Per Share $	—	—	—	—	—	—
Shares Outstanding Mil	—	—	—	—	—	242
Return on Equity %	1.5	10.5	9.9	11.8	7.5	7.4
Net Margin %	1.8	12.1	11.8	11.3	7.7	7.3
Asset Turnover	0.1	0.1	0.1	0.1	0.1	0.1
Financial Leverage	12.8	11.5	11.7	13.9	12.1	12.8

Fiscal Year-End: December

Valuation Ratios	Stock	Rel to Industry	Rel to S&P 500
Price/Earnings	—	—	—
Price/Book	1.7	0.4	0.4
Price/Sales	1.7	0.3	0.6
Price/Cash Flow	—	—	—

Major Fund Holders	% of Fund Assets
Clipper	4.70
FBR Large Cap Financial	3.83
SunAmerica Focused Mid-Cap Growth A	3.64
Morgan Stanley Financial Services B	3.41

Thesis By Dafina Dunmore, 11-21-06 Stock Price as of Analysis: $53.92

Despite its expansive distribution force, we think large amounts of regulatory capital, negative fund flows and fierce competition make it difficult for Ameriprise Financial to generate above-average returns. Our fair value estimate is $51 per share.

The retail brokerage industry has inherent competitive advantages, thanks to the strong relationships developed between advisors and clients. Clients tend to be more loyal to their advisor, with whom they have a relationship, than to the firm itself. Therefore, advisors retain most of the competitive advantage via attractive compensation packages. Brokerage powerhouses like Merrill Lynch and independent advisory unit National Financial Partners poach successful advisors as a method of increasing client assets. Ameriprise has historically used a homegrown approach to expand its advisor force, but is beginning to target experienced advisors. This, and continually purging less productive agents, should lead to increasing productivity.

Although competition is intense, we think Ameriprise offers some differentiating factors. It uses a flexible business model, which allows advisors to build equity in their practice and receive higher payouts in exchange for paying certain business expenses. These advisors stick around longer, resulting in higher client retention. This franchise model somewhat insulates Ameriprise during market downturns because advisors pay certain of their business expenses. Alternatively, it can't fully leverage asset growth in favorable markets.

We think Ameriprise's deeply rooted advice-centric financial planning culture contributes to favorable client retention. Clients who have purchased a financial plan from Ameriprise tend to stick around longer and keep 3 times more assets with the firm. Ameriprise is experiencing greater success with selling financial plans to mass affluent clients, which could spur future asset growth.

Historically poor investment performance contributed to negative flows in Ameriprise's mutual funds. Although we don't expect flows to turn positive until late 2007, the firm is beginning to show signs of improvement. Sales are gaining momentum and redemptions are slowing, thanks to better investment performance. Ameriprise is also building relationships with third-party distributors, which should augment sales growth. However, this will be offset by the cost of these new distribution initiatives and Ameriprise's industry-driven decision to sell nonproprietary funds.

Data as of 12-29-06

Amgen AMGN

	Rating	Fair Value	Last Close	Consider Buy	Consider Sell	Yield %
	★★★★★	$91.00	$68.31	$70.20	$114.00	0.00

Company Profile

Amgen develops and manufactures biotechnology-based human therapeutics. Flagship drugs include red blood cell boosters Epogen and Aranesp, immune system boosters Neupogen and Neulasta, and Enbrel for indications such as rheumatoid arthritis and psoriasis. Amgen received approval for its first cancer therapeutic, Vectibix, in September. It focuses its development efforts on cancer and bone disorders.

Management   Stewardship Grade [C]

CEO Kevin Sharer has brought in some top-level executives from outside and appointed new vice presidents in key areas. The firm's success under Sharer's reign has been unparalleled, and he's been amply rewarded for his efforts. His 2005 salary and bonus totaled nearly $6 million (in line with many high-paid pharma executives and surpassing most biotech execs), and he received 225,000 stock options. Sharer gets personal use of a car and driver, and many on the executive staff have received large retention bonuses and forgivable loans in the past. In September, Sharer replaced former Bristol-Myers Squibb CEO Peter Dolan as chairman of drug industry trade group Pharmaceutical Research and Manufacturers of America. Sharer exercised all of his 1.3 million exercisable options in 2005 and subsequently sold these shares on the open market; we believe this reduces his incentive to act in shareholders' best interests. On the other hand, we applaud Amgen's creation of a corporate venture fund and management's decision to aggressively repurchase shares. The $4.8 billion in share repurchases over the first nine months of 2006 reflects the biotech's enormous cash-generating capabilities.

One Amgen Center Drive
Thousand Oaks, CA 91320-1799
www.Amgen.com

Growth [B+]	2002	2003	2004	2005
Revenue %	37.5	51.3	26.3	17.8
Earnings/Share %	NMF	NMF	7.1	61.9
Book Value/Share %	231.2	-8.8	4.1	8.1
Dividends/Share %	NMF	NMF	NMF	NMF

Profitability [A-]	2003	2004	2005	TTM
Return on Assets %	8.7	8.1	12.5	9.0
Oper Cash Flow $Mil	3,567	3,697	4,911	5,276
- Cap Spending $Mil	1,357	1,336	867	1,099
= Free Cash Flow $Mil	2,210	2,361	4,044	4,177

Financial Health [A]	2003	2004	2005	09-30-06
Long-term Debt $Mil	3,080	3,937	3,957	7,233
Total Equity $Mil	19,389	19,705	20,451	17,721
Debt/Equity Ratio	0.2	0.2	0.2	0.4

Industry	Business Risk	Moat Size	Investment Style	Sector
Biotechnology	Average	Wide	Large Growth	Healthcare

Competition	Market Cap $Mil	12 Mo Trailing Sales $Mil	Price/Cash Flow	Return On Assets%	Debt/Equity	Total Return% 1 Yr	3 Yr
Amgen	79,685	13,704	15.1	9.0	0.4	-13.4	3.1
Johnson & Johnson	191,415	52,252	14.5	18.5	0.0	12.4	10.8
Merck	94,656	22,358	13.0	11.6	0.2	42.7	1.7

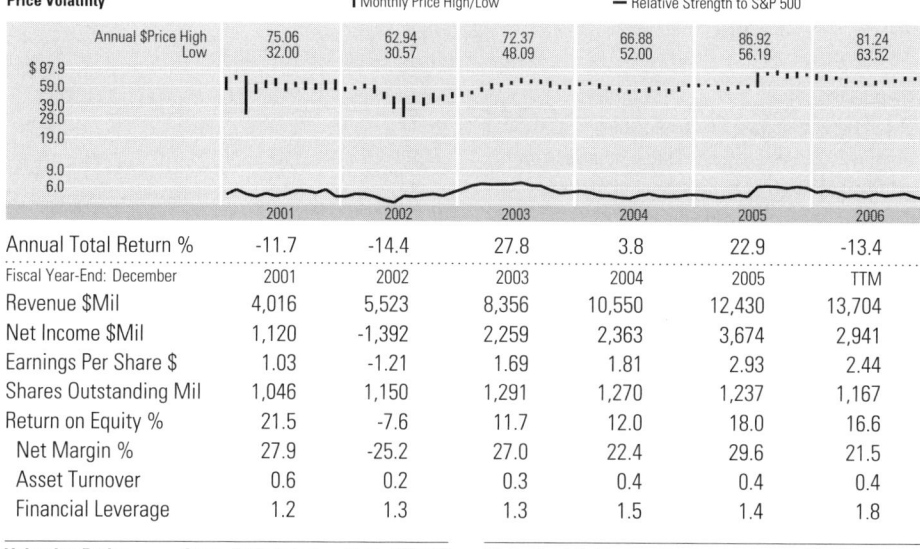

	2001	2002	2003	2004	2005	2006
Annual Total Return %	-11.7	-14.4	27.8	3.8	22.9	-13.4
Fiscal Year-End: December	2001	2002	2003	2004	2005	TTM
Revenue $Mil	4,016	5,523	8,356	10,550	12,430	13,704
Net Income $Mil	1,120	-1,392	2,259	2,363	3,674	2,941
Earnings Per Share $	1.03	-1.21	1.69	1.81	2.93	2.44
Shares Outstanding Mil	1,046	1,150	1,291	1,270	1,237	1,167
Return on Equity %	21.5	-7.6	11.7	12.0	18.0	16.6
Net Margin %	27.9	-25.2	27.0	22.4	29.6	21.5
Asset Turnover	0.6	0.2	0.3	0.4	0.4	0.4
Financial Leverage	1.2	1.3	1.3	1.5	1.4	1.8

Valuation Ratios	Stock	Rel to Industry	Rel to S&P 500
Price/Earnings	28.0	0.6	1.4
Price/Book	4.5	0.6	1.1
Price/Sales	5.8	0.5	2.0
Price/Cash Flow	15.1	0.5	1.0

Major Fund Holders	% of Fund Assets
ProFunds Biotechnology UltraSector Inv	24.24
Rydex Biotechnology Inv	9.92
Integrity Health Sciences A	9.79
Allianz RCM Biotechnology D	8.69

Thesis By Karen Andersen, 12-13-06 Stock Price as of Analysis: $69.84

An impressive lineup of blockbuster drugs places Amgen at the head of the biotech class. Despite ongoing reimbursement concerns and new competition from branded and generic biologics, we believe the firm's competitive advantages are still strong. Amgen's wide economic moat, based on its rich pipeline and solid foundation of approved drugs, helps shield the firm from long-term adversity.

A biotech industry heavyweight, Amgen has historically focused on supportive-care products for kidney disease and cancer. Sales of anemia drugs Epogen and Aranesp should surpass $6 billion in 2006, and Amgen has cornered the $4 billion market for white blood cell boosters with Neupogen and Neulasta. Amgen gained a fifth blockbuster product, arthritis and psoriasis drug Enbrel, with its 2002 acquisition of Immunex. Years of blockbuster sales have led to impressive profitability; in 2005, Amgen achieved 39% operating margins, and free cash flow amounted to 32% of sales, or almost $4 billion.

But new competition could pressure Amgen's profits. Europe recently created an approval pathway for generic biologics, and legislation is being introduced in the United States that could lead to similar changes. Roche is planning to launch branded competition to Amgen's anemia franchise if it receives Food and Drug Administration approval in February, even though Amgen's patent litigation against Roche won't go to trial until September. While these are legitimate hurdles, we think high manufacturing and clinical trial costs will limit the number of generic competitors, and we believe Roche will have a tough time displacing Amgen's entrenched drugs even with a nod from the FDA and a legal win.

A deep pipeline of strong drug candidates will be key to reducing Amgen's reliance on sales of older drugs. We applaud the firm's aggressive funding of research and development, which is set to top $3 billion in 2006. Recently approved cancer drug Vectibix and pipeline candidate denosumab, both from the $2.1 billion Abgenix acquisition, are among the most promising growth drivers. Vectibix sells at a 20% discount to Imclone's Erbitux and appears to offer equivalent efficacy with improved safety and convenience. Denosumab, in Phase III trials for osteoporosis, has demonstrated that it improves bone density better than Merck's $3.2 billion drug Fosamax.

We think Amgen's financial health and strong pipeline bode well for continued stellar returns in the long term.

Anadarko Petroleum APC

Data as of 12-29-06

Rating	Fair Value	Last Close	Consider Buy	Consider Sell	Yield %
★★★★	$55.00	$43.52	$42.40	$68.90	0.83

Industry	Business Risk	Moat Size	Investment Style	Sector
Oil/Gas	Average	Narrow	Large Value	Energy

Company Profile

Thanks to several acquisitions and aggressive internal expansion, Anadarko is one of the largest independent exploration and production companies in North America. In 2006, the firm acquired Kerr-McGee and Western Gas in separate transactions for a combined $23.3 billion. The deals solidify Anadarko's position in the deep-water Gulf of Mexico and the Rockies. Internationally, the firm's operations are primarily concentrated in Algeria.

Management
Stewardship Grade [C]

CEO Jim Hackett earned $7.7 million plus 40,000 options in 2005. We are pleased that bonuses have constituted as much as two thirds of total compensation and are tied to the company's performance. Performance metrics include finding and development costs, operating costs per barrel, production growth, corporate overhead, and safety goals. However, we dislike that Hackett received more than $350,000 in other compensation primarily for personal use of the corporate jet. We aren't big fans of the company's staggered elections for board members and the fact that the majority of director compensation is cash-based. Option grants have typically been less than 1% of shares outstanding. Directors and executives beneficially own 1.2% of outstanding shares, a respectable amount for a company of Anadarko's size. Overall, we give the firm's stewardship practices a C grade.

1201 Lake Robbins Drive
The Woodlands, TX 77380-1046
www.anadarko.com

Competition

	Market Cap $Mil	12 Mo Trailing Sales $Mil	Price/Cash Flow	Return On Assets %	Debt/Equity	Total Return % 1 Yr	Total Return % 3 Yr
Anadarko Petroleum	20,008	9,838	3.9	6.3	0.8	-7.4	20.4
Occidental Petroleum	41,070	17,548	6.4	13.9	0.2	24.3	34.9
Devon Energy	29,649	11,274	4.3	9.4	0.3	8.1	33.7

Price Volatility — Monthly Price High/Low — Relative Strength to S&P 500

Annual $Price High/Low	36.99/21.55	29.28/18.40	25.86/20.14	35.78/24.00	50.71/30.01	56.98/39.51
	2001	2002	2003	2004	2005	2006
Annual Total Return %	-19.7	-15.2	7.5	28.3	47.4	-7.4

Fiscal Year-End: December	2001	2002	2003	2004	2005	TTM
Revenue $Mil	4,718	3,833	5,113	6,079	7,100	9,838
Net Income $Mil	-188	825	1,287	1,601	2,466	3,809
Earnings Per Share $	-0.75	3.21	2.55	3.18	5.20	8.19
Shares Outstanding Mil	251	248	499	500	470	460
Return on Equity %	-3.0	11.8	15.0	17.4	22.5	27.8
Net Margin %	-4.0	21.5	25.2	26.3	34.7	38.7
Asset Turnover	0.3	0.2	0.2	0.3	0.3	0.2
Financial Leverage	2.6	2.6	2.4	2.2	2.1	4.4

Valuation Ratios

	Stock	Rel to Industry	Rel to S&P 500
Price/Earnings	5.5	0.4	0.3
Price/Book	1.5	0.5	0.4
Price/Sales	2.0	1.1	0.7
Price/Cash Flow	3.9	0.5	0.3

Major Fund Holders

	% of Fund Assets
Legg Mason Partners Aggressive Growth A	6.37
Westport R	4.33
ING Partners Legg Mason Pnrs Aggr Gr Ini	3.97
Muhlenkamp	3.46

Growth [C+]

	2002	2003	2004	2005
Revenue %	-18.8	33.4	18.9	16.8
Earnings/Share %	NMF	-20.7	25.0	63.4
Book Value/Share %	6.8	-37.3	7.4	20.4
Dividends/Share %	44.4	35.4	27.3	28.6

Profitability [B]

	2003	2004	2005	TTM
Return on Assets %	6.3	7.9	10.9	6.3
Oper Cash Flow $Mil	3,043	3,207	4,146	5,138
- Cap Spending $Mil	2,772	3,064	3,408	4,239
= Free Cash Flow $Mil	271	143	738	899

Financial Health [C]

	2003	2004	2005	09-30-06
Long-term Debt $Mil	—	3,671	3,555	11,163
Total Equity $Mil	8,599	9,196	10,962	13,726
Debt/Equity Ratio	—	0.4	0.3	0.8

Thesis
By Justin Perucki, CFA, 12-26-06 Stock Price as of Analysis: $42.70

After seeing production decline in 2002 and 2003, Anadarko sold more than 11% of its reserve base in 2004. Most of the reserves that were sold required large capital investments and generated only modest returns. The restructuring freed up capital, allowing Anadarko to develop and expand its existing properties as well as its international portfolio. This strategic shift was sorely needed; Anadarko's exploration-focused strategy and expensive legacy assets had dragged down financial performance. Helped by robust oil and gas prices, returns and cash flow improved dramatically in subsequent years, but performance still lagged management's expectations.

The firm refocused its strategy again in 2006 and purchased Kerr-McGee and Western Gas Resources in separate transactions for a combined $23.3 billion. As a result of the acquisitions, debt increased to 67% of total capital. Management hopes to reduce that figure to a more manageable 40% of total capital by the end of 2007 through asset sales and internally generated cash flow. If cash flow from operations or asset sales is lower than expected, Anadarko may have to tap the equity market to get debt levels in line.

At the end of the day, Anadarko will be roughly the same size company in terms of proved reserves as it was before the transactions, albeit with a very large set of midstream assets. The key difference between the old and new Anadarko is the fact that the firm is now significantly more leveraged to the deep-water Gulf of Mexico and Rocky Mountain regions. The firm also believes the upside potential (i.e., the amount of probable and possible reserves) is much greater. We think Anadarko is making a big bet on natural-gas prices and putting a lot of faith in its ability to convert Kerr-McGee's and Western Gas' probable reserves to proved. If it is successful at exploiting its refined reserve base and commodity prices remain high, returns should be phenomenal. But if growth is lower than expected and commodity prices fall significantly, returns will suffer.

We've awarded Anadarko (and most of its peers) a narrow economic moat rating, mainly because of OPEC. By limiting its members' production, OPEC manipulates oil prices higher. This lifts profitability in what would otherwise be a brutally competitive commodity market. Without OPEC, there would be no moat. With it, profits are handsome, albeit volatile. Anadarko also benefits from the stranded nature of natural gas, which limits imports and keeps prices high.

Data as of 12-29-06

Analog Devices ADI

Rating	Fair Value	Last Close	Consider Buy	Consider Sell	Yield %
★★★★★	$48.00	$32.87	$37.00	$60.10	1.83

Company Profile
Analog Devices makes high-performance analog, mixed-signal, and digital signal processing (DSP) integrated circuits. The firm derives more than two thirds of its revenue from converters and amplifiers and about 20% from DSP products. Its products serve the needs of 60,000 customers worldwide in applications such as cellular base stations, collision avoidance systems in automobiles, digital cameras, high-definition TVs, and multi-slice 3D CAT scanners.

Management   Stewardship Grade [B]
President and CEO Jerald Fishman, a 20-year company vet, has headed Analog Devices since succeeding founder Ray Stata in 1996. Stata still serves an integral role with the firm as chairman of the board. The company has recently reached a tentative settlement with the SEC, which concluded that Analog Devices should have disclosed that options were granted, in two cases, prior to issuance of favorable financial results and that the company priced some options in prior years on dates after the grants rather than before. We view the settlement as a positive step in alleviating investor concerns. Analog Devices' corporate governance is sound, for the most part. Board terms are staggered, however, a practice that we're not particularly fond of. Insiders own about 3% of the firm.

Industry	Business Risk	Moat Size	Investment Style	Sector
Semiconductor	Average	Narrow	Large Growth	Hardware

Competition

	Market Cap $Mil	12 Mo Trailing Sales $Mil	Price/Cash Flow	Return On Assets%	Debt/Equity	Total Return% 1 Yr	3 Yr
Analog Devices	11,242	2,573	18.1	13.8	—	-6.7	-9.4
Texas Instruments	42,736	15,173	16.1	29.3	0.0	-9.8	-0.2
Maxim Integrated Products	9,820	1,749	16.4	15.3	—	-14.1	-13.7

Price Volatility | Monthly Price High/Low   — Relative Strength to S&P 500

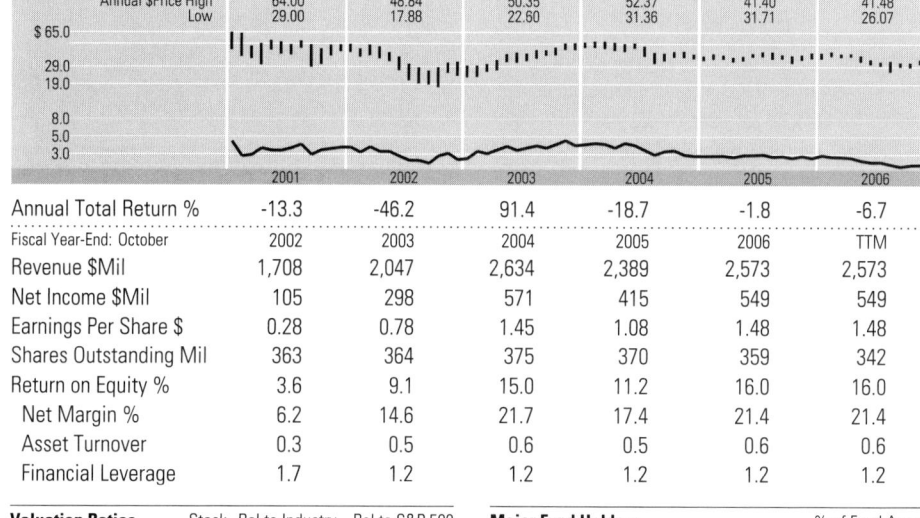

Annual Total Return %	-13.3	-46.2	91.4	-18.7	-1.8	-6.7
Fiscal Year-End: October	2002	2003	2004	2005	2006	TTM
Revenue $Mil	1,708	2,047	2,634	2,389	2,573	2,573
Net Income $Mil	105	298	571	415	549	549
Earnings Per Share $	0.28	0.78	1.45	1.08	1.48	1.48
Shares Outstanding Mil	363	364	375	370	359	342
Return on Equity %	3.6	9.1	15.0	11.2	16.0	16.0
Net Margin %	6.2	14.6	21.7	17.4	21.4	21.4
Asset Turnover	0.3	0.5	0.6	0.5	0.6	0.6
Financial Leverage	1.7	1.2	1.2	1.2	1.2	1.2

Valuation Ratios	Stock	Rel to Industry	Rel to S&P 500
Price/Earnings	22.2	0.8	1.1
Price/Book	3.3	0.9	0.8
Price/Sales	4.4	1.0	1.5
Price/Cash Flow	18.1	1.1	1.2

Major Fund Holders	% of Fund Assets
ACM Convertible Securities	11.82
Fidelity Select Electronics	4.49
VALIC I Science & Technology	3.57
T. Rowe Price Science & Tech	3.38

One Technology Way P.O. Box 9106   www.analog.com
Norwood, MA 02062-9106

Growth [C]	2003	2004	2005	2006
Revenue %	19.9	28.6	-9.3	7.7
Earnings/Share %	178.6	85.9	-25.5	37.0
Book Value/Share %	11.5	12.3	-0.4	-3.7
Dividends/Share %	NMF	NMF	60.0	75.2

Profitability [A]	2004	2005	2006	TTM
Return on Assets %	12.1	9.1	13.8	13.8
Oper Cash Flow $Mil	778	673	621	621
- Cap Spending $Mil	146	85	129	129
= Free Cash Flow $Mil	632	587	492	492

Financial Health [A+]	2004	2005	2006	10-31-06
Long-term Debt $Mil	—	—	—	—
Total Equity $Mil	3,800	3,692	3,436	3,436
Debt/Equity Ratio	—	—	—	—

Thesis By Larry Cao, CFA, 11-29-06 Stock Price as of Analysis: $32.25

Analog Devices has built a strong position in high-performance analog and general-purpose digital signal processing (DSP) components over the last decade.

In recent years, growth of high-performance analog components has outpaced the overall semiconductor industry thanks to a wide array of real world applications across industries. Analog Devices is the market leader in data converters and amplifiers, which combined represent 40% of the high-performance analog chip market.

Analog Devices currently makes 10,000 product models of analog components, serving the needs of 60,000 customers in diverse industries such as communications, computers, consumer electronics, and industrials. The company has built itself into this formidable position by focusing R&D investments on core technology platforms that can be leveraged to develop a large number of standard products. Analog Devices has successfully identified niches where these products can be readily integrated into applications with little additional programming and where demand is not large enough for volume production. The "built-in" benefits of such niches are long product life cycles and benign pricing environments. Stable pricing allows Analog Devices to grow revenue faster than competitors that make commodified volume products. Focused R&D efforts and long product life cycles help the company leverage costs better than those firms involved in customized design.

Consistent profitability is evidence of Analog Devices' market position. The firm's operating margin averaged close to 20% during the last decade. Healthy earnings have also translated into strong cash flow and a stellar balance sheet.

Some end-market and customer-specific issues have dogged Analog Devices in the past couple of years, however. Most of them, such as the weakness in the automatic testing equipment market in 2005, have turned out to be temporary. The industrial sector grew 15% in Analog Devices' fiscal 2006 (which ended in October). The consumer business has also been strong, partly as a result of the firm winning the game console business at Nintendo. We expect the impending PC upgrade cycle to help the company regain its momentum in power management products for the computing end market in the coming years. Analog Devices will remain on the industry's leading edge thanks to its product strength and market position.

Data as of 12-29-06

Anheuser-Busch Companies BUD

	Rating	Fair Value	Last Close	Consider Buy	Consider Sell	Yield %
	★★★★	$57.00	$49.20	$48.60	$74.80	2.30

Company Profile

Anheuser-Busch is the world's largest brewer by total sales. Its domestic beer brands, which include Budweiser, Michelob, Busch, and Natural Light, are produced at 12 breweries in the U.S. The company owns 50% of Grupo Modelo and has made substantial investments in Chinese breweries. It also owns a brewery in the U.K. and licenses its brands to various brewers worldwide. The company owns packaging companies and nine theme parks, including Sea World and Busch Gardens.

Management   Stewardship Grade [A]

Anheuser-Busch has a long record of investing in its business for the long term and catering to shareholders' interests. As of December 2006, CEO August Busch IV is the new face with a familiar name, with former CEO Patrick Stokes moving to chairman and former chairman and longtime CEO August Busch III remaining on the board. We hope that Busch IV will be willing to take the steps necessary, some perhaps drastic, to ensure growth. However, it is unclear just how much power he will ultimately have over large strategic decisions, considering that Stokes and Busch III remain on the board. Busch IV is just 42, but he has been with the company for 21 years and knows the domestic operations very well. He is a bit light on international experience and has no experience leading a large, public company. If the company flounders, questions about the thoroughness of the board's CEO search will probably be raised by an investor base that has become less loyal and more impatient. Busch IV must quickly prove that he brings more than his last name to the table. The company has staggered elections for board members, with directors serving terms of three years, one of the few blemishes on its record. Directors and executives own about 3.8% of shares outstanding.

One Busch Place   www.anheuser-busch.com
St. Louis, MO 63118

Growth [C]	2002	2003	2004	2005
Revenue %	5.1	4.3	5.6	0.7
Earnings/Share %	16.4	12.7	11.7	-15.2
Book Value/Share %	-22.9	-6.7	1.8	29.5
Dividends/Share %	8.7	10.7	12.0	10.8

Profitability [A]	2003	2004	2005	TTM
Return on Assets %	14.1	13.9	11.1	11.9
Oper Cash Flow $Mil	2,971	2,940	2,728	2,807
- Cap Spending $Mil	993	1,090	1,137	800
= Free Cash Flow $Mil	1,978	1,851	1,591	2,007

Financial Health [B]	2003	2004	2005	09-30-06
Long-term Debt $Mil	7,285	8,279	7,972	7,393
Total Equity $Mil	2,712	2,668	3,343	4,344
Debt/Equity Ratio	2.7	3.1	2.4	1.7

Industry	Business Risk	Moat Size	Investment Style	Sector
Alcoholic Beverages	Below Avg	Wide	Large Core	Consumer Goods

Competition	Market Cap $Mil	12 Mo Trailing Sales $Mil	Price/Cash Flow	Return On Assets%	Debt/Equity	Total Return% 1 Yr	3 Yr
Anheuser-Busch Companies	37,826	15,691	13.5	11.9	1.7	17.4	0.1
Diageo PLC ADR	60,493	12,931	21.3	13.8	0.9	40.7	18.0
Molson Coors Brewing Comp	6,595	5,698	7.3	2.4	0.4	16.3	13.0

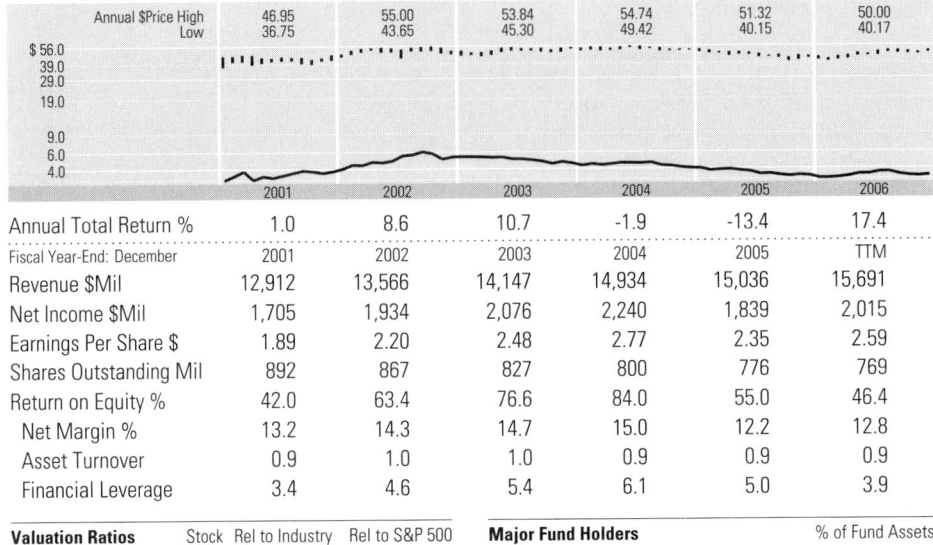

Annual Total Return %	1.0	8.6	10.7	-1.9	-13.4	17.4
Fiscal Year-End: December	2001	2002	2003	2004	2005	TTM
Revenue $Mil	12,912	13,566	14,147	14,934	15,036	15,691
Net Income $Mil	1,705	1,934	2,076	2,240	1,839	2,015
Earnings Per Share $	1.89	2.20	2.48	2.77	2.35	2.59
Shares Outstanding Mil	892	867	827	800	776	769
Return on Equity %	42.0	63.4	76.6	84.0	55.0	46.4
Net Margin %	13.2	14.3	14.7	15.0	12.2	12.8
Asset Turnover	0.9	1.0	1.0	0.9	0.9	0.9
Financial Leverage	3.4	4.6	5.4	6.1	5.0	3.9

Valuation Ratios	Stock	Rel to Industry	Rel to S&P 500	Major Fund Holders	% of Fund Assets
Price/Earnings	19.0	0.7	0.9	Sycuan U.S. Value	4.29
Price/Book	8.7	1.0	2.1	Meehan Focus	4.21
Price/Sales	2.4	0.4	0.8	Foresight Value	4.08
Price/Cash Flow	13.5	0.6	0.9	Primary Trend	3.95

Thesis By Matthew Reilly, 11-17-06 Stock Price as of Analysis: $46.89

Anheuser-Busch has a significant scale advantage in the manufacture and distribution of premium domestic beer. Though the company has developed several powerful brands, most notably Budweiser, we continue to believe that superior distribution capabilities remain its most potent competitive advantage and the largest contributor to its wide economic moat. We do not expect fantastic earnings growth from the company anytime soon. Rather, we expect incremental gains over long periods, making this stock an attractive core holding.

Anheuser-Busch faces an enormous challenge in 2007 and beyond--finding sustainable avenues for growth against a difficult commodity cost environment. Though the company has investments with decent growth prospects, such as a 51% equity interest in Grupo Modelo and Chinese operations, it must improve core domestic revenue growth. To accomplish this, the company can no longer rely on its prowess as a purveyor of premium domestic beer. Anheuser-Busch must use its exclusive distributor base to tap into more high-growth areas of alcoholic beverages in America, which have recently included import and craft beers, wine, and spirits. While growth in each of these categories is prone to a degree of cyclicality and fluctuation, we believe the trend of consumers trading up to prestige brands with cachet and superpremium pricing will not change anytime soon.

The good news is that this trend generally means that the profit pie for the industry as a whole is likely to increase, though some of the gross margin gain will be reduced by investment in marketing to support prestige positioning. The bad news for Anheuser-Busch is that its core brands fall short of this positioning.

We believe the company can compensate and has already taken appropriate steps. It is distributing more import beers, developing more craftlike brands and brews, making minority equity investments in regional brewers, developing a spirits brand, and distributing the quickly growing Monster brand made by Hansen. Management has also said that it will consider acquisitions or product development in any area of the alcoholic beverage market that is experiencing significant growth. We believe this focus on leveraging distribution advantages to maximize a business with already strong cash flow is the best strategy for the company and will bolster results.

Ann Taylor Stores ANN

Data as of 12-29-06

Rating	Fair Value	Last Close	Consider Buy	Consider Sell	Yield %
★★★	$33.00	$32.84	$25.40	$41.30	0.00

Industry	Business Risk	Moat Size	Investment Style	Sector
Clothing Stores	Average	Narrow	Mid Core	Consumer Services

Company Profile
Ann Taylor Stores operates a chain of more than 820 women's clothing stores throughout the United States and Puerto Rico under the names Ann Taylor, Ann Taylor Loft, and Ann Taylor Factory Store. The stores primarily sell career separates, dresses, tops, weekend wear, shoes, and accessories. In 2005, Ann Taylor Loft surpassed the Ann Taylor brand in revenue: Loft made up 48% of total sales and Ann Taylor made up around 42%.

Management
Stewardship Grade [B]

Kay Krill is president and CEO of Ann Taylor. In October 2005, she replaced J. Patrick Spainhour, who had been chairman and CEO since 1996. Krill joined Ann Taylor in 1994 as a vice president of merchandising. She was then selected to lead the development of the Ann Taylor Loft business, until her promotion to president of the company in November 2004. In 2005, Krill's annual compensation was $1.2 million (not including the roughly $6 million in restricted stock, the 245,000 stock options, or the $684,000 long-term incentive plan bonus she was awarded). Given that a significant portion of Krill's total compensation is variable, executive compensation does not seem egregious. We like that a sizable chunk of Krill's pay is in the form of stock, and we believe that it helps to align her incentives with those of shareholders. The CEO and chairman roles are not filled by the same person, and with outsiders representing 8 of 9 board seats, the board is independent. However, directors serve three-year terms, which we frown upon. We believe annual director elections are more shareholder-friendly, giving stockholders the ability to oust underperforming board members in a more timely manner. Overall, transparency is good, and we think Ann Taylor's corporate governance is above average.

142 West 57th Street www.anntaylor.com
New York, NY 10019

Growth [B+]	2003	2004	2005	2006
Revenue %	6.3	15.0	16.7	11.8
Earnings/Share %	178.0	24.6	-38.0	28.4
Book Value/Share %	9.7	15.3	11.6	10.8
Dividends/Share %	NMF	NMF	NMF	NMF

Profitability [B]	2004	2005	2006	TTM
Return on Assets %	8.0	4.8	5.5	9.0
Oper Cash Flow $Mil	208	154	311	338
- Cap Spending $Mil	90	137	188	149
= Free Cash Flow $Mil	118	17	124	189

Financial Health [A]	2004	2005	2006	10-31-06
Long-term Debt $Mil	—	—	—	—
Total Equity $Mil	819	927	1,034	1,121
Debt/Equity Ratio	—	—	—	—

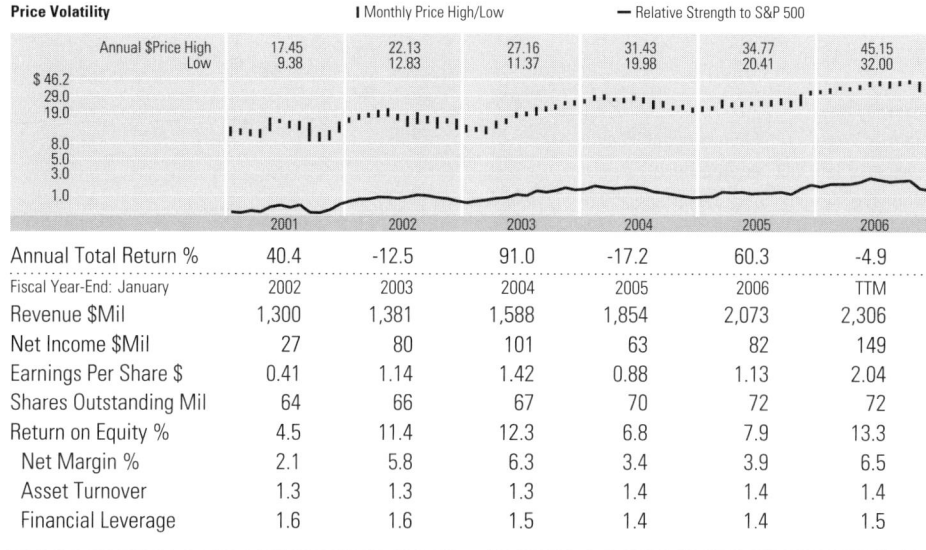

Competition	Market Cap $Mil	12 Mo Trailing Sales $Mil	Price/Cash Flow	Return On Assets %	Debt/Equity	Total Return % 1 Yr	3 Yr
Ann Taylor Stores	2,358	2,306	7.0	9.0	—	-4.9	9.4
Gap	15,807	15,834	8.6	9.7	0.0	12.5	-3.7
Nordstrom	12,682	8,226	11.4	13.5	0.3	33.4	45.3

Price Volatility — Monthly Price High/Low — Relative Strength to S&P 500

	2001	2002	2003	2004	2005	2006
Annual $Price High	17.45	22.13	27.16	31.43	34.77	45.15
Low	9.38	12.83	11.37	19.98	20.41	32.00
Annual Total Return %	40.4	-12.5	91.0	-17.2	60.3	-4.9

Fiscal Year-End: January	2002	2003	2004	2005	2006	TTM
Revenue $Mil	1,300	1,381	1,588	1,854	2,073	2,306
Net Income $Mil	27	80	101	63	82	149
Earnings Per Share $	0.41	1.14	1.42	0.88	1.13	2.04
Shares Outstanding Mil	64	66	67	70	72	72
Return on Equity %	4.5	11.4	12.3	6.8	7.9	13.3
Net Margin %	2.1	5.8	6.3	3.4	3.9	6.5
Asset Turnover	1.3	1.3	1.3	1.4	1.4	1.4
Financial Leverage	1.6	1.6	1.5	1.4	1.4	1.5

Valuation Ratios	Stock	Rel to Industry	Rel to S&P 500
Price/Earnings	16.1	0.8	0.8
Price/Book	2.1	0.5	0.5
Price/Sales	1.0	0.7	0.3
Price/Cash Flow	7.0	0.6	0.5

Major Fund Holders	% of Fund Assets
Undiscovered Mgrs Behavioral Growth Inst	2.35
Performance Leaders Equity Instl	2.22
Azzad Ethical Mid Cap	2.19
ING FMR Mid Cap Growth S	1.87

Thesis By Kimberly Picciola, 11-20-06 Stock Price as of Analysis: $35.94

Ann Taylor is staging a turnaround. After two years of sluggish sales and paltry operating margins, the company is reconnecting with its customers. Management's focus on differentiating between its two apparel concepts, Ann Taylor and Ann Taylor Loft, has led to improved top- and bottom-line performance. With a more targeted merchandise assortment in its two chains, we expect improved financial performance in the near term, but fierce competition will likely limit gains over the long run.

Despite Ann Taylor's recent struggles, the strength of its brand has kept competitors at bay. We think this indicates that Ann Taylor still has a competitive advantage. However, the company's returns on invested capital have deteriorated in the last two years due to the company's disappointing performance. Should returns fall below Ann Taylor's cost of capital, we would reconsider this retailer's narrow economic moat rating.

Ann Taylor has invested heavily in building its store base, particularly the Loft concept, over the past five years. This has helped drive the firm's average double-digit sales growth over the same period. Although we expect continued new-store openings for Loft, we don't think future expansion of this chain can sustain the firm's historic top-line growth rate. We project that new store openings and low-single-digit increases in total same-store sales (sales from stores open at least a year) will result in average top-line growth of 9% annually over the next five years.

While the company has managed to revive its namesake brand while expanding its Loft concept, continually differentiating between these two divisions will be key to minimizing cannibalization. The Ann Taylor line has been repositioned as a brand that offers professional and special-occasion attire, while the Loft concept offers a more casual look. We applaud CEO Kay Krill and her management team for their diligent effort to better understand each brand's customers and more clearly delineate between the merchandise each concept offers.

Despite Ann Taylor's revival, we don't think this specialty retailer is in the clear. The company continues to battle rivals such as Banana Republic and J. Crew, which are in hot pursuit of the consumer shopping for that classic look with a twist. Although the company has put up impressive profit gains in recent quarters, we think it operates in a crowded retail environment. We believe this will make it difficult for Ann Taylor to keep up the positive bottom-line momentum.

Apache APA

Data as of 12-29-06

	Rating	Fair Value	Last Close	Consider Buy	Consider Sell	Yield %
	★★★★	$86.00	$66.51	$66.30	$107.70	0.68

Company Profile
Apache is one of the oil patch's largest independent exploration and production companies. Although most of its wells are in North America, Apache also has operations in the North Sea, Argentina, Australia, and Egypt. The company has about 2.1 billion barrels of oil equivalent in its proven reserves, a little more than half of which is in natural gas. It produces more than 450,000 barrels of oil equivalents a day.

Management
Stewardship Grade [C]

A former World War II bomber pilot, chairman Raymond Plank founded Apache in 1954. Under his leadership, Apache has grown from $250,000 in startup capital to more than $20 billion in assets. After more than 35 years as CEO, Plank stepped down from day-to-day management in mid-2002 and handed the reins to Steven Farris, who has been with the company since 1988. In 2005, Farris took home $5 million in total compensation, relatively low in comparison with the executives at some of Apache's close competitors. We like that the company has stopped paying executives with stock options in favor of restricted stock. But we dislike the shareholder-rights plan and staggered elections for board members. Apache's corporate stewardship is average, in our opinion.

One Post Oak Central 2000 Post Oak Boulevard
Houston, TX 77056-4400   www.apachecorp.com

Growth [C+]	2002	2003	2004	2005
Revenue %	-8.9	63.7	27.3	42.2
Earnings/Share %	-23.9	90.6	46.6	55.9
Book Value/Share %	15.7	23.7	24.0	27.6
Dividends/Share %	57.1	9.0	25.2	30.8

Profitability [A]	2003	2004	2005	TTM
Return on Assets %	9.0	10.7	13.6	12.0
Oper Cash Flow $Mil	2,706	3,232	4,332	4,571
- Cap Spending $Mil	2,960	3,337	3,716	5,326
= Free Cash Flow $Mil	-254	-105	616	-755

Financial Health [A-]	2003	2004	2005	09-30-06
Long-term Debt $Mil	2,327	2,588	2,192	2,189
Total Equity $Mil	6,434	8,106	10,443	12,537
Debt/Equity Ratio	0.4	0.3	0.2	0.2

Industry	Business Risk	Moat Size	Investment Style	Sector
Oil/Gas	Average	Narrow	Large Core	Energy

Competition	Market Cap $Mil	12 Mo Trailing Sales $Mil	Price/Cash Flow	Return On Assets%	Debt/Equity	Total Return% 1 Yr	3 Yr
Apache	21,909	8,424	4.8	12.0	0.2	-2.3	19.0
Occidental Petroleum	41,070	17,548	6.4	13.9	0.2	24.3	34.9
Anadarko Petroleum	20,008	9,838	3.9	6.3	0.8	-7.4	20.4

Price Volatility — Monthly Price High/Low — Relative Strength to S&P 500

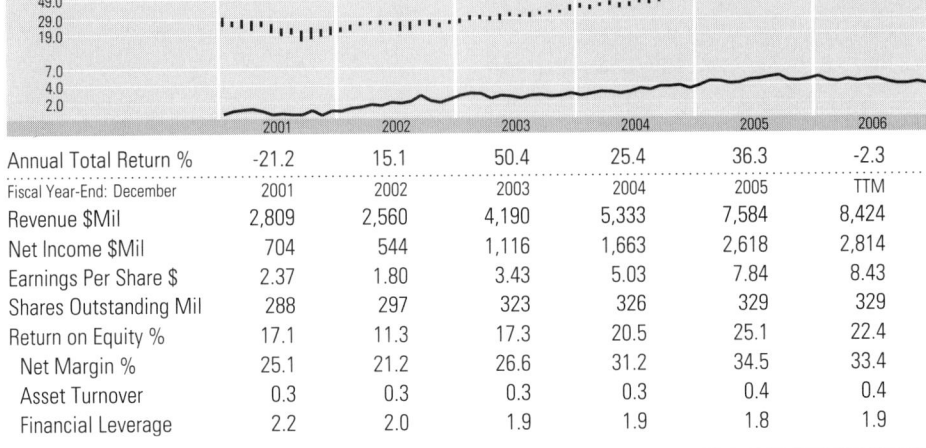

	2001	2002	2003	2004	2005	2006
Annual $Price High	31.49	28.88	41.68	55.16	78.15	76.25
Low	16.57	21.14	26.26	36.79	47.45	56.50
Annual Total Return %	-21.2	15.1	50.4	25.4	36.3	-2.3

Fiscal Year-End: December	2001	2002	2003	2004	2005	TTM
Revenue $Mil	2,809	2,560	4,190	5,333	7,584	8,424
Net Income $Mil	704	544	1,116	1,663	2,618	2,814
Earnings Per Share $	2.37	1.80	3.43	5.03	7.84	8.43
Shares Outstanding Mil	288	297	323	326	329	329
Return on Equity %	17.1	11.3	17.3	20.5	25.1	22.4
Net Margin %	25.1	21.2	26.6	31.2	34.5	33.4
Asset Turnover	0.3	0.3	0.3	0.3	0.4	0.4
Financial Leverage	2.2	2.0	1.9	1.9	1.8	1.9

Valuation Ratios	Stock	Rel to Industry	Rel to S&P 500
Price/Earnings	7.9	0.6	0.4
Price/Book	1.7	0.5	0.4
Price/Sales	2.6	1.4	0.9
Price/Cash Flow	4.8	0.6	0.3

Major Fund Holders	% of Fund Assets
Diamond Hill Select A	5.24
Artisan Opportunistic Value Inv	4.99
Diamond Hill Large Cap A	4.88
Dunham Large Cap Value N	4.86

Thesis
By Justin Perucki, CFA, 10-30-06 Stock Price as of Analysis: $65.32

As a growing exploration and production company, Apache is different from its reserved and more mature peers. Apache has historically chosen to sell stock and reinvest most of its cash flow to expand, instead of buying back shares and paying out a robust dividend. However, with cash flooding in, the firm announced it would repurchase $1 billion worth of stock. Most of Apache's growth has been through purchasing legacy properties piecemeal from the oil majors like BP and ExxonMobil, instead of exploring for reserves itself. Since 2000, Apache's asset base has more than doubled in size.

About 70% of Apache's reserves are in North America. Consequently, the firm's political risk is below average; however, this comes at a price. In general, North American reserves are older and more difficult to produce, resulting in higher fixed costs. This increases the company's leverage to cyclical and volatile commodity energy prices. But Apache is one of the lowest-cost producers in the oil patch, which helps it remain profitable even when commodity prices decline. Over the past three years, Apache's average lifting costs were only $7.30 per barrel of oil equivalent produced.

To complement its North American base, Apache is working hard at expanding its international portfolio. In the past year, most of Apache's success has been in Egypt and the North Sea. Recent discoveries and a new contract with Egyptian General Petroleum Corporation have Apache expecting Egyptian gas production to double in the near future. In the North Sea, Apache is in the midst of a dramatic turnaround of BP's old North Sea properties. Since acquiring the assets in 2003, Apache has slashed lifting costs 50% and increased daily production by 67%. Continued internal growth like this should have a positive impact on Apache's share price.

We've awarded Apache (and most of its peers) a narrow economic moat rating, mainly because of OPEC. By limiting its members' production, OPEC manipulates oil prices higher. This lifts profitability in what would otherwise be a brutally competitive commodity market. Without OPEC, there would be no moat. With it, profits are handsome, albeit volatile.

Data as of 12-29-06

Apollo Group A APOL

Rating	Fair Value	Last Close	Consider Buy	Consider Sell	Yield %
★★★★★	$65.00	$38.97	$50.10	$81.40	0.00

Company Profile
Apollo Group provides postsecondary education to working adults through the University of Phoenix, UOP Online, and the Institute for Professional Development. Its Western International University segment targets younger working adults. Apollo has 259 campuses and learning centers nationwide. At the end of the fiscal fourth quarter of 2006, enrollment at UOP and Axia was 292,996 students. Programs include business, information technology, education, and nursing.

Management
Stewardship Grade [C]

Todd Nelson resigned in January 2006, ending a 19-year career with the firm. He was president, chairman (since 2004), and CEO (since 2001). Brian Mueller was appointed president of Apollo. We are comforted by Mueller's long tenure at Apollo and significant breadth of experience at the firm. He spent a decade heading UOP Online, which has enjoyed tremendous growth. Founder John Sperling takes over as interim executive chairman. Compensation at the firm is reasonable. However, top management receives cash bonuses tied to the board's earnings targets and earns additional bonuses for beating those goals, which may increase shorter-term earnings maneuvering at the expense of longer-term increases in shareholder value. Another negative, Apollo Class A shares have no voting rights. The John Sperling Trust and Peter Sperling (John Sperling's son) control the Class B voting shares, so this is a controlled company; shareholders are along for the ride. Our Stewardship Grade would improve if the company eliminated its staggered board and split the chairman and CEO roles. The company also faces an investigation into its stock option grants, some of which appear to be unusually auspicious. On Oct. 18, the firm announced that its special committee has identified various deficiencies related to option grants, which could lead to financial restatements.

4615 East Elwood Street
Phoenix, AZ 85040
www.apollogrp.edu

Growth [A]	2002	2003	2004	2005
Revenue %	31.2	32.7	34.3	25.2
Earnings/Share %	45.0	49.4	-40.8	210.4
Book Value/Share %	40.7	43.2	-50.9	43.2
Dividends/Share %	NMF	NMF	NMF	NMF

Profitability [A+]	2003	2004	2005	TTM
Return on Assets %	17.5	18.6	34.1	43.5
Oper Cash Flow $Mil	391	545	566	596
- Cap Spending $Mil	57	108	104	75
= Free Cash Flow $Mil	335	437	462	521

Financial Health [A]	2003	2004	2005	02-28-06
Long-term Debt $Mil	—	68	78	85
Total Equity $Mil	1,027	957	707	441
Debt/Equity Ratio	—	0.1	0.1	0.2

Industry	Business Risk	Moat Size	Investment Style	Sector
Education	Average	Wide	Mid Growth	Consumer Services

Competition	Market Cap $Mil	12 Mo Trailing Sales $Mil	Price/Cash Flow	Return On Assets%	Debt/Equity	Total Return% 1 Yr	3 Yr
Apollo Group A	6,733	2,409	11.3	43.5	0.2	-35.5	-17.5
ITT Educational Services	2,746	734	15.0	28.4	—	12.6	12.2
Career Education	2,573	2,042	7.8	9.6	0.0	-26.5	-15.9

Price Volatility | Monthly Price High/Low — Relative Strength to S&P 500

	2001	2002	2003	2004	2005	2006
Annual $Price High	33.31	46.15	73.09	98.01	84.20	63.26
Low	19.33	28.13	40.72	62.55	57.40	33.33
Annual Total Return %	37.3	46.6	54.1	19.0	-25.1	-35.5

Fiscal Year-End: August	2001	2002	2003	2004	2005	TTM
Revenue $Mil	769	1,009	1,340	1,798	2,251	2,409
Net Income $Mil	108	161	247	278	445	459
Earnings Per Share $	0.60	0.87	1.30	0.77	2.39	2.54
Shares Outstanding Mil	—	—	187	356	183	173
Return on Equity %	22.4	23.1	24.1	29.0	62.9	104.1
Net Margin %	14.0	16.0	18.4	15.4	19.8	19.1
Asset Turnover	1.1	1.0	1.0	1.2	1.7	2.3
Financial Leverage	1.5	1.4	1.4	1.6	1.8	2.4

Valuation Ratios	Stock	Rel to Industry	Rel to S&P 500
Price/Earnings	15.3	0.6	0.7
Price/Book	15.3	0.7	3.7
Price/Sales	2.8	0.3	1.0
Price/Cash Flow	11.3	0.7	0.8

Major Fund Holders	% of Fund Assets
Touchstone Sands Capital Select Growth Z	4.08
MassMutual Select Aggressive Growth S	4.06
Black Pearl Focus	3.91
Wasatch Heritage Growth	3.83

Thesis By Kristan Rowland, 10-19-06 Stock Price as of Analysis: $36.80

Apollo's widely recognized University of Phoenix (UOP) is the leader in online education and the largest private university in the country, with more than 300,000 students.

Demographics serve Apollo well. The National Center for Education Statistics estimates that 37% of all students (over 6 million) are older than 24; a large portion of these students are likely to be working, which bodes well for Apollo's growth prospects. Roughly 91% of UOP's student base is 23 and older. Apollo has grown rapidly as it has served this niche, catering specifically to working adults.

Apollo's regional accreditation, recognizable brands, and solid reputation contribute to its wide moat. Its UOP and Western International University are regionally accredited. Accreditation is difficult to obtain and allows UOP and WIU to participate in federal student aid programs (63% and 72% of students participate at each institution, respectively).

Apollo's ability to attract working adults and its students' employers' willingness to support tuition reimbursement for an Apollo education are indications of its solid reputation. About 45% of Apollo's students receive some type of tuition reimbursement from their employers, an indication of the value employers place on an education at an Apollo institution. Also, with a reputation for premier online programs, it attracts adults looking for a good education with flexibility. Competition in online programs has picked up, but Apollo still maintains a sizable lead. Its huge advertising budget and scale, compared with budget-constrained public universities, should help fuel continued growth.

WIU's Axia College (which became part of UOP this spring) is attempting to cater to a younger working adult student and is a welcome growth opportunity for Apollo. The average age of an Axia student is 30 compared with 33 for UOP, and that average age should continue to decline. Apollo counts on a significant portion of the Axia students continuing to pursue their bachelor's degree studies at UOP. Axia's associate's degree is less pricey on a per-class basis to obtain than if the same person enrolled directly into the bachelor's degree at UOP, so effectively, it's a way of discounting the bachelor's degree at UOP and attracting a larger market. Associate's degrees have grown from 3.9% of Apollo's student base in 2004 to about 26% in 2006. We attribute the decline in revenue per student to the growth of Axia. We think this is a good long-term opportunity for Apollo but may continue to put near-term pressure on revenue per student.

Data as of 12-29-06

Apple Computer AAPL

	Rating	Fair Value	Last Close	Consider Buy	Consider Sell	Yield %
	★	$66.00	$84.84	$50.90	$82.70	0.00

Company Profile

Apple Computer designs personal computer hardware, software, and peripherals like the iPod music player. The company makes iMac and PowerMac personal computers and MacBook and iBook portable computers, which use Apple's proprietary operating systems. Apple also designs and sells software for graphics-intensive businesses and consumers interested in digital entertainment. Apple sells its products online as well as through company stores and retail chains.

Industry	Business Risk	Moat Size	Investment Style	Sector
Computer Equip.	Average	Narrow	Large Growth	Hardware

Competition

	Market Cap $Mil	12 Mo Trailing Sales $Mil	Price/Cash Flow	Return On Assets %	Debt/Equity	Total Return % 1 Yr	3 Yr
Apple Computer	72,901	19,315	32.8	11.6	—	18.0	99.8
Hewlett-Packard	112,070	91,658	9.9	7.6	0.1	45.2	22.7
Dell	56,995	56,738	12.2	14.9	0.1	-16.2	-9.9

Management

Stewardship Grade [C]

Cofounder Steve Jobs remains Apple's legendary CEO. He still has a significant stake in the company, so his interests are much in line with investors'. An ongoing stock-option investigation has delayed some financial filings, but investigators have issued a preliminary conclusion that Jobs and the current management team are all clean. Jobs is well supported at Apple by a capable executive management team anchored by COO Tim Cook and CFO Peter Oppenheimer. Shareholder-friendliness remains a sticking point at Apple. Employee stock-option exercises have led to significant growth in shares outstanding the past few years. Apple has ample cash on its balance sheet to mitigate this dilution; the firm's hesitance to buy back its own shares at current valuation levels is of note. Apple expanded its board of directors in 2006 with the addition of Google CEO Eric Schmidt. New board members should help augment the firm's existing leadership as a larger, more complex Apple tackles the new global opportunity of digital entertainment.

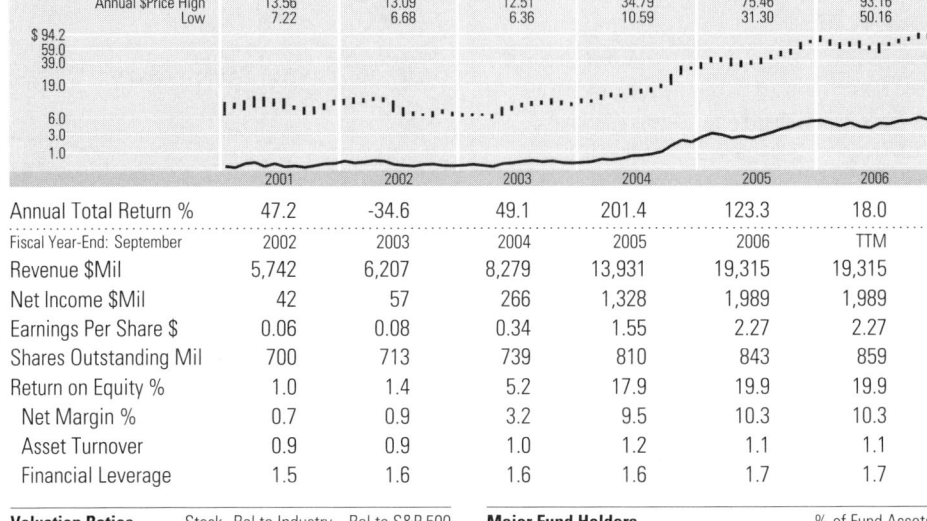

	2001	2002	2003	2004	2005	2006
Annual $Price High	13.56	13.09	12.51	34.79	75.46	93.16
Low	7.22	6.68	6.36	10.59	31.30	50.16
Annual Total Return %	47.2	-34.6	49.1	201.4	123.3	18.0

Fiscal Year-End: September	2002	2003	2004	2005	2006	TTM
Revenue $Mil	5,742	6,207	8,279	13,931	19,315	19,315
Net Income $Mil	42	57	266	1,328	1,989	1,989
Earnings Per Share $	0.06	0.08	0.34	1.55	2.27	2.27
Shares Outstanding Mil	700	713	739	810	843	859
Return on Equity %	1.0	1.4	5.2	17.9	19.9	19.9
Net Margin %	0.7	0.9	3.2	9.5	10.3	10.3
Asset Turnover	0.9	0.9	1.0	1.2	1.1	1.1
Financial Leverage	1.5	1.6	1.6	1.6	1.7	1.7

Valuation Ratios	Stock	Rel to Industry	Rel to S&P 500
Price/Earnings	37.4	1.4	1.8
Price/Book	7.3	1.3	1.8
Price/Sales	3.8	1.5	1.3
Price/Cash Flow	32.8	2.2	2.2

Major Fund Holders	% of Fund Assets
Chicken Little Growth	29.28
Transamerica Premier Focus Inv	11.41
SunAmerica Focused Technology A	8.87
Fidelity Select Computers	7.63

1 Infinite Loop www.apple.com
Cupertino, CA 95014

Growth [A+]	2002	2003	2004	2005
Revenue %	8.1	33.4	68.3	38.6
Earnings/Share %	33.3	325.0	355.9	46.5
Book Value/Share %	1.2	9.5	33.6	31.4
Dividends/Share %	NMF	NMF	NMF	NMF

Profitability [A]	2003	2004	2005	TTM
Return on Assets %	3.3	11.5	11.6	11.6
Oper Cash Flow $Mil	934	2,535	2,220	2,220
- Cap Spending $Mil	176	260	657	657
= Free Cash Flow $Mil	758	2,275	1,563	1,563

Financial Health [A-]	2003	2004	2005	03-31-06
Long-term Debt $Mil	—	—	—	
Total Equity $Mil	5,076	7,428	9,984	9,984
Debt/Equity Ratio	—	—	—	

Thesis By Rod Bare, 11-30-06 Stock Price as of Analysis: $91.66

Apple is king when it comes to making money selling technology to consumers. Its secret is taking complex gadgets like digital music players and computers and making them easy to use. Apple offers unique software and online stores that help customers refuel their toys and their imaginations. This in turn keeps customers coming back to buy better toys.

The resulting virtuous circle has lifted Apple's profit margins to levels rarely seen in the competitive world of consumer technology. How well Apple's economic moat protects shareholders the next few years as competitors, suppliers, and customers pursue their own economic interests will be the key factor that defines this company's potential as a long-term investment.

Apple's revenue drivers are fairly well known. The iPod family remains wildly popular. The new Intel-based Macs offer cutting-edge price/performance attributes, and Apple's software remains critically acclaimed as the best option for most consumers.

It's the profitability trend that's the toughest part of Apple to predict. Strong growth in Apple's high-margin software helps insulate the firm from the margin issues found in tech hardware. However, consumer technology margins are notoriously susceptible to competitive pressures and fickle consumer tastes. Apple's top-line shift to products with short life cycles and fragile margins can offset the positive effects of scale if innovation can't keep pace.

Apple's large cash position also creates a valuation wrinkle that prospective investors may want to consider. About 10%-15% of Apple's earnings per share number comes from the interest earned on the firm's $10 billion cash balance. A popular valuation shortcut involves applying a robust earnings multiple to an EPS number to estimate the value of a share. Investors in a hurry may forget to treat the interest income part of the EPS exercise differently. Ur some may add back an excess cash per share amount without subtracting the interest income from EPS. Our detailed cash-flow approach to valuation avoids double-counting the earning power of the cash.

We respect Apple's technology simplification prowess. We think the firm has innovation advantages that open up opportunities well beyond the personal computer market. Measuring the longevity of this advantage is a challenge, however. Using industry history as a guide, we'd recommend an entry price for this fine firm that contemplates a normalized expected profitability trend.

Data as of 12-29-06

Applebee's International APPB

Rating	Fair Value	Last Close	Consider Buy	Consider Sell	Yield %
★★★★★	$33.00	$24.67	$25.40	$41.30	0.89

Company Profile
The company develops, franchises, and operates restaurants under the Applebee's Neighborhood Grill & Bar brand, the largest casual dining concept in the world. Applebee's offers a full-service lunch and dinner menu with an average check per guest of $10.50-$11.00. As of September 2006, there were 1,884 Applebee's restaurants: 1,372 franchise and 512 company units. The chain has a presence in 49 states and 17 foreign countries.

Management   Stewardship Grade [B]
Applebee's promoted veteran restaurant executive Dave Goebel to CEO in August 2006. He succeeded Lloyd Hill, who held the role for eight years and will continue to serve as chairman of the company. We believe Goebel has the skills and experience to lead the company. He signed up with Applebee's in 2001 as senior vice president of franchise operations and quickly worked his way up the corporate ladder, assuming the role of chief operating officer in 2004 and president in 2005. Prior to joining Applebee's, he had nearly 30 years of general management experience, including 22 years in the restaurant business. As CEO, Goebel's annual compensation will include $650,000 in salary and a potential cash bonus of up to $682,500. He'll also receive a very generous package of restricted stock and stock appreciation rights.

Overall, the executives and directors have demonstrated good stewardship, in our opinion. We especially like the fact that executives are required to own a multiple of their salary in company stock, including 4 times base salary for the CEO. We do, however, take a dim view of staggered board elections and other takeover defenses, which could favor the interests of management over shareholders.

4551 W. 107th Street
Overland Park, KS 66207
www.applebees.com

Growth [B-]	2002	2003	2004	2005
Revenue %	11.4	19.3	12.3	9.4
Earnings/Share %	27.0	17.0	20.9	-4.5
Book Value/Share %	20.1	17.5	12.8	-13.6
Dividends/Share %	12.7	16.8	28.5	233.3

Profitability [A]	2003	2004	2005	TTM
Return on Assets %	14.5	14.7	11.6	9.3
Oper Cash Flow $Mil	176	191	221	172
- Cap Spending $Mil	83	109	139	125
= Free Cash Flow $Mil	93	81	82	47

Financial Health [B+]	2003	2004	2005	09-30-06
Long-term Debt $Mil	21	35	180	184
Total Equity $Mil	453	497	413	479
Debt/Equity Ratio	0.0	0.1	0.4	0.4

Industry	Business Risk	Moat Size	Investment Style	Sector
Restaurants	Average	Narrow	Small Core	Consumer Services

Competition	Market Cap $Mil	12 Mo Trailing Sales $Mil	Price/Cash Flow	Return On Assets%	Debt/Equity	Total Return% 1 Yr	3 Yr
Applebee's International	1,831	1,296	10.7	9.3	0.4	10.2	-0.8
Darden Restaurants	5,898	5,767	9.4	11.2	0.4	4.4	25.2
Brinker International	3,705	4,215	7.8	10.2	0.5	18.2	11.5

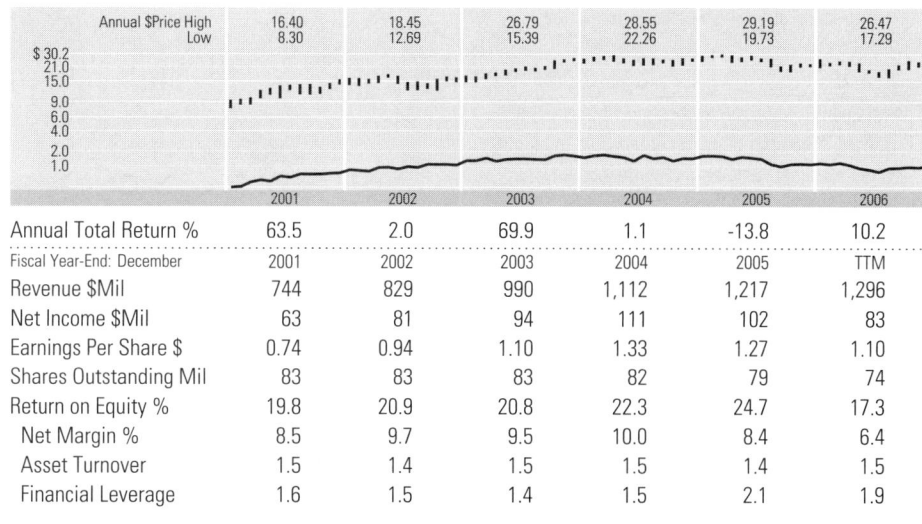

	2001	2002	2003	2004	2005	
Annual $Price High	16.40	18.45	26.79	28.55	29.19	26.47
Low	8.30	12.69	15.39	22.26	19.73	17.29
Annual Total Return %	63.5	2.0	69.9	1.1	-13.8	10.2

Fiscal Year-End: December	2001	2002	2003	2004	2005	TTM
Revenue $Mil	744	829	990	1,112	1,217	1,296
Net Income $Mil	63	81	94	111	102	83
Earnings Per Share $	0.74	0.94	1.10	1.33	1.27	1.10
Shares Outstanding Mil	83	83	83	82	79	74
Return on Equity %	19.8	20.9	20.8	22.3	24.7	17.3
Net Margin %	8.5	9.7	9.5	10.0	8.4	6.4
Asset Turnover	1.5	1.4	1.5	1.5	1.4	1.5
Financial Leverage	1.6	1.5	1.4	1.5	2.1	1.9

Valuation Ratios	Stock	Rel to Industry	Rel to S&P 500
Price/Earnings	22.2	0.8	1.1
Price/Book	3.8	0.7	0.9
Price/Sales	1.4	0.7	0.5
Price/Cash Flow	10.7	0.7	0.7

Major Fund Holders	% of Fund Assets
FMI Common Stock	2.38
Royce Value Service	2.38
Westport Select Cap R	1.85
Saratoga Small Capitalization I	1.84

Thesis By John Owens, CFA, CPA, 11-27-06 Stock Price as of Analysis: $22.57

Despite near-term pressures, we're confident about Applebee's prospects over the long run. The company is benefiting from economies of scale, an alliance with Weight Watchers, and stronger carryout sales. We believe the chain has plenty of room for growth.

In 2006, casual dining hit its roughest patch in more than 15 years. Soaring gas prices, rising interest rates, and weakening consumer confidence led to a widespread decline in guest traffic. We do not believe this difficult environment will persist indefinitely. Furthermore, spending at casual dining restaurants should get a boost in the long run from maturing baby boomers entering their peak earning years, a rise in dual-income families, and a growing desire for convenience in a time-pressed society.

We believe Applebee's is well positioned to capitalize on these favorable long-term trends. The chain dominates the grill and bar segment with more than 1,800 domestic units (about 62% larger than leading rival Chili's and more than twice as big as Ruby Tuesday). This scale provides huge marketing muscle, which contributed to Applebee's impressive run of 31 consecutive quarters of comparable sales growth through the first quarter of 2006.

An exclusive five-year agreement with Weight Watchers gives the chain another edge. The Applebee's menu features 10 Weight Watchers items, with each selection listing calories, fat and fiber grams, and Weight Watchers points. Applebee's has also broadened its customer reach with an increased focus on Carside To Go service, which accounts for about 10% of sales at company-operated units, up from 5% in 2002.

With potential for 3,000 domestic restaurants, Applebee's has substantial opportunity for growth, in our opinion. The management team has proved adept at development, opening at least 100 new restaurants for 13 consecutive years. The company has been particularly successful in seizing a first-mover advantage in small-town locations with a unit design that generates healthy returns. Over the five years ended in 2005, the firm delivered a 22% average return on invested capital.

Despite its strong position, Applebee's still faces challenges. Its customer base skews to a lower income than its rivals', making it more vulnerable in this difficult environment. The chain's comparable sales declined in each of the past seven months, and the performance of some newer restaurants has suffered. Rising development costs have also been a headwind, leading management to scale back openings of company-operated restaurants for 2007.

Applied Materials AMAT

Data as of 12-29-06

	Rating	Fair Value	Last Close	Consider Buy	Consider Sell	Yield %
	★★★	$20.00	$18.45	$15.40	$25.10	0.98

Company Profile

Applied Materials is the world's largest supplier of semiconductor manufacturing equipment. The firm's systems are used in the chemical vapor deposition, physical vapor deposition, and electroplating steps of the chip fabrication process. Applied also supplies etching, ion implantation, chemical mechanical polishing, and wafer- and reticle-inspection systems, as well as critical-dimension measurement and defect-inspection scanning electron microscopes.

Management Stewardship Grade [C]

Michael Splinter took over as Applied's president and CEO in April 2003 after being recruited from Intel, one of Applied's largest customers. Splinter served key roles at Intel during his 20 years there and was executive vice president before taking the helm at Applied. Since becoming CEO, he has successfully navigated Applied from the bottom of an industry downturn and maintained the firm's dominance in the chip equipment market. Applied has long been regarded as having good management depth. However, there has been some turnover, including the departure of former CFO Joseph Bronson for FormFactor following the hiring of an external candidate for CEO. Former CEO James Morgan continues to serve as chairman of the board. Applied's management is highly focused on profitability, paying particular attention to returns on invested capital and free cash flow, and it has been successful in achieving it. The firm initiated a small dividend in fiscal 2005 and has been making substantial stock buybacks to return some of its excess cash to shareholders. Executive compensation is on par with industry standards, and option issuance has become much more reasonable in recent years. As a group, directors and officers collectively own about 1% of Applied's outstanding shares.

3050 Bowers Avenue P.O. Box 58039 www.appliedmaterials.com
Santa Clara, CA 95054

Growth [B+]	2002	2003	2004	2005
Revenue %	-11.6	79.0	-12.7	31.1
Earnings/Share %	NMF	NMF	-6.4	32.9
Book Value/Share %	2.1	9.8	0.8	21.0
Dividends/Share %	NMF	NMF	NMF	166.7

Profitability [A]	2003	2004	2005	TTM
Return on Assets %	11.2	10.7	16.0	16.0
Oper Cash Flow $Mil	1,627	1,247	1,936	1,936
- Cap Spending $Mil	191	200	179	179
= Free Cash Flow $Mil	1,437	1,047	1,756	1,756

Financial Health [A]	2003	2004	2005	07-31-06
Long-term Debt $Mil	410	407	205	205
Total Equity $Mil	9,262	8,929	6,651	6,651
Debt/Equity Ratio	0.0	0.0	0.0	0.0

Industry	Business Risk	Moat Size	Investment Style	Sector
Semiconductor Equip.	Average	Wide	Large Growth	Hardware

Competition	Market Cap $Mil	12 Mo Trailing Sales $Mil	Price/Cash Flow	Return On Assets%	Debt/Equity	Total Return% 1 Yr	3 Yr
Applied Materials	25,696	9,167	13.3	16.0	0.0	3.9	-5.4
KLA-Tencor	9,905	1,982	29.6	8.2	—	1.9	-3.5
Lam Research	7,181	1,642	19.9	14.5	0.3	41.9	16.9

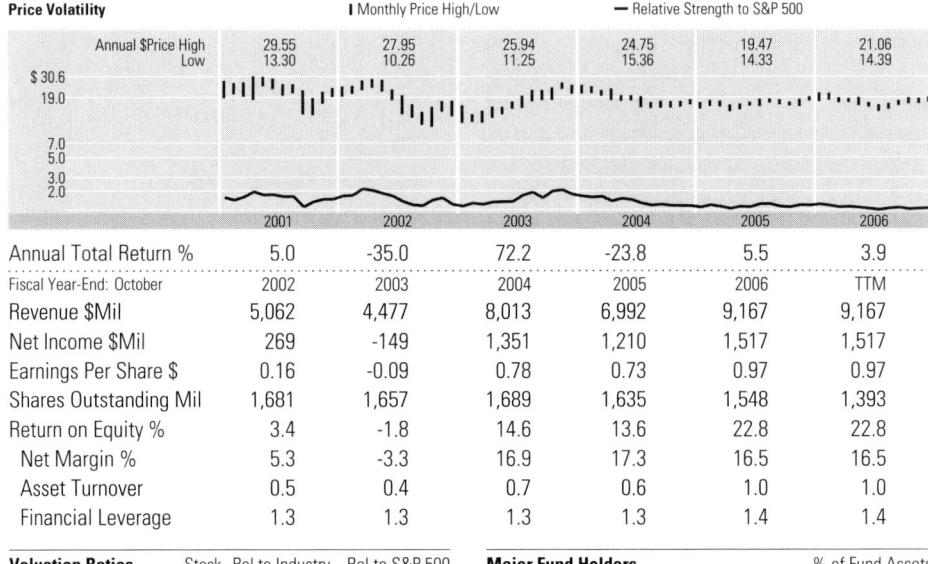

Price Volatility — Monthly Price High/Low — Relative Strength to S&P 500

	2001	2002	2003	2004	2005	2006
Annual $Price High	29.55	27.95	25.94	24.75	19.47	21.06
Low	13.30	10.26	11.25	15.36	14.33	14.39
Annual Total Return %	5.0	-35.0	72.2	-23.8	5.5	3.9

Fiscal Year-End: October	2002	2003	2004	2005	2006	TTM
Revenue $Mil	5,062	4,477	8,013	6,992	9,167	9,167
Net Income $Mil	269	-149	1,351	1,210	1,517	1,517
Earnings Per Share $	0.16	-0.09	0.78	0.73	0.97	0.97
Shares Outstanding Mil	1,681	1,657	1,689	1,635	1,548	1,393
Return on Equity %	3.4	-1.8	14.6	13.6	22.8	22.8
Net Margin %	5.3	-3.3	16.9	17.3	16.5	16.5
Asset Turnover	0.5	0.4	0.7	0.6	1.0	1.0
Financial Leverage	1.3	1.3	1.3	1.3	1.4	1.4

Valuation Ratios	Stock	Rel to Industry	Rel to S&P 500
Price/Earnings	19.0	0.7	0.9
Price/Book	3.9	0.9	1.0
Price/Sales	2.8	0.6	1.0
Price/Cash Flow	13.3	0.7	0.9

Major Fund Holders	% of Fund Assets
Firsthand Technology Leaders	7.04
Fidelity Select Electronics	6.00
Pin Oak Aggressive Stock	5.63
ProFunds Semiconductor UltraSector Inv	4.79

Thesis By Andy Ng, 12-13-06 Stock Price as of Analysis: $17.94

As the giant of the semiconductor equipment industry, Applied Materials has scale and product breadth that is unmatched by its smaller rivals. We think Applied's wide economic moat will allow the firm to maintain its industry-leading position.

Applied provides semiconductor fabrication tools to chipmakers. It is the dominant player in a fragmented industry and, with its broad product portfolio, competes in nearly every segment of the market, giving the firm a near ubiquitous presence in chip production. Applied is the nearest thing to a one-stop shop for chip manufacturers, as competitors are usually specialists in their respective segments. In 2005, the firm had a commanding 14% share in a $34 billion market, according to Gartner.

Applied has a wide moat for several reasons. Its installed base has grown to more than 17,000 tools, and the firm has engineers in nearly every chip manufacturing facility in the world. Applied's scale and trusted name have allowed it to develop close relationships with customers, giving the firm insight into current and future customer technology needs. Further, Applied's substantial resources allow it to compete successfully in various market segments, in aspects ranging from pricing and marketing to research and development. Few firms can rival Applied's $1 billion annual R&D budget. A strong balance sheet gives the company flexibility in a deeply cyclical industry and allows it to enter new markets with relative ease, either through internal development or acquisitions.

Applied also benefits from capacity expansion as chip devices become increasingly prevalent in everyday electronics. Advances in semiconductor technology are also growth drivers for the firm. As chip circuitries increase in complexity, semiconductor fabrication requires more process steps and new manufacturing technologies. Applied provides cutting-edge equipment to chipmakers, which allows them to produce state-of-the-art chips.

The recent acquisition of Applied Films helped pave the way for Applied to enter the emerging solar equipment market. Solar panels and chips share similar manufacturing technologies, allowing Applied to use its core technology expertise. Despite the potential of the solar opportunity (The firm hopes it will contribute about $500 million in sales by 2010), it is too early to tell whether the venture will be an ultimate success. Applied isn't always triumphant in its new endeavors. For example, in late 2005, Applied closed its struggling Etec subsidiary, which it bought for $1.8 billion worth of stock in 2000.

Data as of 12-29-06

Arthur J. Gallagher & Co. AJG

	Rating	Fair Value	Last Close	Consider Buy	Consider Sell	Yield %
	★★★★	$35.00	$29.55	$27.00	$43.90	4.06

Company Profile

More than two thirds of revenue at Arthur J. Gallagher & Co. comes from insurance brokerage. Gallagher advises corporate and institutional clients on managing risk and recommends insurance products from third-party providers. Through its risk-management business, Gallagher processes claims for its clients and provides related services. The financial-services arm invests the firm's extra cash, largely in tax-advantaged ventures.

Management   Stewardship Grade [B]

Gallagher's sales- and service-focused organization is led by dynamic, inspirational leaders. CEO Pat Gallagher took the reins in 1995 from his uncle Bob Gallagher, who served as CEO from 1963 to 1994 and then remained as chairman. With the passing of Bob Gallagher in August 2006, CEO Pat became the company's chairman as well. We frown on the dual chairman and CEO role, but we're holding our Stewardship Grade at a B. Senior officers and directors own roughly $100 million in stock, helping to promote shareholder-friendly governance amidst strenuous anti-takeover defenses. Gallagher pays senior leaders a reasonable amount of annual cash and bonus compensation. We like the pay structure. Annual bonus pay varies with short-term results and appears tailored to individual contributions to firm performance.

Gallagher's business depends on clients' trust in its integrity. When asked how to establish a culture to earn this trust, CEO Pat Gallagher once responded, "If you do something in our organization that violates our integrity, I will kill you." We think this joke reflects serious underlying resolve and that the firm has developed a culture that respects the value of ethical behavior.

Two Pierce Place   www.ajg.com
Itasca, IL 60143-3141

Growth [C+]	2002	2003	2004	2005
Revenue %	20.2	19.6	17.7	3.3
Earnings/Share %	1.4	11.3	26.8	-83.9
Book Value/Share %	39.1	16.0	20.8	-0.5
Dividends/Share %	15.4	20.0	38.9	12.0

Profitability [B+]	2003	2004	2005	TTM
Return on Assets %	5.0	5.8	0.9	3.3
Oper Cash Flow $Mil	229	277	189	—
- Cap Spending $Mil	25	29	23	—
= Free Cash Flow $Mil	—	—	—	—

Financial Health [NA]	2003	2004	2005	09-30-06
Long-term Debt $Mil	—	—	—	—
Total Equity $Mil	619	761	769	846
Debt/Equity Ratio	—	—	—	—

Industry	Business Risk	Moat Size	Investment Style	Sector
Insurance (General)	Average	Narrow	Mid Value	Financial Services

Competition	Market Cap $Mil	12 Mo Trailing Sales $Mil	Price/Cash Flow	Return On Assets %	Debt/ Equity	Total Return% 1 Yr	3 Yr
Arthur J. Gallagher & Co.	2,899	1,495	—	3.3	—	0.0	1.2
Marsh & McLennan Companie	16,897	11,715	—	4.5	—	-1.2	-11.9
Aon	11,113	10,006	—	2.4	—	-0.1	16.2

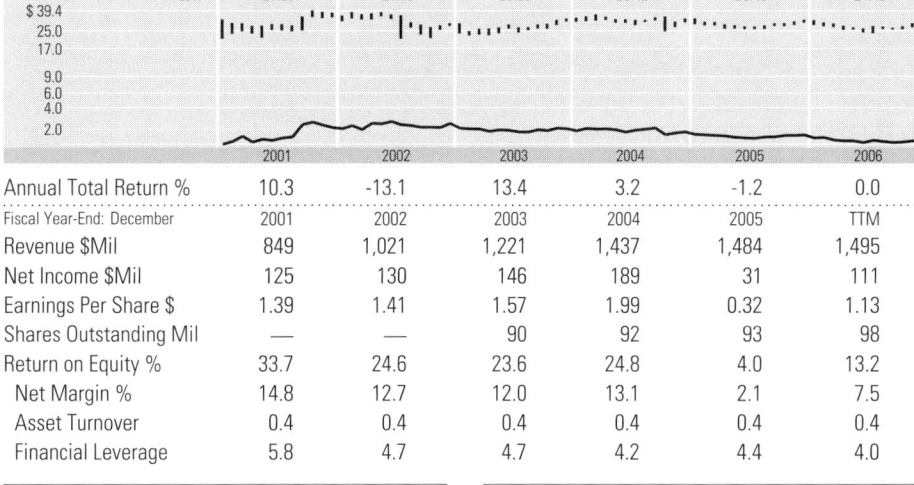

	2001	2002	2003	2004	2005	TTM
Annual Total Return %	10.3	-13.1	13.4	3.2	-1.2	0.0
Fiscal Year-End: December	2001	2002	2003	2004	2005	TTM
Revenue $Mil	849	1,021	1,221	1,437	1,484	1,495
Net Income $Mil	125	130	146	189	31	111
Earnings Per Share $	1.39	1.41	1.57	1.99	0.32	1.13
Shares Outstanding Mil	—	—	90	92	93	98
Return on Equity %	33.7	24.6	23.6	24.8	4.0	13.2
Net Margin %	14.8	12.7	12.0	13.1	2.1	7.5
Asset Turnover	0.4	0.4	0.4	0.4	0.4	0.4
Financial Leverage	5.8	4.7	4.7	4.2	4.4	4.0

Valuation Ratios	Stock	Rel to Industry	Rel to S&P 500	Major Fund Holders	% of Fund Assets
Price/Earnings	25.9	1.7	1.3	AIM Trimark Endeavor A	4.35
Price/Book	3.4	1.7	0.8	Stonebridge Small-Cap Growth	3.69
Price/Sales	1.9	1.1	0.7	Ave Maria Rising Dividend	3.55
Price/Cash Flow	—	—	—	Excelsior Equity Income	3.37

Thesis By Bill Bergman, 11-20-06 Stock Price as of Analysis: $29.14

Arthur J. Gallagher's focus on selling insurance to niche-market clients and its successful development of scale and scope economies garner the firm a narrow economic moat. Our fair value estimate is $35 per share.

Insurance brokerage is a highly competitive business, but Gallagher has built a narrow moat by specializing in more than 20 niches, like shopping centers, universities, public entities, construction contractors, and sports teams. Niche markets can provide relatively high brokerage profitability, but the whole is more than the sum of the parts. Customers increasingly view Gallagher as a valuable solution because it provides efficient one-stop access to a range of insurance coverage and to experts in a variety of risk-management services. These include claims advocacy, appraisal services, risk-control consulting, and alternative risk solutions, like weather derivatives. Gallagher creates scope economies because customers attached to one of these services can benefit from the firm's other specialties more easily than acquiring the services piecemeal. Plus, as the firm spreads increased volume over its backbone infrastructure, its healthy operating margins increase.

We're not typically big fans of acquisitive firms, but Gallagher's acquisitions enhance rather than destroy shareholder value--a rarity. Gallagher executes a disciplined acquisition strategy that expands its range of niche market products, bolstering its scope economies. For Gallagher, organic growth and acquisitions feed off each other. Gallagher can cross-sell its existing products to customers in newly acquired specialty lines, while acquired brokers and their customers can benefit from other services in the Gallagher supermarket. Avoiding acquisition missteps is difficult, but Gallagher has developed expertise to identify, attract, and meld complementary brokers. The firm's acquisition expertise establishes an entry barrier to achieving the scale and scope economies that consolidation can provide.

Gallagher's high-quality claim services further differentiate the firm and enhance its moat. Customers want quick and accurate claim payments without a lot of hassle. Gallagher makes this happen. What mediocre players view as a homely back-office function, winners like Gallagher turn into a key tool for customer satisfaction and longer-term success. Gallagher has also grown external sales in its claims services unit significantly.

Associated Banc-Corp ASBC

Data as of 12-29-06

Rating	Fair Value	Last Close	Consider Buy	Consider Sell	Yield %
★★★	$36.00	$34.88	$30.70	$47.30	3.27

Company Profile

Associated Banc-Corp is a conservative regional bank with about $21 billion in assets. Associated operates more than 320 branch locations primarily in Wisconsin, Minnesota, and Illinois. With its acquisition of First Federal Capital Bank in 2004, Associated added 50 supermarket locations to its distribution network, which improves the convenience with which its customers can bank. The firm's loan portfolio is approximately 60% commercial and 40% consumer loans.

Management   Stewardship Grade [B]

Paul Beideman has served as president and CEO since 2003. Before joining Associated, Beideman was an executive at Mellon Financial. Beideman has exhibited his management capabilities by integrating three sizable acquisitions while controlling expenses. Although not specifically stated as a requirement, a majority of the board members reside within Associated's core geographies of Wisconsin, Minnesota, and Illinois. The board appears to have sufficient understanding of the company's strategy, as the average tenure of the board members is about nine years, with five of the 11 members holding their positions for more than 12 years. Associated continues to maintain a change-in-control plan, which would allow for compensation for the CEO and 29 other senior executives in a takeover. We would view a change in this measure as a positive. We are excited that the company recently adopted a policy to terminate its staggered board structure in favor of an annual election of directors by 2009. We are encouraged that the board will be held accountable to its shareholders on an annual basis. This process will be phased in over the next three years.

1200 Hansen Road
Green Bay, WI 54304
www.associatedbank.com

Growth [B+]	2002	2003	2004	2005
Revenue %	16.1	1.5	4.8	26.3
Earnings/Share %	13.9	10.2	9.8	8.0
Book Value/Share %	15.3	7.7	45.4	0.4
Dividends/Share %	9.3	9.8	10.1	8.5

Profitability [A-]	2003	2004	2005	TTM
Return on Assets %	1.5	1.3	1.4	1.6
Oper Cash Flow $Mil	491	377	338	—
- Cap Spending $Mil	—	—	—	—
= Free Cash Flow $Mil	—	—	—	—

Financial Health [NA]	2003	2004	2005	09-30-06
Long-term Debt $Mil	—	—	—	—
Total Equity $Mil	1,348	2,017	2,325	2,270
Debt/Equity Ratio	—	—	—	—

Industry	Business Risk	Moat Size	Investment Style	Sector
Regional Banks	Below Avg	Narrow	Mid Value	Financial Services

Competition	Market Cap $Mil	12 Mo Trailing Sales $Mil	Price/Cash Flow	Return On Assets%	Debt/Equity	Total Return% 1 Yr	3 Yr
Associated Banc-Corp	4,545	981	—	1.6	—	11.0	10.6
Marshall & Ilsley	12,234	3,189	—	1.4	—	14.4	11.2
Huntington Bancshares	5,641	1,622	—	1.2	—	4.3	5.9

Price Volatility | Monthly Price High/Low — Relative Strength to S&P 500

	2001	2002	2003	2004	2005	2006
Annual $Price High	22.41	25.63	29.00	35.16	35.26	35.27
Low	17.42	18.01	21.33	26.99	28.87	30.10
Annual Total Return %	20.4	9.6	30.7	20.2	1.2	11.0

Fiscal Year-End: December	2001	2002	2003	2004	2005	TTM
Revenue $Mil	618	717	728	763	963	981
Net Income $Mil	180	211	229	258	320	330
Earnings Per Share $	1.63	1.86	2.05	2.25	2.43	2.45
Shares Outstanding Mil	109	112	110	113	131	130
Return on Equity %	16.8	16.6	17.0	12.8	13.8	14.5
Net Margin %	29.1	29.4	31.4	33.9	33.2	33.6
Asset Turnover	0.0	0.0	0.0	0.0	0.0	0.0
Financial Leverage	12.7	11.8	11.3	10.2	9.5	9.2

Valuation Ratios	Stock	Rel to Industry	Rel to S&P 500
Price/Earnings	14.2	0.8	0.7
Price/Book	2.0	0.7	0.5
Price/Sales	4.6	0.8	1.6
Price/Cash Flow	—	—	—

Major Fund Holders	% of Fund Assets
Old Westbury Mid Cap Equity	2.40
WHG SMidCap Inst	2.02
Nicholas Equity Income I	1.97
FMI Focus	1.77

Thesis By Erin Swanson, CFA, 11-28-06 Stock Price as of Analysis: $33.20

Associated Banc-Corp is a conservative bank with an intense focus on credit quality. Thanks to its efficient operating practices, Associated earns above-average returns that we believe are sustainable despite its Midwest footprint.

Although the Midwest suffers from a lack of growth compared with other U.S. regions, Associated has combated this by being extremely efficient. The company uses less than half of its revenue to fund its expenses. We view Associated's performance as particularly impressive considering that it managed to improve profitability while integrating several significant acquisitions.

Credit quality at Associated is not a concern of ours. According to the company, between 1970 and 2005, net charge-offs averaged 0.2% of loans, and in 2005, the bank held enough loan-loss reserves to cover more than 16 years' worth of charge-offs, assuming 2005's level of losses. Although we do not believe this low level of charge-offs is sustainable, we expect that management will continue to exhibit similar discipline as the credit environment tightens.

We are further impressed by Associated's efforts to improve its earnings quality by reducing its use of wholesale funding, which declined to 23% of total funding in September 2006 from 34% in September 2005. The continued flat yield curve increased Associated's funding costs without improving the yields on its longer-term assets. By reducing this funding, net margins improved to 3.63% in the third quarter of 2006 from 3.56% in the year-ago quarter. The fact that the company took on this initiative without incurring a one-time charge is a notable feat, in our opinion.

Finally, evidence suggests that management is a successful integrator. Associated took part in the regional bank industry's consolidation, completing more than 20 acquisitions in the past 15 years in both its core markets as well as new locations, without incurring any significant charges to complete these purchases. Associated's consistent performance produced an average return on tangible equity of 21% for its shareholders.

Associated continues to return value to shareholders through a combination of share repurchases and dividend increases. Its conservative lending policy and consistent performance make Associated an attractive investment candidate with a solid dividend yield.

AstraZeneca PLC ADR AZN

Data as of 12-29-06

Rating	Fair Value	Last Close	Consider Buy	Consider Sell	Yield %
★★★	$51.00	$53.55	$39.30	$63.90	2.63

Company Profile
AstraZeneca is the result of a 1999 merger between Astra of Sweden and Zeneca Group of the United Kingdom. It ranks first in gastrointestinal (ulcer) treatment sales worldwide and has a strong showing in cancer, respiratory, and heart medicines as well. The company's top five drugs in terms of worldwide sales account for more than 50% of total revenue. It sells products in more than 100 countries.

Management
Stewardship Grade [NA]

David Brennan became CEO at the beginning of 2006, taking over from Tom McKillop. Brennan came up through the ranks at AstraZeneca and previously headed the company's North American operations. We like the transparency of AstraZeneca's compensation policies and performance measures, but we wish the firm used long-term return measures in place of earnings per share to determine executive bonuses. Compensation levels seem reasonable given AstraZeneca's position as a large, global pharmaceutical firm, with total cash compensation to the board of directors and top four executives in 2005 totaling $19 million. We're pleased Brennan increased his ownership of AstraZeneca shares by more than 50% in 2005.

15 Stanhope Gate www.astrazeneca.com
London, United Kingdom W1K 1LN

Growth [NA]	2002	2003	2004	2005
Revenue %	10.0	5.7	13.7	11.8
Earnings/Share %	-0.6	7.9	23.2	33.5
Book Value/Share %	18.7	18.6	12.0	-1.7
Dividends/Share %	0.0	3.6	15.2	22.8

Profitability [NA]	2003	2004	2005	TTM
Return on Assets %	12.9	14.4	19.0	19.0
Oper Cash Flow $Mil	3,368	4,817	6,743	6,743
- Cap Spending $Mil	1,282	1,063	810	810
= Free Cash Flow $Mil	2,086	3,754	5,933	5,933

Financial Health [NA]	2003	2004	2005	12-31-05
Long-term Debt $Mil	351	1,127	1,111	1,111
Total Equity $Mil	13,175	14,497	13,691	13,691
Debt/Equity Ratio	0.0	0.1	0.1	0.1

Industry	Business Risk	Moat Size	Investment Style	Sector
Drugs	Average	Wide	Large Growth	Healthcare

Competition

	Market Cap $Mil	12 Mo Trailing Sales $Mil	Price/Cash Flow	Return On Assets %	Debt/ Equity	Total Return% 1 Yr	3 Yr
AstraZeneca PLC ADR	84,438	23,950	12.5	19.0	0.1	13.3	5.4
Pfizer	186,751	52,208	10.5	11.6	0.1	15.2	-7.4
Merck	94,656	22,358	13.0	11.6	0.2	42.7	1.7

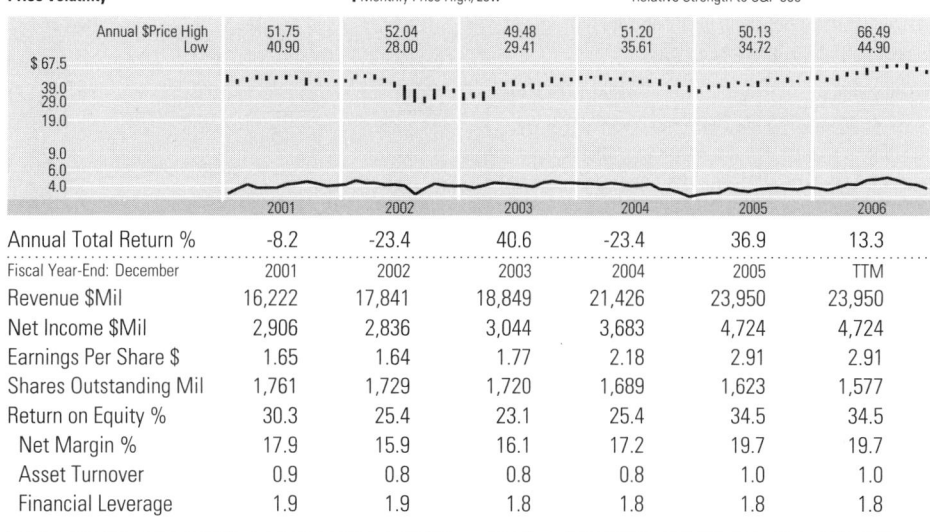

Price Volatility — Monthly Price High/Low — Relative Strength to S&P 500

	2001	2002	2003	2004	2005	2006
Annual $Price High	51.75	52.04	49.48	51.20	50.13	66.49
Low	40.90	28.00	29.41	35.61	34.72	44.90
Annual Total Return %	-8.2	-23.4	40.6	-23.4	36.9	13.3

Fiscal Year-End: December

	2001	2002	2003	2004	2005	TTM
Revenue $Mil	16,222	17,841	18,849	21,426	23,950	23,950
Net Income $Mil	2,906	2,836	3,044	3,683	4,724	4,724
Earnings Per Share $	1.65	1.64	1.77	2.18	2.91	2.91
Shares Outstanding Mil	1,761	1,729	1,720	1,689	1,623	1,577
Return on Equity %	30.3	25.4	23.1	25.4	34.5	34.5
Net Margin %	17.9	15.9	16.1	17.2	19.7	19.7
Asset Turnover	0.9	0.8	0.8	0.8	1.0	1.0
Financial Leverage	1.9	1.9	1.8	1.8	1.8	1.8

Valuation Ratios	Stock	Rel to Industry	Rel to S&P 500
Price/Earnings	18.4	0.8	0.9
Price/Book	6.2	1.1	1.5
Price/Sales	3.5	0.8	1.2
Price/Cash Flow	12.5	0.8	0.9

Major Fund Holders	% of Fund Assets
Fidelity Select Pharmaceuticals	4.78
AMIDEX Cancer Innovation & Healthcare	4.61
ProFunds Europe 30 Svc	4.18
ING Large Cap Growth A	3.91

Thesis By Heather Brilliant, CFA, 12-20-06 Stock Price as of Analysis: $53.80

AstraZeneca has distinguished itself as a leading provider of medicines to combat gastrointestinal diseases, and also boasts an impressive portfolio of drugs in oncology and cardiovascular and respiratory diseases. We think the firm's ability to rebound from major patent expirations and manage costs is a testament to its wide moat.

AstraZeneca is best known for its acid-reflux medicines, the ubiquitously advertised "purple pills" Prilosec and Nexium. Both of these products come from a class of drugs called proton pump inhibitors (PPIs), which help block the stomach acids that cause heartburn. In 2001, the outlook for AstraZeneca's branded drug sales was dire, as Prilosec and several other drugs neared their patent expirations. In response to that crisis, management skillfully introduced a follow-on drug, Nexium, to replace top-selling Prilosec. Today, Nexium is AstraZeneca's top seller.

Thanks to Nexium and other new products, AstraZeneca now enjoys one of the youngest and most diversified drug portfolios in the industry. Crestor for cholesterol and Symbicort for asthma recently reached blockbuster status. In fact, AstraZeneca currently markets 10 blockbuster drugs, each generating more than $1 billion in annual sales, and it faces fewer patent expirations in the next few years than many of its peers. Because AstraZeneca has been able to successfully market several products simultaneously, it is less dependent on a single drug for its future success.

Its drug portfolio is not without problems, though. Toprol-XL, AstraZeneca's product for the treatment of hypertension, is facing patent challenges by generic drug firms. We estimate that Toprol will bring in about $1.7 billion in sales in 2006, and we think that will fall precipitously in 2007 due to generic competition. Further, AstraZeneca's late-stage drug pipeline has suffered several blows in the past year as three drugs have failed to demonstrate adequate efficacy or safety in Phase III clinical trials. As a result, the firm stopped working on all three drugs, and now faces a dearth of products in late-stage development.

However, we think the firm can overcome these challenges. Its earlier-stage pipeline looks solid and was bolstered by its mid-2006 acquisition of Cambridge Antibody Technologies. The firm generates strong returns on invested capital that are easily more than double its cost of capital, and management is committed to returning excess cash to shareholders through dividends and share buybacks.

Data as of 12-29-06

AT&T T

	Rating	Fair Value	Last Close	Consider Buy	Consider Sell	Yield %
	★	$28.00	$35.75	$21.60	$35.10	2.79

Company Profile

AT&T is the dominant local phone company in 13 states, serving about 47 million local phone customers and 8 million high-speed Internet users. The firm also provides phone and data services, such as Web hosting and data transport, to consumers and businesses nationwide, notably large corporations. AT&T also owns 60% of Cingular Wireless, the largest U.S. carrier with nearly 60 million customers, and a directory-publishing business. The firm agreed to acquire BellSouth in March 2006.

Management Stewardship Grade [D]

AT&T's stewardship has improved recently, but we still have concerns about the firm's compensation practices. Edward Whitacre, chairman and CEO since 1990, has earned at least $6 million in annual salary and bonus for each of the past several years. In addition, in 2001 he was given a $10.5 million "special performance and retention" award and stock options worth about $40 million at the time of the grant. His total compensation was nearly $17 million during 2005. In early 2003, the firm attempted to block a shareholder proposal concerning compensation from coming to a vote. Since then, the board has reviewed its compensation policies and made some positive changes. Notably, equity compensation is now in the form of performance units, which pay out only if certain profitability criteria are met. Also, annual cash bonuses are based explicitly on earnings, free cash flow, and customer service, a big improvement from previous practice. However, in 2004, the firm exceeded its targets on all counts, which seems odd to us given that both earnings and free cash flow were down significantly from the previous year. During 2005, the firm paid out the maximum allowed for cash bonuses, which again doesn't jibe with the firm's performance, in our opinion. One big positive is the level of detail AT&T provides in its quarterly earnings releases.

175 E. Houston www.sbc.com
San Antonio, TX 78205-2233

Growth [B]	2002	2003	2004	2005
Revenue %	-5.6	-5.4	0.7	7.5
Earnings/Share %	-18.4	51.5	-30.9	-19.8
Book Value/Share %	3.4	16.0	5.8	33.2
Dividends/Share %	4.3	28.2	-8.6	3.2

Profitability [A-]	2003	2004	2005	TTM
Return on Assets %	8.3	5.3	3.3	4.9
Oper Cash Flow $Bil	13.4	11.0	13.0	15.2
- Cap Spending $Bil	5.2	5.1	5.6	8.0
= Free Cash Flow $Bil	8.2	5.9	7.4	7.2

Financial Health [B]	2003	2004	2005	09-30-06
Long-term Debt $Bil	16.1	21.2	26.1	26.8
Total Equity $Bil	38.2	40.5	54.7	55.4
Debt/Equity Ratio	0.4	0.5	0.5	0.5

Industry	Business Risk	Moat Size	Investment Style	Sector
Telecom Svcs.	Average	Narrow	Large Value	Telecommunication

Competition	Market Cap $Mil	12 Mo Trailing Sales $Mil	Price/Cash Flow	Return On Assets%	Debt/Equity	Total Return% 1 Yr	3 Yr
AT&T	137,384	60,171	9.0	4.9	0.5	51.6	16.3
AT&T	137,384	60,171	9.0	4.9	0.5	51.6	16.3
Verizon Communications	108,723	88,881	4.4	3.7	0.7	34.9	8.0

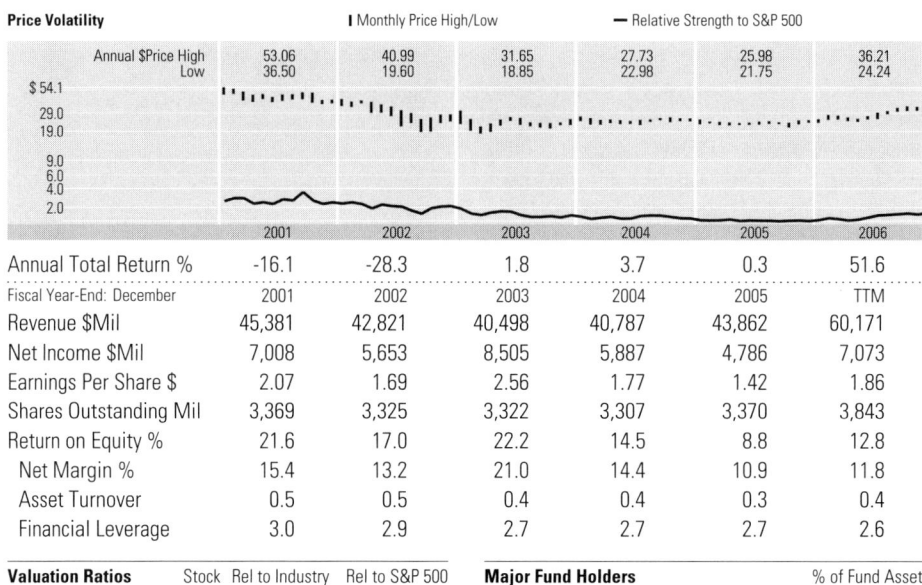

Annual Total Return %	-16.1	-28.3	1.8	3.7	0.3	51.6
Fiscal Year-End: December	2001	2002	2003	2004	2005	TTM
Revenue $Mil	45,381	42,821	40,498	40,787	43,862	60,171
Net Income $Mil	7,008	5,653	8,505	5,887	4,786	7,073
Earnings Per Share $	2.07	1.69	2.56	1.77	1.42	1.86
Shares Outstanding Mil	3,369	3,325	3,322	3,307	3,370	3,843
Return on Equity %	21.6	17.0	22.2	14.5	8.8	12.8
Net Margin %	15.4	13.2	21.0	14.4	10.9	11.8
Asset Turnover	0.5	0.5	0.4	0.4	0.3	0.4
Financial Leverage	3.0	2.9	2.7	2.7	2.7	2.6

Valuation Ratios	Stock	Rel to Industry	Rel to S&P 500
Price/Earnings	19.2	1.0	0.9
Price/Book	2.5	0.6	0.6
Price/Sales	2.3	1.0	0.8
Price/Cash Flow	9.0	1.0	0.6

Major Fund Holders	% of Fund Assets
ProFunds Telecom UltraSector Inv	22.24
Fidelity Select Telecommunications	15.32
Fidelity Advisor Utilities T	14.18
Fidelity Utilities	12.33

Thesis By Michael Hodel, CFA, 12-27-06 Stock Price as of Analysis: $35.42

The new AT&T reaches into almost every facet of the telecom sector. Acquiring BellSouth, a deal we think will close in early 2007, will expand the firm's reach into the Southeast and bring Cingular under direct control. But AT&T will still face several challenges as new technologies and rivals pressure the business.

BellSouth should be the last major piece in the AT&T puzzle. The two firms are closely related, sharing both history and control of Cingular Wireless. With BellSouth, AT&T will serve about 33 million residential local phone customers in a territory with around 50 million households, or 45% of the nation. This size pushes the scale of the combined firm well beyond its closest competitors. Comcast serves about 21.5 million customers in a territory with nearly 42 million households, and Verizon's territory covers about 30 million households. While this scale provides some benefits, the residential fixed-line business, which constitutes around 20% of combined sales, still faces a tough decision that magnifies its impact on the firm: Invest lightly in network upgrades and risk falling short of rivals' capabilities (notably cable) and customer demand, or invest heavily and risk not earning a decent return. Thus far, AT&T has chosen the former, with subpar results, in our view.

Cingular Wireless, about 30% of combined sales, is increasingly our favorite of AT&T's businesses. We think it is one of three firms with the financial resources and scale needed to dominate. With the BellSouth merger, AT&T will own all of Cingular, which will bring it under a single brand and should allow it to coordinate better with the fixed-line business to sell services. With recent consolidation, profitability has improved across the industry, but Cingular's results have been particularly impressive. Margins have steadily expanded while growth has accelerated, in large part a result of improved customer loyalty. Though its performance is still short of Verizon Wireless, we believe Cingular will continue to narrow the gap.

With the acquisition of the old AT&T in late 2005, the new AT&T is now the leader in the business-services and wholesale markets. Technology changes are also altering the way businesses purchase telecom services, but we think AT&T will enjoy several advantages in this market thanks to the reach and capabilities of its networks. The addition of BellSouth further enhances the reach of AT&T's networks and expands the number of customers it is uniquely positioned to serve. We think that the firm will be able to keep customers while reducing costs to support margins.

Data as of 12-29-06

Autodesk ADSK

	Rating	Fair Value	Last Close	Consider Buy	Consider Sell	Yield %
	★★★	$43.00	$40.46	$33.20	$53.90	0.00

Company Profile
Autodesk is the leading vendor of computer-aided software to designers and manufacturers around the world. Its customers are in 160 countries and range from 98% of the Fortune 1000 to single-person architectural firms. Manufacturing, infrastructure, building, media and entertainment, and wireless data services companies use Autodesk software to create, analyze, and manage their digital designs more efficiently, enabling them to complete their projects faster.

Management — Stewardship Grade [A]
In May, Carl Bass took over as CEO from Carol Bartz, who served in the role for 14 years. Bartz is now the company's chairman and will focus on Autodesk's opportunity in the developing world and on its key customer relationships. Bass has held many positions at the company, and we believe he was carefully groomed for his new role. Together, executive directors and officers own roughly 3% of shares, either through direct ownership or options. Although this doesn't constitute substantial ownership on a percentage basis, we believe executive officers have a substantial dollar investment in the firm that aligns their interests with shareholders.

Our Stewardship Grade is an "A," based on the company's transparency, shareholder-friendliness, and stewardship. Our largest gripe with the board had been management's liberal use of employee stock options (13% of shares outstanding at the end of fiscal 2006), but the firm has taken steps to curb such issuance over the past several years. The current investigation into stock option grant backdating is a black eye, and we will reassess our Stewardship Grade once the investigation's results are announced; so far it has been discovered that backdating did occur for broad-based, not just executive-based, grants.

111 McInnis Parkway
San Rafael, CA 94903
www.autodesk.com

Growth [B+]	2003	2004	2005	2006
Revenue %	-12.9	15.4	29.6	23.5
Earnings/Share %	-65.0	271.4	73.1	47.8
Book Value/Share %	6.5	7.6	-2.0	21.5
Dividends/Share %	0.0	0.0	0.0	-75.0

Profitability [A+]	2004	2005	2006	TTM
Return on Assets %	11.8	19.4	24.2	20.9
Oper Cash Flow $Mil	220	373	415	442
- Cap Spending $Mil	26	41	21	26
= Free Cash Flow $Mil	194	332	395	416

Financial Health [A]	2004	2005	2006	04-30-06
Long-term Debt $Mil	—	—	—	—
Total Equity $Mil	622	648	791	846
Debt/Equity Ratio	—	—	—	—

	Industry	Business Risk	Moat Size	Investment Style	Sector
	Business Appl.	Average	Wide	Mid Growth	Software

Competition	Market Cap $Mil	12 Mo Trailing Sales $Mil	Price/Cash Flow	Return On Assets%	Debt/ Equity	Total Return% 1 Yr	3 Yr
Autodesk	9,375	1,604	21.2	20.9	—	-5.8	49.1
Dassault Systemes SA ADR	6,081	1,170	24.7	13.1	—	-5.8	5.3
Parametric Tech	2,012	805	32.4	6.2	—	18.2	22.2

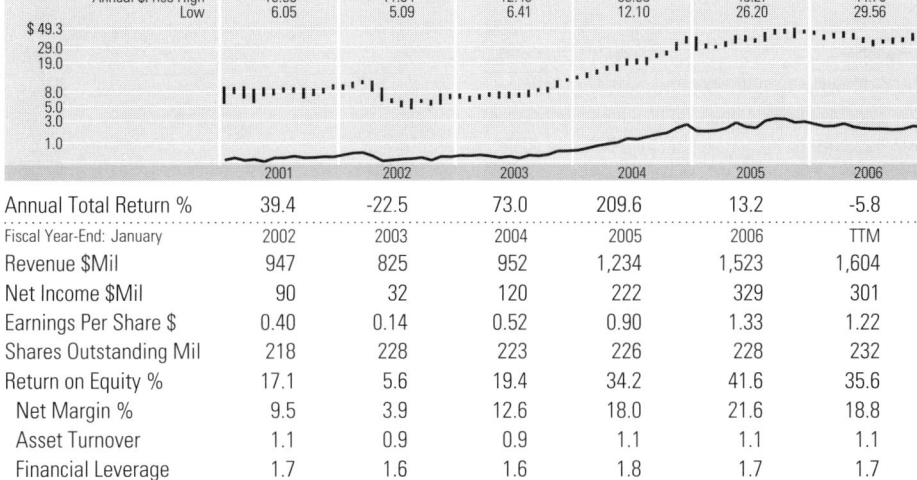

Annual Total Return %	39.4	-22.5	73.0	209.6	13.2	-5.8
Fiscal Year-End: January	2002	2003	2004	2005	2006	TTM
Revenue $Mil	947	825	952	1,234	1,523	1,604
Net Income $Mil	90	32	120	222	329	301
Earnings Per Share $	0.40	0.14	0.52	0.90	1.33	1.22
Shares Outstanding Mil	218	228	223	226	228	232
Return on Equity %	17.1	5.6	19.4	34.2	41.6	35.6
Net Margin %	9.5	3.9	12.6	18.0	21.6	18.8
Asset Turnover	1.1	0.9	0.9	1.1	1.1	1.1
Financial Leverage	1.7	1.6	1.6	1.8	1.7	1.7

Valuation Ratios	Stock	Rel to Industry	Rel to S&P 500
Price/Earnings	33.2	1.1	1.6
Price/Book	11.1	1.3	2.7
Price/Sales	5.8	0.9	2.0
Price/Cash Flow	21.2	0.8	1.5

Major Fund Holders	% of Fund Assets
Parnassus Workplace	5.44
Parnassus Mid-Cap	4.20
Permanent Portfolio Aggressive Growth	3.74
SunAmerica Focused Technology A	3.32

Thesis By Mike Ford-Taggart, CFA, 11-30-06 Stock Price as of Analysis: $41.18

Autodesk has enticing market opportunities, an unusually wide economic moat, and a strong management team.

Autodesk has long dominated mechanical design software with AutoCAD, its flagship product, enabling users to create everything from China's Chengdu hydroelectric dam to the digital coloring in movies. For customers, each annual upgrade of Autodesk products increases productivity and lowers time to market.

Three dramatic changes should continue to drive Autodesk's financial performance for several years. First, instead of buying licenses, customers are increasingly subscribing to Autodesk products to get feature-enhancing add-ons and faster, slightly cheaper upgrades. For Autodesk, subscription revenue is more stable, as it is recognized ratably, and carries fatter gross margins (above 95%) than traditional license revenue. Subscription revenue is now 22% of total firm revenue.

Second, more and more designers want to analyze virtually created products before finalizing them, and 3D software allows for faster, easier, and more robust analysis than 2D software. Since customers are already familiar with Autodesk software, they typically migrate to an Autodesk 3D solution, rather than choosing an altogether new software provider; high economic switching costs once again protect Autodesk's economic moat. For Autodesk, 3D solutions bring in 2-3 times more revenue than 2D solutions, boosting revenue growth and operating efficiency. Only 10% of the installed base is currently using 3D solutions, and we believe that long term, the majority of customers will make the transition, leaving plenty of room for growth.

Third, Autodesk's revenue from developing countries is increasingly strong as the number of designers surges. This growth is not just due to modernization and the buildout of infrastructure. When Autodesk's multinational customers move into an underdeveloped region, they typically insist that their local suppliers and manufacturers also use legitimate Autodesk software. As users switch from pirated software or as they become truly new users, their first purchase is typically the most advanced (and priciest) software package. Less than one third of Autodesk's revenue now comes from the United States, and that proportion will continue to decline.

Increased revenue should improve operating efficiency and cash generation, and we estimate that operating margins can expand 1-2 percentage points every year.

Data as of 12-29-06

Automatic Data Processing ADP

	Rating	Fair Value	Last Close	Consider Buy	Consider Sell	Yield %
	★★★★	$54.00	$49.25	$46.00	$70.90	1.59

Company Profile
ADP is one of the largest providers of computerized transaction processing, data communication, and information services. It is a leader in human resources services such as payroll and tax, and it also provides benefit administration and comprehensive outsourcing services. It serves about 600,000 clients and paid 32 million client employees in fiscal 2006.

Industry	Business Risk	Moat Size	Investment Style	Sector
Data Processing	Below Avg	Wide	Large Core	Business Services

Competition

	Market Cap $Mil	12 Mo Trailing Sales $Mil	Price/Cash Flow	Return On Assets%	Debt/Equity	Total Return% 1 Yr	3 Yr
Automatic Data Processing	27,117	9,177	17.2	6.1	0.0	9.1	8.8
Paychex	15,069	1,785	24.6	8.6	—	5.6	4.1
DST Systems	4,354	2,363	43.6	11.4	2.3	4.5	14.3

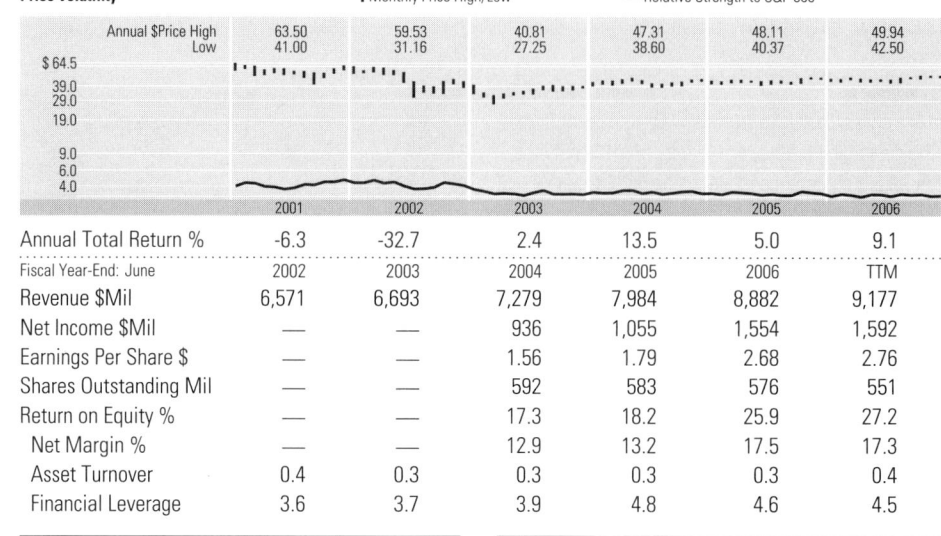

Price Volatility

Annual $Price High Low	63.50 41.00	59.53 31.16	40.81 27.25	47.31 38.60	48.11 40.37	49.94 42.50
	2001	2002	2003	2004	2005	2006
Annual Total Return %	-6.3	-32.7	2.4	13.5	5.0	9.1

Fiscal Year-End: June	2002	2003	2004	2005	2006	TTM
Revenue $Mil	6,571	6,693	7,279	7,984	8,882	9,177
Net Income $Mil	—	—	936	1,055	1,554	1,592
Earnings Per Share $	—	—	1.56	1.79	2.68	2.76
Shares Outstanding Mil	—	—	592	583	576	551
Return on Equity %	—	—	17.3	18.2	25.9	27.2
Net Margin %	—	—	12.9	13.2	17.5	17.3
Asset Turnover	0.4	0.3	0.3	0.3	0.3	0.4
Financial Leverage	3.6	3.7	3.9	4.8	4.6	4.5

Management Stewardship Grade [B]
CEO Gary Butler recently took the reins from Arthur Weinbach, ADP's longtime CEO. We feel comfortable with Butler at the helm given his experience as ADP's president and chief operating officer since 1998. The firm shows good shareholder stewardship, in our opinion. Management compensation is reasonable. We also like that the company sticks to its performance compensation objectives. In 2002 and 2003, Weinbach received annual bonuses that were substantially lower than his target, but he has been rewarded more recently for posting better results. However, we would prefer that annual performance bonuses were not based on metrics such as earnings per share growth, which could lead to some maneuvering. We like that the company offers long-term compensation in the form of restricted-stock units and options to better align management and shareholder interests. It recently instituted a two-year performance window, which began in July, and if performance targets are not met, no shares of restricted stock will be issued, which we like to see. Option issuance was high in 2004, with grants amounting to 3% of shares outstanding. However, grants have become more reasonable and were just 1.5% of shares outstanding in 2005 and 1.6% in 2006, a trend we like to see.

One ADP Boulevard
Roseland, NJ 07068-1728
www.adp.com

Growth [B-]	2003	2004	2005	2006
Revenue %	1.9	8.8	9.7	11.2
Earnings/Share %	—	NMF	14.7	49.7
Book Value/Share %		NMF	8.6	5.7
Dividends/Share %	6.1	13.7	12.0	17.4

Profitability [B+]	2004	2005	2006	TTM
Return on Assets %	4.4	3.8	5.7	6.1
Oper Cash Flow $Mil	1,385	1,433	1,813	1,578
- Cap Spending $Mil	188	187	292	275
= Free Cash Flow $Mil	1,197	1,246	1,520	1,303

Financial Health [B]	2004	2005	2006	09-30-06
Long-term Debt $Mil	76	76	74	74
Total Equity $Mil	5,418	5,784	6,012	5,848
Debt/Equity Ratio	0.0	0.0	0.0	0.0

Valuation Ratios

	Stock	Rel to Industry	Rel to S&P 500
Price/Earnings	25.1	1.1	1.2
Price/Book	4.6	0.9	1.1
Price/Sales	3.0	0.8	1.0
Price/Cash Flow	17.2	0.8	1.2

Major Fund Holders

	% of Fund Assets
JHancock U.S. Global Leaders Gr A	5.15
JHT U.S. Global Leaders Growth Tr Ser I	5.07
JHFunds2 U.S. Global Lead Gr NAV	5.03
Destination Select Equity	4.89

Thesis By Kristan Rowland, 12-08-06 Stock Price as of Analysis: $47.94

ADP is the leader in payroll processing solutions, and it benefits from its position in several ways. It boasts a 30% share of this market, by our estimates, and the firm's large size enables it to benefit from scale economies. Additionally, its fixed cost investment in payroll processing solutions means that each new customer added is hugely profitable and that its returns on invested capital are likely to remain topnotch. Further, it would be prohibitively expensive for a new entrant in this business to match the investment ADP has made in its platform and brand. The unrivaled scale, high entry barriers, and brand recognition all contribute to ADP's wide moat.

ADP's employer services division, which includes payroll services, makes up about two thirds of ADP's revenues and about three quarters of its profits. ADP's employer services unit also enjoys a high level of stability. It serves a diverse base of about 600,000 clients worldwide, so the loss of any one client is immaterial. This helps keep the firm's business risk low. Also, customer retention is high, about 90%, giving ADP a fairly predictable cash-flow stream. Given the amount of information ADP holds for each client, once a customer is entrenched with the firm, it faces high switching costs, another advantage of ADP's business model.

ADP's employer services division has room to grow, but may face some challenges. Untapped market opportunities, especially in the small-business market, and increased outsourcing should drive growth. However, despite the huge opportunity in small business, ADP may find it difficult to penetrate this base. Also, as it attracts more of these small-business clients, ADP may experience more client churn because small-business clients tend to have shorter lives.

ADP's recent decision to spin off its brokerage and securities clearing and outsourcing business is a good one, in our opinion. This allows the firm to focus on its "moaty" payroll processing and human resources solutions business. Its brokerage business has faced challenges. Financial institution mergers have resulted in some pressures as the larger institutions have extracted volume discounts, and industrywide declining revenues per trade have negatively impacted this business as well. We think ADP will benefit as it focuses on client payroll growth and leveraging its current massive client base to cross-sell additional human resources services. The future looks bright for this services provider, in our opinion.

Data as of 12-29-06

AutoNation AN

	Rating	Fair Value	Last Close	Consider Buy	Consider Sell	Yield %
	★★★	$23.00	$21.32	$17.70	$28.80	0.00

Company Profile

AutoNation is the largest automotive dealer in the United States with nearly 300 dealerships in 17 states, primarily in Sunbelt metropolitan areas. New-vehicle sales account for about 60% of revenue; the company also sells used vehicles, parts, and repair services, as well as auto financing. The company (formerly Republic Industries) spun off its waste-management unit (Republic Services) in 1999 and its car-rental businesses (ANC Rental) in 2000.

Management   Stewardship Grade [B]

Michael Jackson became CEO in September 1999 and chairman in 2003, taking the reins from founder Wayne Huizenga, who brought Waste Management and Blockbuster to prominence. Jackson has about three decades of industry sales experience, including many years at Mercedes-Benz USA, where he was CEO from October 1998 to September 1999. Jackson has led AutoNation's strategic shift away from growth and toward greater operating efficiency. We like the fact that a sizable portion of Jackson's total compensation package requires management to achieve performance targets that align management's interests with outside investors. Shareholders have a board advocate in private investor Eddie Lampert of Sears and Kmart fame, whose ESL Investments owns almost 25% of outstanding shares. Lampert heads the company's compensation committee, and is known to be a champion of returns on invested capital over growth. Lampert took some of his chips off the table through a 2006 leveraged stock repurchase program, but he remains a major shareholder.

110 S.E. 6th Street   www.autonation.com
Ft. Lauderdale, FL 33301

Growth [D]	2002	2003	2004	2005
Revenue %	-1.7	0.4	4.2	1.1
Earnings/Share %	72.5	40.3	-4.8	16.4
Book Value/Share %	7.2	12.9	13.6	11.3
Dividends/Share %	NMF	NMF	NMF	NMF

Profitability [B]	2003	2004	2005	TTM
Return on Assets %	5.4	5.0	5.6	3.8
Oper Cash Flow $Mil	481	564	580	529
- Cap Spending $Mil	132	211	142	177
= Free Cash Flow $Mil	349	353	438	352

Financial Health [B]	2003	2004	2005	09-30-06
Long-term Debt $Mil	809	798	484	1,462
Total Equity $Mil	3,950	4,263	4,670	3,660
Debt/Equity Ratio	0.2	0.2	0.1	0.4

Industry	Business Risk	Moat Size	Investment Style	Sector
Auto Retail	Average	Narrow	Mid Value	Consumer Services

Competition	Market Cap $Mil	12 Mo Trailing Sales $Mil	Price/Cash Flow	Return On Assets%	Debt/Equity	Total Return% 1 Yr	3 Yr
AutoNation	4,429	19,384	8.4	3.8	0.4	-1.9	5.8
CarMax	5,729	6,862	62.0	11.3	0.0	93.8	20.7
United Auto Group	2,227	11,189	8.3	2.9	0.7	25.0	17.0

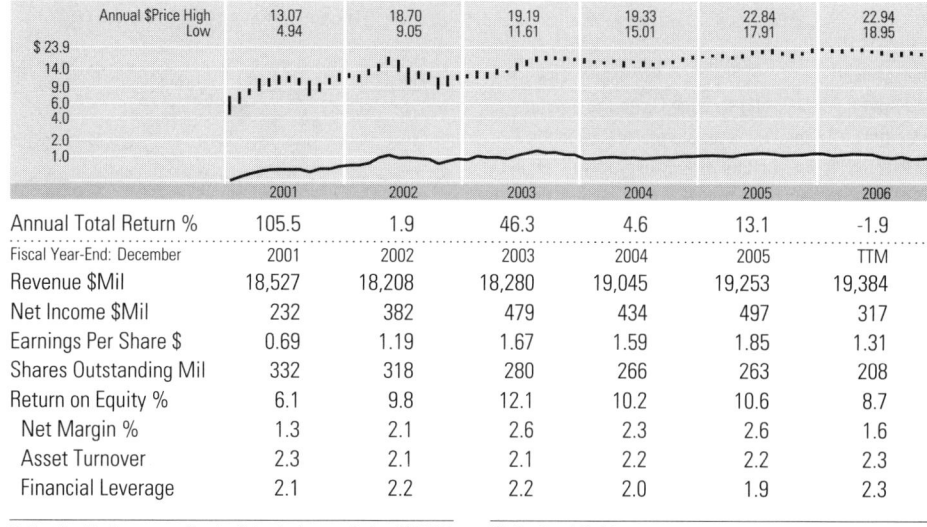

Annual Total Return %	105.5	1.9	46.3	4.6	13.1	-1.9
Fiscal Year-End: December	2001	2002	2003	2004	2005	TTM
Revenue $Mil	18,527	18,208	18,280	19,045	19,253	19,384
Net Income $Mil	232	382	479	434	497	317
Earnings Per Share $	0.69	1.19	1.67	1.59	1.85	1.31
Shares Outstanding Mil	332	318	280	266	263	208
Return on Equity %	6.1	9.8	12.1	10.2	10.6	8.7
Net Margin %	1.3	2.1	2.6	2.3	2.6	1.6
Asset Turnover	2.3	2.1	2.1	2.2	2.2	2.3
Financial Leverage	2.1	2.2	2.2	2.0	1.9	2.3

Valuation Ratios	Stock	Rel to Industry	Rel to S&P 500
Price/Earnings	15.3	0.8	0.7
Price/Book	1.2	0.2	0.3
Price/Sales	0.2	0.2	0.1
Price/Cash Flow	8.4	0.4	0.6

Major Fund Holders	% of Fund Assets
Fidelity Select Automotive	1.91
Wells Fargo Advantage Opportunity Inv	1.41
ING Partners Goldman Sachs Struct Eq Svc	1.41
Volumetric	1.38

Thesis By John Novak, 12-14-06 Stock Price as of Analysis: $20.69

As the country's biggest auto dealership group, AutoNation illustrates a paradox of growing large. On one hand, its size provides economies of scale that have helped the company establish a narrow economic moat. Yet with more than $19 billion in annual sales, AutoNation isn't likely to achieve the kind of growth it enjoyed in the past. Nevertheless, even if revenue growth slows, we think AutoNation's business model should deliver steady profits and ample free cash flow.

While most auto manufacturers face enormous fixed costs that prevent them from earning their cost of capital, auto dealerships have proved they can be good businesses. State franchise laws provide dealers with some protection against competitors and powerful manufacturers. In addition, dealers enjoy access to so-called floor-plan financing, a form of low-cost secured borrowing used to finance expensive vehicle inventories. Finally, the industry remains highly fragmented--we estimate the top 100 dealership groups account for less than 15% of total industry sales--providing an opportunity for consolidators like AutoNation, which can realize economies of scale by spreading fixed costs over a large store base.

For much of the 1990s, AutoNation was one of the industry's most prolific acquirers, but in recent years the company has shifted its focus to improving profitability at existing stores. We think the firm will continue to grow through selective acquisitions, but at much slower pace than it has in the past. For one, AutoNation's size means only very large acquisitions will have a meaningful impact on the company's overall growth rate. In addition, consolidation has reduced the number of large dealership groups available for sale and driven up prices on those that remain. AutoNation has proved to be a disciplined acquisitor, so we don't think it's likely to engage in bidding wars for targets.

Although we expect top-line growth to slow, we think AutoNation will continue to produce steady profits and solid free cash flow. Like most auto retailers, the company generates revenue from multiple sources, and the bulk of operating profits comes from the sale of high-margin parts and services. This aftermarket parts and services businesses are growing areas where we think the firm can focus to improve same-store profitability. Despite potential volatility arising from its exposure to Detroit's struggling Big Three, we think the company's Asian and European dealerships will help stabilize the company.

AutoZone AZO

Data as of 12-29-06

	Rating	Fair Value	Last Close	Consider Buy	Consider Sell	Yield %
	★★★	$115.00	$115.56	$98.00	$151.00	0.00

Industry	Business Risk	Moat Size	Investment Style	Sector
Auto Retail	Below Avg	Narrow	Mid Core	Consumer Services

Company Profile
AutoZone is the largest specialty retailer of automotive parts and accessories to do-it-yourself individuals and professional installers. As of August 2006, the firm had 3,771 stores in the United States and 100 in Mexico. The firm also sells ALLDATA diagnostic and repair software.

Competition

	Market Cap $Mil	12 Mo Trailing Sales $Mil	Price/Cash Flow	Return On Assets %	Debt/Equity	Total Return % 1 Yr	Total Return % 3 Yr
AutoZone	8,167	6,003	10.1	12.6	3.5	26.0	11.1
Genuine Parts	8,082	10,325	22.3	9.5	0.2	11.4	16.3
Advance Auto Parts	3,842	4,265	11.8	9.2	0.4	-17.6	9.7

Management — Stewardship Grade [A]
William Rhodes III, who has been with the firm for more than 10 years, became the fourth CEO in the company's 25-year history after Steve Odland left in 2005. Founder and board member J.R. Hyde III took on the role of chairman. We like that the CEO and chairman roles have been split. Generally, we find that the firm has avoided the common pitfalls of corporate governance, earning it an excellent Stewardship Grade. Directors are elected every year and can only receive half of their compensation in cash, with the rest in stock options. Edward Lampert recently stepped down as a director, but his hedge fund, ESL Investments, still beneficially owns 31% of the common stock. In fiscal 2006, Rhodes earned a $605,077 salary, $567,079 bonus, and 50,000 options, which we view as reasonable. We are pleased to see that part of his variable compensation was tied to returns on invested capital.

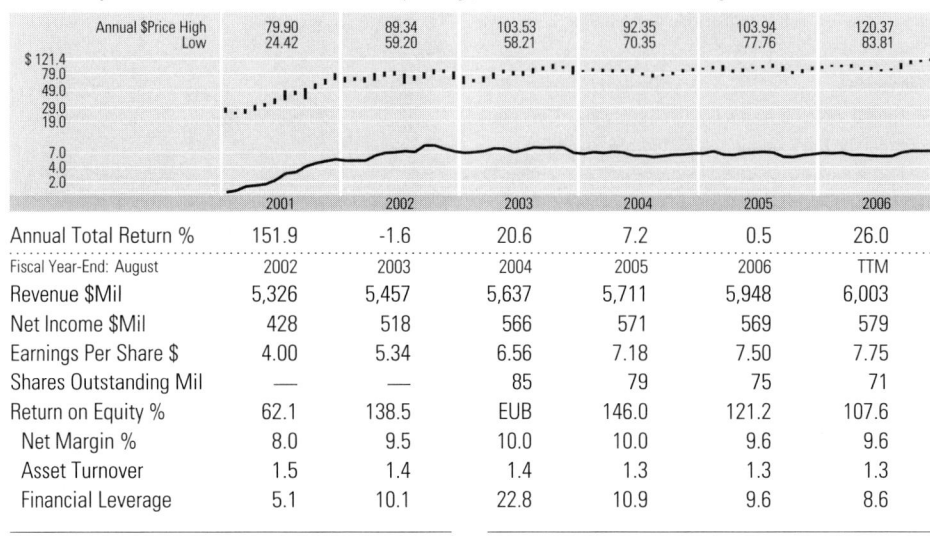

Price Volatility — Monthly Price High/Low — Relative Strength to S&P 500

	2001	2002	2003	2004	2005	2006
Annual $Price High	79.90	89.34	103.53	92.35	103.94	120.37
Low	24.42	59.20	58.21	70.35	77.76	83.81
Annual Total Return %	151.9	-1.6	20.6	7.2	0.5	26.0

Fiscal Year-End: August	2002	2003	2004	2005	2006	TTM
Revenue $Mil	5,326	5,457	5,637	5,711	5,948	6,003
Net Income $Mil	428	518	566	571	569	579
Earnings Per Share $	4.00	5.34	6.56	7.18	7.50	7.75
Shares Outstanding Mil	—	—	85	79	75	71
Return on Equity %	62.1	138.5	EUB	146.0	121.2	107.6
Net Margin %	8.0	9.5	10.0	10.0	9.6	9.6
Asset Turnover	1.5	1.4	1.4	1.3	1.3	1.3
Financial Leverage	5.1	10.1	22.8	10.9	9.6	8.6

Valuation Ratios	Stock	Rel to Industry	Rel to S&P 500
Price/Earnings	14.9	0.8	0.7
Price/Book	15.2	3.0	3.7
Price/Sales	1.4	1.6	0.5
Price/Cash Flow	10.1	0.5	0.7

Major Fund Holders	% of Fund Assets
Fidelity Select Automotive	5.14
SunAmerica Focused Value A	3.53
Legg Mason Special Investment Prim	2.95
Excelsior Mid Cap Value & Restructuring	2.92

123 South Front Street
Memphis, TN 38103
www.autozone.com

Growth [C]	2003	2004	2005	2006
Revenue %	2.5	3.3	1.3	4.2
Earnings/Share %	33.5	22.8	9.5	4.5
Book Value/Share %	-40.1	-48.5	147.6	25.8
Dividends/Share %	NMF	NMF	NMF	NMF

Profitability [A+]	2004	2005	2006	TTM
Return on Assets %	14.5	13.5	12.6	12.6
Oper Cash Flow $Mil	638	648	823	807
- Cap Spending $Mil	185	283	264	257
= Free Cash Flow $Mil	454	365	559	550

Financial Health [B]	2004	2005	2006	08-31-06
Long-term Debt $Mil	1,869	1,862	1,857	1,859
Total Equity $Mil	171	391	470	538
Debt/Equity Ratio	10.9	4.8	4.0	3.5

Thesis By Michelle Chang, 11-09-06   Stock Price as of Analysis: $112.87

AutoZone is the leading retailer in the automotive aftermarket. Competitors are gaining ground, but we think its size still gives AutoZone advantages over its smaller rivals.

AutoZone's stores are more productive, delivering $243 in sales per square foot in fiscal 2006, compared with $220 for O'Reilly Automotive and $208 for Advance Auto Parts in 2005. With the largest store footprint of almost 3,800 U.S. locations, AutoZone has more power in negotiating lower prices from suppliers and more leverage in fixed costs. These factors contributed to a 17% operating margin in fiscal 2006. Second-place O'Reilly is a ways behind at 12%.

Competition is heightening, however. Because of its much larger size, AutoZone has fewer opportunities to increase its footprint. The company has expanded its store base at an average of 5% over the past five years, a slower rate than Advance and O'Reilly.

Another reason AutoZone's growth has lagged competitors' in recent years is its slower expansion into the professional segment. In 2005, commercial sales were 22% of Advance's revenue, while O'Reilly boasts a 50/50 mix between the commercial and consumer segments. AutoZone, however, still largely derives its revenue from the direct-to-consumer business. In fiscal 2006, U.S. direct retail sales totaled $5 billion, or 88% of AutoZone's total domestic parts revenue, with the remainder from professional sales. On average, revenue from the consumer segment has increased by 4% annually over the past five years, about on par with industry trends.

Because sales to professional installers are still a small percentage of AutoZone's business, we see opportunities to grow in this market, where no dominant player exists. The firm holds an advantage with the largest store and distribution network and can leverage this to further its presence among the professional base. AutoZone has increased revenue from this segment by $177 million over the past five years. Professional sales may have hiccuped in the past two years, but we have yet to see a full rollout of company initiatives. The firm has been experimenting in test markets to profitably expand commercial sales.

In the end, AutoZone is still the leader in sales productivity and profitability. While we anticipate incremental improvements from its competitors, those rivals still have some catching up to do.

AvalonBay Communities AVB

Data as of 12-29-06

Rating ★	Fair Value $64.00	Last Close $130.05	Consider Buy $49.40	Consider Sell $80.20	Yield % 2.40

Industry	Business Risk	Moat Size	Investment Style	Sector
REITs	Average	Narrow	Mid Core	Financial Services

Company Profile

AvalonBay Communities is a real estate investment trust that develops, owns, and manages upscale apartment communities. The company owns or has interests in more than 160 communities comprising more than 45,000 apartment units in 10 states and the District of Columbia. AvalonBay also owns development rights to 40 communities with a capacity of more than 12,000 apartment units. Nearly three fourths of rental income is generated in the Northeast and California.

Management   Stewardship Grade [B]

Bryce Blair joined predecessor firm Avalon Properties in 1993, becoming CEO and chairman in 2002. We like that the executive team has an average tenure of 16 years with the firm. Blair received about $1.8 million in salary and bonus in 2005--a reasonable amount, in our opinion. The criteria for calculating cash bonuses reward both risk-taking (growth in funds from operations) and prudence (fixed-charge coverage ratios). We think this discourages management from pursuing projects that may put the dividend at risk. AvalonBay appears to have a strong, independent board; only one employee (the CEO) sits on the board. And, all outside directors, with the exception of the lead director, receive company stock rather than cash as compensation. Directors and executives together own 4% of the common stock.

2900 Eisenhower Avenue Suite 300   www.avalonbay.com
Alexandria, VA 22314

Growth [C+]	2002	2003	2004	2005
Revenue %	2.0	4.5	10.1	9.3
Earnings/Share %	-26.2	67.3	-21.7	44.2
Book Value/Share %	NMF	NMF	NMF	3.4
Dividends/Share %	9.4	0.0	0.0	1.4

Profitability [A]	2003	2004	2005	TTM
Return on Assets %	5.3	4.2	6.1	5.7
Oper Cash Flow $Mil	240	276	307	—
- Cap Spending $Mil	369	498	459	—
= Free Cash Flow $Mil	—	—	—	—

Financial Health [NA]	2003	2004	2005	09-30-06
Long-term Debt $Mil	—	—	—	—
Total Equity $Mil	—	2,385	2,542	2,635
Debt/Equity Ratio	—	—	—	—

Competition

	Market Cap $Mil	12 Mo Trailing Sales $Mil	Price/Cash Flow	Return On Assets%	Debt/ Equity	Total Return% 1 Yr	3 Yr
AvalonBay Communities	9,702	716	—	5.7	—	49.7	45.3
Equity Residential	14,826	2,187	—	5.3	—	34.6	25.5
Archstone-Smith Trust	12,734	1,190	—	6.6	—	43.9	35.1

Price Volatility | Monthly Price High/Low   — Relative Strength to S&P 500

	2001	2002	2003	2004	2005	2006
Annual $Price High	51.90	52.65	49.71	75.93	92.99	134.60
Low	42.45	36.38	35.24	46.72	64.98	88.95
Annual Total Return %	-0.4	-11.9	30.2	65.0	22.8	49.7

Fiscal Year-End: December	2001	2002	2003	2004	2005	TTM
Revenue $Mil	523	534	558	614	671	716
Net Income $Mil	209	156	261	211	314	317
Earnings Per Share $	3.02	2.23	3.73	2.92	4.21	4.21
Shares Outstanding Mil	68	69	69	72	73	75
Return on Equity %	NMF	NMF	NMF	8.8	12.3	12.0
Net Margin %	39.9	29.2	46.8	34.4	46.8	44.3
Asset Turnover	0.1	0.1	0.1	0.1	0.1	0.1
Financial Leverage	—	—	—	2.1	2.0	2.1

Valuation Ratios	Stock	Rel to Industry	Rel to S&P 500
Price/Earnings	67.7	1.4	3.3
Price/Book	3.7	0.9	0.9
Price/Sales	13.5	1.8	4.7
Price/Cash Flow	—	—	—

Major Fund Holders	% of Fund Assets
Principal Inv Real Estate Sec Pfd	6.34
JPMorgan U.S. Real Estate A	6.16
E.I.I. Realty Securities Instl	5.65
Morgan Stanley Real Estate B	5.48

Thesis   By Jeremy Glaser, 10-27-06   Stock Price as of Analysis: $129.49

AvalonBay Communities' luxury apartments have benefited greatly from a softening new home market, which is sending tenants rushing back into rentals. We believe AvalonBay's future is bright--the company is one of the best developers in the business, and its large development pipeline should fuel growth.

Low interest rates and a fear of being left out of the housing boom led to an unprecedented rise in the number of homeowners, forcing AvalonBay to lower rents to retain tenants. This trend started reversing in 2005 as rising mortgage rates and stratospheric housing prices created a large affordability gap between renting and buying. As buyers are priced out of the market, AvalonBay can charge more while increasing occupancy to near-record levels. With job growth looking strong in many of AvalonBay's core markets, we believe the fundamentals for the company should strengthen.

AvalonBay focuses on major coastal markets; its largest holdings are in the Northeast and California. With limited land supply and a bewildering entitlement and permitting process, these regions experience both little growth in multifamily rental supply and high single family housing prices. We believe these factors, combined with immigration growth on the coasts, should drive demand, allowing AvalonBay to increase rents faster than the national average. The downside of this concentration is that AvalonBay's profits are vulnerable to regional downturns in job or population growth.

We like that AvalonBay relies on its development expertise to fuel growth--most apartment real estate investment trusts depend on more costly acquisitions to expand. With almost 4,000 units under construction and 12,000 units in the planning stage, AvalonBay should have no problem growing without paying the high price that apartments currently fetch in the open market. It would be difficult for a competitor to replicate AvalonBay's development pipeline, which gives the company a distinct competitive advantage. We would happily invest in AvalonBay at the right price.

Data as of 12-29-06

Avid Technology AVID

	Rating	Fair Value	Last Close	Consider Buy	Consider Sell	Yield %
	★★★★	$47.00	$37.26	$36.20	$58.90	0.00

Company Profile
Avid sells hardware and software products that help make, manage, and distribute video, film, audio, and 3-D animation content. Its technology is used primarily by film studios, television networks, recording studios, advertising agencies, and government and educational organizations. Projects using the company's tools have received high-profile awards such as Oscars, Emmys, and a Grammy. Avid sells its hardware and software primarily through resellers and distributors.

Management
Stewardship Grade [C]

David Krall has been CEO since April 2000. The board of directors brought in a new management team in 2000 that consisted of several executives from Digidesign, the digital audio firm Avid acquired a few years earlier. This team's recent record has been unsatisfactory: A number of snafus with Pinnacle's acquisition, several botched product transitions, and quality-control issues have tarnished Avid's stellar reputation and undermined investors' confidence in management's abilities. Avid has handed out roughly 4% of its outstanding shares in the form of option grants over the past three years, which we consider to be overly generous. The firm also has several antitakeover provisions in place. Its elections for board of directors are staggered into three classes. Executive compensation is protected in the case of an unsolicited takeover through a change-in-control agreement, and a poison pill exists in the form of a shareholder-rights agreement. We also disapprove of Avid's recent accelerated vesting of certain stock options. This cosmetic accounting trick has no cash impact and only serves to reduce the option grant expense Avid is now required to include on its income statement.

Avid Technology Park One Park West www.avid.com
Tewksbury, MA 01876

Growth [A]	2002	2003	2004	2005
Revenue %	-3.7	12.7	24.9	31.5
Earnings/Share %	NMF	EUB	64.0	-58.0
Book Value/Share %	10.8	53.2	74.8	75.0
Dividends/Share %	NMF	NMF	NMF	NMF

Profitability [B]	2003	2004	2005	TTM
Return on Assets %	11.7	12.4	3.2	2.7
Oper Cash Flow $Mil	59	81	50	33
- Cap Spending $Mil	8	15	18	20
= Free Cash Flow $Mil	51	66	32	14

Financial Health [A]	2003	2004	2005	09-30-06
Long-term Debt $Mil	1	0	0	—
Total Equity $Mil	227	425	840	822
Debt/Equity Ratio	0.0	0.0	0.0	0.0

Industry	Business Risk	Moat Size	Investment Style	Sector
Business Appl.	Average	Narrow	Small Core	Software

Competition

	Market Cap $Mil	12 Mo Trailing Sales $Mil	Price/Cash Flow	Return On Assets%	Debt/ Equity	Total Return% 1 Yr	3 Yr
Avid Technology	1,527	917	46.0	2.7	0.0	-32.0	-8.2
Apple Computer	72,901	19,315	32.8	11.6	—	18.0	99.8
Sony ADR	42,870	66,335	12.1	1.2	0.2	5.5	7.6

Price Volatility
| Monthly Price High/Low   — Relative Strength to S&P 500

Annual $Price High/Low	22.50/6.50	23.47/7.25	59.77/16.76	62.57/38.43	68.35/35.78	59.10/32.05
	2001	2002	2003	2004	2005	2006
Annual Total Return %	-33.4	88.9	109.2	28.6	-11.3	-32.0

Fiscal Year-End: December	2001	2002	2003	2004	2005	TTM
Revenue $Mil	435	419	472	590	775	917
Net Income $Mil	-38	3	41	72	34	28
Earnings Per Share $	-1.49	0.11	1.25	2.05	0.86	0.67
Shares Outstanding Mil	26	27	29	32	38	41
Return on Equity %	-36.4	2.4	18.0	16.9	4.0	3.4
Net Margin %	-8.8	0.7	8.7	12.2	4.4	3.1
Asset Turnover	2.0	1.8	1.4	1.0	0.7	0.9
Financial Leverage	2.1	1.9	1.5	1.4	1.3	1.3

Valuation Ratios	Stock	Rel to Industry	Rel to S&P 500
Price/Earnings	55.6	1.9	2.7
Price/Book	1.9	0.2	0.5
Price/Sales	1.7	0.3	0.6
Price/Cash Flow	46.0	1.8	3.2

Major Fund Holders	% of Fund Assets
Columbia Acorn Select Z	3.72
Brown Advisory Opportunity Instl	3.58
Parnassus Small-Cap	3.52
Ancora Special Opportunity C	3.44

Thesis By Irina Logovinsky, CPA, 11-16-06 Stock Price as of Analysis: $40.11

Avid Technology has developed highly regarded solutions to create and manage media content for the broadcast and entertainment markets. Its products support global news networks and serve as video-editing tools for movie studios and video game developers. But despite its reputation for excellent products, Avid has repeatedly stumbled during major product upgrades. It has also struggled to integrate Pinnacle Systems, a consumer video-editing company, creating headaches for management and an opportunity for rivals to grab market share.

Avid's narrow economic moat stems from high switching costs. Since filmmakers and broadcasters are trained early in their careers to use Avid, the time and cost required to learn a new technology are too extreme to justify switching. In addition, these clients would be hard-pressed to find a comparable combination of cutting-edge hardware and software to satisfy their pressing production needs.

Avid dominates roughly 50% of the market and continues to grow, thanks to an evolution in media technology. Its large clients are upgrading their tape-based equipment to all-digital platforms. The Federal Communications Commission's mandate for high-definition broadcast signals is also inducing these content creators to transition to HD production.

These trends translate into heightened demand for Avid's new generation of products, which the company estimates has penetrated only one third of its client base.

Avid's long-term growth story is marred by a series of self-inflicted wounds. Its ill-executed acquisition of Pinnacle resulted in salesforce troubles that delayed broadcast hardware sales and quality-control problems that allowed the release of a flawed version of consumer software. The maladies of the consumer group might be detrimental to Avid's long-term success if future video editors (current students) avoid Avid because of product-quality concerns.

While the firm is recovering from these gaffes, rivals have taken the opportunity to grab share. Adobe and Apple have compelling offerings in the low- to mid-range video-editing market. We think Apple's Final Cut Pro could also deliver a damaging blow to Avid's high-end video-editing offerings as the product is finding its way to major newsroom editing floors.

Despite these worries, we believe the industry is still in the early stages of the digital and HD transformation, and over the longer term, Avid's topnotch products should outweigh its execution blunders.

Data as of 12-29-06

Avon Products AVP

	Rating	Fair Value	Last Close	Consider Buy	Consider Sell	Yield %
	★★★★	$41.00	$33.04	$31.60	$51.40	2.12

Company Profile
Avon is the world's largest direct seller of cosmetics; its famed "Avon ladies" now number 5 million. Its representatives conduct business in homes and workplaces. More than 65% of the company's sales come from outside the United States. Avon makes most of its own beauty-care products; it plans to expand its jewelry line and add lingerie products as well.

Industry	Business Risk	Moat Size	Investment Style	Sector
Household Products	Average	Wide	Large Growth	Consumer Goods

Competition	Market Cap $Mil	12 Mo Trailing Sales $Mil	Price/Cash Flow	Return On Assets%	Debt/ Equity	Total Return% 1 Yr	3 Yr
Avon Products	14,688	8,540	15.2	8.9	1.3	18.5	1.6
Procter & Gamble	203,656	72,214	16.8	6.8	0.6	13.4	11.3
Unilever NV	46,726	49,679	8.6	10.6	0.8	25.0	12.4

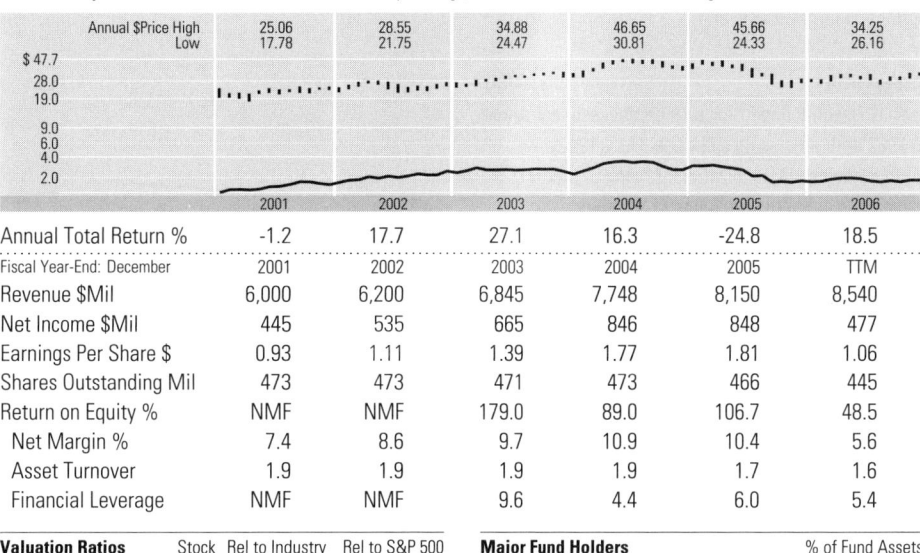

	2001	2002	2003	2004	2005	2006/TTM
Annual Total Return %	-1.2	17.7	27.1	16.3	-24.8	18.5
Fiscal Year-End: December	2001	2002	2003	2004	2005	TTM
Revenue $Mil	6,000	6,200	6,845	7,748	8,150	8,540
Net Income $Mil	445	535	665	846	848	477
Earnings Per Share $	0.93	1.11	1.39	1.77	1.81	1.06
Shares Outstanding Mil	473	473	471	473	466	445
Return on Equity %	NMF	NMF	179.0	89.0	106.7	48.5
Net Margin %	7.4	8.6	9.7	10.9	10.4	5.6
Asset Turnover	1.9	1.9	1.9	1.9	1.7	1.6
Financial Leverage	NMF	NMF	9.6	4.4	6.0	5.4

Management — Stewardship Grade [A]
CEO Andrea Jung orchestrated one turnaround at Avon in 1999 as head of global marketing, but her image has lost a bit of its luster over the past year as the company's turnaround appears to be taking longer than expected. There's a lot riding on Jung's leadership now, particularly with the departure of second-in-command Susan Kropf, who will retire at the end of 2006. In the last fiscal year, Jung received no bonus, a salary of $1.3 million (up slightly from the prior year), and 675,000 stock options that are deep under water. Moreover, the firm expects it will make no payouts under the 2005-07 performance plan it outlined before Avon's problems. We like the fact that bonus awards are actually withheld when financial targets aren't met. Generally speaking, Jung's total compensation is slightly above her peer group average, but we think Avon's compensation policy does a good job of balancing long-term strategic goals with short-term goals like growth in earnings per share. Senior executives are invested in Avon's turnaround, as they are required to own stock valued at 1-5 times their base salaries. Officers and directors own less than 1% of shares outstanding. The firm declassified its three-tier board structure, a move we applaud; now it should separate the chairman and CEO roles.

1345 Avenue of the Americas www.avon.com
New York, NY 10105-0196

Growth [B-]	2002	2003	2004	2005
Revenue %	3.3	10.4	13.2	5.2
Earnings/Share %	20.0	25.2	27.3	2.3
Book Value/Share %	NMF	NMF	156.0	-14.7
Dividends/Share %	5.3	5.0	33.3	17.9

Profitability [A]	2003	2004	2005	TTM
Return on Assets %	18.7	20.4	17.8	8.9
Oper Cash Flow $Mil	745	883	896	964
- Cap Spending $Mil	163	250	207	160
= Free Cash Flow $Mil	583	633	689	805

Financial Health [A]	2003	2004	2005	09-30-06
Long-term Debt $Mil	—	866	767	1,257
Total Equity $Mil	371	950	794	983
Debt/Equity Ratio	—	0.9	1.0	1.3

Valuation Ratios	Stock	Rel to Industry	Rel to S&P 500
Price/Earnings	31.2	1.3	1.5
Price/Book	14.9	2.5	3.6
Price/Sales	1.7	0.6	0.6
Price/Cash Flow	15.2	0.9	1.0

Major Fund Holders	% of Fund Assets
Ashport Large Cap C	5.64
Fidelity Advisor Strategic Growth T	3.35
Payson Total Return	2.78
Northern Large Cap Value	2.39

Thesis By Lauren DeSanto, 12-05-06 Stock Price as of Analysis: $33.88

When times were good, Avon was a bit like the grasshopper, enjoying its time in the sun. It should have been more like the industrious ant, planning for the cold winter. That winter hit midway through 2005, when the firm saw declining North American profits, rapid sales deceleration in emerging markets, and a crucial misstep in its reduced advertising investment. The downturn at Avon has been longer and more pronounced than we anticipated, but we are confident of a turnaround.

Avon operates a direct-sales business model, selling cosmetics products through a global network of representatives. The model is easy to introduce into new markets, and it's incredibly low-cost; reps must pay for the company's advertising catalogs, for example. As growth in markets like Poland and Russia began to take off several years ago, Avon expanded quickly, and with its strong brand and an attractive, entrepreneurial earnings opportunity, it established a beachhead in many new markets.

Growth was explosive for a while. Over the past five years, sales in Avon's European division increased 21% on average. These kinds of growth rates weren't sustainable, however, since more traditional consumer product companies, namely L'Oreal and Procter & Gamble, and other direct-sales companies, like Amway and Oriflame, were also entering these growth markets.

By summer 2005, it was clear Avon was in trouble. In addition to sales deceleration in Central and Eastern Europe, the transition to direct selling in China disrupted Avon's salesforce, which pulled back on placing new orders, while in the United States, rising gas prices started to crimp its customer base's spending. From 2004 to 2005, operating margins declined almost 200 basis points, and they'll probably be down another 300 basis points in 2006.

At this point, we believe the worst is behind Avon. A $500 million restructuring is under way, and it has pared 10% of the workforce, including 25% of the management ranks. Savings from these initiatives are being poured back into advertising, which will increase 50% in 2006. More important, the firm is working to recalibrate the earnings opportunity for its sales reps to keep it competitive. Finally, Avon remains exceedingly well positioned in China with a broad and growing network of direct-sales reps.

It's been a painful year and a half for Avon shareholders, but we believe the firm is getting its house in order and its wide moat is intact. We'd pick up the shares at the right price and hold them for the long haul.

Data as of 12-29-06

Axcan Pharma AXCA

Rating ★★★	Fair Value $15.00	Last Close $14.24	Consider Buy $11.60	Consider Sell $18.80	Yield % 0.00

Company Profile
Axcan, a Canadian-based pharmaceutical company, specializes in marketing therapies for gastrointestinal conditions such as irritable bowel syndrome, liver diseases, and complications from cystic fibrosis. Its salesforce targets GI specialists in North America and Europe with more than 40 products. The firm actively pursues acquisitions and in-licensing deals of complementary products to offer more treatment options to target physicians.

Management   Stewardship Grade [NA]
Leon Gosselin founded Axcan's predecessor company in 1982 and remains its chairman. He led Axcan through the commercialization of many GI products and can be credited with much of the company's success. Gosselin and other insiders owned about 9% of Axcan as of the latest filing. We like to see significant ownership stakes like that because they generally help align insider interests with those of other shareholders. Gosselin handed over day-to-day management to Frank Verwiel in 2005. Verwiel is now Axcan's president and CEO after serving Merck for nearly a decade, most recently as vice president of hypertension in worldwide human health marketing. Since ITAX is no longer viable, Verwiel may have to cut his teeth on product acquisitions to pump up the firm's growth. It remains to be seen if Verwiel possesses that skill.

597 Laurier Blvd.   www.axcan.com
Mont St. Hilaire, QC J3H 6C4

Growth [NA]	2002	2003	2004	2005
Revenue %	27.4	34.8	35.7	3.2
Earnings/Share %	58.1	28.6	52.4	-41.7
Book Value/Share %	20.7	14.0	4.0	11.6
Dividends/Share %	NMF	NMF	NMF	NMF

Profitability [NA]	2003	2004	2005	TTM
Return on Assets %	5.1	8.0	4.1	4.1
Oper Cash Flow $Mil	57	23	68	68
- Cap Spending $Mil	4	13	6	6
= Free Cash Flow $Mil	52	10	61	61

Financial Health [NA]	2003	2004	2005	09-30-05
Long-term Debt $Mil	108	128	126	126
Total Equity $Mil	366	392	418	418
Debt/Equity Ratio	0.3	0.3	0.3	0.3

Industry	Business Risk	Moat Size	Investment Style	Sector
Drugs	Average	Narrow	Small Core	Healthcare

Competition	Market Cap $Mil	12 Mo Trailing Sales $Mil	Price/Cash Flow	Return On Assets%	Debt/ Equity	Total Return% 1 Yr	3 Yr
Axcan Pharma	651	251	9.6	4.1	0.3	-5.9	-3.4
AstraZeneca PLC ADR	84,438	23,950	12.5	19.0	0.1	13.3	5.4
Shire PLC ADR	10,362	1,764	20.8	9.8	0.0	59.8	29.0

Price Volatility | Monthly Price High/Low   — Relative Strength to S&P 500

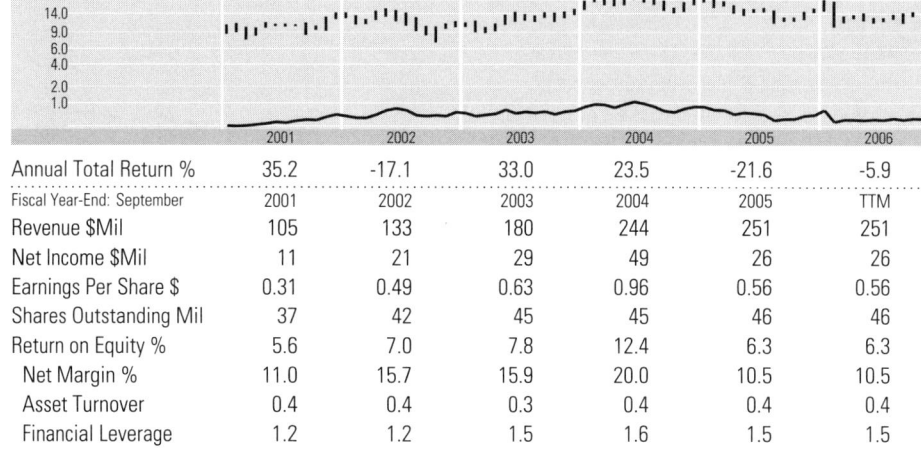

	2001	2002	2003	2004	2005	2006
Annual $Price High	14.54	15.82	15.71	21.80	19.94	18.94
Low	8.31	7.85	9.58	14.43	11.73	10.86
Annual Total Return %	35.2	-17.1	33.0	23.5	-21.6	-5.9
Fiscal Year-End: September	2001	2002	2003	2004	2005	TTM
Revenue $Mil	105	133	180	244	251	251
Net Income $Mil	11	21	29	49	26	26
Earnings Per Share $	0.31	0.49	0.63	0.96	0.56	0.56
Shares Outstanding Mil	37	42	45	45	46	46
Return on Equity %	5.6	7.0	7.8	12.4	6.3	6.3
Net Margin %	11.0	15.7	15.9	20.0	10.5	10.5
Asset Turnover	0.4	0.4	0.3	0.4	0.4	0.4
Financial Leverage	1.2	1.2	1.5	1.6	1.5	1.5

Valuation Ratios	Stock	Rel to Industry	Rel to S&P 500
Price/Earnings	25.4	1.1	1.2
Price/Book	1.6	0.3	0.4
Price/Sales	2.6	0.6	0.9
Price/Cash Flow	9.6	0.6	0.7

Major Fund Holders	% of Fund Assets
Stonebridge Small-Cap Growth	3.21
William Blair Small Cap Growth N	1.11

Thesis By Julie Stralow, CFA, 12-15-06 Stock Price as of Analysis: $14.25

Axcan Pharma specializes in marketing gastroenterology treatments and rakes in lots of free cash flow in the process. Even without a potential blockbuster like ITAX waiting in the wings, we think Axcan should generate returns befitting its narrow moat in the long run.

Axcan has built an economic moat on the back of its specialized salesforce, which targets gastroenterologists in North America and Europe. Like most specialty pharmaceutical companies, this salesforce remains Axcan's most prized possession, as it provides the means to funnel more complementary products to targeted physicians. Axcan's sales representative are highly productive (the average U.S. representative contributes $2.5 million in annual sales) and help Axcan generate returns on invested capital that comfortably exceed its cost of capital.

The firm's existing product lineup includes treatments for inflammatory bowel, liver, and pancreatic diseases. With less than $300 million in annualized sales, moving the needle on Axcan's sales should be relatively easy. However, Axcan's lead product candidate, ITAX for the treatment of functional dyspepsia, failed in Phase III clinical trials. Axcan will not generate any returns on the development costs of ITAX, which at one time promised to double the firm's sales. Also, Axcan faces generic competition as patents on some of its largest products, including URSO for primary biliary cirrhosis and Canasa for ulcerative proctitis, expire in late 2007. This threat could start cutting into Axcan's sales in fiscal 2008. Its other products are relatively mature, too, with growth coming primarily from new formulations or indications.

Axcan needs to inject new products into the mix to offset looming generic threats. The Food and Drug Administration recently approved Pylera to combat the Helicobacter pylori bacteria, which causes most gastric and duodenal ulcers. Axcan aims to capture a significant portion of this $160 million market when it launches Pylera in 2007. Axcan also could use its solid financial position to acquire already marketed or developing products to boost its growth potential. The firm has already entered into one deal targeting a very large potential market for the treatment of gastro-esophageal reflux disease.

So while Axcan may endure some difficult years in the intermediate term, we think its assets should help it capitalize on many GI market opportunities. If it can acquire new growth drivers for a reasonable price, its prospects would substantially improve.

Baker Hughes BHI

	Rating	Fair Value	Last Close	Consider Buy	Consider Sell	Yield %
	★	$59.00	$74.66	$45.50	$73.90	0.70

Data as of 12-29-06

Company Profile
Houston-based Baker Hughes is one of the premier providers to the oil patch, selling products and services related to finding, drilling for, and producing oil and gas. Baker Hughes specializes in downhole tool technologies and is the leading provider of drill bits and related systems. Baker Hughes provides technological know-how to international energy and national oil companies in more than 90 countries.

Management
Stewardship Grade [C]

Michael Wiley retired as chairman and CEO in October 2004. His replacement, Chad Deaton, had been CEO at Hanover Compressor since 2002. Before that, he was the executive vice president at Schlumberger. Deaton's $825,000 salary seems appropriate relative to compensation for CEOs at peer companies. He's also eligible for a performance-based bonus of as much as 100% of his base salary. In the past, the firm has done a fine job of varying executive compensation with the company's performance, and we're confident the practice will continue. Baker Hughes' executives and board members own about 1% of the shares outstanding. We are impressed by the firm's financial discipline during a period of industry optimism; management has bypassed run-of-the-mill projects that don't top its hurdle rate. Although the firm has missed out on the red-hot pressure pumping niche of the oil-service business over the past several years, Baker's top executives have had the foresight to ramp up the firm's Eastern Hemisphere infrastructure. Baker receives a C Stewardship Grade, losing points for not splitting the CEO and chairman positions and requiring a supermajority vote for changes to the bylaws.

3900 Essex Lane Suite 1200 www.bakerhughes.com
Houston, TX 77027

Growth [C-]	2002	2003	2004	2005
Revenue %	-2.8	8.0	16.2	18.2
Earnings/Share %	—	NMF	315.8	62.7
Book Value/Share %	—	NMF	17.9	18.0
Dividends/Share %	0.0	0.0	0.0	3.3

Profitability [B+]	2003	2004	2005	TTM
Return on Assets %	2.0	7.7	11.3	26.8
Oper Cash Flow $Mil	656	784	955	602
- Cap Spending $Mil	404	348	478	761
= Free Cash Flow $Mil	252	436	477	-158

Financial Health [A+]	2003	2004	2005	09-30-06
Long-term Debt $Mil	—	1,086	1,078	1,075
Total Equity $Mil	3,350	3,895	4,698	5,193
Debt/Equity Ratio	—	0.3	0.2	0.2

Industry	Business Risk	Moat Size	Investment Style	Sector
Oil/Gas Svcs.	Average	Narrow	Large Growth	Energy

Competition
	Market Cap $Mil	12 Mo Trailing Sales $Mil	Price/Cash Flow	Return On Assets %	Debt/Equity	Total Return % 1 Yr	3 Yr
Baker Hughes	23,946	8,564	39.8	26.8	0.2	23.7	34.2
Schlumberger	74,416	17,904	17.6	15.6	0.4	31.1	33.6
Halliburton	31,221	22,886	8.5	17.5	0.4	1.1	35.2

Price Volatility — Monthly Price High/Low — Relative Strength to S&P 500

Annual Total Return %	-11.1	-10.4	1.5	34.3	43.8	23.7
Fiscal Year-End: December	2001	2002	2003	2004	2005	TTM
Revenue $Mil	4,981	4,844	5,233	6,080	7,186	8,564
Net Income $Mil	438	169	129	529	878	2,351
Earnings Per Share $	—	—	0.38	1.58	2.57	6.97
Shares Outstanding Mil	—	—	339	335	339	321
Return on Equity %	13.2	5.0	3.8	13.6	18.7	45.3
Net Margin %	8.8	3.5	2.5	8.7	12.2	27.4
Asset Turnover	0.7	0.7	0.8	0.9	0.9	1.0
Financial Leverage	2.0	1.9	1.9	1.8	1.7	1.7

Valuation Ratios	Stock	Rel to Industry	Rel to S&P 500
Price/Earnings	10.8	0.6	0.5
Price/Book	4.6	0.6	1.1
Price/Sales	2.8	0.9	1.0
Price/Cash Flow	39.8	2.5	2.7

Major Fund Holders	% of Fund Assets
Rydex Energy Services Inv	5.22
Monteagle Large Cap Growth	4.46
Fidelity Select Energy Service	4.44
Heritage Capital Appreciation A	4.16

Thesis By Matt Moran, CFA, 12-15-06 Stock Price as of Analysis: $78.25

Baker Hughes is an established competitor in oil services. The firm has dug itself a narrow economic moat by supplying innovative, differentiated technologies since the early 1900s.

Petroleum companies have tapped most of the easy-to-reach oil and gas reserves. Drilling for deposits in high-pressure formations and at greater depths requires advanced oil field equipment. Baker Hughes is one of the oil patch's premier suppliers of products and services, providing such critical components as advanced drill bits, drilling fluids, submersible pumps, and well-measurement devices. Passionate about building shareholder value, the management team understands that differentiated technology is the only road to riches in oil services and is dedicated to maintaining high levels of technological innovation. Baker Hughes enjoys a dominant position in share and technology in several niche markets for advanced drilling systems.

Exploration and production companies lose billions each year in nonproductive drilling time. Baker Hughes is determined to hammer out the inefficiencies in the global hunt for hydrocarbons with a commitment to cutting-edge technology. Hefty research and development investments have boosted new product revenue from less than 15% of total revenue in 2002 to closer to 25% in 2005. Taking a page out of Schlumberger's playbook, Baker Hughes is developing its worldwide training infrastructure in the Eastern Hemisphere, establishing research centers in key international areas. We are confident that closer proximity to essential customers will benefit the bottom line.

In early 2006, Baker Hughes sold its 30% stake in WesternGeco, a leading seismic operation, to Schlumberger, the other owner of the joint venture, for $2.4 billion in cash. We are not surprised that Baker Hughes decided to exit this business, as it has been primarily a Schlumberger project from the get-go. We think Baker Hughes got a fair price for its interest and will use its growing cash hoard to buy back significant amounts of stock.

Although the oil services industry remains highly cyclical, recent developments should improve Baker Hughes' prospects. Thanks to high gas and oil prices over the past several years, Baker Hughes' customers are drowning in cash and desperately need high-end equipment and services. While cyclical lows will create bumps in the road, we expect modest long-term growth for the overall oil services field, and we're confident that Baker Hughes will maintain its share of the market.

Data as of 12-29-06

Bank of America BAC

	Rating	Fair Value	Last Close	Consider Buy	Consider Sell	Yield %
	★★★★	$67.00	$53.39	$51.70	$83.90	3.97

Company Profile

Bank of America is a financial services holding company that provides commercial, retail, and foreign banking services; originates home mortgage loans; and operates full-service and discount securities businesses. It also issues credit cards and provides computer banking services. The company offers securities underwriting and other investment banking services to corporations. Bank of America operates about 5,700 banking offices throughout the United States.

Management — Stewardship Grade [B]

Chairman and CEO Ken Lewis earned his current job in 2001, succeeding his mentor, Hugh McColl, who headed NationsBank and merged it with what was then called BankAmerica. While Lewis began his reign by refocusing B of A on profitable, internal growth, he more recently has taken the bank down an aggressive merger-growth path, with the acquisition of FleetBoston in 2004 and MBNA on Jan. 1, 2006. Though he met with substantial skepticism, he and his management team have executed on their first deal--Fleet--astoundingly well, with B of A blowing past its financial targets laid out at the time of the deal. Additionally, the MBNA deal looks attractive to us; B of A gained a terrific business and paid a fair price. For his troubles, Lewis in 2005 earned $22 million in salary, bonus, restricted stock, options, and perquisites--which is high by any measure, but not out of line with other large financial firms. Fortunately, for such a complex pay package, the company threw in $20,920 worth of tax and financial planning for Lewis. B of A's corporate governance appears relatively good, but it could improve. Our concerns center on the big compensation packages awarded to executives and the fact that Lewis is both chairman and CEO.

Bank of America Corporate Center 100 N. Tryon Street
Charlotte, NC 28255   www.bankofamerica.com

Growth [A-]	2002	2003	2004	2005
Revenue %	-0.4	9.9	29.1	14.6
Earnings/Share %	41.4	20.8	2.0	11.0
Book Value/Share %	7.7	1.5	65.0	-4.8
Dividends/Share %	7.0	18.0	18.1	11.8

Profitability [B+]	2003	2004	2005	TTM
Return on Assets %	1.5	1.3	1.3	1.3
Oper Cash Flow $Mil	23,150	-3,522	-12,223	—
- Cap Spending $Mil	209	863	1,228	—
= Free Cash Flow $Mil	—	—	—	—

Financial Health [NA]	2003	2004	2005	09-30-06
Long-term Debt $Mil	—	—	—	—
Total Equity $Mil	47,926	99,964	101,262	132,771
Debt/Equity Ratio	—	—	—	—

Industry	Business Risk	Moat Size	Investment Style	Sector
International Banks	Average	Wide	Large Value	Financial Services

Competition	Market Cap $Mil	12 Mo Trailing Sales $Mil	Price/Cash Flow	Return On Assets %	Debt/ Equity	Total Return% 1 Yr	Total Return% 3 Yr
Bank of America	239,758	68,368	—	1.3	—	20.7	15.2
Citigroup	273,691	86,566	—	1.3	—	19.6	8.4
J.P. Morgan Chase & Co.	167,551	59,650	—	0.9	—	25.6	13.2

Price Volatility | Monthly Price High/Low   — Relative Strength to S&P 500

Annual $Price	2001	2002	2003	2004	2005	2006
High	32.80	38.55	42.45	47.47	47.44	55.08
Low	22.50	26.98	32.13	38.51	41.13	40.93
Annual Total Return %	42.7	14.5	20.1	21.5	2.4	20.7

Fiscal Year-End: December	2001	2002	2003	2004	2005	TTM
Revenue $Mil	34,638	34,494	37,914	48,965	56,091	68,368
Net Income $Mil	6,787	9,244	10,806	13,931	16,447	19,438
Earnings Per Share $	2.09	2.96	3.57	3.64	4.04	4.32
Shares Outstanding Mil	3,186	3,041	2,977	3,755	4,011	4,491
Return on Equity %	14.0	18.4	22.5	13.9	16.2	14.6
Net Margin %	19.6	26.8	28.5	28.5	29.3	28.4
Asset Turnover	0.1	0.1	0.1	0.0	0.0	0.0
Financial Leverage	12.8	13.2	15.0	11.1	12.8	10.9

Valuation Ratios	Stock	Rel to Industry	Rel to S&P 500
Price/Earnings	12.4	0.7	0.6
Price/Book	1.8	0.7	0.4
Price/Sales	3.5	0.8	1.2
Price/Cash Flow	—	—	—

Major Fund Holders	% of Fund Assets
ProFunds Banks UltraSector Inv	13.10
North Track Dow Jones US Fin 100 A	8.89
Wells Fargo Advantage Spec Fin Serv A	8.59
Morgan Stanley Financial Services B	6.81

Thesis By Craig Woker, CFA, 11-28-06 Stock Price as of Analysis: $54.27

In the annals of Bank of America's more than century of history, the past year certainly will rank among the firm's most bountiful.

B of A has made tremendous strides. It has generated record profits in 2006, consummated a lucrative merger with MBNA, and shaken off the last vestiges of doubt regarding the FleetBoston acquisition. But past laurels are irrelevant to the question of whether success can be repeated in sufficient measure to provide superior future stock performance. We opine that B of A's recently robust growth will continue into 2007, that virtually inevitable net interest margin expansion will propel double-digit income gains for several years thereafter, and that procuring adequate and attractively priced funding--not finding sufficient loan growth--will fast become the firm's primary vexation.

We believe that B of A's future funding constraints--namely, luring in more deposits--will ironically come as a result of one of its greatest advantages, namely that it is already the leading retail bank in the U.S., with double the deposits of its nearest rival. Even as B of A has aggressively courted consumers in their demand for mortgages and credit cards--as well as businesses for their loan needs--the bank itself is finding cheap funding harder to come by. In times past, B of A solved this quandary quite simply by purchasing a competitor and its deposit base. However, a federal cap prohibits banks from purchasing rivals if the combined deposit market share would pierce 10%, which B of A already has. Barring a repeal of this ceiling--or B of A developing some proprietary process for capturing greater market share organically--the firm's deposit growth rate will be only about 5% per annum in future years. In our view, this will present the firm with only three obvious options: 1) Reduce loan growth, 2) Issue higher-cost debt to fund loans, or 3) Deploy resources into investments in riskier or less attractive markets, like buying foreign banks and expanding into brokerage or asset management.

That said, these issues would not give us pause in investing in B of A at attractive prices, as we have accounted for them within our valuation. For a company that offers commodity products and services, B of A is an impressive firm with an attractively profitable business. We estimate 18% returns on invested capital on average over the next five years, and given B of A's strong competitive position, the firm should maintain above-average returns for many years thereafter.

Data as of 12-29-06

Bank of Montreal BMO

	Rating	Fair Value	Last Close	Consider Buy	Consider Sell	Yield %
	★★★	$67.00	$59.19	$51.70	$83.90	3.38

Company Profile
BMO is the fourth-largest Canadian bank in terms of market capitalization. The bank has more than C$310 billion in assets; it operates almost 1,000 branches in Canada under its own name and another 215 in the United States under the Harris Bank brand. The bank also has offices in nine countries outside North America. The oldest bank in Canada, BMO also provides investment banking and wealth-management services.

Management — Stewardship Grade [NA]
Tony Comper was appointed CEO in February 1999, after serving the bank in various positions for more than three decades. In 2005, he took home a base salary of C$1 million and a bonus of C$1.7 million, which we find reasonable. Comper has announced plans to retire by March 2007, with current COO Bill Downe taking his place. Downe has been with BMO for more than two decades and has abundant experience as a leader. We don't expect this change to materially affect the bank's strategy or performance. BMO isn't a one-man show, and Downe will head a very experienced team of professionals. We remain confident in management's ability to keep delivering strong results. We think BMO's corporate governance is in good shape, given that the chairman and CEO positions are separate, the board is nonstaggered, options are being expensed, and option grants aren't excessive. We are also pleased with the bank's financial disclosures, which are detailed and comprehensive.

129 St. Jaques Street
Montreal, QC H2Y 1L6
www.bmo.com

Growth [NA]	2002	2003	2004	2005
Revenue %	4.2	2.5	5.2	1.5
Earnings/Share %	28.4	27.9	5.2	11.2
Book Value/Share %	3.4	-0.9	9.5	8.9
Dividends/Share %	—	—	—	—

Profitability [NA]	2003	2004	2005	TTM
Return on Assets %	0.8	0.8	0.8	0.8
Oper Cash Flow $Mil	485	-5,833	540	—
- Cap Spending $Mil	277	399	511	—
= Free Cash Flow $Mil	—	—	—	—

Financial Health [NA]	2003	2004	2005	10-31-05
Long-term Debt $Mil	—	—	—	—
Total Equity $Mil	10,442	11,731	13,447	13,447
Debt/Equity Ratio	—	—	—	—

Industry	Business Risk	Moat Size	Investment Style	Sector
International Banks	Average	Wide	Large Value	Financial Services

Competition	Market Cap $Mil	12 Mo Trailing Sales $Mil	Price/Cash Flow	Return On Assets%	Debt/Equity	Total Return% 1 Yr	3 Yr
Bank of Montreal	29,638	8,753	—	0.8	—	9.5	15.9
J.P. Morgan Chase & Co.	167,551	59,650	—	0.9	—	25.6	13.2
ABN AMRO Holding NV ADR	60,187	29,071	—	0.5	—	28.9	16.9

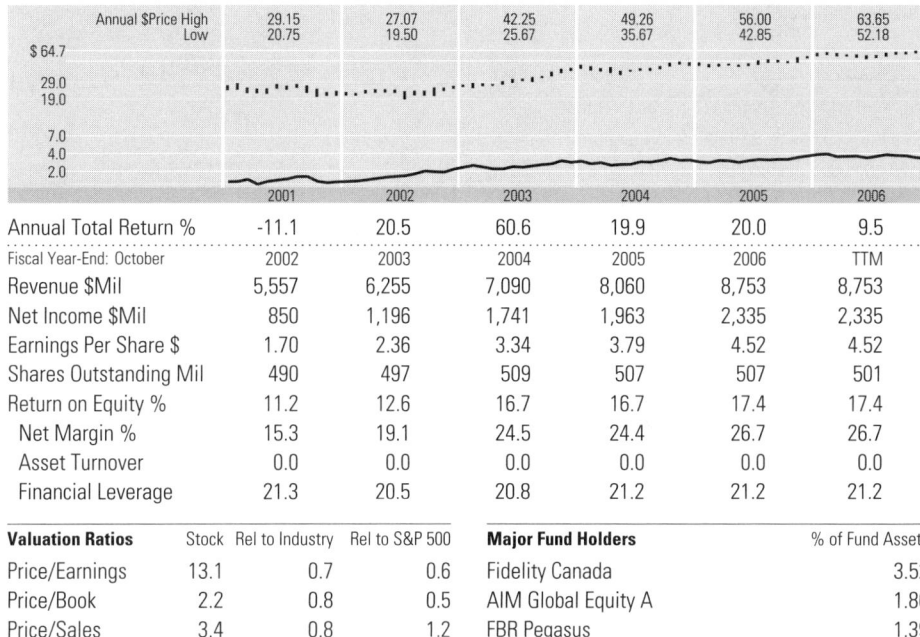

Annual Total Return %	-11.1	20.5	60.6	19.9	20.0	9.5
Fiscal Year-End: October	2002	2003	2004	2005	2006	TTM
Revenue $Mil	5,557	6,255	7,090	8,060	8,753	8,753
Net Income $Mil	850	1,196	1,741	1,963	2,335	2,335
Earnings Per Share $	1.70	2.36	3.34	3.79	4.52	4.52
Shares Outstanding Mil	490	497	509	507	507	501
Return on Equity %	11.2	12.6	16.7	16.7	17.4	17.4
Net Margin %	15.3	19.1	24.5	24.4	26.7	26.7
Asset Turnover	0.0	0.0	0.0	0.0	0.0	0.0
Financial Leverage	21.3	20.5	20.8	21.2	21.2	21.2

Valuation Ratios	Stock	Rel to Industry	Rel to S&P 500
Price/Earnings	13.1	0.7	0.6
Price/Book	2.2	0.8	0.5
Price/Sales	3.4	0.8	1.2
Price/Cash Flow	—	—	—

Major Fund Holders	% of Fund Assets
Fidelity Canada	3.52
AIM Global Equity A	1.80
FBR Pegasus	1.39
Legg Mason Partners Financial Services B	1.30

Thesis By Michael Kon, CFA, 11-30-06 Stock Price as of Analysis: $59.92

Bank of Montreal is a financial supermarket operating in several international locations. However, we think the crown jewel is the Canadian operation, a top-performing franchise that generates vigorous returns.

BMO provides a wide range of financial services to individuals, governments, and corporate clients. In addition to traditional retail and commercial banking, the bank offers investment banking services, wealth-management services, and many other products. More than 75% of BMO's net income comes from Canada, where the bank is a junior member of an oligopoly that dominates the Canadian market. BMO benefits from benign regulation and substantial operational advantages, which garner it a wide economic moat.

Over many years, BMO has built a vast branch and ATM network that spans major parts of Canada. This network crowds bank distribution channels in Canada and protects BMO's earnings from potential competitors. In addition, BMO strives to be a one-stop shop for financial services. The bank's Canadian operation has an integrated business model, which means it provides almost any financial product available in Canada. This has led to noninterest income soaring above 50% of total revenue, a rare level of diversification in the banking world. More important, clients usually purchase multiple products from BMO, which allows the bank to form enduring relationships with clients and further intensify its competitive position.

BMO's investment banking group further differentiates it from peers, in our view. The firm has built a top-ranked bulge-bracket business that leads the market in every product category. We think this has also helped BMO to establish strong relationships with corporate clients and ramp up its corporate lending business. As investment banking contributes 27% of total revenue and 32% of net income, BMO makes more money from this business than almost any other Canadian bank.

One concern, however, is BMO's Harris subsidiary, which operates in the low-growth U.S. Midwest region and faces tough competition. This operation generates 12% return on equity, on average, while in Canada BMO records an impressive 20%. Consequently, we are discouraged by the bank's plan to double its Midwestern footprint through acquisitions. However, we don't think it will significantly diminish the bank's return, given that less than 5% of net income comes from this business.

Data as of 12-29-06

Bank of New York Company BK

	Rating	Fair Value	Last Close	Consider Buy	Consider Sell	Yield %
	★★★★	$48.00	$39.37	$37.00	$60.10	2.18

Company Profile

Bank of New York's primary line of business is securities servicing. It is one of the largest asset custodians in the world. As such, it provides back-office services to financial firms. The company has a loan portfolio geared mainly toward commercial lending. Its asset-management and private banking operation serves wealthy investors in the United States and abroad. The bank has agreed to sell its retail banking operations.

Management   Stewardship Grade [B]

Chairman and CEO Thomas Renyi has led the company's business strategy. A former credit officer, Renyi has been pushing Bank of New York to pare its loan portfolio and focus on fee-generating activities. He won't have his job for much longer, however: Mellon Financial CEO Robert Kelly is poised to take the CEO reins as part of BoNY's merger with Mellon in July 2007. Renyi will remain as chairman of the combined entity for 18 months before retiring. However, BoNY brass will be well-represented in the management ranks of the merged entity, particularly on the asset-servicing side, where BoNY is pre-eminent. In addition, since BoNY will hold 10 board seats to Mellon's eight, BoNY will control the merged company. Renyi has been well paid. In 2005 his total compensation amounted to about $8 million. Shareholders approved a proposal to bar renewal of the poison-pill takeover defense in April 2004. The vote was nonbinding, but the board finally agreed to get rid of the poison pill in February 2005. The board retains the ability to adopt a new takeover defense without prior shareholder approval, however. With a few minor exceptions (staggered board, Renyi holding both the chairman and CEO jobs), corporate governance is generally shareholder-friendly.

One Wall Street 10th Floor   www.bankofny.com
New York, NY 10286

Growth [C+]	2002	2003	2004	2005
Revenue %	-8.5	16.8	12.1	9.1
Earnings/Share %	-31.5	22.6	21.7	9.7
Book Value/Share %	7.9	20.5	7.8	6.9
Dividends/Share %	5.6	0.0	3.9	10.1

Profitability [B+]	2003	2004	2005	TTM
Return on Assets %	1.3	1.5	1.5	1.5
Oper Cash Flow $Mil	3,812	3,358	-1,112	—
- Cap Spending $Mil	129	262	131	—
= Free Cash Flow $Mil	—	—	—	—

Financial Health [NA]	2003	2004	2005	09-30-06
Long-term Debt $Mil	—	—	—	—
Total Equity $Mil	8,428	9,290	9,876	10,467
Debt/Equity Ratio	—	—	—	—

Industry	Business Risk	Moat Size	Investment Style	Sector
International Banks	Average	Wide	Large Core	Financial Services

Competition	Market Cap $Mil	12 Mo Trailing Sales $Mil	Price/Cash Flow	Return On Assets%	Debt/ Equity	Total Return% 1 Yr	3 Yr
Bank of New York Company	41,334	7,308	—	1.5	—	26.9	9.2
Citigroup	273,691	86,566	—	1.3	—	19.6	8.4
J.P. Morgan Chase & Co.	167,551	59,650	—	0.9	—	25.6	13.2

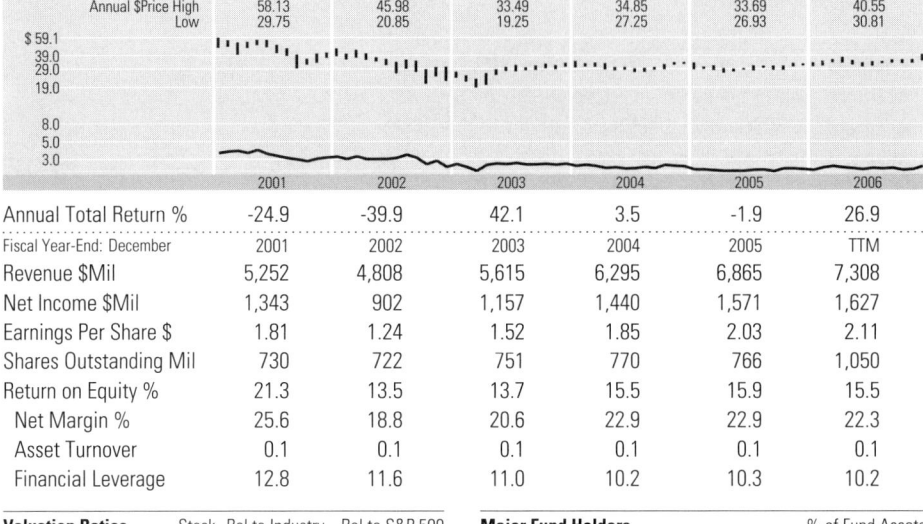

Annual Total Return %	-24.9	-39.9	42.1	3.5	-1.9	26.9
Fiscal Year-End: December	2001	2002	2003	2004	2005	TTM
Revenue $Mil	5,252	4,808	5,615	6,295	6,865	7,308
Net Income $Mil	1,343	902	1,157	1,440	1,571	1,627
Earnings Per Share $	1.81	1.24	1.52	1.85	2.03	2.11
Shares Outstanding Mil	730	722	751	770	766	1,050
Return on Equity %	21.3	13.5	13.7	15.5	15.9	15.5
Net Margin %	25.6	18.8	20.6	22.9	22.9	22.3
Asset Turnover	0.1	0.1	0.1	0.1	0.1	0.1
Financial Leverage	12.8	11.6	11.0	10.2	10.3	10.2

Valuation Ratios	Stock	Rel to Industry	Rel to S&P 500
Price/Earnings	18.8	1.0	0.9
Price/Book	3.9	1.5	1.0
Price/Sales	5.7	1.4	2.0
Price/Cash Flow	—	—	—

Major Fund Holders	% of Fund Assets
Barrett Opportunity	9.24
Burnham Financial Industries A	5.51
Touchstone Diversified Value A	4.57
Constellation Pitcairn Select Value II	4.44

Thesis By Jeffrey Ptak, CPA, CFA, 12-18-06 Stock Price as of Analysis: $39.60

Bank of New York and Mellon Financial's recently announced merger looks like a winner.

Mellon and Bank of New York (BoNY) recently announced that they will merge in mid-2007. The combined entity, to be called Bank of New York Mellon Corporation, will be the leading global custodian and one of the world's largest asset managers.

Both companies gain something from the deal. For instance, scale is vital in the custody business due to the huge technology and personnel outlays needed to service client assets. To that end, Mellon can leverage BoNY's hulking presence in the custody arena--the transaction will nearly quadruple Mellon's assets under custody and fill gaps in its asset-servicing roster where BoNY is pre-eminent, such as corporate trust. As such, the deal will vault Mellon into a market-leadership position.

The deal also should significantly upgrade Bank of New York's asset-management capabilities. Mellon's $1.1 trillion in assets under management (AUM) dwarfs BoNY's recent tally. Moreover, Mellon brings a long roster of well-respected, brisk-selling institutional strategies to the table. With a deeper reservoir of asset-management options to draw upon, BoNY can lessen its dependence on asset-servicing, thereby further diversifying its revenue stream.

Unlike many combinations motivated by rosy projections or vanity, this deal should deliver real synergies. Asset-servicers are well-suited to peddle asset-management products given that custody brings them into near-daily contact with clients' key investment decision-makers. Thus, the combined unit should be better-positioned to pair a more-robust suite of investment management products with low-cost custody solutions. And the projected annual cost savings from the deal--$700 million, to be fully realized by 2010--are wholly attainable given the overlap it creates in certain areas.

To make the deal pay off, both companies will have to integrate systems and meld cultures without roiling clients. Here, too, we think there's cause for guarded optimism. While BoNY will control the merged entity, Mellon CEO Robert Kelly will head it up, and several Mellon executives are slated to assume key posts. This should create greater parity in management's ranks, mitigating the risk of culture clash. In addition, since the deal wasn't priced for perfection, it should relieve the pressure to roar out of the gates in order to rationalize a lofty price, allowing both parties to proceed judiciously with the integration.

Data as of 12-29-06

Bank of Nova Scotia BNS

	Rating	Fair Value	Last Close	Consider Buy	Consider Sell	Yield %
	★★★	$43.00	$44.80	$33.20	$53.90	3.06

Company Profile
With assets of more than C$370 billion, Bank of Nova Scotia is one of the biggest banks in Canada. In its home country, the firm has 972 branches and 2,742 ATMs. It has an additional 1,070 branches and 2,195 ATMs in more than 40 other countries, with its primary focus in Mexico, Central America, and the Caribbean. In Canada, the firm provides retail, corporate, and commercial banking services, as well as investment services and wealth management.

Management
Stewardship Grade [NA]

Richard Waugh was appointed CEO in December 2003. Waugh, who has been with the bank since 1970, succeeded Peter Godsoe and has continued the firm's record of solid performance. We think Waugh's C$9 million in total compensation in 2005 is reasonable compared with peers, and we are pleased by his growing ownership position in the bank. We think corporate governance is good, as the board includes only one insider (Waugh), board members are compensated with stock, and option grants don't seem excessive. We like that on average, more than 30% of senior executive pay is driven by long-term performance. We are also pleased that the bank provides detailed and comprehensive financial disclosures.

Scotia Plaza 44 King Street, 8th Floor
Toronto, ON M5H 1H1
www.scotiabank.ca

Growth [NA]	2001	2002	2003	2004
Revenue %	-4.3	0.2	2.1	12.0
Earnings/Share %	41.8	20.5	11.7	12.7
Book Value/Share %	2.0	6.6	11.1	6.5
Dividends/Share %	—	—	NMF	NMF

Profitability [NA]	2002	2003	2004	TTM
Return on Assets %	1.0	1.0	0.9	0.9
Oper Cash Flow $Mil	732	-2,721	-5,228	—
- Cap Spending $Mil	—	—	—	—
= Free Cash Flow $Mil	—	—	—	—

Financial Health [NA]	2002	2003	2004	10-31-04
Long-term Debt $Mil	—	—	—	—
Total Equity $Mil	12,037	13,629	15,131	15,131
Debt/Equity Ratio	—	—	—	—

Industry	Business Risk	Moat Size	Investment Style	Sector
International Banks	Average	Wide	Large Value	Financial Services

Competition	Market Cap $Mil	12 Mo Trailing Sales $Mil	Price/Cash Flow	Return On Assets%	Debt/ Equity	Total Return% 1 Yr	3 Yr
Bank of Nova Scotia	44,330	10,211	—	0.9	—	16.8	24.5
Royal Bank of Canada	61,039	20,637	—	0.9	—	26.0	29.5
Toronto-Dominion Bank	43,027	11,488	—	1.2	—	15.4	23.9

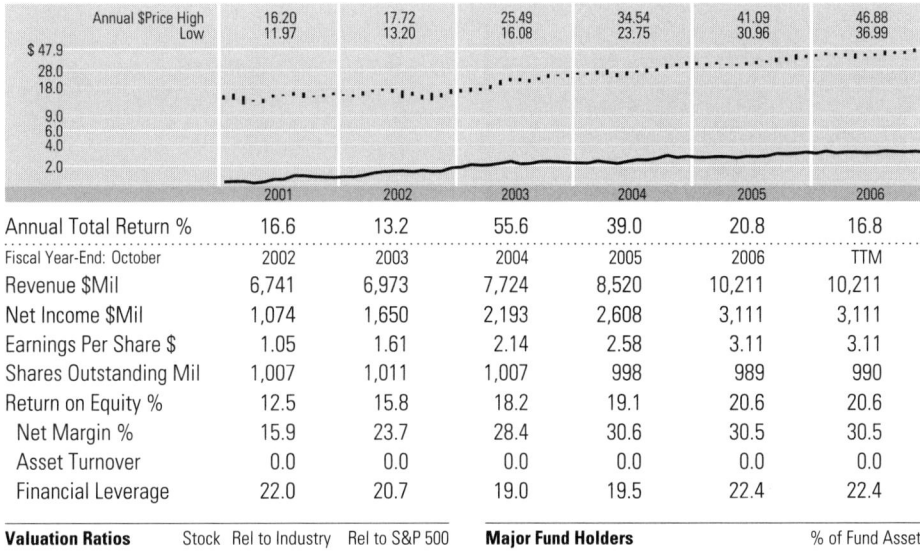

Price Volatility — Monthly Price High/Low — Relative Strength to S&P 500

| Annual $Price High | 16.20 | 17.72 | 25.49 | 34.54 | 41.09 | 46.88 |
| Low | 11.97 | 13.20 | 16.08 | 23.75 | 30.96 | 36.99 |

Annual Total Return %	16.6	13.2	55.6	39.0	20.8	16.8
Fiscal Year-End: October	2002	2003	2004	2005	2006	TTM
Revenue $Mil	6,741	6,973	7,724	8,520	10,211	10,211
Net Income $Mil	1,074	1,650	2,193	2,608	3,111	3,111
Earnings Per Share $	1.05	1.61	2.14	2.58	3.11	3.11
Shares Outstanding Mil	1,007	1,011	1,007	998	989	990
Return on Equity %	12.5	15.8	18.2	19.1	20.6	20.6
Net Margin %	15.9	23.7	28.4	30.6	30.5	30.5
Asset Turnover	0.0	0.0	0.0	0.0	0.0	0.0
Financial Leverage	22.0	20.7	19.0	19.5	22.4	22.4

Valuation Ratios	Stock	Rel to Industry	Rel to S&P 500
Price/Earnings	14.4	0.8	0.7
Price/Book	2.9	1.1	0.7
Price/Sales	4.3	1.0	1.5
Price/Cash Flow	—	—	—

Major Fund Holders	% of Fund Assets
FBR Pegasus	1.97
Citizens Global Equity Stndrd	1.31

Thesis By Michael Kon, CFA, 12-11-06 Stock Price as of Analysis: $45.07

With a dominant position in Canada, Bank of Nova Scotia went on a search for growth in foreign lands. While peers chose to expand in the United States, Scotia has found substantial profits in Latin America.

In addition to traditional retail and commercial banking, Scotia offers investment banking, wealth management, and insurance to individuals, governments, and corporate clients. We think that what differentiates Scotia from other Canadian banks is its international operation, which has contributed, on average, 26% of earnings and generated an impressive 18% return on equity over the past five years.

Instead of following the steps of its Canadian peers in the U.S. market, Scotia has built a beachhead in the less competitive markets of Latin America. The bank has significant market share (more than 6% of deposits) in countries like Mexico, Chile, and Costa Rica, and as these markets consolidate, Scotia is well positioned to buy more competitors and increase its dominance and market power.

In our view, Scotia also can reap significant benefits from its focus on two main geographic regions. Although the bank operates in more than 19 countries, it mainly concentrates on Latin America and Asia. We think this should enable the bank to consolidate back-office operations, thus improving efficiency. As a result, we expect the efficiency ratio--operating expenses as a percentage of revenue--of the international unit, which averaged 64% over the past five years, to decline to an average of 55% over the next five years.

In Canada, Scotia has a well-entrenched branch and ATM network that is part of an oligopoly that dominates the Canadian banking sector. This operation, which contributes about 40% of net income, benefits from a wide economic moat. While facing limited growth opportunities in Canada, this unit managed to generate a 31% return on equity over the past five years, well above the 27% reported by peers. In our opinion, this superior return was achieved thanks to Scotia's prudent interest rate risk management, which helped its net interest margin outpace the peer group by 30 basis points during this period.

In our opinion, Scotia is the best managed of the Canadian banks we cover. We would warmly recommend the shares should a buying opportunity present itself.

BankAtlantic Bancorp A BBX

	Rating	Fair Value	Last Close	Consider Buy	Consider Sell	Yield %
	★★★★	$16.00	$13.81	$12.30	$20.00	1.14

Company Profile
BankAtlantic Bancorp is a financial-services holding company that owns BankAtlantic, a South Florida-based bank, and Ryan Beck, a New Jersey-based investment banking firm. BankAtlantic has 81 stores primarily in the Broward, Miami, Palm Beach, and Tampa areas has and assets of over $6 billion. Ryan Beck, with 43 offices in 14 states, provides individual and institutional clients with asset management, investment banking, and capital market services.

Management
Stewardship Grade [C]

Chairman and CEO Alan B. Levan and vice chairman John E. Abdo are much more businessmen than bankers. They hold the same titles at BFC Corporation, a holding company that owns over 20% of BankAtlantic and controls over 50% of the voting interest in the company. Besides BankAtlantic Bancorp, BFC holds equity stakes in Levitt Corporation, Benihana, and other privately held companies. We are slightly concerned that given these other interests, management is not entirely focused on BankAtlantic; however, the team has showed a successful track record of balancing these diverse responsibilities. Levan became president and CEO of BankAtlantic Bancorp in 1997; he had been president and chairman of BankAtlantic Bank since 1984. Through their personal holdings and BFC, management maintains a substantial equity interest in BankAtlantic. We believe this properly aligns the long-term interests of management and shareholders. We also note that Jarett Levan, Alan's son, is the president of the banking subsidiary and, long-term, he is likely to succeed his father in running the company.

1750 East Sunrise Blvd. www.bankatlantic.com
Ft. Lauderdale, FL 33304

Growth [NA]	2002	2003	2004	2005
Revenue %	—	—	NMF	7.4
Earnings/Share %	24.6	33.3	2.8	-17.1
Book Value/Share %	-14.2	-12.7	11.8	9.1
Dividends/Share %	-12.8	-20.8	77.9	-13.6

Profitability [C]	2003	2004	2005	TTM
Return on Assets %	1.4	1.1	0.9	0.2
Oper Cash Flow $Mil	100	67	57	—
- Cap Spending $Mil	13	48	43	—
= Free Cash Flow $Mil	—	—	—	—

Financial Health [NA]	2003	2004	2005	09-30-06
Long-term Debt $Mil	—	—	—	—
Total Equity $Mil	413	469	516	525
Debt/Equity Ratio	—	—	—	—

Industry	Business Risk	Moat Size	Investment Style	Sector
Regional Banks	Average	Narrow	Small Core	Financial Services

Competition	Market Cap $Mil	12 Mo Trailing Sales $Mil	Price/Cash Flow	Return On Assets%	Debt/Equity	Total Return% 1 Yr	3 Yr
BankAtlantic Bancorp A	844	544	—	0.2	—	-0.3	-1.3
Bank of America	239,758	68,368	—	1.3	—	20.7	15.2
Wachovia	90,049	27,749	—	1.3	—	12.0	11.3

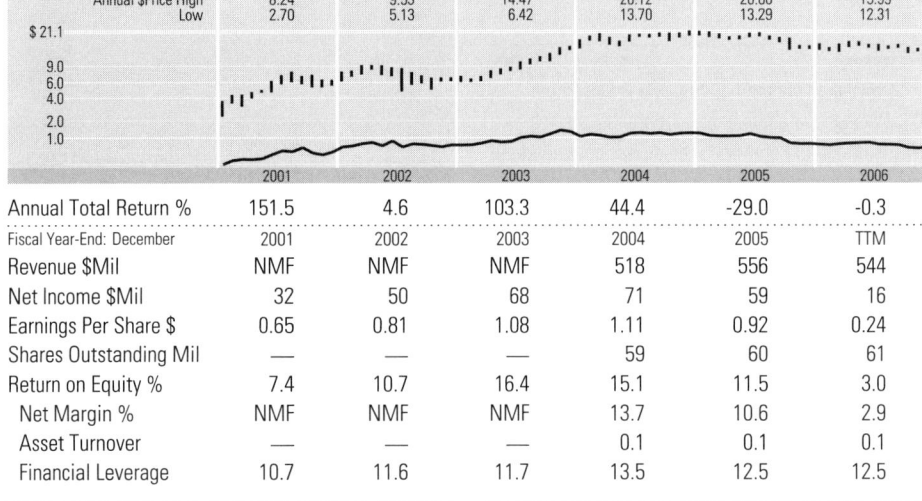

	2001	2002	2003	2004	2005	2006
Annual Total Return %	151.5	4.6	103.3	44.4	-29.0	-0.3
Fiscal Year-End: December	2001	2002	2003	2004	2005	TTM
Revenue $Mil	NMF	NMF	NMF	518	556	544
Net Income $Mil	32	50	68	71	59	16
Earnings Per Share $	0.65	0.81	1.08	1.11	0.92	0.24
Shares Outstanding Mil	—	—	—	59	60	61
Return on Equity %	7.4	10.7	16.4	15.1	11.5	3.0
Net Margin %	NMF	NMF	NMF	13.7	10.6	2.9
Asset Turnover	—	—	—	0.1	0.1	0.1
Financial Leverage	10.7	11.6	11.7	13.5	12.5	12.5

Valuation Ratios	Stock	Rel to Industry	Rel to S&P 500
Price/Earnings	57.5	3.2	2.8
Price/Book	1.6	0.5	0.4
Price/Sales	1.6	0.3	0.6
Price/Cash Flow	—	—	—

Major Fund Holders	% of Fund Assets
TrendStar Small Cap	1.98
Cambiar Conquistador Inv	1.86
Stratton Small-Cap Value	1.71
Becker Small Cap Value Equity	1.52

Thesis By Ryan Lentell, 11-10-06 Stock Price as of Analysis: $13.35

Rising interest rates have slowed BankAtlantic's strategy of acquiring low-cost deposits. Meanwhile, a decrease in investment banking revenues, coupled with increased costs have hurt the company's Ryan Beck segment. Despite its current challenges, we believe this is a well-run financial institution.

Since 2001 BankAtlantic has aimed to increase its low-cost deposits by becoming "Florida's Most Convenient Bank." By replacing higher-cost debt with the lower-cost deposits, the bank seeks to increase net interest margins. With interest rates at historically low levels from 2001 to 2005, this strategy worked remarkably well. Over this period, low-cost deposits grew by 250%. However, in the first nine months of 2006, low-cost deposits have grown by less than 1%. We believe this slowdown is due to the overall banking environment, as consumers have become more sensitive to interest rates, seeking higher returns on their deposits. We do not think the slowdown is a result of any internal change at BankAtlantic.

Despite the tough operating environment, management plans to open 27 stores next year. We think this expansion will surely drive deposit growth, but at a high price, as each store takes approximately 18 months to reach profitability. This almost 30% increase in stores should put significant pressure on earnings over the next few years.

Earlier this year the company filed to sell a portion of the equity in its Ryan Beck unit in an IPO. However, it was later forced to withdraw this IPO plan, thanks to a challenging market environment and the poor financial performance of the unit. Earnings at Ryan Beck have been hurt by costs related to an expansion across all business lines and a slowdown in its investment banking group. Because investment banking is driven by deal flow, we realize this business can be particularly choppy. We believe the group has a strong reputation underwriting small to midsize financial institutions, and we think it will to return to profitability in the near term. However, this unit's sporadic performance will likely make it difficult for BankAtlantic to monetize its investment in Ryan Beck through an IPO for a number of years. We believe a sale to a strategic buyer could be a possibility, but we do not forecast that happening in the short term.

Data as of 12-29-06

Barclays PLC ADR BCS

	Rating	Fair Value	Last Close	Consider Buy	Consider Sell	Yield %
	★★★	$62.00	$58.14	$47.80	$77.70	3.46

Company Profile
Barclays is the third-largest U.K. bank by market capitalization. It has a collection of high-quality businesses: U.K. banking serves retail and business clients in the United Kingdom, Barclays Capital is a debt-focused investment bank, Barclaycard is one of the largest European credit card issuers, and Barclays Global Investors is an asset manager.

Management — Stewardship Grade [NA]
Matthew Barrett stepped down as CEO in September 2004 to become chairman, in a departure from recently formulated corporate-governance guidelines. Former CFO John Varley, whose wife's lineage can be traced back to Barclays' founders, succeeded Barrett as CEO. Executives who lost out to Varley, including Bob Diamond, have been soothed with larger mandates. Diamond now heads investment banking, private banking, and asset management. He has repaid that faith by delivering stupendous profit growth in all three of his charges. Executive pay, while below average for a bank of Barclays' size, is high compared with U.K. peers. The top six directors beneficially own 18.3 million shares. In March 2005, the bank did away with stock options in favor of share awards. We believe both of these factors align management's interests with those of shareholders.

54 Lombard Street
London, United Kingdom EC3P 3AH
www.barclays.com

Growth [NA]	2002	2003	2004	2005
Revenue %	2.7	8.0	98.9	22.9
Earnings/Share %	-9.2	26.0	18.3	5.6
Book Value/Share %	4.1	10.7	-4.7	-0.3
Dividends/Share %	—	—	—	—

Profitability [NA]	2003	2004	2005	TTM
Return on Assets %	0.6	0.6	0.4	0.4
Oper Cash Flow $Mil	-6,213	9,402	-19,162	—
- Cap Spending $Mil	507	967	1,073	—
= Free Cash Flow $Mil	—	—	—	—

Financial Health [NA]	2003	2004	2005	12-31-05
Long-term Debt $Mil	—	—	—	—
Total Equity $Mil	29,239	30,519	30,045	30,045
Debt/Equity Ratio	—	—	—	—

Industry	Business Risk	Moat Size	Investment Style	Sector
International Banks	Average	Wide	Large Value	Financial Services

Competition	Market Cap $Mil	12 Mo Trailing Sales $Mil	Price/Cash Flow	Return On Assets%	Debt/ Equity	Total Return% 1 Yr	3 Yr
Barclays PLC ADR	94,325	31,638	—	0.4	—	44.1	21.5
Citigroup	273,691	86,566	—	1.3	—	19.6	8.4
HSBC Holdings PLC ADR	204,784	49,836	—	1.1	—	18.9	9.5

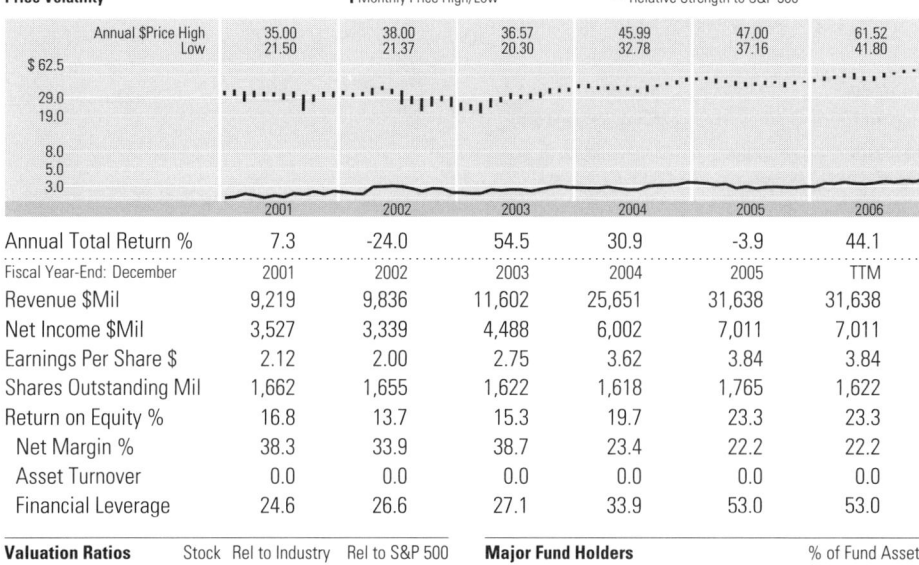

Price Volatility — Monthly Price High/Low — Relative Strength to S&P 500

Annual $Price High/Low	35.00/21.50	38.00/21.37	36.57/20.30	45.99/32.78	47.00/37.16	61.52/41.80
	2001	2002	2003	2004	2005	2006
Annual Total Return %	7.3	-24.0	54.5	30.9	-3.9	44.1

Fiscal Year-End: December	2001	2002	2003	2004	2005	TTM
Revenue $Mil	9,219	9,836	11,602	25,651	31,638	31,638
Net Income $Mil	3,527	3,339	4,488	6,002	7,011	7,011
Earnings Per Share $	2.12	2.00	2.75	3.62	3.84	3.84
Shares Outstanding Mil	1,662	1,655	1,622	1,618	1,765	1,622
Return on Equity %	16.8	13.7	15.3	19.7	23.3	23.3
Net Margin %	38.3	33.9	38.7	23.4	22.2	22.2
Asset Turnover	0.0	0.0	0.0	0.0	0.0	0.0
Financial Leverage	24.6	26.6	27.1	33.9	53.0	53.0

Valuation Ratios	Stock	Rel to Industry	Rel to S&P 500
Price/Earnings	15.1	0.8	0.7
Price/Book	3.1	1.2	0.8
Price/Sales	3.0	0.7	1.0
Price/Cash Flow	—	—	—

Major Fund Holders	% of Fund Assets
Meehan Focus	3.42
Lazard International Equity Sel Instl	3.22
Aston/River Road Dynamic Equity Income N	2.44
FCI Equity	2.11

Thesis By Ganesh Rathnam, 11-14-06 Stock Price as of Analysis: $53.82

Barclays is the second-largest U.K. bank, behind Lloyds TSB. We believe the United Kingdom is an oligopolistic market and, barring severe missteps, the top players will be hard to dislodge. We think Barclays' entrenched businesses--U.K. business and retail banking, Barclaycard, Barclays Capital, and Barclays Global Investors--provide a wide economic moat.

In sharp contrast to the bad rap its retail bank gets, Barclays' business bank is considered the best in the United Kingdom and is the single-largest source of the company's profits. Cost-cutting and aligning relationship managers' compensation with economic value added has boosted profit growth more than 20% annually since 2001. This incentive structure should help the business bank maintain its high returns on capital. With the turnaround complete in the business bank, management has identified areas that need immediate improvement in the retail bank, such as mortgage servicing and customer satisfaction, and has quickly taken big measures to address these issues.

Barclaycard, Europe's biggest card operator and a niche player in the United States, accounts for 12.5% of profits and is another stellar business for Barclays. Although it issues cards at large in Europe, Barclays wisely does not compete head-to-head with MBNA and Capital One in the United States. It relies heavily on affinity programs because of their high spending, above-average credit quality, and customer loyalty. Barclaycard possesses some prestigious franchises, such as exclusive overseas rights to Manchester United brand cards and exclusive access to Harvard alumni. A spike in charge-offs hurt 2005 performance, but the sources for long-term success remain firmly in place.

Perhaps the most exciting part of the company's business is the fast-growing trio of Barclays Capital (23% of profits), Barclays Global Investors (10%), and wealth management (3%). Barclays Capital benefits from a focus on debt-related banking and the solid leadership of Bob Diamond. BGI has $1.5 trillion in assets under management and is the second-largest asset manager in the world. We think the proliferation of exchange-traded funds and Barclays' position as the pre-eminent promoter of them will continue to drive growth. The wealth-management business is benefiting from demographic changes and should remain extremely profitable.

We think Barclays' businesses will continue to deliver economic profits, and we'd invest at a nominal discount to our fair value estimate.

Data as of 12-29-06

Barr Pharmaceuticals BRL

Rating	Fair Value	Last Close	Consider Buy	Consider Sell	Yield %
★★★★	$62.00	$50.12	$47.80	$77.70	0.00

Company Profile
Barr Pharmaceuticals develops, manufactures, and sells generic and branded drugs through operating subsidiaries Barr Laboratories and Duramed Pharmaceuticals. Including Pliva, its product portfolio contains around 120 generic and 19 proprietary pharmaceutical products. In November 2003, Barr launched Seasonale, the first extended-cycle oral contraceptive drug on the market. Barr acquired FEI Women's Health in November 2005 and Pliva in 2006.

Management   Stewardship Grade [A]
Three of Barr's five top executives are lawyers, which emphasizes the importance of legal expertise to the firm. Success at challenging patents defines the company's growth and profit opportunities. As a former patent attorney with more than 10 years in the generic business, CEO and chairman Bruce Downey understands the secret to success. Downey also serves as the chairman of the influential Generic Pharmaceutical Association. Based on his past performance and management style, we consider him one of the industry's top leaders. The poaching of Duramed president Carole Ben-Maimon from leading competitor Teva affirms Barr's commitment to building its research capabilities--and was a positive move, in our opinion. The board of directors is well qualified and has a good balance of skills. Barr reaches the top of our corporate-governance scale with straightforward accounting, objective performance measures, and reasonable compensation. The only knock on the company from a corporate-governance standpoint is the combination of the CEO and chairman duties.

400 Chestnut Ridge Road   www.barrlabs.com
Woodcliff Lake, NJ 07677-7668

Growth [C]	2003	2004	2005	2006
Revenue %	-24.1	45.0	-20.0	25.5
Earnings/Share %	-21.4	-29.0	76.5	53.7
Book Value/Share %	28.5	16.0	19.7	34.6
Dividends/Share %	NMF	NMF	NMF	NMF

Profitability [A+]	2004	2005	2006	TTM
Return on Assets %	9.2	14.4	17.5	16.2
Oper Cash Flow $Mil	258	363	327	448
- Cap Spending $Mil	47	55	61	56
= Free Cash Flow $Mil	211	308	266	392

Financial Health [A+]	2004	2005	2006	06-30-06
Long-term Debt $Mil	32	15	7	7
Total Equity $Mil	1,042	1,234	1,691	1,764
Debt/Equity Ratio	0.0	0.0	0.0	0.0

Industry	Business Risk	Moat Size	Investment Style	Sector
Drugs	Average	Narrow	Mid Core	Healthcare

Competition	Market Cap $Mil	12 Mo Trailing Sales $Mil	Price/Cash Flow	Return On Assets%	Debt/Equity	Total Return% 1 Yr	3 Yr
Barr Pharmaceuticals	5,332	1,336	11.9	16.2	0.0	-19.5	-0.9
Teva Pharmaceutical Indus	20,098	5,250	14.7	10.3	0.3	-27.2	3.1
Mylan Laboratories	4,231	1,359	11.2	12.7	0.7	1.2	-6.5

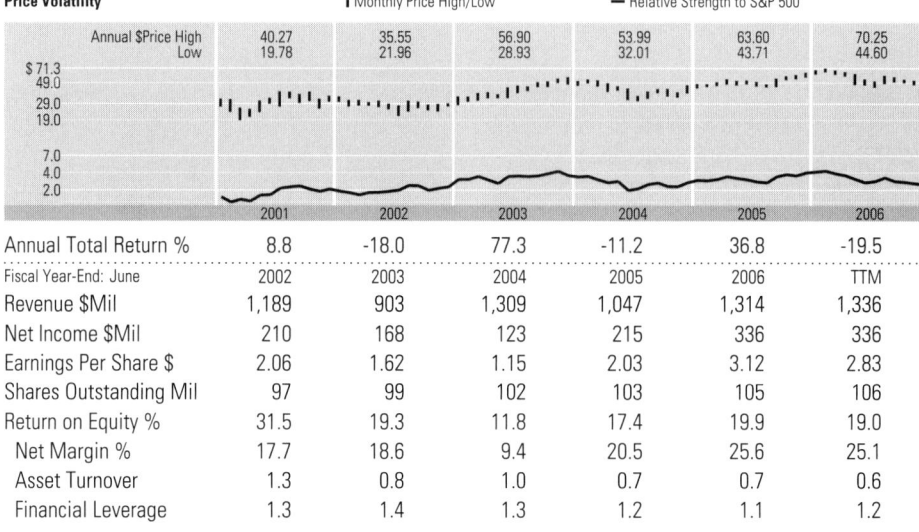

Annual Total Return %	8.8	-18.0	77.3	-11.2	36.8	-19.5
Fiscal Year-End: June	2002	2003	2004	2005	2006	TTM
Revenue $Mil	1,189	903	1,309	1,047	1,314	1,336
Net Income $Mil	210	168	123	215	336	336
Earnings Per Share $	2.06	1.62	1.15	2.03	3.12	2.83
Shares Outstanding Mil	97	99	102	103	105	106
Return on Equity %	31.5	19.3	11.8	17.4	19.9	19.0
Net Margin %	17.7	18.6	9.4	20.5	25.6	25.1
Asset Turnover	1.3	0.8	1.0	0.7	0.7	0.6
Financial Leverage	1.3	1.4	1.3	1.2	1.1	1.2

Valuation Ratios	Stock	Rel to Industry	Rel to S&P 500
Price/Earnings	17.7	0.7	0.9
Price/Book	3.0	0.6	0.7
Price/Sales	4.0	0.9	1.4
Price/Cash Flow	11.9	0.7	0.8

Major Fund Holders	% of Fund Assets
Calvert Capital Accumulation A	3.17
Quaker Mid-Cap Value A	3.15
SunAmerica Biotech/Health A	3.03
Schwab Health Care	2.38

Thesis By Brian Laegeler, CPA, 12-15-06 Stock Price as of Analysis: $51.55

Barr Pharmaceuticals is among our most admired generic drug companies. Higher-than-average research spending has generated innovative products and industry-leading margins. Barr's Pliva acquisition furthers its commitment to research while introducing new platforms for growth.

Barr is best known for its branded women's health innovations such as Seasonale, the first extended-cycle oral contraceptive, or Plan B, an over-the-counter emergency contraceptive. Barr and Watson Pharmaceuticals lead the oral contraceptives market, each with a 30% share. This market presence builds credibility with doctors and increases the productivity of Barr's 250-person specialty salesforce. A careful combination of new products, acquisitions, and line extensions should sustain this leadership for years to come.

In addition to a successful branded franchise, Barr owes its leading gross margins to a solid generic drug portfolio. Eight of its 75 generics are produced exclusively by Barr. Others have difficult-to-produce characteristics, such as extended-release formulations, that limit competition. More than half of Barr's pipeline of anticipated new products have similar defensive characteristics. Croatia-based Pliva brings a European selling platform with 45 generic drugs, some of which are hard-to-make injectables that Barr will introduce in the United States.

Barr sustains its growth by investing in research and development at a rate almost twice the industry average. On the generic side, Barr has 50 applications pending approval. On the branded side, Barr is extending the now generic Seasonale franchise with Seasonique, a related combination drug, and Seasonale Lo, a lower-strength version of Seasonale. Various new women's health and other products, such as an adenovirus vaccine for the U.S. military, are undergoing clinical trials. Pliva gives Barr a leadership position in European generics and generic biologics, two of the industry's most promising frontiers.

Barr lacks the size of Teva or Sandoz (a division of Novartis) and the low-cost structure of India-based Dr. Reddy. However, its robust pipeline and long-term strategy for generic biologics is enough to earn the company a narrow economic moat.

Baxter International BAX

Data as of 12-29-06

Rating ★★	Fair Value $40.00	Last Close $46.39	Consider Buy $30.80	Consider Sell $50.10	Yield % 1.26

Company Profile
Baxter operates in three health-care segments: medication delivery, bioscience, and renal care. Medication delivery remains a key revenue generator, with products like intravenous bags, solutions, and devices to control fluid inflow. Baxter's similarly sized bioscience segment specializes in developing treatments for disorders like hemophilia. The balance of the firm's revenue, about 20%, comes from dialysis equipment for patients with kidney failure.

Management Stewardship Grade [B]
Baxter's turnaround efforts included uprooting management, and we now think the company has above-average stewards at the helm. Robert Parkinson replaced Harry Kraemer as chairman, president, and CEO in 2004 after Kraemer's disappointing tenure. Parkinson has since replaced a slew of top executives, and we praise the company's forthright disclosure practices, more-efficient operations, and realistic growth objectives under Parkinson's team. Parkinson, former president and COO of Abbott Laboratories, is leading Baxter's turnaround efforts with a renewed focus on creating shareholder value. Our relatively minor complaints about stewardship include Baxter's combined chairman and CEO position, staggered board, and hefty director compensation packages. Given the firm's long history, we are not surprised that insiders hold a tiny percentage of Baxter shares. Parkinson and his team remain in the process of accumulating stakes that are substantial multiples of their annual compensation, though.

One Baxter Parkway
Deerfield, IL 60015-4633
www.baxter.com

Growth [C]	2002	2003	2004	2005
Revenue %	10.3	9.9	6.8	3.6
Earnings/Share %	—	NMF	-55.9	141.3
Book Value/Share %	—	NMF	7.7	13.6
Dividends/Share %	0.0	0.0	0.0	0.0

Profitability [A-]	2003	2004	2005	TTM
Return on Assets %	6.3	2.7	7.5	9.0
Oper Cash Flow $Mil	1,426	1,380	1,550	1,657
- Cap Spending $Mil	792	558	444	501
= Free Cash Flow $Mil	634	822	1,106	1,156

Financial Health [A-]	2003	2004	2005	09-30-06
Long-term Debt $Mil	4,421	3,933	2,414	2,680
Total Equity $Mil	3,382	3,705	4,299	6,338
Debt/Equity Ratio	1.3	1.1	0.6	0.4

Industry	Business Risk	Moat Size	Investment Style	Sector
Medical Equip.	Average	Narrow	Large Growth	Healthcare

Competition	Market Cap $Mil	12 Mo Trailing Sales $Mil	Price/Cash Flow	Return On Assets%	Debt/ Equity	Total Return% 1 Yr	3 Yr
Baxter International	30,360	10,106	18.3	9.0	0.4	24.8	17.2
Bayer AG ADR	38,971	34,290	8.9	4.6	—	31.1	26.3
Novo Nordisk ADR	27,072	5,671	18.5	14.8	0.0	51.1	28.4

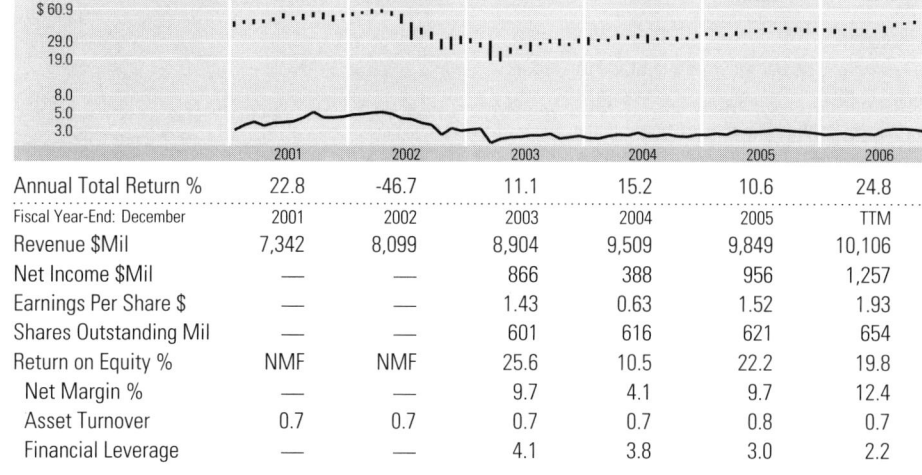

Price Volatility — Monthly Price High/Low — Relative Strength to S&P 500

	2001	2002	2003	2004	2005	2006
Annual $Price High	55.90	59.90	31.32	34.84	41.07	48.54
Low	40.06	24.07	18.18	26.75	33.08	35.12
Annual Total Return %	22.8	-46.7	11.1	15.2	10.6	24.8

Fiscal Year-End: December	2001	2002	2003	2004	2005	TTM
Revenue $Mil	7,342	8,099	8,904	9,509	9,849	10,106
Net Income $Mil	—	—	866	388	956	1,257
Earnings Per Share $	—	—	1.43	0.63	1.52	1.93
Shares Outstanding Mil	—	—	601	616	621	654
Return on Equity %	NMF	NMF	25.6	10.5	22.2	19.8
Net Margin %	—	—	9.7	4.1	9.7	12.4
Asset Turnover	0.7	0.7	0.7	0.7	0.8	0.7
Financial Leverage	—	—	4.1	3.8	3.0	2.2

Valuation Ratios	Stock	Rel to Industry	Rel to S&P 500
Price/Earnings	24.0	0.8	1.2
Price/Book	4.8	0.9	1.2
Price/Sales	3.0	0.6	1.0
Price/Cash Flow	18.3	0.8	1.3

Major Fund Holders	% of Fund Assets
Fidelity Select Medical Equip/Systems	6.37
American Century Focused Growth Inv	4.25
Gartmore Global Health Sci A	4.17
Dreyfus Premier Health Care A	4.05

Thesis By Julie Stralow, CFA, 12-12-06 Stock Price as of Analysis: $44.48

Despite Baxter International's high-profile infusion pump woes, we think transitional efforts over the past few years are paying off and the company remains on the right track.

We think Baxter is about to hit its stride after a few transitional years that have involved significant top management turnover, facility consolidation, and select product divestitures. Baxter's management team is focusing on improving returns on invested capital, and we like what we see so far on the margin and capital-allocation fronts. Management is allocating resources only to its most attractive business opportunities, primarily in select areas of the medication delivery and bioscience segments. Baxter also continues to exit certain businesses where it doesn't have sustainable competitive advantages, like hemodialysis equipment.

Baxter's scale and innovative ability keep competitors at bay in a number of health-care businesses, and the firm serves a wide range of patients through its medication delivery, renal, and bioscience segments. The medication delivery and bioscience segments have gotten the bulk of management's attention recently for very different reasons. The medication delivery segment contains the infusion pumps that have been such a thorn in Baxter's side over the past year. The firm halted sales of the Colleague infusion pump in 2006 because of production and quality-control problems that it is attempting to solve with the cooperation of regulators. Declining sales from a key anesthesia product, propofol, after an assault from generic competition have also hurt this segment's results. These troubles do not erase the firm's moat in medication delivery, though, and Baxter remains a reliable, low-cost provider of essential supplies to caregivers. Management intends to increase returns on invested capital in this segment by introducing innovative drug and nutritional solutions, increasing delivery automation through its systems, and providing manufacturing services for other firms that make injectable treatments.

Resources continue to funnel into the bioscience segment as well, which relies on Baxter's expertise in blood components to develop new treatments for blood-related disorders. Baxter is the leading provider of hemophilia therapies, and it innovates in this area by making these products safer and more effective. The firm also uses its blood-clotting expertise to develop and market products like surgical sealants. We expect this segment to be Baxter's primary growth engine.

BB&T BBT

Data as of 12-29-06

	Rating	Fair Value	Last Close	Consider Buy	Consider Sell	Yield %
	★★★	$49.00	$43.93	$37.80	$61.40	3.64

Industry	Business Risk	Moat Size	Investment Style	Sector
Super Regional Banks	Average	Narrow	Large Value	Financial Services

Company Profile

Operating more than 1,400 branches in 11 southeastern states and Washington, D.C., BB&T is the 10th-largest bank in the United States, assets-wise. Based in Winston-Salem, N.C., BB&T offers commercial and retail banking, residential mortgages, trust, insurance, specialty finance, investment banking, and brokerage. BB&T is primarily focused on retail consumers and small-to-midsized businesses.

Management   Stewardship Grade [B]

We are increasing our Stewardship Grade to a "B" as a result of BB&T's recent upgrades in corporate governance. At the 2006 annual meeting, the company passed an amendment to its bylaws to eliminate its staggered board structure. This follows a change of directors' compensation to include stock options as well as cash in 2005. We like to see the board of directors receive a combination of stock and cash for their services, in order to better align directors' interests with shareholders. We applaud these governance improvements.

CEO and chairman John Allison, 58, has run BB&T since 1989. Starting as a $3 billion local player, Allison built a major regional bank with $118 billion in assets. In our view, it is Allison's vision that created the bank's successful acquisition strategy. Moreover, Allison still has grand ambitions for his bank. He will not be content to see BB&T sit back and enjoy its franchise. We expect Allison to continue to find new ways to add value for shareholders, possibly outside of the traditional banking business and into insurance or other financial services. While Allison is well compensated for his excellent work at BB&T, management pay is reasonable compared with the industry.

200 West Second Street
Winston-Salem, NC 27102
www.bbandt.com

Growth [B-]	2002	2003	2004	2005
Revenue %	13.8	13.1	11.4	7.0
Earnings/Share %	28.3	-23.9	35.3	7.1
Book Value/Share %	15.2	25.2	1.2	3.3
Dividends/Share %	12.2	10.9	9.8	9.0

Profitability [A-]	2003	2004	2005	TTM
Return on Assets %	1.2	1.6	1.5	1.4
Oper Cash Flow $Mil	3,819	3,038	1,759	—
- Cap Spending $Mil	336	460	440	—
= Free Cash Flow $Mil	—	—	—	—

Financial Health [NA]	2003	2004	2005	09-30-06
Long-term Debt $Mil	—	—	—	—
Total Equity $Mil	9,935	10,874	11,129	11,734
Debt/Equity Ratio	—	—	—	—

Competition	Market Cap $Mil	12 Mo Trailing Sales $Mil	Price/Cash Flow	Return On Assets%	Debt/Equity	Total Return% 1 Yr	3 Yr
BB&T	23,763	6,190	—	1.4	—	8.9	8.6
Bank of America	239,758	68,368	—	1.3	—	20.7	15.2
Wachovia	90,049	27,749	—	1.3	—	12.0	11.3

Price Volatility

Annual $Price High	38.84	39.47	39.69	43.25	43.92	44.74
Low	30.25	31.03	30.66	33.02	37.04	38.24
	2001	2002	2003	2004	2005	2006
Annual Total Return %	-0.5	5.7	8.1	12.9	3.4	8.9

Fiscal Year-End: December	2001	2002	2003	2004	2005	TTM
Revenue $Mil	3,814	4,340	4,909	5,467	5,850	6,190
Net Income $Mil	974	1,303	1,065	1,558	1,654	1,707
Earnings Per Share $	2.12	2.72	2.07	2.80	3.00	3.13
Shares Outstanding Mil	453	474	510	553	548	541
Return on Equity %	15.8	17.6	10.7	14.3	14.9	14.5
Net Margin %	25.5	30.0	21.7	28.5	28.3	27.6
Asset Turnover	0.1	0.1	0.1	0.1	0.1	0.1
Financial Leverage	11.5	10.9	9.1	9.2	9.8	10.1

Valuation Ratios	Stock	Rel to Industry	Rel to S&P 500
Price/Earnings	14.0	1.0	0.7
Price/Book	2.0	0.9	0.5
Price/Sales	3.8	1.1	1.3
Price/Cash Flow	—	—	—

Major Fund Holders	% of Fund Assets
Ave Maria Rising Dividend	3.16
Fidelity Select Banking	2.74
Huntington Income-Equity Tr	2.51
JHancock Regional Bank B	2.23

Thesis By Jaime Black, CFA, CPA, 12-14-06 Stock Price as of Analysis:

BB&T is an average bank with a large appetite for acquisition. Although the company is made up of a hodgepodge of financial service companies, we think they work together well.

BB&T could really stand for "Buying Banks & Thrifts." Since 1995, BB&T has purchased 30 banks and thrifts, 57 insurance brokers, 15 specialty lenders, six broker/dealers, and four asset managers. We are pleased to see that BB&T's bank acquisition activity has quieted down in the past three years as the company shows pricing discipline. Management happily discloses that it has talked to several potential targets, but lofty pricing expectations have left these discussions at a standstill. In addition to organic growth, the company's informal target is to increase assets 5% annually through acquisition, but it is not afraid to ignore this target if it's in the best interest of shareholders.

Current CEO John Allison made waves in November 2006 by saying that BB&T will need to complete another merger of equals in the next five to 10 years to survive. The statement is an exaggeration, to say the least. BB&T would not go bankrupt or be unable to compete if it could not find a partner to merge with. But in today's consolidating banking market, management believes that it must continue growing rapidly to stay at the top of the competitive pack. We view Allison's statement as an admission that if BB&T is not an acquirer, it would most likely be a target.

While banking accounts for 83% of BB&T earnings, this ambitious bank has its toes in several other businesses. It owns one of the largest insurance brokerage businesses in the United States, and insurance commissions make up the largest proportion of BB&T's noninterest income. We love this business: It's a great fee generator, it isn't tied to interest rates, and it continues to grow more quickly than the retail banking business. Referrals from the bank's commercial loan department are creating profitable leads for the insurance business.

BB&T's constant acquisitions have dragged profitability from good to average. Returns on equity stand at 15%, primarily due to the large amount of goodwill that acquisitions bring. While we believe that BB&T's returns would quickly improve if it stopped acquiring businesses and focused internally, we cannot see this occurring in the near future.

As we consider management to be fairly disciplined in its acquisition strategy, we would buy the shares at a modest discount to our fair value estimate.

Data as of 12-29-06

Bear Stearns Companies BSC

| | Rating ★ | Fair Value $126.00 | Last Close $162.78 | Consider Buy $97.20 | Consider Sell $157.90 | Yield % 0.69 |

Company Profile
Bear Stearns is the seventh-largest investment bank in the United States. The firm underwrites debt and equity offerings for corporations, packages mortgages and mortgage securities for resale, trades securities, and executes trades in a wide variety of financial securities for professional investors, primarily hedge funds. The company also manages assets for wealthy clients.

Management
Stewardship Grade [B]

The management team at Bear Stearns is homegrown and has a big stake in the company. James Cayne has been chairman and CEO for more than six years and is the company's largest individual shareholder, owning almost 5.6% of the firm through stock, restricted-stock units, and options. At 71, he has yet to announce retirement plans, but his probable successors, Alan Schwartz and Warren Spector, were named presidents and co-COOs in 2001. Spector runs the fixed-income businesses and owns about 0.5% of shares outstanding. Schwartz is the head of investment banking and owns about 1.5% of the shares. All of these executives have been with the firm for decades, presiding over returns on average common equity in the midteens over the last financial market cycle. The executive compensation plan is heavily weighted toward equity ownership, which, combined with the long tenure of the management team, has accounted for the big equity stakes. Employees as a whole own about two fifths of the firm, which generally keeps employee and shareholder interests aligned. However, such high employee ownership may give employees a disproportionate influence over the dispersal of cash flows, and employees could put their own interests slightly ahead of shareholders'.

383 Madison Avenue
New York, NY 10179
www.bearstearns.com

Growth [B]	2002	2003	2004	2005
Revenue %	4.5	16.9	13.7	8.8
Earnings/Share %	51.5	31.7	14.6	5.6
Book Value/Share %	22.8	20.2	20.6	18.0
Dividends/Share %	3.3	19.4	14.9	17.6

Profitability [D+]	2003	2004	2005	TTM
Return on Assets %	0.5	0.5	0.5	0.6
Oper Cash Flow $Mil	-5,217	-2,177	-14,012	—
- Cap Spending $Mil	37	128	203	—
= Free Cash Flow $Mil	—	—	—	—

Financial Health [NA]	2003	2004	2005	08-31-06
Long-term Debt $Mil	—	—	—	—
Total Equity $Mil	6,932	8,543	10,419	11,363
Debt/Equity Ratio	—	—	—	—

Industry	Business Risk	Moat Size	Investment Style	Sector
Securities	Average	Narrow	Large Value	Financial Services

Competition

	Market Cap $Mil	12 Mo Trailing Sales $Mil	Price/Cash Flow	Return On Assets %	Debt/ Equity	Total Return% 1 Yr	3 Yr
Bear Stearns Companies	19,096	8,701	—	0.6	—	42.1	28.0
Citigroup	273,691	86,566	—	1.3	—	19.6	8.4
J.P. Morgan Chase & Co.	167,551	59,650	—	0.9	—	25.6	13.2

Price Volatility

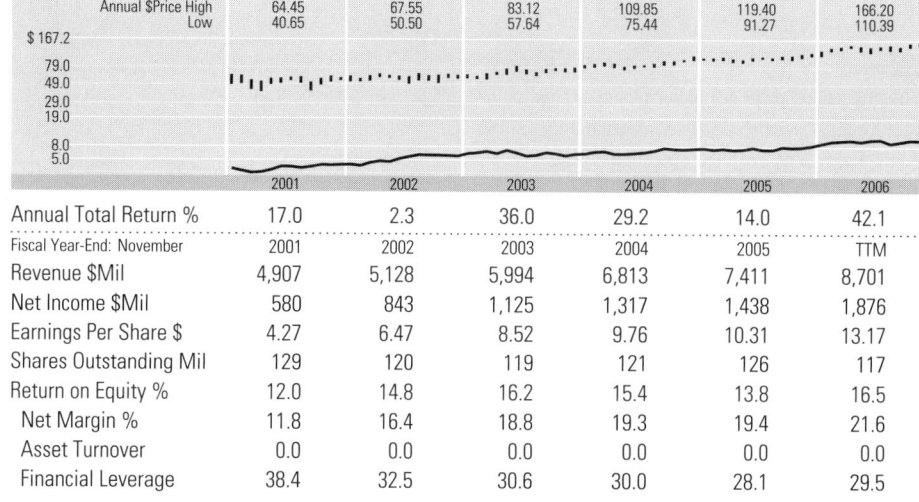

	2001	2002	2003	2004	2005	2006 TTM
Annual Total Return %	17.0	2.3	36.0	29.2	14.0	42.1
Fiscal Year-End: November	2001	2002	2003	2004	2005	TTM
Revenue $Mil	4,907	5,128	5,994	6,813	7,411	8,701
Net Income $Mil	580	843	1,125	1,317	1,438	1,876
Earnings Per Share $	4.27	6.47	8.52	9.76	10.31	13.17
Shares Outstanding Mil	129	120	119	121	126	117
Return on Equity %	12.0	14.8	16.2	15.4	13.8	16.5
Net Margin %	11.8	16.4	18.8	19.3	19.4	21.6
Asset Turnover	0.0	0.0	0.0	0.0	0.0	0.0
Financial Leverage	38.4	32.5	30.6	30.0	28.1	29.5

Valuation Ratios	Stock	Rel to Industry	Rel to S&P 500
Price/Earnings	12.4	0.7	0.6
Price/Book	1.7	0.4	0.4
Price/Sales	2.2	0.5	0.8
Price/Cash Flow	—	—	—

Major Fund Holders	% of Fund Assets
New York Equity	5.01
Constellation Pitcairn Select Value II	4.37
CGM Mutual	4.21
FBR Large Cap Financial	4.08

Thesis By Philip Guziec, 12-14-06 Stock Price as of Analysis: $159.96

Investment banking is a moat-worthy business in which ongoing relationships protect market share and margins. Although revenue can be volatile, growth opportunities abound. Bear Stearns' strength lies in fixed-income products, and its focus is on enabling customer transactions rather than putting its own capital at risk. While rising interest rates may yet affect Bear Stearns, a decline in the stock price could create a nice buying opportunity.

The largest portion of Bear's revenue is derived from underwriting and trading fixed-income securities and mortgages. This area of the securities business has been on a tear as falling interest rates and narrowing credit spreads prompted companies to issue debt and debtholders to trade, driving fixed-income revenue up 24% annually since 2000. The mortgage market has also boomed, and issuance of securities backed by mortgages has grown 41% annually since 2000. Bear has remained a leader in issuing these securities and has vaulted into the top spot in the related league tables. Volatility in foreign-exchange markets has also helped to drive trading profits, which the company books as fixed-income revenue. All told, the fixed-income business represented 44% of the company's revenue in 2006, and proprietary transactions accounted for about three quarters of those percentage points, including profits on the issuance of mortgage securities. We don't expect fixed-income revenue growth to continue at recent levels in the face of flat to rising interest rates, and we're a bit concerned that this business may slow in the near term. However, in the longer run, we think Bear will remain a strong player in the fixed-income and mortgage markets.

Clearing services, or the business of facilitating trades for clients, accounted for 12% of 2006 net revenue. About two thirds of this revenue is derived from net interest income, earned by offering margin loans and loaning stocks to clients. Bear Stearns, Morgan Stanley, and Goldman Sachs collectively provide almost three fourths of all prime brokerage clearing services to hedge funds, and Bear believes it leads this market. Continued hedge fund growth, rising interest rates, and increasing market volatility would all bode well for clearing services, and while the business is also tied to the health of financial markets, little capital is at risk.

Bear also provides merger advisory, equity underwriting, and wealth-management services, all businesses with high returns on investment that add to the bottom line. We like the company's package of businesses and its low-risk focus.

Becton, Dickinson and Company BDX

Data as of 12-29-06

Rating	Fair Value	Last Close	Consider Buy	Consider Sell	Yield %
★★★	$74.00	$70.15	$63.10	$97.20	1.27

Company Profile
Becton, Dickinson is the world's largest manufacturer and distributor of medical surgical products, such as needles, syringes, and sharps-disposal units. The company also manufactures diagnostic instruments and reagents (30% of total sales) and flow cytometry and cell imaging systems (15% of total sales). International revenues account for 52% of the company's business.

Management
Stewardship Grade [C]

We give Becton Dickinson's management a C grade for corporate stewardship despite its great track record for achieving excellent operating results. Our main beef is with the company's generous compensation plan. In 2005 CEO Ed Ludwig took home a package worth more than $7 million, including $1.6 million in stock options. Becton's independent directors are also well-compensated for their services, receiving nearly $180,000 each per year. We consider this level of pay excessive, although we note that two thirds of their compensation is in the form of restricted stock. With the exception of Becton's pay structure, our overall view of the company's corporate governance is positive. We approve of several recently enacted shareholder-friendly initiatives. Becton eliminated its poison pill provision, modified its executive severance arrangements to reduce mandatory post-takeover employment, and required Ludwig to reimburse the company for personal use of Becton's plane. We also approve of the minimum ownership requirements, which mandate the company's executives maintain a certain portion of their compensation in Becton stock. Finally, we agree with Becton's decision to consider long-term performance metrics, such as return on invested capital, in determining executive compensation.

1 Becton Drive
Franklin Lakes, NJ 07417-1880
www.bd.com

Growth [C+]	2003	2004	2005	2006
Revenue %	12.7	10.6	9.7	7.8
Earnings/Share %	15.6	-14.5	56.5	5.8
Book Value/Share %	17.1	8.2	9.5	10.6
Dividends/Share %	2.6	50.0	20.0	19.4

Profitability [A+]	2004	2005	2006	TTM
Return on Assets %	8.1	11.8	11.0	11.0
Oper Cash Flow $Mil	1,103	1,216	1,076	1,076
- Cap Spending $Mil	266	318	459	459
= Free Cash Flow $Mil	837	898	617	617

Financial Health [A]	2004	2005	2006	09-30-06
Long-term Debt $Mil	1,546	1,402	1,227	1,227
Total Equity $Mil	3,037	3,284	3,836	3,836
Debt/Equity Ratio	0.5	0.4	0.3	0.3

Industry	Business Risk	Moat Size	Investment Style	Sector
Medical Equip.	Below Avg	Narrow	Large Core	Healthcare

Competition	Market Cap $Mil	12 Mo Trailing Sales $Mil	Price/Cash Flow	Return On Assets%	Debt/ Equity	Total Return% 1 Yr	3 Yr
Becton, Dickinson and Company	17,302	5,835	16.1	11.0	0.3	18.3	21.1
Roche Holding AG ADR	154,312	28,721	19.1	10.4	0.2	20.4	22.6
Tyco International	60,461	40,960	10.8	5.8	0.3	6.8	5.1

Price Volatility — Monthly Price High/Low — Relative Strength to S&P 500

Annual $Price High/Low	39.25 / 29.96	38.60 / 24.70	41.82 / 28.82	58.18 / 40.90	61.17 / 49.71	74.25 / 58.08
	2001	2002	2003	2004	2005	2006
Annual Total Return %	-3.2	-6.3	35.7	39.7	7.2	18.3

Fiscal Year-End: September	2002	2003	2004	2005	2006	TTM
Revenue $Mil	3,960	4,464	4,935	5,415	5,835	5,835
Net Income $Mil	480	547	467	722	752	752
Earnings Per Share $	1.79	2.07	1.77	2.77	2.93	2.93
Shares Outstanding Mil	259	256	253	252	247	247
Return on Equity %	19.3	19.1	15.4	22.0	19.6	19.6
Net Margin %	12.1	12.3	9.5	13.3	12.9	12.9
Asset Turnover	0.8	0.8	0.9	0.9	0.9	0.9
Financial Leverage	2.0	1.9	1.9	1.9	1.8	1.8

Valuation Ratios	Stock	Rel to Industry	Rel to S&P 500
Price/Earnings	23.8	0.8	1.2
Price/Book	4.5	0.8	1.1
Price/Sales	3.0	0.6	1.0
Price/Cash Flow	16.1	0.7	1.1

Major Fund Holders	% of Fund Assets
Fidelity Select Medical Equip/Systems	6.52
Schwab Health Care	4.87
Schwab Large-Cap Growth Sel	4.09
FMI Large Cap	3.96

Thesis By Alex Morozov, CFA, 11-17-06 Stock Price as of Analysis: $71.24

Becton, Dickinson built its needles and surgical tools empire on experience and innovation. Now, as the surgical segment is slowly maturing, the company is shifting its focus and applying its research and development prowess to advance its rapidly growing diagnostics and biosciences operations.

Becton made a name for itself manufacturing basic surgical instruments: needles, syringes, and scalpels, among others. As the industry evolved, so did the company's products, with many significant technological innovations first introduced at Becton. The recent launch of safety-engineered products designed to prevent injuries is among the firm's latest achievements, these products are now mandatory in most of the hospitals across the U.S. Becton has also been advocating greater use of safety products overseas, and its push is paying off: The firm is seeing switching from traditional to safety-guarded sharps. This trend is particularly evident in developing countries, where the prevalence of infectious diseases makes Becton's single-use, safety-engineered needles and syringes valuable to both nurses and patients.

Safety-engineered products also carry higher margins than traditional sharps and provide Becton with a steady stream of cash flows. The firm reinvests this cash into its rapidly growing diagnostic and flow cytometry product lines. As the needle market becomes saturated, we expect diagnostic and bioscience operations will become the firm's primary growth drivers. The recent acquisition of GeneOhm and the pending purchase of TriPath Imaging exemplify Becton's commitment to growing the diagnostic business. While neither of these deals will move the needle in the short run, as the two companies combined generate under $100 million in sales, they will provide Becton with a pathway into genetic and oncology diagnostics, areas we project to grow at a substantially higher rate than the rest of the business.

Our favorable take on Becton's prospects also stems from our confidence in the firm's management. Becton has a history of allocating its capital wisely and providing shareholders with solid returns on investment. The company's reputation for searching out pockets of growth, along with its sizable manufacturing and distribution infrastructure, convinces us that Becton will be able to fend off competition and continue to defend its narrow moat.

Bed Bath & Beyond BBBY

Data as of 12-29-06

Rating	Fair Value	Last Close	Consider Buy	Consider Sell	Yield %
★★★	$43.00	$38.10	$33.20	$53.90	0.00

Industry	Business Risk	Moat Size	Investment Style	Sector
Furniture Retail	Average	None	Mid Growth	Consumer Services

Company Profile

Bed Bath & Beyond operates retail stores that sell brand-name domestic merchandise and home furnishings--bed linens, bath accessories, kitchen textiles, cookware, dinnerware, glassware, and basic housewares. The company operates about 760 Bed Bath & Beyond stores throughout most of the United States. The company also owns Christmas Tree Shops, a 31-store giftware and household items retailer, and Harmon Stores, a 38-store health- and beauty-care retailer.

Management

Stewardship Grade [**D**]

Warren Eisenberg and Leonard Feinstein cofounded Bed Bath & Beyond in 1971 and serve as cochairmen. Steven Temares, who joined the company in 1992, was promoted to chief executive officer in 2003. The senior managers average more than 20 years with Bed Bath & Beyond, and there has been very little turnover. Management compensation appears to be fairly reasonable. The board of directors consists of Eisenberg, Feinstein, Temares, and seven outside directors. Directors and executive officers own about 6% of the company's common stock, most of which is owned by Eisenberg and Feinstein. The company's corporate stewardship leaves much to be desired. We are not big fans of the staggered board of directors, transactions with related parties, or the high fixed percentage of total compensation for top executives.

650 Liberty Avenue
Union, NJ 07083
www.bedbathandbeyond.com

Growth [**B+**]	2003	2004	2005	2006
Revenue %	25.2	22.2	15.0	12.9
Earnings/Share %	35.1	31.0	26.0	16.4
Book Value/Share %	30.3	35.9	10.3	5.3
Dividends/Share %	NMF	NMF	NMF	NMF

Profitability [**A+**]	2004	2005	2006	TTM
Return on Assets %	13.9	15.8	16.9	15.6
Oper Cash Flow $Mil	544	607	660	647
- Cap Spending $Mil	109	181	220	268
= Free Cash Flow $Mil	435	426	440	380

Financial Health [**A+**]	2004	2005	2006	08-31-06
Long-term Debt $Mil	—	—	—	—
Total Equity $Mil	1,991	2,204	2,262	2,549
Debt/Equity Ratio	—	—	—	—

Competition	Market Cap $Mil	12 Mo Trailing Sales $Mil	Price/Cash Flow	Return On Assets %	Debt/Equity	Total Return% 1 Yr	3 Yr
Bed Bath & Beyond	10,770	6,137	16.6	15.6	—	5.4	-3.5
Williams-Sonoma	3,526	3,687	11.1	10.7	0.0	-26.5	-2.4
Pier 1 Imports	521	1,710	—	-10.7	0.4	-29.5	-32.5

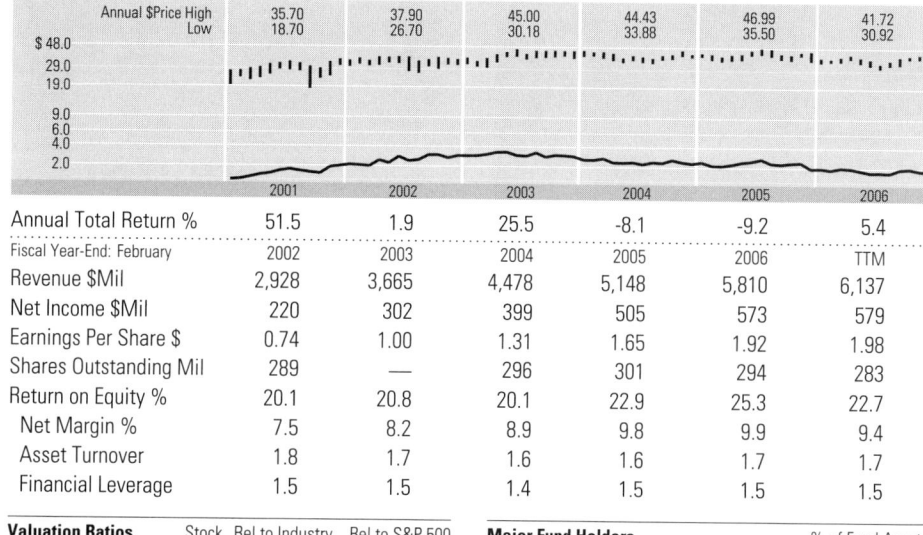

	2002	2003	2004	2005	2006	TTM
Annual Total Return %	51.5	1.9	25.5	-8.1	-9.2	5.4
Fiscal Year-End: February	2002	2003	2004	2005	2006	TTM
Revenue $Mil	2,928	3,665	4,478	5,148	5,810	6,137
Net Income $Mil	220	302	399	505	573	579
Earnings Per Share $	0.74	1.00	1.31	1.65	1.92	1.98
Shares Outstanding Mil	289	—	296	301	294	283
Return on Equity %	20.1	20.8	20.1	22.9	25.3	22.7
Net Margin %	7.5	8.2	8.9	9.8	9.9	9.4
Asset Turnover	1.8	1.7	1.6	1.6	1.7	1.7
Financial Leverage	1.5	1.5	1.4	1.5	1.5	1.5

Valuation Ratios	Stock	Rel to Industry	Rel to S&P 500
Price/Earnings	19.2	1.0	0.9
Price/Book	4.2	1.0	1.0
Price/Sales	1.8	1.3	0.6
Price/Cash Flow	16.6	1.2	1.1

Major Fund Holders	% of Fund Assets
Sequoia	5.73
Black Pearl Focus	4.05
Parnassus	3.91
Parnassus Workplace	3.59

Thesis

By Anthony Chukumba, 11-20-06 Stock Price as of Analysis: $39.84

Bed Bath & Beyond is one of the best-run retailers we follow. Despite competing in the fierce home furnishings industry with specialty stores, department stores, mass merchants, and off-price retailers, the firm continues to perform: Sales have grown at an average of 19% annually over the past five years, and Bed Bath & Beyond's 15.1% operating margin in 2005 is one of the highest in all of retailing. In addition, the company is a strong cash-flow generator, with an average free cash flow/sales ratio over the past five years of 8%, and its returns on invested capital far outpace its weighted average cost of capital, creating shareholder value.

A wide breadth of products makes Bed Bath & Beyond's stores one-stop shopping destinations for housewares. Customers also like the everyday low pricing of the goods, ensuring that they are always getting a fair price, rather than having to wait for a sale before making a purchase. The real secret to Bed Bath & Beyond's success, though, lies in its store-level execution, primarily in merchandising and customer service. Store managers have the autonomy to select 70%-75% of the items offered in the store. Thus, the goods stocked in each store reflect the specific tastes of the people who live nearby.

Bed Bath & Beyond is able to offer such freedom to its store managers because virtually all of them are promoted from within. Thus, store managers have worked for the company for years, soaking in the firm's merchandising strategy, operating model, and distinctive culture. Bed Bath & Beyond also has a relentless focus on customer service which, as we can attest from our frequent visits to stores, directly leads to a better consumer experience. However, although Bed Bath & Beyond does a nearly flawless job in execution, there is nothing about its strategy that is truly unique or that competitors could not copy. Thus, despite the lofty historical profit margins and returns, we do not believe the firm has an economic moat.

As new store growth has begun to slow in the core Bed Bath & Beyond concept, the firm has made two small acquisitions that could present attractive growth prospects. In 2002 the company bought Harmon Stores, a health- and beauty-care retailer, and in 2003 it picked up Christmas Tree Shops, a small giftware and household item retailer. Placing Harmon "shops-in-shops" in Bed Bath & Beyond stores and more aggressively opening new Christmas Tree Shops could provide Bed Bath & Beyond with plenty more years of double-digit top-line growth.

Data as of 12-29-06

Bemis BMS

	Rating	Fair Value	Last Close	Consider Buy	Consider Sell	Yield %
	★★★	$35.00	$33.98	$27.00	$43.90	2.24

Company Profile
Wisconsin-based Bemis is a global leader in the flexible packaging and pressure-sensitive material industries. Representing 80% of sales, flexible packaging includes a portfolio of value-added, proprietary products targeted toward the food, medical device, and personal-care markets. Pressure-sensitive materials, which constitute 20% of sales, include products that are sold to the label, graphic, and technical markets.

Management
Stewardship Grade [B]

Jeffrey H. Curler was appointed president and CEO in 2000 after nearly three decades with Bemis and its subsidiaries. We admire management's strategic approach and ability to make small acquisitions that continue to create value. Corporate governance is sound, in our opinion, highlighted by reasonable management compensation, light option issuance (less than 1% of total shares outstanding), and total executive and director ownership of 6.4% of the outstanding shares. All members of the nominating and compensation committees are independent. On the negative side, board elections are staggered.

Industry	Business Risk	Moat Size	Investment Style	Sector
Packaging	Average	Narrow	Mid Value	Consumer Goods

Competition	Market Cap $Mil	12 Mo Trailing Sales $Mil	Price/Cash Flow	Return On Assets%	Debt/ Equity	Total Return% 1 Yr	3 Yr
Bemis	3,562	3,631	11.3	5.8	0.5	24.9	13.9
Avery Dennison	7,457	5,466	15.3	6.1	0.4	26.1	9.5
Sealed Air	5,234	4,258	12.8	5.4	1.2	16.9	7.4

Price Volatility — Monthly Price High/Low — Relative Strength to S&P 500

	2001	2002	2003	2004	2005	2006
Annual $Price High	26.24	29.12	25.58	29.49	32.50	34.99
Low	14.34	19.70	19.67	23.24	23.20	27.87
Annual Total Return %	50.2	3.0	3.3	19.2	-1.6	24.9

Fiscal Year-End: December	2001	2002	2003	2004	2005	TTM
Revenue $Mil	2,293	2,369	2,635	2,834	3,474	3,631
Net Income $Mil	140	166	147	180	163	180
Earnings Per Share $	1.32	1.54	1.37	1.67	1.51	1.68
Shares Outstanding Mil	106	106	106	107	106	105
Return on Equity %	15.8	17.3	12.9	13.8	12.0	12.0
Net Margin %	6.1	7.0	5.6	6.3	4.7	4.9
Asset Turnover	1.2	1.1	1.1	1.1	1.2	1.2
Financial Leverage	2.2	2.4	2.0	1.9	2.2	2.1

Valuation Ratios	Stock	Rel to Industry	Rel to S&P 500
Price/Earnings	20.2	0.8	1.0
Price/Book	2.4	0.7	0.6
Price/Sales	1.0	1.0	0.3
Price/Cash Flow	11.3	1.0	0.8

Major Fund Holders	% of Fund Assets
Fidelity Select Paper & Forest Prod	5.10
Phoenix Small-Mid Cap X	4.61
FMI Common Stock	3.79
Meridian Equity Income	2.82

One Neenah Center P.O. Box 669 www.bemis.com
Neenah, WI 54956-0669

Growth [A-]	2002	2003	2004	2005
Revenue %	3.3	11.2	7.6	22.6
Earnings/Share %	16.7	-11.0	21.9	-9.6
Book Value/Share %	7.0	18.8	14.5	3.3
Dividends/Share %	4.0	7.7	14.3	12.5

Profitability [B]	2003	2004	2005	TTM
Return on Assets %	6.4	7.2	5.5	5.8
Oper Cash Flow $Mil	311	272	280	315
- Cap Spending $Mil	106	135	187	179
= Free Cash Flow $Mil	205	137	93	136

Financial Health [B]	2003	2004	2005	09-30-06
Long-term Debt $Mil	583	534	790	713
Total Equity $Mil	1,139	1,308	1,349	1,493
Debt/Equity Ratio	0.5	0.4	0.6	0.5

Thesis
By Kevin Walkush, 11-29-06 Stock Price as of Analysis: $33.85

Bemis boasts an exemplary record of innovation and success, which has translated into consistent financial returns for its shareholders.

Bemis is an industry leader in material science, packaging innovation, and customer service. With a product portfolio built upon proprietary technologies, the firm delivers high value-added packaging solutions that satisfy unique customer needs and capture healthy margins. A generous research budget demonstrates this commitment to innovation. Location is also a competitive advantage. Bemis operates plants close to major customers, helping develop symbiotic relationships with customers and increasing switching costs.

Targeting the food-related market has also proved advantageous for Bemis. Because demand and growth for food is relatively stable, the firm is protected from large swings in the economy. Meat and cheese packaging currently represents one of the firm's fastest-growing products. Pricing power has proved instrumental, enabling Bemis to pass along volatile costs for raw materials like resin. Taken together, we believe Bemis has carved out a narrow economic moat around its business.

Stable operating performance is another hallmark at Bemis. Over the past 10 years, Bemis has been consistently successful, posting an average return on invested capital of 12%, well above its cost of capital. This performance has resulted in dividend increases for 23 consecutive years, a remarkable record.

Customer trends have evolved in Bemis' favor. In an effort to differentiate their products, customers are repeatedly trading up--switching to packages that introduce unique and convenient features. The evolution of packaging technology, particularly printing-related capabilities, has also helped eliminate bulk and waste. Thanks to its commitment to research, development, and innovation, Bemis is well positioned to capitalize on both trends.

Bemis' pressure-sensitive material (PSM) segment is less attractive. Representing about 20% of net sales, PSM sales have been a drag on performance. The PSM market is commoditylike and remains troubled by price competition and excess capacity. To combat such issues, Bemis has aggressively consolidated operations and boosted utilization capacity. It is also developing its graphic and technical product areas through investments in technology, hoping to differentiate its product line and capture higher margins.

Data as of 12-29-06

Berkshire Hathaway B BRK.B

Rating	Fair Value	Last Close	Consider Buy	Consider Sell	Yield %
★★★★★	$4550.00	$3666.00	$3877.10	$5973.70	0.00

Company Profile

Diversified holding company Berkshire Hathaway owns and operates more than 65 businesses and also invests widely in undervalued equities and bonds. Berkshire owns large stakes in Coke, Moody's, and American Express. Berkshire is the world's only AAA rated reinsurer; its insurance businesses include Geico, General Re, and National Indemnity. Berkshire also owns stakes in several private businesses, including Medical Protective, Forest River, and Western Plastics.

Management   Stewardship Grade [A]

Chairman and CEO Warren Buffett's decision to begin gifting his Berkshire stake to a group of charitable foundations run by his children and board member Bill Gates does not affect our Stewardship Grade for the firm. In our view, Buffett's interests remain sharply aligned with those of shareholders. In addition, we continue to be impressed by Berkshire's managerial incentives. Berkshire's managers are handsomely rewarded for increasing free cash flows relative to the capital invested, which is exactly what should drive compensation. Berkshire's managers are also rewarded by the opportunity to work for--and be praised by--CEO Warren Buffett, but with a degree of autonomy rarely awarded to the managers of acquired firms. This autonomy also obviates dependence on headquarters, freeing senior management to concentrate on investment opportunities.

Industry	Business Risk	Moat Size	Investment Style	Sector
Insurance (General)	Below Avg	Wide	Large Core	Financial Services

Competition

	Market Cap $Mil	12 Mo Trailing Sales $Mil	Price/Cash Flow	Return On Assets%	Debt/Equity	Total Return% 1 Yr	3 Yr
Berkshire Hathaway B	169,636	97,676	—	5.2	—	24.9	9.4
General Electric	383,564	161,022	12.8	2.5	2.2	9.4	9.0
Swiss Reinsurance ADR	27,461	28,315	—	0.7	—	19.0	9.9

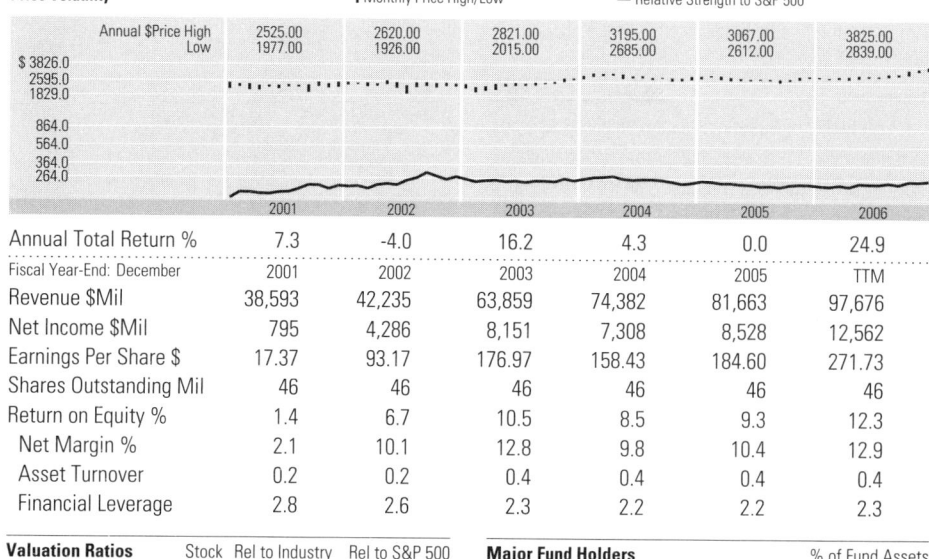

	2001	2002	2003	2004	2005	2006
Annual Total Return %	7.3	-4.0	16.2	4.3	0.0	24.9
Fiscal Year-End: December	2001	2002	2003	2004	2005	TTM
Revenue $Mil	38,593	42,235	63,859	74,382	81,663	97,676
Net Income $Mil	795	4,286	8,151	7,308	8,528	12,562
Earnings Per Share $	17.37	93.17	176.97	158.43	184.60	271.73
Shares Outstanding Mil	46	46	46	46	46	46
Return on Equity %	1.4	6.7	10.5	8.5	9.3	12.3
Net Margin %	2.1	10.1	12.8	9.8	10.4	12.9
Asset Turnover	0.2	0.2	0.4	0.4	0.4	0.4
Financial Leverage	2.8	2.6	2.3	2.2	2.2	2.3

Valuation Ratios	Stock	Rel to Industry	Rel to S&P 500
Price/Earnings	13.5	0.9	0.7
Price/Book	1.7	0.8	0.4
Price/Sales	1.7	1.0	0.6
Price/Cash Flow	—	—	—

Major Fund Holders	% of Fund Assets
Midas Special	19.88
Tilson Focus	13.42
Frank Value	9.93
Meehan Focus	9.05

Thesis By Justin Fuller, CFA, 12-14-06 Stock Price as of Analysis: $3675.00

Near-term concerns continue to weigh on Berkshire's shares, and we think this has created an opportunity for astute investors to augment their holdings at attractive prices.

Executive succession anxiety has plagued Berkshire for years, but we think this is overblown. Warren Buffett is well aware of this concern and has planned to bifurcate his role between CEOs for operations and investments. Buffett has also indicated that Berkshire's board has settled on two people, one to handle each of these roles. While we think that each of these individuals will be exceptionally capable, we also acknowledge that Berkshire's investment returns will likely be lower under their stewardship. That said, since we've already forecasted lower investment returns, and since Berkshire's operating businesses are already well stocked with highly motivated managers who operate autonomously, we think the eventual succession should be relatively painless.

Another concern is a seemingly persistent dearth of investment opportunities, which is partly due to the growth of private equity capital prospecting for acquisitions. We acknowledge this competition has elevated asset prices, but we think Berkshire still gets a look at some great businesses. Many entrepreneurs want a partner like Buffett who will allow them to continue to run their firms autonomously, so we think that they will not only seek out Berkshire, but that they are also potentially willing to take a below-market price for their businesses, which will enhance Berkshire's long-term returns. Plus, Buffett is starting to find more investments offshore, as evidenced by the recent purchase of Israel-based Iscar Metalworking for $4 billion. This transaction could be a watershed event in Berkshire's history, as it has the potential to increase Berkshire's deal flow for years to come.

Finally, despite a benign Atlantic hurricane season in 2006, many are concerned that the Earth is in a period of elevated windstorm activity that will lead to persistently higher losses for reinsurance businesses. While we don't know the answer to this weather question, we do know that Berkshire's Gibraltar-like financial strength allows the conglomerate to command significantly higher prices than the rest of the reinsurance industry. As a result of this competitive advantage--and Berkshire's intense focus on loss control--we expect the conglomerate's catastrophe policies to be profitable over the long haul, even if the storm experience of 2004 or 2005 is repeated at some point down the road.

1440 Kiewit Plaza   www.berkshirehathaway.com
Omaha, NE 68131

Growth [B+]	2002	2003	2004	2005
Revenue %	9.4	51.2	16.5	9.8
Earnings/Share %	436.5	89.9	-10.5	16.5
Book Value/Share %	10.0	21.0	10.5	6.3
Dividends/Share %	NMF	NMF	NMF	NMF

Profitability [A-]	2003	2004	2005	TTM
Return on Assets %	4.5	3.9	4.3	5.2
Oper Cash Flow $Mil	8,341	7,311	9,446	—
- Cap Spending $Mil	1,066	1,278	2,195	—
= Free Cash Flow $Mil	—	—	—	—

Financial Health [NA]	2003	2004	2005	09-30-06
Long-term Debt $Mil	—	—	—	—
Total Equity $Mil	77,596	85,900	91,484	102,244
Debt/Equity Ratio	—	—	—	—

Data as of 12-29-06

Best Buy Co. BBY

Rating	Fair Value	Last Close	Consider Buy	Consider Sell	Yield %
★★★★	$58.00	$49.19	$44.70	$72.70	0.73

Company Profile
Best Buy is the largest specialty retailer of consumer electronics in North America, with approximately 900 stores in the U.S. and Canada. The company sells a variety of merchandise including video and audio equipment, personal computers, and home appliances. Best Buy operates electronics stores in Canada and China under the names Future Shop and Five Star, respectively, and specialty stores Magnolia Home Theater, Pacific Sales Kitchen and Bath, and Geek Squad in the U.S.

Management — Stewardship Grade [B]
We think highly of Best Buy's experienced management team and solid corporate governance. Chairman Richard Schulze founded Best Buy in 1966, and CEO Brad Anderson has been with the firm since 1973, serving as chief executive since 2002. We are pleased that the company has kept the CEO and chairman roles separate. In our opinion, both Schulze and Anderson hold enough stock to closely align their interests with those of shareholders. Schulze still owns about 16% of the company, and the value of Anderson's holdings is a large multiple of his annual compensation. Total management compensation seems reasonable, considering that the company has consistently earned returns well above its cost of capital and that a significant amount of pay is based on the creation of measurable shareholder value. In fiscal 2006, Anderson was paid just over $1 million in salary and nearly $2.7 in annual bonus. We like that the firm keeps non-monetary executive perks to a minimum. We believe the board is sufficiently independent, although we would prefer that all of the directors stood for election every year, rather than serving staggered two-year terms.

7601 Penn Avenue South
Richfield, MN 55423-3645
www.bestbuy.com

Growth [B+]	2003	2004	2005	2006
Revenue %	18.2	17.2	11.8	12.4
Earnings/Share %	-83.1	610.0	38.0	15.8
Book Value/Share %	5.7	25.0	28.6	18.1
Dividends/Share %	NMF	NMF	5.0	9.5

Profitability [B+]	2004	2005	2006	TTM
Return on Assets %	8.1	9.6	9.6	10.0
Oper Cash Flow $Mil	1,387	1,981	1,695	1,861
- Cap Spending $Mil	545	502	648	667
= Free Cash Flow $Mil	842	1,479	1,047	1,194

Financial Health [A+]	2004	2005	2006	08-31-06
Long-term Debt $Mil	—	528	178	184
Total Equity $Mil	3,422	4,449	5,257	5,434
Debt/Equity Ratio	—	0.1	0.0	0.0

Industry	Business Risk	Moat Size	Investment Style	Sector
Electronics Stores	Average	Narrow	Large Growth	Consumer Services

Competition	Market Cap $Mil	12 Mo Trailing Sales $Mil	Price/Cash Flow	Return On Assets %	Debt/ Equity	Total Return % 1 Yr	3 Yr
Best Buy Co.	23,624	32,590	12.7	10.0	0.0	13.9	14.1
Amazon.com	16,254	9,702	27.6	8.9	6.7	-16.3	-8.7
Circuit City Stores	3,325	12,269	11.7	4.1	0.0	-15.6	24.0

Price Volatility — Monthly Price High/Low — Relative Strength to S&P 500

| Annual $Price High | 33.42 | 35.83 | 41.73 | 41.47 | 53.17 | 59.50 |
| Low | 12.39 | 11.33 | 15.77 | 29.25 | 31.93 | 43.32 |

	2001	2002	2003	2004	2005	2006
Annual Total Return %	151.9	-51.4	117.4	14.6	10.8	13.9

Fiscal Year-End: February	2002	2003	2004	2005	2006	TTM
Revenue $Mil	17,711	20,943	24,548	27,433	30,848	32,590
Net Income $Mil	570	99	705	984	1,140	1,246
Earnings Per Share $	1.18	0.20	1.42	1.96	2.27	2.50
Shares Outstanding Mil	475	471	486	490	489	480
Return on Equity %	22.6	3.6	20.6	22.1	21.7	22.9
Net Margin %	3.2	0.5	2.9	3.6	3.7	3.8
Asset Turnover	2.4	2.7	2.8	2.7	2.6	2.6
Financial Leverage	2.9	2.8	2.5	2.3	2.3	2.3

Valuation Ratios	Stock	Rel to Industry	Rel to S&P 500
Price/Earnings	19.7	0.9	1.0
Price/Book	4.3	1.1	1.0
Price/Sales	0.7	1.0	0.2
Price/Cash Flow	12.7	1.0	0.9

Major Fund Holders	% of Fund Assets
Kelmoore Strategy C	5.08
Aston/Veredus Select Growth N	4.16
Brandywine Blue	3.89
Fidelity Select Computers	3.60

Thesis By Brady Lemos, 12-12-06 Stock Price as of Analysis: $51.30

During a time of rapidly advancing technology over the past 20 years, Best Buy built itself into a category killer by offering the latest consumer electronics at low prices in shopper-friendly stores. However, the company has nearly saturated the domestic market, and a number of powerful retailers, including Wal-Mart and Amazon, are intent on stealing share. Faced with these challenges, we believe Best Buy is taking the right steps to differentiate itself from competitors and capitalize on new growth opportunities.

Best Buy's commitment to "customer-centricity" is its most compelling point of differentiation, in our view. By utilizing specially trained sales associates in customized store environments, Best Buy is able to provide a unique shopping experience unmatched by mass merchants and online retailers. Best Buy is also expanding its Geek Squad computer support service and integrating Magnolia high-end home theater departments into many of its stores. Thanks to this differentiated approach to retailing, Best Buy should continue to generate impressive returns on invested capital, justifying a narrow economic moat rating.

Best Buy's merchandising expertise should help it expand internationally and enter new retail categories in the U.S. Most notably, Best Buy's 2006 acquisition of Jiangsu Five Star provided instant access to China's huge consumer electronics market. Wisely mimicking its growth strategy in Canada, Best Buy intends to roll out namesake stores only after careful study of the Chinese market and local customs. Domestically, Best Buy entered the quickly growing premium segment of the home-remodeling market by acquiring Pacific Sales Kitchen and Bath in 2006.

While strategically justifiable, investing in these growth opportunities and customer-service initiatives will pressure profitability. Five Star's gross margin, for example, is roughly half that of Best Buy's domestic stores', and expanding services such as computer support and in-home installation increases store operating expenses. Even if Best Buy is able to differentiate its shopping experience, the presence of low-price competitors like Wal-Mart and Costco will probably keep a lid on industrywide profitability.

Despite a challenging environment, we believe Best Buy is well positioned to remain a destination store among consumer electronics retailers. Best Buy's flexible merchandising platform and willingness to adapt should be valuable assets as the company enters new markets.

Data as of 12-29-06

BG Group PLC ADR BRG

Rating	Fair Value	Last Close	Consider Buy	Consider Sell	Yield %
★★	$57.00	$68.44	$44.00	$71.40	0.93

Company Profile
BG Group is an integrated natural-gas company. The firm explores for and produces primarily natural gas--but also oil--from fields in the U.K. Continental Shelf, Kazakhstan, Trinidad, Egypt, and other areas. BG Group has a liquefied natural gas business that brings natural gas from producing areas to U.S. markets. Finally, the company operates natural-gas pipelines and distribution systems as well as gas-fired electricity generation plants.

Management   Stewardship Grade [NA]
Chairman Robert Wilson has been a director of BG Group since 2002. Wilson comes from Rio Tinto, one of the world's best-run mining companies, where he was chief executive and chairman. Chief executive Frank Chapman has been with BG Group or predecessor British Gas since 1996. Chapman has been in the oil and gas industry for 30 years and has worked at both BP and Royal Dutch Shell. Wilson's total compensation in 2005 was 526,794 pounds (or about $964,000), and Chapman took home about 1.6 million pounds (or about $2.9 million). Management's bonuses are based on earnings per share, return on average capital employed, total shareholder return versus peers, and long-term earnings growth. We're happy to see that management gets rewarded for both short-term performance and long-term value creation. Because BG focuses on return on average capital employed (similar to return on equity), it probably won't pursue growth at the expense of a bloated asset base.

100 Thames Valley Park Drive   www.bg-group.com
Reading, United Kingdom RG6 1PT

Growth [NA]	2002	2003	2004	2005
Revenue %	NMF	37.4	13.3	33.5
Earnings/Share %	NMF	87.9	14.7	72.0
Book Value/Share %	NMF	18.5	12.1	35.7
Dividends/Share %	NMF	—	—	—

Profitability [NA]	2003	2004	2005	TTM
Return on Assets %	9.8	9.9	14.7	14.7
Oper Cash Flow $Mil	2,362	2,173	2,931	2,931
- Cap Spending $Mil	1,281	1,858	1,942	1,942
= Free Cash Flow $Mil	1,081	315	989	989

Financial Health [NA]	2003	2004	2005	12-31-05
Long-term Debt $Mil	1,238	1,637	2,228	2,228
Total Equity $Mil	7,009	8,783	10,659	10,659
Debt/Equity Ratio	0.2	0.2	0.2	0.2

Industry	Business Risk	Moat Size	Investment Style	Sector
Oil/Gas	Average	Narrow	Large Growth	Energy

Competition
	Market Cap $Mil	12 Mo Trailing Sales $Mil	Price/Cash Flow	Return On Assets%	Debt/Equity	Total Return% 1 Yr	3 Yr
BG Group PLC ADR	48,575	9,900	16.6	14.7	0.2	39.0	40.2
Total SA ADR	176,957	153,547	9.6	12.5	0.3	19.2	20.2
ENI SpA ADR	53,896	93,324	2.9	11.6	0.2	27.4	26.4

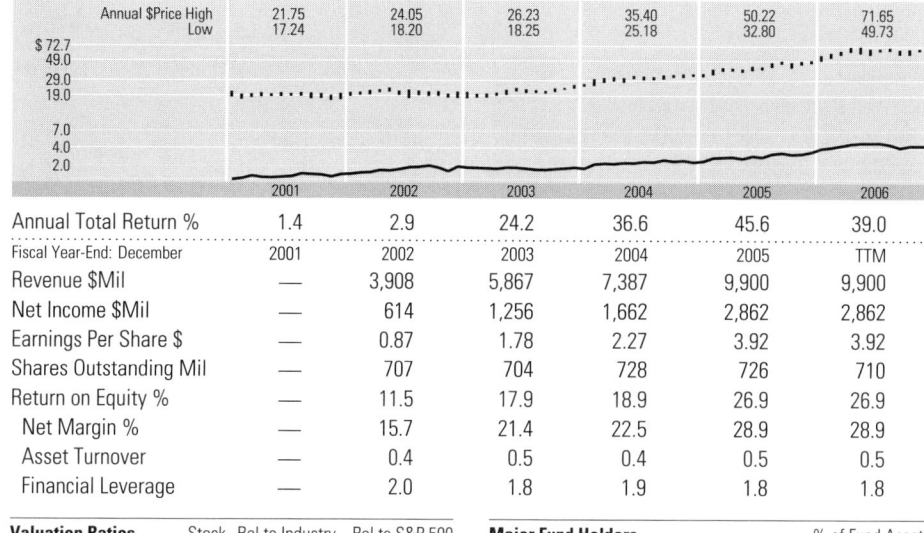

	2001	2002	2003	2004	2005	TTM
Annual Total Return %	1.4	2.9	24.2	36.6	45.6	39.0
Fiscal Year-End: December	2001	2002	2003	2004	2005	TTM
Revenue $Mil	—	3,908	5,867	7,387	9,900	9,900
Net Income $Mil	—	614	1,256	1,662	2,862	2,862
Earnings Per Share $	—	0.87	1.78	2.27	3.92	3.92
Shares Outstanding Mil	—	707	704	728	726	710
Return on Equity %	—	11.5	17.9	18.9	26.9	26.9
Net Margin %	—	15.7	21.4	22.5	28.9	28.9
Asset Turnover	—	0.4	0.5	0.4	0.5	0.5
Financial Leverage	—	2.0	1.8	1.9	1.8	1.8

Valuation Ratios	Stock	Rel to Industry	Rel to S&P 500
Price/Earnings	17.4	1.4	0.8
Price/Book	4.6	1.4	1.1
Price/Sales	4.9	2.6	1.7
Price/Cash Flow	16.6	2.0	1.1

Major Fund Holders	% of Fund Assets
Citizens Global Equity Stndrd	1.39
UMB Scout International	1.25
BlackRock All-Cap Global Resources Inst	1.22

Thesis By Elizabeth Collins, 11-21-06 Stock Price as of Analysis: $67.53

As an integrated natural-gas company, BG Group is set to profit from the growth in global demand.

BG has a diverse array of energy assets, spanning from oil and gas exploration and production (E&P) to local distribution systems and gas-fired power generation. The firm also has a growing liquefied natural gas (LNG) business that can connect gas supplies and markets from distant parts of the world.

We think BG enjoys a narrow economic moat around its businesses. Forty percent of its production comes from the North Sea and feeds the gas-hungry U.K. markets. Thanks to the United Kingdom's healthy demand for gas and declining indigenous production, BG is able to sell gas there at a hefty premium to the price it commands in the rest of the world. Because of the stranded nature of gas--it must be transported by pipe or LNG ship--BG's U.K. production should remain profitable for years to come.

However, BG's economic moat may erode over time. BG's new natural-gas production will be coming from parts of the world such as Egypt and Trinidad. Part of the supply feeds domestic markets, but the serious money comes when BG sells this production to markets in the United States. In LNG form, the gas must be transported at supercool temperatures on special ships. E&P in Egypt and Trinidad may currently be a lucrative proposition, but LNG--almost by design--is turning gas into a global, fungible commodity. There's no reason to believe that other energy companies won't pile aboard the LNG train and compete away any excess profits. That said, building an LNG supply chain can take many years. BG's moat should survive for at least that long.

Besides supplying stranded U.K. markets, BG does have another competitive advantage that's critical to any firm producing a commodity: low operating costs. Even assuming some cost inflation, BG's E&P activities can be profitable at energy prices significantly below current levels.

We put BG in our average risk bucket because it faces some noteworthy threats. Although it has low-cost operations, falling energy prices would eat away at profits. And BG faces some serious political risks. For example, the company recently made its first upstream investment in Nigeria, where oil platforms and pipelines have come under frequent attacks from local militant groups. And Bolivia's move to nationalize its natural resources has depressed the potential value of BG's assets there. We don't think the company faces above-average risk, though, because of its control over costs and its global diversity.

Data as of 12-29-06

Biogen Idec BIIB

	Rating	Fair Value	Last Close	Consider Buy	Consider Sell	Yield %
	★★★	$51.00	$49.19	$39.30	$63.90	0.00

Industry	Business Risk	Moat Size	Investment Style	Sector
Biotechnology	Average	Wide	Large Growth	Healthcare

Company Profile

Biogen Idec was formed by the merger of IDEC Pharmaceuticals and Biogen in November 2003. The firm develops and manufactures biopharmaceutical products that treat cancer and autoimmune diseases. Its products include Avonex, the leading multiple sclerosis drug in the United States, and Rituxan and Zevalin for non-Hodgkin's lymphoma. Genentech and Roche market Rituxan; Biogen Idec markets its other products in the United States and overseas.

Management — Stewardship Grade [B]

There's no shortage of business acumen or scientific expertise on Biogen Idec's executive team and board. James Mullen, Biogen's CEO since 2000, became Biogen Idec's CEO after the merger. Mullen is credited with developing an international salesforce and instilling a more innovative approach to drug development than his predecessor did. Mullen is the only insider on the board after previous executive chairman William Rastetter retired at the beginning of the year. Outsider Bruce Ross, a former Bristol-Myers exec who has sat on Idec's board since 1997, is now nonexecutive chairman. Herb Boyer, known as the father of biotechnology, also serves on the board. Mullen is amply compensated with a $992,000 base salary in 2005, which will increase to $1.0-$1.1 million in 2006, in line with his counterparts at profitable biotech peers. He also received a hefty $1.2 million bonus, 240,000 options with an exercise price of $67, and 80,000 restricted stock units in 2005. We like that the company awards restricted stock to most of its employees, and despite antitakeover defenses and sizable option issues, the company seems relatively shareholder-friendly.

14 Cambridge Center
Cambridge, MA 02142
www.biogenidec.com

Growth [A-]	2002	2003	2004	2005
Revenue %	48.2	68.0	225.6	9.5
Earnings/Share %	44.1	NMF	NMF	571.4
Book Value/Share %	14.7	522.6	-52.0	8.0
Dividends/Share %	NMF	NMF	NMF	NMF

Profitability [C+]	2003	2004	2005	TTM
Return on Assets %	-9.2	0.3	1.9	2.0
Oper Cash Flow $Mil	170	728	890	874
- Cap Spending $Mil	301	361	318	236
= Free Cash Flow $Mil	-131	367	571	638

Financial Health [B]	2003	2004	2005	09-30-06
Long-term Debt $Mil	887	102	43	45
Total Equity $Mil	7,053	6,826	6,906	6,895
Debt/Equity Ratio	0.1	0.0	0.0	0.0

Competition

	Market Cap $Mil	12 Mo Trailing Sales $Mil	Price/Cash Flow	Return On Assets%	Debt/Equity	Total Return% 1 Yr	3 Yr
Biogen Idec	16,583	2,608	19.0	2.0	0.0	8.6	10.0
GlaxoSmithKline PLC ADR	157,300	39,536	14.5	18.7	0.7	8.0	7.6
Genentech	85,511	8,462	42.1	13.4	0.2	-12.3	20.1

Price Volatility

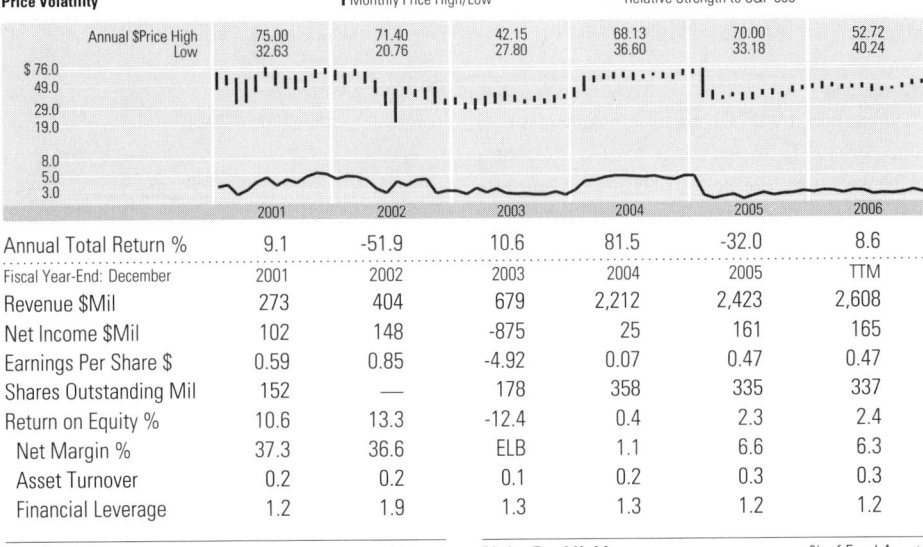

	2001	2002	2003	2004	2005	TTM
Annual Total Return %	9.1	-51.9	10.6	81.5	-32.0	8.6
Fiscal Year-End: December	2001	2002	2003	2004	2005	TTM
Revenue $Mil	273	404	679	2,212	2,423	2,608
Net Income $Mil	102	148	-875	25	161	165
Earnings Per Share $	0.59	0.85	-4.92	0.07	0.47	0.47
Shares Outstanding Mil	152	—	178	358	335	337
Return on Equity %	10.6	13.3	-12.4	0.4	2.3	2.4
Net Margin %	37.3	36.6	ELB	1.1	6.6	6.3
Asset Turnover	0.2	0.2	0.1	0.2	0.3	0.3
Financial Leverage	1.2	1.9	1.3	1.3	1.2	1.2

Valuation Ratios	Stock	Rel to Industry	Rel to S&P 500
Price/Earnings	106.9	2.4	5.2
Price/Book	2.4	0.3	0.6
Price/Sales	6.4	0.6	2.2
Price/Cash Flow	19.0	0.7	1.3

Major Fund Holders	% of Fund Assets
Fidelity Select Biotechnology	6.85
Fidelity Advisor Biotechnology B	6.75
Rydex Biotechnology Inv	5.01
Franklin Biotechnology Discovery A	4.98

Thesis By Jill Kiersky, 11-03-06 Stock Price as of Analysis: $47.52

Despite the troubling start for multiple sclerosis drug Tysabri, we still think Biogen Idec is an attractive company. We believe market exclusivity and strong research capabilities give the firm a wide economic moat, but because of the uncertainty surrounding Tysabri's ability to regain footing and slow market penetration of newer drugs like Zevalin, this biotech still holds many risks.

Biogen Idec boasts a diverse revenue stream focusing on oncology and immunology, with two first-in-class blockbuster drugs. Non-Hodgkin's lymphoma (NHL) drug Rituxan was the first monoclonal antibody approved to treat cancer and has become the standard for treating this disease, the fifth-most common cause of cancer deaths. Rituxan sales were $1.8 billion (which the firm shares with marketing partner Genentech) in 2005 and should expand with new uses in its traditional cancer setting as well as in newly approved autoimmune diseases. Avonex, with sales surpassing $1.6 billion worldwide, has enjoyed the top spot in the multiple sclerosis market. We estimate that, despite competition from Serono's Rebif, Avonex's share will stabilize around 30-35%.

With the third-largest biotech research-and-development budget, Biogen Idec now has the opportunity to repeat its successes. The firm has a decent number of candidates in its product pipeline. To improve its odds of success, the firm also plans to invest $200 million annually to acquire products. The company's acquisition of Fumapharm earlier this year added another drug to the firm's multiple sclerosis franchise prospects, and a collaboration with Alnylam to develop diagnostics and therapies for progressive multifocal leukoencephalopathy could help mitigate Tysabri's risk concerns. While there's no guarantee that this strategy will succeed, the company's selective approach could pay off down the road.

Biogen Idec's manufacturing capabilities widen the firm's moat. Producing biologics is no small feat, especially on a large scale, and the firm now has enough capacity to manufacture its current and new products. Not only should the company exhibit high returns on invested capital, but it has become a partner of choice for smaller firms looking for resources and expertise to bring products to market.

Still, risks abound. Revenue is concentrated with a handful of products, and the company depends heavily on its research pipeline. But given the positive free cash flow and strong growth opportunities, we think the stock is worth a look at the right price.

Data as of 12-29-06

Biomarin Pharmaceutical BMRN

Rating	Fair Value	Last Close	Consider Buy	Consider Sell	Yield %
★★★	$18.00	$16.39	$11.50	$21.70	0.00

Industry	Business Risk	Moat Size	Investment Style	Sector
Biotechnology	Above Avg	Narrow	Small Growth	Healthcare

Company Profile
BioMarin develops and commercializes products to treat rare genetic diseases. The company's two approved products, Aldurazyme and Naglazyme, are both enzyme-replacement therapies for rare lysosomal storage disorders. Genzyme markets Aldurazyme through its joint venture with BioMarin, and BioMarin markets Naglazyme independently. BioMarin has established a collaborative agreement with Serono for pipeline candidates Phenoptin and Phenylase.

Management
Stewardship Grade [B]

BioMarin's management team has seen some shuffling, but we think the current senior executives are well qualified and appropriately compensated. Fredric D. Price resigned from his position as chairman and chief executive officer in 2004, and Jean-Jacques Bienaime took over the position. Bienaime had served as CEO of SangStat Medical and Genencor and has diverse experience in manufacturing and developing biological products. BioMarin's chief medical officer, Emil Kakkis, was one of the original scientists behind the creation of Aldurazyme. Bienaime's $468,000 annual salary seems fair compared with commercial biotech peers. Although annual bonuses have so far been reasonable, we wish the company provided a bit more information as to how these bonuses are determined. BioMarin tends to annually grant options representing more than 3% of shares outstanding, and the more than 8 million options outstanding could have a dilutive effect if exercised.

371 Bel Marin Keys Blvd. Suite 210
Novato, CA 94949

Growth [A+]	2002	2003	2004	2005
Revenue %	NMF	NMF	54.1	37.7
Earnings/Share %	NMF	NMF	NMF	NMF
Book Value/Share %	-52.6	2.8	NMF	NMF
Dividends/Share %	NMF	NMF	NMF	NMF

Profitability [D]	2003	2004	2005	TTM
Return on Assets %	-29.6	-80.5	-38.0	-7.1
Oper Cash Flow $Mil	-43	-51	-63	-58
- Cap Spending $Mil	6	24	3	23
= Free Cash Flow $Mil	-49	-75	-66	-81

Financial Health [F]	2003	2004	2005	09-30-06
Long-term Debt $Mil	—	228	213	293
Total Equity $Mil	118	-68	-77	122
Debt/Equity Ratio	—	ELB	ELB	2.4

Competition

	Market Cap $Mil	12 Mo Trailing Sales $Mil	Price/Cash Flow	Return On Assets%	Debt/ Equity	Total Return% 1 Yr	3 Yr
Biomarin Pharmaceutical	1,497	72	—	-7.1	2.4	52.0	27.5
Genzyme	16,187	3,061	20.5	4.8	0.1	-13.0	7.9
Shire PLC ADR	10,362	1,764	20.8	9.8	0.0	59.8	29.0

Price Volatility

	2001	2002	2003	2004	2005	2006
Annual $Price High	14.40	14.06	13.67	8.87	11.70	18.40
Low	6.56	3.57	5.79	3.87	4.40	10.55
Annual Total Return %	38.7	-47.5	10.1	-17.7	68.7	52.0

Fiscal Year-End: December	2001	2002	2003	2004	2005	TTM
Revenue $Mil	—	—	12	19	26	72
Net Income $Mil	-68	-77	-76	-187	-74	-33
Earnings Per Share $	-1.65	-1.45	-1.22	-2.91	-1.08	-0.42
Shares Outstanding Mil	41	53	62	64	69	91
Return on Equity %	-42.4	-78.6	-64.3	NMF	NMF	-27.1
Net Margin %	NMF	NMF	ELB	ELB	ELB	-46.2
Asset Turnover	0.0	0.0	0.0	0.1	0.1	0.2
Financial Leverage	1.1	1.1	2.2	NMF	NMF	3.8

Valuation Ratios	Stock	Rel to Industry	Rel to S&P 500
Price/Earnings	NMF	—	—
Price/Book	12.3	1.5	3.0
Price/Sales	20.9	1.8	7.2
Price/Cash Flow	—	—	—

Major Fund Holders	% of Fund Assets
SunAmerica Biotech/Health A	2.50
Eaton Vance Worldwide Health Sci A	2.28
BlackRock Health Sciences Ops Inv A	1.85
Navellier Aggressive Micro Cap	1.80

Thesis By Karen Andersen, 12-07-06 Stock Price as of Analysis: $18.04

BioMarin Pharmaceutical has a sharp focus on genetic disease therapeutics. With two products on the market and positive trial results for a third, the future looks bright for this relatively young biotech. We've assigned BioMarin a narrow moat for its expertise in treating rare diseases, which we think creates a solid foundation of competition-free marketed products.

Like its much larger cousin Genzyme, BioMarin develops and commercializes treatments for rare forms of enzyme deficiencies and metabolic disorders. In fact, BioMarin formed a 50/50 joint venture with Genzyme to market its first approved drug, Aldurazyme, for the treatment of mucopolysaccharidosis I (MPS I). There are only 3,000 people in the developed world with this life-threatening disease, and orphan-drug status provides protection from competition.

One of the most challenging aspects of the rare-disease business is locating potential patients; as a result, sales growth is typically slow and steady. For example, Genzyme's Cerezyme reached the market 15 years ago, and sales are just beginning to flatten around $1 billion. Although Aldurazyme serves a slightly smaller market than Cerezyme, we expect sales of the drug, which costs $200,000 per patient annually, to reach $300 million by 2010.

After observing Aldurazyme's commercialization, BioMarin chose to market its second drug independently. Naglazyme, which treats MPS VI, received U.S. approval in 2005 and is being successfully launched internationally. Although the prevalence of MPS VI is lower, the drug sells at a premium to Aldurazyme, and BioMarin stands to recognize the full potential of global sales.

BioMarin's pipeline continues in the rare-disease tradition but could eventually serve a broader market. In 2007, we expect BioMarin to file for approval of Phenoptin to treat mild to moderate phenylketonuria (PKU) and to announce data that will shed light on this drug's potential in the multi-billion dollar hypertension market. Rounding out the pipeline, the firm's severe PKU drug, known as Phenylase, could eventually enable BioMarin to serve the spectrum of PKU patients, given its strong preclinical data.

BioMarin should enjoy steady sales growth from its innovative, life-saving treatments, and we expect it is just a matter of time before this biotech turns a profit. However, we believe recent stock prices already reflect an appropriate bump for Phenoptin's potential outside of PKU, and we're waiting for clinical data before making any bold calls.

Data as of 12-29-06

Blackrock BLK

	Rating	Fair Value	Last Close	Consider Buy	Consider Sell	Yield %
	★	$117.00	$151.90	$90.20	$146.60	1.11

Company Profile
The complexion of BlackRock changed dramatically with the acquisition of Merrill Lynch Investment Managers in the third quarter of 2006. Formerly a bond manager catering primarily to institutional client, the firm now has a large equity platform as well, which it will market to both institutions and retail customers around the globe.

Industry	Business Risk	Moat Size	Investment Style	Sector
Money Mgmt.	Average	Wide	Large Growth	Financial Services

Competition	Market Cap $Mil	12 Mo Trailing Sales $Mil	Price/Cash Flow	Return On Assets%	Debt/ Equity	Total Return% 1 Yr	3 Yr
Blackrock	17,686	1,449	—	1.3	—	41.8	43.1
Allianz SE ADR	82,762	122,351	—	0.5	—	36.9	19.0
Legg Mason	12,491	3,810	—	13.0	—	-20.0	23.0

Price Volatility — Monthly Price High/Low — Relative Strength to S&P 500

Annual $Price High Low	44.50 30.76	47.60 33.55	53.63 39.40	78.24 53.03	113.87 69.38	161.49 105.74
	2001	2002	2003	2004	2005	2006
Annual Total Return %	-0.7	-5.5	35.9	47.6	42.4	41.7

Fiscal Year-End: December	2001	2002	2003	2004	2005	TTM
Revenue $Mil	533	577	598	725	1,191	1,449
Net Income $Mil	107	133	155	143	234	226
Earnings Per Share $	1.65	2.04	2.36	2.17	3.50	3.38
Shares Outstanding Mil	64	65	65	64	64	116
Return on Equity %	22.1	21.0	21.8	18.6	25.4	2.1
Net Margin %	20.2	23.1	26.0	19.7	19.6	15.6
Asset Turnover	0.8	0.7	0.6	0.6	0.6	0.1
Financial Leverage	1.4	1.4	1.4	1.5	2.0	1.7

Valuation Ratios	Stock	Rel to Industry	Rel to S&P 500
Price/Earnings	44.9	1.5	2.2
Price/Book	1.7	0.4	0.4
Price/Sales	12.2	2.0	4.2
Price/Cash Flow	—	—	—

Major Fund Holders	% of Fund Assets
Transamerica Premier Growth Opp Inv	6.39
TA IDEX Transamerica Growth Opport B	5.24
Saratoga Financial Service A	4.96
Sentinel Growth Leaders A	4.14

Management
Stewardship Grade [C]

Laurence D. Fink has been chairman and CEO since BlackRock's formation in 1988. The board has long been dominated by executives connected to PNC Financial Services, which formerly controlled 70% of BlackRock's common stock and 84% of the voting power. But the MLIM deal changed all that. Merrill Lynch now owns 49% of the combined firm, PNC 34%, and the public and BlackRock employees own the remaining 17%. This still puts average shareholders in the minority. However the board now has an unusual structure, with nine independent directors, four BlackRock managers, two Merrill representatives, and two from PNC. The big owners will still call the shots on big-ticket items like a sale of all or part of the company. However, they are required to vote with the independent directors on other matters. Corporate governance still rates a C grade because of the remaining takeover provisions and the fuzziness of compensation guidelines for executives. That said, we have been very impressed by the performance of Fink and his colleagues. Under their leadership, BlackRock has grown from a tiny bond shop into a diversified asset-management powerhouse, while showing tremendous discipline with acquisitions.

40 East 52nd Street www.blackrock.com
New York, NY 10022

Growth [A+]	2002	2003	2004	2005
Revenue %	8.2	3.7	21.2	64.3
Earnings/Share %	23.6	15.7	-8.1	61.3
Book Value/Share %	30.1	11.5	7.5	18.5
Dividends/Share %	NMF	NMF	150.0	20.0

Profitability [A]	2003	2004	2005	TTM
Return on Assets %	16.1	12.5	12.7	1.3
Oper Cash Flow $Mil	180	231	255	—
- Cap Spending $Mil	13	26	55	—
= Free Cash Flow $Mil	—	—	—	—

Financial Health [NA]	2003	2004	2005	06-30-06
Long-term Debt $Mil	—	—	—	—
Total Equity $Mil	713	768	922	10,607
Debt/Equity Ratio	—	—	—	—

Thesis By Rachel Barnard, Ph.D., 12-07-06 Stock Price as of Analysis: $147.82

BlackRock struck a terrific deal with Merrill Lynch, but it still faces challenges ahead.

In our view, this merger is a clear winner for BlackRock shareholders. On the basis of our estimates of the combined value of BlackRock's asset-management business and Merrill's asset-management business, known as Merrill Lynch Investment Managers (MLIM), BlackRock shareholders gained about $11 per share in value through a combination of anticipated cost savings and value that was outright swiped away from the investment banking firm. In the process, BlackRock has suddenly become a much more diversified firm that should not be as susceptible to a potential downturn in fixed-income markets.

BlackRock has historically been a bond shop. It has a good chunk of the institutional fixed-income market sewn up as part of an oligopoly of institutional bond managers. A strong discipline in risk management has been a hallmark of the firm. BlackRock's time-tested strategy and conservative risk profile make its core products appealing to many institutional investors that aren't interested in betting on riskier sectors of the bond market, like junk bonds.

Despite efforts to get into the equity business with the State Street Research acquisition in 2005, fixed income still dominates and is BlackRock's real competitive strength. The equity funds BlackRock inherited from Merrill have not been stellar performers, though MLIM has made strides over the past couple of years to improve its investment performance as well as its operational performance. And BlackRock will be venturing into territory where it does not have a record of success or a core of expertise, as it does in the bond business. This makes us a little uneasy. We have yet to see evidence that the firm has an edge with equities, and we wonder whether it will be able to turn in superior and consistent performance.

Great performance is only one half of what it takes to be successful in investment management, however. The other half is distribution. Here we are confident that Merrill's network of brokers around the world will be able to push BlackRock funds. In fact, this is a core rationale for the Merrill Lynch deal, giving BlackRock a huge retail outlet for its products.

The key to success here will be delivering competitive investment performance that Merrill brokers can sell. If that happens, the deal should be a slam dunk. But we don't believe there is enough evidence of BlackRock's ability to manage equities to hand the trophy out just yet.

Blue Nile NILE

Data as of 12-29-06

Rating	Fair Value	Last Close	Consider Buy	Consider Sell	Yield %
★★★★	$42.00	$36.89	$32.40	$52.60	0.00

Company Profile

Founded in 1999, Blue Nile is an online retailer of diamonds and fine jewelry. Diamond engagement rings accounted for around 72% of its sales in 2005. Through exclusive agreements with suppliers, Blue Nile displays thousands of certified diamonds on its Web site that customers can pair with various settings to customize engagement rings and other diamond jewelry. Blue Nile also sells more than 1,000 styles of rings, earrings, necklaces, and watches.

Management

Stewardship Grade [B]

Mark Vadon founded the company in 1999 and serves as chairman and CEO. Prior to Blue Nile, Vadon worked for management consulting firm Bain & Company. Although his experience running a company outside of Blue Nile is limited, his educational credentials are impressive, and he has surrounded himself with seasoned executives on the board and management team. In 2005, Vadon's annual compensation included a salary of around $328,000 and a bonus of $30,000, which we think is reasonable. We believe his sizable stake in the company (he owns about 10% of the shares outstanding) helps to align his interests with those of shareholders. Executives and directors own 16% of shares outstanding. Management issued around 3% of shares outstanding in stock options in 2005, which we think is bordering excessive. We also frown upon the three-year terms for directors. We think directors should be elected on an annual basis to give shareholders more flexibility in ousting underperforming board members. Although we'd prefer the chairman of the board to be someone other than the CEO of the company, a good majority of the board is independent, which helps to provide the necessary checks and balances. After reviewing the company's 2005 proxy statement, corporate governance is good, in our opinion.

705 5th Avenue South Suite 900
Seattle, WA 98104
www.bluenile.com

Growth [A-]	2002	2003	2004	2005
Revenue %	48.2	78.7	31.3	20.0
Earnings/Share %	NMF	NMF	NMF	NMF
Book Value/Share %	—	—	—	NMF
Dividends/Share %	NMF	NMF	NMF	NMF

Profitability [B]	2003	2004	2005	TTM
Return on Assets %	43.3	7.8	9.5	16.7
Oper Cash Flow $Mil	20	30	31	30
- Cap Spending $Mil	4	1	1	2
= Free Cash Flow $Mil	16	28	30	28

Financial Health [A]	2003	2004	2005	09-30-06
Long-term Debt $Mil	—	—	—	—
Total Equity $Mil	-27	84	82	41
Debt/Equity Ratio	—	—	—	—

Industry	Business Risk	Moat Size	Investment Style	Sector
Jewelry/Accessories	Average	Narrow	Small Growth	Consumer Goods

Competition	Market Cap $Mil	12 Mo Trailing Sales $Mil	Price/Cash Flow	Return On Assets%	Debt/Equity	Total Return% 1 Yr	3 Yr
Blue Nile	591	234	19.5	16.7	—	-8.5	—
Amazon.com	16,254	9,702	27.6	8.9	6.7	-16.3	-8.7
Odimo	1	36	—	ELB	—	-94.1	—

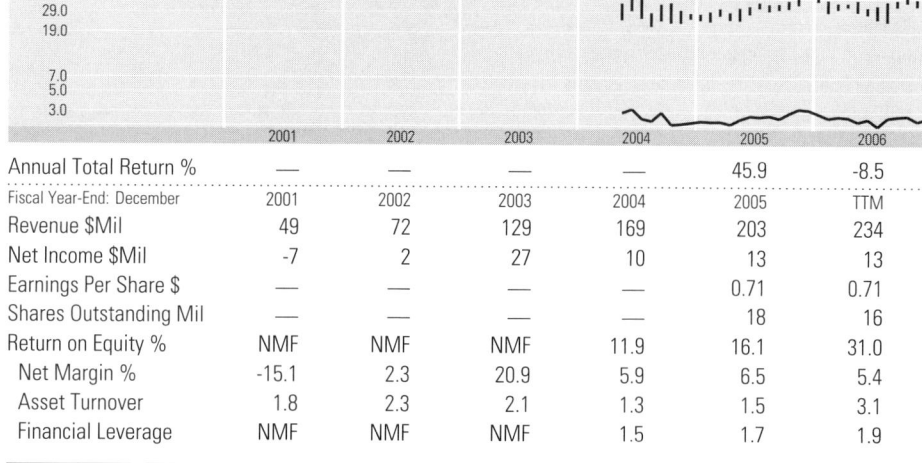

	2001	2002	2003	2004	2005	TTM
Annual Total Return %	—	—	—	—	45.9	-8.5
Fiscal Year-End: December	2001	2002	2003	2004	2005	TTM
Revenue $Mil	49	72	129	169	203	234
Net Income $Mil	-7	2	27	10	13	13
Earnings Per Share $	—	—	—	—	0.71	0.71
Shares Outstanding Mil	—	—	—	—	18	16
Return on Equity %	NMF	NMF	NMF	11.9	16.1	31.0
Net Margin %	-15.1	2.3	20.9	5.9	6.5	5.4
Asset Turnover	1.8	2.3	2.1	1.3	1.5	3.1
Financial Leverage	NMF	NMF	NMF	1.5	1.7	1.9

Valuation Ratios	Stock	Rel to Industry	Rel to S&P 500
Price/Earnings	52.0	1.9	2.5
Price/Book	14.6	1.7	3.6
Price/Sales	2.5	0.6	0.9
Price/Cash Flow	19.5	0.8	1.3

Major Fund Holders	% of Fund Assets
Delaware Pooled Focus Smid-Cap Gr Eq	6.76
Pin Oak Aggressive Stock	4.91
Red Oak Technology Select	3.34
STI Classic Emerging Growth Stock I	2.92

Thesis By Kimberly Picciola, 10-31-06 Stock Price as of Analysis: $38.21

Blue Nile has become a trusted online source for quality custom engagement rings. We believe its exclusive agreements to sell select diamond manufacturers' stones online and a premium brand differentiate this retailer from its competitors. Armed with a business model that gives this purveyor of gems a competitive advantage, we think Blue Nile is well positioned to gain share of the growing online jewelry market.

The key to Blue Nile's success is its agreements with its suppliers. Select diamond manufacturers have arranged to sell their loose diamond inventory online solely through Blue Nile's Web site. This enables diamond manufacturers to sell their goods through a new distribution channel, increasing their inventory turns, or the rate at which the stones are sold. Additionally, the diamond manufacturers benefit from sales data they receive from Blue Nile, allowing them to monitor diamond prices and trends.

As for Blue Nile, linking up with these suppliers enables the firm to offer consumers a vast selection of diamonds at lower prices than most traditional jewelers. Additionally, Blue Nile benefits from the limited investment it makes in diamond inventory. As part of the arrangement, the loose diamond inventory remains on a manufacturer's books until a Blue Nile customer purchases it individually or pairs it with a setting. Thus, Blue Nile receives payment for the diamond from its customer before it pays its supplier. This leads to returns on invested capital that far exceed its cost of capital.

In our opinion, Blue Nile's business model provides it with a narrow economic moat. The exclusive agreements create a barrier to entry for newcomers looking to sell high-quality diamonds online. In addition, there is a cost for a Blue Nile supplier to switch to another online retailer. Suppliers have invested in integrating their systems with Blue Nile's to keep inventory in check, while also benefiting from the sales data they receive regarding current diamond demand.

Although Blue Nile dominates the nascent online jewelry market, risks exist. Maintaining strong supplier relationships is key to the company's future success. Should suppliers end current agreements, Blue Nile would lose its leg up over the competition. Additionally, the cost of diamonds and precious metals has been on the rise, which could pressure Blue Nile's profitability in the near term.

Data as of 12-29-06

Boeing BA

	Rating	Fair Value	Last Close	Consider Buy	Consider Sell	Yield %
	★★★	$95.00	$88.84	$73.30	$119.00	1.35

Company Profile
Boeing is about half plane manufacturer and half defense contractor these days. Integrated Defense Systems, the world's second-largest defense contractor on its own, develops and manufactures military aircraft, missiles, and command, control, communications, computer, and intelligence systems. Boeing Commercial Airplanes competes with Airbus for global dominance of the commercial airplane market. With a third of sales booked abroad, Boeing is America's largest exporter.

Management   Stewardship Grade [B]
We believe that Boeing got its man in chairman and CEO Jim McNerney. Yale University, Harvard Business School, Procter & Gamble, General Electric, and 3M grace his resume and qualify him, in our view, to lead Boeing back from some recent hiccups. If nothing else, McNerney knows how to manufacture more cheaply, and efficient operations are the most likely source of wider margins in the hotly contested commercial airplane duopoly and in the execution of government contracts. James Bell should be even more valuable as CFO after his successful stint as interim CEO, and Jim Albaugh is a strong leader in the defense business. BCA head Alan Mulally left to become the CEO of Ford, but we consider his replacement, Scott Carson, to be quite capable after 34 years at Boeing. The firm compensated McNerney for unvested 3M equity awards to the tune of about $25 million in restricted-stock awards (as valued on July 1, 2005), as well as for a supplemental retirement benefit he forfeited. This is a steep price, but not just anyone can successfully lead the United States' biggest exporter, as some have recently demonstrated. We think McNerney will be worth that price, and we definitely think he will earn his $1.75 million base salary and reasonable bonus scheme.

100 North Riverside   www.boeing.com
Chicago, IL 60606-1596

Growth [D]	2002	2003	2004	2005
Revenue %	-7.1	-6.6	4.4	4.6
Earnings/Share %	—	NMF	158.4	39.1
Book Value/Share %	—	NMF	37.4	-0.8
Dividends/Share %	0.0	0.0	13.2	29.9

Profitability [B-]	2003	2004	2005	TTM
Return on Assets %	1.3	3.3	4.3	2.7
Oper Cash Flow $Mil	2,776	3,504	7,000	7,445
- Cap Spending $Mil	836	1,246	1,547	1,566
= Free Cash Flow $Mil	1,940	2,258	5,453	5,879

Financial Health [B]	2003	2004	2005	09-30-06
Long-term Debt $Mil	—	10,879	9,538	8,549
Total Equity $Mil	8,139	11,286	11,059	11,026
Debt/Equity Ratio	—	1.0	0.9	0.8

Industry	Business Risk	Moat Size	Investment Style	Sector
Aerospace/Defense	Average	Narrow	Large Growth	Industrial Materials

Competition	Market Cap $Mil	12 Mo Trailing Sales $Mil	Price/Cash Flow	Return On Assets %	Debt/Equity	Total Return % 1 Yr	3 Yr
Boeing	70,249	59,114	9.4	2.7	0.8	28.4	30.4
Lockheed Martin	39,028	39,009	11.1	8.1	0.5	47.0	24.1
Northrop Grumman	23,384	30,448	10.9	4.2	0.2	14.6	14.7

Price Volatility | Monthly Price High/Low   — Relative Strength to S&P 500

Annual $Price High Low	69.85 27.60	51.07 28.53	43.35 24.73	58.80 35.90	72.40 49.52	92.05 65.90
	2001	2002	2003	2004	2005	2006
Annual Total Return %	-40.4	-13.4	30.4	24.9	37.9	28.4
Fiscal Year-End: December	2001	2002	2003	2004	2005	TTM
Revenue $Mil	57,970	53,831	50,256	52,457	54,845	59,114
Net Income $Mil	2,827	492	718	1,872	2,572	1,686
Earnings Per Share $	—	—	0.89	2.30	3.20	2.15
Shares Outstanding Mil	—	—	798	803	787	791
Return on Equity %	26.1	6.4	8.8	16.6	23.3	15.3
Net Margin %	4.9	0.9	1.4	3.6	4.7	2.9
Asset Turnover	1.1	1.0	0.9	0.9	0.9	1.0
Financial Leverage	4.7	7.0	6.8	5.0	5.4	5.6

Valuation Ratios	Stock	Rel to Industry	Rel to S&P 500
Price/Earnings	41.1	1.6	2.0
Price/Book	6.4	1.5	1.6
Price/Sales	1.2	0.9	0.4
Price/Cash Flow	9.4	0.7	0.6

Major Fund Holders	% of Fund Assets
Fidelity Select Air Transportation	5.60
Schwab Large-Cap Growth Sel	5.46
IXIS CGM Advisor Targeted Equity A	5.07
Hillman Focused Advantage	4.98

Thesis By Chris Lozier, 12-18-06 Stock Price as of Analysis: $89.56

Boeing has established a lead in widebody jets and is in a good position to strengthen its narrowbody presence. The firm should be the clear winner in its duopoly with Airbus for the next 10 years.

Much of Boeing's recent momentum can be attributed to the expected cyclical upturn in air travel, which still has three to five years to run. We believe, however, that the firm's powerful lineup of commercial airplanes is the primary driver of intrinsic value at Boeing. Importantly, Boeing's order book consists of a much greater mix of higher-margin, widebody planes, helped by strategic missteps at Airbus with both the A340 and the A380.

The low-cost stalwart 737 will continue to constitute the bulk of its deliveries, and the likelihood of both firms launching next-generation narrowbodies within five years appears to be high. We like the prospect of Boeing launching soon, while Airbus struggles to divide its resources among the A350 development and the A380 problems. Those resources include the world's aerospace suppliers, which the duopoly shares, and which have begun to assume airplane development risk in recent years. The spare capacity for Airbus does not currently exist at those firms.

Still, Boeing's greatest market share gains should come from its larger aircraft. The widebody, long-range 777 has experienced renewed success over recent years, and we expect the game-changing 787 Dreamliner to deliver a material, and rare, quality advantage to its airline customers. With a far greater composite constitution than the challenger A350, the 787 should be cheaper to build, fly, and maintain. We also doubt that the A350's extra three inches of fuselage diameter--arguably that plane's only advantage over the 787--will earn a sufficient price premium to justify the expense of design and construction.

Boeing has balanced the temperamental commercial air business with a growing defense segment. Defense revenue of $30.8 billion in 2005 made Boeing the world's second-largest defense contractor. Wins on such key transformational programs as the Future Combat System support Boeing's leadership status in innovation as well. While aggressive Pentagon spending after 9/11 helped offset the struggling commercial aerospace business, those roles are about to reverse. We do not, however, expect defense spending to shrink in the near future, and while some major programs will be winding down (C-17, F-22), we expect others to fill that void (KC-X).

Data as of 12-29-06

Boston Beer Company A SAM

	Rating	Fair Value	Last Close	Consider Buy	Consider Sell	Yield %
	★★★	$33.00	$35.98	$25.40	$41.30	0.00

Company Profile
Boston Beer Company brews specialty beers primarily under the Samuel Adams brand. It is the sixth-largest brewer in the United States, but has less than a 1% share of the domestic beer market. Sam Adams primarily competes with imports and domestic craft and specialty brews, which represent the highest price points. Product offerings include lager, light, and seasonal beers as well as hard cider and alcoholic iced teas.

Management
Stewardship Grade [C]

Boston Beer founder James Koch built the business from scratch in 1985, managing the company through explosive growth into maturity. In 2001, Martin Roper took over as CEO from Koch, who retained his role as chairman. Koch owns 32% of the company and Roper owns 6%. As the sole owner of all Class B shares, Koch elects four of the seven directors and can increase that number at his discretion. Of the four Class B directors, Koch has chosen three insiders, including himself, his father, and Roper. Koch's near-dictatorial powers come at the expense of minority shareholders, though we have not seen any evidence of abuse. Directors stand for election annually. Executive pay is very reasonable, in our opinion, though variable compensation is a relatively low percentage of overall pay. Because Boston Beer is a small company with a strong brand, it is often mentioned as an acquisition target. Given Koch's power, whether to accept or even entertain offers is fully at his whim. Even though public, this is clearly still Koch's company. Management is extremely tight-lipped, and Boston Beer seems to be run more like a private than a public company.

75 Arlington Street
Boston, MA 02116
www.samadams.com

Growth [B-]	2002	2003	2004	2005
Revenue %	15.3	-3.4	4.5	9.7
Earnings/Share %	10.6	34.6	22.9	24.4
Book Value/Share %	2.2	-13.5	30.0	9.7
Dividends/Share %	NMF	NMF	NMF	NMF

Profitability [A]	2003	2004	2005	TTM
Return on Assets %	12.1	11.6	13.1	12.2
Oper Cash Flow $Mil	20	-5	29	31
- Cap Spending $Mil	2	5	14	11
= Free Cash Flow $Mil	19	-9	15	20

Financial Health [B]	2003	2004	2005	09-30-06
Long-term Debt $Mil	—	—	—	—
Total Equity $Mil	63	78	86	103
Debt/Equity Ratio	—	—	—	—

Industry	Business Risk	Moat Size	Investment Style	Sector
Alcoholic Beverages	Average	Narrow	Small Core	Consumer Goods

Competition	Market Cap $Mil	12 Mo Trailing Sales $Mil	Price/Cash Flow	Return On Assets%	Debt/ Equity	Total Return% 1 Yr	3 Yr
Boston Beer Company A	506	277	16.4	12.2	—	43.9	25.4
Anheuser-Busch Companies	37,826	15,691	13.5	11.9	1.7	17.4	0.1
Heineken NV ADR	23,127	13,519	9.9	7.7	0.5	49.8	16.3

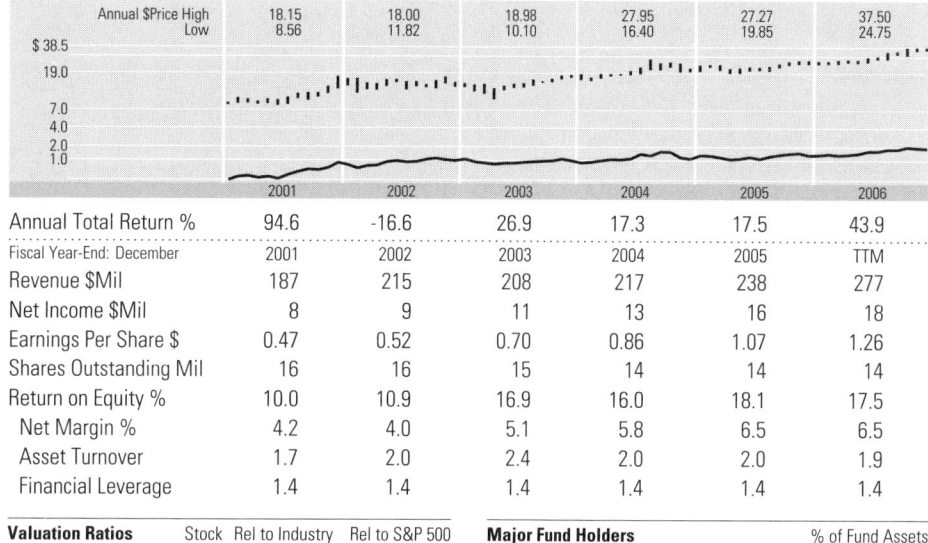

Annual Total Return %	94.6	-16.6	26.9	17.3	17.5	43.9
Fiscal Year-End: December	2001	2002	2003	2004	2005	TTM
Revenue $Mil	187	215	208	217	238	277
Net Income $Mil	8	9	11	13	16	18
Earnings Per Share $	0.47	0.52	0.70	0.86	1.07	1.26
Shares Outstanding Mil	16	16	15	14	14	14
Return on Equity %	10.0	10.9	16.9	16.0	18.1	17.5
Net Margin %	4.2	4.0	5.1	5.8	6.5	6.5
Asset Turnover	1.7	2.0	2.4	2.0	2.0	1.9
Financial Leverage	1.4	1.4	1.4	1.4	1.4	1.4

Valuation Ratios	Stock	Rel to Industry	Rel to S&P 500
Price/Earnings	28.6	1.1	1.4
Price/Book	4.9	0.5	1.2
Price/Sales	1.8	0.3	0.6
Price/Cash Flow	16.4	0.7	1.1

Major Fund Holders	% of Fund Assets
Bjurman, Barry Small Cap Growth	1.33
Allianz CCM Emerging Companies Instl	1.02

Thesis By Matthew Reilly, 12-12-06 Stock Price as of Analysis: $37.20

Boston Beer is a leading domestic craft brewer that uses the strength of its Samuel Adams brand to introduce a variety of specialty and seasonal brews that have struck the right chord with American beer drinkers looking for high-quality new tastes. Though the company is a tiny player in the American beer industry, with a market share of less than 1%, the strength of its brand and its history of generating returns on invested capital that easily beat our estimate of its cost of capital have earned it a narrow economic moat.

The company's returns are very likely to decline in the near future, however, as Boston Beer may need to invest $155-$210 million in a new brewery. The company has relied on contract brewers to fulfill about one third of its volume in recent years, but finding capacity, on the West Coast in particular, will be a challenge in the coming years. If Boston Beer is forced to make the capital expenditures that management has outlined, we estimate that its invested capital base will almost quintuple from current levels.

Boston Beer remains strong in its niche, positioning its brands to compete outside the offerings of megabrands like Budweiser and Miller Lite, but we believe that the large brewers will increasingly target higher-price and luxury offerings as American consumers continue to show a penchant for trading up to superpremium offerings. We also believe that competition from imports, most notably Heineken and Corona (though there are countless others), will remain fierce, as the Corona brand will try to maintain its recent hot streak and Heineken Light has come on strong. To add more pressure, Boston Beer must also fend off competition from increasingly popular spirits and wine, which have taken the lion's share of alcoholic beverage growth in the United States over the past couple of years.

Despite stiff competition, Boston Beer's financial performance has remained strong, as 2005 was a great year and 2006 looks even better. Management has been very reluctant to return profits to shareholders, however, preferring to sit on a cash hoard that may now be used to fund the aforementioned brewery projects.

If the company's new brewery is built, it would ensure Boston Beer's independence for the foreseeable future. But with management giving few details on the brewery's return on investment and long-term costs and benefits, there is a great deal of uncertainty in predicting the future of this shareholder-unfriendly company.

Data as of 12-29-06

Boston Scientific BSX

Rating	Fair Value	Last Close	Consider Buy	Consider Sell	Yield %
★★★★★	$25.00	$17.18	$19.30	$31.30	0.00

Company Profile

Boston Scientific produces less-invasive medical devices that are inserted into the human body through small openings or cuts. It manufactures products for use in angioplasty, blood-clot filtration, cardiac rhythm management, catheter-directed ultrasound imaging, upper gastrointestinal tract tests, and treatment of incontinence. The firm markets its devices to health-care professionals and institutions globally. Foreign sales account for nearly 40% of its total sales.

Management   Stewardship Grade [C]

We give Boston average marks for stewardship and were disappointed by management's complete disregard for existing shareholders' interests as the firm pursued the pricey purchase of Guidant. James Tobin has been president and CEO since 1999; he gained experience from posts at Baxter International and Biogen Idec. We give Tobin credit for the turnaround he engineered at Boston in the late 1990s, and we expect he'll be able to address the remaining quality issues at the newly acquired CRM unit. Additionally, the firm's two founders, who hold substantial stakes in the company's equity, remain highly involved with Boston Scientific. Both John Abele and Peter Nicholas serve on the board of directors, with the latter acting as chairman. However, we believe the Guidant acquisition was a clear demonstration of Boston's board putting management's goals ahead of protecting existing shareholders. Now that the board has proved it would go that far, we are not as confident that it will make shareholder-friendly decisions in the future.

One Boston Scientific Place
Natick, MA 01760-1537   www.bsci.com

Growth [B+]	2002	2003	2004	2005
Revenue %	9.2	19.1	61.8	11.7
Earnings/Share %	NMF	24.4	121.4	-39.5
Book Value/Share %	22.7	14.1	38.4	8.8
Dividends/Share %	NMF	NMF	NMF	NMF

Profitability [B+]	2003	2004	2005	TTM
Return on Assets %	8.3	13.0	7.7	-11.4
Oper Cash Flow $Mil	787	1,804	903	1,990
- Cap Spending $Mil	188	274	341	304
= Free Cash Flow $Mil	599	1,530	562	562

Financial Health [NA]	2003	2004	2005	06-30-06
Long-term Debt $Mil	1,172	1,139	1,864	8,893
Total Equity $Mil	2,862	4,025	4,282	15,016
Debt/Equity Ratio	0.4	0.3	0.4	0.6

Industry	Business Risk	Moat Size	Investment Style	Sector
Medical Equip.	Average	Wide	Large Core	Healthcare

Competition	Market Cap $Mil	12 Mo Trailing Sales $Mil	Price/Cash Flow	Return On Assets %	Debt/ Equity	Total Return % 1 Yr	3 Yr
Boston Scientific	25,323	7,296	12.7	-11.4	0.6	-29.9	-22.0
Johnson & Johnson	191,415	52,252	14.5	18.5	0.0	12.4	10.8
Medtronic	61,597	11,808	24.7	14.2	0.5	-6.3	4.1

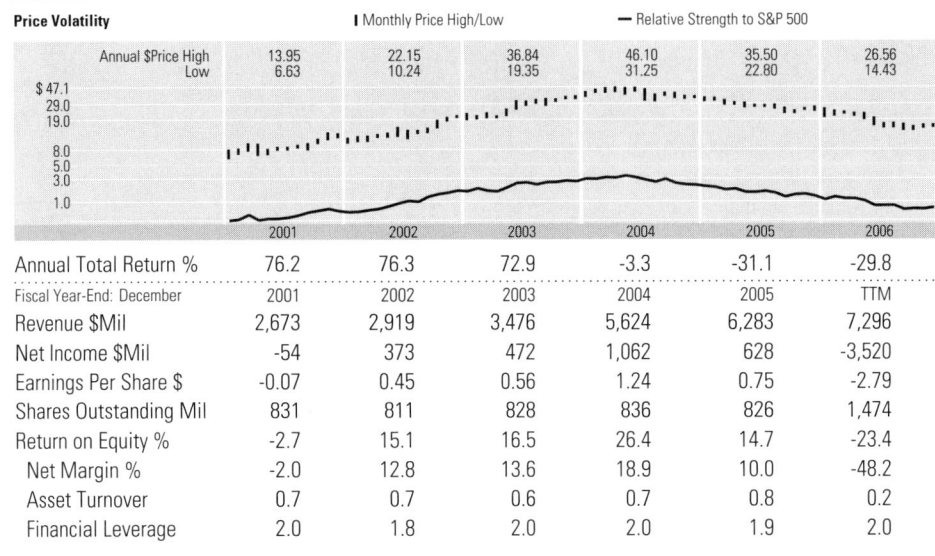

	2001	2002	2003	2004	2005	
Annual $Price High	13.95	22.15	36.84	46.10	35.50	26.56
Low	6.63	10.24	19.35	31.25	22.80	14.43
Annual Total Return %	76.2	76.3	72.9	-3.3	-31.1	-29.8

Fiscal Year-End: December	2001	2002	2003	2004	2005	TTM
Revenue $Mil	2,673	2,919	3,476	5,624	6,283	7,296
Net Income $Mil	-54	373	472	1,062	628	-3,520
Earnings Per Share $	-0.07	0.45	0.56	1.24	0.75	-2.79
Shares Outstanding Mil	831	811	828	836	826	1,474
Return on Equity %	-2.7	15.1	16.5	26.4	14.7	-23.4
Net Margin %	-2.0	12.8	13.6	18.9	10.0	-48.2
Asset Turnover	0.7	0.7	0.6	0.7	0.8	0.2
Financial Leverage	2.0	1.8	2.0	2.0	1.9	2.0

Valuation Ratios	Stock	Rel to Industry	Rel to S&P 500
Price/Earnings	NMF	—	—
Price/Book	1.7	0.3	0.4
Price/Sales	3.5	0.7	1.2
Price/Cash Flow	12.7	0.5	0.9

Major Fund Holders	% of Fund Assets
Integrity Health Sciences A	7.85
Integrity Value A	5.04
Fountainhead Special Value	4.20
Sound Shore	3.77

Thesis By Debbie S. Wang, 12-14-06 Stock Price as of Analysis: $16.47

After completing its expensive purchase of Guidant, medical-device maker Boston Scientific now faces the task of digesting and integrating the new cardiac rhythm management (CRM) business. There may be more short-term turbulence, but we anticipate Boston should hit its stride in the next few years.

Between Guidant's high price tag and its recent product-recall issues, Boston has its work cut out. Boston must not only rectify the quality problems that have dogged Guidant since 2005, but it must also revise guidelines to ensure communications about product issues are handled in a way that is entirely above-board. Further, the series of Guidant recalls has hindered category growth of implantable cardioverter defibrillators (ICDs), which has fallen from the 20% range two years ago to the high single digits. It may take a couple of years before Boston regains the confidence of doctors and sees double-digit growth from ICDs.

Despite potential pitfalls in the near term, we remain upbeat about Boston's longer-term prospects. The addition of Guidant's CRM business has alleviated our earlier concern that the firm was overly reliant on the Taxus stent. We now expect the CRM unit to contribute nearly as much revenue as Boston's stent business, providing some much-needed diversification. We believe Boston's new ICD business should eventually get back on the growth track in 2008, as this large and profitable market remains underpenetrated--only one in three eligible patients has received an ICD, while sudden cardiac arrest causes about 350,000 deaths each year.

Boston has proved to be a fierce competitor when it comes to innovation. The firm already launched its next-generation drug-coated stent in Europe last year, with a domestic launch expected in early 2007. Aside from heart devices, Boston has several new products planned for endoscopy, neuromodulation, and neurovascular intervention. We think the firm will apply its innovation knack to the new CRM business, too.

Lastly, we are confident that Boston management can solve the quality problems it inherited from Guidant. Boston's approach to handling its own massive recall of Taxus stents in 2004 made the best of a bad situation. With a minimum of disruption, the firm managed to pull all potentially affected stents off hospital shelves and replace them with a new product. We think management will scrutinize the new CRM business with a keen eye and make appropriate changes.

BP PLC ADR BP

	Rating	Fair Value	Last Close	Consider Buy	Consider Sell	Yield %
	★★★	$72.00	$67.10	$55.50	$90.20	3.43

Company Profile
London-based BP is the second-largest oil company on the planet behind ExxonMobil. Formed by the 1998 merger of British Petroleum and Amoco, BP boasts proven reserves of 18.3 billion barrels of oil equivalent; in 2005, it produced 4 million barrels per day. BP has refining capacity of 2.8 million barrels per day, operates petrochemical plants, and sells petroleum through 25,200 service stations around the globe.

Management
Stewardship Grade [NA]

John Browne has been BP's chief executive since 1995. Not afraid to make bold moves, Browne has been the driving force behind the company's numerous mergers and acquisitions, including the Amoco purchase that sparked the oil megamergers of recent years, as well as BP's expansion into natural gas and emerging markets like Russia. Under Browne's leadership, BP was the first major oil firm to publicly recognize the risk of rising greenhouse-gas emissions. Browne has had a rough 2006, with lingering issues from the Texas City refinery explosion, pipeline corrosion problems in Alaska, and price-manipulation allegations. There have been management changes in the firm's North American operations, and BP will increase spending to improve safety at its U.S. refineries and Alaskan pipelines.

In 2005, Browne's salary amounted to 1.5 million pounds (or approximately $2.6 million), and his annual bonus was 1.8 million pounds (or roughly $3.2 million). Peter Sutherland has been chairman of BP since 1997, and he received an annual fee of 500,000 pounds (or $910,000) in 2005. We're happy to see that BP splits the chairman and chief executive roles, and in general we think BP has shareholder-friendly practices.

1 St James's Square www.bp.com
London, United Kingdom SW1Y 4PD

Growth [NA]	2002	2003	2004	2005
Revenue %	2.6	-7.9	16.6	24.9
Earnings/Share %	4.7	82.9	38.2	34.1
Book Value/Share %	5.8	0.5	12.5	6.6
Dividends/Share %	44.6	8.5	8.6	25.8

Profitability [NA]	2003	2004	2005	TTM
Return on Assets %	7.3	8.9	10.8	10.8
Oper Cash Flow $Mil	16,303	23,378	26,721	26,721
- Cap Spending $Mil	11,885	12,286	12,281	12,281
= Free Cash Flow $Mil	4,418	11,092	14,440	14,440

Financial Health [NA]	2003	2004	2005	12-31-05
Long-term Debt $Mil	12,869	12,907	10,230	10,230
Total Equity $Mil	70,264	78,235	80,450	80,450
Debt/Equity Ratio	0.2	0.2	0.1	0.1

Industry	Business Risk	Moat Size	Investment Style	Sector
Oil/Gas	Average	Narrow	Large Core	Energy

Competition	Market Cap $Mil	12 Mo Trailing Sales $Mil	Price/Cash Flow	Return On Assets %	Debt/Equity	Total Return% 1 Yr	Total Return% 3 Yr
BP PLC ADR	231,015	239,792	8.6	10.8	0.1	7.9	14.3
ExxonMobil	446,944	386,951	8.8	17.8	0.1	39.1	26.2
Royal Dutch Shell PLC ADR	230,956	306,731	7.7	11.5	0.1	19.3	15.1

Price Volatility
| Monthly Price High/Low — Relative Strength to S&P 500

Annual $Price High/Low	55.20/42.20	53.98/36.25	49.59/34.67	62.10/45.51	72.66/56.60	76.85/63.52
	2001	2002	2003	2004	2005	2006
Annual Total Return %	-0.9	-9.9	26.0	22.1	13.5	7.9

Fiscal Year-End: December	2001	2002	2003	2004	2005	TTM
Revenue $Mil	174,218	178,721	164,653	192,024	239,792	239,792
Net Income $Mil	6,554	6,845	12,618	17,262	22,317	22,317
Earnings Per Share $	1.74	1.83	3.34	4.61	6.18	6.18
Shares Outstanding Mil	3,739	3,734	3,746	3,677	3,568	3,443
Return on Equity %	10.0	9.9	18.0	22.1	27.7	27.7
Net Margin %	3.8	3.8	7.7	9.0	9.3	9.3
Asset Turnover	1.2	1.1	1.0	1.0	1.2	1.2
Financial Leverage	2.2	2.3	2.5	2.5	2.6	2.6

Valuation Ratios	Stock	Rel to Industry	Rel to S&P 500
Price/Earnings	10.9	0.9	0.5
Price/Book	2.9	0.9	0.7
Price/Sales	1.0	0.5	0.3
Price/Cash Flow	8.6	1.0	0.6

Major Fund Holders	% of Fund Assets
ProFunds Europe 30 Svc	7.30
Women's Equity	5.45
Reaves Select Research Instl	4.85
California Investment Euro Gr & Inc Dir	4.65

Thesis By Elizabeth Collins, 12-13-06 Stock Price as of Analysis: $68.59

We like BP's focus on oil and gas exploration and production. Of integrated energy firms' activities, we think E&P offers the best prospects for strong returns.

Compared with peers ExxonMobil and Shell, E&P makes up a larger chunk of BP's business. We think most E&P operations enjoy an economic moat because OPEC helps maintain industrywide profitability. BP is no exception. Plus, the firm's enormous size allows it to pursue projects that are risky but have the potential for huge rewards.

Refining and marketing activities, on the other hand, have less attractive economics. The industry has historically been plagued by periods of excess capacity that lead to weak--or even negative--gross profits. While refining profits should be strong for the next several years, in the long run we don't believe this industry enjoys a defensible economic moat. However, BP does have an important advantage in refining: size. As one of the largest refiners on the planet, BP benefits from economies of scale.

BP has several challenges ahead. In its quest to aggressively grow oil and gas production, the firm will be partnering with foreign governments and national oil companies in politically unstable regions. Although BP's capital resources and technological expertise make it a valuable partner, the upper hand often goes to the foreign governments because they have what matters most: oil and gas resources. BP could find it increasingly difficult to secure production agreements on favorable terms.

A political risk worth highlighting for BP is its exposure to Russia. More than one third of BP's oil production comes from its share of TNK-BP, a leading Russian oil producer. No other supermajor is this dependent on Russian energy. Russia has become notorious for using its vast resources as a political weapon. The dismantling in 2004 of leading Russian oil producer Yukos, plus TNK-BP's own experience with surprise back-tax bills, does nothing to bolster our confidence for BP's investments in this country. Still, BP's strategy of applying technology and management savvy to Russia's enormous resources could bring handsome rewards.

While BP has not shied away from taking large calculated risks, it has avoided higher-cost unconventional developments (such as oil sands in Canada). These projects' profitability is especially dependent on high oil prices. BP's focus on investing in large, potentially high-reward, low-cost oil and gas fields means that profitability depends less on high energy prices.

Data as of 12-29-06

Bristol-Myers Squibb BMY

	Rating	Fair Value	Last Close	Consider Buy	Consider Sell	Yield %
	★★★	$26.00	$26.32	$16.60	$31.40	4.26

Company Profile
Bristol-Myers Squibb produces and sells pharmaceuticals and over-the-counter medicines around the world. Cardiovascular, oncology, diabetes, and anti-infective therapies are the firm's top sellers. Bristol is also investing heavily in biologics, signing multimillion-dollar agreements with Imclone and Medarex. Bristol also sells brand-name nutritional, ostomy, wound-care, and medical imaging products.

Management — Stewardship Grade [C]
Bristol is currently searching for a new CEO to replace Peter Dolan who was ousted after concerns were raised that the botched arrangement with Apotex may have violated a deferred prosecution agreement the company was operating under due to a prior accounting scandal. In the meantime, board member and former Guidant chairman and CEO James Cornelius is serving as interim CEO. We hope the new CEO when hired can help restore credibility that has been lacking following numerous management blunders over the past several years

Bristol had to restate 1999-2002 earnings in 2003 and again in 2004 because it didn't properly recognize revenue. It later admitted to using drug distributors to stuff its inventory channel to meet Wall Street financial forecasts. It has paid hundreds of millions of dollars to settle government investigations for violations ranging from improper marketing practices to infringement of antitrust laws. As part of a settlement with the government, the company decided to separate the roles of CEO and chairman, which we think benefits shareholders providing more checks and balances among executives. We think management also failed in its due diligence while negotiating a $1 billion deal with Imclone Systems, probably overpaying for the investment as a result.

345 Park Avenue   www.bms.com
New York, NY 10154-0037

Growth [D]	2002	2003	2004	2005
Revenue %	-2.4	15.1	3.9	-0.9
Earnings/Share %	—	NMF	-23.9	25.6
Book Value/Share %	—	NMF	3.2	9.9
Dividends/Share %	27.3	-20.0	-25.0	33.3

Profitability [A]	2003	2004	2005	TTM
Return on Assets %	11.3	7.8	10.7	8.2
Oper Cash Flow $Mil	3,512	3,176	1,836	2,169
- Cap Spending $Mil	937	676	738	762
= Free Cash Flow $Mil	2,575	2,500	1,098	1,407

Financial Health [A]	2003	2004	2005	09-30-06
Long-term Debt $Mil	8,522	8,463	8,364	7,837
Total Equity $Mil	9,786	10,202	11,208	11,589
Debt/Equity Ratio	0.9	0.8	0.7	0.7

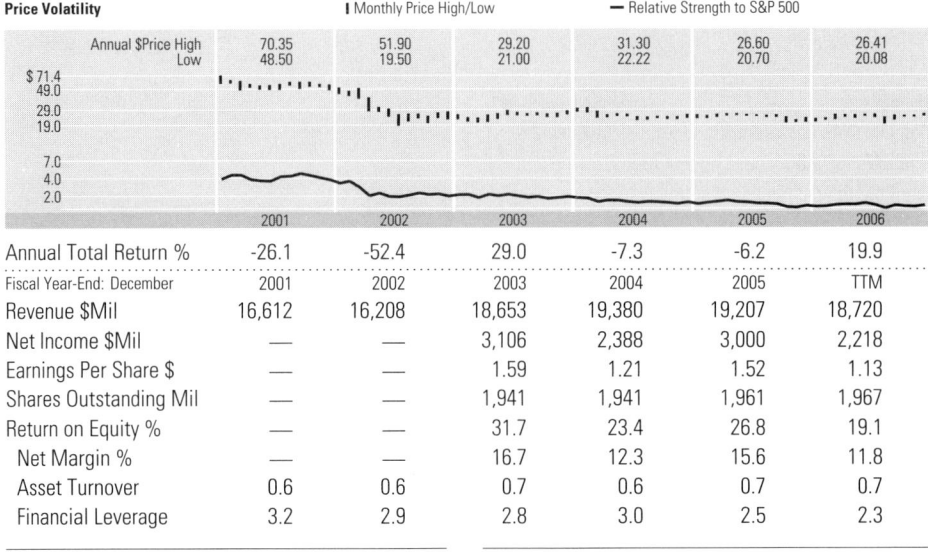

Industry	Business Risk	Moat Size	Investment Style	Sector
Drugs	Above Avg	Wide	Large Core	Healthcare

Competition	Market Cap $Mil	12 Mo Trailing Sales $Mil	Price/Cash Flow	Return On Assets%	Debt/Equity	Total Return% 1 Yr	3 Yr
Bristol-Myers Squibb	51,764	18,720	23.9	8.2	0.7	19.9	0.6
Pfizer	186,751	52,208	10.5	11.6	0.1	15.2	-7.4
GlaxoSmithKline PLC ADR	157,300	39,536	14.5	18.7	0.7	8.0	7.6

	2001	2002	2003	2004	2005	TTM
Annual Total Return %	-26.1	-52.4	29.0	-7.3	-6.2	19.9
Fiscal Year-End: December	2001	2002	2003	2004	2005	TTM
Revenue $Mil	16,612	16,208	18,653	19,380	19,207	18,720
Net Income $Mil	—	—	3,106	2,388	3,000	2,218
Earnings Per Share $	—	—	1.59	1.21	1.52	1.13
Shares Outstanding Mil	—	—	1,941	1,941	1,961	1,967
Return on Equity %	—	—	31.7	23.4	26.8	19.1
Net Margin %	—	—	16.7	12.3	15.6	11.8
Asset Turnover	0.6	0.6	0.7	0.6	0.7	0.7
Financial Leverage	3.2	2.9	2.8	3.0	2.5	2.3

Valuation Ratios	Stock	Rel to Industry	Rel to S&P 500
Price/Earnings	23.3	1.0	1.1
Price/Book	4.5	0.8	1.1
Price/Sales	2.8	0.6	1.0
Price/Cash Flow	23.9	1.5	1.6

Major Fund Holders	% of Fund Assets
Fidelity Select Pharmaceuticals	5.57
ProFunds Pharmaceuticals UltraSector Inv	4.91
Wells Fargo Advantage Spec Health Sci B	4.78
Allianz RCM Health Care D	4.65

Thesis — By Brandon Troegle, 12-20-06 Stock Price as of Analysis: $25.77

Bristol-Myers Squibb is dealing with a host of challenges as expiring patents hurt sales and management missteps continue. New drugs and a developing pipeline leave the company well poised for future growth though.

Bristol has faced significant challenges over the last few years as several of its best-selling drugs, including Pravachol, lost patent protection. This year, its top-selling drug, Plavix, faced earlier than expected generic competition when Canadian drugmaker Apotex introduced a generic version of the anticlotting drug, saying that Bristol's patent, which doesn't expire until 2011, is invalid.

In addition to patent expirations, Bristol has been hurt by a series of management gaffes in the past several years, the most recent being its fumbled strategy in dealing with the generic threat to Plavix. Bristol and Plavix partner Sanofi-Aventis entered into an agreement with Apotex, effectively paying the company to keep its generic version of Plavix off the market for the next several years. When the Federal Trade Commission did not approve of the arrangement, the deal dissolved and Apotex flooded the market with its generic. Bristol succeeded in winning an injunction that halted further sales of the generic, but supplies already in distribution will continue to hurt Plavix sales in the near term, and sales will be permanently hurt if Bristol doesn't prevail in the patent infringement case, which goes to trial in early 2007.

With millions in sales lost because of the maturation of its drug portfolio, Bristol developed a strategy of developing a drug pipeline for unmet medical needs in 10 disease areas. Four new drugs have been launched in the past year, and we expect several of these newly approved drugs and others in the pipeline to provide much-needed top- and bottom-line growth. In particular, we expect Avapro for hypertension, Reyataz and Sustiva for HIV, Abilify for schizophrenia and bipolar disorder, and biologics Erbitux for cancer and Orencia for rheumatoid arthritis to generate significant sales. Bristol also has several promising cancer drugs in late-stage development. Disregarding the pivotal challenge regarding blockbuster Plavix, Bristol does not have any major drugs losing protection until 2011. Meanwhile, the company has other high-margin products including nutritional products, ostomy, wound-care, and medical imaging products provide some stability and dampen the volatility of the company's portfolio.

British American Tobacco PLC ADR BTI

Data as of 12-29-06

Rating	Fair Value	Last Close	Consider Buy	Consider Sell	Yield %
★★★	$60.00	$56.66	$38.20	$72.40	3.06

Company Profile
British American sells more than 300 brands of cigarettes in 180 countries, making it the second-largest tobacco firm in the world, behind Altria. British American's collection of global cigarette brands includes well-known names like Dunhill, Kent, Pall Mall, and Lucky Strike. British American also markets a long list of regional cigarette brands, cigars, roll-your-own tobacco products, and smokeless tobacco. The company holds a 42% economic interest in Reynolds American.

Management
Stewardship Grade [NA]

We give British American credit for having its chairman and CEO positions separated since the retirement of Martin Broughton in 2004. Broughton had been chief executive for 10 years and took over the chairman's role in 1999 following the firm's emergence as a publicly traded company. In 1998, British American Tobacco separated from its parent company, BAT Industries, which also combined its remaining financial-services arm with Zurich Insurance Company to form the Zurich Financial Services Group. The company's current chairman, Jan du Plessis, joined the board of British American Tobacco as a director in 1999 and continues to serve in a nonexecutive role. Paul Adams, who ascended into his role as CEO in July 2004, joined the tobacco firm in 1991 as the regional director of the Asia-Pacific region. He has had a considerable amount of experience in Europe and Asia and is well-suited to manage the firm longer term. Over the years, the management team at British American has been extremely astute at finding and integrating meaningful acquisitions, as well as ferreting out cost savings within its own operations. The company generates a significant amount of free cash flow and has been diligent about returning it to shareholders as dividends and share repurchases.

Globe House 4 Temple Place
London, United Kingdom WC2R 2PG
www.bat.com

Growth [NA]	2002	2003	2004	2005
Revenue %	-3.9	3.8	24.2	-24.7
Earnings/Share %	13.9	-46.7	391.3	-36.1
Book Value/Share %	11.1	-24.9	74.6	12.0
Dividends/Share %	—	—	—	—

Profitability [NA]	2003	2004	2005	TTM
Return on Assets %	3.8	15.7	10.5	10.5
Oper Cash Flow $Mil	3,238	3,600	4,242	4,242
- Cap Spending $Mil	3,737	551	695	695
= Free Cash Flow $Mil	-499	3,049	3,547	3,547

Financial Health [NA]	2003	2004	2005	12-31-05
Long-term Debt $Mil	—	11,910	9,024	9,024
Total Equity $Mil	8,189	11,763	11,857	11,857
Debt/Equity Ratio	—	1.0	0.8	0.8

Industry	Business Risk	Moat Size	Investment Style	Sector
Tobacco	Above Avg	Wide	Large Core	Consumer Goods

Competition

	Market Cap $Mil	12 Mo Trailing Sales $Mil	Price/Cash Flow	Return On Assets%	Debt/Equity	Total Return% 1 Yr	3 Yr
British American Tobacco PLC ADR	59,384	43,778	14.0	10.5	0.8	30.1	32.1
Altria Group	179,868	100,499	12.6	10.5	0.3	19.9	21.8
Imperial Tobacco Group PL	28,814	20,706	16.8	9.6	20.3	35.3	30.0

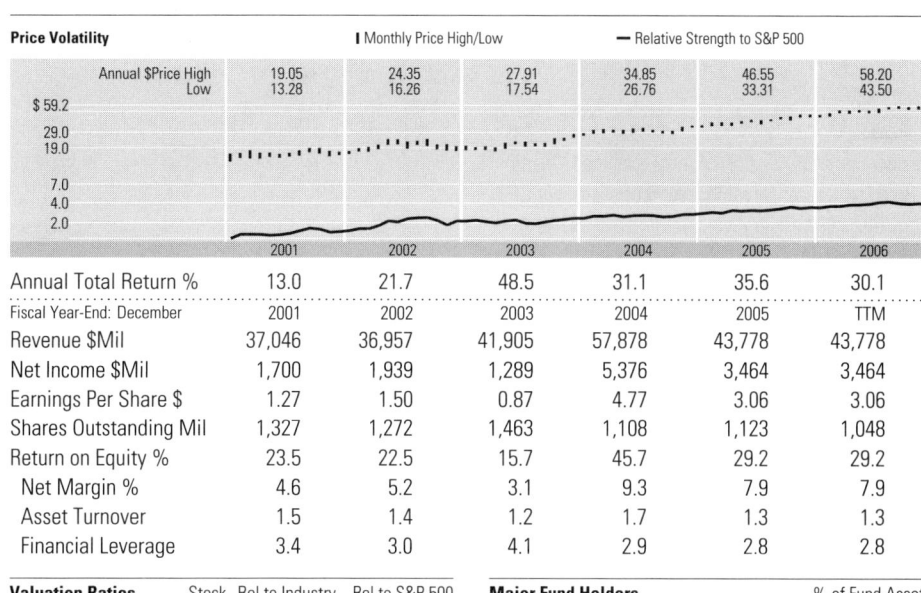

	2001	2002	2003	2004	2005	TTM
Annual Total Return %	13.0	21.7	48.5	31.1	35.6	30.1
Fiscal Year-End: December	2001	2002	2003	2004	2005	TTM
Revenue $Mil	37,046	36,957	41,905	57,878	43,778	43,778
Net Income $Mil	1,700	1,939	1,289	5,376	3,464	3,464
Earnings Per Share $	1.27	1.50	0.87	4.77	3.06	3.06
Shares Outstanding Mil	1,327	1,272	1,463	1,108	1,123	1,048
Return on Equity %	23.5	22.5	15.7	45.7	29.2	29.2
Net Margin %	4.6	5.2	3.1	9.3	7.9	7.9
Asset Turnover	1.5	1.4	1.2	1.7	1.3	1.3
Financial Leverage	3.4	3.0	4.1	2.9	2.8	2.8

Valuation Ratios	Stock	Rel to Industry	Rel to S&P 500
Price/Earnings	18.5	1.0	0.9
Price/Book	5.0	0.2	1.2
Price/Sales	1.4	0.8	0.5
Price/Cash Flow	14.0	1.0	1.0

Major Fund Holders	% of Fund Assets
Vice Fund	3.51
Navellier International Growth A	2.11

Thesis
By Greggory Warren, CFA, 12-06-06 Stock Price as of Analysis: $57.95

Despite generating very few sales or profits from Britain or the United States, British American has emerged as one of the largest tobacco firms in the world. The company produces significant amounts of cash flow and has used it wisely to expand its position in developing and emerging markets. With leading share in most of the developed world, and critical exposure in faster-growing markets in Eastern Europe and Asia, British American has built a significant moat around its operations.

The company has worked relentlessly to bring cigarettes to just about every nook and cranny of the world, selling more than 300 brands of cigarettes in 180 different countries. While British American may not have a dominant international brand, like Marlboro, it has done extremely well with its core group of international brands (Kent, Dunhill, Pall Mall, and Lucky Strike) and has been astute about acquiring local brands that resonate with consumers and provide the company crucial market share.

British American is the dominant seller of cigarettes in Canada, South Africa, and Malaysia, holding greater than 50% share in each of these markets. British American also ranks among the top three players in France, Germany, Italy, and Australia. More importantly, the company has a significant presence in developing and emerging markets, where sales volumes are increasing 2%-3% annually versus the 1%-2% volume declines experienced in its mature markets. Its first-mover advantage in many of these markets has helped British American to secure leading market share in economies that will eventually improve in size and profitability.

The company's focus on rationalizing its manufacturing base, taking most of its production to lower cost markets in Eastern Europe and Asia, has allowed it to improve operating margins over the past few years. While British American's returns on invested capital have trailed those posted by Altria Group, they have remained well above our estimate of the company's cost of capital, reinforcing our wide-moat rating for the firm.

We believe British American's wide moat is further enhanced by the heavy restrictions that exist in most of the world's developed markets on the sale, promotion, and use of tobacco products. This makes it extremely difficult for new companies or brands to develop, leaving market shares fairly static for the established cigarette manufacturers and allowing British American to go after share in the much faster-growing developing and emerging markets.

Data as of 12-29-06

Broadcom BRCM

	Rating	Fair Value	Last Close	Consider Buy	Consider Sell	Yield %
	★★★★	$40.00	$32.31	$25.50	$48.20	0.00

Company Profile

Broadcom develops a diverse array of integrated circuits targeting high-speed networking and broadband applications. The firm's extensive product portfolio includes many of the key components found in devices such as cable modems, set-top boxes, and local area networking (LAN) switches. Broadcom also designs chips for storage networking and wireless equipment, such as servers and mobile handsets. The firm markets its products primarily to top-tier technology firms.

Management   Stewardship Grade [D]

President and CEO Scott McGregor assumed the reins at Broadcom in January 2005, succeeding former CEO Lanny Ross. McGregor joined the firm after several years of heading up the Philips Semiconductor division of Royal Philips Electronics. Company co-founder Henry Samueli remains Broadcom's chairman and chief technical officer. William Ruehle, CFO since 1997, retired in September 2006 amid Broadcom's options award review. Broadcom is one of the more than 100 companies that received an informal inquiry from the SEC with regard to its options granting practices. Preliminary findings indicate that historical earnings have been significantly overstated as a result, although we expect the effect on historical cash flow will be limited. As of November 2006, the company has not completed the restatement. We frown on Broadcom's stock-option exchanges in 2001 and 2003, which wiped out underwater options, and its aggressive use of pro forma accounting. Additional non-shareholder-friendly policies include provisions to prevent takeovers. We think the company's effort at offsetting options dilution with share buybacks to limit total dilution to 2%-3% a year is a step in the right direction.

16215 Alton Parkway   www.broadcom.com
Irvine, CA 92618-3616

Growth [A]	2002	2003	2004	2005
Revenue %	12.6	48.7	49.1	11.3
Earnings/Share %	NMF	NMF	NMF	74.6
Book Value/Share %	-51.4	-16.8	33.4	23.3
Dividends/Share %	NMF	NMF	NMF	NMF

Profitability [D]	2003	2004	2005	TTM
Return on Assets %	-47.6	7.6	11.0	11.0
Oper Cash Flow $Mil	31	502	447	527
- Cap Spending $Mil	48	50	42	49
= Free Cash Flow $Mil	-17	452	405	478

Financial Health [B-]	2003	2004	2005	03-31-06
Long-term Debt $Mil	—	—	—	—
Total Equity $Mil	1,490	2,366	3,145	3,668
Debt/Equity Ratio	—	—	—	—

Industry	Business Risk	Moat Size	Investment Style	Sector
Semiconductor	Above Avg	Narrow	Large Growth	Hardware

Competition

	Market Cap $Mil	12 Mo Trailing Sales $Mil	Price/Cash Flow	Return On Assets%	Debt/Equity	Total Return% 1 Yr	3 Yr
Broadcom	17,619	3,021	33.4	11.0	—	2.8	12.1
Texas Instruments	42,736	15,173	16.1	29.3	0.0	-9.8	-0.2
Marvell Technology	11,230	1,827	29.5	9.5	0.0	-31.6	26.5

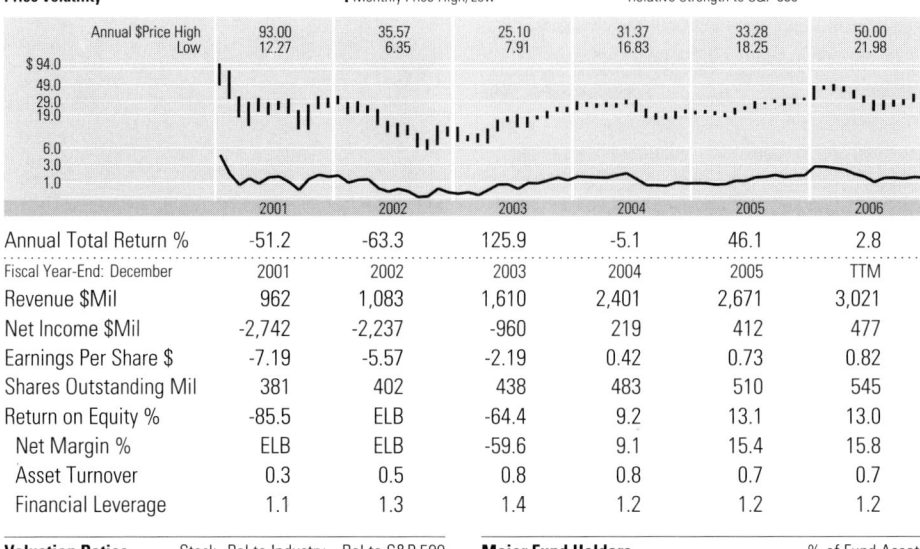

Annual Total Return %	-51.2	-63.3	125.9	-5.1	46.1	2.8
Fiscal Year-End: December	2001	2002	2003	2004	2005	TTM
Revenue $Mil	962	1,083	1,610	2,401	2,671	3,021
Net Income $Mil	-2,742	-2,237	-960	219	412	477
Earnings Per Share $	-7.19	-5.57	-2.19	0.42	0.73	0.82
Shares Outstanding Mil	381	402	438	483	510	545
Return on Equity %	-85.5	ELB	-64.4	9.2	13.1	13.0
Net Margin %	ELB	ELB	-59.6	9.1	15.4	15.8
Asset Turnover	0.3	0.5	0.8	0.8	0.7	0.7
Financial Leverage	1.1	1.3	1.4	1.2	1.2	1.2

Valuation Ratios	Stock	Rel to Industry	Rel to S&P 500
Price/Earnings	39.3	1.4	1.9
Price/Book	4.8	1.3	1.2
Price/Sales	5.8	1.4	2.0
Price/Cash Flow	33.4	2.0	2.3

Major Fund Holders	% of Fund Assets
Fidelity Select Network & Infrastruct	8.12
Fidelity Advisor Electronics T	6.95
Firsthand Technology Leaders	4.68
Turner Concentrated Growth Instl	4.53

Thesis   By Larry Cao, CFA, 11-14-06   Stock Price as of Analysis: $34.05

With a broad product portfolio, we think Broadcom is arguably the best positioned communications chip company today, and at the right price, it is our favorite idea in the sector.

Broadcom offers the enabling technology to connect people at home, at work, and on the go. We think the firm derives its moat from the depth and breadth of its technology portfolio, as well as its strong engineering talent. It has leading positions in cable modems, digital cable TV set-top boxes, high-speed enterprise network switches, wireless local area networks, and Bluetooth products. The firm also is a major supplier of chips for DSL modems, direct broadcasting satellite set-top boxes, voice over Internet protocol, and digital TV. Because Broadcom knows each technology well, it is in a great position to offer integrated solutions such as modems with VoIP capabilities, which is exactly what many of its clients demand. The integrated solution also enhances Broadcom's moat by raising clients' switching costs.

We believe Broadcom's business risk is much lower than that of its peers thanks to the diversification of its technology portfolio. While it is difficult to predict the rate of adoption for any specific technology, Broadcom's management has stayed away from "market timing" and instead focused on building a strong and deep portfolio. For example, Broadcom has lost most of its $300 million server business over the past few years, and certain other business lines were periodically affected by industrywide inventory corrections. However, strength in cable modems in 2003, satellite set-top boxes in 2004, and Bluetooth in 2005, among other areas, more than offset the weaknesses elsewhere and kept Broadcom growing at a 22% compound annual rate in the last five years.

Broadcom's fabless manufacturing strategy also lowers its risk profile. Not having to invest billions in cutting-edge fabrication facilities stabilized Broadcom's gross margin through the typical boom-bust cycle of the semiconductor industry. This allows Broadcom to steadily grow its R&D budgets and focus on advancing its technology advantages.

Broadcom hit a soft patch in the second half of 2006 as a result of end market weaknesses. We believe the issues are temporary and not structural. The industry has become much more disciplined in building capacity and managing inventory, so cycles have become shorter and more moderate. We believe investors who focus on Broadcom's value creation potential will benefit over the long run.

Brookfield Asset Management BAM

Data as of 12-29-06

Rating	Fair Value	Last Close	Consider Buy	Consider Sell	Yield %
★★★	$48.00	$48.18	$37.00	$60.10	1.43

Company Profile
Brookfield Asset Management, formerly known as Brascan, owns and manages office properties, residential developments, and hydroelectric power plants. The company has about $50 billion of assets under management, which are primarily in Canada, the northeastern United States, England, and Brazil.

	Industry	Business Risk	Moat Size	Investment Style	Sector
	Finance	Average	Narrow	Large Growth	Financial Services

Competition

	Market Cap $Mil	12 Mo Trailing Sales $Mil	Price/Cash Flow	Return On Assets %	Debt/ Equity	Total Return % 1 Yr	Total Return % 3 Yr
Brookfield Asset Management	41,886	5,256	—	6.4	—	46.0	54.1
Vornado Realty Trust	17,259	2,696	—	3.4	—	51.1	36.9
SL Green Realty	6,077	496	—	3.0	—	77.7	52.6

Price Volatility
Monthly Price High/Low — Relative Strength to S&P 500

Annual $Price	2001	2002	2003	2004	2005	2006
High	8.38	10.85	13.92	26.77	34.62	50.07
Low	6.22	7.76	8.09	13.53	20.83	31.79
Annual Total Return %	29.2	17.1	53.5	80.7	42.0	46.0

Fiscal Year-End: December	2001	2002	2003	2004	2005	TTM
Revenue $Mil	3,042	3,064	3,370	3,899	5,256	5,256
Net Income $Mil	201	83	232	555	1,662	1,662
Earnings Per Share $	0.19	0.04	0.23	0.60	1.81	1.81
Shares Outstanding Mil	—	—	—	910	895	869
Return on Equity %	3.4	2.2	4.7	16.9	36.8	36.8
Net Margin %	6.6	2.7	6.9	14.2	31.6	31.6
Asset Turnover	0.2	0.2	0.2	0.2	0.2	0.2
Financial Leverage	2.4	3.8	3.3	6.1	5.8	5.8

Management   Stewardship Grade [B]
Overall, Brookfield's stewardship is excellent. Insiders own about 17% of the company, or almost $3 billion worth of shares. We like the split chairman and CEO roles, annual director elections, and the expensing of options. Further, management and directors are required to own a certain amount of stock a few years after gaining their posts, quickly aligning their interests with other shareholders'. We also like the clear performance goals Brookfield spells out for its executives. For instance, CEO Bruce Flatt is measured on the company's ability to increase cash flow from operations and produce high cash returns on equity, both sound financial measures. This scheme awards business fundamentals--not stock price performance--which we find extremely sensible. And we can't fail to mention Brookfield's detailed financial reports and compelling shareholder letters. The only things keeping Brookfield from earning our highest Stewardship Grade are the loans to executives that remain outstanding and the dual-class share structure, which gives Class B shareholders more power than their true economic interest.

Valuation Ratios

	Stock	Rel to Industry	Rel to S&P 500
Price/Earnings	26.6	1.4	1.3
Price/Book	9.3	2.2	2.3
Price/Sales	8.0	1.5	2.8
Price/Cash Flow	—	—	—

Major Fund Holders

	% of Fund Assets
Third Avenue Real Estate Value	8.40
Navellier Top 20 A	6.66
Morgan Stanley Inst Focus Equity A	6.17
Morgan Stanley Focus Growth B	6.07

Thesis By Akash Dave, 10-04-06 Stock Price as of Analysis: $43.90

Brookfield Asset Management is redeploying its assets into funds that it will manage for institutional investors. We view this classic case of resource conversion positively and would gladly invest at a reasonable discount to our fair value estimate.

Brookfield primarily owns trophy office properties and hydroelectric power plants. The company's stellar assets share a number of attractive characteristics. First, they are located in high-barrier-to-entry markets. Second, they require high up-front costs, but minimal ongoing expenditures. Finally, Brookfield collects a contractual revenue stream from the assets, allowing for nonrecourse debt to be placed on them. This type of financing enhances returns for common shareholders without raising the risk profile, as lenders can look only to the asset for remedy. As a result, the company has produced 20% returns on equity over the past five years, by our estimates, earning it a narrow moat.

Like most great companies, Brookfield is adapting to the changing competitive landscape. With an overabundance of institutional capital chasing assets--like Brookfield's--that generate stable income, prices have been driven to dizzying levels. Unable to meet its stringent return requirements, Brookfield has elected to strategically redeploy its resources from outright ownership of assets into joint-venture funds with institutional partners. Brookfield typically takes a 20% stake in the fund and earns a fee for managing the balance of the assets. We believe this fund management model will likely drive returns on equity to an average of 24% over the next five years.

There is no shortage of competition, though. Macquarie, an Australian-based investment bank, and Goldman Sachs are just two of the many large players lining up to run such asset funds. However, we believe Brookfield will hold up well. It already owns a tremendous amount of high-quality assets that can be used to seed its funds. Additionally, investors are likely to pay up for the privilege of investing alongside a proven operator like Brookfield. Finally, institutional capital would prefer to invest alongside managers with meaningful skin in the game, which is the case with Brookfield. For these reasons, we believe that Brookfield should protect its narrow moat, grow its asset management business to scale, and earn economic profits for shareholders.

With high-quality assets and a profitable transition in its midst, we would gladly purchase Brookfield's common shares at a discount to our fair value.

Suite 300, BCE Place, 181 Bay Street PO Box 762
Toronto, ON M5J 2T3   www.brascancorp.com

Growth [NA]

	2002	2003	2004	2005
Revenue %	0.7	10.0	15.7	34.8
Earnings/Share %	-78.5	456.9	159.0	203.0
Book Value/Share %	-66.1	155.4	-27.4	39.4
Dividends/Share %	-2.3	13.6	13.4	8.0

Profitability [NA]

	2003	2004	2005	TTM
Return on Assets %	1.4	2.8	6.4	6.4
Oper Cash Flow $Mil	742	626	683	—
- Cap Spending $Mil	—	23	1,065	—
= Free Cash Flow $Mil	—	—	—	—

Financial Health [NA]

	2003	2004	2005	12-31-05
Long-term Debt $Mil	—	—	—	—
Total Equity $Mil	4,885	3,277	4,514	4,514
Debt/Equity Ratio	—	—	—	—

Data as of 12-29-06

Brown & Brown BRO

	Rating	Fair Value	Last Close	Consider Buy	Consider Sell	Yield %
	★★★	$30.00	$28.21	$23.10	$37.60	0.74

Company Profile

Brown & Brown is the sixth-largest insurance brokerage firm in the United States. It focuses on middle-market clients like professional partnerships and small businesses. Brown's agents act as a liaison between insurance buyers and sellers and receive a commission as compensation for their services. Brown & Brown uses a decentralized operating structure in which each brokerage office is run as a separate profit center subject to uniform firmwide profitability targets.

Management — Stewardship Grade [A]

Our Stewardship Grade for Brown & Brown remains an A. Chairman and CEO J. Hyatt Brown owns about 15% (more than $600 million worth) of Brown's common stock. He became CEO in 1993 and chairman in 1994. We do not look favorably on the chairman and CEO being the same person. However, Brown is nearing retirement, and the firm has achieved outstanding results since he assumed both roles. Plus, the remaining executives and directors own more than 6% of the stock, bringing total insider ownership to about 21%, which we think appropriately aligns their interests with those of shareholders. Brown takes leadership development seriously, dedicating a senior executive to a formal effort to spark and spread leadership qualities the firm has deemed responsible for its success. We think this initiative serves shareholders well. We also like the firm's emphasis on cultivating and maintaining ethical behavior.

220 South Ridgewood Ave.
Daytona Beach, FL 32114
www.bbinsurance.com

Growth [A]	2002	2003	2004	2005
Revenue %	24.9	20.9	17.4	21.5
Earnings/Share %	43.5	31.1	16.3	16.1
Book Value/Share %	108.0	25.7	24.8	21.7
Dividends/Share %	24.9	21.2	19.4	17.2

Profitability [A+]	2003	2004	2005	TTM
Return on Assets %	12.7	10.3	9.4	9.5
Oper Cash Flow $Mil	143	170	215	—
- Cap Spending $Mil	16	10	13	—
= Free Cash Flow $Mil	—	—	—	—

Financial Health [NA]	2003	2004	2005	09-30-06
Long-term Debt $Mil	—	—	—	—
Total Equity $Mil	498	624	764	896
Debt/Equity Ratio	—	—	—	—

Industry	Business Risk	Moat Size	Investment Style	Sector
Insurance (General)	Average	Wide	Mid Growth	Financial Services

Competition	Market Cap $Mil	12 Mo Trailing Sales $Mil	Price/Cash Flow	Return On Assets %	Debt/Equity	Total Return % 1 Yr	3 Yr
Brown & Brown	3,948	860	—	9.5	—	-7.0	20.6
Marsh & McLennan Companie	16,897	11,715	—	4.5	—	-1.2	-11.9
Aon	11,113	10,006	—	2.4	—	-0.1	16.2

Price Volatility — Monthly Price High/Low — Relative Strength to S&P 500

Annual $Price High / Low	15.70 / 7.19	18.50 / 12.00	18.83 / 13.38	23.38 / 16.01	31.90 / 21.00	35.25 / 27.06
	2001	2002	2003	2004	2005	2006
Annual Total Return %	57.1	19.2	1.7	34.5	41.3	-7.0

Fiscal Year-End: December	2001	2002	2003	2004	2005	TTM
Revenue $Mil	365	456	551	647	786	860
Net Income $Mil	54	83	110	129	151	170
Earnings Per Share $	0.43	0.61	0.80	0.93	1.08	1.22
Shares Outstanding Mil	125	134	137	139	138	140
Return on Equity %	30.8	21.2	22.2	20.6	19.7	19.0
Net Margin %	14.8	18.2	20.0	19.9	19.2	19.8
Asset Turnover	0.7	0.6	0.6	0.5	0.5	0.5
Financial Leverage	2.8	1.9	1.7	2.0	2.1	2.0

Valuation Ratios	Stock	Rel to Industry	Rel to S&P 500
Price/Earnings	23.1	1.5	1.1
Price/Book	4.4	2.2	1.1
Price/Sales	4.6	2.7	1.6
Price/Cash Flow	—	—	—

Major Fund Holders	% of Fund Assets
FAM Value Inv	5.65
Hallmark Small-Cap Growth R	3.21
Ave Maria Growth	2.97
FAM Equity-Income Inv	2.73

Thesis By Bill Bergman, 12-04-06 Stock Price as of Analysis: $29.34

Brown & Brown's unique sales and service-oriented growth culture yields the insurance brokerage firm a wide moat. However, we think the best returns from Brown's acquisition strategy are in the past. Our fair value estimate is $30 per share.

The key to understanding Brown's superior historical results lies in a vibrant intangible asset. The firm's leaders have sparked an action-oriented sales and service culture. A cheetah is Brown's unofficial corporate symbol, taking the cover of the firm's annual reports. Brown has a poster with a story noting that every day a gazelle has to get up and start running or it will get eaten, while every day a cheetah has to get up and start running or it will starve to death. The moral is that when you get up, you had better start running. One way Brown puts this into practice is by requiring offices to earn 25% operating margins. If they don't, personnel changes typically ensue.

Brown seeks and attracts talented people, employing carrots as well as sticks. The net result is motivated people seeking out and serving their customers. Brown pays agents twice as much for generating new business as for renewing contracts, which motivates them to seek new opportunities. As a further incentive, successful agents are eligible to participate in a long-term stock program for their retirement--one that can add up to almost 20% of their annual salary. These incentives have helped the company's profit margins to expand and to align agents' interests with those of customers as well as shareholders.

Brown's pursuit of rapid earnings growth has included an aggressive acquisition strategy. From 2002 to 2005, Brown purchased more than 100 independent insurance brokerage firms. Revenue of acquired firms provided roughly two thirds of Brown's overall revenue growth in that time frame. We think the firm employs a responsible due-diligence process, but the best returns on this strategy are probably behind it. We expect heightened competition for acquisitions.

Brown's continued success depends on developing new leaders. To this end, management has invested significantly in a proprietary training program designed to inculcate agents with the Brown & Brown culture and to provide a deep bench of future profit-center managers. This initiative should help ensure the propagation of the firm's culture.

Data as of 12-29-06

Brown-Forman B BF.B

	Rating	Fair Value	Last Close	Consider Buy	Consider Sell	Yield %
	★★★	$68.00	$66.24	$57.90	$89.30	1.73

Company Profile

Founded in 1870, Brown-Forman produces and markets a host of premium spirits and wine brands. Spirits include Jack Daniel's, Southern Comfort, Finlandia, Canadian Mist, and Tuaca. Wines include Fetzer, Bolla, and distribution rights for Korbel. Alcoholic beverages now account for virtually all of the company's revenue and profits, with a negligible portion still coming from Hartmann luggage and a sliver of the company's former consumer durables business.

Management
Stewardship Grade [C]

Holders of Brown-Forman Class B shares, which represent virtually all that are available to the public, have no voting rights. The Brown family controls 70% of Class A voting shares and therefore the company, along with 32% of Class B shares. Management is strongly motivated to create shareholder value, but we never look kindly upon the complete disenfranchisement of a class of shareholders. Directors stand for elections annually, which would be nice if Class B shareholders could vote. Brown-Forman is considered a controlled company and is thus exempt from Sarbanes-Oxley-mandated independent director minimums. The Brown family has not hesitated to take advantage by appointing eight insiders to the 13-member board. Although the Browns have retained complete control over the firm, they haven't shown any sign of abusing the power and have in fact created shareholder value. Executive compensation has a large incentive component and seems reasonable. Paul Varga replaced Owsley Brown II as CEO in August 2005. Varga has been with the company for 18 years, most recently as president and CEO of Brown-Forman Beverages, and the transition has been smooth. Brown remains chairman, splitting the role from the CEO--a move we applaud.

850 Dixie Highway www.brown-forman.com
Louisville, KY 40210

Growth [B+]	2003	2004	2005	2006
Revenue %	10.6	10.9	10.2	9.7
Earnings/Share %	—	NMF	20.9	3.1
Book Value/Share %	—	NMF	19.3	18.4
Dividends/Share %	6.6	10.3	14.4	14.8

Profitability [A+]	2004	2005	2006	TTM
Return on Assets %	10.7	11.6	11.7	14.2
Oper Cash Flow $Mil	304	396	344	385
- Cap Spending $Mil	39	45	52	52
= Free Cash Flow $Mil	265	351	292	333

Financial Health [A+]	2004	2005	2006	10-31-06
Long-term Debt $Mil	—	351	351	354
Total Equity $Mil	1,095	1,310	1,563	1,750
Debt/Equity Ratio	—	0.3	0.2	0.2

Industry	Business Risk	Moat Size	Investment Style	Sector
Alcoholic Beverages	Below Avg	Narrow	Mid Core	Consumer Goods

Competition	Market Cap $Mil	12 Mo Trailing Sales $Mil	Price/Cash Flow	Return On Assets %	Debt/ Equity	Total Return % 1 Yr	3 Yr
Brown-Forman B	8,153	2,606	21.2	14.2	0.2	-3.0	14.4
Diageo PLC ADR	60,493	12,931	21.3	13.8	0.9	40.7	18.0
Constellation Brands A	6,774	4,888	19.5	3.3	1.3	10.6	20.8

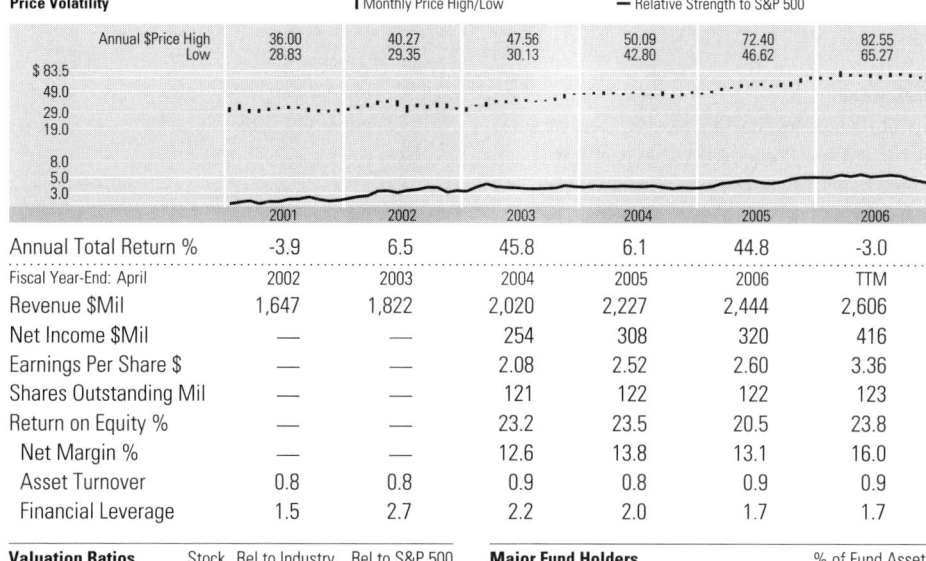

Annual Total Return %	-3.9	6.5	45.8	6.1	44.8	-3.0
Fiscal Year-End: April	2002	2003	2004	2005	2006	TTM
Revenue $Mil	1,647	1,822	2,020	2,227	2,444	2,606
Net Income $Mil	—	—	254	308	320	416
Earnings Per Share $	—	—	2.08	2.52	2.60	3.36
Shares Outstanding Mil	—	—	121	122	122	123
Return on Equity %	—	—	23.2	23.5	20.5	23.8
Net Margin %	—	—	12.6	13.8	13.1	16.0
Asset Turnover	0.8	0.8	0.9	0.8	0.9	0.9
Financial Leverage	1.5	2.7	2.2	2.0	1.7	1.7

Valuation Ratios	Stock	Rel to Industry	Rel to S&P 500
Price/Earnings	19.8	0.8	1.0
Price/Book	4.7	0.5	1.1
Price/Sales	3.1	0.6	1.1
Price/Cash Flow	21.2	0.9	1.5

Major Fund Holders	% of Fund Assets
Van Kampen American Franchise A	2.90
Cookson Peirce Core Equity	2.10
Van Kampen Global Franchise A	1.93
ING Van Kampen Global Franchise S	1.88

Thesis By Matthew Reilly, 12-11-06 Stock Price as of Analysis: $66.50

Now that Brown-Forman has sold the vast majority of its consumer durables business, it is essentially a pure-play premium alcoholic beverage maker. With its brands stronger than ever, consumers continuing to trade up to premium spirits brands, and a management team that we believe is making the right moves, we think Brown Forman makes an excellent long-term holding if bought for the right price.

Brown-Forman has a long history of generating returns on invested capital well in excess of our estimate of its cost of capital. We expect the returns to get even better now that the Lenox anchor has been released from the company's neck, freeing up capital and, more important, managerial resources. Focus on the spirits business is especially important because the international market is consolidating and management must figure out how to most efficiently employ more than $300 million in annual free cash flow; it most recently put some of that to use with the $255 million acquisition of Chambord and the $876 million acquisition of Casa Herradura. Because limited financial details are available for both transactions, it is difficult to gauge whether the company got good values. The brands seem to be strong strategic fits with decent growth prospects, though the deals appear to have been fully priced.

We believe more acquisitions are likely, as the company's net annual sales are only about one fifth of industry leader Diageo's. This lack of scale is a main reason Brown-Forman has only a narrow economic moat, despite its strong returns on invested capital. Also, the firm is still highly dependent on sales of one brand, Jack Daniel's, and we believe a desire for diversification provides a good deal of the impetus behind management's current interest in spirits acquisitions.

It is difficult to predict how long Brown-Forman's halcyon days will last. The company achieved its highest volume growth ever for Jack Daniel's in fiscal 2005 and followed with a strong 2006 in which Jack Daniel's depletions, or sales from wholesalers to retailers, increased 8% and net revenue from the company's ongoing operations was up about 11%. While we do not expect this torrid pace to continue indefinitely, we do expect growth and margins to remain strong over the next few years. Volume and earnings growth have shown deceleration in early fiscal 2007, and with dilution expected from acquisitions over the next couple of years, we think the company's valuation may provide an opportunity for patient, long-term investors.

Data as of 12-29-06

Brunswick BC

	Rating	Fair Value	Last Close	Consider Buy	Consider Sell	Yield %
	★★★★	$37.00	$31.90	$28.50	$46.40	1.88

Company Profile
Brunswick manufactures and markets recreational products. Its marine brands include Mercury and Mariner outboard engines; Mercury MerCruiser stern drives and inboard engines; and Sea Ray, Bayliner, Baja, Boston Whaler, Hatteras, and Princecraft boats. Other leisure brands include Life Fitness, Hammer Strength, and ParaBody fitness equipment and Brunswick bowling and billiard products.

Industry	Business Risk	Moat Size	Investment Style	Sector
Recreation	Average	Narrow	Mid Value	Consumer Goods

Competition

	Market Cap $Mil	12 Mo Trailing Sales $Mil	Price/Cash Flow	Return On Assets%	Debt/Equity	Total Return% 1 Yr	3 Yr
Brunswick	2,929	5,993	8.2	5.7	0.4	-20.1	1.5
Genmar Holdings							
AMBWQ							

Management   Stewardship Grade [B]
In 2005, CEO George Buckley departed to take the helm at 3M, and Dustin McCoy, president of the boating group, took over as chairman and CEO of Brunswick. McCoy was brought to Brunswick by Buckley and had worked with him throughout the firm since 2000. During that time, Brunswick sold noncore businesses and focused on leveraging the firm's strengths in its core boating and recreational markets. McCoy was part of the team that has been largely responsible for modernizing manufacturing, improving process efficiency, and integrating technology across the company's fleet of boats. Once tapped to lead Brunswick, McCoy received a new compensation package that is weighted heavily toward incentive bonus pay. In addition, the board awarded him restricted-stock units that vest in 2009, which will help ensure that his interests are aligned with those of shareholders. We applaud the board for avoiding the use of extravagant stock options, which had been showered on the previous CEO.

Price Volatility
| Monthly Price High/Low   — Relative Strength to S&P 500

	2001	2002	2003	2004	2005	2006
Annual $Price High	25.00	30.01	32.08	49.85	49.77	42.84
Low	14.03	18.30	17.15	31.25	35.00	27.08
Annual Total Return %	35.6	-6.5	63.0	57.5	-16.6	-20.1
Fiscal Year-End: December	2001	2002	2003	2004	2005	TTM
Revenue $Mil	3,371	3,712	4,129	5,229	5,924	5,993
Net Income $Mil	82	78	135	270	385	275
Earnings Per Share $	0.93	0.86	1.47	2.77	3.90	2.86
Shares Outstanding Mil	88	90	91	96	98	92
Return on Equity %	7.4	7.1	10.2	15.8	19.5	13.5
Net Margin %	2.4	2.1	3.3	5.2	6.5	4.6
Asset Turnover	1.1	1.1	1.1	1.2	1.3	1.2
Financial Leverage	2.8	3.0	2.7	2.5	2.3	2.4

Valuation Ratios	Stock	Rel to Industry	Rel to S&P 500
Price/Earnings	9.7	0.5	0.5
Price/Book	1.4	0.3	0.3
Price/Sales	0.5	0.2	0.2
Price/Cash Flow	8.2	0.6	0.6

Major Fund Holders	% of Fund Assets
AIM Mid Cap Basic Value A	2.13
Snow Capital Opportunity A	1.79
Huntington Situs Small Cap Trust	1.58
CastleRock	1.38

One North Field Court
Lake Forest, IL 60045-4811   www.brunswick.com

Growth [B+]	2002	2003	2004	2005
Revenue %	10.1	11.2	26.7	13.3
Earnings/Share %	-7.5	70.9	88.4	40.8
Book Value/Share %	-4.3	19.0	22.2	13.9
Dividends/Share %	0.0	0.0	20.0	0.0

Profitability [B-]	2003	2004	2005	TTM
Return on Assets %	3.8	6.2	8.3	5.7
Oper Cash Flow $Mil	395	415	433	358
- Cap Spending $Mil	160	171	234	223
= Free Cash Flow $Mil	235	244	199	135

Financial Health [B+]	2003	2004	2005	09-30-06
Long-term Debt $Mil	584	728	724	726
Total Equity $Mil	1,323	1,712	1,979	2,039
Debt/Equity Ratio	0.4	0.4	0.4	0.4

Thesis By Marisa E. Thompson, 12-14-06 Stock Price as of Analysis: $32.36

Although scale, a compelling product portfolio, and cost-structure advantages give Brunswick a narrow moat, the firm seems to be entering a cyclical downturn.

Brunswick is a boating behemoth and a leader in marine-related and other recreational markets. Its marine sales eclipse those of its nearest competitor by 5 times, commanding more than 30% market share in boats and more than 50% in engines. Its fitness, bowling, and billiard brands maintain similarly strong positions in their respective markets.

Though the product portfolio has been assembled mostly through acquisitions, the company has elevated its prospects by modernizing manufacturing processes and improving the scale of its production. It is reducing costs by sourcing materials globally and by moving manufacturing overseas for some of its engines and boats. New closed-mold technology lowers emissions from fiberglass hull production and allows the company to scale its capacity in a way that few competitors can afford to replicate. Related efforts to rein in costs by standardizing parts across product lines will pay off over a longer time horizon, since model design turnover occurs every four years.

Although Brunswick is a leader in its markets, it seems to be entering a cyclical downturn. Recently, boat and engine sales have declined markedly, and margins are beginning to suffer as the company is unable to scale back its fixed costs. Some of the weakness in marine engines can be attributed to the tough comparisons with strong sales of higher-emission engines before the government-mandated transition to less-profitable, low-emission versions in 2006.

However, dealer inventory levels remain high in both engines and boats, and the firm is cutting production 20% to maintain low channel inventories toward the end of the model year. The decline in sales has hit most of its boating products, including the highly profitable cruiser segment. The high-end Hatteras and Meridian yachts have yet to see demand slow, but strength in these lower-volume and -margin boats cannot offset the weakness in other categories. Exacerbating Brunswick's ability to sell new boats, used-boat sales continue to make up a growing percentage of total boat sales, from around 50% in the 1970s to above 60% today.

Despite these concerns, Brunswick's long-term prospects are good, considering the depth and breadth of its product offering and management's fiscal discipline.

Data as of 12-29-06

BT Group PLC ADR BT

	Rating	Fair Value	Last Close	Consider Buy	Consider Sell	Yield %
	★★★	$59.00	$59.89	$45.50	$73.90	3.99

Company Profile

BT Group, formerly known as British Telecom, is the largest supplier of fixed-line phone services in Britain. BT is the incumbent and former government-owned monopoly. It controls about 60% of retail voice minutes and 40% of business voice minutes. Sales are split 36% global services, 40% retail, and 24% wholesale, including only external sales from Openreach. "New wave" products now account for 35% of sales. BT is the largest supplier of high-speed Internet lines, including lines it wholesales.

Management
Stewardship Grade [B]

Management has almost completely turned over from the group that led the failed worldwide expansion. Chairman Christopher Bland, CEO Ben Verwaayen, and CFO Hanif Lalani are all new. Former CFO Ian Livingston is now running the retail division. Bland instigated the restructuring, but the rest of the management team seems very much behind him. Bland and Verwaayen have been involved with turnarounds in the past. The board has more independent directors than executive directors. The nonexecutive directors bring a good diversity of backgrounds. One nice thing with many of BT's incentive programs is that a significant portion vests only if BT's total return is in the top quarter of returns compared with a group of European telecom operators. Bland bought 1 million pounds worth of BT stock with his own money when he was named chairman, something we definitely like. For the most part, we think BT's management is quite good; it has put forth a viable strategy and has been a good steward of shareholders' capital. The main area that hurts the firm's stewardship grade is the regular use of write-offs and pro forma numbers that distort comparisons from one year to the next. We would also like to see a portion of the nonexecutive directors' pay come in the form of BT shares.

81 Newgate Street www.btplc.com
London, United Kingdom EC1A 7AJ

Growth [NA]	2003	2004	2005	2006
Revenue %	-8.9	-1.1	-0.5	5.9
Earnings/Share %	160.0	-47.8	30.7	-15.0
Book Value/Share %	NMF	18.6	-98.5	EUB
Dividends/Share %	—	—	—	—

Profitability [NA]	2004	2005	2006	TTM
Return on Assets %	4.9	6.5	6.4	6.4
Oper Cash Flow $Mil	7,635	10,281	9,669	9,669
- Cap Spending $Mil	4,559	5,637	5,277	5,277
= Free Cash Flow $Mil	3,075	4,645	4,392	4,392

Financial Health [NA]	2004	2005	2006	03-31-06
Long-term Debt $Mil	22,593	14,611	14,026	14,026
Total Equity $Mil	5,575	85	2,728	2,728
Debt/Equity Ratio	4.1	172.1	5.1	5.1

Industry	Business Risk	Moat Size	Investment Style	Sector
Telecom Svcs.	Average	Narrow	Large Value	Telecommunication

Competition

	Market Cap $Mil	12 Mo Trailing Sales $Mil	Price/Cash Flow	Return On Assets %	Debt/Equity	Total Return % 1 Yr	3 Yr
BT Group PLC ADR	51,717	35,025	5.3	6.4	5.1	63.6	26.1
France Telecom SA ADR	72,105	61,407	4.3	6.1	1.5	17.7	1.6
NTL	8,234	4,684	6.2	-7.6	1.8	6.1	—

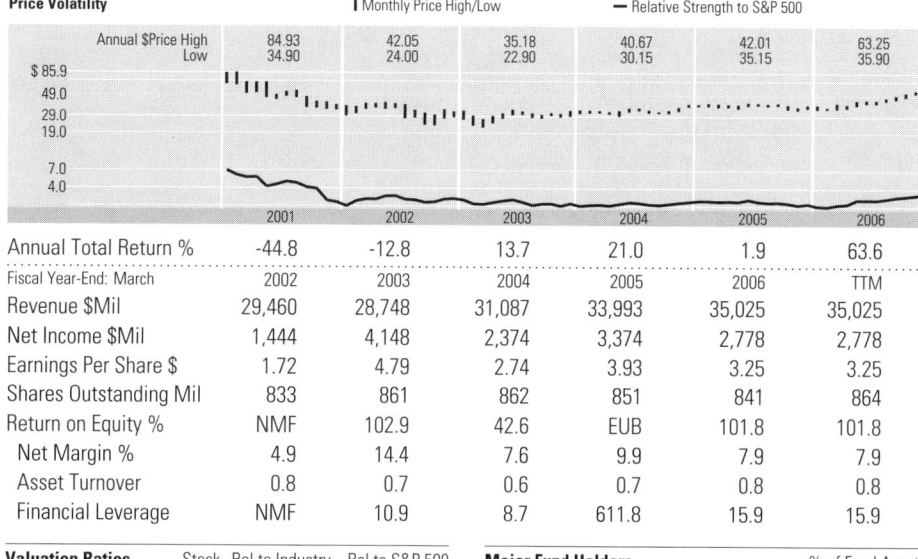

Price Volatility — Monthly Price High/Low — Relative Strength to S&P 500

Annual $Price High / Low	84.93 / 34.90	42.05 / 24.00	35.18 / 22.90	40.67 / 30.15	42.01 / 35.15	63.25 / 35.90
	2001	2002	2003	2004	2005	2006
Annual Total Return %	-44.8	-12.8	13.7	21.0	1.9	63.6

Fiscal Year-End: March	2002	2003	2004	2005	2006	TTM
Revenue $Mil	29,460	28,748	31,087	33,993	35,025	35,025
Net Income $Mil	1,444	4,148	2,374	3,374	2,778	2,778
Earnings Per Share $	1.72	4.79	2.74	3.93	3.25	3.25
Shares Outstanding Mil	833	861	862	851	841	864
Return on Equity %	NMF	102.9	42.6	EUB	101.8	101.8
Net Margin %	4.9	14.4	7.6	9.9	7.9	7.9
Asset Turnover	0.8	0.7	0.6	0.7	0.8	0.8
Financial Leverage	NMF	10.9	8.7	611.8	15.9	15.9

Valuation Ratios	Stock	Rel to Industry	Rel to S&P 500
Price/Earnings	18.4	1.0	0.9
Price/Book	19.0	4.4	4.6
Price/Sales	1.5	0.7	0.5
Price/Cash Flow	5.3	0.6	0.4

Major Fund Holders	% of Fund Assets
ICON Telecommunications & Utilities	3.18
Phoenix Global Utilities A	2.05
Green Century Balanced	1.93
Saratoga International Equity I	1.75

Thesis By Allan C. Nichols, CFA, 11-29-06   Stock Price as of Analysis: $54.69

Recently, BT Group has been ringing up success, with all its major divisions performing well. The regulatory environment in the U.K. has also improved, reducing risks to the firm. With better visibility and higher returns on investment--as it emphasizes the enterprise business and cost-cutting--we now think BT deserves a narrow moat.

The firm's star performers have been its "new wave" businesses, which include networked information technology services, high-speed Internet access, and mobility. These now account for 35% of revenues. The firm has 3 million of its own Internet access customers and another 6.3 million wholesale customers. BT has one of the most extensive enterprise networks in the world, reaching 128 countries. This has allowed it to expand from traditional phone services for large corporations into a systems integrator role. The firm has averaged about 8 billion pounds ($15.2 billion) in new contract wins over each of the last three years. These are long-term contracts, which become more profitable over time. The early contracts are on the upswing to improved profitability, which should lead to further margin expansion and return on investment improvements.

The other area doing well is the wholesale business. It is benefiting from an increased number of competitors using BT's lines to market their own communication services, especially high-speed Internet access. While these new entrants benefit the wholesale side, they increase competition for BT's retail side. However, we think BT has executed well against this increased competition and expect other operators to beat each other up fighting for Internet access customers more than hurting BT.

Wholesale and new wave services have allowed BT to generate sales increases despite the continued decline in the traditional phone business. The fixed-line phone business continues to struggle with new entrants and mobile substitution. However, most of the subscribers the firm is losing are lower-margin customers. BT has been signing its higher-usage customers to bundles of services. In addition, most of the competition has occurred in populated areas, leaving about 40% of the country with minimal competition.

BT has also been busy cutting costs. It is building one of the most advanced Internet Protocol networks in the world, which will allow services to be offered at lower costs. It has also streamlined the number of suppliers allowing better purchasing power and shrinking its own headcount.

Data as of 12-29-06

Buckeye Partners LP BPL

	Rating	Fair Value	Last Close	Consider Buy	Consider Sell	Yield %
	★★★	$51.00	$46.48	$43.50	$67.00	6.51

Company Profile
Buckeye Partners owns and operate refined petroleum pipelines and storage terminals in the United States. Most of the company's assets are found in the Northeast and Midwest, although it also operates terminals and some smaller pipelines in the Southeast and West. Buckeye's pipelines transport a variety of refined petroleum products connecting refineries, storage facilities, other companies' pipelines, and airports.

Industry	Business Risk	Moat Size	Investment Style	Sector
Pipelines	Below Avg	Wide	Small Value	Energy

Competition

	Market Cap $Mil	12 Mo Trailing Sales $Mil	Price/Cash Flow	Return On Assets %	Debt/ Equity	Total Return% 1 Yr	3 Yr
Buckeye Partners LP	1,833	442	12.7	5.2	1.2	17.9	7.3
Kinder Morgan Energy Part	7,797	9,919	6.2	2.7	1.2	7.3	6.8
TEPPCO Partners	3,052	10,039	7.0	3.6	1.0	24.3	7.2

Price Volatility | Monthly Price High/Low   — Relative Strength to S&P 500

Annual $Price High Low	38.10 28.38	40.20 26.50	45.55 33.60	46.00 35.60	50.80 40.93	46.99 40.40
	2001	2002	2003	2004	2005	2006
Annual Total Return %	39.4	9.7	26.1	-0.5	6.1	17.9
Fiscal Year-End: December	2001	2002	2003	2004	2005	TTM
Revenue $Mil	232	247	273	324	408	442
Net Income $Mil	69	71	30	82	99	101
Earnings Per Share $	2.55	2.64	1.05	2.75	2.69	2.61
Shares Outstanding Mil	27	27	28	30	37	39
Return on Equity %	19.7	20.1	8.0	13.6	13.1	12.6
Net Margin %	29.6	28.8	11.0	25.4	24.3	22.9
Asset Turnover	0.3	0.3	0.3	0.2	0.2	0.2
Financial Leverage	2.3	2.4	2.5	2.5	2.4	2.4

Management   Stewardship Grade [C]

Buckeye is organized as a master limited partnership, with its limited partner units traded on the New York Stock Exchange. The partnership underwent a major management change in March 2004 when the general partner, formerly owned by a company controlled by Buckeye's senior management, was sold to the Carlyle/Riverstone Global Energy and Power Fund II. Concurrent with the sale, four key executives and board members left the firm. William Shea Jr. was retained as CEO and given the additional title of chairman of the board of the general partner. While these changes are significant, we think Shea's retention has kept Buckeye's strategy from straying off course. We have some concerns that the new general partner might push for faster growth than the partnership can handle, but that hasn't happened so far. Buckeye, like most other MLPs we cover, earns a "C" Stewardship Grade. The biggest mark against Buckeye is that the MLP form of business does not allow limited partners to have much say in the management of the partnership. Buckeye also gets dinged for having Shea serve as both CEO and chairman and for the relatively small portion of executive and director compensation paid in partnership units.

Valuation Ratios	Stock	Rel to Industry	Rel to S&P 500
Price/Earnings	17.8	0.6	0.9
Price/Book	2.3	0.9	0.6
Price/Sales	4.1	1.9	1.4
Price/Cash Flow	12.7	1.3	0.9

Major Fund Holders   % of Fund Assets

Thesis By Michael Cumming, CFA, 12-20-06 Stock Price as of Analysis: $46.02

A series of acquisitions doubled Buckeye Partners' asset base over the past two years. An expanded network enhances Buckeye's already-wide moat, in our view.

Buckeye sticks to what it knows best--refined-products pipelines and storage terminals--and most of its pipeline acquisitions have been connected to its network, creating the greatest possible synergies. Most of Buckeye's refined-products pipelines are in competitive markets and are allowed to charge market-based rates rather than the inflation-based, regulated rates charged by most other pipelines. Pipeline operators favor market-based rates because they generally rise when regulated rates rise and stay steady when regulated rates fall.

We give Buckeye our wide economic moat rating, which is typical of most pipeline companies we follow. These firms enjoy significant barriers to entry, mainly because of regulatory restrictions but also because of the high cost of building new pipelines. Other forms of transportation such as trucks simply can't compete with pipelines and their low-cost structure. Buckeye earns our below-average-risk rating largely because of the consistent cash flows the company has produced year after year.

Much of Buckeye's growth has come through acquisitions. In 2004, the company bought pipeline and terminal assets from Royal Dutch Shell. In 2005, Buckeye turned around and bought similar assets from ExxonMobil. The company has completed several smaller deals for pipelines and terminals in 2006. We like these deals for several reasons. Most of the acquired assets are attached to Buckeye's legacy network, making the new assets a natural extension of the company's operations. Both Shell and Exxon formerly used these assets for their own operations. The Shell pipelines had spare capacity that Buckeye has opened to other customers, and Buckeye can use spare capacity on its own system to relieve the overflow from the Exxon pipelines. Most important, these acquisitions enabled the company to increase cash distributions to unitholders, which now stand at $3.05 per unit annually. We think more increases are likely as the new assets are fully integrated into Buckeye's system. Our one concern is the relatively high price paid for these assets. Buckeye will have to work hard to fill excess capacity in these pipes and tanks in order to make these deals pay off.

5002 Buckeye Road   www.buckeye.com
Emmaus, PA 18049

Growth [D+]	2002	2003	2004	2005
Revenue %	6.4	10.4	18.5	26.2
Earnings/Share %	3.5	-60.2	161.9	-2.2
Book Value/Share %	1.2	0.3	53.0	1.7
Dividends/Share %	2.0	1.5	3.9	7.1

Profitability [NA]	2003	2004	2005	TTM
Return on Assets %	3.2	5.4	5.5	5.2
Oper Cash Flow $Mil	109	100	142	144
- Cap Spending $Mil	42	73	78	88
= Free Cash Flow $Mil	67	27	65	56

Financial Health [C+]	2003	2004	2005	09-30-06
Long-term Debt $Mil	448	797	899	981
Total Equity $Mil	375	603	756	807
Debt/Equity Ratio	1.2	1.3	1.2	1.2

Data as of 12-29-06

Burlington Northern Santa Fe BNI

Rating	Fair Value	Last Close	Consider Buy	Consider Sell	Yield %
★★★	$82.00	$73.81	$63.20	$102.70	1.22

Industry	Business Risk	Moat Size	Investment Style	Sector
Land Transport	Average	None	Large Core	Business Services

Company Profile
Based in Fort Worth, Texas, Burlington Northern Santa Fe is the second-largest North American railroad, behind Union Pacific, operating a railroad system consisting of 32,000 route miles of track in the western two thirds of the country. The firm is the result of the 1995 merger of Burlington Northern and Santa Fe Pacific. It generates revenue by moving freight such as consumer products, industrial products, coal, and agricultural products throughout its rail network.

Management   Stewardship Grade [B]
Chairman, president, and CEO Matthew Rose, 46, has been in charge at BNSF since late 2000. We think highly of his leadership capabilities and the team he has assembled. After a few lean years, he led the firm in 2004 and 2005 through some of its most substantial internal growth in volume and pricing in years. Rose certainly got paid for the improvement: In 2004, his base salary and bonus totaled $1.2 million, and he also received $9.1 million in time-based restricted stock. In 2005, he received a larger bonus and earned about $9 million through the exercise of stock options. We are not overly troubled by these amounts, though, given our increasing comfort with the sustainability of many of the improvements that have taken place under his watch. From a corporate-governance standpoint, we like the firm's policy of re-electing the full board of directors every year and its elimination of its poison pill, but we do not like the charter and bylaw provisions limiting shareholders' ability to act by written consent or call a special meeting. We also do not agree with the firm's decisions to bestow the chairman and CEO roles on one person, allow blank-check preferred stock, and compensate directors almost entirely in cash.

2650 Lou Menk Drive   www.bnsf.com
Fort Worth, TX 76131-2830

Growth [B]	2002	2003	2004	2005
Revenue %	-2.5	4.8	16.3	18.6
Earnings/Share %	7.0	9.5	-4.1	91.0
Book Value/Share %	4.0	9.2	8.4	0.7
Dividends/Share %	-2.0	12.5	18.5	15.6

Profitability [B]	2003	2004	2005	TTM
Return on Assets %	3.0	2.7	5.1	5.7
Oper Cash Flow $Mil	2,285	2,377	2,609	2,824
- Cap Spending $Mil	1,726	1,527	1,750	2,054
= Free Cash Flow $Mil	559	850	859	770

Financial Health [C+]	2003	2004	2005	09-30-06
Long-term Debt $Mil	6,440	6,051	6,698	6,611
Total Equity $Mil	8,495	9,311	9,508	10,129
Debt/Equity Ratio	0.8	0.7	0.7	0.7

Competition

	Market Cap $Mil	12 Mo Trailing Sales $Mil	Price/Cash Flow	Return On Assets%	Debt/ Equity	Total Return% 1 Yr	3 Yr
Burlington Northern Santa Fe	26,513	14,653	9.4	5.7	0.7	5.5	34.1
Union Pacific	24,820	15,237	8.6	3.9	0.5	15.9	11.9
Canadian National Railway	23,096	5,983	10.3	6.8	0.5	9.0	28.0

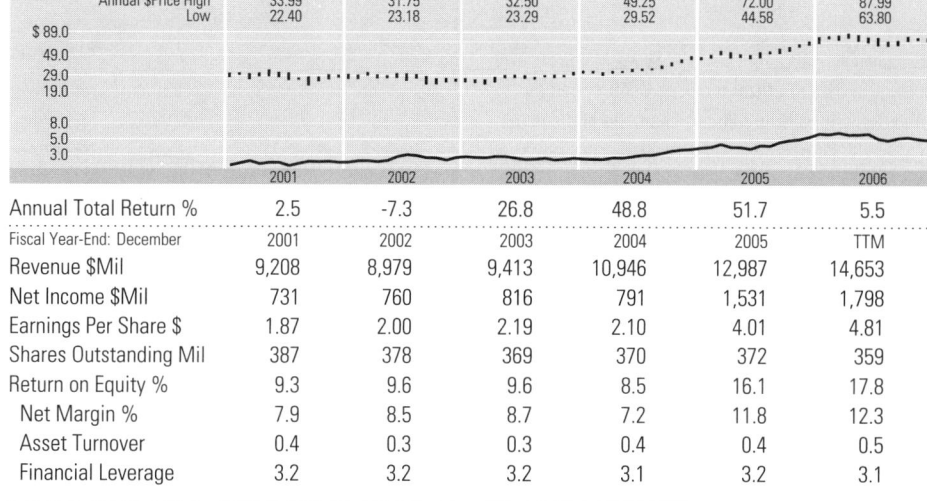

	2001	2002	2003	2004	2005	2006
Annual $Price High	33.99	31.75	32.50	49.25	72.00	87.99
Low	22.40	23.18	23.29	29.52	44.58	63.80
Annual Total Return %	2.5	-7.3	26.8	48.8	51.7	5.5

Fiscal Year-End: December	2001	2002	2003	2004	2005	TTM
Revenue $Mil	9,208	8,979	9,413	10,946	12,987	14,653
Net Income $Mil	731	760	816	791	1,531	1,798
Earnings Per Share $	1.87	2.00	2.19	2.10	4.01	4.81
Shares Outstanding Mil	387	378	369	370	372	359
Return on Equity %	9.3	9.6	9.6	8.5	16.1	17.8
Net Margin %	7.9	8.5	8.7	7.2	11.8	12.3
Asset Turnover	0.4	0.3	0.3	0.4	0.4	0.5
Financial Leverage	3.2	3.2	3.2	3.1	3.2	3.1

Valuation Ratios	Stock	Rel to Industry	Rel to S&P 500
Price/Earnings	15.3	0.9	0.7
Price/Book	2.6	1.1	0.6
Price/Sales	1.8	0.8	0.6
Price/Cash Flow	9.4	0.9	0.6

Major Fund Holders	% of Fund Assets
ING Corporate Leaders Trust B	11.62
Fidelity Select Transportation	6.24
Rydex Transportation Inv	6.17
Marsico Focus	4.48

Thesis By Peter Smith, 11-20-06 Stock Price as of Analysis: $76.65

Burlington Northern Santa Fe is one of the better-operating North American railroads, though not the best. However, its proportion of business from coal, agricultural products, and intermodal--three freight groups that we expect to continue to perform well in an economic downturn--is higher than that of any of its peers, making it one of the railroads we'd like to own over the long haul.

Operating a railroad is not easy, partially because each firm is responsible for its own track. Though that acts as a stellar barrier to entry, railroads spend the highest percentage of sales on capital expenditures of any major North American industry--and almost all of it is for rail maintenance. BNSF is no exception, recently spending about 13%-14% of revenue per year for rail upkeep, and we think this number is likely to average 15% over the long term. Railroads also face the challenge of running a smooth, uncongested network. BNSF hasn't experienced as many problems in this regard as its main competitor, Union Pacific, but its service has been under some pressure lately because of the higher volume moving through its network.

Some rails have fared better than others in the face of these challenges. BNSF has been a solid performer in the past few years, but not the strongest. After some lean years earlier this decade, the firm has made great strides in sales growth and cost reduction. Its operating ratio (expenses as a percentage of revenue) fell below 80% in 2005, a level not reached since 2000. While impressive, the firm is still well behind the most efficient railroad, Canadian National, and a bit behind its Eastern rival, Norfolk Southern.

Growth prospects at BNSF look promising. The coal business should benefit from increasing demand as power plants, seeking an alternative to pricey natural gas, turn to the cheap, low-sulfur coal that BNSF (and Union Pacific) haul. The agricultural division is likely to continue to prosper from strong export demand, and container ships are expected to continue pouring into the Los Angeles/Long Beach port, bolstering BNSF's formidable intermodal franchise. Even if the economy dips in the next few years, these businesses should remain strong.

To retain business from these opportunities, BNSF needs to become more efficient, particularly as it raises prices in the current period of tight freight capacity and as Union Pacific restores fluidity to its network. If the company can match its growth with profitability improvements, then it should be a solid long-term investment.

Data as of 12-29-06

Cadbury Schweppes PLC ADR CSG

	Rating	Fair Value	Last Close	Consider Buy	Consider Sell	Yield %
	★★★★	$49.00	$42.93	$41.80	$64.30	2.19

Company Profile

Cadbury Schweppes manufactures, markets, and distributes confectionery products around the world and nonalcoholic beverages in North America. Its brands include Cadbury, Trebor, Halls, Trident, Dentyne, Hollywood, Bassett's, Dr Pepper, 7 UP, and Snapple. The company has a number-one worldwide position in total confectionery and is number two in chewing gum.

Management Stewardship Grade [NA]

Current CEO Todd Stitzer replaced Cadbury veteran John Sutherland, who remains chairman of the board, in May 2003. Stitzer was previously the company's chief strategy officer and has been with the company for more than 20 years. Stitzer's 2005 base salary of 783,000 pounds (or $1.4 million) and total compensation of 2.4 million pounds ($4.3 million) doesn't appear out of line to us. Stitzer also owns plenty of common stock, and we approve of Cadbury's policy requiring executives to hold 4 times their base salary in company stock. Two thirds of executive pay is variable and linked to company performance. Most of the firm's new annual goals, introduced in October 2006, are not quantified. The only specific target, annual sales growth of 3%-5%, has been set artificially low so it will be easily achieved, or beaten, in most years. In our view, management should be held to a higher standard if it plans to spend 5%-5.5% of sales per year on capital expenditures. We think directors should stand for election annually instead of every three years.

25 Berkeley Square   www.cadburyschweppes.com
London, United Kingdom W1J 6HB

Growth [NA]	2002	2003	2004	2005	
Revenue %	6.8	21.6	-5.5	7.0	
Earnings/Share %	0.7	-33.5	42.0	43.6	
Book Value/Share %	2.9	-8.3	-27.7	33.6	
Dividends/Share %	—	—	—	—	

Profitability [NA]	2003	2004	2005	TTM
Return on Assets %	3.3	5.2	7.5	7.5
Oper Cash Flow $Mil	1,164	1,738	1,990	1,990
- Cap Spending $Mil	466	518	544	544
= Free Cash Flow $Mil	698	1,220	1,446	1,446

Financial Health [NA]	2003	2004	2005	12-31-05
Long-term Debt $Mil	6,604	6,896	5,284	5,284
Total Equity $Mil	5,398	4,423	5,233	5,233
Debt/Equity Ratio	1.2	1.6	1.0	1.0

	Industry	Business Risk	Moat Size	Investment Style	Sector
	Food Mfg.	Below Avg	Wide	Large Value	Consumer Goods

Competition

	Market Cap $Mil	12 Mo Trailing Sales $Mil	Price/Cash Flow	Return On Assets%	Debt/ Equity	Total Return% 1 Yr	3 Yr
Cadbury Schweppes PLC ADR	22,367	11,879	11.2	7.5	1.0	14.7	15.2
Nestle SA ADR	138,417	73,660	16.8	8.8	—	20.9	14.7
Coca-Cola	113,088	23,707	19.6	16.8	0.1	23.1	1.1

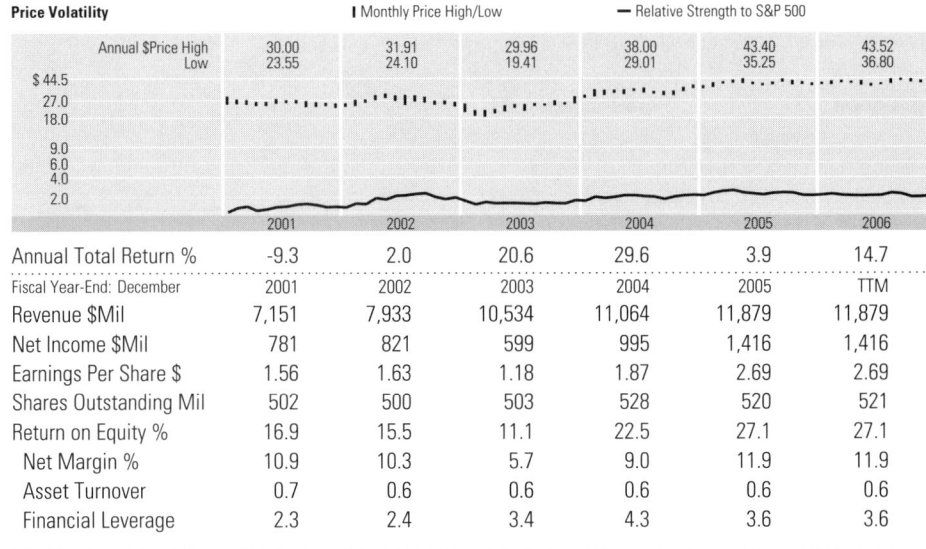

	2001	2002	2003	2004	2005	2006
Annual Total Return %	-9.3	2.0	20.6	29.6	3.9	14.7

Fiscal Year-End: December	2001	2002	2003	2004	2005	TTM
Revenue $Mil	7,151	7,933	10,534	11,064	11,879	11,879
Net Income $Mil	781	821	599	995	1,416	1,416
Earnings Per Share $	1.56	1.63	1.18	1.87	2.69	2.69
Shares Outstanding Mil	502	500	503	528	520	521
Return on Equity %	16.9	15.5	11.1	22.5	27.1	27.1
Net Margin %	10.9	10.3	5.7	9.0	11.9	11.9
Asset Turnover	0.7	0.6	0.6	0.6	0.6	0.6
Financial Leverage	2.3	2.4	3.4	4.3	3.6	3.6

Valuation Ratios	Stock	Rel to Industry	Rel to S&P 500
Price/Earnings	17.6	0.8	0.9
Price/Book	4.3	1.0	1.0
Price/Sales	1.9	1.1	0.7
Price/Cash Flow	11.2	0.7	0.8

Major Fund Holders	% of Fund Assets
Oak Value	5.04
BBH Core Select N	4.07
Phoenix Focused Value A	3.62
FMI Large Cap	3.32

Thesis By Mitchell P. Corwin, CFA, CPA, 11-07-06 Stock Price as of Analysis: $39.96

With 50 transactions since the mid-1980s and 21 transactions from 2000 to 2003, Cadbury Schweppes today reigns as the largest worldwide confectionery company, and the only firm that is a significant player in all three confectionery segments: chocolate, sugar, and gum. This strong platform garners the company a wide economic moat despite a less advantaged regional beverages business.

Having a worldwide leadership position in confectionery makes Cadbury an attractive long-term investment for two reasons. First, unlike many other packaged food categories, confectionery firms can maintain attractive margins due to a lack of considerable private-label penetration, rational competition among a few firms in most markets, and a good number of impulse-driven sales at checkout counters. Second, the confectionery industry is fragmented, with few worldwide players in any given category. Cadbury can rely on developed markets to generate robust profits that it can invest to grow in India, Brazil, and China.

Cadbury can hit all three confectionery segments today because of the 2003 Adams purchase, which vaulted the firm into second place in worldwide chewing gum behind Wrigley. The firm gained strong brands with economies of scale in developed markets, such as the U.S., and the means to expand chewing gum presence in emerging markets.

Cadbury's track record in growing chewing gum sales since the Adams acquisition gives us comfort that it will be able to exploit the long-term opportunity ahead of it in confectionery. Growth in the four primary Adams brands averaged low double digits in 2004 and 2005, and its share of the U.S. chewing gum market has grown more than 500 basis points. We think this performance has demonstrated Cadbury's ability to innovate to drive sales.

Innovation has also been a strong driver of improving performance in Cadbury's beverages business in the Americas, which account for about half of the firm's annual profits. Despite some fine niche brands, such as Dr Pepper, Cadbury's lack of control over much of its distribution and lack of access to fast-growing categories, such as bottled water, place it at a relative disadvantage to Pepsi and Coke. Cadbury's 7 UP brand has yet to fully recover from being pulled from the Pepsi bottling system in favor of Sierra Mist.

Aside from 7 UP, though, Cadbury's beverages business has performed well, and the strong cash flow thrown off by beverages goes a long way in helping to fund a growing confectionery business.

Data as of 12-29-06

Calamos Asset Management A CLMS

	Rating	Fair Value	Last Close	Consider Buy	Consider Sell	Yield %
	★★★	$26.00	$26.83	$20.00	$32.60	1.34

Company Profile

Calamos Investments became a public company in 2004, but its roots go back to 1977, when John Calamos founded the firm specializing in convertible securities. Calamos now manages money for individuals and institutions and primarily distributes its products through intermediaries. The firm manages convertible securities, equities, bonds, and alternative investments in mutual funds and separate accounts.

Management   Stewardship Grade [D]

Chairman and CEO John Calamos Sr. founded his eponymous firm in 1977 and is still in charge. After the IPO, Calamos brought in professional managers to take care of company operations, but John Calamos still guides the firm's direction and serves as co-chief investment officer with his nephew, Nick Calamos. Though Calamos Investments is now public, it resembles a private company in many respects, and it will have to do a better job of looking out for the interests of minority shareholders to earn higher than a "D" Stewardship Grade. The Calamos family owns 77% of the company, so it already calls the shots. However, the family also owns all the Class B shares, which have 10 times the voting rights of the Class A shares that are available to the public. This gives the Calamos family 97% voting control and effectively strips minority shareholders of any voting power.

Family control is also evident in several related-party transactions that we frown upon. Calamos Investments leases its headquarters building and its airplane from businesses privately owned by the Calamos family. These types of arrangements could be abused since John Calamos is essentially leasing from himself (and his relatives) at whatever rate he chooses.

2020 Calamos Court   www.calamos.com
Naperville, IL 60563

Growth [A]	2002	2003	2004	2005
Revenue %	85.5	84.9	92.2	33.8
Earnings/Share %	NMF	NMF	NMF	NMF
Book Value/Share %	—	—	—	NMF
Dividends/Share %	NMF	NMF	NMF	NMF

Profitability [A-]	2003	2004	2005	TTM
Return on Assets %	64.4	20.6	4.4	4.4
Oper Cash Flow $Mil	37	133	224	—
- Cap Spending $Mil	7	10	41	—
= Free Cash Flow $Mil	—	—	—	—

Financial Health [NA]	2003	2004	2005	09-30-06
Long-term Debt $Mil	—	—	—	—
Total Equity $Mil	46	158	186	207
Debt/Equity Ratio	—	—	—	—

Industry	Business Risk	Moat Size	Investment Style	Sector
Money Mgmt.	Average	Wide	Small Core	Financial Services

Competition

	Market Cap $Mil	12 Mo Trailing Sales $Mil	Price/Cash Flow	Return On Assets %	Debt/ Equity	Total Return % 1 Yr	3 Yr
Calamos Asset Management A	621	477	—	4.4	—	-13.7	—
Legg Mason	12,491	3,810	—	13.0	—	-20.0	23.0
T Rowe Price Group	11,539	1,729	—	18.8	—	23.3	23.7

Price Volatility

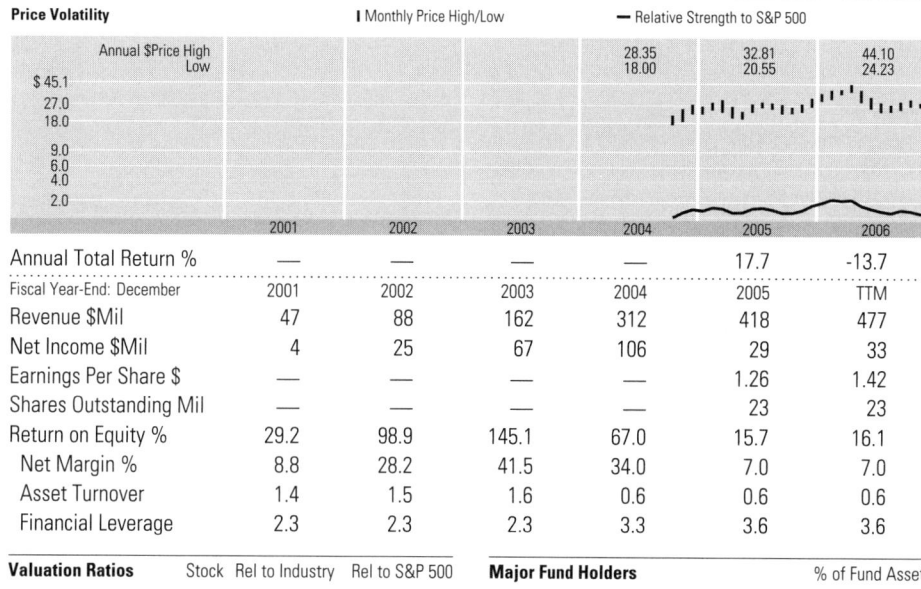

Annual Total Return %	—	—	—	—	17.7	-13.7
Fiscal Year-End: December	2001	2002	2003	2004	2005	TTM
Revenue $Mil	47	88	162	312	418	477
Net Income $Mil	4	25	67	106	29	33
Earnings Per Share $	—	—	—	—	1.26	1.42
Shares Outstanding Mil	—	—	—	—	23	23
Return on Equity %	29.2	98.9	145.1	67.0	15.7	16.1
Net Margin %	8.8	28.2	41.5	34.0	7.0	7.0
Asset Turnover	1.4	1.5	1.6	0.6	0.6	0.6
Financial Leverage	2.3	2.3	2.3	3.3	3.6	3.6

Valuation Ratios	Stock	Rel to Industry	Rel to S&P 500
Price/Earnings	18.9	0.6	0.9
Price/Book	3.0	0.7	0.7
Price/Sales	1.3	0.2	0.4
Price/Cash Flow	—	—	—

Major Fund Holders	% of Fund Assets
Morgan Stanley Financial Services B	3.30
Julius Baer U.S. Smallcap I	2.16
Morgan Stanley Inst Mid Cap Growth	2.03
Morgan Stanley Developing Gr Secs B	2.02

Thesis By Jeffrey Ptak, CPA, CFA, 12-12-06 Stock Price as of Analysis: $27.43

A recognizable brand, distribution heft, and scalable investment model earn Calamos Asset Management a wide moat.

In fairly short order, Calamos has evolved from a convertible-bond investing outpost to a roughly $45 billion complex offering a diversified suite of strategies. To broaden its footprint, the firm has leveraged a number of competitive advantages to the hilt, trenching a wide moat in the process.

Calamos has carved out an enviable niche as a growth and convertible-bond specialist par excellence thanks to the standout performance of its flagship Calamos Growth and Calamos Growth & Income funds. These funds, which recently accounted for more than half of the firm's assets under management, have helped to mold the company's identity and engender loyalty among advisors. Thus, the Calamos name, while once relatively obscure, now registers in the marketplace.

That prominence has paved the way to fruitful marketing alliances. For instance, Calamos entered a pact with Swiss bank Union Bancaire Privee (UBP) in 2006 under which UBP will distribute a Calamos-branded product in Europe. That deal builds on Calamos' strength in the U.S., where it has cultivated profitable relationships with national broker-dealers that act as vital cogs in the distribution chain. Those alliances, in turn, should facilitate Calamos' growth ahead.

While it's unrealistic to expect Calamos to sustain its meteoric recent growth (and, in fact, the company has seen sales decelerate thus far in 2006), its versatile business model should allow it to pivot smoothly into other areas, such as the institutional market as well as the alternative-investments arena. While such shifts have been tough for other retail-focused managers to pull off in the past, Calamos' investment strategy is unusual in its emphasis on risk management, with much of the underlying analytical work performed by computer models. That disciplined, quantitatively oriented ethos is likely to resonate with a risk-conscious clientele like pension funds.

That approach is also eminently scalable, as Calamos need not add scores of analysts to support the new strategies it's seeding. Instead, it can tap into processes and technology already in place, a tack that resembles the approach Calamos has taken when launching retail strategies in the past. The upshot is that Calamos should continue to be able to post operating margins ranging from 45% to 50%.

Data as of 12-29-06

Campbell Soup CPB

	Rating	Fair Value	Last Close	Consider Buy	Consider Sell	Yield %
	★★★	$37.00	$38.89	$31.50	$48.60	1.95

Company Profile

Campbell Soup is the largest seller of soups in the world and a leading producer of juices, sauces, cookies, crackers, salty snacks, and confectionery products. The company's soups are sold under the Campbell's brand globally, as well as under the Erasco and Liebig brands in Europe. Its other key products include Pepperidge Farm cookies and crackers, V8 juice beverages, Pace Mexican sauces, Prego pasta sauces, Arnott's biscuits and salty snacks, and Godiva chocolates.

Management — Stewardship Grade [B]

Dorrance family members, who are direct descendants of John Dorrance (the man who invented the process for turning wet soup into condensed soup), own more than 40% of Campbell Soup, but have left management of the firm to professionals. While the family and its foundation hold 5 of the 16 seats available on the company's board of directors, they have usually acted in the best interest of shareholders, even willing to approve a 30% cut in the dividend in 2001 on the belief that the move was in the long-term interest of the company and investors. Doug Conant, who had the difficult task of persuading the family and minority shareholders that the cut was necessary to fund capital expenditures and expand the marketing budget, has been president and CEO since January 2001. He has more than 25 years of experience in packaged foods, working for competitors like General Mills, Kraft, and Nabisco. While Conant earned less in compensation in fiscal 2006 than he has in prior years, his salary and bonus was paid completely in cash, with performance-driven pay making up a smaller portion of the mix. Benchmarks for management are also more short-term-oriented than we like to see, with sales and earnings growth, market share gains, and total stock return being key determinants.

1 Campbell Place
Camden, NJ 08103-1799
www.campbellsoup.com

Growth [C]	2003	2004	2005	2006
Revenue %	8.9	6.5	-0.5	3.8
Earnings/Share %	13.3	8.3	8.9	8.2
Book Value/Share %	NMF	124.9	44.8	39.0
Dividends/Share %	0.0	0.0	7.9	5.9

Profitability [A]	2004	2005	2006	TTM
Return on Assets %	9.7	10.4	9.7	10.7
Oper Cash Flow $Mil	744	990	1,226	1,025
- Cap Spending $Mil	288	332	309	317
= Free Cash Flow $Mil	456	658	917	708

Financial Health [A-]	2004	2005	2006	10-31-06
Long-term Debt $Mil	2,543	2,542	2,116	2,116
Total Equity $Mil	874	1,270	1,768	1,268
Debt/Equity Ratio	2.9	2.0	1.2	1.7

Industry	Business Risk	Moat Size	Investment Style	Sector
Food Mfg.	Below Avg	Wide	Large Core	Consumer Goods

Competition	Market Cap $Mil	12 Mo Trailing Sales $Mil	Price/Cash Flow	Return On Assets%	Debt/ Equity	Total Return% 1 Yr	3 Yr
Campbell Soup	15,125	7,494	14.8	10.7	1.7	33.4	16.0
Kraft Foods	58,683	34,648	13.9	5.5	0.2	30.5	6.5
General Mills	19,761	11,821	11.5	5.9	0.5	19.9	11.5

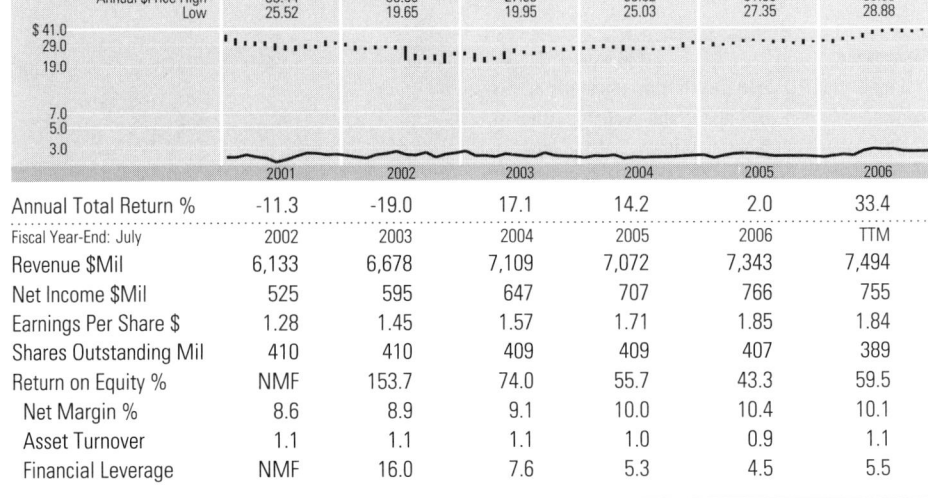

Annual Total Return %	-11.3	-19.0	17.1	14.2	2.0	33.4
Fiscal Year-End: July	2002	2003	2004	2005	2006	TTM
Revenue $Mil	6,133	6,678	7,109	7,072	7,343	7,494
Net Income $Mil	525	595	647	707	766	755
Earnings Per Share $	1.28	1.45	1.57	1.71	1.85	1.84
Shares Outstanding Mil	410	410	409	409	407	389
Return on Equity %	NMF	153.7	74.0	55.7	43.3	59.5
Net Margin %	8.6	8.9	9.1	10.0	10.4	10.1
Asset Turnover	1.1	1.1	1.1	1.0	0.9	1.1
Financial Leverage	NMF	16.0	7.6	5.3	4.5	5.5

Valuation Ratios	Stock	Rel to Industry	Rel to S&P 500
Price/Earnings	21.7	1.0	1.1
Price/Book	11.9	2.6	2.9
Price/Sales	2.0	1.2	0.7
Price/Cash Flow	14.8	1.0	1.0

Major Fund Holders	% of Fund Assets
Cookson Peirce Core Equity	4.46
Schwab Large-Cap Growth Sel	2.76
Westcore Blue Chip	2.62
Berwyn Cornerstone	2.40

Thesis By Greggory Warren, CFA, 11-21-06 Stock Price as of Analysis: $37.68

Campbell Soup is one of only a handful of packaged food firms with a wide moat around its business. The firm has achieved this status through its complete dominance of the soup category in North America. Despite its leading position, Campbell realizes that it needs to continuously invest its profits back into product innovation and marketing in order to stay one step ahead of the competition.

Campbell's wide economic moat is founded on its U.S. soup business, which with its domestic sauce and beverage businesses accounts for 45% of sales and 65% of operating profits. With its namesake brand, Campbell is the largest producer of soups in the United States, outselling the next leading branded soup maker by a margin of nearly 7 to 1. Controlling more than 70% of the $4 billion domestic market for soup has allowed the division to generate 25% operating margins, making it one of the most profitable businesses in the packaged food industry.

Rather than sitting back and collecting profits, Campbell has been on the offensive for much of the past five years. It has committed a significant amount of capital to new products and packaging, in-store displays, and marketing behind its brands. New products and packaging (like the firm's single-serve microwavable soups and low-sodium soups) have driven sales growth higher in the soup aisle, especially with consumers demanding more convenient and healthier meal solutions. Condensed soup sales, which were in decline for much of the past 10 years, increased more than 5% in both 2005 and 2006 following the installation of gravity-fed shelving in most grocery stores in the United States.

While Campbell has also been able to improve the sales of its soups and sauces outside the United States, as well as sales of its Pepperidge Farm and Godiva brands globally, the operating margins for these businesses continue to fall well below those of its domestic soup business. We think this is because Campbell's U.S. soup business is truly unique, with brand equity built up over decades of exposure with American consumers. The disparate brands that make up the remainder of the firm's portfolio lack any real overlap with this business, as well as with one another, limiting Campbell's ability to leverage its core strengths.

Despite these shortcomings, the company's stranglehold on the U.S. soup category and a willingness to spend capital to support its brands make us believe that Campbell Soup will be able to hold its own longer term.

Data as of 12-29-06

Canadian Imperial Bank of Commerce CM

Rating	Fair Value	Last Close	Consider Buy	Consider Sell	Yield %
★★★	$79.00	$84.29	$60.90	$99.00	2.90

Company Profile

CIBC is the fifth-largest bank in Canada, as measured by market capitalization. With more than C$300 billion in assets, the retail banking unit provides deposit and checking services through more than 1,000 branches and issues credit cards and consumer loans. The wealth-management business includes a full-service brokerage and provides trust and asset-management services. CIBC also provides investment banking and corporate banking services.

Management — Stewardship Grade [NA]

CIBC's management and board have come under fire for a perceived lack of foresight. In 2003, the firm settled Securities and Exchange Commission allegations that it helped Enron cook its books; soon afterward, the SEC named the bank as a central facilitator in the mutual fund trading scandal. Gerald McCaughey, who became CEO in August 2005, will try to restore investor confidence by continuing to improve regulatory compliance and corporate governance. McCaughey was appointed president and COO in December 2004 and has been a top executive at CIBC for six years. McCaughey's base salary is set at C$1 million, in line with other Canadian banks. Apart from recent scandals, corporate governance is in fine shape. The chairman and CEO roles are split and option grants are minimal. The board serves nonstaggered one-year terms and is compensated in cash and stock.

Industry	Business Risk	Moat Size	Investment Style	Sector
International Banks	Average	Wide	Large Value	Financial Services

Competition

	Market Cap $Mil	12 Mo Trailing Sales $Mil	Price/Cash Flow	Return On Assets %	Debt/ Equity	Total Return % 1 Yr	3 Yr
Canadian Imperial Bank of Commerce	28,319	9,934	—	0.9	—	32.4	23.2
Royal Bank of Canada	61,039	20,637	—	0.9	—	26.0	29.5
Bank of Nova Scotia	44,330	10,211	—	0.9	—	16.8	24.5

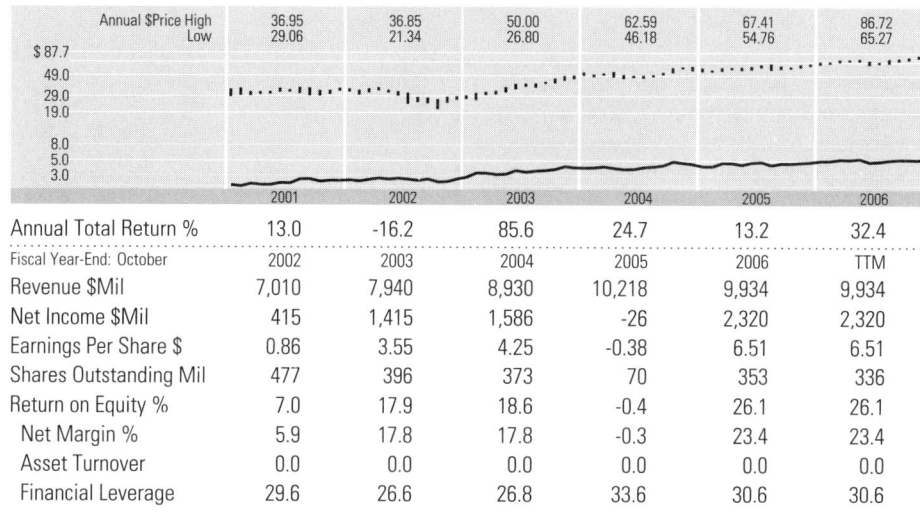

Price Volatility — Monthly Price High/Low — Relative Strength to S&P 500

Annual $Price High/Low	36.95 / 29.06	36.85 / 21.34	50.00 / 26.80	62.59 / 46.18	67.41 / 54.76	86.72 / 65.27
	2001	2002	2003	2004	2005	2006
Annual Total Return %	13.0	-16.2	85.6	24.7	13.2	32.4

Fiscal Year-End: October	2002	2003	2004	2005	2006	TTM
Revenue $Mil	7,010	7,940	8,930	10,218	9,934	9,934
Net Income $Mil	415	1,415	1,586	-26	2,320	2,320
Earnings Per Share $	0.86	3.55	4.25	-0.38	6.51	6.51
Shares Outstanding Mil	477	396	373	70	353	336
Return on Equity %	7.0	17.9	18.6	-0.4	26.1	26.1
Net Margin %	5.9	17.8	17.8	-0.3	23.4	23.4
Asset Turnover	0.0	0.0	0.0	0.0	0.0	0.0
Financial Leverage	29.6	26.6	26.8	33.6	30.6	30.6

Valuation Ratios	Stock	Rel to Industry	Rel to S&P 500
Price/Earnings	12.9	0.7	0.6
Price/Book	3.2	1.2	0.8
Price/Sales	2.9	0.7	1.0
Price/Cash Flow	—	—	—

Major Fund Holders	% of Fund Assets
AXA Enterprise Global Financial Svc A	2.54
Fidelity Canada	2.11
ING Global Equity Dividend A	1.61
Hartford Global Financial Svcs HLS IA	1.46

Commerce Court
Toronto, ON M5L 1A2
www.cibc.com

Growth [NA]	2002	2003	2004	2005
Revenue %	4.8	1.7	5.9	-9.1
Earnings/Share %	283.7	8.1	NMF	NMF
Book Value/Share %	36.9	6.4	331.3	-76.7
Dividends/Share %	—	—	—	NMF

Profitability [NA]	2003	2004	2005	TTM
Return on Assets %	0.7	0.0	0.9	0.9
Oper Cash Flow $Mil	3,576	-89	-6,083	—
- Cap Spending $Mil	178	215	96	—
= Free Cash Flow $Mil	—	—	—	—

Financial Health [NA]	2003	2004	2005	10-31-05
Long-term Debt $Mil	—	—	—	—
Total Equity $Mil	8,522	7,076	8,876	8,876
Debt/Equity Ratio	—	—	—	—

Thesis By Michael Kon, CFA, 12-07-06 Stock Price as of Analysis: $82.56

Although its reputation has gone through the wringer in recent years, Canadian Imperial Bank of Commerce's highly profitable retail business remains intact. We like the recent cleanup the bank has undergone and expect return on equity to quickly bounce back to historical levels.

CIBC offers a variety of financial products and distributes them mainly through a well-entrenched branch and ATM network that spans Canada. The bank also enjoys a benign regulatory environment and is part of an oligopoly that dominates the Canadian banking sector. In our view, this garners the bank a wide economic moat.

We think CIBC stands out for its solid retail banking unit. While peers looked to expand their retail and commercial banking business outside Canada, CIBC refrained from doing any significant acquisitions. Consequently, more than 95% of the bank's retail and commercial banking revenue comes from Canada. This segment has generated a remarkable return on equity of more than 35%, on average, over the past five years. We think this return was due to CIBC's leading position in consumer lending in Canada, which we expect the bank to maintain.

Things have been a bit different at the investment bank. Less than a decade ago, CIBC profited enormously from a buoyant Canadian stock market by establishing a leading position in income trusts--a tax-efficient alternative to publicly traded companies. But then CIBC expanded its deal-making business to the United States. This ended in turmoil, thanks to the Enron and mutual fund trading scandals. In addition to a tarnished reputation and mounting legal bills, CIBC had to book a one-time charge in 2005 of C$2.8 billion, an amount equivalent to 23% of 2004 shareholders' equity.

In response, management was replaced and the bank embarked on a mission to reduce risk by shrinking the merchant banking and large corporate credit portfolios. Nevertheless, CIBC's investment bank remains a bulge-bracket firm in Canada with a dominant market position. We think the lower risk will result in a lower and more stable return on equity for the investment banking unit; the past return of 25%-plus is unlikely to be repeated, and CIBC will probably settle for a stable 15% return for this unit.

We welcome these changes, as we think they should produce consistent profitability that will contribute to, rather than spoil, the excellent performance of the retail banking business.

Data as of 12-29-06

Canadian National Railway CNI

	Rating	Fair Value	Last Close	Consider Buy	Consider Sell	Yield %
	★★★	$45.00	$43.03	$34.70	$56.40	1.35

Company Profile
Based in Montreal, Quebec, Canadian National Railway is the largest railroad in Canada, offering coast-to-coast service. Through its acquisitions of the Wisconsin Central and Illinois Central railroads, the company became a major player in the mid-America market as well. In total, the railroad operates around 19,200 route miles, over which it moves mostly commodities, including industrial products, forest products, grain, coal, sulfur, fertilizer, and automotive products.

Management   Stewardship Grade [A]
Lifelong railroader Hunter Harrison took charge of Canadian National at the start of 2003 and is regarded as one of the best executives in the industry. He joined the firm as COO in 1998 after Canadian National acquired Illinois Central, where Harrison had been CEO. As its CEO, he was responsible for making Illinois Central the most efficient railroad in the business through the framework of a "scheduled" railroad. He brought that ideology to Canadian National, which has helped the firm make huge strides in the last few years. The results don't lie: With Harrison as COO and CEO, Canadian National has handily outperformed its peers in almost every metric, including the all-important operating ratio. We think this will continue to be the case, though competitors may close the gap a bit in the coming years. From a corporate-governance standpoint, the firm is at the top of the heap. As examples, compensation is pretty reasonable (with much of it variable), and directors are re-elected every year. Accordingly, we have given the firm our highest Stewardship Grade.

935 de La Gauchetiere Street West   www.cn.ca
Montreal, QC H3B 2M9

Growth [NA]	2002	2003	2004	2005
Revenue %	8.1	-3.7	11.3	10.6
Earnings/Share %	-24.1	31.9	24.4	27.7
Book Value/Share %	10.3	4.8	10.4	2.8
Dividends/Share %	10.4	16.0	17.1	28.2

Profitability [NA]	2003	2004	2005	TTM
Return on Assets %	4.5	5.2	6.8	6.8
Oper Cash Flow $Mil	1,394	1,647	2,236	2,236
- Cap Spending $Mil	769	2,128	1,159	1,159
= Free Cash Flow $Mil	625	-481	1,077	1,077

Financial Health [NA]	2003	2004	2005	12-31-05
Long-term Debt $Mil	3,236	3,822	3,997	3,997
Total Equity $Mil	6,536	7,737	7,905	7,905
Debt/Equity Ratio	0.5	0.5	0.5	0.5

Industry	Business Risk	Moat Size	Investment Style	Sector
Land Transport	Average	Narrow	Large Growth	Business Services

Competition	Market Cap $Mil	12 Mo Trailing Sales $Mil	Price/Cash Flow	Return On Assets%	Debt/Equity	Total Return% 1 Yr	3 Yr
Canadian National Railway	23,096	5,983	10.3	6.8	0.5	9.0	28.0
Burlington Northern Santa	26,513	14,653	9.4	5.7	0.7	5.5	34.1
Union Pacific	24,820	15,237	8.6	3.9	0.5	15.9	11.9

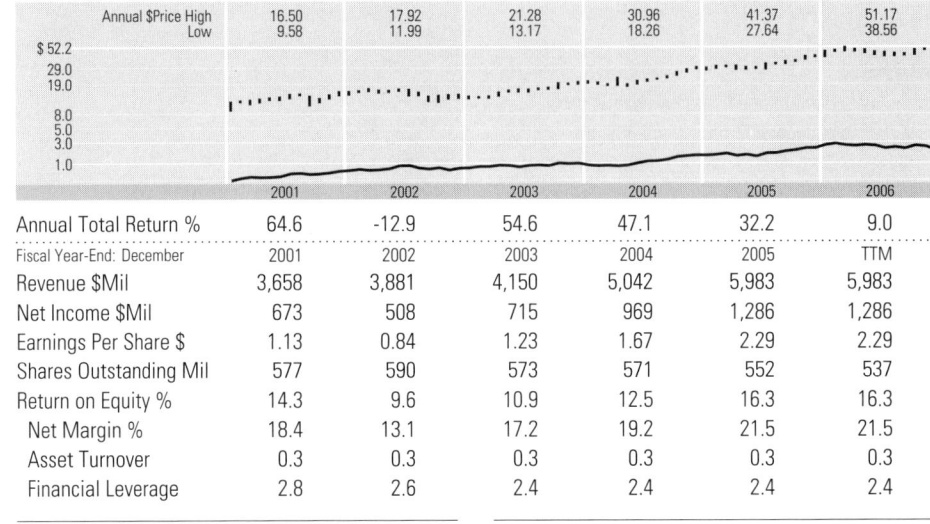

	2001	2002	2003	2004	2005	
Annual Total Return %	64.6	-12.9	54.6	47.1	32.2	9.0
Fiscal Year-End: December	2001	2002	2003	2004	2005	TTM
Revenue $Mil	3,658	3,881	4,150	5,042	5,983	5,983
Net Income $Mil	673	508	715	969	1,286	1,286
Earnings Per Share $	1.13	0.84	1.23	1.67	2.29	2.29
Shares Outstanding Mil	577	590	573	571	552	537
Return on Equity %	14.3	9.6	10.9	12.5	16.3	16.3
Net Margin %	18.4	13.1	17.2	19.2	21.5	21.5
Asset Turnover	0.3	0.3	0.3	0.3	0.3	0.3
Financial Leverage	2.8	2.6	2.4	2.4	2.4	2.4

Valuation Ratios	Stock	Rel to Industry	Rel to S&P 500
Price/Earnings	18.8	1.1	0.9
Price/Book	2.9	1.2	0.7
Price/Sales	3.9	1.8	1.3
Price/Cash Flow	10.3	1.0	0.7

Major Fund Holders	% of Fund Assets
DWS Equity Partners A	5.14
Fidelity Select Transportation	4.90
Fidelity Select Materials	3.71
Pioneer Growth Leaders A	3.43

Thesis By Peter Smith, 11-21-06 Stock Price as of Analysis: $46.71

Despite operating in a tough industry, Canadian National's record of on-time service, consistent profitability, and strong free cash flow make it a solid long-term investment at the right price, in our view.

The railroad industry is notoriously challenging. Each firm is responsible for its own track--as opposed to trucking and water transport firms, for which the government covers highway and waterway maintenance. Though this acts as a stellar barrier to entry, rails spend the highest percentage of sales on capital expenditures of any major North American industry--and almost all of it for track maintenance, not growth. CN is no exception, spending about 16% of revenue per year on average (and closer to 20% in some years). Rails also face the challenge of providing consistent service, as delays in one section can cascade throughout the entire system.

Since becoming a public company in 1995, CN has generated better results than all of its peers in the face of these logistical and economic challenges, consistently churning out more than 10% of its sales as free cash flow (and more like 20% lately). It also has maintained the best operating ratio in the industry by a wide margin--indicating that it can grow with lower incremental costs than its peers. Additionally, it is one of the only rails to earn its cost of capital consistently, a notable achievement given its massive asset base.

CN's outstanding performance can be attributed to its strict adherence to running a "scheduled" railroad, a process instituted in 1998 after the firm's acquisition of Illinois Central. By focusing on the clock rather than the weight or size of the train, CN has significantly improved the efficiency of its operations and, more importantly, its asset utilization. This model has proved to be so successful that several of its peers have followed in its footsteps, but given the complexity of implementing a scheduled railroad, we do not think they will match CN's efficiency anytime soon, if ever. For this reason, we think CN has a narrow economic moat.

After years of cost-cutting, management's focus has now shifted to top-line growth (though it is still cutting costs). In particular, the firm hopes to boost its intermodal volumes, a less cyclical business than the commodities it currently moves, and its forest products business, which should benefit from reconstruction in hurricane-stricken areas along the Gulf Coast.

CN will undoubtedly have stretches during which it is not as efficient, but overall, we suspect that it will remain the most reliable railroad for years to come.

Data as of 12-29-06

Canadian Natural Resources CNQ

Rating	Fair Value	Last Close	Consider Buy	Consider Sell	Yield %
★★★	$53.00	$53.23	$40.90	$66.40	0.50

Company Profile
Calgary-based Canadian Natural Resources is the second-largest natural-gas producer in Canada. In recent years, the addition of international properties in the North Sea and West Africa has boosted oil production to 57% of the total. In 2005, the firm produced 553,000 gross barrels of oil equivalent per day and posted approximately 3.7 billion barrels of gross proved reserves, including oil sands resources.

Management
Stewardship Grade [B]

Canadian Natural does not have a chief executive officer; leadership responsibilities are shared by John Langille, the vice chairman of the board, and Steve Laut, who is president and chief operating officer of the company. Laut recently joined the board of directors as well. In 2005, Langille took home C$325,000 in base salary and C$443,000 in bonus. Laut received a base salary of C$408,000 plus C$1.1 million in bonus. We believe that this compensation is reasonable given Canadian Natural's position within the oil and gas industry. In addition to Langille and Laut, Allan Markin serves as chairman of the board, and Murray Edwards serves as vice chairman. With directors and officers owning a sizable chunk of the company's stock, the interests of management and shareholders are clearly aligned. In our opinion, Canadian Natural's stewardship is good. The company could improve on this metric by providing more details on how managers' bonus amounts are determined.

2500, 855-2 Street S.W. www.cnrl.com
Calgary, AB T2P 4J8

Growth [NA]	2002	2003	2004	2005
Revenue %	21.0	41.8	6.2	33.7
Earnings/Share %	-16.6	134.8	2.8	-25.0
Book Value/Share %	22.7	20.6	25.1	12.9
Dividends/Share %	—	—	—	—

Profitability [NA]	2003	2004	2005	TTM
Return on Assets %	8.7	7.1	4.6	4.6
Oper Cash Flow $Mil	2,174	2,842	3,964	3,964
- Cap Spending $Mil	1,753	3,528	4,413	4,413
= Free Cash Flow $Mil	420	-687	-449	-449

Financial Health [NA]	2003	2004	2005	12-31-05
Long-term Debt $Mil	2,130	2,948	2,838	2,838
Total Equity $Mil	4,656	6,103	7,040	7,040
Debt/Equity Ratio	0.5	0.5	0.4	0.4

Industry	Business Risk	Moat Size	Investment Style	Sector
Oil/Gas	Average	Narrow	Large Growth	Energy

Competition

	Market Cap $Mil	12 Mo Trailing Sales $Mil	Price/Cash Flow	Return On Assets%	Debt/ Equity	Total Return% 1 Yr	3 Yr
Canadian Natural Resources	28,550	7,224	7.2	4.6	0.4	7.8	61.1
EnCana	39,483	14,266	5.3	10.0	0.4	2.6	33.2
Talisman Energy	18,668	6,650	4.6	8.2	0.8	-2.9	39.8

Price Volatility

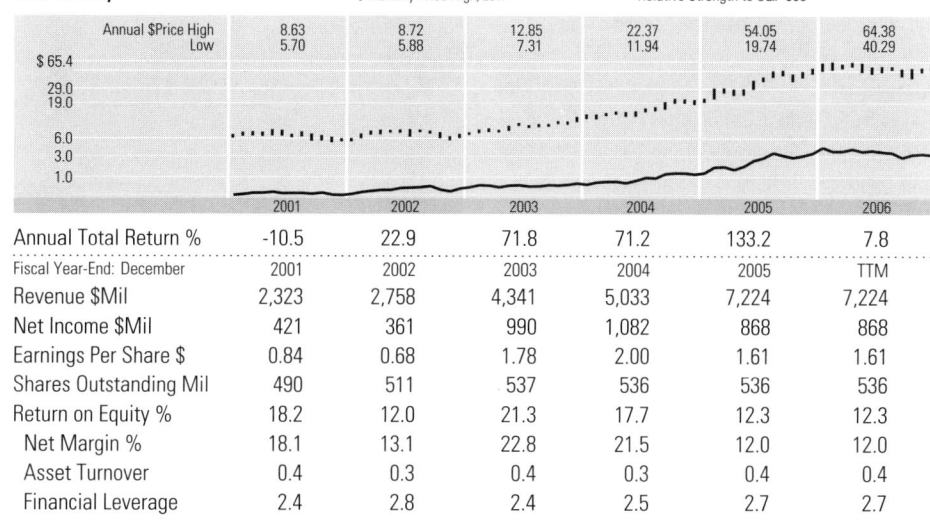

	2001	2002	2003	2004	2005	2006
Annual $Price High	8.63	8.72	12.85	22.37	54.05	64.38
Low	5.70	5.88	7.31	11.94	19.74	40.29
Annual Total Return %	-10.5	22.9	71.8	71.2	133.2	7.8

Fiscal Year-End: December	2001	2002	2003	2004	2005	TTM
Revenue $Mil	2,323	2,758	4,341	5,033	7,224	7,224
Net Income $Mil	421	361	990	1,082	868	868
Earnings Per Share $	0.84	0.68	1.78	2.00	1.61	1.61
Shares Outstanding Mil	490	511	537	536	536	536
Return on Equity %	18.2	12.0	21.3	17.7	12.3	12.3
Net Margin %	18.1	13.1	22.8	21.5	12.0	12.0
Asset Turnover	0.4	0.3	0.4	0.3	0.4	0.4
Financial Leverage	2.4	2.8	2.4	2.5	2.7	2.7

Valuation Ratios	Stock	Rel to Industry	Rel to S&P 500
Price/Earnings	33.0	2.6	1.6
Price/Book	4.1	1.3	1.0
Price/Sales	4.0	2.1	1.4
Price/Cash Flow	7.2	0.8	0.5

Major Fund Holders	% of Fund Assets
Fairholme	12.19
JHFunds2 Natural Resources NAV	5.36
JHancock Large Cap Intrinsic Value A	5.32
Fidelity Select Natural Gas	4.70

Thesis By Elizabeth Collins, 12-13-06   Stock Price as of Analysis: $53.40

By pinning growth to a 40-year investment in Canada's oil-sands resources, Canadian Natural Resources faces a different set of risks than other conventional oil and gas producers.

As Canada's second-largest natural-gas producer, Canadian Natural has profited markedly from increases in North American natural-gas demand and prices. Although Canadian Natural expanded to the North Sea and West Africa in recent years, western Canada still represents the lion's share of production and reserves. Conventional oil and gas resources in the mature western Canadian basin do not offer the promise of long-term production growth, and it is becoming an increasingly tough chore to add reserves there. Although the firm has lots of undeveloped land it can still tap, it has turned increasingly toward heavy oil and unconventional oil sands.

Canadian Natural has large reserves of heavy oil, which has lower value and is more expensive to refine than light oil. Management is attempting to enlarge the market for heavy oil through heavy oil pipeline additions, oil-blending strategies, and the encouragement of heavy oil refining capacity growth. While there is significant marketing risk with heavy oil production, the economics are promising.

The company's long-term strategy is anchored in Alberta's oil sands, and the potential for growth there is huge. Oil sands are hydrocarbon-rich deposits of sand from which thick, heavy oil can be extracted and upgraded into higher-quality crude oil. Having received board sanctioning, the Horizon Oil Sands Project--expected to cost C$10.8 billion--is targeted for startup in 2008. Upon completion of all three phases in 2012, the operation is designed to crank out more than 230,000 barrels of high-quality crude per day for upward of 40 years. Estimated reserves are more than 6 billion barrels, and the project involves no exploration risk whatsoever.

However, we can't ignore the other risks, which are significant. Extracting and upgrading oil from sand is expensive, and project economics are highly sensitive to numerous variables, including volatile natural-gas prices, currency movements, labor costs, and environmental liabilities. While today's lofty oil prices make most oil-sands projects look invincible, high overall costs make the projects susceptible to declining oil prices. With enormous up-front capital costs, there is also risk of cost overruns similar to those that have plagued comparable projects. Still, considering these risks in conjunction with our projected energy prices, we think Horizon will generate decent returns.

Data as of 12-29-06

Capital One Financial COF

	Rating	Fair Value	Last Close	Consider Buy	Consider Sell	Yield %
	★★★	$87.00	$76.82	$55.40	$104.90	0.14

Company Profile

Capital One Financial is a diversified financial institution. It is one of the largest issuers of Visa and MasterCard credit cards in the United States, and now that it has closed its North Fork Bancorp acquisition, it is one of the largest depository institutions in the United States. In addition, the firm has an auto finance segment and a global financial services segment, which includes foreign credit cards and other lending such as small-business loans.

Industry	Business Risk	Moat Size	Investment Style	Sector
Finance	Above Avg	Wide	Large Value	Financial Services

Competition	Market Cap $Mil	12 Mo Trailing Sales $Mil	Price/Cash Flow	Return On Assets%	Debt/ Equity	Total Return% 1 Yr	3 Yr
Capital One Financial	23,411	11,731	—	2.4	—	-11.0	8.6
Citigroup	273,691	86,566	—	1.3	—	19.6	8.4
J.P. Morgan Chase & Co.	167,551	59,650	—	0.9	—	25.6	13.2

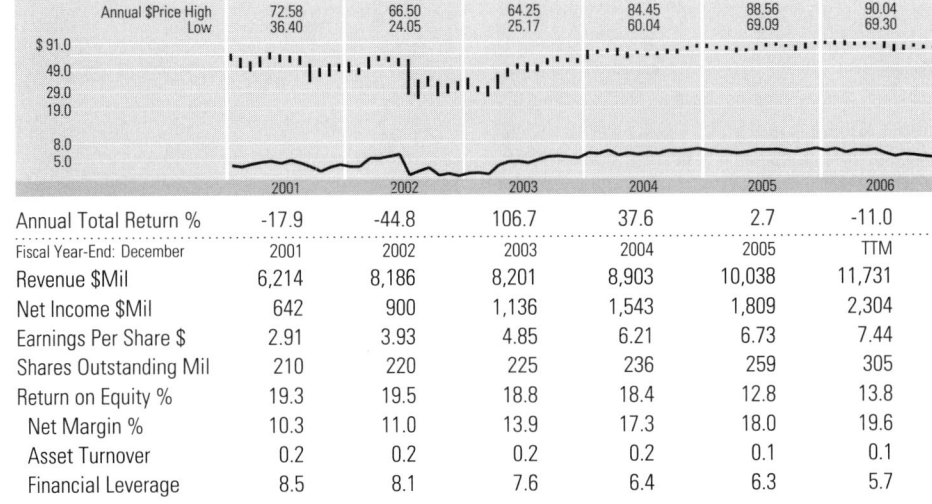

Price Volatility | Monthly Price High/Low — Relative Strength to S&P 500

Annual $Price High/Low	72.58/36.40	66.50/24.05	64.25/25.17	84.45/60.04	88.56/69.09	90.04/69.30
	2001	2002	2003	2004	2005	2006
Annual Total Return %	-17.9	-44.8	106.7	37.6	2.7	-11.0

Fiscal Year-End: December	2001	2002	2003	2004	2005	TTM
Revenue $Mil	6,214	8,186	8,201	8,903	10,038	11,731
Net Income $Mil	642	900	1,136	1,543	1,809	2,304
Earnings Per Share $	2.91	3.93	4.85	6.21	6.73	7.44
Shares Outstanding Mil	210	220	225	236	259	305
Return on Equity %	19.3	19.5	18.8	18.4	12.8	13.8
Net Margin %	10.3	11.0	13.9	17.3	18.0	19.6
Asset Turnover	0.2	0.2	0.2	0.2	0.1	0.1
Financial Leverage	8.5	8.1	7.6	6.4	6.3	5.7

Valuation Ratios	Stock	Rel to Industry	Rel to S&P 500
Price/Earnings	10.3	0.5	0.5
Price/Book	1.4	0.3	0.3
Price/Sales	2.0	0.4	0.7
Price/Cash Flow	—	—	—

Major Fund Holders	% of Fund Assets
Destination Select Equity	6.09
Bridges Investment	5.25
Neuberger Berman Focus Inv	5.16
Constellation Pitcairn Select Value II	4.42

Management Stewardship Grade [B]

Although CEO Richard Fairbank has not received a cash salary or bonus since 1997, he has received large option grants that more than adequately compensate him for performance. When cofounder Nigel Morris left the firm in 2004, he exercised about 3 million options and sold the underlying shares for net proceeds of more than $147 million, a hefty payday by anyone's standards. Because options are such an integral part of executive pay, we were especially pleased that the firm adopted the practice of expensing stock options as of 2003, much earlier than most firms that use options liberally. We take our hats off to management for its diversification efforts, which have proved to be very prescient, given the industrywide slowdown in credit card balances in the United States. We think Fairbank is a visionary who is unafraid to take risks for the sake of protecting the long-term value of the Capital One franchise. While investing alongside a visionary manager requires a certain amount of faith (because if the vision's wrong, the firm suffers), Fairbank has an excellent record, and we think he's doing a good job running Capital One for the benefit of shareholders.

2980 Fairview Park Drive Suite 1300
Falls Church, VA 22042-4525
www.capitalone.com

Growth [B]	2002	2003	2004	2005
Revenue %	31.7	0.2	8.6	12.8
Earnings/Share %	35.1	23.4	28.0	8.4
Book Value/Share %	34.1	28.0	30.6	55.7
Dividends/Share %	0.0	0.0	0.0	0.0

Profitability [A]	2003	2004	2005	TTM
Return on Assets %	2.5	2.9	2.0	2.4
Oper Cash Flow $Mil	2,034	4,514	3,632	—
- Cap Spending $Mil	263	209	160	—
= Free Cash Flow $Mil	—	—	—	—

Financial Health [NA]	2003	2004	2005	09-30-06
Long-term Debt $Mil	—	—	—	—
Total Equity $Mil	6,052	8,388	14,129	16,677
Debt/Equity Ratio	—	—	—	—

Thesis By Ryan Batchelor, CPA, 12-07-06 Stock Price as of Analysis: $76.56

We like Capital One's diversification plan, and we think the firm's proprietary Information Based Strategy (IBS) provides a competitive advantage as the company develops into a more well-rounded consumer finance firm.

In 2002, Capital One switched the focus of its credit card lending from subprime borrowers, who generated generous fee and interest income but were less likely to pay, to higher-quality consumers in the prime segments. More recently, Capital One has been diversifying its revenue and funding by acquiring regional banks: Hibernia in 2005 and North Fork Bancorp in late 2006.

We believe the move into banking makes sense over the long haul for Capital One because it diversifies revenue even more and--more important, in our view--provides a low-cost source of funding, customer deposits, that may be used at the firm's discretion. Given the maturity of the U.S. credit card business, we expect Capital One's long-term growth rate in card balances to be in the mid- to upper single digits, roughly equal to our expectations for its deposit growth. Thus, Capital One should continue to post fat margins from its credit card business, thanks to a new stable source of cheap deposits.

The firm's other segments, global financial services and auto lending, have experienced strong growth over the past several years. We think the long-term outlook for both of these segments is good, particularly for the global financial services segment, which includes, among other things, small-business lending and foreign credit card operations. While this segment has been a recent thorn in the side, thanks primarily to credit issues in the United Kingdom, we have a very positive view of its future, given the diversification benefits this unit provides.

Capital One faces fierce competition in each of its business lines from aggressive competitors. However, its IBS model provides an edge on such formidable foes, in our opinion. The IBS model compiles and processes massive amounts of consumer data to help Capital One make almost all of its business decisions. For example, IBS has been very effective in finding the right products to cross-sell to customers, setting appropriate rates to maximize profits, and determining the best strategies to collect delinquent accounts. The beauty of IBS is that it can be used to develop strategies and optimize profitability in a variety of consumer businesses outside credit cards. We think use of IBS will widen Capital One's moat as the company diversifies into noncredit card products and expands globally.

Data as of 12-29-06

Cardinal Health CAH

	Rating	Fair Value	Last Close	Consider Buy	Consider Sell	Yield %
	★★★★	$78.00	$64.43	$60.10	$97.70	0.51

Company Profile

Cardinal Health serves customers through two sectors--one focused on the company's primary distribution business and the other on manufacturing. Cardinal is a leading distributor of pharmaceutical and medical products to pharmacies and hospitals. It also manufactures and sells proprietary medical products including point-of-use systems that automate the distribution of medicines and supplies in hospitals, infusion delivery devices, and surgical products.

Management   Stewardship Grade [C]

Kerry Clark was named president and CEO in April 2006, replacing Robert Walter, who served as the company's CEO for the last 35 years. Considering Walter was the visionary who built the company, this isn't a small change, but we think there are several positive takeaways. Clark brings operations experience from Procter & Gamble where he served as an executive and board member. His leadership, operational, and international expansion experience should benefit the company. He also brings fresh insight into the company's need to acquire or divest operations.

We have reservations about Cardinal's corporate governance, but the company is sponsoring changes that we think are improving governance. Accounting improprieties uncovered during 2004 led to restatements. The company has since appointed a new CEO, CFO, treasurer, and chief accounting officer; created a chief ethics and compliance officer; and boosted the internal audit staff. Compensation has been high, but we are glad that it is set to decrease and that much of it is tied to performance. Further, the largely independent board sponsored a proposal to move to annual elections for all directors, which we think benefits minority shareholders.

7000 Cardinal Place   www.cardinal.com
Dublin, OH 43017

Growth [B]	2003	2004	2005	2006
Revenue %	10.7	14.1	15.1	9.5
Earnings/Share %	30.0	10.6	-28.1	-3.3
Book Value/Share %	22.3	7.2	8.8	0.4
Dividends/Share %	5.0	14.3	25.0	80.0

Profitability [A-]	2004	2005	2006	TTM
Return on Assets %	7.0	4.8	4.3	4.4
Oper Cash Flow $Mil	2,624	2,843	2,140	2,134
- Cap Spending $Mil	396	554	443	453
= Free Cash Flow $Mil	2,228	2,289	1,697	1,681

Financial Health [B]	2004	2005	2006	09-30-06
Long-term Debt $Mil	2,835	2,320	2,600	2,627
Total Equity $Mil	7,976	8,593	8,491	8,421
Debt/Equity Ratio	0.4	0.3	0.3	0.3

Industry	Business Risk	Moat Size	Investment Style	Sector
Medical Goods/Svcs.	Average	Narrow	Large Core	Healthcare

Competition	Market Cap $Mil	12 Mo Trailing Sales $Mil	Price/Cash Flow	Return On Assets%	Debt/ Equity	Total Return% 1 Yr	3 Yr
Cardinal Health	26,095	83,483	12.2	4.4	0.3	-5.8	2.9
McKesson	15,006	91,798	10.5	3.8	0.3	-1.3	18.7
AmerisourceBergen	9,062	59,478	7.8	2.8	0.3	8.9	18.8

Price Volatility

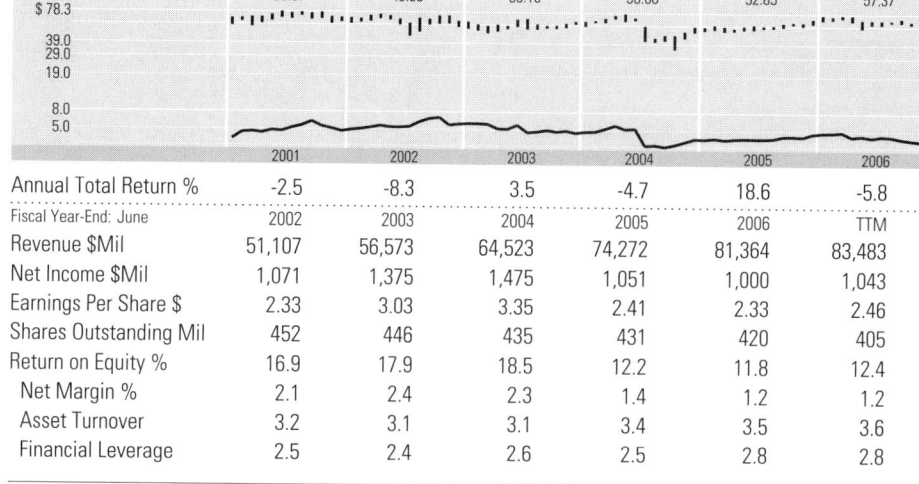

	2001	2002	2003	2004	2005	2006
Annual Total Return %	-2.5	-8.3	3.5	-4.7	18.6	-5.8

Fiscal Year-End: June	2002	2003	2004	2005	2006	TTM
Revenue $Mil	51,107	56,573	64,523	74,272	81,364	83,483
Net Income $Mil	1,071	1,375	1,475	1,051	1,000	1,043
Earnings Per Share $	2.33	3.03	3.35	2.41	2.33	2.46
Shares Outstanding Mil	452	446	435	431	420	405
Return on Equity %	16.9	17.9	18.5	12.2	11.8	12.4
Net Margin %	2.1	2.4	2.3	1.4	1.2	1.2
Asset Turnover	3.2	3.1	3.1	3.4	3.5	3.6
Financial Leverage	2.5	2.4	2.6	2.5	2.8	2.8

Valuation Ratios	Stock	Rel to Industry	Rel to S&P 500
Price/Earnings	20.9	0.9	1.0
Price/Book	3.1	1.0	0.8
Price/Sales	0.3	0.5	0.1
Price/Cash Flow	12.2	0.7	0.8

Major Fund Holders	% of Fund Assets
Fidelity Advisor Dividend Growth T	7.96
Fidelity Dividend Growth	7.83
FMI Large Cap	4.53
Torray	4.51

Thesis By Brandon Troegle, 12-13-06 Stock Price as of Analysis: $65.46

Cardinal Health's broad portfolio of health-care businesses is well-positioned for the long term. The transition to a new pharmaceutical distribution model is complete, and we think the company is making significant changes that should be beneficial.

The majority of Cardinal's revenue and earnings come from its pharmaceutical distribution business. Much of the company's weaker operating performance in 2005 and 2006 related to the industry's transition to a new fee-based model. The transition is complete, and while margins are lower as a result, the division is less capital-intensive now. This division will continue to drive the company's performance, and we think it will enjoy strong revenue growth. While growth is higher in lower-margin bulk sales than direct-to-store sales, we think the resulting margin pressure will be mostly offset by higher-margin generics coming to the market.

Cardinal has refocused its efforts and reorganized the company this year along the lines of distribution and manufacturing. Cardinal's focus on optimizing its portfolio and integrating products and services under the Cardinal brand is crucial after the many acquisitions it has made. New CEO Kerry Clark should bring some fresh ideas to the company, and we think his international operations experience will help as Cardinal tries to grow its Pharmaceutical and Medical Products sector internationally.

The abundance of new management at the company should also help in optimizing the portfolio as they decide whether and how to utilize past acquisitions that overextended the firm. In Clark's first big move, the company announced it will sell its pharmaceutical technologies and services division, which performed poorly in 2006 and has remained under pressure since. Management is also focused on cost controls, and has been closing plants and cutting its workforce in an effort to rein in costs.

We think shareholders should benefit from the company's disciplined capital use and emphasis on returning value to shareholders. It intends to return on average 50% of operating cash flows to shareholders via buybacks and an increasing dividend, use about 25% on capital expenditures, and about 20% on small tuck-in acquisitions. We think this discipline will also guide management in pursuing small acquisitions that enhance Cardinal's current offerings.

With the transition to the new distribution model complete, and the company focused on integrating its services and implementing cost controls, we think Cardinal is well-positioned.

CarMax KMX

Data as of 12-29-06

	Rating	Fair Value	Last Close	Consider Buy	Consider Sell	Yield %
	★★★★	$63.00	$53.63	$48.60	$78.90	0.00

Company Profile
CarMax sells, finances, and services used and new cars through a chain of retail stores. The company was formed in 1993 as a unit of Circuit City and was spun off into an independent company in late 2002. Used-car sales account for about four fifths of revenue while new-car sales, financing, maintenance, and repair services provide the remaining one fifth of sales.

Management Stewardship Grade [B]
Thomas J. Folliard, 41, became CEO and president in 2006 after Austin Ligon, who was part of the team that conceived CarMax, retired. Folliard has been with CarMax since its inception as a unit of Circuit City Stores in 1993. He held various roles in sales, marketing, and operations before becoming executive vice president of store operations in 2001. Although it remains to be seen how Folliard will perform at the helm, we think his knowledge of CarMax's culture and operating model should allow the company to maintain its consistent growth trajectory. In addition, Ligon has agreed to serve as a consultant to CarMax for as long as two years, which we view as a positive, given his long history with the company. Management has proved to be focused on creating long-term shareholder value and not simply growing for the sake of meeting short-term financial targets. This was most evident around 2000-2002, when the company stopped opening new stores to fine-tune its business model and enhance profitability at existing locations. Once same-store sales performance improved, the company resumed opening new locations in late 2002. We dislike CarMax's poison pill and three-tier staggered directorships, which make it difficult for an outside investor to force managerial changes.

4900 Cox Rd.
Glen Allen, VA 23060
www.carmax.com

Growth [B-]	2003	2004	2005	2006
Revenue %	12.3	15.8	14.4	19.0
Earnings/Share %	4.6	20.9	-2.7	29.9
Book Value/Share %	14.4	20.8	18.0	18.7
Dividends/Share %	NMF	NMF	NMF	NMF

Profitability [A]	2004	2005	2006	TTM
Return on Assets %	11.1	8.7	9.9	11.3
Oper Cash Flow $Mil	147	46	122	92
- Cap Spending $Mil	181	230	194	134
= Free Cash Flow $Mil	-34	-184	-72	-41

Financial Health [B]	2004	2005	2006	08-31-06
Long-term Debt $Mil	100	128	135	34
Total Equity $Mil	681	801	960	1,132
Debt/Equity Ratio	0.1	0.2	0.1	0.0

Industry	Business Risk	Moat Size	Investment Style	Sector
Auto Retail	Average	Narrow	Mid Growth	Consumer Services

Competition	Market Cap $Mil	12 Mo Trailing Sales $Mil	Price/Cash Flow	Return On Assets%	Debt/ Equity	Total Return% 1 Yr	3 Yr
CarMax	5,729	6,862	62.0	11.3	0.0	93.8	20.7
AutoNation	4,429	19,384	8.4	3.8	0.4	-1.9	5.8
United Auto Group	2,227	11,189	8.3	2.9	0.7	25.0	17.0

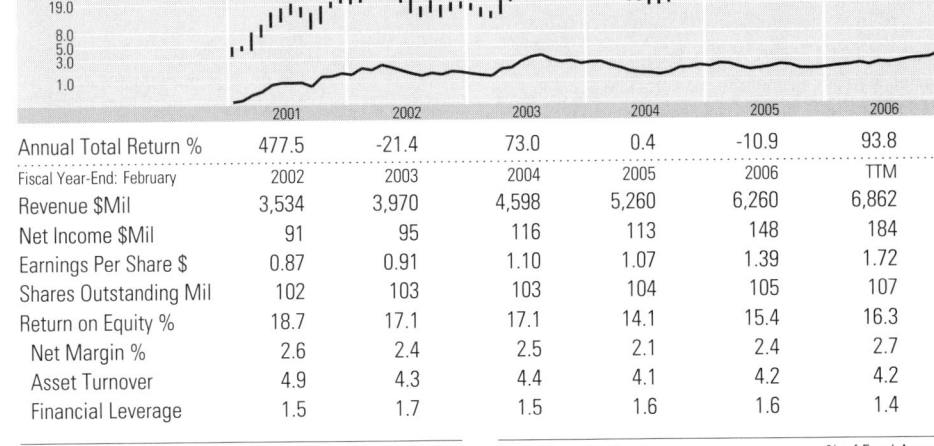

Annual Total Return %	477.5	-21.4	73.0	0.4	-10.9	93.8
Fiscal Year-End: February	2002	2003	2004	2005	2006	TTM
Revenue $Mil	3,534	3,970	4,598	5,260	6,260	6,862
Net Income $Mil	91	95	116	113	148	184
Earnings Per Share $	0.87	0.91	1.10	1.07	1.39	1.72
Shares Outstanding Mil	102	103	103	104	105	107
Return on Equity %	18.7	17.1	17.1	14.1	15.4	16.3
Net Margin %	2.6	2.4	2.5	2.1	2.4	2.7
Asset Turnover	4.9	4.3	4.4	4.1	4.2	4.2
Financial Leverage	1.5	1.7	1.5	1.6	1.6	1.4

Valuation Ratios	Stock	Rel to Industry	Rel to S&P 500	Major Fund Holders	% of Fund Assets
Price/Earnings	31.2	1.7	1.5	The Turnaround	11.13
Price/Book	5.1	1.0	1.2	FBR Small Cap	7.03
Price/Sales	0.8	0.9	0.3	FPA Perennial	4.22
Price/Cash Flow	62.0	3.0	4.2	Camco Investors	4.04

Thesis By John Novak, 12-15-06 Stock Price as of Analysis: $48.90

As CarMax continues to expand, we think the company's prospects are brighter than ever.

In an industry often derided for its high-pressure sales tactics, CarMax's clean and bright stores, highly trained sales staff, and clear, no-haggle pricing policies are helping the company gain market share. CarMax's commission-free compensation system reinforces its customer-focused strategy by ensuring that its staff isn't motivated to squeeze an extra dollar of profit out of each transaction at the expense of customer relationships.

CarMax's unique business model and growing store base provide an edge over the other 66,000 competitors in the highly fragmented used-car industry. For example, it's difficult for franchised new car dealers to copy CarMax's no-haggle policies because they often depend on their considerable negotiating power in used-car transactions to compensate for slim profit margins on new car sales. Meanwhile, local and regional used-car dealers can't match CarMax's vehicle inventory and knowledge of vehicle pricing and demand. Although there's nothing in CarMax's strategy that couldn't be imitated over time, we think the company's brand, business model, and operating experience provides a significant lead over would-be competitors.

With more than 70 stores in 20 states, we think CarMax has plenty of room to grow. The company intends to expand its store count by about 15%-20% annually over the next few years. In regions where it has been operating for several years, we estimate that CarMax has a 10% market share. Yet the company still accounts for less than 1% of total U.S. retail used-car sales, allowing for enormous growth potential. CarMax is also increasing revenues by offering financing, extended warranties, maintenance and repair, and related services.

In addition to considerable top-line growth, we think CarMax's operating margins will expand as its stores mature. We estimate that it takes about four years for a store to mature, and about 45% of CarMax's stores are in that early stage of life. As these several dozen stores age, operating profit margins should increase. In addition, ongoing growth should allow CarMax to more fully leverage its technology and infrastructure investments.

In the short term, weaker consumer spending and hefty new-car incentives could create volatility in the used-car market. Nonetheless, used-car demand has been relatively steady over the long run, and we think CarMax's unique business model creates a compelling long-term story.

Data as of 12-29-06

Carnival CCL

Rating	Fair Value	Last Close	Consider Buy	Consider Sell	Yield %
★★★★	$58.00	$49.05	$44.70	$72.70	2.09

Company Profile
Carnival is the world's largest multiple-night cruise line on the basis of number of passengers and revenue. It serves the cruise market through brands such as Carnival Cruise Lines, Princess, P&O, Cunard, and Costa Cruises; the premium market through Holland America Line; and the luxury market through Windstar Cruises and Seabourn Cruise Line. The lines' itineraries include the Caribbean, Mexican Riviera, South Pacific, Mediterranean, and the Far East.

Management   Stewardship Grade [B]
Micky Arison, son of founder Ted Arison, is the CEO and chairman of Carnival. Starting out as a bingo operator on a cruise ship, Arison has been at the helm since 1979. Management has done a fine job building Carnival's brands and adopting a laserlike focus on controlling costs. The past few years have been very strong ones for the company, and Arison has received some nice paydays. The CEO's compensation package, including restricted-stock grants and options, exceeded $8 million in both 2004 and 2005. (Arison donated almost all of his cumulative $5.3 million cash bonus to hurricane relief efforts.) The 2005 figure includes about $160,000 relating to "personal use of sporting event tickets" and more than $215,000 for the personal use of Carnival's aircraft. The Arison family owns roughly 23% of the combined voting power of the firm, and provisions in the firm's articles of incorporation effectively eliminate the possibility of takeover. We would prefer to see the roles of chairman and CEO separated.

3655 N.W. 87th Avenue   www.carnivalcorp.com
Miami, FL 33178-2428

Growth [A]	2002	2003	2004	2005
Revenue %	-3.6	53.3	44.8	14.0
Earnings/Share %	7.6	-3.6	37.4	20.5
Book Value/Share %	10.4	52.6	1.1	6.6
Dividends/Share %	0.0	4.8	19.3	52.4

Profitability [B+]	2003	2004	2005	TTM
Return on Assets %	4.9	6.7	7.9	7.4
Oper Cash Flow $Mil	1,933	3,216	3,410	3,410
- Cap Spending $Mil	2,516	3,586	1,977	1,977
= Free Cash Flow $Mil	-583	-370	1,433	1,433

Financial Health [A]	2003	2004	2005	08-31-06
Long-term Debt $Mil	6,918	6,291	5,727	6,556
Total Equity $Mil	13,793	15,760	16,972	17,879
Debt/Equity Ratio	0.5	0.4	0.3	0.4

Industry	Business Risk	Moat Size	Investment Style	Sector
Recreation	Average	Narrow	Large Core	Consumer Goods

Competition

	Market Cap $Mil	12 Mo Trailing Sales $Mil	Price/Cash Flow	Return On Assets %	Debt/Equity	Total Return % 1 Yr	3 Yr
Carnival	40,975	11,595	12.0	7.4	0.4	-6.2	9.0
Royal Caribbean Cruises	8,775	5,106	8.5	4.8	0.7	-6.8	7.1

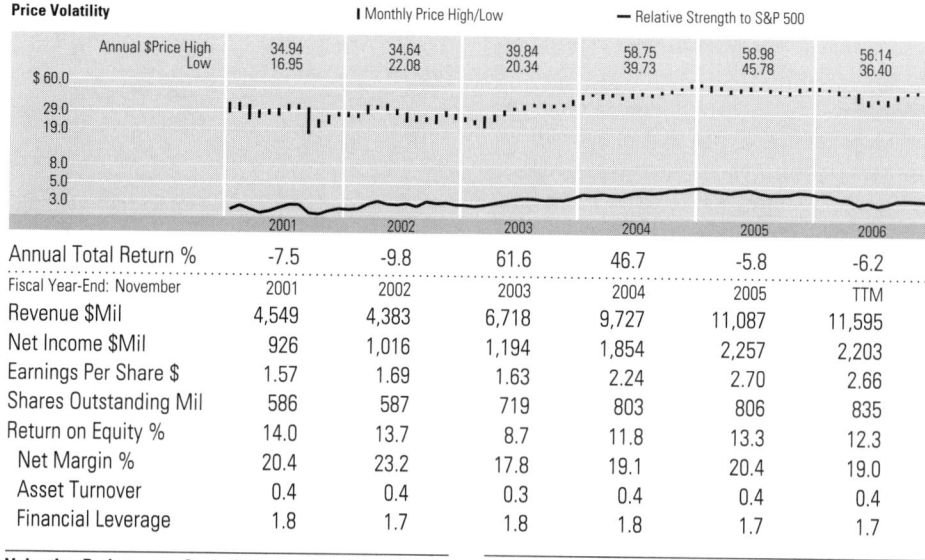

Annual Total Return %	-7.5	-9.8	61.6	46.7	-5.8	-6.2
Fiscal Year-End: November	2001	2002	2003	2004	2005	TTM
Revenue $Mil	4,549	4,383	6,718	9,727	11,087	11,595
Net Income $Mil	926	1,016	1,194	1,854	2,257	2,203
Earnings Per Share $	1.57	1.69	1.63	2.24	2.70	2.66
Shares Outstanding Mil	586	587	719	803	806	835
Return on Equity %	14.0	13.7	8.7	11.8	13.3	12.3
Net Margin %	20.4	23.2	17.8	19.1	20.4	19.0
Asset Turnover	0.4	0.4	0.3	0.4	0.4	0.4
Financial Leverage	1.8	1.7	1.8	1.8	1.7	1.7

Valuation Ratios	Stock	Rel to Industry	Rel to S&P 500
Price/Earnings	18.4	0.9	0.9
Price/Book	2.3	0.4	0.6
Price/Sales	3.5	1.2	1.2
Price/Cash Flow	12.0	0.9	0.8

Major Fund Holders	% of Fund Assets
Destination Select Equity	6.42
Allianz OCC Value Instl	6.24
Ariel Appreciation	4.51
Ariel Focus	4.49

Thesis By Sumit Desai, CFA, 12-06-06   Stock Price as of Analysis: $48.02

Carnival is the largest and most profitable player in an attractive and steadily growing industry. We think the company's size and future prospects give it a narrow moat.

Carnival is the largest cruise provider, with a near 60% market share of the worldwide cruise market. Size is important in this industry, as larger players gain more bargaining power with suppliers and distributors (mostly travel agents), and larger fleets allow companies to spread fixed costs across more ships. Carnival's scale advantages are evident in its results--its operating margins have regularly bested those of number-two player Royal Caribbean by almost 6 percentage points.

Carnival also benefits from sizable barriers to entry, which keep away new cruise providers and protect the company's returns on invested capital. Building a new cruise ship is a costly and lengthy process: New ships cost hundreds of millions of dollars, with no revenue seen for several years. As such, it's very difficult and expensive to achieve the critical mass needed to enjoy scale advantages. Accordingly, the industry resembles a duopoly, with Carnival and Royal Caribbean owning about 85% of the market. We expect the industry to remain concentrated for the foreseeable future.

The cruise industry has grown about 8% annually since 1980, and we expect it to continue growing at a healthy clip. Favorable demographics, notably an aging population, should provide a nice tailwind. Also, attracting first-time cruisers is a key focus for cruise operators; customer satisfaction rates are generally high, so first-timers often become repeat customers. Companies have made strides in broadening the appeal of cruises by making ports more accessible and adding more onboard activities, which have helped lure the younger demographic.

Several factors could take the wind out of Carnival's sails, however. Soaring energy prices have taken a large bite out of the company's profits, with Carnival's fuel costs expected to rise to more than 7% of sales in 2006 from 5% in 2004. The company has offset some of these costs through higher ticket prices and improved cost-management in other areas, but oil prices remain a threat to profits. Further, the cruise industry is driven by supply and demand factors, and irrational building or a price war would lower returns for all industry players. North American industry capacity is expected to grow about 7% annually over the next four years and could result in weaker returns if the capacity expansion coincides with an economic slowdown.

Caterpillar CAT

Data as of 12-29-06

Rating ★★★	Fair Value $66.00	Last Close $61.33	Consider Buy $50.90	Consider Sell $82.70	Yield % 1.79

Industry	Business Risk	Moat Size	Investment Style	Sector
Constr. Machinery	Average	Wide	Large Core	Industrial Materials

Company Profile

Caterpillar manufactures earthmoving, construction, and material-handling machinery and engines. Its products include track and wheel tractors, lift trucks, track and wheel excavators, off-highway trucks, dump trucks, paving equipment, and log loaders. The firm also makes engines used in its own and other manufacturers' machines and in other applications, like power generation. Caterpillar offers financing and insurance services. More than 50% of sales are derived overseas.

Management

Stewardship Grade [B]

Jim Owens took the chairman and CEO reins from Glen Barton in early 2004. Cat executives are typically homegrown, and Owens is no exception, having been with the company since 1972. In addition to Owens' experience, Cat boasts a deep bench of experienced managers who, through the company's highly regarded training program, have held positions in multiple business units and geographic territories throughout their careers. The company does a nice job of spelling out the CEO's goals each year, including financial performance, contact with customers, and product launches. We like the fact that Cat's management sets bold, but achievable goals. Over the past few years, the company has turned to more return-based measures for assessing performance, and we expect this to eventually lead to a shift toward more service-related businesses. Cat implemented a series of corporate governance changes in 1999, including a requirement that all directors except the CEO must be independent. CEOs must also resign from the board when they leave the company. We like the company's opposition to golden parachutes for executives and the decision to dissolve its poison pill in 2005. In an effort to improve its corporate stewardship further, we would also like to see the company eliminate its staggered board terms and separate the CEO and chairman positions.

100 NE Adams Street
Peoria, IL 61629-7310
www.CAT.com

Growth [A-]	2002	2003	2004	2005
Revenue %	-1.6	13.0	32.9	19.9
Earnings/Share %	-0.9	35.7	84.6	40.3
Book Value/Share %	-2.5	9.4	22.5	12.9
Dividends/Share %	1.4	1.4	9.9	16.7

Profitability [B]	2003	2004	2005	TTM
Return on Assets %	3.0	4.7	6.1	6.9
Oper Cash Flow $Mil	-5,611	-3,991	3,113	4,549
- Cap Spending $Mil	1,765	2,114	2,415	2,444
= Free Cash Flow $Mil	-7,376	-6,105	698	2,105

Financial Health [NA]	2003	2004	2005	09-30-06
Long-term Debt $Mil	14,546	15,837	15,677	18,145
Total Equity $Mil	6,078	7,467	8,432	9,028
Debt/Equity Ratio	2.4	2.1	1.9	2.0

Competition

	Market Cap $Mil	12 Mo Trailing Sales $Mil	Price/Cash Flow	Return On Assets%	Debt/ Equity	Total Return% 1 Yr	3 Yr
Caterpillar	39,897	40,177	8.8	6.9	2.0	7.9	16.1
Deere & Company	21,631	22,148	22.2	4.9	1.5	42.3	16.1
Terex	6,568	7,410	15.6	7.3	0.5	117.4	64.7

Price Volatility

	2001	2002	2003	2004	2005	2006
Annual $Price High	28.41	30.00	42.47	49.36	59.88	82.03
Low	19.88	16.88	20.62	34.25	41.31	57.05
Annual Total Return %	13.7	-9.8	86.1	19.8	20.7	7.9

Fiscal Year-End: December	2001	2002	2003	2004	2005	TTM
Revenue $Mil	20,510	20,185	22,807	30,306	36,339	40,177
Net Income $Mil	805	798	1,099	2,035	2,854	3,501
Earnings Per Share $	1.16	1.15	1.56	2.88	4.04	5.10
Shares Outstanding Mil	688	688	691	685	678	651
Return on Equity %	14.3	14.6	18.1	27.3	33.8	38.8
Net Margin %	3.9	4.0	4.8	6.7	7.9	8.7
Asset Turnover	0.7	0.6	0.6	0.7	0.8	0.8
Financial Leverage	5.4	6.0	6.0	5.8	5.6	5.6

Valuation Ratios	Stock	Rel to Industry	Rel to S&P 500
Price/Earnings	12.0	0.9	0.6
Price/Book	4.4	1.0	1.1
Price/Sales	1.0	0.8	0.3
Price/Cash Flow	8.8	0.7	0.6

Major Fund Holders	% of Fund Assets
Chicken Little Growth	7.85
Fidelity Select Construction&Housing	6.74
Integrity Value A	4.94
Fidelity Select Industrial Equipment	4.90

Thesis

By John Kearney, CFA, 12-13-06   Stock Price as of Analysis: $61.49

Acute near-term weakness across Caterpillar's on-highway engines and light construction businesses will temper the impressive growth rates the company has achieved over the past several years. That said, we think this wide-moat company will continue to generate robust economic profits for shareholders over the long term.

Caterpillar's first-rate manufacturing capabilities, unparalleled distribution network, and renowned brand name have solidified its standing as one of the world's premier industrial firms. While Cat competes in a capital-intensive and highly cyclical industry, its pricing capacity, product breath, and diverse customer base have allowed the firm to weather the industry's cyclical highs and lows better than most. Over the last decade, Cat maintained positive earnings during the deepest of trough years, and its average ROIC during this period remained well above of its cost of capital. Even well-regarded rivals like Deere can't make such a claim.

Cat's record sales and profit levels over the last several years have been spurred by revitalized investment out of the mining and energy sectors after two decades of underinvestment. A general recovery across the industrial sector as a whole has also contributed the company's unwavering strength lately. On an aggregate basis, cyclical recoveries have historically had a seven- to eight-year duration. At just four years into the current cycle, Cat should continue profiting from strong business fundamentals in the coming years. However, a weak housing market will undoubtedly curb sales for the company's light construction equipment in 2007. Similarly, the company's on-highway engine business will see a substantial sales decline during the year. This is due to the fact that truck engine demand for 2007 was pulled into earlier periods, ahead of the new engine emissions standards that commence for engines produced after 2006. The declines in light construction and engine sales will offset strength in other product categories during 2007, but Cat's growth trajectory should pick back up in 2008.

While the machine and engine businesses will continue to account for the bulk of Cat's performance, the oft-ignored service-oriented businesses will account for as much as 20% of revenues and 30% of net income by 2010 (versus 15% and 20%, respectively, in 2006). Expansion of Cat's financial services, logistics, and remanufacturing businesses should not only boost margins throughout the cycle, it will also limit the company's downside earnings exposure in the next cyclical slump.

Data as of 12-29-06

CBOT Holdings BOT

| | Rating ★★★★ | Fair Value $193.00 | Last Close $151.47 | Consider Buy $148.80 | Consider Sell $241.80 | Yield % 0.00 |

Company Profile
The Chicago Board of Trade is the world's third-largest derivatives exchange. Founded in 1848 as a commodities marketplace, the firm has since branched out into financial derivatives and went public in 2005. Interest rate-based futures and options, primarily based on U.S. Treasuries, represent 80% of trading volume. The CBOT also has an exclusive license to list futures based on Dow Jones indices, and creates markets for agricultural products and metals as well.

Management
Stewardship Grade [B]

Charles Carey, chairman of the CBOT, guided the firm through its demutualization and public offering. Carey has been a member since 1978 and is a partner in commodity trading firm Henning and Carey. Vice chairman Robert Corvino is also a member of the CBOT. Carey and Corvino work with president and CEO Bernard Dan, who joined the CBOT in 2001 after working at Cargill Investor Services for more than 15 years. We think the management talent and oversight are more than sufficient to run the company well in the face of rapid industry consolidation. Given its board and capital structure and the high percentage of shares owned by members, it's clear that, by design, outside shareholders will have very little influence on the CBOTs decision-making. In more excruciating detail, the board is make up of 17 directors who serve staggered terms and are elected by two groups: 11 by A shareholders and six by the B shareholder. The B shareholder, which is a subsidiary voting trust, also has the right to vote on any board proposal that would impact the "core rights" or members, including the right to trade certain products via open auction market. Most directors are also members.

141 West Jackson Boulevard
Chicago, IL 60604-2994
www.cbot.com

Growth [B+]	2002	2003	2004	2005
Revenue %	22.5	23.7	-0.3	22.7
Earnings/Share %	NMF	NMF	NMF	NMF
Book Value/Share %	—	—	—	—
Dividends/Share %	NMF	NMF	NMF	NMF

Profitability [A+]	2003	2004	2005	TTM
Return on Assets %	6.3	9.1	11.2	18.6
Oper Cash Flow $Mil	114	102	134	—
- Cap Spending $Mil	46	51	40	—
= Free Cash Flow $Mil	—	—	—	—

Financial Health [NA]	2003	2004	2005	09-30-06
Long-term Debt $Mil	—	—	—	—
Total Equity $Mil	251	294	542	671
Debt/Equity Ratio	—	—	—	—

| Industry Securities | Business Risk Average | Moat Size Wide | Investment Style Mid Growth | Sector Financial Services |

Competition

	Market Cap $Mil	12 Mo Trailing Sales $Mil	Price/Cash Flow	Return On Assets %	Debt/ Equity	Total Return % 1 Yr	3 Yr
CBOT Holdings	8,004	582	—	18.6	—	61.6	—
Chicago Mercantile Exchan	17,747	1,062	—	10.9	—	39.5	92.5

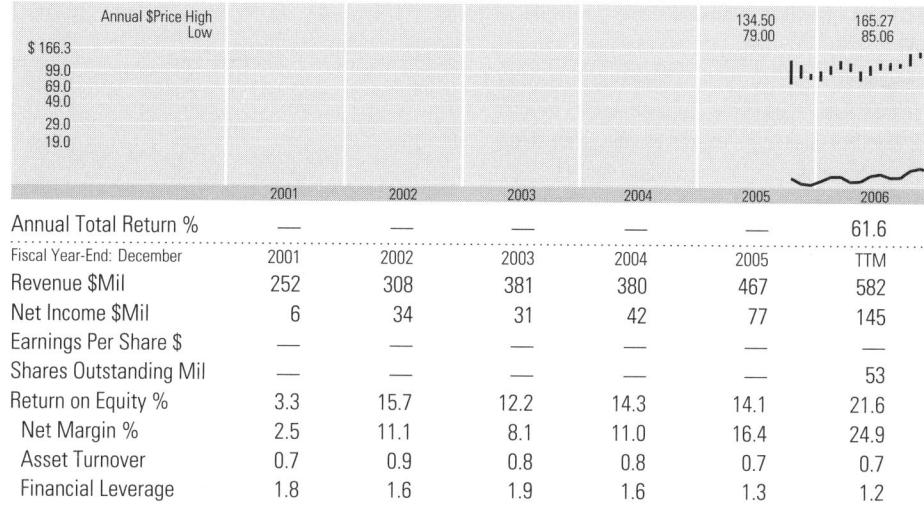

Price Volatility | Monthly Price High/Low — Relative Strength to S&P 500

Fiscal Year-End: December	2001	2002	2003	2004	2005	TTM
Revenue $Mil	252	308	381	380	467	582
Net Income $Mil	6	34	31	42	77	145
Earnings Per Share $	—	—	—	—	—	—
Shares Outstanding Mil	—	—	—	—	—	53
Return on Equity %	3.3	15.7	12.2	14.3	14.1	21.6
Net Margin %	2.5	11.1	8.1	11.0	16.4	24.9
Asset Turnover	0.7	0.9	0.8	0.8	0.7	0.7
Financial Leverage	1.8	1.6	1.9	1.6	1.3	1.2

Valuation Ratios	Stock	Rel to Industry	Rel to S&P 500
Price/Earnings	—	—	—
Price/Book	11.9	2.9	2.9
Price/Sales	13.7	3.2	4.7
Price/Cash Flow	—	—	—

Major Fund Holders	% of Fund Assets
SunAmerica Focused Mid-Cap Value A	4.38
Thornburg Core Growth A	3.61
Ashport Small/Mid Cap C	3.08
Fidelity Select Brokerage & Investmnt	2.76

Thesis By Patrick O'Shaughnessy, 10-16-06 Stock Price as of Analysis: $134.51

After decades of sleepy growth, the exchange industry has recently become a rapidly evolving and dynamic world. Not-for-profits have become public, open outcry has largely given way to electronic trading, exchanges are going global, and consolidation is afoot. The Chicago Board of Trade, like crosstown rival the Chicago Mercantile Exchange, has taken full advantage of these trends for the past several years to increase revenues and earnings at double-digit rates. The CBOT doesn't have some of the advantages that the CME possesses, but nevertheless it owns a wide-moat business and should generate substantial cash flows for its investors in the years to come.

A unique feature about futures contracts is that they can only be settled on the exchange at which they were opened, creating nontransferable pools of liquidity. This property, plus the existence of a strong network effect, makes it very difficult for competing products to achieve the critical mass necessary for survival. For the CBOT, this means that it holds a near monopoly on its listed products. Although it cut prices in the face of competition from Eurex during 2004, we believe that the firm's competitive advantage has proven itself under duress. In fact, the CBOT has been consistently raising prices following the one-time price cut.

The trading of Treasury futures and the 30-day Fed Funds rate, as well as options on these futures, is CBOT's primary earnings driver. Treasury futures are derivatives that allow firms to hedge against interest-rate changes, and they are increasingly attracting speculators. Interest-rate trading represents almost 75% of the firm's trading revenue, so as goes Treasuries trading so goes the exchange. Agriculture futures are the exchange's next most popular offering, with stock index and metals futures and options rounding out its offerings.

The industry dynamics that have led to past strong growth should stick around for awhile and possibly even improve. While the extremely rapid growth that followed the implementation of electronic trading has waned, technology continues to improve and more investors are treating derivatives as an investable asset class. Furthermore, after a two-year lull in interest-rate volatility, an increase in volatility may lead to more trading. Given the firm's bright long-term growth prospects, solid competitive position, and minimal capital investment requirements, we believe that the CBOT's shares would become very attractive at the right price.

CBS B CBS

Data as of 12-29-06

	Rating	Fair Value	Last Close	Consider Buy	Consider Sell	Yield %
	★★★★	$36.00	$31.18	$27.80	$45.10	2.37

Company Profile
Entertainment company CBS Corp. owns CBS and UPN, CBS Radio and its 178 stations, Viacom Outdoor, Simon & Schuster, and King World Productions, home of Jeopardy, the Oprah Winfrey Show, and Wheel of Fortune. CBS also owns 39 television stations. Revenue from these assets was about $14 billion in 2005. CBS is based in New York City and was previously known as Viacom. CBS spun off its cable networks and movie studio in early 2006.

Management
Stewardship Grade [C]

Chairman Sumner Redstone, 82, controls CBS through the 46 million-plus A shares--representing more than 70% of the outstanding voting shares--that his family-owned National Amusements holds (the more liquid B shares don't come with a vote). By the same means, National Amusements also controls Viacom, and Redstone is its chairman, too. Recently, Redstone's daughter Shari has become more active; she's now vice chairman at CBS and Viacom. CEO Les Moonves has played a key role in getting CBS back to the top in network ratings. Moonves doesn't have a lot of experience with radio or outdoor advertising, but he has several lieutenants to help him in these areas. Redstone and Moonves have both been very well compensated over the years, despite low returns on invested capital, below-average revenue growth, and negative shareholder returns. In 2005, Redstone was paid more than $24 million (including restricted shares), while Moonves earned just less. While neither received option grants in 2005, they did each receive more than $4 million in restricted shares, which are supposed to be used to motivate managers; with control of more than 90 million Viacom shares already, we don't think Redstone needs any more motivation. Overall, this group hasn't been a great steward of outside shareholders' capital over the years.

51 West 52nd Street
New York, NY 10019

Growth [C-]	2002	2003	2004	2005
Revenue %	1.6	3.0	7.3	-0.1
Earnings/Share %	NMF	96.3	NMF	NMF
Book Value/Share %	-3.2	1.7	-31.7	-43.8
Dividends/Share %	NMF	NMF	108.3	12.0

Profitability [D]	2003	2004	2005	TTM
Return on Assets %	1.6	-25.7	-16.5	-18.0
Oper Cash Flow $Mil	3,497	3,641	3,537	2,322
- Cap Spending $Mil	234	262	376	377
= Free Cash Flow $Mil	3,263	3,378	3,161	1,946

Financial Health [C]	2003	2004	2005	09-30-06
Long-term Debt $Mil	—	9,352	7,153	7,033
Total Equity $Mil	63,205	42,024	21,737	23,248
Debt/Equity Ratio	—	0.2	0.3	0.3

	Industry	Business Risk	Moat Size	Investment Style	Sector
	Media Conglomerates	Average	Narrow	Large Value	Media

Competition	Market Cap $Mil	12 Mo Trailing Sales $Mil	Price/Cash Flow	Return On Assets%	Debt/Equity	Total Return% 1 Yr	3 Yr
CBS B	24,368	14,650	10.5	-18.0	0.3	33.2	0.6
General Electric	383,564	161,022	12.8	2.5	2.2	9.4	9.0
Time Warner	86,932	44,532	14.4	4.9	0.5	26.4	6.8

Price Volatility — Monthly Price High/Low — Relative Strength to S&P 500

	2001	2002	2003	2004	2005	2006
Annual $Price High	43.94	38.28	35.50	33.24	28.76	32.04
Low	20.80	21.99	24.50	22.20	22.08	23.85
Annual Total Return %	-5.6	-7.7	9.7	-16.5	-8.4	33.2

Fiscal Year-End: December	2001	2002	2003	2004	2005	TTM
Revenue $Mil	12,950	13,163	13,555	14,547	14,536	14,650
Net Income $Mil	-224	726	1,417	-17,462	-7,089	-7,811
Earnings Per Share $	-0.26	0.82	1.61	-20.37	-8.98	-9.81
Shares Outstanding Mil	860	874	875	857	789	782
Return on Equity %	-0.4	1.2	2.2	-41.6	-32.6	-33.6
Net Margin %	-1.7	5.5	10.5	ELB	-48.8	-53.3
Asset Turnover	0.1	0.1	0.2	0.2	0.3	0.3
Financial Leverage	1.5	1.4	1.4	1.6	2.0	1.9

Valuation Ratios	Stock	Rel to Industry	Rel to S&P 500
Price/Earnings	NMF	—	—
Price/Book	1.0	0.3	0.2
Price/Sales	1.7	0.5	0.6
Price/Cash Flow	10.5	0.6	0.7

Major Fund Holders	% of Fund Assets
Boyar Value	4.27
Ariel Appreciation	3.71
Gartmore Worldwide Leaders A	3.48
Primary Trend	3.30

Thesis By Jonathan Schrader, CFA, 11-02-06 Stock Price as of Analysis: $28.73

CBS Corp. owns several valuable properties, including CBS and its station group, Viacom Outdoor, CBS Radio, and publisher Simon & Schuster. As most viewers know, CBS is the most-watched network on television. The CBS station group and Infinity Radio are cash cows, with cash-flow margins topping 50% at many stations. Viacom Outdoor's margins are less than half that, but its position in the out-of-home ad market is very strong. We're not as excited by Simon & Schuster, and we wouldn't mind seeing the company sell it to the highest bidder.

Combined, CBS' properties should generate around $2 billion in free cash flow in 2006. That's a lot of cash that could go to dividends--CBS' current dividend payout is just over $600 million annually--and share repurchases. The vexing questions are how much that cash flow will grow and what CBS will ultimately do with the cash.

Growth in the two biggest businesses, television and radio, will largely drive overall growth for CBS. Declining ratings, growing use of digital video recorders, and an increasing willingness by marketers to shift advertising dollars to newer media will probably continue to stymie CBS' efforts to boost television revenue, easily its most important source of cash flow. CBS Radio's challenges include satellite radio and digital media players, both of which are increasingly popular ways for consumers to entertain themselves without ever clicking on the radio.

CBS is well aware of its challenges and is rethinking the way it does business. While the bulk of CBS' cash flow for the foreseeable future will come from traditional advertising, an increasing portion will come from packaging its content--think CSI and Survivor--for consumption via Internet, telephone, video on demand, and other new media platforms. Deals to distribute CBS content through Google, Yahoo, and Apple's iTunes are promising.

Deals like these could help CBS offset weakness in television and radio advertising. Will they result in double-digit cash flow growth for years to come? Not likely. In our opinion, the best that investors can hope for is 7%-8% growth in the coming years. We hope CBS management will make owning its shares worthwhile by paying out the majority of its cash flow to shareholders. Early results are promising: The firm has been aggressive in raising its dividend payout. However, we'd like to see even more of CBS' cash returned to shareholders, so management isn't tempted to use it for imprudent acquisitions that could ultimately lead to value destruction.

CDW CDWC

Data as of 12-29-06

	Rating	Fair Value	Last Close	Consider Buy	Consider Sell	Yield %
	★★★	$76.00	$70.32	$58.60	$95.20	0.74

Company Profile

CDW is a $6.3 billion high-volume, low-cost distributor of name-brand computer hardware, software, and accessories. The company offers more than 120,000 products and ships orders on a same-day basis. It operates distribution facilities in Vernon Hills, Ill., which is also its headquarters, and Las Vegas. Customers are small to midsize businesses, Fortune 500 companies, and public agencies. Points of sales are through its salesforce, magazines, or the company's Web site.

Management   Stewardship Grade [B]

John A. Edwardson succeeded founder Michael Krasny (who is a director and chairman emeritus) as chairman and CEO in January 2001. Previously, Edwardson was COO and president of United Airlines. Excluding Krasny, managers and directors own about 2% of the company, though 75% of the ownership is in the form of options. Krasny owns 21.5% of CDW shares. Edwardson and Krasny are the only insiders on the board of directors, and corporate governance is good, though we'd prefer to see the chairman and CEO roles split. Executive compensation is reasonable, given that CDW shares have outperformed relevant benchmarks over the past four years, and the compensation policy limits bonus payments to no more than $3 million per year.

200 N. Milwaukee Ave.
Vernon Hills, IL 60061
www.cdw.com

Growth [C+]	2002	2003	2004	2005
Revenue %	7.6	9.4	23.0	9.7
Earnings/Share %	11.1	-3.3	37.4	16.8
Book Value/Share %	20.1	17.4	16.7	5.6
Dividends/Share %	NMF	NMF	20.0	19.4

Profitability [A+]	2003	2004	2005	TTM
Return on Assets %	13.4	15.9	16.5	15.7
Oper Cash Flow $Mil	125	184	304	267
- Cap Spending $Mil	11	22	49	50
= Free Cash Flow $Mil	114	162	255	217

Financial Health [A+]	2003	2004	2005	09-30-06
Long-term Debt $Mil	—	—	—	—
Total Equity $Mil	1,061	1,241	1,265	1,306
Debt/Equity Ratio				

Industry	Business Risk	Moat Size	Investment Style	Sector
Distributors	Average	Narrow	Mid Core	Business Services

Competition

	Market Cap $Mil	12 Mo Trailing Sales $Mil	Price/Cash Flow	Return On Assets%	Debt/Equity	Total Return% 1 Yr	3 Yr
CDW	5,512	6,569	20.6	15.7	—	23.3	6.9
Ingram Micro	3,381	30,461	32.2	3.6	0.2	2.4	8.7
Insight Enterprises	912	3,303	12.6	7.2	0.0	-3.8	0.1

Price Volatility

	2001	2002	2003	2004	2005	2006
Annual $Price High	56.88	60.00	63.65	74.45	66.97	72.18
Low	24.88	40.25	33.88	56.07	51.86	50.28
Annual Total Return %	92.7	-18.4	32.4	15.5	-12.5	23.3

Fiscal Year-End: December	2001	2002	2003	2004	2005	TTM
Revenue $Mil	3,962	4,265	4,665	5,738	6,292	6,569
Net Income $Mil	169	185	175	241	272	283
Earnings Per Share $	1.89	2.10	2.03	2.79	3.26	3.49
Shares Outstanding Mil	86	85	83	83	81	78
Return on Equity %	21.7	20.0	16.5	19.4	21.5	21.7
Net Margin %	4.3	4.3	3.8	4.2	4.3	4.3
Asset Turnover	4.2	3.9	3.6	3.8	3.8	3.6
Financial Leverage	1.2	1.2	1.2	1.2	1.3	1.4

Valuation Ratios	Stock	Rel to Industry	Rel to S&P 500
Price/Earnings	20.1	1.1	1.0
Price/Book	4.2	1.4	1.0
Price/Sales	0.8	0.7	0.3
Price/Cash Flow	20.6	0.7	1.4

Major Fund Holders	% of Fund Assets
FAM Equity-Income Inv	5.41
IXIS Harris Associates Focused Value C	4.58
FPA Perennial	4.40
Black Pearl Focus	4.19

Thesis By Andrew Golomb, 12-08-06 Stock Price as of Analysis: $70.38

CDW's focus on small and medium-size businesses (SMB) has allowed the firm to capture market share and realize impressive financial returns. As customers utilize resellers to solve increasingly complex IT problems, we believe CDW's efforts to increase service offerings will also pay off nicely for investors.

CDW's ability to successfully serve the SMB market has allowed it to thrive. Because CDW's customers are at the departmental, rather than corporate level, they are below the radars of the direct salesforces of large suppliers such as IBM, which reduces price competition. CDW's diverse customer mix also ensures a reliable revenue stream, even during cyclical downturns. With the average invoice around $1,000, most customers place orders that support daily operations--monitors, ink cartridges, printers--and don't require budgetary approval. Because orders are small, CDW does not depend on large deals that could get reduced, delayed, or canceled.

Increasingly, IT managers are utilizing resellers to solve network, storage, and security infrastructure challenges. We like how the $184 million acquisition of enterprise solutions provider Berbee enhances CDW's solution capabilities in these areas. These services are especially important to SMB customers, which have limited expertise or financial resources necessary to solve enterprise problems. By lowering customers' total cost of technology ownership, CDW builds loyalty, which will engender customers to spend a greater portion of their IT budgets with CDW.

This strategy appears to be working. Despite intensifying competition and increasing pricing pressures, revenues have grown 11% over the past five years, well in excess of the industry's 7% growth rate. At the same time, gross margins increased from 13% to 15.5% today. The company typically turns inventory every 17 days, collects receivables every 40 days, and pays suppliers every 17 days. These low working-capital requirements allow the company to generate impressive returns on invested capital hovering around 25%, despite 6.7% operating margins.

We believe CDW's sharp salesforce, growing solution offerings, and impressive working capital management will allow it to compete effectively against other value-added distributors. Given CDW's competitive advantages, solid balance sheet, and strong cash flows, we believe this narrow-moat firm can build its market share and continue to post impressive returns on investment.

Celgene CELG

Data as of 12-29-06

	Rating	Fair Value	Last Close	Consider Buy	Consider Sell	Yield %
	★	$42.00	$57.53	$26.80	$50.70	0.00

Company Profile

Celgene is a biopharmaceutical firm that discovers, develops, and markets therapeutics for the treatment of cancer and immunological diseases. Celgene currently focuses on marketing two drugs; Thalomid, used primarily to treat multiple myeloma, and Revlimid, a less toxic thalidomide derivative, to treat MDS and multiple myeloma. Celgene has acquired discovery capabilities that include cell-signaling pathways and stem-cell research.

Management Stewardship Grade [B]

John Jackson presided as chairman and CEO for nearly a decade. With the approval of Revlimid in December 2005, Celgene announced Jackson's retirement as CEO effective May 2006, but he remains chairman. Jackson led Celgene to profitability in 2003, and has been amply rewarded in both cash and stock options; in 2005, Jackson received roughly $3 million in cash compensation and 1.8 million options. Longtime president and COO Sol Barer replaced Jackson as CEO, and is poised to receive both a $750,000 base salary and 100% target bonus this year; although this seems excessive at first glance, we think the company's performance has been strong enough to justify these hefty salaries. Several well-qualified newcomers arrived in time for Revlimid's launch; Mark Alles, vice president of marketing, joined in 2004 with 11 years of experience at Aventis Oncology. Shawn Tomasello, vice president of sales, joined Celgene in 2005 with 16 years of experience at Genentech. Alles' involvement in the marketing of cancer blockbuster Taxotere and Tomasello's experience leading the salesforce for another cancer blockbuster, Rituxan, make them uniquely qualified for their new roles at Celgene.

7 Powder Horn Drive
Warren, NJ 07059
www.celgene.com

Growth [A+]	2002	2003	2004	2005
Revenue %	18.8	100.0	39.1	42.2
Earnings/Share %	NMF	NMF	87.5	20.0
Book Value/Share %	-44.4	14.4	31.4	32.4
Dividends/Share %	NMF	NMF	NMF	NMF

Profitability [B]	2003	2004	2005	TTM
Return on Assets %	3.2	4.8	5.1	3.3
Oper Cash Flow $Mil	19	156	42	30
- Cap Spending $Mil	11	36	36	45
= Free Cash Flow $Mil	7	120	6	-15

Financial Health [B+]	2003	2004	2005	09-30-06
Long-term Debt $Mil	400	400	400	400
Total Equity $Mil	332	477	636	838
Debt/Equity Ratio	1.2	0.8	0.6	0.5

Industry	Business Risk	Moat Size	Investment Style	Sector
Biotechnology	Above Avg	Narrow	Large Growth	Healthcare

Competition	Market Cap $Mil	12 Mo Trailing Sales $Mil	Price/Cash Flow	Return On Assets%	Debt/Equity	Total Return% 1 Yr	3 Yr
Celgene	20,276	773	EUB	3.3	0.5	77.6	72.0
Amgen	79,685	13,704	15.1	9.0	0.4	-13.4	3.1
Millennium Pharmaceutical	3,445	469	—	-3.9	0.0	12.4	-16.7

Price Volatility

	2001	2002	2003	2004	2005	2006
Annual $Price High	9.72	8.05	12.22	16.29	32.68	60.12
Low	3.60	2.83	5.04	9.37	12.35	31.51
Annual Total Return %	-1.8	-32.7	109.0	18.2	144.3	77.6

Fiscal Year-End: December	2001	2002	2003	2004	2005	TTM
Revenue $Mil	114	136	271	378	537	773
Net Income $Mil	-2	-90	26	53	64	50
Earnings Per Share $	-0.01	-0.29	0.08	0.15	0.18	0.14
Shares Outstanding Mil	191	312	321	330	335	352
Return on Equity %	-0.6	-32.1	7.7	11.1	10.0	6.0
Net Margin %	-1.7	-66.7	9.5	14.0	11.9	6.5
Asset Turnover	0.3	0.4	0.3	0.3	0.4	0.5
Financial Leverage	1.1	1.2	2.5	2.3	2.0	1.8

Valuation Ratios	Stock	Rel to Industry	Rel to S&P 500
Price/Earnings	EUB	—	—
Price/Book	24.2	3.0	5.9
Price/Sales	26.2	2.3	9.0
Price/Cash Flow	EUB	—	—

Major Fund Holders	% of Fund Assets
Allianz RCM Biotechnology D	9.83
Franklin Biotechnology Discovery A	8.56
Fidelity Advisor Biotechnology B	7.90
Victory Focused Growth A	7.79

Thesis By Karen Andersen, 12-19-06 Stock Price as of Analysis: $59.62

Celgene is in the process of establishing itself as a global biopharmaceutical leader in cancer and immunoinflammatory conditions. The company's sales and marketing teams have been in the midst of an aggressive launch, as Revlimid received FDA approval in two indications within a six-month period. We expect nothing less than blockbuster status for Revlimid and have assigned Celgene a narrow moat, based on the company's competitive advantage and expertise in immunomodulatory drugs.

Celgene's ability to fund Revlimid's development came from an unlikely source. Thalidomide, marketed as Thalomid, is an off-patent drug that caused thousands of birth defects in the 1950s. When Celgene obtained FDA approval for Thalomid in 1998 to treat a rare complication of leprosy, it also patented the STEPS program to restrict distribution of this potentially toxic drug. Because Thalomid's toxicity and STEPS have thus far prevented generic competition, the drug turned Celgene profitable in 2003 and brought in roughly $400 million in 2005 sales (mostly off-label to treat multiple myeloma), about three quarters of Celgene's total revenue.

Although Celgene finally received approval for Thalomid in multiple myeloma, most of the company's hopes are pinned on Revlimid, a thalidomide-derived drug. Revlimid received approval for myelodysplastic syndrome at the end of 2005 and relapsed multiple myeloma in mid-2006. Although Thalomid will remain an important part of multiple-myeloma therapy, it should take a backseat to Revlimid's lower toxicity and increased potency. Given the high cost of treatment, we think Revlimid sales will reach $2.6 billion by 2010.

Celgene's strongest competition comes from Millennium's relapsed multiple myeloma drug Velcade. We think that Revlimid's potency should give it an edge for new patients, but that Velcade's combinability will help it maintain a strong position in subsequent treatments of this frequently relapsing disease. These two drugs could also face off in lymphoma, as Revlimid is being studied in Velcade's approved mantle cell lymphoma indication, and both drugs are being studied in combination with Genentech's lymphoma blockbuster Rituxan.

We expect several years of stellar returns from Celgene. Revlimid is being developed in a laundry list of new indications, and the company's diverse pipeline gives us reason to believe in this biotech's longevity and competitive advantages. At current prices, however, Celgene's shares incorporate this optimistic outlook.

Cemex SAB de CV ADR CX

Data as of 12-29-06

Rating	Fair Value	Last Close	Consider Buy	Consider Sell	Yield %
★★★★★	$45.00	$33.88	$34.70	$56.40	0.00

Company Profile
Cemex purchased RMC in March 2005 and is now proposing an acquisition of Rinker. The combined firm would be one of the largest cement, ready-mix, and aggregate producers in the world. Cement would contribute nearly 60% of operating profit before depreciation and amortization (EBITDA), while the rest would come from aggregates, concrete, and other sources. Mexico would produce only one fourth of EBITDA, while the United States would contribute about 40%.

Management
Stewardship Grade [NA]

We're big fans of Cemex's bold management team, headed by Lorenzo Zambrano. Management has excelled by identifying acquisition targets and not overpaying for them. Cemex then leverages best practices across the organization and wrings out substantial cost savings in acquired companies. Cemex is not hesitant to make big up-front investments that may hurt near-term results but will add value in the long run. One of Zambrano's first moves as CEO was to invest heavily in technology infrastructure, which was costly but ultimately paid off in spades; thanks to a more efficient delivery system for ready-mix concrete, Cemex was able to reduce its truck fleet by 35%. Financial disclosure is very good and corporate-governance practices are sound, especially compared with some of the firm's home-country peers. Management stabilizes financial results by instituting natural hedges against currency fluctuation (locating production near demand), balancing supply and demand through global cement trading, matching the currency of its debts against those of its cash receipts, and hedging away some of its Mexican peso risk. Also, the company has a strong record of talent development; Cemex has a deep bench.

Av. Ricardo Margain Zozaya 325
San Pedro Garza Ga, Mexico 66265
www.cemex.com

Growth [NA]	2002	2003	2004	2005
Revenue %	-2.0	7.3	6.1	86.9
Earnings/Share %	-56.4	8.8	87.8	54.7
Book Value/Share %	-15.8	-12.4	9.8	20.6
Dividends/Share %	—	—	—	—

Profitability [NA]	2003	2004	2005	TTM
Return on Assets %	4.1	7.8	7.9	7.9
Oper Cash Flow $Mil	1,664	2,209	3,367	3,367
- Cap Spending $Mil	418	430	774	774
= Free Cash Flow $Mil	1,246	1,779	2,594	2,594

Financial Health [NA]	2003	2004	2005	12-31-05
Long-term Debt $Mil	4,622	4,645	8,164	8,164
Total Equity $Mil	6,894	7,812	10,200	10,200
Debt/Equity Ratio	0.7	0.6	0.8	0.8

Industry	Business Risk	Moat Size	Investment Style	Sector
Building Materials	Average	Narrow	Large Core	Industrial Materials

Competition
	Market Cap $Mil	12 Mo Trailing Sales $Mil	Price/Cash Flow	Return On Assets%	Debt/Equity	Total Return% 1 Yr	3 Yr
Cemex SAB de CV ADR	26,008	15,094	7.7	7.9	0.8	14.2	40.0
Lafarge ADR	26,187	19,997	11.1	5.4	0.7	69.7	21.5
Holcim							

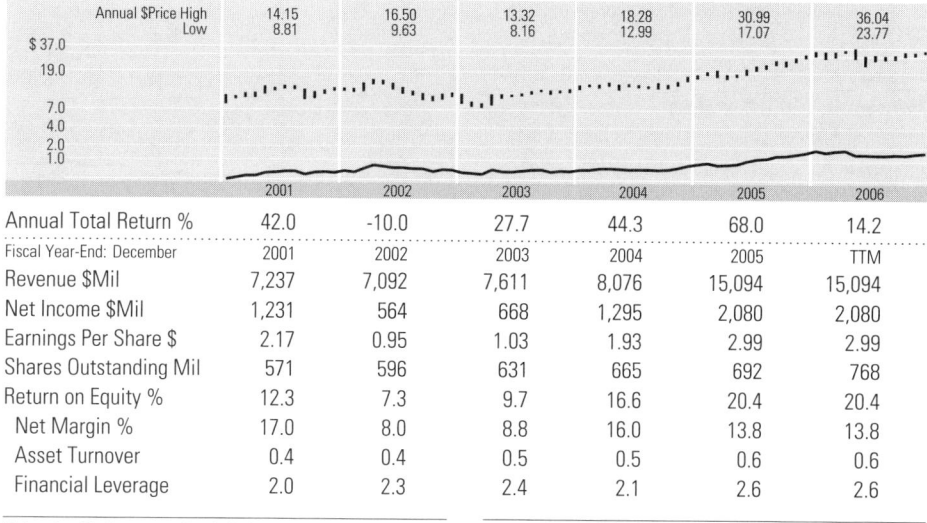

Price Volatility — Monthly Price High/Low — Relative Strength to S&P 500

Annual $Price High/Low	14.15/8.81	16.50/9.63	13.32/8.16	18.28/12.99	30.99/17.07	36.04/23.77
	2001	2002	2003	2004	2005	2006
Annual Total Return %	42.0	-10.0	27.7	44.3	68.0	14.2

Fiscal Year-End: December	2001	2002	2003	2004	2005	TTM
Revenue $Mil	7,237	7,092	7,611	8,076	15,094	15,094
Net Income $Mil	1,231	564	668	1,295	2,080	2,080
Earnings Per Share $	2.17	0.95	1.03	1.93	2.99	2.99
Shares Outstanding Mil	571	596	631	665	692	768
Return on Equity %	12.3	7.3	9.7	16.6	20.4	20.4
Net Margin %	17.0	8.0	8.8	16.0	13.8	13.8
Asset Turnover	0.4	0.4	0.5	0.5	0.6	0.6
Financial Leverage	2.0	2.3	2.4	2.1	2.6	2.6

Valuation Ratios	Stock	Rel to Industry	Rel to S&P 500
Price/Earnings	11.3	0.7	0.5
Price/Book	2.6	0.7	0.6
Price/Sales	1.7	1.2	0.6
Price/Cash Flow	7.7	0.7	0.5

Major Fund Holders	% of Fund Assets
Fidelity Latin America	5.77
Fidelity Advisor Latin America A	5.74
Atlantic Whitehall Multi-Cap Globl Val I	5.11
Longleaf Partners International	5.07

Thesis By Matthew Warren, 11-01-06 Stock Price as of Analysis: $30.56

Cemex's assets would be nearly impossible to replicate. This narrow-moat firm enjoys enviable positions in some of the world's most attractive markets, and its seasoned management team boasts one of the lowest-cost structures in the industry.

While similar grades of cement are essentially commodities, transport costs act as a barrier to entry for incumbents in geographically protected markets. The cost structures at the cement plant as well as the distribution level--Cemex is a leader in both, thanks in part to its flexible energy strategy and advanced logistical capabilities--determine the baseline economics in a market. If production costs are lower in another region, this disparity can be profitably arbitraged only as long as transport costs don't chew up the difference.

While waterborne transport is by far the cheapest, this service has doubled in price over recent years because of tight ship supply and escalating fuel costs. Despite this, cement continues to be traded among coastal regions to alleviate supply and demand imbalances. As one of the industry's largest cement traders, Cemex benefits not only from its well-protected inland plants, but from seeking out underserved markets as an outlet for highly profitable incremental production.

Another barrier to trade involves government intervention, often in the form of quotas or tariffs. In fact, Cemex will be a prime beneficiary of the unwinding of one such situation. The U.S. and Mexican governments have negotiated a reduction and eventual elimination of long-standing limits on Mexican cement imports. Because U.S. demand has long outstripped domestic supply, Asian plants have filled the gap. If Cemex can supplant a portion of this business with its Mexican cement, the additional volume and attendant operating leverage could yield quite a windfall.

Cemex has a long-running record of using the steady and substantial cash flows from its Mexican operations to support the cheap debt necessary to opportunistically acquire competitors around the globe. With Mexican population centers largely landlocked, Cemex has captured more than 50% of the market. And because self-construction is so prevalent, the firm has amassed a substantial brand and distribution advantage, which allows for prolific margins on bagged cement. Now a global powerhouse, Cemex is well positioned in an increasingly oligopolistic industry.

Data as of 12-29-06

Centex CTX

	Rating	Fair Value	Last Close	Consider Buy	Consider Sell	Yield %
	★★★★	$64.00	$56.27	$49.40	$80.20	0.28

Company Profile

Founded more than 50 years ago, Centex is a homebuilder providing turnkey homes, along with financial and construction services. The company has operations in more than 86 markets in 25 states. In fiscal 2006, Centex sold 39,232 homes to entry-level, move-up, second-home, and resort buyers, at an average price of about $304,000. Homebuilding accounts for about 85% of revenues, while construction and financial services make up the rest.

Management — Stewardship Grade [A]

Chairman and CEO Timothy Eller, a 33-year Centex veteran, succeeded Laurence Hirsch as head of the company in April 2004. Eller has been with Centex through various business cycles and has been associated with many of the technology innovations that have led to improving operating margins. He owns 2.5% of the company's stock. We like the criteria used in awarding cash bonuses and options, which include targets for earnings growth, customer satisfaction, and margin improvement. The fact that Centex has been voluntarily expensing options since 2003 is also a feather in management's cap, in our opinion. The company has a stock-ownership requirement for the most highly paid executives, resulting in total insider ownership of about 6% of the common stock. We believe the board is fairly independent, with only two affiliated directors out of the 11 members. We like that two thirds of directors' fees are in the form of stock options and restricted stock, and that the company recently let its poison pill expire. Still, we think the $300,000 annual director's compensation is steep relative to peers'. Additionally, we prefer annual rather than staggered board elections.

2728 N. Harwood
Dallas, TX 75201-1516
www.centex.com

Growth [A]	2003	2004	2005	2006
Revenue %	17.7	21.5	19.6	23.4
Earnings/Share %	44.1	45.1	19.4	27.1
Book Value/Share %	24.4	11.9	37.1	16.7
Dividends/Share %	0.0	37.5	45.5	0.0

Profitability [B]	2004	2005	2006	TTM
Return on Assets %	5.1	5.1	6.0	7.1
Oper Cash Flow $Mil	711	-368	-933	-367
- Cap Spending $Mil	54	43	92	74
= Free Cash Flow $Mil	657	-411	-1,025	-441

Financial Health [C]	2004	2005	2006	09-30-06
Long-term Debt $Mil	3,994	4,804	6,059	6,255
Total Equity $Mil	3,050	4,281	5,012	5,097
Debt/Equity Ratio	1.3	1.1	1.2	1.2

Industry	Business Risk	Moat Size	Investment Style	Sector
Home Building	Average	Narrow	Mid Core	Consumer Services

Competition	Market Cap $Mil	12 Mo Trailing Sales $Mil	Price/Cash Flow	Return On Assets%	Debt/Equity	Total Return% 1 Yr	3 Yr
Centex	6,679	14,672	—	7.1	1.2	-21.1	6.5
DR Horton	8,306	15,051	—	8.3	0.8	-24.4	9.9
Pulte Homes	8,432	15,017	—	9.1	0.5	-15.4	13.8

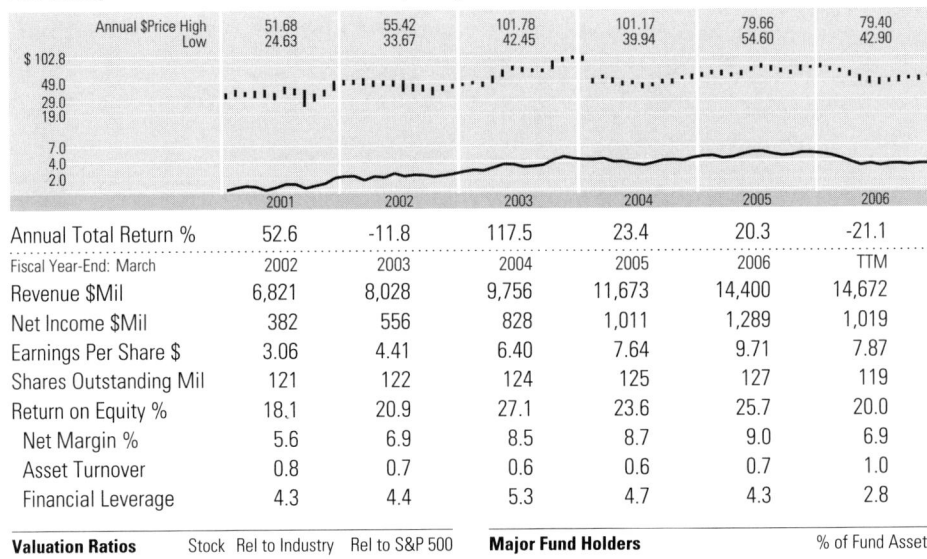

Annual Total Return %	52.6	-11.8	117.5	23.4	20.3	-21.1
Fiscal Year-End: March	2002	2003	2004	2005	2006	TTM
Revenue $Mil	6,821	8,028	9,756	11,673	14,400	14,672
Net Income $Mil	382	556	828	1,011	1,289	1,019
Earnings Per Share $	3.06	4.41	6.40	7.64	9.71	7.87
Shares Outstanding Mil	121	122	124	125	127	119
Return on Equity %	18.1	20.9	27.1	23.6	25.7	20.0
Net Margin %	5.6	6.9	8.5	8.7	9.0	6.9
Asset Turnover	0.8	0.7	0.6	0.6	0.7	1.0
Financial Leverage	4.3	4.4	5.3	4.7	4.3	2.8

Valuation Ratios	Stock	Rel to Industry	Rel to S&P 500
Price/Earnings	7.7	0.9	0.4
Price/Book	1.3	0.7	0.3
Price/Sales	0.5	0.6	0.2
Price/Cash Flow	—	—	—

Major Fund Holders	% of Fund Assets
Hotchkis and Wiley Core Value I	3.85
ING Partners OpCap Balanced Val Svc	3.48
Oppenheimer Quest Balanced A	3.16
Allianz OCC Equity Premium Strategy I	3.12

Thesis By Eric Landry, 12-18-06 Stock Price as of Analysis: $55.60

As a top-five builder with operations throughout the United States, Centex enjoys the spoils of being a pretty big fish in several different ponds. This plus laser-like focus on customer satisfaction has helped it differentiate its brand and produce sizable returns. Yet because this narrow-moat builder may currently be a bit overloaded with land, the next couple of years may be tough going.

Centex has done a good job of carving out a reputation for quality in an industry not traditionally know for such. Aside from Pulte, no other large builder was ranked higher in this year's JD Power customer satisfaction survey. The company placed first in 13 of the 34 markets surveyed, up from 10 first-place finishes a year ago. The benefits are tangible, as the company can point first-time customers to evidence that a Centex house is a good investment, while at the same time creating a potential repeat customer for its move-up, luxury, or active adult product several years hence. By placing such an emphasis on delighting buyers, Centex has done a good job of creating the closest thing homebuilders have to a captive customer.

With operations in 86 markets strewn across 25 states and the District of Columbia, Centex operates in virtually all of the country's high-growth markets. Though less so in today's pervasive softness, such diversification is usually effective in hedging against regional economic slumps like the one currently gripping Michigan. The problem, however, is that Centex is dominant in only a few of these markets. As of the end of 2005, it was a top-five builder in only one of the country's 10 largest markets (Dallas), and only four of the top 20. Compare this to similar sized competitor Pulte, which is a top-five builder in nine of the top 10 markets, or Lennar, a top-five builder in six of the top 10. It's likely these rivals get better pricing from subcontractors and are able to spread infrastructure costs over more units.

Up through fiscal 2006, management has been furiously optioning land, in what we think was an attempt to increase the company's local scale. The result is that inventories ballooned from $5.6 billion at the end of fiscal 2004 to $10.4 billion today. Total lots will now satisfy 7.4 years of orders, up from 6.4 in the same quarter in 2004. With home prices and unit volumes flat to down in most markets for what could be a sustained period, Centex will likely have to walk away from many options underwritten in recent years. Fortunately, because some options are refundable, paring inventory won't be as painful for Centex than for some others.

Data as of 12-29-06

Centurytel CTL

	Rating	Fair Value	Last Close	Consider Buy	Consider Sell	Yield %
	★★	$37.00	$43.66	$28.50	$46.40	0.57

Company Profile

CenturyTel provides local phone service to about 2.2 million lines in 21 states. It was built via a string of acquisitions over the past several decades, the largest and most recent being the 2002 purchase of 675,000 phone lines from Verizon. Nearly two thirds of the firm's lines are in Wisconsin, Missouri, Alabama, and Arkansas. The company also provides long-distance and Internet-access services and resells satellite TV and wireless services to its local phone customers.

Management   Stewardship Grade [C]

We think CenturyTel's stewardship is a bit below average. Our biggest concern is that, in addition to formal takeover defenses, an entrenched minority appears to control the firm. Shares owned continuously by one person since May 1987 are entitled to 10 votes per share. About 7% of shares outstanding currently qualify, giving these holders 43% voting control as of early 2006, up from 39% the previous year, a result of share repurchases. Much of this voting power is held in an employee stock-ownership program, and we think this voting structure could serve to entrench management. Also, nine of the 12 directors have served for a decade or longer, and four are current or former employees of the firm. Clarke Williams founded CenturyTel in the 1940s and built the firm into one of the largest independent phone companies in the nation. Glen Post, who has been with the company since 1976 and has been CEO since 1992, assumed the chairmanship upon Williams' death in 2002. We prefer the CEO and chairman roles to be separated. We think Post has done a good job of running the business, but his compensation is very generous. He was paid $2.3 million in salary, bonus, tax reimbursements, and other compensation during 2005 and received 20% of the firm's total option grant. He also was granted $2 million of restricted stock.

100 CenturyTel Drive   www.centurytel.com
Monroe, LA 71203

Growth [C-]	2002	2003	2004	2005
Revenue %	17.4	20.1	1.7	3.0
Earnings/Share %	132.8	-58.1	2.6	3.3
Book Value/Share %	31.7	9.8	2.7	10.5
Dividends/Share %	5.0	4.8	4.5	4.3

Profitability [A-]	2003	2004	2005	TTM
Return on Assets %	4.4	4.3	4.3	5.1
Oper Cash Flow $Mil	1,068	956	965	854
- Cap Spending $Mil	378	385	415	346
= Free Cash Flow $Mil	690	571	550	508

Financial Health [B+]	2003	2004	2005	09-30-06
Long-term Debt $Mil	3,109	2,762	2,376	2,418
Total Equity $Mil	3,471	3,402	3,609	3,298
Debt/Equity Ratio	0.9	0.8	0.7	0.7

Industry	Business Risk	Moat Size	Investment Style	Sector
Telecom Svcs.	Average	Narrow	Mid Value	Telecommunication

Competition	Market Cap $Mil	12 Mo Trailing Sales $Mil	Price/Cash Flow	Return On Assets%	Debt/Equity	Total Return% 1 Yr	3 Yr
Centurytel	5,012	2,461	5.9	5.1	0.7	32.5	10.8
Verizon Communications	108,723	88,881	4.4	3.7	0.7	34.9	8.0
Qwest Communications Inte	16,023	13,915	6.0	-0.6	NMF	48.1	25.7

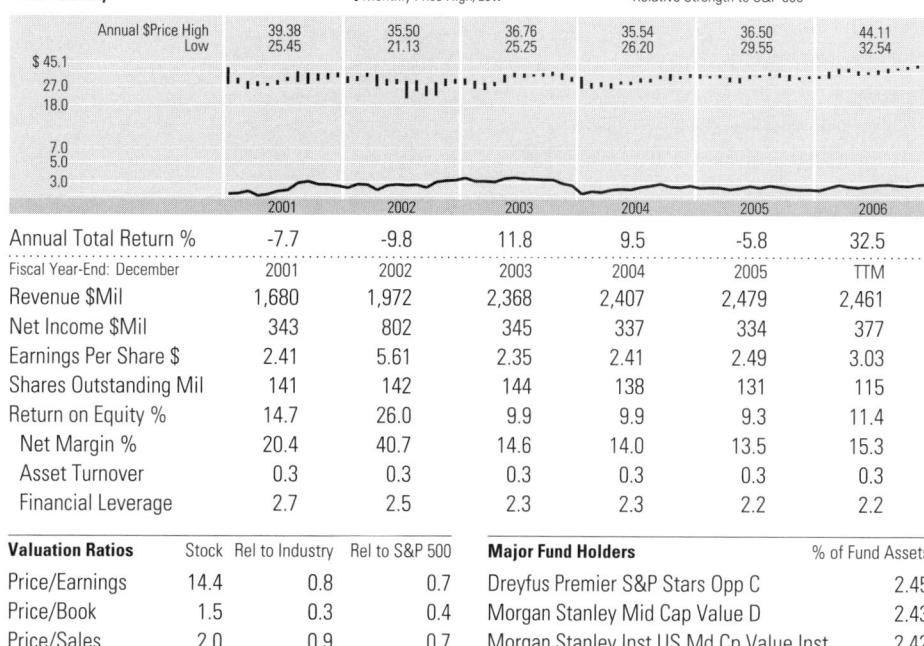

	2001	2002	2003	2004	2005	2006
Annual Total Return %	-7.7	-9.8	11.8	9.5	-5.8	32.5

Fiscal Year-End: December	2001	2002	2003	2004	2005	TTM
Revenue $Mil	1,680	1,972	2,368	2,407	2,479	2,461
Net Income $Mil	343	802	345	337	334	377
Earnings Per Share $	2.41	5.61	2.35	2.41	2.49	3.03
Shares Outstanding Mil	141	142	144	138	131	115
Return on Equity %	14.7	26.0	9.9	9.9	9.3	11.4
Net Margin %	20.4	40.7	14.6	14.0	13.5	15.3
Asset Turnover	0.3	0.3	0.3	0.3	0.3	0.3
Financial Leverage	2.7	2.5	2.3	2.3	2.2	2.2

Valuation Ratios	Stock	Rel to Industry	Rel to S&P 500
Price/Earnings	14.4	0.8	0.7
Price/Book	1.5	0.3	0.4
Price/Sales	2.0	0.9	0.7
Price/Cash Flow	5.9	0.6	0.4

Major Fund Holders	% of Fund Assets
Dreyfus Premier S&P Stars Opp C	2.45
Morgan Stanley Mid Cap Value D	2.43
Morgan Stanley Inst US Md Cp Value Inst	2.42
Van Kampen American Value A	2.41

Thesis By Michael Hodel, CFA, 10-25-06 Stock Price as of Analysis: $41.00

We expect CenturyTel will continue to lose customers over the next few years, pressuring revenue and margins, as competition increases and newer means of communicating take hold. But we still think the firm is better prepared than many of its peers to meet future challenges, and we expect it to continue generating strong cash flow.

The territories in which CenturyTel offers phone services are typically sparsely populated; the firm serves an average 13 phone lines per square mile, about one fourth the national average. As a result, CenturyTel's markets haven't attracted as much competition as more urban areas. The primary competition for fixed-line phone service comes from wireless and cable companies. Wireless substitution--customers turning to wireless as their only phone--has been the biggest driver of customer losses in recent years. But only about 20% of CenturyTel's customers can get phone service from a cable company today. We expect this percentage to rise, but we think around half of the firm's customers will never have the option to switch to cable for fixed-line calling. As a result, CenturyTel's customer losses compare well with those at the larger phone companies.

We do think competition from wireless and cable firms will hurt CenturyTel's customer base over time, particularly as voice over Internet protocol (VoIP) gains popularity and wireless coverage improves. Also, customers are increasingly replacing phone lines with high-speed Internet access services. The best defense against cable competitors, in our view, is high-speed Internet access, and CenturyTel has done a nice job of accelerating the pace at which it is adding customers. However, this business generates lower margins than traditional phone service.

The steady change in technology and customer preferences threatens to deal a major blow to CenturyTel's profitability. Per-minute network access fees from other carriers generate about one fourth of CenturyTel's revenue. As the firm loses phone customers and customers shift calling to VoIP and other means of communicating, its ability to earn this high-margin revenue stream is diminished. Also, regulators are debating the future of access fees and subsidies, another high-margin revenue stream that generates about 15% of revenue.

Despite the increase in competition, we think CenturyTel will continue to benefit from the stability of its markets. Its financial position, which is stronger than many peers, should also enable the firm to compete effectively.

CH Robinson Worldwide CHRW

Data as of 12-29-06

	Rating	Fair Value	Last Close	Consider Buy	Consider Sell	Yield %
	★★★	$45.00	$40.89	$34.70	$56.40	1.39

Company Profile
Based in Eden Prairie, Minn., CH Robinson provides transportation and logistics services through a network of more than 170 offices across North America, Europe, and South America. It has contracts with more than 30,000 trucking firms for access to dry vans, temperature-controlled vans, containers, and flatbed trailers and provides air, ocean, and customs brokerage services. The firm also sources fresh produce and partners with railroads to provide intermodal transportation.

Management
Stewardship Grade [B]

Chairman and CEO John Wiehoff, 44, has led CH Robinson since 2002 and has played a central role in developing and implementing the firm's growth strategies. The company has done quite well since he took charge, and we expect its success to continue under his watch, though growth is likely to slow from its recent torrid pace. We see some pluses and minuses in corporate governance. On the plus side, management is reasonably compensated (Wiehoff earned a total of around $6.25 million in salary, bonus, and stock gains over the past four years). We also like that Wiehoff has a stake in the firm, owning about 0.5% of shares outstanding (worth about $43 million). On the minus side, the firm has a number of antitakeover provisions in place. These include a poison pill, staggered election of directors, and a provision requiring a supermajority to approve a merger. In addition, shareholders may not call special meetings, nor can they act by written consent. Also, the firm recently named Wiehoff chairman; we'd prefer to see the chairman and CEO positions held by separate individuals. While the firm has certainly done well enough of late to render these concerns moot, shareholders must hope a time doesn't come when they become more of a problem.

8100 Mitchell Road
Eden Prairie, MN 55344-2248
www.chrobinson.com

Growth [A]	2002	2003	2004	2005
Revenue %	6.6	9.7	20.1	31.0
Earnings/Share %	10.6	20.2	26.4	46.8
Book Value/Share %	18.7	22.0	18.3	24.5
Dividends/Share %	23.8	38.5	41.7	39.2

Profitability [A+]	2003	2004	2005	TTM
Return on Assets %	11.8	12.7	14.6	16.0
Oper Cash Flow $Mil	109	156	229	306
- Cap Spending $Mil	9	35	22	39
= Free Cash Flow $Mil	101	121	207	267

Financial Health [A]	2003	2004	2005	09-30-06
Long-term Debt $Mil	—	—	—	—
Total Equity $Mil	519	621	780	917
Debt/Equity Ratio	—	—	—	—

Industry	Business Risk	Moat Size	Investment Style	Sector
Transportation	Average	Wide	Mid Growth	Business Services

Competition	Market Cap $Mil	12 Mo Trailing Sales $Mil	Price/Cash Flow	Return On Assets%	Debt/Equity	Total Return% 1 Yr	3 Yr
CH Robinson Worldwide	7,121	6,497	23.3	16.0	—	11.9	30.7
Expeditors International	8,633	4,486	23.3	15.2	—	20.5	30.2
UTi Worldwide	2,885	3,338	22.5	5.9	0.3	-3.2	32.6

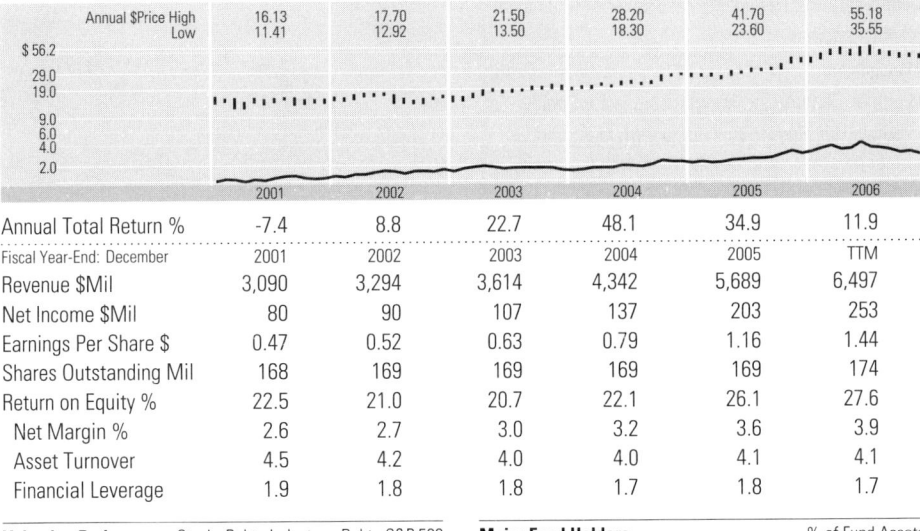

	2001	2002	2003	2004	2005	2006
Annual Total Return %	-7.4	8.8	22.7	48.1	34.9	11.9

Fiscal Year-End: December	2001	2002	2003	2004	2005	TTM
Revenue $Mil	3,090	3,294	3,614	4,342	5,689	6,497
Net Income $Mil	80	90	107	137	203	253
Earnings Per Share $	0.47	0.52	0.63	0.79	1.16	1.44
Shares Outstanding Mil	168	169	169	169	169	174
Return on Equity %	22.5	21.0	20.7	22.1	26.1	27.6
Net Margin %	2.6	2.7	3.0	3.2	3.6	3.9
Asset Turnover	4.5	4.2	4.0	4.0	4.1	4.1
Financial Leverage	1.9	1.8	1.8	1.7	1.8	1.7

Valuation Ratios	Stock	Rel to Industry	Rel to S&P 500
Price/Earnings	28.4	1.4	1.4
Price/Book	7.8	1.8	1.9
Price/Sales	1.1	0.7	0.4
Price/Cash Flow	23.3	1.6	1.6

Major Fund Holders	% of Fund Assets
Fidelity Select Air Transportation	6.03
Delaware Pooled Focus Smid-Cap Gr Eq	4.93
Transamerica Premier Growth Opp Inv	4.05
Fidelity Select Transportation	3.96

Thesis By Peter Smith, 11-17-06 Stock Price as of Analysis: $43.59

CH Robinson dominates truck brokerage. Its leading market position, enviable business model, and long-standing relationships make it a company for long-term investors to consider.

Robinson has its hands in a few businesses, but its bread and butter is truck brokerage. The firm maintains the largest network of truck capacity in the country, offering a value proposition to both shippers and carriers. For shippers, Robinson manages every aspect of a cargo transaction via on-the-spot transactions as well as longer-term contracts, simplifying the process by acting as a single point of contact. It also offers better rates, thanks to its bulk-capacity purchasing, wide selection of carriers, and multimodal offerings.

For carriers, Robinson helps reduce empty miles by providing a load when a carrier can't attract one on its own. That offering is particularly important for small carriers that need to keep their trucks full in order to compete with larger firms like JB Hunt. Small carriers can also leverage Robinson's extensive tracking technology to get at business that would be unavailable to them otherwise.

Unlike many trucking firms, Robinson does not own any trucks. Rather than worry about keeping its own trucks loaded with freight, it focuses on keeping its customers' trucks loaded. This non-asset-based business model is ideal, as most of its costs are variable. As demand for trucking services rises and falls, Robinson simply purchases more or less capacity to resell, avoiding the boom and bust cycles that plague many asset-based trucking firms.

Robinson isn't the only firm in truck brokerage, but with returns on invested capital routinely in the 20%-30% range, it is the most profitable. It has a 100-year history of brokering cargo shipments, resulting in two major competitive advantages. First, it has the largest network in a business where scale counts. No one can match its nationwide scope, and as its network expands, its ability to drive down prices only increases, driving up the value of its service. This network effect makes it very difficult for competitors to chip away at its business. Second, Robinson has built up local knowledge and long-standing relationships with truckers and shippers, an amorphous network that would not be easy to replicate. These two advantages are the sources of the firm's wide moat.

Though competition is heating up in truck brokerage, making growth harder to come by, we expect CH Robinson to continue to reap above-average profits for years to come.

Data as of 12-29-06

Charles River Laboratories International CRL

Rating	Fair Value	Last Close	Consider Buy	Consider Sell	Yield %
★★★★	$51.00	$43.25	$39.30	$63.90	0.00

Company Profile
Charles River Laboratories is the world's largest provider of animal research models, such as purpose-bred rats and mice, to pharmaceutical and biotechnology companies. The firm also performs preclinical studies required prior to human trials—including toxicology, pathology, and drug metabolism testing—and conducts Phase I clinical trials at its recently acquired operations in the U.K. and the U.S.

Management
Stewardship Grade [B]

We don't have many complaints about Charles River's corporate governance practices and assign it a "B" Stewardship Grade. However, our faith in management's decision-making stumbled a bit following the company's disappointing foray into the Phase II-IV business. The firm's eagerness to become a full-spectrum contract research organization with no prior experience in late-stage clinical trials resulted in a major error that destroyed $200 million of shareholder capital. We are willing to give this management team and CEO James Foster the benefit of the doubt for now; they have done a tremendous job turning Charles River into the world's premier provider of research models and preclinical services. We think the firm has established acceptable compensation policies, and we applaud its executive ownership guidelines, which require top executives to hold significant stock positions worth many multiples of their annual salaries. We also like Charles River's shift toward granting restricted stock in lieu of options; we think this practice better aligns management interests with shareholders.

251 Ballardvale Street
Wilmington, MA 01887
www.criver.com

Growth [A-]	2002	2003	2004	2005
Revenue %	19.1	10.7	25.0	46.3
Earnings/Share %	32.5	54.7	2.4	16.7
Book Value/Share %	15.5	25.8	189.8	-8.5
Dividends/Share %	NMF	NMF	NMF	NMF

Profitability [B+]	2003	2004	2005	TTM
Return on Assets %	10.0	3.4	5.6	-1.6
Oper Cash Flow $Mil	124	185	237	195
- Cap Spending $Mil	33	45	96	126
= Free Cash Flow $Mil	91	139	141	69

Financial Health [A-]	2003	2004	2005	09-30-06
Long-term Debt $Mil	186	606	260	577
Total Equity $Mil	465	1,473	1,827	1,554
Debt/Equity Ratio	0.4	0.4	0.1	0.4

Industry	Business Risk	Moat Size	Investment Style	Sector
Research Svcs.	Average	Narrow	Mid Core	Healthcare

Competition	Market Cap $Mil	12 Mo Trailing Sales $Mil	Price/Cash Flow	Return On Assets %	Debt/ Equity	Total Return % 1 Yr	3 Yr
Charles River Laboratories International	2,893	1,174	14.8	-1.6	0.4	2.1	8.3
Pharmaceutical Product De	3,777	1,196	21.9	11.4	0.1	4.3	34.3
Covance	3,769	1,390	15.2	10.9	—	21.3	30.1

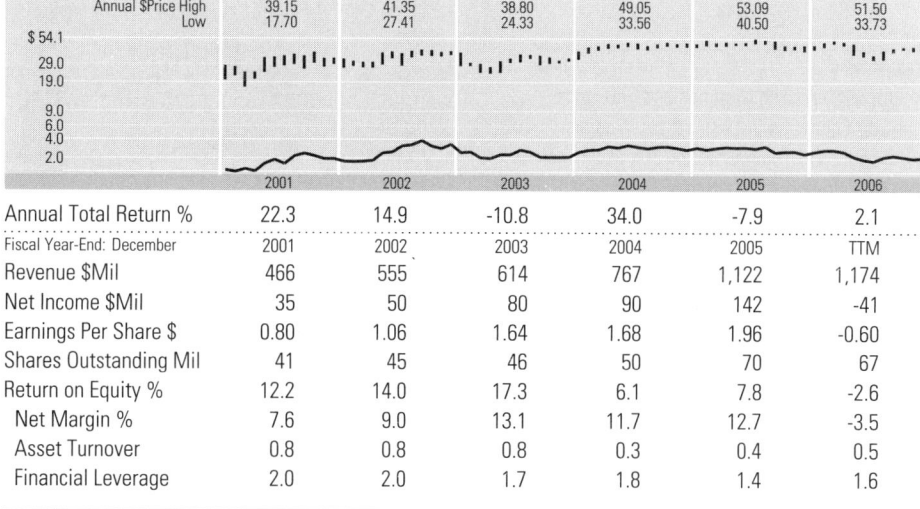

Price Volatility — Monthly Price High/Low — Relative Strength to S&P 500

	2001	2002	2003	2004	2005	2006
Annual $Price High	39.15	41.35	38.80	49.05	53.09	51.50
Low	17.70	27.41	24.33	33.56	40.50	33.73
Annual Total Return %	22.3	14.9	-10.8	34.0	-7.9	2.1

Fiscal Year-End: December	2001	2002	2003	2004	2005	TTM
Revenue $Mil	466	555	614	767	1,122	1,174
Net Income $Mil	35	50	80	90	142	-41
Earnings Per Share $	0.80	1.06	1.64	1.68	1.96	-0.60
Shares Outstanding Mil	41	45	46	50	70	67
Return on Equity %	12.2	14.0	17.3	6.1	7.8	-2.6
Net Margin %	7.6	9.0	13.1	11.7	12.7	-3.5
Asset Turnover	0.8	0.8	0.8	0.3	0.4	0.5
Financial Leverage	2.0	2.0	1.7	1.8	1.4	1.6

Valuation Ratios	Stock	Rel to Industry	Rel to S&P 500
Price/Earnings	NMF	—	—
Price/Book	1.9	0.5	0.5
Price/Sales	2.5	0.7	0.9
Price/Cash Flow	14.8	0.7	1.0

Major Fund Holders	% of Fund Assets
Genomics Y	4.82
FPA Perennial	3.97
Live Oak Health Sciences	3.67
FPA Paramount	3.64

Thesis By Alex Morozov, CFA, 11-06-06 Stock Price as of Analysis: $42.60

The Inveresk acquisition turned out to be a costly lapse in judgment from an otherwise credible management team, but our opinion of Charles River's core business remains positive.

Charles River is the world's largest provider of animal research models (lab animals) for drug development. The company is also involved in preclinical and early-stage clinical trials, which account for 52% of its revenue. In 2004 the firm made an attempt to penetrate the late-stage development business through the acquisition of Inveresk. However, it was unable to achieve meaningful growth and profitability and decided to sell its Phase II-IV operations to Kendle. While the Inveresk acquisition proved to be a costly error, it did allow the firm to expand its preclinical and early-stage operations, which we view as the primary future growth drivers.

The firm's preclinical services are growing rapidly. Large drug developers do not consider these studies, particularly toxicology, to be a core competency and increasingly outsource them to contract research organizations. As one of the very few contract research organizations with expertise and infrastructure capable of addressing this growing demand, Charles River stands to benefit considerably from this trend. The toxicology market alone is estimated to be worth $5-$6 billion; with 75% of those studies still performed in-house, the firm has an ample room to increase its revenue in this business.

The research model segment doesn't have the growth characteristics of its preclinical counterpart, but it is mostly insulated from competition. The firm is the only global supplier of research models and provides nearly 50% of all animals used in drug development worldwide. Charles River built its dominant presence by consistently producing high-quality colonies of mice and rats with specific genetic characteristics as required by its clients. This proven track record allows the firm to charge prices that are 10%-20% above the competition, which in turn translates into operating margins in excess of 30%. Since these animals have short lifespans, customers need to replace them often, giving the firm a predictable stream of recurring revenues.

We believe Charles River has built a narrow moat around its preclinical and research model segment businesses. With only a handful of competitors, substantial infrastructure requirements for new entrants, and rapidly growing demand for the firm's services, we think Charles River will produce excess returns on invested capital for the long run.

Data as of 12-29-06

Checkfree CKFR

Rating	Fair Value	Last Close	Consider Buy	Consider Sell	Yield %
★★★★★	$55.00	$40.16	$42.40	$68.90	0.00

Company Profile
Founded in 1981, CheckFree is the leading provider of electronic bill presentment and payment services. CheckFree processed 905 million payment transactions and delivered 140 million e-bills in 2005, giving it about 75% of the e-bill market. CheckFree also offers portfolio-management services to financial institutions and provides software to facilitate and process electronic payments.

Industry	Business Risk	Moat Size	Investment Style	Sector
Systems/Security	Average	Wide	Mid Growth	Software

Competition

	Market Cap $Mil	12 Mo Trailing Sales $Mil	Price/Cash Flow	Return On Assets %	Debt/ Equity	Total Return% 1 Yr	3 Yr
Checkfree	3,555	894	16.3	7.6	0.0	-12.5	13.4
Metavante							

Management   Stewardship Grade [D]
Peter Kight has been chairman and CEO since founding CheckFree in 1981. He received more than $1 million in cash compensation last fiscal year, as well as restricted stock worth $840,000 and 72,000 options. He owns about 7.1% of the firm's shares, and Mark Johnson, the board's vice chairman, owns about 1.2%. The combined holdings of other directors and executives total less than 1%. Microsoft, one of the firm's clients, owns roughly 9.5% of CheckFree. We don't like the way CheckFree distributes options. Kight received 42% of all options granted last year. Given his sizable stake in the company, we think Kight's interests are already aligned with the interests of other shareholders. We'd prefer to see more options filter down the management ranks. Overall, CheckFree gets poor marks for stewardship. We think the firm overuses one-time charges. CheckFree also loses points for exchanging deep out-of-the-money options for restricted stock in 2003. The firm could improve its score by splitting the chairman and CEO roles and removing antitakeover provisions. We'd also like to see the firm begin compensating directors with stock instead of cash. CheckFree's directors can choose to be compensated in cash, stock, or some combination of the two. Only two of the firm's six nonemployee directors have chosen to be compensated with stock.

4411 East Jones Bridge Road   www.checkfree.com
Norcross, GA 30092

Growth [B]	2003	2004	2005	2006
Revenue %	12.7	10.0	25.1	17.3
Earnings/Share %	NMF	NMF	354.5	172.0
Book Value/Share %	-3.9	-5.4	5.3	11.0
Dividends/Share %	NMF	NMF	NMF	NMF

Profitability [B]	2004	2005	2006	TTM
Return on Assets %	0.7	3.0	7.2	7.6
Oper Cash Flow $Mil	171	206	214	218
- Cap Spending $Mil	3	2	1	1
= Free Cash Flow $Mil	168	204	213	217

Financial Health [B-]	2004	2005	2006	09-30-06
Long-term Debt $Mil	—	25	28	39
Total Equity $Mil	1,299	1,336	1,484	1,423
Debt/Equity Ratio	—	0.0	0.0	0.0

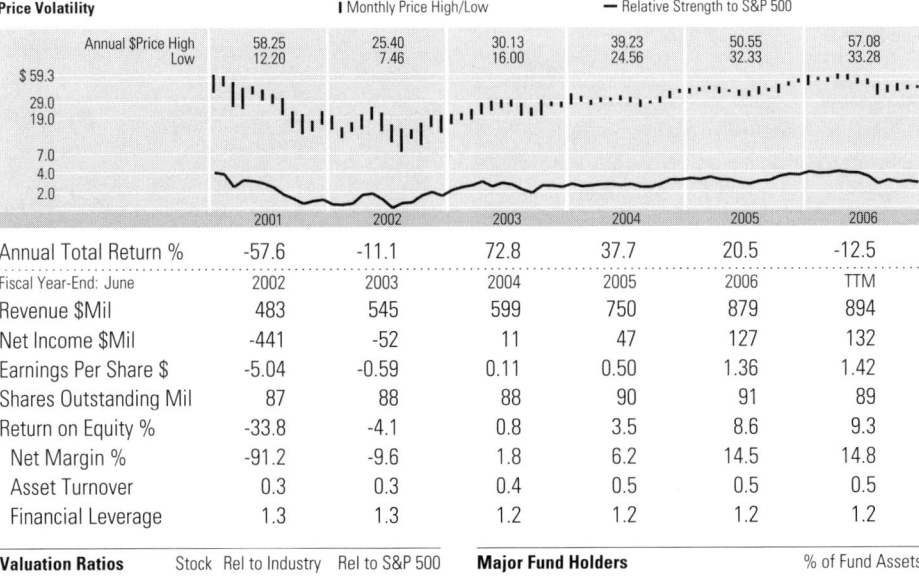

Price Volatility — Monthly Price High/Low — Relative Strength to S&P 500

| Annual $Price High | 58.25 | 25.40 | 30.13 | 39.23 | 50.55 | 57.08 |
| Low | 12.20 | 7.46 | 16.00 | 24.56 | 32.33 | 33.28 |

	2001	2002	2003	2004	2005	2006
Annual Total Return %	-57.6	-11.1	72.8	37.7	20.5	-12.5
Fiscal Year-End: June	2002	2003	2004	2005	2006	TTM
Revenue $Mil	483	545	599	750	879	894
Net Income $Mil	-441	-52	11	47	127	132
Earnings Per Share $	-5.04	-0.59	0.11	0.50	1.36	1.42
Shares Outstanding Mil	87	88	88	90	91	89
Return on Equity %	-33.8	-4.1	0.8	3.5	8.6	9.3
Net Margin %	-91.2	-9.6	1.8	6.2	14.5	14.8
Asset Turnover	0.3	0.3	0.4	0.5	0.5	0.5
Financial Leverage	1.3	1.3	1.2	1.2	1.2	1.2

Valuation Ratios	Stock	Rel to Industry	Rel to S&P 500
Price/Earnings	29.7	0.6	1.4
Price/Book	2.5	0.6	0.6
Price/Sales	4.0	0.7	1.4
Price/Cash Flow	16.3	0.8	1.1

Major Fund Holders	% of Fund Assets
Kinetics Internet	9.66
Waddell & Reed Adv Science & Tech A	3.70
Ivy Science & Technology C	3.67
Goldman Sachs Tollkeeper A	3.35

Thesis By Mark Weber, 10-23-06   Stock Price as of Analysis: $43.89

CheckFree's transaction-processing business has great growth prospects and is surrounded by a wide economic moat.

CheckFree is the leading firm in the electronic bill-payment and -presentment (EBPP) market. The firm handles online billing functions for a variety of billers, such as utilities, and for e-bill consolidators, primarily banks, that collect consumers' bills in one online location. Banks recognize that EBPP cuts costs and boosts customer retention, and they are taking measures to boost consumers' use of online banking and bill payment. As a result, CheckFree's revenue has surged in recent years, rising from $310 million in 2000 to almost $760 million last year. We think there is still plenty of room to grow. Consumers in the United States paid only 26% of their bills electronically in 2005, up from 20% in 2004. Moreover, consumers received only 18% of their bills via the Internet in 2005.

We also think CheckFree enjoys competitive advantages that are sustainable enough to earn a wide-moat rating. The firm's economic moat is a product of scale and network economics. CheckFree's costs are largely fixed, and the firm handles almost 5 times as many transactions as its nearest competitor, generating unmatched economies of scale. As a result, CheckFree can offer lower prices than the competition. The firm shares some of the benefits from its scale economies with customers, offering generous volume-based discounts. We think this is a good strategy that keeps clients happy and encourages them to market online banking to consumers. Moreover, the volume discounts haven't kept CheckFree from expanding gross margins 140 basis points over the past two years.

CheckFree is also the hub of an expanding bill-presentment network that rivals will have a hard time duplicating. Over the past several years, CheckFree has done the grunt work necessary to establish electronic bill-presentment linkages with most of the nation's largest billers. As banks and billers expand their bill-presentment offerings, they could go through the long and difficult process of establishing their own links. Given the number of parties involved, however, we think it makes a lot more sense to just hook up to CheckFree. Each institution that connects to the firm's bill-presentment service will make the network more valuable to all the other parties, widening CheckFree's moat even further.

Data as of 12-29-06

Chevron CVX

	Rating	Fair Value	Last Close	Consider Buy	Consider Sell	Yield %
	★★★	$77.00	$73.53	$59.40	$96.50	2.73

Company Profile

The current Chevron was created by the 2001 merger of Chevron and Texaco. The second-largest U.S. oil company, Chevron operates across all segments of the oil and gas industry in more than 180 countries. At the end of 2005, the firm booked proved oil and gas reserves totaling 11.3 billion barrels of oil equivalent, production of 2.4 million barrels a day, refining capacity of 2.2 million barrels a day, and a retail distribution network consisting of 26,500 service stations.

Management

Stewardship Grade [B]

Chevron veteran David O'Reilly continued as chairman and CEO following the merger with Texaco. O'Reilly rose through the Chevron ranks for more than 30 years and was a vice president for most of the 1990s. Although there were hiccups along the way, O'Reilly successfully combined two midsize oil players into a top-tier energy firm. Late in 2004, O'Reilly appointed as vice chairman Peter Robertson, an executive from the firm's exploration and production unit, putting him in a position to replace O'Reilly whenever that time comes. In 2005, O'Reilly received cash compensation worth $8.8 million and 425,000 stock options. We give Chevron's board the thumbs-up for significantly reducing bonuses in 2002 after the firm's tough year. The executives and directors as a group own or have options on roughly 0.2% of the outstanding shares, which is typical for a company of Chevron's size and age.

6001 Bollinger Canyon Road
San Ramon, CA 94583-2324
www.chevrontexaco.com

Growth [C]	2002	2003	2004	2005
Revenue %	-6.8	23.1	28.1	27.6
Earnings/Share %	-65.8	556.6	80.5	4.1
Book Value/Share %	-7.6	18.1	22.0	36.4
Dividends/Share %	5.7	2.1	7.0	14.4

Profitability [B+]	2003	2004	2005	TTM
Return on Assets %	8.9	14.3	11.2	13.1
Oper Cash Flow $Mil	12,315	14,690	20,105	24,517
- Cap Spending $Mil	5,625	6,310	8,701	12,892
= Free Cash Flow $Mil	6,690	8,380	11,404	11,625

Financial Health [A+]	2003	2004	2005	09-30-06
Long-term Debt $Mil	10,894	10,456	12,131	8,104
Total Equity $Mil	36,295	45,230	62,676	69,602
Debt/Equity Ratio	0.3	0.2	0.2	0.1

Industry	Business Risk	Moat Size	Investment Style	Sector
Oil/Gas	Average	Narrow	Large Value	Energy

Competition	Market Cap $Mil	12 Mo Trailing Sales $Mil	Price/Cash Flow	Return On Assets%	Debt/ Equity	Total Return% 1 Yr	3 Yr
Chevron	160,294	216,166	6.5	13.1	0.1	33.8	23.5
ExxonMobil	446,944	386,951	8.8	17.8	0.1	39.1	26.2
BP PLC ADR	231,015	239,792	8.6	10.8	0.1	7.9	14.3

Price Volatility

| Annual $Price High | 49.25 | 45.80 | 43.50 | 56.07 | 65.98 | 76.20 |
| Low | 39.22 | 32.71 | 30.67 | 42.00 | 49.50 | 53.76 |

	2001	2002	2003	2004	2005	2006
Annual Total Return %	9.3	-23.1	35.4	25.6	11.5	33.8

Fiscal Year-End: December	2001	2002	2003	2004	2005	TTM
Revenue $Mil	105,702	98,537	121,277	155,300	198,200	216,166
Net Income $Mil	3,288	1,132	7,230	13,328	14,099	17,510
Earnings Per Share $	1.55	0.53	3.48	6.28	6.54	7.92
Shares Outstanding Mil	2,121	2,136	2,078	2,116	2,143	2,180
Return on Equity %	9.7	3.6	19.9	29.5	22.5	25.2
Net Margin %	3.1	1.1	6.0	8.6	7.1	8.1
Asset Turnover	1.4	1.3	1.5	1.7	1.6	1.6
Financial Leverage	2.3	2.4	2.2	2.1	2.0	1.9

Valuation Ratios	Stock	Rel to Industry	Rel to S&P 500
Price/Earnings	9.3	0.7	0.5
Price/Book	2.3	0.7	0.6
Price/Sales	0.7	0.4	0.2
Price/Cash Flow	6.5	0.8	0.4

Major Fund Holders	% of Fund Assets
Profunds UltraSector Oil & Gas Inv	7.83
ING Corporate Leaders Trust B	6.34
Vanguard Energy	5.81
Waddell & Reed Adv Accumulative A	5.37

Thesis By Justin Perucki, CFA, 12-08-06 Stock Price as of Analysis: $72.83

Since its merger with Texaco in 2001, Chevron has dumped its least profitable upstream and downstream assets, positioned itself to capture refining profits in the fast-growing Asian market, and made sweeping changes to the way it manages downstream operations.

Even so, recent oil and gas production figures have not been stellar. Since 2001, production has declined an average of 2.5% per year. Unable to wring ever-increasing amounts from mature producing regions in North America and the North Sea, Chevron relies heavily on its international portfolio for production growth. However, these projects have long lead times and often experience delays and cost overruns.

Nevertheless, we think these international projects will pay off generously. Large oil fields in Kazakhstan and offshore production in West Africa are two of the key development areas that should propel growth over the next several years. The company is also building an integrated global gas business with investments in gas-to-liquid (GTL) and liquefied natural gas (LNG) projects. While growth prospects abroad are much better than at home, political uncertainty abounds in many of the areas where production is increasing, which materially heightens the firm's risk profile. Consider that 27% of proved reserves are in Kazakhstan.

Like all of its peers, Chevron faces the increasingly onerous task of adding new reserves to replace those pulled from the ground. Unlike most of its large peers, Chevron has explicitly raised the oil price it uses to evaluate the economics of prospective new projects (from $15-$25 per barrel to $20-$30). This effectively increases the number of projects that Chevron would see as profitable ventures, and we expect the firm to boost exploration spending in order to keep the oil flowing. That said, Chevron runs the risk of overinvesting. Large energy projects can take upward of a decade to go from conception to initial production. If prices fall significantly from current levels, returns on capital could suffer.

We've awarded Chevron our narrow-moat rating. Due to the integrated nature of the company--it has production and refining operations--Chevron's returns are more stable than that of a pure play oil producer or refiner. Moreover, Chevron benefits from OPEC's influence on oil prices, which keeps prices and profits artificially high. These factors ensure that Chevron's returns on capital exceed its cost of capital over the course of the industry cycle.

Data as of 12-29-06

Chicago Mercantile Exchange Holdings CME

Rating	Fair Value	Last Close	Consider Buy	Consider Sell	Yield %
★★★★	$627.00	$509.75	$483.50	$785.60	0.49

Company Profile

The Chicago Mercantile Exchange is the world's largest futures exchange, with 883 million futures contracts traded in 2005. The combined CME Group had over 1.4 billion contracts traded in 2005. The firm offers both open-outcry trading pits as well as electronic trading. Major product categories include interest rate futures, equity-index-based futures, foreign currencies, and commodities.

Management — Stewardship Grade [B]

The management team of the CME Group will largely look the same as it does for the Merc today. Bernie Dan, CEO of CBOT, will stay on as a special advisor, and Charles Carey, chairman of CBOT, will serve as vice chairman of the combined firm. Craig Donohue, CEO of the Merc since January 2004, will continue to serve in the same role for the CME Group. Terry Duffy has served as chairman at the Merc since April 2002, and has been a member of the exchange for more than 20 years. The board's senior statesman is Leo Melamed, who serves as chairman emeritus and senior policy advisor. Melamed has been a member of the firm for more than 45 years. In general we are pleased with the firm on the corporate governance front. Stock options have been expensed since the Merc went public in 2002, and issuance has been reasonably low. Bonus pools are based on the company's ability to generate cash earnings, a practice that we applaud.

30 South Wacker Drive
Chicago, IL 60606-7499
www.cme.com

Growth [A]	2002	2003	2004	2005
Revenue %	17.1	18.3	36.9	25.4
Earnings/Share %	NMF	NMF	77.2	38.1
Book Value/Share %	—	NMF	42.3	36.0
Dividends/Share %	NMF	NMF	65.1	76.9

Profitability [A]	2003	2004	2005	TTM
Return on Assets %	2.5	7.7	7.7	10.9
Oper Cash Flow $Mil	191	329	392	—
- Cap Spending $Mil	—	—	—	—
= Free Cash Flow $Mil	—	—	—	—

Financial Health [NA]	2003	2004	2005	09-30-06
Long-term Debt $Mil	—	—	—	—
Total Equity $Mil	563	813	1,119	1,421
Debt/Equity Ratio	—	—	—	—

Industry	Business Risk	Moat Size	Investment Style	Sector
Securities	Average	Wide	Large Growth	Financial Services

Competition

	Market Cap $Mil	12 Mo Trailing Sales $Mil	Price/Cash Flow	Return On Assets%	Debt/Equity	Total Return% 1 Yr	3 Yr
Chicago Mercantile Exchange Holdings	17,747	1,062	—	10.9	—	39.5	92.5
CBOT Holdings	8,004	582	—	18.6	—	61.6	—
LIFFE							

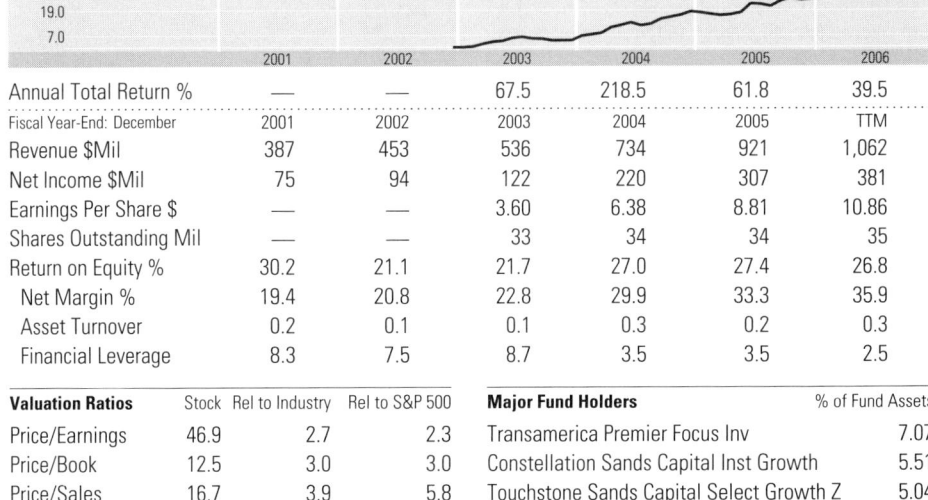

Price Volatility | Monthly Price High/Low — Relative Strength to S&P 500

Annual $Price High/Low			45.50 / 38.90	79.30 / 41.35	229.80 / 72.36	396.90 / 163.80	557.97 / 354.50
	2001	2002	2003	2004	2005	2006
Annual Total Return %	—	—	67.5	218.5	61.8	39.5

Fiscal Year-End: December	2001	2002	2003	2004	2005	TTM
Revenue $Mil	387	453	536	734	921	1,062
Net Income $Mil	75	94	122	220	307	381
Earnings Per Share $	—	—	3.60	6.38	8.81	10.86
Shares Outstanding Mil	—	—	33	34	34	35
Return on Equity %	30.2	21.1	21.7	27.0	27.4	26.8
Net Margin %	19.4	20.8	22.8	29.9	33.3	35.9
Asset Turnover	0.2	0.1	0.1	0.3	0.2	0.3
Financial Leverage	8.3	7.5	8.7	3.5	3.5	2.5

Valuation Ratios	Stock	Rel to Industry	Rel to S&P 500
Price/Earnings	46.9	2.7	2.3
Price/Book	12.5	3.0	3.0
Price/Sales	16.7	3.9	5.8
Price/Cash Flow	—	—	—

Major Fund Holders	% of Fund Assets
Transamerica Premier Focus Inv	7.07
Constellation Sands Capital Inst Growth	5.51
Touchstone Sands Capital Select Growth Z	5.04
Victory Focused Growth A	4.89

Thesis By Patrick O'Shaughnessy, 10-23-06 Stock Price as of Analysis: $503.25

We think the future looks bright for the Chicago Mercantile Exchange, and the recently announced acquisition of the Chicago Board of Trade only serves to widen its moat. The combined entity will be the largest and most diversified derivatives exchange in the world. We expect strong earnings growth for years to come, and at the right price, we believe this firm merits a spot in investors' portfolios.

The "Merc," as it is commonly known, was founded in 1898 as the Chicago Egg and Butter Board. It's come a long way since those days, though, and has developed a reputation as an innovator in the industry. The firm became the first exchange to introduce financial futures contracts, cash-settled futures contracts, and global electronic trading of derivatives. Its history of leading the way is a big reason why it is now the largest futures exchange in the world.

Being the biggest guy on the block is typically a good thing, and even better when that block happens to be an industry that lends itself to natural monopolies. Two counterparties to a futures contract must make periodic settlement payments via a clearinghouse, and they close out their positions using the same clearinghouse. Since the Merc runs its own clearing operations, its contracts cannot be transferred to another exchange. The result is that the Merc's competitors have been and will continue to be unable to steal liquidity or market share.

With the acquisition of the CBOT, the future CME Group appears to have further solidified its industry leadership position. Management has estimated cost savings to run at $125 million a year as a result of eliminating overhead, consolidating facilities, and reducing technology costs. While growth benefits from the merger are very speculative at this point, it stands to reason that the combined firm, with its broad product offering, cutting-edge trading platform, and large customer base, would become an attractive partner for foreign and smaller exchanges.

As with any acquisition, there is a chance that the CBOT purchase could fall through for regulatory or other reasons. We view this risk as minimal. Another potential complication stems from the Merc's relationship with the New York Mercantile Exchange (NYMEX), whose energy products are traded on the CME Globex platform. The CBOT competes against the NYMEX in the metals arena, and it remains to be seen how this conflict will be resolved. We believe the Merc will work through these issues, however, and the merger should only improve the firm's already-strong position.

Chico's FAS CHS

Data as of 12-29-06

Rating	Fair Value	Last Close	Consider Buy	Consider Sell	Yield %
★★★★	$27.00	$20.69	$20.80	$33.80	0.00

Company Profile
Chico's is a specialty retailer providing private-label clothing and accessories to women through four distinct concepts and more than 825 stores. Its Chico's concept provides casual, relaxed clothing to women 35 and older; White House | Black Market offers more contemporary clothes in shades of black and white to women in their mid-20s and older; Soma provides a line of intimate apparel to Chico's core customers; and Fitigues offers luxury sportswear for the family.

Management
Stewardship Grade [B]

Scott Edmonds is CEO and president. After serving in several roles for 10 years, he replaced Marvin Gralnick in September 2003. Gralnick, who founded the company with his wife, Helen, in 1983, is chairman of the board of directors. In 2005, Edmonds' annual compensation was nearly $3.4 million, excluding options, a 72% increase from his compensation in 2004. Although this was a hefty increase from the prior year, his base salary grew only 11%, with the remainder of the jump in compensation coming from a performance-based bonus. Given the company's stellar record under his leadership as well as the fact that the majority of his annual compensation is variable, we think his pay is reasonable. Although Edmonds owns less than 1% of the total shares outstanding, we think he owns a large enough stake to align his interests with those of shareholders. The board has staggered classes, with directors serving three-year terms. We frown upon staggered terms because it makes it more difficult for shareholders to oust underperforming members in a timely manner. In general, transparency regarding the company's operations is very good, and we think Chico's corporate governance is good.

11215 Metro Parkway www.chicos.com
Fort Myers, FL 33912

Growth [A]	2003	2004	2005	2006
Revenue %	40.5	44.7	38.8	31.7
Earnings/Share %	56.0	46.2	36.8	35.9
Book Value/Share %	65.0	52.0	45.3	42.2
Dividends/Share %	NMF	NMF	NMF	NMF

Profitability [A+]	2004	2005	2006	TTM
Return on Assets %	21.3	19.7	19.4	18.6
Oper Cash Flow $Mil	145	224	268	267
- Cap Spending $Mil	52	93	148	226
= Free Cash Flow $Mil	93	131	121	41

Financial Health [A+]	2004	2005	2006	10-31-06
Long-term Debt $Mil	—	—	—	—
Total Equity $Mil	375	561	806	782
Debt/Equity Ratio	—	—	—	—

Industry	Business Risk	Moat Size	Investment Style	Sector
Clothing Stores	Average	Narrow	Mid Growth	Consumer Services

Competition
	Market Cap $Mil	12 Mo Trailing Sales $Mil	Price/Cash Flow	Return On Assets %	Debt/Equity	Total Return % 1 Yr	3 Yr
Chico's FAS	3,636	1,576	13.6	18.6	—	-52.9	4.1
Ann Taylor Stores	2,358	2,306	7.0	9.0	—	-4.9	9.4
Coldwater Creek	2,282	981	23.2	10.2	—	20.5	93.0

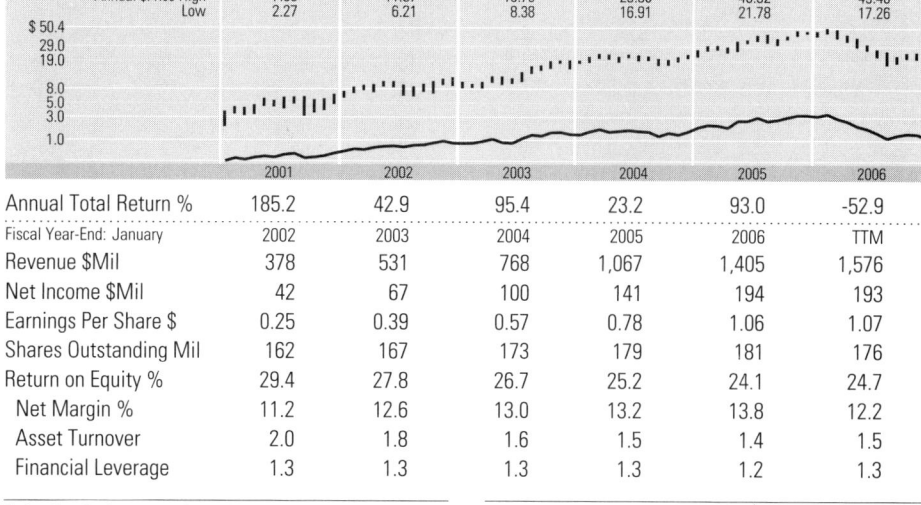

Price Volatility — Monthly Price High/Low — Relative Strength to S&P 500

	2001	2002	2003	2004	2005	2006
Annual $Price High	7.00	11.87	19.70	23.80	46.32	49.40
Low	2.27	6.21	8.38	16.91	21.78	17.26
Annual Total Return %	185.2	42.9	95.4	23.2	93.0	-52.9

Fiscal Year-End: January	2002	2003	2004	2005	2006	TTM
Revenue $Mil	378	531	768	1,067	1,405	1,576
Net Income $Mil	42	67	100	141	194	193
Earnings Per Share $	0.25	0.39	0.57	0.78	1.06	1.07
Shares Outstanding Mil	162	167	173	179	181	176
Return on Equity %	29.4	27.8	26.7	25.2	24.1	24.7
Net Margin %	11.2	12.6	13.0	13.2	13.8	12.2
Asset Turnover	2.0	1.8	1.6	1.5	1.4	1.5
Financial Leverage	1.3	1.3	1.3	1.3	1.2	1.3

Valuation Ratios	Stock	Rel to Industry	Rel to S&P 500
Price/Earnings	19.3	1.0	0.9
Price/Book	4.7	1.1	1.1
Price/Sales	2.3	1.6	0.8
Price/Cash Flow	13.6	1.1	0.9

Major Fund Holders	% of Fund Assets
Bender Growth C	3.39
Calvert Capital Accumulation A	2.65
Aston/ABN AMRO Mid Cap Growth N	2.55
Baird MidCap Inst	2.43

Thesis By Kimberly Picciola, 11-20-06 Stock Price as of Analysis: $24.04

We think it is going to be a rough couple of years for Chico's. This specialty retailer had been hitting the ball out of the park year after year with double-digit increases in same-store sales and operating profits. However, its namesake brand has hit a slump and is not inspiring its loyal customers to purchase the latest accessory or piece of apparel like it has done so consistently in the past.

Stale marketing campaigns and poor merchandising have stunted sales at Chico's stores. We believe this slowdown coupled with investments the company is making in its younger concepts will pressure profitability in the near term. The issues at its namesake stores are fixable, in our opinion; however, the real question is whether the company's newer concepts--White House | Black Market, Soma, and Fitigues--can contribute to the company's sales and profitability growth as the Chico's brand matures. In time, we believe they will and would gladly purchase shares of this retailer at the right price.

Despite its recent struggles, we remain impressed by the strength of the Chico's brand, which continues to increase its share of the underserved market of women 35 and older. Permanent members of Chico's loyalty program, Passport Club, accounted for roughly 77% of the brand's revenue in 2005. We expect the growth of this maturing brand will slow over the next five years but believe the growing demographic will contribute to positive same-store sales increases in the future.

With the Chico's brand maturing, future growth lies in the White House | Black Market and Soma concepts. White House | Black Market is a contemporary line targeting women in their mid-20s and older. We think its Black Book loyalty program will help drive top-line growth and believe increased markups to consumers and reduced sourcing costs will narrow the gap between its merchandise margins and Chico's. As for Soma, we think this intimate apparel line, which targets the Chico's customer, is a move in the right direction. We believe the heavy investments required to scale the business in the near term will start to pay off in 2008.

Although we think this specialty retailer can make a comeback, risks exist. Its newer concepts may not contribute to the company's future growth like we are expecting. Additionally, the competition for share of the baby boomer's wallet is heating up. Coldwater Creek is expanding at a rapid pace, and Gap is moving forward with its latest concept, Forth & Towne.

Data as of 12-29-06

Chipotle Mexican Grill A CMG

Rating	Fair Value	Last Close	Consider Buy	Consider Sell	Yield %
★★★	$51.00	$57.00	$39.30	$63.90	0.0

Company Profile

Chipotle operates around 530 restaurants. Its strategy is to offer a simple menu of high-quality burritos, tacos, and salads, which use a selection of a dozen core ingredients. Food is assembled on a line in full view of patrons, there is no table service, and the decor is sparse. However, given a basic price point of about $8 for an entree and a drink, we think Chipotle is more comparable to fast casual restaurants than to traditional fast food restaurants.

Management Stewardship Grade [B]

Chipotle's management team has a great deal of experience with the company and in the restaurant industry. CEO Steve Ells, who holds a degree from the Culinary Institute of America, founded Chipotle in 1993. President and COO Montgomery Moran formally joined the firm in early 2005 but has long served as Chipotle's general counsel. CFO Jack Hartung, a two-decade veteran of McDonald's, has been with Chipotle since 2002. The company hasn't developed a corporate-governance record yet, but we think it is off to a good start. Directors are elected every year and serve one-year terms. Management compensation looks reasonable, and there aren't any worrisome related-party transactions. As of October 2006, McDonald's no longer held a voting or economic interest in Chipotle.

1543 Wazee Street Suite 200 www.chipotle.com
Denver, CO 80202

Growth [A]	2002	2003	2004	2005
Revenue %	55.5	54.2	49.2	33.3
Earnings/Share %	NMF	NMF	NMF	NMF
Book Value/Share %	—	—	—	—
Dividends/Share %	NMF	NMF	NMF	143.8

Profitability [D+]	2003	2004	2005	TTM
Return on Assets %	-3.1	1.9	9.6	6.1
Oper Cash Flow $Mil	22	40	77	98
- Cap Spending $Mil	86	96	83	92
= Free Cash Flow $Mil	-64	-56	-6	6

Financial Health [C-]	2003	2004	2005	09-30-06
Long-term Debt $Mil	—	—	—	—
Total Equity $Mil	191	263	309	454
Debt/Equity Ratio	—	—	—	—

Industry	Business Risk	Moat Size	Investment Style	Sector
Restaurants	Average	None	Small Growth	Consumer Services

Competition	Market Cap $Mil	12 Mo Trailing Sales $Mil	Price/Cash Flow	Return On Assets %	Debt/Equity	Total Return % 1 Yr	3 Yr
Chipotle Mexican Grill A	1,860	777	18.9	6.1	—	—	—
McDonald's	54,825	21,790	13.3	9.4	0.6	34.6	23.9
Yum Brands	15,586	9,444	12.9	13.7	1.5	26.8	21.6

Price Volatility | Monthly Price High/Low   — Relative Strength to S&P 500

Annual Total Return %	—	—	—	—	—	—
Fiscal Year-End: December	2001	2002	2003	2004	2005	TTM
Revenue $Mil	132	205	316	471	628	777
Net Income $Mil	-24	-17	-8	6	38	35
Earnings Per Share $	—	—	—	—	—	—
Shares Outstanding Mil	—	—	—	—	—	33
Return on Equity %	-19.4	-10.7	-4.0	2.3	12.2	7.7
Net Margin %	-18.2	-8.4	-2.4	1.3	6.0	4.5
Asset Turnover	0.9	1.1	1.3	1.4	1.6	1.4
Financial Leverage	1.2	1.2	1.3	1.3	1.3	1.3

Valuation Ratios	Stock	Rel to Industry	Rel to S&P 500
Price/Earnings	—	—	—
Price/Book	4.1	0.7	1.0
Price/Sales	2.4	1.2	0.8
Price/Cash Flow	18.9	1.3	1.3

Major Fund Holders	% of Fund Assets
IPO Plus Aftermarket	5.25
SunAmerica Focused Gr A	3.87
Aston/Veredus Aggressive Growth N	3.54
DWS Small Cap Growth A	2.20

Thesis By Joseph Beaulieu,   Stock Price as of Analysis:

Chipotle Mexican Grill has a strong restaurant concept, and on the basis of current market penetration of comparable fast food and fast casual restaurants, we think it can expand from around 500 stores to more than 2,000. The company is positioned at the intersection of several prominent trends, including a growing emphasis on healthy eating, the increasing popularity of Mexican-inspired cuisine, a growing percentage of household food budgets being spent in restaurants, and the increasing market share of fast casual restaurants at the expense of lower-end traditional fast food outlets.

Chipotle's simple, Mexican-inspired menu has several advantages. Food preparation takes place on an assembly line in full view of customers, who customize their order as it moves down the line. This makes it relatively easy for the company to train new employees and keeps the ingredient list fairly short while still allowing for a large number of meal choices. It also keeps the line moving quickly. We think the large number of choices combined with short wait times will help drive more frequent customer visits.

The firm's business model has been tested over 12 years, and we think its expansion strategy is likely to succeed. Corporate parent McDonald's MCD saw Chipotle's potential in 1998, acquired it, and guided it through its early growth stages. Now that McDonald's has exited the business, we'll be interested to see if Chipotle can maintain its steady growth trajectory.

While we think this exit increases execution risk, we are more concerned about the more tangible benefits that Chipotle received from McDonald's. Chipotle piggybacked on its parent's relationships with its suppliers, getting a better deal on everything from soda concentrate to credit card processing. This lent it economies of scale far beyond what its size would otherwise suggest. We're pleased that management has reassured investors that it does not expect major changes to supplier agreements or its cost structure, but we'll be watching gross margins for any backsliding.

There are some other significant risks besides the end of the Golden Arches relationship. First, the restaurant industry is not conducive to long-term competitive advantages. There are low barriers to entry, no switching costs for customers, and intense rivalry between existing firms. Second, Chipotle would be especially vulnerable to a change in customer preferences, especially since it does not have any alternative restaurant concepts.

Data as of 12-29-06

Cimarex Energy XEC

Rating	Fair Value	Last Close	Consider Buy	Consider Sell	Yield %
★★★★★	$59.00	$36.50	$45.50	$73.90	0.44

Industry	Business Risk	Moat Size	Investment Style	Sector
Oil/Gas	Average	Narrow	Mid Value	Energy

Company Profile

Denver-based Cimarex was created in 2002 when it spun off from Helmerich & Payne and subsequently acquired Key Production. Cimarex explores for and produces oil and natural gas. At the end of 2005, it reported proven reserves of 1,393 billion cubic feet of natural-gas equivalent, with average daily production of 354 million cubic feet. About 72% of proven reserves are natural gas. Most of Cimarex's reserves are in Oklahoma, Texas, and Kansas.

Management

Stewardship Grade [B]

F.H. Merelli has been chairman, president, and CEO since Cimarex's founding in 2002. He has more than 30 years of industry experience. Before Cimarex, he held the same titles at Key Production. When Cimarex was spun off from its parent, Helmerich & Payne, it also acquired Key Production. Many of Key's executives retained leadership positions at Cimarex after the acquisition. Excluding substantial stock awards granted during the creation of Cimarex, management compensation is average compared with other oil and gas firms of similar size. All told, management owns about 3% of the outstanding stock. Management's respectable equity stake, focus on generating excess returns on capital, and conservative business practices lead us to believe shareholders' interests are being protected.

707 Seventeeth Street Suite 3300 www.cimarex.com
Denver, CO 80202

Growth [A]	2002	2003	2004	2005
Revenue %	NMF	102.7	45.9	135.4
Earnings/Share %	NMF	69.5	61.7	36.5
Book Value/Share %	NMF	-14.3	30.6	136.5
Dividends/Share %	NMF	NMF	NMF	NMF

Profitability [A-]	2003	2004	2005	TTM
Return on Assets %	11.7	13.9	7.9	9.9
Oper Cash Flow $Mil	206	356	705	964
- Cap Spending $Mil	161	282	634	1,041
= Free Cash Flow $Mil	46	74	71	-77

Financial Health [A-]	2003	2004	2005	09-30-06
Long-term Debt $Mil	—	0	352	400
Total Equity $Mil	535	701	2,595	2,907
Debt/Equity Ratio	—	0.0	0.1	0.1

Competition	Market Cap $Mil	12 Mo Trailing Sales $Mil	Price/Cash Flow	Return On Assets%	Debt/ Equity	Total Return% 1 Yr	3 Yr
Cimarex Energy	3,024	1,401	3.1	9.9	0.1	-14.8	10.3
Devon Energy	29,649	11,274	4.3	9.4	0.3	8.1	33.7
Anadarko Petroleum	20,008	9,838	3.9	6.3	0.8	-7.4	20.4

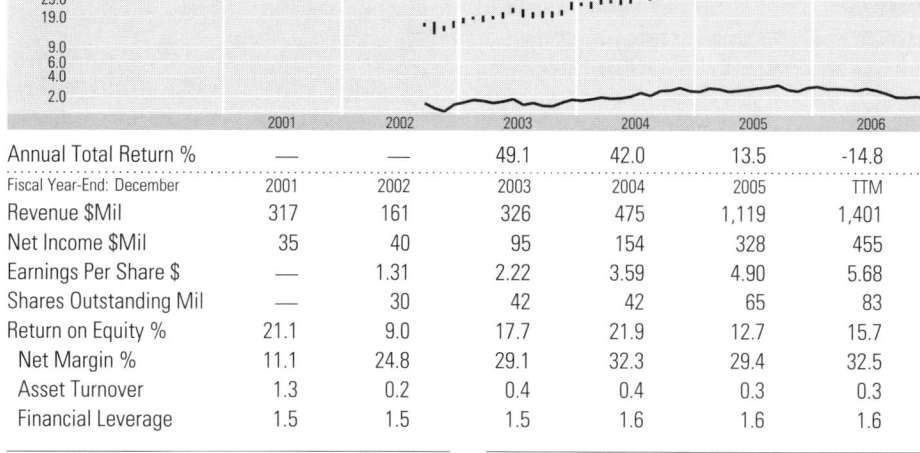

Price Volatility

	2001	2002	2003	2004	2005	2006
Annual $Price High			18.00	28.14	41.45	46.31	47.80
Low			13.23	17.07	24.05	33.35	32.56
Annual Total Return %	—	—	49.1	42.0	13.5	-14.8

Fiscal Year-End: December	2001	2002	2003	2004	2005	TTM
Revenue $Mil	317	161	326	475	1,119	1,401
Net Income $Mil	35	40	95	154	328	455
Earnings Per Share $	—	1.31	2.22	3.59	4.90	5.68
Shares Outstanding Mil	—	30	42	42	65	83
Return on Equity %	21.1	9.0	17.7	21.9	12.7	15.7
Net Margin %	11.1	24.8	29.1	32.3	29.4	32.5
Asset Turnover	1.3	0.2	0.4	0.4	0.3	0.3
Financial Leverage	1.5	1.5	1.5	1.6	1.6	1.6

Valuation Ratios	Stock	Rel to Industry	Rel to S&P 500
Price/Earnings	6.4	0.5	0.3
Price/Book	1.0	0.3	0.2
Price/Sales	2.2	1.2	0.8
Price/Cash Flow	3.1	0.4	0.2

Major Fund Holders	% of Fund Assets
Diamond Hill Small Cap A	3.72
Diamond Hill Small-Mid Cap I	3.71
Akros Absolute Return	2.96
Diamond Hill Select A	2.72

Thesis

By Justin Perucki, CFA, 12-11-06 Stock Price as of Analysis: $37.35

Cimarex is different from many of the other exploration and production companies we cover. Its focus on returns on invested capital, as opposed to many other firms' obsession with quickly boosting reserves, is a refreshing change.

Cimarex's primary talent and strategy center on the drill bit. The company shuns unconventional projects like coal bed methane and sets its sights on conventional basins in the Mid-Continent, Texas, and Gulf of Mexico. Because its desire to earn high returns trumps its desire to expand reserves, the firm is lured to projects with sound economics in these areas that its competitors would probably avoid. As a result, Cimarex isn't likely to be one of the fastest-growing E&P companies, but it does have a decent shot at adding shareholder value over time. One of the potential risks in this strategy is that the firm may occasionally run low on new drilling prospects. Consequently, it may feel the itch to make acquisitions to replenish its portfolio.

An example is Cimarex's 2005 purchase of Magnum Hunter. Although the deal fits Cimarex's strategy geologically--it adds conventional oil and gas assets in areas where the firm already operates--we question the timing and the price paid. We initially saw little margin for error in this transaction, though the deal looks much better using our higher natural-gas price assumptions. To add considerable value for shareholders, though, we think oil and gas prices will need to stay high for some time and Cimarex's drilling program will need to deliver. Cimarex has control over its drilling program, and its record is good. However, oil and gas prices are out of its hands.

The Magnum Hunter transaction really raises the stakes at Cimarex, in our view. If oil and gas prices decline for an extended period, the deal could become quite costly. Also, Cimarex's drilling capabilities will be put to the test over the next few years. As the firm weathers these risks, it will also have to contend with integrating Magnum Hunter's properties and personnel into its own.

We believe Cimarex has a narrow moat. The firm principally benefits from the stranded nature of natural gas, which inhibits cheap natural-gas imports from outside North America. Management's strong determination to generate excess returns on invested capital helps ensure shareholders' capital is used efficiently. Although oil represents only about 25% of the production mix, Cimarex still benefits from OPEC's influence on oil prices.

Data as of 12-29-06

Cintas CTAS

	Rating	Fair Value	Last Close	Consider Buy	Consider Sell	Yield %
	★★★	$45.00	$39.71	$34.70	$56.40	0.88

Company Profile

Cintas is the leader of the uniform industry. Boasting more than 700,000 customers, it designs, manufactures, rents, and sells uniforms to businesses in various industries, and roughly 5 million employees in these industries wear its uniforms every day. Cintas also provides ancillary products such as entrance mats, restroom supplies, first-aid and safety products and services, and document-management services.

Industry	Business Risk	Moat Size	Investment Style	Sector
Business Support	Average	Wide	Mid Core	Business Services

Competition

	Market Cap $Mil	12 Mo Trailing Sales $Mil	Price/Cash Flow	Return On Assets%	Debt/ Equity	Total Return% 1 Yr	3 Yr
Cintas	6,376	3,494	13.5	9.9	0.3	-2.6	-6.7
Aramark	6,029	11,621	10.3	5.0	1.2	21.5	9.0
G & K Services A	833	896	12.1	4.3	0.4	-0.6	2.0

Management — Stewardship Grade [A]

Scott Farmer, 47, has been CEO since 2003 and has served Cintas for more than 20 years. His father, Richard Farmer, is Cintas' founder, former CEO, current chairman, and the largest shareholder, owning 11% of shares outstanding. Cintas' management ranks highly as a shareholder steward. Salaries are very reasonable and bonuses are variable. In 2004, bonuses were virtually eliminated because earnings grew less than 10%. We also appreciate the firm's detailed disclosure of incentive criteria, which are evenly weighted between operating profit and earnings per share targets. Over the past three years, less than 1% of shares outstanding have been granted as options, and the top five executives combined received less than 5% of this figure. Overall operating performance has been commendable--revenue, income, and dividends have increased annually for more than two decades, and return on invested capital is solid. Attenuating our view of management is Richard Farmer's somewhat excessive compensation as chairman and plurality voting for directors. Shareholder proposals in 2005 addressed both of these concerns, but a majority vote was not reached. We're also not fond Cintas' investment in an aircraft owned by Richard Farmer.

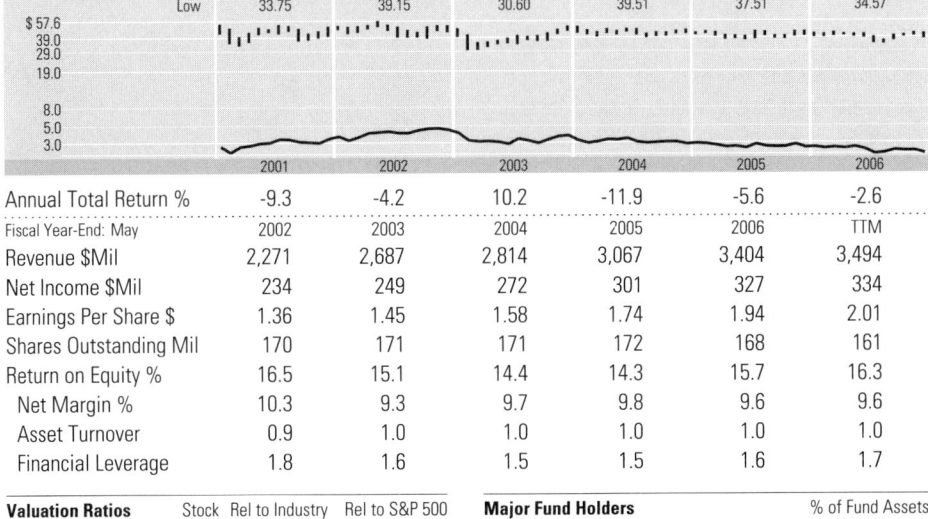

	2001	2002	2003	2004	2005	2006
Annual $Price High	53.25	56.62	50.68	50.35	45.50	44.30
Low	33.75	39.15	30.60	39.51	37.51	34.57
Annual Total Return %	-9.3	-4.2	10.2	-11.9	-5.6	-2.6

Fiscal Year-End: May	2002	2003	2004	2005	2006	TTM
Revenue $Mil	2,271	2,687	2,814	3,067	3,404	3,494
Net Income $Mil	234	249	272	301	327	334
Earnings Per Share $	1.36	1.45	1.58	1.74	1.94	2.01
Shares Outstanding Mil	170	171	171	172	168	161
Return on Equity %	16.5	15.1	14.4	14.3	15.7	16.3
Net Margin %	10.3	9.3	9.7	9.8	9.6	9.6
Asset Turnover	0.9	1.0	1.0	1.0	1.0	1.0
Financial Leverage	1.8	1.6	1.5	1.5	1.6	1.7

Valuation Ratios	Stock	Rel to Industry	Rel to S&P 500
Price/Earnings	19.8	0.7	1.0
Price/Book	3.1	0.7	0.8
Price/Sales	1.8	0.4	0.6
Price/Cash Flow	13.5	0.7	0.9

Major Fund Holders	% of Fund Assets
Principal Inv MidCap Blend Pfd	3.49
FMI Large Cap	3.37
Black Pearl Focus	3.31
Pioneer Small and Mid Cap Growth A	3.26

6800 Cintas Boulevard P.O. Box 625737 www.cintas.com
Cincinnati, OH 45262-5737

Growth [C]	2003	2004	2005	2006
Revenue %	18.3	4.7	9.0	11.0
Earnings/Share %	6.6	9.0	10.1	11.5
Book Value/Share %	15.9	14.4	11.2	1.6
Dividends/Share %	8.0	7.4	10.3	9.4

Profitability [A]	2004	2005	2006	TTM
Return on Assets %	9.7	9.8	9.6	9.9
Oper Cash Flow $Mil	510	414	462	471
- Cap Spending $Mil	113	141	157	157
= Free Cash Flow $Mil	397	273	305	314

Financial Health [A]	2004	2005	2006	08-31-06
Long-term Debt $Mil	474	465	794	627
Total Equity $Mil	1,888	2,104	2,088	2,051
Debt/Equity Ratio	0.3	0.2	0.4	0.3

Thesis By Joel Bloomer, 11-07-06 Stock Price as of Analysis: $41.39

Cintas is a wide-moat firm that specializes in route-oriented, repeatable business services. After achieving dominant market share in the uniform rental market, Cintas hopes to leverage its economies of scale in new businesses with similar operating models.

Cintas benefits from significant scale advantages. The firm is the leading player in the uniform rental business, with about 30% share, while three companies--G&K Services, Aramark, and UniFirst --constitute another 40% of the $7 billion U.S. market. Cintas' substantial size advantage allows for better volume discounts from suppliers while keeping overhead costs low as a percentage of sales. As a result, Cintas enjoys an operating margin that is about 50% higher than its closest competitor. Further augmenting Cintas' wide moat is an extremely fragmented base of 700,000 customers, none contributing more than 1% of total revenue. This lopsided relationship with clients gives Cintas the bargaining power to structure favorable long-term contracts that allow for annual price increases.

Cintas' massive customer base offers attractive cross-selling opportunities. As the uniform business matures, Cintas is expanding its portfolio of non-rental services (25% of revenue), which mostly consist of uniform sales, first aid and safety, and document management. Cintas' customers already outsource certain functions and, therefore, may be receptive to new service offerings. Although these ancillary businesses are not as profitable as rentals, return on investment should improve as these new offerings gain scale, and Cintas' salespeople become familiar with new products.

Investors in Cintas face two primary risks--Cintas' acquisitions in new lines of business and employee discontent. Cintas has proved itself capable of integrating acquisitions, having purchased nearly 80 companies in the past two years. However, new additions are increasingly focused on non-rental businesses, Cintas' core competency. Another risk is the potential for unions to grow beyond their current 2% of Cintas' 30,000 employees, which could hurt profitability. Lastly, pending litigation related to discrimination and wage disputes might result in material judgments. The potential liability is presently unknown, according to the company.

Despite these concerns, we derive great comfort from management's admirable record: It has produced 37 consecutive years of revenue and income growth along with 23 years of dividend increases. We're confident that Cintas' moat will remain intact.

Data as of 12-29-06

Cisco Systems CSCO

	Rating	Fair Value	Last Close	Consider Buy	Consider Sell	Yield %
	★★★	$30.00	$27.33	$23.10	$37.60	0.00

Company Profile

Cisco Systems is the world's leading supplier of data-networking equipment and software. Its products include routers, switches, access equipment, and network-management software that allow data communication among dispersed computer networks. The firm has also entered newer markets, such as home networking, security devices, storage technology, and Internet-based telephony. Services account for about 16% of sales.

Industry	Business Risk	Moat Size	Investment Style	Sector
Data Networking	Average	Wide	Large Growth	Hardware

Competition

	Market Cap $Mil	12 Mo Trailing Sales $Mil	Price/Cash Flow	Return On Assets%	Debt/ Equity	Total Return% 1 Yr	3 Yr
Cisco Systems	165,967	30,118	18.9	13.2	0.3	59.6	4.1
Nortel Networks	11,591	11,078	—	-12.1	3.4	-12.7	-15.9
Juniper Networks	10,715	2,182	18.1	4.4	0.1	-15.1	-1.3

Management   Stewardship Grade [B]

Cisco has one of the deepest management benches in the technology industry, in our opinion, and notwithstanding its liberal use of stock options, Cisco's management has a solid track record of execution and corporate stewardship. John Chambers has been CEO since 1995. Most top managers, including Chambers, have sales or manufacturing backgrounds. After forgoing a salary for several years, Chambers' annual salary has been $350,000, with a $1.3 million bonus, for the past two years as the company struggled. He has typically taken home a big slug of options each year, though he received none during fiscal 2004. In total, Chambers holds about 30 million options and shares, which should keep his interests aligned with shareholders'. The biggest knock against Cisco's management is its massive use of stock options to compensate employees: The firm gave options equal to nearly 3% of shares outstanding during fiscal 2006. Cisco's option expense lowers our fair value estimate by nearly 15%. While the firm is now mandated to expense options on its income statement, it still clings to reporting pro forma results excluding the impact of options.

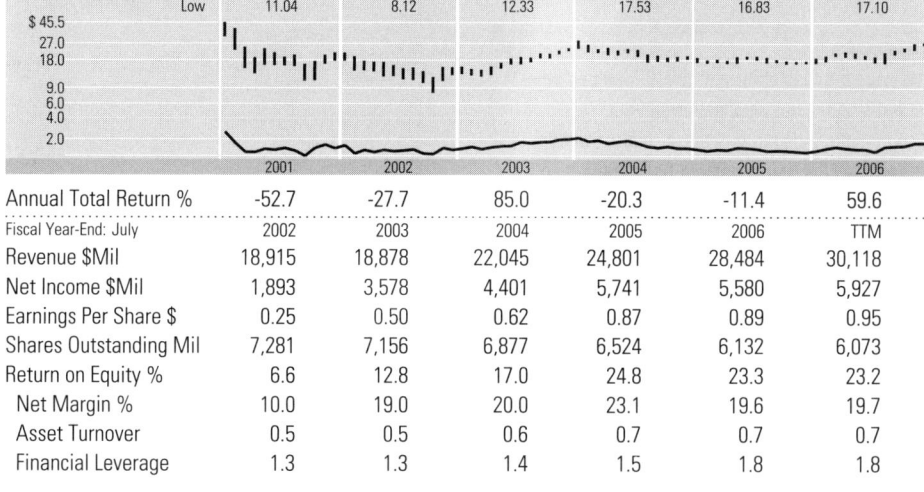

Price Volatility | Monthly Price High/Low   — Relative Strength to S&P 500

	2001	2002	2003	2004	2005	2006
Annual $Price High	44.50	21.84	24.60	29.39	20.25	27.96
Low	11.04	8.12	12.33	17.53	16.83	17.10
Annual Total Return %	-52.7	-27.7	85.0	-20.3	-11.4	59.6

Fiscal Year-End: July	2002	2003	2004	2005	2006	TTM
Revenue $Mil	18,915	18,878	22,045	24,801	28,484	30,118
Net Income $Mil	1,893	3,578	4,401	5,741	5,580	5,927
Earnings Per Share $	0.25	0.50	0.62	0.87	0.89	0.95
Shares Outstanding Mil	7,281	7,156	6,877	6,524	6,132	6,073
Return on Equity %	6.6	12.8	17.0	24.8	23.3	23.2
Net Margin %	10.0	19.0	20.0	23.1	19.6	19.7
Asset Turnover	0.5	0.5	0.6	0.7	0.7	0.7
Financial Leverage	1.3	1.3	1.4	1.5	1.8	1.8

Valuation Ratios	Stock	Rel to Industry	Rel to S&P 500
Price/Earnings	28.8	1.0	1.4
Price/Book	6.5	1.1	1.6
Price/Sales	5.5	1.0	1.9
Price/Cash Flow	18.9	1.0	1.3

Major Fund Holders	% of Fund Assets
Rydex Internet Inv	9.73
White Oak Select Growth	7.45
Rydex Telecommunications Inv	7.28
Managers 20 A	7.22

170 West Tasman Drive   www.cisco.com
San Jose, CA 95134-1706

Growth [B+]	2003	2004	2005	2006
Revenue %	-0.2	16.8	12.5	14.9
Earnings/Share %	100.0	24.0	40.3	2.3
Book Value/Share %	3.5	-7.1	-3.5	8.6
Dividends/Share %	NMF	NMF	NMF	NMF

Profitability [A+]	2004	2005	2006	TTM
Return on Assets %	12.4	16.9	12.9	13.2
Oper Cash Flow $Mil	6,962	7,568	7,899	8,768
- Cap Spending $Mil	613	692	772	771
= Free Cash Flow $Mil	6,349	6,876	7,127	7,997

Financial Health [A-]	2004	2005	2006	10-31-06
Long-term Debt $Mil	—	0	6,332	6,455
Total Equity $Mil	25,826	23,174	23,912	25,529
Debt/Equity Ratio	—	0.0	0.3	0.3

Thesis By John Slack, 11-09-06   Stock Price as of Analysis: $26.71

Cisco is the 800-pound gorilla of the data-networking industry, and with its recent acquisition of Scientific-Atlanta, we believe the firm is poised to extend its leadership into the market for video delivery as well. We would buy this wide-moat tech stalwart at a discount to our fair value estimate.

Cisco's scale and large installed base of enterprise customers is the source of its competitive advantage. As data has become a mission-critical component of business, customers prefer well-established, trusted vendors and are loath to switch to an unproven vendor. Cisco has translated its first-mover advantage into greater than 50% market share in the routing and switching markets and greater than 90% share in a number of key midrange segments of the corporate router market.

Cisco is building upon its dominance in switching and routing by moving into a number of high-growth markets that are natural extensions of its product line, such as security, storage, wireless networking, Internet-based telephony (or VoIP), and video. The firm's acquisition of Scientific-Atlanta meshes well with its end-to-end networking strategy, in our opinion, as managing video traffic has become an increasingly important component of networks. Offering end-to-end networking products allows Cisco to integrate additional functionality into its routers and switches--such as VoIP capability and security features--that not only help insulate it from pricing pressures, but also help "pull" the sales of additional products. The downside is that Cisco is now competing on numerous fronts, often against entrenched competitors.

The scale and breadth of Cisco's product line also drive its industry-leading margins and cash flow. The company uses its clout to demand the best component pricing available. It also uses its scale to fund key software and chipset development internally. Cisco spent more on R&D in fiscal 2004 than its rivals Nortel, Lucent, and Juniper combined.

We don't see any challengers to Cisco's dominant position in the networking equipment market. If anything, we believe Cisco's moat is widening, as evidenced by the company's share gains in most of its growth areas, and with the addition of Scientific-Atlanta, we believe the firm is poised to extend its leadership into the market for video delivery as well. Although we doubt the shares will return to the upward trajectory of the late 1990s, we believe the company's ability to throw off cash will be rewarded by the market over the long run.

Data as of 12-29-06

CIT Group CIT

	Rating	Fair Value	Last Close	Consider Buy	Consider Sell	Yield %
	★★★	$60.00	$55.77	$46.30	$75.20	1.43

Company Profile
CIT Group, founded in 1908, provides commercial and consumer financing and leasing services. The company provides a wide range of financing products to small, midsize, and larger companies in a variety of different industries, and home loan and student loan products to consumers. The firm managed almost $72 billion in assets as of Sept. 30, 2006.

Industry	Business Risk	Moat Size	Investment Style	Sector
Finance	Average	Narrow	Mid Value	Financial Services

Competition

	Market Cap $Mil	12 Mo Trailing Sales $Mil	Price/Cash Flow	Return On Assets%	Debt/ Equity	Total Return% 1 Yr	3 Yr
CIT Group	11,059	3,953	—	1.4	—	9.5	17.6
General Electric	383,564	161,022	12.8	2.5	2.2	9.4	9.0
Citigroup	273,691	86,566	—	1.3	—	19.6	8.4

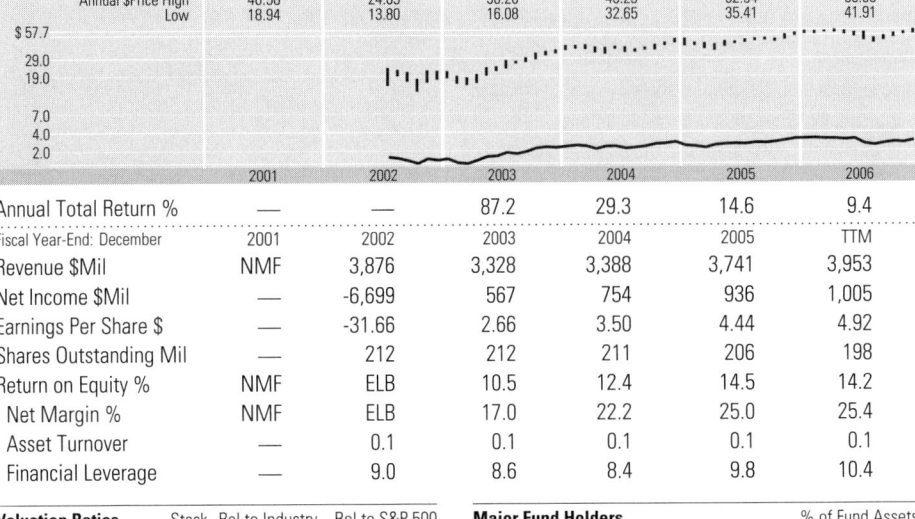

Price Volatility | Monthly Price High/Low — Relative Strength to S&P 500

Annual $Price High / Low			40.56 / 18.94	24.05 / 13.80	36.20 / 16.08	46.23 / 32.65	52.94 / 35.41	56.66 / 41.91
			2001	2002	2003	2004	2005	2006
Annual Total Return %			—	—	87.2	29.3	14.6	9.4
Fiscal Year-End: December			2001	2002	2003	2004	2005	TTM
Revenue $Mil			NMF	3,876	3,328	3,388	3,741	3,953
Net Income $Mil			—	-6,699	567	754	936	1,005
Earnings Per Share $			—	-31.66	2.66	3.50	4.44	4.92
Shares Outstanding Mil			—	212	212	211	206	198
Return on Equity %			NMF	ELB	10.5	12.4	14.5	14.2
Net Margin %			NMF	ELB	17.0	22.2	25.0	25.4
Asset Turnover			—	0.1	0.1	0.1	0.1	0.1
Financial Leverage			—	9.0	8.6	8.4	9.8	10.4

Management — Stewardship Grade [B]

We were big fans of former CEO Al Gamper, who retired in 2004, but we also haven't been disappointed thus far with his successor, current CEO Jeffrey Peek. CIT management has a reputation for being honest and grounded, maintaining a focus on the long term. Although management has recently begun providing annual earnings guidance--something that did not happen with Gamper--the firm still primarily focuses on long-term metrics and its strategies for achieving company goals, which we applaud. Management compensation is generous but not excessive, and the firm does not give away exorbitant amounts of options. CIT has been a good steward of shareholder capital in the past, and we see no reason the future should be any different. We're particularly fond of management's strict focus on achieving strong returns on invested capital in each of its various business segments. If a specific segment is not expected to generate the level of long-term returns that the firm requires, management will not hesitate to sell it and reinvest the freed-up capital into higher-return businesses. We think this type of capital-allocation discipline will serve investors well over the long run.

1 CIT Drive
Livingston, NJ 07039
www.citgroup.com

Growth [C-]	2002	2003	2004	2005
Revenue %	NMF	-14.1	1.8	10.4
Earnings/Share %	NMF	NMF	31.6	26.9
Book Value/Share %	NMF	12.6	11.1	9.0
Dividends/Share %	NMF	NMF	-13.3	17.3

Profitability [D-]	2003	2004	2005	TTM
Return on Assets %	1.2	1.5	1.5	1.4
Oper Cash Flow $Mil	2,482	1,618	2,913	—
- Cap Spending $Mil	2,096	1,489	2,359	—
= Free Cash Flow $Mil	—	—	—	—

Financial Health [NA]	2003	2004	2005	09-30-06
Long-term Debt $Mil	—	—	—	—
Total Equity $Mil	5,394	6,055	6,463	7,059
Debt/Equity Ratio	—	—	—	—

Valuation Ratios	Stock	Rel to Industry	Rel to S&P 500
Price/Earnings	11.3	0.6	0.5
Price/Book	1.6	0.4	0.4
Price/Sales	2.8	0.5	1.0
Price/Cash Flow	—	—	—

Major Fund Holders	% of Fund Assets
FBR Large Cap Financial	3.78
Kirr Marbach Partners Value	3.33
CastleRock	3.23
Aston/ABN AMRO Mid Cap Growth N	3.13

Thesis By Ryan Batchelor, CPA, 12-11-06 Stock Price as of Analysis: $53.10

With a 98-year history, CIT has intimate industry knowledge and long-standing client relationships that help it succeed. We think this finance company is around to stay, and we believe it will earn strong returns over the long haul.

CIT has the broad product line and experience to compete in almost any type of commercial financing, and it is now moving into certain segments of consumer financing, as well. The company is split into two main groups, specialty finance (SF) and commercial finance (CF). The firm's SF group provides leasing solutions and small-business loans to companies, and home loans and student loans to consumers. CIT is the largest small-business administration lender in the country. Some of the notable specialties in the CF group include aircraft and train leasing, factoring (purchase and collection of accounts receivable), and lending, leasing, and banking services to middle-market companies.

The firm's experience and strong relationships with customers are a potent deterrent for competitors and potential upstarts. CIT's customers, which generally consist of small and midsize companies, have proved to be very profitable when proper credit discipline is adhered to. This discipline has helped the company sail through some very stormy times without ever posting an operating loss. When credit losses do occur, CIT is diligent in recovering as much as possible. The result is a historical charge-off rate of less than 1% of loans outstanding.

In recent years, the number of finance companies has shrunk, thanks to consolidation among larger players and the departure of smaller, insolvent players. This is generally a plus for CIT because, as a survivor, the firm has greater market power. However, because of the economy's strength, banks--the historical lifeblood for small and midsize firms--have become more interested in CIT's customers, and price competition has intensified. To combat this trend, CIT takes a very personal, high-touch approach to its customer relationships--often lending to businesses in difficult times when others won't. As a result, companies have tended to be more loyal to CIT rather than jumping to the next cheapest deal.

CIT is poised to succeed, in our opinion. The company has recently moved into student loans--a business we think very highly of--and has plans to aggressively court clients in the ever-growing health-care industry. We also like management's cost-cutting plans and emphasis on increasing returns on equity, which we believe demonstrate the firm's focus on delivering value to shareholders.

Morningstar Stocks 500

Data as of 12-29-06

Citigroup C

	Rating	Fair Value	Last Close	Consider Buy	Consider Sell	Yield %
	★★★	$60.00	$55.70	$46.30	$75.20	3.52

Company Profile
Citigroup is one of the world's largest and most diverse financial-services companies. It is at or near the top of virtually all its product categories, including credit cards, consumer finance, retail banking, corporate lending, investment banking, and brokerage. The firm operates in more than 100 countries.

Management
Stewardship Grade [B]

Charles Prince became the top executive of Citigroup in October 2003 after the legendary Sanford Weill decided to elevate his chosen successor. After Weill fully retired, Prince added the chairmanship in April 2005--a move we frown upon due to stewardship issues that can arise from consolidating the two offices. If Citi doesn't start to show better growth in 2007, Prince could come under greater pressure from shareholders, some of whom have already started to murmur about the need to break up the conglomerate to enhance shareholder value or agitate for a broader management shakeup than just putting Robert Druskin into the vacant COO role, as occurred in late 2006. Prince pocketed $23 million in total compensation in 2005; this includes salary, bonus, perquisites, restricted stock, and options. Though high by any standard, this level of compensation is in line with other large financial institutions.

399 Park Avenue www.citigroup.com
New York, NY 10043

Growth [C+]	2002	2003	2004	2005
Revenue %	7.5	8.1	11.2	5.0
Earnings/Share %	8.1	16.3	-4.7	45.7
Book Value/Share %	6.7	12.5	10.2	4.0
Dividends/Share %	16.7	57.1	45.5	10.0

Profitability [A]	2003	2004	2005	TTM
Return on Assets %	1.4	1.1	1.6	1.3
Oper Cash Flow $Mil	-14,862	-2,276	31,845	—
- Cap Spending $Mil	2,354	3,011	3,724	—
= Free Cash Flow $Mil	—	—	—	—

Financial Health [NA]	2003	2004	2005	09-30-06
Long-term Debt $Mil	—	—	—	—
Total Equity $Mil	98,014	108,166	111,412	116,865
Debt/Equity Ratio	—	—	—	—

Industry	Business Risk	Moat Size	Investment Style	Sector
International Banks	Average	Wide	Large Value	Financial Services

Competition	Market Cap $Mil	12 Mo Trailing Sales $Mil	Price/Cash Flow	Return On Assets%	Debt/ Equity	Total Return% 1 Yr	3 Yr
Citigroup	273,691	86,566	—	1.3	—	19.6	8.4
Bank of America	239,758	68,368	—	1.3	—	20.7	15.2
J.P. Morgan Chase & Co.	167,551	59,650	—	0.9	—	25.6	13.2

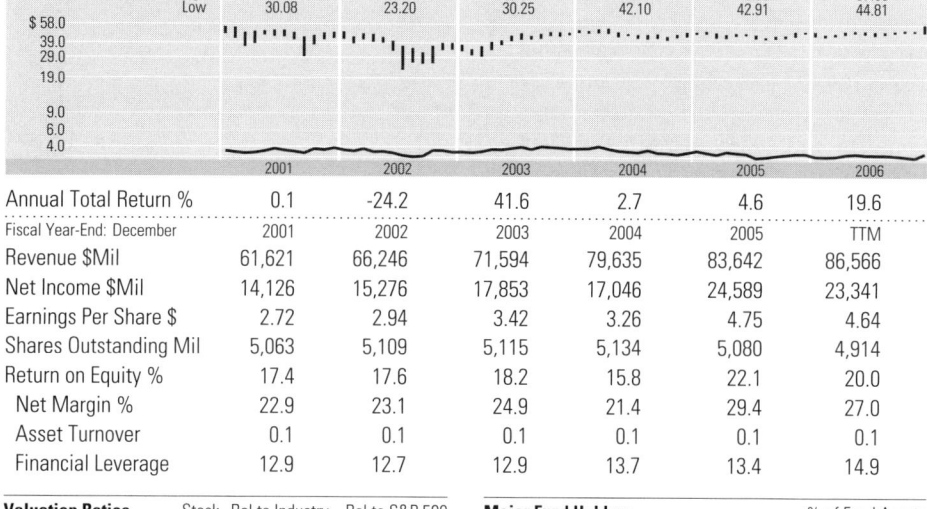

	2001	2002	2003	2004	2005	TTM
Annual Total Return %	0.1	-24.2	41.6	2.7	4.6	19.6
Fiscal Year-End: December	2001	2002	2003	2004	2005	TTM
Revenue $Mil	61,621	66,246	71,594	79,635	83,642	86,566
Net Income $Mil	14,126	15,276	17,853	17,046	24,589	23,341
Earnings Per Share $	2.72	2.94	3.42	3.26	4.75	4.64
Shares Outstanding Mil	5,063	5,109	5,115	5,134	5,080	4,914
Return on Equity %	17.4	17.6	18.2	15.8	22.1	20.0
Net Margin %	22.9	23.1	24.9	21.4	29.4	27.0
Asset Turnover	0.1	0.1	0.1	0.1	0.1	0.1
Financial Leverage	12.9	12.7	12.9	13.7	13.4	14.9

Valuation Ratios	Stock	Rel to Industry	Rel to S&P 500
Price/Earnings	13.3	0.7	0.6
Price/Book	2.3	0.9	0.6
Price/Sales	3.2	0.8	1.1
Price/Cash Flow	—	—	—

Major Fund Holders	% of Fund Assets
ProFunds Banks UltraSector Inv	13.39
North Track Dow Jones US Fin 100 A	9.41
Wells Fargo Advantage Spec Fin Serv A	8.35
AIM Financial Services Inv	8.15

Thesis By Craig Woker, CFA, 12-14-06 Stock Price as of Analysis: $53.11

Citigroup is in the midst of a transformation. Once known for industry-shaping mega-mergers and consistently robust double-digit income growth, Citi has slowed down to focus on squeezing out internal efficiencies. This isn't exciting stuff, but it can make for some solid value creation. Plus, because of the attractive markets around the globe in which the firm operates, a slower-growth Citi should still look like a robust performer compared with many U.S. banks.

There is little question that Citi is an impressive firm. Even if this conglomerate were broken up, most of its units could earn wide moat ratings on their own. But although we've talked over the years about this firm's competitive edges, this analysis of strategic minutiae can overlook two equally important points--factors that are likely to drive results over the next couple of years. First, while Citigroup is a U.S.-based bank, the firm is a truly global business, with correspondingly higher embedded growth prospects. So, just because Citi's growth will inevitably slow, it won't come to a grinding halt. Second, because of the company's global footprint (100-plus countries) and the fungible nature of its assets, Citi has historically ferreted out exceptional loan yields around the world--a head start toward above-average returns on capital.

Citi derives almost half of its profits outside the U.S., and this proportion will grow with time. On average, worldwide nominal GDP growth has averaged a couple of percentage points higher than the U.S. over the past decade, and this spread is likely to remain for the foreseeable future. Because banking growth generally keeps pace with local economic growth, Citi should be able to generate respectable organic expansion in loans and deposits (7%-8%) just by keeping pace with the relative economic expansion of the countries in which it operates.

Additionally, just because Citi offers thousands of products around the globe doesn't mean that profits are watered down for the sake of revenue diversity. To the contrary, Citi has typically generated yields--even on a risk-adjusted basis--that most banks can only covet. For example, Citi has earned a 9.6% rate on its loans since the company's formation in the late 1990s. In other words, it earns about 20%-25% more on its major product than the average U.S. bank. Though some of this yield advantage has typically been lost because of Citi's relatively weak base of no-interest deposits, the firm's current expansion of retail banking should only aide its cause.

Data as of 12-29-06

Citizens Communications CZN

	Rating	Fair Value	Last Close	Consider Buy	Consider Sell	Yield %
	★★★	$13.00	$14.37	$10.00	$16.30	6.96

	Industry	Business Risk	Moat Size	Investment Style	Sector
	Telecom Svcs.	Average	Narrow	Mid Value	Telecommunication

Company Profile
Citizens Communications serves about 2.1 million phone lines and 365,000 high-speed Internet access customers under the Frontier brand in 24 states. About 40% of customers are in New York, with a bit more than half of those in the Rochester area. These businesses were acquired from Global Crossing, Verizon, and a handful of smaller companies. The firm agreed to sell its competitive local phone company, Electric Lightwave, and acquire Commonwealth Telephone during 2006.

Management   Stewardship Grade [C]
Leonard Tow, who amassed his fortune in the cable business, took control of Citizens in 1989 and shaped it into a telecom firm. Tow resigned as CEO effective with the announcement of the firm's new dividend policy in 2004 and later surrendered the chairman title as well. We weren't fond of Citizens' corporate governance under Tow, but the situation appears to be improving. All but four of the firm's 13 directors have been appointed since Tow's departure. Among the directors who have left is an individual whose law firm has done extensive business with Citizens. The executive ranks have also seen considerable turnover since 2004. We like the fact that CEO Maggie Wilderotter's compensation includes a large restricted-stock component. The firm also issues very few stock options generally, using restricted stock for most employees. Wilderotter took the chairman title as well in December 2005. We would have preferred the firm give this role to a separate individual. Wilderotter spent two years as a vice president at Microsoft but had worked extensively in the cable and wireless businesses before that. She held the top spot at interactive television firm Wink for six years until it was sold to Liberty Media.

3 High Ridge Park
Stamford, CT 06905
www.czn.net

Growth [D]	2002	2003	2004	2005
Revenue %	8.7	-8.4	-10.6	-0.3
Earnings/Share %	NMF	NMF	-64.1	160.9
Book Value/Share %	-49.4	15.6	-9.9	-28.9
Dividends/Share %	NMF	NMF	NMF	-60.0

Profitability [B-]	2003	2004	2005	TTM
Return on Assets %	2.5	1.1	3.2	5.8
Oper Cash Flow $Mil	742	711	844	835
- Cap Spending $Mil	277	275	268	265
= Free Cash Flow $Mil	465	436	576	569

Financial Health [D+]	2003	2004	2005	09-30-06
Long-term Debt $Mil	4,196	4,267	3,999	3,948
Total Equity $Mil	1,415	1,362	1,042	983
Debt/Equity Ratio	3.0	3.1	3.8	4.0

Competition

	Market Cap $Mil	12 Mo Trailing Sales $Mil	Price/Cash Flow	Return On Assets%	Debt/Equity	Total Return% 1 Yr	3 Yr
Citizens Communications	4,626	2,184	5.5	5.8	4.0	26.6	17.5
AT&T	137,384	60,171	9.0	4.9	0.5	51.6	16.3
Verizon Communications	108,723	88,881	4.4	3.7	0.7	34.9	8.0

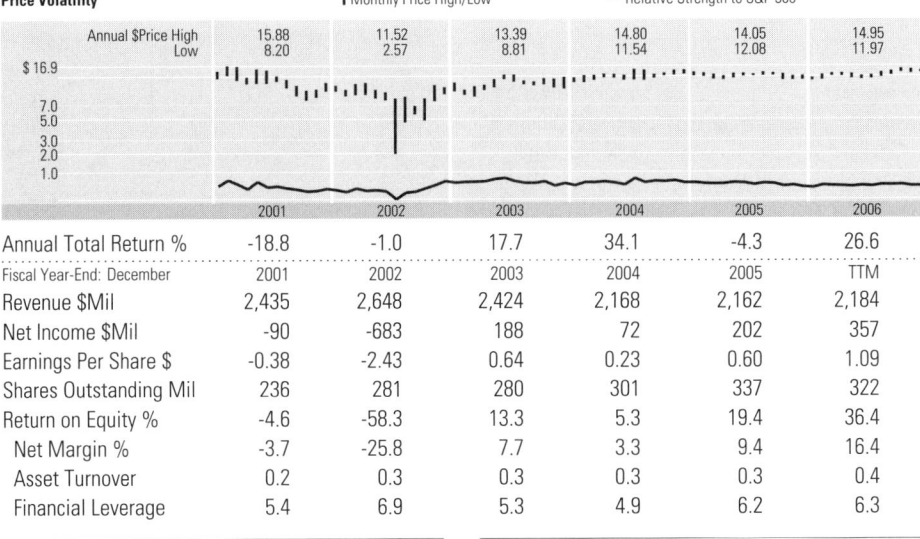

Price Volatility — Monthly Price High/Low — Relative Strength to S&P 500

	2001	2002	2003	2004	2005	2006
Annual $Price High	15.88	11.52	13.39	14.80	14.05	14.95
Low	8.20	2.57	8.81	11.54	12.08	11.97
Annual Total Return %	-18.8	-1.0	17.7	34.1	-4.3	26.6

Fiscal Year-End: December	2001	2002	2003	2004	2005	TTM
Revenue $Mil	2,435	2,648	2,424	2,168	2,162	2,184
Net Income $Mil	-90	-683	188	72	202	357
Earnings Per Share $	-0.38	-2.43	0.64	0.23	0.60	1.09
Shares Outstanding Mil	236	281	280	301	337	322
Return on Equity %	-4.6	-58.3	13.3	5.3	19.4	36.4
Net Margin %	-3.7	-25.8	7.7	3.3	9.4	16.4
Asset Turnover	0.2	0.3	0.3	0.3	0.3	0.4
Financial Leverage	5.4	6.9	5.3	4.9	6.2	6.3

Valuation Ratios	Stock	Rel to Industry	Rel to S&P 500
Price/Earnings	17.1	0.9	0.8
Price/Book	4.7	1.1	1.1
Price/Sales	2.1	0.9	0.7
Price/Cash Flow	5.5	0.6	0.4

Major Fund Holders	% of Fund Assets
Reaves Select Research Instl	4.08
Pioneer Classic Balanced A	2.39
Kirr Marbach Partners Value	2.28
FMC Strategic Value	2.23

Thesis By Michael Hodel, CFA, 12-08-06 Stock Price as of Analysis: $14.06

Citizens' financial position, in terms of both leverage and cash flow committed to pay dividends, is better than many rural phone companies. We also like the firm's decision to acquire Commonwealth, a business that we believe embodies the benefits of rural markets and was available at a reasonable price. We remain concerned that growing competition will limit growth and pressure profitability.

Rural phone companies like Citizens have garnered attention in recent years as safe havens in the telecom industry. The revenue opportunity in small markets often isn't large enough to attract as much attention from rivals, and regulations can provide more insulation from competition than in urban areas. Wireless service is also sometimes spotty, making substitution for fixed-line service less attractive. As a result, Citizens has historically generated steady cash flow, which it uses to support a fairly large debt load and pay a large dividend.

Our fear with the rural telecom companies is that competition is increasing and less-profitable services are taking the place of higher-margin revenues. Citizens, in particular, faces more competition than many small phone companies because it serves Rochester, N.Y., a market that, thanks to its size, has attracted more interest from rivals. Rochester, which accounts for about 20% of Citizens' business, is a Time Warner market, and the cable giant has offered phone service there since 2004. We think Citizens has prepared better than most rural peers for increased competition, aggressively offering high-speed Internet access. In Rochester, specifically, the firm has slowed the rate at which it is losing customers recently.

Across all of Citizens' markets, though, customer losses continue to accelerate. Cable companies are pushing out into smaller markets, using discounts on packages of services to generate growth and fend off satellite competitors. In response, Citizens has been ratcheting up promotions and discounts. We also think the firm will need to increase capital spending over time to maintain its ability to match the competition. We are concerned that the firm may hold back on necessary spending in order to fund the dividend, buy back shares, and pay down debt.

Citizens earns about 22% of its revenue from subsidies and regulated fees other carriers pay to use its network. These revenue streams deliver exceptionally high margins. Though actions that hurt rural carriers are politically unpopular today, an adverse regulatory change could hurt the firm. Changes in either the competitive or regulatory arena could hinder Citizens' ability to sustain its dividend.

Data as of 12-29-06

City National CYN

Rating	Fair Value	Last Close	Consider Buy	Consider Sell	Yield %
★★★	$74.00	$71.20	$57.10	$92.70	2.30

Company Profile
Based in Beverly Hills, Calif., City National is a regional bank with more than $14 billion in assets, catering to individuals with $1 million or more in assets and small to midsize companies with annual revenue of $5-$250 million. The bank offers traditional lending and deposit products, combined with wealth-management, brokerage, international banking, and trust services.

Management Stewardship Grade [B]
CEO Russell Goldsmith has run the bank since 1995, and the results speak for themselves. With a strong California economy helping business, City National has outperformed its peers in growth of assets, revenue, and net income. Goldsmith is handsomely rewarded for the bank's performance, in our opinion, raking in more than $3 million in total compensation in 2005, 26% of which was stock awards. While one could argue that the bank's results merit this pay package, his compensation is significantly above that of peer banks. Although City National does have separate individuals as chairman and CEO, they are father and son. Together they beneficially own 18% of the outstanding shares. Although this ownership is not 100% directly controlled by these two people, it should make the individual investor wary. City National hasn't historically expensed stock options, but in 2003, it began issuing increasing amounts of restricted stock, which is expensed. The 10-member board of directors serves staggered three-year terms and is required to own a threshold amount of bank stock.

City National Center 400 North Roxbury Drive www.cnb.com
Beverly Hills, CA 90210

Growth [C+]	2002	2003	2004	2005
Revenue %	16.8	4.6	5.5	12.4
Earnings/Share %	20.3	4.5	8.6	13.9
Book Value/Share %	19.7	12.6	8.7	8.2
Dividends/Share %	5.4	24.4	32.0	12.5

Profitability [A]	2003	2004	2005	TTM
Return on Assets %	1.4	1.5	1.6	1.6
Oper Cash Flow $Mil	237	194	286	—
- Cap Spending $Mil	18	23	33	—
= Free Cash Flow $Mil	—	—	—	—

Financial Health [NA]	2003	2004	2005	09-30-06
Long-term Debt $Mil	—	—	—	—
Total Equity $Mil	1,219	1,349	1,458	1,458
Debt/Equity Ratio	—	—	—	—

Industry	Business Risk	Moat Size	Investment Style	Sector
Regional Banks	Average	Narrow	Mid Value	Financial Services

Competition
	Market Cap $Mil	12 Mo Trailing Sales $Mil	Price/Cash Flow	Return On Assets%	Debt/ Equity	Total Return% 1 Yr	3 Yr
City National	3,612	846	—	1.6	—	0.6	6.9
Bank of America	239,758	68,368	—	1.3	—	20.7	15.2
Wells Fargo	120,049	34,770	—	1.7	—	16.8	10.4

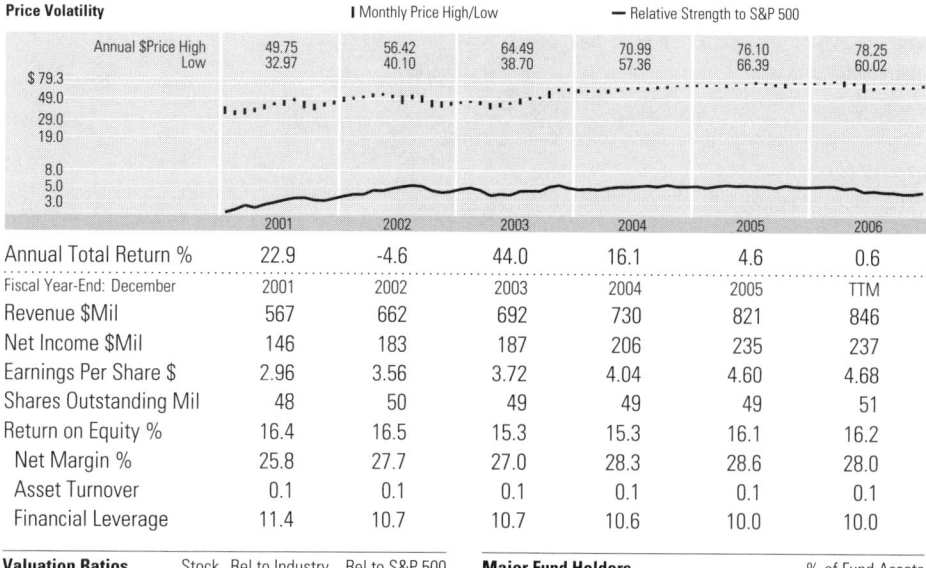

	2001	2002	2003	2004	2005	2006
Annual $Price High	49.75	56.42	64.49	70.99	76.10	78.25
Low	32.97	40.10	38.70	57.36	66.39	60.02
Annual Total Return %	22.9	-4.6	44.0	16.1	4.6	0.6

Fiscal Year-End: December	2001	2002	2003	2004	2005	TTM
Revenue $Mil	567	662	692	730	821	846
Net Income $Mil	146	183	187	206	235	237
Earnings Per Share $	2.96	3.56	3.72	4.04	4.60	4.68
Shares Outstanding Mil	48	50	49	49	49	51
Return on Equity %	16.4	16.5	15.3	15.3	16.1	16.2
Net Margin %	25.8	27.7	27.0	28.3	28.6	28.0
Asset Turnover	0.1	0.1	0.1	0.1	0.1	0.1
Financial Leverage	11.4	10.7	10.7	10.6	10.0	10.0

Valuation Ratios	Stock	Rel to Industry	Rel to S&P 500
Price/Earnings	15.2	0.8	0.7
Price/Book	2.5	0.8	0.6
Price/Sales	4.3	0.7	1.5
Price/Cash Flow	—	—	—

Major Fund Holders	% of Fund Assets
Ancora Bancshares D	6.11
Hallmark Mid-Cap Growth I	2.42
Hallmark Informed Investors Growth R	2.33
Allianz RCM Financial Services Instl	2.13

Thesis By Michael Kon, CFA, 12-04-06 Stock Price as of Analysis: $68.96

City National's focus on affluent individuals and their businesses produces pleasing returns to owners. We see plenty of untapped growth outside its current footprint.

City National provides retail banking services through a network of branches in California. The bank has also established a presence in New York City and is in the process of acquiring a bank in Nevada. In addition to retail banking, City National offers investment and trust services and banking solutions for international trade. The bank differentiates itself by targeting wealthy individuals with more than $1 million in assets and small to midsize businesses with established revenue of $1 million to $250 million.

We think the focus on affluent individuals is one of the bank's main strengths. City National's clients typically have a solid asset base and generate a high level of annual income. Clients also enjoy minimal delinquencies, which translates into a low level of loan losses for City National. Net charge-offs of gross loans have averaged 0.22% over the past 10 years. Moreover, serving affluent individuals requires a degree of personal touch. This basically means that City National's bankers form relationships with their clients and in many cases with their families and the businesses that they own. These relationships, in our view, further widen City National's economic moat.

Another important advantage is the bank's attractive deposit base. Unlike peers that fund a large chunk of their assets with expensive certificate deposits, City National enjoys an abundant supply of cheap funding. Affluent clients flood the bank with boatloads of noninterest deposits, the cheapest funding source available for banks. Noninterest deposits account for more than 50% of total deposits, compared with a peer average of about 25%. Combine the bank's average loan yields with very cheap deposits, and you get industry-leading net interest margins, averaging 4.7% over the past five years.

The bank also keeps a tight rein on operational expenses. The efficiency ratio hovers near a respectable 53%, which is, on average, 150 basis points below peers'. This, combined with an industry-leading NIM, results in a peer-superior return on average equity of about 18% over the past 10 years.

We think City National's ability to serve its niche market translates into solid returns for investors, and we'd snap up shares given the right price.

Data as of 12-29-06

Clear Channel Outdoor Holdings CCO

	Rating	Fair Value	Last Close	Consider Buy	Consider Sell	Yield %
	★	$20.00	$27.91	$15.40	$25.10	0.0

Industry	Business Risk	Moat Size	Investment Style	Sector
Advertising	Average	Narrow	Mid Growth	Business Services

Company Profile

Clear Channel Outdoor was formed through a series of acquisitions of smaller outdoor companies, with most of the heavy acquisition activity taking place between 1997 and 2002. The company has two segments: U.S. and international. In the United States, billboards (73% of segment sales) contribute higher profit margins than street furniture and transit displays. Billboards and street furniture represent 44% and 34% of sales, respectively, in the international segment.

Management Stewardship Grade [C]

In evaluating Clear Channel Outdoor's corporate governance, we place heavy emphasis on the management team of the parent company, Clear Channel, which holds 90% of the shares. In October 2006, the board of directors announced that it is evaluating various strategic alternatives, which could involve completely spinning off the remaining 90% of Clear Channel Outdoor or an outright sale of the outdoor business to another company. We think the company's corporate governance has room for improvement. Mark Mays serves as CEO of both the parent and the outdoor company. Most of our issues with Clear Channel revolve around the way the firm is essentially family-managed. Three members of the Mays family occupy the positions of chairman, CEO, and CFO of the parent company. We don't like the fact that each of these executives has a seven-year employment contract with automatic daily extensions. The contracts also allow for generous severance and change-in-control payments, which are triggered if the CEO title is held by someone other than these three members of the Mays clan.

200 East Basse Road www.clearchanneloutdoor.com
San Antonio, TX 78209

Growth [C]	2002	2003	2004	2005
Revenue %	6.4	16.9	12.5	9.0
Earnings/Share %	NMF	NMF	NMF	NMF
Book Value/Share %	—	—	—	—
Dividends/Share %	—	—	—	—

Profitability [D]	2003	2004	2005	TTM
Return on Assets %	-0.7	-3.0	1.3	2.5
Oper Cash Flow $Mil	433	492	510	560
- Cap Spending $Mil	249	176	208	242
= Free Cash Flow $Mil	184	316	302	318

Financial Health [D]	2003	2004	2005	09-30-06
Long-term Debt $Mil	70	30	87	105
Total Equity $Mil	2,760	2,730	1,209	1,445
Debt/Equity Ratio	0.0	0.0	0.1	0.1

Competition	Market Cap $Mil	12 Mo Trailing Sales $Mil	Price/Cash Flow	Return On Assets%	Debt/Equity	Total Return% 1 Yr	3 Yr
Clear Channel Outdoor Holdings	9,894	2,802	17.7	2.5	0.1	39.9	—
Omnicom Group	17,866	11,100	10.6	5.1	0.8	24.1	7.5
WPP Group PLC ADR	16,984	9,809	11.1	2.9	0.4	27.4	12.6

Price Volatility — Monthly Price High/Low — Relative Strength to S&P 500

	2001	2002	2003	2004	2005	2006
Annual $Price High/Low					20.40 / 17.75	28.13 / 18.49
Annual Total Return %	—	—	—	—	—	39.9

Fiscal Year-End: December	2001	2002	2003	2004	2005	TTM
Revenue $Mil	1,748	1,860	2,175	2,447	2,666	2,802
Net Income $Mil	-281	-3,583	-35	-155	62	128
Earnings Per Share $	—	—	—	—	—	—
Shares Outstanding Mil	—	—	—	—	—	354
Return on Equity %	-5.2	ELB	-1.3	-5.7	5.1	8.9
Net Margin %	-16.1	ELB	-1.6	-6.4	2.3	4.6
Asset Turnover	0.2	0.4	0.4	0.5	0.5	0.5
Financial Leverage	1.4	1.9	1.9	1.9	4.1	3.6

Valuation Ratios	Stock	Rel to Industry	Rel to S&P 500
Price/Earnings	—	—	—
Price/Book	6.8	1.4	1.7
Price/Sales	3.5	0.8	1.2
Price/Cash Flow	17.7	1.3	1.2

Major Fund Holders	% of Fund Assets
VALIC II Mid Cap Growth	1.16
SunAmerica Tax Managed Equity C	1.13
Oppenheimer Small & Mid Cap Value A	1.04

Thesis By Michael Corty, CFA, 11-08-06 Stock Price as of Analysis: $24.99

We think Clear Channel Outdoor's prospects in the United States (46% of sales and 65% of cash flow) are bright, thanks to industry concentration and a favorable regulatory environment. The top three players--Clear Channel, Viacom, and Lamar Advertising--control 65% of the U.S. billboard market, while the Highway Beautification Act of 1965 limits the number of new billboards that can be built, cementing Clear Channel's position in existing markets and giving the company pricing power with advertisers.

We think Clear Channel participates in one of the few "old media" businesses with solid growth prospects. Outdoor advertising revenue in the United States has increased at a 7% clip over the past decade, according to the Outdoor Advertising Association of America. Billboards are an effective way to build brands at a relatively low price per thousand viewer impressions. Additionally, we think the outdoor business model is shielded from disruptive technologies that have fragmented the audiences of other traditional media platforms like newspapers and television. As long as people continue to commute to work, we don't see a viable substitute or an emerging threat to outdoor advertising.

We are big fans of Clear Channel's domestic assets; however, we have some concerns about its international operations. Structural differences in the economics of the business mean that Clear Channel's profitability overseas is less than half that in the U.S. A key difference is that outside the U.S., outdoor advertisers are often not allowed to own the lease permit. Thus, the permit owners often take a big share of profits through revenue-sharing and minimum guaranteed payment arrangements.

Some more specific concerns involve England and France, which together contribute about 50% of Clear Channel's international sales. In England, the issues are structural. For example, billboard contracts can be as short as a few weeks, crimping profit margins as Clear Channel absorbs the cost of frequently changing the billboard content. (U.S. billboard contracts usually run between six and 12 months). Additionally, the national ad buyers have consolidated to four major players, which makes rate increases difficult. In France, the company has undergone a restructuring in each of the past two years in response to overcapacity and a lackluster economy.

While Clear Channel's international business isn't nearly as attractive as its U.S. operations, we'd still buy the shares at our 5-star price.

Data as of 12-29-06

Clorox CLX

	Rating	Fair Value	Last Close	Consider Buy	Consider Sell	Yield %
	★★★	$61.00	$64.15	$52.00	$80.10	1.81

Company Profile

Clorox mainly produces chlorine and nonchlorine bleaches, food products, and cleansers. The company also makes other well-known consumer products, including Pine-Sol and Formula 409 household cleansers, S.O.S. soap pads, Glad plastic wrap, and Kingsford and Match Light charcoal products. In addition, it produces Liquid-Plumr drain openers, Brita water filters, Armor All automotive-cleaning products, and STP automotive additives.

Management Stewardship Grade [B]

In September 2005, Donald Knauss, president of North American operations for Coca-Cola, was appointed chairman and CEO. He is the first outsider to take the helm of Clorox. In Knauss, Clorox taps a leader with strong brand expertise and a record of working with domestic retailers. This experience will come in handy, given the intense cost pressures and competitive categories that Clorox faces. Knauss received $500,000 in cash to sign on with the firm. He will receive a base salary of $950,000 and an annual cash bonus ranging from 115% to 200% of his annual base salary, determined by financial targets for earnings per share, sales growth, and working capital. This compensation is about standard for consumer product companies, but we think the minimum for cash bonuses should be 0%. We also believe the additional $50,000 in loss protection he received for the sale of his Atlanta home is a bit excessive. The CEO must hold stock equal to 4 times his or her base salary while other executive officers' holdings must be 3 times base salary. Insiders own less than 1.0% of shares outstanding. We like that directors at Clorox are elected annually, but we think the firm took a step backward when it chose to hire Knauss as both chairman and CEO, roles we believe should remain separated.

1221 Broadway www.clorox.com
Oakland, CA 94612-1888

Growth [C+]	2003	2004	2005	2006
Revenue %	3.3	4.4	5.4	5.8
Earnings/Share %	62.8	14.8	138.7	-52.5
Book Value/Share %	-5.4	30.7	NMF	NMF
Dividends/Share %	4.8	22.7	1.9	3.6

Profitability [A]	2004	2005	2006	TTM
Return on Assets %	14.3	30.3	12.3	12.6
Oper Cash Flow $Mil	899	765	522	714
- Cap Spending $Mil	170	151	180	174
= Free Cash Flow $Mil	729	614	342	540

Financial Health [C+]	2004	2005	2006	09-30-06
Long-term Debt $Mil	475	2,122	1,966	1,965
Total Equity $Mil	1,540	-553	-156	-55
Debt/Equity Ratio	0.3	ELB	ELB	NMF

Industry	Business Risk	Moat Size	Investment Style	Sector
Household Products	Below Avg	Narrow	Mid Core	Consumer Goods

Competition	Market Cap $Mil	12 Mo Trailing Sales $Mil	Price/Cash Flow	Return On Assets%	Debt/Equity	Total Return% 1 Yr	3 Yr
Clorox	9,739	4,701	13.6	12.6	NMF	14.9	12.6
Procter & Gamble	203,656	72,214	16.8	6.8	0.6	13.4	11.3
Unilever NV	46,726	49,679	8.6	10.6	0.8	25.0	12.4

Price Volatility | Monthly Price High/Low — Relative Strength to S&P 500

Annual $Price High/Low	40.85/29.95	47.95/31.92	49.16/37.40	59.45/46.50	66.04/52.50	66.00/56.17
	2001	2002	2003	2004	2005	2006
Annual Total Return %	14.2	6.5	20.4	23.9	-1.6	14.9

Fiscal Year-End: June	2002	2003	2004	2005	2006	TTM
Revenue $Mil	3,859	3,986	4,162	4,388	4,644	4,701
Net Income $Mil	322	493	549	1,096	444	447
Earnings Per Share $	1.37	2.23	2.56	6.11	2.90	2.92
Shares Outstanding Mil	232	218	212	177	151	152
Return on Equity %	23.6	40.6	35.6	NMF	NMF	NMF
Net Margin %	8.3	12.4	13.2	25.0	9.6	9.5
Asset Turnover	1.1	1.1	1.1	1.2	1.3	1.3
Financial Leverage	2.6	3.0	2.5	NMF	NMF	NMF

Valuation Ratios	Stock	Rel to Industry	Rel to S&P 500
Price/Earnings	22.0	0.9	1.1
Price/Book	—	—	—
Price/Sales	2.1	0.8	0.7
Price/Cash Flow	13.6	0.8	0.9

Major Fund Holders	% of Fund Assets
Madison Mosaic Mid-Cap	3.49
Pioneer Growth Leaders A	3.45
Pioneer Small and Mid Cap Growth A	2.89
Commerce Value Instl	2.58

Thesis By Lauren DeSanto, 12-04-06 Stock Price as of Analysis: $64.44

In the household staple arena, Clorox cleans up with its leading cleaners, salad dressings, and charcoals. The company is a solid, if unexciting, performer that has demonstrated it can deliver new products in staid categories and drive strong returns on invested capital.

The company competes primarily in the contentious household cleaning aisle, armed with Clorox and other brands, including Formula 409, Pine-Sol, and Tilex. We believe its narrow economic moat derives from its domination of the bleach category, where it claims more than 50% U.S. share and a name that has become almost synonymous with bleach. The company has leveraged its stranglehold on this category to introduce a wider variety of higher-margin cleaning products, like its toilet wand and bath and shower wand. Given its strong brand equity, we expect Clorox will prosper in this steadily growing category, particularly since consumer demand for convenient cleaning products, even those at higher prices, appears unquenchable.

Clorox manufactures other household brands across a disparate lineup of categories, including Glad bags, Hidden Valley salad dressings, Kingsford Charcoal, and STP auto-care products. It competes with much larger Procter & Gamble, Unilever, Reckitt Benckiser, S.C. Johnson, and Kraft in these categories and battles for the number-one or -two market share position. In the face of retailer consolidation, holding one of these slots is paramount to preventing the loss of shelf space to private-label offerings.

In our opinion, the greatest threat for Clorox is essentially how the firm manages the increased costs for its raw-material inputs. It has successfully passed through price increases to offset some of these increased costs, but these moves have also resulted in volume declines. Some of this is to be expected initially, but any prolonged volume weakness could quickly undermine its operating leverage, especially considering it is only recently coming off its 2004 restructuring. Also, Clorox has a long record of introducing innovative new products, but the need for dynamic offerings is never-ending, and knockoffs seem to be reaching the shelves even faster.

These issues don't cause us to doubt Clorox's long-term prospects, however, and the firm still remains very underpenetrated in international markets. So while blockbuster growth probably isn't in the cards, we'll take the consistent, above-average returns we believe Clorox can deliver in its stable categories.

Data as of 12-29-06

CNOOC ADR CEO

	Rating	Fair Value	Last Close	Consider Buy	Consider Sell	Yield %
	★★	$79.00	$94.63	$50.30	$95.30	2.99

Industry	Business Risk	Moat Size	Investment Style	Sector
Oil/Gas	Above Avg	Narrow	Large Value	Energy

Company Profile

CNOOC holds the dominant presence in oil and gas exploration and production in offshore China and is the only company approved to enter into production-sharing contracts with foreign energy companies for offshore developments. The firm had proven oil and gas reserves of 2.4 billion barrels of oil equivalent (BOE) and production of 422,000 BOE per day in 2005. It was carved out of the former state oil company and is majority-owned by the Chinese government.

Management   Stewardship Grade [NA]

Despite any claims made by the company, CNOOC is effectively controlled by the Chinese central government, which owns CNOOC's parent company and thus 70% of CNOOC. Government approval is required for nearly any activity that the company would want to undertake, from drilling new wells to setting prices. CNOOC has expressed a desire to have the government reduce its stake in the company in order to reduce political obstacles to any overseas acquisitions. All of CNOOC's top managers have long careers in the Chinese energy industry, and compensation is very reasonable. Management has gained valuable experience with offshore operations through production-sharing contracts with major international oil companies. CNOOC has used the expertise garnered by these arrangements to undertake several independent projects.

65th Floor, Bank of China Tower One Garden Road
Hong Kong, China   www.cnoocltd.com

Competition

	Market Cap $Mil	12 Mo Trailing Sales $Mil	Price/Cash Flow	Return On Assets%	Debt/ Equity	Total Return% 1 Yr	3 Yr
CNOOC ADR	38,850	8,462	9.9	21.7	0.2	44.1	35.1
ExxonMobil	446,944	386,951	8.8	17.8	0.1	39.1	26.2
PetroChina Company ADR	252,026	67,281	10.1	17.6	0.1	79.1	36.5

Price Volatility

Annual $Price High	22.00	30.66	46.89	58.95	77.60	94.98
Low	15.70	19.00	24.90	34.40	49.20	66.86

	2001	2002	2003	2004	2005	2006 TTM
Annual Total Return %	—	38.4	61.4	39.7	30.2	44.1
Fiscal Year-End: December	2001	2002	2003	2004	2005	TTM
Revenue $Mil	2,514	3,181	4,940	6,661	8,462	8,462
Net Income $Mil	961	1,111	1,387	1,947	3,085	3,085
Earnings Per Share $	—	2.65	3.38	4.70	7.43	7.43
Shares Outstanding Mil	—	418	411	414	408	411
Return on Equity %	23.9	22.9	24.7	28.6	33.8	33.8
Net Margin %	38.2	34.9	28.1	29.2	36.5	36.5
Asset Turnover	0.5	0.4	0.6	0.6	0.6	0.6
Financial Leverage	1.3	1.5	1.6	1.7	1.6	1.6

Valuation Ratios	Stock	Rel to Industry	Rel to S&P 500
Price/Earnings	12.7	1.0	0.6
Price/Book	4.3	1.3	1.0
Price/Sales	4.6	2.4	1.6
Price/Cash Flow	9.9	1.2	0.7

Major Fund Holders	% of Fund Assets
CGM Focus	4.08
Mundoval	3.11
U.S. Global Investors China Reg Opp	2.92
TCW Emerging Markets Eq I	2.16

Growth [NA]	2002	2003	2004	2005
Revenue %	26.7	55.3	34.9	25.8
Earnings/Share %	NMF	27.3	39.3	56.4
Book Value/Share %	NMF	17.5	20.5	30.0
Dividends/Share %	—	—	—	—

Profitability [NA]	2003	2004	2005	TTM
Return on Assets %	15.7	17.2	21.7	21.7
Oper Cash Flow $Mil	2,149	2,693	3,917	3,917
- Cap Spending $Mil	1,492	2,246	2,128	2,128
= Free Cash Flow $Mil	657	447	1,789	1,789

Financial Health [NA]	2003	2004	2005	12-31-05
Long-term Debt $Mil	982	2,072	2,052	2,052
Total Equity $Mil	5,604	6,809	9,121	9,121
Debt/Equity Ratio	0.2	0.3	0.2	0.2

Thesis By Michael Cumming, CFA, 11-20-06 Stock Price as of Analysis: $85.14

An attractive production profile and high energy prices make CNOOC a compelling investment opportunity.

CNOOC is a pure play in the upstream segment of the energy sector. All of its operations are focused on exploration for and production of oil and natural gas, with more than 90% of production coming from fields offshore China. CNOOC specializes in deep-water production and is the only Chinese oil company allowed to enter into production-sharing contracts with foreign firms, which helps reduce its risk associated with an individual project. Without exposure to refining or other low-margin businesses, CNOOC has produced an average return on invested capital of 20% over the past four years, easily beating its cost of capital of 11.4%. All of the company's fields are relatively young and should produce ample supplies of oil and gas for many years.

Like most industries in China, the energy industry is highly regulated. Investment is tightly controlled, serving to protect CNOOC, Sinopec, and PetroChina from any serious domestic competition. Although government regulation and the beneficial effects of the OPEC cartel provide an economic moat around CNOOC's business, the commodity nature of the company's products prompts us to give the firm and its Chinese peers only a narrow moat rating. Any reductions in regulation connected to China's entry into the World Trade Organization could create a much more competitive environment for CNOOC and its Chinese peers, though we don't anticipate any major changes in exploration and production regulations anytime soon.

Greater-than-expected political heat led CNOOC to abandon its bid for U.S.-based Unocal, allowing Chevron to win the bidding war. This was CNOOC's largest attempt to acquire non-Chinese assets, but was certainly not the last. In fact, the company has secured stakes in Nigerian and Kenyan oil projects in 2006. Overseas operations carry new risks for the large Chinese oil companies, given their lack of experience in completing major acquisitions and operating outside China. In addition, record nominal oil and natural-gas prices have pushed the price for acquiring energy reserves very high. A drop in oil and natural-gas prices could be catastrophic for any firm acquiring assets today. On the other hand, of the large Chinese energy companies, CNOOC is the best equipped to make such deals, given its experience in joint ventures that develop natural gas off the coasts of Australia and Indonesia.

Coach COH

Data as of 12-29-06

Rating	Fair Value	Last Close	Consider Buy	Consider Sell	Yield %
★★	$38.00	$42.96	$29.30	$47.60	0.00

Company Profile
Coach is a specialty retailer focused on providing premium everyday accessories in an assortment of styles and materials. Its products include handbags, wallets, watches, footwear, and other accessories. Although more than 50% of sales come from its 200-plus U.S. retail stores and more than 80 outlet stores, Coach also sells its products through department stores, international shops, the Internet, and its catalog.

Management
Stewardship Grade [B]

Lew Frankfort has served as chairman and CEO since 1995 and helped lead the firm through its initial public offering in October 2000. He has more than 25 years of experience at Coach. In recent years, he has revitalized the Coach brand and assembled a topnotch management team to lead this effort. His annual salary and bonus in 2006 was just shy of $3 million, and he realized $57 million in gains from the exercise of stock options; he also received a significant grant of restricted stock and some additional option grants. While this is a tidy sum, we note that the stock is trading at around 16 times its 2000 IPO price (all under Frankfort's watch), and a large portion of his compensation comes from stock options, which align his interests with shareholders'. In recent years, Coach has granted more than 3% of shares annually as options, which we view as excessive, because it dilutes the value for current shareholders. A majority of Coach's board is independent, and officers and directors own nearly 4% of the shares outstanding. We believe management does a good job of providing transparency around the business. Overall, corporate governance is good, in our opinion.

516 West 34th Street
New York, NY 10001
www.coach.com

Growth [A]	2003	2004	2005	2006
Revenue %	32.5	38.6	29.5	23.4
Earnings/Share %	66.7	77.1	48.4	38.0
Book Value/Share %	57.9	77.4	30.6	12.8
Dividends/Share %	NMF	NMF	NMF	NMF

Profitability [A+]	2004	2005	2006	TTM
Return on Assets %	22.4	26.2	30.4	31.4
Oper Cash Flow $Mil	359	476	597	623
- Cap Spending $Mil	74	95	134	148
= Free Cash Flow $Mil	286	381	463	474

Financial Health [A+]	2004	2005	2006	09-30-06
Long-term Debt $Mil	3	3	3	3
Total Equity $Mil	796	1,056	1,189	1,192
Debt/Equity Ratio	0.0	0.0	0.0	0.0

Industry	Business Risk	Moat Size	Investment Style	Sector
Jewelry/Accessories	Average	Narrow	Large Growth	Consumer Goods

Competition	Market Cap $Mil	12 Mo Trailing Sales $Mil	Price/Cash Flow	Return On Assets%	Debt/ Equity	Total Return% 1 Yr	3 Yr
Coach	15,787	2,216	25.4	31.4	0.0	28.9	32.5
Kenneth Cole Productions	480	535	11.0	7.5	—	-3.1	-4.1

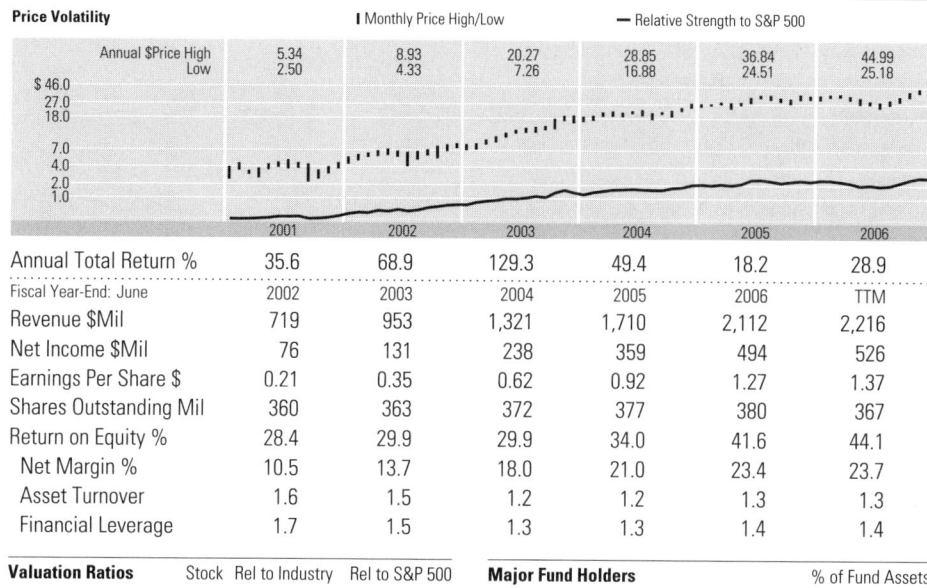

Price Volatility — Monthly Price High/Low — Relative Strength to S&P 500

Annual $Price High/Low	5.34/2.50	8.93/4.33	20.27/7.26	28.85/16.88	36.84/24.51	44.99/25.18
	2001	2002	2003	2004	2005	2006
Annual Total Return %	35.6	68.9	129.3	49.4	18.2	28.9

Fiscal Year-End: June	2002	2003	2004	2005	2006	TTM
Revenue $Mil	719	953	1,321	1,710	2,112	2,216
Net Income $Mil	76	131	238	359	494	526
Earnings Per Share $	0.21	0.35	0.62	0.92	1.27	1.37
Shares Outstanding Mil	360	363	372	377	380	367
Return on Equity %	28.4	29.9	29.9	34.0	41.6	44.1
Net Margin %	10.5	13.7	18.0	21.0	23.4	23.7
Asset Turnover	1.6	1.5	1.2	1.2	1.3	1.3
Financial Leverage	1.7	1.5	1.3	1.3	1.4	1.4

Valuation Ratios	Stock	Rel to Industry	Rel to S&P 500
Price/Earnings	31.4	1.2	1.5
Price/Book	13.2	1.6	3.2
Price/Sales	7.1	1.6	2.4
Price/Cash Flow	25.4	1.0	1.7

Major Fund Holders	% of Fund Assets
Westcore Select	5.11
Manor Growth	4.76
Turner Concentrated Growth Instl	4.54
Excelsior Large Cap Growth	4.46

Thesis
By Kimberly Picciola, 10-31-06 Stock Price as of Analysis: $39.64

Coach has experienced remarkable growth domestically over the past five years, but we think international expansion, particularly in Asia, will be key to future growth. Coach has created a niche in the accessory market with its "accessible luxury" products. The Coach brand has been well received in Japan, where consumers crave fashion, and we think there are opportunities for it to increase its presence in China over time. Although we expect Coach's rate of growth will slow over the next five years, we think there remain ample expansion opportunities that could support 14% average annual top-line growth.

Coach has garnered the largest share of the growing, highly fragmented premium handbag and accessory market in the United States. As a market leader, we think Coach has built a narrow economic moat. Its frequent introductions and innovative merchandise offerings drive demand for its products, which fill a void between moderate brands and designer labels. Despite the fashion risk inherent in Coach's trendy products, this specialty retailer consistently generates returns on invested capital in excess of our estimate of its cost of capital, furthering our case that it has a sustainable competitive advantage.

While we don't believe Coach can maintain the average 29% annual top-line growth rate it has posted over the past five years, we do think expansion opportunities exist. Coach has increased its domestic distribution in recent years, with the majority of growth attributable to new store openings and double-digit increases in same-store sales (sales from stores open at least a year). The company plans to further penetrate the domestic market, with a long-term target of roughly 400 retail stores.

We think the most compelling growth opportunity for Coach over the next five years will be its foray into new and existing international markets. In 2005, Coach bought out its Japanese partner's stake in Coach Japan, and it is now accelerating expansion efforts there. Japanese consumers are willing to pay a premium for luxury goods, so capitalizing on this market is key. Additionally, we think China will present another avenue of growth for this retailer down the road.

Although Coach has a stellar track record, risk exists. The firm depends on hitting the latest fashion trends. Merchandising missteps could stunt top-line growth and pressure margins. Also, given that the firm's assortment of goods includes more premium priced products, we think Coach risks alienating its customer looking for "accessible luxury."

Coca-Cola KO

Data as of 12-29-06

Rating	Fair Value	Last Close	Consider Buy	Consider Sell	Yield %
★★★★	$55.00	$48.25	$46.90	$72.20	2.57

Industry	Business Risk	Moat Size	Investment Style	Sector
Beverage Mfg.	Below Avg	Wide	Large Core	Consumer Goods

Company Profile

Coke is the world's largest beverage company. It manufactures, distributes, and markets soft drink concentrates under brand names including Coca-Cola, Sprite, and Fanta. Noncarbonated brands include Minute Maid, Dasani, and Powerade. Coke's offerings encompass 400 brands. The company's products are sold in more than 200 countries through an extensive network of independent and company-owned bottlers. About 71% of 2005 sales were derived outside North America.

Management
Stewardship Grade [C]

Neville Isdell is the third CEO to take the helm since the death of Roberto Goizueta in 1997, and investors can only hope that he fares better than his two predecessors. Coke has been furiously trying to build executive depth since Isdell took over in June 2004, and we believe it has done a decent job reducing a deficit of managerial talent. Most of the management team is relatively new or serving in a new capacity. Executive compensation, especially stock-based, has been chronically overgenerous, in our opinion, with severance packages for unsuccessful and short-tenured executives particularly galling. The equity accounting used for many of Coke's bottling investments (51 unconsolidated stakes) understates the capital requirements and overstates the margins of the company's operations. We also do not like that Isdell serves as both chairman and CEO. On a more positive note, Coke's directors, which we believe are adequately independent, stand for elections annually. Berkshire Hathaway owns more than 8% of the company's shares, but its iconic chairman, Warren Buffett, left Coke's board in 2006. The average age of Coke's 11 board members is older than 67, with the youngest member 61. We think the board could use some youthful views to complement its silver-haired wisdom.

One Coca-Cola Plaza
Atlanta, GA 30313
www.coca-cola.com

Competition

	Market Cap $Mil	12 Mo Trailing Sales $Mil	Price/Cash Flow	Return On Assets%	Debt/Equity	Total Return% 1 Yr	3 Yr
Coca-Cola	113,088	23,707	19.6	16.8	0.1	23.1	1.1
Nestle SA ADR	138,417	73,660	16.8	8.8	—	20.9	14.7
PepsiCo	102,712	34,850	18.4	15.4	0.2	7.9	12.4

Price Volatility

	2001	2002	2003	2004	2005	2006
Annual $Price High	62.19	57.90	50.90	53.50	45.26	49.35
Low	42.40	42.90	37.01	38.30	40.31	39.36
Annual Total Return %	-21.5	-5.5	18.2	-16.1	-0.7	23.1

Fiscal Year-End: December	2001	2002	2003	2004	2005	TTM
Revenue $Mil	17,374	19,394	20,857	21,742	23,104	23,707
Net Income $Mil	3,969	3,050	4,347	4,847	4,872	5,266
Earnings Per Share $	1.60	1.23	1.77	2.00	2.04	2.24
Shares Outstanding Mil	2,481	2,480	2,456	2,424	2,388	2,344
Return on Equity %	34.9	25.8	30.9	30.4	29.8	29.3
Net Margin %	22.8	15.7	20.8	22.3	21.1	22.2
Asset Turnover	0.8	0.8	0.8	0.7	0.8	0.8
Financial Leverage	2.0	2.1	1.9	2.0	1.8	1.7

Valuation Ratios	Stock	Rel to Industry	Rel to S&P 500
Price/Earnings	21.5	1.0	1.0
Price/Book	6.3	1.1	1.5
Price/Sales	4.8	1.4	1.7
Price/Cash Flow	19.6	1.1	1.3

Major Fund Holders	% of Fund Assets
Yacktman Focused	11.65
Yacktman	9.50
Wisdom Inv	8.79
ProFunds Consumer Goods UltraSector Inv	6.14

Growth [C+]	2002	2003	2004	2005
Revenue %	11.6	7.5	4.2	6.3
Earnings/Share %	-23.1	43.9	13.0	2.0
Book Value/Share %	3.9	20.6	14.6	4.2
Dividends/Share %	11.1	10.0	13.6	12.0

Profitability [A+]	2003	2004	2005	TTM
Return on Assets %	15.9	15.4	16.6	16.8
Oper Cash Flow $Mil	5,456	5,968	6,423	5,777
- Cap Spending $Mil	812	755	899	1,226
= Free Cash Flow $Mil	4,644	5,213	5,524	4,551

Financial Health [A+]	2003	2004	2005	09-30-06
Long-term Debt $Mil	—	1,157	1,154	1,242
Total Equity $Mil	14,090	15,935	16,355	18,000
Debt/Equity Ratio	—	0.1	0.1	0.1

Thesis
By Matthew Reilly, 12-11-06 Stock Price as of Analysis: $48.81

The secret formula for Coca-Cola is not currently the basis for the company's wide economic moat. With a number of close cola imitators and competitors throughout the globe, the uniqueness of Coke's blend won't inevitably lead to financial success, in our opinion. Rather, the company must continue to better leverage its two main competitive advantages--its powerful brands supported by large advertising dollars and its unrivaled international beverage distribution infrastructure--to continue recent promising top-line results.

We think Coke's management has finally accepted these simple truths, and we are encouraged by the initial steps the company has taken to transform from the risk-averse, aimless soft drink giant that Neville Isdell inherited in mid-2004. The company's most important improvements have come through increasing advertising, improving managerial depth and morale within the company, and embracing the reality of the need for any mature 21st century consumer product company to constantly innovate (and assume the inherent risk). Coke has also realized, grudgingly and at a painfully slow rate, that it needs to understand and cater to consumers' beverage needs. The firm can no longer push the same old products into new frontiers; with operations in more than 200 countries, frontiers are running out.

After decades of international expansion, Coke products account for about 10% of total worldwide nonalcoholic beverage volume--a large portion, but leaving plenty of opportunity. Coke aims to capitalize by increasing per capita consumption of its products around the globe, especially in emerging markets. We believe it can still expand carbonated soft drink volume in several markets, but it must also leverage its infrastructure to sell more noncarbonated beverages, even if this transformation is suboptimally belated. Coke held on to its carbonated soft drink-centric vision of the world for much too long, blinded by past success and the profitability of the product category, though management now claims that it can maintain margins with products like sports and energy drinks. We only question what took it so long to figure this out.

Coke must become a true innovator rather than a responder. Products like Godiva ready-to-drink coffees and Gold Peak premium iced teas came to the party several years too late, missing much of the growth in their categories and vital opportunities to build brand equity. We think Coke's distribution infrastructure, anchored by its bottlers, secures its moat, but management must better prevent stagnant waters.

Colgate-Palmolive CL

Data as of 12-29-06

Rating	Fair Value	Last Close	Consider Buy	Consider Sell	Yield %
★★★	$63.00	$65.24	$53.70	$82.70	1.92

Industry	Business Risk	Moat Size	Investment Style	Sector
Household Products	Below Avg	Wide	Large Core	Consumer Goods

Company Profile

Colgate-Palmolive is one of the world's largest consumer product companies. In addition to its namesake toothpaste and detergents, the firm manufactures shampoos, shower gels, deodorants, and shaving products. It also owns specialty pet-food maker Hill's, which sells its products through veterinarians and specialty pet retailers. Colgate products are sold around the world; about three fourths of sales come from outside the United States.

Management   Stewardship Grade [B]

As CEO since 1984, Reuben Mark has one of the longest tenures of any consumer product chief executive. He's also held the role of chairman since 1986, and his imprint on Colgate has been undeniable. At times the succession plan at Colgate has been murky, but COO Ian Cook is now expected to assume the CEO role in 2007, with Mark remaining chairman. Mark has beneficial ownership of 5.7 million shares and 5.2 million stock options. In 2005, he earned a salary plus bonus of $5.3 million, an increase of 66% from 2004 and above average for his consumer product peers. He received a restricted-stock award of 187,074 shares in 2005 as an incentive to stay with the firm during the management transition. We're not big fans of the high levels of compensation that Mark has been awarded over the years, especially the added encouragements to stay during Colgate's leadership changeover. We doubt that there is any real risk to Mark leaving, so this award seems excessive. The firm reduced option grants in favor of restricted-stock awards and eliminated its shareholder-rights plan--two positive developments, in our view. Officers and directors as a group own 3.6% of outstanding shares.

300 Park Avenue   www.colgate.com
New York, NY 10022-7499

Growth [B-]	2002	2003	2004	2005
Revenue %	2.3	6.6	6.9	7.7
Earnings/Share %	15.9	12.3	-5.3	4.3
Book Value/Share %	-94.4	EUB	65.8	15.6
Dividends/Share %	6.7	25.0	6.7	15.6

Profitability [A+]	2003	2004	2005	TTM
Return on Assets %	19.0	15.3	15.9	14.3
Oper Cash Flow $Mil	1,768	1,754	1,784	1,849
- Cap Spending $Mil	302	348	389	383
= Free Cash Flow $Mil	1,466	1,406	1,395	1,466

Financial Health [A-]	2003	2004	2005	09-30-06
Long-term Debt $Mil	2,685	3,090	2,918	3,126
Total Equity $Mil	594	971	1,096	1,404
Debt/Equity Ratio	4.5	3.2	2.7	2.2

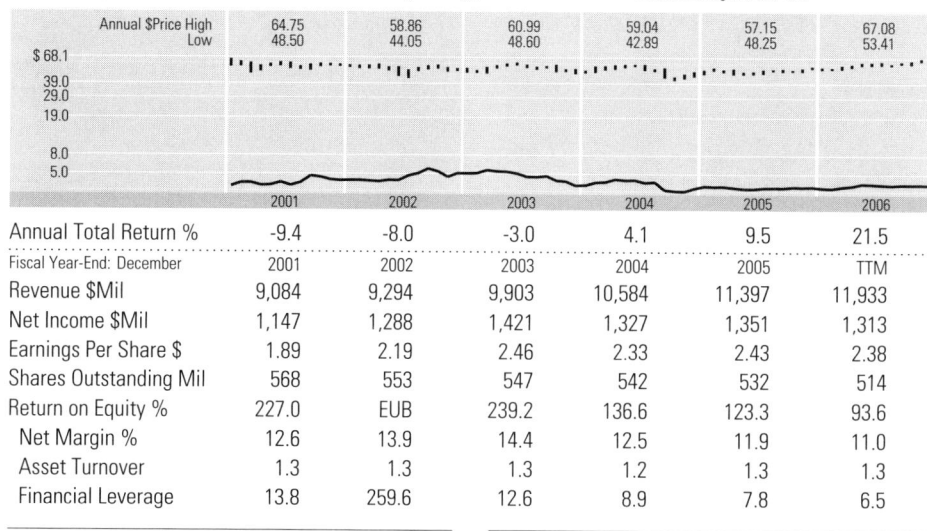

Competition	Market Cap $Mil	12 Mo Trailing Sales $Mil	Price/Cash Flow	Return On Assets%	Debt/ Equity	Total Return% 1 Yr	3 Yr
Colgate-Palmolive	33,554	11,933	18.1	14.3	2.2	21.5	11.8
Procter & Gamble	203,656	72,214	16.8	6.8	0.6	13.4	11.3
Unilever NV	46,726	49,679	8.6	10.6	0.8	25.0	12.4

	2001	2002	2003	2004	2005	2006
Annual $Price High	64.75	58.86	60.99	59.04	57.15	67.08
Low	48.50	44.05	48.60	42.89	48.25	53.41
Annual Total Return %	-9.4	-8.0	-3.0	4.1	9.5	21.5
Fiscal Year-End: December	2001	2002	2003	2004	2005	TTM
Revenue $Mil	9,084	9,294	9,903	10,584	11,397	11,933
Net Income $Mil	1,147	1,288	1,421	1,327	1,351	1,313
Earnings Per Share $	1.89	2.19	2.46	2.33	2.43	2.38
Shares Outstanding Mil	568	553	547	542	532	514
Return on Equity %	227.0	EUB	239.2	136.6	123.3	93.6
Net Margin %	12.6	13.9	14.4	12.5	11.9	11.0
Asset Turnover	1.3	1.3	1.3	1.2	1.3	1.3
Financial Leverage	13.8	259.6	12.6	8.9	7.8	6.5

Valuation Ratios	Stock	Rel to Industry	Rel to S&P 500
Price/Earnings	27.4	1.1	1.3
Price/Book	23.9	4.0	5.8
Price/Sales	2.8	1.0	1.0
Price/Cash Flow	18.1	1.0	1.2

Major Fund Holders	% of Fund Assets
Ivy Large Cap Growth A	4.74
Waddell & Reed Adv Vanguard A	4.73
Ameristock	4.50
Pioneer AmPac Growth A	4.19

Thesis By Lauren DeSanto, 11-27-06   Stock Price as of Analysis: $65.01

Colgate-Palmolive stock has staged a remarkable comeback in the past two years, though we'd argue that the company never left. A restructuring initiative launched in 2004 helped set the stage for leaner operations and a renewed advertising investment behind its core oral-care category. The company manufactures products other than toothpaste, including deodorant, hand and dish soap, and pet food, but it is relentless in its pursuit of leading market share in oral care.

We believe this focus on oral care gives Colgate the advantage it needs to compete with a much larger Procter & Gamble and its Crest brand. Colgate and Crest fight neck and neck for market share in the United States, though globally Colgate leads with a 40% share. Crest is a leading brand for P&G, but Colgate's eponymous brand is its bread and butter, not one of 22 other top brands across a wide variety of categories. With so much on the line in the toothpaste aisle, Colgate has been able to exploit P&G's occasional lack of focus and inability to find consistent growth in the segment.

The dynamic could change, however, with P&G's new Crest Pro-Health product and its associated $100 million in advertising support. Colgate Total has been the leading toothpaste since its launch in 1998, but Pro Health appears designed to change that. We don't know how the battle will play out, but Colgate is pretty scrappy, and with 200 years of experience under its belt, we're willing to bet it will continue to do well in the category despite new P&G products.

Most of Colgate's non-oral-care products are sold in categories that are adjacent to oral care, offering retail distribution synergies. They are fragmented categories where Colgate can still compete successfully with brands like Speed Stick and Softsoap. The firm has been smart enough to know how to differentiate itself--for example, by selling its Hill's Science Diet pet food only through veterinarians--as well as when it should quit a category, as with its laundry detergent business, where it realized it couldn't profitably compete with P&G.

Some might argue that Colgate needs to diversify, but we believe that its narrow band of categories is a source of strength and a terrific example of how a highly diversified product lineup isn't the only path to stellar performance in the consumer product arena. Colgate's management team won't be distracted from its oral-care focus, making this a wide-moat firm to own for the long haul.

Data as of 12-29-06

Comcast A CMCSA

Rating	Fair Value	Last Close	Consider Buy	Consider Sell	Yield %
★★★	$38.00	$42.33	$29.30	$47.60	0.00

Industry	Business Risk	Moat Size	Investment Style	Sector
Cable TV	Average	Wide	Large Growth	Media

Company Profile

Comcast is the largest operator in the cable industry. The firm's networks reach about 46 million households, with 23.3 million customers signing up for at least basic cable service. In addition to cable, the firm offers high-speed Internet access and phone service. The five largest markets Comcast serves are Philadelphia, Chicago, San Francisco, Seattle, and Boston. The firm also owns interests in a handful of cable networks, including E! and The Golf Channel.

Management — Stewardship Grade [C]

The biggest issue we have with Comcast's stewardship is that the founding Roberts family owns all of the supervoting Class B shares, thereby holding 33% voting control of the firm. Holders of Class A shares have the remainder of voting power, while holders of Class A Special shares are not entitled to vote on corporate matters. The Roberts' voting power can't be diluted under the firm's articles of incorporation--the number of Class A votes per share adjusts to maintain Class B voting power. Investing alongside the Roberts has historically been rewarding for minority shareholders, but we still don't like to see control of the firm concentrated in this manner. President and CEO Brian Roberts took the chairman spot from C. Michael Armstrong, the former CEO of AT&T, in May 2004; we would prefer these roles were separated. Roberts is well paid: Cash compensation totaled $12.8 million in 2005, and he was awarded $5.6 million of restricted stock and 425,000 options. We view this level of compensation as excessive given Roberts' stake in the firm. COO Stephen Burke and Brian's father Ralph, who heads two board committees, are also very highly paid. Bonuses in the past have been based largely on the firm's cash flow, a feature we like, but the board has very wide discretion in determining performance goals under a new bonus plan adopted in 2006.

1500 Market Street
Philadelphia, PA 19102-2148
www.comcast.com

Growth [A-]	2002	2003	2004	2005
Revenue %	36.5	126.5	10.7	9.6
Earnings/Share %	NMF	NMF	-70.1	-2.3
Book Value/Share %	133.6	-47.1	-0.8	-0.9
Dividends/Share %	NMF	NMF	NMF	NMF

Profitability [B-]	2003	2004	2005	TTM
Return on Assets %	3.0	0.9	0.9	2.1
Oper Cash Flow $Mil	2,854	5,930	4,922	6,114
- Cap Spending $Mil	4,161	3,660	3,621	3,919
= Free Cash Flow $Mil	-1,307	2,270	1,301	2,195

Financial Health [B-]	2003	2004	2005	09-30-06
Long-term Debt $Mil	23,835	20,093	21,682	26,446
Total Equity $Mil	41,662	41,422	40,219	40,722
Debt/Equity Ratio	0.6	0.5	0.5	0.6

Competition	Market Cap $Mil	12 Mo Trailing Sales $Mil	Price/Cash Flow	Return On Assets %	Debt/Equity	Total Return % 1 Yr	3 Yr
Comcast A	88,095	24,531	14.4	2.1	0.6	63.3	8.7
Verizon Communications	108,723	88,881	4.4	3.7	0.7	34.9	8.0
DirecTV	30,516	14,168	11.5	8.3	0.5	76.6	15.9

Price Volatility — Monthly Price High/Low — Relative Strength to S&P 500

Annual $Price High/Low	45.81/31.85	37.55/17.05	34.77/23.42	36.50/26.25	34.50/25.80	43.41/25.35
	2001	2002	2003	2004	2005	2006
Annual Total Return %	-12.9	-34.5	39.1	1.5	-22.1	63.3

Fiscal Year-End: December	2001	2002	2003	2004	2005	TTM
Revenue $Mil	5,937	8,102	18,348	20,307	22,255	24,531
Net Income $Mil	609	-274	3,240	970	928	2,276
Earnings Per Share $	0.63	-0.25	1.44	0.43	0.42	1.07
Shares Outstanding Mil	952	1,096	2,250	2,256	2,210	2,081
Return on Equity %	4.2	-0.7	7.8	2.3	2.3	5.6
Net Margin %	10.3	-3.4	17.7	4.8	4.2	9.3
Asset Turnover	0.2	0.1	0.2	0.2	0.2	0.2
Financial Leverage	2.6	3.0	2.6	2.5	2.6	2.7

Valuation Ratios	Stock	Rel to Industry	Rel to S&P 500
Price/Earnings	45.0	1.3	2.2
Price/Book	2.2	0.2	0.5
Price/Sales	3.6	1.1	1.2
Price/Cash Flow	14.4	0.9	1.0

Major Fund Holders	% of Fund Assets
Fidelity Utilities	7.62
ICON Consumer Discretionary	6.32
SunAmerica Focused Large Cap Gr A	5.79
Holland Balanced	5.12

Thesis By Michael Hodel, CFA, 10-24-06 Stock Price as of Analysis: $39.01

Comcast's performance recently has demonstrated the capabilities of its network. The firm has also completed additional steps, most notably the Adelphia transaction, to further enhance its competitive position. We would love to own the shares of this wide-moat firm.

We think Comcast's ability to distribute content and provide communications services is unparalleled in the industry and is unlikely to be matched anytime soon. With the closing of the Adelphia transaction and a couple of smaller deals, the firm's cable networks reach around 46 million U.S. homes--about 40% of the total--and serve 23.3 million customers, 50% larger than its nearest pay-TV competitor. Only AT&T, assuming its acquisition of BellSouth goes through, has a fixed-line network that reaches more homes or serves more customers. Comcast has also used recent transactions to expand its control of certain markets where it's dominant, like Boston.

The firm's major markets are spread across the territories of the major phone companies, each of which has taken a different approach to upgrading networks and providing services. Verizon, the nation's second-largest phone company, has ambitious plans, but it is rolling out new services relatively slowly. AT&T hopes to move more quickly, but it is using less advanced technology, and we question its ability to provide a superior service to Comcast's. We think the trade-off between deployment speed and ability these firms face illustrates the strong position Comcast enjoys. The firm has aggressively rolled out phone service during 2006 and now claims around 2 million customers. With the percentage of television customers who also subscribe to Comcast high-speed Internet access service approaching 45%, we think the firm is clearly expanding and cementing its relationship with customers. The firm has seen the benefits of bundling services already, as television customer losses--today almost entirely the result of satellite competition--have slowed sharply during the past year.

The television and video distribution market continues to evolve as the Internet gains prominence We think Comcast's size gives it an advantage in acquiring content and that customers benefit from the firm's ability to negotiate programming fees paid to media giants like Viacom and Disney. Comcast also has a hand in creating content, particularly regional sports programming in larger markets, and has been a leader in working with content providers to bring a large library of content to its video-on-demand service.

Data as of 12-29-06

Comerica CMA

	Rating	Fair Value	Last Close	Consider Buy	Consider Sell	Yield %
	★★★	$66.00	$58.68	$50.90	$82.70	4.02

Company Profile

Comerica is a $58 billion asset bank with headquarters in Michigan. The company has been expanding its presence throughout faster-growing U.S. markets. Its California, Nevada, Colorado, Arizona, Washington, Texas, and Florida markets combine to make up nearly 48% of its loan portfolio. Comerica operates a total of 395 branches throughout its markets.

Industry	Business Risk	Moat Size	Investment Style	Sector
Regional Banks	Average	Narrow	Mid Value	Financial Services

Competition

	Market Cap $Mil	12 Mo Trailing Sales $Mil	Price/Cash Flow	Return On Assets%	Debt/Equity	Total Return% 1 Yr	3 Yr
Comerica	9,322	2,904	—	1.4	—	7.8	5.8
ABN AMRO Holding NV ADR	60,187	29,071	—	0.5	—	28.9	16.9
Fifth Third Bancorp	22,842	5,431	—	1.4	—	13.0	-8.1

Management Stewardship Grade [B]

Ralph Babb stepped up from CFO to president and CEO in 2002, just as the company began restructuring its balance sheet to eliminate its problem loans while still expanding in its promising footprint. Babb has made a series of tough choices, but after all the headwinds, he has positioned the company to return to its former glory. Comerica's credit performance has reached pre-restructuring levels, and its return on equity is improving. For this work, Babb has been paid handsomely. Even though the 17% earnings increase in 2005 was almost all related to provisioning, Babb's paycheck, excluding stock options, increased 51%, to $3.8 million. We like the fact that Babb is required to own 5 times his base salary in stock, but owns stock equivalent to 52 times his salary. Other executive officers are required to own 1-5 times their base salaries invested in Comerica stock. This gives the management a stake in the company and helps align its interests with shareholders'.

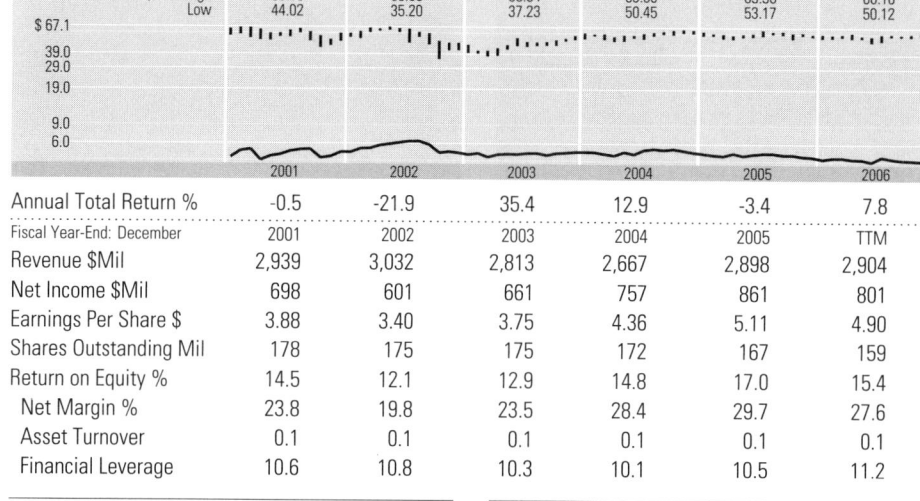

	2001	2002	2003	2004	2005	2006
Annual Total Return %	-0.5	-21.9	35.4	12.9	-3.4	7.8
Fiscal Year-End: December	2001	2002	2003	2004	2005	TTM
Revenue $Mil	2,939	3,032	2,813	2,667	2,898	2,904
Net Income $Mil	698	601	661	757	861	801
Earnings Per Share $	3.88	3.40	3.75	4.36	5.11	4.90
Shares Outstanding Mil	178	175	175	172	167	159
Return on Equity %	14.5	12.1	12.9	14.8	17.0	15.4
Net Margin %	23.8	19.8	23.5	28.4	29.7	27.6
Asset Turnover	0.1	0.1	0.1	0.1	0.1	0.1
Financial Leverage	10.6	10.8	10.3	10.1	10.5	11.2

Valuation Ratios	Stock	Rel to Industry	Rel to S&P 500
Price/Earnings	11.8	0.7	0.6
Price/Book	1.8	0.6	0.4
Price/Sales	3.2	0.6	1.1
Price/Cash Flow	—	—	—

Major Fund Holders	% of Fund Assets
FBR Large Cap Financial	3.78
Quant Long/Short Ordinary	2.81
Schwab Financial Services	2.79
Diamond Hill Financial Long-Short A	2.77

Comerica Tower at Detroit Center 500 Woodward Avenue, MC 3391
Detroit, MI 48226-3509   www.comerica.com

Growth [D+]	2002	2003	2004	2005
Revenue %	3.2	-7.2	-5.2	8.7
Earnings/Share %	-12.4	10.3	16.3	17.2
Book Value/Share %	4.7	3.6	1.4	2.3
Dividends/Share %	9.1	4.2	4.0	5.8

Profitability [B+]	2003	2004	2005	TTM
Return on Assets %	1.3	1.5	1.6	1.4
Oper Cash Flow $Mil	1,321	1,028	846	—
- Cap Spending $Mil	—	95	132	—
= Free Cash Flow $Mil	—	—	—	—

Financial Health [NA]	2003	2004	2005	09-30-06
Long-term Debt $Mil	—	—	—	—
Total Equity $Mil	5,110	5,105	5,068	5,208
Debt/Equity Ratio	—	—	—	—

Thesis By Jaime Black, CFA, CPA, 11-28-06 Stock Price as of Analysis: $57.76

After a few years of distraction, Comerica is focusing on its best asset: its commercial lending business. We would snap up its shares at the right price.

Comerica is primarily a commercial lender. But with most of its branches in Michigan, growth opportunities were limited. As a result, the company began looking outside its home market for growth; these new markets now make up 48% of total loans. We expect its attractive California, Arizona, Texas, and Florida markets to continue to grow rapidly. We like Comerica's determination to build its presence in these markets, after its attempt at acquiring a foothold flopped and resulted in a few years of nasty restructurings.

On the surface, Comerica has a strong deposit base. The $45 billion deposit base--with 33% being noninterest-bearing--is capable of funding nearly all of the company's loan portfolio cheaply. However, about $5.5 billion of the company's deposit base is from the financial services division, a unit that takes title and escrow deposits that the company pays for in three ways: making normal market-driven interest payments, offering free escrow accounting and other normally fee-generating services, or lending at below-market rates. So, despite a healthy amount of seemingly no-cost deposits, Comerica "pays" through forgone income generation. These deposits, and their associated costs, depend on residential real estate transactions. As a result, they have dropped nearly in half in the past year because of a slower housing market, forcing Comerica to fund more of its loan growth with higher-cost certificates of deposit.

Although the market views Comerica's $11.5 billion in auto-related loan exposure with fear, we believe the true risk is far smaller. As a business bank with headquarters in Michigan, Comerica is one of the leading lenders to the auto industry. But the majority of its auto loan portfolio--15% of total loans--is actually the highly profitable, highly collateralized, low-risk financing of car dealer inventory, a great business to have. Only 4% of Comerica's total loan portfolio is to suppliers dependent on the struggling American car manufacturers. We are wary of this portion of the portfolio, but take comfort that it is closely monitored and heavily reserved. While we wish the company were not quite so exposed to the volatile auto industry, we believe it has positioned itself well overall.

Comerica's prospects look bright, and we would invest with an appropriate margin of safety.

Commerce Bancorp NJ CBH

Data as of 12-29-06

Rating	Fair Value	Last Close	Consider Buy	Consider Sell	Yield %
★★★	$36.00	$35.27	$27.80	$45.10	1.36

Industry	Business Risk	Moat Size	Investment Style	Sector
Regional Banks	Average	Narrow	Mid Core	Financial Services

Company Profile
Commerce is a rapidly growing bank with an expected 440 branches in New Jersey, New York, Philadelphia, Washington, D.C., and Western Florida by the end of 2006. With $43 billion in assets as of Sept. 30, Commerce increased assets 36% annually over the past five years. The company concentrates on gathering low-cost deposits, using the proceeds to fund its loan portfolio and its large securities portfolio.

Management
Stewardship Grade [D]

We give Commerce a D for stewardship, but we must point out the firm is attempting to change at least some of its policies and is on its way to earning a solid C if it continues down this path. We cringe at some of the company's related-party transactions and the millions of dollars CEO and chairman Vernon Hill and his top executives receive. In April 2005, Hill's outsized base salary of $2.5 million was cut to $1 million. No bonuses were awarded in 2005, and stock option grants, while still extremely generous, declined to 2% of shares outstanding from 3%. Hill owns $91 million of in-the-money options, and the top four managers combine to have $150 million of in-the-money options. Hill is no longer involved in leasing sites to Commerce from his real estate partnership. However, his wife's design firm earned $7.5 million in fees in 2005 after earning $6.4 million in 2004. Since the design of the branches is a part of what makes Commerce unique, we are willing to be a bit generous on this particular related-party transaction. The bottom line: Commerce's stewardship is mediocre, and although it's improving, we will wait to see if the leopard has really changed its spots.

Commerce Atrium 1701 Route 70 East www.commerceonline.com
Cherry Hill, NJ 08034-5400

Growth [A-]	2002	2003	2004	2005
Revenue %	38.8	31.1	28.0	14.6
Earnings/Share %	35.1	26.5	26.4	-1.2
Book Value/Share %	38.6	31.2	17.1	32.3
Dividends/Share %	9.0	10.0	15.2	15.8

Profitability [C]	2003	2004	2005	TTM
Return on Assets %	0.9	0.9	0.7	0.7
Oper Cash Flow $Mil	495	484	705	—
- Cap Spending $Mil	300	340	424	—
= Free Cash Flow $Mil	—	—	—	—

Financial Health [NA]	2003	2004	2005	09-30-06
Long-term Debt $Mil	—	—	—	—
Total Equity $Mil	1,277	1,666	2,309	2,715
Debt/Equity Ratio	—	—	—	—

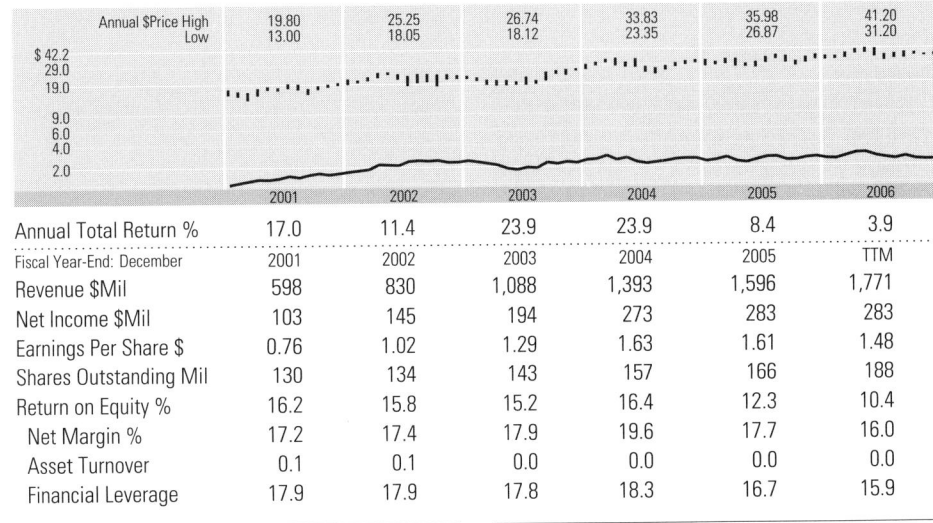

Competition	Market Cap $Mil	12 Mo Trailing Sales $Mil	Price/Cash Flow	Return On Assets%	Debt/ Equity	Total Return% 1 Yr	3 Yr
Commerce Bancorp NJ	6,614	1,771	—	0.7	—	3.9	11.0
Bank of America	239,758	68,368	—	1.3	—	20.7	15.2
J.P. Morgan Chase & Co.	167,551	59,650	—	0.9	—	25.6	13.2

	2001	2002	2003	2004	2005	2006
Annual $Price High	19.80	25.25	26.74	33.83	35.98	41.20
Low	13.00	18.05	18.12	23.35	26.87	31.20
Annual Total Return %	17.0	11.4	23.9	23.9	8.4	3.9

Fiscal Year-End: December	2001	2002	2003	2004	2005	TTM
Revenue $Mil	598	830	1,088	1,393	1,596	1,771
Net Income $Mil	103	145	194	273	283	283
Earnings Per Share $	0.76	1.02	1.29	1.63	1.61	1.48
Shares Outstanding Mil	130	134	143	157	166	188
Return on Equity %	16.2	15.8	15.2	16.4	12.3	10.4
Net Margin %	17.2	17.4	17.9	19.6	17.7	16.0
Asset Turnover	0.1	0.1	0.0	0.0	0.0	0.0
Financial Leverage	17.9	17.9	17.8	18.3	16.7	15.9

Valuation Ratios	Stock	Rel to Industry	Rel to S&P 500
Price/Earnings	23.8	1.3	1.2
Price/Book	2.4	0.8	0.6
Price/Sales	3.7	0.6	1.3
Price/Cash Flow	—	—	—

Major Fund Holders	% of Fund Assets
The Turnaround	13.41
Davis Financial A	4.82
Biondo Growth Inv	4.82
JHT Financial Services Trust Ser I	4.19

Thesis By Jaime Black, CFA, CPA, 11-28-06 Stock Price as of Analysis: $34.91

Commerce uses its easy-to-access branches in metropolitan areas to attract low-cost deposits. The firm has exploited this deceptively simple strategy, becoming one of the fastest-growing banks in the United States. We love this story, despite some serious reservations about its management.

After having initial doubts, we believe Commerce has the ability to find enough locations and attractive markets for its planned branch expansion. The company expects to open 67 branches in 2006 and 100 a year by 2009. Commerce has already identified and entered markets that will support an estimated 950 branches, which will take the company out to 2011 before needing to look for another market. Given Commerce's willingness to pay high prices for good locations, we believe the company will find the real estate for its branches.

Commerce is serious about its "America's Most Convenient Bank" motto. The company must constantly come up with new perks, since many of its ideas are easily copied. However, like Southwest Airlines, no other company has been able to replicate all the little items that make this company special. It is ingrained in the culture to put the customer first. For example, Commerce refunds all foreign ATM fees for customers who have a $2,500 minimum balance and offers free self-serve coin-counting machines, compared with Coinstar, which charges an 8.9% fee for cashing in change.

Commerce's model comes at a high cost. The company spent a whopping 73% of revenues on operating costs in the first nine months of 2006. Banks in Commerce's peer group average operating costs of 55% of revenues. We believe Commerce's high expenses are a necessary evil to its strategy. Part of the high cost is the drag on newly opened branches, which are more expensive than typical banking branches due to their premium locations. But the majority of costs is from all the little perks that draw in the deposits which give the company its advantage.

Commerce concentrates on deposit growth to drive its earnings growth. Its model is designed to draw in as many deposits as it can, and it works wonderfully. Commerce's 10-year-old branches are increasing their deposit base by 15% annually, compared with an industry average of 4%. With deposits growing much faster than loans, Commerce has the ability to buy longer-maturity securities with higher yields. However, the continued flat yield curve has temporarily eliminated this advantage.

We couldn't be more impressed with Commerce.

Data as of 12-29-06

Companhia Vale Do Rio Doce RIO

Rating ★	Fair Value $21.00	Last Close $29.74	Consider Buy $13.40	Consider Sell $25.30	Yield % 1.77

Industry	Business Risk	Moat Size	Investment Style	Sector
Steel/Iron	Above Avg	Narrow	Large Core	Industrial Materials

Company Profile

Incorporated in 1942, Companhia Vale do Rio Doce was privatized in 1997. CVRD's business is divided into mining, rail, and electric power generation. The company, which mines bauxite and produces aluminum, potash, and kaolin, is the world's largest exporter of iron ore; it is also a major supplier of manganese and ferroalloys. CVRD's railway network is responsible for two thirds of all Brazilian rail freight. CVRD recently acquired nickel miner Canico Resources.

Management   Stewardship Grade [NA]

Formerly in charge of the Banco Bradesco capital markets division, Roger Agnelli became chief executive officer of CVRD in 2001. An economist by training, Agnelli was the chairman of CVRD from May 2000 to July 2001. In 2005, CVRD paid about $14.1 million in aggregate to its executive officers and about $477,100 to its directors. Executive officers and directors as a group own 41,161 common shares and 231,889 preferred shares. CVRD was privatized in 1997 when Valepar acquired a 53.3% stake from the Brazilian government. CVRD has common and preferred shares and 3 golden shares. Golden shares are owned by the Brazilian government and entitle it to significant veto power. Because of its share ownership, Valepar can control the outcome of most actions requiring shareholder approval--something small investors should be wary about.

Av. Graca Aranha 26, 18 Andar Castelo   www.cvrd.com.br
Rio de Janeiro, Brazil 20005-900

Growth [NA]	2002	2003	2004	2005
Revenue %	4.8	29.8	50.8	58.6
Earnings/Share %	NMF	NMF	66.4	88.3
Book Value/Share %	—	NMF	62.5	58.3
Dividends/Share %	NMF	258.5	65.8	-24.2

Profitability [NA]	2003	2004	2005	TTM
Return on Assets %	13.5	16.4	21.4	21.4
Oper Cash Flow $Mil	1,757	3,471	5,161	5,161
- Cap Spending $Mil	1,543	2,022	3,977	3,977
= Free Cash Flow $Mil	214	1,449	1,184	1,184

Financial Health [NA]	2003	2004	2005	12-31-05
Long-term Debt $Mil	2,771	3,232	3,715	3,715
Total Equity $Mil	3,829	6,215	9,827	9,827
Debt/Equity Ratio	0.7	0.5	0.4	0.4

Competition

	Market Cap $Mil	12 Mo Trailing Sales $Mil	Price/Cash Flow	Return On Assets%	Debt/Equity	Total Return% 1 Yr	3 Yr
Companhia Vale Do Rio Doce	68,492	12,792	13.3	21.4	0.4	47.8	49.9
Rio Tinto PLC ADR	81,024	19,033	11.7	18.4	0.2	20.7	27.5
BHP Billiton ADR	69,482	32,153	6.6	21.7	0.3	21.2	31.3

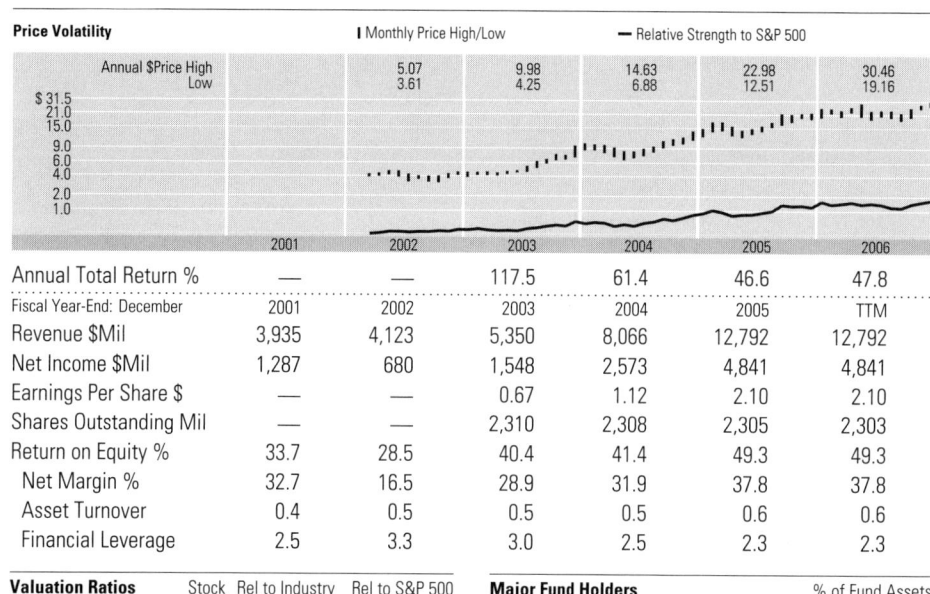

Price Volatility — Monthly Price High/Low — Relative Strength to S&P 500

Annual $Price High/Low	5.07/3.61	9.98/4.25	14.63/6.88	22.98/12.51	30.46/19.16

Annual Total Return %	—	—	117.5	61.4	46.6	47.8
Fiscal Year-End: December	2001	2002	2003	2004	2005	TTM
Revenue $Mil	3,935	4,123	5,350	8,066	12,792	12,792
Net Income $Mil	1,287	680	1,548	2,573	4,841	4,841
Earnings Per Share $	—	—	0.67	1.12	2.10	2.10
Shares Outstanding Mil	—	—	2,310	2,308	2,305	2,303
Return on Equity %	33.7	28.5	40.4	41.4	49.3	49.3
Net Margin %	32.7	16.5	28.9	31.9	37.8	37.8
Asset Turnover	0.4	0.5	0.5	0.5	0.6	0.6
Financial Leverage	2.5	3.3	3.0	2.5	2.3	2.3

Valuation Ratios	Stock	Rel to Industry	Rel to S&P 500
Price/Earnings	14.2	1.1	0.7
Price/Book	7.0	1.4	1.7
Price/Sales	5.4	2.1	1.9
Price/Cash Flow	13.3	1.0	0.9

Major Fund Holders	% of Fund Assets
T. Rowe Price Latin America	5.21
RiverSource Emerging Markets A	4.68
Janus Overseas	4.01
Janus Adviser International Growth S	4.00

Thesis By Parvathy Krishnan, CFA, 12-11-06 Stock Price as of Analysis: $29.47

Surging worldwide demand for iron ore, most notably from China, has pushed Companhia Vale do Rio Doce (CVRD) to new heights. As the largest exporter of iron ore and a significant producer of other base metals, CVRD has been a primary beneficiary of a rising tide that has boosted all metal producers over the past three years. But the company still remains susceptible to downturns in the notoriously cyclical commodity pricing cycle, so we would urge investors to proceed with caution when considering these risky shares.

CVRD's bread and butter--and the source of more than 63% of its revenue--is iron. Three producers control about 70% of the global iron ore trade: CVRD, Rio Tinto, and BHP Billiton. The fact that CVRD has the largest share in a highly concentrated market enables it to earn returns on invested capital above its cost of capital--over the past four years they've averaged 23.3%, comfortably above our calculated cost of capital of 9.9%. The firm's market share, competitive cost structure, iron ore quality, and near monopoly on rail freight in Brazil constitute a narrow economic moat, in our opinion.

CVRD's goal is to become one of the world's largest diversified mining companies. This concerns us because it is difficult, if not impossible, to maintain a competitive edge in several different commodity businesses at once. We think the edge that CVRD enjoys in iron ore will be diluted by the company's diversification into nickel and other commodities. We therefore expect its returns on invested capital to shrink.

We are also concerned about the impact that expansion will have on the balance sheet. With demand and prices at record levels, CVRD has enjoyed a few good years and is spending all its extra cash--and then some--on expansion projects. The capital expenditure budget for 2006 is a record $4.6 billion, and the company will spend about $17 billion to acquire Inco. As a result, we expect that CVRD's debt/capitalization ratio will worsen from its 2005 level, which was already high at 32%.

When the market turns south, CVRD might be left high and dry with idle capacity and a heavy debt burden. The situation could be made even worse by Brazil's regulatory instability. As is often the case in emerging economies, significant changes in fiscal, monetary, and international trade policies are quite common and could hurt CVRD's business. These issues, along with the cyclicality inherent in the industry, land CVRD in the above-average-risk category.

Data as of 12-29-06

Compass Minerals International CMP

Rating	Fair Value	Last Close	Consider Buy	Consider Sell	Yield %
★★★★★	$41.00	$31.56	$31.60	$51.40	3.87

Company Profile
Compass Minerals mines and sells various salts. The firm bills itself as North America's largest producer of rock salt, used for highway de-icing. It also mines and sells salt suitable for trade uses, including water softening and human consumption (table salt). Compass operates extensively in North America and the United Kingdom, and runs the world's largest salt mine, in Goderich, Ontario, and the largest salt mine in the U.K., in Winsford, Cheshire.

Management   Stewardship Grade [B]
Angelo Brisimitzakis took the reigns from Michael Ducey in May 2006, and we think he is a worthy successor. Ducey led the company through the initial years admirably, focusing on operational improvements to create value for shareholders. Brisimitzakis brings more strategic vision to the company. His background in specialty chemicals has given him appreciation of the stability of the rock salt industry. While he wants Compass to grow through product and geographic expansion, he is keenly aware of the economics and role that Compass plays in the salt industry. Ducey's total compensation was $1.4 million in 2005 and $1.3 million in 2003. He owns 1.8% of the company's stock. While we like the management team's principles, there are two main reasons why our Stewardship Grade for Compass is not an A. First, the board of directors is staggered. It will take two annual meetings of stockholders to change a majority of the board. Second, in the first half of 2005, management acknowledged the inadequacy of internal controls with regard to reporting of tax-related items on the financial statements, and it has initiated steps to address this issue.

8300 College Blvd. www.compassminerals.com
Overland Park, KS 66210

Growth [C]	2002	2003	2004	2005
Revenue %	-4.7	20.6	15.6	16.0
Earnings/Share %	NMF	NMF	NMF	-38.2
Book Value/Share %	—	—	NMF	NMF
Dividends/Share %	NMF	NMF	NMF	17.3

Profitability [B]	2003	2004	2005	TTM
Return on Assets %	5.7	6.9	4.1	6.3
Oper Cash Flow $Mil	69	100	88	97
- Cap Spending $Mil	21	27	32	37
= Free Cash Flow $Mil	49	73	56	60

Financial Health [B-]	2003	2004	2005	09-30-06
Long-term Debt $Mil	—	583	612	569
Total Equity $Mil	-128	-88	-79	-74
Debt/Equity Ratio	—	ELB	ELB	NMF

Industry	Business Risk	Moat Size	Investment Style	Sector
Mining (Nonmetal)	Average	Narrow	Small Value	Industrial Materials

Competition
	Market Cap $Mil	12 Mo Trailing Sales $Mil	Price/Cash Flow	Return On Assets %	Debt/Equity	Total Return % 1 Yr	3 Yr
Compass Minerals International	1,012	733	10.4	6.3	NMF	34.5	36.0
Rohm and Haas	11,166	8,300	11.6	7.1	0.4	8.4	9.0
Cargill (private)							

Price Volatility
Monthly Price High/Low — Relative Strength to S&P 500

	2001	2002	2003	2004	2005	2006
Annual $Price High				14.45	24.40	26.83	34.69
Low				13.00	14.00	21.58	21.98

Annual Total Return %	—	—	—	77.9	6.0	34.5
Fiscal Year-End: December	2001	2002	2003	2004	2005	TTM
Revenue $Mil	482	459	554	640	742	733
Net Income $Mil	28	6	39	50	31	42
Earnings Per Share $	—	—	—	1.57	0.97	1.30
Shares Outstanding Mil	—	—	—	31	32	32
Return on Equity %	NMF	NMF	NMF	NMF	NMF	NMF
Net Margin %	5.8	1.4	7.1	7.8	4.2	5.8
Asset Turnover	0.7	0.7	0.8	0.9	1.0	1.1
Financial Leverage	NMF	NMF	NMF	NMF	NMF	NMF

Valuation Ratios	Stock	Rel to Industry	Rel to S&P 500
Price/Earnings	27.0	1.5	1.3
Price/Book	—	—	—
Price/Sales	1.4	0.4	0.5
Price/Cash Flow	10.4	0.7	0.7

Major Fund Holders	% of Fund Assets
Integrity Growth & Income A Load Waived	3.98
Calvert Small Cap Value A	3.89
Calvert Mid Cap Value A	3.12
Fidelity Small Cap Retirement	2.84

Thesis By Parvathy Krishnan, CFA, 11-03-06 Stock Price as of Analysis: $30.56

With a history of steady price increases driving revenue growth and enviable cost advantages over its rivals, we think Compass is exactly the simple and boring, yet profitable and sometimes undervalued, business that Warren Buffett would love.

The salt industry is characterized by stable demand and steady price increases across various grades, resulting in strong, consistent cash flows. Compass is the second-largest producer of salt in North America. This leadership position in a stable, solid industry leads us to believe Compass has a narrow economic moat. The firm generates good free cash flow, and its moat is evidenced by exceptional returns on invested capital. The average ROIC over the past three years is 15.9%, comfortably above the company's cost of capital, which we estimate to be 8.8%

Compass has a significant cost advantage over its rivals. Its Goderich, Ontario, mine is not only the largest salt mine in the world in terms of reserves, but the structure of the ore body gives Compass a 30%-40% cost advantage over other mines. Two other factors contribute to lower the cost of the delivered product. First, Goderich has its own port on Lake Huron, so rock salt gets on a ship directly from the mine. This is a major advantage over land-locked mines as water transportation of salt is about 50% less expensive than road or rail transportation. Second, the company has built a network of 72 depots close to the extensive water network of the Midwest, where salt is stored before being transported by rail or road to the customer. It also helps that the company targets the Midwest, where snowfall is more consistent than in other parts of the continent.

A cursory glance at Compass' financial statements may raise some initial concerns, but we believe these challenges are both manageable and often overblown. High interest rates on the company's debt and exposure to weather anomalies make the company's present cash flows seem more volatile than we anticipate the near future to be. Much of the company's legacy debt, the aftermath of a leveraged buyout, becomes callable soon, and we expect refinancings to significantly lower both interest expenses and the company's cost of capital. Weather variance is increasingly mitigated by flexible labor agreements at Goderich and new CEO Angelo Brisimitzakis' focus on growing sales of other products. Sulfate of potash and general trade segments are expected to grow significantly through innovations that leverage the company's strengths.

Data as of 12-29-06

ConocoPhillips COP

Rating	Fair Value	Last Close	Consider Buy	Consider Sell	Yield %
★★★	$73.00	$71.95	$56.30	$91.50	2.00

Company Profile

ConocoPhillips was created by the August 2002 merger of midsize oil firms Conoco and Phillips. It is the third-largest oil company and the second-largest refiner in the United States. For 2005, the Houston-based company posted proved reserves of 9.5 billion oil equivalent barrels, daily production of 1.6 million barrels, and refining capacity of 2.6 million barrels per day. The company also has midstream natural-gas, petrochemical, and retail service station operations.

Management   Stewardship Grade [C]

Management comes roughly equally from Conoco and Phillips. CEO James Mulva was the CEO of Phillips and assumed the additional role of chairman when former chairman Archie Dunham retired in 2004. We would prefer that these roles were kept separate. Mulva has proved himself a skilled deal maker and oversaw the successful combination of Conoco and Phillips. He has aggressively pursued growth opportunities, as evidenced by the firm's bold move into Russia and the Burlington acquisition. In 2005, Mulva earned $31.1 million, the bulk of which was performance-related. On top of this, he received 392,800 stock options. Although generous, total compensation is par for companies of ConocoPhillips' size. We like that performance-based compensation is primarily determined by total shareholder return and returns on invested capital relative to the firm's peer group. Directors and executive officers beneficially own 13.6 million shares, a fair amount given ConocoPhillips' size.

600 North Dairy Ashford Road www.phillips66.com
Houston, TX 77079

Growth [B]	2002	2003	2004	2005
Revenue %	129.8	83.7	30.3	33.9
Earnings/Share %	NMF	NMF	67.9	64.7
Book Value/Share %	25.3	-17.8	21.6	22.1
Dividends/Share %	5.7	10.1	9.8	31.8

Profitability [B]	2003	2004	2005	TTM
Return on Assets %	5.7	8.8	12.6	9.8
Oper Cash Flow $Mil	9,356	11,959	17,628	20,554
- Cap Spending $Mil	6,169	9,496	11,620	14,560
= Free Cash Flow $Mil	3,187	2,463	6,008	5,994

Financial Health [A-]	2003	2004	2005	09-30-06
Long-term Debt $Mil	19,943	18,264	15,349	29,360
Total Equity $Mil	34,366	42,723	52,731	80,476
Debt/Equity Ratio	0.6	0.4	0.3	0.4

Industry	Business Risk	Moat Size	Investment Style	Sector
Oil/Gas	Average	Narrow	Large Value	Energy

Competition	Market Cap $Mil	12 Mo Trailing Sales $Mil	Price/Cash Flow	Return On Assets%	Debt/ Equity	Total Return% 1 Yr	3 Yr
ConocoPhillips	118,413	198,161	5.8	9.8	0.4	26.5	33.0
ExxonMobil	446,944	386,951	8.8	17.8	0.1	39.1	26.2
Total SA ADR	176,957	153,547	9.6	12.5	0.3	19.2	20.2

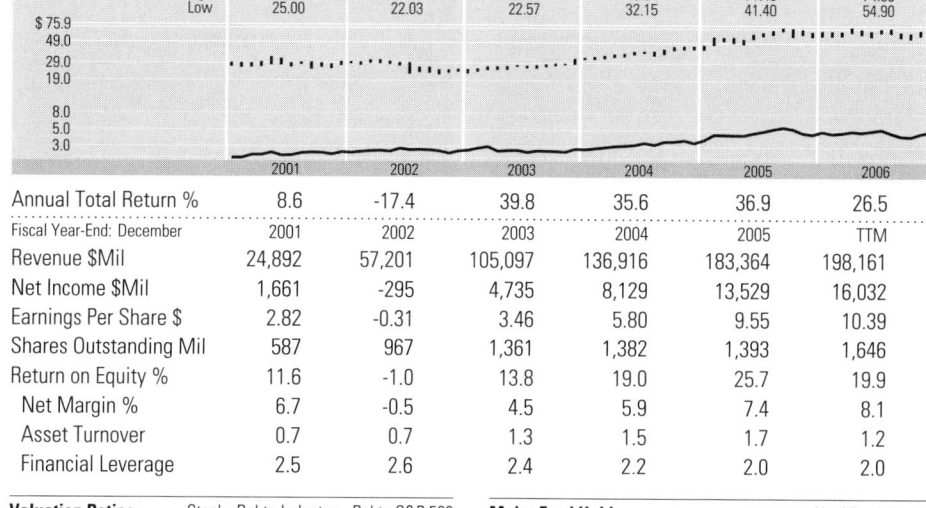

	2001	2002	2003	2004	2005	2006/TTM
Annual Total Return %	8.6	-17.4	39.8	35.6	36.9	26.5
Revenue $Mil	24,892	57,201	105,097	136,916	183,364	198,161
Net Income $Mil	1,661	-295	4,735	8,129	13,529	16,032
Earnings Per Share $	2.82	-0.31	3.46	5.80	9.55	10.39
Shares Outstanding Mil	587	967	1,361	1,382	1,393	1,646
Return on Equity %	11.6	-1.0	13.8	19.0	25.7	19.9
Net Margin %	6.7	-0.5	4.5	5.9	7.4	8.1
Asset Turnover	0.7	0.7	1.3	1.5	1.7	1.2
Financial Leverage	2.5	2.6	2.4	2.2	2.0	2.0

Valuation Ratios	Stock	Rel to Industry	Rel to S&P 500
Price/Earnings	6.9	0.5	0.3
Price/Book	1.5	0.5	0.4
Price/Sales	0.6	0.3	0.2
Price/Cash Flow	5.8	0.7	0.4

Major Fund Holders	% of Fund Assets
DWS Dreman Concentrated Value A	8.02
Clipper	7.70
Integrity Value A	7.14
SunAmerica Focused Large Cap Value A	6.60

Thesis By Justin Perucki, CFA, 12-08-06 Stock Price as of Analysis: $71.04

The 2002 merger of Conoco and Phillips has proved rewarding for investors. Now the third-largest energy company in the United States, ConocoPhillips has shed billions of dollars in underperforming assets and achieved merger synergies well beyond those initially promised. While its recent acquisition of Burlington Resources brings it closer in size to domestic peers ExxonMobil and Chevron, ConocoPhillips still trails in terms of oil and gas reserves and production.

With almost 80% of its oil and gas production drawn from reserves in North America and Europe, ConocoPhillips is fighting the high production decline rates inherent in these mature regions. Although we think ConocoPhillips paid a hefty price for Burlington, it provides a much-needed boost to the firm's North American operations. The company is also pushing ahead with its strategy of expanding production in new, higher-risk areas. With large investments in Venezuela, Asia, and the Middle East, a pipeline of projects is set to come onstream over the next few years that will shift the geographic mix and help lift production.

The company also has made a risky bet in Russia. Late in 2004, ConocoPhillips purchased a noncontrolling stake in one of Russia's largest energy players, Lukoil. The deal grants access to Russia's large energy resources. Although we are uneasy about the risks, the purchase delivers a significant boost to reserves at a reasonable price. We think ConocoPhillips needed to make a bold move, and there aren't many politically stable places left to do that. ConocoPhillips holds a 20% equity stake in Lukoil.

Even with sky-high energy prices boosting profits from the upstream exploration and production segment, the refining segment has stolen the spotlight lately. Over the past two years, rising demand for refined products has tested the limits of U.S. refining capacity. As one of the largest refiners in the United States, ConocoPhillips has benefited from rising throughput, robust refining margins, and fat discounts on low-quality crude-oil feedstocks. While capacity constraints are likely to lend support over the near to medium term, refining remains a highly cyclical industry and provides few opportunities for companies to establish sustainable competitive advantages.

Data as of 12-29-06

Consolidated Edison ED

	Rating	Fair Value	Last Close	Consider Buy	Consider Sell	Yield %
	★★★	$49.00	$48.07	$41.80	$64.30	4.79

Company Profile
Consolidated Edison is a holding company for two regulated utilities (Con Ed of New York and O&R) that provide steam, natural gas, and electricity to customers in southeastern New York--including New York City--and parts of New Jersey and Pennsylvania. The company's electric utility operations generate 70% of Con Ed's operating revenue.

Industry	Business Risk	Moat Size	Investment Style	Sector
Electric Utilities	Below Avg	Narrow	Large Value	Utilities

Competition

	Market Cap $Mil	12 Mo Trailing Sales $Mil	Price/Cash Flow	Return On Assets%	Debt/Equity	Total Return% 1 Yr	3 Yr
Consolidated Edison	12,344	12,481	15.0	3.0	1.0	9.1	9.3
KeySpan	7,218	7,793	8.6	3.1	0.9	21.0	8.8
Energy East	3,663	5,385	20.0	2.2	1.4	14.2	7.7

Price Volatility
| Monthly Price High/Low — Relative Strength to S&P 500

Annual $Price High	43.37	45.40	46.02	45.59	49.29	49.28
Low	31.44	32.70	36.56	37.23	41.10	41.17
	2001	2002	2003	2004	2005	2006
Annual Total Return %	10.9	11.8	6.3	7.3	11.3	9.1

Fiscal Year-End: December

	2001	2002	2003	2004	2005	TTM
Revenue $Mil	9,389	8,502	9,808	9,758	11,690	12,481
Net Income $Mil	682	646	528	537	719	674
Earnings Per Share $	3.21	3.02	2.38	2.27	2.94	2.72
Shares Outstanding Mil	212	213	221	236	244	257
Return on Equity %	11.6	10.9	8.0	7.6	9.8	9.8
Net Margin %	7.3	7.6	5.4	5.5	6.2	5.4
Asset Turnover	0.5	0.4	0.5	0.4	0.5	0.6
Financial Leverage	3.0	3.3	3.2	3.2	3.4	3.3

Management
Stewardship Grade [**B**]

Kevin Burke, formerly a lawyer and chief operating officer at Con Ed, became CEO of the firm in 2005 and was elected chairman in 2006. Burke, whose rise to Con Ed's top position spans more than 30 years, replaced now-retired Eugene McGrath. We think Burke's extensive history at Con Ed will serve him well in executing the firm's time-proven model as a conservative, financially sound, regulated utility. Con Ed's shareholder friendliness compares favorably with that of other companies in our universe. Executive compensation is in line with the industry average and incentive pay is based on a number of shareholder-oriented performance metrics, including return on equity and dividend payouts. We think target stock ownership levels of 3 times base salary for the CEO and 2 times for other officers will help align management and shareholder interests. Directors are partly compensated via stock-based incentives, and all are elected annually. Although these policies serve shareholders' interests, we think the company missed an opportunity to further strengthen its stewardship practices by permanently separating the chairman and CEO positions. Instead, the company elected Burke as chairman in early 2006.

4 Irving Place
New York, NY 10003
www.conedison.com

Growth [B]
	2002	2003	2004	2005
Revenue %	-9.4	15.4	-0.5	19.8
Earnings/Share %	-5.9	-21.2	-4.6	29.5
Book Value/Share %	0.0	8.1	-0.3	0.2
Dividends/Share %	0.9	0.9	0.9	0.9

Profitability [B]
	2003	2004	2005	TTM
Return on Assets %	2.5	2.4	2.9	3.0
Oper Cash Flow $Mil	1,309	1,311	793	824
- Cap Spending $Mil	1,398	1,397	1,636	1,879
= Free Cash Flow $Mil	-89	-86	-843	-1,055

Financial Health [C-]
	2003	2004	2005	09-30-06
Long-term Debt $Mil	6,733	6,594	7,428	6,782
Total Equity $Mil	6,636	7,054	7,310	6,846
Debt/Equity Ratio	1.0	0.9	1.0	1.0

Valuation Ratios

	Stock	Rel to Industry	Rel to S&P 500
Price/Earnings	17.5	1.0	0.8
Price/Book	1.8	0.5	0.4
Price/Sales	1.0	0.6	0.3
Price/Cash Flow	15.0	1.3	1.0

Major Fund Holders

	% of Fund Assets
ING Corporate Leaders Trust B	2.43
Federated Strategic Value C	2.06
Phoenix Global Utilities A	2.02
American Century Equity Income Inv	1.97

Thesis By Ryan McLean, 12-14-06 Stock Price as of Analysis: $49.13

Consolidated Edison's traditional "wires and pipes" business may lack the allure of the city it serves, but we think the firm deserves investors' consideration. Dependable earnings and dividends make this 200-year-old utility a solid income-producing investment. What's more, Con Ed's supportive regulatory relationships and natural monopoly status should enable it to steadily grow payouts.

Four fifths of operating revenues and virtually all of earnings flow from the firm's regulated segment, Con Edison of New York. By means of its vast transmission and distribution network--much of which is underground--this entity delivers purchased electricity and natural gas to customers throughout New York City. Orange & Rockland Utilities (O&R)--an electric and gas utility that serves nearby areas--contributes the remainder of Con Ed's income. We think these utilities' regulated earnings, coupled with their difficult-to-reproduce delivery infrastructures, earn Con Ed a narrow economic moat rating and below-average business risk rating. While we like Con Ed's focus on its stalwart utilities, we are less cheerful about its determination to retain a handful of unprofitable competitive energy businesses. Still, these segments' overall impact on earnings is minor.

Aging infrastructure and demand growth are driving a substantial capital investment program at Con Ed. From 2007 to 2008, the firm will invest $3.5 billion in infrastructure--about 50% above historical levels. The firm's industry-leading customer reliability has helped it secure regulatory approval for a rate base expansion that reflects these outlays. Even after recent blackouts, the firm is 9 times more reliable than the national average. Given this backdrop, we think regulators will allow Con Ed to reap an assured return on its rate base well into the future.

Con Edison's commitment to its basic strategy has allowed it to navigate the waters of deregulation more stably than some of its utility peers. The company has increased dividends consecutively each year for over three decades. At our fair value estimate, Con Ed's current dividend yield is 4.7%--well above an industry average closer to 3.5%. Despite heavy capital outlays in the years ahead, we expect the firm will remain free-cash-flow positive. On a less encouraging note, we do not anticipate improved returns on invested capital, which should hover around the firm's cost of capital for the foreseeable future.

Costco Wholesale COST

Data as of 12-29-06

Rating	Fair Value	Last Close	Consider Buy	Consider Sell	Yield %
★★★	$51.00	$52.87	$39.30	$63.90	0.96

Company Profile
Costco Wholesale operates membership warehouses that offer a limited selection of nationally branded and selected private-label products in a wide range of merchandise categories at low prices. The company's stores average 139,000 square feet and offer goods in a no-frills, self-service environment. Costco operates about 490 warehouses in the United States and six other countries and has 48 million club members.

Management
Stewardship Grade [A]

President and CEO James Sinegal and chairman Jeffrey Brotman cofounded Costco in 1983. Virtually all of the senior executives have been with the company for several years. The board of directors comprises Sinegal, Brotman, two other senior executives, and 10 outside directors, including Charles Munger of Berkshire Hathaway fame. Executive officers and directors own just over 2% of the company's common stock. Costco's corporate stewardship is excellent, including very reasonable management compensation, voluntary expensing of stock options, and a high level of communication and transparency with the financial community. Having said that, we are not fans of the company's staggered board of directors.

999 Lake Drive www.costco.com
Issaquah, WA 98027

Growth [B+]	2002	2003	2004	2005
Revenue %	9.7	15.4	10.1	13.6
Earnings/Share %	3.4	20.9	17.8	5.5
Book Value/Share %	15.5	14.9	13.9	4.7
Dividends/Share %	NMF	NMF	115.0	14.0

Profitability [B+]	2003	2004	2005	TTM
Return on Assets %	5.8	6.4	6.3	6.3
Oper Cash Flow $Mil	1,507	2,096	1,776	1,827
- Cap Spending $Mil	706	995	1,213	—
= Free Cash Flow $Mil	1,391	781	615	—

Financial Health [NA]	2003	2004	2005	08-31-06
Long-term Debt $Mil	994	711	215	215
Total Equity $Mil	7,625	8,881	9,143	9,143
Debt/Equity Ratio	0.1	0.1	0.0	0.0

Industry	Business Risk	Moat Size	Investment Style	Sector
Discount Stores	Average	Narrow	Large Core	Consumer Services

Competition

	Market Cap $Mil	12 Mo Trailing Sales $Mil	Price/Cash Flow	Return On Assets %	Debt/Equity	Total Return % 1 Yr	3 Yr
Costco Wholesale	24,229	60,151	13.3	6.3	0.0	7.9	14.3
Wal-Mart Stores	192,479	339,150	9.8	7.2	0.5	0.1	-2.9
BJ's Wholesale Club	2,002	8,236	9.6	5.5	0.0	5.2	11.7

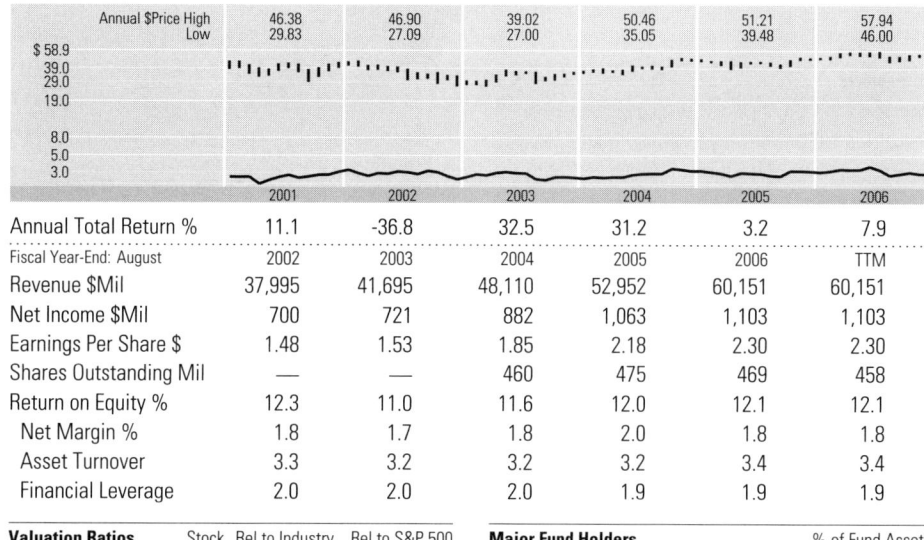

	2001	2002	2003	2004	2005	2006
Annual $Price High	46.38	46.90	39.02	50.46	51.21	57.94
Low	29.83	27.09	27.00	35.05	39.48	46.00
Annual Total Return %	11.1	-36.8	32.5	31.2	3.2	7.9

Fiscal Year-End: August	2002	2003	2004	2005	2006	TTM
Revenue $Mil	37,995	41,695	48,110	52,952	60,151	60,151
Net Income $Mil	700	721	882	1,063	1,103	1,103
Earnings Per Share $	1.48	1.53	1.85	2.18	2.30	2.30
Shares Outstanding Mil	—	—	460	475	469	458
Return on Equity %	12.3	11.0	11.6	12.0	12.1	12.1
Net Margin %	1.8	1.7	1.8	2.0	1.8	1.8
Asset Turnover	3.3	3.2	3.2	3.2	3.4	3.4
Financial Leverage	2.0	2.0	2.0	1.9	1.9	1.9

Valuation Ratios	Stock	Rel to Industry	Rel to S&P 500
Price/Earnings	23.0	1.1	1.1
Price/Book	2.7	0.7	0.7
Price/Sales	0.4	0.5	0.1
Price/Cash Flow	13.3	1.1	0.9

Major Fund Holders	% of Fund Assets
Clipper	6.94
MMA Praxis Core Stock B	4.18
Tilson Dividend	4.10
Destination Select Equity	3.96

Thesis
By Anthony Chukumba, 10-16-06 Stock Price as of Analysis: $52.98

Costco Wholesale dominates the growing niche of warehouse club retailing. The company offers its club members food items, household goods, electronics, and apparel in a no-frills, self-service warehouse format. Costco prides itself on selling its limited selection of wares in each product category at prices that are well below those of traditional supermarkets and discounters. While Costco's profit margins are extremely low, with operating margins routinely less than 3%, the firm's high inventory turns lead to returns on invested capital that are well in excess of our estimate of its weighted average cost of capital. We believe that Costco's strong brand name, leverage with suppliers and prime real estate locations provide it with a narrow economic moat.

Costco has steadily grown by opening new warehouse clubs and increasing the sales at its older locations. Over the past five years, the firm has averaged 6% annual new store growth, with openings both in the U.S. and abroad. Costco plans on opening an additional 35 clubs in 2007. The company has also continued to generate healthy comparable-store sales, or comps (sales at stores open at least a year), primarily through expanding its merchandise offerings and adding more "treasure hunt" items into the stores, such as jewelry and large-screen televisions. The average Costco store generated a whopping $127 million in sales last year, an increase of over 25% compared with an average of $101 million in 2001.

Costco has also been one of the few retailers to successfully compete with behemoth Wal-Mart. Costco's stores generate over 50% more annual sales on average than Sam's Club stores, and its comps regularly outpace its peers'. The firm's higher store productivity is due to two factors: better merchandising and superior customer service, due to its better-paid, more-loyal employees. Costco's top managers truly view its employees as partners in its success, rather than just expendable assets.

Costco's store-level workforce is one of the best in retailing. This is due to high wages (the average hourly wage at Costco is $17, versus $10 at Wal-Mart) and generous benefits (for example, Costco workers pay 10% of health premiums versus 33% at Wal-Mart and a retail average of 23%). The pay and benefits for Costco employees lead directly to lower employee turnover (17% a year), lower recruiting and training costs, and a more highly motivated workforce. All of this leads to superior customer service--vastly better than consumers receive at Sam's Club or the local supermarket.

Countrywide Financial CFC

Data as of 12-29-06

	Rating	Fair Value	Last Close	Consider Buy	Consider Sell	Yield %
	★★★	$46.00	$42.45	$35.50	$57.60	1.41

Company Profile
Countrywide Financial is one of the leading mortgage issuers and servicers in the United States. It primarily originates single-family mortgage loans and sells them in the secondary market, retaining the servicing rights. The company also has a retail banking subsidiary, as well as other nonmortgage segments like insurance and capital markets.

Industry	Business Risk	Moat Size	Investment Style	Sector
Savings & Loans	Average	Narrow	Large Value	Financial Services

Competition

	Market Cap $Mil	12 Mo Trailing Sales $Mil	Price/Cash Flow	Return On Assets%	Debt/ Equity	Total Return% 1 Yr	3 Yr
Countrywide Financial	26,365	11,251	—	1.4	—	26.2	21.3
Bank of America	239,758	68,368	—	1.3	—	20.7	15.2
Wells Fargo	120,049	34,770	—	1.7	—	16.8	10.4

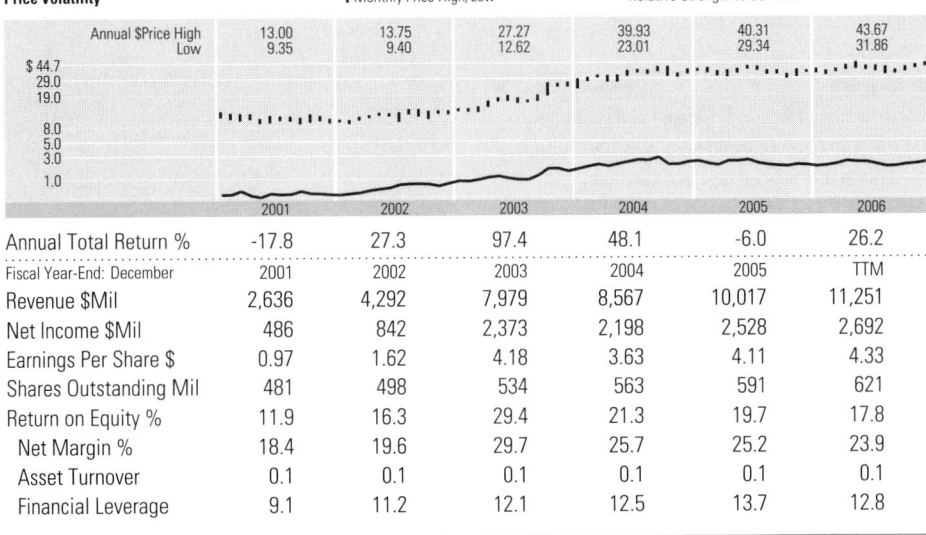

Price Volatility | Monthly Price High/Low — Relative Strength to S&P 500

Annual $Price	2001	2002	2003	2004	2005	2006
High	13.00	13.75	27.27	39.93	40.31	43.67
Low	9.35	9.40	12.62	23.01	29.34	31.86
Annual Total Return %	-17.8	27.3	97.4	48.1	-6.0	26.2

Fiscal Year-End: December	2001	2002	2003	2004	2005	TTM
Revenue $Mil	2,636	4,292	7,979	8,567	10,017	11,251
Net Income $Mil	486	842	2,373	2,198	2,528	2,692
Earnings Per Share $	0.97	1.62	4.18	3.63	4.11	4.33
Shares Outstanding Mil	481	498	534	563	591	621
Return on Equity %	11.9	16.3	29.4	21.3	19.7	17.8
Net Margin %	18.4	19.6	29.7	25.7	25.2	23.9
Asset Turnover	0.1	0.1	0.1	0.1	0.1	0.1
Financial Leverage	9.1	11.2	12.1	12.5	13.7	12.8

Management — Stewardship Grade [C]
Chairman and CEO Angelo Mozilo cofounded the company in 1969. Mozilo is generally regarded as a visionary leader, and we think his vision usually turns out to be correct. We like the steps Countrywide has taken under his leadership in diversifying the firm's revenue base and focusing on businesses that are complementary to mortgage banking, such as mortgage servicing and retail banking. We've seen this management team sacrifice short-term profits for the sake of better long-term returns, which we applaud. Plus, the company keeps its shareholders well informed. Management takes pains to explain the mortgage business in simple terms and provides the data needed to understand the business drivers and the complex accounting that accompanies mortgage banking. The top brass also maintain significant ownership stakes in the company--Mozilo owns almost 2% of the total shares--which we like to see. Despite these noble traits, management has helped itself to shareholders' cash. Top management compensation (both cash and noncash) seems too high, in our opinion, even in light of Countrywide's outstanding recent performance. Additionally, options granted over the past several years have approached 3% of outstanding shares annually, which is more than we'd like to see.

Valuation Ratios	Stock	Rel to Industry	Rel to S&P 500
Price/Earnings	9.8	0.5	0.5
Price/Book	1.7	1.0	0.4
Price/Sales	2.3	0.5	0.8
Price/Cash Flow	—	—	—

Major Fund Holders	% of Fund Assets
Weitz Hickory	7.29
Weitz Value	6.61
Weitz Partners Value	6.58
Weitz Partners III Opportunity	6.19

4500 Park Granada
Calabasas, CA 91302
www.countrywide.com

Growth [B+]	2002	2003	2004	2005
Revenue %	122.0	85.9	7.4	16.9
Earnings/Share %	105.1	158.0	-13.2	13.2
Book Value/Share %	32.2	43.4	19.6	22.3
Dividends/Share %	90.0	-22.4	149.8	60.2

Profitability [B+]	2003	2004	2005	TTM
Return on Assets %	2.4	1.7	1.4	1.4
Oper Cash Flow $Mil	-10,552	-5,459	-11,701	—
- Cap Spending $Mil	261	342	476	—
= Free Cash Flow $Mil	—	—	—	—

Financial Health [NA]	2003	2004	2005	09-30-06
Long-term Debt $Mil	—	—	—	—
Total Equity $Mil	8,085	10,310	12,816	15,099
Debt/Equity Ratio	—	—	—	—

Thesis
By Ryan Batchelor, CPA, 12-01-06 Stock Price as of Analysis: $39.97

Although the housing slowdown that we've anticipated for several years has finally arrived, we believe Countrywide has a strong long-term future as the largest mortgage bank in the country.

Like other mortgage bankers, Countrywide books large gains by originating high volumes of mortgage loans and then quickly selling the loans in the secondary market for a profit. During the mortgage boom of the past several years, the firm has grown to be one of the largest mortgage originators and servicers--which involves billing, payment processing, and related services--of mortgages in the country, with respective market shares of about 15% and 12% through the first three quarters of 2006. Additionally, the firm's banking segment has grown from a negligible size in 2001 to one of the top 20 banks in the country, based on total assets. We think Countrywide has sustainable competitive advantages in its servicing and banking segments; thus, we've awarded the firm a narrow moat rating.

We're particularly impressed by the firm's mortgage servicing portfolio, which amounted to about $1.24 trillion as of September 2006. We think mortgage servicing is a good business that provides very stable cash flows; we expect about $5 billion in cash flows from servicing during 2006 alone. The largest players in servicing also enjoy the highest profitability because they can spread the fixed costs of servicing over a larger pool of customers (economies of scale). Additionally, by servicing a mortgage, Countrywide can develop a valuable customer relationship, which provides a "stickiness" factor, in our opinion, because the firm would be the most convenient and familiar choice for a customer's future mortgage banking needs.

The firm's banking operations are also impressive, in our opinion. Basically, the bank grows by adding banking kiosks and banking experts to its established home loan branches. This is a very low-cost structure, which allows the firm to offer higher-than-average rates on its deposit products (primarily CDs) and still earn healthy profits.

Despite these positives, Countrywide's origination franchise is still at the mercy of factors beyond its control--mainly fluctuating interest rates--which results in volatile demand for mortgages. We expect industrywide originations to decrease about 14% in 2006 and another 25% in 2007, which may stunt Countrywide's near-term earnings growth. However, we think Countrywide has a very strong long-term future, so we're not too concerned about any short-term stumbles.

 Stocks 500

Data as of 12-29-06

Covance CVD

	Rating	Fair Value	Last Close	Consider Buy	Consider Sell	Yield %
	★★★	$60.00	$58.91	$46.30	$75.20	0.00

Company Profile

With total revenue exceeding $1 billion, Covance is the largest publicly traded provider of drug-development services to the pharmaceutical and biotech industries. Its business is split between the early-stage segment, which includes toxicology, pharmaceutical chemistry, and pharmacology services, and late-stage development services, which include Covance's central lab operations and late-phase clinical studies. Foreign operations account for one third of total revenue.

Management
Stewardship Grade [B]

Covance's succession plan was completed at the end of 2005, when Christopher Kuebler resigned as chairman and Joseph Herring took over both the CEO and chairman roles. As anticipated, the transition has been smooth; Herring knows Covance's business inside and out, having been involved with the company for more than 10 years, including three years as president and COO. We continue to view the company's policies as shareholder-friendly and stick to our above-average Stewardship Grade. We are comfortable with the company's compensation policies, which appear to be driven by performance. We also like the use of restricted stock instead of options to reward top executives. Restricted stock aligns the interests of managers and shareholders; exposing managers to downside encourages them to consider risk as well as reward. We would, however, prefer Covance to abandon its staggered board structure and separate the chairman and CEO roles.

210 Carnegie Center
Princeton, NJ 08540
www.covance.com

Growth [B]	2002	2003	2004	2005
Revenue %	3.2	5.4	8.4	18.4
Earnings/Share %	30.4	17.5	25.6	23.7
Book Value/Share %	22.5	28.6	10.4	16.2
Dividends/Share %	NMF	NMF	NMF	NMF

Profitability [A+]	2003	2004	2005	TTM
Return on Assets %	9.4	10.6	11.3	10.9
Oper Cash Flow $Mil	140	163	182	248
- Cap Spending $Mil	63	73	153	131
= Free Cash Flow $Mil	78	90	29	117

Financial Health [A]	2003	2004	2005	09-30-06
Long-term Debt $Mil	—	—	—	—
Total Equity $Mil	564	638	732	907
Debt/Equity Ratio	—	—	—	—

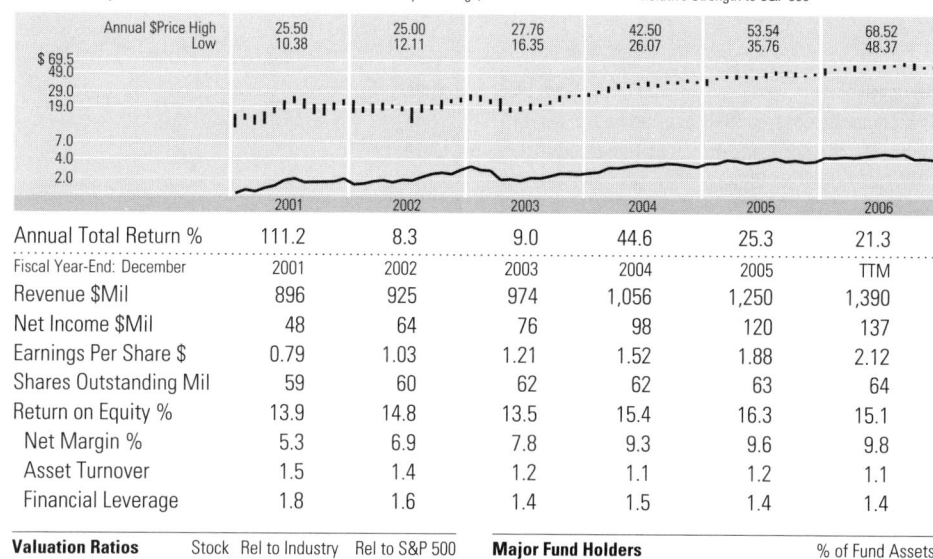

Industry	Business Risk	Moat Size	Investment Style	Sector
Research Svcs.	Average	Narrow	Mid Growth	Healthcare

Competition	Market Cap $Mil	12 Mo Trailing Sales $Mil	Price/Cash Flow	Return On Assets %	Debt/ Equity	Total Return% 1 Yr	3 Yr
Covance	3,769	1,390	15.2	10.9	—	21.3	30.1
Pharmaceutical Product De	3,777	1,196	21.9	11.4	0.1	4.3	34.3
Charles River Laboratorie	2,893	1,174	14.8	-1.6	0.4	2.1	8.3

	2001	2002	2003	2004	2005	2006
Annual Total Return %	111.2	8.3	9.0	44.6	25.3	21.3

Fiscal Year-End: December	2001	2002	2003	2004	2005	TTM
Revenue $Mil	896	925	974	1,056	1,250	1,390
Net Income $Mil	48	64	76	98	120	137
Earnings Per Share $	0.79	1.03	1.21	1.52	1.88	2.12
Shares Outstanding Mil	59	60	62	62	63	64
Return on Equity %	13.9	14.8	13.5	15.4	16.3	15.1
Net Margin %	5.3	6.9	7.8	9.3	9.6	9.8
Asset Turnover	1.5	1.4	1.2	1.1	1.2	1.1
Financial Leverage	1.8	1.6	1.4	1.5	1.4	1.4

Valuation Ratios	Stock	Rel to Industry	Rel to S&P 500	Major Fund Holders	% of Fund Assets
Price/Earnings	27.8	0.9	1.3	Security Select 25 A	4.21
Price/Book	4.2	1.1	1.0	Ashport Small/Mid Cap C	4.05
Price/Sales	2.7	0.8	0.9	Chase Mid Cap Growth A	3.93
Price/Cash Flow	15.2	0.8	1.0	UMB Scout Growth	3.34

Thesis By Alex Morozov, CFA, 12-07-06 Stock Price as of Analysis: $61.45

The future looks bright for Covance. The contract research industry is booming, fueled by increasing growth in outsourcing by pharmaceutical and biotech companies. This growth is particularly evident in the market segments where Covance holds leading positions: preclinical toxicology and central lab services.

Covance offers a range of services unmatched in the industry, providing drug-development services to biotech and pharmaceutical companies. The firm is a leader in preclinical toxicology, which studies the effects of drugs on animals, clinical pharmacology, which includes first-in-human trials, and central lab services. Covance's goal is to be involved with the entire process of drug development, from initial preclinical studies to postapproval marketing services. The firm's dominant presence in essentially every stage of the process enables its customers to outsource complete drug-development projects to Covance.

A diversified revenue base allows Covance to capture market growth irrespective of which stages of development are strong at a particular time. The company's business is split almost evenly between its early- and late-stage segments, which provides a cushion in the event of unexpected late-stage cancellations or a dry spell in early-stage drug research. Covance continues to increase its presence in the clinical pharmacology segment. This business is less vulnerable to cancellations, as fewer projects get withdrawn in the early phases of development and individual contracts typically carry a smaller dollar value than late-stage clinical trial deals. The firm has also been successful in diversifying its customer base and lining up large contracts in its toxicology segment. We consider toxicology a significant growth opportunity for Covance. In our opinion, big pharmaceutical companies face higher costs and capacity underutilization issues associated with in-house toxicology departments. To free up sparsely used facilities and personnel, we expect they will increasingly look to outsource these efforts to contract research organizations (CROs).

Industry conditions remain highly favorable. Drug development is a long and costly process, and an increasing number of pharmaceutical and biotech companies outsource some or all of this to CROs. The industry is expected to grow 12%-13% annually, and we expect Covance to surpass such growth. The company has positioned itself as a leader through its wide array of services, global presence, and strong client relationships.

CVS CVS

Data as of 12-29-06

Rating	Fair Value	Last Close	Consider Buy	Consider Sell	Yield %
★★★	$32.00	$30.91	$24.70	$40.10	0.50

Company Profile
CVS is the largest drugstore operator in the United States, with 6,200 retail and specialty stores in 43 states and the District of Columbia. Prescription drugs account for about 70% of total sales. The remainder of sales include nonprescription drugs, health and beauty items, toiletries, food, beverages, and general merchandise. The firm operates its own pharmacy benefit management service.

Management   Stewardship Grade [C]
CVS' corporate governance is a mixed bag, in our view. CEO, chairman, and president Thomas Ryan began his career at CVS as a pharmacist and rose through the ranks. We prefer that companies separate the CEO and chairman positions. Ryan's total compensation in 2005, which included salary, bonus, restricted stock, options, and other items, totaled $25.7 million. That amount was excessive, in our opinion, and we don't approve of the multiple retention bonuses he has received. We also don't like shareholders footing the bill for Ryan's personal travel aboard the corporate jet. Ryan holds plenty of CVS stock, so his interests should be aligned well with those of shareholders. We are concerned about the generous payouts to executives in the event of a transaction that seems to shield the company from potential bidders. Board members are evenly compensated with salary and stock, and each member stands for election annually, which we like.

One CVS Drive
Woonsocket, RI 02895
www.cvs.com

Growth [A]	2002	2003	2004	2005
Revenue %	8.7	10.0	15.1	21.0
Earnings/Share %	75.0	17.7	6.8	31.8
Book Value/Share %	14.2	15.9	15.0	18.2
Dividends/Share %	0.0	0.0	15.3	9.3

Profitability [B+]	2003	2004	2005	TTM
Return on Assets %	7.9	6.2	7.9	6.4
Oper Cash Flow $Mil	969	914	1,612	1,754
- Cap Spending $Mil	1,122	1,348	1,495	1,471
= Free Cash Flow $Mil	-153	-434	117	283

Financial Health [B-]	2003	2004	2005	09-30-06
Long-term Debt $Mil	753	1,926	1,594	3,280
Total Equity $Mil	5,779	6,759	8,109	9,219
Debt/Equity Ratio	0.1	0.3	0.2	0.4

Industry	Business Risk	Moat Size	Investment Style	Sector
Specialty Retail	Average	Narrow	Large Growth	Consumer Services

Competition	Market Cap $Mil	12 Mo Trailing Sales $Mil	Price/Cash Flow	Return On Assets%	Debt/Equity	Total Return% 1 Yr	3 Yr
CVS	25,456	41,480	14.5	6.4	0.4	17.6	20.7
Walgreen	46,048	47,409	18.9	10.2	—	4.4	9.3
Rite Aid	2,895	17,542	12.0	17.4	2.2	56.3	-2.9

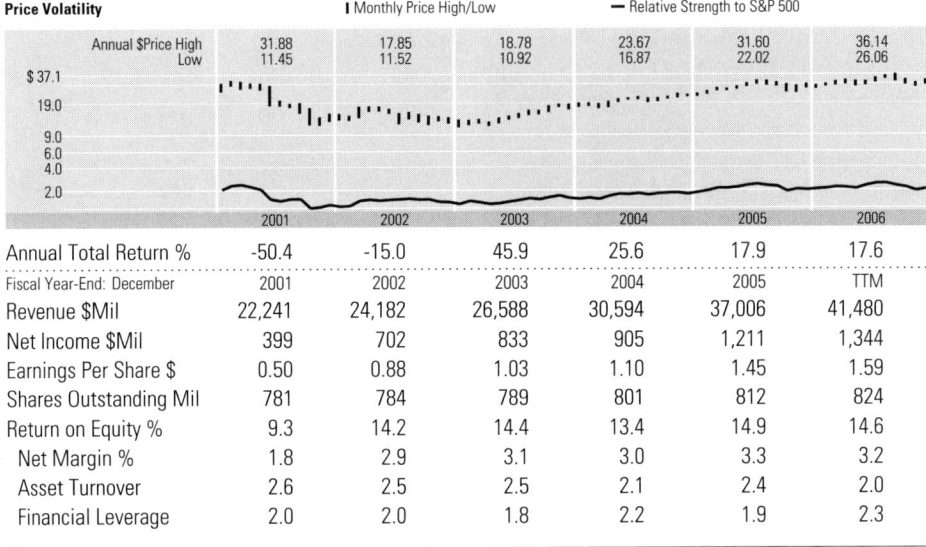

	2001	2002	2003	2004	2005	2006
Annual Total Return %	-50.4	-15.0	45.9	25.6	17.9	17.6

Fiscal Year-End: December	2001	2002	2003	2004	2005	TTM
Revenue $Mil	22,241	24,182	26,588	30,594	37,006	41,480
Net Income $Mil	399	702	833	905	1,211	1,344
Earnings Per Share $	0.50	0.88	1.03	1.10	1.45	1.59
Shares Outstanding Mil	781	784	789	801	812	824
Return on Equity %	9.3	14.2	14.4	13.4	14.9	14.6
Net Margin %	1.8	2.9	3.1	3.0	3.3	3.2
Asset Turnover	2.6	2.5	2.5	2.1	2.4	2.0
Financial Leverage	2.0	2.0	1.8	2.2	1.9	2.3

Valuation Ratios	Stock	Rel to Industry	Rel to S&P 500
Price/Earnings	19.4	0.8	0.9
Price/Book	2.8	0.7	0.7
Price/Sales	0.6	0.6	0.2
Price/Cash Flow	14.5	0.8	1.0

Major Fund Holders	% of Fund Assets
IXIS CGM Advisor Targeted Equity A	5.50
Victory Focused Growth A	5.46
Wells Fargo Advantage Endeavor Select A	4.59
CGM Mutual	4.41

Thesis   By Mitchell P. Corwin, CFA, CPA, 11-21-06 Stock Price as of Analysis: $28.08

There are positives and negatives associated with the announced merger of CVS and Caremark, but we believe it will ultimately create shareholder value through unrivaled economies of scale in purchasing and a more compelling offering to health plan sponsors. CVS sees its future as providing more holistic pharmacy services; access to payers in order to influence plan design is necessary to fulfill that strategy. In addition, the company will also gain a better foothold in fast-growing areas of prescription drug spending, such as specialty pharmacy and disease management.

While there are strategic benefits to the merger, we see some risks as well. Pharmacy benefit managers like Caremark face challenges as their customers demand more transparency. PBMs have profited for years on the rebates they receive from drug manufacturers, which are at risk. Newer competitors have offered less price ambiguity. In addition, at-risk insurers that have been outsourcing prescription drug plan management to PBMs could themselves enter the business. Acquiring a PBM business now may not be attractive.

If the combination is as compelling as advertised, we expect other retail chains, most notably Walgreen, to respond. The larger chains can't allow CVS to gain a competitive advantage that may direct customers away from their pharmacies via incentives to plan participants. Other retail chains could follow CVS' lead, limiting the merger's long-term benefits.

The cost savings promised by CVS, mostly derived from purchasing synergies, seem achievable, and the aforementioned incentives to plan participants could boost store traffic. The recent Eckerd and Savon/Osco acquisitions gave CVS a coast-to-coast presence in attractive markets. At 6,200 stores, the firm is the largest drugstore chain, and its existing economies of scale give it significant competitive advantages over smaller operators.

As one of two dominant retail chains, CVS remains poised to benefit from continued favorable demographics and trends shaping growth in prescription drug spending. An aging baby boomer population, increased use of pharmaceuticals as a solution for health-care needs, the Medicare prescription drug benefit, and more generic drug introductions should all provide strong tailwinds for the prescription drug providers over the next decade.

It is because of these strong industry tailwinds and CVS' favorable position in retail that we remain positive on the company's long-term prospects and maintain our narrow moat rating.

Danaher DHR

Data as of 12-29-06

	Rating	Fair Value	Last Close	Consider Buy	Consider Sell	Yield %
	★★★	$78.00	$72.44	$60.10	$97.70	0.11

Industry	Business Risk	Moat Size	Investment Style	Sector
Electric Equip.	Average	Narrow	Large Growth	Industrial Materials

Company Profile
Danaher is a diversified manufacturer, housing more than 40 industrial brands in three segments. Its professional instrumentation segment produces electronic, medical, and water-test equipment. Its industrial technology segment produces precision motors and controls, product-identification equipment, and other niche products. Its tool and component division makes Sears' Craftsman line of hand tools, Matco tools for professional mechanics, and other store-branded tools.

Management
Stewardship Grade [B]

Danaher was founded by Steven and Mitchell Rales in the early 1980s. Combined, they own almost 22% of outstanding stock, and both remain on the nine-member board. Steven Rales is the chairman, and six members are independent. Board members and senior management collectively own a significant chunk of the company, indicating strong alignment with minority holders. Lawrence Culp replaced George Sherman, who led the firm's transformation from toolmaker to industrial conglomerate, as CEO in 2001. Culp has experience with acquisitions and the implementation of the Danaher Business System. While we're comforted that the board is in the same boat as minority holders, wed prefer more transparency in the incentive compensation structure. Executive officers' variable cash compensation is based on undisclosed personal objectives and growth in earnings per share. Equity awards are based on peer benchmarks; undisclosed contributions to growth, development, and success of the company; individual performance; level of management. We'd be more comfortable if performance benchmarks were more explicitly stated and if a return on capital measure were mentioned prominently.

2099 Pennsylvania Ave. NW 12th Floor www.danaher.com
Washington, DC 20006-1813

Growth [A]	2002	2003	2004	2005
Revenue %	21.0	15.7	30.1	15.9
Earnings/Share %	-6.5	79.8	36.1	20.0
Book Value/Share %	29.5	17.8	24.1	9.7
Dividends/Share %	12.5	11.1	15.0	21.7

Profitability [A]	2003	2004	2005	TTM
Return on Assets %	7.8	8.8	9.8	8.7
Oper Cash Flow $Mil	862	1,033	1,204	1,385
- Cap Spending $Mil	80	116	121	133
= Free Cash Flow $Mil	781	917	1,083	1,252

Financial Health [A]	2003	2004	2005	09-30-06
Long-term Debt $Mil	1,284	926	858	2,262
Total Equity $Mil	3,647	4,620	5,080	6,151
Debt/Equity Ratio	0.4	0.2	0.2	0.4

Competition	Market Cap $Mil	12 Mo Trailing Sales $Mil	Price/Cash Flow	Return On Assets%	Debt/Equity	Total Return% 1 Yr	3 Yr
Danaher	22,297	9,200	16.1	8.7	0.4	30.0	17.0
Illinois Tool Works	26,184	13,798	14.5	12.7	0.1	6.7	5.3
Cooper Industries	14,345	5,029	22.1	3.9	0.3	26.0	18.7

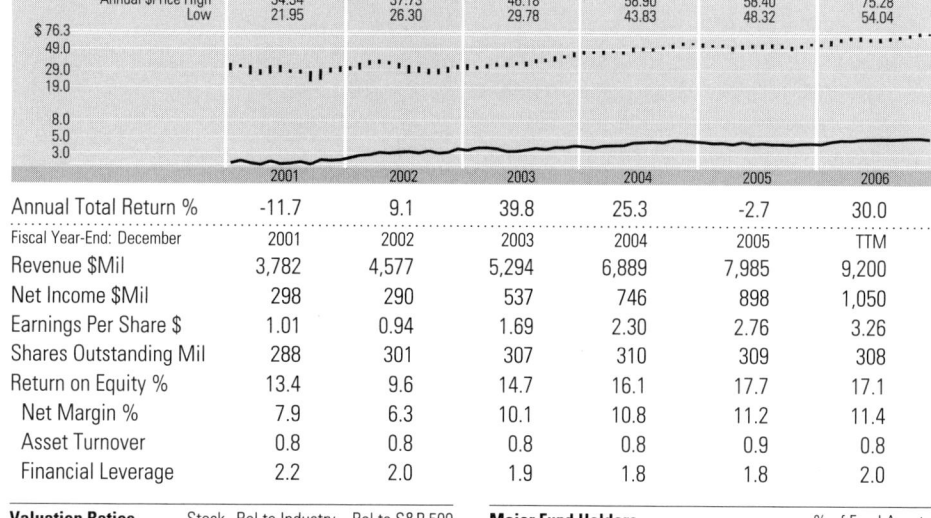

	2001	2002	2003	2004	2005	TTM
Annual Total Return %	-11.7	9.1	39.8	25.3	-2.7	30.0
Fiscal Year-End: December	2001	2002	2003	2004	2005	TTM
Revenue $Mil	3,782	4,577	5,294	6,889	7,985	9,200
Net Income $Mil	298	290	537	746	898	1,050
Earnings Per Share $	1.01	0.94	1.69	2.30	2.76	3.26
Shares Outstanding Mil	288	301	307	310	309	308
Return on Equity %	13.4	9.6	14.7	16.1	17.7	17.1
Net Margin %	7.9	6.3	10.1	10.8	11.2	11.4
Asset Turnover	0.8	0.8	0.8	0.8	0.9	0.8
Financial Leverage	2.2	2.0	1.9	1.8	1.8	2.0

Valuation Ratios	Stock	Rel to Industry	Rel to S&P 500
Price/Earnings	22.2	1.0	1.1
Price/Book	3.6	1.0	0.9
Price/Sales	2.4	1.0	0.8
Price/Cash Flow	16.1	1.1	1.1

Major Fund Holders	% of Fund Assets
Fidelity Select Construction&Housing	6.45
Neuberger Berman Guardian Inv	4.94
Neuberger Berman Socially Resp Inv	4.89
Ashport Large Cap C	4.19

Thesis By Tom D'Amore, CFA, 11-15-06 Stock Price as of Analysis: $73.41

Danaher is an industrial consolidator and integrator par excellence. Its management team has a proven record of delivering double-digit earnings growth through a combination of internal growth and acquisitions. We put Danaher in the upper echelon of our multi-industrial coverage group and encourage investors to take a close look at this gem.

Danaher has an all-weather earnings growth strategy that starts with an efficient operating system. The firm deftly deploys the Danaher Business System of continuous manufacturing improvement to reduce costs and increase profitability in its stable of core businesses. The power of the DBS is backed up by excellent operating performance metrics. Operating margins presently approach 16% and are at the high end of the range for the multi-industry companies we follow. Return on invested capital has averaged 17% over the past five years, handily exceeding a cost of capital of 9.3%. Free cash flow is also superb. The company generated $1 billion in free cash flow in 2005, an impressive 14% of sales and 120% of net income.

Danaher uses its efficient base of businesses to support an aggressive acquisition program to further leverage growth. The company takes the robust cash generated from its core businesses to fund its acquisitions and uses the DBS to seamlessly integrate them. Danaher's growth strategy has been a resounding success. Over the past five years, earnings have increased at a compound rate of 20% on compound sales growth of 16%.

Danaher's recently completed purchase of Sybron Dental, its largest acquisition to date, is an excellent case study for its acquisition strategy. Sybron produces light equipment for the professional dental market and has a substantial consumable component. Danaher is leveraging Sybron's established market position with its proven DBS operating model to reduce costs and increase profitability. We expect Danaher to continue focusing on the medical and dental markets for future acquisitions, given their high-profit-margin and high-growth characteristics. The medical technology segment now represents 15% of total sales, up from the low single digits three years ago.

With a sales base just one fourth of other premier industrial consolidators, such as United Technologies and Illinois Tool Works, Danaher has plenty of room to grow and offers substantial capital appreciation potential to investors, in our opinion.

Data as of 12-29-06

Darden Restaurants DRI

	Rating	Fair Value	Last Close	Consider Buy	Consider Sell	Yield %
	★★★	$44.00	$40.17	$37.50	$57.80	1.07

Company Profile

In 1968, Bill Darden opened the first Red Lobster, which eventually grew into Darden Restaurants, a portfolio of 1,431 casual dining restaurants in the United States and Canada. Chains include the flagship Red Lobster (683 units) and Olive Garden (584 units) as well as newer concepts, including Smokey Bones (127 units), Bahama Breeze (32 units), and Season 52 (five units).

Management   Stewardship Grade [B]

Joe Lee, who had been with the company since 1968, when he managed the first Red Lobster restaurant, stepped down as CEO in December 2004 and as chairman in November 2005. The board promoted Clarence Otis, formerly president of the now-floundering Smokey Bones, to succeed Lee in the top two roles, which we believe should be split for better corporate governance. For fiscal 2006, Lee was paid $1.9 million in salary plus bonus, which we view as reasonable compensation, especially given the company's solid performance in a challenging year for casual dining. He was also awarded a generous package of restricted stock and options.

We like that directors are required to hold at least $250,000 in Darden stock and that executives must also hold a multiple of their base salary in the company's shares (6 times base salary for the CEO). The board and management collectively own about 4% of the company. Overall, they have demonstrated good stewardship, but we do take a dim view of Darden's poison pill and other antitakeover measures, which we believe favor the interests of management over shareholders.

5900 Lake Ellenor Drive   www.darden.com
Orlando, FL 32809

Growth [C+]	2003	2004	2005	2006
Revenue %	6.6	7.5	5.5	8.4
Earnings/Share %	0.0	5.5	32.8	21.3
Book Value/Share %	8.8	9.2	12.5	0.7
Dividends/Share %	49.8	0.0	0.0	400.0

Profitability [A]	2004	2005	2006	TTM
Return on Assets %	8.2	9.9	11.2	11.2
Oper Cash Flow $Mil	525	583	717	626
- Cap Spending $Mil	354	329	338	353
= Free Cash Flow $Mil	171	254	379	273

Financial Health [B+]	2004	2005	2006	08-31-06
Long-term Debt $Mil	653	350	495	494
Total Equity $Mil	1,175	1,273	1,230	1,265
Debt/Equity Ratio	0.6	0.3	0.4	0.4

Industry	Business Risk	Moat Size	Investment Style	Sector
Restaurants	Below Avg	Narrow	Mid Core	Consumer Services

Competition	Market Cap $Mil	12 Mo Trailing Sales $Mil	Price/Cash Flow	Return On Assets %	Debt/Equity	Total Return % 1 Yr	3 Yr
Darden Restaurants	5,898	5,767	9.4	11.2	0.4	4.4	25.2
Brinker International	3,705	4,215	7.8	10.2	0.5	18.2	11.5
OSI Restaurant Partners	2,918	3,770	9.2	5.8	0.2	-4.4	-2.5

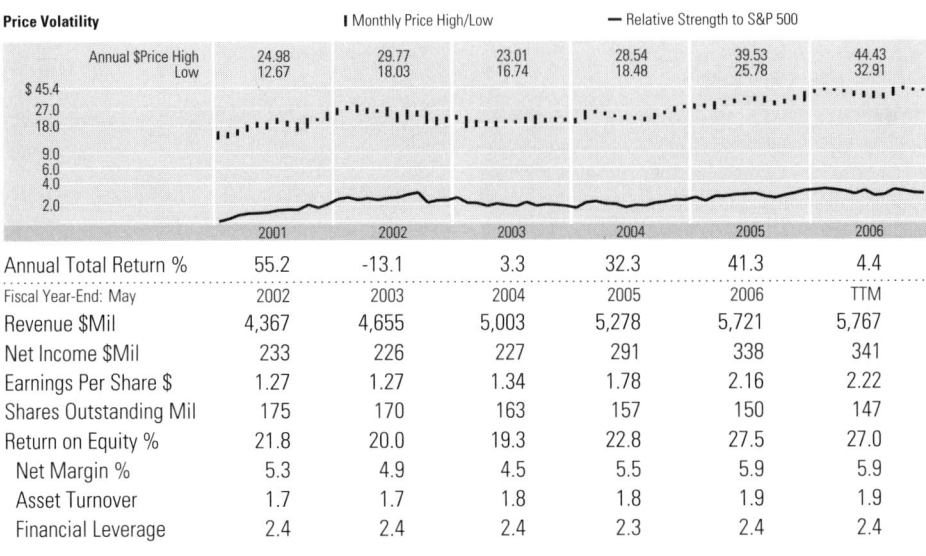

	2002	2003	2004	2005	2006	TTM
Annual Total Return %	55.2	-13.1	3.3	32.3	41.3	4.4
Fiscal Year-End: May	2002	2003	2004	2005	2006	TTM
Revenue $Mil	4,367	4,655	5,003	5,278	5,721	5,767
Net Income $Mil	233	226	227	291	338	341
Earnings Per Share $	1.27	1.27	1.34	1.78	2.16	2.22
Shares Outstanding Mil	175	170	163	157	150	147
Return on Equity %	21.8	20.0	19.3	22.8	27.5	27.0
Net Margin %	5.3	4.9	4.5	5.5	5.9	5.9
Asset Turnover	1.7	1.7	1.8	1.8	1.9	1.9
Financial Leverage	2.4	2.4	2.4	2.3	2.4	2.4

Valuation Ratios	Stock	Rel to Industry	Rel to S&P 500
Price/Earnings	18.1	0.7	0.9
Price/Book	4.7	0.8	1.1
Price/Sales	1.0	0.5	0.3
Price/Cash Flow	9.4	0.6	0.6

Major Fund Holders	% of Fund Assets
Westport Select Cap R	3.26
Chaconia Income & Growth	2.85
Westcore Mid-Cap Value	2.38
James Equity	2.21

Thesis By John Owens, CFA, CPA, 11-22-06 Stock Price as of Analysis: $41.46

Despite near-term pressures, we're confident about the future of casual dining and believe that Darden will remain a leader in the industry. We believe the company is poised for further growth over the long run, thanks to its leading brands (Olive Garden and Red Lobster), strong management, and scale advantages.

In 2006, casual dining hit its roughest patch in more than 15 years. Soaring gas prices, rising interest rates, and weakening consumer confidence led to a widespread decline in guest traffic. Darden, however, has held up relatively well, with Olive Garden extending its streak of positive same-restaurant sales growth to 48 quarters. Darden's other flagship chain, Red Lobster, delivered positive growth in seven of the past eight quarters. We attribute these chains' resilient performances to their strong guest loyalty and compelling value-oriented offerings, which still provide a good margin. We also credit management for aggressively driving unnecessary costs out of the business. As a result, Darden was able to deliver impressive earnings per share growth of over 20% last fiscal year, despite the difficult industry conditions.

In our view, the challenging macro environment will not persist indefinitely. Spending at casual dining restaurants should get a boost in the long run from maturing baby boomers entering their peak earning years, a rise in dual-income families, and a growing desire for convenience in a time-pressed society. As one of just two casual dining firms with a moat, Darden is well positioned to capitalize on these favorable long-term trends. Olive Garden and Red Lobster each delivered total annual sales of $2.6 billion last fiscal year. This scale provides tremendous buying power (especially for seafood) and allows its brands to leverage the efficiency of national advertising.

The firm does face some challenges as it attempts to expand its younger concepts. Bahama Breeze has struggled to achieve sufficient returns on sales. The company shut down six of these Caribbean-inspired restaurants in 2004 and has put further expansion on hold as it attempts to hone the concept's unit economics. Darden is also overhauling its Smokey Bones brand, which saw its same-restaurant sales fall 3.7% last fiscal year and 8.6% in the first quarter of the current fiscal year. Management is considering possible changes to its name, menu, and restaurant design, in an effort to broaden its appeal and to increase the frequency of guest visits.

© 2007 Morningstar, Inc. All rights reserved. Intended for United States residents only, this report is for information purposes and should not be considered a solicitation to buy or sell any security. Download your free reports at http://www.morningstar.com/goto/2007Stocks500

 Stocks 500

DCP Midstream Partners LP DPM

Data as of 12-29-06

Rating	Fair Value	Last Close	Consider Buy	Consider Sell	Yield %
★★★	$33.00	$34.55	$25.40	$41.30	3.56

Company Profile

DCP Midstream Partners LP is a midstream master limited partnership that gathers, processes, transports, and markets natural gas and natural gas liquids in Louisiana and Texas and operates wholesale propane distribution terminals in the Northeastern U.S. DCP's flagship assets include its PELICO intrastate system, Minden and Ada gathering systems and processing plants, and ownership stakes in three natural gas liquids pipelines.

Management   Stewardship Grade [D]

DCP Midstream Partners is managed and controlled by its general partner, DCP Midstream GP LLC, a private company wholly owned by Duke Energy Field Services, which is a joint venture between Duke Energy and ConocoPhillips. Mark Borer, a longtime DEFS executive, was appointed CEO in November 2006. Beginning in January 2007, when Duke Energy completes the spin-off of its gas business into Spectra Energy, Fred Fowler, Spectra's president and CEO, will become the chairman of the board of DCP's general partner. There are tremendous advantages in having such a tight linkage between DCP and DEFS, including benefiting from DEFS' dominant industry position, sharing strategic plans, and enjoying asset drop-downs. However, the close relationship between the companies also raises some concerns, especially since DCP is a master limited partnership. Because of how MLPs are structured, common unitholders have virtually no say in the management or operations of the company and cannot provide adequate safeguards against DEFS' interests being served at the expense of DCP's unaffiliated unitholders. We think that this close relationship, when combined with other related-party transactions, is enough reason to give DCP a "D" Stewardship Grade, slightly lower than the "C" most MLPs receive.

370 17th Street Suite 2775
Denver, CO 80202

Growth [D-]	2002	2003	2004	2005
Revenue %	-14.6	59.9	7.2	54.0
Earnings/Share %	NMF	NMF	NMF	NMF
Book Value/Share %	—	—	—	—
Dividends/Share %	NMF	NMF	NMF	NMF

Profitability [NA]	2003	2004	2005	TTM
Return on Assets %	4.2	0.0	1.1	8.0
Oper Cash Flow $Mil	31	26	76	85
- Cap Spending $Mil	3	3	8	14
= Free Cash Flow $Mil	28	23	68	71

Financial Health [B-]	2003	2004	2005	09-30-06
Long-term Debt $Mil	—	0	210	190
Total Equity $Mil	201	198	107	124
Debt/Equity Ratio	—	0.0	2.0	1.5

Industry	Business Risk	Moat Size	Investment Style	Sector
Pipelines	Average	Narrow	Small Core	Energy

Competition	Market Cap $Mil	12 Mo Trailing Sales $Mil	Price/Cash Flow	Return On Assets %	Debt/Equity	Total Return% 1 Yr	3 Yr
DCP Midstream Partners LP	365	591	4.3	8.0	1.5	47.1	—
Energy Transfer Partners	5,999	7,859	11.0	7.3	1.6	65.5	47.7
Crosstex Energy	1,456	3,414	39.0	3.1	2.8	55.0	54.0

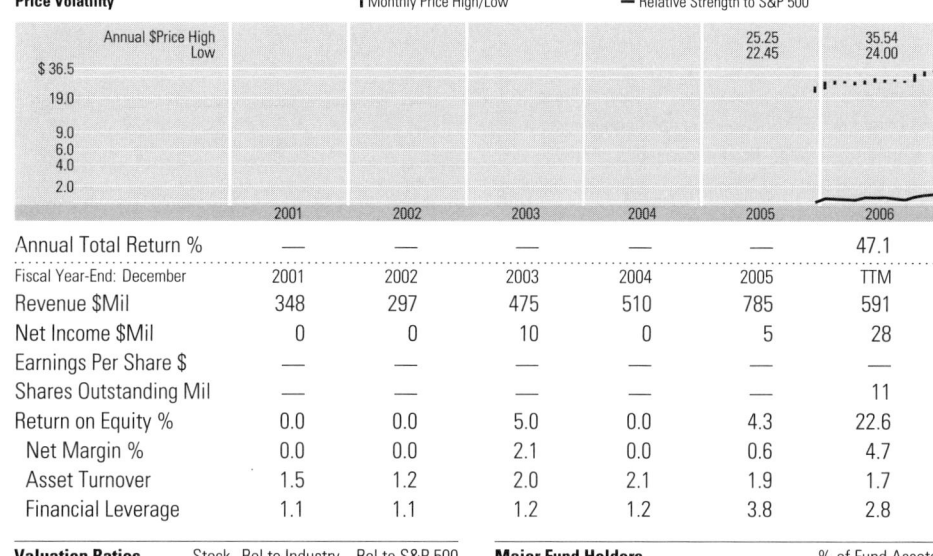

	2001	2002	2003	2004	2005	2006
Annual Total Return %	—	—	—	—	—	47.1
Fiscal Year-End: December	2001	2002	2003	2004	2005	TTM
Revenue $Mil	348	297	475	510	785	591
Net Income $Mil	0	0	10	0	5	28
Earnings Per Share $	—	—	—	—	—	—
Shares Outstanding Mil	—	—	—	—	—	11
Return on Equity %	0.0	0.0	5.0	0.0	4.3	22.6
Net Margin %	0.0	0.0	2.1	0.0	0.6	4.7
Asset Turnover	1.5	1.2	2.0	2.1	1.9	1.7
Financial Leverage	1.1	1.1	1.2	1.2	3.8	2.8

Valuation Ratios	Stock	Rel to Industry	Rel to S&P 500
Price/Earnings	—	—	—
Price/Book	2.9	1.2	0.7
Price/Sales	0.6	0.3	0.2
Price/Cash Flow	4.3	0.4	0.3

Major Fund Holders	% of Fund Assets

Thesis By Jason Stevens, 12-20-06 Stock Price as of Analysis: $33.80

Spun off from Duke Energy Field Services (DEFS) in 2005, DCP Midstream Partners is a newer master limited partnership (MLP) with a small but profitable asset base, steady cash flows, and attractive growth prospects.

The partnership's natural-gas asset base in northern Louisiana generates stable cash flows and is attractively located in an area with continued drilling. The Minden and Ada gathering systems collect gas from almost 700 receipt points and deliver it to two processing plants, where impurities and natural-gas liquids (NGLs) are removed. DCP's PELICO system gathers and transports pipeline-quality gas from producers and the partnership's processing plants to market hubs and interstate pipelines. Drilling activity in the Vernon field ensures continued volume, though DCP must compete with companies like Regency for new production. We also like that the Minden processing plant feeds NGLs into the Black Lake pipeline, which is 45% owned by DCP Partners and ships NGLs to storage and markets in Texas.

DEFS, the general partner of DCP and a joint venture between Duke Energy and ConocoPhillips, is experienced with the MLP structure (from its previous ownership of the general partner of TEPPCO), understands firsthand the cost-of-capital advantages inherent in MLPs, and is committed to spinning assets down into DCP. In October 2006, DEFS sold its wholesale propane business to DCP for $77 million, and committed to another $250 million in asset sales to DCP during 2007, which will help DCP to grow faster than many of its peers.

As an MLP, DCP does not pay corporate taxes and can acquire and operate assets at a lower cost of capital than DEFS. And because DCP is in its "low splits," or lowest level of general partner compensation, it can compete effectively for assets with more-mature MLPs with higher costs of capital. For investors, DCP's low splits also mean that a greater share of total cash distributions accrue to common unitholders rather than to the general partner. DCP is on track to end 2006 with a distribution coverage ratio better than 1.6, which compares favorably with the industry target of 1.1, leaving plenty of room to raise distributions faster than its peers. And because of its cost of capital advantage, DCP can finance accretive growth projects more cheaply than established MLPs, further boosting cash available for distributions. The caveat is that any new projects or acquisitions must be cash-flow accretive.

Data as of 12-29-06

Deere & Company DE

Rating	Fair Value	Last Close	Consider Buy	Consider Sell	Yield %
★★★	$90.00	$95.07	$69.40	$112.80	1.69

Company Profile
Deere manufactures agricultural, industrial, forestry, and lawn-care equipment. Products include tractors, harvesters, sprayers, mowers, excavators, loaders, diesel engines, utility transport vehicles, and machinery components. Deere's credit subsidiaries provide financing and leasing services to aid in the purchase of new and used equipment.

Management — Stewardship Grade [A]
Chairman and CEO Robert Lane has been leading the company since 2000. The team working under Lane is composed of longtime employees, most with decades of company experience. Relations with the unions are quite good, and there hasn't been a major strike at the company since 1987. We find Deere's management to be shareholder-friendly and have awarded the firm a Stewardship Grade of A. The company's financial disclosure is topnotch, and 11 of the 12 board members are independent. We like that management's bonuses are performance-based and that there is a history of significant bonus reduction when performance targets haven't been met. We applaud Deere's focus on returns in excess of its cost of capital. Management has set some lofty goals with regards to this measure, and shareholders will be well rewarded if the company can hit these targets.

One John Deere Place
Moline, IL 61265
www.johndeere.com

Growth [C]	2003	2004	2005	2006
Revenue %	11.7	29.3	10.3	4.5
Earnings/Share %	98.5	110.6	5.6	22.3
Book Value/Share %	24.6	53.9	10.0	14.2
Dividends/Share %	0.0	20.5	14.2	28.9

Profitability [B]	2004	2005	2006	TTM
Return on Assets %	4.9	4.3	4.9	4.9
Oper Cash Flow $Mil	496	1,217	973	973
- Cap Spending $Mil	364	513	766	766
= Free Cash Flow $Mil	132	704	207	207

Financial Health [B-]	2004	2005	2006	07-31-06
Long-term Debt $Mil	11,090	11,739	11,584	11,584
Total Equity $Mil	6,393	6,852	7,491	7,491
Debt/Equity Ratio	1.7	1.7	1.5	1.5

Industry	Business Risk	Moat Size	Investment Style	Sector
Ag. Machinery	Average	Narrow	Large Core	Industrial Materials

Competition	Market Cap $Mil	12 Mo Trailing Sales $Mil	Price/Cash Flow	Return On Assets%	Debt/ Equity	Total Return% 1 Yr	3 Yr
Deere & Company	21,631	22,148	22.2	4.9	1.5	42.3	16.1
Caterpillar	39,897	40,177	8.8	6.9	2.0	7.9	16.1
Kubota ADR	12,077	9,327	15.5	6.0	0.3	9.9	31.3

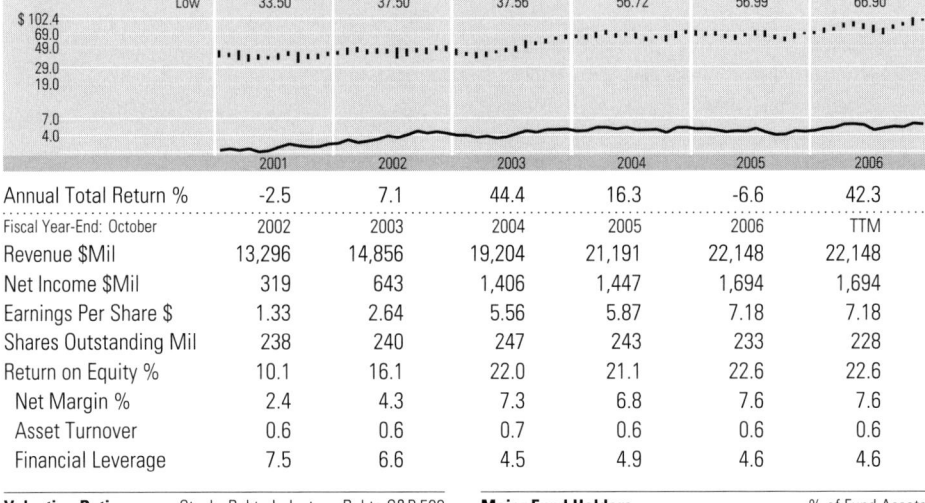

Price Volatility — Monthly Price High/Low — Relative Strength to S&P 500

	2001	2002	2003	2004	2005	2006
Annual $Price High	46.13	51.60	67.41	74.93	74.41	101.40
Low	33.50	37.50	37.56	56.72	56.99	66.90
Annual Total Return %	-2.5	7.1	44.4	16.3	-6.6	42.3

Fiscal Year-End: October	2002	2003	2004	2005	2006	TTM
Revenue $Mil	13,296	14,856	19,204	21,191	22,148	22,148
Net Income $Mil	319	643	1,406	1,447	1,694	1,694
Earnings Per Share $	1.33	2.64	5.56	5.87	7.18	7.18
Shares Outstanding Mil	238	240	247	243	233	228
Return on Equity %	10.1	16.1	22.0	21.1	22.6	22.6
Net Margin %	2.4	4.3	7.3	6.8	7.6	7.6
Asset Turnover	0.6	0.6	0.7	0.6	0.6	0.6
Financial Leverage	7.5	6.6	4.5	4.9	4.6	4.6

Valuation Ratios	Stock	Rel to Industry	Rel to S&P 500
Price/Earnings	15.4	0.8	0.7
Price/Book	2.9	1.2	0.7
Price/Sales	1.0	1.0	0.3
Price/Cash Flow	22.2	1.3	1.5

Major Fund Holders	% of Fund Assets
Fidelity Select Industrial Equipment	3.90
Pioneer Classic Balanced A	2.87
Turner Concentrated Growth Instl	2.70
HGK Equity Value	2.61

Thesis By John Kearney, CFA, 11-27-06 Stock Price as of Analysis:

Over the past 170 years, the John Deere moniker has come to symbolize a standard of quality that has enabled the firm to dredge an economic moat in the highly consolidated agricultural equipment market. It has also allowed the manufacturer to capitalize on this brand strength by expanding into other markets. We think Deere's strong brand name and operating proficiency will continue to harvest healthy returns for investors.

Deere holds roughly 50% of the North American ag equipment market, the world's largest. Much of the company's North American success is tied to its reputation for quality, which has been furthered by an extensive dealer network. This network can quickly source parts for Deere equipment and make repairs, which are huge selling points for farmers who need to minimize equipment downtime during the planting and harvesting seasons. In Western Europe and South America, Deere faces more entrenched competition from CNH Global and AGCO. On the whole, though, a strong balance sheet allows Deere to whether ag downturns better than its competitors, while its superior operating performance facilitates above-average returns during cyclical upturns.

Farm equipment sales are the backbone of Deere's operations, but cash flow from the company's construction and forestry segment helps offset the cyclicality of the ag equipment business. The construction market is susceptible to its own cycles, but they tend to move more in step with the general economy than the volatile ag cycles. Deere has more than 50% of the forestry market, but it is more of a secondary player in construction. Nonetheless, the company has garnered a sizable slice of the construction market, where it now generates its highest margins and a third of its operating profit.

Like Deere's other businesses, the commercial and consumer equipment segment has positioned itself as the high-quality, premium-price brand for lawn-care equipment and utility vehicles. While we are not convinced Deere can leverage its brand strength in the high-volume and low-margin consumer market to the same degree it has in its other markets, we think the commercial side of this business offers some attractive prospects. We think the segment's consistent cash flow generation will also help mute the impact of downturns in the ag business.

Dell DELL

Data as of 12-29-06

	Rating	Fair Value	Last Close	Consider Buy	Consider Sell	Yield %
	★★★★★	$34.00	$25.09	$26.20	$42.60	0.00

Industry	Business Risk	Moat Size	Investment Style	Sector
Computer Equip.	Average	Wide	Large Growth	Hardware

Company Profile
Dell designs and distributes a wide range of computer systems and services worldwide. Products include enterprise systems (such as servers, storage, workstations and networking), client systems (such as notebook and desktop systems, printing and imaging systems, software and peripherals), and other services. The company sells its products directly to customers, which include corporate, government, and education accounts, small to medium-sized businesses, and individuals.

Management
Stewardship Grade [D]

There is a deep management bench at Dell. Kevin Rollins became CEO in 2004 and has shared overall operating responsibility with Michael Dell, the company founder. Rollins has 11 years of experience with the company. The average tenure for other senior executives is 10 years. Donald Carty, former CEO of American Airlines' parent company AMR, is the new CFO as of 2007. Many positions have shared responsibility, which minimizes the risk of any individual departure. Such deep company and industry experience should serve them well as they continue to expand their business model worldwide. While the company professes an incentive compensation plan that rewards the achievement of company goals, historical pay from lucrative stock options has been extensive. The company has paid a cumulative $10 billion over the last seven fiscal years to prevent dilution from employee stock options. Also, missing two straight quarterly SEC filings is a bit disturbing as the company deals with the ongoing SEC probe into certain accounting and financial reporting matters.

807 Las Cimas Parkway Building 2
Austin, TX 78746
www.dell.com

Growth [B]	2003	2004	2005	2006
Revenue %	13.6	17.1	18.7	13.6
Earnings/Share %	73.9	26.3	16.8	23.7
Book Value/Share %	6.0	30.5	4.9	-32.9
Dividends/Share %	NMF	NMF	NMF	NMF

Profitability [A+]	2004	2005	2006	TTM
Return on Assets %	13.7	13.1	15.5	14.9
Oper Cash Flow $Mil	3,670	5,310	4,839	4,671
- Cap Spending $Mil	329	525	728	769
= Free Cash Flow $Mil	3,341	4,785	4,111	3,902

Financial Health [B]	2004	2005	2006 04-30-06
Long-term Debt $Mil	505	505	504	503
Total Equity $Mil	6,280	6,485	4,129	3,374
Debt/Equity Ratio	0.1	0.1	0.1	0.1

Competition

	Market Cap $Mil	12 Mo Trailing Sales $Mil	Price/Cash Flow	Return On Assets%	Debt/Equity	Total Return% 1 Yr	3 Yr
Dell	56,995	56,738	12.2	14.9	0.1	-16.2	-9.9
Hewlett-Packard	112,070	91,658	9.9	7.6	0.1	45.2	22.7
Sun Microsystems	19,020	13,068	29.7	-5.7	0.1	29.4	4.9

Price Volatility
| Monthly Price High/Low — Relative Strength to S&P 500

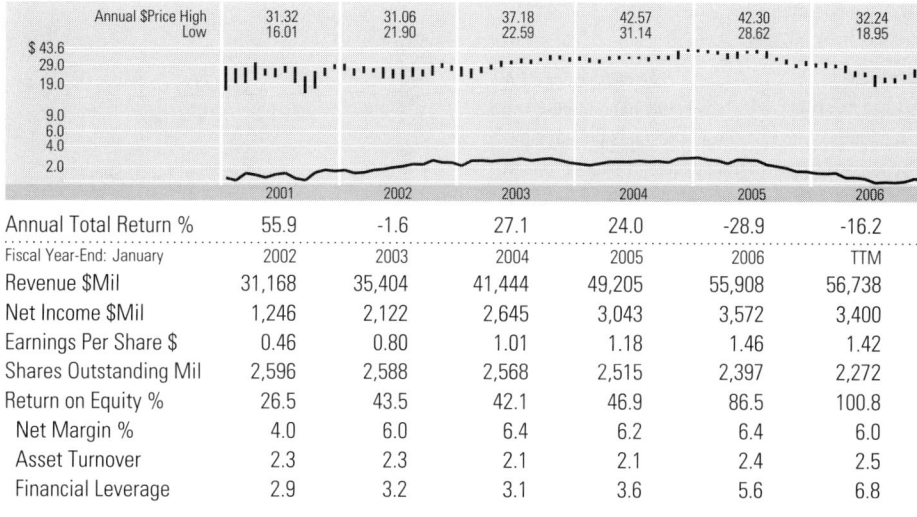

| Annual $Price High | 31.32 | 31.06 | 37.18 | 42.57 | 42.30 | 32.24 |
| Low | 16.01 | 21.90 | 22.59 | 31.14 | 28.62 | 18.95 |

	2001	2002	2003	2004	2005	2006
Annual Total Return %	55.9	-1.6	27.1	24.0	-28.9	-16.2

Fiscal Year-End: January	2002	2003	2004	2005	2006	TTM
Revenue $Mil	31,168	35,404	41,444	49,205	55,908	56,738
Net Income $Mil	1,246	2,122	2,645	3,043	3,572	3,400
Earnings Per Share $	0.46	0.80	1.01	1.18	1.46	1.42
Shares Outstanding Mil	2,596	2,588	2,568	2,515	2,397	2,272
Return on Equity %	26.5	43.5	42.1	46.9	86.5	100.8
Net Margin %	4.0	6.0	6.4	6.2	6.4	6.0
Asset Turnover	2.3	2.3	2.1	2.1	2.4	2.5
Financial Leverage	2.9	3.2	3.1	3.6	5.6	6.8

Valuation Ratios	Stock	Rel to Industry	Rel to S&P 500
Price/Earnings	17.7	0.7	0.9
Price/Book	16.9	3.0	4.1
Price/Sales	1.0	0.4	0.3
Price/Cash Flow	12.2	0.8	0.8

Major Fund Holders	% of Fund Assets
Longleaf Partners	9.42
Janus Global Opportunities	8.55
Longleaf Partners International	8.45
Brown Advisory Opportunity Instl	6.50

Thesis By Rick Hanna, 12-20-06 Stock Price as of Analysis: $25.77

Dell is a company in transition, facing slowing PC growth and increasing competition. We believe that Dell will meet this challenge by expanding internationally and growing non-PC revenue such as enterprise hardware (servers and storage) and enhanced services.

World-class supply chain efficiencies have provided Dell with a wide economic moat. The company holds substantial negotiating power and earns favorable terms from its component suppliers. It holds inventory an average of five days, while competitors average 15 days. Furthermore, customers pay Dell in approximately 36 days, while Dell pays suppliers in 75 days, enabling Dell to receive cash before paying. Dell's control of the supply chain and working capital management have provided the company with the highest operating margins and returns on capital in the PC industry.

Despite Dell's advantages, it has recently struggled. Gross margins have declined over 1 percentage point as it lowered prices in an attempt to gain market share. Operating margins have been squeezed by investments in customer service. We think these investments are wise, as Dell's highly regarded customer satisfaction had been declining. We think the problems the company experienced in 2006 are mostly short term, however. Strategically, the company maintains its focus on high-margin segments of enterprise customers, which should receive a boost from corporations upgrading their systems for the new Microsoft operating system.

We believe Dell's biggest growth opportunity is international expansion. Dell consistently has gained share in virtually every product category and every geographic region over the last 10 years. The top PC manufacturers have captured nearly two thirds of the overall market growth, as their scale and distribution have given them a competitive advantage. Dell has more than doubled its share in the Asia/Pacific region over the last five years, exceeding even the growth rate of Lenovo. Overall, we project non-U.S. revenue will grow at twice the rate and represent a larger percentage than U.S. revenue for Dell over the next five years.

In spite of a slowing PC market, the next growth thrust for Dell is to bundle additional products and services with PC hardware. Non-PC categories now represent more than one third of Dell's consolidated revenue and have grown almost 3 times faster than the PC segment. We expect the company's operating margin to increase from the growth of these higher-margin segments.

Data as of 12-29-06

Devon Energy DVN

	Rating	Fair Value	Last Close	Consider Buy	Consider Sell	Yield %
	★★★★★	$93.00	$67.08	$71.70	$116.50	0.67

Industry	Business Risk	Moat Size	Investment Style	Sector
Oil/Gas	Average	Narrow	Large Value	Energy

Company Profile
Devon Energy as we know it today was formed in 2003 from the merger of Devon and Ocean Energy. It is now one of the largest independent exploration and production companies based in the United States. In 2005, the firm produced 680 billion cubic feet of natural gas and 70 million barrels of oil equivalent. Devon's reserves are 65% natural gas and almost entirely in North America. Midstream and marketing operations accounted for about 17% of total revenues in 2005.

Management   Stewardship Grade [C]
CEO and chairman J. Larry Nichols and his father co-founded Devon in 1971. Nichols has presided over the company's growth from a small, regional firm into America's largest independent exploration and production company. In 2005, Nichols earned $7 million plus options, which was a bit less than CEOs earned at many peer companies. We were happy to see that the majority of Nichols' compensation was variable. However, we wish the board would explicitly disclose its executive compensation criteria rather than providing a host of possible metrics. We also dislike that the CEO and chairman roles are not split and that director elections are staggered. Directors and executives hold a respectable $420 million in Devon stock, assuming a stock price of $70. Overall, Devon has average stewardship practices.

Competition	Market Cap $Mil	12 Mo Trailing Sales $Mil	Price/Cash Flow	Return On Assets%	Debt/ Equity	Total Return% 1 Yr	3 Yr
Devon Energy	29,649	11,274	4.3	9.4	0.3	8.1	33.7
Occidental Petroleum	41,070	17,548	6.4	13.9	0.2	24.3	34.9
Apache	21,909	8,424	4.8	12.0	0.2	-2.3	19.0

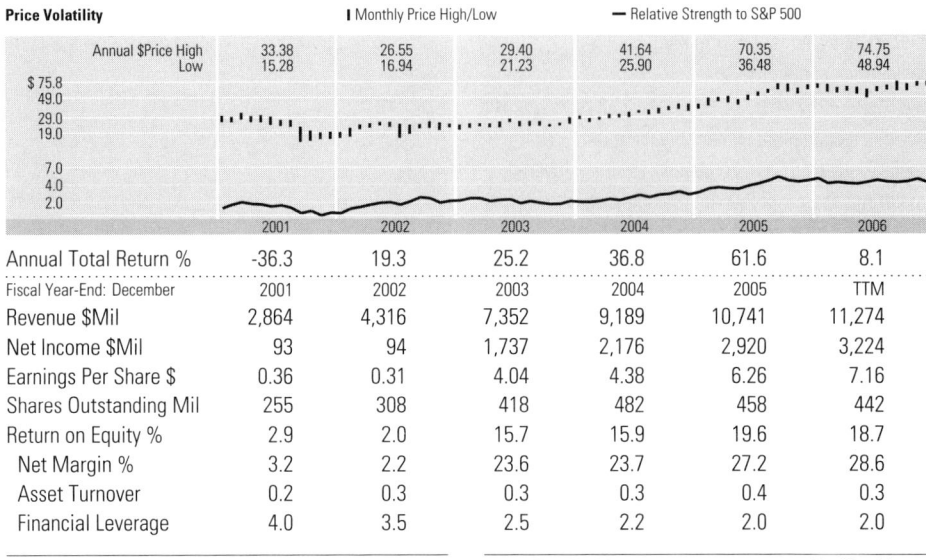

Price Volatility — Monthly Price High/Low — Relative Strength to S&P 500

	2001	2002	2003	2004	2005	2006
Annual $Price High	33.38	26.55	29.40	41.64	70.35	74.75
Low	15.28	16.94	21.23	25.90	36.48	48.94
Annual Total Return %	-36.3	19.3	25.2	36.8	61.6	8.1

Fiscal Year-End: December	2001	2002	2003	2004	2005	TTM
Revenue $Mil	2,864	4,316	7,352	9,189	10,741	11,274
Net Income $Mil	93	94	1,737	2,176	2,920	3,224
Earnings Per Share $	0.36	0.31	4.04	4.38	6.26	7.16
Shares Outstanding Mil	255	308	418	482	458	442
Return on Equity %	2.9	2.0	15.7	15.9	19.6	18.7
Net Margin %	3.2	2.2	23.6	23.7	27.2	28.6
Asset Turnover	0.2	0.3	0.3	0.3	0.4	0.3
Financial Leverage	4.0	3.5	2.5	2.2	2.0	2.0

Valuation Ratios	Stock	Rel to Industry	Rel to S&P 500
Price/Earnings	9.4	0.7	0.5
Price/Book	1.7	0.5	0.4
Price/Sales	2.6	1.4	0.9
Price/Cash Flow	4.3	0.5	0.3

Major Fund Holders	% of Fund Assets
Diamond Hill Select A	5.79
Diamond Hill Large Cap A	5.12
Excelsior Mid Cap Value & Restructuring	4.20
Concorde Value	3.95

Thesis By Justin Perucki, CFA, 11-08-06 Stock Price as of Analysis: $69.38

Devon is one of the largest U.S.-based independent oil and natural-gas companies. With about 90% of its reserves and production in North America, Devon has a lower risk profile than some of its more internationally focused competitors. Moreover, Devon's proximity to the U.S. market should allow the firm to enjoy robust sales and higher-than-average margins for the foreseeable future, because large-scale liquefied natural-gas importation is still a few years away.

Historically, Devon has expanded its reserve base through acquisitions rather than through the drill bit. The acquisitions greatly expanded its reserves, but they came at a price. Since 1998, shares outstanding almost tripled, long-term debt grew from $886 million to $8.5 billion, and goodwill went from zero to $5.5 billion. Over the same period, the firm generated free cash flow only twice. We don't generally favor companies that grow through acquisitions, but we're willing to make an exception in Devon's case. The firm chose its acquisitions carefully, focusing on gas reserves and, for the most part, buying at reasonable prices during industry downturns. Devon also seems to know when to sell properties. The company sold 14% of its proved reserves for more than $2.3 billion in 2005. Devon used the proceeds to repurchase shares and pay down debt.

Devon has an eclectic group of assets. In the United States, the firm is one of the five largest leaseholders of promising deep-water Gulf of Mexico properties, it is also the largest leaseholder and producer in the prodigious Barnett Shale deposit around Fort Worth, Texas. In addition to its traditional oil and gas assets in Canada, Devon also has a stake in the Alberta oil sands. The firm has a 100% working interest in Jackfish, a steam-assisted gravity drilling project that is slated to commence production in the latter half of 2007. International properties only make up about 10% of Devon's reserve base, but key projects in Brazil and Azerbaijan are expected to contribute more than 60,000 barrels of oil equivalent per day by 2007.

Like many exploration and production companies, Devon gets a narrow moat rating because of OPEC's influence on petroleum prices. By establishing quotas and restricting production, the cartel limits competition and keeps prices high enough for Devon to earn an economic profit. The firm also benefits from the stranded nature of natural gas, which limits imports and keeps prices high.

20 North Broadway Suite 1500 www.devonenergy.com
Oklahoma City, OK 73102-8260

Growth [C]	2002	2003	2004	2005
Revenue %	50.7	70.3	25.0	16.9
Earnings/Share %	-15.3	EUB	8.4	42.9
Book Value/Share %	19.7	70.3	7.0	15.8
Dividends/Share %	0.0	0.0	100.0	50.0

Profitability [B-]	2003	2004	2005	TTM
Return on Assets %	6.4	7.2	9.6	9.4
Oper Cash Flow $Mil	3,768	4,816	5,612	6,842
- Cap Spending $Mil	2,587	3,103	4,090	7,313
= Free Cash Flow $Mil	1,181	1,713	1,522	-471

Financial Health [A+]	2003	2004	2005	09-30-06
Long-term Debt $Mil	8,580	7,724	6,575	5,962
Total Equity $Mil	11,055	13,673	14,861	17,216
Debt/Equity Ratio	0.8	0.6	0.4	0.3

Data as of 12-29-06

DeVry DV

	Rating	Fair Value	Last Close	Consider Buy	Consider Sell	Yield %
	★★★	$30.00	$28.00	$23.10	$37.60	0.18

Company Profile
DeVry operates three segments: DeVry University, Ross University, and Professional and Training. DeVry offers undergraduate programs in business and technology and graduate courses in business. Undergraduate revenue was 65% of 2006 revenue. DeVry offers undergraduate and graduate programs at 23 campuses and 58 smaller locations. Ross University is its medical and veterinary school in Dominica. DeVry also prepares candidates for various professional certification examinations.

Management
Stewardship Grade [C]

Daniel Hamburger succeeds Ron Taylor as DeVry's CEO. Hamburger has been with DeVry since 2002, most recently as its COO, and has worked closely with Taylor for the past few years. We expect a smooth transition. Corporate stewardship is average, in our opinion. Management as a whole owns an impressive 17.5% of outstanding shares, with chairman Dennis Keller owning 12.8%, enough to align their interests with shareholders. Compensation seems reasonable; however, bonus compensation is based on certain performance metrics that are a bit vague. Taylor's annual bonus increased significantly in 2006. We feel the increase was appropriate given the company's performance in 2006 compared with 2005 and the firm's investments for long-term growth. In addition, the company relies on stock options as the primary long-term incentive vehicle; however, we would prefer the company used restricted shares to better align management's interests with shareholders'. In late 2004, the board adopted a shareholder-rights plan, which would make it more difficult for a party to acquire the firm, even if it would benefit shareholders. Eliminating this rights plan and DeVry's staggered board would serve to improve DeVry's corporate stewardship.

One Tower Lane Suite 1000 www.devry.com
Oakbrook Terrace, IL 60181

Growth [C-]	2003	2004	2005	2006
Revenue %	4.9	15.5	-0.5	7.9
Earnings/Share %	-8.4	-14.9	-64.9	134.6
Book Value/Share %	18.1	15.2	8.8	7.9
Dividends/Share %	NMF	NMF	NMF	NMF

Profitability [B]	2004	2005	2006	TTM
Return on Assets %	5.9	2.0	4.9	6.3
Oper Cash Flow $Mil	—	87	91	127
- Cap Spending $Mil	43	43	25	28
= Free Cash Flow $Mil	—	44	66	98

Financial Health [A]	2004	2005	2006	06-30-06
Long-term Debt $Mil	—	175	65	—
Total Equity $Mil	482	513	565	587
Debt/Equity Ratio	—	0.3	0.1	0.1

Industry	Business Risk	Moat Size	Investment Style	Sector
Education	Average	Wide	Mid Growth	Consumer Services

Competition

	Market Cap $Mil	12 Mo Trailing Sales $Mil	Price/Cash Flow	Return On Assets%	Debt/ Equity	Total Return% 1 Yr	3 Yr
DeVry	1,983	867	15.7	6.3	0.1	40.3	3.9
Washington Post Co	7,167	3,813	13.1	6.9	0.1	-1.5	-1.0
Apollo Group A	6,733	2,409	11.3	43.5	0.2	-35.5	-17.5

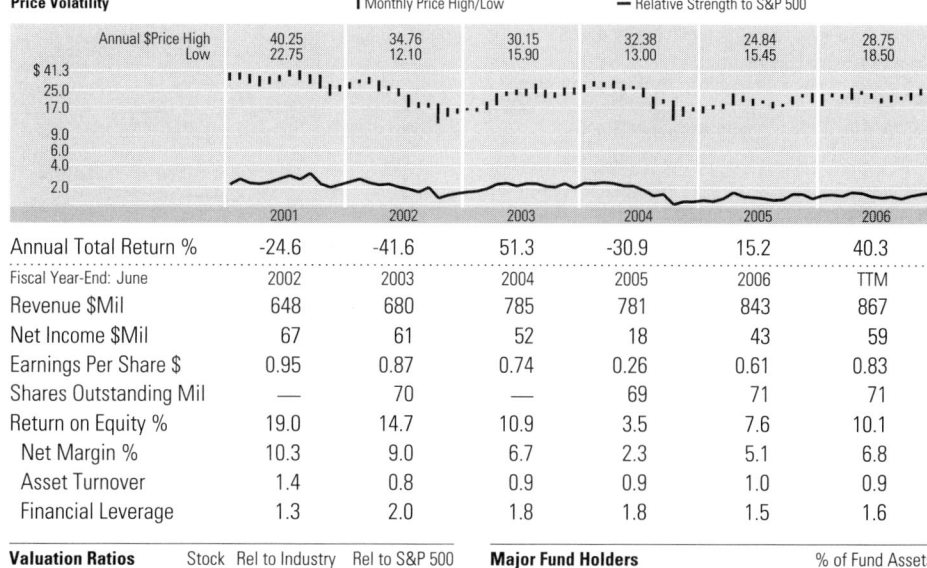

Annual Total Return %	-24.6	-41.6	51.3	-30.9	15.2	40.3
Fiscal Year-End: June	2002	2003	2004	2005	2006	TTM
Revenue $Mil	648	680	785	781	843	867
Net Income $Mil	67	61	52	18	43	59
Earnings Per Share $	0.95	0.87	0.74	0.26	0.61	0.83
Shares Outstanding Mil	—	70	—	69	71	71
Return on Equity %	19.0	14.7	10.9	3.5	7.6	10.1
Net Margin %	10.3	9.0	6.7	2.3	5.1	6.8
Asset Turnover	1.4	0.8	0.9	0.9	1.0	0.9
Financial Leverage	1.3	2.0	1.8	1.8	1.5	1.6

Valuation Ratios	Stock	Rel to Industry	Rel to S&P 500
Price/Earnings	33.7	1.4	1.6
Price/Book	3.4	0.2	0.8
Price/Sales	2.3	0.2	0.8
Price/Cash Flow	15.7	1.0	1.1

Major Fund Holders	% of Fund Assets
Westport Select Cap R	2.41
Baron Capital Asset Ins	2.22
Fidelity Advisor Mid Cap T	2.15
SunAmerica Focused Small-Cap Growth A	1.98

Thesis By Kristan Rowland, 11-22-06 Stock Price as of Analysis: $26.12

DeVry is a leader in for-profit postsecondary education, and it should benefit from several broad-based trends. Enrollment in postsecondary education is expected to increase 13% from 2004 to 2014, according to the National Center for Education Statistics (NCES). This growth is partly driven by the large echo-boom generation graduating from high school and should help fuel DeVry's enrollment growth. Also, the percentage of high school graduates enrolling in postsecondary education is near its peak at 66.7%, a result of a postsecondary education's importance in today's service-based economy. DeVry boasts numerous programs for recent high school graduates, so it should stand to benefit from this growth.

DeVry should also benefit from the growth of working adults returning to school who see the value of postsecondary education. U.S. Census Bureau statistics show that college graduates earn nearly double those with only a high school diploma. Also, the unemployment rate among Americans with a college degree is about half that of those without a degree. In 2005, the NCES estimated that 40% of all college students were at least 25 years old, and this demographic has been the fastest-growing part of DeVry's enrollments. This trend should continue to benefit DeVry, which offers flexible course schedules, online courses, convenient locations, and career-oriented programs in relatively growth-oriented areas of the economy.

DeVry also enjoys regional accreditation, an indication of a quality institution. Students can receive government financial aid only after an institution has been accredited. The accreditation process can take years to complete and contributes to education firms' moats. It takes even longer for a school to obtain regional accreditation, a factor that contributes to DeVry's wide moat.

DeVry's outlook should continue to brighten. It boasts a strong reputation for providing high-quality technology programs. A solid technology career outlook should help drive more enrollments. Also, DeVry's diversification into health-care programs, with Ross University and Chamberlain College of Nursing, should prove positive given the need for health-care professionals, which should also benefit enrollment growth. Nine of the top 10 fastest-growing occupations are in health care or information technology. Given DeVry's programs, solid reputation, and career-oriented education, we think these trends should fuel enrollment growth and solid future results for DeVry.

Diageo PLC ADR DEO

Rating	Fair Value	Last Close	Consider Buy	Consider Sell	Yield %
★★★	$86.00	$79.31	$73.30	$112.90	2.86

Company Profile

The product of a merger between Grand Metropolitan and Guinness in 1997, Diageo is the world's leading producer of branded premium spirits. It also produces and markets beer and wine. Brands include Guinness stout, Smirnoff vodka, Tanqueray and Gordon's gins, Captain Morgan rum, Bailey's Irish Cream, and Johnnie Walker scotch. Diageo also owns 34% of upscale champagne and cognac maker Moet Hennessy, a subsidiary of French luxury goods maker Moet Hennessy-Louis Vuitton.

Management
Stewardship Grade [NA]

Paul Walsh, a veteran who started at Grand Metropolitan in 1982 and spent a decade running Pillsbury, stepped into the CEO role in 2000. Walsh has been the driving force behind Diageo's strategy to shed noncore businesses in order to focus on spirits. Lord James Blyth, retired chairman of Boots Company, became Diageo's chairman in July 2000 and presides over its 10-member board. We applaud the separation of the chairman and CEO roles, and the fact that Diageo's board is composed of eight independent members. We don't see any alarming red flags in corporate governance. Compensation levels seem consistent with those at comparable companies, and about 75% of compensation is variable, based on both annual and longer-term performance. We like the structure of the company's Total Shareholder Return incentive plan, which awards Diageo shares based on the company's total return to shareholders relative to a peer group. Management and shareholder interests appear well-aligned. The board seems sufficiently independent, with only two inside directors. However, directors do not stand for elections annually, and we think the company could strengthen its governance policy by removing staggered board elections.

8 Henrietta Place
London, United Kingdom W1G 0NB
www.diageo.com

Growth [NA]	2003	2004	2005	2006
Revenue %	-14.9	-4.2	-24.9	8.7
Earnings/Share %	-66.6	186.9	-1.5	48.7
Book Value/Share %	787.8	-92.1	8.4	7.1
Dividends/Share %	—	—	—	—

Profitability [NA]	2004	2005	2006	TTM
Return on Assets %	9.4	10.2	13.8	13.8
Oper Cash Flow $Mil	3,094	3,194	2,841	2,841
- Cap Spending $Mil	565	544	458	458
= Free Cash Flow $Mil	2,529	2,650	2,383	2,383

Financial Health [NA]	2004	2005	2006	06-30-06
Long-term Debt $Mil	6,227	6,685	7,275	7,275
Total Equity $Mil	7,605	8,411	8,511	8,511
Debt/Equity Ratio	0.8	0.8	0.9	0.9

	Industry	Business Risk	Moat Size	Investment Style	Sector
	Alcoholic Beverages	Below Avg	Wide	Large Core	Consumer Goods

Competition	Market Cap $Mil	12 Mo Trailing Sales $Mil	Price/Cash Flow	Return On Assets%	Debt/Equity	Total Return% 1 Yr	3 Yr
Diageo PLC ADR	60,493	12,931	21.3	13.8	0.9	40.7	18.0
Brown-Forman B	8,153	2,606	21.2	14.2	0.2	-3.0	14.4
Constellation Brands A	6,774	4,888	19.5	3.3	1.3	10.6	20.8

Price Volatility — Monthly Price High/Low — Relative Strength to S&P 500

	2001	2002	2003	2004	2005	2006
Annual $Price High	46.35	55.40	53.09	58.05	61.63	80.20
Low	36.63	40.75	37.55	48.21	54.45	58.30
Annual Total Return %	8.0	-2.6	25.4	13.8	4.5	40.7

Fiscal Year-End: June	2002	2003	2004	2005	2006	TTM
Revenue $Mil	15,732	14,632	15,367	12,365	12,931	12,931
Net Income $Mil	2,293	79	2,406	2,591	3,500	3,500
Earnings Per Share $	2.77	1.01	3.17	3.35	4.79	4.79
Shares Outstanding Mil	829	78	758	774	731	763
Return on Equity %	22.7	0.9	31.6	30.8	41.1	41.1
Net Margin %	14.6	0.5	15.7	21.0	27.1	27.1
Asset Turnover	0.6	0.6	0.6	0.5	0.5	0.5
Financial Leverage	2.7	2.8	3.4	3.0	3.0	3.0

Valuation Ratios	Stock	Rel to Industry	Rel to S&P 500
Price/Earnings	16.6	0.6	0.8
Price/Book	7.1	0.8	1.7
Price/Sales	4.7	0.9	1.6
Price/Cash Flow	21.3	1.0	1.5

Major Fund Holders	% of Fund Assets
Meehan Focus	4.90
Vice Fund	4.37
FMI Large Cap	3.72
Tweedy, Browne American Value	3.66

Thesis By Matthew Reilly, 12-12-06 Stock Price as of Analysis: $78.13

Diageo is the largest spirits maker in the world, boasting nine of the world's top 20 brands. Spirits make up about 75% of the company's revenue, with beer constituting 20% and wine the remainder. The company puts it marketing muscle to work on a global scale behind such leading brands as Smirnoff, Johnnie Walker, Jose Cuervo, Guinness, and Captain Morgan. We believe that the strength of the company's brands, its worldwide scale, and its shrewd, shareholder-focused management will deliver steady financial results, making the company an attractive long-term holding.

Diageo's scale advantage is not as great as a few years ago due to consolidation in the spirits industry. The sale and split of Allied Domecq has vaulted Pernod Ricard to the number-two spot, but the new Pernod's annual revenue still amounts to only about 60% of Diageo's. Many of Pernod's brands are also local or national, which we believe puts Pernod at a competitive disadvantage to Diageo's global brands. With the spirits industry continuing to consolidate and the globalization of the international community accelerating, global scalability has become increasingly important.

The American market is vital to Diageo's performance, and the company's performance should be enhanced by its exclusive distributor base. There also appears to be no end in sight to the secular trend of American consumers trading up to premium and above spirits brands, where the majority of Diageo's products are positioned.

Like many consumer-products companies, Diageo's European operations have struggled lately, and we think that consumer spending will remain tight in the near future. We think the company has borne the brunt of severe volume drops already, and it has wisely redeployed marketing funds.

A large portion of the marketing funds have been redirected to Diageo's international division, encompassing operations in several emerging markets. Strong performance in markets such as Brazil and China helped this division increase organic revenue 13% in fiscal 2006. Comparable operating margins contracted due to marketing investments, but we think Diageo is wisely using these funds to expand its moat in attractive and dynamic markets.

While margin expansion is unlikely--and in some senses undesirable due to the constant need to reinvest marketing funds to keep the premium positioning of its brands--the company still manages to make operating margins in excess of 28%, a level we feel is sustainable for the foreseeable future.

Data as of 12-29-06

The DirecTV Group DTV

Rating ★★	Fair Value $20.00	Last Close $24.94	Consider Buy $15.40	Consider Sell $25.10	Yield % 0.00

Company Profile

The DirecTV Group is the largest satellite television provider in the United States, with 15.7 million customers. The firm also owns satellite operations in Latin America: 74% of Sky Brazil, 41% of Sky Mexico, and 100% of PanAmericana, which covers much of the region. These businesses serve about 4 million customers combined. DirecTV sold its stake in PanAmSat, set-top box manufacturing assets, and set-top box software business in 2004. It sold Hughes Network Systems in 2005.

Management   Stewardship Grade [C]

News Corporation plans to transfer its 38.5% stake in DirecTV (plus cash and other News assets) to John Malone's Liberty Media for Liberty's stake in News. The swap is expected to be completed in mid-2007. We expect Malone, a cable industry pioneer, will replace News chairman Rupert Murdoch as chairman of DirecTV. Malone will also likely remake DirecTV's board: Of its 11 members, nine have been appointed since News took over in 2003 and four have direct News ties. We think the relationship between DirecTV and a larger shareholder (whether News or Liberty) is the biggest knock against the firm's stewardship, as it creates a major takeover defense and could present potential conflicts of interest. CEO and board member Chase Carey was a longtime News executive, but he is expected to remain at the helm following the Liberty deal, which should make for a smooth transition. The executive team is very highly compensated--Carey took home $5 million in salary and bonus during 2005. The compensation structure is based largely on customer growth, which we think could push the firm to pursue strategies that don't create long-term value. The recent trouble stemming from the addition of customers with poor credit histories illustrates this point. Management's decision to tighten credit policies is encouraging, though. Also, we like the firm's financial disclosure.

2250 East Imperial Highway   www.hughes.com
El Segundo, CA 90245

Growth [A]	2002	2003	2004	2005
Revenue %	9.2	14.5	21.2	15.9
Earnings/Share %	—	NMF	NMF	NMF
Book Value/Share %	—	NMF	-21.5	4.5
Dividends/Share %	NMF	NMF	NMF	NMF

Profitability [C-]	2003	2004	2005	TTM
Return on Assets %	-1.9	-13.6	2.1	8.3
Oper Cash Flow $Mil	787	229	1,172	2,643
- Cap Spending $Mil	747	1,023	889	1,562
= Free Cash Flow $Mil	40	-795	283	1,081

Financial Health [C-]	2003	2004	2005	09-30-06
Long-term Debt $Mil	—	2,410	3,405	3,398
Total Equity $Mil	9,631	7,507	7,940	6,210
Debt/Equity Ratio	—	0.3	0.4	0.5

Industry	Business Risk	Moat Size	Investment Style	Sector
Cable TV	Average	Narrow	Large Growth	Media

Competition	Market Cap $Mil	12 Mo Trailing Sales $Mil	Price/Cash Flow	Return On Assets%	Debt/ Equity	Total Return% 1 Yr	3 Yr
DirecTV	30,516	14,168	11.5	8.3	0.5	76.6	15.9
AT&T	137,384	60,171	9.0	4.9	0.5	51.6	16.3
Comcast A	88,095	24,531	14.4	2.1	0.6	63.3	8.7

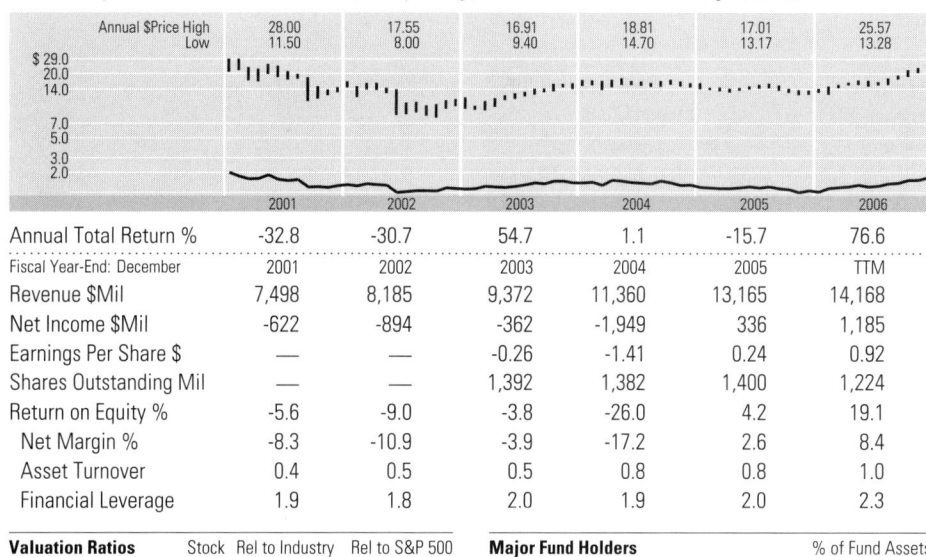

Price Volatility — Monthly Price High/Low — Relative Strength to S&P 500

	2001	2002	2003	2004	2005	2006
Annual $Price High	28.00	17.55	16.91	18.81	17.01	25.57
Low	11.50	8.00	9.40	14.70	13.17	13.28
Annual Total Return %	-32.8	-30.7	54.7	1.1	-15.7	76.6

Fiscal Year-End: December	2001	2002	2003	2004	2005	TTM
Revenue $Mil	7,498	8,185	9,372	11,360	13,165	14,168
Net Income $Mil	-622	-894	-362	-1,949	336	1,185
Earnings Per Share $	—	—	-0.26	-1.41	0.24	0.92
Shares Outstanding Mil	—	—	1,392	1,382	1,400	1,224
Return on Equity %	-5.6	-9.0	-3.8	-26.0	4.2	19.1
Net Margin %	-8.3	-10.9	-3.9	-17.2	2.6	8.4
Asset Turnover	0.4	0.5	0.5	0.8	0.8	1.0
Financial Leverage	1.9	1.8	2.0	1.9	2.0	2.3

Valuation Ratios	Stock	Rel to Industry	Rel to S&P 500
Price/Earnings	27.1	0.8	1.3
Price/Book	4.9	0.4	1.2
Price/Sales	2.2	0.7	0.8
Price/Cash Flow	11.5	0.7	0.8

Major Fund Holders	% of Fund Assets
Longleaf Partners	5.53
Thornburg Core Growth A	3.22
JHFunds2 Core Equity NAV	3.17
JHT Core Equity Trust Ser I	3.16

Thesis By Michael Hodel, CFA, 12-22-06 Stock Price as of Analysis: $24.55

Recently, DirecTV's growth has slowed more rapidly than we had expected. We still, however, expect the firm to play an important role in the pay-television industry, allowing it to generate solid cash flow.

Although it will soon no longer own DirecTV, News Corp and the management team it installed has done much since late-2003 to reinvigorate the firm, focusing its attention on the satellite television business. The firm has also made some missteps along the way, though, notably aggressively going after customers with poor credit. While customer growth was strong through 2005, the percentage of customers disconnecting service or being disconnected (churn) has also spiked. Spending heavily to win new customers--the average cost per new addition exceeds $650--who can't or won't pay is clearly a poor investment. DirecTV has tightened credit policies and instituted an equipment leasing program similar to rival EchoStar's, but churn has remained high, eroding customer growth.

We think churn and growth will improve as the new policies take hold, but we expect that the competition will make it harder for DirecTV to win and keep customers. The cable companies are in the initial stages of rolling out phone service, giving these firms another tool--in addition to Internet access--to attract customers. The nation's two largest cable companies, Comcast and Time Warner Cable, have added scale recently, carving up Adelphia, a far weaker competitor. Finally, phone companies are also rolling out television service. DirecTV is considering new means of countering the competition, such as using WiMax to offer Internet access, but we're skeptical that this will have much impact.

Despite the competition, we still think satellite TV will serve a sizable niche over time. The cable and phone companies underserve a meaningful chunk of the country in rural areas. AT&T and Verizon, the nation's largest phone companies, plan to upgrade only a bit more than half their networks. DirecTV has also positioned itself as a premier provider of TV service--as its industry-leading $72 average monthly customer bill attests. The firm's nationwide platform makes it a good partner for niche content.

Our central thesis on DirecTV remains the same: The firm has adequate scale to generate strong cash flow growth as customer growth slows. We've already seen margins improve recently as spending on customer acquisition has fallen. The average customer still stays with the firm about five years, and we think the firm can maintain its customer base while further reducing acquisition costs.

Data as of 12-29-06

Discovery Holding Company A DISCA

	Rating	Fair Value	Last Close	Consider Buy	Consider Sell	Yield %
	★★★	$16.00	$16.09	$12.30	$20.00	0.00

Company Profile
Discovery Holding Company owns Ascent Media and a 50% stake in Discovery Communications. Ascent Media provides creative and technical services for the media and entertainment industries. Discovery is a leading provider of nonfiction entertainment through The Discovery Channel, TLC, Animal Planet, The Travel Channel, and other cable networks. Discovery reaches more than 1 billion subscribers globally.

Management
Stewardship Grade [F]

We think Discovery Holding Company, in its current structure, has poor corporate governance. It has numerous takeover defenses, including the ability to issue "blank check" preferred stock to increase the number of shares outstanding, staggered board elections, large majority voting requirements for certain actions (including mergers and acquisitions), and the existence of authorized and unissued stock, which could be issued to anyone friendly to current management. We're pleased that John C. Malone, DHC's chairman and CEO (roles we'd like to see split between two individuals) has a material stake in the company, but his 89.6% ownership of supervoting Series B shares gives him about a third of its voting power, enough to block corporate actions. We have issues with the corporate governance at Discovery, too. Cox Communications and Advance/Newhouse, Discovery's other owners, have the ability to block any activity at Discovery that may benefit DHC's shareholders. Currently, DHC doesn't have access to the cash that Discovery generates, and it won't unless the other owners agree to let Discovery pay dividends. We've also noticed that disclosure regarding Discovery has gotten worse since DHC's spin-off.

12300 Liberty Boulevard
Englewood, CO 80112

Growth [C]	2002	2003	2004	2005
Revenue %	-9.0	-6.2	24.7	10.0
Earnings/Share %	NMF	NMF	NMF	NMF
Book Value/Share %	—	—	—	—
Dividends/Share %	NMF	NMF	NMF	NMF

Profitability [C]	2003	2004	2005	TTM
Return on Assets %	-1.0	1.2	0.6	-0.7
Oper Cash Flow $Mil	30	84	85	73
- Cap Spending $Mil	26	49	91	67
= Free Cash Flow $Mil	4	35	-5	5

Financial Health [C]	2003	2004	2005	06-30-06
Long-term Debt $Mil	—	—	—	—
Total Equity $Mil	4,260	4,347	4,575	4,540
Debt/Equity Ratio	—	—	—	—

Industry	Business Risk	Moat Size	Investment Style	Sector
Media Conglomerates	Average	Narrow	Mid Growth	Media

Competition	Market Cap $Mil	12 Mo Trailing Sales $Mil	Price/Cash Flow	Return On Assets%	Debt/ Equity	Total Return% 1 Yr	3 Yr
Discovery Holding Company A	4,508	663	62.1	-0.7	—	6.2	—
Walt Disney	70,886	34,285	11.7	5.6	0.3	44.3	14.2
Viacom B	28,691	10,598	23.7	5.9	0.1	-0.3	—

Price Volatility | Monthly Price High/Low   — Relative Strength to S&P 500

Annual $Price High/Low: 2005: 18.50/13.00; 2006: 16.96/12.81

	2001	2002	2003	2004	2005	2006
Annual Total Return %	—	—	—	—	—	6.2
Fiscal Year-End: December	2001	2002	2003	2004	2005	TTM
Revenue $Mil	593	539	506	631	695	663
Net Income $Mil	-608	-129	-52	66	33	-40
Earnings Per Share $	—	—	—	—	—	—
Shares Outstanding Mil	—	—	—	—	—	280
Return on Equity %	-17.0	-3.6	-1.2	1.5	0.7	-0.9
Net Margin %	ELB	-24.0	-10.4	10.5	4.8	-6.0
Asset Turnover	0.1	0.1	0.1	0.1	0.1	0.1
Financial Leverage	1.5	1.5	1.3	1.3	1.3	1.3

Valuation Ratios	Stock	Rel to Industry	Rel to S&P 500
Price/Earnings	—	—	—
Price/Book	1.0	0.3	0.2
Price/Sales	6.8	1.9	2.3
Price/Cash Flow	62.1	3.7	4.3

Major Fund Holders	% of Fund Assets
Longleaf Partners Small-Cap	5.39
IXIS Harris Associates Focused Value C	3.21
Madison Mosaic Mid-Cap	3.07
FMC Select	2.90

Thesis By James M. Walden, CFA, 11-14-06 Stock Price as of Analysis: $15.32

The bulk of the value of Discovery Holding Company (DHC) comes from its 50% stake in Discovery Communications (Discovery), which holds the attractive Discovery Channel, TLC, Animal Planet, Travel Channel, and Discovery Health Channel cable networks, as well as several emerging networks. In our opinion, one of Discovery's strong advantages comes from its massive library of nonfiction content. We think Discovery's content, presented largely in documentary form, has strong universal appeal, transcending cultures and languages. As a result, Discovery is able to effectively repurpose its content to more than a billion subscription units in about 160 countries; such a large global footprint catches the eyes of advertisers.

We think anyone trying to take a large share of Discovery's niche faces significant barriers to entry; it would be quite a task to attempt to match Discovery's programming library, which it has been building up since The Discovery Channel began airing in 1985. We think Discovery has dug itself an economic moat, and because we estimate that DHC's investment in Discovery accounts for about 80% of DHC's value, we think DHC has an economic moat.

But even with Discovery's competitive advantages, which translate into impressive profitability, we think its moat is only narrow; advertisers and consumers have an ever-increasing number of ways to spend their dollars and time, respectively. Another reason DHC's overall moat isn't wider is the Ascent Media business, which provides creative and technical services for the entertainment and media industries. Ascent operates in a very competitive environment, and it's eked out an operating profit in only one of the past several years. We don't think it has any kind of economic moat.

We're big fans of Discovery's assets; so is media mogul John Malone, DHC's CEO and chairman. Malone has made no secret of his desire to own all of Discovery. But because of the current tax environment relating to the 2005 tax-free spin-off of DHC from Liberty Media (Malone's other media company), his hands are currently tied. When this clears up, we think Malone will make a move. Our concern is that his desire to own all of Discovery may cause him to pay too much for the other half, which we believe makes it all the more important to have an appropriate margin of safety before investing in DHC. If the shares were available to us at an appropriate discount, we'd be happy owning them.

 Stocks 500

Data as of 12-29-06

Dominion Resources D

	Rating	Fair Value	Last Close	Consider Buy	Consider Sell	Yield %
	★★★	$85.00	$83.84	$65.50	$106.50	3.29

Company Profile
Dominion is an integrated energy company. Its 28,100-megawatt electricity-generation fleet provides electricity to utility and unregulated customers. The company has gas and electric transmission lines and a liquefied natural-gas import terminal. Dominion distributes electricity in Virginia and North Carolina and gas in Ohio, Pennsylvania, and West Virginia. The company also produces natural gas and oil and has 6 trillion cubic feet equivalent of proved reserves.

Management
Stewardship Grade [B]

Thomas Capps, longtime CEO and chairman of the board, stepped down as CEO in December 2005 but still heads the board. Thomas Farrell is now president and CEO. He's been with Dominion since 1995 and has held several executive management positions at the company. Farrell is also on the board of directors and holds about 800,000 shares either outright or through options. This puts Farrell's potential stake in Dominion around $80 million and closely aligns his interests with shareholders'. We're happy to see that meaningful stock ownership is required: Top executives must own 3-8 times their salary in stock. Another positive for Dominion's shareholders is the firm's stance on at-risk compensation--officers didn't receive annual bonuses in 2004 because Dominion didn't meet aggressive internal goals. This indicates that Dominion's incentive compensation plan is more than just a name. Also, the new long-term incentive plan for executives is based on shareholder returns and ROICs. Now roughly 50% of senior management's compensation is performance-based, which we definitely approve of. Our main concern with the company's stewardship is the firm's extensive use of perks: Top executives' benefits include company cars, luncheon club memberships, home security systems, and personal use of the company plane.

120 Tredegar Street
Richmond, VA 23219
www.dom.com

Growth [A-]	2002	2003	2004	2005
Revenue %	-3.3	18.4	15.7	28.9
Earnings/Share %	124.2	-79.3	278.0	-20.6
Book Value/Share %	7.1	-8.4	1.9	-12.7
Dividends/Share %	0.0	0.0	0.8	3.1

Profitability [C-]	2003	2004	2005	TTM
Return on Assets %	0.7	2.8	2.0	3.2
Oper Cash Flow $Mil	2,350	2,770	2,623	3,611
- Cap Spending $Mil	3,438	2,750	3,358	3,814
= Free Cash Flow $Mil	-1,088	20	-735	-203

Financial Health [C]	2003	2004	2005	09-30-06
Long-term Debt $Mil	—	15,507	14,653	14,372
Total Equity $Mil	10,795	11,426	10,397	13,548
Debt/Equity Ratio	—	1.4	1.4	1.1

Industry	Business Risk	Moat Size	Investment Style	Sector
Electric Utilities	Average	Narrow	Large Value	Utilities

Competition	Market Cap $Mil	12 Mo Trailing Sales $Mil	Price/Cash Flow	Return On Assets%	Debt/Equity	Total Return% 1 Yr	3 Yr
Dominion Resources	29,656	17,641	8.2	3.2	1.1	12.6	13.6
Exelon	41,525	15,798	10.1	0.4	1.2	19.8	27.3
Southern	28,133	14,494	11.6	3.7	1.1	11.7	12.0

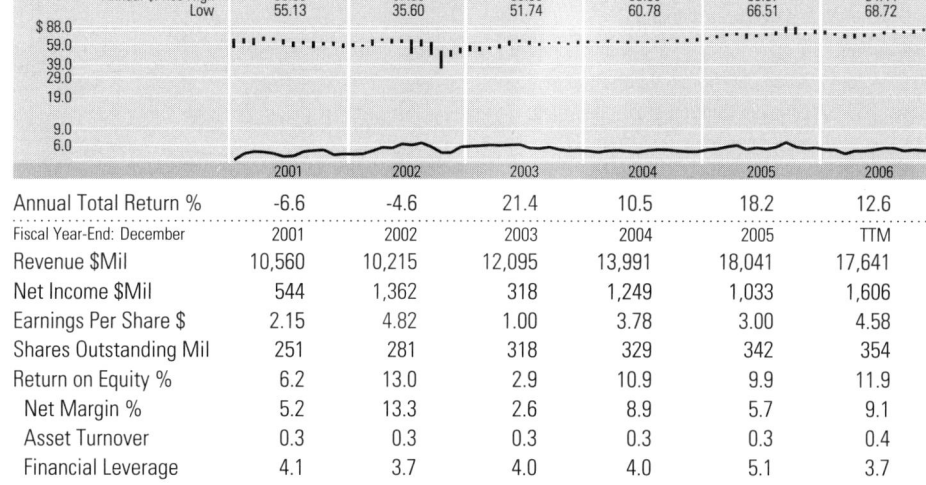

	2001	2002	2003	2004	2005	2006
Annual $Price High	69.99	67.06	65.95	68.85	86.97	84.44
Low	55.13	35.60	51.74	60.78	66.51	68.72
Annual Total Return %	-6.6	-4.6	21.4	10.5	18.2	12.6

Fiscal Year-End: December	2001	2002	2003	2004	2005	TTM
Revenue $Mil	10,560	10,215	12,095	13,991	18,041	17,641
Net Income $Mil	544	1,362	318	1,249	1,033	1,606
Earnings Per Share $	2.15	4.82	1.00	3.78	3.00	4.58
Shares Outstanding Mil	251	281	318	329	342	354
Return on Equity %	6.2	13.0	2.9	10.9	9.9	11.9
Net Margin %	5.2	13.3	2.6	8.9	5.7	9.1
Asset Turnover	0.3	0.3	0.3	0.3	0.3	0.4
Financial Leverage	4.1	3.7	4.0	4.0	5.1	3.7

Valuation Ratios	Stock	Rel to Industry	Rel to S&P 500
Price/Earnings	18.3	1.0	0.9
Price/Book	2.2	0.6	0.5
Price/Sales	1.7	0.9	0.6
Price/Cash Flow	8.2	0.7	0.6

Major Fund Holders	% of Fund Assets
Putnam Utilities Growth & Income A	5.39
Allianz OCC Value Instl	4.97
Franklin Utilities A	4.74
MainStay ICAP Select Equity I	4.18

Thesis By Jason Stevens, 12-13-06 Stock Price as of Analysis: $82.64

In previous reports we've pointed out that Dominion's hedging strategy may not be the best tool for achieving one of its stated aims--reduced earnings volatility. Now it seems the company has decided to address the root cause rather than the symptom, and has placed a for-sale sign on the bulk of its exploration and production properties. We think this is a great move that not only will help the company generate more predictable earnings but also allow management to focus on capturing real value from growth opportunities in its core businesses.

Over the past several years Dominion has become a significant player in the U.S. oil and gas patch, but its successes have increased rather than lessened the company's earnings volatility and required Dominion to put on complicated hedges that lock in the sales price of its oil and gas production. In the current rising price environment, this means that only a small portion of Dominion's production benefits from higher market prices, and, at the same time, the company is left exposed to higher production costs that tend to follow rising commodity prices. The decision to sell most of its exploration and production operations presents Dominion with the chance to exit this business gracefully, and possibly even at premium valuations.

Another benefit that we like is that the proceeds of any sale will be used to pay down debt and buy back shares. The benefit to shareholders of a buyback would depend on the buyback price Dominion offers and is hard to quantify now. But by paying down debt, Dominion will be able to improve its credit metrics and reduce its cost of future borrowing, which will, in turn, make potential future growth projects more affordable. That's the kind of thinking we applaud, especially because we like each of Dominion's continuing operations: generation, delivery, and energy infrastructure.

We particularly like the latter two businesses, as electricity and natural-gas distribution utilities enjoy regulated monopolies, and the company's pipelines and liquefied natural gas terminal are protected from competition by their scale economies and the need for regulatory approval for new projects. We think these businesses are well positioned to earn economic profits. And Dominion's generation fleet, while exposed to competitive forces, enjoys favorable positioning as a low-cost producer given the company's nuclear and coal-fired generating fleet. In our view, selling its E&P operations and focusing on its core businesses will help Dominion create lasting shareholder value.

Data as of 12-29-06

Donaldson DCI

	Rating	Fair Value	Last Close	Consider Buy	Consider Sell	Yield %
	★★	$29.00	$34.71	$22.40	$36.30	0.98

Company Profile

Donaldson manufactures air- and liquid-filtration products in two segments. The engine product segment, which accounts for about 60% of revenue, produces intake and exhaust systems for diesel-powered heavy equipment and trucks. The industrial product segment manufactures air-filtration systems for gas turbines, factory air-purification systems, disk drives, and other industrial applications. Sales are split about evenly between North America and overseas markets.

Management   Stewardship Grade [B]

Bill Cook took over as CEO from Bill Van Dyke in August 2004. A company veteran of 20-plus years, Cook has held several positions, including CFO, head of international operations, and head of marketing. As a whole, Donaldson's managers are well aligned with shareholders, as evidenced by a well-thought-out compensation structure. Every executive officer is required to own 5-10 times his or her salary in company stock, and option grants as well as cash compensation are reasonable. By focusing on expanding aftermarket and international sales, Cook aims to maintain the company's impressive record of sales growth. Besides accruing additional profits, these efforts also help diversify revenue and smooth out cyclical first-fit sales, which are tied to the lumpy sales patterns of truck and off-road equipment makers. With its PowerCore investment, the company has once again proved its technological prowess and long-term focus, which should benefit shareholders for years to come.

1400 West 94th Street   www.donaldson.com
Minneapolis, MN 55431

Growth [C]	2003	2004	2005	2006
Revenue %	8.2	16.1	12.8	6.2
Earnings/Share %	10.5	12.4	7.6	22.0
Book Value/Share %	17.8	23.7	-1.1	6.3
Dividends/Share %	12.9	17.1	14.6	36.2

Profitability [A+]	2004	2005	2006	TTM
Return on Assets %	10.6	9.9	11.8	11.7
Oper Cash Flow $Mil	118	143	157	157
- Cap Spending $Mil	48	55	81	81
= Free Cash Flow $Mil	70	88	75	75

Financial Health [A]	2004	2005	2006	10-31-06
Long-term Debt $Mil	71	103	100	96
Total Equity $Mil	549	525	547	584
Debt/Equity Ratio	0.1	0.2	0.2	0.2

Industry	Business Risk	Moat Size	Investment Style	Sector
Environ. Control	Average	Narrow	Mid Core	Business Services

Competition	Market Cap $Mil	12 Mo Trailing Sales $Mil	Price/Cash Flow	Return On Assets%	Debt/ Equity	Total Return% 1 Yr	3 Yr
Donaldson	2,801	1,737	17.9	11.7	0.2	10.2	6.7
Cummins	6,200	11,082	6.3	9.1	0.3	33.2	36.4
Pall	4,229	2,085	16.3	5.7	0.5	30.6	10.5

Price Volatility | Monthly Price High/Low   — Relative Strength to S&P 500

Annual $Price High/Low	20.17/12.23	22.50/14.96	30.75/16.09	34.45/25.05	33.90/28.60	38.97/30.16
	2001	2002	2003	2004	2005	2006
Annual Total Return %	41.0	-6.5	65.7	11.0	-1.5	10.2

Fiscal Year-End: July	2002	2003	2004	2005	2006	TTM
Revenue $Mil	1,126	1,218	1,415	1,596	1,694	1,737
Net Income $Mil	87	95	106	111	132	136
Earnings Per Share $	0.95	1.05	1.18	1.27	1.55	1.61
Shares Outstanding Mil	88	87	88	85	83	81
Return on Equity %	22.7	21.3	19.4	21.1	24.2	23.3
Net Margin %	7.7	7.8	7.5	6.9	7.8	7.8
Asset Turnover	1.3	1.4	1.4	1.4	1.5	1.5
Financial Leverage	2.2	2.0	1.8	2.1	2.1	2.0

Valuation Ratios	Stock	Rel to Industry	Rel to S&P 500
Price/Earnings	21.6	0.7	1.0
Price/Book	4.8	0.7	1.2
Price/Sales	1.6	1.5	0.6
Price/Cash Flow	17.9	1.6	1.2

Major Fund Holders	% of Fund Assets
Mairs & Power Growth	3.28
Ave Maria Growth	2.84
FAM Equity-Income Inv	2.41
Phoenix Small-Mid Cap X	2.33

Thesis By Matthew Warren, 12-14-06 Stock Price as of Analysis: $35.32

Donaldson is aiming to increase its historically weak share of the diesel aftermarket, since replacement filter sales come with higher margins and help insulate this narrow-moat firm from its cyclical first-fit markets.

Donaldson has built a commanding position in several air- and liquid-filtration markets. Its products filter air, oil, and exhaust in diesel engines used to power tractor-trailers and off-road equipment. Its filters are also used in factory air purification, compressed gas filtration, gas turbine air intakes, and disk drive filters. As the number-one or -two player in most of its markets, Donaldson is able to reinvest in product development and productivity efforts to protect its lead.

Donaldson has vastly expanded its markets. Since 1990, the company has posted 9% compound annual revenue growth by moving beyond its U.S.-based diesel engine heritage. By entering markets with similar performance requirements and taking share overseas, Donaldson has diversified its revenue stream and outgrown its industrial peers.

Much of this success derives from Donaldson's engineering prowess and history of bringing new technologies to market. Despite the disappointing loss of Caterpillar's heavy-duty truck emission business, which Cat decided to bring in-house, Donaldson managed to win new business from two other manufacturers for next-generation trucks due out in 2007. The firm's emission equipment is also being retrofitted on many bus fleets around the country. Donaldson is well positioned to continue increasing its content per engine as stepped-up regulations take effect in 2009 and 2010.

Donaldson's new PowerCore air-filtration technology is also gaining traction in several end markets. Though this new technology--which provides the same filtration capability in a much smaller package--will allow Donaldson to boost margins on its original-equipment manufacturer sales (filters installed at the factory), the product will have a bigger effect on the aftermarket. Previously, as products matured, aftermarket sales would be siphoned away by the copycat competition. With PowerCore, the patented replacement filters should lock in a longer tail of recurring revenue.

Donaldson has an impressive history of top-line growth, but it is nevertheless exposed to some cyclical end markets. Tractor, off-road equipment, and gas turbine makers usually face deep cycles. That said, Donaldson has numerous opportunities on the horizon.

Data as of 12-29-06

Dover DOV

	Rating	Fair Value	Last Close	Consider Buy	Consider Sell	Yield %
	★★★	$53.00	$49.02	$40.90	$66.40	1.45

Company Profile
Dover is an industrial conglomerate composed of 50 operating companies that sell to industrial and commercial markets. Products include industrial ink-jet printers, commercial coolers and freezers, heat-transfer products, tractor cabs, bearings, oil and gas exploration tools, garbage-truck parts, automatic teller machines, circuit assembly and test equipment, and many other diverse product lines.

Management
Stewardship Grade [**B**]

New CEO Ron Hoffman took the helm of Dover from Thomas Reece at the end of 2004. Reece remains chairman of the board. Hoffman, just the fifth CEO since the company's founding in 1955, recently headed the firm's recourses segment. At about 100 employees, Dover's worldwide corporate staff is extremely small, reinforcing the company's long history of decentralized operations. Unit and segment heads' annual compensation is based upon the performance of their units as measured by earnings growth, return on investment, and operating metrics. Management is also awarded cash and stock incentives that are deferred for three years and based upon meeting goals within that period. Nine of Dover's 11 board members are independent. Approximately 60% of each non-employee board member's $120,000 annual compensation is awarded in company stock, aligning them with shareholders.

280 Park Avenue
New York, NY 10017
www.dovercorporation.com

Growth [**B+**]	2002	2003	2004	2005
Revenue %	-4.4	8.9	25.2	16.5
Earnings/Share %	NMF	NMF	40.3	23.8
Book Value/Share %	—	NMF	13.2	6.9
Dividends/Share %	3.8	5.6	8.8	6.5

Profitability [**A**]	2003	2004	2005	TTM
Return on Assets %	5.7	7.2	7.8	7.6
Oper Cash Flow $Mil	575	578	660	925
- Cap Spending $Mil	90	103	152	201
= Free Cash Flow $Mil	485	475	507	723

Financial Health [**A-**]	2003	2004	2005	09-30-06
Long-term Debt $Mil	—	753	1,344	1,491
Total Equity $Mil	2,743	3,119	3,330	3,796
Debt/Equity Ratio	—	0.2	0.4	0.4

Industry	Business Risk	Moat Size	Investment Style	Sector
Diversified	Average	Narrow	Mid Core	Industrial Materials

Competition	Market Cap $Mil	12 Mo Trailing Sales $Mil	Price/Cash Flow	Return On Assets%	Debt/ Equity	Total Return% 1 Yr	3 Yr
Dover	10,008	6,969	10.8	7.6	0.4	22.9	9.2
Danaher	22,297	9,200	16.1	8.7	0.4	30.0	17.0
Ingersoll-Rand A	11,997	11,232	12.8	9.4	0.2	-1.4	6.9

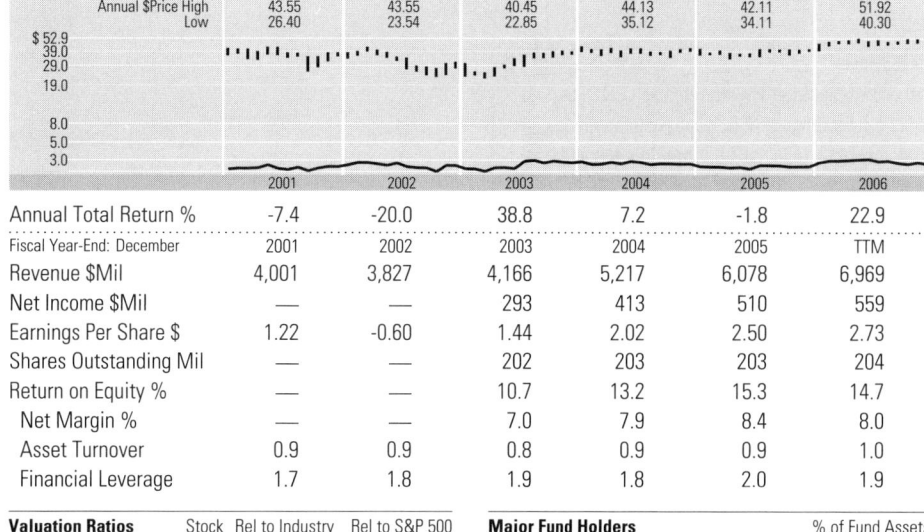

	2001	2002	2003	2004	2005	2006
Annual $Price High	43.55	43.55	40.45	44.13	42.11	51.92
Low	26.40	23.54	22.85	35.12	34.11	40.30
Annual Total Return %	-7.4	-20.0	38.8	7.2	-1.8	22.9

Fiscal Year-End: December	2001	2002	2003	2004	2005	TTM
Revenue $Mil	4,001	3,827	4,166	5,217	6,078	6,969
Net Income $Mil	—	—	293	413	510	559
Earnings Per Share $	1.22	-0.60	1.44	2.02	2.50	2.73
Shares Outstanding Mil	—	—	202	203	203	204
Return on Equity %	—	—	10.7	13.2	15.3	14.7
Net Margin %	—	—	7.0	7.9	8.4	8.0
Asset Turnover	0.9	0.9	0.8	0.9	0.9	1.0
Financial Leverage	1.7	1.8	1.9	1.8	2.0	1.9

Valuation Ratios	Stock	Rel to Industry	Rel to S&P 500
Price/Earnings	16.9	0.9	0.8
Price/Book	2.6	0.8	0.6
Price/Sales	1.4	0.8	0.5
Price/Cash Flow	10.8	0.8	0.7

Major Fund Holders	% of Fund Assets
Brown Advisory Opportunity Instl	5.05
Westcore Select	4.66
Federated MDT Mid Cap Growth A	4.59
GE Premier Growth Equity A	3.90

Thesis
By Tom D'Amore, CFA, 12-12-06 Stock Price as of Analysis: $49.17

As a classic industrial conglomerate, Dover uses its portfolio of niche businesses to smooth out revenue and earnings swings. A recently completed business portfolio upgrade should accelerate earnings growth and returns on capital.

Dover has an impressive long-term performance track record. For example, it boasts a 50-year history of consecutive dividend increases, the fourth-longest streak on the New York Stock Exchange. The firm favors a decentralized management structure, giving individual managers maximum autonomy in running their independent units. Using this strategy, Dover generated earnings growth at a compounded rate of 10% over the 10-year period ending in 2005.

Despite these favorable results, performance faltered over the 2000-03 period, and returns on capital dipped to just 4% in 2002. Dover's new CEO Ron Hoffman has been hard at work upgrading Dover's stable of approximately 50 industrial business units. Over the last two years, Hoffman has completed the acquisition of 20 businesses with approximately $1.2 billion in annual sales and estimated operating profit margins of 12%-14%. The acquisitions replace lost earnings power from 15 discontinued businesses that produced $1 billion in sales annually, but generated average operating margins of just 5%. We like Dover's trade-up to higher-margin businesses as it drives higher returns on capital.

Robust cash flow is another Dover hallmark. Dover keeps close tabs on its working capital and capital expenditures. As a result, free cash flow from operations has exceeded reported income every year since 2002. We expect rich free cash flow generation to fund continued expansion through a combination of organic growth and acquisitions.

We also like Dover's new focused performance monitoring program. Hoffman has selected five key metrics as key performance targets: inventory turns, annual earnings growth, operating margins, working capital efficiency, and return on investment. We think these indicators give a balanced picture of the value-creating characteristics of Dover's businesses and will help management to identify laggard units for corrective action.

Due to the portfolio upgrade and increased attention to key performance targets, we project that Dover's growth and returns on investment will accelerate over the next several years. For example, we forecast operating margins of 14% in 2006, up over 200 basis points from 2005.

Data as of 12-29-06

Dow Jones & Company DJ

	Rating	Fair Value	Last Close	Consider Buy	Consider Sell	Yield %
	★★★	$35.00	$38.00	$27.00	$43.90	2.63

Company Profile
Dow Jones publishes The Wall Street Journal and its international and online editions, Barron's and the Far Eastern Economic Review. It also runs Dow Jones Newswires, Dow Jones Indexes, MarketWatch, and the Ottaway group of community newspapers. Its organizational structure includes three segments: consumer media, enterprise media and local media.

Industry	Business Risk	Moat Size	Investment Style	Sector
Media Conglomerates	Average	Wide	Mid Core	Media

Competition

	Market Cap $Mil	12 Mo Trailing Sales $Mil	Price/Cash Flow	Return On Assets%	Debt/ Equity	Total Return% 1 Yr	3 Yr
Dow Jones & Company	3,170	1,853	—	12.7	0.8	10.1	-5.9
Gannett	14,167	7,880	9.8	6.9	0.7	1.9	-10.5
New York Times A	3,503	3,392	12.7	3.9	0.5	-5.3	-18.1

Management Stewardship Grade [D]
Richard F. Zannino took the reins as CEO in January 2006, succeeding Peter R. Kann, who began his career at Dow Jones as an intern in 1963 and had been chairman and CEO since 1991. (Kann has retained his chairman role.) In 2004, Kann took home $1.8 million in salary and bonus, along with another $1.0 million of long-term compensation, excluding options; we think that package was reasonable. While Kann's personal stake in Dow Jones is less than 1%, the rest of the directors and executives own more than 15% of the company's Class A shares. However, supervoting Class B shares provide the Bancroft family with control of the company; as a result, the interests of outside shareholders come second. We're disappointed by the company's history of allocating shareholder capital. In the late 1980s, Dow Jones bought financial information service Telerate for $1.6 billion, the largest acquisition for the company at the time. In our opinion, Dow Jones paid too much for it; in 1998, the company sold the unprofitable business for only $510 million.

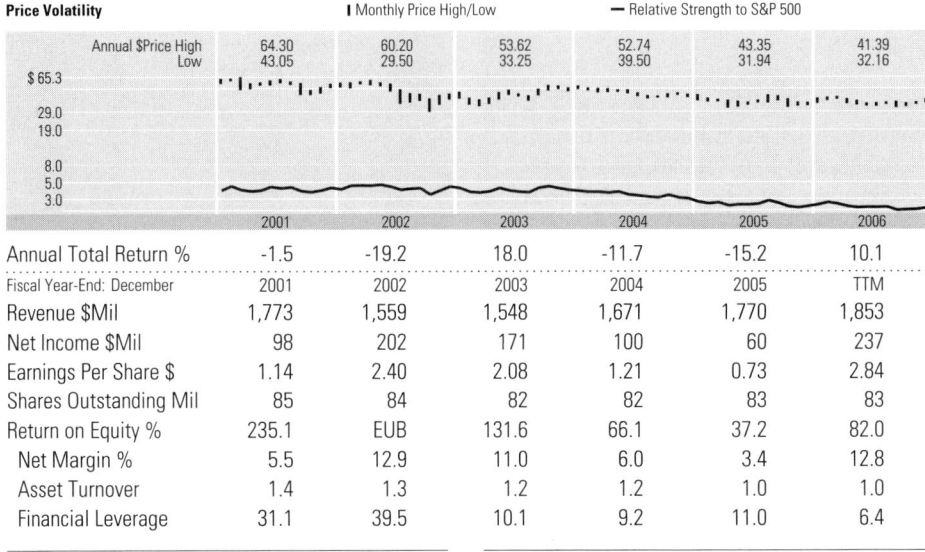

Price Volatility		Monthly Price High/Low		— Relative Strength to S&P 500		
Annual $Price High	64.30	60.20	53.62	52.74	43.35	41.39
Low	43.05	29.50	33.25	39.50	31.94	32.16
	2001	2002	2003	2004	2005	2006
Annual Total Return %	-1.5	-19.2	18.0	-11.7	-15.2	10.1
Fiscal Year-End: December	2001	2002	2003	2004	2005	TTM
Revenue $Mil	1,773	1,559	1,548	1,671	1,770	1,853
Net Income $Mil	98	202	171	100	60	237
Earnings Per Share $	1.14	2.40	2.08	1.21	0.73	2.84
Shares Outstanding Mil	85	84	82	82	83	83
Return on Equity %	235.1	EUB	131.6	66.1	37.2	82.0
Net Margin %	5.5	12.9	11.0	6.0	3.4	12.8
Asset Turnover	1.4	1.3	1.2	1.2	1.0	1.0
Financial Leverage	31.1	39.5	10.1	9.2	11.0	6.4

Valuation Ratios	Stock	Rel to Industry	Rel to S&P 500
Price/Earnings	21.2	0.8	1.0
Price/Book	11.0	3.3	2.7
Price/Sales	1.7	0.5	0.6
Price/Cash Flow	—	—	—

Major Fund Holders	% of Fund Assets
SunAmerica Focused Dividend Strat C	3.06
Hotchkis and Wiley Mid-Cap Value I	2.98
CM Advisers	2.41
Boyar Value	2.07

200 Liberty Street
New York, NY 10281
www.dowjones.com

Growth [C]	2002	2003	2004	2005
Revenue %	-12.1	-0.7	7.9	5.9
Earnings/Share %	110.5	-13.3	-41.8	-39.7
Book Value/Share %	-24.9	334.2	15.7	7.2
Dividends/Share %	0.0	0.0	0.0	0.0

Profitability [A]	2003	2004	2005	TTM
Return on Assets %	13.1	7.2	3.4	12.7
Oper Cash Flow $Mil	220	252	198	-1
- Cap Spending $Mil	56	76	65	84
= Free Cash Flow $Mil	164	176	132	-85

Financial Health [B]	2003	2004	2005	09-30-06
Long-term Debt $Mil	153	136	225	225
Total Equity $Mil	130	151	162	289
Debt/Equity Ratio	1.2	0.9	1.4	0.8

Thesis By James M. Walden, CFA, 12-18-06 Stock Price as of Analysis: $38.23

In our opinion, Dow Jones has one of the widest economic moats of all the media companies that we cover. Its moat comes from the rich business content provided by its nearly 2,000-member staff dedicated to business and financial news. (For perspective, this dwarfs the entire New York Times newsroom staff of about 1,200.) We believe the timely delivery of such extensive coverage and analysis of current business headlines through its flagship publication, The Wall Street Journal, puts the paper at a competitive advantage over other publications that provide in-depth yet less immediate business news, such as BusinessWeek, Forbes, and Fortune magazines.

Despite the Journal having provided timely information for business professionals for more than 100 years, management isn't shy about taking bold initiatives to keep it fresh and to improve its financial position. Historically, the Journal has relied heavily on business-to-business (B2B) advertising. But when the tech bubble burst in early 2000, the Journal's ad revenue plummeted over each of the next few years, largely from less spending from players in the tech and financial-services industries. To mitigate its dependence on B2B advertising, management launched the Weekend Edition of the Journal at the end of 2005. About 60% of the Weekend Edition's ads are targeted at consumers, which should provide a buffer if any particular business industry falters.

The print Journal remains the company's crown jewel, in our view, but we think Dow Jones has done an excellent job traversing the changing media landscape lately. In early 2005, Dow Jones completed its acquisition of MarketWatch in what proved to be almost uncanny timing. The deal was considered rather expensive at the time, but the acquisition tripled Dow Jones' online audience and almost doubled its online revenue, just as consumption of media over the Internet surged. We also think Dow Jones has met success taking its Journal franchise to the Web, too. Its online Journal reached about 800,000 paying subscribers in 2006, giving it a paid "circulation" larger than every U.S. paper other than USAToday, The New York Times, and the print Journal. In our estimate, these online investments have helped provide a valuable source of diversification for the company. In fact, once the acquisition of Factiva is completed, about 40% of Dow Jones' revenue will be from online sources and business-information sources (i.e., not newspapers), a percentage that we expect will increase over the next several years.

Data as of 12-29-06

DR Horton DHI

	Rating	Fair Value	Last Close	Consider Buy	Consider Sell	Yield %
	★★★	$29.00	$26.49	$22.40	$36.30	1.89

Company Profile

DR Horton, the largest homebuilder in the country based on homes sold, operates in 83 markets across 27 states in the Mid-Atlantic, Midwest, Southeast, Southwest, and West. In fiscal 2006, the company sold 53,099 homes, at an average price of $274,000, to entry-level, first-time move-up, and active-adult buyers. DR Horton also offers mortgage, title insurance, and closing services to its homebuyers.

Management — Stewardship Grade [C]

DR Horton was founded in 1978 by current chairman Donald R. Horton. His near-9% stake (the combined Horton family owns about 12%) provides good alignment with minority shareholders. Donald Tomnitz, the current CEO, has had operational control since 2000. Four of the seven board members are independent, with CFO Bill Wheat joining Horton and Tomnitz as the only nonindependent members. Variable cash compensation is based upon quarterly pretax income levels, while equity grants such as options are based upon a mix of several financial metrics. It's not clear, however, which are used in calculating grant amounts. We also feel that the company's relatively limited use of off-balance-sheet financing aids investors in determining the company's true financial health. Management has thus far foregone the use of off-balance-sheet financing vehicles such as joint ventures. DR Horton's only significant contractual obligation not represented on the balance sheet is $129 million in specific performance clauses related to land options. Everything else is pretty much captured on the balance sheet, something not every other builder can claim.

301 Commerce Street Suite 500 www.drhorton.com
Fort Worth, TX 76102

Growth [B+]	2002	2003	2004	2005
Revenue %	29.5	24.2	27.9	8.6
Earnings/Share %	42.7	50.9	49.5	-15.6
Book Value/Share %	23.2	26.6	34.2	21.2
Dividends/Share %	39.6	59.3	43.0	43.1

Profitability [A-]	2003	2004	2005	TTM
Return on Assets %	10.9	11.8	8.3	8.3
Oper Cash Flow $Mil	-423	-621	-1,191	-1,191
- Cap Spending $Mil	55	68	83	83
= Free Cash Flow $Mil	-478	-689	-1,274	-1,274

Financial Health [C]	2003	2004	2005	06-30-06
Long-term Debt $Mil	3,007	3,660	4,887	4,887
Total Equity $Mil	3,961	5,360	6,453	6,453
Debt/Equity Ratio	0.8	0.7	0.8	0.8

Industry	Business Risk	Moat Size	Investment Style	Sector
Home Building	Average	Narrow	Mid Value	Consumer Services

Competition	Market Cap $Mil	12 Mo Trailing Sales $Mil	Price/Cash Flow	Return On Assets %	Debt/ Equity	Total Return % 1 Yr	3 Yr
DR Horton	8,306	15,051	—	8.3	0.8	-24.4	9.9
Pulte Homes	8,432	15,017	—	9.1	0.5	-15.4	13.8
Lennar	8,313	17,031	25.7	11.0	0.4	-12.9	5.0

Price Volatility |Monthly Price High/Low   — Relative Strength to S&P 500

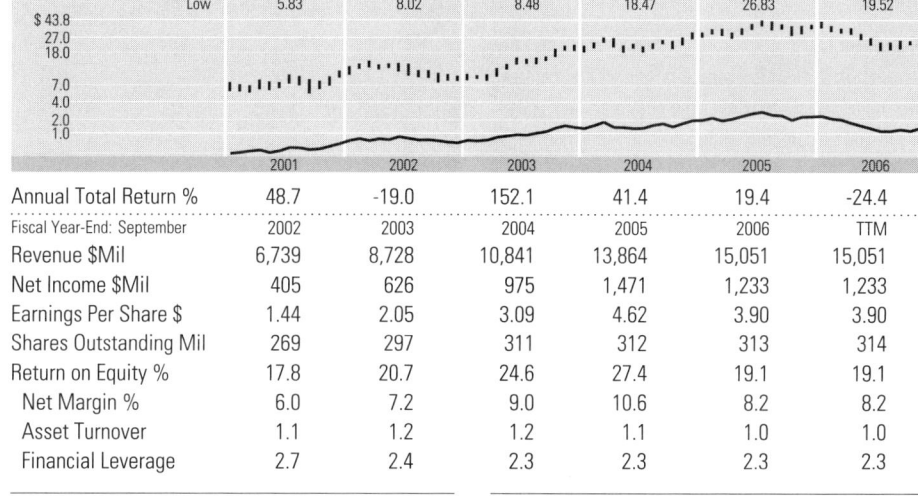

Annual $Price High Low	11.17 5.83	14.58 8.02	22.68 8.48	31.41 18.47	42.82 26.83	41.66 19.52
	2001	2002	2003	2004	2005	2006
Annual Total Return %	48.7	-19.0	152.1	41.4	19.4	-24.4

Fiscal Year-End: September	2002	2003	2004	2005	2006	TTM
Revenue $Mil	6,739	8,728	10,841	13,864	15,051	15,051
Net Income $Mil	405	626	975	1,471	1,233	1,233
Earnings Per Share $	1.44	2.05	3.09	4.62	3.90	3.90
Shares Outstanding Mil	269	297	311	312	313	314
Return on Equity %	17.8	20.7	24.6	27.4	19.1	19.1
Net Margin %	6.0	7.2	9.0	10.6	8.2	8.2
Asset Turnover	1.1	1.2	1.2	1.1	1.0	1.0
Financial Leverage	2.7	2.4	2.3	2.3	2.3	2.3

Valuation Ratios	Stock	Rel to Industry	Rel to S&P 500
Price/Earnings	6.8	0.8	0.3
Price/Book	1.3	0.7	0.3
Price/Sales	0.6	0.7	0.2
Price/Cash Flow	—	—	—

Major Fund Holders	% of Fund Assets
Hillman Focused Advantage	4.99
TCW Focused Equities N	4.73
TCW Equities I	4.23
Fidelity Select Construction&Housing	3.91

Thesis   By Eric Landry, 11-14-06   Stock Price as of Analysis: $24.50

Long-term fundamentals look encouraging for DR Horton's narrow-moat, low-cost business model. The next couple of years, however, will be very difficult even for the best operators.

DR Horton likes to compare itself to retailing giant Wal-Mart. And why not: It, too, caters to value-conscious consumers such as first-time and first-time move-up buyers; it's the largest homebuilder in the nation in terms of units; and instead of blanketing the country with unrelated discrete communities, it prefers to build outward from areas in which it already has an established infrastructure (a strategy made famous by Wal-Mart). This "satellite" strategy allows DR Horton to enter a smaller region (typically within a short driving distance of an established operation) with a fraction of the overhead otherwise required because administrative functions are performed at the regional hub. Scale in materials procurement combined with this lower overhead allows DR Horton to compete with smaller builders in markets that are unattractive to other large production operators.

By using this "clustering" strategy in 82 markets spread across 27 states, DR Horton can allocate resources to the most profitable regions and, importantly, de-emphasize weaker ones. Increased market share is one result, as weaker builders wedded to a single region sometimes go out of business during downturns. Though the benefit is partially muted by the industry's lack of entry barriers, DR Horton has successfully grown its market share from about 1% in 1997 to somewhere around 4% last year.

Due in part to the aforementioned advantages, DR Horton's three-year growth rate of unit closings is tops among the largest builders. And while its average selling price is among the lowest of the big guys (only KB Home is lower), its operating margin is among the highest, indicating its market share gains aren't at the expense of profitability.

That said, we believe the entire industry is in for a couple of very lean years. Speculative buying by investors and second-home buyers that helped fuel above-trend pricing and unit growth for the past few years has recently turned into a torrent of supply. Inventories of unsold homes in formerly hot markets are at historically high levels and could take anywhere from months to years to burn off. Worse yet, affordability ratios are at unprecedented lows in several regions, and it could take several years of flat to declining prices to get back into alignment.

Dun & Bradstreet DNB

Data as of 12-29-06

Rating	Fair Value	Last Close	Consider Buy	Consider Sell	Yield %
★★	$64.00	$82.79	$54.50	$84.00	0.00

Industry	Business Risk	Moat Size	Investment Style	Sector
Business/Online Svcs.	Below Avg	Wide	Mid Core	Business Services

Company Profile
The information in Dun & Bradstreet's database of more than 100 million companies is used by its customers for risk management, researching sales prospects, and generating direct mailing lists. The Hoover's Web site, acquired by D&B in 2003, allows users to research companies, executives, and industries. D&B's international segment has offices in 13 countries.

Management
Stewardship Grade [C]

Stewardship at D&B is average on the whole. Former COO Steven Alesio took over the chairman and CEO roles in 2005, replacing Allan Loren in a planned succession. Alesio joined D&B in 2001, and his promotion signaled an ongoing commitment to the strategies pursued by the company over the past five years. Alesio's total compensation of $6.9 million in 2005 was fairly generous, in our opinion. While we give management credit for returning most of its free cash flow to stockholders, we'd prefer that the company start paying a dividend to reduce management's discretion. We'd also like to see management and directors increase their ownership stakes, as they currently hold only 2% of outstanding shares. In addition, D&B's Stewardship Grade could be improved if the firm separated the chairman and CEO titles, dropped antitakeover defenses, and eased up on the constant restructuring charges.

103 JFK Parkway
Short Hills, NJ 07078
www.dnb.com

Competition

	Market Cap $Mil	12 Mo Trailing Sales $Mil	Price/Cash Flow	Return On Assets %	Debt/ Equity	Total Return % 1 Yr	3 Yr
Dun & Bradstreet	5,084	1,503	15.1	16.5	5.2	23.6	18.4
Equifax	5,080	1,518	14.3	14.5	0.5	7.3	19.7
Acxiom	1,992	1,377	5.1	5.5	1.6	12.5	11.8

Price Volatility

Year	2001	2002	2003	2004	2005	2006
Annual $Price High	36.90	43.40	50.81	60.80	68.00	84.98
Low	20.99	28.26	32.31	47.85	54.90	65.03
Annual Total Return %	36.4	-2.3	47.0	17.6	12.3	23.6

Fiscal Year-End: December	2001	2002	2003	2004	2005	TTM
Revenue $Mil	1,305	1,276	1,386	1,414	1,444	1,503
Net Income $Mil	150	143	175	212	221	240
Earnings Per Share $	1.84	1.87	2.30	2.90	3.19	3.59
Shares Outstanding Mil	79	74	74	70	67	61
Return on Equity %	NMF	NMF	EUB	EUB	EUB	EUB
Net Margin %	11.5	11.2	12.6	15.0	15.3	16.0
Asset Turnover	0.9	0.8	0.9	0.9	0.9	1.0
Financial Leverage	NMF	NMF	33.6	30.2	20.8	18.7

Valuation Ratios	Stock	Rel to Industry	Rel to S&P 500
Price/Earnings	23.1	0.4	1.1
Price/Book	65.5	7.2	16.0
Price/Sales	3.4	0.3	1.2
Price/Cash Flow	15.1	0.4	1.0

Major Fund Holders	% of Fund Assets
Davis Financial A	7.20
Oakmark Select I	4.19
Calvert Mid Cap Value A	3.52
Regions Morgan Keegan Sel MidCap Value A	3.48

Growth [D]

	2002	2003	2004	2005
Revenue %	-2.2	8.7	2.0	2.1
Earnings/Share %	1.6	23.0	26.1	10.0
Book Value/Share %	NMF	NMF	16.3	50.8
Dividends/Share %	NMF	NMF	NMF	NMF

Profitability [A+]

	2003	2004	2005	TTM
Return on Assets %	10.7	13.0	13.7	16.5
Oper Cash Flow $Mil	236	268	262	338
- Cap Spending $Mil	11	12	6	10
= Free Cash Flow $Mil	225	256	256	327

Financial Health [A-]

	2003	2004	2005	09-30-06
Long-term Debt $Mil	300	300	0	400
Total Equity $Mil	48	54	78	-188
Debt/Equity Ratio	6.2	5.5	0.0	5.2

Thesis
By Brett Horn, 11-16-06   Stock Price as of Analysis: $82.00

Dun & Bradstreet has some very attractive qualities. Its database of information on more than 100 million companies makes it a wide-moat firm with solid margins and minimal reinvestment needs. The company is a free cash flow machine and, better yet, it returns most of this cash to stockholders, rather than using it to expand into less attractive lines of business.

Through its 165-year history, D&B has built a database of information that would be incredibly difficult for any other competitor to replicate, protecting its solid profit margins. This established position also gives D&B an information-gathering edge; companies are willing to provide private information since they know that helping D&B improve its database enhances the information D&B can provide to them.

D&B converts its database information into revenue in two ways. The risk-management segment, which accounts for 66% of revenue, sells information to businesses that use the payment histories in D&B reports to decide whether to extend credit to other companies. The sales and marketing segment, which accounts for 27% of revenue, sells information to companies for researching sales prospects or generating direct mailing lists.

D&B's market position is established, and with 90% of S&P 500 companies already using its services, domestic revenue growth is hard to come by. International markets offer some opportunities, but the company is reluctant to invest capital in countries where it cannot quickly achieve a dominant market position, preferring to simply partner with the leading provider. Hoover's, acquired in 2003, was a good fit and offered a new platform for growth through its Web site. Still, single-digit internal revenue growth is about all that we can reasonably expect.

Given limited opportunities for top-line growth, management has focused on reducing costs to boost its bottom line. Management has been remarkably successful in driving down costs, increasing the operating margin (excluding restructuring charges) from 17% to 27% over the past five years by shedding underperforming businesses, migrating customers to Internet distribution, and reducing head count.

Because of D&B's wide moat and established market position, we would gladly buy the shares at an adequate discount to our fair value estimate.

Eaton ETN

Data as of 12-29-06

Rating	Fair Value	Last Close	Consider Buy	Consider Sell	Yield %
★★★	$75.00	$75.14	$57.80	$94.00	1.97

Company Profile
Eaton designs and manufactures hydraulic systems, electrical power control devices, automotive engine air and powertrain control systems, and drivetrain and fuel systems for trucks. Common products include automotive engine valves, truck transmissions, electrical switch gear, and flight control systems. With $11.1 billion in 2005 sales, the company holds significant share in most of its niche markets.

Industry	Business Risk	Moat Size	Investment Style	Sector
Electric Equip.	Average	Narrow	Large Value	Industrial Materials

Competition

	Market Cap $Mil	12 Mo Trailing Sales $Mil	Price/Cash Flow	Return On Assets%	Debt/ Equity	Total Return% 1 Yr	3 Yr
Eaton	11,196	12,181	7.8	8.2	0.4	14.4	14.3
Emerson Electric	35,376	20,133	14.1	9.9	0.4	20.7	13.5
Parker Hannifin	9,066	9,824	10.5	8.5	0.2	18.0	10.3

Management — Stewardship Grade [C]
Sandy Cutler has been running the show since 2000. He leads a 10-member board, nine of whom are independent. Elections are staggered. We're impressed that Cutler has been able to institute restructuring activities and adhere to the company's strategic plan laid out in 2000. Eaton's corporate-governance policies are a mixed bag, in our opinion. We found no significant related transactions with board members, and base salaries are reasonable. Annual cash incentives are based on cash-flow return on investment, growth in earnings per share, and individual or business unit performance. No payments are made unless the company exceeds an undisclosed predetermined amount of cash-flow return on investment. Long-term incentives are awarded in two components: cash payments based on four-year performance horizons (earnings per share and cash flow returns) and stock options. However, in 2002 the board changed the performance criteria on which so-called phantom share unit awards were based because of what it termed "significant adverse changes in the global economy," essentially allowing higher incentive awards during a rough period for shareholders. This, along with the staggered board elections, is the primary reason for the firm's C Stewardship Grade.

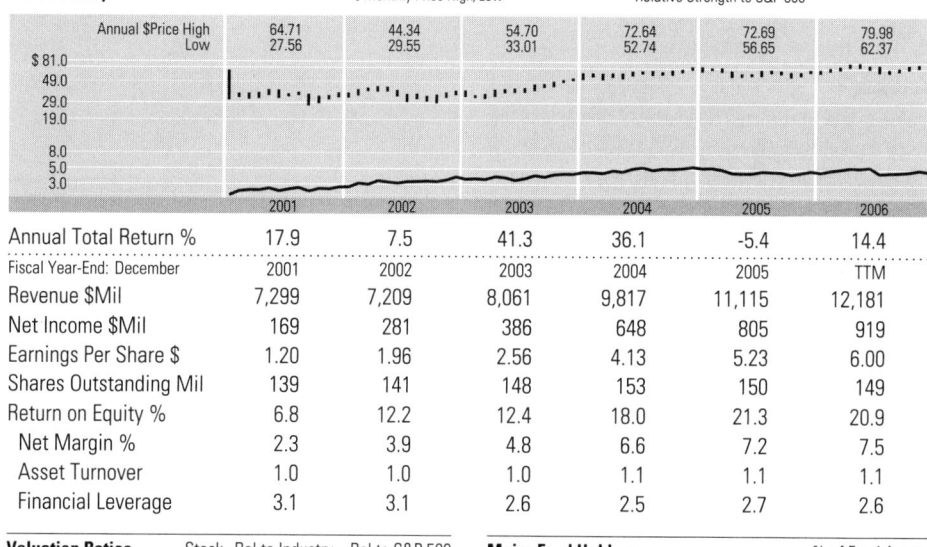

Price Volatility

	Annual $Price High Low	64.71 27.56	44.34 29.55	54.70 33.01	72.64 52.74	72.69 56.65	79.98 62.37
Annual Total Return %		17.9	7.5	41.3	36.1	-5.4	14.4
Fiscal Year-End: December		2001	2002	2003	2004	2005	TTM
Revenue $Mil		7,299	7,209	8,061	9,817	11,115	12,181
Net Income $Mil		169	281	386	648	805	919
Earnings Per Share $		1.20	1.96	2.56	4.13	5.23	6.00
Shares Outstanding Mil		139	141	148	153	150	149
Return on Equity %		6.8	12.2	12.4	18.0	21.3	20.9
Net Margin %		2.3	3.9	4.8	6.6	7.2	7.5
Asset Turnover		1.0	1.0	1.0	1.1	1.1	1.1
Financial Leverage		3.1	3.1	2.6	2.5	2.7	2.6

Valuation Ratios

	Stock	Rel to Industry	Rel to S&P 500
Price/Earnings	13.0	0.6	0.6
Price/Book	2.6	0.7	0.6
Price/Sales	0.9	0.4	0.3
Price/Cash Flow	7.8	0.6	0.5

Major Fund Holders

	% of Fund Assets
Fidelity Select Automotive	2.98
AIM Opportunities II A	2.82
Quaker Core Value A	2.56
HGK Equity Value	2.33

Eaton Center 1111 Superior Avenue www.eaton.com
Cleveland, OH 44114-2584

Growth [B]

	2002	2003	2004	2005
Revenue %	-1.2	11.8	21.8	13.2
Earnings/Share %	64.0	30.6	61.3	26.6
Book Value/Share %	-8.3	28.7	11.2	6.8
Dividends/Share %	0.0	4.5	2.7	31.2

Profitability [B+]

	2003	2004	2005	TTM
Return on Assets %	4.7	7.1	7.9	8.2
Oper Cash Flow $Mil	874	838	1,135	1,440
- Cap Spending $Mil	273	330	363	354
= Free Cash Flow $Mil	601	508	772	1,086

Financial Health [B+]

	2003	2004	2005	09-30-06
Long-term Debt $Mil	1,651	1,734	1,830	1,770
Total Equity $Mil	3,117	3,606	3,778	4,388
Debt/Equity Ratio	0.5	0.5	0.5	0.4

Thesis By John Kearney, CFA, 11-03-06 Stock Price as of Analysis: $71.44

The effectiveness of Eaton's attempt to become a more cyclically stable entity will be tested by a looming market malaise in the company's early-cycle residential electric, automotive, and heavy-duty truck businesses. However, with the bulk of the company's revenue stream now dispersed evenly across the economic cycle, we think Eaton will continue to increase shareholder value over the coming years by leaning on the strength of its mid- and late-cycle businesses.

Over the past several years, Eaton has been transforming itself from a vehicle component supplier into a diversified industrial firm. The company divested itself of nearly half of its revenue base by exiting its underperforming automotive and truck businesses. It subsequently allocated more capital to the fluid power and electrical markets, where management saw better growth and less cyclicality. Eaton now generates roughly two thirds of its revenue from the sale of fluid power (hydraulics) and electrical products. With its exposure to late-cycle markets like the nonresidential construction market (through its electrical business) and the commercial aerospace market (through its fluid power business), Eaton has transformed itself into a truly diversified entity.

While the fluid power and electrical businesses are now the largest components of the company's revenue stream, Eaton's truck business--the world's leading manufacturer of truck drivetrain systems and components--is arguably one of the company's most important divisions. Eaton has never increased earnings during a year in which the heavy-duty truck industry experienced a downturn. This is not an encouraging harbinger for the company over the near term, given that the heavy-duty truck market is expected to fall 40% in 2007 as a result of the expensive emission standards that will be required on all new heavy-duty trucks. However, with its more balanced product portfolio and end-market exposure, Eaton will not be as susceptible to a trucking downturn as it has been in prior periods.

The automotive business has historically been the most profitable segment, but it too will face some headwinds over the near term. The auto market has been weakening over the past several years and is expected to be down again this year. Despite the operating hurdles facing its legacy automotive and truck businesses, we think Eaton will achieve earnings growth in both 2006 and 2007, validating the success of its diversification strategy.

Data as of 12-29-06

Eaton Vance EV

	Rating	Fair Value	Last Close	Consider Buy	Consider Sell	Yield %
	★★★	$33.00	$33.01	$25.40	$41.30	1.27

Industry	Business Risk	Moat Size	Investment Style	Sector
Money Mgmt.	Average	Wide	Mid Growth	Financial Services

Company Profile
Eaton Vance creates, markets, and manages investment assets. Once known for municipal-bond products, the firm now specializes in managing a broad array of tax-managed funds and separate accounts. Eaton Vance is the largest manager of bank-loan funds, exchange funds, and tax-managed equity funds.

Competition	Market Cap $Mil	12 Mo Trailing Sales $Mil	Price/Cash Flow	Return On Assets%	Debt/ Equity	Total Return% 1 Yr	Total Return% 3 Yr
Eaton Vance	4,194	832	—	24.9	—	22.5	23.4
Franklin Resources	27,932	5,051	—	13.3	—	17.8	30.3
Blackrock	17,686	1,449	—	1.3	—	41.8	43.1

Price Volatility — Monthly Price High/Low — Relative Strength to S&P 500

Annual $Price High/Low	19.61/13.25	20.50/11.28	18.75/11.51	26.20/16.39	28.16/21.90	33.51/23.83
	2001	2002	2003	2004	2005	2006
Annual Total Return %	11.1	-19.8	31.3	44.4	6.4	22.5

Fiscal Year-End: October

	2001	2002	2003	2004	2005	TTM
Revenue $Mil	503	523	523	662	753	832
Net Income $Mil	116	121	106	139	160	180
Earnings Per Share $	0.80	0.85	0.75	0.99	1.13	1.29
Shares Outstanding Mil	137	138	138	135	132	127
Return on Equity %	38.5	32.5	25.5	30.9	35.1	36.1
Net Margin %	23.1	23.1	20.3	21.0	21.2	21.6
Asset Turnover	0.7	0.8	0.8	0.9	1.1	1.2
Financial Leverage	2.2	1.7	1.6	1.7	1.5	1.5

Management — Stewardship Grade [B]
Chairman and CEO James Hawkes has changed Eaton Vance from a stodgy bond shop into a well-diversified asset manager in an attractive niche. The former aerospace engineer says the transition wasn't rocket science, but it looks smart in retrospect; Eaton Vance has outperformed all of its rivals, in terms of total return to shareholders, over the past five and 10 years. Hawkes began his career with Eaton Vance in the 1970s and came up through the ranks. In January 2006, chief investment officer Thomas Faust was formally named as heir apparent to Hawkes. Eaton Vance's retirement policy requires Hawkes to step down Oct. 31, 2007. Faust will have big shoes to fill as Hawkes has had a truly remarkable tenure at the firm. Both men are part of a small group of company executives that owns 100% of the voting shares. Eaton Vance has an excellent record of responsible governance, but the fact that shareholders essentially have no voice leaves open the possibility that management could abuse its power. The company distributes options liberally, to the tune of 3.8% of shares in 2005.

Valuation Ratios	Stock	Rel to Industry	Rel to S&P 500
Price/Earnings	25.6	0.8	1.2
Price/Book	8.4	2.0	2.0
Price/Sales	5.0	0.8	1.7
Price/Cash Flow	—	—	—

Major Fund Holders	% of Fund Assets
Phoenix Small-Mid Cap X	4.86
Jennison Financial Services A	4.03
Dividend Growth Trust Rising Div Grwth A	2.87
Baird MidCap Inst	2.83

Thesis By Rachel Barnard, Ph.D., 11-22-06 Stock Price as of Analysis: $31.65

With its recent performance, Eaton Vance has put to bed any doubt that it can bring in new assets without offering closed-end funds.

Eaton Vance raised $3 billion in 2004 and $4.6 billion in fiscal 2005 by rolling out closed-end funds, which raise money up front and then trade on an exchange. Unlike open-end funds, investors cannot sell their shares back to Eaton Vance, meaning that the firm keeps managing all the assets it has raised. Recent closed-end fund offerings include municipal-bond funds, bank-loan funds, and high-income equity funds.

Though its other products have taken a backseat in recent years, they have made up almost 100% of net new sales in the past year, proving that Eaton Vance has plenty of popular products to sell even without closed-end funds. The firm continues to raise new money in open-end funds, retail managed accounts, and institutional separate accounts. Municipal-bond funds, a core strength for the firm, have been selling well as retail investors have shown interest in fixed-income products with longer durations.

The firm is making progress toward its goal of being a leader in tax-efficient managed accounts for wealthy investors. These accounts allow investors to own a basket of securities--much like a mutual fund--but instead of owning shares in a fund, investors own the individual securities. This allows a small degree of customization and can also minimize tax liabilities. Plus, it offers a certain cachet for wealthy investors who like exclusive products. Eaton Vance now manages $9.5 billion in these accounts. This has been a growth area in money management, and Eaton Vance already has a considerable presence in the market. Parametric Portfolio Associates, acquired in 2003, gives it further capabilities to manage customized accounts in a tax-efficient way.

Eaton Vance has also recently completed a significant buildout of its institutional salesforce. It should be able to leverage its long records in numerous products, including bank-loan funds, to build more institutional sales. This could come in handy now that the demand for closed-end funds has died down and institutional sales have been weak.

The firm paid off all of its remaining debt in August. For the time being, it plans to keep its balance sheet debt-free in case any juicy acquisition opportunities come its way. We think this is a wise move, as Eaton Vance's record of sensible and well-priced acquisitions gives us confidence that the firm will use its dry powder wisely.

255 State Street, Boston, MA 02109 www.eatonvance.com

Growth [B]	2002	2003	2004	2005
Revenue %	4.1	0.0	26.5	13.8
Earnings/Share %	6.3	-11.8	32.0	14.1
Book Value/Share %	25.9	12.5	8.9	0.4
Dividends/Share %	17.9	34.3	37.5	-12.7

Profitability [A+]	2003	2004	2005	TTM
Return on Assets %	16.1	18.7	22.8	24.9
Oper Cash Flow $Mil	44	117	108	—
- Cap Spending $Mil	1	4	3	—
= Free Cash Flow $Mil	—	—	—	—

Financial Health [NA]	2003	2004	2005	07-31-06
Long-term Debt $Mil	—	—	—	—
Total Equity $Mil	416	450	455	497
Debt/Equity Ratio	—	—	—	—

Data as of 12-29-06

eBay EBAY

	Rating	Fair Value	Last Close	Consider Buy	Consider Sell	Yield %
	★★★★★	$45.00	$30.07	$38.30	$59.10	0.00

Company Profile

EBay provides an online trading platform for buyers and sellers of a wide variety of items, such as used cars, consumer electronics, computers, clothing, and books. The firm has a presence in 33 markets, including the U.S., Germany, the U.K., France, Italy, Korea, and China. EBay has more than 210 million users, including nearly 80 million active users. The company also has an online payment service, PayPal, and an Internet communications business, Skype.

Industry	Business Risk	Moat Size	Investment Style	Sector
Online Retail	Below Avg	Wide	Large Growth	Consumer Services

Competition

	Market Cap $Mil	12 Mo Trailing Sales $Mil	Price/Cash Flow	Return On Assets%	Debt/ Equity	Total Return% 1 Yr	3 Yr
eBay	41,921	5,579	19.5	7.9	—	-30.4	-1.5
Google	140,979	9,319	42.4	15.4	0.0	11.0	—
Yahoo	34,740	6,224	20.6	11.0	0.1	-34.8	4.0

Management   Stewardship Grade [B]

Meg Whitman has been president and CEO since February 1998, successfully leading eBay through the dot-com boom, bust, and recovery. At the height of the boom, she boldly pledged that the company would achieve $3 billion in revenue by 2005 (compared with just $431 million in sales in 2000); eBay achieved the target a year early. In 2005, Whitman was paid a reasonable $2.7 million in salary and bonus. She also received 550,000 options and more than $400,000 in perks, including personal use of the corporate aircraft. We like that executive officers and directors are required to hold a multiple of their annual base salary or retainer in eBay stock (5 times in the case of the CEO). Management and the board beneficially own about 18% of the stock, including a 14% stake for chairman and founder Pierre Omidyar and 2% for Whitman. These executives and directors have a decent record of doing right by shareholders, including providing excellent disclosure. We do, however, take a dim view of the staggered board elections and executives' personal use of the company aircraft. We also frown on the sizable option compensation in recent years, which diluted shareholders' ownership. However, the top five executives received just 7% of the option grants in 2005.

2145 Hamilton Avenue
San Jose, CA 95125
www.ebay.com

Price Volatility

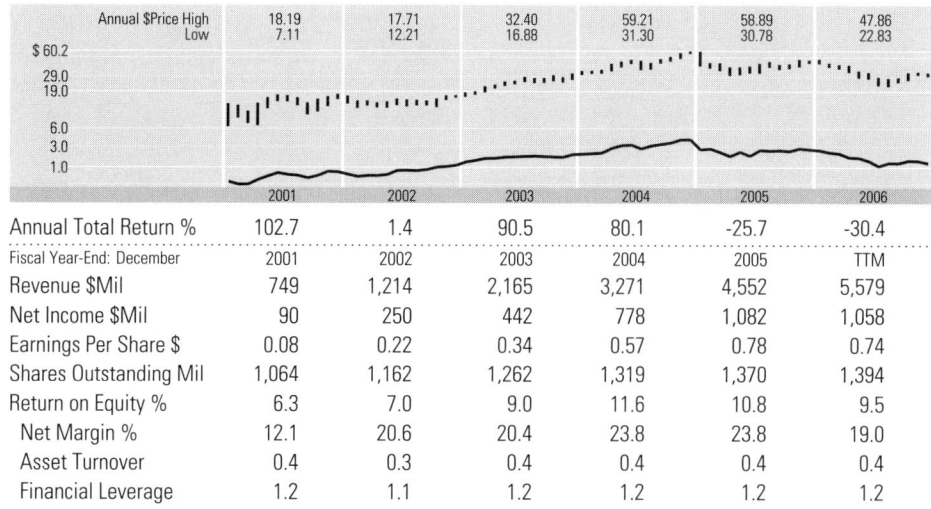

	2001	2002	2003	2004	2005	2006/TTM
Annual $Price High	18.19	17.71	32.40	59.21	58.89	47.86
Low	7.11	12.21	16.88	31.30	30.78	22.83
Annual Total Return %	102.7	1.4	90.5	80.1	-25.7	-30.4

Fiscal Year-End: December

	2001	2002	2003	2004	2005	TTM
Revenue $Mil	749	1,214	2,165	3,271	4,552	5,579
Net Income $Mil	90	250	442	778	1,082	1,058
Earnings Per Share $	0.08	0.22	0.34	0.57	0.78	0.74
Shares Outstanding Mil	1,064	1,162	1,262	1,319	1,370	1,394
Return on Equity %	6.3	7.0	9.0	11.6	10.8	9.5
Net Margin %	12.1	20.6	20.4	23.8	23.8	19.0
Asset Turnover	0.4	0.3	0.4	0.4	0.4	0.4
Financial Leverage	1.2	1.1	1.2	1.2	1.2	1.2

Valuation Ratios	Stock	Rel to Industry	Rel to S&P 500
Price/Earnings	40.6	0.9	2.0
Price/Book	3.8	0.2	0.9
Price/Sales	7.5	1.6	2.6
Price/Cash Flow	19.5	1.0	1.3

Major Fund Holders	% of Fund Assets
Fidelity Advisor Growth Opport T	8.50
Delaware Select Growth A	6.34
Delaware Pooled All-Cap Growth Equity	6.25
ProFunds Internet UltraSector Inv	5.87

Growth [A]	2002	2003	2004	2005
Revenue %	62.1	78.3	51.1	39.2
Earnings/Share %	168.8	58.1	67.6	36.8
Book Value/Share %	142.3	23.2	30.8	47.0
Dividends/Share %	NMF	NMF	NMF	NMF

Profitability [B+]	2003	2004	2005	TTM
Return on Assets %	7.6	9.7	9.2	7.9
Oper Cash Flow $Mil	874	1,285	2,010	2,148
- Cap Spending $Mil	365	293	338	517
= Free Cash Flow $Mil	509	992	1,672	1,631

Financial Health [A+]	2003	2004	2005	09-30-06
Long-term Debt $Mil	124	—	—	—
Total Equity $Mil	4,896	6,728	10,048	11,103
Debt/Equity Ratio	0.0	—	—	—

Thesis By John Owens, CFA, CPA, 11-22-06   Stock Price as of Analysis: $33.87

With a strong network of users, continued innovation, and strategic alliances, eBay has built a very wide moat. The company has ample opportunity to expand overseas, but faces tough competition in Asia. We believe PayPal has excellent prospects, while the acquisition of Skype might just pay off.

EBay benefits from a powerful network effect. As more buyers and sellers transact in its marketplace, the network becomes more valuable. Today, the 11-year-old firm boasts more than 210 million users. Tapping into this demand, sellers listed more than 1.9 billion items on eBay in 2005, which led to $44.3 billion in gross merchandise volume.

New features and formats, including Buy It Now and eBay stores, have also contributed to the company's success. The recently launched eBay Express, which offers a faster and easier way to shop for newer fixed-price items, could further boost sales. Its initial results have been encouraging, with buyers who have shopped at both eBay.com and Express spending nearly 25% more than those who have yet to try Express. Partnerships with Yahoo in the United States and Google abroad could also open the door for eBay to generate more advertising revenue.

Overseas expansion is another strategic priority. Led by dominant positions in the United Kingdom and Germany, international marketplaces now represent about 36% of eBay's revenue. Yet, the company has been losing market share in South Korea to Gmarket and has fallen a tad behind Alibaba's Taobao in China (both are part owned by Yahoo). Its loss to Yahoo in Japan shows that eBay isn't unbeatable.

Perhaps the company's greatest opportunity lies with PayPal. The online payment service has secured more than 120 million accounts, and the volume of payments through its system totaled $27.5 billion in 2005. While the business has significant scope to strengthen its penetration on eBay, its addressable market off eBay is about 10 times larger.

Management hopes Skype, acquired in 2005, will be another success. The Internet communications company, which has gained more than 130 million users in under three years, is experiencing rapid growth but is incurring significant startup losses as management focuses on expanding the network. Over time, we believe the business should generate more meaningful revenue and profits from SkypeIn and SkypeOut (calls to and from landlines and mobiles), voice mail and other services, and hardware loyalties. Skype could also help to accelerate sales on eBay and to monetize the lead-generation businesses, like Shopping.com and Rent.com.

© 2007 Morningstar, Inc. All rights reserved. Intended for United States residents only, this report is for information purposes and should not be considered a solicitation to buy or sell any security. Download your free reports at http://www.morningstar.com/goto/2007Stocks500

EchoStar Communications DISH

	Rating	Fair Value	Last Close	Consider Buy	Consider Sell	Yield %
	★★	$33.00	$38.03	$25.40	$41.30	0.00

Industry	Business Risk	Moat Size	Investment Style	Sector
Cable TV	Average	Narrow	Large Growth	Media

Company Profile
Providing satellite television service generates about 95% of EchoStar's revenue. The company serves about 12.8 million customers, offering more than 2,000 television and audio channels, including local channels in about 170 markets. This service is provided via the firm's network of 11 owned and three leased satellites. The remainder of the firm's business is primarily selling set-top boxes.

Competition

	Market Cap $Mil	12 Mo Trailing Sales $Mil	Price/Cash Flow	Return On Assets%	Debt/ Equity	Total Return% 1 Yr	3 Yr
EchoStar Communications	16,923	9,398	8.0	6.3	NMF	39.9	4.8
Comcast A	88,095	24,531	14.4	2.1	0.6	63.3	8.7
Time Warner	86,932	44,532	14.4	4.9	0.5	26.4	6.8

Management   Stewardship Grade [B]
CEO Charlie Ergen, his wife, Cantey Ergen, and executive vice president James DeFranco founded EchoStar in 1980 and sit on the 10-member board. The Ergens, directly and via family trusts, own more than half the company, including all the supervoting Class B shares, giving them 92% voting control (73% excluding the trusts). We aren't fans of supervoting share classes, and this is the biggest factor weighing on our Stewardship Grade. However, the Ergens have based most of their prosperity on increasing the value of EchoStar stock. Charlie Ergen has received a modest base salary and no bonus in recent years. EchoStar doesn't pay executives large base salaries and has rarely awarded top executives bonuses. The firm recently instituted a cash bonus program, but maximum bonuses are equal to base salaries. EchoStar has historically not issued many options, and a big chunk of past grants don't vest unless the firm achieves certain long-term targets. This compensation system lends credence to comments the CEO regularly makes regarding the importance of return on investment. Option issuance was heavier in 2005 and 2004 than in the past, though still within reason. However, 9% of the 2005 grant and 20% of the 2004 grant went to Charlie Ergen. This concentration seems odd, given his existing stake in the company.

9601 South Meridian Boulevard   www.echostar.com
Englewood, CO 80112

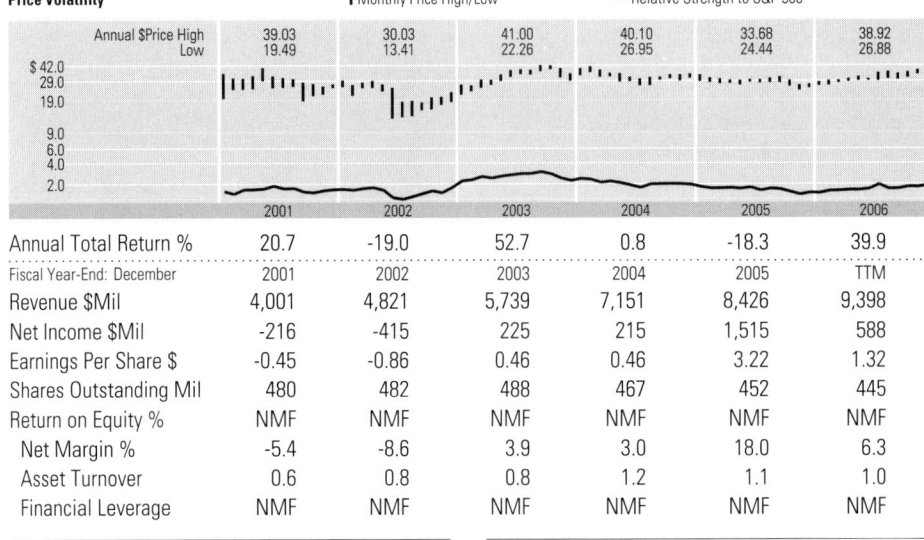

Price Volatility

Fiscal Year-End: December	2001	2002	2003	2004	2005	TTM
Annual Total Return %	20.7	-19.0	52.7	0.8	-18.3	39.9
Revenue $Mil	4,001	4,821	5,739	7,151	8,426	9,398
Net Income $Mil	-216	-415	225	215	1,515	588
Earnings Per Share $	-0.45	-0.86	0.46	0.46	3.22	1.32
Shares Outstanding Mil	480	482	488	467	452	445
Return on Equity %	NMF	NMF	NMF	NMF	NMF	NMF
Net Margin %	-5.4	-8.6	3.9	3.0	18.0	6.3
Asset Turnover	0.6	0.8	0.8	1.2	1.1	1.0
Financial Leverage	NMF	NMF	NMF	NMF	NMF	NMF

Valuation Ratios	Stock	Rel to Industry	Rel to S&P 500
Price/Earnings	28.8	0.8	1.4
Price/Book	—	—	—
Price/Sales	1.8	0.5	0.6
Price/Cash Flow	8.0	0.5	0.5

Major Fund Holders	% of Fund Assets
Fairholme	9.60
Fidelity Select Defense & Aerospace	5.92
Nicholas Liberty	4.33
Black Pearl Focus	3.78

Growth [A]

	2002	2003	2004	2005
Revenue %	20.5	19.1	24.6	17.8
Earnings/Share %	NMF	NMF	0.0	600.0
Book Value/Share %	NMF	NMF	NMF	NMF
Dividends/Share %	NMF	NMF	NMF	NMF

Profitability [B]

	2003	2004	2005	TTM
Return on Assets %	3.0	3.6	20.4	6.3
Oper Cash Flow $Mil	576	1,001	1,774	2,111
- Cap Spending $Mil	322	981	1,506	1,543
= Free Cash Flow $Mil	254	21	268	568

Financial Health [B]

	2003	2004	2005	09-30-06
Long-term Debt $Mil	5,499	6,036	6,127	7,221
Total Equity $Mil	-1,033	-2,078	-867	-365
Debt/Equity Ratio	ELB	ELB	ELB	NMF

Thesis   By Michael Hodel, CFA, 11-14-06   Stock Price as of Analysis: $36.28

With little exception, EchoStar has run a steady business over the years, focusing on costs and carving out a niche as the price leader in pay television. Though the industry continues to evolve, we believe EchoStar will remain a strong competitor.

The hallmark of EchoStar's management team is a focus on return on investment and the related attention paid to costs. The two biggest costs of providing TV service are fees paid to cable networks and equipment that goes in customers' homes. EchoStar has taken a hard line with cable networks in negotiations, and it isn't afraid to drop channels for a time to boost its position. A growing customer base gives the firm increased leverage over content suppliers. To help reduce the cost of equipment in customers' homes, EchoStar pioneered a leasing plan, recently mimicked by rival DirecTV, to recapture equipment after a customer discontinues service. We think this cost focus gives the firm an enduring advantage in serving many customers.

EchoStar already generates strong returns on capital, by our calculation, and we expect profitability to continue increasing as the business matures. Management hasn't been afraid to sacrifice profits today for longer-term gain. For example, it sharply increased advertising recently, which, combined with a few modest missteps at DirecTV, has allowed EchoStar to gain market share. The firm has also increased spending on customer service, pressuring margins but helping to retain subscribers. Holding on to customers is critical to profitability, given the high cost of adding new ones, so this effort should benefit the firm.

Increasing competition remains the biggest threat to EchoStar, in our view. Cable firms have turned their attention to improving the quality of their video service while adding Internet access and phone service. As a result, cable companies in aggregate are holding on to customers better than they were a couple of years ago. Arguably the biggest change is the entrance of a handful of phone companies into the TV business. We don't believe this will have a huge impact on EchoStar, though. AT&T and Verizon, the nation's largest phone companies, plan to offer the service to only about half their customers, rolled out over the next few years. Satellite will probably remain the only alternative to cable--or the only option at all--for a large chunk of the country for some time. We expect EchoStar will continue to run a tight ship, allowing it to maintain its appeal to more price-sensitive customers.

Data as of 12-29-06

Ecolab ECL

Rating	Fair Value	Last Close	Consider Buy	Consider Sell	Yield %
★★★★	$50.00	$45.20	$42.60	$65.60	0.92

Company Profile

Ecolab produces and sells cleaning products and services to institutional, hospitality, and industrial customers. The company's products include detergent, vehicle-care, and pest-elimination products, among others. Ecolab's major customers are restaurants, hotels, hospitals, and schools. The firm has a strong international presence: Almost half of its revenue comes from abroad.

Management   Stewardship Grade [C]

Douglas Baker took over as chairman and CEO after Al Schuman retired in July 2004. Though we're disappointed that Ecolab is not keeping the CEO and chairman roles separate, we have confidence in Baker's ability to lead Ecolab. Baker joined the company 16 years ago and most recently served as COO. We are not big fans of Ecolab's compensation policies, which include performance bonuses based on easily manipulated numbers like earnings per share. That said, executive pay is reasonable, with Baker earning an annual salary of $700,000. We also give management credit for its ability to create economic profits. For example, Ecolab has booked an impressive 11-year streak of returns on equity of more than 20%. We like that directors and officers collectively own 2.4% of total shares outstanding, as of the firm's last proxy filing. We view the board's staggered structure as a slight negative, but we like that each director's $135,000 annual salary is paid through a combination of cash and company stock.

370 Wabasha Street North   www.ecolab.com
St. Paul, MN 55102-1390

Growth [C]	2002	2003	2004	2005
Revenue %	46.7	10.5	11.2	8.4
Earnings/Share %	4.2	32.0	10.1	12.8
Book Value/Share %	39.5	17.3	22.8	3.0
Dividends/Share %	4.8	8.2	10.1	10.7

Profitability [A]	2003	2004	2005	TTM
Return on Assets %	8.1	7.6	8.4	8.8
Oper Cash Flow $Mil	524	571	590	573
- Cap Spending $Mil	212	276	269	284
= Free Cash Flow $Mil	312	295	321	288

Financial Health [A]	2003	2004	2005	09-30-06
Long-term Debt $Mil	604	645	519	543
Total Equity $Mil	1,321	1,598	1,649	1,763
Debt/Equity Ratio	0.5	0.4	0.3	0.3

Industry	Business Risk	Moat Size	Investment Style	Sector
Chemicals	Below Avg	Narrow	Large Growth	Industrial Materials

Competition

	Market Cap $Mil	12 Mo Trailing Sales $Mil	Price/Cash Flow	Return On Assets %	Debt/Equity	Total Return % 1 Yr	3 Yr
Ecolab	11,352	4,766	19.8	8.8	0.3	25.9	19.9
Procter & Gamble	203,656	72,214	16.8	6.8	0.6	13.4	11.3
Clorox	9,739	4,701	13.6	12.6	NMF	14.9	12.6

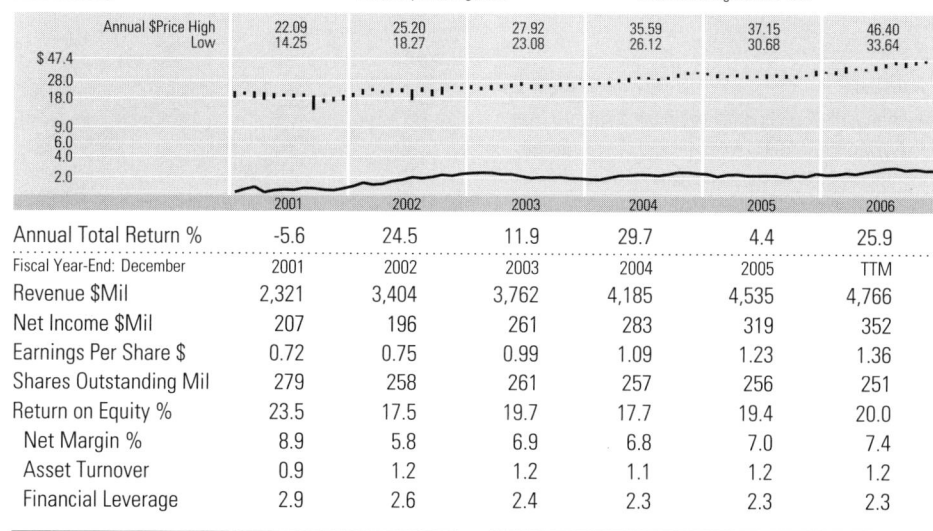

Price Volatility — Monthly Price High/Low — Relative Strength to S&P 500

	2001	2002	2003	2004	2005	2006
Annual $Price High	22.09	25.20	27.92	35.59	37.15	46.40
Low	14.25	18.27	23.08	26.12	30.68	33.64
Annual Total Return %	-5.6	24.5	11.9	29.7	4.4	25.9

Fiscal Year-End: December	2001	2002	2003	2004	2005	TTM
Revenue $Mil	2,321	3,404	3,762	4,185	4,535	4,766
Net Income $Mil	207	196	261	283	319	352
Earnings Per Share $	0.72	0.75	0.99	1.09	1.23	1.36
Shares Outstanding Mil	279	258	261	257	256	251
Return on Equity %	23.5	17.5	19.7	17.7	19.4	20.0
Net Margin %	8.9	5.8	6.9	6.8	7.0	7.4
Asset Turnover	0.9	1.2	1.2	1.1	1.2	1.2
Financial Leverage	2.9	2.6	2.4	2.3	2.3	2.3

Valuation Ratios	Stock	Rel to Industry	Rel to S&P 500
Price/Earnings	33.2	1.8	1.6
Price/Book	6.4	1.9	1.6
Price/Sales	2.4	1.4	0.8
Price/Cash Flow	19.8	1.3	1.4

Major Fund Holders	% of Fund Assets
Fidelity Select Environmental	7.71
Mairs & Power Growth	3.54
Jensen J	3.26
Badgley Growth	3.01

Thesis By Ben Johnson, 12-12-06 Stock Price as of Analysis: $45.17

Ecolab mops the floor with its competition in the industrial and institutional cleaning and sanitation business. We think this narrow-moat firm will continue to earn attractive returns for years to come.

Ecolab's primary advantage is scale. The firm generated $4.5 billion in sales in 2005, or 11% of the $39 billion worldwide industrial and institutional market. Its next-closest rival, JohnsonDiversey, had sales of $3 billion in 2005, and early in 2006 announced that it would no longer provide direct service to its customers. This leaves Ecolab as the lone provider with the scale and the breadth of service offerings to effectively serve the largest players in the restaurant and hospitality industry.

The company's salesforce provides some serious muscle. This is a motivated bunch, with many salespeople earning as much as 75% of their annual compensation in the form of variable pay. These reps make monthly stops at each client site to ensure that the company's products are working correctly and being used properly. This high-touch service is extremely valuable to customers who typically lack the time to train personnel and monitor and repair their equipment. From Ecolab's perspective, these visits allow its people to be the first responders to any client issues, providing the chance to capitalize on incremental revenue opportunities.

Ecolab's customer retention rate hovers around 90%. This speaks not only to the firm's outstanding service, but also to its admirable business model. Many of the company's products are consumables that could be easily purchased from any number of manufacturers. Where it sets itself apart is by providing its customers with specialized dispensing and application equipment that is only compatible with Ecolab-branded consumables. This makes for more-efficient use of consumables by the customer and, importantly, creates substantial switching costs.

Ecolab's overseas operations are a bit rougher around the edges. The firm's international salespeople are not quite as eager as their U.S.-based colleagues and have a more limited menu of service offerings to present to their clients. Also, differences in regulations and conventions between countries make managing the number of stock-keeping units in the overseas catalog extremely difficult. However, an ongoing effort to rationalize SKU counts, more vigorous training of the salesforce, and a growing service offering should bring the performance of the firm's foreign operations in line with those at home.

Data as of 12-29-06

Educate EEEE

Rating	Fair Value	Last Close	Consider Buy	Consider Sell	Yield %
★★★	$8.00	$7.12	$6.20	$10.00	0.00

Industry	Business Risk	Moat Size	Investment Style	Sector
Education	Average	Narrow	Small Core	Consumer Services

Company Profile

Educate owns the Sylvan Learning and Hooked on Phonics brands. In the United States, Educate operates about 250 learning centers in about 180 territories while its franchisees operate another 880 in 730 territories. Educate also provides tutoring services to special-needs students and has more than 1,000 owned or franchised tutoring centers (Schulerhilfe) in Europe. The company is based in Baltimore.

Competition

	Market Cap $Mil	12 Mo Trailing Sales $Mil	Price/Cash Flow	Return On Assets%	Debt/ Equity	Total Return% 1 Yr	3 Yr
Educate	306	353	140.6	-1.2	0.0	-39.7	—
Washington Post Co	7,167	3,813	13.1	6.9	0.1	-1.5	-1.0
Princeton Review	146	136	19.4	-6.5	0.0	2.5	-18.7

Management Stewardship Grade [C]

Chairman and CEO Christopher Hoehn-Saric has been with Sylvan since 1991, when he and board member Doug Becker merged their company--KEE Systems--into Sylvan. At the time, Hoehn-Saric was 30 and Becker was 25, and each had already made millions by selling a technology-related business they started years earlier. Both Hoehn-Saric and Becker are entrepreneurs by nature and have made lots of money and overseen fantastic growth wherever they've gone. Their aggressiveness and vision have sometimes resulted in their getting ahead of the market. Not content with gradually expanding what was a very good tutoring business, the two eventually added international secondary institutions, an online testing business, and a large venture-investing fund to Sylvan's portfolio of assets. In 2003, Hoehn-Saric and Becker split the company in two, with Becker leaving Sylvan to oversee the higher-education assets (Laureate Education) and Hoehn-Saric assuming the helm of the newly formed Educate. Management has had some significant missteps recently, and we're watching closely to see if it can right the ship quickly. Further missteps could shake our faith in management and prompt us to raise our required margin of safety.

1001 Fleet Street
Baltimore, MD 21202
www.educate-inc.com

Price Volatility

	2001	2002	2003	2004	2005	2006
Annual $Price High				14.09	17.11	13.47
Low				11.10	9.96	5.06
Annual Total Return %	—	—	—	—	-10.9	-39.7

Fiscal Year-End: December

	2001	2002	2003	2004	2005	TTM
Revenue $Mil	181	216	236	273	330	353
Net Income $Mil	—	—	—	6	15	-6
Earnings Per Share $	—	—	—	—	0.35	-0.14
Shares Outstanding Mil	—	—	—	—	43	43
Return on Equity %	NMF	NMF	NMF	3.2	7.3	-2.6
Net Margin %	—	—	—	2.3	4.7	-1.6
Asset Turnover	1.7	1.6	0.7	0.7	0.7	0.8
Financial Leverage	—	—	—	1.9	2.1	2.2

Valuation Ratios

	Stock	Rel to Industry	Rel to S&P 500
Price/Earnings	NMF	—	—
Price/Book	1.4	0.1	0.3
Price/Sales	0.9	0.1	0.3
Price/Cash Flow	140.6	9.2	9.6

Major Fund Holders

	% of Fund Assets
AIM Trimark Small Companies A	2.75
Buffalo Micro Cap	2.24
Calvert Small Cap Value A	1.58

Growth [B]

	2002	2003	2004	2005
Revenue %	19.2	8.9	15.9	21.0
Earnings/Share %	NMF	NMF	NMF	NMF
Book Value/Share %	—	—	—	NMF
Dividends/Share %	NMF	NMF	NMF	NMF

Profitability [NA]

	2003	2004	2005	TTM
Return on Assets %	—	1.7	3.4	-1.2
Oper Cash Flow $Mil	7	24	11	2
- Cap Spending $Mil	4	5	12	13
= Free Cash Flow $Mil	3	19	-2	-11

Financial Health [NA]

	2003	2004	2005	06-30-06
Long-term Debt $Mil	—	120	160	2
Total Equity $Mil	—	198	212	214
Debt/Equity Ratio	—	0.6	0.8	0.0

Thesis By Jonathan Schrader, CFA, 10-27-06 Stock Price as of Analysis: $7.64

Educate owns two of the best-known brands in K-12 education: Sylvan Learning and Hooked on Phonics. Educate has traditionally exploited the Sylvan brand by franchising territories to third parties. Franchisees had to pay an up-front fee and purchase curriculum and other supplies from Educate, but most revenue came from a very high-margin royalty stream of 8%. The more franchisees Sylvan had, the higher its royalty stream.

Recently, Educate altered its business model; much growth now comes from acquiring existing franchisees and building company-owned learning centers. First, by acquiring existing territories, Educate can book all the revenue earned in those territories, not just the 8% royalty. This is an immediate, big boost to Educate's top line.

Educate's sales also get a boost for two to three years after an acquisition. The franchised territories that Educate buys, on average, produce about $530,000 in sales annually, while Educate-owned territories generate $860,000 annually. After buying formerly franchised territories, Educate introduces best practices--longer hours and weekend openings, for example--that typically move revenue up toward the level of company-owned territories.

There is more to Educate than Sylvan Learning, though. The company recently purchased the Hooked on Phonics brand, long known for its television infomercials. Educate has shelved the infomercials and plans to make Hooked on Phonics the focus of an aggressive push into the consumer product market. Educate's strategy includes distribution through major retailers like Wal-Mart, Amazon.com, and Toys 'R' Us. The market for these products could be significant, especially given Educate's plan to use the "Hooked on" name for math, foreign language, and other nonreading subjects. The risk is that in building the consumer product business--with which the firm has little previous experience--Educate's management loses focus. We've already seen evidence of this in the first half of 2006.

Despite recent struggles, we like Educate's prospects. There are still more than 700 franchised territories that the company could eventually acquire--it owned just 178 as of March--and Educate thinks there is a possibility for 1,000 more territories in North America. Monetizing the well-known but still small Hooked on Phonics brand could provide another lucrative income stream in the coming years.

Data as of 12-29-06

Electronic Arts ERTS

	Rating	Fair Value	Last Close	Consider Buy	Consider Sell	Yield %
	★★★★	$61.00	$50.36	$47.00	$76.40	0.00

Company Profile
Electronic Arts creates and distributes interactive entertainment software for a variety of hardware platforms, including PC, PlayStation, Xbox, and Nintendo systems. During fiscal 2005, the firm published 32 new internally developed titles and co-published an additional 11 new titles. EA generates about half its revenue internationally.

Management
Stewardship Grade [B]

Chairman and CEO Lawrence Probst has been with Electronic Arts since 1984 and has served as CEO since 1991. V. Paul Lee started with the firm in 1991 and was named president in 2005. Management has a great record of generating returns well in excess of the firm's cost of capital. Over the past eight years, EA's return on invested capital has averaged 45%. Executive compensation appears reasonable, and bonuses are tied to performance. Probst and several senior executives did not receive an incentive bonus in fiscal 2005 as certain targets were not met. EA's Stewardship Grade is bolstered by the lack of a poison pill, a nonstaggered board of directors, and meaningful stock ownership by the CEO. Hurting EA's grade are generous annual option grants, which have averaged more than 3% of total shares outstanding over the past three years.

209 Redwood Shores Parkway www.ea.com
Redwood City, CA 94065-1175

Growth [C]	2003	2004	2005	2006
Revenue %	43.9	19.1	5.8	-5.7
Earnings/Share %	208.6	73.1	-15.0	-52.8
Book Value/Share %	42.6	42.7	27.1	-1.9
Dividends/Share %	NMF	NMF	NMF	NMF

Profitability [A]	2004	2005	2006	TTM
Return on Assets %	16.7	11.5	5.4	4.1
Oper Cash Flow $Mil	669	634	596	571
- Cap Spending $Mil	90	126	123	153
= Free Cash Flow $Mil	579	508	473	418

Financial Health [A+]	2004	2005	2006	09-30-06
Long-term Debt $Mil	—	—	—	—
Total Equity $Mil	2,678	3,498	3,408	3,591
Debt/Equity Ratio	—	—	—	—

Industry	Business Risk	Moat Size	Investment Style	Sector
Entertain./Ed. Media	Average	Wide	Large Growth	Software

Competition	Market Cap $Mil	12 Mo Trailing Sales $Mil	Price/Cash Flow	Return On Assets%	Debt/Equity	Total Return% 1 Yr	3 Yr
Electronic Arts	15,536	3,107	27.2	4.1	—	-3.7	1.9
Activision	4,834	1,415	124.5	1.9	—	25.5	34.8
THQ	2,092	787	EUB	3.1	—	36.4	41.9

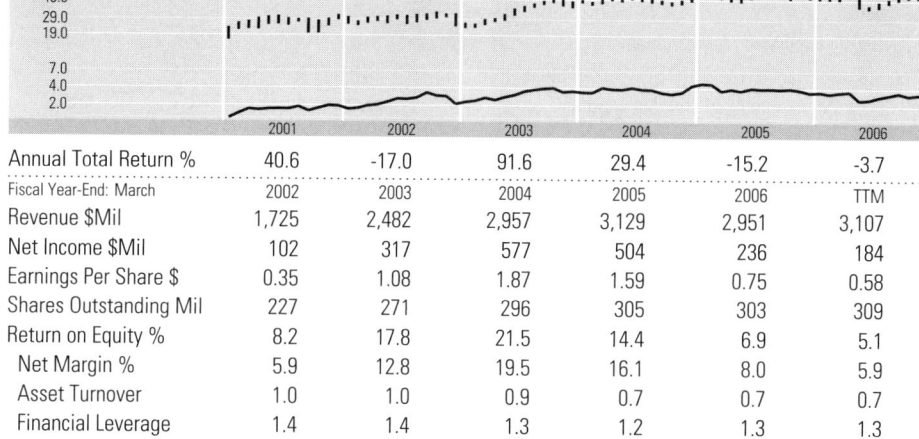

Annual Total Return %	40.6	-17.0	91.6	29.4	-15.2	-3.7

Fiscal Year-End: March	2002	2003	2004	2005	2006	TTM
Revenue $Mil	1,725	2,482	2,957	3,129	2,951	3,107
Net Income $Mil	102	317	577	504	236	184
Earnings Per Share $	0.35	1.08	1.87	1.59	0.75	0.58
Shares Outstanding Mil	227	271	296	305	303	309
Return on Equity %	8.2	17.8	21.5	14.4	6.9	5.1
Net Margin %	5.9	12.8	19.5	16.1	8.0	5.9
Asset Turnover	1.0	1.0	0.9	0.7	0.7	0.7
Financial Leverage	1.4	1.4	1.3	1.2	1.3	1.3

Valuation Ratios	Stock	Rel to Industry	Rel to S&P 500
Price/Earnings	86.8	1.0	4.2
Price/Book	4.3	1.0	1.0
Price/Sales	5.0	1.0	1.7
Price/Cash Flow	27.2	0.6	1.9

Major Fund Holders	% of Fund Assets
AXA Enterprise Large Cap Growth A LW	8.16
Goldman Sachs Tollkeeper A	4.98
BlackRock Global Technology A	4.66
Brown Advisory Opportunity Instl	4.64

Thesis By Norman Young, 11-06-06 Stock Price as of Analysis: $59.25

Electronic Arts' rock-solid balance sheet, healthy free cash flows, and exclusive licenses place the firm in a competitive position that is the envy of rivals.

As the leading video game maker, EA should ride a wave of industry growth as gaming continues to move from a niche market to a mainstream form of entertainment. Industry growth has been impressive, with sales increasing from $3.7 billion in 1996 to $7.3 billion in 2004. We expect this trend to continue as the first generation of gamers enter their 30s armed with more disposable income and a desire to continue gaming. Additionally, we think technological advances like better graphics and faster Internet connections are enticing new customers to consider gaming for the first time.

We think EA also holds many sustainable competitive advantages. The firm is consistently one of the top three providers of games to the console and PC markets, and more recently it has been the market-share leader in the PlayStation 2, Xbox, and PC segments. With the nearest pure-play competitor having one third of EA's sales volume, we believe the firm leverages its size to ensure wide distribution of its titles and to attract the top developers in the industry.

By investing heavily in its products ($2.3 billion was spent on research and development over the past five years) and making exclusive licensing deals with top properties like the NFL, EA has created a significant barrier to entry. The firm's top four franchises each have generated more than $1 billion in cumulative sales, which lands EA squarely on top of the industry's blockbuster lists. EA also has been successful in introducing new games. From 2001 to 2005, the firm has seen its number of platinum titles (games that have sold more than 1 million units) increase to 31 from 13. Activision has the next highest total with 10.

However, the game industry is dogged by cyclicality. Revenue and margins typically take a big hit when the next generation of gaming consoles is introduced, an event that occurs about every five to six years. Game makers are forced to cut prices on old titles, while sales on new games lag until a critical mass of consoles can be sold. EA hopes to avoid the worst of the transition as it continues to produce titles for legacy (PS2, Xbox) and next generation systems concurrently. Because the Xbox 360 was released a year before Sony's PS3 and Nintendo's Wii, EA has been able to develop next generation titles while still catering to the current generation market.

Eli Lilly & Company LLY

Data as of 12-29-06

Rating	Fair Value	Last Close	Consider Buy	Consider Sell	Yield %
★★★★	$61.00	$52.10	$47.00	$76.40	3.07

Industry	Business Risk	Moat Size	Investment Style	Sector
Drugs	Average	Wide	Large Core	Healthcare

Company Profile

Eli Lilly produces pharmaceuticals for human and animal use. Its products include anti-infectives, diabetes-care products, central nervous system drugs, cardiovascular products, and oncolytic drugs. The company's major drugs include schizophrenia drug Zyprexa, osteoporosis medicine Evista, oncology treatment Gemzar, and Humalog insulin for diabetes. Almost half of its sales are to markets outside the United States.

Management — Stewardship Grade [B]

We give Lilly high marks for management and corporate governance. The company has performed well under the leadership of chairman and CEO Sidney Taurel, who has kept the focus on research and away from distracting mergers or controversy. The board is well balanced, with leaders from academia, science, and business. The company requires 75% of its board members to be independent and maintains rigorous procedures for nominating members to its special committees. Incentive compensation is based on well-defined specific performance objectives and includes an economic value-added metric and an aftertax profit measure of capital-allocation efficiency. Only the combined chairman and CEO position keeps us from awarding our top grade for corporate governance.

Lilly Corporate Center
Indianapolis, IN 46285
www.lilly.com

Growth [C]	2002	2003	2004	2005
Revenue %	-4.0	13.6	10.1	5.7
Earnings/Share %	-2.0	-5.2	-30.0	9.0
Book Value/Share %	17.2	18.3	10.8	-1.5
Dividends/Share %	10.7	8.1	6.0	7.0

Profitability [A]	2003	2004	2005	TTM
Return on Assets %	11.8	7.3	8.1	13.5
Oper Cash Flow $Mil	3,647	2,870	1,914	2,933
- Cap Spending $Mil	1,707	1,898	1,298	1,087
= Free Cash Flow $Mil	1,940	971	616	1,845

Financial Health [A]	2003	2004	2005	09-30-06
Long-term Debt $Mil	4,688	4,492	5,764	4,553
Total Equity $Mil	9,765	10,920	10,792	13,055
Debt/Equity Ratio	0.5	0.4	0.5	0.3

Competition

	Market Cap $Mil	12 Mo Trailing Sales $Mil	Price/Cash Flow	Return On Assets %	Debt/Equity	Total Return % 1 Yr	Total Return % 3 Yr
Eli Lilly & Company	58,956	15,325	20.1	13.5	0.3	-5.2	-7.5
Merck	94,656	22,358	13.0	11.6	0.2	42.7	1.7
Bristol-Myers Squibb	51,764	18,720	23.9	8.2	0.7	19.9	0.6

Price Volatility

Annual $Price High Low	95.00 / 70.01	81.09 / 43.90	73.89 / 52.77	76.95 / 50.34	60.98 / 49.47	59.24 / 50.19
	2001	2002	2003	2004	2005	2006
Annual Total Return %	-14.4	-17.6	13.1	-17.6	2.5	-5.2

Fiscal Year-End: December	2001	2002	2003	2004	2005	TTM
Revenue $Mil	11,543	11,078	12,583	13,858	14,645	15,325
Net Income $Mil	2,780	2,708	2,561	1,810	1,980	3,231
Earnings Per Share $	2.55	2.50	2.37	1.66	1.81	2.97
Shares Outstanding Mil	1,078	1,079	1,076	1,084	1,088	1,132
Return on Equity %	39.1	32.7	26.2	16.6	18.3	24.8
Net Margin %	24.1	24.4	20.4	13.1	13.5	21.1
Asset Turnover	0.7	0.6	0.6	0.6	0.6	0.6
Financial Leverage	2.3	2.3	2.2	2.3	2.3	1.8

Valuation Ratios	Stock	Rel to Industry	Rel to S&P 500
Price/Earnings	17.4	0.7	0.8
Price/Book	4.5	0.8	1.1
Price/Sales	3.8	0.9	1.3
Price/Cash Flow	20.1	1.2	1.4

Major Fund Holders	% of Fund Assets
Fidelity Select Pharmaceuticals	5.39
ProFunds Pharmaceuticals UltraSector Inv	5.22
Firsthand Health Sciences	5.00
Touchstone Family Heritage(R) A	4.96

Thesis   By Heather Brilliant, CFA, 12-15-06   Stock Price as of Analysis: $54.52

Eli Lilly's long-term commitment to research and development has helped the company dig a wide economic moat. With a slew of recent product introductions and a solid pipeline in development, the firm should remain a leader in the pharmaceutical industry for years to come.

The past five years have benefited from the strength of Lilly's research capabilities, with nine new products reaching the market over that period. Because of the company's rigorous vetting process, most of these drugs have the potential to generate more than $1 billion in peak annual sales. Recently introduced drugs that are products of Lilly's internal research include Forteo for osteoporosis and Strattera for attention-deficit hyperactivity disorder, both of which meet the company's goals of developing innovative or best-in-class treatments. Lilly has been able to turn out such a large number of products with blockbuster potential because it consistently invests around 20% of sales in R&D, more than the 14%-18% its competitors typically spend to find and develop new drugs.

The company has also turned to external sources of new drugs, namely in-licensing from and partnering with smaller biotechnology firms. A recent example is Byetta, a new treatment for Type 2 diabetes that was developed by Amylin and recently received Food and Drug Administration approval. Byetta is a novel treatment for a disease that affects about 18 million people in the United States alone. Lilly is also working with Alkermes to develop inhalable insulin. These partnerships should help breathe new life into Lilly's leading diabetes franchise.

Lilly's new products constituted almost 20% of 2005 sales and are on track to account for about one fourth of sales in 2006. However, its current products and pipeline are not enough to insulate it from the ills that plague the pharmaceutical industry. As governments around the world place increasing focus on reducing health-care costs, drug companies like Lilly will probably continue to face pressure to lower prices. This could come in the form of direct government intervention or greater pressure from generic competitors, both of which have presented challenges in recent years.

However, Lilly's commitment to R&D has helped it stay on the cutting edge, providing novel or best-in-class treatments for a well-defined group of diseases. While there will be bumps along the way, we think Lilly will remain a top player among pharmaceutical firms.

Data as of 12-29-06

Embarq EQ

	Rating	Fair Value	Last Close	Consider Buy	Consider Sell	Yield %
	★★★	$58.00	$52.56	$44.70	$72.70	1.90

Industry	Business Risk	Moat Size	Investment Style	Sector
Telecom Svcs.	Average	Narrow	Mid Value	Telecommunication

Company Profile

Embarq was spun out of Sprint Nextel in May 2006. The firm provides local phone service to about 7 million lines across 18 states, including several larger markets like Las Vegas and Orlando. In addition to phone service, Embarq serves nearly 1 million high-speed Internet access customers, about 146,000 television customers via a resale agreement with satellite operator EchoStar, and about 25,000 wireless customers via an agreement with Sprint Nextel.

Management   Stewardship Grade [C]

Embarq's management team was put in place during the summer of 2005, primarily with former Sprint executives. Chairman and CEO Daniel Hesse is an exception, though, having joined Sprint Nextel in June 2005 to head the local phone unit. He had served as CEO of AT&T Wireless in the late 1990s and most recently headed Terabeam, a wireless equipment firm. COO Michael Fuller had served as president of the local phone unit for nearly 10 years and had been with Sprint and its predecessor for more than 30 years. We liked Sprint Nextel's stewardship for the most part, with executive compensation our biggest complaint. We have similar concerns at Embarq. Hesse receives a base salary in excess of $900,000 and can receive a bonus of up to $2.3 million. The firm's bonus plan is based in part on revenue and operating income before depreciation and amortization (EBITDA), which can be inflated at the expense of long-term performance and more easily manipulated than other financial measures. Hesse will also receive more than $10 million of restricted stock. In addition, we don't like that the same person holds the CEO and chairman positions. The firm also has several takeover defenses, including a staggered board and poison pill. A takeover is unlikely until at least 2008 for tax reasons.

554 West 110th Street
Overland Park, KS 66211

Growth [D+]	2002	2003	2004	2005
Revenue %	-4.5	-1.5	-0.3	1.9
Earnings/Share %	NMF	NMF	NMF	NMF
Book Value/Share %	—	—	—	—
Dividends/Share %	NMF	NMF	NMF	NMF

Profitability [A]	2003	2004	2005	TTM
Return on Assets %	16.8	9.8	9.5	7.5
Oper Cash Flow $Mil	1,804	2,064	1,904	2,135
- Cap Spending $Mil	1,118	975	828	994
= Free Cash Flow $Mil	686	1,089	1,076	1,141

Financial Health [C+]	2003	2004	2005	09-30-06
Long-term Debt $Mil	—	1,125	1,123	6,506
Total Equity $Mil	4,889	4,960	4,852	-191
Debt/Equity Ratio	—	0.2	0.2	1.3

Competition

	Market Cap $Mil	12 Mo Trailing Sales $Mil	Price/Cash Flow	Return On Assets%	Debt/Equity	Total Return% 1 Yr	3 Yr
Embarq	7,857	6,349	3.7	7.5	1.3	—	—
AT&T	137,384	60,171	9.0	4.9	0.5	51.6	16.3
Verizon Communications	108,723	88,881	4.4	3.7	0.7	34.9	8.0

Price Volatility — Monthly Price High/Low — Relative Strength to S&P 500

Annual $Price High/Low: 53.32 / 38.81

Annual Total Return %	2001	2002	2003	2004	2005	2006
	—	—	—	—	—	—

Fiscal Year-End: December	2001	2002	2003	2004	2005	TTM
Revenue $Mil	6,547	6,250	6,159	6,139	6,254	6,349
Net Income $Mil	—	—	1,554	917	878	745
Earnings Per Share $	—	—	—	—	—	—
Shares Outstanding Mil	—	—	—	—	—	149
Return on Equity %	—	—	31.8	18.5	18.1	15.4
Net Margin %	—	—	25.2	14.9	14.0	11.7
Asset Turnover	0.7	0.7	0.7	0.7	0.7	0.6
Financial Leverage	2.1	2.2	1.9	1.9	1.9	2.0

Valuation Ratios	Stock	Rel to Industry	Rel to S&P 500
Price/Earnings	—	—	—
Price/Book	1.6	0.4	0.4
Price/Sales	1.2	0.5	0.4
Price/Cash Flow	3.7	0.4	0.3

Major Fund Holders	% of Fund Assets
SunAmerica Focused Dividend Strat C	3.27
DWS Communications A	2.79
MFS Mid Cap Value A	2.53
Phoenix Pathfinder A	2.26

Thesis By Michael Hodel, CFA,   Stock Price as of Analysis:

Embarq, the fifth-largest local phone company in the U.S., shares traits of both the larger, more urban regional Bells and smaller rural phone companies. We think this position, coupled with a relatively strong balance sheet and realistic dividend payout, make the firm worth owning.

The distinction between rural and urban markets in the telecom industry is important. Urban markets are likely to have a strong cable competitor and several wireless carriers vying to steal customers. Rural markets are typically much less competitive, but are also more dependent on subsidies and access charges paid by long-distance carriers. A bit more than half of Embarq's customers are located in urban areas, including several rapidly growing markets.

Smaller phone companies typically cite the percentage of customers able to receive phone service from cable companies as a gauge of the level of competition faced. As we would expect, the percentage at Embarq is high--about 55% today and expected to reach somewhere around 80% over time. We aren't impressed with the work the firm has done thus far to counter the competition. Specifically, the firm has been slow to roll out and promote high-speed Internet access service: About one in six Embarq residential phone customers subscribes to the service, well below urban peers, regional Bells like AT&T T, and many rural carriers we follow. We view Internet access as a critical service to increase customer loyalty and help preserve phone revenues.

We expect Embarq to be more competitive as a stand-alone firm, with management focused solely on the local phone business. The firm has done a good job, in our opinion, of planning for the spin-off, getting the brand in place, and sharpening its service offerings. For example, in the business-services market, which we expect to be a source of stability in the future, the firm has pushed its salesforce to focus on smaller businesses rather than the large enterprises Sprint had traditionally targeted. Embarq's ubiquitous networks in the markets it serves should give it a strong advantage in serving smaller customers. Also, we think the firm will have an advantage integrating wireless and fixed-line services thanks to its relationship with Sprint Nextel S.

Thanks to its dominant market position and the relative stability of its more rural markets, Embarq generates strong cash flow. The firm's flexibility to use that cash flow to strengthen the business is much greater than most rural carriers we follow because it enjoys a much stronger balance sheet and has committed to pay a much smaller dividend.

Data as of 12-29-06

EMC EMC

	Rating	Fair Value	Last Close	Consider Buy	Consider Sell	Yield %
	★★★★★	$19.00	$13.20	$14.70	$23.80	0.00

Company Profile

EMC is a leading provider of hardware, software, and services for enterprise network storage. Its legacy was built on leading-edge proprietary storage hardware. Over the past couple of years, the company has increased its focus on its software and services segments, which now generate more than 50% of overall revenue. About 50% of sales are through partners including original-equipment manufacturers and resellers like Dell.

Management   Stewardship Grade [D]

Joe Tucci has been CEO since January 2001. He has also taken over as chairman of the board, replacing Michael Ruettgers, who was CEO from 1992 to 2001 and had also served as chairman or executive chairman since 2001. David Goulden took over as CFO from Bill Teuber, who was promoted to vice chairman in 2006. We believe that Tucci and the rest of the management team are talented leaders; however, we have several concerns with respect to overall stewardship and corporate governance. EMC has leased real estate from a management company that is beneficially owned by John Egan, a director of the company. Egan is also related to another board member, Paul Fitzgerald. Additionally, several employees are related to Egan or the management team. While we have no reason to believe that the board of directors' and management's interests are misaligned with shareholders', we think the company could make several strides toward improving overall corporate governance.

176 South Street   www.emc.com
Hopkinton, MA 01748

Growth [B]	2002	2003	2004	2005
Revenue %	-23.3	14.7	32.0	17.4
Earnings/Share %	NMF	NMF	63.6	30.6
Book Value/Share %	-11.6	58.6	-1.3	5.1
Dividends/Share %	NMF	NMF	NMF	NMF

Profitability [B]	2003	2004	2005	TTM
Return on Assets %	3.5	5.6	6.7	5.4
Oper Cash Flow $Mil	1,521	2,102	2,216	2,085
- Cap Spending $Mil	369	371	601	688
= Free Cash Flow $Mil	1,153	1,731	1,615	1,396

Financial Health [B+]	2003	2004	2005	09-30-06
Long-term Debt $Mil	130	128	127	0
Total Equity $Mil	10,885	11,523	12,065	10,961
Debt/Equity Ratio	0.0	0.0	0.0	0.0

Industry	Business Risk	Moat Size	Investment Style	Sector
Computer Equip.	Average	Narrow	Large Growth	Hardware

Competition	Market Cap $Mil	12 Mo Trailing Sales $Mil	Price/Cash Flow	Return On Assets%	Debt/Equity	Total Return% 1 Yr	3 Yr
EMC	29,072	10,651	13.9	5.4	0.0	-3.1	-0.1
IBM	146,342	89,593	9.8	8.8	0.4	19.8	3.0
Hewlett-Packard	112,070	91,658	9.9	7.6	0.1	45.2	22.7

Price Volatility | Monthly Price High/Low   — Relative Strength to S&P 500

	2001	2002	2003	2004	2005	2006
Annual $Price High	80.23	17.97	14.65	15.80	15.09	14.75
Low	10.01	3.67	5.98	9.24	11.10	9.44
Annual Total Return %	-79.4	-54.3	110.4	15.1	-8.4	-3.1

Fiscal Year-End: December	2001	2002	2003	2004	2005	TTM
Revenue $Mil	7,091	5,438	6,237	8,229	9,664	10,651
Net Income $Mil	-508	-119	496	871	1,133	984
Earnings Per Share $	-0.23	-0.05	0.22	0.36	0.47	0.43
Shares Outstanding Mil	2,207	2,374	2,255	2,420	2,361	2,202
Return on Equity %	-6.7	-1.6	4.6	7.6	9.4	9.0
Net Margin %	-7.2	-2.2	8.0	10.6	11.7	9.2
Asset Turnover	0.7	0.6	0.4	0.5	0.6	0.6
Financial Leverage	1.3	1.3	1.3	1.3	1.4	1.6

Valuation Ratios	Stock	Rel to Industry	Rel to S&P 500
Price/Earnings	30.7	1.1	1.5
Price/Book	2.7	0.5	0.7
Price/Sales	2.7	1.0	0.9
Price/Cash Flow	13.9	0.9	1.0

Major Fund Holders	% of Fund Assets
Hillman Focused Advantage	5.14
Old Mutual Focused Z	4.99
Fidelity Select Computers	4.31
Old Mutual Large Cap Z	4.21

Thesis By Rick Summer, CFA, CPA, 10-18-06 Stock Price as of Analysis: $12.18

Storage is one of the few developed market segments that we expect to grow more quickly than the overall technology industry. In our opinion, EMC is the company that will best capitalize on the growth and transformation in storage.

EMC has successfully evolved from a company providing leading-edge storage "islands" to a full-service company helping customers expand their storage capabilities while helping them simplify the resulting complexity. Historically, companies flocked to major storage vendors like EMC simply because they needed more storage to hold their spawning files of data. Over time, larger storage networks and new business requirements (e.g., compliance) created a need to build intelligent software on top of the storage hardware to manage this complexity. EMC recognized these needs early; more than 50% of revenue comes from software and services, compared with less than 30% a few years ago. We believe that EMC's ability to build and support total storage offerings (including hardware, software, and services) will solidify its hold on customers' IT spending.

EMC's narrow economic moat centers on its large installed customer base and focus on product integration and support. While storage hardware standards have become more open, we believe customers look to EMC to provide better software management and integration services for their evolving storage needs. EMC's customers have significant integration requirements, and it is easier and cheaper for them to buy more products and services from EMC than from rivals like IBM and Hitachi. Furthermore, chief information officers are typically risk-averse; they are more likely to depend on EMC for their existing storage needs than choose a new vendor and risk disrupting their networks.

We are encouraged by EMC's effort to look outside its own organization for growth. Most notably, the sales partnership with Dell has helped EMC reach double-digit growth in its midrange storage segment. Furthermore, an aggressive acquisition strategy has helped to move the company into adjacent and faster-growing markets. VMware, a $200 million acquisition, represents more than 6% of revenue and is still growing more than 50% annually. It adds at least $3 to our fair value estimate. We are impressed by EMC's position in the storage industry and believe in the investments the company has made in its sales channels and software products.

Emerson Electric EMR

Data as of 12-29-06

	Rating	Fair Value	Last Close	Consider Buy	Consider Sell	Yield %
	★★★	$43.00	$44.09	$36.60	$56.50	2.11

Company Profile
Emerson manages five business segments: process management (23% of sales), industrial automation (18%), network power (21%), climate technologies (17%), and tools and appliances (21%). Primary products include motors, drives, valves, switches, test equipment, air conditioning compressors, garbage disposals, electric tools, and home storage solutions.

Industry	Business Risk	Moat Size	Investment Style	Sector
Electric Equip.	Below Avg	Narrow	Large Core	Industrial Materials

Competition

	Market Cap $Mil	12 Mo Trailing Sales $Mil	Price/Cash Flow	Return On Assets%	Debt/ Equity	Total Return% 1 Yr	3 Yr
Emerson Electric	35,376	20,133	14.1	9.9	0.4	20.7	13.5
Siemens AG ADR	87,817	107,241	14.4	3.2	0.5	17.3	8.8
Honeywell International	36,939	30,367	13.2	6.2	0.3	24.1	13.2

Price Volatility
Monthly Price High/Low — Relative Strength to S&P 500

Annual $Price High/Low	39.63 / 22.02	33.03 / 20.89	32.50 / 21.89	35.44 / 28.11	38.92 / 30.35	45.21 / 36.78
$46.2 / 29.0 / 19.0 / 7.0 / 5.0 / 3.0	2001	2002	2003	2004	2005	2006
Annual Total Return %	-25.7	-8.3	31.3	11.1	9.2	20.7

Fiscal Year-End: September	2002	2003	2004	2005	2006	TTM
Revenue $Mil	13,748	13,958	15,615	17,305	20,133	20,133
Net Income $Mil	122	1,089	1,257	1,422	1,845	1,845
Earnings Per Share $	0.15	1.30	1.49	1.70	2.24	2.24
Shares Outstanding Mil	841	838	838	829	816	802
Return on Equity %	2.1	16.9	17.4	19.2	22.6	22.6
Net Margin %	0.9	7.8	8.1	8.2	9.2	9.2
Asset Turnover	0.9	0.9	1.0	1.0	1.1	1.1
Financial Leverage	2.5	2.4	2.3	2.3	2.3	2.3

Management   Stewardship Grade [B]
Emerson emphatically states that it strongly supports long-term shareholder value creation and has an excellent track record of backing up this claim. Management's goal is to return at least 50% of cash flows to shareholders in the form of dividends or share buybacks. Dividends have been steadily increased since the 1950s. CEO David Farr took the helm in 2000. Farr demonstrated his focus on long-term value creation in 2000 by opting to incur costs to improve Emerson's business and allowing earnings to decline after 43 consecutive years of increases. Emerson's 16-member board includes 11 independent directors. Emerson expensed options before new GAAP rules required it this year. Compensation is based on management's ability to achieve clear targets set by the board. One negative is that Farr holds both the CEO and chairman titles.

Valuation Ratios	Stock	Rel to Industry	Rel to S&P 500
Price/Earnings	19.7	0.9	1.0
Price/Book	4.3	1.2	1.0
Price/Sales	1.8	0.8	0.6
Price/Cash Flow	14.1	1.0	1.0

Major Fund Holders	% of Fund Assets
Fidelity Select Industrial Equipment	5.26
Jensen J	5.03
Pioneer AmPac Growth A	4.14
Mairs & Power Growth	4.13

8000 West Florissant Avenue P.O. Box 4100
St. Louis, MO 63136   www.gotoemerson.com

Growth [B]	2003	2004	2005	2006
Revenue %	1.5	11.9	10.8	16.3
Earnings/Share %	793.1	15.1	14.1	31.8
Book Value/Share %	12.6	11.7	3.1	11.9
Dividends/Share %	1.3	1.9	3.8	7.2

Profitability [A]	2004	2005	2006	TTM
Return on Assets %	7.7	8.3	9.9	9.9
Oper Cash Flow $Mil	2,216	2,187	2,512	2,512
- Cap Spending $Mil	400	518	601	601
= Free Cash Flow $Mil	1,816	1,669	1,911	1,911

Financial Health [A]	2004	2005	2006	09-30-06
Long-term Debt $Mil	3,136	3,128	3,128	3,128
Total Equity $Mil	7,238	7,400	8,154	8,154
Debt/Equity Ratio	0.4	0.4	0.4	0.4

Thesis By Tom D'Amore, CFA, 12-14-06 Stock Price as of Analysis: $43.00

Emerson offers investors a portfolio of respected industrial businesses that generate stable returns under the stewardship of a top-shelf management team. We think Emerson is one of the better value creators in the industrial sector and would eagerly pick up the shares at a modest discount to our fair value estimate.

Emerson boasts well-known brand names, and its products are associated with a high level of craftsmanship and superior customer support. Its reputation for quality helps Emerson maintain profit margins and increase its market share against lower-cost competitors.

Emerson's financial returns are a picture of stability. Over the last 10 years, sales have increased at a compounded annual rate of 6% and earnings at 5%. Dividends, an important measure of earnings quality, have increased every year since 1956 at a rate in line with earnings. The company's returns on invested capital have averaged a respectable 12%, exceeding the company's 9% cost of capital.

We think Emerson's management deserves credit for deftly positioning the company to serve the competitive industrial products market. For example, aggressive cost-cutting has helped lift operating profit margins 400 basis points since 2003. Product innovation and aggressive marketing practices have also been top priorities. We estimate that approximately 40% of Emerson's sales this year will come from products introduced in the last five years. We think that management's effort are paying off in the form of higher returns on invested capital (ROIC). We forecast ROIC will increase to the high teens this year, up from the 10-year average in the low teens.

Management also deserves credit for salvaging a poorly timed business expansion in network power equipment just prior to a market collapse in 2001. The network power business is now Emerson's fastest-growing segment thanks to sizzling end-market conditions.

We think Emerson's management has demonstrated a noteworthy commitment to shareholder value creation. Management devotes as much time and resources to evaluating strategic divestitures as it does to acquisitions. CEO Dave Farr has committed to carefully reviewing all of Emerson's individual businesses periodically and culling underperformers. Farr has set a goal of generating $1 billion in fresh capital from the sale of underperforming or noncore businesses over the next several years. This level of discipline in capital allocation is rare among industrial companies.

Empresa Brasileira ADR ERJ

Data as of 12-29-06

	Rating	Fair Value	Last Close	Consider Buy	Consider Sell	Yield %
	★★★	$44.00	$41.43	$28.00	$53.10	1.97

Industry	Business Risk	Moat Size	Investment Style	Sector
Aerospace/Defense	Above Avg	Narrow	Large Core	Industrial Materials

Company Profile
Based in Sao Paulo, Brazil, Embraer shares the global duopoly for small commercial aircraft with Bombardier of Canada. Regional jets ranging from 50 to 120 seats account for about 75% of the firm's revenue. The firm also produces aircraft for military and corporate aviation, as well as aircraft systems and structural components. Embraer employs about 17,000 people.

Competition

	Market Cap $Mil	12 Mo Trailing Sales $Mil	Price/Cash Flow	Return On Assets%	Debt/ Equity	Total Return% 1 Yr	3 Yr
Empresa Brasileira ADR	7,440	—	—	—	—	8.2	8.5
Boeing	70,249	59,114	9.4	2.7	0.8	28.4	30.4
Airbus							

Management   Stewardship Grade [NA]
CEO Mauricio Botelho has led the company since its privatization in 1995 and successfully transformed Embraer from a defense manufacturer into one of the largest commercial jet manufacturers in the world. While Botelho has proved a savvy manager, his background as an engineer ensures that the company maintains an eye toward constant innovation. We think the recent appointment of Frederico Curado to succeed Botelho in 2007 bodes well for the firm's future, since Curado has been instrumental in driving market share gains for the commercial aircraft segment and has a wealth of experience, including roles in manufacturing, procurement, technology, contracts, and sales. While most Brazilian companies have a two-tier share structure, subordinating foreign investors, Embraer is an exception. The firm recently remodeled its capital structure, converting preferred shares into common and evenly distributing voting rights. We applaud the company's efforts to bring its corporate governance more in line with international standards. Still, the government maintains its golden share, which gives it the right to stop foreign firms from gaining a majority stake in the company. Embraer paid out 63% of its earnings in dividends last year, which far exceeded the mandatory payout ratio as governed by Brazilian law.

Av. Brigadeiro Faria Lima, 2170, P.C. 29   www.embraer.com.br
Sao Jose dos Campos, Brazil 12227-901

Growth [NA]	2001	2002	2003	2004
Revenue %	6.0	-13.7	-15.1	60.5
Earnings/Share %	NMF	NMF	-40.8	177.8
Book Value/Share %	—	NMF	14.9	23.5
Dividends/Share %	407.3	-25.1	-50.9	194.8

Profitability [NA]	2002	2003	2004	TTM
Return on Assets %	5.2	2.2	6.3	—
Oper Cash Flow $Mil	576	240	3	—
- Cap Spending $Mil	111	65	50	—
= Free Cash Flow $Mil	465	175	-47	—

Financial Health [NA]	2002	2003	2004	12-31-04
Long-term Debt $Mil	878	113	105	105
Total Equity $Mil	406	481	598	598
Debt/Equity Ratio	2.2	0.2	0.2	—

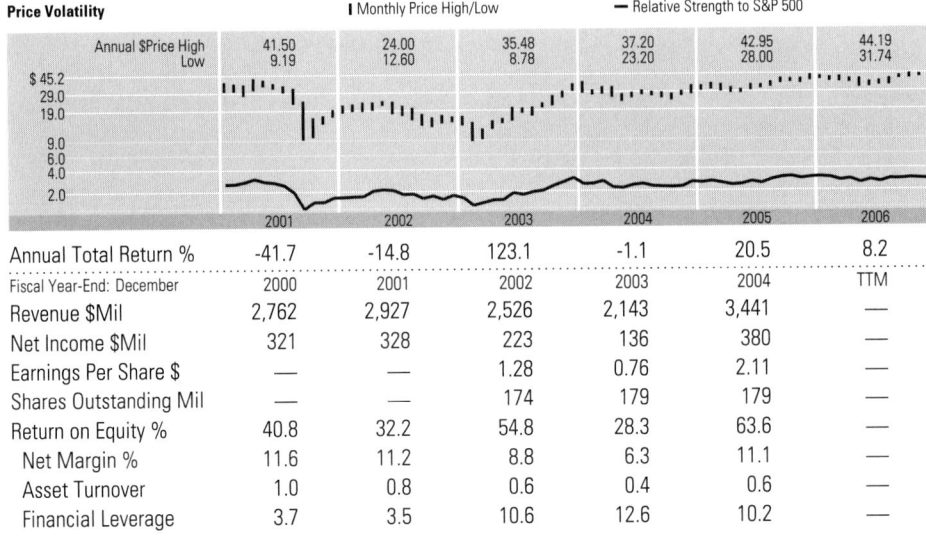

Annual Total Return %	-41.7	-14.8	123.1	-1.1	20.5	8.2
Fiscal Year-End: December	2000	2001	2002	2003	2004	TTM
Revenue $Mil	2,762	2,927	2,526	2,143	3,441	—
Net Income $Mil	321	328	223	136	380	—
Earnings Per Share $	—	—	1.28	0.76	2.11	—
Shares Outstanding Mil	—	—	174	179	179	—
Return on Equity %	40.8	32.2	54.8	28.3	63.6	—
Net Margin %	11.6	11.2	8.8	6.3	11.1	—
Asset Turnover	1.0	0.8	0.6	0.4	0.6	—
Financial Leverage	3.7	3.5	10.6	12.6	10.2	—

Valuation Ratios	Stock	Rel to Industry	Rel to S&P 500
Price/Earnings	—	—	—
Price/Book	—	—	—
Price/Sales	—	—	—
Price/Cash Flow	—	—	—

Major Fund Holders	% of Fund Assets
CGM Focus	3.74
Excelsior Mid Cap Value & Restructuring	3.58
Dreyfus Midcap Value	2.94
Franklin Mid Cap Value A	2.44

Thesis By Marisa E. Thompson, 12-14-06 Stock Price as of Analysis: $43.44

Embraer's latest offering gives it the edge over competitor Bombardier.

Founded by the Brazilian government in 1969, now-private Embraer has grown into one of the largest manufacturers of regional jets, sharing a virtual duopoly with Bombardier. Thanks to its engineering investments and cost advantages, Embraer has increased its market share to almost 50%. The firm is positioned to take further share of the regional market, which is trending toward larger aircraft. Bombardier's product line currently tops out at the 90-seat CRJ900 regional jet, while Embraer produces the Embraer 190, which has 93-106 seats, and the Embraer 195, with 106-118 seats. These planes have a longer reach, with the ability to fly more than 2,500 miles without refueling.

Although Embraer has fought its way into the market, other potential entrants would find engineering and financing barriers too high. Embraer developed its technology over the past 35 years and had huge financial sponsorship from the Brazilian government along the way. Additionally, aircraft manufacturers Boeing and Airbus have virtually bowed out of the regional jet market, focusing on the race for superjumbo jets. Though Chinese aircraft manufacturer Harbin could try to make a run, Embraer has chosen to work alongside the company in a joint venture, better securing its long-term position as Chinese manufacturing increases.

Embraer sits in an enviable position in the regional jet market, but the business jet market is a whole other ball game. Embraer has a relatively small position in the market and must battle five other well-capitalized manufacturers. Additionally, the end markets for business jets are more fragmented, adding to selling costs. Still Embraer benefits from its low-cost manufacturing base and has a new set of business jets due out in 2008.

Embraer and other manufacturers are benefiting from global growth in aircraft sales, but the next downturn could bring an end to the party, leaving manufacturers with hundreds of canceled orders. The recent aerospace upturn may actually prove to be more prolonged than past cycles thanks to growth in emerging markets and the prospects of an extended fleet replacement cycle in mature markets. Just in case, though, Embraer is building up its maintenance and repair business, which will help take the sting out of the next slowdown while enabling it to get closer to its customers and stay on top of their evolving needs.

Data as of 12-29-06

Energy Transfer Equity LP ETE

Rating	Fair Value	Last Close	Consider Buy	Consider Sell	Yield %
★★★★★	$39.00	$31.40	$33.20	$51.20	0.94

Company Profile

Energy Transfer Equity LP owns the general partner interests, incentive distribution rights, and about 25% of the outstanding limited partner interests of Energy Transfer Partners. ETP is a master limited partnership primarily engaged in natural-gas transportation and storage and also is the third-largest retail marketer of propane in the United States, serving more than a million customers in 41 states.

Management

Stewardship Grade [NA]

Despite a labyrinthine ownership structure involving multiple levels of limited and general partnerships, Energy Transfer is ultimately the brainchild of Ray Davis and Kelcy Warren, who are co-CEOs and co-chairmen of the general partner of Energy Transfer Partners. Energy Transfer Equity owns equity stakes in and effectively controls this private entity. Energy Transfer Equity is itself a limited partnership, and its general partner, LE GP LLC, is owned by Davis, Warren, and a private investment fund. Davis and Warren are co-chairmen of the board, and John McReynolds is president and CFO. While we dislike the complexity of the ownership structure, we do like the management of Davis and Warren, who have more than five decades of combined business experience in the energy industry and have demonstrated a knack for increasing earnings through new projects and deal-making. From a stewardship perspective, the limited partner structure provides few unitholder rights and almost no real voice in the management of the company. For instance, any unaffiliated owner that accumulates more than 20% of outstanding units loses voting rights on any matter. While we may like the company's operational management, we think it rates a D when it comes to stewardship.

2828 Woodside Street
Dallas, TX 75204
www.energytransfer.com

Growth [B]	2003	2004	2005	2006
Revenue %	NMF	NMF	162.8	27.4
Earnings/Share %	NMF	NMF	NMF	NMF
Book Value/Share %	—	—	—	—
Dividends/Share %	NMF	NMF	NMF	NMF

Profitability [NA]	2004	2005	2006	TTM
Return on Assets %	15.6	3.0	1.8	1.8
Oper Cash Flow $Mil	122	38	311	311
- Cap Spending $Mil	110	196	680	680
= Free Cash Flow $Mil	12	-158	-369	-369

Financial Health [D]	2004	2005	2006	08-31-06
Long-term Debt $Mil	1,071	2,278	3,206	3,206
Total Equity $Mil	364	-89	46	46
Debt/Equity Ratio	2.9	ELB	70.0	70.0

Industry	Business Risk	Moat Size	Investment Style	Sector
Oil/Gas Svcs.	Below Average		Mid Growth	Energy

Competition	Market Cap $Mil	12 Mo Trailing Sales $Mil	Price/Cash Flow	Return On Assets %	Debt/ Equity	Total Return% 1 Yr	3 Yr
Energy Transfer Equity LP	6,595	7,859	21.2	1.8	70.0	—	—
Kinder Morgan	14,177	9,788	9.2	2.5	2.7	19.2	26.3
Enterprise GP Holdings LP	3,286	14,421	2.6	0.7	7.1	1.4	—

Price Volatility | Monthly Price High/Low — Relative Strength to S&P 500

Fiscal Year-End: August	2002	2003	2004	2005	2006	TTM
Revenue $Mil	—	—	2,347	6,169	7,859	7,859
Net Income $Mil	—	—	446	146	107	107
Earnings Per Share $	—	—	—	—	—	—
Shares Outstanding Mil	—	—	—	—	—	210
Return on Equity %	—	—	122.4	NMF	232.5	232.5
Net Margin %	—	—	19.0	2.4	1.4	1.4
Asset Turnover	—	—	0.8	1.3	1.3	1.3
Financial Leverage	—	—	7.9	NMF	129.3	129.3

Valuation Ratios	Stock	Rel to Industry	Rel to S&P 500
Price/Earnings	—	—	—
Price/Book	143.9	20.3	35.1
Price/Sales	0.8	0.3	0.3
Price/Cash Flow	21.2	1.3	1.5

Major Fund Holders	% of Fund Assets
Gartmore Global Natural Resources A	1.98
Royce Dividend Value Service	1.84
Jennison Utility B	1.37

Thesis By Jason Stevens, 12-20-06 Stock Price as of Analysis: $30.55

We're big fans of Energy Transfer Partners ETP and think that the initial public offering of its general partner, Energy Transfer Equity, presents an attractive opportunity for investors who are interested in natural-gas pipeline plays and are looking more for growth than yield.

Through ETP, ETE operates an impressive network of 12,000 miles of natural-gas gathering and transportation pipelines across Texas and is the third-largest retail propane business in the nation, with more than a million customers in 41 states. Recent projects that are building takeaway capacity for Barnett Shale producers will drive growth over the next few years. As we expected, ETP's acquisitive tendencies were demonstrated again with the acquisition of Southern Union's SUG Transwestern pipeline, which should enhance the optionality the partnership can offer to producers.

Because it now holds 100% of the incentive distribution rights (IDRs) of ETP, Energy Transfer Equity will see its share of total distributions from ETP increase over time, and ETE's distributions to unitholders will grow more rapidly than will ETP's. Incentive distribution rights are used by master limited partnerships (MLPs) to align the interests of general partners and limited partner unitholders and entitle their holders to an increasing share of total distributions as the overall level of distribution payments increases. On the basis of ETP's current quarterly distribution of $0.75 per unit, ETE receives 33.8% of the total cash payout, and as ETP's distributions rise, the percentage of the total payout ETE receives also increases. For instance, a 10% increase in ETP's quarterly distribution results in a 19.6% increase in cash received by ETE and boosts its share to 35.7% of total distributions, by our calculations.

So while ETE's current annualized 3.2% yield at our fair value estimate may be low compared with those of standard MLPs, which typically fall in the 6%-10% range, ETE affords investors the chance to leverage the growth of the underlying business. As new projects increase ETP's cash available for distributions, ETE's unitholders will benefit from the leverage provided by the general partner's ownership of ETP's incentive distribution rights and will see their cash distributions grow faster than those of common unitholders of ETP. All else being equal, this should translate to greater stock price appreciation for ETE relative to ETP, at the price of a lower distribution yield.

Energy Transfer Partners ETP

Data as of 12-29-06

Rating	Fair Value	Last Close	Consider Buy	Consider Sell	Yield %
★★★★★	$69.00	$54.10	$58.80	$90.60	3.65

Company Profile
Energy Transfer Partners is a master limited partnership primarily engaged in natural-gas transportation and storage. The partnership operates more than 12,000 miles of natural-gas gathering and intrastate transportation pipelines in Texas and Louisiana, and the 2,500-mile Transwestern interstate pipeline. Also, Energy Transfer Partners is the third-largest retail marketer of propane in the United States, serving more than a million customers in 41 states.

Management
Stewardship Grade [C]

Ray Davis and Kelcy Warren are co-CEOs and co-chairmen of Energy Transfer's general partner. Under the master limited partnership structure, the general partner manages the day-to-day operations of Energy Transfer. Davis and Warren have more than five decades of combined business experience in the energy industry. The general partner holds "incentive distribution rights," which means it will receive an increasing percentage of the quarterly cash distributions after the minimum quarterly distribution has been paid. This motivates the general partner to increase distributions well above the current annualized payout of $3.00 per unit, and limited partner unitholders will benefit from these potential increases. Our key stewardship concerns are management oversight and transparency. Only three of 13 board members are independent, and the complex ownership structure of the firm makes it difficult to identify who ultimately controls the company. Also, Energy Transfer's partnership agreement contains provisions that make it extremely difficult to remove current management.

2838 Woodside Street www.heritagepropane.com
Dallas, TX 75204

Growth [A]	2002	2003	2004	2005
Revenue %	23.6	310.7	162.8	27.4
Earnings/Share %	616.0	93.3	50.3	21.2
Book Value/Share %	24.2	108.4	-20.9	20.2
Dividends/Share %	0.5	7.8	30.9	42.2

Profitability [C+]	2003	2004	2005	TTM
Return on Assets %	3.9	6.9	7.3	7.3
Oper Cash Flow $Mil	163	169	544	544
- Cap Spending $Mil	110	196	680	680
= Free Cash Flow $Mil	53	-27	-136	-136

Financial Health [C]	2003	2004	2005	05-31-06
Long-term Debt $Mil	1,071	1,676	2,589	2,589
Total Equity $Mil	720	1,277	1,654	1,654
Debt/Equity Ratio	1.5	1.3	1.6	1.6

Industry	Business Risk	Moat Size	Investment Style	Sector
Oil/Gas	Below Avg	Narrow	Mid Core	Energy

Competition	Market Cap $Mil	12 Mo Trailing Sales $Mil	Price/Cash Flow	Return On Assets%	Debt/ Equity	Total Return% 1 Yr	3 Yr
Energy Transfer Partners	5,999	7,859	11.0	7.3	1.6	65.5	47.7
Enterprise Products Partn	12,514	14,421	9.8	3.5	0.8	29.2	13.3
Enbridge Energy LP	2,466	6,930	8.5	5.2	1.0	21.7	7.4

Price Volatility | Monthly Price High/Low — Relative Strength to S&P 500

	2001	2002	2003	2004	2005	2006
Annual $Price High	15.50	14.95	21.33	29.75	39.09	56.00
Low	10.81	11.25	13.80	17.25	26.92	33.55
Annual Total Return %	47.7	4.3	58.0	51.4	24.6	65.5

Fiscal Year-End: August	2002	2003	2004	2005	2006	TTM
Revenue $Mil	462	571	2,347	6,169	7,859	7,859
Net Income $Mil	4	30	90	304	397	397
Earnings Per Share $	0.13	0.90	1.73	2.60	3.15	3.15
Shares Outstanding Mil	32	33	52	117	126	111
Return on Equity %	2.3	13.5	12.5	23.8	24.0	24.0
Net Margin %	0.9	5.2	3.8	4.9	5.1	5.1
Asset Turnover	0.6	0.8	1.0	1.4	1.4	1.4
Financial Leverage	4.2	3.3	3.2	3.5	3.3	3.3

Valuation Ratios	Stock	Rel to Industry	Rel to S&P 500
Price/Earnings	17.2	1.4	0.8
Price/Book	3.6	1.1	0.9
Price/Sales	0.0	0.4	0.3
Price/Cash Flow	11.0	1.3	0.8

Major Fund Holders	% of Fund Assets
Diamond Hill Strategic Income A	1.84
Huntington Dividend Capture Tr	1.74
AIM Opportunities II A	1.20
AIM Global Equity A	1.17

Thesis By Jason Stevens, 12-20-06 Stock Price as of Analysis: $53.09

We think Energy Transfer Partners will reap the benefits during 2007 and onward of two key strategic moves. First, full-throttle investment in Barnett Shale takeaway capacity will begin to have an increasing impact on earnings, and second, the partnership's first foray into interstate transportation will more than pay for itself. This partnership operates one of the best natural-gas transportation systems in the industry, in our view, and because of this and its strong growth prospects, generous cash distributions, and below-average risk, we think this may be one of the most attractive MLP stocks in our coverage.

The Barnett Shale continues to be the hottest natural-gas play in the country, and, in our opinion, Energy Transfer Partners is in the best position among pipeline operators to benefit from production growth. The partnership anticipates completing a 42-inch pipe by March that will significantly increase its throughput capacity and provide shippers with access to major Eastern markets. Equally important, the new pipe will free up the partnership's Oasis line to bring gas east from its newly acquired Transwestern pipeline. Transwestern, which Energy Transfer purchased from Southern Union in 2006, is an interstate pipeline that stretches from the California-Arizona border east into the Permian and Anadarko basins, with an expansion line running from the San Juan basin south into the main line. We think this is a near-perfect complement to Energy Transfer's Texas intrastate pipeline system and expect the partnership to be able to expand its footprint rapidly because of the deal.

One of the industry trends we are watching is the potential for a capacity glut developing in northern Louisiana. Several other pipeline firms, notably Boardwalk and Regency, are also developing projects to bring gas east from Texas and north from the Gulf, and we suspect that the Carthage and Perryville markets will become saturated at some point, depressing prices there. Energy Transfer's proposed new venture with Kinder Morgan (the Midcontinent Express Pipeline) looks to leapfrog these congested markets, offering producers additional access to Northeastern and Southeastern markets. When combined with Transwestern, which offers access to markets in the Western U.S., you've got a pipeline system that enables producers to sell into whichever market offers the best price for gas at any given time.

We've been fans of Energy Transfer's strategic vision since its inception, and believe that deals like this will continue to keep it one step ahead of the midstream pack.

Data as of 12-29-06

Enersis ADR ENI

	Rating	Fair Value	Last Close	Consider Buy	Consider Sell	Yield %
	★★★	$15.00	$16.00	$9.60	$18.10	1.25

Industry	Business Risk	Moat Size	Investment Style	Sector
Electric Utilities	Above Avg	Narrow	Large Growth	Utilities

Company Profile

Enersis holds a diversified portfolio of assets with electricity generation and distribution interests in Chile, Argentina, Brazil, Colombia, and Peru. Its generation subsidiary, the largest private-sector generation company in Latin America, accounts for roughly 50% of Enersis' operating income. The distribution subsidiaries account for the remaining 50%. Endesa acquired control of Enersis in 1999 and now owns 60% of the company.

Management

Stewardship Grade [NA]

With its 60% equity stake in Enersis, Endesa controls the shareholder electoral power of the company's board. The management team is appointed by and serves at the discretion of the board. Thus, Endesa effectively controls the management team as well. A number of Enersis' directors and executives were previously employed by or have strong ties to Endesa. For instance, Enersis' new CEO, Ignacio Antonanzas, comes from Endesa, where he had served as the general deputy director of strategy. He replaces Mario Valcarce, a 20-year veteran of the Endesa-Enersis organization, who had served as Enersis' CEO since 2003 and is moving on to serve as the chairman of Endesa Chile's board of directors. Chilean law does not permit staggered terms, so Enersis' seven directors serve three-year terms that expire concurrently. And though as a controlled company (since Endesa has a majority stake), Enersis is not required to meet the standard NYSE independence requirements, its audit committee is comprised of three independent directors. The company also has a directors' committee, as required by Chilean law, which is chaired by a director who does not represent the interests of Enersis' controlling owner.

Santa Rosa 76 Piso 16 www.enersis.com
Santiago, Chile

Growth [NA]	2002	2003	2004	2005
Revenue %	-18.7	-6.0	12.0	13.9
Earnings/Share %	—	—	—	—
Book Value/Share %	—	—	—	—
Dividends/Share %	—	—	—	—

Profitability [NA]	2003	2004	2005	TTM
Return on Assets %	0.1	0.4	0.6	0.6
Oper Cash Flow $Mil	869	1,031	1,587	1,587
- Cap Spending $Mil	391	444	564	564
= Free Cash Flow $Mil	477	588	1,023	1,023

Financial Health [NA]	2003	2004	2005	12-31-05
Long-term Debt $Mil	—	6,077	5,173	5,173
Total Equity $Mil	4,383	4,752	5,045	5,045
Debt/Equity Ratio	—	1.3	1.0	1.0

Competition

	Market Cap $Mil	12 Mo Trailing Sales $Mil	Price/Cash Flow	Return On Assets%	Debt/Equity	Total Return% 1 Yr	3 Yr
Enersis ADR	10,448	5,710	6.6	0.6	1.0	47.7	29.8
AES	14,639	12,205	5.8	1.1	5.8	39.2	32.5
Companhia Energetica de M	7,812	3,056	10.9	8.0	0.5	34.7	44.6

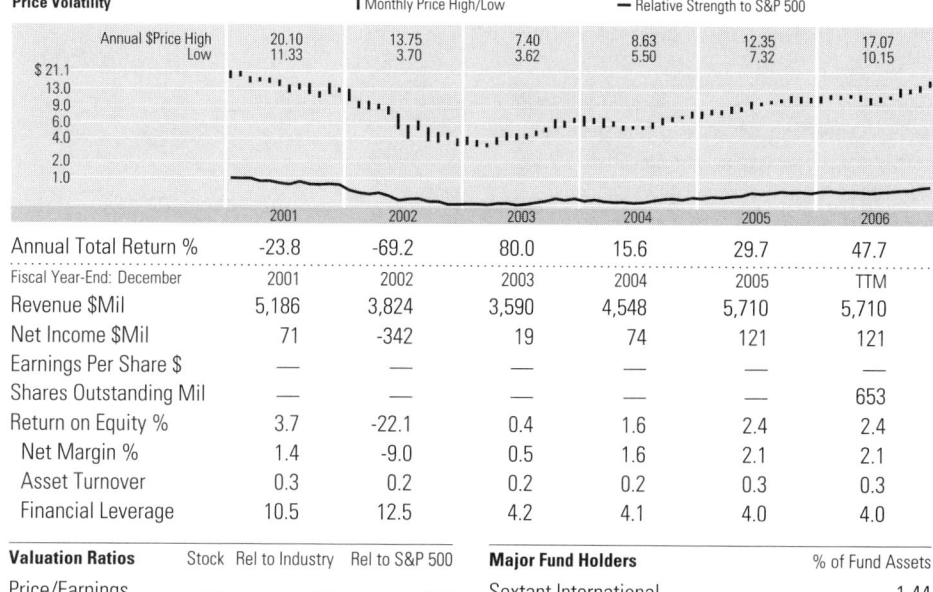

	2001	2002	2003	2004	2005	2006/TTM
Annual Total Return %	-23.8	-69.2	80.0	15.6	29.7	47.7
Fiscal Year-End: December	2001	2002	2003	2004	2005	TTM
Revenue $Mil	5,186	3,824	3,590	4,548	5,710	5,710
Net Income $Mil	71	-342	19	74	121	121
Earnings Per Share $	—	—	—	—	—	—
Shares Outstanding Mil	—	—	—	—	—	653
Return on Equity %	3.7	-22.1	0.4	1.6	2.4	2.4
Net Margin %	1.4	-9.0	0.5	1.6	2.1	2.1
Asset Turnover	0.3	0.2	0.2	0.2	0.3	0.3
Financial Leverage	10.5	12.5	4.2	4.1	4.0	4.0

Valuation Ratios	Stock	Rel to Industry	Rel to S&P 500
Price/Earnings	—	—	—
Price/Book	2.1	0.6	0.5
Price/Sales	1.8	1.0	0.6
Price/Cash Flow	6.6	0.6	0.5

Major Fund Holders	% of Fund Assets
Sextant International	1.44

Thesis By Jason Stevens, 12-15-06 Stock Price as of Analysis: $16.32

Enersis is literally a South American powerhouse. The company generates and distributes electricity in Chile, Argentina, Brazil, Colombia, and Peru. As these economies grow, end users require an increasing supply of electricity, and Enersis is up to the task of meeting the growing demand. However, its success depends on the growth and stability of each country's economy, and that dependency introduces an above-average risk that we urge potential investors to consider carefully.

Enersis makes money on two fronts: distributing and generating electricity. We like the company's narrow-moat distribution business, which focuses on delivering electricity to more than 10 million customers in five dense urban markets across South America; this business expects to see demand growth of 6%-7% annually. While each separate market presents unique challenges, we're comforted that management has identified tactical improvements, such as clamping down on energy losses and focusing on efficient operations, that should result in improving operating margins.

We think that the company's generating business will be able to increase electricity sales about 5% annually on strong demand growth and will see higher margins because of a structural shift toward market pricing across much of South America.

Although we like Enersis' growth prospects and emphasis on operating efficiencies, we are concerned about the large mismatch between the company's dollar-denominated debt and its local currency earnings. About 50% of total debt is denominated in U.S. dollars, and only 20% of 2005 revenue was dollar-denominated or -linked. While this ensures that Enersis has more than enough dollar-denominated revenue to meet the current portion of its debt obligations, a devaluation of any of the currencies in which Enersis operates would be problematic, as the relative cost of debt would soar. We would normally argue that Enersis' diversification across several South American countries limits the harm that any one country's crisis could inflict, but crises in this region tend to be contagious. Therefore, we don't think Enersis' presence across several countries provides much diversification benefit.

Because electricity demand is highly correlated with GDP growth, we think owning shares of Enersis is a great way for investors seeking broad exposure to South America to participate in the growth of the region. However, given the inherent risks, we'd urge investors to buy shares only with a significant margin of safety.

ENI SpA ADR E

Data as of 12-29-06

Rating	Fair Value	Last Close	Consider Buy	Consider Sell	Yield %
★★★	$67.00	$67.28	$51.70	$83.90	4.68

Industry	Business Risk	Moat Size	Investment Style	Sector
Oil/Gas	Average	Narrow	Large Value	Energy

Company Profile
Rome-based Eni explores for and produces oil and natural gas in Italy and abroad. It holds proven reserves of 6.8 billion equivalent barrels of oil and gas, produces 1.7 million barrels a day, has the ability to refine roughly 701,000 barrels a day, and has a network of 6,282 retail service stations. One of the more diversified major energy companies, Eni also has operations in oil field services, petrochemicals, natural-gas distribution, and electricity generation.

Management
Stewardship Grade [NA]

The Italian government holds a "golden share" in Eni that gives it special veto powers for certain transactions, such as mergers. Although the government controls only 30% of the company, politicians appoint a majority of board members, as well as the chief executive. We regard this influence as less than ideal, since the Italian government could pursue interests that conflict with those of minority investors. The recent political appointment of Paolo Scaroni as chief executive raises eyebrows, despite evidence of Scaroni's business acumen, because of his lack of experience in the oil and gas sector. Scaroni replaced Vittorio Mincato, who oversaw the company's noteworthy upstream growth over the past six years. Scaroni's most recent position was as CEO of Enel, Italy's leading electric utility. We're concerned that Scaroni will take the company in a different direction than Mincato had envisioned, with heavier investments in the gas and power division. While gas and power operations carry lower risk than the firm's other segments, we don't think there's as great an opportunity for excess returns, given the deregulation of the Italian market. Indeed, the company is already facing scrutiny over possible abuse of its dominant market position.

Piazzale Enrico Mattei 1 www.eni.it
Rome, Italy I-00144

Growth [NA]	2002	2003	2004	2005
Revenue %	-1.7	6.9	12.4	26.5
Earnings/Share %	-39.4	23.3	26.4	25.1
Book Value/Share %	-2.3	3.1	24.6	12.6
Dividends/Share %	0.0	0.0	20.0	22.2

Profitability [NA]	2003	2004	2005	TTM
Return on Assets %	7.4	9.4	11.6	11.6
Oper Cash Flow $Mil	12,126	15,528	18,703	18,703
- Cap Spending $Mil	8,784	8,429	8,212	8,212
= Free Cash Flow $Mil	3,342	7,099	10,491	10,491

Financial Health [NA]	2003	2004	2005	12-31-05
Long-term Debt $Mil	10,420	10,421	9,111	9,111
Total Equity $Mil	33,370	48,685	46,687	46,687
Debt/Equity Ratio	0.3	0.2	0.2	0.2

Competition	Market Cap $Mil	12 Mo Trailing Sales $Mil	Price/Cash Flow	Return On Assets%	Debt/Equity	Total Return% 1 Yr	3 Yr
ENI SpA ADR	53,896	93,324	2.9	11.6	0.2	27.4	26.4
Total SA ADR	176,957	153,547	9.6	12.5	0.3	19.2	20.2
BG Group PLC ADR	48,575	9,900	16.6	14.7	0.2	39.0	40.2

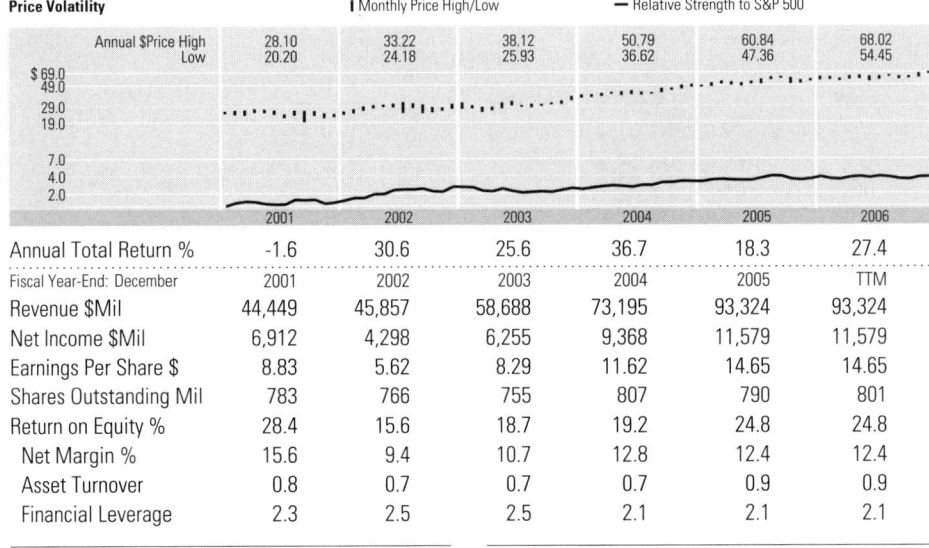

Price Volatility — Monthly Price High/Low — Relative Strength to S&P 500

	2001	2002	2003	2004	2005	2006
Annual $Price High	28.10	33.22	38.12	50.79	60.84	68.02
Low	20.20	24.18	25.93	36.62	47.36	54.45
Annual Total Return %	-1.6	30.6	25.6	36.7	18.3	27.4

Fiscal Year-End: December	2001	2002	2003	2004	2005	TTM
Revenue $Mil	44,449	45,857	58,688	73,195	93,324	93,324
Net Income $Mil	6,912	4,298	6,255	9,368	11,579	11,579
Earnings Per Share $	8.83	5.62	8.29	11.62	14.65	14.65
Shares Outstanding Mil	783	766	755	807	790	801
Return on Equity %	28.4	15.6	18.7	19.2	24.8	24.8
Net Margin %	15.6	9.4	10.7	12.8	12.4	12.4
Asset Turnover	0.8	0.7	0.7	0.7	0.9	0.9
Financial Leverage	2.3	2.5	2.5	2.1	2.1	2.1

Valuation Ratios	Stock	Rel to Industry	Rel to S&P 500
Price/Earnings	4.6	0.4	0.2
Price/Book	1.2	0.4	0.3
Price/Sales	0.6	0.3	0.2
Price/Cash Flow	2.9	0.3	0.2

Major Fund Holders	% of Fund Assets
Thornburg Investment Income Builder A	3.30
Fidelity International Value	2.85
Munder Energy A	2.79
Vanguard Energy	2.75

Thesis By Elizabeth Collins, 11-22-06 Stock Price as of Analysis: $64.09

Although Eni faces deregulation of the Italian gas market, it still has one of the most attractive development portfolios in the oil patch.

By several metrics, Eni is the sixth-largest integrated oil company in the world. Spawned by the privatization of Italy's national oil and gas company, Eni represents an amalgamation of numerous business segments combined to form one vertically integrated European powerhouse. While the firm still lacks the scale and cost advantages of supermajors like ExxonMobil, BP, and Royal Dutch Shell, Eni's smaller size and attractive portfolio of prospects offer superior production growth potential, in our opinion.

Eni is seeking to boost its stature in international energy. Increasing emphasis on upstream oil and gas exploration and production has yielded an impressive collection of development projects in places like Libya, Algeria, Nigeria, and Angola that are set to deliver well-above-average production growth over the next several years. Eni is also leading efforts to tap the colossal Kashagan oil field under the Caspian Sea. Hailed as the most significant find in decades, this project is expected to attain a production rate of 1.2 million barrels per day.

Geopolitical factors permit Eni to operate where other Western players face greater political opposition--namely North Africa and the Middle East. With nearly half of proved reserves and production stemming from North and West Africa, Eni's geographic exposure is geared toward regions with greater growth potential, but correspondingly higher political risk. Lower exposure to mature North American and European basins means that Eni must struggle less with declining production from existing fields.

Eni still has its core gas and power-distribution businesses in Europe. Previously supported by monopoly power in Italy, these legacy businesses have been quite profitable and have helped Eni generate impressive returns on invested capital. However, as the forces of deregulation take hold, Eni is being obliged to scale down these operations and compete vigorously with other players. We expect returns to shrink as a result. To mitigate this effect, the firm has taken stakes in several gas distributors outside Italy and is planning increased gas sales to other European nations.

Despite Eni's weaker competitive position against the dominant oil giants, we believe the company will post adequate returns over the balance of the cycle. Still, we'll watch closely for signs that government influence is leading the firm in the wrong direction.

Stocks 500

Data as of 12-29-06

Enterprise GP Holdings LP EPE

Rating	Fair Value	Last Close	Consider Buy	Consider Sell	Yield %
★★★★	$43.00	$36.97	$33.20	$53.90	3.30

Company Profile
Enterprise GP Holdings owns the general partner stake in Enterprise Products Partners, a Houston-based master limited partnership that transports and processes energy-related commodities, primarily natural gas and natural-gas liquids. The majority of its pipelines and processing plants are concentrated along the Gulf Coast. As a partnership, Enterprise GP pays no corporate income tax; its tax burden flows through to individual stockholders.

Management   Stewardship Grade [B]
The Enterprise family of companies is essentially controlled by Dan Duncan. He owns a majority of EPCO, a private company that controls Enterprise GP, which in turn manages the operations of Enterprise Products. Enterprise GP is itself organized as an MLP, but its general partner, EPCO, does not receive incentive distributions. Instead, EPCO receives distributions from Enterprise GP in the same proportion as those allocated to limited partners. EPCO also controls TEPPCO, another midstream energy master limited partnership. We're a bit uncomfortable with this relationship because it presents all sorts of potential self-dealing conflicts; we think it would be much cleaner if TEPPCO and Enterprise were merged. While Duncan is chairman of the board, most of the day-to-day operations are managed by vice chairman O.S. Andras and Robert Phillips, who assumed the CEO role from Andras in February 2005. Management has proved to be relatively frugal: Phillips was paid total cash compensation of $875,000 in 2005 plus equity compensation totaling more than $600,000, much less than many of his peers in the energy sector. In 2005, Enterprise's top executives once again received restricted units and options that exceeded 50% of their base salaries.

2727 North Loop West Suite 101   www.enterprisegp.com
Houston, TX 77008-1044

Growth [A-]	2002	2003	2004	2005
Revenue %	NMF	49.1	55.6	47.3
Earnings/Share %	NMF	NMF	NMF	NMF
Book Value/Share %	—	—	—	—
Dividends/Share %	NMF	NMF	NMF	NMF

Profitability [NA]	2003	2004	2005	TTM
Return on Assets %	0.3	0.3	0.4	0.7
Oper Cash Flow $Mil	427	388	614	1,258
- Cap Spending $Mil	147	156	864	1,133
= Free Cash Flow $Mil	280	233	-250	125

Financial Health [D-]	2003	2004	2005	09-30-06
Long-term Debt $Mil	—	4,629	4,968	5,040
Total Equity $Mil	36	74	715	712
Debt/Equity Ratio	—	62.5	6.9	7.1

Industry	Business Risk	Moat Size	Investment Style	Sector
Natural Gas	Average	Narrow	Mid Growth	Utilities

Competition

	Market Cap $Mil	12 Mo Trailing Sales $Mil	Price/Cash Flow	Return On Assets %	Debt/Equity	Total Return % 1 Yr	3 Yr
Enterprise GP Holdings LP	3,286	14,421	2.6	0.7	7.1	1.4	—
Williams Companies	15,576	12,719	9.3	0.9	1.2	14.4	40.0
Enbridge	12,009	6,986	16.1	3.1	1.9	13.7	21.9

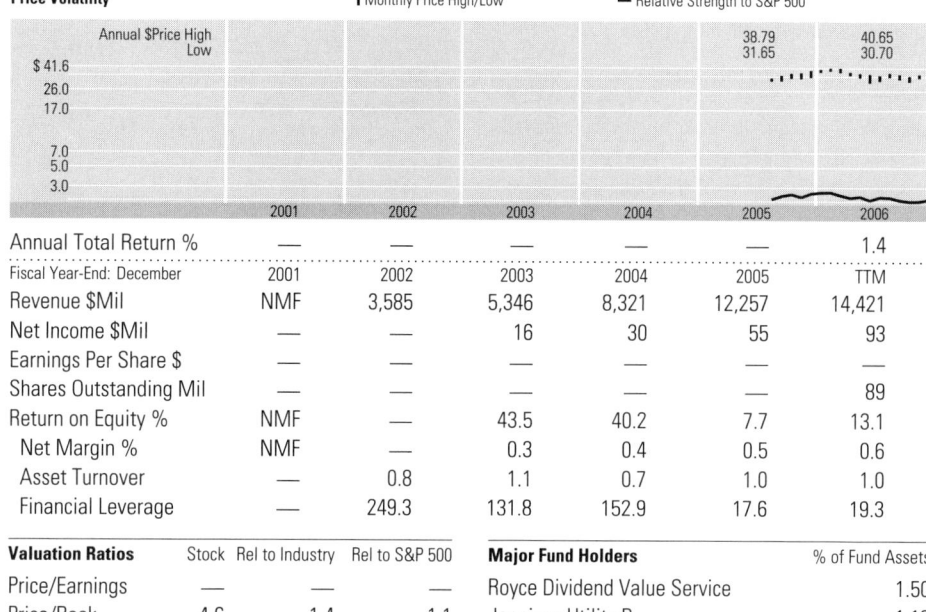

Annual Total Return %	—	—	—	—	—	1.4
Fiscal Year-End: December	2001	2002	2003	2004	2005	TTM
Revenue $Mil	NMF	3,585	5,346	8,321	12,257	14,421
Net Income $Mil	—	—	16	30	55	93
Earnings Per Share $	—	—	—	—	—	—
Shares Outstanding Mil	—	—	—	—	—	89
Return on Equity %	NMF	—	43.5	40.2	7.7	13.1
Net Margin %	NMF	—	0.3	0.4	0.5	0.6
Asset Turnover	—	0.8	1.1	0.7	1.0	1.0
Financial Leverage	—	249.3	131.8	152.9	17.6	19.3

Valuation Ratios	Stock	Rel to Industry	Rel to S&P 500
Price/Earnings	—	—	—
Price/Book	4.6	1.4	1.1
Price/Sales	0.2	0.2	0.1
Price/Cash Flow	2.6	0.2	0.2

Major Fund Holders	% of Fund Assets
Royce Dividend Value Service	1.50
Jennison Utility B	1.19

Thesis By Michael Cumming, CFA, 12-20-06 Stock Price as of Analysis: $36.91

Enterprise GP Holdings offers investors the opportunity to invest in the nation's largest pipeline master limited partnership (MLP) but with more upside potential than owning units of its subsidiary, Enterprise Products Partners.

Enterprise GP controls the general partner of Enterprise Products, a limited partnership that owns pipelines and storage terminals primarily in the Gulf Coast region. With the general partner interest come two important benefits. Enterprise GP controls the management of Enterprise Products and has incentive distribution rights, which is a fancy way of saying that as cash payments to owners of Enterprise Products increase, Enterprise GP gets an even bigger slice of the pie. As it stands now, Enterprise GP gets 25% of any new distributable cash flow even though it owns only 2% of the company.

While we like the size and operational diversity of Enterprise's network, the position of the network is what really excites us. With a presence in the Rockies, the Barnett Shale region in Texas, and all along the Gulf Coast, Enterprise has found ample opportunity to initiate organic growth projects to transport and process the increasing amounts of natural gas and natural-gas liquids (NGL) being produced in these areas. Two projects stand out.

First, the Independence platform and pipeline off the coast of Louisiana will gather and transport up to 1 billion cubic feet per day (bcf/d) of natural gas from its deep-water position. Second, the company recently announced plans to build a new pipeline through the Barnett Shale that will carry 1.1 bcf/d of natural gas to Sherman, Texas. There it will connect with a new pipeline being built by Boardwalk Pipeline Partners that will provide access to a variety of delivery points in the southeast and northeast U.S. In all, the company plans to spend nearly $4 billion in capital expenditures from 2006 through 2008.

Beyond the current plans, additional growth opportunities will likely present themselves over the next five years. Production in the Barnett Shale should continue to expand, which will require additional processing and transportation capacity. The company's processing and NGL pipelines in the Rockies should stay busy, and capacity expansion is not out of the question. In addition, Enterprise's strong presence along the Gulf Coast could benefit from liquefied-natural-gas imports and new offshore production as producers search for hydrocarbons in deeper and deeper waters.

Data as of 12-29-06

EOG Resources EOG

	Rating	Fair Value	Last Close	Consider Buy	Consider Sell	Yield %
	★★★★	$77.00	$62.45	$59.40	$96.50	0.35

Company Profile
EOG Resources is one of the largest independent natural-gas producers in the United States. About 85% of its production in gas and 85% of its total production comes from the U.S. and Canada. At year-end, the company had total reserves of 6.2 trillion cubic feet of gas equivalent and was producing over 1.5 billion cubic feet of gas equivalent a day. EOG Resources changed its name from Enron Oil and Gas when its spin-off from Enron was completed in 1999.

Management
Stewardship Grade [B]

Though EOG can trace its lineage to Enron, its current management does not appear to have had anything to do with the funny business that brought Enron down. Mark Papa has been at EOG and its predecessor companies for more than 20 years; he became chairman and CEO at the time of EOG's independence from Enron in 1999. In 2005, Papa took home $3.4 million in cash compensation and restricted stock. We like that the firm relies on a mix of cash bonuses, restricted stock, and stock options to compensate its executives. Executive bonuses are based on reinvestment rate of return, production growth, reserve replacement, finding costs, and stock price performance in relation to the firm's peer group. In addition, individual cash bonuses are capped at $2 million. We like that the firm has tempered its use of stock options over the past three years. The firm also earns kudos for its minimum stock ownership requirement for senior managers, which ranges from 1 times base salary for vice presidents to 5 times base salary for the CEO. We believe EOG has above-average stewardship practices.

333 Clay Street Suite 4200 www.eogresources.com
Houston, TX 77002-7361

Growth [B]	2002	2003	2004	2005
Revenue %	-33.9	59.4	30.2	59.4
Earnings/Share %	-80.6	462.5	43.3	98.8
Book Value/Share %	10.4	26.8	34.2	44.4
Dividends/Share %	3.2	12.5	27.8	30.4

Profitability [A]	2003	2004	2005	TTM
Return on Assets %	8.8	10.6	16.2	16.5
Oper Cash Flow $Mil	1,249	1,444	2,369	2,845
- Cap Spending $Mil	1,246	1,417	1,725	2,454
= Free Cash Flow $Mil	4	28	645	391

Financial Health [A+]	2003	2004	2005	09-30-06
Long-term Debt $Mil	1,109	1,078	859	705
Total Equity $Mil	2,075	2,847	4,217	5,375
Debt/Equity Ratio	0.5	0.4	0.2	0.1

Industry	Business Risk	Moat Size	Investment Style	Sector
Oil/Gas	Average	Narrow	Large Core	Energy

Competition	Market Cap $Mil	12 Mo Trailing Sales $Mil	Price/Cash Flow	Return On Assets%	Debt/Equity	Total Return% 1 Yr	3 Yr
EOG Resources	15,205	4,186	5.3	16.5	0.1	-14.6	40.2
Occidental Petroleum	41,070	17,548	6.4	13.9	0.2	24.3	34.9
Devon Energy	29,649	11,274	4.3	9.4	0.3	8.1	33.7

Price Volatility — Monthly Price High/Low — Relative Strength to S&P 500

	2001	2002	2003	2004	2005	2006
Annual $Price High/Low	27.75/12.90	22.08/15.01	23.76/17.85	38.25/21.23	82.00/32.05	86.91/56.31
Annual Total Return %	-28.2	2.5	16.2	55.2	106.3	-14.6
Fiscal Year-End: December	2001	2002	2003	2004	2005	TTM
Revenue $Mil	1,655	1,095	1,745	2,271	3,620	4,186
Net Income $Mil	388	76	419	614	1,252	1,513
Earnings Per Share $	1.65	0.32	1.80	2.58	5.13	6.16
Shares Outstanding Mil	231	231	229	233	239	243
Return on Equity %	25.9	4.6	20.2	21.6	29.7	28.2
Net Margin %	23.4	7.0	24.0	27.0	34.6	36.2
Asset Turnover	0.5	0.3	0.4	0.4	0.5	0.5
Financial Leverage	2.3	2.3	2.3	2.0	1.8	1.7

Valuation Ratios	Stock	Rel to Industry	Rel to S&P 500
Price/Earnings	10.1	0.8	0.5
Price/Book	2.8	0.9	0.7
Price/Sales	3.6	1.9	1.2
Price/Cash Flow	5.3	0.6	0.4

Major Fund Holders	% of Fund Assets
Westport R	5.34
Blackrock Natural Resources B	3.56
Masters' Select Equity	3.38
Stratton Multi Cap	3.30

Thesis By Justin Perucki, CFA, 11-07-06 Stock Price as of Analysis: $66.25

EOG focuses on natural-gas exploration and production in North America. About 85% of its production is natural gas, with the balance primarily oil. A similarly large percentage of its production is done in the United States and Canada, with the rest mostly in Trinidad.

EOG has historically shunned acquisitions, preferring to find and develop reserves on its own. Although its production growth hasn't been as impressive as some of its competitors, EOG operates one of the lowest-cost asset bases in the industry. The firm's low-cost structure helps improve its odds of remaining profitable even during the bottom of the industry cycle. Moreover, by minimizing capital costs and operational costs, EOG enjoys solid returns on capital. EOG's returns on capital over the past five years have averaged north of 20%, by our calculations.

Recently, EOG has been aggressively targeting unconventional natural-gas deposits. With 504,000 acres, EOG is one of the largest lease holders in the prodigious Barnett Shale, which is around Fort Worth, Texas. Like most unconventional resource plays, the natural-gas deposits in the Barnett are well-defined, but extracting large amounts of natural gas from the area was not economical until a few years ago. Thanks to high natural-gas prices and technological advances like horizontal drilling, the Barnett Shale is now one of the hottest areas in North American natural gas.

EOG has been ramping up its drilling program in the area, and production growth has been accelerating. However, we are more impressed with the firm's ability to keep costs in check in an escalating price environment. One way EOG has been able to minimize costs has been by cutting in half the time it takes to drill a well, enabling the firm to drill twice as many wells in the same amount of time. The Barnett Shale should be a substantial value driver for the firm for many years. Management is hoping to apply the knowledge it is acquiring from the Barnett Shale to other shale resources plays as well: EOG is evaluating five other shale-based plays that could materially increase the firm's reserves over the next two years.

The proximity of EOG's producing properties to the thirsty American market is a distinct advantage. Unlike oil, natural gas is very difficult to transport outside a pipeline network, and imports from resource-rich places such as the Middle East are currently negligible. Natural-gas prices, as a result, are kept artificially high.

Data as of 12-29-06

Equifax EFX

	Rating	Fair Value	Last Close	Consider Buy	Consider Sell	Yield %
	★★★	$37.00	$40.60	$28.50	$46.40	0.39

Company Profile

Equifax collects, organizes, and manages various types of financial, demographic, and marketing information. Consumers access their credit reports through Equifax, and Equifax enables businesses to make credit and service decisions, manage their risk, and develop marketing strategies. It is one of the nation's largest credit-reporting agencies, boasting information on more than 400 million consumers and businesses worldwide.

Management Stewardship Grade [C]

CEO and chairman Richard Smith joined Equifax in September 2005, when Thomas Chapman retired. Before joining Equifax, Smith spent two decades with General Electric, most recently as COO of GE Insurance Solutions. Smith received a generous compensation package of $1.3 million in base salary and a bonus targeted at 1 times his salary. He also received 75,000 options and 50,000 restricted-stock units upon joining the firm. Moreover, to replace potential compensation he forfeited by leaving GE, Equifax paid Smith a $2.7 million bonus and awarded him an additional $1.2 million in restricted stock. Overall, Equifax gets average marks for stewardship. The firm could improve its score by trimming takeover defenses, putting all directors up for re-election every year, separating the chairman and CEO roles, and providing more information about how the CEO's performance-based bonus is determined.

1550 Peachtree Street, N.W. www.equifax.com
Atlanta, GA 30309

Growth [C]	2002	2003	2004	2005
Revenue %	-0.1	10.5	5.1	13.4
Earnings/Share %	—	NMF	46.7	5.7
Book Value/Share %	—	NMF	45.2	57.6
Dividends/Share %	-64.4	0.0	37.5	36.4

Profitability [A+]	2003	2004	2005	TTM
Return on Assets %	10.6	15.1	13.5	14.5
Oper Cash Flow $Mil	294	309	338	356
- Cap Spending $Mil	14	17	17	18
= Free Cash Flow $Mil	280	293	321	338

Financial Health [A]	2003	2004	2005	09-30-06
Long-term Debt $Mil	663	399	464	417
Total Equity $Mil	372	524	820	918
Debt/Equity Ratio	1.8	0.8	0.6	0.5

Industry	Business Risk	Moat Size	Investment Style	Sector
Business Support	Average	Wide	Mid Core	Business Services

Competition	Market Cap $Mil	12 Mo Trailing Sales $Mil	Price/Cash Flow	Return On Assets%	Debt/Equity	Total Return% 1 Yr	3 Yr
Equifax	5,080	1,518	14.3	14.5	0.5	7.3	19.7
First American	3,932	8,360	—	6.4	—	-8.6	12.4
Fair Isaac	2,349	825	11.8	7.8	0.0	-7.8	8.1

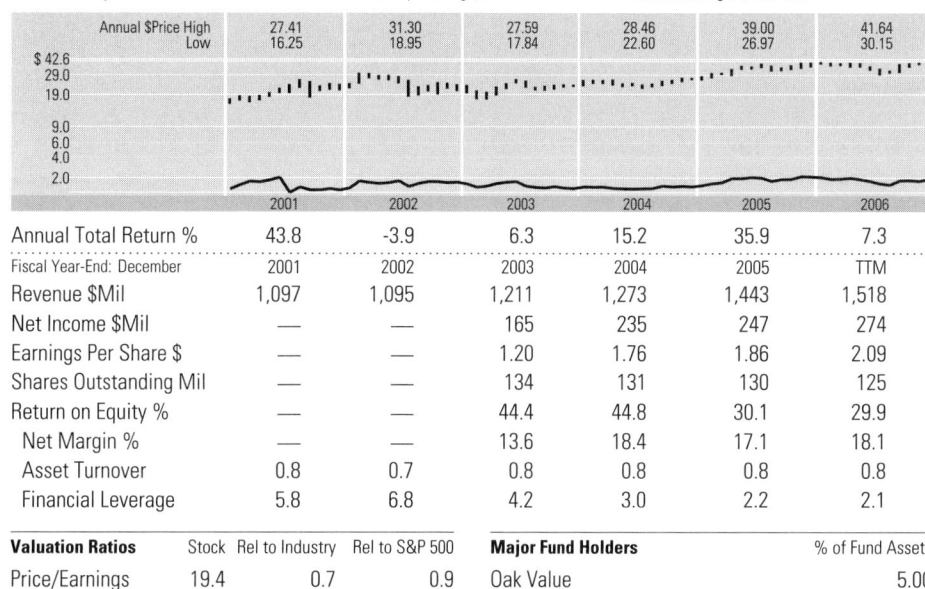

	2001	2002	2003	2004	2005	2006
Annual Total Return %	43.8	-3.9	6.3	15.2	35.9	7.3
Fiscal Year-End: December	2001	2002	2003	2004	2005	TTM
Revenue $Mil	1,097	1,095	1,211	1,273	1,443	1,518
Net Income $Mil	—	—	165	235	247	274
Earnings Per Share $	—	—	1.20	1.76	1.86	2.09
Shares Outstanding Mil	—	—	134	131	130	125
Return on Equity %	—	—	44.4	44.8	30.1	29.9
Net Margin %	—	—	13.6	18.4	17.1	18.1
Asset Turnover	0.8	0.7	0.8	0.8	0.8	0.8
Financial Leverage	5.8	6.8	4.2	3.0	2.2	2.1

Valuation Ratios	Stock	Rel to Industry	Rel to S&P 500
Price/Earnings	19.4	0.7	0.9
Price/Book	5.5	1.3	1.3
Price/Sales	3.3	0.7	1.1
Price/Cash Flow	14.3	0.8	1.0

Major Fund Holders	% of Fund Assets
Oak Value	5.00
Jensen J	3.79
Regions Morgan Keegan Sel MidCap Value A	2.81
Legacy Multi-Cap Core Equity Tr	2.79

Thesis By Mark Weber, 10-19-06 Stock Price as of Analysis: $36.92

Although Equifax's core credit-reporting business squares off against two big rivals, we think the firm has a wide moat.

Equifax's most valuable asset is its database of credit histories on more than 400 million consumers and businesses worldwide. Financial institutions use credit histories to make lending decisions. Equifax shares the credit information market with two well-matched competitors: Experian and TransUnion. Given the high barriers to entry, we expect the triumvirate to rule the credit-reporting business for the foreseeable future.

The credit information industry's economics are compelling. Banks typically pull reports from multiple databases, so there's plenty of business to go around, keeping competition from crushing returns. The presence of two large rivals in the marketplace hasn't kept Equifax from earning returns on capital almost 3 times larger than its cost of capital.

Moreover, managing a database and providing credit information is a highly scalable business with few incremental costs. The firm's North American credit-reporting segment generates operating margins higher than 40%, driving companywide operating margins close to 30%. Equifax's core credit data business requires very little capital reinvestment, resulting in enviable free cash flows. Over the past five years, the firm's free cash has consistently been around 20% of sales.

Although we don't expect much growth from the firm's core North American credit business, Equifax does have some attractive growth opportunities elsewhere. The company holds a dominant position in several Latin American countries where credit reporting is still in its infancy. Latin American operations, however, produced less than 9% of the firm's revenue last year. Equifax's North American segment, which generates more than 80% of total revenue and almost all of the firm's operating income, will continue to drive the firm's performance for the foreseeable future.

Equifax's small-business credit scores also offer a promising avenue for growth. Revenue from small-business scores has grown sixfold since 2003, but still makes up only 1% of total sales. We expect the unit to enjoy phenomenal growth for several years, rising above 5% of total revenue by 2010. Equifax's small-business database is proprietary, unique to the industry, and would be difficult to replicate. Banks are hungry for a way to better assess small-business loan risks, and Equifax is perfectly positioned to fulfill that need.

Data as of 12-29-06

Equity Residential EQR

	Rating	Fair Value	Last Close	Consider Buy	Consider Sell	Yield %
	★	$35.00	$50.75	$29.80	$46.00	3.53

Company Profile

Equity Residential is the largest publicly traded apartment real estate investment trust by both units owned and market capitalization. The company owns or has an interest in about 950 multifamily residential properties comprising more than 200,000 apartments in 33 states. Its top five markets by net operating income are Boston, Atlanta, South Florida, San Francisco, and Los Angeles.

Management
Stewardship Grade [A]

Legendary real estate investor Sam Zell founded Equity Residential in 1969, took it public in 1993, and remains the chairman. The company has seen high CEO turnover in the past four years: In 2006, David Neithercut took over from Bruce Duncan, who had become CEO at the beginning of 2003 after longtime CEO Douglas Crocker retired. Neithercut was previously president of the company, and we think that the succession has gone smoothly. Duncan received around $1.8 million in total compensation in 2005, a reasonable amount considering the company's performance. All trustees and executive officers together own 7% of the firm, which should align their interests with those of other shareholders.

Two North Riverside Plaza www.eqr.com
Chicago, IL 60606

Growth [C+]	2002	2003	2004	2005
Revenue %	-2.0	1.4	10.9	11.5
Earnings/Share %	-11.9	31.4	-4.5	88.5
Book Value/Share %	-5.4	-3.7	-13.9	7.7
Dividends/Share %	3.0	0.0	0.0	0.6

Profitability [A]	2003	2004	2005	TTM
Return on Assets %	3.7	3.3	5.7	5.3
Oper Cash Flow $Mil	744	718	714	—
- Cap Spending $Mil	809	1,171	2,676	—
= Free Cash Flow $Mil	—	—	—	—

Financial Health [NA]	2003	2004	2005	09-30-06
Long-term Debt $Mil	—	—	—	—
Total Equity $Mil	5,015	4,436	4,891	5,137
Debt/Equity Ratio	—	—	—	—

Industry	Business Risk	Moat Size	Investment Style	Sector
REITs	Below Avg	Narrow	Large Value	Financial Services

Competition	Market Cap $Mil	12 Mo Trailing Sales $Mil	Price/Cash Flow	Return On Assets %	Debt/ Equity	Total Return % 1 Yr	3 Yr
Equity Residential	14,826	2,187	—	5.3	—	34.6	25.5
Archstone-Smith Trust	12,734	1,190	—	6.6	—	43.9	35.1
AvalonBay Communities	9,702	716	—	5.7	—	49.7	45.3

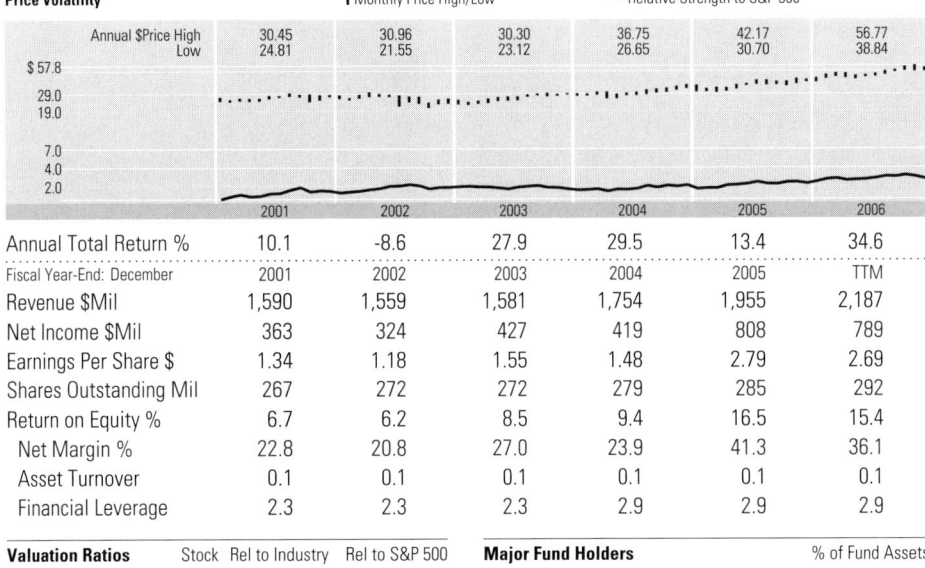

	2001	2002	2003	2004	2005	2006
Annual Total Return %	10.1	-8.6	27.9	29.5	13.4	34.6
Fiscal Year-End: December	2001	2002	2003	2004	2005	TTM
Revenue $Mil	1,590	1,559	1,581	1,754	1,955	2,187
Net Income $Mil	363	324	427	419	808	789
Earnings Per Share $	1.34	1.18	1.55	1.48	2.79	2.69
Shares Outstanding Mil	267	272	272	279	285	292
Return on Equity %	6.7	6.2	8.5	9.4	16.5	15.4
Net Margin %	22.8	20.8	27.0	23.9	41.3	36.1
Asset Turnover	0.1	0.1	0.1	0.1	0.1	0.1
Financial Leverage	2.3	2.3	2.3	2.9	2.9	2.9

Valuation Ratios	Stock	Rel to Industry	Rel to S&P 500	Major Fund Holders	% of Fund Assets
Price/Earnings	115.3	2.4	5.6	Fidelity Advisor Real Estate A	7.42
Price/Book	2.9	0.7	0.7	Fidelity Real Estate Investment	6.93
Price/Sales	6.8	0.9	2.3	SSgA Tuckerman Active REIT	6.73
Price/Cash Flow	—	—	—	Adelante U.S. Real Estate Secs Y	6.16

Thesis By Jeremy Glaser, 12-11-06 Stock Price as of Analysis: $52.95

Equity Residential's massive collection of apartments has generated a steady income stream for years. We think that the recent slowdown in the housing market, which has pushed up demand for rental apartments, will lead to even stronger growth in the future.

When interest rates were low many would-be apartment dwellers bought homes out of fear of missing out on rising markets. As residents moved out, Equity Residential was forced to cut rents to keep its apartments occupied, leading to years of soft growth. Fortunately for Equity Residential, its broad national exposure and condo conversion business softened the blow.

Equity Residential used this buying frenzy as an opportunity to reshape its portfolio. In the past, the company spent considerable energy building a national presence, with apartments in nearly every major market in the United States. But, in the past five years, it has sold properties in slowing markets like the Midwest to focus on markets with high barriers to entry, such as New York and Washington. As investors willingly paid stratospheric prices to snap up condos--even in secondary markets--Equity Residential secured attractive valuations for its properties, reinvesting the proceeds into higher-growth opportunities. We think this reworked portfolio will drive growth for years to come.

Now that apartment fundamentals are turning in Equity Residential's favor, the firm is ready to profit. High home prices combined with less favorable mortgage terms are making renting more attractive than owning. As a result, Equity Residential is increasing occupancies, raising rent, reducing concessions, and passing on a larger share of utility costs to tenants. Even though a slow housing market is killing off the firm's condo business, we believe the increased attractiveness of its core rental business will more than make up for the lost revenue.

The company is also benefiting from a lull in the supply of apartments. A large number of luxury rental buildings were converted to condominiums in the past five years, and almost all new construction in that period was focused on condos and single-family homes. Additionally, sky-high construction costs and challenging permitting processes are preventing a flood of new construction from hitting the rental market. Even if condos built for sale are put up for rent, we believe it will be a long time before supply catches up to demand. Equity Residential is in the pole position to profit from the strong rental market.

Data as of 12-29-06

Estee Lauder A EL

Rating ★★★	Fair Value $41.00	Last Close $40.82	Consider Buy $31.60	Consider Sell $51.40	Yield % 1.23

Company Profile
Estee Lauder manufactures skin-care, makeup, fragrance, and hair-care products. Its products are sold in more than 130 countries and territories and include brand names like Estee Lauder, Clinique, Prescriptives, and Origins. The firm also makes men's skin-care and fragrance products sold mainly under the Aramis brand name. Lauder's women's fragrances include Beautiful, White Linen, Pleasures, and Clinique Happy.

Management   Stewardship Grade [C]
Estee Lauder's grandson, William Lauder, assumed the helm as CEO in July 2004. William's father, Leonard Lauder, is chairman, and his uncle Ronald, his mother, Evelyn, and cousins Aerin and Jane also work for the firm. Family members have about 83.1% of the voting power of the company via ownership of Class B common stock. Directors and officers own 14.3% of Class A shares. We dislike the discrepancy between management control and economic interest reflected in these two share classes. With the sway that the family has over the company, shareholder concerns are more likely to take a back seat. The Lauder family's interests are certainly well aligned with the firm, but shareholder returns over the last five years have still been subpar. William Lauder was paid $3.0 million in salary and bonus in 2006, 8.5% less than the previous year, for failing to meet revenue and earnings goals. He also received $1.1 million in restricted stock during the year, which strikes us as a bit much. With so much of his and his family's wealth tied up in Estee Lauder, we question the effectiveness of these additional awards.

767 Fifth Avenue   www.elcompanies.com
New York, NY 10153

Growth [C+]	2003	2004	2005	2006
Revenue %	8.1	13.7	9.4	2.9
Earnings/Share %	80.0	17.5	20.3	-37.1
Book Value/Share %	5.2	33.7	-1.1	0.3
Dividends/Share %	0.0	50.0	33.3	0.0

Profitability [B+]	2004	2005	2006	TTM
Return on Assets %	9.2	10.5	6.5	6.2
Oper Cash Flow $Mil	673	478	710	704
- Cap Spending $Mil	212	230	261	282
= Free Cash Flow $Mil	461	249	449	422

Financial Health [A-]	2004	2005	2006	09-30-06
Long-term Debt $Mil	—	451	432	439
Total Equity $Mil	1,734	1,693	1,622	1,589
Debt/Equity Ratio	—	0.3	0.3	0.3

Industry	Business Risk	Moat Size	Investment Style	Sector
Household Products	Average	Narrow	Mid Core	Consumer Goods

Competition	Market Cap $Mil	12 Mo Trailing Sales $Mil	Price/Cash Flow	Return On Assets%	Debt/ Equity	Total Return% 1 Yr	3 Yr
Estee Lauder A	8,522	6,560	12.1	6.2	0.3	23.4	3.0
Procter & Gamble	203,656	72,214	16.8	6.8	0.6	13.4	11.3
L'Oreal ADR	62,617	18,198	23.9	8.7	0.0	35.8	7.4

Price Volatility | Monthly Price High/Low — Relative Strength to S&P 500

Annual $Price High Low	44.35 29.85	38.80 25.20	40.20 25.75	49.34 37.50	47.50 29.98	43.60 32.79
	2001	2002	2003	2004	2005	2006
Annual Total Return %	-26.4	-16.8	49.9	17.6	-26.0	23.4

Fiscal Year-End: June	2002	2003	2004	2005	2006	TTM
Revenue $Mil	4,672	5,050	5,742	6,280	6,464	6,560
Net Income $Mil	192	320	342	406	244	244
Earnings Per Share $	0.70	1.26	1.48	1.78	1.12	1.13
Shares Outstanding Mil	270	252	228	226	214	209
Return on Equity %	13.1	22.5	19.7	24.0	15.1	15.4
Net Margin %	4.1	6.3	6.0	6.5	3.8	3.7
Asset Turnover	1.4	1.5	1.5	1.6	1.7	1.7
Financial Leverage	2.3	2.4	2.1	2.3	2.3	2.5

Valuation Ratios	Stock	Rel to Industry	Rel to S&P 500	Major Fund Holders	% of Fund Assets
Price/Earnings	27.6	1.1	1.3	Sycuan U.S. Value	4.16
Price/Book	5.4	0.9	1.3	IXIS Harris Associates Focused Value C	3.98
Price/Sales	1.3	0.5	0.4	Van Kampen American Franchise A	2.92
Price/Cash Flow	12.1	0.7	0.8	AIM Mid Cap Core Equity A	2.75

Thesis By Lauren DeSanto, 12-05-06 Stock Price as of Analysis: $41.98

We're big believers in the power of luxury and aspirational brands and their ability to entice consumers to trade up. Estee Lauder has a stable of these prestige brands, which have given it a narrow economic moat, but its reliance on a consolidating department store retail channel has dealt the shares a setback over the past year.

Estee Lauder's brands define the prestige segment in beauty care. The firm has crafted aspirational hair-care, skin-care, makeup, and fragrance brands for all types of consumers and protected them over the years by controlling their distribution. Clinique, Estee Lauder, and La Mer are found at department stores, for example, while Aveda and MAC have stand-alone stores. The brands' sales outlets have been fundamental to the prestige image the firm cultivates.

Unfortunately for Estee Lauder, changes in U.S. consumer shopping habits that have been building for several years came to a head in the form of dramatic department store consolidation. So far, Federated's acquisition of May has resulted in 75 department store closures and lost revenue of $70 million for Estee Lauder's fiscal 2006. These closures have hurt the core Estee Lauder and Clinique brands, which rely heavily on department store cosmetics counters for distribution. Compounding the problems associated with these changes at retail has been management's poor initial assessment of their impact. More store closures are likely to follow in 2007, and we expect stability in the channel is still another year or more out.

We remain positive about Estee Lauder over the long term, however, because it relies less and less on that channel. Roughly 37% of sales come from North American department stores now, compared with 46% four years ago. More important, the firm's core competence is in creating and nurturing prestige brands, not just the brands themselves. This means that even when some brands, like Estee Lauder, risk being out of date with many consumers, the firm has in its lineup other fast-growing, niche brands--like MAC, Bobbi Brown, and Aveda--with a lot of potential. We believe the firm's brands will continue to be relevant to consumers as Estee Lauder balances the need to build out alternative points of distribution to compensate for department store sales declines with retaining the cachet so essential to its brands. In the meantime, the firm continues to earn returns on invested capital that exceed our estimate of its cost of capital. We would look for a discount to our fair value estimate before investing.

Data as of 12-29-06

Expedia EXPE

	Rating	Fair Value	Last Close	Consider Buy	Consider Sell	Yield %
	★★★★★	$30.00	$20.98	$23.10	$37.60	0.00

Industry	Business Risk	Moat Size	Investment Style	Sector
Online Retail	Average	Narrow	Mid Core	Consumer Services

Company Profile
Expedia is the world's largest online travel agency, with over $15 billion in gross bookings during 2005. The firm's brands include Expedia.com, Hotels.com, Hotwire, and TripAdvisor. In early 2005, the company increased its ownership of Chinese online travel agent eLong to 59%, making it a wholly owned subsidiary of Expedia. In 2005, Expedia generated more than 20% of sales from its international operations. Expedia was spun off from parent IAC/InterActiveCorp in August 2005.

Management
Stewardship Grade [NA]

Dara Khosrowshahi was appointed CEO of Expedia after the company was spun off from its former parent, IAC/InterActiveCorp. Prior to his current role, Khosrowshahi served in various executive positions within IAC. Barry Diller remains chairman of Expedia, in addition to his role as CEO and chairman of IAC. We're not fans of Expedia's dual-class ownership structure, as each B-class share gives its owner 10 votes compared with only one vote per common share. By owning 100% of the B-class shares (including those owned by Liberty Media L, over which Diller has voting control), Diller controls slightly more than 50% of the total voting power, leaving minority shareholders with little say in the strategy and business proceedings of Expedia. That said, we have no reason to expect any wrongdoings and admire management's willingness to sacrifice short-term results to create value over the long haul.

3150 139th Avenue SE
Bellevue, WA 98005
www.expedia.com

Growth [C+]	2002	2003	2004	2005
Revenue %	179.4	56.1	-21.2	15.0
Earnings/Share %	NMF	NMF	NMF	NMF
Book Value/Share %	—	—	—	—
Dividends/Share %	NMF	NMF	NMF	NMF

Profitability [C]	2003	2004	2005	TTM
Return on Assets %	1.3	1.7	2.9	2.4
Oper Cash Flow $Mil	644	803	850	653
- Cap Spending $Mil	46	53	52	79
= Free Cash Flow $Mil	598	749	798	574

Financial Health [A]	2003	2004	2005	09-30-06
Long-term Debt $Mil	—	—	—	500
Total Equity $Mil	7,554	8,153	5,734	5,794
Debt/Equity Ratio	—	—	—	0.1

Competition	Market Cap $Mil	12 Mo Trailing Sales $Mil	Price/Cash Flow	Return On Assets%	Debt/Equity	Total Return% 1 Yr	3 Yr
Expedia	6,947	2,201	10.6	2.4	0.1	-12.4	—
Sabre Holdings CD	4,221	2,789	11.9	2.9	0.6	34.7	16.1

Price Volatility | Monthly Price High/Low — Relative Strength to S&P 500

	2001	2002	2003	2004	2005	2006
Annual Total Return %	—	—	—	—	—	-12.4
Fiscal Year-End: December	2001	2002	2003	2004	2005	TTM
Revenue $Mil	536	1,499	2,340	1,843	2,119	2,201
Net Income $Mil	9	77	111	163	229	203
Earnings Per Share $	—	—	—	—	—	—
Shares Outstanding Mil	—	—	—	—	—	331
Return on Equity %	3.9	3.7	1.5	2.0	4.0	3.5
Net Margin %	1.7	5.1	4.8	8.9	10.8	9.2
Asset Turnover	0.8	0.5	0.3	0.2	0.3	0.3
Financial Leverage	2.9	1.6	1.2	1.2	1.4	1.4

Valuation Ratios	Stock	Rel to Industry	Rel to S&P 500
Price/Earnings	—	—	—
Price/Book	1.2	0.1	0.3
Price/Sales	3.2	0.7	1.1
Price/Cash Flow	10.6	0.6	0.7

Major Fund Holders	% of Fund Assets
Janus Global Opportunities	3.47
Red Oak Technology Select	3.25
Pin Oak Aggressive Stock	3.10
Legg Mason Special Investment Prim	3.04

Thesis By Sumit Desai, CFA, 12-15-06 Stock Price as of Analysis: $20.65

Expedia has set itself apart from its peers in the cutthroat online travel market. Although competition is heating up, we like Expedia's chances of remaining on top.

The online travel arena is crowded, with several players fighting for a piece of the consumer's travel budget. Online travel agents (OTAs) negotiate wholesale rates with travel suppliers (airlines and hotels) and sell at a markup, while pocketing the difference. Initially, travel suppliers were eager to use OTAs to help sell inventory. In recent years, however, hotels and airlines--boosted by an improved economy and improving occupancy rates--have begun selling inventory through their own Web sites and reducing allocations to OTAs.

Expedia has separated itself from the pack, however, with several competitive advantages. Expedia is almost twice as big as its closest competitor, with a near-40% market share of U.S. online leisure bookings. The company uses its size to negotiate lower wholesale prices from suppliers, and, because Expedia is the largest OTA, more suppliers are likely to distribute through the firm. The lower costs lead to higher margins than competitors, and the diverse inventory attracts even more customers to Expedia's sites, leading to favorable network economics and an uphill battle for competing OTAs.

In response to competition, Expedia is focusing on differentiating its product offerings. For example, the company is focusing on offering higher-margin vacation packages, which are difficult for suppliers and meta-search firms to duplicate. Expedia also benefits from the vast amount of user reviews on its various Web sites. User reviews are often the last feature viewed on Expedia's site before a purchase is made, demonstrating the importance consumers often place on this feature. Expedia's user reviews also benefit from the network effect. As more users write reviews, other customers are more likely to book on Expedia and leave additional user reviews.

We also have high hopes for Expedia's international expansion for several reasons. First, online travel penetration has yet to reach the levels seen in the U.S. In Europe, only 14% of travel was booked online during 2005, compared with almost 30% in the States. As Expedia and other OTAs increase their marketing in Europe, we expect online travel bookings to increase rapidly. Expedia should also benefit from a more fragmented travel market in Europe and Asia, since smaller hotels hold less bargaining power and look to large OTAs as attractive marketing partners.

Data as of 12-29-06

Expeditors International of Washington EXPD

	Rating	Fair Value	Last Close	Consider Buy	Consider Sell	Yield %
	★★★★★	$56.00	$40.50	$47.70	$73.50	0.54

Company Profile

Based in Seattle, Expeditors is primarily a consolidator and secondarily a forwarder of international air and ocean freight. It buys cargo space in bulk and resells it to customers needing shipping services. Expeditors also provides customs brokerage and other related logistics services. Its freight brokerage business primarily involves shipments to and from Asia, the United States, and Europe, with the first two constituting the bulk of business.

Management   Stewardship Grade [A]

Expeditors is exceptionally well managed, in our opinion, and earns our highest Stewardship Grade. Chairman and CEO Peter Rose has led the company for almost 20 years, and we think he has done a fantastic job. He has helped build a firm that is among the most profitable in the industry, with a strong record of internal growth on his watch. He has also steered the firm away from potentially disastrous acquisitions, something that has hampered many of the firm's peers. We also like that several of his lieutenants came from other international freight forwarders and are generally a pretty experienced bunch. We are particularly enamored with the company's unique compensation structure and candid disclosure. Executives earn very small fixed salaries, while the variable component is based on operating profit. This philosophy provides an incentive to maximize profitability and extends down to each branch manager, which spills over to the rank-and-file employees, who also share in the bonus pool. From a corporate-governance standpoint, we like what we see, though we would prefer to have the chairman and CEO positions held by separate individuals. Given the firm's laudable record of creating shareholder value, however, we're not terribly concerned.

1015 Third Avenue 12th Floor   www.expd.com
Seattle, WA 98104

Growth [A-]	2002	2003	2004	2005
Revenue %	22.0	14.3	26.4	17.6
Earnings/Share %	15.7	8.7	25.9	39.0
Book Value/Share %	26.3	23.6	23.0	12.3
Dividends/Share %	20.0	33.3	37.5	36.4

Profitability [A+]	2003	2004	2005	TTM
Return on Assets %	11.7	11.4	14.0	15.2
Oper Cash Flow $Mil	114	193	280	370
- Cap Spending $Mil	21	66	91	156
= Free Cash Flow $Mil	94	126	189	214

Financial Health [A]	2003	2004	2005	09-30-06
Long-term Debt $Mil	—	—	—	—
Total Equity $Mil	646	807	914	1,022
Debt/Equity Ratio	—	—	—	—

Industry	Business Risk	Moat Size	Investment Style	Sector
Transportation	Below Avg	Wide	Mid Growth	Business Services

Competition	Market Cap $Mil	12 Mo Trailing Sales $Mil	Price/Cash Flow	Return On Assets %	Debt/ Equity	Total Return % 1 Yr	3 Yr
Expeditors International of Washington	8,633	4,486	23.3	15.2	—	20.5	30.2
United Parcel Service B	80,494	46,873	15.1	11.4	0.2	1.8	2.4
FedEx	33,307	33,132	9.4	8.1	0.2	5.4	17.4

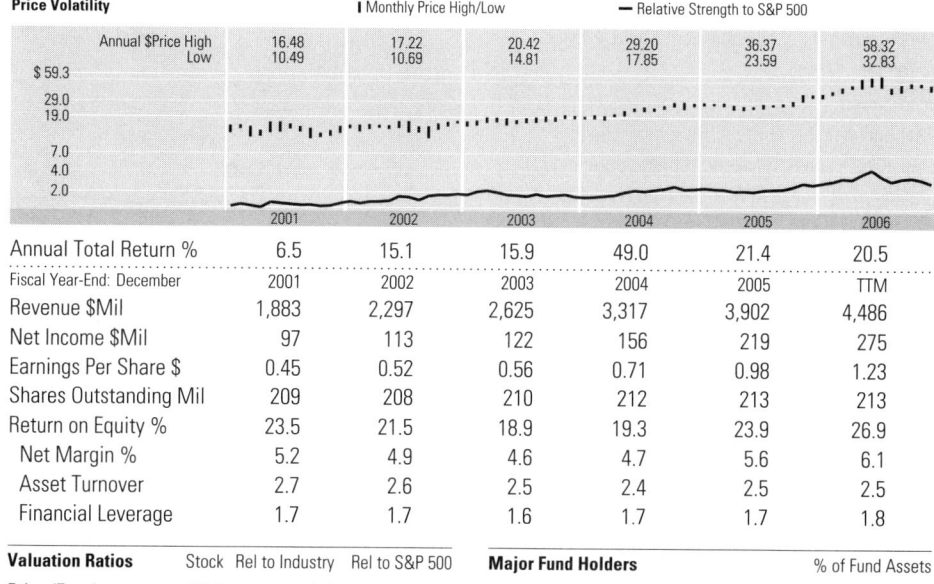

	2001	2002	2003	2004	2005	2006
Annual Total Return %	6.5	15.1	15.9	49.0	21.4	20.5
Fiscal Year-End: December	2001	2002	2003	2004	2005	TTM
Revenue $Mil	1,883	2,297	2,625	3,317	3,902	4,486
Net Income $Mil	97	113	122	156	219	275
Earnings Per Share $	0.45	0.52	0.56	0.71	0.98	1.23
Shares Outstanding Mil	209	208	210	212	213	213
Return on Equity %	23.5	21.5	18.9	19.3	23.9	26.9
Net Margin %	5.2	4.9	4.6	4.7	5.6	6.1
Asset Turnover	2.7	2.6	2.5	2.4	2.5	2.5
Financial Leverage	1.7	1.7	1.6	1.7	1.7	1.8

Valuation Ratios	Stock	Rel to Industry	Rel to S&P 500
Price/Earnings	32.9	1.6	1.6
Price/Book	8.5	1.9	2.1
Price/Sales	1.9	1.3	0.7
Price/Cash Flow	23.3	1.6	1.6

Major Fund Holders	% of Fund Assets
Fidelity Select Air Transportation	8.86
Kinetics Internet	7.30
Fidelity Select Transportation	4.76
Transamerica Premier Growth Opp Inv	4.62

Thesis By Peter Smith, 10-30-06 Stock Price as of Analysis: $48.66

Expeditors is one of the top companies in a pretty attractive industry.

Expeditors is a third-party logistics provider, which means it brokers freight transactions but does not actually move the goods itself, so it owns few assets. It acts primarily as a consolidator and secondarily as a forwarder of international air and ocean freight. As a consolidator, it purchases cargo space from airlines and ocean carriers and resells it to shippers at a lower price than they could obtain on their own. Once it has the cargo, it combines shipments into optimally sized (economically speaking) pallets and containers for shipment, creating value for itself in the process.

As a forwarder, Expeditors plays a similar role, but instead of prebuying cargo space and consolidating shipments, it simply "forwards" cargo to airlines and ocean carriers. Forwarding is less profitable than consolidation, so the company plays this role only when a given route does not yield sufficient volume for consolidation. In either case, the value for shippers is a lower shipping rate and wider carrier selection, while carriers get access to a broader array of shippers and freight.

In addition, Expeditors offers ancillary logistics services that add further value for shippers. Shippers are willing to pay Expeditors for its expertise in, say, customs brokerage to speed up a transaction and avoid the hassle. In fact, Expeditors is so good at these services that other freight forwarders occasionally hire the company for these segments of their transactions.

Non-asset-based firms such as Expeditors have among the highest returns on invested capital in the transportation industry, and competition is heating up as companies try to grab a piece of the pie. We believe Expeditors has several competitive advantages that increase its customers' willingness to pay, earning the firm our wide moat rating. Its global network, customer relationships, unique compensation structure that discourages frivolous spending, and sophisticated IT system would be challenging to duplicate. The firm also creates value partially through scale (by consolidating shipments), which might discourage a new entrant.

We think the firm has plenty of room to grow as more and more shippers streamline their logistics operations. We also expect the firm to continue to perform well in a slowing economy because it will have greater purchasing leverage with transportation providers. Despite increasing competition, Expeditors should continue to exhibit industry-leading growth and returns in the coming years.

Data as of 12-29-06

ExxonMobil XOM

	Rating	Fair Value	Last Close	Consider Buy	Consider Sell	Yield %
	★★★	$79.00	$76.63	$67.30	$103.70	1.67

Company Profile
The product of the 1999 marriage of energy giants Exxon and Mobil, ExxonMobil is the largest firm in the oil and gas industry and among the largest companies on the planet. ExxonMobil does business in almost every segment of the oil industry. In 2005, hydrocarbon production and oil refining capacity amounted to 4.2 million and 6.4 million barrels per day, respectively. ExxonMobil has proven reserves of 22 billion barrels of oil equivalent and a presence in more than 200 countries.

Management
Stewardship Grade [B]

After spending his entire 42-year career with ExxonMobil, Lee R. Raymond retired at the end of 2005. Former president Rex Tillerson is now in charge. Known for his fierce negotiation skills, we view Tillerson as a worthy successor, and expect the same conservative, high-return strategy that characterized Raymond's tenure to continue to be the Exxon mantra. We don't have 2005 compensation figures yet, but in 2004, Raymond's pay was just over $10 million, including salary, bonuses, and other compensation. He also received $28 million worth of restricted stock, but no stock options. Raymond's total compensation is among the highest in the energy sector, but he also headed the company that had the largest profits in the world last year. As a group, executives and directors own or have options on less than 0.4% of the total outstanding shares, not uncommon for a company of this age and size. While we think the company's financial disclosure is a bit weak and we'd prefer to see the chairmanship split from the CEO role, it would be very tough to argue that management hasn't provided good stewardship over time.

5959 Las Colinas Boulevard www.exxonmobil.com
Irving, TX 75039-2298

Growth [C-]	2002	2003	2004	2005
Revenue %	-3.7	22.8	20.8	24.4
Earnings/Share %	-24.0	92.3	20.4	46.8
Book Value/Share %	3.6	23.5	15.7	12.4
Dividends/Share %	1.1	6.5	8.2	7.5

Profitability [A+]	2003	2004	2005	TTM
Return on Assets %	12.3	13.0	17.3	17.8
Oper Cash Flow $Mil	28,498	40,551	48,138	50,814
- Cap Spending $Mil	12,859	11,986	13,839	15,200
= Free Cash Flow $Mil	15,639	28,565	34,299	35,614

Financial Health [A+]	2003	2004	2005	09-30-06
Long-term Debt $Mil	4,756	5,013	6,220	6,464
Total Equity $Mil	89,915	101,756	111,186	116,593
Debt/Equity Ratio	0.1	0.0	0.1	0.1

Industry	Business Risk	Moat Size	Investment Style	Sector
Oil/Gas	Below Avg	Wide	Large Core	Energy

Competition	Market Cap $Mil	12 Mo Trailing Sales $Mil	Price/Cash Flow	Return On Assets %	Debt/ Equity	Total Return% 1 Yr	3 Yr
ExxonMobil	446,944	386,951	8.8	17.8	0.1	39.1	26.2
BP PLC ADR	231,015	239,792	8.6	10.8	0.1	7.9	14.3
Royal Dutch Shell PLC ADR	230,956	306,731	7.7	11.5	0.1	19.3	15.1

Price Volatility — Monthly Price High/Low — Relative Strength to S&P 500

	2001	2002	2003	2004	2005	2006
Annual $Price High	45.84	44.54	41.13	52.05	65.96	79.00
Low	35.01	29.86	31.58	39.91	49.25	56.17
Annual Total Return %	-7.6	-8.9	20.6	28.0	11.8	39.1

Fiscal Year-End: December	2001	2002	2003	2004	2005	TTM
Revenue $Mil	208,715	200,949	246,738	298,035	370,680	386,951
Net Income $Mil	15,320	11,460	21,510	25,330	36,130	39,960
Earnings Per Share $	2.21	1.68	3.23	3.89	5.71	6.57
Shares Outstanding Mil	—	—	6,639	6,478	6,273	5,832
Return on Equity %	20.9	15.4	23.9	24.9	32.5	34.3
Net Margin %	7.3	5.7	8.7	8.5	9.7	10.3
Asset Turnover	1.5	1.3	1.4	1.5	1.8	1.7
Financial Leverage	2.0	2.0	1.9	1.9	1.9	1.9

Valuation Ratios	Stock	Rel to Industry	Rel to S&P 500
Price/Earnings	11.7	0.9	0.6
Price/Book	3.8	1.2	0.9
Price/Sales	1.2	0.6	0.4
Price/Cash Flow	8.8	1.0	0.6

Major Fund Holders	% of Fund Assets
Profunds UltraSector Oil & Gas Inv	21.83
ING Corporate Leaders Trust B	18.57
Putnam Global Natural Resources A	11.16
Copley	9.46

Thesis By Justin Perucki, CFA, 12-08-06 Stock Price as of Analysis: $75.50

We think ExxonMobil's massive scale and unrelenting pursuit of operational efficiency create a competitive advantage that the firm can bank on, no matter what path energy prices take.

Joining in the oil megamergers of the late 1990s, Exxon and Mobil combined to form the company we know today. Any way you slice them, the figures are impressive. In 2005, ExxonMobil registered revenue of $359 billion and staggering profits of $36 billion, greater than any other publicly traded firm in history. With more cash than debt and an 87-year-old AAA credit rating, the company's financial strength is almost unrivaled.

Underpinning this record of financial success is a culture of operational excellence and a conservative, disciplined approach to capital allocation, which former CEO Lee R. Raymond labeled as "boringly consistent." Compared with closest peers BP and Royal Dutch Shell, downstream refining, petrochemical, and lubricant operations make up a larger chunk of ExxonMobil's business. Although we don't view these industries as having attractive long-run economics, the scale and degree of integration that ExxonMobil achieves create opportunities for logistics efficiencies and product-flow optimization upon which the firm capitalizes. This allows the company to generate consistently superior returns.

In the oil field, ExxonMobil is making large investments that will shift its oil and gas production mix. While there's a lot of life left in large yet mature producing areas in North America and Europe, firm output in these geographies will steadily give way to rising production in more politically sensitive regions like West Africa, the Middle East, and Russia. Carving out its stake in the burgeoning global market for liquefied natural gas, ExxonMobil is exercising its forte and building a vast, integrated network.

Despite its industry-leading position, ExxonMobil has several challenges ahead. Its hulking size means growth will be increasingly harder to come by. In looking to work with foreign governments and national oil companies, the firm must ensure its status as a valued partner. Often targeted as environmental enemy number one, its environmental risks will not disappear anytime soon.

Despite being a price taker in a commodity market, ExxonMobil gets our wide moat rating because it consistently earns returns that exceed both its own cost of capital and the returns posted by its peers by a significant margin over the course of the cycle.

F5 Networks FFIV

Data as of 12-29-06

Rating	Fair Value	Last Close	Consider Buy	Consider Sell	Yield %
★★★	$72.00	$74.21	$45.90	$86.80	0.00

Company Profile
F5 Networks provides products that help manage growing network traffic, application complexity, and security concerns. F5's customer base has evolved from an initial focus on Internet service providers, Web hosters, and e-commerce sites to a current emphasis on the corporate IT market. Customers include Deutsche Telekom, Citigroup, eBay, General Electric, and General Motors.

Industry	Business Risk	Moat Size	Investment Style	Sector
Data Networking	Above Avg	Narrow	Mid Growth	Hardware

Competition

	Market Cap $Mil	12 Mo Trailing Sales $Mil	Price/Cash Flow	Return On Assets %	Debt/ Equity	Total Return % 1 Yr	3 Yr
F5 Networks	3,050	394	24.3	9.0	—	29.8	41.8
Cisco Systems	165,967	30,118	18.9	13.2	0.3	59.6	4.1
Nortel Networks	11,591	11,078	—	-12.1	3.4	-12.7	-15.9

Management Stewardship Grade [B]

Most of F5's corporate governance practices have been solid, but, like many other companies, the firm is embroiled in an investigation over its stock option granting practices. John McAdam, who previously ran IBM's Web server division, was brought in as president and CEO in 2000. McAdam and his senior management team did a good job weathering the downturn in information-technology spending. We think McAdam was fairly compensated in 2005, earning roughly $900,000 in combined salary and bonus. While top management owns only about 4% of the common stock, it holds a substantial number of options. However, management has the authority to initiate anti-takeover provisions, which could limit certain rights of shareholders. With the close of its fiscal year in September, the company noted that it had "substantially completed" its internal investigation into its past option granting practices and that it anticipates it will need to record up to $30 million in additional stock-based compensation expenses dating back to 1999, and does not expect the restatements to affect its cash or revenue position. While the company's past granting practices are troubling, we believe the company has been forthright and thorough in its disclosure and option investigation.

401 Elliott Avenue West www.F5.com
Seattle, WA 98119

Growth [A+]	2002	2003	2004	2005
Revenue %	7.0	47.7	64.4	40.0
Earnings/Share %	NMF	EUB	19.8	31.4
Book Value/Share %	5.3	118.4	38.8	25.1
Dividends/Share %	NMF	NMF	NMF	NMF

Profitability [A-]	2003	2004	2005	TTM
Return on Assets %	10.1	8.7	9.0	9.0
Oper Cash Flow $Mil	41	85	125	125
- Cap Spending $Mil	6	9	21	21
= Free Cash Flow $Mil	35	76	104	104

Financial Health [A+]	2003	2004	2005	03-31-06
Long-term Debt $Mil	—	—	—	—
Total Equity $Mil	308	460	616	616
Debt/Equity Ratio	—	—	—	—

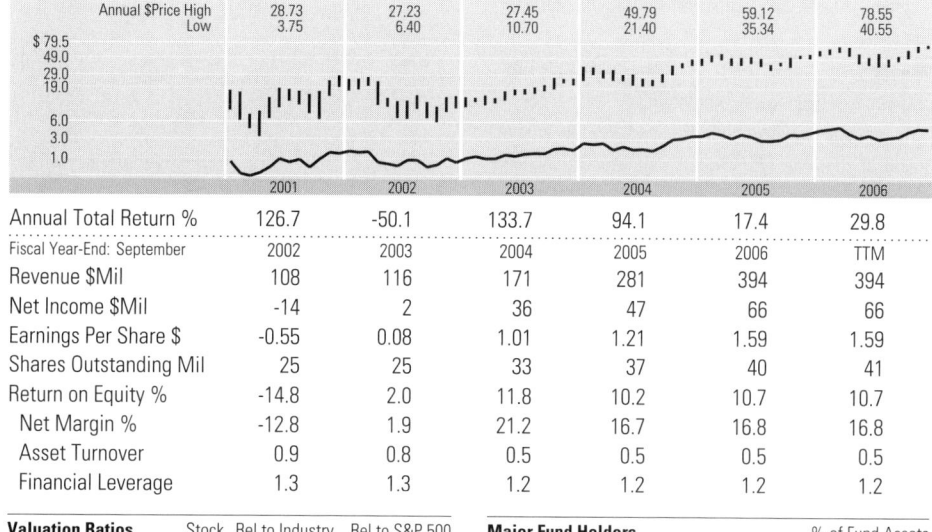

Price Volatility

	2001	2002	2003	2004	2005	2006
Annual $Price High	28.73	27.23	27.45	49.79	59.12	78.55
Low	3.75	6.40	10.70	21.40	35.34	40.55
Annual Total Return %	126.7	-50.1	133.7	94.1	17.4	29.8

Fiscal Year-End: September	2002	2003	2004	2005	2006	TTM
Revenue $Mil	108	116	171	281	394	394
Net Income $Mil	-14	2	36	47	66	66
Earnings Per Share $	-0.55	0.08	1.01	1.21	1.59	1.59
Shares Outstanding Mil	25	25	33	37	40	41
Return on Equity %	-14.8	2.0	11.8	10.2	10.7	10.7
Net Margin %	-12.8	1.9	21.2	16.7	16.8	16.8
Asset Turnover	0.9	0.8	0.5	0.5	0.5	0.5
Financial Leverage	1.3	1.3	1.2	1.2	1.2	1.2

Valuation Ratios	Stock	Rel to Industry	Rel to S&P 500
Price/Earnings	46.7	1.6	2.3
Price/Book	4.9	0.8	1.2
Price/Sales	7.7	1.4	2.7
Price/Cash Flow	24.3	1.2	1.7

Major Fund Holders	% of Fund Assets
Turner New Enterprise	3.94
STI Classic Emerging Growth Stock I	3.90
William Blair Mid Cap Growth N	3.24
William Blair Small-Mid Cap Growth I	2.70

Thesis By John Slack, 10-26-06 Stock Price as of Analysis: $66.65

As corporations move mission-critical applications and services to the Internet, efficiently prioritizing network traffic becomes imperative. F5 Networks' differentiated approach to network traffic management has allowed it to gain share from larger rivals like Cisco. We like the company's growth prospects and strategy.

As companies move more functionality online, network traffic has become increasingly complex, giving rise to a new category of network hardware called application switches. These devices examine each data packet to optimize traffic movement across the network. Customers save money by using a less expensive application switch instead of processor power embedded in servers or routers, while increasing network security and efficiency. F5 is a key player in this market; its switches essentially act as traffic cops to deliver maximum efficiency, throughput, and availability on the network.

Over the past several years, F5 has doubled its share of the application switch market--largely at Cisco's expense--by emphasizing a software-based approach to traffic management. F5's application switches consist of the firm's iControl software running on off-the-rack hardware. The high software content of its switches gives F5 industry-leading gross margins, above 75%. The company is able to control its costs by purchasing commodity hardware components and focusing on software development. Recently, F5 has made several small acquisitions in the network security area and plans to integrate this additional functionality into its switches.

The real competitive advantage of F5's switches lies in the iControl software. F5 has taken what we believe is a truly differentiated step in opening its software source code to outside vendors so they can modify their software to speed application performance. This adaptability has led to sales to would-be competitors like Dell, Hewlett-Packard, and IBM for use in their switches and blade server systems. More important, software developers like Microsoft, Oracle, and IBM have optimized many of their Web-based applications to run over F5's switches. These companies have become a lucrative sales channel for F5, driving more than 40% of new sales.

We think the company can improve margins while still enjoying robust sales growth over the next few years, but we do have concerns. Larger competitors like Cisco could, and probably will, integrate many of F5's features into their own products.

Data as of 12-29-06

Fair Isaac FIC

	Rating	Fair Value	Last Close	Consider Buy	Consider Sell	Yield %
	★★★	$44.00	$40.65	$33.90	$55.10	0.20

Industry	Business Risk	Moat Size	Investment Style	Sector
Data Processing	Average	Narrow	Mid Core	Business Services

Company Profile

Fair Isaac provides products and services that help businesses automate and improve decisions. With those tools, companies can target and acquire customers more efficiently, reduce fraud and credit losses, lower operating expenses, and enter new markets more profitably. Fair Isaac's customers are predominantly financial services companies but also include insurers, retailers, telecommunications providers, health-care organizations, and government agencies.

Competition

	Market Cap $Mil	12 Mo Trailing Sales $Mil	Price/Cash Flow	Return On Assets%	Debt/Equity	Total Return% 1 Yr	3 Yr
Fair Isaac	2,349	825	11.8	7.8	0.0	-7.8	8.1
Automatic Data Processing	27,117	9,177	17.2	6.1	0.0	9.1	8.8
Equifax	5,080	1,518	14.3	14.5	0.5	7.3	19.7

Management — Stewardship Grade [B]

CEO Thomas Grudnowski abruptly resigned his post with Fair Isaac in November. He has been replaced on an interim basis by CFO Charles Osborne. Grudnowski joined the company in 1999 after a long career with Accenture. A. George Battle, Fair Isaac's chairman, is also an Accenture alumnus, having spent almost three decades with the consultancy. Given their backgrounds, we aren't surprised that Fair Isaac has put a lot of emphasis on expanding its professional and consulting services. Despite Grudnowski's departure, the board and acting CEO do not plan to change Fair Isaac's strategic direction. We like the firm's compensation policy. Grudnowski's 2005 cash compensation totaled $1.5 million, mostly in the form of a performance-based bonus. In 2004, Grudnowski received no bonus and no base salary adjustment because the firm only partially achieved targeted objectives. Directors and executives as a whole own about 6.3% of the company. The firm's stewardship practices are sound. We particularly like that Fair Isaac allows cumulative voting for directors, which gives shareholders one vote per share multiplied by the number of directors. Cumulative voting empowers minority shareholders and is a practice we'd like more companies to adopt.

Price Volatility

Annual $Price High	31.07	29.61	43.12	41.53	48.47	47.89
Low	13.43	19.43	28.00	23.70	32.26	32.51
	2001	2002	2003	2004	2005	2006
Annual Total Return %	85.6	1.8	15.3	12.2	20.7	-7.8

Fiscal Year-End: September	2002	2003	2004	2005	2006	TTM
Revenue $Mil	392	629	706	799	825	825
Net Income $Mil	18	107	103	135	103	103
Earnings Per Share $	0.32	1.40	1.31	1.86	1.59	1.59
Shares Outstanding Mil	55	72	70	67	63	58
Return on Equity %	1.8	12.6	11.2	16.7	13.4	13.4
Net Margin %	4.6	17.0	14.6	16.8	12.5	12.5
Asset Turnover	0.3	0.4	0.5	0.6	0.6	0.6
Financial Leverage	1.3	1.8	1.6	1.7	1.7	1.7

Valuation Ratios	Stock	Rel to Industry	Rel to S&P 500
Price/Earnings	25.6	1.1	1.2
Price/Book	3.1	0.6	0.8
Price/Sales	2.8	0.8	1.0
Price/Cash Flow	11.8	0.6	0.8

Major Fund Holders	% of Fund Assets
Phoenix Small-Mid Cap X	4.62
Fidelity Select IT Services	4.32
BB&T Special Opportunities Equity A	3.33
Brown Capital Mgmt Small Co Instl	2.51

901 Marquette Ave. Suite 3200
Minneapolis, MN 55402
www.fairisaac.com

Growth [C-]	2003	2004	2005	2006
Revenue %	60.4	12.2	13.1	3.3
Earnings/Share %	337.5	-6.4	42.0	-14.5
Book Value/Share %	-36.3	5.2	-4.7	6.3
Dividends/Share %	19.8	25.2	20.1	0.0

Profitability [A-]	2004	2005	2006	TTM
Return on Assets %	7.1	10.0	7.8	7.8
Oper Cash Flow $Mil	199	214	199	199
- Cap Spending $Mil	23	16	31	31
= Free Cash Flow $Mil	176	198	168	168

Financial Health [A]	2004	2005	2006	09-30-06
Long-term Debt $Mil	400	400	0	0
Total Equity $Mil	916	805	770	770
Debt/Equity Ratio	0.4	0.5	0.0	0.0

Thesis By Mark Weber, CFA, 11-27-06 Stock Price as of Analysis: $41.34

Affirming high school algebra teachers' repeated claims that "this stuff really is useful," Fair Isaac turns mathematical formulas into cold, hard cash.

Fair Isaac is best known for the FICO credit scores it generates on every American with a credit history. Credit scoring's share of overall revenue has declined in recent years, falling from 38% in 2001 to 21% last year. Even so, the scoring operation is Fair Isaac's crown jewel and generated 55% of total operating earnings in 2006. Because FICO's reinvestment needs are minimal, the segment also generates more than its fair share of the firm's cash flow.

The FICO score does have a rival in the Vantage Score recently introduced by the big credit bureaus. We think the FICO business is surrounded by a wide moat that will protect its enviable returns on capital. FICO scores are used in the vast majority of lending and credit decisions made in the United States. Competitors face high barriers to entry. Fair Isaac has been refining FICO scores for more than three decades, giving it a big head start over would-be rivals. Competitors would have to convince lenders that their scores are as reliable as Fair Isaac's--a tall order, considering that financial institutions have been successfully using FICO scores since 1970.

However, the credit score market is mature, forcing Fair Isaac to pursue growth in new markets. The firm has introduced software and data-management products aimed at the telecommunications, insurance, health-care, and retail industries. Fair Isaac faces stiff competition in these markets, including heavy-hitters such as SAS, Oracle, and Acxiom. Although Fair Isaac's new products are solidly profitable, we don't think they will yield returns anywhere near those enjoyed by the credit score business.

We do think Falcon, the firm's credit card fraud-detection program, boasts a wide moat. More than 65% of the world's card transactions are routed through Falcon, which is a distinct competitive advantage. The program gets slightly better with each transaction, making it hard for rivals to offer an equally effective product.

We expect the share of total revenue from fraud solutions to grow from 9% in 2005 to 16% by 2010 and estimate that its share of operating income is far larger than its share of overall sales. Combining Falcon with FICO, we think that more than half the firm's operating income is protected by a wide moat. However, we don't think Fair Isaac's other products enjoy similar competitive advantages. As a result, we award the overall company a narrow moat.

Data as of 12-29-06

Fairfax Financial Holdings FFH

Rating	Fair Value	Last Close	Consider Buy	Consider Sell	Yield %
★★★	$275.00	$198.50	$143.00	$338.00	0.00

Company Profile
Toronto-based insurance conglomerate Fairfax Financial Holdings owns a wide range of insurance, reinsurance, and brokerage firms across Europe, Hong Kong, the United States, and Canada. Major products include property-casualty insurance, specialty insurance, health insurance, and reinsurance. Major subsidiaries include Crum & Forster, Odyssey Re, and Northbridge Financial. Fairfax shares trade on the Toronto and New York exchanges.

Industry	Business Risk	Moat Size	Investment Style	Sector
Insurance (General)	Speculative	Narrow	Mid Value	Financial Services

Competition

	Market Cap $Mil	12 Mo Trailing Sales $Mil	Price/Cash Flow	Return On Assets %	Debt/Equity	Total Return % 1 Yr	3 Yr
Fairfax Financial Holdings	3,705	5,878	—	-1.8	—	38.5	4.9
HSBC Holdings PLC ADR	204,784	49,836	—	1.1	—	18.9	9.5
Royal Bank of Canada	61,039	20,637	—	0.9	—	26.0	29.5

Management — Stewardship Grade [C]
We typically avoid highly leveraged insurers, but we think Fairfax management's talent and high ownership stake--more than $70 million--is likely to rectify the firm's current problems and create significant value over the long term, especially as management delivers on its commitment to deleverage the firm. CEO Prem Watsa is paid a flat C$600,000 annual salary, which we think is a steal. In addition, management owns more than 10% of the shares, but controls 55.3% of the votes, thanks to exclusive ownership of all 1.5 million multiple voting shares. We generally frown upon controls that exceed economic interest, but given Watsa's long-term performance and shareholder orientation, this isn't a huge concern. Executive bonuses are paid in stock, which is expected to be held for the long term.

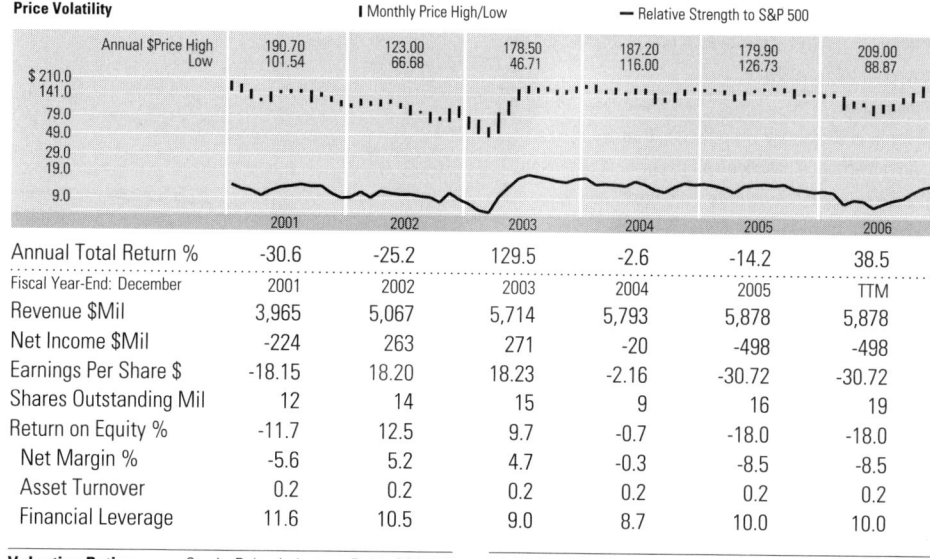

	2001	2002	2003	2004	2005	2006
Annual Total Return %	-30.6	-25.2	129.5	-2.6	-14.2	38.5

Fiscal Year-End: December

	2001	2002	2003	2004	2005	TTM
Revenue $Mil	3,965	5,067	5,714	5,793	5,878	5,878
Net Income $Mil	-224	263	271	-20	-498	-498
Earnings Per Share $	-18.15	18.20	18.23	-2.16	-30.72	-30.72
Shares Outstanding Mil	12	14	15	9	16	19
Return on Equity %	-11.7	12.5	9.7	-0.7	-18.0	-18.0
Net Margin %	-5.6	5.2	4.7	-0.3	-8.5	-8.5
Asset Turnover	0.2	0.2	0.2	0.2	0.2	0.2
Financial Leverage	11.6	10.5	9.0	8.7	10.0	10.0

Valuation Ratios

	Stock	Rel to Industry	Rel to S&P 500
Price/Earnings	NMF	—	—
Price/Book	1.3	0.7	0.3
Price/Sales	0.6	0.4	0.2
Price/Cash Flow	—	—	—

Major Fund Holders

	% of Fund Assets
Torray	4.18
Torray Institutional	4.09
Longleaf Partners International	3.84
Longleaf Partners Small-Cap	3.59

Thesis By Justin Fuller, CFA, 12-14-06 Stock Price as of Analysis: $200.25

We think leveraged investment vehicle Fairfax Financial is a promising option for long-term investors. But because leverage amplifies gains and losses, we'd recommend Fairfax only to investors who don't mind a few bumps during a lengthy ascent.

Since its 1985 inception, Fairfax has used debt to buy other insurers, then used these operations to fund a burgeoning investment portfolio. Because Fairfax's float--insurance premiums invested until claims are paid--has been a sizable multiple of its equity, shareholders have earned leveraged investment returns. For the first 15 years, this strategy generated pleasing results, as the float produced by Fairfax's stable of insurers came at relatively low cost, while the investment portfolio delivered outstanding leveraged returns.

But about eight years ago, Fairfax had a misstep. It used debt and reinsurance indemnities to acquire several troubled insurers, believing its expertise could substantially improve their performance. Disastrous results ensued, as surprisingly heavy casualty losses quickly accumulated, forcing Fairfax to sell assets and discontinue several acquirees. Worse still, a liquidity crunch wreaked financial havoc when legacy operations couldn't finance the losses or service the extra debt, while most reinsurance benefits were a decade away. This debacle magnetized short-sellers, who bet heavily against the stock, surmising that continued losses and elevated leverage would ultimately bankrupt Fairfax.

Fairfax remains at risk today, but management's ongoing repair work has made its recovery prospects appealing. For example, Fairfax has extended the bulk of its debt maturities until 2012 and recently canceled a major reinsurance contract with Swiss Re. We think these moves have improved Fairfax's financial position and liquidity, as management will be able to forgo funding losses in its problematic European run-off operation for about 18 months.

What's more, since 2004 Fairfax has raised more than $900 million of equity, which includes the firm's sale of 9 million shares of its Odyssey Re subsidiary. In our view, these actions have improved Fairfax's financial health and positioned its ongoing businesses for profitable growth--but at the cost of heavily diluting existing shareholders. Finally--since it can ill afford additional losses--Fairfax has hedged its investments by short-selling the S&P 500 and buying credit default protection and put options for its bonds. Despite this defensive stance, we think Fairfax could still grow its book value by almost 10% annually.

---

95 Wellington Street Suite 800
Toronto, ON M5J 2N7
www.fairfax.ca

Growth [NA]

	2002	2003	2004	2005
Revenue %	-17.3	12.8	1.4	1.5
Earnings/Share %	NMF	0.2	NMF	NMF
Book Value/Share %	-40.7	28.0	77.0	-48.4
Dividends/Share %	NMF	NMF	45.7	0.0

Profitability [NA]

	2003	2004	2005	TTM
Return on Assets %	1.1	-0.1	-1.8	-1.8
Oper Cash Flow $Mil	392	111	628	—
- Cap Spending $Mil	30	37	21	—
= Free Cash Flow $Mil	—	—	—	—

Financial Health [NA]

	2003	2004	2005	12-31-05
Long-term Debt $Mil	—	—	—	—
Total Equity $Mil	2,781	3,034	2,769	2,769
Debt/Equity Ratio	—	—	—	—

Fastenal FAST

Data as of 12-29-06

Rating	Fair Value	Last Close	Consider Buy	Consider Sell	Yield %
★★★★★	$53.00	$35.88	$45.20	$69.60	1.12

Company Profile
Fastenal supplies customers, including manufacturers and commercial contractors, with 271,000 varieties of fasteners and 310,000 general-purpose maintenance, repair, and operations products. The company utilizes 12 North American distribution centers and an in-house truck fleet to facilitate five deliveries per week to roughly 85% of its 1,700-plus company-owned stores. Fastenal's over 6,700 store employees receive incentive compensation based on new account development.

Management
Stewardship Grade [A]

Fastenal is extremely shareholder-friendly. It has good governance practices on paper, and its actions speak louder than its words. Free cash flow is reinvested in value-creating growth. Top executives are all paid similar amounts, with an emphasis on cash incentives. No stock options have been issued over the past two years. This company is downright frugal compared with its peers. Five out of nine board members are independent, and directors and officers own almost 17% of the company, aligning owners' and managers' interests. This is one of relatively few companies in our coverage universe that receives an A for corporate stewardship. We are most impressed that these managers set out with a differentiated strategy and continue to execute, year after year. Not only have new store rollouts been successful, but management is relentless in its efforts to continuously improve the appearance and efficiency of existing stores. While opportunities for new store locations will eventually diminish, Fastenal is in the early innings of taking share in the roughly $140 billion MRO industry.

2001 Theurer Blvd www.fastenal.com
Winona, MN 55987-1500

Growth [A-]	2002	2003	2004	2005
Revenue %	10.7	9.9	24.5	23.0
Earnings/Share %	8.7	11.0	55.0	27.9
Book Value/Share %	18.7	15.0	18.1	15.0
Dividends/Share %	11.1	320.0	90.5	55.0

Profitability [A+]	2003	2004	2005	TTM
Return on Assets %	12.9	16.9	18.7	19.3
Oper Cash Flow $Mil	91	57	122	126
- Cap Spending $Mil	—	53	66	87
= Free Cash Flow $Mil	—	5	56	39

Financial Health [A+]	2003	2004	2005	09-30-06
Long-term Debt $Mil	—	—	—	—
Total Equity $Mil	577	684	784	872
Debt/Equity Ratio	—	—	—	—

Industry	Business Risk	Moat Size	Investment Style	Sector
Distributors	Below Avg	Wide	Mid Growth	Business Services

Competition

	Market Cap $Mil	12 Mo Trailing Sales $Mil	Price/Cash Flow	Return On Assets %	Debt/Equity	Total Return % 1 Yr	3 Yr
Fastenal	5,416	1,745	43.0	19.3	—	-7.4	13.9
Home Depot	81,961	90,061	12.5	11.6	0.2	1.0	6.0
W.W. Grainger	6,017	5,812	13.0	12.6	0.0	-0.1	15.6

Price Volatility

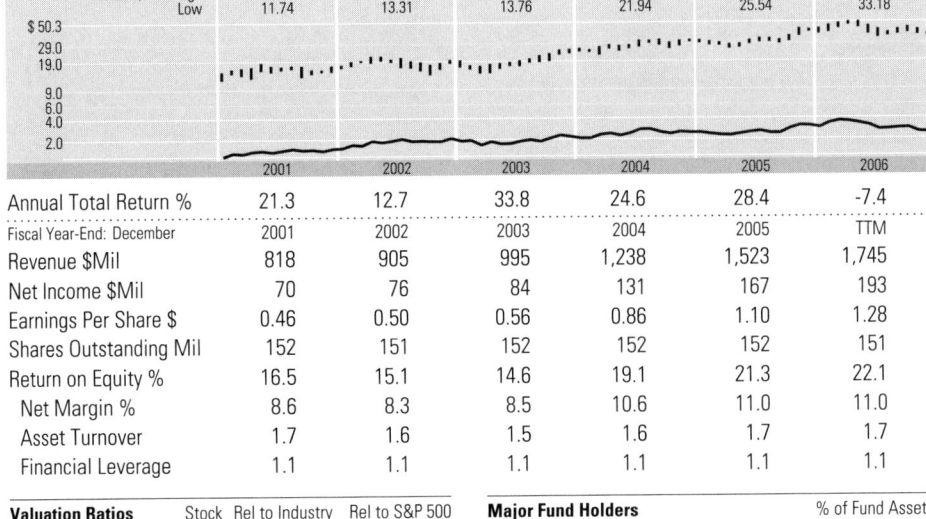

Monthly Price High/Low — Relative Strength to S&P 500

| Annual $Price High | 18.25 | 21.68 | 25.50 | 32.25 | 41.96 | 49.32 |
| Low | 11.74 | 13.31 | 13.76 | 21.94 | 25.54 | 33.18 |

	2001	2002	2003	2004	2005	2006
Annual Total Return %	21.3	12.7	33.8	24.6	28.4	-7.4
Fiscal Year-End: December	2001	2002	2003	2004	2005	TTM
Revenue $Mil	818	905	995	1,238	1,523	1,745
Net Income $Mil	70	76	84	131	167	193
Earnings Per Share $	0.46	0.50	0.56	0.86	1.10	1.28
Shares Outstanding Mil	152	151	152	152	152	151
Return on Equity %	16.5	15.1	14.6	19.1	21.3	22.1
Net Margin %	8.6	8.3	8.5	10.6	11.0	11.0
Asset Turnover	1.7	1.6	1.5	1.6	1.7	1.7
Financial Leverage	1.1	1.1	1.1	1.1	1.1	1.1

Valuation Ratios	Stock	Rel to Industry	Rel to S&P 500
Price/Earnings	28.0	1.5	1.4
Price/Book	6.2	2.1	1.5
Price/Sales	3.1	2.6	1.1
Price/Cash Flow	43.0	1.5	2.9

Major Fund Holders	% of Fund Assets
FMI Provident Trust Strategy	5.86
Delaware Pooled Focus Smid-Cap Gr Eq	4.87
Sequoia	4.69
Transamerica Premier Growth Opp Inv	3.79

Thesis By Matthew Warren, 12-15-06 Stock Price as of Analysis: $35.50

Fastenal has leveraged its vast product selection and efficient distribution network into decades of profitable growth. This wide-moat firm continues to turn out new stores, dominate the fastener niche, and take share in a fragmented market.

As the name suggests, this company sells fasteners--everything from nuts and bolts to screws and anchors. By offering more than a quarter million types of fasteners (and a similar variety of maintenance, repair, and operations--or MRO--products) through its 1,700-plus stores, Fastenal provides far more selection and convenience than broad-line or regional distributors. Also, the company's 12 North American distribution centers and in-house truck fleet provide a highly efficient path to market, especially for heavy fasteners, which are expensive to ship via parcel carriers.

The company's diminutive products are easily stocked in smallish stores on less-than-prime real estate. These low-rent facilities allow Fastenal to focus its investments on breadth of inventory and a skilled salesforce, which receives commissions for drumming up business from local factories and contractors. This time-tested approach enables stores to reach profitability within a year, followed by four additional years of rapid growth before maturity.

Even more impressive is the fact that mature stores have averaged 9% same-store sales growth over the past nine years.

With its proven business model, Fastenal continues to roll out new stores, expanding its network 15% annually. Despite this rapid growth, the company's impressive margins actually understate the firm's true earnings power. Once Fastenal stores saturate the landscape, which we expect to be many years off, earnings pressure resulting from underleveraged new stores would abate. In the meantime, Fastenal is adding density in underserved markets, further pressuring regional competitors.

Each new store adds to Fastenal's advantage as the largest fastener-focused industrial distributor. Volume growth adds to the company's buying power, and new storefronts help leverage existing transportation and distribution assets. Never resting on its laurels, the firm recently embarked on a second initiative aimed at improving store layouts. Fastenal's vast footprint and consistent offerings are salable attributes when pitching national and government accounts. As these customers consolidate vendors in search of lower costs, Fastenal and its brethren--MRO distributors with scale advantages or differentiated offerings--will continue to steal market share.

Data as of 12-29-06

Federated Investors B FII

	Rating	Fair Value	Last Close	Consider Buy	Consider Sell	Yield %
	★★★★★	$46.00	$33.78	$35.50	$57.60	2.04

Company Profile
Federated Investors provides asset management and related financial services. The company manages primarily money market assets, but also offers fixed-income and equity mutual funds that account for about one third of assets under management. Federated distributes its retail products through banks, brokers, and other investment advisers and also sells to the institutional market.

Industry	Business Risk	Moat Size	Investment Style	Sector
Money Mgmt.	Average	Wide	Mid Core	Financial Services

Competition

	Market Cap $Mil	12 Mo Trailing Sales $Mil	Price/Cash Flow	Return On Assets %	Debt/ Equity	Total Return % 1 Yr	3 Yr
Federated Investors B	3,548	971	—	24.1	—	-6.9	7.3
Bank of America	239,758	68,368	—	1.3	—	20.7	15.2
Merrill Lynch & Company	82,298	32,796	—	0.8	—	39.3	18.6

Management   Stewardship Grade [C]
Federated is run by members of the Donahue family, who control all of the voting stock. Founder John Donahue is still with the company as chairman. He handed the CEO title to his son J. Christopher Donahue in 1998. Another son, Thomas, is CFO. As a group, the board of directors--which includes both John and Chris Donahue--owns more than 14% of the firm's outstanding stock. Salaries and bonuses are fairly modest, so the executives generate most of their personal wealth from owning the firm's shares. Several Donahues have been selling shares recently, though family ownership still remains high enough to give management a powerful incentive to look out for shareholders. The firm's voting stock (Class A) is all held by a trust for the benefit of the Donahue family. Other investors can buy the nonvoting (Class B) shares. We would like to see all shares get equal voting rights, but after discussing this with the CEO, we don't think this will happen. Management wants to maintain control of the firm. However, holders of Class A shares do not have absolute power. The bylaws mandate that B shareholders must consent to any merger, sale, or liquidation of the company.

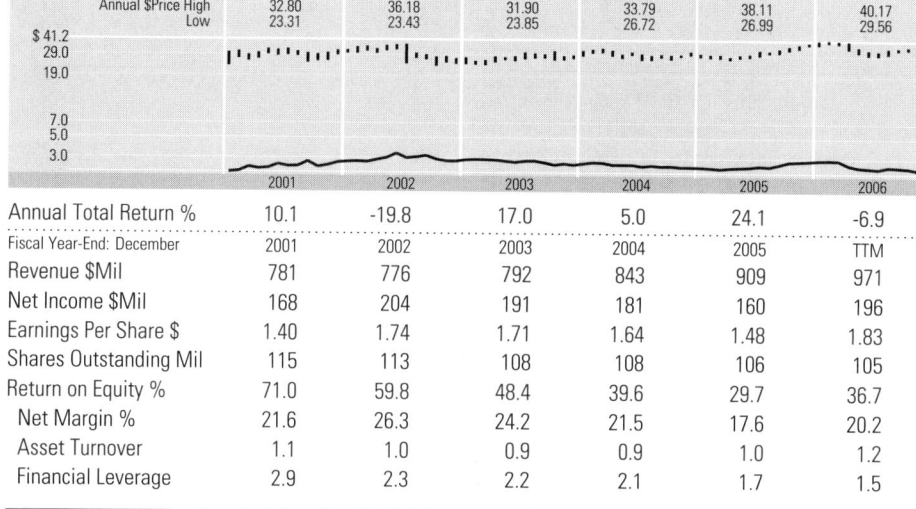

Price Volatility — Monthly Price High/Low — Relative Strength to S&P 500

	2001	2002	2003	2004	2005	2006
Annual $Price High	32.80	36.18	31.90	33.79	38.11	40.17
Low	23.31	23.43	23.85	26.72	26.99	29.56
Annual Total Return %	10.1	-19.8	17.0	5.0	24.1	-6.9
Fiscal Year-End: December	2001	2002	2003	2004	2005	TTM
Revenue $Mil	781	776	792	843	909	971
Net Income $Mil	168	204	191	181	160	196
Earnings Per Share $	1.40	1.74	1.71	1.64	1.48	1.83
Shares Outstanding Mil	115	113	108	108	106	105
Return on Equity %	71.0	59.8	48.4	39.6	29.7	36.7
Net Margin %	21.6	26.3	24.2	21.5	17.6	20.2
Asset Turnover	1.1	1.0	0.9	0.9	1.0	1.2
Financial Leverage	2.9	2.3	2.2	2.1	1.7	1.5

Valuation Ratios	Stock	Rel to Industry	Rel to S&P 500
Price/Earnings	18.9	0.6	0.9
Price/Book	6.6	1.5	1.6
Price/Sales	3.7	0.6	1.3
Price/Cash Flow	—	—	—

Major Fund Holders	% of Fund Assets
FAM Equity-Income Inv	5.52
FAM Value Inv	3.49
Tweedy, Browne American Value	3.44
Pioneer Small and Mid Cap Growth A	3.44

Thesis By Rachel Barnard, Ph.D., 12-11-06 Stock Price as of Analysis: $33.23

We're fans of Federated's business model because of its economic moat and resulting high returns on capital.

Federated makes its money primarily from the fees it charges on the investment products it manages. Unlike banks and many other financial services firms, it can do this without a large balance sheet and without borrowing. Its economic moat is also a product of its position as one of the largest providers of money market funds, representing about 7% of the total market share in these investments and affording the firm huge economies of scale.

The environment for money market funds is looking brighter now than it did earlier in the year. The Federal Reserve has paused in raising interest rates, and this should drive considerable asset inflows into Federated's institutional money market funds. As the underlying assets in the money funds reprice and stabilize, the yields on these funds should beat other short-term vehicles available to investors. In the past, this has resulted in large inflows for Federated, and we have already seen flows pick up in the third quarter. The Fed could, of course, decide to raise rates further, delaying the big benefits for Federated. But once the Fed stops tightening for any length of time, we expect Federated to have large net money market inflows and to gain additional market share as it has over the past five years.

We are less optimistic about the firm's equity business, however. The Kaufmann fund has been a perennial outperformer, but many other portfolios have been inconsistent or downright lousy performers. This has contributed to the equity outflows in recent quarters. The equity division has been retooled to make its funds into institutional-quality offerings, meaning more risk controls and less deviation from the benchmarks. It's too early to tell what the results will be, but we expect the equity lineup to add higher volatility to the firm's asset base.

To augment its equity capabilities, Federated recently purchased a quantitative equity manager, MDT Advisors. The acquisition represents an excellent opportunity, in our view. Quantitative products are extremely popular right now, and MDT has an enviable performance record. We believe Federated's marketing muscle will help get these products to market more effectively, and we expect MDT to add to its $7.1 billion of assets under management over the next few quarters. We think that this shop may have the potential to be another Kaufmann for Federated.

Federated Investors Tower   www.federatedinvestors.com
Pittsburgh, PA 15222-3779

Growth [C]	2002	2003	2004	2005
Revenue %	-0.7	2.1	6.4	7.8
Earnings/Share %	24.3	-1.7	-4.1	-9.8
Book Value/Share %	47.7	21.5	17.2	20.4
Dividends/Share %	24.0	36.9	39.4	38.9

Profitability [A+]	2003	2004	2005	TTM
Return on Assets %	21.8	19.0	17.9	24.1
Oper Cash Flow $Mil	249	297	186	—
- Cap Spending $Mil	6	6	2	—
= Free Cash Flow $Mil	—	—	—	—

Financial Health [NA]	2003	2004	2005	09-30-06
Long-term Debt $Mil	—	—	—	—
Total Equity $Mil	396	458	540	534
Debt/Equity Ratio	—	—	—	—

Data as of 12-29-06

FedEx FDX

	Rating	Fair Value	Last Close	Consider Buy	Consider Sell	Yield %
	★★★	$122.00	$108.62	$94.10	$152.90	0.32

Company Profile

Based in Memphis, Tenn., FedEx uses airplanes and trucks to transport goods around the globe. Services offered by FedEx companies include worldwide express document and parcel delivery, ground small-package delivery, less-than-truckload freight delivery, freight forwarding, and customs brokerage, as well as trade facilitation, document management, and other commercial services.

Management Stewardship Grade [C]

We have mixed feelings about FedEx management. On one hand, Fred Smith, the company's chairman and CEO, is an industry visionary, having virtually created the small-package delivery industry in the early 1970s when he founded FedEx. Through a combination of organic growth and risky strategic acquisitions, he has built an enviable global logistics network that would be nearly impossible to replicate. On the other hand, we have several corporate-governance concerns. Including value realized from stock option exercises (Smith realized $30 million from stock options alone in 2004), Smith has received a higher total compensation over the last five years than any other CEO in the transportation sector. The firm has questionable related-party transactions, including marketing agreements with the Washington Redskins, of which Smith is a 10% owner, and the Memphis Grizzlies, which is partly owned by a board member. In addition, the chairman and CEO positions are held by the same person, and the firm is sometimes aggressive with its expected long-term rate of return on assets in its pension. On the plus side, the firm recently repealed the supermajority voting provision of its bylaws, lifting our Stewardship Grade to C from D.

942 South Shady Grove Road www.fedex.com
Memphis, TN 38120

Growth [B-]	2003	2004	2005	2006
Revenue %	9.1	9.9	18.8	10.0
Earnings/Share %	17.1	0.7	71.0	23.5
Book Value/Share %	11.5	10.0	18.0	19.0
Dividends/Share %	NMF	10.0	27.3	14.3

Profitability [A-]	2004	2005	2006	TTM
Return on Assets %	4.4	7.1	8.0	8.1
Oper Cash Flow $Mil	3,020	3,117	3,676	3,558
- Cap Spending $Mil	1,271	2,236	2,518	2,546
= Free Cash Flow $Mil	1,749	881	1,158	1,012

Financial Health [A]	2004	2005	2006	08-31-06
Long-term Debt $Mil	2,837	2,427	1,592	2,090
Total Equity $Mil	8,036	9,588	11,511	12,021
Debt/Equity Ratio	0.4	0.3	0.1	0.2

Industry	Business Risk	Moat Size	Investment Style	Sector
Transportation	Average	Narrow	Large Core	Business Services

Competition	Market Cap $Mil	12 Mo Trailing Sales $Mil	Price/Cash Flow	Return On Assets%	Debt/Equity	Total Return% 1 Yr	Total Return% 3 Yr
FedEx	33,307	33,132	9.4	8.1	0.2	5.4	17.4
United Parcel Service B	80,494	46,873	15.1	11.4	0.2	1.8	2.4
TNT NV ADR	20,678	12,654	16.8	8.3	0.3	41.0	25.8

Price Volatility

	Annual $Price High Low	53.48 33.15	61.35 42.80	78.05 47.76	100.92 64.84	105.82 76.81	120.01 96.50
		2001	2002	2003	2004	2005	2006
Annual Total Return %		29.8	4.8	24.9	46.4	5.3	5.4
Fiscal Year-End: May		2002	2003	2004	2005	2006	TTM
Revenue $Mil		20,607	22,487	24,710	29,363	32,294	33,132
Net Income $Mil		710	830	838	1,449	1,806	1,942
Earnings Per Share $		2.34	2.74	2.76	4.72	5.83	6.26
Shares Outstanding Mil		298	297	299	301	304	307
Return on Equity %		10.8	11.4	10.4	15.1	15.7	16.2
Net Margin %		3.4	3.7	3.4	4.9	5.6	5.9
Asset Turnover		1.5	1.5	1.3	1.4	1.4	1.4
Financial Leverage		2.1	2.1	2.4	2.1	2.0	2.0

Valuation Ratios	Stock	Rel to Industry	Rel to S&P 500
Price/Earnings	17.4	0.8	0.8
Price/Book	2.8	0.6	0.7
Price/Sales	1.0	0.7	0.3
Price/Cash Flow	9.4	0.7	0.6

Major Fund Holders	% of Fund Assets
Rydex Transportation Inv	7.17
Hillman Focused Advantage	5.49
Security Select 25 A	5.38
Vanguard PRIMECAP	4.85

Thesis By Peter Smith, 11-09-06 Stock Price as of Analysis: $113.48

Over its 35-year history, FedEx has gradually built a formidable global transportation network, one that now handles more than 6 million shipments daily. Despite the firm's scale, however, its profits have been a bit underwhelming. In order to compete more effectively against rival UPS, FedEx must capture more value from its unique network.

FedEx's goal is to meet all consumer and business shipping needs. Through its four divisions--Express, Ground, Freight, and Kinko's--the firm can move any sized package to any destination per a customer's desired timetable. Many, including the Federal Reserve, view its results as an indicator of global economic health.

The firm's traditional strength has been express delivery, which involves the rapid transport of packages by aircraft, both domestically and internationally. Express hasn't been very profitable, though, and doesn't meet all customer needs. In response, the firm has expanded its domestic ground capabilities (a more profitable, but slower-growing niche dominated by UPS) as well as its less than truckload (LTL) freight network, logistics offerings, and document-management services (Kinko's).

FedEx has a few notable competitive advantages. In its ground business, it classifies drivers as "independent contractors" rather than "employees," which prevents them from unionizing and enables FedEx to adjust its labor force more easily. UPS, which is unionized, would likely adopt the same model if it could do so without facing a stiff backlash. FedEx's Freight division is also an advantage: It is also not unionized, it is among the most profitable LTL carriers in the industry, and it focuses on the regional market (which is growing much faster than the national market). Plus, UPS only recently became a competitor in the market with its purchase of less-profitable Overnite.

Despite these advantages, UPS is still more profitable in aggregate. Though UPS' greater mix of higher-margin ground business explains part of the disparity, FedEx's historical focus on expansion over profitability is the main driver, in our opinion. This has changed recently, however, with management embarking on several profit-enhancing initiatives: increasing the mix of high-margin international volumes, culling unprofitable business, and gaining share in the domestic ground market. The firm has improved margins in the last two years, but if a weaker economy makes it harder for FedEx to be so selective about freight, profitability improvement may prove more elusive.

Fomento Economico Mexicano SAB ADR FMX

Data as of 12-29-06

Rating ★★★

Fair Value	Last Close	Consider Buy	Consider Sell	Yield %
$123.00	$115.76	$94.80	$154.10	0.67

Company Profile
Femsa is made up of four holding companies: Coca-Cola Femsa is the largest Coke bottler in Latin America and the second-largest in the world; Femsa Cerveza brews beers like Tecate and Dos Equis; Femsa Comercio owns the Oxxo chain of convenience stores, which is growing rapidly. Other operations include packaging and logistics. Femsa owns 53.7% of Coke Femsa and controls a majority of the voting shares. All other operations are 100%-owned by Femsa.

Management
Stewardship Grade [NA]

Femsa is controlled by a voting trust, composed mainly of five wealthy Mexican families. The trust controls 70% of the stock with full voting rights and owns 36% of the capital stock. The trust votes in a unified block and can elect a majority of the board of directors and substantially control all matters decided by shareholders. The board currently consists of 19 directors who, though elected for only one-year terms, remain on the board until a successor is elected to replace them--effectively making their terms indefinite. The controlling families are descended from Femsa founders and include Eugenio Garza Laguera, director and honorary chairman for life. The board is full of his relatives, both close and distant. His son-in-law, Jose Antonio Fernandez, has been CEO since 1995 and chairman since 2001. Femsa's performance has significantly improved under Fernandez, but minority shareholders essentially have no power, and we see little independence on the board. Like many large Mexican companies, Femsa's ownership structure is overly complex and riddled with various subsidiaries. The company's disclosure on director and executive compensation is limited, as it provides only aggregate figures.

General Anaya 601 Poniente, Colonia Bella Vista, Monterrey, Mexico 64410
www.femsa.com

Growth [NA]	2002	2003	2004	2005
Revenue %	5.2	37.5	17.4	9.0
Earnings/Share %	-16.9	5.6	77.2	-13.9
Book Value/Share %	-1.2	46.6	0.5	25.9
Dividends/Share %	—	—	—	—

Profitability [NA]	2003	2004	2005	TTM
Return on Assets %	4.6	8.0	6.5	6.5
Oper Cash Flow $Mil	908	1,469	1,273	1,273
- Cap Spending $Mil	—	—	—	—
= Free Cash Flow $Mil	—	—	—	—

Financial Health [NA]	2003	2004	2005	12-31-05
Long-term Debt $Mil	3,238	3,336	2,758	2,758
Total Equity $Mil	4,482	4,793	6,233	6,233
Debt/Equity Ratio	0.7	0.7	0.4	0.4

Industry	Business Risk	Moat Size	Investment Style	Sector
Beverage Mfg.	Average	Narrow	Large Growth	Consumer Goods

Competition

	Market Cap $Mil	12 Mo Trailing Sales $Mil	Price/Cash Flow	Return On Assets%	Debt/Equity	Total Return% 1 Yr	3 Yr
Fomento Economico Mexicano SAB ADR	10,475	9,794	8.2	6.5	0.4	61.3	47.8
Companhia de Bebidas das	32,148	6,491	19.0	4.4	0.4	32.2	43.3
Pepsi Bottling Group	7,295	12,627	6.3	3.6	2.1	9.4	9.7

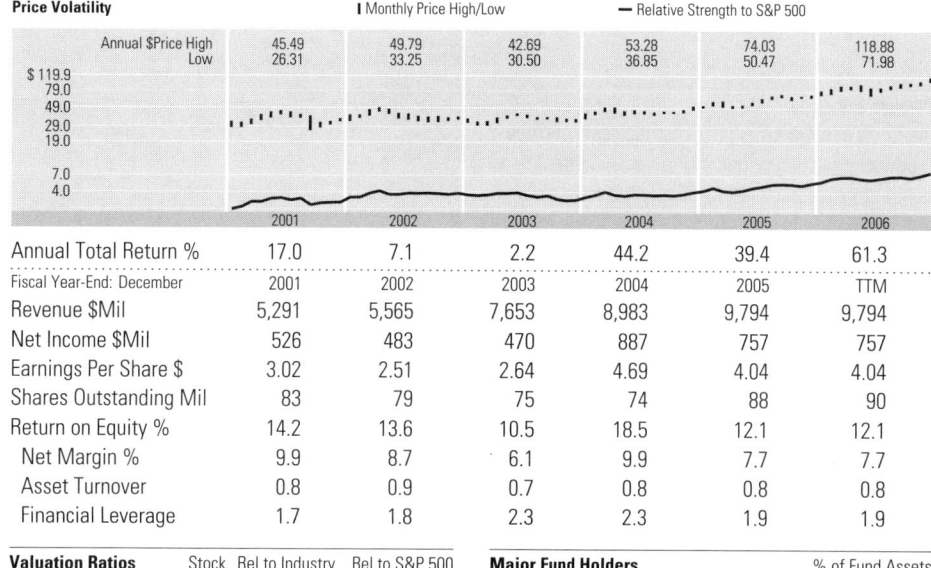

Price Volatility — Monthly Price High/Low — Relative Strength to S&P 500

Annual $Price High / Low	45.49 / 26.31	49.79 / 33.25	42.69 / 30.50	53.28 / 36.85	74.03 / 50.47	118.88 / 71.98
	2001	2002	2003	2004	2005	2006
Annual Total Return %	17.0	7.1	2.2	44.2	39.4	61.3

Fiscal Year-End: December

	2001	2002	2003	2004	2005	TTM
Revenue $Mil	5,291	5,565	7,653	8,983	9,794	9,794
Net Income $Mil	526	483	470	887	757	757
Earnings Per Share $	3.02	2.51	2.64	4.69	4.04	4.04
Shares Outstanding Mil	83	79	75	74	88	90
Return on Equity %	14.2	13.6	10.5	18.5	12.1	12.1
Net Margin %	9.9	8.7	6.1	9.9	7.7	7.7
Asset Turnover	0.8	0.9	0.7	0.8	0.8	0.8
Financial Leverage	1.7	1.8	2.3	2.3	1.9	1.9

Valuation Ratios	Stock	Rel to Industry	Rel to S&P 500
Price/Earnings	29.0	1.3	1.4
Price/Book	1.7	0.3	0.4
Price/Sales	1.1	0.3	0.4
Price/Cash Flow	8.2	0.5	0.6

Major Fund Holders	% of Fund Assets
DWS Latin America Equity S	3.70
Fidelity Latin America	2.98
Fidelity Advisor Latin America A	2.96
JPMorgan Emerging Mkts Instl	2.51

Thesis
By Matthew Reilly, 12-15-06 Stock Price as of Analysis:

Femsa maintains strong market positions in several Latin American beverage markets and a dominant chain of convenience stores in Mexico. Although we think the company has built a moat with these operations, our concerns regarding the long-term legality of exclusive relationships with retailers in Mexico and the general instability of several countries where Femsa operates limit the moat to narrow.

Femsa owns 54% of Coca-Cola Femsa, a bottler with operations in Mexico and several Latin American countries. This is one of the most efficient and profitable bottlers in the world, capitalizing on the strength of the Coke brand in its markets, the fragmentation of its retailer base, and low but increasing per capita consumption that is complemented by favorable demographic trends. Coke Femsa's growth prospects are significantly better than Coke bottlers with exposure to more mature markets, such as Coca-Cola Enterprises faces in North America and Western Europe, but this opportunity comes with the risk of several unstable political and economic climates.

Femsa also constitutes half of the Mexican beer duopoly through Femsa Cerveza, brewing brands such as Tecate and Dos Equis. With iconic brands domestically (though again this is reinforced by exclusive retail arrangements) and bright export opportunities, we think Femsa Cerveza has both a defensible business model and decent growth prospects. However, we feel that all of Femsa's beverage operations will have difficulty maintaining margins in the near term, as sky-high commodity costs, especially for aluminum and sweeteners, will make maintaining profitability extremely challenging. Over time, though, we expect these cost to be passed through to end consumers, meaning margins and volume will come back into equilibrium.

Femsa also owns Oxxo, a rapidly growing chain of Mexican convenience stores that provide a friendly outlet for the company's beverages. The chain now has more stores than any other retailer in Mexico, and it is setting the standard for modern retail operations in Mexico. Oxxo is in many cases building distribution and IT infrastructure as it continues to grow, expertise that may prove to be of increasing value as other retailers modernize and expand. We see Oxxo's store count and value continuing to increase very rapidly over the next few years, and we believe that it could be spun off at some point to shareholders, providing a very nice return.

Data as of 12-29-06

Fidelity National Financial FNF

Rating	Fair Value	Last Close	Consider Buy	Consider Sell	Yield %
★★★	$25.00	$23.88	$19.30	$31.30	4.90

Company Profile
Fidelity National Financial owns five title insurance underwriters, a specialty insurance company, a 40% interest in a claims management company, and other assets including a tree farm. Fidelity is the second-largest title insurance underwriter and holds a dominant share of the commercial title insurance market.

Industry	Business Risk	Moat Size	Investment Style	Sector
Insurance (Title)	Average	Narrow	Mid Value	Financial Services

Competition

	Market Cap $Mil	12 Mo Trailing Sales $Mil	Price/Cash Flow	Return On Assets%	Debt/Equity	Total Return% 1 Yr	Total Return% 3 Yr
Fidelity National Financial	4,163	6,048	—	6.9	—	3.5	—
First American	3,932	8,360	—	6.4	—	-8.6	12.4
LandAmerica Financial Gro	1,119	4,028	—	2.8	—	2.4	7.8

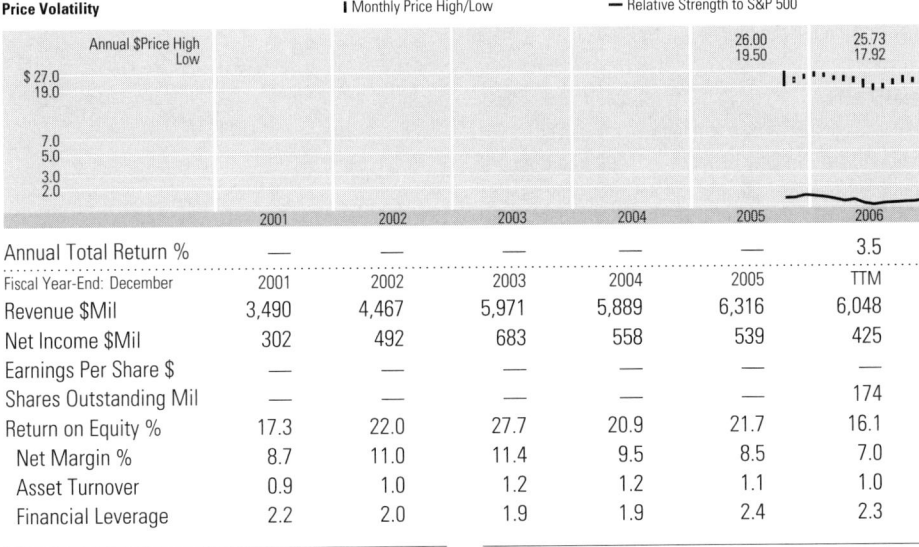

Price Volatility — Monthly Price High/Low — Relative Strength to S&P 500

Annual Total Return %	—	—	—	—	—	3.5
Fiscal Year-End: December	2001	2002	2003	2004	2005	TTM
Revenue $Mil	3,490	4,467	5,971	5,889	6,316	6,048
Net Income $Mil	302	492	683	558	539	425
Earnings Per Share $	—	—	—	—	—	—
Shares Outstanding Mil	—	—	—	—	—	174
Return on Equity %	17.3	22.0	27.7	20.9	21.7	16.1
Net Margin %	8.7	11.0	11.4	9.5	8.5	7.0
Asset Turnover	0.9	1.0	1.2	1.2	1.1	1.0
Financial Leverage	2.2	2.0	1.9	1.9	2.4	2.3

Management Stewardship Grade [C]
The firm's asset shuffling has cost the company fees to advisors and has distracted management from day-to-day execution. Astoundingly, chairman and CEO Bill Foley was awarded $19 million solely for completing the restructuring, which we frown upon. Other members of the executive management team were also rewarded in the same vein, though not to the same extent. We believe this smacks of reward for activity over shareholder-value creation. We also wonder how management can be rewarded for what it has admitted was a misstep (last year's spin-off of the title company). We think management is focused on short-term market valuation instead of working to widen the firm's moat. The chairman and CEO positions are occupied by the same person. Excluding the chairman, the board collectively owns less than 1% of the outstanding shares of the company. We've cut our Stewardship Grade to C, and it wouldn't take much to reduce it further.

Valuation Ratios	Stock	Rel to Industry	Rel to S&P 500
Price/Earnings	—	—	—
Price/Book	1.6	1.1	0.4
Price/Sales	0.7	1.2	0.2
Price/Cash Flow	—	—	—

Major Fund Holders	% of Fund Assets
Tilson Dividend	4.71
Artisan Opportunistic Value Inv	2.77
Dreyfus Midcap Value	2.31
Managers AMG FQ Tx-Mgd U.S. Eq Inst	2.19

601 Riverside Avenue
Jacksonville, FL 32204

Growth [C]	2002	2003	2004	2005
Revenue %	28.0	33.7	-1.4	7.2
Earnings/Share %	NMF	NMF	NMF	NMF
Book Value/Share %	—	—	—	—
Dividends/Share %	NMF	NMF	NMF	NMF

Profitability [A]	2003	2004	2005	TTM
Return on Assets %	14.3	11.0	9.1	6.9
Oper Cash Flow $Mil	853	646	697	—
- Cap Spending $Mil	82	77	92	—
= Free Cash Flow $Mil	—	—	—	—

Financial Health [NA]	2003	2004	2005	06-30-06
Long-term Debt $Mil	—	—	—	—
Total Equity $Mil	2,469	2,677	2,480	2,636
Debt/Equity Ratio	—	—	—	—

Thesis   By Jim Ryan, 11-10-06   Stock Price as of Analysis:

Fidelity National Financial's title insurance companies are endowed with the narrowest of moats, in our view. Our fair value estimate is $25 per share.

After six years of acquisitions, spin-offs, mergers, and restructuring, Fidelity is back to where it started: a title insurer with a few small investments in other businesses. Since the acquisition of Chicago Title six years ago, Fidelity has been a dominant force in title insurance and has benefited from the housing explosion. However, Fidelity suffers from two problems: aggressive competition and high fixed costs. It has surrendered market share over the past three years, which cuts into profitability in the scale-sensitive title insurance business. Archrival First American has made dramatic gains nationally and internationally and now challenges Fidelity's long-held stronghold, commercial title insurance, the most profitable segment of the business. In residential markets, First American is outpacing Fidelity in ancillary services, which are needed to compete for business from national lenders.

High fixed costs resulting from the need to maintain production and closing facilities, as well as the need to keep a staff of experts employed, reduces the firm's ability to adjust its cost structure as market conditions change. Even worse, the firm lacks pricing power, and we think margins will decline.

What little moat protection Fidelity enjoys stems from its ownership of the real estate database it has built over the years. Even that is threatened as more counties come online with open access to property records. Fidelity's national presence is a double-edged sword. While it may grant the firm favor with certain large, national customers, it also is expensive to maintain, particularly in slow markets.

Fidelity has investments in other businesses, but we're not convinced they add much value. Home warranty insurance tends to follow the real estate cycle, and flood processing is a lumpy business influenced by weather cycles. Personal lines, such as automobile and homeowners insurance, require scale to achieve good returns, and Fidelity is an insignificant presence in these fields. What's more, after a few good years of respectable pricing, personal lines have softened.

In the last restructuring, the appraisal business and control of the title plants went with Fidelity National Information Systems. While Fidelity National may be able to instill cooperation between FNF and FIS in the short run, a change in control of FIS could be devastating to FNF.

Data as of 12-29-06

Fifth Third Bancorp FITB

	Rating	Fair Value	Last Close	Consider Buy	Consider Sell	Yield %
	★★★	$44.00	$40.93	$33.90	$55.10	3.86

Industry	Business Risk	Moat Size	Investment Style	Sector
Super Regional Banks	Average	Narrow	Large Value	Financial Services

Company Profile

With about $106 billion in assets, Fifth Third offers commercial and retail banking throughout the Midwest. The bank has 1,100 branches and 2,200 ATMs in eight states. Additionally, the bank's electronic processing segment handles more than 9 billion transactions annually. In 2004, Fifth Third bought First National Bankshares, significantly building its presence in Florida.

Competition

	Market Cap $Mil	12 Mo Trailing Sales $Mil	Price/Cash Flow	Return On Assets%	Debt/Equity	Total Return% 1 Yr	3 Yr
Fifth Third Bancorp	22,842	5,431	—	1.4	—	13.0	-8.1
US Bancorp	63,617	13,499	—	2.2	—	26.3	11.8
KeyCorp	15,272	5,038	—	1.3	—	21.0	14.1

Management Stewardship Grade [B]

We give management a poor review for recent performance, although we believe the bank is still governed with the best interests of shareholders in mind. Despite a solid long-term record of results, the bank has had numerous missteps in recent years. The management team--still led by CEO George Schaefer--recently reorganized. Poor balance sheet management led to one of the most expensive balance sheet restructurings--as well as the departure of CFO Mark Graf--we've seen. But despite the revenue hit, Fifth Third retained its cost-conscious culture, and we believe the bank will experience some positive operating leverage when revenue growth returns. The bank hired a new CFO in 2006, along with a COO and a treasurer. Accountability for results, while localized with every manager, holds true at the very top: After two years of reduced bonuses, Schaefer received no 2005 bonus given the bank's bottom-line performance. We approve of the bank's retroactive adoption of expensing options, although we were disappointed to see Schaefer add the chairman title (we prefer the chairman and CEO roles to be separated). This recent move pushed Fifth Third's corporate Stewardship Grade down to a B.

38 Fountain Square Plaza www.53.com
Cincinnati, OH 45263

Growth [D]	2002	2003	2004	2005
Revenue %	15.7	10.4	1.7	-0.2
Earnings/Share %	48.4	4.0	-6.6	3.4
Book Value/Share %	10.0	4.4	5.0	7.7
Dividends/Share %	18.1	15.3	15.9	11.5

Profitability [A]	2003	2004	2005	TTM
Return on Assets %	1.8	1.6	1.5	1.4
Oper Cash Flow $Mil	8,115	3,495	4,186	—
- Cap Spending $Mil	10,935	8,140	10,333	—
= Free Cash Flow $Mil	—	—	—	—

Financial Health [NA]	2003	2004	2005	09-30-06
Long-term Debt $Mil	—	—	—	—
Total Equity $Mil	8,658	8,915	9,437	10,013
Debt/Equity Ratio	—	—	—	—

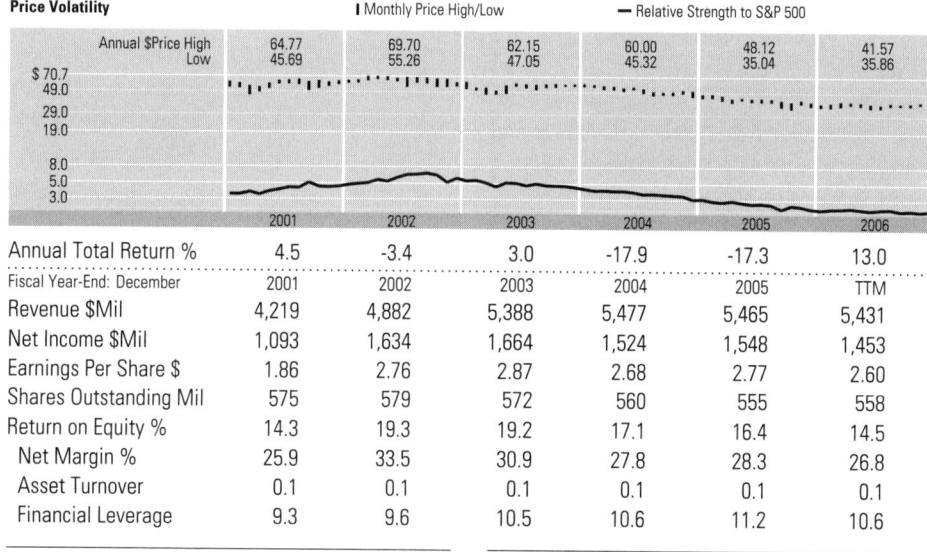

Price Volatility — Monthly Price High/Low — Relative Strength to S&P 500

Annual $Price High/Low	64.77/45.69	69.70/55.26	62.15/47.05	60.00/45.32	48.12/35.04	41.57/35.86

	2001	2002	2003	2004	2005	2006
Annual Total Return %	4.5	-3.4	3.0	-17.9	-17.3	13.0
Fiscal Year-End: December	2001	2002	2003	2004	2005	TTM
Revenue $Mil	4,219	4,882	5,388	5,477	5,465	5,431
Net Income $Mil	1,093	1,634	1,664	1,524	1,548	1,453
Earnings Per Share $	1.86	2.76	2.87	2.68	2.77	2.60
Shares Outstanding Mil	575	579	572	560	555	558
Return on Equity %	14.3	19.3	19.2	17.1	16.4	14.5
Net Margin %	25.9	33.5	30.9	27.8	28.3	26.8
Asset Turnover	0.1	0.1	0.1	0.1	0.1	0.1
Financial Leverage	9.3	9.6	10.5	10.6	11.2	10.6

Valuation Ratios	Stock	Rel to Industry	Rel to S&P 500
Price/Earnings	15.7	1.2	0.8
Price/Book	2.3	1.0	0.6
Price/Sales	4.2	1.2	1.4
Price/Cash Flow	—	—	—

Major Fund Holders	% of Fund Assets
T. Rowe Price Financial Services	4.44
AIM Financial Services Inv	3.61
Philadelphia	3.59
Phoenix Focused Value A	3.48

Thesis By Jim Callahan, CFA, 10-20-06 Stock Price as of Analysis: $39.37

We believe Fifth Third's moat has shrunk, but a recently reorganized management should improve upon the bank's recent results.

Fifth Third's moat remains, but a wide moat it is not. Historically, Fifth Third's decentralized banking model, strict cost controls, and strong sales culture have earned it a dominating share in small towns and an entry point into larger metropolitan markets. Its 1,100 branches are entrenched in small and midsize markets where the forecasted population growth is running at about half the national average. Competitors have shunned these demographics, allowing Fifth Third to consistently generate double-digit earnings growth and returns on equity in the high teens.

However, the bank has underperformed in recent years due to both internal and external factors. When interest rates were at multi-decade lows in 2003, Fifth Third was burned badly by balance sheet mismanagement as it reached for yield with its investment securities portfolio. With new executive management supporting CEO George Schaefer and the slow but painful whittling down of the bloated portfolio, we believe the worst of the balance sheet mismanagement is over.

There's no denying the increased competition Fifth Third faces. Regional competitors National City and KeyCorp have stepped up their retail banking offerings during recent years, with the increased competition forcing Fifth Third's cost of deposits higher. Although we believe Fifth Third can survive within the slow-growth Midwestern markets, its biggest challenge will remain the strong competition for deposits within its home regions.

That said, Fifth Third's business model remains intact. Through its current crisis, Fifth Third has done a good job of keeping expenses in check, in our opinion. When its recent growth resumes, we expect Fifth Third will remain one of the more efficient operators among the large banks. Further, the bank's payment processing unit and healthy credit quality provide it with future bottom-line growth.

With all the negative press, we'd still keep an eye on Fifth Third. Despite its lowest net interest margin on record, the bank still generates a 55% efficiency ratio and 15% returns on invested capital--metrics that other average banks long to achieve. Therefore, at the right price, we believe the shares offer an attractive risk/reward profile for patient investors.

First American FAF

Data as of 12-29-06

Rating	Fair Value	Last Close	Consider Buy	Consider Sell	Yield %
★★★★★	$61.00	$40.68	$47.00	$76.40	1.77

Industry	Business Risk	Moat Size	Investment Style	Sector
Insurance (Title)	Average	Narrow	Mid Value	Financial Services

Company Profile

Diversified information services firm First American provides real estate data and analysis. The company is currently the largest title insurer in the United States. First American is expanding beyond real estate transactions by investing in business information and related products and services. The firm also has a larger international footprint than its competitors. First American owns about 80% of First Advantage, a risk mitigation and screening firm.

Management — Stewardship Grade [A]

As of Dec. 1, 2006, the directors of First American are still investigating the possible backdating of options. Backdating options is dishonest and not shareholder friendly. However, because the board has yet to uncover and release all the facts, we will wait until the investigation is complete before revising (if necessary) the firm's current A Stewardship Grade.

The team at First American deserves credit for conceiving and executing a farsighted strategy to transform its business. About 20 years ago, title insurance was a fragmented and regionalized labor-intensive business. Profits were far less abundant. First American's team was blessed with the foresight to aggressively consolidate smaller rivals and invest heavily in technology to move the business into the electronic age. This foresight helped First American emerge as an industry leader and also establish important first-mover advantages in adjacent property information markets, like title imaging. We attribute part of this success to management's powerful incentive to compound the value of the firm. First American's management owns about 5.1% of the shares, which equates to about a $200 million stake. Management consistently buys back shares at a price below our fair value estimate, which creates value for shareholders'.

1 First American Way
Santa Ana, CA 92707-5913
www.firstam.com

Growth [A]	2002	2003	2004	2005
Revenue %	25.4	32.1	8.2	19.9
Earnings/Share %	28.6	78.8	-26.6	29.8
Book Value/Share %	13.4	27.9	24.2	13.9
Dividends/Share %	25.9	47.1	20.0	20.0

Profitability [A+]	2003	2004	2005	TTM
Return on Assets %	8.8	5.6	6.4	6.4
Oper Cash Flow $Mil	830	679	921	—
- Cap Spending $Mil	99	202	201	—
= Free Cash Flow $Mil	—	—	—	—

Financial Health [NA]	2003	2004	2005	03-31-06
Long-term Debt $Mil	—	—	—	—
Total Equity $Mil	1,880	2,464	3,007	3,050
Debt/Equity Ratio	—	—	—	—

Competition

	Market Cap $Mil	12 Mo Trailing Sales $Mil	Price/Cash Flow	Return On Assets%	Debt/Equity	Total Return% 1 Yr	3 Yr
First American	3,932	8,360	—	6.4	—	-8.6	12.4
Old Republic Internationa	5,366	3,883	—	4.2	—	13.9	8.7
Fidelity National Financi	4,163	6,048	—	6.9	—	3.5	—

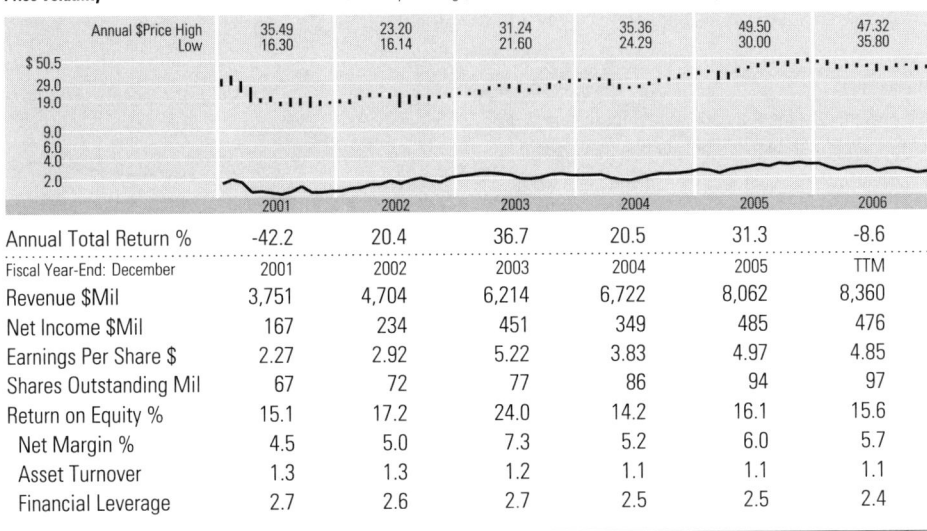

	2001	2002	2003	2004	2005	TTM
Annual Total Return %	-42.2	20.4	36.7	20.5	31.3	-8.6
Revenue $Mil	3,751	4,704	6,214	6,722	8,062	8,360
Net Income $Mil	167	234	451	349	485	476
Earnings Per Share $	2.27	2.92	5.22	3.83	4.97	4.85
Shares Outstanding Mil	67	72	77	86	94	97
Return on Equity %	15.1	17.2	24.0	14.2	16.1	15.6
Net Margin %	4.5	5.0	7.3	5.2	6.0	5.7
Asset Turnover	1.3	1.3	1.2	1.1	1.1	1.1
Financial Leverage	2.7	2.6	2.7	2.5	2.5	2.4

Valuation Ratios	Stock	Rel to Industry	Rel to S&P 500
Price/Earnings	8.4	0.8	0.4
Price/Book	1.3	0.9	0.3
Price/Sales	0.5	0.8	0.2
Price/Cash Flow	—	—	—

Major Fund Holders	% of Fund Assets
Fidelity Select Home Finance	2.98
Wasatch Core Growth	2.15
FPA Perennial	1.94
FPA Paramount	1.78

Thesis By Jim Ryan, 12-06-06 Stock Price as of Analysis: $40.29

First American's narrow moat originates in the vast array of services the company provides and in a favored treatment from state regulatory authorities. We think its shares are worth $61 each.

First American is gradually transforming itself into a global provider of real estate information services. Thirty years ago the company was a network of fragmented title insurance offices and agencies. Today, in addition to being the largest provider of title insurance and closing services, First American markets mortgage and property information and specialty insurance. Risk mitigation and business solutions are offered via majority-owned First Advantage Corporation. Combined, these offerings provide a valuable suite of services to large, national mortgage lenders. What's more, the data that feeds these services are a platform to offer information to other non-real-estate businesses. For example, auto dealers seeking credit information on potential buyers regularly use First Advantage credit services.

State insurance regulations also protect First American. In most states, premium rates and coverages are regulated in one form or another, which insulates the company from price wars and excessive policy liability. Even better for First American are the licensing requirements that protect title insurers against new entrants. States require a monoline license to issue title policies, which pre-empts new competitors from opening shop.

First American is an industry leader in international operations. Leading title insurance operations in Canada, Mexico, and some European countries help to diversify revenue. First American has also shifted costs for title production on properties in America to countries like India. We consider this a somewhat mixed blessing. While the cost savings are attractive, we worry that some of the firm's expertise in title assessment could be diluted.

The downside for First American is the cyclical nature of the business. Most of its revenue is still dependent on the volume of real estate transactions, which is volatile. First American must maintain production and closing facilities, and it is limited in cutting highly trained staff. Thus, in a downturn, the firm's costs remain high while revenue declines, harming profitability. Fortunately, First American's reliance on cyclical title revenue is shifting to information services, a higher-margin business. For the first three quarters of 2006, about half of pretax income was from title operations as opposed to two-thirds for the same period of 2005.

Data as of 12-29-06

First Data FDC

	Rating	Fair Value	Last Close	Consider Buy	Consider Sell	Yield %
	★★★	$23.00	$25.52	$17.70	$28.80	0.82

Industry	Business Risk	Moat Size	Investment Style	Sector
Data Processing	Average	Wide	Large Core	Business Services

Company Profile
First Data's commercial services segment provides processing services that allow merchants to accept debit and credit cards. The company had 4.6 million merchant customers and processed 25.2 billion transactions in 2005. Its STAR network also processes ATM transactions. First Data's financial institution services segment provides processing and account management services to issuers of credit cards. Approximately 19% of First Data's revenue is generated internationally.

Management   Stewardship Grade [D]
First Data's previous CEO and chairman, Charles Fote, resigned in late 2005, citing personal reasons. We think that Fote's exit package was overly generous and evidence of the company's tendency to overpay its executives. First Data accelerated restricted stock grants worth $4.3 million for Fote and has retained him as a part-time consultant, paying him an annual fee of $1.1 million, a figure equivalent to the salary he earned as the company's CEO. Ric Duques, who had handed off the chairman and CEO roles to Fote in 2003 and had previously held them since 1989, has resumed those roles until a replacement can be found. Given the temporary nature of Duques' leadership role, it is unlikely that First Data will make any big moves until a successor is in place. Duques is instead focused on improving operating results in First Data's existing businesses, primarily the struggling financial institutions segment. First Data's Stewardship Grade could be improved by separating the chairman and CEO roles, removing the staggered terms of its board of directors, and weaning itself off of constant restructuring charges.

6200 South Quebec Street
Greenwood Village, CO 80111
www.firstdatacorp.com

Growth [C+]	2002	2003	2004	2005
Revenue %	13.6	12.0	19.2	4.8
Earnings/Share %	NMF	16.8	18.6	-9.4
Book Value/Share %	NMF	-0.1	95.6	1.9
Dividends/Share %	75.0	14.3	0.0	200.0

Profitability [A-]	2003	2004	2005	TTM
Return on Assets %	5.5	5.7	4.6	4.4
Oper Cash Flow $Mil	1,996	2,338	2,219	2,332
- Cap Spending $Mil	162	177	225	212
= Free Cash Flow $Mil	1,834	2,161	1,994	2,120

Financial Health [B]	2003	2004	2005	09-30-06
Long-term Debt $Mil	3,575	4,606	5,356	4,506
Total Equity $Mil	4,047	8,886	8,457	10,255
Debt/Equity Ratio	0.9	0.5	0.6	0.4

Competition
	Market Cap $Mil	12 Mo Trailing Sales $Mil	Price/Cash Flow	Return On Assets %	Debt/Equity	Total Return% 1 Yr	3 Yr
First Data	19,543	10,806	8.4	4.4	0.4	9.9	5.6
American Express	73,094	26,507	—	2.9	—	19.1	14.2
Total System Services	5,197	1,704	15.2	13.9	0.0	35.0	-3.9

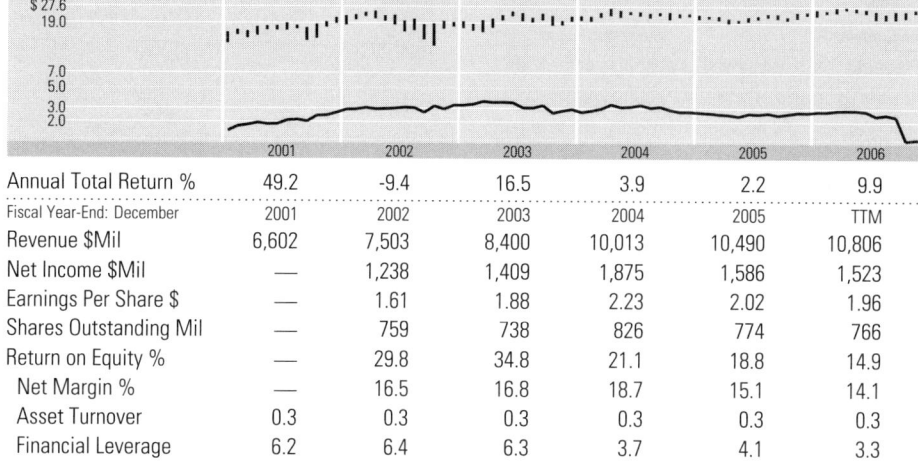

	2001	2002	2003	2004	2005	2006
Annual Total Return %	49.2	-9.4	16.5	3.9	2.2	9.9

Fiscal Year-End: December	2001	2002	2003	2004	2005	TTM
Revenue $Mil	6,602	7,503	8,400	10,013	10,490	10,806
Net Income $Mil	—	1,238	1,409	1,875	1,586	1,523
Earnings Per Share $	—	1.61	1.88	2.23	2.02	1.96
Shares Outstanding Mil	—	759	738	826	774	766
Return on Equity %	—	29.8	34.8	21.1	18.8	14.9
Net Margin %	—	16.5	16.8	18.7	15.1	14.1
Asset Turnover	0.3	0.3	0.3	0.3	0.3	0.3
Financial Leverage	6.2	6.4	6.3	3.7	4.1	3.3

Valuation Ratios	Stock	Rel to Industry	Rel to S&P 500
Price/Earnings	12.3	0.5	0.6
Price/Book	1.9	0.4	0.5
Price/Sales	1.8	0.5	0.6
Price/Cash Flow	8.4	0.4	0.6

Major Fund Holders	% of Fund Assets
Fidelity Select IT Services	11.93
Strategic Partners Concentrated Growth M	5.23
Oakmark Select I	5.02
Heritage Capital Appreciation A	5.00

Thesis By Brett Horn, 12-08-06 Stock Price as of Analysis: $25.28

While this payment processing titan has gone through some difficulties and big changes lately, spinning off Western Union in September, we think its wide moat is intact. First Data's dominant market share in credit and debit card processing positions the company to continue to exploit consumers' increasing preference for using plastic, in our opinion.

First Data's main business is credit and debit card processing. Its commercial services segment accounts for approximately 71% of its revenues. First Data is the undisputed market leader, processing 49% of credit and debit card transactions in the U.S. either directly or through alliances with its banking partners. Its closest competitor, Bank of America Merchant Services, handles only 16%. Because a large portion of the costs associated with processing payments are fixed, scale matters, and First Data's market position represents a long-term competitive advantage. First Data's lower cost structure allows it to undercut its competitors on price while still maintaining healthy margins.

Additionally, First Data's commercial services business benefits from the shift toward credit and debit cards and away from cash and checks. The volume of credit and debit card transactions in the U.S. increased 8% and 19% in 2005, respectively. With cash and checks still used in about half of all transactions in the U.S., this trend continues to provide opportunities for growth.

First Data's financial institutions segment, which provides processing and account management services and accounts for 19% of revenues, has struggled lately. Concentration among card issuers is increasing with the 10 largest issuers now accounting for 88% of U.S. credit card outstandings. This concentration gives them greater pricing power and has led some issuers to take their processing in-house. Over the past couple of years, First Data has lost a number of high-profile accounts due to issuers taking processing in-house and to the market leader, Total System Services. First Data did post one success lately, winning Sears' private-label card business. However, in our opinion, the fact that First Data considered selling this business in 2005 indicates that the growth prospects are limited.

Commercial services remains the main driver of First Data's results, and the long-term fundamentals of this business are intact. We would gladly buy First Data's shares at a reasonable discount to our fair value estimate, despite the poor outlook in the financial institution segment and the spin-off of Western Union's attractive money transfer business.

First Horizon National FHN

Data as of 12-29-06

	Rating	Fair Value	Last Close	Consider Buy	Consider Sell	Yield %
	★★★★	$52.00	$41.78	$40.10	$65.20	4.31

Industry	Business Risk	Moat Size	Investment Style	Sector
Regional Banks	Average	Narrow	Mid Value	Financial Services

Company Profile

First Horizon operates three businesses. Its $23.2 billion asset banking business has a dominant market share in its home state of Tennessee as well as an emerging presence in Mississippi, Georgia, Texas, and Virginia. First Horizon operates a nationwide mortgage brokerage office, where the company originates, sells, and services residential mortgages. Finally, the company runs a capital markets business specializing in fixed-income security sales and equity research.

Management   Stewardship Grade [B]

J. Kenneth Glass has served as chairman since 2004 and chief executive officer since 2002. Prior to heading up the holding company, Glass held several executive positions at First Tennessee, the banking division of First Horizon. During his tenure, Glass has achieved tremendous growth while increasing the company's return on equity to the enviable level of 19% in 2005. Glass and the rest of the executive managers' compensation is based on long-term wealth creation, which should help align their interests with shareholders'. Glass is the only insider on the 12-person board. Outside directors are paid through a combination of cash and restricted stock that is vested over 10 years. Directors are also able to take stock options in lieu of cash compensation. Overall, the management and board of directors are pretty shareholder friendly, actively returning excess capital to shareholders through its generous dividend payouts and share buybacks. The company used $100 million from the recent sale of the merchant processing business to repurchase shares instead of plowing it back into the business. Management has stated that it will not reinvest capital into the business without first checking to see if returning the money to shareholders is a better deal.

165 Madison Avenue
Memphis, TN 38103
www.firstTennessee.com

Growth [D+]	2002	2003	2004	2005
Revenue %	—	NMF	-10.3	7.4
Earnings/Share %	19.4	25.3	-2.2	-4.0
Book Value/Share %	15.5	11.4	10.0	12.9
Dividends/Share %	15.4	23.8	25.4	6.7

Profitability [A]	2003	2004	2005	TTM
Return on Assets %	1.9	1.5	1.2	1.3
Oper Cash Flow $Mil	2,481	-53	499	—
- Cap Spending $Mil	150	79	96	—
= Free Cash Flow $Mil	—	—	—	—

Financial Health [NA]	2003	2004	2005	09-30-06
Long-term Debt $Mil	—	—	—	—
Total Equity $Mil	1,890	2,041	2,312	2,511
Debt/Equity Ratio	—	—	—	—

Competition	Market Cap $Mil	12 Mo Trailing Sales $Mil	Price/Cash Flow	Return On Assets%	Debt/ Equity	Total Return% 1 Yr	3 Yr
First Horizon National	5,200	2,275	—	1.3	—	13.7	2.9
Wachovia	90,049	27,749	—	1.3	—	12.0	11.3
SunTrust Banks	29,907	8,070	—	1.2	—	19.8	9.4

Price Volatility

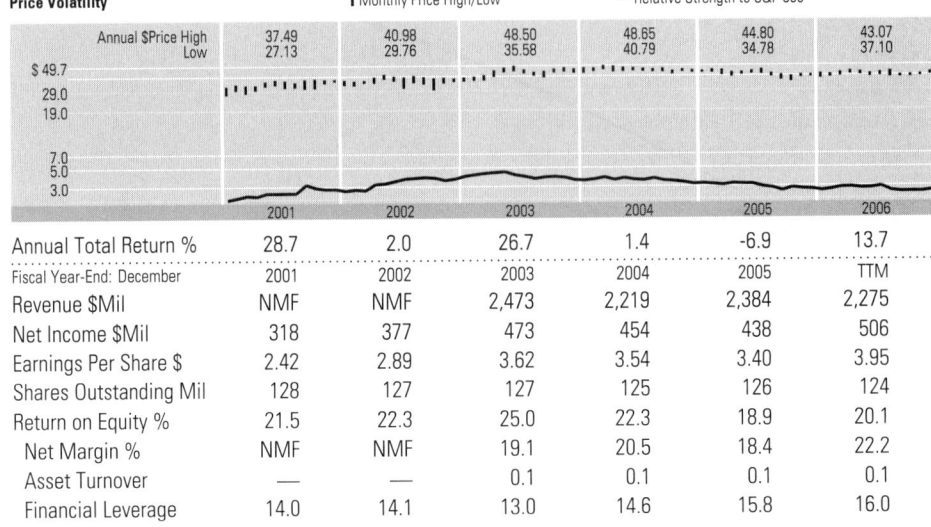

Monthly Price High/Low — Relative Strength to S&P 500

Annual $Price High	37.49	40.98	48.50	48.65	44.80	43.07
Low	27.13	29.76	35.58	40.79	34.78	37.10
	2001	2002	2003	2004	2005	2006

	2001	2002	2003	2004	2005	TTM
Annual Total Return %	28.7	2.0	26.7	1.4	-6.9	13.7
Fiscal Year-End: December						
Revenue $Mil	NMF	NMF	2,473	2,219	2,384	2,275
Net Income $Mil	318	377	473	454	438	506
Earnings Per Share $	2.42	2.89	3.62	3.54	3.40	3.95
Shares Outstanding Mil	128	127	127	125	126	124
Return on Equity %	21.5	22.3	25.0	22.3	18.9	20.1
Net Margin %	NMF	NMF	19.1	20.5	18.4	22.2
Asset Turnover	—	—	0.1	0.1	0.1	0.1
Financial Leverage	14.0	14.1	13.0	14.6	15.8	16.0

Valuation Ratios	Stock	Rel to Industry	Rel to S&P 500
Price/Earnings	17.4	1.0	0.8
Price/Book	2.1	0.7	0.5
Price/Sales	2.3	0.4	0.8
Price/Cash Flow	—	—	—

Major Fund Holders	% of Fund Assets
T. Rowe Price Financial Services	3.04
JHancock Regional Bank B	2.40
Federated Strategic Value C	2.15
FMC Select	2.05

Thesis By Jaime Black, CFA, CPA, 11-30-06 Stock Price as of Analysis: $39.86

First Horizon is molding its business model for the long run. Two of First Horizon's businesses--mortgage banking and capital markets--are cyclical and tend to have some rather volatile results, but it's the company's traditional banking business that gets us all warm and fuzzy inside, making this bank one of our favorite opportunities.

First Horizon's retail and commercial bank has a dominating position in its home state of Tennessee, with 20.6% deposit share, up from 15.5% in 2002. We are truly impressed with this phenomenal growth considering that it was accomplished without a single in-state acquisition. Instead, the company took advantage of consolidation in the Tennessee market, which left First Horizon as the only large in-state bank, an angle the company played up in its advertising. First Horizon was hugely rewarded for extending its hours and becoming more convenient for its customers. The bank increased earnings by more than 20% annually between 2002 and 2005. While growth has since slowed, we believe that First Horizon's bank will continue to post industry-leading returns while growing at an above-average rate.

After five boom years, First Horizon's nationwide mortgage banking business--the origination, sale, and subsequent servicing of mortgages--is now facing a challenging time. Due to some very messy accounting rules, profits for the mortgage business are extremely volatile, with interest-rate levels and the volume of transactions significantly affecting accounting profits. However, the accounting profits do not adequately reflect the health of the business. Mortgage banking produces large volumes of free cash flow throughout the cycle. As a result of the cooling housing market, we predict that the mortgage banking segment's accounting profits will struggle in the short term, but over the long run it is a great income generator.

First Horizon's capital markets business contributed just 4% of the company's earnings in 2005, or $15.7 million. In 2003, the capital markets business accounted for 21% of total earnings. The decline is due to lower fixed-income sale fees, as a result of the flat yield curve. The decline in earnings is a result of temporary external forces; going forward, we expect this business to contribute 13% of First Horizon's income from continuing operations.

First Horizon's prospects are bright. Despite a short-term rough patch from its two cyclical businesses, the company's fundamentals are strong, and we would gladly own it for the long haul.

FirstEnergy FE

Data as of 12-29-06

Rating	Fair Value	Last Close	Consider Buy	Consider Sell	Yield %
★★★	$59.00	$60.30	$45.50	$73.90	2.99

Industry	Business Risk	Moat Size	Investment Style	Sector
Electric Utilities	Average	Narrow	Large Value	Utilities

Company Profile

FirstEnergy owns seven electric utility operating companies serving about 4 million customers in Ohio, Pennsylvania, and New Jersey. The company's 13,387 megawatts of power-generation assets are 55% coal-based and 28% nuclear-based, with the rest being a combination of hydro, oil, and natural gas. More than 90% of the company's output is sold via fixed-price contracts.

Management Stewardship Grade [C]

Mismanagement for an extended period is largely responsible for FirstEnergy's woes of the past few years, but the story is improving. President and CEO Anthony Alexander has been with FirstEnergy since 1972. In 2005, he took home just over $3.6 million in total compensation, above average for the industry. While we think he and other senior executives were handsomely compensated for managing a utility of FirstEnergy's size and complexity, we like that management maintains a decent ownership stake in the company, aligning its interests with shareholders'. Management recently made the shareholder-friendly decision to do away with the firm's shareholder-rights plan, a poison pill that could deter potential suitors. In addition, management has indicated it would not adopt a new poison pill unless the plan was first approved by shareholders. These moves not only help the company earn a fair Stewardship Grade but also could translate into real value following the repeal of the Public Utilities Holding Company Act (PUHCA). PUHCA's repeal opens the door to merger-and-acquisition activity that was previously difficult in the utility industry, and eliminating merger deterrents could create substantial value for FirstEnergy shareholders.

76 South Main Street www.firstenergycorp.com
Akron, OH 44308-1890

Growth [D]	2002	2003	2004	2005
Revenue %	61.3	1.4	6.5	-0.6
Earnings/Share %	-33.1	-26.1	92.1	-2.2
Book Value/Share %	-23.9	21.0	-4.1	6.6
Dividends/Share %	0.0	0.0	0.0	11.2

Profitability [C]	2003	2004	2005	TTM
Return on Assets %	1.3	2.8	2.7	3.6
Oper Cash Flow $Mil	1,777	1,892	2,220	1,547
- Cap Spending $Mil	856	846	1,208	1,442
= Free Cash Flow $Mil	921	1,046	1,012	105

Financial Health [B+]	2003	2004	2005	09-30-06
Long-term Debt $Mil	—	10,949	9,006	8,760
Total Equity $Mil	8,290	8,590	9,188	9,208
Debt/Equity Ratio	—	1.3	1.0	1.0

Competition

	Market Cap $Mil	12 Mo Trailing Sales $Mil	Price/Cash Flow	Return On Assets%	Debt/Equity	Total Return% 1 Yr	3 Yr
FirstEnergy	19,248	11,923	12.4	3.6	1.0	27.3	23.9
Exelon	41,525	15,798	10.1	0.4	1.2	19.8	27.3
FPL Group	22,026	15,251	48.8	3.5	1.0	35.5	23.0

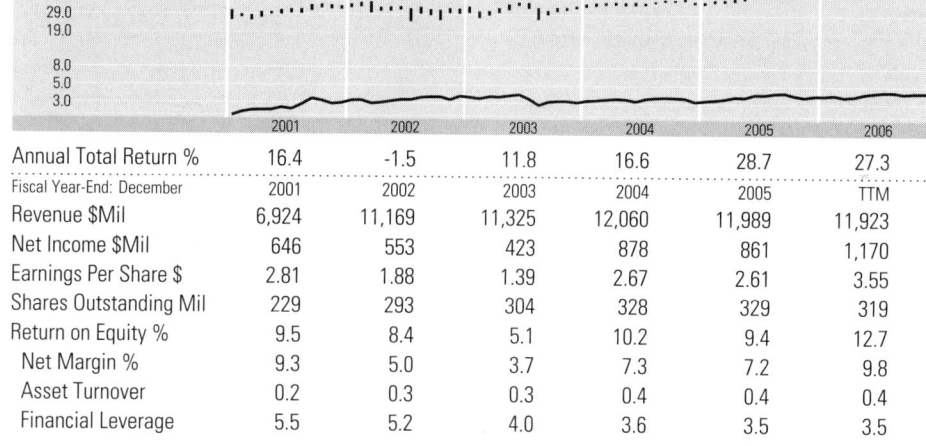

Price Volatility — Monthly Price High/Low — Relative Strength to S&P 500

	2001	2002	2003	2004	2005	2006
Annual $Price High	36.98	39.12	38.90	43.41	53.36	61.70
Low	25.10	24.85	26.20	35.20	37.70	47.75
Annual Total Return %	16.4	-1.5	11.8	16.6	28.7	27.3

Fiscal Year-End: December	2001	2002	2003	2004	2005	TTM
Revenue $Mil	6,924	11,169	11,325	12,060	11,989	11,923
Net Income $Mil	646	553	423	878	861	1,170
Earnings Per Share $	2.81	1.88	1.39	2.67	2.61	3.55
Shares Outstanding Mil	229	293	304	328	329	319
Return on Equity %	9.5	8.4	5.1	10.2	9.4	12.7
Net Margin %	9.3	5.0	3.7	7.3	7.2	9.8
Asset Turnover	0.2	0.3	0.3	0.4	0.4	0.4
Financial Leverage	5.5	5.2	4.0	3.6	3.5	3.5

Valuation Ratios	Stock	Rel to Industry	Rel to S&P 500
Price/Earnings	16.6	0.9	0.8
Price/Book	2.1	0.6	0.5
Price/Sales	1.6	0.9	0.6
Price/Cash Flow	12.4	1.1	0.8

Major Fund Holders	% of Fund Assets
Cohen & Steers Utility A	6.29
Franklin Utilities A	4.54
Phoenix Global Utilities A	4.41
Putnam Utilities Growth & Income A	3.81

Thesis By Paul Justice, CFA, 12-15-06 Stock Price as of Analysis: $60.85

After addressing its operational woes, FirstEnergy is a substantially better investment prospect than it was two years ago. A deregulating Ohio market gives this stock a higher risk profile, but the company's total return prospects are also improving.

FirstEnergy started the new millennium with major operational failures in 2002 and 2003. The first was the immediate lockdown of the firm's Davis-Besse nuclear power plant after inspectors found significant corrosion on a reactor head caused by boric acid. A large-scale governmental investigation identified numerous flaws in safety procedures at the facility. The shutdown raised FirstEnergy's incremental costs and deprived the company of a valuable source of cheap, base-load power. The second operational failure was the August 2003 blackout that enveloped the Northeast. A report fingered FirstEnergy as responsible for three of the five causes of the blackout: improper line maintenance, computer problems, and the slow response of human operators.

But FirstEnergy recently turned a corner. It restarted the Davis-Besse power plant in early 2004, allowing the company to enjoy the facility's low-cost power again. Also, FirstEnergy has taken steps to raise operating efficiency across its nuclear fleet by standardizing its reporting and control systems, hiring experienced talent from other nuclear utilities, and benchmarking the best practices of other operators in the industry. We think these actions will go a long way in helping FirstEnergy meet its goal of raising nuclear fleet utilization to 90%.

Low-cost generation earns FirstEnergy a narrow economic moat, even in the face of deregulation. While deregulation brings additional competitive risks into the mix, we believe that the company's earnings will grow fast enough to make the trade-off attractive to investors. The company has the advantage of owning coal-fired power plants that are already environmentally compliant and can utilize a wide range of coal types. This flexible, low-cost position means that FirstEnergy is well suited to weather the price caps in place in its major markets of Ohio and Pennsylvania.

FirstEnergy increased its dividend to $1.80 per share on an annualized basis, meeting its long-run target payout ratio of 50%-60%. At our fair value estimate, the dividend would yield 3.1%, which is slightly below average for our utility stock universe. We believe the dividend is safe and offers appealing growth prospects for income investors.

Data as of 12-29-06

Fiserv FISV

	Rating	Fair Value	Last Close	Consider Buy	Consider Sell	Yield %
	★★★	$49.00	$52.42	$37.80	$61.40	0.00

Industry	Business Risk	Moat Size	Investment Style	Sector
Data Processing	Average	Wide	Mid Growth	Business Services

Company Profile

Fiserv's roots go back to 1984, when former CEO Leslie Muma spun his processing division out of a Florida savings and loan and merged it with First Data Processing. Since its initial public offering in 1986, Fiserv has made more than 130 acquisitions and has grown into the nation's largest provider of core processing services to banks and credit unions. More recently, the firm has expanded into insurance processing and health-plan management services.

Management — Stewardship Grade [C]

Jeffery Yabuki joined Fiserv as president and CEO in December 2005, when Leslie Muma retired. Muma is a tough act to follow. He became Fiserv's COO when the firm was founded, took the helm in 1999, and guided the company from small player to industry juggernaut. Yabuki has spent the last six years as a top executive at H&R Block. Before that, he spent 12 years with American Express and managed that firm's tax and business services unit. Kenneth Jensen, Fiserv's executive vice president and CFO since 1986, will retire this summer. He will be replaced by Tom Hirsch, the company's controller. Fiserv gets average marks for stewardship. We like that executives and directors own 6% of the firm's stock, and that the single largest shareholder, Donald Dillon, is chairman of the board. Moreover, compensation levels are reasonable and largely tied to performance. However, the main performance metric is earnings per share, which could give management an incentive to focus on short-term EPS numbers instead of creating shareholder value over the long term. In addition to linking compensation to long-term value creation, Fiserv could improve its Stewardship Grade by removing takeover defenses.

255 Fiserv Drive
Brookfield, WI 53045
www.fiserv.com

Growth [B]	2002	2003	2004	2005
Revenue %	18.1	22.4	27.5	8.8
Earnings/Share %	25.7	17.5	18.6	41.4
Book Value/Share %	12.0	19.5	15.4	-0.6
Dividends/Share %	NMF	NMF	NMF	NMF

Profitability [A-]	2003	2004	2005	TTM
Return on Assets %	4.4	4.5	8.6	8.0
Oper Cash Flow $Mil	596	698	597	657
- Cap Spending $Mil	139	161	165	205
= Free Cash Flow $Mil	457	537	432	452

Financial Health [A-]	2003	2004	2005	09-30-06
Long-term Debt $Mil	699	505	595	829
Total Equity $Mil	2,200	2,564	2,466	2,447
Debt/Equity Ratio	0.3	0.2	0.2	0.3

Competition	Market Cap $Mil	12 Mo Trailing Sales $Mil	Price/Cash Flow	Return On Assets %	Debt/Equity	Total Return% 1 Yr	Total Return% 3 Yr
Fiserv	9,078	4,425	13.8	8.0	0.3	21.2	10.3
Fidelity National Financi	4,163	6,048	—	6.9	—	3.5	—
Jack Henry & Associates	1,941	606	15.8	11.2	—	13.3	2.2

Price Volatility

| Monthly Price High/Low — Relative Strength to S&P 500

Annual $Price High	44.61	47.24	40.77	41.01	46.89	53.60
Low	29.08	22.50	27.23	32.20	36.33	40.29
	2001	2002	2003	2004	2005	2006

	2001	2002	2003	2004	2005	TTM
Annual Total Return %	33.8	-19.8	16.5	1.6	7.7	21.1
Fiscal Year-End: December						
Revenue $Mil	2,024	2,389	2,925	3,730	4,059	4,425
Net Income $Mil	208	266	315	378	516	494
Earnings Per Share $	1.09	1.37	1.61	1.91	2.70	2.73
Shares Outstanding Mil	188	191	193	195	188	173
Return on Equity %	13.0	14.6	14.3	14.7	20.9	20.2
Net Margin %	10.3	11.1	10.8	10.1	12.7	11.2
Asset Turnover	0.4	0.4	0.4	0.4	0.7	0.7
Financial Leverage	3.3	3.5	3.3	3.3	2.4	2.5

Valuation Ratios	Stock	Rel to Industry	Rel to S&P 500
Price/Earnings	19.5	0.8	0.9
Price/Book	3.7	0.7	0.9
Price/Sales	2.1	0.6	0.7
Price/Cash Flow	13.8	0.7	0.9

Major Fund Holders	% of Fund Assets
Black Pearl Focus	4.81
Madison Mosaic Mid-Cap	3.78
Pioneer Small and Mid Cap Growth A	3.52
BBH Core Select N	3.50

Thesis By Mark Weber, CFA, 11-27-06 Stock Price as of Analysis: $51.11

We like the economics of Fiserv's main bank-processing business. However, we think the firm's health-plan management segment is far less attractive. Moreover, Fiserv is looking to that less-attractive segment to fuel growth.

Fiserv provides a wide range of data-processing services to financial institutions, insurance providers, and other companies. The firm's backbone, however, is its account-processing products for banks, credit unions, and other financial institutions, which generated more than 82.5% of 2005 revenue. In particular, Fiserv handles banks' core functions, including keeping track of deposits, withdrawals, and loan payments.

The bank-processing business enjoys a wide economic moat. Banks are reluctant to risk disrupting account-processing functions without a compelling reason. The transition from one processor to another can take more than a year and requires retraining bank staff, as well as the conversion of archived transactions to the new system.

Clients rarely leave Fiserv. The processor loses only 1% of its clients annually on average, typically because the client has been acquired by a non-Fiserv bank or has gone out of business. Fiserv's client base provides a captive market for cross-selling ancillary products like Internet banking applications, check-imaging solutions, fraud-prevention products, and customer-relationship management software.

Fiserv generates substantial free cash flow (cash from operations less capital expenditures)--an astounding 17% of sales on average over the past five years. Free cash flow is great, but we aren't convinced management uses it wisely. Fiserv has completed more than 130 acquisitions over the past 20 years. Early acquisitions focused on other bank processors and produced beneficial economies of scale. More recently, however, Fiserv has been acquiring its way into health-plan management, a business with lower profit margins than the firm's other operations. Moreover, Fiserv lacks a competitive advantage in the health-plan management market. The company's new rivals, including Aetna, UnitedHealth Group, and Cigna, bundle plan-management services with their preferred provider organizations, a service Fiserv doesn't offer. Instead of pursuing growth in new industries, we'd rather see the firm return some of its ample cash flow to shareholders through larger share repurchases or by initiating a dividend.

Forest Laboratories FRX

Data as of 12-29-06

Rating	★★
Fair Value	$42.00
Last Close	$50.60
Consider Buy	$32.40
Consider Sell	$52.60
Yield %	0.00

Industry	Business Risk	Moat Size	Investment Style	Sector
Drugs	Average	Narrow	Large Growth	Healthcare

Company Profile

A leading player in branded, generic, and over-the-counter pharmaceuticals, Forest Laboratories develops, manufactures, and markets drugs in the central nervous system, cardiovascular, respiratory, and endocrinology therapeutic areas. Its top sellers include Lexapro for depression, Namenda for Alzheimer's disease, and Benicar for hypertension. Forest sells primarily in the United States but also has a presence in the United Kingdom and Ireland.

Management Stewardship Grade [B]

We believe that Forest's corporate governance is above average, thanks to excellent disclosure, straightforward accounting, and management ownership. However, the company loses points by combining the CEO and chairman duties. A former attorney, chairman and CEO Howard Solomon has headed Forest since 1977 and led the firm to profitability by focusing on highly specialized niche products. He's responsible for Forest's European drug-licensing strategy and wisely used Celexa proceeds to build a healthy cash surplus. President and COO Kenneth Goodman could be heir apparent, but there is no official news on succession planning, even though Solomon is 77. Executives are rooted in the company, and the board of directors (43% of whom are current or prior insiders) have adopted golden parachutes and a poison pill to fight off takeover attempts. Excess cash is currently used to repurchase shares, which is a shareholder-friendly allocation of capital only if shares are purchased at a discount to our fair value estimate.

909 Third Avenue www.forestlaboratories.com
New York, NY 10022-4731

Growth [D+]	2003	2004	2005	2006
Revenue %	40.9	20.1	15.2	-8.5
Earnings/Share %	82.4	17.5	15.4	-7.6
Book Value/Share %	43.4	37.5	-2.6	-5.7
Dividends/Share %	NMF	NMF	NMF	NMF

Profitability [A+]	2004	2005	2006	TTM
Return on Assets %	19.1	22.6	22.7	21.8
Oper Cash Flow $Mil	628	926	597	986
- Cap Spending $Mil	102	89	55	44
= Free Cash Flow $Mil	527	837	542	942

Financial Health [A+]	2004	2005	2006	06-30-06
Long-term Debt $Mil	—	—	—	—
Total Equity $Mil	3,256	3,132	2,698	2,832
Debt/Equity Ratio	—	—	—	—

Competition

	Market Cap $Mil	12 Mo Trailing Sales $Mil	Price/Cash Flow	Return On Assets%	Debt/Equity	Total Return% 1 Yr	Total Return% 3 Yr
Forest Laboratories	16,026	2,965	16.3	21.8	—	24.4	-6.6
Pfizer	186,751	52,208	10.5	11.6	0.1	15.2	-7.4
Wyeth	68,574	19,877	23.4	11.3	0.6	12.9	8.2

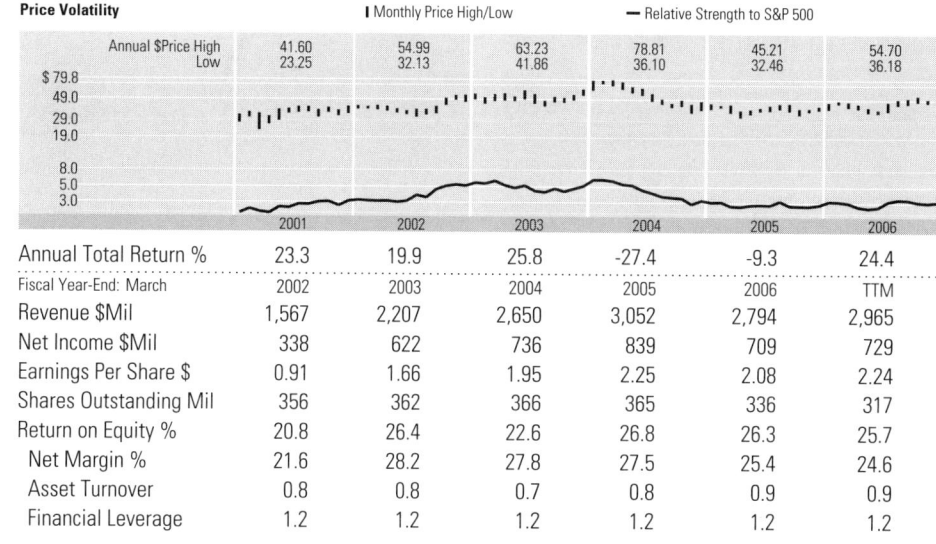

Price Volatility — Monthly Price High/Low — Relative Strength to S&P 500

Annual $Price High/Low	41.60 / 23.25	54.99 / 32.13	63.23 / 41.86	78.81 / 36.10	45.21 / 32.46	54.70 / 36.18
	2001	2002	2003	2004	2005	2006
Annual Total Return %	23.3	19.9	25.8	-27.4	-9.3	24.4

Fiscal Year-End: March	2002	2003	2004	2005	2006	TTM
Revenue $Mil	1,567	2,207	2,650	3,052	2,794	2,965
Net Income $Mil	338	622	736	839	709	729
Earnings Per Share $	0.91	1.66	1.95	2.25	2.08	2.24
Shares Outstanding Mil	356	362	366	365	336	317
Return on Equity %	20.8	26.4	22.6	26.8	26.3	25.7
Net Margin %	21.6	28.2	27.8	27.5	25.4	24.6
Asset Turnover	0.8	0.8	0.7	0.8	0.9	0.9
Financial Leverage	1.2	1.2	1.2	1.2	1.2	1.2

Valuation Ratios	Stock	Rel to Industry	Rel to S&P 500
Price/Earnings	22.6	0.9	1.1
Price/Book	5.7	1.1	1.4
Price/Sales	5.4	1.2	1.9
Price/Cash Flow	16.3	1.0	1.1

Major Fund Holders	% of Fund Assets
Fountainhead Special Value	5.86
ING Partners Legg Mason Pnrs Aggr Gr Ini	5.81
Prasad Growth	4.05
Legg Mason Partners Aggressive Growth A	3.87

Thesis By Brian Laegeler, CPA, 10-19-06 Stock Price as of Analysis: $51.67

Forest Laboratories' 3,000-person direct salesforce is the envy of smaller, research-based firms. We're betting its size and reputation will attract a new generation of licensing deals to replace revenue lost to upcoming generic competition. Given the company's limited drug-discovery efforts, it must in-license to survive.

Forest's three largest drugs constitute 85% of its sales and have made impressive inroads into the highly competitive central nervous system (CNS) and cardiovascular categories. Lexapro is positioned to become the second largest SSRI (selective serotonin reuptake inhibitor) antidepressant in terms of sales, now that Pfizer's Zoloft faces generic competition. Namenda is the only drug approved for moderate to late-stage Alzheimer's disease and is on its way to becoming a billion-dollar drug. Benicar continues to gain share in the crowded antihypertensive market.

Despite the inevitable patent expirations of these products, we think Forest's size and reputation will safeguard its position as a leading specialty marketer. A $3 billion annual revenue base provides Forest the financial flexibility to outbid direct competitors like King Pharmaceuticals and Shire for attractive in-licensing deals. Forest has a highly reputable salesforce with broad national reach, making it a preferred partner for such transactions. These factors help explain Forest's 25%-plus historical returns on invested capital and support our expectation that they will continue.

Forest's current pipeline is limited to a few small to midsize opportunities. Late-stage candidates milnacipran for fibromyalgia and nebivolol for high blood pressure are perhaps the most meaningful potential contributors. Desmoteplase, an early-stage candidate for stroke, also has significant potential. Forest continues to explore new indications for existing drugs, but it requires additional in-licensing opportunities to fill the revenue hole left by $2 billion Lexapro when its patent expires in early 2012.

Despite its heavy reliance on Lexapro over the next five years, Forest appears to have the size and reputation to fill even the largest of revenue gaps through business development. This established position is rare in the specialty pharmaceutical industry and is worthy of a narrow moat rating, in our view.

Forward Air FWRD

Data as of 12-29-06

Rating ★★★★★	Fair Value $40.00	Last Close $28.93	Consider Buy $30.80	Consider Sell $50.10	Yield % 0.97

Industry	Business Risk	Moat Size	Investment Style	Sector
Land Transport	Average	Wide	Small Core	Business Services

Company Profile

Forward Air provides ground cargo transportation services. It specializes in handling large freight shipments requiring delivery in one to five days among its 81 terminals at or near major airports in North America, which are linked through a central sorting facility in Ohio as well as regional hubs. The firm mostly serves freight forwarders and airlines and does not market its services directly to shippers. It also provides logistics services such as truckload brokerage.

Management — Stewardship Grade [B]

President and CEO Bruce Campbell has done an excellent job leading Forward Air since 2003, when he took over from Scott Niswonger, one of the firm's founders. Niswonger remained chairman until 2005, when he stepped down from that position as well. We applaud Campbell for retaining a search firm rather than assuming the chairman role himself. (We prefer that the CEO and chairman positions be held by separate individuals.) Other corporate-governance provisions we like include the firm's policies of re-electing its full board of directors annually and ensuring that the audit and nominating committees are free of insiders. Management compensation is reasonable, which we also like. There are three things that concern us, however: First, we don't like the firm's poison pill--the board has authority to issue blank-check preferred stock and can determine voting, dividend, and other rights. Specifically, this stock can be placed with friendly investors to prevent a takeover. Second, we also do not approve of the firm's recent decision to accelerate the vesting of stock options, enabling it to avoid a future expense on its income statement. Third, we would like to see the firm raise its meager dividend rather than buy back shares, which management seems to prefer.

430 Airport Rd
Greeneville, TN 37745
www.forwardair.com

Growth [C]

	2002	2003	2004	2005
Revenue %	-0.6	6.8	16.8	13.7
Earnings/Share %	9.6	21.5	32.9	32.4
Book Value/Share %	11.9	27.0	22.2	0.2
Dividends/Share %	NMF	NMF	NMF	NMF

Profitability [A+]

	2003	2004	2005	TTM
Return on Assets %	14.7	16.0	21.1	23.6
Oper Cash Flow $Mil	33	37	51	56
- Cap Spending $Mil	3	11	22	24
= Free Cash Flow $Mil	30	26	29	31

Financial Health [A+]

	2003	2004	2005	09-30-06
Long-term Debt $Mil	1	1	1	1
Total Equity $Mil	148	181	179	177
Debt/Equity Ratio	0.0	0.0	0.0	0.0

Competition

	Market Cap $Mil	12 Mo Trailing Sales $Mil	Price/Cash Flow	Return On Assets%	Debt/ Equity	Total Return% 1 Yr	Total Return% 3 Yr
Forward Air	881	349	15.9	23.6	0.0	-20.4	16.0
United Parcel Service B	80,494	46,873	15.1	11.4	0.2	1.8	2.4
FedEx	33,307	33,132	9.4	8.1	0.2	5.4	17.4

Price Volatility

	2001	2002	2003	2004	2005	2006
Annual $Price High	29.46	23.67	21.33	31.50	40.93	43.67
Low	13.55	10.93	12.12	18.33	22.02	28.86
Annual Total Return %	-9.1	-42.8	41.7	62.5	23.9	-20.4

Fiscal Year-End: December

	2001	2002	2003	2004	2005	TTM
Revenue $Mil	228	226	242	282	321	349
Net Income $Mil	20	22	26	34	45	49
Earnings Per Share $	0.59	0.65	0.79	1.05	1.39	1.55
Shares Outstanding Mil	32	32	32	32	32	30
Return on Equity %	18.7	18.3	17.5	19.0	25.1	27.6
Net Margin %	8.7	9.6	10.7	12.2	14.0	14.0
Asset Turnover	1.7	1.6	1.4	1.3	1.5	1.7
Financial Leverage	1.3	1.2	1.2	1.2	1.2	1.2

Valuation Ratios

	Stock	Rel to Industry	Rel to S&P 500
Price/Earnings	18.7	1.1	0.9
Price/Book	5.0	2.1	1.2
Price/Sales	2.5	1.1	0.9
Price/Cash Flow	15.9	1.6	1.1

Major Fund Holders

	% of Fund Assets
EV Atlanta Capital Small-Cap I	2.84
River Oak Discovery	2.79
PF NB Fasciano Small Equity A	2.12
Allegiant Small Cap Core I	1.77

Thesis By Peter Smith, 10-24-06 Stock Price as of Analysis: $31.97

Forward Air is the market leader in a niche of the freight transportation industry that its competitors can't seem to crack, though they are trying. This has translated into impressive profitability and boatloads of free cash flow, making Forward Air the kind of company we'd want to own.

Like less-than-truckload carriers such as YRC Worldwide, Forward Air consolidates shipments from multiple shippers on a single truck and runs them through a hub-and-spoke network--but that is where the similarities end. All of Forward Air's 81 terminals are at or near airports throughout North America, giving the firm access to freight that might otherwise move in the air. Additionally, its customers are not the shippers themselves, but freight forwarders, integrators, and airlines.

Another difference is that Forward Air does not own any of the trucks that move its freight, instead contracting with owner-operators for trucks and leasing its terminals and trailers. This asset-light business model frees management from worrying about keeping trucks loaded with freight when the economy goes south, but gives it the flexibility to increase capacity during the good times. Forward Air can get away with this because it does not handle the pickup or delivery of goods, so its routes are shorter and more predictable--exactly what owner-operators want.

Such a seemingly simple business model raises the question of why others haven't entered the fray and competed away profits. Some have tried, but their lack of scale and know-how prevented them from matching Forward Air's service level. As a result, they couldn't attract the same volume of freight or charge profitable prices--a vicious cycle. Forward Air went through years of losses in order to build sufficient scale in its network to turn a profit, and any potential competitor would have to do the same. Also, Forward Air now has enough volume to warrant point-to-point truckload shipments without any stops in between, further reducing costs. This competitive position, along with its technology and network, is the source of Forward Air's wide economic moat.

Nevertheless, Forward Air's niche is becoming more crowded. Kitty Hawk is trying to build a comparable airport-to-airport network, and freight forwarder EGL is marketing its airport-to-airport network more aggressively to outsiders (it had previously been used mostly for internal business). Though these entrants could see modest success, we still expect Forward Air to continue to dominate its profitable niche for the foreseeable future.

France Telecom SA ADR FTE

Data as of 12-29-06

Rating ★★★★	Fair Value $34.00	Last Close $27.70	Consider Buy $26.20	Consider Sell $42.60	Yield % 4.49

Industry	Business Risk	Moat Size	Investment Style	Sector
Telecom Svcs.	Average	Narrow	Large Value	Telecommunication

Company Profile
France Telecom is the incumbent telephone operator in France. FT now has less than 68% of the local market and 48% of the cellular market. The firm also has large wireless shares in the U.K., Spain, Poland, and other countries, with a total of 92.6 million subscribers. Fixed and cellular clients generate 85% of sales. FT also owns an Internet service and an international corporate telecom service, which have been integrated with the wireless service under the Orange brand.

Management
Stewardship Grade [NA]

Didier Lombard was named chairman and CEO in February 2005 after former CEO Thierry Breton was named France's finance minister. Lombard was previously senior executive vice president of the Technologies, Strategic Partnerships and New Usages group at France Telecom and worked with Breton in devising the firm's restructuring plan, based on 15 billion euros in cost savings via the TOP program, 15 billion euros in new equity, and 15 billion euros in debt refinancing. The restructuring plan is ahead of schedule, and FT is no longer facing a cash crunch. Gervais Pellissier was named CFO in February 2006; prior to that, he was chairman and CEO of Bull, a French information technology company. Sanjiv Ahuja, Orange's CEO, was very involved with that division's growth, even before his promotion to lead it. We do have a few corporate governance complaints. We would like to see the chairman and CEO roles separated. And although we are pleased to see the number of directors from the government reduced, we are concerned that as long as the French government is a significant FT shareholder (it owns a 32.5% stake), the firm may be used to implement political policies, such as increased employment, rather than run for all shareholders. A takeover of the company from any entity that is not acceptable to the government is also prevented.

6, place d'Alleray Cedex 15 www.francetelecom.fr
Paris, France 75505

Growth [NA]	2002	2003	2004	2005
Revenue %	8.4	-1.1	0.1	6.2
Earnings/Share %	NMF	NMF	-23.8	80.3
Book Value/Share %	NMF	NMF	12.0	46.4
Dividends/Share %	—	—	—	—

Profitability [NA]	2003	2004	2005	TTM
Return on Assets %	2.9	2.9	6.1	6.1
Oper Cash Flow $Mil	12,681	15,773	16,747	16,747
- Cap Spending $Mil	5,714	6,386	7,691	7,691
= Free Cash Flow $Mil	6,966	9,386	9,056	9,056

Financial Health [NA]	2003	2004	2005	12-31-05
Long-term Debt $Mil	48,455	58,621	50,757	50,757
Total Equity $Mil	15,033	24,223	33,855	33,855
Debt/Equity Ratio	3.2	2.4	1.5	1.5

Competition

	Market Cap $Mil	12 Mo Trailing Sales $Mil	Price/Cash Flow	Return On Assets%	Debt/ Equity	Total Return% 1 Yr	3 Yr
France Telecom SA ADR	72,105	61,407	4.3	6.1	1.5	17.7	1.6
Vodafone Group PLC ADR	127,867	52,679	6.0	-17.6	0.2	34.1	6.3
Deutsche Telekom AG ADR	76,405	74,638	4.1	4.6	—	15.0	1.8

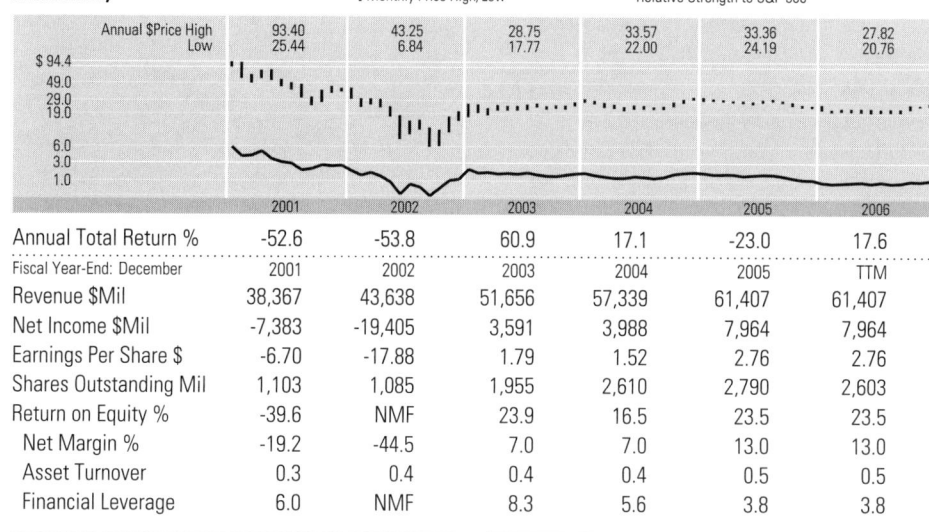

	2001	2002	2003	2004	2005	TTM
Annual Total Return %	-52.6	-53.8	60.9	17.1	-23.0	17.6
Fiscal Year-End: December	2001	2002	2003	2004	2005	TTM
Revenue $Mil	38,367	43,638	51,656	57,339	61,407	61,407
Net Income $Mil	-7,383	-19,405	3,591	3,988	7,964	7,964
Earnings Per Share $	-6.70	-17.88	1.79	1.52	2.76	2.76
Shares Outstanding Mil	1,103	1,085	1,955	2,610	2,790	2,603
Return on Equity %	-39.6	NMF	23.9	16.5	23.5	23.5
Net Margin %	-19.2	-44.5	7.0	7.0	13.0	13.0
Asset Turnover	0.3	0.4	0.4	0.4	0.5	0.5
Financial Leverage	6.0	NMF	8.3	5.6	3.8	3.8

Valuation Ratios	Stock	Rel to Industry	Rel to S&P 500
Price/Earnings	10.1	0.5	0.5
Price/Book	2.1	0.5	0.5
Price/Sales	1.2	0.5	0.4
Price/Cash Flow	4.3	0.5	0.3

Major Fund Holders	% of Fund Assets
ICON Telecommunications & Utilities	2.28
1st Source Monogram Long/Short	1.34
Commonwealth Global	1.04
California Investment Euro Gr & Inc Dir	1.02

Thesis
By Allan C. Nichols, CFA, 12-15-06 Stock Price as of Analysis: $27.41

Despite a slowdown in France Telecom's revenue growth, we still like the company. The firm has been successfully moving into Internet-based services, and we think it has an under appreciated emerging-markets wireless portfolio.

Despite giving us the term laissez-faire, France isn't the poster child for a deregulated economy. However, the French market for high-speed Internet access and voice over Internet protocol is possibly the most competitive in the world.

FT competitor Iliad has been leading the competitive charge, with 2.1 million Internet access subscribers who also use its service for VoIP calling. FT has responded by cannibalizing its traditional phone customers. It now has 5.5 million high-speed Internet customers, with 53% taking VoIP service and expects that about 30% of France's fixed-line market will be using VoIP by the end of 2006.

However, Iliad and most competitors still rely on FT's network to carry part or all of the transmission of their services. This allows FT to continue to earn some revenue even from customers it loses. VoIP generates less revenue than traditional phone service, but costs less to provide. While this isn't a full offset, when added to continued cost-cutting, we expect FT's operating margins to hold fairly steady.

Even more important though, is the cash the firm generates. The beauty of large incumbent telecom operators is they throw off tons of cash. Because of legacy networks the firms built, they have large depreciation charges. This means as revenue growth slows, the firm's net income is hurt more than cash flow. We continue to expect the revenue from FT's fixed-line business to decline, but the cash flow to remain substantial. The firm has generated a return on capital around 17%, evidence that its entrenched position and scale economies provide the company with a narrow moat.

We also think the firm will be able to grow its wireless business. We particularly like its position in emerging markets and don't think this is appreciated by the stock market. FT has 32.3 million subscribers--out of 92.6 million--in its "rest of world" category, a figure that grew 29% over the past year. We expect this segment to grow significantly faster than the rest of the business.

FT is also taking what it has learned in France into other countries. It now has 3.7 million high-speed Internet access customers outside of France and is the leading VoIP provider in the U.K. FT has also moved into other services; it serves 421,000 television customers via the Internet.

Franklin Resources BEN

Data as of 12-29-06

	Rating	Fair Value	Last Close	Consider Buy	Consider Sell	Yield %
	★	$77.00	$110.17	$59.40	$96.50	0.46

Industry	Business Risk	Moat Size	Investment Style	Sector
Money Mgmt.	Average	Wide	Large Growth	Financial Services

Company Profile

Franklin Resources serves retail, institutional, and high-net-worth clients with mutual fund and separate-account products. It sells its retail products exclusively through advisor channels but has a direct salesforce for institutional products. Franklin Templeton mutual funds, which recently accounted for roughly 70% of the firm's managed assets, specialize in fixed-income, hybrid, and value-oriented equity funds. The Fiduciary Trust business serves institutional and high-net-worth investors.

Management   Stewardship Grade [A]

Franklin has been run by the Johnson family since 1947. The family still owns nearly 35% of the stock and holds three of the director positions. Chairman Charles B. Johnson stepped down as CEO in 2004. He still receives generous compensation and benefits for serving as chairman. His son, Greg Johnson, and Martin Flanagan (no relation) took over as co-CEOs, and this arrangement lasted until August 2005 when Flanagan left the firm to lead Amvescap. Greg Johnson is now sole CEO. His fiscal 2005 compensation came in at $6.9 million, which was in line with other asset-management executives. Though Greg Johnson does not own a large stake in the company, his father and uncle recently owned nearly one third of outstanding shares. We think this gives him ample motivation to look out for the interests of shareholders.

One Franklin Parkway
San Mateo, CA 94403
www.frk.com

Competition

	Market Cap $Mil	12 Mo Trailing Sales $Mil	Price/Cash Flow	Return On Assets%	Debt/ Equity	Total Return% 1 Yr	3 Yr
Franklin Resources	27,932	5,051	—	13.3	—	17.8	30.3
Mellon Financial	17,360	5,092	—	2.0	—	26.0	12.3
Marsh & McLennan Companie	16,897	11,715	—	4.5	—	-1.2	-11.9

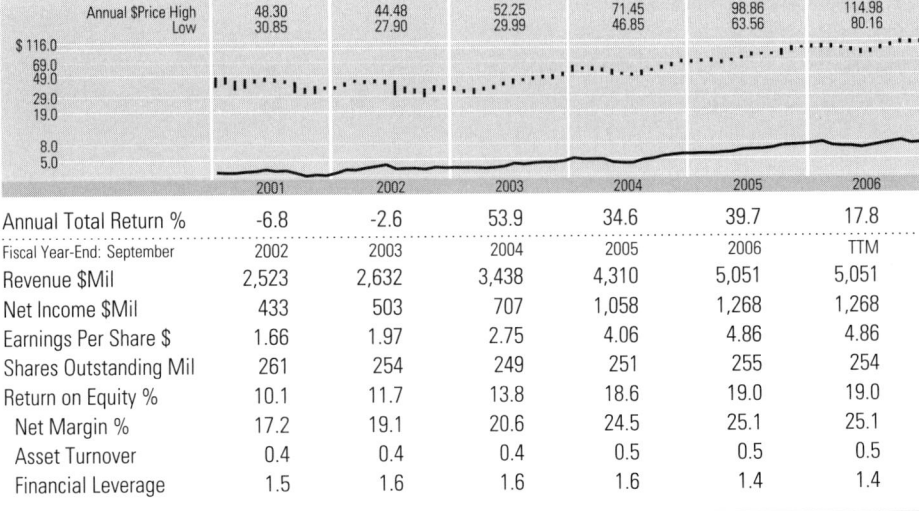

	2001	2002	2003	2004	2005	2006
Annual Total Return %	-6.8	-2.6	53.9	34.6	39.7	17.8
Fiscal Year-End: September	2002	2003	2004	2005	2006	TTM
Revenue $Mil	2,523	2,632	3,438	4,310	5,051	5,051
Net Income $Mil	433	503	707	1,058	1,268	1,268
Earnings Per Share $	1.66	1.97	2.75	4.06	4.86	4.86
Shares Outstanding Mil	261	254	249	251	255	254
Return on Equity %	10.1	11.7	13.8	18.6	19.0	19.0
Net Margin %	17.2	19.1	20.6	24.5	25.1	25.1
Asset Turnover	0.4	0.4	0.4	0.5	0.5	0.5
Financial Leverage	1.5	1.6	1.6	1.6	1.4	1.4

Valuation Ratios	Stock	Rel to Industry	Rel to S&P 500
Price/Earnings	22.7	0.7	1.1
Price/Book	4.2	1.0	1.0
Price/Sales	5.5	0.9	1.9
Price/Cash Flow	—	—	—

Major Fund Holders	% of Fund Assets
FMI Provident Trust Strategy	5.35
Fidelity Select Brokerage & Investmnt	5.06
Allianz RCM Financial Services Instl	5.05
Schwab Financial Services	4.92

Growth [A]	2002	2003	2004	2005
Revenue %	4.3	30.6	25.4	17.2
Earnings/Share %	18.7	39.6	47.6	19.7
Book Value/Share %	3.2	17.7	9.8	17.5
Dividends/Share %	7.3	40.7	478.3	-80.0

Profitability [A+]	2003	2004	2005	TTM
Return on Assets %	8.6	11.9	13.3	13.3
Oper Cash Flow $Mil	930	850	1,278	—
- Cap Spending $Mil	21	75	69	—
= Free Cash Flow $Mil	—	—	—	—

Financial Health [NA]	2003	2004	2005	06-30-06
Long-term Debt $Mil	—	—	—	—
Total Equity $Mil	5,107	5,684	6,685	6,685
Debt/Equity Ratio	—	—	—	—

Thesis By Jeffrey Ptak, CPA, CFA, 12-13-06 Stock Price as of Analysis: $112.31

Franklin Resources' scale, strong brands, and diversified asset base earn it a wide moat.

Franklin stands apart from the crowd in one obvious respect--size. With nearly $600 billion in assets under management, the firm can spread its predominately fixed-cost base across a wider expanse, explaining why many Franklin funds boast below-average expense ratios. Since this cost advantage gives many funds a built-in head start versus peers, Franklin's portfolio managers have the luxury of taking on less risk than rivals. This has helped to keep volatility in check, which, in turn, has served to further stabilize the firm's asset base, as investors are less inclined to jump in or bail out of funds absent jarring performance changes.

Yet, perhaps the single greatest stabilizing factor is Franklin's suite of well-respected brands, including Templeton and Mutual Series. While these imprints specialize in different styles, each tends to share an affinity for stodgy, price-conscious, low-turnover investing that has generally translated to steady long-term performance. That, in turn, has engendered loyalty from advisors, fueled additional interest, and paved the way to fruitful marketing alliances.

Franklin's asset base is also well-balanced across asset classes, styles, locales, products, and customer types. Recently, more than half of the firm's assets under management were invested in stock strategies (roughly 40% in foreign-stock strategies), about one fourth was in fixed-income strategies, and the balance was in hybrid strategies. And while retail investors still make up the bulk of Franklin's business, institutional and high-net-worth assets now constitute about one third of the firm's book. Moreover, with roughly 15% of assets invested in strategies domiciled outside of the U.S., Franklin has a formidable and growing presence abroad. This gives the firm a leg up in courting an increasingly affluent foreign clientele, particularly in emerging countries.

The virtues of that well-balanced attack have been on display in recent years: The Templeton strategies and hybrid funds, such as Franklin Income, have raked in assets at a prodigious clip amid investors' heightened demand for foreign exposure and income. And while some of Templeton's growth strategies have lagged amid stylistic headwinds, the firm has enjoyed strong flows into its deep-value-oriented Mutual series products.

With more than $3 billion in cash on its balance sheet, Franklin also enjoys ample financial flexibility. The key will be how wisely management deploys that hoard.

Data as of 12-29-06

Gamco Investors GBL

Rating	Fair Value	Last Close	Consider Buy	Consider Sell	Yield %
★★★★	$44.00	$38.46	$33.90	$55.10	0.31

Company Profile

Gamco Investors manages money for institutions, mutual fund investors, and individual high-net-worth clients. The majority of Gamco's assets under management are invested in equities, both in the United States and abroad. Equity securities account for more than 90% of managed assets. Gamco also has a hedge fund business and an institutional brokerage.

Industry	Business Risk	Moat Size	Investment Style	Sector
Money Mgmt.	Average	Wide	Small Value	Financial Services

Competition

	Market Cap $Mil	12 Mo Trailing Sales $Mil	Price/Cash Flow	Return On Assets%	Debt/ Equity	Total Return% 1 Yr	3 Yr
Gamco Investors	1,086	250	—	8.5	—	-11.4	-0.5
Franklin Resources	27,932	5,051	—	13.3	—	17.8	30.3
Legg Mason	12,491	3,810	—	13.0	—	-20.0	23.0

Price Volatility

	2001	2002	2003	2004	2005	2006
Annual $Price High	48.90	44.45	40.80	50.50	49.20	49.05
Low	27.75	24.40	25.60	37.22	38.60	32.82
Annual Total Return %	30.2	-30.5	32.6	26.5	-10.1	-11.4

Fiscal Year-End: December

	2001	2002	2003	2004	2005	TTM
Revenue $Mil	224	210	207	255	252	250
Net Income $Mil	61	53	50	63	63	64
Earnings Per Share $	2.03	1.76	1.65	2.06	2.09	2.19
Shares Outstanding Mil	30	30	30	30	30	28
Return on Equity %	22.2	16.6	13.2	18.7	14.9	15.4
Net Margin %	27.2	25.4	24.0	24.5	25.1	25.6
Asset Turnover	0.5	0.4	0.3	0.4	0.4	0.3
Financial Leverage	1.8	1.8	1.9	2.1	1.7	1.8

Management — Stewardship Grade [D]

Celebrity fund manager Mario Gabelli has been chairman, CEO, and chief investment officer of the company and its predecessors since its inception in 1976. He has complete control of the firm through a private company, which owns more than 80% of Gamco Investors stock. This company also owns special Class B shares, which have 10 times the voting power of regular Class A shares. In addition to this tight grip, the bylaws have strong antitakeover provisions, virtually guaranteeing that the firm will not change hands. Gabelli makes far more than any CEO in the asset-management industry and is one of the world's highest-paid executives. His compensation totaled $55.5 million in 2005, which amounted to 22% of revenue. This is enormous by any standard. Gamco has well earned its Stewardship Grade of D, which reflects the company's general failure to consistently place shareholder interests front and center.

Valuation Ratios

	Stock	Rel to Industry	Rel to S&P 500
Price/Earnings	17.6	0.6	0.9
Price/Book	2.6	0.6	0.6
Price/Sales	4.3	0.7	1.5
Price/Cash Flow	—	—	—

Major Fund Holders

	% of Fund Assets
Phoenix Small-Cap Growth A	3.37
Phoenix All-Cap Growth A	1.89
JohnsonFamily Small Cap Value	1.71
Royce Dividend Value Service	1.19

One Corporate Center
Rye, NY 10580-1422
www.gabelli.com

Growth [D]

	2002	2003	2004	2005
Revenue %	-6.4	-1.2	23.0	-1.1
Earnings/Share %	-13.3	-6.3	24.8	1.5
Book Value/Share %	16.1	17.9	-11.9	26.8
Dividends/Share %	NMF	NMF	8700.0	-94.9

Profitability [A+]

	2003	2004	2005	TTM
Return on Assets %	6.8	9.0	8.8	8.5
Oper Cash Flow $Mil	38	-24	-34	—
- Cap Spending $Mil	—	—	—	—
= Free Cash Flow $Mil	—	—	—	—

Financial Health [NA]

	2003	2004	2005	09-30-06
Long-term Debt $Mil	—	—	—	—
Total Equity $Mil	378	335	424	418
Debt/Equity Ratio	—	—	—	—

Thesis
By Jeffrey Ptak, CPA, CFA, 12-14-06 Stock Price as of Analysis: $38.33

Headline risk shouldn't threaten Gamco Investors' durably profitable business model.

Gamco Investors manages roughly $27 billion in assets for retail and institutional investors and specializes in a brand of value investing that founder and CEO Mario Gabelli has helped to popularize. Generally speaking, Gabelli's stature and recognizability have been pivotal in fueling interest in Gamco's products, thereby attracting new assets.

Yet, Gabelli has been more a hindrance than a help lately. He continues to catch flak for his outsize pay package ($55.5 million in 2005) and until recently had been embroiled in a civil suit alleging that he orchestrated fraudulent purchases of wireless spectrum from the federal government. He also recently settled a messy dispute with his former partners concerning the value of their stake in a private partnership that controls Gamco.

In addition, business has been weak recently: Gamco has suffered net outflows across virtually every segment of its business thus far in 2006, and performance has been lackluster, with most funds lagging typical peers over the trailing five-year period.

Unease over Gabelli's reputation and performance is natural--he's Gamco's chief decision-maker, runs the lion's share of the firm's assets, and serves as its most-potent marketing tool. In short, the success of Gamco's operating model hinges on Gabelli's reputation and advocacy of the company's strategies.

While success might seem like a stretch in light of Gabelli's recent missteps, there's an enduringly attractive business here. With Gabelli doing most of the investing and marketing, the company doesn't typically have to make big outlays for investment staff or distribution. That's translated into heady returns on invested capital as assets have risen.

Profits would suffer amid a torrent of outflows, but we don't think that's especially likely, as Gabelli has carved out a nice niche as one of value investing's foremost practitioners. While recent weakness in the telecom and media industries--longtime Gabelli favorites--has weighed on results, Gabelli's impressive long-term record should ensure that Gamco's products remain on investors' radar screen.

That said, our fair value estimate doesn't call for assets under management to grow by leaps and bounds: We assume that Gamco's bond assets under management will evaporate while institutional equity assets continue to leave. We're banking on market appreciation to be the primary driver of asset growth.

Data as of 12-29-06

Gannett GCI

	Rating	Fair Value	Last Close	Consider Buy	Consider Sell	Yield %
	★★★	$65.00	$60.46	$50.10	$81.40	1.99

Industry	Business Risk	Moat Size	Investment Style	Sector
Media Conglomerates	Average	Narrow	Large Value	Media

Company Profile

Gannett is a leading international news and information company that publishes about 90 daily newspapers in the U.S., including USA Today, the nation's largest-selling daily newspaper. The company also owns almost 1,000 non-daily publications in the U.S. and USA Weekend, a weekly newspaper magazine. Subsidiary Newsquest is the United Kingdom's second-largest regional newspaper company. Gannett operates more than 20 TV stations in the U.S. and more than 130 Internet sites.

Management   Stewardship Grade [D]

Craig A. Dubow became president and CEO in 2005 when Douglas H. McCorkindale stepped down from his post. McCorkindale retained his chairman role. Excluding his stock-option grants (which Gannett doesn't expense yet), McCorkindale received total compensation of $5.8 million in 2004, a package at the high end of the industry range. Considering the size of the company, we don't think his compensation was outlandish, but Gannett's stock performance has roughly mirrored its competitors' over the past several years. We're disappointed to see staggered board elections and generous golden parachutes, which don't benefit shareholders. Also, Gannett has entered into a consulting agreement with a former executive that includes a generous salary and lavish perks, in our opinion--another knock against the company's stewardship.

7950 Jones Branch Drive www.gannett.com
McLean, VA 22107-0910

Growth [B-]	2002	2003	2004	2005
Revenue %	2.0	4.5	10.1	4.3
Earnings/Share %	—	NMF	10.3	2.6
Book Value/Share %	—	NMF	-1.7	0.7
Dividends/Share %	4.4	4.3	6.1	7.7

Profitability [A]	2003	2004	2005	TTM
Return on Assets %	8.2	8.5	7.9	6.9
Oper Cash Flow $Mil	1,481	1,586	1,432	1,447
- Cap Spending $Mil	281	280	263	236
= Free Cash Flow $Mil	1,200	1,306	1,169	1,211

Financial Health [A-]	2003	2004	2005	09-30-06
Long-term Debt $Mil	3,835	4,608	5,438	5,495
Total Equity $Mil	8,423	8,164	7,571	8,346
Debt/Equity Ratio	0.5	0.6	0.7	0.7

Competition	Market Cap $Mil	12 Mo Trailing Sales $Mil	Price/Cash Flow	Return On Assets %	Debt/Equity	Total Return % 1 Yr	Total Return % 3 Yr
Gannett	14,167	7,880	9.8	6.9	0.7	1.9	-10.5
Tribune	7,353	5,527	13.2	3.4	0.9	4.2	-14.1
Washington Post Co	7,167	3,813	13.1	6.9	0.1	-1.5	-1.0

Price Volatility — Monthly Price High/Low — Relative Strength to S&P 500

	2001	2002	2003	2004	2005	2006
Annual $Price High	71.14	79.90	89.63	91.38	82.41	64.97
Low	53.00	62.76	66.70	78.84	58.37	51.65
Annual Total Return %	8.1	8.1	25.8	-7.2	-24.7	1.9

Fiscal Year-End: December	2001	2002	2003	2004	2005	TTM
Revenue $Mil	6,204	6,330	6,616	7,284	7,599	7,880
Net Income $Mil	—	—	1,211	1,317	1,245	1,151
Earnings Per Share $	—	—	4.46	4.92	5.05	4.83
Shares Outstanding Mil	—	—	270	265	245	234
Return on Equity %	—	—	14.4	16.1	16.4	13.8
Net Margin %	—	—	18.3	18.1	16.4	14.6
Asset Turnover	0.5	0.5	0.5	0.5	0.5	0.5
Financial Leverage	2.3	2.0	1.7	1.9	2.1	2.0

Valuation Ratios	Stock	Rel to Industry	Rel to S&P 500
Price/Earnings	12.5	0.5	0.6
Price/Book	1.7	0.5	0.4
Price/Sales	1.8	0.5	0.6
Price/Cash Flow	9.8	0.6	0.7

Major Fund Holders	% of Fund Assets
Destination Select Equity	6.00
CM Advisers	4.12
Sycuan U.S. Value	4.11
Ariel Appreciation	3.85

Thesis By James M. Walden, CFA, 12-18-06 Stock Price as of Analysis: $61.04

Part of Gannett's economic moat comes from its flagship newspaper, USA Today. With circulation of about 2.3 million, USA Today is the largest-selling daily paper in the United States. In our opinion, USA Today's strong brand and wide distribution provide an attractive means for advertisers to reach a broad, national audience, making it more attractive than many other papers. In fact, USA Today increased revenue by about 1% in 2005, while the entire industry saw revenue from printed national ads slip 2% during the same time, according to figures provided by the Newspaper Association of America. Given the high up-front costs associated with launching a newspaper and the maturity of the industry, we think it's very unlikely USA Today will ever see competition from another national paper.

While USA Today is Gannett's largest publication, it also owns about 90 other daily papers and about 1,000 non-daily titles, providing a total circulation that makes Gannett the largest newspaper company in the United States and a bellwether for the industry. And the industry is currently going through some tough times. We expect total industry ad revenue to show a small dip in 2006, despite strong online ad-revenue growth. This would be the first annual decline since 2002, the tail end of the last economic recession in the U.S. However, a significant amount of the industry's current challenges comes from the Internet. Increased broadband penetration has changed the way individuals consume media, including news. As a result, advertisers have flocked to the Internet. According to PricewaterhouseCoopers, online advertising revenue grew 30% in the U.S. in 2005 alone, while dollars from printed newspaper ads inched up only 2%, lower than its historical rate of about 3%-4%.

We think Gannett is doing a commendable job with its efforts to adapt to the changing media and advertising landscape. In our opinion, the best example is its continued investment in CareerBuilder, which it co-owns with Tribune and McClatchy. The results are evident: In 2006, CareerBuilder overtook rival online recruiter Monster in revenue, unique traffic, and job postings in North America. We also think Gannett is doing the right thing by continuing to invest in its newspapers' and TV stations' Web sites. Currently, Gannett's sites boast 24 million unique visitors in aggregate, reaching more than 15% of the Internet audience, according to Nielsen/NetRatings. We expect the Internet will be an even more important medium for Gannett going forward.

Data as of 12-29-06

Gap GPS

	Rating	Fair Value	Last Close	Consider Buy	Consider Sell	Yield %
	★★★★	$23.00	$19.50	$14.70	$27.70	1.64

Company Profile
Gap is a specialty retailer whose stores sell casual apparel for men, women, and children under private-label brand names. These brands are marketed under the Gap, GapKids, babyGap, Banana Republic, Old Navy, and Forth and Towne names. The company operates more than 3,000 stores throughout the United States, Canada, Western Europe, and Japan. Virtually all stores are leased.

Industry	Business Risk	Moat Size	Investment Style	Sector
Clothing Stores	Above Avg	Narrow	Large Core	Consumer Services

Competition

	Market Cap $Mil	12 Mo Trailing Sales $Mil	Price/Cash Flow	Return On Assets%	Debt/ Equity	Total Return% 1 Yr	3 Yr
Gap	15,807	15,834	8.6	9.7	0.0	12.5	-3.7
Target	49,000	56,727	11.3	6.9	0.6	4.7	15.6
Limited Brands	11,510	10,188	16.3	11.4	0.7	32.5	22.8

Management   Stewardship Grade [A]
Disney veteran Paul Pressler joined the company as president and CEO in September 2002, bringing CFO Byron Pollitt on board from Disney six months later. They have done a great job of getting the company's finances under control, and of managing profitability and cash flows during a period of declining sales. However, turnover at the top of the two biggest chains--Gap and Old Navy--is worrisome. We think that corporate governance is fine. The board is elected every year and is sufficiently independent, with plenty of relevant retail and consumer experience. Executive and board compensation is disclosed in high detail, and while Pressler's initial option grant was enormous, executive compensation has been reasonable in recent years. He did not receive a bonus in 2005, due to the company's weak performance.

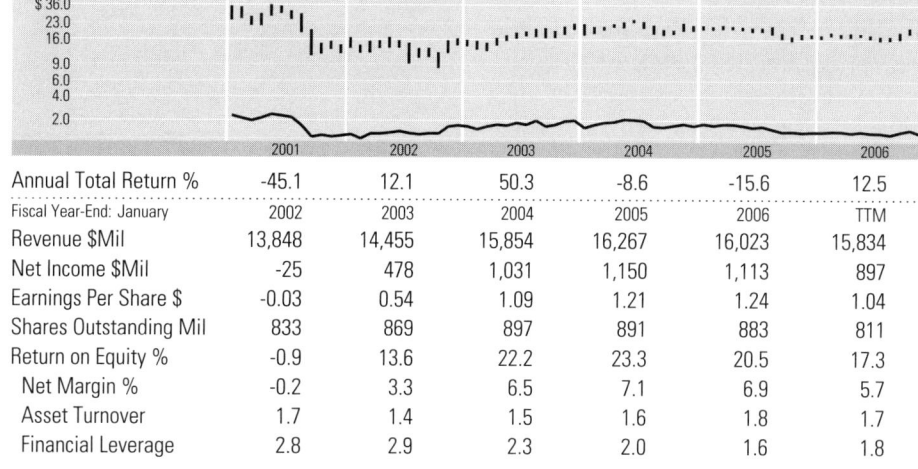

Price Volatility
Monthly Price High/Low — Relative Strength to S&P 500

Annual $Price High/Low	34.98/11.12	17.14/8.35	23.47/12.45	25.72/18.12	22.70/15.90	21.39/15.91
	2001	2002	2003	2004	2005	2006
Annual Total Return %	-45.1	12.1	50.3	-8.6	-15.6	12.5
Fiscal Year-End: January	2002	2003	2004	2005	2006	TTM
Revenue $Mil	13,848	14,455	15,854	16,267	16,023	15,834
Net Income $Mil	-25	478	1,031	1,150	1,113	897
Earnings Per Share $	-0.03	0.54	1.09	1.21	1.24	1.04
Shares Outstanding Mil	833	869	897	891	883	811
Return on Equity %	-0.9	13.6	22.2	23.3	20.5	17.3
Net Margin %	-0.2	3.3	6.5	7.1	6.9	5.7
Asset Turnover	1.7	1.4	1.5	1.6	1.8	1.7
Financial Leverage	2.8	2.9	2.3	2.0	1.6	1.8

Valuation Ratios	Stock	Rel to Industry	Rel to S&P 500
Price/Earnings	18.8	0.9	0.9
Price/Book	3.0	0.7	0.7
Price/Sales	1.0	0.7	0.3
Price/Cash Flow	8.6	0.7	0.6

Major Fund Holders	% of Fund Assets
Snow Capital Opportunity A	4.14
Wells Fargo Advantage Large Co Core A	3.75
Wells Fargo Advantage Growth and Inc Inv	3.72
Matrix Advisors Value	3.28

Two Folsom St. www.gapinc.com
San Francisco, CA 94105

Growth [D]	2003	2004	2005	2006
Revenue %	4.4	9.7	2.6	-1.5
Earnings/Share %	NMF	101.9	11.0	2.5
Book Value/Share %	15.3	23.4	5.7	16.4
Dividends/Share %	0.0	0.0	0.0	127.7

Profitability [B+]	2004	2005	2006	TTM
Return on Assets %	9.6	11.4	12.6	9.7
Oper Cash Flow $Mil	2,160	1,597	1,551	1,843
- Cap Spending $Mil	261	419	600	558
= Free Cash Flow $Mil	1,899	1,178	951	1,285

Financial Health [A+]	2004	2005	2006	10-31-06
Long-term Debt $Mil	2,487	1,886	513	188
Total Equity $Mil	4,648	4,936	5,425	5,193
Debt/Equity Ratio	0.5	0.4	0.1	0.0

Thesis   By Joseph Beaulieu, 12-14-06   Stock Price as of Analysis: $20.28

Gap's turnaround is coming more slowly than we would like, although strong improvements at Banana Republic, positive developments at Gap, and a management overhaul at Old Navy suggest that the company has correctly identified the root of its problems and is headed in the right direction. However, it seems to be headed there at a snail's pace. We've been bullish on the shares for some time now, and the stock has actually performed fairly well over the course of 2006. But problems at Old Navy have soured our view on the company somewhat.

We think that the core of Paul Pressler's strategy for managing the company's three brands (Banana Republic, Gap, and Old Navy) was sound. He inherited three chains whose most obvious differentiating factor was price, and a key challenge was to establish more distinct identities for each brand so that each would draw from a different group of customers, thereby limiting cannibalization across the chains. But the execution of the strategy was flawed. It took far too long for the company to implement the more youth-oriented identity of the Gap chain. Additionally, Banana Republic moved too far into trendy fashions, and Old Navy moved too far into commodity discount clothing.

Banana Republic appears to be back on track. Its product mix has shifted back to the dressy-casual styles its customers prefer, and as a result, same-store sales are back into positive territory. We think that the Gap chain is positioned for a similar rebound, but the company has only recently begun converting stores to the new trendier look. We think the merchandise looks better than it has in years, but this hasn't yet translated to improved sales.

Old Navy isn't on the mend yet, however. The stores aren't in great shape, and the chain has to resort to deep discounts to move merchandise. This, plus the cluttered and promotional atmosphere of the stores, is making the brand look low-end, in our opinion. Same-store sales and merchandise margins have weakened, and we don't believe that new brand president Dawn Robertson has yet made much progress in reducing these trends.

We think that Gap has a lot of potential, but we also see it as a riskier-than-average investment. It has taken a long time for the core Gap stores to find their direction, and now that Old Navy is on the rocks, we're not enthused by the potential for another drawn-out turnaround effort.

Genentech DNA

Data as of 12-29-06

	Rating	Fair Value	Last Close	Consider Buy	Consider Sell	Yield %
	★★★	$86.00	$81.13	$66.30	$107.70	0.00

Industry	Business Risk	Moat Size	Investment Style	Sector
Biotechnology	Average	Wide	Large Growth	Healthcare

Company Profile

Genentech, a Roche subsidiary, develops and produces pharmaceuticals. Products include treatments for breast cancer, colorectal cancer, lung cancer, asthma, non-Hodgkin's lymphoma, and cystic fibrosis. The firm also manufactures growth hormones for children and adults and a declotting enzyme (Activase) used to treat strokes. Genentech is developing drugs to treat cancers as well as immunological, cardiovascular, and neurodegenerative diseases.

Management   Stewardship Grade [C]

Genentech head Arthur Levinson is credited with helping the company develop a diverse product pipeline. Swiss drug giant Roche owns 56% of the firm and holds three of the seven board seats. Viewing Herb Boyer (often regarded as the father of biotechnology and a Genentech founder) as an outsider, more than 50% of the board are insiders. The company's top 11 board members and executives combined hold 6.5 million exercisable options, but they own only 65,000 shares (0.006% of the shares outstanding). So although the upside potential is huge for the executive team, the potential downside is negligible. Antitakeover defenses in the form of poison pills and golden parachutes also lower our Stewardship Grade, as does the relationship with Roche, which gives the larger parent certain product rights that might not be in the best interest of Genentech shareholders. Offsetting some of those negatives, however, Genentech employees receive the lion's share of option grants, and we appreciate the company's good disclosure of information.

Competition

	Market Cap $Mil	12 Mo Trailing Sales $Mil	Price/Cash Flow	Return On Assets%	Debt/ Equity	Total Return% 1 Yr	3 Yr
Genentech	85,511	8,462	42.1	13.4	0.2	-12.3	20.1
Johnson & Johnson	191,415	52,252	14.5	18.5	0.0	12.4	10.8
Celgene	20,276	773	EUB	3.3	0.5	77.6	72.0

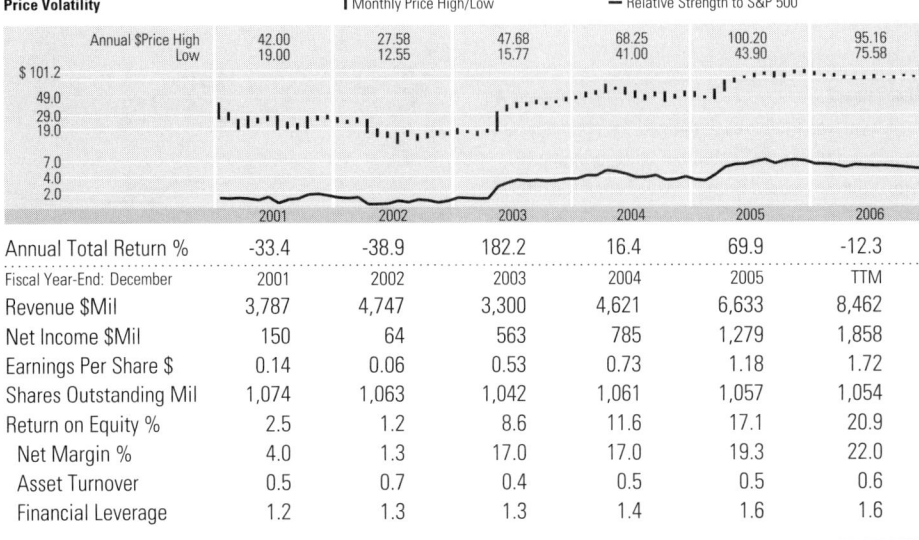

	2001	2002	2003	2004	2005	2006
Annual $Price High	42.00	27.58	47.68	68.25	100.20	95.16
Low	19.00	12.55	15.77	41.00	43.90	75.58
Annual Total Return %	-33.4	-38.9	182.2	16.4	69.9	-12.3

Fiscal Year-End: December

	2001	2002	2003	2004	2005	TTM
Revenue $Mil	3,787	4,747	3,300	4,621	6,633	8,462
Net Income $Mil	150	64	563	785	1,279	1,858
Earnings Per Share $	0.14	0.06	0.53	0.73	1.18	1.72
Shares Outstanding Mil	1,074	1,063	1,042	1,061	1,057	1,054
Return on Equity %	2.5	1.2	8.6	11.6	17.1	20.9
Net Margin %	4.0	1.3	17.0	17.0	19.3	22.0
Asset Turnover	0.5	0.7	0.4	0.5	0.5	0.6
Financial Leverage	1.2	1.3	1.3	1.4	1.6	1.6

Valuation Ratios	Stock	Rel to Industry	Rel to S&P 500
Price/Earnings	47.2	1.1	2.3
Price/Book	9.6	1.2	2.3
Price/Sales	10.1	0.9	3.5
Price/Cash Flow	42.1	1.5	2.9

Major Fund Holders	% of Fund Assets
AMIDEX Cancer Innovation & Healthcare	20.57
Genomics Y	14.28
ProFunds Biotechnology UltraSector Inv	11.04
Rydex Biotechnology Inv	10.08

Thesis   By Jill Kiersky, 11-16-06   Stock Price as of Analysis: $80.72

Genentech remains one of our favorite biotech companies. Its novel cancer treatments and strong research-and-development capabilities have led to annual revenue near $7 billion, making it the second-largest biotech firm in the United States. We expect the company to develop innovative products in the near future, but we remain cognizant of the risk that any of its products in development could fail.

With five product approvals since mid-2003, including two groundbreaking cancer therapies, the company has diversified its revenue stream and should enjoy strong sales and profit growth. Genentech's flagship cancer therapies, Rituxan and Herceptin, provide more than one third of the company's revenue. These products bring in more than $2.5 billion annually, don't cost much to produce (gross margins were 82% of product sales in 2005), and have long patent lives.

Now that Avastin (the first antiangiogenic therapy approved by the Food and Drug Administration), Tarceva for lung cancer, and Lucentis for wet age-related macular degeneration are on the market, Genentech has proved that innovation is its modus operandi. (We think the company's ability to pump out innovative products after 30 years in business is exceptional.) The market size for colon cancer, Avastin's approved market, could reach $8 billion. Our $3.5 billion sales estimate by 2010 is more conservative than most analysts' estimates, and if Avastin proves efficacious in other cancers, such as lung and ovarian, there is additional sales potential for the already-impressive drug. We expect Tarceva and Lucentis to also provide a strong sales boost despite their more competitive landscapes.

With a solid commercial lineup on top of a strong pipeline, Genentech has leveraged its operations into a highly scalable business. Operating margins have improved from 18% in 2002 to around 30% as the firm spreads its research and overhead costs over a quickly growing sales base. Returns on capital in the mid-20s and rising still far exceed its cost of capital. Furthermore, Genentech's large biologic manufacturing capabilities make it a partner of choice for smaller biotechs needing a development partner, which in turn helps Genentech find more promising drug candidates for its pipeline.

Genentech has had a long and impressive streak of good fortune, but drug development is probability-based, and odds are that a biotech company will witness a setback at some point, even a firm as strong as Genentech.

1 DNA Way
South San Francisc, CA 94080-4990
www.gene.com

Growth [A]	2002	2003	2004	2005
Revenue %	25.4	-30.5	40.0	43.5
Earnings/Share %	-57.1	783.3	37.7	61.6
Book Value/Share %	-8.9	22.4	2.7	9.2
Dividends/Share %	NMF	NMF	NMF	NMF

Profitability [A-]	2003	2004	2005	TTM
Return on Assets %	6.4	8.3	10.5	13.4
Oper Cash Flow $Mil	1,242	1,195	2,364	2,031
- Cap Spending $Mil	322	650	1,400	1,181
= Free Cash Flow $Mil	920	545	964	850

Financial Health [A]	2003	2004	2005	09-30-06
Long-term Debt $Mil	—	412	2,083	2,164
Total Equity $Mil	6,520	6,782	7,470	8,890
Debt/Equity Ratio	—	0.1	0.3	0.2

Data as of 12-29-06

General Dynamics GD

	Rating	Fair Value	Last Close	Consider Buy	Consider Sell	Yield %
	★★★	$70.00	$74.35	$54.00	$87.70	1.20

Company Profile

General Dynamics is a defense and aerospace manufacturer of ships, armored vehicles, information systems, and business jets with a growing information technology services practice. Contracts include nuclear submarines, naval destroyers, battle tanks, and surveillance and communication systems. About two thirds of sales are to the U.S. government, making GD the smallest of the five major U.S. defense contractors. The firm is based in Falls Church, Va., and employs about 81,000 people.

Management Stewardship Grade [A]

We think General Dynamics has the best management team in our defense coverage universe. Nicholas Chabraja, whose contract has been renewed through 2008, has been chairman and CEO since 1997. Hugh Redd was elected by the board in 2006 to become CFO, replacing the retiring Michael Mancuso. Redd seems a worthy replacement, having held numerous financial positions over his 20 years at GD, and he must be held in high esteem by Chabraja, who is undoubtedly thinking of succession planning. Chabraja is largely responsible for steering GD into a clear leadership position among large defense contractors, and we will watch closely for signs of an emerging successor to lead this wide-moat firm. Chabraja is the only insider on the firm's 12-member board. Directors James Crown and Charles Goodman together control about 6% of the shares. We think this makes for a productive balance of power between the CEO and shareholders' representatives on the board. Chabraja is increasingly well paid but not egregiously so, in our opinion. In 2005, he earned $4.7 million as well as restricted-stock awards with an estimated value of $5.5 million. While executive compensation is generous across the board at GD, a substantial portion is stock-based, and variable compensation is tied to meaningful long-term shareholder value creation.

2941 Fairview Park Drive Suite 100   www.generaldynamics.com
Falls Church, VA 22042-4153

Growth [B+]	2002	2003	2004	2005
Revenue %	15.0	19.5	17.1	11.1
Earnings/Share %	-2.8	-44.2	20.8	18.6
Book Value/Share %	14.8	-42.0	20.0	12.8
Dividends/Share %	7.3	6.8	11.1	11.4

Profitability [A]	2003	2004	2005	TTM
Return on Assets %	6.2	7.0	7.5	8.6
Oper Cash Flow $Mil	1,721	1,800	2,056	2,227
- Cap Spending $Mil	220	264	279	318
= Free Cash Flow $Mil	1,501	1,536	1,777	1,909

Financial Health [A]	2003	2004	2005	09-30-06
Long-term Debt $Mil	—	3,291	2,781	2,778
Total Equity $Mil	5,921	7,189	8,145	9,472
Debt/Equity Ratio	—	0.5	0.3	0.3

Industry	Business Risk	Moat Size	Investment Style	Sector
Aerospace/Defense	Average	Wide	Large Core	Industrial Materials

Competition	Market Cap $Mil	12 Mo Trailing Sales $Mil	Price/Cash Flow	Return On Assets%	Debt/ Equity	Total Return% 1 Yr	3 Yr
General Dynamics	30,085	23,582	13.5	8.6	0.3	32.2	20.1
Boeing	70,249	59,114	9.4	2.7	0.8	28.4	30.4
Lockheed Martin	39,028	39,009	11.1	8.1	0.5	47.0	24.1

Price Volatility | Monthly Price High/Low   — Relative Strength to S&P 500

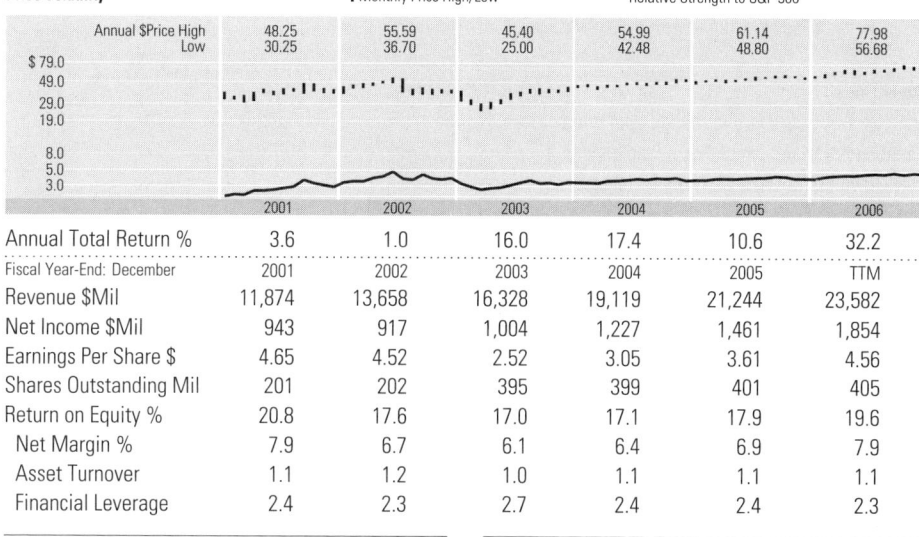

	2001	2002	2003	2004	2005	2006
Annual $Price High	48.25	55.59	45.40	54.99	61.14	77.98
Low	30.25	36.70	25.00	42.48	48.80	56.68
Annual Total Return %	3.6	1.0	16.0	17.4	10.6	32.2
Fiscal Year-End: December	2001	2002	2003	2004	2005	TTM
Revenue $Mil	11,874	13,658	16,328	19,119	21,244	23,582
Net Income $Mil	943	917	1,004	1,227	1,461	1,854
Earnings Per Share $	4.65	4.52	2.52	3.05	3.61	4.56
Shares Outstanding Mil	201	202	395	399	401	405
Return on Equity %	20.8	17.6	17.0	17.1	17.9	19.6
Net Margin %	7.9	6.7	6.1	6.4	6.9	7.9
Asset Turnover	1.1	1.2	1.0	1.1	1.1	1.1
Financial Leverage	2.4	2.3	2.7	2.4	2.4	2.3

Valuation Ratios	Stock	Rel to Industry	Rel to S&P 500
Price/Earnings	18.2	0.7	0.9
Price/Book	3.2	0.7	0.8
Price/Sales	1.3	1.0	0.4
Price/Cash Flow	13.5	1.0	0.9

Major Fund Holders	% of Fund Assets
Fidelity Select Defense & Aerospace	7.33
Fidelity Select Air Transportation	6.72
Barrett Opportunity	4.95
First Eagle Fund of America Y	3.97

Thesis By Chris Lozier, 10-19-06   Stock Price as of Analysis: $72.45

Outstanding leadership, a strong defense portfolio, a leading position in business jets, and a unique culture of efficiency make General Dynamics our only wide-moat defense contractor.

Led by CEO Nicholas Chabraja, GD has far outpaced its peers in the requisite transformation from bloated legacy defense giant to lean, flexible, and extremely cost-conscious firm. While rivals like Lockheed Martin are now closing the gap, GD continues to create superior wealth compared with its peers. The firm has delivered returns on invested capital averaging nearly 16% since 1997, exceeding our estimate of its weighted average cost of capital by 5.5 percentage points. In contrast, ROICs of the other four major defense players, on average, approximately equaled their respective WACCs during this time.

With disciplined asset allocation, GD has meticulously developed leading positions in key military markets. It is one of two firms that will meet the shipbuilding needs of the U.S. Navy. High-value, long-term programs such as the Virginia-class submarine and the Aegis Destroyer should provide many years of steady cash flow. GD has also become a dominant supplier of land combat vehicles, having delivered more than 8,000 Abrams tanks, which it continues to upgrade. Indicative of this ongoing revenue stream, total backlog was about $42 billion at the end of 2005.

Rather than relying solely on legacy programs, however, GD is also at the forefront of the military transformation that geopolitics demand and technology enables. The firm is converting four Trident-class submarines into delivery platforms for cruise missiles and special operations forces. It is also supplying the Army with the new tank substitute: the more deployable wheeled Stryker combat vehicles. Its development contract for the Army's tactical Warfighter Information Network gives GD a strong foothold in information systems, for which spending should be very strong over the next decade.

By acquiring Gulfstream in 1999, GD diversified its cash flow streams and acquired a business with higher margins than most of its defense businesses. Gulfstream owns about 25% of the worldwide business jet market and faces only four major competitors. This scale and its position at the high end of the market have enabled Gulfstream to deliver an average operating margin of almost 15% over the past five years. Textron's and Raytheon's business jet units averaged 10.7% and negative 5.3%, respectively, during this time.

Data as of 12-29-06

General Electric GE

Rating	Fair Value	Last Close	Consider Buy	Consider Sell	Yield %
★★★	$38.00	$37.21	$29.30	$47.60	2.77

Company Profile
Based in Fairfield, Conn., GE is a massive conglomerate with leading positions in an array of industries, including energy, transportation, health care, media, and consumer products. It also offers a wide variety of commercial and consumer finance products, such as credit cards, through its financial-services division. As a nod to its longevity, GE is the only surviving member of the original 12 stocks in the 1896 Dow Jones Industrial Average.

Management
Stewardship Grade [B]

GE is known for the strength and depth of its management team, which has a long history of creating value for key stakeholders: employees, customers, and investors. As a testament to its depth, several former executives have gone on to lead other large companies (Home Depot CEO Bob Nardelli and Boeing CEO Jim McNerney are former GE executives). Management talent is particularly important at GE; investors could get similar portfolio exposure via a mutual fund or ETF, but choose not to do so based largely on management's strength in creating value through strategic capital allocation. Current CEO Jeff Immelt has led the company for about five years, and his tenure to date has been characterized by a stronger balance sheet (GECS' debt is no longer supported by the parent company, for instance), significant acquisition spending, and the divestiture of most of the firm's insurance businesses. The firm's stock performance has been underwhelming, but we think Immelt's long-term growth focus will ultimately bear fruit. Overall, we're satisfied with GE's corporate governance practices but would prefer to see Immelt's variable compensation more closely linked to return on invested capital, as that metric provides a better proxy for corporate stewardship than operating cash flow.

3135 Easton Turnpike
Fairfield, CT 06828-0001
www.ge.com

Growth [B]	2002	2003	2004	2005
Revenue %	5.9	-0.9	19.1	11.3
Earnings/Share %	2.9	7.1	6.6	-4.3
Book Value/Share %	16.7	23.7	34.4	-2.9
Dividends/Share %	10.6	5.5	6.5	11.0

Profitability [B]	2003	2004	2005	TTM
Return on Assets %	2.4	2.2	2.4	2.5
Oper Cash Flow $Bil	29.2	36.5	37.6	30.1
- Cap Spending $Bil	9.8	13.1	14.4	15.8
= Free Cash Flow $Bil	19.5	23.4	23.2	14.3

Financial Health [B]	2003	2004	2005	09-30-06
Long-term Debt $Bil	170.3	207.9	212.3	242.9
Total Equity $Bil	79.6	110.8	109.4	111.4
Debt/Equity Ratio	2.1	1.9	1.9	2.2

Industry	Business Risk	Moat Size	Investment Style	Sector
Electric Equip.	Average	Wide	Large Core	Industrial Materials

Competition	Market Cap $Mil	12 Mo Trailing Sales $Mil	Price/Cash Flow	Return On Assets %	Debt/ Equity	Total Return % 1 Yr	3 Yr
General Electric	383,564	161,022	12.8	2.5	2.2	9.4	9.0
Siemens AG ADR	87,817	107,241	14.4	3.2	0.5	17.3	8.8
United Technologies	62,748	46,303	14.6	7.0	0.4	13.7	11.6

Price Volatility

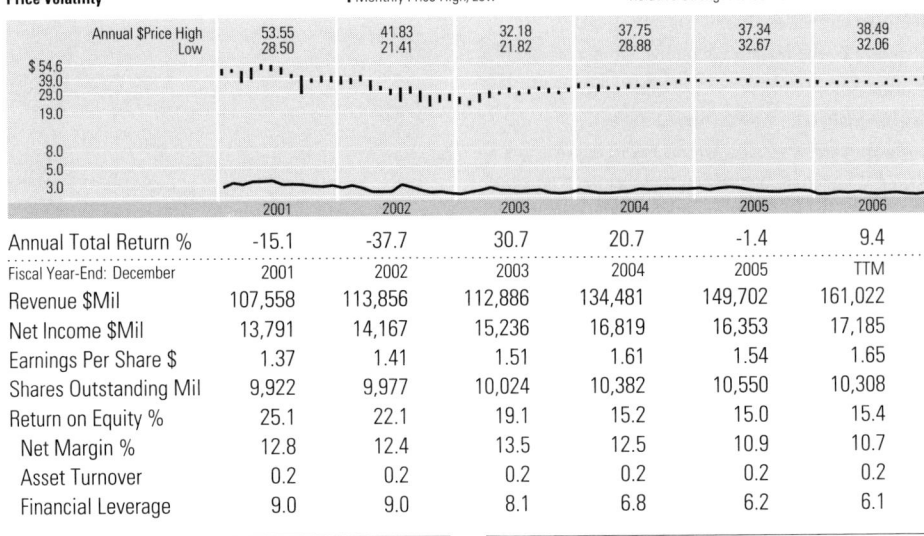

	2001	2002	2003	2004	2005	2006
Annual $Price High	53.55	41.83	32.18	37.75	37.34	38.49
Low	28.50	21.41	21.82	28.88	32.67	32.06
Annual Total Return %	-15.1	-37.7	30.7	20.7	-1.4	9.4

Fiscal Year-End: December	2001	2002	2003	2004	2005	TTM
Revenue $Mil	107,558	113,856	112,886	134,481	149,702	161,022
Net Income $Mil	13,791	14,167	15,236	16,819	16,353	17,185
Earnings Per Share $	1.37	1.41	1.51	1.61	1.54	1.65
Shares Outstanding Mil	9,922	9,977	10,024	10,382	10,550	10,308
Return on Equity %	25.1	22.1	19.1	15.2	15.0	15.4
Net Margin %	12.8	12.4	13.5	12.5	10.9	10.7
Asset Turnover	0.2	0.2	0.2	0.2	0.2	0.2
Financial Leverage	9.0	9.0	8.1	6.8	6.2	6.1

Valuation Ratios	Stock	Rel to Industry	Rel to S&P 500
Price/Earnings	19.8	0.9	1.0
Price/Book	3.4	1.0	0.8
Price/Sales	2.4	1.0	0.8
Price/Cash Flow	12.8	0.9	0.9

Major Fund Holders	% of Fund Assets
ICON Industrials	15.52
ProFunds Industrial Ultra Sector Inv	15.02
Old Mutual Focused Z	8.15
Fidelity Advisor Industrials A	8.12

Thesis By Peter Smith, 12-14-06 Stock Price as of Analysis: $36.21

GE's vast array of businesses and complex financial reporting make it a company few investors appreciate. Peeling away the layers, however, reveals a world-class firm whose short- and long-cycle businesses are poised for solid long-term growth, in our view.

GE is a diversified conglomerate with leadership positions in a variety of industries. Many people associate GE strictly with its consumer products (light bulbs, kitchen appliances, etc.), not knowing that it also manufactures locomotives, medical imaging equipment, aircraft engines, and gas turbines, while also dabbling in the media industry and a few other businesses. For good measure, GE Capital Services (GECS) is one of the largest banks in the world, in the same league as industry titans such as Citigroup.

While former CEO Jack Welch focused largely on cutting costs, current CEO Jeff Immelt seeks to produce robust revenue growth in order to boost profits. In this regard, we believe GE has several opportunities. The firm has been a technological leader since its inception, and this reputation still rings true today; its substantial research-and-development spending is typically 3%-4% of industrial sales. The firm's "ecomagination" initiative, in particular, aims to develop products that are more environmentally friendly, something management views as one of its largest business opportunities going forward.

Management also views emerging markets as a source of future growth. Less than 50% of total sales come from outside of the United States, so management hopes to penetrate these fast-growing markets further, especially in infrastructure businesses such as energy. A third growth opportunity for GE is in servicing the various products it manufactures. True, GE isn't the first company to notice the steady high margins in product service/repair, but the lengthy useful lives of many of its products (engines and turbines in particular) make it an opportunity that GE must target aggressively in order to produce revenue growth.

Despite these opportunities, GE has faced a few challenges in recent years. After a series of hurricane-related losses, GECS has been steadily divesting insurance assets in order to make room for better-returning investments. The firm also faced a slowdown in its energy business that cut revenues by over 20% from 2002 to 2003. Nevertheless, we believe the pieces are falling into place for solid long-term growth. As long as it can execute on its strategies, the future looks pretty bright for GE.

Data as of 12-29-06

General Mills GIS

	Rating	Fair Value	Last Close	Consider Buy	Consider Sell	Yield %
	★★★	$57.00	$57.60	$48.60	$74.80	2.40

Company Profile

General Mills is one of the largest packaged food companies in the United States. It produces ready-to-eat breakfast cereals, refrigerated dough and other baking items, snack and convenience foods, frozen vegetables, yogurt, and beverages. Well-known brands include Cheerios, Lucky Charms, Wheaties, Chex, Betty Crocker, Pillsbury, Gold Medal, Green Giant, Hamburger Helper, Old El Paso, Pop Secret, Colombo, and Yoplait. U.S. sales account for 85% of total annual revenue.

Management   Stewardship Grade [C]

Steve Sanger has been chairman and CEO of General Mills since 1995. He joined the company in 1974 and had served as head of several different business units, including the yogurt and cereal divisions, before accepting the top job. While executive pay is performance-based with explicit stock ownership targets for senior executives, we have to question the 35% increase Sanger saw in his total compensation package for fiscal 2006. Despite the fact that year-end bonuses are supposed to be tied to four equally weighted measures (earnings per share growth, operating profit growth, net sales growth, and improvement in return on invested capital), it looks like last year's payout was tied more directly to earnings growth than to any of the other benchmarks. General Mills' financial statements have been littered with restructuring and merger-related charges over the years, which have clouded the operating picture. Management has also been reluctant to offer explicit guidance about future charges that might be incurred as part of its ongoing reorganization of the firm. While General Mills does disclose information on its operating segments, the level of clarity and consistency provided is poor compared with its peers.

Number One General Mills Boulevard   www.generalmills.com
Minneapolis, MN 55426-1348

Growth [C-]	2003	2004	2005	2006
Revenue %	32.2	5.4	1.6	3.5
Earnings/Share %	81.3	7.0	18.5	-5.8
Book Value/Share %	5.7	16.9	9.0	8.9
Dividends/Share %	0.0	0.0	12.7	8.1

Profitability [B]	2004	2005	2006	TTM
Return on Assets %	5.7	6.9	6.0	5.9
Oper Cash Flow $Mil	1,461	1,711	1,771	1,717
- Cap Spending $Mil	628	434	360	376
= Free Cash Flow $Mil	833	1,277	1,411	1,341

Financial Health [B]	2004	2005	2006	08-31-06
Long-term Debt $Mil	7,410	4,255	2,415	2,406
Total Equity $Mil	5,248	5,676	5,772	5,330
Debt/Equity Ratio	1.4	0.8	0.4	0.5

Industry	Business Risk	Moat Size	Investment Style	Sector
Food Mfg.	Below Avg	Narrow	Large Core	Consumer Goods

Competition

	Market Cap $Mil	12 Mo Trailing Sales $Mil	Price/Cash Flow	Return On Assets%	Debt/Equity	Total Return% 1 Yr	3 Yr
General Mills	19,761	11,821	11.5	5.9	0.5	19.9	11.5
Kraft Foods	58,683	34,648	13.9	5.5	0.2	30.5	6.5
Groupe Danone ADR	43,070	16,309	18.6	9.2	1.0	57.3	28.9

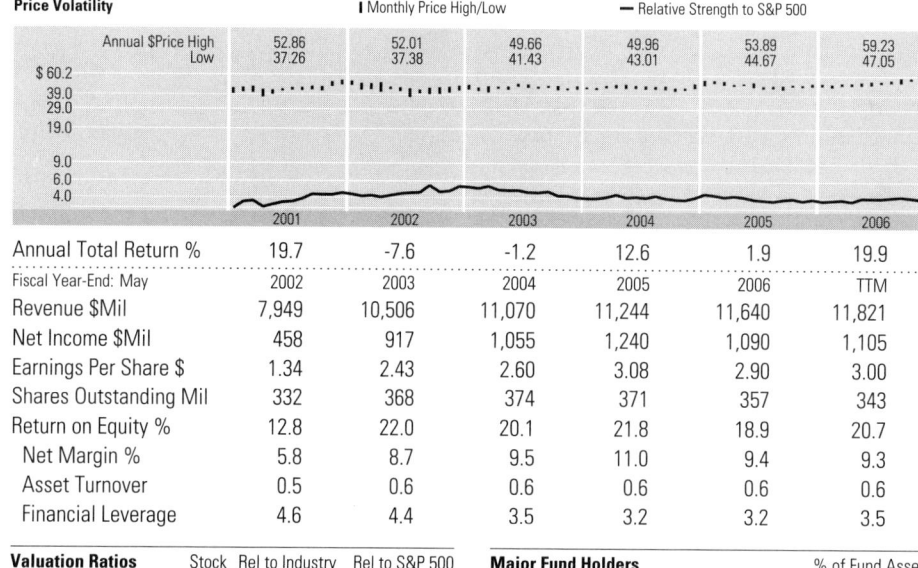

Price Volatility — Monthly Price High/Low — Relative Strength to S&P 500

Annual $Price High/Low	52.86/37.26	52.01/37.38	49.66/41.43	49.96/43.01	53.89/44.67	59.23/47.05
	2001	2002	2003	2004	2005	2006
Annual Total Return %	19.7	-7.6	-1.2	12.6	1.9	19.9

Fiscal Year-End: May	2002	2003	2004	2005	2006	TTM
Revenue $Mil	7,949	10,506	11,070	11,244	11,640	11,821
Net Income $Mil	458	917	1,055	1,240	1,090	1,105
Earnings Per Share $	1.34	2.43	2.60	3.08	2.90	3.00
Shares Outstanding Mil	332	368	374	371	357	343
Return on Equity %	12.8	22.0	20.1	21.8	18.9	20.7
Net Margin %	5.8	8.7	9.5	11.0	9.4	9.3
Asset Turnover	0.5	0.6	0.6	0.6	0.6	0.6
Financial Leverage	4.6	4.4	3.5	3.2	3.2	3.5

Valuation Ratios	Stock	Rel to Industry	Rel to S&P 500
Price/Earnings	19.2	0.9	0.9
Price/Book	3.7	0.8	0.9
Price/Sales	1.7	1.0	0.6
Price/Cash Flow	11.5	0.8	0.8

Major Fund Holders	% of Fund Assets
BNY Hamilton Large Cap Value Instl	3.64
Mairs & Power Growth	3.42
Fidelity Select Consumer Staples	3.11
Primary Trend	3.10

Thesis By Greggory Warren, CFA, 12-08-06 Stock Price as of Analysis: $57.32

After four difficult years of restructuring following the acquisition of Pillsbury, General Mills appears to finally be on track to deliver sustainable sales and earnings growth longer term. The company has emerged with a much stronger portfolio, which management believes it can sustain with increased product innovation and marketing, especially in categories that are on trend with consumers.

The company's key goal for fiscal 2007 has been to improve U.S. sales of ready-to-eat cereal and Pillsbury products. With Kellogg holding one third of the domestic market for cereal, General Mills 30%, and Quaker (owned by PepsiCo) and Post (owned by Kraft) another 30% between them, expansion opportunities for the category are limited. More rational pricing and product innovation, though, have allowed the group to improve sales and profitability, and General Mills believes this trend will continue longer term. Meanwhile, the joint venture with Nestle, Cereal Partners Worldwide, has allowed General Mills to pursue more attractive growth opportunities outside the United States.

With Pillsbury, the biggest hurdle has been overcoming the disarray that accompanied the initial acquisition. Because of antitrust concerns, the deal was hung up for 18 months, with General Mills forfeiting the rights to Pillsbury baking mixes and ready-to-spread frostings in order to get Federal Trade Commission approval. Higher-margin sales to the food-service channel never materialized, and the company struggled with the low-carbohydrate diet craze that hurt the market for packaged foods. New product development, increased marketing, and expansion into alternate channels have allowed General Mills to improve the positioning of the Pillsbury brand longer term, with most of these efforts expected to bear fruit this year.

Although Danone has been able to grab additional market share with its purchase of Stonyfield Farms and the introduction of probiotic brands to the yogurt category, General Mills continues to generate strong sales growth with Yoplait. The company has also held its own in the canned soup aisle, where Campbell Soup has succeeded in rejuvenating sales of its condensed soup line. In both cases, General Mills has benefited from the increased awareness its competitors have brought to these categories, and we believe increased product innovation and marketing behind its own brands will allow General Mills to continue to tap into that success longer term.

Data as of 12-29-06

Gen-Probe GPRO

	Rating	Fair Value	Last Close	Consider Buy	Consider Sell	Yield %
	★★★	$53.00	$52.37	$40.90	$66.40	0.00

Company Profile
Gen-Probe manufactures and markets NAT-based products used in the clinical diagnoses of infectious diseases such as HIV and hepatitis C, blood screening, and industrial testing. The company distributes its blood screening assays worldwide through Chiron, recently acquired by Novartis.

Industry	Business Risk	Moat Size	Investment Style	Sector
Research Svcs.	Average	Narrow	Mid Growth	Healthcare

Competition

	Market Cap $Mil	12 Mo Trailing Sales $Mil	Price/Cash Flow	Return On Assets %	Debt/Equity	Total Return % 1 Yr	3 Yr
Gen-Probe	2,727	352	30.4	10.1	—	7.3	12.8
Roche Holding AG ADR	154,312	28,721	19.1	10.4	0.2	20.4	22.6
Abbott Laboratories	74,763	22,306	14.0	9.5	0.5	26.9	3.9

Management Stewardship Grade [C]
We give Gen-Probe a C Stewardship Grade, but we are encouraged by the recent changes to the firm's corporate governance policies. Gen-Probe eliminated its poison pill provision and instituted a minimum ownership requirement for executives, which in our opinion promotes long-term thinking. We remain impressed with the company's board composition, which includes several seasoned industry veterans, and we like that the majority of its executives have been with the firm for many years. In our opinion, this management team has done a tremendous job creating shareholder value, as evidenced by high historical returns on capital, but we have a few reservations regarding the company's compensation policy. Options account for 12% of the outstanding stock, which means that current investors would experience 12% dilution in the event of exercise. We also believe the severance agreement signed with CEO Henry Nordhoff provides for a payout above the industry norm, and we frown on the company's staggered board structure.

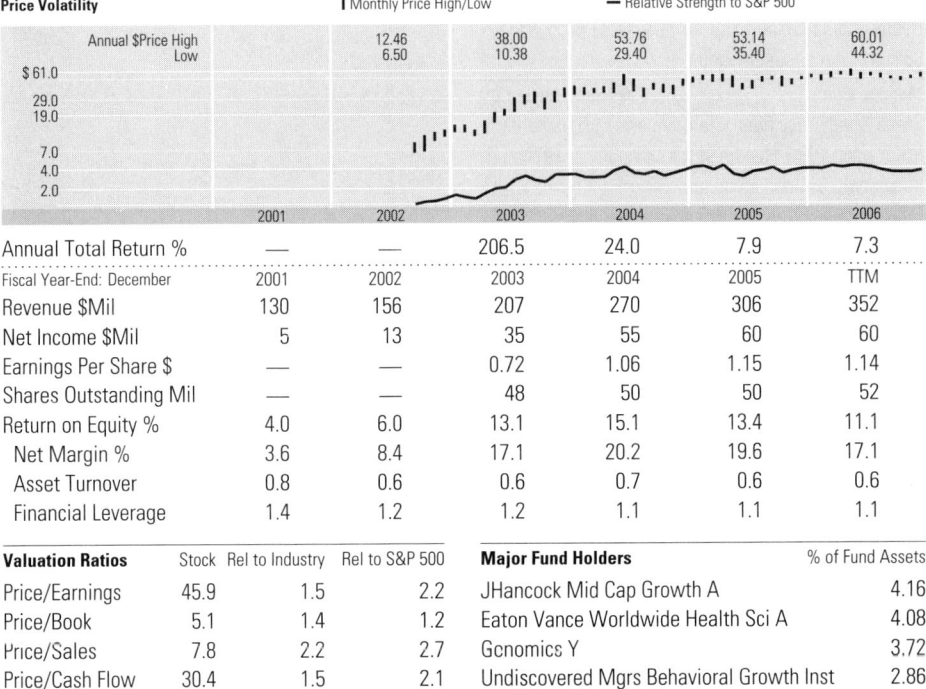

Annual Total Return %	—	—	206.5	24.0	7.9	7.3
Fiscal Year-End: December	2001	2002	2003	2004	2005	TTM
Revenue $Mil	130	156	207	270	306	352
Net Income $Mil	5	13	35	55	60	60
Earnings Per Share $	—	—	0.72	1.06	1.15	1.14
Shares Outstanding Mil	—	—	48	50	50	52
Return on Equity %	4.0	6.0	13.1	15.1	13.4	11.1
Net Margin %	3.6	8.4	17.1	20.2	19.6	17.1
Asset Turnover	0.8	0.6	0.6	0.7	0.6	0.6
Financial Leverage	1.4	1.2	1.2	1.1	1.1	1.1

Valuation Ratios	Stock	Rel to Industry	Rel to S&P 500
Price/Earnings	45.9	1.5	2.2
Price/Book	5.1	1.4	1.2
Price/Sales	7.8	2.2	2.7
Price/Cash Flow	30.4	1.5	2.1

Major Fund Holders	% of Fund Assets
JHancock Mid Cap Growth A	4.16
Eaton Vance Worldwide Health Sci A	4.08
Genomics Y	3.72
Undiscovered Mgrs Behavioral Growth Inst	2.86

Thesis By Alex Morozov, CFA, 12-13-06 Stock Price as of Analysis: $53.02

Nucleic acid testing (NAT) has transformed the clinical diagnostic industry, and Gen-Probe has been on the forefront of the revolution.

Gen-Probe's NAT-based screens represent a significant upgrade over traditional laboratory testing methods, as they enable more rapid and accurate detection of target organisms in the blood screening and clinical diagnostics markets. Gen-Probe dominates the domestic blood testing market, as 80% of the U.S. blood supply is screened with the company's assays. However, we think that the growth lies in Europe and Asia, markets presently ruled by Roche Diagnostics. With an eye on these markets, Gen-Probe has recently launched a new Procleix Ultrio assay, which combines the existing HIV/hepatitis C product with a test for hepatitis B. In our opinion, the new Ultrio assay may help Gen-Probe take a bite out of Roche's dominant position and allow the company to strengthen its presence overseas.

Gen-Probe's clinical diagnostic revenues are derived from sales of products that test for chlamydia and gonorrhea. The company has built a strong franchise in sexually transmitted disease (STD) testing, primarily through its technological know-how and shrewd marketing strategy of bundling several tests into one assay. We believe this segment will continue to present tremendous growth opportunities for Gen-Probe, both domestically and abroad. Furthermore, the company continues to seek expansion opportunities elsewhere within clinical diagnostics. We think Gen-Probe's foray into oncology with its PCA3 technology, which screens for prostate cancer, could be a very successful venture.

We are also encouraged by the strong demand for Gen-Probe's Tigris platform, which allows customers to automate the entire NAT screening process, a feature previously not available in the industry. Gen-Probe currently distributes the platform at no profit, but should benefit from sales of high-margin reagents for use with Tigris, if approved.

While Tigris placements have been healthy, Abbott and Becton, Dickinson have launched systems designed to compete with Tigris. We believe Gen-Probe's significant installed base, Tigris' technological advantages, and the company's leading position in NAT assays will enable Gen-Probe to fend off the competition. We would be concerned, however, if the company continues to experience setbacks in the FDA approval process, as it may allow competitors to catch up.

10210 Genetic Center Drive
San Diego, CA 92121-4362

Growth [B]	2002	2003	2004	2005
Revenue %	19.9	33.2	30.2	13.4
Earnings/Share %	NMF	NMF	47.2	8.5
Book Value/Share %	—	NMF	27.3	22.1
Dividends/Share %	NMF	NMF	NMF	NMF

Profitability [A]	2003	2004	2005	TTM
Return on Assets %	10.9	13.3	11.8	10.1
Oper Cash Flow $Mil	53	62	86	90
- Cap Spending $Mil	12	26	45	56
= Free Cash Flow $Mil	40	36	40	34

Financial Health [A+]	2003	2004	2005	09-30-06
Long-term Debt $Mil	—	—	—	—
Total Equity $Mil	270	361	447	539
Debt/Equity Ratio	—	—	—	—

Genuine Parts GPC

Data as of 12-29-06

Rating	Fair Value	Last Close	Consider Buy	Consider Sell	Yield %
★★★	$48.00	$47.43	$40.90	$63.00	2.85

Industry	Business Risk	Moat Size	Investment Style	Sector
Auto Retail	Below Avg	Narrow	Mid Value	Consumer Services

Company Profile

Genuine Parts is a distributor of automotive replacement parts, industrial replacement parts, office products, and electrical/electronic materials. The company operates from roughly 1,900 locations in the United States, Canada, and Mexico. Its auto-parts group is the largest division and offers more than 300,000 parts. This group consists of 58 distribution centers, serving about 5,800 NAPA Auto Parts stores, of which almost 1,000 are company-owned.

Management

Stewardship Grade [B]

In August 2004, Thomas Gallagher became the fourth CEO in Genuine Parts' history. In February 2005, he assumed the role of chairman. Having served for more than a decade as COO, Gallagher offers continuity in the leadership of a similarly seasoned management team. Executive compensation is generally in line with industry practices and is heavily weighted toward incentive compensation, which we regard as a plus. That said, we would prefer to see return on capital metrics play a more prominent role alongside annual cash-flow targets. Additional concerns include the relatively light insider ownership at the firm and the interlocking board relationship between Gallagher and J. Hicks Lanier; the former serves on the board of Oxford Industries, of which the latter is CEO and chairman. This type of relationship could impair the independence of Lanier, who also serves as chairman of the compensation, nominating, and governance committee. We are, however, encouraged that the board acted to terminate its shareholder-rights plan and proposed the annual election of directors beginning in 2007.

2999 Circle 75 Parkway
Atlanta, GA 30339
www.genpt.com

Growth [C]	2002	2003	2004	2005
Revenue %	0.5	2.3	7.7	7.5
Earnings/Share %	NMF	NMF	17.8	11.1
Book Value/Share %	-8.5	7.0	9.5	6.4
Dividends/Share %	1.8	1.7	1.7	4.2

Profitability [B]	2003	2004	2005	TTM
Return on Assets %	8.1	8.9	9.2	9.5
Oper Cash Flow $Mil	402	555	441	363
- Cap Spending $Mil	74	72	86	120
= Free Cash Flow $Mil	328	483	355	243

Financial Health [A]	2003	2004	2005	09-30-06
Long-term Debt $Mil	625	500	500	500
Total Equity $Mil	2,312	2,544	2,694	2,785
Debt/Equity Ratio	0.3	0.2	0.2	0.2

Competition

	Market Cap $Mil	12 Mo Trailing Sales $Mil	Price/Cash Flow	Return On Assets %	Debt/Equity	Total Return % 1 Yr	Total Return % 3 Yr
Genuine Parts	8,082	10,325	22.3	9.5	0.2	11.4	16.3
AutoZone	8,167	6,003	10.1	12.6	3.5	26.0	11.1
W.W. Grainger	6,017	5,812	13.0	12.6	0.0	-0.1	15.6

Price Volatility

	2001	2002	2003	2004	2005	2006
Annual $Price High	37.88	38.80	33.70	44.32	46.64	48.34
Low	23.91	27.10	27.20	32.03	40.75	40.00
Annual Total Return %	45.5	-13.2	11.9	36.9	2.6	11.4

Fiscal Year-End: December	2001	2002	2003	2004	2005	TTM
Revenue $Mil	8,221	8,259	8,449	9,097	9,783	10,325
Net Income $Mil	297	-28	334	396	437	465
Earnings Per Share $	1.71	-0.16	1.91	2.25	2.50	2.69
Shares Outstanding Mil	173	172	174	175	174	170
Return on Equity %	12.7	-1.3	14.4	15.5	16.2	16.7
Net Margin %	3.6	-0.3	4.0	4.3	4.5	4.5
Asset Turnover	2.0	2.0	2.0	2.0	2.1	2.1
Financial Leverage	1.8	1.9	1.8	1.8	1.8	1.8

Valuation Ratios	Stock	Rel to Industry	Rel to S&P 500
Price/Earnings	17.6	1.0	0.9
Price/Book	2.9	0.6	0.7
Price/Sales	0.8	0.9	0.3
Price/Cash Flow	22.3	1.1	1.5

Major Fund Holders	% of Fund Assets
Ave Maria Rising Dividend	3.30
Fidelity Select Automotive	3.16
Meridian Equity Income	2.78
CRM Mid Cap Value Instl	2.46

Thesis

By Matthew Warren, 10-16-06 Stock Price as of Analysis: $45.01

Despite the tame growth prospects that Genuine Parts' mature end markets offer, we are impressed by the company's solid returns on capital and shareholder-friendly asset allocation. We think the firm's competitive advantages amount to a narrow economic moat.

Genuine Parts enjoys a leading 7%-8% share of the fragmented market for auto-parts distribution, which accounts for about 50% of its sales. Unlike the do-it-yourself parts market dominated by retailers like AutoZone, Genuine Parts' customers are predominantly professional installers who are on the clock, face limited repair bay space, and require the timely delivery of a wide variety of high-quality parts. The firm's highly regarded NAPA brand, vast store and distribution network, and megafleet of delivery trucks are unmatched by retailers, and we expect Genuine Parts to continue gaining market share. While margins in this segment have slowly eroded from 11% in 1995 to just under 8% in 2005 because of heightened competition, we expect this pattern to reverse course as Johnson Industries--an ill-fated acquisition--is sold or disbanded.

Genuine Parts also runs a maintenance, repair, and operations (MRO) supply business that accounted for 29% of 2005 revenue and specializes in selling critical replacement parts to heavy industrial concerns. These customers also demand timely delivery of a wide variety of specialized products to minimize production downtime. While sales in this segment tend to closely track the industrial cycle, Genuine Parts' sheer scale (with 1.5 times the sales of Applied Industrial Technologies, the closest competitor with a similar product set), numerous branch locations, and niche product focus make for relatively steady margins and attractive returns.

We have bigger concerns about the firm's office product wholesaling business, even though its second-place market position has produced above-corporate-average profit margins. Big-box office supply retailers are tough customers, and they continue to expand their store bases and steal business from Genuine Parts' smaller retail and direct sales customers. The bigger they get, the more sense it makes for them to direct-source and private-label more products from manufacturers, with whom increased volume strengthens negotiations. This logic does not apply for slower-turning products, though, and we expect one-stop shopping for these items from effective, well-stocked middlemen like Genuine Parts will continue apace.

Data as of 12-29-06

Genzyme GENZ

	Rating	Fair Value	Last Close	Consider Buy	Consider Sell	Yield %
	★★★★	$71.00	$61.58	$54.70	$89.00	0.00

Company Profile
Genzyme focuses on developing, manufacturing, and marketing products to treat genetic disorders and other chronic debilitating diseases. The company's broad product and service portfolio addresses genetic diseases, kidney failure, organ transplant, orthopedics, diagnostic and predictive testing, and oncology. The Ilex and Bone Care acquisitions expanded Genzyme's renal and oncology segments, while the recent AnorMED acquisition will build on its transplant business.

Management
Stewardship Grade [B]

Genzyme has received better marks for corporate governance since it eliminated its tracking-stock structure in 2003; tracking stocks aren't required to have separate boards, creating the potential for misaligned incentives. Henri Termeer has led Genzyme for more than 20 years and is a board member of BIO and PhRMA, the drug industry's leading lobbying organizations. Termeer certainly deserves much of the credit for the company's success. We think his 2005 salary and bonus of just over $3 million is reasonable for a profitable biotech, and we appreciate the company's emphasis on both corporate and individual strategic accomplishments in determining cash bonuses. Cash bonuses at Genzyme are also not guaranteed--Genzyme did not meet its corporate goals in 2002, and no cash bonuses were awarded for company performance. However, the company's wide use of stock options to compensate employees potentially dilutes shareholder value; for example, Termeer continues to receive healthy stock-option grants, such as the 425,000 options granted in 2005. The vast majority of his compensation in 2005 came from stock option exercises; he sold more than 600,000 shares of stock and realized gains of $33 million.

500 Kendall St.
Cambridge, MA 02142
www.genzyme.com

Growth [A-]	2002	2003	2004	2005
Revenue %	8.7	28.9	28.4	24.2
Earnings/Share %	—	—	NMF	345.9
Book Value/Share %	—	—	NMF	2.8
Dividends/Share %	NMF	NMF	NMF	NMF

Profitability [B-]	2003	2004	2005	TTM
Return on Assets %	-1.4	1.4	6.4	4.8
Oper Cash Flow $Mil	388	578	732	789
- Cap Spending $Mil	260	187	192	297
= Free Cash Flow $Mil	128	390	539	492

Financial Health [A]	2003	2004	2005	09-30-06
Long-term Debt $Mil	1,415	811	816	811
Total Equity $Mil	2,936	4,380	5,150	5,785
Debt/Equity Ratio	0.5	0.2	0.2	0.1

	Industry	Business Risk	Moat Size	Investment Style	Sector
	Biotechnology	Average	Wide	Large Growth	Healthcare

Competition	Market Cap $Mil	12 Mo Trailing Sales $Mil	Price/Cash Flow	Return On Assets %	Debt/Equity	Total Return % 1 Yr	3 Yr
Genzyme	16,187	3,061	20.5	4.8	0.1	-13.0	7.9
Amgen	79,685	13,704	15.1	9.0	0.4	-13.4	3.1
Abbott Laboratories	74,763	22,306	14.0	9.5	0.5	26.9	3.9

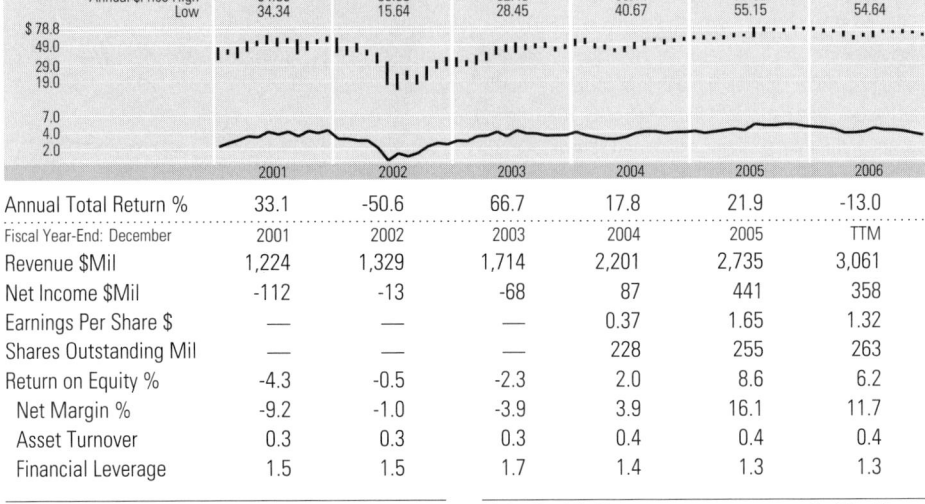

	2001	2002	2003	2004	2005	2006
Annual $Price High	64.00	59.86	52.45	59.14	77.82	75.34
Low	34.34	15.64	28.45	40.67	55.15	54.64
Annual Total Return %	33.1	-50.6	66.7	17.8	21.9	-13.0

Fiscal Year-End: December	2001	2002	2003	2004	2005	TTM
Revenue $Mil	1,224	1,329	1,714	2,201	2,735	3,061
Net Income $Mil	-112	-13	-68	87	441	358
Earnings Per Share $	—	—	—	0.37	1.65	1.32
Shares Outstanding Mil	—	—	—	228	255	263
Return on Equity %	-4.3	-0.5	-2.3	2.0	8.6	6.2
Net Margin %	-9.2	-1.0	-3.9	3.9	16.1	11.7
Asset Turnover	0.3	0.3	0.3	0.4	0.4	0.4
Financial Leverage	1.5	1.5	1.7	1.4	1.3	1.3

Valuation Ratios	Stock	Rel to Industry	Rel to S&P 500
Price/Earnings	46.7	1.1	2.3
Price/Book	2.8	0.3	0.7
Price/Sales	5.3	0.5	1.8
Price/Cash Flow	20.5	0.7	1.4

Major Fund Holders	% of Fund Assets
ACM Convertible Securities	18.18
Franklin Biotechnology Discovery A	7.84
SunAmerica Biotech/Health A	6.43
Integrity Health Sciences A	6.21

Thesis By Karen Andersen, 10-27-06 Stock Price as of Analysis: $68.72

Genzyme has strengthened and diversified its business through innovation, acquisitions, and global expansion. While rare-disease drug Cerezyme and kidney-disease treatment Renagel have made this biotech a success, we see strong potential outside of these core products. Given Genzyme's evolution, we're upgrading its moat to wide from narrow.

Genzyme has achieved unparalleled success in the treatment of ultra-rare diseases, challenging markets that require significant up-front investment and address fewer than 10,000 patients globally. Market exclusivity and wide insurance coverage mean Genzyme can charge $200,000 for a year's supply; its breakthrough therapeutic Cerezyme, prescribed for Gaucher disease, brought in $930 million in 2005.

Despite Cerezyme's near-blockbuster sales, other forms of enzyme-replacement therapies are contributing to the therapeutic segment's impressive operating margins, which exceeded 60% in the first half of 2006. Fabrazyme is set to achieve $350 million in sales in 2006, and newly approved Pompe disease treatment Myozyme brought in $20 million during its first full quarter on the market. We're also starting to see the fruits of Genzyme's innovative research within the field of rare genetic diseases; a novel oral drug in Phase II trials could eventually eliminate the need for enzyme replacement, which involves costly manufacturing and requires patients to endure hours of drug infusions.

Most of the balance of Genzyme's profits come from its renal disease segment, led by sales of kidney-failure drug Renagel. Despite Renagel's long tenure on the market, sales remain strong, thanks to Medicare prescription drug coverage and a reduced mortality benefit in certain patients. With a second-generation Renagel to be approved next year and vitamin D therapy Hectorol complementing these treatments, we think this segment should see 19% average annual sales growth over the next five years.

Although the stability of the therapeutic and renal segments forms the foundation for our wide moat, Genzyme's future competitive advantage also stems from a strong, diverse product pipeline. Severe diarrhea treatment tolevamer and stem cell mobilizer Mozobil could reach the market in 2008, and Genzyme's marketed cancer antibody Campath has the potential to receive approval to enter the $4 billion multiple sclerosis market shortly thereafter. Although we think returns on invested capital will continue to hover around the 12% mark for another couple of years, Genzyme's solid product portfolio should push them toward 20% over the long term.

Data as of 12-29-06

Gerdau SA ADR PN GGB

	Rating	Fair Value	Last Close	Consider Buy	Consider Sell	Yield %
	★★★★	$20.00	$16.00	$12.70	$24.10	3.72

Company Profile
Gerdau is the largest producer of long steel in the Americas. It operates 26 minimills, mainly in Brazil and the United States, producing more than 16 million tons of steel annually. Gerdau also operates Acominas, an integrated steel producer with 2 million tons of crude steel production annually. The company's products are mainly used by the construction and general manufacturing industries.

Management
Stewardship Grade [NA]

The Gerdau family controls the company through its holding company, Metalurgica Gerdau. Unlike many family-run Brazilian businesses, Gerdau appears to be a refreshingly open, well-managed enterprise where controlling interests seem to have minority shareholders' well-being in mind. Management has an excellent record of buying struggling assets at attractive prices and turning these businesses around. As an ADR, Gerdau doesn't have to disclose management compensation, making it difficult for us to comment on whether the family members and other members of management are being fairly compensated. Although the Gerdau family owns only 43% of the company's outstanding shares, it controls 91% of the voting capital.

Av. Joao XXIII, 6777 Santa Cruz
Rio de Janeiro, Brazil 23560-900
www.gerdau.com.br

Growth [NA]	2002	2003	2004	2005
Revenue %	36.0	38.8	53.4	27.9
Earnings/Share %	38.1	119.2	128.9	-3.4
Book Value/Share %	-36.4	362.5	8.2	38.7
Dividends/Share %	11.7	80.2	71.4	78.8

Profitability [NA]	2003	2004	2005	TTM
Return on Assets %	10.7	16.9	12.0	12.0
Oper Cash Flow $Mil	611	1,071	345	345
- Cap Spending $Mil	298	441	697	697
= Free Cash Flow $Mil	314	630	-352	-352

Financial Health [NA]	2003	2004	2005	12-31-05
Long-term Debt $Mil	—	1,625	2,647	2,647
Total Equity $Mil	1,403	1,506	2,087	2,087
Debt/Equity Ratio	—	1.1	1.3	1.3

Industry	Business Risk	Moat Size	Investment Style	Sector
Steel/Iron	Above Avg	Narrow	Large Value	Industrial Materials

Competition	Market Cap $Mil	12 Mo Trailing Sales $Mil	Price/Cash Flow	Return On Assets%	Debt/Equity	Total Return% 1 Yr	3 Yr
Gerdau SA ADR PN	10,681	8,894	31.0	12.0	1.3	49.5	58.8
Mittal Steel Co NV	29,697	28,132	7.5	10.8	0.9	62.5	68.8
Nucor	16,514	14,490	7.9	21.4	0.2	70.7	61.9

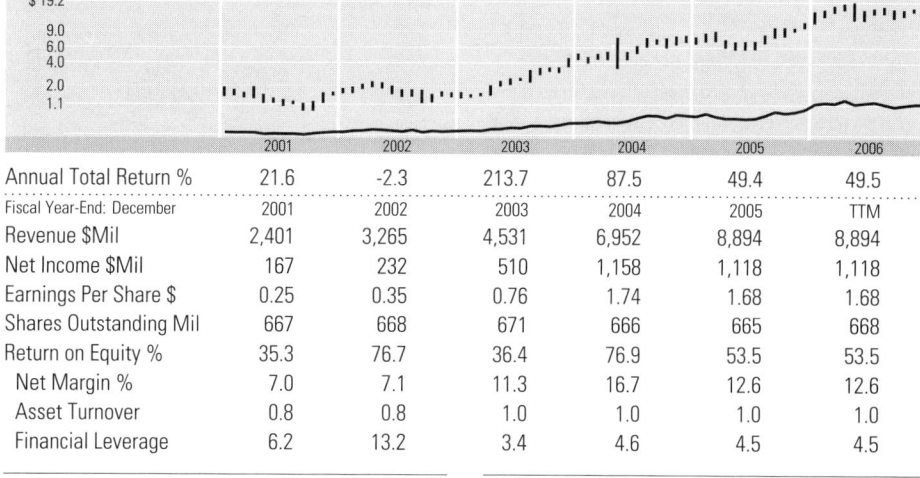

	2001	2002	2003	2004	2005	2006/TTM
Annual Total Return %	21.6	-2.3	213.7	87.5	49.4	49.5
Revenue $Mil	2,401	3,265	4,531	6,952	8,894	8,894
Net Income $Mil	167	232	510	1,158	1,118	1,118
Earnings Per Share $	0.25	0.35	0.76	1.74	1.68	1.68
Shares Outstanding Mil	667	668	671	666	665	668
Return on Equity %	35.3	76.7	36.4	76.9	53.5	53.5
Net Margin %	7.0	7.1	11.3	16.7	12.6	12.6
Asset Turnover	0.8	0.8	1.0	1.0	1.0	1.0
Financial Leverage	6.2	13.2	3.4	4.6	4.5	4.5

Valuation Ratios	Stock	Rel to Industry	Rel to S&P 500
Price/Earnings	9.5	0.7	0.5
Price/Book	5.1	1.0	1.2
Price/Sales	1.2	0.5	0.4
Price/Cash Flow	31.0	2.4	2.1

Major Fund Holders	% of Fund Assets
Quant Emerging Markets Ord	1.14

Thesis
By Scott Burns, 11-13-06 Stock Price as of Analysis: $15.11

Brazilian minimill Gerdau enjoys cost advantages in energy, raw materials, and labor that make it one of the lowest-cost steel producers in the world. These competitive advantages give the company a narrow economic moat, but concerns about the stability of the Brazilian economy and currency prompt us to seek a wide margin of safety to our fair value estimate before we would consider investing.

Brazil provides a unique operating environment for a minimill like Gerdau. Minimills consume tremendous amounts of electricity during the melt process. Brazil's significant hydroelectric generation capabilities provide Gerdau with a power source that costs a fraction of what competitors must pay. Additionally, Brazil has some of the richest iron ore deposits in the world. Ore is expensive to transport, so proximity to such a rich and abundant source is a significant cost advantage. Throw cheap labor on top of this, and it's no surprise that Gerdau's operating profit per ton is twice that of U.S. steel leader Nucor.

Gerdau also operates the second-largest minimill in the United States. The company entered the U.S. market in an effort to hedge against the periodic tariffs that its Brazilian exports faced and to locate production closer to customers. Although the U.S. operations don't enjoy the same cost advantages as their Brazilian counterparts, they are still competitive with other domestic minimills and have the advantage of being able to source iron slabs from Brazil to help offset high scrap prices. As a result of the U.S. operations and exports from the Brazilian unit, Gerdau has lowered its dependence on Brazil, which accounted for only 27% of revenue in 2005.

As good as Gerdau is at making steel, investing in this company still holds some inherent risks. For one, steel is a cyclical business that relies on the construction, auto, and appliance industries to drive demand. Global overcapacity and protectionist activities can wreak havoc on supply and demand. In addition, there are general risks facing any company based in Brazil. The country's political system, economy, and currency are fairly unstable and often cause swings in the performance of Gerdau's operations and stock.

We think geographic diversification and its status as a low-cost producer put Gerdau in a better position than most steel and Brazilian companies to weather the volatility. Investors in the developing markets could do a lot worse than Gerdau, in our opinion.

Data as of 12-29-06

Getty Images GYI

	Rating	Fair Value	Last Close	Consider Buy	Consider Sell	Yield %
	★★★★★	$69.00	$42.82	$53.20	$86.50	0.00

Industry	Business Risk	Moat Size	Investment Style	Sector
Business Support	Average	Wide	Mid Growth	Business Services

Company Profile

Getty licenses photographs and film to a global customer base. Its growing image inventory includes stock and editorial photographs. Its customers include advertising and design agencies, publishers, and corporate in-house advertising and communications departments. Through direct and indirect salesforces it services clients in more than 100 countries.

Competition

	Market Cap $Mil	12 Mo Trailing Sales $Mil	Price/Cash Flow	Return On Assets%	Debt/Equity	Total Return% 1 Yr	Total Return% 3 Yr
Getty Images	2,559	790	9.9	8.5	0.2	-52.0	-5.2
Zefa							
Corbis							

Price Volatility

| Monthly Price High/Low — Relative Strength to S&P 500

| Annual $Price High | 37.25 | 38.48 | 51.00 | 70.30 | 95.43 | 90.58 |
| Low | 9.15 | 13.19 | 25.80 | 47.15 | 64.42 | 41.21 |

	2001	2002	2003	2004	2005	2006
Annual Total Return %	-28.2	32.9	64.1	37.3	29.7	-52.0

Fiscal Year-End: December	2001	2002	2003	2004	2005	TTM
Revenue $Mil	451	463	523	622	734	790
Net Income $Mil	-95	21	64	107	150	142
Earnings Per Share $	-1.84	0.39	1.11	1.72	2.28	2.24
Shares Outstanding Mil	52	54	55	59	62	60
Return on Equity %	-15.9	3.2	7.7	10.0	12.0	11.6
Net Margin %	-21.1	4.6	12.2	17.1	20.4	18.0
Asset Turnover	0.5	0.5	0.4	0.4	0.4	0.5
Financial Leverage	1.7	1.5	1.5	1.4	1.3	1.4

Valuation Ratios	Stock	Rel to Industry	Rel to S&P 500
Price/Earnings	19.1	0.7	0.9
Price/Book	2.1	0.5	0.5
Price/Sales	3.2	0.7	1.1
Price/Cash Flow	9.9	0.5	0.7

Major Fund Holders	% of Fund Assets
Brown Advisory Opportunity Instl	4.70
SunAmerica Focused Technology A	2.87
Baron iOpportunity	2.73
Brown Advisory Small-Cap Growth I	2.42

Management Stewardship Grade [C]

Getty was founded by Mark Getty and Jonathan Klein. After several years as an executive, Getty now serves as nonexecutive chairman of the company, and day-to-day leadership now falls to Klein, the firm's CEO, who also sits on the board of directors. Under Klein's leadership, Getty has done an excellent job of both consolidating the fragmented business-to-business imagery market and advancing the sector. In 2005, Klein's total compensation was $1.6 million, not including 350,000 stock options, which basically replaced the 344,000 options Klein exercised in 2005 for a total gain of $19 million. Klein also gained $32 million from option exercises in 2004. As of March 1, 2006, Klein and Getty each held about 1.8% of shares outstanding. In total, the firm's senior management and board held 4.4%, while Getty Investments, which Mark Getty chairs, owned more than 16% of the company. We aren't fond of the steps the company has taken to protect itself from being acquired, including a staggered board of directors, because we believe these measures can limit input from outside shareholders.

601 N. 34th Street
Seattle, WA 98103
www.gettyimages.com

Growth [B-]	2002	2003	2004	2005
Revenue %	2.7	13.0	19.0	17.9
Earnings/Share %	NMF	184.6	55.0	32.6
Book Value/Share %	4.8	19.4	18.3	10.4
Dividends/Share %	NMF	NMF	NMF	NMF

Profitability [B]	2003	2004	2005	TTM
Return on Assets %	5.2	7.3	9.0	8.5
Oper Cash Flow $Mil	158	203	257	257
- Cap Spending $Mil	35	37	58	63
= Free Cash Flow $Mil	123	166	200	195

Financial Health [A+]	2003	2004	2005	06-30-06
Long-term Debt $Mil	265	265	—	265
Total Equity $Mil	836	1,063	1,243	1,225
Debt/Equity Ratio	0.3	0.2	—	0.2

Thesis By Jonathan Schrader, CFA, 12-18-06 Stock Price as of Analysis: $43.63

Getty Images's stock imagery business generates loads of excess cash for its shareholders. Increasing competition at the lower end of the market, however, has presented new challenges. We think that Getty's moat is wide enough to withstand these new pressures, allowing the company to continue to generate excess returns for many more years, albeit with a slower growth rate than the company has enjoyed in the past.

Chairman Mark Getty and CEO Jonathan Klein founded Getty Images in 1995 after recognizing that the image-distribution market was ripe for consolidation. Getty and Klein used their experience as investment bankers to make a series of acquisitions that quickly made Getty Images one of the biggest players in the market.

This scale alone would have provided Getty with significant competitive advantages, but it was Getty's move to digitize its images and distribute them online that propelled the firm to its current dominance. The image-distribution market--especially at the higher end of the market--naturally lends itself to dominance by a small number of players, since it's much more efficient for the advertising agencies that buy images to deal with just a few suppliers with very large inventories of images than several firms with small inventories.

Getty's aggressive move to bulk up its collections made it one of the first places that ad agencies would turn to find an image--because of the size and quality of its collections--while its move to Web distribution made it much easier for customers to find the perfect image. Getty's success in efficiently providing the perfect image begot more success, attracting more buyers (and photographers) to Getty, boosting its margins and providing the firm with additional capital for acquisitions. Because of its strength, smaller rivals soon clamored to get distribution through Getty's Web site, further increasing Getty's importance to both image buyers and sellers.

We think that Getty still has many good years ahead of it, although we suspect that competition at the lower end of the market (where image quality and rights clearance isn't as important) will likely lead to slower growth in the near term. Most of this competition comes from micropayment Web sites, which sell images for as little as $1. While growth in micropayment may slow Getty's sales growth in the short term, Getty's acquisition of iStockphoto.com, the largest micropayment Web site, should allow Getty to benefit from the long-term growth of this market.

Gilead Sciences GILD

Rating	Fair Value	Last Close	Consider Buy	Consider Sell	Yield %
★★★	$57.00	$64.93	$36.30	$68.70	0.00

Company Profile

Gilead Sciences develops and produces therapeutics for life-threatening infectious diseases. The company currently has four products--Viread, Emtriva, combination pill Truvada, and triple combination Atripla--in its HIV franchise, as well as Hepsera for hepatitis B. The recent acquisitions of Corus Pharma and Myogen have broadened the focus of Gilead's pipeline to include pulmonary and cardiovascular indications.

Management   Stewardship Grade [C]

John Martin replaced Gilead's founder, Michael Riordan, as CEO in 1996. Martin was previously Bristol-Myers' director of antiviral chemistry and has more than a quarter century of experience in the field. Martin is the only insider on the board, which has an independent chairman. The board is quite diverse, and we like that management is rewarded for things like R&D progress rather than earnings per share. Martin began prescheduling monthly option exercises in September, which alleviates any concerns over the timing and size of these actions. While we expect Martin to exercise close to half a million options during 2006, we feel he has retained a respectable level of ownership in the firm. We also applaud recent efforts to keep option issuance below 3% of shares outstanding; however, with 22 million options exercisable at the end of the third quarter, shareholders are vulnerable to dilution. Gilead's dramatic reduction in volatility assumptions in 2004 (which makes 2006 stock-option expenses less of a jolt to the bottom line) seems unjustified. Executive compensation is above average for the company's peer group, but so is performance.

333 Lakeside Drive   www.gilead.com
Foster City, CA 94404

Growth [A]	2002	2003	2004	2005
Revenue %	99.7	85.9	52.6	53.1
Earnings/Share %	34.6	NMF	NMF	73.7
Book Value/Share %	23.2	80.8	64.4	55.2
Dividends/Share %	NMF	NMF	NMF	NMF

Profitability [A]	2003	2004	2005	TTM
Return on Assets %	-4.6	20.8	21.6	14.3
Oper Cash Flow $Mil	235	511	715	1,084
- Cap Spending $Mil	537	51	48	88
= Free Cash Flow $Mil	-303	460	667	996

Financial Health [A]	2003	2004	2005	09-30-06
Long-term Debt $Mil	345	0	241	1,380
Total Equity $Mil	1,003	1,871	3,028	3,299
Debt/Equity Ratio	0.3	0.0	0.1	0.4

Industry	Business Risk	Moat Size	Investment Style	Sector
Biotechnology	Above Avg	Narrow	Large Growth	Healthcare

Competition

	Market Cap $Mil	12 Mo Trailing Sales $Mil	Price/Cash Flow	Return On Assets%	Debt/Equity	Total Return% 1 Yr	3 Yr
Gilead Sciences	29,857	2,736	27.5	14.3	0.4	23.5	30.8
GlaxoSmithKline PLC ADR	157,300	39,536	14.5	18.7	0.7	8.0	7.6
Abbott Laboratories	74,763	22,306	14.0	9.5	0.5	26.9	3.9

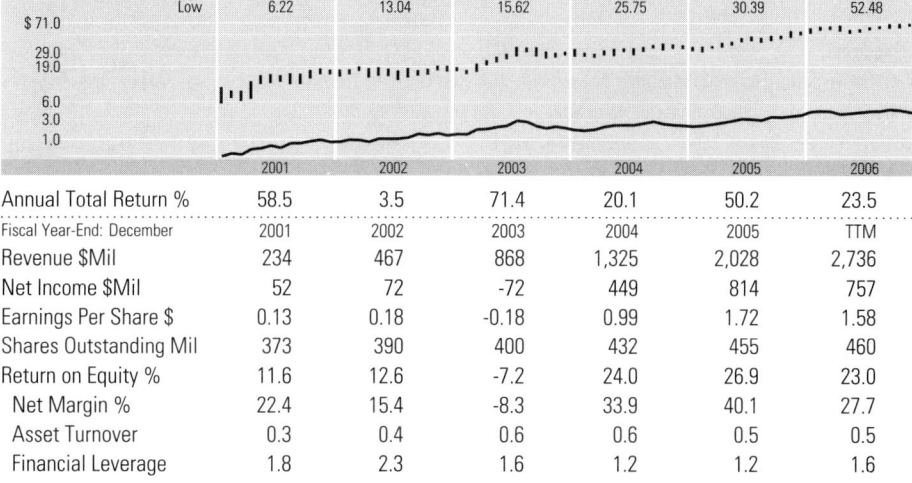

Price Volatility — Monthly Price High/Low — Relative Strength to S&P 500

Annual $Price High/Low	18.42/6.22	20.00/13.04	35.31/15.62	39.10/25.75	56.51/30.39	70.00/52.48
	2001	2002	2003	2004	2005	2006
Annual Total Return %	58.5	3.5	71.4	20.1	50.2	23.5

Fiscal Year-End: December	2001	2002	2003	2004	2005	TTM
Revenue $Mil	234	467	868	1,325	2,028	2,736
Net Income $Mil	52	72	-72	449	814	757
Earnings Per Share $	0.13	0.18	-0.18	0.99	1.72	1.58
Shares Outstanding Mil	373	390	400	432	455	460
Return on Equity %	11.6	12.6	-7.2	24.0	26.9	23.0
Net Margin %	22.4	15.4	-8.3	33.9	40.1	27.7
Asset Turnover	0.3	0.4	0.6	0.6	0.5	0.5
Financial Leverage	1.8	2.3	1.6	1.2	1.2	1.6

Valuation Ratios	Stock	Rel to Industry	Rel to S&P 500
Price/Earnings	41.1	0.9	2.0
Price/Book	9.1	1.1	2.2
Price/Sales	10.9	0.9	3.8
Price/Cash Flow	27.5	1.0	1.9

Major Fund Holders	% of Fund Assets
ACM Convertible Securities	18.55
AMIDEX Cancer Innovation & Healthcare	10.76
ProFunds Biotechnology UltraSector Inv	8.39
Allianz RCM Biotechnology D	7.41

Thesis By Karen Andersen, 12-15-06 Stock Price as of Analysis: $64.49

The global success of Gilead Sciences' HIV franchise has boosted the company to sustainable and impressive profitability. The recent launch of the all-in-one pill Atripla only reinforces Gilead's dominance in this highly competitive field. With its bold $2.5 billion acquisition of Myogen, Gilead is taking a big step toward diversifying its portfolio. While we don't think current share prices fully incorporate the regulatory risks that Gilead faces, approval of Myogen's lead drug candidates and continuing strong Tamiflu royalties could push Gilead into wide-moat territory.

Gilead's HIV franchise, which accounted for 70% of revenue during the first nine months of 2006, is the heart of the firm's product portfolio. Viread, Emtriva, and combo drug Truvada are part of the Department of Health and Human Services' preferred HIV treatment regimen, one of many reasons that sales of Gilead's HIV drugs are poised to surpass $2 billion in 2006, a sizable chunk of the $7 billion HIV antiviral market. The baton has now been passed to Atripla, the all-in-one triple combination pill approved in July that combines Truvada with Bristol Myers-Squibb's Sustiva. Although the pill's ingredients aren't novel, we believe the creation of a one-pill option will expand Gilead's market share significantly; Atripla's convenience reduces the likelihood of missed doses and subsequent drug resistance, which makes doctors more comfortable prescribing it at an earlier stage of the disease.

At first glance, Gilead's acquisition of Myogen appeared to come out of left field. Myogen's two cardiovascular drug candidates aim to serve vastly different markets from Gilead's familiar infectious disease territory, but we see several parallels. Ambrisentan, which could be approved by mid-2007 to treat pulmonary arterial hypertension, appears safer and more convenient than its alternatives, and its approval should aid efforts to improve diagnosis rates and expand the market. As combination therapy becomes more prevalent, a niche salesforce should help Gilead capitalize on its experience with similar developments in HIV.

Gilead has translated successful products into a strong, profitable business, as demonstrated by its $740 million in operating cash flows over the first nine months of 2006. We're also encouraged by the potential of Gilead's early-stage pipeline outside of recent acquisitions, which includes novel HIV and hepatitis C drugs. However, a growing amount of Gilead's value is wrapped up in its pipeline, which keeps our risk rating at above average.

Given Imaging GIVN

	Rating	Fair Value	Last Close	Consider Buy	Consider Sell	Yield %
	★★★★	$25.00	$19.35	$19.30	$31.30	0.00

Company Profile
Based in Israel, Given Imaging develops, manufactures, and markets patient-friendly systems for diagnosing gastrointestinal disorders. The firm's main product is the capsule endoscope system, which consists of a disposable miniaturized video camera enclosed in a capsule that patients swallow, a data recorder that receives images transmitted wirelessly, and a workstation where the digital images can be viewed.

Management   Stewardship Grade [NA]
Given has experienced considerable management turnover in the last couple of years. Homi Shamir replaced founder Gavriel Meron as president and CEO in spring 2006. Given's CFO and president of the U.S. division also joined the firm within the last 18 months. While the departure of a founder often sets the stage for turbulence, we believe new CEO Shamir brings the right type of global imaging experience from his previous post at Eastman Kodak to help Given embark on its next stage of growth on the global stage. Chairman Doron Birger has become the continuity on the board. The seven-member board includes six independent directors who bring to the table wide-ranging experience with venture capital, cardiac devices, and auditing. Chairman Birger also owns approximately 24% of the company, which reassures us that the board is heavily invested in Given's future and should act carefully to protect shareholder interests. The firm has historically hewn to reasonable compensation policies for its top executives, and we're hopeful this pattern has held true for Shamir's compensation package.

13 HaYetzira Street New Industrial Park POB 258
Yoqneam, Israel 20692   www.givenimaging.com

Growth [NA]	2002	2003	2004	2005
Revenue %	510.7	40.3	60.4	33.5
Earnings/Share %	NMF	NMF	NMF	110.0
Book Value/Share %	NMF	-17.1	84.9	3.1
Dividends/Share %	NMF	NMF	NMF	NMF

Profitability [NA]	2003	2004	2005	TTM
Return on Assets %	-17.3	2.3	4.3	4.3
Oper Cash Flow $Mil	-9	12	13	13
- Cap Spending $Mil	3	3	8	8
= Free Cash Flow $Mil	-11	9	6	6

Financial Health [NA]	2003	2004	2005	12-31-05
Long-term Debt $Mil	0	0	0	0
Total Equity $Mil	45	95	102	102
Debt/Equity Ratio	0.0	0.0	0.0	0.0

	Industry	Business Risk	Moat Size	Investment Style	Sector
	Medical Equip.	Average	Narrow	Small Growth	Healthcare

Competition	Market Cap $Mil	12 Mo Trailing Sales $Mil	Price/Cash Flow	Return On Assets%	Debt/ Equity	Total Return% 1 Yr	3 Yr
Given Imaging	541	87	40.1	4.3	0.0	-25.9	2.7
Siemens AG ADR	87,817	107,241	14.4	3.2	0.5	17.3	8.8
Philips Electronics NV AD	45,147	38,062	17.3	8.9	0.2	22.8	9.8

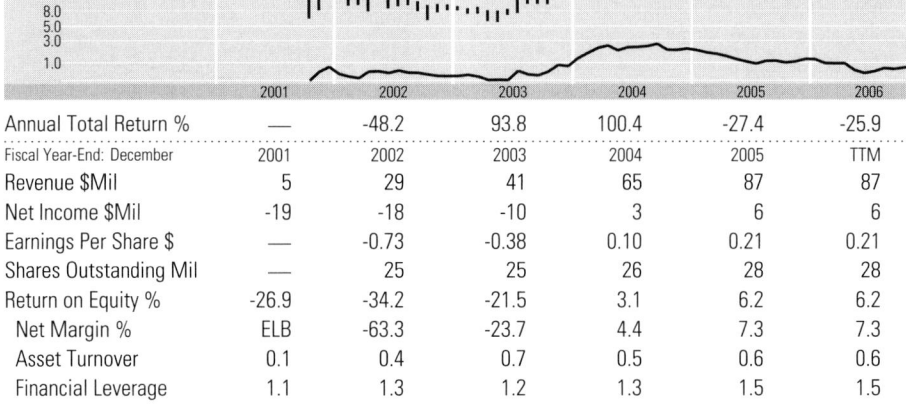

Annual Total Return %	—	-48.2	93.8	100.4	-27.4	-25.9
Fiscal Year-End: December	2001	2002	2003	2004	2005	TTM
Revenue $Mil	5	29	41	65	87	87
Net Income $Mil	-19	-18	-10	3	6	6
Earnings Per Share $	—	-0.73	-0.38	0.10	0.21	0.21
Shares Outstanding Mil	—	25	25	26	28	28
Return on Equity %	-26.9	-34.2	-21.5	3.1	6.2	6.2
Net Margin %	ELB	-63.3	-23.7	4.4	7.3	7.3
Asset Turnover	0.1	0.4	0.7	0.5	0.6	0.6
Financial Leverage	1.1	1.3	1.2	1.3	1.5	1.5

Valuation Ratios	Stock	Rel to Industry	Rel to S&P 500
Price/Earnings	92.1	3.2	4.5
Price/Book	5.3	1.0	1.3
Price/Sales	6.2	1.3	2.1
Price/Cash Flow	40.1	1.7	2.7

Major Fund Holders	% of Fund Assets
Stonebridge Small-Cap Growth	4.62
ING AllianceBernstein Mid Cap Growth S	3.03
AllianceBernstein Mid-Cap Growth A	3.00

Thesis By Debbie S. Wang, 11-02-06 Stock Price as of Analysis: $21.66

Though innovation in the world of medical devices often yields evolutionary improvements, Given Imaging's debut product could spark a revolution in gastrointestinal (GI) diagnostic procedures.

After receiving regulatory approval in 2001, Given was the first to introduce a small-bowel capsule endoscope system. Using Israeli missile technology, Given scientists have created a miniature wireless video camera that a patient can swallow. Over the course of eight hours, this tiny battery-powered camera takes pictures of the inside of the gastrointestinal tract and transmits the images to a data recorder worn around the waist. The doctor later downloads the data files onto a workstation in the office to look at the images for signs of lesions, bleeding, inflammation, or other disorders.

This method of endoscopy offers several key advantages over more traditional methods of imaging the GI tract. First, the capsule can travel the entire length of the intestines. Traditional endoscopy can only reach the top third of the small intestine, and the remaining 20 feet can be accessed only through abdominal surgery. Further, the PillCam SB allows patients to go about their regular routines while it snaps pictures of their insides, in contrast with traditional (and highly invasive) endoscopy and colonoscopy, both of which involve patient discomfort and sedation. Lastly, clinical data suggest that the Pill Cam SB allows doctors to reach a diagnosis in 71% of cases, compared with 41% for the traditional methods--making it substantially more valuable to doctors.

Given has not eased up on its research and development; it continues to develop more GI-focused diagnostic tools. The firm is conducting clinical trials (and has already received regulatory clearance in Europe) for its new PillCam COLON product, an ingestible video capsule for colonoscopies. This product would allow Given to tap into a far larger market of 5-7 million Americans who have that procedure each year. The firm also received domestic regulatory approval for its new PillCam ESO for imaging the esophagus.

While the future looks bright for Given, insurance reimbursement remains a major challenge, especially in Europe, and could heavily influence how quickly sales might grow. Additionally, Olympus has made strides in developing a competitive capsule, which could enter the U.S. market in the next year. Nonetheless, we like what Given has done so far, and we expect that it should benefit as gastroenterologists adopt this new technology.

Data as of 12-29-06

GlaxoSmithKline PLC ADR GSK

	Rating	Fair Value	Last Close	Consider Buy	Consider Sell	Yield %
	★★★★	$63.00	$52.76	$48.60	$78.90	3.29

Company Profile

GlaxoSmithKline is the second-largest pharmaceutical company in the world. It competes in a myriad of pharmaceutical sectors, including the central nervous system, respiratory, and antiviral areas. Glaxo also produces vaccines and consumer products including Aquafresh toothpaste and smoking-control aid Nicoderm. Prescription-drug sales account for about 85% of revenue. U.S. consumers generate about half of its sales.

Management

Stewardship Grade [NA]

Dr. Jean-Pierre Garnier has been CEO since 2000. He came from SmithKline Beecham, one of the legacy firms that now constitute GlaxoSmithKline. With a Ph.D. in pharmacology and many years of pharmaceutical experience, we think Garnier is well suited to lead the world's second-largest pharmaceutical firm. However, Garnier is scheduled to retire in May 2008, so Glaxo will need to find a replacement in short order. We're pleased to see that Glaxo's chairman and CEO roles are separate, which tends to be more common in the U.K. We also like the firm's share-ownership guidelines and tempered use of options (relative to U.S. companies). For example, the CEO must own an amount of stock equivalent to 4 times his or her salary; other top execs have a 2-3 times salary requirement, and options don't count toward the goal.

980 Great West Road
Brentford, United Kingdom TW8 9GS
www.gsk.com

Growth [NA]	2002	2003	2004	2005
Revenue %	3.5	1.1	-6.8	8.4
Earnings/Share %	32.3	16.5	-11.6	20.6
Book Value/Share %	-7.6	-21.5	11.7	28.6
Dividends/Share %	—	—	—	—

Profitability [NA]	2003	2004	2005	TTM
Return on Assets %	19.4	16.6	18.7	18.7
Oper Cash Flow $Mil	7,945	8,989	10,875	10,875
- Cap Spending $Mil	1,560	1,433	1,648	1,648
= Free Cash Flow $Mil	6,385	7,556	9,227	9,227

Financial Health [NA]	2003	2004	2005	12-31-05
Long-term Debt $Mil	6,934	8,425	9,088	9,088
Total Equity $Mil	9,034	11,008	12,605	12,605
Debt/Equity Ratio	0.8	0.8	0.7	0.7

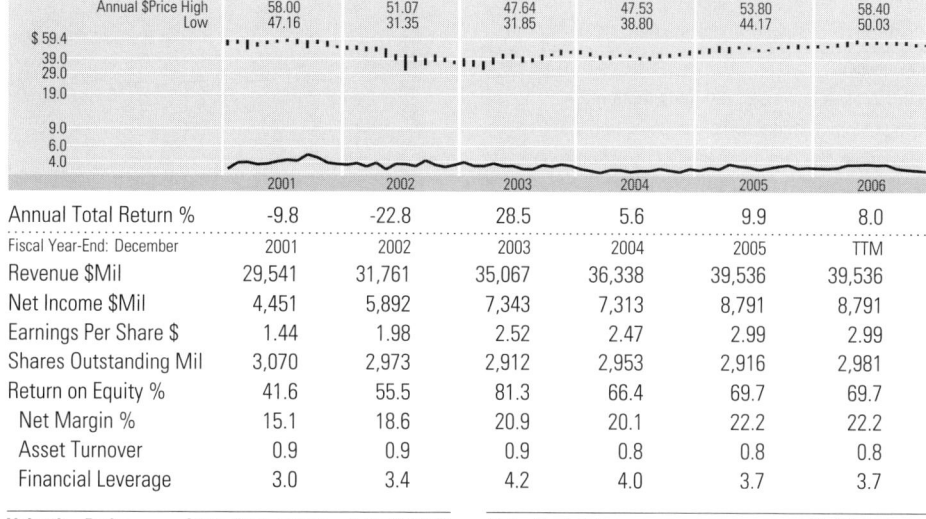

	Industry	Business Risk	Moat Size	Investment Style	Sector
	Drugs	Average	Wide	Large Core	Healthcare

Competition	Market Cap $Mil	12 Mo Trailing Sales $Mil	Price/Cash Flow	Return On Assets%	Debt/ Equity	Total Return% 1 Yr	3 Yr
GlaxoSmithKline PLC ADR	157,300	39,536	14.5	18.7	0.7	8.0	7.6
Pfizer	186,751	52,208	10.5	11.6	0.1	15.2	-7.4
AstraZeneca PLC ADR	84,438	23,950	12.5	19.0	0.1	13.3	5.4

	2001	2002	2003	2004	2005	2006
Annual $Price High	58.00	51.07	47.64	47.53	53.80	58.40
Low	47.16	31.35	31.85	38.80	44.17	50.03
Annual Total Return %	-9.8	-22.8	28.5	5.6	9.9	8.0

Fiscal Year-End: December	2001	2002	2003	2004	2005	TTM
Revenue $Mil	29,541	31,761	35,067	36,338	39,536	39,536
Net Income $Mil	4,451	5,892	7,343	7,313	8,791	8,791
Earnings Per Share $	1.44	1.98	2.52	2.47	2.99	2.99
Shares Outstanding Mil	3,070	2,973	2,912	2,953	2,916	2,981
Return on Equity %	41.6	55.5	81.3	66.4	69.7	69.7
Net Margin %	15.1	18.6	20.9	20.1	22.2	22.2
Asset Turnover	0.9	0.9	0.9	0.8	0.8	0.8
Financial Leverage	3.0	3.4	4.2	4.0	3.7	3.7

Valuation Ratios	Stock	Rel to Industry	Rel to S&P 500
Price/Earnings	17.6	0.7	0.9
Price/Book	12.5	2.3	3.0
Price/Sales	4.0	0.9	1.4
Price/Cash Flow	14.5	0.9	1.0

Major Fund Holders	% of Fund Assets
Kinetics Medical	6.82
AMIDEX Cancer Innovation & Healthcare	5.89
ProFunds Europe 30 Svc	5.41
Fidelity Select Pharmaceuticals	4.48

Thesis

By Heather Brilliant, CFA, 11-06-06 Stock Price as of Analysis: $53.75

GlaxoSmithKline has amassed an impressive lineup of pharmaceutical offerings. While the firm has several blockbusters in its portfolio, its revenue comes from a wide variety of drugs, insulating it from the generic competition risks that most of its competitors face.

Glaxo markets one of the broadest product lines in the industry. The firm's drug portfolio is balanced across a wide variety of therapeutic classes, and it has amassed solid offerings in diabetes care, respiratory diseases, and anti-viral medications, just to name a few. With a strong pipeline in oncology drugs and a large vaccine offering, we think the firm's breadth will continue to improve. It's largest drug in terms of sales, Advair for asthma, constitutes just 15% of sales, insulating Glaxo from the reliance on blockbusters that plagues competitors.

We also think Glaxo has proved adept at product life-cycle management, or extending the life of branded products beyond initial patent expiration through the development of improved formulations, such as extended-release versions of its drugs. For example, the firm recently received approval for Coreg CR, a once-a-day oral medication for heart failure that will now compete in the hypertension market. While the underlying U.S. patent on Coreg will expire in 2007, we expect Glaxo to gain a few years of market exclusivity with its new controlled-release version of the drug.

Even more important, Glaxo has amassed a broad pipeline of drugs in each stage of clinical development that should ensure solid revenue growth in the future. The firm has three drugs currently pending a decision from the Food and Drug Administration, and a handful more that it expects to file within the next year. The firm has organized its research-and-development efforts by therapeutic area, and each group is charged with advancing the best compounds in a given class of drugs. This can include in-licensing promising drugs from outside firms, or internal development. Such openness to partnering with other firms has boosted Glaxo's product portfolio, with drugs such as Lexiva for HIV and Boniva for osteoporosis coming from partner firms.

Although we believe Glaxo is well-positioned within the pharmaceutical industry, regulatory and generic competition risks will undoubtedly continue to rear their ugly heads from time to time. Glaxo will have to continue fighting off numerous challenges to its patents and improve efficiency to maintain high returns on capital.

Data as of 12-29-06

Global Cash Access Holdings GCA

Rating	Fair Value	Last Close	Consider Buy	Consider Sell	Yield %
★★★★	$20.00	$16.23	$12.70	$24.10	0.00

Company Profile
Global Cash Access provides casino patrons with access to cash in establishments in the United States, Canada, the United Kingdom, and the Caribbean. It operates machines that allow users to access cash in bank accounts through ATM transactions, and it facilitates point-of-sale debit card withdrawals and credit card cash advances. The company also provides consumer credit data to casinos for use in credit decisions and provides check-cashing services to casino patrons.

Management   Stewardship Grade [B]
We don't see any major red flags related to stewardship. Management compensation looks reasonable, the chairman and CEO positions aren't held by the same individual, and there is only one share class. Given the continued majority ownership of the shares by the pre-IPO owners and the close relationship between GCA and other entities controlled by its majority owners, there is the risk that smaller investors won't have much of a say in the way the business is run, but we see no signs of abuse. We'd prefer that the whole board stand for election every year, but since the board largely consists of company owners, it wouldn't make much difference at this point.

Industry	Business Risk	Moat Size	Investment Style	Sector
Data Processing	Above Avg	Narrow	Small Core	Business Services

Competition	Market Cap $Mil	12 Mo Trailing Sales $Mil	Price/Cash Flow	Return On Assets%	Debt/ Equity	Total Return% 1 Yr	3 Yr
Global Cash Access Holdings	1,336	522	—	4.7	—	11.2	—
Automatic Data Processing	27,117	9,177	17.2	6.1	0.0	9.1	8.8
First Data	19,543	10,806	8.4	4.4	0.4	9.9	5.6

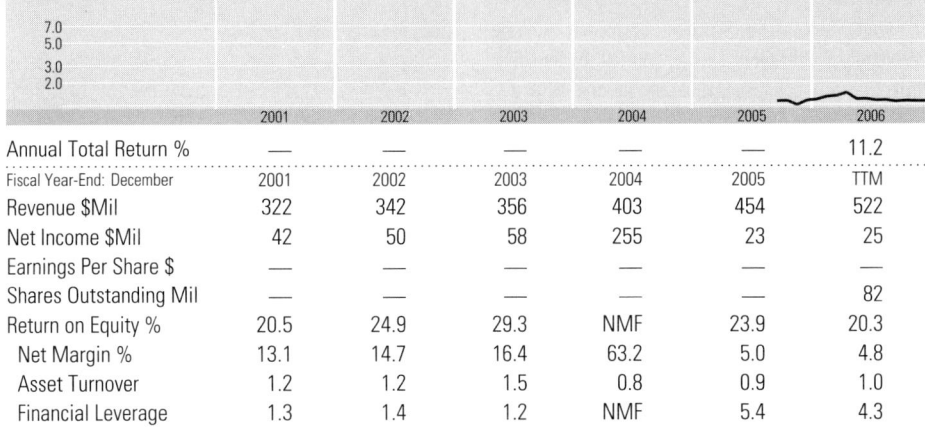

Fiscal Year-End: December	2001	2002	2003	2004	2005	TTM
Revenue $Mil	322	342	356	403	454	522
Net Income $Mil	42	50	58	255	23	25
Earnings Per Share $	—	—	—	—	—	—
Shares Outstanding Mil	—	—	—	—	—	82
Return on Equity %	20.5	24.9	29.3	NMF	23.9	20.3
Net Margin %	13.1	14.7	16.4	63.2	5.0	4.8
Asset Turnover	1.2	1.2	1.5	0.8	0.9	1.0
Financial Leverage	1.3	1.4	1.2	NMF	5.4	4.3

Valuation Ratios	Stock	Rel to Industry	Rel to S&P 500	Major Fund Holders	% of Fund Assets
Price/Earnings	—	—	—	Delaware Pooled Focus Smid-Cap Gr Eq	4.50
Price/Book	10.8	2.1	2.6	Delaware Select Growth A	3.13
Price/Sales	2.6	0.7	0.9	Delaware Pooled All-Cap Growth Equity	3.13
Price/Cash Flow	—	—	—	Fidelity Select IT Services	2.03

Thesis   By Sumit Desai, CFA, 11-03-06   Stock Price as of Analysis: $16.34

Global Cash Access has built the dominant franchise in casino-related cash access services. We like this narrow-moat firm's prospects.

GCA is 8 times larger than its nearest competitor and counts the 10 largest casinos in the United States as customers. For its ATM services, revenue is driven by transaction volume, as GCA earns a flat fee every time a customer uses one of its machines. Transaction volume has increased more than 11% annually since 2002, allowing GCA's ATM revenue to grow about 15% over this time. For cash-advance services, GCA earns a percentage of the amount dispensed, so sales are driven by both volume and the dollar amount of each transaction. Since 2002, the average cash-advance transaction has increased to $516 from $439, causing sales to grow about 9% over the past three years. For both types of services, GCA's cost structure largely consists of fees and commissions it pays to casinos, banks, and credit card associations.

GCA's moat is based on its exclusive contracts and close integration with casino operators and its wide breadth of services, many of which are difficult to duplicate. GCA locks its customers up for three- to five-year contracts and installs its own cash-dispensing machines and systems directly into the casino, making it difficult for rivals to steal business. As a result, GCA enjoys a customer retention rate of nearly 97%. It also uses decades' worth of customer transaction history to build an extensive database of gambling and spending habits and sells this data to casinos for marketing purposes. GCA's customer data are especially valuable since they indicate a patron's activity across various casinos, as opposed to just one property. This information is difficult for any competitor to duplicate, given the time involved and extent of GCA's data.

GCA's gross margins have plunged recently, as renewed contracts have included higher fees to casinos. However, we see several factors that can offset this. In our opinion, much of the decline was caused by a large wave of consolidation in the gaming industry, giving casinos more bargaining power over suppliers. However, most of GCA's large customers are now signed under new long-term contracts with fixed terms, so margin pressure should be minimized. We also think the company's growth prospects will help mitigate further margin compression. Since GCA's contracts are for all of a customer's properties, the company will benefit as its customers enter new gaming jurisdictions domestically and abroad.

3525 East Post Road Suite 120   www.globalcashaccess.com
Las Vegas, NV 89120

Growth [B-]	2002	2003	2004	2005
Revenue %	6.3	4.0	13.3	12.7
Earnings/Share %	NMF	NMF	NMF	NMF
Book Value/Share %	—	—	—	—
Dividends/Share %	NMF	NMF	NMF	NMF

Profitability [A]	2003	2004	2005	TTM
Return on Assets %	24.0	51.3	4.4	4.7
Oper Cash Flow $Mil	33	75	37	—
- Cap Spending $Mil	6	3	7	—
= Free Cash Flow $Mil	—	—	—	—

Financial Health [NA]	2003	2004	2005	09-30-06
Long-term Debt $Mil	—	—	—	—
Total Equity $Mil	199	-57	94	124
Debt/Equity Ratio	—	—	—	—

Data as of 12-29-06

Goldman Sachs Group GS

Rating	Fair Value	Last Close	Consider Buy	Consider Sell	Yield %
★★	$161.00	$199.35	$124.10	$201.70	0.65

Company Profile
Goldman Sachs is a premier financial-services firm catering to institutions and wealthy individuals. It has three divisions. The investment-banking group focuses on corporate-advisory and underwriting services. The trading and principal investments group consists of the trading desks and the merchant bank. The asset-management and securities-services group is responsible for managing mutual funds and client portfolios and servicing client transactions.

Management — Stewardship Grade [B]
Lloyd Blankfein recently replaced Henry Paulson as CEO when Paulson left to become secretary of the treasury. Blankfein had been COO since 1994 and came up through the trading ranks at Goldman. We don't expect much of a change under his leadership. Managerial ranks at Goldman are stable, strong, and deep. When senior executives do leave the firm, they historically have done so on an individual basis and not in a mass exodus. Transitions are known for their orderliness. Blankfein is backed by Robert Steel and Robert Kaplan. In an attempt to improve corporate governance, Goldman has stopped staggered board elections. Compensation is high across Wall Street but is typically well aligned with performance, and Goldman Sachs is no exception.

85 Broad Street
New York, NY 10004
www.gs.com

Growth [A]	2002	2003	2004	2005
Revenue %	-11.5	14.5	28.3	20.6
Earnings/Share %	-5.4	45.7	52.0	25.7
Book Value/Share %	7.7	16.6	16.3	6.8
Dividends/Share %	0.0	54.2	35.1	0.0

Profitability [C]	2003	2004	2005	TTM
Return on Assets %	0.7	0.9	0.8	1.0
Oper Cash Flow $Mil	-16,739	-33,391	-12,413	—
- Cap Spending $Mil	856	829	1,421	—
= Free Cash Flow $Mil	—	—	—	—

Financial Health [NA]	2003	2004	2005	08-31-06
Long-term Debt $Mil	—	—	—	—
Total Equity $Mil	21,632	25,079	26,252	30,393
Debt/Equity Ratio	—	—	—	—

Industry	Business Risk	Moat Size	Investment Style	Sector
Securities	Average	Wide	Large Growth	Financial Services

Competition	Market Cap $Mil	12 Mo Trailing Sales $Mil	Price/Cash Flow	Return On Assets %	Debt/Equity	Total Return % 1 Yr	Total Return % 3 Yr
Goldman Sachs Group	84,890	34,181	—	1.0	—	57.4	28.3
Citigroup	273,691	86,566	—	1.3	—	19.6	8.4
J.P. Morgan Chase & Co.	167,551	59,650	—	0.9	—	25.6	13.2

Price Volatility
| Monthly Price High/Low — Relative Strength to S&P 500

	2001	2002	2003	2004	2005	2006
Annual $Price High	120.00	97.25	100.00	110.88	134.99	206.70
Low	63.27	58.57	61.05	83.29	94.75	124.23
Annual Total Return %	-12.8	-26.1	46.3	6.5	23.9	57.4

Fiscal Year-End: November	2001	2002	2003	2004	2005	TTM
Revenue $Mil	15,811	13,986	16,012	20,550	24,782	34,181
Net Income $Mil	2,310	2,114	3,005	4,553	5,609	7,918
Earnings Per Share $	4.26	4.03	5.87	8.92	11.21	16.44
Shares Outstanding Mil	510	495	489	490	478	426
Return on Equity %	12.7	11.1	13.9	18.2	21.4	26.1
Net Margin %	14.6	15.1	18.8	22.2	22.6	23.2
Asset Turnover	0.1	0.0	0.0	0.0	0.0	0.0
Financial Leverage	17.1	18.7	18.7	21.2	26.9	26.3

Valuation Ratios	Stock	Rel to Industry	Rel to S&P 500
Price/Earnings	12.1	0.7	0.6
Price/Book	2.8	0.7	0.7
Price/Sales	2.5	0.6	0.9
Price/Cash Flow	—	—	—

Major Fund Holders	% of Fund Assets
Wells Fargo Advantage Large Co Growth Ad	9.54
Marsico Growth	5.82
Marsico Focus	5.74
JHT Financial Services Trust Ser I	5.70

Thesis By Philip Guziec, 12-15-06 Stock Price as of Analysis: $199.84

Goldman Sachs is the gold standard among investment banks. We expect solid performance in the long run, and investors with a stomach for volatility might consider the shares during one of the dark periods that are nearly inevitable in the financial markets.

Goldman has successfully capitalized on its brand and reputation. It maintains top market share in its advisory and underwriting business, keeps unusually low turnover among its banker staff, and has increased fee-based businesses like asset management. The company has also generated solid returns on its investment and trading portfolio. It is this brand and history, along with the associated senior-level relationships and financial expertise, that create the company's wide moat. However, all of these businesses tend to perform in tandem, and financial markets are notoriously volatile, so investors should expect a bumpy ride.

Because the firm's advisory, brokerage, and underwriting businesses don't require much capital, Goldman has had to find places to put its prodigious earnings to work. Since its initial public offering in 1999, Goldman has more than doubled its tangible equity, the result of plowing much of its earnings into expanding other businesses.

One example of this expansion is asset management, where the Goldman Sachs name is a premium brand that comes in handy for gathering assets from wealthy clients. However, the trading and principal investments segment has grown the most; the company's large equity and debt trading operations provided a base for plowing earnings into rapidly growing derivatives trading activities. This segment has ballooned to more than half of revenue and as much as three fourths of operating income.

The trading and principal investments portfolio produces interest income from the interest-bearing holdings in the portfolio, profits from the trading spreads between selling and buying prices for securities, and gains from Goldman's good investments. However, the firm is also exposed to losses on its bad investments and volatility as the value of the securities in the portfolio goes up and down with movements in the financial markets.

Even though returns can be great in the long run, trading profits can be volatile, and the potholes in the road can be huge. However, even the big losses are unlikely to be fatal for the firm and could provide great buying opportunities for those waiting for a chance to get a piece of Goldman Sachs.

Data as of 12-29-06

Google GOOG

	Rating	Fair Value	Last Close	Consider Buy	Consider Sell	Yield %
	★	$315.00	$460.48	$242.90	$394.70	0.00

Industry	Business Risk	Moat Size	Investment Style	Sector
Business/Online Svcs.	Average	Narrow	Large Growth	Business Services

Company Profile
Google provides a free search engine for users to find content about virtually any topic. The company auctions advertising to its large customer base and places the ads on its Web sites as well as content providers' sites that are part of the Google network. In this network, the company splits the advertising revenue with Google network members. Less than 40% of revenues and less than 10% of operating profits are generated by Google's network of content partners.

Management
Stewardship Grade [C]

Larry Page and Sergey Brin founded Google in 1998 and now lead the company as a triumvirate with Eric Schmidt, who has been CEO since 2001. Schmidt had previously been CEO of Novell and chief technology officer of Sun Microsystems. Many have heralded the unorthodox decision making led by this three-person committee, but we question its sustainability, particularly if Schmidt were to leave. Page, Brin, and Schmidt have more than two thirds of the equity voting rights as of the last proxy filing, thanks to a dual-class structure. This disproportionate voting power is a significant risk for the remaining equity shareholders. We believe Schmidt plays a critical role in the success of the company that highlights the talents of each of the leaders. Currently, we think that the company is a bit too generous in its stock plan--the stock plan has set aside more than 5% of the outstanding equity for employee stock grants. Additionally, we believe management could be more forthcoming with regard to its long-term strategy and operating metrics of the business.

1600 Amphitheatre Parkway www.google.com
Mountain View, CA 94043

Growth [A+]	2002	2003	2004	2005
Revenue %	408.5	233.5	117.6	92.5
Earnings/Share %	NMF	NMF	NMF	NMF
Book Value/Share %	—	—	—	NMF
Dividends/Share %	NMF	NMF	NMF	NMF

Profitability [A]	2003	2004	2005	TTM
Return on Assets %	12.1	12.0	14.3	15.4
Oper Cash Flow $Mil	395	977	2,459	3,328
- Cap Spending $Mil	177	319	838	1,782
= Free Cash Flow $Mil	219	658	1,621	1,546

Financial Health [A+]	2003	2004	2005	09-30-06
Long-term Debt $Mil	—	6	2	—
Total Equity $Mil	589	2,929	9,419	14,397
Debt/Equity Ratio	—	0.0	0.0	0.0

Competition	Market Cap $Mil	12 Mo Trailing Sales $Mil	Price/Cash Flow	Return On Assets%	Debt/Equity	Total Return% 1 Yr	3 Yr
Google	140,979	9,319	42.4	15.4	0.0	11.0	—
Yahoo	34,740	6,224	20.6	11.0	0.1	-34.8	4.0
IAC/InterActiveCorp	11,864	6,568	13.2	2.2	0.1	31.3	0.2

Price Volatility

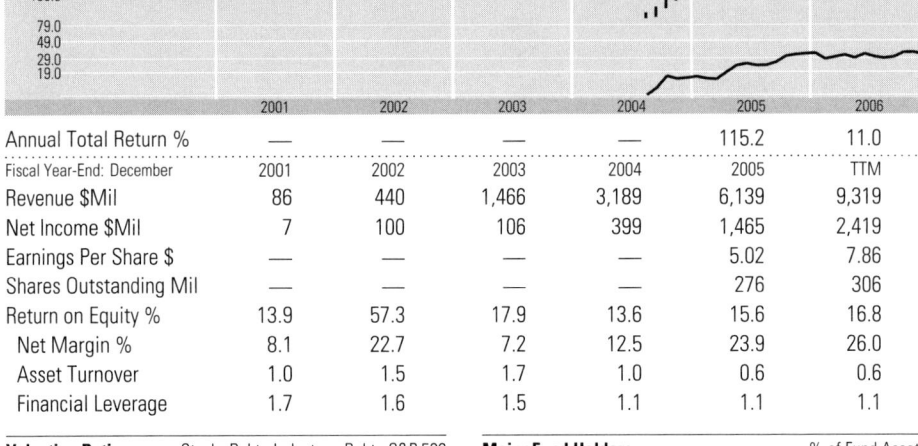

	2001	2002	2003	2004	2005	2006
Annual Total Return %	—	—	—	—	115.2	11.0

Fiscal Year-End: December	2001	2002	2003	2004	2005	TTM
Revenue $Mil	86	440	1,466	3,189	6,139	9,319
Net Income $Mil	7	100	106	399	1,465	2,419
Earnings Per Share $	—	—	—	—	5.02	7.86
Shares Outstanding Mil	—	—	—	—	276	306
Return on Equity %	13.9	57.3	17.9	13.6	15.6	16.8
Net Margin %	8.1	22.7	7.2	12.5	23.9	26.0
Asset Turnover	1.0	1.5	1.7	1.0	0.6	0.6
Financial Leverage	1.7	1.6	1.5	1.1	1.1	1.1

Valuation Ratios	Stock	Rel to Industry	Rel to S&P 500	Major Fund Holders	% of Fund Assets
Price/Earnings	58.6	1.1	2.8	Fidelity Advisor Growth Opport T	11.94
Price/Book	9.8	1.1	2.4	Constellation Sands Capital Inst Growth	11.50
Price/Sales	15.1	1.2	5.2	Touchstone Sands Capital Select Growth Z	9.76
Price/Cash Flow	42.4	1.0	2.9	Fidelity Select Software & Comp	9.55

Thesis By Rick Summer, CFA, CPA, 10-24-06 Stock Price as of Analysis: $473.31

When it comes to Internet search, Google is the runaway leader. However, we expect powerful content owners and other competitors will lead the next phase of growth in sales of online advertising.

Google makes almost 100% of its money from selling online advertising. When someone uses its search engine, Google displays ads based on the keywords or phrases used for the search. If the user then clicks on an ad (a click-through), the advertiser pays Google based on an agreed-upon price per click. Google has a network of advertising customers that place ads on its Web sites and content partners' sites. Site traffic drives click-throughs, which drive revenue.

While accurate numbers are difficult to obtain, we estimate Google's market share of Internet searches to be twice as large as its nearest competitor, Yahoo. Google's market dominance will be tough to challenge as users have very little incentive to switch search engines. Still, Google's dominance is far from certain. In the 1990s, users were happy to switch away from leading search engines, including HotBot and Lycos. Switching costs are more psychological than economic.

We are skeptical that Google will translate its dominance in search into new products. We acknowledge that Google is the dominant delivery channel for online advertising today. However, we believe competition will intensify as advertisers look to enhance their marketing capabilities to include entertainment, co-branding, and rich media advertisements. Consequently, non-search advertising on the Internet will grow more quickly, in our opinion. As Google looks to new delivery channels for advertising (e.g., online video), we believe the company may be squeezed out by many of the incumbent competitors, such as advertising agencies and content owners. In short, we believe significant content owners such as MySpace will command a greater share of the advertising dollar and will be less generous in sharing those revenues as the market matures.

By 2008, we expect Google's growth rate to be less than half of its 2006 growth rate. Admittedly, we have been surprised by Yahoo's inability to launch a counterattack in 2006--we question whether its new advertising platform (Panama) will level the playing field in 2007. However, the true value of Google lies beyond what happens in 2007. We think Google's potential will be constrained by the growth of searches on the Internet and the increasing number of choices advertisers have to reach their audience.

Graco GGG

Data as of 12-29-06

Rating	Fair Value	Last Close	Consider Buy	Consider Sell	Yield %
★★★	$43.00	$39.62	$33.20	$53.90	1.46

Industry	Business Risk	Moat Size	Investment Style	Sector
Machinery	Average	Narrow	Mid Growth	Industrial Materials

Company Profile

Graco makes systems and equipment that move, measure, mix, proportion, control, dispense, and spray a wide variety of fluids and viscous materials; the company makes handling sticky fluids easier and more reliable. Its industrial and automotive segment focuses on factory paint and adhesive applications. The contractor segment makes spray equipment for professional painters. The third segment, oil-lubrication equipment, makes up less than 10% of total sales.

Management   Stewardship Grade [B]

Chairman and CEO David Roberts joined Graco in 2001 from The Marmon Group, where he ran a portfolio of manufacturing companies. He is the only insider on the board, and all key committees are staffed with independent directors. Management pay is in line with industry practices, and directors and executives as a group own roughly 2.7% of shares outstanding, helping align their interests with those of outside shareholders. We are most impressed, however, by management's excellent stewardship of shareholder capital. Excess funds are used for dividends, share buybacks, and sensible acquisitions. With limited capital needs and significant operating leverage, any growth that Graco can muster--notably from emerging economies--will have an outsize effect on the bottom line.

Competition

	Market Cap $Mil	12 Mo Trailing Sales $Mil	Price/Cash Flow	Return On Assets%	Debt/Equity	Total Return% 1 Yr	3 Yr
Graco	2,664	799	16.7	28.8	—	10.1	17.4
Illinois Tool Works	26,184	13,798	14.5	12.7	0.1	6.7	5.3
Ingersoll-Rand A	11,997	11,232	12.8	9.4	0.2	-1.4	6.9

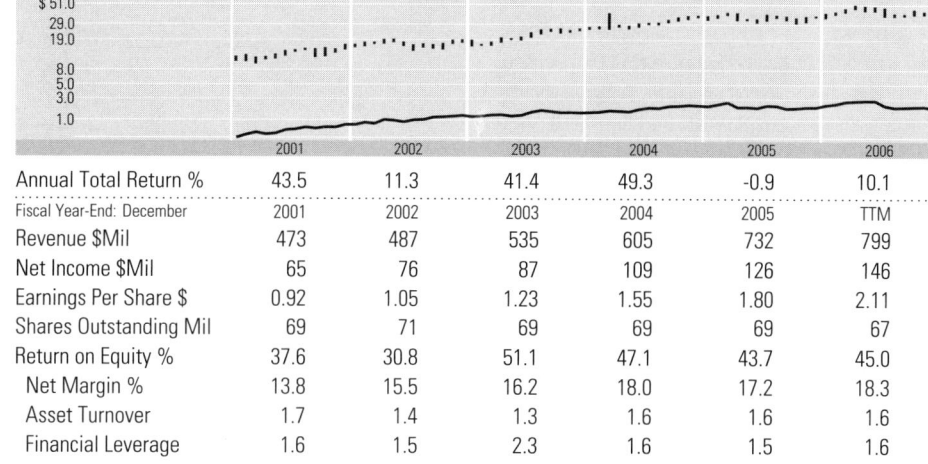

Price Volatility — Monthly Price High/Low — Relative Strength to S&P 500

Annual $Price High/Low	17.71 / 10.33	20.38 / 14.75	27.15 / 16.68	40.26 / 26.34	41.10 / 31.00	50.00 / 35.52
	2001	2002	2003	2004	2005	2006
Annual Total Return %	43.5	11.3	41.4	49.3	-0.9	10.1

Fiscal Year-End: December	2001	2002	2003	2004	2005	TTM
Revenue $Mil	473	487	535	605	732	799
Net Income $Mil	65	76	87	109	126	146
Earnings Per Share $	0.92	1.05	1.23	1.55	1.80	2.11
Shares Outstanding Mil	69	71	69	69	69	67
Return on Equity %	37.6	30.8	51.1	47.1	43.7	45.0
Net Margin %	13.8	15.5	16.2	18.0	17.2	18.3
Asset Turnover	1.7	1.4	1.3	1.6	1.6	1.6
Financial Leverage	1.6	1.5	2.3	1.6	1.5	1.6

Valuation Ratios	Stock	Rel to Industry	Rel to S&P 500
Price/Earnings	18.8	0.9	0.9
Price/Book	8.2	2.6	2.0
Price/Sales	3.3	2.1	1.1
Price/Cash Flow	16.7	0.9	1.1

Major Fund Holders	% of Fund Assets
Delaware Pooled Focus Smid-Cap Gr Eq	4.38
Ave Maria Opportunity	3.36
Mairs & Power Growth	3.17
Calvert Capital Accumulation A	3.03

Thesis By Matthew Warren, 12-14-06 Stock Price as of Analysis: $41.06

Graco makes equipment used to handle all kinds of sticky situations, from spraying pizza sauce in a food-processing plant to paint in an auto factory. This narrow-moat firm fiercely protects its technological advantage.

Users of viscous materials--professional painters, manufacturers, and quick-lube companies--are likely to use Graco equipment. The finishing touch provided by Graco equipment--furniture stain, for example--is highly visible to the end user, yet represents only a small portion of production costs. Graco maintains an impeccable record of precision performance, which facilitates premium pricing in this niche industry.

To maintain its cachet with demanding customers, Graco regularly reinvests 3%-4% of its revenue in research and development. The results speak for themselves. For example, Graco's paint-circulation equipment is used in 80% of worldwide auto production, a dominant position that allows the firm to capture industry growth around the globe. Regular product advancements stave off commoditization and drive replacement business from existing customers.

Because of the relatively small size of its markets, new entrants could never achieve sales figures that would justify the investment required to match Graco's capabilities. The larger threat comes from industry players like Illinois Tool Works, Ingersoll-Rand, and Nordson --all of which run somewhat similar businesses and would like to siphon off share. Graco's position elicits such envy because of its stellar returns: Operating margins continue to march beyond 25%. Aside from dominant market share and the resulting scale benefits, Graco controls costs by stressing lean manufacturing techniques and efficiency gains at the corporate office.

Also, this business quite naturally fits the razor-and-blade business model. Spraying abrasive fluids through a plastic gun creates constant wear and tear. Consumable parts and accessories, which make up 40% of total sales, contribute higher margins and help smooth out cyclical demand for the firm's products. For the customer, diligent maintenance ensures consistent performance and prevents costly waste of material. Though small in the grand scheme, Graco posts giant returns.

---

88 - 11th Avenue Northeast
Minneapolis, MN 55413   www.graco.com

Growth [B]	2002	2003	2004	2005
Revenue %	3.0	9.9	13.1	20.9
Earnings/Share %	13.8	17.5	26.0	16.1
Book Value/Share %	38.7	-29.1	36.7	25.0
Dividends/Share %	9.9	12.5	751.3	-72.2

Profitability [A+]	2003	2004	2005	TTM
Return on Assets %	21.8	29.2	28.2	28.8
Oper Cash Flow $Mil	110	123	153	160
- Cap Spending $Mil	16	19	21	20
= Free Cash Flow $Mil	94	104	133	140

Financial Health [A+]	2003	2004	2005	09-30-06
Long-term Debt $Mil	—	—	—	—
Total Equity $Mil	170	231	288	325
Debt/Equity Ratio	—	—	—	—

Data as of 12-29-06

Groupe Danone ADR DA

	Rating	Fair Value	Last Close	Consider Buy	Consider Sell	Yield %
	★★★	$33.00	$32.60	$25.40	$41.30	1.24

Company Profile

Danone is a global packaged food company domiciled in France. It produces fresh dairy products, bottled water, and cookies and crackers. Danone's portfolio of brands includes Danone/Dannon fresh dairy products, LU biscuits, Evian and Volvic bottled still water, and Wahaha and Aqua packaged water in China and Indonesia, respectively. Danone receives 62% of its sales from Europe, 17% from Asia, and the remainder from North and South America.

Management   Stewardship Grade [NA]

Franck Riboud has been chairman and CEO of Danone since 1996. He succeeded his father, Antoine Riboud, who over the course of 30 years transformed French glass manufacturer BSN into one of the largest packaged food companies in the world. During the past decade, Franck has been dismantling most of what his father built, focusing Danone on fresh dairy, biscuits, and water. He was an early proponent of shareholder value in a country that came late to the idea that companies should act in the best interest of their owners. That may have become irrelevant in 2005, though, when Danone became the subject of takeover rumors that had the French government up in arms and management looking for ways to protect itself from a hostile bid. We believe this sort of economic nationalism can only be detrimental to Danone and its shareholders as it deters possible bidders (depriving shareholders of potential gains) and raises the possibility that Danone could miss out on the next stage of global consolidation among the packaged food firms. Holders of the company's U.S.-traded ADRs have just one fifth of a share of the French company for each depository receipt in their portfolio and no voting rights.

17, Boulevard Haussmann   www.danone.fr
Paris, France 75009

Growth [NA]	2002	2003	2004	2005
Revenue %	-6.3	-3.1	-6.5	6.1
Earnings/Share %	873.2	-31.8	-44.4	227.9
Book Value/Share %	-14.4	-1.1	-3.0	25.5
Dividends/Share %	11.7	7.0	9.8	25.9

Profitability [NA]	2003	2004	2005	TTM
Return on Assets %	5.3	2.5	9.2	9.2
Oper Cash Flow $Mil	1,851	2,104	2,313	2,313
- Cap Spending $Mil	608	646	760	760
= Free Cash Flow $Mil	1,243	1,458	1,553	1,553

Financial Health [NA]	2003	2004	2005	12-31-05
Long-term Debt $Mil	5,214	9,147	6,776	6,776
Total Equity $Mil	6,030	6,173	6,692	6,692
Debt/Equity Ratio	0.9	1.5	1.0	1.0

Industry	Business Risk	Moat Size	Investment Style	Sector
Food Mfg.	Average	Narrow	Large Growth	Consumer Goods

Competition	Market Cap $Mil	12 Mo Trailing Sales $Mil	Price/Cash Flow	Return On Assets%	Debt/Equity	Total Return% 1 Yr	3 Yr
Groupe Danone ADR	43,070	16,309	18.6	9.2	1.0	57.3	28.9
Nestle SA ADR	138,417	73,660	16.8	8.8	—	20.9	14.7
Kraft Foods	58,683	34,648	13.9	5.5	0.2	30.5	6.5

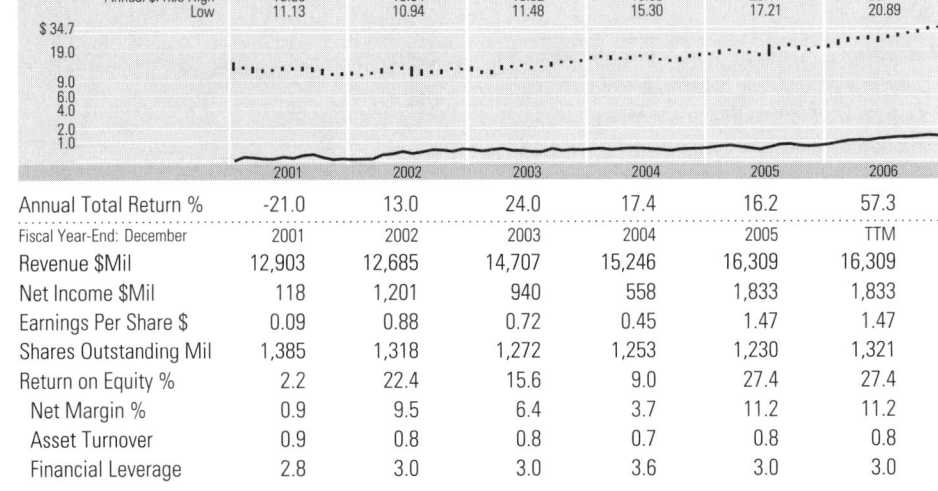

Annual $Price High	15.50	13.94	16.32	18.58	23.17	33.74
Low	11.13	10.94	11.48	15.30	17.21	20.89
	2001	2002	2003	2004	2005	2006
Annual Total Return %	-21.0	13.0	24.0	17.4	16.2	57.3
Fiscal Year-End: December	2001	2002	2003	2004	2005	TTM
Revenue $Mil	12,903	12,685	14,707	15,246	16,309	16,309
Net Income $Mil	118	1,201	940	558	1,833	1,833
Earnings Per Share $	0.09	0.88	0.72	0.45	1.47	1.47
Shares Outstanding Mil	1,385	1,318	1,272	1,253	1,230	1,321
Return on Equity %	2.2	22.4	15.6	9.0	27.4	27.4
Net Margin %	0.9	9.5	6.4	3.7	11.2	11.2
Asset Turnover	0.9	0.8	0.8	0.7	0.8	0.8
Financial Leverage	2.8	3.0	3.0	3.6	3.0	3.0

Valuation Ratios	Stock	Rel to Industry	Rel to S&P 500
Price/Earnings	22.2	1.0	1.1
Price/Book	6.4	1.4	1.6
Price/Sales	2.6	1.5	0.9
Price/Cash Flow	18.6	1.2	1.3

Major Fund Holders	% of Fund Assets
Dreyfus Premier Worldwide Growth A	4.03
Dean Large Cap Value A	2.37
Hallmark International Equity R	1.92
Navellier International Growth A	1.91

Thesis By Greggory Warren, CFA, 12-05-06 Stock Price as of Analysis: $32.95

Despite receiving a majority of its sales and operating profits from slower-growing economies in Europe and North America, Danone has found a formula for success in the highly competitive packaged food market. By focusing on just three key categories--fresh dairy, bottled water, and cookies and crackers--Danone has been able to generate above-average sales growth through increased product innovation and expansion into emerging and developing markets.

Danone is a powerhouse in the categories where it competes. It is the largest global producer of yogurt, the second-largest seller of bottled water by dollar revenue, and the second-largest producer of cookies and crackers in the world. With strong brands like Danone/Dannon, Evian, and LU, the firm has built a fairly solid moat around its operations. We believe that the only thing keeping Danone from earning a wide moat is the lack of consistency in its profitability and free cash flow generation over the years. While much of this was due to restructuring efforts, we would prefer to see Danone's operating margins at the same level as its two closest competitors, Kraft Foods and General Mills.

Danone is well on its way toward reaching that goal, having generated 6.0% annual top-line growth during the past two years, as well as improving its operating margins from 12.5% to 13.6%. New product introductions have been the key driver of the sales growth and profitability improvement, especially in the firm's more mature markets in Europe and North America. The successful launch of probiotic yogurt brands Activia and Actimel in these markets has allowed Danone to post double-digit sales gains in its fresh dairy operating segment over the past two years.

In bottled water, Danone has taken full advantage of its first-mover advantage in China and Indonesia, two of Asia's three largest emerging market economies. Having locked up key distribution assets in these critical markets, Danone has emerged as the leading provider of bottled water in the region. While cookies and crackers has been a lackluster category for Danone the past couple of years, sales growth actually turned positive in 2006, with improvements in the company's European markets helping lift the segment's operating margins to more normal levels.

With a focus on just three key categories, we believe Danone has the right strategy to succeed longer term, and we consider it to be one of the best-positioned firms in the packaged food industry.

H & R Block HRB

Data as of 12-29-06

Rating	Fair Value	Last Close	Consider Buy	Consider Sell	Yield %
★★★	$25.00	$23.04	$15.90	$30.20	2.26

Company Profile
H&R Block is best known as the leader in paid tax preparation. It also provides financial advisory and brokerage services as well as mortgage products and services. Its business services segment provides payroll and benefit administration and retirement plan administration services to middle-market companies. Tax operations make up about half of the firm's revenue, while the mortgage segment accounts just over one fourth. Block received a bank charter in May 2006.

Management   Stewardship Grade [C]
Mark Ernst has been CEO since 2001. He has been behind the vision of H&R Block as a diversified financial services provider--a vision about which we remain skeptical, given the poor cross-selling between tax services and the investment services business, which continues to lose money. Block's corporate stewardship is average, in our opinion. The firm's accounting is complex, and it has undergone some restatements. A staggered board and short-term incentive compensation based on various metrics (revenue, diluted earnings per share, pretax earnings, and business-unit-specific metrics) could lead to more short-term maneuvering and less value for long-term shareholders. The company also has a shareholder-rights plan, which could be unfavorable to shareholders in the event of a takeover. We would prefer the company to split the chairman and CEO roles. We look favorably on the reduction of Enrst's 2006 annual bonus award to $355,696 (from $394,292 in 2005 and $865,477 in 2004) under the executive performance plan, as well as the fact that he declined such an award. We thought this was appropriate given the firm's mediocre results in 2006.

4400 Main Street   www.hrblock.com
Kansas City, MO 64111

Growth [C]	2003	2004	2005	2006
Revenue %	12.7	13.9	4.1	10.2
Earnings/Share %	11.1	47.7	-3.6	-20.5
Book Value/Share %	-57.3	238.2	10.1	11.4
Dividends/Share %	11.1	11.4	10.3	12.8

Profitability [A-]	2004	2005	2006	TTM
Return on Assets %	13.3	11.3	8.2	5.1
Oper Cash Flow $Mil	852	514	586	100
- Cap Spending $Mil	124	209	251	268
= Free Cash Flow $Mil	729	304	335	-167

Financial Health [B]	2004	2005	2006	07-31-06
Long-term Debt $Mil	546	923	418	412
Total Equity $Mil	1,897	1,949	2,148	1,629
Debt/Equity Ratio	0.3	0.5	0.2	0.3

Industry	Business Risk	Moat Size	Investment Style	Sector
Personal Svcs.	Above Avg	Wide	Mid Core	Consumer Services

Competition
	Market Cap $Mil	12 Mo Trailing Sales $Mil	Price/Cash Flow	Return On Assets%	Debt/Equity	Total Return% 1 Yr	3 Yr
H & R Block	7,426	4,757	74.1	5.1	0.3	-4.0	-4.3
American Express	73,094	26,507	—	2.9	—	19.1	14.2
Intuit	10,637	2,400	13.0	14.2	0.0	14.5	5.3

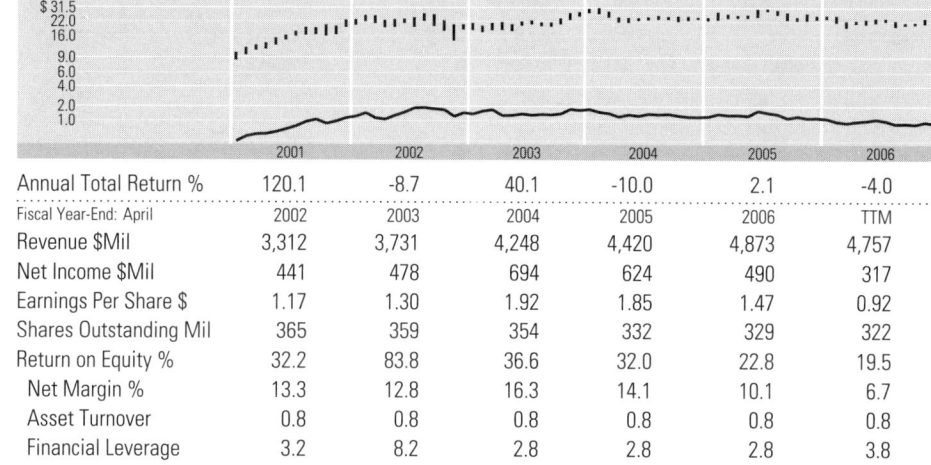

Annual Total Return %	120.1	-8.7	40.1	-10.0	2.1	-4.0
Fiscal Year-End: April	2002	2003	2004	2005	2006	TTM
Revenue $Mil	3,312	3,731	4,248	4,420	4,873	4,757
Net Income $Mil	441	478	694	624	490	317
Earnings Per Share $	1.17	1.30	1.92	1.85	1.47	0.92
Shares Outstanding Mil	365	359	354	332	329	322
Return on Equity %	32.2	83.8	36.6	32.0	22.8	19.5
Net Margin %	13.3	12.8	16.3	14.1	10.1	6.7
Asset Turnover	0.8	0.8	0.8	0.8	0.8	0.8
Financial Leverage	3.2	8.2	2.8	2.8	2.8	3.8

Valuation Ratios	Stock	Rel to Industry	Rel to S&P 500
Price/Earnings	25.0	1.0	1.2
Price/Book	4.6	1.2	1.1
Price/Sales	1.6	0.7	0.6
Price/Cash Flow	74.1	2.5	5.1

Major Fund Holders	% of Fund Assets
Oakmark Select I	5.71
Ariel Focus	5.28
T. Rowe Price Financial Services	4.27
SunAmerica Focused Dividend Strat C	3.24

Thesis By Kristan Rowland, 11-22-06 Stock Price as of Analysis: $24.01

H&R Block is the leader in the paid tax-preparation business. We base our wide-moat rating on this business, given its well-known brand, dominant market position, and unmatched scale. In fiscal 2006, it served roughly 19.5 million clients in the United States and represented roughly 15.7% of the Internal Revenue Service's estimate of total individual tax returns filed, making it the industry leader.

Despite this industry-leading position, however, tax client growth has been disappointing over the past several years. Block's volume of tax returns prepared has generally stagnated as a result of competition from traditional independent tax preparers, tough rivals like Jackson Hewitt and Liberty Tax, free online filing, and digital tax products from Intuit. Even though growth in Block's company and franchise-owned locations was 12.6% and 9% in 2005 and 2006, respectively, client growth in those service mediums was flat in 2005 and down 2% in 2006. The strategy of attracting new clients does not seem to be working. Gains in digital tax and international helped Block eke out a 2.5% increase in its client base in 2006, but the gains in digital tax were largely due to discounting.

Block's mortgage services segment has seen better days, and we think the no-moat business will continue to face challenges. This is Block's second-largest business, accounting for just over one fourth of its revenue and more than one third of its profit. The majority of the loans it originates, services, securitizes, and sells are subprime (higher credit risk). This market attracted loads of mortgage lenders because of its attractive profits, and margins have shrunk as a result of hefty competition and an increased cost of funds caused by higher interest rates. Rising rates are a risk to mortgage origination growth, as people may decide not to purchase real estate. Also, Block could also face higher delinquencies on the loans it retains as rates increase, which could pressure margins.

Block acquired Olde Discount Corporation as part of its strategy to become a one-stop financial shop, but this business continues to lose money. We think the company's broad financial services strategy is flawed, and we don't think cross-selling opportunities will garner much fruit. Account growth was 6% in 2006, only because of the Express IRA product. The number of accounts (assuming an account equals one client) represents just 4% of the firm's U.S. tax clients, even after six years.

H.J. Heinz HNZ

Data as of 12-29-06

Rating	Fair Value	Last Close	Consider Buy	Consider Sell	Yield %
★★	$40.00	$45.01	$30.80	$50.10	3.00

Company Profile

Heinz is a global producer and marketer of packaged foods. Its principal products include ketchup, condiments and sauces, frozen foods, soups, baby food, beans, and tuna. The Heinz brand can be found on everything from ketchup to baked beans and baby food. Other well-known brands include Ore-Ida (french fries) and Classico (pasta sauce). With operations in Europe, Latin America, and the Asia-Pacific region, Heinz receives close to 60% of its sales from outside the U.S.

Management   Stewardship Grade [C]

Bill Johnson has been president and CEO of Heinz since April 1998. He became chairman in September 2000. As only the sixth CEO in Heinz's 133-year history, Johnson has certainly left his mark. In fiscal 1998, the company generated $9.2 billion in sales and $1.5 billion in operating profits. Heinz finished fiscal 2006 with $8.6 billion in sales and $1.0 billion in operating profits. Despite having sold more than 25% of the company during that time, which helped to improve the mix of Heinz's product portfolio longer term, management came under assault in 2006 from activist investor Nelson Peltz, who faulted management for the poor performance of the company's stock during the past eight years. Having gained two seats on the Heinz board, Peltz believes he can convince management to adopt his plans for improving shareholder returns, which include cutting costs, leveraging up the balance sheet, and repurchasing shares. While we don't blame investors for their impatience with the current management team, we believe that some of Peltz's recommendation would do significant damage to the company longer term. We remain concerned about the presence of the activist investor on the board, believing that it may cause more near-term disruption than good for Heinz and its shareholders.

600 Grant Street   www.heinz.com
Pittsburgh, PA 15219

Growth [C+]	2003	2004	2005	2006
Revenue %	7.5	0.8	6.3	6.7
Earnings/Share %	—	NMF	-6.2	-11.3
Book Value/Share %	—	NMF	37.8	-18.6
Dividends/Share %	-7.6	-27.3	5.6	5.3

Profitability [B+]	2004	2005	2006	TTM
Return on Assets %	8.1	7.1	6.6	6.6
Oper Cash Flow $Mil	1,249	1,161	1,075	946
- Cap Spending $Mil	232	241	231	221
= Free Cash Flow $Mil	1,017	920	844	725

Financial Health [B]	2004	2005	2006	10-31-06
Long-term Debt $Mil	—	4,122	4,357	4,508
Total Equity $Mil	1,894	2,602	2,049	2,234
Debt/Equity Ratio	—	1.6	2.1	2.0

Industry	Business Risk	Moat Size	Investment Style	Sector
Food Mfg.	Average	Narrow	Large Value	Consumer Goods

Competition	Market Cap $Mil	12 Mo Trailing Sales $Mil	Price/Cash Flow	Return On Assets%	Debt/Equity	Total Return% 1 Yr	3 Yr
H.J. Heinz	14,830	8,878	15.7	6.6	2.0	37.9	11.3
Nestle SA ADR	138,417	73,660	16.8	8.8	—	20.9	14.7
Kraft Foods	58,683	34,648	13.9	5.5	0.2	30.5	6.5

Price Volatility | Monthly Price High/Low   — Relative Strength to S&P 500

Annual $Price High/Low	44.22/34.04	40.11/27.31	36.82/28.90	40.61/34.53	39.13/33.64	46.75/33.42
	2001	2002	2003	2004	2005	2006
Annual Total Return %	-9.6	-9.2	14.5	10.3	-10.6	37.9

Fiscal Year-End: April	2002	2003	2004	2005	2006	TTM
Revenue $Mil	7,041	7,567	7,626	8,103	8,643	8,878
Net Income $Mil	—	—	804	753	646	670
Earnings Per Share $	—	—	2.27	2.13	1.89	2.00
Shares Outstanding Mil	—	—	351	350	340	329
Return on Equity %	—	—	42.5	28.9	31.5	30.0
Net Margin %	—	—	10.5	9.3	7.5	7.5
Asset Turnover	0.7	0.8	0.8	0.8	0.9	0.9
Financial Leverage	6.0	7.7	5.2	4.1	4.8	4.6

Valuation Ratios	Stock	Rel to Industry	Rel to S&P 500
Price/Earnings	28.7	1.3	1.4
Price/Book	6.6	1.5	1.6
Price/Sales	1.7	1.0	0.6
Price/Cash Flow	15.7	1.0	1.1

Major Fund Holders	% of Fund Assets
Calvert Mid Cap Value A	3.22
Delaware Large Cap Value A	2.96
Delaware Value A	2.96
Gabelli Woodland Sm Cp Value AAA	2.75

Thesis By Greggory Warren, CFA, 11-17-06 Stock Price as of Analysis: $43.94

H.J. Heinz is the undisputed leader of the ketchup category worldwide. The company has dominant market share in just about every country where it competes. The strength of the Heinz brand has allowed the firm to expand its iconic trademark beyond ketchup into other food categories. From ketchup to baked beans to baby food, the Heinz brand generates more than $3 billion in global sales each year.

If its namesake brand were the only thing the company sold, Heinz would be a wide-moat firm. But the company has more than 70 other brands in its portfolio, most of which offer no significant competitive advantage. Built up through decades of acquisitions, these products have struggled to play a supporting role for the company. While Heinz has been diligent about identifying and selling noncore brands and product lines, the effort has dragged down operating results and shareholder returns over much of the past eight years.

This opened the door for activist investor Nelson Peltz, who managed to gain two seats on the company's board of directors in 2006 following an expensive proxy fight with Heinz's management team. Peltz believes that the company's poor returns are the result of a faulty business strategy, and that significant cuts in the firm's overhead, a leveraging up of the balance sheet, and significant share repurchases will prove to be beneficial to shareholders. He also questions the firm's investments in developing and emerging markets, which he believes are a distraction from management's focus on its core markets in Europe and North America.

While some of the blame for Heinz's poor performance can be placed with management, the real culprit has been the rapidly changing nature of the packaged food industry over the past eight years. Wal-Mart has become a major player in the grocery business, and retail consolidation has stripped the packaged food firms of most of their pricing power. Ultimately, we don't believe that the two seats Peltz gained on the company's board will do much to change these dynamics, and we're concerned that his presence may cause more near-term disruption than good.

Longer term, we expect Heinz will continue to focus on expanding sales in its core categories and markets, and we believe that its presence in developing and emerging markets--like Russia, India, China, and Indonesia--will be critical to the growth of the firm.

Data as of 12-29-06

Halliburton HAL

	Rating	Fair Value	Last Close	Consider Buy	Consider Sell	Yield %
	★	$23.00	$31.05	$17.70	$28.80	0.97

Company Profile

Houston-based Halliburton operates in the energy and construction industries. Its energy services group makes drilling equipment and provides maintenance, testing, and data-processing services for oil and gas companies. Halliburton's KBR unit provides engineering, design, and construction services for projects like power and chemical plants. Halliburton will sell a small portion of KBR in an IPO and spin off its remaining ownership in early 2007.

Management — Stewardship Grade [C]

David Lesar became CEO and chairman after current U.S. Vice President Dick Cheney, who had been CEO for five years, resigned to run for office in 2000. Although he has sold more than 2 million shares in the past 12 months, we were pleased to see that Lesar still owns 1.7 million shares, a sizable stake. We commend the current management team for its insistence on shedding the KBR unit. Although KBR generates a lot of revenue, the division never made much money for Halliburton and was a public relations nightmare. We hope the top brass uses the KBR proceeds to reinvest in its world-class services business. Lingering issues related to the company's operations in Iran and Nigeria and a recently settled SEC investigation into the firm's accounting practices leave a bad taste in our mouth. However, we did increase our Stewardship Grade to fair from poor as a result of Lesar's excellent job articulating Halliburton's ambitious growth initiatives. He has surrounded himself with very capable lieutenants, further deepening an already talented executive bench.

5 Houston Center 1401 McKinney, Suite 2400
Houston, TX 77010   www.halliburton.com

Growth [D]	2002	2003	2004	2005
Revenue %	-3.6	29.4	25.8	2.6
Earnings/Share %	NMF	NMF	NMF	NMF
Book Value/Share %	-25.4	-29.1	52.7	37.6
Dividends/Share %	0.0	0.0	0.0	0.0

Profitability [C-]	2003	2004	2005	TTM
Return on Assets %	-5.3	-6.2	15.7	17.5
Oper Cash Flow $Mil	-775	928	701	3,691
- Cap Spending $Mil	515	575	651	796
= Free Cash Flow $Mil	-1,290	353	50	2,895

Financial Health [B+]	2003	2004	2005	09-30-06
Long-term Debt $Mil	—	3,593	2,813	2,745
Total Equity $Mil	2,547	3,932	6,372	7,089
Debt/Equity Ratio	—	0.9	0.4	0.4

Industry	Business Risk	Moat Size	Investment Style	Sector
Oil/Gas Svcs.	Average	Narrow	Large Growth	Energy

Competition	Market Cap $Mil	12 Mo Trailing Sales $Mil	Price/Cash Flow	Return On Assets %	Debt/ Equity	Total Return% 1 Yr	3 Yr
Halliburton	31,221	22,886	8.5	17.5	0.4	1.1	35.2
Schlumberger	74,416	17,904	17.6	15.6	0.4	31.1	33.6
Baker Hughes	23,946	8,564	39.8	26.8	0.2	23.7	34.2

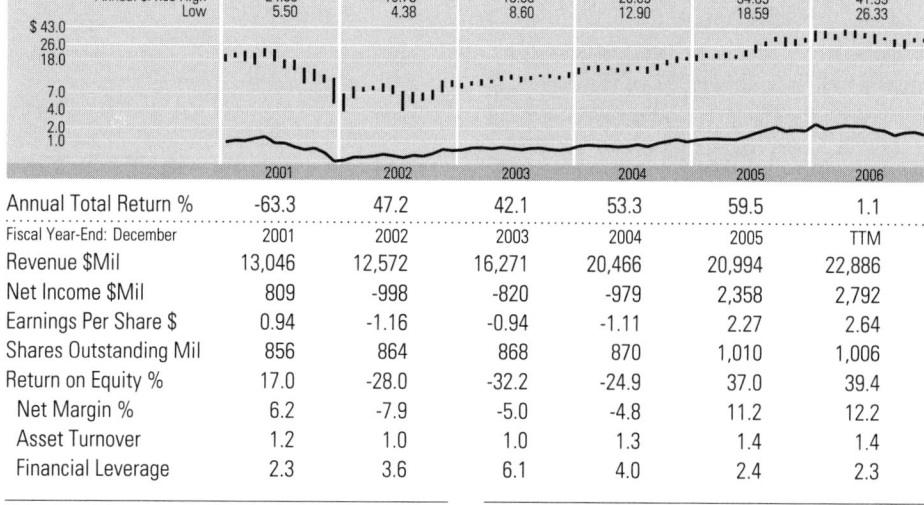

Price Volatility — Monthly Price High/Low — Relative Strength to S&P 500

	2001	2002	2003	2004	2005	2006
Annual $Price High	24.63	10.73	13.60	20.85	34.89	41.99
Low	5.50	4.38	8.60	12.90	18.59	26.33
Annual Total Return %	-63.3	47.2	42.1	53.3	59.5	1.1
Fiscal Year-End: December	2001	2002	2003	2004	2005	TTM
Revenue $Mil	13,046	12,572	16,271	20,466	20,994	22,886
Net Income $Mil	809	-998	-820	-979	2,358	2,792
Earnings Per Share $	0.94	-1.16	-0.94	-1.11	2.27	2.64
Shares Outstanding Mil	856	864	868	870	1,010	1,006
Return on Equity %	17.0	-28.0	-32.2	-24.9	37.0	39.4
Net Margin %	6.2	-7.9	-5.0	-4.8	11.2	12.2
Asset Turnover	1.2	1.0	1.0	1.3	1.4	1.4
Financial Leverage	2.3	3.6	6.1	4.0	2.4	2.3

Valuation Ratios	Stock	Rel to Industry	Rel to S&P 500
Price/Earnings	12.0	0.7	0.6
Price/Book	4.4	0.6	1.1
Price/Sales	1.4	0.5	0.5
Price/Cash Flow	8.5	0.5	0.6

Major Fund Holders	% of Fund Assets
Rydex Energy Services Inv	6.57
Fidelity Select Energy	6.08
Fidelity Select Industrial Equipment	5.78
Fidelity Select Energy Service	5.56

Thesis By Matt Moran, CFA, 11-06-06 Stock Price as of Analysis: $32.52

Halliburton's oil services business is rock-solid, but it comes with a lot of baggage. Fortunately for investors, the firm has decided to shed its low-margin, high-profile KBR segment.

Halliburton's oil services division is benefiting from the rekindled love affair between global energy companies and North American natural gas. Technological advances, along with soaring natural-gas prices, have encouraged operators to reconsider searching for North American natural gas trapped in unconventional places such as coal, tight sandstone, and shale. Although natural-gas prices have weakened recently, the majority of Halliburton's customers are established operators committed to unconventional projects and confident of the long-term appeal of natural-gas. Armed with the industry's most advanced pressure pumping equipment, Halliburton has had little trouble raising prices in the past few years as operators desperately tried to get their gas to market.

KBR is responsible for roughly half of Halliburton's revenue, but adds almost nothing to the bottom line. KBR is a heavy hitter in global engineering and construction (its energy and chemical business) and is also a leading government contractor (its government and infrastructure business). According to the firm, the E&C segment is responsible for constructing nearly half of the world's operating liquefied natural-gas production capacity over the past 30 years and is likely to emerge as a huge winner in the global energy infrastructure buildout. The G&I business, as one of the world's largest government contractors, competes for major defense and civil infrastructure projects around the globe. Although KBR's units have a bright outlook for top-line growth, these businesses just don't make much money.

While KBR's operating margins peak below 5%, Halliburton's oil services division posts margins topping 25%. The oil services division has had no trouble raising prices, and we think topnotch technology will allow Halliburton to maintain pricing power in most operating environments. Oil and gas production companies have accumulated a lot of cash, thanks to high commodity prices, and we're confident that much of that money will find its way to oil services firms over the next few years.

We are relieved Halliburton has finally decided to discard KBR, and we are convinced the oil services division remains stronger than ever. Freed from its KBR shackles, Halliburton should thrive as a technological leader in the oil patch.

Hansen Natural HANS

Data as of 12-29-06

	Rating	Fair Value	Last Close	Consider Buy	Consider Sell	Yield %
	★★★★	$46.00	$33.68	$29.30	$55.50	0.00

Industry	Business Risk	Moat Size	Investment Style	Sector
Beverage Mfg.	Above Avg	Narrow	Mid Growth	Consumer Goods

Company Profile

Hansen develops, markets, sells, and, on a very limited scale, distributes "alternative" beverages including energy drinks under the Monster Energy, Lost, Rumba, and Joker Mad Energy brands; natural sodas under the Hansen's and Blue Sky brands; and a variety of noncarbonated beverages including juices and smoothies. Energy drinks have grown explosively since Monster's 2002 introduction and accounted for 77% of revenue and almost 95% of operating income in 2005.

Management   Stewardship Grade [A]

Rodney Sacks serves as both CEO and chairman of the board, roles we prefer to see separated. Sacks has been CEO since 1990 and chairman since 1992. Sacks received a salary of $257,250 in 2005, which we consider reasonable. Hilton Schlosberg serves as CFO and vice chairman. An investor group led by Sacks purchased Hansen in 1992, four years after the firm filed for bankruptcy. Primarily a purveyor of juices and natural sodas until 1997, when it first dabbled with energy drinks, the company developed a runaway hit with the 2002 introduction of Monster Energy. Option grants have been highly skewed to top management, mostly Sacks and Schlosberg, but shareholders cannot be anything but ecstatic with the job management has done creating value since the introduction of Monster, and their riches have been well earned. Sacks claims beneficial ownership of about 6% of the company including exercisable options and shares held in trusts, and disclaims beneficial ownership of another 15% that is held in trusts where he serves as general partner along with Schlosberg, who also claims beneficial ownership of about 6%. Hansen recently received a letter from the SEC regarding its stock option grants, which does not itself indicate a violation, though we will monitor the situation carefully.

1010 Railroad Street
Corona, CA 92882
www.hansens.com

Growth [A+]	2002	2003	2004	2005
Revenue %	14.1	19.9	63.4	93.5
Earnings/Share %	3.7	89.5	212.5	201.2
Book Value/Share %	15.8	19.6	51.9	109.6
Dividends/Share %	NMF	NMF	NMF	NMF

Profitability [A+]	2003	2004	2005	TTM
Return on Assets %	12.4	24.9	38.3	33.1
Oper Cash Flow $Mil	5	20	55	67
- Cap Spending $Mil	2	1	2	3
= Free Cash Flow $Mil	4	19	53	64

Financial Health [A]	2003	2004	2005	06-30-06
Long-term Debt $Mil	0	0	0	0
Total Equity $Mil	35	59	126	198
Debt/Equity Ratio	0.0	0.0	0.0	0.0

Competition

	Market Cap $Mil	12 Mo Trailing Sales $Mil	Price/Cash Flow	Return On Assets%	Debt/Equity	Total Return% 1 Yr	3 Yr
Hansen Natural	3,060	479	46.0	33.1	0.0	70.9	219.3
Nestle SA ADR	138,417	73,660	16.8	8.8	—	20.9	14.7
Coca-Cola	113,088	23,707	19.6	16.8	0.1	23.1	1.1

Price Volatility

| Monthly Price High/Low — Relative Strength to S&P 500

Annual $Price High/Low	0.55/0.32	0.58/0.38	1.18/0.40	4.60/0.95	22.07/4.05	52.72/19.40
	2001	2002	2003	2004	2005	2006
Annual Total Return %	8.2	0.6	99.4	332.2	332.9	70.9

Fiscal Year-End: December

	2001	2002	2003	2004	2005	TTM
Revenue $Mil	81	92	110	180	349	479
Net Income $Mil	3	3	6	20	63	88
Earnings Per Share $	0.04	0.04	0.07	0.22	0.65	0.90
Shares Outstanding Mil	79	80	81	85	88	91
Return on Equity %	11.9	10.7	16.9	34.8	50.0	44.5
Net Margin %	3.7	3.3	5.4	11.3	18.0	18.4
Asset Turnover	2.1	2.3	2.3	2.2	2.1	1.8
Financial Leverage	1.5	1.4	1.4	1.4	1.3	1.3

Valuation Ratios	Stock	Rel to Industry	Rel to S&P 500
Price/Earnings	37.5	1.7	1.8
Price/Book	15.5	2.7	3.8
Price/Sales	6.4	1.9	2.2
Price/Cash Flow	46.0	2.6	3.2

Major Fund Holders	% of Fund Assets
CGM Capital Development	5.11
Navellier Top 20 A	4.15
Phoenix Small-Cap Growth A	3.74
Ashport Small/Mid Cap C	3.34

Thesis By Matthew Reilly, 11-30-06 Stock Price as of Analysis: $28.13

From its introduction in April 2002, Hansen's Monster has grown to be the second-largest energy drink brand in American behind Red Bull. The brand is taking share on an almost daily basis in the energy category, an impressive feat considering that the category is growing 60%-80% annually because of a hip category image, shrewd marketing, and perceived functionality. The category is also growing rapidly because it is relatively small, with our best estimate putting the domestic retail market around $3 billion in 2005.

Hansen has a beautiful business model. It does not make any of its products, instead outsourcing production to third-party manufacturers. This serves to keep capital requirements low and returns on invested capital at astronomical levels--we estimate 2005 returns at 125%, more than doubling the already-impressive result from 2004. With such strong returns and a powerful brand in Monster, we think that Hansen's has quickly built an economic moat.

We think that Hansen's moat is narrow because the company is a relative gnat in a beverage world dominated by Coke and PepsiCo, which are now aggressively promoting their own brands in the high-margin energy category. If energy drinks are considered carbonated soft drinks--and the blurring of categorical lines is certainly a recurring theme--then Hansen's share of the American market is well under 1%. With this lack of scale and no dedicated bottling and distribution base such as that enjoyed by larger players, gaining distribution for its products has been the largest issue the company has faced. But as Monster has continued to grow in popularity, Hansen has been able to trade up its distributor base, recently signing a deal with Anheuser-Busch to leverage its powerful distributor base and expanding distribution into Mexico with Cadbury Bebidas.

Management has indicated that it intends to use the excess cash it has generated over the past few years, or possibly stock, to acquire brands it can funnel through its hard-earned distribution network. This seems a reasonable plan to us; now that Hansen's distributor relationships are in place and seem to be improving every day, it makes sense to leverage them as much as possible, especially with the long-term prospects for the energy drink market largely unknown. Management must choose its investments very carefully, however. We think that Hansen has enough cash to contemplate a dividend when the dust starts to settle but, for now, it should concentrate on continuing its phenomenal growth.

Data as of 12-29-06

Harley-Davidson HOG

	Rating	Fair Value	Last Close	Consider Buy	Consider Sell	Yield %
	★★★	$64.00	$70.47	$49.40	$80.20	1.15

Company Profile

Harley-Davidson manufactures motorcycles, parts, and accessories. Its motorcycles are powered by V-twin engines ranging from 883 to 1,584 cubic centimeters of displacement. It markets motorcycles under distinct product families including Softail, Sportster, Dyna, Touring and VRSC, as well as the Buell brand. It also sells Harley-Davidson branded motorcycle accessories and clothing. The Harley-Davidson Financial Services subsidiary offers financing for customers and dealers.

Management   Stewardship Grade [B]

2006 marks the first full year of leadership under James Ziemer--a 33-year veteran--who was promoted to CEO from CFO, a position he held for 10 years. He replaced Jeffrey Bleustein, who had been with Harley-Davidson for nearly 30 years. Harley's management team once championed a strategy of restricting supply to maintain pricing, brand cachet, and manufacturing capacity utilization, which resulted in outstanding financial performance since the buyout. Supply and demand have now come into balance, necessitating more focus on marketing and design to fit the niches of different customers. Recently, management has become more aggressive in returning cash to shareholders, buying back $2.5 billion in stock and increasing the dividend over 300% since 2003. Management has been astute in allocating capital to share repurchases when the market has undervalued the company in the past, and it could continue to add value if it can duplicate this feat in the future. Executives and directors own less than 1.5% of the company's outstanding shares.

3700 West Juneau Avenue   www.harley-davidson.com
Milwaukee, WI 53208

Growth [B]	2002	2003	2004	2005
Revenue %	19.9	14.0	8.5	6.6
Earnings/Share %	32.9	31.6	20.0	13.7
Book Value/Share %	27.4	32.9	11.7	1.0
Dividends/Share %	17.4	44.4	107.7	54.3

Profitability [A+]	2003	2004	2005	TTM
Return on Assets %	15.5	16.2	18.3	20.3
Oper Cash Flow $Mil	663	832	961	1,060
- Cap Spending $Mil	227	214	198	214
= Free Cash Flow $Mil	435	619	762	846

Financial Health [A+]	2003	2004	2005	09-30-06
Long-term Debt $Mil	—	—	—	—
Total Equity $Mil	2,958	3,218	3,084	2,846
Debt/Equity Ratio	—	—	—	—

	Industry	Business Risk	Moat Size	Investment Style	Sector
	Recreation	Average	Wide	Large Growth	Consumer Goods

Competition

	Market Cap $Mil	12 Mo Trailing Sales $Mil	Price/Cash Flow	Return On Assets%	Debt/ Equity	Total Return% 1 Yr	3 Yr
Harley-Davidson	18,261	6,008	17.2	20.3	—	38.8	15.6
Honda Motor ADR	72,206	87,921	14.1	5.9	0.5	39.2	22.1
Ducati Motor Holding SpA	190	402	3.6	-9.4	1.1	35.5	-4.6

Price Volatility

Annual $Price High	55.98	57.25	52.50	63.75	62.49	75.87
Low	32.00	42.69	35.50	45.20	44.40	47.86
	2001	2002	2003	2004	2005	2006
Annual Total Return %	37.0	-14.7	3.3	28.7	-14.2	38.8

Fiscal Year-End: December

	2001	2002	2003	2004	2005	TTM
Revenue $Mil	3,588	4,302	4,904	5,320	5,674	6,008
Net Income $Mil	438	580	761	890	960	1,021
Earnings Per Share $	1.43	1.90	2.50	3.00	3.41	3.80
Shares Outstanding Mil	302	302	302	295	281	259
Return on Equity %	24.9	26.0	25.7	27.6	31.1	35.9
Net Margin %	12.2	13.5	15.5	16.7	16.9	17.0
Asset Turnover	1.2	1.1	1.0	1.0	1.1	1.2
Financial Leverage	1.8	1.7	1.7	1.7	1.7	1.8

Valuation Ratios	Stock	Rel to Industry	Rel to S&P 500
Price/Earnings	18.5	0.9	0.9
Price/Book	6.4	1.2	1.6
Price/Sales	3.0	1.0	1.0
Price/Cash Flow	17.2	1.3	1.2

Major Fund Holders	% of Fund Assets
Blue Chip Investor	6.20
Clipper	5.52
Oak Value	5.46
Van Kampen American Franchise A	4.35

Thesis By Marisa E. Thompson, 10-23-06 Stock Price as of Analysis: $68.56

Harley-Davidson's business model has dream-like qualities--a wide-moat brand with returns on invested capital that exceed 30% per year. However, Harley-Davidson's core demographic is aging, and the company must depend more on growth from abroad.

Harley-Davidson posts stellar returns on invested capital thanks to its brand image and the economics of motorcycle manufacturing. With each bike, Harley-Davidson sells an image crowning the free-riding lifestyle. Few other firms can claim that their logo is tattooed on the bodies of loyal admirers. This image explains why the company can sell their bikes for an average 10% premium to foreign brands. In order to churn out these motorbikes, the company does not need to make huge capital investments, and the cost of labor and materials is only a fraction of the wholesale price.

The business model is solid and management is executing well, but growth in Harley-Davidson's core demographic has begun to slow. The company targets consumers aged 35-65, but the core Harley riders reside in the 35-50 age group. After riding the wave of demand from affluent baby boomers, this tailwind is diminishing. Already, sales growth has slowed from 18% (on average) during 1998-2003 to less than 8% over the past three years.

Since domestic sales growth is slowing, the company must increasingly rely on international sales. Management has revamped its model lineup and distribution to meet the needs of the more performance-oriented European customer. In addition, the company just authorized a new Harley-Davidson dealership in China. Already efforts are paying off now that 22% of units sold are exported internationally compared with 18% a few years ago.

To address changing demographics, the firm is targeting customers more precisely. Harley has added many specialized bikes to its lineup, bringing to 38 the number of models offered, with plans for additional introductions. Catering to older riders, the firm has upgraded its touring line and has shifted its production mix to these more stable, comfortable bikes capable of long-distance travel. To attract the next generation of young riders, Harley created the V-Rod and Street Rod series. Also, the firm continues to upgrade engines and features--the latest upgrade made electronic fuel injection standard on all models--while holding price increases to less than 2%.

These efforts to keep sales and profits on track require more capital, and Harley likely must reinvest more to weather the generational storm.

Data as of 12-29-06

Harrah's Entertainment HET

	Rating	Fair Value	Last Close	Consider Buy	Consider Sell	Yield %
	★★★	$82.00	$82.72	$63.20	$102.70	1.84

Company Profile
Harrah's is the world's largest casino operator. Following its acquisitions of Caesars (June 2005) and Horseshoe (July 2004), it owns or operates more than 40 casinos across 12 states and three countries. The firm manages several Native American casinos. The $9 billion Caesars acquisition boosted Harrah's customer database from 28 million to 40 million names. About 85% of revenue comes from gaming operations, compared with 50% or less for Harrah's more Vegas-centric peers.

Management   Stewardship Grade [B]
We think Harrah's has a strong management team. Gary Loveman, a former Harvard Business School professor, took the helm in 2003 and has brought a fresh, retail-like perspective to the industry. Along with ex-CEO Phil Satre, he has done a nice job of building Harrah's brand (and fostering brand loyalty) through database mining, targeted marketing, and topnotch customer service. Harrah's has solid corporate governance, with numerous independent directors and people with strong finance backgrounds on its audit committee. The firm does have a staggered board, though, and its executives are paid well. Loveman received $5.3 million in salary and bonus in 2005 (up from $3.3 million the previous year), as well as 1,000,000 options (20% of the total number granted to employees). Executive bonus compensation is tied to earnings, returns on invested capital, and customer-satisfaction improvement.

One Harrah's Court
Las Vegas, NV 89119
www.harrahs.com

Growth [A+]	2002	2003	2004	2005
Revenue %	13.0	5.4	15.2	56.3
Earnings/Share %	14.4	28.0	23.0	-51.8
Book Value/Share %	8.9	21.5	14.6	108.5
Dividends/Share %	NMF	NMF	110.0	9.9

Profitability [C+]	2003	2004	2005	TTM
Return on Assets %	4.4	4.3	1.2	1.6
Oper Cash Flow $Mil	667	791	615	1,359
- Cap Spending $Mil	384	654	1,160	1,975
= Free Cash Flow $Mil	283	137	-545	-615

Financial Health [C+]	2003	2004	2005	09-30-06
Long-term Debt $Mil	—	5,151	11,039	10,726
Total Equity $Mil	1,738	2,035	5,665	6,073
Debt/Equity Ratio	—	2.5	1.9	1.8

Industry	Business Risk	Moat Size	Investment Style	Sector
Gambling/Casinos	Average	Narrow	Large Core	Consumer Services

Competition	Market Cap $Mil	12 Mo Trailing Sales $Mil	Price/Cash Flow	Return On Assets%	Debt/Equity	Total Return% 1 Yr	3 Yr
Harrah's Entertainment	15,388	9,439	11.3	1.6	1.8	18.6	21.7
MGM Mirage	16,125	7,451	13.9	2.5	3.7	56.4	45.5
Boyd Gaming	3,913	2,359	9.2	2.9	2.2	-3.7	41.3

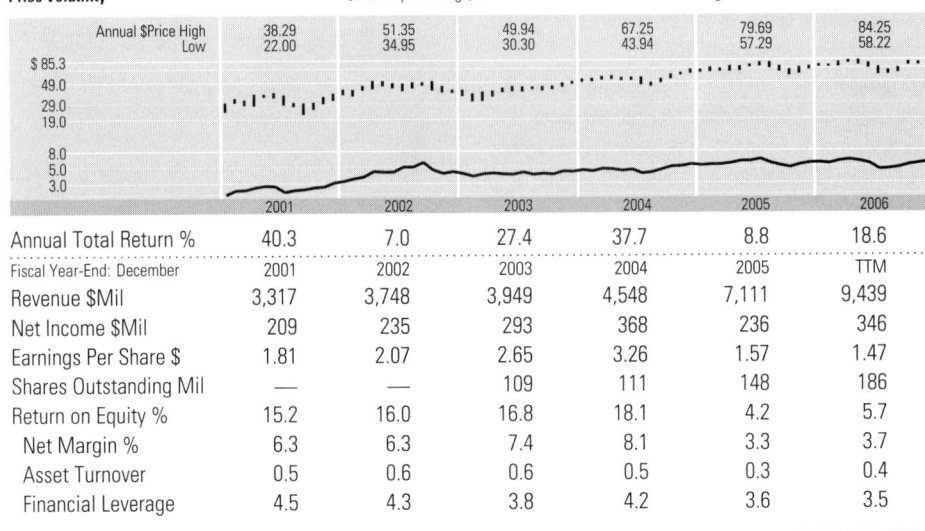

	2001	2002	2003	2004	2005	2006
Annual Total Return %	40.3	7.0	27.4	37.7	8.8	18.6
Fiscal Year-End: December	2001	2002	2003	2004	2005	TTM
Revenue $Mil	3,317	3,748	3,949	4,548	7,111	9,439
Net Income $Mil	209	235	293	368	236	346
Earnings Per Share $	1.81	2.07	2.65	3.26	1.57	1.47
Shares Outstanding Mil	—	—	109	111	148	186
Return on Equity %	15.2	16.0	16.8	18.1	4.2	5.7
Net Margin %	6.3	6.3	7.4	8.1	3.3	3.7
Asset Turnover	0.5	0.6	0.6	0.5	0.3	0.4
Financial Leverage	4.5	4.3	3.8	4.2	3.6	3.5

Valuation Ratios	Stock	Rel to Industry	Rel to S&P 500
Price/Earnings	43.5	0.9	2.1
Price/Book	2.5	0.3	0.6
Price/Sales	1.6	0.2	0.6
Price/Cash Flow	11.3	0.5	0.8

Major Fund Holders	% of Fund Assets
Heritage Capital Appreciation A	5.55
AIM Leisure Inv	5.50
QCM Absolute Return	4.69
Janus Aspen Forty Instl	4.35

Thesis   By Sumit Desai, CFA, 12-20-06   Stock Price as of Analysis: $82.69

Harrah's Entertainment earns a narrow moat, thanks to its strong customer loyalty and geographic diversification.

Unlike many casino operators that target high rollers, Harrah's focuses on the midtier, frequent gamblers. These customers are less costly to attract and generally do not require the lavish amenities offered at competing casinos. As a result, Harrah's earns about 85% of its revenue from gaming activities (versus about 40% at MGM Grand) and the company's returns on invested capital rank among the best in the industry.

Harrah's loyalty program, combined with its geographic diversity, also create a network effect unique within the gaming industry. Through its Total Rewards card program, which boasts almost 40 million members, Harrah's encourages customers to visit its properties no matter where in the country they are. The firm's efforts to foster brand loyalty have yielded nice returns: Cross-market play (gaming by customers away from their "home" casino) now accounts for about 30% of total revenue, up from 18% in 2000. Moreover, Harrah's has accumulated a vast database of customer information, which it uses to design highly targeted marketing promotions.

With 40 properties spread across 12 states and three countries, Harrah's also has one of the most geographically diverse property portfolios of all the operators. This broad footprint enhances the company's push to increase cross-market play and also helps to smooth out volatility in any one gaming jurisdiction. Geographic diversity does have some drawbacks, though, including erratic regulation and stiff competition. Gaming tax increases in states like Illinois and Indiana have strained the firm's profitability in recent years, while Harrah's faces stiff competition in its Midwestern markets from the likes of Ameristar and Penn National Gaming.

That's a key reason we like the $9.3 billion mega-merger with Caesars in 2005. The acquisition increased Harrah's exposure to regions with stable tax structures, like Las Vegas and Atlantic City. Further, the network nature of Harrah's business model should boost results at the legacy Caesars' properties. Within the first year of the deal, Harrah's increased Caesars' rated play (gamblers enrolled in a loyalty program) to about 79% of gaming revenue from 70% before the purchase. Finally, the company now has over 300 acres of land smack in the middle of the Las Vegas Strip, giving Harrah's the option for a large-scale redevelopment to compete with other mega-casinos being built by MGM and Boyd.

Data as of 12-29-06

Hawaiian Electric Industries HE

Rating	Fair Value	Last Close	Consider Buy	Consider Sell	Yield %
★★★	$28.00	$27.15	$23.90	$36.80	4.57

Company Profile
Hawaiian Electric Industries is a utility holding company. The firm owns and operates three vertically integrated utilities that together supply electricity to 93% of Hawaii's residents. In addition to its principal electric utility business, the company engages in banking. Its American Savings Bank (ASB) subsidiary is the third-largest bank in Hawaii, operating 65 branch offices and a network of automated teller machines.

Management Stewardship Grade [B]
In May 2006, Constance Lau was named president and CEO of Hawaiian Electric Industries. She also serves as chairman of Hawaiian Electric Company and chairman, president, and CEO of American Savings Bank. We think Lau's varied experience on both the utility and banking sides of the business will serve her well as head of the consolidated entity. Hawaiian Electric scores well in terms of shareholder friendliness. Officer compensation is below the industry average and includes a significant portion of "at-risk" (performance-based) pay. Executive performance measures include target returns on equity, a goal we favor over mere EPS objectives. We think minimum stock ownership levels--at 2.5 times base salary for the CEO, 1.5 times base salary for other executives, and 5 times annual cash payouts for directors--help align management's interests with shareholders'. We applaud the company's policy of compensating board members largely through share awards instead of just cash, and commend the recent separation of the CEO and chairman positions. While these policies are helpful, we think Hawaiian Electric's stewardship could be further enhanced by the elimination of staggered board terms.

900 Richards Street
Honolulu, HI 96813
www.hei.com

Growth [NA]	2002	2003	2004	2005
Revenue %	-4.3	7.7	8.0	15.2
Earnings/Share %	31.7	-6.2	-9.2	13.0
Book Value/Share %	5.0	1.1	5.1	-1.7
Dividends/Share %	0.0	0.0	0.0	0.0

Profitability [C-]	2003	2004	2005	TTM
Return on Assets %	1.2	1.1	1.3	4.0
Oper Cash Flow $Mil	241	244	218	247
- Cap Spending $Mil	163	215	224	218
= Free Cash Flow $Mil	78	29	-5	28

Financial Health [A]	2003	2004	2005	09-30-06
Long-term Debt $Mil	—	2,155	2,078	766
Total Equity $Mil	1,089	1,211	1,217	1,072
Debt/Equity Ratio	—	1.8	1.7	0.7

Industry	Business Risk	Moat Size	Investment Style	Sector
Electric Utilities	Below Avg	Narrow	Mid Value	Utilities

Competition	Market Cap $Mil	12 Mo Trailing Sales $Mil	Price/Cash Flow	Return On Assets%	Debt/ Equity	Total Return% 1 Yr	3 Yr
Hawaiian Electric Industries	2,556	NMF	10.4	4.0	0.7	9.8	9.7
Pinnacle West Capital	5,061	3,292	20.8	2.7	0.9	27.0	12.6
Sierra Pacific Resources	3,718	3,332	12.2	3.1	1.6	29.1	31.4

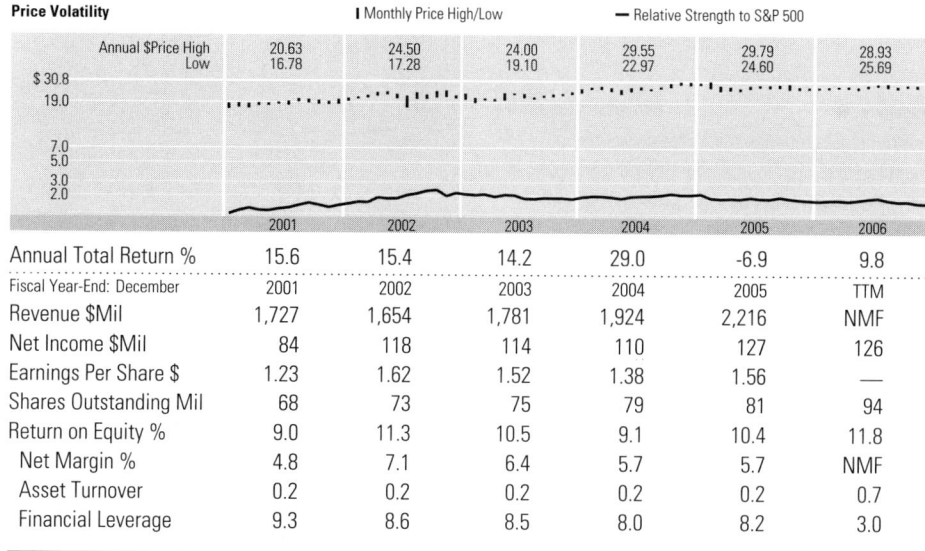

Price Volatility | Monthly Price High/Low — Relative Strength to S&P 500

	2001	2002	2003	2004	2005	2006
Annual $Price High	20.63	24.50	24.00	29.55	29.79	28.93
Low	16.78	17.28	19.10	22.97	24.60	25.69
Annual Total Return %	15.6	15.4	14.2	29.0	-6.9	9.8

Fiscal Year-End: December	2001	2002	2003	2004	2005	TTM
Revenue $Mil	1,727	1,654	1,781	1,924	2,216	NMF
Net Income $Mil	84	118	114	110	127	126
Earnings Per Share $	1.23	1.62	1.52	1.38	1.56	—
Shares Outstanding Mil	68	73	75	79	81	94
Return on Equity %	9.0	11.3	10.5	9.1	10.4	11.8
Net Margin %	4.8	7.1	6.4	5.7	5.7	NMF
Asset Turnover	0.2	0.2	0.2	0.2	0.2	0.7
Financial Leverage	9.3	8.6	8.5	8.0	8.2	3.0

Valuation Ratios	Stock	Rel to Industry	Rel to S&P 500
Price/Earnings	17.3	1.0	0.8
Price/Book	2.4	0.6	0.6
Price/Sales	1.2	0.7	0.4
Price/Cash Flow	10.4	0.9	0.7

Major Fund Holders	% of Fund Assets
Philadelphia	2.23
Fifth Third Small Cap Value Instl	1.01

Thesis By Ryan McLean, 11-01-06 Stock Price as of Analysis: $27.91

Hawaiian Electric's two business segments--electric utilities and banking--form an odd but attractive pair. While we see room for improvement on the electric utility side, we believe the company's overall strengths outweigh the weaknesses. For investors seeking low-risk exposure to the state of Hawaii's above-average economic growth, we think Hawaiian Electric is a reasonable bet.

Hawaiian Electric derives almost two thirds of its earnings from its narrow-moat, below-average-risk electric utility segment. Given Hawaii's geographic isolation and the firm's role in producing and delivering electricity to 93% of the state's population, regulators have shunned reform. Despite its dominant position, the firm's realized returns have fallen short of allowed levels. This is partly due to regulatory lag, and partly to demand growth that has outpaced generation capacity. Rising demand has forced the firm to run its generation facilities longer and harder than it otherwise would, driving up operation and maintenance expenses. To address this problem, several expansion projects are under way, and two major rate cases are currently on the table. These developments should help true up returns closer to allowed levels.

American Savings Bank (ASB), which Hawaiian Electric acquired in 1998, accounts for the remaining third of the company's earnings. Formerly a thrift, ASB has diversified into commercial banking and real estate, and is now the state's third-largest bank. Despite a flattening yield curve, ASB has managed to attract deposits and achieve net margin expansion. A prolonged flattening of the yield curve, however, would pose a serious risk to the bank. Customers seeking higher yields may choose to withdraw their funds, forcing ASB to cut prices and spend more on advertising. Such challenges aside, we like the bank's high-quality loan portfolio, solid cash flow generation, and steady interest margin.

With strong interest coverage and a conservative capital structure, Hawaiian Electric is financially sound. We expect positive free cash flow generation to steadily increase in the years ahead. On a less encouraging note, we expect returns on invested capital will continue to approximate the firm's cost of capital. Finally, while the firm's dividend currently yields a decent 4.4%, the company aims to reduce its payout ratio from historical levels as high as 80% to a more sustainable 65%. As such, investors should not expect any dividend increases for the foreseeable future.

Heartland Payment Systems HPY

	Rating	Fair Value	Last Close	Consider Buy	Consider Sell	Yield %
	★★★	$31.00	$28.25	$19.80	$37.40	0.18

Company Profile
Heartland provides payment-processing services that allow merchants to accept debit and credit cards. Heartland has 128,000 merchant clients and is the third-largest independent merchant processor, handling 2% of the purchase volume in the United States.

Industry	Business Risk	Moat Size	Investment Style	Sector
Data Processing	Above Avg	Narrow	Small Growth	Business Services

Competition

	Market Cap $Mil	12 Mo Trailing Sales $Mil	Price/Cash Flow	Return On Assets%	Debt/ Equity	Total Return% 1 Yr	3 Yr
Heartland Payment Systems	1,050	1,036	—	11.2	0.2	30.7	—
First Data	19,543	10,806	8.4	4.4	0.4	9.9	5.6
Global Payments	3,712	944	18.3	13.0	0.0	-0.5	25.2

Price Volatility
Monthly Price High/Low — Relative Strength to S&P 500

Annual $Price High/Low: 2005: 27.73/20.77, 2006: 29.90/21.22

Annual Total Return %	—	—	—	—	—	30.7
Fiscal Year-End: December	2001	2002	2003	2004	2005	TTM
Revenue $Mil	283	341	422	603	835	1,036
Net Income $Mil	-19	-2	10	5	14	26
Earnings Per Share $	—	—	—	—	—	—
Shares Outstanding Mil	—	—	—	—	—	37
Return on Equity %	NMF	NMF	NMF	75.4	17.9	20.0
Net Margin %	-6.6	-0.5	2.4	0.8	1.7	2.5
Asset Turnover	5.1	5.2	4.2	4.5	4.6	4.4
Financial Leverage	NMF	NMF	NMF	22.0	2.3	1.8

Management
Stewardship Grade [C]

Heartland gets average marks for stewardship. Chairman and CEO Bob Carr founded the company in 1997. He has 25 years of experience in the payment-processing industry and is seen as an innovator. Carr maintains a controlling interest, owning 51% of outstanding shares. His compensation in 2005 totaled only $450,000, with no restricted-stock or option grants or company-paid perks. However, option grants to other employees have been a little too high, in our opinion, totaling almost 4% of outstanding shares in 2005. We would like to see more industry experience on the board, as four of the six directors come from private-equity firms that hold stakes in the company. Heartland's Stewardship Grade could also be improved by basing management bonuses on specified performance criteria.

Valuation Ratios	Stock	Rel to Industry	Rel to S&P 500
Price/Earnings	—	—	—
Price/Book	8.0	1.6	2.0
Price/Sales	1.0	0.3	0.3
Price/Cash Flow	—	—	—

Major Fund Holders	% of Fund Assets
Baird SmallCap Inst	2.38
SunAmerica Growth Opportunities A	2.34
Masters' Select Smaller Companies	2.10
Julius Baer U.S. Microcap A	1.61

Thesis By Brett Horn, 10-27-06 Stock Price as of Analysis: $26.73

With a 47% compound annual revenue growth rate over the past five years, Heartland Payment Systems has achieved success in the payment-processing industry by adhering to a simple rule: Treat customers fairly.

Heartland has differentiated itself from its competitors by positioning itself as a merchant-friendly processor. Bob Carr founded the company in 1997 on the belief that the overly complex pricing practices of other processors created an opportunity. Heartland strives to make its pricing as transparent as possible and provide statements that merchants can understand, eschewing hidden fees and markups on interchange rates. Heartland has even published a merchant bill of rights, laying out what clients should expect from their payment processor. The fact that the company's growth has significantly outpaced the industry's indicates that merchants prefer Heartland's straightforward approach. Heartland's positive reputation among merchants creates a sustainable competitive advantage, in our opinion.

Heartland should also benefit from the development and implementation of internal front- and back-end processing systems. Before 2005, Heartland depended on third-party processors' systems. By the end of the second quarter of 2006, Heartland had converted substantially all of its clients to its back-end system, Passport, and about 62% of its clients have been converted to its front-end system, HPS Exchange. The conversion to HPS Exchange will take some more time as the company has yet to develop applications for all of the industries it serves. The rollout of the Passport and HPS Exchange systems increases operating leverage, as Heartland will no longer pay fees to use an outside system, and it should drive margin improvement as the company grows. Additionally, once fully fleshed out, these systems will provide a servicing advantage as they incorporate features previously available only to larger merchants and offer better functionality than other processors' more dated systems.

Heartland should continue to rack up impressive sales and margin growth. While its lack of scale relative to industry titan First Data will make moving beyond the small-merchant niche impossible, in our opinion, Heartland estimates that it has only 5% market share among small merchants, giving it plenty of room to grow.

---

90 Nassau Street
Princeton, NJ 08542
www.heartlandpaymentsystems.com

Growth [A+]	2002	2003	2004	2005
Revenue %	20.3	24.0	42.8	38.5
Earnings/Share %	NMF	NMF	NMF	NMF
Book Value/Share %	—	—	—	—
Dividends/Share %	NMF	NMF	NMF	NMF

Profitability [C]	2003	2004	2005	TTM
Return on Assets %	10.2	3.4	7.9	11.2
Oper Cash Flow $Mil	12	18	-25	-36
- Cap Spending $Mil	4	9	12	13
= Free Cash Flow $Mil	8	9	-37	-49

Financial Health [C]	2003	2004	2005	06-30-06
Long-term Debt $Mil	12	26	18	21
Total Equity $Mil	-41	6	80	131
Debt/Equity Ratio	ELB	4.2	0.2	0.2

Expand Your Investing Horizons with These Other Morningstar Annuals!

Morningstar® ETFs 150™

We've improved and expanded this essential ETF research tool. We now cover 150 ETFs and provide the Morningstar Rating for every ETF. Plus, you'll find nearly 100 additional pages of helpful editorial guidance. Articles help you determine which ETFs will give you optimal exposure to the part of the market you're looking to track. They explain how to avoid common ETF-investing mistakes. You'll find out how to blend ETFs into your existing portfolio and much more!

- ▶ Exclusive! Best time to buy or sell
- ▶ Nearly 100 pages of "how-to" guidance

January 2007. Softbound. 8 1/2" x 11". Approx. 235 pages. $35 (plus $4.95 S&H).

Morningstar® Funds 500™

Reduce your portfolio's risk and benefit from the investment expertise of the best mutual fund managers in the business. Our fund reports cover the biggest and most popular mutual funds, and contain critical year-end information and written commentary by a Morningstar analyst. These reports are the industry standards—the same full-page reports relied upon by financial professionals.

- ▶ Analyst guidance in every report
- ▶ Best funds for 2007

January 2007. Softbound. 8 1/2" X 11". Approx. 600 pages. $35 ($4.95 S&H).

Examine both annuals risk-free for 30 days.

Additional Reports Available Free!
Order either book now and gain access to additional Morningstar ETF Reports or Morningstar Fund Reports of your choice. Access up to 50 of our 2,000 Fund Reports or all of our ETF Reports any time in 2007—you decide when!

To order, call toll-free 866-608-9570
Mention code AS5-INS-7A

MORNINGSTAR®

Get Fresh Stock Ideas All Year Long—Free

Access updated analysis and research on up to 50 online stock reports any time in 2007. It's fast, easy, and completely free to you.

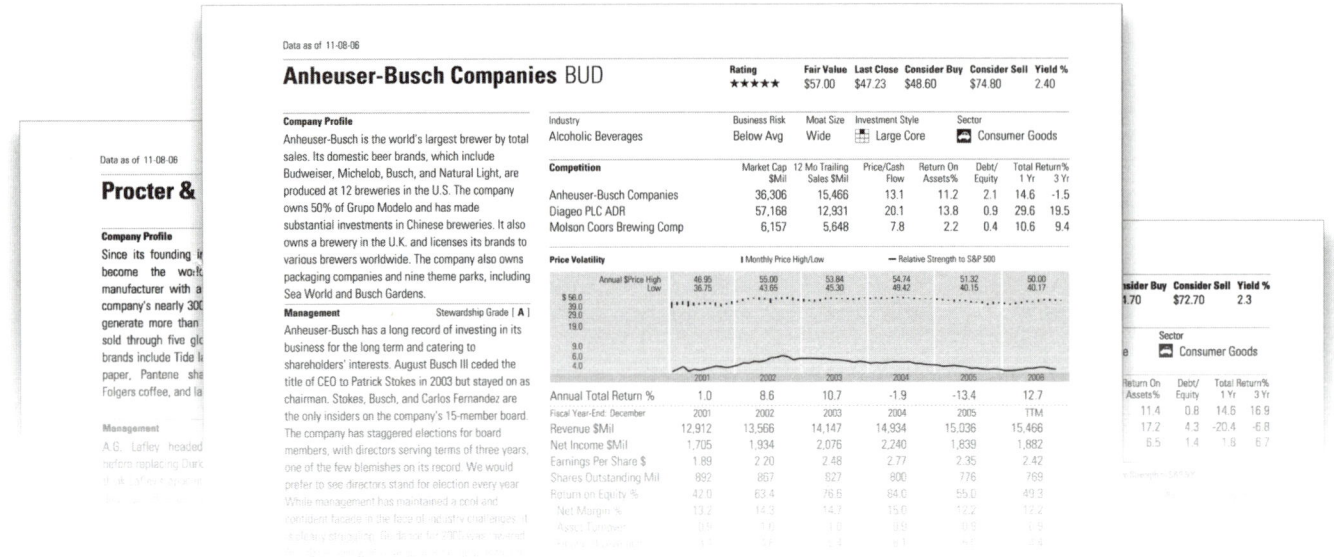

Thank you for purchasing *Morningstar Stocks 500*. In addition to the reports contained here, you have free access to 50 more of our 1,800 Stock Reports at any time during 2007. You decide when and what Stock Reports you want to download!

Note that you will be asked to register if you are not already registered for one of Morningstar's online services. This process takes only a minute, does not require a credit card, and is absolutely free.

Online stock information includes:

▶ The latest Morningstar Ratings—updated daily!

▶ Updated fair value estimates

▶ Consider Buying/Consider Selling prices

▶ Economic moat ratings

▶ Fresh Analyst Reports

▶ And more!

When you're ready to access your free Stock Reports, visit this Web address:

www.morningstar.com/goto/2007Stocks500

Thank You for Choosing Morningstar!

Data as of 12-29-06

Hershey Company HSY

	Rating	Fair Value	Last Close	Consider Buy	Consider Sell	Yield %
	★★★	$55.00	$49.80	$46.90	$72.20	2.07

Company Profile

The Hershey Company is the largest North American manufacturer of chocolate and nonchocolate confectionery products. The company markets brands including Hershey's, Reese's, Hershey's Kisses, Kit Kat, Almond Joy, Mounds, York, Jolly Rancher, Twizzlers, Ice Breakers, and Bubble Yum. The company derives about 11% of its sales internationally.

Industry	Business Risk	Moat Size	Investment Style	Sector
Food Mfg.	Below Avg	Wide	Large Core	Consumer Goods

Competition

	Market Cap $Mil	12 Mo Trailing Sales $Mil	Price/Cash Flow	Return On Assets %	Debt/Equity	Total Return % 1 Yr	3 Yr
Hershey Company	11,546	4,951	16.7	12.6	1.5	-8.1	11.1
Nestle SA ADR	138,417	73,660	16.8	8.8	—	20.9	14.7
Cadbury Schweppes PLC ADR	22,367	11,879	11.2	7.5	1.0	14.7	15.2

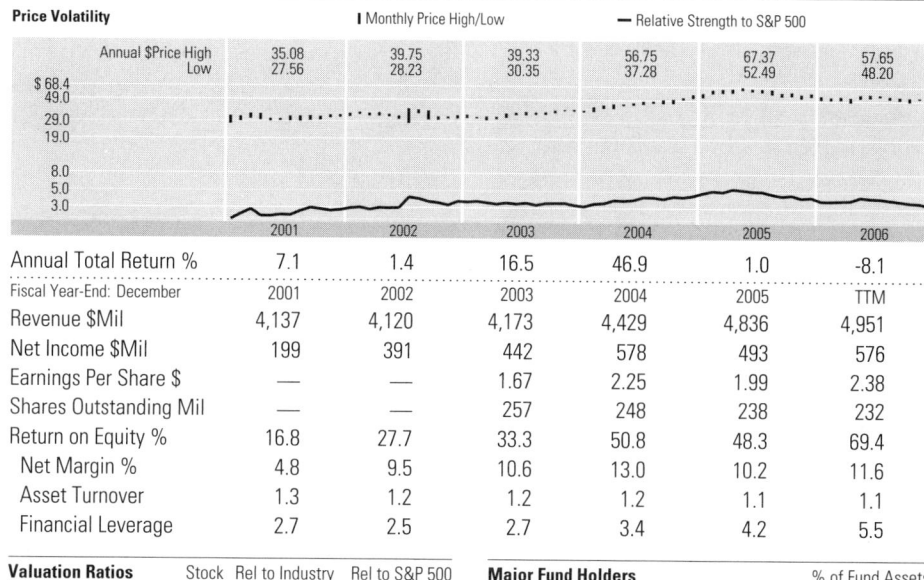

	2001	2002	2003	2004	2005	2006
Annual Total Return %	7.1	1.4	16.5	46.9	1.0	-8.1
Fiscal Year-End: December	2001	2002	2003	2004	2005	TTM
Revenue $Mil	4,137	4,120	4,173	4,429	4,836	4,951
Net Income $Mil	199	391	442	578	493	576
Earnings Per Share $	—	—	1.67	2.25	1.99	2.38
Shares Outstanding Mil	—	—	257	248	238	232
Return on Equity %	16.8	27.7	33.3	50.8	48.3	69.4
Net Margin %	4.8	9.5	10.6	13.0	10.2	11.6
Asset Turnover	1.3	1.2	1.2	1.2	1.1	1.1
Financial Leverage	2.7	2.5	2.7	3.4	4.2	5.5

Management Stewardship Grade [C]

Hershey is ultimately controlled by the Milton Hershey Trust, which owns Class B 10-to-1 supervoting shares that, when combined with its 7% ownership of common stock shares, give the trust 79% voting power and 31% ownership. We don't like these types of dual share classes that limit the rights of minority shareholders. In addition, the company and the trust have butted heads in the past. In 2002, the trust tried to force the sale of the company. Overall, we think very highly of Hershey's management. CEO Rick Lenny has done an excellent job focusing the company's efforts on its key brands, establishing strong relationships with impulse-oriented convenience and drug stores, and making operations more efficient. Although we're impressed by Lenny's leadership, we still think Hershey should separate its CEO and chairman positions. We aren't troubled by Lenny's $3.5 million of salary and bonus earned in 2005. He has plenty of skin in the game, with options worth about $30 million and more than 330,000 aggregate shares of common and restricted stock. Directors are elected on an annual basis, but only two are elected by common shareholders. We do like that directors are required to hold common stock worth 3 times the sum of their annual retainer and restricted-stock grant.

Valuation Ratios	Stock	Rel to Industry	Rel to S&P 500
Price/Earnings	20.9	1.0	1.0
Price/Book	13.9	3.1	3.4
Price/Sales	2.3	1.4	0.8
Price/Cash Flow	16.7	1.1	1.1

Major Fund Holders	% of Fund Assets
Biondo Growth Inv	3.90
SunAmerica New Century A	2.42
Sparrow Growth A	2.40
FCI Equity	2.26

100 Crystal A Drive www.hersheys.com
Hershey, PA 17033

Growth [C]	2002	2003	2004	2005
Revenue %	-0.4	1.3	6.2	9.2
Earnings/Share %	—	NMF	34.7	-11.6
Book Value/Share %	—	NMF	-11.6	-6.9
Dividends/Share %	8.2	14.7	15.6	11.4

Profitability [A]	2003	2004	2005	TTM
Return on Assets %	12.3	15.2	11.5	12.6
Oper Cash Flow $Mil	584	788	462	693
- Cap Spending $Mil	237	196	194	175
= Free Cash Flow $Mil	347	592	267	518

Financial Health [C]	2003	2004	2005	09-30-06
Long-term Debt $Mil	968	691	943	1,255
Total Equity $Mil	1,326	1,137	1,021	830
Debt/Equity Ratio	0.7	0.6	0.9	1.5

Thesis By Mitchell P. Corwin, CFA, CPA, 12-12-06 Stock Price as of Analysis: $50.10

Hershey's iconic brands and unmatched economies of scale in manufacturing and distribution should enable the firm to maintain its leading domestic confectionery position and robust margins. However, with about 90% of its sales in the U.S., more than modest earnings growth will be a challenge.

A drawn-out transition away from limited edition and line extensions, more aggressive competition from Mars, and Wal-Mart's inventory tightening all have been responsible for Hershey's anemic top-line growth in 2006. Most significant was the firm's de-emphasis on limited editions and line extensions. Those products not only were incremental to Hershey's top line but also effectively promoted the company's core brands.

With gains from that strategy likely fully realized, Hershey is aiming to achieve more sustainable growth by broadening its product portfolio around platforms such as snacks and premium chocolate. While that strategy makes sense, the heavier promotional and advertising efforts the firm has recently initiated are likely not temporary.

Since 2001, advertising as a percentage of sales has dropped by nearly 2 percentage points. While some ad dollars have shifted to promotions, which are accounted for as a reduction of sales, the decline is still significant. Hershey spends much less on advertising than other industry participants. To support core products and new platforms, we believe the firm will need to narrow that gap.

We are comfortable that Hershey will find a sustainable rate of advertising and promotion that will enable it to achieve its long-term organic sales growth objective of 3%-4%. However, the company's target of operating margin expansion of 70-90 basis points is overly ambitious, in our view. A mix shift favoring higher-margin products, such as single-serve bars, should help. However, we feel the company will have to invest annually to grow, whether that is in increased advertising or boosting its salesforce. This will likely mitigate some of the anticipated margin expansion.

Because we are skeptical about Hershey's long-term financial goals, our estimate of annual profit growth is lower than the company's expectations. However, we still have a more favorable view of the company's long-term prospects compared with other packaged food firms because many confectionery products are sold on impulse, and private-label penetration is relatively weak. Thus, we think Hershey will maintain high margins and returns on invested capital.

Data as of 12-29-06

Hewlett-Packard HPQ

	Rating	Fair Value	Last Close	Consider Buy	Consider Sell	Yield %
	★	$30.00	$41.19	$23.10	$37.60	0.78

Company Profile
Hewlett-Packard designs and distributes computer products to a wide range of business and individual customers around the globe. HP's products include printers, personal computers, servers, enterprise storage, handheld devices, and consumer electronics such as flat-panel TVs. The company also provides installation and consulting services and offers software programs focused on the management of corporate IT networks. HP purchased Compaq in an all-stock deal in 2002.

Management
Stewardship Grade [B]

President and CEO Mark Hurd joined HP in March 2005 after a 25-year career at NCR, where he orchestrated a very successful turnaround by forcing the various divisions to focus on execution instead of breaking up the firm and selling underperformers. His focus on asset efficiency and profits are now key parts of HP's strategy. Cathie Lesjak, the company's treasurer, will be taking over as CFO when Bob Wayman retires at the end of 2007. HP veteran Anne Livermore, who runs the servers and storage business, has made great strides in shoring up her group's flagging product portfolio and winning business. Vyomesh Joshi is the head of the all-important printing and imaging group, and has held a variety of engineering and managerial positions in this segment going back to 1980. He has preserved HP's dominant market position in the face of heightened competition and has his business poised for growth. Our only corporate governance complaints are the golden parachute plans for executives and a bevy of antitakeover provisions. HP shareholders are restricted from calling special meetings, and the firm carries a poison pill in the form of blank-check preferred stock, which enables HP's board to issue voting stock and fend off unwelcome takeover bids.

3000 Hanover Street
Palo Alto, CA 94304
www.hp.com

Growth [C+]	2002	2003	2004	2005
Revenue %	29.1	9.4	8.5	5.7
Earnings/Share %	NMF	38.6	-28.7	165.9
Book Value/Share %	-14.6	0.1	2.9	5.5
Dividends/Share %	0.0	0.0	0.0	0.0

Profitability [A-]	2003	2004	2005	TTM
Return on Assets %	4.6	3.1	7.6	7.6
Oper Cash Flow $Mil	5,088	8,028	11,353	11,353
- Cap Spending $Mil	2,126	1,995	2,536	2,536
= Free Cash Flow $Mil	2,962	6,033	8,817	8,817

Financial Health [B+]	2003	2004	2005	07-31-06
Long-term Debt $Mil	4,623	3,392	2,490	2,490
Total Equity $Mil	37,564	37,176	38,144	38,144
Debt/Equity Ratio	0.1	0.1	0.1	0.1

Industry	Business Risk	Moat Size	Investment Style	Sector
Computer Equip.	Average	Narrow	Large Core	Hardware

Competition	Market Cap $Mil	12 Mo Trailing Sales $Mil	Price/Cash Flow	Return On Assets%	Debt/Equity	Total Return% 1 Yr	3 Yr
Hewlett-Packard	112,070	91,658	9.9	7.6	0.1	45.2	22.7
IBM	146,342	89,593	9.8	8.8	0.4	19.8	3.0
Dell	56,995	56,738	12.2	14.9	0.1	-16.2	-9.9

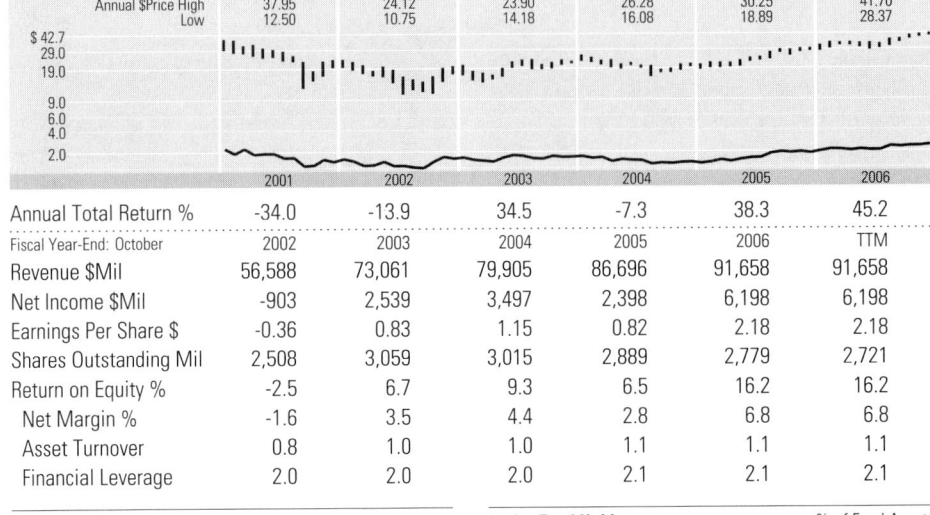

Annual Total Return %	-34.0	-13.9	34.5	-7.3	38.3	45.2
Fiscal Year-End: October	2002	2003	2004	2005	2006	TTM
Revenue $Mil	56,588	73,061	79,905	86,696	91,658	91,658
Net Income $Mil	-903	2,539	3,497	2,398	6,198	6,198
Earnings Per Share $	-0.36	0.83	1.15	0.82	2.18	2.18
Shares Outstanding Mil	2,508	3,059	3,015	2,889	2,779	2,721
Return on Equity %	-2.5	6.7	9.3	6.5	16.2	16.2
Net Margin %	-1.6	3.5	4.4	2.8	6.8	6.8
Asset Turnover	0.8	1.0	1.0	1.1	1.1	1.1
Financial Leverage	2.0	2.0	2.0	2.1	2.1	2.1

Valuation Ratios	Stock	Rel to Industry	Rel to S&P 500	Major Fund Holders	% of Fund Assets
Price/Earnings	18.9	0.7	0.9	Hartford Global Technology HLS IA	9.33
Price/Book	2.9	0.5	0.7	Hartford Global Technology A	9.30
Price/Sales	1.2	0.5	0.4	Fidelity Select Computers	7.55
Price/Cash Flow	9.9	0.7	0.7	Schwab Technology	6.57

Thesis By Mark E. Lanyon, CFA, 12-18-06 Stock Price as of Analysis: $40.03

A margin-focused management team is steadily improving profitability at Hewlett-Packard. Although recent fundamental improvements are impressive, this company's exposure to mature businesses and lack of compelling growth opportunities make us only lukewarm on its long-term prospects.

The chief driver of HP's recent resurgence is a comprehensive restructuring started by former CEO Carly Fiorina and continued by her replacement, Mark Hurd. Hurd started his tenure at HP by eliminating 14,500 jobs (10% of the workforce) and is now reducing global real estate and working to improve HP's supply-chain efficiency. Operating expenses (SG&A and R&D) have declined as a percentage of sales each year since fiscal 2001, and HP's operating margin excluding restructuring charges has jumped from 4.7% in fiscal 2002 to nearly 7% last year. Its returns on invested capital excluding goodwill jumped from 5% in 2001 to over 20% last year.

We believe HP's exposure to commoditied hardware offerings will be a check to any cost savings over the longer term, however. Its personal systems group (31% of sales), which primarily sells desktop and notebook PCs, should continue to experience painful pricing pressure. The server and storage business (19% of sales) also experiences tough competition from IBM and EMC that keeps a lid on profits. HP's gross margin is proof of these struggles, dropping nearly every year since 1999, from 30% to 23% last year. The increasingly commodified nature of PC and server markets and the emergence of low-cost Asian competitors such as Lenovo and Acer should continue to pressure HP's margins. HP's crown jewel printer segment (29% of sales), a moaty business if we have ever seen one, should continue to generate the lion's share of this company's operating profits. It has effectively subsidized HP's less-profitable divisions, delivering $14 billion in operating profits since 2002 versus less than $10 billion for the company as a whole.

HP's growth prospects are also modest due to its huge market share in mature or declining businesses. The company expects only low-single-digit sales growth for almost every division except its software group (only 1% of sales in 2005), which has engaged in multiple acquisitions to strengthen its network and storage management tools.

Managers can cut only so much fat before hitting muscle. HP's fundamental performance could continue to pick up over the near term, but we think its long-term results will be beholden to the negative forces pressuring its business' largest parts.

Data as of 12-29-06

Hilton Hotels HLT

	Rating	Fair Value	Last Close	Consider Buy	Consider Sell	Yield %
	★	$26.00	$34.90	$20.00	$32.60	0.46

Industry	Business Risk	Moat Size	Investment Style	Sector
Hotels	Average	Narrow	Large Growth	Consumer Services

Company Profile

Hilton Hotels owns or operates nearly 2,400 hotels in 50 countries with brand names such as Hilton, Doubletree, Embassy Suites, Hampton Inn, and Homewood Suites. Hilton owns several marquee hotel properties like the Waldorf=Astoria in New York and the Hilton Hawaiian Village. The company also sells timeshares under the Hilton Grand Vacations name.

Competition

	Market Cap $Mil	12 Mo Trailing Sales $Mil	Price/Cash Flow	Return On Assets%	Debt/ Equity	Total Return% 1 Yr	3 Yr
Hilton Hotels	13,493	7,013	42.8	2.8	2.4	45.6	27.7
Marriott International A	18,868	11,720	20.9	7.5	0.6	43.4	28.2
Starwood Hotels & Resorts	13,250	5,923	58.1	10.7	0.9	21.8	31.0

Management   Stewardship Grade [C]

Stephen Bollenbach took over as president and CEO of Hilton in 1996, when the long-tenured Barron Hilton retired. Corporate restructuring is Bollenbach's forte. He was CEO of Host Marriott from 1993 to 1995, after playing a key role in engineering its spin-off from Marriott. As CFO of Disney in 1995-96, he helped manage the acquisition of ABC/Cap Cities. These experiences made Bollenbach ideal to handle Hilton's 1999 Promus acquisition and the 1998 spin-off of Caesars Entertainment, as well as its ongoing divestiture of owned properties. He's been well paid for his efforts: As CEO, Bollenbach has collected a whopping 10 million options, in addition to earning at least $2 million in total compensation per year since 2000 ($3 million in 2005). All executive insiders collectively own about 8% of the firm, with Barron Hilton claiming 6% of total shares outstanding.

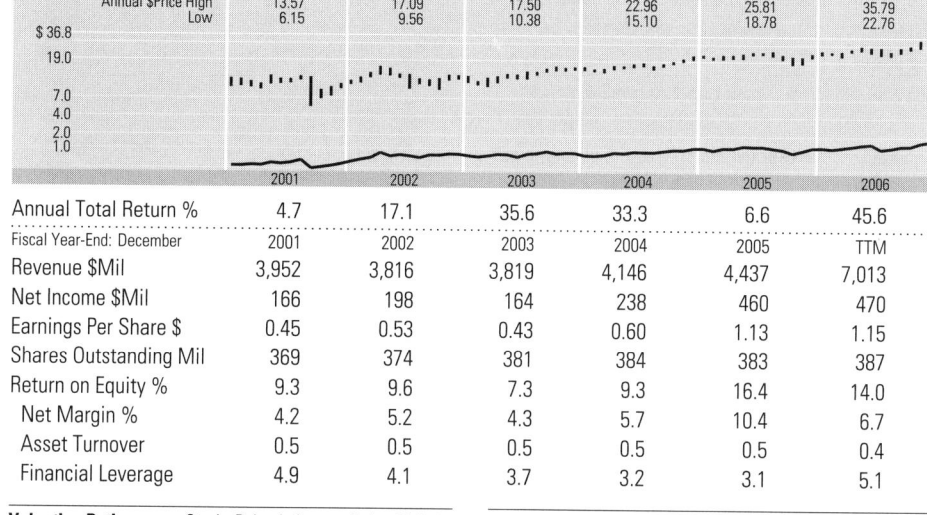

Price Volatility
Monthly Price High/Low — Relative Strength to S&P 500

	2001	2002	2003	2004	2005	2006
Annual $Price High	13.57	17.09	17.50	22.96	25.81	35.79
Low	6.15	9.56	10.38	15.10	18.78	22.76
Annual Total Return %	4.7	17.1	35.6	33.3	6.6	45.6
Fiscal Year-End: December	2001	2002	2003	2004	2005	TTM
Revenue $Mil	3,952	3,816	3,819	4,146	4,437	7,013
Net Income $Mil	166	198	164	238	460	470
Earnings Per Share $	0.45	0.53	0.43	0.60	1.13	1.15
Shares Outstanding Mil	369	374	381	384	383	387
Return on Equity %	9.3	9.6	7.3	9.3	16.4	14.0
Net Margin %	4.2	5.2	4.3	5.7	10.4	6.7
Asset Turnover	0.5	0.5	0.5	0.5	0.5	0.4
Financial Leverage	4.9	4.1	3.7	3.2	3.1	5.1

Valuation Ratios

	Stock	Rel to Industry	Rel to S&P 500
Price/Earnings	30.3	1.2	1.5
Price/Book	4.0	0.7	1.0
Price/Sales	1.9	0.6	0.7
Price/Cash Flow	42.8	1.2	2.9

Major Fund Holders

	% of Fund Assets
Midas Special	14.80
Alpine U.S. Real Estate Equity	7.20
Schneider Value	4.53
ING Van Kampen Real Estate S	4.15

9336 Civic Center Dr.
Beverly Hills, CA 90210
www.hilton.com

Growth [A]	2002	2003	2004	2005
Revenue %	-3.4	0.1	8.6	7.0
Earnings/Share %	17.8	-18.9	39.5	88.3
Book Value/Share %	13.7	6.8	10.3	6.7
Dividends/Share %	0.0	0.0	0.0	50.0

Profitability [C+]	2003	2004	2005	TTM
Return on Assets %	2.0	2.9	5.3	2.8
Oper Cash Flow $Mil	380	548	486	315
- Cap Spending $Mil	202	178	423	458
= Free Cash Flow $Mil	178	370	63	-143

Financial Health [C]	2003	2004	2005	09-30-06
Long-term Debt $Mil	—	3,633	3,572	7,902
Total Equity $Mil	2,239	2,568	2,811	3,356
Debt/Equity Ratio	—	1.4	1.3	2.4

Thesis   By Jeremy Glaser, 10-18-06   Stock Price as of Analysis: $29.32

A reunification with its overseas partner gives Hilton Hotels a chance to explore international opportunities while enjoying a resurgent North American lodging market.

Forty years after splitting, Hilton Hotels reclaimed Hilton International for $6 billion in early 2006. The purchase diversifies Hilton Hotels' portfolio and allows the company to participate in the booming Asian and Middle East markets. Additionally, regaining full worldwide brand ownership should help Hilton compete more effectively with Marriott International and Starwood Hotels & Resorts. Although we are disappointed that Hilton increased its leverage--the deal is almost entirely debt-financed--we believe the firm improved its long-term growth prospects at a reasonable price.

Hilton is also recharging its business model by shedding many of the risks associated with hotel ownership. The company has been selling properties to third parties while retaining lucrative management contracts. Hilton receives a fixed management fee, which cushions the downside, and earns incentive bonuses for meeting certain profit targets, which captures a portion of the upside from owning hotels. We believe the decision to sell is a net positive, even though by franchising and managing rather than owning properties Hilton may not fully benefit from industry rallies, such as the current eruption of business travel. However, we are comfortable with Hilton potentially leaving some money on the table in exchange for insulation from a sudden drop-off in travel.

The acquisition of Hilton International is not without problems, though. Hilton International had been much less aggressive in selling its hotels, receiving about 40% of earnings from owned hotels. To remedy this, management plans to sell many of its international properties, using the proceeds to pay down debt and reinvest in the Hilton brand. We think this reinvestment is critical for Hilton, as the company is losing share in the crucial midscale sector and has fallen behind rivals in entering the luxury market. Hilton is banking on its Conrad brand to capture a slice of the fragmented luxury segment. Additionally, it expects improved marketing and designs for Hampton Inn and Hilton Garden Inn to keep up with aggressive moves by competing brands like Marriott's Courtyard and Starwood's aloft.

Notwithstanding the competition, we think Hilton is an iconic lodging brand that still resonates with travelers. We would invest at a reasonable discount to our fair value estimate.

Data as of 12-29-06

Home Depot HD

	Rating	Fair Value	Last Close	Consider Buy	Consider Sell	Yield %
	★★★★	$44.00	$40.16	$37.50	$57.80	1.68

Industry	Business Risk	Moat Size	Investment Style	Sector
Home Supply	Below Avg	Wide	Large Core	Consumer Services

Company Profile

Home Depot is the world's largest home-improvement retailer. The company's Home Depot stores offer building materials, home-improvement supplies, and lawn and garden products, primarily to do-it-yourselfers. The firm also operates stores that offer design, renovation, landscaping, and flooring products, and it distributes products and sells installation services to businesses and governments. Home Depot operates about 2,100 stores in the United States, Canada, and Mexico.

Management   Stewardship Grade [D]

Bob Nardelli joined Home Depot as president and CEO in 2000 after being passed over for the top job at General Electric. Nardelli added the title of chairman in 2002. Nardelli has definitively placed his stamp on senior management, as many of Home Depot's present senior executives were hired after he arrived, including two of his former colleagues from GE. The board of directors comprises Nardelli, one of the company's cofounders, and nine outside directors, most of whom have extensive senior-executive-level experience. We reduced our corporate Stewardship Grade for Home Depot to a D from a C following the company's display of blatant disrespect for its shareholders at its last shareholder meeting. In addition, management compensation is excessive--Nardelli received almost $30 million last year in salary, bonuses, restricted stock, and other compensation, not to mention a 590,000-share stock-option grant. We are also not big fans of the fact that Nardelli is both CEO and chairman. Insiders own 1.5% of Home Depot's common stock.

Competition

	Market Cap $Mil	12 Mo Trailing Sales $Mil	Price/Cash Flow	Return On Assets%	Debt/Equity	Total Return% 1 Yr	3 Yr
Home Depot	81,961	90,061	12.5	11.6	0.2	1.0	6.0
Lowe's Companies	47,435	47,330	11.5	11.7	0.3	-6.1	5.3
Sears Holdings	25,845	52,810	15.4	4.3	0.3	45.4	94.0

Price Volatility | Monthly Price High/Low — Relative Strength to S&P 500

| Annual $Price High | 53.73 | 52.60 | 37.89 | 44.30 | 43.98 | 43.95 |
| Low | 30.00 | 23.01 | 20.10 | 32.34 | 34.56 | 32.85 |

	2001	2002	2003	2004	2005	2006
Annual Total Return %	12.1	-52.7	49.4	21.5	-4.3	1.0

Fiscal Year-End: January	2002	2003	2004	2005	2006	TTM
Revenue $Mil	53,553	58,247	64,816	73,094	81,511	90,061
Net Income $Mil	3,044	3,664	4,304	5,001	5,838	6,121
Earnings Per Share $	1.29	1.56	1.88	2.26	2.72	2.93
Shares Outstanding Mil	—	—	2,289	2,203	2,138	2,041
Return on Equity %	16.8	18.5	19.2	20.7	21.7	22.1
Net Margin %	5.7	6.3	6.6	6.8	7.2	6.8
Asset Turnover	2.0	1.9	1.9	1.9	1.8	1.7
Financial Leverage	1.5	1.5	1.5	1.6	1.7	1.9

Valuation Ratios	Stock	Rel to Industry	Rel to S&P 500
Price/Earnings	13.7	1.0	0.7
Price/Book	3.0	1.0	0.7
Price/Sales	0.9	1.0	0.3
Price/Cash Flow	12.5	1.0	0.9

Major Fund Holders	% of Fund Assets
GMO U.S. Quality Equity IV	6.82
Fidelity Select Construction&Housing	5.86
Fidelity Dividend Growth	5.21
Hillman Focused Advantage	5.04

Thesis By Anthony Chukumba, 11-20-06 Stock Price as of Analysis: $38.41

Home Depot is the world's largest home-improvement retailer. Selling home-improvement products is a very competitive business. In addition to warehouse home-improvement stores, Home Depot competes with traditional hardware, plumbing, electrical, and home-supply retailers and lumberyards. Home Depot built up brand-name recognition and a loyal customer base by being the first firm to open large-format stores nationwide. This helped Home Depot build a wide economic moat.

Throughout most of the 1990s, Home Depot generated 20%-plus annual revenue and earnings growth as it opened new stores across the country. However, increased competition with Lowe's Companies, management miscues, and the saturation of the home-improvement retailing market have slowed Home Depot's growth the last few years. Home Depot has taken several steps lately to improve results, including attempting to make its stores more inviting to female shoppers and improving customer service.

Home Depot has also centralized its product purchases, allowing it to better leverage its purchasing power, as well as extract more favorable payment terms from suppliers. Early results of these changes have been positive, as Home Depot has improved its comparable-store sales (sales at stores open at least a year) and boosted profit margins and returns on invested capital. The company's free cash flow/sales ratio has also improved, and it has returned most of the cash it has generated the last few years back to its shareholders through share repurchases and cash dividends.

Home Depot is aggressively pursuing additional avenues for growth. Recent efforts to build multilevel stores in urban areas and to increase sales of installation services as well as sales to contractors have been very promising. Home Depot has started to expand internationally, through acquisitions and organic growth in Mexico and Canada, and has also begun exploring opening stores in China.

Our primary concern with Home Depot relates to the company's recent expansion into the contractor supply business, mainly through acquisitions. We worry that Home Depot could have problems integrating the acquired companies, which could lead management to take its eye off the ball at the core retail stores. For example, Home Depot recently announced plans to slow new store growth significantly over the next few years as it accelerates the growth of the contractor supply business.

2455 Paces Ferry Road N.W.   www.homedepot.com
Atlanta, GA 30339-4024

Growth [A]	2003	2004	2005	2006
Revenue %	8.8	11.3	12.8	11.5
Earnings/Share %	20.9	20.5	20.2	20.4
Book Value/Share %	10.0	16.1	11.5	14.8
Dividends/Share %	23.5	23.8	25.0	23.1

Profitability [A+]	2004	2005	2006	TTM
Return on Assets %	12.5	12.8	13.1	11.6
Oper Cash Flow $Mil	6,545	6,904	6,484	6,555
- Cap Spending $Mil	3,508	3,948	3,881	3,538
= Free Cash Flow $Mil	3,037	2,956	2,603	3,017

Financial Health [A-]	2004	2005	2006	10-31-06
Long-term Debt $Mil	856	2,148	2,672	6,671
Total Equity $Mil	22,407	24,158	26,909	27,758
Debt/Equity Ratio	0.0	0.1	0.1	0.2

Honeywell International HON

Data as of 12-29-06

Rating ★★	Fair Value $37.00	Last Close $45.24	Consider Buy $28.50	Consider Sell $46.40	Yield % 2.01

Company Profile
Honeywell operates four major business segments: aerospace (36% of sales), automation products for process controls, sensing instruments, and safety and security products (33%), specialty materials (16%), and transportation products (15%).

Management
Stewardship Grade [C]

CEO Dave Cote took over in 2002. We give him high marks for reinvigorating Honeywell's culture. Cote has implemented measures to more closely tie employee appraisals and incentive awards to productivity contributions. Before joining Honeywell, Cote was CEO of TRW; before that, he was CEO of GE Appliances. Despite his success, we think Honeywell's board has been overly generous in awarding compensation. Cote has earned in excess of $17 million in each of the past three years. We would prefer to see pay more closely tied to each year's performance. We like Honeywell's annual elections for board members.

101 Columbia Road P.O. Box 4000 www.honeywell.com
Morristown, NJ 07962-2497

Growth [C]	2002	2003	2004	2005
Revenue %	-5.8	3.7	10.8	8.0
Earnings/Share %	NMF	470.4	-3.2	30.2
Book Value/Share %	—	—	NMF	0.8
Dividends/Share %	0.0	0.0	0.0	10.0

Profitability [NA]	2003	2004	2005	TTM
Return on Assets %	—	4.1	5.1	6.2
Oper Cash Flow $Mil	2,199	2,253	2,442	2,809
- Cap Spending $Mil	655	629	684	661
= Free Cash Flow $Mil	1,544	1,624	1,758	2,148

Financial Health [C]	2003	2004	2005	09-30-06
Long-term Debt $Mil	—	4,069	3,082	3,909
Total Equity $Mil	10,729	11,252	11,254	11,321
Debt/Equity Ratio	—	0.4	0.3	0.3

Industry	Business Risk	Moat Size	Investment Style	Sector
Diversified	Average	Narrow	Large Core	Industrial Materials

Competition
	Market Cap $Mil	12 Mo Trailing Sales $Mil	Price/Cash Flow	Return On Assets%	Debt/Equity	Total Return% 1 Yr	3 Yr
Honeywell International	36,939	30,367	13.2	6.2	0.3	24.1	13.2
General Electric	383,564	161,022	12.8	2.5	2.2	9.4	9.0
United Technologies	62,748	46,303	14.6	7.0	0.4	13.7	11.6

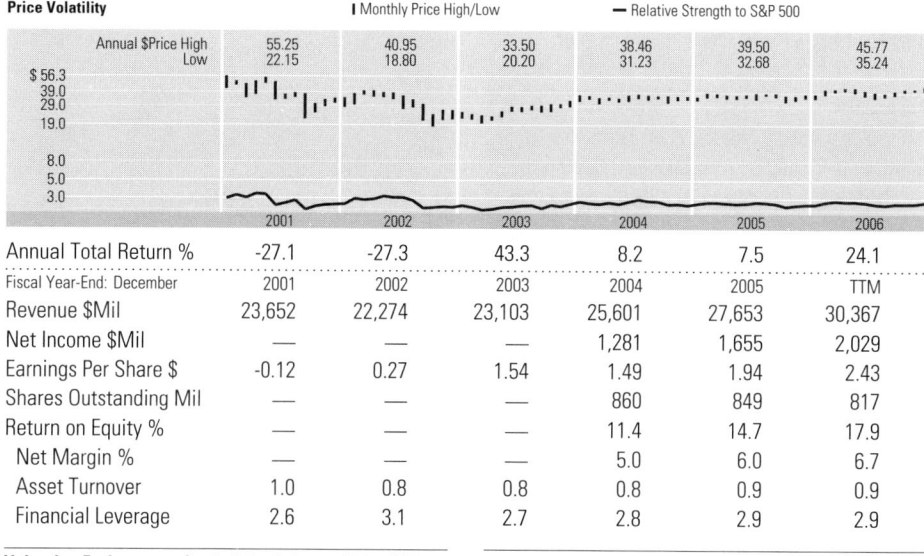

	2001	2002	2003	2004	2005	TTM
Annual Total Return %	-27.1	-27.3	43.3	8.2	7.5	24.1
Revenue $Mil	23,652	22,274	23,103	25,601	27,653	30,367
Net Income $Mil	—	—	—	1,281	1,655	2,029
Earnings Per Share $	-0.12	0.27	1.54	1.49	1.94	2.43
Shares Outstanding Mil	—	—	—	860	849	817
Return on Equity %	—	—	—	11.4	14.7	17.9
Net Margin %	—	—	—	5.0	6.0	6.7
Asset Turnover	1.0	0.8	0.8	0.8	0.9	0.9
Financial Leverage	2.6	3.1	2.7	2.8	2.9	2.9

Valuation Ratios	Stock	Rel to Industry	Rel to S&P 500
Price/Earnings	18.7	1.0	0.9
Price/Book	3.3	1.0	0.8
Price/Sales	1.2	0.7	0.4
Price/Cash Flow	13.2	1.0	0.9

Major Fund Holders	% of Fund Assets
Fidelity Select Industrial Equipment	6.23
Giordano	4.38
BlackRock Legacy Inv A	4.34
Fidelity Blue Chip Value	4.01

Thesis By Tom D'Amore, CFA, 12-13-06 Stock Price as of Analysis: $41.86

After significant efforts by management to reinvigorate its multiple lines of business, operating performance at Honeywell has begun to turn around. Profit margins are improving, cash flow is up, debt ratios are declining, and returns on invested capital are increasing.

Under the leadership of CEO Dave Cote, Honeywell has fostered a culture of performance. Appraisal and incentive processes have been revised to better reflect productivity contributions. Product management has been refocused to serve customer satisfaction. Cote has also raised the octane of the company's proprietary Six Sigma productivity program and standardized its implementation across all major business lines. As a result, sales per employee are up 25% since 2002. Honeywell's operating margins are also on the march. We forecast operating margins of about 9.5% in 2006, up 2 percentage points since Cote's arrival in 2002.

In addition to upgrading its operating productivity, Honeywell has made changes to its portfolio of businesses to boost sales growth. Recent acquisitions include faster-growing businesses in the energy, security, and transportation safety sectors.

Honeywell's higher-growth profile is paying off. We forecast free cash flow of $2.1 billion in 2006, up 70% from just three years ago. We expect returns on invested capital to reach 14% in 2006, up from 6% in 2003 and handily exceeding the company's 10% cost of capital. Higher cash flows have also elevated Honeywell's shareholder equity while allowing its debt to remain essentially unchanged despite recent acquisitions. As a result, we expect Honeywell's debt/equity ratio to decline below 25% at the end of 2006 from about 50% in 2002.

Despite the advances in productivity and cash generation, we see some chinks in Honeywell's armor. We believe the firm's traditional stronghold in process control automation is losing market share to more-innovative competitors. Market share growth in the transportation division appears to be slowing as a result of shifts in end customer preferences for more fuel-efficient vehicles that are less likely to use Honeywell's power-enhancing turbo-boosting technology. Honeywell also continues to bleed cash from its lingering asbestos liability. We expect the company to pay out at least $1 billion over the next five years before the liability is resolved.

Data as of 12-29-06

Hospira HSP

	Rating	Fair Value	Last Close	Consider Buy	Consider Sell	Yield %
	★★★★	$43.00	$33.58	$33.20	$53.90	0.00

Company Profile
Hospira is one of the largest global specialty pharmaceutical and medication-delivery companies. It offers generic injectable drugs primarily to U.S. hospitals, integrated medication-delivery systems that provide infusion therapy and pain management, and contract-manufacturing services to biopharmaceutical companies. Hospira was spun off from Abbott Laboratories in April 2004 and plans to purchase Mayne Pharma for $2 billion in 2007.

Management   Stewardship Grade [B]
With several Abbott veterans on its team, Hospira enjoys an unusually deep management talent pool. CEO Chris Begley was formerly Abbott's senior vice president of hospital products--the business that spun off as Hospira--and boasts 30 years of hospital industry experience. Another Abbott veteran, COO Terrence Kearney brings a multidisciplinary background covering various operating and financial roles since 1979. CFO Thomas Werner was recruited from outside the firm in August 2006 following the completion of the spinoff. Werner's broad financial experience both in and out of health care should serve Hospira well as a stand-alone company. Given its short history as a public company, overall corporate stewardship of shareholders' interests has been good. We give Hospira credit for being a former Abbott division when rating areas such as accounting and internal controls. Transparency and communication with shareholders have been sufficient to date. The only major related-party transactions are with Abbott, which should decrease over time. Management compensation looks reasonable by industry standards, and a modest corporate headquarters indicates management is focused on cost containment.

275 North Field Drive   www.hospira.com
Lake Forest, IL 60045

Growth [D]	2002	2003	2004	2005
Revenue %	3.5	0.8	0.8	-0.7
Earnings/Share %	NMF	NMF	NMF	NMF
Book Value/Share %	—	—	—	NMF
Dividends/Share %	NMF	NMF	NMF	NMF

Profitability [A]	2003	2004	2005	TTM
Return on Assets %	11.6	12.9	8.4	7.8
Oper Cash Flow $Mil	368	387	571	432
- Cap Spending $Mil	197	229	256	250
= Free Cash Flow $Mil	171	158	315	181

Financial Health [A-]	2003	2004	2005	06-30-06
Long-term Debt $Mil	0	699	695	690
Total Equity $Mil	1,453	984	1,328	1,317
Debt/Equity Ratio	0.0	0.7	0.5	0.5

Industry	Business Risk	Moat Size	Investment Style	Sector
Drugs	Average	Narrow	Mid Core	Healthcare

Competition	Market Cap $Mil	12 Mo Trailing Sales $Mil	Price/Cash Flow	Return On Assets%	Debt/Equity	Total Return% 1 Yr	3 Yr
Hospira	5,232	2,628	12.1	7.8	0.5	-21.5	—
Baxter International	30,360	10,106	18.3	9.0	0.4	24.8	17.2
Teva Pharmaceutical Indus	20,098	5,250	14.7	10.3	0.3	-27.2	3.1

Price Volatility | Monthly Price High/Low   — Relative Strength to S&P 500

	2001	2002	2003	2004	2005	2006
Annual $Price High					34.86	45.10	47.99
Low					24.02	28.35	31.15
Annual Total Return %	—	—	—	—	27.7	-21.5

Fiscal Year-End: December	2001	2002	2003	2004	2005	TTM
Revenue $Mil	2,514	2,603	2,624	2,645	2,627	2,628
Net Income $Mil	273	247	260	302	236	217
Earnings Per Share $	—	—	—	—	1.46	1.34
Shares Outstanding Mil	—	—	—	—	159	156
Return on Equity %	18.7	18.5	17.9	30.6	17.7	16.5
Net Margin %	10.8	9.5	9.9	11.4	9.0	8.3
Asset Turnover	1.2	1.2	1.2	1.1	0.9	0.9
Financial Leverage	1.5	1.6	1.5	2.4	2.1	2.1

Valuation Ratios	Stock	Rel to Industry	Rel to S&P 500
Price/Earnings	25.1	1.0	1.2
Price/Book	4.0	0.7	1.0
Price/Sales	2.0	0.5	0.7
Price/Cash Flow	12.1	0.7	0.8

Major Fund Holders	% of Fund Assets
Synovus Mid Cap Value Instl	3.54
Phoenix Fundamental Growth A	3.03
Dreyfus Premier MidCap Value A	2.41
Dreyfus Midcap Value	2.30

Thesis By Brian Laegeler, CPA, 12-13-06   Stock Price as of Analysis: $33.83

Hospira's short history as a public company understates its established track record in the hospital supply market. The company boasts formidable competitive advantages in drug delivery systems and generic injectable drugs that make Hospira worth consideration at the right price.

Hospira built a 30% market share in drug delivery systems during the decades prior to its 2004 spinoff from Abbott Laboratories. The company maintains around 400,000 long-lived drug pumps within U.S. hospitals. This installed equipment base generates recurring demand for the company's exclusive high-margin consumables. Customers are loyal because the pumps are an integral component to overall hospital information systems; minor innovations are generally not enough to switch brands. An exception to the rule, the temporary absence of a competitor (due to regulatory issues) has allowed Hospira to add some competitive accounts. We only expect low-to-mid single-digit growth rates from this mature category, but the business is durable enough to make it attractive even with modest growth.

Generic injectable drugs is another defensible business for Hospira. Compared with easy-to-make generic pills, injectables require complex factories, specialized distribution, and innovative packaging. Hospira typically encounters six to nine competitors after an injectable's patent expires compared with 10 to 20 players in the pill market. Fewer competitors means higher margins and market share in another important product category for U.S. hospitals. The acquisition of Mayne Pharma adds an international selling platform as well as oncology expertise from which the firm can grow.

Hospira inherited a contract manufacturing business, which we like despite its recent troubles, from Abbott. The increasing pace of patent expirations should deliver higher sales to leading outsourced service providers like Hospira. The business comes in waves, though, and it will undergo a downturn in 2007 due to the loss of certain product lines in the absence of new business. While contract manufacturing doesn't have the same competitive barriers as drug delivery or generic injectables, potential double-digit growth could provide upside over the longer term.

HSBC Holdings PLC ADR HBC

Data as of 12-29-06

Rating	Fair Value	Last Close	Consider Buy	Consider Sell	Yield %
★★★	$97.00	$91.65	$74.80	$121.50	4.15

Company Profile

HSBC is one of the largest banks in the world, with a pedigree reaching back to mid-19th century Hong Kong. Based in London, the bank has 9,800 offices in 77 countries and more than $1.5 trillion in assets. The bank's activities are concentrated in four main divisions: corporate investment banking and markets, personal financial services, commercial banking, and private banking.

Management   Stewardship Grade [NA]

We anticipate little change in HSBC's strategy despite the retirement of Sir John Bond. Stephen Green, CEO since 2003, succeeds Bond as chairman while Michael Geoghegan, a 33-year HSBC veteran, succeeds Green as CEO. We believe HSBC's management is the gold standard for corporate leadership and ownership management. Performance is measured by economic profits and total shareholder return. Cost control is almost an obsession. HSBC has cultivated a deep bench of managerial talent by providing incentives that produce unusually long tenure with the bank. The top 40 managers have an astounding 800 years of collective experience. Management compensation is very nominal, given the size of HSBC. Green draws a base salary of 1.25 million pounds while Geoghegan takes home 1 million pounds. Cash bonuses of as much as 250% of base salary are discretionary and based on achieving individual and group performance goals. Option grants are very conservative. Given HSBC's huge market capitalization, insider ownership of stock, while substantial, is still below 1% of shares outstanding.

8 Canada Square
London, United Kingdom E14 5HQ
www.hsbc.com

Growth [NA]	2002	2003	2004	2005
Revenue %	5.0	65.6	76.4	10.3
Earnings/Share %	24.5	25.8	41.0	15.4
Book Value/Share %	12.9	28.7	-0.4	12.0
Dividends/Share %	4.2	38.4	-8.0	9.5

Profitability [NA]	2003	2004	2005	TTM
Return on Assets %	0.8	1.1	1.1	1.1
Oper Cash Flow $Mil	22,675	59,897	7,021	—
- Cap Spending $Mil	1,981	2,830	2,887	—
= Free Cash Flow $Mil	—	—	—	—

Financial Health [NA]	2003	2004	2005	12-31-05
Long-term Debt $Mil	—	—	—	—
Total Equity $Mil	74,473	85,522	92,432	92,432
Debt/Equity Ratio	—	—	—	—

Industry	Business Risk	Moat Size	Investment Style	Sector
International Banks	Average	Wide	Large Core	Financial Services

Competition

	Market Cap $Mil	12 Mo Trailing Sales $Mil	Price/Cash Flow	Return On Assets %	Debt/Equity	Total Return % 1 Yr	3 Yr
HSBC Holdings PLC ADR	204,784	49,836	—	1.1	—	18.9	9.5
Citigroup	273,691	86,566	—	1.3	—	19.6	8.4
Bank of America	239,758	68,368	—	1.3	—	20.7	15.2

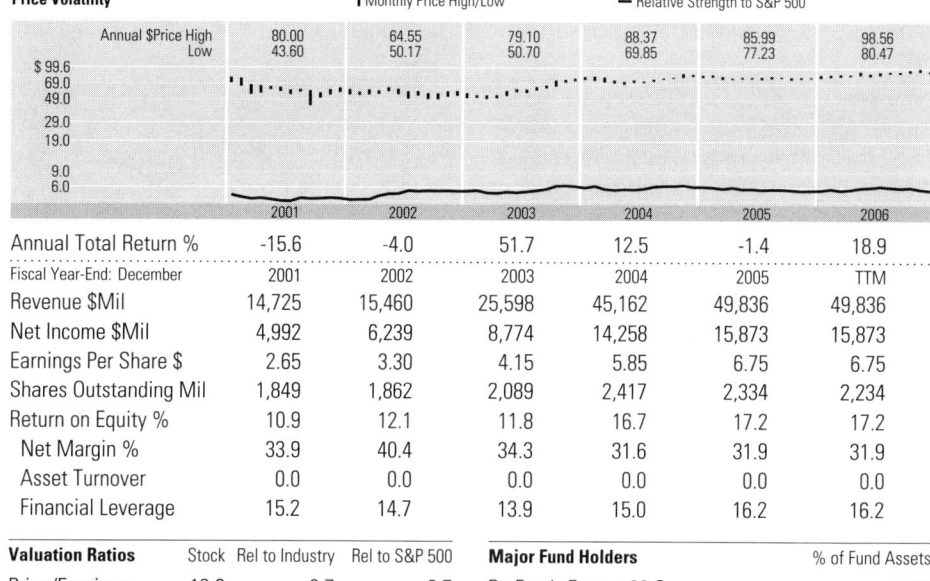

	2001	2002	2003	2004	2005	2006
Annual Total Return %	-15.6	-4.0	51.7	12.5	-1.4	18.9

Fiscal Year-End: December	2001	2002	2003	2004	2005	TTM
Revenue $Mil	14,725	15,460	25,598	45,162	49,836	49,836
Net Income $Mil	4,992	6,239	8,774	14,258	15,873	15,873
Earnings Per Share $	2.65	3.30	4.15	5.85	6.75	6.75
Shares Outstanding Mil	1,849	1,862	2,089	2,417	2,334	2,234
Return on Equity %	10.9	12.1	11.8	16.7	17.2	17.2
Net Margin %	33.9	40.4	34.3	31.6	31.9	31.9
Asset Turnover	0.0	0.0	0.0	0.0	0.0	0.0
Financial Leverage	15.2	14.7	13.9	15.0	16.2	16.2

Valuation Ratios	Stock	Rel to Industry	Rel to S&P 500
Price/Earnings	13.6	0.7	0.7
Price/Book	2.2	0.8	0.5
Price/Sales	4.1	1.0	1.4
Price/Cash Flow	—	—	—

Major Fund Holders	% of Fund Assets
ProFunds Europe 30 Svc	6.41
California Investment Euro Gr & Inc Dir	4.24
Lazard International Equity Sel Instl	4.03
Guinness Atkinson Asia Pacific Dividend	3.92

Thesis By Ganesh Rathnam, 11-14-06 Stock Price as of Analysis: $95.27

HSBC possesses the traits we want in an elite global bank: It has a corporate culture that is obsessed with providing superior service, determined to cut unnecessary costs, and focused on economic profits and total shareholder returns. We'd gladly invest in this stellar global bank at the right price.

In our opinion, HSBC's competitive advantage stems from its unique geographic footprint, scale, diversity of business, and corporate culture. While the banking industry is rapidly consolidating worldwide, few global banks operate in all the areas that HSBC does, such as Hong Kong, the United Kingdom, the United States, Latin America, and Asia. This geographic spread enables the bank to offer cheaper and better service to multinational corporations operating in rapidly growing Asian and Latin American economies. The diversity has fetched the bank more than 120 million retail customers and 2.5 million business clients, giving it considerable scale advantages over competitors. Businesses like retail banking, commercial banking, wealth management, and a subcustody business in emerging markets give HSBC diverse income streams while providing a comprehensive set of services to clients. Lastly, the ability of managers to leverage years of international experience and assemble crack teams from within the bank to execute in a new environment gives HSBC an intangible advantage when moving into a new market.

The bank also excels in developing sound strategies to deepen its moat. For example, after the acquisition of Household International in the United States, the bank sought to build a deposit base to fund Household's consumer business. It rapidly increased its branch network and launched HSBC Direct, an online savings product offering higher interest rates, and rapidly mobilized $3 billion in its first year. Despite being the largest bank in Hong Kong, it acquired a 62% stake in Hang Seng, the third-largest bank, and cemented its domination of that market. This move also ensures that HSBC services a larger portion of trade flows into and out of China that come via Hong Kong, a safer way to play China's growth.

Businesses like credit card issuing and management, wealth management, and subcustody for hedge funds investing in developing countries give HSBC a rapidly growing fee income stream. A disciplined and deep management bench ensures continuance of strategy and a commitment to delivering shareholder value despite Sir John Bond's retirement.

Data as of 12-29-06

IAC/InterActiveCorp IACI

Rating	Fair Value	Last Close	Consider Buy	Consider Sell	Yield %
★★★★	$42.00	$37.16	$32.40	$52.60	0.00

Company Profile

IAC is a diversified commerce and media firm. The Home Shopping Network is its biggest business, placing IAC in the sweet spot of televised direct marketing. HSN is followed in size by ticketing giant Ticketmaster. Other brands include LendingTree, Match.com, Ask.com (acquired in July 2005), timeshare exchange Interval International, and local services such as Citysearch, Evite, and ServiceMagic. IAC spun off its Expedia travel business in August 2005.

Management   Stewardship Grade [C]

We have assigned a "C" stewardship grade to IAC. Buying shares in the company is essentially a bet that CEO Barry Diller can create value over time. Diller owns about 26% of the Class A shares outstanding but also has full voting power over the company's Class B shares, giving him complete control over the direction of the company. This means that minority shareholders are essentially along for the ride. We like this management team's willingness to focus on the long-term profitability of the company, even if it's at the expense of short-term gains. Executive compensation at IAC is based on a variety of factors, including growth in operating income before amortization. We have no major qualms with IAC's compensation practices; however, we think the almost $700,000 in personal aircraft use that Diller received in 2005 is a tad generous. That said, we like that Diller's large ownership stake means he has a vested interest in IAC's long-term success.

Industry	Business Risk	Moat Size	Investment Style	Sector
Online Retail	Average	Narrow	Large Core	Consumer Services

Competition

	Market Cap $Mil	12 Mo Trailing Sales $Mil	Price/Cash Flow	Return On Assets%	Debt/Equity	Total Return% 1 Yr	3 Yr
IAC/InterActiveCorp	11,864	6,568	13.2	2.2	0.1	31.3	0.2
Google	140,979	9,319	42.4	15.4	0.0	11.0	—
Yahoo	34,740	6,224	20.6	11.0	0.1	-34.8	4.0

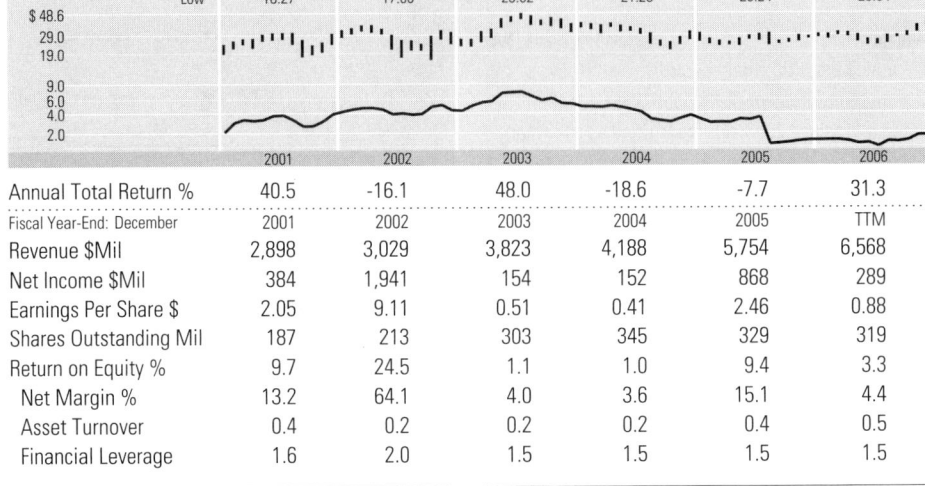

	2001	2002	2003	2004	2005	2006
Annual Total Return %	40.5	-16.1	48.0	-18.6	-7.7	31.3
Fiscal Year-End: December	2001	2002	2003	2004	2005	TTM
Revenue $Mil	2,898	3,029	3,823	4,188	5,754	6,568
Net Income $Mil	384	1,941	154	152	868	289
Earnings Per Share $	2.05	9.11	0.51	0.41	2.46	0.88
Shares Outstanding Mil	187	213	303	345	329	319
Return on Equity %	9.7	24.5	1.1	1.0	9.4	3.3
Net Margin %	13.2	64.1	4.0	3.6	15.1	4.4
Asset Turnover	0.4	0.2	0.2	0.2	0.4	0.5
Financial Leverage	1.6	2.0	1.5	1.5	1.5	1.5

Valuation Ratios	Stock	Rel to Industry	Rel to S&P 500
Price/Earnings	40.4	0.9	2.0
Price/Book	1.4	0.1	0.3
Price/Sales	1.8	0.4	0.6
Price/Cash Flow	13.2	0.7	0.9

Major Fund Holders	% of Fund Assets
Janus Global Opportunities	5.61
Legg Mason Growth Trust Primary	4.88
Pin Oak Aggressive Stock	4.42
ProFunds Internet UltraSector Inv	3.96

Thesis By Sumit Desai, 10-19-06 Stock Price as of Analysis: $29.75

IAC/InterActiveCorp (IAC) is shifting from an Internet holding company to a finely-tuned, integrated Internet company. We like this narrow-moat firm's chances of succeeding.

IAC is well positioned to capitalize on the massive number of transactions migrating online. The firm is home to well known names such as Ticketmaster and Home Shopping Network (HSN) as well as some of the Internet's choicest properties, like Match.com, LendingTree, and Ask.com. IAC's businesses all share attractive economics, including significant operating leverage and network effect benefits.

Until recently, IAC lacked a clear strategy--the result of hundreds of acquisitions, spin-offs, and divestitures over the past several years. Each of the firm's businesses was operated separately with few synergies or sharing of resources. This changed, in our opinion, with IAC's acquisition of Ask.com in 2005. We expect this purchase will lead to a mutually beneficial relationship between Ask.com and IAC's pre-existing companies. For example, each of IAC's sites can carry an Ask.com search box, leading to higher search volumes (and revenue) for Ask.com. Further, Ask.com can position its search results to generate higher traffic to IAC's other sites. This is especially beneficial for IAC's niche sites like Citysearch and its various real estate sites.

However, this strategy has risks. IAC is sacrificing Ask.com's profits in the short run in order to gain scale and market share over the long run. The company is investing heavily in marketing and infrastructure in order to increase its awareness with consumers. While we applaud management's long-term focus and think it will eventually succeed, this strategy faces an uphill battle. The company competes directly with entrenched competitors with significantly more market share, like Google and Yahoo, and any missteps would further extend the payback period on IAC's Ask.com investment.

Still, these risks are tempered by IAC's ability to generate gobs of cash. The company's two largest businesses, retailing (primarily HSN) and Ticketmaster make up more than half of the company's total revenues. HSN is the number-two player in the interactive retailing market, providing retailers with enormous reach, free advertising, and instant customer feedback. Ticketmaster, meanwhile, dominates the online ticketing market (66% share) and is the go-to channel for venues looking to fill their seats. We expect these companies to help IAC achieve free cash flow margins in the midteens over the next five years.

152 West 57th Street   www.iac.com
New York, NY 10019

Growth [A+]	2002	2003	2004	2005
Revenue %	4.5	26.2	9.5	37.4
Earnings/Share %	344.4	-94.4	-19.6	500.0
Book Value/Share %	76.5	28.0	-17.2	-33.7
Dividends/Share %	NMF	NMF	NMF	NMF

Profitability [B-]	2003	2004	2005	TTM
Return on Assets %	0.7	0.7	6.2	2.2
Oper Cash Flow $Mil	621	504	-72	899
- Cap Spending $Mil	139	168	241	245
= Free Cash Flow $Mil	482	336	-314	654

Financial Health [A]	2003	2004	2005	09-30-06
Long-term Debt $Mil	1,118	797	959	872
Total Equity $Mil	14,416	14,605	9,231	8,735
Debt/Equity Ratio	0.1	0.1	0.1	0.1

Data as of 12-29-06

IBM IBM

	Rating	Fair Value	Last Close	Consider Buy	Consider Sell	Yield %
	★★★	$94.00	$97.15	$80.10	$123.40	1.13

Company Profile

IBM is the biggest computer equipment vendor and IT services provider in the world. It designs computer systems, peripherals, and software and provides related services. The company's computer systems offerings include personal computers, high-end through low-end servers, storage systems, and electronic subsystems. IBM is also a leader in middleware, software that allows different computer systems to communicate. IBM's business outsourcing segment is growing in importance.

Management   Stewardship Grade [B]

IBM's CEO is former president and chief operating officer Samuel Palmisano, an IBM lifer. Palmisano rose through the ranks to head the global services division and won the top job in 2002. His services experience continues to benefit IBM as the firm works hard to fine-tune the profitability and resource-allocation issues that come with expanding such a complex business. CFO Mark Loughridge is from IBM's profitable global financing unit. Corporate governance is decent: no staggered board elections, good stock ownership by the team, and good financial disclosure. One item to monitor is IBM's accounting policies. We measure corporate accounting practices in terms of aggressiveness, and IBM is one firm that has historically been on the more aggressive side in how it accounts for postretirement liabilities, intellectual property, asset sales, and service contract recognition. Outside scrutiny historically determines that IBM is within the rules, but new regulations could leave the firm with less earnings-smoothing ability. We'd like to think IBM will take the high road should tempting situations arise.

Industry	Business Risk	Moat Size	Investment Style	Sector
Computer Equip.	Below Avg	Wide	Large Core	Hardware

Competition

	Market Cap $Mil	12 Mo Trailing Sales $Mil	Price/Cash Flow	Return On Assets%	Debt/ Equity	Total Return% 1 Yr	3 Yr
IBM	146,342	89,593	9.8	8.8	0.4	19.8	3.0
Hewlett-Packard	112,070	91,658	9.9	7.6	0.1	45.2	22.7
Oracle	89,050	15,203	18.9	12.2	0.4	40.4	9.3

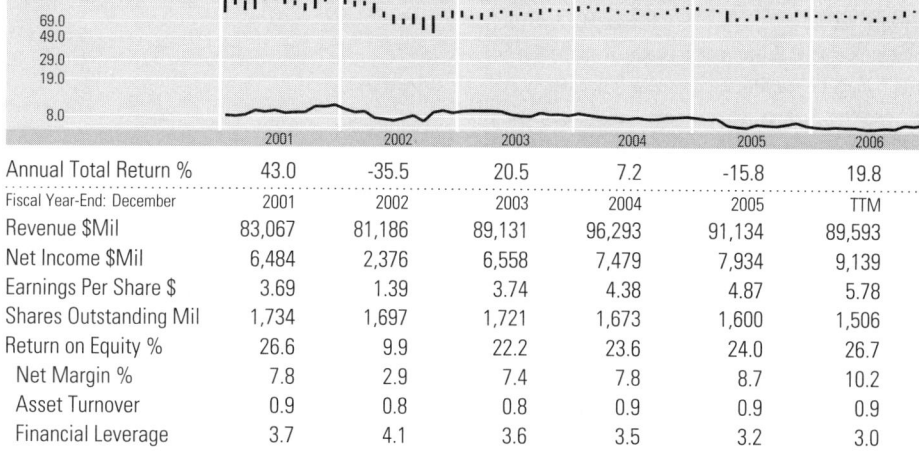

	2001	2002	2003	2004	2005	2006
Annual Total Return %	43.0	-35.5	20.5	7.2	-15.8	19.8
Fiscal Year-End: December	2001	2002	2003	2004	2005	TTM
Revenue $Mil	83,067	81,186	89,131	96,293	91,134	89,593
Net Income $Mil	6,484	2,376	6,558	7,479	7,934	9,139
Earnings Per Share $	3.69	1.39	3.74	4.38	4.87	5.78
Shares Outstanding Mil	1,734	1,697	1,721	1,673	1,600	1,506
Return on Equity %	26.6	9.9	22.2	23.6	24.0	26.7
Net Margin %	7.8	2.9	7.4	7.8	8.7	10.2
Asset Turnover	0.9	0.8	0.8	0.9	0.9	0.9
Financial Leverage	3.7	4.1	3.6	3.5	3.2	3.0

Valuation Ratios	Stock	Rel to Industry	Rel to S&P 500
Price/Earnings	16.8	0.6	0.8
Price/Book	4.3	0.8	1.0
Price/Sales	1.6	0.6	0.6
Price/Cash Flow	9.8	0.6	0.7

Major Fund Holders	% of Fund Assets
Ariel Focus	6.50
ICON Information Technology	6.11
E*TRADE Technology Index	5.30
Legg Mason Partners Technology B	5.28

Thesis By Rod Bare, 12-01-06 Stock Price as of Analysis: $91.25

IBM is one of the few technology firms remaining that can deliver a complete hardware, software, services, and financing package to clients worldwide. This valuable capability is a key reason IBM should continue to deliver solid profitability even as some of its end markets slip into slow-growth maturity.

The firm's global services group, responsible for half of overall revenue, is key to IBM's future in several important ways. The group's mission is to deliver the best solution possible for the client's budget, even if some components are non-IBM. By shifting the focus from pushing the product line to helping clients solve complex IT issues, the IBM services model improves customer relationships and generates several cross-selling opportunities. One key opportunity taking shape is IBM's ability to take over a customer's entire business process, like the systems and personnel related to accounting, HR, or network security. IBM can use its best-practices knowledge to tweak the unit to peak efficiency, aiming to give the client more bang for the buck.

IBM continues to improve its software business as revenue grows and margins widen. The firm has made several key investments to bolster its middleware solutions, spending more than $4 billion on software acquisitions through the summer of 2006 alone. Most of IBM's middleware installed base functions as a valuable annuity, with ongoing maintenance and upgrade revenue. Other software solutions, such as network security, help open the door for global services to sell additional consulting or outsourcing business. Software also has relatively high margins compared with hardware and services; strength here can offset weakness elsewhere.

Computer hardware remains an interesting area to watch. Revenue volatility continues, thanks to ongoing product-refresh cycles. The overall trend should be low-single-digit growth as customer preferences shift and competition increases in this consolidating market. An interesting area to watch on the hardware side is IBM's growing partnership with Network Appliance, a leading network storage company. NetApp is a key player in the fast-growing distributed storage market, and its impressive software and hardware assets are a nice addition to the menu for the global services group.

The international market remains a source of opportunity for IBM. Despite pockets of weakness in Western Europe, IBM is well positioned in growth areas like China, India, and Russia; investments in these regions should balance maturity in other markets.

One New Orchard Road
Armonk, NY 10504
www.ibm.com

Growth [D]	2002	2003	2004	2005
Revenue %	-2.3	9.8	8.0	-5.4
Earnings/Share %	-62.3	169.1	17.1	11.2
Book Value/Share %	1.8	19.4	10.2	9.5
Dividends/Share %	7.3	6.8	11.1	11.4

Profitability [A]	2003	2004	2005	TTM
Return on Assets %	6.2	6.7	7.5	8.8
Oper Cash Flow $Mil	14,537	15,349	14,914	14,914
- Cap Spending $Mil	4,393	4,368	3,842	3,842
= Free Cash Flow $Mil	10,144	10,981	11,072	11,072

Financial Health [B+]	2003	2004	2005	09-30-06
Long-term Debt $Mil	—	14,828	15,425	13,436
Total Equity $Mil	29,531	31,688	33,098	34,248
Debt/Equity Ratio	—	0.5	0.5	0.4

Data as of 12-29-06

Idexx Laboratories IDXX

	Rating	Fair Value	Last Close	Consider Buy	Consider Sell	Yield %
	★★★	$73.00	$79.30	$62.20	$95.80	0.00

Company Profile

Idexx Laboratories primarily develops, manufactures, and distributes diagnostic products, equipment, and services for pets and livestock. Its key product lines include single-use canine and feline test kits that veterinarians can use in the office, laboratory equipment for blood-panel analysis, veterinary pharmaceuticals, and tests to detect and manage disease in livestock. Idexx gets about 34% of its revenue from outside the United States.

Management   Stewardship Grade [B]

Idexx gets a good Stewardship Grade in our books. After a long, deliberate search, Idexx found a new CEO and chairman in Jonathan Ayers at the beginning of 2002. Ayers spent seven years leading the Carrier unit at United Technologies, another firm that has earned an above-average Stewardship Grade. We're enthusiastic about the level of detailed disclosure the company provides, as well as the preponderance of outsiders on Idexx's eight-member board. We like that the CEO is required to report on succession planning to the board at least annually. Importantly, the firm recently changed its stock incentive compensation plan to emphasize restricted stock over the stock options it used in the past. Also, we're impressed that Ayers has exchanged some of his cash bonus for deferred shares. Although his equity stake remains lower than we'd like to see (not uncommon for recently arrived CEOs), we like that he chose shares over the immediate gratification of cash. This suggests he's thinking and acting more like an owner than a mercenary.

One Idexx Drive
Westbrook, ME 04092-2041   www.idexx.com

Growth [B]	2002	2003	2004	2005
Revenue %	6.9	15.3	15.4	16.2
Earnings/Share %	19.3	22.3	37.7	5.0
Book Value/Share %	11.7	17.9	-3.4	-2.4
Dividends/Share %	NMF	NMF	NMF	NMF

Profitability [A+]	2003	2004	2005	TTM
Return on Assets %	10.9	15.2	15.9	17.0
Oper Cash Flow $Mil	117	95	117	111
- Cap Spending $Mil	20	32	27	43
= Free Cash Flow $Mil	98	64	90	68

Financial Health [A]	2003	2004	2005	09-30-06
Long-term Debt $Mil	0	1	0	7
Total Equity $Mil	413	398	369	388
Debt/Equity Ratio	0.0	0.0	0.0	0.0

Industry	Business Risk	Moat Size	Investment Style	Sector
Drugs	Below Avg	Narrow	Mid Growth	Healthcare

Competition	Market Cap $Mil	12 Mo Trailing Sales $Mil	Price/Cash Flow	Return On Assets%	Debt/ Equity	Total Return% 1 Yr	3 Yr
Idexx Laboratories	2,482	714	22.3	17.0	0.0	10.2	19.1
VCA Antech	2,688	958	23.4	11.0	0.9	14.2	27.7

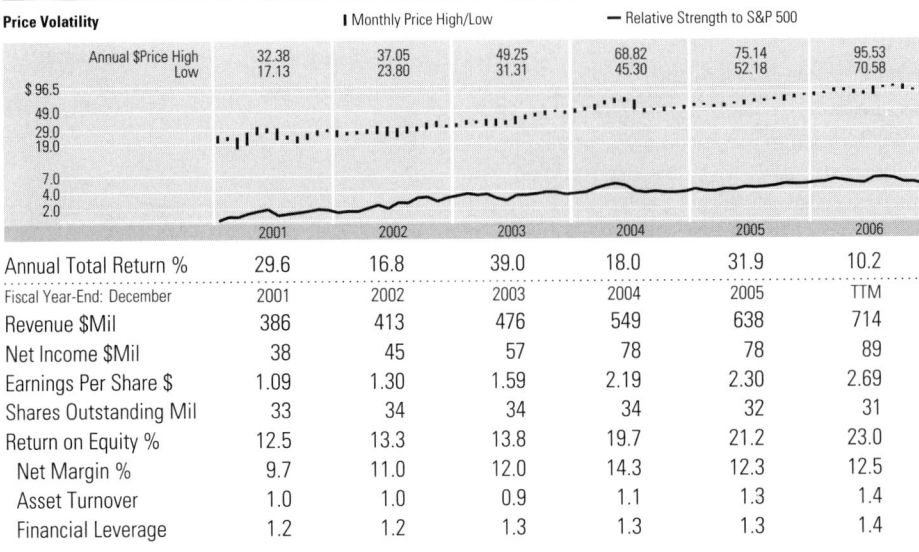

Price Volatility — Monthly Price High/Low — Relative Strength to S&P 500

	2001	2002	2003	2004	2005	2006
Annual $Price High	32.38	37.05	49.25	68.82	75.14	95.53
Low	17.13	23.80	31.31	45.30	52.18	70.58
Annual Total Return %	29.6	16.8	39.0	18.0	31.9	10.2

Fiscal Year-End: December	2001	2002	2003	2004	2005	TTM
Revenue $Mil	386	413	476	549	638	714
Net Income $Mil	38	45	57	78	78	89
Earnings Per Share $	1.09	1.30	1.59	2.19	2.30	2.69
Shares Outstanding Mil	33	34	34	34	32	31
Return on Equity %	12.5	13.3	13.8	19.7	21.2	23.0
Net Margin %	9.7	11.0	12.0	14.3	12.3	12.5
Asset Turnover	1.0	1.0	0.9	1.1	1.3	1.4
Financial Leverage	1.2	1.2	1.3	1.3	1.3	1.4

Valuation Ratios	Stock	Rel to Industry	Rel to S&P 500
Price/Earnings	29.5	1.2	1.4
Price/Book	6.4	1.2	1.6
Price/Sales	3.5	0.8	1.2
Price/Cash Flow	22.3	1.4	1.5

Major Fund Holders	% of Fund Assets
Payden Small Cap Leaders	6.46
Sequoia	4.18
Ashport Small/Mid Cap C	3.86
DF Dent Premier Growth	2.96

Thesis   By Debbie S. Wang, 12-15-06   Stock Price as of Analysis: $81.80

Idexx Laboratories focuses on creating small advantages and has quietly increased its scale and reach in the veterinary diagnostic lab business to build a narrow economic moat.

Idexx offers a large range of diagnostic test kits, lab equipment and instruments, and testing services to animal hospitals, as well as for livestock. Along with other pet-oriented companies, Idexx is well positioned to benefit from two key trends, as about 80% of its total revenue comes from the pet market. First, pet ownership continues to grow, with 63% of U.S. households owning pets in 2005 compared with 56% in 1988. Further, pet owners have demonstrated greater willingness to spend more on their companion animals--animal lovers doubled spending on pet products and services in the past decade.

Although Idexx isn't the overwhelming market leader in every product line, it has established a substantial footprint in key areas where it can offer a compelling product advantage and then extend its reach by offering a greater breadth of complementary products. For example, Idexx has carved out a leadership position in single-use test kits for in-office use. These premium-price, high-margin products offer vets and pet owners the convenience of test results in approximately 10 minutes; many routine and recurring diagnostics have switched from outside labs to the kits. Idexx also maintains a number-two position in off-site lab testing, another area that continues to see double-digit growth.

Idexx's ability to sniff out opportunities to build a better mousetrap also crosses over to its smaller water-testing and livestock-testing businesses. Local municipalities are often required to routinely test water supplies for dangerous levels of bacteria; Idexx offers a unique test that can detect two of the most common bacterial contaminants and is easier and faster to use than traditional testing methods. This has allowed the firm to capture more than 60% of the water market.

Idexx has also developed a simpler, streamlined test to detect bovine spongiform encephalopathy (BSE, or mad-cow disease). Even though U.S. demand for this test remains small, international markets such as Europe and Japan offer potential, as both are committed to testing cattle on a widespread basis. While these segments haven't seen growth as robust as that of the pet business, they generally offer fatter margins. We like the innovation Idexx has demonstrated, and we expect more.

Illinois Tool Works ITW

Data as of 12-29-06

Rating	Fair Value	Last Close	Consider Buy	Consider Sell	Yield %
★★★	$50.00	$46.19	$38.60	$62.60	1.62

Company Profile

Illinois Tool Works' 700 autonomous subsidiaries operate in 45 countries in two groups: engineered products (short-cycle industrial goods such as fasteners, adhesives, and construction tools) and specialty systems (industrial machinery, food equipment, and packaging systems). ITW's target markets are diverse and include the automotive, food-service, construction, and general manufacturing sectors. The company also has a small investment and leasing arm.

Management Stewardship Grade [B]

In 2005, David Speer became ITW's fifth CEO since the firm went public in the early 1960s. A 27-year company veteran, he has spent most of his time managing various businesses in the firm's construction divisions. His tenure at the company is about equal to that of the average senior manager, illustrating the high level of experience throughout the organization. We're impressed by the company's lean management structure. Headquarters maintains a staff of less than 200 people, and unit managers are only three steps from the CEO. Helping to manage the disparate operations are eight executive vice presidents, each responsible for more than $1 billion in revenue. The company's governance policies are good. Board elections are not staggered, compensation is not egregious, and financials are conservatively stated (the company started expensing option awards in 2005). Annual bonuses are based on net income and "predetermined management goals" such as succession planning, corporate governance, cost reduction, market penetration, and acquisition planning. Though return on invested capital isn't mentioned in the 2004 proxy statement as being a component of annual bonus criteria, management tells us it is. Stock incentive awards are based on an officer's position in the company and his or her ability to effect long-term growth and profitability.

3600 West Lake Avenue www.itw.com
Glenview, IL 60025-5811

Growth [C+]	2002	2003	2004	2005
Revenue %	1.9	6.0	16.9	10.1
Earnings/Share %	-12.2	43.7	32.2	18.5
Book Value/Share %	9.3	18.5	-2.1	5.0
Dividends/Share %	7.1	4.4	10.6	17.3

Profitability [A+]	2003	2004	2005	TTM
Return on Assets %	9.1	11.8	13.1	12.7
Oper Cash Flow $Mil	1,369	1,532	1,847	1,806
- Cap Spending $Mil	258	283	293	300
= Free Cash Flow $Mil	1,110	1,249	1,553	1,506

Financial Health [A+]	2003	2004	2005	09-30-06
Long-term Debt $Mil	920	921	958	964
Total Equity $Mil	7,874	7,628	7,547	8,711
Debt/Equity Ratio	0.1	0.1	0.1	0.1

Industry	Business Risk	Moat Size	Investment Style	Sector
Machinery	Average	Narrow	Large Core	Industrial Materials

Competition

	Market Cap $Mil	12 Mo Trailing Sales $Mil	Price/Cash Flow	Return On Assets %	Debt/Equity	Total Return % 1 Yr	3 Yr
Illinois Tool Works	26,184	13,798	14.5	12.7	0.1	6.7	5.3
Danaher	22,297	9,200	16.1	8.7	0.4	30.0	17.0
Dover	10,008	6,969	10.8	7.6	0.4	22.9	9.2

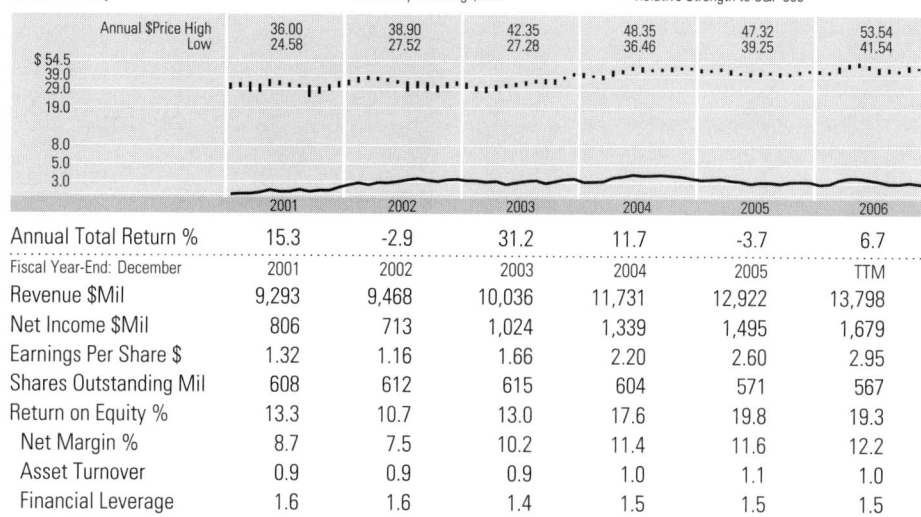

	2001	2002	2003	2004	2005	2006
Annual $Price High	36.00	38.90	42.35	48.35	47.32	53.54
Low	24.58	27.52	27.28	36.46	39.25	41.54
Annual Total Return %	15.3	-2.9	31.2	11.7	-3.7	6.7

Fiscal Year-End: December	2001	2002	2003	2004	2005	TTM
Revenue $Mil	9,293	9,468	10,036	11,731	12,922	13,798
Net Income $Mil	806	713	1,024	1,339	1,495	1,679
Earnings Per Share $	1.32	1.16	1.66	2.20	2.60	2.95
Shares Outstanding Mil	608	612	615	604	571	567
Return on Equity %	13.3	10.7	13.0	17.6	19.8	19.3
Net Margin %	8.7	7.5	10.2	11.4	11.6	12.2
Asset Turnover	0.9	0.9	0.9	1.0	1.1	1.0
Financial Leverage	1.6	1.6	1.4	1.5	1.5	1.5

Valuation Ratios	Stock	Rel to Industry	Rel to S&P 500
Price/Earnings	15.7	0.8	0.8
Price/Book	3.0	1.0	0.7
Price/Sales	1.9	1.2	0.7
Price/Cash Flow	14.5	0.8	1.0

Major Fund Holders	% of Fund Assets
Blue Chip Investor	4.43
FMI Provident Trust Strategy	3.59
Concorde Value	3.47
HSBC Investor Growth & Income I	3.38

Thesis By John Kearney, CFA, 12-04-06 Stock Price as of Analysis: $47.27

Illinois Tool Works' growth-by-acquisition strategy is hardly a unique concept to the diversified industrial sector. It's the company's mastery of the 80/20 principle and its unconventional acquisition integration approach that separate ITW from the rest of the pack.

For the last 20 years, ITW has managed its business around the basic tenet that 80% of a firm's profits come from 20% of its customers--dubbed the 80/20 rule. By streamlining its 700-plus business units with the 80/20 principle, ITW has been able to manage its most profitable customers and products with laser-like precision. Though not the first or only firm to implement the concept, ITW has become one of the most successful practitioners of the 80/20 model, having recorded 13% annual earnings growth over the last decade and an average 15% return on invested capital.

ITW's success is not due simply to its proficiency in applying the 80/20 rule to its legacy businesses, but rather its ability to employ the demanding process across newly acquired businesses. After making an acquisition, ITW breaks the newly acquired entity into several small, autonomous business units, each with its own salesforce, engineering team, and manufacturing line. This decentralized operating structure is the antithesis of the typical industrial acquirer's philosophy of consolidating activities into centralized operations to reduce expenses. However, ITW's methodology complements the 80/20 principle by keeping each business close to the core customers, which in turn allows the company to serve the needs of its most profitable customers more effectively than a larger, more centralized business.

Acquisitions have played (and will continue to play) an important role in augmenting ITW's earnings growth. The company completes around 28 acquisitions a year, paying roughly 1 times sales for the targeted business (roughly $32 million per acquisition). The company focuses on niche markets where it feels it can differentiate itself and expand margins with its disciplined business model. On average, ITW has been able to double the operating margins of its acquired businesses by increasing margins from 10% to nearly 20% in just five years.

It's hard to argue with ITW's track record on the acquisition front and the effectiveness of its focused operating process. The question going forward will be whether or not ITW will be able to maintain its torrid acquisition pace at prices that will continue to generate economic value for shareholders.

Imperial Oil IMO

Data as of 12-29-06

Rating	Fair Value	Last Close	Consider Buy	Consider Sell	Yield %
★★★	$38.00	$36.83	$29.30	$47.60	0.77

Industry	Business Risk	Moat Size	Investment Style	Sector
Oil/Gas	Average	Narrow	Large Core	Energy

Company Profile
Imperial Oil is Canada's largest integrated oil company and is 70% owned by ExxonMobil. It is involved in upstream oil and gas exploration and production as well as downstream refining, distribution, and chemicals production. With abundant oil sands resources, Imperial produces about 317,000 barrels of oil equivalent per day. It has refining capacity of 502,000 barrels per day and sells petroleum products through a network of 2,000 Esso-branded retail outlets.

Management   Stewardship Grade [B]
Imperial Oil is an affiliate of ExxonMobil, which owns 69.6% of Imperial's shares. This relationship is quite beneficial to Imperial, which has access to ExxonMobil's research, international skills, and economies of scale for procurement. Tim J. Hearn has been chairman, president, and CEO of Imperial since 2002, and he has worked at either Imperial or ExxonMobil for nearly four decades. In 2005, Hearn received a base salary of C$1.1 million, and C$2.2 million in bonus, other compensation, and long-term incentive payouts. He was also awarded C$7.5 million worth of restricted stock or deferred shares. We don't think this is excessive for this type of company, and the incentive-based pay reflects a record year in which Imperial's profits reached C$2.6 billion. Although we would prefer that the firm divide the CEO and chairman role, we like the fact that Imperial's management has demonstrated a long-term focus and even avoids quarterly management conference calls. By our calculations, returns on invested capital have averaged 19% over the past six years, which is among the best in the oil patch.

111 St. Clair Avenue West
Toronto, ON M5W 1K3
www.imperialoil.ca

Growth [NA]	2002	2003	2004	2005
Revenue %	-1.5	13.0	17.4	24.0
Earnings/Share %	2.9	-94.7	25.4	32.2
Book Value/Share %	17.8	-95.7	18.8	9.5
Dividends/Share %	—	—	—	—

Profitability [NA]	2003	2004	2005	TTM
Return on Assets %	12.6	13.5	16.1	19.7
Oper Cash Flow $Mil	1,571	2,550	2,852	3,310
- Cap Spending $Mil	1,045	1,060	1,183	1,082
= Free Cash Flow $Mil	525	1,491	1,669	2,228

Financial Health [NA]	2003	2004	2005	09-30-06
Long-term Debt $Mil	666	1,577	2,215	1,369
Total Equity $Mil	4,298	5,268	5,669	6,532
Debt/Equity Ratio	0.2	0.3	0.4	0.2

Competition

	Market Cap $Mil	12 Mo Trailing Sales $Mil	Price/Cash Flow	Return On Assets%	Debt/ Equity	Total Return% 1 Yr	3 Yr
Imperial Oil	35,457	23,051	10.7	19.7	0.2	11.8	36.1
Suncor Energy	36,114	9,162	18.1	7.8	0.5	25.4	46.5
Petro-Canada	21,141	13,867	6.4	8.4	0.3	3.2	18.8

Price Volatility
Monthly Price High/Low — Relative Strength to S&P 500

Annual $Price High Low	9.82 7.53	10.62 8.00	14.92 9.42	20.82 14.11	39.14 18.27	40.38 29.99
	2001	2002	2003	2004	2005	2006
Annual Total Return %	8.2	4.9	57.6	35.6	69.3	11.8

Fiscal Year-End: December	2001	2002	2003	2004	2005	TTM
Revenue $Mil	11,102	10,729	13,467	17,256	22,973	23,051
Net Income $Mil	792	771	1,203	1,580	2,149	2,830
Earnings Per Share $	2.01	2.03	0.12	0.16	0.23	0.98
Shares Outstanding Mil	393	379	10,021	9,635	9,222	963
Return on Equity %	29.1	24.8	28.0	30.0	37.9	43.3
Net Margin %	7.1	7.2	8.9	9.2	9.4	12.3
Asset Turnover	1.6	1.4	1.4	1.5	1.7	1.6
Financial Leverage	2.5	2.4	2.2	2.2	2.3	2.2

Valuation Ratios	Stock	Rel to Industry	Rel to S&P 500
Price/Earnings	37.4	2.9	1.8
Price/Book	5.4	1.7	1.3
Price/Sales	1.5	0.8	0.5
Price/Cash Flow	10.7	1.3	0.7

Major Fund Holders	% of Fund Assets
Harding Loevner International Equity	2.22
UMB Scout Stock	1.99
Excelsior Energy & Nat Resources	1.71
Fidelity Canada	1.59

Thesis   By Elizabeth Collins, 11-21-06   Stock Price as of Analysis: $36.80

Imperial Oil's history of generating sizable returns and dividend growth is enviable. But as the firm wades deeper into Alberta's expensive oil sands, its dependence on high oil prices is increasing. Even so, we think oil prices are likely to stay high enough, and we like Imperial's prospects.

As conventional oil and gas reserves decline in Canada, Imperial is focusing on its long-term oil sands projects. Oil sands are a mixture of oil, sand, and clay from which low-quality oil is extracted and upgraded into higher-quality crude oil. Oil sands accounted for 56% of Imperial's 2005 total energy production, and that percentage is set to rise. Imperial is also Canada's largest refiner.

Compared with conventional oil production, extracting and upgrading oil from sand is expensive. If oil prices do drop sharply, oil sands producers will be the first to feel the pinch. Technological and process improvements should lower per-barrel costs, but how much those savings will be and how soon they will be realized is highly uncertain. Oil sands production also requires massive capital outlays, which is why Cold Lake and Syncrude, Imperial's two large oil sands projects, are being developed in stages. Syncrude, an oil sands consortium in which Imperial has a 25% stake, has been dogged by cost overruns and delays that will take a big bite out of returns. Natural gas is also a key ingredient in the energy-intensive oil sands process, making long-term supply of low-cost natural gas a challenging critical success factor.

High per-barrel costs, large up-front capital expenditures, and dependence on natural gas make oil sands projects risky, but looking long term, we think oil prices are likely to stay strong enough for these projects to pan out. In fact, the company has submitted plans for the Kearl oil sands project to regulators for approval. Imperial has other energy prospects that should also yield results, namely undeveloped conventional oil and gas resources in the Mackenzie Delta and Atlantic offshore. Barring a substantial oil price dip, we think Imperial should continue to generate strong cash flows.

Furthermore, we like the advantages that come with being majority owned by ExxonMobil. Financial backing and a corresponding AAA credit rating give Imperial a lower debt cost than many of its peers. ExxonMobil is further able to lend research and engineering capabilities and procurement advantages. And with operations exclusively in Canada, Imperial avoids a lot of messy political uncertainty of operating in less stable regions.

Data as of 12-29-06

Imperial Tobacco Group PLC ADR ITY

Rating	Fair Value	Last Close	Consider Buy	Consider Sell	Yield %
★★★	$70.00	$79.03	$44.60	$84.40	2.66

Company Profile

Imperial Tobacco is the top seller of cigarettes in the United Kingdom and the fifth-largest manufacturer of tobacco products worldwide. Imperial markets its cigarettes under the Lambert & Butler, Richmond, Embassy, Superkings, Davidoff, and West brands. The firm is a top seller in the roll-your-own tobacco market with its Drum loose tobacco brand and Rizla rolling papers. Imperial also sells Amphora and St. Bruno pipe tobaccos and cigars under the Classic brand.

Management Stewardship Grade [NA]

Gareth Davis has been CEO of Imperial Tobacco since the company's 1996 spin-off from Hanson, a British conglomerate that sold everything from coal to whirlpool baths. Davis joined Imperial in 1972 and has been instrumental in the company's expansion program, aimed at acquiring international tobacco assets that would lessen the firm's exposure to a declining U.K. cigarette market. Management has been extremely astute at finding and integrating meaningful acquisitions, as well as at ferreting out cost savings within its own operations. Imperial is also dedicated to creating shareholder value and adheres to a strict return on capital discipline throughout the organization. The company's only significant non-shareholder-friendly move over the past 10 years involved the issuance of deeply discounted rights in connection with its 2002 acquisition of Reemtsma, which diluted the share base more than 15%. After repairing the company's credit profile (which suffered when Imperial secured 3.6 billion British pounds in credit lines to use for the purchase of Reemtsma) with the rating agencies, management has moved forward with a share-repurchase program that should enhance shareholder value longer term.

P.O. Box 244 Southville www.imperial-tobacco.com
Bristol, United Kingdom BS99-7UJ

Growth [NA]	2002	2003	2004	2005
Revenue %	40.2	37.6	-3.6	2.3
Earnings/Share %	-27.4	41.9	5.7	28.4
Book Value/Share %	NMF	NMF	130.5	3.2
Dividends/Share %	14.6	27.3	19.0	12.0

Profitability [NA]	2003	2004	2005	TTM
Return on Assets %	5.8	6.8	9.6	9.6
Oper Cash Flow $Mil	662	1,405	1,720	1,720
- Cap Spending $Mil	131	182	166	166
= Free Cash Flow $Mil	531	1,223	1,555	1,555

Financial Health [NA]	2003	2004	2005	09-30-05
Long-term Debt $Mil	5,808	5,834	4,988	4,988
Total Equity $Mil	98	243	246	246
Debt/Equity Ratio	59.1	24.0	20.3	20.3

Industry	Business Risk	Moat Size	Investment Style	Sector
Tobacco	Above Avg	Wide	 Large Core	Consumer Goods

Competition

	Market Cap $Mil	12 Mo Trailing Sales $Mil	Price/Cash Flow	Return On Assets %	Debt/Equity	Total Return % 1 Yr	3 Yr
Imperial Tobacco Group PLC ADR	28,814	20,706	16.8	9.6	20.3	35.3	30.0
Altria Group	179,868	100,499	12.6	10.5	0.3	19.9	21.8
British American Tobacco	59,384	43,778	14.0	10.5	0.8	30.1	32.1

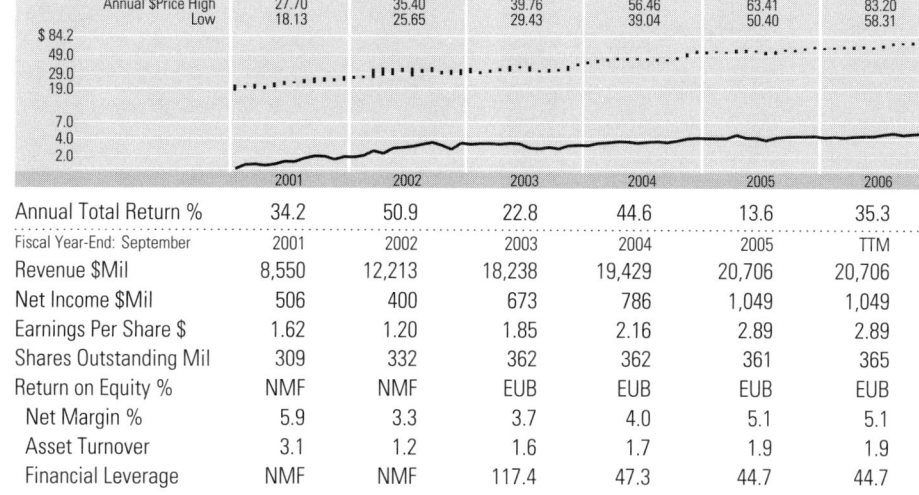

	2001	2002	2003	2004	2005	TTM
Annual Total Return %	34.2	50.9	22.8	44.6	13.6	35.3
Fiscal Year-End: September	2001	2002	2003	2004	2005	TTM
Revenue $Mil	8,550	12,213	18,238	19,429	20,706	20,706
Net Income $Mil	506	400	673	786	1,049	1,049
Earnings Per Share $	1.62	1.20	1.85	2.16	2.89	2.89
Shares Outstanding Mil	309	332	362	362	361	365
Return on Equity %	NMF	NMF	EUB	EUB	EUB	EUB
Net Margin %	5.9	3.3	3.7	4.0	5.1	5.1
Asset Turnover	3.1	1.2	1.6	1.7	1.9	1.9
Financial Leverage	NMF	NMF	117.4	47.3	44.7	44.7

Valuation Ratios	Stock	Rel to Industry	Rel to S&P 500
Price/Earnings	27.3	1.5	1.3
Price/Book	117.3	5.7	28.6
Price/Sales	1.4	0.8	0.5
Price/Cash Flow	16.8	1.3	1.2

Major Fund Holders	% of Fund Assets
Old Mutual Barrow Hanley Value Z	3.60
American Independence Stock I	3.48
Vice Fund	3.42
Lazard International Equity Sel Instl	2.65

Thesis By Greggory Warren, CFA, 12-06-06 Stock Price as of Analysis: $79.40

Even with high excise taxes and declining cigarette consumption in its core markets, Imperial generates significant amounts of cash flow from its tobacco operations. A prudent allocator of capital, Imperial has made meaningful acquisitions and returned excess cash to shareholders in the form of dividends and share repurchases. Given the threat posed by international tobacco litigation and the influence governments have over the sale and use of tobacco products worldwide, Imperial does have a higher risk profile than most other packaged goods firms.

With cigarette consumption declining 4% per year on average in the United Kingdom, Imperial has looked to other tobacco markets for sales and earnings growth. Over the past decade, the firm has focused on acquisitions that expanded the geographic reach of its operations. This reduced Imperial's exposure to the United Kingdom from 50% of sales and 65% of operating profits in 1999 to just 26% of sales and 38% of profits in 2006. More importantly, it increased the amount of sales Imperial receives from faster-growing markets in Eastern Europe, the Middle East, and sub-Saharan Africa.

Imperial's largest deal was the 2002 purchase of Reemtsma, which made it the second-largest cigarette producer in Germany and gave it a foothold in Eastern Europe and Southeast Asia. While the German cigarette market is not much different from the United Kingdom, the company saw a huge opportunity to improve profitability at Reemtsma. In just the past three years, Imperial has improved operating margins at the acquired firm from less than 30% to around 45% through a keen focus on better product mix and cost-cutting initiatives.

While some of this improvement may wane this year as higher taxes are imposed on roll-your-own tobacco products in Germany, we feel that the turnaround at Reemtsma speaks volumes about management's ability to find and integrate meaningful acquisitions in both mature and emerging markets. It also shows that Imperial is willing to sacrifice profitability in the near term if it believes it will enhance the cash flow characteristics of the business longer term.

With heavy restrictions on the promotion and use of tobacco products in Western Europe making it difficult for new companies or brands to develop, and Imperial increasing its market share in key emerging markets through acquisitions, we feel that the firm should be able to retain its wide-moat status and continue to generate significant amounts of cash flow for investors longer term.

Data as of 12-29-06

Infosys Technologies ADR INFY

	Rating	Fair Value	Last Close	Consider Buy	Consider Sell	Yield %
	★★	$48.00	$54.56	$37.00	$60.10	0.93

Industry	Business Risk	Moat Size	Investment Style	Sector
Business Appl.	Average	Narrow	Large Growth	Software

Company Profile

Founded in 1981 by seven software engineers with the equivalent of $250, Infosys has become the poster child of the New India and is one of the world's largest IT services firms. Based in Bangalore, the firm offers a full range of IT services: from application maintenance to management consulting. Though known best for its offshore work, a full 30% of revenues come from onsite and near-shore assignments. In fiscal 2006, North American clients constituted 71% of sales and operating income.

Management

Stewardship Grade [NA]

Non-executive chairman and chief mentor Narayana Murthy stepped down from active involvement with the firm in August 2006 when he reached the firm's mandatory retirement age of 60. Murthy was one of the firm's founders and built a reputation of fostering strong corporate governance, in addition to being credited with Infosys' amazing rise as a global IT titan. In fiscal 2006, Murthy's total compensation was an ascetic $93,500. He owns about 16 million shares (about $865 million). CEO Nandan Nilekani, another founder and the second pillar of Infosys' success, was compensated $92,500 in fiscal 2006. He owns more than 10 million shares. President and COO S. Gopalakrishnan has jointly run the firm since 1981 with Murthy and Nilekani.

Infosys has long served as a model for Indian corporate transparency and became the first among its peers to grant employee stock options. Top executives receive no options or restricted-stock grants. Infosys was the first Indian company to list its shares on the Nasdaq exchange and is one of the first foreign firms to meet U.S. Sarbanes-Oxley requirements. There are no material related-party transactions. The firm does provide loans for employees (though not for the purpose of stock purchases), which we ascribe more to the state of Indian banking than to anything untoward.

Electronics City Hosur Road www.infosys.com
Bangalore, India 560 100

Growth [NA]	2002	2003	2004	2005
Revenue %	38.3	41.0	49.8	35.2
Earnings/Share %	17.7	38.4	50.5	31.6
Book Value/Share %	40.2	52.1	27.5	45.6
Dividends/Share %	59.1	22.4	434.7	-63.8

Profitability [NA]	2003	2004	2005	TTM
Return on Assets %	23.9	28.8	26.9	26.9
Oper Cash Flow $Mil	372	344	599	599
- Cap Spending $Mil	93	186	246	246
= Free Cash Flow $Mil	279	158	353	353

Financial Health [NA]	2003	2004	2005	03-31-05
Long-term Debt $Mil	—	—	—	—
Total Equity $Mil	953	1,253	1,837	1,837
Debt/Equity Ratio	—	—	—	—

Competition	Market Cap $Mil	12 Mo Trailing Sales $Mil	Price/Cash Flow	Return On Assets%	Debt/ Equity	Total Return% 1 Yr	3 Yr
Infosys Technologies ADR	29,525	2,152	49.3	26.9	—	36.8	31.5
IBM	146,342	89,593	9.8	8.8	0.4	19.8	3.0
Accenture	28,867	18,852	11.7	11.3	0.0	29.3	13.4

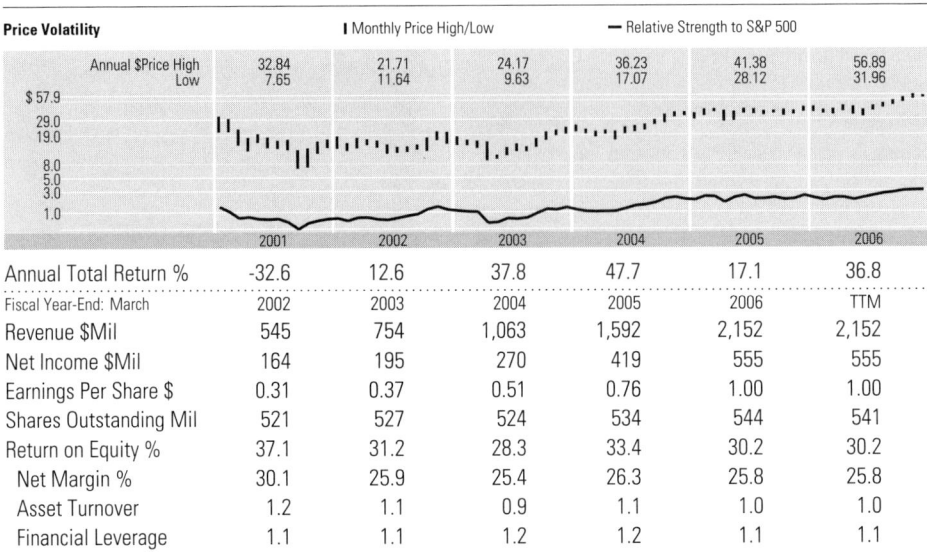

	2001	2002	2003	2004	2005	2006
Annual $Price High	32.84	21.71	24.17	36.23	41.38	56.89
Low	7.65	11.64	9.63	17.07	28.12	31.96
Annual Total Return %	-32.6	12.6	37.8	47.7	17.1	36.8

Fiscal Year-End: March	2002	2003	2004	2005	2006	TTM
Revenue $Mil	545	754	1,063	1,592	2,152	2,152
Net Income $Mil	164	195	270	419	555	555
Earnings Per Share $	0.31	0.37	0.51	0.76	1.00	1.00
Shares Outstanding Mil	521	527	524	534	544	541
Return on Equity %	37.1	31.2	28.3	33.4	30.2	30.2
Net Margin %	30.1	25.9	25.4	26.3	25.8	25.8
Asset Turnover	1.2	1.1	0.9	1.1	1.0	1.0
Financial Leverage	1.1	1.1	1.2	1.2	1.1	1.1

Valuation Ratios	Stock	Rel to Industry	Rel to S&P 500
Price/Earnings	54.6	1.8	2.7
Price/Book	16.1	1.9	3.9
Price/Sales	13.7	2.1	4.7
Price/Cash Flow	49.3	2.0	3.4

Major Fund Holders	% of Fund Assets
Boyle Marathon	4.07
American Century Legacy Foc Lg Cap Inv	3.72
BlackRock Focus Twenty B	3.39
Calamos International Growth A	3.16

Thesis By Mike Ford-Taggart, CFA, 12-14-06 Stock Price as of Analysis: $55.22

The well-known story on Infosys is that various crises will manifest next year or the following year and cripple the firm's torrid growth and profitability. But next year never seems to arrive for Infosys. Instead, its reputation for high-quality project deliverance combined with its imbedded cost advantages help the firm stay ahead of the global competition.

Concerns about Infosys' future growth and profitability are not unfounded. Non-Indian information technology (IT) firms have set up shop in India, challenging Infosys' labor-cost advantages and straining India's resource of IT professionals. The firm's move into higher-end IT offerings creates the need to hire increasing numbers of higher-paid non-Indians who can work onsite at client offices. Increased competition, brought about by rivals' response to the firm's expansion, necessitates increased sales and marketing expenses. Eventually, revenue and profit growth will have to slow as overall revenue begins to dwarf incremental revenue.

We believe, though, that such concerns tend to be overblown. Despite the growing scarcity of IT professionals, Infosys still hires at will: Indeed, only 1.5% of applicants eventually get hired, and even fewer complete their mandatory training. Because Infosys professionals are paid above industry norms, ill effects of wage inflation and attrition have been muted: Salaries still increase sharply every year, but they don't pay "catch up" bonuses like some rivals; attrition levels around 13% are near the industry's lows. Increased costs from higher-end offerings and larger contracts will, we believe, pay off in the long term. No firm can expand forever, but Infosys continues to delay the inevitable by increasing the breadth of its offerings, expanding abroad, and garnering its share of the Indian IT services market.

The often-overshadowed story on Infosys is how it has transitioned to a high-benefit provider. Adherence to disciplined processes, refined over 25 years and across thousands of projects, has engendered a sterling reputation built around high-quality delivery, transparent contract pricing, and sophisticated, industry-tailored solutions. If you think this is fluff, consider that 95% of revenues in fiscal 2006 came from repeat business with existing clients. The number of clients contributing greater than $50 million in annual revenue has increased to 12 as of September 2006 from five in March 2005, suggesting that the world's largest companies are increasingly placing their trust and their IT budgets with Infosys. This alone should allay misplaced fears of a pending slowdown.

Data as of 12-29-06

Ingersoll-Rand A IR

	Rating	Fair Value	Last Close	Consider Buy	Consider Sell	Yield %
	★★★★	$44.00	$39.13	$33.90	$55.10	1.74

Company Profile
Ingersoll-Rand manufactures construction machinery, refrigeration systems, road-building equipment, mechanical locks, electronic security systems, golf cars, and several other products. It has five segments: compact vehicle technologies, climate-control technologies, construction technologies, industrial technologies, and security technologies. The company's strongest brands include Bobcat, Thermo King, Club Car, Schlage, Hussmann, Ingersoll-Rand, and Montabert.

Management   Stewardship Grade [B]
Herbert Henkel, who became CEO in 1999, leads a board of 11 members, nine of whom are independent. Executive compensation is mostly variable and aligned with share performance; on average, a considerable amount of compensation is linked to growth, return on capital, and share appreciation. We find Ingersoll-Rand maintains good governance policies in several areas. There are no material related-party transactions, and the fact that shareholders' cumulative voting rights were relinquished in 2004 doesn't bother us too much. The board was also declassified, so all directors are elected annually. Director compensation is variable, with more than half of each director's $110,000 in annual compensation awarded in share equivalents. However, a poison pill exists, and share ownership among independent directors is light. The largest stake including stock and deferred share units (shares earned and vested under the director compensation plan) is in the $2 million range.

Clarendon House 2 Church Street   www.ingersoll-rand.com
Hamilton, Bermuda HM 11

Growth [B-]	2002	2003	2004	2005
Revenue %	2.6	8.8	13.9	12.3
Earnings/Share %	—	NMF	85.6	-11.0
Book Value/Share %	—	NMF	25.2	3.5
Dividends/Share %	0.0	5.9	22.2	29.5

Profitability [A]	2003	2004	2005	TTM
Return on Assets %	6.0	10.7	9.0	9.4
Oper Cash Flow $Mil	138	753	843	938
- Cap Spending $Mil	99	109	112	152
= Free Cash Flow $Mil	39	645	731	786

Financial Health [A]	2003	2004	2005	09-30-06
Long-term Debt $Mil	1,518	1,268	1,184	1,171
Total Equity $Mil	4,493	5,734	5,762	5,680
Debt/Equity Ratio	0.3	0.2	0.2	0.2

Industry	Business Risk	Moat Size	Investment Style	Sector
Machinery	Average	None	Large Core	Industrial Materials

Competition

	Market Cap $Mil	12 Mo Trailing Sales $Mil	Price/Cash Flow	Return On Assets%	Debt/Equity	Total Return % 1 Yr	3 Yr
Ingersoll-Rand A	11,997	11,232	12.8	9.4	0.2	-1.4	6.9
United Technologies	62,748	46,303	14.6	7.0	0.4	13.7	11.6
Caterpillar	39,897	40,177	8.8	6.9	2.0	7.9	16.1

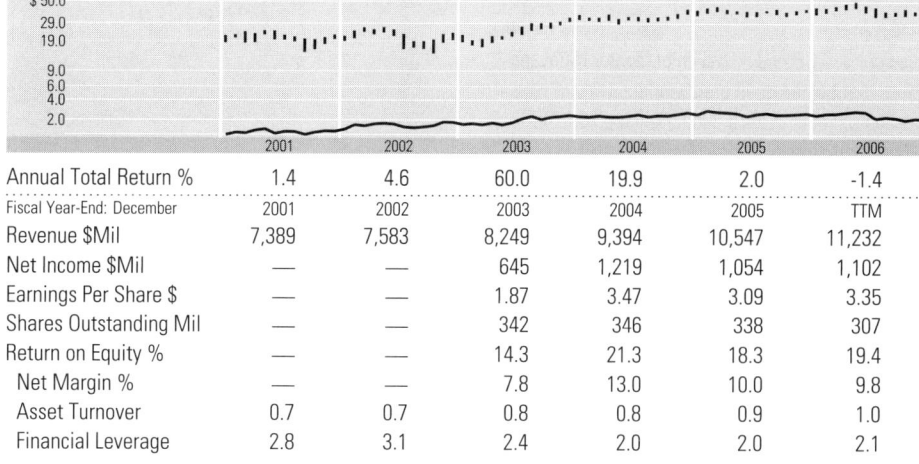

Price Volatility — Monthly Price High/Low — Relative Strength to S&P 500

Annual $Price High Low	25.14 15.20	27.20 14.85	34.10 17.26	41.45 29.52	43.96 35.13	49.00 34.95
	2001	2002	2003	2004	2005	2006
Annual Total Return %	1.4	4.6	60.0	19.9	2.0	-1.4

Fiscal Year-End: December	2001	2002	2003	2004	2005	TTM
Revenue $Mil	7,389	7,583	8,249	9,394	10,547	11,232
Net Income $Mil	—	—	645	1,219	1,054	1,102
Earnings Per Share $	—	—	1.87	3.47	3.09	3.35
Shares Outstanding Mil	—	—	342	346	338	307
Return on Equity %	—	—	14.3	21.3	18.3	19.4
Net Margin %	—	—	7.8	13.0	10.0	9.8
Asset Turnover	0.7	0.7	0.8	0.8	0.9	1.0
Financial Leverage	2.8	3.1	2.4	2.0	2.0	2.1

Valuation Ratios	Stock	Rel to Industry	Rel to S&P 500
Price/Earnings	11.6	0.6	0.6
Price/Book	2.1	0.7	0.5
Price/Sales	1.1	0.7	0.4
Price/Cash Flow	12.8	0.7	0.9

Major Fund Holders	% of Fund Assets
Snow Capital Opportunity A	3.28
New River Core Equity	3.17
Payson Total Return	3.04
RSI Retirement Trust Value Equity	2.98

Thesis By John Kearney, CFA, 12-05-06 Stock Price as of Analysis: $38.87

A revamped product portfolio has helped Ingersoll-Rand transform itself from a cyclical capital-goods manufacturer into a diversified industrial firm. We believe that IR's new business mix will prove more resilient to market downturns and will create long-term economic returns for shareholders. If the company is able to confirm our thesis by continuing to post sustainable operating results and potentially carve itself a moat, we think the shares could deliver heady returns to investors.

Ingersoll-Rand serves a number of varying end-markets with products ranging from dead-bolt locks to compact skid-steer loaders. The company's roots were established in the heavy construction and mining equipment markets more than 130 years ago, but over the last decade the company has reduced or eliminated its exposure to these cyclical industries by replacing more than half of its revenue base with less-volatile, and in some cases more-profitable, businesses. New business forays have included a move into the compact vehicles market with Bobcat skid-steer loaders and Club Car golf carts, as well as the climate-control industry with the acquisition of Thermo King's transport refrigeration business and Hussmann's refrigeration display case business.

Acquisitions figure to play a continued role in IR's growth strategy. So-called 'bolt-on" acquisitions will be made to IR's existing business platforms and will be entirely financed with free cash flow, so as not to increase the company's debt load. Management believes that it can double the company's 4%-6% organic growth rate with this bolt-on acquisition strategy, which will be used to fill geographic gaps and increase IR's recurring revenue streams (aftermarket parts and services). These revenue streams carry 20%-plus operating margins but only account for 21% of consolidated revenues.

Each of Ingersoll-Rand's business platforms is well positioned over the next several years with solid brands, well-managed operations, and identifiable growth opportunities. Impending weakness in the residential construction market could stymie growth in Bobcat construction equipment and Schlage safety locks. However, we see this as a potential opportunity for IR to prove its chops as a self-described diversified industrial firm by leveraging its diverse end market exposures to withstand a cyclical downturn. If its new product portfolio proves effective in helping IR overcome its historic cyclicality, we think the market will take notice and reward shareholders.

Intel INTC

Data as of 12-29-06

	Rating	Fair Value	Last Close	Consider Buy	Consider Sell	Yield %
	★★★	$21.00	$20.25	$16.20	$26.30	1.98

Company Profile
Intel is the largest chipmaker in the world. It develops and manufactures microprocessors and platform solutions for the global PC market. Intel pioneered the x86 architecture for microprocessors. It also produces flash memory products.

Industry	Business Risk	Moat Size	Investment Style	Sector
Semiconductor	Average	Wide	Large Growth	Hardware

Competition

	Market Cap $Mil	12 Mo Trailing Sales $Mil	Price/Cash Flow	Return On Assets%	Debt/Equity	Total Return% 1 Yr	3 Yr
Intel	116,762	35,889	11.5	12.8	0.1	-17.2	-13.1
NVIDIA	13,159	2,824	22.6	15.2	—	102.5	47.5
Advanced Micro Devices	11,164	5,714	7.2	6.0	0.1	-33.5	11.1

Management Stewardship Grade [B]
President and CEO Paul Otellini became CEO in 2005. Before that he had been president and COO as well as a board member since 2002. He joined Intel in 1974 after getting his MBA from UC Berkeley. Andy Bryant, executive vice president and chief financial and enterprise services officer, joined Intel in 1981 as controller for the commercial memory systems operation and held various finance positions. He previously worked for Ford and Chrysler. Craig Barrett became chairman in 2005 after serving as CEO for seven years. Before joining Intel in 1974, Barrett was an associate professor at Stanford University. We like the separation of the chairman and CEO positions. The outside director compensation consists of cash as well as an equity-based component. We don't like the company's poison-pill provisions, which basically allow the board to adopt antitakeover arrangements without shareholder approval

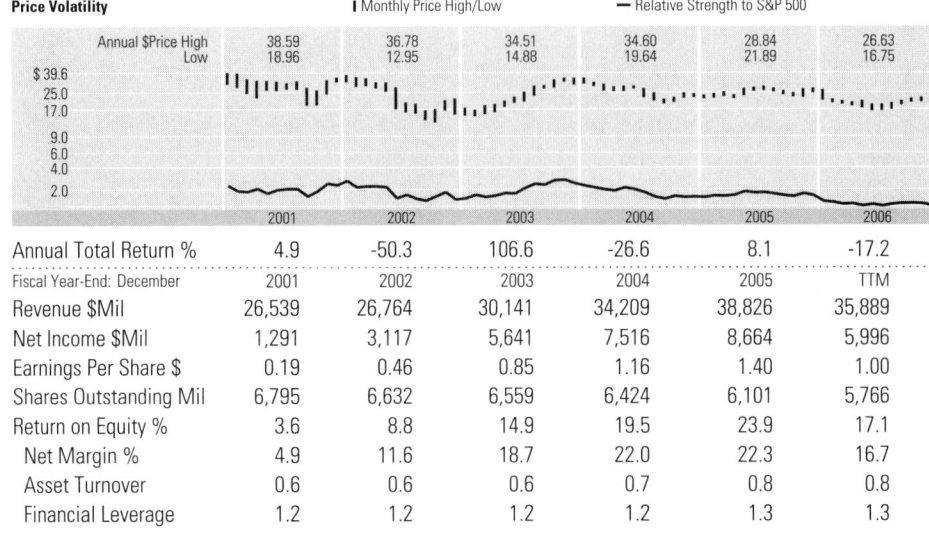

Annual Total Return %	4.9	-50.3	106.6	-26.6	8.1	-17.2
Fiscal Year-End: December	2001	2002	2003	2004	2005	TTM
Revenue $Mil	26,539	26,764	30,141	34,209	38,826	35,889
Net Income $Mil	1,291	3,117	5,641	7,516	8,664	5,996
Earnings Per Share $	0.19	0.46	0.85	1.16	1.40	1.00
Shares Outstanding Mil	6,795	6,632	6,559	6,424	6,101	5,766
Return on Equity %	3.6	8.8	14.9	19.5	23.9	17.1
Net Margin %	4.9	11.6	18.7	22.0	22.3	16.7
Asset Turnover	0.6	0.6	0.6	0.7	0.8	0.8
Financial Leverage	1.2	1.2	1.2	1.2	1.3	1.3

Valuation Ratios	Stock	Rel to Industry	Rel to S&P 500
Price/Earnings	20.3	0.7	1.0
Price/Book	3.3	0.9	0.8
Price/Sales	3.3	0.8	1.1
Price/Cash Flow	11.5	0.7	0.8

Major Fund Holders	% of Fund Assets
ProFunds Semiconductor UltraSector Inv	20.11
Integrity Technology A	9.22
Rydex Electronics Inv	8.94
ICON Information Technology	7.60

2200 Mission College Boulevard
Santa Clara, CA 95052-8119
www.intel.com

Growth [C]	2002	2003	2004	2005
Revenue %	0.8	12.6	13.5	13.5
Earnings/Share %	142.1	84.8	36.5	20.7
Book Value/Share %	-0.7	8.9	4.4	-1.8
Dividends/Share %	0.0	0.0	100.0	100.0

Profitability [A+]	2003	2004	2005	TTM
Return on Assets %	12.0	15.6	17.9	12.8
Oper Cash Flow $Mil	11,515	13,119	14,823	10,147
- Cap Spending $Mil	3,656	3,843	5,818	6,022
= Free Cash Flow $Mil	7,859	9,276	9,005	4,125

Financial Health [A]	2003	2004	2005	09-30-06
Long-term Debt $Mil	936	703	2,106	2,060
Total Equity $Mil	37,846	38,579	36,182	35,017
Debt/Equity Ratio	0.0	0.0	0.1	0.1

Thesis By Larry Cao, CFA, 10-20-06 Stock Price as of Analysis: $21.33

Besides Microsoft, Intel is arguably the company that benefited the most from Bill Gates' vision of a computer on every desk and in every home. With its dominant position in the microprocessor industry, Intel remains the king of chip land.

Intel's depth of design and manufacturing expertise has largely gone unrivaled since the firm introduced the first microprocessor in 1974. Intel's engineers consistently turned cofounder Gordon Moore's insight into reality, churning out generations of successful microprocessors. Intel has stayed at the forefront of processing technology, allowing it to produce chips at a low cost. Its commercial success enables the company to invest in the largest research and development program and most cutting-edge facilities in the industry.

Intel's strategy of bundling auxiliary chips that are designed to work with its microprocessors has been the key to success. The platform strategy was a major boon to PC manufacturers, saving them time and resources in developing new personal computers. The strategy also allowed Intel to use older manufacturing facilities in the production of these auxiliary chips. Intel's Centrino mobile platform is widely credited for its dominance in notebooks.

The downside of dominance is that potential is limited by the industry. Worldwide PC sales growth has come down from the 20%-30% seen in the 1990s to single digits in recent years. Intel's growth has slowed with the industry, and its foray outside PCs has met with limited success.

Also, competition with Advanced Micro Devices has really heated up. AMD's biggest coup came in 2005, when the firm's dual-core processors wowed the industry with an innovative architecture that boosted performance with lower power consumption. Intel took back the performance lead with its latest lineup, but we believe it will be increasingly more difficult for Intel to offer products with the kind of price performance edge it enjoyed historically. Customers agree: They used to pay twice as much for an Intel chip as for a similar AMD chip. Now they pay only 50% more.

Despite slowing PC growth and heightened competition, we still like Intel. The PC industry is poised for better growth. Innovative new processors, coinciding with the launch of Microsoft Vista, will give end users strong incentives to upgrade. Beyond that, the mighty research and manufacturing organization should give investors comfort that Intel will be Intel for years to come.

Data as of 12-29-06

IntercontinentalExchange ICE

Rating	Fair Value	Last Close	Consider Buy	Consider Sell	Yield %
★★★	$110.00	$107.90	$70.10	$132.70	0.00

Company Profile

IntercontinentalExchange Inc. is an all-electronic energy exchange for futures and over-the-counter contracts, earning fees for matching trades. Formed in May 2000, the exchange (commonly known as ICE) has grown rapidly by acquiring several smaller energy exchanges, most notably the International Petroleum Exchange in 2001, and converting them to an electronic platform. It is best known for its Brent Crude futures contract.

Management
Stewardship Grade [B]

Chairman and CEO Jeffrey C. Sprecher started the growth of the firm by purchasing Continental Power Exchange in 1997 following a 14-year career in the power industry. He owns almost 5% of the company, enough to keep his interests well aligned with shareholders' but not enough to give him complete control of the company. President and COO Charles Vice has a background in the energy industry and started at Continental Power Exchange in 1994. Compensation levels are in line with the industry and the performance of ICE. We think the executive team as a whole has the background in both energy and financial exchanges necessary to successfully lead the growth of the company. ICE rates a B on our corporate stewardship scale.

2100 RiverEdge Parkway Suite 500   /www.theice.com
Atlanta, GA 30328

Growth [A-]	2002	2003	2004	2005
Revenue %	87.7	-25.3	15.6	43.8
Earnings/Share %	NMF	NMF	NMF	NMF
Book Value/Share %	—	—	—	—
Dividends/Share %	NMF	NMF	NMF	NMF

Profitability [B]	2003	2004	2005	TTM
Return on Assets %	9.3	10.6	-7.9	16.3
Oper Cash Flow $Mil	27	40	50	—
- Cap Spending $Mil	2	2	9	—
= Free Cash Flow $Mil	—	—	—	—

Financial Health [NA]	2003	2004	2005	09-30-06
Long-term Debt $Mil	—	—	—	—
Total Equity $Mil	101	132	233	379
Debt/Equity Ratio	—	—	—	—

Industry	Business Risk	Moat Size	Investment Style	Sector
Securities	Above Avg	Wide	Mid Growth	Financial Services

Competition

	Market Cap $Mil	12 Mo Trailing Sales $Mil	Price/Cash Flow	Return On Assets%	Debt/Equity	Total Return% 1 Yr	3 Yr
IntercontinentalExchange	6,198	260	—	16.3	—	196.8	—
Morgan Stanley	86,198	32,195	—	0.8	—	45.9	14.8
Goldman Sachs Group	84,890	34,181	—	1.0	—	57.4	28.3

Price Volatility | Monthly Price High/Low   — Relative Strength to S&P 500

	2001	2002	2003	2004	2005	2006
Annual $Price High / Low					44.21 / 31.27	113.85 / 36.00

	2001	2002	2003	2004	2005	TTM
Annual Total Return %	—	—	—	—	—	196.8
Fiscal Year-End: December	2001	2002	2003	2004	2005	TTM
Revenue $Mil	67	125	94	108	156	260
Net Income $Mil	8	20	20	22	-21	68
Earnings Per Share $	—	—	—	—	—	—
Shares Outstanding Mil	—	—	—	—	—	57
Return on Equity %	39.8	40.6	19.8	16.6	-9.0	18.0
Net Margin %	11.6	16.2	21.3	20.2	-13.4	26.4
Asset Turnover	0.5	0.7	0.4	0.5	0.6	0.6
Financial Leverage	6.9	3.4	2.1	1.6	1.1	1.1

Valuation Ratios	Stock	Rel to Industry	Rel to S&P 500
Price/Earnings	—	—	—
Price/Book	16.3	4.0	4.0
Price/Sales	23.9	5.6	8.2
Price/Cash Flow	—	—	—

Major Fund Holders	% of Fund Assets
IPO Plus Aftermarket	5.82
Jennison Financial Services A	5.33
Constellation Sands Capital Inst Growth	3.68
Delaware Pooled Focus Smid-Cap Gr Eq	3.56

Thesis By Patrick O'Shaughnessy, 12-12-06 Stock Price as of Analysis:

IntercontinentalExchange (ICE) is an all-electronic marketplace for futures and over-the-counter (OTC) energy contracts. Through a series of acquisitions and innovations, the company has developed into a leading energy exchange, essentially creating a duopoly with recently public NYMEX. ICE's success in creating a highly liquid marketplace for its products has earned the firm a wide moat.

Exchanges are an attractive industry due to their network effects, meaning that the value of their service increases as more and more people use that service. Investors flock to where liquidity exists and are hesitant to try new exchanges where it may be much more difficult to enter or exit a position. This effect tends to create natural moats around ICE's products. One of the few catalysts that can alter futures markets, however, is technology. Innovations that can increase price transparency, liquidity, and ease of trading can, in fact, steal share. ICE has taken advantage of both the network effect and a first-mover advantage by beating NYMEX to the electronic marketplace, and its growth and market share gains reflect this.

ICE's management team has made several intelligent moves that further strengthened its position. Its electronic exchange has created a low-cost and scalable operating structure that eliminates the need for membership and enables Internet-based trading. ICE's purchase of the New York Board of Trade (NYBOT) is another example of the firm's strong leadership and should be highly value-creating. It gives NYBOT, currently a floor-based soft commodity futures exchange, an entry point into electronic and OTC trading, which should significantly accelerate its growth. It also provides ICE with clearing capabilities that will allow it to capture more value from each trade.

2006 has been a very successful year for ICE. The firm's introduction of West Texas crude trading has exceeded expectations, and the exchange now claims 50% market share in global crude futures. With NYBOT's members expected to approve the acquisition soon, 2007 is lining up to be successful as well. The challenge for ICE will be to sustain its innovation and growth while also protecting its market share gains from a now-public and electronic NYMEX. On balance, we expect it to do so, but we'd recommend a fairly large margin of safety before purchasing shares.

Data as of 12-29-06

International Game Tech IGT

	Rating	Fair Value	Last Close	Consider Buy	Consider Sell	Yield %
	★★★	$44.00	$46.20	$33.90	$55.10	1.10

Company Profile

International Game Technology is the world's largest manufacturer of casino gaming machines and related systems. Half of its revenue comes from selling slots outright--IGT makes about 70% of the casino games operating in North America. The other half comes from proprietary gaming systems, like progressive jackpots. Recent innovations include games based on TV shows and cashless ticketing systems. IGT is licensed to operate in every significant gaming jurisdiction worldwide.

Management   Stewardship Grade [B]

We like IGT's management team and think it has done a solid job serving the company's shareholders. T.J. Matthews was named CEO of IGT in 2003 and added the chairman title in 2005. We'd prefer the company split the CEO and chairman roles, but overall corporate governance policies are still sound. Prior to his role as CEO, Matthews was COO for two years and was also CEO of Anchor Gaming, which IGT acquired in 2001. Matthews is surrounded by a talented managerial bench, and directors and officers of the company own a combined 2.2% of the shares outstanding, as of the most recent proxy filing. CEO compensation is based primarily on the company's goals for operating income growth. Although we would prefer to see pay tied to a metric like returns on invested capital, we still think management has shareholders' best interests at heart. The company has done a remarkable job buying back shares on the cheap, and ROICs are well above the company's cost of capital, despite several acquisitions over the past decade.

9295 Prototype Drive
Reno, NV 89521
www.igt.com

Growth [D+]	2002	2003	2004	2005
Revenue %	23.1	16.8	-4.2	5.6
Earnings/Share %	36.7	22.2	-9.1	11.7
Book Value/Share %	11.7	14.5	-1.9	10.3
Dividends/Share %	NMF	71.4	60.0	5.2

Profitability [A]	2003	2004	2005	TTM
Return on Assets %	12.6	11.3	12.1	12.1
Oper Cash Flow $Mil	624	726	624	624
- Cap Spending $Mil	211	239	311	311
= Free Cash Flow $Mil	413	488	314	314

Financial Health [A+]	2003	2004	2005	06-30-06
Long-term Debt $Mil	1,302	702	577	577
Total Equity $Mil	1,977	1,906	2,042	2,042
Debt/Equity Ratio	0.7	0.4	0.3	0.3

Industry	Business Risk	Moat Size	Investment Style	Sector
Gambling/Casinos	Average	Wide	Large Growth	Consumer Services

Competition	Market Cap $Mil	12 Mo Trailing Sales $Mil	Price/Cash Flow	Return On Assets%	Debt/Equity	Total Return% 1 Yr	3 Yr
International Game Tech	15,492	2,512	24.8	12.1	0.3	52.1	11.0
WMS Industries	1,126	457	10.5	6.2	0.3	38.9	10.4
Shuffle Master	915	150	26.9	3.3	—	4.2	19.6

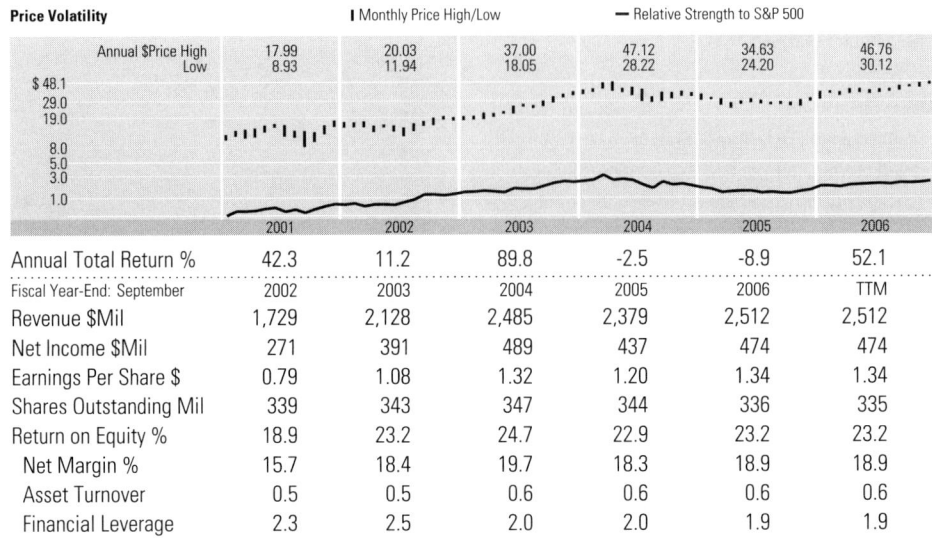

	2001	2002	2003	2004	2005	2006
Annual $Price High	17.99	20.03	37.00	47.12	34.63	46.76
Low	8.93	11.94	18.05	28.22	24.20	30.12
Annual Total Return %	42.3	11.2	89.8	-2.5	-8.9	52.1

Fiscal Year-End: September	2002	2003	2004	2005	2006	TTM
Revenue $Mil	1,729	2,128	2,485	2,379	2,512	2,512
Net Income $Mil	271	391	489	437	474	474
Earnings Per Share $	0.79	1.08	1.32	1.20	1.34	1.34
Shares Outstanding Mil	339	343	347	344	336	335
Return on Equity %	18.9	23.2	24.7	22.9	23.2	23.2
Net Margin %	15.7	18.4	19.7	18.3	18.9	18.9
Asset Turnover	0.5	0.5	0.6	0.6	0.6	0.6
Financial Leverage	2.3	2.5	2.0	2.0	1.9	1.9

Valuation Ratios	Stock	Rel to Industry	Rel to S&P 500
Price/Earnings	34.5	0.7	1.7
Price/Book	7.6	0.8	1.9
Price/Sales	6.2	0.9	2.1
Price/Cash Flow	24.8	1.0	1.7

Major Fund Holders	% of Fund Assets
Fidelity Select Leisure	4.65
T. Rowe Price Media & Telecom	4.03
Turner Concentrated Growth Instl	3.77
Delaware Large Cap Growth Instl	3.76

Thesis By Sumit Desai, 10-25-06 Stock Price as of Analysis: $42.25

International Game Technology benefits from research-and-development prowess, barriers to entry, and low-cost advantages. At the right price, we'd happily bet on this wide-moat company.

IGT is the largest manufacturer of slot machines, enjoying a near 70% share of the North American slot market. IGT earns attractive returns on invested capital (about 26% on average over the past three years) thanks to both industry dynamics and company-specific competitive advantages. The slot machine industry is highly regulated, and the rigorous licensing processes involved help keep new entrants away. We also like that casinos are relatively price insensitive, as a typical slot machine pays for itself within just a few months. This gives IGT and other slot makers significant pricing power. Further, IGT's leading market share gives the company a sizable scale advantage. For example, IGT spends more than double its nearest competitor on research and development, allowing the company to consistently stay one step ahead of others in its field in terms game content and technology.

After years of torrid sales growth, IGT's top line has stumbled recently due to a slowdown in the cashless slot replacement market. Cashless slots were wildly popular with casinos, since the machines allowed for more-efficient cash-handling and experienced less downtime. We're not concerned by the recent slowdown, however, as we see several factors contributing to another wave of strong demand. First, we like the prospects of IGT's server-based gaming products, which should hit the market between 2008 and 2009. Server-based slots allow casinos to download different games onto their machines or adjust betting limits based on the time of day, customer traffic, or other factors. The company should also see robust demand from new gaming jurisdictions, including Pennsylvania, New York, and Florida. Pennsylvania alone is expected to add about 60,000 slot machines over the next couple of years, and we expect IGT to receive a large portion of these orders.

While IGT's product sales are often lumpy, its leased-machine business can help mitigate these cycles. Half of IGT's revenue comes from proprietary gaming systems that the firm leases to customers in exchange for a piece of the action, typically 20% of the net win or 3%-4% of gross wagers. This recurring revenue stream, combined with IGT's knack for developing new game themes, should help the company maintain its leadership for the foreseeable future.

Data as of 12-29-06

International Speedway A ISCA

Rating ★★★★	Fair Value $63.00	Last Close $51.04	Consider Buy $48.60	Consider Sell $78.90	Yield % 0.16

Company Profile

International Speedway is a leading promoter of motor-sports entertainment activities in the U.S. It operates 12 tracks including the mecca, Daytona International Speedway in Daytona, Fla.--also the location of the firm's headquarters. Although its mainstay is a steady supply of Nextel Cup stock car races, International Speedway hosts truck, motorcycle, and other competitions as well. The France family has controlled both Nascar and International Speedway since inception.

Management   Stewardship Grade [C]

Management mostly consists of the France family, which also owns Nascar, the sanctioning body responsible for most of Speedway's revenue. The family has a 30% equity stake and 62% of the voting power, thanks to a dual-share-class structure. William France Jr., son of Bill France Sr. (founder of International Speedway), has been a director since 1958 and is chairman of the board. James France, William's brother, has been CEO since 2003. Brian France, William's son and a director since 1994, has been Nascar's chairman and CEO since 2003. Although these relationships are disconcerting at first, we believe the France family has proved itself to be a good management team. In addition, if shareholders wanted to gain voting power, they could purchase B shares over the counter. Option issuance is not a concern at International Speedway--variable incentives are provided using reasonable bonuses and restricted shares. Tempering our view are staggered director elections and a charter provision that allows for voting preferred share issuance without shareholder approval.

1801 West International Speedway Bouleva
Daytona Beach, FL 32120-2801   www.iscmotorsports.com

Growth [B]	2002	2003	2004	2005
Revenue %	4.4	4.7	18.0	14.2
Earnings/Share %	NMF	NMF	48.5	1.7
Book Value/Share %	-39.9	16.4	21.6	17.7
Dividends/Share %	0.0	0.0	0.0	0.0

Profitability [C-]	2003	2004	2005	TTM
Return on Assets %	8.1	9.7	8.9	8.3
Oper Cash Flow $Mil	195	226	147	258
- Cap Spending $Mil	73	135	249	127
= Free Cash Flow $Mil	122	91	-102	131

Financial Health [B]	2003	2004	2005	08-31-06
Long-term Debt $Mil	75	369	368	368
Total Equity $Mil	726	882	1,040	1,147
Debt/Equity Ratio	0.1	0.4	0.4	0.3

Industry	Business Risk	Moat Size	Investment Style	Sector
Recreation	Average	Wide	Mid Core	Consumer Goods

Competition	Market Cap $Mil	12 Mo Trailing Sales $Mil	Price/Cash Flow	Return On Assets%	Debt/ Equity	Total Return% 1 Yr	3 Yr
International Speedway A	2,724	782	10.6	8.3	0.3	6.7	4.8
Speedway Motor Sports	1,681	573	14.3	7.4	0.5	11.8	11.1
Dover Motorsports	193	92	12.9	1.7	0.4	-12.1	15.3

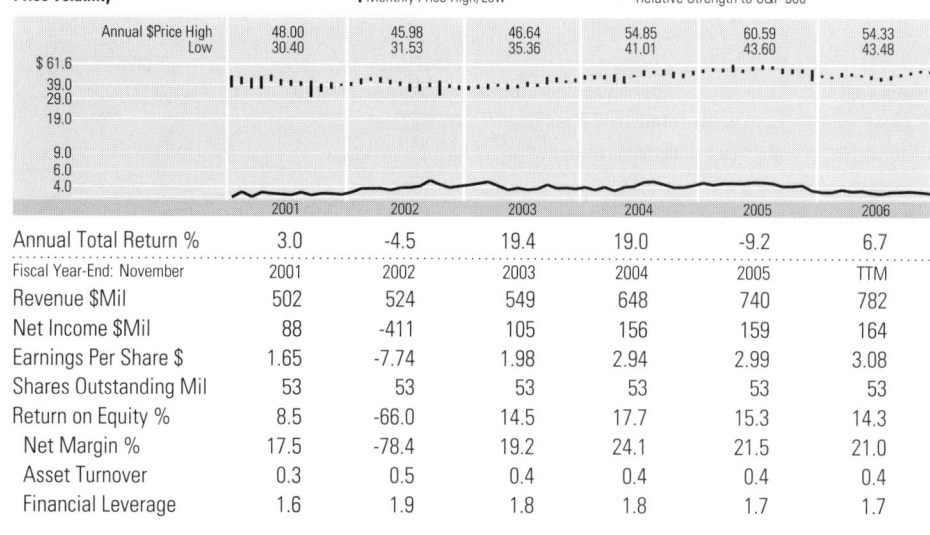

Annual Total Return %	3.0	-4.5	19.4	19.0	-9.2	6.7
Fiscal Year-End: November	2001	2002	2003	2004	2005	TTM
Revenue $Mil	502	524	549	648	740	782
Net Income $Mil	88	-411	105	156	159	164
Earnings Per Share $	1.65	-7.74	1.98	2.94	2.99	3.08
Shares Outstanding Mil	53	53	53	53	53	53
Return on Equity %	8.5	-66.0	14.5	17.7	15.3	14.3
Net Margin %	17.5	-78.4	19.2	24.1	21.5	21.0
Asset Turnover	0.3	0.5	0.4	0.4	0.4	0.4
Financial Leverage	1.6	1.9	1.8	1.8	1.7	1.7

Valuation Ratios	Stock	Rel to Industry	Rel to S&P 500	Major Fund Holders	% of Fund Assets
Price/Earnings	16.6	0.8	0.8	FAM Equity-Income Inv	5.23
Price/Book	2.4	0.4	0.6	Intrepid Small Cap	5.21
Price/Sales	3.5	1.2	1.2	Pioneer AmPac Growth A	2.77
Price/Cash Flow	10.6	0.8	0.7	Intrepid Capital	2.65

Thesis   By Joel Bloomer, 12-05-06   Stock Price as of Analysis: $53.51

International Speedway's wide moat is protected by large barriers to entry, formidable intangible assets, and long-term contracts with media outlets.

International Speedway, or ISC, has family ties to Nascar, which governs the most well-known racing circuits. We think this generates value and augments ISC's moat, as it creates barriers to entry. ISC has the most tracks and is usually first in line when races are allocated, especially for the most profitable and widely followed Nextel Cup dates. This allows ISC to confidently invest in its venues knowing that the events will follow.

In our opinion, Nascar is the Major League Baseball of racing, while tracks like ISC's Daytona International Speedway are the Wrigley Field of racetracks: valuable intangible assets. Nascar has been expanding its fan base quickly for more than 50 years and touts patrons as loyal as those of other major sports organizations. Despite having more than 100,000 seats at four of its tracks--in addition to spectator capacity in the infield--ISC still fills every seat for its marquee events at hefty ticket prices.

However, unlike Wrigley, Daytona and other racetracks like it aren't restricted by historical landmark status. As demand grows, ISC adds grandstand seats, luxury suites, and merchandise points to its stadiums, making the construction of competing tracks much less attractive. Plus, unlike other professional sports, capitalism and marketing run wild in Nascar, generating a very high-margin sponsorship revenue stream. These advantages lead to good returns on invested capital.

Nascar's long-term contracts with major networks, radio stations, and publications solidify ISC's market-leading position. The most notable of these is the eight-year TV deal signed in late 2005 that guarantees a certain percentage of revenue for networks, winning driving teams, and hosting racetracks. All three parties have the common vested interest of endearing Nascar to its fans. In addition, as Nascar and its constituents become more revered, advertising dollars should grow commensurately. The result is a network effect that keeps competitors at bay and returns high.

ISC is not without risk. Antitrust sentiment has surfaced recently in an attempt to traverse the company's economic moat, which could lead to races being more widely spread among tracks not owned by ISC. However, we believe ISC and Nascar have attained their vaunted status by providing a superior product, and we expect them to remain the primary draw in racing.

Data as of 12-29-06

Intuit INTU

	Rating	Fair Value	Last Close	Consider Buy	Consider Sell	Yield %
	★★★	$33.00	$30.51	$25.40	$41.30	0.00

Company Profile

Intuit is well known for its software products, such as Quicken for managing personal finances, TurboTax for preparing tax returns, and QuickBooks for small-business accounting. The firm is further branching out into the small-business market, targeting additional needs of small businesses with credit-card processing services.

Industry	Business Risk	Moat Size	Investment Style	Sector
Business Appl.	Average	Wide	Mid Growth	Software

Competition

	Market Cap $Mil	12 Mo Trailing Sales $Mil	Price/Cash Flow	Return On Assets%	Debt/ Equity	Total Return% 1 Yr	3 Yr
Intuit	10,637	2,400	13.0	14.2	0.0	14.5	5.3
Microsoft	293,538	45,352	20.8	19.8	—	15.8	7.6
H & R Block	7,426	4,757	74.1	5.1	0.3	-4.0	-4.3

Price Volatility

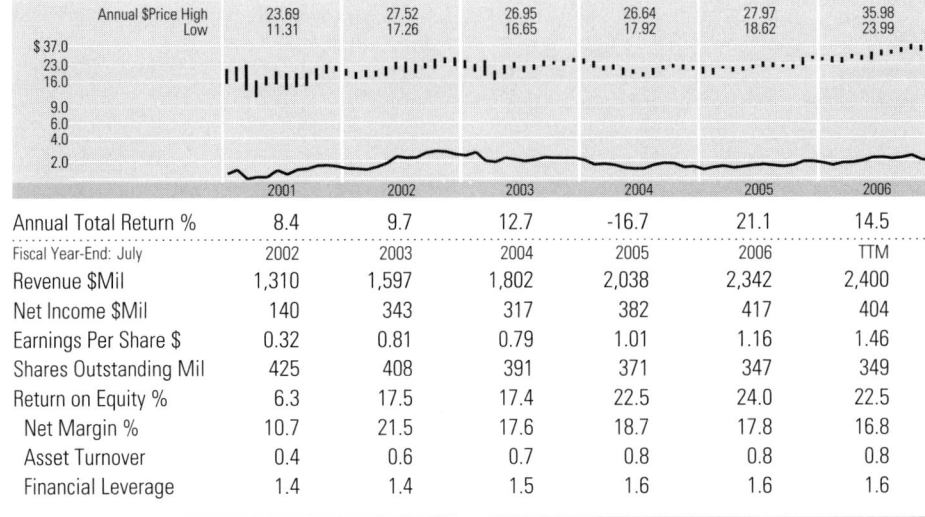

	2001	2002	2003	2004	2005	2006
Annual $Price High	23.69	27.52	26.95	26.64	27.97	35.98
Low	11.31	17.26	16.65	17.92	18.62	23.99
Annual Total Return %	8.4	9.7	12.7	-16.7	21.1	14.5

Fiscal Year-End: July	2002	2003	2004	2005	2006	TTM
Revenue $Mil	1,310	1,597	1,802	2,038	2,342	2,400
Net Income $Mil	140	343	317	382	417	404
Earnings Per Share $	0.32	0.81	0.79	1.01	1.16	1.46
Shares Outstanding Mil	425	408	391	371	347	349
Return on Equity %	6.3	17.5	17.4	22.5	24.0	22.5
Net Margin %	10.7	21.5	17.6	18.7	17.8	16.8
Asset Turnover	0.4	0.6	0.7	0.8	0.8	0.8
Financial Leverage	1.4	1.4	1.5	1.6	1.6	1.6

Management   Stewardship Grade [B]

CEO Stephen Bennett, formerly of General Electric, has turned Intuit around by selling underperforming divisions and refocusing on small businesses. Co-founder and former CEO Scott Cook remains actively involved at Intuit. Intuit named Kiran Patel as CFO, replacing Brad Henske, who's now running the consumer tax business. Management depth did take a hit in 2005 when the highly regarded Lorrie Norrington left to be the CEO of Shopping.com, which was later acquired by eBay. For the most part, Intuit has good stewardship, receiving a grade of B. The board of directors is not staggered, and executives' stock ownership is adequate. We had taken issue with loans made to executives, but Intuit has since stopped that practice.

Valuation Ratios	Stock	Rel to Industry	Rel to S&P 500
Price/Earnings	22.1	0.7	1.1
Price/Book	5.9	0.7	1.4
Price/Sales	4.4	0.7	1.5
Price/Cash Flow	13.0	0.5	0.9

Major Fund Holders	% of Fund Assets
Black Pearl Focus	5.51
Delaware Pooled Large-Cap Growth Eqty	3.74
Delaware Large Cap Growth Instl	3.70
Schwab Large-Cap Growth Sel	3.62

Thesis By Irina Logovinsky, CPA, 11-17-06 Stock Price as of Analysis:

When it comes to accounting software, Intuit has no equal. The company has built a loyal customer base for its Quicken and TurboTax (personal finance and tax) and QuickBooks (small-business accounting) products, which simplify difficult and unpleasant tasks like preparing tax returns and keeping accounting records.

Intuit's franchise is protected by a wide moat based on high switching costs. Once customers become familiar with a product, the time it takes to learn a new application and to transfer data makes it uneconomical to switch to a competing product. Such switching costs lay the foundation of Intuit's competitive advantage and serve as a deterrent for new challengers.

In spite of its dominant market share, Intuit continues to get bigger. The company grows along with its 3.5 million small-business clients who buy QuickBooks upgrades as their needs become more complex. And with 600,000 new small businesses formed every year and 24 million already in existence, Intuit still has room to grow. On the TurboTax front, its potential is equally good. In 2006, TurboTax was used to file 20 million tax returns out of 134 million, representing only 15% of the total market. Intuit's strategy is to go after nonusers, the pen-and-pencil filers, and to disrupt more expensive alternatives such as the H&R Block franchise.

The story of Intuit would not be complete without mentioning Microsoft, which for years has been trying to usurp Intuit's customers. Naysayers point out that Microsoft could be able to lure Intuit's users with a product that integrates better with its Office suite. We think this threat has little merit, since customers primarily demand a simple application--something that Intuit delivers better than anybody else--and integration with Microsoft Office is only a secondary concern. Nevertheless, Microsoft does take a toll on Intuit's margins, as Intuit has to pour more resources into R&D and marketing to defend its turf.

The TurboTax market, however, is vulnerable to Free File Alliance, a free tax-filing offering from the IRS and 20 tax software companies. This offering is available for taxpayers who make less than $50,000 annually, which is 70% of all the tax-filing population. Although Intuit claims that eligible Free-File consumers are willing to pay for TurboTax because it saves time on data entry, Free File could curb TurboTax growth in the long run.

Despite Intuit's market dominance and potential pitfalls in the tax market, we think the firm will continue to grow, albeit at a slower clip.

2700 Coast Avenue
Mountain View, CA 94043
www.intuit.com

Growth [B]	2003	2004	2005	2006
Revenue %	21.9	12.8	13.1	14.9
Earnings/Share %	153.1	-2.5	27.8	14.9
Book Value/Share %	-8.3	-2.1	-1.2	7.8
Dividends/Share %	NMF	NMF	NMF	NMF

Profitability [A+]	2004	2005	2006	TTM
Return on Assets %	11.6	14.0	15.1	14.2
Oper Cash Flow $Mil	553	590	595	816
- Cap Spending $Mil	118	70	82	86
= Free Cash Flow $Mil	435	520	513	730

Financial Health [A]	2004	2005	2006	07-31-06
Long-term Debt $Mil	16	18	15	15
Total Equity $Mil	1,822	1,695	1,738	1,798
Debt/Equity Ratio	0.0	0.0	0.0	0.0

 Stocks 500

Iowa Telecommunications Services IWA

Data as of 12-29-06

Rating	★★★
Fair Value	$18.00
Last Close	$19.71
Consider Buy	$11.50
Consider Sell	$21.70
Yield %	8.22

Industry	Telecom Svcs.
Business Risk	Above Avg
Moat Size	Narrow
Investment Style	Small Value
Sector	Telecommunication

Company Profile

Iowa Telecom provides local phone and other fixed-line telecom services to residential and business customers in rural Iowa. As the incumbent phone company in about 440 different communities, it provides local service to over 230,000 lines. It also provides long-distance service to 145,000 customers and Internet access (DSL and dial-up) to 76,000 customers. Iowa Telecom operates a competitive local phone business serving 22,000 additional lines outside its incumbent service territory.

Management   Stewardship Grade [B]

Chief executive officer and chairman Alan Wells has been with the company since its founding in 1999, originally serving as chief operating officer. Before joining Iowa Telecom, Wells was chief financial officer of MidAmerican Energy, an Iowa-based electric and gas utility. Iowa Network Services, a consortium of 127 independent rural phone companies, created Iowa Telecom for the purpose of acquiring the Iowa assets of GTE (now Verizon). The organization and its subsidiaries remain the largest shareholder, collectively holding nearly 20% of shares outstanding. Iowa Telecom has operated as a public company for only two years, but corporate governance during that time has been solid. Still, we would like to see the chairman and CEO positions split, which we think would foster better oversight and stewardship. We also fault the company for staggering the election of directors, which can be used as a takeover defense.

115 South 2nd Avenue West   www.iowatelecom.com
Newton, IA 50208

Growth [D]	2002	2003	2004	2005
Revenue %	-0.3	1.1	11.0	1.5
Earnings/Share %	NMF	NMF	NMF	NMF
Book Value/Share %	—	—	—	NMF
Dividends/Share %	NMF	NMF	NMF	825.7

Profitability [C+]	2003	2004	2005	TTM
Return on Assets %	2.1	8.2	5.4	4.9
Oper Cash Flow $Mil	80	77	97	96
- Cap Spending $Mil	24	35	30	27
= Free Cash Flow $Mil	56	42	67	69

Financial Health [B]	2003	2004	2005	06-30-06
Long-term Debt $Mil	605	478	478	478
Total Equity $Mil	77	276	281	275
Debt/Equity Ratio	7.9	1.7	1.7	1.7

Competition

	Market Cap $Mil	12 Mo Trailing Sales $Mil	Price/Cash Flow	Return On Assets%	Debt/Equity	Total Return% 1 Yr	Total Return% 3 Yr
Iowa Telecommunications Services	625	232	6.5	4.9	1.7	38.3	—
Qwest Communications Inte	16,023	13,915	6.0	-0.6	NMF	48.1	25.7
United States Cellular	6,069	3,266	9.5	3.0	0.4	40.9	25.6

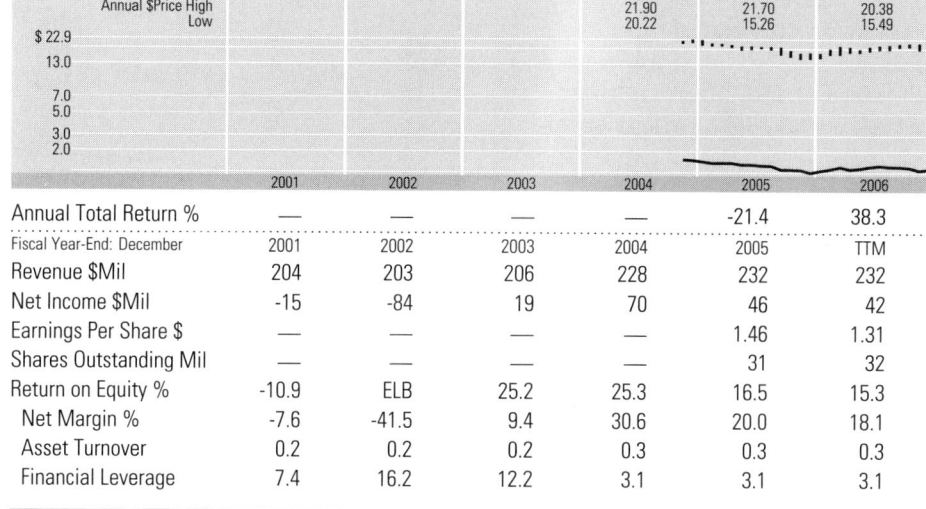

	2001	2002	2003	2004	2005	2006
Annual $Price High					21.90 / 20.22	21.70 / 15.26	20.38 / 15.49

Annual Total Return %	—	—	—	—	-21.4	38.3
Fiscal Year-End: December	2001	2002	2003	2004	2005	TTM
Revenue $Mil	204	203	206	228	232	232
Net Income $Mil	-15	-84	19	70	46	42
Earnings Per Share $	—	—	—	—	1.46	1.31
Shares Outstanding Mil	—	—	—	—	31	32
Return on Equity %	-10.9	ELB	25.2	25.3	16.5	15.3
Net Margin %	-7.6	-41.5	9.4	30.6	20.0	18.1
Asset Turnover	0.2	0.2	0.2	0.3	0.3	0.3
Financial Leverage	7.4	16.2	12.2	3.1	3.1	3.1

Valuation Ratios	Stock	Rel to Industry	Rel to S&P 500
Price/Earnings	15.0	0.8	0.7
Price/Book	2.3	0.5	0.6
Price/Sales	2.7	1.2	0.9
Price/Cash Flow	6.5	0.7	0.4

Major Fund Holders	% of Fund Assets
Calvert Small Cap Value A	2.67
Fifth Third Small Cap Value Instl	2.01
Waddell & Reed Advisors Dividend Inc A	1.11
American Century Mid Cap Value Inv	1.09

Thesis By Patrick Elgrably, CFA, 12-05-06 Stock Price as of Analysis: $18.88

Iowa Telecom's high-yielding dividend is enticing, and recent regulatory developments have been favorable. Nevertheless, we anticipate cable competition will soon be introduced in many of the company's markets, which may further accelerate the rural phone service provider's fixed-line losses.

Competition in Iowa Telecom's incumbent markets has traditionally been modest given the company's deep rural focus. The challenging economics of serving low-density populations and Iowa Telecom's established local presence create considerable barriers to entry. As a result, the company is the sole provider of fixed-line phone service in 85% of its incumbent territories, and we estimate 85% of households covered subscribe to its service.

Iowa Telecom is susceptible to the competitive dynamics affecting the industry. Like most local phone companies in the United States, wireless substitution and customers trading in second lines for high-speed Internet access services have generated fixed-line customer losses. However, Iowa Telecom is losing a larger percentage of its local phone customers than most other rural carriers. Iowa Telecom has offset fixed-line losses in its traditional markets by offering additional services, thereby improving its average revenue per access line. For instance, the company's network is capable of providing DSL Internet access service to about 75% of customers. Iowa Telecom has made other basic improvements such as adding long-distance service and enhanced calling features (i.e., voicemail, caller ID, and call waiting).

To date, Iowa Telecom has been spared another significant source of competitive pressure affecting the industry--Internet-based voice services offered by cable companies. That luxury, however, may soon dissipate. We expect Mediacom, the dominant cable provider in Iowa, will start offering phone service to Iowa Telecom's customers in the near future. Such an event will likely generate incremental customer losses at Iowa Telecom, albeit moderately. Mediacom's footprint overlaps with only a third of Iowa Telecom's territory. Further, only about half of the households in Mediacom's markets subscribe to its video services, significantly limiting the potential threat.

Iowa Telecom's healthy cash flows, disciplined capital spending, and minimal tax payments allow the company to pay out a large dividend. Longer term, however, we fear the large dividend may impede Iowa Telecom's willingness to make the necessary investments to keep pace with competitors.

Iron Mountain IRM

Data as of 12-29-06

	Rating	Fair Value	Last Close	Consider Buy	Consider Sell	Yield %
	★★★★	$30.67	$27.56	$26.10	$40.30	0.00

Company Profile
Iron Mountain stores paper, film, and digital materials for 150,000 clients in the United States, Europe, Latin America, and Asia. The bulk of Iron Mountain's revenue comes from physical storage--paper and film records--and ancillary services such as retrieval, delivery, and shredding; storage of digital information accounts for the rest. International sales will become more relevant, thanks to the acquisition of Europe's largest document-storage business from Hays.

Management Stewardship Grade [A]
Richard Reese has been CEO since 1981 and chairman since 1995. Reese is an experienced operator and maintains a team of capable managers. On the physical-record side of the business, most executives and managers have been with the firm for more than 10 years; executives in the digital services unit are newer. Management is aggressive in attacking new market opportunities and has continually reinvested in the business. On one hand, this has fueled double-digit revenue growth (including acquisitions); on the other hand, the company has had a more difficult time managing the integration and overhead costs. Opening up too many investment fronts has led to deteriorating returns on invested capital. Despite these issues, which we think can be worked out over the long run, the company's stewardship is excellent. Management and directors own 13.6% of the firm's equity. In addition to meaningful equity stakes held by top management, other practices contributing to Iron Mountain's high Stewardship Grade are annual elections for its board of directors and variable compensation based on long-term goals. Shareholders are in good company since significant equity stakes are held by such respected investors as Buffett's Berkshire Hathaway and Davis Advisors.

745 Atlantic Ave. www.ironmountain.com
Boston, MA 02111

Growth [B]	2002	2003	2004	2005
Revenue %	11.2	13.9	21.1	14.3
Earnings/Share %	NMF	43.4	10.8	16.7
Book Value/Share %	3.4	11.4	13.8	11.2
Dividends/Share %	NMF	NMF	NMF	NMF

Profitability [C+]	2003	2004	2005	TTM
Return on Assets %	2.2	2.1	2.3	2.3
Oper Cash Flow $Mil	289	305	377	378
- Cap Spending $Mil	204	232	272	342
= Free Cash Flow $Mil	84	73	105	35

Financial Health [C]	2003	2004	2005	06-30-06
Long-term Debt $Mil	1,974	2,439	2,504	2,575
Total Equity $Mil	1,066	1,219	1,370	1,504
Debt/Equity Ratio	1.9	2.0	1.8	1.7

Industry	Business Risk	Moat Size	Investment Style	Sector
Business Support	Below Avg	Wide	Mid Growth	Business Services

Competition	Market Cap $Mil	12 Mo Trailing Sales $Mil	Price/Cash Flow	Return On Assets%	Debt/ Equity	Total Return% 1 Yr	3 Yr
Iron Mountain	5,474	2,279	14.5	2.3	1.7	-2.1	16.5
Crown Worldwide							
Recall							

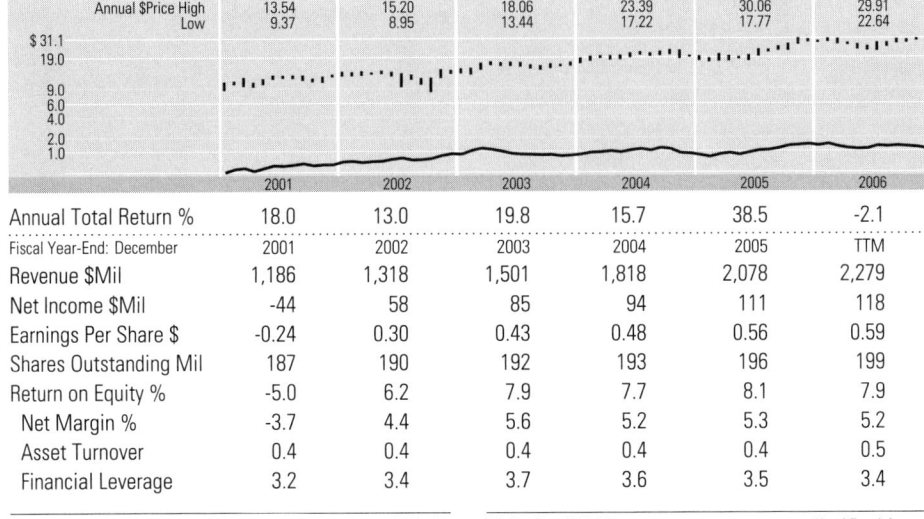

	2001	2002	2003	2004	2005	
Annual Total Return %	18.0	13.0	19.8	15.7	38.5	-2.1
Fiscal Year-End: December	2001	2002	2003	2004	2005	TTM
Revenue $Mil	1,186	1,318	1,501	1,818	2,078	2,279
Net Income $Mil	-44	58	85	94	111	118
Earnings Per Share $	-0.24	0.30	0.43	0.48	0.56	0.59
Shares Outstanding Mil	187	190	192	193	196	199
Return on Equity %	-5.0	6.2	7.9	7.7	8.1	7.9
Net Margin %	-3.7	4.4	5.6	5.2	5.3	5.2
Asset Turnover	0.4	0.4	0.4	0.4	0.4	0.5
Financial Leverage	3.2	3.4	3.7	3.6	3.5	3.4

Valuation Ratios	Stock	Rel to Industry	Rel to S&P 500
Price/Earnings	45.5	1.7	2.2
Price/Book	3.6	0.8	0.9
Price/Sales	2.4	0.5	0.8
Price/Cash Flow	14.5	0.8	1.0

Major Fund Holders	% of Fund Assets
Needham Aggressive Growth	3.10
DF Dent Premier Growth	2.99
Morgan Stanley Inst Mid Cap Growth	2.94
Morgan Stanley Developing Gr Secs B	2.92

Thesis By Marisa E. Thompson, 11-28-06 Stock Price as of Analysis: $43.11

As the global leader in records management, Iron Mountain benefits from an annuitylike revenue stream.

With the proliferation of global communication and increased regulation, the volume of records generated by companies has ballooned, necessitating management by outside vendors such as Iron Mountain. Iron Mountain's recurring revenue stream, which makes up 56% of total revenues and has increased over 70 consecutive quarters, derives from the fees it charges customers to store records. Customers are "sticky" because it's costly to move thousands of boxes out of warehouses. Therefore, as customers generate more records, Iron Mountain doesn't have to compete for incremental business, leading to high-single-digit internal revenue growth.

Iron Mountain is constantly investing in future opportunities. With the acquisitions of Connected and LiveVault, the firm has transformed itself from just a physical-records manager to one that can also handle digital records, providing server backup and recovery. In addition, Iron Mountain is building infrastructure to handle digital archiving for e-mails, a business that provides a wellspring of recurring revenue and one in which the firm has started to gain traction as a trusted provider to most of the large investment banks. The company has invested globally to increase its footprint and provide service to its multinational customers. Through joint ventures, acquisitions, and internal growth, Iron Mountain has expanded its operations into 24 countries in Europe, Latin America, and the Asia Pacific. More recently, management formed a government-services unit as federal rules now allow private companies to manage these records.

However, Iron Mountain's continual investment has actually depressed returns on capital. The capital expenditure requirements of the business are large because each additional box requires the company to find or build more space. As a result, capital expenditures average 13%-15% of revenue. Additionally, the plethora of acquisitions over the past 10 years, totaling $1.8 billion, drags down returns on capital, especially when considering goodwill. The new digital business has a selling cost structure of 27% of revenue compared with 5% for the physical business.

Still, Iron Mountain is the 800-pound gorilla in the business with a largely recurring, noncyclical revenue stream. Investments, especially in the more scalable digital business, should pay off in the long run, but near-term margin pressures remain.

Data as of 12-29-06

J.P. Morgan Chase & Co. JPM

	Rating	Fair Value	Last Close	Consider Buy	Consider Sell	Yield %
	★★★★	$61.00	$48.30	$47.00	$76.40	2.82

Company Profile
J.P. Morgan Chase is one of the top three bank holding companies in the United States, based on assets. It is the top corporate syndicated lender and operates banking offices globally. It is also a large investment bank specializing in debt markets, and it operates large units focused on securities custody, trust banking, credit cards, venture capital, and asset management.

Industry	Business Risk	Moat Size	Investment Style	Sector
International Banks	Average	Wide	Large Value	Financial Services

Competition

	Market Cap $Mil	12 Mo Trailing Sales $Mil	Price/Cash Flow	Return On Assets%	Debt/Equity	Total Return% 1 Yr	3 Yr
J.P. Morgan Chase & Co.	167,551	59,650	—	0.9	—	25.6	13.2
Citigroup	273,691	86,566	—	1.3	—	19.6	8.4
Bank of America	239,758	68,368	—	1.3	—	20.7	15.2

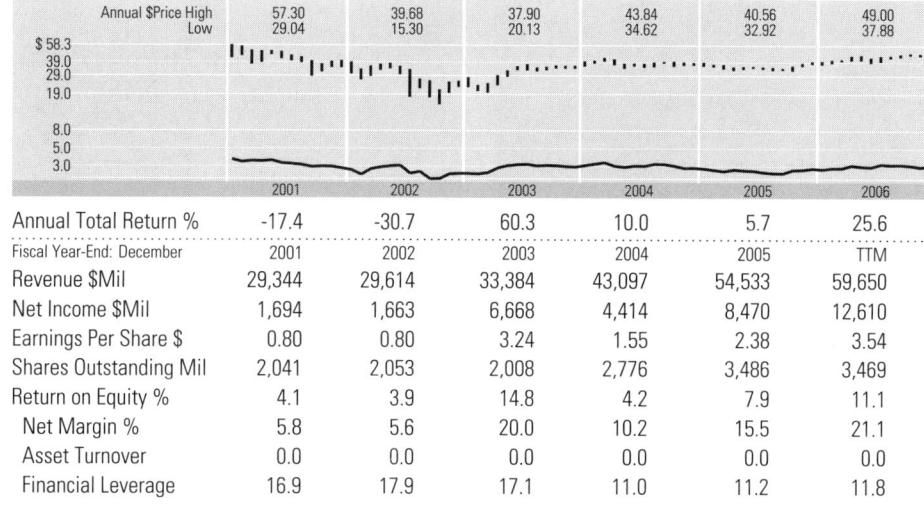

	2001	2002	2003	2004	2005	2006
Annual Total Return %	-17.4	-30.7	60.3	10.0	5.7	25.6

Fiscal Year-End: December	2001	2002	2003	2004	2005	TTM
Revenue $Mil	29,344	29,614	33,384	43,097	54,533	59,650
Net Income $Mil	1,694	1,663	6,668	4,414	8,470	12,610
Earnings Per Share $	0.80	0.80	3.24	1.55	2.38	3.54
Shares Outstanding Mil	2,041	2,053	2,008	2,776	3,486	3,469
Return on Equity %	4.1	3.9	14.8	4.2	7.9	11.1
Net Margin %	5.8	5.6	20.0	10.2	15.5	21.1
Asset Turnover	0.0	0.0	0.0	0.0	0.0	0.0
Financial Leverage	16.9	17.9	17.1	11.0	11.2	11.8

Management   Stewardship Grade [A]
Jamie Dimon--who was Morningstar's 2002 CEO of the Year for his work at Bank One--took over as CEO of J.P. Morgan Chase at the start of this year. We've liked the improvement that has occurred since Morgan merged with Bank One and began adopting its better corporate-governance standards. That said, the firm seems to have taken a step back by letting Dimon assume chairman duties--as well as his present CEO hat--after the retirement of William Harrison at the end of 2006. While Dimon no doubt has generated good results as a manager, we favor companies keeping the chairman and CEO offices separate to ensure consistent oversight. Thus, we have lowered our Stewardship Grade to a B. This downgrade notwithstanding, Dimon does appear to be a pretty smart capital allocator, displaying a good grasp of how shareholder value is created. As such, he seeks out attractive businesses that also have the ability to earn an above-average return on capital over the long term. His shareholder letters over the years have been appropriately apologetic in regard to any business unit that had not lived up to its full potential in a given year, while outlining detailed plans for how the business unit could eventually be a long-range value driver for the firm.

Valuation Ratios	Stock	Rel to Industry	Rel to S&P 500
Price/Earnings	13.7	0.7	0.7
Price/Book	1.5	0.6	0.4
Price/Sales	2.8	0.7	1.0
Price/Cash Flow	—	—	—

Major Fund Holders	% of Fund Assets
ProFunds Banks UltraSector Inv	8.83
AIM Financial Services Inv	8.72
Senbanc	7.62
North Track Dow Jones US Fin 100 A	5.80

Thesis By Craig Woker, CFA, 12-14-06 Stock Price as of Analysis: $47.95

J.P. Morgan Chase has made tremendous progress in its turnaround. Still, while we like the firm's prospects, it is clear that much more work remains.

Over the past couple of years, Morgan has evolved from a bank generating mediocre profits to one that is starting to show a glimmer of promise. Its aggregation of very good businesses is starting to demonstrate its true earnings potential, multibillion-dollar merger and litigation charges are fading into memory, and cost-control efforts have taken hold. Still, even this improved performance is nothing to brag about. For 2006, the firm will generate a return on equity of only 12%, by our estimate. This is 5-10 percentage points lower than the industry's best performers. Hard-charging CEO Jamie Dimon says he is targeting a consistent 20% ROE. We like Morgan's prospects, but not that much; our forecast calls for the firm to reach a peak ROE of 17% in 2010.

Regardless, Morgan must improve two operations, in our view, if it wants to boost profitability. These divisions are investment banking (specifically trading) and retail. Of J.P. Morgan's six divisions, these are the most important, as they account for half of revenue, but they are also arguably the weakest. By the firm's capital allocation methods, the investment bank generated just a 17% ROE in the first three quarters of 2006, which isn't bad except that peers have been doing much better in the midst of a sectorwide upswing. While I-banking fees--which require little capital--have increased at a 30%-40% rate, the firm's trading operations have not re-ascended to the levels of five years ago when looked at relative to assets committed, much less the performance of the middle to late 1990s. In our view, this is due to Morgan's lower risk tolerance over the last three or so years versus prior times. For Morgan to achieve its goal of a cycle-average 20% ROE in this division, we believe that it must successfully take greater volatility risk, much as rivals have done.

Within retail banking, Morgan is wisely seeking to improve customer service and upgrade and standardize the look of its 2,600-location branch network. These branches, branded under the Chase name, had been assembled via five megamergers over the past 15 years. Because of underinvestment, many of them looked dowdy, particularly in New York. This allowed aggressive competitors to chisel away market share, a trend that should now slow.

Overall, we like Morgan's prospects. The firm has boosted the performance of other business units, and we believe the remaining ones will follow suit.

270 Park Avenue
New York, NY 10017
www.jpmorganchase.com

Growth [A]	2002	2003	2004	2005
Revenue %	0.9	12.7	29.1	26.5
Earnings/Share %	0.0	305.0	-52.2	53.5
Book Value/Share %	4.9	7.8	68.6	-18.6
Dividends/Share %	1.5	0.0	0.0	0.0

Profitability [D]	2003	2004	2005	TTM
Return on Assets %	0.9	0.4	0.7	0.9
Oper Cash Flow $Mil	14,601	-21,805	-24,227	—
- Cap Spending $Mil	—	—	—	—
= Free Cash Flow $Mil	—	—	—	—

Financial Health [NA]	2003	2004	2005	09-30-06
Long-term Debt $Mil	—	—	—	—
Total Equity $Mil	45,145	105,314	107,072	113,561
Debt/Equity Ratio	—	—	—	—

Jack Henry & Associates JKHY

Data as of 12-29-06

Rating	Fair Value	Last Close	Consider Buy	Consider Sell	Yield %
★★★★	$25.00	$21.40	$21.30	$32.80	1.03

Industry	Business Risk	Moat Size	Investment Style	Sector
Data Processing	Below Avg	Wide	Small Core	Business Services

Company Profile
Jack Henry provides core processing services for banks and credit unions on an in-house or outsourced basis. In addition, Jack Henry leverages its core processing relationships to sell customer service, sales management, business banking, Internet banking, electronic funds transfer, asset management, and document imaging products. The company also purchases and resells the hardware necessary to run its systems.

Management   Stewardship Grade [B]
Stewardship at Jack Henry is good on the whole. The company was founded by Jack Henry and Jerry Hall in 1976. Both founders maintain seats on the board, and Jack's son, Michael, is the chairman. The management team is very stable, and the top five executives have been with Jack Henry for 18 years on average. The Henry family and Hall continue to hold significant ownership stakes, and total management and director holdings are substantial at 14% of outstanding shares. Jack Prim was promoted to CEO in 2004, the first time someone outside the Henry family has held the position. Management's pay is very reasonable, with Prim earning total compensation of only $456,000 in fiscal 2006. Although we don't like that managements' bonuses are tied to earnings per share, a number that is easily manipulated, the fact that management hasn't received bonuses in the last three years suggests it is playing fair. We'd like to see more outsiders and more banking industry experience on the board. Of the seven directors, only four are outsiders, and only one has direct banking experience.

663 Highway 60 P.O. Box 807
Monett, MO 65708
www.jackhenry.com

Competition

	Market Cap $Mil	12 Mo Trailing Sales $Mil	Price/Cash Flow	Return On Assets %	Debt/ Equity	Total Return % 1 Yr	3 Yr
Jack Henry & Associates	1,941	606	15.8	11.2	—	13.3	2.2
Fiserv	9,078	4,425	13.8	8.0	0.3	21.2	10.3
Fidelity National Financi	4,163	6,048	—	6.9	—	3.5	—

Price Volatility | Monthly Price High/Low   — Relative Strength to S&P 500

Annual $Price High/Low	33.24 / 18.56	24.49 / 7.24	22.04 / 9.90	21.00 / 17.17	21.96 / 15.35	23.77 / 17.40
	2001	2002	2003	2004	2005	2006
Annual Total Return %	-29.4	-44.4	72.5	-2.4	-3.2	13.3

Fiscal Year-End: June	2002	2003	2004	2005	2006	TTM
Revenue $Mil	397	405	467	536	592	606
Net Income $Mil	57	49	62	76	90	92
Earnings Per Share $	0.62	0.55	0.68	0.81	0.96	0.98
Shares Outstanding Mil	89	88	89	91	92	91
Return on Equity %	16.7	13.5	14.1	14.6	15.6	16.0
Net Margin %	14.4	12.2	13.3	14.1	15.2	15.2
Asset Turnover	0.8	0.7	0.7	0.7	0.7	0.7
Financial Leverage	1.4	1.5	1.5	1.6	1.6	1.4

Valuation Ratios

	Stock	Rel to Industry	Rel to S&P 500
Price/Earnings	21.8	0.9	1.1
Price/Book	3.4	0.7	0.8
Price/Sales	3.2	0.9	1.1
Price/Cash Flow	15.8	0.8	1.1

Major Fund Holders

	% of Fund Assets
Phoenix Small-Mid Cap X	4.61
Calvert Mid Cap Value A	2.61
First Focus Growth Opportunities Inst	2.30
EV Atlanta Capital Small-Cap I	2.13

Growth [C]

	2003	2004	2005	2006
Revenue %	2.0	15.5	14.6	10.5
Earnings/Share %	-11.3	23.6	19.1	18.5
Book Value/Share %	9.8	18.9	14.8	10.7
Dividends/Share %	7.7	7.1	13.3	17.6

Profitability [A]

	2004	2005	2006	TTM
Return on Assets %	9.5	9.3	9.9	11.2
Oper Cash Flow $Mil	113	108	169	123
- Cap Spending $Mil	49	58	45	45
= Free Cash Flow $Mil	64	50	124	78

Financial Health [A+]

	2004	2005	2006	09-30-06
Long-term Debt $Mil	—	—	—	—
Total Equity $Mil	443	517	575	576
Debt/Equity Ratio	—	—	—	—

Thesis By Brett Horn, 11-22-06 Stock Price as of Analysis: $22.63

Jack Henry provides core processing services for banks, the nuts and bolts systems that banks need to maintain their deposit and loan accounts and post daily transactions. Banks are reluctant to switch their core processing provider, creating a wide moat for the company's business. This protects Jack Henry's enviable returns on invested capital, which have averaged 20% over the last five years, well above its cost of capital.

Given the integral nature of core processing to their operations, banks are reluctant to switch their systems. Beyond the potential for interruptions, converting to a new system would require the banks to retrain employees. Customers typically sign five- to seven-year contracts with Jack Henry, and attrition is very low, only about 3% annually, with the bulk of lost customers due to acquisitions by another bank.

Jack Henry has three sources of revenue. The first is license revenue, which accounted for only 14% of sales, but 32% of gross profit. The majority of the costs associated with software applications are associated with initial development, and license revenue drops almost completely to the bottom line. However, license revenue historically has been somewhat erratic due to its one-time nature. Margins in the service and support segment, which accounts for 46% of revenue and 60% of gross profit, are much lower but still healthy, and the revenue from this part of the business is recurring and stable due to low customer attrition. Additionally, margins in this segment have been improving based on the scalability of the business. Finally, Jack Henry also purchases and resells the hardware necessary to run its systems, but this accounts for only 10% of revenue and 9% of gross profit.

Jack Henry leverages its core processing relationships with its existing customer base to cross-sell ancillary products such as Internet banking and electronic funds transfer. Through its acquisitions and internal development, Jack Henry essentially has a complete portfolio of products to address banks' needs.

While there is some concern that consolidation in the banking industry may create a more difficult growth environment for Jack Henry going forward, this trend has been in place for the last decade. Jack Henry has been able to grow despite bank consolidation by tying prices to customer banks' size, so its growth is more closely related to total industry asset growth, rather than the number of banks.

Based on the firm's wide moat, we'd gladly buy the shares at a reasonable discount to our fair value.

Data as of 12-29-06

Jacobs Engineering Group JEC

	Rating	Fair Value	Last Close	Consider Buy	Consider Sell	Yield %
	★★	$68.00	$81.54	$52.40	$85.20	0.00

Company Profile
Jacobs Engineering Group provides construction, engineering, and consulting services to a variety of industries. The company markets its services to government agencies as well as companies in industries such as energy, pharmaceuticals, and chemicals. More than a third of revenue comes from the oil and gas industry, and another 20% is tied to federal government projects.

Management Stewardship Grade [B]
Jacobs' deep and experienced management team is led by Craig Martin, who took the reins in April 2006 following the retirement of longtime CEO Noel Watson. Martin is only the third person to hold the CEO title since the firm was founded by Joseph Jacobs in 1947. The company scores relatively well on corporate governance. Compensation is high but not egregious, and bonuses are not paid unless the firm earns a minimum pretax return on equity, which we view as a very reasonable performance benchmark. Moreover, when performance at the company slipped in 2004, executive bonuses actually declined, which we think is appropriate but see less often than we'd like. Further, management compensation consists of salary, bonus, and options, so shareholders are not directly paying for frippery like loans to executives, company cars, or golf club memberships. No golden-parachute plans are in place to save the skin of the top brass at the expense of shareholders. Option issuance has been quite reasonable, averaging about 2% of shares outstanding over the past five years. One corporate-governance blotch is the firm's staggered board of directors.

1111 South Arroyo Parkway www.jacobs.com
Pasadena, CA 91105

Growth [A-]	2003	2004	2005	2006
Revenue %	1.3	-0.5	22.7	31.7
Earnings/Share %	14.6	-0.9	-0.4	46.0
Book Value/Share %	20.0	17.4	13.2	19.1
Dividends/Share %	NMF	NMF	NMF	NMF

Profitability [A]	2004	2005	2006	TTM
Return on Assets %	6.2	5.5	6.9	6.9
Oper Cash Flow $Mil	88	150	224	224
- Cap Spending $Mil	37	—	—	—
= Free Cash Flow $Mil	51	—	—	—

Financial Health [NA]	2004	2005	2006	09-30-06
Long-term Debt $Mil	79	90	78	78
Total Equity $Mil	1,005	1,166	1,423	1,423
Debt/Equity Ratio	0.1	0.1	0.1	0.1

Industry	Business Risk	Moat Size	Investment Style	Sector
Engineering/Constr.	Average	Narrow	Mid Growth	Business Services

Competition	Market Cap $Mil	12 Mo Trailing Sales $Mil	Price/Cash Flow	Return On Assets%	Debt/Equity	Total Return% 1 Yr	3 Yr
Jacobs Engineering Group	4,816	7,421	21.5	6.9	0.1	20.1	19.9
Fluor	7,189	14,408	—	5.1	0.1	6.7	29.3
Shaw Group	2,696	4,776	—	2.0	0.1	15.2	35.8

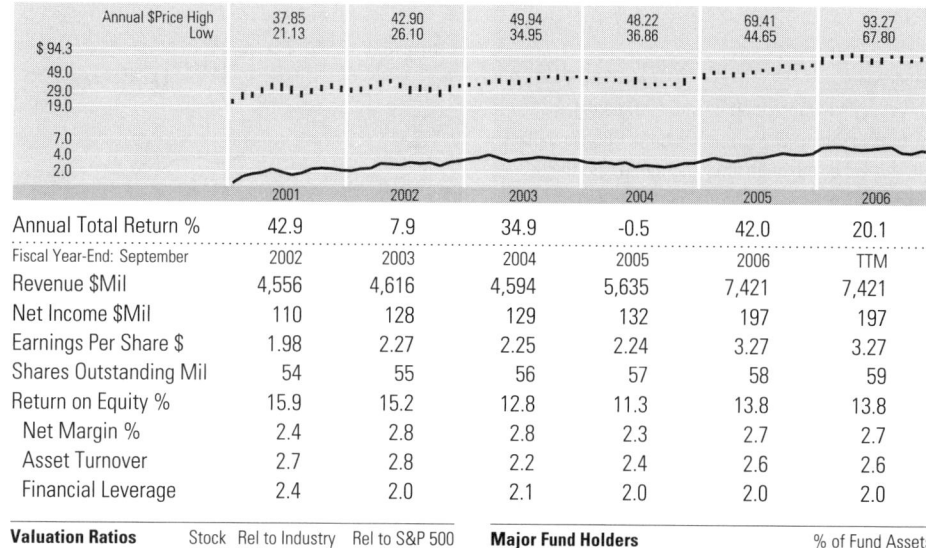

	2001	2002	2003	2004	2005	2006
Annual Total Return %	42.9	7.9	34.9	-0.5	42.0	20.1

Fiscal Year-End: September	2002	2003	2004	2005	2006	TTM
Revenue $Mil	4,556	4,616	4,594	5,635	7,421	7,421
Net Income $Mil	110	128	129	132	197	197
Earnings Per Share $	1.98	2.27	2.25	2.24	3.27	3.27
Shares Outstanding Mil	54	55	56	57	58	59
Return on Equity %	15.9	15.2	12.8	11.3	13.8	13.8
Net Margin %	2.4	2.8	2.8	2.3	2.7	2.7
Asset Turnover	2.7	2.8	2.2	2.4	2.6	2.6
Financial Leverage	2.4	2.0	2.1	2.0	2.0	2.0

Valuation Ratios	Stock	Rel to Industry	Rel to S&P 500
Price/Earnings	24.9	0.7	1.2
Price/Book	3.4	0.9	0.8
Price/Sales	0.6	0.7	0.2
Price/Cash Flow	21.5	1.5	1.5

Major Fund Holders	% of Fund Assets
Transamerica Premier Growth Opp Inv	4.94
FMI Provident Trust Strategy	4.58
TA IDEX Transamerica Balanced A	4.48
Transamerica Premier Balanced Inv	4.36

Thesis By John Kearney, CFA, 11-03-06 Stock Price as of Analysis: $78.80

Jacobs Engineering Group's highly disciplined and differentiated business model has created unparalleled value compared with more transaction-oriented peers. Jacobs has carved out a narrow economic moat for itself in the engineering and construction (E&C) industry, which we've viewed as intensely competitive and cyclically challenged.

While Jacobs is not immune to E&C cyclicality, we think it is capable of weathering these cyclical turns better than most. The company's operating strength and stability is derived from its diverse client mix and, more important, its relationship-based approach to serving those clients. Jacobs generates 80% of its business from 30-40 core customers, with whom it has worked on numerous projects over a span of as long as 50 years. Unlike the majority of its peers, Jacobs largely abstains from engaging in one-time transaction-based projects that involve competitive bidding for fixed-price contracts. Though some fixed-price contracts can be highly profitable, most add the risk of cost overruns. Consequently, Jacobs focuses almost exclusively on cost-reimbursable contracts, where its downside exposure is protected.

Jacobs' relationship-based business model has two fundamental advantages: The company can leverage its close relationships by cross-selling other services to clients on a particular project, and it can win repeat business by building customer loyalty, which allows it to avoid incurring marketing expenses. Some of those savings can be passed on to the client, but of even more value to the customer is Jacobs' ability to more aptly serve that client, thanks to an acute understanding of its core customers' needs.

The internal growth generated by Jacobs' relationship-based model has been complemented by the company's ability to integrate value-added acquisitions into its model to boost profitability growth. Over each of the past 10 years, Jacobs has generated returns on invested capital in excess of its cost of capital and has increased earnings per share at a compound annual rate of 15%. Historically, one third of Jacobs' annual growth rate has come from acquisition growth, and we expect acquisitions to play an equally important role in the future. However, we expect management to maintain its strict policy of avoiding any transaction that is not compatible with its business model and not immediately accretive to shareholder value.

Data as of 12-29-06

Janus Capital Group JNS

	Rating	Fair Value	Last Close	Consider Buy	Consider Sell	Yield %
	★★★	$21.00	$21.59	$13.40	$25.30	0.19

Company Profile

Janus Capital Group is an asset-management firm that has historically been a specialist in growth-equity mutual funds. The firm also has a growing quantitative equity business in subsidiary INTECH. Janus sells its investment products to retail consumers and institutions or through retirement plans. The firm owns a small printing business, which it acquired in an asset swap with DST.

Industry	Business Risk	Moat Size	Investment Style	Sector
Money Mgmt.	Above Avg	Narrow	Mid Core	Financial Services

Competition	Market Cap $Mil	12 Mo Trailing Sales $Mil	Price/Cash Flow	Return On Assets%	Debt/Equity	Total Return% 1 Yr	3 Yr
Janus Capital Group	4,279	1,008	—	2.9	—	16.1	9.2
Marsh & McLennan Companie	16,897	11,715	—	4.5	—	-1.2	-11.9
T Rowe Price Group	11,539	1,729	—	18.8	—	23.3	23.7

Price Volatility — Monthly Price High/Low — Relative Strength to S&P 500

Annual $Price High	46.63	29.22	19.00	17.90	20.59	24.20
Low	18.20	8.97	9.46	12.60	12.75	15.50
	2001	2002	2003	2004	2005	2006
Annual Total Return %	-30.9	-51.8	25.8	2.7	11.1	16.1
Fiscal Year-End: December	2001	2002	2003	2004	2005	TTM
Revenue $Mil	1,537	1,123	995	1,011	953	1,008
Net Income $Mil	297	77	943	170	88	107
Earnings Per Share $	1.27	0.35	4.11	0.73	0.40	0.51
Shares Outstanding Mil	220	221	228	232	220	198
Return on Equity %	21.6	5.1	35.2	6.2	3.4	4.5
Net Margin %	19.3	6.9	94.8	16.8	9.2	10.6
Asset Turnover	0.5	0.3	0.2	0.3	0.3	0.3
Financial Leverage	2.5	2.2	1.6	1.4	1.4	1.5

Valuation Ratios	Stock	Rel to Industry	Rel to S&P 500
Price/Earnings	42.3	1.4	2.1
Price/Book	1.8	0.4	0.4
Price/Sales	4.2	0.7	1.4
Price/Cash Flow	—	—	—

Major Fund Holders	% of Fund Assets
Ariel	4.49
Maxim Ariel SmallCap Value	3.96
FIMCO Select	3.54
Ariel Appreciation	3.52

Management Stewardship Grade [D]

Janus has had more than its share of management shuffles in recent years, and we hope CEO Gary Black will remain at the helm long enough to turn things around. Black took over in January 2006 from chairman Steve Scheid, who acted as interim CEO after Mark Whiston abruptly resigned in 2004. Whiston replaced a largely ineffective and inept series of managers whose bad decisions left Janus with a struggling fund lineup and a truckload of debt. The market-timing violations occurred on Whiston's watch, calling into question his commitment to customer-friendly business practices and ultimately leading to his resignation. Even so, he took home $13.9 million in compensation and severance in 2004. Good corporate governance has never been a strong suit at Janus, which, during its restructuring, awarded huge paydays to portfolio managers and executives (with accelerated vesting of stock awards). Black and Scheid took home very large paychecks in 2005 despite the continuing problem of asset outflows. Including options, Black earned $5.9 million and Scheid pulled down $6.4 million. This is comparable with the $6.9 million that Franklin's Greg Johnson earned in what was a fantastic year for his company. We think Black and Scheid have their work cut out for them to grow into the compensation they are collecting.

100 Fillmore Street
Denver, CO 64105
www.janus.com

Growth [D]	2002	2003	2004	2005
Revenue %	-26.9	-11.4	1.6	-5.7
Earnings/Share %	-72.4	EUB	-82.2	-45.2
Book Value/Share %	17.3	69.5	0.9	-0.1
Dividends/Share %	25.0	-20.0	0.0	0.0

Profitability [B+]	2003	2004	2005	TTM
Return on Assets %	21.8	4.5	2.4	2.9
Oper Cash Flow $Mil	260	-10	273	—
- Cap Spending $Mil	24	27	24	—
= Free Cash Flow $Mil	—	—	—	—

Financial Health [NA]	2003	2004	2005	09-30-06
Long-term Debt $Mil	—	—	—	—
Total Equity $Mil	2,678	2,735	2,581	2,371
Debt/Equity Ratio	—	—	—	—

Thesis By Rachel Barnard, Ph.D., 11-08-06 Stock Price as of Analysis: $19.48

We're encouraged by the new focus at Janus. CEO Gary Black is taking Janus back to its roots as a growth-stock manager and envisions the firm as a boutique asset manager specializing in growth investing. He also recognizes the burgeoning importance of INTECH, the brand name for Janus' best-selling quantitative equity products. Janus will focus on selling these two strategies through financial intermediaries (brokers, financial advisors, etc.) and downplay its historical focus on direct retail sales.

Janus has encountered a daunting series of setbacks in recent years. Its growth-equity funds were out of favor during the bear market, causing the firm to bleed assets at an alarming clip. Just as the equity markets rebounded in 2003, the firm became embroiled in the mutual fund scandal. Janus admitted to allowing market-timing in its funds; it essentially let hedge funds siphon off profits that belonged to long-term fundholders in return for a kickback.

The final settlement over the market-timing allegations cost Janus more than $100 million in penalties and restitution and is a continuing burden because of the mandated fee reductions on the firm's funds. Even with the settlement behind it, Janus' growth funds--the firm's bread and butter--are still losing assets as investors pull their money out.

But Janus is not about to roll over and play dead. INTECH products have been selling like hotcakes. This quantitative strategy has the capacity to triple its current assets without adding much in the way of costs; incremental margins are above 50% of sales. On the growth-equity front, performance is improving now that the disastrous 2000 numbers are less of a factor in the long-term record. More than 40% of Janus funds now have 4- or 5-star Morningstar ratings, better than the peer average of 33%.

Janus is also beefing up its salesforce dedicated to financial advisors. Eighty percent of funds outside retirement plans are sold through advisors, so Janus is wise to target the highest-volume sales channel. In addition, the firm plans a new branding initiative to tout the performance of its funds, recognizing that the recent investment record alone is failing to drive new flows into its growth funds.

While we are more optimistic about the company than we have been in years, we still caution investors that the market will dictate the terms of growth for Janus. We recommend a large margin of safety before investing.

Data as of 12-29-06

JB Hunt Transport Services JBHT

Rating	Fair Value	Last Close	Consider Buy	Consider Sell	Yield %
★★★★	$24.00	$20.77	$18.50	$30.10	1.54

Company Profile

Based in Lowell, Ark., J.B. Hunt uses its fleet of trucks and a large staff of drivers to deliver goods in whole truckloads across North America. The company also partners with railroads to offer intermodal service, and it offers dedicated truck and driver combinations under contract. J.B. Hunt is one of the largest transportation logistics providers in the country and serves a variety of industries, including retail, beverage, consumer goods, food, paper, and manufacturing.

Management   Stewardship Grade [B]

In the past few years, J.B. Hunt went through an impressive transformation from a floundering, unfocused, and barely profitable operation to the premier publicly traded truckload company. We credit this transformation to current management, particularly CEO Kirk Thompson, and the firm's focus on cost-cutting and yield management. We generally like what we see from a corporate-governance standpoint: The positions of CEO and chairman are separate, there is no poison pill in place, and the major committees (audit and compensation) are composed entirely of independent directors. The independent board sets forth ownership targets for executives at various levels, expressed as a multiple of annual salary; moreover, the board explicitly strives to increase the variable, or at-risk, portion of executives' salaries as responsibilities increase. We would prefer, however, that the full board of directors be elected annually instead of at staggered terms. Founder Johnnie Bryan Hunt Sr. ("J.B. Hunt") recently passed away, fueling speculation that the company could be bought out since he owned approximately 21% of the company. Investors should be aware (but not overly concerned) that his wife still serves as a director and corporate secretary, and their son is also a director.

615 J.B. Hunt Corporate Drive   www.jbhunt.com
Lowell, AR 72745

Growth [B-]	2002	2003	2004	2005
Revenue %	7.0	8.3	14.5	12.3
Earnings/Share %	43.5	77.3	50.4	45.5
Book Value/Share %	17.4	14.5	20.2	-2.6
Dividends/Share %	NMF	NMF	NMF	433.3

Profitability [A]	2003	2004	2005	TTM
Return on Assets %	7.0	9.7	13.4	13.3
Oper Cash Flow $Mil	333	405	332	332
- Cap Spending $Mil	—	—	204	204
= Free Cash Flow $Mil	—	—	128	128

Financial Health [NA]	2003	2004	2005	09-30-06
Long-term Debt $Mil	—	0	124	166
Total Equity $Mil	703	861	817	703
Debt/Equity Ratio	—	0.0	0.2	0.2

Industry	Business Risk	Moat Size	Investment Style	Sector
Transportation	Average	Narrow	Mid Core	Business Services

Competition	Market Cap $Mil	12 Mo Trailing Sales $Mil	Price/Cash Flow	Return On Assets %	Debt/ Equity	Total Return % 1 Yr	3 Yr
JB Hunt Transport Services	2,997	3,335	9.0	13.3	0.2	-6.9	16.0
Landstar System	2,172	2,703	24.0	19.2	0.5	-8.3	26.7
Swift Transportation	1,968	3,235	4.9	7.1	0.2	29.4	7.3

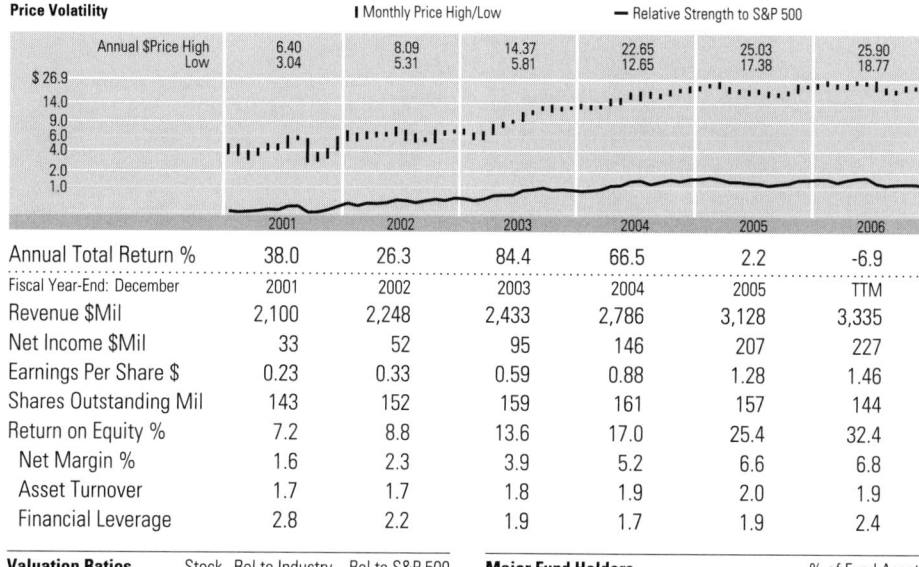

	2001	2002	2003	2004	2005	2006
Annual Total Return %	38.0	26.3	84.4	66.5	2.2	-6.9
Fiscal Year-End: December	2001	2002	2003	2004	2005	TTM
Revenue $Mil	2,100	2,248	2,433	2,786	3,128	3,335
Net Income $Mil	33	52	95	146	207	227
Earnings Per Share $	0.23	0.33	0.59	0.88	1.28	1.46
Shares Outstanding Mil	143	152	159	161	157	144
Return on Equity %	7.2	8.8	13.6	17.0	25.4	32.4
Net Margin %	1.6	2.3	3.9	5.2	6.6	6.8
Asset Turnover	1.7	1.7	1.8	1.9	2.0	1.9
Financial Leverage	2.8	2.2	1.9	1.7	1.9	2.4

Valuation Ratios	Stock	Rel to Industry	Rel to S&P 500
Price/Earnings	14.2	0.7	0.7
Price/Book	4.3	1.0	1.0
Price/Sales	0.9	0.6	0.3
Price/Cash Flow	9.0	0.6	0.6

Major Fund Holders	% of Fund Assets
Franklin Mid Cap Value A	2.75
Heartland Select Value	2.45
Rydex Transportation Inv	2.16
Heritage Mid Cap Stock A	2.02

Thesis   By Peter Smith, 12-13-06   Stock Price as of Analysis: $21.00

We think J.B. Hunt's profitable suite of services will continue to create economic value.

J.B. Hunt has three equal-size segments: truck, intermodal, and dedicated contract services. The truck division operates on the truckload (TL) side of the industry. Unlike less-than-truckload (LTL) carriers that transport shipments for multiple customers in the same trailer, truckload carriers move full loads of goods, each for a single customer. Both types of carriers require significant assets (trucks), however, that cannot easily be pared in weaker economic times. This inflexibility has resulted in lower long-run returns for both TL and LTL firms than those of non-asset-based and asset-light peers.

The intermodal division leaves the bulk of the hauling process to railroads, but provides the assets (shipping containers) and transports them to and from the rail yards. Intermodal shipping is expected to continue to grow, which will help offset cyclicality in the truck division. The third division, dedicated contract services, establishes three- to five-year contracts with shippers looking to outsource their private fleets. These longer-term contracts also help insulate the firm from heavily cyclical freight demand.

Having the three divisions--and ample experience with each--under one roof provides the firm with a key competitive advantage. By offering multiple transportation methods, J.B. Hunt can determine the cheapest option from point A to point B. Plus, shippers--particularly big-box retailers--are increasingly reducing the number of vendors they use, which bodes well for a one-stop shop like J.B. Hunt. The next step would be to expand into freight forwarding, a strategic move that crafty rival Schneider National has already made.

Global trade growth has increased demand for trucking services, and a shortage of qualified truck drivers has worked in the industry's favor by limiting fleet expansions. This tight supply-demand dynamic has enabled carriers to raise prices and improve utilization rates, two keys for success. It has also had some negative effects, though, as carriers have lost market share to railroads and grappled with higher driver costs. Rising costs for insurance, fuel, and engines have also rained on the parade. Strong GDP growth has helped mitigate these issues, but when the economy inevitably goes south, price competition will pick up and the good times will end in a hurry.

Though an investment in J.B. Hunt is not without risk, we think its position as a one-stop shop will help keep it a step ahead of the competition.

Data as of 12-29-06

JetBlue Airways JBLU

Rating	Fair Value	Last Close	Consider Buy	Consider Sell	Yield %
★	$6.00	$14.20	$3.80	$7.20	0.00

Company Profile
JetBlue is a low-cost airline that offers high-quality service, including assigned seating and in-flight entertainment. Based at New York's JFK airport, JetBlue serves short- and long-haul routes throughout the U.S. with a fleet of about 95 Airbus A320 aircraft and 25 Embraer 190 regional jets. The firm has plans to take delivery of at least 100 new Embraer 190s and 80 new A320s over the next eight years. JetBlue went public in 2002 and employs about 9,200 people.

Management   Stewardship Grade [A]
The strong culture built and nurtured by founder and CEO David Neeleman is crucial to JetBlue's success. Neeleman seeks to maintain a dynamic and innovative culture while bringing the humanity back to air travel. As a result, JetBlue employees not only get high marks for customer service but also are among the most productive. Neeleman and his seasoned team have loads of experience, and they understand the evolving airline business as well as anyone. President and COO David Barger ran Continental's Newark hub for several years. CFO John Owen, who used to buy planes for Southwest, brings experience key to executing JetBlue's low-cost model. We are particularly impressed by management's sense of corporate stewardship. The top three officers all had the same $200,000 salary the past three years and refused their bonuses in 2005 when JetBlue's net income turned negative. Neeleman still owns 6.2% of the company and declined a generous option grant when the firm went public so he could give more to employees.

118-29 Queens Boulevard   www.jetblue.com
Forest Hills, NY 11375

Growth [A]	2002	2003	2004	2005
Revenue %	97.8	57.2	26.8	34.5
Earnings/Share %	NMF	NMF	-56.3	NMF
Book Value/Share %	—	NMF	10.2	29.0
Dividends/Share %	NMF	NMF	NMF	NMF

Profitability [B-]	2003	2004	2005	TTM
Return on Assets %	4.7	1.6	-0.5	-1.4
Oper Cash Flow $Mil	287	199	170	233
- Cap Spending $Mil	733	797	1,124	1,212
= Free Cash Flow $Mil	-446	-598	-954	-979

Financial Health [C]	2003	2004	2005	09-30-06
Long-term Debt $Mil	—	1,396	2,103	2,338
Total Equity $Mil	670	754	911	917
Debt/Equity Ratio	—	1.9	2.3	2.6

Industry	Business Risk	Moat Size	Investment Style	Sector
Air Transport	Above Avg	Narrow	Mid Growth	Business Services

Competition	Market Cap $Mil	12 Mo Trailing Sales $Mil	Price/Cash Flow	Return On Assets%	Debt/Equity	Total Return% 1 Yr	3 Yr
JetBlue Airways	2,495	2,176	10.7	-1.4	2.6	-7.7	-7.3
Southwest Airlines	12,131	8,798	8.6	4.1	0.2	-6.7	-1.2
AMR	6,482	22,334	3.8	-1.3	NMF	36.0	32.5

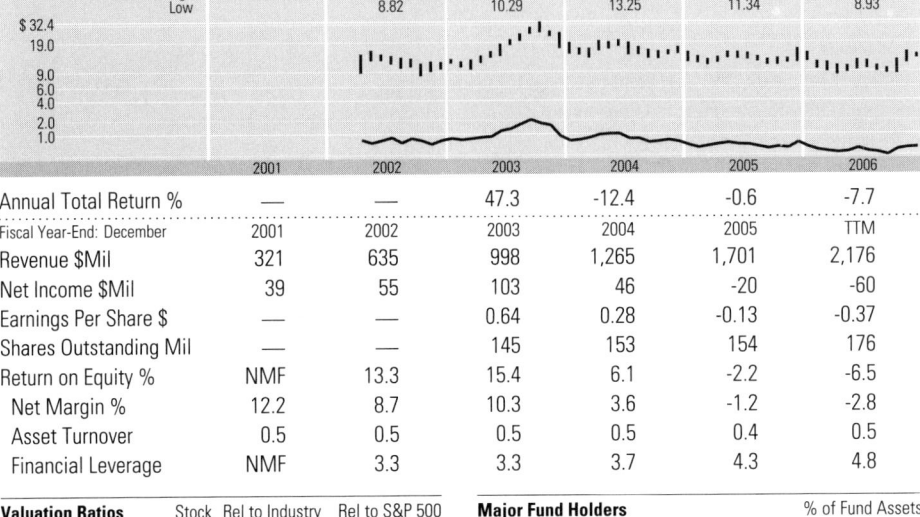

Price Volatility — Monthly Price High/Low — Relative Strength to S&P 500

Annual $Price High/Low		16.34 / 8.82	31.43 / 10.29	20.67 / 13.25	16.85 / 11.34	15.60 / 8.93
	2001	2002	2003	2004	2005	2006
Annual Total Return %	—	—	47.3	-12.4	-0.6	-7.7
Fiscal Year-End: December	2001	2002	2003	2004	2005	TTM
Revenue $Mil	321	635	998	1,265	1,701	2,176
Net Income $Mil	39	55	103	46	-20	-60
Earnings Per Share $	—	—	0.64	0.28	-0.13	-0.37
Shares Outstanding Mil	—	—	145	153	154	176
Return on Equity %	NMF	13.3	15.4	6.1	-2.2	-6.5
Net Margin %	12.2	8.7	10.3	3.6	-1.2	-2.8
Asset Turnover	0.5	0.5	0.5	0.5	0.4	0.5
Financial Leverage	NMF	3.3	3.3	3.7	4.3	4.8

Valuation Ratios	Stock	Rel to Industry	Rel to S&P 500
Price/Earnings	NMF	—	—
Price/Book	2.7	0.7	0.7
Price/Sales	1.1	0.7	0.4
Price/Cash Flow	10.7	1.1	0.7

Major Fund Holders	% of Fund Assets
The Turnaround	10.99
Thornburg Core Growth A	3.01
Fidelity Select Air Transportation	2.96
Fidelity Select Transportation	2.80

Thesis By Marisa E. Thompson, 12-15-06 Stock Price as of Analysis: $13.77

JetBlue benefits from a strong management team, low-cost structure, and superb culture. However, margins will continue to come under pressure from high oil prices and expenses that reflect the growing pains of a young airline.

The airline industry has become more commodified than ever, and it follows that airlines with the lowest-cost structures will be the most profitable. JetBlue is one of those airlines. When adjusted for the average length of its flights, the young company's unit cost is modestly higher than that of perennial cost leader Southwest Airlines. All JetBlue passengers fly ticketless, and the company sells most of its fares through its own Web site, thus reducing ticket-distribution expenses. Most importantly, the company has low labor expenses while generating excellent productivity from its workers.

Some of JetBlue's cost advantages will eventually erode, however. For one, the firm recently began flying 100-seat Embraer 190s. With the Embraer 190, JetBlue intends to target regional routes with higher pricing yields, but the yields might not entirely offset the higher unit costs associated with this smaller plane. Plus, JetBlue will incur incremental pilot training and maintenance costs with the addition of this second airplane type to its fleet of Airbus A320s. In general, as its young fleet of airplanes ages, more frequent and thorough maintenance will add to unit costs. JetBlue's labor expenses will grow as the workforce accumulates tenure, and JetBlue is not immune to the threat of unionization, particularly if profit-sharing and employee stock-purchase plans deliver less-than-stellar compensation. The likely end result, even if airline ticket prices return to healthy levels, is a long-run average operating margin in the high single digits, a far cry from the high-teen margins that used to inspire JetBlue mania.

The airline has plenty of opportunity to expand its top line, and management has demonstrated a rare ability to add new routes while maintaining and even improving load factors. However, JetBlue's fleet plan may outstrip the availability of additional attractive routes. In fact, management has already put the brakes on its growth plans, deferring many deliveries and pushing back options even further into the future. Furthermore, management remains haunted by the fact that, unlike low-cost rivals AirTran and Southwest, it was not aggressive enough in employing fuel hedges.

Data as of 12-29-06

John Wiley & Sons A JW.A

	Rating	Fair Value	Last Close	Consider Buy	Consider Sell	Yield %
	★★★	$39.00	$38.47	$33.20	$51.20	1.01

Company Profile

John Wiley is a global publisher of print and electronic products, with about 40% of its sales coming from outside the United States. The scientific, technical, and medical segment, which generates the highest profit margin, contributes about 38% of global revenue. The professional/trade segment includes a wide spectrum of categories and brands and contributes about 43% of revenue; Wiley's higher-education segment represents the other 19%.

Management   Stewardship Grade [B]

Overall, we think management serves shareholders well. Wiley's Stewardship Grade takes a hit because of its split share classes. Wiley family members own about 5% of Class A and 75% of Class B shares. (Class B shares have 10 times the voting power of Class A shares.) The company's long history of producing attractive returns on invested capital gives us confidence in the family's control over the firm. CEO William Pesce began his current role in 1998 after a long stint as Wiley's chief operating officer. Pesce earned total cash compensation of $2 million and restricted stock worth $2.5 million in 2006. Over the past two years, stock-option grants represented about 1.5% of outstanding shares--a reasonable amount, in our opinion.

111 River Street   www.wiley.com
Hoboken, NJ 07030

Growth [B-]	2003	2004	2005	2006
Revenue %	16.3	8.1	5.5	7.2
Earnings/Share %	51.6	2.2	-4.3	37.0
Book Value/Share %	23.8	21.1	-3.1	5.5
Dividends/Share %	11.1	30.0	15.4	20.0

Profitability [A]	2004	2005	2006	TTM
Return on Assets %	8.9	8.1	10.8	10.6
Oper Cash Flow $Mil	212	243	243	224
- Cap Spending $Mil	29	27	21	25
= Free Cash Flow $Mil	183	217	221	199

Financial Health [A]	2004	2005	2006	10-31-06
Long-term Debt $Mil	200	196	160	208
Total Equity $Mil	415	397	402	461
Debt/Equity Ratio	0.5	0.5	0.4	0.5

Industry	Business Risk	Moat Size	Investment Style	Sector
Publishing	Below Avg	Wide	Small Core	Media

Competition	Market Cap $Mil	12 Mo Trailing Sales $Mil	Price/Cash Flow	Return On Assets%	Debt/Equity	Total Return% 1 Yr	3 Yr
John Wiley & Sons A	1,811	1,093	8.1	10.6	0.5	-0.4	14.6
McGraw-Hill Companies	24,093	6,202	14.9	14.1	0.0	33.4	26.9
Scholastic	1,514	2,120	6.4	2.1	0.2	25.7	2.5

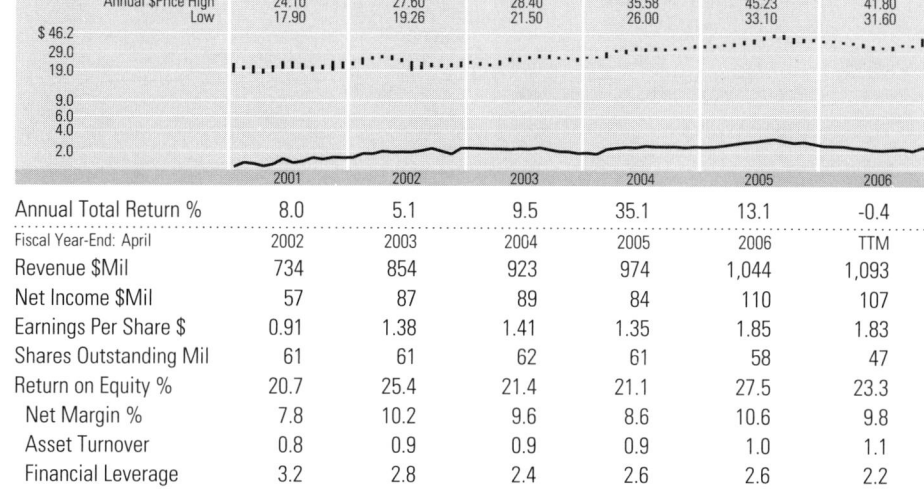

	2002	2003	2004	2005	2006	TTM
Annual Total Return %	8.0	5.1	9.5	35.1	13.1	-0.4
Fiscal Year-End: April	2002	2003	2004	2005	2006	TTM
Revenue $Mil	734	854	923	974	1,044	1,093
Net Income $Mil	57	87	89	84	110	107
Earnings Per Share $	0.91	1.38	1.41	1.35	1.85	1.83
Shares Outstanding Mil	61	61	62	61	58	47
Return on Equity %	20.7	25.4	21.4	21.1	27.5	23.3
Net Margin %	7.8	10.2	9.6	8.6	10.6	9.8
Asset Turnover	0.8	0.9	0.9	0.9	1.0	1.1
Financial Leverage	3.2	2.8	2.4	2.6	2.6	2.2

Valuation Ratios	Stock	Rel to Industry	Rel to S&P 500
Price/Earnings	21.0	0.8	1.0
Price/Book	3.9	0.6	1.0
Price/Sales	1.7	0.6	0.6
Price/Cash Flow	8.1	0.6	0.6

Major Fund Holders	% of Fund Assets
FAM Equity-Income Inv	5.69
Integrity Growth & Income A Load Waived	5.66
FAM Value Inv	2.34
Timothy Plan Patriot C	2.30

Thesis By Michael Corty, CFA, 12-14-06 Stock Price as of Analysis: $39.00

John Wiley has carved out a valuable franchise in each of its three publishing businesses. its most attractive enterprise is the science, technical, and medical (STM) segment, and we think the company is taking steps to widen its economic moat.

The STM business is a lucrative niche of the publishing industry. A majority of Wiley's STM customers are academic and institutional libraries that consider Wiley's journals and books to be must-have content. For example, scientists and engineers rely upon the Journal of Applied Polymer Science in their research endeavors. We think Wiley's relationships within the academic community (developed through its college textbook business) give the company an edge in securing content for its journals--it published 8% more journal pages in fiscal 2006 than in the previous year. The company licenses its STM content with multiyear contracts, and the high regard for its product is evidenced by operating margins that exceed 40%.

Wiley improved its competitive position by developing a proprietary online-distribution infrastructure, Wiley InterScience. A majority of STM content is now accessed online, and the InterScience platform has become a hub of valuable research material. Aggregating its content online has generated incremental revenue for Wiley, as third-party journals are willing to exchange a share of subscription revenue for distribution through Wiley's platform.

In November 2006, Wiley entered into a definitive agreement to acquire Blackwell Publishing, a privately held British academic publisher with valuable journal content in the medical, physical sciences, and humanities fields. This $1 billion all-cash deal is Wiley's largest acquisition to date and will double Wiley's STM revenue base of $380 million. The combined entity will have greater priority with customers, as it will become the third-largest player in the STM niche.

We like that Wiley is making a large investment in its most profitable business. Furthermore, we're inclined to trust that management has made a value-adding deal for shareholders, given Wiley's history of wise capital allocation and its demonstrated patience in pursuing acquisitions. Wiley's last significant acquisition--Hungry Minds in 2001--has proved to be a winner, adding valuable brands like Frommer's and For Dummies to the consumer publishing business.

Data as of 12-29-06

Johnson & Johnson JNJ

	Rating	Fair Value	Last Close	Consider Buy	Consider Sell	Yield %
	★★★★	$76.00	$66.02	$64.80	$99.80	2.20

Industry	Business Risk	Moat Size	Investment Style	Sector
Drugs	Below Avg	Wide	Large Core	Healthcare

Company Profile

Johnson & Johnson is a diversified health-care company with three divisions: pharmaceutical, medical devices and diagnostics, and consumer. Even after J&J's acquisition of Pfizer's consumer health unit, pharmaceutical will remain the largest division, constituting about 40% of expected 2006 revenue. Medical devices and diagnostics will account for about 36%. The remaining 24% comes from well-known consumer products such as Band-Aids, Johnson's Baby Shampoo, and Tylenol.

Management   Stewardship Grade [B]

Bill Weldon has been chairman and CEO since 2002. Weldon is only the sixth chairman in J&J's 117-year history. Weldon started with J&J as a sales representative right out of college. He ran the endosurgery and pharma units before ascending to the top job. J&J's board has consistently been rated one of the best in America, and the firm regularly earns one of the top spots on Fortune's Most Admired Companies list. J&J's long-term management incentive plan is innovative: The value of the awards is not determined (or awarded) until retirement and is fully performance-driven. We wish the firm would separate the chairman and CEO roles, however. J&J has had some management turnover lately, with CFO Bob Darretta and head of DePuy Bill McComb announcing departures in 2006. We're not too concerned, though, as we think strong management runs deep at this highly decentralized firm.

One Johnson & Johnson Plaza   www.jnj.com
New Brunswick, NJ 08933

Competition

	Market Cap $Mil	12 Mo Trailing Sales $Mil	Price/Cash Flow	Return On Assets%	Debt/Equity	Total Return% 1 Yr	3 Yr
Johnson & Johnson	191,415	52,252	14.5	18.5	0.0	12.4	10.8
Novartis AG ADR	134,175	32,526	16.6	10.6	0.0	11.3	9.6
Merck	94,656	22,358	13.0	11.6	0.2	42.7	1.7

Price Volatility

	Annual $Price High/Low					
	60.97 / 40.25	65.85 / 41.50	59.08 / 48.05	64.25 / 49.25	69.99 / 59.76	69.41 / 56.65
	2001	2002	2003	2004	2005	2006
Annual Total Return %	14.0	-7.9	-2.1	25.2	-3.4	12.4

Fiscal Year-End: December	2001	2002	2003	2004	2005	TTM
Revenue $Mil	32,317	36,298	41,862	47,348	50,514	52,252
Net Income $Mil	5,668	6,597	7,197	8,509	10,411	11,331
Earnings Per Share $	1.84	2.16	2.40	2.84	3.46	3.80
Shares Outstanding Mil	3,031	2,999	2,974	2,965	2,975	2,899
Return on Equity %	23.4	29.1	26.8	26.7	27.5	27.9
Net Margin %	17.5	18.2	17.2	18.0	20.6	21.7
Asset Turnover	0.8	0.9	0.9	0.9	0.9	0.9
Financial Leverage	1.6	1.8	1.8	1.7	1.5	1.5

Valuation Ratios	Stock	Rel to Industry	Rel to S&P 500
Price/Earnings	17.4	0.7	0.8
Price/Book	4.7	0.9	1.1
Price/Sales	3.7	0.8	1.3
Price/Cash Flow	14.5	0.9	1.0

Major Fund Holders	% of Fund Assets
ProFunds Pharmaceuticals UltraSector Inv	17.36
North Track DJ US Hlth Care 100 A	9.94
Fidelity Select Medical Equip/Systems	9.49
Profunds UltraSector Health Care Inv	8.31

Growth [C+]	2002	2003	2004	2005
Revenue %	12.3	15.3	13.1	6.7
Earnings/Share %	17.4	11.1	18.3	21.8
Book Value/Share %	-5.5	20.6	18.5	18.5
Dividends/Share %	13.6	16.4	18.4	16.4

Profitability [A+]	2003	2004	2005	TTM
Return on Assets %	14.9	16.0	17.9	18.5
Oper Cash Flow $Mil	10,595	11,131	11,877	13,206
- Cap Spending $Mil	2,262	2,175	2,632	2,749
= Free Cash Flow $Mil	8,333	8,956	9,245	10,457

Financial Health [A+]	2003	2004	2005	09-30-06
Long-term Debt $Mil	2,955	2,565	2,017	2,007
Total Equity $Mil	26,869	31,813	37,871	40,573
Debt/Equity Ratio	0.1	0.1	0.1	0.0

Thesis By Heather Brilliant, CFA, 12-15-06 Stock Price as of Analysis: $66.29

While Johnson & Johnson has encountered some challenges in its pharmaceutical business, we're confident it can emerge unscathed thanks to a solid research pipeline, diverse revenue base, and exceptional cash flow generation.

J&J aims to be a leader in each business in which it operates, and this goal permeates the organization. The company has achieved this in numerous markets, claiming the number-one or -two position in medical devices, over-the-counter medicines (including its pending acquisition of Pfizer's consumer products business), and several pharmaceutical markets. Its businesses are well-positioned to benefit from demographic shifts, including the aging population in the U.S. and Europe and rising spending power in many developing countries.

More than 40% of J&J's revenue currently comes from its pharmaceutical group, with eight drugs each bringing in more than $1 billion in sales. The firm's treatments for schizophrenia, anemia, and rheumatoid arthritis each contribute mightily to revenue. While competition from other branded products and generic alternatives threatens to erode J&J's position in several pharmaceutical markets over the coming years, we think the firm's increasing commitment to research and development and astute in-licensing abilities will help it weather this potential storm. The company has more than 15 new drugs in late-stage development, several of which have blockbuster potential, and an impressive pipeline of compounds in the earlier stages of development.

Further, J&J is unique among pharmaceutical firms in that more than half of its revenue comes from other areas, namely medical devices and consumer health-care products. We expect these businesses will grow faster than the firm's pharmaceutical division over the coming years, and will therefore increase as a proportion of J&J's revenues and profits. Businesses such as orthopedic device maker DePuy and coronary stent division Cordis continue to develop innovative products and lead their respective markets.

This diverse revenue base has helped insulate J&J from the highs and lows that affect its pharmaceutical competitors from time to time. As a result of this and its acquisition strategy, the firm has reported more than 70 years of sales growth and churns out free cash flow (operating cash flow less capital expenditures) reaching almost 20% of sales. This excellent cash generation has enabled the firm to grow its dividend for the past 44 years, a trend we expect to continue.

Data as of 12-29-06

Johnson Controls JCI

	Rating	Fair Value	Last Close	Consider Buy	Consider Sell	Yield %
	★★★	$80.00	$85.92	$61.70	$100.20	1.36

Company Profile

Johnson Controls operates in three distinct business segments: automotive interiors, vehicle batteries, and building controls and services. Globally, the firm employs 120,000 people. Sales are about $32 billion with auto parts and batteries making up about 60% of the total and building controls and services contributing the remaining 40% of revenue. Johnson bought York International, a provider of building mechanical equipment and services, for $3.2 billion in August 2005.

Management   Stewardship Grade [B]

CEO John Barth and his senior team have done an admirable job of leading Johnson Controls through several years of brutal industry conditions. Barth has been CEO since October 2002. Prior to assuming the company's top job, he was COO and a member of the board of directors since 1997. The company is managed with an eye on creating shareholder value, and sales, net income, and dividend payouts have all increased steadily for the past two decades. Although JCI's acquisitions strategy introduces new risks, the company is an accomplished acquirer and most of its investments increase shareholder value. Management's compensation consists of a base salary and short- and long-term cash and stock bonuses. Although total compensation is generous, we like the fact that incentives are based on criteria linked to the long-term performance of the company. We also like the steps the firm took in 2005 to improve transparency by disclosing separate financial information for its battery segment. While Johnson Controls focuses on creating shareholder value, we dislike the company's staggered directorships, which make it difficult for an outside investor to influence the company.

5757 North Green Bay Avenue   www.johnsoncontrols.com
Milwaukee, WI 53201

Growth [A-]	2002	2003	2004	2005
Revenue %	12.7	16.2	11.7	17.3
Earnings/Share %	13.2	17.8	10.4	11.8
Book Value/Share %	22.5	19.2	15.2	20.0
Dividends/Share %	9.1	25.0	11.1	12.0

Profitability [A-]	2003	2004	2005	TTM
Return on Assets %	5.5	5.6	4.7	4.7
Oper Cash Flow $Mil	1,303	927	1,417	1,417
- Cap Spending $Mil	784	664	711	711
= Free Cash Flow $Mil	520	263	706	706

Financial Health [C+]	2003	2004	2005	06-30-06
Long-term Debt $Mil	1,631	1,578	4,166	4,166
Total Equity $Mil	5,206	6,058	7,355	7,355
Debt/Equity Ratio	0.3	0.3	0.6	0.6

Industry	Business Risk	Moat Size	Investment Style	Sector
AutoParts	Average	Narrow	Large Core	Industrial Materials

Competition

	Market Cap $Mil	12 Mo Trailing Sales $Mil	Price/Cash Flow	Return On Assets%	Debt/Equity	Total Return% 1 Yr	3 Yr
Johnson Controls	16,822	32,235	11.9	4.7	0.6	19.6	16.0
Magna International A	8,714	22,811	5.1	5.2	0.1	14.2	1.8
Lear	1,990	17,956	4.5	-7.9	2.1	4.9	-20.3

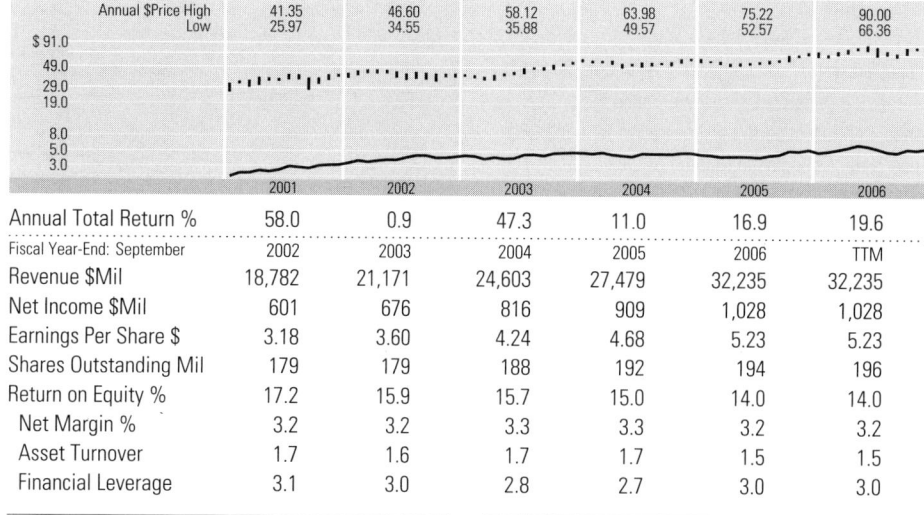

	2001	2002	2003	2004	2005	2006
Annual $Price High	41.35	46.60	58.12	63.98	75.22	90.00
Low	25.97	34.55	35.88	49.57	52.57	66.36
Annual Total Return %	58.0	0.9	47.3	11.0	16.9	19.6

Fiscal Year-End: September	2002	2003	2004	2005	2006	TTM
Revenue $Mil	18,782	21,171	24,603	27,479	32,235	32,235
Net Income $Mil	601	676	816	909	1,028	1,028
Earnings Per Share $	3.18	3.60	4.24	4.68	5.23	5.23
Shares Outstanding Mil	179	179	188	192	194	196
Return on Equity %	17.2	15.9	15.7	15.0	14.0	14.0
Net Margin %	3.2	3.2	3.3	3.3	3.2	3.2
Asset Turnover	1.7	1.6	1.7	1.7	1.5	1.5
Financial Leverage	3.1	3.0	2.8	2.7	3.0	3.0

Valuation Ratios	Stock	Rel to Industry	Rel to S&P 500
Price/Earnings	16.4	1.0	0.8
Price/Book	2.3	0.9	0.6
Price/Sales	0.5	0.6	0.2
Price/Cash Flow	11.9	1.0	0.8

Major Fund Holders	% of Fund Assets
Fidelity Select Automotive	5.68
Hallmark Strategic Growth I	3.18
Crawford Dividend Growth I	3.07
Hallmark Large-Cap Growth R	2.86

Thesis   By John Novak, 12-13-06   Stock Price as of Analysis: $82.61

Despite tough competition across its entire portfolio, Johnson Controls (JCI) is a market leader in the industries in which it competes, and we think the company's operating expertise, global footprint, and healthy balance sheet leave the firm well-positioned for the long term. Smart acquisitions have further improved the outlook by reducing the firm's reliance on the struggling domestic auto sector.

The 2005 acquisition of York International nearly doubled the size of JCI's building controls and services unit. While the building systems industry is highly competitive and prone to cyclical swings, JCI's focus on selling replacement systems and maintenance services should damp the volatility of new construction activity. The trend toward higher oil and gas prices (which have crushed the company's traditional auto business) should provide additional opportunities as customers look for solutions to rein in skyrocketing energy costs.

Recent acquisitions have vaulted JCI into the top rungs of the world's vehicle battery makers. Unlike the company's other automotive businesses, which are dependent on new car production, about 80% of the segment revenues come from the relatively stable market for replacement batteries. Demand for batteries in mature Western countries should remain steady, and JCI is well-positioned to take advantage of fast-growing emerging markets such as China and Eastern Europe, where vehicle ownership rates are expected to soar for the next decade. In addition, the company is working on the next generation of batteries for the small, but rapidly expanding, hybrid electric vehicle market.

With JCI's diversification efforts attracting attention, it's possible to forget that the company remains one the world's largest auto parts makers. While we don't think the turmoil in the U.S. auto industry will subside anytime soon, JCI's interiors business is well-positioned to prosper in the long run. To cope with the downturn in Detroit and meet demand in fast-growing emerging markets, JCI is reducing its North American manufacturing capacity, shifting operations to low-cost countries, and winning business with Asian and European customers. Ultimately, we think these steps should help the segment's operating margins rebound toward historical norms over the next few years. What's more, JCI's healthy balance sheet should provide the flexibility to make strategic investments while cash-strapped competitors are forced scale back ambitions as they fight for survival.

Data as of 12-29-06

Jones Apparel Group JNY

	Rating	Fair Value	Last Close	Consider Buy	Consider Sell	Yield %
	★★★	$34.00	$33.43	$26.20	$42.60	1.50

Industry	Business Risk	Moat Size	Investment Style	Sector
Apparel Makers	Average	Narrow	Mid Value	Consumer Goods

Company Profile
Jones Apparel Group designs and produces women's sportswear, suits, dresses, and shoes. The company markets its products under the Jones New York, Anne Klein, Kasper, Bandolino, and Nine West names. The company sells its products through major department stores, specialty retailers, and direct-mail catalog companies throughout North America. It also operates its own specialty retail stores, including Barneys New York.

Management   Stewardship Grade [C]
Overall, we think corporate governance is fair at Jones. Peter Boneparth has been president and CEO since 2002. He replaced founder Sidney Kimmel, who led the company from 1975 to 2002. Kimmel is now chairman of the board and owns 1.8% of the shares outstanding. Boneparth owns 2.2% of the outstanding shares. Although bonuses for executives were pared back in 2005 due to the company's poor performance, we continue to think executive compensation is excessive. Boneparth earned nearly $4 million in annual compensation (including a $1.2 million bonus) and received roughly $3.7 million in restricted stock. Although Jones scores poorly in executive compensation, the company does have a number of shareholder-friendly policies. We applaud the board for electing members on an annual basis, splitting the role of chairman and CEO, and providing relatively good disclosure despite a number of acquisitions. We are impressed with Jones' latest addition to the board, Allen Questrom, who is well respected in the retail industry as the former CEO of Federated and most recently as the leader of J.C. Penney's successful turnaround.

250 Rittenhouse Circle Keystone Park www.jny.com
Bristol, PA 19007

Growth [D+]	2002	2003	2004	2005
Revenue %	5.9	0.8	6.3	9.1
Earnings/Share %	29.7	5.1	-3.6	-3.8
Book Value/Share %	16.3	12.2	9.7	6.4
Dividends/Share %	NMF	NMF	125.0	22.2

Profitability [B]	2003	2004	2005	TTM
Return on Assets %	7.8	6.6	6.0	4.1
Oper Cash Flow $Mil	455	462	427	487
- Cap Spending $Mil	53	57	88	142
= Free Cash Flow $Mil	402	405	340	345

Financial Health [A-]	2003	2004	2005	09-30-06
Long-term Debt $Mil	835	1,017	790	790
Total Equity $Mil	2,538	2,654	2,666	2,574
Debt/Equity Ratio	0.3	0.4	0.3	0.3

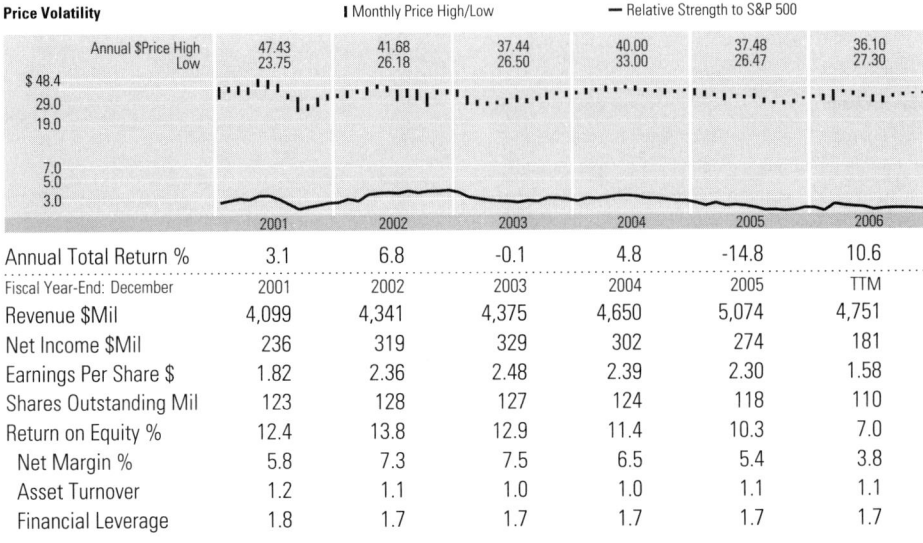

Competition
	Market Cap $Mil	12 Mo Trailing Sales $Mil	Price/Cash Flow	Return On Assets%	Debt/ Equity	Total Return% 1 Yr	3 Yr
Jones Apparel Group	3,686	4,751	7.6	4.1	0.3	10.6	0.3
Liz Claiborne	4,454	4,865	11.0	7.3	0.3	22.1	8.2

Annual Total Return %	3.1	6.8	-0.1	4.8	-14.8	10.6
Fiscal Year-End: December	2001	2002	2003	2004	2005	TTM
Revenue $Mil	4,099	4,341	4,375	4,650	5,074	4,751
Net Income $Mil	236	319	329	302	274	181
Earnings Per Share $	1.82	2.36	2.48	2.39	2.30	1.58
Shares Outstanding Mil	123	128	127	124	118	110
Return on Equity %	12.4	13.8	12.9	11.4	10.3	7.0
Net Margin %	5.8	7.3	7.5	6.5	5.4	3.8
Asset Turnover	1.2	1.1	1.0	1.0	1.1	1.1
Financial Leverage	1.8	1.7	1.7	1.7	1.7	1.7

Valuation Ratios	Stock	Rel to Industry	Rel to S&P 500
Price/Earnings	21.3	0.9	1.0
Price/Book	1.4	0.4	0.3
Price/Sales	0.8	0.4	0.3
Price/Cash Flow	7.6	0.5	0.5

Major Fund Holders	% of Fund Assets
Penn Avenue Event-Driven Inv	3.11
Wells Fargo Advantage C&B Mid Cap Val D	2.40
Hotchkis and Wiley Mid-Cap Value I	2.33
MassMutual Select Mid-Cap Value S	2.17

Thesis By Kimberly Picciola, 11-28-06 Stock Price as of Analysis: $33.40

After evaluating strategic alternatives for Jones Apparel Group, the board has decided not to sell the company. Although it is somewhat of a concern that the company did not receive an offer it believed was worth pursuing, we don't think the board was desperate to make a deal. In the near term, we believe management's decision to move forward with its current restructuring strategy will result in improved operating performance. However, we remain wary of the firm's long-term growth prospects. We think consolidation in the department store channel and the firm's exposure to moderate brands will limit future gains.

Despite its recent top-line struggles, Jones has well-established relationships with key department store chains, like Federated. We believe these relationships coupled with its multi-channel, multi-brand portfolio give it a leg up on the competition. Yet, an increased exposure to moderate brands, which have less pricing power, and declining returns on invested capital are worrisome. We think it is too soon to strip Jones of its narrow moat rating; however, it is teetering between narrow and no moat.

Acquisitions have been the main growth driver for Jones in recent years. While this approach has enabled Jones to fill out its portfolio and increase the top line, we don't think growth through acquisition is sustainable over the long run. Additionally, integrating acquisitions can be costly. Operating margins have been lumpy over the past five years, in part because of Jones' acquisitive approach.

Despite its diversification strategy, Jones remains heavily dependent on traditional department stores, which are consolidating. As specialty retailers and discounters have grown in popularity, traditional mall-based department stores have struggled. Federated's acquisition of May has made the combined entity one of Jones' largest customers, accounting for roughly 19% of its revenue in 2005. Although acquisitions like Barneys and Nine West have helped Jones diversify into specialty retail, we believe the firm's significant exposure to the department store channel will slow top-line growth.

In addition, midtier department store chains are incorporating more exclusive merchandise into their offerings to differentiate themselves from competitors, which could further pressure top-line growth for Jones. Federated plans to roll out its private-label brands in former May stores, and Sears is overhauling its apparel business, which may include a boost in its private-label offering.

Data as of 12-29-06

Jones Lang LaSalle JLL

Rating	Fair Value	Last Close	Consider Buy	Consider Sell	Yield %
★	$66.00	$92.17	$50.90	$82.70	0.65

Company Profile

Jones Lang LaSalle was created in 1999 from the merger of Jones Lang Wootton, a 220-year-old London-based company, and LaSalle Partners, a leading Chicago-based real estate manager. With more than 900 million square feet under management and a nearly $37 billion real estate fund, Jones Lang LaSalle is one of the world's leading property and real estate money managers. The company has operations in 50 countries including China, Japan, France, and the United Kingdom.

Management
Stewardship Grade [**B**]

We believe Jones Lang LaSalle has one of the best management teams in the business, bolstered by its global expertise in real estate and its smart succession planning. President and CEO Colin Dyer took the top position in August 2004 and has used his international experience in the retail business to expand the firm's client roster. Executive vice president, CFO, and COO Lauralee Martin came on board four years ago after five years in leadership at Heller Financial, a commercial finance company. Jones Lang LaSalle deserves kudos for its well-defined compensation strategy. Based on three performance objectives, executives can earn restricted stock awards on top of their annual salaries. In 2005, Dyer netted about $4.4 million, including restricted stock awards, which was consistent with the company's surge in revenue and profits. We were pleased with Jones Lang's recent decision to declassify the board and elect board members annually. Directors and officers have a 1.2% stake in the firm, a rather low holding, in our opinion.

200 East Randolph Drive
Chicago, IL 60601
www.joneslanglasalle.com

Growth [A-]	2002	2003	2004	2005
Revenue %	-4.1	9.5	23.9	19.2
Earnings/Share %	NMF	31.8	75.0	59.2
Book Value/Share %	10.6	16.3	15.8	4.5
Dividends/Share %	NMF	NMF	NMF	NMF

Profitability [A]	2003	2004	2005	TTM
Return on Assets %	3.8	6.3	9.0	10.8
Oper Cash Flow $Mil	110	161	121	—
- Cap Spending $Mil	19	28	40	—
= Free Cash Flow $Mil	—	—	—	—

Financial Health [NA]	2003	2004	2005	09-30-06
Long-term Debt $Mil	—	—	—	—
Total Equity $Mil	431	508	536	674
Debt/Equity Ratio	—	—	—	—

Industry	Business Risk	Moat Size	Investment Style	Sector
Real Estate	Average	Narrow	Mid Growth	Financial Services

Competition

	Market Cap $Mil	12 Mo Trailing Sales $Mil	Price/Cash Flow	Return On Assets%	Debt/ Equity	Total Return% 1 Yr	3 Yr
Jones Lang LaSalle	3,366	1,808	—	10.8	—	84.3	64.7
CB Richard Ellis Group	7,425	3,217	—	10.6	—	69.2	—
Kennedy-Wilson	151	—	—	—	—	55.8	54.7

Price Volatility

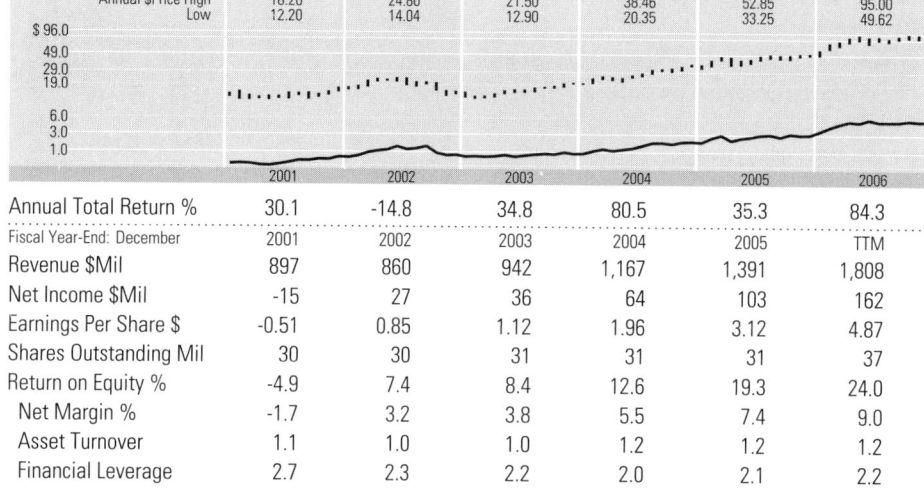

	2001	2002	2003	2004	2005	2006
Annual $Price High	18.20	24.80	21.50	38.46	52.85	95.00
Low	12.20	14.04	12.90	20.35	33.25	49.62
Annual Total Return %	30.1	-14.8	34.8	80.5	35.3	84.3

Fiscal Year-End: December	2001	2002	2003	2004	2005	TTM
Revenue $Mil	897	860	942	1,167	1,391	1,808
Net Income $Mil	-15	27	36	64	103	162
Earnings Per Share $	-0.51	0.85	1.12	1.96	3.12	4.87
Shares Outstanding Mil	30	30	31	31	31	37
Return on Equity %	-4.9	7.4	8.4	12.6	19.3	24.0
Net Margin %	-1.7	3.2	3.8	5.5	7.4	9.0
Asset Turnover	1.1	1.0	1.0	1.2	1.2	1.2
Financial Leverage	2.7	2.3	2.2	2.0	2.1	2.2

Valuation Ratios	Stock	Rel to Industry	Rel to S&P 500
Price/Earnings	18.9	0.7	0.9
Price/Book	5.0	0.8	1.2
Price/Sales	1.9	0.1	0.7
Price/Cash Flow	—	—	—

Major Fund Holders	% of Fund Assets
Maxim Ariel SmallCap Value	4.59
Ariel	4.25
Navellier Fundamental A	2.81
Loomis Sayles Aggressive Growth Ret	2.44

Thesis By Heather Smith, 10-20-06 Stock Price as of Analysis:

Thanks to a churning economy and a red-hot real estate market, Jones Lang LaSalle has broken company records for profits and revenue. We believe the firm's run is not over yet, as it successfully expands its money management business, which should prop profits even if the commercial real estate market cools.

Three powerful trends--the increasing globalization of business, the outsourcing of corporate real estate services, and surging interest in real estate as an investment--should boost Jones Lang's future results. With operations in more than 100 markets, the company has few equals. As more firms seek to grow internationally, companies like Jones Lang can be a single source for all their real estate needs. The company's primary business consists of brokering commercial real estate transactions, helping clients handle the real estate aspect of outsourcing, and managing properties after purchase. Though real estate is typically one of the largest assets on most firms' balance sheets, it usually isn't a core competency. This has hastened the outsourcing of corporate real estate services, and Jones Lang has been a prime beneficiary. The company's large research team, which offers comprehensive market analysis and individual sector expertise, gives the firm an edge relative to competitors.

Jones Lang is also benefiting from real estate's relative safety, which attracts institutional and high-net-worth investor participation in property investment. The company's money-management division invests in real estate assets with these third parties, collecting annual fees based on a percentage of assets and square feet under management. This annuitylike revenue stream is relatively inexpensive to maintain and now constitutes about 40% of operating income, reducing the cyclicality associated with real estate services. We believe that the money-management segment will grow even faster as institutional investors shift a larger portion of their portfolios to real estate.

We believe these long-term trends underpin the commercial real estate market, preventing the large downturn affecting the residential real estate market. Jones Lang Lasalle is a major beneficiary of the record investment activity in international property markets, especially Asia and Europe. Additionally, Jones Lang's defensive business model gives us confidence the firm can navigate a slowdown in the commercial real estate market.

Data as of 12-29-06

Juniper Networks JNPR

	Rating	Fair Value	Last Close	Consider Buy	Consider Sell	Yield %
	★★★★	$22.00	$18.94	$17.00	$27.60	0.00

Industry	Business Risk	Moat Size	Investment Style	Sector
Data Networking	Average	Narrow	Mid Growth	Hardware

Company Profile

Juniper focuses on high-performance routers and serving those who use them: mainly telecom carriers, but also large organizations with demanding requirements. The brains of Juniper's routers--customized chips and software--have been designed with carrier requirements in mind. Over the past several years, Juniper has entered the corporate networking enterprise market and sells a security and application traffic-management products in addition to its routers.

Management   Stewardship Grade [B]

Juniper's governance has historically been fairly solid, but, like many other companies, the firm is embroiled in an investigation over its stock-option granting practices. Juniper's heavy reliance on stock options as a compensation tool has long been our major governance ding against the company. The company's independent investigation into the matter has reached a preliminary conclusion that certain option grant dates did differ from the recorded date. With its investigation largely complete the company hopes to file audited financials within the next couple of quarters.

Though the company saw significant turnover in its upper management ranks in 2005, Juniper has one of the deepest management benches in the communications-equipment industry, in our opinion. CEO since 1996, Scott Kriens co founded StrataCom, a carrier switching firm that became one of Cisco's best acquisitions. Many employees came from StrataCom or Cisco and managed the impressive feat of building a Cisco-compatible operating system. Kriens took a page from StrataCom's playbook by persuading potential competitors (and customers) to become Juniper investors and marketing partners. Kriens holds just under 3% of the outstanding shares. Juniper's cofounder, Pradeep Sindhu, serves as chief technical officer and vice chairman of the board.

1194 N. Mathilda Ave.   www.juniper.net
Sunnyvale, CA 94089

Growth [A]	2002	2003	2004	2005
Revenue %	-38.4	28.3	90.5	54.5
Earnings/Share %	NMF	NMF	177.8	136.0
Book Value/Share %	36.5	-11.8	207.7	4.2
Dividends/Share %	NMF	NMF	NMF	NMF

Profitability [B-]	2003	2004	2005	TTM
Return on Assets %	1.6	1.9	4.4	4.4
Oper Cash Flow $Mil	179	439	643	592
- Cap Spending $Mil	19	63	98	94
= Free Cash Flow $Mil	159	376	545	498

Financial Health [A+]	2003	2004	2005	03-31-06
Long-term Debt $Mil	542	400	400	400
Total Equity $Mil	1,562	5,993	6,900	6,920
Debt/Equity Ratio	0.3	0.1	0.1	0.1

Competition	Market Cap $Mil	12 Mo Trailing Sales $Mil	Price/Cash Flow	Return On Assets%	Debt/ Equity	Total Return% 1 Yr	3 Yr
Juniper Networks	10,715	2,182	18.1	4.4	0.1	-15.1	-1.3
Cisco Systems	165,967	30,118	18.9	13.2	0.3	59.6	4.1
Nortel Networks	11,591	11,078	—	-12.1	3.4	-12.7	-15.9

Price Volatility

Annual $Price High	145.00	23.01	19.38	31.25	27.65	22.63
Low	8.90	4.15	6.80	18.68	19.65	12.09

	2001	2002	2003	2004	2005	2006
Annual Total Return %	-85.0	-64.1	174.7	45.6	-18.0	-15.1
Fiscal Year-End: December	2001	2002	2003	2004	2005	TTM
Revenue $Mil	887	547	701	1,336	2,064	2,182
Net Income $Mil	-13	-120	39	136	354	354
Earnings Per Share $	-0.04	-0.34	0.09	0.25	0.59	0.59
Shares Outstanding Mil	335	352	392	485	553	566
Return on Equity %	-1.3	-8.4	2.5	2.3	5.1	5.1
Net Margin %	-1.5	-21.9	5.6	10.2	17.2	16.2
Asset Turnover	0.4	0.2	0.3	0.2	0.3	0.3
Financial Leverage	2.4	1.8	1.5	1.2	1.2	1.2

Valuation Ratios	Stock	Rel to Industry	Rel to S&P 500
Price/Earnings	32.1	1.1	1.6
Price/Book	1.5	0.2	0.4
Price/Sales	4.9	0.9	1.7
Price/Cash Flow	18.1	0.9	1.2

Major Fund Holders	% of Fund Assets
Pin Oak Aggressive Stock	5.50
AllianceBernstein Mid-Cap Growth A	4.84
ING AllianceBernstein Mid Cap Growth S	4.83
Managers 20 A	4.49

Thesis By John Slack, 12-14-06 Stock Price as of Analysis: $20.37

After seeing Cisco claw back market share in the routing market in 2006, we believe that Juniper's reinvigorated product line should allow the company to post solid growth and throw off considerable amounts of cash over the next few years.

The move by carriers to a Internet-protocol-based network infrastructure continues to be one of the dominant themes driving telecom service provider--or carrier--network spending, and Juniper is well positioned in this market with its focus on carrier-class routing. Rather than adapting existing routers to carriers' needs, Juniper routers were designed with the quality of service that carriers demand from day one. The strength of its product line allowed Juniper to quickly take share from Cisco, which for many years was the only game in town.

Together, Cisco and Juniper dominate the carrier router market, sharing a virtual duopoly with Cisco claiming roughly a 60% share to Juniper's 30%. Juniper now claims the 25 largest service providers worldwide as customers. Cisco, however, didn't stand idle as Juniper took share and launched its new carrier-class router, the CRS-1, in 2005, which helped Cisco win back some market share in the carrier market in 2006. This share loss was exacerbated by the fact that a number of Juniper's routers lacked Ethernet capability, which has become a major area of carrier spending growth. Juniper has recently launched a number of new routers with Ethernet capability, which should benefit the firm.

Juniper has used its success in the carrier router market to broaden its product line--both through acquisitions and internal development--into other high-priority investment areas for carriers, such as application switching and network security. Juniper's moves into these adjacent markets also marked the firm's first serious foray outside the carrier routing market into the much larger market for corporate network equipment.

While these moves Juniper's significantly increases the firm's addressable market, but also raises a number of risks for the company. The company continues to struggle with gaining mindshare versus Cisco with corporate technology purchasing managers. Although some enterprises are demanding the carrier-quality features of Juniper's routers, the corporate market is extremely competitive, and it remains to be seen if its successes against Cisco can be repeated in Cisco's core market. Still, Juniper's position in the core router market should enable it to generate solid margins and returns on capital.

Data as of 12-29-06

Kellogg K

Rating	Fair Value	Last Close	Consider Buy	Consider Sell	Yield %
★★★	$50.00	$50.06	$42.60	$65.60	2.27

Industry	Business Risk	Moat Size	Investment Style	Sector
Food Mfg.	Below Avg	Narrow	Large Core	Consumer Goods

Company Profile

Kellogg is the world's largest producer of breakfast cereals and a leading producer of other convenience foods, including cookies, crackers, toaster pastries, cereal bars, frozen waffles, and meat alternatives. The company markets well-known cereal brands like Special K, Frosted Flakes, Corn Flakes, Rice Krispies, Froot Loops, Raisin Bran, Corn Pops, and Apple Jacks. Other top selling food brands include Pop-Tarts, Eggo, Cheez-It, Keebler, and Morningstar Farms.

Competition

	Market Cap $Mil	12 Mo Trailing Sales $Mil	Price/Cash Flow	Return On Assets%	Debt/Equity	Total Return% 1 Yr	3 Yr
Kellogg	19,941	10,717	17.8	9.1	1.2	18.6	12.5
Kraft Foods	58,683	34,648	13.9	5.5	0.2	30.5	6.5
General Mills	19,761	11,821	11.5	5.9	0.5	19.9	11.5

Management Stewardship Grade [B]

While we are encouraged by Kellogg's move to split up the chairman and CEO roles at the firm, this will not have a significant impact on our Stewardship Grade for the company. We do, however, view the advancement of David Mackay, the company's current chief operating officer, to the role of president and CEO as a big positive longer term. One of the few concerns we've had with Kellogg over the past year was that its current CEO, Jim Jenness, lacked the operating experience necessary to run a large packaged foods firm. While the 20-plus years that Jenness spent with Leo Burnett, the firm that handles the majority of Kellogg's advertising, were critical to the formation of the company's long-term sustainable growth plan, we felt there were too many unanswered questions about his ability to run Kellogg through both good times and bad. This is not the case with Mackay, who has spent much of the past 20 years on the front lines, holding numerous management and leadership positions in Australia, Europe, and the United States. His strong understanding of the company's operations has earned him considerable praise, and as an insider, he is likely to ease some of the discontent that arose in the management ranks at Kellogg when Jenness took the top job in 2005.

Price Volatility

Monthly Price High/Low — Relative Strength to S&P 500

Annual $Price High/Low	33.65/24.25	37.00/29.02	38.57/27.85	45.32/37.00	46.99/42.35	50.95/42.41
	2001	2002	2003	2004	2005	2006
Annual Total Return %	18.8	17.2	14.5	20.1	-0.9	18.6

Fiscal Year-End: December

	2001	2002	2003	2004	2005	TTM
Revenue $Mil	7,548	8,304	8,812	9,614	10,177	10,717
Net Income $Mil	474	721	787	891	980	1,014
Earnings Per Share $	1.16	1.75	1.92	2.14	2.36	2.53
Shares Outstanding Mil	405	407	408	412	412	398
Return on Equity %	54.3	80.5	54.5	39.5	42.9	41.1
Net Margin %	6.3	8.7	8.9	9.3	9.6	9.5
Asset Turnover	0.7	0.8	0.9	0.9	1.0	1.0
Financial Leverage	11.6	11.2	6.9	4.7	4.6	4.5

Valuation Ratios	Stock	Rel to Industry	Rel to S&P 500
Price/Earnings	19.8	0.9	1.0
Price/Book	8.1	1.8	2.0
Price/Sales	1.9	1.1	0.7
Price/Cash Flow	17.8	1.2	1.2

Major Fund Holders	% of Fund Assets
Van Kampen American Franchise A	5.97
W.P. Stewart & Co Growth	4.89
Sycuan U.S. Value	4.22
Fidelity Select Consumer Staples	3.93

One Kellogg Square P.O. Box 3599 www.kelloggcompany.com
Battle Creek, MI 49016-3599

Growth [B-]	2002	2003	2004	2005
Revenue %	10.0	6.1	9.1	5.9
Earnings/Share %	50.9	9.7	11.5	10.3
Book Value/Share %	1.8	62.0	54.1	1.4
Dividends/Share %	0.0	0.0	0.0	5.0

Profitability [A-]	2003	2004	2005	TTM
Return on Assets %	7.9	8.4	9.3	9.1
Oper Cash Flow $Mil	1,171	1,229	1,143	1,121
- Cap Spending $Mil	247	279	374	416
= Free Cash Flow $Mil	924	950	769	705

Financial Health [B-]	2003	2004	2005	09-30-06
Long-term Debt $Mil	4,265	3,893	3,703	3,053
Total Equity $Mil	1,443	2,257	2,284	2,467
Debt/Equity Ratio	3.0	1.7	1.6	1.2

Thesis By Greggory Warren, CFA, 11-17-06 Stock Price as of Analysis: $50.15

We believe that Kellogg is one of the better positioned companies in the packaged foods industry, with leading brands in growing categories that are relevant to consumers. The company has reinvested much of its excess profits back into the business, allowing it to generate above-average sales and earnings growth for a packaged foods firm. With a strong focus on product innovation and brand building, Kellogg should be able to maintain the narrow moat it has around its business.

While Kellogg may compete in only a few categories, the company's commitment to new products and marketing, and an ability to leverage several of its brands across its portfolio, has allowed the firm to capture leading market share in almost all of the categories in which it competes. In ready-to-eat cereal, which generated half of Kellogg's annual revenues last year, the company captured 33% of the market--both domestically and internationally. More importantly, Kellogg garnered more than 50% of the sales tied to new product launches in the ready-to-eat cereal category over the past three years.

Kellogg holds the top spot in the wholesome snack bar category, having leveraged top cereal brands like Special K into market-leading products in this high-growth category. Kellogg could not have done this, though, without the direct-store-delivery system that it picked up five years ago when it acquired Keebler, the second-largest domestic producer of cookies and crackers. Kellogg remains the category-killer in toaster pastries, with its well-known Pop-Tart brand holding an 86% share in the category last year in North America.

The commitment to new products and brand building has not only expanded its share of the markets in which it competes, but has also helped to improve the firm's product mix and profit margins. Kellogg has also worked hard to reduce the amount of capital it has tied up in inventories and receivables, while increasing the amount of time it takes to make payments to its suppliers. This frees up cash that can be invested back into the business or returned to shareholders through dividends or share repurchases.

With a focus on sustainable growth, and a significant presence in categories that are still growing, Kellogg is in an enviable position within the packaged foods group. Strong brands and a solid direct-store-delivery network allow the company to acquire prime shelf space at retailers and charge premium prices for its products, further cementing the firm's narrow moat.

Data as of 12-29-06

KeyCorp KEY

	Rating	Fair Value	Last Close	Consider Buy	Consider Sell	Yield %
	★★★	$34.00	$38.03	$26.20	$42.60	4.54

Company Profile
Based in Cleveland, KeyCorp offers retail and commercial banking, investment management, and investment banking products in branches across 12 states. Nonbank businesses include Victory Capital Management and recently acquired Austin Capital Management. As of September 2006, the bank had over $96 billion in assets and more than 20,000 employees.

Industry	Business Risk	Moat Size	Investment Style	Sector
Super Regional Banks	Average	Narrow	Large Value	Financial Services

Competition

	Market Cap $Mil	12 Mo Trailing Sales $Mil	Price/Cash Flow	Return On Assets%	Debt/Equity	Total Return% 1 Yr	Total Return% 3 Yr
KeyCorp	15,272	5,038	—	1.3	—	21.0	14.1
US Bancorp	63,617	13,499	—	2.2	—	26.3	11.8
Fifth Third Bancorp	22,842	5,431	—	1.4	—	13.0	-8.1

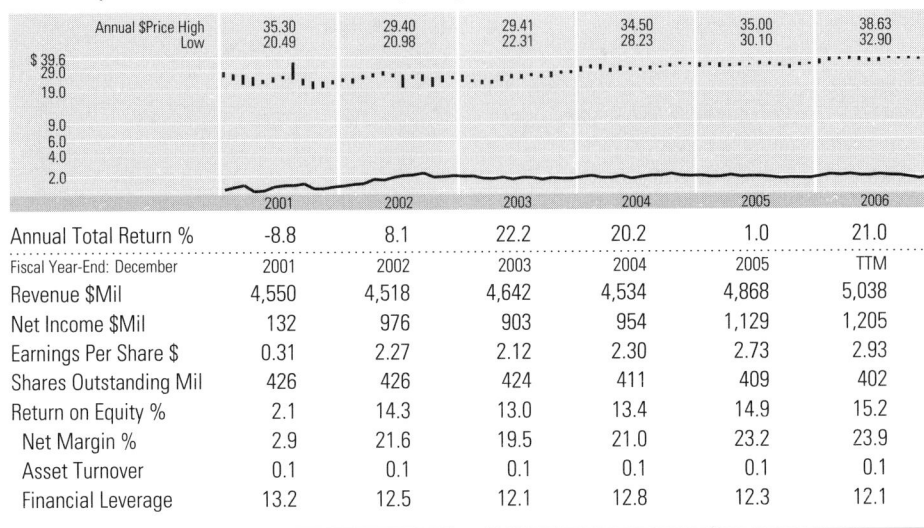

Price Volatility — Monthly Price High/Low — Relative Strength to S&P 500

	2001	2002	2003	2004	2005	2006
Annual $Price High	35.30	29.40	29.41	34.50	35.00	38.63
Low	20.49	20.98	22.31	28.23	30.10	32.90
Annual Total Return %	-8.8	8.1	22.2	20.2	1.0	21.0

Fiscal Year-End: December	2001	2002	2003	2004	2005	TTM
Revenue $Mil	4,550	4,518	4,642	4,534	4,868	5,038
Net Income $Mil	132	976	903	954	1,129	1,205
Earnings Per Share $	0.31	2.27	2.12	2.30	2.73	2.93
Shares Outstanding Mil	426	426	424	411	409	402
Return on Equity %	2.1	14.3	13.0	13.4	14.9	15.2
Net Margin %	2.9	21.6	19.5	21.0	23.2	23.9
Asset Turnover	0.1	0.1	0.1	0.1	0.1	0.1
Financial Leverage	13.2	12.5	12.1	12.8	12.3	12.1

Management Stewardship Grade [C]
Chairman and CEO Henry Meyer has been busy in recent years, and we believe investors are starting to see the fruits of his labor. Meyer led the cost-cutting efforts and restored the bank's credibility, in our opinion. Throughout the restructuring, we believe management kept shareholder interests high on the priority list. Since 1999, however, management has been inconsistent in meeting its long-term goal of 16%-18% annual returns on equity and annual per-share earnings growth of 8%-10%. The next priority will be to generate profit growth from the stronger balance sheet, and we like what we see from the retail-banking segment. Tim King, head of retail banking, has revitalized the consumer banking group by hiring some of his former Wells Fargo colleagues as well as Bank One and US Bancorp executives. Corporate governance measures appear on par with the industry average, as evidenced by our Stewardship Grade. Aside from staggered terms for directors, a poison pill, and Meyer's dual role of chairman and CEO, we believe this bank is run with shareholder interests in mind. Lastly, dividend growth has remained solid at 5.4% compounded annually since 2000.

127 Public Square
Cleveland, OH 44114-1306
www.key.com

Growth [D+]	2002	2003	2004	2005
Revenue %	-0.7	2.7	-2.3	7.4
Earnings/Share %	632.3	-6.6	8.5	18.7
Book Value/Share %	10.0	2.9	4.9	7.1
Dividends/Share %	1.7	1.7	1.6	4.8

Profitability [C]	2003	2004	2005	TTM
Return on Assets %	1.1	1.1	1.2	1.3
Oper Cash Flow $Mil	907	-215	2,168	—
- Cap Spending $Mil	95	102	155	—
= Free Cash Flow $Mil	—	—	—	—

Financial Health [NA]	2003	2004	2005	09-30-06
Long-term Debt $Mil	—	—	—	—
Total Equity $Mil	6,969	7,117	7,598	7,947
Debt/Equity Ratio	—	—	—	—

Valuation Ratios	Stock	Rel to Industry	Rel to S&P 500
Price/Earnings	13.0	1.0	0.6
Price/Book	1.9	0.9	0.5
Price/Sales	3.0	0.9	1.0
Price/Cash Flow	—	—	—

Major Fund Holders	% of Fund Assets
Senbanc	7.29
Schwab Financial Services	4.34
FBR Large Cap Financial	4.14
Allianz NFJ Dividend Value Instl	2.23

Thesis By Jim Callahan, CFA, 10-19-06 Stock Price as of Analysis: $37.58

KeyCorp has come a long way, but we still see room for improvement.

Key's corporate and investment banking provides most of the company's profits, and this segment is benefiting from the cyclical upturn in commercial lending. Although the pace of commercial loan growth has slowed a bit, we still expect midsingle-digit growth to drive the portfolio in 2006. We believe Key's long-standing relationships and built-out commercial product menu are serving it well. For example, Key's commercial real estate loans are leading to growth in related products, while the equipment leasing business it acquired in 2004 is generating both healthy sales and prospective clients for other corporate services. Finally, although Key's asset management subsidiary, Victory Capital Management, continues to post asset gains, we see little translation into fee revenue.

Performance in the bank's retail division continues to impress us. Although Key's retail banking segment accounts for only 30% of loans, it generates over half of Key's revenue and 42% of net income. Any shift in an organization's culture takes time, but we believe Key's retail employees are delivering results thanks to a change in management, a new decentralized structure, investments in technology and training, and revamped incentive structures. Recent results show strong deposit growth, with core deposits now accounting for over 60% of total funding. Given the continued interest-rate pressure, we're pleased with Key's profitability within the competitive Midwest marketplace. That said, returns on invested capital, although improving, still fall short of the bank's competition.

Like many banks at the time, KeyCorp's poor operating performance during the 2001-02 recession forced some significant changes. After incurring some large restructuring charges, Key exited some lending markets and improved underwriting processes. We believe the resulting bank's credit quality remains strong, but we'll keep an eye on the bank's reserve levels. At 1.4% of total loans, Key's loss reserves appear to be healthy. The bank's lower risk profile has also allowed it to book smaller loss provisions relative to charge-offs, providing a boost to net income.

We believe Key's next challenge is taking the sales and service bank it has developed and turning it into a profit-generating operation for its shareholders. Patient investors should look for a margin of safety before investing.

Data as of 12-29-06

Kimberly-Clark KMB

	Rating	Fair Value	Last Close	Consider Buy	Consider Sell	Yield %
	★★★	$67.00	$67.95	$57.10	$88.00	2.88

Company Profile

Kimberly-Clark manufactures paper and synthetic health and hygiene products worldwide. Organized into four global business segments, the company sells a variety of products, including bathroom tissue, diapers, napkins, and paper towels, to consumers and businesses. Its brands include Kleenex, Cottonelle, Scott, Kotex, and Huggies. The company also makes health-care products like surgical gowns, face masks, and infection-control and respiratory products.

Management — Stewardship Grade [B]

Chairman and CEO Thomas Falk's focus at Kimberly-Clark has been on cost-cutting and new product development. In 2005, he received a salary and bonus of $2.4 million, a decrease of roughly 30% from the previous year, since the company fell short of its financial objectives for the year. We think his salary and bonus are on par with his consumer product peers. However, he has also received more than $10.2 million in restricted-stock awards in the past two years, which seems a bit rich. Salaries are targeted toward the middle of the consumer product group, and bonuses are paid according to sales, earnings per share, returns on invested capital, and strategic goals. Key managers must own stock in an amount equal to 3 times their annual salary; for Falk the ratio is 6 times his salary. He owns 1.7 million shares, and officers and directors own less than 1% of shares outstanding. Kimberly-Clark has a staggered board of directors; we would prefer to see them elected annually. We also think the chairman and CEO roles should be separated to foster better corporate governance. Kimberly-Clark has had numerous financial restatements over the years but we don't believe it's an indication that the firm is being overly aggressive in its accounting practices.

P.O. Box 619100
Dallas, TX 75261-9100
www.kimberly-clark.com

Growth [C+]	2002	2003	2004	2005
Revenue %	2.4	6.0	7.5	5.4
Earnings/Share %	6.6	3.4	8.4	-9.1
Book Value/Share %	2.6	22.4	0.0	-12.6
Dividends/Share %	7.1	13.3	17.6	12.5

Profitability [A]	2003	2004	2005	TTM
Return on Assets %	10.1	10.6	9.6	8.3
Oper Cash Flow $Mil	2,552	2,726	2,312	2,443
- Cap Spending $Mil	873	535	710	897
= Free Cash Flow $Mil	1,679	2,191	1,602	1,546

Financial Health [B+]	2003	2004	2005	09-30-06
Long-term Debt $Mil	2,734	2,298	2,595	2,272
Total Equity $Mil	6,766	6,630	5,558	5,967
Debt/Equity Ratio	0.4	0.3	0.5	0.4

Industry	Business Risk	Moat Size	Investment Style	Sector
Household Products	Below Avg	Narrow	Large Value	Consumer Goods

Competition	Market Cap $Mil	12 Mo Trailing Sales $Mil	Price/Cash Flow	Return On Assets%	Debt/ Equity	Total Return % 1 Yr	3 Yr
Kimberly-Clark	31,142	16,449	12.7	8.3	0.4	17.5	8.7
Procter & Gamble	203,656	72,214	16.8	6.8	0.6	13.4	11.3
Johnson & Johnson	191,415	52,252	14.5	18.5	0.0	12.4	10.8

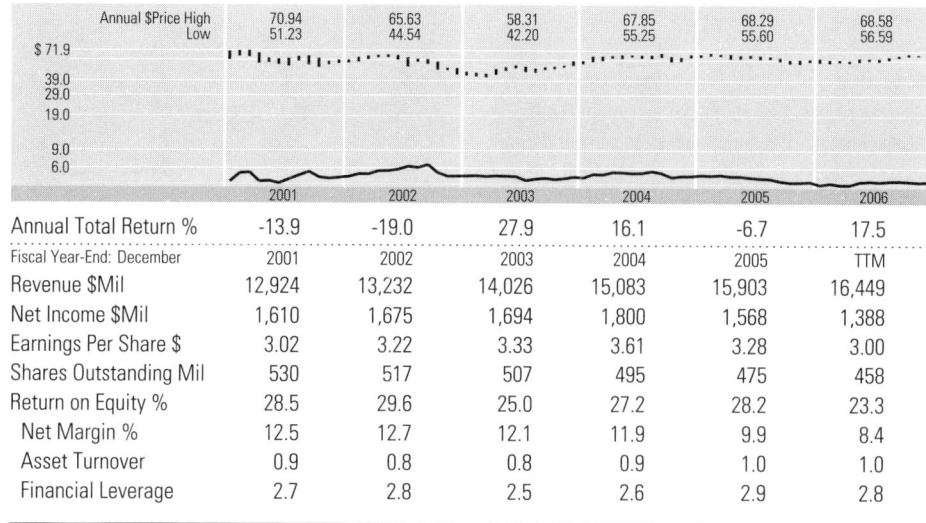

Price Volatility — Monthly Price High/Low — Relative Strength to S&P 500

Annual $Price High	70.94	65.63	58.31	67.85	68.29	68.58
Low	51.23	44.54	42.20	55.25	55.60	56.59
	2001	2002	2003	2004	2005	2006
Annual Total Return %	-13.9	-19.0	27.9	16.1	-6.7	17.5

Fiscal Year-End: December	2001	2002	2003	2004	2005	TTM
Revenue $Mil	12,924	13,232	14,026	15,083	15,903	16,449
Net Income $Mil	1,610	1,675	1,694	1,800	1,568	1,388
Earnings Per Share $	3.02	3.22	3.33	3.61	3.28	3.00
Shares Outstanding Mil	530	517	507	495	475	458
Return on Equity %	28.5	29.6	25.0	27.2	28.2	23.3
Net Margin %	12.5	12.7	12.1	11.9	9.9	8.4
Asset Turnover	0.9	0.8	0.8	0.9	1.0	1.0
Financial Leverage	2.7	2.8	2.5	2.6	2.9	2.8

Valuation Ratios	Stock	Rel to Industry	Rel to S&P 500
Price/Earnings	22.4	0.9	1.1
Price/Book	5.2	0.9	1.3
Price/Sales	1.9	0.7	0.7
Price/Cash Flow	12.7	0.7	0.9

Major Fund Holders	% of Fund Assets
Van Kampen American Franchise A	7.03
Fidelity Select Paper & Forest Prod	4.91
GJMB Growth	4.82
CM Advisers	4.18

Thesis By Lauren DeSanto, 11-20-06 Stock Price as of Analysis: $66.31

Keeping babies' bottoms clean is a tough business. Just ask Kimberly-Clark, which battles Procter & Gamble for a share of the roughly $21 billion global diaper market. While diapers are only about 10%-12% of Kimberly's total sales, we think the category is representative of others in which Kimberly competes: The economics are looking more and more commoditylike to us.

Kimberly's Huggies diapers have earned number-two market share over more than 30 years via innovation and brand extensions. Clearly the firm can give P&G's Pampers a run for the money, but we are concerned that the premium these brands have historically commanded in the category is waning.

Parents choose a diaper brand for a variety of reasons, but judging by the jockeying of P&G, Kimberly, and private-label competitors, price is definitely a concern. Raw-material increases have driven up diaper manufacturing costs, but when private-label competitors held the line on pricing at the end of 2005, they forced both P&G and Kimberly to roll back their increases. This kind of pricing dynamic, the improved quality of private-label diapers, and the short period during which parents shop for diapers all work against brands in the category, in our opinion.

Kimberly's other products, including facial tissue, toilet paper, baby wipes, and incontinence care products, are also susceptible to private-label competition. Kimberly has many products with a value positioning in their categories, which can be good when consumers are looking to save money, as long as a performance advantage over private-label products remains intact to justify the brand. So far for Kimberly, this seems to be the case. Product improvements have helped the firm exploit profitable niches in its categories, but it needs to create another breakthrough category like its Huggies Pull-Ups training pants more than 10 years ago. We see the need for innovation in Kimberly's returns on invested capital, which have eroded over the years.

Kimberly has some strong brands, like Kleenex, Scott, and Kotex, and it has a restructuring plan aimed at generating $300-$350 million in annual pretax savings by 2009. With some of these funds invested back into research and product development, Kimberly should be able to accelerate growth in developing markets, as it's done in its Mexican subsidiary. We expect the diaper business to be messy for some time, though, so we'd look for a discount to our fair value estimate before investing.

© 2007 Morningstar, Inc. All rights reserved. Intended for United States residents only, this report is for information purposes and should not be considered a solicitation to buy or sell any security. Download your free reports at http://www.morningstar.com/goto/2007Stocks500

Kinder Morgan Energy Partners KMP

Data as of 12-29-06

Rating	Fair Value	Last Close	Consider Buy	Consider Sell	Yield %
★★★	$52.00	$47.90	$44.30	$68.30	6.74

Industry	Business Risk	Moat Size	Investment Style	Sector
Pipelines	Below Avg	Wide	Mid Value	Energy

Company Profile

Kinder Morgan Energy Partners (KMP) is a master limited partnership that consolidates fixed assets used to transport energy commodities. It owns and operates more than 25,000 miles of pipelines for oil and natural-gas transport. It also owns nearly 100 processing terminals that can handle and store liquids, gases, and dry bulk materials such as coal. As a partnership, KMP pays no corporate income tax, but its tax burden flows through to individual unitholders.

Management — Stewardship Grade [A]

We think founder Richard Kinder is one of the best CEOs in energy. That may sound strange, considering that Kinder was president of Enron until 1996, but he left well before the funny business began. We admire that Kinder is the lowest-paid CEO of any major public corporation. Since the firm's founding, his only compensation has been his $1 annual salary. As the largest shareholder, his personal fortune rises and falls with those of the firm's limited partners. All other executives have their base salaries capped at $200,000, and cash bonuses in 2005 were all under $1.1 million. KMP is organized as a master limited partnership, which allows the company to avoid paying most income taxes but pushes tax responsibilities to investors. We give KMP a Stewardship Grade of "A," reflecting the company's shareholder-friendly policies and outstanding disclosure.

Competition

	Market Cap $Mil	12 Mo Trailing Sales $Mil	Price/Cash Flow	Return On Assets%	Debt/ Equity	Total Return% 1 Yr	3 Yr
Kinder Morgan Energy Partners	7,797	9,919	6.2	2.7	1.2	7.3	6.8
Williams Companies	15,576	12,719	9.3	0.9	1.2	14.4	40.0
Enterprise Products Partn	12,514	14,421	9.8	3.5	0.8	29.2	13.3

Price Volatility

	2001	2002	2003	2004	2005	2006
Annual $Price High	39.65	38.89	49.95	49.27	55.20	52.32
Low	25.19	24.00	33.51	37.65	42.77	42.80
Annual Total Return %	42.4	-0.7	50.1	-4.3	14.8	7.3

Fiscal Year-End: December	2001	2002	2003	2004	2005	TTM
Revenue $Mil	2,947	4,237	6,624	7,933	9,787	9,919
Net Income $Mil	240	338	371	436	335	320
Earnings Per Share $	1.56	1.96	2.00	2.22	1.58	1.42
Shares Outstanding Mil	154	172	185	197	212	163
Return on Equity %	7.7	10.1	10.8	11.5	9.6	8.6
Net Margin %	8.2	8.0	5.6	5.5	3.4	3.2
Asset Turnover	0.4	0.5	0.7	0.8	0.8	0.8
Financial Leverage	2.2	2.5	2.7	2.8	3.4	3.2

Valuation Ratios	Stock	Rel to Industry	Rel to S&P 500
Price/Earnings	33.7	1.2	1.6
Price/Book	2.1	0.8	0.5
Price/Sales	0.8	0.4	0.3
Price/Cash Flow	6.2	0.6	0.4

Major Fund Holders	% of Fund Assets
Flex-funds Total Return Utilities	3.82
Camco Investors	2.07
Strategic Dividend I	1.68

500 Dallas Street Suite 1000 www.kindermorgan.com
Houston, TX 77002

Growth [C]	2002	2003	2004	2005
Revenue %	43.8	56.3	19.8	23.4
Earnings/Share %	25.6	2.0	11.0	-28.8
Book Value/Share %	-3.7	-4.8	4.4	-14.6
Dividends/Share %	15.1	9.1	9.1	9.3

Profitability [C+]	2003	2004	2005	TTM
Return on Assets %	4.1	4.1	2.8	2.7
Oper Cash Flow $Mil	769	1,155	1,289	1,267
- Cap Spending $Mil	577	747	863	1,017
= Free Cash Flow $Mil	192	408	426	249

Financial Health [C]	2003	2004	2005	09-30-06
Long-term Debt $Mil	4,438	4,853	5,319	4,432
Total Equity $Mil	3,427	3,793	3,494	3,730
Debt/Equity Ratio	1.3	1.3	1.5	1.2

Thesis By Michael Cumming, CFA, 12-20-06 Stock Price as of Analysis: $48.11

It is not just the high, tax-advantaged yield that attracts us to Kinder Morgan Energy Partners. KMP owns stable assets that generate substantial free cash flow largely insulated from swings in commodity prices.

We've given KMP a wide-moat rating because of its high-quality asset base and history of producing returns that exceed the company's cost of capital. The company's network of pipelines and storage terminals create multiple pickup and delivery options for potential customers, which make the network more attractive than other companies' pipelines. KMP also seems to remain one step ahead of the competition, anticipating the need for new infrastructure and completing more profitable projects than any other company in the midstream sector.

KMP is the premier "roll-up" in the energy transportation and storage industry. Beyond acquisitions, significant opportunities for internal growth exist, as demand for moving energy should grow as the economy expands. KMP expects it can increase its partnership distributions near 8% per year on average from internal opportunities alone.

We also like Kinder's management. Enron would've been much better off had it not strayed from its core businesses after parting ways with Richard Kinder. CEO Kinder does not receive any compensation beyond his $1 annual salary. He got his stake in KMP the old-fashioned way--he bought it--and makes money purely from increasing per-share cash flow and distributions. We are extremely impressed by how well top management's interests are aligned with public owners' interests.

While there is much to admire about KMP, future growth will be more difficult than the explosive growth the company has experienced in the past. This is due to the structure of its partnership agreement. At current cash-flow levels, limited partners split all additional cash flow 50-50 with the general partner, owned by parent Kinder Morgan. Combined with its nearly 20% economic interest in KMP, KMI has a claim on over half of KMP's cash flow. We don't think this spread is onerous today, given management's success in expanding and running the company, but this structure increases the firm's incremental cost of capital, making long-term unit distribution growth harder. The upside to this cash-flow split with KMI is that it reduces risk. This is because limited partners would bear only half the downside on anything but the most severe cash-flow interruption.

Data as of 12-29-06

Kinetic Concepts KCI

Rating	Fair Value	Last Close	Consider Buy	Consider Sell	Yield %
★★★	$37.00	$39.55	$23.60	$44.60	0.00

Company Profile

Kinetic Concepts designs, manufactures, and markets wound-care systems and therapeutic surfaces. Deep wounds are often slow to heal and prone to infection. KCI rents vacuum-assisted closure devices and sells proprietary foam dressings to promote better wound healing. KCI's other products include therapeutic beds and surfaces. Customers are primarily hospitals, extended-care facilities, and home health-care providers.

Management   Stewardship Grade [C]

KCI just recruited a new president and CEO. Cathy Burzik has taken the reins from Denny Ware, who did an excellent job managing the firm's explosive growth since 2000. Burzik will face a different set of challenges including a changing competitive landscape for the VAC product set. While this is her first role as CEO of a public company, she is a seasoned executive within the life science and medical device industries. Burzik's most recent experience was as president of Applera's Applied Biosystems group, and she's previously headed up divisions at Johnson & Johnson and Eastman Kodak. We think KCI remains in capable hands and continue to give the firm a C Stewardship Grade. James Leininger founded KCI in 1976 and remains on the board with a 17% stake in KCI. KCI emerged from private hands in 2004 after a leveraged buyout in 1997, and the company still carries debt as a result of its previous ownership structure. This debt load may hinder management's flexibility in pursuing acquisitions or implementing defensive strategies.

8023 Vantage Drive
San Antonio, TX 78230

Growth [B+]	2002	2003	2004	2005
Revenue %	27.3	31.6	30.0	21.8
Earnings/Share %	NMF	NMF	NMF	NMF
Book Value/Share %	—	—	—	NMF
Dividends/Share %	NMF	NMF	NMF	NMF

Profitability [A+]	2003	2004	2005	TTM
Return on Assets %	9.0	4.2	16.0	24.2
Oper Cash Flow $Mil	280	188	238	257
- Cap Spending $Mil	76	93	94	94
= Free Cash Flow $Mil	204	95	144	163

Financial Health [A]	2003	2004	2005	09-30-06
Long-term Debt $Mil	679	443	293	226
Total Equity $Mil	-507	51	191	296
Debt/Equity Ratio	ELB	8.7	1.5	0.8

Industry	Business Risk	Moat Size	Investment Style	Sector
Medical Equip.	Above Avg	Narrow	Mid Growth	Healthcare

Competition	Market Cap $Mil	12 Mo Trailing Sales $Mil	Price/Cash Flow	Return On Assets%	Debt/ Equity	Total Return% 1 Yr	3 Yr
Kinetic Concepts	2,760	1,322	10.8	24.2	0.8	-0.5	—
Smith & Nephew ADR	9,845	2,568	36.7	11.3	0.1	14.2	8.8
Hillenbrand Industries	3,498	1,963	120.2	11.3	0.3	17.6	-0.7

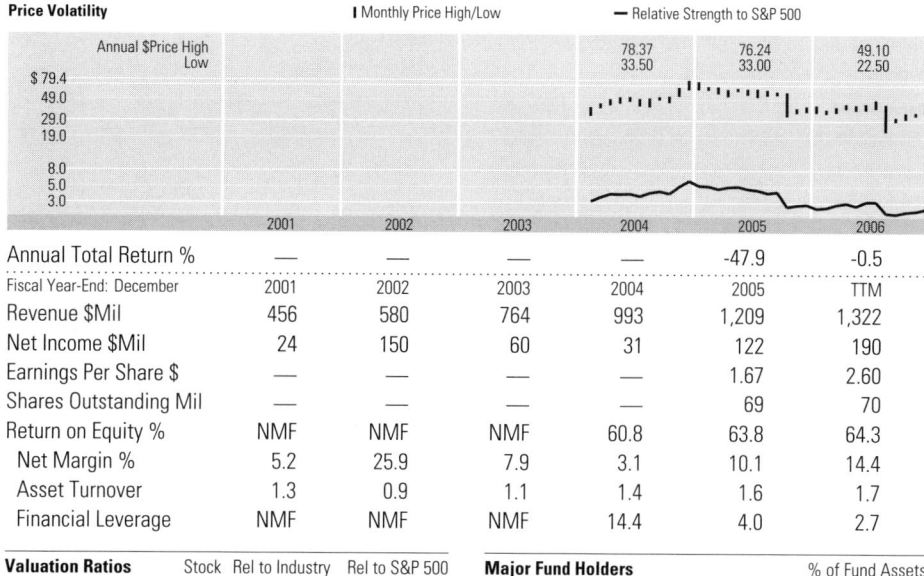

	2001	2002	2003	2004	2005	2006
Annual Total Return %	—	—	—	—	-47.9	-0.5
Fiscal Year-End: December	2001	2002	2003	2004	2005	TTM
Revenue $Mil	456	580	764	993	1,209	1,322
Net Income $Mil	24	150	60	31	122	190
Earnings Per Share $	—	—	—	—	1.67	2.60
Shares Outstanding Mil	—	—	—	—	69	70
Return on Equity %	NMF	NMF	NMF	60.8	63.8	64.3
Net Margin %	5.2	25.9	7.9	3.1	10.1	14.4
Asset Turnover	1.3	0.9	1.1	1.4	1.6	1.7
Financial Leverage	NMF	NMF	NMF	14.4	4.0	2.7

Valuation Ratios	Stock	Rel to Industry	Rel to S&P 500
Price/Earnings	15.2	0.5	0.7
Price/Book	9.3	1.7	2.3
Price/Sales	2.1	0.4	0.7
Price/Cash Flow	10.8	0.5	0.7

Major Fund Holders	% of Fund Assets
Fountainhead Special Value	6.94
AIM Trimark Small Companies A	5.35
Schwartz Value	5.01
Ave Maria Opportunity	4.78

Thesis By Julie Stralow, CFA, 12-11-06 Stock Price as of Analysis: $38.84

Kinetic Concepts could face significant pressure on its VAC wound closure systems after a jury ruled a similar product may stay on the market. Pressure could come in the form of reimbursement rate cuts or new entrants. However, we still think the firm sports a narrow economic moat and wouldn't count KCI out on its ability to compete effectively in this market.

KCI pioneered negative pressure wound therapy with its VAC systems. These systems consist of two major parts--rented pressure generators and consumable foam dressings. VAC products have been used on more than 1 million difficult-to-treat wounds around the world. Typical wounds treated with VAC systems include diabetic foot ulcers, bed sores, surgical openings, and major trauma. VAC devices use suction to quickly pull wound edges together, remove fluid and infectious particles, and promote healing through healthy tissue growth.

KCI has held a near-monopoly position with its VAC devices since receiving U.S. regulatory approval in 1995. Competitors have been held at bay with KCI's patent portfolio, wide third-party reimbursement, compelling clinical data, and large service network. However, a recent jury decision suggests VAC's competitive landscape will likely change over the next few years with the introduction of similar devices. A jury decided a similar product from rival BlueSky Medical does not infringe on KCI's patents, so BlueSky can keep marketing it. Other copycats may enter as well and compete away profits. Also, the Centers for Medicare and Medicaid Services (CMS) put BlueSky's product in the same reimbursement category as KCI's VAC in late 2005, setting up pricing competition with BlueSky's cheaper device. Other third parties could follow CMS' lead, and if BlueSky's product gains acceptance with more third-party payers, reimbursement rate declines could pressure KCI's VAC sales. VAC devices generate about three quarters of KCI's total sales.

We still think KCI has a leg up on BlueSky with its VAC systems in terms of product quality, clinical evidence, and a large service and support network; other new entrants may find it difficult to compete with KCI based on those factors, too. We also admire KCI's ability to continually improve the VAC product set by adding differentiating features like medication delivery. This ability to enhance VAC's effectiveness only raises the hurdle for other providers vying for caregiver attention. That may be an onerous task for firms wishing to compete with KCI's VAC systems.

Data as of 12-29-06

KLA-Tencor KLAC

	Rating	Fair Value	Last Close	Consider Buy	Consider Sell	Yield %
	★★★	$48.00	$49.75	$37.00	$60.10	0.97

Company Profile
KLA-Tencor designs and manufactures yield-management and process-monitoring systems for the semiconductor industry. The systems are used to analyze the manufacturing process at various steps in a product's development. The firm's laser-scanning products are used for wafer qualification, process monitoring, and equipment monitoring. KLA-Tencor also provides systems for optical metrology, e-beam metrology, and scanning electron microscope inspection.

Management
Stewardship Grade [C]

CEO Rick Wallace took the helm in January 2006; he was previously president and COO. Wallace joined KLA in 1988 and has successfully headed several major divisions during his tenure, including the reticle and photomask inspection division and the wafer inspection group. Management has long recognized that the firm's competitive advantages lie in its technological lead and is focused maintaining on it. KLA was willing to spend large sums on research and development during the severe industry downturn in 2002-03, even as competitors cut back, to further its technological edge. Relative to other chip equipment makers, KLA's executive cash compensation looks reasonable and is performance-oriented. However, option grants are generous and accounted for about 5% of shares outstanding in fiscal 2005. The firm has a stated policy of using share buybacks to prevent dilution from option issuance. KLA has been engulfed by the options backdating scandal afflicting many public companies. A special committee of the firm's board of directors has concluded that past stock-option backdating did indeed occur, principally from July 1997 to June 2002. As a result, the firm is restating past financial results and has been late with its regulatory filings.

160 Rio Robles
San Jose, CA 95134
www.kla-tencor.com

Growth [C+]	2002	2003	2004	2005
Revenue %	-22.2	-19.2	13.1	39.3
Earnings/Share %	223.5	-36.4	72.9	91.7
Book Value/Share %	15.7	9.4	15.4	16.0
Dividends/Share %	NMF	NMF	NMF	NMF

Profitability [A]	2003	2004	2005	TTM
Return on Assets %	4.8	6.9	11.7	8.2
Oper Cash Flow $Mil	246	350	507	335
- Cap Spending $Mil	134	56	60	64
= Free Cash Flow $Mil	112	294	447	271

Financial Health [A]	2003	2004	2005	03-31-06
Long-term Debt $Mil	—	—	—	—
Total Equity $Mil	2,216	2,628	3,045	3,413
Debt/Equity Ratio	—	—	—	—

Industry	Business Risk	Moat Size	Investment Style	Sector
Semiconductor Equip.	Average	Wide	Mid Growth	Hardware

Competition	Market Cap $Mil	12 Mo Trailing Sales $Mil	Price/Cash Flow	Return On Assets%	Debt/Equity	Total Return% 1 Yr	3 Yr
KLA-Tencor	9,905	1,982	29.6	8.2	—	1.9	-3.5
Applied Materials	25,696	9,167	13.3	16.0	0.0	3.9	-5.4
Hitachi ADR	21,004	83,989	3.4	0.4	0.6	-6.4	1.7

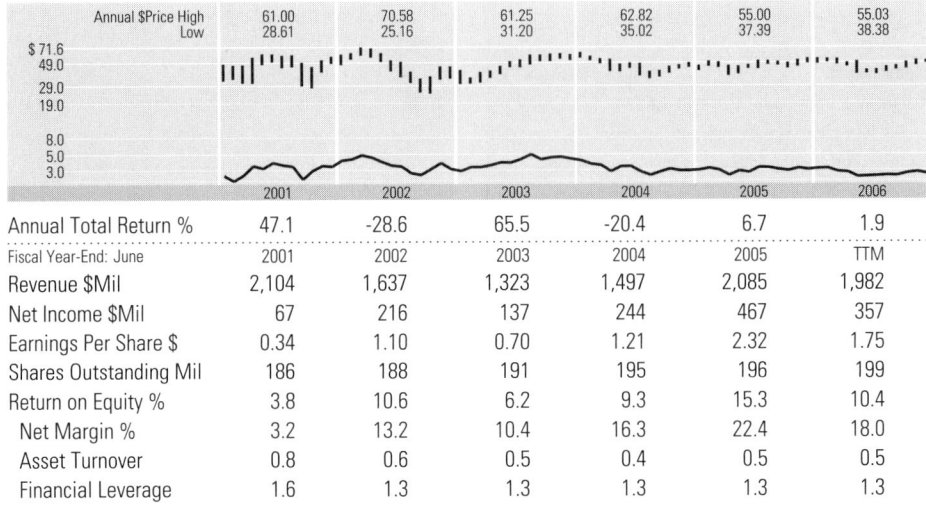

Price Volatility — Monthly Price High/Low — Relative Strength to S&P 500

Annual $Price High	61.00	70.58	61.25	62.82	55.00	55.03
Low	28.61	25.16	31.20	35.02	37.39	38.38

	2001	2002	2003	2004	2005	2006
Annual Total Return %	47.1	-28.6	65.5	-20.4	6.7	1.9

Fiscal Year-End: June	2001	2002	2003	2004	2005	TTM
Revenue $Mil	2,104	1,637	1,323	1,497	2,085	1,982
Net Income $Mil	67	216	137	244	467	357
Earnings Per Share $	0.34	1.10	0.70	1.21	2.32	1.75
Shares Outstanding Mil	186	188	191	195	196	199
Return on Equity %	3.8	10.6	6.2	9.3	15.3	10.4
Net Margin %	3.2	13.2	10.4	16.3	22.4	18.0
Asset Turnover	0.8	0.6	0.5	0.4	0.5	0.5
Financial Leverage	1.6	1.3	1.3	1.3	1.3	1.3

Valuation Ratios	Stock	Rel to Industry	Rel to S&P 500
Price/Earnings	28.4	1.0	1.4
Price/Book	2.9	0.7	0.7
Price/Sales	5.0	1.1	1.7
Price/Cash Flow	29.6	1.6	2.0

Major Fund Holders	% of Fund Assets
Fidelity Advisor Electronics T	6.79
Pin Oak Aggressive Stock	4.88
Fidelity Select Electronics	4.78
Turner Concentrated Growth Instl	4.12

Thesis By Andy Ng, 12-15-06 Stock Price as of Analysis: $50.36

KLA-Tencor dominates a highly attractive segment of the chip equipment industry. The top provider of process diagnostic and control tools is in a favorable position to benefit from advances in semiconductor technology.

Chipmakers use PDC tools to measure and detect defects during semiconductor production and to identify and correct the problem sources; this lowers costs by reducing the number of faulty chips produced. Customers rely on KLA's tools to accelerate the manufacturing ramp to full production of new chip designs and factory startups, as well as to maintain high yields for devices already in production to maximize profitability.

KLA leads the PDC market with over 50% share and has a wide economic moat for several reasons. KLA's vast experience in PDC--gained from an installed based of 20,000 tools and having engineers in every chip-manufacturing facility--has allowed the firm to build its leading technical expertise and extensive database, which are significant competitive advantages. Further, KLA's dominant position gives it an advantage in maintaining its technological edge. The firm has the largest research and development budget in the PDC market ($340 million in fiscal 2005) and its close working relationships with customers give the firm insight into future PDC needs of the semiconductor industry.

The moat is certainly evident in KLA's superb financial performance. From fiscal 2001 to 2005, operating margins averaged 19% and average returns on invested capital were above 20%. Even in fiscal 2003, during the depths of the worst downturn in the industry's history, KLA still posted a profit of $216 million and an operating margin of 10.5%. Faced with few credible rivals, KLA has some room to charge a premium for its highly proprietary products, which help chipmakers save considerable time and money.

KLA is capable of growing faster than the broader semiconductor equipment market in the years ahead. As manufacturing technologies continue to produce smaller and more complex semiconductor circuits, defect detection will play an increasingly critical role in successful chip production. PDC as a percentage of total chip equipment spending has been steadily rising, from 5% in the 1990s to 11% in 2000, and is now about 15%. This trend is certainly to continue as chipmakers continue to push the technology envelope over time. With its wide moat, we think KLA is poised to benefit from the PDC market's bright prospects.

Data as of 12-29-06

Kohl's KSS

	Rating	Fair Value	Last Close	Consider Buy	Consider Sell	Yield %
	★	$53.00	$68.43	$40.90	$66.40	0.00

Company Profile

Kohl's operates more than 750 specialty department stores across the United States. Targeting middle-income customers, the stores feature moderately priced, nationally known brands of apparel, shoes, accessories, and housewares. In addition to national-brand merchandise, the stores also offer private-label goods (which constitute about 25% of total sales) in many departments.

Management Stewardship Grade [C]

R. Lawrence Montgomery has been CEO since 1999. He and president Kevin Mansell started working at Kohl's in the 1980s. Although Montgomery owns less than 1% of the total shares outstanding, he does own more than 2 times his cash compensation, which we think helps align his interests with those of shareholders. In 2005, Montgomery's annual compensation was $1.6 million. While his 2005 compensation was up 60% over 2004 because of a $613,000 performance-based bonus, we think the increase is reasonable given the company's improved results. In comparison, his annual compensation increased by less than 1% from 2003 to 2004, and he did not receive a bonus in 2004 due to the firm's lackluster performance. While there is a long-term compensation component to Montgomery's salary, the company's proxy statement does not clearly outline the long-term targets that he must meet to receive this compensation. A majority of the board is independent, but six of the 13 members are current or former executives of the company. The board is structured with staggered elections, so directors serve three-year terms. We believe directors should be elected on an annual basis because it gives shareholders the ability to oust underperforming members in a more timely manner. Overall, we think corporate governance is satisfactory.

N56 W17000 Ridgewood Drive   www.kohls.com
Menomonee Falls, WI 53051-5660

Growth [A]	2003	2004	2005	2006
Revenue %	21.8	12.7	13.8	14.5
Earnings/Share %	29.6	-9.1	28.3	19.1
Book Value/Share %	24.7	19.1	19.1	17.8
Dividends/Share %	NMF	NMF	NMF	NMF

Profitability [A]	2004	2005	2006	TTM
Return on Assets %	8.2	8.8	9.2	10.5
Oper Cash Flow $Mil	740	937	882	3,009
- Cap Spending $Mil	832	890	799	1,074
= Free Cash Flow $Mil	-92	47	82	1,935

Financial Health [A-]	2004	2005	2006	10-31-06
Long-term Debt $Mil	1,076	1,103	1,046	1,040
Total Equity $Mil	4,212	5,034	5,957	5,529
Debt/Equity Ratio	0.3	0.2	0.2	0.2

Industry	Business Risk	Moat Size	Investment Style	Sector
Discount Stores	Average	Narrow	Large Growth	Consumer Services

Competition	Market Cap $Mil	12 Mo Trailing Sales $Mil	Price/Cash Flow	Return On Assets%	Debt/ Equity	Total Return% 1 Yr	3 Yr
Kohl's	22,378	14,765	7.4	10.5	0.2	40.8	16.0
Target	49,000	56,727	11.3	6.9	0.6	4.7	15.6
Sears Holdings	25,845	52,810	15.4	4.3	0.3	45.4	94.0

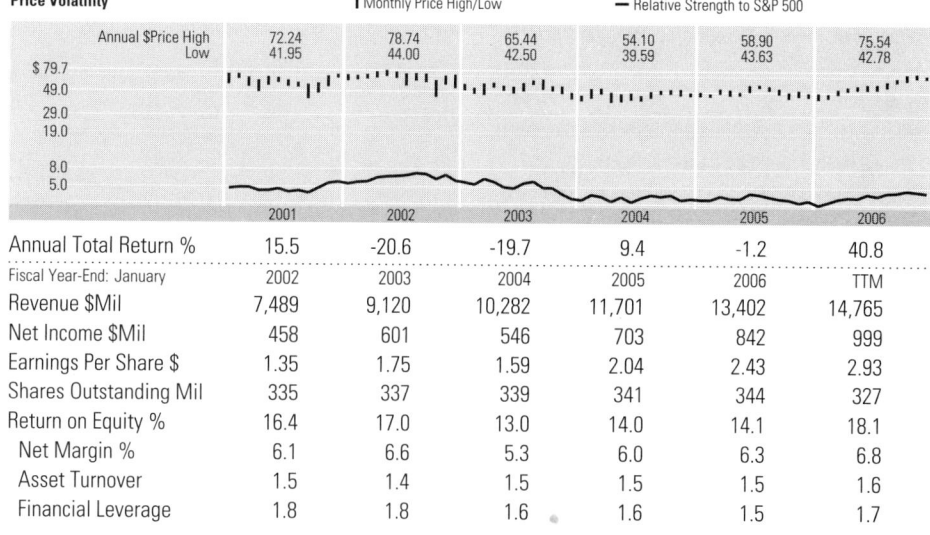

	2002	2003	2004	2005	2006	TTM
Annual Total Return %	15.5	-20.6	-19.7	9.4	-1.2	40.8
Fiscal Year-End: January	2002	2003	2004	2005	2006	TTM
Revenue $Mil	7,489	9,120	10,282	11,701	13,402	14,765
Net Income $Mil	458	601	546	703	842	999
Earnings Per Share $	1.35	1.75	1.59	2.04	2.43	2.93
Shares Outstanding Mil	335	337	339	341	344	327
Return on Equity %	16.4	17.0	13.0	14.0	14.1	18.1
Net Margin %	6.1	6.6	5.3	6.0	6.3	6.8
Asset Turnover	1.5	1.4	1.5	1.5	1.5	1.6
Financial Leverage	1.8	1.8	1.6	1.6	1.5	1.7

Valuation Ratios	Stock	Rel to Industry	Rel to S&P 500
Price/Earnings	23.4	1.1	1.1
Price/Book	4.0	1.1	1.0
Price/Sales	1.5	1.9	0.5
Price/Cash Flow	7.4	0.6	0.5

Major Fund Holders	% of Fund Assets
BB&T Mid Cap Value I	4.22
Brandywine	4.20
ICON Consumer Discretionary	4.12
Manor Growth	3.75

Thesis By Kimberly Picciola, 11-20-06 Stock Price as of Analysis: $71.68

Having shed its credit card business in the first part of 2006, Kohl's is focused on running its retail business. By offering fashionable apparel and home furnishings at value-based prices, this chain has carved out a niche between discounters, such as Wal-Mart, and midtier department stores, like Federated. Although we think it is difficult for retailers to develop a sustainable competitive advantage, we believe Kohl's low-cost approach and its ability to generate returns on invested capital in the high teens support this retailer's narrow economic moat.

With plans to expand its store base by more than 50% over the next four years, the growth story continues for Kohl's. In addition to growth through new store openings, we believe Kohl's will continue to steal share from struggling competitors like Sears, and we think same-store sales (sales from stores open at least a year) will increase in the low single digits over the next five years. We like the company's expansion strategy, which entails opening multiple stores in a single market. This enables Kohl's to distribute the marketing and advertising costs to enter a new market across multiple stores.

In addition to getting more bang for its buck from its new store opening strategy, we expect the company will leverage its increasing size and efficient store operations to grow operating profits at a faster rate than sales. Kohl's off-mall big box stores are less costly to run than traditional mall-based department stores. With cheaper rent expense and fewer employees required to operate each store, Kohl's low-cost model enables this retailer to earn double-digit operating margins, which is impressive for a big box chain.

Despite the growth potential, risks exist. The company faces stiff competition from the likes of Target and Wal-Mart, which are focused on enhancing their apparel offerings. Additionally, J.C. Penney has made a complete turnaround, and Federated has big plans for its national chain of Macy's stores. We expect Kohl's will continue to grow its share of the market, but it will face a tougher battle as more retailers compete for its customers.

While we expect some fashion missteps given Kohl's reliance on predicting fashion trends, we think this retailer has positioned itself well and will continue to be a popular destination for consumers looking for quality, fashionable merchandise at affordable prices.

Data as of 12-29-06

Kraft Foods KFT

	Rating	Fair Value	Last Close	Consider Buy	Consider Sell	Yield %
	★★★	$35.00	$35.70	$29.80	$46.00	2.69

Company Profile

Kraft Foods is the largest packaged food company in North America and the second largest in the world. With such powerful brands as Kraft, Nabisco, Oscar Mayer, Maxwell House, Post, and Philadelphia cream cheese, as well as an extensive portfolio of other well-known products, the company generates more than $30 billion in annual sales. Altria, the parent company of Philip Morris USA and Philip Morris International, owns 87% of Kraft's common stock.

Management Stewardship Grade [C]

The hiring of Irene Rosenfeld as CEO marks the end of what has been a muddled period of leadership at Kraft, which began with the appointment of co-CEOs during the company's initial public offering in June 2001. While Betsy Holden and Roger Deromedi were strong leaders of their own individual business units before the company went public, neither demonstrated an ability to lead Kraft through the vagaries of being a publicly traded firm. We can only hope that Rosenfeld, who until recently was chairman and CEO of the Frito-Lay division of PepsiCo, brings a better sense of leadership and transparency to the struggling packaged food giant. That said, it remains to be seen how much of what Rosenfeld learned with Frito-Lay, which we believe has been one of the few packaged food firms that has gotten it right over the past 10 years, can be applied to the ailing Kraft. We are also concerned that Rosenfeld spent more than 20 years with Kraft and General Foods before taking the top job at Frito-Lay in September 2004. While we are firm believers that change starts from the inside, Rosenfeld may be too deeply rooted in the culture that created many of the problems Kraft faces today.

Three Lakes Drive
Northfield, IL 60093

Growth [C]	2002	2003	2004	2005
Revenue %	1.8	4.3	5.5	6.0
Earnings/Share %	NMF	2.6	-22.9	0.0
Book Value/Share %	NMF	10.6	5.5	0.2
Dividends/Share %	115.4	17.9	16.7	13.0

Profitability [B]	2003	2004	2005	TTM
Return on Assets %	5.9	4.4	4.6	5.5
Oper Cash Flow $Mil	4,119	4,008	3,464	4,222
- Cap Spending $Mil	1,085	1,006	1,171	1,074
= Free Cash Flow $Mil	3,034	3,002	2,293	3,148

Financial Health [B]	2003	2004	2005	06-30-06
Long-term Debt $Mil	11,591	9,723	8,475	7,081
Total Equity $Mil	28,530	29,911	29,593	30,398
Debt/Equity Ratio	0.4	0.3	0.3	0.2

Industry	Business Risk	Moat Size	Investment Style	Sector
Food Mfg.	Below Avg	Narrow	Large Value	Consumer Goods

Competition	Market Cap $Mil	12 Mo Trailing Sales $Mil	Price/Cash Flow	Return On Assets %	Debt/ Equity	Total Return % 1 Yr	3 Yr
Kraft Foods	58,683	34,648	13.9	5.5	0.2	30.5	6.5
Nestle SA ADR	138,417	73,660	16.8	8.8	—	20.9	14.7
Groupe Danone ADR	43,070	16,309	18.6	9.2	1.0	57.3	28.9

Price Volatility — Monthly Price High/Low — Relative Strength to S&P 500

Annual $Price High/Low	35.57 / 29.50	43.95 / 32.50	39.40 / 26.38	36.06 / 29.45	35.65 / 27.88	36.67 / 27.44
	2001	2002	2003	2004	2005	2006
Annual Total Return %	—	16.1	-15.4	13.2	-18.6	30.5

Fiscal Year-End: December	2001	2002	2003	2004	2005	TTM
Revenue $Mil	28,731	29,248	30,498	32,168	34,113	34,648
Net Income $Mil	1,882	3,394	3,476	2,665	2,632	3,209
Earnings Per Share $	—	1.96	2.01	1.55	1.55	1.93
Shares Outstanding Mil	—	1,732	1,729	1,708	1,687	1,644
Return on Equity %	8.0	13.1	12.2	8.9	8.9	10.6
Net Margin %	6.6	11.6	11.4	8.3	7.7	9.3
Asset Turnover	0.5	0.5	0.5	0.5	0.6	0.6
Financial Leverage	2.4	2.2	2.1	2.0	1.9	1.9

Valuation Ratios	Stock	Rel to Industry	Rel to S&P 500
Price/Earnings	18.4	0.8	0.9
Price/Book	1.9	0.4	0.5
Price/Sales	1.7	1.0	0.6
Price/Cash Flow	13.9	0.9	1.0

Major Fund Holders	% of Fund Assets
Yacktman Focused	3.72
Rydex Consumer Products Inv	3.56
Yacktman	3.47
SunAmerica Focused Dividend Strat C	3.21

Thesis By Greggory Warren, CFA, 12-11-06 Stock Price as of Analysis: $34.95

If it weren't in the packaged food industry, Kraft might be a wide-moat firm. But poor industry dynamics and a hefty amount of goodwill from acquisitions have limited the firm to a narrow moat rating. Kraft does generate a significant amount of cash flow, though, which it routinely returns to shareholders as dividends and share repurchases. At the right price, the company's shares could prove to be a worthwhile investment.

Kraft is an indispensable partner for retailers in a world where shelf space is relegated to just number-one and number-two branded products and a private-label alternative. The company's brands hold the top spot in over 70% of the categories where they compete, both domestically and internationally, and tend to define their categories. Imagine a supermarket without Oreo cookies or DiGiorno pizza, and you have some idea of the kind of power Kraft's brands have with retailers and consumers.

Despite the leadership position Kraft enjoys at retail, several of its key categories have become commodified, with consumers no longer willing to pay up for the benefit once associated with its brands. This trend has been most pronounced in its cheese, where the company faces stiff competition from privately held Sargento and private-label offerings, which are often just as good in quality but priced at a significant discount to their branded counterparts.

Kraft has also struggled with product innovation and has been noticeably absent in some of the fastest-growing categories in the industry, like organic and ethnic foods. Part of this stems from the sheer size of its operations, which makes it harder for a successful new product launch or the acquisition of a niche food manufacturer to have a meaningful impact on sales and profitability.

With a new CEO in place and the company currently engaged in a far-reaching review of its product portfolio, we expect to see some significant changes at the packaged food giant in the year ahead. This could include asset disposals and additional restructuring charges, all of which will be aimed at improving the mix of products at Kraft longer term. A more narrowly focused portfolio, with capital allocated more judiciously on product innovation and marketing, should help the company produce more consistent sales and earnings results. This is critical, given the fact that Kraft is in the process of being spun out from Altria and must demonstrate to a new round of investors why they should hold on to the stock longer term.

Data as of 12-29-06

Laboratory Corp of America LH

Rating	Fair Value	Last Close	Consider Buy	Consider Sell	Yield %
★★	$64.00	$73.47	$49.40	$80.20	0.00

Company Profile

Laboratory Corporation of America provides clinical diagnostic testing services to hospitals, physicians and other health-care providers. Through a network of 36 laboratories and 1,300 service sites, LabCorp has captured nearly 22% of the independent clinical labs market.

Industry	Business Risk	Moat Size	Investment Style	Sector
Diagnostics	Average	Narrow	Mid Core	Healthcare

Competition

	Market Cap $Mil	12 Mo Trailing Sales $Mil	Price/Cash Flow	Return On Assets%	Debt/Equity	Total Return% 1 Yr	3 Yr
Laboratory Corp of America	9,213	3,515	14.8	10.0	0.3	36.4	25.2
Quest Diagnostics	10,338	6,194	10.9	9.9	0.4	3.7	14.4

Management   Stewardship Grade [B]

LabCorp's long-standing CEO Thomas Mac Mahon is retiring at the end of 2006 and will be replaced by COO David King. While Mac Mahon has been instrumental in turning LabCorp into an industry giant, we think he is leaving the company in good hands. King has been involved with LabCorp since 2001 and has solid knowledge of the business, having served as the company's COO and vice president of strategic planning and development. Our take on the company's corporate governance is unchanged. We think this management team has shown its commitment to creating shareholder value by consistently generating excess returns on capital for shareholders. While the number of options issued to top executives seems a bit high, and we would prefer if the CEO and chairman roles were separated, our overall impression is positive. We like LabCorp's shareholder-friendly policy to elect its directors annually, and the compensation packages appear to be driven by performance. We also like that insiders jointly own approximately 2.2 million shares of LabCorp.

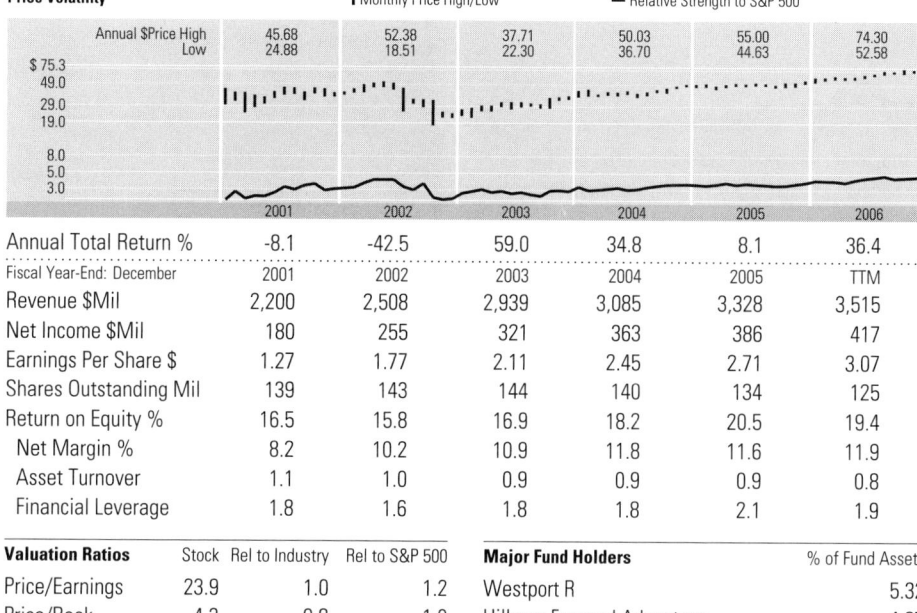

Price Volatility

Annual $Price High Low	45.68 24.88	52.38 18.51	37.71 22.30	50.03 36.70	55.00 44.63	74.30 52.58
	2001	2002	2003	2004	2005	2006
Annual Total Return %	-8.1	-42.5	59.0	34.8	8.1	36.4

Fiscal Year-End: December	2001	2002	2003	2004	2005	TTM
Revenue $Mil	2,200	2,508	2,939	3,085	3,328	3,515
Net Income $Mil	180	255	321	363	386	417
Earnings Per Share $	1.27	1.77	2.11	2.45	2.71	3.07
Shares Outstanding Mil	139	143	144	140	134	125
Return on Equity %	16.5	15.8	16.9	18.2	20.5	19.4
Net Margin %	8.2	10.2	10.9	11.8	11.6	11.9
Asset Turnover	1.1	1.0	0.9	0.9	0.9	0.8
Financial Leverage	1.8	1.6	1.8	1.8	2.1	1.9

Valuation Ratios	Stock	Rel to Industry	Rel to S&P 500
Price/Earnings	23.9	1.0	1.2
Price/Book	4.3	0.8	1.0
Price/Sales	2.6	0.6	0.9
Price/Cash Flow	14.8	0.9	1.0

Major Fund Holders	% of Fund Assets
Westport R	5.32
Hillman Focused Advantage	4.97
Navellier Top 20 A	4.71
Tilson Dividend	4.64

Thesis By Alex Morozov, CFA, 12-12-06 Stock Price as of Analysis: $72.00

Laboratory Corporation of America looks well-positioned to benefit from the aging population and increasing demand for specialized testing. We like management's ability to grow revenue organically and through strategic acquisitions, while preserving healthy margins and operating cash flows.

LabCorp is one of two sizable players in what is otherwise a fragmented industry. While Quest Diagnostics is presently the largest player in the field, LabCorp's leading position in specialized testing, which includes oncology and gene-based testing, should bode well for its future growth prospects. LabCorp posted double-digit growth in this segment in 2005, and we expect the company to continue to rely on specialized testing for future expansion. However, while LabCorp has been able to grow this segment, it has yet to capitalize on the higher margins that this business typically exhibits. We believe the investment LabCorp has made in its salesforce and the integration of the US LABS and Esoterix acquisitions should help the firm improve its margins over time.

Growth in routine testing, such as blood and urine analyses, has lagged the explosiveness exhibited by the specialty (or esoteric) segment, but we anticipate that routine testing could experience a small boost.

Cytyc's ThinPrep Imaging System, which LabCorp uses in its labs, now accounts for 38% of all liquid-based pap smears ordered and should continue to grow due to its higher accuracy. LabCorp should also benefit from higher pricing per test, which we estimate will grow in the low single digits in 2006. Additionally, the company has been successful replacing lower-margin capped contracts with fee-for-service arrangements, which should further improve LabCorp's profitability.

Another area that LabCorp has targeted for growth is the managed-care business. LabCorp's national presence, vast expertise, and significant scale advantages fit well with managed care providers' strategy to reduce the amount of work performed and billed by smaller, less efficient laboratories. LabCorp's exclusive agreements with UnitedHealth and WellPoint underscore the firm's intent to become a preferred provider of laboratory services to managed care organizations (MCOs), which could prove to be a major source of future revenue expansion. However, we are concerned that the long duration and vast geographic scope of these agreements could give MCOs substantial bargaining powers, which may result in lower prices and deteriorating profitability for LabCorp.

358 South Main Street
Burlington, NC 27215
www.labcorp.com

Growth [C]	2002	2003	2004	2005
Revenue %	14.0	17.2	4.9	7.9
Earnings/Share %	39.4	19.2	16.1	10.6
Book Value/Share %	45.9	11.2	8.3	-1.9
Dividends/Share %	NMF	NMF	NMF	NMF

Profitability [A+]	2003	2004	2005	TTM
Return on Assets %	9.4	10.0	10.0	10.0
Oper Cash Flow $Mil	564	538	574	623
- Cap Spending $Mil	84	95	94	90
= Free Cash Flow $Mil	481	443	481	533

Financial Health [B+]	2003	2004	2005	09-30-06
Long-term Debt $Mil	—	889	605	603
Total Equity $Mil	1,896	1,999	1,886	2,145
Debt/Equity Ratio	—	0.4	0.3	0.3

Lee Enterprises LEE

Data as of 12-29-06

	Rating	Fair Value	Last Close	Consider Buy	Consider Sell	Yield %
	★★★	$29.00	$31.06	$22.40	$36.30	2.32

Industry	Business Risk	Moat Size	Investment Style	Sector
Publishing	Average	Narrow	Small Value	Media

Company Profile

Lee Enterprises is a premier publisher of newspapers in midsize markets, with 51 dailies and a joint interest in five others, a rapidly growing online business, and more than 300 weekly newspapers and specialty publications in 23 states. Lee's newspapers have a circulation of 1.6 million daily and 1.9 million Sunday, reaching more than 4 million readers daily.

Competition

	Market Cap $Mil	12 Mo Trailing Sales $Mil	Price/Cash Flow	Return On Assets %	Debt/ Equity	Total Return % 1 Yr	3 Yr
Lee Enterprises	1,430	1,129	7.3	2.1	1.5	-13.7	-9.0
McClatchy A	3,545	1,577	17.4	1.9	0.7	-25.5	-13.3
Journal Communications A	887	776	8.4	5.7	0.5	-7.6	-10.4

Price Volatility | Monthly Price High/Low — Relative Strength to S&P 500

Annual $Price High Low	37.60 26.94	40.09 28.90	44.15 30.35	49.83 43.35	46.06 36.36	37.43 22.98
	2001	2002	2003	2004	2005	2006
Annual Total Return %	24.5	-6.0	32.6	7.2	-18.5	-13.7

Fiscal Year-End: September	2002	2003	2004	2005	2006	TTM
Revenue $Mil	477	606	643	819	1,129	1,129
Net Income $Mil	80	78	86	78	71	71
Earnings Per Share $	1.80	1.75	1.91	1.70	1.56	1.56
Shares Outstanding Mil	44	44	45	46	45	46
Return on Equity %	10.7	9.7	9.8	8.4	7.2	7.2
Net Margin %	16.8	12.9	13.4	9.6	6.3	6.3
Asset Turnover	0.3	0.4	0.5	0.2	0.3	0.3
Financial Leverage	2.0	1.8	1.6	3.7	3.4	3.4

Valuation Ratios	Stock	Rel to Industry	Rel to S&P 500
Price/Earnings	19.9	0.7	1.0
Price/Book	1.4	0.2	0.3
Price/Sales	1.3	0.5	0.4
Price/Cash Flow	7.3	0.5	0.5

Major Fund Holders	% of Fund Assets
Calvert Small Cap Value A	3.11
Maxim Ariel SmallCap Value	2.65
Ariel	2.51
AHA Socially Responsible Equity I	2.29

Management

Stewardship Grade [C]

Mary Junck was elected chairman, CEO, and president of Lee Enterprises in 2002 after being with the company since 1999. Her previous stints include executive vice president at the Times Mirror Company and publisher and CEO of The Baltimore Sun. In 2005, Junck took home a salary and bonus of $1.9 million, along with $3.2 million of restricted stock and 45,000 stock options. We think her pay package is reasonable, especially considering the successful integration of two large acquisitions. We're also pleased that Lee had been expensing stock options well before it was required. However, we do have some concerns. Class B supervoting stock and staggered board elections are to shareholders' disadvantage. We'd also prefer the executive officers and directors to have more of a stake in the company; as a group, they own just 2.5% of the common stock (excluding director Gregory P. Schermer's 7.6% ownership of the Class B shares). Moreover, we would like to see Junck relinquish some of her titles. Overall, though, we think she has done a commendable job with this newspaper publisher.

201 N. Harrison Street Suite 600
Davenport, IA 52801
www.lee.net

Growth [A+]	2002	2003	2004	2005
Revenue %	27.3	6.1	27.3	37.8
Earnings/Share %	-2.8	9.1	-11.0	-8.2
Book Value/Share %	7.4	8.2	4.4	7.4
Dividends/Share %	0.0	5.9	0.0	0.0

Profitability [B]	2003	2004	2005	TTM
Return on Assets %	6.1	2.3	2.1	2.1
Oper Cash Flow $Mil	122	152	197	197
- Cap Spending $Mil	18	24	33	33
= Free Cash Flow $Mil	103	128	165	165

Financial Health [C]	2003	2004	2005	06-30-06
Long-term Debt $Mil	202	1,706	1,510	1,510
Total Equity $Mil	877	936	991	991
Debt/Equity Ratio	0.2	1.8	1.5	1.5

Thesis By James M. Walden, CFA, 12-18-06 Stock Price as of Analysis: $30.50

We think Lee Enterprises has surrounded itself with an economic moat by assembling a portfolio of local papers primarily in small and midsize markets. We believe that newspapers in these communities dominate their particular markets, serving as a bigger source of news and information than those in larger markets. As a result, local advertisers flock to them.

While Lee owns the dominant media franchise in many of its markets, it still has exposure to the same trends that affect the overall newspaper industry, and over the last several periods, it's felt the impact of increased media consumption and advertising over the Internet. In fiscal 2006, Lee's advertising revenue inched up 0.8% (pro forma for the full inclusion of Pulitzer, which it acquired in June 2005), due in part to the Internet stealing some of Lee's thunder. In contrast, ad revenue spent on the Web in the United States is expected to be up about 24% in calendar 2006, according to PricewaterhouseCoopers. But we think the Internet will have a smaller effect on Lee than many of its peers because of Lee's focus on smaller markets. Papers in many of the publisher's smaller markets have little competition from classified-ad Web sites, and volatile national ads make up only 7% of Lee's total printed ads, about half of the total industry's exposure, according to figures provided by the Newspaper Association of America.

Lee is pushing back impressively with its own Internet initiatives, in our opinion. The company is investing heavily in its newspapers' Web sites, with evident results: In fiscal 2006, Lee's online revenue was up 40.3% over fiscal 2005 (pro forma for the full inclusion of Pulitzer). And in 2006, a consortium of newspaper publishers, including Lee, formed what we consider to be a very strategic alliance with Yahoo. Initially, the agreement will allow Lee to sell help-wanted ads on Yahoo's HotJobs site. We think it could become an even more attractive agreement because, eventually, Lee and the other publishers will collaborate with Yahoo on other projects, such as local search, which should provide an even tighter lock on their markets.

Legg Mason LM

Data as of 12-29-06

Rating	Fair Value	Last Close	Consider Buy	Consider Sell	Yield %
★★★★	$114.00	$95.05	$87.90	$142.80	0.82

Company Profile

Legg Mason started life as a regional brokerage, but asset management became a larger and larger part of the business over the years. In June 2005, Legg finally took the plunge and swapped its brokerage for Citigroup's asset-management operation. Now all of its revenue will come from money management. With these new assets, and the addition of a fund-of-hedge-funds business, Legg is one of the largest asset managers in the world.

Management

Stewardship Grade [C]

No one could accuse Legg Mason of being stingy with compensation. Chairman and CEO Chip Mason is one of the highest-paid executives in the asset-management industry. Mason pulled down more than $14 million in compensation during fiscal 2006, not counting the 500,000 options he received that year worth a cool $21.2 million. But Mason has arguably earned an outsize paycheck with his excellent stewardship of Legg Mason over the years, and the recent Citigroup deal adds another feather to his cap. He owns more than 2% of the firm's shares after the dilution from the deal. In March 2006, the firm finally announced the selection of a likely successor to Mason: James W. Hirschmann became Legg Mason's president on May 1, 2006. He comes from Legg Mason's bond group, Western Asset Management. Though Mason has not announced plans to retire and is doing an excellent job shepherding the company, we are pleased that Legg now has an heir apparent. This should ensure management continuity whenever Mason, now 69, decides to hang up his CEO shoes. Corporate governance overall has been fair, though the firm has done a few things that we frown on, like issuing Mason two special bonuses to pay off loans from the company.

100 Light Street
Baltimore, MD 21202
www.leggmason.com

Growth [A+]	2003	2004	2005	2006
Revenue %	12.1	43.6	36.2	68.4
Earnings/Share %	22.8	48.9	33.2	149.3
Book Value/Share %	13.2	19.3	42.8	127.0
Dividends/Share %	10.2	30.3	47.3	25.5

Profitability [A+]	2004	2005	2006	TTM
Return on Assets %	4.1	5.0	12.3	13.0
Oper Cash Flow $Mil	268	366	545	—
- Cap Spending $Mil	—	—	—	—
= Free Cash Flow $Mil	—	—	—	—

Financial Health [NA]	2004	2005	2006	09-30-06
Long-term Debt $Mil	—	—	—	—
Total Equity $Mil	1,560	2,293	5,850	6,207
Debt/Equity Ratio	—	—	—	—

Industry	Business Risk	Moat Size	Investment Style	Sector
Money Mgmt.	Average	Wide	Large Growth	Financial Services

Competition	Market Cap $Mil	12 Mo Trailing Sales $Mil	Price/Cash Flow	Return On Assets%	Debt/Equity	Total Return% 1 Yr	3 Yr
Legg Mason	12,491	3,810	—	13.0	—	-20.0	23.0
Allianz SE ADR	82,762	122,351	—	0.5	—	36.9	19.0
Franklin Resources	27,932	5,051	—	13.3	—	17.8	30.3

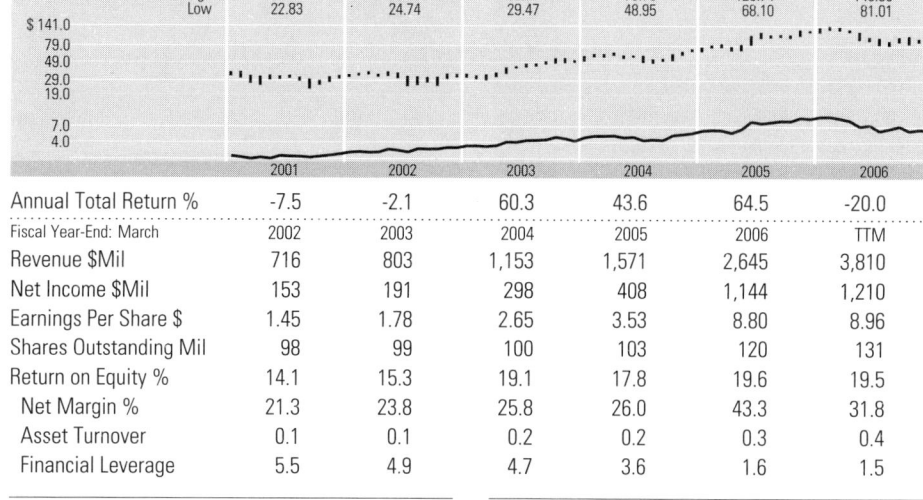

Price Volatility — Monthly Price High/Low — Relative Strength to S&P 500

Annual $Price High / Low	37.99 / 22.83	38.10 / 24.74	56.77 / 29.47	73.70 / 48.95	126.74 / 68.10	140.00 / 81.01
	2001	2002	2003	2004	2005	2006
Annual Total Return %	-7.5	-2.1	60.3	43.6	64.5	-20.0

Fiscal Year-End: March	2002	2003	2004	2005	2006	TTM
Revenue $Mil	716	803	1,153	1,571	2,645	3,810
Net Income $Mil	153	191	298	408	1,144	1,210
Earnings Per Share $	1.45	1.78	2.65	3.53	8.80	8.96
Shares Outstanding Mil	98	99	100	103	120	131
Return on Equity %	14.1	15.3	19.1	17.8	19.6	19.5
Net Margin %	21.3	23.8	25.8	26.0	43.3	31.8
Asset Turnover	0.1	0.1	0.2	0.2	0.3	0.4
Financial Leverage	5.5	4.9	4.7	3.6	1.6	1.5

Valuation Ratios	Stock	Rel to Industry	Rel to S&P 500
Price/Earnings	24.1	0.8	1.2
Price/Book	2.0	0.5	0.5
Price/Sales	3.3	0.5	1.1
Price/Cash Flow	—	—	—

Major Fund Holders	% of Fund Assets
Destination Select Equity	4.77
AllianceBernstein Growth B	4.75
CGM Focus	4.24
Midas Special	3.64

Thesis

By Jeffrey Ptak, CPA, CFA, 12-15-06 Stock Price as of Analysis: $96.06

Though Legg Mason's transformation into a pure-play asset manager hasn't gone without a hitch, we still think management can pull it off.

Recent months have been a slog for Legg Mason. In December 2005, Legg closed its landmark deal with Citigroup by exchanging its private client and capital markets businesses for Citi's asset management unit. In so doing, Legg bit off a big piece--$437 billion in new assets, roughly doubling its asset base in one fell swoop. With those assets came an array of challenges, not the least of which was ensuring that Legg retained the acquired Citi assets amid any flux that the merger created. Yet, a relatively soft first half of fiscal 2007--which was marred by higher-than-expected asset outflows from Citi-managed accounts--have brought those concerns into even sharper pitch.

Nevertheless, investors should take a deep breath: Since Legg was able to buy the Citi assets for a song--the price came to roughly 0.80% of assets under management, skirting the norm for such purchases--the deal wasn't priced for perfection to begin with. Thus, the recent asset run-off, while unwelcome, doesn't undercut the economics of the deal, which is made even more-compelling by the prospect of looming cost cuts. In addition, a large chunk of the recent outflows stemmed from clients defecting from various Citi liquidity strategies (amid poaching by rivals), which tend to be lower-yielding assets anyway. By contrast, there have been scant signs of widespread outflows from Citi's more-lucrative equity strategies.

In short, the strategic and economic rationale for the deal appears very much intact. Legg has culled the remaining dead wood from its business--its more-capital-intensive private client and capital markets operations--and replaced it with scalable, profitable assets in an area that it knows well: asset management. What's more, Legg will be able to harness Citi's gigantic broker network as part of the deal, giving it far-greater distribution heft.

Even before this deal, we thought highly of Legg, whose stable includes a number of respected asset managers, including Royce and Western Asset, spanning the retail, institutional, and high-net-worth markets and virtually all asset classes. While Citi's unit lacks the cachet of those names, the deal will extend Legg's reach into segments and locales that have eluded it in the past. This should stimulate growth and widen operating margins without meaningfully increasing the company's invested-capital base.

Lehman Brothers Holdings LEH

Data as of 12-29-06

	Rating	Fair Value	Last Close	Consider Buy	Consider Sell	Yield %
	★	$61.00	$78.12	$47.00	$76.40	0.61

Industry	Business Risk	Moat Size	Investment Style	Sector
Securities	Average	Narrow	Large Core	Financial Services

Company Profile
Lehman Brothers is a global financial services firm with three primary divisions. The investment banking division caters to corporate, institutional, and government clients around the world. The capital markets division provides securities trading and financing for institutions. The investment management unit includes asset-management operations and offers financial solutions to wealthy individuals.

Management — Stewardship Grade [B]
Richard Fuld is closely associated with Lehman, and not only as co-chairman and CEO. In 1984, as a bond trader, he fought tooth and nail to stop American Express' takeover of Lehman. Ten years later, when American Express sold Lehman to the public, Fuld was the firm's CEO and champion. Today he owns just over 2% of the stock. Supporting Fuld is Joseph Gregory, president and COO, who has been with Lehman since 1994 and is the firm's second-largest individual shareholder. The board serves staggered terms, and eight of the 10 directors are deemed independent. Compensation is high, but normal for the industry.

Competition

	Market Cap $Mil	12 Mo Trailing Sales $Mil	Price/Cash Flow	Return On Assets%	Debt/ Equity	Total Return% 1 Yr	Total Return% 3 Yr
Lehman Brothers Holdings	41,408	16,740	—	0.8	—	22.7	27.5
Citigroup	273,691	86,566	—	1.3	—	19.6	8.4
J.P. Morgan Chase & Co.	167,551	59,650	—	0.9	—	25.6	13.2

Price Volatility
Monthly Price High/Low — Relative Strength to S&P 500

Annual $Price High/Low	43.10 / 21.75	34.95 / 21.24	38.85 / 25.08	44.86 / 33.63	66.58 / 42.71	78.89 / 58.37
	2001	2002	2003	2004	2005	2006
Annual Total Return %	-0.8	-19.7	46.0	14.2	47.7	22.7

Fiscal Year-End: November	2001	2002	2003	2004	2005	TTM
Revenue $Mil	6,736	6,155	8,647	11,576	14,630	16,740
Net Income $Mil	1,161	906	1,649	2,297	3,191	3,762
Earnings Per Share $	2.19	1.74	3.18	3.95	5.44	6.48
Shares Outstanding Mil	487	491	492	550	556	530
Return on Equity %	15.0	11.0	12.5	16.9	20.3	21.7
Net Margin %	17.2	14.7	19.1	19.8	21.8	22.5
Asset Turnover	0.0	0.0	0.0	0.0	0.0	0.0
Financial Leverage	31.9	31.6	23.7	26.3	26.1	27.4

Valuation Ratios	Stock	Rel to Industry	Rel to S&P 500
Price/Earnings	12.2	0.7	0.6
Price/Book	2.4	0.6	0.6
Price/Sales	2.5	0.6	0.9
Price/Cash Flow	—	—	—

Major Fund Holders	% of Fund Assets
Legg Mason Partners Aggressive Growth A	9.52
Concorde Value	6.09
ING Partners Legg Mason Pnrs Aggr Gr Ini	5.43
CGM Mutual	5.37

Thesis By Philip Guziec, 12-12-06 Stock Price as of Analysis: $76.67

One of the smaller investment banks on Wall Street, Lehman has been trying to retain its independence by expanding beyond its historical strength in debt markets. We think the moat-worthy characteristics of investment banking and the firm's reputation for disciplined deployment of capital will generate solid returns for investors, if the shares can be had at the right price.

Lehman has been investing in its equity, corporate advisory, and asset-management businesses, but it still generates almost 60% of revenue from fixed income--three fourths of capital markets net revenue comes from fixed income, and almost half of its investment banking business comes from debt underwriting. However, Lehman has a broad range of debt products, from traditional corporate bonds to highly sophisticated leveraged finance, credit-linked obligations, mortgage-backed securitizations, and interest rate derivatives. This diverse product scope should provide some consistency to Lehman's fixed-income revenue stream, regardless of the interest rate environment, although we're wary of a slowdown in the mortgage business.

Another reason for diversification efforts is the firm's dependence on trading operations for more than half of its noninterest revenue. Other investment banks face this same situation, and most are pursuing additional, more consistent revenue streams.

In search of stable revenue, Lehman acquired asset manager Neuberger Berman in 2003. Because Lehman was spun out from American Express in 1994 without a brokerage or asset-management group, it was forced to build these businesses from scratch. Neuberger Berman filled the remaining hole, boosting assets under management to roughly $170 billion from $9 billion in 2002. This move helped boost recurring revenue from asset management to more than 7% of net revenue.

Lehman has also repositioned itself in its equity and advisory businesses over the past several years. The firm took advantage of the bear market to strengthen its equities business. It hired teams of disaffected bankers from traditional powerhouses, as well as senior salespeople and traders, especially in Asia and Japan. Recent expansion has also served to make Lehman a significant player in Europe and Asia.

Diversification has provided Lehman a breadth of offerings on par with the likes of Goldman Sachs and Morgan Stanley. Now the firm's challenge is to continue expanding its diversified businesses while retaining profitability.

---

745 Seventh Avenue
New York, NY 10019
www.lehman.com

Growth [A]	2002	2003	2004	2005
Revenue %	-8.6	40.5	33.9	26.4
Earnings/Share %	-20.8	83.0	24.4	37.6
Book Value/Share %	7.8	60.7	-8.0	14.5
Dividends/Share %	28.6	33.3	33.3	25.0

Profitability [D+]	2003	2004	2005	TTM
Return on Assets %	0.5	0.6	0.8	0.8
Oper Cash Flow $Mil	1,896	-11,484	-7,488	—
- Cap Spending $Mil	451	401	409	—
= Free Cash Flow $Mil	—	—	—	—

Financial Health [NA]	2003	2004	2005	08-31-06
Long-term Debt $Mil	—	—	—	—
Total Equity $Mil	13,174	13,575	15,699	17,301
Debt/Equity Ratio	—	—	—	—

Data as of 12-29-06

Lennar LEN

Rating	Fair Value	Last Close	Consider Buy	Consider Sell	Yield %
★★★★	$60.00	$52.46	$46.30	$75.20	1.22

Company Profile

Lennar, one of the largest homebuilders in the United States, operates in more than 40 markets in 15 states and focuses on first-time buyers, move-up buyers, and active adults (those older than 55). The average selling price of Lennar's homes was $311,000 last year, up from $272,000 in 2004. A small financial-services division, accounting for less than 8% of operating earnings, provides mortgages, title insurance, and other financial services primarily to Lennar home buyers.

Management   Stewardship Grade [D]

Lennar's executive team is headed by president and CEO Stuart Miller, who has been a senior executive at the company for 20 years and CEO since 1997, when he took over for his father, Leonard. From 1997 through 2005, the younger Miller was also chairman of LNR Property Group, the company's former commercial development arm (it was spun out in 1997) and current joint-venture partner. When LNR was bought by Cerberus Capital last year, Miller relinquished the chairmanship and received a 20% interest in the private equity group. Through a separate class of shares (the Miller family controls 65% of the B shares, which enjoy 10 times the voting power of A shares), the Millers control 47% of Lennar's voting stock, ensuring control over the board. The company's incentive compensation is based upon a myriad of factors, including net income, return on capital or net assets, customer satisfaction, growth, and corporate governance. Last year, Miller's incentive compensation was calculated as a percentage of pretax earnings that is based upon the return on capital attained. In order to reach the maximum percentage (1%), however, specified customer satisfaction and earnings per share hurdles needed to be cleared; needless to say, all goals were met.

700 Northwest 107th Avenue   www.lennar.com
Miami, FL 33172

Growth [A+]	2002	2003	2004	2005
Revenue %	21.1	23.1	17.9	32.1
Earnings/Share %	-35.7	165.0	22.6	44.4
Book Value/Share %	-33.8	181.4	21.0	30.5
Dividends/Share %	0.0	528.5	257.6	11.7

Profitability [A]	2003	2004	2005	TTM
Return on Assets %	11.1	10.3	10.8	11.0
Oper Cash Flow $Mil	581	420	323	323
- Cap Spending $Mil	—	—	—	—
= Free Cash Flow $Mil	—	—	—	—

Financial Health [NA]	2003	2004	2005	08-31-06
Long-term Debt $Mil	—	2,021	2,593	—
Total Equity $Mil	3,264	4,053	5,251	5,931
Debt/Equity Ratio	—	0.5	0.5	0.4

Industry	Business Risk	Moat Size	Investment Style	Sector
Home Building	Average	Narrow	Mid Value	Consumer Services

Competition	Market Cap $Mil	12 Mo Trailing Sales $Mil	Price/Cash Flow	Return On Assets %	Debt/ Equity	Total Return % 1 Yr	3 Yr
Lennar	8,313	17,031	25.7	11.0	0.4	-12.9	5.0
DR Horton	8,306	15,051	—	8.3	0.8	-24.4	9.9
Pulte Homes	8,432	15,017	—	9.1	0.5	-15.4	13.8

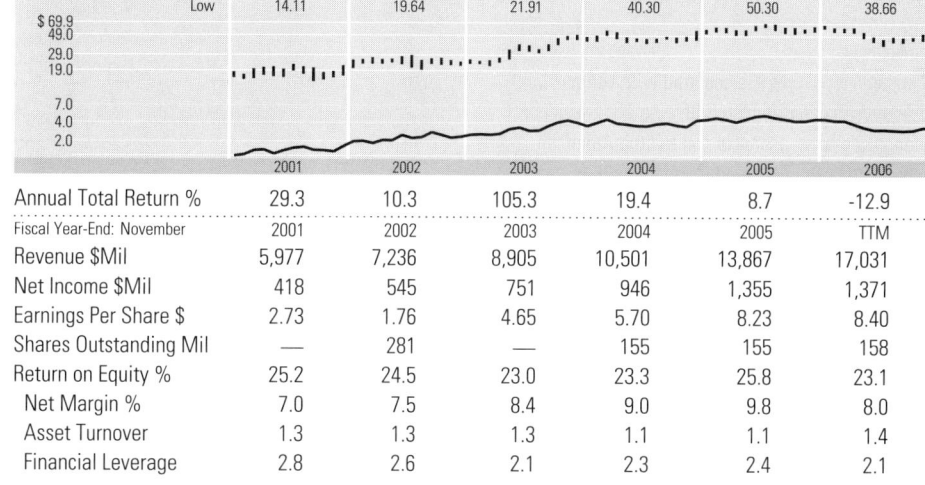

Price Volatility — Monthly Price High/Low — Relative Strength to S&P 500

Annual $Price High/Low	22.67 / 14.11	29.08 / 19.64	50.90 / 21.91	57.20 / 40.30	68.86 / 50.30	66.44 / 38.66

	2001	2002	2003	2004	2005	2006
Annual Total Return %	29.3	10.3	105.3	19.4	8.7	-12.9

Fiscal Year-End: November	2001	2002	2003	2004	2005	TTM
Revenue $Mil	5,977	7,236	8,905	10,501	13,867	17,031
Net Income $Mil	418	545	751	946	1,355	1,371
Earnings Per Share $	2.73	1.76	4.65	5.70	8.23	8.40
Shares Outstanding Mil	—	281	—	155	155	158
Return on Equity %	25.2	24.5	23.0	23.3	25.8	23.1
Net Margin %	7.0	7.5	8.4	9.0	9.8	8.0
Asset Turnover	1.3	1.3	1.3	1.1	1.1	1.4
Financial Leverage	2.8	2.6	2.1	2.3	2.4	2.1

Valuation Ratios	Stock	Rel to Industry	Rel to S&P 500
Price/Earnings	6.2	0.7	0.3
Price/Book	1.4	0.8	0.3
Price/Sales	0.5	0.6	0.2
Price/Cash Flow	25.7	1.3	1.8

Major Fund Holders	% of Fund Assets
Alpine U.S. Real Estate Equity	4.59
SunAmerica Focused Large Cap Gr A	4.57
Allianz OCC Value Instl	4.37
Midas Special	3.84

Thesis By Eric Landry, 12-26-06 Stock Price as of Analysis: $51.25

With more than 42,000 closings and almost $14 billion in revenue in 2005, Lennar is the country's fourth-largest homebuilder. We think this narrow-moat firm is fairly well positioned to benefit from its bountiful holdings of raw dirt in several land-constrained markets once the industry rebounds. But before it does, the company likely will churn through plenty of less-profitable land currently sitting on its balance sheet.

As in most real estate businesses, success in homebuilding depends mostly upon location. Skills in vertical construction are widely dispersed throughout the industry, making the so-called "sticks and bricks" almost a pure commodity. In turn, builders are forced to compete on the basis of their land expertise. Those that secure land in attractive locations at the lowest cost to eventual buyers usually win. Lennar knows this, which is why it has chosen to completely separate its land procurement unit from construction. Each function requires a different skill set, and people in each have very different incentives. This differs from many other builders that delegate responsibility on a regional basis without delineating between land procurement and construction.

Another hallmark of Lennar is its use of joint ventures to control massive tracts of land. With an investment of $1.5 billion, Lennar is a partner in some of the largest redevelopments in the country. Projects such as Newhall Ranch and the El Toro Marine base in land-constrained California will keep the pipeline stocked for years. Yet the risks are not insignificant. Lennar is on the hook for repayment guarantees of $1.2 billion if the JVs default, while several of its current financial ratios are skewed to the better because the entities aren't consolidated.

Lennar is also unique in that it is currently maintaining a full production schedule at the expense of gross margins. The company has explained that its "even flow" production system demands that production be balanced evenly throughout the cycle. We think, however, that by selling houses at cost or below in some regions, management is trying to run through some land it wishes it never purchased during the late stages of the boom period. More than most other builders, Lennar seems to be operating with a sense of urgency as it tries to reduce inventory and produce as much cash as possible. Essentially, management has made the decision that by ridding itself of expensive land before other builders (most still have plenty), Lennar can be more opportunistic later in the downturn.

Data as of 12-29-06

Leucadia National LUK

	Rating	Fair Value	Last Close	Consider Buy	Consider Sell	Yield %
	★★★	$26.00	$28.20	$20.00	$32.60	0.89

Company Profile
Managers Ian Cumming and Joseph Steinberg acquired control of investment company Leucadia National in 1978. Leucadia buys out-of-favor assets at discounts to intrinsic value and then works to improve and extract value from those assets. Leucadia's current holdings include real estate developer HomeFed, the Pine Ridge and Archery Summit wineries, and several other public and private companies.

Management   Stewardship Grade [B]
A Leucadia investment is essentially a vote of confidence in chairman Ian Cumming and president Joseph Steinberg, as much of the firm's value depends on their investment acumen. In a business where managerial aptitude is the critical determinant of value creation, these two have excelled. Their extraordinary investment skill and discipline have delivered impressive results for more than 25 years. In addition, Cumming and Steinberg own 25% of Leucadia, which sharply aligns their interests with shareholders', in our opinion. Executive compensation is similarly aligned. As a result of Leucadia's low returns in recent years, Cumming and Steinberg continued to receive modest $650,000 salaries.

Industry	Business Risk	Moat Size	Investment Style	Sector
Diversified	Average	Narrow	Mid Core	Industrial Materials

Competition	Market Cap $Mil	12 Mo Trailing Sales $Mil	Price/Cash Flow	Return On Assets%	Debt/ Equity	Total Return% 1 Yr	3 Yr
Leucadia National	6,100	1,259	—	8.4	—	19.9	23.1
American Capital Strategi	6,578	620	—	8.5	—	39.3	27.2
Allied Capital	4,763	433	—	11.8	—	20.6	14.9

Price Volatility | Monthly Price High/Low   — Relative Strength to S&P 500

Annual $Price High Low	11.90 8.77	13.42 9.21	15.40 10.86	23.50 15.02	24.64 16.20	32.62 23.26
	2001	2002	2003	2004	2005	2006
Annual Total Return %	-17.8	30.1	24.3	51.5	3.0	19.9
Fiscal Year-End: December	2001	2002	2003	2004	2005	TTM
Revenue $Mil	370	235	314	638	1,041	1,259
Net Income $Mil	-8	162	97	146	1,636	436
Earnings Per Share $	-0.09	1.92	0.53	0.67	7.14	1.93
Shares Outstanding Mil	83	83	183	214	216	216
Return on Equity %	-0.6	10.5	4.5	6.4	44.7	11.4
Net Margin %	-2.0	68.7	30.9	22.8	157.1	34.7
Asset Turnover	0.2	0.1	0.1	0.1	0.2	0.2
Financial Leverage	2.1	1.7	2.1	2.1	1.4	1.4

Valuation Ratios	Stock	Rel to Industry	Rel to S&P 500
Price/Earnings	57.0	3.1	2.8
Price/Book	1.6	0.5	0.4
Price/Sales	4.8	2.7	1.7
Price/Cash Flow	—	—	—

Major Fund Holders	% of Fund Assets

315 Park Avenue South   www.leucadia-nyc.com
New York, NY 10010-3607

Growth [A+]	2002	2003	2004	2005
Revenue %	-36.4	33.4	103.4	63.2
Earnings/Share %	NMF	-72.7	27.6	964.9
Book Value/Share %	27.2	-36.7	-9.9	53.5
Dividends/Share %	0.0	0.0	49.9	0.0

Profitability [A]	2003	2004	2005	TTM
Return on Assets %	2.2	3.0	31.1	8.4
Oper Cash Flow $Mil	-23	68	321	—
- Cap Spending $Mil	154	120	162	—
= Free Cash Flow $Mil	—	—	—	—

Financial Health [NA]	2003	2004	2005	09-30-06
Long-term Debt $Mil	—	—	—	—
Total Equity $Mil	2,134	2,259	3,662	3,825
Debt/Equity Ratio	—	—	—	—

Thesis By Justin Fuller, CFA, 12-13-06 Stock Price as of Analysis: $27.59

Ian Cumming and Joseph Steinberg, Leucadia National's savvy management team, strive to purchase out-of-favor assets at steep discounts to fair value, then work to extract value. Historically, this strategy has generated handsome shareholder returns and, in our opinion, garners a narrow economic moat.

Leucadia's moat originates in managerial skill and its strict discipline of not overpaying for acquisitions. The investment conglomerate seeks to purchase companies that provide products or services with low obsolescence risk, and often finds acquisition candidates in disheveled companies that others have given up for dead. These opportunities are often available at bargain prices. Once acquisitions are consummated, Leucadia's team works to extract value by slashing costs and improving the consistency and quality of each company's products and services. In addition, many acquisitions come to Leucadia with huge operating losses that management can use as a tax shield to shelter profits earned in other investments, further enhancing shareholder returns.

Even though we like this strategy, we continue to think that Leucadia is overcapitalized, and we expect the investment conglomerate's returns to remain in the midsingle digits until Cumming and Steinberg can begin to deploy Leucadia's cash hoard into new investments. On this front, we're optimistic.

At the firm's last annual meeting, Cumming and Steinberg said they are starting to see some attractive investments in the domestic energy industry as well as some international opportunities. Over the past year, Leucadia has invested $60 million in Goober Drilling, $90.8 million in a project to rebuild the Hard Rock Hotel & Casino in Biloxi, Miss., about $200 million in the equity of Eastman Chemical, $50 million in a partnership to invest in Japanese equities, and $400 million in start-up Australian iron ore producer Fortescue Metals Group.

We are pleased by these $800 million of new investments, but since Leucadia's cash hoard remains at about $2.15 billion--approximately $10 per share--we still think shareholder returns will remain low in the near term. In addition, we don't expect Leucadia to aggressively buy back shares or pay a large dividend, as it could render many of the firm's tax credits worthless. That said, we'd rather Leucadia keep its powder dry than overpay for an acquisition. Should there be any tumult in the public or private equity markets, we'd gladly have the team at Leucadia investing on our behalf.

Data as of 12-29-06

Lexmark International LXK

Rating	Fair Value	Last Close	Consider Buy	Consider Sell	Yield %
★	$53.00	$73.20	$40.90	$66.40	0.00

Industry	Business Risk	Moat Size	Investment Style	Sector
Computer Equip.	Average	Narrow	Mid Core	Hardware

Company Profile
Based in Lexington, Ky., Lexmark International is the fourth-largest manufacturer of laser and ink-jet printers as well as associated consumable supplies for offices and homes. The sales split between business and consumer products is fairly even. Revenue is also evenly split between printer hardware and supplies. International sales are about 55% of the total.

Management — Stewardship Grade [C]
Paul J. Curlander has been chairman and CEO since April 1999 and was with IBM for 17 years before the computer giant spun off Lexmark in 1991. He is aided by CFO John Gamble Jr., the former CFO of semiconductor maker Agere Systems. The leadership seems capable, but we have been disappointed by management's slow response to quickly changing conditions in the consumer sector. Lexmark's corporate governance is adequate but could stand some improvement. Executive compensation is reasonable for a company this size, and we were happy to see that Curlander's 2005 bonus was cut to $160,000 from $1.4 million after the company's disastrous performance that year. Nevertheless, compensation targets are based on a basket of measurements such as revenue, cash flow cycle, returns on invested capital, and earnings per share growth, which makes it difficult for us to understand how compensation goals are set and met. Lexmark has a staggered board of directors and a change-in-control agreement that rewards senior managers in the case of a hostile takeover. Executive ownership is barely adequate, with directors and executive officers as a group owning 3.5% of the company.

One Lexmark Centre Drive www.lexmark.com
Lexington, KY 40550

Growth [C-]	2002	2003	2004	2005
Revenue %	6.1	9.1	11.8	-1.7
Earnings/Share %	36.1	19.7	28.1	-32.0
Book Value/Share %	2.1	51.8	25.5	-25.6
Dividends/Share %	NMF	NMF	NMF	NMF

Profitability [A+]	2003	2004	2005	TTM
Return on Assets %	12.7	13.8	10.7	11.1
Oper Cash Flow $Mil	748	775	576	750
- Cap Spending $Mil	94	198	201	193
= Free Cash Flow $Mil	654	577	375	557

Financial Health [B]	2003	2004	2005	09-30-06
Long-term Debt $Mil	149	150	150	150
Total Equity $Mil	1,643	2,083	1,429	1,010
Debt/Equity Ratio	0.1	0.1	0.1	0.1

Competition

	Market Cap $Mil	12 Mo Trailing Sales $Mil	Price/Cash Flow	Return On Assets%	Debt/Equity	Total Return% 1 Yr	3 Yr
Lexmark International	7,168	5,104	9.6	11.1	0.1	63.3	-2.2
Hewlett-Packard	112,070	91,658	9.9	7.6	0.1	45.2	22.7
Canon ADR	75,441	34,222	13.7	10.2	0.0	46.7	23.0

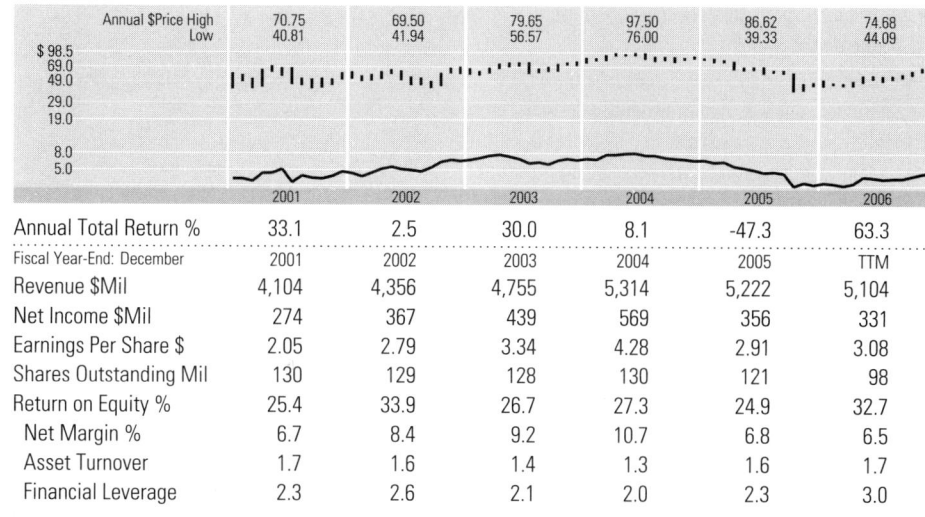

	2001	2002	2003	2004	2005	2006
Annual $Price High	70.75	69.50	79.65	97.50	86.62	74.68
Low	40.81	41.94	56.57	76.00	39.33	44.09
Annual Total Return %	33.1	2.5	30.0	8.1	-47.3	63.3

Fiscal Year-End: December	2001	2002	2003	2004	2005	TTM
Revenue $Mil	4,104	4,356	4,755	5,314	5,222	5,104
Net Income $Mil	274	367	439	569	356	331
Earnings Per Share $	2.05	2.79	3.34	4.28	2.91	3.08
Shares Outstanding Mil	130	129	128	130	121	98
Return on Equity %	25.4	33.9	26.7	27.3	24.9	32.7
Net Margin %	6.7	8.4	9.2	10.7	6.8	6.5
Asset Turnover	1.7	1.6	1.4	1.3	1.6	1.7
Financial Leverage	2.3	2.6	2.1	2.0	2.3	3.0

Valuation Ratios	Stock	Rel to Industry	Rel to S&P 500
Price/Earnings	23.8	0.9	1.2
Price/Book	7.1	1.2	1.7
Price/Sales	1.4	0.5	0.5
Price/Cash Flow	9.6	0.6	0.7

Major Fund Holders	% of Fund Assets
Evergreen Omega A	4.05
ING Evergreen Omega S	4.00
Evergreen Large Company Growth B	3.22
Aston/Optimum Mid Cap N	3.06

Thesis By Irina Logovinsky, CPA, 11-15-06 Stock Price as of Analysis: $66.98

Lexmark International is a $5 billion printer company with a narrow economic moat, thanks to a large number of installed printers generating high-margin supply sales. Its competitive strength is improving from a year ago, when the absence of key products and fierce price competition almost wiped out earnings in its consumer group. But although Lexmark's consumer business is back on track, its enterprise segment faces worsening conditions.

The enterprise business is Lexmark's strongest suit. Substantial expertise in several industries (retail, finance, etc.) enables the firm to win large and lucrative orders generating close to 75% of its profits. In the past year, though, the segment's operating margin has declined by 3 percentage points, to 20%, as a result of rapid price erosion in its color laser equipment. In addition, the market shift toward low-end, less profitable laser machines is pressuring earnings. We find these trends especially worrisome, since this division drives the firm's excess returns on capital.

Most of Lexmark's recent problems had been in the consumer sector. Tough competition from Hewlett-Packard and consumer demand for multifunctional photo printers led to a decline in sales of Lexmark printers that lacked these desirable features. This erosion of the installed base had a perceptible consequence on the sales of replacement ink, the most profitable part of Lexmark's business model. An original-equipment manufacturer relationship with Dell brought another problem. Although the partnership generated incremental printer sales, the bundling of Lexmark's printers with Dell's PCs did not turn out to be a profitable strategy, as these sales did not produce meaningful ink revenue.

We are encouraged by Lexmark's attempt to reorient its consumer segment in order to profit from the evolution of print technology. The firm's research and development has churned out multifunctional photo printers (which can also copy, scan, and fax) to replace single-function machines. Lexmark's color laser technology is also winning over consumers. Since color products require more supplies, profits in this segment are much healthier than for black and white. As the new-generation machines grow in the product mix, the firm's profit margins should climb back to low double digits.

With its consumer group in recovery mode, Lexmark needs to address mounting pressures in the enterprise segment if it wishes to remain near the top of the document equipment world.

Data as of 12-29-06

Linear Technology LLTC

	Rating	Fair Value	Last Close	Consider Buy	Consider Sell	Yield %
	★★★★★	$45.00	$30.32	$34.70	$56.40	1.98

Company Profile
Linear Technology designs and manufactures high-performance analog integrated circuits. Its 7,500-plus semiconductor products target functions like power management and signal processing in a variety of electronic systems. Typical applications for Linear's chips include mobile handsets, PCs, and industrial instrumentation. Linear markets its products to more than 15,000 device manufacturers across the globe, generating roughly 70% of sales outside the United States.

Management
Stewardship Grade [B]

Company cofounder Bob Swanson stepped down as CEO in early 2005 and was succeeded by former COO Lothar Maier. Swanson, a well-respected industry vet with deep roots in the analog chip sector, remains as executive chairman. Maier is an experienced semiconductor executive, having served in various management roles at Cypress Semiconductor before joining Linear as COO in April 1999. Rounding out the management team is CFO Paul Coghlan and president Dave Bell. Executive cash compensation is fairly conservative, in our view, while stock-option issuance is somewhat more generous, albeit not egregious by industry standards. Profit-sharing is a large part of Linear's compensation, which is good because it aligns the interests of employees with company performance.

Industry	Business Risk	Moat Size	Investment Style	Sector
Semiconductor	Average	Wide	Mid Growth	Hardware

Competition
	Market Cap $Mil	12 Mo Trailing Sales $Mil	Price/Cash Flow	Return On Assets%	Debt/Equity	Total Return% 1 Yr	3 Yr
Linear Technology	9,064	1,129	17.8	18.4	—	-14.4	-9.0
Texas Instruments	42,736	15,173	16.1	29.3	0.0	-9.8	-0.2
Analog Devices	11,242	2,573	18.1	13.8	—	-6.7	-9.4

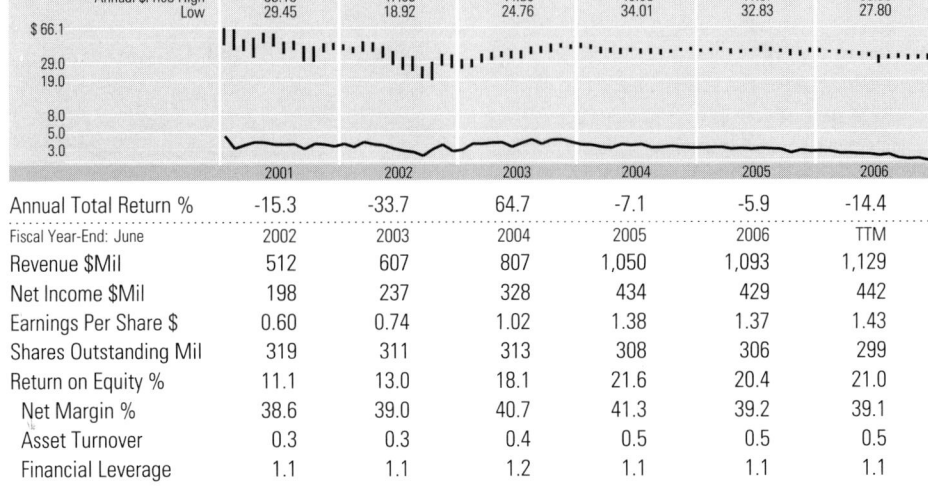

Annual Total Return %	-15.3	-33.7	64.7	-7.1	-5.9	-14.4
Fiscal Year-End: June	2002	2003	2004	2005	2006	TTM
Revenue $Mil	512	607	807	1,050	1,093	1,129
Net Income $Mil	198	237	328	434	429	442
Earnings Per Share $	0.60	0.74	1.02	1.38	1.37	1.43
Shares Outstanding Mil	319	311	313	308	306	299
Return on Equity %	11.1	13.0	18.1	21.6	20.4	21.0
Net Margin %	38.6	39.0	40.7	41.3	39.2	39.1
Asset Turnover	0.3	0.3	0.4	0.5	0.5	0.5
Financial Leverage	1.1	1.1	1.2	1.1	1.1	1.1

Valuation Ratios	Stock	Rel to Industry	Rel to S&P 500
Price/Earnings	21.2	0.8	1.0
Price/Book	4.3	1.2	1.0
Price/Sales	8.0	1.9	2.8
Price/Cash Flow	17.8	1.1	1.2

Major Fund Holders	% of Fund Assets
Pin Oak Aggressive Stock	4.65
Goldman Sachs Tollkeeper A	4.51
Pioneer Growth Leaders A	4.16
Fidelity Select Electronics	3.25

1630 McCarthy Boulevard
Milpitas, CA 95035
www.linear.com

Growth [B-]	2003	2004	2005	2006
Revenue %	18.4	33.1	30.0	4.1
Earnings/Share %	23.3	37.8	35.3	-0.7
Book Value/Share %	5.0	-0.9	13.4	5.4
Dividends/Share %	23.5	33.3	28.6	38.9

Profitability [A+]	2004	2005	2006	TTM
Return on Assets %	15.7	19.0	17.9	18.4
Oper Cash Flow $Mil	458	493	510	509
- Cap Spending $Mil	21	62	69	78
= Free Cash Flow $Mil	437	431	441	430

Financial Health [A+]	2004	2005	2006	09-30-06
Long-term Debt $Mil	—	—	—	—
Total Equity $Mil	1,811	2,007	2,104	2,109
Debt/Equity Ratio	—	—	—	—

Thesis By Larry Cao, CFA, 11-21-06 Stock Price as of Analysis: $33.09

Linear Technology is a perfect candidate for investors looking for a high-quality company through which to participate in the chip industry without the typically high risk.

Analog chip design expertise and processing technologies coupled with flawless execution afford the company a wide economic moat. Analog chip design is more labor-intensive, making the chips more proprietary. Linear has clearly demonstrated its grasp of premium power management circuits. The company has also focused on factory production since its early days.

Linear differentiates itself from other successful semiconductor firm with its relentless focus on profitability. Management seeks to identify opportunities early on and be first to market with its proprietary products. Linear gets premium pricing because there is often less competition in these new niches, and products typically compete on performance rather than pricing in the early stage. Over the product cycle, which is more than 10 years in some cases, Linear capitalizes on its proprietary processes to achieve cost-efficiency. It also derives a third of its revenue from the industrial sector, where lower individual order size and long product cycles give sellers a structural advantage.

With high margins and stable returns on invested capital, Linear's financials can easily be mistaken for those of a top-tier software company. In fiscal 2006, Linear achieved an operating margin of 52% (before deducting stock-option expenses) and a return on assets of 18%. Not only does its profitability outshine chip industry peers', it also surpasses that of software giants Microsoft and Oracle.

While we are impressed by Linear's record of maintaining high margins, the high profitability hurdle for taking on projects may ultimately hinder growth. An example is the handset market. Linear's products are more suitable for feature-rich third-generation phones than low-end phones. Even though 3G phones are expected to take off worldwide, growth is tepid at the moment. While we think investor concerns about Linear's below-industry growth rate over the past two years are overblown, we do note the firm's limitation at growing beyond the high-margin niche that it dominates.

Linear is one of the best-run semiconductor companies. We believe its dominance in the high-margin segment of the high-performance analog business coupled with management's focus on profitability will serve long-term investors well.

Liz Claiborne LIZ

	Rating	Fair Value	Last Close	Consider Buy	Consider Sell	Yield %
	★★★★	$50.00	$43.46	$38.60	$62.60	0.52

Company Profile
Liz Claiborne designs clothing and related items. Its products are sold under brand names like Liz Claiborne, Elisabeth, Sigrid Olsen, Dana Buchman, Juicy Couture, Crazy Horse, Lucky Brand, Enyce, and Mexx. With around 74% of its business in wholesale, the apparel manufacturer distributes its products through third-party retailers, including traditional department stores. The remaining 26% of Liz's sales come from its specialty shops and outlets.

Management
Stewardship Grade [B]

Paul Charron, CEO since 1995, is stepping down to be replaced by Johnson & Johnson veteran William McComb. Despite McComb's apparent lack of apparel industry experience, we think he brings strong leadership and global brand-building expertise to Liz Claiborne. These skills should help the apparel company pursue its multibrand growth strategy, which includes the likelihood of future acquisitions. At the end of 2006, longtime director Kay Koplovitz will take the chairman role. Overall, we think Liz's corporate governance is good. Management compensation is about par for the industry. We like that a significant portion of Charron's compensation was variable (based on company targets like returns on invested capital) and part of his total compensation came from equity, aligning his incentives with shareholders'. In our opinion, management does a thorough job of discussing the business on a quarterly basis, and we applaud it for its exceptional disclosure. As a group, executives and directors own 2.5% of Liz Claiborne's outstanding shares, including Charron's 1.5% stake. While we think electing directors annually as opposed to every three years would be more shareholder-friendly, the majority of the board is independent, and the most important committees are run by independent directors.

1441 Broadway
New York, NY 10018
www.lizclaiborne.com

Growth [C]	2002	2003	2004	2005	
Revenue %	7.8	14.1	9.2	4.6	
Earnings/Share %	18.0	18.1	11.8	3.2	
Book Value/Share %	19.4	19.7	14.5	12.7	
Dividends/Share %	0.0	0.0	0.0	0.0	
Profitability [A]		2003	2004	2005	TTM
Return on Assets %		10.7	10.4	10.1	7.3
Oper Cash Flow $Mil		419	457	441	405
- Cap Spending $Mil		97	134	140	155
= Free Cash Flow $Mil		322	323	300	250
Financial Health [A]		2003	2004	2005	09-30-06
Long-term Debt $Mil		440	485	418	677
Total Equity $Mil		1,578	1,812	2,003	2,042
Debt/Equity Ratio		0.3	0.3	0.2	0.3

Industry: Apparel Makers | Business Risk: Average | Moat Size: Narrow | Investment Style: Mid Value | Sector: Consumer Goods

Competition

	Market Cap $Mil	12 Mo Trailing Sales $Mil	Price/Cash Flow	Return On Assets %	Debt/Equity	Total Return % 1 Yr	3 Yr
Liz Claiborne	4,454	4,865	11.0	7.3	0.3	22.1	8.2
VF	9,174	6,912	20.5	9.7	0.2	52.0	27.2
Jones Apparel Group	3,686	4,751	7.6	4.1	0.3	10.6	0.3

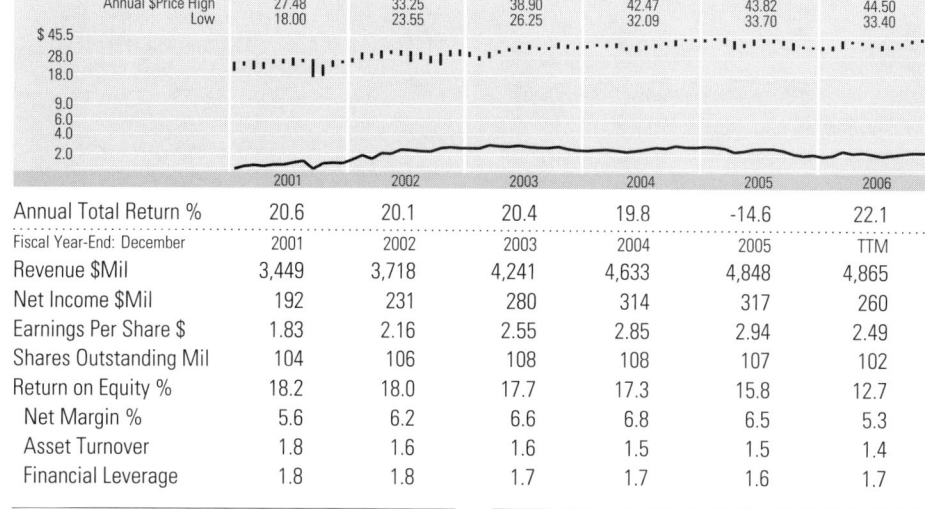

	2001	2002	2003	2004	2005	2006
Annual $Price High	27.48	33.25	38.90	42.47	43.82	44.50
Low	18.00	23.55	26.25	32.09	33.70	33.40
Annual Total Return %	20.6	20.1	20.4	19.8	-14.6	22.1
Fiscal Year-End: December	2001	2002	2003	2004	2005	TTM
Revenue $Mil	3,449	3,718	4,241	4,633	4,848	4,865
Net Income $Mil	192	231	280	314	317	260
Earnings Per Share $	1.83	2.16	2.55	2.85	2.94	2.49
Shares Outstanding Mil	104	106	108	108	107	102
Return on Equity %	18.2	18.0	17.7	17.3	15.8	12.7
Net Margin %	5.6	6.2	6.6	6.8	6.5	5.3
Asset Turnover	1.8	1.6	1.6	1.5	1.5	1.4
Financial Leverage	1.8	1.8	1.7	1.7	1.6	1.7

Valuation Ratios	Stock	Rel to Industry	Rel to S&P 500
Price/Earnings	17.5	0.7	0.8
Price/Book	2.2	0.6	0.5
Price/Sales	0.9	0.5	0.3
Price/Cash Flow	11.0	0.7	0.8

Major Fund Holders	% of Fund Assets
AIM Trimark Endeavor A	5.16
IXIS Harris Associates Focused Value C	4.66
Foresight Value	3.82
FMI Common Stock	3.79

Thesis By Kimberly Picciola, 10-30-06 Stock Price as of Analysis: $41.71

Liz Claiborne has developed a diverse portfolio of brands that it distributes through department stores and specialty retail shops in the United States and abroad. While we expect some turbulence in the short term as a result of consolidation in the domestic department store sector and longtime CEO Paul Charron's retirement, we think the apparel manufacturer's assortment of quality brands and scale will enable Liz to overcome these near-term challenges.

In recent years, Liz has expanded beyond its namesake label through acquisitions of brands like Dana Buchman, Juicy Couture, and European-based Mexx. While growth through acquisitions can be risky, Liz's management team has repeatedly demonstrated its ability to successfully integrate new brands into its business. Management's keen eye for buying niche brands with untapped revenue potential, like Juicy Couture, has also boosted the company's internal sales growth.

We think Liz's diverse portfolio of brands gives the firm a leg up over the competition. Additionally, its low-cost structure and strong relationships with the major department stores have enabled it to build a narrow economic moat. These competitive advantages should enable Liz to continue earning returns on invested capital that exceed our estimate of its cost of capital.

Although we are impressed by Liz's ability to develop an economic moat, a number of risks exist. The domestic retail environment is highly competitive, which has resulted in consolidation among midtier department stores, most notably Federated and May. While Liz has expanded beyond the department store sector by opening individual retail shops, wholesale sales continue to make up nearly three fourths of Liz's total business. In addition to closing stores, chains like Federated are increasing their focus on private-label merchandise to better differentiate themselves from competitors, which will pressure Liz's top line.

Another concern is the retirement of CEO Paul Charron at the end of 2006. In his 11-plus years leading the company, he has been instrumental in reinventing the organization by building a portfolio of brands and expanding beyond the department store channel. In addition to his departure, there has been a fair amount of turnover in senior executives.

Lloyds TSB Group PLC ADR LYG

Data as of 12-29-06

Rating ★★★	Fair Value $49.00	Last Close $45.33	Consider Buy $37.80	Consider Sell $61.40	Yield % 5.38

Industry	Business Risk	Moat Size	Investment Style	Sector
International Banks	Average	Wide	Large Value	Financial Services

Company Profile
London-based Lloyds TSB Group is a financial services firm operating primarily in the United Kingdom. The bank has three divisions. The retail unit provides traditional banking services to individuals through 2,100 offices in the United Kingdom. The insurance unit offers a variety of products, primarily through the Scottish Widows brand. The wholesale and international banking unit was restructured in 2003, with most of the international businesses sold.

Management
Stewardship Grade [NA]

Maarten van den Bergh stepped down as chairman in May 2006 following a five-year tenure. He was replaced by Victor Blank. Eric Daniels was hired in 2001, initially heading up the retail banking unit before becoming CEO in June 2003. Daniels' career includes 25 years as a banker at Citigroup and a stint as CEO at Zona Financiera, an online financial-services startup in Latin America that folded after one year. Since becoming CEO, Daniels has unleashed a massive restructuring and divestiture program throughout the bank so that it can better perform in its core markets. We believe management has adopted shareholder-friendly policies. Executive compensation at the bank is modest by U.S. standards and tied to achieving performance targets and beating the total shareholder returns of peer banks. Option grants are nominal, preventing dilution by greater than 10% over 10 years.

71 Lombard Street
London, United Kingdom EC3P 3BS
www.lloydstsb.com

Growth [NA]	2002	2003	2004	2005
Revenue %	0.0	11.5	94.6	17.9
Earnings/Share %	-20.0	81.6	-26.9	4.0
Book Value/Share %	-23.9	22.6	19.9	-8.9
Dividends/Share %	—	—	—	—

Profitability [NA]	2003	2004	2005	TTM
Return on Assets %	1.2	0.8	0.9	0.9
Oper Cash Flow $Mil	-2,255	22,207	-604	—
- Cap Spending $Mil	1,272	2,845	3,364	—
= Free Cash Flow $Mil	—	—	—	—

Financial Health [NA]	2003	2004	2005	12-31-05
Long-term Debt $Mil	—	—	—	—
Total Equity $Mil	17,186	22,458	18,328	18,328
Debt/Equity Ratio	—	—	—	—

Competition

	Market Cap $Mil	12 Mo Trailing Sales $Mil	Price/Cash Flow	Return On Assets %	Debt/Equity	Total Return% 1 Yr	3 Yr
Lloyds TSB Group PLC ADR	63,492	41,482	—	0.9	—	43.0	19.3
HSBC Holdings PLC ADR	204,784	49,836	—	1.1	—	18.9	9.5
Barclays PLC ADR	94,325	31,638	—	0.4	—	44.1	21.5

Price Volatility
| Monthly Price High/Low — Relative Strength to S&P 500

	2001	2002	2003	2004	2005	2006
Annual $Price High	46.00	48.85	32.75	37.03	39.51	45.52
Low	33.25	27.42	19.20	29.40	31.05	33.80
Annual Total Return %	2.8	-33.1	24.5	22.2	-1.5	43.0

Fiscal Year-End: December	2001	2002	2003	2004	2005	TTM
Revenue $Mil	12,815	13,307	16,205	35,060	41,482	41,482
Net Income $Mil	3,302	2,773	5,435	4,471	4,664	4,664
Earnings Per Share $	2.31	1.92	3.80	3.09	3.23	3.23
Shares Outstanding Mil	1,417	1,442	1,425	1,436	1,432	1,401
Return on Equity %	22.1	21.6	31.6	19.9	25.4	25.4
Net Margin %	25.8	20.8	33.5	12.8	11.2	11.2
Asset Turnover	0.0	0.0	0.0	0.1	0.1	0.1
Financial Leverage	22.8	31.8	26.2	24.4	29.1	29.1

Valuation Ratios	Stock	Rel to Industry	Rel to S&P 500
Price/Earnings	14.0	0.8	0.7
Price/Book	3.5	1.3	0.9
Price/Sales	1.5	0.4	0.5
Price/Cash Flow	—	—	—

Major Fund Holders	% of Fund Assets
Maxim INVESCO ADR	2.04
California Investment Euro Gr & Inc Dir	1.48
Commonwealth Global	1.25
Lazard International Equity Sel Instl	1.03

Thesis
By Ganesh Rathnam, 11-07-06   Stock Price as of Analysis: $42.74

Lloyds TSB's turnaround is almost complete. The retail bank's customer base, increasing switching costs, and scale bestow Lloyds with a wide economic moat, in our opinion. We would rush to invest at an appropriate discount to our fair value estimate.

Lloyds sold its noncore and international operations to concentrate on what it does best: retail banking in the United Kingdom. Lloyds has an unmatched retail banking franchise, with a 22% market share and arguably the best retail distribution channel in the United Kingdom. While financial products are commodities, the bank is increasing switching costs by striving to increase the number of retail products a customer buys from Lloyds. An early investment in a state-of-the-art customer-management system helps sales personnel identify appropriate products to sell to a particular customer. In our opinion, this strategy is very capital-efficient. Incremental costs incurred to sell new products to existing customers are negligible, so returns on capital receive a boost.

Lloyds is also intent on improving its business banking franchise. Although it has a 19% share of the small- and medium-size enterprise market (less than 2 million pounds in annual sales), that share falls precipitously as customer size increases. Lloyds has just a 7% share among FTSE 100-size companies. Big corporations prefer to do business with investment banks because the latter offer more sophisticated products and services. While Lloyds isn't trying to change its stripes, it realizes the value of its business banking franchise in keeping overall funding costs low. Management hired a dedicated team to develop a suite of products in ancillary areas like foreign exchange and derivatives, so that Lloyds can maintain, if not gain, share in business banking.

In our opinion, Lloyds' focus on capital efficiency is the key to its high returns. Scottish Widows, Lloyds' insurance arm, amply demonstrates this focus. Widows has always had a strong underwriting culture. However, its products weren't capital efficient. Lloyds applied its banking-style capital-management discipline to Widows, resulting in 15% profit growth in 2005 while reducing capital by 1 billion pounds.

A shareholder-friendly management team--which is committed to delivering economic profits, maintaining a healthy dividend, and generating returns on equity above 20%--rounds out Lloyds' attractions. We would gladly partner with this management team at the right price.

Lockheed Martin LMT

Data as of 12-29-06

	Rating	Fair Value	Last Close	Consider Buy	Consider Sell	Yield %
	★★★	$92.00	$92.07	$70.90	$115.30	1.36

Company Profile

Lockheed is the world's largest defense contractor, with 2005 sales of $37.2 billion. It operates through three segments--aeronautics, space, and systems and information technology--to develop aerospace, defense, computing, and communications systems for U.S. and foreign governments. In 2005, U.S. government contracts accounted for 85% of the firm's revenue. Based in Bethesda, Md., Lockheed employs about 135,000 people.

Management Stewardship Grade [B]

Robert Stevens has been president and CEO since August 2004 and was elected chairman of the board in April 2005. We like what we have seen from Stevens and CFO Chris Kubasik, a rising star in the defense community. The two have instilled in Lockheed a renewed focus on return on invested capital. Business is shifting to an inherently higher ROIC mix, but management also seems to be allocating capital with more discipline as well as incorporating related measurements into its executive pay scheme. We agree that measuring ROIC encourages the right behavior, and we believe that overall stewardship at Lockheed is strong. Perhaps more important, we believe the philosophy of doing more with less is trickling down through the entire organization, and this is what ultimately will make Lockheed's operational efficiency more like Dell's and less like that of the bloated bureaucracy that is the Department of Defense.

Stevens, his executives, and the board members have significant skin in the game. Together, the 25 directors and executives own about 0.6% of outstanding shares, which, at our fair value estimate, equates to about $216 million. We generally prefer that the same individual not serve as both chairman and CEO, but we think Lockheed's corporate governance is otherwise solid.

6801 Rockledge Drive www.lockheedmartin.com
Bethesda, MD 20817-1877

Growth [C]	2002	2003	2004	2005
Revenue %	10.8	19.7	11.6	4.7
Earnings/Share %	NMF	110.8	20.9	44.9
Book Value/Share %	-12.7	15.3	4.5	12.6
Dividends/Share %	0.0	31.8	56.9	15.4

Profitability [B-]	2003	2004	2005	TTM
Return on Assets %	4.0	5.0	6.6	8.1
Oper Cash Flow $Mil	1,809	2,924	3,194	3,506
- Cap Spending $Mil	687	769	865	956
= Free Cash Flow $Mil	1,122	2,155	2,329	2,550

Financial Health [A-]	2003	2004	2005	09-30-06
Long-term Debt $Mil	6,072	5,104	4,784	4,403
Total Equity $Mil	6,756	7,021	7,867	8,083
Debt/Equity Ratio	0.9	0.7	0.6	0.5

Industry	Business Risk	Moat Size	Investment Style	Sector
Aerospace/Defense	Average	Wide	Large Core	Industrial Materials

Competition	Market Cap $Mil	12 Mo Trailing Sales $Mil	Price/Cash Flow	Return On Assets%	Debt/Equity	Total Return% 1 Yr	3 Yr
Lockheed Martin	39,028	39,009	11.1	8.1	0.5	47.0	24.1
Boeing	70,249	59,114	9.4	2.7	0.8	28.4	30.4
Honeywell International	36,939	30,367	13.2	6.2	0.3	24.1	13.2

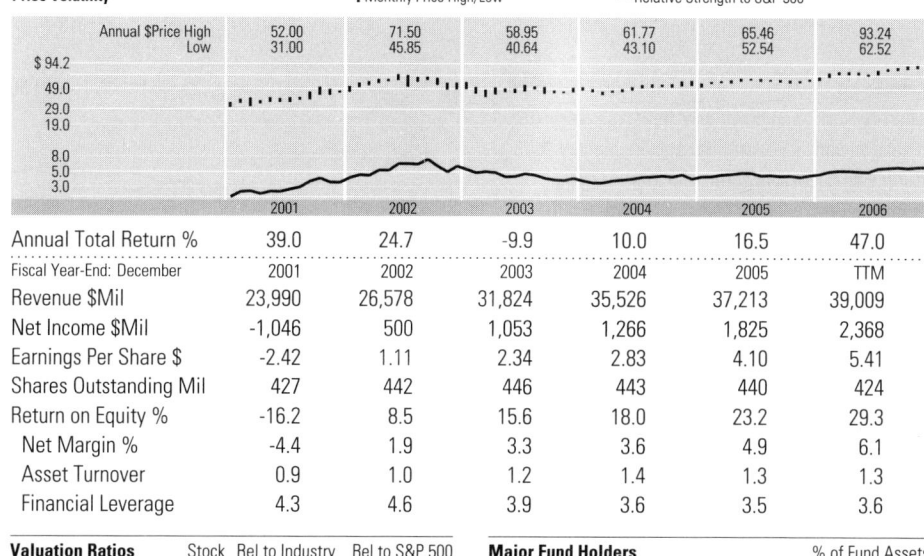

	2001	2002	2003	2004	2005	TTM
Annual Total Return %	39.0	24.7	-9.9	10.0	16.5	47.0
Fiscal Year-End: December	2001	2002	2003	2004	2005	TTM
Revenue $Mil	23,990	26,578	31,824	35,526	37,213	39,009
Net Income $Mil	-1,046	500	1,053	1,266	1,825	2,368
Earnings Per Share $	-2.42	1.11	2.34	2.83	4.10	5.41
Shares Outstanding Mil	427	442	446	443	440	424
Return on Equity %	-16.2	8.5	15.6	18.0	23.2	29.3
Net Margin %	-4.4	1.9	3.3	3.6	4.9	6.1
Asset Turnover	0.9	1.0	1.2	1.4	1.3	1.3
Financial Leverage	4.3	4.6	3.9	3.6	3.5	3.6

Valuation Ratios	Stock	Rel to Industry	Rel to S&P 500
Price/Earnings	17.0	0.7	0.8
Price/Book	4.8	1.1	1.2
Price/Sales	1.0	0.8	0.3
Price/Cash Flow	11.1	0.8	0.8

Major Fund Holders	% of Fund Assets
Schwab Large-Cap Growth Sel	4.93
Navellier Top 20 A	4.80
Chase Growth	4.52
Concorde Value	4.40

Thesis By Chris Lozier, 12-18-06 Stock Price as of Analysis: $90.18

Lockheed Martin's fundamentally improved returns on invested capital, combined with a slew of other traits that are extremely hard to replicate, have earned the firm a wide economic moat rating.

We start with what had already constituted a narrow moat for Lockheed. First, the firm is the largest player in a heavily concentrated military industry, with nearly 20% more in revenue than its next-largest competitor. This size enables the firm to spread fixed costs across more programs while better utilizing its increasingly flexible asset base. Second, more than half of Lockheed's roughly 135,000 employees have security clearances. These uniquely qualified workers are necessary for much of the sensitive government work for which the firm competes, and demand for cleared labor will probably continue to outpace supply.

The company is also many years ahead of most competitors on the long and shallow learning curves of missiles, space exploration, launch vehicles, combat electronics, and military airframes, to name but a few. Extremely high barriers to entry protect most of these businesses, and so competition for copious work should remain concentrated. Finally, Lockheed enjoys an extremely long and mostly smooth relationship with the federal government, from which it earns 85% of its revenues. Major-league defense contractors number only five, and Lockheed's ties to the customer are as strong as anyone's.

With the high fixed costs, risky developmental programs, and contractual margin caps that characterize the defense business, what is it that now makes Lockheed a wide moat firm? Fundamentally, Lockheed has learned under current leadership how to translate these advantages into economic profits. Management started with more-disciplined asset allocation on its part. It has maintained discipline in acquisitions while skillfully expanding its asset-light IT, systems integration, and consulting businesses. It has returned piles of cash to shareholders by repurchasing stock at what we believe to be cheap prices. Management then worked on improving program execution by making the company leaner and by wringing greater efficiencies from design and manufacturing processes.

Most importantly, leadership has changed the firm's culture to one of working for ROIC. While easier said than done at a large defense contractor, 2005 ROIC reached nearly 14%, and we expect this metric to remain in the teens for the next 15-20 years, regardless of defense spending volatility.

Data as of 12-29-06

Lowe's Companies LOW

	Rating	Fair Value	Last Close	Consider Buy	Consider Sell	Yield %
	★★★	$33.00	$31.15	$28.10	$43.30	0.51

Company Profile
Lowe's Companies is the second-largest home-improvement retailer in the world, with an emphasis on do-it-yourself and commercial business customers. The company's stores offer products and services for home improvement, home decor, home maintenance, home repair, and remodeling and maintenance of commercial buildings. Lowe's operates over 1,250 stores in 49 states.

Management
Stewardship Grade [B]

Robert Niblock, who previously served as president of Lowe's, became CEO and chairman in January 2005 after his predecessor retired. Senior managers average several years of experience with the company. We have always been impressed by the management team, with its depth of knowledge of the home-improvement retailing business and its high level of commitment to the corporate vision. The board of directors comprises Niblock and 10 outside directors. Lowe's corporate stewardship is slightly above average. Management compensation strikes us as a bit excessive, with the top five executives collecting more than $2 million each in salary, bonuses, restricted-stock awards, and other compensation in 2005--not to mention generous stock-option grants. We're also not big fans of the staggered board of directors, or the fact that Niblock is both chairman and CEO. Executive officers and directors own less than 1% of Lowe's common stock.

1000 Lowe's Boulevard www.lowes.com
Mooresville, NC 28117

Growth [A]	2003	2004	2005	2006
Revenue %	20.3	18.1	18.2	18.6
Earnings/Share %	51.2	22.6	18.9	27.7
Book Value/Share %	24.5	23.0	13.7	24.6
Dividends/Share %	9.5	29.4	36.4	46.7

Profitability [A]	2004	2005	2006	TTM
Return on Assets %	9.9	10.3	11.2	11.7
Oper Cash Flow $Mil	3,034	3,073	3,842	4,125
- Cap Spending $Mil	2,345	2,927	3,379	3,826
= Free Cash Flow $Mil	689	146	463	299

Financial Health [A]	2004	2005	2006	07-31-06
Long-term Debt $Mil	3,678	3,060	3,499	4,337
Total Equity $Mil	10,216	11,535	14,339	15,086
Debt/Equity Ratio	0.4	0.3	0.2	0.3

Industry	Business Risk	Moat Size	Investment Style	Sector
Home Supply	Below Avg	Wide	Large Growth	Consumer Services

Competition	Market Cap $Mil	12 Mo Trailing Sales $Mil	Price/Cash Flow	Return On Assets%	Debt/Equity	Total Return% 1 Yr	3 Yr
Lowe's Companies	47,435	47,330	11.5	11.7	0.3	-6.1	5.3
Home Depot	81,961	90,061	12.5	11.6	0.2	1.0	6.0
Sears Holdings	25,845	52,810	15.4	4.3	0.3	45.4	94.0

Price Volatility | Monthly Price High/Low   — Relative Strength to S&P 500

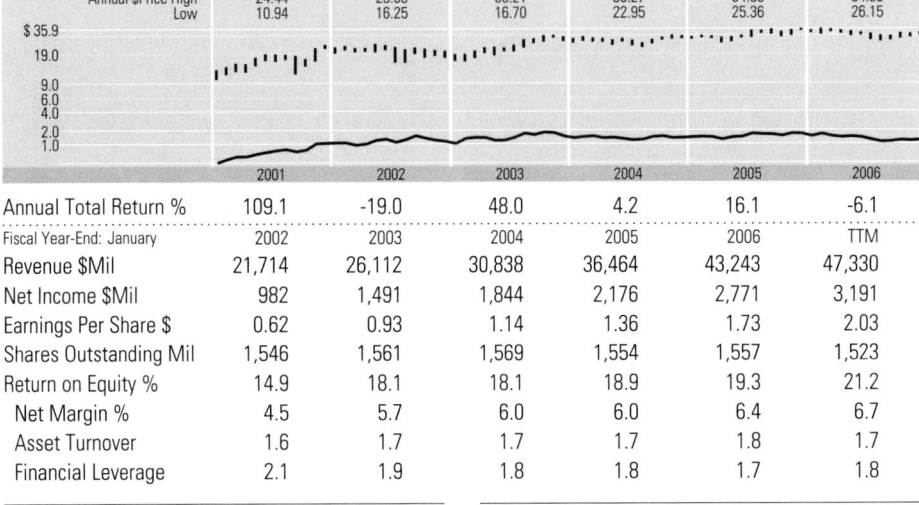

	2001	2002	2003	2004	2005	2006
Annual Total Return %	109.1	-19.0	48.0	4.2	16.1	-6.1

Fiscal Year-End: January	2002	2003	2004	2005	2006	TTM
Revenue $Mil	21,714	26,112	30,838	36,464	43,243	47,330
Net Income $Mil	982	1,491	1,844	2,176	2,771	3,191
Earnings Per Share $	0.62	0.93	1.14	1.36	1.73	2.03
Shares Outstanding Mil	1,546	1,561	1,569	1,554	1,557	1,523
Return on Equity %	14.9	18.1	18.1	18.9	19.3	21.2
Net Margin %	4.5	5.7	6.0	6.0	6.4	6.7
Asset Turnover	1.6	1.7	1.7	1.7	1.8	1.7
Financial Leverage	2.1	1.9	1.8	1.8	1.7	1.8

Valuation Ratios	Stock	Rel to Industry	Rel to S&P 500
Price/Earnings	15.3	1.1	0.7
Price/Book	3.1	1.0	0.8
Price/Sales	1.0	1.1	0.3
Price/Cash Flow	11.5	0.9	0.8

Major Fund Holders	% of Fund Assets
GMO U.S. Quality Equity IV	5.49
Constellation Sands Capital Inst Growth	4.54
Touchstone Sands Capital Select Growth Z	4.33
FMI Provident Trust Strategy	4.07

Thesis By Anthony Chukumba, 10-16-06 Stock Price as of Analysis: $31.14

Lowe's Companies has one of the widest moats and best management teams of any retailer that we follow. The company's large stores, which provide a one-stop home-improvement shopping destination, are bright, clean, and easy to shop, with plenty of staffers ready and willing to help. This unique store model, combined with Lowe's prime locations, brand name recognition and enormous supplier leverage, has allowed the firm to consistently generate outsized profits and returns on invested capital, which we expect to continue far into the future. For example, Lowe's nearly 11% operating margin is one of the highest in hardlines retailing.

Lowe's is planning on sticking to its core strategy of aggressively opening new stores in the U.S. and will expand into Canada in 2007. This is a stark contrast to its larger foe Home Depot, which has begun to expand into the industrial supply business. Thus, we view Lowe's future growth prospects to be less risky, because it is simply sticking to its knitting. Lowe's still has far fewer stores than Home Depot, and its stores' superior shopping experience allow them to prosper even in locations where they overlap with a Home Depot. The firm has also made major investments in installed sales, special orders, and sales to contractors to continue to drive store productivity and profit margin expansion.

We have been very impressed with Lowe's management team, which we view as extremely dedicated to and knowledgeable about the business, as well as shareholder friendly. We believe that top management's annual compensation is quite modest given the company's impressive track record. We also like the fact that Lowe's regularly returns cash to shareholders through share repurchases and cash dividends.

Our only major worries about Lowe's are the effects of a slowing housing market and increased competition from Home Depot. Much of Lowe's future expansion is planned for California, Florida, and the Northeast. We believe that due to aggressive new home building and price appreciation the last few years, these markets are very susceptible to a prolonged housing slowdown, which would hurt the results of Lowe's stores in these markets. In addition, after years of underinvesting in its stores and neglecting its spotty customer service, Home Depot has a renewed focus on these areas. This could lead to increased competition, especially as Lowe's opens more stores in major metropolitan areas, Home Depot's historical stronghold.

M & T Bank MTB

Data as of 12-29-06

Rating	Fair Value	Last Close	Consider Buy	Consider Sell	Yield %
★★★	$113.00	$122.16	$87.10	$141.60	1.84

Company Profile
Based in Buffalo, N.Y., M&T Bank has $56 billion in assets. The company operates more than 660 full-service banking branches in New York, Pennsylvania, Virginia, West Virginia, Maryland, and Delaware. The company also operates mortgage offices in 16 other states. M&T is the 18th-largest commercial bank in the United States.

Industry	Business Risk	Moat Size	Investment Style	Sector
Regional Banks	Average	Narrow	Large Core	Financial Services

Competition

	Market Cap $Mil	12 Mo Trailing Sales $Mil	Price/Cash Flow	Return On Assets%	Debt/Equity	Total Return% 1 Yr	3 Yr
M & T Bank	13,519	2,838	—	1.5	—	14.2	9.6
Bank of America	239,758	68,368	—	1.3	—	20.7	15.2
J.P. Morgan Chase & Co.	167,551	59,650	—	0.9	—	25.6	13.2

Management   Stewardship Grade [A]
M&T Bank is a shining example of excellent corporate governance, earning an A Stewardship Grade. Bob Sadler will retire as CEO at the end of 2006, after taking the helm from chairman Bob Wilmers in June 2005. Wilmers will temporarily return to the CEO job as Mark Czarnecki and Michael Pinto take new leadership roles as president and vice chairman, respectively. We believe the transition will go smoothly and expect one of newly promoted leaders will step into the CEO role sometime in 2007. We love that 20.5% of M&T is owned by its employees and directors. This large ownership is typical in a small bank but not one of the top 20 in the United States, and it helps align employees' interests with those of outside shareholders. Allied Irish Bank, former owner of Allfirst, maintains a 24% stake in M&T. M&T agreed to protect Allied Irish's ownership through several provisions, including guaranteeing board seats and seeking permission before issuing shares that could dilute Allied Irish's stake in the company. We do not think Allied Irish's stake will harm shareholders, but it might act as a takeover deterrent. Finally, we can't end a discussion about M&T's shareholders without mentioning that 6% of the shares outstanding are owned by Warren Buffett's Berkshire Hathaway.

One M&T Plaza 5th Floor www.mandtbank.com
Buffalo, NY 14203

Growth [C]	2002	2003	2004	2005
Revenue %	NMF	38.1	10.2	2.5
Earnings/Share %	33.5	3.6	21.2	12.2
Book Value/Share %	11.9	46.9	-3.5	6.3
Dividends/Share %	5.0	14.3	33.3	9.4

Profitability [B]	2003	2004	2005	TTM
Return on Assets %	1.2	1.4	1.4	1.5
Oper Cash Flow $Mil	1,216	724	298	—
- Cap Spending $Mil	32	32	27	—
= Free Cash Flow $Mil	—	—	—	—

Financial Health [NA]	2003	2004	2005	09-30-06
Long-term Debt $Mil	—	—	—	—
Total Equity $Mil	5,717	5,730	5,876	6,151
Debt/Equity Ratio	—	—	—	—

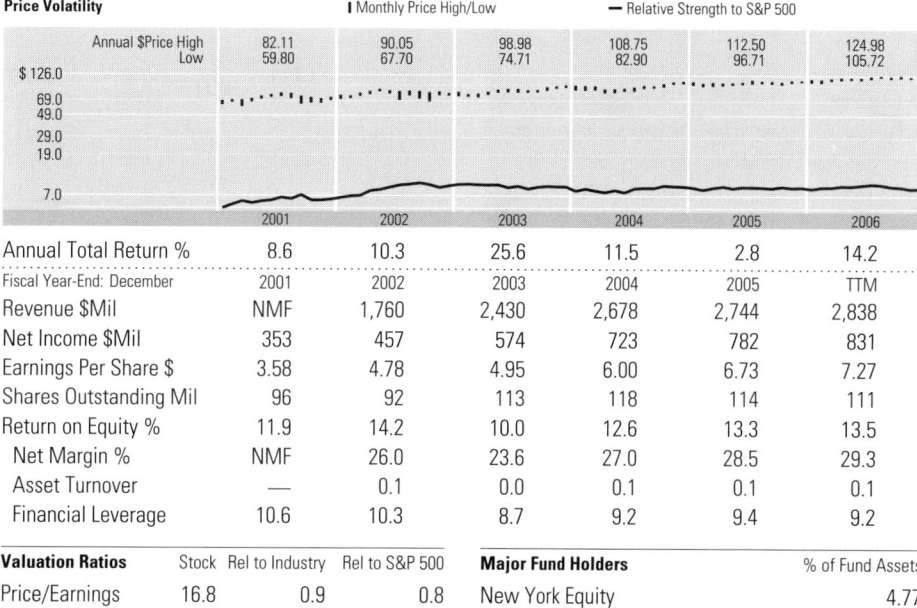

Price Volatility
Monthly Price High/Low — Relative Strength to S&P 500

	2001	2002	2003	2004	2005	2006
Annual $Price High	82.11	90.05	98.98	108.75	112.50	124.98
Low	59.80	67.70	74.71	82.90	96.71	105.72
Annual Total Return %	8.6	10.3	25.6	11.5	2.8	14.2
Fiscal Year-End: December	2001	2002	2003	2004	2005	TTM
Revenue $Mil	NMF	1,760	2,430	2,678	2,744	2,838
Net Income $Mil	353	457	574	723	782	831
Earnings Per Share $	3.58	4.78	4.95	6.00	6.73	7.27
Shares Outstanding Mil	96	92	113	118	114	111
Return on Equity %	11.9	14.2	10.0	12.6	13.3	13.5
Net Margin %	NMF	26.0	23.6	27.0	28.5	29.3
Asset Turnover	—	0.1	0.0	0.1	0.1	0.1
Financial Leverage	10.6	10.3	8.7	9.2	9.4	9.2

Valuation Ratios	Stock	Rel to Industry	Rel to S&P 500
Price/Earnings	16.8	0.9	0.8
Price/Book	2.2	0.7	0.5
Price/Sales	4.8	0.8	1.7
Price/Cash Flow	—	—	—

Major Fund Holders	% of Fund Assets
New York Equity	4.77
Saratoga Financial Service A	3.22
Fidelity Select Banking	2.72
JHancock Regional Bank B	2.40

Thesis By Jaime Black, CFA, CPA, 11-28-06 Stock Price as of Analysis: $117.81

M&T Bank is the ultimate example of a consistent strategy and a smart management team succeeding despite a weak market. This Buffalo, N.Y.-based bank is an expert at client relationships and is opportunistic in its expansion.

We marvel at M&T's ability to increase earnings per share 14% annually over the past five years, given its footprint. Nearly 60% of the company's deposits are generated from western and central New York, where the population has declined 2% over the past 10 years. The leading industry in this region, manufacturing, has been in decline for decades with no end in sight. M&T has continued to flourish in this market by taking share and finding new methods to provide more services to its customers.

M&T's Mid-Atlantic expansion will be the main source of growth for the foreseeable future. In 2003, M&T purchased Allfirst, giving it $17 billion in assets and more than 200 branches in the region. M&T successfully integrated Allfirst into its franchise and is working to build its reputation and increase the penetration of these branches. Currently only 2% of M&T's Mid-Atlantic customers have mortgages through the company, compared with 10% in its New York region. On the commercial side, only 22% of its Mid-Atlantic customers use M&T's merchant services, compared with 37% in New York. If M&T is able to bring its Mid-Atlantic production up to the level of its legacy branches, income from the average retail household will increase 11%, and income from the average middle-market client will increase 44%, or more than $26,000 annually per client.

We love that M&T is disciplined and opportunistic with its acquisitions. Former CEO Bob Wilmers picked up Allfirst on the cheap as a result of a scandal. Newly minted CEO Robert Sadler has already proved his ability to jump quickly at a good opportunity. In the second quarter of 2006, M&T purchased 21 branches from Citibank. These upstate New York branches provided M&T with $1 billion of deposits, which the company used to pay down its wholesale borrowings and improve its net interest margin. The new branches give M&T the top market share in upstate New York.

Given that M&T's management team has consistently proved its ability to grow in a tough environment and take advantage of expansion opportunities when available, we would join Warren Buffett, whose Berkshire Hathaway owns 6% of the company, as shareholders of this bank at an appropriate discount to our fair value estimate.

Data as of 12-29-06

Macrovision MVSN

	Rating	Fair Value	Last Close	Consider Buy	Consider Sell	Yield %
	★★	$23.00	$28.26	$17.70	$28.80	0.00

Industry	Business Risk	Moat Size	Investment Style	Sector
Business Appl.	Average	Narrow	Small Growth	Software

Company Profile
Founded in 1983, Macrovision has two key segments. The entertainment technology unit develops and licenses copy protection and digital rights management technology for CDs, DVDs, pay-per-view/video-on-demand programs, and PC games. The software technology unit provides solutions to help software vendors and end users manage licensing. Customers include movie studios, record labels, PC game vendors, and hardware manufacturers.

Management
Stewardship Grade [C]

Cofounder John Ryan helped invent Macrovision's core video copy protection technology. He was the chief executive officer from 1995 until 2001 and has been the chairman since 1991. Ryan owns 2.2% of outstanding shares (or roughly $30 million worth of stock). Fred Amoroso, a former advisor to investment firm Warburg Pincus, joined Macrovision in July 2005 as president and CEO. His base compensation of $500,000 is very reasonable, in our opinion. He was awarded options to purchase 500,000 shares of stock upon being hired, and he will receive options to purchase 250,000 more shares in each of 2006, 2007, and 2008. We believe Ryan's and Amoroso's interests are aligned with shareholders. We do ding the board's stewardship for excessive option issuance and management's highlighting of pro forma (referred to as non-GAAP) performance in press releases. In 2005, option issuance was greater than 6% of outstanding shares. Fortunately, management is now forced to expense such compensation. Management tends to highlight margins excluding several expenses, which is legal but--in our opinion--can be misleading. We believe management should report the figures and allow investors to do their own math and reach their own conclusions.

2830 De La Cruz Boulevard
Santa Clara, CA 95050
www.macrovision.com

Growth [B]	2002	2003	2004	2005
Revenue %	3.5	25.5	41.9	11.6
Earnings/Share %	-35.1	125.0	35.2	-41.1
Book Value/Share %	-4.0	16.0	15.8	5.2
Dividends/Share %	NMF	NMF	NMF	NMF

Profitability [A-]	2003	2004	2005	TTM
Return on Assets %	7.0	8.1	4.4	2.8
Oper Cash Flow $Mil	59	60	55	80
- Cap Spending $Mil	3	5	9	12
= Free Cash Flow $Mil	56	55	46	67

Financial Health [B]	2003	2004	2005	09-30-06
Long-term Debt $Mil	—	—	—	240
Total Equity $Mil	341	398	428	425
Debt/Equity Ratio	—	—	—	0.6

Competition

	Market Cap $Mil	12 Mo Trailing Sales $Mil	Price/Cash Flow	Return On Assets%	Debt/Equity	Total Return% 1 Yr	3 Yr
Macrovision	1,448	234	18.1	2.8	0.6	68.9	6.8
Microsoft	293,538	45,352	20.8	19.8	—	15.8	7.6
Apple Computer	72,901	19,315	32.8	11.6	—	18.0	99.8

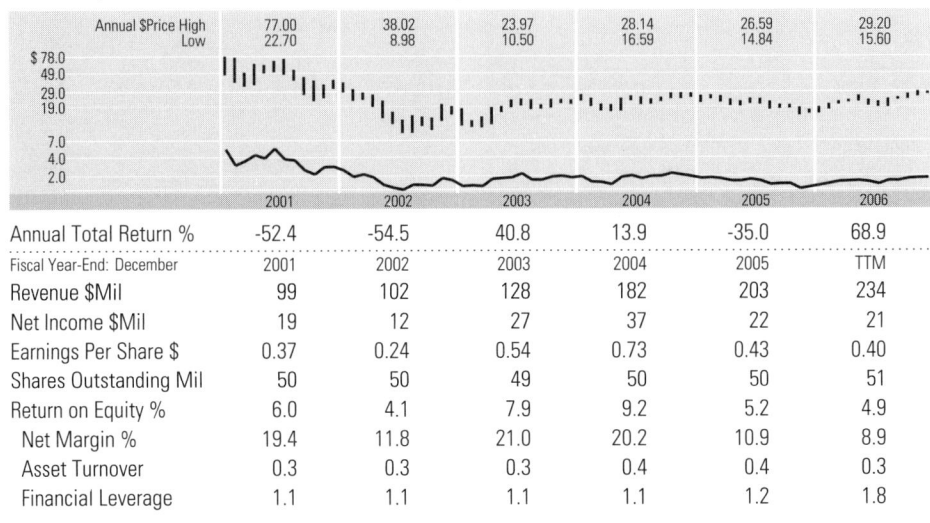

Price Volatility — Monthly Price High/Low — Relative Strength to S&P 500

Annual $Price High	77.00	38.02	23.97	28.14	26.59	29.20
Low	22.70	8.98	10.50	16.59	14.84	15.60
	2001	2002	2003	2004	2005	2006
Annual Total Return %	-52.4	-54.5	40.8	13.9	-35.0	68.9

Fiscal Year-End: December	2001	2002	2003	2004	2005	TTM
Revenue $Mil	99	102	128	182	203	234
Net Income $Mil	19	12	27	37	22	21
Earnings Per Share $	0.37	0.24	0.54	0.73	0.43	0.40
Shares Outstanding Mil	50	50	49	50	50	51
Return on Equity %	6.0	4.1	7.9	9.2	5.2	4.9
Net Margin %	19.4	11.8	21.0	20.2	10.9	8.9
Asset Turnover	0.3	0.3	0.3	0.4	0.4	0.3
Financial Leverage	1.1	1.1	1.1	1.1	1.2	1.8

Valuation Ratios	Stock	Rel to Industry	Rel to S&P 500
Price/Earnings	70.7	2.4	3.4
Price/Book	3.4	0.4	0.8
Price/Sales	6.2	0.9	2.1
Price/Cash Flow	18.1	0.7	1.2

Major Fund Holders	% of Fund Assets
Transamerica Premier Focus Inv	5.96
JHancock Technology A	4.64
Brown Capital Mgmt Small Co Instl	4.44
Pioneer Mid-Cap Growth A	4.22

Thesis
By Mike Ford-Taggart, CFA, 11-22-06 Stock Price as of Analysis: $28.60

It's easy to get excited about the evolution of entertainment content distribution, how consumers access such content, and Macrovision's role in the underlying technology. More difficult is arguing that Macrovision has a wide economic moat to protect it from the changing end markets. We are decreasing our moat rating to narrow from wide.

Macrovision's management did a great job carving out a wide moat--a sustainable competitive advantage--around the task of protecting the intellectual property written onto physical formats (DVDs and CDs). Its role as the leading crusader against digital piracy has been well publicized. Unfortunately for Macrovision, the world of DVDs is undergoing a significant change. Most analysts focus on declining sales of DVDs as Macrovision's bugaboo, and management seemingly has set this focus up as its favorite straw man. But the real issue is how Macrovision competes in the new world of the recordable protection market. So far, management's execution has been okay. Revenue growth remains stellar, up nearly 22% year over year through the first nine months of 2006.

That Macrovision's end markets are changing significantly is readily apparent. Consumers want to purchase entertainment content or software programs on the Internet. They want their content now; they do not want to go out and purchase or wait for the delivery of a DVD or a CD. Entertainment content providers and software publishers are considering ways to protect their intellectual property while giving their customers what they want.

To respond to such change, Macrovision is using the economics of its existing business for acquisition capital and its deep relationships for sales calls. But the real response has been a strategic repositioning involving overpriced acquisitions ($161 million for four firms, with $108 million going to goodwill) starting in 2004 that have had no discernable effect on increasing profit growth commensurately. Essentially, the firm is replacing slowing profit growth with acquired profits, which is a sure sign that the wide moat has diminished.

Another item that cools our heels is stock-based compensation. Morningstar believes stock-based compensation should be viewed as the expense that it is. Macrovision's financials show that so far in 2006, such compensation is equal to roughly 7.2% of revenue. This is extremely high, in our view, but consistent with the firm's practice of granting large amounts of options to employees.

Data as of 12-29-06

Magellan Midstream Holdings LP MGG

	Rating	Fair Value	Last Close	Consider Buy	Consider Sell	Yield %
	★★★	$25.00	$22.30	$21.30	$32.80	2.50

Company Profile
Magellan Midstream Holdings LP is a master limited partnership that owns the general partner of Magellan Midstream Partners, which operates pipelines and storage terminals for refined petroleum products and ammonia in the central United States. The partnership's pipeline network runs north from the Gulf of Mexico to end markets in Illinois, Minnesota, and Colorado.

Industry	Business Risk	Moat Size	Investment Style	Sector
Pipelines	Below Average	Wide	Small Growth	Energy

Competition

	Market Cap $Mil	12 Mo Trailing Sales $Mil	Price/Cash Flow	Return On Assets%	Debt/Equity	Total Return% 1 Yr	Total Return% 3 Yr
Magellan Midstream Holdings LP	1,397	1,217	7.0	1.4	NMF	—	—
TransCanada	17,029	5,061	10.8	4.8	1.5	15.1	21.4
Williams Companies	15,576	12,719	9.3	0.9	1.2	14.4	40.0

Management   Stewardship Grade [C]
Chairman and CEO Don Wellendorf provides stable and competent guidance for Magellan, holding both offices at the general partner and the limited partner companies. He has been a member of the executive team since Magellan's predecessor company was spun off from Williams in 2000, and CEO of the general partner since 2002. The board has six members, including Wellendorf. Only one of them qualifies as independent per NYSE rules; the remaining four members represent Madison Dearborn and Riverstone, private-equity firms that own MGG's general partner. Magellan gets a C grade for stewardship, in line with other MLPs. Because of the MLP structure, common unitholders do not have the same degree of control and voting rights as shareholders in a standard corporation would. For example, it would require a 67% supermajority of common unitholders to remove the general partner, but MGG's general partner owns 64.9% of the units, making such a move challenging without the approval of the general partner.

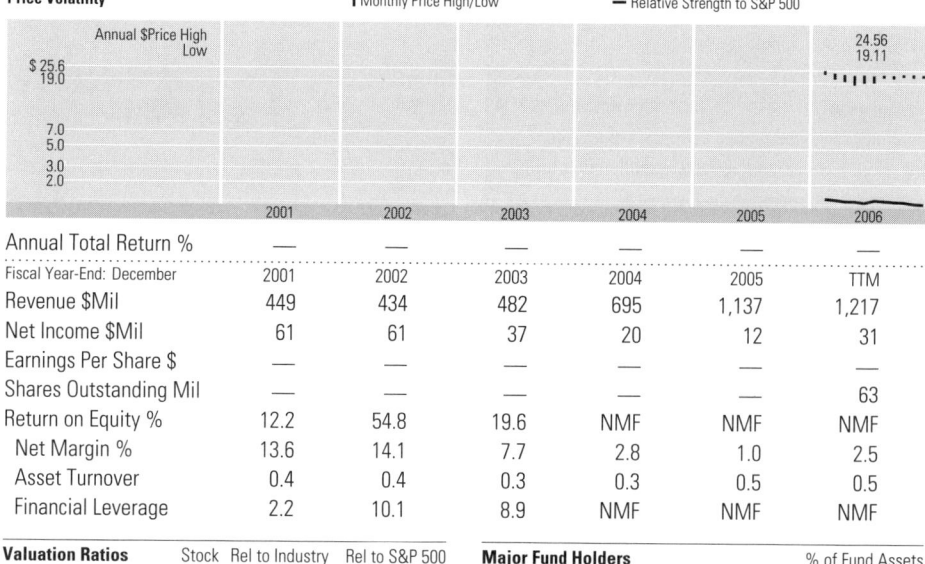

Price Volatility — Monthly Price High/Low — Relative Strength to S&P 500

Annual $Price High/Low: 2006: 24.56 / 19.11

Fiscal Year-End: December	2001	2002	2003	2004	2005	TTM
Revenue $Mil	449	434	482	695	1,137	1,217
Net Income $Mil	61	61	37	20	12	31
Earnings Per Share $	—	—	—	—	—	—
Shares Outstanding Mil	—	—	—	—	—	63
Return on Equity %	12.2	54.8	19.6	NMF	NMF	NMF
Net Margin %	13.6	14.1	7.7	2.8	1.0	2.5
Asset Turnover	0.4	0.4	0.3	0.3	0.5	0.5
Financial Leverage	2.2	10.1	8.9	NMF	NMF	NMF

Valuation Ratios

	Stock	Rel to Industry	Rel to S&P 500
Price/Earnings	—	—	—
Price/Book	—	—	—
Price/Sales	1.1	0.5	0.4
Price/Cash Flow	7.0	0.7	0.5

Major Fund Holders
	% of Fund Assets
DWS Equity Partners A	1.78
Royce Dividend Value Service	1.51

1 Williams Center
Tulsa, OK 74172

Growth [B-]

	2002	2003	2004	2005
Revenue %	-3.1	10.9	44.3	63.5
Earnings/Share %	NMF	NMF	NMF	NMF
Book Value/Share %	—	—	—	—
Dividends/Share %	NMF	NMF	NMF	NMF

Profitability [NA]

	2003	2004	2005	TTM
Return on Assets %	2.2	0.9	0.5	1.4
Oper Cash Flow $Mil	147	221	223	201
- Cap Spending $Mil	48	576	104	147
= Free Cash Flow $Mil	99	-354	120	54

Financial Health [D]

	2003	2004	2005	09-30-06
Long-term Debt $Mil	745	1,019	787	805
Total Equity $Mil	190	-43	-215	-222
Debt/Equity Ratio	3.9	ELB	ELB	NMF

Thesis By Jason Stevens, 12-20-06 Stock Price as of Analysis: $22.02

A key trend among master limited partnerships (MLPs) in 2006 has been the public offering of general partners of MLPs. The IPO of Magellan Midstream Partners' MMP general partner, Magellan Midstream Holdings (MGG), has provided investors who are seeking energy infrastructure exposure with an attractive option, given the stability of MMP's underlying business model and the growth prospects inherent in publicly traded general partnerships.

MGG has no assets or business operations other than its ownership of the general partner and incentive distribution rights of MMP. Because of the structure of MLPs, this is a nice arrangement. MLPs pay out 100% of available cash each quarter in the form of a cash distribution to partners. General partners are entitled to receive 2% of the total cash paid out, and to encourage them to continue to increase distributions, general partners also receive incentive distributions on a sliding scale. In the case of MMP, distributions have reached what is called the "high splits," which means that together with their incentive distributions, general partners receive fully half of all cash paid out as distributions over a certain threshold. Based on MMP's most recently announced distribution of $0.59 per unit, general partner MGG stands to receive about 28% of the total cash payout. As distributions at MMP continue their 20-quarter streak of quarterly increases, MGG's share of the total payout will only increase.

For investors in MGG, the bottom line is that so long as MMP continues to increase its distributions, MGG's distributions will also increase, and at a faster rate. In fact, the partnership calculates that a 10% increase in MMP's distributions will result in a 29% increase in distributions received by MGG. This leverage factor benefits MGG unitholders, since MGG pays out 99.9% of available cash to its unitholders each quarter. (MGG's general partner receives the remaining 0.01%.)

Investors have a choice with Magellan: buy units of MMP for their attractive yield (5.2% at our fair value estimate) or buy units of MGG for their lower yield (3.6% at our fair value estimate) but greater growth prospects. Either investment is based on the underlying performance of Magellan's core petroleum products pipelines and terminals, which we think will continue to generate strong returns on invested capital.

Data as of 12-29-06

Manulife Financial MFC

	Rating	Fair Value	Last Close	Consider Buy	Consider Sell	Yield %
	★★	$29.00	$33.79	$22.40	$36.30	1.90

Company Profile
After merging with John Hancock Financial Services, Canadian-based Manulife became the second-largest life insurer in North America. Manulife provides a wide range of financial products and services, including individual life insurance, group life and health insurance, pension products, annuities, and mutual funds. In addition to Canada, the firm sells its products in the United States and Asia--primarily in Hong Kong and Japan.

Management   Stewardship Grade [NA]
Dominic D'Alessandro has been CEO of Manulife since 1994. He earned about $13 million in total compensation in 2005, which we think is fair, given the company's performance during the period. D'Alessandro owns about $10 million of Manulife stock, which we think is enough to align his interests with shareholders'. Manulife has done well under D'Alessandro--shareholders have enjoyed a 28% average annual return since the firm's initial public offering.

Industry	Business Risk	Moat Size	Investment Style	Sector
Insurance (General)	Average	Narrow	Large Core	Financial Services

Competition	Market Cap $Mil	12 Mo Trailing Sales $Mil	Price/Cash Flow	Return On Assets%	Debt/Equity	Total Return% 1 Yr	3 Yr
Manulife Financial	53,527	26,485	—	1.8	—	17.2	30.2
American International Gr	186,296	110,593	—	1.2	—	6.1	3.2
AXA ADR	75,518	131,481	—	0.8	—	30.7	26.9

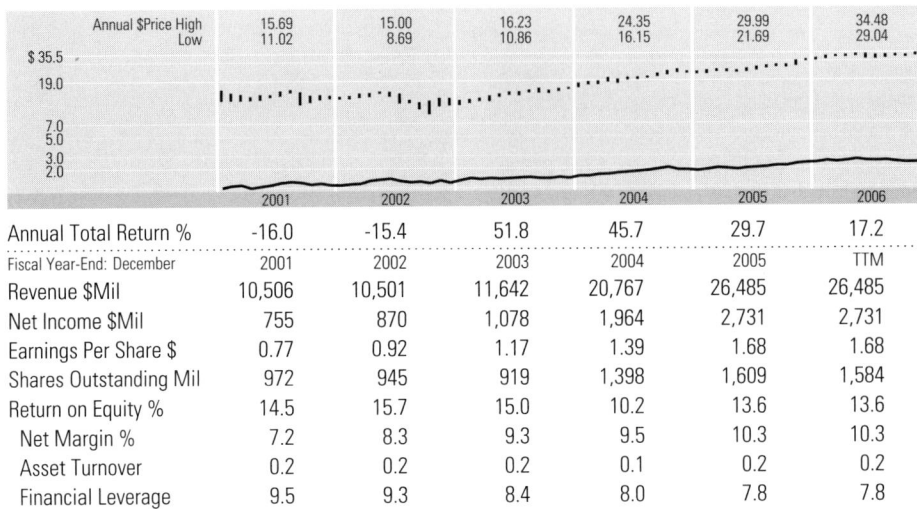

	2001	2002	2003	2004	2005	TTM
Annual Total Return %	-16.0	-15.4	51.8	45.7	29.7	17.2
Fiscal Year-End: December	2001	2002	2003	2004	2005	TTM
Revenue $Mil	10,506	10,501	11,642	20,767	26,485	26,485
Net Income $Mil	755	870	1,078	1,964	2,731	2,731
Earnings Per Share $	0.77	0.92	1.17	1.39	1.68	1.68
Shares Outstanding Mil	972	945	919	1,398	1,609	1,584
Return on Equity %	14.5	15.7	15.0	10.2	13.6	13.6
Net Margin %	7.2	8.3	9.3	9.5	10.3	10.3
Asset Turnover	0.2	0.2	0.2	0.1	0.2	0.2
Financial Leverage	9.5	9.3	8.4	8.0	7.8	7.8

Valuation Ratios	Stock	Rel to Industry	Rel to S&P 500
Price/Earnings	20.1	1.3	1.0
Price/Book	2.7	1.4	0.7
Price/Sales	2.0	1.2	0.7
Price/Cash Flow	—	—	—

Major Fund Holders	% of Fund Assets
Fidelity Canada	4.98
Cookson Peirce Core Equity	2.44
Leuthold Select Industries	2.17
ING International Capital Appreciation I	1.81

Thesis By Dafina Dunmore, 11-22-06 Stock Price as of Analysis: $33.33

Manulife boasts an impressive distribution force in the United States, Canada, and Asia. This gives the firm tremendous scale and earns it a narrow economic moat, in our opinion. Our fair value estimate is $29 per share.

Manulife's vast agent distribution network helps the firm win customers and earns it the narrowest of moats. In general, life insurance products are not actively sought by consumers; they are sold by life insurance agents. We think this places a great deal of importance on life insurance firms' distribution channels. Manulife enjoys one of the largest independent agencies in Canada, and its John Hancock acquisition gives it strong name recognition in the United States. The insurer also benefits from a robust distribution force in Asia that boasts more than 22,000 agents.

Thanks to the John Hancock acquisition, Manulife generates more than half of its earnings from wealth-management and life insurance products in the United States. After successfully integrating John Hancock, Manulife has continuously expanded its share of the highly fragmented variable annuity market from 2.9% in 2004 to 3.3%. We expect industry sales to slow, given the saturation of savvy guarantee products. However, we think Manulife can maintain its market share. Canadian equity markets are more important to the adequacy of Manulife's reserves than U.S. market performance because variable annuity funds are not reinsured as they are in the United States.

The long-term care industry, where Manulife is a market leader, continues to be challenging and unpredictable. However, we think the innovation and simplicity of Manulife's products will allow it to expand this business relative to its peers.

Manulife is well positioned to benefit from the rapidly growing and lightly penetrated Asian life insurance market. However, China has been a tough insurance market for most foreign companies, as the top three domestic players retain a 95% market share. Along with American International Group, Manulife is one of the best-positioned foreign insurers to take advantage of the robust market opportunity, in our opinion, given its massive distribution force and strong distribution relationship with the world's largest bank, Mitsubishi UFJ Financial Group.

200 Bloor Street East
Toronto, ON M4W 1E5
www.manulife.com

Growth [NA]	2002	2003	2004	2005
Revenue %	1.9	-0.2	63.4	18.8
Earnings/Share %	21.0	14.9	9.4	12.4
Book Value/Share %	8.7	9.0	63.6	-11.9
Dividends/Share %	—	—	—	—

Profitability [NA]	2003	2004	2005	TTM
Return on Assets %	1.8	1.3	1.8	1.8
Oper Cash Flow $Mil	1,873	4,216	6,776	—
- Cap Spending $Mil	—	—	—	—
= Free Cash Flow $Mil	—	—	—	—

Financial Health [NA]	2003	2004	2005	12-31-05
Long-term Debt $Mil	—	—	—	—
Total Equity $Mil	7,177	19,251	20,037	20,037
Debt/Equity Ratio	—	—	—	—

Data as of 12-29-06

Markel MKL

	Rating	Fair Value	Last Close	Consider Buy	Consider Sell	Yield %
	★★★	$525.00	$480.10	$404.80	$657.80	0.00

Industry	Business Risk	Moat Size	Investment Style	Sector
Insurance (Property)	Average	Narrow	Mid Value	Financial Services

Company Profile

Markel sells specialty insurance, which covers unusual risks that competitors won't insure. Its excess and surplus products include restaurant, bar, and product-liability insurance. Its specialty-admitted products cover summer camps, yachts, and sports camps. Markel International covers difficult-to-insure risks like marine cargo, prize indemnity, and computer crime; it also owns a Lloyd's of London syndicate. Products are sold through independent brokers.

Management   Stewardship Grade [A]

We think Markel is one of the best-managed insurers. Its incentive structure is commendable, and we see this repeatedly manifested in disciplined and patient underwriting and investment decisions. Executive bonuses are awarded on the basis of five-year average compound growth in book value per share. This mandates value creation; book value growth demands strong underwriting and investing results. Management must clear a high bar—no bonus is paid if book value growth is less than 11%. A 250% bonus requires 24% compound growth, which would make Markel 3 times larger. Directors and executives collectively own about 10% of the company, so they have a strong and compounding incentive to create shareholder value.

4521 Highwoods Parkway   www.markelcorp.com
Glen Allen, VA 23060-6148

Growth [D+]	2002	2003	2004	2005
Revenue %	26.7	18.2	8.1	-2.7
Earnings/Share %	NMF	60.9	33.3	-9.8
Book Value/Share %	-7.4	17.1	19.3	3.8
Dividends/Share %	NMF	NMF	NMF	NMF

Profitability [C-]	2003	2004	2005	TTM
Return on Assets %	1.4	1.8	1.5	3.9
Oper Cash Flow $Mil	631	691	551	—
- Cap Spending $Mil	8	7	29	—
= Free Cash Flow $Mil	—	—	—	—

Financial Health [NA]	2003	2004	2005	09-30-06
Long-term Debt $Mil				
Total Equity $Mil	1,382	1,657	1,705	1,975
Debt/Equity Ratio	—	—	—	—

Competition

	Market Cap $Mil	12 Mo Trailing Sales $Mil	Price/Cash Flow	Return On Assets %	Debt/Equity	Total Return % 1 Yr	3 Yr
Markel	4,639	2,448	—	3.9	—	51.4	23.4
St. Paul Travelers Compan	37,047	24,802	—	2.8	—	22.9	13.7
ZURRY							

Price Volatility

	2001	2002	2003	2004	2005	2006
Annual $Price High	213.25	222.03	279.00	365.00	373.00	494.00
Low	159.75	171.10	201.50	252.00	307.41	315.50
Annual Total Return %	-0.7	14.4	23.4	43.6	-12.9	51.4

Fiscal Year-End: December	2001	2002	2003	2004	2005	TTM
Revenue $Mil	1,397	1,770	2,092	2,262	2,200	2,448
Net Income $Mil	-126	75	123	165	148	394
Earnings Per Share $	-14.73	7.65	12.31	16.41	14.80	39.52
Shares Outstanding Mil	9	10	10	10	10	10
Return on Equity %	-11.6	6.5	8.9	10.0	8.7	20.0
Net Margin %	-9.0	4.3	5.9	7.3	6.7	16.1
Asset Turnover	0.2	0.2	0.2	0.2	0.2	0.2
Financial Leverage	5.9	6.4	6.2	5.7	5.8	5.1

Valuation Ratios	Stock	Rel to Industry	Rel to S&P 500
Price/Earnings	12.1	0.8	0.6
Price/Book	2.3	1.4	0.6
Price/Sales	1.9	1.4	0.7
Price/Cash Flow	—	—	—

Major Fund Holders	% of Fund Assets
FBR Small Cap	11.62
Wisdom Inv	7.10
Maxim Ariel SmallCap Value	5.55
Ariel	4.85

Thesis By Justin Fuller, CFA, 12-11-06 Stock Price as of Analysis: $456.49

Markel's expert underwriting and keen investment acumen have delivered pleasing long-term returns for shareholders and, in our opinion, garner the insurer a narrow economic moat. We think Markel shares are worth $525 each.

Markel's underwriters focus on developing expertise in speciality insurance products that are too small or too difficult for many larger rivals to underwrite. As a result, Markel's policies are somewhat sheltered from the fierce pricing competition that often plagues standard insurance markets. And since Markel's underwriters have long had a beachhead in speciality insurance, many clients value their expertise, which helps the insurer earn small price premiums.

In addition, since more than 30% of each underwriter's total compensation is contingent upon the product generating underwriting profits, underwriters are compelled to refuse business that doesn't meet Markel's rigid pricing criteria. Not surprisingly, in six out of the last 10 years—which include three years of heavy catastrophe losses—Markel's combined ratio was below 100%.

Markel augments its solid underwriting with a prudent investment style that has helped management to expand book value per share at an average of 28% annually over the past decade. We are particularly impressed by management's approach to equity investments, where it seeks to purchase attractively priced businesses with good returns on capital, talented management, and ample reinvestment opportunities. Since its time horizon is measured in decades, not months, the firm can afford to be patient and invest only when the iron is hot. And because of its long holding period, Markel benefits from the effects of compounding, providing an even bigger boost to book value growth.

Management's success in public equity investments has led Markel to begin making private-equity investments, recently acquiring an interest in First Market Bank and AMF Bakery Systems. We think transactions in private companies are often made at lower valuations, which fosters higher expected returns for long-term owners. In addition, we think these investments will help Markel to build relationships with executives who share the firm's long-term outlook, which we expect will lead Markel to other attractive investment opportunities, albeit not immediately. If this strategy sounds reminiscent of Berkshire Hathaway's long-ago tilt toward private investments, that's because it is—and in our view, that's great.

Marriott International A MAR

Data as of 12-29-06

	Rating	Fair Value	Last Close	Consider Buy	Consider Sell	Yield %
	★	$37.00	$47.72	$28.50	$46.40	0.50

Industry	Business Risk	Moat Size	Investment Style	Sector
Hotels	Average	Narrow	Large Growth	Consumer Services

Company Profile
Marriott International's rapid expansion overseas has made it one of the most recognized hotels in the world. The firm franchises or operates more than 2,800 hotels comprising almost 510,000 rooms in 67 countries. Marriott's brands--including Ritz-Carlton, Renaissance, Marriott Hotels & Resorts, Residence Inn, Courtyard, Fairfield Inn, SpringHill Suites, and TownePlace Suites--cover a wide spectrum of customer tastes.

Management — Stewardship Grade [B]
Marriott management prefers to keep the chief executive role in the family. J.W. Marriott Jr. took over the title from his father in 1972, after about two decades of internal management experience. He owns about 13% of shares outstanding, and all executives combined own about 15% of the company. He made more than $2.5 million in total compensation in 2005, which was an increase of about 8% from the prior year. We think the raise is justified, as Marriott's operations in 2005 showed substantial improvement. The CEO is 73 but has yet to announce any formal plans to retire. His possible successors include COO William Shaw. Management is committed to improving corporate governance by initiating annual elections of board members and majority voting.

10400 Fernwood Road
Bethesda, MD 20817
www.marriott.com

Competition

	Market Cap $Mil	12 Mo Trailing Sales $Mil	Price/Cash Flow	Return On Assets%	Debt/Equity	Total Return% 1 Yr	3 Yr
Marriott International A	18,868	11,720	20.9	7.5	0.6	43.4	28.2
Hilton Hotels	13,493	7,013	42.8	2.8	2.4	45.6	27.7
Starwood Hotels & Resorts	13,250	5,923	58.1	10.7	0.9	21.8	31.0

Price Volatility
Monthly Price High/Low — Relative Strength to S&P 500

Annual $Price High/Low	25.25 / 13.65	23.23 / 13.13	23.60 / 14.28	32.00 / 20.32	35.39 / 29.01	48.31 / 32.32
	2001	2002	2003	2004	2005	2006
Annual Total Return %	-3.2	-18.5	41.6	37.2	7.0	43.4

Fiscal Year-End: December	2001	2002	2003	2004	2005	TTM
Revenue $Mil	7,768	8,415	9,014	10,099	11,550	11,720
Net Income $Mil	236	277	502	596	669	625
Earnings Per Share $	0.92	1.10	1.03	1.24	1.45	1.41
Shares Outstanding Mil	—	—	465	453	433	395
Return on Equity %	6.8	7.8	13.1	14.6	20.6	23.1
Net Margin %	3.0	3.3	5.6	5.9	5.8	5.3
Asset Turnover	0.9	1.0	1.1	1.2	1.4	1.4
Financial Leverage	2.6	2.3	2.1	2.1	2.6	3.1

Valuation Ratios	Stock	Rel to Industry	Rel to S&P 500
Price/Earnings	28.9	1.2	1.4
Price/Book	7.0	1.2	1.7
Price/Sales	1.6	0.5	0.6
Price/Cash Flow	20.9	0.6	1.4

Major Fund Holders	% of Fund Assets
Wells Fargo Advantage Endeavor Select A	4.34
W.P. Stewart & Co Growth	3.85
William Blair Large Cap Growth N	3.83
TA IDEX Transamerica Balanced A	3.56

Growth [B-]

	2002	2003	2004	2005
Revenue %	8.3	7.1	12.0	14.4
Earnings/Share %	19.6	-6.8	21.0	16.5
Book Value/Share %	4.7	-44.8	8.3	-17.3
Dividends/Share %	7.8	7.3	11.9	21.2

Profitability [B]

	2003	2004	2005	TTM
Return on Assets %	6.1	6.9	7.8	7.5
Oper Cash Flow $Mil	403	891	837	901
- Cap Spending $Mil	210	181	780	373
= Free Cash Flow $Mil	193	710	57	528

Financial Health [B-]

	2003	2004	2005	08-31-06
Long-term Debt $Mil	—	836	1,681	1,622
Total Equity $Mil	3,838	4,081	3,252	2,702
Debt/Equity Ratio	—	0.2	0.5	0.6

Thesis By Jeremy Glaser, 12-08-06 Stock Price as of Analysis: $46.39

Marriott International's premier brands and experienced management team make it one of the best firms in the business. Low capital requirements, a booming travel market, and an aggressive push into international markets has put the company on solid footing for the coming years.

Marriott signs long-term management contracts in lieu of owning hotels outright, alleviating many of the fixed costs that plague competitors with ownership models. For example, the arrangement with partner Host Hotels & Resorts keeps properties on Host's balance sheet while Marriott collects the management fees. Managing properties is lower risk than owning, since the long-term agreement guarantees a base fee through thick and thin. Incentive fees, which are earned when hotels reach certain profitability thresholds, allow Marriott to capture some of the upside of a bustling economy.

From Residence Inn to Ritz-Carlton, Marriott controls some of the strongest brands in the industry. Travelers are drawn to the familiarity of the properties and by the Marriott Rewards loyalty program, which is one of the industry's largest. The company has leveraged strong brand recognition in the United States to expand overseas: More than 15% of total rooms are outside of the Americas, up from next to nothing in the early 1990s. Over the next three years, management plans to increase international rooms by 35% as the firm makes further inroads into growing Asian and consolidating European markets. Successful foreign expansion will be crucial to the firm's growth, since many of these new rooms will be in lucrative full-service hotels, a market that is largely mature in North America.

Copious amounts of free cash flow allow Marriott great flexibility to finance new opportunities internally. We are heartened to see Marriott's commitment to keeping its brands fresh by shedding failing properties and further polishing the luxury Ritz-Carlton and midscale Courtyard brands. Investment in the Marriott Vacation Club time-share business sparked growth during three years of weak travel.

However, we still believe Marriott should move cautiously with time-shares, as the industry is becoming increasingly competitive and time-shares require a larger cash outlay than the scalable management business. We are encouraged that Marriott is committed to building future time-shares in joint ventures, which will reduce capital requirements and spread risk. Marriott's business has proved it can endure the worst industry conditions.

Data as of 12-29-06

Marsh & McLennan Companies MMC

Rating ★★★★★	Fair Value $43.00	Last Close $30.66	Consider Buy $33.20	Consider Sell $53.90	Yield % 2.22

Company Profile
Marsh & McLennan is a professional services firm that offers risk management advice and transaction services via four major operating units. Marsh Inc. provides risk and insurance services, Putnam offers investment-management services to institutional and individual investors, Mercer Consulting supplies a variety of human resources and other consulting services, and Kroll provides investigative and security consulting services.

Management   Stewardship Grade [B]
We think Marsh & McLennan has developed a great leadership team. CEO Michael Cherkasky and other leaders have done a remarkable job addressing regulatory issues. We believe the current leadership team is also well-suited for the growth period that lies ahead. We are pleased with some recent governance enhancements, which include minimum ownership targets for officers and directors. Anti-takeover defenses like a staggered board remain blemishes, but we like the CEO. We base our B Stewardship Grade on the firm as it exists today, not as it existed entering the 2004 crisis.

Senior officers and directors as a group hold roughly $25 million in stock, and retain an indirect interest (via options) in another $125 million. The total comes to less than 1% of Marsh & McLennan's market capitalization. We'd like the managers to have a larger stake in the firm. However, we think it is satisfactory at this stage of recovery from the 2004 crisis. New senior leaders have not had much time to accumulate a large stake, but other incentives work to align management's interests with shareholders'. For example, Brian Storms, a charismatic and forceful arrival now leading Marsh, has a high share of his potential compensation linked to financial performance.

1166 Avenue Of The Americas   www.mmc.com
New York, NY 10036

Growth [D+]	2002	2003	2004	2005
Revenue %	5.3	10.8	5.0	-0.9
Earnings/Share %	44.1	14.7	-88.3	124.2
Book Value/Share %	-0.2	10.4	-4.7	3.6
Dividends/Share %	5.8	36.7	-33.6	-31.5

Profitability [B+]	2003	2004	2005	TTM
Return on Assets %	10.2	1.0	2.3	4.5
Oper Cash Flow $Mil	1,867	2,069	399	—
- Cap Spending $Mil	436	376	345	—
= Free Cash Flow $Mil	—	—	—	—

Financial Health [NA]	2003	2004	2005	09-30-06
Long-term Debt $Mil	—	—	—	—
Total Equity $Mil	5,451	5,056	5,360	6,204
Debt/Equity Ratio	—	—	—	—

Industry Insurance (General)	Business Risk Average	Moat Size Wide	Investment Style Large Core	Sector Financial Services

Competition

	Market Cap $Mil	12 Mo Trailing Sales $Mil	Price/Cash Flow	Return On Assets%	Debt/ Equity	Total Return% 1 Yr	3 Yr
Marsh & McLennan Companies	16,897	11,715	—	4.5	—	-1.2	-11.9
Franklin Resources	27,932	5,051	—	13.3	—	17.8	30.3
Aon	11,113	10,006	—	2.4	—	-0.1	16.2

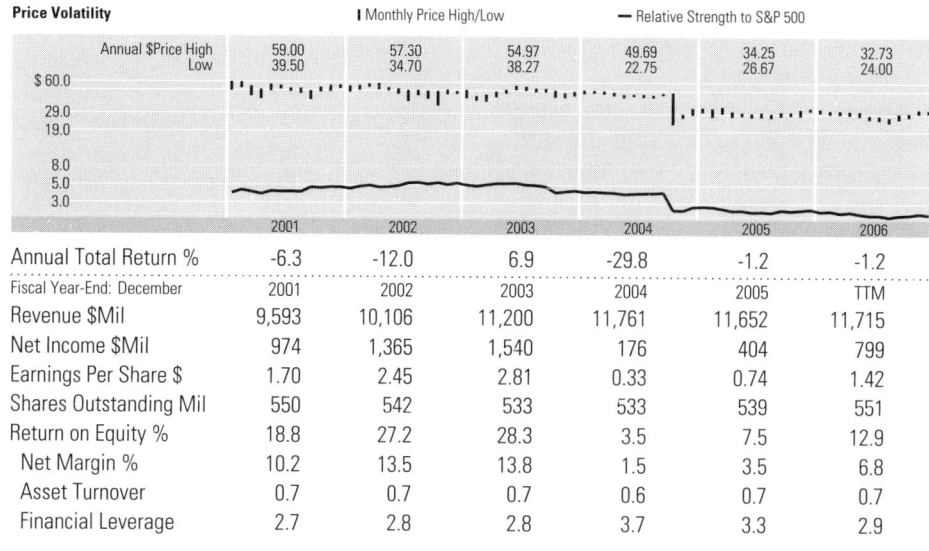

	2001	2002	2003	2004	2005	TTM
Annual Total Return %	-6.3	-12.0	6.9	-29.8	-1.2	-1.2
Fiscal Year-End: December	2001	2002	2003	2004	2005	TTM
Revenue $Mil	9,593	10,106	11,200	11,761	11,652	11,715
Net Income $Mil	974	1,365	1,540	176	404	799
Earnings Per Share $	1.70	2.45	2.81	0.33	0.74	1.42
Shares Outstanding Mil	550	542	533	533	539	551
Return on Equity %	18.8	27.2	28.3	3.5	7.5	12.9
Net Margin %	10.2	13.5	13.8	1.5	3.5	6.8
Asset Turnover	0.7	0.7	0.7	0.6	0.7	0.7
Financial Leverage	2.7	2.8	2.8	3.7	3.3	2.9

Valuation Ratios	Stock	Rel to Industry	Rel to S&P 500
Price/Earnings	28.7	1.9	1.4
Price/Book	2.7	1.4	0.7
Price/Sales	1.4	0.8	0.5
Price/Cash Flow	—	—	—

Major Fund Holders	% of Fund Assets
Dreyfus Premier Select J	4.94
Legg Mason Partners Capital I	4.58
Dreyfus Premier Blue Chip J	4.10
AIM Financial Services Inv	3.74

Thesis By Bill Bergman, 12-15-06 Stock Price as of Analysis:

As Marsh & McLennan's recovery from regulatory woes continues, we think its wide moat--owing to brand leverage and the firm's broad perspective on solving customer risk management problems--has been reinforced by new, motivated leadership. Our fair value estimate is $43 per share.

Marsh & McLennan has built one of the largest risk management services firms in the world. In recent years, investigations into insurance industry compensation methods and mutual fund trading practices prompted a regulatory crisis for many firms. For Marsh & McLennan, a civil suit from the New York attorney general included charges of bid-rigging, prompting significant changes in business methods as well as senior management turnover. New leadership initiatives have borne fruit in recent renewed sales momentum and margin expansion. Returns should improve in years ahead.

Over the past decade, Marsh & McLennan has developed healthy underlying synergies among its insurance brokerage and consulting brands. For example, customers are attached to insurance broker Marsh, in part, by the human resources and specialty consulting services purchased from Mercer. The 2004 crisis slashed into these synergies. It proved especially untimely for the mid-2004 acquisition of Kroll, a unique security services firm and a great fit with other subsidiaries. Yet, a sufficient mass of customers remain attached, and the firm is winning new business again. Communication and data systems have been a key to exploiting cross-selling synergies, and Marsh & McLennan's operations people provide a competitive advantage.

Marsh retains fundamental competitive strengths in its industry expertise and customer focus. It works to understand the risk management needs of its individual clients at least as well as it knows insurance products. Marsh stresses "pull" solutions to attract and retain customers, not "pushing" sales of standardized policies. We like the broad perspective, which helps it find creative new revenue sources and to react and prosper amidst competitive threats. Traditionally focused on larger customers, Marsh has a well-organized initiative to penetrate the middle market. It won't be easy, but we believe this is another positive recent development.

Marsh & McLennan has explored the possibility of selling Putnam, its investment management subsidiary. This is a relatively profitable business, but we believe any synergies with other units are limited. Asset outflows have recently ceased, and the time is ripe for a possible sale.

Martin Marietta Materials MLM

Data as of 12-29-06

	Rating	Fair Value	Last Close	Consider Buy	Consider Sell	Yield %
	★★★	$98.00	$103.91	$75.60	$122.80	0.97

Company Profile

Martin Marietta, a leading aggregate producer in the United States, has a strong presence in the Southeast, Central, and Midwest regions. The company's 100 distribution sites support long-haul rail and water transport of aggregates--rocks, sand, and gravel used mostly in concrete and asphalt paving. Its smaller specialty product segment--less than 10% of sales--produces magnesia-based chemicals, dolomitic lime used to produce steel, and structural composite products.

Management   Stewardship Grade [B]

Stephen Zelnak, Martin Marietta's CEO since 1993, used acquisitions to achieve a leading market position in a very fragmented industry (the largest five producers account for roughly one fourth of the market). Zelnak is also chairman of the board, presiding over the remaining independent members. Management pay is in line with industry practices and provides a reasonable balance between salary and variable compensation. Management and directors own 2% of outstanding shares, helping align their interest with those of outside shareholders. Regarding execution, we are most impressed with management's ability to streamline operations in acquired companies. Over the past couple of years, Martin Marietta has enjoyed significant margin expansion due to both pricing and efficiency gains. Numerous projects have paid off, especially the firm's forays into Nova Scotia and the Bahamas, which are remotely serving coastal markets by water transport. Deeming most recent acquisition opportunities overpriced, management has stepped up its return of cash to shareholders, which we highly encourage.

2710 Wycliff Road
Raleigh, NC 27607-3033
www.martinmarietta.com

Growth [B-]	2002	2003	2004	2005
Revenue %	1.0	6.1	6.1	16.1
Earnings/Share %	-19.2	7.9	39.3	53.4
Book Value/Share %	4.5	3.8	3.1	4.6
Dividends/Share %	3.6	19.0	10.1	13.2

Profitability [A-]	2003	2004	2005	TTM
Return on Assets %	4.0	5.5	7.9	9.1
Oper Cash Flow $Mil	277	267	318	319
- Cap Spending $Mil	121	163	221	278
= Free Cash Flow $Mil	157	103	96	42

Financial Health [A]	2003	2004	2005	09-30-06
Long-term Debt $Mil	717	714	709	580
Total Equity $Mil	1,130	1,153	1,174	1,262
Debt/Equity Ratio	0.6	0.6	0.6	0.5

Industry	Business Risk	Moat Size	Investment Style	Sector
Mining (Nonmetal)	Average	Narrow	Mid Growth	Industrial Materials

Competition	Market Cap $Mil	12 Mo Trailing Sales $Mil	Price/Cash Flow	Return On Assets%	Debt/ Equity	Total Return% 1 Yr	3 Yr
Martin Marietta Materials	4,691	2,185	14.7	9.1	0.5	36.9	32.6
Rinker Group ADR	12,933	5,108	13.7	16.7	0.3	28.6	48.6
Vulcan Materials	8,486	3,281	15.1	13.0	0.2	35.1	26.4

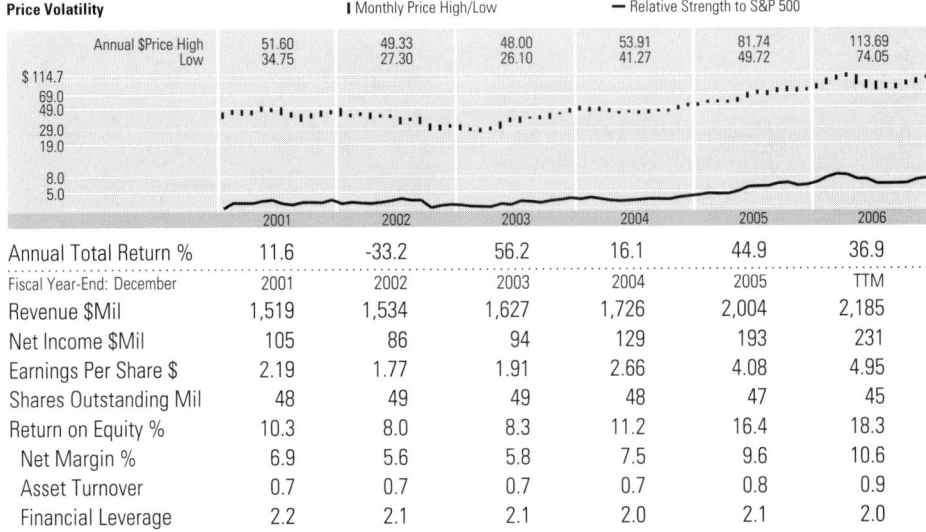

Price Volatility — Monthly Price High/Low — Relative Strength to S&P 500

| Annual $Price High | 51.60 | 49.33 | 48.00 | 53.91 | 81.74 | 113.69 |
| Low | 34.75 | 27.30 | 26.10 | 41.27 | 49.72 | 74.05 |

	2001	2002	2003	2004	2005	2006
Annual Total Return %	11.6	-33.2	56.2	16.1	44.9	36.9

Fiscal Year-End: December

	2001	2002	2003	2004	2005	TTM
Revenue $Mil	1,519	1,534	1,627	1,726	2,004	2,185
Net Income $Mil	105	86	94	129	193	231
Earnings Per Share $	2.19	1.77	1.91	2.66	4.08	4.95
Shares Outstanding Mil	48	49	49	48	47	45
Return on Equity %	10.3	8.0	8.3	11.2	16.4	18.3
Net Margin %	6.9	5.6	5.8	7.5	9.6	10.6
Asset Turnover	0.7	0.7	0.7	0.7	0.8	0.9
Financial Leverage	2.2	2.1	2.1	2.0	2.1	2.0

Valuation Ratios	Stock	Rel to Industry	Rel to S&P 500
Price/Earnings	21.1	1.2	1.0
Price/Book	3.7	0.9	0.9
Price/Sales	2.1	0.6	0.7
Price/Cash Flow	14.7	1.0	1.0

Major Fund Holders	% of Fund Assets
SunAmerica Focused Mid-Cap Value A	5.36
FAM Equity-Income Inv	2.80
SunAmerica Focused Mid-Cap Growth A	2.61
Azzad Ethical Mid Cap	2.51

Thesis By Matthew Warren, 12-14-06 Stock Price as of Analysis: $100.75

The quarry business exhibits sound fundamentals including significant entry barriers, pricing power, and steady demand. Because Martin Marietta also enjoys scale benefits, we think it is protected by a narrow economic moat.

Barriers to entry in the aggregate business can be nearly insurmountable because strategically located quarries are difficult to replicate. NIMBY--not in my back yard--objections are pervasive, as community groups are loath to accept a quarry's noise, dust, and traffic. Even if a potential entrant successfully negotiates the multiyear permitting process, substantial up-front investments are required to fund capital equipment and site development.

Well-entrenched players also benefit from the incentive to source from the nearest quarry. The economics are simple: Aggregates cost about $7 per ton--an average that varies widely between regions depending on local scarcity--at the plant site but incur an additional $0.10-$0.15 per ton for every mile traveled by truck. Transport costs effectively reduce a quarry's prime market to a 50-mile radius. And with three fourths of the firm's business derived from local projects, supply constraints typically lead to substantial pricing power.

But not all markets are geologically blessed with plentiful stone deposits, and regions facing shortages, like the coastal Southeast, are forced to use long-haul distribution. One fourth of Martin Marietta's aggregate volumes reach these markets by rail or water, moving through one of the industry's largest distribution networks, comprising 100 facilities. These incremental sales enable Martin Marietta to better utilize existing quarry capacity. The problem lies in the added exposure to cyclical swings in transportation costs and availability.

Aggregate shipments exhibit much less volatility than other construction-supply businesses because half of sales are tied to public infrastructure projects including highways. These aggregate-intensive endeavors are politically popular because of the numerous jobs they create and the tangible benefits they provide to constituents. Also, dedicated federal funding from gasoline taxes--which require state matching funds--is marching ever higher, providing an anchor of support for large project planners. Additional state and local funds are more directly tied to tax receipts and are therefore more cyclical in nature. Relatively steady demand and pricing power protect aggregate producers from the losses commonly faced by asset-intensive businesses during downturns.

Data as of 12-29-06

MasterCard MA

Rating	Fair Value	Last Close	Consider Buy	Consider Sell	Yield %
★★★	$105.00	$98.49	$81.00	$131.60	0.09

Company Profile

MasterCard manages a group of global payment card brands, including MasterCard, Maestro, and Cirrus, which it licenses to financial institutions that issue cards to their customers. The firm acts as the payment processor by facilitating the authorization, clearing, and settlement of transactions on its proprietary networks. At the end of 2005, there were almost 750 million MasterCard-branded cards issued, which generated about $1.7 trillion of transactions during the year.

Management   Stewardship Grade [C]

CEO Robert Selander has been at the helm of MasterCard since 1997. We think management will need to prove its mettle over the next few years as it deals with the tricky transition from being a bank-owned association to a publicly held, profit-focused enterprise. Plus, according to industry data, MasterCard has not gained market share over the past few years in an industry where we think market share matters, so we are hesitant to heap praise on the management team. We also have some reservations about the firm's governance and ownership structure. Outside investors now own roughly 49% of the equity and 83% of the voting power. But we believe this voting power is toothless for any major corporate decisions, given the various supermajority voting provisions and antitakeover measures the firm has elected. MasterCard's former owners, the member banks, also retained a nonvoting equity stake of about 41% and the power to elect three directors. Because these banks are MasterCard's customers, we see inherent conflicts of interest in the structure. The firm also established a charitable foundation that owns the remaining 10% of the outstanding stock and controls the remaining 17% of the voting power. We believe this foundation was simply another way for MasterCard to keep control of the firm close to home.

2000 Purchase Street
Purchase, NY 10577
www.mastercard.com

Growth [B]	2002	2003	2004	2005
Revenue %	17.4	17.9	16.2	13.3
Earnings/Share %	NMF	NMF	NMF	NMF
Book Value/Share %	—	—	—	—
Dividends/Share %	NMF	NMF	NMF	NMF

Profitability [B-]	2003	2004	2005	TTM
Return on Assets %	-13.3	7.3	7.2	-0.9
Oper Cash Flow $Mil	190	344	273	371
- Cap Spending $Mil	76	31	44	55
= Free Cash Flow $Mil	114	313	229	316

Financial Health [A]	2003	2004	2005	09-30-06
Long-term Debt $Mil	746	698	645	677
Total Equity $Mil	699	975	1,169	2,320
Debt/Equity Ratio	1.1	0.7	0.6	0.3

Industry	Business Risk	Moat Size	Investment Style	Sector
Data Processing	Average	Wide	Large Growth	Business Services

Competition	Market Cap $Mil	12 Mo Trailing Sales $Mil	Price/Cash Flow	Return On Assets%	Debt/ Equity	Total Return% 1 Yr	3 Yr
MasterCard	13,293	3,203	35.8	-0.9	0.3	—	—
Morgan Stanley	86,198	32,195	—	0.8	—	45.9	14.8
American Express	73,094	26,507	—	2.9	—	19.1	14.2

Price Volatility — Monthly Price High/Low — Relative Strength to S&P 500

Annual $Price High/Low: 108.60 / 40.20

Annual Total Return %	2001	2002	2003	2004	2005	2006
	—	—	—	—	—	—

Fiscal Year-End: December	2001	2002	2003	2004	2005	TTM
Revenue $Mil	1,611	1,892	2,231	2,593	2,938	3,203
Net Income $Mil	142	116	-386	238	267	-44
Earnings Per Share $	—	—	—	—	—	—
Shares Outstanding Mil	—	—	—	—	—	135
Return on Equity %	23.4	11.4	-55.2	24.4	22.8	-1.9
Net Margin %	8.8	6.2	-17.3	9.2	9.1	-1.4
Asset Turnover	1.1	0.8	0.8	0.8	0.8	0.7
Financial Leverage	2.5	2.2	4.2	3.3	3.2	2.1

Valuation Ratios	Stock	Rel to Industry	Rel to S&P 500
Price/Earnings	—	—	—
Price/Book	5.7	1.1	1.4
Price/Sales	4.2	1.2	1.4
Price/Cash Flow	35.8	1.7	2.5

Major Fund Holders	% of Fund Assets
Destination Select Equity	3.79
RS Core Equity A	3.62
Markman Core Growth	2.88
Old Mutual Focused Z	2.84

Thesis By Ryan Batchelor, CPA, 12-12-06 Stock Price as of Analysis: $95.75

We think the strength of MasterCard's business model transcends its legal issues. The firm competes in the very attractive global consumer payment market, which should provide it with ample growth opportunities over the long term.

We view MasterCard as a brand and a transaction processor, and we're big fans of both things. The firm receives more than 70% of its revenue from its processing functions (operations fees), and the remainder comes from assessments it charges its members to use the MasterCard brand.

MasterCard has an impressive global brand, in our opinion, bolstered by its worldwide "Priceless" marketing campaign. In our view, one of the greatest benefits of its brand strength is that MasterCard is maintaining most of its pricing power, even though its customers--generally the banks that issue cards--are getting larger and gaining more bargaining power, thanks to consolidation. We believe the firm will make up for any concessions it provides to large customers by charging higher fees to its remaining customers, which don't possess as much bargaining power.

We also like the processing business, which performs functions like authorizing charges and clearing and settling the payments between merchants' and consumers' banks. MasterCard charges various fees for performing these services, which have averaged about $0.15 per transaction during 2006. These fees are analogous to a small tax that MasterCard receives every time a consumer swipes his or her card. And we believe that consumers worldwide will be swiping their cards more than ever.

We see the global payment industry continuing to move away from cash and checks, which have historically dominated, toward electronic forms of payment, including cards. We believe this shift, along with increased acceptance of cards for almost any type of payment, paints a picture of a very fertile field of long-term growth for MasterCard.

Despite its strengths, MasterCard faces some serious legal issues. Most of the lawsuits relate to alleged anticompetitive behavior by the firm in determining "interchange fees"--fees that merchants pay to the card-issuing banks--and by allegedly stifling competition by not allowing competitors like American Express and Morgan Stanley's Discover to issue their cards through banks that issue MasterCards. We've estimated the exposure to these legal issues in our valuation model, which shaves about 10% off the value of the firm.

© 2007 Morningstar, Inc. All rights reserved. Intended for United States residents only, this report is for information purposes and should not be considered a solicitation to buy or sell any security. Download your free reports at http://www.morningstar.com/goto/2007Stocks500

Data as of 12-29-06

Maxim Integrated Products MXIM

	Rating	Fair Value	Last Close	Consider Buy	Consider Sell	Yield %
	★★★★★	$52.00	$30.62	$40.10	$65.20	1.84

Company Profile
Maxim Integrated Products makes high-performance analog and mixed-signal integrated circuits. The firm's extensive portfolio of products serves a host of analog-intensive applications, including power management and data conversion. Maxim supplies its diverse array of about 5,000 circuits to a broad base of customers in end markets including communications, computing, and industrial. Roughly 70% of the firm's sales are based outside the United States.

Management
Stewardship Grade [B]

Company founder John Gifford has been president, chairman, and CEO since Maxim's inception in 1983. Gifford is an esteemed semiconductor industry veteran, having cofounded Advanced Micro Devices before starting Maxim. Executive base salaries are very modest compared with industry norms, as a large percentage of pay is tied to performance through bonuses and stock-option grants. This sort of performance pay structure is appealing to us, but we find Maxim's stock-option issuance to be a bit more liberal than some of its chip peers'. Maxim is one of the many companies that has been under investigation by the Securities and Exchange Commission and the state of California for its option-granting practices. The company had not filed its September-quarter financials as of early December.

120 San Gabriel Drive
Sunnyvale, CA 94086
www.maxim-ic.com

Growth [C]	2002	2003	2004	2005	
Revenue %	-35.0	12.5	24.8	16.2	
Earnings/Share %	-21.5	24.7	31.9	31.7	
Book Value/Share %	-15.9	24.1	-0.8	25.0	
Dividends/Share %	NMF	NMF	300.0	18.8	

Profitability [A+]	2003	2004	2005	TTM
Return on Assets %	13.1	16.5	18.0	15.3
Oper Cash Flow $Mil	582	695	699	598
- Cap Spending $Mil	84	232	132	117
= Free Cash Flow $Mil	498	464	567	482

Financial Health [A+]	2003	2004	2005	03-31-06
Long-term Debt $Mil	—	—	—	—
Total Equity $Mil	2,070	2,112	2,584	2,608
Debt/Equity Ratio	—	—	—	—

Industry	Business Risk	Moat Size	Investment Style	Sector
Semiconductor	Average	Wide	Mid Growth	Hardware

Competition	Market Cap $Mil	12 Mo Trailing Sales $Mil	Price/Cash Flow	Return On Assets%	Debt/ Equity	Total Return% 1 Yr	3 Yr
Maxim Integrated Products	9,820	1,749	16.4	15.3	—	-14.1	-13.7
Texas Instruments	42,736	15,173	16.1	29.3	0.0	-9.8	-0.2
STMicroelectronics NV	16,457	8,882	9.2	2.1	0.0	3.0	-11.7

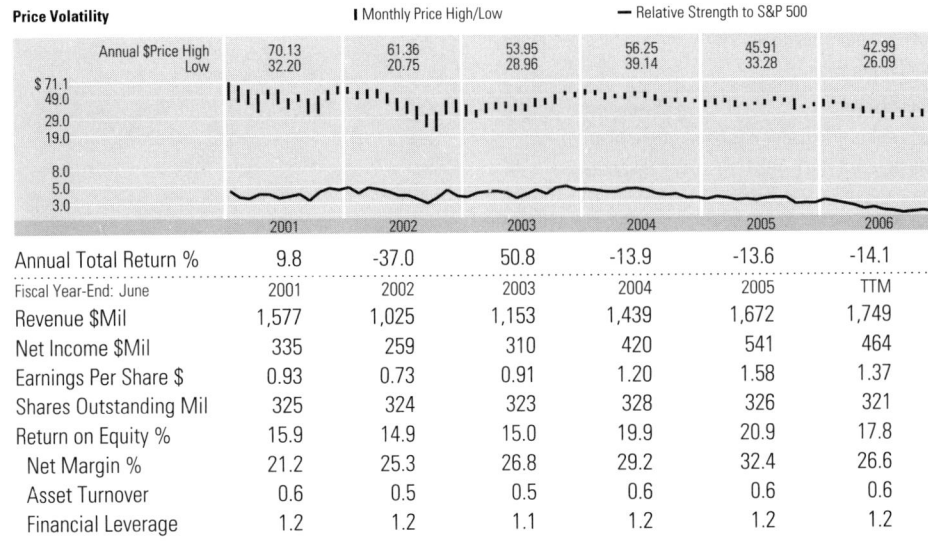

	2001	2002	2003	2004	2005	2006
Annual Total Return %	9.8	-37.0	50.8	-13.9	-13.6	-14.1
Fiscal Year-End: June	2001	2002	2003	2004	2005	TTM
Revenue $Mil	1,577	1,025	1,153	1,439	1,672	1,749
Net Income $Mil	335	259	310	420	541	464
Earnings Per Share $	0.93	0.73	0.91	1.20	1.58	1.37
Shares Outstanding Mil	325	324	323	328	326	321
Return on Equity %	15.9	14.9	15.0	19.9	20.9	17.8
Net Margin %	21.2	25.3	26.8	29.2	32.4	26.6
Asset Turnover	0.6	0.5	0.5	0.6	0.6	0.6
Financial Leverage	1.2	1.2	1.1	1.2	1.2	1.2

Valuation Ratios	Stock	Rel to Industry	Rel to S&P 500
Price/Earnings	22.4	0.8	1.1
Price/Book	3.8	1.1	0.9
Price/Sales	5.6	1.3	1.9
Price/Cash Flow	16.4	1.0	1.1

Major Fund Holders	% of Fund Assets
Fidelity Select Electronics	5.17
Fidelity Advisor Electronics T	4.96
Pin Oak Aggressive Stock	4.72
Managers 20 A	4.51

Thesis By Larry Cao, CFA, 12-13-06 Stock Price as of Analysis: $30.28

Investors looking for a semiconductor company that has rivaled Microsoft in profitability and growth need search no further.

Sophisticated chip design expertise coupled with balanced exposure to profitable niches across end markets affords Maxim Integrated Products a wide economic moat. The high-performance analog (HPA) segment is, in our view, the most attractive of the semiconductor industry, and Maxim is a clear leader in the power management area of the HPA business. Analog chip design is more labor-intensive because analog engineers do not have the equivalent of the electronic design tools that their digital peers do. The fact that major U.S. research universities haven't trained sufficient numbers of analog engineers for two decades only made these workers more valuable. As a pioneer in the HPA business, Maxim's portfolio of analog products and corps of analog engineers are the envy of the industry. The proprietary nature of analog design and long life cycle of analog chips make Maxim's product prowess last even longer. This is reflected by Maxim's industry-leading margins sustained across multiple industry cycles.

Maxim's integrated approach to product design and its continuous focus on innovation are key to an impressive growth trajectory. The company has institutionalized a new product development and launch process, showing an aptitude for identifying and capturing growth opportunities. Its integrated solutions help clients reduce design cost and time to market of their products. They are typically smaller, more power-efficient, and less costly than the chips they replace. Maxim's technical strength allowed the firm to bring these products to market ahead of the competition, further setting it apart from the crowd. In addition, management has initiated a strategy of focusing on the top 20 clients worldwide in an attempt to integrate further into clients' design processes.

We like Maxim's balanced approach to profitability and growth. The firm invests heavily in research and development to retain its lead in high-margin markets and at the same time continuously expands its presence in fast-growing markets like flat-panel displays and portable electronics. Its broad exposure to all key end markets reduces volatility in its revenue stream, lowering its risk profile. We believe long-term investors who can look beyond temporary sentiment changes in the stock market will be handsomely rewarded.

Data as of 12-29-06

MBIA MBI

	Rating	Fair Value	Last Close	Consider Buy	Consider Sell	Yield %
	★★★	$76.00	$73.06	$48.40	$91.70	1.70

Company Profile
MBIA provides financial guaranty insurance for municipal bonds and asset-backed securities. It offers an unconditional guarantee to repay the principal and interest on these securities if the issuer defaults. MBIA insures bonds sold in the primary and secondary markets, as well as those held in unit investment trusts and by mutual funds. Many MBIA customers are secure public-sector entities.

Management Stewardship Grade [B]
Senior management of MBIA is experienced and competent. We commend them for their prudent pricing and underwriting approach. However, given the lackluster performance of the business last year, we do not endorse the sizable cash bonuses paid in 2005 to the most senior managers. In our view, management's annual incentive compensation should reflect the fortunes of shareholders. Other than that, MBIA is a shareholder-friendly company in almost all other respects. MBIA's CEO must own stock worth 5 times his salary, while other senior officers must own amounts in the range of 3-4 times their salaries. As a consequence, directors and officers collectively own 4% of MBIA stock (about $350 million worth), which we consider an appropriate stake. In 2005, management repurchased 5.9 million shares at an average price of $57.88. This is substantially lower than our fair value estimate, and we think it is an excellent way to create value for shareholders.

Industry	Business Risk	Moat Size	Investment Style	Sector
Insurance (General)	Above Avg	Narrow	Mid Value	Financial Services

Competition
	Market Cap $Mil	12 Mo Trailing Sales $Mil	Price/Cash Flow	Return On Assets%	Debt/Equity	Total Return% 1 Yr	3 Yr
MBIA	9,849	2,617	—	2.2	—	23.9	9.3
Ambac Financial Group	9,450	1,845	—	4.2	—	16.5	9.6
PMI Group	3,747	1,171	—	7.6	—	15.4	8.8

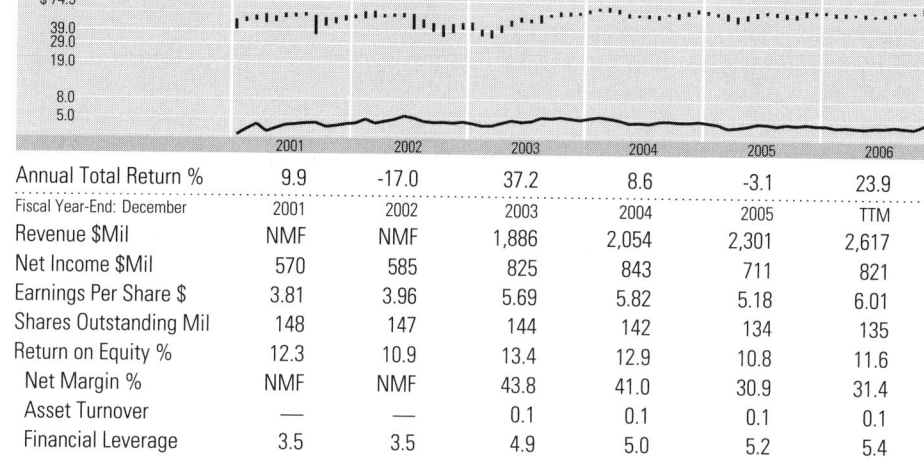

	2001	2002	2003	2004	2005	2006
Annual Total Return %	9.9	-17.0	37.2	8.6	-3.1	23.9
Fiscal Year-End: December	2001	2002	2003	2004	2005	TTM
Revenue $Mil	NMF	NMF	1,886	2,054	2,301	2,617
Net Income $Mil	570	585	825	843	711	821
Earnings Per Share $	3.81	3.96	5.69	5.82	5.18	6.01
Shares Outstanding Mil	148	147	144	142	134	135
Return on Equity %	12.3	10.9	13.4	12.9	10.8	11.6
Net Margin %	NMF	NMF	43.8	41.0	30.9	31.4
Asset Turnover	—	—	0.1	0.1	0.1	0.1
Financial Leverage	3.5	3.5	4.9	5.0	5.2	5.4

Valuation Ratios	Stock	Rel to Industry	Rel to S&P 500
Price/Earnings	12.2	0.8	0.6
Price/Book	1.4	0.7	0.3
Price/Sales	3.8	2.2	1.3
Price/Cash Flow	—	—	—

Major Fund Holders	% of Fund Assets
Matthew 25	7.94
CastleRock	7.76
Allianz OCC Value Instl	4.12
Hartford Global Financial Svcs HLS IA	3.89

113 King Street
Armonk, NY 10504
www.mbia.com

Growth [B]	2002	2003	2004	2005
Revenue %	—	NMF	8.9	12.0
Earnings/Share %	3.9	43.7	2.3	-11.0
Book Value/Share %	16.9	16.7	6.8	6.1
Dividends/Share %	13.3	17.6	20.0	16.7

Profitability [A]	2003	2004	2005	TTM
Return on Assets %	2.7	2.6	2.1	2.2
Oper Cash Flow $Mil	1,026	889	781	—
- Cap Spending $Mil	11	9	9	—
= Free Cash Flow $Mil	—	—	—	—

Financial Health [NA]	2003	2004	2005	09-30-06
Long-term Debt $Mil	—	—	—	—
Total Equity $Mil	6,150	6,559	6,592	7,057
Debt/Equity Ratio	—	—	—	—

Thesis By Jim Ryan, 11-16-06 Stock Price as of Analysis: $67.10

Long-term contracts, high entry barriers derived from AAA credit, and unique underwriting skill endow MBIA with a narrow economic moat and a prized risk-management reputation. Our fair value estimate is $76 per share.

MBIA's AAA credit rating was difficult to obtain, as it requires long-demonstrated risk-management prowess and a fortresslike balance sheet. Historically, few guarantors have been AAA rated, which has deterred many entrants due to capital requirements. As capital markets prefer AAA rated credit, MBIA received prime consideration on all new business opportunities. Furthermore, its primary product, insured municipal-bond obligations, provided real value as the cost savings were greater due to the value provided via MBIA guarantees. Expansion into other structured credit vehicles outside of its main product line further enriched corporate coffers, which produced enviable returns.

However, today there are seven AAA rated financial guarantors, and the field is getting crowded. To the detriment of MBIA, there is no cost to switch to its competitors nor does MBIA bring much to the table that the competition cannot match (of course, the competition is in the same boat). The end result is a changing market that demands more risk assumption at a lower cost. MBIA has stubbornly refused to play this game, but if the spreads don't increase sometime soon, it will have to decide to meet the market or lose share, which decreases future earned premium. To add to its woes, tight credit spreads have narrowed the size of the market as some debt self insures, while more competition, outside of the financial guaranty industry, has emerged.

Fortunately for MBIA, it benefits from a huge book of business written over the past 20 years. And Investment Management Services has demonstrated strong revenue growth, albeit at lower margins. The risk here is that MBIA is invading another space with even more competition. However, MBIA has a leg up with a portion of the market due to its existing relationships with municipal-bond trustees.

The bottom line is that competitors are chipping away at MBIA's moat. Competition has lowered return on equity to about 11% this year from 14% in 2003. Add to that the increasing risk MBIA has assumed in pursuing other sources of revenue and negative headlines over past alleged indiscretions, and the outlook darkens. We believe the market is welcoming newcomers and that MBIA's competitive advantage is weakening.

Data as of 12-29-06

McCormick & Company MKC

Rating	Fair Value	Last Close	Consider Buy	Consider Sell	Yield %
★★	$35.00	$38.56	$29.80	$46.00	1.92

Company Profile
McCormick is the global leader in manufacturing, marketing, and distributing spices, herbs, extracts, seasonings, and other flavorings. McCormick serves a customer base that includes top quick-serve restaurants, retail grocery chains, and packaged food processors, with about 40% of sales in international markets. Some of the company's best-known brands include McCormick, Old Bay, Zatarain's, and Thai Kitchen.

Management   Stewardship Grade [B]
Bob Lawless has been president of McCormick since 1996, CEO since 1997, and chairman since 1999. He started as a distribution manager for McCormick in 1977 and quickly moved up the ranks. Although we like to see the CEO and chairman positions split between two people for better corporate governance, we are encouraged by Lawless' focus on using long-term metrics like economic value added and returns on invested capital to measure company performance. We like that management's variable pay structure is truly variable; executives were paid less in 2005 to reflect the company's flat performance. McCormick has been working on reducing the number of seats that top management holds on the board. Currently, four key executives sit on the board, but over time, the firm expects to have just one person from inside the company serving as a director. The company's use of cash flow to make acquisitions, increase the dividend, and repurchase shares has served shareholders well. However, we think McCormick could improve its voting structure. Currently, there are two different share classes, with the majority of the voting rights held by employees and members of the founding family. Overall, we are encouraged by McCormick's corporate-governance initiatives.

18 Loveton Circle P.O Box 6000   www.mccormick.com
Sparks, MD 21152

Growth [D+]	2002	2003	2004	2005
Revenue %	-7.8	11.0	11.3	2.6
Earnings/Share %	20.0	17.5	2.7	2.6
Book Value/Share %	25.1	27.7	18.9	-7.9
Dividends/Share %	5.0	9.5	21.7	14.3

Profitability [A]	2003	2004	2005	TTM
Return on Assets %	9.8	9.1	9.5	8.4
Oper Cash Flow $Mil	202	350	339	331
- Cap Spending $Mil	92	70	74	85
= Free Cash Flow $Mil	110	280	265	246

Financial Health [B]	2003	2004	2005	08-31-06
Long-term Debt $Mil	449	465	464	566
Total Equity $Mil	755	890	800	917
Debt/Equity Ratio	0.6	0.5	0.6	0.6

Industry	Business Risk	Moat Size	Investment Style	Sector
Food Mfg.	Below Avg	Wide	Mid Core	Consumer Goods

Competition	Market Cap $Mil	12 Mo Trailing Sales $Mil	Price/Cash Flow	Return On Assets%	Debt/ Equity	Total Return% 1 Yr	3 Yr
McCormick & Company	5,067	2,650	15.3	8.4	0.6	27.3	11.0
International Flavors & F	4,409	2,043	16.1	7.5	0.5	49.7	14.8
Givaudan SA							

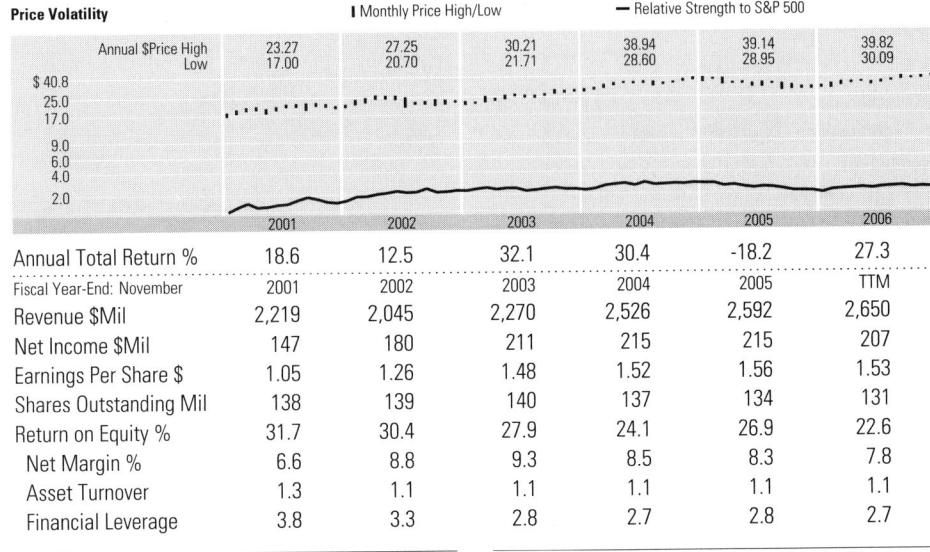

	2001	2002	2003	2004	2005	2006
Annual Total Return %	18.6	12.5	32.1	30.4	-18.2	27.3
Fiscal Year-End: November	2001	2002	2003	2004	2005	TTM
Revenue $Mil	2,219	2,045	2,270	2,526	2,592	2,650
Net Income $Mil	147	180	211	215	215	207
Earnings Per Share $	1.05	1.26	1.48	1.52	1.56	1.53
Shares Outstanding Mil	138	139	140	137	134	131
Return on Equity %	31.7	30.4	27.9	24.1	26.9	22.6
Net Margin %	6.6	8.8	9.3	8.5	8.3	7.8
Asset Turnover	1.3	1.1	1.1	1.1	1.1	1.1
Financial Leverage	3.8	3.3	2.8	2.7	2.8	2.7

Valuation Ratios	Stock	Rel to Industry	Rel to S&P 500
Price/Earnings	25.2	1.2	1.2
Price/Book	5.5	1.2	1.3
Price/Sales	1.9	1.1	0.7
Price/Cash Flow	15.3	1.0	1.0

Major Fund Holders	% of Fund Assets
Van Kampen Exchange	5.28
Van Kampen American Franchise A	3.47
Ave Maria Growth	2.88
Cookson Peirce Core Equity	2.48

Thesis   By Ann Gilpin, 12-04-06 Stock Price as of Analysis: $39.13

McCormick's dominant scale and command over the spice and seasoning market make for a wide economic moat.

McCormick controls half of the market for spices and seasonings in North America and is more than twice the size of its next-largest competitor. With leading brands like McCormick and Old Bay, the company has maintained solid sales growth and profitability in its category. Most supermarkets carry just one full line of branded spices and seasonings, and McCormick has secured contracts (renewable over three- to five-year spans) with more than 90% of the retail grocers in North America.

McCormick's domination of the spice and seasoning market stems from one of the biggest problems facing consumer packaged goods companies: private labels. Many consumers choose the less expensive private-label offerings, which make up 15% of the spice and seasoning market. However, McCormick is also the largest producer of private-label spices and seasonings in North America. This allows it to limit the threat posed by private labels, ensuring that no other company gains enough scale in this segment to significantly affect the pricing of McCormick's branded offerings.

McCormick is also a leading supplier to industrial consumers. In the United States, McCormick supplies 9 of the top 10 quick-serve restaurants and 19 of the top 20 food companies. The company is one of only a handful of global firms that have expertise across all flavor disciplines, making it a one-stop shop for packaged food companies and restaurant chains looking for new flavors or textures to add to their products.

To spur sales growth, McCormick has looked to product innovation and acquisitions. The company is revitalizing its U.S. spice business with contemporary labels, new flip-top caps, and gravity-fed merchandising systems. McCormick plans to have gravity-fed spice racks installed in more than 3,000 grocery stores by the end of 2006, which should improve product awareness and sales, much as it did for Campbell's line of condensed soups. McCormick also acquired Thai Kitchen and Simply Asia, both of which are well positioned in the fast-growing Asian packaged food category. Additionally, the company has unveiled a three-year restructuring plan that will reduce the number of industrial customers and products it supplies by about 25%. While sales may take a hit in the short run and restructuring charges will crimp operating margins, the restructuring plan will benefit McCormick's bottom line longer term.

Data as of 12-29-06

McDonald's MCD

Rating ★★★	Fair Value $43.00	Last Close $44.33	Consider Buy $36.60	Consider Sell $56.50	Yield % 2.26

Company Profile

McDonald's is the world's largest restaurant chain, with more than 30,000 restaurants in over 100 countries. More than 8,000 are operated by the company; the remainder are run by franchisees, licensees, and affiliates. The company also operates the fast-casual chain Boston Market in the United States and has a minority ownership in U.K.-based Pret A Manger.

Industry	Business Risk	Moat Size	Investment Style	Sector
Restaurants	Below Avg	Narrow	Large Core	Consumer Services

Competition

	Market Cap $Mil	12 Mo Trailing Sales $Mil	Price/Cash Flow	Return On Assets%	Debt/ Equity	Total Return% 1 Yr	3 Yr
McDonald's	54,825	21,790	13.3	9.4	0.6	34.6	23.9
Yum Brands	15,586	9,444	12.9	13.7	1.5	26.8	21.6
Wendy's International	3,905	3,777	9.5	4.2	0.3	30.5	24.9

Management — Stewardship Grade [A]

Jim Skinner is the company's third CEO since McDonald's began its turnaround effort in 2003. (Jim Cantalupo died of a heart attack in April 2004, and his successor, Charlie Bell, resigned in November of that year after being diagnosed with colon cancer.) Skinner, who also serves as vice chairman, has been with the company for 35 years and previously held leadership positions in every restaurant geography of the company. We expect Skinner to continue the successful execution of the company's Plan to Win strategy. He will also need to focus on leadership development, given the turnover in the executive suite. In 2005, Skinner was paid $1.1 million in salary and a $2 million bonus, which we view as reasonable, given another year of solid performance from the company. We like that Skinner and other officers are expected to hold a multiple of their salary in company stock, which gives them ample incentive to increase shareholder value. Overall, the executives and directors have demonstrated good stewardship, but we do frown upon the company's staggered board, blank-check preferred stock, and other antitakeover measures, which we believe favor the interests of management over shareholders.

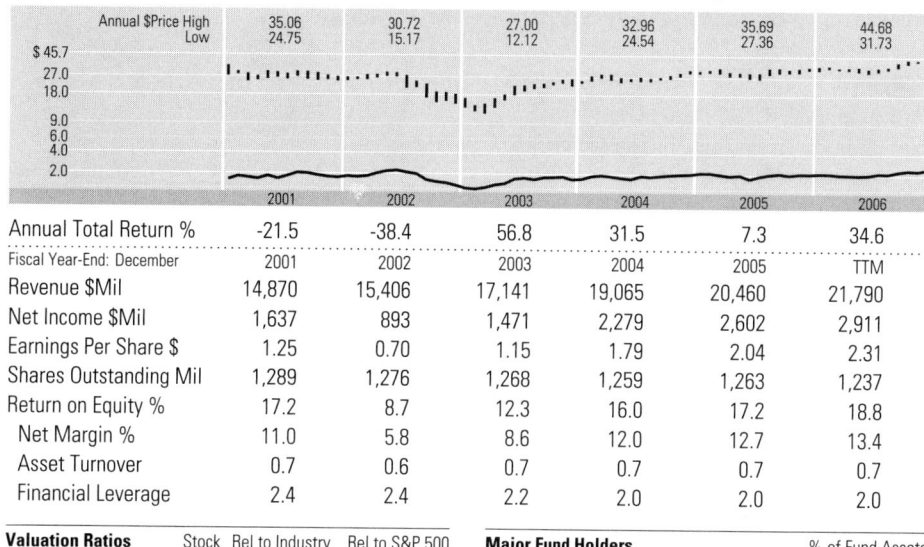

Price Volatility | Monthly Price High/Low — Relative Strength to S&P 500

Annual $Price High/Low	35.06 / 24.75	30.72 / 15.17	27.00 / 12.12	32.96 / 24.54	35.69 / 27.36	44.68 / 31.73
	2001	2002	2003	2004	2005	2006
Annual Total Return %	-21.5	-38.4	56.8	31.5	7.3	34.6

Fiscal Year-End: December	2001	2002	2003	2004	2005	TTM
Revenue $Mil	14,870	15,406	17,141	19,065	20,460	21,790
Net Income $Mil	1,637	893	1,471	2,279	2,602	2,911
Earnings Per Share $	1.25	0.70	1.15	1.79	2.04	2.31
Shares Outstanding Mil	1,289	1,276	1,268	1,259	1,263	1,237
Return on Equity %	17.2	8.7	12.3	16.0	17.2	18.8
Net Margin %	11.0	5.8	8.6	12.0	12.7	13.4
Asset Turnover	0.7	0.6	0.7	0.7	0.7	0.7
Financial Leverage	2.4	2.4	2.2	2.0	2.0	2.0

Valuation Ratios	Stock	Rel to Industry	Rel to S&P 500
Price/Earnings	19.2	0.7	0.9
Price/Book	3.5	0.6	0.9
Price/Sales	2.5	1.3	0.9
Price/Cash Flow	13.3	0.9	0.9

Major Fund Holders	% of Fund Assets
Tilson Focus	13.95
Oakmark Select I	5.46
Fidelity Select Consumer Staples	5.28
IXIS Harris Associates Large Cap Value A	5.15

McDonald's Plaza
Oak Brook, IL 60523
www.mcdonalds.com

Growth [B-]	2002	2003	2004	2005
Revenue %	3.6	11.3	11.2	7.3
Earnings/Share %	-44.0	64.3	55.7	14.0
Book Value/Share %	11.2	16.2	19.1	6.4
Dividends/Share %	4.4	70.2	37.5	21.8

Profitability [B+]	2003	2004	2005	TTM
Return on Assets %	5.7	8.2	8.7	9.4
Oper Cash Flow $Mil	3,269	3,904	4,337	4,133
- Cap Spending $Mil	1,307	1,419	1,607	1,719
= Free Cash Flow $Mil	1,961	2,484	2,730	2,414

Financial Health [A+]	2003	2004	2005	09-30-06
Long-term Debt $Mil	9,343	8,357	8,937	8,569
Total Equity $Mil	11,982	14,202	15,146	15,526
Debt/Equity Ratio	0.8	0.6	0.6	0.6

Thesis By John Owens, CFA, CPA, 10-16-06 Stock Price as of Analysis:

We believe McDonald's will strengthen its leadership position in the fast-food sector. Management's efforts to revitalize the brand are resonating with customers in the United States and are beginning to gain traction in Europe (these markets each contribute about one third of total revenue). The company also has excellent growth prospects in China.

In 2003, McDonald's shifted its focus from rapid unit growth to generating more sales from existing restaurants. As part of its "Plan to Win," the restaurant chain introduced several new menu items, including salads and chicken offerings, which gave its customers more reasons to visit, more often. The company also launched the popular "I'm lovin' it" marketing campaign.

In the United States, these new initiatives helped to drive 7% average annual growth in comparable sales over the past three years. We believe further innovation, including the recent launch of premium coffee, will spur additional top-line growth. Management's continued efforts to optimize the drive-through business (which accounts for 65% of domestic sales), extend hours of operation, and remodel restaurants with a more modern decor should also contribute to higher sales.

The turnaround in Europe has taken more time. Same-restaurant sales fell 1% in 2003 and grew less than 3% in the following two years. Then, management began to employ some of the same strategies and tactics in Europe that were successful in the United States. Recent results have been encouraging, with Europe's comparable sales up 5.3% year to date through September.

The company also has the opportunity to expand in emerging markets like China. With a growing middle class and automobile ownership on the rise there, McDonald's opened its first drive-through in China in November 2005 and aims for 120 by the end of 2008. The recently launched rice burger has been a hit with Chinese customers and is being rolled out to other Asian markets.

McDonald's still faces some challenges. The restaurant industry remains highly competitive. Many rivals, including Burger King, Wendy's, and CKE Restaurants, are aggressively targeting fast food's heavy users with indulgent items. Meanwhile, the iconic McDonald's receives more blame for rising obesity, which has been especially damaging to its reputation in the United Kingdom. Under such public scrutiny, a more timid McDonald's could lose some of its hard-core customers to its unabashed competitors.

Data as of 12-29-06

McGraw-Hill Companies MHP

Rating	Fair Value	Last Close	Consider Buy	Consider Sell	Yield %
★★	$58.00	$68.02	$49.40	$76.10	1.07

Company Profile

McGraw-Hill is an information services company. The financial services division, which generates 68% of the company's operating profit, offers ratings and analytics to the worldwide securities market. The education division sells its products to all grade levels, from elementary school to universities. The media division includes market-leading brands such as BusinessWeek magazine and J.D. Power and Associates.

Management   Stewardship Grade [B]

We think McGraw-Hill has reasonable corporate-governance policies. Harold McGraw III has been chairman since 2000 and president and CEO since 1998. He joined the company in 1980, working his way up through a variety of positions, including stints at each of the firm's three operating units. The stock and the company have performed well under his watch. Most of his wealth has come from long-term compensation in the form of options and restricted shares. In our opinion, the company's executives are well compensated, as three executive officers under McGraw III each received total cash compensation in excess of $2 million in 2005. In each of the past two years, the company's option grants represented about 3% of outstanding shares, which is higher than we'd prefer to see. McGraw-Hill has spent more than $5.5 billion on share repurchases and dividends since 1996.

1221 Avenue Of The Americas   www.mcgraw-hill.com
New York, NY 10020

Growth [B]	2002	2003	2004	2005
Revenue %	3.8	3.9	7.4	14.3
Earnings/Share %	54.2	-39.5	9.5	12.8
Book Value/Share %	17.7	-40.1	16.3	5.3
Dividends/Share %	4.1	5.9	11.1	10.0

Profitability [A]	2003	2004	2005	TTM
Return on Assets %	12.9	12.9	13.2	14.1
Oper Cash Flow $Mil	1,382	1,063	1,560	1,613
- Cap Spending $Mil	115	139	120	104
= Free Cash Flow $Mil	1,267	924	1,440	1,509

Financial Health [A]	2003	2004	2005	09-30-06
Long-term Debt $Mil	—	1	0	0
Total Equity $Mil	2,557	2,985	3,113	2,606
Debt/Equity Ratio	—	0.0	0.0	0.0

Industry	Business Risk	Moat Size	Investment Style	Sector
Publishing	Below Avg	Wide	Large Growth	Media

Competition	Market Cap $Mil	12 Mo Trailing Sales $Mil	Price/Cash Flow	Return On Assets%	Debt/Equity	Total Return% 1 Yr	3 Yr
McGraw-Hill Companies	24,093	6,202	14.9	14.1	0.0	33.4	26.9
Moody's	19,323	1,920	26.4	54.1	7.8	12.9	32.2
Reed Elsevier PLC ADR	14,060	0	—	22.8	—	20.6	12.5

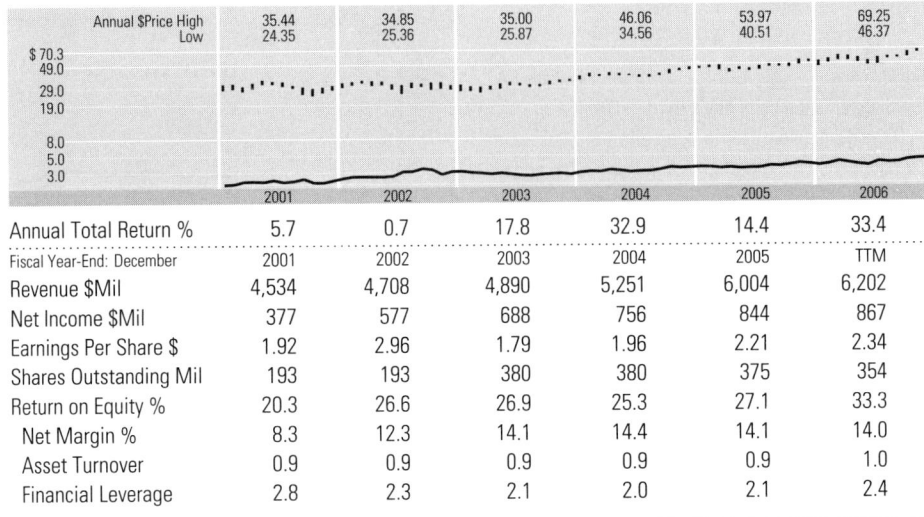

Price Volatility — Monthly Price High/Low — Relative Strength to S&P 500

Annual $Price High	35.44	34.85	35.00	46.06	53.97	69.25
Low	24.35	25.36	25.87	34.56	40.51	46.37
	2001	2002	2003	2004	2005	2006
Annual Total Return %	5.7	0.7	17.8	32.9	14.4	33.4

Fiscal Year-End: December	2001	2002	2003	2004	2005	TTM
Revenue $Mil	4,534	4,708	4,890	5,251	6,004	6,202
Net Income $Mil	377	577	688	756	844	867
Earnings Per Share $	1.92	2.96	1.79	1.96	2.21	2.34
Shares Outstanding Mil	193	193	380	380	375	354
Return on Equity %	20.3	26.6	26.9	25.3	27.1	33.3
Net Margin %	8.3	12.3	14.1	14.4	14.1	14.0
Asset Turnover	0.9	0.9	0.9	0.9	0.9	1.0
Financial Leverage	2.8	2.3	2.1	2.0	2.1	2.4

Valuation Ratios	Stock	Rel to Industry	Rel to S&P 500
Price/Earnings	29.1	1.1	1.4
Price/Book	9.2	1.5	2.2
Price/Sales	3.9	1.4	1.3
Price/Cash Flow	14.9	1.0	1.0

Major Fund Holders	% of Fund Assets
Fidelity Select Multimedia	7.26
Strategic Partners Concentrated Growth M	6.19
Heritage Capital Appreciation A	5.55
Jensen J	5.47

Thesis By Michael Corty, CFA, 12-14-06 Stock Price as of Analysis: $68.92

McGraw-Hill has two great businesses and is poised for continued success. We wouldn't hesitate to invest in this firm's shares at the right price.

We can't think of a much better business than the Standard & Poor's credit-rating franchise, which benefits from operating in a long-standing duopoly with Moody's. On average, debt issuances are required to have two independent ratings. S&P essentially acts as a toll collector on publicly issued debt that flows through its rating pipeline. Recent legislation that calls for additional competition will have little impact on S&P's dominant market share, in our opinion. The company rates more than 90% of U.S. debt issuance, and we wouldn't be surprised if it holds a similar share in 2016.

McGraw-Hill has used its powerful S&P brand name to forge into other areas of financial services. We believe most of its nonrating operations drag down the segment's lofty 42% operating margins; however, the licensing of its S&P brand name for equity indexes and other investment vehicles like exchange-traded funds generates fatter margins than issuing credit ratings. For example, the company generates fees based on the trading volume and level of assets in underlying S&P index-based ETF assets, which have grown to $162 billion from $36 billion in 2000. With minimal costs associated with this licensing, most of this incremental revenue falls directly to the bottom line.

While often overshadowed by the more profitable financial segment, McGraw-Hill's education business has an enviable competitive position and solid growth prospects, in our opinion. McGraw-Hill, Pearson, and Reed Elsevier dominate the U.S. elementary-high school publishing and testing market. Almost half of textbook sales come from adoption states, which means public school districts must purchase materials that have been adopted at the state level in order to qualify for state funding. Creating and customizing an educational program for individual states requires deep pockets and well-established brands, so we believe competition is limited to the existing market leaders. McGraw-Hill usually gets its fair share of the new adoption market; it captured 33% of the new state adoption spending in 2005.

The education business in on pace to generate negative sales growth in 2006, thanks to a slow year in state adoptions. However, we expect ample growth in the el-hi publishing market over the next three years, and we think McGraw-Hill is well positioned to land its share of these dollars.

Data as of 12-29-06

Medtronic MDT

	Rating	Fair Value	Last Close	Consider Buy	Consider Sell	Yield %
	★★★★★	$64.00	$53.51	$54.50	$84.00	0.77

Company Profile

One of the largest medical-device companies, Medtronic develops and manufactures therapeutic medical devices for chronic diseases. Its implantable products include pacemakers, heart valves, stents, insulin pumps, and artificial spinal discs. The company markets its products to health-care institutions and physicians in the United States and overseas. Foreign sales account for about 33% of the company's total sales.

Management   Stewardship Grade [A]

Medtronic gets above-average marks for its stewardship. After joining Medtronic from Abbott Laboratories in 1992, Arthur D. Collins Jr. became chief executive in May 2001 and chairman in April 2002. He shares credit for broadening Medtronic's product lines, strengthening its competitive position, and overseeing investments made in the late 1990s that have really paid off for the company. We believe he has the vision to allocate resources with the goal of making Medtronic into a stronger competitor. We like that Medtronic's 10-member board is heavily weighted toward outsiders who bring a great deal of public health, academic, and cardiac health-care experience to the table. Collins is the only insider on the board. Executive compensation is in line with that of comparable companies and is based on meeting target goals for diluted earnings per share, revenue growth, and return on assets.

710 Medtronic Parkway www.medtronic.com
Minneapolis, MN 55432

Growth [B]	2003	2004	2005	2006
Revenue %	19.6	18.6	10.6	12.3
Earnings/Share %	62.5	23.1	-7.5	41.2
Book Value/Share %	22.9	15.4	15.7	-10.2
Dividends/Share %	8.7	16.0	15.6	14.9

Profitability [A+]	2004	2005	2006	TTM
Return on Assets %	13.9	10.9	13.0	14.2
Oper Cash Flow $Mil	2,846	2,819	2,207	2,495
- Cap Spending $Mil	425	452	407	429
= Free Cash Flow $Mil	2,421	2,367	1,800	2,066

Financial Health [A]	2004	2005	2006	10-31-06
Long-term Debt $Mil	1	1,973	5,486	5,581
Total Equity $Mil	9,077	10,450	9,383	10,277
Debt/Equity Ratio	0.0	0.2	0.6	0.5

Industry	Business Risk	Moat Size	Investment Style	Sector
Medical Equip.	Below Avg	Wide	Large Growth	Healthcare

Competition

	Market Cap $Mil	12 Mo Trailing Sales $Mil	Price/Cash Flow	Return On Assets%	Debt/ Equity	Total Return% 1 Yr	3 Yr
Medtronic	61,597	11,808	24.7	14.2	0.5	-6.3	4.1
Johnson & Johnson	191,415	52,252	14.5	18.5	0.0	12.4	10.8
Boston Scientific	25,323	7,296	12.7	-11.4	0.6	-29.9	-22.0

Price Volatility

	2001	2002	2003	2004	2005	2006
Annual $Price High	60.81	51.21	52.92	53.70	58.91	59.87
Low	36.75	32.50	42.15	43.99	48.70	42.37
Annual Total Return %	-14.8	-10.3	7.2	2.7	16.7	-6.3

Fiscal Year-End: April	2002	2003	2004	2005	2006	TTM
Revenue $Mil	6,411	7,665	9,087	10,055	11,292	11,808
Net Income $Mil	984	1,600	1,959	1,804	2,547	2,690
Earnings Per Share $	0.80	1.30	1.60	1.48	2.09	2.26
Shares Outstanding Mil	1,215	1,221	1,217	1,211	1,207	1,151
Return on Equity %	15.3	20.2	21.6	17.3	27.1	26.2
Net Margin %	15.3	20.9	21.6	17.9	22.6	22.8
Asset Turnover	0.6	0.6	0.6	0.6	0.6	0.6
Financial Leverage	1.7	1.6	1.6	1.6	2.1	1.8

Valuation Ratios	Stock	Rel to Industry	Rel to S&P 500
Price/Earnings	23.7	0.8	1.2
Price/Book	6.0	1.1	1.5
Price/Sales	5.2	1.1	1.8
Price/Cash Flow	24.7	1.0	1.7

Major Fund Holders	% of Fund Assets
Saratoga Health & Biotechnology B	6.76
Live Oak Health Sciences	6.50
Wells Fargo Advantage Large Co Growth Ad	6.37
Biondo Growth Inv	6.02

Thesis   By Debbie S. Wang, 11-21-06   Stock Price as of Analysis: $53.55

With its diversified portfolio and strategy to develop products for a wide range of chronic diseases, Medtronic is well positioned to take advantage of new trends in disease management.

This wide-moat company's vision is to establish a significant presence in chronic diseases, in addition to its historical stronghold in heart disease. Investments in neurological, diabetes, and spinal products from the mid- to late 1990s have paid off in spades, offering new revenue streams and taking some pressure off heart products. Revenue from those three product areas inched up from 25% of total sales in fiscal 2000 to 35% in fiscal 2006. Compared with its peers, Medtronic relies less on any single type of product and is better able to weather glitches in the development or approval process for any particular new device.

We're impressed by the firm's persistent ability to innovate, and by how it's often first to market with new products. For instance, Medtronic's promising new spinal bone graft product remains the only one of its kind on the market. Because this novel device contains recombinant bone protein that induces the patient to grow new bone, it is considered superior to traditional lumbar-fusion procedures--it's less invasive and spares patients the stress of grafting bone from other body parts. The firm already has a second bone morphogenic product in development. Additionally, Medtronic is one of the leaders in developing sensors that constantly monitor blood sugar levels in diabetics. Sensors that measure blood glucose 280 times a day would offer a significant advantage over the traditional four-times-a-day finger pricks that most diabetics perform to monitor blood sugar, leading to better blood sugar control and fewer disease complications. Medtronic is also leading the way to create monitors that work automatically with insulin pumps to release insulin at the appropriate times. This brings Medtronic one step closer to an artificial pancreas--the holy grail of diabetes care devices.

But even the most innovative companies may stumble on occasion. Medtronic's late start in developing a drug-coated stent has been a disappointment. We don't expect the firm to enter the U.S. market with its own stent until 2007, long after rivals Boston Scientific and Johnson & Johnson have established footprints in that market. In the meantime, Medtronic continues to generate strong free cash flow and returns on invested capital in the low 20s, and we expect to see more of the same going forward.

Mellon Financial MEL

Data as of 12-29-06

	Rating	Fair Value	Last Close	Consider Buy	Consider Sell	Yield %
	★★★★	$50.00	$42.15	$38.60	$62.60	2.04

Company Profile

Mellon Financial offers banking, asset-management, and back-office asset-processing services to institutions and wealthy individuals. Once a banking organization spanning the Northeast, the firm dropped most of its retail banking operations to focus on fee-based services and significantly reduced its lending operations. In 2005, Mellon sold its human resources outsourcing business. The bank now concentrates on investment management and trust and custody services.

Management   Stewardship Grade [C]

Chairman and CEO Robert P. Kelly, who took over in February 2006 from Mellon veteran Martin McGuinn, hasn't wasted any time in leaving his mark on the company: In December 2006, Mellon unveiled plans to merge with its larger custody rival, Bank of New York, in a deal that will create an asset-servicing and investment-management colossus. Kelly will serve as CEO of the merged entity. BoNY chief Thomas Renyi will serve as chairman of the merged company for 18 months before retiring. Kelly won't be alone in the merged company's management ranks, as several other members of Mellon brass are being tapped to run key divisions. Merger aside, Mellon earns a C grade for corporate stewardship due to a few shortcomings. We thought McGuinn's severance payments were astonishingly high at $19.3 million. Board elections are staggered, meaning it would take three years to replace the entire board. We would also like to see the demise of the poison pill. Mellon says that it will review these two takeover defenses in the coming year and plans to recommend de-staggering its board. It also appears poised to get rid of the poison pill. Should these things transpire, Mellon's Stewardship Grade would improve.

One Mellon Center
Pittsburgh, PA 15258-0001
www.mellon.com

Growth [C]	2002	2003	2004	2005
Revenue %	28.4	-0.6	-0.5	13.3
Earnings/Share %	-43.8	5.2	15.3	-0.5
Book Value/Share %	5.8	11.6	12.5	3.7
Dividends/Share %	-40.2	16.3	22.8	11.4

Profitability [A]	2003	2004	2005	TTM
Return on Assets %	2.1	2.1	2.0	2.0
Oper Cash Flow $Mil	866	1,701	953	—
- Cap Spending $Mil	133	165	174	—
= Free Cash Flow $Mil	—	—	—	—

Financial Health [NA]	2003	2004	2005	09-30-06
Long-term Debt $Mil	—	—	—	—
Total Equity $Mil	3,702	4,102	4,202	4,495
Debt/Equity Ratio	—	—	—	—

Industry	Business Risk	Moat Size	Investment Style	Sector
International Banks	Average	Wide	Large Core	Financial Services

Competition	Market Cap $Mil	12 Mo Trailing Sales $Mil	Price/Cash Flow	Return On Assets%	Debt/Equity	Total Return% 1 Yr	Total Return% 3 Yr
Mellon Financial	17,360	5,092	—	2.0	—	26.0	12.3
J.P. Morgan Chase & Co.	167,551	59,650	—	0.9	—	25.6	13.2
Bank of New York Company	41,334	7,308	—	1.5	—	26.9	9.2

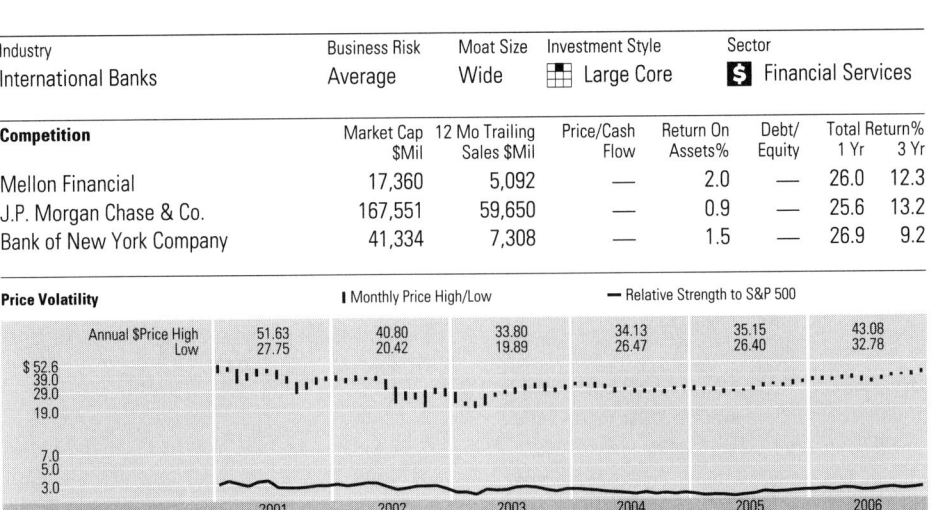

Price Volatility — Monthly Price High/Low — Relative Strength to S&P 500

	2001	2002	2003	2004	2005	2006
Annual $Price High	51.63	40.80	33.80	34.13	35.15	43.08
Low	27.75	20.42	19.89	26.47	26.40	32.78
Annual Total Return %	-22.0	-29.5	25.6	-0.8	13.1	26.0

Fiscal Year-End: December	2001	2002	2003	2004	2005	TTM
Revenue $Mil	3,321	4,264	4,239	4,218	4,781	5,092
Net Income $Mil	1,318	682	701	796	782	869
Earnings Per Share $	2.76	1.55	1.63	1.88	1.87	2.10
Shares Outstanding Mil	472	437	427	419	416	412
Return on Equity %	37.9	20.1	18.9	19.4	18.6	19.3
Net Margin %	39.7	16.0	16.5	18.9	16.4	17.1
Asset Turnover	0.1	0.1	0.1	0.1	0.1	0.1
Financial Leverage	10.2	10.7	9.2	9.0	9.2	9.5

Valuation Ratios	Stock	Rel to Industry	Rel to S&P 500
Price/Earnings	20.3	1.1	1.0
Price/Book	3.9	1.5	1.0
Price/Sales	3.4	0.8	1.2
Price/Cash Flow	—	—	—

Major Fund Holders	% of Fund Assets
Saratoga Financial Service A	4.33
Foresight Value	4.20
MFS Strategic Value A	4.10
Schwab Financial Services	3.33

Thesis By Jeffrey Ptak, CPA, CFA, 12-18-06 Stock Price as of Analysis: $42.45

Bank of New York and Mellon Financial's recently announced merger looks like a winner.

Mellon and Bank of New York (BoNY) recently announced that they will merge in mid-2007. The combined entity, to be called Bank of New York Mellon Corporation, will be the leading global custodian and one of the world's largest asset managers.

Both companies gain something from the deal. For instance, scale is vital in the custody business due to the huge technology and personnel outlays needed to service client assets. To that end, Mellon can leverage BoNY's hulking presence in the custody arena--the transaction will nearly quadruple Mellon's assets under custody and fill gaps in its asset-servicing roster where BoNY is pre-eminent, such as corporate trust. As such, the deal will vault Mellon into a market-leadership position.

The deal also should significantly upgrade Bank of New York's asset-management capabilities. Mellon's $1.1 trillion in assets under management (AUM) dwarfs BoNY's recent tally. Moreover, Mellon brings a long roster of well-respected, brisk-selling institutional strategies to the table. With a deeper reservoir of asset-management options to draw upon, BoNY can lessen its dependence on asset-servicing, thereby further diversifying its revenue stream.

Unlike many combinations motivated by rosy projections or vanity, this deal should deliver real synergies. Asset-servicers are well-suited to peddle asset-management products given that custody brings them into near-daily contact with clients' key investment decision-makers. Thus, the combined unit should be better-positioned to pair a more-robust suite of investment management products with low-cost custody solutions. And the projected annual cost savings from the deal--$700 million, to be fully realized by 2010--are wholly attainable given the overlap it creates in certain areas.

To make the deal pay off, both companies will have to integrate systems and meld cultures without roiling clients. Here, too, we think there's cause for guarded optimism. While BoNY will control the merged entity, Mellon CEO Robert Kelly will head it up, and several Mellon executives are slated to assume key posts. This should create greater parity in management's ranks, mitigating the risk of culture clash. In addition, since the deal wasn't priced for perfection, it should relieve the pressure to roar out of the gates in order to rationalize a lofty price, allowing both parties to proceed judiciously with the integration.

Merck MRK

Data as of 12-29-06

Rating	Fair Value	Last Close	Consider Buy	Consider Sell	Yield %
★★★	$38.00	$43.60	$24.20	$45.80	3.49

Industry	Business Risk	Moat Size	Investment Style	Sector
Drugs	Above Avg	Wide	Large Value	Healthcare

Company Profile
Merck makes pharmaceutical products to treat conditions in a number of therapeutic areas, including cardiovascular disease, asthma, infections, and osteoporosis. The company also has a substantial vaccines business, with treatments to prevent hepatitis B and pediatric diseases as well as HPV and shingles. About 60% of the company's sales are generated in the United States.

Competition

	Market Cap $Mil	12 Mo Trailing Sales $Mil	Price/Cash Flow	Return On Assets %	Debt/ Equity	Total Return % 1 Yr	3 Yr
Merck	94,656	22,358	13.0	11.6	0.2	42.7	1.7
Pfizer	186,751	52,208	10.5	11.6	0.1	15.2	-7.4
Eli Lilly & Company	58,956	15,325	20.1	13.5	0.3	-5.2	-7.5

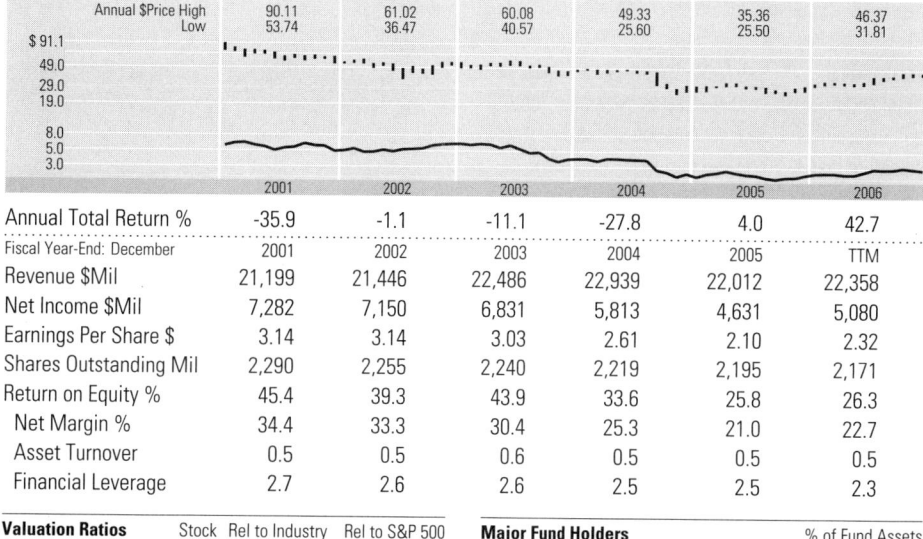

Price Volatility — Monthly Price High/Low — Relative Strength to S&P 500

Annual $Price High Low	90.11 / 53.74	61.02 / 36.47	60.08 / 40.57	49.33 / 25.60	35.36 / 25.50	46.37 / 31.81
	2001	2002	2003	2004	2005	2006
Annual Total Return %	-35.9	-1.1	-11.1	-27.8	4.0	42.7

Fiscal Year-End: December	2001	2002	2003	2004	2005	TTM
Revenue $Mil	21,199	21,446	22,486	22,939	22,012	22,358
Net Income $Mil	7,282	7,150	6,831	5,813	4,631	5,080
Earnings Per Share $	3.14	3.14	3.03	2.61	2.10	2.32
Shares Outstanding Mil	2,290	2,255	2,240	2,219	2,195	2,171
Return on Equity %	45.4	39.3	43.9	33.6	25.8	26.3
Net Margin %	34.4	33.3	30.4	25.3	21.0	22.7
Asset Turnover	0.5	0.5	0.6	0.5	0.5	0.5
Financial Leverage	2.7	2.6	2.6	2.5	2.5	2.3

Management — Stewardship Grade [B]
Richard Clark was appointed CEO in May 2005. He is a longtime Merck employee who has held numerous posts at the company, including CEO of former subsidiary Medco Health Solutions and president of the manufacturing division. A three-member executive committee of independent board members currently acts as chairman, a situation the firm views as temporary so Clark can learn the ropes in his new position. Peter Kim, a renowned research scientist from the Massachusetts Institute of Technology, joined Merck in 2002 as president of Merck Research Labs. Kim was instrumental in Merck's acquisition of biotech firm Rosetta Inpharmatics and has significantly increased Merck's willingness to work with external firms to enhance its research pipeline. Merck's board is packed with current and retired CEOs, which can lead to quid pro quo compensation packages for top executives but lends valuable strategic-planning experience. Merck recently shifted from staggered to annual elections of its board members, and empowers minority shareholders by allowing cumulative voting for board members.

Valuation Ratios

	Stock	Rel to Industry	Rel to S&P 500
Price/Earnings	18.8	0.8	0.9
Price/Book	4.9	0.9	1.2
Price/Sales	4.2	1.0	1.4
Price/Cash Flow	13.0	0.8	0.9

Major Fund Holders

	% of Fund Assets
Fidelity Select Pharmaceuticals	11.05
Integrity Health Sciences A	9.81
ProFunds Pharmaceuticals UltraSector Inv	7.83
Allianz RCM Health Care D	7.36

One Merck Drive
Whitehouse Station, NJ 08889-0100
www.merck.com

Growth [D]

	2002	2003	2004	2005
Revenue %	1.2	4.9	2.0	-4.0
Earnings/Share %	0.0	-3.5	-13.9	-19.5
Book Value/Share %	15.5	-13.6	12.3	4.7
Dividends/Share %	2.9	2.8	2.7	1.3

Profitability [A+]

	2003	2004	2005	TTM
Return on Assets %	16.8	13.7	10.3	11.6
Oper Cash Flow $Mil	8,427	8,799	7,609	7,254
- Cap Spending $Mil	1,916	1,726	1,403	1,091
= Free Cash Flow $Mil	6,511	7,073	6,206	6,163

Financial Health [A+]

	2003	2004	2005	09-30-06
Long-term Debt $Mil	—	4,692	5,126	4,790
Total Equity $Mil	15,576	17,288	17,917	19,285
Debt/Equity Ratio	—	0.3	0.3	0.2

Thesis
By Heather Brilliant, CFA, 11-16-06 Stock Price as of Analysis: $44.65

At first glance, it's not hard to turn your back on Merck, with products comprising almost half of its 2005 revenue losing patent protection during the next five years and litigation related to Vioxx that will continue long into the future. However, we see a diamond in the rough, with an improving pipeline of potential new drugs and a management team focused on improving efficiency and reducing costs.

To be sure, Merck has had a difficult couple of years, and things are going to get worse before they get better. Cholesterol treatment Zocor, which generated more than $4 billion in sales for Merck during 2005, lost patent protection earlier this year and is facing an onslaught of generic competition. While it is still reeling from this, Fosamax for osteoporosis and Cosopt for glaucoma will face generic competitors in 2008. Further, anti-hypertensive Cozaar, which generated $3 billion in sales in 2005, will lose patent protection in 2010.

Fortunately, this historical research and development powerhouse has a few tricks up its sleeve. Merck recently received approval for Januvia for diabetes and Gardasil, a vaccine to protect young women from human papillomavirus (HPV), the virus that causes cervical cancer. We think these drugs each have the potential to generate more than $1 billion in annual sales for Merck after a few years on the market. Its late-stage pipeline also holds several promising drugs, including Gaboxadol for insomnia and innovative treatments for cholesterol and HIV. Additionally, the company now has more than 40 compounds in earlier stages of development, an improvement of more than 50% from just a few years ago. Much of this improvement is due to Merck's increasing willingness to look outside its own doors for research opportunities, and we expect in-licensing and small acquisitions to continue to fuel growth in the firm's pipeline.

On top of the revenues generated by these new products, Merck's joint ventures with other drug companies should generate critical income to help the firm navigate these transition years. Merck receives a substantial royalty on the blockbuster proton pump inhibitor Nexium, sold by AstraZeneca. In addition, Merck co-markets the highly successful cholesterol medicines Zetia and Vytorin with Schering-Plough.

While things are looking up at Merck, the firm is in the process of navigating a major legal mess with Vioxx. We estimate Merck will pay hundreds of millions of dollars in legal expenses for the next decade.

Data as of 12-29-06

Merrill Lynch & Company MER

	Rating	Fair Value	Last Close	Consider Buy	Consider Sell	Yield %
	★	$71.00	$93.10	$54.70	$89.00	1.07

Company Profile
Merrill Lynch is one of the largest financial-services firms in the world, with offices in 36 countries. It has three primary divisions. Global markets and investment banking focuses on capital markets, institutional brokerage, and investment banking services. The global private client unit serves individual investors around the world. Merrill Lynch is swapping its investment management business for a nearly 50% stake of BlackRock.

Management
Stewardship Grade [B]

Stanley O'Neal was named CEO in December 2002, but his ascendancy was clear when he became president in July 2001. The first CEO in Merrill's history without a broker pedigree, O'Neal rose through the ranks as a debt banker. He started cutting costs upon his arrival, largely by trimming underproducing brokers. It remains hard to tell if removing a big chunk of brokerage capacity at the bottom of a market trough was a needed cost discipline, or if money was left on the table during the following recovery as a result. O'Neal has developed a deep bench of capable executives, including Bob McCann, a former rival he wooed back to the fold. The 10-member board of directors serves staggered terms and is largely independent, with O'Neal the only Merrill employee. Executive compensation and overall options issuance are high, but in line with industry norms. Directors and executive officers as a group own less than 1% of the company, but O'Neal's 1 million shares of stock and 3 million share total ownership, including options, should be enough to keep his interests aligned with those of shareholders.

4 World Financial Center
New York, NY 10080
www.ml.com

Growth [B]	2002	2003	2004	2005
Revenue %	-14.7	8.3	10.8	17.9
Earnings/Share %	NMF	118.6	13.2	17.8
Book Value/Share %	3.1	15.3	4.1	9.9
Dividends/Share %	0.0	0.0	0.0	18.8

Profitability [D]	2003	2004	2005	TTM
Return on Assets %	0.8	0.7	0.7	0.8
Oper Cash Flow $Mil	8,656	-14,941	-25,658	—
- Cap Spending $Mil	—	—	—	—
= Free Cash Flow $Mil	—	—	—	—

Financial Health [NA]	2003	2004	2005	09-30-06
Long-term Debt $Mil	—	—	—	—
Total Equity $Mil	28,884	30,740	32,927	35,504
Debt/Equity Ratio	—	—	—	—

Industry	Business Risk	Moat Size	Investment Style	Sector
Securities	Average	Wide	Large Core	Financial Services

Competition	Market Cap $Mil	12 Mo Trailing Sales $Mil	Price/Cash Flow	Return On Assets %	Debt/ Equity	Total Return % 1 Yr	3 Yr
Merrill Lynch & Company	82,298	32,796	—	0.8	—	39.3	18.6
Citigroup	273,691	86,566	—	1.3	—	19.6	8.4
J.P. Morgan Chase & Co.	167,551	59,650	—	0.9	—	25.6	13.2

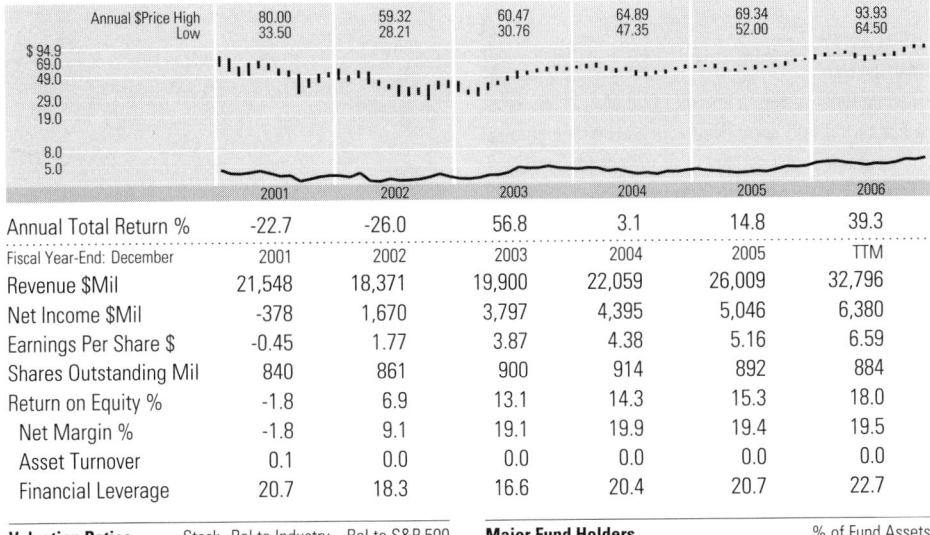

	2001	2002	2003	2004	2005	2006
Annual $Price High	80.00	59.32	60.47	64.89	69.34	93.93
Low	33.50	28.21	30.76	47.35	52.00	64.50
Annual Total Return %	-22.7	-26.0	56.8	3.1	14.8	39.3

Fiscal Year-End: December	2001	2002	2003	2004	2005	TTM
Revenue $Mil	21,548	18,371	19,900	22,059	26,009	32,796
Net Income $Mil	-378	1,670	3,797	4,395	5,046	6,380
Earnings Per Share $	-0.45	1.77	3.87	4.38	5.16	6.59
Shares Outstanding Mil	840	861	900	914	892	884
Return on Equity %	-1.8	6.9	13.1	14.3	15.3	18.0
Net Margin %	-1.8	9.1	19.1	19.9	19.4	19.5
Asset Turnover	0.1	0.0	0.0	0.0	0.0	0.0
Financial Leverage	20.7	18.3	16.6	20.4	20.7	22.7

Valuation Ratios	Stock	Rel to Industry	Rel to S&P 500
Price/Earnings	14.1	0.8	0.7
Price/Book	2.3	0.6	0.6
Price/Sales	2.5	0.6	0.9
Price/Cash Flow	—	—	—

Major Fund Holders	% of Fund Assets
Neuberger Berman Focus Inv	5.95
IXIS CGM Advisor Targeted Equity A	5.84
CGM Focus	5.35
JHT Financial Services Trust Ser I	5.05

Thesis By Philip Guziec, 12-14-06 Stock Price as of Analysis: $90.64

Merrill Lynch has the largest book value of the investment banks, funding a top-tier advisory and underwriting business, a top-tier brokerage, and a stake in BlackRock, an asset management business. After the weak capital markets of 2000-02, the company embarked on a cost-cutting mission, emerging leaner and meaner. Now the firm is seeking to expand and diversify this well-run package of moat-worthy businesses.

The advisory and underwriting businesses (investment banking) remain perennially near the top of the league tables across the board; the Merrill Lynch brand and senior banker relationships keep market share remarkably consistent over the long term. However, the capital markets business dwarfs banking, with about 3 times the revenue, and is a bigger driver of the company's value. The underwriting, advisory, and capital markets businesses have performed well in strong financial markets. Expansion efforts here have been focused on increasing prime brokerage (providing loans and market access to hedge funds).

The unit that separates Merrill from its Wall Street peers is the retail brokerage, or private client unit. This group is the largest brokerage on Wall Street, controlling close to $1.4 trillion in client assets, and its competitive advantage is evident. The average financial advisor brings in around three quarters of a million dollars, while the pretax margin has expanded to the high teens, compared with 12% in 2002. These results compare favorably with Morgan Stanley's average revenue of about a half million per advisor and single digit pretax margins. The expansion plan for this business unit is to broaden the suite of everyday financial products, including bank deposits. The firm isn't above buying advisors and bringing them into the fold through training, as evidenced by its recent acquisition of 500-advisor firm Advest.

Merrill spun off its investment management group, swapping about $540 billion in assets under management for a 49.8% stake in topnotch asset manager BlackRock--a deal that will about double BlackRock's size. The move made strategic sense, eliminating the perceived conflict of interest from having brokers hawk in-house funds. The unit provided less than 8% of the firm's profits in 2005, and we think Merrill got slightly less than fair value for the business, resulting in a small drop in our fair value estimate.

Data as of 12-29-06

Metropolitan Life Insurance MET

Rating ★★★	Fair Value $59.00	Last Close $59.01	Consider Buy $45.50	Consider Sell $73.90	Yield % 1.00

Company Profile

MetLife provides myriad insurance and financial services to individual and institutional customers through several distribution channels. The firm offers life insurance, annuities, and individual automobile and homeowner's insurance, as well as group insurance, reinsurance, and retirement and savings products and services to corporations and institutions. MetLife is a leading insurance provider in several foreign markets, including Mexico, Argentina, and Chile.

Management   Stewardship Grade [B]

In 2006, C. Robert Henrikson was unanimously elected MetLife's chairman and CEO after more than 33 years with MetLife. Henrikson has held numerous executive positions including president and chief operating officer. We think management is compensated fairly based on its performance and in comparison with its peer group. Henrikson owns $22 million in MetLife stock, which we think is sufficient to align his interests with those of shareholders. The board of directors retains the voting power on 39% of outstanding shares, which were allocated to eligible policyholders when the company demutualized. This gives the board de facto control.

200 Park Avenue
New York, NY 10010-3690

Growth [B+]	2002	2003	2004	2005
Revenue %	6.5	8.1	10.3	15.4
Earnings/Share %	254.8	33.6	24.2	68.8
Book Value/Share %	13.2	18.8	6.7	27.6
Dividends/Share %	5.0	9.5	100.0	13.0

Profitability [D]	2003	2004	2005	TTM
Return on Assets %	0.7	0.8	1.0	0.6
Oper Cash Flow $Mil	6,127	6,510	8,005	—
- Cap Spending $Mil	—	—	—	—
= Free Cash Flow $Mil	—	—	—	—

Financial Health [NA]	2003	2004	2005	09-30-06
Long-term Debt $Mil	—	—	—	—
Total Equity $Mil	21,149	22,824	29,100	31,609
Debt/Equity Ratio	—	—	—	—

Industry	Business Risk	Moat Size	Investment Style	Sector
Insurance (Life)	Average	Narrow	Large Value	Financial Services

Competition

	Market Cap $Mil	12 Mo Trailing Sales $Mil	Price/Cash Flow	Return On Assets%	Debt/ Equity	Total Return% 1 Yr	3 Yr
Metropolitan Life Insurance	44,861	47,120	—	0.6	—	21.7	22.0
American International Gr	186,296	110,593	—	1.2	—	6.1	3.2
Merrill Lynch & Company	82,298	32,796	—	0.8	—	39.3	18.6

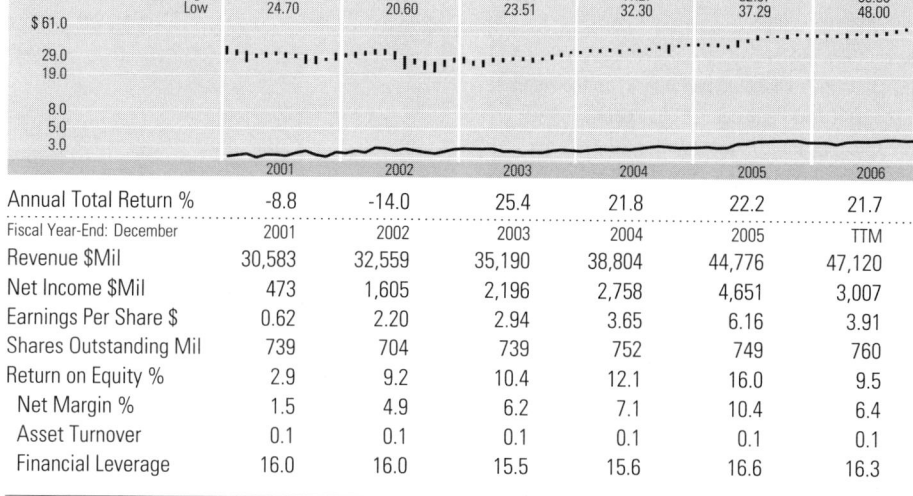

	2001	2002	2003	2004	2005	TTM
Annual Total Return %	-8.8	-14.0	25.4	21.8	22.2	21.7
Fiscal Year-End: December	2001	2002	2003	2004	2005	TTM
Revenue $Mil	30,583	32,559	35,190	38,804	44,776	47,120
Net Income $Mil	473	1,605	2,196	2,758	4,651	3,007
Earnings Per Share $	0.62	2.20	2.94	3.65	6.16	3.91
Shares Outstanding Mil	739	704	739	752	749	760
Return on Equity %	2.9	9.2	10.4	12.1	16.0	9.5
Net Margin %	1.5	4.9	6.2	7.1	10.4	6.4
Asset Turnover	0.1	0.1	0.1	0.1	0.1	0.1
Financial Leverage	16.0	16.0	15.5	15.6	16.6	16.3

Valuation Ratios	Stock	Rel to Industry	Rel to S&P 500
Price/Earnings	15.8	0.6	0.8
Price/Book	1.4	0.4	0.3
Price/Sales	1.0	0.4	0.3
Price/Cash Flow	—	—	—

Major Fund Holders	% of Fund Assets
Fidelity Select Insurance	5.48
Schwab Core Equity	4.53
Schwab Financial Services	4.46
Rochdale Large Value	4.05

Thesis By Dafina Dunmore, CFA, 12-07-06 Stock Price as of Analysis: $57.54

MetLife boasts a powerful brand, robust multichannel distribution, and tremendous scale economies, which allow it to spread its costs over a large book of business. MetLife uses this leverage to further invest in its brand and first-class technology to operate its cost-efficient group insurance business. We think this endows the insurer with a narrow economic moat. Our fair value estimate is $59 per share.

MetLife has one of the most recognizable brands in the life insurance industry, and we think Snoopy helps the insurer win both retail and institutional business. While it's no secret that people want to do business with firms they know, that is not enough to win new business. A large, diversified distribution network allows MetLife to reach its clients through multiple channels.

The Travelers acquisition augments MetLife's tremendous scale in the group insurance business. MetLife's operational platform allows it to add new business with little incremental cost, and its online administration ensures simplicity and efficiency for employers. This contributes to the near 20% returns on equity in the employer-sponsored business, although we think increased competition will drive profits down. Management has increased its focus on the small business market, where competition is less intense.

The voluntary benefits market--where employees pay all or a portion of the premium--continues to grow, as employers struggle with rising health-care costs. MetLife's existing employer relationships gives it tremendous cross-selling ability. These supplemental benefits also afford MetLife reduced earnings volatility via diversification of businesses.

MetLife's individual business contributes about 40% of its profits, but clings to a slim competitive advantage. The insurer continues to endure spread compression in its life insurance and fixed annuity business. We think an unrelenting inverted, or flat, yield curve could further pressure MetLife's margins during 2007.

MetLife has an enviable position in international markets, which was augmented by the Travelers deal. Prior to the acquisition, MetLife enjoyed a satisfactory presence in emerging markets while Travelers possessed relationships in more developed markets. This combination yields an international platform with solid earnings generation and sound growth potential.

Data as of 12-29-06

MGIC Investment MTG

	Rating	Fair Value	Last Close	Consider Buy	Consider Sell	Yield %
	★★★★	$76.00	$62.54	$58.60	$95.20	1.60

Company Profile
With more than $165 billion of insured loans, MGIC is the largest U.S. mortgage insurer. MGIC's client base includes more than 13,800 master policyholders, and the firm insures more than 1.2 million mortgages. MGIC's mortgage insurance protects lenders against higher default rates on homes purchased with less than a 20% down payment. MGIC owns 46% of C-BASS, which invests in credit-sensitive mortgages, and 34% of Sherman Financial, an investor in delinquent credit cards.

Management
Stewardship Grade [A]

MGIC's management could be forgiven for feeling as if the cards it was dealt came from a deck stacked with jokers. Record-low interest rates, the rise of lender captives, and massive market share loss to piggyback loans have made this decade challenging and consistently pressured the stock price. However, we think management has reacted intelligently, especially by continually repurchasing shares at attractive prices. During 2005, MGIC repurchased about 9% of its shares outstanding. However, the shares remained attractively valued and the balance sheet overcapitalized, so management continued buying back the firm's stock throughout 2006, repurchasing another 5.9 million shares at an average price of $63. As these purchases were at prices below our fair value estimate, we think they created appreciable value for shareholders. We think management's healthy financial stake in the firm fostered this laudable stewardship. Collectively, directors and officers own about 1.14% of MGIC, a $65 million investment. Plus, the CEO and directors must own shares exceeding 5 times the value of their annual cash compensation. Even better, return on equity is the primary metric in the managers' cash bonus plan.

250 East Kilbourn Avenue
Milwaukee, WI 53202
www.mgic.com

Growth [D-]	2002	2003	2004	2005
Revenue %	12.9	13.5	-4.3	-5.3
Earnings/Share %	1.9	-17.4	12.8	20.4
Book Value/Share %	16.3	17.7	9.9	6.8
Dividends/Share %	0.0	12.5	100.0	133.3

Profitability [A]	2003	2004	2005	TTM
Return on Assets %	8.3	8.7	9.9	8.8
Oper Cash Flow $Mil	687	559	508	—
- Cap Spending $Mil	—	—	—	—
= Free Cash Flow $Mil	—	—	—	—

Financial Health [NA]	2003	2004	2005	09-30-06
Long-term Debt $Mil	—	—	—	—
Total Equity $Mil	3,797	4,144	4,165	4,220
Debt/Equity Ratio	—	—	—	—

Industry	Business Risk	Moat Size	Investment Style	Sector
Insurance (Property)	Average	Narrow	Mid Value	Financial Services

Competition	Market Cap $Mil	12 Mo Trailing Sales $Mil	Price/Cash Flow	Return On Assets%	Debt/ Equity	Total Return% 1 Yr	3 Yr
MGIC Investment	5,192	1,473	—	8.8	—	-3.4	4.5
Radian Group	4,344	1,279	—	6.8	—	-7.9	3.8
PMI Group	3,747	1,171	—	7.6	—	15.4	8.8

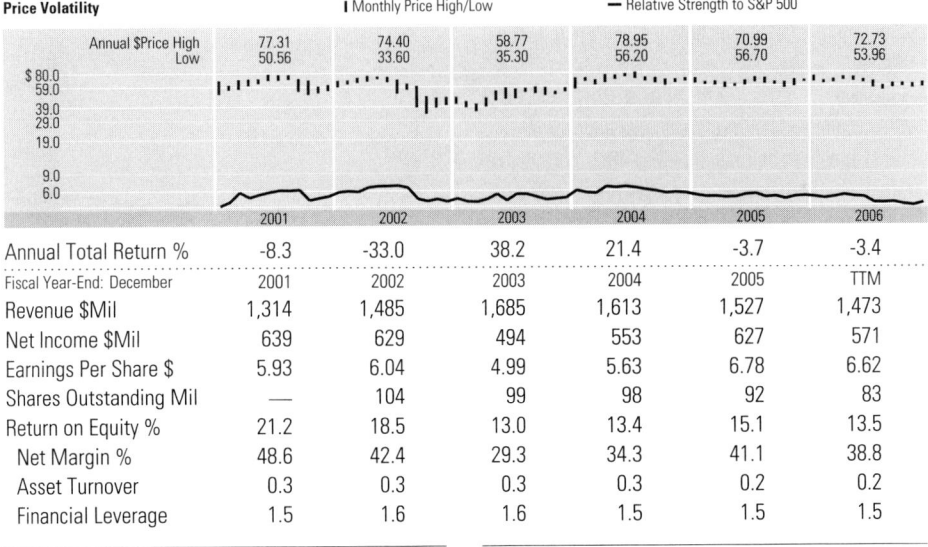

	2001	2002	2003	2004	2005	2006
Annual $Price High	77.31	74.40	58.77	78.95	70.99	72.73
Low	50.56	33.60	35.30	56.20	56.70	53.96
Annual Total Return %	-8.3	-33.0	38.2	21.4	-3.7	-3.4

Fiscal Year-End: December	2001	2002	2003	2004	2005	TTM
Revenue $Mil	1,314	1,485	1,685	1,613	1,527	1,473
Net Income $Mil	639	629	494	553	627	571
Earnings Per Share $	5.93	6.04	4.99	5.63	6.78	6.62
Shares Outstanding Mil	—	104	99	98	92	83
Return on Equity %	21.2	18.5	13.0	13.4	15.1	13.5
Net Margin %	48.6	42.4	29.3	34.3	41.1	38.8
Asset Turnover	0.3	0.3	0.3	0.3	0.2	0.2
Financial Leverage	1.5	1.6	1.6	1.5	1.5	1.5

Valuation Ratios	Stock	Rel to Industry	Rel to S&P 500
Price/Earnings	9.4	0.7	0.5
Price/Book	1.2	0.7	0.3
Price/Sales	3.5	2.5	1.2
Price/Cash Flow	—	—	—

Major Fund Holders	% of Fund Assets
Fidelity Select Home Finance	4.21
FMI Focus	2.97
Madison Mosaic Investors	2.74
CastleRock	2.66

Thesis By Jim Ryan, 11-15-06 Stock Price as of Analysis: $60.50

We believe lender consolidation has tarnished the luster on MGIC's crown via the rise of captives and competition from piggyback mortgages. We think MGIC shares are worth $76 each.

MGIC's clients--the rapidly consolidating mortgage originators--have flexed their muscles and breached the firm's moat. Despite MGIC's initial resistence, lagging market share resulted in the firm allowing lenders to establish captives--private insurers--to reinsure MGIC's portfolio. To win mortgage insurance business from these lenders, MGIC must cede as much as 40% of its traditional flow channel insurance premium to the captive in return for protection against large losses. Because lenders established a loss rate well above historical levels, the net effect is a reinsurance policy that pays MGIC only in dire times of mortgage defaults. We suspect that while some of the costs of captive reinsurance cut into MGIC's margins, the better part of it is passed on to the mortgage borrower. After all, it's the borrower who pays, not the lender.

During the mortgage market explosion of the early 2000s, MGIC, as well as all other mortgage guarantors, lost about 40%-50% of potential new business to piggyback loans. These mortgages are structured as an 80% first mortgage, 10% home-equity loan, and 10% down payment (or some variant thereof) to avoid non-tax-deductible mortgage insurance. This was partially a cyclical problem, as low interest rates and risk perceptions temporarily reduced the interest rate spread between first and second mortgages, making home-equity loans cheaper than mortgage insurance in many instances. While rising interest rates will lessen this problem, it won't go away--lenders earn attractive profits from selling home-equity loans, but nothing for selling mortgage insurance. We think the market will settle somewhere in the middle range of the historic 5%-10% rate of piggyback mortgages and the levels reached in the mortgage boom. That would add about $100 million in additional annual revenue to the mortgage insurance market of which MGIC would garner a large slice of the bigger pie.

MGIC missed a golden opportunity to protect its moat through international expansion. The company must now play catch-up to Genworth and PMI Group, which have made significant inroads into Australia, Canada, and other foreign markets. MGIC has filed to issue mortgage insurance in Canada next year but it's far behind the competition.

Data as of 12-29-06

MGM Mirage MGM

	Rating	Fair Value	Last Close	Consider Buy	Consider Sell	Yield %
	★★★	$54.00	$57.35	$41.60	$67.70	0.00

Company Profile

MGM Mirage owns and operates casinos in Nevada, Mississippi, and Michigan. MGM acquired Mandalay Resort Group in 2005, adding casinos such as Mandalay Bay, Luxor, and Excalibur to its portfolio, which already included the likes of the Bellagio, MGM Grand, New York-New York, Mirage, and Treasure Island. The firm also owns a 50% interest in the Borgata in Atlantic City and a joint venture in Macau. MGM is also constructing the $7 billion Project City Center on the Strip.

Management   Stewardship Grade [C]

Kirk Kerkorian, 88, has a long, illustrious record in the gaming industry and holds more than 55% of the stock through his investment vehicle Tracinda Corp. MGM has a deep, well-respected management team, headed by chairman and CEO Terrence Lanni. The superb profit margins posted across the company's property portfolio speak to management's proficiency at operating casinos. MGM's executives are very well paid for its performance. In 2005, Lanni received more than $8 million in salary and bonus (up from $5.4 million in 2004) as well as a large slug of option grants, while his top three officers each cleared close to $6 million. Variable compensation in 2005 was based on the company meeting set operating income targets. While we like that compensation is based on performance, we'd prefer a metric more tailored to drive value creation, such as returns on invested capital. This is especially important for a capital-intensive business such as MGM's.

3600 Las Vegas Boulevard South   www.mgmmirage.com
Las Vegas, NV 89109

Growth [A+]	2002	2003	2004	2005
Revenue %	1.5	2.8	9.7	52.9
Earnings/Share %	71.7	-11.5	77.6	4.9
Book Value/Share %	5.8	1.0	14.8	13.9
Dividends/Share %	NMF	NMF	NMF	NMF

Profitability [C]	2003	2004	2005	TTM
Return on Assets %	2.3	3.7	2.1	2.5
Oper Cash Flow $Mil	741	829	1,183	1,161
- Cap Spending $Mil	550	703	760	1,716
= Free Cash Flow $Mil	191	126	423	EUB

Financial Health [C-]	2003	2004	2005	09-30-06
Long-term Debt $Mil	5,645	5,613	12,551	13,171
Total Equity $Mil	2,534	2,772	3,235	3,541
Debt/Equity Ratio	2.2	2.0	3.9	3.7

Industry	Business Risk	Moat Size	Investment Style	Sector
Gambling/Casinos	Average	Narrow	Large Growth	Consumer Services

Competition

	Market Cap $Mil	12 Mo Trailing Sales $Mil	Price/Cash Flow	Return On Assets%	Debt/Equity	Total Return% 1 Yr	3 Yr
MGM Mirage	16,125	7,451	13.9	2.5	3.7	56.4	45.5
Harrah's Entertainment	15,388	9,439	11.3	1.6	1.8	18.6	21.7
AZR							

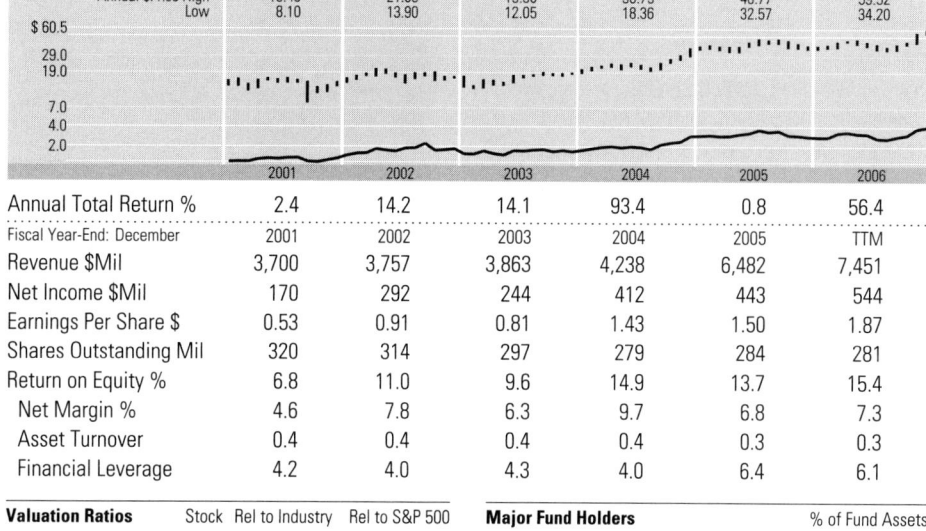

Price Volatility — Monthly Price High/Low — Relative Strength to S&P 500

	2001	2002	2003	2004	2005	2006
Annual $Price High	16.43	21.00	19.30	36.75	46.77	59.52
Low	8.10	13.90	12.05	18.36	32.57	34.20
Annual Total Return %	2.4	14.2	14.1	93.4	0.8	56.4
Fiscal Year-End: December	2001	2002	2003	2004	2005	TTM
Revenue $Mil	3,700	3,757	3,863	4,238	6,482	7,451
Net Income $Mil	170	292	244	412	443	544
Earnings Per Share $	0.53	0.91	0.81	1.43	1.50	1.87
Shares Outstanding Mil	320	314	297	279	284	281
Return on Equity %	6.8	11.0	9.6	14.9	13.7	15.4
Net Margin %	4.6	7.8	6.3	9.7	6.8	7.3
Asset Turnover	0.4	0.4	0.4	0.4	0.3	0.3
Financial Leverage	4.2	4.0	4.3	4.0	6.4	6.1

Valuation Ratios	Stock	Rel to Industry	Rel to S&P 500
Price/Earnings	30.7	0.7	1.5
Price/Book	4.6	0.5	1.1
Price/Sales	2.2	0.3	0.8
Price/Cash Flow	13.9	0.6	1.0

Major Fund Holders	% of Fund Assets
Delaware Large Cap Growth Instl	3.41
Delaware Pooled Large-Cap Growth Eqty	3.25
Delaware U.S. Growth A	3.21
Vice Fund	3.19

Thesis By Sumit Desai, CFA, 11-21-06 Stock Price as of Analysis: $49.00

MGM owns some of the most attractive properties in the gaming industry, including the Bellagio, Mandalay Bay, and MGM Grand. In our opinion, MGM's competitive position and future prospects earn it a narrow moat.

MGM solidified its presence on the Las Vegas Strip with its $7 billion purchase of Mandalay Bay in 2005. As a result of the deal, MGM now earns 80% of its revenue from its Strip properties. In addition, it controls 50% of the hotel rooms, 37% of all slots, and 32% of the table games on the Strip. The acquisition also boosted MGM's footprint in the Las Vegas conventions market. This business is important because it helps fill rooms during the otherwise slow mid-week periods. Accordingly, MGM's average hotel occupancy rates generally range in the mid- to high-90s and are usually above the average rate for the overall Las Vegas market.

MGM is embarking on two new projects, both of which should give a significant boost to the company's top line. First is City Center, a $7 billion mega-casino that will include a 4,000-room casino resort, two luxury condominium buildings, two boutique hotels, and about 470,000 square feet of retail and entertainment space. The timing of this project is less than ideal, as its late-2009 opening will coincide with the completion of almost $20 billion of other new hotel and casino construction projects in Las Vegas. We're not too worried by this, however, and believe the market will absorb this capacity over time. Through 2010, the number of hotel rooms in Las Vegas is expected to grow at about a 5% annual rate--in line with historical growth rates since 1970. So long as the number of visitors to Las Vegas grows at the same clip (it has for the past 35 years), we think MGM should earn a respectable return on its investment.

MGM's second major project is its 50% interest in MGM Grand Macau, slated to open in late 2007. The growth prospects for this region, just south of mainland China, are exciting. Over 100 million people live within 3 hours of Macau but only 18.7 million people visited the region in 2005, versus about 39 million visitors in Vegas. Despite fewer visitors, Macau generates almost the same amount of gaming revenue as the Vegas Strip and is set to grow much faster over the next several years. Fueling this growth are Macau's prime geographic location, a booming middle class in China, and loosened Chinese travel restrictions. We think the region can generate as much as $10 billion in gaming revenue by 2010 and expect MGM to participate in this growth.

Data as of 12-29-06

Microsoft MSFT

	Rating	Fair Value	Last Close	Consider Buy	Consider Sell	Yield %
	★★★★	$34.00	$29.86	$29.00	$44.60	1.24

Company Profile

Microsoft develops the Windows operating system and the Office suite of productivity software. Windows and Office account for roughly 60% of Microsoft's revenue, with another 25% coming from software for enterprise servers. The firm's other businesses include the Xbox video game console, MSN Internet service, business software, and software for mobile devices.

Industry	Business Risk	Moat Size	Investment Style	Sector
Business Appl.	Below Avg	Wide	Large Growth	Software

Competition

	Market Cap $Mil	12 Mo Trailing Sales $Mil	Price/Cash Flow	Return On Assets %	Debt/Equity	Total Return % 1 Yr	3 Yr
Microsoft	293,538	45,352	20.8	19.8	—	15.8	7.6
IBM	146,342	89,593	9.8	8.8	0.4	19.8	3.0
Google	140,979	9,319	42.4	15.4	0.0	11.0	—

Price Volatility — Monthly Price High/Low — Relative Strength to S&P 500

Annual $Price High	38.08	35.31	30.00	30.20	28.25	30.26
Low	21.44	20.71	22.55	24.01	23.82	21.46

	2001	2002	2003	2004	2005	2006
Annual Total Return %	52.8	-22.0	6.8	9.0	-0.9	15.8

Fiscal Year-End: June	2002	2003	2004	2005	2006	TTM
Revenue $Mil	28,365	32,187	36,835	39,788	44,282	45,352
Net Income $Mil	5,355	7,531	8,168	12,254	12,599	12,936
Earnings Per Share $	0.48	0.69	0.75	1.12	1.20	1.26
Shares Outstanding Mil	—	10,759	10,747	10,844	10,412	9,830
Return on Equity %	9.8	11.6	10.9	25.5	31.4	35.8
Net Margin %	18.9	23.4	22.2	30.8	28.5	28.5
Asset Turnover	0.4	0.4	0.4	0.6	0.6	0.7
Financial Leverage	1.3	1.3	1.3	1.5	1.7	1.8

Management

Stewardship Grade [A]

Chairman Bill Gates and CEO Steve Ballmer are two of the brightest minds in technology. Ray Ozzie, Microsoft's new chief technical officer, will also play an important role in shaping the firm's strategy. As evidenced by the firm's continuing record of excellent returns on invested capital, management has done a superb job of transitioning Microsoft from a hypergrowth company to a mature technology giant. Although returns have declined in recent years as the firm has entered new markets outside Windows and Office, Microsoft still earned a very respectable 60% ROIC in fiscal 2005. Management also takes corporate governance seriously. Gates and Ballmer own about 10% and 4% of Microsoft, respectively, and neither has taken any stock options in the past decade. We think this level of ownership clearly aligns management's interests with those of outside shareholders. Executive compensation is below that of other large technology firms. In addition, the replacement of employee stock options with restricted-stock grants earns Microsoft a high Stewardship Grade.

Valuation Ratios	Stock	Rel to Industry	Rel to S&P 500
Price/Earnings	23.7	0.8	1.2
Price/Book	8.1	1.0	2.0
Price/Sales	6.5	1.0	2.2
Price/Cash Flow	20.8	0.8	1.4

Major Fund Holders	% of Fund Assets
ICON Information Technology	12.02
Old Mutual Focused Z	11.12
Tilson Focus	9.52
E*TRADE Technology Index	9.43

One Microsoft Way www.microsoft.com
Redmond, WA 98052-6399

Growth [B]	2003	2004	2005	2006
Revenue %	13.5	14.4	8.0	11.3
Earnings/Share %	43.8	8.7	49.3	7.1
Book Value/Share %	21.0	15.5	-36.0	-13.1
Dividends/Share %	NMF	100.0	1975.0	-89.8

Profitability [A+]	2004	2005	2006	TTM
Return on Assets %	8.7	17.3	18.1	19.8
Oper Cash Flow $Bil	14.6	16.6	14.4	14.1
- Cap Spending $Bil	1.1	0.8	1.6	1.8
= Free Cash Flow $Bil	13.5	15.8	12.8	12.4

Financial Health [A]	2004	2005	2006	09-30-06
Long-term Debt $Bil	—	—	—	—
Total Equity $Bil	74.8	48.1	40.1	36.1
Debt/Equity Ratio	—	—	—	—

Thesis By Toan Tran, 12-15-06 Stock Price as of Analysis: $30.19

With Windows Vista and Office 2007 on the horizon, Microsoft is at the cusp of a strong product introduction cycle that will add another chapter to the firm's long history of growth. In addition, Microsoft is prudently investing to ensure that there are many more chapters ahead for the world's largest software company.

Although Microsoft has ventured into other markets, the majority of its revenue and profits still flow from two exceptional franchises: the Windows operating system and Office productivity suite. These two businesses place Microsoft in the enviable position of collecting a toll on almost every personal computer system. Operating margins for both businesses average more than 70%, and they generate a significant portion of Microsoft's $15 billion of annual free cash flow. Microsoft's competitive position is also very defensible, thanks to the powerful network effects associated with an almost universally adopted operating system and suite of productivity software.

Microsoft has conquered much of the software world, but disruptive change is a hallmark of the technology industry. Microsoft must now prepare for a software-as-a-service (SaaS) world, where software is delivered on-demand over the Internet and paid for with traditional licenses, subscription fees, or even advertising. The success of Salesforce.com is a prime example of the allure of SaaS to enterprise customers, and it's not a stretch to see that Google could eventually release a Web-based competitor to Office. Microsoft is acutely aware of the threats and opportunities posed by what Bill Gates has called the "coming services wave," and the firm is willing to sacrifice near-term profitability to address it. We think this is absolutely the right decision. The industry is changing, and if Microsoft does not adapt, its competitive advantages will one day disappear.

SaaS brings a new set of challenges, but we believe Microsoft is one of the few firms with the resources to compete effectively. The infrastructure cost required to provision SaaS on a large scale could total in the billions, and this will be a significant barrier to entry. While Microsoft is not always an innovator and its first attempts often fail, the firm's persistence is impressive. We think this long-term perspective, coupled with unmatched financial resources, will serve Microsoft well in the years ahead.

Millennium Pharmaceuticals MLNM

Data as of 12-29-06

	Rating	Fair Value	Last Close	Consider Buy	Consider Sell	Yield %
	★★★	$11.00	$10.90	$7.00	$13.30	0.00

Company Profile

Millennium discovers and develops biopharmaceuticals to treat cancer, cardiovascular disease, and inflammatory conditions. The firm markets Velcade for multiple myeloma and mantle cell lymphoma in the U.S., and will begin copromoting the drug within the U.S. in 2007 with its former U.S. partner, Johnson & Johnson. Millennium returned the distribution rights for cardiovascular disease drug Integrilin to Schering-Plough, but will continue to receive substantial royalties.

Management

Stewardship Grade [D]

In July 2005, Mark Levin ended his 12-year career as head of Millennium and was replaced by Deborah Dunsire, a pharmaceutical veteran who took part in the launch of cancer drug Gleevec while she was at Novartis. Her considerable oncology experience should help the company make the most of Velcade, but we are disappointed by the price of her arrival; her annual salary and cash bonus amount to $1.4 million, double that of the former CEO. Add the 400,000 shares of stock she was given, $300,000 signing bonus, and 450,000 stock options, and we are even more disappointed. Christophe Bianchi's employment package is equally generous for a company otherwise preoccupied with reducing expenses. A Sanofi-Aventis veteran with 17 years of U.S. pharmaceutical experience, Bianchi joined Millennium as executive vice president of commercial operations in 2006 for annual cash compensation of roughly $600,000, as well as 200,000 options, 30,000 shares of restricted stock, a $100,000 tax-deferred account, and $60,000 in additional bonuses. The company also consistently points to non-GAAP earnings that exclude habitual restructuring, amortization, and stock-option compensation expenses, a habit that makes us skeptical of the merit behind any management profitability goals.

40 Landsdowne Street
Cambridge, MA 02139
www.mlnm.com

Growth [D+]	2002	2003	2004	2005
Revenue %	43.4	22.8	3.3	24.6
Earnings/Share %	NMF	NMF	NMF	NMF
Book Value/Share %	45.7	-19.5	-11.3	-9.3
Dividends/Share %	NMF	NMF	NMF	NMF

Profitability [C+]	2003	2004	2005	TTM
Return on Assets %	-16.1	-9.2	-7.8	-3.9
Oper Cash Flow $Mil	-221	-173	-57	-33
- Cap Spending $Mil	52	50	12	11
= Free Cash Flow $Mil	-274	-223	-69	-44

Financial Health [C]	2003	2004	2005	09-30-06
Long-term Debt $Mil	193	186	176	75
Total Equity $Mil	2,502	2,273	2,102	2,114
Debt/Equity Ratio	0.1	0.1	0.1	0.0

Industry	Business Risk	Moat Size	Investment Style	Sector
Biotechnology	Above Avg	Narrow	Mid Growth	Healthcare

Competition	Market Cap $Mil	12 Mo Trailing Sales $Mil	Price/Cash Flow	Return On Assets%	Debt/Equity	Total Return% 1 Yr	3 Yr
Millennium Pharmaceuticals	3,445	469	—	-3.9	0.0	12.4	-16.7
Genentech	85,511	8,462	42.1	13.4	0.2	-12.3	20.1
Celgene	20,276	773	EUB	3.3	0.5	77.6	72.0

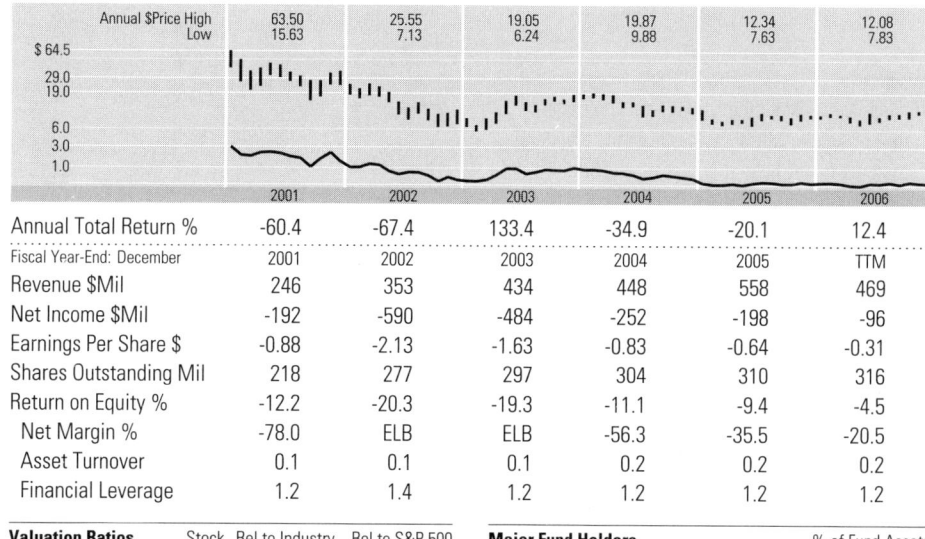

	2001	2002	2003	2004	2005	2006
Annual Total Return %	-60.4	-67.4	133.4	-34.9	-20.1	12.4

Fiscal Year-End: December	2001	2002	2003	2004	2005	TTM
Revenue $Mil	246	353	434	448	558	469
Net Income $Mil	-192	-590	-484	-252	-198	-96
Earnings Per Share $	-0.88	-2.13	-1.63	-0.83	-0.64	-0.31
Shares Outstanding Mil	218	277	297	304	310	316
Return on Equity %	-12.2	-20.3	-19.3	-11.1	-9.4	-4.5
Net Margin %	-78.0	ELB	ELB	-56.3	-35.5	-20.5
Asset Turnover	0.1	0.1	0.1	0.2	0.2	0.2
Financial Leverage	1.2	1.4	1.2	1.2	1.2	1.2

Valuation Ratios	Stock	Rel to Industry	Rel to S&P 500
Price/Earnings	NMF	—	—
Price/Book	1.6	0.2	0.4
Price/Sales	7.3	0.6	2.5
Price/Cash Flow	—	—	—

Major Fund Holders	% of Fund Assets
Eaton Vance Worldwide Health Sci A	3.64
Kinetics Medical	2.30
Rydex Biotechnology Inv	2.19
First Eagle Fund of America Y	1.90

Thesis By Karen Andersen, 12-15-06 Stock Price as of Analysis: $11.53

Millennium Pharmaceuticals markets its sole drug, Velcade, as the leading treatment for relapsed multiple myeloma and as a new option for some lymphoma patients. However, multiple myeloma has turned into a highly competitive cancer niche, and Millennium's pipeline, which regularly falters before hitting late-stage trials, doesn't provide any relief from the company's high-risk, one-drug profile.

Millennium discovers and develops drugs using a genomics-based research platform. Historically, the bulk of Millennium's revenue came from alliances with large pharmaceutical partners and sales of its acquired cardiovascular disease drug Integrilin. Shortly after Deborah Dunsire's arrival as CEO, Millennium smartly returned Integrilin rights to its marketing partner Schering-Plough. This removed a slow-growth product from the company's revenue stream but also provides significant royalties to contribute to pipeline development.

Millennium's first internally developed product, Velcade, reached the market in 2003 as a novel drug to treat relapsed multiple myeloma. Velcade enjoys a sizable market share approaching 50% in second- and third-line treatment and U.S. sales should surpass $200 million in 2006. However, strong competition could prevent Millennium from extending its use to newly diagnosed patients. Celgene's Thalomid has been used for years to treat multiple myeloma, and the company has now received approval for Revlimid, an improved version of Thalomid with fewer side effects and better efficacy. Phase III data currently indicates that Revlimid is the more effective drug in newly diagnosed patients, which should limit Velcade's ability to expand its 10% market share in this patient group.

Velcade is also being studied in several areas outside of multiple myeloma, and it was recently approved for a rare but aggressive form of blood cancer known as mantle cell lymphoma. While Millennium is also hoping to piggyback on the use of Genentech's antibody Rituxan in other, more common forms of lymphoma, we're not optimistic that the combination will prove significantly more effective than Rituxan alone.

Millennium's pipeline outside of multiple myeloma is growing, and the company has several cancer and inflammation-related drugs in early-stage clinical trials, but success outside multiple myeloma is still a gamble, and we're waiting for more data before becoming too enthusiastic about Millennium's prospects.

Data as of 12-29-06

Mittal Steel Co NV MT

	Rating	Fair Value	Last Close	Consider Buy	Consider Sell	Yield %
	★★★	$45.00	$42.18	$34.70	$56.40	1.19

Company Profile
Arcelor Mittal is the world's largest steel producer. The company produces steel in 27 countries and has the capacity to produce more than 115 million tons of steel annually. Arcelor Mittal also operates several iron mines, coal mines, coke plants and the largest European metal distribution system. The company produces a mixture of both long and flat steel and operates both integrated and mini-mill operations.

Industry	Business Risk	Moat Size	Investment Style	Sector
Steel/Iron	Average	Narrow	Large Core	Industrial Materials

Competition

	Market Cap $Mil	12 Mo Trailing Sales $Mil	Price/Cash Flow	Return On Assets%	Debt/Equity	Total Return% 1 Yr	3 Yr
Mittal Steel Co NV	29,697	28,132	7.5	10.8	0.9	62.5	68.8
Posco ADR	26,486	25,544	5.0	14.5	0.1	67.0	35.0
Nucor	16,514	14,490	7.9	21.4	0.2	70.7	61.9

Price Volatility

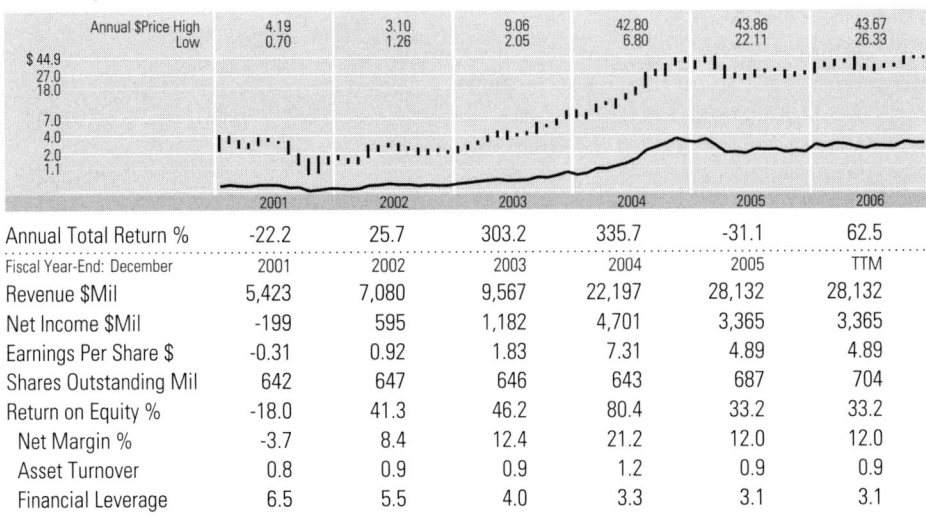

| Annual $Price High | 4.19 | 3.10 | 9.06 | 42.80 | 43.86 | 43.67 |
| Low | 0.70 | 1.26 | 2.05 | 6.80 | 22.11 | 26.33 |

	2001	2002	2003	2004	2005	2006
Annual Total Return %	-22.2	25.7	303.2	335.7	-31.1	62.5

Fiscal Year-End: December	2001	2002	2003	2004	2005	TTM
Revenue $Mil	5,423	7,080	9,567	22,197	28,132	28,132
Net Income $Mil	-199	595	1,182	4,701	3,365	3,365
Earnings Per Share $	-0.31	0.92	1.83	7.31	4.89	4.89
Shares Outstanding Mil	642	647	646	643	687	704
Return on Equity %	-18.0	41.3	46.2	80.4	33.2	33.2
Net Margin %	-3.7	8.4	12.4	21.2	12.0	12.0
Asset Turnover	0.8	0.9	0.9	1.2	0.9	0.9
Financial Leverage	6.5	5.5	4.0	3.3	3.1	3.1

Management
Stewardship Grade [NA]

Although we consider the Mittal family to be "in charge" of Arcelor Mittal, it's far from the unilateral position the family held at predecessor Mittal. Owning just under 50% of the stock, Lakshmi Mittal and son Aditya have retained the positions of President of the Board and CFO, respectively. Former Arcelor Chairman Joseph Kinsch will take over as Chairman of Arcelor Mittal with the understanding that he will eventually cede the position to Lakshmi Mittal. Roland Junck has assumed the post of CEO. We'll see how long he holds onto it once the Mittal family has more formal control of the company. That could take up to five years given the standstill agreement that they signed as part of the merger agreement. The overall board membership is composed of six former board members from Arcelor, six from Mittal (including famed financier Wilbur Ross), three minority shareholder representatives and three employee representatives. Overall, the board counts eight independent members. We have a high overall regard for the Mittal family's stewardship and we gained respect for Kinsch's focus on maximizing shareholder value for Arcelor shareholders during the merger negotiation.

Valuation Ratios	Stock	Rel to Industry	Rel to S&P 500
Price/Earnings	8.6	0.7	0.4
Price/Book	2.9	0.6	0.7
Price/Sales	1.1	0.4	0.4
Price/Cash Flow	7.5	0.6	0.5

Major Fund Holders	% of Fund Assets
Legg Mason Opportunity Prim	4.31
JHFunds2 Natural Resources NAV	2.29
ProFunds Europe 30 Svc	2.03
Van Eck Global Hard Assets A	1.92

15th Floor, Hofplein 20
Rotterdam, Netherlands 3032 AC
www.ispat.com

Growth [NA]	2002	2003	2004	2005
Revenue %	30.6	35.1	132.0	26.7
Earnings/Share %	—	NMF	299.5	-33.1
Book Value/Share %	—	NMF	129.3	62.3
Dividends/Share %	NMF	NMF	NMF	NMF

Profitability [NA]	2003	2004	2005	TTM
Return on Assets %	11.7	24.5	10.8	10.8
Oper Cash Flow $Mil	1,438	4,611	3,974	3,974
- Cap Spending $Mil	421	898	1,181	1,181
= Free Cash Flow $Mil	1,017	3,713	2,793	2,793

Financial Health [NA]	2003	2004	2005	12-31-05
Long-term Debt $Mil	2,406	2,448	9,335	9,335
Total Equity $Mil	2,561	5,846	10,150	10,150
Debt/Equity Ratio	0.9	0.4	0.9	0.9

Thesis
By Scott Burns, 12-05-06 Stock Price as of Analysis: $41.80

The new Arcelor Mittal is a powerful combination that has changed the landscape of the global steel industry. Although the recent merger created some new challenges, we feel that Arcelor Mittal's narrow moat has only strengthened as a result of the merger.

Mittal's hostile bid for Arcelor in early 2006 led to the creation of the worlds largest steel producer with dominant market share in every geographic region except East Asia. As the only truly global steel producer, the company is uniquely positioned to read and respond to changing market demands and to serve an increasingly global base of manufacturers.

Arcelor Mittals portfolio of assets is balanced not only geographically, but also across the quality and cost spectrums. In North America and Western Europe, the company possesses the technological know-how to produce the metal demanded by high-end users such as automobile and appliance makers. In developing areas, the company has some of the most cost-competitive facilities in the world. Going forward, Arcelor Mittal will enjoy billions of dollars in synergies as technology is transferred to developing regions and low-cost raw steel is supplied to developed regions for finishing.

In terms of vertical integration, the combination diluted the self-sufficient position that predecessor Mittal enjoyed in terms of raw materials like iron ore, coal and coke. Arcelor Mittal will still internally generate 47% of its own iron ore needs (a high proportion for any producer) but this is still half of what Mittal produced on its own. We expect the company to continue to seek opportunities to regain its lost raw material self-sufficiency.

On the other end of the integration spectrum, Arcelor did contribute a distribution network that more or less dominates Europe. Control over the supply-chain should allow Arcelor Mittal to better gauge demand--and consequently production--in its European markets. Management has stated that they would like to explore replicating this model in North America and may be looking to acquire one of the large distribution firms located there.

Overall, scale, diversification and vertical integration won't eliminate the cyclicality that the company faces, but it should provide a much smoother ride for investors than steel companies have traditionally generated. As with any large merger, there are going to be challenges integrating operations and cultures. Still, Arcelor Mittal is really the culmination of a decade long industry consolidation process and we feel that management is more than up to the task.

Mohawk Industries MHK

Data as of 12-29-06

	Rating	Fair Value	Last Close	Consider Buy	Consider Sell	Yield %
	★★★★	$95.00	$74.86	$73.30	$119.00	0.00

Company Profile
Mohawk Industries manufactures flooring products including carpets, tiles, resilient, hardwood, and laminate. It markets its products under various brands that include Aladdin, Mohawk Home, Bigelow, Karastan, and Custom Weave. Mohawk distributes these goods through a variety of retail and wholesale channels for use in the construction and renovation of homes, offices, hospitals, schools, and government buildings.

Management
Stewardship Grade [B]

Overall, the company gets relatively high marks for its corporate governance practices. Good qualities include a reasonable executive compensation framework, no antitakeover measures, and no related-party transactions. Staggered director terms and a lack of separation between the CEO and chairman positions, however, keep the company from earning our highest Stewardship Grade. We think Jeffrey Lorberbaum has done a splendid job of growing the company during his five-year tenure as CEO. He has been particularly adept at identifying value-enhancing acquisitions and seamlessly integrating the acquired firms into the Mohawk portfolio. And with a 20% ownership stake in the company, we also like the fact that Lorberbaum's interests appear to be closely aligned to those of his fellow shareholders.

Industry	Business Risk	Moat Size	Investment Style	Sector
Textiles	Average	Narrow	Mid Value	Consumer Goods

Competition

	Market Cap $Mil	12 Mo Trailing Sales $Mil	Price/Cash Flow	Return On Assets%	Debt/ Equity	Total Return% 1 Yr	3 Yr
Mohawk Industries	5,070	7,812	6.5	4.8	0.7	-13.9	1.7
Interface A	779	1,014	15.9	0.0	2.4	73.0	34.5
Dixie Group	163	339	12.4	2.6	0.7	-8.3	16.3

Price Volatility

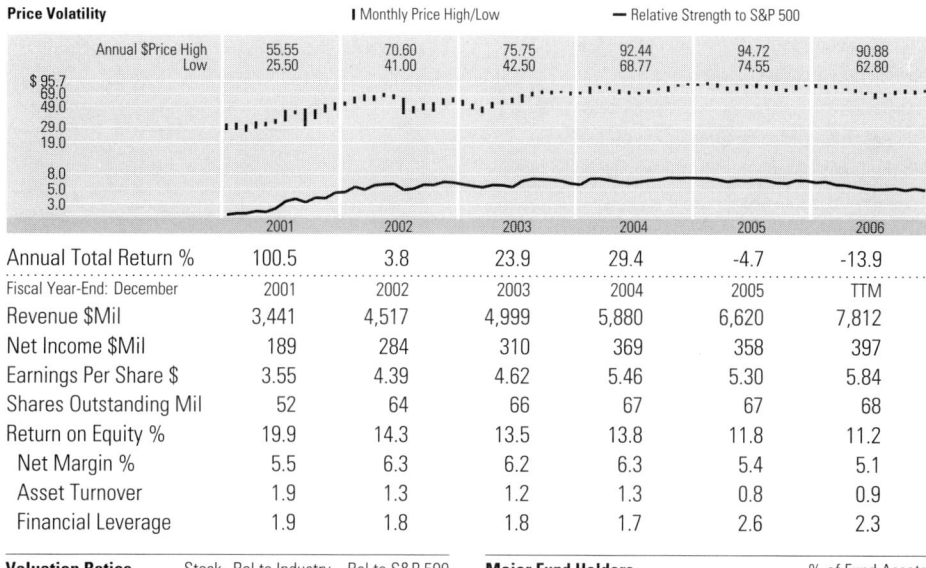

Annual Total Return %	100.5	3.8	23.9	29.4	-4.7	-13.9
Fiscal Year-End: December	2001	2002	2003	2004	2005	TTM
Revenue $Mil	3,441	4,517	4,999	5,880	6,620	7,812
Net Income $Mil	189	284	310	369	358	397
Earnings Per Share $	3.55	4.39	4.62	5.46	5.30	5.84
Shares Outstanding Mil	52	64	66	67	67	68
Return on Equity %	19.9	14.3	13.5	13.8	11.8	11.2
Net Margin %	5.5	6.3	6.2	6.3	5.4	5.1
Asset Turnover	1.9	1.3	1.2	1.3	0.8	0.9
Financial Leverage	1.9	1.8	1.8	1.7	2.6	2.3

Valuation Ratios	Stock	Rel to Industry	Rel to S&P 500	Major Fund Holders	% of Fund Assets
Price/Earnings	12.8	1.0	0.6	Sequoia	7.31
Price/Book	1.4	0.7	0.3	Wisdom Inv	5.13
Price/Sales	0.6	0.9	0.2	Fairholme	4.74
Price/Cash Flow	6.5	0.7	0.4	Ariel Appreciation	3.77

Thesis By John Kearney, CFA, 11-20-06 Stock Price as of Analysis: $76.07

Mohawk Industries has steadily become a commanding force in the $22 billion floor covering market. The breadth and depth of the company's distribution system remain unrivaled by its peers and will allow Mohawk to continue to bolster its share in the market, in our opinion.

Due to continued consolidation over the years, the U.S. flooring industry has become a virtual duopoly with more than 40% of the market now controlled by Mohawk Industries and Berkshire Hathaway's Shaw Industries. No other competitor has more than a single-digit percentage share of the floor covering market. Mohawk Industries is the leading producer of floor covering products for residential and commercial applications in the U.S. Consistent with its strategy to be a diversified total flooring company, Mohawk is entrenched in every floor covering category and at every price range.

Over the last decade, Mohawk has steadily increased its share of the flooring market through a series of well-executed and strategic acquisitions, including Dal-Tile in 2002. We think the company's late-2005 acquisition of Unilin Holdings will be equally successful in helping the firm expand its market position, as well as fueling continued earnings expansion in the modestly growing flooring industry. Unilin is the global leader in laminate flooring, one of the latest and fastest-growing segments of the flooring market. Mohawk will use its relationship with more than 30,000 vendors and its superior distribution capabilities to accelerate the penetration rate of Unilin's products in the U.S., where laminate flooring is quickly gaining in popularity and growing at a double-digit rate. Given the success rate management has achieved with its previous acquisitions (as illustrated by the company's relatively consistent double-digit ROICs over the last decade), we have a high degree of confidence that the Unilin acquisition will be accretive to shareholder value as well.

While Mohawk has been impacted by the housing slowdown, the company is not as susceptible to new home builds as is often perceived. In fact, 60% of the company's sales are derived from the replacement market, which has historically shown its greatest strength when the new construction market softened. Therefore, as long as consumer confidence and discretionary spending remain relatively strong, we think Mohawk will be able to generate adequate sales and profitability growth while at the same time strengthening its position in the consolidated flooring market.

P.O. Box 12069 160 S. Industrial Boulevard www.mohawkind.com
Calhoun, GA 30701

Growth [A+]	2002	2003	2004	2005
Revenue %	31.3	10.7	17.6	12.6
Earnings/Share %	23.7	5.2	18.2	-2.9
Book Value/Share %	71.4	11.9	15.4	13.4
Dividends/Share %	NMF	NMF	NMF	NMF

Profitability [B]	2003	2004	2005	TTM
Return on Assets %	7.4	8.4	4.5	4.8
Oper Cash Flow $Mil	309	243	562	780
- Cap Spending $Mil	115	107	247	221
= Free Cash Flow $Mil	195	136	314	559

Financial Health [C]	2003	2004	2005	09-30-06
Long-term Debt $Mil	709	700	3,195	2,439
Total Equity $Mil	2,298	2,666	3,027	3,531
Debt/Equity Ratio	0.3	0.3	1.1	0.7

Molson Coors Brewing Company TAP

Data as of 12-29-06

Rating	Fair Value	Last Close	Consider Buy	Consider Sell	Yield %
★★★	$76.00	$76.44	$58.60	$95.20	1.68

Company Profile
Molson Coors is the fifth-largest brewer in the world. Major brands include Coors Light, Molson Canadian, Carling, Blue Moon, Killian's, Zima, Caffrey's, Worthington's, and Keystone. Its largest markets by volume are America (56%), the U.K. (26%), and Canada (18%). Broken down by comparable operating profit, the company's largest operations are Canada (57%), America (31%), and the U.K. (12%). The company recently sold its majority interest in Brazilian brewer Kaiser.

Management
Stewardship Grade [C]

Voting control of Molson Coors is split into thirds, with the Coors family, the Molson family, and a block of publicly available stock having roughly equal voting power. With the Coorses and Molsons agreeing to vote in a bloc concerning most matters, minority shareholders have essentially no power. A dual-class voting structure gives the families control disproportionate to their economic stakes, and the NYSE considers Molson Coors "controlled," meaning the firm is exempt from independent director minimums. Predictably, Molson and Coors family members dominate the 15-member board, with the Coorses and Molsons each appointing six directors and the public only three--the families have currently chosen to leave one seat vacant. Directors and executive officers own about 79% of Class A shares (which retain superior voting rights) and about 22% of Class B shares outstanding. The company has retained dual headquarters in Golden, Colo., and Montreal. Eric Molson is chairman of the company, and Coors' Leo Kiely serves as CEO. Recent management compensation has been reasonable, with Kiely making a base salary well under $1 million in 2005. The company's structure is overly complex as a result of the merger and should be simplified, though this seems easier said than done, given legalities.

311 Tenth Street
Golden, CO 80401
www.coors.com

Growth [A-]	2002	2003	2004	2005
Revenue %	55.4	5.9	7.6	27.9
Earnings/Share %	33.5	7.9	8.8	-67.4
Book Value/Share %	4.8	28.9	22.0	57.9
Dividends/Share %	2.5	0.0	0.0	56.1

Profitability [C+]	2003	2004	2005	TTM
Return on Assets %	3.9	4.2	1.1	2.4
Oper Cash Flow $Mil	529	500	422	904
- Cap Spending $Mil	240	212	406	489
= Free Cash Flow $Mil	288	288	16	416

Financial Health [C+]	2003	2004	2005	09-30-06
Long-term Debt $Mil	1,160	894	2,137	2,177
Total Equity $Mil	1,267	1,601	5,325	5,872
Debt/Equity Ratio	0.9	0.6	0.4	0.4

Industry	Business Risk	Moat Size	Investment Style	Sector
Alcoholic Beverages	Average	Narrow	Mid Value	Consumer Goods

Competition	Market Cap $Mil	12 Mo Trailing Sales $Mil	Price/Cash Flow	Return On Assets%	Debt/ Equity	Total Return% 1 Yr	3 Yr
Molson Coors Brewing Company	6,595	5,698	7.3	2.4	0.4	16.3	13.0
Diageo PLC ADR	60,493	12,931	21.3	13.8	0.9	40.7	18.0
Anheuser-Busch Companies	37,826	15,691	13.5	11.9	1.7	17.4	0.1

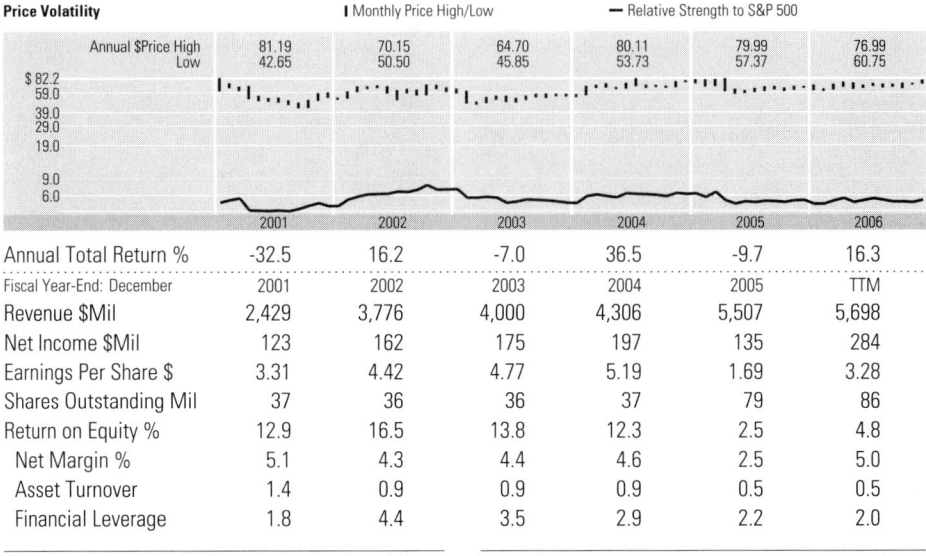

	2001	2002	2003	2004	2005	2006
Annual $Price High	81.19	70.15	64.70	80.11	79.99	76.99
Low	42.65	50.50	45.85	53.73	57.37	60.75
Annual Total Return %	-32.5	16.2	-7.0	36.5	-9.7	16.3

Fiscal Year-End: December	2001	2002	2003	2004	2005	TTM
Revenue $Mil	2,429	3,776	4,000	4,306	5,507	5,698
Net Income $Mil	123	162	175	197	135	284
Earnings Per Share $	3.31	4.42	4.77	5.19	1.69	3.28
Shares Outstanding Mil	37	36	36	37	79	86
Return on Equity %	12.9	16.5	13.8	12.3	2.5	4.8
Net Margin %	5.1	4.3	4.4	4.6	2.5	5.0
Asset Turnover	1.4	0.9	0.9	0.9	0.5	0.5
Financial Leverage	1.8	4.4	3.5	2.9	2.2	2.0

Valuation Ratios	Stock	Rel to Industry	Rel to S&P 500
Price/Earnings	22.5	0.9	1.1
Price/Book	1.1	0.1	0.3
Price/Sales	1.2	0.2	0.4
Price/Cash Flow	7.3	0.3	0.5

Major Fund Holders	% of Fund Assets
Longleaf Partners International	4.68
Longleaf Partners Small-Cap	4.27
High Pointe Select Value	3.73
AIM Mid Cap Basic Value A	3.49

Thesis
By Matthew Reilly, 12-15-06 Stock Price as of Analysis: $73.90

Molson Coors is the world's fifth-largest brewer by volume but faces very difficult market conditions in the United States, Canada, and Europe. Because the company has well-known, established brands and formidable Canadian market share along with significant market shares in the United States and Europe, we have assigned it a narrow moat.

We applaud the firm's recent decision to throw in the towel and sell the majority of its interest in a Brazilian operation that has been a disaster since day one, but Molson Coors still faces the prospect of very low volume growth in its core markets. American beer shipment volume, for example, has grown at less than 1% annually over the past 10 years. Wine, spirits, imported beers, and craft brews have taken the lion's share of recent American alcoholic beverage growth. The pricing environments also remain difficult in Molson Coors' three main markets, as brewers, which face high fixed costs, are loath to give up any volume in an overall flat market, even in a highly inflationary commodity environment.

Though Molson Coors has gained scale through its recent merger, it does not dominate its main markets. In America, it competes with Anheuser-Busch, which controls about 49% of the domestic market compared with Molson Coors' 11%. Molson Coors is thus in the position of battling a larger, more efficient rival for a customer base that is not growing substantially.

The company's competitive position in Canada is stronger, but many facets of the market are worrisome. The company is the largest brewer by volume in the market, which is essentially a duopoly along with AmBev, a company that is majority owned by InBev, the world's largest brewer. Though still large, Molson Coors' market share has been steadily declining over the past few years, with deep-discount brewers taking volume from the company's flagship Molson Canadian brand. AmBev has proved that profitability can improve despite a difficult market, and Molson is showing slow improvement.

Compared with the United Kingdom, however, the beer markets in Canada and the United States are a day at the beach. In 2004, the firm's U.K. operations had operating income of about $146 million, but this declined to about $82 million in 2005, though there has been improvement in 2006. A mix shift to off-premise consumption, cash-strapped consumers, and a competitive pricing environment all contributed to the dismal results. We see this market, and the company's overall results, improving incrementally over the next few years, but we do not expect a sudden turnaround.

Data as of 12-29-06

Monsanto Company MON

	Rating	Fair Value	Last Close	Consider Buy	Consider Sell	Yield %
	★★★	$52.00	$52.53	$40.10	$65.20	0.76

Company Profile

Monsanto is the world's leading producer of seeds. The company's seeds and genomics division combines advanced breeding and biotechnology traits to produce high-value-added seeds for corn, soybeans, cotton, fruits, vegetables, and other crops. The agricultural productivity segment produces a number of herbicides including Roundup. This segment also creates products that increase the output of dairy cows and the nutritional value of swine.

Industry	Business Risk	Moat Size	Investment Style	Sector
Agrochemical	Average	Narrow	Large Growth	Industrial Materials

Competition

	Market Cap $Mil	12 Mo Trailing Sales $Mil	Price/Cash Flow	Return On Assets %	Debt/ Equity	Total Return % 1 Yr	3 Yr
Monsanto Company	28,540	7,344	17.0	5.9	0.3	36.8	56.0
DuPont De Nemours E.I.	44,804	26,972	12.9	7.1	0.6	18.6	5.7
Dow Chemical	38,112	48,805	9.9	8.3	0.5	-5.4	2.3

Management Stewardship Grade [B]

We assign Monsanto a Stewardship Grade of B. Hugh Grant was named chairman and CEO in 2003, and we feel he is leading Monsanto in the right direction. Grant has been with Monsanto for 24 years, last serving as COO for three years. In fiscal 2005, Grant earned a salary and bonus of $3.2 million and options to purchase 225,310 shares. Executive pay is based on a variety of factors, including growth in cash flow, sales, and earnings per share. We like that seven out of nine board members are independent and that directors receive half of their $150,000 annual retainer in the form of deferred common stock. However, we're not fans of the staggered board structure or the combined CEO and chairman position. Monsanto requires executives to own a multiple of their base salary in stock. In total, directors and officers own slightly less than 1% of the company. In our opinion, Monsanto's managerial bench is deep with talented executives, all of whom have worked in the agriculture field for several decades, have a deep understanding of the business and are committed to maintaining the firm's dominant position in the industry.

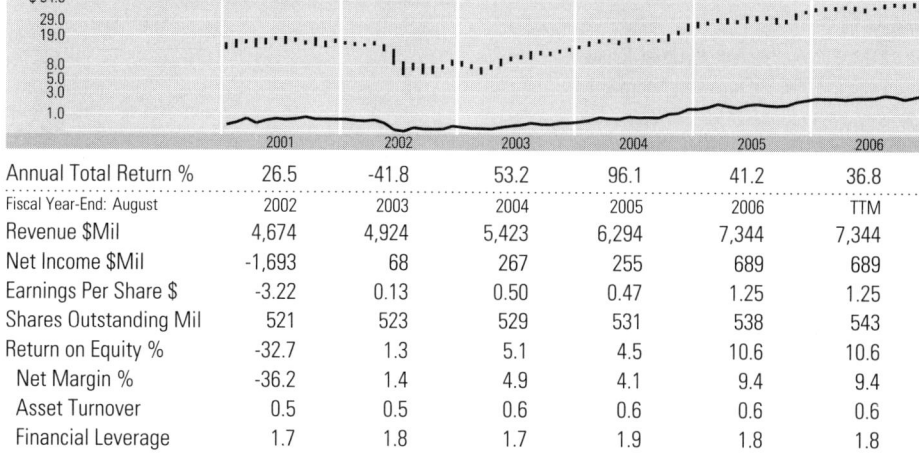

Annual Total Return %	26.5	-41.8	53.2	96.1	41.2	36.8
Fiscal Year-End: August	2002	2003	2004	2005	2006	TTM
Revenue $Mil	4,674	4,924	5,423	6,294	7,344	7,344
Net Income $Mil	-1,693	68	267	255	689	689
Earnings Per Share $	-3.22	0.13	0.50	0.47	1.25	1.25
Shares Outstanding Mil	521	523	529	531	538	543
Return on Equity %	-32.7	1.3	5.1	4.5	10.6	10.6
Net Margin %	-36.2	1.4	4.9	4.1	9.4	9.4
Asset Turnover	0.5	0.5	0.6	0.6	0.6	0.6
Financial Leverage	1.7	1.8	1.7	1.9	1.8	1.8

Valuation Ratios	Stock	Rel to Industry	Rel to S&P 500	Major Fund Holders	% of Fund Assets
Price/Earnings	41.4	1.1	2.0	Fidelity Select Chemicals	6.92
Price/Book	4.4	1.0	1.1	Morgan Stanley Focus Growth B	5.54
Price/Sales	3.9	1.1	1.3	Morgan Stanley Inst Focus Equity A	5.48
Price/Cash Flow	17.0	1.0	1.2	Van Kampen Equity Growth A	5.32

Thesis By Ben Johnson, 12-12-06 Stock Price as of Analysis: $48.10

Monsanto is the cream of the crop in the agricultural seed business. Over the past two decades, the firm has invested billions in developing its breeding and genetic modification (GM) technologies. This massive investment has created an enormous library of genetic information that has yielded the company's current product offerings and fuels its impressive R&D pipeline. Monsanto's technological leadership should allow this narrow-moat company to lead the pack for years to come.

Monsanto's core competency is research and development. The firm has stuck to its guns longer than any competitor in the GM seed business, consistently pouring around 10% of sales into R&D. As a result, Monsanto has lapped the competition in the race to bring premium seeds to the market. In most cases, competitive technologies from DuPont and Syngenta lag Monsanto by a few generations. It would take a major slowdown at Monsanto and some serious leapfrogging by the competition to level the playing field--something we doubt will happen anytime soon.

Any farmer's ultimate goal is not unlike that of an investor: maximize return and minimize risk. To achieve this, farmers must diversify their (genetic) portfolios and, where possible, hedge against known risks. Monsanto's broad base of genetic material allows farmers to diversify their crops, while GM technology provides a hedge against known risks such as weed and insect infestation. Monsanto has combined the forces of breeding and biotechnology to allow farmers to achieve their maximum risk-adjusted return. Because of this, farmers have been happy to pony up for Monsanto's premium seeds, and the firm has profited enormously as a result.

With costs that are mostly fixed, Monsanto is able to benefit from high operating leverage. Each additional acre of market share that the firm captures adds a good deal to the company's bottom line. Furthermore, as the company has begun to "stack" its traits, offering seeds possessing multiple GM technologies, it has also been stacking its profits. These topnotch seeds cost no more to produce than any ordinary seed variety and increase the premium that farmers are willing to pay. The recent introduction of triple stacked traits in corn and the pending introduction of a quadruple stacked corn variety in 2008 are proof positive of the firm's stronghold on innovation and bright prospects for future growth.

800 North Lindbergh Boulevard www.monsanto.com
St. Louis, MO 63167

Growth [C]	2003	2004	2005	2006	
Revenue %	5.3	10.1	16.1	16.7	
Earnings/Share %	NMF	280.8	-5.1	166.0	
Book Value/Share %	0.1	-1.1	6.1	14.4	
Dividends/Share %	-22.9	44.6	22.4	17.6	

Profitability [C]	2004	2005	2006	TTM
Return on Assets %	2.9	2.4	5.9	5.9
Oper Cash Flow $Mil	1,261	1,737	1,674	1,674
- Cap Spending $Mil	210	281	370	370
= Free Cash Flow $Mil	1,051	1,456	1,304	1,304

Financial Health [B-]	2004	2005	2006	08-31-06
Long-term Debt $Mil	1,075	1,458	1,639	1,639
Total Equity $Mil	5,258	5,613	6,525	6,525
Debt/Equity Ratio	0.2	0.3	0.3	0.3

Monster Worldwide MNST

Data as of 12-29-06

	Rating	Fair Value	Last Close	Consider Buy	Consider Sell	Yield %
	★	$35.00	$46.64	$27.00	$43.90	0.00

Company Profile
Founded in 1967, Monster Worldwide is the parent company of Monster, a leading global online property that provides recruitment services in North America, Europe, and the Asia Pacific region. Its offerings include searchable job postings, a resume database, and career-management content and advice. Monster Worldwide also has an advertising and communications segment, which designs recruitment advertisements.

Management   Stewardship Grade [D]
William M. Pastore became CEO of Monster Worldwide in 2006. He replaced Andrew J. McKelvey, who founded Monster Worldwide's predecessor in 1967, when McKelvey resigned in the midst of an investigation related to options backdating. In 2005, McKelvey earned a base salary of $1 million plus a cash and stock bonus of $1.8 million. Aside from the options situation, we think his compensation was reasonable, but the rest of Monster's corporate stewardship profile is littered with unattractive characteristics. Monster didn't expense options until it was required to, and it has a history of being too generous with them. (Options granted in 2004 were more than 5% of the company's average diluted count.) It also seems that shareholders take a back seat to insiders' interests: Antitakeover provisions allow the board to issue senior preferred stock without the consent of common shareholders, the company pays rent to a business owned by three directors, and the firm sold its order-fulfillment business to a company majority-owned by one of Monster's directors.

622 Third Ave
New York, NY 10017
www.tmp.com

Growth [B]	2002	2003	2004	2005
Revenue %	-21.7	-1.9	37.0	30.5
Earnings/Share %	NMF	NMF	NMF	41.0
Book Value/Share %	-32.8	-42.8	51.0	16.8
Dividends/Share %	NMF	NMF	NMF	NMF

Profitability [C-]	2003	2004	2005	TTM
Return on Assets %	-7.3	4.7	6.4	7.3
Oper Cash Flow $Mil	17	93	222	256
- Cap Spending $Mil	19	17	40	43
= Free Cash Flow $Mil	-2	76	182	214

Financial Health [C+]	2003	2004	2005	03-31-06
Long-term Debt $Mil	—	34	16	3
Total Equity $Mil	468	756	920	1,019
Debt/Equity Ratio	—	0.0	0.0	0.0

Industry	Business Risk	Moat Size	Investment Style	Sector
Advertising	Average	Narrow	Mid Growth	Business Services

Competition	Market Cap $Mil	12 Mo Trailing Sales $Mil	Price/Cash Flow	Return On Assets%	Debt/Equity	Total Return% 1 Yr	3 Yr
Monster Worldwide	5,987	1,050	23.3	7.3	0.0	14.3	27.9
Yahoo	34,740	6,224	20.6	11.0	0.1	-34.8	4.0
Manpower	6,365	17,138	20.0	5.2	0.3	62.5	17.7

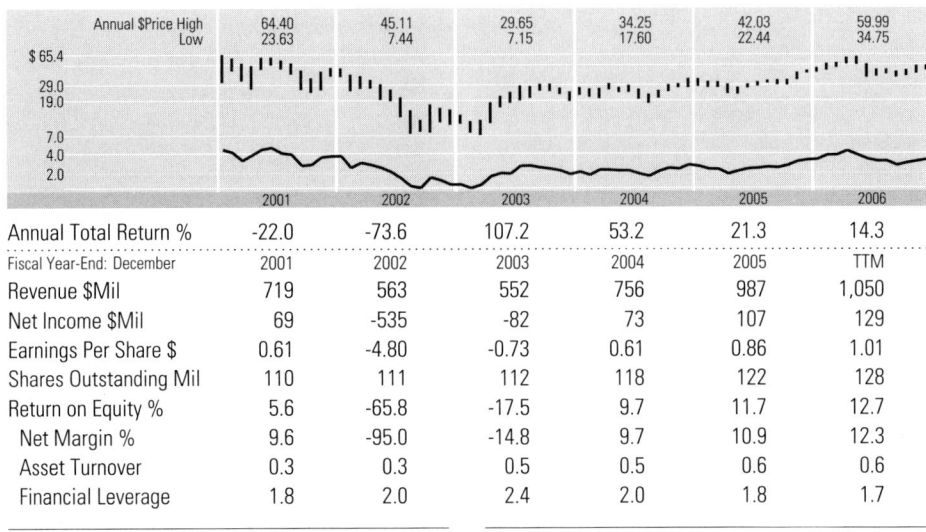

	2001	2002	2003	2004	2005	2006
Annual $Price High	64.40	45.11	29.65	34.25	42.03	59.99
Low	23.63	7.44	7.15	17.60	22.44	34.75
Annual Total Return %	-22.0	-73.6	107.2	53.2	21.3	14.3

Fiscal Year-End: December	2001	2002	2003	2004	2005	TTM
Revenue $Mil	719	563	552	756	987	1,050
Net Income $Mil	69	-535	-82	73	107	129
Earnings Per Share $	0.61	-4.80	-0.73	0.61	0.86	1.01
Shares Outstanding Mil	110	111	112	118	122	128
Return on Equity %	5.6	-65.8	-17.5	9.7	11.7	12.7
Net Margin %	9.6	-95.0	-14.8	9.7	10.9	12.3
Asset Turnover	0.3	0.3	0.5	0.5	0.6	0.6
Financial Leverage	1.8	2.0	2.4	2.0	1.8	1.7

Valuation Ratios	Stock	Rel to Industry	Rel to S&P 500
Price/Earnings	45.7	1.8	2.2
Price/Book	5.9	1.2	1.4
Price/Sales	5.7	1.2	2.0
Price/Cash Flow	23.3	1.7	1.6

Major Fund Holders	% of Fund Assets
Munder Internet A	4.00
T. Rowe Price Instl Global Equity	3.53
T. Rowe Price Global Stock	3.28
Firsthand e-Commerce	3.21

Thesis By James M. Walden, CFA, 12-11-06 Stock Price as of Analysis: $44.99

Monster Worldwide is the global leader in the attractive online job recruiting industry, and we think it's doing the right things to capitalize on this profitable niche.

One of Monster's greatest assets is its powerful brand. Over the past few years, management has spent hundreds of millions of dollars on building up Monster's brand with expensive campaigns like Super Bowl ads. The firm has funneled almost 20% of annual sales into marketing and promotion expenses.

While some criticize such high marketing outlays, we think they are the catalyst for the network effect that the company enjoys. Its strong brand recognition causes job seekers to post their resumes on Monster. Companies that want access to such a large candidate pool will pay up to post jobs on its sites and for access to Monster's resume database. As the number of job postings from potential employers increases, even more potential hires post their resumes. (Monster can receive around 50,000 new and updated resumes each day, which contributes mightily to its database of about 40 million.) In our opinion, this effect contributes to Monster's narrow economic moat.

These competitive advantages should allow the company to prosper from favorable industry trends. Information provided by research firm IDC suggests that spending on online recruiting in the United States will increase at an average annual rate of almost 21% through 2009. In our opinion, international markets hold even more potential. While we expect Monster to continue to spend a chunk on its branding, much of this incremental business should flow through to the bottom line. As Monster takes advantage of such opportunity, it should create shareholder value with returns on invested capital even greater than the 18.6% realized in 2005.

Monster still faces stiff competition, though, which keeps its moat width in check. Traditional adversaries like newspapers and headhunters still loom large, especially in local markets. And Monster squares off against other online recruiters like CareerBuilder (an online property owned by newspaper publishers Gannett, McClatchy, and Tribune) and Yahoo's HotJobs. These channels are not mutually exclusive, though; an employer may post a job opportunity through several channels, benefiting companies like Monster, which can offer significant reach. We like this company's story and would gladly invest in its shares at the appropriate discount to our fair value estimate.

Data as of 12-29-06

Moody's MCO

Rating ★★	Fair Value $57.00	Last Close $69.06	Consider Buy $48.60	Consider Sell $74.80	Yield % 0.41

Company Profile

Moody's publishes credit opinions, research, and ratings on fixed-income securities, issuers of securities, and other credit obligations. It has offices in 18 countries and is expanding into developing markets through joint ventures or affiliations with local rating agencies. Customers include corporate and governmental issuers of securities as well as investors, depositors, creditors, investment banks, commercial banks, and other financial intermediaries.

Management Stewardship Grade [B]

Moody's corporate-governance policies rate well, in our opinion. Ray McDaniel became CEO and chairman in May 2005. We'd prefer to see these two roles split. McDaniel has 18 years of experience at the company and has served as president of its rating business since 2001. In each of the past three years, stock-option grants represented less than 2% of outstanding shares, a reasonable amount, in our view. Management has been opportunistic in its share buybacks, scooping up 67 million shares (about 23% of outstanding shares) at an average price of $27 since the firm went public in October 2000. The company recently announced it will add systematic buybacks to its opportunistic share repurchases as a way of returning more capital to shareholders. We think the company can afford to increase its paltry dividend, which currently yields about 0.3%.

99 Church Street www.moodys.com
New York, NY 10007

Growth [B+]	2002	2003	2004	2005
Revenue %	28.4	21.8	15.4	20.4
Earnings/Share %	39.4	29.3	17.6	31.4
Book Value/Share %	NMF	NMF	NMF	-2.9
Dividends/Share %	0.0	0.0	66.7	16.7

Profitability [A+]	2003	2004	2005	TTM
Return on Assets %	37.9	30.6	38.5	54.1
Oper Cash Flow $Mil	467	526	708	731
- Cap Spending $Mil	18	21	31	34
= Free Cash Flow $Mil	449	505	677	697

Financial Health [A+]	2003	2004	2005	09-30-06
Long-term Debt $Mil	—	0	300	300
Total Equity $Mil	-32	318	309	39
Debt/Equity Ratio	—	0.0	1.0	7.8

Industry	Business Risk	Moat Size	Investment Style	Sector
Business Support	Below Avg	Wide	Large Growth	Business Services

Competition	Market Cap $Mil	12 Mo Trailing Sales $Mil	Price/Cash Flow	Return On Assets%	Debt/ Equity	Total Return% 1 Yr	3 Yr
Moody's	19,323	1,920	26.4	54.1	7.8	12.9	32.2
McGraw-Hill Companies	24,093	6,202	14.9	14.1	0.0	33.4	26.9

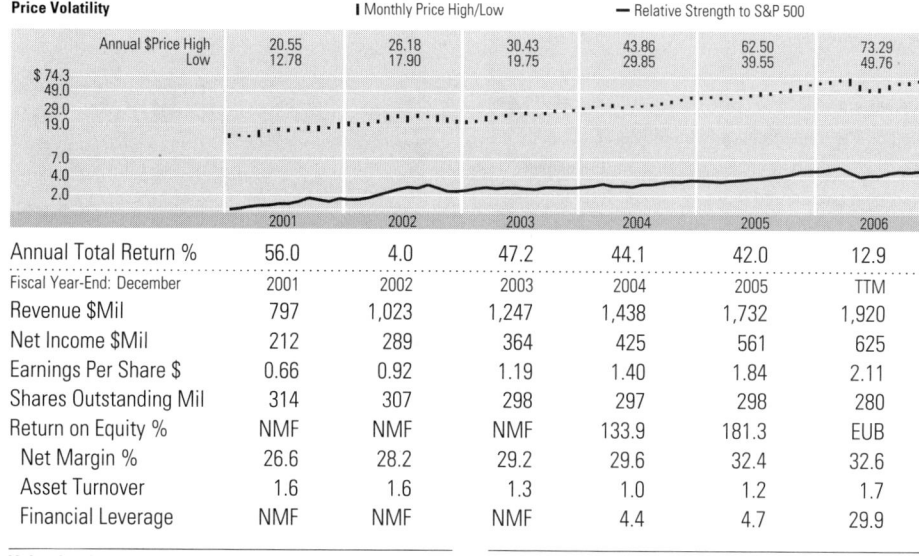

	2001	2002	2003	2004	2005	2006
Annual Total Return %	56.0	4.0	47.2	44.1	42.0	12.9
Fiscal Year-End: December	2001	2002	2003	2004	2005	TTM
Revenue $Mil	797	1,023	1,247	1,438	1,732	1,920
Net Income $Mil	212	289	364	425	561	625
Earnings Per Share $	0.66	0.92	1.19	1.40	1.84	2.11
Shares Outstanding Mil	314	307	298	297	298	280
Return on Equity %	NMF	NMF	NMF	133.9	181.3	EUB
Net Margin %	26.6	28.2	29.2	29.6	32.4	32.6
Asset Turnover	1.6	1.6	1.3	1.0	1.2	1.7
Financial Leverage	NMF	NMF	NMF	4.4	4.7	29.9

Valuation Ratios	Stock	Rel to Industry	Rel to S&P 500
Price/Earnings	32.7	1.2	1.6
Price/Book	EUB	—	—
Price/Sales	10.1	2.1	3.5
Price/Cash Flow	26.4	1.4	1.8

Major Fund Holders	% of Fund Assets
Davis Financial A	6.20
JHT Financial Services Trust Ser I	5.77
Fidelity Select IT Services	4.51
Morgan Stanley Focus Growth B	4.49

Thesis By Michael Corty, CFA, 12-07-06 Stock Price as of Analysis: $70.01

Moody's has a wide economic moat around its credit-rating franchise, and we don't see any significant threats to its competitive position.

The Credit Rating Agency Reform Act is a new law that reduces the regulatory hurdles necessary for firms looking to enter the industry. Crafters of this legislation think the law can eventually break up the current duopoly of Moody's and Standard & Poor's (S&P), a division of McGraw-Hill, each of which hold about 40% of the credit-rating market.

In our opinion, allowing additional firms to issue credit ratings won't impact Moody's market share, as there is little incentive for debt issuers to pay a new entrant. Most debt products require two independent ratings, and both debt issuers and investors want to use as few rating agencies as possible. Debt issuers want to limit their time spent with credit analysts, and investors favor fewer voices to many, because excessive competition could lead debt issuers to choose the agency that provides the highest rating or the lowest price.

Due to its enviable position in the industry, Moody's simply acts as a toll collector on publicly issued debt that flows through its ratings pipeline. It takes a small cut ($100,000 on a $250 million plain-vanilla corporate bond), and borrowers accept the charge as a cost of accessing the public markets. The company does not control the amount of debt coming to market, but fortunately for Moody's, global debt issuance has increased at a 22% annual average clip over the past five years.

Along with robust issuance growth, the variety and complexity of debt products continues to expand. Moody's leverages its expertise to evaluate these more complex debt offerings, and even better for the firm, it can charge a higher rate for evaluating such products--as much as three times the rate for a plain-vanilla bond offering.

Looking ahead, we think Moody's has ample opportunities for international expansion. For example, its European revenue has grown at a 32% average annual clip (compared with 19% in the U.S.) from 2000 to 2005. Foreign borrowers are increasingly raising funds in the public market (in lieu of bank loans) and are starting to embrace the more complex offerings that have become popular in the U.S. In our opinion, a bulk of Moody's future sales growth will come from overseas markets.

Data as of 12-29-06

Morgan Stanley MS

	Rating	Fair Value	Last Close	Consider Buy	Consider Sell	Yield %
	★★★	$83.00	$81.43	$64.00	$104.00	1.33

Industry	Business Risk	Moat Size	Investment Style	Sector
Securities	Average	Wide	Large Core	Financial Services

Company Profile

Morgan Stanley is one of the world's largest financial-services firms. It has four operating divisions. The institutional securities group focuses on capital markets activities. The individual investor unit is the brokerage arm. The investment-management arm is responsible for the firm's mutual funds and institutional separate accounts. The credit services group operates the Discover credit card.

Competition

	Market Cap $Mil	12 Mo Trailing Sales $Mil	Price/Cash Flow	Return On Assets%	Debt/ Equity	Total Return% 1 Yr	3 Yr
Morgan Stanley	86,198	32,195	—	0.8	—	45.9	14.8
Citigroup	273,691	86,566	—	1.3	—	19.6	8.4
J.P. Morgan Chase & Co.	167,551	59,650	—	0.9	—	25.6	13.2

Management Stewardship Grade [B]

Being on the management team of Morgan Stanley in 2005 must have been like living in a martini shaker. The drama culminated in the ouster of CEO Philip Purcell, who came from the Dean Witter business and led years of underperformance at the firm, while irritating enough senior staff at the firm to cause a mass exodus. He had just reorganized the executive team when the board of directors showed him the door, and some of his recently promoted allies went with him. Former Morgan head John Mack returned to the firm as CEO after a 2001 departure. Mack has been rebuilding the management ranks during 2006, luring many senior staff into returning, promoting a number from within, and hiring new blood. Recently the firm hired James Gorman, former president of Merrill Lynch's Global Private Client Group, to fix the troubled retail brokerage group.

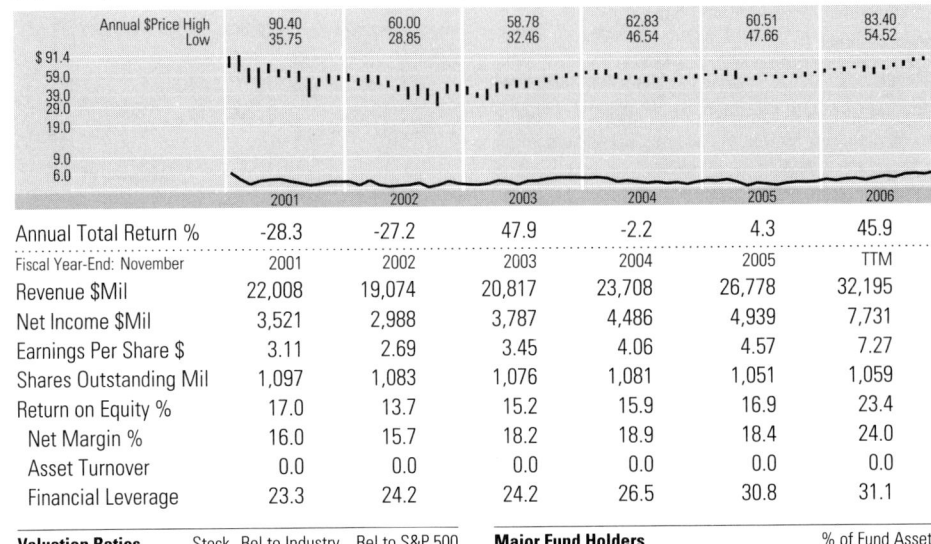

Price Volatility — Monthly Price High/Low — Relative Strength to S&P 500

Annual $Price High Low	90.40 35.75	60.00 28.85	58.78 32.46	62.83 46.54	60.51 47.66	83.40 54.52
	2001	2002	2003	2004	2005	2006
Annual Total Return %	-28.3	-27.2	47.9	-2.2	4.3	45.9

Fiscal Year-End: November	2001	2002	2003	2004	2005	TTM
Revenue $Mil	22,008	19,074	20,817	23,708	26,778	32,195
Net Income $Mil	3,521	2,988	3,787	4,486	4,939	7,731
Earnings Per Share $	3.11	2.69	3.45	4.06	4.57	7.27
Shares Outstanding Mil	1,097	1,083	1,076	1,081	1,051	1,059
Return on Equity %	17.0	13.7	15.2	15.9	16.9	23.4
Net Margin %	16.0	15.7	18.2	18.9	18.4	24.0
Asset Turnover	0.0	0.0	0.0	0.0	0.0	0.0
Financial Leverage	23.3	24.2	24.2	26.5	30.8	31.1

Valuation Ratios	Stock	Rel to Industry	Rel to S&P 500	Major Fund Holders	% of Fund Assets
Price/Earnings	12.3	0.7	0.6	Fidelity Select Brokerage & Investmnt	5.91
Price/Book	2.6	0.6	0.6	CGM Focus	5.41
Price/Sales	2.7	0.6	0.9	IXIS CGM Advisor Targeted Equity A	5.06
Price/Cash Flow	—	—	—	Principal Inv Ptr LgCap Value I Inst	4.94

1585 Broadway www.morganstanley.com
New York, NY 10036-8293

Growth [B-]	2002	2003	2004	2005
Revenue %	-13.3	9.1	13.9	12.9
Earnings/Share %	-13.5	28.3	17.7	12.6
Book Value/Share %	7.7	15.0	12.7	5.8
Dividends/Share %	0.0	0.0	8.7	8.0

Profitability [C]	2003	2004	2005	TTM
Return on Assets %	0.6	0.6	0.6	0.8
Oper Cash Flow $Mil	10,527	-27,458	-31,352	—
- Cap Spending $Mil	—	—	—	—
= Free Cash Flow $Mil	—	—	—	—

Financial Health [NA]	2003	2004	2005	08-31-06
Long-term Debt $Mil	—	—	—	—
Total Equity $Mil	24,867	28,206	29,182	33,072
Debt/Equity Ratio	—	—	—	—

Thesis By Philip Guziec, 12-15-06 Stock Price as of Analysis: $79.26

Morgan Stanley is a diversified investment bank, recently freed from the clutches of an overly conservative management team. The firm is bruised and battered, but nothing is broken. We think the new management team under John Mack will be able to right the ship and eventually hoist more sail. We'd be happy to get a piece of this fallen angel at the right price.

Despite a lot of headlines about its smaller businesses, the firm is still primarily an institutional investment bank. About half of revenue and two thirds of profits come from investment banking and trading. Investment banking, operating with reasonable autonomy, has been performing solidly, remaining perennially near the top of the league tables in mergers and acquisitions and underwriting. However, in 2005, several of the top brass headed for the door amid management restructuring. Some bankers have returned, and we think the remaining senior staff's relationships and the company brand should allow the investment banking business to maintain its competitive position. Growth in the trading operation has been hamstrung by an overly risk-averse management team, but we think loosening the reins here should allow for rapid improvement.

Morgan's other businesses do not have the same storied history. The company's retail producers, largely former Dean Witter brokers, bring in fewer commissions on average than Merrill Lynch or even the former American Express brokerage, Ameriprise. The investment-management unit has fewer client assets than it did in 2000, while competitors like Goldman Sachs never skipped a beat, increasing assets significantly since 2000. We think management and incentive changes and the expansion of product offerings can lead to significant improvements in the retail businesses.

The credit services unit contains Discover card, a small fish in the slowing credit card industry. However, a Department of Justice decision has opened up the market for cobranded cards, which should create another path to get Discover cards into a greater number of wallets. The unit also partnered with GE Finance to issue the Wal-Mart Discover card. While Morgan won't maintain the accounts, it will earn a fee every time a transaction is processed over its network.

We think near-term investments in the firm may delay the acceleration of earnings growth, but we expect solid improvements in Morgan's return on equity in the coming years, driven by strengthening of

Motorola MOT

Data as of 12-29-06

Rating	Fair Value	Last Close	Consider Buy	Consider Sell	Yield %
★★★★	$25.00	$20.56	$19.30	$31.30	0.92

Industry	Business Risk	Moat Size	Investment Style	Sector
Wireless Equip.	Average	Narrow	Large Core	Hardware

Company Profile
Motorola provides integrated communications solutions for the wireless, wireline, and cable markets. It is the second-largest supplier of mobile phones worldwide (which account for more than 65% of sales) and a leading supplier of mobile and cable infrastructure equipment, set-top boxes, and cable modems. In the past several years, Motorola has become a more focused vendor of communications equipment by shedding its semiconductor unit and automotive electronics business.

Management
Stewardship Grade [C]

We think Motorola is a prime example of how new leadership can reinvigorate a technology company. The hiring of Ed Zander in early 2004 as CEO provided much-needed vision in the executive suite, and the firm has been re-energized under his watch. Before coming to Motorola, Zander spent 15 years at Sun Microsystems, where he was president from 1998 to 2002. Not only is he confident in the direction the business is heading, but he isn't becoming complacent from recent success. It's clear to us that he has brought the healthy paranoia he learned in Silicon Valley to Motorola's culture. We believe management deserves credit for the strides it has made in getting its financial house in order since the telecom bubble. In 2003, Motorola had six divisions, all operating relatively independently. Today, it has three divisions, one purchasing department and largely centralized research and development. Its capital-intensive and highly cyclical semiconductor unit was spun off in 2004. It sold its stagnant, low-margin automotive business in 2006 and merged its network and government enterprise businesses into one unit. Motorola's improved operating picture has led to strong free cash flow generation. The company is using this cash to clean up its balance sheet by cutting its debt and returning cash to shareholders via a share buyback, its first ever.

1303 E. Algonquin Road
Schaumburg, IL 60196
www.motorola.com

Growth [B+]	2002	2003	2004	2005
Revenue %	-11.5	-1.1	35.3	17.6
Earnings/Share %	NMF	NMF	68.4	182.8
Book Value/Share %	-20.4	9.5	3.1	18.4
Dividends/Share %	0.0	0.0	0.0	0.0

Profitability [B]	2003	2004	2005	TTM
Return on Assets %	3.3	5.0	12.8	11.3
Oper Cash Flow $Mil	1,991	3,066	4,605	4,886
- Cap Spending $Mil	344	494	583	587
= Free Cash Flow $Mil	1,647	2,572	4,022	4,299

Financial Health [B]	2003	2004	2005	09-30-06
Long-term Debt $Mil	—	4,581	3,806	3,780
Total Equity $Mil	12,689	13,331	16,673	17,138
Debt/Equity Ratio	—	0.3	0.2	0.2

Competition

	Market Cap $Mil	12 Mo Trailing Sales $Mil	Price/Cash Flow	Return On Assets %	Debt/Equity	Total Return % 1 Yr	3 Yr
Motorola	49,703	42,707	10.2	11.3	0.2	-8.2	17.6
Nokia ADR	90,097	42,815	17.4	17.1	0.0	13.4	8.2
Alcatel Lucent ADR	20,314	16,448	19.1	4.8	0.1	16.6	3.4

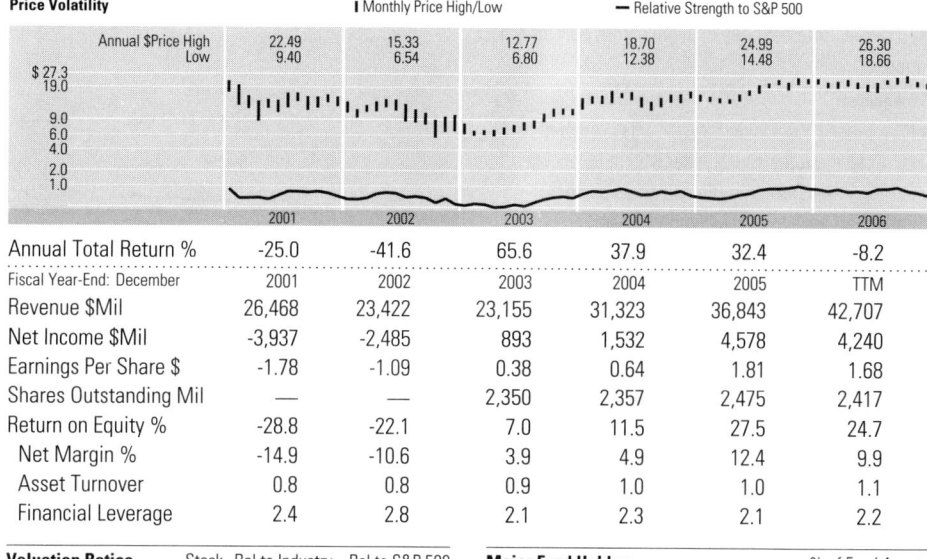

Price Volatility — Monthly Price High/Low — Relative Strength to S&P 500

Annual $Price High	22.49	15.33	12.77	18.70	24.99	26.30
Low	9.40	6.54	6.80	12.38	14.48	18.66
	2001	2002	2003	2004	2005	2006
Annual Total Return %	-25.0	-41.6	65.6	37.9	32.4	-8.2

Fiscal Year-End: December	2001	2002	2003	2004	2005	TTM
Revenue $Mil	26,468	23,422	23,155	31,323	36,843	42,707
Net Income $Mil	-3,937	-2,485	893	1,532	4,578	4,240
Earnings Per Share $	-1.78	-1.09	0.38	0.64	1.81	1.68
Shares Outstanding Mil	—	—	2,350	2,357	2,475	2,417
Return on Equity %	-28.8	-22.1	7.0	11.5	27.5	24.7
Net Margin %	-14.9	-10.6	3.9	4.9	12.4	9.9
Asset Turnover	0.8	0.8	0.9	1.0	1.0	1.1
Financial Leverage	2.4	2.8	2.1	2.3	2.1	2.2

Valuation Ratios	Stock	Rel to Industry	Rel to S&P 500
Price/Earnings	13.0	0.6	0.6
Price/Book	2.9	0.6	0.7
Price/Sales	1.2	0.3	0.4
Price/Cash Flow	10.2	0.5	0.7

Major Fund Holders	% of Fund Assets
Fidelity Select Wireless	7.92
Fidelity Advisor Communications Equip T	6.98
Monetta Select Technology	6.64
Oppenheimer Quest Balanced A	6.61

Thesis By John Slack, 12-19-06 Stock Price as of Analysis: $20.49

Motorola has reinvented itself over the past few years. This transformation, coupled with our belief that scale is imperative for success in the handset business, is significant enough that we believe the company now has an economic moat.

After years of struggles, once-stodgy Motorola has refocused on its complementary handset and telecom infrastructure businesses while shedding its slower-growing, more capital-intensive businesses like its automotive division and semiconductor unit Freescale. These moves have resulted not only in an impressive transformation of the company's culture and morale, but also a financial turnaround that we believe is sustainable.

With nearly 1 billion wireless handsets expected to ship worldwide in 2006, supply-chain management, procurement, and distribution are imperative for success, and we believe scale creates sustainable advantages and competitive barriers to entry. Motorola and industry leader Nokia have it, and no one else comes close. Motorola closed the third quarter with a 22.5% share of the global market--up nearly 9 percentage points from 2003 and nearly double the share of number-three vendor Samsung. Motorola's Razr family of phones may have garnered headlines and propelled growth, but the company is also making the right moves to cement its position in the handset market.

Scale allows Motorola to extract the best terms from suppliers and ensures that its orders are filled ahead of rivals', which is important when components are in tight supply. Distribution is arguably even more important, particularly from an emerging market perspective. This is best illustrated by Nokia, which hasn't really had a solid handset lineup in three years but is still able to gain share by the brute force of its distribution system in India and China. Motorola has smartly used its newfound scale and profitability over the past two years to invest heavily in distribution in developing markets.

The capstone of the turnaround has been Motorola's financial performance. Nearly every financial metric has shown considerable improvement over the past three years. Operating margins, after being negative in 2002, are now roughly 13%. Returns on invested capital have steadily improved to nearly 30%, well in excess of Motorola's cost of capital. The balance sheet is now pristine, with a debt/capital ratio of 20% and more than $10 billion in net cash. What's more, the company is free cash flow positive, recently increased its dividend, and is buying back shares.

MSC Industrial Direct Co. MSM

Data as of 12-29-06

Rating	Fair Value	Last Close	Consider Buy	Consider Sell	Yield %
★★★★★	$60.00	$39.15	$46.30	$75.20	1.43

Company Profile
MSC Industrial Direct markets more than 500,000 maintenance, repair, and operations products to a variety of domestic companies. Products like machine tool consumables, abrasives, measuring instruments, electrical supplies, and safety equipment are sold through direct-mail catalogs and the Internet. MSC's 90 branch offices are home base to more than 500 field salespeople, and its four distribution centers are used to facilitate next-day delivery across 80% of the nation.

Management   Stewardship Grade [B]
In November 2005, David Sandler was promoted to CEO, replacing large shareholder Mitchell Jacobson, who will remain as chairman and serve as an experienced advisor to the company. Sandler, who joined MSC when it acquired the company he founded, had been chief operating officer for the past five years. Because he had already been charged with day-to-day operations and was significantly involved in all strategic decisions, we are confident that the company will maintain its long-term focus. As of the 2005 annual proxy, Jacobson still enjoys a roughly 20% economic interest in the company and controls 51% of the firm's votes through Class B shares. Class A shareholders are simply along for the ride. However, we are not overly concerned by this, as management has proved its shareholder-friendliness with its actions. MSC has stepped up its return of capital to shareholders by raising the dividend, handing out a special dividend, and buying back shares. Management compensation provides a nice balance of cash salary, incentive compensation, stock options, and restricted stock. Four of the seven board members are independent, and they staff all key committees.

75 Maxess Road
Melville, NY 11747
www.mscdirect.com

Growth [B]	2003	2004	2005	2006
Revenue %	6.4	13.1	15.1	19.8
Earnings/Share %	51.0	51.9	37.6	24.2
Book Value/Share %	13.5	18.1	-14.7	23.2
Dividends/Share %	NMF	480.0	569.0	-72.2

Profitability [A]	2004	2005	2006	TTM
Return on Assets %	11.1	17.2	13.4	13.4
Oper Cash Flow $Mil	67	125	134	134
- Cap Spending $Mil	9	11	23	23
= Free Cash Flow $Mil	58	114	111	111

Financial Health [A-]	2004	2005	2006	08-31-06
Long-term Debt $Mil	1	1	193	193
Total Equity $Mil	618	530	639	639
Debt/Equity Ratio	0.0	0.0	0.3	0.3

Industry	Business Risk	Moat Size	Investment Style	Sector
Distributors	Average	Narrow	Mid Growth	Business Services

Competition	Market Cap $Mil	12 Mo Trailing Sales $Mil	Price/Cash Flow	Return On Assets%	Debt/Equity	Total Return% 1 Yr	3 Yr
MSC Industrial Direct Co.	2,622	1,318	19.6	13.4	0.3	-1.5	15.4
W.W. Grainger	6,017	5,812	13.0	12.6	0.0	-0.1	15.6
Fastenal	5,416	1,745	43.0	19.3	—	-7.4	13.9

Price Volatility — Monthly Price High/Low — Relative Strength to S&P 500

	2001	2002	2003	2004	2005	2006
Annual $Price High	20.49	24.36	28.19	37.00	40.73	55.80
Low	13.90	9.30	15.65	26.39	26.30	37.23
Annual Total Return %	9.3	-10.1	55.6	32.3	18.0	-1.5

Fiscal Year-End: August	2002	2003	2004	2005	2006	TTM
Revenue $Mil	794	845	955	1,100	1,318	1,318
Net Income $Mil	36	52	81	112	136	136
Earnings Per Share $	0.51	0.77	1.17	1.61	2.00	2.00
Shares Outstanding Mil	69	67	67	68	67	67
Return on Equity %	7.7	10.2	13.1	21.2	21.3	21.3
Net Margin %	4.6	6.2	8.5	10.2	10.4	10.4
Asset Turnover	1.4	1.4	1.3	1.7	1.3	1.3
Financial Leverage	1.2	1.2	1.2	1.2	1.6	1.6

Valuation Ratios	Stock	Rel to Industry	Rel to S&P 500
Price/Earnings	19.6	1.1	1.0
Price/Book	4.1	1.4	1.0
Price/Sales	2.0	1.7	0.7
Price/Cash Flow	19.6	0.7	1.3

Major Fund Holders	% of Fund Assets
Roxbury Mid Cap Instl	2.64
Wasatch Core Growth	2.63
MFS New Endeavor A	2.40
UBS U.S. Mid Cap Growth Y	2.33

Thesis By Matthew Warren, 12-15-06 Stock Price as of Analysis: $38.56

Though MSC Industrial Direct isn't the largest in its industry--Home Depot Supply holds a substantial sales advantage--its direct-distribution model provides the lowest-cost route to market.

MSC distributes industrial supplies through field salespeople, catalogs, and the Internet. While Home Depot Supply and Grainger's multichannel strategies include branch stores that stock high-volume items, MSC's direct approach--similar to a few other industry players like larger rival McMaster-Carr--is fairly disruptive. By stocking 500,000 less-than-common items for next-day delivery (compared with 115,000 at Grainger), MSC provides unmatched selection and quick turnaround. In fact, the company offers customers $50 if it fails on its same-day-shipping promise. Despite its higher inventory carrying costs, it is increasingly clear that MSC is a low cost provider.

Further, we expect MSC to experience strong internal growth as the industry consolidates. Currently, the top dozen or so distributors control 15%-20% of the market, but this will change as domestic companies attempt to cut costs in the face of stepped up global competition. MSC estimates that indirect costs associated with maintenance, repair, and operations (MRO) purchases represent roughly 35% of total spending. For many customers, the simple solution is to reduce the number of supplier relationships--and associated complexity costs--and stop wasting time comparing prices of infrequently purchased items. Typically, this process involves choosing from the industry's top players. A major contract win--alongside Grainger--to supply all of the U.S. Postal Service's MRO needs highlights the appeal of MSC's model.

As MSC continues to grow, the extreme operating leverage in the business model is shining through. The firm posted incremental operating margins--additional operating profit per additional dollar of sales--above 30% over the past three years. Underlying these impressive metrics are the company's limited investment requirements. MSC will continue to leverage its fixed asset base by filling out and then expanding existing warehouses and using its estimated 80% of unused IT capacity. And because most of MSC's sales typically involve items with high value/weight ratios, the firm relies solely on third-party transportation, the cost of which is passed along to customers. Lastly, management has a proven track record of shareholder-friendly capital allocation decisions--no small point considering MSC's growing free cash flows.

Municipal Mortgage & Equity LLC MMA

Data as of 12-29-06

Rating	Fair Value	Last Close	Consider Buy	Consider Sell	Yield %
★★★	$31.00	$32.20	$23.90	$38.80	6.21

Industry	Business Risk	Moat Size	Investment Style	Sector
Finance	Average	Narrow	Small Value	Financial Services

Company Profile

Municipal Mortgage & Equity (MuniMae) provides financing for housing projects in several ways. The firm invests primarily in tax-exempt bonds, earning money on the spread between its funding costs and the tax-free interest it receives. After a 2003 acquisition, MuniMae's model became more fee-oriented, with roughly half of its revenue coming from fees related to originating loans, managing low-income housing tax credit syndications, and performing other asset management.

Management Stewardship Grade [C]

We think MuniMae has a good management team. CEO Michael Falcone is relatively new to his position but not to MuniMae. He's been with the firm since its inception, along with chairman and former CEO Mark Joseph. We are impressed by the management team's candor with us in explaining the firm's strengths and weaknesses, and with the conservative way they run the business. Directors and officers own more than 5% of the company, aligning management's interests with shareholders', in our opinion. We'd prefer to see no conflicts--or even potential conflicts--of interest, so we're wary of MuniMae's numerous ties to Shelter Group, a real estate firm in which Joseph is a partner. However, executive compensation seems reasonable, and option issuance is low. Management also provides the cash available for distribution performance metric, which we think is the best indicator of its performance and its dividend safety. Our Stewardship Grade reflects the stumbles the firm has had in its accounting and its slowness in reporting its results. We think both of these concerns are being addressed, and we're pleased with the steps MuniMae is taking to improve its disclosures and produce timely financial reports. However, we'd expect nothing less from a public company, especially a firm that's as difficult to understand as MuniMae.

621 E. Pratt Street 3rd Floor
Baltimore, MD 21202-3140
www.munimaemidland.com

Growth [A]

	2002	2003	2004	2005
Revenue %	8.3	19.2	46.7	27.6
Earnings/Share %	-7.8	114.7	-33.3	69.1
Book Value/Share %	3.0	11.7	-7.6	4.0
Dividends/Share %	2.3	2.3	3.1	4.3

Profitability [B+]

	2003	2004	2005	TTM
Return on Assets %	2.7	1.4	2.3	2.1
Oper Cash Flow $Mil	40	94	47	—
- Cap Spending $Mil	2	7	8	—
= Free Cash Flow $Mil	—	—	—	—

Financial Health [NA]

	2003	2004	2005	03-31-06
Long-term Debt $Mil	—	—	—	—
Total Equity $Mil	625	677	768	774
Debt/Equity Ratio	—	—	—	—

Competition

	Market Cap $Mil	12 Mo Trailing Sales $Mil	Price/Cash Flow	Return On Assets %	Debt/ Equity	Total Return% 1 Yr	3 Yr
Municipal Mortgage & Equity LLC	1,240	302	—	2.1	—	34.1	17.8
Indymac Bancorp	3,201	1,321	—	1.3	—	20.8	19.7
CharterMac	1,101	338	—	0.3	—	10.2	8.6

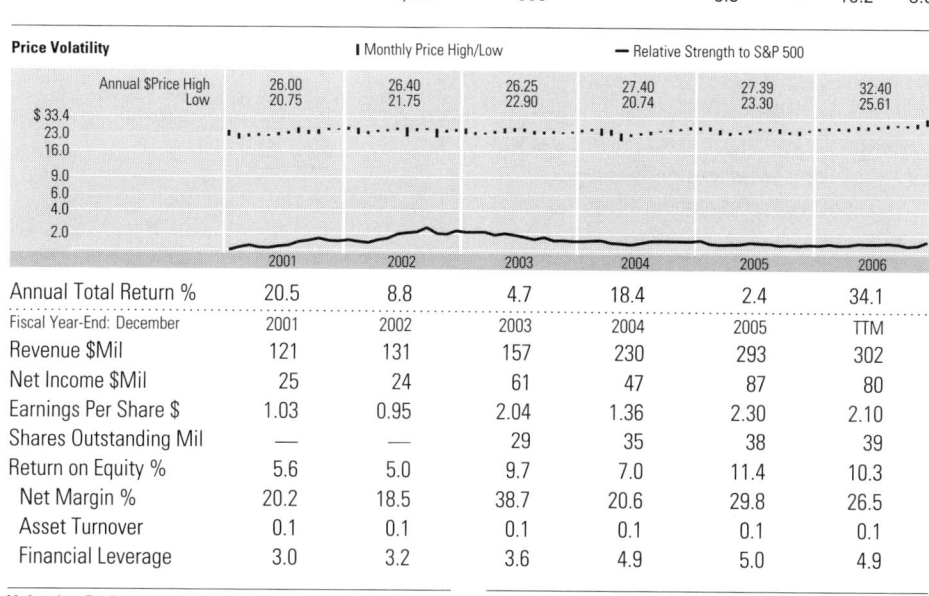

Price Volatility — Monthly Price High/Low — Relative Strength to S&P 500

	2001	2002	2003	2004	2005	2006
Annual $Price High	26.00	26.40	26.25	27.40	27.39	32.40
Low	20.75	21.75	22.90	20.74	23.30	25.61
Annual Total Return %	20.5	8.8	4.7	18.4	2.4	34.1

Fiscal Year-End: December	2001	2002	2003	2004	2005	TTM
Revenue $Mil	121	131	157	230	293	302
Net Income $Mil	25	24	61	47	87	80
Earnings Per Share $	1.03	0.95	2.04	1.36	2.30	2.10
Shares Outstanding Mil	—	—	29	35	38	39
Return on Equity %	5.6	5.0	9.7	7.0	11.4	10.3
Net Margin %	20.2	18.5	38.7	20.6	29.8	26.5
Asset Turnover	0.1	0.1	0.1	0.1	0.1	0.1
Financial Leverage	3.0	3.2	3.6	4.9	5.0	4.9

Valuation Ratios

	Stock	Rel to Industry	Rel to S&P 500
Price/Earnings	17.4	0.9	0.8
Price/Book	1.6	0.4	0.4
Price/Sales	4.1	0.8	1.4
Price/Cash Flow	—	—	—

Major Fund Holders % of Fund Assets

Thesis By Ryan Batchelor, CPA, 12-05-06 Stock Price as of Analysis: $29.00

Municipal Mortgage & Equity, known as MuniMae, seeks to be the one-stop shop for developers of multifamily housing and a premier real estate finance company. At the right price, we think its shares could be attractive to income-hungry investors, especially those in higher tax brackets.

MuniMae can be thought of as two main businesses: a multifamily-housing lender and a fee-generating tax credit syndicator. Since 1986, the company has provided financing to developers of multifamily housing and other real estate properties. The financing--generally in the form of municipal bonds--is subject to credit risk, but the bonds are secured by both the properties and the rental income from the properties' tenants, so credit losses are generally minimal. In addition to originating municipal bonds, the company occasionally purchases other real estate-related bonds on the secondary market for investment purposes. Traditionally, the majority of the firm's profits (roughly 75% in recent years) are tax-exempt; thus, a similar portion of MuniMae's dividend is tax-free for shareholders, a big plus for investors in high tax brackets.

More recently, however, MuniMae has moved beyond its core interest spread businesses. Its recent purchases include Housing and Community Investing (HCI), a tax credit syndicator, in 2003; MONY Realty Capital, a real estate investment management firm, and Glaser Financial, an Upper Midwest commercial mortgage banker, in 2005; and most recently Renewable Ventures, a clean energy financier that also benefits from government tax credits.

The HCI deal was particularly impressive, in our opinion. Through the HCI purchase, MuniMae has become a market leader in the tax credit syndication business. This business is based on low-income housing tax credits, which developers receive from the government as an incentive to build affordable housing. Because these credits are of limited value to developers but represent great value to corporations with higher tax burdens, the developers sell the credits to MuniMae, which then pools the credits together for the benefit of corporate investors. MuniMae earns an up-front syndication fee at the onset and an ongoing asset-management fee for managing the pooled funds.

By offering both tax credit equity and its traditional debt products, MuniMae has diversified its income stream. It also works as a one-stop shop, because the two products are very complementary for capital-hungry developers.

Data as of 12-29-06

Nalco Holding NLC

Rating	Fair Value	Last Close	Consider Buy	Consider Sell	Yield %
★★★	$21.00	$20.46	$13.40	$25.30	0.00

Company Profile

Based in Naperville, Ill., Nalco provides water treatment services and chemicals for businesses looking to become more efficient. These services include anti-corrosion techniques, paper-making process improvements, and upstream and downstream energy services. The company holds the largest share in the water services and chemical market. A majority of Nalco's sales are outside the U.S., and the company owns plants all over the world.

Management Stewardship Grade [B]

CEO William Joyce joined Nalco in 2003, a year before industry-services company Suez spun the company out in a private-equity-backed leveraged buyout. Previously, he had served with competitor Hercules and chemical manufacturer Union Carbide (a division of Dow Chemical) in management roles. Joyce's base pay--at $1 million--seems reasonable to us, and we like that he already owns over 2% of shares outstanding. Also, as evidence that incentive compensation is appropriately performance-based, management didn't receive bonuses in 2005 due to missed EBITDA targets. We're impressed that Joyce has been able to curb Nalco's previously frivolous spending; when the company was private, it built a lavish headquarters and set up an incredibly inefficient purchasing network. He and his team have put in cost saving measures that should expand Nalco's profitability and help reduce debt. The firms that took Nalco public--Blackstone, Apollo, and Goldman Sachs --together still own 13% of shares, and they each have a member on the board. However, we don't like that, as both CEO and chairman, Joyce has considerable power, which could be used to favor projects that run contrary to shareholders' interest. All together, we rate Nalco's stewardship a B.

1601 West Diehl Road www.nalco.com
Naperville, IL 60563

Growth [C]	2002	2003	2004	2005
Revenue %	0.9	4.6	9.6	9.2
Earnings/Share %	NMF	NMF	NMF	NMF
Book Value/Share %	—	—	—	NMF
Dividends/Share %	NMF	NMF	NMF	NMF

Profitability [C]	2003	2004	2005	TTM
Return on Assets %	-3.0	-2.3	0.9	1.5
Oper Cash Flow $Mil	233	238	200	231
- Cap Spending $Mil	—	92	75	89
= Free Cash Flow $Mil	—	146	125	142

Financial Health [F]	2003	2004	2005	09-30-06
Long-term Debt $Mil	—	3,425	3,244	3,060
Total Equity $Mil	1,069	710	706	818
Debt/Equity Ratio	—	4.8	4.6	3.7

Industry	Business Risk	Moat Size	Investment Style	Sector
Chemicals	Above Avg	Narrow	Mid Core	Industrial Materials

Competition

	Market Cap $Mil	12 Mo Trailing Sales $Mil	Price/Cash Flow	Return On Assets%	Debt/ Equity	Total Return% 1 Yr	3 Yr
Nalco Holding	2,927	3,519	12.7	1.5	3.7	15.5	—
General Electric	383,564	161,022	12.8	2.5	2.2	9.4	9.0
Ciba Specialty Chemicals	4,601	6,000	13.9	-2.6	0.8	7.0	-1.4

Price Volatility | Monthly Price High/Low — Relative Strength to S&P 500

Annual $Price High/Low: 2004: 20.24/15.15 2005: 22.03/14.25 2006: 21.19/15.83

Fiscal Year-End: December	2001	2002	2003	2004	2005	TTM
Annual Total Return %	—	—	—	—	-9.3	15.5
Revenue $Mil	2,620	2,644	2,767	3,033	3,312	3,519
Net Income $Mil	-84	128	-182	-139	48	86
Earnings Per Share $	—	—	—	—	0.33	0.60
Shares Outstanding Mil	—	—	—	—	141	143
Return on Equity %	-2.2	3.6	-17.1	-19.5	6.8	10.5
Net Margin %	-3.2	4.9	-6.6	-4.6	1.4	2.4
Asset Turnover	0.4	0.4	0.4	0.5	0.6	0.6
Financial Leverage	1.7	1.8	5.8	8.4	7.9	6.8

Valuation Ratios	Stock	Rel to Industry	Rel to S&P 500
Price/Earnings	34.1	1.9	1.7
Price/Book	3.6	1.1	0.9
Price/Sales	0.8	0.5	0.3
Price/Cash Flow	12.7	0.8	0.9

Major Fund Holders	% of Fund Assets
BB&T Special Opportunities Equity A	4.17
Atlantic Whitehall Equity Income I	2.23
JHT Value Trust Ser I	2.22
Morgan Stanley Mid Cap Value D	2.16

Thesis By Adam Fleck, 11-14-06 Stock Price as of Analysis: $20.04

Nalco's superior products and high customer switching costs will enable it to hold competitors at bay for many years, in our opinion.

Nalco is the largest player in the water treatment market, serving about 16% of a market that reached $17.7 billion in 2005. The company operates in three segments (industrial/institutional, energy, and paper), but its water treatment solutions run across all of its business lines. With thousands of patents, the company has separated itself from competitors through superior product innovation. As the rest of the market struggles to keep up, Nalco continues to introduce specific solutions for each client that have helped create "sticky" customers. As a result, Nalco engineers at a customer's plant can leverage Nalco's position to generate a high level of incremental sales. Furthermore, while many of the firm's clients operate in cyclical industries, Nalco's services are in demand regardless of the economy, stabilizing the company's growth.

Future growth for Nalco will likely stem from emerging markets and energy services. Foreign markets currently offer similar profitability to domestic operations, and we think Nalco will be able to leverage its higher level of technology to gain further pricing power. Volume should grow as well, since paper-making (which is very water-intensive) in China is expected to double by 2008. Similarly, we believe the upstream energy segment, which services pre-refinery oil companies (including drillers), will see impressive growth. High oil prices have made difficult-to-reach oil economically feasible, and Nalco's products improve the efficiency of these processes.

Though Nalco's growth prospects look positive, ineffective operating practices have been the bane of the company. To address this issue, the company has centralized most of its previously dispersed purchasing departments while reorganizing its sales and service staff, improving efficiency. Though Nalco has had difficulty reaching its savings goal of $75 million, we expect substantial margin improvement to take place nevertheless.

The major risk we see for Nalco going forward is its high debt level--stemming from its spin-off from Suez in 2003. However, management is focused on using all available free cash flow to reduce this leverage. Further mitigating this risk, the company's debt level doesn't mature until 2010. Overall, we think that Nalco's narrow moat and growth potential make it a long-term investment worth watching.

Data as of 12-29-06

Nasdaq Stock Market NDAQ

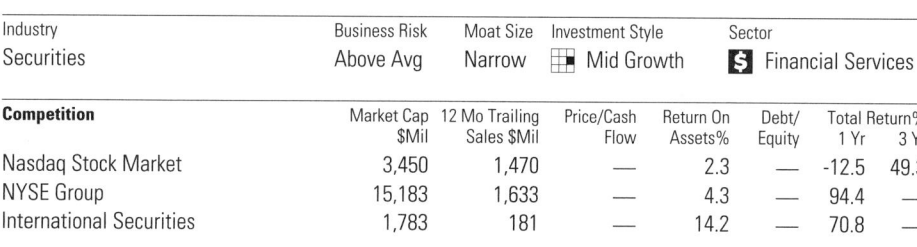

Rating	Fair Value	Last Close	Consider Buy	Consider Sell	Yield %
★★★★★	$52.00	$30.79	$33.10	$62.70	0.00

Industry	Business Risk	Moat Size	Investment Style	Sector
Securities	Above Avg	Narrow	Mid Growth	Financial Services

Company Profile

The Nasdaq Stock Market was founded in 1971 to trade over-the-counter securities, and now it is the listing home to 3,200 companies worth more than $3.8 trillion and about one third of U.S. equity transactions by volume. The firm trades stocks listed on multiple venues, including the NYSE; the 2005 acquisition of Instinet made the company the second-biggest player among U.S. exchanges. Nasdaq also generates revenue from data-feed services.

Management   Stewardship Grade [B]

President and CEO Robert Greifeld joined the Nasdaq from SunGard Data Systems in 2003, where he had experience in automated clearing. The remaining management team came from a mixture of different securities exchange businesses and is fairly young, with the oldest being Edward Knight, who's in his 50s. We think the executive team has the collective experience to run the organization and successfully integrate Instinet. However, we expect the coming years to include dramatic changes in securities markets and fast-paced integrations, and Greifeld will have to be a strong and decisive leader to maximize the company's value during this time. Greifeld's compensation is big, but not out of line for financial services, with most of the compensation coming from bonus or restricted stock. The bonus is tied to operating income, which should be a reasonable incentive structure for the coming years of industry consolidation. Another incentive tool for the management team is option vesting, which can be accelerated by achieving performance goals.

1 Liberty Plaza
New York, NY 10006
www.nasdaq.com

Growth [A-]	2002	2003	2004	2005
Revenue %	-7.2	-25.1	-8.4	62.8
Earnings/Share %	NMF	NMF	NMF	NMF
Book Value/Share %	—	NMF	-15.5	464.7
Dividends/Share %	NMF	NMF	NMF	NMF

Profitability [F]	2003	2004	2005	TTM
Return on Assets %	-13.4	-0.2	2.7	2.3
Oper Cash Flow $Mil	105	117	121	—
- Cap Spending $Mil	32	26	25	—
= Free Cash Flow $Mil	—	—	—	—

Financial Health [NA]	2003	2004	2005	09-30-06
Long-term Debt $Mil	—	—	—	—
Total Equity $Mil	27	26	158	1,317
Debt/Equity Ratio	—	—	—	—

Competition

	Market Cap $Mil	12 Mo Trailing Sales $Mil	Price/Cash Flow	Return On Assets%	Debt/Equity	Total Return% 1 Yr	3 Yr
Nasdaq Stock Market	3,450	1,470	—	2.3	—	-12.5	49.3
NYSE Group	15,183	1,633	—	4.3	—	94.4	—
International Securities	1,783	181	—	14.2	—	70.8	—

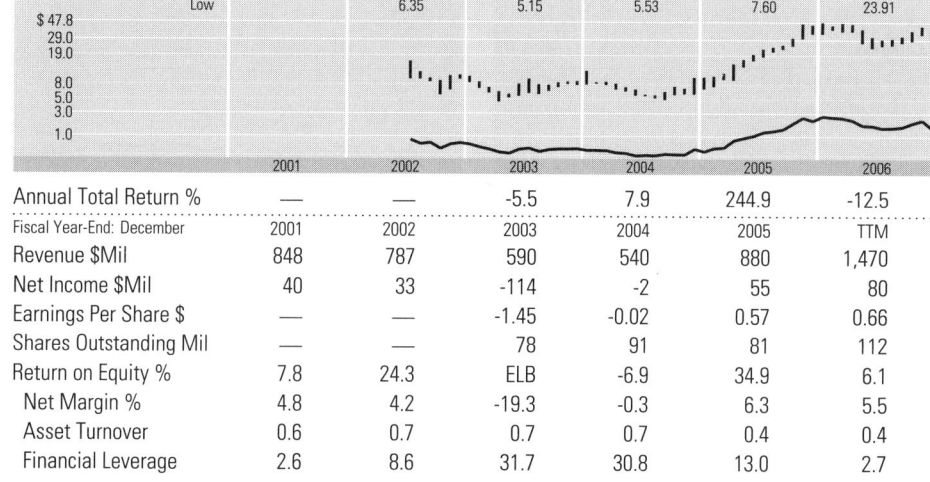

Annual Total Return %	—	—	-5.5	7.9	244.9	-12.5
Fiscal Year-End: December	2001	2002	2003	2004	2005	TTM
Revenue $Mil	848	787	590	540	880	1,470
Net Income $Mil	40	33	-114	-2	55	80
Earnings Per Share $	—	—	-1.45	-0.02	0.57	0.66
Shares Outstanding Mil	—	—	78	91	81	112
Return on Equity %	7.8	24.3	ELB	-6.9	34.9	6.1
Net Margin %	4.8	4.2	-19.3	-0.3	6.3	5.5
Asset Turnover	0.6	0.7	0.7	0.7	0.4	0.4
Financial Leverage	2.6	8.6	31.7	30.8	13.0	2.7

Valuation Ratios	Stock	Rel to Industry	Rel to S&P 500
Price/Earnings	46.7	2.7	2.3
Price/Book	2.6	0.6	0.6
Price/Sales	2.3	0.5	0.8
Price/Cash Flow	—	—	—

Major Fund Holders	% of Fund Assets
Kinetics Small Cap Opportunities	4.99
JHancock Financial Industries A	4.11
Timothy Plan Aggressive Growth A	3.78
ING AllianceBernstein Mid Cap Growth S	3.35

Thesis By Patrick O'Shaughnessy, 12-15-06 Stock Price as of Analysis: $35.55

Just when Nasdaq CEO Robert Greifeld believes he has all the leaks plugged, more seem to spring up. Nasdaq likely thought that it could breathe easy after the firm and the New York Stock Exchange bought all of their major competitors, but the threat of new challengers once again threatens to siphon market share. While we still believe Nasdaq possesses a narrow moat, Greifeld must aggressively fend off competition and chart a course to more-friendly seas.

Stock exchanges primarily make money in two ways: from listing stocks and from facilitating trading activity. For years, virtually all shares that were listed on Nasdaq traded there, but regulatory changes in the 1990s allowed for decoupling of the trading venue from the listing venue. The exchange is still very attractive for high-tech firms, and it owns a wide moat around its listing business, but Nasdaq faces a renewed assault on its trading business. Several investment banks and other firms, wary of the higher transaction fees a Nasdaq/NYSE duopoly could create, have supported a new round of competitors, regional exchanges, and off-exchange matching networks. These venues are once again threatening to steal market share and pressure Nasdaq's trading fees.

Nasdaq does have a few things in its favor. Above all, trading in equities continues to increase at a steady clip, and it provides a solid foundation for Nasdaq's growth. The Instinet acquisition gives the firm the fastest trading system, an important element in keeping hyperactive traders happy. The exchange also has the largest pools of liquidity in its listed stocks, which should help protect its market share and is the source of its narrow moat. Lastly, Nasdaq is poised to steal share in NYSE-listed stocks as the NYSE migrates to electronic trading.

Like NYSE, Nasdaq is also looking to offset its risks in the U.S. by expanding internationally; in Nasdaq's case, through purchasing the London Stock Exchange. Such a purchase is a double-edged sword, however. Although it would provide scale and globalization benefits, the London Stock Exchange is itself becoming increasingly susceptible to new competition in Europe and lacks the diversification of other European exchanges. Furthermore, if Nasdaq is to complete the acquisition it will have to pay a hefty price and take on substantial new debt. All in all, Nasdaq faces significant challenges and is not as well-positioned as several of its exchange brethren, including NYSE. Given its risks, we would wait for a large margin of safety before investing in Nasdaq.

Data as of 12-29-06

National City NCC

	Rating	Fair Value	Last Close	Consider Buy	Consider Sell	Yield %
	★★★★	$43.00	$36.56	$33.20	$53.90	4.16

Company Profile

National City is a financial holding company with more than $138 billion in assets. The bank operates more than 1,245 branches and 1,968 ATMs across Ohio, Illinois, Indiana, Kentucky, Michigan, Missouri, and Pennsylvania. The bank is expanding its footprint beyond the Midwest through two recently announced acquisitions in Florida, which will add another 92 branches to its mix. National City's loan portfolio is 60% consumer and 40% commercial.

Management   Stewardship Grade [B]

David Daberko--chairman and CEO since 1995--has more than 37 years with National City, making him a valuable asset with extensive knowledge and experience. Daberko's efforts include refocusing the bank's attention on its retail banking franchise and away from more cyclical businesses, such as mortgage originations. Corporate governance is a priority for this Midwest bank, in our opinion, as National City ensures that its board is operating in the best interests of the bank and its shareholders. For example, none of National City's directors is allowed to serve on more than four other public company boards. This is a good measure to have in place, as it helps to prevent directors from spreading themselves too thin. In addition, National City instituted a policy in 1996 requiring each board member to beneficially own at least 12,000 shares within the first three years as a director. We are particularly pleased that the entire board is held accountable to shareholders annually, as every director stands for election each year.

1900 East Ninth Street www.nationalcity.com
Cleveland, OH 44114-3484

Growth [D]	2002	2003	2004	2005
Revenue %	6.9	21.3	11.9	-9.8
Earnings/Share %	3.5	46.0	25.7	-28.3
Book Value/Share %	9.8	14.0	31.3	-1.1
Dividends/Share %	3.4	4.2	7.2	7.5

Profitability [B+]	2003	2004	2005	TTM
Return on Assets %	1.9	2.0	1.4	1.3
Oper Cash Flow $Mil	12,822	5,021	6,464	—
- Cap Spending $Mil	297	146	190	—
= Free Cash Flow $Mil	—	—	—	—

Financial Health [NA]	2003	2004	2005	09-30-06
Long-term Debt $Mil	—	—	—	—
Total Equity $Mil	9,329	12,804	12,613	12,902
Debt/Equity Ratio	—	—	—	—

Industry	Business Risk	Moat Size	Investment Style	Sector
Super Regional Banks	Average	Narrow	Large Value	Financial Services

Competition	Market Cap $Mil	12 Mo Trailing Sales $Mil	Price/Cash Flow	Return On Assets %	Debt/ Equity	Total Return % 1 Yr	Total Return % 3 Yr
National City	22,015	7,757	—	1.3	—	13.7	7.2
US Bancorp	63,617	13,499	—	2.2	—	26.3	11.8
Fifth Third Bancorp	22,842	5,431	—	1.4	—	13.0	-8.1

Price Volatility | Monthly Price High/Low   — Relative Strength to S&P 500

Annual $Price High/Low	32.70 / 23.70	33.75 / 24.60	34.97 / 26.53	39.66 / 32.14	40.00 / 29.75	38.04 / 33.26
	2001	2002	2003	2004	2005	2006
Annual Total Return %	6.0	-2.6	29.4	14.9	-6.8	13.7

Fiscal Year-End: December	2001	2002	2003	2004	2005	TTM
Revenue $Mil	6,117	6,539	7,929	8,873	8,000	7,757
Net Income $Mil	1,388	1,447	2,117	2,780	1,985	1,856
Earnings Per Share $	2.27	2.35	3.43	4.31	3.09	3.00
Shares Outstanding Mil	604	—	612	636	634	602
Return on Equity %	18.8	17.7	22.7	21.7	15.7	14.4
Net Margin %	22.7	22.1	26.7	31.3	24.8	23.9
Asset Turnover	0.1	0.1	0.1	0.1	0.1	0.1
Financial Leverage	14.3	14.5	12.2	10.9	11.3	10.7

Valuation Ratios	Stock	Rel to Industry	Rel to S&P 500
Price/Earnings	12.2	0.9	0.6
Price/Book	1.7	0.8	0.4
Price/Sales	2.8	0.8	1.0
Price/Cash Flow	—	—	—

Major Fund Holders	% of Fund Assets
Senbanc	5.79
FBR Large Cap Financial	3.73
Highmark Core Equity Fid	3.00
Huntington Income-Equity Tr	2.88

Thesis By Erin Swanson, CFA, 11-29-06 Stock Price as of Analysis: $36.61

National City is the dominant bank in Ohio, a claim to fame we wouldn't write home about given the market's difficult characteristics. In our opinion, National City's future success depends on its ability to export its model beyond the Midwest.

The Ohio market is not known for rapid economic growth, which means National City will need to take its show on the road. The bank is successfully expanding in Midwest metro markets, such as St. Louis, Cincinnati, and Chicago. But National City's true test is whether its model is strong and flexible enough to gain share in other regions of the country with different demographics. National City recently announced two acquisitions in the Florida market--its first move outside its core Midwest footprint. However, we are troubled that these two acquisitions did not satisfy management's appetite for challenges, as the company contends it's open to putting more on its plate despite the potential strain on the rest of its business.

We are encouraged by management's efforts to lower the bank's overall risk profile, most recently through the sale of its First Franklin business. First Franklin is an originator of nonprime residential mortgages focusing on the California market. We believe the complexity and skepticism surrounding National City's foray into subprime lending prevented National City's stock price from reflecting the value of this business. Following the completion of the First Franklin sale, National City's revenue base will be more subject to spread income and, subsequently, changes in interest rates. We expect the contribution of noninterest income as a percentage of net revenue to fall to 36% by 2010, down from 45% on average over the past five years.

Despite the elimination of First Franklin, National City will continue to be heavily exposed to the U.S. real estate market--more than 60% of the bank's loan portfolio. However, we believe management's experience in this market and the bank's conservative lending process will enable it to weather any storms arising in the slowing housing market. We are further comforted that National City continues to sell a majority of its mortgage loan production in the secondary market and adequately reserves for losses on the loans it retains.

National City continues to reinvest in its business and return value to shareholders through share repurchases and increased dividends. We are encouraged by the steps management is taking to refocus the business and lower its risk profile, and we'd be buyers at an appropriate margin of safety.

Network Appliance NTAP

Data as of 12-29-06

Rating	Fair Value	Last Close	Consider Buy	Consider Sell	Yield %
★	$31.00	$39.28	$23.90	$38.80	0.00

Industry	Business Risk	Moat Size	Investment Style	Sector
Computer Equip.	Average	Narrow	Large Growth	Hardware

Company Profile

NetApp sells hardware, software, and services for customers to store and manage critical data across their networks. The company was an early pioneer in building storage hardware that could easily attach to a customer's existing network as a simple "storage appliance." Today, NetApp supports network and storage protocols that allow customers to unify storage networks and support new applications for disaster recovery and business continuity.

Competition

	Market Cap $Mil	12 Mo Trailing Sales $Mil	Price/Cash Flow	Return On Assets %	Debt/ Equity	Total Return % 1 Yr	3 Yr
Network Appliance	14,684	2,409	20.5	8.3	0.0	45.5	23.7
IBM	146,342	89,593	9.8	8.8	0.4	19.8	3.0
Hewlett-Packard	112,070	91,658	9.9	7.6	0.1	45.2	22.7

Management   Stewardship Grade [C]

Dan Warmenhoven has been at the helm of the company as CEO since 1994. Prior to joining NetApp, he worked at Network Equipment Technologies as CEO and also spent 13 years at IBM. David Hitz and James Lau, who founded NetApp in 1992, still remain as key members of the management team. We consider Hitz's and Lau's involvement to be crucial in helping to keep NetApp at the forefront of innovation in the storage industry. We are encouraged by directors' and executive officers' equity ownership of approximately 8% of the company. Additionally, Warmenhoven and CFO Steven Gomo own a combined 4.5% of NetApp's equity. We are less excited about the company's options policy, which we feel is transferring too much of the shareholders' value to employees. Historically, NetApp has typically given away about 5% of equity every year as options. We believe option compensation should be pared down closer to 3% of overall equity.

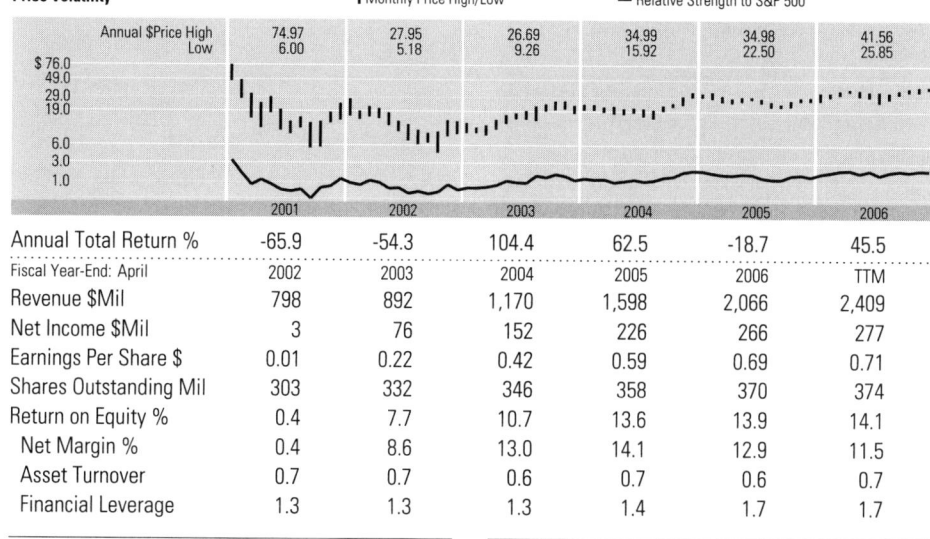

Price Volatility — Monthly Price High/Low — Relative Strength to S&P 500

Annual $Price High / Low	74.97 / 6.00	27.95 / 5.18	26.69 / 9.26	34.99 / 15.92	34.98 / 22.50	41.56 / 25.85
	2001	2002	2003	2004	2005	2006
Annual Total Return %	-65.9	-54.3	104.4	62.5	-18.7	45.5

Fiscal Year-End: April	2002	2003	2004	2005	2006	TTM
Revenue $Mil	798	892	1,170	1,598	2,066	2,409
Net Income $Mil	3	76	152	226	266	277
Earnings Per Share $	0.01	0.22	0.42	0.59	0.69	0.71
Shares Outstanding Mil	303	332	346	358	370	374
Return on Equity %	0.4	7.7	10.7	13.6	13.9	14.1
Net Margin %	0.4	8.6	13.0	14.1	12.9	11.5
Asset Turnover	0.7	0.7	0.6	0.7	0.6	0.7
Financial Leverage	1.3	1.3	1.3	1.4	1.7	1.7

Valuation Ratios	Stock	Rel to Industry	Rel to S&P 500
Price/Earnings	55.3	2.1	2.7
Price/Book	7.5	1.3	1.8
Price/Sales	6.1	2.3	2.1
Price/Cash Flow	20.5	1.3	1.4

Major Fund Holders	% of Fund Assets
TCW Select Equities I	6.57
Bender Growth C	5.55
AXA Enterprise Equity A	5.52
ING Large Cap Growth A	4.71

Thesis By Rick Summer, CFA, CPA, 12-18-06 Stock Price as of Analysis: $40.65

Network Appliance's (NetApp's) storage products are not only technically advanced; they are also in the fastest-growing segments of the storage industry.

NetApp has proved itself to be a nimble developer of technically advanced storage technology, and a savvy acquirer of firms that round out its broader storage solution. While NetApp continues to marry ease of use and innovative storage technology, the company has acquired companies that allow for advanced storage management, provisioning, and security. As storage records proliferate, customers look to storage vendors to control costs by managing complexity. For example, intelligent software can allow customers to move storage records to a cheaper part of the storage network when needs change, saving money and improving performance.

New advances in storage are being driven by software that unifies enterprise storage networks, regardless of technology or vendor. Although most of the revenues in the storage industry flow to EMC, IBM, Hitachi Data Systems, and HP, NetApp is a leader in the distributed storage segment. We feel the company's primary advantage comes from its software that enables customers to use a greater portion of unused storage.

The company's growth is driven by its concentration in the fastest-growing segments of the storage industry as well as a strategy providing for aggressive product upgrades. NetApp is the largest vendor of network-attached storage, which we expect to grow in the midteens. Additionally, the company is an early adopter of storage based on Internet technologies, the highest-growth segment of the storage industry. The company also upgrades products, almost forcing the upgrade on customers by abandoning support for old products. While this strategy may ultimately create some customer backlash, we believe switching costs are too great for customers to look elsewhere.

Our only concern is the company's dependence on its indirect sales channels to fuel revenue growth. More than 50% of sales are through systems integrators and other partners, and we expect that percentage to increase over time. We are encouraged, however, by the company's continued progress in the sales channel. We are most excited about a partnership with IBM. IBM is selling NetApp hardware into a new customer base, which we believe will be almost 4% of revenues in 2007.

---

495 East Java Drive
Sunnyvale, CA 94089
www.netapp.com

Growth [A+]	2003	2004	2005	2006
Revenue %	11.7	31.2	36.6	29.3
Earnings/Share %	EUB	90.9	40.5	16.9
Book Value/Share %	0.4	37.7	11.0	14.8
Dividends/Share %	NMF	NMF	NMF	NMF

Profitability [A]	2004	2005	2006	TTM
Return on Assets %	8.1	9.5	8.2	8.3
Oper Cash Flow $Mil	313	462	554	716
- Cap Spending $Mil	49	94	133	146
= Free Cash Flow $Mil	264	369	421	570

Financial Health [A-]	2004	2005	2006	10-31-06
Long-term Debt $Mil	5	4	138	78
Total Equity $Mil	1,416	1,661	1,923	1,963
Debt/Equity Ratio	0.0	0.0	0.1	0.0

New Jersey Resources NJR

Data as of 12-29-06

Rating	Fair Value	Last Close	Consider Buy	Consider Sell	Yield %
★★★★	$56.00	$48.58	$47.70	$73.50	3.01

Industry	Business Risk	Moat Size	Investment Style	Sector
Natural Gas	Below Avg	Narrow	Small Value	Utilities

Company Profile

New Jersey Resources is a holding company that provides retail and wholesale energy services to customers in New Jersey. Its regulated utility, New Jersey Natural Gas, is one of the fastest-growing local distribution companies in the United States and accounts for roughly 70% of NJR's profits. New Jersey Resources also controls a nonregulated wholesale energy services business, as well as several other nonregulated energy-related subsidiaries.

Management   Stewardship Grade [B]

New Jersey Resources ranks relatively high in terms of shareholder stewardship. Members of management are required to own a substantial amount of shares, closely aligning their interests with shareholders'. Executive compensation is in line with what we expect at a company of NJR's size, and we give CEO Laurence Downes additional credit for turning down his $300,000 performance bonus in 2006. Downes was authorized to receive the bonus based on 2005 consolidated results that exceeded prespecified goals, but elected to forgo the bonus because NJNG, the company's regulated subsidiary, did not meet its earnings target in fiscal 2005. This move, in addition to more timely disclosure of all of the company's financial statements with its quarterly earnings release, has led to the company's B Stewardship Grade. However, we would still prefer to see nonstaggered board terms and a separation of the chairman and CEO positions at New Jersey Resources. That being said, Downes has done a tremendous job in both of these roles by conservatively and effectively managing the business. In his 10 years at the company's helm, NJR has delivered compounded annual returns of more than 11% to shareholders.

1415 Wyckoff Road
Wall, NJ 07719
www.njliving.com

Growth [C]	2003	2004	2005	2006
Revenue %	39.0	-0.4	24.3	4.8
Earnings/Share %	13.9	7.1	6.3	3.3
Book Value/Share %	14.7	9.4	-6.7	42.6
Dividends/Share %	3.3	4.8	4.6	5.9

Profitability [A]	2004	2005	2006	TTM
Return on Assets %	3.8	3.3	3.3	3.3
Oper Cash Flow $Mil	-50	205	-23	-23
- Cap Spending $Mil	74	54	59	59
= Free Cash Flow $Mil	-124	150	-82	-82

Financial Health [D]	2004	2005	2006	09-30-06
Long-term Debt $Mil	316	317	332	332
Total Equity $Mil	468	438	622	622
Debt/Equity Ratio	0.7	0.7	0.5	0.5

Competition

	Market Cap $Mil	12 Mo Trailing Sales $Mil	Price/Cash Flow	Return On Assets%	Debt/ Equity	Total Return% 1 Yr	3 Yr
New Jersey Resources	1,345	3,300	—	3.3	0.5	19.6	11.2
Sempra Energy	14,692	12,673	12.1	5.6	0.6	28.1	26.2
Atmos Energy	2,611	6,152	8.4	2.6	1.3	27.6	14.0

Price Volatility

	2001	2002	2003	2004	2005	2006
Annual $Price High	32.53	33.60	39.54	44.55	49.34	53.16
Low	24.84	24.35	30.01	36.50	40.68	41.49
Annual Total Return %	12.7	5.2	26.3	16.3	-0.3	19.6

Fiscal Year-End: September	2002	2003	2004	2005	2006	TTM
Revenue $Mil	1,830	2,543	2,534	3,148	3,300	3,300
Net Income $Mil	57	65	72	76	79	79
Earnings Per Share $	2.09	2.38	2.55	2.71	2.80	2.80
Shares Outstanding Mil	27	27	28	28	28	28
Return on Equity %	15.7	15.6	15.3	17.4	12.6	12.6
Net Margin %	3.1	2.6	2.8	2.4	2.4	2.4
Asset Turnover	1.3	1.6	1.4	1.4	1.4	1.4
Financial Leverage	4.0	3.8	4.0	5.3	3.9	3.9

Valuation Ratios	Stock	Rel to Industry	Rel to S&P 500
Price/Earnings	17.4	1.1	0.8
Price/Book	2.2	0.7	0.5
Price/Sales	0.4	0.4	0.1
Price/Cash Flow	—	—	—

Major Fund Holders	% of Fund Assets
Queens Road Small Cap Value	2.64
Copley	2.43
Morgan Stanley Utilities B	2.04
Van Kampen Utility A	1.98

Thesis By Paul Justice, CFA, 12-15-06 Stock Price as of Analysis: $50.40

New Jersey Resources is one of the most well-managed and financially secure companies on our utility coverage list. Its long-standing ability to drive consistent earnings- and dividend-growth underscores why we would need only a small margin of safety before aggressively acquiring these shares.

New Jersey Natural Gas--the company's regulated distribution business--accounts for the bulk of NJR's earnings and has been the driving force behind the company's earnings stability and growth. NJNG is one of the fastest-growing local distribution companies in the United States with customer growth averaging roughly 3% over the last 10 years--twice the industry average. Population growth in NJNG's service territory has been the foundation of the company's impressive growth, but it has also benefited from customers converting from competing fuels to natural gas.

Due in large part to above-average customer growth, NJNG has been able to manage its business without relying on rate-base increases for earnings growth. While its rate structure allows NJNG to capture an 11.5% return on equity and to pass through natural-gas costs to its customers, the company has not received a base rate increase in 11 years. Despite this, NJNG continues to consistently increase its profitability. Given the constructive relationship the company has forged with state regulators through its exemplary service record, we see little from a regulatory standpoint that would jeopardize NJR's future returns.

Regulated utilities like NJNG have a natural monopoly over their respective service areas as competitors would be hard-pressed to put new pipes in the ground. To maintain quality service at a reasonable price, regulators intervene to establish allowed rates of return that balance the need for shareholders to earn a reasonable risk-adjusted market rate of return while keeping costs to the public as low as possible. The monopoly and capped returns combine to warrant a narrow-moat rating for utilities.

We expect NJR's regulated business to remain the primary component of future earnings, but expansion of the company's nonregulated wholesale energy business has been increasingly important to NJR's profitability and growth lately. We think this business could provide additional growth going forward, especially if today's strong demand environment continues to strain natural-gas supplies, allowing the company to extract even more value from its portfolio of storage and transportation capacity.

Data as of 12-29-06

New York Times A NYT

	Rating	Fair Value	Last Close	Consider Buy	Consider Sell	Yield %
	★★★	$22.00	$24.36	$17.00	$27.60	2.83

Company Profile
New York Times is a leading media company. Properties include The New York Times, the International Herald Tribune, The Boston Globe, 15 regional newspapers, and around 35 Web sites, including NYTimes.com, Boston.com, and About.com.

Industry	Business Risk	Moat Size	Investment Style	Sector
Media Conglomerates	Average	Narrow	Mid Value	Media

Competition

	Market Cap $Mil	12 Mo Trailing Sales $Mil	Price/Cash Flow	Return On Assets%	Debt/Equity	Total Return% 1 Yr	3 Yr
New York Times A	3,503	3,392	12.7	3.9	0.5	-5.3	-18.1
Gannett	14,167	7,880	9.8	6.9	0.7	1.9	-10.5
Tribune	7,353	5,527	13.2	3.4	0.9	4.2	-14.1

Management — Stewardship Grade [C]
Janet L. Robinson became president and CEO in 2005. She was formerly senior vice president of newspaper operations and president and general manager of The New York Times. In 2005, Robinson received annual compensation of $1.5 million, along with $2 million worth of restricted stock and an additional 149,000 options. In our opinion, Robinson's pay package seems reasonable. However, we have other issues with the company's governance. The board is controlled by the Ochs-Sulzberger family (Arthur Ochs-Sulzberger is publisher of The New York Times and chairman of the board), which through a trust owns the majority of the Class B shares, allowing it to elect 70% of the directors via staggered board elections. While we appreciate the family's efforts to protect the journalistic excellence of the company, the dual-class structure puts the interests of outside shareholders behind the family's.

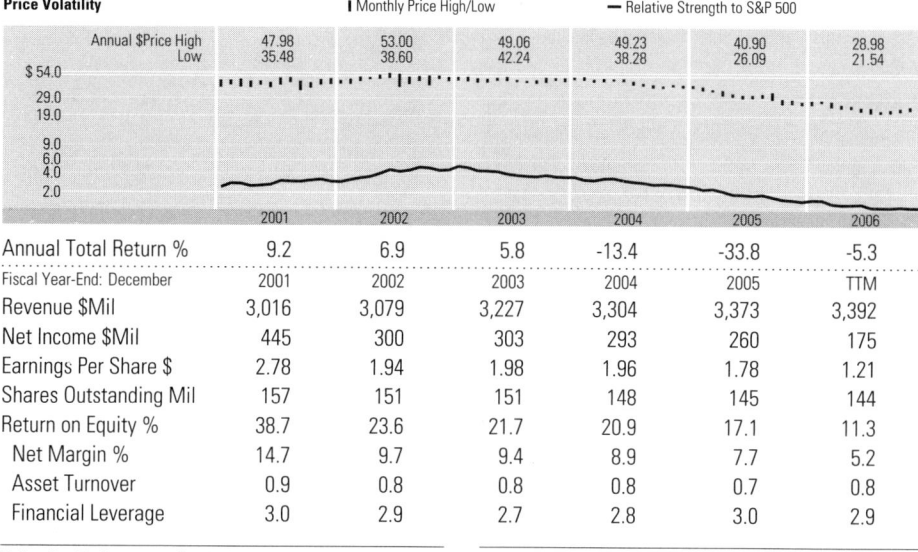

Annual $Price High/Low	47.98 / 35.48	53.00 / 38.60	49.06 / 42.24	49.23 / 38.28	40.90 / 26.09	28.98 / 21.54
	2001	2002	2003	2004	2005	2006
Annual Total Return %	9.2	6.9	5.8	-13.4	-33.8	-5.3
Fiscal Year-End: December	2001	2002	2003	2004	2005	TTM
Revenue $Mil	3,016	3,079	3,227	3,304	3,373	3,392
Net Income $Mil	445	300	303	293	260	175
Earnings Per Share $	2.78	1.94	1.98	1.96	1.78	1.21
Shares Outstanding Mil	157	151	151	148	145	144
Return on Equity %	38.7	23.6	21.7	20.9	17.1	11.3
Net Margin %	14.7	9.7	9.4	8.9	7.7	5.2
Asset Turnover	0.9	0.8	0.8	0.8	0.7	0.8
Financial Leverage	3.0	2.9	2.7	2.8	3.0	2.9

Valuation Ratios	Stock	Rel to Industry	Rel to S&P 500
Price/Earnings	19.6	0.8	1.0
Price/Book	2.3	0.7	0.6
Price/Sales	1.0	0.3	0.3
Price/Cash Flow	12.7	0.8	0.9

Major Fund Holders	% of Fund Assets
Van Kampen American Franchise A	4.67
Aston/Optimum Mid Cap N	3.58
MFS Strategic Value A	3.29
ING Midcap Value A	2.13

229 West 43rd Street www.nytco.com
New York, NY 10036

Growth [C]	2002	2003	2004	2005
Revenue %	2.1	4.8	2.4	2.1
Earnings/Share %	-30.2	2.1	-1.0	-9.2
Book Value/Share %	14.3	10.9	3.0	10.7
Dividends/Share %	8.2	7.5	7.0	6.6

Profitability [A]	2003	2004	2005	TTM
Return on Assets %	8.0	7.4	5.7	3.9
Oper Cash Flow $Mil	466	444	294	276
- Cap Spending $Mil	121	188	221	286
= Free Cash Flow $Mil	345	256	73	-10

Financial Health [B]	2003	2004	2005	09-30-06
Long-term Debt $Mil	726	471	898	796
Total Equity $Mil	1,392	1,401	1,516	1,543
Debt/Equity Ratio	0.5	0.3	0.6	0.5

Thesis By James M. Walden, CFA, 12-18-06 Stock Price as of Analysis: $24.10

We think The New York Times Company earns its economic moat from the high-quality content of its flagship paper, which has earned it the reputation of the nation's newspaper of record. The New York Times' newsroom houses more writers, editors, and photographers than any other national newspaper, which we believe allows the newspaper to provide more in-depth analysis on national and international stories than its peers. In fact, the Times has won more than 90 Pulitzers, roughly twice the amount won by The Washington Post.

Despite the accolades the paper has received for its newsroom efforts, the Times' journalistic excellence has done little recently to help the company's overall financial results. In our opinion, the blame falls squarely on the shoulders of the company's New England Media Group, which houses The Boston Globe. In 2005, revenue at the New England Media Group fell 3.6% from the year before, driven by lower ad and circulation revenue; we expect the group's revenue to drop an additional 7%-8% in 2006. Part of the Globe's recent struggles come from a sluggish economy in Massachusetts and the loss of advertising revenue when Federated Department Stores acquired May, which had a presence in Boston with its landmark Filene's department store. Going forward, our biggest concern for the Globe is the Internet. According to researcher comScore Media Metrix (as reported by The Wall Street Journal), 76% of Boston households have high-speed Internet, ranking it third among U.S. cities with the highest broadband penetration. We believe this makes the Globe much more susceptible to changing viewer habits and advertising trends than other newspapers.

The New York Times Company is fighting back with its own Internet offensive. In 2005, it acquired About.com, an online property that offers guides to various subjects, to diversify its revenue streams. It also launched TimesSelect, which offers exclusive online access to op-ed pieces and the Times' archives. We estimate that initial annual revenue from TimesSelect was less than $10 million--a relatively small component of the company's total--but we also estimate incremental costs to be minimal, allowing most of the revenue to flow to the bottom line. In our opinion, the Times is one of the few newspapers that can monetize its content online in such a way.

Data as of 12-29-06

News Corporation NWS

	Rating	Fair Value	Last Close	Consider Buy	Consider Sell	Yield %
	★★★	$21.00	$22.26	$17.90	$27.60	0.45

Company Profile
News Corporation has eight units. Filmed entertainment produces films and TV shows. Television runs Fox, 35 TV stations, and Star. Cable network programming operates several networks. Direct-broadcast satellite television transmits programming to subscribers in Italy. Magazines and inserts prints ad material. Newspapers publishes Australian, U.K., and U.S. papers. Book publishing is HarperCollins. Various other businesses include MySpace.com.

Management
Stewardship Grade [C]

Chairman and CEO Rupert Murdoch is considered a legend in the media world, after building his family's small newspaper firm into one of the largest media conglomerates on Earth. Murdoch wants his family to remain in charge at News Corp. once he retires, and with the 2005 departure of older son Lachlan, it looks like younger son James, currently the CEO of News Corp.-owned BSkyB, is the logical choice. Helping the Murdochs manage News Corp. is the highly respected Peter Chernin, president and chief operating officer, who made about $28 million in salary, bonus, and perks in 2005 and was also given options on 500,000 shares. Chernin is a board member and, as of late 2005, held 9 million options but almost no actual shares. Murdoch's pay included a base salary of $4.5 million and an $18.9 million bonus, but no options. We appreciate that Murdoch wasn't given additional options, as he and his family already own about 30% of the firm. Outside of the Murdoch family, News Corp.'s directors and officers own relatively few shares in the company. In the past, News Corp. has moved to limit the influence of outside investors, including the introduction of a poison pill. We'd like to see the board more firmly dedicated to the rights of non-Murdoch shareholders.

1211 Avenue of Americas
New York, NY 10036
www.newscorp.com

Growth [C+]	2001	2002	2003	2004
Revenue %	NMF	19.7	14.7	6.2
Earnings/Share %	NMF	-4.9	25.9	4.1
Book Value/Share %	NMF	-28.0	27.6	-2.6
Dividends/Share %	NMF	103.4	8.0	101.2

Profitability [B]	2002	2003	2004	TTM
Return on Assets %	3.2	3.9	4.1	6.2
Oper Cash Flow $Mil	2,395	3,371	3,257	3,257
- Cap Spending $Mil	—	—	—	—
= Free Cash Flow $Mil	—	—	—	—

Financial Health [NA]	2002	2003	2004	03-31-05
Long-term Debt $Mil	9,080	10,087	11,385	11,394
Total Equity $Mil	20,875	29,377	29,874	30,695
Debt/Equity Ratio	0.4	0.3	0.4	0.4

Industry	Business Risk	Moat Size	Investment Style	Sector
Media Conglomerates	Below Avg	Narrow	Large Core	Media

Competition	Market Cap $Mil	12 Mo Trailing Sales $Mil	Price/Cash Flow	Return On Assets%	Debt/ Equity	Total Return% 1 Yr	3 Yr
News Corporation	70,411	25,559	21.6	6.2	0.4	34.8	7.2
Time Warner	86,932	44,532	14.4	4.9	0.5	26.4	6.8
Walt Disney	70,886	34,285	11.7	5.6	0.3	44.3	14.2

Price Volatility — Monthly Price High/Low — Relative Strength to S&P 500

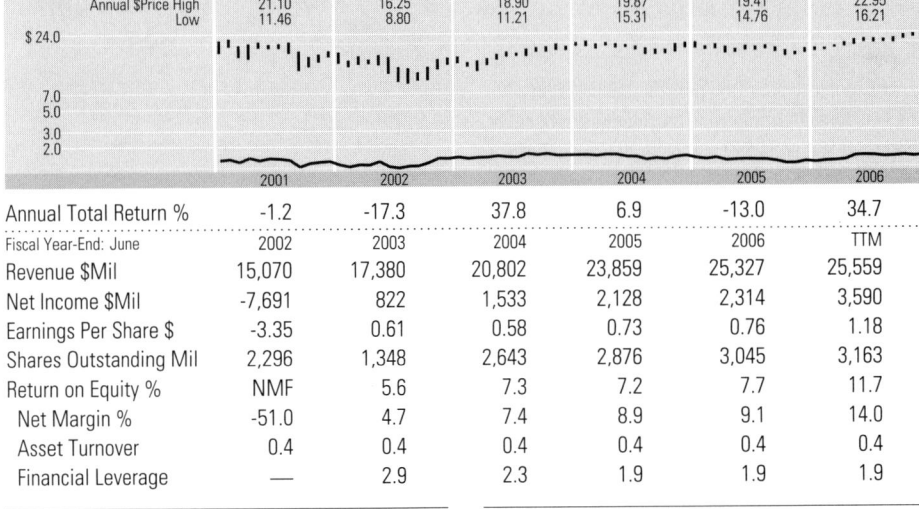

Annual $Price High/Low	21.10 / 11.46	16.25 / 8.80	18.90 / 11.21	19.87 / 15.31	19.41 / 14.76	22.95 / 16.21
Annual Total Return %	-1.2	-17.3	37.8	6.9	-13.0	34.7

Fiscal Year-End: June	2002	2003	2004	2005	2006	TTM
Revenue $Mil	15,070	17,380	20,802	23,859	25,327	25,559
Net Income $Mil	-7,691	822	1,533	2,128	2,314	3,590
Earnings Per Share $	-3.35	0.61	0.58	0.73	0.76	1.18
Shares Outstanding Mil	2,296	1,348	2,643	2,876	3,045	3,163
Return on Equity %	NMF	5.6	7.3	7.2	7.7	11.7
Net Margin %	-51.0	4.7	7.4	8.9	9.1	14.0
Asset Turnover	0.4	0.4	0.4	0.4	0.4	0.4
Financial Leverage	—	2.9	2.3	1.9	1.9	1.9

Valuation Ratios	Stock	Rel to Industry	Rel to S&P 500
Price/Earnings	22.0	0.9	1.1
Price/Book	2.3	0.7	0.6
Price/Sales	2.8	0.8	1.0
Price/Cash Flow	21.6	1.3	1.5

Major Fund Holders	% of Fund Assets
Sycuan U.S. Value	5.22
Longleaf Partners International	4.86
Manor Growth	3.01
Legg Mason Partners Fundamental Value A	2.85

Thesis By Jonathan Schrader, CFA, 11-09-06 Stock Price as of Analysis: $22.04

From humble beginnings as a newspaper publisher in Australia, News Corporation has grown into one of the biggest media companies on the planet, thanks to the efforts of CEO and chairman Rupert Murdoch, who owns almost 30% of the company's voting stock. Today, News Corp. controls many "old media" businesses, including newspapers, movie and television studios, television stations, cable networks, and satellite television providers.

Thanks to recent acquisitions, especially its 2005 purchase of MySpace parent Intermix Media for $580 million in cash, News Corp. has also become a major player in "new media." This business and geographic diversification--with assets in Asia, Europe, South America, Australia, and North America--puts News Corp. in a position to weather challenging economic times relatively well.

Not only do we like News Corp.'s diversification, we also like its assets. While the market in general has soured on old media assets, we like the generous cash flow that newspapers, television stations, and the like generate. While it's true that the Internet has made increasing sales difficult for media distributors, we're not ready to write their obituaries, especially for those assets that are in the hands of more aggressive operators like Murdoch. If managed deftly, growth at MySpace could make up for weakness at News Corp.'s traditional media operations.

Additionally, News Corp. controls some topnotch content, including a large library of movies and television series. While the success of MySpace shows that just about anyone today can create content and post it online, producing high-quality content that advertisers and consumers are consistently willing to pay big dollars for is still not easy, and it's very expensive. Because of this, we think News Corp. has a sizable economic moat.

However, we estimate that the firm's total return on invested capital (including goodwill from acquisitions) is below its weighted average cost of capital, thanks to a long series of overly rich acquisitions that made News Corp. the behemoth that it is today. Future deals could result in further value destruction, which isn't necessarily a problem for Murdoch, who is now worth billions, but would be for anyone providing fresh equity capital to the company. We'd rather the company avoid any big deals and instead focus on building its library of content and making the properties that it already owns the best in their class.

Data as of 12-29-06

Nike B NKE

	Rating	Fair Value	Last Close	Consider Buy	Consider Sell	Yield %
	★★★	$105.00	$99.03	$81.00	$131.60	1.31

Company Profile
Nike is the world's largest athletic footwear and apparel brand. International sales to more than 160 countries around the world account for over half of the company's total revenue. Primarily a wholesaler, Nike also operates about 400 retail stores domestically and abroad. Nike owns several footwear and accessory brands including Cole Haan, Jordan, Converse, Starter, Bauer, and Hurley.

Management   Stewardship Grade [B]
Mark Parker was named CEO in 2006 following the resignation of William Perez, who clashed with founder and chairman Phil Knight. We think Nike is in good hands with Parker at the helm. A Nike employee for nearly 30 years, most recently serving as copresident with Charlie Denson, Parker brings plenty of industry experience. Perhaps just as crucially, he arrives fully wired into Nike's unique company culture, an obstacle that outsider Perez could not overcome. We are confident Parker and Knight are capable of leading Nike through its latest growth cycle and maintaining its market dominance. Knight has sold some of his Nike stock since stepping down as CEO, yet still owns about 40% of the company with his Class A and B shares. Even though Knight is entitled to elect the majority of the directors, we believe the board is sufficiently independent; nine of the 11 directors are outsiders. In fiscal 2006, Parker was paid $2.4 million in salary and bonus and was awarded another $3.5 million worth of restricted stock, stock options, and other incentive compensation as part of his employment contract. Overall, executive compensation is reasonable for this industry, and corporate governance appears to be sound.

One Bowerman Drive   www.nikebiz.com
Beaverton, OR 97005-6453

Growth [B+]	2003	2004	2005	2006
Revenue %	8.1	14.5	12.1	8.8
Earnings/Share %	-27.5	98.3	27.6	17.9
Book Value/Share %	5.5	19.1	17.6	14.2
Dividends/Share %	8.3	30.8	32.4	24.4

Profitability [A+]	2004	2005	2006	TTM
Return on Assets %	12.0	13.8	14.1	14.0
Oper Cash Flow $Mil	1,519	1,571	1,668	1,638
- Cap Spending $Mil	215	257	334	348
= Free Cash Flow $Mil	1,304	1,314	1,334	1,291

Financial Health [A+]	2004	2005	2006	08-31-06
Long-term Debt $Mil	682	687	411	380
Total Equity $Mil	4,782	5,644	6,285	6,221
Debt/Equity Ratio	0.1	0.1	0.1	0.1

Industry	Business Risk	Moat Size	Investment Style	Sector
Shoes	Average	Narrow	Large Growth	Consumer Goods

Competition	Market Cap $Mil	12 Mo Trailing Sales $Mil	Price/Cash Flow	Return On Assets %	Debt/ Equity	Total Return % 1 Yr	3 Yr
Nike B	24,827	15,287	15.2	14.0	0.1	15.8	15.0
Under Armour A	2,403	383	—	11.6	0.0	31.7	—
Timberland	1,971	1,545	14.2	12.9	—	-3.0	6.9

Price Volatility | Monthly Price High/Low   — Relative Strength to S&P 500

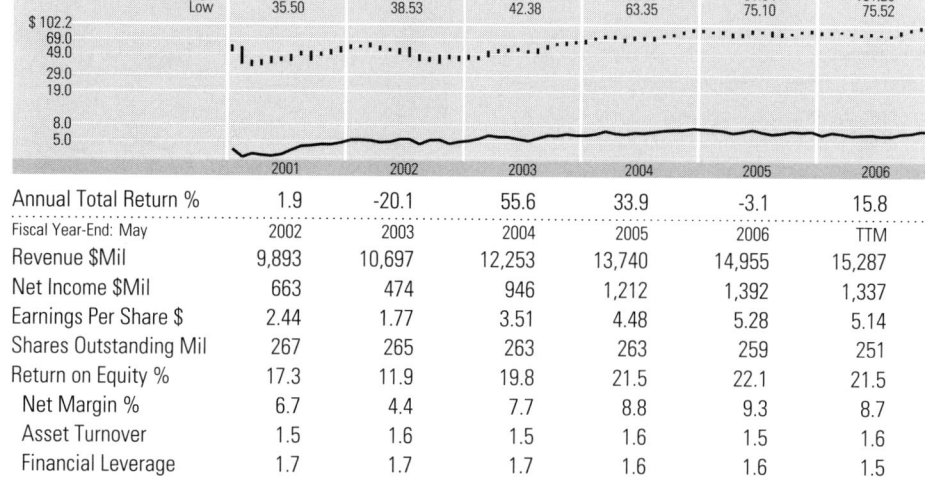

Annual $Price High	60.06	64.28	68.54	92.43	91.54	101.20
Low	35.50	38.53	42.38	63.35	75.10	75.52
	2001	2002	2003	2004	2005	2006
Annual Total Return %	1.9	-20.1	55.6	33.9	-3.1	15.8

Fiscal Year-End: May	2002	2003	2004	2005	2006	TTM
Revenue $Mil	9,893	10,697	12,253	13,740	14,955	15,287
Net Income $Mil	663	474	946	1,212	1,392	1,337
Earnings Per Share $	2.44	1.77	3.51	4.48	5.28	5.14
Shares Outstanding Mil	267	265	263	263	259	251
Return on Equity %	17.3	11.9	19.8	21.5	22.1	21.5
Net Margin %	6.7	4.4	7.7	8.8	9.3	8.7
Asset Turnover	1.5	1.6	1.5	1.6	1.5	1.6
Financial Leverage	1.7	1.7	1.7	1.6	1.6	1.5

Valuation Ratios	Stock	Rel to Industry	Rel to S&P 500
Price/Earnings	19.3	1.0	0.9
Price/Book	4.0	0.4	1.0
Price/Sales	1.6	0.6	0.6
Price/Cash Flow	15.2	0.9	1.0

Major Fund Holders	% of Fund Assets
Artisan Opportunistic Value Inv	5.07
Blue Chip Investor	5.05
Sycuan U.S. Value	4.52
William Blair Large Cap Growth N	4.42

Thesis   By Brady Lemos, 12-11-06   Stock Price as of Analysis: $97.45

Promising growth opportunities, global scale advantages, and a history of product innovation position Nike to maintain market dominance in athletic apparel and footwear. We believe that Nike's iconic image, in addition to its diversified product portfolio and global presence, is a competitive advantage rivals cannot match. This brand prestige should help the firm earn returns on invested capital well in excess of its cost of capital. We've awarded Nike only a narrow economic moat, however, to account for low customer switching costs.

Vital to the firm's growth strategy is international expansion, and World Cup 2006 provided the ideal stage to showcase the Nike brand to an estimated 1 billion viewers around the globe. Sales of replica jerseys and boots helped expand Nike's soccer division into a $1.5 billion business, more than double its size following World Cup 2002. We expect Nike to deepen its penetration of the massive soccer markets in Europe and South America through athlete endorsements and club licensing deals.

The exploding popularity of basketball in Asia provides another avenue for growth in China, where Nike is already the top-selling brand and business has more than doubled over the past two years. The Beijing 2008 Olympics should spark sales even higher. Domestically, Nike entered the low-price sneaker business in 2005 by introducing Starter footwear into Wal-Mart. We believe this foray into the mass channel offers significant growth potential without diluting the premium Nike brand.

Nike is partnering with leaders in other industries, like media and technology, to stimulate innovative marketing and product design. In 2006, Nike teamed with Google to create its Joga Bonito online soccer community and with Apple to develop its Nike+ training software for iPod. Both projects provide Nike with proprietary platforms for growth.

Even the best-run apparel companies are susceptible to unfavorable industry trends, however. In 2006, for example, the firm struggled in Europe, where fads favoring low-profile shoes from vendors like Puma hurt demand for Nike's higher-price sneakers. Fortunately for Nike, expansion in other regions like China and South America more than offset weak performance in softer markets. Furthermore, Nike's new low-profile footwear collection has been well received by consumers. While certain risks are largely unavoidable, Nike has demonstrated that its diverse product offering and global reach can provide a mitigating buffer unequaled in the industry.

Nokia ADR NOK

Data as of 12-29-06

	Rating	Fair Value	Last Close	Consider Buy	Consider Sell	Yield %
	★★★	$21.00	$20.32	$16.20	$26.30	2.21

Company Profile
Nokia is the world's top maker of mobile phones; it sold 265 million handsets during 2005 and exited the year with a 33% global market share. Europe accounted for 36% of handset sales, while 33% came from Asia and 17% from the Americas. Mobile phones account for 82% of Nokia's sales; the company's other main business is supplying telecom infrastructure gear to wireless carriers.

Management
Stewardship Grade [A]

Nokia has a history of solid stewardship and corporate governance. As planned, Nokia veteran Olli-Pekka Kallasvuo replaced longtime chairman and CEO Jorma Ollila in mid-2006. Ollila has long been regarded as a superstar CEO and was credited with reversing Nokia's fortunes in the early 1990s by transforming it into a wireless-only company. But we believe such success also led to complacency and stands as part of the reason Nokia was caught flat-footed as demand shifted in recent years. We believe Kallasvuo, a quiet executive who is known for his attention to cost-cutting, will refocus Nokia on compelling low-cost handsets. Management has occasionally been guilty of not delivering on inflated expectations. The firm is stingy in issuing options; at the end of 2002, options represented less than 5% of the outstanding share count. Compared with Nokia's peers in the tech industry, management is also modestly compensated: Ollila took home just 2.6 million euros in pay in 2003, and only one other executive cleared 1 million. Management's overall ownership stake in the firm is very small, representing less than 1% of total equity.

Keilalahdentie 4 PO Box 226
Espoo, Finland 02150
www.nokia.com

Growth [NA]	2002	2003	2004	2005
Revenue %	-3.8	-1.6	-0.5	16.4
Earnings/Share %	54.3	4.2	-6.8	20.3
Book Value/Share %	17.5	0.7	3.1	-8.9
Dividends/Share %	—	—	—	—

Profitability [NA]	2003	2004	2005	TTM
Return on Assets %	13.3	12.8	17.1	17.1
Oper Cash Flow $Mil	5,882	5,395	5,189	5,189
- Cap Spending $Mil	728	806	952	952
= Free Cash Flow $Mil	5,154	4,589	4,238	4,238

Financial Health [NA]	2003	2004	2005	12-31-05
Long-term Debt $Mil	25	26	25	25
Total Equity $Mil	18,068	19,725	14,714	14,714
Debt/Equity Ratio	0.0	0.0	0.0	0.0

Industry	Business Risk	Moat Size	Investment Style	Sector
Wireless Equip.	Average	Narrow	Large Core	Hardware

Competition	Market Cap $Mil	12 Mo Trailing Sales $Mil	Price/Cash Flow	Return On Assets%	Debt/Equity	Total Return% 1 Yr	3 Yr
Nokia ADR	90,097	42,815	17.4	17.1	0.0	13.4	8.2
Motorola	49,703	42,707	10.2	11.3	0.2	-8.2	17.6
Nortel Networks	11,591	11,078	—	-12.1	3.4	-12.7	-15.9

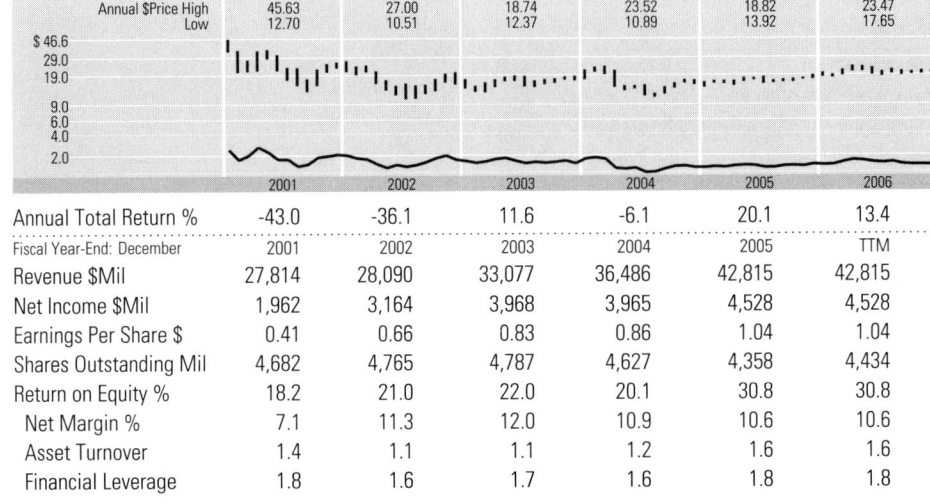

	2001	2002	2003	2004	2005	2006
Annual Total Return %	-43.0	-36.1	11.6	-6.1	20.1	13.4

Fiscal Year-End: December	2001	2002	2003	2004	2005	TTM
Revenue $Mil	27,814	28,090	33,077	36,486	42,815	42,815
Net Income $Mil	1,962	3,164	3,968	3,965	4,528	4,528
Earnings Per Share $	0.41	0.66	0.83	0.86	1.04	1.04
Shares Outstanding Mil	4,682	4,765	4,787	4,627	4,358	4,434
Return on Equity %	18.2	21.0	22.0	20.1	30.8	30.8
Net Margin %	7.1	11.3	12.0	10.9	10.6	10.6
Asset Turnover	1.4	1.1	1.1	1.2	1.6	1.6
Financial Leverage	1.8	1.6	1.7	1.6	1.8	1.8

Valuation Ratios	Stock	Rel to Industry	Rel to S&P 500
Price/Earnings	19.6	0.9	1.0
Price/Book	6.1	1.2	1.5
Price/Sales	2.1	0.6	0.7
Price/Cash Flow	17.4	0.9	1.2

Major Fund Holders	% of Fund Assets
Legg Mason Growth Trust Primary	5.55
Rydex Telecommunications Inv	4.85
Neuberger Berman Focus Inv	4.54
Fidelity Select Wireless	4.50

Thesis By John Slack, 12-07-06 Stock Price as of Analysis: $20.32

With the handset market maturing in most of the developed world, vendors are increasingly turning to emerging markets for growth. We believe Nokia's leadership position in emerging economies, coupled with its ability to generate substantial free cash flow, merits attention from investors.

Nokia's 35% share of the global wireless handset market is well ahead of its closest rival, Motorola, which has a 22% share. Nokia's size gives the company considerable economies of scale and the greatest pricing flexibility in the industry. With nearly 1 billion wireless handsets expected to ship worldwide in 2006, we think supply chain management, procurement, and distribution are imperative for success. Nokia's scale allows it to extract the best terms from suppliers and assures that its orders are filled ahead of rivals', which is important when components are in tight supply.

Nokia stumbled in 2004 and the first half of 2005, when it missed shifts in demand toward clamshell-style phones and camera phones, which culminated in market share losses for the firm. In our view, Nokia's dominance bred complacency, but we believe that a fresh management team should help reinvigorate the company. It has since recovered its share losses by revamping its high-end handset lineup and by flexing its considerable muscle in developing countries. Nokia's efficiency and pricing power allow it to be one of the only companies that can profitably compete in developing countries, and it has built deep distribution channels in key markets, which has bolstered Nokia's share to over 40% in the developing world.

However, Nokia's strong handset volumes have come at the expense of operating margins as the company struggles with a product mix skewed toward low-end (and lower-margin) phones. After bottoming at 12% in the second quarter of 2005, handset margins have rebounded to just over 13%. We think a refreshed product lineup at both the high and low ends, coupled with a tight rein on costs, should allow Nokia's margins to rebound to the midteens over the next year, within shouting distance of the company's new 15% margin target.

Outside its handset business, Nokia has significantly reinvented its networks business through its joint venture with Siemens. We believe that the combination is a smart way for Nokia to gain much-needed scale in its infrastructure business, which, over time, should allow it to improve margins through cost reductions and improved sourcing.

Norfolk Southern NSC

Data as of 12-29-06

Rating ★★★★	Fair Value $60.00	Last Close $50.29	Consider Buy $46.30	Consider Sell $75.20	Yield % 1.35

Company Profile

Based in Norfolk, Va., Norfolk Southern is one of two major rail carriers in the Eastern United States (the other is CSX). The firm transports a variety of goods—including chemicals, agricultural products, metals, paper/forest products, coal, and automobiles—over its 21,500 miles of track. It also derives a large portion of its business from intermodal transport, which involves moving goods via multiple methods, including rail, ship, and truck.

Management — Stewardship Grade [B]

Charles "Wick" Moorman recently took over the chairman and CEO positions from longtime leader David Goode. Moorman had been groomed for the position for quite some time, so the transition was smooth and uneventful. Goode had been chairman and CEO since 1992, and while his record was mixed, his term did end positively. The firm's fluid network, the product of several years of engineering, enabled it to capitalize on recent strong rail demand, earning Goode the 2005 Railroader of the Year award from industry trade journal Railway Age. Moorman's background is in technology; he was president of the firm's Thoroughbred Technology and Telecommunications division from 1999 to 2004 and, before that, vice president of information technology. We expect the firm under his leadership to continue to prioritize the use of technology to optimize network operations. We are curious how he will handle the capital-spending budget in the coming years, as it has been restrained of late and shippers will probably lobby for additional capacity now that the firm is earning a decent return on its capital. As for corporate governance, compensation is reasonable, but we'd prefer to see the full board re-elected annually and the chairman and CEO positions held by separate individuals.

Three Commercial Place
Norfolk, VA 23510-9227
www.nscorp.com

Growth [B]	2002	2003	2004	2005
Revenue %	1.6	3.2	13.0	16.6
Earnings/Share %	21.6	16.1	68.6	34.6
Book Value/Share %	5.8	7.1	11.9	12.8
Dividends/Share %	33.3	-6.3	20.0	33.3

Profitability [B]	2003	2004	2005	TTM
Return on Assets %	2.6	3.7	5.0	5.6
Oper Cash Flow $Mil	1,054	1,661	2,105	2,220
- Cap Spending $Mil	720	1,041	1,025	1,309
= Free Cash Flow $Mil	334	620	1,080	911

Financial Health [B]	2003	2004	2005	06-30-06
Long-term Debt $Mil	6,800	6,863	6,616	6,141
Total Equity $Mil	6,976	7,990	9,289	9,579
Debt/Equity Ratio	1.0	0.9	0.7	0.6

Industry	Business Risk	Moat Size	Investment Style	Sector
Land Transport	Average	None	Large Core	Business Services

Competition	Market Cap $Mil	12 Mo Trailing Sales $Mil	Price/Cash Flow	Return On Assets%	Debt/Equity	Total Return% 1 Yr	3 Yr
Norfolk Southern	19,960	9,345	9.0	5.6	0.6	13.7	29.8
Burlington Northern Santa	26,513	14,653	9.4	5.7	0.7	5.5	34.1
Union Pacific	24,820	15,237	8.6	3.9	0.5	15.9	11.9

Price Volatility — Monthly Price High/Low — Relative Strength to S&P 500

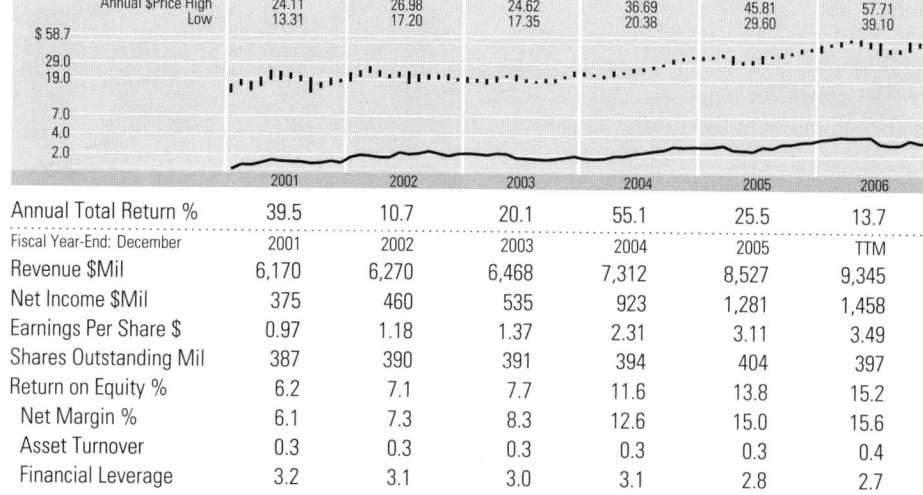

	2001	2002	2003	2004	2005	2006
Annual $Price High	24.11	26.98	24.62	36.69	45.81	57.71
Low	13.31	17.20	17.35	20.38	29.60	39.10
Annual Total Return %	39.5	10.7	20.1	55.1	25.5	13.7

Fiscal Year-End: December

	2001	2002	2003	2004	2005	TTM
Revenue $Mil	6,170	6,270	6,468	7,312	8,527	9,345
Net Income $Mil	375	460	535	923	1,281	1,458
Earnings Per Share $	0.97	1.18	1.37	2.31	3.11	3.49
Shares Outstanding Mil	387	390	391	394	404	397
Return on Equity %	6.2	7.1	7.7	11.6	13.8	15.2
Net Margin %	6.1	7.3	8.3	12.6	15.0	15.6
Asset Turnover	0.3	0.3	0.3	0.3	0.3	0.4
Financial Leverage	3.2	3.1	3.0	3.1	2.8	2.7

Valuation Ratios	Stock	Rel to Industry	Rel to S&P 500
Price/Earnings	14.4	0.8	0.7
Price/Book	2.1	0.9	0.5
Price/Sales	2.1	1.0	0.7
Price/Cash Flow	9.0	0.9	0.6

Major Fund Holders	% of Fund Assets
Rydex Transportation Inv	5.58
Fidelity Select Transportation	5.44
Hallmark Strategic Growth I	3.37
Manor	3.06

Thesis By Peter Smith, 10-25-06 Stock Price as of Analysis: $53.73

Norfolk Southern's impressive profitability, reputation for on-time service, and strong free cash flow generation make it a railroad we'd want to own.

Operating a railroad is a challenge, partly because each rail company is responsible for building and maintaining its own track. Though that acts as a stellar barrier to entry, rail companies have to reinvest a substantial portion of their revenue annually on capital expenditures, with much of it going strictly toward track maintenance. Norfolk Southern has reduced capital expenditures in recent years to 11%-12% of sales, resulting in industry-leading free cash flow that it has used to reduce its hefty debt load. While we believe the firm will continue to generate strong free cash flow in the coming years, we expect capital spending as a percentage of sales to increase.

Another challenge railroads face is providing consistent on-time service. Norfolk Southern has been one of the best performers in this regard, handling increasing volumes much better than some of its rail peers. Its secret weapon is its Thoroughbred Operating Plan ("TOP"), a multi-phase project gradually implemented over the last few years. Through the use of sophisticated technology and an assortment of process tweaks, TOP has produced substantial improvements in service reliability and consistency.

As a result of TOP, the firm is enjoying a historically low operating ratio (operating expenses as a percentage of revenue). At 75.5% for 2005, Norfolk's ratio was far superior to that of its Eastern counterpart, CSX, and second only to industry leader Canadian National. Norfolk Southern just about earned its cost of capital in 2005, and we expect it to earn some excess return in the next few years. For this to continue, the company must maintain reliable service, which will help make price increases stick.

Lately, the railroad industry has enjoyed its best pricing environment since it was deregulated in 1980. Recent growth in global trade, secular growth trends in the coal and grain industries, and a severe truck driver shortage (preventing trucking firms from flexing up capacity to meet demand) have resulted in unprecedented demand for rail service. This favorable dynamic won't last forever, though, as one of the factors currently benefiting the industry will inevitably turn the other direction. When the music stops, we'd prefer to own a railroad, like Norfolk Southern, that has sufficiently strong operational and financial characteristics to continue to succeed in a less auspicious environment.

Data as of 12-29-06

Nortel Networks NT

Rating	Fair Value	Last Close	Consider Buy	Consider Sell	Yield %
★★★	$30.00	$26.73	$19.10	$36.20	0.00

Company Profile
Canada-based Nortel Networks manufactures telecommunication equipment for telecom service providers, cable network operators, corporations, governments, and universities. Its products include central office switching systems, optical networking gear, and wireless infrastructure equipment. Wireless networks have typically accounted for more than 50% of sales, with enterprise, wireline, and optical networks constituting most of the remainder.

Management   Stewardship Grade [NA]
Nortel is looking to put its history of checkered corporate governance behind it with the hiring of Mike Zafirovski as its president and CEO. We view this as a major positive. Zafirovski, who had been president and COO of Motorola, was instrumental in leading the turnaround in Motorola's handset business, and we believe he brings a strategic vision and confidence to Nortel that was lacking during former CEO Bill Owens' tenure. Owens was instrumental in helping stabilize the company after its accounting fiasco, but we viewed him as a crisis manager and administrator and believe he lacked the tech industry savvy and operating experience necessary to turn around a ship as large as Nortel. New management has a mammoth undertaking: The firm is losing share across nearly every product line, and its research and development has been woefully unproductive over the past five years. The board continues to investigate the accounting problems at the firm. We applaud Nortel's recent move to pursue legal action against the aforementioned fired executives in an effort to have them return bonuses paid during the period of accounting fraud. Before the firings, option grants were fairly egalitarian, with top executives receiving less than 2% of the options granted in 2002.

8200 Dixie Road Suite 100   www.nortel.com
Brampton, ON L6T 5P6

Growth [NA]	2002	2003	2004	2005
Revenue %	-43.0	-7.5	-4.2	10.6
Earnings/Share %	NMF	NMF	NMF	NMF
Book Value/Share %	-48.4	14.3	-1.0	-79.5
Dividends/Share %	NMF	NMF	NMF	NMF

Profitability [NA]	2003	2004	2005	TTM
Return on Assets %	1.7	-1.2	-14.2	-12.1
Oper Cash Flow $Mil	-140	-179	-180	-211
- Cap Spending $Mil	169	276	258	342
= Free Cash Flow $Mil	-309	-455	-438	-553

Financial Health [NA]	2003	2004	2005	09-30-06
Long-term Debt $Mil	—	3,852	2,439	4,446
Total Equity $Mil	3,719	3,640	786	1,315
Debt/Equity Ratio	—	1.1	3.1	3.4

Industry	Business Risk	Moat Size	Investment Style	Sector
Wireline Equip.	Above Avg	Narrow	Large Core	Hardware

Competition	Market Cap $Mil	12 Mo Trailing Sales $Mil	Price/Cash Flow	Return On Assets%	Debt/ Equity	Total Return% 1 Yr	3 Yr
Nortel Networks	11,591	11,078	—	-12.1	3.4	-12.7	-15.9
Cisco Systems	165,967	30,118	18.9	13.2	0.3	59.6	4.1
Ciena	2,340	522	—	-14.5	1.2	33.3	-16.0

Price Volatility

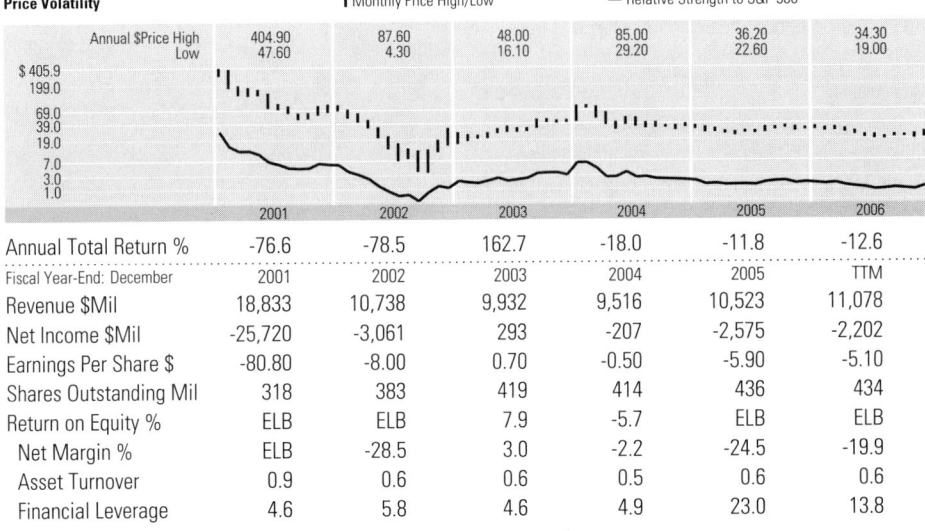

	2001	2002	2003	2004	2005	TTM
Annual $Price High	404.90	87.60	48.00	85.00	36.20	34.30
Low	47.60	4.30	16.10	29.20	22.60	19.00
Annual Total Return %	-76.6	-78.5	162.7	-18.0	-11.8	-12.6
Fiscal Year-End: December	2001	2002	2003	2004	2005	TTM
Revenue $Mil	18,833	10,738	9,932	9,516	10,523	11,078
Net Income $Mil	-25,720	-3,061	293	-207	-2,575	-2,202
Earnings Per Share $	-80.80	-8.00	0.70	-0.50	-5.90	-5.10
Shares Outstanding Mil	318	383	419	414	436	434
Return on Equity %	ELB	ELB	7.9	-5.7	ELB	ELB
Net Margin %	ELB	-28.5	3.0	-2.2	-24.5	-19.9
Asset Turnover	0.9	0.6	0.6	0.5	0.6	0.6
Financial Leverage	4.6	5.8	4.6	4.9	23.0	13.8

Valuation Ratios	Stock	Rel to Industry	Rel to S&P 500
Price/Earnings	NMF	—	—
Price/Book	8.8	1.9	2.1
Price/Sales	1.0	0.2	0.3
Price/Cash Flow	—	—	—

Major Fund Holders	% of Fund Assets
Constellation JSAM Large Cap Value	4.76
Fidelity Advisor Communications Equip T	4.65
Touchstone Large Cap Value A	4.40
MFS Strategic Value A	4.00

Thesis By John Slack, 11-30-06 Stock Price as of Analysis: $21.50

Nortel is hoping to put its accounting fiasco behind it, but we remain concerned that the turmoil of the past couple of years has consumed management's attention at the expense of operational execution. While a recently revamped management team should help reinvigorate the company, we would look for a healthy discount to our fair value estimate until we see improved evidence of execution.

During the bubble years, Nortel cobbled together what was arguably one of the strongest and broadest product lineups in the communications equipment industry. The firm views itself as a jack of all trades, selling cutting-edge equipment to nearly every communications equipment end market. This broad exposure is a blessing and a curse. Nortel's legacy product offerings in circuit-based equipment have come under pressure as these markets have contracted; the firm has tried to offset this by using its strong carrier relationships to sell higher-growth wireless and Internet-based technologies. It's also the leading optical-networking vendor in the long-haul and metro markets. This segment has poor near-term prospects, but it should be a good source of growth because most new networks will eventually use these products at their core. While Nortel's jack-of-all-trades strategy may have worked in the past, recently the firm has been losing ground to sharply focused competitors such as Cisco in networking and Ericsson in wireless equipment.

The distraction caused by the company's accounting woes played a part in this slide, but management hasn't made any moves to improve our confidence in its ability to execute a turnaround. Furthermore, rather than concentrating acquisition and research and development dollars on growth areas of equipment spending--as its competitors have done--Nortel instead spent nearly $450 million to buy PEC Solutions to gain entry to the U.S. government IT systems integration market. This is not a natural strategic path for Nortel and adds merger integration risk to the complications confronting the company.

We believe Nortel's best prospects lie outside its traditional carrier customers. Sales of network equipment to corporate customers account for 25% of the firm's total revenue. Nortel has refocused its noncarrier business on Internet-based phone systems. To this end, it has formed an alliance with Microsoft and launched a new sales program focused on the small-business market. While these moves make sense to us, it remains to be seen how well Nortel can compete head-to-head with Cisco in the latter firm's core market.

Northern Trust NTRS

Data as of 12-29-06

Rating ★★★	Fair Value $59.00	Last Close $60.69	Consider Buy $45.50	Consider Sell $73.90	Yield % 1.55

Company Profile
Northern Trust began by specializing in asset management for affluent individuals. It is still committed to that mission and intends to aggressively expand its wealth-management business. Northern Trust also provides custody, asset administration, and investment services to institutions, corporations, and private clients. More than 70% of Northern Trust's revenue comes from fees for these services; the balance is interest income from lending operations.

Management
Stewardship Grade [B]

William Osborn, a 35-year Northern veteran, has been chairman and CEO since 1995. Steven Fradkin was named CFO in 2004. Business heads at the Northern tend to be longtime employees who have made the rounds at the bank's various divisions. Executive compensation is generous, but right in line with the Northern's trust bank peers. Executives own sizable chunks of stock, much of which is a result of the generous option policy. The board reads like a Who's Who of the Chicago business community. Corporate governance is generally shareholder-friendly. We have a few reservations, however, leading to our B grade. Northern has a poison pill that we believe is not in the best interest of shareholders. In addition, the firm granted 2.4 million stock options in February 2005 that vested fully about a month later. This accelerated vesting period means that the Northern did not have to include the expense of these options in its financial statements when it began expensing option grants. In our opinion, this has the effect of hiding compensation expenses from shareholders by not including them on the GAAP financial statements, and we frown on this practice. But in general, we look favorably on the bank's stewardship and are pleased to see some large shareholders sitting on the board.

50 South La Salle Street
Chicago, IL 60675
www.northerntrust.com

Growth [C+]
	2002	2003	2004	2005
Revenue %	-6.4	1.2	8.7	15.5
Earnings/Share %	-6.6	-8.6	26.1	16.3
Book Value/Share %	10.1	6.7	8.7	9.9
Dividends/Share %	7.1	2.9	11.4	10.3

Profitability [B]
	2003	2004	2005	TTM
Return on Assets %	1.0	1.1	1.1	1.2
Oper Cash Flow $Mil	419	654	585	—
- Cap Spending $Mil	82	49	86	—
= Free Cash Flow $Mil	—	—	—	—

Financial Health [NA]
	2003	2004	2005	09-30-06
Long-term Debt $Mil	—	—	—	—
Total Equity $Mil	3,055	3,296	3,601	3,936
Debt/Equity Ratio	—	—	—	—

Industry	Business Risk	Moat Size	Investment Style	Sector
International Banks	Average	Wide	Large Core	Financial Services

Competition
	Market Cap $Mil	12 Mo Trailing Sales $Mil	Price/Cash Flow	Return On Assets%	Debt/Equity	Total Return% 1 Yr	3 Yr
Northern Trust	13,230	2,913	—	1.2	—	19.1	11.4
J.P. Morgan Chase & Co.	167,551	59,650	—	0.9	—	25.6	13.2
Bank of New York Company	41,334	7,308	—	1.5	—	26.9	9.2

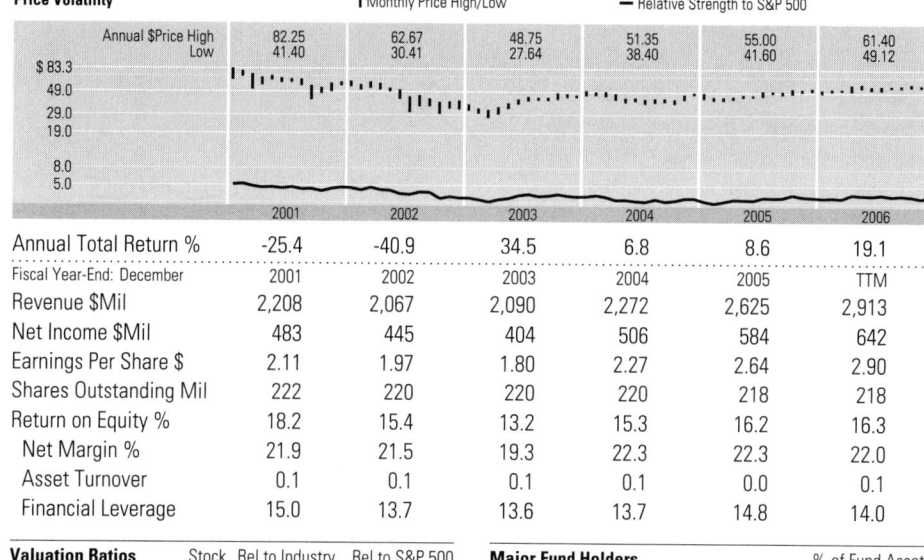

Price Volatility — Monthly Price High/Low — Relative Strength to S&P 500

	2001	2002	2003	2004	2005	2006
Annual $Price High	82.25	62.67	48.75	51.35	55.00	61.40
Low	41.40	30.41	27.64	38.40	41.60	49.12
Annual Total Return %	-25.4	-40.9	34.5	6.8	8.6	19.1

Fiscal Year-End: December	2001	2002	2003	2004	2005	TTM
Revenue $Mil	2,208	2,067	2,090	2,272	2,625	2,913
Net Income $Mil	483	445	404	506	584	642
Earnings Per Share $	2.11	1.97	1.80	2.27	2.64	2.90
Shares Outstanding Mil	222	220	220	220	218	218
Return on Equity %	18.2	15.4	13.2	15.3	16.2	16.3
Net Margin %	21.9	21.5	19.3	22.3	22.3	22.0
Asset Turnover	0.1	0.1	0.1	0.1	0.0	0.1
Financial Leverage	15.0	13.7	13.6	13.7	14.8	14.0

Valuation Ratios
	Stock	Rel to Industry	Rel to S&P 500
Price/Earnings	20.9	1.1	1.0
Price/Book	3.4	1.3	0.8
Price/Sales	4.5	1.1	1.6
Price/Cash Flow	—	—	—

Major Fund Holders
	% of Fund Assets
Schwab Financial Services	4.87
Ariel Appreciation	4.49
Crawford Dividend Growth I	3.45
Bryce Capital Growth	3.45

Thesis By Jeffrey Ptak, CPA, CFA, 12-06-06 Stock Price as of Analysis: $57.38

A venerable name in the wealth management business, Northern Trust's clear-cut competitive advantages should endure, in our opinion.

Northern Trust is perhaps best known as a reserve of the wealthy. The reputation is well deserved: The Northern is not only one of the largest personal trust banks in the U.S., with more than $350 billion in assets under management or custody, but also the banker to some of the world's richest families. To wit, the firm estimates it serves roughly 24% of the richest families profiled annually in the Forbes 400.

The Northern has garnered that following in a few ways. First, it boasts one of the longest track records in the private banking world, dating back to 1889. In addition, unlike diversified financial services firms that peddle wealth management services alongside credit cards and other retail products, the Northern has remained true to its wealth management roots, thereby cementing its reputation as a committed wealth counselor. Taken together, these factors have served to deepen client loyalty and breed referrals of new customers attracted by the firm's pedigree.

The Northern's immersive service model has also conferred enduring client relationships. Rather than provide asset management services a la carte, the company strives to envelop clients with solutions that run the gamut of the wealth management spectrum, from asset safekeeping to establishment of trusts, asset management, and even management of family businesses. What's more, by catering to the needs of successive generations of a given family, the firm is able to deeply entwine itself within wealthy clients' financial affairs. In so doing, the firm forges durable bonds with customers, which aid retention and facilitate up-sales of additional services.

There's also a wide moat around the Northern's institutional asset servicing and investment management businesses. With more than $3 trillion in assets under administration, the company boasts the scale needed to compete in the custody business. What's more, its global footprint puts it in the hunt to win foreign mandates, which are becoming a bigger piece of the asset servicing pie. While custody business isn't lucrative in its own right, it provides frequent entree to decision-makers at large institutions and, thus, often yields cross-sales. The Northern has parlayed that access into additional, more-profitable assignments, such as asset management, where the company's faculty for quantitative investing and cash management and acumen in technical areas such as asset/liability matching keep it in strong demand.

Data as of 12-29-06

Northrop Grumman NOC

	Rating	Fair Value	Last Close	Consider Buy	Consider Sell	Yield %
	★★★	$64.00	$67.70	$49.40	$80.20	1.71

Industry	Business Risk	Moat Size	Investment Style	Sector
Aerospace/Defense	Average	Narrow	Large Value	Industrial Materials

Company Profile
Northrop Grumman operates through seven business segments and deals in a wide range of products, systems, and solutions. The firm produces satellites, lasers, electronics, radar, precision weapons, aircraft, and ships. Key systems with which Northrop is involved include aircraft carriers, submarines, the B-2 stealth bomber, and the Global Hawk unmanned aircraft. Headquartered in Los Angeles, Northrop employs about 120,000 people.

Competition

	Market Cap $Mil	12 Mo Trailing Sales $Mil	Price/Cash Flow	Return On Assets%	Debt/Equity	Total Return% 1 Yr	Total Return% 3 Yr
Northrop Grumman	23,384	30,448	10.9	4.2	0.2	14.6	14.7
Boeing	70,249	59,114	9.4	2.7	0.8	28.4	30.4
United Technologies	62,748	46,303	14.6	7.0	0.4	13.7	11.6

Management — Stewardship Grade [B]
Northrop's management team is experienced and smart, starting with chairman and CEO Dr. Ronald Sugar, who has more than 20 years' service in the defense business. We've also been impressed by relatively young Wes Bush, who has been CFO since January 2005. Beyond these two, the executive team brings with it many decades of industry know-how. The 10-person board consists of nine independent directors and Sugar. It includes distinguished public servants who provide "customer intimacy" in the arcane defense-spending process: a former commander in chief of the Strategic Air Command, a former congressman who served on the Armed Services and Appropriations committees, and a retired Navy admiral. We like that the board, which also includes the former TRW chairman, a former commissioner with the Securities and Exchange Commission, and other business experts, has set out more investor-friendly goals for management than just completing acquisitions. We were happy to see Northrop cancel its antitakeover poison pill in 2003, and we like that shareholders declassified the board structure at their 2005 annual meeting. Executive compensation aligns management with shareholders, and together, executives and directors own approximately $30 million worth of the firm.

1840 Century Park East
Los Angeles, CA 90067-2199
www.northropgrumman.com

Growth [C]
	2002	2003	2004	2005
Revenue %	31.9	51.6	13.1	2.9
Earnings/Share %	—	NMF	28.0	29.6
Book Value/Share %	—	NMF	8.2	1.1
Dividends/Share %	0.0	0.0	11.3	13.5

Profitability [B]
	2003	2004	2005	TTM
Return on Assets %	2.6	3.3	4.1	4.2
Oper Cash Flow $Mil	798	1,936	2,627	2,145
- Cap Spending $Mil	637	672	824	798
= Free Cash Flow $Mil	161	1,264	1,803	1,347

Financial Health [A]
	2003	2004	2005	09-30-06
Long-term Debt $Mil	5,410	5,116	3,881	3,796
Total Equity $Mil	15,785	16,700	16,828	17,330
Debt/Equity Ratio	0.3	0.3	0.2	0.2

Price Volatility

	2001	2002	2003	2004	2005	2006
Annual $Price High	55.28	67.50	50.55	58.15	60.26	71.37
Low	38.20	43.60	39.14	46.91	51.10	59.10
Annual Total Return %	23.7	-2.4	0.3	15.7	12.6	14.6

Fiscal Year-End: December	2001	2002	2003	2004	2005	TTM
Revenue $Mil	13,199	17,406	26,396	29,853	30,721	30,448
Net Income $Mil	—	—	866	1,084	1,400	1,420
Earnings Per Share $	—	—	2.32	2.97	3.85	4.01
Shares Outstanding Mil	—	—	370	360	356	345
Return on Equity %	—	—	5.5	6.5	8.3	8.2
Net Margin %	—	—	3.3	3.6	4.6	4.7
Asset Turnover	0.6	0.4	0.8	0.9	0.9	0.9
Financial Leverage	2.8	3.0	2.1	2.0	2.0	2.0

Valuation Ratios
	Stock	Rel to Industry	Rel to S&P 500
Price/Earnings	16.7	0.7	0.8
Price/Book	1.3	0.3	0.3
Price/Sales	0.8	0.6	0.3
Price/Cash Flow	10.9	0.8	0.7

Major Fund Holders
	% of Fund Assets
Highmark Core Equity Fid	3.14
HSBC Investor Value I	3.01
Old Mutual Barrow Hanley Value Z	2.99
MegaTrends	2.95

Thesis
By Chris Lozier, 12-18-06 Stock Price as of Analysis: $66.79

Northrop Grumman has a narrow moat but is not yet capable of sustaining economic profits when times are tough.

Largely through acquisitions, Northrop has become the third-largest player in the highly concentrated defense industry. The firm recorded $30.7 billion in sales in 2005 and ended the year with a backlog of more than $56 billion. As one of only five prime contractors that collectively own 50%-70% of the U.S. defense market, Northrop faces only a few competitors in each of its segments. This is a key ingredient to the firm's narrow economic moat.

Northrop has amassed a diversified portfolio that should help ensure solid cash flows in the future. Customers include all four branches of the U.S. military, numerous federal agencies, and many foreign militaries. Products and services range from submarines to systems integration for the IRS. Legacy programs like the F-16 fire-control radar will provide aftermarket business for years to come as Northrop services its huge installed base of ships, planes, and other systems. Highly specialized capabilities and assets, like its satellite payload technologies and the world's only private nuclear aircraft carrier refueling station, make the future of some programs all but certain for Northrop. And in addition to all that, Northrop has won contracts in many of the military's most forward-looking programs, such as missile defense, unmanned aerial vehicles, and network-centric command and control systems.

Size and diversity notwithstanding, Northrop is more susceptible than its peers to defense cuts. With its massive price tag, high profile, and the public perception of a spotty testing and development record, missile defense may remain on the chopping block for as long as it lives. Shipbuilding has also become a regular target for budget cuts due to the military's current challenges. Decelerating defense spending may already have manifested itself in Northrop's 2005 backlog shrinkage, but we expect defense spending to continue growing, albeit at a more modest rate.

Lastly, Northrop's buying spree has piled copious goodwill onto the balance sheet and dragged ROIC below the firm's cost of capital. We prefer the more recent trend of better margins and less capital investment, greatly improved free cash flow generation, and management's smart allocation of that cash. With today's level of uncertainty in Pentagon spending, however, there is time to wait and see if that trend continues.

Novartis AG ADR NVS

Data as of 12-29-06

Rating	Fair Value	Last Close	Consider Buy	Consider Sell	Yield %
★★★★★	$73.00	$57.44	$62.20	$95.80	1.56

Industry	Business Risk	Moat Size	Investment Style	Sector
Drugs	Below Avg	Wide	Large Growth	Healthcare

Company Profile

Novartis manufactures and markets a variety of branded pharmaceutical, generic, and consumer-related products. Within branded drugs, Novartis has strong franchises in oncology and cardiovascular products, among others. Consumer health-care brands include such familiar names as Ex-Lax, Maalox, Lamisil, and Gerber. Its Ciba-Geigy division makes disposable contact lenses as well as health products for domesticated animals and livestock.

Management

Stewardship Grade [NA]

Daniel Vasella, a Swiss doctor, inherited the top job at Novartis while still in his early 40s following the 1996 merger of two primary competitors, Sandoz and Ciba-Geigy. Vasella is the architect of the current Novartis business model. After the merger, he turned the stodgy Ciba-Geigy on its head by ordering a massive restructuring that included layoffs and the institution of performance-based incentives at all levels. Vasella also dramatically expanded the company's American presence by doubling the salesforce and moving global research facilities to Boston. U.S. sales increased from 19% of total sales in 1998 to 46% in 2005.

Competition

	Market Cap $Mil	12 Mo Trailing Sales $Mil	Price/Cash Flow	Return On Assets%	Debt/ Equity	Total Return% 1 Yr	3 Yr
Novartis AG ADR	134,175	32,526	16.6	10.6	0.0	11.3	9.6
Johnson & Johnson	191,415	52,252	14.5	18.5	0.0	12.4	10.8
Pfizer	186,751	52,208	10.5	11.6	0.1	15.2	-7.4

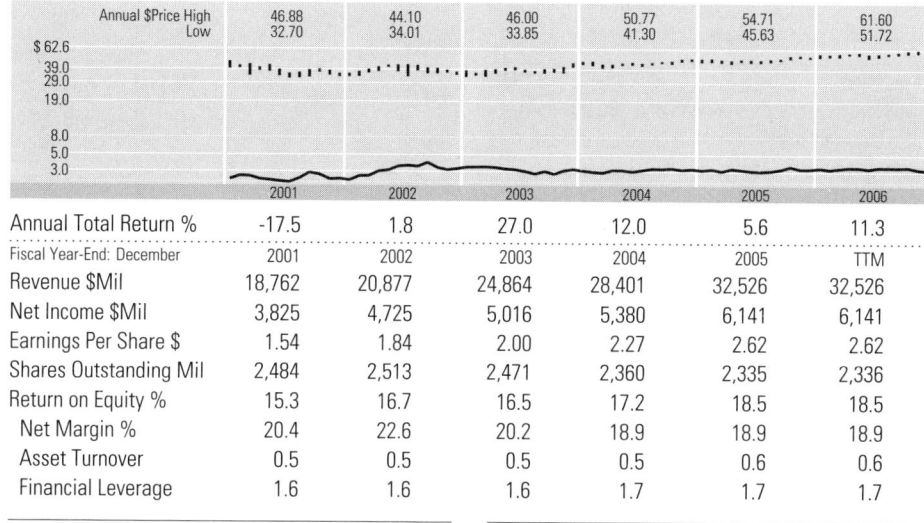

Price Volatility — Monthly Price High/Low — Relative Strength to S&P 500

	2001	2002	2003	2004	2005	2006
Annual $Price High	46.88	44.10	46.00	50.77	54.71	61.60
Low	32.70	34.01	33.85	41.30	45.63	51.72
Annual Total Return %	-17.5	1.8	27.0	12.0	5.6	11.3

Fiscal Year-End: December	2001	2002	2003	2004	2005	TTM
Revenue $Mil	18,762	20,877	24,864	28,401	32,526	32,526
Net Income $Mil	3,825	4,725	5,016	5,380	6,141	6,141
Earnings Per Share $	1.54	1.84	2.00	2.27	2.62	2.62
Shares Outstanding Mil	2,484	2,513	2,471	2,360	2,335	2,336
Return on Equity %	15.3	16.7	16.5	17.2	18.5	18.5
Net Margin %	20.4	22.6	20.2	18.9	18.9	18.9
Asset Turnover	0.5	0.5	0.5	0.5	0.6	0.6
Financial Leverage	1.6	1.6	1.6	1.7	1.7	1.7

Valuation Ratios	Stock	Rel to Industry	Rel to S&P 500
Price/Earnings	21.9	0.9	1.1
Price/Book	4.0	0.7	1.0
Price/Sales	4.1	0.9	1.4
Price/Cash Flow	16.6	1.0	1.1

Major Fund Holders	% of Fund Assets
Kinetics Medical	7.60
Fidelity Select Pharmaceuticals	6.41
MainStay ICAP Select Equity I	5.56
ProFunds Europe 30 Svc	5.27

Thesis By Heather Brilliant, CFA, 10-16-06 Stock Price as of Analysis: $57.54

A world-class generics franchise and one of the strongest pipelines in the industry position Novartis at the head of the class when it comes to large pharmaceutical firms. To top it off, the company has fewer sales at risk from patent expirations over the next several years than most of its peers. With several products on the verge of reaching the market, Novartis is well-positioned to continue its above-industry growth in the coming years.

Novartis has built itself into a leader in pharmaceuticals and generics through a series of acquisitions over the past 10 years. The company was formed with the merger of Ciba-Geigy and Sandoz in 1996, and continues to acquire companies in key areas, most recently strengthening its position in biotechnology and vaccines with the purchase of Chiron. While an acquisitive strategy does not always create value, we think Novartis has carefully selected its targets and generated strategic benefits and cost savings that have helped the firm consistently earn returns on capital well above its cost of capital.

The firm's strong product portfolio is a testament to this ability to gain complementary assets from varying businesses. Historically, the pharmaceutical and generics industries have been at odds, each trying to win a larger share of the profits from manufacturing drugs in a zero-sum game. But at Novartis, these two businesses not only coexist, they feed off each other. Its pharmaceutical business has the inside scoop on how to protect its patents from generic challengers, and Sandoz has exceptional manufacturing expertise in difficult-to-make drugs. Further, as growth slows in the branded drug market, Sandoz is well-positioned to benefit from the double-digit growth we expect in the generic drug industry. Market-leading drugs like Diovan for hypertension and Gleevec for leukemia should also help Novartis' branded pharmaceutical business to grow faster than its peers.

Novartis' biggest upcoming challenge is one any big pharma firm would love to have: It must manage the rollout of a slew of new drugs that could receive regulatory approval in the U.S. and Europe in the next year. Aclasta for osteoporosis, diabetes treatment Galvus, and hypertension drug Rasilez could be blockbusters if approved, and Novartis has about 50 total drugs in late-stage development that could reach the market in the coming three to five years. While not all of these products will receive regulatory approval, the odds are stacked in Novartis' favor that it will continue to generate exceptional returns.

Lichtstrasse 35 Postfach
Basel, Switzerland CH-4056
www.novartis.com

Growth [NA]	2002	2003	2004	2005
Revenue %	11.3	19.1	14.2	14.5
Earnings/Share %	19.5	8.7	13.5	15.4
Book Value/Share %	9.5	10.2	8.9	7.1
Dividends/Share %	NMF	34.1	31.3	10.6

Profitability [NA]	2003	2004	2005	TTM
Return on Assets %	10.2	10.3	10.6	10.6
Oper Cash Flow $Mil	6,652	6,595	8,080	8,080
- Cap Spending $Mil	1,329	1,269	1,188	1,188
= Free Cash Flow $Mil	5,323	5,326	6,892	6,892

Financial Health [NA]	2003	2004	2005	12-31-05
Long-term Debt $Mil	3,191	2,736	1,319	1,319
Total Equity $Mil	30,429	31,315	33,164	33,164
Debt/Equity Ratio	0.1	0.1	0.0	0.0

Novo Nordisk ADR NVO

Data as of 12-29-06

	Rating	Fair Value	Last Close	Consider Buy	Consider Sell	Yield %
	★★	$69.00	$83.63	$53.20	$86.50	1.16

Company Profile
Novo Nordisk, a Denmark-based health-care company with roots dating back to the 1920s, earned its reputation as a leading provider of diabetes-care products. It offers a comprehensive portfolio of insulin therapies, insulin administrators, and one major oral treatment. The company has branched out slightly from its diabetes base and also offers hemophilia and other hormone-based therapies.

Management
Stewardship Grade [NA]

Novo Nordisk splits its chairman and CEO positions, which we like. Lars Rebien Sorensen was named president and CEO in 2000 after Novo Nordisk was split from Novozymes. Outsider Sten Scheibye was recently named chairman. The most striking aspect of the company's management structure continues to be its dominance by insiders. More than half of the board is composed of current and former insiders of Novo Nordisk; four of those are nonexecutive insiders elected by Danish employees as required by that country's law. Also, Novo A/S, Novo Nordisk's parent company, wields over 50% of the voting power without commensurate shares. Based on this insider-dominated setup, we believe that minority voting interests could be disregarded easily. We think that the firm rewards executives with reasonable compensation. However, we'd prefer to see pay for performance rather than fixed pay. Most executive compensation comes in the form of salaries, benefits, and pension contributions, rather than stock and bonuses.

Novo Alle www.novonordisk.com
Bagsvaerd, Denmark DK-2880

Growth [NA]	2002	2003	2004	2005
Revenue %	5.9	3.9	11.0	16.3
Earnings/Share %	5.6	20.7	4.8	20.2
Book Value/Share %	13.5	10.5	8.1	7.2
Dividends/Share %	7.5	22.2	9.1	25.0

Profitability [NA]	2003	2004	2005	TTM
Return on Assets %	12.5	12.2	14.8	14.8
Oper Cash Flow $Mil	926	1,266	1,463	1,463
- Cap Spending $Mil	370	524	655	655
= Free Cash Flow $Mil	556	742	808	808

Financial Health [NA]	2003	2004	2005	12-31-05
Long-term Debt $Mil	127	218	198	198
Total Equity $Mil	4,178	4,863	4,379	4,379
Debt/Equity Ratio	0.0	0.0	0.0	0.0

Industry	Business Risk	Moat Size	Investment Style	Sector
Drugs	Average	Wide	Large Growth	Healthcare

Competition	Market Cap $Mil	12 Mo Trailing Sales $Mil	Price/Cash Flow	Return On Assets%	Debt/ Equity	Total Return% 1 Yr	3 Yr
Novo Nordisk ADR	27,072	5,671	18.5	14.8	0.0	51.1	28.4
Sanofi-Aventis ADR	129,397	35,705	16.2	2.7	0.1	7.3	9.2
Eli Lilly & Company	58,956	15,325	20.1	13.5	0.3	-5.2	-7.5

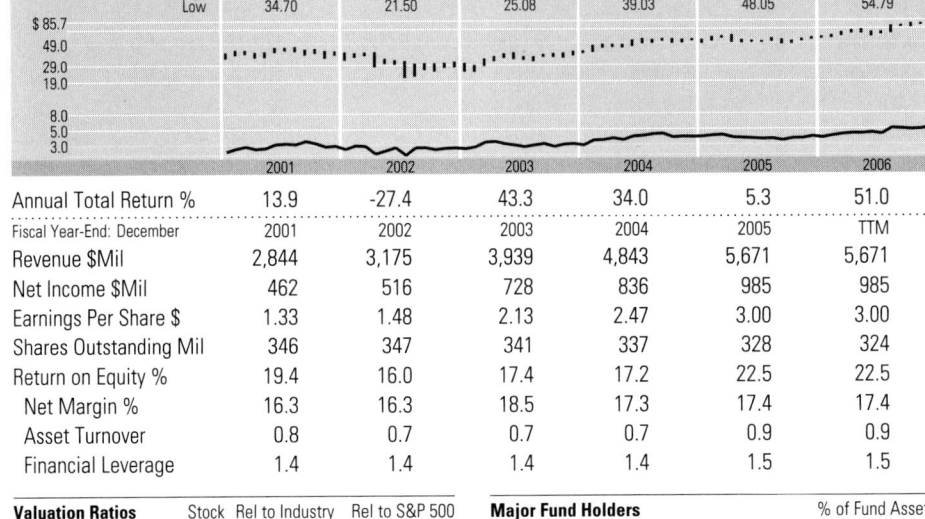

Price Volatility — Monthly Price High/Low — Relative Strength to S&P 500

	2001	2002	2003	2004	2005	2006
Annual $Price High	46.30	40.60	41.13	55.28	60.10	84.65
Low	34.70	21.50	25.08	39.03	48.05	54.79
Annual Total Return %	13.9	-27.4	43.3	34.0	5.3	51.0

Fiscal Year-End: December	2001	2002	2003	2004	2005	TTM
Revenue $Mil	2,844	3,175	3,939	4,843	5,671	5,671
Net Income $Mil	462	516	728	836	985	985
Earnings Per Share $	1.33	1.48	2.13	2.47	3.00	3.00
Shares Outstanding Mil	346	347	341	337	328	324
Return on Equity %	19.4	16.0	17.4	17.2	22.5	22.5
Net Margin %	16.3	16.3	18.5	17.3	17.4	17.4
Asset Turnover	0.8	0.7	0.7	0.7	0.9	0.9
Financial Leverage	1.4	1.4	1.4	1.4	1.5	1.5

Valuation Ratios	Stock	Rel to Industry	Rel to S&P 500
Price/Earnings	27.9	1.2	1.4
Price/Book	6.2	1.1	1.5
Price/Sales	4.8	1.1	1.7
Price/Cash Flow	18.5	1.1	1.3

Major Fund Holders	% of Fund Assets
Navellier International Growth A	3.48
Excelsior Equity Opportunities	2.71
Excelsior Blended Equity	1.74
Dreyfus Premier Alpha Growth C	1.58

Thesis By Julie Stralow, CFA, 10-30-06 Stock Price as of Analysis: $74.67

Novo Nordisk dominates attractive hemophilia and hormone-based treatment niches. We admire its ability to introduce novel treatments in these fields to consistently generate returns far exceeding capital costs. We expect more of the same from Novo Nordisk in the future.

Diabetes remains one of the most prevalent diseases around the world. With expanding waistlines and an aging population in the developed world, the disease appears destined to only grow in prevalence. Novo Nordisk remains uniquely positioned to benefit from diabetes growth as the leading treatment provider. Its prowess lies in injectables where it sells human insulin and premium-priced analogs. Insulin-analogs help patients more accurately control blood sugar throughout the day. As the only provider of a full analog spectrum (long-acting, intermediate-acting, and rapid-acting), Novo Nordisk remains at the forefront of this fast-growing diabetes niche. It aims to capitalize on this advantage by rapidly expanding its U.S. salesforce in conjunction with the 2006 Levemir (long-acting analog) launch.

The firm isn't resting on its laurels either. Novo Nordisk has two late-stage product candidates that could serve as alternatives to traditional insulin treatments. The company remains firmly entrenched in the inhaled insulin battle with a product candidate in Phase III trials. An effective inhaled treatment could capture diagnosed patients unwilling to seek injected treatments, so inhaled insulin could significantly grow the diabetes market. It remains unclear which firm will win this battle in the long run, though, as Pfizer's Exubera has the first-mover advantage, and other product candidates may present more convenient dosing or device characteristics if approved. Liraglutide is the firm's response to Eli Lilly's Byetta; liraglutide is in Phase III trials as a daily injection to spur pancreas insulin production, which could delay the need for intensive insulin treatments.

Novo Nordisk complements these diabetes opportunities with a highly profitable mix of hemophilia, human growth hormone, and hormone replacement therapies. NovoSeven, the firm's hemophilia offering, provides the bulk of these sales and is being tested in other indications like hemorrhagic strokes and trauma. Its midteens growth rate continues to impress as does the firm's human growth hormone product that continues to grow rapidly. We think Novo Nordisk's opportunities in these areas and diabetes should keep sales growing at a healthy clip for the foreseeable future.

Nucor NUE

	Rating	Fair Value	Last Close	Consider Buy	Consider Sell	Yield %
	★★★	$49.00	$54.66	$37.80	$61.40	0.73

Company Profile

Nucor is the largest steel producer in the United States. As a minimill, it uses scrap as its primary input instead of the raw iron ore used by the integrated mills. Total capacity at the end of 2005 was about 20 million tons. The sales mix consists of sheet, structural, bar, and plate steel, with sheet occupying roughly half of all production. End markets are nonresidential construction and, to a lesser extent, oil and gas exploration rigs, automobiles, and appliances.

Management   Stewardship Grade [A]

Nucor boasts one of the most efficient management structures in the industry. Total nonproduction employees number 1,700, and CEO Dan DiMicco is only two layers removed from the shop floor. In contrast, the CEO of U.S. Steel is at least four layers away. Nucor's culture and entrepreneurial attitude at every level of the corporate ladder is one of the keys to this firm's success. The firm also exhibits exemplary corporate governance, which has earned it an A stewardship grade. Seven of eight board members are independent, and incentive plans are based on return on equity. Bonuses are paid only when the company meets its targets, even in years when the entire industry is in a trough. Financial and operating disclosure is topnotch, and management runs the company as a shareholder would. Management uses a disciplined approach to acquisitions and doesn't participate in the "special charge" charade. All expenses are absorbed into operating income, and there are no related-party transactions.

2100 Rexford Road
Charlotte, NC 28211   www.nucor.com

Growth [A]	2002	2003	2004	2005
Revenue %	10.8	30.5	81.6	11.6
Earnings/Share %	42.8	-61.4	EUB	17.7
Book Value/Share %	5.0	0.6	45.0	24.7
Dividends/Share %	11.8	5.3	17.5	293.6

Profitability [A]	2003	2004	2005	TTM
Return on Assets %	1.4	18.3	18.4	21.4
Oper Cash Flow $Mil	494	1,025	2,137	2,100
- Cap Spending $Mil	215	286	331	349
= Free Cash Flow $Mil	278	739	1,805	1,751

Financial Health [NA]	2003	2004	2005	09-30-06
Long-term Debt $Mil	—	1,611	1,603	922
Total Equity $Mil	2,342	3,456	4,280	4,665
Debt/Equity Ratio	—	0.5	0.4	0.2

Industry	Business Risk	Moat Size	Investment Style	Sector
Steel/Iron	Average	Narrow	Large Value	Industrial Materials

Competition	Market Cap $Mil	12 Mo Trailing Sales $Mil	Price/Cash Flow	Return On Assets %	Debt/Equity	Total Return % 1 Yr	3 Yr
Nucor	16,514	14,490	7.9	21.4	0.2	70.7	61.9
Mittal Steel Co NV	29,697	28,132	7.5	10.8	0.9	62.5	68.8
United States Steel	8,665	15,411	6.3	11.2	0.3	53.6	28.3

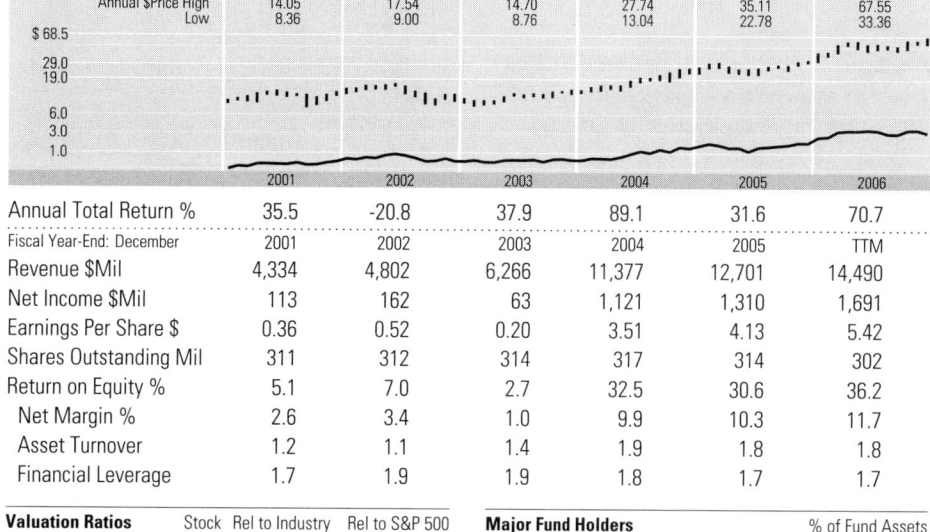

Annual Total Return %	35.5	-20.8	37.9	89.1	31.6	70.7
Fiscal Year-End: December	2001	2002	2003	2004	2005	TTM
Revenue $Mil	4,334	4,802	6,266	11,377	12,701	14,490
Net Income $Mil	113	162	63	1,121	1,310	1,691
Earnings Per Share $	0.36	0.52	0.20	3.51	4.13	5.42
Shares Outstanding Mil	311	312	314	317	314	302
Return on Equity %	5.1	7.0	2.7	32.5	30.6	36.2
Net Margin %	2.6	3.4	1.0	9.9	10.3	11.7
Asset Turnover	1.2	1.1	1.4	1.9	1.8	1.8
Financial Leverage	1.7	1.9	1.9	1.8	1.7	1.7

Valuation Ratios	Stock	Rel to Industry	Rel to S&P 500	Major Fund Holders	% of Fund Assets
Price/Earnings	10.1	0.8	0.5	Cookson Peirce Core Equity	4.22
Price/Book	3.5	0.7	0.9	SunAmerica Focused Large Cap Value A	3.90
Price/Sales	1.1	0.4	0.4	Guinness Atkinson Global Innovators	3.77
Price/Cash Flow	7.9	0.6	0.5	Hallmark Large-Cap Growth R	3.24

Thesis   By Scott Burns, 12-15-06   Stock Price as of Analysis: $59.28

Amid a renaissance in the oft-maligned steel industry, Nucor's size, operating efficiency, disciplined management, and innovation have made the company one of the success stories of the domestic steel sector. These advantages allow the narrow-moat firm to effectively compete in an inherently volatile industry and have established it as a force to be reckoned with in the steel-producing world.

In a history marked by booms and busts, the steel industry is in the midst of an unprecedented boom, and Nucor is riding this wave as well as any other steel producer. Since 2003, Nucor's quarterly results have not only been record quarters, but often would have been record "years" prior to this period. Soaring prices and volumes led to net income of over $1 billion the past two years compared with only $62 million in 2003.

Although Nucor's recent performance has been nothing short of remarkable, we do consider it more the exception than the rule. Still, there have been significant changes in the domestic steel industry, not least of which has been its consolidation. Nucor, U.S. Steel, and Mittal Steel are now the big three domestic steel producers and control nearly 70% of domestic production. This consolidation of production should help lessen the volatility that has typified the steel industry over the past 15 years.

The biggest contributor to Nucor's success has been the company's celebrated operating model. Nucor's nonunion workforce is paid largely with incentive bonuses based on productivity measures and overall company performance. The motivated workforce combined with the inherent cost advantages of being a minimill has established Nucor as the low-cost producer in the United States. As a result of its cost position, Nucor hasn't posted a losing quarter since 1966. This is an impressive feat, considering that more than 30 steel companies have gone bankrupt over the past five years.

Additionally, Nucor's management has shown incredible discipline through the years. The company uses cash during the up cycles to reduce debt and build cash reserves. During down cycles, Nucor buys assets from bankrupt competitors for a fraction of their initial cost. In addition to keeping debt low, this strategy boosts overall shareholder returns.

We expect Nucor to continue being a leading innovator in the steel world. The company is developing a viable scrap substitute product, and its low-cost Castrip technology has the potential to revolutionize steelmaking.

Nuveen Investments JNC

Data as of 12-29-06

	Rating	Fair Value	Last Close	Consider Buy	Consider Sell	Yield %
	★★★	$53.00	$51.88	$45.20	$69.60	1.79

Company Profile
Nuveen Investments is diversifying away from its core municipal-bond products and has developed specialties in income-oriented funds and separate accounts for high-net-worth investors. Nuveen manages growth and value equity, taxable and tax-free fixed-income, and hedge funds. The company is a leader in closed-end fixed-income funds.

Management
Stewardship Grade [B]

Nuveen became a fully independent company in 2005 after St. Paul Travelers Companies, which owned 79% of the stock, was forced to sell its holdings in order to bolster its reserves. We think Nuveen shareholders should be happy with the consequent changes. Because of St. Paul's majority ownership, Nuveen had been saddled with Byzantine voting rules and dual share classes, which gave St. Paul the ability to call all the shots. Now Nuveen has one share class, and all shares have identical voting rights. Director terms are staggered, which could help to prevent takeovers. Otherwise, we think the changes in the board structure are favorable. Management compensation is generous, though not excessive compared with other asset-management firms. Despite new accounting rules that require stock options to be expensed, Nuveen is still a lavish issuer of stock-option compensation, which represents around 3% of outstanding shares annually.

333 West Wacker Drive
Chicago, IL 60606
www.nuveen.com

Growth [B+]	2002	2003	2004	2005
Revenue %	6.8	14.0	11.9	16.5
Earnings/Share %	13.1	16.5	15.6	22.1
Book Value/Share %	-1.2	23.8	22.0	-70.1
Dividends/Share %	7.1	12.0	23.2	13.0

Profitability [A+]	2003	2004	2005	TTM
Return on Assets %	14.1	14.6	15.9	15.5
Oper Cash Flow $Mil	203	192	209	—
- Cap Spending $Mil	7	6	13	—
= Free Cash Flow $Mil	—	—	—	—

Financial Health [NA]	2003	2004	2005	09-30-06
Long-term Debt $Mil	—	—	—	—
Total Equity $Mil	479	585	157	262
Debt/Equity Ratio	—	—	—	—

Industry	Business Risk	Moat Size	Investment Style	Sector
Money Mgmt.	Below Avg	Wide	Mid Growth	Financial Services

Competition	Market Cap $Mil	12 Mo Trailing Sales $Mil	Price/Cash Flow	Return On Assets %	Debt/Equity	Total Return % 1 Yr	3 Yr
Nuveen Investments	4,085	671	—	15.5	—	24.1	27.5
Franklin Resources	27,932	5,051	—	13.3	—	17.8	30.3
Legg Mason	12,491	3,810	—	13.0	—	-20.0	23.0

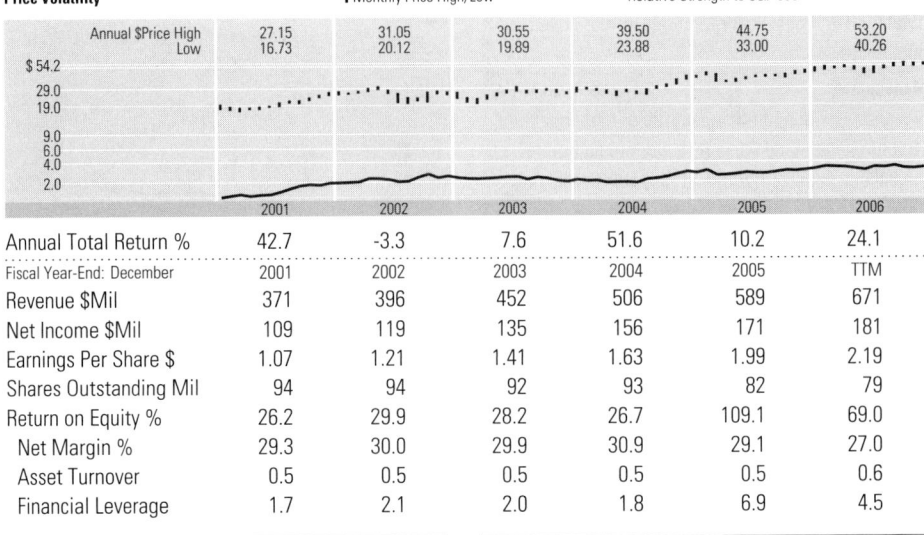

	2001	2002	2003	2004	2005	2006
Annual $Price High	27.15	31.05	30.55	39.50	44.75	53.20
Low	16.73	20.12	19.89	23.88	33.00	40.26
Annual Total Return %	42.7	-3.3	7.6	51.6	10.2	24.1

Fiscal Year-End: December	2001	2002	2003	2004	2005	TTM
Revenue $Mil	371	396	452	506	589	671
Net Income $Mil	109	119	135	156	171	181
Earnings Per Share $	1.07	1.21	1.41	1.63	1.99	2.19
Shares Outstanding Mil	94	94	92	93	82	79
Return on Equity %	26.2	29.9	28.2	26.7	109.1	69.0
Net Margin %	29.3	30.0	29.9	30.9	29.1	27.0
Asset Turnover	0.5	0.5	0.5	0.5	0.5	0.6
Financial Leverage	1.7	2.1	2.0	1.8	6.9	4.5

Valuation Ratios	Stock	Rel to Industry	Rel to S&P 500
Price/Earnings	23.7	0.8	1.2
Price/Book	15.6	3.6	3.8
Price/Sales	6.1	1.0	2.1
Price/Cash Flow	—	—	—

Major Fund Holders	% of Fund Assets
River Oak Discovery	3.24
Kinetics Small Cap Opportunities	2.88
Columbia Acorn Select Z	2.36
Roxbury Mid Cap Instl	2.10

Thesis By Rachel Barnard, Ph.D., 10-19-06 Stock Price as of Analysis: $47.99

Nuveen's focus on new product development should ensure that the best is yet to come.

Unlike many of its peers who favor growth by acquisition, Nuveen prefers to develop products internally. Closed-end fund offerings are an obvious outlet for this strategy, but Nuveen is also working on a range of mutual funds and separate account products. We believe the firm is wise to use its deep pockets and broad expertise to grow internally.

A series of acquisitions in a wide range of asset classes has turned Nuveen into the highly diversified firm it is today. The firm's days as just a municipal-bond specialist are now in the rearview mirror. Today, less than half of all assets under management are still in municipal bonds. Muni bonds are tax-free fixed-income products that offer a steady stream of income with relatively low risk. They are a favorite of wealthy investors seeking tax breaks. Although muni bonds aren't sexy, they sell well in almost any market, and Nuveen has steadily increased its muni assets nearly every year.

Nuveen has added to its strength in muni bonds over the years by taking on growth and value equity funds, hedge funds, and real estate funds, among others. In October 2005, the firm completed its acquisition of another growth equity manager, Santa Barbara Asset Management.

Branching out like this has its advantages. It gives Nuveen some bench strength. When one asset class isn't selling well, the company has plenty of other products to hawk. As a case in point, Rittenhouse has struggled recently, as its specialty--growth equities--has been out of favor since growth stocks flopped in 2001. This led to outflows from Rittenhouse over the past several years. However, value equity products have been selling extremely well, as have bonds and hedge funds.

Nuveen also specializes in closed-end funds, which has proved to be a winning strategy. Closed-end funds are mutual funds whose shares trade on an exchange. Investors wishing to sell their shares do not sell them back to the fund company, as in open-end funds, but sell them to another investor instead, much like a stock. Closed-end funds are a great deal for fund companies because they never have to redeem shares once they sell them. Nuveen continues to collect management fees on all outstanding shares.

In 2006, Nuveen showcased a relatively new niche for it: international and global products. The new Tradewinds subsidiary, formerly part of NWQ, now accounts for a large part of the net flows.

Data as of 12-29-06

NYSE Group NYX

	Rating	Fair Value	Last Close	Consider Buy	Consider Sell	Yield %
	★★★★	$128.00	$97.20	$81.60	$154.40	0.00

Industry	Business Risk	Moat Size	Investment Style	Sector
Securities	Above Avg	Narrow	Large Growth	Financial Services

Company Profile

NYSE Group was formed by the merger of the New York Stock Exchange and Archipelago Holdings. Following its anticipated 2007 merger with Euronext, the firm will be known as NYSE Euronext. The combined company will provide listing services for U.S. and international companies and offer trading venues for stocks, bonds, options, and futures. The company also makes money by selling its market data.

Management

Stewardship Grade [B]

John Thain, the NYSE's CEO since 2004, will continue to lead the combined NYSE Euronext. Thain replaced Dick Grasso, who was ousted in 2003 after a political imbroglio surrounding his oversize pay package. Thain had been COO and a board member at Goldman Sachs before coming to NYSE, and we believe he possesses the temperament, experience, and industry contacts to successfully lead the firm. The chairman of the combined firm will be Jan-Michiel Hessels, the current Euronext supervisory board chairman. NYSE's current chairman, Marshall Carter, will assume a deputy chairman role at the combined company, and Euronext's current CEO will become deputy CEO. This allocation of responsibility should help create a smooth integration of the two firms. Corporate governance at NYSE remains a concern. Under the pretense of protecting the markets as a national asset, the NYSE lists provisions to deter a change in control as a risk to investing in the shares. These include antitakeover provisions, such as an 80% supermajority requirement for company bylaw changes and a 10% voting power limit for any individual shareholder.

100 South Wacker Drive Suite 1800
Chicago, IL 60606
www.archipelago.com

Growth [D]	2002	2003	2004	2005
Revenue %	-3.1	2.1	-1.3	3.1
Earnings/Share %	NMF	NMF	NMF	NMF
Book Value/Share %	—	—	—	—
Dividends/Share %	NMF	NMF	NMF	NMF

Profitability [B]	2003	2004	2005	TTM
Return on Assets %	3.0	1.5	1.8	4.3
Oper Cash Flow $Mil	121	64	264	—
- Cap Spending $Mil	77	85	106	—
= Free Cash Flow $Mil	—	—	—	—

Financial Health [NA]	2003	2004	2005	06-30-06
Long-term Debt $Mil	—	—	—	—
Total Equity $Mil	728	767	799	1,603
Debt/Equity Ratio	—	—	—	—

Competition	Market Cap $Mil	12 Mo Trailing Sales $Mil	Price/Cash Flow	Return On Assets %	Debt/Equity	Total Return % 1 Yr	3 Yr
NYSE Group	15,183	1,633	—	4.3	—	94.4	—
Chicago Mercantile Exchan	17,747	1,062	—	10.9	—	39.5	92.5
Nasdaq Stock Market	3,450	1,470	—	2.3	—	-12.5	49.3

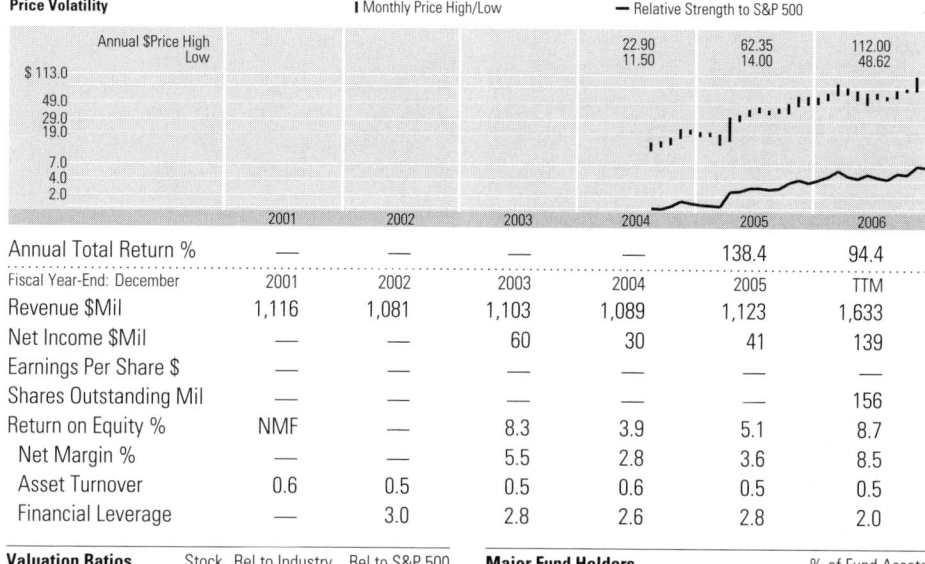

	2001	2002	2003	2004	2005	2006
Annual Total Return %	—	—	—	—	138.4	94.4

Fiscal Year-End: December	2001	2002	2003	2004	2005	TTM
Revenue $Mil	1,116	1,081	1,103	1,089	1,123	1,633
Net Income $Mil	—	—	60	30	41	139
Earnings Per Share $	—	—	—	—	—	—
Shares Outstanding Mil	—	—	—	—	—	156
Return on Equity %	NMF	—	8.3	3.9	5.1	8.7
Net Margin %	—	—	5.5	2.8	3.6	8.5
Asset Turnover	0.6	0.5	0.5	0.6	0.5	0.5
Financial Leverage	—	3.0	2.8	2.6	2.8	2.0

Valuation Ratios	Stock	Rel to Industry	Rel to S&P 500
Price/Earnings	—	—	—
Price/Book	9.5	2.3	2.3
Price/Sales	9.3	2.2	3.2
Price/Cash Flow	—	—	—

Major Fund Holders	% of Fund Assets
Kinetics Internet	7.65
SunAmerica Focused Mid-Cap Value A	5.28
Kinetics Paradigm	4.33
Ivy Capital Appreciation A	4.22

Thesis By Patrick O'Shaughnessy, 11-21-06 Stock Price as of Analysis: $104.60

The times they are a-changin' for the New York Stock Exchange. NYSE Group, as it is now known, is leading the industry consolidation charge and soon will facilitate trading in stocks, bonds, options, and futures across two continents. Partially as a result, and despite the industry's shift away from floor-based trading, we believe NYSE has been able to retain its narrow moat. Mergers with Archipelago and Euronext should create significant shareholder value, and we believe the firm's growth story is still in its early chapters.

The New York Stock Exchange's roots go back to 1792, when a group of traders met under a buttonwood tree near Wall Street to create America's first-ever exchange; 214 years later, the founders would hardly recognize what their idea has evolved into. The exchange went public in March 2006 via a merger with Archipelago, in the process changing its name to NYSE Group and gaining electronic trading capability as well as a stock option exchange. In May 2006 the firm announced another merger, this time with Euronext, a multicountry European exchange that trades financial future contracts as well as stocks. We view it as very likely that the deal closes in early 2007.

NYSE's recent changes highlight the upside potential of its business. By consolidating, the firm is taking advantage of the operating leverage inherent in its business model, especially as it shifts from floor-based trading to more scalable electronic platforms. Diversifying revenue streams reduces the firm's dependence on any one market and offers new trading opportunities, while adding a futures exchange benefits from the more monopolylike characteristics of that business. Lastly, by expanding internationally, NYSE is expanding its market in terms of both traders and trading hours.

Electronic trading represents a threat as well as an opportunity because it increases the portability of liquidity away from the listing exchange. We still believe NYSE's existing liquidity pools provide the firm's stock exchange business with a narrow moat. However, in addition to existing competition from regional stock exchanges and electronic communication networks, several option exchanges and investment banks have begun competing as well. Off-exchange trading venues also pose an increasing challenge, and we expect that NYSE will ultimately lose some share in the stock exchange business. Nevertheless, strong trading demand combined with the firm's diversification and wide moats around its listing and futures businesses bode well.

Data as of 12-29-06

Occidental Petroleum OXY

Rating	Fair Value	Last Close	Consider Buy	Consider Sell	Yield %
★★★	$52.00	$48.83	$40.10	$65.20	1.64

Industry	Business Risk	Moat Size	Investment Style	Sector
Oil/Gas	Average	Narrow	Large Value	Energy

Company Profile
Based in Los Angeles, Occidental Petroleum is an independent oil and gas producer with operations in the United States, the Middle East, and Latin America. Beyond finding and producing hydrocarbons, the firm also has a chemical-manufacturing business. At the end of 2005, Occidental had 2.7 billion equivalent barrels of proved reserves in the ground, about 80% of which is crude oil.

Management   Stewardship Grade [C]
Ray Irani has been chairman and CEO since 1990. Even considering Occidental's above-average performance over the past few years, to say the firm's executives are well compensated would be an understatement. In 2005, the top five executives earned $81 million in cash and restricted stock plus option grants for 1.5 million shares. Irani alone received $49 million plus rights to 700,000 shares. Although we think compensation is egregious, we do like that most of it is incentive-based, in the form of restricted shares, stock options, and variable cash bonuses. Executives and directors beneficially own 1.5% of total shares outstanding, with 84% of their claim in the form of options. We like that the firm elected to begin expensing options earlier than required. Corporate performance objectives include maximizing free cash flow, minimizing costs, and generating top returns on capital. Except for excessive executive pay, Occidental has above-average stewardship practices.

10889 Wilshire Boulevard   www.oxy.com
Los Angeles, CA 90024-4201

Growth [C]	2002	2003	2004	2005
Revenue %	-9.5	27.5	23.0	33.8
Earnings/Share %	-15.5	-24.7	62.9	101.7
Book Value/Share %	10.5	-38.8	28.8	39.8
Dividends/Share %	0.0	4.0	5.8	17.3

Profitability [A]	2003	2004	2005	TTM
Return on Assets %	8.4	12.0	20.2	13.9
Oper Cash Flow $Mil	3,074	3,878	5,337	6,382
- Cap Spending $Mil	1,600	1,843	2,423	2,832
= Free Cash Flow $Mil	1,474	2,035	2,914	3,550

Financial Health [A+]	2003	2004	2005	09-30-06
Long-term Debt $Mil	—	3,345	2,873	2,847
Total Equity $Mil	7,929	10,550	15,032	18,858
Debt/Equity Ratio	—	0.3	0.2	0.2

Competition	Market Cap $Mil	12 Mo Trailing Sales $Mil	Price/Cash Flow	Return On Assets%	Debt/Equity	Total Return% 1 Yr	3 Yr
Occidental Petroleum	41,070	17,548	6.4	13.9	0.2	24.3	34.9
ConocoPhillips	118,413	198,161	5.8	9.8	0.4	26.5	33.0
Marathon Oil	32,516	69,006	5.0	17.6	0.2	54.7	44.1

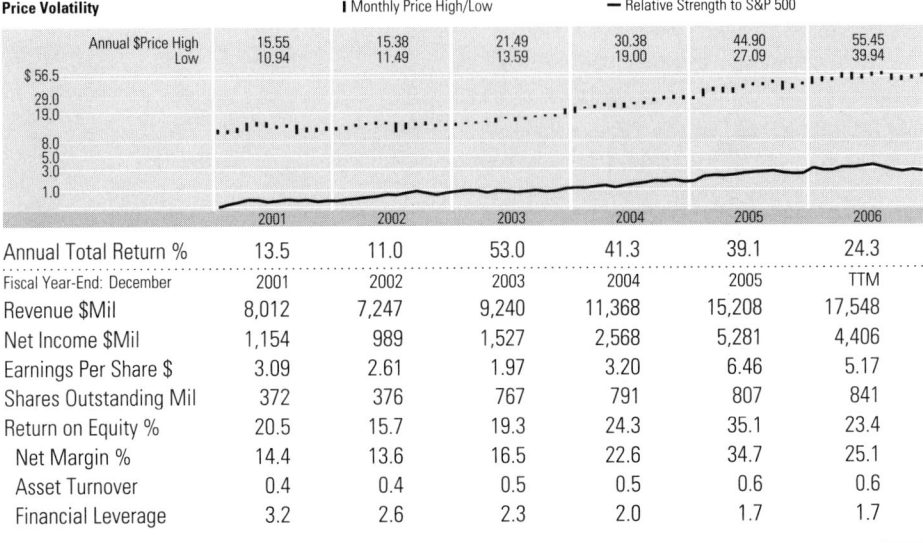

	2001	2002	2003	2004	2005	2006
Annual $Price High	15.55	15.38	21.49	30.38	44.90	55.45
Low	10.94	11.49	13.59	19.00	27.09	39.94
Annual Total Return %	13.5	11.0	53.0	41.3	39.1	24.3

Fiscal Year-End: December	2001	2002	2003	2004	2005	TTM
Revenue $Mil	8,012	7,247	9,240	11,368	15,208	17,548
Net Income $Mil	1,154	989	1,527	2,568	5,281	4,406
Earnings Per Share $	3.09	2.61	1.97	3.20	6.46	5.17
Shares Outstanding Mil	372	376	767	791	807	841
Return on Equity %	20.5	15.7	19.3	24.3	35.1	23.4
Net Margin %	14.4	13.6	16.5	22.6	34.7	25.1
Asset Turnover	0.4	0.4	0.5	0.5	0.6	0.6
Financial Leverage	3.2	2.6	2.3	2.0	1.7	1.7

Valuation Ratios	Stock	Rel to Industry	Rel to S&P 500
Price/Earnings	8.6	0.7	0.4
Price/Book	2.2	0.7	0.5
Price/Sales	2.3	1.2	0.8
Price/Cash Flow	6.4	0.8	0.4

Major Fund Holders	% of Fund Assets
Gartmore Global Natural Resources A	7.03
CGM Mutual	4.79
Putnam Global Natural Resources A	4.61
AIM Energy Inv	4.40

Thesis By Justin Perucki, CFA, 12-08-06 Stock Price as of Analysis: $49.51

Occidental's main line of business is finding and producing oil and gas. Primarily located in the United States, Occidental's reserves are 80% crude oil. The firm's fields in California and the Permian Basin are large, but with all the easily available resources already drilled, production growth is minimal. However, Occidental has arguably become the world's expert on advanced recovery methods. These techniques help offset production declines for a short period and boost ultimate recovery from a field. Although the up-front investment can be large, these projects require little maintenance capital. Consequently, these fields generate an abundance of cash, which Occidental uses to fund its international growth projects.

Occidental is heading back to Libya after leaving nearly 20 years ago when the U.S. government imposed economic sanctions on the country. In addition to the exploration blocks the firm was awarded last year, Occidental has received approval from the Libyan National Oil Corporation to return to its previously owned assets. Libya is appealing because of its plentiful undeveloped reserves, its close proximity to the European market, and the quality of its reserves. Libyan oil reserves primarily consist of high-quality light sweet crude, which sells at a premium to other crude grades because it is easier to refine. We are not big fans of the agreements that Occidental has in place that require the firm to pay the majority of profits generated from these fields to the Libyan government, but this is the cost of having international operations in the oil patch.

By concentrating on a relatively small number of geographical areas, Occidental has produced solid results. Although the company received some help from rising energy prices, its returns on capital have been well above its cost of capital as well as the industry average returns. We expect Occidental to continue generating excess returns for the foreseeable future.

With no significant refining and marketing operations to act as ballast when energy prices are low, Occidental's profits are more volatile than those of integrated competitors. Luckily for Occidental, OPEC's effort to ensure profits for its member countries benefits the entire oil patch. Because of this, we've given Occidental a narrow economic moat rating, despite its commodity business.

Odyssey Re Holdings ORH

Data as of 12-29-06

Rating	Fair Value	Last Close	Consider Buy	Consider Sell	Yield %
★★★	$36.00	$37.30	$22.90	$43.40	0.34

Industry	Business Risk	Moat Size	Investment Style	Sector
Reinsurance	Above Avg	Narrow	Mid Value	Financial Services

Company Profile

Odyssey Re is a New York-based reinsurance carrier that serves a worldwide client base, although more than 50% of its sales originate in North America. The firm offers property-casualty coverage as well as many specialized risk-protection products, including professional liability, marine, and aerospace coverage. The firm also markets via the Lloyd's of London market through an investment in its Newline subsidiary. Fairfax Financial Holdings owns the majority of Odyssey Re.

Management   Stewardship Grade [B]

Odyssey has a well-seasoned management team. CEO Andrew Barnard has more than 25 years' experience as a reinsurance executive, the last eight as the head of Odyssey and its predecessors. Before joining Odyssey, he had a seven-year stint as the chief underwriting officer of Transatlantic Holdings. Barnard earned a $1 million salary and $5.5 million of restricted stock awards in 2005, on top of a $6 million cash payment from a new employment agreement. While this compensation package does align his interests with those of shareholders, we think it is somewhat generous. In addition, considering Fairfax's majority ownership of Odyssey, we continue to think that Prem Watsa, Odyssey's chairman and Fairfax's CEO, will have the final say on strategy. However, given Watsa's large indirect ownership of Odyssey (Watsa has more than 90% of his net wealth in Fairfax stock) and his shareholder-friendliness, we are not concerned.

140 Broadway 39th Floor
New York, NY 10005

Growth [C]	2002	2003	2004	2005
Revenue %	70.6	35.4	12.9	-1.2
Earnings/Share %	NMF	18.3	-19.1	NMF
Book Value/Share %	NMF	28.7	16.1	10.5
Dividends/Share %	300.0	6.3	17.8	0.0

Profitability [B]	2003	2004	2005	TTM
Return on Assets %	3.8	2.6	-1.2	3.9
Oper Cash Flow $Mil	564	594	397	—
- Cap Spending $Mil	—	—	—	—
= Free Cash Flow $Mil	—	—	—	—

Financial Health [NA]	2003	2004	2005	06-30-06
Long-term Debt $Mil	—	—	—	—
Total Equity $Mil	1,348	1,555	1,623	2,008
Debt/Equity Ratio	—	—	—	—

Competition

	Market Cap $Mil	12 Mo Trailing Sales $Mil	Price/Cash Flow	Return On Assets%	Debt/Equity	Total Return% 1 Yr	3 Yr
Odyssey Re Holdings	2,654	2,866	—	3.9	—	49.4	19.1
ACE	19,755	13,047	—	2.8	—	15.4	15.9
XL Capital	12,993	9,748	—	-1.8	—	9.3	0.1

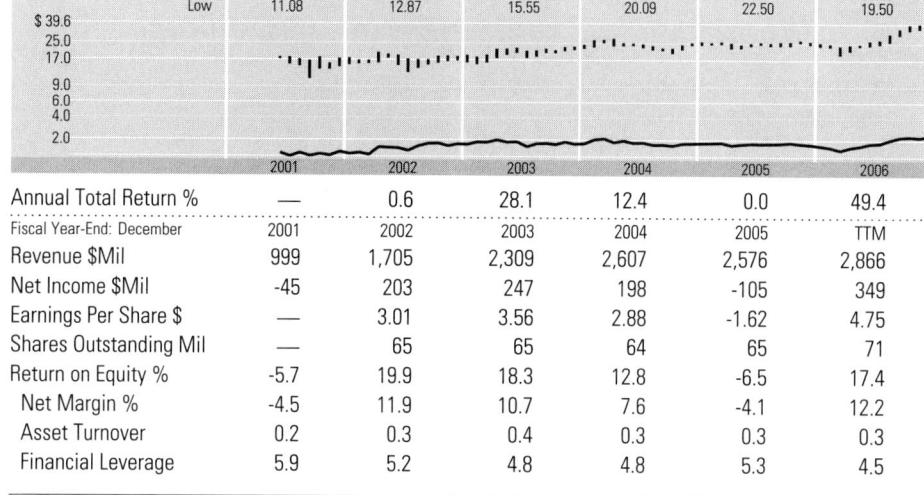

Price Volatility | Monthly Price High/Low — Relative Strength to S&P 500

Annual $Price High/Low	18.18/11.08	20.25/12.87	23.29/15.55	27.80/20.09	26.92/22.50	38.65/19.50
Annual Total Return %	—	0.6	28.1	12.4	0.0	49.4

Fiscal Year-End: December	2001	2002	2003	2004	2005	TTM
Revenue $Mil	999	1,705	2,309	2,607	2,576	2,866
Net Income $Mil	-45	203	247	198	-105	349
Earnings Per Share $	—	3.01	3.56	2.88	-1.62	4.75
Shares Outstanding Mil	—	65	65	64	65	71
Return on Equity %	-5.7	19.9	18.3	12.8	-6.5	17.4
Net Margin %	-4.5	11.9	10.7	7.6	-4.1	12.2
Asset Turnover	0.2	0.3	0.4	0.3	0.3	0.3
Financial Leverage	5.9	5.2	4.8	4.8	5.3	4.5

Valuation Ratios	Stock	Rel to Industry	Rel to S&P 500
Price/Earnings	7.9	0.6	0.4
Price/Book	1.3	0.9	0.3
Price/Sales	0.9	0.5	0.3
Price/Cash Flow	—	—	—

Major Fund Holders	% of Fund Assets
Madison Mosaic Mid-Cap	3.03
CNI Charter RCB Sm Cap Val R	2.82
Legg Mason U.S. Small Cap Value Prim	1.43
HighMark Cognitive Value M	1.18

Thesis By Justin Fuller, CFA, 12-11-06 Stock Price as of Analysis: $34.35

Odyssey Re combines a focus on reinsurance market timing with impressive investment returns to deliver pleasing results for shareholders. Our fair value estimate is $36 per share.

Odyssey aims to time the reinsurance market by expanding premiums when pricing is attractive and contracting as prices fall. For example, in 1999 and 2000, when reinsurance prices were extremely low--and were apt to produce underwriting losses rather than profits--Odyssey wrote only about $0.67 of premium for each $1 of equity. This low operating leverage was important, as Odyssey was able to contain its underwriting losses and bide its time until industrywide pricing became attractive.

In 2001, severe catastrophe losses created a dearth of industry capacity, sending reinsurance prices skyward. For about three years, overall prices remained strong, so Odyssey leveraged up and wrote almost $1.50 of premium for each $1 of equity. This was a boon for shareholders as the higher-priced business delivered good underwriting profits, and the additional operating leverage magnified the effect on Odyssey's bottom line. Now that property reinsurance rates are at attractive levels, we expect Odyssey to again exploit this opportunity.

While we like Odyssey's approach to timing the reinsurance market, it is not without risk. Elevated operating leverage is the quintessential double-edge sword. Should Odyssey maintain its leverage as pricing deteriorates or misprice some business, losses could quickly mount. In a worst-case scenario, we could envision Odyssey having to write more poorly priced business just to pay the claims on its existing contracts--a virtual death spiral for a reinsurer. However, we think this scenario is highly unlikely, as Odyssey has a trump card in its back pocket.

Odyssey's access to parent Fairfax Financial's investment arm, Hamblin Watsa, endows a valuable investing advantage. Since 1985, Hamblin Watsa has compounded its subsidiaries' investment portfolios at a 34% annual rate. Since 1999, it has compounded Odyssey's investment portfolio by a still-decent 22% annual rate. Not only do these impressive investment results boost shareholder returns, but they can also help shelter Odyssey's results should the firm accept some poorly priced business. While we'd hate to see investment results used like this, we do think it offers investors an additional margin of safety.

In our view, Odyssey could be a compelling investment at the right margin of safety.

Data as of 12-29-06

Omnicom Group OMC

Rating	Fair Value	Last Close	Consider Buy	Consider Sell	Yield %
★★★	$95.00	$104.54	$73.30	$119.00	0.96

Company Profile
Omnicom is a holding company of advertising and marketing firms that operate in more than 100 countries with more than 5,000 clients. Its businesses focus on traditional media advertising and more than 30 marketing services, including customer-relationship management, public relations, and specialty communications.

Industry	Business Risk	Moat Size	Investment Style	Sector
Advertising	Average	Narrow	Large Core	Business Services

Competition	Market Cap $Mil	12 Mo Trailing Sales $Mil	Price/Cash Flow	Return On Assets%	Debt/ Equity	Total Return% 1 Yr	3 Yr
Omnicom Group	17,866	11,100	10.6	5.1	0.8	24.1	7.5
WPP Group PLC ADR	16,984	9,809	11.1	2.9	0.4	27.4	12.6
Interpublic Group of Comp	5,400	6,209	—	-1.5	1.2	26.8	-7.6

Management   Stewardship Grade [B]
John Wren is Omnicom's CEO and president, and he is also a director. He received $1 million in base salary and a $4.4 million bonus in 2005, while also gaining about $10 million from the exercise of stock options. Neither Wren nor any of Omnicom's officers received option grants in 2005. As of April 2006, Wren held 1.6% of shares outstanding. All officers and directors combined own less than 4% of the company. Wren has traditionally been very involved in Omnicom's day-to-day operations, especially regarding strategy and finance, but gives the heads of Omnicom's agencies plenty of autonomy in running their businesses, a strategy that has paid off over time. Jean-Marie Dru (head of TBWA Worldwide), Chuck Brymer (CEO at DDB Worldwide), Andrew Robertson (head of BBDO), and Randall Weisenburger (executive vice president and CFO) are other key executives at Omnicom. Wren's predecessor, Bruce Crawford, is now chairman of Omnicom's board.

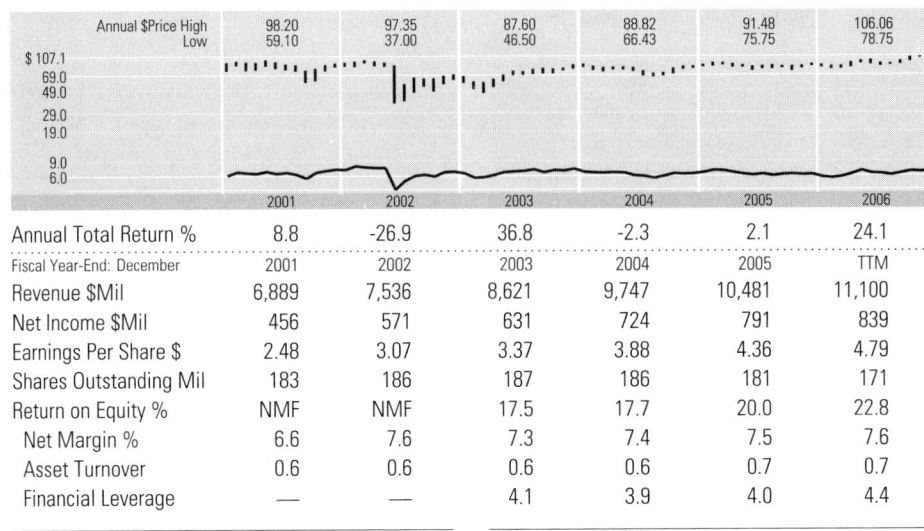

Price Volatility — Monthly Price High/Low — Relative Strength to S&P 500

Annual $Price High Low	98.20 59.10	97.35 37.00	87.60 46.50	88.82 66.43	91.48 75.75	106.06 78.75
	2001	2002	2003	2004	2005	2006
Annual Total Return %	8.8	-26.9	36.8	-2.3	2.1	24.1

Fiscal Year-End: December	2001	2002	2003	2004	2005	TTM
Revenue $Mil	6,889	7,536	8,621	9,747	10,481	11,100
Net Income $Mil	456	571	631	724	791	839
Earnings Per Share $	2.48	3.07	3.37	3.88	4.36	4.79
Shares Outstanding Mil	183	186	187	186	181	171
Return on Equity %	NMF	NMF	17.5	17.7	20.0	22.8
Net Margin %	6.6	7.6	7.3	7.4	7.5	7.6
Asset Turnover	0.6	0.6	0.6	0.6	0.7	0.7
Financial Leverage	—	—	4.1	3.9	4.0	4.4

Valuation Ratios	Stock	Rel to Industry	Rel to S&P 500
Price/Earnings	21.8	0.8	1.1
Price/Book	4.8	1.0	1.2
Price/Sales	1.6	0.3	0.6
Price/Cash Flow	10.6	0.8	0.7

Major Fund Holders	% of Fund Assets
AIM Leisure Inv	5.91
Fidelity Select Multimedia	5.63
Jensen J	5.02
Pioneer Growth Leaders A	5.01

437 Madison Ave   www.omnicomgroup.com
New York, NY 10022

Growth [C+]	2002	2003	2004	2005
Revenue %	9.4	14.4	13.1	7.5
Earnings/Share %	23.8	9.8	15.1	12.4
Book Value/Share %	NMF	NMF	13.7	-0.5
Dividends/Share %	3.2	0.0	12.5	2.8

Profitability [B+]	2003	2004	2005	TTM
Return on Assets %	4.3	4.5	5.0	5.1
Oper Cash Flow $Mil	1,054	1,288	991	1,686
- Cap Spending $Mil	141	160	163	180
= Free Cash Flow $Mil	913	1,128	829	1,506

Financial Health [B]	2003	2004	2005	09-30-06
Long-term Debt $Mil	2,537	2,358	2,358	3,055
Total Equity $Mil	3,603	4,079	3,948	3,687
Debt/Equity Ratio	0.7	0.6	0.6	0.8

Thesis By Jonathan Schrader, CFA, 10-25-06 Stock Price as of Analysis:

Omnicom is in the business of helping companies communicate. Well, that's not exactly correct. Omnicom is actually a holding company that over the years has acquired hundreds of companies that are in the business of helping companies communicate. Thanks to these acquisitions, Omnicom is now the largest marketing services firm in the world, offering its 5,000 clients in more than 100 countries dozens of services, from advertising creation to media buying to public relations, and almost anything in between.

While most people think of the major holding companies, including Omnicom peers WPP Group and Interpublic Group, as advertising firms, traditional advertising now contributes less than half of Omnicom's sales (43% in 2005, to be exact). Providing customer-relationship management services to clients generates a hefty 35% of Omnicom's revenue, while the balance comes from public relations and specialty communications.

Omnicom's diversification strategy has been led by CEO John Wren, one of the most respected leaders in the business. Wren typically takes a hands-off approach when it comes to the agencies in Omnicom's portfolio, but he is very active in making strategic and financing decisions with respect to Omnicom's growth. Wren is likely to agree to many more acquisitions, albeit smaller ones than those of the past. Asia, and China in particular, is an area that Omnicom is focusing on for growth.

Wren has also been working to make his three global ad agencies look more like mini holding companies, each able to provide a full portfolio of services to current and potential clients. We like this strategy, given the strength of Omnicom's agency portfolio. DDB Worldwide and BBDO Worldwide are two of the most-recognized and most-honored agencies in the world. Omnicom's third global agency, TBWA Worldwide, has also garnered a reputation for the quality of its work and was recognized as the most-awarded agency in the world in 2005 by the Gunn Report.

Because Omnicom's individual agencies are so strong, the firm has typically been able to retain even dissatisfied clients by moving them to a sibling agency. This has kept Omnicom's sales growing even in challenging times. While there will probably be more challenges--especially from economic weakness--we think Omnicom has many good years ahead of it and can continue to earn incremental returns on investment that are well above its cost of capital. Because of this, we'd be happy to buy its stock, if we could get it at a 5-star price.

Data as of 12-29-06

ONEOK Partners LP OKS

	Rating	Fair Value	Last Close	Consider Buy	Consider Sell	Yield %
	★★★	$58.00	$63.34	$49.40	$76.10	5.68

Company Profile
Oneok Partners gathers, processes, and transports natural gas. The partnership's interstate pipelines carry nearly one fifth of the gas exported from Canada to the United States, while its large gathering and processing operations serve Texas, Oklahoma, Kansas, and the High Plains region. As a partnership, Oneok Partners pays no corporate income tax; its tax burden flows through to individual unitholders.

Industry	Business Risk	Moat Size	Investment Style	Sector
Pipelines	Below Avg	Wide	Mid Value	Energy

Competition

	Market Cap $Mil	12 Mo Trailing Sales $Mil	Price/Cash Flow	Return On Assets%	Debt/Equity	Total Return% 1 Yr	3 Yr
ONEOK Partners LP	2,939	3,730	5.8	6.7	0.9	61.8	26.3
Enterprise Products Partn	12,514	14,421	9.8	3.5	0.8	29.2	13.3
Kinder Morgan Energy Part	7,797	9,919	6.2	2.7	1.2	7.3	6.8

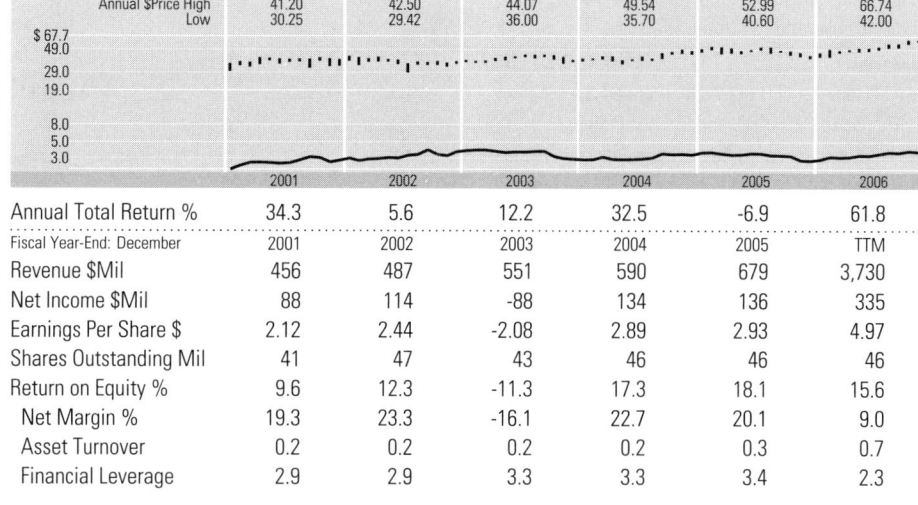

Price Volatility — Monthly Price High/Low — Relative Strength to S&P 500

	2001	2002	2003	2004	2005	2006
Annual $Price High	41.20	42.50	44.07	49.54	52.99	66.74
Low	30.25	29.42	36.00	35.70	40.60	42.00

	2001	2002	2003	2004	2005	TTM
Annual Total Return %	34.3	5.6	12.2	32.5	-6.9	61.8
Fiscal Year-End: December						
Revenue $Mil	456	487	551	590	679	3,730
Net Income $Mil	88	114	-88	134	136	335
Earnings Per Share $	2.12	2.44	-2.08	2.89	2.93	4.97
Shares Outstanding Mil	41	47	43	46	46	46
Return on Equity %	9.6	12.3	-11.3	17.3	18.1	15.6
Net Margin %	19.3	23.3	-16.1	22.7	20.1	9.0
Asset Turnover	0.2	0.2	0.2	0.2	0.3	0.7
Financial Leverage	2.9	2.9	3.3	3.3	3.4	2.3

Management
Stewardship Grade [**C**]

Oneok owns 45.7% of Oneok Partners, including the general partnership interest, giving Oneok control over the partnership. With the change in control, Oneok executives now hold the top posts at Oneok Partners; most of the old Northern Border managers have been given new responsibilities within the partnership. David Kyle has been president of Oneok since its formation in 1997 and has been chairman and CEO since 2000. He now serves as CEO of Oneok Partners as well. We gave Oneok Partners a Stewardship Grade of C, the same as most of the other master limited partnerships we cover. An MLP's grade is hurt by the lack of limited-partner input into the management of the partnership. We will closely monitor any other governance changes made by Oneok over the next few months and adjust our Stewardship Grade accordingly.

Valuation Ratios	Stock	Rel to Industry	Rel to S&P 500
Price/Earnings	12.8	0.4	0.6
Price/Book	1.4	0.6	0.3
Price/Sales	0.8	0.4	0.3
Price/Cash Flow	5.8	0.6	0.4

Major Fund Holders	% of Fund Assets
Westwood Income AAA	1.34

13710 FNB Parkway www.northernborderpartners.com
Omaha, NE 68124-1000

Growth [A+]	2002	2003	2004	2005
Revenue %	6.8	13.1	7.2	14.9
Earnings/Share %	15.1	NMF	NMF	1.4
Book Value/Share %	-10.1	-7.1	-9.5	-3.3
Dividends/Share %	7.1	0.0	0.0	0.0

Profitability [NA]	2003	2004	2005	TTM
Return on Assets %	-3.4	5.3	5.4	6.7
Oper Cash Flow $Mil	225	245	267	503
- Cap Spending $Mil	30	43	60	135
= Free Cash Flow $Mil	194	201	207	367

Financial Health [B-]	2003	2004	2005	09-30-06
Long-term Debt $Mil	1,408	1,325	1,353	2,023
Total Equity $Mil	785	774	750	2,144
Debt/Equity Ratio	1.8	1.7	1.8	0.9

Thesis
By Michael Cumming, CFA, 12-20-06 Stock Price as of Analysis: $65.31

For several years, the Enron cloud that lingered over Northern Border Partners prevented the pipeline partnership from pursuing acquisitions or major expansions. As a result, distributions to unitholders remained stagnant for four years, causing many investors to look at other opportunities in midstream energy.

The days of stagnation are over. Oneok assumed control of Northern Border's general partner from Enron in September 2004. In April 2006, Oneok bought out TransCanada to become the sole general partner and changed the name of the partnership to Oneok Partners. In return, TransCanada affiliate TC Pipelines gets an additional 20% stake in the Northern Border Pipeline, and TransCanada will become the operator of the pipeline in April 2007. At the same time, Oneok sold most of its midstream assets to Oneok Partners in a deal that more than doubles the size of the partnership. We think this deal will benefit both Oneok entities. Oneok Partners finally has the growth opportunities it needs to increase distributions to long-suffering unitholders. Oneok will benefit from the tax protections available from the master limited partnership structure while retaining a 45.7% interest in the partnership and an even larger share of cash flows through its general partner incentive rights.

After these transactions, Oneok Partners operates a much more diverse set of assets. While the partnership's old assets consisted of about three fourths interstate pipelines and one fourth gathering and processing concentrated in the Northern Plains, the new asset mix includes a larger exposure to gathering and processing and natural-gas liquids (NGLs). In addition, all of the new assets are in Texas, Oklahoma, and Kansas, giving the firm greater geographic diversification. We hold natural-gas gathering and processing in lower regard than long-haul pipelines because the business is somewhat cyclical. If price differentials between natural gas and NGLs compress, removing the liquids becomes less economical and thus processing revenue declines. This greater exposure to gathering and processing reduces Oneok Partners' moat, but not by enough for us to change our rating at this time.

We are attracted to pipelines because of their wide economic moats. Rights of way do not come easily, and regulators do not give their approval to new systems or expansions unless there is a demonstrated economic need. Plus, with tariffs regulated, customers have little incentive to switch.

Oracle ORCL

Data as of 12-29-06

	Rating	Fair Value	Last Close	Consider Buy	Consider Sell	Yield %
	★★★★	$22.00	$17.14	$17.00	$27.60	0.00

Company Profile
Oracle is a $14 billion (in revenue) enterprise software company. Approximately half of the company's revenue comes from sales of new software licenses, while the remainder comes from software maintenance and professional services. Although database products put Oracle on the map, the company also sells an array of middleware, applications, and business intelligence software. The company has spent more than $20 billion acquiring companies over the past three years.

Management
Stewardship Grade [B]

Larry Ellison, the CEO of Oracle, founded the company in 1977. Safra Catz, CFO, and Charles Phillips, president, are extremely capable executives who also serve as Ellison's trusted lieutenants. We are pleased that Ellison owns more than 20% of the company in the form of direct shares (as opposed to only through stock options), strongly indicating his alignment with the remaining shareholders. However, there are several stewardship issues that are less than optimal. In spite of his considerable wealth and equity stake, Ellison has been paid more than $6 million in annual cash compensation as well as stock appreciation rights representing 8.5 million shares over the past two years. Although we view this compensation as excessive, we recognize that he is a critical force driving strategy and operations of the company. Additionally, Oracle conducts business with several entities wholly or partially owned by Ellison (including a flight services company for use of a corporate jet). While we have no reason to believe that Oracle is paying more than fair value for these services, we believe some of these arrangements might lead to a misalignment of shareholders and managements interests.

500 Oracle Parkway
Redwood City, CA 94065
www.oracle.com

Growth [B+]	2003	2004	2005	2006
Revenue %	-2.0	7.2	16.2	21.9
Earnings/Share %	10.3	16.3	10.0	16.4
Book Value/Share %	9.8	26.6	38.5	37.6
Dividends/Share %	NMF	NMF	NMF	NMF

Profitability [A]	2004	2005	2006	TTM
Return on Assets %	21.0	14.0	11.6	12.2
Oper Cash Flow $Mil	3,195	3,552	4,541	4,706
- Cap Spending $Mil	189	188	236	233
= Free Cash Flow $Mil	3,006	3,364	4,305	4,473

Financial Health [B+]	2004	2005	2006	08-31-06
Long-term Debt $Mil	163	159	5,735	5,737
Total Equity $Mil	7,995	10,837	15,012	14,899
Debt/Equity Ratio	0.0	0.0	0.4	0.4

Industry	Business Risk	Moat Size	Investment Style	Sector
Business Appl.	Average	Wide	Large Growth	Software

Competition	Market Cap $Mil	12 Mo Trailing Sales $Mil	Price/Cash Flow	Return On Assets %	Debt/Equity	Total Return % 1 Yr	3 Yr
Oracle	89,050	15,203	18.9	12.2	0.4	40.4	9.3
Microsoft	293,538	45,352	20.8	19.8	—	15.8	7.6
IBM	146,342	89,593	9.8	8.8	0.4	19.8	3.0

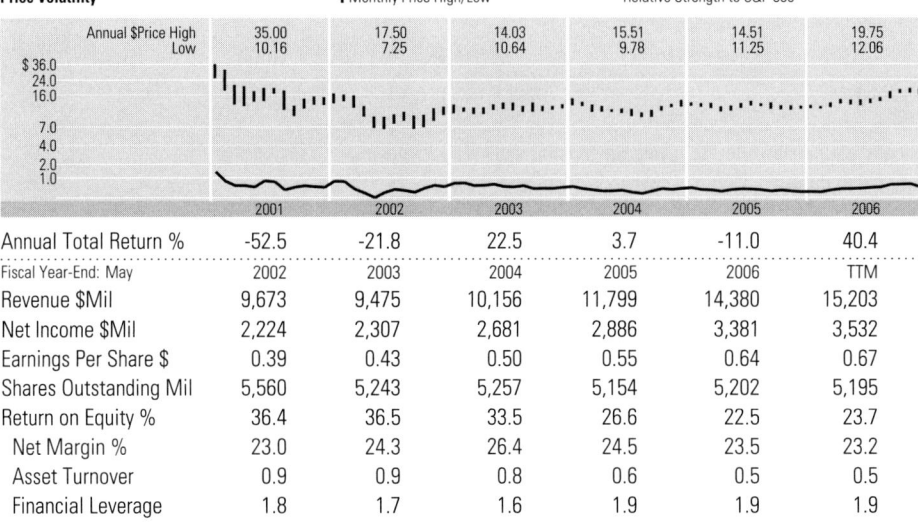

	2001	2002	2003	2004	2005	2006
Annual $Price High	35.00	17.50	14.03	15.51	14.51	19.75
Low	10.16	7.25	10.64	9.78	11.25	12.06
Annual Total Return %	-52.5	-21.8	22.5	3.7	-11.0	40.4

Fiscal Year-End: May	2002	2003	2004	2005	2006	TTM
Revenue $Mil	9,673	9,475	10,156	11,799	14,380	15,203
Net Income $Mil	2,224	2,307	2,681	2,886	3,381	3,532
Earnings Per Share $	0.39	0.43	0.50	0.55	0.64	0.67
Shares Outstanding Mil	5,560	5,243	5,257	5,154	5,202	5,195
Return on Equity %	36.4	36.5	33.5	26.6	22.5	23.7
Net Margin %	23.0	24.3	26.4	24.5	23.5	23.2
Asset Turnover	0.9	0.9	0.8	0.6	0.5	0.5
Financial Leverage	1.8	1.7	1.6	1.9	1.9	1.9

Valuation Ratios	Stock	Rel to Industry	Rel to S&P 500
Price/Earnings	25.6	0.9	1.2
Price/Book	6.0	0.7	1.5
Price/Sales	5.9	0.9	2.0
Price/Cash Flow	18.9	0.8	1.3

Major Fund Holders	% of Fund Assets
Oak Value	4.62
ICON Information Technology	4.59
Concorde Value	4.44
Fidelity Select Software & Comp	4.39

Thesis By Rick Summer, CFA, CPA, 12-05-06 Stock Price as of Analysis: $18.86

After shrewdly outmaneuvering competition in the 1990s, Oracle leaped to the front of the pack in the market for database software. In the 2000s, the company is making even larger bets, swallowing billions of dollars worth of software companies. Although this strategy would be treacherous for many companies, we are encouraged by early results and expect Oracle to continue its record of success.

Oracle has spent more than $20 billion on software acquisitions since 2003, moving beyond its core database business and launching an offensive against competitor SAP. Oracle has acquired widely deployed software applications such as PeopleSoft and Siebel Systems and their massive base of customers. The company has not merely acquired customers in the hopes of holding onto lucrative software maintenance revenues--its customers are also upgrading applications and purchasing new licenses, showing surprising growth.

Furthermore, Oracle is attempting to develop products for an emerging industry segment called services-oriented architecture. Services-oriented architecture solutions help save customers time and expense connecting and reconnecting their application islands. For example, connecting an order management system to inventory management would become as easy as rerouting a trip on a map. To be frank, we are skeptical that Oracle's promised services-oriented architecture solution (called Fusion) consists of anything beyond marketing presentations today--real products are probably two years away. Still, we believe that Oracle's solid customer standing affords the company the luxury of reacting slowly to industry trends; customers will wait for an Oracle product if they believe it is "coming soon."

In spite of Oracle's advantages, a few stumbling blocks may disrupt Oracles business model. Although customer switching costs in the database market (where Oracle is the largest provider ahead of IBM and Microsoft) provide a wide economic moat, we believe that customers have tired of paying steep prices for software maintenance. Companies like TomorrowNow (owned by SAP) sell support for Oracle owned applications at substantial discounts, forcing Oracle to discount some of its own maintenance rates..

In spite of new dynamics in the software industry, we believe Oracle has been re-energized by competition and is successfully finding new growth in areas beyond the database market. We would welcome a chance to invest in this software giant.

Data as of 12-29-06

Oshkosh Truck OSK

	Rating	Fair Value	Last Close	Consider Buy	Consider Sell	Yield %
	★★★	$48.00	$48.42	$37.00	$60.10	0.83

Company Profile

Oshkosh manufactures an extensive range of severe-duty specialty trucks and truck bodies, including fire engines, aerial work platforms, ambulances, refuse trucks, and military vehicles. After the acquisition of JLG, its four business segments--fire and emergency, commercial, defense, and access equipment--will account for roughly 15%, 15%, 30%, and 40% of revenue, respectively. Oshkosh is the U.S. Department of Defense's leading supplier of tactical trucks.

Management   Stewardship Grade [B]

CEO and chairman Bob Bohn has worked alongside CFO Charlie Szews since the mid-1990s, when Oshkosh was primarily a defense supplier. Management soon began a quest to diversify the company by becoming a major player in attractive specialty truck markets such as refuse trucks, cement mixers, and fire trucks. The acquisition-based strategy has been nearly flawless, and the stock price has responded, rising from $2 per share in 1997 to above $60 at one point in 2006. In 2005, Bohn received 75% of his total compensation in the form of bonuses, long-term restricted stock, and stock options. We'd like to see his vested interest in the company a bit higher than 1%. We like that Oshkosh's board of directors is re-elected every year and that it decided to transition from two classes of stock to just one in 2005. Overall, management does an excellent job of providing guidance and disclosure about past, present, and future issues in all of its segments.

2307 Oregon Street P.O. Box 2566   www.oshkoshtruck.com
Oshkosh, WI 54903-2566

Growth [A-]	2003	2004	2005	2006
Revenue %	10.5	17.5	30.8	15.8
Earnings/Share %	25.6	45.4	38.9	26.6
Book Value/Share %	25.3	19.5	25.8	28.0
Dividends/Share %	8.3	39.1	70.0	66.0

Profitability [A]	2004	2005	2006	TTM
Return on Assets %	7.8	9.3	9.7	9.7
Oper Cash Flow $Mil	135	212	177	177
- Cap Spending $Mil	30	43	56	56
= Free Cash Flow $Mil	105	169	121	121

Financial Health [A-]	2004	2005	2006	09-30-06
Long-term Debt $Mil	3	3	2	2
Total Equity $Mil	636	819	1,062	1,062
Debt/Equity Ratio	0.0	0.0	0.0	0.0

Industry	Business Risk	Moat Size	Investment Style	Sector
Truck Makers	Average	Narrow	Mid Core	Industrial Materials

Competition	Market Cap $Mil	12 Mo Trailing Sales $Mil	Price/Cash Flow	Return On Assets %	Debt/Equity	Total Return% 1 Yr	3 Yr
Oshkosh Truck	3,572	3,427	20.1	9.7	0.0	9.5	24.2
DaimlerChrysler AG	62,526	187,555	4.0	1.5	—	24.3	14.0
Federal Signal	765	1,208	15.8	-1.7	0.8	8.5	-1.8

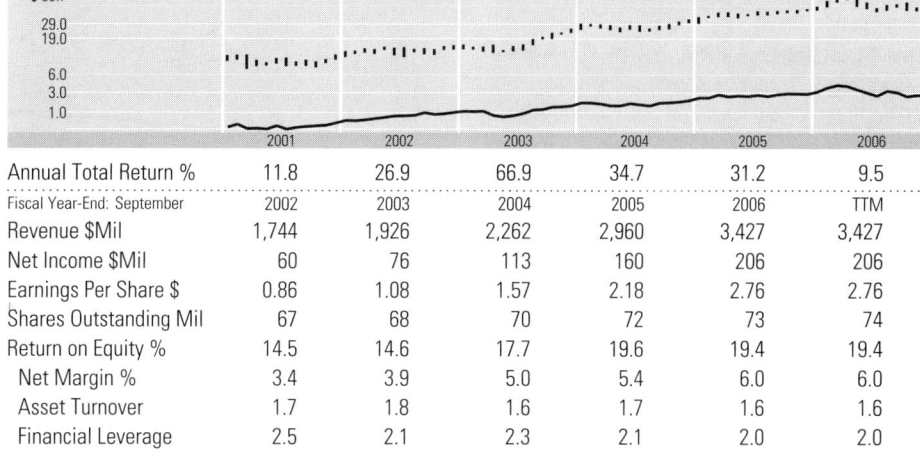

	2002	2003	2004	2005	2006	TTM
Annual Total Return %	11.8	26.9	66.9	34.7	31.2	9.5
Fiscal Year-End: September	2002	2003	2004	2005	2006	TTM
Revenue $Mil	1,744	1,926	2,262	2,960	3,427	3,427
Net Income $Mil	60	76	113	160	206	206
Earnings Per Share $	0.86	1.08	1.57	2.18	2.76	2.76
Shares Outstanding Mil	67	68	70	72	73	74
Return on Equity %	14.5	14.6	17.7	19.6	19.4	19.4
Net Margin %	3.4	3.9	5.0	5.4	6.0	6.0
Asset Turnover	1.7	1.8	1.6	1.7	1.6	1.6
Financial Leverage	2.5	2.1	2.3	2.1	2.0	2.0

Valuation Ratios	Stock	Rel to Industry	Rel to S&P 500
Price/Earnings	17.5	1.1	0.8
Price/Book	3.4	1.1	0.8
Price/Sales	1.0	1.1	0.3
Price/Cash Flow	20.1	1.6	1.4

Major Fund Holders	% of Fund Assets
Westcore Select	5.01
DWS Mid Cap Growth Inst	3.18
Franklin Mid Cap Value A	2.83
JHT Dynamic Growth Trust Ser I	2.78

Thesis   By Ben Butwin, 10-18-06 Stock Price as of Analysis: $51.30

Oshkosh Truck is benefiting directly from the massive defense budget, but this narrow-moat firm is also taking steps to ensure that its revenue will be diverse enough to allow it to survive an eventual curtailment in government spending.

Oshkosh has engineered its moat through a record of successful accretive acquisitions in specialty truck markets. By only acquiring the number-one or -two brand in a given sector, Oshkosh has built an empire of niche-market suppliers that outshine smaller competitors through shared production platforms, combined purchasing power, and extensive distribution networks.

The company's most dominant division is its defense segment, which has sold vehicles to the Department of Defense for more than 80 years. Oshkosh is reaping the benefits of Operation Iraqi Freedom through exclusive government contracts that are usually three to five years long. We expect that by 2008 or 2009, the atypical demand on which the segment has coasted for the past few years will slow significantly. The results should not be too catastrophic, however, thanks to steady parts, service, and remanufacturing revenue, as well as the military's unceasing demand for high-tech vehicle innovations.

Still, the eventual abatement of military spending has forced Oshkosh to focus more on generating growth from other sources. While bolt-on purchases are possible, the best opportunities lie in other growing specialty truck markets that Oshkosh does not yet dominate. Its most recent (and largest) acquisition, aerial work platform manufacturer JLG Industries, will nearly double annual sales and should cut defense spending from 40% of revenue to 30%.

Filling out its product range is a high priority, but we're glad to see that Oshkosh is committed to internal improvements as well. Major progress is occurring in the firm's commercial segment, where margins have lagged other divisions. Turning around its European refuse business will be based solely on cost reductions through product and process redesigns. This suggests to us that its current troubles are internal--not based on unattractive industry fundamentals--and therefore fixable.

Oshkosh is an above-average company with superior competitive positioning, in our eyes. Still, uncertainty surrounds future defense revenue and the extent of recovery in the commercial segment. Long-term investors who can stomach these risks should keep Oshkosh in mind, but not overpay amid the strong tailwinds of hot defense spending.

Data as of 12-29-06

PACCAR PCAR

	Rating	Fair Value	Last Close	Consider Buy	Consider Sell	Yield %
	★★★	$61.00	$64.90	$47.00	$76.40	1.18

Company Profile

PACCAR makes medium-duty (Class 6-7) and heavy-duty (Class 8) trucks under the Peterbilt and Kenworth names in the U.S. and the DAF and Foden names in Western Europe. Its Class 8 market share is around 25% in the U.S. and 14% in Europe. The firm's financial segment provides services such as financing arrangements and full-service leasing to dealers and customers. PACCAR also sells aftermarket truck parts (about 12% of sales) and manufactures industrial winches (1%).

Management
Stewardship Grade [C]

One dollar invested in PACCAR 10 years ago would be worth nearly 7 times as much today. CEO and chairman Mark Pigott, who is just the fourth CEO in the company's 100-year history, owns about 1.5% of PACCAR's stock; executives as a group own nearly 7%. Pigott earned $1.25 million in 2005 and about 2.5 times that amount in bonuses and long-term incentive payouts. We think this is fair compensation, given PACCAR's phenomenal record. We approve of the firm's conservative accounting practices, but we believe that management could afford to give a bit more color regarding negative performance aspects and provide more disclosure of business details in general. We're not fans of the company's staggered board of directors (three of whom could be considered insiders) and poison-pill provision (which was not approved by shareholders). We did enjoy learning that PACCAR matches its employees' 401(k) contributions in company stock.

Industry	Business Risk	Moat Size	Investment Style	Sector
Truck Makers	Average	Narrow	Large Core	Industrial Materials

Competition	Market Cap $Mil	12 Mo Trailing Sales $Mil	Price/Cash Flow	Return On Assets%	Debt/ Equity	Total Return% 1 Yr	3 Yr
PACCAR	16,116	15,860	10.0	9.2	0.7	46.9	25.3
DaimlerChrysler AG	62,526	187,555	4.0	1.5	—	24.3	14.0
Navistar International	2,344	—	—	—	—	16.8	-10.9

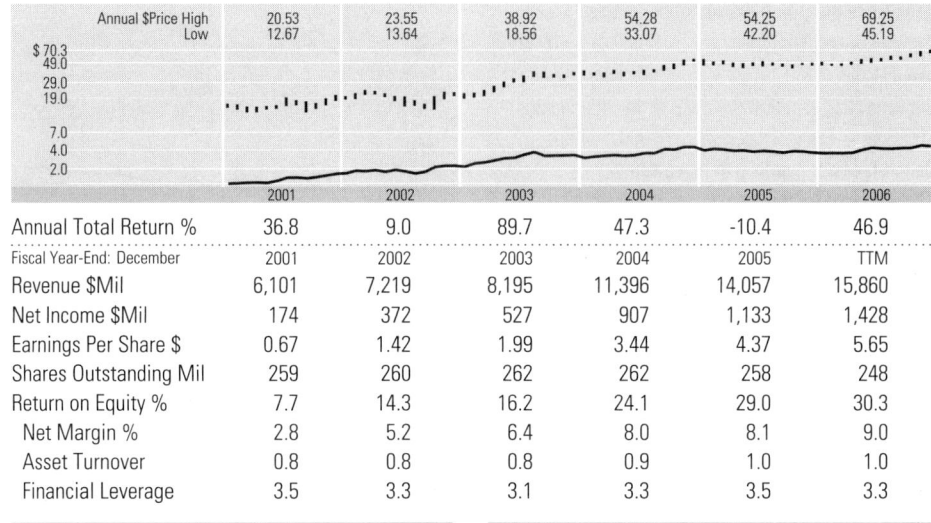

	2001	2002	2003	2004	2005	2006
Annual Total Return %	36.8	9.0	89.7	47.3	-10.4	46.9
Fiscal Year-End: December	2001	2002	2003	2004	2005	TTM
Revenue $Mil	6,101	7,219	8,195	11,396	14,057	15,860
Net Income $Mil	174	372	527	907	1,133	1,428
Earnings Per Share $	0.67	1.42	1.99	3.44	4.37	5.65
Shares Outstanding Mil	259	260	262	262	258	248
Return on Equity %	7.7	14.3	16.2	24.1	29.0	30.3
Net Margin %	2.8	5.2	6.4	8.0	8.1	9.0
Asset Turnover	0.8	0.8	0.8	0.9	1.0	1.0
Financial Leverage	3.5	3.3	3.1	3.3	3.5	3.3

Valuation Ratios	Stock	Rel to Industry	Rel to S&P 500
Price/Earnings	11.5	0.7	0.6
Price/Book	3.4	1.1	0.8
Price/Sales	1.0	1.1	0.3
Price/Cash Flow	10.0	0.8	0.7

Major Fund Holders	% of Fund Assets
BB&T Special Opportunities Equity A	4.04
Blue Chip Investor	3.69
American Century Legacy Foc Lg Cap Inv	3.43
Pioneer Equity Income A	3.16

777 - 106th Ave. N.E.
Bellevue, WA 98004
www.paccar.com

Growth [A]	2002	2003	2004	2005
Revenue %	18.3	13.5	39.1	23.4
Earnings/Share %	113.0	40.4	72.6	27.1
Book Value/Share %	14.8	23.8	16.1	5.5
Dividends/Share %	55.2	37.3	100.2	4.4

Profitability [A-]	2003	2004	2005	TTM
Return on Assets %	5.3	7.4	8.3	9.2
Oper Cash Flow $Mil	778	891	987	1,610
- Cap Spending $Mil	369	634	849	869
= Free Cash Flow $Mil	409	258	138	741

Financial Health [B]	2003	2004	2005	09-30-06
Long-term Debt $Mil	1,557	2,314	2,678	3,216
Total Equity $Mil	3,246	3,762	3,901	4,714
Debt/Equity Ratio	0.5	0.6	0.7	0.7

Thesis By Ben Butwin, 10-24-06 Stock Price as of Analysis: $60.86

PACCAR consistently outshines its peers via its quality products, manufacturing efficiency, and technological superiority. We'd be comfortable holding this company's shares for the long haul.

PACCAR's narrow moat stems from a variety of competitive advantages, the most prominent being its brand strength. Its Kenworth and Peterbilt names in North America and DAF and Foden brands in Europe represent the highest-quality medium- and heavy-duty trucks money can buy. Each truck is customized to order, mixes driver comfort with the latest technology, and boasts a longer life cycle than competing trucks. These factors allow PACCAR to keep its customers and maintain substantial pricing premiums over rivals.

The company's de jure competitors include other truck makers such as Navistar, Volvo, and Freightliner. Yet PACCAR's market dominance and commitment to excellence give the firm a new set of de facto peers, in its eyes. It benchmarks its working-capital management after Dell, mimics Toyota's quality standards, and constantly partners and competes with high-tech firms like Microsoft.

In fact, PACCAR is one of the world's most technologically advanced companies, regardless of industry. The firm pours unparalleled amounts of capital into cutting-edge research like radio-frequency identification, satellite imagery, and Six Sigma. It was recently awarded the National Medal of Technology for developing lighter, more-aerodynamic trucks that have reduced fuel consumption and increased productivity in the trucking industry.

The list of PACCAR's advantages goes on. The firm's aggressive management of its production rates and cost structure have made it the most efficient manufacturer in the business. It generates sales from a diverse geographic base, owns numerous patents, enjoys intimate dealer and supplier relationships, and obtains a growing portion of its sales from its lucrative financial services and aftermarket parts businesses. The result? Returns on capital well in excess of 20%, 67 straight years of profits, and double-digit annual growth in revenue and profits.

However, PACCAR's future is not without its uncertainties. Stricter engine emission laws in 2007 and 2010 will cause volume to drop significantly, making the cyclical waters of the industry more difficult to navigate. But if investors can handle some short-term market fluctuations, we believe PACCAR, with its squeaky-clean balance sheet, healthy dividend, and proven brand name, has the potential for persistent long-term shareholder value creation.

Panera Bread PNRA

Rating ★★★★
Fair Value $66.00
Last Close $55.91
Consider Buy $50.90
Consider Sell $82.70
Yield % 0.00

Industry: Restaurants
Business Risk: Average
Moat Size: None
Investment Style: Small Growth
Sector: Consumer Services

Company Profile
Panera Bread Company owns and franchises bakery-cafes, which specialize in freshly baked goods, made-to-order sandwiches, soups, salads, and custom-roasted coffees. Targeting suburban dwellers and workers, the bakery-cafes are principally located in suburban strip malls and regional malls in 37 states. As of September 2006, there were 976 Panera Bread bakery-cafes open, of which 353 are company-owned and 623 are franchised.

Management
Stewardship Grade [**C**]

Chairman and CEO Ron Shaich has overseen major expansion at Panera since the company he co-founded, Au Bon Pain, bought it in 1993. (The Au Bon Pain unit was subsequently sold in 1999.) Under his leadership, the Panera concept has grown from 20 bakery-cafes in the St. Louis area to more than 1,000 units across America. In 2005, Shaich was paid a salary plus bonus of $1.1 million, which is reasonable compensation, in our view. He also received a very generous package of restricted stock and options, resulting in about 6% beneficial ownership of the company. We do take exception to shareholders footing the bill for his personal chartered air travel, which totaled around $164,000 over the past three years. We're also unimpressed by several measures taken by Shaich and his board to limit the powers of outside shareholders, including a dual-class structure, staggered board elections, a poison pill, and other takeover defenses. We'd also prefer for the roles of chairman and CEO to be split. On the other hand, stockholders have fared very well under these arrangements, with the shares rising more than fivefold over the five years ended in 2005.

6710 Clayton Rd
Richmond Heights, MO 63117
www.panerabread.com

Growth [**A+**]	2002	2003	2004	2005
Revenue %	40.3	28.9	31.7	33.6
Earnings/Share %	61.4	40.8	25.0	32.0
Book Value/Share %	22.9	26.1	22.8	28.2
Dividends/Share %	NMF	NMF	NMF	NMF

Profitability [**A**]	2003	2004	2005	TTM
Return on Assets %	11.8	11.9	11.9	11.5
Oper Cash Flow $Mil	73	84	111	97
- Cap Spending $Mil	46	80	82	99
= Free Cash Flow $Mil	27	4	29	-2

Financial Health [**A**]	2003	2004	2005	09-30-06
Long-term Debt $Mil	—	—	—	—
Total Equity $Mil	194	241	317	371
Debt/Equity Ratio	—	—	—	—

Competition

	Market Cap $Mil	12 Mo Trailing Sales $Mil	Price/Cash Flow	Return On Assets %	Debt/Equity	Total Return% 1 Yr	3 Yr
Panera Bread	1,768	769	18.3	11.5	—	-14.9	12.3
McDonald's	54,825	21,790	13.3	9.4	0.6	34.6	23.9
Starbucks	26,737	7,787	23.6	12.7	0.0	18.0	29.1

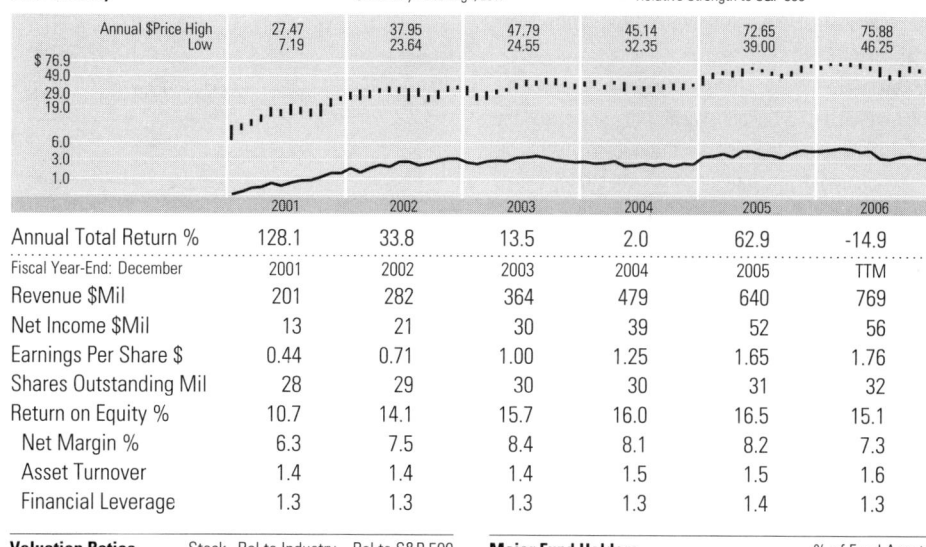

Price Volatility — Monthly Price High/Low — Relative Strength to S&P 500

	2001	2002	2003	2004	2005	2006
Annual $Price High	27.47	37.95	47.79	45.14	72.65	75.88
Low	7.19	23.64	24.55	32.35	39.00	46.25
Annual Total Return %	128.1	33.8	13.5	2.0	62.9	-14.9

Fiscal Year-End: December	2001	2002	2003	2004	2005	TTM
Revenue $Mil	201	282	364	479	640	769
Net Income $Mil	13	21	30	39	52	56
Earnings Per Share $	0.44	0.71	1.00	1.25	1.65	1.76
Shares Outstanding Mil	28	29	30	30	31	32
Return on Equity %	10.7	14.1	15.7	16.0	16.5	15.1
Net Margin %	6.3	7.5	8.4	8.1	8.2	7.3
Asset Turnover	1.4	1.4	1.4	1.5	1.5	1.6
Financial Leverage	1.3	1.3	1.3	1.3	1.4	1.3

Valuation Ratios	Stock	Rel to Industry	Rel to S&P 500
Price/Earnings	31.8	1.2	1.5
Price/Book	4.8	0.8	1.2
Price/Sales	2.3	1.1	0.8
Price/Cash Flow	18.3	1.2	1.3

Major Fund Holders	% of Fund Assets
Bender Growth C	4.45
Payden Small Cap Leaders	3.43
Oberweis Mid-Cap	2.88
North Track Geneva Growth A	2.14

Thesis By John Owens, CFA, CPA, 12-11-06 Stock Price as of Analysis: $56.74

In our opinion, Panera Bread has carved out a lucrative niche between fast food and casual dining. We've been impressed with the chain's ability to grow sales beyond the busy lunch period and see ample opportunity for expansion. Its success, however, has not gone unnoticed, and rivals are now responding more aggressively.

Panera is well known for its fresh artisan breads, and its menu includes distinctive items, like a bistro steak salad and a turkey artichoke panini. The concept also differentiates itself from fast-food fare by serving its meals with silverware on china, while providing a faster speed of service than casual dining restaurants. With an average check of around $8 (just a couple of bucks more than a meal at McDonald's and a few dollars less than the average check at Applebee's before tip), Panera offers its customers a compelling value, in our opinion.

Many of its locations incorporate the warmth of a fireplace and cozy seating areas as well as gathering spots for small groups. Panera's cafes also offer free wireless Internet access. All of this encourages customers to hang out and spend more on coffee, pastries, and sweets. In 2005, Panera introduced egg souffles, which helped fuel growth in morning sales. The company also recently launched Crispani (a hand-crafted pizza made with fresh, all-natural toppings and a flatbread crust) to boost evening business, and initial results have been encouraging. Panera's average annual sales now exceed $2 million per unit, more than any other major fast-food rival.

Given these strong unit economics, we think the chain of more than 1,000 bakery-cafes has ample opportunity for expansion. By comparison, McDonald's, Starbucks, and Applebees are presently about 15 times, 8 times, and 2 times larger, respectively, than Panera, based on number of U.S. locations. The chain could build out to nearly 5,000 domestic units if it could match the density of its home market in St. Louis, where it continues to add new bakery-cafes. Panera is also expanding into Canada in 2007.

The company, however, is facing increasing competition from fast-food chains. For example, McDonald's now serves premium chicken sandwiches and gourmet coffee and is "re-imaging" its restaurants with a more upscale decor. Starbucks is also making a strong push, rolling out warm breakfast sandwiches and expanding its lunch offering. Casual dining chains like Applebee's are heavily promoting value items and improving their convenience proposition with more focus on "to go" orders.

Parker Hannifin PH

Data as of 12-29-06

	Rating	Fair Value	Last Close	Consider Buy	Consider Sell	Yield %
	★★★	$82.00	$76.88	$63.20	$102.70	1.28

Industry	Business Risk	Moat Size	Investment Style	Sector
Machinery	Average	Narrow	Mid Value	Industrial Materials

Company Profile

Parker Hannifin is a diversified manufacturing firm that provides motion and control components and systems. It operates in four business segments: industrials in North America and the rest of the world, aerospace, and climate and controls. The core industrial and aerospace segments have key product categories ranging from hydraulics, fluid connectors, filtration, and automation to flight control systems and components. Parker has nearly 8,200 distributors in 87 countries.

Management   Stewardship Grade [B]

Chairman and CEO Donald Washkewicz and president and COO Nick Vande Steeg are the chief architects of the company's restructuring and growth strategies. Parker operates a decentralized organizational model. The four business segments are divided into eight product categories, each headed by a group president. We like that 12 out of 15 board members are independent. However, direct ownership among independent board members is light, with the exception of retired CEO Duane Collins. Management's incentive structure seems to be aligned well with shareholders' interests, and the compensation committee is headed by an independent board member. The annual cash incentive compensation is based on free cash flow margins and returns on net assets, with an added bonus for increased internal sales targets. Long-term incentives include stock and options, and the metrics are structured around compound annual revenue growth, earnings per share growth, and return on invested capital. Incentive compensation has been tied to business and individual performance, but we would like to see more of it tied to longer-term value-creation metrics.

6035 Parkland Boulevard   www.phstock.com
Cleveland, OH 44124-4141

Growth [B+]	2003	2004	2005	2006
Revenue %	1.2	10.7	17.2	16.3
Earnings/Share %	50.0	73.2	72.5	11.0
Book Value/Share %	-2.9	16.3	10.5	26.6
Dividends/Share %	2.8	2.7	2.6	17.9

Profitability [A-]	2004	2005	2006	TTM
Return on Assets %	5.6	8.8	8.2	8.5
Oper Cash Flow $Mil	662	854	955	861
- Cap Spending $Mil	138	155	198	213
= Free Cash Flow $Mil	524	699	757	648

Financial Health [A]	2004	2005	2006	09-30-06
Long-term Debt $Mil	954	938	1,059	1,046
Total Equity $Mil	2,982	3,340	4,241	4,270
Debt/Equity Ratio	0.3	0.3	0.3	0.2

Competition

	Market Cap $Mil	12 Mo Trailing Sales $Mil	Price/Cash Flow	Return On Assets%	Debt/Equity	Total Return% 1 Yr	3 Yr
Parker Hannifin	9,066	9,824	10.5	8.5	0.2	18.0	10.3
Honeywell International	36,939	30,367	13.2	6.2	0.3	24.1	13.2
Eaton	11,196	12,181	7.8	8.2	0.4	14.4	14.3

Price Volatility | Monthly Price High/Low   — Relative Strength to S&P 500

Annual $Price High	50.10	54.88	59.80	78.42	76.23	88.00
Low	30.40	34.52	35.82	51.73	56.80	65.16
	2001	2002	2003	2004	2005	2006
Annual Total Return %	5.8	2.1	31.2	28.9	-11.7	18.0

Fiscal Year-End: June	2002	2003	2004	2005	2006	TTM
Revenue $Mil	6,149	6,222	6,888	8,069	9,386	9,824
Net Income $Mil	130	196	346	605	673	711
Earnings Per Share $	1.12	1.68	2.91	5.02	5.57	5.89
Shares Outstanding Mil	115	116	118	119	119	118
Return on Equity %	5.0	7.8	11.6	18.1	15.9	16.7
Net Margin %	2.1	3.2	5.0	7.5	7.2	7.2
Asset Turnover	1.1	1.0	1.1	1.2	1.1	1.2
Financial Leverage	2.2	2.4	2.1	2.1	1.9	1.9

Valuation Ratios	Stock	Rel to Industry	Rel to S&P 500
Price/Earnings	13.2	0.7	0.6
Price/Book	2.1	0.7	0.5
Price/Sales	0.9	0.6	0.3
Price/Cash Flow	10.5	0.6	0.7

Major Fund Holders	% of Fund Assets
Fort Pitt Capital Total Return	2.84
Homestead Value	2.82
Permanent Portfolio Aggressive Growth	2.52
Stratton Multi Cap	2.37

Thesis   By Ramesh Poola, Ph.D., 10-18-06   Stock Price as of Analysis: $83.06

Parker Hannifin has returned to its historical profitability and demonstrated its ability to create shareholder value. Although the company operates in a highly fragmented and cyclical industrial sector, its wide distribution network, swift response to customer needs, and successful acquisitions help it secure a narrow economic moat.

Parker is not a technical leader and therefore relies on supply-chain management and customer service to drive profits. Over the past several years, the company has initiated several efficiency improvements aimed at not only withstanding down cycles but also improving overall long-term profitability. As a result of these efforts, it has reduced the number of inventory days from about 77 to 56. By rationalizing its asset base, Parker has been able to increase its return on sales from about 7% to 12%.

Supply-chain management is only part of Parker's recipe for success. Leveraging its inventory expertise, Parker can deliver parts more quickly than its competitors. Furthermore, Parker's superior service has deepened its customer relationships, allowing the firm to increase volume and take market share. As a result of these distinct competitive advantages, operating margins improved steadily from 5% in 2002 to 10.2% in 2005.

While its distribution network helps keep Parker ahead of its competition, internal growth has benefited from shifting the product mix to higher-margin aftermarket and aerospace businesses. Aerospace-related sales already account for 19% of operating income, and we believe both revenue and profits will benefit from strong demand from the sector over the next several years.

Notwithstanding these improvements, Parker's internal growth is rather limited at the modest--but predictable--level of 4%-5% over the course of a full cycle. Despite this, management has a goal of 10% annual sales growth, with the expectation that acquisitions will pick up the slack. We believe Parker is a good acquisitor because it targets small to medium-size acquisitions that fill its product gaps and geographically diversify it away from North American industrial markets. For example, its 60% equity stake in Japan-based Taiyo not only increases its global presence but also provides access to hydraulics and pneumatic technologies. Parker's return on invested capital (with goodwill) steadily increased from 5.6% in 2002 to 12.2% in 2005, demonstrating the company's success in acquiring the right targets at the right price.

Data as of 12-29-06

Patterson Companies PDCO

	Rating ★★★	Fair Value $36.00	Last Close $35.51	Consider Buy $27.80	Consider Sell $45.10	Yield % 0.00

Company Profile
Patterson Companies is a specialty distributor of supplies and equipment to the dental (75% of sales), medical (12%), and veterinary (13%) markets. The company markets and sells its products and services through 1,800 sales representatives. Sales of consumables, such as X-ray film, sterilization and anaesthetic products, toothbrushes and other dental accessories, accounted for 64% of revenue, with large equipment sales and maintenance services contributing the remainder.

Management — Stewardship Grade [C]
We are becoming concerned with the growing turnover among the company's top management. Jeff Webster, longtime president of the company's veterinary unit, is the latest high-ranking executive to leave Patterson. His resignation completes the circle, as now all three divisions have replaced their top executives in the span of nine months. We are particularly concerned with Webster's departure, as he has been Webster Veterinary's executive for over 20 years, well before the business was acquired by Patterson. We are also uneasy with the company's board composition. While five out of seven board members are independent, one of the independent members, Ron Ezerski, served as the company's CFO until his retirement in 1999. The company's staggered board elections add to our discomfort. On the positive side, we believe the compensation structure is fair and performance-driven. We also like the high executive ownership stakes and approve of the use of restricted stock in lieu of stock options.

1031 Mendota Heights Road
St. Paul, MN 55120-1419
www.pattersondental.com

Growth [B-]	2003	2004	2005	2006
Revenue %	17.1	18.9	23.0	8.0
Earnings/Share %	25.0	23.4	22.2	8.3
Book Value/Share %	22.6	25.1	25.9	22.8
Dividends/Share %	NMF	NMF	NMF	NMF

Profitability [A]	2004	2005	2006	TTM
Return on Assets %	9.4	10.9	10.4	10.8
Oper Cash Flow $Mil	198	207	164	179
- Cap Spending $Mil	20	32	49	32
= Free Cash Flow $Mil	178	176	115	147

Financial Health [A]	2004	2005	2006	10-31-06
Long-term Debt $Mil	480	302	210	200
Total Equity $Mil	802	1,015	1,243	1,242
Debt/Equity Ratio	0.6	0.3	0.2	0.2

Industry	Business Risk	Moat Size	Investment Style	Sector
Medical Goods/Svcs.	Average	Narrow	Mid Growth	Healthcare

Competition	Market Cap $Mil	12 Mo Trailing Sales $Mil	Price/Cash Flow	Return On Assets %	Debt/ Equity	Total Return% 1 Yr	3 Yr
Patterson Companies	4,941	2,727	27.7	10.8	0.2	6.3	4.1
Henry Schein	4,338	4,997	19.4	5.9	0.3	12.2	13.6
PSS World Medical	1,322	1,687	20.0	6.3	0.4	31.6	17.0

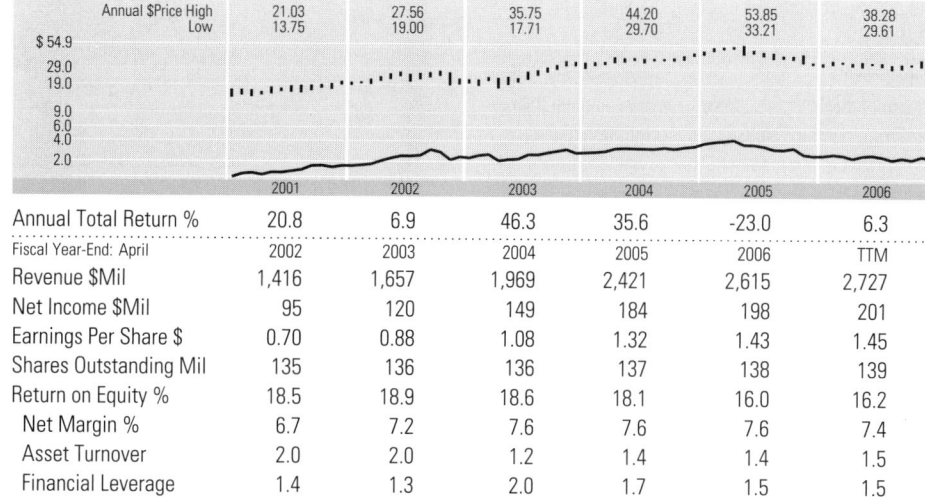

	2001	2002	2003	2004	2005	2006
Annual $Price High	21.03	27.56	35.75	44.20	53.85	38.28
Low	13.75	19.00	17.71	29.70	33.21	29.61
Annual Total Return %	20.8	6.9	46.3	35.6	-23.0	6.3

Fiscal Year-End: April	2002	2003	2004	2005	2006	TTM
Revenue $Mil	1,416	1,657	1,969	2,421	2,615	2,727
Net Income $Mil	95	120	149	184	198	201
Earnings Per Share $	0.70	0.88	1.08	1.32	1.43	1.45
Shares Outstanding Mil	135	136	136	137	138	139
Return on Equity %	18.5	18.9	18.6	18.1	16.0	16.2
Net Margin %	6.7	7.2	7.6	7.6	7.6	7.4
Asset Turnover	2.0	2.0	1.2	1.4	1.4	1.5
Financial Leverage	1.4	1.3	2.0	1.7	1.5	1.5

Valuation Ratios	Stock	Rel to Industry	Rel to S&P 500	Major Fund Holders	% of Fund Assets
Price/Earnings	24.5	1.1	1.2	Jensen J	3.70
Price/Book	4.0	1.3	1.0	Parnassus Mid-Cap	3.44
Price/Sales	1.8	3.0	0.6	Madison Mosaic Mid-Cap	3.11
Price/Cash Flow	27.7	1.6	1.9	Janus Global Opportunities	2.83

Thesis By Alex Morozov, CFA, 12-05-06 Stock Price as of Analysis: $38.13

While Patterson Companies continues to rely on its stalwart dental segment for the bulk of sales, its expansion into the veterinary and medical fields opens up promising avenues for future growth. Its increasing presence in these markets should boost Patterson's sales and allow the company to leverage its distribution infrastructure across all three operating segments.

Patterson's bread and butter is its dental distribution operations. Along with Henry Schein, the company is one of the two largest North American distributors of dental equipment and consumables. Through its massive salesforce of 1,500 representatives, Patterson is involved in the purchasing decisions of 120,000 dentists in the U.S. and Canada. The company's successful penetration of this market (the firm's share has increased from 23% in 1998 to 32% presently) is primarily a result of Patterson's value-added service approach. The firm's broad product offering features standard consumable supplies, an extensive line of basic and high-tech equipment, as well as support software, financing, and back-office services. This full-service approach fosters client relationships and allows Patterson to charge prices above the competition.

The company has been successful in transcribing its dental operating model to the veterinary segment. Despite being a relative newcomer, Patterson has the second-largest share in this market, and operations are growing in excess of 10% annually (nearly double the market growth rate). We think that this segment offers significant expansion opportunities, as Patterson's name, large salesforce, broad line of equipment, and vast distribution network give the firm an advantage over smaller competitors, such as MWI Veterinary. We also think growth in this segment will allow Patterson to further consolidate its distribution facilities and provide the company with additional cost advantages over Schein.

Although the vet division has exceeded expectations, the medical segment's results had been disappointing until recently. Patterson was having difficulty improving on its leading position in this market, despite favorable industry conditions. To inject life into this segment, the company replaced the management team and is investing heavily in salesforce and product-line expansion. These measures appear to be working, with the medical operations enjoying low-double-digit growth for the first time in the company's history.

Data as of 12-29-06

Paychex PAYX

	Rating	Fair Value	Last Close	Consider Buy	Consider Sell	Yield %
	★★★	$43.00	$39.54	$36.60	$56.50	1.75

Industry	Business Risk	Moat Size	Investment Style	Sector
Data Processing	Below Avg	Wide	Large Growth	Business Services

Company Profile

Paychex provides payroll, human resources, and benefits outsourcing solutions predominantly to small and medium-size businesses. Payroll represents the heart of Paychex and includes services such as payroll processing, payroll tax administration, and employee pay services like direct deposit. Paychex offers its services to about 100 of the largest markets in the U.S. and Germany, and serves just over 543,000 clients, making it one of the leading providers.

Management   Stewardship Grade [A]

Jonathan Judge is Paychex's CEO. He assumed the role from founder Tom Golisano in October 2004. Judge most recently was CEO of Crystal Decisions and previously served as general manager of IBM's personal computer division after holding various management positions within IBM. Paychex has a sound management team and good corporate stewardship. Chairman Tom Golisano founded the company in 1971 and owns 10% of shares outstanding. Directors and officers own a total of 11.4% of shares outstanding, enough to align their interests with those of shareholders. Stock option grants are reasonable, averaging less than 1% of shares outstanding over the past few years. The company expects to continue to grant stock options amounting to roughly 1% of shares outstanding going forward, a fair amount, in our opinion. We like the firm's annual election of its board of directors and its split chairman and CEO roles.

---

911 Panorama Trail South   www.paychex.com
Rochester, NY 14625-2396

Growth [B]	2003	2004	2005	2006
Revenue %	15.1	17.8	11.7	15.9
Earnings/Share %	6.8	2.6	21.3	25.8
Book Value/Share %	16.6	10.7	15.0	19.2
Dividends/Share %	4.8	6.8	8.5	19.6

Profitability [A]	2004	2005	2006	TTM
Return on Assets %	7.7	8.0	8.4	8.6
Oper Cash Flow $Mil	389	467	569	613
- Cap Spending $Mil	51	71	81	82
= Free Cash Flow $Mil	338	396	488	531

Financial Health [A-]	2004	2005	2006	08-31-06
Long-term Debt $Mil	—	—	—	—
Total Equity $Mil	1,200	1,386	1,655	1,828
Debt/Equity Ratio	—	—	—	—

Competition	Market Cap $Mil	12 Mo Trailing Sales $Mil	Price/Cash Flow	Return On Assets%	Debt/ Equity	Total Return% 1 Yr	Total Return% 3 Yr
Paychex	15,069	1,785	24.6	8.6	—	5.6	4.1
Automatic Data Processing	27,117	9,177	17.2	6.1	0.0	9.1	8.8
Intuit	10,637	2,400	13.0	14.2	0.0	14.5	5.3

Price Volatility
Monthly Price High/Low — Relative Strength to S&P 500

Annual $Price High/Low	51.00 / 28.27	42.15 / 20.39	40.54 / 23.76	39.12 / 28.83	43.37 / 28.60	42.37 / 32.98
	2001	2002	2003	2004	2005	2006

Annual Total Return %	-27.2	-19.2	35.3	-7.1	13.7	5.6

Fiscal Year-End: May	2002	2003	2004	2005	2006	TTM
Revenue $Mil	955	1,099	1,294	1,445	1,675	1,785
Net Income $Mil	275	293	303	369	465	505
Earnings Per Share $	0.73	0.78	0.80	0.97	1.22	1.32
Shares Outstanding Mil	376	376	379	380	378	381
Return on Equity %	29.7	27.2	25.2	26.6	28.1	27.6
Net Margin %	28.7	26.7	23.4	25.5	27.8	28.3
Asset Turnover	0.3	0.3	0.3	0.3	0.3	0.3
Financial Leverage	3.2	3.4	3.3	3.3	3.4	3.2

Valuation Ratios	Stock	Rel to Industry	Rel to S&P 500
Price/Earnings	30.0	1.3	1.5
Price/Book	8.2	1.6	2.0
Price/Sales	8.4	2.3	2.9
Price/Cash Flow	24.6	1.2	1.7

Major Fund Holders	% of Fund Assets
Fidelity Select IT Services	7.50
The MP 63	4.48
William Blair Large Cap Growth N	4.15
William Blair Mid Cap Growth N	3.85

Thesis   By Kristan Rowland, 12-05-06   Stock Price as of Analysis: $39.62

Paychex is the leading payroll and human-resources services firm for small businesses, and it enjoys a wide moat due to its scale and high barriers to entry. It boasts a highly developed operating infrastructure, giving the firm a sound platform to execute its strategy. Its average core client has only 17 employees, and a new player would find the costs to acquire these small clients to be quite high. Each additional client it adds to this platform is highly profitable as most of its costs are fixed. Over the past 11 years, Paychex's operating margins have increased nicely (from 19% in 1995 to about 39% in 2006), a result of its scalable model.

Paychex benefits from its massive client base of small businesses in several ways. No single client represents a material portion of its revenue and switching costs are high, which gives it some pricing power. Also a result of high switching costs, it enjoys client retention of about 80%, giving Paychex good future cash-flow visibility. Small-business owners that outsource payroll generally don't like the hassle of keeping abreast of tax changes, etc., so once Paychex has an employer's financial information, the client usually sticks with it. The majority of its client losses occur as they go out of business. Paychex's ancillary offerings, including time and attendance systems, should help increase revenues and retention, as its clients depend on the firm for more key services. Its 543,000-strong client base should provide ample opportunities for generating revenues from these other services.

According to management, Paychex's potential market comprises 7.6 million businesses, which provides a large client-expansion opportunity. We forecast only 4% net new client growth over the next few years, versus management's long-term goal of 5%. Paychex's net client growth has been modest the past three years at 3.1%, 3.4%, and 4%, respectively. Two headwinds for Paychex include replacing 20% of its client base annually and penetrating the small business market. Paychex largely relies on referrals (66%) for new business.

Low interest rates over the past few years put a damper on operating margin expansion, but this trend has changed with Federal Reserve rate increases. The funds rate dipped as low as 1% in 2004 but now stands at 5.25%, and Paychex's operating margins fell to 33.5% in 2004 but have recovered to over 40%. We forecast further improvement as Paychex adds more clients and generates more revenues from its existing client base.

Data as of 12-29-06

PepsiCo PEP

	Rating	Fair Value	Last Close	Consider Buy	Consider Sell	Yield %
	★★★★	$74.00	$62.55	$63.10	$97.20	1.86

Company Profile

PepsiCo produces snack foods, which account for 58% of revenue, through its Frito-Lay division. Brands include Lay's, Ruffles, Fritos, and Doritos. The company also produces beverages, which account for 37% of revenue. Brands include Pepsi-Cola, Diet Pepsi, Mountain Dew, Gatorade, Aquafina, and Tropicana. Coffee and tea drinks are produced through joint ventures with Starbucks and Unilever. About 5% of PepsiCo's sales come from oatmeal and branded grain (Quaker) products.

Management   Stewardship Grade [B]

Indra Nooyi became CEO in October 2006 and former CEO Steve Reinemund will relinquish his role as chairman in May 2007. We think Nooyi is an excellent choice to replace Reinemund as CEO, though she may need to rein in some of her outspoken ways now that she's in the spotlight. That other large consumer product companies, such as Kraft, Sara Lee, and ConAgra, have chosen former PepsiCo managers as their CEOs does not surprise us, as PepsiCo routinely sets the bar for excellence in packaged food and beverages and seems to constantly be one step in front of its rivals. The company has a strong managerial bench, and recent turnover does not worry us, and we have a strong suspicion that the brain drain will continue as other consumer product firms will likely raid PepsiCo's well-stocked cupboard. Management salaries are generally reasonable overall, with a large portion of total compensation variable and performance-based. PepsiCo's corporate governance is fairly strong, and we hope that the CEO and chairman roles will stay permanently separated when Reinemund retires in May. We think the company's relationship with its bottlers is a bit of a worry because, in our opinion, PepsiCo effectively controls these entities, yet does not consolidate their operations on its books.

700 Anderson Hill Road   www.pepsico.com
Purchase, NY 10577-1444

Growth [B+]	2002	2003	2004	2005
Revenue %	6.8	7.4	8.5	11.3
Earnings/Share %	—	NMF	19.0	-2.0
Book Value/Share %	—	NMF	14.9	6.6
Dividends/Share %	3.5	5.9	34.9	18.8

Profitability [A+]	2003	2004	2005	TTM
Return on Assets %	14.1	15.1	12.9	15.4
Oper Cash Flow $Mil	4,328	5,054	5,852	5,586
- Cap Spending $Mil	1,345	1,387	1,736	2,070
= Free Cash Flow $Mil	2,983	3,667	4,116	3,516

Financial Health [A+]	2003	2004	2005	09-30-06
Long-term Debt $Mil	1,702	2,397	2,313	2,528
Total Equity $Mil	11,833	13,482	14,210	15,967
Debt/Equity Ratio	0.1	0.2	0.2	0.2

Industry	Business Risk	Moat Size	Investment Style	Sector
Beverage Mfg.	Below Avg	Wide	Large Core	Consumer Goods

Competition	Market Cap $Mil	12 Mo Trailing Sales $Mil	Price/Cash Flow	Return On Assets%	Debt/ Equity	Total Return% 1 Yr	3 Yr
PepsiCo	102,712	34,850	18.4	15.4	0.2	7.9	12.4
Coca-Cola	113,088	23,707	19.6	16.8	0.1	23.1	1.1
Cadbury Schweppes PLC ADR	22,367	11,879	11.2	7.5	1.0	14.7	15.2

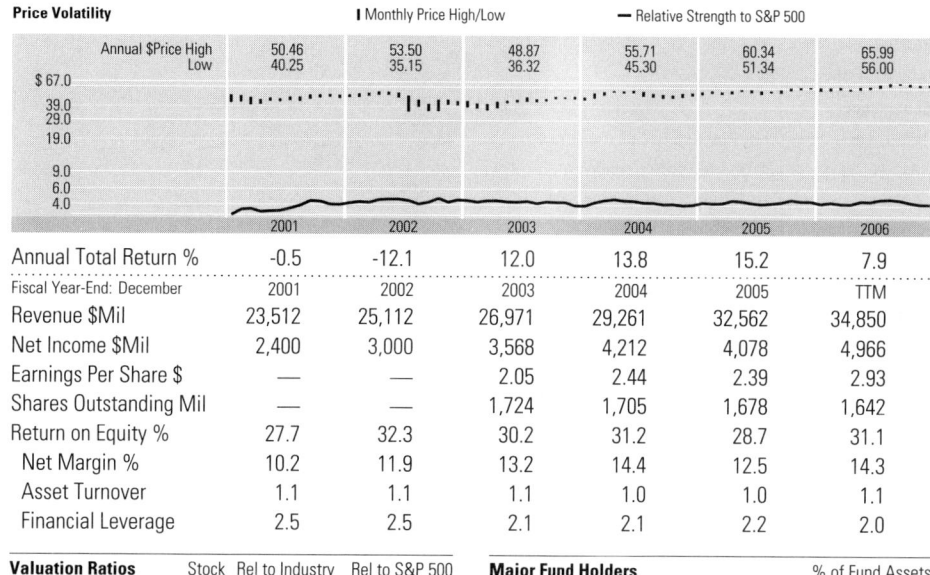

Price Volatility — Monthly Price High/Low — Relative Strength to S&P 500

	2001	2002	2003	2004	2005	2006
Annual $Price High	50.46	53.50	48.87	55.71	60.34	65.99
Low	40.25	35.15	36.32	45.30	51.34	56.00
Annual Total Return %	-0.5	-12.1	12.0	13.8	15.2	7.9

Fiscal Year-End: December	2001	2002	2003	2004	2005	TTM
Revenue $Mil	23,512	25,112	26,971	29,261	32,562	34,850
Net Income $Mil	2,400	3,000	3,568	4,212	4,078	4,966
Earnings Per Share $	—	—	2.05	2.44	2.39	2.93
Shares Outstanding Mil	—	—	1,724	1,705	1,678	1,642
Return on Equity %	27.7	32.3	30.2	31.2	28.7	31.1
Net Margin %	10.2	11.9	13.2	14.4	12.5	14.3
Asset Turnover	1.1	1.1	1.1	1.0	1.0	1.1
Financial Leverage	2.5	2.5	2.1	2.1	2.2	2.0

Valuation Ratios	Stock	Rel to Industry	Rel to S&P 500
Price/Earnings	21.3	1.0	1.0
Price/Book	6.4	1.1	1.6
Price/Sales	2.9	0.9	1.0
Price/Cash Flow	18.4	1.1	1.3

Major Fund Holders	% of Fund Assets
ProFunds Consumer Goods UltraSector Inv	6.65
Fidelity Advisor Consumer Disc A	5.42
Fidelity Select Consumer Staples	5.27
JHFunds2 U.S. Global Lead Gr NAV	5.02

Thesis By Matthew Reilly, 11-27-06 Stock Price as of Analysis: $61.50

PepsiCo sets the standard for consumer products companies, deriving sales and profit growth from its dominant position in salty snacks and its formidable presence in beverages. The company's international prospects remain bright, and we think that its moat is among the largest of any consumer product manufacturer.

PepsiCo has recently excelled in every facet of the game consumer products companies play. This starts at the top, with excellent management, a strong grasp of changing consumer tastes and preferences, and a relentless commitment to innovation. The balancing act between pricing and volume is usually close to optimally performed by PepsiCo, and in most competitive situations the company simply wins.

This is not to say everything is ducky. PepsiCo likely will face a difficult commodity cost environment in 2007, with price of many inputs such as corn (used both in salty snacks and to make sweeteners), aluminum, and PET resin at or near all-time highs. However, we have seen the company navigate difficult price-increase versus volume-drop trade-offs in the past, and we have no reason to doubt its competence now.

Another area of concern regarding PepsiCo is that many of its products can accurately be labeled "junk" food. While health and wellness trends have changed over the past few years, we think that PepsiCo functions best and most profitably when it delivers the consumers the products that they demand. PepsiCo has expanded its arsenal of healthier products in recent years, and it also has brands such as Dole, Quaker, and Tropicana that enjoy reputations for being healthy. We think that changing consumer tastes favor the nimble and forward thinking, and therefore PepsiCo.

We also believe that international operations will continue to see margin expansion. PepsiCo International should continue to solidify its position as the dominant international salty snack maker and increase beverage volumes in markets with attractive growth prospects. The international unit has delivered fantastic results over the past few years, as operating margins increased from 11.7% in 2002 to 14.1% in 2005 and revenue increased by almost 14% annually, and 2006 has seen no slowdown.

PepsiCo's innovation pipeline for 2007 seems extremely strong, from soft drinks to Flat Earth vegetable and fruit chips, and the company has done a good job increasing its presence with growing retailers such as Whole Foods. We think that the rationale for investing in PepsiCo is intact.

PetroChina Company ADR PTR

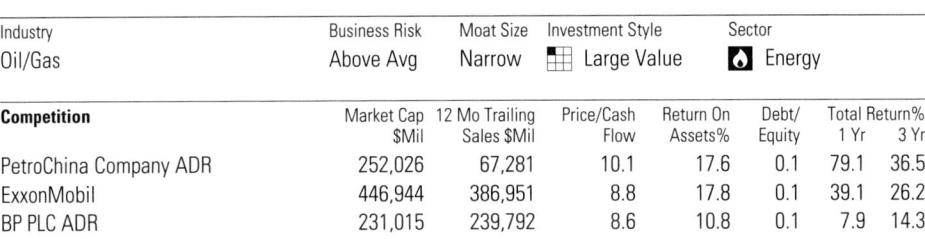

	Rating	Fair Value	Last Close	Consider Buy	Consider Sell	Yield %
	★	$104.00	$140.78	$66.30	$125.40	3.40

Industry	Business Risk	Moat Size	Investment Style	Sector
Oil/Gas	Above Avg	Narrow	Large Value	Energy

Company Profile

PetroChina was established in 1999 when state-owned China National Petroleum was restructured into three companies. In addition to finding and developing oil and gas, PetroChina owns and operates refineries, storage facilities, chemical factories, and China's largest pipeline network. The vast majority of PetroChina's operations are located in mainland China, though it is beginning to expand internationally with investments in markets such as Indonesia and Canada.

Management   Stewardship Grade [NA]

The Chinese government owns 90% of the firm's Class A shares, which do not trade publicly, and is in a position to elect PetroChina's board. Several board members seem to have been chosen for their government and Communist Party ties, not their stock ownership or business experience, which is just one indication of how the government's interests may conflict with minority shareholders' interests. Moreover, China's nascent corporate law does not offer the same shareholder rights and protections found in many other jurisdictions. We like aspects of the firm's compensation policy. One fourth of the top executives' compensation comes from salary, while another 25% comes in a performance-based bonus. Half of the executives' compensation is from stock-appreciation rights, which is a cash bonus based on growth in the firm's stock price. However, stock-appreciation rights do not carry any downside risk, so executive pay is not affected if the share price falls. We'd prefer to see actual stock ownership.

World Tower, 16 Andelu   www.petrochina.com.cn
Beijing, China 100011

Growth [NA]	2002	2003	2004	2005
Revenue %	—	NMF	28.0	39.0
Earnings/Share %	3.8	48.1	47.5	27.1
Book Value/Share %	8.2	10.4	18.9	20.3
Dividends/Share %	—	—	—	—

Profitability [NA]	2003	2004	2005	TTM
Return on Assets %	12.9	16.9	17.6	17.6
Oper Cash Flow $Mil	16,836	17,092	24,840	24,840
- Cap Spending $Mil	10,083	11,344	14,526	14,526
= Free Cash Flow $Mil	6,753	5,747	10,314	10,314

Financial Health [NA]	2003	2004	2005	12-31-05
Long-term Debt $Mil	6,224	5,386	5,523	5,523
Total Equity $Mil	44,257	53,434	67,369	67,369
Debt/Equity Ratio	0.1	0.1	0.1	0.1

Competition	Market Cap $Mil	12 Mo Trailing Sales $Mil	Price/Cash Flow	Return On Assets %	Debt/ Equity	Total Return% 1 Yr	3 Yr
PetroChina Company ADR	252,026	67,281	10.1	17.6	0.1	79.1	36.5
ExxonMobil	446,944	386,951	8.8	17.8	0.1	39.1	26.2
BP PLC ADR	231,015	239,792	8.6	10.8	0.1	7.9	14.3

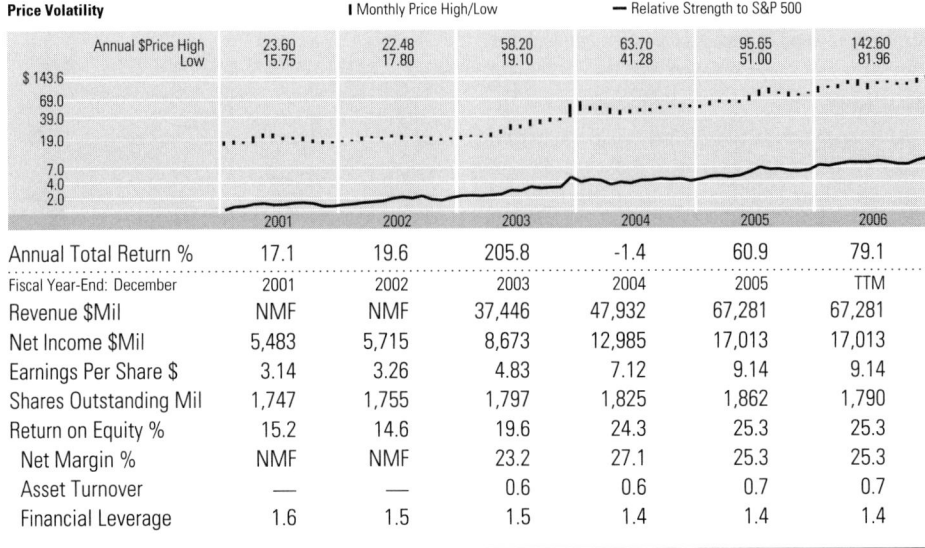

	2001	2002	2003	2004	2005	2006
Annual $Price High	23.60	22.48	58.20	63.70	95.65	142.60
Low	15.75	17.80	19.10	41.28	51.00	81.96
Annual Total Return %	17.1	19.6	205.8	-1.4	60.9	79.1

Fiscal Year-End: December	2001	2002	2003	2004	2005	TTM
Revenue $Mil	NMF	NMF	37,446	47,932	67,281	67,281
Net Income $Mil	5,483	5,715	8,673	12,985	17,013	17,013
Earnings Per Share $	3.14	3.26	4.83	7.12	9.14	9.14
Shares Outstanding Mil	1,747	1,755	1,797	1,825	1,862	1,790
Return on Equity %	15.2	14.6	19.6	24.3	25.3	25.3
Net Margin %	NMF	NMF	23.2	27.1	25.3	25.3
Asset Turnover	—	—	0.6	0.6	0.7	0.7
Financial Leverage	1.6	1.5	1.5	1.4	1.4	1.4

Valuation Ratios	Stock	Rel to Industry	Rel to S&P 500
Price/Earnings	15.4	1.2	0.7
Price/Book	3.7	1.2	0.9
Price/Sales	3.7	1.9	1.3
Price/Cash Flow	10.1	1.2	0.7

Major Fund Holders	% of Fund Assets
Quaker Core Equity A	3.98
Quaker Small Cap Growth I	3.83
ICON Energy	3.41
U.S. Global Investors China Reg Opp	3.02

Thesis By Michael Cumming, CFA, 11-21-06 Stock Price as of Analysis: $115.76

PetroChina dominates a protected, growing market that includes one sixth of the world's population. This narrow-moat giant should remain highly profitable for many years to come.

PetroChina is the largest of the three publicly traded Chinese oil companies and is affiliated with the largest state-owned oil company in China, China National Petroleum (CNPC). PetroChina has a significant presence in all aspects of the Chinese energy sector, from major exploration and production operations to the largest network of retail outlets. It has used this position to generate healthy free cash flow and profits throughout its existence. The firm's protected market has grown exponentially in recent years; China accounted for 45% of the growth in world oil demand between 2000 and 2004.

Continuing its run of strong performance will be more difficult going forward. Domestic energy supplies have proved insufficient to satisfy China's voracious demand growth, which will force PetroChina to develop an increasing portion of its oil and natural gas from foreign sources. This is where PetroChina's relationship with its parent comes in handy: CNPC acquires foreign reserves, then sells portions of only the best properties to PetroChina. So long as CNPC places value in boosting PetroChina's profits, PetroChina should be able to grow its foreign reserve base at reasonable prices. Finding enough foreign reserves to move the needle for such a large company could be difficult, though.

Further challenges will come from competition in PetroChina's home market, which will be gradually opened to foreign firms as part of the reforms mandated by China's accession into the World Trade Organization. Beginning in 2007, foreign firms will be allowed to own retail filling stations outside of joint ventures with Chinese companies; other changes could come later. We doubt that exploration and production--where PetroChina makes most of its profits--will be fully opened to foreign competition anytime soon, so loss of market share downstream is not a big concern.

PetroChina's reliance on the growth of the Chinese market could later haunt the company. All of PetroChina's production is consumed domestically, making the firm entirely dependent on China. The company will suffer if China's economy falters, which we think is a distinct possibility. Moreover, with the state owning 90% of its stock and mandating much of the firm's capital spending, we doubt PetroChina will be able to mitigate the impact of an economic downturn with cuts in personnel and investments.

Data as of 12-29-06

Petroleo Brasileiro ADR PBR

Rating	Fair Value	Last Close	Consider Buy	Consider Sell	Yield %
★	$78.00	$102.99	$49.70	$94.10	3.70

Industry	Business Risk	Moat Size	Investment Style	Sector
Oil/Gas	Above Avg	Narrow	Large Value	Energy

Company Profile

Petrobras is an integrated energy firm controlled by the Brazilian government. At the end of 2005, the firm posted proven reserves of 11.8 billion barrels of oil equivalent (boe) with average daily production of 2.2 million boe. Petrobras' daily refining capacity is greater than 2 million barrels, representing more than 98% of Brazil's total refining capacity. The company also has 7,000 retail outlets in Brazil.

Management Stewardship Grade [NA]

The Brazilian government owns a majority of the voting shares of Petrobras, and thus controls the selection of Petrobras' management. As such, management is prone to change with each new government. The current team is no exception. Chairman Dilma Vana Rousseff and newly appointed president and CEO Jose Sergio Gabrielli de Azevedo have extensive resumes in bureaucracy and academia. Petrobras' strategy has also undergone many revisions, depending on the reigning political leadership. Individual investors in Petrobras are minority shareholders with the Brazilian government. At Petrobras, it is quite possible that the creation of long-term value for shareholders will take a back seat to Brazil's social and political agendas.

Av. Republica do Chile 65, 23 Andar Centro
Rio de Janeiro, Brazil 20031-912 www.petrobras.com.br

Growth [NA]	2002	2003	2004	2005
Revenue %	-7.9	36.7	24.3	46.6
Earnings/Share %	-33.6	181.7	-6.0	67.4
Book Value/Share %	-39.7	93.8	32.2	59.0
Dividends/Share %	-29.8	60.1	-5.4	-13.2

Profitability [NA]	2003	2004	2005	TTM
Return on Assets %	12.2	9.8	13.2	13.2
Oper Cash Flow $Mil	8,569	8,155	15,115	15,115
- Cap Spending $Mil	6,551	7,718	10,365	10,365
= Free Cash Flow $Mil	2,018	437	4,750	4,750

Financial Health [NA]	2003	2004	2005	12-31-05
Long-term Debt $Mil	11,888	13,214	12,518	12,518
Total Equity $Mil	13,363	17,734	28,145	28,145
Debt/Equity Ratio	0.9	0.7	0.4	0.4

Competition

	Market Cap $Mil	12 Mo Trailing Sales $Mil	Price/Cash Flow	Return On Assets %	Debt/Equity	Total Return % 1 Yr	3 Yr
Petroleo Brasileiro ADR	112,932	56,324	7.5	13.2	0.4	51.1	56.8
PetroChina Company ADR	252,026	67,281	10.1	17.6	0.1	79.1	36.5
China Petroleum & Chemica	80,321	100,284	8.6	8.0	0.3	92.3	26.9

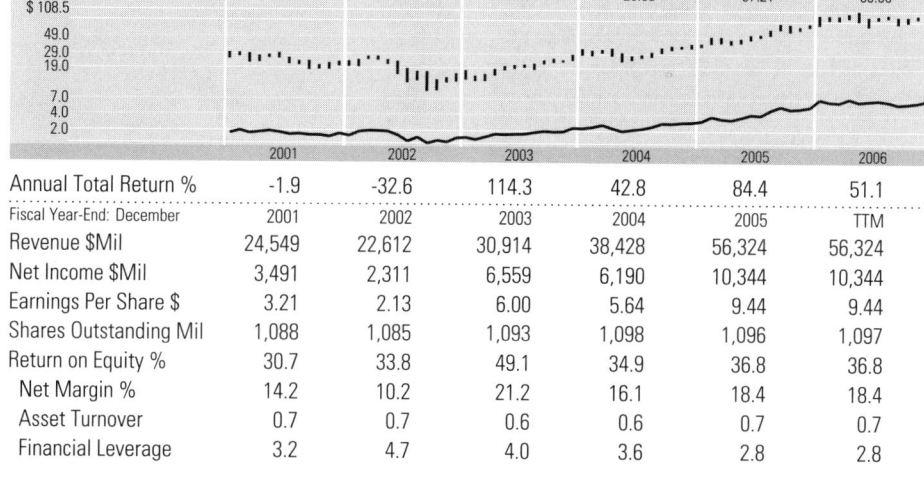

Price Volatility — Monthly Price High/Low — Relative Strength to S&P 500

	2001	2002	2003	2004	2005	2006
Annual $Price High	30.50	27.42	29.35	40.57	74.20	107.45
Low	18.01	9.34	12.84	23.69	37.21	69.00
Annual Total Return %	-1.9	-32.6	114.3	42.8	84.4	51.1

Fiscal Year-End: December	2001	2002	2003	2004	2005	TTM
Revenue $Mil	24,549	22,612	30,914	38,428	56,324	56,324
Net Income $Mil	3,491	2,311	6,559	6,190	10,344	10,344
Earnings Per Share $	3.21	2.13	6.00	5.64	9.44	9.44
Shares Outstanding Mil	1,088	1,085	1,093	1,098	1,096	1,097
Return on Equity %	30.7	33.8	49.1	34.9	36.8	36.8
Net Margin %	14.2	10.2	21.2	16.1	18.4	18.4
Asset Turnover	0.7	0.7	0.6	0.6	0.7	0.7
Financial Leverage	3.2	4.7	4.0	3.6	2.8	2.8

Valuation Ratios	Stock	Rel to Industry	Rel to S&P 500
Price/Earnings	11.1	0.9	0.5
Price/Book	4.0	1.3	1.0
Price/Sales	2.0	1.1	0.7
Price/Cash Flow	7.5	0.9	0.5

Major Fund Holders	% of Fund Assets
T. Rowe Price Latin America	8.33
Dunham Emerging Markets Stock N	5.78
Fidelity Latin America	5.24
Fidelity Advisor Latin America A	5.21

Thesis By Elizabeth Collins, 11-27-06 Stock Price as of Analysis: $89.08

Despite its upstream focus and large competitive advantage, Petrobras carries more risk than the typical integrated energy company. Most of Petrobras' valuable upstream assets are in a developing country, Brazil, so investors should expect volatility.

We like that the lion's share of Petrobras' operating profit comes from the upstream operation. Of all the businesses run by integrated energy firms, we think upstream operations offer the best long-term profit potential. OPEC uses its hefty market power to influence global oil supplies, promoting the health of nearly all upstream producers. Thus, we award Petrobras a narrow economic moat rating. Petrobras also has a huge competitive advantage: It has exclusive rights to harvest oil from its existing upstream properties. And, the company has noteworthy deep-water expertise.

However, being based in Brazil has repercussions. In 1995, Brazil began taking strides to increase competition in its oil industry, and Petrobras officially lost its government-sponsored monopoly. Yet the government still regularly interferes in energy markets. This partial deregulation has led to three major drawbacks for the firm.

First, in valuing a company's upstream business, location and mobility of reserves are key. About 90% of Petrobras' reserves are in Brazil. Because of government interference, Petrobras is sometimes forced to sell products below international market prices. If government intervention worsens, Petrobras' average selling prices could slip or its costs could rise, in which case we might have to reduce our moat rating.

Second, foreign and private competition in Brazil has increased over the past decade. Although the pace has been slower than one might expect (Petrobras' strategic advantage has forced rivals to fight an uphill battle), the government's move to encourage competition is being felt. When refined product prices slump in Brazil, Petrobras' competitors are free to export products to receive better prices. But Petrobras adheres to a policy of social obligation to supply Brazilian demand below market prices during these times. In the past, Petrobras was compensated for this. Today, it's not so lucky.

Third, the government controls the majority of Petrobras' voting stock. As such, Petrobras' management and strategy will probably change with each new administration, and we think individual shareholders' interests will take a back seat to the government's.

Data as of 12-29-06

PetSmart PETM

	Rating	Fair Value	Last Close	Consider Buy	Consider Sell	Yield %
	★★★★	$34.00	$28.86	$26.20	$42.60	0.42

Company Profile

PetSmart sells pet food, supplies, and professional services. It operates more than 885 North American stores, which range in size from 19,000 to 27,000 square feet and are generally located near major shopping centers. It also reaches customers through mail-order catalogs and its Web site. PetSmart is the largest provider of grooming and pet-training services in the United States. Vet care is also available in about two thirds of its stores, mostly through a strategic relationship with Banfield.

Management   Stewardship Grade [B]

Philip Francis has served as CEO since March 1998 and was named chairman in September 1999. We believe these roles should be split for better corporate governance. In fiscal 2005, Francis was paid a salary and bonus of $1.8 million, which we viewed as reasonable, given his excellent long-term record. In the five years that ended in fiscal 2005, total shareholder returns exceeded 530%. The CEO was also awarded a generous package of $1.4 million in restricted stock and 95,000 options.

Overall, the board and management have demonstrated good stewardship. We like the fact that directors and officers are now required to own a multiple of their annual retainer/base salary in company stock, including 5 times for board members and the CEO. However, we think directors should be subject to election annually, rather than every three years. We also take a dim view of the company's poison pill and other takeover defenses, which could favor the interests of management over shareholders.

19601 North 27th Avenue www.petsmart.com
Phoenix, AZ 85027

Growth [B+]	2003	2004	2005	2006
Revenue %	7.8	11.1	12.4	11.8
Earnings/Share %	96.4	54.5	23.5	19.0
Book Value/Share %	74.3	20.3	16.9	-0.8
Dividends/Share %	NMF	NMF	200.0	0.0

Profitability [B+]	2004	2005	2006	TTM
Return on Assets %	8.8	9.4	9.8	8.8
Oper Cash Flow $Mil	219	256	342	313
- Cap Spending $Mil	159	144	166	198
= Free Cash Flow $Mil	60	113	177	114

Financial Health [A]	2004	2005	2006	10-31-06
Long-term Debt $Mil	—	244	352	421
Total Equity $Mil	817	974	941	948
Debt/Equity Ratio	—	0.3	0.4	0.4

Industry	Business Risk	Moat Size	Investment Style	Sector
Specialty Retail	Average	Narrow	Mid Growth	Consumer Services

Competition	Market Cap $Mil	12 Mo Trailing Sales $Mil	Price/Cash Flow	Return On Assets%	Debt/ Equity	Total Return% 1 Yr	3 Yr
PetSmart	3,917	4,118	12.5	8.8	0.4	13.0	7.2
Wal-Mart Stores	192,479	339,150	9.8	7.2	0.5	0.1	-2.9
Target	49,000	56,727	11.3	6.9	0.6	4.7	15.6

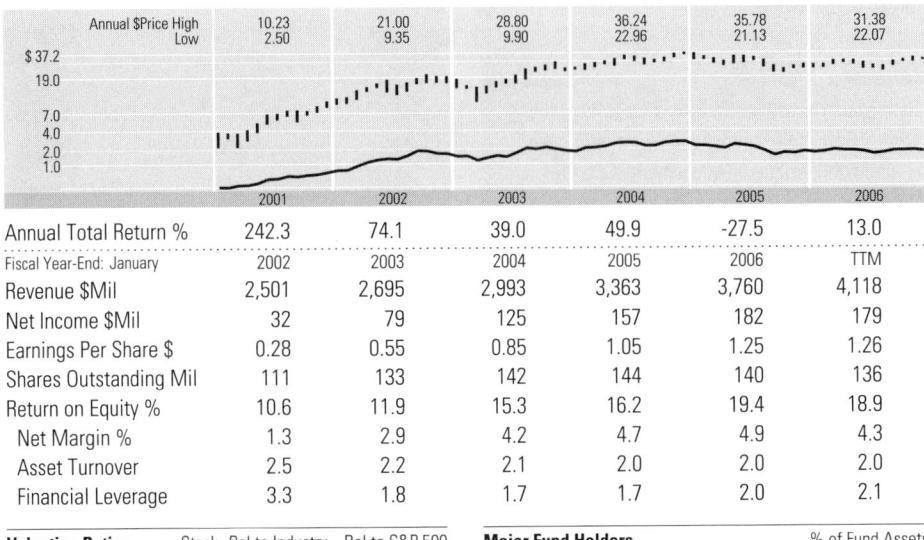

	2001	2002	2003	2004	2005	2006
Annual $Price High	10.23	21.00	28.80	36.24	35.78	31.38
Low	2.50	9.35	9.90	22.96	21.13	22.07
Annual Total Return %	242.3	74.1	39.0	49.9	-27.5	13.0

Fiscal Year-End: January	2002	2003	2004	2005	2006	TTM
Revenue $Mil	2,501	2,695	2,993	3,363	3,760	4,118
Net Income $Mil	32	79	125	157	182	179
Earnings Per Share $	0.28	0.55	0.85	1.05	1.25	1.26
Shares Outstanding Mil	111	133	142	144	140	136
Return on Equity %	10.6	11.9	15.3	16.2	19.4	18.9
Net Margin %	1.3	2.9	4.2	4.7	4.9	4.3
Asset Turnover	2.5	2.2	2.1	2.0	2.0	2.0
Financial Leverage	3.3	1.8	1.7	1.7	2.0	2.1

Valuation Ratios	Stock	Rel to Industry	Rel to S&P 500
Price/Earnings	22.9	1.0	1.1
Price/Book	4.1	1.1	1.0
Price/Sales	1.0	1.0	0.3
Price/Cash Flow	12.5	0.7	0.9

Major Fund Holders	% of Fund Assets
Brown Advisory Opportunity Instl	5.19
Brown Advisory Small-Cap Growth I	2.79
Dreyfus Premier S&P Stars T	2.48
Phoenix Fundamental Growth A	2.28

Thesis By John Owens, CFA, CPA, 12-11-06 Stock Price as of Analysis: $29.63

We believe PetSmart will strengthen its leadership position over the debt-loaded Petco. While competition from big box retailers is on the rise, the company's unmatched range of product and services should continue to drive customer traffic to its stores. We're also optimistic about PetSmart's fast-growing services business.

Following its buyout, PetSmart's rival, Petco, is now highly levered, with $1.35 billion of debt, representing about two thirds of its total capital. As a result, the company needs to focus on paying down debt, which should mean a slower pace of expansion and less investment in its stores. It is also possible that Petco will be less aggressive on pricing. (PetSmart already offers prices about 10% lower than those of Petco and other pet specialty shops).

So we believe Petco, under its new ownership structure, poses less of a threat to PetSmart. Due to this changing competitive dynamic, PetSmart's management has decided to accelerate investments in its stores, supply chain, and information technology. We like the fact that the company is willing to sacrifice some profits in the near term to improve its competitive advantage, which we believe should lead to increased earnings over the long run.

PetSmart, however, does face growing competition from Target and Wal-Mart. Both have expanded their pet sections over the years. Target recently launched its own brand of premium pet food named LIFELong. The cheap chic retailer also offers collars, leashes, apparel, and other pet supplies from fashion designers like Isaac Mizrahi and Michael Graves. Wal-Mart, which already has the number-one-selling dry dog food (Ol' Roy), is also going upscale, with its recent rollout premium pet food brand Natural Life.

Still, these big box retailers do not offer PetSmart's premium brands and owners are generally reluctant to switch their pet's main dish. The company's superstores also sell a much broader range of pet products and offer grooming, training, and even vet care at most locations, all of which are not available at the big-box retailers. Another differentiating factor is PetsHotels, in-store dog and cat boarding facilities. PetSmart now envisions an ultimate construction of 435 PetsHotels, up from its initial projection of 300. Management estimates that PetSmart stores which add a PetsHotel should be able to generate 29% more revenue and nearly double the pretax income (versus stores without boarding facilities) within five years' time.

Data as of 12-29-06

Pfizer PFE

	Rating	Fair Value	Last Close	Consider Buy	Consider Sell	Yield %
	★★★	$29.00	$25.90	$22.40	$36.30	3.71

Industry	Business Risk	Moat Size	Investment Style	Sector
Drugs	Average	Wide	Large Value	Healthcare

Company Profile

Pfizer is the world's largest pharmaceutical firm, with annual sales near $50 billion. After the sale of its consumer health-care division to J&J, prescription drugs will account for more than 90% of sales. Top sellers include cholesterol-lowering Lipitor, antidepressant Zoloft, Viagra for impotence, and Norvasc for hypertension. Recently approved drugs with blockbuster potential include oncology drug Sutent and Lyrica for epilepsy and some types of neuropathic pain.

Management   Stewardship Grade [C]

Pfizer named Jeffrey Kindler to the CEO post in July 2006, replacing Hank McKinnell almost two years before McKinnell's expected mandatory retirement in early 2008. McKinnell will remain chairman of the board until February 2007. We expect the transition will be relatively smooth, as Kindler has been on the executive committee at Pfizer since 2002, when he joined the company. With his background in corporate law, Kindler brings little direct pharmaceutical experience compared with 35-year Pfizer veteran McKinnell. However, with the industry increasingly having to focus on patent challenges and other legal and regulatory issues, we think Kindler could prove to be well suited for the job. In 2005, Pfizer instituted annual elections for every board member, which we believe is more shareholder-friendly than the previous staggered elections. Accounting transparency is not ideal, largely because of financial distortions caused by frequent acquisitions. Kindler has taken some initial steps to make information on the firm's pipeline more available to investors, which gives us hope that transparency overall will improve under his leadership.

235 East 42nd Street
New York, NY 10017-5755
www.pfizer.com

Growth [C]	2002	2003	2004	2005
Revenue %	11.6	38.5	17.4	-2.3
Earnings/Share %	19.7	-63.0	175.9	-26.8
Book Value/Share %	11.4	182.9	-1.1	-1.2
Dividends/Share %	18.2	15.4	13.3	11.8

Profitability [A]	2003	2004	2005	TTM
Return on Assets %	3.3	9.2	6.9	11.6
Oper Cash Flow $Mil	11,727	16,340	14,733	17,855
- Cap Spending $Mil	2,629	2,601	2,106	2,051
= Free Cash Flow $Mil	9,098	13,739	12,627	15,804

Financial Health [A+]	2003	2004	2005	09-30-06
Long-term Debt $Mil	5,755	7,279	6,347	5,561
Total Equity $Mil	65,377	68,085	65,458	69,566
Debt/Equity Ratio	0.1	0.1	0.1	0.1

Competition	Market Cap $Mil	12 Mo Trailing Sales $Mil	Price/Cash Flow	Return On Assets%	Debt/ Equity	Total Return% 1 Yr	3 Yr
Pfizer	186,751	52,208	10.5	11.6	0.1	15.2	-7.4
GlaxoSmithKline PLC ADR	157,300	39,536	14.5	18.7	0.7	8.0	7.6
Merck	94,656	22,358	13.0	11.6	0.2	42.7	1.7

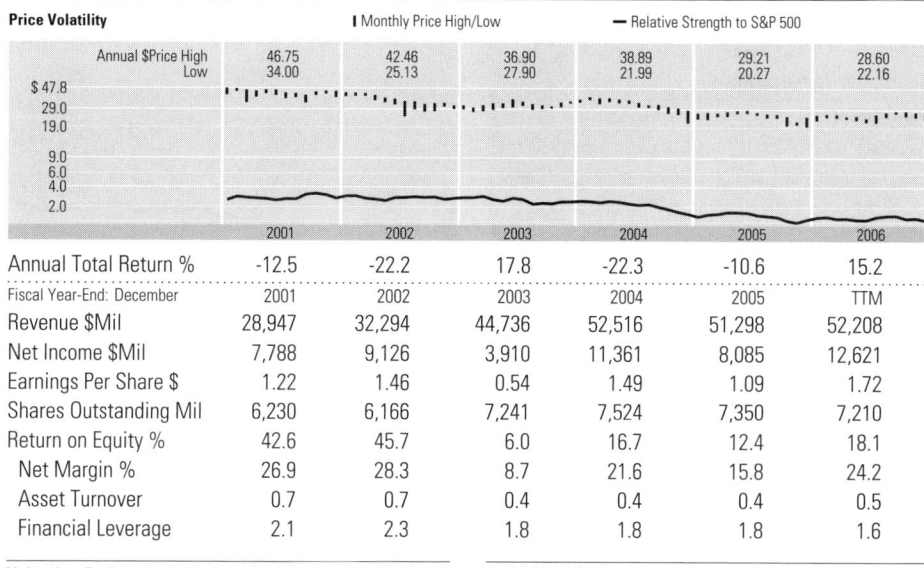

	2001	2002	2003	2004	2005	2006
Annual $Price High	46.75	42.46	36.90	38.89	29.21	28.60
Low	34.00	25.13	27.90	21.99	20.27	22.16
Annual Total Return %	-12.5	-22.2	17.8	-22.3	-10.6	15.2

Fiscal Year-End: December	2001	2002	2003	2004	2005	TTM
Revenue $Mil	28,947	32,294	44,736	52,516	51,298	52,208
Net Income $Mil	7,788	9,126	3,910	11,361	8,085	12,621
Earnings Per Share $	1.22	1.46	0.54	1.49	1.09	1.72
Shares Outstanding Mil	6,230	6,166	7,241	7,524	7,350	7,210
Return on Equity %	42.6	45.7	6.0	16.7	12.4	18.1
Net Margin %	26.9	28.3	8.7	21.6	15.8	24.2
Asset Turnover	0.7	0.7	0.4	0.4	0.4	0.5
Financial Leverage	2.1	2.3	1.8	1.8	1.8	1.6

Valuation Ratios	Stock	Rel to Industry	Rel to S&P 500
Price/Earnings	15.1	0.6	0.7
Price/Book	2.7	0.5	0.7
Price/Sales	3.6	0.8	1.2
Price/Cash Flow	10.5	0.6	0.7

Major Fund Holders	% of Fund Assets
ProFunds Pharmaceuticals UltraSector Inv	16.76
North Track DJ US Hlth Care 100 A	10.55
Fidelity Select Pharmaceuticals	10.33
Fidelity Select Health Care	9.24

Thesis By Heather Brilliant, CFA, 12-04-06   Stock Price as of Analysis: $24.90

In an industry where size matters, Pfizer dominates the landscape. As the largest pharmaceutical company in the world, Pfizer has the resources to invest more than its competitors--in research and development as well as marketing. This unmatched heft, combined with a broad portfolio of patent-protected drugs, has helped Pfizer build a wide moat around its business.

Being the biggest has conferred certain advantages upon Pfizer. Drug development is largely a numbers game; the more products in the pipeline, the better a firm's chances of getting one of them approved by the Food and Drug Administration. Pfizer has more than 150 drugs in its pipeline and has filed with the FDA for 15 new drug approvals in the past four years. Several of these products have recently received regulatory approval, including cancer drug Sutent and Chantix for smoking cessation, each of which could generate more than $1 billion in annual revenue within the next five years.

Pfizer's investment in drug development doesn't stop once the drug is approved. The firm spends mightily on continuing studies to demonstrate clinical superiority of its products to competing drugs. The results of these studies serve as fodder for Pfizer's industry-leading salesforce. With topnotch drugs in its portfolio and more dollars to allocate to marketing and ongoing studies than any other firm, Pfizer will continue to rule the roost, in our opinion.

However, some major clouds are on the horizon. Several of Pfizer's best-performing drugs, including antidepressant Zoloft, antibacterial treatment Zithromax, and Neurontin for epilepsy, have already lost patent protection and are facing generic competition. Worse, almost all of Pfizer's current portfolio of 10 blockbuster drugs will face a similar fate at some point during the next five years, including cholesterol treatment Lipitor, which currently brings in more than $12 billion in annual sales.

Despite the significant risks involved in surviving such an onslaught of generic competition, we think Pfizer is up to the challenge. We expect several of its pipeline drugs, if approved, to make major contributions to future sales. And with more than $10 billion in annual free cash flow, Pfizer should be able to complement its internal research with in-licensed products and acquisitions.

Data as of 12-29-06

Pharmaceutical Product Development PPDI

	Rating	Fair Value	Last Close	Consider Buy	Consider Sell	Yield %
	★★★	$32.00	$32.22	$24.70	$40.10	0.25

Company Profile

Pharmaceutical Product Development provides clinical research services to pharmaceutical and biotech companies. Through its network of 62 offices in 28 countries, PPD is one of the largest global CROs. The company's business is split in two segments: contract research and development, which accounts for 90% of total revenue, and discovery science, which includes biomarker discovery and compound development. The company derives 30% of its sales outside the United States.

Management   Stewardship Grade [B]

Founder Fred Eshelman has been CEO since 1990 and vice chairman since 1993. Eshelman controls roughly 9% of the outstanding shares of PPD, and directors and executives as a group hold 13%. While we like to see such significant insider ownership, we note that the executives, including Eshelman, have sold more than 700,000 shares in the past six months alone, reaping substantial benefits from the stock's appreciation. Our overall view of the compensation structure is positive: While we think the executive pay and severance packages are rich, PPD's strong cash flows and healthy returns on capital warrant a higher level of compensation. We also give kudos to the management team for its decision to forgo bonuses in 2003 because of slower growth in the company's core business. We like that all directors are elected simultaneously, rather than in staggered terms.

3151 South 17th Street   www.PPDI.com
Wilmington, NC 28412

Growth [B+]	2002	2003	2004	2005
Revenue %	32.1	19.4	15.7	23.3
Earnings/Share %	-23.4	13.9	112.2	29.9
Book Value/Share %	37.3	14.2	23.2	14.1
Dividends/Share %	NMF	NMF	NMF	NMF

Profitability [A]	2003	2004	2005	TTM
Return on Assets %	5.9	10.1	11.4	11.4
Oper Cash Flow $Mil	14	179	191	172
- Cap Spending $Mil	32	49	110	127
= Free Cash Flow $Mil	-18	131	81	45

Financial Health [A]	2003	2004	2005	09-30-06
Long-term Debt $Mil	6	6	23	56
Total Equity $Mil	513	635	742	892
Debt/Equity Ratio	0.0	0.0	0.0	0.1

Industry	Business Risk	Moat Size	Investment Style	Sector
Research Svcs.	Average	Narrow	Mid Growth	Healthcare

Competition	Market Cap $Mil	12 Mo Trailing Sales $Mil	Price/Cash Flow	Return On Assets%	Debt/Equity	Total Return% 1 Yr	3 Yr
Pharmaceutical Product Development	3,777	1,196	21.9	11.4	0.1	4.3	34.3
Covance	3,769	1,390	15.2	10.9	—	21.3	30.1
ICON PLC ADR	1,048	—	—	—	—	83.3	20.3

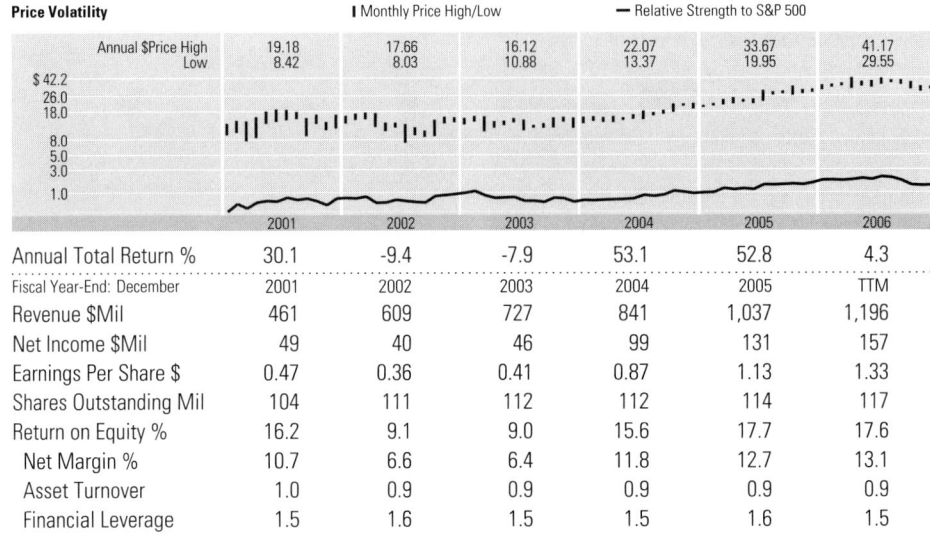

	2001	2002	2003	2004	2005	TTM
Annual Total Return %	30.1	-9.4	-7.9	53.1	52.8	4.3
Fiscal Year-End: December	2001	2002	2003	2004	2005	TTM
Revenue $Mil	461	609	727	841	1,037	1,196
Net Income $Mil	49	40	46	99	131	157
Earnings Per Share $	0.47	0.36	0.41	0.87	1.13	1.33
Shares Outstanding Mil	104	111	112	112	114	117
Return on Equity %	16.2	9.1	9.0	15.6	17.7	17.6
Net Margin %	10.7	6.6	6.4	11.8	12.7	13.1
Asset Turnover	1.0	0.9	0.9	0.9	0.9	0.9
Financial Leverage	1.5	1.6	1.5	1.5	1.6	1.5

Valuation Ratios	Stock	Rel to Industry	Rel to S&P 500	Major Fund Holders	% of Fund Assets
Price/Earnings	24.2	0.8	1.2	Harbor Small Cap Value Instl	3.59
Price/Book	4.2	1.1	1.0	Chase Mid Cap Growth A	3.55
Price/Sales	3.2	0.9	1.1	Sextant Growth	3.48
Price/Cash Flow	21.9	1.1	1.5	Allegiant Small Cap Core I	3.24

Thesis By Alex Morozov, CFA, 12-12-06 Stock Price as of Analysis: $32.49

Pharmaceutical Product Development's clinical development segment is firing on all cylinders. The company is positioned as a leader in late-stage clinical trials and should continue to benefit from favorable industry trends. However, we are taking a wait-and-see approach to the company's compound discovery business.

PPD operates in the contract research industry, which is not overly glamorous but is increasingly instrumental in drug development. While pharmaceutical companies are responsible for the ultimate success of their drugs, companies like PPD and Covance are often hired to do a significant portion of the actual development work. Limited internal development capacity and cost constraints increasingly push pharmaceutical companies to outsource a portion of their development work to contract research organizations (CROs). PPD zeroes in on the most lucrative segment of the drug-development process: late-stage clinical trials.

The number of drugs entering late-stage studies has not changed much over the past 10 years, but the level of complexity associated with Phase III trials has. Many clinical trials now require thousands more patients, an increasing amount of tests per subject, and a significant amount of regulatory work. PPD is one of few CROs that can accommodate these demands, thanks to its massive global infrastructure and vast experience in late-stage drug development. PPD's backlog, which is an indicator of future revenue, continues to grow rapidly, giving us confidence in our forecast for strong revenue growth over the next several years. We also expect healthy profitability in this segment. While the late-stage business is susceptible to early cancellations, it also enjoys the highest returns.

Our excitement over the company's clinical development prospects is tempered by the uncertainty associated with its compound discovery and development segment. This business has yet to show long-term viability and exposes PPD to drug approval risk, which is not inherent to the firm's core business. While we think this business offers potential upside, we would caution against getting overly excited about its prospects.

PPD's global capabilities and its long history of execution have made it one of the largest CROs in the world. The industry is expected to grow 12% annually for the next five years, and we feel confident that PPD possesses strengths that will allow it to outpace the industry and grab a larger share of the market.

Philadelphia Consolidated Holding PHLY

Data as of 12-29-06

Rating	Fair Value	Last Close	Consider Buy	Consider Sell	Yield %
★	$31.00	$44.56	$23.90	$38.80	0.00

Company Profile
Philadelphia Consolidated offers commercial, property, and casualty insurance. Commercial products--covering autos and business needs--contribute 76% of sales. Personal homeowners' insurance brings in a further 8%, and specialty products--insuring professional liability--add the remaining 16%. Philadelphia's insurance is sold by independent agents, who are supported by 36 regional offices, and direct and Internet sales.

Management
Stewardship Grade [A]

Philadelphia earns our highest Stewardship Grade. Cofounder James Maguire has been chairman since inception and is responsible for much of Philadelphia's success. His son, James Maguire Jr., has been CEO since 1996 and is perpetuating the family's value-creating talent. He brings more than 20 years of industry experience, including an executive role with American International Group. Maguire Jr. earned about $2.8 million in 2005, which we think is reasonable. Directors and officers collectively own close to 19% of the shares, which we think is the best incentive for good performance. The managers are owners, and Philadelphia is shareholder-friendly, in our view.

One Bala Plaza Suite 100
Bala Cynwyd, PA 19004
www.phly.com

Growth [A]	2002	2003	2004	2005
Revenue %	34.8	36.9	32.2	28.4
Earnings/Share %	-21.9	82.7	31.4	78.3
Book Value/Share %	-15.8	13.2	15.3	20.7
Dividends/Share %	NMF	NMF	NMF	NMF

Profitability [A+]	2003	2004	2005	TTM
Return on Assets %	3.3	3.4	5.4	7.3
Oper Cash Flow $Mil	299	391	431	—
- Cap Spending $Mil	7	8	7	—
= Free Cash Flow $Mil	—	—	—	—

Financial Health [NA]	2003	2004	2005	09-30-06
Long-term Debt $Mil	—	—	—	—
Total Equity $Mil	546	644	816	1,074
Debt/Equity Ratio	—	—	—	—

Industry	Business Risk	Moat Size	Investment Style	Sector
Insurance (Property)	Average	Narrow	Mid Core	Financial Services

Competition

	Market Cap $Mil	12 Mo Trailing Sales $Mil	Price/Cash Flow	Return On Assets%	Debt/Equity	Total Return% 1 Yr	3 Yr
Philadelphia Consolidated Holding	3,139	1,197	—	7.3	—	38.3	40.5
American International Gr	186,296	110,593	—	1.2	—	6.1	3.2
St. Paul Travelers Compan	37,047	24,802	—	2.8	—	22.9	13.7

Price Volatility

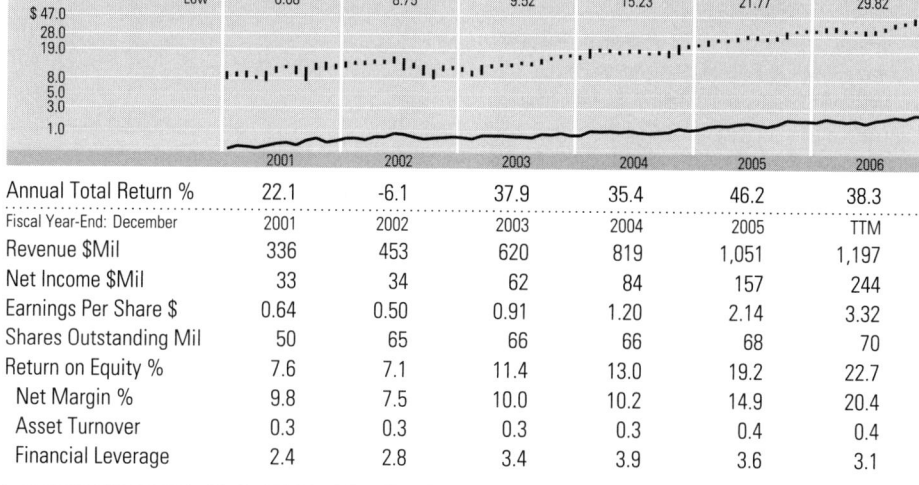

Annual Total Return %	22.1	-6.1	37.9	35.4	46.2	38.3
Fiscal Year-End: December	2001	2002	2003	2004	2005	TTM
Revenue $Mil	336	453	620	819	1,051	1,197
Net Income $Mil	33	34	62	84	157	244
Earnings Per Share $	0.64	0.50	0.91	1.20	2.14	3.32
Shares Outstanding Mil	50	65	66	66	68	70
Return on Equity %	7.6	7.1	11.4	13.0	19.2	22.7
Net Margin %	9.8	7.5	10.0	10.2	14.9	20.4
Asset Turnover	0.3	0.3	0.3	0.3	0.4	0.4
Financial Leverage	2.4	2.8	3.4	3.9	3.6	3.1

Valuation Ratios	Stock	Rel to Industry	Rel to S&P 500
Price/Earnings	13.4	0.9	0.7
Price/Book	2.9	1.7	0.7
Price/Sales	2.6	1.9	0.9
Price/Cash Flow	—	—	—

Major Fund Holders	% of Fund Assets
Phoenix Small-Mid Cap X	3.77
JHT Small Cap Trust Ser I	3.73
Excelsior Small Cap	3.66
JHFunds2 Small Cap NAV	3.62

Thesis By Matt Nellans, 11-15-06 Stock Price as of Analysis: $45.48

We admire Philadelphia Consolidated's underwriting discipline and niche market strategy and think the insurer enjoys a narrow moat. Our fair value estimate is $31 per share.

It's difficult to find a chink in Philadelphia's armor. Chairman James Maguire started the firm in 1962, and his family still owns almost 19%. In the past decade, premium volume increased 28% per year while return on equity averaged 16%--with sparing debt use. Not surprisingly, the stock price climbed 26% per year over that period. These results suggest Philadelphia benefited from a powerful competitive advantage. However, our moat rating is prospective, and we think the insurer falls short of a wide moat.

Philadelphia controls its largest and most uncertain cost, claims, better than most insurers. We are impressed by the firm's dedication to underwriting and think its underwriting prowess is the source of its narrow moat. Policies are sold before the true cost is known, and undisciplined underwriting can offset the balance of the firm's profit efforts. Philadelphia's underwriting margin was close to 10% over the past decade, which places it at the head of the underwriting class. In our view, the insurer's stellar underwriting is a result of management's large stake. Because managers risk their personal net worth, we think it's unlikely shareholders' capital will be destroyed via shabby underwriting. However, the firm's savvy risk selection and pricing are the result of seasoned managers executing daily. This advantage, though powerful in the short run, can erode over time.

Philadelphia's niche-market underwriting knowledge and experience are costly to replicate, creating modest entry barriers. However, few potential policyholders seek out the insurer to buy insurance. Instead, Philadelphia relies on its agents to gather new clients and retain current clients. Over time, policyholders tend to gravitate to the lowest-price policy, in our view. Philadelphia's agents, when faced with the prospect of lost business, will either press for lower prices or advise the policyholder to switch to a cheaper insurer. This constant pricing pressure coupled with minimal switching costs plays a large role in our hesitancy to award a wide moat. However, Philadelphia compensates for this weakness by allowing its best agents to share equally in underwriting profits. In our opinion, this system lures productive agents to Philadelphia and offers a strong incentive for the agent to submit profitable risks.

Data as of 12-29-06

Pitney Bowes PBI

	Rating	Fair Value	Last Close	Consider Buy	Consider Sell	Yield %
	★★★	$46.00	$46.19	$39.20	$60.40	2.77

Company Profile
Pitney Bowes is the world's largest provider of postage meters and mailing equipment with over 2 million customers worldwide. The firm offers a number of related services for both large and small clients including mailroom and document management outsourcing, outgoing mail presorting (for postage discounts), and customer tracking technologies. Pitney Bowes also coordinates targeted marketing materials that get sent to customers who fill out certain government forms.

Industry	Business Risk	Moat Size	Investment Style	Sector
Office Equip.	Below Avg	Wide	Mid Value	Industrial Materials

Competition

	Market Cap $Mil	12 Mo Trailing Sales $Mil	Price/Cash Flow	Return On Assets%	Debt/Equity	Total Return% 1 Yr	3 Yr
Pitney Bowes	10,249	5,737	22.8	0.6	3.5	12.6	7.5
Xerox	16,361	15,766	10.7	5.5	0.7	15.7	7.6
Iron Mountain	5,474	2,279	14.5	2.3	1.7	-2.1	16.5

Management Stewardship Grade [C]
The Pitney Bowes management team, headed by chairman and CEO Michael Critelli since 1997, has nicely navigated through a number of challenges within the company and the industry. We like the fact that Critelli has taken initiatives to exit Pitney Bowes' noncore businesses. The firm has leased airplanes and other machinery in the past, and it finally spun off its noncore financing arm this year. We think Critelli's $2.8 million compensation package in 2005 was a bit generous given the stock's underperformance that year. We would also like to see greater executive ownership in the company, which helps to align management's goals with the creation of long-term shareholder value. Executive officers and directors own only 1.6% cumulatively. Director elections are staggered, which could make swift company changes difficult. In addition, Critelli acts as both CEO and chairman, which could present a conflict of interest when it comes to the objective evaluation of management performance.

Price Volatility

	2001	2002	2003	2004	2005	2006
Annual $Price High	43.65	44.41	42.74	46.97	47.50	47.97
Low	31.25	28.55	29.45	38.88	40.34	40.18
Annual Total Return %	19.8	-10.4	28.5	17.2	-6.1	12.6
Fiscal Year-End: December	2001	2002	2003	2004	2005	TTM
Revenue $Mil	4,122	4,410	4,577	4,957	5,492	5,737
Net Income $Mil	488	476	498	481	527	53
Earnings Per Share $	1.97	1.97	2.11	2.05	2.27	0.23
Shares Outstanding Mil	245	239	234	231	229	222
Return on Equity %	54.9	55.8	45.9	37.3	40.5	5.5
Net Margin %	11.8	10.8	10.9	9.7	9.6	0.9
Asset Turnover	0.5	0.5	0.5	0.5	0.5	0.6
Financial Leverage	9.3	10.3	8.2	7.9	8.2	9.9

Valuation Ratios	Stock	Rel to Industry	Rel to S&P 500
Price/Earnings	19.4	1.1	0.9
Price/Book	10.7	2.4	2.6
Price/Sales	1.8	1.6	0.6
Price/Cash Flow	22.8	1.4	1.6

Major Fund Holders	% of Fund Assets
Ariel Appreciation	4.89
Osterweis	3.02
Harbor Large Cap Value Instl	2.94
Buffalo Balanced	2.82

1 Elmcroft Road www.pb.com
Stamford, CT 06926-0700

Growth [C]	2002	2003	2004	2005
Revenue %	7.0	3.8	8.3	10.8
Earnings/Share %	0.0	7.1	-2.8	10.7
Book Value/Share %	-1.7	30.4	19.5	2.0
Dividends/Share %	1.7	1.7	1.7	1.6

Profitability [A-]	2003	2004	2005	TTM
Return on Assets %	5.6	4.7	5.0	0.6
Oper Cash Flow $Mil	851	945	540	450
- Cap Spending $Mil	286	317	292	320
= Free Cash Flow $Mil	566	628	248	130

Financial Health [C+]	2003	2004	2005	06-30-06
Long-term Debt $Mil	2,841	3,165	3,850	3,349
Total Equity $Mil	1,086	1,289	1,301	956
Debt/Equity Ratio	2.6	2.5	3.0	3.5

Thesis By Karen Yiu, 12-07-06 Stock Price as of Analysis: $46.36

A maturing postage meter industry has motivated Pitney Bowes to pursue growth through other methods. We think this wide-moat incumbent offers a base of recurring cash flow that can keep the business stable as it focuses on newly acquired operations.

The postage meter industry is showing signs of age, but its sturdy position could provide a jumping-off point for new growth opportunities. Since Pitney Bowes initiated the first secure postage printing machine in the 1920s, the company has benefited from faithful U.S. meter adoption, rapid international expansion, and the popularity of direct marketing. Finding a sizable business that doesn't already lease a postage meter might be tough these days, but Pitney's customer base is relatively stable and still generates significant cash flow for the firm. Pitney Bowes already dominates the meter market with a 62% global market share while competing aggressively with Neopost and Francotyp-Postalia in Europe. Future growth in this area might come from emerging mail markets like India, Japan, and South America, where governments and businesses can benefit from the company's experience with postal processes.

The acquisition of niche businesses presents a much better growth opportunity but may take time to affect overall firm growth. Within the past three years, Pitney Bowes has acquired 10 businesses with an average $63 million price tag in areas ranging from litigation document services to direct-mail marketing. The overall theme revolves around broadening Pitney Bowes' exposure to the spectrum of businesses related to document handling and the postal system. Although the incremental revenue streams from these new operations have a small impact now, Pitney hopes that this investment will lead to a beneficial mix shift over the next few years. Cross-selling to Pitney Bowes' huge client base has become a top priority and a motivating factor for its acquisitions of mail software and presorting services. It has also taken steps to provide document management consulting for large clients, essentially competing against Xerox and Iron Mountain. These new sources of revenue come at the expense of lower margins, but the contribution to operating profits is most helpful as the legacy meter business slows.

Although Pitney Bowes' entry into new markets puts its high margins at risk, we think this is a logical step for a firm that wants to stay on its toes in the fast-paced tech industry.

Data as of 12-29-06

Plains All American Pipeline LP PAA

Rating	Fair Value	Last Close	Consider Buy	Consider Sell	Yield %
★★★★	$61.00	$51.20	$47.00	$76.40	5.61

Company Profile

Plains All American Pipeline is a master limited partnership that operates a network of crude-oil pipelines, terminals, and related businesses in the United States and Canada. The partnership's prized asset is its Cushing interchange, which will have a total storage capacity of 7.4 million barrels when the current expansion is completed. In addition to crude-oil transportation, the company trades in the crude oil it transports to earn a small margin.

Management
Stewardship Grade [B]

Plains was established as a subsidiary of Plains Resources to control the pipeline business of the Plains family of companies. As a master limited partnership, the parent company receives a greater percentage of excess cash from Plains as cash flow per unit increases, providing the incentive to grow smartly and not just for growth's sake. The management ranks are filled with longtime Plains employees, starting with CEO and chairman Greg Armstrong and continuing through the majority of the company's senior officers. We think this organizational continuity has helped Plains recognize business opportunities and trends, and we're full of respect for this team. We also like that a portion of directors' pay is tied to long-term unit prices, and that the company provides detailed data with its quarterly reports. While Plains earns a slightly higher stewardship grade than many of the MLPs that we cover, we ding the firm for having the same person serve as CEO and chairman and for the severely limited power of limited partners under the MLP structure.

333 Clay Street Suite 1600 www.paalp.com
Houston, TX 77002

Growth [C+]	2002	2003	2004	2005
Revenue %	22.1	50.2	66.6	48.6
Earnings/Share %	—	NMF	89.0	43.9
Book Value/Share %	—	NMF	17.7	7.6
Dividends/Share %	8.3	3.6	5.3	11.8

Profitability [NA]	2003	2004	2005	TTM
Return on Assets %	2.5	3.8	4.8	4.3
Oper Cash Flow $Mil	115	104	24	292
- Cap Spending $Mil	65	117	164	265
= Free Cash Flow $Mil	50	-13	-140	27

Financial Health [D]	2003	2004	2005	09-30-06
Long-term Debt $Mil	519	949	952	1,200
Total Equity $Mil	747	1,039	1,294	1,793
Debt/Equity Ratio	0.7	0.9	0.7	0.7

Industry	Business Risk	Moat Size	Investment Style	Sector
Pipelines	Average	Narrow	Mid Value	Energy

Competition

	Market Cap $Mil	12 Mo Trailing Sales $Mil	Price/Cash Flow	Return On Assets%	Debt/ Equity	Total Return% 1 Yr	3 Yr
Plains All American Pipeline LP	4,147	26,767	14.2	4.3	0.7	38.0	24.0
Kinder Morgan Energy Part	7,797	9,919	6.2	2.7	1.2	7.3	6.8
Magellan Midstream Partne	2,562	1,217	13.3	7.1	1.0	27.9	23.0

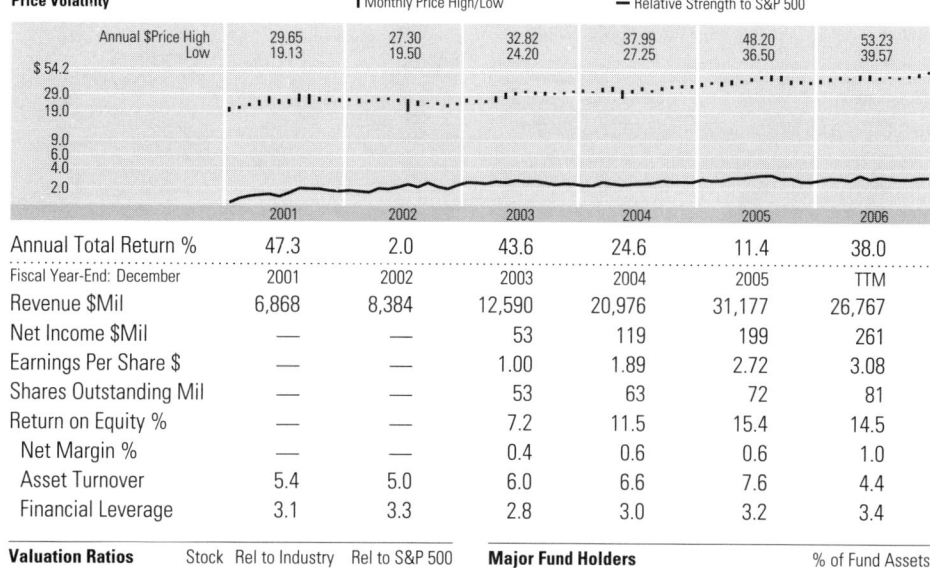

Price Volatility — Monthly Price High/Low — Relative Strength to S&P 500

	2001	2002	2003	2004	2005	2006
Annual $Price High	29.65	27.30	32.82	37.99	48.20	53.23
Low	19.13	19.50	24.20	27.25	36.50	39.57
Annual Total Return %	47.3	2.0	43.6	24.6	11.4	38.0

Fiscal Year-End: December	2001	2002	2003	2004	2005	TTM
Revenue $Mil	6,868	8,384	12,590	20,976	31,177	26,767
Net Income $Mil	—	—	53	119	199	261
Earnings Per Share $	—	—	1.00	1.89	2.72	3.08
Shares Outstanding Mil	—	—	53	63	72	81
Return on Equity %	—	—	7.2	11.5	15.4	14.5
Net Margin %	—	—	0.4	0.6	0.6	1.0
Asset Turnover	5.4	5.0	6.0	6.6	7.6	4.4
Financial Leverage	3.1	3.3	2.8	3.0	3.2	3.4

Valuation Ratios	Stock	Rel to Industry	Rel to S&P 500
Price/Earnings	17.1	0.6	0.8
Price/Book	2.3	0.9	0.6
Price/Sales	0.2	0.1	0.1
Price/Cash Flow	14.2	1.4	1.0

Major Fund Holders	% of Fund Assets
Dividend Growth Trust Rising Div Grwth A	2.19
1st Source Monogram Long/Short	1.78
Lighthouse Opportunity	1.78
Diamond Hill Strategic Income A	1.44

Thesis By Jason Stevens, 12-20-06 Stock Price as of Analysis: $51.14

In 2006, Plains All American Pipeline used its checkbook to significantly broaden both its geographic footprint and its asset mix, closing on $2.7 billion in acquisitions, including the $2.4 billion merger with Pacific Energy Partners. While these strategic moves have taken the partnership into new territory, we think they will pay off nicely for unitholders.

We've long admired how Plains built a competitive advantage by focusing on the Midwest's need for crude oil. The region is landlocked and has almost no oil production, yet its refineries require 3 million barrels of crude-oil feedstocks per day to supply the Midwest with gasoline and other refined products. Through a series of deals, Plains created an impressive network of gathering and transportation pipelines, storage assets, and terminals that is ideally situated to funnel crude from the Gulf, Mid-Continent producers, and Canada into the Midwest. This asset network generates a steadily growing stream of fee-based revenue, which the company amplifies through its gathering and marketing operations.

With its acquisition of Pacific Energy, Plains can extend this model to the West Coast and the Rockies. The West Coast became a net importer of oil in 1993, and its appetite has only grown more voracious as California's main producing region, the San Joaquin Valley, has seen production decline. Recognizing the region's need for secure crude-oil supplies, Pacific Energy, whose pipelines already supply Los Angeles area refiners with domestic crude, began constructing a massive crude-oil terminal at the Port of Los Angeles that will be able to handle 250,000 barrels of crude a day and provide storage capacity of 3 million barrels. We think that Plains will combine the fee-based pipeline, terminaling, and storage operations with its expertise in gathering and marketing crude oil, which in turn will optimize the earnings potential of Pacific Energy's assets.

And while less profound in size, we note that in 2006 Plains extended its operations from crude oil and into refined products, liquefied petroleum gas (LPG), and natural-gas storage. With crude oil the partnership has proved to be a more than competent operator of hard assets and has parlayed its expertise into a significant marketing business. We think Plains' entry into complementary businesses is the first step toward replicating a similar model throughout the midstream sector and should serve notice to other MLPs that there's a new competitor in town.

PNC Financial Services Group PNC

Data as of 12-29-06

Rating ★★★	Fair Value $76.00	Last Close $74.04	Consider Buy $58.60	Consider Sell $95.20	Yield % 2.90

Industry	Business Risk	Moat Size	Investment Style	Sector
Super Regional Banks	Average	Narrow	Large Value	Financial Services

Company Profile

PNC has four business lines: retail banking, commercial banking, PFPC, and BlackRock. PNC's 874 bank branches are located primarily in the Mid-Atlantic region. PFPC is one of the nation's largest mutual fund processors, while PNC's 34% stake in BlackRock gives it one of the leading institutional fixed-income asset managers in the country. PNC will add 246 branches to its impressive franchise via its pending acquisition of Mercantile Bankshares.

Management
Stewardship Grade [B]

Now that we no longer punish the company for the 2001 restatement of earnings, we give PNC a B Stewardship Grade. While we still penalize the firm for combining the CEO and chairman jobs under James Rohr and the continued existence of a poison pill, we are impressed by its overall stewardship. PNC issues an impressive amount of disclosure every year, walking the investor through each business line in a clear and easy-to-follow manner. The company similarly attempts to answer questions about management and director compensation in a straightforward way. We like that the company requires its directors and executive officers to hold a minimum amount of PNC stock. This helps align management's motives with common shareholders'.

One PNC Plaza 249 Fifth Avenue www.pnc.com
Pittsburgh, PA 15222-2707

Growth [B-]	2002	2003	2004	2005
Revenue %	9.8	-2.6	5.3	14.2
Earnings/Share %	229.4	-14.5	18.6	8.1
Book Value/Share %	23.5	-2.0	-44.2	11.9
Dividends/Share %	0.0	1.0	3.1	0.0

Profitability [B]	2003	2004	2005	TTM
Return on Assets %	1.5	1.5	1.4	2.6
Oper Cash Flow $Mil	1,706	463	-676	—
- Cap Spending $Mil	—	—	—	—
= Free Cash Flow $Mil	—	—	—	—

Financial Health [NA]	2003	2004	2005	09-30-06
Long-term Debt $Mil	—	—	—	—
Total Equity $Mil	13,281	7,473	8,563	10,758
Debt/Equity Ratio	—	—	—	—

Competition

	Market Cap $Mil	12 Mo Trailing Sales $Mil	Price/Cash Flow	Return On Assets %	Debt/ Equity	Total Return % 1 Yr	3 Yr
PNC Financial Services Group	21,754	8,735	—	2.6	—	23.6	14.7
Fifth Third Bancorp	22,842	5,431	—	1.4	—	13.0	-8.1
Mellon Financial	17,360	5,092	—	2.0	—	26.0	12.3

Price Volatility
Monthly Price High/Low — Relative Strength to S&P 500

	2001	2002	2003	2004	2005	2006
Annual $Price High	75.75	62.80	55.55	59.79	65.66	75.15
Low	51.14	32.70	41.63	48.90	49.35	61.78
Annual Total Return %	-20.7	-22.4	36.2	8.9	11.7	23.6

Fiscal Year-End: December	2001	2002	2003	2004	2005	TTM
Revenue $Mil	4,914	5,394	5,253	5,532	6,316	8,735
Net Income $Mil	377	1,184	1,001	1,197	1,325	2,574
Earnings Per Share $	1.26	4.15	3.55	4.21	4.55	8.66
Shares Outstanding Mil	297	283	280	282	286	294
Return on Equity %	3.2	8.6	7.5	16.0	15.5	23.9
Net Margin %	7.7	22.0	19.1	21.6	21.0	29.5
Asset Turnover	0.1	0.1	0.1	0.1	0.1	0.1
Financial Leverage	6.0	4.8	5.1	10.7	10.7	9.2

Valuation Ratios	Stock	Rel to Industry	Rel to S&P 500
Price/Earnings	8.6	0.6	0.4
Price/Book	2.0	0.9	0.5
Price/Sales	2.5	0.7	0.9
Price/Cash Flow	—	—	—

Major Fund Holders	% of Fund Assets
Fidelity Select Banking	4.95
Midas Special	4.41
Schwab Financial Services	4.32
Tweedy, Browne American Value	4.14

Thesis
By Jaime Black, CFA, CPA, 11-28-06 Stock Price as of Analysis: $69.60

We think PNC Financial Services Group has developed a great banking business, although it is almost overshadowed by the even better-performing BlackRock unit.

After an impressive job of integrating the scandal-ridden Riggs Bank, PNC is taking on a new challenge with its proposed acquisition of Mercantile Bankshares. The purchase would complement PNC's current footprint, filling the geographic void between PNC's Pennsylvania and Delaware markets and the branches it acquired from Riggs in Washington, D.C. Mercantile's major asset is its fast-growing, low-cost branch network in and around Washington. Its purchase replaces PNC's planned de novo expansion in the area, although the price paid is a bit steep, in our opinion.

PNC will face some integration challenges. Mercantile operates as a supercommunity bank; it has 12 affiliate banks, each with its own management and board of directors. PNC will need to completely change the management structure in order to mold Mercantile into its more centralized model and consolidate the separate banking charters. In the process, PNC will need to be careful not to damage the lower-cost operating culture that makes Mercantile so attractive.

PNC is getting its expenses under control. It has been working its way through a cost-saving initiative that began in 2005. The plan is to eliminate 3,000 positions, add revenue opportunities, and save an estimated $300 million. Before this program, PNC's operating expenses at the bank level were nearly 69% of total revenue, higher than most of its competition. Since the plan's introduction, the expense/revenue ratio has declined to 66%; while this is still higher than average, it is acceptable, given PNC's high-touch customer service and fee-generating businesses.

Excluding BlackRock, PNC earns about 57% of its revenue from noninterest income sources. Fee-generating businesses are prized in the banking industry for lowering dependency on the yield curve. PNC earns its fees from a combination of traditional charges on deposits and revenue from its asset-management processing business, PFPC. The processing business makes up 30% of noninterest income, excluding BlackRock, and 6% of earnings. PFPC is one of the largest mutual fund processors in this scale business, and we expect it to continue to grow steadily.

We would buy this bank at an appropriate margin of safety to our fair value estimate.

Data as of 12-29-06

Posco ADR PKX

	Rating	Fair Value	Last Close	Consider Buy	Consider Sell	Yield %
	★★★	$75.00	$82.67	$57.80	$94.00	0.00

Industry	Business Risk	Moat Size	Investment Style	Sector
Steel/Iron	Average	Narrow	Large Value	Industrial Materials

Company Profile

Posco is the third-largest steel producer in the world. The company produces more than 29 million tons of product, mainly in its two South Korean mills. The company also operates several joint ventures, including three in China and one in the United States. Posco mostly produces varying qualities of flat-rolled steel, including basic hot-rolled, cold-rolled, galvanized, and stainless steel. The company was privatized by the Korean government in 2000.

Management

Stewardship Grade [NA]

Posco has worked very hard to distinguish itself from most Korean companies in terms of corporate governance. Nine out of 15 directors are outsiders, including one known for his shareholder advocacy. Incestuous company ownership and deals are rampant in many Korean firms. Since privatization, Posco has refrained from investing in unrelated businesses and has done a pretty good job of jettisoning most of its minority holdings. Although we'd rather management returned more of the company's cash flow to shareholders in the form of dividends and stock buybacks, we recognize that the company's hands are somewhat tied with regard to its role in the Korean economy. Overall, we like management's efforts to make this company as transparent as possible. The average Posco executive has been with the firm for more than 30 years, and the company boasts a deep bench of experienced managers. Given the relatively high quality of corporate stewardship, we are surprised that the directors and executives hold fewer than 8,000 shares of stock combined, though they do hold a larger interest in the form of stock options.

892 Daechi-4-dong Gangnam-gu
Seoul, South Korea
www.posco.co.kr

Growth [NA]	2002	2003	2004	2005
Revenue %	9.4	23.9	34.8	9.7
Earnings/Share %	28.3	84.3	92.6	7.3
Book Value/Share %	13.7	12.7	24.7	23.7
Dividends/Share %	—	—	—	—

Profitability [NA]	2003	2004	2005	TTM
Return on Assets %	9.6	14.4	14.5	14.5
Oper Cash Flow $Mil	2,929	4,303	5,305	5,305
- Cap Spending $Mil	1,087	1,970	3,264	3,264
= Free Cash Flow $Mil	1,842	2,332	2,041	2,041

Financial Health [NA]	2003	2004	2005	12-31-05
Long-term Debt $Mil	2,471	1,958	1,108	1,108
Total Equity $Mil	11,090	15,643	19,464	19,464
Debt/Equity Ratio	0.2	0.1	0.1	0.1

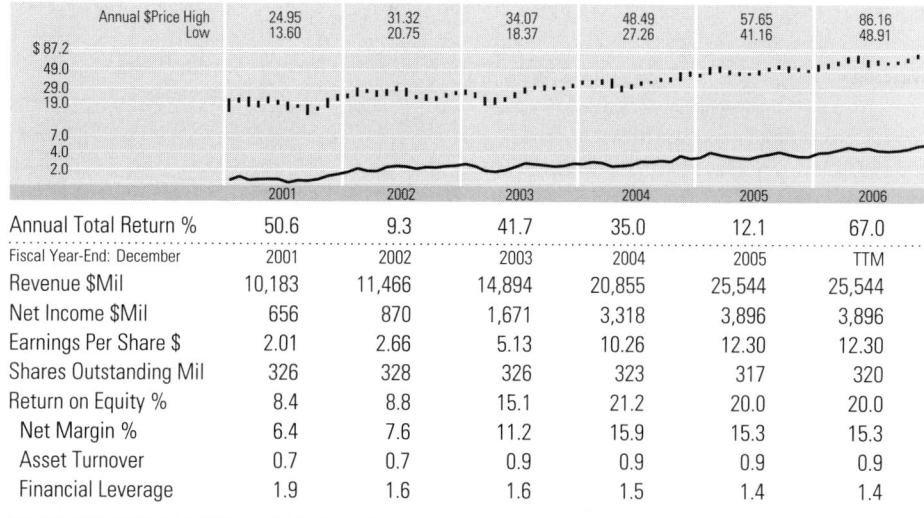

Competition	Market Cap $Mil	12 Mo Trailing Sales $Mil	Price/Cash Flow	Return On Assets %	Debt/ Equity	Total Return% 1 Yr	3 Yr
Posco ADR	26,486	25,544	5.0	14.5	0.1	67.0	35.0
Mittal Steel Co NV	29,697	28,132	7.5	10.8	0.9	62.5	68.8
Nucor	16,514	14,490	7.9	21.4	0.2	70.7	61.9

	2001	2002	2003	2004	2005	2006
Annual $Price High	24.95	31.32	34.07	48.49	57.65	86.16
Low	13.60	20.75	18.37	27.26	41.16	48.91
Annual Total Return %	50.6	9.3	41.7	35.0	12.1	67.0

Fiscal Year-End: December	2001	2002	2003	2004	2005	TTM
Revenue $Mil	10,183	11,466	14,894	20,855	25,544	25,544
Net Income $Mil	656	870	1,671	3,318	3,896	3,896
Earnings Per Share $	2.01	2.66	5.13	10.26	12.30	12.30
Shares Outstanding Mil	326	328	326	323	317	320
Return on Equity %	8.4	8.8	15.1	21.2	20.0	20.0
Net Margin %	6.4	7.6	11.2	15.9	15.3	15.3
Asset Turnover	0.7	0.7	0.9	0.9	0.9	0.9
Financial Leverage	1.9	1.6	1.6	1.5	1.4	1.4

Valuation Ratios	Stock	Rel to Industry	Rel to S&P 500
Price/Earnings	6.7	0.5	0.3
Price/Book	1.4	0.3	0.3
Price/Sales	1.0	0.4	0.3
Price/Cash Flow	5.0	0.4	0.3

Major Fund Holders	% of Fund Assets
SunAmerica Focused Value A	5.27
ICON Materials	2.63
Third Avenue Value	2.49
MFS Emerging Markets Equity A	1.90

Thesis By Scott Burns, 10-18-06 Stock Price as of Analysis: $67.23

Steel is a fickle industry, and it's rare to find a producer that demonstrates strong and consistent cash flows in good times and bad. Posco is one of these rare companies and is an investment worth considering at the right price, in our opinion.

Posco dominates the Korean flat-rolled market and controls an estimated 75% of the country's production. In addition, the Korean economy is very insular, and customers generally prefer domestic products over imports. We hypothesize that this offers the company a degree of insulation from the ebbs and flows of the global steel market. Operating like a virtual monopoly, Posco has been a cash cow since it was privatized in 2000. From 2000 to 2004, Posco averaged $1.45 billion of free cash flow per year and boasted an average free cash flow margin of nearly 9%.

Posco is one of the lowest-cost steel producers in the world. The company benefits from having some of the most technologically advanced mills in the world, a labor force that works six days a week, and captive power plants and port facilities. As a result, Posco routinely posts operating margins above 15%.

The company also benefits from its proximity to the largest steel-consuming nation in the world, China. Shipping steel to China takes only one day for Posco, and the shipping costs are a fraction of those for other low-cost producers in countries such as Brazil and Russia. Although Chinese steel production has grown exponentially in the past few years, much of it is low-quality steel, and the country still needs the advanced materials that Posco produces.

If Posco has a weak spot, it's the reliance on imported raw materials such as iron ore and coal. The Korean peninsula is far from flush with these commodities, so Posco relies mainly on mines in Australia and Brazil for these supplies. Recent merger activity combined with insatiable Chinese raw-material demand has given mining companies unprecedented pricing power. Prices for iron ore alone rose 70% in 2005. Posco is not taking this lying down and was one of the first steel producers to seek mining acquisitions and partnerships over the past few years. So far, the company has been able to pass these costs on to customers, but it needs to continue addressing this concern.

In addition to its operating excellence, Posco has an investment-grade balance sheet and pays a nice dividend. Investors looking to diversify into some international holdings could do a lot worse than Posco.

Potash Corp of Saskatchewan POT

Data as of 12-29-06

Rating	Fair Value	Last Close	Consider Buy	Consider Sell	Yield %
★	$115.00	$143.48	$88.70	$144.10	0.42

Company Profile
Potash Corporation of Saskatchewan's three main products--potash, phosphate, and nitrogen--are used in fertilizers, animal feed, and industrial applications. In North America, the company sells to retailers, cooperatives, and distributors, which then sell the products to farmers. The company mines potash at seven locations in Canada and one in Chile. Phosphate and nitrogen are produced from 12 facilities in the United States and South America.

Management
Stewardship Grade [A]

In our opinion, PCS' management does a decent job in a very tough industry. President and chief executive officer William J. Doyle has been in the fertilizer industry for 30 years. He became CEO in 1999 after having served on Potash's management team for 12 years. Doyle is also on the boards of Canpotex and The Fertilizer Institute. In our opinion, PCS has commendable corporate-governance policies. For example, the company has split the CEO and chairman roles, and each board member is subject to re-election each year. Further, the company has expensed stock options since 2003. We think PCS' compensation policies are sound and view Doyle's salary and bonus as reasonable. We also give the company kudos for the detailed information it provides in its regulatory filings and on its Web site. This information increases the company's transparency and indicates a shareholder-friendly management team.

Suite 500 122-1st Avenue South www.potashcorp.com
Saskatoon, SK S7K 7G3

Growth [NA]	2002	2003	2004	2005
Revenue %	-6.9	45.1	15.9	18.6
Earnings/Share %	-55.6	NMF	NMF	81.1
Book Value/Share %	0.7	88.1	14.1	-11.0
Dividends/Share %	0.0	0.0	5.0	14.3

Profitability [NA]	2003	2004	2005	TTM
Return on Assets %	-2.8	5.8	10.1	9.8
Oper Cash Flow $Mil	382	658	865	444
- Cap Spending $Mil	151	221	383	521
= Free Cash Flow $Mil	231	438	482	-77

Financial Health [NA]	2003	2004	2005	09-30-06
Long-term Debt $Mil	1,269	1,259	1,258	857
Total Equity $Mil	1,974	2,386	2,133	2,575
Debt/Equity Ratio	0.6	0.5	0.6	0.3

Industry	Business Risk	Moat Size	Investment Style	Sector
Mining (Nonmetal)	Average	Narrow	Large Growth	Industrial Materials

Competition

	Market Cap $Mil	12 Mo Trailing Sales $Mil	Price/Cash Flow	Return On Assets %	Debt/Equity	Total Return % 1 Yr	3 Yr
Potash Corp of Saskatchewan	14,951	3,674	33.7	9.8	0.3	80.0	50.4
Norsk Hydro ASA ADR	38,359	27,146	9.0	7.3	0.2	51.6	38.5
The Mosaic Company	9,357	5,191	26.8	-1.1	0.6	46.0	—

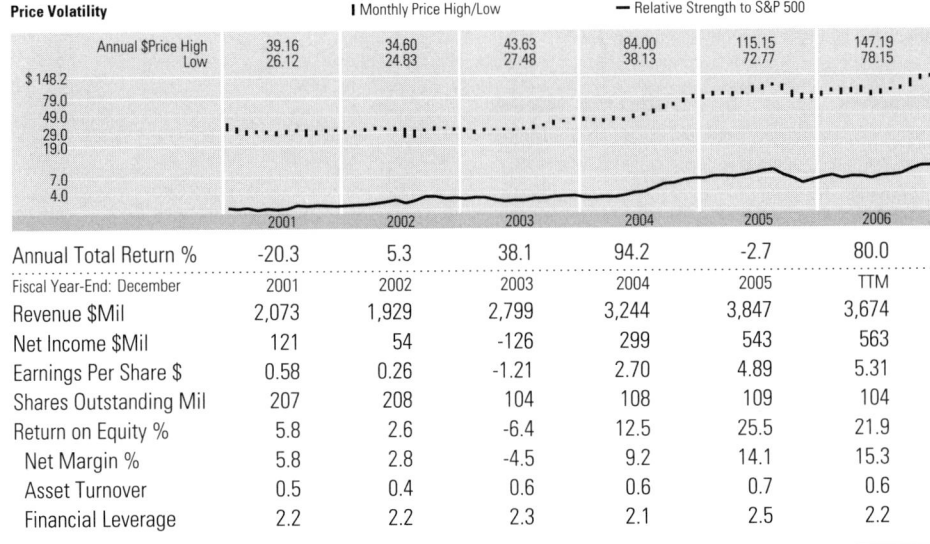

	2001	2002	2003	2004	2005	TTM
Annual Total Return %	-20.3	5.3	38.1	94.2	-2.7	80.0
Revenue $Mil	2,073	1,929	2,799	3,244	3,847	3,674
Net Income $Mil	121	54	-126	299	543	563
Earnings Per Share $	0.58	0.26	-1.21	2.70	4.89	5.31
Shares Outstanding Mil	207	208	104	108	109	104
Return on Equity %	5.8	2.6	-6.4	12.5	25.5	21.9
Net Margin %	5.8	2.8	-4.5	9.2	14.1	15.3
Asset Turnover	0.5	0.4	0.6	0.6	0.7	0.6
Financial Leverage	2.2	2.2	2.3	2.1	2.5	2.2

Fiscal Year-End: December

Valuation Ratios	Stock	Rel to Industry	Rel to S&P 500
Price/Earnings	27.0	1.5	1.3
Price/Book	5.8	1.5	1.4
Price/Sales	4.1	1.2	1.4
Price/Cash Flow	33.7	2.4	2.3

Major Fund Holders	% of Fund Assets
Janus Aspen International Grth Instl	5.69
Janus Overseas	5.48
Janus Adviser International Growth S	5.35
Janus Twenty	3.57

Thesis By Ben Johnson, 11-29-06 Stock Price as of Analysis: $141.22

Control of more than 75% of the world's excess potash production capacity gives Potash Corporation of Saskatchewan the ability to almost single-handedly manage the global balance of supply and demand for potash and, in our opinion, results in a narrow economic moat.

PCS is the world's largest producer of potash, a key element in plant nutrition used by farmers worldwide. Though it's a commodity producer, the firm has a unique position with attractive dynamics atypical of undifferentiated industries. Most commodity markets have low barriers to entry, allowing new producers to easily enter the market during periods of profitability. This influx typically creates a supply overhang and crushes margins. However, PCS' evenhanded control over the majority of excess capacity and the substantial investment required for greenfield production make for an industry dynamic uncharacteristic of commodity markets.

As tight supply and demand balances cause potash margins to expand, new entrants are actually deterred. A world-scale mine capable of producing 2 million metric tons of potash per year would require a capital investment of roughly $1.5 billion and, barring any significant disruptions, take five years to reach full capacity. PCS can bring its excess capacity online at a fraction of the cost and far more quickly than it would take to develop a new mine. This capability keeps irrational competitors at bay and allows PCS to match supply to demand at its discretion.

PCS is also a major producer of nitrogen fertilizers. While making nitrogen fertilizers is a relatively unattractive business, PCS' attractive cost structure makes this segment a perennial contributor to the bottom line. The bulk of the company's basic nitrogen products are produced at its Trinidad facility, which benefits from long-term contracts for cheap natural gas and proximity to the North American mainland. These factors make the Trinidad site the low-cost provider to its northern neighbors and mean steady profitability for PCS.

The firm's equity portfolio has grown by leaps and bounds in recent years. PCS holds substantial stakes in Arab Potash Company, Israel Chemicals Ltd., Sinochem, and SQM. These investments mark the firm's entree to what would it would like to develop into controlling stakes, and they provide substantial intangible benefits as well. For instance, being an active owner of Sinofert, China's largest fertilizer distributor, allows PCS to keep its fingers on the pulse of the world's largest fertilizer market.

Data as of 12-29-06

Praxair PX

Rating	Fair Value	Last Close	Consider Buy	Consider Sell	Yield %
★★★	$54.00	$59.33	$41.60	$67.70	1.69

Industry	Business Risk	Moat Size	Investment Style	Sector
Chemicals	Average	Narrow	Large Core	Industrial Materials

Company Profile

Praxair is the largest industrial-gas company in the Americas and one of the largest worldwide. It produces atmospheric gases (oxygen, nitrogen, argon) primarily through cryogenic air separation, process gases (hydrogen, carbon dioxide, helium), and high-performance surface coatings. Praxair serves a variety of industries, including steel, chemicals, electronics, energy, food and beverage, health care, and manufacturing. The firm was spun off from Union Carbide in 1992.

Management   Stewardship Grade [B]

Dennis Reilley, who took over as CEO in March 2000, has done a fine job maximizing the potential of the business. He has improved discipline in the bidding process by focusing on 11 core geographies--which leads to density advantages including a competitive cost structure and solid reliability--and sticking to an impressive hurdle rate. These efforts--along with healthier end markets--are paying off with higher returns on capital. Reilley has also been successful raising prices in an industry benefiting from meaningful consolidation. He will step down as CEO at the end of the year, but will remain as chairman until April 30, 2007. Stephen Angel, who joined the firm in 2001 after a long career at General Electric, became president, COO, and a director of the board earlier this year. He'll step up to fill the top job in January and the role of chairman upon Reilley's retirement. Praxair is on a roll in terms of winning new business and improving returns on its existing portfolio. Corporate-governance practices and financial disclosure are solid. We are also pleased with the company's use of cash from operations, which has been apportioned to fund growth through discretionary capital expenditures and acquisitions, as well as funding a growing dividend and share buybacks.

39 Old Ridgebury Rd. www.praxair.com
Danbury, CT 06810-5113

Growth [B]	2002	2003	2004	2005
Revenue %	-0.6	9.5	17.5	16.1
Earnings/Share %	-5.3	42.7	18.6	4.8
Book Value/Share %	-6.0	31.7	16.3	8.8
Dividends/Share %	11.8	20.4	31.1	20.0

Profitability [A]	2003	2004	2005	TTM
Return on Assets %	7.0	7.1	6.9	8.5
Oper Cash Flow $Mil	1,137	1,243	1,475	1,565
- Cap Spending $Mil	983	668	877	1,079
= Free Cash Flow $Mil	154	575	598	486

Financial Health [A-]	2003	2004	2005	09-30-06
Long-term Debt $Mil	2,661	2,876	2,926	4,329
Total Equity $Mil	3,088	3,608	3,902	4,494
Debt/Equity Ratio	0.9	0.8	0.8	1.0

Competition

	Market Cap $Mil	12 Mo Trailing Sales $Mil	Price/Cash Flow	Return On Assets %	Debt/ Equity	Total Return % 1 Yr	3 Yr
Praxair	19,158	8,221	12.2	8.5	1.0	14.0	18.2
Air Products and Chemical	15,246	8,850	1.2	6.5	0.5	21.2	12.4
Airgas	3,207	3,013	9.1	5.3	0.6	24.1	24.8

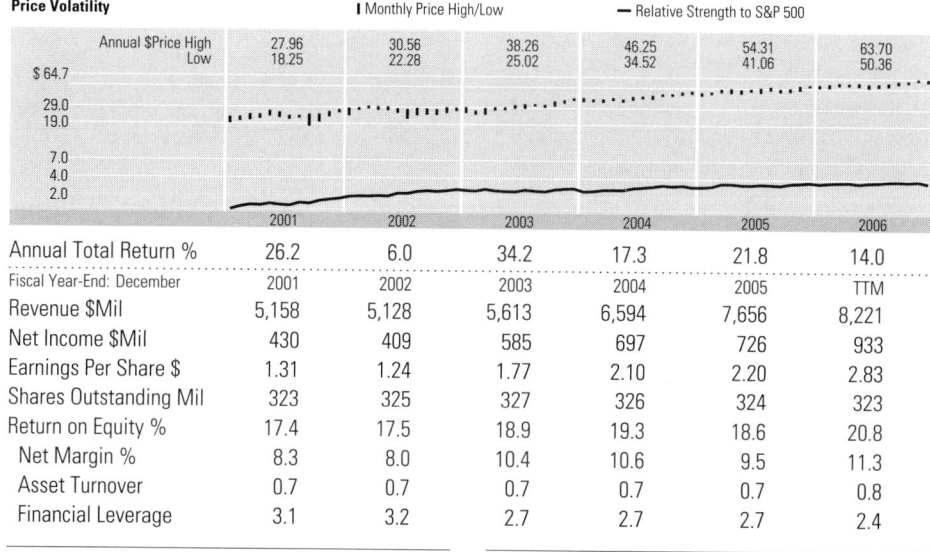

	2001	2002	2003	2004	2005	2006
Annual Total Return %	26.2	6.0	34.2	17.3	21.8	14.0

Fiscal Year-End: December	2001	2002	2003	2004	2005	TTM
Revenue $Mil	5,158	5,128	5,613	6,594	7,656	8,221
Net Income $Mil	430	409	585	697	726	933
Earnings Per Share $	1.31	1.24	1.77	2.10	2.20	2.83
Shares Outstanding Mil	323	325	327	326	324	323
Return on Equity %	17.4	17.5	18.9	19.3	18.6	20.8
Net Margin %	8.3	8.0	10.4	10.6	9.5	11.3
Asset Turnover	0.7	0.7	0.7	0.7	0.7	0.8
Financial Leverage	3.1	3.2	2.7	2.7	2.7	2.4

Valuation Ratios	Stock	Rel to Industry	Rel to S&P 500
Price/Earnings	20.8	1.1	1.0
Price/Book	4.3	1.3	1.0
Price/Sales	2.3	1.4	0.8
Price/Cash Flow	12.2	0.8	0.8

Major Fund Holders	% of Fund Assets
Oak Value	6.87
ING Corporate Leaders Trust B	5.91
Westport R	5.85
ICON Materials	5.37

Thesis By Matthew Warren, 12-15-06 Stock Price as of Analysis: $62.22

While some might decry Praxair as plodding and sedate, this narrow-moat firm is a disciplined leader in an industry with attractive fundamentals.

Praxair is one of the world's largest industrial-gas companies, producing everything from medical-grade oxygen to the hydrogen used to remove sulfur from crude oil. While gases of similar purity are essentially commodities, prohibitive transport costs make this a largely regional game, with density serving as a key advantage. A string of mergers has pared the industry to a handful of global players, with various geographic strongholds. And because gases represent only a fraction of final production costs, customers are not overly price-sensitive, especially since unreliable gas supply can torpedo operations.

Roughly one fourth of Praxair's gas sales are to sizable customers from onsite plants. By doing away with transport costs, Praxair offers better pricing and reliability, especially when serving the customer from redundant facilities via pipeline. Despite the significant up-front investment, these projects are compelling because they offer steady sales--contracts include long-term take-or-pay clauses mandating minimum purchases--and margins that are protected by the ability to pass along fluctuating electricity and natural-gas costs. When it comes time to renew, Praxair can bid much more aggressively than a competitor that must build a new plant. This virtually ensures continuity over the life of the customer's facility.

Praxair also serves the merchant market by engaging in piggybacking--selling unused coproducts to off-site customers. Coproducts result when Praxair is contracted to build an air separation plant for a customer that requires only one of the three main atmospheric gases: oxygen, nitrogen, or argon. Liquefied merchant gas, which generates a third of gas sales, is delivered by Praxair's truck fleet to rental tanks located at the customer's facility. Though these shorter-duration contracts provide less protection from cyclical demand, they allow Praxair to leverage existing investments.

The balance of Praxair's gas sales are derived from the packaged-gas market, which involves taking bulk gas and repackaging it into high-pressure cylinders for smaller-scale users. While the oligopolistic and vertically integrated European packaged-gas market offers substantial returns, the U.S. equivalent is highly fragmented and competitive. As one of the only vertically integrated players in the United States, Praxair stands to benefit from consolidation in this distribution channel.

Precision Castparts PCP

Data as of 12-29-06

Rating	Fair Value	Last Close	Consider Buy	Consider Sell	Yield %
★★★	$82.00	$78.28	$63.20	$102.70	0.15

Company Profile
Precision makes complex metal components for aerospace, power generation, automotive, and other industrial applications. Its investment castings are essential to jet engine and gas turbine functionality, while its forged products and fastener systems are found in such critical areas as aircraft wing structures, bulkheads, and engine-to-wing connections. Precision Castparts has annual sales of $3.5 billion and employs more than 16,000 people worldwide.

Management
Stewardship Grade [B]

Precision's management is gifted at identifying and integrating acquisitions, effecting synergies across the board, and taking out costs quarter after quarter. Much of this operational proficiency has been driven by GE alumnus Mark Donegan, who joined the company in 1985 and became CEO in August 2002. Donegan has been highly rewarded for the company's success over the years and ranks among the most highly paid public executives. In fiscal 2006, Donegan took home about $2.33 million in salary and bonus and 260,000 stock options, which added more than $8 million to his total compensation package. Overall, we think Precision is well managed and that recent accounting issues are now behind the company. Corporate-governance policies are sound, but we would prefer to see the firm separate the chairman and CEO roles and disarm its takeover defenses, which include sizable severance packages for top management in the event of a buyout.

4650 S.W. Macadam Avenue Suite 440 www.precast.com
Portland, OR 97239-4252

Growth [A]	2003	2004	2005	2006
Revenue %	-17.5	5.8	52.6	21.5
Earnings/Share %	185.4	-12.8	NMF	NMF
Book Value/Share %	8.6	48.4	-29.4	50.4
Dividends/Share %	0.0	0.0	0.0	75.0

Profitability [B]	2004	2005	2006	TTM
Return on Assets %	3.1	0.0	9.3	9.8
Oper Cash Flow $Mil	143	354	231	419
- Cap Spending $Mil	56	62	99	133
= Free Cash Flow $Mil	87	292	132	286

Financial Health [B+]	2004	2005	2006	09-30-06
Long-term Debt $Mil	—	799	600	796
Total Equity $Mil	1,715	1,780	2,141	2,458
Debt/Equity Ratio	—	0.4	0.3	0.3

Industry	Business Risk	Moat Size	Investment Style	Sector
Metal Products	Average	Narrow	Mid Growth	Industrial Materials

Competition	Market Cap $Mil	12 Mo Trailing Sales $Mil	Price/Cash Flow	Return On Assets %	Debt/ Equity	Total Return % 1 Yr	3 Yr
Precision Castparts	10,623	4,258	25.4	9.8	0.3	51.4	51.4
Alcoa	26,022	29,666	11.4	5.8	0.3	3.5	-5.3
Ladish Company	527	346	—	7.4	0.3	65.9	65.0

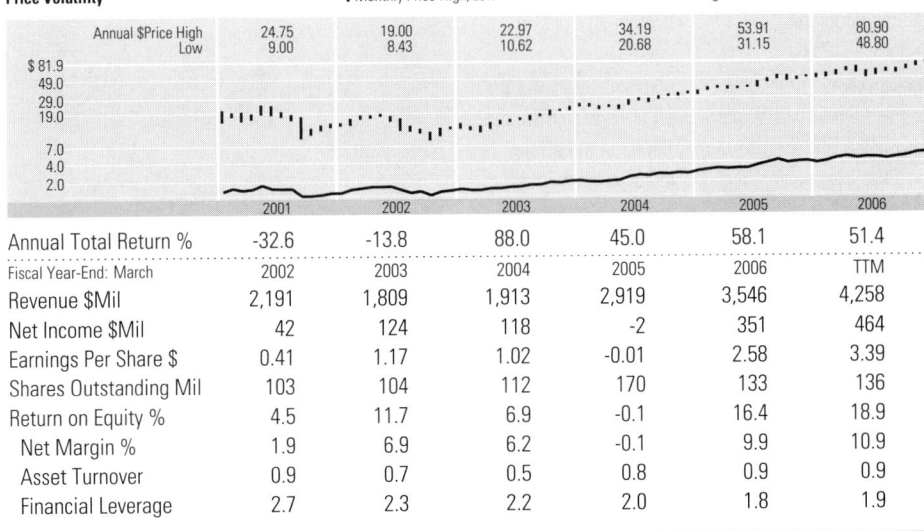

	2001	2002	2003	2004	2005	2006
Annual $Price High	24.75	19.00	22.97	34.19	53.91	80.90
Low	9.00	8.43	10.62	20.68	31.15	48.80
Annual Total Return %	-32.6	-13.8	88.0	45.0	58.1	51.4

Fiscal Year-End: March	2002	2003	2004	2005	2006	TTM
Revenue $Mil	2,191	1,809	1,913	2,919	3,546	4,258
Net Income $Mil	42	124	118	-2	351	464
Earnings Per Share $	0.41	1.17	1.02	-0.01	2.58	3.39
Shares Outstanding Mil	103	104	112	170	133	136
Return on Equity %	4.5	11.7	6.9	-0.1	16.4	18.9
Net Margin %	1.9	6.9	6.2	-0.1	9.9	10.9
Asset Turnover	0.9	0.7	0.5	0.8	0.9	0.9
Financial Leverage	2.7	2.3	2.2	2.0	1.8	1.9

Valuation Ratios	Stock	Rel to Industry	Rel to S&P 500
Price/Earnings	24.0	1.3	1.2
Price/Book	4.3	1.3	1.0
Price/Sales	2.5	1.4	0.9
Price/Cash Flow	25.4	1.6	1.7

Major Fund Holders	% of Fund Assets
Fidelity Select Air Transportation	7.60
Westport R	6.87
Fidelity Select Defense & Aerospace	6.72
Gartmore Mid Cap Growth Leaders D	5.56

Thesis By Brian Nelson, 10-25-06 Stock Price as of Analysis: $67.86

Precision Castparts is the low-cost leader in the aerospace metal-forming industry. Its operational flexibility and deep-rooted customer relationships create a narrow moat around its business.

Precision makes investment castings (45% of fiscal 2006 sales), forged products (25%), fastener systems (23%), and industrial products (7%) and sells them primarily to the commercial and military aerospace and power generation markets. The firm's highly complex castings are used in aircraft jet engines and power turbines to maintain their structural integrity under intense thermal conditions. Since its castings use proprietary technologies and are critical to engine functionality, Precision's customers--General Electric, Rolls Royce, and United Technologies--are reluctant to seek out unproven suppliers. This conservatism shuts the door on potential new entrants; the firm's largest customer, GE, has bought Precision's castings for more than four decades.

Leveraging its existing customer base, Precision has eclipsed Alcoa's Howmet unit as the market share leader and complemented its core casting business with acquisitions in aerospace fasteners and forged products. Given its dominance, Precision is ideally positioned to benefit from a multiyear cyclical upswing in aerospace demand as foreign carriers expand capacity to accommodate global airline traffic growth and as domestic airlines upgrade to more fuel-efficient planes. Thanks to continued share gains, the firm is also poised to benefit from increased dollar content on Boeing's and Airbus' next-generation aircraft, which use more expensive casting technology than prior models.

The cyclicality of the aerospace industry (59% of sales) and Precision's lack of pricing power--thanks to its oligopolistic customer base--remain enduring challenges for the company. However, Precision has some advantages that prop up results when others succumb to fading cyclical demand and price concessions. Management's tightfisted operational philosophy has preserved operating margins in the 10%-16% range in each of the past 10 years--a consistency that has escaped competitors. Precision's fully integrated supply chain, from raw material to forged product or casting, should mitigate gyrations in input costs, and its growing aftermarket business should hedge against slowing aircraft orders during economic downturns. These defenses, along with Precision's unique position in the aerospace industry, earn the company a narrow moat, in our opinion.

Data as of 12-29-06

Procter & Gamble PG

	Rating	Fair Value	Last Close	Consider Buy	Consider Sell	Yield %
	★★★	$67.00	$64.27	$57.10	$88.00	1.88

Company Profile

Since its founding in 1837, Procter & Gamble has become the world's largest consumer-products manufacturer, with a lineup of famous brands. The company's nearly 300 brands are sold through five global business units and include Tide laundry detergent, Charmin toilet paper, Pantene shampoo, Cover Girl cosmetics, Folgers coffee, and Iams pet food. The company completed its acquisition of Gillette in October 2005.

Management   Stewardship Grade [B]

A.G. Lafley became CEO in June 2000, and he also serves as chairman of the board, roles we'd prefer to see separated. In fiscal 2006 Lafley was paid a salary and bonus of $5.2 million, the same as 2005 and toward the higher end of his consumer-products peer group. It's Lafley's long-term compensation that is a bit off the charts, in our opinion, as he received $8.5 million in stock options and $5.0 million in restricted stock during the year. We like seeing CEOs with ownership in their companies, but Lafley now owns stock valued at more than 24 times his base salary, and we're skeptical of the motivational impact of additional grants. The largess wasn't limited to Lafley, though, as Jim Kilts received $15.6 million in stock options as part of his employment agreement following the merger with Gillette. Generally speaking, P&G does a good job of putting most executive compensation into at-risk incentive programs tied to long-term performance, and the firm's executive compensation plan was restructured to include metrics linked to the successful integration of Gillette. Officers and directors own less than 1% of shares outstanding. P&G has a staggered board of directors but is slowly phasing it out in favor of annual elections by 2008.

One Procter & Gamble Plaza   www.pg.com
Cincinnati, OH 45202

Growth [A+]	2003	2004	2005	2006
Revenue %	7.8	18.5	10.4	20.2
Earnings/Share %	22.3	29.4	15.0	4.3
Book Value/Share %	18.0	7.5	-4.5	200.9
Dividends/Share %	7.9	13.7	10.5	11.7

Profitability [A-]	2004	2005	2006	TTM
Return on Assets %	10.8	11.3	6.4	6.8
Oper Cash Flow $Mil	9,355	8,679	11,375	12,157
- Cap Spending $Mil	2,024	2,181	2,667	2,836
= Free Cash Flow $Mil	7,331	6,498	8,708	9,321

Financial Health [A]	2004	2005	2006	09-30-06
Long-term Debt $Mil	—	12,887	35,976	35,727
Total Equity $Mil	18,190	16,992	61,457	62,373
Debt/Equity Ratio	—	0.8	0.6	0.6

Industry	Business Risk	Moat Size	Investment Style	Sector
Household Products	Below Avg	Wide	Large Core	Consumer Goods

Competition

	Market Cap $Mil	12 Mo Trailing Sales $Mil	Price/Cash Flow	Return On Assets %	Debt/Equity	Total Return % 1 Yr	3 Yr
Procter & Gamble	203,656	72,214	16.8	6.8	0.6	13.4	11.3
Unilever NV	46,726	49,679	8.6	10.6	0.8	25.0	12.4
Colgate-Palmolive	33,554	11,933	18.1	14.3	2.2	21.5	11.8

Price Volatility

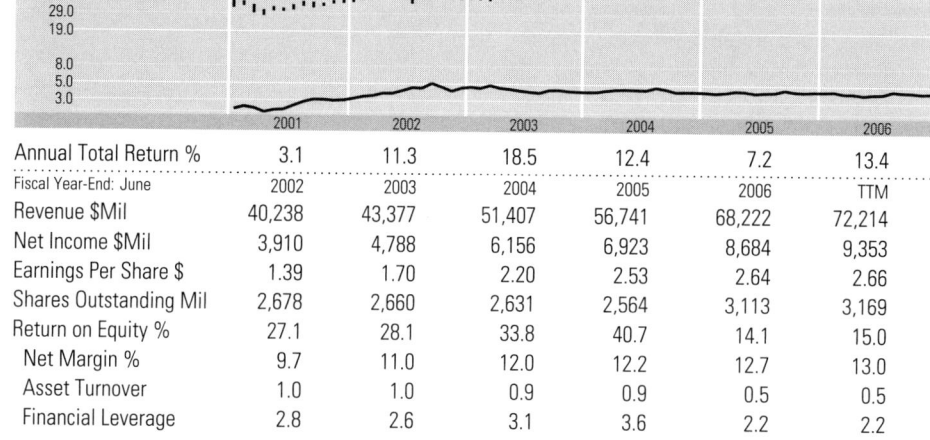

Annual Total Return %	3.1	11.3	18.5	12.4	7.2	13.4
Fiscal Year-End: June	2002	2003	2004	2005	2006	TTM
Revenue $Mil	40,238	43,377	51,407	56,741	68,222	72,214
Net Income $Mil	3,910	4,788	6,156	6,923	8,684	9,353
Earnings Per Share $	1.39	1.70	2.20	2.53	2.64	2.66
Shares Outstanding Mil	2,678	2,660	2,631	2,564	3,113	3,169
Return on Equity %	27.1	28.1	33.8	40.7	14.1	15.0
Net Margin %	9.7	11.0	12.0	12.2	12.7	13.0
Asset Turnover	1.0	1.0	0.9	0.9	0.5	0.5
Financial Leverage	2.8	2.6	3.1	3.6	2.2	2.2

Valuation Ratios	Stock	Rel to Industry	Rel to S&P 500
Price/Earnings	24.2	1.0	1.2
Price/Book	3.3	0.5	0.8
Price/Sales	2.8	1.0	1.0
Price/Cash Flow	16.8	0.9	1.2

Major Fund Holders	% of Fund Assets
ProFunds Consumer Goods UltraSector Inv	11.69
Wisdom Inv	9.19
W.P. Stewart & Co Growth	6.97
Rydex Consumer Products Inv	6.81

Thesis By Lauren DeSanto, 12-07-06 Stock Price as of Analysis: $63.80

In the consumer-products industry, moats don't get any wider than Procter & Gamble's, and its acquisition of Gillette in 2005 only reinforced its barricade.

P&G is a consumer-products behemoth with sales topping $70 billion worldwide, fueled by 22 brands each with sales in excess of $1 billion. While a handful of rivals give P&G a run for its money in specific categories, particularly Colgate in toothpaste, Kimberly-Clark in diapers, and L'Oreal in beauty care, no other single company can stack up against P&G's entire broad product portfolio. When categories face the risk of becoming commoditized, like laundry care, P&G manages to maintain margins, and sales, with a steady stream of new product introductions or brand extensions, such as "Tide with a Touch of Downy," that help it hold or grow market share and keep competitors at bay. Time and time again, P&G has also been a leader in pricing or has used its scale advantage to push pricing to unprofitable levels for its competition.

Underpinning all that P&G does is a focus on brands and market research that we believe is unparalleled. P&G utilizes its consumer research to help foster emotional connections to its brands and learn ways it can promote consumption and new habits. Whether it's disposable Swiffer wipes for quick cleaning or Pringles single-serve snack packs, P&G excels at responding to, and creating, consumer needs. We don't see any threat to P&G's consumer-driven brands anytime soon, but there are some chinks in the firm's armor.

We believe that P&G will be challenged to increase sales since it needs to add several billion dollars to its top line just to achieve midsingle-digit sales growth. Despite a push into higher-growth beauty-care segments, where competition is quite heated, it still operates in many slow-growth categories such as laundry care. Similarly, while P&G still has an opportunity to build out Gillette's distribution in developing markets, growth in these markets is starting to cool somewhat. Meanwhile, in mature markets, discount retailers and private-label manufacturers are only becoming more entrenched. For these reasons, we've forecasted sales growth for the firm of 5%, at the low end of the company's expectations.

We may not expect blockbuster growth from P&G, but that doesn't keep it from being one of our favorite companies. With the Gillette integration on track, and very healthy returns on invested capital, this is a stock for the long haul.

Progressive PGR

Data as of 12-29-06

Rating	Fair Value	Last Close	Consider Buy	Consider Sell	Yield %
★★★	$26.00	$24.22	$20.00	$32.60	0.14

Industry	Business Risk	Moat Size	Investment Style	Sector
Insurance (Property)	Average	Wide	Large Value	Financial Services

Company Profile

Progressive underwrites private and commercial auto insurance for 12 million customers and is the third-largest auto insurer in the United States. The company markets Drive Insurance policies through more than 30,000 independent insurance agencies in the United States and Canada. Direct-marketed policies, sold under the Progressive brand online and via phone, represents about 33% of total in-force policies, while agent-marketed policies represent the remaining two thirds.

Management Stewardship Grade [A]

The team at Progressive walks the walk. Directors and officers collectively own about 8.2% of the firm, thanks to chairman Peter Lewis' 6.7% stake. The short-term incentive compensation plan is straightforward and rewards good results but not mediocrity. CEO Glenn Renwick earned $2.4 million cash in 2005, plus $7.5 million in restricted stock. About half of these restricted shares expire in 2014 (Renwick receives $0) unless the firm produces $17.5 billion in premiums and a 96% combined ratio in a 12-month period. Premium volume needs to increase only about 2.8% each year to achieve the goal by 2014. However, because the shares vest upon reaching this goal, Renwick has strong incentive to increase premium volume as rapidly as possible while earning a sizable underwriting profit. Progressive's managers focus on widening the firm's moat and are worth every penny, in our view. Altogether Progressive is a shareholder-friendly firm, in our opinion, and easily earns our highest Stewardship Grade.

6300 Wilson Mills Road www.progressive.com
Mayfield Village, OH 44143

Growth [B-]	2002	2003	2004	2005
Revenue %	24.1	27.9	15.9	3.8
Earnings/Share %	63.4	90.3	34.1	-8.5
Book Value/Share %	16.8	35.0	4.6	28.2
Dividends/Share %	4.3	4.1	9.5	8.7

Profitability [A+]	2003	2004	2005	TTM
Return on Assets %	7.7	9.6	7.4	7.7
Oper Cash Flow $Mil	2,437	2,663	1,994	—
- Cap Spending $Mil	171	192	219	—
= Free Cash Flow $Mil	—	—	—	—

Financial Health [NA]	2003	2004	2005	09-30-06
Long-term Debt $Mil	—	—	—	—
Total Equity $Mil	5,031	5,155	6,108	6,714
Debt/Equity Ratio	—	—	—	—

Competition

	Market Cap $Mil	12 Mo Trailing Sales $Mil	Price/Cash Flow	Return On Assets%	Debt/ Equity	Total Return% 1 Yr	Total Return% 3 Yr
Progressive	18,448	14,692	—	7.7	—	-16.9	5.7
Berkshire Hathaway B	169,636	97,676	—	5.2	—	24.9	9.4
Allstate	40,690	35,639	—	3.0	—	23.4	17.2

Price Volatility

Annual $Price High	12.65	15.12	20.96	24.32	31.23	29.77
Low	6.84	11.19	11.56	18.28	20.35	22.18
	2001	2002	2003	2004	2005	2006
Annual Total Return %	44.4	-0.1	68.7	1.6	37.8	-16.9

Fiscal Year-End: December	2001	2002	2003	2004	2005	TTM
Revenue $Mil	7,488	9,294	11,892	13,782	14,303	14,692
Net Income $Mil	411	667	1,255	1,649	1,394	1,528
Earnings Per Share $	0.46	0.75	1.42	1.91	1.75	1.94
Shares Outstanding Mil	885	875	867	852	788	762
Return on Equity %	12.7	17.7	25.0	32.0	22.8	22.8
Net Margin %	5.5	7.2	10.6	12.0	9.7	10.4
Asset Turnover	0.7	0.7	0.7	0.8	0.8	0.7
Financial Leverage	3.4	3.6	3.2	3.3	3.1	3.0

Valuation Ratios	Stock	Rel to Industry	Rel to S&P 500
Price/Earnings	12.5	0.9	0.6
Price/Book	2.7	1.6	0.7
Price/Sales	1.3	0.9	0.4
Price/Cash Flow	—	—	—

Major Fund Holders	% of Fund Assets
Sequoia	15.62
AXA Enterprise Equity A	6.92
TCW Select Equities I	6.11
Ameristock	3.62

Thesis By Jim Ryan, 12-01-06 Stock Price as of Analysis: $22.49

Progressive's underwriting insights, advanced technology, and strong claims service are making its auto insurance more than just a commodity--and compounding the firm's already-wide moat. We think the stock is worth $26 per share.

We believe Progressive's success originates in its underwriting prowess, the source of its widening moat. Progressive can apply greater underwriting insight more finely and much faster than competitors. This is critical, as it caps the firm's largest expense--claim payments--and makes it one of the lowest-cost providers in the market. Progressive's low prices are the key reason the firm's growth outpaces the industry. Drivers must buy auto insurance, and the cost is a significant portion of most household budgets, so many hunt ruthlessly for low prices. Progressive can consistently offer some of the cheapest insurance around, at prices at which competitors struggle to be profitable, so it often makes the short list.

Progressive's management has described the firm as a technology company disguised as an insurer, and we agree. Auto-accident frequency and cost data are widely available and used by insurers, but no competitor can match the pricing insights Progressive's sophisticated automated underwriting algorithms enable. Better still, based on voluminous data, Progressive's "statistics factory" enables much more finely segmented pricing that helps the firm match quotes with demand. It also provides the capability to rapidly detect mispricing, which helps Progressive keep pace with loss trends. Rivals can't easily replicate Progressive's insights and speed, so they concede an advantage on their largest cost.

Quality service is right behind pricing in achieving customer satisfaction. Progressive's good claims service differentiates the firm from the pack and helps it retain policyholders and reduce costs. Progressive falters in other service areas beyond claims, however. In recent J.D. Power auto insurance satisfaction surveys, the firm ranks near the bottom in achieving overall customer satisfaction. Bundled services, particularly homeowners insurance, is an important factor in acquiring and retaining customers. Progressive lacked this capability until recently, when it inked a deal to broker homeowner insurance with an independent provider. While Progressive doesn't receive an economic benefit from the relationship, it's an important step to help increase customer satisfaction, in our view.

ProLogis Trust PLD

Data as of 12-29-06

	Rating	Fair Value	Last Close	Consider Buy	Consider Sell	Yield %
	★	$46.00	$60.77	$35.50	$57.60	2.63

Company Profile
ProLogis is a real estate investment trust that owns and manages industrial distribution facilities. The firm owns more than 2,400 properties in 81 markets in North America (76% of leasable area), Europe (19%), and Asia (5%). ProLogis manages and has an ownership stake in 13 property funds with nearly $11 billion in assets under management; fees from managing the funds constitute about half of the company's operating income.

Management Stewardship Grade [B]
Company veteran Jeffrey Schwartz succeeded CEO Dane Brooksher in early 2005. Brooksher retained the chairman title. We like ProLogis' decentralized management structure; regional presidents are responsible for investments and operations in each geographical area, mitigating any negative effects of changes at the top. Schwartz was paid nearly $1.2 million in salary and bonus in 2005. ProLogis' board is fairly independent--nine of the 12 members are outsiders--and the company's directors are elected annually. The company recently added Nelson Rising, former chairman and CEO of Catellus, to its board. Insiders own a little over 2% of the firm's common stock.

14100 East 35th Place
Aurora, CO 80011
www.prologis.com

Growth [C-]	2002	2003	2004	2005
Revenue %	20.8	-1.9	26.9	-0.1
Earnings/Share %	144.9	-3.3	-6.9	63.0
Book Value/Share %	4.8	4.7	-12.3	66.4
Dividends/Share %	2.9	1.4	1.4	1.4

Profitability [A-]	2003	2004	2005	TTM
Return on Assets %	3.3	2.9	2.8	4.2
Oper Cash Flow $Mil	367	559	498	—
- Cap Spending $Mil	23	25	27	—
= Free Cash Flow $Mil	—	—	—	—

Financial Health [NA]	2003	2004	2005	09-30-06
Long-term Debt $Mil	—	—	—	—
Total Equity $Mil	3,059	2,752	5,138	5,543
Debt/Equity Ratio	—	—	—	—

Industry	Business Risk	Moat Size	Investment Style	Sector
REITs	Average	Narrow	Large Value	Financial Services

Competition	Market Cap $Mil	12 Mo Trailing Sales $Mil	Price/Cash Flow	Return On Assets %	Debt/ Equity	Total Return % 1 Yr	3 Yr
ProLogis Trust	15,037	2,288	—	4.2	—	34.0	28.5
AMB Property	5,235	751	—	3.5	—	23.3	26.1
First Industrial Realty T	2,101	410	—	2.8	—	30.1	20.0

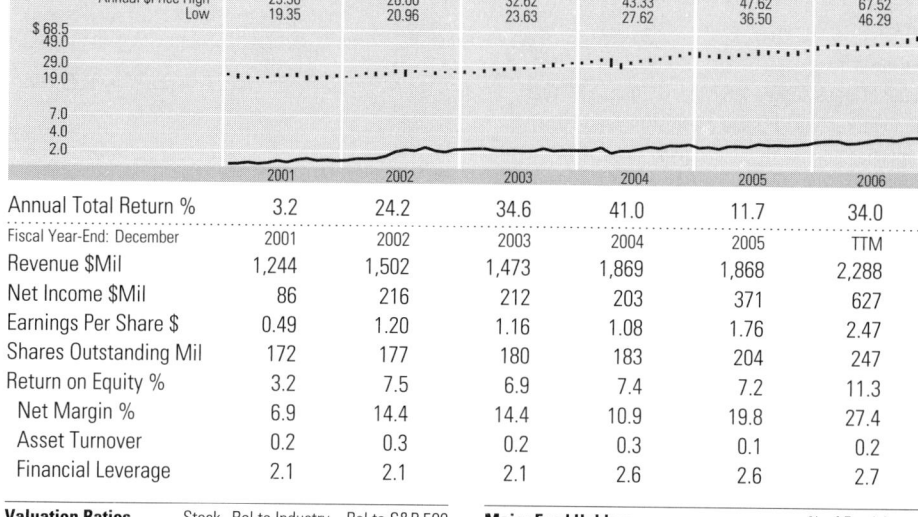

Price Volatility — Monthly Price High/Low — Relative Strength to S&P 500

	2001	2002	2003	2004	2005	TTM
Annual Total Return %	3.2	24.2	34.6	41.0	11.7	34.0
Fiscal Year-End: December	2001	2002	2003	2004	2005	TTM
Revenue $Mil	1,244	1,502	1,473	1,869	1,868	2,288
Net Income $Mil	86	216	212	203	371	627
Earnings Per Share $	0.49	1.20	1.16	1.08	1.76	2.47
Shares Outstanding Mil	172	177	180	183	204	247
Return on Equity %	3.2	7.5	6.9	7.4	7.2	11.3
Net Margin %	6.9	14.4	14.4	10.9	19.8	27.4
Asset Turnover	0.2	0.3	0.2	0.3	0.1	0.2
Financial Leverage	2.1	2.1	2.1	2.6	2.6	2.7

Valuation Ratios	Stock	Rel to Industry	Rel to S&P 500
Price/Earnings	34.3	0.7	1.7
Price/Book	2.7	0.7	0.7
Price/Sales	6.6	0.9	2.3
Price/Cash Flow	—	—	—

Major Fund Holders	% of Fund Assets
Third Avenue Real Estate Value	9.86
Fidelity Real Estate Investment	8.66
Aston/ABN AMRO Real Estate N	8.18
SSgA Tuckerman Active REIT	7.69

Thesis By Heather Smith, 10-20-06 Stock Price as of Analysis: $60.81

ProLogis Trust is an industrial property landlord with a global mind-set. The firm's self-funding platform provides capital for new development, enabling it to outpace the competition in terms of expansion. With the global economy humming, we believe ProLogis will continue to enjoy solid profits and dividend growth. We would consider purchasing the shares at a reasonable margin of safety to our fair value estimate.

ProLogis' business consists of two different parts: property management and property funds. The latter is unique to a real estate investment trust and reflects management's innovative approach to growth. Because a REIT must distribute at least 90% of its taxable income as dividends, it cannot reinvest much in operations. This leaves raising capital via the equity markets as its main funding option, which can be costly and dilutive to shareholders.

ProLogis gets around this problem by setting up property funds with institutional investors. The company contributes development properties to the funds, making it both a minority owner and a managing partner. This arrangement gives ProLogis three sources of income--development profits, rental revenue, and management fees--that supplement its bread-and-butter business of property management.

The multiple income streams also give ProLogis an internal source of funding, serving to lower its overall cost of capital. Finally, the strategy diminishes the risk associated with new projects; 90% of the properties contributed to the funds meet published criteria, reducing speculative development.

With this innovative funding strategy, ProLogis' footprint now extends to 17 countries. It is one of the only industrial REITs to offer a global network of distribution facilities--a fact that has not been lost on customers. The company's ability to respond to each tenant's needs quickly and cost-effectively explains its high customer-retention rate. Additionally, the recent Catellus Development acquisition should further strengthen client relationships. We believe this is a savvy move, as Catellus' attractive industrial portfolio--with higher occupancies, newer buildings, and a concentration in high-growth markets--will enhance the firm's asset quality.

We believe ProLogis is a high-quality REIT with a smart business model that drives measures of profitability, such as return on equity, consistently higher. The company offers not only a handsome dividend, but also an impressive collection of assets in some of the most desirable markets in the world.

Data as of 12-29-06

Pulte Homes PHM

	Rating	Fair Value	Last Close	Consider Buy	Consider Sell	Yield %
	★★★	$37.00	$33.12	$28.50	$46.40	0.48

Industry	Business Risk	Moat Size	Investment Style	Sector
Home Building	Average	Narrow	Mid Core	Consumer Services

Company Profile

Pulte Homes sold 45,600 homes in 2005, making it the second-largest homebuilder in the nation by units as well as total revenue. The company is a top five builder in 15 of the 20 largest metropolitan areas, with operations in all the fast-growing states. Under its Del Webb and Sun City brands, Pulte is one of the leading builders of active-adult homes for people 55 and older. A small financial subsidiary provides mortgage and title services mainly to Pulte homebuyers.

Management
Stewardship Grade [B]

Richard Dugas succeeded Mark O'Brien, a 21-year Pulte veteran, as CEO and president in mid-2003. Dugas has been with the company since 1994, working his way up from president of the company's Southeastern coastal region to executive vice president and chief operating officer. Chairman William Pulte founded the company more than 50 years ago and remains a 16% shareholder with no outstanding options. All directors and executives together own almost 19% of the company, including exercisable options. Only two of the 12 board members are affiliated with the company, and board elections are staggered. Nonexecutive members earn $50,000 annually in addition to 7,000 options and 3,600 restricted shares. We like that senior executive's annual incentive compensation is based in part on the achievement of return on equity objectives. With such strong performance throughout the entire industry, top brass was well compensated in 2005.

100 Bloomfield Hills Parkway Suite 300
Bloomfield Hills, MI 48304
www.pulte.com

Growth [A]	2002	2003	2004	2005
Revenue %	35.9	21.2	30.5	27.6
Earnings/Share %	22.7	34.8	52.8	49.9
Book Value/Share %	-1.2	22.3	26.9	30.6
Dividends/Share %	0.0	-25.0	233.3	30.0

Profitability [A-]	2003	2004	2005	TTM
Return on Assets %	7.7	9.5	11.4	9.1
Oper Cash Flow $Mil	-302	-692	19	-749
- Cap Spending $Mil	39	75	89	106
= Free Cash Flow $Mil	-341	-767	-70	-855

Financial Health [B-]	2003	2004	2005	09-30-06
Long-term Debt $Mil	2,151	2,862	3,387	3,538
Total Equity $Mil	3,448	4,522	5,957	6,567
Debt/Equity Ratio	0.6	0.6	0.6	0.5

Competition	Market Cap $Mil	12 Mo Trailing Sales $Mil	Price/Cash Flow	Return On Assets %	Debt/ Equity	Total Return% 1 Yr	3 Yr
Pulte Homes	8,432	15,017	—	9.1	0.5	-15.4	13.8
DR Horton	8,306	15,051	—	8.3	0.8	-24.4	9.9
Lennar	8,313	17,031	25.7	11.0	0.4	-12.9	5.0

Price Volatility — Monthly Price High/Low — Relative Strength to S&P 500

Annual $Price High/Low	12.56/6.53	14.94/9.06	24.49/11.36	32.50/20.00	48.23/30.01	44.70/26.02
	2001	2002	2003	2004	2005	2006
Annual Total Return %	6.4	7.5	96.0	36.8	23.8	-15.4

Fiscal Year-End: December	2001	2002	2003	2004	2005	TTM
Revenue $Mil	5,354	7,276	8,821	11,514	14,695	15,017
Net Income $Mil	301	454	625	987	1,492	1,270
Earnings Per Share $	1.50	1.84	2.48	3.79	5.68	4.88
Shares Outstanding Mil	197	241	244	252	255	255
Return on Equity %	13.2	16.4	18.1	21.8	25.0	19.3
Net Margin %	5.6	6.2	7.1	8.6	10.2	8.5
Asset Turnover	0.9	1.1	1.1	1.1	1.1	1.1
Financial Leverage	2.5	2.5	2.3	2.3	2.2	2.1

Valuation Ratios	Stock	Rel to Industry	Rel to S&P 500
Price/Earnings	7.0	0.8	0.3
Price/Book	1.3	0.7	0.3
Price/Sales	0.6	0.7	0.2
Price/Cash Flow	—	—	—

Major Fund Holders	% of Fund Assets
Granum Value	8.07
Alpine U.S. Real Estate Equity	4.00
Fidelity Select Construction&Housing	3.46
Morgan Stanley Focus Growth B	3.21

Thesis By Eric Landry, 12-18-06 Stock Price as of Analysis: $32.93

With almost 46,000 closings in 2005, Pulte is one of homebuilding's 800-pound gorillas. But size isn't the only thing going for this narrow-moat builder. The company also has a fair degree of brand recognition and is well positioned to take advantage of significant demographic tailwinds.

In an industry not known for high customer satisfaction, Pulte has managed to gain a reputation as a very high-quality builder. In the 2006 J.D. Power new homebuilder customer satisfaction study, the company's brands (Pulte Homes, Del Webb, and DiVosta) placed first in 14 of the 30 markets it participated in and second in 12 markets. In total, Pulte placed in the top three in 28 of the 30 markets, besting all other large builders in this widely followed index. The benefits are significant, as this allows the company some degree of brand power in what is essentially a commodity business. Though not overwhelming, it also improves customer captivity somewhat, as satisfied customers are likely to remember pleasant experiences as they progress through first-time, move-up, and then finally active-adult home purchases, all of which are served by Pulte. Though we don't want to overplay the advantages of one large builder over the others in an industry that doesn't allow for significant competitive divergences, it's likely that Pulte enjoys some mild competitive edges.

A big part of Pulte's success revolves around Del Webb. Acquired in 2001 for about $1.7 billion, the unit is probably the most widely recognized brand in the active-adult space. The deal has proved to be a home run for shareholders as folks reaching retirement age flock to Del Webb's age-restricted communities. Not withstanding the current downturn, we think demand for this product will be strong for at least the next decade, thanks to a baby boom tidal wave that produced roughly 76 million births from 1946 through 1964, 52% more than the prior 19-year period. The oldest of that group, now entering their 60s, are prime Del Webb consumers, while roughly the other half of the boomers (those born between 1956 and 1964, when births jumped to an average of 4.2 million annually) should provide even more demand in coming years.

Still, the next couple of years are going to be tough. We estimate the homebuilding industry in aggregate was overbuilt by around 1 million units over the past three years. With annual demand around double that, it's going to take awhile before the market is back to equilibrium.

Data as of 12-29-06

Qualcomm QCOM

Rating	Fair Value	Last Close	Consider Buy	Consider Sell	Yield %
★★★★	$46.00	$37.79	$35.50	$57.60	1.19

Company Profile
Qualcomm pioneered code-division multiple access technology, a digital platform used in cellular phones, telecom equipment, and satellite base stations. As a result, Qualcomm is the world's leading designer and supplier of CDMA chipsets and system software; it licenses CDMA technology to many companies. The firm's OmniTRACS systems provide satellite communication, position location, and location management for trucking fleets.

Management
Stewardship Grade [A]

Despite the tight control the Jacobs family has had over the company, Qualcomm gets solid corporate governance marks due to excellent disclosures and recent strides to improve board transparency. Qualcomm's founder and chairman, Irwin Jacobs, recently passed the CEO reins to his son Paul Jacobs, who has been with the company nearly 15 years, most recently serving as the president of the wireless and Internet group. Other Jacobs family members are also executives, and the Jacobs family owns roughly 3% of the firm. With Irwin Jacobs stepping down from day-to-day activities, the company moved to deepen its management bench by elevating Steven Altman to president. Altman has been with Qualcomm for more than 15 years and spearheaded the company's aggressive intellectual-property licensing strategy. Qualcomm's management is well seasoned, as most executive officers have been with the firm for eight to 10 years. The firm's corporate governance is decent, for the most part. Including options, management pay is at the high end for the industry. But this is arguably warranted, given the company's above-average performance. In addition, the company eliminated its staggered board of directors earlier this year. Each director will now stand for election annually.

5775 Morehouse Drive
San Diego, CA 92121-1714
www.qualcomm.com

Growth [A+]	2003	2004	2005	2006
Revenue %	32.0	26.9	16.3	32.7
Earnings/Share %	131.8	102.0	22.3	14.3
Book Value/Share %	42.2	23.5	13.0	19.6
Dividends/Share %	NMF	123.5	68.4	31.3

Profitability [A+]	2004	2005	2006	TTM
Return on Assets %	15.9	17.2	16.2	16.2
Oper Cash Flow $Mil	2,481	2,686	3,253	3,253
- Cap Spending $Mil	332	576	685	685
= Free Cash Flow $Mil	2,149	2,110	2,568	2,568

Financial Health [A+]	2004	2005	2006	09-30-06
Long-term Debt $Mil	—	—	—	—
Total Equity $Mil	9,664	11,119	13,406	13,406
Debt/Equity Ratio	—	—	—	—

Industry	Business Risk	Moat Size	Investment Style	Sector
Wireless Equip.	Average	Wide	Large Growth	Hardware

Competition

	Market Cap $Mil	12 Mo Trailing Sales $Mil	Price/Cash Flow	Return On Assets %	Debt/Equity	Total Return % 1 Yr	3 Yr
Qualcomm	62,450	7,526	19.2	16.2	—	-11.3	13.1
Nokia ADR	90,097	42,815	17.4	17.1	0.0	13.4	8.2
Texas Instruments	42,736	15,173	16.1	29.3	0.0	-9.8	-0.2

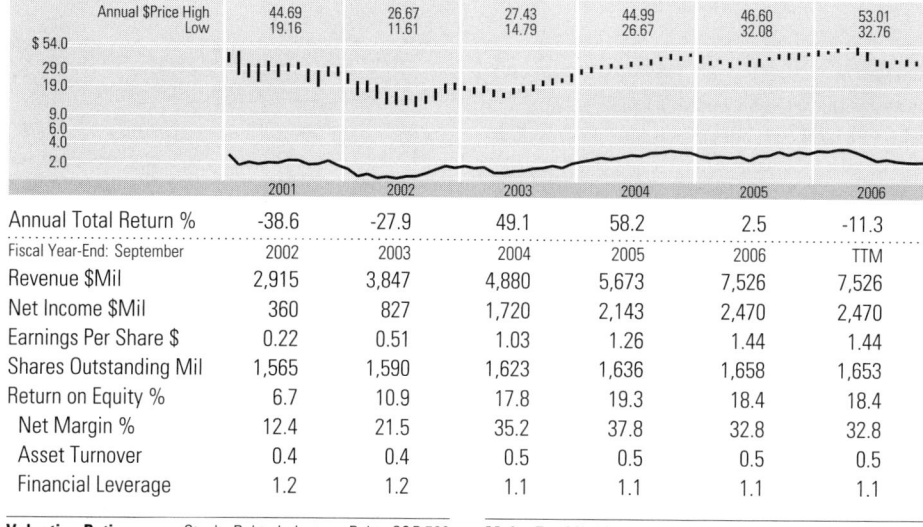

Price Volatility — Monthly Price High/Low, Relative Strength to S&P 500

	2001	2002	2003	2004	2005	2006
Annual $Price High	44.69	26.67	27.43	44.99	46.60	53.01
Low	19.16	11.61	14.79	26.67	32.08	32.76
Annual Total Return %	-38.6	-27.9	49.1	58.2	2.5	-11.3

Fiscal Year-End: September	2002	2003	2004	2005	2006	TTM
Revenue $Mil	2,915	3,847	4,880	5,673	7,526	7,526
Net Income $Mil	360	827	1,720	2,143	2,470	2,470
Earnings Per Share $	0.22	0.51	1.03	1.26	1.44	1.44
Shares Outstanding Mil	1,565	1,590	1,623	1,636	1,658	1,653
Return on Equity %	6.7	10.9	17.8	19.3	18.4	18.4
Net Margin %	12.4	21.5	35.2	37.8	32.8	32.8
Asset Turnover	0.4	0.4	0.5	0.5	0.5	0.5
Financial Leverage	1.2	1.2	1.1	1.1	1.1	1.1

Valuation Ratios	Stock	Rel to Industry	Rel to S&P 500
Price/Earnings	26.2	1.2	1.3
Price/Book	4.7	1.0	1.1
Price/Sales	8.3	2.3	2.9
Price/Cash Flow	19.2	1.0	1.3

Major Fund Holders	% of Fund Assets
ACM Convertible Securities	14.87
Fidelity Select Wireless	8.73
Fidelity Select Communications Equip	7.78
Fidelity Advisor Communications Equip T	7.75

Thesis
By John Slack, 11-22-06 Stock Price as of Analysis: $37.35

Qualcomm is in the enviable position of owning much of the intellectual property behind one of the dominant standards in the communications industry: code-division multiple access (CDMA) wireless technology. While the company's royalty agreements have come under increased scrutiny lately, we still believe the company stands to benefit from increased adoption of CDMA technology globally, and we would recommend this wide-moat stock at a modest discount to our fair value estimate.

Qualcomm's competitive advantage stems from its extensive patent portfolio and intellectual property relating to CDMA technology, one of two major wireless protocols used around the world. The firm's business model capitalizes on the use of CDMA from primarily two revenue streams. The first is through the design and manufacture of chipsets for CDMA phones. The other source of revenue is collecting royalties for the use of its CDMA patents. The firm collects a one-time licensing fee and then reaps a low-single-digit percentage cut of the selling price of each CDMA phone sold. This toll-bridge quality--the firm's economic moat--is the main reason to get excited about Qualcomm.

Qualcomm stands to be the prime beneficiary as the wireless industry migrates to the next-generation technology--often called third-generation or 3G. This is because both 3G standards--cdma2000 and W-CDMA--are derivations of CDMA, meaning Qualcomm will be entitled to royalties on nearly every handset sold. We estimate that the transition to 3G handsets will effectively quadruple Qualcomm's addressable market as wireless subscribers using GSM technology--the dominant technology in much of world--migrate to Qualcomm-based 3G technology. In addition, 3G phones should be more expensive than existing models, which will help slow the decline in handset prices, boosting Qualcomm's royalty revenues.

Over the past year, Qualcomm has seen pushback from a number of its patent licensees, which have argued that the company's royalty rates are too high. A number of firms--most notably Nokia and Texas Instruments --have complained to regulators that Qualcomm does not offer some of its patents on reasonable terms and offers lower royalty rates to handset customers that buy Qualcomm chips. One remedy, which we would applaud, would be for Qualcomm to spin off its chip business. While it will likely take years to sort out in the courts, Qualcomm's legal team has been remarkably effective at enforcing its patents in the past.

Data as of 12-29-06

Quest Diagnostics DGX

	Rating	Fair Value	Last Close	Consider Buy	Consider Sell	Yield %
	★★★	$57.00	$53.00	$44.00	$71.40	0.74

Company Profile
Quest Diagnostics is a leading provider of laboratory testing services, with more than $5.5 billion in revenue generated in 2005. The firm's clinical testing segment accounts for roughly 92% of sales. The remainder is attributable to clinical-trial testing services and to the recently acquired risk-assessment services business.

Industry	Business Risk	Moat Size	Investment Style	Sector
Diagnostics	Average	Narrow	Mid Core	Healthcare

Competition	Market Cap $Mil	12 Mo Trailing Sales $Mil	Price/Cash Flow	Return On Assets%	Debt/ Equity	Total Return% 1 Yr	3 Yr
Quest Diagnostics	10,338	6,194	10.9	9.9	0.4	3.7	14.4
Laboratory Corp of Americ SP	9,213	3,515	14.8	10.0	0.3	36.4	25.2

Management Stewardship Grade [B]
We assign Quest a B Stewardship Grade. Surya Mohapatra has been with the firm since 1999 as COO and took over as chairman and CEO in 2004 following the retirement of Kenneth Freeman. Most of the company's top management has been with the firm since the inception, which speaks highly of Quest's ability to retain its employees. Our view on management compensation is mixed. While we think the cash compensation received by the top executives is reasonable, the sizable option packages Mohapatra received in 2004 and 2005 seem excessive. We would also prefer if executive bonuses were tied to long-term performance targets, such as return on invested capital, in lieu of current earnings per share and revenue benchmarks. We believe the present bonus structure encourages decisions that are more short-term oriented. We would also like to see the chairman and CEO roles separated, as well as annual director elections instead of the current three-year terms.

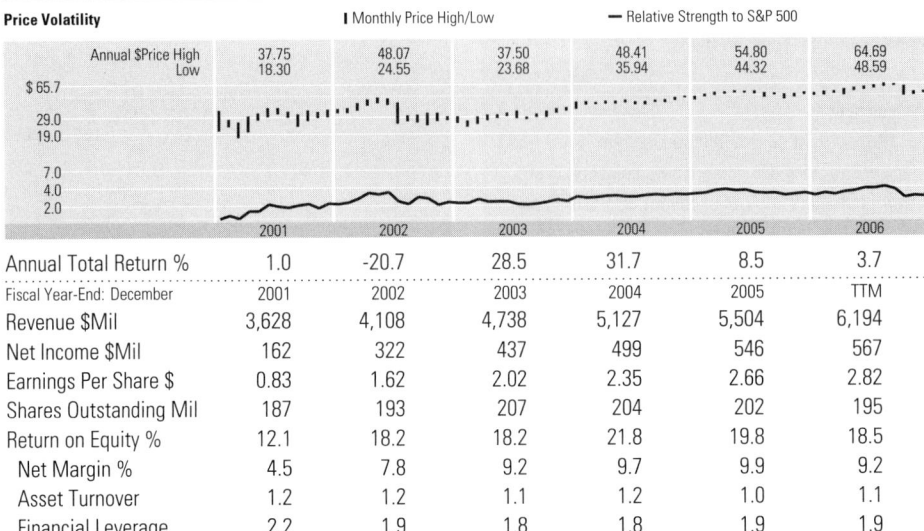

Price Volatility — Monthly Price High/Low — Relative Strength to S&P 500

Annual $Price High	37.75	48.07	37.50	48.41	54.80	64.69
Low	18.30	24.55	23.68	35.94	44.32	48.59
	2001	2002	2003	2004	2005	2006
Annual Total Return %	1.0	-20.7	28.5	31.7	8.5	3.7

Fiscal Year-End: December	2001	2002	2003	2004	2005	TTM
Revenue $Mil	3,628	4,108	4,738	5,127	5,504	6,194
Net Income $Mil	162	322	437	499	546	567
Earnings Per Share $	0.83	1.62	2.02	2.35	2.66	2.82
Shares Outstanding Mil	187	193	207	204	202	195
Return on Equity %	12.1	18.2	18.2	21.8	19.8	18.5
Net Margin %	4.5	7.8	9.2	9.7	9.9	9.2
Asset Turnover	1.2	1.2	1.1	1.2	1.0	1.1
Financial Leverage	2.2	1.9	1.8	1.8	1.9	1.9

Valuation Ratios	Stock	Rel to Industry	Rel to S&P 500
Price/Earnings	17.8	0.7	0.9
Price/Book	3.4	0.6	0.8
Price/Sales	1.7	0.4	0.6
Price/Cash Flow	10.9	0.7	0.7

Major Fund Holders	% of Fund Assets
Federated MDT Mid Cap Growth A	4.15
Pax World Growth	4.09
American Century Legacy Foc Lg Cap Inv	3.39
Badgley Growth	3.24

1290 Wall Street West www.questdiagnostics.com
Lyndhurst, NJ 07071

Growth [B-]	2002	2003	2004	2005
Revenue %	13.2	15.3	8.2	7.4
Earnings/Share %	94.6	25.1	16.3	13.2
Book Value/Share %	29.8	24.9	-2.7	24.9
Dividends/Share %	NMF	NMF	NMF	15.0

Profitability [A]	2003	2004	2005	TTM
Return on Assets %	10.2	11.9	10.3	9.9
Oper Cash Flow $Mil	663	799	852	949
- Cap Spending $Mil	175	176	224	179
= Free Cash Flow $Mil	488	623	627	770

Financial Health [A-]	2003	2004	2005	09-30-06
Long-term Debt $Mil	1,029	724	1,255	1,239
Total Equity $Mil	2,395	2,289	2,763	3,069
Debt/Equity Ratio	0.4	0.3	0.5	0.4

Thesis By Alex Morozov, CFA, 12-13-06 Stock Price as of Analysis: $52.54

Quest Diagnostics continues to expand its revenue base and generate steady and healthy operating cash flows. Its core diagnostic business is strong, driven by growth in specialty testing and economies of scale.

Quest and Laboratory Corporation of America operate in the independent diagnostic services industry essentially as a duopoly; the two industry giants jointly control more than 50% of the market. Quest is the largest player in the field and a leader across all major product lines. It has built an enormous infrastructure, with more than 2,000 patient service centers nationwide, and continues to expand its reach by acquiring smaller regional labs.

Quest's business benefits from the aging population and increases in health-care spending. Over the past few years, the company's operations have shown steady growth in the number of tests provided and the price charged per test. The latter is particularly remarkable, given that a significant portion of the company's contracts with managed-care providers include price caps. Faster growth in higher-priced genetic and other complex tests has contributed to the overall price improvement.

The company's next step is to show that its laboratory testing service is not a commodity. Quest is putting significant effort into expanding its product offering, retraining its personnel, and investing in new information technology. The firm is rolling out its Web-based physician portal in an effort to improve physician loyalty. We agree with management's assessment that once physicians are trained to use the company's platform, they are more likely to refer patients to Quest. Such differentiation efforts, along with the company's large infrastructure, scientific know-how, and commitment to quality, should provide Quest with a competitive advantage over smaller rivals for years to come.

However, LabCorp is intensifying its efforts to unseat Quest from its leadership position and in the process could be altering the competitive landscape of the diagnostic industry. LabCorp's recent agreement with UnitedHealth signals that managed-care providers could be increasingly looking toward long-term exclusive contracts to induce more favorable terms. This move could result in a fierce bidding process, which may shift bargaining power to insurance companies, erode profits, and result in deterioration in quality, as each competitor may have fewer incentives to keep quality high.

Data as of 12-29-06

Raytheon RTN

	Rating	Fair Value	Last Close	Consider Buy	Consider Sell	Yield %
	★★★	$50.00	$52.80	$38.60	$62.60	1.82

Company Profile
Raytheon is the fourth-largest defense company in the United States, with 2005 revenue of $21.9 billion. It operates through six segments and competes predominantly in the areas of missile defense, precision engagement, homeland defense, and intelligence, surveillance, and reconnaissance. Sales to the U.S. government account for about 75% of the company's total sales. Raytheon is based in Waltham, Mass., and employs about 80,000 people.

Management
Stewardship Grade [B]

Bill Swanson became president in 2002, CEO in July 2003, and chairman in January 2004. We tend to favor managers with long tenures, and we love the fact that Swanson's career at Raytheon began in 1972. His increasingly well-known "Swanson's Unwritten Rules of Management" and the kudos this collection of thoughts has received from the likes of Warren Buffett make us like him even more. We also think Swanson understands how to improve operations, starting with his comprehensive 2003 program review and the $226 million in charges he took against 10 underperforming contracts. Swanson is the only nonindependent director on the firm's 11-member board. Shareholders should continue to benefit from management's use of cash to repurchase shares, retire debt, and increase dividends, which it did again in 2006 by 9%. Our misgivings about corporate governance at Raytheon are few and, in some cases, diminishing. We prefer that separate individuals serve as chairman and CEO, and the use of one-time charges is becoming decreasingly frequent as the engineering and construction debacle starts to fade into the past. We raised our Stewardship Grade to a B when shareholders voted in favor of moving to a nonclassified board structure at the 2005 annual meeting.

870 Winter Street
Waltham, MA 02451
www.raytheon.com

Growth [C]	2002	2003	2004	2005
Revenue %	4.6	8.0	11.8	8.1
Earnings/Share %	NMF	NMF	6.8	104.3
Book Value/Share %	-30.9	1.5	7.7	-0.7
Dividends/Share %	0.0	0.0	0.0	10.0

Profitability [C]	2003	2004	2005	TTM
Return on Assets %	1.5	1.7	3.6	4.8
Oper Cash Flow $Mil	2,034	2,071	2,515	2,419
- Cap Spending $Mil	428	363	338	328
= Free Cash Flow $Mil	1,606	1,708	2,177	2,091

Financial Health [A-]	2003	2004	2005	09-30-06
Long-term Debt $Mil	7,376	4,637	3,969	3,401
Total Equity $Mil	9,162	10,551	10,709	11,380
Debt/Equity Ratio	0.8	0.4	0.4	0.3

Industry	Business Risk	Moat Size	Investment Style	Sector
Aerospace/Defense	Average	Narrow	Large Core	Industrial Materials

Competition	Market Cap $Mil	12 Mo Trailing Sales $Mil	Price/Cash Flow	Return On Assets%	Debt/ Equity	Total Return% 1 Yr	3 Yr
Raytheon	23,476	22,766	9.7	4.8	0.3	34.2	23.6
Boeing	70,249	59,114	9.4	2.7	0.8	28.4	30.4
Lockheed Martin	39,028	39,009	11.1	8.1	0.5	47.0	24.1

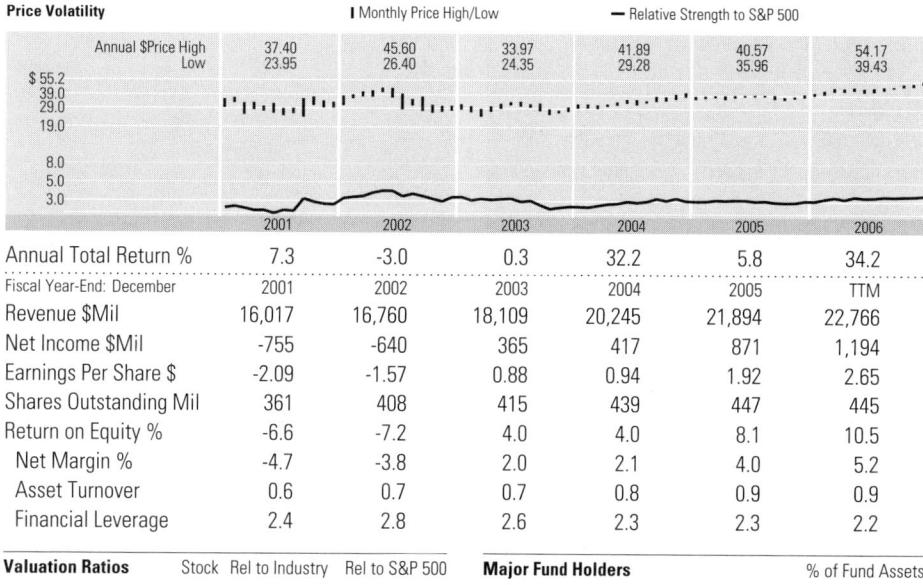

Price Volatility — Monthly Price High/Low — Relative Strength to S&P 500

	2001	2002	2003	2004	2005	2006
Annual $Price High	37.40	45.60	33.97	41.89	40.57	54.17
Low	23.95	26.40	24.35	29.28	35.96	39.43
Annual Total Return %	7.3	-3.0	0.3	32.2	5.8	34.2

Fiscal Year-End: December	2001	2002	2003	2004	2005	TTM
Revenue $Mil	16,017	16,760	18,109	20,245	21,894	22,766
Net Income $Mil	-755	-640	365	417	871	1,194
Earnings Per Share $	-2.09	-1.57	0.88	0.94	1.92	2.65
Shares Outstanding Mil	361	408	415	439	447	445
Return on Equity %	-6.6	-7.2	4.0	4.0	8.1	10.5
Net Margin %	-4.7	-3.8	2.0	2.1	4.0	5.2
Asset Turnover	0.6	0.7	0.7	0.8	0.9	0.9
Financial Leverage	2.4	2.8	2.6	2.3	2.3	2.2

Valuation Ratios	Stock	Rel to Industry	Rel to S&P 500
Price/Earnings	19.7	0.8	1.0
Price/Book	2.1	0.5	0.5
Price/Sales	1.0	0.8	0.3
Price/Cash Flow	9.7	0.7	0.7

Major Fund Holders	% of Fund Assets
Fidelity Select Defense & Aerospace	7.18
Integrity Growth & Income A Load Waived	5.59
SunAmerica Focused Large Cap Value A	3.59
Nuveen Santa Barbara Dividend Growth A	3.20

Thesis By Chris Lozier, 12-26-06 Stock Price as of Analysis: $53.45

A "program-agnostic" business model, size, and extensive weapons system expertise make Raytheon a good bet to dole out steady cash flows for years to come. The sale of its struggling airplane business should only help make cash flow stronger.

Raytheon mitigates its dependence on individual programs or platforms by primarily competing as a subcontractor to put its systems on many types of aircraft, ships, and combat vehicles. When enormous programs like the F/A-22 get scaled back, lead contractors take proportional top-line hits, but Raytheon is far less affected and can often translate its technology to other platforms. Raytheon's business is diversified across thousands of contracts, which are about equally divided between cost-plus and fixed-price deals. No program accounts for more than 4% of total sales, and the firm counts foreign governments, numerous U.S. federal agencies, and all four branches of the military as customers.

Raytheon's core strengths are well aligned with the military's transformation into a more agile and networked force. The firm has decades of experience developing precision munitions, missiles, radar systems, and other sensors, and should continue to win its share of contracts in these growth areas. Market leadership in missile detection and guidance technology has already earned the firm an extensive role in developing a ballistic missile defense system for the United States and its allies. Contract wins have also been steady on thousands of smaller programs that are Raytheon's lifeblood.

Raytheon's narrow moat should translate to solid growth (by defense industry standards) and wider margins over the next few years. Unprofitable and noncore divisions have been sold, including Raytheon Aircraft Company (sale should close in the first half of 2007), and CEO Bill Swanson is aggressively pushing a return on invested capital philosophy down the ranks of the firm.

We have several concerns, however. First, defense spending should continue to flatten out with mounting federal deficit pressures and the eventual drawdown of U.S. engagements in Iraq and Afghanistan. We don't foresee a meaningful decline in spending levels and, in fact, the ongoing reset of military assets will require heady spending for years after we pull our troops. Still, we expect low-single-digit growth at Raytheon over the next 10 years. Second, government budgets are fickle, and Raytheon is not immune. Finally, Raytheon is burdened by severely underfunded pension plans that will drain cash for many years.

Data as of 12-29-06

Regency Energy Partners LP RGNC

Rating	Fair Value	Last Close	Consider Buy	Consider Sell	Yield %
★★★	$28.00	$27.15	$21.60	$35.10	3.47

Industry	Business Risk	Moat Size	Investment Style	Sector
Natural Gas	Average	Narrow	Small Growth	Utilities

Company Profile
Regency is a midstream operator with natural-gas gathering, processing, and transportation assets spread across northern Louisiana, west Texas, and the Mid-Continent region of Kansas, Oklahoma, and Texas, with 11 treating and processing plants and more than 4,800 miles of gathering and transportation pipelines connecting with more than 2,800 active wells. The company became a publicly traded master limited partnership on Jan. 31, 2006.

Management
Stewardship Grade [D]

CEO and chairman James Hunt has more than 15 years of experience in energy investment banking and was previously CEO of exploration and production company Cenergy Corporation and offshore drilling contractor Diamond M Company. COO Michael Williams hails from Energy Transfer Partners ETP, where he was in charge of operations and engineering. The two bring deep financial and operational experience to the partnership; Hunt has extensive merger and acquisition and financing experience from his long tenure in energy investment banking, and Williams draws on more than 25 years in the midstream natural-gas business. Hunt and Williams, together with the other members of the management team, personally own 6.6% of Regency's limited partner units. Four out of the nine board members are principals with HM Capital Partners, the private-equity fund that took Regency public. HM Capital Partners controls Regency's general partner and owns 66% of the limited partner's common and subordinated units. The remaining five board members qualify as independent. Because of the MLP structure, common unitholders do not have the same degree of control and voting rights as shareholders in a standard corporation would. For example, it would require a 66% supermajority of common unitholders to remove

1700 Pacific Suite 2900　　www.regencyenergy.com
Dallas, TX 75201

Growth [B]	2002	2003	2004	2005
Revenue %	NMF	NMF	157.4	44.2
Earnings/Share %	NMF	NMF	NMF	NMF
Book Value/Share %	—	—	—	—
Dividends/Share %	NMF	NMF	NMF	NMF

Profitability [NA]	2003	2004	2005	TTM
Return on Assets %	3.8	4.4	-1.7	-2.7
Oper Cash Flow $Mil	6	27	31	36
- Cap Spending $Mil	4	17	151	165
= Free Cash Flow $Mil	3	10	-120	-129

Financial Health [F]	2003	2004	2005	09-30-06
Long-term Debt $Mil	55	248	358	611
Total Equity $Mil	60	177	170	217
Debt/Equity Ratio	0.9	1.4	2.1	2.8

Competition

	Market Cap $Mil	12 Mo Trailing Sales $Mil	Price/Cash Flow	Return On Assets%	Debt/ Equity	Total Return% 1 Yr	3 Yr
Regency Energy Partners LP	1,269	931	35.5	-2.7	2.8	—	—
Energy Transfer Partners	5,999	7,859	11.0	7.3	1.6	65.5	47.7
Crosstex Energy LP	1,293	3,487	17.7	-0.2	1.2	24.0	30.6

Price Volatility ｜ Monthly Price High/Low　— Relative Strength to S&P 500

Annual $Price High/Low: 27.60 / 19.17 (2006)

Annual Total Return %	—	—	—	—	—	—
Fiscal Year-End: December	2001	2002	2003	2004	2005	TTM
Revenue $Mil	—	—	187	480	693	931
Net Income $Mil	—	—	6	21	-11	-26
Earnings Per Share $	—	—	—	—	—	—
Shares Outstanding Mil	—	—	—	—	—	47
Return on Equity %	—	—	10.3	12.1	-6.6	-12.1
Net Margin %	—	—	3.3	4.5	-1.6	-2.8
Asset Turnover	—	—	1.1	1.0	1.1	1.0
Financial Leverage	—	—	2.7	2.7	3.9	4.4

Valuation Ratios	Stock	Rel to Industry	Rel to S&P 500
Price/Earnings	—	—	—
Price/Book	5.9	1.8	1.4
Price/Sales	1.4	1.4	0.5
Price/Cash Flow	35.5	3.1	2.4

Major Fund Holders % of Fund Assets

Thesis By Jason Stevens, 12-20-06 Stock Price as of Analysis: $27.05

With the acquisition of TexStar Field Services in the rearview mirror, Regency Energy Partners' prospects look favorable. We are increasingly comfortable with this midstream natural-gas operator and think that the partnership is gaining critical mass, but we remain a bit leery of the company's decision to pursue a deal with an affiliate of its general partner.

The $360 million acquisition of TexStar's natural-gas gathering, processing, and treating assets in south and east Texas appears to be a smart strategic move that will bulk up Regency's gathering segment. The deal adds two more Texas producing regions to Regency's current presence in west Texas, north Louisiana, and the Mid-Continent region, increasing system capacity by 415 million cubic feet per day, and includes an existing relationship with a producer.

However, both TexStar and its anchor producer, BlackBrush, are affiliate companies of Regency's general partner, the private equity firm HM Capital Partners. We tend to frown on related-party transactions because it is not always clear that investors get the best deal. While Regency claims the acquisition was negotiated at arm's length, we have some cause for concern. TexStar was formed in order to purchase underutilized assets in areas where BlackBrush operated, suggesting that the managers of both firms collaborated on strategy and operations. By agreeing to have Regency acquire TexStar, the general partner is in effect cashing out its position in TexStar while retaining complete control over its operations, and enjoying a share of future cash flows to boot. The deal should be cash-flow accretive and help the company to increase distributions, but for individual investors, it isn't completely clear that this deal was the best use of $360 million.

And while the TexStar deal will boost Regency's gathering and processing operations, we're also excited about the partnership's completion of a $140 million capital project to expand and extend its main pipeline system, which we view as a solid step toward generating robust cash flows going forward. The pipeline system enhancements relieve prior bottlenecks, bumping throughput capacity from 200 million to 800 million cubic feet per day, and now connect to the three largest producing fields in Louisiana. This will allow the partnership to quadruple the volume of natural gas it ships, generating substantially more fee-based revenue with no direct commodity price exposure and deepening the partnership's narrow economic moat.

Data as of 12-29-06

Reliance Steel and Aluminum RS

	Rating	Fair Value	Last Close	Consider Buy	Consider Sell	Yield %
	★★★★	$45.00	$39.38	$34.70	$56.40	0.56

Company Profile

Reliance Steel and Aluminum is a holding company that owns more than 100 businesses across the United States, making it one of the two largest metal service centers in America. It provides products to the manufacturing, construction, transportation, aerospace, and semiconductor industries. About 55% of the metal it obtains (mainly steel and aluminum) is sent in small quantities right to manufacturers; the remaining 45% is processed to meet customer specifications.

Management

Stewardship Grade [A]

Nearly all of Reliance's senior managers and directors have been with the company for the long haul. Former CEO and current chairman Joe Crider has been with the firm for more than 30 years; the CFO and COO also have long tenures with the company. CEO David Hannah has been employed by Reliance since 1981, well before it went public in 1994. Our Stewardship Grade of A rewards Reliance for its exemplary corporate governance and shareholder-friendliness. Since taking the helm in 1999, Hannah has impressively guided Reliance through the ever-volatile steel industry and led shareholders to gains of over 300%. The company has demonstrated effective management of its 160-plus service center locations, allowing plant managers a high degree of autonomy while continually looking to squeeze greater efficiency out of them. Reliance lacks a poison-pill provision, which would dilute shareholder value in the event of a takeover. The company's cumulative voting policy also gives shareholders more voting power when electing directors. Finally, since Hannah's personal stake in Reliance is likely worth more than 5 times his 2005 cash compensation, we believe his interests are well-aligned with shareholders'.

350 South Grand Avenue Suite 5100 www.rsac.com
Los Angeles, CA 90071

Growth [A+]	2002	2003	2004	2005
Revenue %	5.3	7.9	56.3	14.4
Earnings/Share %	-25.8	-43.7	385.0	19.7
Book Value/Share %	-6.5	-47.0	23.4	23.8
Dividends/Share %	0.0	0.0	8.3	46.2

Profitability [A-]	2003	2004	2005	TTM
Return on Assets %	2.5	10.9	11.6	9.1
Oper Cash Flow $Mil	108	122	272	119
- Cap Spending $Mil	21	36	54	104
= Free Cash Flow $Mil	87	86	218	14

Financial Health [C+]	2003	2004	2005	09-30-06
Long-term Debt $Mil	469	381	307	1,158
Total Equity $Mil	648	823	1,030	1,673
Debt/Equity Ratio	0.7	0.5	0.3	0.7

Industry	Business Risk	Moat Size	Investment Style	Sector
Metal Products	Average	Narrow	Mid Value	Industrial Materials

Competition	Market Cap $Mil	12 Mo Trailing Sales $Mil	Price/Cash Flow	Return On Assets%	Debt/ Equity	Total Return% 1 Yr	3 Yr
Reliance Steel and Aluminum	2,974	5,042	25.1	9.1	0.7	29.6	32.6
Worthington Industries	1,574	2,982	EUB	8.1	0.3	-4.2	3.3
Ryerson	659	5,798	—	3.1	1.7	4.0	32.0

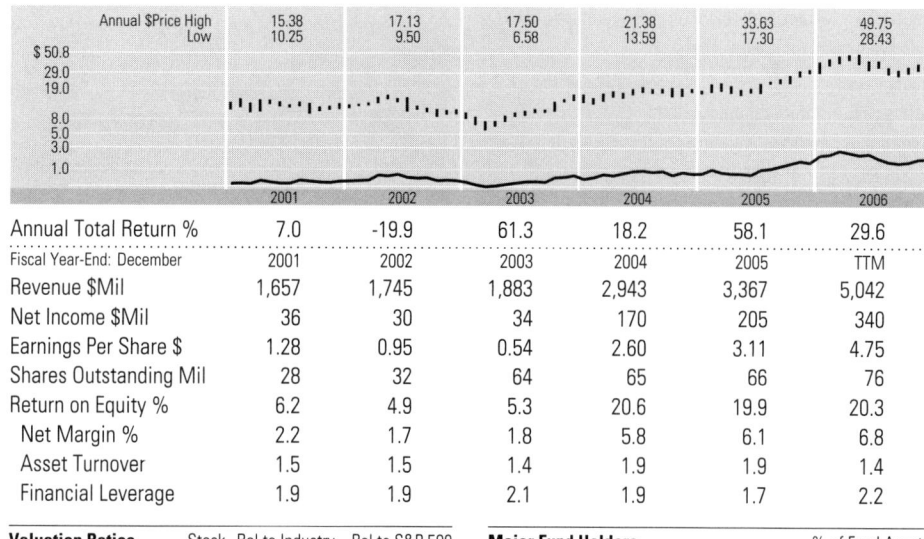

	2001	2002	2003	2004	2005	2006/TTM
Annual Total Return %	7.0	-19.9	61.3	18.2	58.1	29.6
Revenue $Mil	1,657	1,745	1,883	2,943	3,367	5,042
Net Income $Mil	36	30	34	170	205	340
Earnings Per Share $	1.28	0.95	0.54	2.60	3.11	4.75
Shares Outstanding Mil	28	32	64	65	66	76
Return on Equity %	6.2	4.9	5.3	20.6	19.9	20.3
Net Margin %	2.2	1.7	1.8	5.8	6.1	6.8
Asset Turnover	1.5	1.5	1.4	1.9	1.9	1.4
Financial Leverage	1.9	1.9	2.1	1.9	1.7	2.2

Valuation Ratios	Stock	Rel to Industry	Rel to S&P 500
Price/Earnings	8.3	0.4	0.4
Price/Book	1.8	0.5	0.4
Price/Sales	0.6	0.3	0.2
Price/Cash Flow	25.1	1.5	1.7

Major Fund Holders	% of Fund Assets
Hennessy Cornerstone Growth	2.01
Managers AMG FQ Tx-Mgd U.S. Eq Inst	1.83
Penn Street Advisors Sector Rotational A	1.81
Calvert Capital Accumulation A	1.73

Thesis By Ben Butwin, 12-08-06 Stock Price as of Analysis: $40.42

Reliance distributes primarily steel and aluminum to manufacturing firms whose supply needs are too small to enable them to buy directly from metal producers. We think this narrow-moat firm has a favorable business model compared with its rivals.

Metal distribution is a mature, fragmented, and competitive industry. Even with plenty of consolidation over the past two decades, Reliance and its largest rivals, including the comparably sized Ryerson, make up just a small percentage of the market. Local, independent mom-and-pop centers are still fierce competitors in every geography.

Internal sales growth rarely exceeds 5% for even the best-run metal distributors, so Reliance looks for additional growth through acquisitions, having completed more than 30 since going public in 1994. The largest is its recent purchase of Earle M. Jorgensen, which has boosted annual sales from $3.4 billion to well more than $5 billion. Because of its ability to provide subsidiaries with more capital and better sourcing, Reliance adds value through these acquisitions while expanding its geographical reach, product range, and customer line.

The ability to integrate acquisitions is just one of many aspects of Reliance's operations that we like. While most rivals have a few large, centralized plants, Reliance maintains a local, decentralized strategy. Nearly all of its customers are within 200 miles of one of its service centers, allowing custom order delivery within 24 hours of receipt. Prompt service results in better inventory management--Reliance turns its inventory around 6 times per year compared with the industry average of about 5. The company makes more money than its peers by getting more metal in and out the door.

In addition, Reliance adds value to the supply chain through order customization and a diverse product base. While some metal is held as inventory and passed on without modification, much of it is processed to meet specifications, which saves valuable time and labor expense for customers. Because it offers more than 90,000 products to customers in various industries, Reliance doesn't depend on one type of metal or a handful of buyers.

By offering a broad array of products, value-added customization, and quick delivery, Reliance keeps its customers "sticky" without needing to enter into long-term binding contracts, as many of its competitors do. This enables it to immediately pass through price increases caused by rising commodity costs and maintain solid profitability throughout the economic cycle.

Data as of 12-29-06

Renaissance Re Holdings RNR

	Rating	Fair Value	Last Close	Consider Buy	Consider Sell	Yield %
	★★★★	$75.00	$60.00	$47.80	$90.50	1.40

Company Profile
Renaissance Re is a Bermuda-based reinsurer formed in 1993. Ren Re offers a range of property-catastrophe reinsurance products, catastrophe-exposed individual risk protection, and specialty reinsurance for risks that include workers' compensation, personal accidents, aviation, and terrorism. Most risks are short-tail, which means losses are identified within a few years. Direct insurance coverage has taken a growing share of Ren Re's product mix in recent years.

Management
Stewardship Grade [B]

Cofounder and then-chairman and CEO Jim Stanard resigned in late 2005 amidst a continuing regulatory probe. He was replaced as CEO by cofounder Neill Currie. Stanard's loss is significant, but Ren Re has developed a wide and deep executive talent pool, and we are encouraged that Stanard still owns about $250 million of Ren Re stock. The firm has added outside talent to its management ranks, including in the compliance area, to respond to concerns in recent industry investigations.

In our view, the managers' stake in the firm and the incentive scheme align their interest with shareholders'. Current and former directors and officers own about $400 million of the outstanding common stock, more than 10% of the firm. We approve of the firm's compensation plan. Variable pay is thoughtfully developed to include annual as well as long-term results.

We like Ren Re's commitment to people throughout the firm. The firm's internal "leadership development institute" is evidence of a bona fide effort in this regard. Ren Re sparks an atmosphere of continual learning and enthusiasm for applying knowledge, which we think will improve the firm's risk selection over time.

Renaissance House 8-12 East Broadway www.renre.com
Pembroke, Bermuda HM 19

Growth [B-]	2004	2005	2006	2007
Revenue %	NMF	50.4	14.5	5.6
Earnings/Share %	75.7	64.0	-78.3	NMF
Book Value/Share %	NMF	38.0	1.6	-16.6
Dividends/Share %	6.3	5.9	-5.0	40.4

Profitability [B]	2005	2006	2007	TTM
Return on Assets %	12.8	2.4	-4.1	4.6
Oper Cash Flow $Mil	821	518	336	—
- Cap Spending $Mil	—	—	—	—
= Free Cash Flow $Mil	—	—	—	—

Financial Health [NA]	2005	2006	2007	09-30-06
Long-term Debt $Mil	—	—	—	—
Total Equity $Mil	2,085	2,144	1,754	2,297
Debt/Equity Ratio	—	—	—	—

Industry	Business Risk	Moat Size	Investment Style	Sector
Reinsurance	Above Avg	Wide	 Mid Value	Financial Services

Competition	Market Cap $Mil	12 Mo Trailing Sales $Mil	Price/Cash Flow	Return On Assets%	Debt/ Equity	Total Return% 1 Yr	3 Yr
Renaissance Re Holdings	4,328	1,854	—	4.6	—	38.3	8.2
XL Capital	12,993	9,748	—	-1.8	—	9.3	0.1
Transatlantic Holdings	4,097	3,929	—	2.3	—	-6.8	-0.5

Price Volatility   ▮ Monthly Price High/Low   — Relative Strength to S&P 500

Annual $Price High	34.83	44.10	50.00	56.63	52.19	61.14
Low	20.70	28.76	34.03	46.61	34.50	40.56

	2001	2002	2003	2004	2005	2006
Annual Total Return %	24.4	26.5	25.6	7.4	-13.8	38.3
Fiscal Year-End: December	2001	2002	2003	2004	2005	TTM
Revenue $Mil	NMF	910	1,369	1,568	1,656	1,854
Net Income $Mil	185	365	606	133	-281	350
Earnings Per Share $	2.96	5.20	8.53	1.85	-3.99	4.81
Shares Outstanding Mil	—	68	69	70	71	72
Return on Equity %	NMF	24.5	29.1	6.2	-16.0	15.2
Net Margin %	NMF	40.1	44.3	8.5	-17.0	18.9
Asset Turnover	—	0.2	0.3	0.3	0.2	0.2
Financial Leverage	—	2.5	2.3	2.6	3.9	3.3

Valuation Ratios	Stock	Rel to Industry	Rel to S&P 500
Price/Earnings	12.5	1.0	0.6
Price/Book	1.9	1.4	0.5
Price/Sales	2.3	1.4	0.8
Price/Cash Flow	—	—	—

Major Fund Holders	% of Fund Assets
Integrity Growth & Income A Load Waived	5.80
CGM Capital Development	5.51
High Pointe Small Cap Equity	3.74
BlackRock Global Financial Svcs B	3.53

Thesis By Bill Bergman, 12-04-06 Stock Price as of Analysis: $59.90

Ren Re is one of our favorite reinsurers. The firm has engineered a wide moat by coupling a dedication to industry-standard customer service with the development of superior underwriting and pricing insights. Our fair value estimate is $75 per share.

Ren Re's hard-earned reputation for accurate and rapid claim payments keeps the firm in good graces with brokers and clients. It would take time for a less-established reinsurer to earn this respect. Ren Re's service offering incorporates wide, deep knowledge of industry practice and market conditions. Ren Re shares its analysis of current market conditions and future expectations in ways that brokers and primary insurers value. For example, as the severity of the 2005 hurricane season unfolded, Ren Re was positioned to quickly understand the specific implications the widespread damage had for its primary insurer clients and their brokers, and wrote additional specialty "live-cat" and backup coverage late in the year. Ren Re's level of customer service distinguishes it not only from the mediocre crowd, but also from the good reinsurers.

Ren Re's proprietary catastrophe loss models and current conditions monitoring are also critical to its success. The firm recognizes the drawbacks of blind reliance on modeling and strives to continually adjust and use its models to improve accountable human decision-making as well as the information services provided to clients. Ren Re's analysis of its models led the firm to pull in its sails in a timely fashion in 2005, which helped the company avoid the larger loss, as a percentage of equity, that afflicted several competitors. Even better, the models are designed to help underwriters assess the incremental return on equity and capital requirement of each new contract, enabling decision-makers to accept or reject business on that basis. In its core catastrophe markets, Ren Re targets market share gains opportunistically, not blindly or continually.

Ren Re isn't satisfied with mere underwriting excellence. The team exploits its specialist knowledge to further boost returns on capital. The firm seeks to expand into adjacent markets where it can profitably employ its expertise, such as specialty reinsurance markets that competitors shun because the risks are harder to price and individual risk markets that support rigorous pricing analysis. Best of all, Ren Re underwrites reinsurance for other firms on an outsourced basis. This lets it earn additional fees with minor incremental investment, which further increases returns on capital.

Data as of 12-29-06

Republic Services A RSG

	Rating	Fair Value	Last Close	Consider Buy	Consider Sell	Yield %
	★★★★	$46.00	$40.67	$39.20	$60.40	1.48

Company Profile
Republic is the third-largest provider of solid-waste management in the United States, with 6% market share. The firm provides services for commercial, industrial, and residential customers in 21 states, handling waste from curbside to the point of disposal. It owns or operates 92 transfer stations, 59 solid waste landfills, and 32 recycling facilities. Republic operates primarily in the high-growth Sunbelt markets, including Florida, Georgia, Nevada, California, and Texas.

Management Stewardship Grade [B]

Chairman and CEO James O'Connor joined the company in 1998, after serving in various managerial roles in 26 years at Waste Management. O'Connor's expertise is augmented by a highly talented and seasoned management team that boasts, on average, 24 years' experience in the solid waste industry. Although O'Connor took home a sizable $4 million in salary, bonus, and restricted stock in 2005, we think Republic's compensation program is shareholder-friendly, linking incentive pay at both the corporate and field management levels to free cash flow growth and return on capital targets. Management prides itself on being predictable, and we believe its capital-deployment strategy is disciplined. Republic uses its excess cash to buy back company stock and pay a healthy dividend and will only pursue acquisitions that exceed its low-double-digit hurdle rate for returns on invested capital. Corporate-governance policies are sound, although we would prefer that management own a larger stake in the company. Top executives including O'Connor continue to authorize buybacks with shareholder money, but opt to cash in options themselves, now collectively owning less than 1% of Republic's shares outstanding. Bill Gates' Cascade Investment LLC owns more than 13% of Republic's outstanding shares.

110 S.E. 6th Street 28th Floor
Ft. Lauderdale, FL 33301

Growth [C]	2002	2003	2004	2005
Revenue %	4.8	6.5	7.6	5.8
Earnings/Share %	97.3	-23.6	39.1	14.4
Book Value/Share %	10.7	4.3	2.1	-8.0
Dividends/Share %	NMF	NMF	200.0	44.4

Profitability [B+]	2003	2004	2005	TTM
Return on Assets %	3.9	5.3	5.6	6.1
Oper Cash Flow $Mil	601	666	768	575
- Cap Spending $Mil	273	284	329	321
= Free Cash Flow $Mil	327	383	439	254

Financial Health [B]	2003	2004	2005	09-30-06
Long-term Debt $Mil	1,289	1,352	1,472	1,665
Total Equity $Mil	1,905	1,873	1,606	1,434
Debt/Equity Ratio	0.7	0.7	0.9	1.2

	Industry	Business Risk	Moat Size	Investment Style	Sector
	Waste Management	Below Avg	Narrow	Mid Core	Business Services

Competition	Market Cap $Mil	12 Mo Trailing Sales $Mil	Price/Cash Flow	Return On Assets%	Debt/ Equity	Total Return% 1 Yr	3 Yr
Republic Services A	5,307	3,043	9.2	6.1	1.2	9.9	17.6
Waste Management	19,672	13,452	7.8	5.7	1.3	24.2	10.1
Allied Waste Industries	4,523	6,003	6.4	1.2	2.5	40.6	-4.0

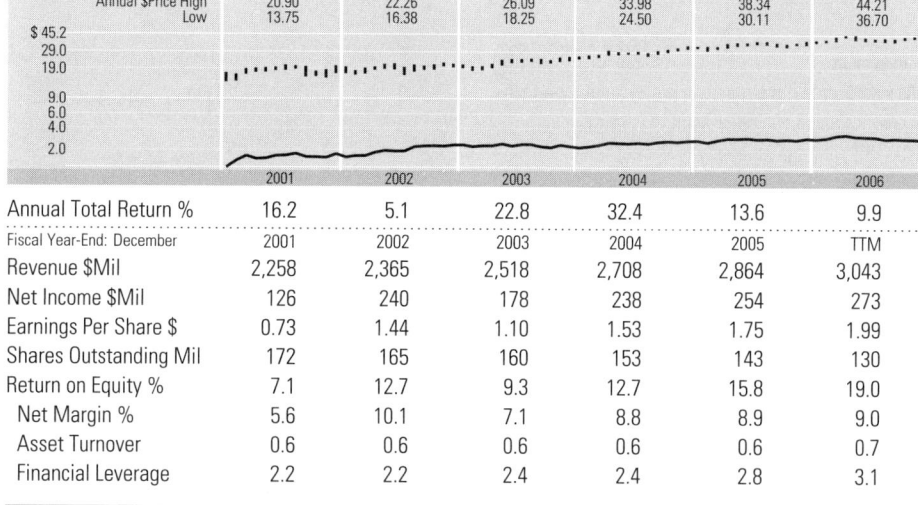

Annual Total Return %	16.2	5.1	22.8	32.4	13.6	9.9
Fiscal Year-End: December	2001	2002	2003	2004	2005	TTM
Revenue $Mil	2,258	2,365	2,518	2,708	2,864	3,043
Net Income $Mil	126	240	178	238	254	273
Earnings Per Share $	0.73	1.44	1.10	1.53	1.75	1.99
Shares Outstanding Mil	172	165	160	153	143	130
Return on Equity %	7.1	12.7	9.3	12.7	15.8	19.0
Net Margin %	5.6	10.1	7.1	8.8	8.9	9.0
Asset Turnover	0.6	0.6	0.6	0.6	0.6	0.7
Financial Leverage	2.2	2.2	2.4	2.4	2.8	3.1

Valuation Ratios	Stock	Rel to Industry	Rel to S&P 500
Price/Earnings	20.4	0.9	1.0
Price/Book	3.7	1.1	0.9
Price/Sales	1.7	0.9	0.6
Price/Cash Flow	9.2	0.9	0.6

Major Fund Holders	% of Fund Assets
Fidelity Select Environmental	5.13
SunAmerica Focused Mid-Cap Growth A	3.41
Regions Morgan Keegan Sel MidCap Value A	3.15
Heritage Diversified Growth A	2.66

Thesis By Brian Nelson, 11-28-06 Stock Price as of Analysis: $41.70

Although Republic Services doesn't have the landfill capacity of its larger rivals, its focus on high-growth markets and the industry's renewed emphasis on improving pricing should contribute to solid cash generation for many years to come.

We believe landfill ownership is the key long-term competitive advantage in the solid waste industry. Constructing a landfill requires considerable capital investment, managerial experience, and environmental permits and zoning approvals, which are often opposed by various parties, including politicians and citizens' groups. Since the barriers to developing a new landfill are high, waste firms with substantial disposal assets often control pricing and, in some isolated markets, charge hefty landfill fees (tipping fees) to waste collectors lacking viable alternatives.

As available landfill space dwindles and becomes more valuable, we expect tipping fees to escalate, further separating the economics of waste companies with lasting landfill capacity from those without. This concept underlies our industry thesis, which favors garbage haulers that not only own a vast network of landfills but also minimize third-party tipping fees through highly integrated operations, as measured by a firm's internalization rate (the percentage of company-collected waste that is dumped in company-owned landfills).

Despite doubling its percentage of disposal revenue to 20% of revenue since 1998, Republic ranks third among public companies in landfill ownership and total disposal capacity, with 59 solid waste landfills and nearly 1.8 billion cubic yards of disposal capacity. Republic's internalization rate has increased to 57% in 2005 from 40% in 1998, but still lags that of the other three waste haulers we cover: Waste Management (66%), Allied Waste (73%), and Waste Connections (69%).

Although Republic's not the largest or most vertically integrated trash hauler, we still ascribe it a narrow economic moat because of its respectable landfill network and long-term, exclusive franchise contracts (8-30 years). Not only do these regional deals insulate the firm from competition in about 40% of its revenue base, but they also contribute solid operating margins (20%-plus). Its unique competitive strategy that target the faster-growing Sunbelt states (67% of revenue) should also help the firm generate higher waste volume growth than its larger brethren. Finally, we think Republic is poised to benefit from improved pricing driven by a renewed industrywide focus on return on capital.

Data as of 12-29-06

Research in Motion RIMM

	Rating	Fair Value	Last Close	Consider Buy	Consider Sell	Yield %
	★★	$110.00	$127.78	$70.10	$132.70	0.00

Company Profile

Ontario-based Research in Motion designs, manufactures, and markets BlackBerry devices for wide-area wireless mobile communications globally. By developing integrated hardware, software, and services that support multiple wireless network standards, the company provides platforms and solutions for seamless, secure access to information, including e-mail, phone, and Internet- and intranet-based corporate data applications.

Industry	Business Risk	Moat Size	Investment Style	Sector
Computer Equip.	Above Avg	Narrow	Large Growth	Hardware

Competition

	Market Cap $Mil	12 Mo Trailing Sales $Mil	Price/Cash Flow	Return On Assets%	Debt/ Equity	Total Return% 1 Yr	3 Yr
Research in Motion	23,767	2,066	EUB	16.5	0.0	93.6	54.5
IBM	146,342	89,593	9.8	8.8	0.4	19.8	3.0
Hewlett-Packard	112,070	91,658	9.9	7.6	0.1	45.2	22.7

Management — Stewardship Grade [B]

RIM's corporate governance is pretty solid for a tech company. Executive compensation is relatively restrained, and the company tends not to award outlandish bonuses or option grants. Jim Balsillie and RIM founder Mike Lazaridis share the CEO position and together hold roughly 13% of the firm's stock. Balsillie, who is also chairman, joined RIM in 1992 and is responsible for directing the company's strategy and business development. Lazaridis is president and oversees research and development and product development. Both Lazaridis and Balsillie were paid just under $400,000 in each of the past few years and did not receive bonuses or option grants. Most of the management team at RIM has been in place since before the company's 1997 IPO and helped pioneer the market for wireless e-mail devices. As a whole, top executives and board members control around 15% of the shares. Option grants have not been excessive historically. Some critics have labeled RIM's management arrogant or naive in its approach to negotiating the patent lawsuit, but we believe management took a high-risk but principled stand. RIM recently announced that it had conducted a voluntary review of its stock-option granting policies, and its initial findings are that GAAP earnings from 1997 to the present would be reduced by $25-$45 million.

295 Phillip Street
Waterloo, ON N2L 3W8
www.rim.com

Growth [NA]	2003	2004	2005	2006
Revenue %	4.3	93.9	127.1	53.0
Earnings/Share %	NMF	NMF	251.6	79.8
Book Value/Share %	-18.0	125.9	-1.6	1.2
Dividends/Share %	NMF	NMF	NMF	NMF

Profitability [NA]	2004	2005	2006	TTM
Return on Assets %	2.7	8.1	16.5	16.5
Oper Cash Flow $Mil	64	278	150	150
- Cap Spending $Mil	22	109	179	179
= Free Cash Flow $Mil	42	169	-29	-29

Financial Health [NA]	2004	2005	2006	02-28-06
Long-term Debt $Mil	6	7	7	7
Total Equity $Mil	1,722	1,984	1,999	1,999
Debt/Equity Ratio	0.0	0.0	0.0	0.0

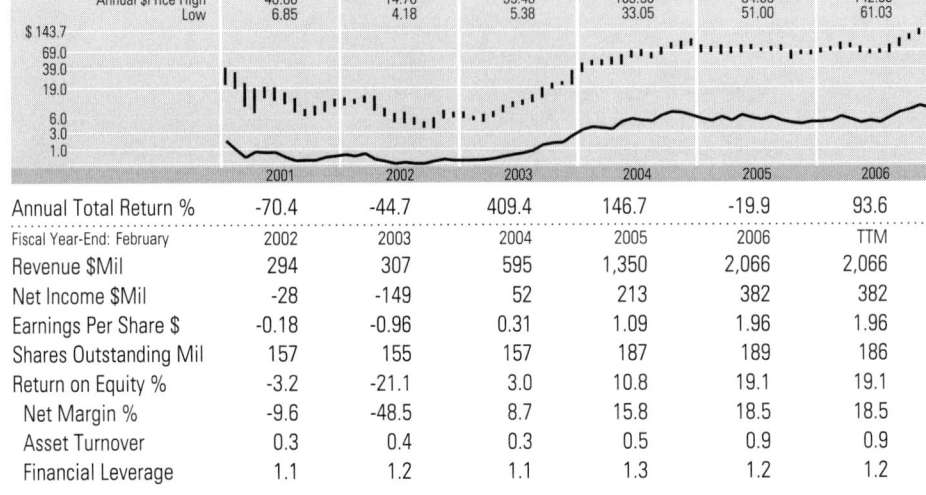

Price Volatility		Monthly Price High/Low	— Relative Strength to S&P 500			
Annual $Price High	40.00	14.78	35.48	103.56	84.55	142.66
Low	6.85	4.18	5.38	33.05	51.00	61.03

	2001	2002	2003	2004	2005	2006
Annual Total Return %	-70.4	-44.7	409.4	146.7	-19.9	93.6
Fiscal Year-End: February	2002	2003	2004	2005	2006	TTM
Revenue $Mil	294	307	595	1,350	2,066	2,066
Net Income $Mil	-28	-149	52	213	382	382
Earnings Per Share $	-0.18	-0.96	0.31	1.09	1.96	1.96
Shares Outstanding Mil	157	155	157	187	189	186
Return on Equity %	-3.2	-21.1	3.0	10.8	19.1	19.1
Net Margin %	-9.6	-48.5	8.7	15.8	18.5	18.5
Asset Turnover	0.3	0.4	0.3	0.5	0.9	0.9
Financial Leverage	1.1	1.2	1.1	1.3	1.2	1.2

Valuation Ratios	Stock	Rel to Industry	Rel to S&P 500
Price/Earnings	65.2	2.4	3.2
Price/Book	11.9	2.1	2.9
Price/Sales	11.5	4.4	4.0
Price/Cash Flow	EUB	—	—

Major Fund Holders	% of Fund Assets
Waddell & Reed Adv Science & Tech A	5.92
Ivy Science & Technology C	5.84
Turner New Enterprise	4.79
Aston/Montag & Caldwell Growth N	4.61

Thesis By John Slack, 12-08-06 Stock Price as of Analysis: $127.69

Research in Motion's BlackBerry wireless platform is the de facto standard in mobile enterprise data. With its legal distractions now behind it and a slew of new devices in the pipeline, we believe the company can extend its leadership position in providing wireless data solutions to corporations.

We believe RIM's extensive carrier and enterprise relationships and first-mover advantage in the market for wireless data systems give the company a narrow moat. RIM's proprietary end-to-end wireless data platform, which includes hardware, software, and service, provides the robustness and security that enterprise customers demand. RIM has strengthened its position by beginning to license the BlackBerry platform to wireless carriers, equipment manufacturers, and application developers. Most of the major hardware vendors, including Motorola, Palm, and Nokia, have licensed RIM's platform and carriers are now allowing access to the BlackBerry system over non-RIM devices. In addition, the firm has established third-party application software-development agreements with Oracle, Bloomberg, and IBM.

About 70% of RIM's revenue currently comes from the sales of BlackBerry devices, but we expect an increasing proportion of revenue to come from two areas: service billing and licensing of the RIM platform. While RIM's device sales garner the lion's share of attention, we believe the company differentiates itself from the competition with the service component of its business. Unlike most other smartphones, BlackBerry users also generate recurring revenue through a subscription model in which carriers pay RIM. This service and licensing revenue amounts to a high-margin annuity stream. The company generates monthly service revenue of $7-$10 for enterprise users and $3-$5 for BlackBerry Web client users, and it sells software licenses for the BlackBerry platform to wireless equipment vendors and third-party software developers.

RIM has more than 6.25 million subscribers, but this barely scratches the surface of demand for wireless e-mail, in our view. RIM is not alone in its designs on wireless e-mail, but we believe this market is large enough for multiple players. Competitive pressures have increased over the past year as devices that include wireless e-mail have proliferated. Nokia and Motorola have entered the market with quality devices. In addition, Microsoft has incorporated wireless e-mail into its Windows Mobile software, which syncs with Windows e-mail servers without buying additional software.

Data as of 12-29-06

ResMed RMD

	Rating	Fair Value	Last Close	Consider Buy	Consider Sell	Yield %
	★★	$41.00	$49.22	$31.60	$51.40	0.00

Industry	Business Risk	Moat Size	Investment Style	Sector
Medical Equip.	Average	Narrow	Mid Growth	Healthcare

Company Profile
ResMed develops, manufactures, and distributes medical devices, such as airflow generators and masks, to treat breathing disorders. It recently acquired a ventilation firm, but its primary focus remains sleep-disordered breathing. ResMed's reach is truly global with distribution capabilities in more than 65 countries through wholly owned and independent firms. Most of its manufacturing capacity remains in Australia, where it was founded.

Management   Stewardship Grade [B]
We give ResMed a good Stewardship Grade. We like that founder Peter Farrell remains with the company, though we'd prefer the chairman and CEO roles he occupies to be split. Farrell founded ResMed and owns about 2% of the company, which should align his interests with those of other shareholders. His track record of creating shareholder value at ResMed and high growth in both revenue and profits impresses us. Given Farrell's age, we think ResMed could experience a significant leadership transition sooner rather than later. His leadership will definitely be missed when he chooses to retire. The complaints we have about ResMed's stewardship include a staggered board of directors and some extremely generous perks, in our opinion, for top executives. The perks include personal use of the company's leased aircraft, exclusive use of an expensive car for Farrell, club memberships, and luxurious personal travel benefits. We typically don't think shareholders should pay for benefits like these and worry they could get out of hand in terms of value or pervasiveness.

14040 Danielson St.   www.resmed.com
Poway, CA 92064-6857

Growth [A]	2003	2004	2005	2006
Revenue %	34.1	24.0	25.4	42.7
Earnings/Share %	20.9	22.6	11.7	27.5
Book Value/Share %	47.2	23.5	29.5	45.8
Dividends/Share %	NMF	NMF	NMF	NMF

Profitability [A]	2004	2005	2006	TTM
Return on Assets %	10.4	8.4	8.8	9.4
Oper Cash Flow $Mil	77	71	99	109
- Cap Spending $Mil	57	40	103	91
= Free Cash Flow $Mil	19	31	-4	18

Financial Health [A]	2004	2005	2006	09-30-06
Long-term Debt $Mil	113	59	116	115
Total Equity $Mil	361	474	738	771
Debt/Equity Ratio	0.3	0.1	0.2	0.2

Competition	Market Cap $Mil	12 Mo Trailing Sales $Mil	Price/Cash Flow	Return On Assets %	Debt/ Equity	Total Return % 1 Yr	3 Yr
ResMed	3,743	643	34.3	9.4	0.2	28.5	32.8
Tyco International	60,461	40,960	10.8	5.8	0.3	6.8	5.1
Respironics	3,019	1,073	28.9	9.8	0.0	1.8	19.0

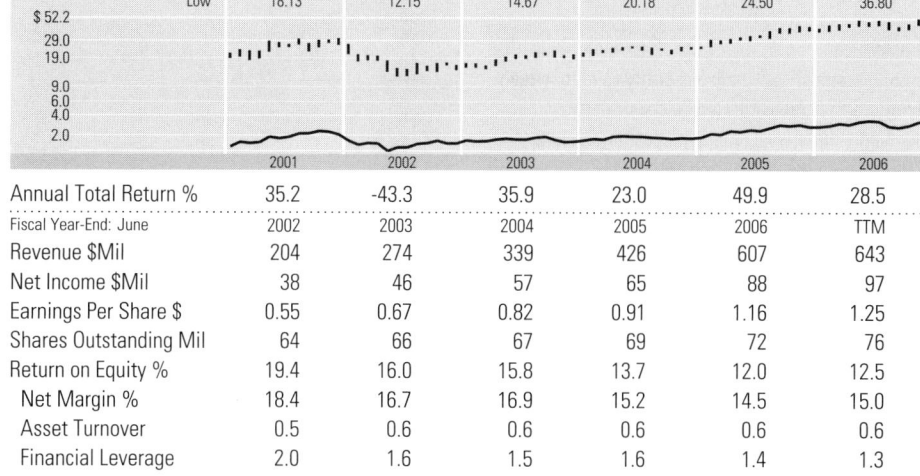

Price Volatility | Monthly Price High/Low — Relative Strength to S&P 500

| Annual $Price High Low | 31.10 18.13 | 26.96 12.15 | 23.35 14.67 | 26.00 20.18 | 42.81 24.50 | 51.17 36.80 |

	2001	2002	2003	2004	2005	2006
Annual Total Return %	35.2	-43.3	35.9	23.0	49.9	28.5

Fiscal Year-End: June	2002	2003	2004	2005	2006	TTM
Revenue $Mil	204	274	339	426	607	643
Net Income $Mil	38	46	57	65	88	97
Earnings Per Share $	0.55	0.67	0.82	0.91	1.16	1.25
Shares Outstanding Mil	64	66	67	69	72	76
Return on Equity %	19.4	16.0	15.8	13.7	12.0	12.5
Net Margin %	18.4	16.7	16.9	15.2	14.5	15.0
Asset Turnover	0.5	0.6	0.6	0.6	0.6	0.6
Financial Leverage	2.0	1.6	1.5	1.6	1.4	1.3

Valuation Ratios	Stock	Rel to Industry	Rel to S&P 500
Price/Earnings	39.4	1.3	1.9
Price/Book	4.9	0.9	1.2
Price/Sales	5.8	1.2	2.0
Price/Cash Flow	34.3	1.4	2.3

Major Fund Holders	% of Fund Assets
Aston/ABN AMRO Mid Cap Growth N	2.95
William Blair Tax-Managed Growth I	2.89
Baird MidCap Inst	2.58
Pioneer Small and Mid Cap Growth A	2.46

Thesis By Julie Stralow, CFA, 10-31-06 Stock Price as of Analysis: $43.99

ResMed's sleep-disordered breathing business remains a financial dream.

Sleep-disordered breathing, including obstructive sleep apnea, remains a huge medical problem that often goes unnoticed and untreated by patients and even physicians. Studies suggests that as many as one out of every five U.S. adults suffers from some form of obstructive sleep apnea, but the vast majority remain undiagnosed and untreated. One reason is that typical symptoms--like snoring and excessive daytime sleepiness--can be vague and relatively benign. These low-key symptoms allow many sufferers to fly under the radar screen even during a typical physician examination. Also, treatment compliance can suffer if diagnosed patients balk at uncomfortable changes to their sleep routine.

ResMed is helping lead the charge on obstructive sleep apnea and should benefit from exceptional growth for years to come by serving this huge potential marketplace. The firm is spearheading educational efforts for physicians and the public, but its greatest contributions come from developing increasingly effective and comfortable noninvasive treatment options. ResMed provides the airflow generators, masks, nasal pillows, and other accessories needed to noninvasively prop open a person's respiratory pathway and prevent apnea events during sleep.

Lately, ResMed has launched several innovative products, including the S8 airflow generators and Mirage Swift nasal pillows, that are turbocharging the firm's growth. Demand for the nasal pillows in particular has been extremely high. The invasiveness of an airflow device plays an especially important role in patient compliance, and ResMed's new nasal pillows have greatly improved patient comfort without sacrificing treatment quality, as measured by the airflow intake needed to keep a patient's airway open.

Like any medical-device company, ResMed's long-term success will depend on its ability to continue innovating. It will be pushed by competitors, especially Respironics, but we think there's plenty of room in this large marketplace for several firms to succeed. ResMed continues to up the innovation ante with new product introductions, and we think it should remain an influential leader of this market for the foreseeable future. We really admire ResMed as a company, and think this firm is poised for continued success in the sleep apnea market.

Data as of 12-29-06

Resources Global Professionals RECN

	Rating	Fair Value	Last Close	Consider Buy	Consider Sell	Yield %
	★	$23.00	$31.84	$17.70	$28.80	0.00

Company Profile
Resources Global Professionals is an international professional services firm that provides accounting and finance, risk-management and internal audit, information technology, human resources, and supply-chain management professionals to clients on a project basis. It operates out of 79 offices around the world, serving more than 2,100 clients from a broad range of industries. About 20% of its revenue is generated outside the United States.

Management
Stewardship Grade [C]

Resources Global was founded in 1996 by a team at Deloitte & Touche, led by CEO Donald Murray. Founding members include CFO Stephen Giusto and executive vice president Karen Ferguson. In 1999, they completed a management-led buyout, as they were unable to offer certain accounting services because of the regulatory constraints of being part of a Big Four firm. They became independent and increased the scope of services available to clients. Returns on invested capital have been impressive and show that the management team has done a good job of leading the firm. The company has granted a considerable amount of options, amounting to 6.29%, 4.98%, 8.22%, 3.67%, and 3.97% of shares outstanding in 2002, 2003, 2004, 2005, and 2006, respectively. The company has said it intends to target 4%-5%, which is still high, in our opinion, and contributes to our average Stewardship Grade for the firm. Our grade would also be higher if the entire board of directors went from staggered to annual elections, if the chairman and CEO roles were split, and if the firm abandoned its shareholder-rights plan, which makes it more difficult for the company to be acquired.

695 Town Center Drive Suite 600   www.resourcesglobal.com
Costa Mesa, CA 92626

Growth [B+]	2003	2004	2005	2006
Revenue %	11.2	62.5	63.7	17.9
Earnings/Share %	-5.2	81.8	122.0	5.4
Book Value/Share %	18.3	26.6	32.7	24.6
Dividends/Share %	NMF	NMF	NMF	NMF

Profitability [A+]	2004	2005	2006	TTM
Return on Assets %	10.8	17.5	15.2	14.4
Oper Cash Flow $Mil	19	67	71	70
- Cap Spending $Mil	3	4	21	22
= Free Cash Flow $Mil	16	63	50	48

Financial Health [A+]	2004	2005	2006	08-31-06
Long-term Debt $Mil	—	—	—	—
Total Equity $Mil	180	248	317	323
Debt/Equity Ratio	—	—	—	—

	Industry	Business Risk	Moat Size	Investment Style	Sector
	Employment	Average	Narrow	Small Growth	Business Services

Competition
	Market Cap $Mil	12 Mo Trailing Sales $Mil	Price/Cash Flow	Return On Assets%	Debt/Equity	Total Return% 1 Yr	3 Yr
Resources Global Professionals	1,530	649	21.8	14.4	—	22.0	31.8
Adecco SA ADR	12,751	22,920	34.2	7.0	0.3	50.3	3.5
Robert Half International	6,220	3,838	16.1	19.0	0.0	-1.2	17.1

Price Volatility
Annual $Price High	17.13	15.08	14.67	27.82	31.50	32.59
Low	8.13	5.21	8.06	13.66	17.40	22.35
	2001	2002	2003	2004	2005	2006
Annual Total Return %	38.6	-11.9	17.7	98.9	-3.8	21.9

Fiscal Year-End: May	2002	2003	2004	2005	2006	TTM
Revenue $Mil	182	202	328	538	634	649
Net Income $Mil	13	13	24	56	61	56
Earnings Per Share $	0.29	0.28	0.50	1.11	1.17	1.10
Shares Outstanding Mil	42	44	46	47	48	48
Return on Equity %	11.7	9.4	13.5	22.6	19.1	17.5
Net Margin %	7.3	6.2	7.4	10.4	9.6	8.7
Asset Turnover	1.4	1.3	1.5	1.7	1.6	1.7
Financial Leverage	1.2	1.2	1.3	1.3	1.3	1.2

Valuation Ratios	Stock	Rel to Industry	Rel to S&P 500
Price/Earnings	28.9	1.2	1.4
Price/Book	4.7	1.1	1.1
Price/Sales	2.4	2.7	0.8
Price/Cash Flow	21.8	0.9	1.5

Major Fund Holders	% of Fund Assets
Phoenix Small-Cap Growth A	3.29
Wells Fargo Advantage Small Cap Growth A	2.76
TCW Growth Equities I	2.33
TCW Small Cap Growth I	2.14

Thesis   By Kristan Rowland, 12-05-06   Stock Price as of Analysis: $28.10

Resources Global Professionals provides experienced, highly skilled business professionals on a project basis. Areas served by the company address markets in the billions, providing ample opportunity for growth.

Resources Global's narrow moat is based on its reputation, client relationships, and strong returns on invested capital (22% on average since 2000), well in excess of the firm's cost of capital. The firm has retained more than 90% of its top 50 clients since 2003, which is evidence of its quality work. More proof of its good reputation lies in its cross-selling efforts. In the first quarter of fiscal 2007, roughly three fourths of Resources Global's top 50 clients retained the firm for more than one of its services, which also demonstrates strong customer loyalty.

Resources Global's recent growth has been hindered by falling year-two and -three Sarbanes-Oxley compliance work, as competition has heated up and corporations have sought ways to cut compliance costs. Sarbanes-Oxley reforms drove much of the explosive growth in 2004 and 2005, but resource-audit-solutions demand has softened, and competition from Big Four firms has increased, which has led to some pricing pressure. Lower pricing may continue, which could inhibit Resources Global's growth.

Despite this challenge, Resources Global has done a good job diversifying away from Sarbanes-Oxley-related business. Its other revenue sources posted 29% growth in the most recent first quarter, accounting for 76% of sales, up from 60% about a year ago. We believe sales of those other services will continue to be important areas of growth for the firm as the company leverages its relationships with clients and cross-sells other services. It has already shown a solid ability to cross-sell its services, so we believe it will continue to successfully execute this strategy.

Resources Global's future continues to be bright, but it could face challenges related to the tight supply of finance and accounting professionals. The firm may have to compensate its workers more than firms that offer a steady salary and job security--its professionals are only paid when working on a project. Also, Resources Global could face margin pressure if it is unable to pass along the higher pay it must dole out to attract these professionals. We like this topnotch firm but would wait for a margin of safety before making an investment.

Respironics RESP

Data as of 12-29-06

Rating	Fair Value	Last Close	Consider Buy	Consider Sell	Yield %
★★★	$39.00	$37.75	$30.10	$48.90	0.00

Company Profile
Respironics develops and manufactures medical devices for respiratory ailments. The firm generates the majority of its sales from equipment and masks that treat sleep apnea. Ventilation systems, particularly noninvasive tools, represent its second-largest segment. Two others--children's medical ventures and respiratory drug delivery--remain new, potentially large opportunities that complement the firm's expertise in sleep and respiratory treatments.

Management   Stewardship Grade [C]
We give Respironics a fair Stewardship Grade. Founder Gerald McGinnis heads the board while John Miclot, a transplant from Respironics' acquisition of Healthdyne in 1998, leads the executive team as president and CEO. Miclot's transition from executive at an acquisition target to Respironics' leader is not unique. Respironics has retained several Healthdyne veterans in its top management team while four of the firm's directors were once executives at acquired firms. This retention suggests management quality and continuity play an important role when considering acquisition targets. However, given the prominence of acquisitions to its strategy, restructuring charges often obscure Respironics' financial results, hurting the firm's transparency portion of our Stewardship Grade. Also, insiders only own about 3% of the firm including options, which is relatively meager, given the founder's continued involvement on the board. Considering that ownership profile, we are surprised by the significant influence of current and former insiders on the board and the firm's extensive takeover defenses, which could limit outside influence at Respironics. Executives take home reasonable cash pay packages, but their option packages raise our eyebrows somewhat.

1010 Murry Ridge Lane
Murrysville, PA 15668-8525
www.respironics.com

Growth [B]	2003	2004	2005	2006
Revenue %	27.3	20.6	20.0	14.8
Earnings/Share %	13.3	35.3	27.2	16.2
Book Value/Share %	8.5	17.9	18.5	19.6
Dividends/Share %	NMF	NMF	NMF	NMF

Profitability [A]	2004	2005	2006	TTM
Return on Assets %	9.1	9.6	9.8	9.8
Oper Cash Flow $Mil	141	135	93	105
- Cap Spending $Mil	51	62	58	64
= Free Cash Flow $Mil	90	73	34	40

Financial Health [A+]	2004	2005	2006	06-30-06
Long-term Debt $Mil	27	29	27	26
Total Equity $Mil	519	628	764	796
Debt/Equity Ratio	0.1	0.0	0.0	0.0

Industry	Business Risk	Moat Size	Investment Style	Sector
Medical Equip.	Average	Narrow	Mid Growth	Healthcare

Competition	Market Cap $Mil	12 Mo Trailing Sales $Mil	Price/Cash Flow	Return On Assets%	Debt/Equity	Total Return% 1 Yr	3 Yr
Respironics	3,019	1,073	28.9	9.8	0.0	1.8	19.0
Tyco International	60,461	40,960	10.8	5.8	0.3	6.8	5.1
ResMed	3,743	643	34.3	9.4	0.2	28.5	32.8

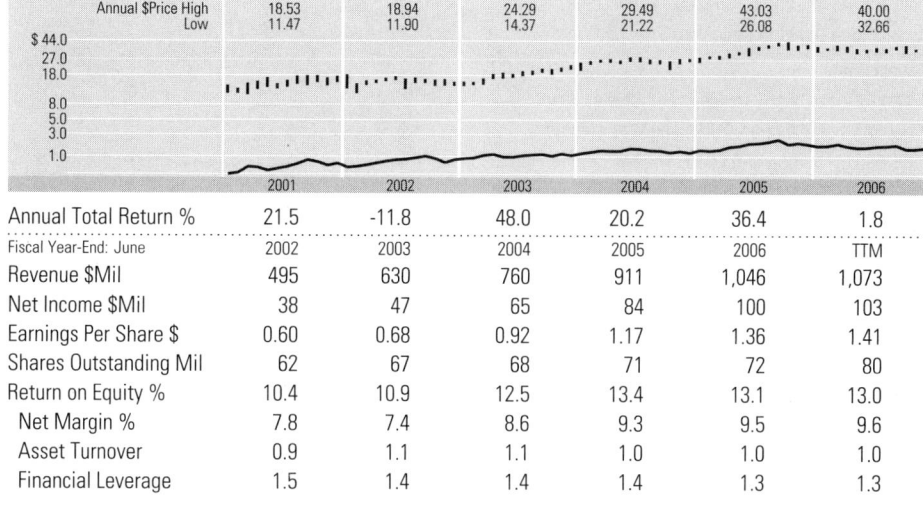

	2001	2002	2003	2004	2005	2006
Annual $Price High	18.53	18.94	24.29	29.49	43.03	40.00
Low	11.47	11.90	14.37	21.22	26.08	32.66
Annual Total Return %	21.5	-11.8	48.0	20.2	36.4	1.8

Fiscal Year-End: June	2002	2003	2004	2005	2006	TTM
Revenue $Mil	495	630	760	911	1,046	1,073
Net Income $Mil	38	47	65	84	100	103
Earnings Per Share $	0.60	0.68	0.92	1.17	1.36	1.41
Shares Outstanding Mil	62	67	68	71	72	80
Return on Equity %	10.4	10.9	12.5	13.4	13.1	13.0
Net Margin %	7.8	7.4	8.6	9.3	9.5	9.6
Asset Turnover	0.9	1.1	1.1	1.0	1.0	1.0
Financial Leverage	1.5	1.4	1.4	1.4	1.3	1.3

Valuation Ratios	Stock	Rel to Industry	Rel to S&P 500
Price/Earnings	26.8	0.9	1.3
Price/Book	3.8	0.7	0.9
Price/Sales	2.8	0.6	1.0
Price/Cash Flow	28.9	1.2	2.0

Major Fund Holders	% of Fund Assets
HSBC Investor Opportunity A	3.36
HSBC Investor Small Cap Equity	3.36
SunAmerica Focused Mid-Cap Growth A	3.10
Rochdale Darwin	2.97

Thesis By Julie Stralow, CFA, 12-05-06 Stock Price as of Analysis: $37.12

Respironics has dug a narrow moat around leading respiratory device positions, and we think its marketing muscle and development skills will keep it at the forefront of these niches for the long run.

The firm's foundation lies in sleep apnea devices, which provide more than half of sales. Respironics launched the first continuous positive airway pressure system in the 1980s and remains a leading force in this market. The firm provides the two major components of sleep apnea treatment--airflow generators and masks--and competes primarily with ResMed. ResMed has been exploiting some key technological advantages recently, which we think has hurt Respironics' growth in this niche.

However, we definitely don't think Respironics is down for the count in sleep apnea. This market remains underpenetrated with many untreated patients. If Respironics and ResMed focus on increasing public awareness of sleep apnea, enhancing physician tools to diagnose at-risk patients, and improving device offerings, both firms can succeed. Also, the value of Respironics' marketing team, especially in the United States, should not be underestimated. Even with technical advantages, ResMed has faced a tough battle against Respironics' topnotch salesforce, which has blanketed the United States with its systems. Respironics' brand names remain synonymous with sleep apnea treatments even through this period of lagging technology.

Respironics hasn't placed all its eggs in one basket, either. It offers a plethora of ventilation systems to help patients breathe better. We remain particularly excited about its noninvasive ventilation systems, a field that Respironics dominates. These systems help patients maintain part of their breathing function, which can create a more comfortable and affordable health-care process. Respironics is attacking other respiratory problems by pioneering several products for premature infants and offering better ways to deliver inhaled drugs. These offerings continue to expand the firm's long-term revenue and profit potential.

The firm's ability to innovate also helps it lead respiratory device niches. Respironics uses its expertise in harnessing airflow to solve a variety of respiratory ailments, and we continue think it will expand into other areas by tapping into this expertise. With innovative and marketing capabilities in spades, Respironics should continue to excel in its chosen niches.

Reynolds American RAI

Data as of 12-29-06

	Rating	Fair Value	Last Close	Consider Buy	Consider Sell	Yield %
	★★★	$63.00	$65.47	$40.10	$76.00	4.20

Company Profile
Reynolds American is the second-largest domestic producer of cigarettes. Its product portfolio includes such well-known brands as Camel, Kool, Doral, Winston, and Salem. Through the acquisition of Conwood, Reynolds is now the second-largest domestic producer of smokeless tobacco products. Conwood's key brands are Kodiak, a premium smokeless product, and Grizzly, the fastest-growing discount brand. British American Tobacco has a 42% ownership interest in Reynolds American.

Management
Stewardship Grade [C]

Susan Ivey has been president and CEO of Reynolds American since January 2004; she was elected chairman of the board in 2006. She held the top job at Brown & Williamson (a subsidiary of British American Tobacco) before it was merged with R.J. Reynolds to form Reynolds American. At Brown & Williamson, Ivey used cost-cutting programs and productivity enhancements to improve margins and free up capital needed to support the firm's top brands. The same strategy has been installed at Reynolds, which is focused mainly on its two key cigarette brands, Camel and Kool. The purchase of Conwood, the second-largest domestic smokeless tobacco producer, provides Reynolds with much needed top-line growth and profits that (so far) have not been breached by tobacco litigation. Executive compensation appears to be reasonable, with pay tied more directly to performance-based measures than fixed salary. Current management, including the board of directors, owns less than 1% of Reynolds' total outstanding shares. Ultimately, we'd like to see management have more skin in the game, and we expect this statistic to improve over time. Certain standstill provisions and transfer restrictions, as well as golden-parachute plans for top management, act as significant takeover defenses for the firm.

401 North Main Street P.O. Box 2866 www.rjrholdings.com
Winston-Salem, NC 27102-2866

Growth [B+]	2002	2003	2004	2005
Revenue %	-0.9	-15.2	22.2	28.3
Earnings/Share %	NMF	NMF	NMF	14.4
Book Value/Share %	-7.7	-51.2	51.7	-19.8
Dividends/Share %	12.9	2.0	0.0	10.5

Profitability [D+]	2003	2004	2005	TTM
Return on Assets %	-35.6	4.8	7.2	7.5
Oper Cash Flow $Mil	581	736	1,273	1,450
- Cap Spending $Mil	70	92	105	136
= Free Cash Flow $Mil	511	644	1,168	1,314

Financial Health [D+]	2003	2004	2005	09-30-06
Long-term Debt $Mil	1,671	1,595	1,558	4,394
Total Equity $Mil	3,057	6,176	6,553	6,999
Debt/Equity Ratio	0.5	0.3	0.2	0.6

Industry	Business Risk	Moat Size	Investment Style	Sector
Tobacco	Above Avg	Narrow	Large Value	Consumer Goods

Competition	Market Cap $Mil	12 Mo Trailing Sales $Mil	Price/Cash Flow	Return On Assets%	Debt/Equity	Total Return% 1 Yr	3 Yr
Reynolds American	19,353	8,488	13.3	7.5	0.6	43.9	38.3
Altria Group	179,868	100,499	12.6	10.5	0.3	19.9	21.8
UST	9,364	1,840	16.0	38.2	9.6	49.5	23.8

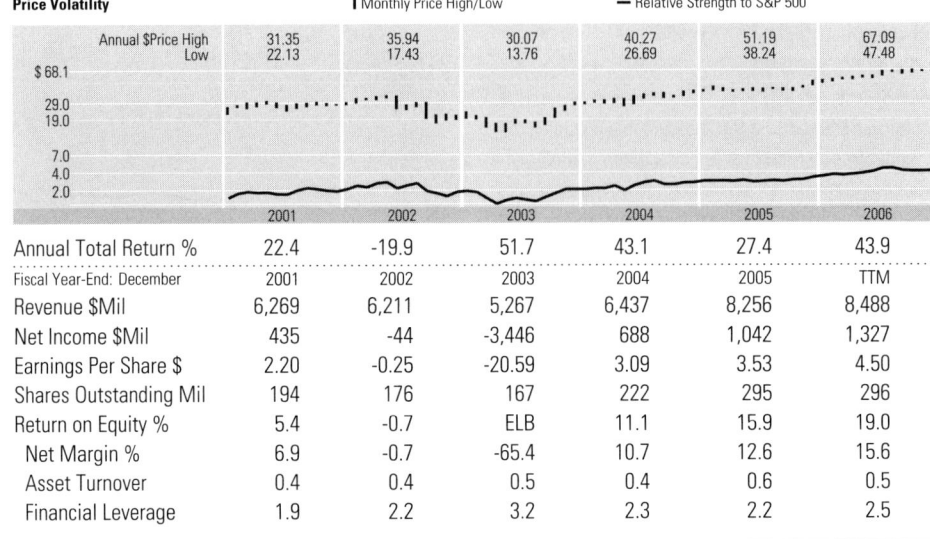

	2001	2002	2003	2004	2005	2006/TTM
Annual Total Return %	22.4	-19.9	51.7	43.1	27.4	43.9
Revenue $Mil	6,269	6,211	5,267	6,437	8,256	8,488
Net Income $Mil	435	-44	-3,446	688	1,042	1,327
Earnings Per Share $	2.20	-0.25	-20.59	3.09	3.53	4.50
Shares Outstanding Mil	194	176	167	222	295	296
Return on Equity %	5.4	-0.7	ELB	11.1	15.9	19.0
Net Margin %	6.9	-0.7	-65.4	10.7	12.6	15.6
Asset Turnover	0.4	0.4	0.5	0.4	0.6	0.5
Financial Leverage	1.9	2.2	3.2	2.3	2.2	2.5

Valuation Ratios	Stock	Rel to Industry	Rel to S&P 500
Price/Earnings	16.1	0.9	0.8
Price/Book	2.8	0.1	0.7
Price/Sales	2.3	1.3	0.8
Price/Cash Flow	13.3	1.0	0.9

Major Fund Holders	% of Fund Assets
Midas Special	6.19
Van Kampen American Franchise A	4.75
SunAmerica Focused Dividend Strat C	3.08
Vice Fund	3.05

Thesis By Greggory Warren, CFA, 12-12-06 Stock Price as of Analysis: $64.61

We are impressed by Reynolds American's recent moves to invigorate its portfolio. While we were skeptical at first, the company's focus on its top two cigarette brands has been a moderate success. The acquisition of Conwood, the second-largest domestic producer of smokeless tobacco, only adds to the positive product mix shift and should enhance profitability longer term. While the future is certainly looking brighter for Reynolds, we'd still require a significant margin of safety before purchasing the shares, given the litigious nature of the domestic tobacco industry. Reynolds is the second-largest producer of cigarettes in the United States, with more than $8 billion in annual sales and 30% of the market. Given the cartellike environment of the domestic cigarette industry, Reynolds should have a significant moat around its business. However, the rapid growth of deep-discount brands, as well as a lack of scale in premium brands, has made the environment extremely difficult for the firm to navigate.

Hoping to improve its position, Reynolds is betting its future in cigarettes on just two key brands. Camel and Kool, which generate more than one third of the company's annual sales, get almost all of Reynolds' annual marketing support for cigarettes, while the firm's other brands are managed for cash. The company believes improved sales and market share for these two key brands will offset losses in the rest of its portfolio.

The Conwood acquisition is also meant to enhance product mix and profitability. Sales of smokeless tobacco products have been increasing around 5% per year, with Conwood experiencing double-digit sales gains, driven by the strength of its dominant discount brand, Grizzly. The deal provides Reynolds with leading market share in the discount segment and production assets that would have taken years to develop, had the firm decided to enter the category on its own. The profit margins for smokeless tobacco are also significantly higher than those generated by Reynolds' cigarette franchise, with the cash flows from the business currently untouched by tobacco litigation.

While there is some concern that the $3.5 billion price that Reynolds paid for Conwood was expensive, we believe the improvement in the firm's sales and profit mix, as well as a lower estimated cost of capital, only increases the likelihood that the company will generate excess returns longer term--albeit still significantly below those produced by its peers.

 Stocks 500

Data as of 12-29-06

Robert Half International RHI

Rating	Fair Value	Last Close	Consider Buy	Consider Sell	Yield %
★★	$32.00	$37.12	$27.30	$42.00	0.86

Company Profile

Robert Half provides temporary staffing, project placement, and permanent placement services for professionals. It markets its services through a variety of brands that specialize in placing professionals in specific industries. Its areas of expertise include accounting, finance, law, marketing and design, information technology, and administrative functions. It also provides internal audit and risk consulting services through its Protiviti unit.

Management   Stewardship Grade [A]

CEO Max Messmer and CFO Keith Waddell have headed Robert Half since the late 1980s, when Messmer led a friendly buyout of founder Bob Half. The company has remained faithful to the strategy management began articulating in 1988, and that has paid off. For the past 15 years, returns on invested capital have averaged an impressive 17.5%, and the stock has logged impressive returns. The successful acquisition of Protiviti shows management's foresight in industry trends. Corporate stewardship at Robert Half is very good, in our opinion. Insiders own a significant stake in the company; Messmer owns 3.5%, while all executive officers and directors own about 12.5%, which helps to align their interests with those of shareholders. Option grants are distributed throughout the organization and have averaged a modest 0.7% of shares outstanding over each of the past three years. We would prefer the company eliminated using earnings per share for purposes of calculating bonuses, since it could encourage short-term maneuvering. However, the company does stipulate that the metric is determined without regard for mergers, acquisitions, dispositions, and material restructurings, which gives us some comfort.

2884 Sand Hill Road Suite 200
Menlo Park, CA 94025
www.rhi.com

Growth [B+]	2002	2003	2004	2005
Revenue %	-22.3	3.7	35.5	24.8
Earnings/Share %	-98.5	300.0	EUB	72.2
Book Value/Share %	-22.9	43.7	3.8	8.3
Dividends/Share %	NMF	NMF	NMF	55.6

Profitability [A]	2003	2004	2005	TTM
Return on Assets %	0.6	11.7	18.0	19.0
Oper Cash Flow $Mil	113	162	328	387
- Cap Spending $Mil	37	33	62	85
= Free Cash Flow $Mil	76	129	266	302

Financial Health [A+]	2003	2004	2005	09-30-06
Long-term Debt $Mil	—	2	3	4
Total Equity $Mil	789	912	971	987
Debt/Equity Ratio	—	0.0	0.0	0.0

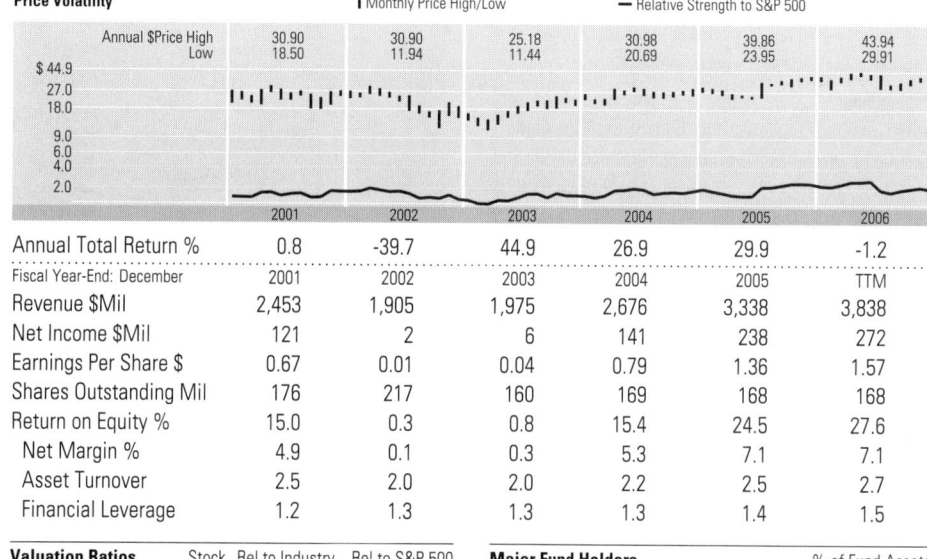

Industry	Business Risk	Moat Size	Investment Style	Sector
Employment	Below Avg	Narrow	Mid Growth	Business Services

Competition	Market Cap $Mil	12 Mo Trailing Sales $Mil	Price/Cash Flow	Return On Assets%	Debt/ Equity	Total Return% 1 Yr	3 Yr
Robert Half International	6,220	3,838	16.1	19.0	0.0	-1.2	17.1
Adecco SA ADR	12,751	22,920	34.2	7.0	0.3	50.3	3.5
Manpower	6,365	17,138	20.0	5.2	0.3	62.5	17.7

	2001	2002	2003	2004	2005	2006
Annual $Price High	30.90	30.90	25.18	30.98	39.86	43.94
Low	18.50	11.94	11.44	20.69	23.95	29.91
Annual Total Return %	0.8	-39.7	44.9	26.9	29.9	-1.2

Fiscal Year-End: December	2001	2002	2003	2004	2005	TTM
Revenue $Mil	2,453	1,905	1,975	2,676	3,338	3,838
Net Income $Mil	121	2	6	141	238	272
Earnings Per Share $	0.67	0.01	0.04	0.79	1.36	1.57
Shares Outstanding Mil	176	217	160	169	168	168
Return on Equity %	15.0	0.3	0.8	15.4	24.5	27.6
Net Margin %	4.9	0.1	0.3	5.3	7.1	7.1
Asset Turnover	2.5	2.0	2.0	2.2	2.5	2.7
Financial Leverage	1.2	1.3	1.3	1.3	1.4	1.5

Valuation Ratios	Stock	Rel to Industry	Rel to S&P 500
Price/Earnings	23.6	1.0	1.1
Price/Book	6.3	1.5	1.5
Price/Sales	1.6	1.8	0.6
Price/Cash Flow	16.1	0.7	1.1

Major Fund Holders	% of Fund Assets
FMI Provident Trust Strategy	4.67
Phoenix Dynamic Growth A	3.50
Fidelity Select IT Services	3.13
Manor Growth	3.00

Thesis By Kristan Rowland, 10-27-06 Stock Price as of Analysis: $36.71

Robert Half is the leading firm in specialty professional staffing. It provides temporary and full-time professional workers in fast-growing areas like finance, accounting, and information technology.

The firm has a solid narrow moat for several reasons. It boasts a stellar reputation in its specialty staffing areas, with its nearly 60-year operating history and expertise in placing individuals in various areas. It also benefits from scale and a strong network effect--workers go to Half for the best selection of jobs, and companies turn to Half for the greatest selection of candidates. Reputation and scale are also important in attracting strong internal staff. Successful recruiters work for Half because of the flow of candidates and relationships with corporations. They know that opportunities abound at Half. We think the firm's scale and reputation will continue to provide it with growth opportunities over the long term.

General industry trends are working in Robert Half's favor. In most advanced economies, temporary workers make up less than 2% of the workforce. Many countries have been easing restrictions on temporary labor to encourage economic growth. In some countries, this is often the only way firms can obtain labor cost flexibility, as stringent laws can make it extremely difficult to hire and fire permanent workers. Also, the looming talent shortage as baby boomers retire should make Robert Half an even more important resource for many companies. As the available pie grows, Robert Half should stand to benefit with its well-known brands.

Robert Half has performed well, considering it operates in a highly competitive market with relatively low barriers to entry. Competition varies by market, as customers tend to use firms with offices in proximity to their own to ensure a reliable supply of workers. Robert Half's strategy has proved fruitful, as returns on invested capital have averaged 17.5% over the past 15 years, well ahead of its cost of capital.

The future holds challenges, however. Large staffing firms like Manpower and Adecco both compete in the professional staffing market. These firms and other competition could mean pressure on Robert Half's gross margins, and its returns on invested capital could suffer. However, given Robert Half's reputation, scale, and sizable lead, we think the firm remains in an enviable position. With the looming talent shortage, we think companies will choose to maintain their relationships with Half as an important source for their hiring needs.

Rockwell Automation ROK

Data as of 12-29-06

	Rating	Fair Value	Last Close	Consider Buy	Consider Sell	Yield %
	★★★	$64.00	$61.08	$49.40	$80.20	1.58

Company Profile
Rockwell produces industrial process-control equipment designed to make the factory floor more efficient. It makes products that control, measure, and monitor processes ranging from beverage production to heavy-equipment manufacturing. Products include motor starters, signaling devices, relays, sensors, and motors. After selling its power systems segment, control systems will be the firm's sole line of business. Rockwell's most recognized brand is Allen-Bradley in controllers.

Management
Stewardship Grade [B]

Keith Nosbusch took over the CEO title in 2004 and became chairman in 2005. Nosbusch began his career with Rockwell subsidiary Allen-Bradley. Nosbusch was one of the key players in Rockwell's successful development of Logix, the company's marquee automation system. He heads a 10-member board, eight of whom are independent. We're impressed by the manner in which senior management runs the company in general and its focus on long-term value creation specifically. We applaud the company's decision to sell its power systems division in order to more efficiently allocate capital and enhance shareholder value. The company's governance policies are solid. Board members do have some skin in the game (though not an overwhelming amount), and management's annual cash incentives include a return on capital component. Annual bonuses are based on revenue, earnings per share, free cash flow, and pretax return on invested capital.

Industry	Business Risk	Moat Size	Investment Style	Sector
Electric Equip.	Average	Narrow	Mid Core	Industrial Materials

Competition	Market Cap $Mil	12 Mo Trailing Sales $Mil	Price/Cash Flow	Return On Assets%	Debt/ Equity	Total Return% 1 Yr	3 Yr
Rockwell Automation	10,394	5,561	24.4	12.8	0.4	4.8	22.7
General Electric	383,564	161,022	12.8	2.5	2.2	9.4	9.0
Siemens AG ADR	87,817	107,241	14.4	3.2	0.5	17.3	8.8

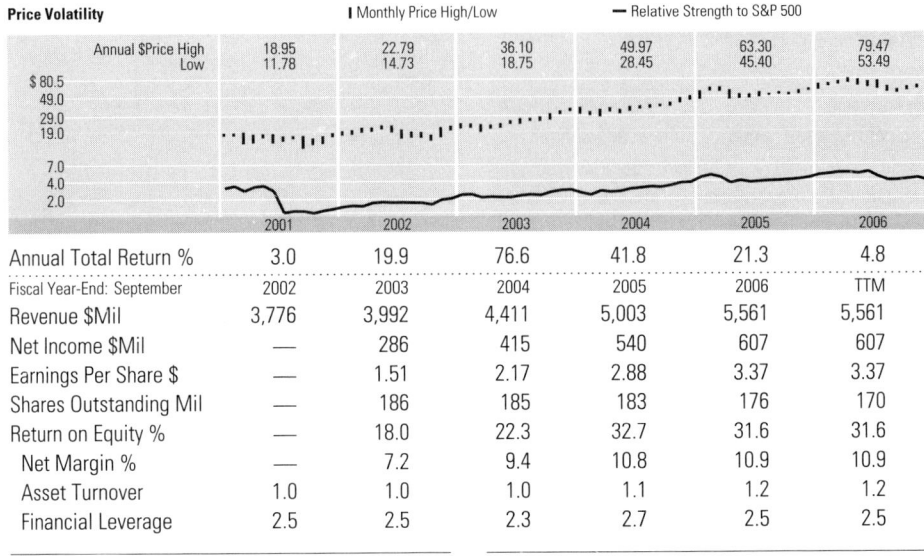

Price Volatility — Monthly Price High/Low — Relative Strength to S&P 500

Annual Total Return %	3.0	19.9	76.6	41.8	21.3	4.8
Fiscal Year-End: September	2002	2003	2004	2005	2006	TTM
Revenue $Mil	3,776	3,992	4,411	5,003	5,561	5,561
Net Income $Mil	—	286	415	540	607	607
Earnings Per Share $	—	1.51	2.17	2.88	3.37	3.37
Shares Outstanding Mil	—	186	185	183	176	170
Return on Equity %	—	18.0	22.3	32.7	31.6	31.6
Net Margin %	—	7.2	9.4	10.8	10.9	10.9
Asset Turnover	1.0	1.0	1.0	1.1	1.2	1.2
Financial Leverage	2.5	2.5	2.3	2.7	2.5	2.5

Valuation Ratios	Stock	Rel to Industry	Rel to S&P 500
Price/Earnings	17.5	0.8	0.8
Price/Book	5.4	1.5	1.3
Price/Sales	1.9	0.8	0.7
Price/Cash Flow	24.4	1.7	1.7

Major Fund Holders	% of Fund Assets
FMI Provident Trust Strategy	6.17
Quaker Capital Opportunities A	3.97
Stratton Multi Cap	3.54
Hallmark Large-Cap Growth R	3.06

1201 South 2nd Street www.rockwellautomation.com
Milwaukee, WI 53204

Growth [B-]	2002	2003	2004	2005
Revenue %	5.7	10.5	13.4	11.2
Earnings/Share %	NMF	43.7	32.7	17.0
Book Value/Share %	NMF	16.3	-9.6	21.1
Dividends/Share %	0.0	0.0	18.2	15.4

Profitability [A+]	2003	2004	2005	TTM
Return on Assets %	9.8	11.9	12.8	12.8
Oper Cash Flow $Mil	597	639	426	426
- Cap Spending $Mil	98	124	150	150
= Free Cash Flow $Mil	499	515	276	276

Financial Health [A]	2003	2004	2005	06-30-06
Long-term Debt $Mil	758	748	748	748
Total Equity $Mil	1,861	1,649	1,918	1,918
Debt/Equity Ratio	0.4	0.5	0.4	0.4

Thesis By Tom D'Amore, CFA, 11-07-06 Stock Price as of Analysis: $63.20

Rockwell, a premier supplier of high-margin industrial products, has a track record of generating robust cash flows that are consistently passed on to shareholders. We think that long-term investors in this narrow-moat company can expect a handsome return on their investment.

We can sum up Rockwell's approach to serving the industrial market in these words: focus, focus, focus. Rockwell specializes in a single line of business: factory automation. While many industrial companies seek to mimic the success of industry bellwether General Electric by simultaneously pursuing a variety of distinct business lines, Rockwell has emphatically decided to place a stake in the ground to establish itself as a premier supplier of factory automation systems and controls.

Factory automation is a market poised for healthy long-term growth. The global market pressure on manufacturers to wring out efficiencies in their operations is a long-term secular trend that is driving Rockwell's top line. Rockwell's leading brand, Allen-Bradley, is associated with high reliability and innovation in the market. Rockwell recently introduced a next-generation factory control platform, Logix. Logix offers customers the advantage of increased flexibility to fine-tune production lines at a lower price point. Driven by 20%-plus sales growth from Logix, the total top line increased by double digits in the last two years and is headed for a solid increase in fiscal 2006. Over the past couple of years, sales have grown faster than the industry's average, indicating that Rockwell is increasing its market share in the $30 billion factory automation market. Operating margins also are rising due to increased scale from higher sales. Return on capital, approaching 20% this year, is among the best in the industrial group.

We're impressed with Rockwell's commitment to efficient capital allocation. The company announced the sale of its only non-automation business line, power systems, in late 2006. The business has been performing well, and Rockwell decided to divest it in order to concentrate on its core factory automation business.

Rockwell has an excellent track record of returning cash generated from its business to shareholders. Over the last five years, the company has returned approximately 75% of its free cash flow to shareholders in the form of either dividends or share buybacks.

Data as of 12-29-06

Rockwell Collins COL

	Rating	Fair Value	Last Close	Consider Buy	Consider Sell	Yield %
	★★★	$58.00	$63.29	$44.70	$72.70	0.95

Company Profile
Rockwell Collins is a worldwide provider of communication and aviation electronics for the military and commercial aerospace markets. Its commercial segment sells products for both the flight deck and the cabin of commercial and business aircraft. The government segment designs and manufactures avionics as well as communication and navigation electronics for ground and shipboard defense systems. Collins is based in Cedar Rapids, Iowa, and employs about 14,000 workers.

Management
Stewardship Grade [B]

Clayton Jones has been CEO of Rockwell since the spin-off in 2001, and we believe his leadership is a driving force behind the company's success. A former Air Force pilot, Jones has been at the firm for more than 20 years and runs a very tight operation. He aims to increase efficiencies and is keenly focused on returns on capital. During his tenure, the firm has well exceeded its cost of capital, posting 14% average returns. Even better, at 56, Jones is relatively young and should be at the helm creating value for years to come. Some other managers have been at the firm for more than 20 years, which should provide steady leadership during inevitable cyclical swings in end markets. Organizational culture is important, since management squeezes out inefficiencies and finds ways for groups to collaborate, thus increasing shareholder returns. When pricing military products, management opts to use fixed-price contracts, which impose more fiscal discipline. Aside from staggered director elections and Jones' dual CEO-chairman role, Rockwell's corporate governance is excellent, and we applaud the compensation committee's inclusion of shareholder returns to compute performance metrics. We were also pleased to see the board modify long-term incentives by using fewer stock options and more multiyear performance shares.

400 Collins Road N.E.
Cedar Rapids, IA 52498
www.rockwellcollins.com

Growth [B]	2002	2003	2004	2005
Revenue %	2.0	15.3	17.6	12.1
Earnings/Share %	11.7	16.8	31.7	24.1
Book Value/Share %	-13.8	36.2	-17.0	32.3
Dividends/Share %	0.0	8.3	23.1	16.7

Profitability [A+]	2003	2004	2005	TTM
Return on Assets %	10.5	12.6	14.6	14.6
Oper Cash Flow $Mil	399	574	595	595
- Cap Spending $Mil	92	111	144	144
= Free Cash Flow $Mil	307	463	451	451

Financial Health [B+]	2003	2004	2005	06-30-06
Long-term Debt $Mil	201	200	245	245
Total Equity $Mil	1,133	939	1,206	1,206
Debt/Equity Ratio	0.2	0.2	0.2	0.2

Industry	Business Risk	Moat Size	Investment Style	Sector
Aerospace/Defense	Average	Narrow	Mid Growth	Industrial Materials

Competition
	Market Cap $Mil	12 Mo Trailing Sales $Mil	Price/Cash Flow	Return On Assets%	Debt/Equity	Total Return% 1 Yr	3 Yr
Rockwell Collins	10,582	3,863	17.8	14.6	0.2	37.7	30.6
Matsushita Electric Indus	48,067	78,926	9.4	2.0	0.1	4.7	13.7
Honeywell International	36,939	30,367	13.2	6.2	0.3	24.1	13.2

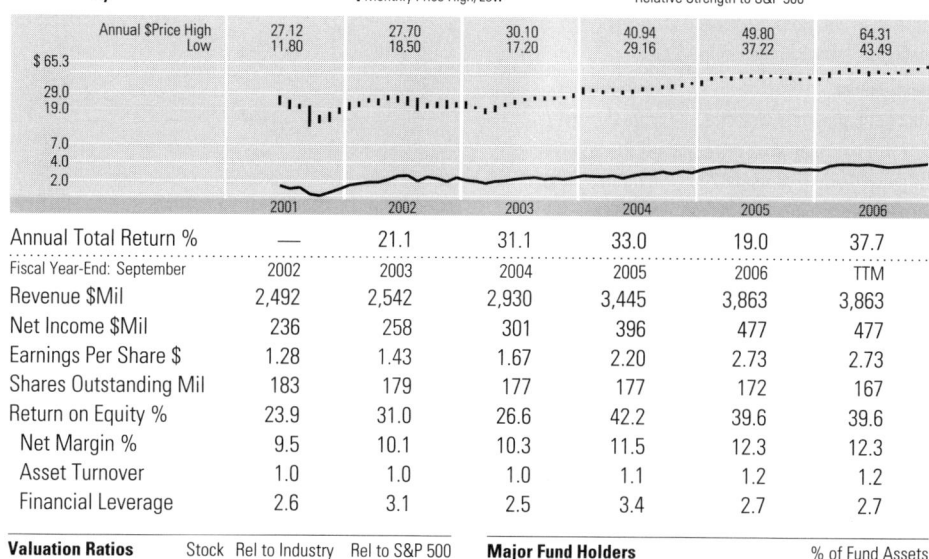

Annual Total Return %	—	21.1	31.1	33.0	19.0	37.7

Fiscal Year-End: September	2002	2003	2004	2005	2006	TTM
Revenue $Mil	2,492	2,542	2,930	3,445	3,863	3,863
Net Income $Mil	236	258	301	396	477	477
Earnings Per Share $	1.28	1.43	1.67	2.20	2.73	2.73
Shares Outstanding Mil	183	179	177	177	172	167
Return on Equity %	23.9	31.0	26.6	42.2	39.6	39.6
Net Margin %	9.5	10.1	10.3	11.5	12.3	12.3
Asset Turnover	1.0	1.0	1.0	1.1	1.2	1.2
Financial Leverage	2.6	3.1	2.5	3.4	2.7	2.7

Valuation Ratios	Stock	Rel to Industry	Rel to S&P 500
Price/Earnings	23.2	0.9	1.1
Price/Book	8.8	2.0	2.1
Price/Sales	2.7	2.1	0.9
Price/Cash Flow	17.8	1.3	1.2

Major Fund Holders	% of Fund Assets
Fidelity Select Air Transportation	7.86
Fidelity Select Defense & Aerospace	6.87
Brandywine Blue	3.53
Capital Management Mid-Cap Instl	3.40

Thesis By Marisa E. Thompson, 11-01-06 Stock Price as of Analysis: $57.75

With systems that span the avionics gamut, including flight decks, simulators, and data links, Rockwell Collins is positioned to capitalize on continued global aerospace growth and an increasingly networked military.

Rockwell maintains a diversified position in military and commercial aviation projects with products on major platforms including the Boeing 787 Dreamliner, Sikorsky helicopters, and the joint tactical radio system. Since Rockwell was spun off in 2001, its military sales have grown 14% per year, thanks to increased spending for advanced communication systems in light of operations in Iraq as well as initiatives to lay the groundwork for future combat systems. Commercial segment revenue has taken awhile to recover since the downturn in 2002 but grew 11% last fiscal year, thanks to a global aerospace boom and Rockwell's superior suite of avionics equipment.

Rockwell maintains research and development efficiencies that are difficult for rivals to replicate. Once Rockwell has developed a system for military use, it leverages that technological expertise to build similar commercial systems. In this way, government spending on military aerospace systems subsidizes innovation on the commercial side. For example, the weather radar system provided to Boeing and Airbus is the same one used by KC-135 airplane tankers.

Rockwell also takes a disciplined approach to capital allocation. The firm discontinued investment in the next generation of in-flight entertainment systems for wide-body jets, since management believes that it can get higher returns investing in data systems (including e-mail and broadcast TV) for business jet customers. And instead of making large, cumbersome acquisitions, the firm targets 8% annual growth from internal projects and completes small, bolt-on acquisitions to augment growth by 1-2 percentage points. These efforts have helped the firm post high-double-digit operating margins and 14% returns on capital over the past five years.

Despite prudent capital allocation and increasing efficiencies, Rockwell cannot escape the realities of the aerospace cycle. The last time the party came to an end in 2002, commercial original-equipment manufacturer sales fell 21%. Rockwell's growth depends on the strong 10-year backlog for 787s, and if global events halt sales, the firm's diverse platforms and less-cyclical government business might not offset the loss. Still, its systems expertise and scale make Rockwell a formidable competitor among large aerospace and defense firms.

Ross Stores ROST

Data as of 12-29-06

Rating ★★	Fair Value $26.00	Last Close $29.30	Consider Buy $20.00	Consider Sell $32.60	Yield % 0.82

Industry	Business Risk	Moat Size	Investment Style	Sector
Clothing Stores	Average	Narrow	Mid Core	Consumer Services

Company Profile
Ross Stores is the nation's second-largest off-price retailer of brand-name apparel and home accessories. The company offers merchandise at prices that are generally 20%-60% below the regular prices of most department and specialty stores. The company recently rolled out dd's Discounts, an offprice retailer of apparel and home fashions targeted to lower-income households. The company operates more than 700 Ross stores and 20-plus dd's Discounts stores in the United States.

Management
Stewardship Grade [C]

Michael Balmuth is vice chairman, president, and CEO. He has been with the company in various roles for more than 15 years. In 2005, Balmuth's annual compensation was $1.6 million, and he was granted $8 million in restricted stock. Relative to the company's peers, we think executive compensation is excessive, with 2004 being the exception. The company failed to meet its pretax earnings targets in 2004; therefore, top executives did not receive a bonus. Balmuth owns less than 1% of common shares outstanding; all executives and directors own 3.3%. Although Balmuth's stake is less than 1% of shares outstanding, it is greater than 2 times his cash compensation, which we think helps to align his interests with those of shareholders. The majority of the board is independent, with two former Ross CEOs as directors. Norman Ferber, who was CEO from 1993 through 1996, is chairman. Our only concern about the board is that directors serve three-year terms as opposed to standing for re-election each year. We think that electing board members on an annual basis is more shareholder-friendly, giving the stock owners more flexibility in ousting underperforming directors. Overall, we think corporate governance is average.

8333 Central Ave.
Newark, CA 94560-3433
www.rossstores.com

Growth [B+]	2003	2004	2005	2006
Revenue %	18.2	11.0	8.1	16.6
Earnings/Share %	31.6	17.6	-23.1	20.4
Book Value/Share %	20.6	21.4	4.7	11.9
Dividends/Share %	11.7	21.0	47.6	23.5

Profitability [A]	2004	2005	2006	TTM
Return on Assets %	13.5	9.8	10.3	10.3
Oper Cash Flow $Mil	321	298	375	441
- Cap Spending $Mil	153	150	176	217
= Free Cash Flow $Mil	169	149	199	224

Financial Health [A-]	2004	2005	2006	10-31-06
Long-term Debt $Mil	50	50	0	0
Total Equity $Mil	753	766	836	859
Debt/Equity Ratio	0.1	0.1	0.0	0.0

Competition	Market Cap $Mil	12 Mo Trailing Sales $Mil	Price/Cash Flow	Return On Assets %	Debt/Equity	Total Return % 1 Yr	Total Return % 3 Yr
Ross Stores	4,095	5,373	9.3	10.3	0.0	2.3	4.7
TJX Companies	12,979	17,102	11.5	13.0	0.4	24.1	10.7
Men's Wearhouse	2,024	1,822	13.2	10.8	0.3	30.7	33.3

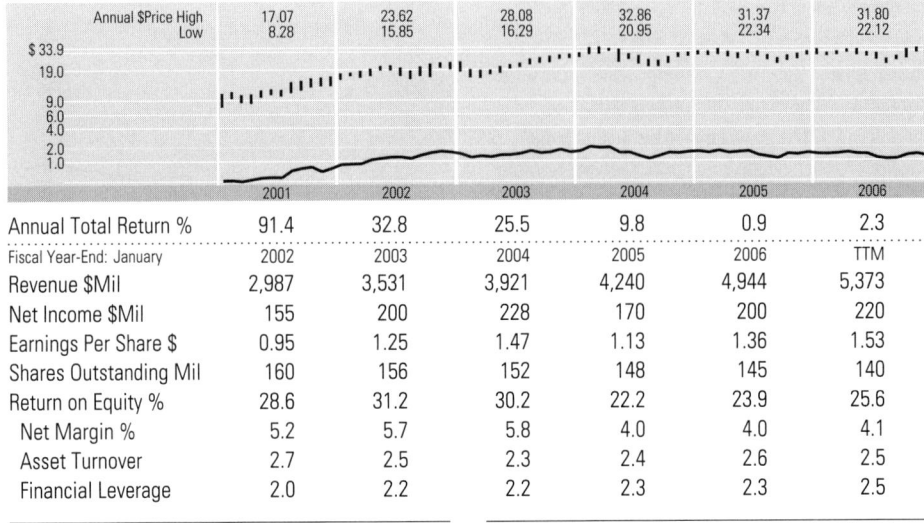

Price Volatility — Monthly Price High/Low — Relative Strength to S&P 500

Annual $Price High Low	17.07 8.28	23.62 15.85	28.08 16.29	32.86 20.95	31.37 22.34	31.80 22.12
	2001	2002	2003	2004	2005	2006
Annual Total Return %	91.4	32.8	25.5	9.8	0.9	2.3

Fiscal Year-End: January	2002	2003	2004	2005	2006	TTM
Revenue $Mil	2,987	3,531	3,921	4,240	4,944	5,373
Net Income $Mil	155	200	228	170	200	220
Earnings Per Share $	0.95	1.25	1.47	1.13	1.36	1.53
Shares Outstanding Mil	160	156	152	148	145	140
Return on Equity %	28.6	31.2	30.2	22.2	23.9	25.6
Net Margin %	5.2	5.7	5.8	4.0	4.0	4.1
Asset Turnover	2.7	2.5	2.3	2.4	2.6	2.5
Financial Leverage	2.0	2.2	2.2	2.3	2.3	2.5

Valuation Ratios	Stock	Rel to Industry	Rel to S&P 500
Price/Earnings	19.2	1.0	0.9
Price/Book	4.8	1.1	1.2
Price/Sales	0.8	0.6	0.3
Price/Cash Flow	9.3	0.7	0.6

Major Fund Holders	% of Fund Assets
FAM Equity-Income Inv	5.69
AIM Trimark Endeavor A	4.06
Ave Maria Rising Dividend	3.41
Calvert Capital Accumulation A	3.27

Thesis By Kimberly Picciola, 11-20-06 Stock Price as of Analysis: $30.32

Execution issues continue to plague Ross Stores. In 2004, it was a botched systems implementation; in 2005, actual inventory differed from expected inventory because of system issues from the prior year and a loss of in-store product. Midway through 2006, merchandising misses pressured top- and bottom-line growth. While we think Ross has room to grow, our optimism is tempered by a lack of faith in management's ability to execute. In our discounted cash-flow model, we factor in a slow recovery from recent operational mishaps.

Despite recent missteps, Ross has carved out a niche in the highly competitive retail environment by offering brand-name apparel at prices that are 20%-60% lower than at traditional department and specialty stores. We think the long-standing relationships that Ross has developed with key apparel manufacturers are critical to its success. These relationships have created a barrier to entry for new competitors and allowed Ross to offer a wide assortment of branded apparel and home furnishings at rock-bottom prices. Additionally, with little capital required to operate its no-frill stores, the company has consistently generated healthy returns on invested capital, furthering our case that Ross has built a narrow economic moat.

Given that Ross' revenue is less than a third of off-price leader TJX Companies', we think growth opportunities exist. On average, total revenue has increased 13% annually over the past five years, driven by new store openings and increases in same-store sales. We expect annual store growth will average in the high single digits over the next five years as the company expands its namesake stores and continues to roll out its lower-priced concept, dd's Discounts.

While we believe Ross Stores has room to expand, we are concerned that there will be more bumps in the road. Each year a new operational issue pops up, leaving us less confident in management's ability to overcome obstacles along the way. Additionally, suppliers are becoming more adept at managing their inventory, putting pressure on operating margins. We think operating margins will improve over the next five years as Ross works through its internal challenges. However, given the continued operational blunders, we don't anticipate they will return to historical levels anytime soon.

Data as of 12-29-06

Royal Bank of Canada RY

Rating	Fair Value	Last Close	Consider Buy	Consider Sell	Yield %
★★	$41.00	$47.65	$31.60	$51.40	2.65

Company Profile

Royal is the largest bank in Canada with about C$475 billion in assets and 1,400 branches—primarily located in Canada and the southeastern U.S. The bank serves more than 14 million customers in North America and 30 other countries across the globe. Royal provides traditional banking services to retail and corporate customers. Other product offerings include insurance, wealth management, and capital markets services.

Management   Stewardship Grade [B]

Management and corporate governance at Royal are solid. CEO Gordon Nixon was appointed in August 2001, and prior to that, had served the bank for more than 27 years in different positions. Executive compensation is in line with peers, and incentive pay is tied to targets such as return on equity and earnings-per-share growth. We also like that stock option issuance isn't excessive, and we are pleased with the bank's financial disclosures, which are detailed and comprehensive.

Industry	Business Risk	Moat Size	Investment Style	Sector
International Banks	Average	Wide	Large Core	Financial Services

Competition

	Market Cap $Mil	12 Mo Trailing Sales $Mil	Price/Cash Flow	Return On Assets%	Debt/ Equity	Total Return% 1 Yr	3 Yr
Royal Bank of Canada	61,039	20,637	—	0.9	—	26.0	29.5
Bank of Nova Scotia	44,330	10,211	—	0.9	—	16.8	24.5
Toronto-Dominion Bank	43,027	11,488	—	1.2	—	15.4	23.9

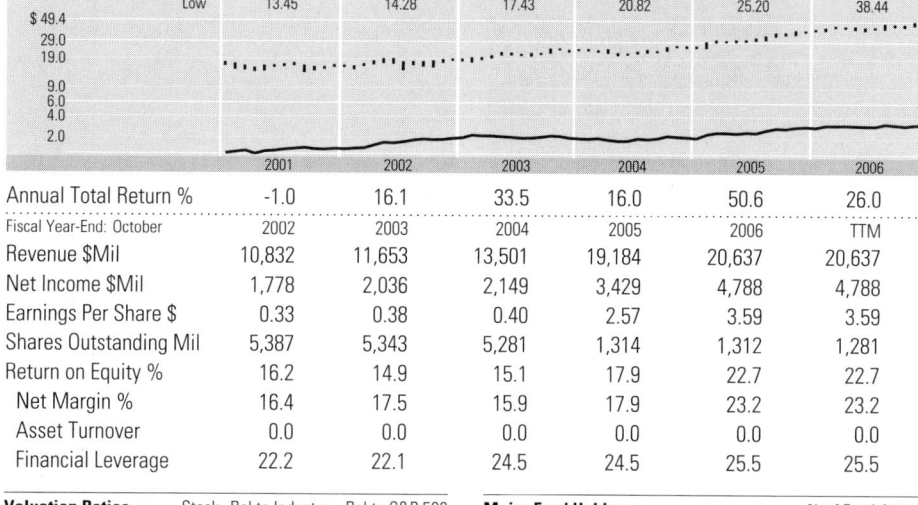

Price Volatility — Monthly Price High/Low — Relative Strength to S&P 500

	2002	2003	2004	2005	2006	
Annual $Price High	17.56	19.29	25.03	26.95	39.18	48.41
Low	13.45	14.28	17.43	20.82	25.20	38.44
Annual Total Return %	-1.0	16.1	33.5	16.0	50.6	26.0
Fiscal Year-End: October	2002	2003	2004	2005	2006	TTM
Revenue $Mil	10,832	11,653	13,501	19,184	20,637	20,637
Net Income $Mil	1,778	2,036	2,149	3,429	4,788	4,788
Earnings Per Share $	0.33	0.38	0.40	2.57	3.59	3.59
Shares Outstanding Mil	5,387	5,343	5,281	1,314	1,312	1,281
Return on Equity %	16.2	14.9	15.1	17.9	22.7	22.7
Net Margin %	16.4	17.5	15.9	17.9	23.2	23.2
Asset Turnover	0.0	0.0	0.0	0.0	0.0	0.0
Financial Leverage	22.2	22.1	24.5	24.5	25.5	25.5

Valuation Ratios	Stock	Rel to Industry	Rel to S&P 500
Price/Earnings	13.2	0.7	0.6
Price/Book	2.9	1.1	0.7
Price/Sales	3.0	0.7	1.0
Price/Cash Flow	—	—	—

Major Fund Holders	% of Fund Assets
Fidelity Canada	4.27
Brown Capital Mgmt Intern Equity Inst	2.62
Gartmore Global Financial A	2.55
Legg Mason Partners Financial Services B	1.36

200 Bay Street   www.rbc.com
Toronto, ON M5J 2J5

Growth [NA]	2003	2004	2005	2006
Revenue %	-0.4	4.8	7.8	7.6
Earnings/Share %	6.6	-3.6	386.0	39.7
Book Value/Share %	5.4	-3.0	342.7	10.1
Dividends/Share %	—	—	NMF	30.9

Profitability [NA]	2004	2005	2006	TTM
Return on Assets %	0.6	0.7	0.9	0.9
Oper Cash Flow $Mil	1,464	-29,527	-14,996	—
- Cap Spending $Mil	333	383	511	—
= Free Cash Flow $Mil	—	—	—	—

Financial Health [NA]	2004	2005	2006	10-31-06
Long-term Debt $Mil	—	—	—	
Total Equity $Mil	14,239	19,147	21,073	21,073
Debt/Equity Ratio	—	—	—	

Thesis By Michael Kon, CFA, 12-01-06 Stock Price as of Analysis: $46.90

Royal Bank of Canada (Royal) is the largest bank in Canada by assets. But size isn't the only thing Royal has to offer. The bank is also a top performer, which produces extremely attractive returns for shareholders.

Royal has the largest branch and ATM network in Canada. The bank operates as a "financial supermarket," offering clients a wide variety of financial products and services. Royal also enjoys a benign regulatory environment and leads an oligopoly that dominates the Canadian banking sector. We think these advantages garner the bank a wide economic moat.

One of Royal's many strengths, in our opinion, is its diversified stream of revenue, which results in lower dependence on spread-based income and hence lower sensitivity to interest rate changes. Revenue diversification comes from many lines of business such as investment banking and trading. Royal is the most diversified bank in Canada as it typically books noninterest income of more than 63% of total revenue, compared with an average of 55% for Canadian peers and 48% for U.S. peers. We expect diversification to remain a key strength in the future.

Royal also leads the Canadian banking industry in wealth management and insurance. Wealth management, which typically accounts for about 20% of total revenue, includes the manufacturing and distribution of asset management products. The bank leverages its vast distribution channels to sell its services to existing and new clients. This has worked out very well as the bank grew assets under management in Canada by 20% annually, on average, over the past three years. Royal also expanded its mutual fund market share by about 300 basis points to an impressive 11%, the only bank in Canada with a double-digit share. As the growth in this industry slows, we expect Royal to further gain share at the expense of weaker players.

Royal's U.S. retail banking business is its Achilles' heel. The bank faces tough competition in its U.S. footprint and, unlike in Canada, doesn't have any significant advantages. We think the U.S. operation is a high-risk/low-return business compared with its Canadian operation. However, since it contributes less than 10% to net income, we don't think it jeopardizes the hefty returns this bank typically generates.

Data as of 12-29-06

Royal Caribbean Cruises RCL

Rating	Fair Value	Last Close	Consider Buy	Consider Sell	Yield %
★★★★★	$55.00	$41.38	$42.40	$68.90	1.45

Company Profile

Royal Caribbean Cruises is the second-largest cruise operator worldwide. It operates 29 ships with more than 60,000 berths under the Royal Caribbean International and Celebrity Cruises brands. The firm's cruise liners serve about 160 destinations in the Caribbean, Bahamas, Mexico, Alaska, Europe, Bermuda, the Panama Canal, Hawaii, and East Asia. The company will steadily expand its fleet starting in 2007.

Management Stewardship Grade [B]

Richard Fain has been chairman and CEO since 1988. Fain has worked in the shipping industry for more than 25 years. After a period of aggressive expansion, management has been more judicious with its spending in recent years. Given recent industry consolidation, we expect more-rational decision-making to lead to higher returns. We also applaud management for cleaning up Royal Caribbean's balance sheet, which is now the healthiest it has been since 2000.

Corporate-governance policies are generally solid, though we disapprove of the staggered board and would prefer to see the roles of CEO and chairman separated. Control of the company effectively rests with the Wilhelmsen, Pritzker, and Ofer families, which alone can decide all matters requiring shareholder approval. Relative to peers, executive compensation is reasonable, in our view.

1050 Caribbean Way   www.royalcaribbean.com
Miami, FL 33132

Growth [B]	2002	2003	2004	2005
Revenue %	9.2	10.2	20.4	7.6
Earnings/Share %	35.6	-20.7	59.2	44.2
Book Value/Share %	5.5	4.9	6.1	10.6
Dividends/Share %	0.0	0.0	0.0	7.7

Profitability [B-]	2003	2004	2005	TTM
Return on Assets %	2.5	4.0	6.4	4.8
Oper Cash Flow $Mil	858	1,077	1,111	1,036
- Cap Spending $Mil	1,030	631	430	1,129
= Free Cash Flow $Mil	-172	446	681	-93

Financial Health [B]	2003	2004	2005	09-30-06
Long-term Debt $Mil	5,521	4,827	3,554	4,182
Total Equity $Mil	4,263	4,805	5,554	6,043
Debt/Equity Ratio	1.3	1.0	0.6	0.7

Industry	Business Risk	Moat Size	Investment Style	Sector
Recreation	Average	Narrow	Mid Value	Consumer Goods

Competition	Market Cap $Mil	12 Mo Trailing Sales $Mil	Price/Cash Flow	Return On Assets%	Debt/ Equity	Total Return% 1 Yr	3 Yr
Royal Caribbean Cruises	8,775	5,106	8.5	4.8	0.7	-6.8	7.1
Carnival	40,975	11,595	12.0	7.4	0.4	-6.2	9.0
NCL Holdings ASA							

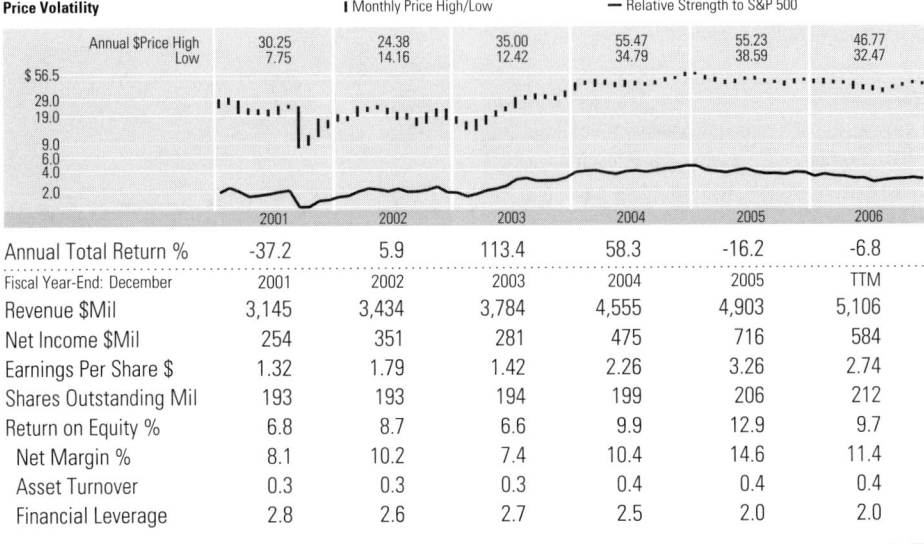

	2001	2002	2003	2004	2005	2006
Annual Total Return %	-37.2	5.9	113.4	58.3	-16.2	-6.8
Fiscal Year-End: December	2001	2002	2003	2004	2005	TTM
Revenue $Mil	3,145	3,434	3,784	4,555	4,903	5,106
Net Income $Mil	254	351	281	475	716	584
Earnings Per Share $	1.32	1.79	1.42	2.26	3.26	2.74
Shares Outstanding Mil	193	193	194	199	206	212
Return on Equity %	6.8	8.7	6.6	9.9	12.9	9.7
Net Margin %	8.1	10.2	7.4	10.4	14.6	11.4
Asset Turnover	0.3	0.3	0.3	0.4	0.4	0.4
Financial Leverage	2.8	2.6	2.7	2.5	2.0	2.0

Valuation Ratios	Stock	Rel to Industry	Rel to S&P 500
Price/Earnings	15.1	0.8	0.7
Price/Book	1.5	0.3	0.4
Price/Sales	1.7	0.6	0.6
Price/Cash Flow	8.5	0.7	0.6

Major Fund Holders	% of Fund Assets
ING Partners OpCap Balanced Val Svc	4.43
Oppenheimer Quest Balanced A	3.88
Allianz OCC Renaissance C	3.14
Meridian Growth	2.60

Thesis By Sumit Desai, CFA, 12-06-06 Stock Price as of Analysis: $41.45

Royal Caribbean is the second-largest player in an attractive industry. We think the company has what it takes to succeed over the long term.

Royal Caribbean enjoys a near 25% market share of the global cruise industry, making it the second largest cruise provider, behind Carnival (60% share). We think the cruise industry will remain concentrated in the future, as sizable barriers to entry have historically kept away new entrants. Building a new cruise ship is a costly and lengthy process: New ships cost hundreds of millions of dollars, with no revenue seen for several years. As such, it's very difficult and expensive to achieve the critical mass needed to enjoy scale advantages.

Size is important in this industry, as larger players gain more bargaining power with suppliers and distributors, and larger fleets allow companies to spread fixed costs across more ships. Size advantages become clear with a comparison between Royal and Carnival. Although Royal regularly turns in strong financial results, its 16% average operating margin over the past five years is almost 600 basis points lower than Carnival's.

We think there is plenty of room in the cruise industry for Royal and Carnival to maintain their respective levels of profitability. The cruise industry has grown about 8% annually since 1980, and we expect it to continue growing at a healthy clip. Favorable demographics, notably an aging population, should provide a nice tailwind. Also, attracting first-time cruisers is a key focus for cruise operators; customer satisfaction rates are generally high, so first-timers often become repeat customers. Companies have made strides in broadening the appeal of cruises by making ports more accessible and adding more onboard activities, which have helped lure the younger demographic.

Although Royal's long-term picture is attractive, there are some short-term risks. Soaring energy prices have taken a large bite out of the company's profits, with Royal's fuel costs expected to rise to more than 8% of sales in 2006 from 5% in 2004. The company has offset some of these costs through higher ticket prices and improved cost-management in other areas, but oil prices remain a vulnerability. Further, the cruise industry is driven by supply and demand factors, and irrational building or a price war would lower returns for all industry players. North American industry capacity is expected to grow about 7% annually over the next four years, and could result in weaker returns for all players if the building coincides with an economic slowdown.

Data as of 12-29-06

Royal Dutch Shell PLC ADR A RDS.A

Rating	Fair Value	Last Close	Consider Buy	Consider Sell	Yield %
★★★	$73.00	$70.79	$62.20	$95.80	3.46

Company Profile

Royal Dutch Shell's global integrated operations cover the spectrum in oil and gas. The third-largest global oil player, Shell is considered a supermajor, along with ExxonMobil and BP. Royal Dutch Shell has 11.5 billion barrels of oil and gas reserves, daily production of 3.5 million barrels of oil equivalent, the capacity to refine 4 million barrels a day, and about 45,000 service stations. Other businesses include chemicals and liquefied natural-gas infrastructure.

Management
Stewardship Grade [NA]

Shell's reserves debacle brought to light serious stewardship gaps that the company is earnestly trying to remedy by overhauling management systems. For the past century, Royal Dutch and Shell Transport had jointly appointed directors to the Shell board and rotated the chairmanship among representatives of the two parent firms. In July 2005, these two holding companies merged into a single entity. Triggered by Shell's reserves issues, the change should simplify the management structure, streamline decision-making, and increase accountability. We're pleased to see that the firm is also revamping its remuneration policies, eliminating the use of stock options and creating long-term incentive plans that better align the interests of management and shareholders. We think the changes will be effective at restoring investor confidence, but new systems and processes will take time to implement and become effective. The new firm is headed by CEO Jeroen van der Veer, who was chief executive of Royal Dutch/Shell Group and a nonexecutive chairman. Van der Veer joined the group in 1971 and has been a managing director since 1997. In our view, he has done an effective job steering Shell's ship since the departure of former chairman Philip Watts, who was ousted following the reserves write-down.

Carel van Bylandtlaan 30
The Hague, Netherlands 2596 HR
www.shell.com

Growth [NA]	2002	2003	2004	2005
Revenue %	23.2	19.1	34.3	15.1
Earnings/Share %	—	—	NMF	38.0
Book Value/Share %	—	—	NMF	8.3
Dividends/Share %	12.0	23.5	8.0	43.6

Profitability [NA]	2003	2004	2005	TTM
Return on Assets %	7.3	9.9	11.5	11.5
Oper Cash Flow $Mil	21,719	26,537	30,113	30,113
- Cap Spending $Mil	12,252	13,566	15,904	15,904
= Free Cash Flow $Mil	9,467	12,971	14,209	14,209

Financial Health [NA]	2003	2004	2005	12-31-05
Long-term Debt $Mil	9,100	8,858	7,578	7,578
Total Equity $Mil	72,497	91,363	97,924	97,924
Debt/Equity Ratio	0.1	0.1	0.1	0.1

Industry	Business Risk	Moat Size	Investment Style	Sector
Oil/Gas	Below Avg	Narrow	Large Value	Energy

Competition

	Market Cap $Mil	12 Mo Trailing Sales $Mil	Price/Cash Flow	Return On Assets %	Debt/Equity	Total Return % 1 Yr	3 Yr
Royal Dutch Shell PLC ADR A	230,956	306,731	7.7	11.5	0.1	19.3	15.1
ExxonMobil	446,944	386,951	8.8	17.8	0.1	39.1	26.2
BP PLC ADR	231,015	239,792	8.6	10.8	0.1	7.9	14.3

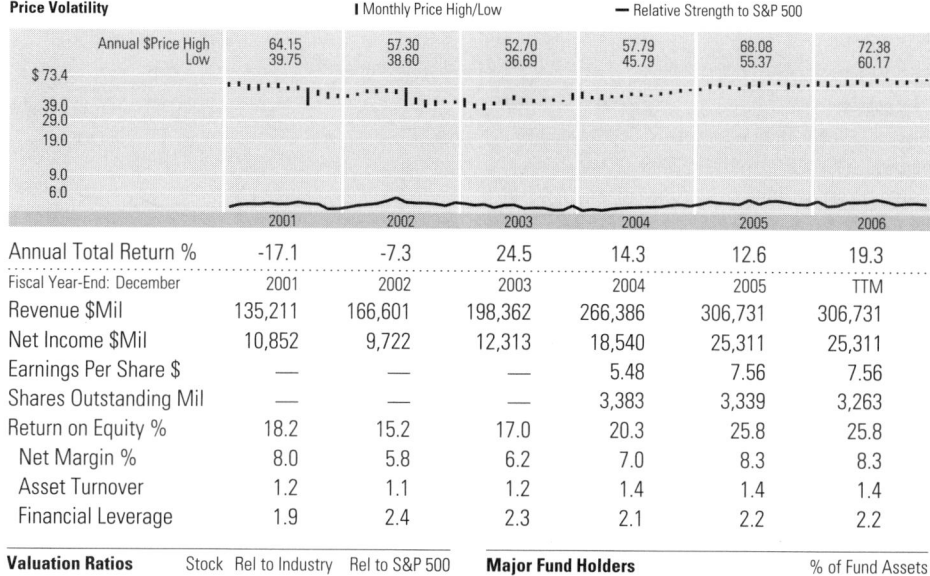

Price Volatility — Monthly Price High/Low — Relative Strength to S&P 500

Annual $Price High / Low	64.15 / 39.75	57.30 / 38.60	52.70 / 36.69	57.79 / 45.79	68.08 / 55.37	72.38 / 60.17

	2001	2002	2003	2004	2005	2006
Annual Total Return %	-17.1	-7.3	24.5	14.3	12.6	19.3

Fiscal Year-End: December	2001	2002	2003	2004	2005	TTM
Revenue $Mil	135,211	166,601	198,362	266,386	306,731	306,731
Net Income $Mil	10,852	9,722	12,313	18,540	25,311	25,311
Earnings Per Share $	—	—	—	5.48	7.56	7.56
Shares Outstanding Mil	—	—	—	3,383	3,339	3,263
Return on Equity %	18.2	15.2	17.0	20.3	25.8	25.8
Net Margin %	8.0	5.8	6.2	7.0	8.3	8.3
Asset Turnover	1.2	1.1	1.2	1.4	1.4	1.4
Financial Leverage	1.9	2.4	2.3	2.1	2.2	2.2

Valuation Ratios	Stock	Rel to Industry	Rel to S&P 500
Price/Earnings	9.2	0.7	0.4
Price/Book	2.4	0.7	0.6
Price/Sales	0.8	0.4	0.3
Price/Cash Flow	7.7	0.9	0.5

Major Fund Holders	% of Fund Assets
Barrett Opportunity	9.30
Integrity Growth & Income A Load Waived	5.29
ProFunds Europe 30 Svc	4.99
Rydex Energy Inv	3.62

Thesis By Elizabeth Collins, 12-13-06 Stock Price as of Analysis: $70.88

In the wake of large downward reserves revisions, Royal Dutch Shell has seen its competitive position weaken. However, it remains an attractive business, thanks to strong company fundamentals.

In January 2004, Shell stunned investors with a sharp downward revision to its proven oil and gas reserves, ultimately slashing the figure by one third. The incident highlighted fundamental weakness in the firm's most profitable segment, exploration and production. In light of the revised data, Shell's reserve life index (the ratio of proved reserves to annual production) sits at a measly 9 years, compared with 14 for ExxonMobil and 12 for BP. Although Shell's short-term outlook is relatively unaffected, the longer-term implications are serious. In the years to come, as the firm replaces depleted reserves, it faces an uphill battle relative to its larger peers.

Shell has emerged from the incident bruised but not beaten. To restore investor confidence, management attacked weak internal controls, revamped the compensation scheme, and simplified the organizational structure. Management also responded with a strategy designed to regain lost ground, which we think can work, albeit gradually. The objective is to rebuild the reserve base and expand the upstream segment. To do this, Shell needs to commit to a prolonged period of heightened investment to book more oil and gas reserves than it produces. With increased emphasis on natural gas and unconventional oil, Shell has increased exploration spending and is targeting production growth in politically challenging areas like Russia, West Africa, and the Middle East.

We're concerned that management will get impatient. Given stiff competition for energy resources and long project lead times, we think management could be tempted to buy its way out of trouble, shoring up reserves with a large acquisition. This could be facilitated by Shell's hefty cash hoard and substantial debt capacity. In today's market of high energy prices, we don't think there are many deals to be had, and paying too much for more reserves won't add shareholder value.

Nonetheless, we expect Shell to continue generating solid returns. Despite the reserves setback, Shell benefits from huge economies of scale, has made progress with cost-cutting initiatives in recent years, and has not had an unprofitable year in decades. Further, few competitors can rival Shell's technology and engineering expertise. These capabilities will help the firm as it pursues more-complex energy projects.

Data as of 12-29-06

Ryanair Holdings PLC ADR RYAAY

	Rating	Fair Value	Last Close	Consider Buy	Consider Sell	Yield %
	★	$54.00	$81.50	$41.60	$67.70	0.00

Industry	Business Risk	Moat Size	Investment Style	Sector
Air Transport	Average	Narrow	Large Growth	Business Services

Company Profile

Ryanair operates the largest low-fare scheduled passenger airline in Europe, serving primarily short-haul, point-to-point routes. The firm has more than a dozen base airports and serves more than 100 cities across 21 European countries. With 3,000 employees, the firm operates more than 100 Boeing 737 jets. Ryanair's U.S.-listed ADRs consist of bundles of five Dublin/London-traded shares.

Management
Stewardship Grade [NA]

Michael O'Leary, Ryanair's dynamic CEO, recently announced his plan to retire in 2008. O'Leary has been the architect of Ryanair's low-cost strategy and has headed the most successful team to implement a Southwest model in the deregulated European markets. As a result of O'Leary's leadership, Ryanair's performance has outstripped all competitors in Europe and arguably even Southwest itself. O'Leary has been outspoken against his critics who claim that the company has negotiated illegal concessions from airports and has denigrated air travel to the detriment of the customer. O'Leary views the airline industry as a pure commodity and has been unapologetic in nickel-and-diming customers, charging them fees for excess baggage and anything else nonessential. Though we believe that O'Leary has been instrumental in shaping the airline, we don't see his departure leading to the demise of the company, and his largely handpicked executive management team will continue to carry out the same mission. Executive compensation is consistent with that of similar U.S. airlines, and directors and officers own a combined 7.8% of outstanding shares. O'Leary owns about 6% of ordinary shares.

Dublin Airport
Dublin, Ireland
www.ryanair.ie

Growth [NA]	2003	2004	2005	2006
Revenue %	35.0	27.5	22.8	28.3
Earnings/Share %	53.7	-13.6	35.7	8.4
Book Value/Share %	19.6	17.4	19.4	13.7
Dividends/Share %	NMF	NMF	NMF	NMF

Profitability [NA]	2004	2005	2006	TTM
Return on Assets %	6.7	7.1	6.7	6.7
Oper Cash Flow $Mil	537	643	748	748
- Cap Spending $Mil	385	795	669	669
= Free Cash Flow $Mil	152	-152	79	79

Financial Health [NA]	2004	2005	2006	03-31-06
Long-term Debt $Mil	1,064	1,680	1,837	1,837
Total Equity $Mil	1,775	2,253	2,400	2,400
Debt/Equity Ratio	0.6	0.7	0.8	0.8

Competition	Market Cap $Mil	12 Mo Trailing Sales $Mil	Price/Cash Flow	Return On Assets%	Debt/Equity	Total Return% 1 Yr	3 Yr
Ryanair Holdings PLC ADR	12,568	2,073	16.8	6.7	0.8	45.6	16.6
British Airways PLC	11,693	15,283	4.9	3.9	1.9	79.6	35.7
AMR	6,482	22,334	3.8	-1.3	NMF	36.0	32.5

Price Volatility — Monthly Price High/Low — Relative Strength to S&P 500

Annual $Price High	32.25	48.20	53.04	58.23	57.93	82.22
Low	16.50	27.63	32.88	25.98	39.33	46.47
	2001	2002	2003	2004	2005	2006

Annual Total Return %	15.1	22.2	29.4	-19.6	37.4	45.6
Fiscal Year-End: March	2002	2003	2004	2005	2006	TTM
Revenue $Mil	551	824	1,248	1,659	2,073	2,073
Net Income $Mil	133	234	240	352	376	376
Earnings Per Share $	0.90	1.53	1.57	2.31	2.43	2.43
Shares Outstanding Mil	146	151	151	152	153	154
Return on Equity %	15.2	17.5	13.5	15.6	15.7	15.7
Net Margin %	24.1	28.4	19.2	21.2	18.1	18.1
Asset Turnover	0.3	0.3	0.3	0.3	0.4	0.4
Financial Leverage	1.9	2.0	2.0	2.2	2.3	2.3

Valuation Ratios	Stock	Rel to Industry	Rel to S&P 500
Price/Earnings	33.5	1.8	1.6
Price/Book	5.2	1.3	1.3
Price/Sales	6.1	3.8	2.1
Price/Cash Flow	16.8	1.7	1.2

Major Fund Holders	% of Fund Assets
AIM Trimark A	3.10
Atlantic Whitehall Multi-Cap Globl Val I	3.07
AIM Trimark Endeavor A	2.76
Seligman International Growth A	1.40

Thesis By Marisa E. Thompson, 12-14-06 Stock Price as of Analysis: $78.08

In the highly commodified airline business, low unit operating costs are synonymous with profitability. With the lowest cost structure of any European airline, Ryanair has sustained profitability despite rampant fuel prices and, consequently, it earns our narrow economic moat rating.

Ryanair has built low costs into every aspect of its operations. The airline flies just one type of airplane, the Boeing 737, affording greater flexibility and savings on training and maintenance. The company flies its planes to second-tier airports where it has been able to save on fees, especially by negotiating with the local airport authority. Ryanair will open service only to airports where it can maintain its industry-leading, 25-minute turnaround, which increases the utilization of its airplanes. Ryanair also contains labor expenses by emphasizing productivity-based pay. In contrast to most other airlines, where union contracts lock in pay regardless of actual hours in the cockpit, over 40% of Ryanair pilots' total compensation is based on such variables as number of hours or sectors flown. Ryanair's flight attendants are compensated partially by commissions on the merchandise that they sell on the airplane during flight.

The company's industry-leading profitability is not only driven by low operating costs but also by ancillary, high-margin revenue. Ryanair's flight attendants are motivated to sell all kinds of products on each flight, from food and drinks to in-flight entertainment to calling cards and even merchandise. The airline also entered into an agreement with MBNA to offer a branded credit card. Plus, Ryanair has leveraged the high traffic on its Web sites to promote rental cars and hotels. Ancillary activities like these account for over 15% of Ryanair's revenue and enabled the firm to achieve operating margins around 20% while low-cost airlines in the U.S. struggled to post just 8% operating margins.

While there are many untapped locales where Ryanair's low-fare service is in demand, the company's ambitious expansion strategy has met resistance. Europe's regulatory framework is strict, and Ryanair is embroiled in a legal battle concerning discounts it receives from some public airports. The airports in some countries, France in particular, maintain high taxes, thus limiting Ryanair's market presence and protecting incumbents. The Dublin airport authority and Ryanair are currently battling over terminal expansion plans, which, as formulated right now, would increase the fees for airlines that want to expand to take advantage of new gates.

Salesforce.com CRM

Data as of 12-29-06

Rating	Fair Value	Last Close	Consider Buy	Consider Sell	Yield %
★★★	$34.00	$36.45	$26.20	$42.60	0.00

Company Profile
Salesforce.com provides subscription-based customer relationship management software. The company hosts the applications and "rents" the software to enterprises on a per-user basis via one- to four-year contracts. The company provides software, hosting, and support but contracts with third parties for actual hosting and delivery. The company has more than 500,000 paying subscribers.

Management Stewardship Grade [C]
Marc Benioff has been chairman and CEO since cofounding the company in 1999. He served in various sales, product-management, and marketing roles at the executive level at Oracle from 1986 to 1999. He owns more than 25% of the outstanding equity and will receive a $10 annual salary with no opportunity for bonus or options in 2006. We applaud Benioff's efforts to align his interests with those of shareholders, but we think the roles of CEO and chairman should be separated. The equity incentive plan provides for future annual employee compensation ranging between 3.5% and 5% of the outstanding equity over the next three years. We believe this overpays the employees at the expense of the shareholders. However, in light of Benioff's compensation structure, we believe the interests of shareholders, management, and the board of directors are appropriately aligned.

1 Market Street Suite 300
San Francisco, CA 94105
www.salesforce.com

Growth [A+]	2003	2004	2005	2006
Revenue %	127.5	88.3	83.7	75.7
Earnings/Share %	NMF	NMF	NMF	NMF
Book Value/Share %	—	—	—	NMF
Dividends/Share %	NMF	NMF	NMF	NMF

Profitability [D+]	2004	2005	2006	TTM
Return on Assets %	4.0	2.6	6.6	1.1
Oper Cash Flow $Mil	22	56	96	112
- Cap Spending $Mil	3	4	23	20
= Free Cash Flow $Mil	19	52	72	92

Financial Health [B]	2004	2005	2006	10-31-06
Long-term Debt $Mil	0	1	0	0
Total Equity $Mil	-46	145	196	256
Debt/Equity Ratio	0.0	0.0	0.0	0.0

Industry	Business Risk	Moat Size	Investment Style	Sector
Business Appl.	Average	Narrow	Mid Growth	Software

Competition

	Market Cap $Mil	12 Mo Trailing Sales $Mil	Price/Cash Flow	Return On Assets %	Debt/Equity	Total Return % 1 Yr	3 Yr
Salesforce.com	4,137	444	36.8	1.1	0.0	13.7	—
Microsoft	293,538	45,352	20.8	19.8	—	15.8	7.6
Oracle	89,050	15,203	18.9	12.2	0.4	40.4	9.3

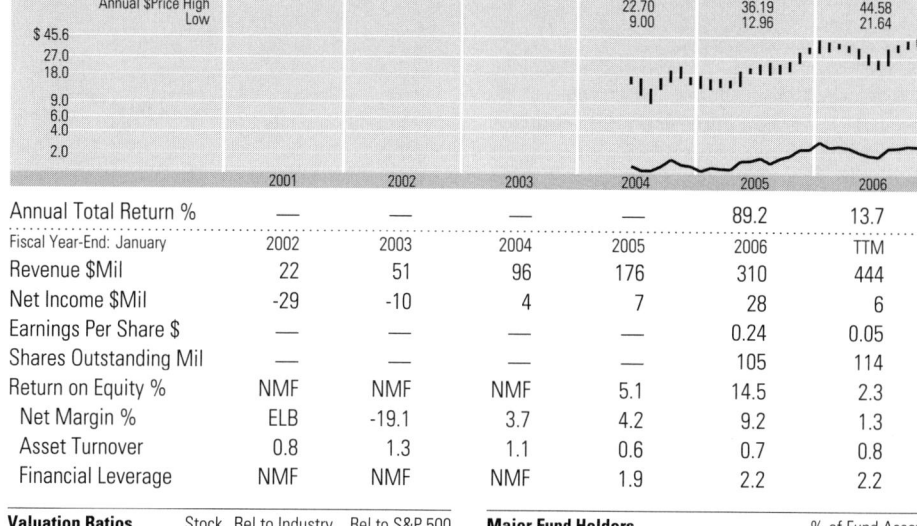

Price Volatility — Monthly Price High/Low — Relative Strength to S&P 500

	2001	2002	2003	2004	2005	2006
Annual Total Return %	—	—	—	—	89.2	13.7

Fiscal Year-End: January	2002	2003	2004	2005	2006	TTM
Revenue $Mil	22	51	96	176	310	444
Net Income $Mil	-29	-10	4	7	28	6
Earnings Per Share $	—	—	—	—	0.24	0.05
Shares Outstanding Mil	—	—	—	—	105	114
Return on Equity %	NMF	NMF	NMF	5.1	14.5	2.3
Net Margin %	ELB	-19.1	3.7	4.2	9.2	1.3
Asset Turnover	0.8	1.3	1.1	0.6	0.7	0.8
Financial Leverage	NMF	NMF	NMF	1.9	2.2	2.2

Valuation Ratios	Stock	Rel to Industry	Rel to S&P 500
Price/Earnings	EUB	—	—
Price/Book	16.1	1.9	3.9
Price/Sales	9.3	1.4	3.2
Price/Cash Flow	36.8	1.5	2.5

Major Fund Holders	% of Fund Assets
AXA Enterprise Equity A	5.28
Black Oak Emerging Technology	4.32
Turner Concentrated Growth Instl	4.08
Goldman Sachs Tollkeeper A	3.59

Thesis By Rick Summer, CFA, CPA, 12-14-06 Stock Price as of Analysis: $39.96

Salesforce.com is making bold moves to cement its leading share in software as a service, the fastest-growing segment in the software industry.

Salesforce.com manages proprietary software in its own data center, helping its customers avoid the cost of managing a complex hardware and software environment. Instead of large up-front license fees, customers pay annual subscriptions, realizing a predictable and stable return on investment while shortening deployment time from months to weeks. The company's highly successful customer relationship management product has helped Salesforce.com become a leading player in software as a service. We believe customers will continue adopting new on-demand applications, and Salesforce.com will benefit.

In our view, the company's most innovative strategy is driven by its AppExchange platform. Through AppExchange, third-party software developers can deliver (and sell) their own applications to customers. Salesforce.com offers an extremely innovative development platform that allows for complex transactions (such as writing to a database), which are critical requirements for large enterprise customers. We think solving this complexity will inject additional growth into the hosted software industry. Most important, Salesforce.com has the ability to own the standard in this new software world, much in the way Microsoft has standardized the software platform for desktop computers. If successful, this strategy will give Salesforce.com an overwhelming competitive advantage, in our opinion.

On-demand software has attracted the attention of numerous rivals. Large software companies like Oracle and SAP and smaller players like RightNow and NetSuite have competing offerings. Entrenched enterprise providers are conflicted about terminating existing maintenance and support agreements and replacing them with on-demand offerings. Revenue growth is likely to slow as SAP and Oracle respond, but we think Salesforce.com will continue to be in the pole position. If the company has any series of missteps, however, this advantage may disappear.

Salesforce.com's narrow economic moat is built on a product leadership position and a large customer base. By solving complex problems and moving toward a platform strategy, this firm is the most significant software company of the past decade, in our view. Salesforce.com is setting the standard in software as a service.

SanDisk SNDK

Data as of 12-29-06

	Rating	Fair Value	Last Close	Consider Buy	Consider Sell	Yield %
	★★★★	$57.00	$43.03	$36.30	$68.70	0.00

Company Profile
SanDisk is the leading maker of flash memory cards. The firm's products are used in a number of consumer electronic devices including digital cameras, multimedia cellular phones, and USB flash drives. SanDisk generates the bulk of its revenue through retail channels, which number greater than 100,000 storefronts worldwide. SanDisk also develops flash memory standards internally, earning royalty revenue on its patented technologies.

Management
Stewardship Grade [B]

SanDisk founder, chairman, and CEO Eli Harari has steered the firm since its inception in 1988. Harari has more than 30 years of experience in the electronics industry, having served in various operational and technological development roles. He has more than 100 U.S. and foreign patents in the field of flash memory technology. President Sanjay Mehrotra is a co-founder of SanDisk. His industry experience includes engineering and management positions at Intel and Integrated Device Technology. CFO Judy Bruner joined the company in 2004. She served as CFO of palmOne from 1999 through 2004. Prior to that, she held various financial positions at Hewlett-Packard, Ridge Computers, and 3Com. Insiders own about 5% of the firm.

140 Caspian Court
Sunnyvale, CA 94089
www.sandisk.com

Growth [A]	2002	2003	2004	2005	
Revenue %	47.8	99.5	64.6	29.8	
Earnings/Share %	NMF	308.0	41.2	38.9	
Book Value/Share %	-11.6	109.1	14.4	24.7	
Dividends/Share %	NMF	NMF	NMF	NMF	

Profitability [B]	2003	2004	2005	TTM
Return on Assets %	8.3	11.5	12.4	7.3
Oper Cash Flow $Mil	273	228	481	482
- Cap Spending $Mil	55	126	134	177
= Free Cash Flow $Mil	218	102	346	305

Financial Health [B+]	2003	2004	2005	09-30-06
Long-term Debt $Mil	150	—	—	1,150
Total Equity $Mil	1,516	1,940	2,524	3,313
Debt/Equity Ratio	0.1	—	—	0.3

Industry	Business Risk	Moat Size	Investment Style	Sector
Semiconductor	Above Avg	Narrow	Mid Growth	Hardware

Competition	Market Cap $Mil	12 Mo Trailing Sales $Mil	Price/Cash Flow	Return On Assets%	Debt/ Equity	Total Return% 1 Yr	3 Yr
SanDisk	8,464	2,844	17.6	7.3	0.3	-31.5	11.4
Sony ADR	42,870	66,335	12.1	1.2	0.2	5.5	7.6
Micron Technology	10,532	5,272	5.2	3.3	0.1	4.9	0.5

Price Volatility | Monthly Price High/Low — Relative Strength to S&P 500

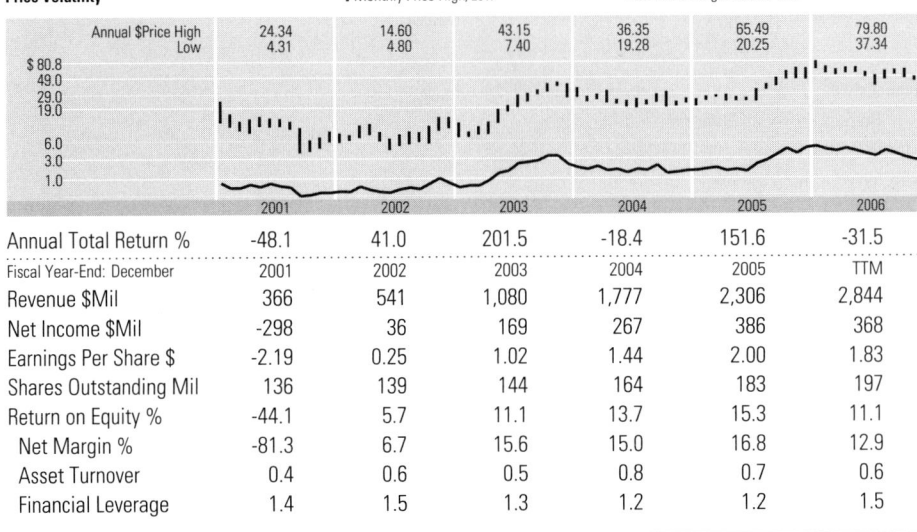

	2001	2002	2003	2004	2005	2006
Annual $Price High	24.34	14.60	43.15	36.35	65.49	79.80
Low	4.31	4.80	7.40	19.28	20.25	37.34
Annual Total Return %	-48.1	41.0	201.5	-18.4	151.6	-31.5

Fiscal Year-End: December	2001	2002	2003	2004	2005	TTM
Revenue $Mil	366	541	1,080	1,777	2,306	2,844
Net Income $Mil	-298	36	169	267	386	368
Earnings Per Share $	-2.19	0.25	1.02	1.44	2.00	1.83
Shares Outstanding Mil	136	139	144	164	183	197
Return on Equity %	-44.1	5.7	11.1	13.7	15.3	11.1
Net Margin %	-81.3	6.7	15.6	15.0	16.8	12.9
Asset Turnover	0.4	0.6	0.5	0.8	0.7	0.6
Financial Leverage	1.4	1.5	1.3	1.2	1.2	1.5

Valuation Ratios	Stock	Rel to Industry	Rel to S&P 500
Price/Earnings	23.5	0.8	1.1
Price/Book	2.6	0.7	0.6
Price/Sales	3.0	0.7	1.0
Price/Cash Flow	17.6	1.1	1.2

Major Fund Holders	% of Fund Assets
Transamerica Premier Focus Inv	6.05
Delaware Select Growth A	5.75
Delaware Pooled All-Cap Growth Equity	5.73
MFS Technology A	5.01

Thesis By Larry Cao, CFA, 11-30-06 Stock Price as of Analysis: $44.40

By pursuing cost leadership and a vertically integrated business model, SanDisk, the world's largest flash memory card maker, has built a narrow economic moat in a highly competitive industry.

Cost leadership is the basis for long-term success in any commodity business. SanDisk battled the price decline of flash memory, averaging 30% per year since the late 1990s, by staying ahead of the curve in developing and implementing new technology. At its joint venture with Toshiba, SanDisk makes memory chips using the most advanced manufacturing technologies. The firm makes smaller chips out of larger wafers, giving it a significant edge on the competition in terms of higher productivity and lower cost. With the largest share of flash memory card shipments, SanDisk is one of the very few companies in the world that can potentially realize the full benefit of owning and operating their own fabs. Smaller competitors have to buy all their memory chips from suppliers at a much higher price.

An integrated business model also differentiates the company because it helps the firm get a better gauge of end-market demand and plan capacity expansion accordingly. SanDisk makes memory chips, packages them, and sells them through electronics retailers or specialty retailers depending on the type of product. Sony is the second-largest flash memory card maker and Panasonic the third, which indicates how important the distribution channel and brand image are in this business. We believe the weaker position of chipmakers STMicro and Infineon in the flash business can largely be attributed to their lack of exposure to the retail sector.

Despite the dramatic growth of flash memory products and SanDisk's competitive positioning in the industry, investors should carefully consider the risk involved. The biggest risk is the many challenges investors face in valuing such a high-growth and intensely competitive business. For example, unit growth estimates for the industry range from 120% to over 200%; pricing has long followed a downward trend of negative 30% a year but is expected to decline 70% in 2006. Any valuation approach will be highly sensitive to such wild swings. The market has also attracted the attention of other chipmakers, including Intel, making competition potentially more intense down the road.

We believe SanDisk is the most competitive player in the flash memory market. Given its cost advantage, royalty stream, and aspiration, we think the firm will emerge as the eventual winner in this industry.

Data as of 12-29-06

Sanofi-Aventis ADR SNY

	Rating	Fair Value	Last Close	Consider Buy	Consider Sell	Yield %
	★★★	$48.00	$46.17	$37.00	$60.10	2.09

Company Profile

Sanofi-Aventis was formed by a merger of two France-based pharmaceutical companies, Sanofi-Synthelabo and Aventis, creating the world's third-largest pharmaceutical firm. The company concentrates its research in oncology, cardiovascular disease, and vaccines, as well as central nervous system disorders and diabetes. Of total revenue, 35% comes from the United States and 44% from Europe.

Management

Stewardship Grade [NA]

CEO Jean-Francois Dehecq came from Sanofi-Synthelabo and has been with Sanofi since its creation in 1973. Gerard Le Fur is senior vice president of scientific and medical affairs and came from Sanofi as well. Sanofi has decided to split the board management between these two men, with Dehecq remaining as president of the board and Le Fur holding the position of director general. Major shareholders of the new entity are French oil conglomerate Total and cosmetic company L'Oreal, which own 19% and 17% of the voting shares outstanding, respectively. The board comprises Dehecq plus 16 directors, 10 of whom are considered independent.

174, avenue de France www.sanofi-synthelabo.com
Paris, France 75013

Growth [NA]	2002	2003	2004	2005
Revenue %	14.8	8.1	95.5	81.2
Earnings/Share %	NMF	NMF	-26.4	-22.6
Book Value/Share %	—	NMF	405.0	-23.2
Dividends/Share %	—	NMF	17.6	26.7

Profitability [NA]	2003	2004	2005	TTM
Return on Assets %	19.1	2.1	2.7	2.7
Oper Cash Flow $Mil	2,537	5,030	8,012	8,012
- Cap Spending $Mil	416	937	1,431	1,431
= Free Cash Flow $Mil	2,121	4,093	6,581	6,581

Financial Health [NA]	2003	2004	2005	12-31-05
Long-term Debt $Mil	66	11,855	5,655	5,655
Total Equity $Mil	7,904	56,881	55,745	55,745
Debt/Equity Ratio	0.0	0.2	0.1	0.1

Industry	Business Risk	Moat Size	Investment Style	Sector
Drugs	Average	Wide	Large Core	Healthcare

Competition	Market Cap $Mil	12 Mo Trailing Sales $Mil	Price/Cash Flow	Return On Assets %	Debt/Equity	Total Return% 1 Yr	3 Yr
Sanofi-Aventis ADR	129,397	35,705	16.2	2.7	0.1	7.3	9.2
Pfizer	186,751	52,208	10.5	11.6	0.1	15.2	-7.4
Novartis AG ADR	134,175	32,526	16.6	10.6	0.0	11.3	9.6

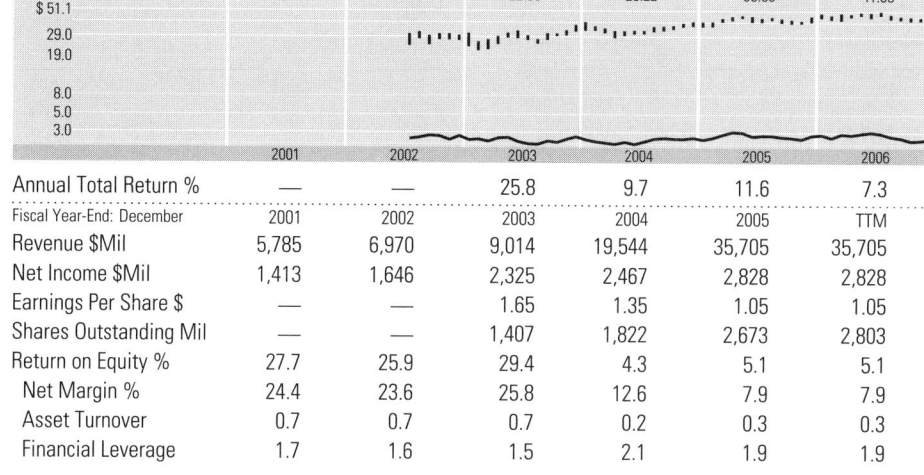

		2001	2002	2003	2004	2005	TTM
Annual Total Return %		—	—	25.8	9.7	11.6	7.3
Fiscal Year-End: December		2001	2002	2003	2004	2005	TTM
Revenue $Mil		5,785	6,970	9,014	19,544	35,705	35,705
Net Income $Mil		1,413	1,646	2,325	2,467	2,828	2,828
Earnings Per Share $		—	—	1.65	1.35	1.05	1.05
Shares Outstanding Mil		—	—	1,407	1,822	2,673	2,803
Return on Equity %		27.7	25.9	29.4	4.3	5.1	5.1
Net Margin %		24.4	23.6	25.8	12.6	7.9	7.9
Asset Turnover		0.7	0.7	0.7	0.2	0.3	0.3
Financial Leverage		1.7	1.6	1.5	2.1	1.9	1.9

Valuation Ratios	Stock	Rel to Industry	Rel to S&P 500	Major Fund Holders	% of Fund Assets
Price/Earnings	43.9	1.8	2.1	Oppenheimer Quest Balanced A	4.98
Price/Book	2.3	0.4	0.6	ProFunds Europe 30 Svc	4.72
Price/Sales	3.6	0.8	1.2	Quaker Capital Opportunities A	4.42
Price/Cash Flow	16.2	1.0	1.1	Constellation JSAM Large Cap Value	4.40

Thesis By Heather Brilliant, CFA, 12-14-06 Stock Price as of Analysis: $45.80

Sanofi-Aventis continues to solidify its wide moat with strong innovation and development of patent-protected products sold around the world. Despite generic competition issues surrounding some of its drugs, we're still big fans of this company's solid business model.

Sanofi is the product of many mergers, most recently that of French drug powerhouses Sanofi-Synthelabo and Aventis. The firm boasts an enviable product portfolio of drugs that are leaders in their respective markets, including Lovenox for preventing blood clots, sleep aid Ambien, and oncology drugs Eloxatin and Taxotere. Sanofi has also established itself as one of the largest providers of vaccines, a business that has experienced tremendous growth in recent years.

Innovation doesn't stop at vaccines; the firm has one of the strongest drug pipelines in the industry, with robust potential products in all phases of development. The firm has more than 10 products in Phase III clinical trials or pending regulatory review in various markets around the world. One such product, Acomplia, was recently approved in Europe and addresses obesity in patients at risk for diabetes or heart disease. The drug received an approvable letter in the United States and could receive Food and Drug Administration approval in mid-2007. Sanofi also has products in late-stage development that could each generate hundreds of millions of dollars in sales treating diseases like asthma, depression, and various cancers.

This strong portfolio of products in development will be crucial for Sanofi in the coming years, because it is facing generic competition with several of its largest products. Allergy medicine Allegra and diabetes treatment Amaryl are already facing generic rivals, and several more of the company's largest 15 drugs will lose patent protection in the next few years. Worse, generic manufacturer Apotex threatens to erode Plavix's market share in the United States. Plavix, a megablockbuster blood thinner that Sanofi markets with partner Bristol-Myers Squibb, brought in more than $6 billion in worldwide sales in 2005. While the loss of patent protection in the United States would hurt Bristol-Myers more, since Bristol markets the drug there, Sanofi stands to lose hundreds of millions of dollars in royalties and shared profits from the drug.

The near term may be challenging, but regardless of the outcome of the Plavix litigation, we think Sanofi's strong pipeline of new products can help the firm overcome the threat of generic competition.

Data as of 12-29-06

Sara Lee SLE

	Rating	Fair Value	Last Close	Consider Buy	Consider Sell	Yield %
	★★★	$15.00	$17.03	$11.60	$18.80	3.49

Company Profile
Sara Lee is a global seller of packaged foods and household and personal products. The company's branded food portfolio includes Sara Lee frozen and baked goods, Earth Grains breads, Hillshire Farm packaged meats, Jimmy Dean sausages, and Ball Park hot dogs. Sara Lee also produces specialty coffees and teas. The firm's household product line includes Ambi Pur air fresheners and Kiwi shoe-care products, with body care products sold overseas under the Sanex banner.

Management — Stewardship Grade [D]
Brenda Barnes has been chairman and CEO of Sara Lee since October 2005. She joined the company as president and COO in July 2004 and became CEO in February 2005. Prior to joining Sara Lee, Barnes worked for PepsiCola North America for over 20 years, serving as president and CEO of that company from 1996 until 1998. While we believe that Barnes was the change agent Sara Lee needed to transform itself from a struggling conglomeration of poor-performing businesses into a more focused operating entity, we feel that the firm's lack of exposure in categories that matter to consumers will limit her ability to turn the company around. Management has also lost a significant amount of credibility since announcing the firm's restructuring in early 2005, primarily by promising too much to equity and debt stakeholders--especially with regard to long-term growth and profitability targets--and then reducing those commitments as the transformation progressed. Given the performance of Sara Lee operations, the returns on invested capital, and the stock's price since Brenda Barnes took over as the CEO, we believe that there has been a large mismatch between the pay that she and other top executives have received and the value that they have created (or, in this case, failed to create).

Three First National Plaza Suite 4600 www.saralee.com
Chicago, IL 60602-4260

Growth [D+]	2003	2004	2005	2006
Revenue %	2.8	6.5	0.9	-0.5
Earnings/Share %	17.1	10.4	-43.4	-20.0
Book Value/Share %	NMF	NMF	NMF	-7.1
Dividends/Share %	3.4	22.0	4.0	1.3

Profitability [B]	2004	2005	2006	TTM
Return on Assets %	8.5	5.0	3.8	6.9
Oper Cash Flow $Mil	2,042	1,350	1,232	847
- Cap Spending $Mil	530	538	625	651
= Free Cash Flow $Mil	1,512	812	607	196

Financial Health [A-]	2004	2005	2006	09-30-06
Long-term Debt $Mil	—	4,112	3,807	3,005
Total Equity $Mil	—	2,732	2,449	2,720
Debt/Equity Ratio	—	1.5	1.6	1.1

Industry	Business Risk	Moat Size	Investment Style	Sector
Food Mfg.	Average	None	Large Value	Consumer Goods

Competition	Market Cap $Mil	12 Mo Trailing Sales $Mil	Price/Cash Flow	Return On Assets %	Debt/ Equity	Total Return % 1 Yr	3 Yr
Sara Lee	12,719	16,072	15.0	6.9	1.1	10.0	1.6
Kraft Foods	58,683	34,648	13.9	5.5	0.2	30.5	6.5
Unilever NV	46,726	49,679	8.6	10.6	0.8	25.0	12.4

Price Volatility — Monthly Price High/Low — Relative Strength to S&P 500

Annual $Price High	21.08	20.31	19.68	20.86	21.30	17.23
Low	15.55	13.76	13.84	17.18	14.74	13.54
	2001	2002	2003	2004	2005	2006

Annual Total Return %	-6.5	4.7	0.5	15.6	-18.0	10.0
Fiscal Year-End: June	2002	2003	2004	2005	2006	TTM
Revenue $Mil	14,519	14,919	15,892	16,029	15,944	16,072
Net Income $Mil	1,010	1,174	1,272	719	555	821
Earnings Per Share $	1.23	1.44	1.59	0.90	0.72	1.07
Shares Outstanding Mil	795	788	790	790	771	747
Return on Equity %	NMF	NMF	NMF	26.3	22.7	30.2
Net Margin %	7.0	7.9	8.0	4.5	3.5	5.1
Asset Turnover	1.1	1.0	1.1	1.1	1.1	1.3
Financial Leverage	—	—	—	5.2	5.9	4.4

Valuation Ratios	Stock	Rel to Industry	Rel to S&P 500
Price/Earnings	23.0	1.1	1.1
Price/Book	4.7	1.0	1.1
Price/Sales	0.8	0.5	0.3
Price/Cash Flow	15.0	1.0	1.0

Major Fund Holders	% of Fund Assets
Ameristock	4.09
Phoenix Mid-Cap Value A	3.67
ING Large Cap Value A	2.80
State Farm Equity A Legacy	2.45

Thesis By Greggory Warren, CFA, 11-27-06 Stock Price as of Analysis: $16.20

With a portfolio full of marginal products that are unlikely to benefit from any additional spending on innovation and brand building, and the firm still struggling to centralize many of its core operations, we believe that it will be extremely difficult for Sara Lee to reverse its fortunes longer term.

Despite having a portfolio of leading brands, Sara Lee has been unable to generate consistent sales and earnings growth for much of the past decade. While some of this can be attributed to increased competition in the packaged foods industry, the majority of the shortfall has been due to the commodified nature of many of the firm's product lines, as well as the decentralized nature of its operations.

Over the past couple of years, Sara Lee has divested several of its poorer-performing product lines and made efforts to centralize many of the functions involved with its disparate collection of businesses. The restructuring has narrowed the company's product portfolio down to just three key divisions--food and beverage, foodservice, and international--and freed up over $3.5 billion that the firm plans to use to pay down debt, repurchase shares, and improve its operations.

By focusing on a much smaller portfolio of products, Sara Lee believes that it will be able to generate more consistent sales and earnings growth over the longer term. The problem with this strategy, though, is that the company does not possess a portfolio of brands that are capable of generating significant improvements in sales and profitability.

While its Sara Lee, Earth Grains, Hillshire Farm, Jimmy Dean, and Kiwi brands might hold market-leading positions, most of these products exist in categories that have become commodified, with consumers no longer willing to pay up for the "benefit" that was once associated with the brands. This trend has been most pronounced in packaged meats and fresh-baked bread, where competition has been fierce and consumer sales are driven more by price than by brand loyalty.

Despite having some semblance of a narrow moat in its household and body-care businesses overseas, the heavy concentration of the remainder of the firm's brand portfolio in poor product categories leaves Sara Lee with no significant economic moat over the longer term. Even with the additional spending that the company has dedicated to product innovation and brand marketing, Sara Lee will struggle to generate consistent sales and earnings growth, let alone remain competitive with its peers.

Sasol ADR SSL

Data as of 12-29-06

	Rating	Fair Value	Last Close	Consider Buy	Consider Sell	Yield %
	★★★	$32.00	$36.90	$20.40	$38.60	2.74

Industry	Business Risk	Moat Size	Investment Style	Sector
Chemicals	Above Avg	Narrow	Large Core	Industrial Materials

Company Profile
Sasol is a vertically integrated oil and gas business with substantial chemical operations. Although it is based in South Africa, the firm has operations in Europe, Asia, and the Americas. On the oil and gas side, Sasol primarily converts coal to diesel and refines oil. The company's chemical operations use the synthetic-fuel process to convert the byproducts from its refining and synthetic-fuel operations into a variety of chemicals.

Management — Stewardship Grade [NA]
Pat Davies took over as CEO from nonexecutive chairman Pieter Cox in June 2005. Cox has been with firm since 1975, he was previously responsible for the globalization of the firm's GTL technology. Cox's 2005 total compensation was about 9 million rand, which, at an exchange rate of 6.5 South African rand per U.S. dollar, is about $1.4 million. Davies earned about 4.6 million rand, or about $708,000, in 2005. Directors and senior executives beneficially own less than 1% of outstanding shares. Sasol has excellent financial disclosure compared with others in the industry.

1 Sturdee Avenue
Rosebank, South Africa 2196
www.sasol.com

Competition

	Market Cap $Mil	12 Mo Trailing Sales $Mil	Price/Cash Flow	Return On Assets%	Debt/Equity	Total Return% 1 Yr	3 Yr
Sasol ADR	22,984	9,525	7.9	13.5	0.3	6.6	40.6
Royal Dutch Shell PLC ADR	230,956	306,731	7.7	11.5	0.1	19.3	15.1
Chevron	160,294	216,166	6.5	13.1	0.1	33.8	23.5

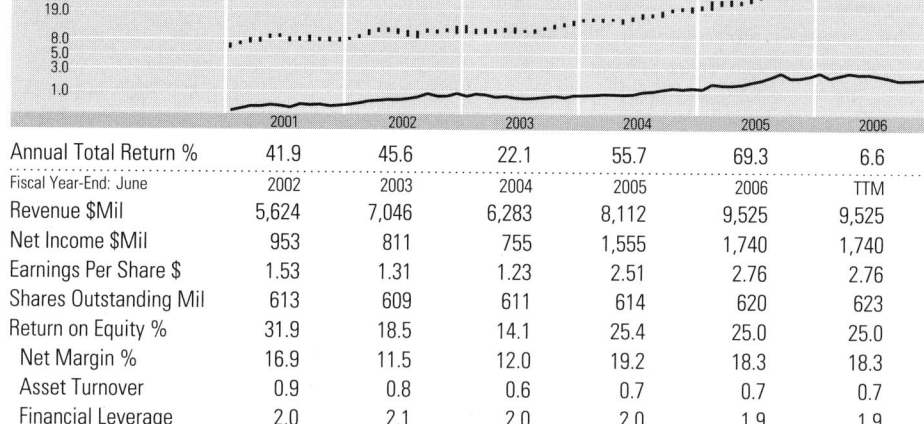

Price Volatility — Monthly Price High/Low — Relative Strength to S&P 500

Annual $Price High/Low	10.01 / 6.50	12.75 / 8.36	14.96 / 10.20	22.00 / 13.64	39.37 / 19.95	46.31 / 29.54
	2001	2002	2003	2004	2005	2006
Annual Total Return %	41.9	45.6	22.1	55.7	69.3	6.6

Fiscal Year-End: June	2002	2003	2004	2005	2006	TTM
Revenue $Mil	5,624	7,046	6,283	8,112	9,525	9,525
Net Income $Mil	953	811	755	1,555	1,740	1,740
Earnings Per Share $	1.53	1.31	1.23	2.51	2.76	2.76
Shares Outstanding Mil	613	609	611	614	620	623
Return on Equity %	31.9	18.5	14.1	25.4	25.0	25.0
Net Margin %	16.9	11.5	12.0	19.2	18.3	18.3
Asset Turnover	0.9	0.8	0.6	0.7	0.7	0.7
Financial Leverage	2.0	2.1	2.0	2.0	1.9	1.9

Valuation Ratios	Stock	Rel to Industry	Rel to S&P 500
Price/Earnings	10.7	0.6	0.5
Price/Book	3.3	1.0	0.8
Price/Sales	2.4	1.4	0.8
Price/Cash Flow	7.9	0.5	0.5

Major Fund Holders	% of Fund Assets
JHancock Large Cap Intrinsic Value A	4.91
Security Large Cap Value A	2.45
JHancock Technology A	2.09
TCW Emerging Markets Eq I	1.92

Growth [NA]	2003	2004	2005	2006
Revenue %	14.6	-31.6	16.2	22.0
Earnings/Share %	-21.5	-27.9	83.3	14.6
Book Value/Share %	6.9	3.8	20.1	22.0
Dividends/Share %	0.0	0.0	20.0	31.5

Profitability [NA]	2004	2005	2006	TTM
Return on Assets %	6.9	12.9	13.5	13.5
Oper Cash Flow $Mil	1,396	2,256	2,906	2,906
- Cap Spending $Mil	1,211	1,625	1,494	1,494
= Free Cash Flow $Mil	185	631	1,412	1,412

Financial Health [NA]	2004	2005	2006	06-30-06
Long-term Debt $Mil	—	1,855	1,815	1,815
Total Equity $Mil	5,361	6,129	6,969	6,969
Debt/Equity Ratio	—	0.3	0.3	0.3

Thesis By Justin Perucki, CFA, 12-11-06 Stock Price as of Analysis: $36.27

With minuscule margins and intense cyclicality, manufacturing chemicals is generally unattractive. However, for Sasol, chemical manufacturing mitigates the impact of oil and gas cycles and provides an end market for most of the byproducts from its synthetic-gas production and oil refining. The firm also leverages its synthetic-gas technology to create the various chemicals, minimizing costs and enabling the firm to earn small but adequate returns on this business.

Sasol recently expanded its technology for converting natural gas to diesel fuel (GTL). In its gaseous state, natural gas can only be transported via pipeline. However, most of the world's gas reserves are in the Middle East, far from the big energy users. By converting natural gas to diesel fuel, producers can ship the fuel to energy consumers like China and the United States. Sasol has had success in South Africa with this process and is partnering with Chevron to build GTL facilities in Qatar and Nigeria. In June, the partnership's first facility in Qatar commenced operations.

Assuming that natural-gas feedstock can be acquired for less than $1 per thousand cubic feet (mcf), GTL is currently economical at oil prices around $15-$20 per barrel. We think that GTL provides a significant growth opportunity, as an estimated 2,500 trillion cubic feet of stranded natural gas is waiting to be recovered. But GTL projects will have to compete for natural gas with LNG liquefaction terminals and chemical plants that are also being built in the Middle East, which could cause prices to increase, raising the break-even price point for GTL. Our oil price forecast is well above the $20 benchmark, so even if natural-gas prices were to rise substantially, Sasol can still generate an attractive rate of return on these projects, in our opinion.

Sasol is currently involved in a slew of coal to liquid (CTL) feasibility studies across the globe, but we are several years away from seeing a large-scale CTL project for several reasons. First, coal still carries a stigma due to the less-than-ideal environmental effects of burning it. Second, the infrastructure necessary to convert coal to diesel and then transport it must still be built. Third, at $30-$40 per barrel of oil, the break-even price point for CTL is higher than traditionally produced oil, GTL, and the Canadian oil sands. With an estimated 1 trillion tons in coal reserves or 164 years worth of supply based on current consumption, CTL should be an important alternative fuel source in the future, however.

Data as of 12-29-06

Schering-Plough SGP

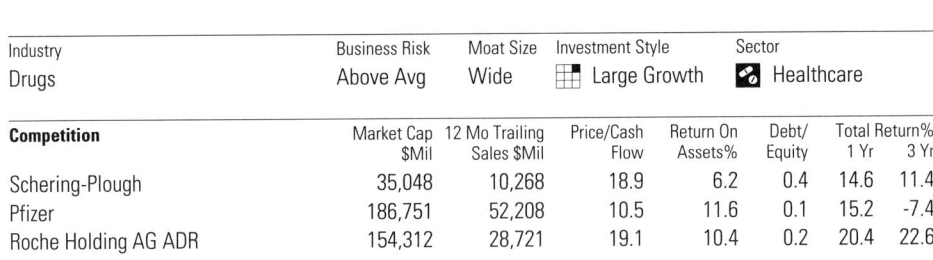

	Rating	Fair Value	Last Close	Consider Buy	Consider Sell	Yield %
	★★★	$27.00	$23.64	$17.20	$32.60	0.93

Company Profile

Schering-Plough manufactures and markets a variety of health-care products, including prescription and over-the-counter drugs, animal-health and foot-care products. Its largest internal product is Remicade for autoimmune diseases, which it markets outside the United States. It sells blockbuster cholesterol drugs Zetia and Vytorin through a joint venture with Merck. Pharmaceuticals account for 80% of total sales; 60% of revenue comes from overseas.

Management

Stewardship Grade [C]

Fred Hassan was named chairman and CEO in April 2003 after running Pharmacia for six years. He's credited with turning Pharmacia around by installing new executives and reining in costs. Hassan has done the same at Schering-Plough, having brought in several senior managers over the past few years--some from Pharmacia. Hassan has served on the boards of several companies and also ran the pharma department at Wyeth and Sandoz (now part of Novartis). He has a science education and a Harvard MBA. His cash compensation of $5.8 million in 2005, excluding sizable restricted stock and option grants, seems particularly rich since the firm hasn't earned its cost of capital since Hassan became CEO. We think annual option grants of more than 1 million shares for the past two years are egregious as well. While we're pleased to see the board uses various measures of performance in determining incentive compensation, stock, and options, we'd prefer if return-oriented measures such as return on capital were used in place of EPS growth. Schering-Plough's board is light on medical research-related members, with just Hassan and one other board member having any experience in this industry. On a positive note, the firm recently moved to elect directors annually instead of every three years.

2000 Galloping Hill Road www.schering-plough.com
Kenilworth, NJ 07033

Growth [D+]	2002	2003	2004	2005
Revenue %	4.3	-18.1	-0.7	14.9
Earnings/Share %	1.5	NMF	NMF	NMF
Book Value/Share %	14.2	-13.4	-12.7	-6.6
Dividends/Share %	8.1	-15.7	-61.1	0.0

Profitability [B]	2003	2004	2005	TTM
Return on Assets %	-0.6	-6.2	1.2	6.2
Oper Cash Flow $Mil	601	-154	882	1,851
- Cap Spending $Mil	711	489	478	450
= Free Cash Flow $Mil	-110	-643	404	1,401

Financial Health [B]	2003	2004	2005	09-30-06
Long-term Debt $Mil	2,410	2,392	2,399	2,413
Total Equity $Mil	7,337	6,118	5,949	6,814
Debt/Equity Ratio	0.3	0.4	0.4	0.4

Industry	Business Risk	Moat Size	Investment Style	Sector
Drugs	Above Avg	Wide	Large Growth	Healthcare

Competition	Market Cap $Mil	12 Mo Trailing Sales $Mil	Price/Cash Flow	Return On Assets%	Debt/Equity	Total Return% 1 Yr	3 Yr
Schering-Plough	35,048	10,268	18.9	6.2	0.4	14.6	11.4
Pfizer	186,751	52,208	10.5	11.6	0.1	15.2	-7.4
Roche Holding AG ADR	154,312	28,721	19.1	10.4	0.2	20.4	22.6

Price Volatility

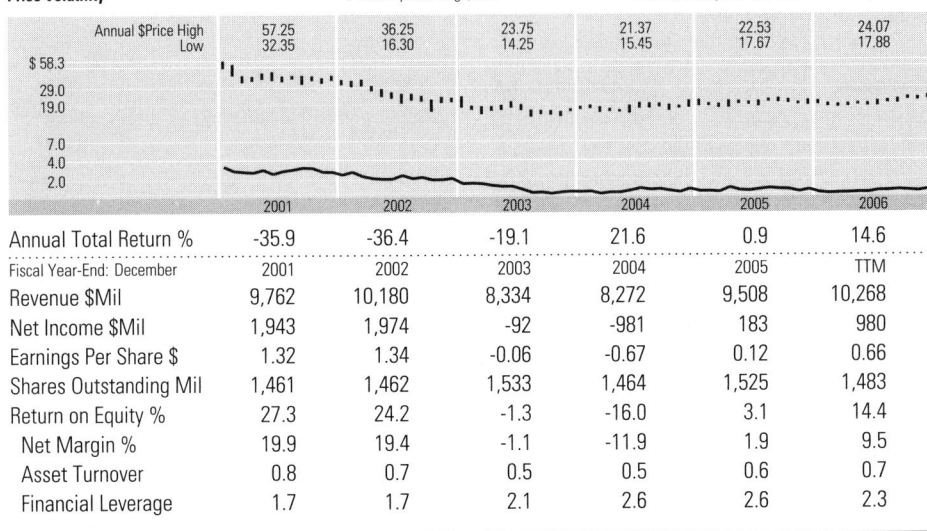

	2001	2002	2003	2004	2005	2006
Annual $Price High	57.25	36.25	23.75	21.37	22.53	24.07
Low	32.35	16.30	14.25	15.45	17.67	17.88
Annual Total Return %	-35.9	-36.4	-19.1	21.6	0.9	14.6

Fiscal Year-End: December	2001	2002	2003	2004	2005	TTM
Revenue $Mil	9,762	10,180	8,334	8,272	9,508	10,268
Net Income $Mil	1,943	1,974	-92	-981	183	980
Earnings Per Share $	1.32	1.34	-0.06	-0.67	0.12	0.66
Shares Outstanding Mil	1,461	1,462	1,533	1,464	1,525	1,483
Return on Equity %	27.3	24.2	-1.3	-16.0	3.1	14.4
Net Margin %	19.9	19.4	-1.1	-11.9	1.9	9.5
Asset Turnover	0.8	0.7	0.5	0.5	0.6	0.7
Financial Leverage	1.7	1.7	2.1	2.6	2.6	2.3

Valuation Ratios	Stock	Rel to Industry	Rel to S&P 500
Price/Earnings	36.9	1.5	1.8
Price/Book	5.1	0.9	1.2
Price/Sales	3.4	0.8	1.2
Price/Cash Flow	18.9	1.2	1.3

Major Fund Holders	% of Fund Assets
Hartford Global Health A	5.24
SunAmerica Biotech/Health A	5.13
Van Kampen Exchange	4.97
Vanguard Health Care	4.65

Thesis By Heather Brilliant, CFA, 12-13-06 Stock Price as of Analysis: $23.30

While Schering-Plough's late-stage product pipeline is not very robust at this point, we think income from its cholesterol joint venture with Merck should provide plenty of cash flow to fund upcoming investment opportunities.

Without any groundbreaking new drugs in late-stage development, Schering-Plough's revenue will continue to rely on existing drugs for the next few years. That puts it in a better position than some of its competitors, though, because the firm is not overly reliant on a few drugs for revenue and faces fewer patent expirations. A growing income stream from its joint venture with Merck should continue to add to Schering-Plough's resources. Zetia and Vytorin are already highly successful cholesterol drugs, and we expect continued growth from these products to boost Schering-Plough's bottom line.

The company has been working on reducing its cost structure and improving efficiency for the past several years. Although it has struggled just to cover its expenses in recent years, we think the firm will benefit handsomely from any increase in revenues, because a greater percentage of each additional dollar it generates should fall to the bottom line. Some of the drugs in its portfolio are growing strongly and should help Schering-Plough improve its operating margins in the coming years. For example, we expect it will generate more than $1 billion in 2006 sales from the international rights to Johnson & Johnson's Remicade for autoimmune diseases.

Its portfolio of currently marketed drugs should give Schering-Plough some time to bolster its pipeline, and we think it will need to work on doing so expeditiously. Its late-stage pipeline is extremely thin, and we don't see much coming down the pipe from earlier research efforts, either. Schering-Plough has just 20 drugs in early-stage development, and we think potential products in Phase I have smaller than a 20% chance of reaching the market (due to historical drug development failure rates), so we expect only four of those drugs will be approved in the future. Schering-Plough does have a handful of potential new products in Phase II that could help bolster sales in 2010 and beyond, but we think only one has blockbuster potential.

The firm's weak internal pipeline is exacerbated by its relative lack of cash to spend on acquisitions. Schering-Plough does not have the large cash war chest many of its competitors benefit from. However, we expect the firm to generate more cash in the coming years, which should bolster its ability to invest in research and acquisitions.

Data as of 12-29-06

Schlumberger SLB

Rating	Fair Value	Last Close	Consider Buy	Consider Sell	Yield %
★	$30.00	$63.16	$23.10	$37.60	0.79

Industry	Business Risk	Moat Size	Investment Style	Sector
Oil/Gas Svcs.	Average	Narrow	Large Growth	Energy

Company Profile

New York City-based Schlumberger is one of the world's largest oil field services firms. It provides services related to seismic surveys, drilling, well completion, and oil production optimization, and operates in more than 100 countries. The firm acquired a host of non-oil-field segments in recent years, but it has systematically sold these segments since 2002, refocusing on its core oil services businesses.

Management   Stewardship Grade [C]

Andrew Gould became chairman and CEO in February 2003 after almost 30 years with Schlumberger. He replaced Eaun Baird, who had been at the helm since 1986. Toward the end of his tenure, Baird led the firm into a variety of non-oil-field-services businesses. Gould spent his first year as CEO refocusing Schlumberger on its core operations and selling many of the non-oilfield segments. Gould's cash compensation in 2005 was $3.7 million, and he received options on 400,000 shares, which is in line with compensation levels at peer firms. Schlumberger's executives and board members as a group beneficially own more than 3% of the outstanding shares, which is more than most of the oil services firms we follow. Gould has done a noteworthy job driving technological innovation at Schlumberger and reinvigorating the company. The company also keeps overall option grants well below 1% of shares outstanding. Schlumberger's Stewardship Grade would be improved if the company split the CEO and chairman role and laid out clearer goals for executive compensation.

153 East 53 Street 57th Floor   www.slb.com
New York, NY 10172

Growth [C]	2002	2003	2004	2005
Revenue %	-11.0	3.7	14.6	24.6
Earnings/Share %	NMF	NMF	213.8	78.4
Book Value/Share %	32.0	-48.2	2.1	22.8
Dividends/Share %	0.0	0.0	0.0	11.9

Profitability [C]	2003	2004	2005	TTM
Return on Assets %	1.9	7.6	12.2	15.6
Oper Cash Flow $Mil	2,015	1,846	3,004	4,226
- Cap Spending $Mil	872	1,216	1,593	2,113
= Free Cash Flow $Mil	1,144	630	1,411	2,113

Financial Health [A]	2003	2004	2005	09-30-06
Long-term Debt $Mil	6,097	3,944	3,591	3,931
Total Equity $Mil	5,881	6,117	7,592	9,599
Debt/Equity Ratio	1.0	0.6	0.5	0.4

Competition

	Market Cap $Mil	12 Mo Trailing Sales $Mil	Price/Cash Flow	Return On Assets %	Debt/ Equity	Total Return % 1 Yr	3 Yr
Schlumberger	74,416	17,904	17.6	15.6	0.4	31.1	33.6
Halliburton	31,221	22,886	8.5	17.5	0.4	1.1	35.2
Baker Hughes	23,946	8,564	39.8	26.8	0.2	23.7	34.2

Price Volatility | Monthly Price High/Low   — Relative Strength to S&P 500

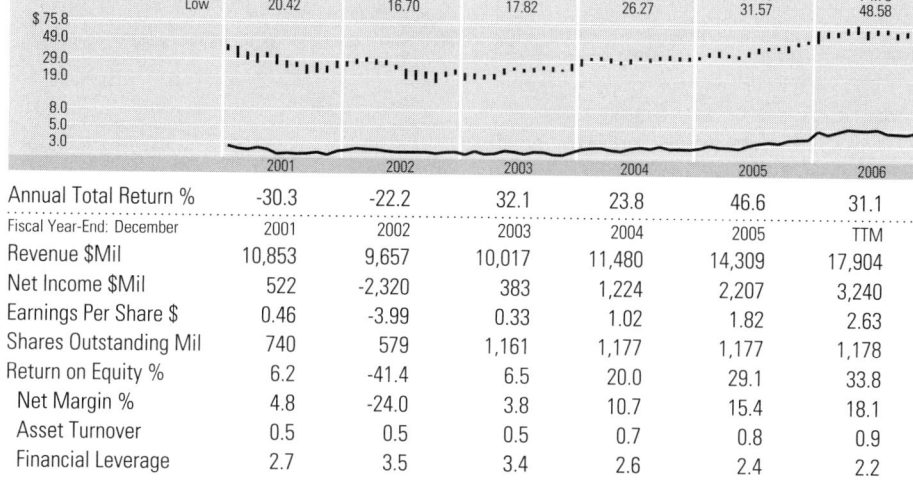

	2001	2002	2003	2004	2005	2006
Annual $Price High	41.41	31.22	28.12	34.95	51.49	74.75
Low	20.42	16.70	17.82	26.27	31.57	48.58
Annual Total Return %	-30.3	-22.2	32.1	23.8	46.6	31.1

Fiscal Year-End: December	2001	2002	2003	2004	2005	TTM
Revenue $Mil	10,853	9,657	10,017	11,480	14,309	17,904
Net Income $Mil	522	-2,320	383	1,224	2,207	3,240
Earnings Per Share $	0.46	-3.99	0.33	1.02	1.82	2.63
Shares Outstanding Mil	740	579	1,161	1,177	1,177	1,178
Return on Equity %	6.2	-41.4	6.5	20.0	29.1	33.8
Net Margin %	4.8	-24.0	3.8	10.7	15.4	18.1
Asset Turnover	0.5	0.5	0.5	0.7	0.8	0.9
Financial Leverage	2.7	3.5	3.4	2.6	2.4	2.2

Valuation Ratios	Stock	Rel to Industry	Rel to S&P 500
Price/Earnings	24.0	1.3	1.2
Price/Book	7.8	1.1	1.9
Price/Sales	4.2	1.4	1.4
Price/Cash Flow	17.6	1.1	1.2

Major Fund Holders	% of Fund Assets
Rydex Energy Services Inv	9.68
TCW Select Equities I	6.65
Fidelity Select Energy Service	5.78
CGM Focus	5.76

Thesis   By Matt Moran, CFA, 10-20-06   Stock Price as of Analysis: $60.10

Schlumberger combines unmatched technological expertise with vast geographical diversity to dominate the oil service industry. Schlumberger's world-class portfolio of services will benefit from heightened demand throughout the remainder of the decade as the energy industry desperately tries to quench the world's growing thirst for hydrocarbons.

Schlumberger provides products and services to oil and gas exploration and production firms. Its offerings run the gamut from capital-intensive well-completion services to consulting and project management. Surging oil and gas consumption, led by Chinese and Indian demand, has caught the industry off-guard. Decades of underinvestment in production has led to dwindling reserves and antiquated service equipment. Spending more on R&D than its three closest competitors combined, Schlumberger will benefit as the world looks for oil and gas in obscure and unusual places.

Schlumberger is uniquely positioned as an oil service provider. The company made the decision 30 years ago to globalize its workforce, placing research centers and technology hubs in strategically important locations. Possessing local technical talent not only accelerates the introduction of new technologies, but it also creates a sense of goodwill between the firm and potentially unfriendly governments (think Yukos). With the majority of the world's oil and gas reserves controlled by eastern-hemisphere national oil companies, demand for Schlumberger's exceptional technology will continue to grow.

Schlumberger's decision in early 2006 to acquire the 30% of WesternGeco owned by Baker Hughes (Schlumberger owned the other 70%) for $2.4 billion in cash positions the firm as the undisputed leader in seismic technology. Although Schlumberger might have paid a tad too much, we like Schlumberger's confidence in WesternGeco's potential. We are inclined to agree with Schlumberger that operators must find new sources of oil and gas to replace their rapidly dwindling reserves.

With 70% of today's oil production coming from fields more than 30 years old, the world will increasingly depend on technology to maximize unconventional reserves. Schlumberger has paved the way in this regard--advancing techniques in many disciplines including directional drilling, advanced fracturing, and seismology. Schlumberger's commitment to technological innovation in the oil patch leads us to believe that the firm has a narrow economic moat.

© 2007 Morningstar, Inc. All rights reserved. Intended for United States residents only, this report is for information purposes and should not be considered a solicitation to buy or sell any security. Download your free reports at http://www.morningstar.com/goto/2007Stocks500

Data as of 12-29-06

Sealed Air SEE

	Rating	Fair Value	Last Close	Consider Buy	Consider Sell	Yield %
	★★★	$68.00	$64.92	$52.40	$85.20	0.92

Company Profile
Sealed Air is divided into two segments: food packaging and protective and specialty packaging. In food packaging, its Cryovac line protects various meat and vegetable products as they pass through the supply chain. In protective packaging, its Bubble Wrap, Jiffy packaging, and Instapak products (among others) are used to secure industrial and retail goods as they travel to the end user. Related equipment revenue makes up 10% of sales.

Management — Stewardship Grade [A]
We're big fans of Sealed Air's management, whose stewardship of capital has been quite impressive. CEO William Hickey, who took the reins in March 2000, has shown a commitment to generating free cash flow and building shareholder value. Faced with rising plastic resin costs, management has steadily increased prices (and reduced other costs) without major volume pressures, which should pay off handsomely as cost pressures subside. Management pay is in line with industry practices, and directors and executive officers together own roughly 2% of outstanding shares, helping align their interests with those of shareholders. There is no question that Sealed Air has recently faced numerous obstacles. While the short-term effects from these efforts only serve to offset some of the raw-material cost pressures, we have little doubt that shareholders will be rewarded with solid earnings and cash flow growth once resin prices stabilize or decline.

Park 80 East www.sealedair.com
Saddle Brook, NJ 07663-5291

Growth [B-]	2002	2003	2004	2005
Revenue %	4.5	10.2	7.5	7.6
Earnings/Share %	NMF	NMF	14.2	19.6
Book Value/Share %	4.3	19.3	17.6	5.2
Dividends/Share %	NMF	NMF	NMF	NMF

Profitability [C]	2003	2004	2005	TTM
Return on Assets %	4.0	4.4	5.3	5.4
Oper Cash Flow $Mil	470	436	358	410
- Cap Spending $Mil	124	103	97	141
= Free Cash Flow $Mil	345	334	261	269

Financial Health [B]	2003	2004	2005	09-30-06
Long-term Debt $Mil	2,260	2,088	1,813	1,825
Total Equity $Mil	1,124	1,334	1,392	1,551
Debt/Equity Ratio	2.0	1.6	1.3	1.2

Industry	Business Risk	Moat Size	Investment Style	Sector
Packaging	Average	Narrow	Mid Core	Consumer Goods

Competition	Market Cap $Mil	12 Mo Trailing Sales $Mil	Price/Cash Flow	Return On Assets%	Debt/Equity	Total Return% 1 Yr	3 Yr
Sealed Air	5,234	4,258	12.8	5.4	1.2	16.9	7.4
Alcoa	26,022	29,666	11.4	5.8	0.3	3.5	-5.3
Alcan	18,330	21,589	6.9	2.2	0.5	20.8	6.2

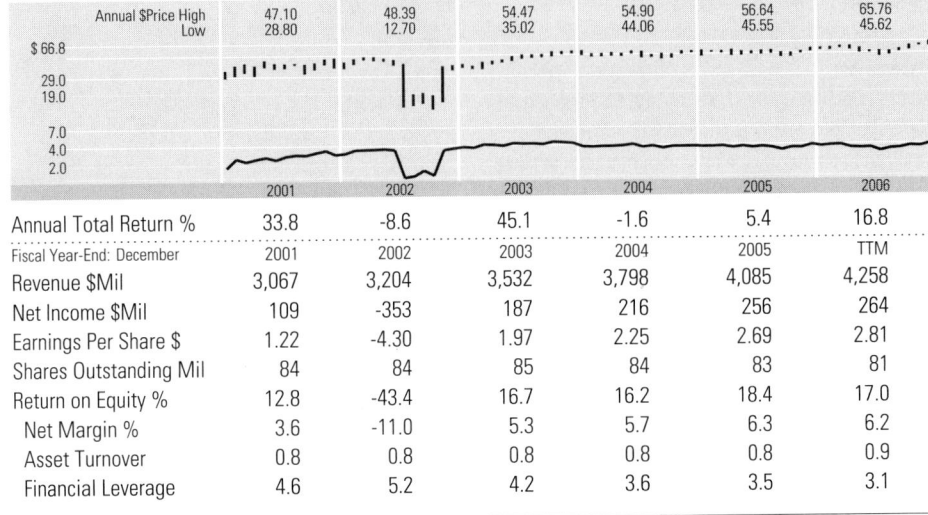

Price Volatility — Monthly Price High/Low — Relative Strength to S&P 500

	2001	2002	2003	2004	2005	2006
Annual $Price High	47.10	48.39	54.47	54.90	56.64	65.76
Low	28.80	12.70	35.02	44.06	45.55	45.62
Annual Total Return %	33.8	-8.6	45.1	-1.6	5.4	16.8

Fiscal Year-End: December	2001	2002	2003	2004	2005	TTM
Revenue $Mil	3,067	3,204	3,532	3,798	4,085	4,258
Net Income $Mil	109	-353	187	216	256	264
Earnings Per Share $	1.22	-4.30	1.97	2.25	2.69	2.81
Shares Outstanding Mil	84	84	85	84	83	81
Return on Equity %	12.8	-43.4	16.7	16.2	18.4	17.0
Net Margin %	3.6	-11.0	5.3	5.7	6.3	6.2
Asset Turnover	0.8	0.8	0.8	0.8	0.8	0.9
Financial Leverage	4.6	5.2	4.2	3.6	3.5	3.1

Valuation Ratios	Stock	Rel to Industry	Rel to S&P 500
Price/Earnings	23.1	0.9	1.1
Price/Book	3.4	1.0	0.8
Price/Sales	1.2	1.2	0.4
Price/Cash Flow	12.8	1.2	0.9

Major Fund Holders	% of Fund Assets
Fidelity Select Paper & Forest Prod	5.35
Concorde Value	3.23
Davis Financial A	2.70
Morgan Stanley Mid Cap Value D	2.64

Thesis By Matthew Warren, 12-15-06 Stock Price as of Analysis: $63.11

Sealed Air's plastic packaging protects delicate or perishable items as they pass through the supply chain. By shielding its customers from losses, this narrow-moat firm enjoys pricing power as a result.

To capture the reward of high-margin consumable sales (resulting from daily use), Sealed Air leverages its industry-leading research and development team to solve its customers' problems. On the protective packaging side of the business, this involves developing customized equipment, if necessary, that can be integrated into the customer's production line to ensure products are adequately protected against breakage. Not only does the firm act as packaging consultant, but its maintenance technicians are on call to ensure limited loss of production time. Although equipment sales represent only 10% of sales, this up-front investment fosters goodwill and sets up a profitable annuity stream.

In Sealed Air's food packaging business, the industry's largest team of food scientists works to introduce innovative products, such as case-ready beef packaging, which allowed Wal-Mart to circumvent the cost of in-house (and traditionally unionized) butchers commonly used by grocers. Once Sealed Air equipment is adopted, consumable sales correlate directly with volume at its food-processing customers. When prices of a given protein rise, sales tend to trail off, but they are generally replaced by consumption of alternate proteins.

Sealed Air generates much better returns than companies providing alternative packaging products, especially paper-based solutions. Sealed Air's plastic packaging materials offer vital protection but cost far less than the product itself. For high-end goods such as stereo speakers, the firm's breakthrough Instapak line employs foam that molds precisely to the contours of the product. Further, by reducing box sizes, Sealed Air products cut indirect costs, including shipping, handling, and storage. By delivering quantifiable value to customers, Sealed Air benefits from premium pricing. Combined with the firm's cost advantages arising from economies of scale, this generates substantial returns, after setting aside funds for reinvestment.

It is also difficult for a competitor to match Sealed Air's global reach. The company's 121 manufacturing sites in 51 countries--located near end-market demand--allow the firm to overcome the cost-prohibitive nature of shipping bulky, lightweight materials. This barrier to entry becomes increasingly difficult to penetrate in a niche market.

SEI Investments SEIC

Data as of 12-29-06

Rating	Fair Value	Last Close	Consider Buy	Consider Sell	Yield %
★	$44.00	$59.56	$37.50	$57.80	0.40

Company Profile

SEI Investments sells software and outsourcing services for back-office operations at financial companies. Almost half of its business comes from banks and trusts that purchase these services. The other half comes from being a "manager of managers," packaging diversified suites of asset-management products for financial advisors, and providing investment-processing services to institutions and money managers. SEI also owns 43% of hedge fund LSV Asset Management.

Management   Stewardship Grade [B]

Chairman and CEO Alfred West founded SEI when he was still a business student at Wharton in 1968. Since then, the business has changed dramatically but kept its focus on technology for banks. West's vision has shaped SEI into the firm it is today, and he deserves much of the credit for positioning SEI to take advantage of market trends. West owns 20% of the company, giving him a huge incentive to make prudent decisions. In 2004, West stepped down from the compensation committee, which is now populated by independent directors. Executives at SEI are fairly modestly paid, particularly in comparison with others in asset management. Directors and officers own about 37% of the company's shares, some of these resulting from a generous stock-compensation policy. In general, corporate governance is shareholder-friendly. Our only objections are to West having both the chairman and CEO roles, and to several takeover defenses that the company has in place, including a staggered board and a poison pill.

1 Freedom Valley Drive www.seic.com
Oaks, PA 19456-1100

Growth [B+]	2002	2003	2004	2005
Revenue %	-4.3	1.1	8.8	11.7
Earnings/Share %	14.7	5.6	21.2	14.4
Book Value/Share %	9.3	30.2	13.9	7.2
Dividends/Share %	88.9	-58.8	314.3	-24.1

Profitability [A+]	2003	2004	2005	TTM
Return on Assets %	24.1	27.5	28.7	23.0
Oper Cash Flow $Mil	178	187	214	323
- Cap Spending $Mil	24	14	16	26
= Free Cash Flow $Mil	154	172	199	298

Financial Health [A+]	2003	2004	2005	09-30-06
Long-term Debt $Mil	24	14	9	70
Total Equity $Mil	364	404	422	575
Debt/Equity Ratio	0.1	0.0	0.0	0.1

Industry	Business Risk	Moat Size	Investment Style	Sector
Business Support	Below Avg	Wide	Mid Growth	Business Services

Competition

	Market Cap $Mil	12 Mo Trailing Sales $Mil	Price/Cash Flow	Return On Assets%	Debt/Equity	Total Return% 1 Yr	3 Yr
SEI Investments	5,891	1,064	18.2	23.0	0.1	61.7	26.0
Bank of New York Company	41,334	7,308	—	1.5	—	26.9	9.2
First Data	19,543	10,806	8.4	4.4	0.4	9.9	5.6

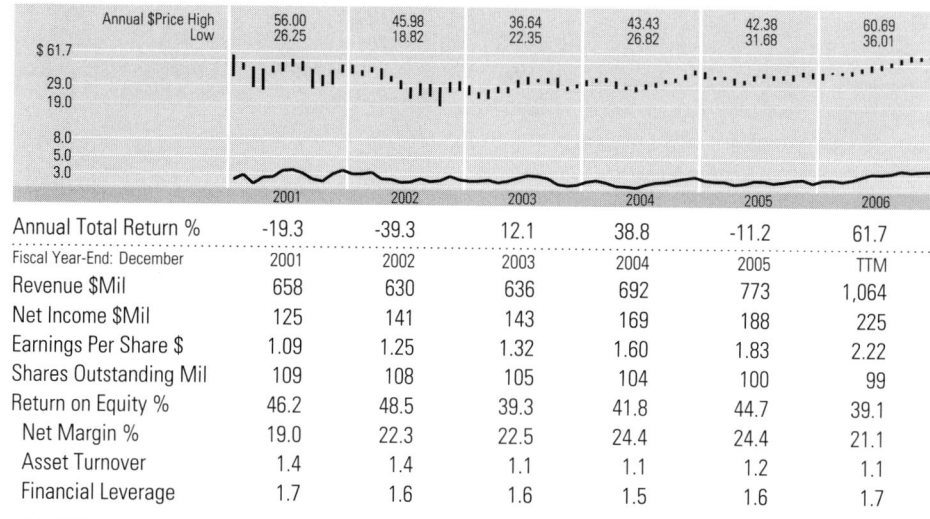

	2001	2002	2003	2004	2005	TTM
Annual Total Return %	-19.3	-39.3	12.1	38.8	-11.2	61.7
Revenue $Mil	658	630	636	692	773	1,064
Net Income $Mil	125	141	143	169	188	225
Earnings Per Share $	1.09	1.25	1.32	1.60	1.83	2.22
Shares Outstanding Mil	109	108	105	104	100	99
Return on Equity %	46.2	48.5	39.3	41.8	44.7	39.1
Net Margin %	19.0	22.3	22.5	24.4	24.4	21.1
Asset Turnover	1.4	1.4	1.1	1.1	1.2	1.1
Financial Leverage	1.7	1.6	1.6	1.5	1.6	1.7

Valuation Ratios	Stock	Rel to Industry	Rel to S&P 500
Price/Earnings	26.8	1.0	1.3
Price/Book	10.2	2.3	2.5
Price/Sales	5.5	1.1	1.9
Price/Cash Flow	18.2	1.0	1.2

Major Fund Holders	% of Fund Assets
Royce Dividend Value Service	4.70
Royce Select I Inv	4.29
Old Westbury Mid Cap Equity	3.58
UMB Scout Growth	3.40

Thesis By Jeffrey Ptak, CPA, CFA, 12-15-06 Stock Price as of Analysis: $59.95

While a makeover doesn't seem to be in order for SEI Investments' wide-moat business, relentless innovation has long been management's calling card.

SEI's business has traditionally been premised on taking on duties that others--principally private banks, advisors, and money managers--couldn't or wouldn't perform themselves. Those chores include a host of back-office tasks that ensure that transactions are properly processed and accounted for as well as middle-office compliance and asset-management functions. SEI recently had more than $160 billion in assets under management, with much of that attributable to intermediaries who have effectively opted to let SEI invest their clients' money in various multimanager products that it offers.

Demand for SEI's services is not surprising: The back office is among the most capital-intensive parts of a wealth manager's business, and such tasks often fall outside what a wealth manager would consider its circle of competence. These firms are only too happy to outsource these functions to a party boasting the necessary resources and expertise. Enter SEI, which boasts those attributes in spades.

Once scaled, this is an impressively profitable business: SEI's returns on invested capital have routinely exceeded 30%, thanks to robust operating margins and efficiency (sales have more than doubled invested capital, on average, in recent years). Tall barriers to entry--represented by the large outlay any upstart must make to simply gain a foothold--have helped to keep competitors at bay. Meanwhile, the recurring nature of SEI's business, most of which is tied to assets under administration, has kept growth on a relatively steady upward arc. That's given management an ample supply of free cash flow to reinvest in the business, research and development in particular.

Against that backdrop, management's push to reinvent the company comes as little surprise. CEO Al West has led the effort to devise a fully immersive "life and wealth" strategy that gives clients a suite of solutions spanning the front, middle, and back offices. The approach is predicated on the notion that clients are increasingly demanding a fully integrated approach to wealth management, with soft, lifestyle-oriented goals being paramount.

We think this strategy holds great promise, as it essentially repackages the company's existing capabilities without degrading its ability to serve current clients. SEI should be able to widen the market for its services while also peddling additional services to existing clients.

Data as of 12-29-06

Siemens AG ADR SI

	Rating	Fair Value	Last Close	Consider Buy	Consider Sell	Yield %
	★★	$80.00	$98.55	$61.70	$100.20	1.59

Company Profile

A true conglomerate, Siemens comprises 13 separate business segments. On a pro forma basis as of June, the primary markets the company serves include industrial business systems and services (31% of sales), power generation (20%), transportation and automotive products (19%), health care (14%), and building and lighting products (12%). A finance subsidiary augments pretax income by an incremental 10%.

Management Stewardship Grade [NA]

Like all German companies, Siemens has imposed strict oversight on management. As required by German law, Siemens has a two-tier corporate-governance structure consisting of a managing board and a supervisory board, which oversees its managing board. The supervisory board has 20 members, with half the members elected by the shareholders and the other half elected by the employees. In January 2005, Siemens replaced its longtime CEO with a much younger and energetic manager, Klaus Kleinfeld. We give Kleinfeld high marks so far for taking decisive action to reorient Siemens' portfolio of businesses toward higher growth. We give management lower marks for not taking more aggressive action against allegations of corruption in a number of its operating units that emerged in 2006. German authorities are investigating at least six Siemens managers on allegations that they approved bribes to secure lucrative contracts. Top Siemens management waited weeks after the official investigation by German authorities before launching a probe of its internal controls conducted by outside auditors and attorneys.

Wittelsbacherplatz 2 www.siemens.com
Munich, Germany D-80333

Growth [NA]	2002	2003	2004	2005
Revenue %	-11.6	-5.4	7.4	15.7
Earnings/Share %	-5.8	33.1	-33.9	34.7
Book Value/Share %	0.9	8.2	1.1	7.9
Dividends/Share %	—	—	—	—

Profitability [NA]	2003	2004	2005	TTM
Return on Assets %	4.2	2.7	3.2	3.2
Oper Cash Flow $Mil	6,110	3,944	6,117	6,117
- Cap Spending $Mil	3,324	4,478	4,875	4,875
= Free Cash Flow $Mil	2,786	-534	1,242	1,242

Financial Health [NA]	2003	2004	2005	09-30-05
Long-term Debt $Mil	12,080	10,164	17,178	17,178
Total Equity $Mil	33,154	32,671	37,572	37,572
Debt/Equity Ratio	0.4	0.3	0.5	0.5

Industry	Business Risk	Moat Size	Investment Style	Sector
Wireline Equip.	Average	Narrow	Large Core	Hardware

Competition	Market Cap $Mil	12 Mo Trailing Sales $Mil	Price/Cash Flow	Return On Assets%	Debt/Equity	Total Return% 1 Yr	3 Yr
Siemens AG ADR	87,817	107,241	14.4	3.2	0.5	17.3	8.8
General Electric	383,564	161,022	12.8	2.5	2.2	9.4	9.0
Philips Electronics NV AD	45,147	38,062	17.3	8.9	0.2	22.8	9.8

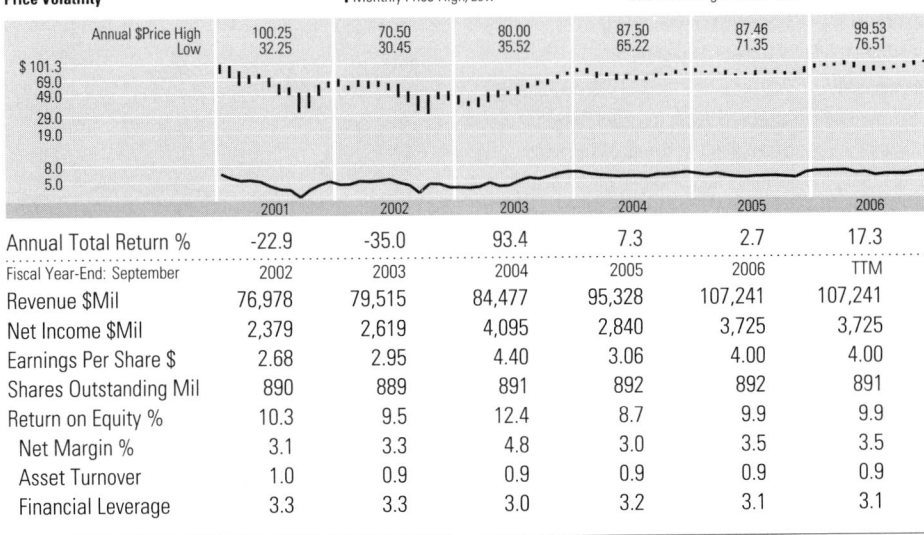

Price Volatility | Monthly Price High/Low — Relative Strength to S&P 500

	2001	2002	2003	2004	2005	2006
Annual $Price High	100.25	70.50	80.00	87.50	87.46	99.53
Low	32.25	30.45	35.52	65.22	71.35	76.51
Annual Total Return %	-22.9	-35.0	93.4	7.3	2.7	17.3

Fiscal Year-End: September	2002	2003	2004	2005	2006	TTM
Revenue $Mil	76,978	79,515	84,477	95,328	107,241	107,241
Net Income $Mil	2,379	2,619	4,095	2,840	3,725	3,725
Earnings Per Share $	2.68	2.95	4.40	3.06	4.00	4.00
Shares Outstanding Mil	890	889	891	892	892	891
Return on Equity %	10.3	9.5	12.4	8.7	9.9	9.9
Net Margin %	3.1	3.3	4.8	3.0	3.5	3.5
Asset Turnover	1.0	0.9	0.9	0.9	0.9	0.9
Financial Leverage	3.3	3.3	3.0	3.2	3.1	3.1

Valuation Ratios	Stock	Rel to Industry	Rel to S&P 500
Price/Earnings	24.2	1.0	1.2
Price/Book	2.3	0.5	0.6
Price/Sales	0.8	0.2	0.3
Price/Cash Flow	14.4	0.9	1.0

Major Fund Holders	% of Fund Assets
MassMutual Premier Value L	6.03
Oppenheimer Quest Value A	5.89
Oppenheimer Value A	5.87
VALIC I Value	5.82

Thesis By Tom D'Amore, CFA, 12-12-06 Stock Price as of Analysis: $97.52

Siemens appears to have been run as a colossal public works project for the past decade. Profit maximization seemed to take a backseat to uncontrolled business and workforce expansion. While Siemens has recently deployed a productivity improvement program to reverse its long-running slide in profitability, we're not ready to give it full credit for a turnaround. We think the company is still in too many businesses and has a long way to go to achieve market-competitive profitability.

Similar to German brethren Bayer and DaimlerChrysler, Siemens' competitive position deteriorated in the 1990s as powerful unions pushed up labor costs and management complacency became the order of the day. At the end of 2004, Siemens comprised 13 largely disparate lines of business, plus a finance subsidiary. Profitability and returns suffered mightily as a result. Operating profit and returns on invested capital over the past five years have averaged 4.9% and 0%, respectively.

New CEO Klaus Kleinfeld has endeavored to address this underperformance by adopting an American-style strategic reorientation program aimed at upgrading Siemens' stable of businesses to provide sustainable total sales growth of approximately 5%-6% and boost profit margins to about 7%. Kleinfeld has made progress in shedding some troubled businesses and adding others with more sales horsepower. The sale of the mobile phone business eliminated one problem unit, and the joint venture with Nokia, combining the two companies' volatile communications networking gear businesses, should eliminate another.

Kleinfeld has opened Siemens' pocketbook by acquiring more growth-oriented businesses. In 2006, the company spent a total of 5.7 billion euros acquiring specialty diagnostic product maker Diagnostic Products and the diagnostic equipment business of Bayer. Both businesses generate operating margins in the high teens and should help Siemens lift its overall profitability and boost returns.

Despite the recent activity, we think it's too soon to say that management's efforts to reinvigorate Siemens' productivity are bearing fruit. The business services unit continues to bleed red ink, and the transportation and automotive units are barely profitable. Operating margins trail leaner competitors by 6-7 percentage points. We don't think it's impossible for management to turn this German battleship around, but we think it has a lot more work to do.

Data as of 12-29-06

Sigma-Aldrich SIAL

Rating ★★★★	Fair Value $45.00	Last Close $38.86	Consider Buy $34.70	Consider Sell $56.40	Yield % 1.08

Company Profile

Sigma-Aldrich is a leading producer and supplier of research biochemicals, organic chemicals, and fine chemicals. Sigma's products are sold to universities, government institutions, and biotechnology and pharmaceutical companies, as well as other industrial and high-tech firms. It sells more than 100,000 chemical products--45,000 of which are proprietary--through various catalogs and over the Internet.

Management   Stewardship Grade [B]

We like the management team's candor and willingness to return cash to shareholders. Sigma recently appointed former COO Jai Nagarkatti as CEO, replacing David Harvey, who remains chairman after retiring as CEO. We expect a seamless transition, as Nagarkatti has historically played a direct role in setting the company's long-term strategy. In 2005, Harvey earned what we consider a reasonable salary and bonus of slightly more than $1.3 million, in addition to options to purchase 50,000 shares. In his position as COO, Nagarkatti earned $811,000 in salary and bonus. We like that senior executives are required to own a multiple of their salary in company stock. We applaud management for its capital-allocation skills; despite a large cash balance, the company has refrained from overpaying for acquisitions in a pricey market. The company has also done a remarkable job of creating value through share buybacks.

3050 Spruce Street
St. Louis, MO 63103
www.sigma-aldrich.com

Growth [B-]	2002	2003	2004	2005
Revenue %	8.3	7.5	8.6	18.3
Earnings/Share %	-4.8	52.2	23.2	12.6
Book Value/Share %	11.6	16.7	23.9	3.3
Dividends/Share %	39.3	44.9	36.0	11.8

Profitability [A+]	2003	2004	2005	TTM
Return on Assets %	12.5	13.3	12.1	11.3
Oper Cash Flow $Mil	309	324	281	291
- Cap Spending $Mil	58	70	92	68
= Free Cash Flow $Mil	251	254	188	223

Financial Health [A]	2003	2004	2005	09-30-06
Long-term Debt $Mil	176	177	283	238
Total Equity $Mil	999	1,212	1,233	1,349
Debt/Equity Ratio	0.2	0.1	0.2	0.2

Industry	Business Risk	Moat Size	Investment Style	Sector
Chemicals	Average	Narrow	Mid Core	Industrial Materials

Competition

	Market Cap $Mil	12 Mo Trailing Sales $Mil	Price/Cash Flow	Return On Assets%	Debt/ Equity	Total Return% 1 Yr	3 Yr
Sigma-Aldrich	5,125	1,744	17.6	11.3	0.2	24.3	11.7
Invitrogen	3,328	1,238	14.4	2.8	0.5	-15.1	-6.6
PerkinElmer	2,792	1,480	22.6	10.5	0.1	-4.4	9.7

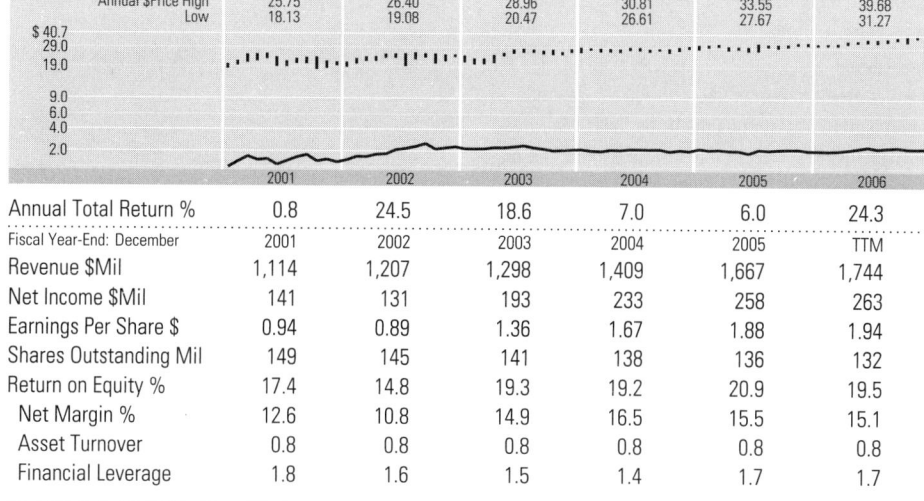

Price Volatility — Monthly Price High/Low — Relative Strength to S&P 500

	2001	2002	2003	2004	2005	2006
Annual $Price High	25.75	26.40	28.96	30.81	33.55	39.68
Low	18.13	19.08	20.47	26.61	27.67	31.27
Annual Total Return %	0.8	24.5	18.6	7.0	6.0	24.3

Fiscal Year-End: December	2001	2002	2003	2004	2005	TTM
Revenue $Mil	1,114	1,207	1,298	1,409	1,667	1,744
Net Income $Mil	141	131	193	233	258	263
Earnings Per Share $	0.94	0.89	1.36	1.67	1.88	1.94
Shares Outstanding Mil	149	145	141	138	136	132
Return on Equity %	17.4	14.8	19.3	19.2	20.9	19.5
Net Margin %	12.6	10.8	14.9	16.5	15.5	15.1
Asset Turnover	0.8	0.8	0.8	0.8	0.8	0.8
Financial Leverage	1.8	1.6	1.5	1.4	1.7	1.7

Valuation Ratios	Stock	Rel to Industry	Rel to S&P 500
Price/Earnings	20.0	1.1	1.0
Price/Book	3.8	1.2	0.9
Price/Sales	2.9	1.7	1.0
Price/Cash Flow	17.6	1.2	1.2

Major Fund Holders	% of Fund Assets
Pioneer Small and Mid Cap Growth A	3.49
TrendStar American Endeavor	3.49
State Farm Growth	3.18
AIM Mid Cap Core Equity A	3.04

Thesis By Ben Johnson, 12-18-06 Stock Price as of Analysis: $78.78

Sigma Aldrich is a cut above its chemical cohorts. The firm's substantial pricing power and topnotch sales and distribution model have helped it earn steady profits for more than a decade. We think that this narrow-moat firm's winning streak will continue for years to come.

The majority of Sigma's products are consumables used in a wide variety of processes, ranging from the lab bench to the manufacturing facility. The company's customers typically spend only 5% of their total budgets on these items, making demand highly inelastic. This allows Sigma to effectively manage prices in response to changes in its own cost structure, thereby maintaining steady profitability. Furthermore, the firm has more than 1 million individual customers, none of which accounts for more than 3% of total sales or has much power in negotiating prices.

Although many of the 145,000 products that Sigma offers are widely available through other distributors, the firm has been extremely successful in developing customer loyalty. Much of this success can be attributed to Sigma's best in class Web portal. The site is as much a research and learning tool for customers as it is a distribution channel.

Many customers come to the site without even knowing what they require for a particular trial or experiment. The breadth and depth of the site's content and its user-friendly interfaces allow customers to drill down to precisely the product they need. As a testament to the site's value to customers, more than one third of total research sales are now initiated online, a substantial jump from zero just five years ago.

A typical research scientist orders supplies just days in advance of anticipated need. Sigma keeps an expansive inventory that allows it to fulfill orders from these time-sensitive customers as quickly as possible. The firm has a 95% success rate in shipping orders the day they are placed. This has been a critical component of the firm's success in driving customer loyalty. However, keeping such a large inventory ties up a good chunk of capital and stifles the firm's cash flows. The firm's average inventory holding period was a lengthy 246 days in 2005. To the firm's credit, though, this number has declined on a yearly basis since 1999, when it stood at 311 days, and there should be room for further improvement.

SLM SLM

Data as of 12-29-06

	Rating	Fair Value	Last Close	Consider Buy	Consider Sell	Yield %
	★★★★	$57.00	$48.77	$48.60	$74.80	1.99

Industry	Business Risk	Moat Size	Investment Style	Sector
Finance	Below Avg	Wide	Large Growth	Financial Services

Company Profile
SLM, known as Sallie Mae, was formed in 1972 as a government-sponsored enterprise (GSE) to provide a secondary market for affordable student loans. The company shed its GSE status in late 2004, well ahead of its original 2008 deadline. Sallie funds a mix of federally guaranteed and private student loans. Most revenue comes from interest payments and loan servicing fees. The firm also operates collection agencies to help return uncollected loans to federal, and its own, coffers.

Management   Stewardship Grade [A]
We give credit to former CEO and current chairman Albert Lord for recognizing the value Sallie Mae was missing, taking control of the firm via winning a proxy vote, and rewarding shareholders by privatizing the firm away from its previous status as a government-sponsored enterprise. CEO Tim Fitzpatrick has worked closely with Lord throughout this process, and we hold the entire management team in high regard. The company's financial disclosures are excellent. The firm provides a great deal of salient information with every quarterly earnings release, and its regulatory filings contain good explanations of areas that may confuse investors and analysts alike. We also like the firm's disclosure of what it deems to be its "core" earnings, which exclude nonrecurring income like securitization and derivatives gains/losses, thus making the firm's core performance more understandable. We aren't thrilled to see the heavy use of stock options; annual option grants have often been 5% of shares outstanding. However, to offset any dilution, the company aggressively buys back its stock, resulting in a net decrease in shares in each of the past several years.

11600 Sallie Mae Drive   www.salliemae.com
Reston, VA 20193

Growth [D]	2002	2003	2004	2005
Revenue %	—	NMF	21.1	-8.6
Earnings/Share %	115.8	93.9	27.0	-24.5
Book Value/Share %	25.0	24.5	21.2	15.9
Dividends/Share %	17.3	80.0	45.1	14.9

Profitability [A-]	2003	2004	2005	TTM
Return on Assets %	2.4	2.3	1.4	1.4
Oper Cash Flow $Mil	894	-317	-699	—
- Cap Spending $Mil	—	—	—	—
= Free Cash Flow $Mil	—	—	—	—

Financial Health [NA]	2003	2004	2005	09-30-06
Long-term Debt $Mil	—	—	—	—
Total Equity $Mil	2,465	2,937	3,226	3,938
Debt/Equity Ratio	—	—	—	—

Competition

	Market Cap $Mil	12 Mo Trailing Sales $Mil	Price/Cash Flow	Return On Assets%	Debt/ Equity	Total Return% 1 Yr	3 Yr
SLM	19,935	4,063	—	1.4	—	-9.8	11.6
Citigroup	273,691	86,566	—	1.3	—	19.6	8.4
Bank of America	239,758	68,368	—	1.3	—	20.7	15.2

Price Volatility

Annual $Price High	29.32	35.65	42.92	54.44	56.48	58.35
Low	18.63	25.67	33.73	36.43	45.56	44.65
	2001	2002	2003	2004	2005	2006
Annual Total Return %	24.7	24.7	10.3	44.2	4.9	-9.8

Fiscal Year-End: December	2001	2002	2003	2004	2005	TTM
Revenue $Mil	NMF	NMF	3,125	3,784	3,459	4,063
Net Income $Mil	384	792	1,522	1,902	1,360	1,536
Earnings Per Share $	0.76	1.64	3.18	4.04	3.05	3.51
Shares Outstanding Mil	492	469	452	436	419	409
Return on Equity %	23.0	39.6	61.7	64.7	42.2	39.0
Net Margin %	NMF	NMF	48.7	50.3	39.3	37.8
Asset Turnover	—	—	0.0	0.0	0.0	0.0
Financial Leverage	31.6	26.6	26.2	28.6	30.8	27.2

Valuation Ratios	Stock	Rel to Industry	Rel to S&P 500
Price/Earnings	13.9	0.7	0.7
Price/Book	5.1	1.2	1.2
Price/Sales	4.9	0.9	1.7
Price/Cash Flow	—	—	—

Major Fund Holders	% of Fund Assets
TCW Select Equities I	5.46
Ivy Large Cap Growth A	4.96
Waddell & Reed Adv Vanguard A	4.94
AXA Enterprise Equity A	4.70

Thesis   By Ryan Batchelor, CPA, 12-13-06   Stock Price as of Analysis: $48.61

SLM, better known as Sallie Mae, is the dominant player in the attractive student loan market. Because of its attractiveness, we've seen an increase in market competition, but we believe Sallie's wide moat should protect its profits over the long haul.

Sallie Mae serves the economically insensitive market for student loans. Federally guaranteed student loans are an extremely attractive asset for lenders. By virtue of its guarantee, the government almost completely eliminates credit risk from federal loans. Interest rate risk is also mitigated by the government, which effectively guarantees fixed spreads over market interest rates. Adding to the attractiveness of this market, the demand for federally guaranteed loans--like Stafford loans--has been very steady and should remain robust because of the below-market interest rates students pay. In addition, the total cost of a higher education continues to outpace inflation, and national enrollment is expected to grow, leading to what we think is a nirvanalike growth story for lenders.

These attractive economics are not hidden from Sallie Mae's competitors, and we've seen heavy competition from incumbents and upstarts alike who are vying for students' business. As a result, promotions and borrower incentives have increased throughout the industry, which pressures its overall profitability. Despite these threats, we think that Sallie has a huge competitive advantage as the largest lender, thanks to inherent economies of scale in its business that allow it to be the low-cost leader in originating, funding, and servicing student loans. The firm also has entrenched relationships with more than 6,000 schools and a huge salesforce that gives it a leg up against the competition, in our opinion.

Additionally, because the limits for federal loans have not increased commensurately with the costs of higher education, more students have been forced to seek nonguaranteed private loans to close the funding gap. Thus, Sallie is in a great position to offer its private loans to borrowers, and this has resulted in an average annual growth rate in its private loan portfolio of almost 40% since 2001. Private loans are also roughly 3 times more profitable than federal loans, thanks to higher interest rates, even after adjusting for credit risk.

The firm's nonlending businesses, primarily in its debt management and collections businesses, are also growing rapidly. Although these fee-based businesses have a more volatile revenue stream than guaranteed student loans, we believe that these segments will enhance Sallie's long-term growth.

Data as of 12-29-06

Smith & Nephew ADR SNN

Rating	Fair Value	Last Close	Consider Buy	Consider Sell	Yield %
★★★	$51.00	$52.33	$39.30	$63.90	0.98

Company Profile

Smith & Nephew is a U.K.-based company with a 150-year history. Orthopedic devices account for about half of sales; major orthopedic offerings include knee and hip implants and tools to set bone fractures. The balance of the firm's sales comes almost equally from two other units. Smith & Nephew's endoscopy unit offers tools to help physicians perform minimally invasive joint surgeries. The firm's advanced wound-management business offers dressings and other devices.

Management   Stewardship Grade [NA]

Christopher O'Donnell has reigned as CEO at Smith & Nephew for nearly a decade. We think S&N executives receive generous salaries, benefits, and stock-based compensation. Also, while a majority of the directors are not current or former S&N executives, they make a healthy living by merely serving on the board. We typically don't like this sort of arrangement, since it makes us question the independence of board members, some of whom pull in six-figure salaries (in dollars) for their service. Since top insiders, including executives and directors, own less than 1% of Smith & Nephew, we do not think inside interests are naturally aligned with those of other shareholders either. John Buchanan, former CFO of another major U.K.-based firm, BP, serves as the board's chairman.

Industry	Business Risk	Moat Size	Investment Style	Sector
Medical Equip.	Average	Narrow	Mid Growth	Healthcare

Competition

	Market Cap $Mil	12 Mo Trailing Sales $Mil	Price/Cash Flow	Return On Assets%	Debt/ Equity	Total Return% 1 Yr	3 Yr
Smith & Nephew ADR	9,845	2,568	36.7	11.3	0.1	14.2	8.8
Johnson & Johnson	191,415	52,252	14.5	18.5	0.0	12.4	10.8
Stryker	22,439	5,221	25.1	14.1	0.0	24.5	9.9

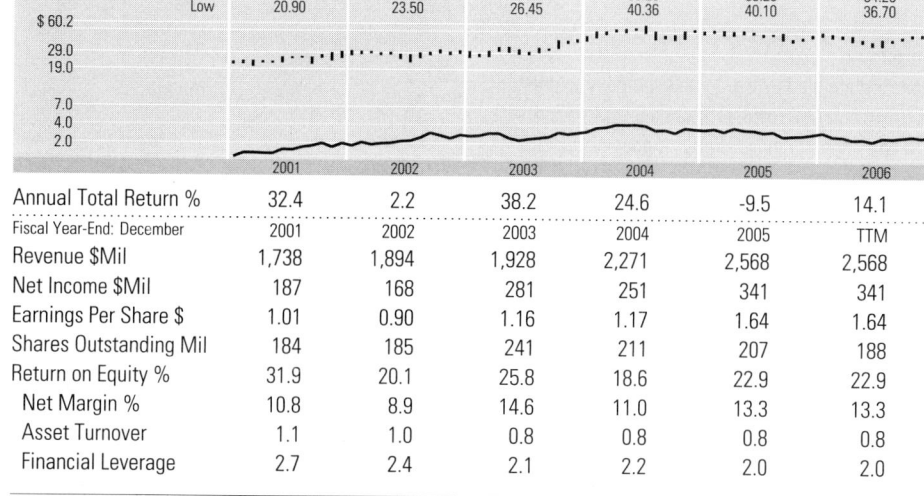

	2001	2002	2003	2004	2005	2006
Annual Total Return %	32.4	2.2	38.2	24.6	-9.5	14.1
Fiscal Year-End: December	2001	2002	2003	2004	2005	TTM
Revenue $Mil	1,738	1,894	1,928	2,271	2,568	2,568
Net Income $Mil	187	168	281	251	341	341
Earnings Per Share $	1.01	0.90	1.16	1.17	1.64	1.64
Shares Outstanding Mil	184	185	241	211	207	188
Return on Equity %	31.9	20.1	25.8	18.6	22.9	22.9
Net Margin %	10.8	8.9	14.6	11.0	13.3	13.3
Asset Turnover	1.1	1.0	0.8	0.8	0.8	0.8
Financial Leverage	2.7	2.4	2.1	2.2	2.0	2.0

Valuation Ratios	Stock	Rel to Industry	Rel to S&P 500
Price/Earnings	29.0	1.0	1.4
Price/Book	6.6	1.2	1.6
Price/Sales	3.8	0.8	1.3
Price/Cash Flow	36.7	1.5	2.5

Major Fund Holders	% of Fund Assets
Texas Capital Value & Growth A	1.08

Thesis By Julie Stralow, CFA, 12-14-06 Stock Price as of Analysis: $47.28

Smith & Nephew competes in one of the most attractive health-care niches, orthopedic medical devices. However, it remains a weaker competitor in that niche, and we think S&N's other businesses dilute its attractiveness.

Orthopedic implants, primarily knees and hips, account for about half of the firm's sales. S&N benefits from the attractive qualities of this niche, including high entry barriers and growing demand from an aging and increasingly active population. Perhaps the most important factor affecting this niche's attractiveness is its sticky physician relationships, which are nurtured over years of training and even consultations during procedures. Procedure outcomes are dramatically influenced by physician expertise with implants, making surgeons particularly loyal to a supplier's devices.

Physician loyalty remains a double-edge sword for S&N, though. S&N claims less than 10% market share in orthopedic implants, and it seems difficult to convince physicians who use other suppliers to switch to S&N's devices. So far, top competitors, including Stryker, Johnson & Johnson, and Zimmer, have done a good job of fending off smaller firms like S&N, and we don't expect industry dynamics to change much without further consolidation.

We think that S&N's other businesses remain less attractive than its orthopedic business. S&N is a leading provider of arthroscopy tools that help physicians perform minimally invasive joint repairs, and new product launches planned in this segment should accelerate intermediate-term growth. However, we think customer switching costs are lower here than in orthopedics, and companies with more resources than S&N could chip away at its advantages in this business.

S&N's advanced wound-management business, which primarily consists of advanced dressings for hard-to-heal wounds, is much less enticing than the orthopedic segment. These products remain difficult to differentiate, and S&N generates much lower margins in this business than in its other segments. Also, more technically advanced devices, including Kinetic Concepts' vacuum-assisted closure devices, are stealing share from more conventional wound-treatment products, making it difficult for S&N to expand this business.

Given its current position in orthopedics and mix from other revenue, we think S&N possesses a narrow economic moat versus its typically wide-moat competitors. We'll continue to make this distinction unless S&N's revenue mix shifts substantially.

---

15 Adam Street www.smith-nephew.com
London, United Kingdom WC2N 6LA

Growth [NA]	2002	2003	2004	2005
Revenue %	4.9	-6.8	5.9	12.7
Earnings/Share %	-13.8	18.1	-9.2	39.5
Book Value/Share %	27.3	-9.1	30.3	26.6
Dividends/Share %	—	—	—	—

Profitability [NA]	2003	2004	2005	TTM
Return on Assets %	12.1	8.6	11.3	11.3
Oper Cash Flow $Mil	260	353	268	268
- Cap Spending $Mil	119	185	203	203
= Free Cash Flow $Mil	141	167	66	66

Financial Health [NA]	2003	2004	2005	12-31-05
Long-term Debt $Mil	195	294	212	212
Total Equity $Mil	1,089	1,350	1,488	1,488
Debt/Equity Ratio	0.2	0.2	0.1	0.1

Data as of 12-29-06

Smithfield Foods SFD

Rating	Fair Value	Last Close	Consider Buy	Consider Sell	Yield %
★★★★	$31.00	$25.66	$19.80	$37.40	0.00

Company Profile
Smithfield is the world's largest hog producer and pork processor, raising more than 15 million hogs and processing more than 27 million hogs per year. Around half of all pork revenue comes from value-added packaged meats, which are the focus of recent acquisitions and central to the company's long-term strategy. Smithfield is also the fifth-largest beef processor in the United States, capturing about 6% of the annual domestic slaughter.

Industry	Business Risk	Moat Size	Investment Style	Sector
Food Mfg.	Above Avg	Narrow	Mid Value	Consumer Goods

Competition

	Market Cap $Mil	12 Mo Trailing Sales $Mil	Price/Cash Flow	Return On Assets%	Debt/ Equity	Total Return% 1 Yr	3 Yr
Smithfield Foods	2,870	11,183	8.6	2.1	1.3	-16.1	7.9
ConAgra Foods	13,758	11,594	10.6	2.9	0.7	38.1	5.4
Tyson Foods A	5,838	25,583	30.1	-0.4	0.7	-2.8	8.7

Price Volatility

	2001	2002	2003	2004	2005	2006
Annual $Price High	26.85	26.25	25.75	31.15	34.64	31.10
Low	13.60	14.60	16.87	20.10	25.69	24.89
Annual Total Return %	45.0	-10.0	4.3	42.9	3.4	-16.1

Fiscal Year-End: April	2002	2003	2004	2005	2006	TTM
Revenue $Mil	6,554	7,075	9,178	11,248	11,404	11,183
Net Income $Mil	197	26	227	296	173	141
Earnings Per Share $	1.78	0.24	2.03	2.64	1.54	1.26
Shares Outstanding Mil	—	—	110	111	111	112
Return on Equity %	14.4	2.0	14.2	15.6	8.5	6.7
Net Margin %	3.0	0.4	2.5	2.6	1.5	1.3
Asset Turnover	1.7	1.7	1.9	1.9	1.8	1.6
Financial Leverage	2.9	3.3	3.0	3.0	3.0	3.3

Management
Stewardship Grade [B]

While we are glad to see Smithfield finally split its chairman and CEO roles, promoting president and COO Larry Pope to the CEO post, it does not have a meaningful impact on our corporate-governance grade for the firm. For 31 years, Joseph Luter served as both chairman and CEO, and while Pope's experience in Smithfield's operations exceeds 25 years, it remains to be seen if he can navigate the company through the issues it faces today. Pope has big shoes to fill as shareholders have done well under Luter, with the stock posting a 26% compound annual rate of return during his tenure. Under Luter's management, Smithfield went on an aggressive acquisition spree, buying up more than 53 companies in the past 25 years. Pope intends to continue this trend, especially with branded meat acquisitions in Europe and the offer for Premium Standard Farms. The company continues to gain market share, but this has not come without controversy. In defense of local hog producers, both U.S. senators from Iowa along with the National Farmers Union are protesting the proposed acquisition of Premium Standard Farms and are calling on the Justice Department to find Smithfield in violation of antitrust laws.

Valuation Ratios	Stock	Rel to Industry	Rel to S&P 500
Price/Earnings	17.6	0.8	0.9
Price/Book	1.4	0.3	0.3
Price/Sales	0.3	0.2	0.1
Price/Cash Flow	8.6	0.6	0.6

Major Fund Holders	% of Fund Assets
New River Small Cap	4.84
BB&T Special Opportunities Equity A	4.00
Queens Road Small Cap Value	2.72
Legg Mason Classic Valuation Prim	2.71

200 Commerce Street
Smithfield, VA 23430

Growth [C+]	2003	2004	2005	2006
Revenue %	7.9	29.7	22.6	1.4
Earnings/Share %	-86.5	745.8	30.0	-41.7
Book Value/Share %	-3.8	20.6	18.6	6.7
Dividends/Share %	NMF	NMF	NMF	NMF

Profitability [C+]	2004	2005	2006	TTM
Return on Assets %	4.7	5.1	2.8	2.1
Oper Cash Flow $Mil	320	95	503	332
- Cap Spending $Mil	134	199	391	461
= Free Cash Flow $Mil	186	-105	111	-130

Financial Health [C]	2004	2005	2006	10-31-06
Long-term Debt $Mil	1,697	2,152	2,314	2,814
Total Equity $Mil	1,599	1,901	2,028	2,105
Debt/Equity Ratio	1.1	1.1	1.1	1.3

Thesis
By Ann Gilpin, 12-05-06 Stock Price as of Analysis: $26.95

Smithfield Foods is the nation's leading producer of hogs and processor of pork products. Acquisitions and the introduction of value-added meats have allowed the company to maintain its narrow economic moat. However, volatile swings in commodity cycles can have deleterious effects on revenue and profits.

In an industry where companies struggle to establish competitive advantages, Smithfield has built a narrow moat around its business, primarily through its unrivaled scale and genetically superior hogs. Smithfield accounts for 13% of total U.S. hog production, 3 times more than its nearest competitor. It is also the largest domestic processor of pork products, handling more than 26% of the annual slaughter in the United States. Its closest competitor, Tyson, handles 18%. In addition, Smithfield owns a proprietary line of genetically superior hogs, which are leaner and more cost-efficient to raise than standard hogs. By supplying 53% of the hogs used in its pork processing operations, Smithfield has greater control over input costs and product quality.

Smithfield hopes to maintain its moat through acquisitions and by moving up the value chain into packaged meats, which traditionally carry much higher profit margins than fresh pork products. Recently acquired brands from ConAgra and Sara Lee should help the company cement its presence in packaged meats and alleviate some of the impact of commodity price swings. Smithfield is also awaiting regulatory approval to acquire Premium Standard Farms. If approved, the acquisition would increase Smithfield's breeding inventory by 50%, to 1 million sows, giving the company control of nearly 20% of the nation's hogs. Opposition to the deal includes U.S. senators from Iowa, the National Farmers Union, and smaller-scale hog producers, who claim that Smithfield's acquisition would violate antitrust laws and create a monopoly.

In the end, Smithfield is in an industry heavily influenced by commodity price volatility. With animal feed constituting 60%-65% of the total cost of raising hogs and corn constituting roughly 85% of a pig's diet, corn prices have a significant impact on end market hog prices. Recent increases in ethanol production have caused corn prices to skyrocket to a 10-year high, and many meat processors have seen their profits crimped as a result. With ethanol production expected to increase over the next 18 months, we anticipate even more swings in the price of this key input.

Sony ADR SNE

Data as of 12-29-06

	Rating	Fair Value	Last Close	Consider Buy	Consider Sell	Yield %
	★★★★	$50.00	$42.83	$38.60	$62.60	0.50

Company Profile
Sony manufactures consumer electronics and has entertainment operations. Its electronic products include televisions, camcorders, CD and DVD players, video game consoles, digital cameras, and computers. Sony's entertainment assets include Columbia TriStar Motion Pictures, Sony Pictures Classics, Columbia and Epic Records, PlayStation, and several television shows. Sony derives about three fourths of its revenue from outside Japan.

Management
Stewardship Grade [NA]

Sir Howard Stringer, an outsider relative to corporate history, is Sony's CEO. Stringer was previously head of Sony's entertainment and America operations, where he was instrumental in improving group performance. Stringer's lack of product development and engineering experience is offset by new president Dr. Ryoji Chubachi, an engineer by training who is also the CEO of the important electronics division. Corporate governance seems adequate. Sony's large board and complex management structure look unwieldy from the outside, but the board has proved it can take bold steps (such as promoting outsider Stringer to CEO) when the firm needs it. The corporate governance provisions under the Japanese Commercial Code encourage a strong board with a clear executive oversight mandate, and Sony has taken steps to strengthen governance beyond what the code requires.

6-7-35 Kita-Shinagawa Shinagawa-ku www.sony.co.jp
Tokyo, Japan 141-0001

Growth [NA]	2003	2004	2005	2006
Revenue %	-1.4	0.3	-4.5	4.4
Earnings/Share %	609.1	-26.4	81.7	-26.1
Book Value/Share %	-9.6	0.1	18.5	9.4
Dividends/Share %	—	—	—	—

Profitability [NA]	2004	2005	2006	TTM
Return on Assets %	0.9	1.7	1.2	1.2
Oper Cash Flow $Mil	5,568	6,024	3,548	3,548
- Cap Spending $Mil	3,761	4,222	4,104	4,104
= Free Cash Flow $Mil	1,807	1,802	-556	-556

Financial Health [NA]	2004	2005	2006	03-31-06
Long-term Debt $Mil	7,361	6,313	6,505	6,505
Total Equity $Mil	22,510	26,688	27,246	27,246
Debt/Equity Ratio	0.3	0.2	0.2	0.2

Industry	Business Risk	Moat Size	Investment Style	Sector
Audio/Video Equip.	Average	Narrow	Large Growth	Consumer Goods

Competition	Market Cap $Mil	12 Mo Trailing Sales $Mil	Price/Cash Flow	Return On Assets%	Debt/Equity	Total Return% 1 Yr	3 Yr
Sony ADR	42,870	66,335	12.1	1.2	0.2	5.5	7.6
Microsoft	293,538	45,352	20.8	19.8	—	15.8	7.6
Apple Computer	72,901	19,315	32.8	11.6	—	18.0	99.8

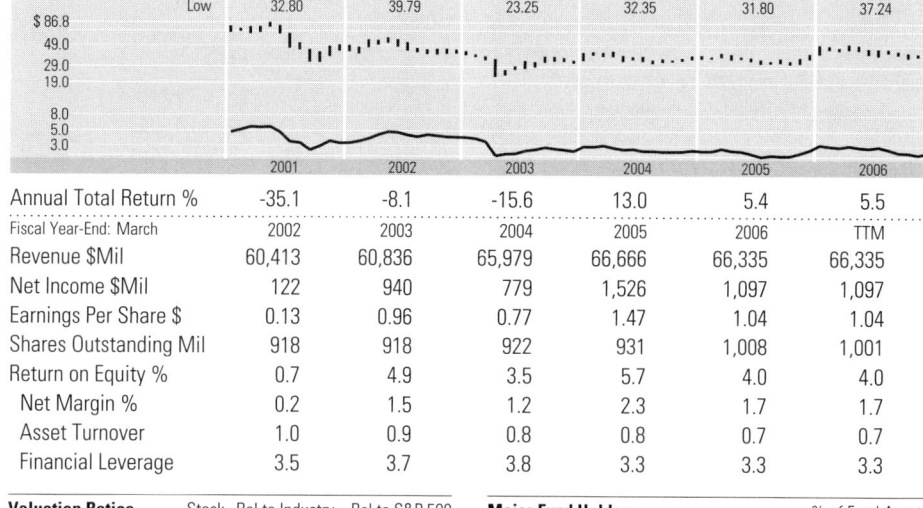

Price Volatility — Monthly Price High/Low — Relative Strength to S&P 500

Annual $Price High/Low	85.75/32.80	59.95/39.79	43.40/23.25	43.67/32.35	41.81/31.80	52.29/37.24
	2001	2002	2003	2004	2005	2006
Annual Total Return %	-35.1	-8.1	-15.6	13.0	5.4	5.5

Fiscal Year-End: March	2002	2003	2004	2005	2006	TTM
Revenue $Mil	60,413	60,836	65,979	66,666	66,335	66,335
Net Income $Mil	122	940	779	1,526	1,097	1,097
Earnings Per Share $	0.13	0.96	0.77	1.47	1.04	1.04
Shares Outstanding Mil	918	918	922	931	1,008	1,001
Return on Equity %	0.7	4.9	3.5	5.7	4.0	4.0
Net Margin %	0.2	1.5	1.2	2.3	1.7	1.7
Asset Turnover	1.0	0.9	0.8	0.8	0.7	0.7
Financial Leverage	3.5	3.7	3.8	3.3	3.3	3.3

Valuation Ratios	Stock	Rel to Industry	Rel to S&P 500
Price/Earnings	41.3	1.5	2.0
Price/Book	1.6	0.7	0.4
Price/Sales	0.6	0.5	0.2
Price/Cash Flow	12.1	0.8	0.8

Major Fund Holders	% of Fund Assets
FBR Pegasus	3.51
Guinness Atkinson Global Innovators	3.42
Dodge & Cox Stock	2.46
FBR Large Cap Technology	2.24

Thesis
By Rod Bare, 12-07-06 Stock Price as of Analysis: $39.90

Sony is a $65 billion consumer-electronics giant with a rich history of success in TVs, music players, and video games. Sony's dominance has faded in recent years but the firm is working hard to fix the situation. We think the successful completion of several cost-cutting initiatives and the cultivation of some key investments should reveal a firm with upside.

Success breeding complacency is what derailed Sony. The firm was slow to capitalize on emerging trends in digitization as music and video content moved from tape to hard drives. Where trends were identified, internal divisions created competing products that unwittingly sabotaged each other and confused the marketplace. Sony left the door wide open for nimbler competitors to seize opportunity in key areas.

Sony identified the challenges and started restructuring a few years ago. The firm began streamlining manufacturing operations in audio, CRT televisions, and semiconductors two years ago, but more work remains. Simultaneously, the company started investing in next-generation products with the help of some unlikely partners. Sony has now made key investments in flat-panel televisions (with Samsung), multi-core processors (with IBM), music (with BMG), movies (with MGM), and smartphones (with Ericsson). Even Sony's mighty gaming division relies on a tricky partnership for key hardware components related to a next-generation DVD technology (called Blu-ray), and the care and feeding of the game developer eco-system can be a test.

Thankfully, these investments look well-positioned to start paying dividends. Sony's Bravia line of flat-panel televisions is a growing success. Sony Ericsson phones have leading market share among profitable high-end customer segments, and Walkman phones are showing real promise. Sales of the PlayStation Portable video game player are robust, and the PlayStation 3 is selling well, when it's available. More importantly, these investments have partners with skin in the game. They represent an intriguing consortium of tech-savvy allies with a very Sony-friendly set of incentives.

Sony isn't done yet, however, and this is where the key risk resides. Howard Stringer, Sony's CEO, is an outsider tasked with completing a substantial set of cost-cutting and team-building projects across this global behemoth. Backing out one-time positives and negatives in recent financials reveals some encouraging improvements, but the operational, cultural, and financial ramifications of this effort remain hard to quantify.

Southern SO

Data as of 12-29-06

Rating	Fair Value	Last Close	Consider Buy	Consider Sell	Yield %
★★★	$38.00	$36.86	$32.40	$49.90	4.16

Company Profile
Southern generates and distributes electricity and provides related services. It owns five electric utilities in Alabama, Georgia, Florida, and Mississippi and has nearly 39,000 megawatts of generating capacity, the majority of which is from coal-fired plants. Southern sells this electricity to its 3.5 million retail and half a million commercial customers. With more than 500,000 shareholders, Southern is one of the most widely held stocks in the country.

Management
Stewardship Grade [B]

Southern's management team has historically comprised a highly capable and conservative group of individuals. The best compliment to its industry-leading management depth is the large number of C-level executives running other utilities who trace their roots back to Southern. Management has fostered a culture of industry-leading returns and customer satisfaction, all the while earning above-average marks in shareholder stewardship. David Ratcliffe was appointed CEO in July 2004. He has been with the company for 33 years and most recently was the CEO of Georgia Power and Mississippi Power, two of Southern's five regulated subsidiaries. The company doesn't appear to engage in aggressive accounting, and executive compensation is roughly in line with that of its peer group. Ratcliffe received $3.7 million of total compensation during 2004--most of which was tied to his performance-based bonus and other long-term compensation.

270 Peachtree St., N.W.
Atlanta, GA 30303
www.southerncompany.com

Growth [B]	2002	2003	2004	2005
Revenue %	2.9	5.5	6.5	15.6
Earnings/Share %	—	NMF	2.0	3.4
Book Value/Share %	—	NMF	4.5	3.5
Dividends/Share %	1.1	2.2	2.2	4.2

Profitability [A+]	2003	2004	2005	TTM
Return on Assets %	4.2	4.1	4.0	3.7
Oper Cash Flow $Mil	3,071	2,695	2,530	2,430
- Cap Spending $Mil	1,964	2,022	2,370	2,854
= Free Cash Flow $Mil	1,107	673	160	-424

Financial Health [B]	2003	2004	2005	09-30-06
Long-term Debt $Mil	10,164	12,449	12,846	12,883
Total Equity $Mil	9,648	10,278	10,689	11,286
Debt/Equity Ratio	1.1	1.2	1.2	1.1

Industry	Business Risk	Moat Size	Investment Style	Sector
Electric Utilities	Below Avg	Narrow	Large Value	Utilities

Competition	Market Cap $Mil	12 Mo Trailing Sales $Mil	Price/Cash Flow	Return On Assets%	Debt/Equity	Total Return% 1 Yr	3 Yr
Southern	28,133	14,494	11.6	3.7	1.1	11.7	12.0
Dominion Resources	29,656	17,641	8.2	3.2	1.1	12.6	13.6
FPL Group	22,026	15,251	48.8	3.5	1.0	35.5	23.0

Price Volatility — Monthly Price High/Low — Relative Strength to S&P 500

Annual $Price High / Low	26.00 / 16.10	31.14 / 23.22	32.00 / 27.00	33.96 / 27.44	36.47 / 31.14	37.40 / 30.49
Annual Total Return %	33.2	17.6	11.8	16.2	7.6	11.7

Fiscal Year-End: December	2001	2002	2003	2004	2005	TTM
Revenue $Mil	10,155	10,447	11,018	11,729	13,554	14,494
Net Income $Mil	1,262	1,318	1,474	1,532	1,591	1,544
Earnings Per Share $	—	—	2.02	2.06	2.13	2.07
Shares Outstanding Mil	—	—	726	740	743	763
Return on Equity %	15.8	15.1	15.3	14.9	14.9	13.7
Net Margin %	12.4	12.6	13.4	13.1	11.7	10.7
Asset Turnover	0.3	0.3	0.3	0.3	0.3	0.3
Financial Leverage	4.0	3.9	3.6	3.6	3.7	3.7

Valuation Ratios	Stock	Rel to Industry	Rel to S&P 500
Price/Earnings	17.8	1.0	0.9
Price/Book	2.5	0.7	0.6
Price/Sales	1.9	1.1	0.7
Price/Cash Flow	11.6	1.0	0.8

Major Fund Holders	% of Fund Assets
Phoenix Global Utilities A	3.97
ProFunds Utilities UltraSector Inv	3.60
Cohen & Steers Utility A	3.56
Franklin Utilities A	3.33

Thesis By Paul Justice, CFA, 12-18-06 Stock Price as of Analysis: $37.04

We believe Southern Company has all of the traits traditional utility investors desire. Its strong earnings growth prospects, rock-solid financial condition, and favorable regulatory relationships justify its place as a core holding in most income investors' portfolios.

In general, regulated utilities succeed financially based on the growth and prosperity of their underlying customer base. Due to a constructive regulatory environment, Southern has been able to capitalize nicely on the steadily growing electric demand prevalent in the Southeast. The company's customer growth has averaged around 1.8% a year for the past decade, while increasing electricity demand provides an additional 2% of growth annually. This customer and demand growth has translated into an appealing partner to Southern's massive 41,000-megawatt generation fleet. The company's low-cost nuclear and coal-fired power plants have kept energy prices for its regulated customers 15% below the national average. This low-cost structure and Southern's reputation for reliability and customer service have kept the company in the good graces of its regulators.

In addition to its core regulated utility businesses, Southern generates roughly 15% of its consolidated income from competitive power supply. However, unlike the typical merchant energy provider, Southern Power operates under a very conservative framework. Southern Power builds a plant only when it has a long-term contract in place with a customer to purchase the power. The contracts have an average life of 13 years, and all of the contracted counterparties have an investment-grade rating; 90% are rated single A or better. The company insulates itself from cost volatility by charging a fixed price and making volatile variable costs the responsibility of its counterparties. This eliminates Southern's exposure to fuel risk or spark-spread risk, making the wholesale business's risk profile only slightly higher than that of its regulated utility and substantially lower than that of most merchant utilities.

Strong growth, reliable cash flow, and financial integrity underscore our affinity for Southern's dividend. Already yielding 4.1% on our fair value estimate, we think the dividend can grow between 4% and 6% per year going forward.

Southwest Airlines LUV

Data as of 12-29-06

	Rating	Fair Value	Last Close	Consider Buy	Consider Sell	Yield %
	★★★	$16.00	$15.32	$12.30	$20.00	0.12

Company Profile
Commercial airline Southwest was founded in 1971 and provides passenger and freight transportation throughout the United States. The airline specializes in short-haul routes, using a point-to-point network as opposed to a hub-and-spoke model. Its fleet consists of more than 475 Boeing 737 aircraft, and the firm employs more than 32,000 people. Passenger transportation generates almost all revenue.

Management
Stewardship Grade [A]

In the summer of 2004, CFO Gary Kelly was named as CEO to succeed Jim Parker, who, citing personal reasons, stepped aside after three years at the helm. At the same time, Southwest veteran Laura Wright took over as CFO. Both Kelly and Wright have been at Southwest since the late 1980s, so the transition reflected the airline's commitment to promote from within the firm. Over their first year as CEO and CFO, this management duo maintained discipline and bottom-line focus when most airlines struggled to survive, and delivered cost savings even excluding Southwest's fuel hedges. In addition, Kelly has kept competitors guessing about his latest moves since the airline has expanded at airports once thought to be out of range for traditional low-cost carriers. In the quest to grow Southwest and undercut rivals, Kelly has expanded to Denver, Pittsburgh, and, most recently, Washington-Dulles. To save cash, executives at Southwest make a little less than some of their peers, but they receive generous option grants and deferred compensation. Management's disclosure is forthright. Annual incentive bonuses are awarded to executive officers based on years of service, level of responsibility, teamwork, and companywide profitability. Management collectively owns 1.1% of shares outstanding.

P.O. Box 36611
Dallas, TX 75235-1611
www.southwest.com

Growth [B]	2002	2003	2004	2005
Revenue %	-0.6	7.5	10.0	16.1
Earnings/Share %	-52.4	80.0	-29.6	76.3
Book Value/Share %	11.3	12.1	8.7	21.7
Dividends/Share %	0.0	0.0	0.0	0.0

Profitability [B]	2003	2004	2005	TTM
Return on Assets %	4.5	2.8	3.9	4.1
Oper Cash Flow $Mil	1,336	1,157	2,229	1,405
- Cap Spending $Mil	1,238	1,775	1,210	1,314
= Free Cash Flow $Mil	98	-618	1,019	91

Financial Health [A]	2003	2004	2005	09-30-06
Long-term Debt $Mil	—	1,700	1,394	1,275
Total Equity $Mil	5,052	5,524	6,675	6,624
Debt/Equity Ratio	—	0.3	0.2	0.2

Industry	Business Risk	Moat Size	Investment Style	Sector
Air Transport	Average	Narrow	Large Growth	Business Services

Competition	Market Cap $Mil	12 Mo Trailing Sales $Mil	Price/Cash Flow	Return On Assets%	Debt/Equity	Total Return% 1 Yr	3 Yr
Southwest Airlines	12,131	8,798	8.6	4.1	0.2	-6.7	-1.2
AMR	6,482	22,334	3.8	-1.3	NMF	36.0	32.5
Continental Airlines B	3,717	12,816	4.1	2.9	6.7	93.7	35.0

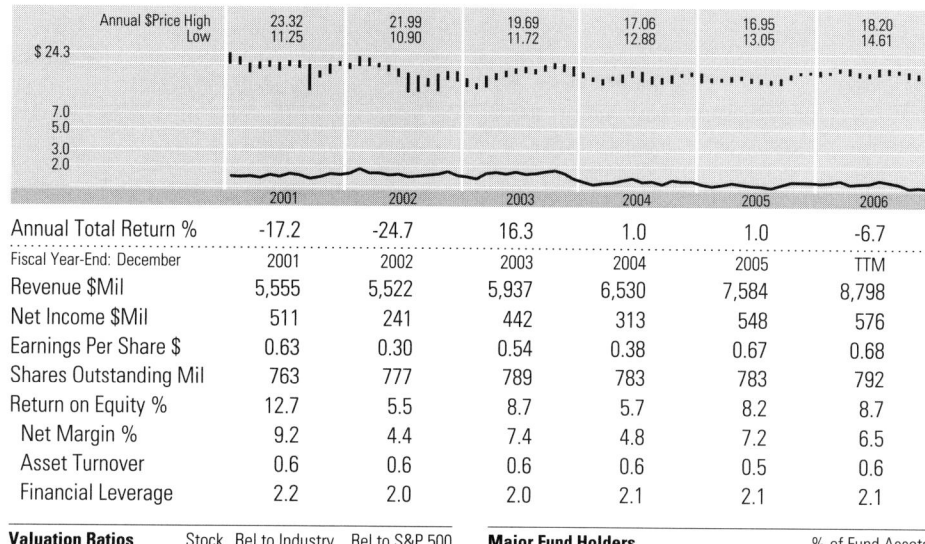

Price Volatility — Monthly Price High/Low — Relative Strength to S&P 500

Annual $Price High Low	23.32 / 11.25	21.99 / 10.90	19.69 / 11.72	17.06 / 12.88	16.95 / 13.05	18.20 / 14.61
	2001	2002	2003	2004	2005	2006

	2001	2002	2003	2004	2005	TTM
Annual Total Return %	-17.2	-24.7	16.3	1.0	1.0	-6.7
Fiscal Year-End: December	2001	2002	2003	2004	2005	TTM
Revenue $Mil	5,555	5,522	5,937	6,530	7,584	8,798
Net Income $Mil	511	241	442	313	548	576
Earnings Per Share $	0.63	0.30	0.54	0.38	0.67	0.68
Shares Outstanding Mil	763	777	789	783	783	792
Return on Equity %	12.7	5.5	8.7	5.7	8.2	8.7
Net Margin %	9.2	4.4	7.4	4.8	7.2	6.5
Asset Turnover	0.6	0.6	0.6	0.6	0.5	0.6
Financial Leverage	2.2	2.0	2.0	2.1	2.1	2.1

Valuation Ratios	Stock	Rel to Industry	Rel to S&P 500
Price/Earnings	22.5	1.2	1.1
Price/Book	1.8	0.5	0.4
Price/Sales	1.4	0.9	0.5
Price/Cash Flow	8.6	0.9	0.6

Major Fund Holders	% of Fund Assets
Rydex Transportation Inv	3.99
Homestead Value	2.93
Rice Hall James Mid-Cap Inv	2.82
Bridgeway Aggressive Investors 1	2.45

Thesis
By Marisa E. Thompson, 12-15-06 Stock Price as of Analysis: $15.89

Southwest is built for profitability in an industry where bankruptcy has become commonplace.

Southwest is the low-cost leader of the airline industry because it uses assets more efficiently than competitors and employs a highly productive workforce. Excluding fuel costs and adjusting for the average length of flights, Southwest's cost per available seat mile is 10% lower than its nearest competitor's.

Southwest's culture emphasizes thrift, and all employees are rewarded for cost-reduction efforts in the form of potential stock appreciation and profit sharing. At the same time, Southwest has rationalized its workforce by consolidating its reservations center and offering early-retirement plans to qualified employees. The result: The number of employees per aircraft is approaching almost 70, one of the lowest in the industry.

Southwest is also known for its streamlined gate procedures, which allow employees to turn around planes faster and fly aircraft more often per day than the competition. Southwest offers frequent, short-haul flights to less-crowded airports enabling the airline to save on airport fees and avoid congestion that would otherwise slow down its operations. Southwest saves on pilot training and maintenance costs by using just one aircraft type, the Boeing 737. The company has extensively invested in technology across the spectrum of its operations, from revenue management to maintenance procedures to ticket distribution.

Southwest is well-positioned to expand, especially if competitors' positions weaken. Southwest maintains the most flexibility in its capital structure, which means it has the financial wherewithal to rapidly enter new markets. When ATA Airlines sought bankruptcy protection, Southwest bought gates from the firm and expanded its presence in Chicago. Southwest also established new service in Philadelphia and Pittsburgh after US Airways pared down its presence in those cities. Furthermore, Southwest's financial strength means that it is well-positioned to purchase assets that might be shed as legacy carriers continue to consolidate.

Because legacy carriers are emerging stronger from bankruptcy and other low-cost carriers are gaining market share, Southwest will have to continue to execute well to extend its unparalleled track record. Aiding this cause is the indisputable fact that the company's operations are built to offer the one competitive advantage that matters most in the commodified airline industry: the lowest fares.

Data as of 12-29-06

Sprint Nextel S

	Rating	Fair Value	Last Close	Consider Buy	Consider Sell	Yield %
	★★★★★	$28.00	$18.89	$21.60	$35.10	0.53

Company Profile
Sprint Nextel is the third-largest carrier in the United States, serving 46 million customers directly and 6 million via resellers. About 15% of sales come from the long-distance unit, which provides fixed-line phone and data services. The firm spun off its fixed-line local phone business on May 18, 2006. The firm has been acquiring affiliated carriers recently, including Nextel Partners.

Management   Stewardship Grade [B]
Sprint Nextel had split management responsibilities between executives of the former companies. CEO Gary Forsee took the top spot at Sprint in March 2003, leaving BellSouth, where he was head of domestic operations. Forsee had also previously served as chairman of Cingular. Nextel CEO Tim Donahue became executive chairman after the merger, but he will retire at the end of 2006. Forsee will become chairman and, while we usually prefer to see the chairman and CEO positions split, we like the fact that one person will be responsible for making tough decisions. Further putting Sprint's direction on Forsee's shoulders, COO Len Lauer was let go in August 2006 and not replaced. Our biggest complaint about Sprint's corporate governance is the level of executive pay. Forsee received about $20 million in total compensation during 2005, and Donahue received about $8 million during the last five months of the year, which now looks very high given the problems the firm has had. Overall, though, we think Sprint Nextel's governance is better than average. We like that the firm appoints a lead outside director each year and has adopted strict independence guidelines. Also, goals for executive compensation should balance long-term and short-term performance well. The firm also has minimum stock ownership requirements for executives and directors.

P.O. Box 7997
Shawnee Mission, KS 66207-0997
www.sprint.com

Growth [A]	2002	2003	2004	2005
Revenue %	4.4	-1.8	4.7	26.4
Earnings/Share %	—	NMF	NMF	NMF
Book Value/Share %	—	NMF	0.4	172.1
Dividends/Share %	0.0	0.0	0.0	-40.0

Profitability [C]	2003	2004	2005	TTM
Return on Assets %	3.0	-2.5	1.7	1.3
Oper Cash Flow $Mil	6,535	6,625	10,678	12,360
- Cap Spending $Mil	3,797	3,980	5,057	7,294
= Free Cash Flow $Mil	2,738	2,645	5,621	5,066

Financial Health [A]	2003	2004	2005	09-30-06
Long-term Debt $Mil	—	15,916	20,632	19,643
Total Equity $Mil	13,113	13,521	51,937	52,815
Debt/Equity Ratio	—	1.2	0.4	0.4

Industry	Business Risk	Moat Size	Investment Style	Sector
Wireless Svcs.	Average	Narrow	Large Value	Telecommunication

Competition	Market Cap $Mil	12 Mo Trailing Sales $Mil	Price/Cash Flow	Return On Assets %	Debt/ Equity	Total Return % 1 Yr	3 Yr
Sprint Nextel	53,177	46,267	4.3	1.3	0.4	-10.4	10.1
AT&T	137,384	60,171	9.0	4.9	0.5	51.6	16.3
Verizon Communications	108,723	88,881	4.4	3.7	0.7	34.9	8.0

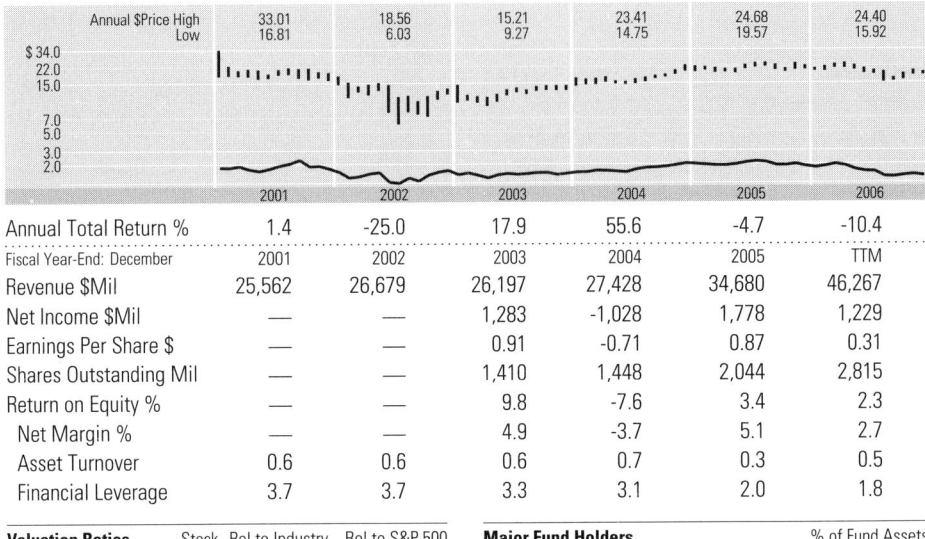

Price Volatility — Monthly Price High/Low — Relative Strength to S&P 500

	2001	2002	2003	2004	2005	2006
Annual $Price High	33.01	18.56	15.21	23.41	24.68	24.40
Low	16.81	6.03	9.27	14.75	19.57	15.92
Annual Total Return %	1.4	-25.0	17.9	55.6	-4.7	-10.4

Fiscal Year-End: December	2001	2002	2003	2004	2005	TTM
Revenue $Mil	25,562	26,679	26,197	27,428	34,680	46,267
Net Income $Mil	—	—	1,283	-1,028	1,778	1,229
Earnings Per Share $	—	—	0.91	-0.71	0.87	0.31
Shares Outstanding Mil	—	—	1,410	1,448	2,044	2,815
Return on Equity %	—	—	9.8	-7.6	3.4	2.3
Net Margin %	—	—	4.9	-3.7	5.1	2.7
Asset Turnover	0.6	0.6	0.6	0.7	0.3	0.5
Financial Leverage	3.7	3.7	3.3	3.1	2.0	1.8

Valuation Ratios	Stock	Rel to Industry	Rel to S&P 500
Price/Earnings	29.1	1.2	1.4
Price/Book	1.0	0.3	0.2
Price/Sales	1.1	0.3	0.4
Price/Cash Flow	4.3	0.5	0.3

Major Fund Holders	% of Fund Assets
Profunds UltraSector Mobile Telecomm Inv	32.84
Fidelity Advisor Utilities T	6.95
Fidelity Select Wireless	6.94
Fidelity Select Utilities Growth	6.72

Thesis By Michael Hodel, CFA, 12-18-06 Stock Price as of Analysis: $19.24

The wireless industry has seen major consolidation in recent years, and our thesis has been that the three largest operators--Verizon Wireless, Cingular, and Sprint Nextel, will prosper because their resources far outstrip those of other industry players. Yet Sprint has languished during 2006 while Verizon and Cingular have surged ahead. We believe the firm's problems are temporary, though, and that Sprint's advantages will shine through over the long run.

With three large carriers controlling more than three quarters of the wireless market, we've been expecting competition to ease, allowing profitability across the industry to continue improving. This seems to be happening, as pricing has stabilized, customer growth remains strong, and margins at several carriers, especially Cingular, have improved. Sprint, on the other hand, has actually seen a net loss of high-value postpaid customers recently, as defections rise. Sprint's marketing has been confusing, the firm let the quality of the Nextel network slip, and it's been slow to adopt popular handset models. Sprint's performance will probably get worse before it gets better, but we think management has taken the right steps to improve the business. The firm has tightened credit policies, stopped adding customers in markets where capacity is tight, continued investing in the network, sharpened advertising, and introduced dual-mode phones.

We think Sprint has natural advantages that will make management's efforts worthwhile. Size creates several advantages in the wireless industry, providing operating benefits, such as marketing scale and broader network coverage, that reduce the cost of providing service. With over 50 million customers, Sprint is over twice the size of Deutsche Telekom's T-Mobile unit, the fourth-largest nationwide carrier. Sprint, Verizon, and Cingular also have deep wireless spectrum positions, which have allowed them to offer higher-speed data services. T-Mobile recently acquired additional spectrum as well, but it will take time for that firm to match its larger peers.

Sprint has some unique attributes that we believe bolster its competitive position. Unlike its larger rivals, Sprint is a wireless pure play since shedding its fixed-line business, allowing the firm to serve as a partner in the cable industry's efforts to offer phone service. Also, Sprint is using its considerable spectrum holdings to deploy WiMax technology, a next-generation technology that will bolster its data capabilities. Finally, the firm has a large base of loyal small-business customers still on the Nextel network.

St. Jude Medical STJ

Rating: ★★★ | **Fair Value:** $41.00 | **Last Close:** $36.56 | **Consider Buy:** $31.60 | **Consider Sell:** $51.40 | **Yield %:** 0.00

Data as of 12-29-06

Company Profile
St. Jude Medical manufactures cardiovascular medical devices, including the world's most widely used mechanical heart valve. Its products include tissue heart valves, catheters, pacemakers, implantable cardioverter defibrillators, and vascular closure devices for catheterization procedures. St. Jude sells its products to hospitals and heart-surgery centers in the United States and abroad. Foreign sales make up about 35% of the company's total sales.

Management
Stewardship Grade [C]

Chairman, president, and CEO Daniel Starks smoothly stepped into his leadership roles in May 2004. Starks has a long history with St. Jude and hasn't instituted many major changes in the strategy set by his predecessor, Terry Shepherd. The nine-member board consists mainly of independent directors--Starks is the only St. Jude insider. The firm gets only middling marks for overall stewardship, however. We believe CEO compensation at St. Jude is too generous, and to add insult to injury, the compensation committee has recommended a 10% increase in Starks' base salary for 2006. We like that Starks has a respectable 2.3% stake in the company but were dismayed to see that he received a too-generous 4.5% share of all options granted last year. Board members can elect to receive 100% of their compensation in cash. We'd rather see directors receive substantial equity stakes to better align their interest with those of shareholders. This is a particular issue with St. Jude, from our view, because five of the eight independent directors have joined the board only in the last five years and have not built up meaningful equity stakes.

One Lillehei Plaza
St. Paul, MN 55117
www.sjm.com

Growth [A-]	2002	2003	2004	2005
Revenue %	18.0	21.5	18.7	27.1
Earnings/Share %	55.7	20.5	20.9	-5.5
Book Value/Share %	29.5	0.4	44.7	21.7
Dividends/Share %	NMF	NMF	NMF	NMF

Profitability [A]	2003	2004	2005	TTM
Return on Assets %	13.2	12.7	8.1	8.5
Oper Cash Flow $Mil	474	604	716	652
- Cap Spending $Mil	50	89	159	250
= Free Cash Flow $Mil	425	515	558	402

Financial Health [A]	2003	2004	2005	09-30-06
Long-term Debt $Mil	352	235	177	358
Total Equity $Mil	1,602	2,334	2,883	2,762
Debt/Equity Ratio	0.2	0.1	0.1	0.1

Industry: Medical Equip. | **Business Risk:** Average | **Moat Size:** Narrow | **Investment Style:** Large Growth | **Sector:** Healthcare

Competition

	Market Cap $Mil	12 Mo Trailing Sales $Mil	Price/Cash Flow	Return On Assets%	Debt/Equity	Total Return% 1 Yr	3 Yr
St. Jude Medical	12,923	3,229	19.8	8.5	0.1	-27.2	6.3
Medtronic	61,597	11,808	24.7	14.2	0.5	-6.3	4.1
Boston Scientific	25,323	7,296	12.7	-11.4	0.6	-29.9	-22.0

Price Volatility

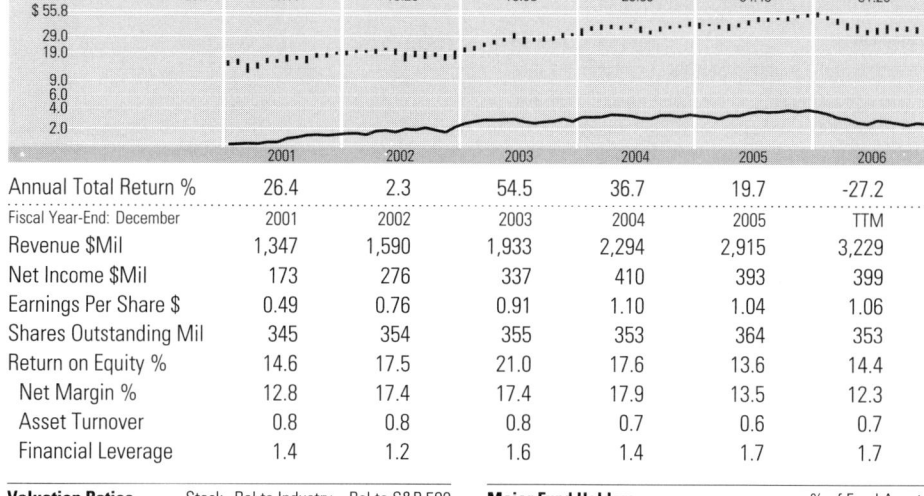

	2001	2002	2003	2004	2005	2006
Annual $Price High	19.51	21.56	32.00	42.90	52.80	54.75
Low	11.11	15.28	19.38	29.90	34.48	31.20
Annual Total Return %	26.4	2.3	54.5	36.7	19.7	-27.2
Fiscal Year-End: December	2001	2002	2003	2004	2005	TTM
Revenue $Mil	1,347	1,590	1,933	2,294	2,915	3,229
Net Income $Mil	173	276	337	410	393	399
Earnings Per Share $	0.49	0.76	0.91	1.10	1.04	1.06
Shares Outstanding Mil	345	354	355	353	364	353
Return on Equity %	14.6	17.5	21.0	17.6	13.6	14.4
Net Margin %	12.8	17.4	17.4	17.9	13.5	12.3
Asset Turnover	0.8	0.8	0.8	0.7	0.6	0.7
Financial Leverage	1.4	1.2	1.6	1.4	1.7	1.7

Valuation Ratios	Stock	Rel to Industry	Rel to S&P 500
Price/Earnings	34.5	1.2	1.7
Price/Book	4.7	0.9	1.1
Price/Sales	4.0	0.9	1.4
Price/Cash Flow	19.8	0.8	1.4

Major Fund Holders	% of Fund Assets
Fidelity Aggressive Growth	5.32
Fidelity Advisor Aggressive Gr A	5.28
AXA Enterprise Large Cap Growth A LW	4.23
Fidelity Select Medical Equip/Systems	3.90

Thesis By Debbie S. Wang, 11-08-06 Stock Price as of Analysis: $33.67

St. Jude Medical benefits from the device industry's high barriers to entry and has dug more of an economic moat for itself.

Originally known as a pioneer in mechanical heart valves, St. Jude branched out considerably with various acquisitions. Diversification has been the key to the firm's growth over the past few years, allowing it to tap into robust markets for implantable cardioverter defibrillators while mechanical heart valve sales continue to decline and tissue valves gain favor. In 2005, cardiac-rhythm management devices accounted for about 75% of total sales, with heart valves contributing only 8%. In addition, St. Jude's purchase of Advanced Neuromodulation Systems offers a substantial footprint in the fast-growing billion-dollar neurostimulation market.

Though sales of implantable cardioverter defibrillators and related cardiac-resynchronization devices saw double-digit growth rates from 2003 through 2005, the market has hit some speed bumps lately thanks to a competitor's extensive product recalls. Nonetheless, St. Jude has taken advantage of competitive stumbles to grab market share, and we believe it's well-positioned to compete once demand for implantable cardioverter defibrillators recovers. We're also excited about St. Jude's Angio-Seal device, which seals the femoral artery following catheterization procedures such as angiograms. This device allows patients to move about more freely and potentially leave the medical facility earlier, and nurses find it easier and safer than the old method of applying manual pressure.

With these products in St. Jude's portfolio, sales growth has leaped into the double digits in the past four years, and operating margins have improved by about 600 basis points since 2001 (excluding special charges). Management has strengthened St. Jude, but the firm remains one beat behind market leaders Medtronic and Boston Scientific, often trailing on innovation. For example, St. Jude didn't get regulatory approval for its cardiac-resynchronization device until mid-2004, while competitors' devices have been on the market since mid-2002. St. Jude's position as a follower rather than a leader is also reflected in its gross margins, which are consistently 200 basis points lower than those of its larger cardiac-rhythm management rivals.

Still, we think there's plenty of room in this growing industry for all three competitors. Even if larger rivals hold an edge on the technology front, St. Jude has done a good job of catching up and giving its competitors a run for their money.

Data as of 12-29-06

Starbucks SBUX

	Rating	Fair Value	Last Close	Consider Buy	Consider Sell	Yield %
	★★★	$35.00	$35.42	$27.00	$43.90	0.00

Industry	Business Risk	Moat Size	Investment Style	Sector
Restaurants	Average	Narrow	Large Growth	Consumer Services

Company Profile

Starbucks has 12,440 stores worldwide, which sell coffee, espresso, tea, and cold blended drinks. The stores offer food, whole bean coffee, coffee-making equipment, a line of CDs, and other merchandise. The firm sells its coffee (under the Starbucks, Seattle's Best, and Torrefazione Italia brands) and Tazo Tea to grocery stores and warehouse clubs. Through joint ventures and other agreements, the company produces and sells branded bottled frappuccino and espresso drinks, ice creams, and liqueurs.

Management   Stewardship Grade [C]

Howard Schultz founded Starbucks in 1985 and has served as its chairman since inception and was also CEO until 2000. Under his leadership, the company has expanded to more than 12,000 stores in 37 countries. CEO James Donald joined Starbucks in 2002 as president of North America and was promoted to his current role in April 2005. Previously, Donald served as chairman and CEO of Pathmark Stores for seven years and held a variety of senior management positions with Albertson's, Safeway, and Wal-Mart.

In fiscal 2005, the chairman and CEO earned a salary plus bonus of $3.6 million and $2.7 million, respectively. Schultz, who beneficially owns 4.1% of Starbucks, also received a very generous package of 1.0 million options, while Donald garnered 800,000 options. Shareholders also had to dole out nearly $1 million for Schultz' personal use of the company aircraft, security services, and other benefits in fiscal 2005. While we were encouraged that the company recently declassified its board, we do not approve of its other takeover defenses, including blank check preferred stock.

2401 Utah Avenue South   www.starbucks.com
Seattle, WA 98134

Growth [A+]	2002	2003	2004	2005
Revenue %	23.9	29.9	20.3	22.3
Earnings/Share %	26.9	42.4	29.8	16.4
Book Value/Share %	21.7	15.9	-13.6	8.7
Dividends/Share %	NMF	NMF	NMF	NMF

Profitability [A]	2003	2004	2005	TTM
Return on Assets %	11.5	14.1	12.7	12.7
Oper Cash Flow $Mil	863	923	1,132	1,132
- Cap Spending $Mil	417	644	771	771
= Free Cash Flow $Mil	446	279	360	360

Financial Health [A]	2003	2004	2005	06-30-06
Long-term Debt $Mil	—	3	2	2
Total Equity $Mil	2,470	2,090	2,229	2,229
Debt/Equity Ratio	—	0.0	0.0	0.0

Competition

	Market Cap $Mil	12 Mo Trailing Sales $Mil	Price/Cash Flow	Return On Assets%	Debt/Equity	Total Return% 1 Yr	3 Yr
Starbucks	26,737	7,787	23.6	12.7	0.0	18.0	29.1
McDonald's	54,825	21,790	13.3	9.4	0.6	34.6	23.9
Tim Hortons	5,581	1,597	20.7	12.5	0.4	—	—

Price Volatility
| Monthly Price High/Low — Relative Strength to S&P 500

Annual $Price High / Low	12.83 / 6.73	12.85 / 9.22	16.72 / 9.81	32.13 / 16.45	32.46 / 22.29	40.01 / 28.72
	2001	2002	2003	2004	2005	2006
Annual Total Return %	-13.9	7.0	62.7	88.1	-3.8	18.0

Fiscal Year-End: September	2002	2003	2004	2005	2006	TTM
Revenue $Mil	3,289	4,076	5,294	6,369	7,787	7,787
Net Income $Mil	210	265	389	494	564	564
Earnings Per Share $	0.26	0.33	0.47	0.61	0.71	0.71
Shares Outstanding Mil	809	780	794	785	763	755
Return on Equity %	12.3	12.8	15.7	23.7	25.3	25.3
Net Margin %	6.4	6.5	7.3	7.8	7.2	7.2
Asset Turnover	1.5	1.5	1.6	1.8	1.8	1.8
Financial Leverage	1.3	1.3	1.4	1.7	2.0	2.0

Valuation Ratios	Stock	Rel to Industry	Rel to S&P 500
Price/Earnings	49.9	1.8	2.4
Price/Book	12.0	2.1	2.9
Price/Sales	3.4	1.7	1.2
Price/Cash Flow	23.6	1.6	1.6

Major Fund Holders	% of Fund Assets
Constellation Sands Capital Inst Growth	8.11
Touchstone Sands Capital Select Growth Z	8.01
MassMutual Select Aggressive Growth S	6.54
Bender Growth C	5.00

Thesis   By John Owens, CFA, CPA, 11-22-06   Stock Price as of Analysis: $36.38

Starbucks is a juggernaut in the specialty coffee retail market, with one of the most recognized and respected brands in the world. The company still has substantial growth opportunities in the U.S. and abroad, but competition outside of the sector is on the rise.

With more than $6 billion of domestic sales last fiscal year, Starbucks has a leading share of the $11 billion U.S. specialty coffee retail market. The Seattle-based company has over 8,800 domestic locations, while the number two chain, Caribou Coffee, has fewer than 500 stores. Furthermore, the coffee giant is strengthening its position, with plans for at least 1,700 domestic openings in fiscal 2007.

We attribute the company's dominance to the powerful Starbucks brand. Its cafes do not sell just a cup of coffee, but an experience. Starbucks baristas, who often greet their regulars by name, hand-craft and customize each customer's drink, with over 55,000 beverage combinations currently available. The stylish cafes, with their eclectic music (available for sale on CDs in stores) and Wi-Fi access, also offer its customers a "third place," an alternative to the home or office where they can relax or work.

The Starbucks brand also resonates with customers abroad. The chain now has more than 3,600 stores in 37 foreign countries, including some with well established cafe cultures like Austria and France. Starbucks has also been embraced in tea-drinking China, with more than 400 units on the mainland, Hong Kong, and Taiwan.

Based on the growing popularity of the brand, we believe Starbucks could eventually expand to 20,000 domestic stores by further penetrating urban and suburban areas and by expanding into smaller towns and off-highway locations. The increasing use of drive-throughs and new breakfast and lunch offerings should also provide a boost to unit volumes, leading to even higher returns on invested capital. We also believe that Starbucks could match its domestic potential in foreign countries, with China ultimately becoming its second-largest market.

Starbucks still faces some challenges. McDonalds and other fast-food chains have rolled out premium roast coffee, and Dunkin' Donuts and Tim Horton's are aggressively expanding, with an increasing focus on coffee and other beverages. We also think the rapidly growing Panera chain offers a competing "third place" for Starbucks' customers. So, we'd still recommend a significant discount to our fair value estimate before investing.

Data as of 12-29-06

Starwood Hotels & Resorts Worldwide HOT

Rating ★★★	Fair Value $57.00	Last Close $62.50	Consider Buy $44.00	Consider Sell $71.40	Yield % 1.34

Company Profile
Starwood owns, leases, or has a majority stake in more than 100 hotels and resorts. As a hotel manager, it runs close to 400 hotels on behalf of third-party owners. Additionally, the firm receives franchise fees from more than 300 hotels. Altogether, Starwood owns, manages, or franchises about 258,000 rooms in 100 countries, under the Sheraton, Westin, St. Regis, W, and Four Points brand names. Sheraton accounts for about half of the rooms.

Management   Stewardship Grade [C]
We are comfortable with CEO Steve Heyer at the helm. His experience as the former chief operating officer at Coca-Cola and on the operating committee at Time Warner gives him the necessary background to continue the innovative branding needed as the firm focuses more on management contracts. His salary and bonus of around $3.5 million is in line with industry peers. He was also awarded $1 million of restricted stock, which should keep his interests aligned with shareholders'. Starwood had been very generous with stock options in the past, granting more than 3% of shares outstanding in 2004. But now that the firm must expense these options, it has moved to a more shareholder-friendly practice of issuing restricted stock to executives.

1111 Westchester Avenue   www.starwoodhotels.com
White Plains, NY 10604

Growth [C]	2002	2003	2004	2005
Revenue %	-1.0	0.9	15.9	11.3
Earnings/Share %	—	NMF	22.7	2.2
Book Value/Share %	—	NMF	6.2	4.1
Dividends/Share %	5.0	0.0	0.0	0.0

Profitability [B]	2003	2004	2005	TTM
Return on Assets %	2.6	3.2	3.4	10.7
Oper Cash Flow $Mil	766	578	764	228
- Cap Spending $Mil	302	333	464	402
= Free Cash Flow $Mil	464	245	300	-174

Financial Health [B-]	2003	2004	2005	12-31-05
Long-term Debt $Mil	4,393	3,823	2,926	2,345
Total Equity $Mil	4,326	4,788	5,211	2,750
Debt/Equity Ratio	1.0	0.8	0.6	0.9

Industry	Business Risk	Moat Size	Investment Style	Sector
Hotels	Average	Narrow	Large Growth	Consumer Services

Competition	Market Cap $Mil	12 Mo Trailing Sales $Mil	Price/Cash Flow	Return On Assets %	Debt/ Equity	Total Return % 1 Yr	3 Yr
Starwood Hotels & Resorts Worldwide	13,250	5,923	58.1	10.7	0.9	21.8	31.0
Marriott International A	18,868	11,720	20.9	7.5	0.6	43.4	28.2
Hilton Hotels	13,493	7,013	42.8	2.8	2.4	45.6	27.7

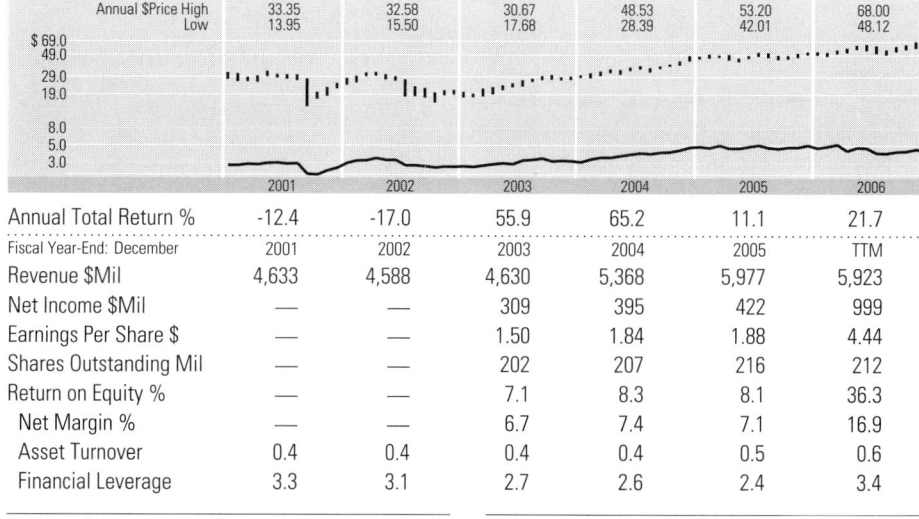

	2001	2002	2003	2004	2005	2006
Annual $Price High	33.35	32.58	30.67	48.53	53.20	68.00
Low	13.95	15.50	17.68	28.39	42.01	48.12
Annual Total Return %	-12.4	-17.0	55.9	65.2	11.1	21.7
Fiscal Year-End: December	2001	2002	2003	2004	2005	TTM
Revenue $Mil	4,633	4,588	4,630	5,368	5,977	5,923
Net Income $Mil	—	—	309	395	422	999
Earnings Per Share $	—	—	1.50	1.84	1.88	4.44
Shares Outstanding Mil	—	—	202	207	216	212
Return on Equity %	—	—	7.1	8.3	8.1	36.3
Net Margin %	—	—	6.7	7.4	7.1	16.9
Asset Turnover	0.4	0.4	0.4	0.4	0.5	0.6
Financial Leverage	3.3	3.1	2.7	2.6	2.4	3.4

Valuation Ratios	Stock	Rel to Industry	Rel to S&P 500
Price/Earnings	13.1	0.5	0.6
Price/Book	4.8	0.8	1.2
Price/Sales	2.2	0.7	0.8
Price/Cash Flow	58.1	1.6	4.0

Major Fund Holders	% of Fund Assets
Fidelity Real Estate Investment	8.12
Alpine U.S. Real Estate Equity	6.42
ING Van Kampen Real Estate S	5.98
Strategic Partners Real Estate Sec A	5.79

Thesis By Jeremy Glaser, 10-18-06 Stock Price as of Analysis: $62.14

Starwood's focus on branding and urban locations has boosted this narrow-moat firm in a resurgent travel market. Additionally, recent asset sales should reduce earnings volatility by making lucrative management contracts a larger part of the business, and they have prepared the firm for any future downturns.

Five luxury urban brands--Sheraton, Westin, The Luxury Collection, St. Regis, and the internally developed W--produce more than 75% of Starwood's cash flows. The company believes in constant improvement, and has engineered significant renovation and repositioning of its brands--the Sheraton and Westin in particular--in order to capture meaningful market share. The W brand is also proving to be a huge success and is attracting a flurry of developer interest. The company is also launching a new midscale hotel brand, aloft, in 2007. These roadside hotels are aimed at travelers who are both style and budget conscious. We think now is a great time to launch this brand to capture the growing demand for suburban midscale hotels.

Starwood is focusing on management contracts to stabilize its core earnings in order to combat the cyclicality of the hotel industry. We believe that the recent sale of nearly $4 billion of hotel properties to Host Hotels is a good step in this direction. Starwood maintains long-term management contracts on these properties, which provide a base fee plus an incentive fee when the company meets certain profitability goals. The contracts produce a more stable income stream, while still allowing Starwood to participate in industry upturns via incentive fees. Although the sale of these properties will initially reduce revenue, we think this is a smart move by Starwood in the long run.

Starwood has mined growth both internally and externally through new segments and brand acquisitions. Starwood is cashing in on a high-growth segment of the travel market by developing time-share vacation resorts and condominium residences for sale. This business accounted for about 18% of Starwood's 2005 revenue and is growing rapidly. We are concerned, however, that this business requires a substantial capital outlay, which makes it riskier than the firm's management business.

We think Starwood has one of the highest-quality portfolios of brands in the business. Given a reasonable margin of safety to our fair value estimate, we would happily check into this stock.

State Street STT

	Rating	Fair Value	Last Close	Consider Buy	Consider Sell	Yield %
	★★	$57.00	$67.44	$44.00	$71.40	1.19

Data as of 12-29-06

Company Profile
State Street primarily provides back-office services for mutual fund companies and other institutional clients such as investment managers, corporations, and pension funds. Clients look to State Street for custody and also management of their assets, the firm's core services. The company also offers services such as foreign exchange, cash management, credit, and electronic trading to help customers negotiate complex global financial markets efficiently.

Management
Stewardship Grade [B]

Ronald Logue became chairman and CEO when David Spina abruptly stepped down in 2004. Spina had been CEO since 2000 and had a long career at the bank behind him. Logue has only been with State Street since 1990, but he proved his mettle by doing an excellent job at integrating the Deutsche Bank purchase. He has pledged to keep State Street on the same course that Spina had set. Executives are well-compensated. Logue pulled in $8.2 million in annual compensation during 2005, plus another estimated $4.3 million in stock options. This put him ahead of all his peers in the group of trust and custody banks. He will have to prove he's worth it by delivering for shareholders in 2006 and beyond. Directors and management collectively own less than 1% of the total shares outstanding. The firm has a poison pill in place, but this is largely superfluous given Massachusetts' stringent antitakeover laws. An acquirer seeking to take control of a company must win majority shareholder approval before purchasing more than 20% of the shares. This virtually ensures State Street's continued independence unless the board chooses to sell.

225 Franklin Street www.statestreet.com
Boston, MA 02110

Growth [B-]	2002	2003	2004	2005
Revenue %	14.9	7.7	4.6	10.5
Earnings/Share %	63.2	-30.6	9.3	6.4
Book Value/Share %	25.7	17.1	6.0	4.7
Dividends/Share %	18.5	16.7	14.3	12.5

Profitability [C]	2003	2004	2005	TTM
Return on Assets %	0.8	0.8	0.9	0.9
Oper Cash Flow $Mil	1,489	416	2,483	—
- Cap Spending $Mil	324	336	314	—
= Free Cash Flow $Mil	—	—	—	—

Financial Health [NA]	2003	2004	2005	09-30-06
Long-term Debt $Mil	—	—	—	—
Total Equity $Mil	5,747	6,159	6,367	7,015
Debt/Equity Ratio	—	—	—	—

Industry	Business Risk	Moat Size	Investment Style	Sector
International Banks	Average	Wide	Large Core	Financial Services

Competition	Market Cap $Mil	12 Mo Trailing Sales $Mil	Price/Cash Flow	Return On Assets%	Debt/Equity	Total Return % 1 Yr	3 Yr
State Street	22,395	6,105	—	0.9	—	23.2	10.9
J.P. Morgan Chase & Co.	167,551	59,650	—	0.9	—	25.6	13.2
Bank of New York Company	41,334	7,308	—	1.5	—	26.9	9.2

Price Volatility | Monthly Price High/Low — Relative Strength to S&P 500

| Annual $Price High | 63.93 | 58.36 | 53.63 | 56.90 | 59.80 | 68.56 |
| Low | 36.25 | 32.11 | 31.29 | 39.91 | 40.62 | 54.39 |

	2001	2002	2003	2004	2005	2006
Annual Total Return %	-15.1	-24.5	35.4	-4.4	14.5	23.2
Fiscal Year-End: December	2001	2002	2003	2004	2005	TTM
Revenue $Mil	3,827	4,396	4,734	4,951	5,473	6,105
Net Income $Mil	628	1,015	722	798	838	1,046
Earnings Per Share $	1.90	3.10	2.15	2.35	2.50	3.12
Shares Outstanding Mil	324	323	331	335	331	332
Return on Equity %	16.3	21.2	12.6	13.0	13.2	14.9
Net Margin %	16.4	23.1	15.3	16.1	15.3	17.1
Asset Turnover	0.1	0.1	0.1	0.1	0.1	0.1
Financial Leverage	18.2	17.9	15.2	15.3	15.4	16.0

Valuation Ratios	Stock	Rel to Industry	Rel to S&P 500
Price/Earnings	21.8	1.2	1.1
Price/Book	3.2	1.2	0.8
Price/Sales	3.7	0.9	1.3
Price/Cash Flow	—	—	—

Major Fund Holders	% of Fund Assets
Pioneer AmPac Growth A	5.25
Pioneer Growth Leaders A	4.62
GE Premier Growth Equity A	4.21
GE Instl Premier Growth Equity Inv	4.20

Thesis By Jeffrey Ptak, CPA, CFA, 12-06-06 Stock Price as of Analysis: $64.60

After dabbling in the corporate lending and trust businesses, State Street has gotten back to basics lately. Management has made several recent acquisitions aimed at beefing up the firm's presence in faster-growing segments of the asset custody business, such as hedge funds and global custody. It has also shed the company's noncore corporate and personal trust units, among other divestitures. Thus, custody and asset management account for the lion's share of revenue and profits anew.

This focused tack makes sense. Scale is vital in the custody business, where back-office functions like transaction-processing and security-pricing entail high fixed costs. With the successful integration of its recently acquired units, State Street stands as one of the largest custodians in the world. In addition, by zeroing in on asset management and custody, management can sharpen its focus on profitability instead of growth for growth's sake. Further, the company's hedge-fund, separate account, and global custody efforts should position it to support one-stop shopping, a key advantage given that demand for back-office solutions is likely to increasingly transcend product type and borders.

With the vast majority of revenue and profit tied to fees that the company levies on assets under management or custody, State Street's success will hinge on its ability to gather assets while keeping a lid on expenses. Here, too, we're encouraged, as State Street's presence abroad should help it exploit the trend toward back-office outsourcing among foreign banks and wealth managers. What's more, the company's asset management unit is a big player in the surging ETF market and boasts considerable name recognition among institutional investors, which have come to rely on its passively managed strategies. On the expense front, management has done a good job of reining in compensation and occupancy costs, reinforcing our confidence in its streamlined strategy.

While switching costs are formidable in the asset-servicing business given the potential disruption any back-office change can cause, State Street still must lock horns with competing global custodians, most notably including Bank of New York and Mellon Financial, which recently announced plans to merge. As such, service quality is likely to remain a key potential differentiator, explaining why personnel and technology outlays will likely make additional operating leverage difficult to achieve.

Data as of 12-29-06

Steel Dynamics STLD

	Rating	Fair Value	Last Close	Consider Buy	Consider Sell	Yield %
	★★★	$32.00	$32.45	$24.70	$40.10	1.08

Company Profile
SDI operates steelmaking minimills in the Midwest and Southeast. Its 4.2 million tons of production capability is split mainly between flat-rolled and steel bar products. About 60% of the company's flat-rolled production consists of high-margin specialty products such as thin-gauge and galvanized steel. The company also operates a scrap substitute facility that manufactures liquid pig iron for use in the company's mills.

Industry	Business Risk	Moat Size	Investment Style	Sector
Steel/Iron	Average	Narrow	Mid Value	Industrial Materials

Competition

	Market Cap $Mil	12 Mo Trailing Sales $Mil	Price/Cash Flow	Return On Assets%	Debt/ Equity	Total Return% 1 Yr	3 Yr
Steel Dynamics	2,981	2,969	7.7	16.1	0.3	86.0	41.6
Mittal Steel Co NV	29,697	28,132	7.5	10.8	0.9	62.5	68.8
Posco ADR	26,486	25,544	5.0	14.5	0.1	67.0	35.0

Management   Stewardship Grade [A]
Steel Dynamics was founded by former Nucor plant manager Keith Busse, along with other financial investors. Busse is a disciple of highly regarded former Nucor CEO Ken Iverson. Like Nucor, SDI employs a culture that provides productivity and cost-reduction incentives for all employees in the form of cash bonuses and options. Management has shown that it has a clear, controlled strategy to develop this business and that it can tighten the belt and cut costs when it has to. We like that insiders own 18% of the company. The directors with the largest stakes represent the private-capital firms that originally financed SDI. The fact that these funds retained a large portion of their ownership is a strong vote of confidence for this company's potential. Management runs SDI from the perspective of a shareholder, and Busse and his team are looking to generate returns on their investment through stock appreciation rather than corporate perks and bloated salaries. We hold SDI's corporate governance in high regard and have awarded the company a Stewardship Grade of A.

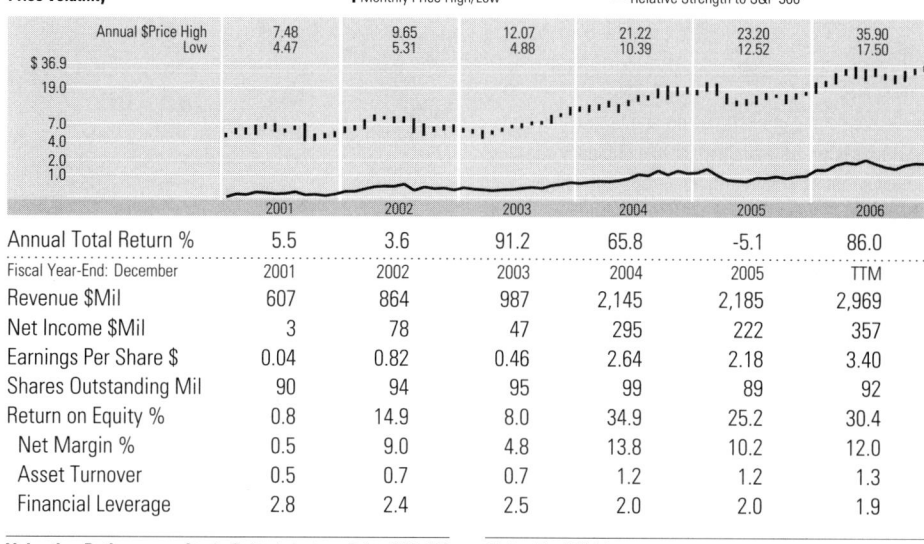

Price Volatility

Annual Total Return %	5.5	3.6	91.2	65.8	-5.1	86.0
Fiscal Year-End: December	2001	2002	2003	2004	2005	TTM
Revenue $Mil	607	864	987	2,145	2,185	2,969
Net Income $Mil	3	78	47	295	222	357
Earnings Per Share $	0.04	0.82	0.46	2.64	2.18	3.40
Shares Outstanding Mil	90	94	95	99	89	92
Return on Equity %	0.8	14.9	8.0	34.9	25.2	30.4
Net Margin %	0.5	9.0	4.8	13.8	10.2	12.0
Asset Turnover	0.5	0.7	0.7	1.2	1.2	1.3
Financial Leverage	2.8	2.4	2.5	2.0	2.0	1.9

Valuation Ratios

	Stock	Rel to Industry	Rel to S&P 500
Price/Earnings	9.6	0.7	0.5
Price/Book	2.5	0.5	0.6
Price/Sales	1.0	0.4	0.3
Price/Cash Flow	7.7	0.6	0.5

Major Fund Holders

	% of Fund Assets
Quaker Mid-Cap Value A	2.40
Navellier Fundamental A	2.30
JHancock Mid Cap Equity A	1.84
Putnam Capital Opportunities A	1.82

6714 Pointe Inverness Way Suite 200   www.steeldynamics.com
Fort Wayne, IN 46804

Growth [A-]	2002	2003	2004	2005
Revenue %	42.4	14.2	117.3	1.9
Earnings/Share %	EUB	-44.5	479.1	-17.5
Book Value/Share %	17.9	3.2	33.4	14.2
Dividends/Share %	NMF	NMF	NMF	60.0

Profitability [A]	2003	2004	2005	TTM
Return on Assets %	3.3	17.0	12.6	16.1
Oper Cash Flow $Mil	128	248	311	389
- Cap Spending $Mil	137	102	63	102
= Free Cash Flow $Mil	-10	146	247	287

Financial Health [A]	2003	2004	2005	09-30-06
Long-term Debt $Mil	592	442	438	402
Total Equity $Mil	587	847	880	1,173
Debt/Equity Ratio	1.0	0.5	0.5	0.3

Thesis   By Scott Burns, 12-15-06 Stock Price as of Analysis: $33.05

Amid a renaissance in the oft-maligned steel industry, Steel Dynamics (SDI) stands out as one of the lowest-cost, most efficient domestic steel producers. SDI's new mills and niche strategy generate strong returns and anchor a narrow economic moat.

The steel industry is in the midst of an unprecedented boom, and SDI is riding this wave as well as any other steel producer. Starting with the second quarter of 2004, SDI's quarterly results were not only record quarters, but often would have been record years prior to this period. Soaring prices led to massive operating leverage, and SDI has regularly posted double digit operating margins since.

We consider much of this remarkable performance to be more the exception than the rule. However, SDI has shown the ability to generate returns even when market conditions aren't ideal. As a minimill, SDI enjoys advantages over integrated steel mills like United States Steel, including lower energy, raw-material, and labor costs. Operating efficiencies also set SDI apart from the pack. Because its minimills are relatively new, SDI needs shorter lead times to fill orders and experiences less maintenance downtime than most mills.

SDI's flexibility enables the company to pursue higher-margin niche products. For instance, SDI has integrated its production lines so that the product can roll right off presses into various coating operations. SDI saves customers as much as $20 per ton in transportation costs by directly coating and painting products rather than shipping them to a different mill for processing.

Recently, SDI has reaped the rewards of its operating model in the form of record cash flow. Management has been shrewdly using this cash to pay down debt, make selective and accretive acquisitions, and to fund brownfield expansion projects at its current facilities. The company also began paying a dividend and has been actively buying back shares at what we consider to be attractive prices. Finally, although the company's Messabi Nugget scrap substitute program suffered a huge setback, we expect SDI to continue investing in scrap substitute programs as it looks for ways to control its largest input cost.

For all of SDI's considerable advantages, we would exercise caution with this stock. After all, the steel industry has a history of boom and bust cycles that can test even the strongest companies.

Stericycle SRCL

Data as of 12-29-06

Rating	Fair Value	Last Close	Consider Buy	Consider Sell	Yield %
★★	$66.00	$75.50	$50.90	$82.70	0.00

Company Profile
Stericycle is the largest medical-waste company in North America, collecting, transporting, and treating medical waste for 346,000 customers. The firm also offers consulting services that help its customers comply with regulatory standards. In 1999, Stericycle purchased the medical-waste business of Browning-Ferris, tripling its revenue. Stericycle's proprietary electrothermal deactivation technology uses low-frequency radio waves to destroy infectious pathogens.

Management
Stewardship Grade [B]

Stericycle's management has done a terrific job. Led by Mark Miller, CEO since 1992, the company has proved adept at integrating numerous acquisitions without compromising profitability or returns on capital. We've been impressed by management's willingness to discontinue large accounts that are generating unsatisfactory margins, sacrificing revenue to improve overall profitability. Management has a significant stake in the company. Directors and executive officers collectively own about 7% of outstanding shares; Miller himself owns about 3%, as does chairman Jack Schuler. Both Miller and Schuler previously held senior-level positions at pharmaceutical and health-care firm Abbott Laboratories before joining Stericycle.

28161 North Keith Drive
Lake Forest, IL 60045
www.stericycle.com

Growth [A-]	2002	2003	2004	2005
Revenue %	11.8	12.9	13.9	18.1
Earnings/Share %	188.6	41.6	18.2	-12.4
Book Value/Share %	30.5	22.8	20.8	7.4
Dividends/Share %	NMF	NMF	NMF	NMF

Profitability [A-]	2003	2004	2005	TTM
Return on Assets %	9.3	9.4	6.4	5.9
Oper Cash Flow $Mil	124	115	94	118
- Cap Spending $Mil	21	33	26	32
= Free Cash Flow $Mil	103	81	68	86

Financial Health [B]	2003	2004	2005	09-30-06
Long-term Debt $Mil	163	190	349	423
Total Equity $Mil	408	495	522	605
Debt/Equity Ratio	0.4	0.4	0.7	0.7

Industry	Business Risk	Moat Size	Investment Style	Sector
Waste Management	Average	Wide	Mid Growth	Business Services

Competition	Market Cap $Mil	12 Mo Trailing Sales $Mil	Price/Cash Flow	Return On Assets%	Debt/ Equity	Total Return% 1 Yr	3 Yr
Stericycle	3,351	747	28.4	5.9	0.7	28.2	16.6
Waste Management	19,672	13,452	7.8	5.7	1.3	24.2	10.1
Republic Services A	5,307	3,043	9.2	6.1	1.2	9.9	17.6

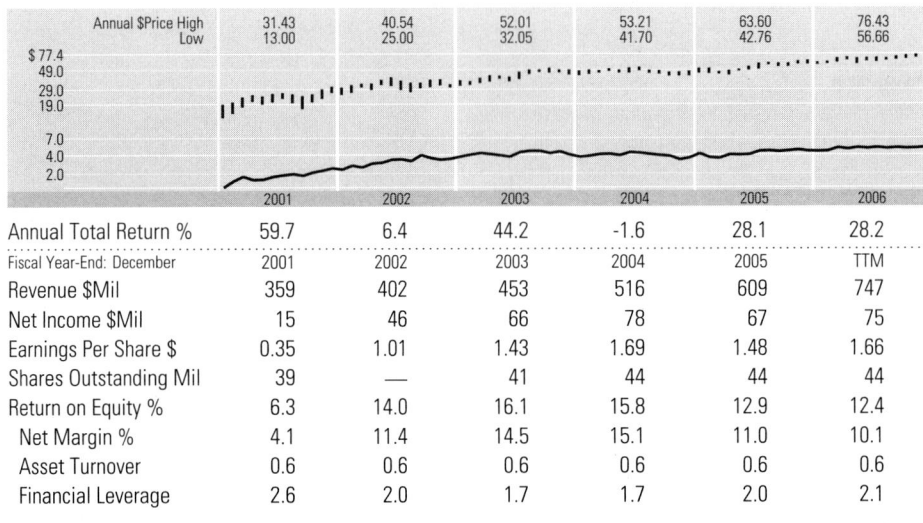

Price Volatility — Monthly Price High/Low — Relative Strength to S&P 500

	2001	2002	2003	2004	2005	2006
Annual $Price High	31.43	40.54	52.01	53.21	63.60	76.43
Low	13.00	25.00	32.05	41.70	42.76	56.66
Annual Total Return %	59.7	6.4	44.2	-1.6	28.1	28.2

Fiscal Year-End: December	2001	2002	2003	2004	2005	TTM
Revenue $Mil	359	402	453	516	609	747
Net Income $Mil	15	46	66	78	67	75
Earnings Per Share $	0.35	1.01	1.43	1.69	1.48	1.66
Shares Outstanding Mil	39	—	41	44	44	44
Return on Equity %	6.3	14.0	16.1	15.8	12.9	12.4
Net Margin %	4.1	11.4	14.5	15.1	11.0	10.1
Asset Turnover	0.6	0.6	0.6	0.6	0.6	0.6
Financial Leverage	2.6	2.0	1.7	1.7	2.0	2.1

Valuation Ratios	Stock	Rel to Industry	Rel to S&P 500
Price/Earnings	45.5	1.9	2.2
Price/Book	5.5	1.6	1.3
Price/Sales	4.5	2.4	1.6
Price/Cash Flow	28.4	2.8	1.9

Major Fund Holders	% of Fund Assets
Eagle Growth	6.91
Fidelity Select Environmental	5.11
Chase Mid Cap Growth A	3.47
BNY Hamilton Small Cap Core Equity Instl	3.44

Thesis By Brian Nelson, 10-27-06 Stock Price as of Analysis: $70.46

Stericycle's nondiscretionary service, dominant market position, low-cost operations, and vertically integrated network create a wide economic moat around its business.

Through numerous acquisitions, including Browning-Ferris' medical-waste operations in November 1999 (which tripled its revenue), Stericycle has become a dominant player, with 16% market share--15 times the size of the next-largest competitor. Its unrivaled scale, geographic reach, and integrated operations have enabled the firm to become the industry's low-cost operator, since few additional expenses are required to add customers to existing truck routes. Increased collection route density and waste volume leverage have helped Stericycle put up the industry's best operating margins (25%-30%) in recent years.

Such strong returns have attracted new entrants, such as Waste Management in early 2005, but competition will probably fall short of shoveling dirt into Stericycle's wide moat. Political opposition and stringent federal regulation requiring the proper handling/disposal of medical waste (it cannot just be left on the curbside) impede new entrants and render Stericycle's existing network of 45 treatment centers nearly impossible to duplicate. Its patented and environment-friendly electrothermal deactivation treatment technology makes attaining new permits for treatment facilities easier, further separating it from competitors. Since customers are responsible for their medical waste from generation to disposal (and could face hefty fines for mishandled waste), Stericycle's reputation for quality and safety--as evidenced by 95%-plus customer retention rates--is yet another advantage that shuts the door on unproven rivals.

What's more, Stericycle is poised to generate solid internal growth and margin expansion in coming years through the continued addition of higher-margin, low-volume customers (outpatient clinics, medical and dental offices, and so on). Small customers fear the hefty fines related to noncompliance and cannot economically justify building out their own waste-treatment facilities. As a result, Stericycle garners solid pricing and lofty gross margins (55%-60%) from these accounts--which have skyrocketed to 63% of sales in 2005 from just over 30% in 1996. We expect this favorable mix shift to continue as the health-care industry moves to smaller, less-expensive patient-care facilities to assuage cost-containment pressures.

Strayer Education STRA

Data as of 12-29-06

	Rating	Fair Value	Last Close	Consider Buy	Consider Sell	Yield %
	★★★	$117.00	$106.05	$90.20	$146.60	1.00

Company Profile

Strayer Education is a for-profit, postsecondary education company. It dates back to 1892, when it was called Strayer's Business College of Baltimore City. Since then, it has expanded to 43 campuses, mostly in the Mid-Atlantic region, close to its roots. It offers a predominantly business-oriented and information-technology curriculum, and 93% of its students pursue associate, bachelor's, and master's degrees.

Management   Stewardship Grade [B]

We like Strayer's management team and good corporate stewardship. Robert Silberman has been chairman of the board since February 2003 and CEO since March 2001. The management team joined in 2001 when the company underwent a recapitalization and invested significantly in its online infrastructure, a strategy that has proved very fruitful. Since then growth has accelerated and average returns on invested capital have more than doubled. Silberman owns 3.6% of shares outstanding, while all executives and directors collectively own 5.5%, enough to align their interests with those of shareholders. Of some concern, Silberman received a whopping 36% of all options granted in 2005. However, option grants overall are very modest at just 1.65%, 0.56%, and 1.88% of total shares outstanding in 2003, 2004, and 2005, respectively. We like that management is responsive to shareholders and focuses on long-term returns on invested capital instead of earnings. We give kudos to management for helping to keep the firm out of regulatory trouble, unlike many of its peers. Our Stewardship Grade would increase if the company split the chairman and CEO roles.

1100 Wilson Blvd. Suite 2500   www.strayereducation.com
Arlington, VA 22209

Growth [B+]	2002	2003	2004	2005
Revenue %	25.7	26.0	24.6	20.4
Earnings/Share %	14.8	27.5	20.7	19.0
Book Value/Share %	NMF	326.3	290.3	0.6
Dividends/Share %	0.0	0.0	55.8	54.3

Profitability [A+]	2003	2004	2005	TTM
Return on Assets %	15.6	19.0	21.3	19.6
Oper Cash Flow $Mil	49	58	55	60
- Cap Spending $Mil	7	11	12	11
= Free Cash Flow $Mil	42	47	43	48

Financial Health [A+]	2003	2004	2005	09-30-06
Long-term Debt $Mil	—	—	—	—
Total Equity $Mil	33	149	152	166
Debt/Equity Ratio	—	—	—	—

Industry	Business Risk	Moat Size	Investment Style	Sector
Education	Average	Wide	Small Growth	Consumer Services

Competition

	Market Cap $Mil	12 Mo Trailing Sales $Mil	Price/Cash Flow	Return On Assets%	Debt/Equity	Total Return% 1 Yr	3 Yr
Strayer Education	1,523	251	25.5	19.6	—	14.3	0.4
Apollo Group A	6,733	2,409	11.3	43.5	0.2	-35.5	-17.5
DeVry	1,983	867	15.7	6.3	0.1	40.3	3.9

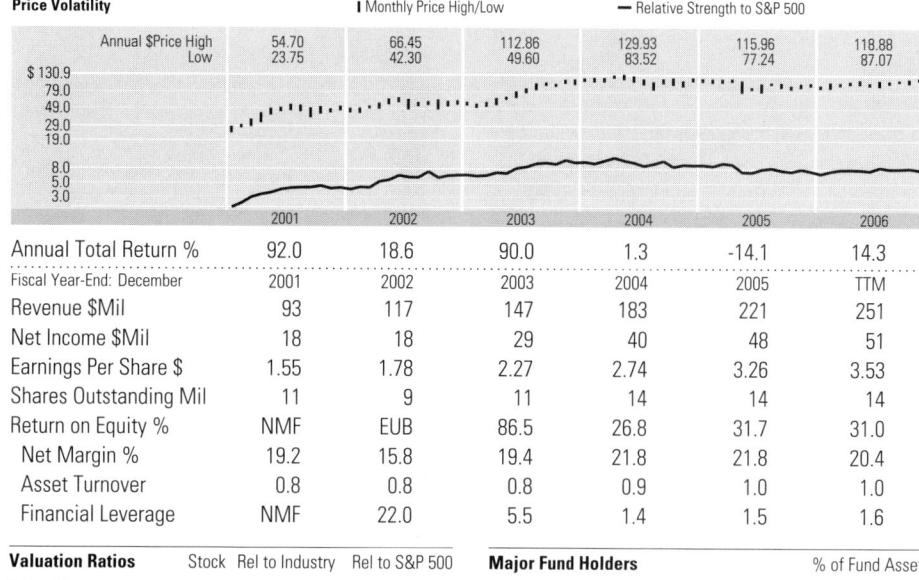

Annual $Price High	54.70	66.45	112.86	129.93	115.96	118.88
Low	23.75	42.30	49.60	83.52	77.24	87.07
	2001	2002	2003	2004	2005	2006
Annual Total Return %	92.0	18.6	90.0	1.3	-14.1	14.3
Fiscal Year-End: December	2001	2002	2003	2004	2005	TTM
Revenue $Mil	93	117	147	183	221	251
Net Income $Mil	18	18	29	40	48	51
Earnings Per Share $	1.55	1.78	2.27	2.74	3.26	3.53
Shares Outstanding Mil	11	9	11	14	14	14
Return on Equity %	NMF	EUB	86.5	26.8	31.7	31.0
Net Margin %	19.2	15.8	19.4	21.8	21.8	20.4
Asset Turnover	0.8	0.8	0.8	0.9	1.0	1.0
Financial Leverage	NMF	22.0	5.5	1.4	1.5	1.6

Valuation Ratios	Stock	Rel to Industry	Rel to S&P 500
Price/Earnings	30.0	1.2	1.5
Price/Book	9.2	0.4	2.2
Price/Sales	6.1	0.6	2.1
Price/Cash Flow	25.5	1.7	1.7

Major Fund Holders	% of Fund Assets
Transamerica Premier Focus Inv	5.14
Delaware Pooled Focus Smid-Cap Gr Eq	4.75
Calvert Capital Accumulation A	3.36
Morgan Stanley Inst Small Co Gr A	3.04

Thesis By Kristan Rowland, 10-16-06 Stock Price as of Analysis: $109.56

Strayer Education enjoys high returns on invested capital, strong operating leverage, and robust free cash flow.

For-profit education is a good business. Wide-moat firms like Apollo Group and Strayer have generated returns on invested capital north of 90% by targeting an underserved adult market. We think Strayer will keep generating returns well in excess of its cost of capital, thanks to its solid reputation and the industry's high barriers to entry. The firm's established brand gives it an edge over any potential startups. It offers curriculum in core areas like business administration and information technology, and 81% of its students earn bachelor's and master's degrees, which are pricier to obtain. In addition, Strayer has passed along tuition price increases of about 5% per year without any trouble, boosting growth.

Top-flight firms like Strayer possess regional accreditation, which is difficult to obtain and contributes to their economic moat. Membership follows a period of candidacy lasting as long as five years, and periodic reviews are required for continued accreditation. Regional accreditation also is indicative of quality. Regional accreditation standards often transcend local and state requirements for universities that are authorized at only the state level. It is also key in evaluating transfers of credit and applications to graduate schools, aspects important to many students. Furthermore, it allows institutions like Strayer to tap into federal student-aid programs, expanding the pool of students that it can attract. About 70% of its revenue is derived from federal financial-aid programs, still well below the 90% limit permitted for a for-profit education company.

Competition for students could hurt Strayer's margins over the long term. Traditional schools have added more programs with flexible schedules at lower tuition levels to capitalize on the adult market opportunity. However, because the market is so large and underserved, we think there's more than enough opportunity for incumbents like Strayer to keep growing very profitably.

Strayer should further benefit from U.S. economic trends, including the increasing awareness of the benefits of a college education, the rise of the knowledge-based economy, and adults returning to school. Also, shrinking budgets of traditional colleges and universities, along with capacity constraints at traditional institutions, should allow many of the for-profits, like Strayer, to grow at impressive rates.

Data as of 12-29-06

Stryker SYK

	Rating	Fair Value	Last Close	Consider Buy	Consider Sell	Yield %
	★★★	$51.00	$55.11	$43.50	$67.00	0.40

Company Profile

Stryker develops, manufactures, and markets medical devices and equipment for use primarily in orthopedic procedures. The firm generates most of its revenue from reconstructive implants like knees and hips. Stryker also offers a range of operating room equipment and tools used for orthopedic and other procedures. Hospital beds, stretchers, and rehabilitation services account for the rest of Stryker's sales.

Industry	Business Risk	Moat Size	Investment Style	Sector
Medical Equip.	Below Avg	Wide	Large Growth	Healthcare

Competition

	Market Cap $Mil	12 Mo Trailing Sales $Mil	Price/Cash Flow	Return On Assets%	Debt/ Equity	Total Return% 1 Yr	3 Yr
Stryker	22,439	5,221	25.1	14.1	0.0	24.5	9.9
Johnson & Johnson	191,415	52,252	14.5	18.5	0.0	12.4	10.8
Zimmer Holdings	18,705	3,410	17.9	13.4	0.0	16.2	3.8

Price Volatility

	2001	2002	2003	2004	2005	2006
Annual $Price High	31.60	33.73	42.68	57.66	56.32	55.92
Low	21.65	21.93	29.83	40.30	39.74	39.77
Annual Total Return %	15.6	15.2	26.9	13.7	-7.7	24.5

Fiscal Year-End: December	2001	2002	2003	2004	2005	TTM
Revenue $Mil	2,602	3,012	3,625	4,262	4,872	5,221
Net Income $Mil	267	346	454	466	675	760
Earnings Per Share $	0.67	0.85	1.11	1.14	1.64	1.85
Shares Outstanding Mil	387	395	398	401	404	407
Return on Equity %	25.3	23.1	21.0	16.9	20.8	19.0
Net Margin %	10.3	11.5	12.5	10.9	13.9	14.6
Asset Turnover	1.1	1.1	1.1	1.0	1.0	1.0
Financial Leverage	2.3	1.9	1.5	1.5	1.5	1.4

Management   Stewardship Grade [C]

We give Stryker a fair Stewardship Grade. Chairman John Brown stepped down as CEO in 2005 after a very successful run spanning nearly three decades. He continues to own about 5% of Stryker, which should align him with other shareholders. In a better stewardship environment, we'd expect Brown's $1 billion stake at recent prices plus associated dividends to be enough incentive for him to continue striving for Stryker's success. We question his need for hefty cash compensation ($1 million in 2005 and $500,000 in 2006) as chairman. Maybe board members are loath to rein in Brown's compensation given their healthy pay packages of $110,000 and 8,000 options annually. Stephen MacMillan stepped into the CEO role after Brown retired. He's a relative newcomer to Stryker, joining the firm in 2003 after executive-level stints at large pharmaceutical and consumer-goods firms. This is MacMillan's first time in the CEO position, and we think the transition from Brown to MacMillan has been smooth so far. Stryker's founding family also remains very influential with a 20% stake through various trusts and a board seat. Advisory committee members for those trusts own an additional 6% of Stryker through other means.

2725 Fairfield Road
Kalamazoo, MI 49002
www.stryker.com

Growth [B]	2002	2003	2004	2005
Revenue %	15.7	20.4	17.6	14.3
Earnings/Share %	26.9	30.6	2.7	43.9
Book Value/Share %	39.0	43.1	27.7	17.2
Dividends/Share %	20.0	16.7	28.6	22.2

Profitability [A+]	2003	2004	2005	TTM
Return on Assets %	14.4	11.4	13.7	14.1
Oper Cash Flow $Mil	649	593	864	893
- Cap Spending $Mil	145	188	272	239
= Free Cash Flow $Mil	504	406	592	655

Financial Health [A+]	2003	2004	2005	09-30-06
Long-term Debt $Mil	19	1	184	1
Total Equity $Mil	2,155	2,752	3,252	3,991
Debt/Equity Ratio	0.0	0.0	0.1	0.0

Valuation Ratios	Stock	Rel to Industry	Rel to S&P 500
Price/Earnings	29.8	1.0	1.4
Price/Book	5.6	1.0	1.4
Price/Sales	4.3	0.9	1.5
Price/Cash Flow	25.1	1.0	1.7

Major Fund Holders	% of Fund Assets
Jensen J	5.24
Biondo Growth Inv	4.91
Live Oak Health Sciences	4.85
Pioneer AmPac Growth A	4.85

Thesis By Julie Stralow, CFA, 12-13-06 Stock Price as of Analysis: $55.45

As a leading provider of orthopedic devices, surgical equipment, and medical furniture, Stryker generates excellent returns on invested capital. This key health-care facility supplier has dug a wide economic moat and faces below-average risks, in our opinion.

We think Stryker pursues attractive niches within the health-care industry. We especially like its top-tier position in the highly profitable orthopedic implant market, which possesses high entry barriers and sticky customer relationships. The firm has led the charge in ceramic-on-ceramic hip replacements; these implants exhibit lower wear, and therefore longer life expectancy, than metal-on-metal or metal-on-plastic options. Stryker also remains focused on relatively higher growth opportunities in the orthopedic implant market, including spine treatments and orthobiologics.

Stryker doesn't just stop at implant devices. It also outfits surgical suites and regular hospital rooms with various tools and equipment. Stryker remains particularly prolific in the operating room with products including cutting tools, medical video equipment, and irrigation devices. These tools often complement its orthopedic devices and greatly improve the efficiency of surgical procedures. Stryker is even a top provider of medical beds and emergency equipment like stretchers. While not as fundamentally attractive as implants, these offerings grow at fast rates, and Stryker's continued prowess in this niche makes the firm an indispensable supplier to the medical community.

Potential headwinds loom for health-care suppliers like Stryker, though. As medical costs seem to continually spiral out of control, third-party payers are taking aim at some of the most profitable procedures, including orthopedic reconstruction. These rates may have to be cut to support the higher unit volumes expected during the next couple of decades. With potential rate changes, Stryker and other medical suppliers may have to improve their own manufacturing or material costs in order to maintain existing returns on invested capital.

Even if some pricing pressure ensues, we still think returns will continue to exceed capital costs many times over at Stryker. Long-term demand trends look promising in the firm's chosen niches, and we think Stryker possesses the right tools to benefit from those growth opportunities.

Data as of 12-29-06

Student Loan STU

Company Profile
Student Loan is 80% owned by Citigroup and was a Citibank division until it listed on the New York Stock Exchange in 1992. Student Loan provides educational loans, principally government-backed, to students and parents; it is one of the largest originators and holders of government-backed student loans in the United States.

Management Stewardship Grade [B]
We think CEO--and recently appointed chairman--Michael Reardon runs a pretty tight ship. Nonetheless, we would like to see Reardon take a position in Student Loan stock. Directors and officers collectively own just 4,400 of the 20 million shares outstanding--not enough, in our opinion. This is a little surprising, given the firm's attractive economics, but we think we know why: Management participates in Citigroup's incentive program, rather than a separate one for Student Loan. We don't think the lack of management ownership should concern investors too much because the management team seems to follow investor-friendly practices. For instance, the firm pays an above-average dividend and it typically increases its dividend commensurately with increases in net income. Student Loan does not issue options, so shareholders need not worry about their ownership stakes being diluted. Also, because there is no Wall Street coverage of the firm, the management team devotes its time almost exclusively to managing the business, rather than analysts' expectations, which we view as a clear plus.

750 Washington Blvd. www.studentloan.com
Stamford, CT 06901

Growth [B+]	2002	2003	2004	2005
Revenue %	NMF	NMF	27.2	7.7
Earnings/Share %	29.5	21.0	34.3	8.4
Book Value/Share %	17.3	21.8	23.2	18.7
Dividends/Share %	0.0	10.0	16.9	20.0

Profitability [C+]	2003	2004	2005	TTM
Return on Assets %	0.9	1.1	1.2	1.2
Oper Cash Flow $Mil	-1,203	383	211	—
- Cap Spending $Mil	25	24	12	—
= Free Cash Flow $Mil	—	—	—	—

Financial Health [NA]	2003	2004	2005	09-30-06
Long-term Debt $Mil	—	—	—	—
Total Equity $Mil	931	1,147	1,362	1,519
Debt/Equity Ratio	—	—	—	—

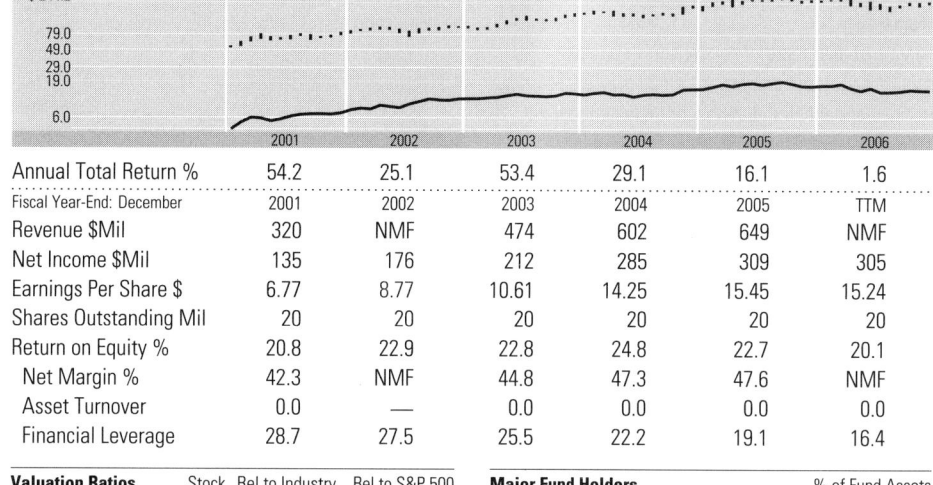

	Rating	Fair Value	Last Close	Consider Buy	Consider Sell	Yield %
	★★★★	$235.00	$207.30	$200.20	$308.50	2.40

Industry	Business Risk	Moat Size	Investment Style	Sector
Finance	Below Avg	Narrow	Mid Core	Financial Services

Competition

	Market Cap $Mil	12 Mo Trailing Sales $Mil	Price/Cash Flow	Return On Assets%	Debt/ Equity	Total Return% 1 Yr	3 Yr
Student Loan	4,146	NMF	—	1.2	—	1.6	15.8
Bank of America	239,758	68,368	—	1.3	—	20.7	15.2
Wells Fargo	120,049	34,770	—	1.7	—	16.8	10.4

	2001	2002	2003	2004	2005	2006
Annual Total Return %	54.2	25.1	53.4	29.1	16.1	1.6
Fiscal Year-End: December	2001	2002	2003	2004	2005	TTM
Revenue $Mil	320	NMF	474	602	649	NMF
Net Income $Mil	135	176	212	285	309	305
Earnings Per Share $	6.77	8.77	10.61	14.25	15.45	15.24
Shares Outstanding Mil	20	20	20	20	20	20
Return on Equity %	20.8	22.9	22.8	24.8	22.7	20.1
Net Margin %	42.3	NMF	44.8	47.3	47.6	NMF
Asset Turnover	0.0	—	0.0	0.0	0.0	0.0
Financial Leverage	28.7	27.5	25.5	22.2	19.1	16.4

Valuation Ratios	Stock	Rel to Industry	Rel to S&P 500
Price/Earnings	13.6	0.7	0.7
Price/Book	2.7	0.6	0.7
Price/Sales	6.4	1.2	2.2
Price/Cash Flow	—	—	—

Major Fund Holders	% of Fund Assets
Artisan Opportunistic Value Inv	4.42
Artisan Mid Cap Value	4.19
Ave Maria Catholic Values	3.27
Schwartz Value	2.99

Thesis By Ryan Batchelor, CPA, 12-13-06 Stock Price as of Analysis: $200.62

Student Loan is an attractive narrow-moat company that is lightly traded and has very little exposure on Wall Street. Thus, about the only thing that moves the share price is the firm's performance, which makes this a great investment candidate, in our view.

For large lenders like Student Loan and Sallie Mae, the federally guaranteed student loan business is extremely attractive. Student loan growth is insensitive to economic conditions; students enroll in both good and bad economies. Also, there is very little interest-rate risk or credit risk, thanks to governmental subsidies and guarantees.

To protect lenders against fluctuating interest rates, the government provides lenders with a guaranteed spread on loans over and above a variable interest rate. When interest rates rise, lenders maintain a steady interest margin because of government subsidies. In the past, lenders received an even bigger boost in low-rate environments, thanks to floor income, which was essentially a payment from the government to lenders when their cost of funds dropped below the rate students were charged (the floor rate). Floor income has essentially gone away now, thanks to new governmental rules, so recent profits have taken a hit. However, most of the government subsidies remain, and we think the future for student lending still looks extremely bright.

The overall outlook for student loan growth remains strong as the costs of higher education continue to rise, resulting in students using loans to finance their education. Additionally, because Congress has not increased loan limits in step with tuition costs, the market for private student loans has seen double-digit growth in recent years as students seek ways to fill the funding gap. While we expect the limits for federally guaranteed loans to rise over time, there's ample opportunity for lenders like Student Loan to see continued loan expansion in private loan portfolios, which are extremely profitable.

Citigroup's majority ownership presents some pros and cons. Because Citi owns 80% of this firm, Student Loan has access to low-cost borrowings, world-class lending experience, and a great pipeline of federal and private student loan originations. However, the stock is relatively illiquid, with only about 12,000 shares trading hands daily. We believe this makes Student Loan unattractive to institutional investors and explains the lack of Wall Street coverage. For investors who are undeterred by this, we think Student Loan would make a solid holding.

Data as of 12-29-06

Suburban Propane Partners SPH

	Rating	Fair Value	Last Close	Consider Buy	Consider Sell	Yield %
	★★★	$38.00	$38.01	$29.30	$47.60	6.64

Company Profile
Suburban Propane Partners distributes propane to about 830,000 customers primarily in the East Coast and West Coast regions of the United States. It also distributes fuel oil and other refined fuels to about 136,000 customers in the Northeastern United States. Other operations include natural-gas and electricity marketing in the deregulated markets of New York and Pennsylvania and installation and service of heating, ventilation, and air conditioning equipment.

Management   Stewardship Grade [C]
A five-member board of supervisors oversees Suburban. Three members are elected by unitholders, and two are appointed by the management-owned general partner. Mark Alexander is one of the appointed board members and also acts as CEO, a post he has held since 1996. Michael Dunn is the other appointed member and is also the president of the partnership. Dunn was promoted to president in May 2005 from senior vice president of corporate development. In 2006, Alexander earned $1,392,011, including $906,013 in bonuses, which seems reasonable to us. Furthermore, we are pleased to see that Alexander beneficially owns 1,055,010 Suburban Propane units, worth $40 million at current prices.

In August 2006, Suburban announced its intention to acquire its general partner's incentive distribution rights and interests in Suburban and its operations for 2.3 million common units. As a result of this transaction, the general partner will no longer have a 15% claim on future distribution growth. This removes the management team's disproportionate share of distribution growth, placing the team in the same boat as common unitholders. When the proposed transaction occurs, common unitholders would elect all members of the board of supervisors.

240 Route 10 West   www.suburbanpropane.com
Whippany, NJ 07981

Growth [D+]	2003	2004	2005	2006
Revenue %	15.7	77.8	23.9	2.6
Earnings/Share %	-12.3	-4.3	NMF	NMF
Book Value/Share %	323.2	73.8	-53.9	27.4
Dividends/Share %	2.2	3.2	2.6	3.3

Profitability [B]	2004	2005	2006	TTM
Return on Assets %	5.3	-0.8	9.2	9.2
Oper Cash Flow $Mil	93	39	170	170
- Cap Spending $Mil	27	29	23	23
= Free Cash Flow $Mil	67	10	147	147

Financial Health [C+]	2004	2005	2006	06-30-06
Long-term Debt $Mil	473	548	548	548
Total Equity $Mil	167	78	103	103
Debt/Equity Ratio	2.8	7.0	5.3	5.3

Industry	Business Risk	Moat Size	Investment Style	Sector
Oil/Gas Products	Average	Narrow	Small Value	Energy

Competition	Market Cap $Mil	12 Mo Trailing Sales $Mil	Price/Cash Flow	Return On Assets%	Debt/Equity	Total Return% 1 Yr	3 Yr
Suburban Propane Partners	1,152	1,662	6.8	9.2	5.3	57.0	14.6
Energy Transfer Partners	5,999	7,859	11.0	7.3	1.6	65.5	47.7
AmeriGas Partners	1,848	2,119	10.4	5.6	4.3	24.0	13.3

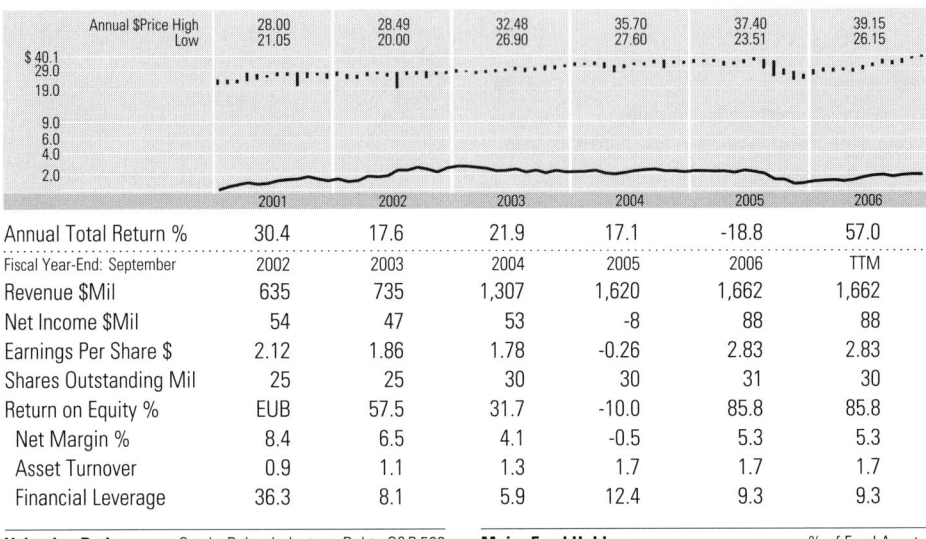

Annual Total Return %	30.4	17.6	21.9	17.1	-18.8	57.0
Fiscal Year-End: September	2002	2003	2004	2005	2006	TTM
Revenue $Mil	635	735	1,307	1,620	1,662	1,662
Net Income $Mil	54	47	53	-8	88	88
Earnings Per Share $	2.12	1.86	1.78	-0.26	2.83	2.83
Shares Outstanding Mil	25	25	30	30	31	30
Return on Equity %	EUB	57.5	31.7	-10.0	85.8	85.8
Net Margin %	8.4	6.5	4.1	-0.5	5.3	5.3
Asset Turnover	0.9	1.1	1.3	1.7	1.7	1.7
Financial Leverage	36.3	8.1	5.9	12.4	9.3	9.3

Valuation Ratios	Stock	Rel to Industry	Rel to S&P 500
Price/Earnings	13.4	0.9	0.7
Price/Book	11.2	4.0	2.7
Price/Sales	0.7	0.4	0.2
Price/Cash Flow	6.8	0.8	0.5

Major Fund Holders	% of Fund Assets
WM Small Cap Value I	1.09

Thesis By Michael Tian, 12-15-06 Stock Price as of Analysis: $38.49

Suburban's core propane-distribution business enjoys high customer switching costs and generates strong returns on invested capital. However, the firm's fuel oil distribution business has less-attractive economics. Suburban's units would yield 7% at our fair value estimate, which makes them attractive to income-oriented investors, in our opinion.

Suburban's propane customers have little incentive to switch, either to other fuels or to other providers. Most customers live in rural areas where natural-gas service isn't available. And since most home appliances are designed for a specific type of fuel, switching from propane to other fuels would be costly. Also, most customers don't own their storage tanks; they lease the tanks from Suburban. Switching providers is a pain because arrangements must be made for the new company to swap tanks with the existing provider. As a result of these hefty switching costs, it would take a substantial price differential to motivate Suburban's customers to leave.

While Suburban's propane customers aren't likely to defect, they are sensitive to prices and weather. Consumers conserve fuel when prices and temperatures are high, and more will be unable to pay as heating costs rise. When these events occur, Suburban's sales volume and profits suffer.

Fuel oil distribution--which generates about 10% of Suburban's gross profits--isn't as attractive as propane. Switching costs are smaller, but attractive pricing, good service, and customer inertia should aid retention. After suffering painful losses in 2005, Suburban "fired" its unprofitable customers and discontinued its price cap program. Performance should improve in the future.

The firm also took steps to improve its profitability. First, it shifted away from less profitable wholesale, industrial, and agricultural propane customers. In addition, Suburban laid off 350 employees, mostly in the HVAC business, and decreased delivery-fleet size. These cost cuts should boost profitability, but hopefully not at the expense of quality customer service.

Propane and fuel oil are both mature industries. Therefore, Suburban's growth depends largely on acquisitions. Firms that use acquisitions to drive growth make us nervous: Competition for targets can result in overpaying, and integration problems can lead to uninspiring financial results. Suburban's Agway deal is a superb example of these risks.

We're huge fans of Suburban's propane business, but the fuel oil segment and any future acquisitions make us wary.

Data as of 12-29-06

Suncor Energy SU

Rating	Fair Value	Last Close	Consider Buy	Consider Sell	Yield %
★	$62.00	$78.91	$47.80	$77.70	0.34

Industry	Business Risk	Moat Size	Investment Style	Sector
Oil/Gas	Average	Narrow	Large Growth	Energy

Company Profile
Calgary-based Suncor Energy produces and refines oil from Alberta's oil sands. A pioneer in oil sands production, Suncor produced an average of 206,000 barrels of oil equivalent per day in 2005. Although the firm has some conventional oil and gas reserves, estimated recoverable oil sand resources approach 11 billion barrels. The firm's downstream assets include two refineries in Ontario and Colorado with total capacity of 160,000 barrels per day.

Competition

	Market Cap $Mil	12 Mo Trailing Sales $Mil	Price/Cash Flow	Return On Assets %	Debt/ Equity	Total Return % 1 Yr	3 Yr
Suncor Energy	36,114	9,162	18.1	7.8	0.5	25.4	46.5
Imperial Oil	35,457	23,051	10.7	19.7	0.2	11.8	36.1
Canadian Natural Resource	28,550	7,224	7.2	4.6	0.4	7.8	61.1

Management Stewardship Grade [A]
Suncor chairman James Shaw is also the founder and chairman of Shaw Communications. CEO Richard George has been with Suncor for more than 10 years and has more than 25 years of industry experience. Compared with peers in the oil and gas industry, Suncor's executive compensation is not unusual. George's performance as CEO is measured against explicitly outlined goals, and variable pay makes up a large portion of total executive compensation. Overall, Suncor's management holds a nominal position in the firm's stock. We'd prefer management to have more skin in the game; however, a small stake like this is not uncommon for a larger firm in the oil industry. Looking at Suncor's overall stewardship, we see no major issues that cause us concern.

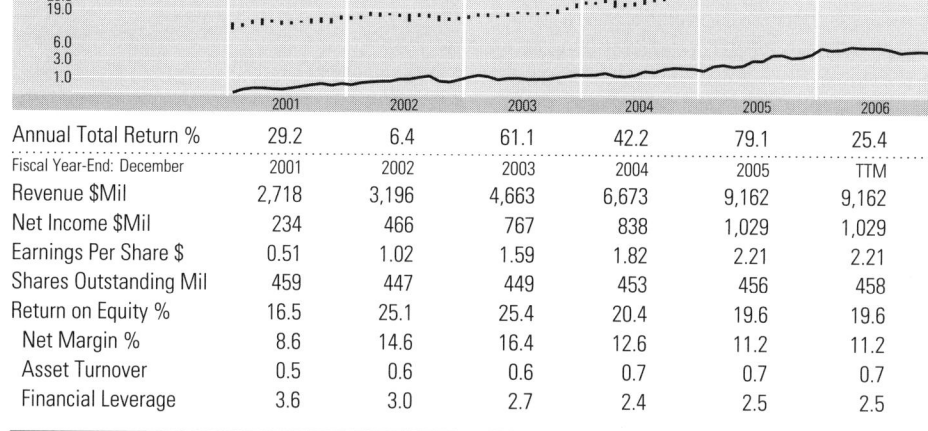

Price Volatility — Monthly Price High/Low — Relative Strength to S&P 500

	2001	2002	2003	2004	2005	2006
Annual $Price High	16.80	18.91	25.42	36.15	66.00	89.88
Low	10.50	13.95	15.32	22.55	31.33	63.13
Annual Total Return %	29.2	6.4	61.1	42.2	79.1	25.4

Fiscal Year-End: December

	2001	2002	2003	2004	2005	TTM
Revenue $Mil	2,718	3,196	4,663	6,673	9,162	9,162
Net Income $Mil	234	466	767	838	1,029	1,029
Earnings Per Share $	0.51	1.02	1.59	1.82	2.21	2.21
Shares Outstanding Mil	459	447	449	453	456	458
Return on Equity %	16.5	25.1	25.4	20.4	19.6	19.6
Net Margin %	8.6	14.6	16.4	12.6	11.2	11.2
Asset Turnover	0.5	0.6	0.6	0.7	0.7	0.7
Financial Leverage	3.6	3.0	2.7	2.4	2.5	2.5

Valuation Ratios	Stock	Rel to Industry	Rel to S&P 500
Price/Earnings	35.8	2.8	1.7
Price/Book	6.9	2.2	1.7
Price/Sales	3.9	2.1	1.3
Price/Cash Flow	18.1	2.1	1.2

Major Fund Holders	% of Fund Assets
JHancock Large Cap Equity A	5.51
JHancock Large Cap Intrinsic Value A	5.18
Saratoga Energy & Basic Materials A	4.68
Allianz RCM Global Resources Instl	4.33

Box 38 112-4th Avenue S.W. www.suncor.com
Calgary, AB T2P 2V5

Growth [NA]	2002	2003	2004	2005
Revenue %	19.8	31.4	31.1	27.9
Earnings/Share %	106.4	40.4	4.4	13.1
Book Value/Share %	32.7	25.6	31.9	23.2
Dividends/Share %	0.0	13.5	19.2	4.3

Profitability [NA]	2003	2004	2005	TTM
Return on Assets %	9.4	8.5	7.8	7.8
Oper Cash Flow $Mil	1,537	1,690	2,001	2,001
- Cap Spending $Mil	—	—	—	—
= Free Cash Flow $Mil	—	—	—	—

Financial Health [NA]	2003	2004	2005	12-31-05
Long-term Debt $Mil	—	1,848	2,570	2,570
Total Equity $Mil	3,018	4,101	5,239	5,239
Debt/Equity Ratio	—	0.5	0.5	0.5

Thesis By Elizabeth Collins, 12-13-06 Stock Price as of Analysis: $79.70

Suncor Energy is almost entirely focused on wringing oil from Alberta's vast oil sands. High oil prices create a rosy outlook for these projects, but a sharp drop would crash the party. Although we think Suncor is better positioned than many others playing in the oil sand box, we're mindful of the high costs and large risks associated with extracting oil from sand.

Oil sands are mostly a mixture of thick, heavy oil and sand from which the oil must be extracted and upgraded into higher-quality crude oil. Suncor primarily uses open-pit mining techniques to collect the oil sand, although future production growth will also come from in situ techniques used to tap deeper resources. This involves drilling pairs of horizontal wells and injecting steam to separate the oil from the sand.

Unlike most of its oil sands peers, Suncor's strategy is entirely geared toward the oil sands. The firm's refining and natural-gas businesses are strategic investments used to support the company's oil sands operations. Through a steady series of expansion projects, Suncor aims to boost production capacity from 260,000 barrels per day to more than half a million barrels per day by 2012. Because the resources are concentrated in one spot, there are no exploration costs, and the oil sands offer a visible, steady production growth opportunity. Growth depends more on how quickly massive investments can be made in the required infrastructure.

Whatever the method, extracting and upgrading oil from sand is expensive, and higher costs per barrel make Suncor more susceptible than conventional producers to a decline in oil prices. Technological developments are likely to lower per-barrel costs, but how much and how soon is highly uncertain. Also, with enormous up-front capital outlays, there is a significant risk of capital cost creep. Suncor's last major expansion, at a final cost of C$3.4 billion, was 70% over the original budget. We don't expect to see further blunders of this magnitude, but risk remains.

Numerous other factors increase the risk involved in oil sands production. Natural gas is a large variable cost, and a long-term, low-cost supply of gas is critical to keeping a lid on costs. Another big issue is the ecological impact of harvesting the oil sands, which has the potential to bring substantial environmental liabilities. Furthermore, events such as fires and harsh winter weather can prompt costly unplanned downtime.

Suncor can thrive under ideal circumstances, much like those today. Even with much lower oil prices, we would expect the firm to generate decent returns.

SunTrust Banks STI

Data as of 12-29-06

	Rating	Fair Value	Last Close	Consider Buy	Consider Sell	Yield %
	★★★	$83.00	$84.45	$70.70	$109.00	2.89

Industry	Business Risk	Moat Size	Investment Style	Sector
Super Regional Banks	Below Avg	Narrow	Large Value	Financial Services

Company Profile

With $181 billion in assets, SunTrust is the eighth-largest bank in the United States. It operates 1,792 branches in the attractive Southeastern United States. More than 20% of SunTrust's branches are located within a retail outlet, including 102 inside Wal-Mart. With headquarters in Atlanta, SunTrust helped Coke go public in 1919. In the process, SunTrust acquired a stake in the soft drink company that now totals 48 million shares.

Management

Stewardship Grade [B]

As a result of the recent announcement that Phil Humann will retire as CEO but stay on as chairman (thus separating the two positions), we've raised our Stewardship Grade to a B. For the past eight years, Humann preached patience to Wall Street, saying that the company would improve its performance and live up to its promises. After years of waiting, investors' patience wore thin and Humann announced his retirement as CEO effective Jan. 1, 2007. COO James Wells, 60, will become the new CEO. We do not believe this represents a major change. Wells has been in the upper management of SunTrust since 1998, as a part of the Crestar acquisition. He has been ingrained in the conservative culture and its current strategy. Wells will be under pressure from the board and Wall Street to show improved performance. He might be given enough room to sell a few businesses, but we believe a major strategic shift is unlikely.

303 Peachtree Street, NE
Atlanta, GA 30308
www.suntrust.com

Growth [B+]	2002	2003	2004	2005
Revenue %	1.9	2.0	11.8	23.0
Earnings/Share %	-1.3	1.5	9.7	5.4
Book Value/Share %	7.0	12.6	52.7	-11.9
Dividends/Share %	7.5	4.7	11.1	10.0

Profitability [B-]	2003	2004	2005	TTM
Return on Assets %	1.1	1.0	1.1	1.2
Oper Cash Flow $Mil	4,114	1,180	-4,719	—
- Cap Spending $Mil	158	238	202	—
= Free Cash Flow $Mil	—	—	—	—

Financial Health [NA]	2003	2004	2005	09-30-06
Long-term Debt $Mil	—	—	—	—
Total Equity $Mil	9,731	15,987	16,887	18,089
Debt/Equity Ratio	—	—	—	—

Competition

	Market Cap $Mil	12 Mo Trailing Sales $Mil	Price/Cash Flow	Return On Assets %	Debt/Equity	Total Return % 1 Yr	3 Yr
SunTrust Banks	29,907	8,070	—	1.2	—	19.8	9.4
Bank of America	239,758	68,368	—	1.3	—	20.7	15.2
Wachovia	90,049	27,749	—	1.3	—	12.0	11.3

Price Volatility

Annual $Price High / Low	72.35 / 57.29	70.20 / 51.55	71.73 / 51.44	76.65 / 61.27	75.77 / 65.32	85.64 / 69.68
	2001	2002	2003	2004	2005	2006
Annual Total Return %	2.0	-6.7	29.4	6.4	1.5	19.8

Fiscal Year-End: December	2001	2002	2003	2004	2005	TTM
Revenue $Mil	5,408	5,513	5,623	6,290	7,734	8,070
Net Income $Mil	1,376	1,332	1,332	1,573	1,987	2,130
Earnings Per Share $	4.72	4.66	4.73	5.19	5.47	5.85
Shares Outstanding Mil	288	283	278	300	359	354
Return on Equity %	16.5	15.2	13.7	9.8	11.8	11.8
Net Margin %	25.4	24.2	23.7	25.0	25.7	26.4
Asset Turnover	0.1	0.0	0.0	0.0	0.0	0.0
Financial Leverage	12.5	13.4	12.9	9.9	10.6	10.1

Valuation Ratios	Stock	Rel to Industry	Rel to S&P 500
Price/Earnings	14.4	1.1	0.7
Price/Book	1.7	0.8	0.4
Price/Sales	3.7	1.1	1.3
Price/Cash Flow	—	—	—

Major Fund Holders	% of Fund Assets
T. Rowe Price Financial Services	4.74
Westport R	3.44
Phoenix Value Equity A	3.30
JHancock Regional Bank B	3.14

Thesis
By Jaime Black, CFA, CPA, 12-12-06 Stock Price as of Analysis: $84.11

Despite a commendable past and great potential for growth, SunTrust has become a mediocre performer. We have a hard time seeing this bank returning to its former glory.

SunTrust is one of the larger regional banks operating in the attractive Southeastern United States. Projected population growth over the next five years for its markets averages nearly 10% and will bring with it economic growth and new deposits. The bank is investing in the infrastructure necessary to maintain its share of the growing markets.

While SunTrust has many opportunities to grow, it has failed to capitalize on these opportunities profitably. Returns on equity, which used to run an admirable 18%-20%, have dipped down to around 12%. The bank's struggles are most evident in the compressed net interest margin, which has declined from 3.55% in 2000 to 2.93% in the third quarter of 2006. While we can blame part of this decline on the change in interest rates, we believe mismanagement of the balance sheet is the primary reason for the decline. Retiring CEO Phil Humann admitted in 2003 that it was his asset-liability management decisions that caused the net interest margin to decline. If long-term interest rates would rise above short-term interest rates, SunTrust's net interest margin would gradually improve. Even with no change in interest rates, the recent focus on capital management leads us to believe that SunTrust's profitability will improve slowly throughout 2007 and 2008.

However, we have doubts that SunTrust can return to past levels of profitability. The bank changed its branching strategy after the 2004 purchase of National Commerce. It began concentrating on small branches within retail stores--now 20% of total branches--as a major avenue of growth. These branches cost a fraction of a full-scale branch to build and run, but they do not generate the real estate loans or commercial relationships that SunTrust finds so profitable. These branches attract lower-income customers who do not meet SunTrust's conservative underwriting criteria, eliminating most of the potential loan-related revenue. As a result, the potential profit is almost entirely on the deposit side. Even with lower operating costs, these branches could be a drag on overall returns.

Despite the potential associated with its geographic footprint, we would hesitate to own SunTrust until it can demonstrate an ability to convert growth into higher profitability.

Data as of 12-29-06

Synchronoss Technologies SNCR

Rating	Fair Value	Last Close	Consider Buy	Consider Sell	Yield %
★★★★	$18.00	$13.72	$11.50	$21.70	0.00

Company Profile

Synchronoss acts as the middleman between communication service providers' back-end systems and their customers (both consumer and business). The firm's ActivationNow platform is used by most large U.S. wireless, wireline, cable, and VoIP providers to take, manage, provision, and bill orders and other transactions from communication service provider (CSP) clients. The client list includes Cablevision, Cingular, Comcast, Level 3, Time Warner Cable, and Vonage.

Management
Stewardship Grade [NA]

Stephen Waldis is the chairman and chief executive officer. Prior to this, he served as the chief operating officer of Vertek, a private telecom consulting firm. In 2000, Vertek spun off Synchronoss as a stand-alone company. Both Waldis and Vertek remain as significant investors in Synchronoss. The company's early success can be attributed to Waldis' foresight that CSPs needed to automate their client processes more efficiently and his relationships with CSP executives.

Compensation is reasonable, in our opinion. In 2005, Waldis earned $900,000, and his key executives earned less than $500,000 each. At this point in the firm's early life as a public company, options issuance has not been egregious. Executive officers and directors still own about 39% of the shares after the initial public offering. The original venture capital investors own another 30%.

We were bothered by one related-party transaction, however: Several top executives owned 18.7% of Omniglobe, a data-entry firm based in India. In 2005, Synchronoss conducted $8 million of business with Omniglobe. Distributions from Omniglobe to investors provided a 161% return on the executives' investment. We were pleased to see that shortly after Synchronoss' IPO, the executives gave up their stake in Omniglobe.

750 Route 202 South, Suite 600
Bridgewater, NJ 08807
www.synchronoss.com

Growth [A]	2002	2003	2004	2005
Revenue %	45.6	102.2	64.3	99.4
Earnings/Share %	NMF	NMF	NMF	NMF
Book Value/Share %	—	—	—	—
Dividends/Share %	NMF	NMF	NMF	NMF

Profitability [C-]	2003	2004	2005	TTM
Return on Assets %	-4.8	-0.2	30.8	12.5
Oper Cash Flow $Mil	0	-2	8	8
- Cap Spending $Mil	2	3	2	4
= Free Cash Flow $Mil	-2	-5	6	4

Financial Health [B+]	2003	2004	2005	06-30-06
Long-term Debt $Mil	—	1	1	0
Total Equity $Mil	-18	-18	-5	91
Debt/Equity Ratio	—	ELB	ELB	0.0

Industry	Business Risk	Moat Size	Investment Style	Sector
Business Support	Above Average		Small Growth	Business Services

Competition

	Market Cap $Mil	12 Mo Trailing Sales $Mil	Price/Cash Flow	Return On Assets%	Debt/ Equity	Total Return% 1 Yr	3 Yr
Synchronoss Technologies	439	67	54.1	12.5	0.0	—	—
Accenture	28,867	18,852	11.7	11.3	0.0	29.3	13.4
VeriSign	5,896	1,596	11.1	11.7	—	9.8	13.8

Price Volatility — Monthly Price High/Low — Relative Strength to S&P 500

Annual $Price High/Low: 15.85 / 6.25 (2006)

Annual Total Return %	—	—	—	—	—	
Fiscal Year-End: December	2001	2002	2003	2004	2005	TTM
Revenue $Mil	6	8	17	27	54	67
Net Income $Mil	-10	-6	-1	0	12	12
Earnings Per Share $	—	—	—	—	—	—
Shares Outstanding Mil	—	—	—	—	—	32
Return on Equity %	NMF	NMF	NMF	NMF	NMF	13.8
Net Margin %	ELB	-74.4	-6.5	-0.2	22.9	18.6
Asset Turnover	0.2	0.4	0.7	1.2	1.3	0.7
Financial Leverage	NMF	NMF	NMF	NMF	NMF	1.1

Valuation Ratios	Stock	Rel to Industry	Rel to S&P 500
Price/Earnings	—	—	—
Price/Book	4.8	1.1	1.2
Price/Sales	6.5	1.3	2.2
Price/Cash Flow	54.1	2.8	3.7

Major Fund Holders	% of Fund Assets
SM&R Alger Technology A	2.64
DWS Micro Cap Inst	1.69
Northpointe Small Cap Growth Inst	1.31

Thesis By Mike Ford-Taggart, CFA, 11-16-06 Stock Price as of Analysis: $10.15

If you believe that consumers will continue moving their telecom service to nontraditional telecom providers--like voice over Internet protocol (VoIP) and cable multi-system operators (MSOs)--Synchronoss is the company for you. Synchronoss is a veritable mutual fund of the VoIP industry.

Approximately 3.5 million U.S. homes had VoIP telephony service at the end of 2005, and research firm IDC estimates that 27 million homes will use VoIP telephony in 2009. Other consultants agree that the adoption will increase over the next few years. Synchronoss is closely tied to this growth via a diverse list of customers, which allow it to benefit from the broader consumer trend, regardless of operator.

But Synchronoss is not a one-trick pony. Initially, it provided customer fulfillment services to AT&T Wireless. Synchronoss was able to broaden its capabilities and apply them to a wide variety of other services. When Cingular acquired AT&T Wireless, Cingular scrapped its own in-house fulfillment systems and switched to Synchronoss' platform. Its ActivationNow platform simplifies technologically complex processes through automation and integration of disparate back-end systems. Importantly, Synchronoss has never lost a customer.

Perhaps the most enticing aspect of Synchronoss is its revenue model. Approximately 85% of its revenues come from processing transactions, for which Synchronoss charges anywhere from $1 to $20 per transaction depending on type. The trends toward seamless mobility, bundled services, and real-time content activation are all favorable. So, every time a Synchronoss client's end customer completes a transaction (switches phone companies, adopts VoIP phone service, or downloads a service or product on the mobile phone), Synchronoss rings the register.

Synchronoss does have blemishes. For example, roughly two thirds of Synchronoss' revenues come from Cingular Wireless. The risk is that Cingular stops using Synchronoss' platform, which we view as highly unlikely given the enormous switching costs to save what would be an immaterial amount of money for Cingular.

We believe Synchronoss has deep relationships in attractive, quickly growing industries. At the right price, it might be time to back up the truck.

Synovus Financial SNV

Data as of 12-29-06

	Rating	Fair Value	Last Close	Consider Buy	Consider Sell	Yield %
	★★★	$31.00	$30.83	$23.90	$38.80	2.53

Company Profile
Synovus Financial is the parent company of 40 small community banks throughout Georgia, Alabama, Florida, Tennessee, and South Carolina. The company's decentralized banking segment has approximately $31 billion in assets. In addition, the company owns 81% of Total System Services, a publicly traded entity, which accounts for approximately 35% of net income. Total System Services is one of two major players in the outsourced credit card processing market.

Management   Stewardship Grade [B]
Synovus is slowly completing a five-year management transition. The company has moved managers around to give the necessary experience to future leaders while current leaders are still there to guide them. The company last shuffled its management in late 2006 when CEO Richard Anthony was named chairman, replacing Jim Blanchard, who will become a regular board member. We are disappointed to see the CEO and chairman jobs combined after they were separated earlier in the transition plan. However, we admire the company's methodical process of seasoning the management team; it gives a clear indication that the company is planning for its future as an independent bank, unlike so many of its peers with CEOs over 60 and no succession planning. The board of directors is quite large at 20 members, with three current or former senior managers on it. We like the fact that insider ownership is high at 5.5%, with three board members owning in excess of 1% of the shares outstanding. We believe that this will help align the directors' and managers' motives with that of ordinary shareholders.

901 Front Avenue P.O. Box 120   www.synovus.com
Columbus, GA 31902

Growth [A-]	2002	2003	2004	2005
Revenue %	8.8	9.2	11.7	21.2
Earnings/Share %	15.2	5.8	10.2	16.3
Book Value/Share %	18.3	9.3	15.3	9.9
Dividends/Share %	15.7	11.9	5.0	5.3

Profitability [A+]	2003	2004	2005	TTM
Return on Assets %	1.8	1.7	1.9	1.8
Oper Cash Flow $Mil	722	796	620	—
- Cap Spending $Mil	184	111	107	—
= Free Cash Flow $Mil	—	—	—	—

Financial Health [NA]	2003	2004	2005	09-30-06
Long-term Debt $Mil	—	—	—	—
Total Equity $Mil	2,245	2,641	2,949	3,564
Debt/Equity Ratio	—	—	—	—

Industry	Business Risk	Moat Size	Investment Style	Sector
Regional Banks	Average	Wide	Mid Core	Financial Services

Competition	Market Cap $Mil	12 Mo Trailing Sales $Mil	Price/Cash Flow	Return On Assets%	Debt/ Equity	Total Return% 1 Yr	3 Yr
Synovus Financial	10,019	3,138	—	1.8	—	17.3	5.5
Bank of America	239,758	68,368	—	1.3	—	20.7	15.2
Wachovia	90,049	27,749	—	1.3	—	12.0	11.3

Price Volatility
Monthly Price High/Low — Relative Strength to S&P 500

Annual $Price High/Low	34.74 / 22.75	31.93 / 16.48	29.25 / 17.25	29.09 / 22.50	30.10 / 26.30	31.13 / 25.74
	2001	2002	2003	2004	2005	2006
Annual Total Return %	-5.2	-20.6	53.3	1.5	-3.0	17.3

Fiscal Year-End: December	2001	2002	2003	2004	2005	TTM
Revenue $Mil	1,794	1,952	2,132	2,382	2,887	3,138
Net Income $Mil	312	365	389	437	516	579
Earnings Per Share $	1.05	1.21	1.28	1.41	1.64	1.81
Shares Outstanding Mil	291	297	301	308	311	325
Return on Equity %	18.4	17.9	17.3	16.5	17.5	16.2
Net Margin %	17.4	18.7	18.2	18.4	17.9	18.4
Asset Turnover	0.1	0.1	0.1	0.1	0.1	0.1
Financial Leverage	9.8	9.3	9.6	9.5	9.4	8.8

Valuation Ratios	Stock	Rel to Industry	Rel to S&P 500
Price/Earnings	17.0	0.9	0.8
Price/Book	2.8	0.9	0.7
Price/Sales	3.2	0.6	1.1
Price/Cash Flow	—	—	—

Major Fund Holders	% of Fund Assets
T. Rowe Price Financial Services	3.78
Madison Mosaic Mid-Cap	3.61
Constellation HLAM Large Cap Quality St	3.43
Ave Maria Rising Dividend	2.98

Thesis By Jaime Black, CFA, CPA, 12-01-06 Stock Price as of Analysis: $29.95

Synovus is really two businesses in one. The company operates a highly successful super-community banking operation and it owns 81% of Total System Services, a large publicly traded financial processor. Total System Services accounts for approximately 35% of Synovus' net income.

Synovus is one of the most successful decentralized banks in the U.S. It is the parent company of 40 community banks--each with a different name--but with a common operating system and similar products. It does not consolidate its banks into one large regional bank because it likes to have the small-town feel and personal touch that community banks impart. So, each of the 40 banks has its own president, local board, and local decision making on most loans. Synovus is often listed by community banks as a tough competitor and role model for the "super-community" banking style--a major compliment.

Despite its decentralized system, which results in a thicker layer of management and a larger bureaucracy, Synovus has lower operating costs than most competitors. As a percentage of net revenues, operating costs hover around 50%, compared to the mid-50s for its local community bank competitors.

Synovus has just completed its retail improvement initiative and is already seeing the benefits. The cultures of the 40 affiliate banks were not changed, but the company trained its employees to look for more referral opportunities and put a new emphasis on the retail relationship at historically commercial-oriented banks. This has resulted in strong retail deposit growth and an increase in the number of products per household served.

Synovus has started an initiative to gain more share of its commercial customers' total banking business. The company is a strong commercial real estate lender, accounting for 62% of the company's total loan portfolio. However, Synovus also has a wide array of other commercial lending and cash management products that many of its customers are not using. As a result, Synovus is targeting its current customers, looking to leverage its existing commercial real estate lending relationship into a complete commercial banking relationship. We believe Synovus will be successful in it efforts and like the idea that it will lower its dependence on the Southeast U.S. commercial real estate market.

With such a strong bank and its ownership of wide-moat Total System Services, we would jump at an opportunity to own this company at an appropriate discount to our fair value estimate.

© 2007 Morningstar, Inc. All rights reserved. Intended for United States residents only, this report is for information purposes and should not be considered a solicitation to buy or sell any security. Download your free reports at http://www.morningstar.com/goto/2007Stocks500

 Stocks 500

Data as of 12-29-06

Sysco SYY

Rating	Fair Value	Last Close	Consider Buy	Consider Sell	Yield %
★★★	$38.00	$36.76	$32.40	$49.90	1.85

Industry	Business Risk	Moat Size	Investment Style	Sector
Food Wholesale	Below Avg	Wide	Large Growth	Consumer Services

Company Profile

Sysco is the largest provider of food-service products in the United States and Canada, distributing more than 300,000 products to 400,000 restaurants, schools, hotels, health-care institutions, and other food-service customers. Restaurants account for two thirds of Sysco's annual sales, with independents contributing 55% of restaurant sales and chains making up the rest. The company's SYGMA Network focuses on chain restaurants, with Wendy's being its largest customer.

Management

Stewardship Grade [B]

Richard Schnieders has been chairman and CEO of Sysco since January 2003. He has been with the company since 1982, serving as president from July 2000 through December 2002 and as chief operating officer from January 2000 through December 2002. We believe that Sysco's management has done right by its shareholders over the years, generating above-average results in what has traditionally been a low-margin, low-return business, and regularly returning cash to investors in the form of dividends and share repurchases. Executive compensation has been fairly consistent over the years, with the firm providing much greater details about salary and bonus packages than many other publicly traded companies. Most long-term compensation is in the form of restricted stock instead of options, and total employee options granted in fiscal 2006 were less than 2% of the company's diluted shares outstanding. Sysco does lose some points, though, for having the chairman and CEO roles held by the same person, as well as for having a staggered board of directors. We believe that investors would be better served longer term if the company were to separate the chairman and CEO roles, and were to hold annual elections for all members of its board of directors, rather than just four out of 12 each year.

1390 Enclave Parkway www.sysco.com
Houston, TX 77077-2099

Growth [C+]	2003	2004	2005	2006
Revenue %	11.9	12.2	3.2	7.7
Earnings/Share %	16.8	16.1	7.3	-7.5
Book Value/Share %	5.2	16.2	8.9	15.1
Dividends/Share %	25.0	52.5	-4.9	-15.5

Profitability [A]	2004	2005	2006	TTM
Return on Assets %	11.6	11.6	9.5	9.0
Oper Cash Flow $Mil	1,191	1,192	1,124	1,101
- Cap Spending $Mil	530	390	515	536
= Free Cash Flow $Mil	661	802	609	564

Financial Health [B+]	2004	2005	2006	06-30-06
Long-term Debt $Mil	1,231	956	1,627	1,739
Total Equity $Mil	2,565	2,759	3,052	3,147
Debt/Equity Ratio	0.5	0.3	0.5	0.6

Competition

	Market Cap $Mil	12 Mo Trailing Sales $Mil	Price/Cash Flow	Return On Assets%	Debt/Equity	Total Return% 1 Yr	3 Yr
Sysco	22,722	33,290	20.6	9.0	0.6	21.0	1.5
Koninklijke Ahold NV ADR	16,455	55,719	6.9	0.8	—	40.5	11.9
Performance Food Group	964	5,787	—	3.6	0.0	-2.6	-8.2

Price Volatility — Monthly Price High/Low — Relative Strength to S&P 500

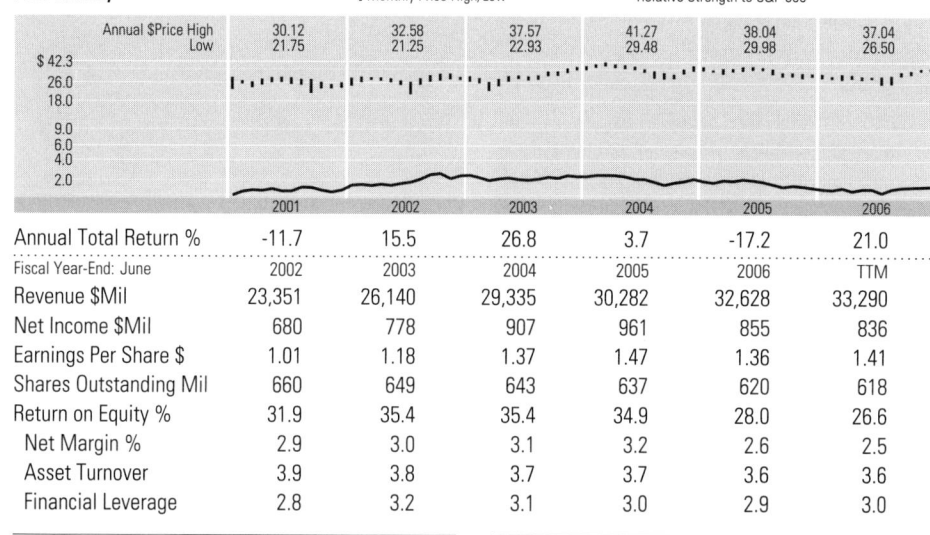

Annual Total Return %	-11.7	15.5	26.8	3.7	-17.2	21.0
Fiscal Year-End: June	2002	2003	2004	2005	2006	TTM
Revenue $Mil	23,351	26,140	29,335	30,282	32,628	33,290
Net Income $Mil	680	778	907	961	855	836
Earnings Per Share $	1.01	1.18	1.37	1.47	1.36	1.41
Shares Outstanding Mil	660	649	643	637	620	618
Return on Equity %	31.9	35.4	35.4	34.9	28.0	26.6
Net Margin %	2.9	3.0	3.1	3.2	2.6	2.5
Asset Turnover	3.9	3.8	3.7	3.7	3.6	3.6
Financial Leverage	2.8	3.2	3.1	3.0	2.9	3.0

Valuation Ratios	Stock	Rel to Industry	Rel to S&P 500
Price/Earnings	26.1	1.0	1.3
Price/Book	7.2	1.3	1.8
Price/Sales	0.7	1.2	0.2
Price/Cash Flow	20.6	0.9	1.4

Major Fund Holders	% of Fund Assets
Brown Advisory Opportunity Instl	5.54
Meehan Focus	4.30
JHancock U.S. Global Leaders Gr A	4.27
JHFunds2 U.S. Global Lead Gr NAV	4.22

Thesis By Greggory Warren, CFA, 12-11-06 Stock Price as of Analysis: $36.12

Despite controlling just 15% of the market, Sysco is the dominant food-service distributor in North America. To cement this leading position within the industry, the company generates impressive returns in what has traditionally been a low-margin business, utilizing economies of scale, prudent investments in technology, and a cadre of marketing associates armed with a portfolio of its own branded products. Sysco exhibits the very traits we look for in wide-moat companies.

Think of Sysco as a grocery store for the restaurant industry, only it delivers (along with 3,000 other broadline suppliers in the U.S. and Canada). Being the market leader in such a highly fragmented industry allows Sysco to grab share from weaker rivals and gives it prime access to new customers and acquisitions. With more than $210 billion in total food-service sales up for grabs in North America, and the restaurant industry is expected to grow by at least 4% annually longer term, Sysco is well positioned to take full advantage of its peers.

We believe part of Sysco's success stems from its unparalleled economies of scale. The food distribution business has high fixed costs, so only companies capable of spreading those expenses over a larger base will generate above-average returns.

Over the past 30 years, Sysco has methodically built out its distribution network, reaching just about every corner in North America and producing returns that are 3 times greater than its closest competitors'.

Investments in technology and its distribution network have allowed Sysco to lower procurement and delivery costs and have cemented the company's position as the low-cost provider in the industry. Sysco also has more than 8,000 marketing associates, averaging 52 customers per sales rep, while its closest competitors, U.S. Foodservice and Performance Food Group, average between 60 and 70 accounts per associate.

What truly distinguishes Sysco from its peers, though, is the company's portfolio of 40,000 private-label and specialty product offerings. Nearly half of the firm's annual sales come from these higher-margin products, which meet the growing need within the industry for quality products at reasonable prices.

While Sysco's advantages are tremendous, we think internal sales growth is likely to slow, as the company has already picked up some of the best pieces of business in the industry. Even with slower growth, though, we wouldn't bet against Sysco's distinct competitive advantages longer term.

Data as of 12-29-06

T Rowe Price Group TROW

	Rating	Fair Value	Last Close	Consider Buy	Consider Sell	Yield %
	★★	$36.00	$43.77	$27.80	$45.10	1.35

Company Profile
T. Rowe Price Group manages assets for individuals through mutual funds and for institutions in separate portfolios. It has a family of more than 80 stock, bond, and money market funds with low expenses. It also offers discount-brokerage and trust services, retirement accounts, and investment-management services. Fund managers are guided by the company's investment philosophy of controlling risk, resulting in relatively stable fund returns.

Management
Stewardship Grade [A]

George A. Roche has been chairman and president of T. Rowe Price since 1997. He and his executive team run a clean and ethical company, explaining its "A" Stock Stewardship Grade. T. Rowe traditionally has been run by a group of top officers (the management committee) who consult one another before making major decisions. Roche is slated to retire at the end of 2006. His successor, James Kennedy, hails from the management committee. Though Roche will be a tough act to follow, as T. Rowe has prospered under his watch, we don't expect Kennedy to chart a markedly different course than his predecessors. Management and board members pull down moderate paychecks. However, stock-option grants have been particularly lavish, with much of the benefit accruing to top officers. Stock options have helped management to gain a small ownership stake in the company, but many board members own little or no stock because they are compensated with cash and options only. Nevertheless, unlike many other companies that curbed their issuance of options once it became mandatory to expense options compensation under GAAP, T. Rowe has shown no signs of slowing down. This at least lends credence to the notion that the firm wasn't using options solely to game the system in order to goose earnings.

100 East Pratt Street
Baltimore, MD 21202
www.troweprice.com

Growth [B+]	2002	2003	2004	2005
Revenue %	-7.1	7.7	28.3	18.4
Earnings/Share %	0.0	-41.8	41.8	25.5
Book Value/Share %	6.3	-41.8	22.2	17.8
Dividends/Share %	6.6	7.7	14.3	21.5

Profitability [A+]	2003	2004	2005	TTM
Return on Assets %	14.7	17.5	18.7	18.8
Oper Cash Flow $Mil	297	374	539	—
- Cap Spending $Mil	32	43	52	—
= Free Cash Flow $Mil	—	—	—	—

Financial Health [NA]	2003	2004	2005	09-30-06
Long-term Debt $Mil	—	—	—	—
Total Equity $Mil	1,329	1,697	2,036	2,266
Debt/Equity Ratio	—	—	—	—

Industry	Business Risk	Moat Size	Investment Style	Sector
Money Mgmt.	Average	Wide	Large Growth	Financial Services

Competition	Market Cap $Mil	12 Mo Trailing Sales $Mil	Price/Cash Flow	Return On Assets%	Debt/Equity	Total Return% 1 Yr	3 Yr
T Rowe Price Group	11,539	1,729	—	18.8	—	23.3	23.7
Franklin Resources	27,932	5,051	—	13.3	—	17.8	30.3
Legg Mason	12,491	3,810	—	13.0	—	-20.0	23.0

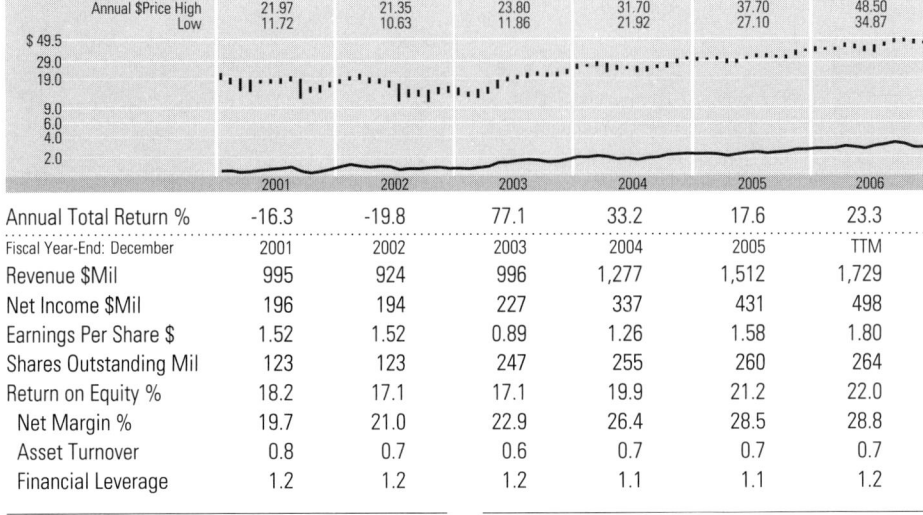

	2001	2002	2003	2004	2005	2006
Annual Total Return %	-16.3	-19.8	77.1	33.2	17.6	23.3
Fiscal Year-End: December	2001	2002	2003	2004	2005	TTM
Revenue $Mil	995	924	996	1,277	1,512	1,729
Net Income $Mil	196	194	227	337	431	498
Earnings Per Share $	1.52	1.52	0.89	1.26	1.58	1.80
Shares Outstanding Mil	123	123	247	255	260	264
Return on Equity %	18.2	17.1	17.1	19.9	21.2	22.0
Net Margin %	19.7	21.0	22.9	26.4	28.5	28.8
Asset Turnover	0.8	0.7	0.6	0.7	0.7	0.7
Financial Leverage	1.2	1.2	1.2	1.1	1.1	1.2

Valuation Ratios	Stock	Rel to Industry	Rel to S&P 500
Price/Earnings	24.4	0.8	1.2
Price/Book	5.1	1.2	1.2
Price/Sales	6.7	1.1	2.3
Price/Cash Flow	—	—	—

Major Fund Holders	% of Fund Assets
Pioneer AmPac Growth A	5.16
FMI Provident Trust Strategy	5.10
JHT Financial Services Trust Ser I	5.08
Jensen J	4.73

Thesis By Jeffrey Ptak, CPA, CFA, 12-11-06 Stock Price as of Analysis: $44.59

T. Rowe Price's strong recent results underscore the qualities that make it one of our favorite asset managers.

T. Rowe has continued to grow briskly this year: Investment advisory fees for the year through Sept. 30, 2006, rose 21% over the year-ago period thanks to a 20.1% increase in average assets under management (AUM). Importantly, a big chunk of the AUM jump came from investors pumping new money into T. Rowe's strategies, a sign that it continues to gain market share. What's more, inflows remain well-dispersed across a relatively wide range of products, including U.S. stock, foreign stock, and fixed-income strategies, and distribution channels. In short, these results reinforce the attributes--a respected brand, well-balanced investment lineup, and enviable scale--that set T. Rowe apart from competitors, earning it a wide moat.

T. Rowe has done an exemplary job building its brand. The firm eschews flash in favor of a stodgy emphasis on long-term investment success. Thus, it has tended to attract investors who share its long-term orientation. This, in turn, has helped to keep the firm's asset base stable, ensuring that its managers can focus on running money. What's more, T. Rowe has taken care to foster teamwork among its investment staff rather than pursue a "star-manager" tack. This, too, has helped to keep the focus off of personalities and squarely on the firm as a whole.

T. Rowe's portfolio managers have held up their end of the bargain, as evidenced by the overall strength of T. Rowe's investment lineup: Its average fund carries a 4-star Morningstar Rating.

The company has leveraged that broad-based strength in various ways. For one, it's a force to be reckoned with in the defined contribution business, where the firm's pedigree and luminous product roster make it a favorite among plan sponsors and participants. In addition, its "Target Retirement" funds of funds, which package multiple T. Rowe strategies in a single product, essentially capitalize on the brand's strength and investors' comfort with the firm's overall investment capabilities. These offerings have been a huge hit and now account for a big share of the inflows into T. Rowe's mutual funds.

That success has attracted a broad cross-section of investors. Thus, T. Rowe finds itself in the enviable position of sitting atop more than $300 billion in AUM. That scale should ensure that the fund's expenses remain below the industry norm and pave the way to continued strong profitability, with operating margins consistently topping 35%.

Data as of 12-29-06

Taiwan Semiconductor ADR TSM

Rating	Fair Value	Last Close	Consider Buy	Consider Sell	Yield %
★★★	$9.50	$10.93	$6.10	$11.50	3.51

Company Profile
TSMC manufactures semiconductor chips for semiconductor chip companies seeking to outsource some or all of their production. The chips are used in a variety of applications related to computers, communications, and industrial and consumer goods. The majority of sales come from semiconductor firms that do not have their own manufacturing capabilities. TSMC was founded in 1987.

Industry	Business Risk	Moat Size	Investment Style	Sector
Semiconductor	Above Avg	Narrow	Large Core	Hardware

Competition

	Market Cap $Mil	12 Mo Trailing Sales $Mil	Price/Cash Flow	Return On Assets%	Debt/Equity	Total Return% 1 Yr	3 Yr
Taiwan Semiconductor Manufacturing ADR	55,682	8,264	11.4	18.4	0.1	18.8	11.3
IBM	146,342	89,593	9.8	8.8	0.4	19.8	3.0
United Microelectronics A	13,293	3,110	9.5	2.1	0.2	15.3	-5.7

Management   Stewardship Grade [NA]
Corporate stewardship at Taiwan Semi is mediocre, on the basis of the information we have. In July 2005, Rick Tsai became CEO, replacing Morris Chang, who remains as chairman. Tsai has more than 20 years of experience in the semiconductor business, and prior to his promotion, he had been TSMC's president and COO since mid-2001. We applaud the division of the chairman and CEO titles between two people. However, we would like to see greater director and executive ownership, as board members, supervisors, and executives together own less than 1% of shares outstanding. While executives can receive bonuses in cash, stock, or options, directors and supervisors are paid solely in cash. In addition, the exact breakout of compensation is lacking in the detail we normally like to see with regard to salaries for the top executive officers and the percentage of variable versus fixed compensation. From the information provided, compensation and benefits for executives, directors, and supervisors amounted to NT$1.9 billion in 2005, compared with NT$557 million in 2004. As of 2005, Philips PHG was TSMC's largest shareholder, with a 16% ownership stake. Philips' interests may not be aligned with those of outside shareholders.

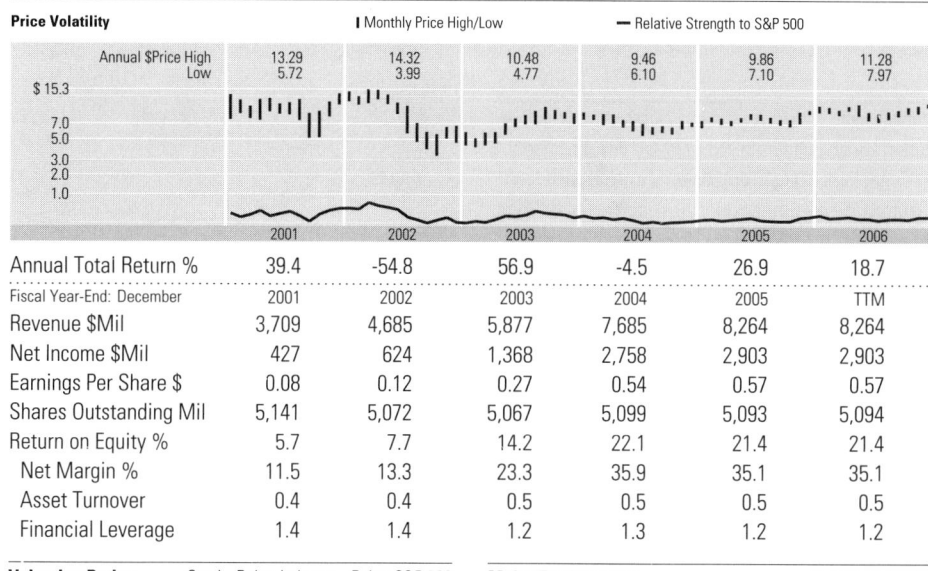

Price Volatility
| Monthly Price High/Low — Relative Strength to S&P 500

Annual $Price High/Low	13.29 / 5.72	14.32 / 3.99	10.48 / 4.77	9.46 / 6.10	9.86 / 7.10	11.28 / 7.97
	2001	2002	2003	2004	2005	2006
Annual Total Return %	39.4	-54.8	56.9	-4.5	26.9	18.7

Fiscal Year-End: December	2001	2002	2003	2004	2005	TTM
Revenue $Mil	3,709	4,685	5,877	7,685	8,264	8,264
Net Income $Mil	427	624	1,368	2,758	2,903	2,903
Earnings Per Share $	0.08	0.12	0.27	0.54	0.57	0.57
Shares Outstanding Mil	5,141	5,072	5,067	5,099	5,093	5,094
Return on Equity %	5.7	7.7	14.2	22.1	21.4	21.4
Net Margin %	11.5	13.3	23.3	35.9	35.1	35.1
Asset Turnover	0.4	0.4	0.5	0.5	0.5	0.5
Financial Leverage	1.4	1.4	1.2	1.3	1.2	1.2

Valuation Ratios	Stock	Rel to Industry	Rel to S&P 500
Price/Earnings	19.2	0.7	0.9
Price/Book	4.1	1.1	1.0
Price/Sales	6.7	1.6	2.3
Price/Cash Flow	11.4	0.7	0.8

Major Fund Holders	% of Fund Assets
Firsthand Global Technology	6.90
Firsthand Technology Leaders	6.41
Pioneer Independence P	4.39
BB&T Equity Income A	3.82

No. 8, Li-Hsin Road 6 Hsinchu Science Park www.tsmc.com.tw
Hsinchu, Taiwan

Growth [NA]	2002	2003	2004	2005
Revenue %	28.9	25.1	26.7	3.6
Earnings/Share %	51.2	119.5	93.9	1.6
Book Value/Share %	8.5	16.8	20.3	12.0
Dividends/Share %	—	—	—	—

Profitability [NA]	2003	2004	2005	TTM
Return on Assets %	11.5	17.7	18.4	18.4
Oper Cash Flow $Mil	3,359	4,576	4,868	4,868
- Cap Spending $Mil	1,096	2,423	2,476	2,476
= Free Cash Flow $Mil	2,263	2,153	2,391	2,391

Financial Health [NA]	2003	2004	2005	12-31-05
Long-term Debt $Mil	1,234	936	890	890
Total Equity $Mil	9,652	12,478	13,543	13,543
Debt/Equity Ratio	0.1	0.1	0.1	0.1

Thesis By Andy Ng, 12-12-06 Stock Price as of Analysis: $10.69

Taiwan Semiconductor Manufacturing (TSMC) is the dominant player in the semiconductor foundry market. Although its large scale offers a competitive advantage, the firm has to periodically endure downturns that afflict the cyclical chip industry.

TSMC is the top provider of outsourced semiconductor manufacturing services to chip companies, with 49% market share in 2005, according to IC Insights. The firm has benefited from favorable industry trends in recent years, as the rising costs of building modern chip fabrication facilities (now about $3-$5 billion) have become prohibitive for many semiconductor companies. As a result, there has been a gradual shift in the semiconductor industry toward fabless business models, where chip designs are outsourced to foundries for fabrication. Even some integrated chip firms now contract out a portion of the manufacturing to better manage their capital spending needs.

As the leading foundry player, TSMC has major scale advantages that its rivals lack. The firm has substantial resources to invest heavily in R&D and cutting-edge equipment in order to stay at the forefront of semiconductor technology and maintain the most efficient manufacturing processes. With revenue more than twice that of its nearest competitor, United Microelectronics (UMC), TSMC is better positioned to absorb expenses than the rest of the players in the foundry market. In addition, the firm can afford to offer more diverse and complex services to customers than competitors can.

Despite its strong market position, TSMC is exposed to the cycles that characterize the semiconductor industry. The large capital investments needed to stay ahead technologically and the high fixed costs that typify the foundry business mean that during downturns, TSMC is burdened with overcapacity and lower profits. Nevertheless, TSMC must continue to sustain R&D and capital spending during these depressed periods or risk losing its competitive edge.

TSMC will have to confront mounting competition in the years ahead, particularly from Chinese firms like Semiconductor Manufacturing International. There currently are Taiwanese restrictions on advanced chip investments in China, which limit TSMC's opportunities in the flourishing Chinese semiconductor industry. The competition from rising and existing foundry players, which include UMC and Chartered, will pressure pricing over time.

Target TGT

Data as of 12-29-06

Rating ★★★★	Fair Value $65.00	Last Close $57.05	Consider Buy $55.40	Consider Sell $85.30	Yield % 0.77

Company Profile
Target operates large-format discount stores that sell name-brand and private-label family apparel, home decor items, food, and everyday consumables. It operates 1,494 of its smaller-format discount stores and 177 SuperTarget stores, which are much larger and feature a greater selection of groceries and consumables.

Management Stewardship Grade [A]
Robert Ulrich joined the company in 1967, became chairman and CEO of Target stores in 1987, and assumed his present position as chairman and CEO of Target Corp. in 1994. Corporate governance appears sound; the board includes a number of independent directors with considerable (and relevant) experience. Management compensation is in line with industry norms, and is largely based on the economic value created for shareholders. The company is open to shareholder proposals and board nominations. Additionally, we are pleased that Target continues to return value to shareholders through share repurchases. Our only criticisms of the firm's corporate governance are the staggered board elections and the fact that the CEO and chairman positions aren't held by different people.

1000 Nicollet Mall www.targetcorp.com
Minneapolis, MN 55403

Growth [A-]	2003	2004	2005	2006
Revenue %	13.3	12.3	11.5	12.3
Earnings/Share %	NMF	10.7	78.2	-22.8
Book Value/Share %	NMF	16.4	18.0	11.8
Dividends/Share %	9.1	8.3	15.4	20.0

Profitability [B+]	2004	2005	2006	TTM
Return on Assets %	5.8	9.9	6.9	6.9
Oper Cash Flow $Mil	3,213	3,808	4,451	4,343
- Cap Spending $Mil	2,738	3,068	3,388	3,735
= Free Cash Flow $Mil	475	740	1,063	608

Financial Health [B+]	2004	2005	2006	10-31-06
Long-term Debt $Mil	10,155	9,034	9,119	9,123
Total Equity $Mil	11,132	13,029	14,205	14,800
Debt/Equity Ratio	0.9	0.7	0.6	0.6

Industry	Business Risk	Moat Size	Investment Style	Sector
Discount Stores	Below Avg	Narrow	Large Growth	Consumer Services

Competition	Market Cap $Mil	12 Mo Trailing Sales $Mil	Price/Cash Flow	Return On Assets%	Debt/ Equity	Total Return% 1 Yr	3 Yr
Target	49,000	56,727	11.3	6.9	0.6	4.7	15.6
Wal-Mart Stores	192,479	339,150	9.8	7.2	0.5	0.1	-2.9
Sears Holdings	25,845	52,810	15.4	4.3	0.3	45.4	94.0

Price Volatility | Monthly Price High/Low   — Relative Strength to S&P 500

Annual $Price High/Low	41.74 / 26.00	46.15 / 24.90	41.79 / 25.60	54.14 / 36.65	60.00 / 45.55	60.34 / 44.70
	2001	2002	2003	2004	2005	2006
Annual Total Return %	28.0	-26.5	29.0	36.1	6.6	4.7

Fiscal Year-End: January	2002	2003	2004	2005	2006	TTM
Revenue $Mil	33,021	37,410	42,025	46,839	52,620	56,727
Net Income $Mil	1,340	1,623	1,809	3,198	2,408	2,607
Earnings Per Share $	—	1.78	1.97	3.51	2.71	2.98
Shares Outstanding Mil	—	907	909	903	882	859
Return on Equity %	17.0	17.1	16.3	24.5	17.0	17.6
Net Margin %	4.1	4.3	4.3	6.8	4.6	4.6
Asset Turnover	1.7	1.5	1.3	1.5	1.5	1.5
Financial Leverage	2.5	2.6	2.8	2.5	2.5	2.6

Valuation Ratios	Stock	Rel to Industry	Rel to S&P 500
Price/Earnings	19.1	0.9	0.9
Price/Book	3.3	0.9	0.8
Price/Sales	0.9	1.1	0.3
Price/Cash Flow	11.3	0.9	0.8

Major Fund Holders	% of Fund Assets
W.P. Stewart & Co Growth	7.53
Fidelity Select Retailing	5.14
BlackRock Exchange Blackrock	4.67
Pioneer Growth Leaders A	4.50

Thesis By Joseph Beaulieu, 12-11-06 Stock Price as of Analysis: $58.34

It is difficult for mass-market and discount retailers to develop long-term competitive advantages, but through smart merchandising and attention to shoppers' experience, we think that Target is one of the few such companies that can claim an economic moat.

Target differentiates itself through style. The stores are clean and spacious, with wide aisles and relatively little in the way of intrusive in-store advertising and end-caps. The company specializes in attractive yet inexpensive clothing and housewares (dubbed "cheap chic"), and sells many exclusive product lines developed by trendy designers. Target regularly brings in new lines of merchandise to keep the selection fresh, giving customers a reason to shop often.

This differentiation from other discount retailers has allowed Target to reel in a more affluent customer base and to avoid having to go head-to-head with Wal-Mart. While Target and Wal-Mart are often portrayed as direct rivals, we don't see it that way. They certainly bump up against each other on the margins, but we think the fact that they target different customer segments has allowed Target to thrive even as Wal-Mart bloodied other competitors. In fact, Wal-Mart's first attempts to emulate Target's cheap-chic fashions were met by consumers with mixed (at best) results.

In addition to providing some protection from Wal-Mart, Target's more affluent customer base has allowed Target to report strong results as other mass retailers and discount stores struggled. While high energy prices (among other things) put a crimp in some consumers' spending and brought Wal-Mart's same-store sales growth to a near halt, Target's comps remained relatively strong. Given the discretionary nature of much of its merchandise, Target could be hit pretty hard in a broad-based economic downturn, but we think it is hedging that risk by increasing the percentage of food and other consumables in its product mix.

Eventually, we think that one or more rivals will learn to copy Target's winning formula, creating more competition in the cheap-chic category. Additionally, as Target moves further into the grocery business, margins could be pressured as it competes with a myriad of other players on commodity products. So despite the strength of Target's current position, we've awarded the company only a narrow economic moat rating. But for the foreseeable future, we don't see any direct threat to Target's dominance of higher-end discounting.

TCF Financial TCB

Company Profile
Minnesota-based TCF Financial is a regional bank operating in six Midwestern states, with more than $13.8 billion in total assets. The bank offers heightened customer service and convenience in its 456 branches, 254 of which are in supermarkets. The bank plans to enter Arizona in 2006 with the opening of several consumer loan production offices. TCF is a secured lender and offers a typical suite of deposit products as well as investment and insurance services.

Management   Stewardship Grade [A]
We think TCF has solid corporate-governance practices. Chairman William Cooper has created significant value for shareholders in his tenure, serving as CEO from 1985 to 2005. The bank has posted much higher returns on assets and equity than other banks over the past 10 years, and the shares have handily outperformed the S&P 500. Excess capital has been used to increase dividends and reduce the diluted share count by about 25% since 1997. Cooper handed the CEO reins to COO and president Lynn Nagorske at the beginning of 2006, but will remain chairman through 2008. Nagorske has been working with Cooper since 1987, so we don't anticipate any major changes in the bank's strategy. Cooper owns 3% of the bank's outstanding shares (Nagorske owns about 0.98%) and his compensation is reasonable (he has received the same base salary since 1997) and well deserved, in our opinion. The 11-member board serves staggered three-year terms, and directors are compensated in both cash and stock.

200 Lake Street East Mail Code EX0-03-A   www.tcfexpress.com
Wayzata, MN 55391-1693

Growth [D+]	2002	2003	2004	2005
Revenue %	7.8	-2.0	9.1	1.4
Earnings/Share %	16.7	-2.9	21.6	7.5
Book Value/Share %	10.6	-1.6	7.6	7.7
Dividends/Share %	15.0	13.0	15.4	13.3

Profitability [A+]	2003	2004	2005	TTM
Return on Assets %	1.9	2.1	2.0	1.8
Oper Cash Flow $Mil	437	443	153	—
- Cap Spending $Mil	580	782	915	—
= Free Cash Flow $Mil	—	—	—	—

Financial Health [NA]	2003	2004	2005	09-30-06
Long-term Debt $Mil	—	—	—	—
Total Equity $Mil	917	958	998	1,031
Debt/Equity Ratio	—	—	—	—

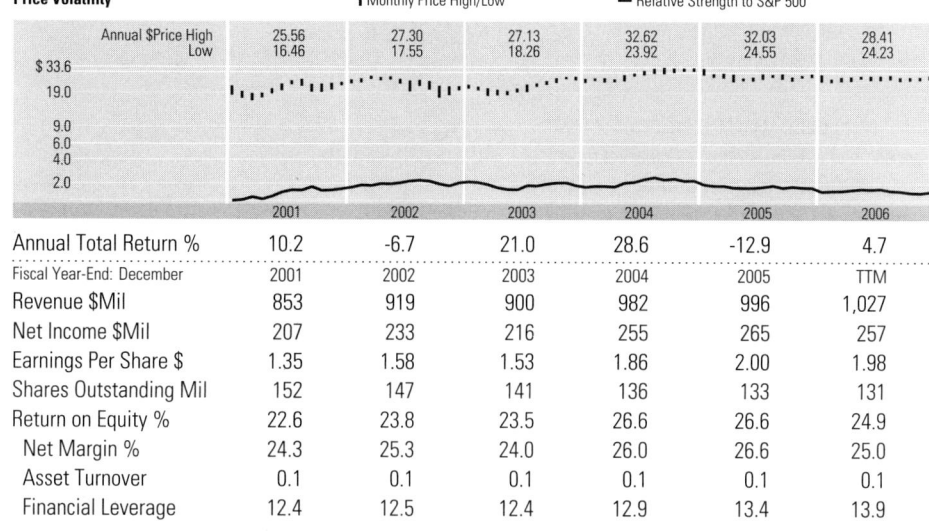

	Rating	Fair Value	Last Close	Consider Buy	Consider Sell	Yield %
	★★★	$29.00	$27.42	$22.40	$36.30	3.36

Industry	Business Risk	Moat Size	Investment Style	Sector
Regional Banks	Average	Narrow	Mid Value	Financial Services

Competition	Market Cap $Mil	12 Mo Trailing Sales $Mil	Price/Cash Flow	Return On Assets%	Debt/Equity	Total Return% 1 Yr	3 Yr
TCF Financial	3,590	1,027	—	1.8	—	4.7	6.3
J.P. Morgan Chase & Co.	167,551	59,650	—	0.9	—	25.6	13.2
Wells Fargo	120,049	34,770	—	1.7	—	16.8	10.4

Annual Total Return %	10.2	-6.7	21.0	28.6	-12.9	4.7
Fiscal Year-End: December	2001	2002	2003	2004	2005	TTM
Revenue $Mil	853	919	900	982	996	1,027
Net Income $Mil	207	233	216	255	265	257
Earnings Per Share $	1.35	1.58	1.53	1.86	2.00	1.98
Shares Outstanding Mil	152	147	141	136	133	131
Return on Equity %	22.6	23.8	23.5	26.6	26.6	24.9
Net Margin %	24.3	25.3	24.0	26.0	26.6	25.0
Asset Turnover	0.1	0.1	0.1	0.1	0.1	0.1
Financial Leverage	12.4	12.5	12.4	12.9	13.4	13.9

Valuation Ratios	Stock	Rel to Industry	Rel to S&P 500
Price/Earnings	13.8	0.8	0.7
Price/Book	3.5	1.2	0.9
Price/Sales	3.5	0.6	1.2
Price/Cash Flow	—	—	—

Major Fund Holders	% of Fund Assets
T. Rowe Price Financial Services	4.94
FAM Equity-Income Inv	3.74
Ave Maria Rising Dividend	3.40
Touchstone Family Heritage(R) A	3.34

Thesis By Michael Kon, CFA, 12-04-06 Stock Price as of Analysis: $26.41

We think TCF's twist to customer convenience differentiates the bank from rivals. The result is very pleasing for both customers and owners.

TCF provides retail and commercial banking services in several Midwestern states. The bank markets itself as the convenient banking choice for the average Joe, leaving other banks to squabble over high-net-worth individuals. We think this differentiates the bank and provides it with a narrow economic moat.

While some banks view convenience as low banking fees, TCF mainly interprets it as being available for customers. The bank's most notable initiative in this area was to open its branches 12 hours a day, 7 days a week, including holidays (except Christmas). We think that in a somewhat commodified banking sector, this move allows TCF to differentiate itself from its rivals, which makes it easier to attract new customers and keep attrition rates low.

In addition, more than 50% of TCF's branches are in supermarkets. While this is very convenient for customers, who can shop and bank at the same location, it has several other benefits for TCF. First, these branches are in high-traffic areas, which makes it easier for TCF to attract customers of other banks and gather deposits. Furthermore, since industry experts estimate that it costs about 4 times less to build a supermarket branch, TCF has built a branch network that is significantly disproportionate to its size. While banks with similar assets typically operate 150-200 branches, TCF has about 450 branches (more than 50% in supermarkets). We think such a large network enables TCF to reach more customers and entrench its position.

TCF also stands out in its ability to produce fee income. Unlike many banks that see deposits as a source of funding, TCF views them as a profit center to generate additional income. This approach results in service charges and fees of 25% of net revenue, compared with less than 15% at peers. Moreover, service charges on deposits have pushed noninterest revenue in 2005 to a staggering 47% of net revenue, compared with only 35% at peers. What's most impressive to us is that TCF earns more in fees on deposits than the interest it pays on those same deposits. This basically means that instead of earning interest, depositors are paying TCF to hold their money for them.

In an industry where differentiation is hard to achieve, TCF's business model stands out.

Telecom Corporation of New Zealand ADR NZT

Data as of 12-29-06

Rating: ★★★

Fair Value	Last Close	Consider Buy	Consider Sell	Yield %
$30.00	$26.92	$23.10	$37.60	6.46

Company Profile
Telecom Corporation of New Zealand is the dominant telecom service provider in its namesake country of about 4 million people. The firm claims the vast majority of the fixed-line phone business, serving about 1.4 million residential and 300,000 business customers. It also serves 1.8 million wireless customers, about 45% of the market. The firm entered Australia via acquisition in 1999; Australian subsidiary AAPT generates a bit less than one fourth of revenue.

Management
Stewardship Grade [NA]

CEO Theresa Gattung and her management team have come under fire for not anticipating recent regulatory changes, but she has maintained the board's support and will remain in her current position for at least the next year. Gattung has headed Telecom since 1999, joining the firm more than a decade ago in a marketing role after holding a similar position with the Bank of New Zealand. She is well paid, receiving total cash compensation of NZ$1.9 million (US$1.3 million) in fiscal 2006. Half of the aftertax amount of her bonus must be used to purchase restricted stock, a feature we like. Former CEO Roderick Deane resigned the chairman position following the announcement of the regulatory changes. Wayne Boyd, an outsider who has sat on numerous boards at New Zealand firms, took the chairman spot. Five large shareholders own about a third of Telecom's shares, though none holds more than 7%. The New Zealand government holds the "Kiwi share," a single share that gives it the right to obligate Telecom to provide service to most consumers at a standard rate.

68 Jervois Quay P.O. Box 570
Wellington, New Zealand
www.telecom.co.nz

Growth [NA]	2003	2004	2005	2006
Revenue %	-6.1	3.6	7.7	0.2
Earnings/Share %	NMF	2.6	25.6	NMF
Book Value/Share %	NMF	NMF	9.7	-56.6
Dividends/Share %	—	—	—	—

Profitability [NA]	2004	2005	2006	TTM
Return on Assets %	9.9	12.7	-7.8	-7.8
Oper Cash Flow $Mil	1,044	1,166	1,205	1,205
- Cap Spending $Mil	389	477	492	492
= Free Cash Flow $Mil	654	690	714	714

Financial Health [NA]	2004	2005	2006	06-30-06
Long-term Debt $Mil	2,176	2,079	1,514	1,514
Total Equity $Mil	1,397	1,728	632	632
Debt/Equity Ratio	1.6	1.2	2.4	2.4

Industry	Business Risk	Moat Size	Investment Style	Sector
Telecom Svcs.	Average	Narrow	Large Value	Telecommunication

Competition	Market Cap $Mil	12 Mo Trailing Sales $Mil	Price/Cash Flow	Return On Assets%	Debt/ Equity	Total Return% 1 Yr	3 Yr
Telecom Corporation of New Zealand ADR	6,599	3,879	5.5	-7.8	2.4	-8.2	6.8
Vodafone Group PLC ADR	127,867	52,679	6.0	-17.6	0.2	34.1	6.3
Telstra Corporation ADR	40,764	16,899	6.7	12.0	0.0	24.9	3.9

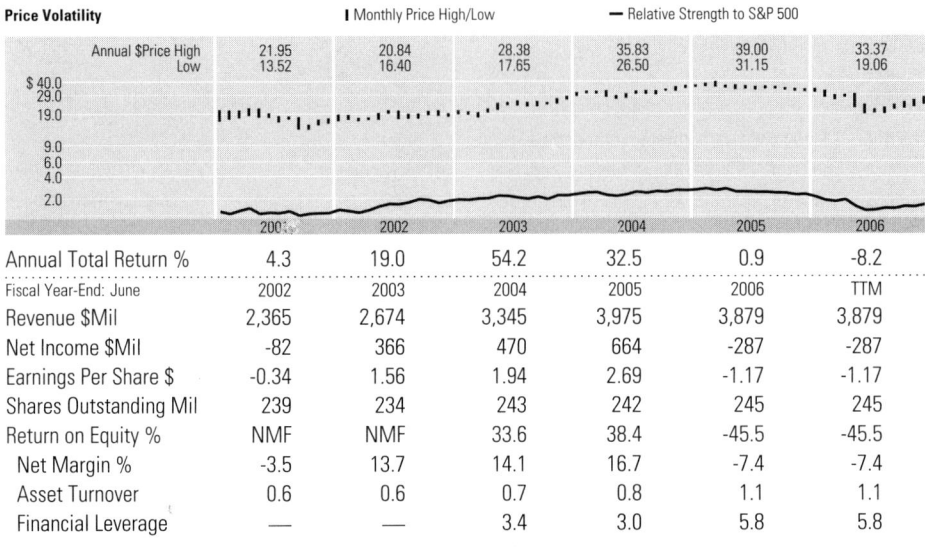

	2002	2003	2004	2005	2006	TTM
Annual Total Return %	4.3	19.0	54.2	32.5	0.9	-8.2
Fiscal Year-End: June	2002	2003	2004	2005	2006	TTM
Revenue $Mil	2,365	2,674	3,345	3,975	3,879	3,879
Net Income $Mil	-82	366	470	664	-287	-287
Earnings Per Share $	-0.34	1.56	1.94	2.69	-1.17	-1.17
Shares Outstanding Mil	239	234	243	242	245	245
Return on Equity %	NMF	NMF	33.6	38.4	-45.5	-45.5
Net Margin %	-3.5	13.7	14.1	16.7	-7.4	-7.4
Asset Turnover	0.6	0.6	0.7	0.8	1.1	1.1
Financial Leverage	—	—	3.4	3.0	5.8	5.8

Valuation Ratios	Stock	Rel to Industry	Rel to S&P 500
Price/Earnings	NMF	—	—
Price/Book	10.4	2.4	2.5
Price/Sales	1.7	0.7	0.6
Price/Cash Flow	5.5	0.6	0.4

Major Fund Holders	% of Fund Assets
Integrity Growth & Income A Load Waived	4.35
Phoenix Global Utilities A	1.84
Sextant International	1.13

Thesis
By Michael Hodel, CFA, 12-12-06 Stock Price as of Analysis: $26.00

Telecom Corporation of New Zealand enjoys a dominant market position and stable cash flows. In May, the government announced plans to further open the firm's networks to competition, leaving a cloud of uncertainty over Telecom and punishing its share price. However, we think its assets make the firm an indispensable part of the nation's economy and infrastructure, giving it a big advantage.

When Telecom was privatized in 1990, the government completely deregulated the industry. New entrants have had little room to maneuver, and Telecom still holds the vast majority of the fixed-line market; this business, despite some pockets of pricing pressure, generates margins and cash flow on par with the best in the world. The regulatory environment in New Zealand has evolved slowly over the years, but it received a big jolt in 2006. The government is splitting Telecom into three operating units: network access, wholesale, and retail. The network access business will have to treat rivals and Telecom's retail unit equally, allowing rivals better rates and service when purchasing unbundled local loops (the wire connecting customers' homes and businesses to the network).

Even with these regulatory changes, we think Telecom will remain dominant. Unlike some markets, including the United States, no major rival, such as a cable company, owns a duplicative network. Competitors will need to make sizable investments hoping that regulation doesn't shift again or that technology doesn't change dramatically. They will also be offering similar services as Telecom, leaving them to compete on price and service with the far larger incumbent.

We think the bigger threat to Telecom is changing wireless technology. The firm's wireless performance had been weak in recent years, despite facing only one rival, Vodafone. Telecom has greatly improved its wireless business recently, though, and has been growing faster than Vodafone for the past year or so. It seems Telecom has learned to compete here, and with around 90% of the population already subscribing to wireless service, we think it is unlikely another firm will enter the market on a broad scale. Still, new wireless technologies could make it possible to attack Telecom's fixed-line data business.

Australia, a market Telecom entered in 1999, is a major concern. The firm has struggled--not only against Telstra, as one would expect, but also against other upstarts. The entry into Australia has severely reduced the firm's overall profitability, yet Telecom remains dedicated to investing in this market.

Data as of 12-29-06

Telefonica SA ADR TEF

	Rating	Fair Value	Last Close	Consider Buy	Consider Sell	Yield %
	★★★★	$78.00	$63.75	$60.10	$97.70	3.24

Company Profile

Telefonica is the incumbent fixed-line and wireless telephone operator in Spain and the Czech Republic. It has the most wireless subscribers in the U.K. and a big position in Germany. It has substantial fixed and wireless assets in Latin America, where over half its customers reside. However, they provide only about 35% of its revenue and 34% of its operating profit before depreciation and amortization. Telefonica also owns stakes in Portugal Telecom and China Netcom.

Management
Stewardship Grade [NA]

Cesar Alierta came in as chairman and CEO in August 2000 to replace Juan Villalonga, who resigned under pressure after overpaying for Endemol and Lycos and making questionable insider trades. Alierta was formerly CEO of Tabacalera, a tobacco firm he led in a merger with Seita. He has strong capital markets experience. Alierta has brought in many new managers to help run the various divisions. Initially, he kept the focus on growth in Latin America, strengthened the firm's ties with Portugal Telecom by merging the two companies' Brazilian cellular operations into Vivo, and was cognizant of prices paid for acquisitions. Recently, Alierta has expanded into other parts of the world and has been willing to pay up for admittance, acting somewhat like Villalonga in the late 1990s. We think the acquisition of O2 weakens management's credibility. We had been concerned for some time about Telefonica's increasingly acquisitive tendencies, but were assured that Telefonica's A bond credit rating was sacrosanct. That went out the window with the O2 acquisition, though, as Standard & Poor's cut its rating to BBB+. Alierta has also thinned the management ranks, and there is some concern he is becoming too powerful. Salaries and option grants seem reasonable for a firm of Telefonica's size.

Gran Via, 28
Madrid, Spain E-28013
www.telefonica.es

Growth [NA]	2002	2003	2004	2005
Revenue %	-8.6	-0.4	8.0	25.1
Earnings/Share %	NMF	NMF	50.6	43.3
Book Value/Share %	-32.1	-2.8	-40.7	26.2
Dividends/Share %	—	—	—	—

Profitability [NA]	2003	2004	2005	TTM
Return on Assets %	3.2	5.3	6.9	6.9
Oper Cash Flow $Mil	10,294	12,585	13,949	13,949
- Cap Spending $Mil	—	4,633	5,681	5,681
= Free Cash Flow $Mil	—	7,952	8,268	8,268

Financial Health [NA]	2003	2004	2005	12-31-05
Long-term Debt $Mil	22,117	23,962	29,961	29,961
Total Equity $Mil	20,946	14,301	15,159	15,159
Debt/Equity Ratio	1.1	1.7	2.0	2.0

Industry	Business Risk	Moat Size	Investment Style	Sector
Telecom Svcs.	Average	Narrow	Large Growth	Telecommunication

Competition

	Market Cap $Mil	12 Mo Trailing Sales $Mil	Price/Cash Flow	Return On Assets%	Debt/ Equity	Total Return% 1 Yr	3 Yr
Telefonica SA ADR	104,574	49,213	7.5	6.9	2.0	47.1	17.7
America Movil SA ADR	81,952	16,897	14.6	13.8	0.6	55.5	68.9
Deutsche Telekom AG ADR	76,405	74,638	4.1	4.6	—	15.0	1.8

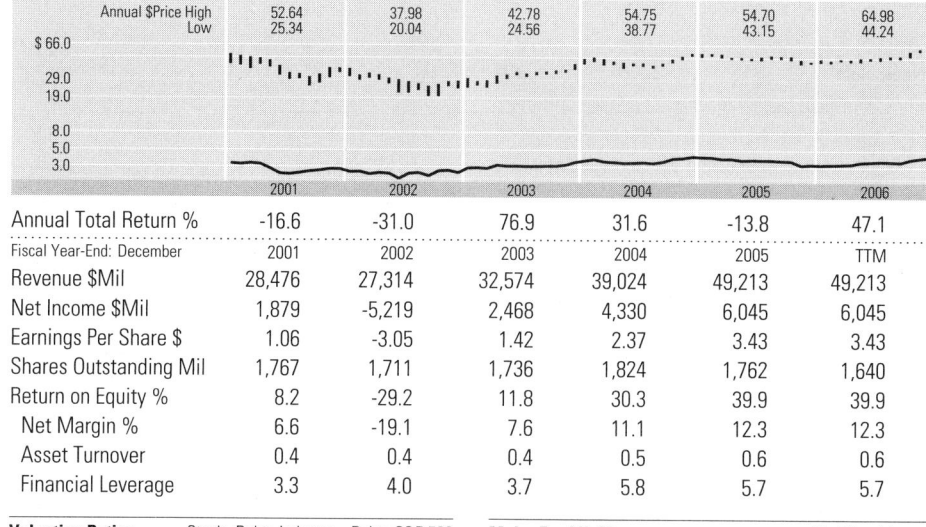

Annual Total Return %	-16.6	-31.0	76.9	31.6	-13.8	47.1
Fiscal Year-End: December	2001	2002	2003	2004	2005	TTM
Revenue $Mil	28,476	27,314	32,574	39,024	49,213	49,213
Net Income $Mil	1,879	-5,219	2,468	4,330	6,045	6,045
Earnings Per Share $	1.06	-3.05	1.42	2.37	3.43	3.43
Shares Outstanding Mil	1,767	1,711	1,736	1,824	1,762	1,640
Return on Equity %	8.2	-29.2	11.8	30.3	39.9	39.9
Net Margin %	6.6	-19.1	7.6	11.1	12.3	12.3
Asset Turnover	0.4	0.4	0.4	0.5	0.6	0.6
Financial Leverage	3.3	4.0	3.7	5.8	5.7	5.7

Valuation Ratios	Stock	Rel to Industry	Rel to S&P 500
Price/Earnings	18.6	1.0	0.9
Price/Book	6.9	1.6	1.7
Price/Sales	2.1	0.9	0.7
Price/Cash Flow	7.5	0.8	0.5

Major Fund Holders	% of Fund Assets
Hartford Global Comm HLS IA	4.09
Hartford Global Communications A	3.94
ICON Telecommunications & Utilities	3.57
Cambiar International Equity Inv	3.24

Thesis By Allan C. Nichols, CFA, 12-13-06 Stock Price as of Analysis: $64.89

With the acquisitions of O2, Cesky Telecom, and Colombia Telecom in the past year, Telefonica has become the third-largest wireless operator in the world, behind only China Mobile and Vodafone. The fixed-line, Internet access, and pay television businesses add to Telefonica's size, giving it the scale to provide cost advantages. And its name recognition, particularly in Spanish- and Portuguese-speaking markets, enables it to earn high returns on capital, which we think provide Telefonica with a narrow moat.

Telefonica has done a great job of integrating O2, which has performed better than we expected. It continues to add new subscribers in the U.K. significantly faster than the other wireless operators. Telefonica has also reduced costs in the rest of the firm, enabling operating margins to remain near previous levels despite the lower margins generated at O2.

However, Telefonica does not have a monopoly on growth. A string of mergers in the European telecom industry is creating continent-wide giants that are also gaining economies of scale. The mergers are pushing the firms into direct competition in many markets. With Telefonica having entered the U.K. and Germany via the O2 acquisition, we expect more aggressive responses from Deutsche Telekom and Vodafone, which have large operations in both nations.

In Spain, Telefonica has enjoyed strong margins as it has historically had less competition than other markets, which has been a key to its success. But consolidation is now hitting close to home with France Telecom having acquired Amena, the second-largest fixed-line and third-largest wireless operator in the country. Also, the two largest Spanish cable companies have merged, which should increase competition for fixed-line and mobile telephone and high-speed Internet access customers.

Meanwhile in Latin America, America Movil and Telecom Italia have become more aggressive, slowing Telefonica's growth, particularly in Brazil. Vivo, Telefonica's Brazilian wireless joint venture with Portugal Telecom, has seen its market share drop to 30% from 40% since the beginning of 2005. The Latin American fixed-line business continues to grow, but at a slower rate. However, outside of Brazil, many countries are becoming wireless duopolies of Telefonica and America Movil, and in our experience, wireless duopolies are very profitable for both firms over time.

Data as of 12-29-06

Telefonos de Mexico SA de CV ADR TMX

Rating	Fair Value	Last Close	Consider Buy	Consider Sell	Yield %
★★★	$30.00	$28.26	$23.10	$37.60	2.60

Company Profile

Telefonos de Mexico offers fixed-line local and long-distance phone and Internet services in Mexico. While the firm says it only has 25% of local phone customers in the nation--a figure that includes wireless--it dominates the fixed-line business, controlling about 95% of local lines. The firm also holds about 75% of the domestic and international long-distance markets. Telmex has expanded into Latin America with operations in Brazil, Chile, Argentina, Peru, and Colombia.

Management   Stewardship Grade [NA]

Carlos Slim Helu bought a controlling stake in Telmex when it was privatized from the Mexican government in 1990. As chairman, he did a wonderful job of running the business, upgrading the network and bringing telephony to millions while also making shareholders money--and making himself the richest person in Latin America. He stepped down as chairman in 2004 to allow his son, Carlos Slim Domit, to take the role. Slim Helu remains honorary lifetime chairman and Telmex's largest shareholder. Slim Domit worked with his father since the privatization, and has also been president of Sanborn Hermanos, the family's retail business. Jaime Chico Pardo, who was CEO for 12 years, was recently made chairman along with Slim Domit. The new CEO is Hector Slim Seade--a nephew of Slim Helu--who has been director of operational support at Telmex since 1995. The firm has voting and nonvoting share classes, which allow Slim Helu to control the company, though his 44% total ownership would provide him with effective control anyway. We don't like multiple class shares, but there has been no evidence of Slim Helu abusing his position at the expense of other shareholders. AT&T also owns 21% of the voting shares. Telmex has many dealings with other companies controlled by Slim Helu, and there is no way to be sure the dealings are all at arm's length.

Parque Via 190 Colonia Cuauhtemoc   www.telmex.com
Mexico City, Mexico 06599

Growth [NA]	2002	2003	2004	2005
Revenue %	-4.4	0.0	12.2	12.6
Earnings/Share %	-14.0	14.0	24.3	3.9
Book Value/Share %	24.4	29.4	35.8	3.0
Dividends/Share %	—	—	—	—

Profitability [NA]	2003	2004	2005	TTM
Return on Assets %	12.6	11.5	11.6	11.6
Oper Cash Flow $Mil	2,648	5,842	4,751	4,751
- Cap Spending $Mil	1,001	1,877	2,174	2,174
= Free Cash Flow $Mil	1,648	3,965	2,576	2,576

Financial Health [NA]	2003	2004	2005	12-31-05
Long-term Debt $Mil	—	7,223	7,269	7,269
Total Equity $Mil	7,702	9,913	10,329	10,329
Debt/Equity Ratio	—	0.7	0.7	0.7

Industry	Business Risk	Moat Size	Investment Style · Sector
Telecom Svcs.	Average	Narrow	Large Core · Telecommunication

Competition	Market Cap $Mil	12 Mo Trailing Sales $Mil	Price/Cash Flow	Return On Assets %	Debt/ Equity	Total Return% 1 Yr	3 Yr
Telefonos de Mexico SA de CV ADR	31,150	15,116	6.6	11.6	0.7	18.2	23.9
Telefonica SA ADR	104,574	49,213	7.5	6.9	2.0	47.1	17.7
America Movil SA ADR	81,952	16,897	14.6	13.8	0.6	55.5	68.9

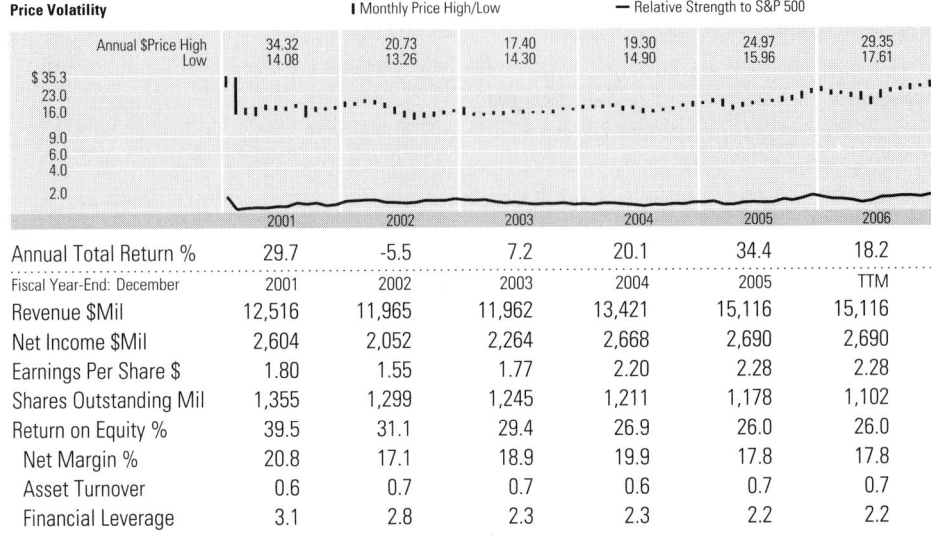

	2001	2002	2003	2004	2005	TTM
Annual Total Return %	29.7	-5.5	7.2	20.1	34.4	18.2
Fiscal Year-End: December						
Revenue $Mil	12,516	11,965	11,962	13,421	15,116	15,116
Net Income $Mil	2,604	2,052	2,264	2,668	2,690	2,690
Earnings Per Share $	1.80	1.55	1.77	2.20	2.28	2.28
Shares Outstanding Mil	1,355	1,299	1,245	1,211	1,178	1,102
Return on Equity %	39.5	31.1	29.4	26.9	26.0	26.0
Net Margin %	20.8	17.1	18.9	19.9	17.8	17.8
Asset Turnover	0.6	0.7	0.7	0.6	0.7	0.7
Financial Leverage	3.1	2.8	2.3	2.3	2.2	2.2

Valuation Ratios	Stock	Rel to Industry	Rel to S&P 500
Price/Earnings	12.4	0.7	0.6
Price/Book	3.0	0.7	0.7
Price/Sales	2.1	0.9	0.7
Price/Cash Flow	6.6	0.7	0.5

Major Fund Holders	% of Fund Assets
Mundoval	3.19
ICON Telecommunications & Utilities	2.24
Columbia Global Value B	2.21
Delaware Intl Value Equity A	2.00

Thesis By Allan C. Nichols, CFA, 11-16-06 Stock Price as of Analysis: $26.80

We love Telefonos de Mexico's high margins, high returns on capital, acquisition discipline, and management. Fixed-line telephone growth prospects in Mexico are limited, however, and competition elsewhere is much more intense.

Telmex dominates Mexico's local and long-distance telephone market with over 95% of the fixed-line market. However, to convince the Mexican telephone regulator that it doesn't have market power, Telmex points out that it has only 25% of the telephone market including cell phones. But because of the high costs of wireless, Telmex still carries more than 80% of all local usage minutes. Wireless services cost more on a per-minute basis and have higher taxes than fixed-line phone calls. While this cost difference is likely to diminish, we expect it to continue for some time. Telmex's domination, combined with efficient operations, has created high margins, high returns, and a narrow moat.

However, the growth in Mexico's phone markets is almost all on the wireless side. Telmex is still adding some prepaid fixed-line subscribers, but it has found that many rarely use these phones and has actually been purging lines that cost more to maintain than they generate in revenue. We expect revenue from new lines and new services will be insufficient to offset price declines in the fixed-line market in Mexico.

In order to grow its revenues, Telmex continues to turn to the rest of Latin America--particularly Brazil. The firm just finished its tender offer for Embratel, and now owns 96.4% of it. Non-Mexican operations now account for 27% of the firm's revenues. These businesses are growing, with Embratel's revenue up 8.2% year over year and Colombia up 47.6%. These countries are more competitive as Telmex is now the newcomer instead of the incumbent. However, Telmex's primary focus is on business customers, and its broad international presence makes a compelling argument for companies operating in more than one country, which we expect will allow these markets to continue to drive Telmex's growth.

We also expect non-Mexican countries to drive margin improvement. From 1999 to 2005 Telmex's operating margins steadily declined, but 2006 appears to be the year of change. The non-Mexican countries have improved operating margins by about 3 percentage points in 2006, which is sufficient to offset the lower margins generated by Mexico's prepaid fixed-line customers. Telmex remains one of the most profitable telecom companies in the world.

Data as of 12-29-06

Tellabs TLAB

	Rating	Fair Value	Last Close	Consider Buy	Consider Sell	Yield %
	★★★★	$12.00	$10.26	$9.30	$15.00	0.00

Company Profile
Tellabs manufactures digital transmission systems telecom-service providers use to manage traffic on their networks. Its primary products are digital cross-connect systems--which carriers use to make networks work more efficiently--and optical access equipment--which carriers are installing to provide faster broadband access. The firm also makes voice quality-enhancement products, and optical-networking gear. Tellabs has a large installed base and a solid reputation with major telecom carriers.

Industry	Business Risk	Moat Size	Investment Style	Sector
Wireline Equip.	Average	Narrow	Mid Core	Hardware

Competition

	Market Cap $Mil	12 Mo Trailing Sales $Mil	Price/Cash Flow	Return On Assets %	Debt/ Equity	Total Return % 1 Yr	3 Yr
Tellabs	4,533	2,108	14.2	6.9	—	-5.9	7.1
Nortel Networks	11,591	11,078	—	-12.1	3.4	-12.7	-15.9
Ciena	2,340	522	—	-14.5	1.2	33.3	-16.0

Management   Stewardship Grade [C]
Although management execution has been strong over the past couple years, Tellabs' heavy issuance of stock options gives it only an average Stewardship Grade. CEO Krish Prabhu, who joined Tellabs in early 2004, stepped into some big shoes: His predecessor, Michael Birck, founded Tellabs in 1974 and returned to the CEO role after former CEO Richard Notebaert departed for Qwest. Birck remained on as chairman and controls nearly 8% of Tellabs' shares. Prabhu is a good match, because he served in a variety of roles at Alcatel, one of Tellabs' key competitors. From 1997 to 1999 he led Alcatel's U.S. operations, and from 1999 to 2001 he was chief operating officer at Alcatel's telecom unit. We believe Prabhu's experience with Alcatel's access business has been invaluable to Tellabs as it integrates the acquisition of AFC. Most senior Tellabs managers have long tenures, which should counter what may seem like a revolving door in the CEO's office over the past five years.

Management compensation does not seem excessive, with high-level executives earning salaries and option grants on par with their counterparts at other telecom-equipment firms. Stock option expense is high; under the new accounting rules for options, we estimate that option expense lowered net income by about 25% in 2006.

One Tellabs Center 1415 W. Diehl Road   www.tellabs.com
Naperville, IL 60563

Growth [A]	2002	2003	2004	2005
Revenue %	-40.1	-25.6	25.6	52.9
Earnings/Share %	NMF	NMF	NMF	NMF
Book Value/Share %	-6.7	-4.2	23.3	-5.0
Dividends/Share %	NMF	NMF	NMF	NMF

Profitability [B-]	2003	2004	2005	TTM
Return on Assets %	-9.3	-0.8	5.0	6.9
Oper Cash Flow $Mil	150	215	258	320
- Cap Spending $Mil	17	41	62	76
= Free Cash Flow $Mil	133	173	197	244

Financial Health [C+]	2003	2004	2005	09-30-06
Long-term Debt $Mil	—	—	—	—
Total Equity $Mil	2,219	2,797	2,815	2,918
Debt/Equity Ratio	—	—	—	—

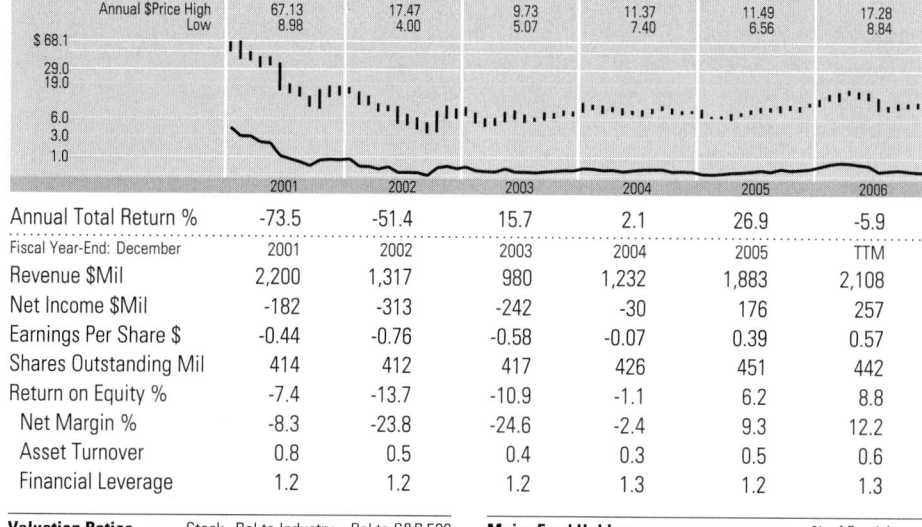

Price Volatility
Monthly Price High/Low — Relative Strength to S&P 500

Annual $Price High/Low	67.13/8.98	17.47/4.00	9.73/5.07	11.37/7.40	11.49/6.56	17.28/8.84
	2001	2002	2003	2004	2005	2006
Annual Total Return %	-73.5	-51.4	15.7	2.1	26.9	-5.9

Fiscal Year-End: December	2001	2002	2003	2004	2005	TTM
Revenue $Mil	2,200	1,317	980	1,232	1,883	2,108
Net Income $Mil	-182	-313	-242	-30	176	257
Earnings Per Share $	-0.44	-0.76	-0.58	-0.07	0.39	0.57
Shares Outstanding Mil	414	412	417	426	451	442
Return on Equity %	-7.4	-13.7	-10.9	-1.1	6.2	8.8
Net Margin %	-8.3	-23.8	-24.6	-2.4	9.3	12.2
Asset Turnover	0.8	0.5	0.4	0.3	0.5	0.6
Financial Leverage	1.2	1.2	1.2	1.3	1.2	1.3

Valuation Ratios	Stock	Rel to Industry	Rel to S&P 500
Price/Earnings	18.0	0.7	0.9
Price/Book	1.6	0.3	0.4
Price/Sales	2.2	0.4	0.8
Price/Cash Flow	14.2	0.9	1.0

Major Fund Holders	% of Fund Assets
Columbia Acorn Select Z	5.58
Quaker Mid-Cap Value A	1.86
Volumetric	1.79
RS MidCap Opportunities A	1.60

Thesis By John Slack, 12-15-06 Stock Price as of Analysis: $10.57

Tellabs has carved out a niche as a provider of a few key telecom equipment products. While the firm's concentrated sales to a handful of carriers creates a great deal of volatility in the firm's revenues and shares, we believe that its exposure to favorable areas of telecom-equipment spending warrant the attention of investors, at the right price.

Tellabs has built a large share in the niche markets of the telecom-equipment industry by providing products that are easily integrated into carriers' networks while offering next-generation functionality. The company has a focused portfolio of products, notably digital cross-connects and optical access equipment, that telecom carriers need to upgrade networks and make them more efficient.

Cross-connects, which represent nearly 30% of sales, are used by carriers to manage bandwidth needs and groom traffic. Tellabs has seen a resurgence in demand for its cross-connects, as wireless carriers ready their networks for the increased call volumes and, especially, data traffic on next-generation wireless networks. The company's sales cycle typically involves large up-front sales of lower-margin equipment chassis that are then followed by years of high-margin add-on business, such as linecards that expand capacity and value-added software feature packs--the most recent being Ethernet functionality.

Tellabs entered the access-equipment market via its acquisition of Advanced Fiber Communications (AFC) in 2004. The market for access equipment has been one of the healthiest areas of growth in the telecom-equipment market over the past few years, as carriers such as Verizon and AT&T push their fiber networks closer to customers. We viewed Tellabs' move into the access-equipment market as a logical extension, adding a strong suite of optical access products to its traditional transport products.

Our concerns about the company stem from the fact that sales tend to be very concentrated and lumpy. In our opinion, equipment expenditures typically move in a step-function pattern. Investment lulls are followed by increases in spending as new capacity is added, which should benefit Tellabs down the road. Another area of concern it that the strength in Tellabs' high-margin cross-connect business will start to fade as newer network technologies begin to ship in volume. Recent deployments and carrier trials of some of Tellabs' newer optical transport products and Tellabs' ability to extend the viability of its cross-connects through software add-ons make us more comfortable that it can manage this transition.

TEPPCO Partners TPP

Data as of 12-29-06

Rating	Fair Value	Last Close	Consider Buy	Consider Sell	Yield %
★★★	$43.00	$40.31	$36.60	$56.50	6.70

Company Profile
Houston-based TEPPCO is a master limited partnership that owns three operating segments: upstream, midstream, and downstream. The upstream segment transports crude oil and other unfinished products. The midstream segment gathers and transports natural gas. The downstream segment transports and stores refined products. TEPPCO owns about 11,600 miles of pipeline; its longest routes connect the Gulf of Mexico to the Northeastern United States.

Management   Stewardship Grade [B]
EPCO, a company controlled by Dan Duncan that also owns the general partner of Enterprise Products Partners, purchased TEPPCO's general partner from Duke Energy and ConocoPhillips in February 2005. We don't anticipate any big changes to TEPPCO's strategy, since it was well run before the change in ownership. Jerry Thompson is the newly elected president and CEO of the general partnership. He joins the team after a 35-year career at CITGO, where he was most recently COO. Our Stewardship Grade for the company is a B rather than the C most master limited partnerships receive, primarily because of the recent elimination of the high incentive distribution rights split. We think this move is in unitholders' best interests, as it will direct a greater share of future cash flows to limited partners. While limited partners still do not have direct input into management decisions, a problem common to all master limited partnerships, we view this proposal as a way to share more of the benefits of ownership with common unitholders. The biggest issue we now have with the partnership's stewardship is the lack of executive and director ownership of partnership units. The partnership uses a "phantom unit" plan to compensate executives, but we would prefer to see actual unit ownership.

2929 Allen Parkway P.O. Box 2521
Houston, TX 77252-2521
www.teppco.com

Growth [B]	2002	2003	2004	2005
Revenue %	-8.8	31.3	40.0	44.6
Earnings/Share %	—	NMF	6.1	9.6
Book Value/Share %	—	NMF	-11.7	13.4
Dividends/Share %	9.3	6.4	5.5	1.4

Profitability [C]	2003	2004	2005	TTM
Return on Assets %	2.9	3.1	3.1	3.6
Oper Cash Flow $Mil	242	267	255	438
- Cap Spending $Mil	168	168	333	209
= Free Cash Flow $Mil	74	100	-78	229

Financial Health [C]	2003	2004	2005	09-30-06
Long-term Debt $Mil	—	1,480	1,525	1,472
Total Equity $Mil	1,103	1,047	1,263	1,415
Debt/Equity Ratio	—	1.4	1.2	1.0

Industry	Business Risk	Moat Size	Investment Style	Sector
Pipelines	Below Avg	Wide	Mid Value	Energy

Competition	Market Cap $Mil	12 Mo Trailing Sales $Mil	Price/Cash Flow	Return On Assets%	Debt/Equity	Total Return% 1 Yr	3 Yr
TEPPCO Partners	3,052	10,039	7.0	3.6	1.0	24.3	7.2
Williams Companies	15,576	12,719	9.3	0.9	1.2	14.4	40.0
Enterprise Products Partn	12,514	14,421	9.8	3.5	0.8	29.2	13.3

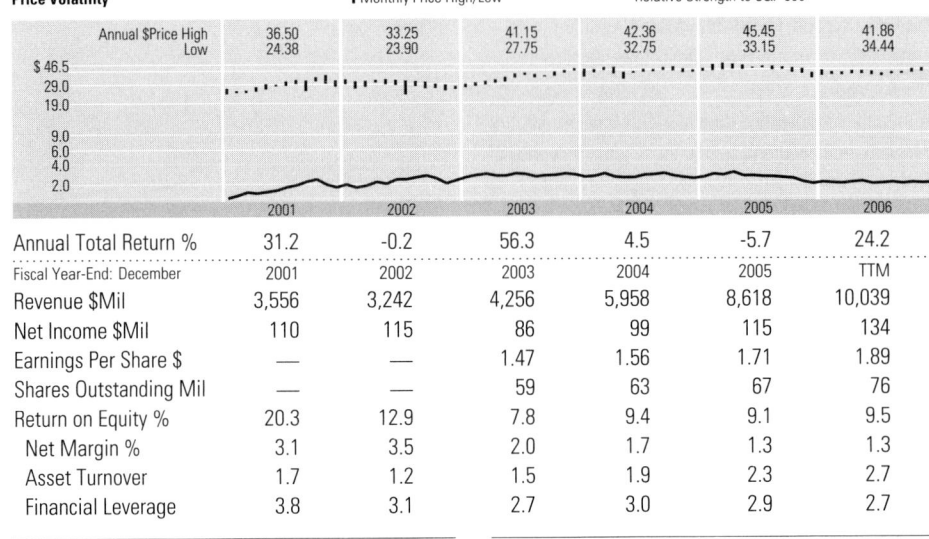

Price Volatility — Monthly Price High/Low — Relative Strength to S&P 500

	2001	2002	2003	2004	2005	2006
Annual $Price High	36.50	33.25	41.15	42.36	45.45	41.86
Low	24.38	23.90	27.75	32.75	33.15	34.44
Annual Total Return %	31.2	-0.2	56.3	4.5	-5.7	24.2
Fiscal Year-End: December	2001	2002	2003	2004	2005	TTM
Revenue $Mil	3,556	3,242	4,256	5,958	8,618	10,039
Net Income $Mil	110	115	86	99	115	134
Earnings Per Share $	—	—	1.47	1.56	1.71	1.89
Shares Outstanding Mil	—	—	59	63	67	76
Return on Equity %	20.3	12.9	7.8	9.4	9.1	9.5
Net Margin %	3.1	3.5	2.0	1.7	1.3	1.3
Asset Turnover	1.7	1.2	1.5	1.9	2.3	2.7
Financial Leverage	3.8	3.1	2.7	3.0	2.9	2.7

Valuation Ratios	Stock	Rel to Industry	Rel to S&P 500
Price/Earnings	23.3	0.8	1.1
Price/Book	2.2	0.9	0.5
Price/Sales	0.3	0.1	0.1
Price/Cash Flow	7.0	0.7	0.5

Major Fund Holders	% of Fund Assets
Akros Absolute Return	1.44

Thesis   By Jason Stevens, 12-20-06   Stock Price as of Analysis: $40.65

TEPPCO Partners offers the sort of consistent results and high cash distributions that are the hallmark of pipeline companies organized as master limited partnerships. We would consider buying units of this partnership to benefit from the company's sustainable growth prospects and high distribution yield.

During 2006 the partnership announced a joint venture with Enterprise Products Partners that will own the Jonah Gas Gathering System that taps the Jonah and Pinedale natural-gas fields in Wyoming. The two partnerships plan to expand system capacity from the current 1.5 billion cubic feet per day to 2.4 bcfd by the end of 2007 and will split the costs of expansion 50/50. By the end of Phase V, TEPPCO will retain an 80% interest in the venture; Enterprise will hold the remaining 20% and serve as operator. We think this is a good arrangement for TEPPCO, as Enterprise is particularly adept at developing and operating gas gathering assets, and we believe both companies will benefit from Enterprise's stewardship. TEPPCO expects the Phase V expansion to cost $415 million and expects to contribute $119 million toward the project in 2006. On top of this, the partnership is pursuing another $195 million in growth projects in 2006. We expect these expenditures to deliver strong cash-flow growth, which should enable the partnership to boost annual distributions at a high-single-digit rate compared with the 1.4%-2.0% increases we've seen recently.

Another factor that, in our opinion, will enable the company to raise distributions at a faster clip is the recent vote to eliminate the highest level of incentive distributions received by the partnership's general partner. By eliminating the highest split, the partnership will be able to avoid a huge drain on future cash flows and instead be able to raise distributions and invest in growth projects, which in turn set the stage for greater distributions.

We think TEPPCO common units carry below-average risk compared with the rest of our coverage universe. The partnership has produced consistent growth in operating income and cash flow over the past five years. Although TEPPCO actively buys and sells some of the oil that travels in its pipeline, it insulates itself from commodity price exposure by simultaneously entering into buy and sell contracts. In any case, the oil marketing business makes up only a very small portion of TEPPCO's operating income.

Data as of 12-29-06

Ternium SA ADR TX

	Rating	Fair Value	Last Close	Consider Buy	Consider Sell	Yield %
	★★★★	$35.00	$29.54	$22.30	$42.20	0.00

Company Profile

Ternium is a Luxembourg-based holding company that owns steel manufacturing operations in Argentina, Venezuela, and Mexico. These firms manufacture, process, and distribute flat and long steel as well as value-added products like cold-rolled coils, prepainted sheets, steel bars, and wire rod. Between 50% and 60% of Ternium's sales come from Central and South America, where it dominates the local markets. The rest of its steel is sold in North America, Europe, and elsewhere.

Management   Stewardship Grade [NA]

Ternium's chairman Paolo Rocca is CEO of the Techint Group, an international group of companies for which Ternium officially holds its investments in Sidor, Siderar, and Hylsamex. The Techint Group is controlled by San Faustin, which is ultimately controlled by Rocca & Partners. Rocca & Partners, through a long, complex chain of ownership, indirectly controls more than 70% of the company's outstanding shares and is able to elect the majority of Ternium's board members. It also has the power to determine the results of most shareholder issues, such as dividend policy (Ternium currently pays no dividends). The ADSs offered in the firm's IPO represent less than 13% of its outstanding shares. CEO Daniel A. Novegil and his fellow directors and executive officers do not beneficially own any stake in the company, but we can forgive this for the time being, as Ternium is a young, newly restructured entity.

46A Avenue John F. Kennedy 2nd Floor www.ternium.com
, Luxembourg L-1855

Growth [NA]	2002	2003	2004	2005
Revenue %	NMF	NMF	51.3	178.2
Earnings/Share %	NMF	NMF	NMF	NMF
Book Value/Share %	—	—	—	—
Dividends/Share %	NMF	NMF	NMF	NMF

Profitability [NA]	2003	2004	2005	TTM
Return on Assets %	16.3	28.3	12.4	12.4
Oper Cash Flow $Mil	346	518	1,262	1,262
- Cap Spending $Mil	34	93	245	245
= Free Cash Flow $Mil	312	425	1,018	1,018

Financial Health [NA]	2003	2004	2005	12-31-05
Long-term Debt $Mil	284	1	2,400	2,400
Total Equity $Mil	1,252	1,772	3,576	3,576
Debt/Equity Ratio	0.2	0.0	0.7	0.7

	Industry	Business Risk	Moat Size	Investment Style	Sector
	Steel/Iron	Above Avg	Narrow		Industrial Materials

Competition

	Market Cap $Mil	12 Mo Trailing Sales $Mil	Price/Cash Flow	Return On Assets%	Debt/Equity	Total Return% 1 Yr	3 Yr
Ternium SA ADR	5,922	4,448	4.7	12.4	0.7	—	—
Mittal Steel Co NV	29,697	28,132	7.5	10.8	0.9	62.5	68.8
Gerdau SA ADR PN	10,681	8,894	31.0	12.0	1.3	49.5	58.8

Price Volatility

Annual $Price High/Low: 30.50 / 19.91

Fiscal Year-End: December	2001	2002	2003	2004	2005	TTM
Annual Total Return %	—	—	—	—	—	—
Revenue $Mil	—	—	1,057	1,599	4,448	4,448
Net Income $Mil	—	—	357	748	1,073	1,073
Earnings Per Share $	—	—	—	—	—	—
Shares Outstanding Mil	—	—	—	—	—	200
Return on Equity %	—	—	28.5	42.2	30.0	30.0
Net Margin %	—	—	33.7	46.8	24.1	24.1
Asset Turnover	—	—	0.5	0.6	0.5	0.5
Financial Leverage	—	—	1.7	1.5	2.4	2.4

Valuation Ratios	Stock	Rel to Industry	Rel to S&P 500
Price/Earnings	—	—	—
Price/Book	1.7	0.3	0.4
Price/Sales	1.3	0.5	0.4
Price/Cash Flow	4.7	0.4	0.3

Major Fund Holders	% of Fund Assets
American Century Emerging Markets Inv	1.07
Gartmore Emerging Markets A	1.04

Thesis By Ben Butwin, 11-07-06 Stock Price as of Analysis: $24.82

Ternium's steel manufacturing operations consist of one wide-moat, one narrow-moat, and one no-moat subsidiary, in our opinion. While our risk rating for the firm is above average, we believe this roll-up's strong market share and cheap access to labor and raw materials will lead to impressive results.

In February 2005, Ternium acquired Amazonia, a holding company that owns a 70% stake in Venezuela's largest steel producer, Sidor. Sidor faces no domestic competition for flat steel, a market in which it claims 95% share, and has very few local rivals for its long steel products. The company's virtual monopoly in its home country is the result of Venezuela's antidumping laws on imported steel from countries such as Brazil and Russia. This enables it to maintain advantageous pricing while deterring new entrants. Sidor's wide moat is evident in its operating margins, which can total 40% and reached 18% even in 2003, an abysmal year for steel.

Ternium's narrow-moat subsidiary, Siderar, is the largest steel maker in Argentina and also dominates its local markets. However, free trade agreements between Argentina and three of its neighbors have existed since the 1990s and have lifted or reduced many import tariffs that stood to keep Siderar's competition at bay. Thus, strong, low-cost Brazilian firms such as Gerdau and CSN have been able to steal some market share. Still, Siderar's operating margins remain solid, ranging from 20% to 30%.

Six months before its IPO, Ternium acquired one of Mexico's largest minimills, Hylsamex. Mexico's steel market is more competitive than that of Argentina or Venezuela and offers less protection from imports, which account for 25% of domestic consumption. This has translated into lower profitability and more-volatile financial results; Hylsamex lost money in 2003 while achieving 20% operating margins the following two years. We believe the attractiveness of this purchase lies in the two iron ore mines that Hylsamex owns, from which Ternium can now obtain raw materials at favorable pricing.

Interested investors need to be aware of the major risks Ternium faces. The Chavez regime in Venezuela, which owns 20% of Sidor, could intervene at any time in its quest to secure control of the economy, ensure cheap raw materials, and redistribute wealth. Exchange-rate fluctuations, high inflation, common recessions, and recent energy crises also make Ternium's future cash flows a bit more uncertain. Yet we think risk-aware investors looking for an industrial market leader with strong profit potential should give Ternium some consideration at the right discount.

Tessera Technologies TSRA

Data as of 12-29-06

Rating	Fair Value	Last Close	Consider Buy	Consider Sell	Yield %
★★	$33.00	$40.34	$25.40	$41.30	0.00

Company Profile
Tessera licenses chip package technology to the semiconductor industry. Tessera's chip-scale technology enables manufacturers to assemble chips in packages that are almost as small as the chip itself. The firm's multichip package technology allows manufacturers to vertically stack multiple chips in a single package. Tessera's technology is licensed by more than 50 companies and is incorporated into many applications, including cell phones, MP3 players, and digital cameras.

Management
Stewardship Grade [B]

Bruce McWilliams has been CEO, president, and a board member since 1999 and became chairman in 2002. McWilliams initiated Tessera's transformation into a pure intellectual-property- and services-based company by selling the firm's Singapore manufacturing plant in 1999. Before joining Tessera, McWilliams held executive positions at Flextronics and two technology firms he co-founded. CFO Charlie Webster joined Tessera in August 2006. Prior to Tessera, Webster had held the position of corporate vice president, finance and treasury, at semiconductor equipment firm KLA-Tencor. Webster also previously held posts at engineering company Bechtel Group and Nexant, an energy consulting firm.

Management compensation appears reasonable, and we like that a substantial portion of the total cash compensation is tied to a performance-based bonus. As a group, management and the board hold about 5% of Tessera's shares. The total number of stock options and restricted stock awards granted was less than 3% of shares outstanding in 2005.

3099 Orchard Drive
San Jose, CA 95134
www.tessera.com

Growth [A+]	2002	2003	2004	2005
Revenue %	4.6	32.0	94.9	30.2
Earnings/Share %	NMF	NMF	NMF	-48.0
Book Value/Share %	—	—	NMF	30.1
Dividends/Share %	NMF	NMF	NMF	NMF

Profitability [C+]	2003	2004	2005	TTM
Return on Assets %	4.5	42.3	16.5	18.2
Oper Cash Flow $Mil	12	36	52	93
- Cap Spending $Mil	1	2	4	3
= Free Cash Flow $Mil	10	34	48	90

Financial Health [A+]	2003	2004	2005	06-30-06
Long-term Debt $Mil	—	—	—	—
Total Equity $Mil	66	135	180	246
Debt/Equity Ratio	—	—	—	—

Industry	Business Risk	Moat Size	Investment Style	Sector
Semiconductor Equip.	Average	Narrow	Small Growth	Hardware

Competition

	Market Cap $Mil	12 Mo Trailing Sales $Mil	Price/Cash Flow	Return On Assets%	Debt/Equity	Total Return% 1 Yr	3 Yr
Tessera Technologies	1,894	183	20.4	18.2	—	56.1	28.0
Applied Materials	25,696	9,167	13.3	16.0	0.0	3.9	-5.4
ASML Holding NV	11,937	3,167	13.4	8.7	0.2	22.7	6.3

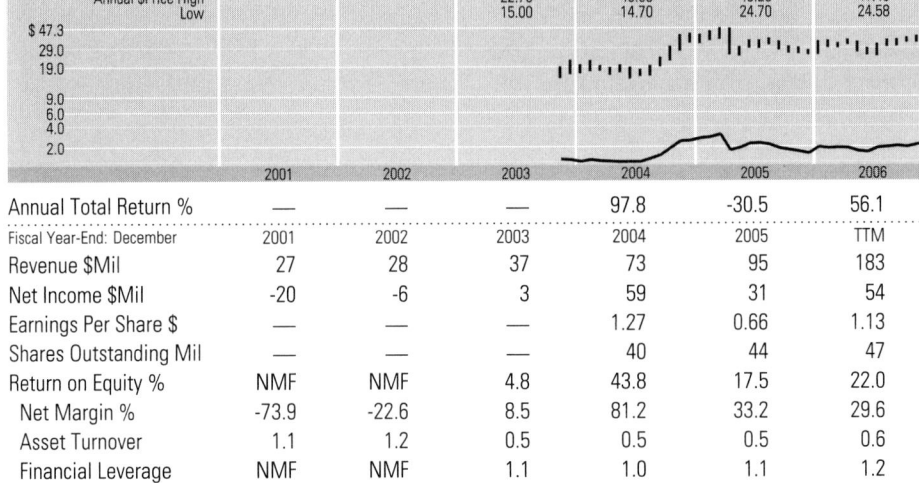

Price Volatility — Monthly Price High/Low — Relative Strength to S&P 500

	2001	2002	2003	2004	2005	2006
Annual $Price High/Low			22.70 / 15.00	40.99 / 14.70	46.28 / 24.70	41.40 / 24.58
Annual Total Return %	—	—	—	97.8	-30.5	56.1

Fiscal Year-End: December	2001	2002	2003	2004	2005	TTM
Revenue $Mil	27	28	37	73	95	183
Net Income $Mil	-20	-6	3	59	31	54
Earnings Per Share $	—	—	—	1.27	0.66	1.13
Shares Outstanding Mil	—	—	—	40	44	47
Return on Equity %	NMF	NMF	4.8	43.8	17.5	22.0
Net Margin %	-73.9	-22.6	8.5	81.2	33.2	29.6
Asset Turnover	1.1	1.2	0.5	0.5	0.5	0.6
Financial Leverage	NMF	NMF	1.1	1.0	1.1	1.2

Valuation Ratios	Stock	Rel to Industry	Rel to S&P 500
Price/Earnings	35.7	1.3	1.7
Price/Book	7.7	1.8	1.9
Price/Sales	10.3	2.3	3.6
Price/Cash Flow	20.4	1.1	1.4

Major Fund Holders	% of Fund Assets
Goldman Sachs Tollkeeper A	5.72
SunAmerica Focused Gr A	2.76
Alger MidCap Growth B	2.65
TCM Small Cap Growth	2.54

Thesis
By Andy Ng, 10-24-06 Stock Price as of Analysis: $34.03

Prospects are bright for Tessera's technology licensing business, but the firm faces litigation risk and has a difficult-to-forecast growth trajectory.

The evolution of semiconductor devices has required technological advances in the packaging used to assemble chips into their final form. Tessera's package miniaturization technologies offer size and performance advantages over traditional packages. The firm receives royalties on every chip produced that uses its technology, which makes for a lucrative, tollbooth-like business. Tessera has a broad portfolio of over 350 patents and counts the world's largest chipmakers among its more than 50 licensees.

Tessera has a narrow moat based on its patents and industry adoption of its products. The firm estimates that more than 100 companies in the semiconductor supply chain have invested in infrastructures that support Tessera's technology. This deters licensees from moving to alternative technologies, since it would be difficult and expensive to switch. Tessera's broad patent portfolio creates a barrier that would make it challenging and costly for licensees to design substitutes around the patents. Also, there would be little incentive for licensees to do so, given that the royalty fees amount to an insignificant percentage of overall device costs.

Tessera's financial performance has been superb, with returns on invested capital far exceeding its cost of capital. Tessera generates substantial free cash flow, which amounted to an impressive $48 million (about 50% of sales) in 2005. As an intellectual-property-based company, Tessera requires minimal capital investment and pockets each incremental dollar of royalties received as pure profit.

Growth prospects are bright for Tessera. The firm's solutions should continue to proliferate because of the constant drive toward faster and smaller semiconductor devices. Through its transaction with Shellcase and recent acquisition of Digital Optics, Tessera has added cutting-edge intellectual property to its portfolio. This, combined the firm's R&D efforts, will equip Tessera with next-generation technologies required to sustain and grow its business.

Tessera currently has a pending patent-infringement lawsuit against a number of chipmakers. Although Tessera has been successful at litigating its claims in the past, the lawsuit still poses a risk. Further, with the first of its patents expiring in 2009 and the potential threat of competing technologies, Tessera must remain innovative to ensure that its technologies continue to be adopted in the future.

Data as of 12-29-06

Teva Pharmaceutical Industries ADR TEVA

Rating	Fair Value	Last Close	Consider Buy	Consider Sell	Yield %
★★★	$34.00	$31.08	$26.20	$42.60	0.82

Company Profile
Established in 1901 as a drug wholesaler, Teva has become the world's largest generic drug company. Based in Israel, Teva develops, manufactures, and commercializes generic and branded drugs. Teva supplies raw materials to competitors through its bulk pharmaceutical business. On the branded side, Teva produces Copaxone, a multiple sclerosis therapy with annual sales of around $1.2 billion, although only a portion of this amount is recognized as revenue to Teva.

Management
Stewardship Grade [A]

Teva has demonstrated excellent corporate governance. Other than not disclosing individual executive compensation, the company has all the little things that matter for a high Stewardship Grade, such as straightforward accounting, the separation of the CEO and chairman duties, and meaningful insider ownership. The management team also offers a high degree of continuity, so we have no reason to think that things will change. A Teva officer since 1995, Israel Makov has served as president and CEO since April 2002. Makov will stay on as a consultant for at least two years after the newly appointed CEO, Shlomo Yanai, takes the top spot in 2007. Yanai was recruited as an outsider, recently leading Makhteshim Agan Industries, an Israel-based maker of generic pesticides. However, many of Teva's top executives--like the president of Teva North America, William Fletcher--have been with the company for decades. The previous CEO and 25-year Teva veteran, Eli Hurvitz, remains chairman. Capital allocation seems appropriate, as management plows excess cash flow into internal research efforts, value-adding acquisitions, and a modest dividend.

5 Basel St. P.O. Box 3190
Petach Tikva, Israel 49131
www.tevapharm.com

Growth [NA]	2002	2003	2004	2005
Revenue %	21.2	30.1	46.5	9.4
Earnings/Share %	49.0	52.6	-56.9	218.0
Book Value/Share %	33.9	63.0	47.1	10.3
Dividends/Share %	47.8	56.4	38.8	36.8

Profitability [NA]	2003	2004	2005	TTM
Return on Assets %	11.7	3.4	10.3	10.3
Oper Cash Flow $Mil	627	1,246	1,370	1,370
- Cap Spending $Mil	208	311	310	310
= Free Cash Flow $Mil	419	935	1,060	1,060

Financial Health [NA]	2003	2004	2005	12-31-05
Long-term Debt $Mil	815	1,728	1,773	1,773
Total Equity $Mil	3,289	5,389	6,042	6,042
Debt/Equity Ratio	0.2	0.3	0.3	0.3

Industry	Business Risk	Moat Size	Investment Style	Sector
Drugs	Average	Narrow	Large Growth	Healthcare

Competition

	Market Cap $Mil	12 Mo Trailing Sales $Mil	Price/Cash Flow	Return On Assets %	Debt/ Equity	Total Return% 1 Yr	3 Yr
Teva Pharmaceutical Industries ADR	20,098	5,250	14.7	10.3	0.3	-27.2	3.1
Novartis AG ADR	134,175	32,526	16.6	10.6	0.0	11.3	9.6
Barr Pharmaceuticals	5,332	1,336	11.9	16.2	0.0	-19.5	-0.9

Price Volatility

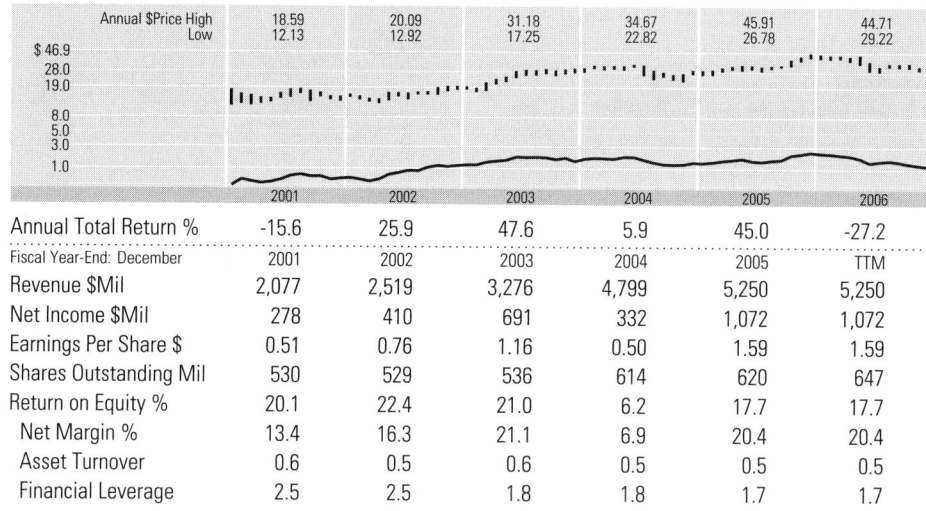

	2001	2002	2003	2004	2005	2006
Annual $Price High	18.59	20.09	31.18	34.67	45.91	44.71
Low	12.13	12.92	17.25	22.82	26.78	29.22
Annual Total Return %	-15.6	25.9	47.6	5.9	45.0	-27.2

Fiscal Year-End: December	2001	2002	2003	2004	2005	TTM
Revenue $Mil	2,077	2,519	3,276	4,799	5,250	5,250
Net Income $Mil	278	410	691	332	1,072	1,072
Earnings Per Share $	0.51	0.76	1.16	0.50	1.59	1.59
Shares Outstanding Mil	530	529	536	614	620	647
Return on Equity %	20.1	22.4	21.0	6.2	17.7	17.7
Net Margin %	13.4	16.3	21.1	6.9	20.4	20.4
Asset Turnover	0.6	0.5	0.6	0.5	0.5	0.5
Financial Leverage	2.5	2.5	1.8	1.8	1.7	1.7

Valuation Ratios	Stock	Rel to Industry	Rel to S&P 500
Price/Earnings	19.5	0.8	0.9
Price/Book	3.3	0.6	0.8
Price/Sales	3.8	0.9	1.3
Price/Cash Flow	14.7	0.9	1.0

Major Fund Holders	% of Fund Assets
AMIDEX35 Israel	13.13
Saratoga Health & Biotechnology B	7.18
Live Oak Health Sciences	6.63
Managers 20 A	5.29

Thesis By Brian Laegeler, CPA, 10-25-06 Stock Price as of Analysis: $33.59

Until recently, Teva Pharmaceutical was the undisputed leader of the generic drug industry. With about 4 times the sales of its next-largest public competitor, Teva maintained excess returns on capital through low costs, customer loyalty, and significant reinvestment. Today, big pharma innovators like Pfizer and Merck pose a serious threat to Teva's cost leadership.

Teva discovered early that the best way to survive the commodified generic drug industry was to get big. Size allows Teva to squeeze more pennies out of every revenue dollar, providing the financial flexibility to beat its competitors on price. For example, after the company fully absorbs recently acquired Ivax, we estimate it will spend only 23 cents per dollar of revenue on operating expenses, while its next three largest public competitors spend, on average, 28 cents per dollar.

Teva has distanced itself from its peers in terms of quality as well. In 2003, Teva purchased Sicor, one of the few leading providers of hard-to-make injectables. The 2005 Ivax acquisition further boosted Teva's technology base with leading respiratory and oncology portfolios. As a globally diversified company, Ivax also gave Teva an instant leadership position in important growth markets like Russia, France, and Mexico. On the branded drug side, Teva researchers developed Copaxone, a leading multiple sclerosis therapy that now accounts for 8% of sales.

While Teva continues to lead the generic drug players, the entry of big pharma effectively neutralizes Teva's primary advantage: cost. Firms like Pfizer can make generic versions of their existing drugs at minimal marginal expense. Further, branded companies can launch a generic drug a few weeks early to lock in customers prior to patent expiration. This blocks firms like Teva from capturing significant market share on large upcoming products and removes the possibility of distributing an authorized generic. Recently, at least four big pharma firms have dedicated resources to this in-house generic strategy, a pattern we expect will stunt Teva's growth as others follow suit.

Big pharma's participation in generic drugs forever changes the industry. While branded drug behemoths are unlikely to encroach upon Teva's existing products, we believe they will increasingly compete on new generic launches. Instead of leading the pack, Teva may have to settle for the crumbs big pharma leaves behind.

Texas Instruments TXN

Data as of 12-29-06

	Rating	Fair Value	Last Close	Consider Buy	Consider Sell	Yield %
	★★★★	$34.00	$28.80	$26.20	$42.60	0.45

Company Profile
Texas Instruments designs and manufactures a wide range of semiconductor products. The firm's product portfolio, which includes digital, analog, and mixed-signal integrated circuits, targets various end-market applications like mobile handsets, networking equipment, and PC peripherals. TI also produces educational devices such as financial and scientific calculators. TI's global operations derive nearly 80% of sales from overseas customers.

Management   Stewardship Grade [A]
A 25-year TI veteran, former COO Richard Templeton assumed the roles of CEO and president in mid-2004, succeeding Thomas Engibous. Engibous, TI's chief since 1996, remains as chairman of the board. In our view, corporate governance at TI is extremely sound and highly favorable to the interests of common shareholders. Executive cash compensation is relatively modest, given TI's scale, while stock-option grants have generally tracked below those of industry peers. Also, we are encouraged by management's forthcoming disclosure of business information and its growing emphasis on returning shareholder value through a combination of dividends and share repurchases.

12500 TI Boulevard P.O. Box 660199   www.ti.com
Dallas, TX 75266-0199

Growth [B]	2002	2003	2004	2005
Revenue %	2.2	17.3	27.9	6.5
Earnings/Share %	NMF	NMF	54.4	32.4
Book Value/Share %	-12.0	7.9	9.4	-3.1
Dividends/Share %	0.0	0.0	4.3	18.1

Profitability [A]	2003	2004	2005	TTM
Return on Assets %	7.7	11.4	15.4	29.3
Oper Cash Flow $Mil	2,151	3,146	3,772	2,652
- Cap Spending $Mil	800	1,298	1,330	1,434
= Free Cash Flow $Mil	1,351	1,848	2,442	1,218

Financial Health [A+]	2003	2004	2005	09-30-06
Long-term Debt $Mil	395	368	360	0
Total Equity $Mil	11,864	13,063	11,937	12,027
Debt/Equity Ratio	0.0	0.0	0.0	0.0

Industry	Business Risk	Moat Size	Investment Style	Sector
Semiconductor	Average	Narrow	Large Growth	Hardware

Competition	Market Cap $Mil	12 Mo Trailing Sales $Mil	Price/Cash Flow	Return On Assets%	Debt/Equity	Total Return% 1 Yr	3 Yr
Texas Instruments	42,736	15,173	16.1	29.3	0.0	-9.8	-0.2
Analog Devices	11,242	2,573	18.1	13.8	—	-6.7	-9.4
Maxim Integrated Products	9,820	1,749	16.4	15.3	—	-14.1	-13.7

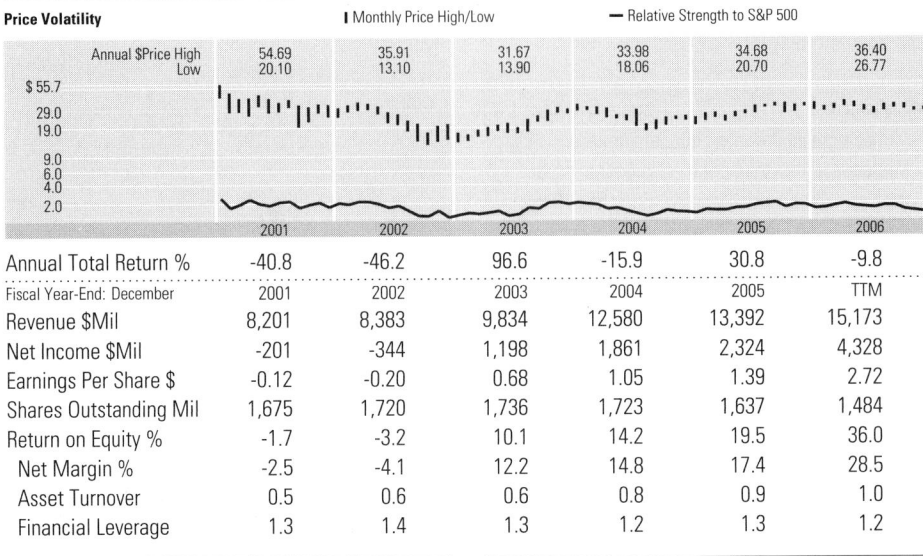

Price Volatility — Monthly Price High/Low — Relative Strength to S&P 500

	2001	2002	2003	2004	2005	2006
Annual $Price High	54.69	35.91	31.67	33.98	34.68	36.40
Low	20.10	13.10	13.90	18.06	20.70	26.77
Annual Total Return %	-40.8	-46.2	96.6	-15.9	30.8	-9.8

Fiscal Year-End: December	2001	2002	2003	2004	2005	TTM
Revenue $Mil	8,201	8,383	9,834	12,580	13,392	15,173
Net Income $Mil	-201	-344	1,198	1,861	2,324	4,328
Earnings Per Share $	-0.12	-0.20	0.68	1.05	1.39	2.72
Shares Outstanding Mil	1,675	1,720	1,736	1,723	1,637	1,484
Return on Equity %	-1.7	-3.2	10.1	14.2	19.5	36.0
Net Margin %	-2.5	-4.1	12.2	14.8	17.4	28.5
Asset Turnover	0.5	0.6	0.6	0.8	0.9	1.0
Financial Leverage	1.3	1.4	1.3	1.2	1.3	1.2

Valuation Ratios	Stock	Rel to Industry	Rel to S&P 500
Price/Earnings	16.8	0.6	0.8
Price/Book	3.6	1.0	0.9
Price/Sales	2.8	0.7	1.0
Price/Cash Flow	16.1	1.0	1.1

Major Fund Holders	% of Fund Assets
ProFunds Semiconductor UltraSector Inv	8.93
Integrity Technology A	6.38
Firsthand Technology Leaders	5.85
Schwab Technology	5.21

Thesis By Larry Cao, CFA, 12-13-06 Stock Price as of Analysis: $29.43

Mobile phones have become the second-largest end market for chipmakers, and arguably the most coveted, thanks to impressive growth. Texas Instruments, the second-largest chipmaker in the United States, has leveraged its technology leadership in this high-switching-cost business and captured the lion's share of the market. In our opinion, differentiated technology and switching costs are at the core of TI's economic moat.

TI built its leading position in digital signal processors (DSPs)--specialized microprocessors for digital audio and image signal processing--and high-performance analog chips through successful research and development investments and acquisitions. At a rate of more than $2 billion a year, TI has one of the highest R&D budgets in the industry. Acquisitions have bolstered the firm's position with additional engineering talent and technology. TI's analog franchise, for example, is largely built on acquired firms like Burr-Brown.

First-mover advantages and switching costs are important factors behind TI's success. Handsets have to satisfy extensive qualification requirements by carriers, making the cost of switching chip vendors formidable. First movers in this type of business are rarely displaced. This is why even companies like Intel, Broadcom, and Marvell have either exited the industry or are still trying hard to gain a foothold.

TI's mutually beneficial relationships with clients are the envy of the industry. As the mainstream cell phone market matures, feature-rich third-generation cell phones and low-end basic cell phones have come to dominate. Japan was the first 3G market to take off in the world. There TI has worked closely with NTT DoCoMo and consistently upgraded its popular multimedia chip for the wireless firm. Technology based on this development now ships to six of the top seven 3G cell phone makers in the world. For Nokia's low-end cell phone, TI custom-developed a single-chip integrated solution that replaced multiple chips by other vendors. Both products should continue to drive TI's revenue growth in the coming years. These close relationships also opened doors for TI to cross-sell analog and other semiconductor components.

Although demand growth for mobile phone semiconductors may have passed its peak, we continue to like the firm's long-term growth potential. TI's leading position in technology and manufacturing capability, close relationships with clients, and financial discipline have made it one of the top chipmakers in the world.

Data as of 12-29-06

Textron TXT

	Rating	Fair Value	Last Close	Consider Buy	Consider Sell	Yield %
	★★★	$90.00	$93.77	$69.40	$112.80	1.65

Company Profile

Textron is a global multi-industry company with about 37,000 employees in 33 countries. It operates through four business segments: designing and manufacturing rotary-wing aircraft for defense and commercial use (Bell); business jets (Cessna); and golf carts, turf-care equipment, plastic fuel systems, wire and cable installation equipment, and industrial pumps and gears (industrial). The firm also has a commercial finance segment.

Management

Stewardship Grade [B]

Lewis Campbell has been with Textron since 1992, serving as COO for six years before becoming CEO in 1998. He has brought a wealth of industrial experience to this multi-industry company, having spent 24 years with General Motors. His recently completed transformation is already boosting margins, and management now exercises greater discipline in considering acquisitions. We are particularly fond of management's focus on returns on invested capital, and we were also happy to see the firm sell the fastening system business. While we were disappointed that myriad efforts failed to turn that business around, we think the divestiture was one of the best asset-allocation decisions management has made. Executive compensation is largely variable and, similar to the firm's capital-allocation strategy, is based at least partly on return on invested capital. The 12-member board consists of Campbell and 11 independent directors. We would prefer to see executives and officers own more than their collective 1.1% of outstanding shares. The only factors keeping Textron from earning an A Stewardship Grade, however, are its staggered directors and Campbell's dual role as chairman and CEO.

40 Westminster Street www.textron.com
Providence, RI 02903

Growth [C]	2002	2003	2004	2005
Revenue %	-15.4	-6.6	3.3	20.7
Earnings/Share %	—	NMF	38.1	-42.9
Book Value/Share %	—	NMF	-3.3	-8.0
Dividends/Share %	0.0	0.0	1.9	5.7

Profitability [B-]	2003	2004	2005	TTM
Return on Assets %	1.7	2.3	1.2	3.0
Oper Cash Flow $Mil	975	950	1,036	815
- Cap Spending $Mil	263	250	365	387
= Free Cash Flow $Mil	712	700	671	428

Financial Health [C+]	2003	2004	2005	09-30-06
Long-term Debt $Mil	—	6,133	7,079	8,406
Total Equity $Mil	3,690	3,642	3,266	3,031
Debt/Equity Ratio	—	1.7	2.2	2.8

Industry	Business Risk	Moat Size	Investment Style	Sector
Aerospace/Defense	Average	Narrow	Large Core	Industrial Materials

Competition

	Market Cap $Mil	12 Mo Trailing Sales $Mil	Price/Cash Flow	Return On Assets%	Debt/ Equity	Total Return% 1 Yr	3 Yr
Textron	11,763	10,990	14.4	3.0	2.8	23.9	20.2
Boeing	70,249	59,114	9.4	2.7	0.8	28.4	30.4
United Technologies	62,748	46,303	14.6	7.0	0.4	13.7	11.6

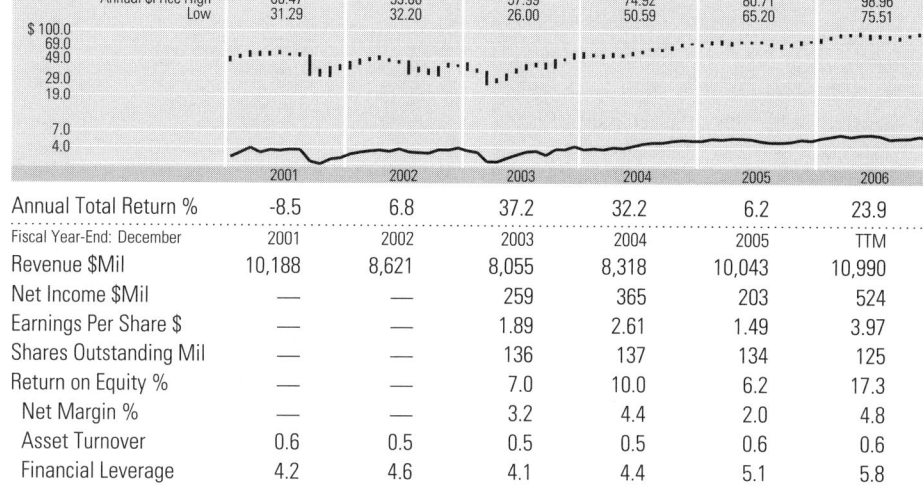

	2001	2002	2003	2004	2005	2006
Annual $Price High	60.47	53.60	57.99	74.92	80.71	98.96
Low	31.29	32.20	26.00	50.59	65.20	75.51
Annual Total Return %	-8.5	6.8	37.2	32.2	6.2	23.9
Fiscal Year-End: December	2001	2002	2003	2004	2005	TTM
Revenue $Mil	10,188	8,621	8,055	8,318	10,043	10,990
Net Income $Mil	—	—	259	365	203	524
Earnings Per Share $	—	—	1.89	2.61	1.49	3.97
Shares Outstanding Mil	—	—	136	137	134	125
Return on Equity %	—	—	7.0	10.0	6.2	17.3
Net Margin %	—	—	3.2	4.4	2.0	4.8
Asset Turnover	0.6	0.5	0.5	0.5	0.6	0.6
Financial Leverage	4.2	4.6	4.1	4.4	5.1	5.8

Valuation Ratios	Stock	Rel to Industry	Rel to S&P 500
Price/Earnings	18.2	0.7	0.9
Price/Book	3.9	0.9	1.0
Price/Sales	1.1	0.8	0.4
Price/Cash Flow	14.4	1.1	1.0

Major Fund Holders	% of Fund Assets
Quaker Capital Opportunities A	4.24
American Century Focused Growth Inv	4.24
Quaker Core Equity A	4.00
WesMark Growth	3.65

Thesis By Chris Lozier, 12-13-06 Stock Price as of Analysis: $95.41

Having divested itself of an abysmal commodity fastener business, Textron is focused on its two narrow-moat aerospace businesses and a collection of smaller, well-positioned industrial brands that have room for internal improvement. With a leaner portfolio and substantial installed bases, this firm should remain an industry leader for years.

While the name Textron may not be widely known, Cessna and Bell are household words in the world of private airplanes and helicopters. Cessna has delivered about 80% more business jets than its closest competitor over the last 10 years, and one out of three operating helicopters in the world is a Bell. These global markets are highly concentrated oligopolies, so each business competes with only a few major players. What's more, each is well positioned to take advantage of strong markets. Cessna's order backlog has grown to more than twice 2005 sales, while Bell's has eclipsed the $3.3 billion mark versus 2005 sales of $2.9 billion. Notably, Bell is on the production teams of both the V-22 Osprey tiltrotor and the US101, which will be the next presidential helicopter.

Textron's industrial segment, now slightly less than a third of manufacturing sales, is itself composed of robust brands in concentrated markets. Kautex is a leader in the rapidly growing plastic fuel-system market, and E-Z-GO owns about half of the $1 billion golf cart market, all of which it shares with only two competitors. Jacobsen competes with only two major rivals for professional turf maintenance. Still, Textron has become increasingly reliant on its aerospace franchises for income, with Cessna and Bell accounting for nearly 90% of manufacturing operating profits.

We remain confident that margin expansion will materialize where it's needed most, in the industrial segment. Management has reduced its workforce, sold noncore businesses, realigned the remaining units, and outsourced or rationalized certain production activities. In 2005, as operating margins expanded at Bell and Cessna, the industrial segment saw its already-thin margins shrink further. High raw-material costs and weak sales volume were the major culprits, though the firm did maintain some pricing power with its excellent brands. Results have been slightly better in 2006, and we expect margins to approach 6% in 2007. We think weak performers in this segment could be pared over the next few years as management remains focused on returns on invested capital.

THQ. THQI

Data as of 12-29-06

	Rating	Fair Value	Last Close	Consider Buy	Consider Sell	Yield %
	★★★	$36.00	$32.52	$27.80	$45.10	0.00

Industry	Business Risk	Moat Size	Investment Style	Sector
Entertain./Ed. Media	Average	None	Mid Growth	Software

Company Profile

THQ sells video games built for the major video game consoles, personal computers, and wireless devices. The company's titles include sports, action, strategy, children's, adventure, and driving games. THQ either licenses the themes and characters for its games from third parties or develops them in-house. The products are primarily sold through retailers such as Wal-Mart and Toys 'R' Us.

Management Stewardship Grade [C]

Brian Farrell has been president and CEO since 1995 and has served in many roles since joining THQ in 1991. Farrell was paid $604,000 in salary and $601,999 in a cash bonus for fiscal 2006, both reasonable in our opinion. However, the company's Stewardship Grade suffered due to Farrell's excessive severance package and opaque performance package metrics. But Farrell does control just more than 2% of the equity, which should help align his interests with that of other shareholders.

THQ does grant options a little too freely, in our opinion, giving away just more than 5% of outstanding shares in fiscal 2006. The company's Stewardship Grade is further lowered to a "C" because of an options backdating investigation which has delayed SEC filings. As a result of these delays, the company also faces de-listing by Nasdaq. We are pleased, however, that the company has a nonstaggered board of directors, which increases accountability.

27001 Agoura Road Suite 325
Calabasas Hills, CA 91301
www.thq.com

Growth [B-]	2003	2004	2005	2006
Revenue %	26.8	33.4	18.1	6.6
Earnings/Share %	-68.3	187.5	69.6	-50.0
Book Value/Share %	-10.0	11.8	21.1	5.3
Dividends/Share %	NMF	NMF	NMF	NMF

Profitability [B+]	2004	2005	2006	TTM
Return on Assets %	6.8	8.4	4.0	3.1
Oper Cash Flow $Mil	71	60	43	6
- Cap Spending $Mil	8	17	23	19
= Free Cash Flow $Mil	64	44	20	-14

Financial Health [A]	2004	2005	2006	06-30-06
Long-term Debt $Mil	—	—	—	—
Total Equity $Mil	439	549	631	623
Debt/Equity Ratio	—	—	—	—

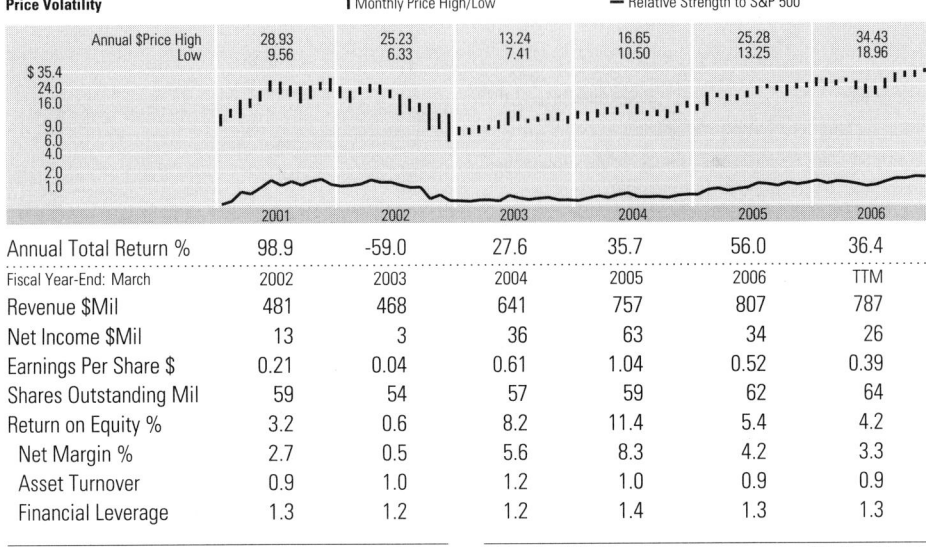

Competition	Market Cap $Mil	12 Mo Trailing Sales $Mil	Price/Cash Flow	Return On Assets%	Debt/Equity	Total Return% 1 Yr	3 Yr
THQ	2,092	787	EUB	3.1	—	36.4	41.9
Electronic Arts	15,536	3,107	27.2	4.1	—	-3.7	1.9
Activision	4,834	1,415	124.5	1.9	—	25.5	34.8

Price Volatility — Monthly Price High/Low — Relative Strength to S&P 500

Annual $Price High	28.93	25.23	13.24	16.65	25.28	34.43
Low	9.56	6.33	7.41	10.50	13.25	18.96
	2001	2002	2003	2004	2005	2006
Annual Total Return %	98.9	-59.0	27.6	35.7	56.0	36.4

Fiscal Year-End: March	2002	2003	2004	2005	2006	TTM
Revenue $Mil	481	468	641	757	807	787
Net Income $Mil	13	3	36	63	34	26
Earnings Per Share $	0.21	0.04	0.61	1.04	0.52	0.39
Shares Outstanding Mil	59	54	57	59	62	64
Return on Equity %	3.2	0.6	8.2	11.4	5.4	4.2
Net Margin %	2.7	0.5	5.6	8.3	4.2	3.3
Asset Turnover	0.9	1.0	1.2	1.0	0.9	0.9
Financial Leverage	1.3	1.2	1.2	1.4	1.3	1.3

Valuation Ratios	Stock	Rel to Industry	Rel to S&P 500
Price/Earnings	83.4	1.0	4.0
Price/Book	3.4	0.8	0.8
Price/Sales	2.7	0.5	0.9
Price/Cash Flow	EUB	—	—

Major Fund Holders	% of Fund Assets
River Oak Discovery	3.08
Aston/ABN AMRO Mid Cap Growth N	3.07
Undiscovered Mgrs Behavioral Growth Inst	2.91
Julius Baer U.S. Smallcap I	1.91

Thesis By Norman Young, 12-20-06 Stock Price as of Analysis: $32.37

Over time, video games have made the transition from the realm of socially awkward teenagers to mainstream entertainment. With ties to popular culture and other mainstream fare, game publisher THQ's success embodies this transition. The company's focus on family-friendly titles gives it a compelling competitive advantage in the industry.

The idea that the popularity of video games has moved beyond niche status is borne out by statistics. Industry sales topped $10 billion in 2005, with more than 60% of all Americans playing video games. Of these gamers, almost half are women, and the average age of gamers has steadily climbed to 33. What is sometimes lost in the statistics is the introduction of children to video games. The introduction often begins at an early age through the purchase of family-friendly titles tied to popular movies and cartoon characters.

As the leading third-party developer of children's video games, we believe that THQ has succeeded by catering to this niche. While other developers battle for teen and adult gamers, the firm has been quietly cornering the market in games geared toward children. With exclusive licenses with Pixar, World Wrestling Entertainment, and others, the company has a steady supply of titles tied to popular movies or television shows. THQ pays higher royalties with licensed games, but the built-in marketing from the release of Pixar or Disney features reduces THQ's own marketing costs. For example, a version of THQ's game Cars, based on Pixar's blockbuster movie, was released in conjunction with the DVD release of the movie. The Cars game has sold more than 4 million copies in fiscal 2006. Approximately half of the company's total revenues comes from similarly licensed titles.

The risk of losing licensed content has forced management to tweak its strategy. This has improved THQ's competitive position by forcing it to develop more in-house titles. Furthermore, because franchises developed in-house are more profitable, THQ has an additional incentive to create its own content. This year, THQ released Saints Row, which has a look and feel similar to Take-Two Interactive's wildly popular Grand Theft Auto series. Sales results are encouraging, and this proved that THQ has the scale and resources to develop its own content, in our opinion. We believe THQ is on the cusp of having a narrow moat, should it create more successful franchises with its own content.

We believe that THQ is a well-diversified publisher with room to grow.

Data as of 12-29-06

Tiffany TIF

	Rating	Fair Value	Last Close	Consider Buy	Consider Sell	Yield %
	★★★	$36.00	$39.24	$27.80	$45.10	0.97

Company Profile

Tiffany is an international jeweler and specialty retailer. It designs and sells fine jewelry in addition to china, fashion accessories, timepieces, fragrances, and gift items through more than 150 retail stores in the United States and abroad. It also offers its trademarked merchandise on its Web site and through its catalog. Tiffany has expanded into selling non-Tiffany-brand items through its Little Switzerland and Iridesse stores.

Management   Stewardship Grade [C]

CEO and chairman Michael Kowalski has been with the company for more than 20 years. Since replacing veteran William Chaney in 1999, Kowalski has led Tiffany to average annual revenue growth of 11% and has expanded into new markets. He owns a 1% stake in the company, which helps to align his interests with shareholders', in our opinion. In 2005, Kowalski received annual compensation (not including stock options) just shy of $3 million, with more than half in the form of a bonus. This is quite a contrast to 2004, when Kowalski's annual compensation (not including stock options) was $1 million and he did not receive an annual bonus because earnings goals were not met. We applaud the board for not granting bonuses to Kowalski and the other members of the executive team in 2004, given Tiffany's poor performance. However, we think the board's disclosure of the performance metrics that drive management's incentive compensation is lacking. While we would like to see the chairman and CEO roles separated, the majority of the board is independent, and directors must be elected each year. With policies that give shareholders a voice, reasonable executive compensation, and good transparency in financial performance, we see no corporate-governance red flags here.

727 Fifth Avenue
New York, NY 10022   www.tiffany.com

Growth [B]	2003	2004	2005	2006
Revenue %	6.2	17.2	10.2	8.6
Earnings/Share %	11.3	13.3	41.4	-14.6
Book Value/Share %	18.5	21.3	16.0	9.8
Dividends/Share %	0.0	18.8	21.1	30.4

Profitability [A]	2004	2005	2006	TTM
Return on Assets %	9.0	11.4	9.2	9.0
Oper Cash Flow $Mil	284	131	263	191
- Cap Spending $Mil	273	142	157	179
= Free Cash Flow $Mil	11	-11	106	13

Financial Health [B+]	2004	2005	2006	10-31-06
Long-term Debt $Mil	393	398	427	417
Total Equity $Mil	1,468	1,701	1,831	1,687
Debt/Equity Ratio	0.3	0.2	0.2	0.2

Industry	Business Risk	Moat Size	Investment Style	Sector
Jewelry/Accessories	Average	Narrow	Mid Core	Consumer Goods

Competition

	Market Cap $Mil	12 Mo Trailing Sales $Mil	Price/Cash Flow	Return On Assets %	Debt/ Equity	Total Return % 1 Yr	3 Yr
Tiffany	5,311	2,520	27.8	9.0	0.2	3.6	-2.6
Signet Group PLC ADR	4,086	3,182	20.1	9.2	0.0	29.9	11.6
Zale	1,371	2,444	EUB	2.9	0.5	12.2	2.4

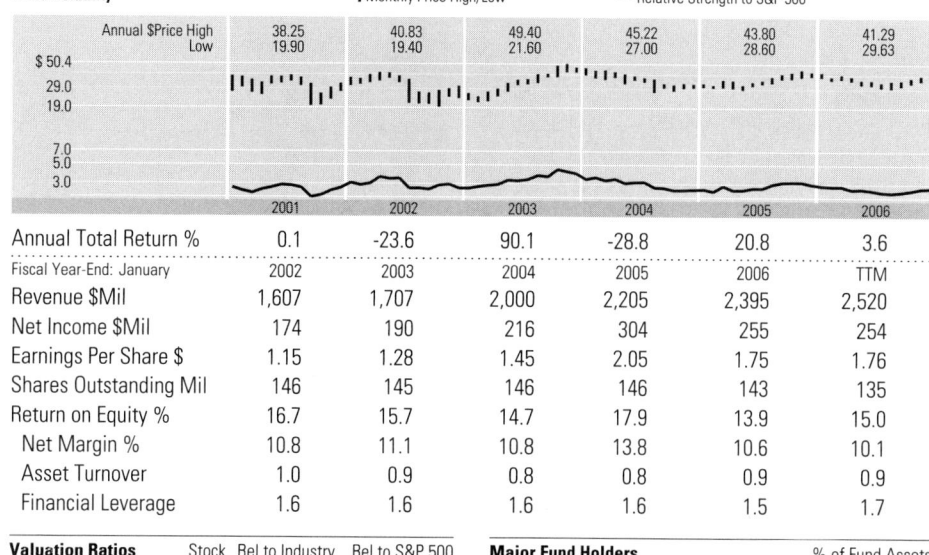

Annual $Price High	38.25	40.83	49.40	45.22	43.80	41.29
Low	19.90	19.40	21.60	27.00	28.60	29.63
	2001	2002	2003	2004	2005	2006
Annual Total Return %	0.1	-23.6	90.1	-28.8	20.8	3.6

Fiscal Year-End: January	2002	2003	2004	2005	2006	TTM
Revenue $Mil	1,607	1,707	2,000	2,205	2,395	2,520
Net Income $Mil	174	190	216	304	255	254
Earnings Per Share $	1.15	1.28	1.45	2.05	1.75	1.76
Shares Outstanding Mil	146	145	146	146	143	135
Return on Equity %	16.7	15.7	14.7	17.9	13.9	15.0
Net Margin %	10.8	11.1	10.8	13.8	10.6	10.1
Asset Turnover	1.0	0.9	0.8	0.8	0.9	0.9
Financial Leverage	1.6	1.6	1.6	1.6	1.5	1.7

Valuation Ratios	Stock	Rel to Industry	Rel to S&P 500
Price/Earnings	22.3	0.8	1.1
Price/Book	3.1	0.4	0.8
Price/Sales	2.1	0.5	0.7
Price/Cash Flow	27.8	1.1	1.9

Major Fund Holders	% of Fund Assets
TrendStar American Endeavor	4.87
Pin Oak Aggressive Stock	4.01
MassMutual Select Focused Value S	3.33
BB&T Large Cap I	3.17

Thesis   By Kimberly Picciola, 11-28-06   Stock Price as of Analysis: $35.93

Tiffany is known for its uniquely designed, quality crafted, high-end pieces of jewelry. With its brand cachet and its distinct products, we think Tiffany has developed a narrow economic moat. Despite high precious metal costs, which have pressured merchandise margins in recent quarters, we think the luxury jeweler is well positioned to increase revenues and improve profitability over the long run.

Tiffany's revenues have grown an average of 8% annually over the past five years. New store openings, increases in same-store sales (sales from stores open at least a year), and the expansion and remodel of its Fifth Avenue flagship store in New York have contributed to the company's top-line growth. Tiffany is continuing to update its product offering. For example, the company recently collaborated with world-renown architect Frank Gehry to add a more contemporary line to its exclusive product offering, and it is also rolling out a pearl-only concept, Iridesse.

While product innovation and the strong demand for luxury goods has helped boost Tiffany's sales in the domestic market, the company has experienced ups and downs in Japan. A few years ago, Tiffany turned off the Japanese consumer due in part to a product mix that included too much silver. The jeweler is focused on reconnecting with those customers by updating its product assortment, launching more targeted marketing campaigns, and sprucing up existing stores. We are encouraged that business in Japan has somewhat stabilized in recent quarters, indicating that the investments are starting to pay off.

Despite fairly consistent top-line growth in recent years, Tiffany's profits have been lumpy. High precious metal costs have pressured merchandise margins, and returns on invested capital have taken an added hit due to the company's decision to invest in its supply chain infrastructure. We believe profit margins should expand as precious metal costs stabilize down the road and expect returns on invested capital to improve as the investment in its infrastructure starts to pay off.

An improved competitive positioning will be necessary to combat strengthening rivals. De Beers has opened its own retail stores in the U.S. through a partnership with LVMH (Moet Hennessy Louis Vuitton). Additionally, online jeweler Blue Nile is expanding its share of the diamond engagement ring market. Consumers may opt to try something outside the little blue box, which could hamper Tiffany's future growth.

Data as of 12-29-06

Tim Hortons THI

	Rating	Fair Value	Last Close	Consider Buy	Consider Sell	Yield %
	★	$22.00	$28.96	$17.00	$27.60	0.43

Industry	Business Risk	Moat Size	Investment Style	Sector
Restaurants	Average	Narrow	Mid Growth	Consumer Services

Company Profile

On the basis of systemwide sales and number of units, Tim Hortons is the largest quick-service restaurant chain in Canada, with 2,637 restaurants (98% of which are franchised). In the United States, the company has 305 restaurants (80% franchised) in 10 states, primarily in the Northeast and Midwest. Its menu features premium-blend coffee and other beverages, fresh sandwiches, and freshly baked goods, including doughnuts, bagels, muffins, cookies, croissants, and pastries.

Management
Stewardship Grade [NA]

After 13 years with Dairy Queen Canada, Paul House joined Tim Hortons as its vice president of marketing in 1985. He was promoted to COO in 1993, president in 1995, and CEO in 2005. House leads an experienced management team, with executives averaging more than 12 years with the company. In 2005, he received C$1.4 million in salary plus bonus, 29,269 shares of Wendy's restricted stock, and C$0.3 million under the company's pension and retirement plans. We believe this represents reasonable compensation. We like the fact that officers and directors will be required to hold a multiple of their annual salary/compensation in Tim Hortons' stock (including 3 times salary for executive officers). We do not, however, approve of the company's staggered board, poison pill, and other takeover defenses and frown upon a couple of related-party transactions.

874 Sinclair Rd. www.timhortons.com
Oakville, ON L6K 2Y1

Growth [B]	2002	2003	2004	2005
Revenue %	14.4	10.6	14.2	10.7
Earnings/Share %	NMF	NMF	NMF	NMF
Book Value/Share %	—	—	—	—
Dividends/Share %	NMF	NMF	NMF	NMF

Profitability [A]	2003	2004	2005	TTM
Return on Assets %	10.1	11.7	12.0	12.5
Oper Cash Flow $Mil	147	401	378	269
- Cap Spending $Mil	132	198	219	199
= Free Cash Flow $Mil	15	203	159	70

Financial Health [A+]	2003	2004	2005	12-31-05
Long-term Debt $Mil	—	247	88	393
Total Equity $Mil	843	1,022	39	1,020
Debt/Equity Ratio	—	0.2	2.2	0.4

Competition

	Market Cap $Mil	12 Mo Trailing Sales $Mil	Price/Cash Flow	Return On Assets%	Debt/Equity	Total Return% 1 Yr	3 Yr
Tim Hortons	5,581	1,597	20.7	12.5	0.4	—	—
McDonald's	54,825	21,790	13.3	9.4	0.6	34.6	23.9
Starbucks	26,737	7,787	23.6	12.7	0.0	18.0	29.1

Price Volatility
Monthly Price High/Low — Relative Strength to S&P 500

Annual $Price High / Low: 33.00 / 23.79

Annual Total Return %	—	—	—	—	—	—
Fiscal Year-End: December	2001	2002	2003	2004	2005	TTM
Revenue $Mil	926	1,060	1,172	1,338	1,482	1,597
Net Income $Mil	132	133	156	205	191	208
Earnings Per Share $	—	—	—	—	—	—
Shares Outstanding Mil	—	—	—	—	—	193
Return on Equity %	38.3	14.4	18.5	20.1	EUB	20.4
Net Margin %	14.3	12.5	13.3	15.3	12.9	13.0
Asset Turnover	0.7	0.6	0.8	0.8	0.9	1.0
Financial Leverage	3.6	1.8	1.8	1.7	40.6	1.6

Valuation Ratios	Stock	Rel to Industry	Rel to S&P 500
Price/Earnings	—	—	—
Price/Book	5.5	0.9	1.3
Price/Sales	3.5	1.8	1.2
Price/Cash Flow	20.7	1.4	1.4

Major Fund Holders	% of Fund Assets
IPO Plus Aftermarket	5.19
AIM Trimark Endeavor A	1.58
Lord Abbett Large-Cap Growth A	1.50
Rydex Leisure Inv	1.46

Thesis By John Owens, CFA, CPA, Stock Price as of Analysis:

Tim Hortons (affectionately called Tim's or Timmy's by its customers) is the leading fast food chain in Canada, with a highly iconic brand. We believe the company still has a lot of room for growth in its home market. Tim's could also become a stronger regional player in the United States, but it will not be easy, as the brand is not as well known and competition is on the rise.

With around C$3.5 billion of systemwide sales in Canada last year, Tim Hortons' chain of more than 2,600 domestic restaurants has a 24% share of that country's fast food market, trumping heavyweight McDonald's MCD, which accounts for 18%. No other competitor has more than 6%. Furthermore, Tim's is strengthening its position, with plans for 140-150 openings in 2006.

We attribute the firm's dominance to its powerful brand, which has become a national institution. Tim's is best known for its coffee (which represents nearly half of its restaurant sales in Canada), so much so that the "double-double"--its phrase for a coffee with two creams and two sugars--was added to the Canadian Oxford dictionary in 2004. The chain also offers doughnuts and other baked goods, soups, sandwiches, specialty teas, and flavored cappuccinos. This broad menu and the freshness and consistency of its products, thanks to a proprietary baking system, give its guests plenty of reasons to visit; about half of the chain's Canadian customers pop in four or more times per week. Advertising, sponsorship, and community programs have also bolstered the firm's down-home, Canadiana image.

Given the chain's popularity, we believe Tim Hortons could expand to around 4,000 domestic units. Growth prospects are particularly strong in western Canada and Quebec, where Tim's penetration measures around 18,000 and 24,000 persons per restaurant, respectively. This compares with about 6,000 persons per restaurant in the Atlantic region and 8,000 in Ontario. Management also sees opportunities in certain high-traffic metropolitan locations.

In the United States, the company aims to grow from around 300 units to 500 by the end of 2008. Tim's has been building its brand south of the border for more than two decades; it has had some success in Buffalo, Detroit, and Columbus, but has not fared as well in New England, a Dunkin' Donuts stronghold. While we think its persistence will eventually pay off, competitive pressures are increasing, as McDonald's and other fast food chains have rolled out premium-roast coffee.

Data as of 12-29-06

Timberland TBL

	Rating	Fair Value	Last Close	Consider Buy	Consider Sell	Yield %
	★★★	$35.00	$31.58	$27.00	$43.90	0.00

Industry	Business Risk	Moat Size	Investment Style	Sector
Shoes	Average	Narrow	Mid Core	Consumer Goods

Company Profile

Timberland designs and markets outdoor-inspired footwear, apparel, and accessories. Its primary products include hiking boots, work boots, casual shoes, and outerwear for men and women. Timberland products are sold through department stores, specialty shops, and company-operated factory outlets and retail locations throughout the world. In addition to its namesake brand, Timberland owns the SmartWool, Mion, Howies, and GoLite labels.

Management
Stewardship Grade [C]

When Jeffrey Swartz was named president and CEO in 1998, he became the third generation of his family to run the firm. Since then, revenue has risen 80%, thanks to acquisitions, brand extensions, and international expansion. In 2005, Timberland paid Swartz just over $2 million in salary, bonus, and other compensation. He was also given $4.6 million worth of restricted stock as part of a long-term incentive program. Timberland's executive compensation seems generous to us, although we like that a significant portion is contingent on meeting long-term profit growth targets. Sidney Swartz, Jeffrey's father, is chairman of the board. Together, the Swartz family owns about 4% of the publicly traded Class A shares but controls about 70% of the voting power with its Class B shares. We believe dual-class systems like this limit the influence of minority shareholders. Despite Timberland's controlled company status, we think the board is sufficiently independent--nine of the 11 directors are outsiders, and each board member is up for re-election annually.

200 Domain Drive
Stratham, NH 03885
www.timberland.com

Growth [C-]	2002	2003	2004	2005
Revenue %	0.6	12.7	11.8	4.3
Earnings/Share %	-6.0	29.7	32.5	13.6
Book Value/Share %	9.4	20.3	22.1	8.8
Dividends/Share %	NMF	NMF	NMF	NMF

Profitability [A+]	2003	2004	2005	TTM
Return on Assets %	18.4	20.2	20.9	12.9
Oper Cash Flow $Mil	199	185	182	139
- Cap Spending $Mil	25	24	26	32
= Free Cash Flow $Mil	174	161	156	106

Financial Health [A]	2003	2004	2005	09-30-06
Long-term Debt $Mil	—	—	—	—
Total Equity $Mil	428	512	528	537
Debt/Equity Ratio	—	—	—	—

Competition

	Market Cap $Mil	12 Mo Trailing Sales $Mil	Price/Cash Flow	Return On Assets%	Debt/Equity	Total Return% 1 Yr	3 Yr
Timberland	1,971	1,545	14.2	12.9	—	-3.0	6.9
Nike B	24,827	15,287	15.2	14.0	0.1	15.8	15.0
Columbia Sportswear	1,994	1,240	20.0	11.8	0.0	17.0	0.6

Price Volatility
Monthly Price High/Low — Relative Strength to S&P 500

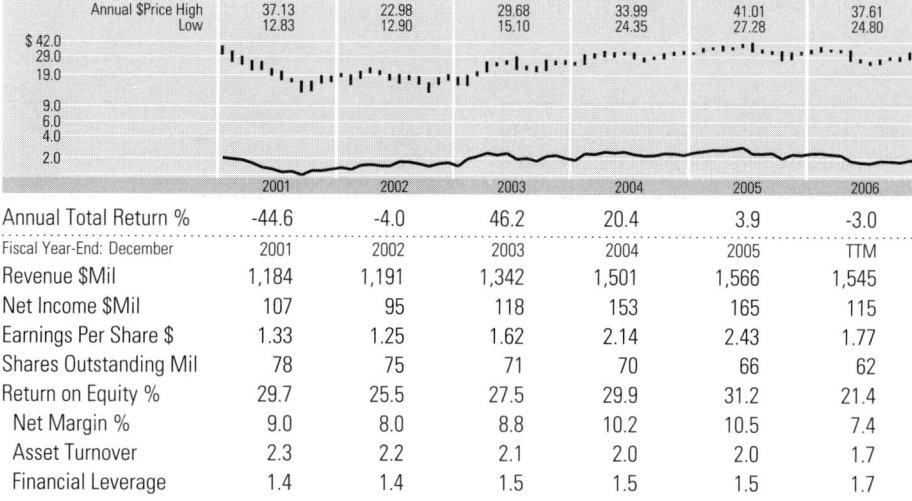

	2001	2002	2003	2004	2005	2006
Annual $Price High	37.13	22.98	29.68	33.99	41.01	37.61
Low	12.83	12.90	15.10	24.35	27.28	24.80
Annual Total Return %	-44.6	-4.0	46.2	20.4	3.9	-3.0

Fiscal Year-End: December	2001	2002	2003	2004	2005	TTM
Revenue $Mil	1,184	1,191	1,342	1,501	1,566	1,545
Net Income $Mil	107	95	118	153	165	115
Earnings Per Share $	1.33	1.25	1.62	2.14	2.43	1.77
Shares Outstanding Mil	78	75	71	70	66	62
Return on Equity %	29.7	25.5	27.5	29.9	31.2	21.4
Net Margin %	9.0	8.0	8.8	10.2	10.5	7.4
Asset Turnover	2.3	2.2	2.1	2.0	2.0	1.7
Financial Leverage	1.4	1.4	1.5	1.5	1.5	1.7

Valuation Ratios	Stock	Rel to Industry	Rel to S&P 500
Price/Earnings	17.8	0.9	0.9
Price/Book	3.7	0.4	0.9
Price/Sales	1.3	0.4	0.4
Price/Cash Flow	14.2	0.9	1.0

Major Fund Holders	% of Fund Assets
IXIS Harris Associates Focused Value C	4.50
High Pointe Small Cap Equity	3.02
Fidelity Small Cap Retirement	2.67
Boston Trust Small Cap	2.06

Thesis
By Brady Lemos, 12-14-06 Stock Price as of Analysis: $32.39

Timberland made its name decades ago by producing high-quality boots and rugged outdoor wear and has never strayed too far from what it knows best. This disciplined merchandising has helped Timberland obtain roughly one third of the domestic outdoor footwear market and build a narrow economic moat. We expect Timberland to be a dominant player in the outdoor footwear market for the foreseeable future, but cyclical returns are unavoidable in this industry.

While shifting fashion trends have pressured boot sales in the United States in 2006, we believe that a lack of product innovation and an inability to tailor products for a diverse consumer base have been the most significant impediments to growth. Consequently, we are encouraged that Timberland has strengthened its design team and localized merchandising to target specific consumers domestically and abroad. New brands like SmartWool and Mion should help stimulate product innovation even further.

We also like that Timberland will stop distributing some of its most popular boots to lower-tier retailers and its own outlet stores. Disciplined distribution should elevate the Timberland brand and boost sales at prime retailers. We do not anticipate a quick recovery, however. Challenging U.S. market conditions, particularly in the crucial urban segment, could continue to hamper boot sales in 2007.

Timberland's profits will also be hurt by European Union-imposed duties on certain leather shoes imported from China and Vietnam. We expect duties to be in place through 2008, although renegotiated limits may be enforced longer. Timberland imports about 25% of its footwear from China and Vietnam to Europe, so these duties will have a meaningful impact on profits, especially if they are in place for an extended period. In addition, reactive shifts in product sourcing to lower-taxed yet potentially less-efficient manufacturers in Asia and elsewhere could lead to higher material and wage costs.

Despite a number of near-term challenges, Timberland remains a well-positioned and financially strong company. We believe the firm has differentiated itself by cultivating a premium image through selective distribution, targeted marketing, and concept shops at retailers. Timberland's ability to maintain this brand cachet has helped it consistently earn a return on invested capital well in excess of our estimate of its cost of capital.

Time Warner TWX

Data as of 12-29-06

	Rating	Fair Value	Last Close	Consider Buy	Consider Sell	Yield %
	★★★	$20.00	$21.78	$17.00	$26.30	0.96

Company Profile

Filmed entertainment, including Warner Bros. Entertainment, is Time Warner's largest business, followed by cable networks, which runs HBO, TNT, and TBS. The firm owns most of Time Warner Cable, one of the biggest cable companies in the U.S. The firm's AOL unit is the largest provider of dialup Internet access in the U.S. and operates a very popular Web site. The firm's publishing unit is the biggest in the world, with titles including People, Time, and Fortune.

Management
Stewardship Grade [C]

Time Warner CEO and chairman Dick Parsons--a trained lawyer with a lengthy record of government service--replaced Gerald Levin several years ago amid accounting restatements, SEC investigations, and shareholder litigation, most of which related to the AOL acquisition. Parsons pulled Time Warner through the turmoil; however, we're not sure that he has what it takes to unlock significant value at Time Warner. Even with his adroit political skills, Parsons hasn't been successful in getting the great businesses that make up Time Warner to cooperate in order to maximize value. Despite this, Parsons has been well-rewarded for his efforts at Time Warner. In 2005, he received a $1.5 million base salary, $7.5 million bonus, and 830,000 shares of restricted stock and options. Jeffrey Bewkes, who became well-known for success at the helm of HBO, was elevated to the position of president and chief operating officer of Time Warner at the end of 2005. Now that Don Logan--former head of Time Warner's media and communications groups--has retired, Parsons and Bewkes are the two most important decision-makers at midtown Manhattan's plush Time Warner Center, which, at $1.7 billion, is the most expensive building complex in the U.S.

One Time Warner Center
New York, NY 10019
www.timewarner.com

Growth [B-]	2002	2003	2004	2005
Revenue %	8.7	6.8	6.4	3.7
Earnings/Share %	NMF	NMF	26.3	-13.9
Book Value/Share %	-65.0	2.1	7.1	2.9
Dividends/Share %	NMF	NMF	NMF	NMF

Profitability [D]	2003	2004	2005	TTM
Return on Assets %	2.2	2.7	2.4	4.9
Oper Cash Flow $Mil	6,601	6,618	4,965	6,018
- Cap Spending $Mil	2,887	3,024	3,246	3,720
= Free Cash Flow $Mil	3,714	3,594	1,719	2,298

Financial Health [D+]	2003	2004	2005	09-30-06
Long-term Debt $Mil	23,458	20,703	20,238	33,255
Total Equity $Mil	56,213	60,771	62,715	61,780
Debt/Equity Ratio	0.4	0.3	0.3	0.5

Industry	Business Risk	Moat Size	Investment Style	Sector
Media Conglomerates	Below Avg	Narrow	Large Core	Media

Competition	Market Cap $Mil	12 Mo Trailing Sales $Mil	Price/Cash Flow	Return On Assets%	Debt/ Equity	Total Return% 1 Yr	3 Yr
Time Warner	86,932	44,532	14.4	4.9	0.5	26.4	6.8
Microsoft	293,538	45,352	20.8	19.8	—	15.8	7.6
Walt Disney	70,886	34,285	11.7	5.6	0.3	44.3	14.2

Fiscal Year-End: December	2001	2002	2003	2004	2005	TTM
Annual Total Return %	-7.8	-59.2	37.3	8.1	-9.8	26.4
Revenue $Mil	34,096	37,060	39,563	42,089	43,652	44,532
Net Income $Mil	-5,860	-97,217	2,639	3,364	2,905	6,337
Earnings Per Share $	-1.32	-21.82	0.57	0.72	0.62	1.45
Shares Outstanding Mil	4,439	4,455	4,473	4,546	4,685	3,991
Return on Equity %	-3.9	ELB	4.7	5.5	4.6	10.3
Net Margin %	-17.2	ELB	6.7	8.0	6.7	14.2
Asset Turnover	0.2	0.3	0.3	0.3	0.4	0.3
Financial Leverage	1.4	2.2	2.2	2.0	2.0	2.1

Valuation Ratios	Stock	Rel to Industry	Rel to S&P 500
Price/Earnings	19.1	0.8	0.9
Price/Book	1.4	0.4	0.3
Price/Sales	2.0	0.6	0.7
Price/Cash Flow	14.4	0.9	1.0

Major Fund Holders	% of Fund Assets
Rydex Internet Inv	6.61
Valley Forge	6.30
FMI Large Cap	5.79
Oak Value	5.28

Thesis
By Jonathan Schrader, CFA, 11-01-06 Stock Price as of Analysis: $19.77

Time Warner owns many of the best properties in media. Individually, these businesses--including Time Warner Cable, HBO, Time, Warner Bros., and AOL--often shine, but as a whole, the company has often disappointed. Because of this, we've come to temper our enthusiasm for Time Warner and its shares, despite the firm's obvious potential.

The media sector has not been hospitable to equity investors over the past several years, and perhaps no shareholder group has as much cause for complaint as Time Warner's. Over the past five years (as of Oct. 31, 2006), Time Warner's shares have dropped 10% annually, while the S&P 500 has gained about 7% (including dividends). Since 2001 when Time Warner merged with AOL, Time Warner has paid out billions to settle lawsuits related to AOL's accounting, written off more than $100 billion (with a "B") in assets, and tried to put the pain of the AOL deal behind it by officially dropping "AOL" from its name.

That's a rough five years, but even before the AOL deal, Time Warner--formed in 1989 by the merger of Time Inc.'s publishing assets with Warner Communications' film, television, music, and cable assets--wasn't known for its management excellence or its business practices. Rather, in-fighting, territorialism, and underachievement followed in the wake of the 1989 merger, and although current management has made strides in getting Time Warner's businesses to get along, we think that there is still much work to be done.

Despite Time Warner's great assets, historically there has been relatively little sharing of content or services across businesses, even when such moves would make perfect business sense and potentially result in increased shareholder value. A fitting example is the failure to-date to make AOL.com the leading broadband portal given that Time Warner owns one of the largest cable companies in the country and some of the most compelling content around. Beyond AOL, other efforts to embrace digital media haven't fared very well, either.

While we have tempered our expectations for Time Warner, we still feel that it is a sleeping giant, with the capacity to take advantage of the low-cost distribution and interactivity that broadband Internet provides. If the firm's leadership can get all of its horses moving in the same direction and embrace rather than shrink from the Internet, Time Warner's future could be very bright, and our fair value estimate could prove too conservative.

TJX Companies TJX

Data as of 12-29-06

	Rating	Fair Value	Last Close	Consider Buy	Consider Sell	Yield %
	★★★	$27.00	$28.52	$20.80	$33.80	0.95

Industry	Business Risk	Moat Size	Investment Style	Sector
Clothing Stores	Average	Narrow	Large Core	Consumer Services

Company Profile

TJX Companies is the nation's largest off-price retailer of brand-name apparel and home fashions. TJX offers family apparel through its T.J. Maxx, Marshalls, A.J. Wright, Winners, and T.K. Maxx chains and home fashions through its HomeGoods and HomeSense stores. In December 2003, TJX acquired Bob's Stores, a value-oriented branded-apparel retailer. TJX operates more than 2,400 stores in the United States, Canada, the United Kingdom, and Ireland.

Management   Stewardship Grade [B]

Bernard Cammarata, who has been chairman of the board since 1999 and led the company for nearly 25 years, is serving as interim CEO. The company has ended its search for Cammarata's replacement, with Carol Meyrowitz slated to take over the role starting in January 2007. We think Meyrowitz is a logical choice given her vast experience with the company since joining in 1983. Most recently, she served as president of TJX, returning in October 2005 after a few months' stint at a private equity firm. Since the return of Cammarata and Meyrowitz, a number of positive changes have taken place. For starters, executive compensation is more reasonable. Cammarata and other top executives took a 10% pay cut at the start of 2005. His base salary in 2006 will be $900,000 with performance-based incentives in the form of equity instead of cash to better align his interests with those of shareholders. Board members no longer serve three-year terms and are elected annually. We think this is more shareholder friendly, allowing stockholders to oust underperforming directors in a more timely manner. Overall, the company has made significant progress in its stewardship, and we are raising our rating from average to above average given the recent changes.

770 Cochituate Road   www.tjx.com
Framingham, MA 01701

Growth [B]	2003	2004	2005	2006
Revenue %	11.9	11.2	11.9	7.7
Earnings/Share %	7.7	18.4	4.3	16.5
Book Value/Share %	9.1	16.4	11.9	11.5
Dividends/Share %	28.6	20.0	25.9	32.4

Profitability [A+]	2004	2005	2006	TTM
Return on Assets %	13.9	12.0	12.6	13.0
Oper Cash Flow $Mil	768	1,077	1,158	1,128
- Cap Spending $Mil	409	429	496	386
= Free Cash Flow $Mil	359	648	662	742

Financial Health [A]	2004	2005	2006	10-31-06
Long-term Debt $Mil	—	599	807	818
Total Equity $Mil	1,627	1,747	1,893	2,174
Debt/Equity Ratio	—	0.3	0.4	0.4

Competition

	Market Cap $Mil	12 Mo Trailing Sales $Mil	Price/Cash Flow	Return On Assets%	Debt/Equity	Total Return% 1 Yr	3 Yr
TJX Companies	12,979	17,102	11.5	13.0	0.4	24.1	10.7
Ross Stores	4,095	5,373	9.3	10.3	0.0	2.3	4.7
Men's Wearhouse	2,024	1,822	13.2	10.8	0.3	30.7	33.3

Price Volatility

	2001	2002	2003	2004	2005	2006
Annual $Price High	20.30	22.45	23.70	26.82	25.96	29.84
Low	13.56	15.30	15.54	20.64	19.95	22.16
Annual Total Return %	44.4	-1.5	13.8	14.8	-6.7	24.1

Fiscal Year-End: January	2002	2003	2004	2005	2006	TTM
Revenue $Mil	10,709	11,981	13,328	14,913	16,058	17,102
Net Income $Mil	513	539	609	610	690	821
Earnings Per Share $	0.91	0.98	1.16	1.21	1.41	1.71
Shares Outstanding Mil	—	—	508	488	467	455
Return on Equity %	37.3	36.8	37.5	34.9	36.5	37.8
Net Margin %	4.8	4.5	4.6	4.1	4.3	4.8
Asset Turnover	3.0	3.0	3.0	2.9	2.9	2.7
Financial Leverage	2.6	2.7	2.7	2.9	2.9	2.9

Valuation Ratios	Stock	Rel to Industry	Rel to S&P 500
Price/Earnings	16.7	0.8	0.8
Price/Book	6.0	1.4	1.5
Price/Sales	0.8	0.6	0.3
Price/Cash Flow	11.5	0.9	0.8

Major Fund Holders	% of Fund Assets
Sequoia	6.41
Brandywine Blue	4.41
FMI Large Cap	4.38
Brandywine	4.03

Thesis   By Kimberly Picciola, 12-07-06   Stock Price as of Analysis: $27.81

TJX dominates off-price retailing. Its base of over 2,400 stores worldwide makes it an attractive outlet for apparel manufacturers looking to dispose of excess inventory. By developing relationships with key apparel manufacturers such as Polo Ralph Lauren and Liz Claiborne, TJX is able to buy brand-name goods at rock bottom prices, passing the savings on to consumers. These vendor relationships give TJX a leg up over its competitors, in our opinion, and is the basis for its narrow economic moat.

While TJX's competitive advantage has kept rivals at bay, the company has had its share of internal challenges recently. In 2005, poor merchandising led to sluggish sales, compelling the company to shift much of its focus away from new-store growth and more toward improving performance in its existing stores. In addition, Edmond English resigned from his role as CEO and chairman of the board, and former CEO Ben Cammarata stepped in to run the show.

Although 2005 was rocky, we think interim CEO Cammarata is making progress. First, he has reinforced the basics of off-price selling (encouraging buyers to purchase merchandise closer to the point at which it will be sold in TJX's stores). This allows buyers to pay more competitive prices while ensuring the merchandise is in line with current trends.

Second, he has contained expenses by eliminating jobs and cutting senior executives' pay by 10%. Finally, he has focused on improving the performance of the company's newer concepts, including Home Goods and A.J. Wrights.

The more recent concepts have put a drag on the company's operating margin, which has declined over the past five years. Additionally, suppliers are becoming more adept at managing their inventory and apparel prices are falling, giving TJX little room for profit expansion in its more mature businesses. Thus, its larger, more established divisions have posted stagnant operating margins in recent years, doing little to compensate for the added startup costs associated with the new concepts.

Although operating margins in the core Marmaxx business (which includes T.J. Maxx and Marshalls) have come under pressure in recent years, they continue to be upward of 9%. So, despite the pressure on profits, the firm continues to generate returns on invested capital in excess of our estimated cost of capital. We believe the core off-price apparel business remains strong, and we're still optimistic that the poor performance of the firm's new concepts will improve. Over the long run, we think TJX will continue to generate shareholder value.

Data as of 12-29-06

Toll Brothers TOL

Rating	Fair Value	Last Close	Consider Buy	Consider Sell	Yield %
★★★	$32.00	$32.23	$24.70	$40.10	0.00

Company Profile

Founded more than 35 years ago, Toll Brothers is the nation's largest homebuilder catering exclusively to affluent customers. The average selling price for the company's homes is in the upper $600,000s. Toll serves the move-up, empty-nester, active-adult, and second-home markets in 21 states. In fiscal 2006, the company built 8,601 homes, almost double 2000's 4,358 deliveries.

Industry	Business Risk	Moat Size	Investment Style	Sector
Home Building	Average	Narrow	Mid Core	Consumer Services

Competition

	Market Cap $Mil	12 Mo Trailing Sales $Mil	Price/Cash Flow	Return On Assets %	Debt/Equity	Total Return % 1 Yr	3 Yr
Toll Brothers	4,947	6,335	—	11.2	0.7	-7.0	18.8
DR Horton	8,306	15,051	—	8.3	0.8	-24.4	9.9
Pulte Homes	8,432	15,017	—	9.1	0.5	-15.4	13.8

Management   Stewardship Grade [C]

Brothers Robert and Bruce Toll founded Toll Brothers more than 35 years ago. Robert has been the CEO since inception, while Bruce retired from active management in 1998. Both remain major stakeholders in the company, and all insiders together beneficially own more than 26% of the shares. We like that CEO Bob Toll, COO Zvi Barzilay, and CFO Joel Rassman have been working together for 20-plus years. On top of $1.3 million in salary, variable compensation for Bob Toll is based on a percentage of the company's earnings before taxes, ranging from 1.5% to 3.5% depending on return on equity thresholds. Using this formula, the CEO received a whopping $27 million bonus in 2005. Options, which are doled out to senior executives with no constant criteria governing the amounts, represent a significant percentage of compensation. At the end of 2005, there were 26 million options outstanding, or almost 18% of the beginning basic shares. Lastly, though generally immaterial, the company is involved in several related-party transactions with multiple board members. Arrangements span from a commercial real estate partnership with senior management to jet rental from a company owned by the CEO. The aggregate of these minor issues results in a C Stewardship Grade for Toll.

3103 Philmont Avenue   www.tollbrothers.com
Huntingdon Valley, PA 19006-4298

Growth [A+]	2002	2003	2004	2005
Revenue %	4.9	19.1	40.0	50.0
Earnings/Share %	5.8	17.8	46.5	89.7
Book Value/Share %	27.2	30.3	21.0	38.6
Dividends/Share %	NMF	NMF	NMF	NMF

Profitability [A]	2003	2004	2005	TTM
Return on Assets %	6.9	8.3	12.7	11.2
Oper Cash Flow $Mil	-45	124	335	-101
- Cap Spending $Mil	15	20	43	44
= Free Cash Flow $Mil	-60	103	292	-145

Financial Health [B+]	2003	2004	2005	07-31-06
Long-term Debt $Mil	—	1,728	1,830	2,291
Total Equity $Mil	1,477	1,920	2,764	3,232
Debt/Equity Ratio	—	0.9	0.7	0.7

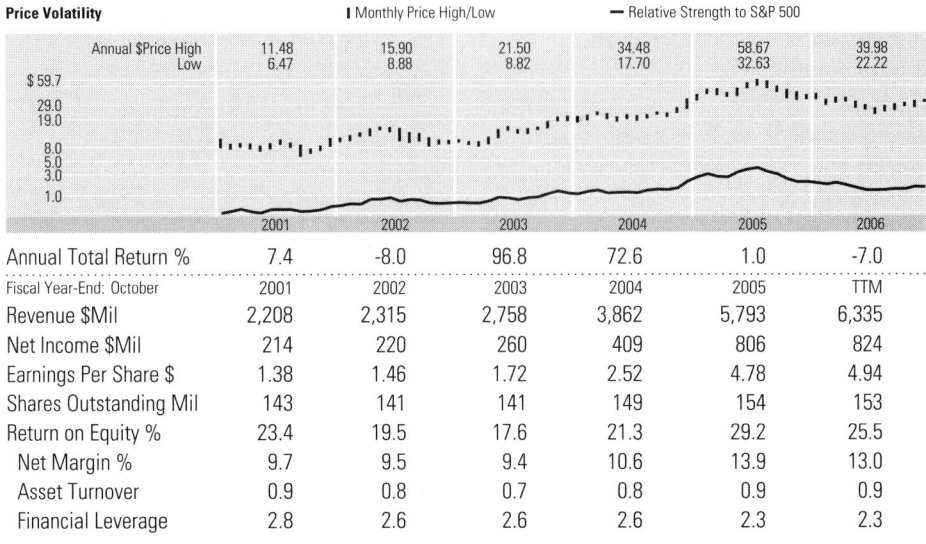

Price Volatility | Monthly Price High/Low   — Relative Strength to S&P 500

Annual $Price High Low	11.48 6.47	15.90 8.88	21.50 8.82	34.48 17.70	58.67 32.63	39.98 22.22
	2001	2002	2003	2004	2005	2006
Annual Total Return %	7.4	-8.0	96.8	72.6	1.0	-7.0

Fiscal Year-End: October	2001	2002	2003	2004	2005	TTM
Revenue $Mil	2,208	2,315	2,758	3,862	5,793	6,335
Net Income $Mil	214	220	260	409	806	824
Earnings Per Share $	1.38	1.46	1.72	2.52	4.78	4.94
Shares Outstanding Mil	143	141	141	149	154	153
Return on Equity %	23.4	19.5	17.6	21.3	29.2	25.5
Net Margin %	9.7	9.5	9.4	10.6	13.9	13.0
Asset Turnover	0.9	0.8	0.7	0.8	0.9	0.9
Financial Leverage	2.8	2.6	2.6	2.6	2.3	2.3

Valuation Ratios	Stock	Rel to Industry	Rel to S&P 500
Price/Earnings	6.5	0.8	0.3
Price/Book	1.5	0.8	0.4
Price/Sales	0.8	1.0	0.3
Price/Cash Flow	—	—	—

Major Fund Holders	% of Fund Assets
Alpine U.S. Real Estate Equity	5.32
New River Core Equity	2.64
Calamos Value A	2.37
IMS Capital Value	2.24

Thesis By Eric Landry, 12-06-06   Stock Price as of Analysis: $33.01

As the largest homebuilder operating exclusively in the high-end luxury market, Toll Brothers has several long-term trends working in its favor. Even though the near term promises to be rocky, we think this narrow-moat builder will create plenty of shareholder value over the coming decade.

Toll has positioned itself to profit handsomely from the growing ranks of America's wealthy households. At nearly 18 million in 2004, the number of households earning at least $100,000 annually was up 64% over the past 15 years, or about triple the increase in overall households. Though the typical Toll Brothers house is out of reach for the lower end of that demographic, the company is positioned perfectly to profit from the baby boomer generation, a segment that is now in its highest earning years. Stretching from 1946 to 1964, the baby boom period witnessed roughly 76 million births, or 52% more than the prior 19-year period. The oldest of the group, now entering their 60s, have helped fuel Toll's 25% annual revenue growth over the past decade. More important, roughly the other half of the boomers (those born between 1956 and 1964, when births jumped to an average of 4.2 million annually) is just entering Toll's strike zone and should provide ample demand for several more years.

Toll's ability to take raw land through the entitlement process is a considerable advantage, in our opinion. The company operates mostly in affluent, land-restricted communities, where NIMBY (not in my back yard) protests are intense. Well-organized opponents are often able to delay the permitting process for as long as a decade in some cases, and shut it down completely in others. Builders without the legal and political savvy to combat these groups are usually frozen out. Yet this is the type of environment Toll has operated in for years, allowing the firm to build valuable expertise. Also, by spreading the cost of these drawn-out battles over thousands of units, Toll is able to wait it out and still generate strong profits where others can't.

Even with these advantages, however, the near term promises to be difficult. Demand from second-home buyers and speculators, which drove record revenue and margins in 2005, is turning into a torrent of supply. Unit orders are off more than 50%, and how long it will take to burn off the excess is anybody's guess. But given the aforementioned trends, coupled with the fact that the company operates in extremely land-constrained markets, the ordeal may be shorter than some think.

Data as of 12-29-06

Torchmark TMK

Rating	Fair Value	Last Close	Consider Buy	Consider Sell	Yield %
★★★	$63.00	$63.76	$48.60	$78.90	0.75

Company Profile

Torchmark sells individual life and health insurance through niche distribution units. The life segment markets term and whole-life contracts; the health segment mainly offers Medicare supplement, cancer, and other supplemental health policies. Torchmark markets insurance directly to consumers and through agents to the middle-income market, unions, and active and retired military officers.

Management

Stewardship Grade [B]

Mark McAndrew, 52, was elected chairman and CEO of Torchmark in 2005 after C.B. Hudson resigned. McAndrew has been with the insurer since 1980, filling such managerial roles as chairman of insurance operations. McAndrew earned $1.5 million in total compensation during 2005 and owns approximately $41 million of Torchmark stock, which is enough to align his interests with shareholders', in our opinion. We think Torchmark is a good example of how an insurance company should be managed thanks to first-rate underwriting discipline and the firm's transparency.

2001 3rd Avenue South www.torchmarkcorp.com
Birmingham, AL 35233

Growth [C]	2002	2003	2004	2005
Revenue %	2.0	6.2	4.8	1.8
Earnings/Share %	12.4	17.3	12.3	11.7
Book Value/Share %	19.3	18.8	8.8	6.0
Dividends/Share %	0.0	5.6	15.8	0.0

Profitability [A+]	2003	2004	2005	TTM
Return on Assets %	3.2	3.3	3.4	3.4
Oper Cash Flow $Mil	741	767	857	—
- Cap Spending $Mil	4	—	—	—
= Free Cash Flow $Mil	—	—	—	—

Financial Health [NA]	2003	2004	2005	10-31-05
Long-term Debt $Mil	—	—	—	—
Total Equity $Mil	3,240	3,420	3,433	3,365
Debt/Equity Ratio	—	—	—	—

Industry	Business Risk	Moat Size	Investment Style	Sector
Insurance (Life)	Average	Narrow	Mid Value	Financial Services

Competition

	Market Cap $Mil	12 Mo Trailing Sales $Mil	Price/Cash Flow	Return On Assets%	Debt/ Equity	Total Return% 1 Yr	3 Yr
Torchmark	6,253	3,333	—	3.4	—	15.6	12.8
UnitedHealth Group	72,374	51,787	11.9	7.7	0.4	-13.5	22.2
Conseco	3,036	4,402	—	0.4	—	-13.8	-2.7

Price Volatility

	2001	2002	2003	2004	2005	2006
Annual $Price High	43.25	42.17	45.75	57.57	57.50	64.59
Low	32.56	30.02	33.00	44.61	50.05	53.91
Annual Total Return %	3.3	-6.2	25.9	26.5	-1.9	15.6

Fiscal Year-End: December	2001	2002	2003	2004	2005	TTM
Revenue $Mil	2,707	2,761	2,931	3,072	3,126	3,333
Net Income $Mil	357	383	430	469	495	502
Earnings Per Share $	2.83	3.18	3.73	4.19	4.68	4.90
Shares Outstanding Mil	125	120	115	110	105	98
Return on Equity %	14.3	13.4	13.3	13.7	14.4	14.9
Net Margin %	13.2	13.9	14.7	15.3	15.8	15.1
Asset Turnover	0.2	0.2	0.2	0.2	0.2	0.2
Financial Leverage	5.0	4.3	4.2	4.2	4.3	4.4

Valuation Ratios	Stock	Rel to Industry	Rel to S&P 500
Price/Earnings	13.0	0.5	0.6
Price/Book	1.9	0.6	0.5
Price/Sales	1.9	0.8	0.7
Price/Cash Flow	—	—	—

Major Fund Holders	% of Fund Assets
Century Shares Trust Instl	4.39
Tweedy, Browne American Value	2.99
JHancock Classic Value A	2.83
Constellation Pitcairn Select Value II	2.80

Thesis By Dafina Dunmore, 10-20-06 Stock Price as of Analysis: $62.54

Torchmark is in an elite field of life insurers that earn a profit notwithstanding investment income. This, along with a lean cost structure, yields Torchmark a narrow economic moat, in our opinion. Our fair value estimate is $63 per share.

Management's willingness to sacrifice sales of irrationally priced products to protect its profitability is the crux of Torchmark's narrow moat. Torchmark's niche focus and lean cost structure offer an edge over competitors. The insurer generates almost 30% of its life insurance underwriting profit via direct mail. The direct marketing strategy endows Torchmark with a 6% expense ratio, one of the lowest-cost structures in the industry. Though still attractive, margins on this business are lower than other channels due to higher acquisition costs on certain products.

Torchmark's American Income subsidiary, which accounts for 32% of life insurance underwriting profit, is one of only two "union-label" life insurance companies targeting union membership. Cultivating new sales in this segment has been a challenge, as management continues to deal with the fallout from its decision to modify agent compensation a couple of years ago. To spur new sales, management has increased its recruitment efforts, which is finally paying off. We expect this trend to continue through 2007.

Unlike most insurers, agents in Torchmark's Liberty National unit were historically paid a salary for servicing existing customers, which resulted in low agent productivity and lackluster sales. Management's recent restructuring of this division to incentive-based compensation and the elimination of its servicing component should bode well for profitable growth.

Supplemental health insurance makes up almost 35% of Torchmark's underwriting income, including Part D prescription drug coverage. The insurer's career agency remains impressive with favorable agent and sales growth but its independent agency remains challenged. Torchmark is undergoing a product mix shift away from Medical Supplement products to limited-benefit products, which have slightly higher acquisition costs. This should result in modestly lower margins in the future.

Torchmark generates higher margins on Part D than its peers by pricing to higher profitability targets and boasting lower expense ratios. Loss ratios continue to trend lower than expected.

Data as of 12-29-06

Toronto-Dominion Bank TD

	Rating	Fair Value	Last Close	Consider Buy	Consider Sell	Yield %
	★★★	$58.00	$59.87	$44.70	$72.70	1.44

Company Profile
Toronto-Dominion Bank is the third-largest bank in Canada in terms of market capitalization. The bank, which has more than C$390 billion in assets, offers traditional banking products to retail and corporate clients. TD has significant insurance, wealth-management, and capital markets operations, and its controlling stake in Maine-based TD Banknorth provides exposure to the U.S. market. The bank also owns a sizable stake in discount broker TD Ameriprise.

Management
Stewardship Grade [NA]

Ed Clark was named CEO in 2000, after TD acquired Canada Trust Financial Services. He has more than two decades of retail banking experience. In 2005, Clark took home C$3.15 million in base salary and bonus, which is in line with peers. We like that Clark has a sizable ownership stake in the bank that amounts to more than 30 times his annual base salary. In our view, corporate governance is good: The chairman and CEO positions are separate, the board is nonstaggered, and option grants aren't excessive. We also like that the board is highly independent, as only 2 out of 16 directors are not independent. We are pleased with the bank's financial disclosures, which are detailed and comprehensive.

Industry	Business Risk	Moat Size	Investment Style	Sector
International Banks	Average	Wide	Large Core	Financial Services

Competition	Market Cap $Mil	12 Mo Trailing Sales $Mil	Price/Cash Flow	Return On Assets%	Debt/Equity	Total Return% 1 Yr	3 Yr
Toronto-Dominion Bank	43,027	11,488	—	1.2	—	15.4	23.9
Royal Bank of Canada	61,039	20,637	—	0.9	—	26.0	29.5
Bank of Nova Scotia	44,330	10,211	—	0.9	—	16.8	24.5

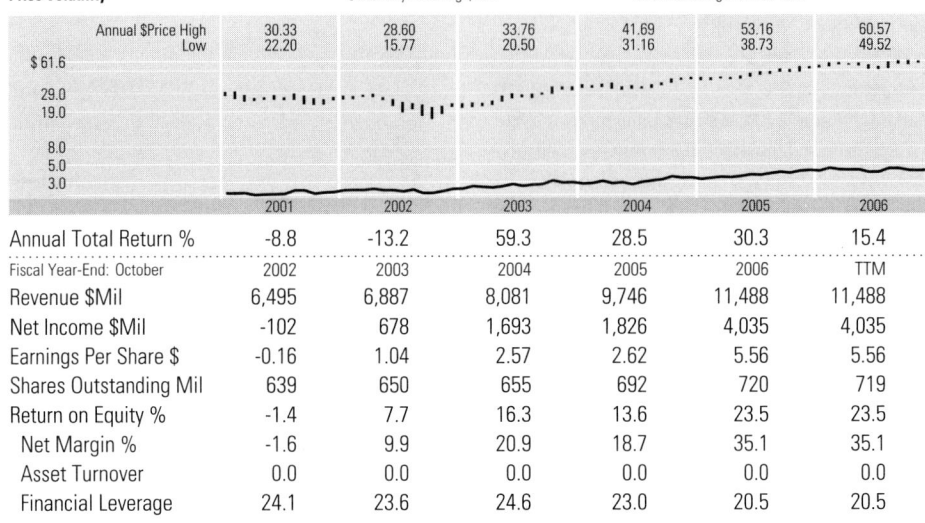

Annual Total Return %	-8.8	-13.2	59.3	28.5	30.3	15.4
Fiscal Year-End: October	2002	2003	2004	2005	2006	TTM
Revenue $Mil	6,495	6,887	8,081	9,746	11,488	11,488
Net Income $Mil	-102	678	1,693	1,826	4,035	4,035
Earnings Per Share $	-0.16	1.04	2.57	2.62	5.56	5.56
Shares Outstanding Mil	639	650	655	692	720	719
Return on Equity %	-1.4	7.7	16.3	13.6	23.5	23.5
Net Margin %	-1.6	9.9	20.9	18.7	35.1	35.1
Asset Turnover	0.0	0.0	0.0	0.0	0.0	0.0
Financial Leverage	24.1	23.6	24.6	23.0	20.5	20.5

Valuation Ratios	Stock	Rel to Industry	Rel to S&P 500
Price/Earnings	10.8	0.6	0.5
Price/Book	2.5	1.0	0.6
Price/Sales	3.7	0.9	1.3
Price/Cash Flow	—	—	—

Major Fund Holders	% of Fund Assets
Fidelity Canada	3.84
Eaton Vance Dividend Income A	1.45
UBS International Equity Y	1.18
Sextant International	1.05

Thesis By Michael Kon, CFA, 12-08-06 Stock Price as of Analysis: $58.70

Toronto-Dominion's Canadian operation is a solid performer that produces very attractive returns on equity. Recent acquisitions in the United States might spur growth, but we doubt returns will match those in Canada.

The heart of TD's operation is the Canadian personal and commercial banking business that accounts for about 55% of total revenue. The bank operates a well-entrenched branch network that spans Canada and differentiates itself from peers by focusing on customer service. The most notable initiative in this area was offering extended branch hours. While better service usually comes with higher costs, TD has managed to keep its costs in line with peers, and although the return on equity over the past five years was slightly below the peer group average, it was still an impressive 20%.

We think this high return was achieved thanks to the bank's business model of being a one-stop shop for financial services in Canada. This strategy enabled the bank to sell multiple products to each client, thus forming enduring relationships with customers and increasing their switching costs. In our view, as more clients buy several different products from TD, the likelihood of their switching to a different financial services provider declines. We think these advantages garner TD a wide economic moat.

We are less excited about the bank's recent U.S. inroads. In 2005, after years of mulling a U.S. entrance strategy, the bank settled on the purchase of a majority stake in one of the largest banks based in New England, Banknorth (now TD Banknorth). As opposed to peers that prefer a more hands-on approach, TD didn't take Banknorth private but only purchased a majority stake and kept its management intact. Since we think Banknorth is a well-managed bank, we like that this unit is managed locally and will remain independent, even though it limits the possibility for synergies between the two banks.

Our the main issue with the U.S. expansion is the potential return on equity. This operation offers TD solid growth opportunities, mainly through acquisitions, but Banknorth operates in a highly competitive environment, which makes it extremely hard to generate a return of more than 15%, much lower than the 20% TD usually generates in Canada. We would watch out for further U.S. expansion, as it might dilute the lofty returns earned in Canada.

P.O. Box 1 Toronto-Dominion Centre www.tdbank.ca
Toronto, ON M5K-1A2

Growth [NA]	2002	2003	2004	2005
Revenue %	-1.8	6.1	11.6	10.1
Earnings/Share %	NMF	124.5	-5.6	98.1
Book Value/Share %	-2.1	8.9	18.4	16.1
Dividends/Share %	—	—	—	—

Profitability [NA]	2003	2004	2005	TTM
Return on Assets %	0.7	0.6	1.2	1.2
Oper Cash Flow $Mil	-6,832	4,311	-5,598	—
- Cap Spending $Mil	—	—	—	—
= Free Cash Flow $Mil	—	—	—	—

Financial Health [NA]	2003	2004	2005	10-31-05
Long-term Debt $Mil	—	—	—	—
Total Equity $Mil	10,384	13,446	17,149	17,149
Debt/Equity Ratio	—	—	—	—

Data as of 12-29-06

Total SA ADR TOT

	Rating ★★★	Fair Value $70.00	Last Close $71.92	Consider Buy $54.00	Consider Sell $87.70	Yield % 2.99

Industry	Business Risk	Moat Size	Investment Style	Sector
Oil/Gas	Average	Narrow	Large Value	Energy

Company Profile

Total is one of the largest companies in the oil and gas industry. It became an industry heavyweight when French firm Total merged with Belgian firm Petrofina in 1999. The two then combined with French firm Elf Aquitaine in 2000. In 2005, Total boasted 11 billion barrels of oil equivalent in reserves, production of 2.5 million barrels per day, and the ability to refine 2.7 million barrels per day. The company also operates a network of roughly 17,000 service stations.

Management   Stewardship Grade [NA]

Thierry Desmarest has been chairman and chief executive officer since 1995. Under his watch, Total's oil and gas production has grown at a remarkable clip. Desmarest also guided the firm through the Petrofina and Elf Aquitaine acquisitions, which turned Total into one of the largest oil companies on the planet. Using 2005 average exchange rates, Desmarest's total compensation last year was roughly $3.9 million. His ownership stake in the company amounts to about $20.5 million, based on the current market price and exchange rate. Since Desmarest's ownership stake is worth much more than his annual salary, we believe his interests should be closely aligned with shareholders'. The company's other directors are compensated primarily with cash and do not have a significant equity stake. We think directors make better company stewards when they have more skin in the game. An employee investment fund holds 2.6% of Total shares and 5.1% of the voting rights. The fund also has one representative on the board of directors.

2, Place de la Coupole La Defense 6   www.total.com
Courbevoie, France 92400

Growth [NA]	2002	2003	2004	2005
Revenue %	-2.6	2.1	-4.0	22.0
Earnings/Share %	-19.3	24.0	62.0	16.0
Book Value/Share %	-1.4	-0.8	8.8	30.9
Dividends/Share %	7.9	14.6	14.9	20.0

Profitability [NA]	2003	2004	2005	TTM
Return on Assets %	7.9	11.7	12.5	12.5
Oper Cash Flow $Mil	13,985	18,214	18,369	18,369
- Cap Spending $Mil	8,655	11,061	14,019	14,019
= Free Cash Flow $Mil	5,330	7,153	4,350	4,350

Financial Health [NA]	2003	2004	2005	12-31-05
Long-term Debt $Mil	12,229	15,464	16,420	16,420
Total Equity $Mil	38,008	44,408	49,385	49,385
Debt/Equity Ratio	0.3	0.3	0.3	0.3

Competition

	Market Cap $Mil	12 Mo Trailing Sales $Mil	Price/Cash Flow	Return On Assets%	Debt/ Equity	Total Return% 1 Yr	3 Yr
Total SA ADR	176,957	153,547	9.6	12.5	0.3	19.2	20.2
ExxonMobil	446,944	386,951	8.8	17.8	0.1	39.1	26.2
BP PLC ADR	231,015	239,792	8.6	10.8	0.1	7.9	14.3

Price Volatility

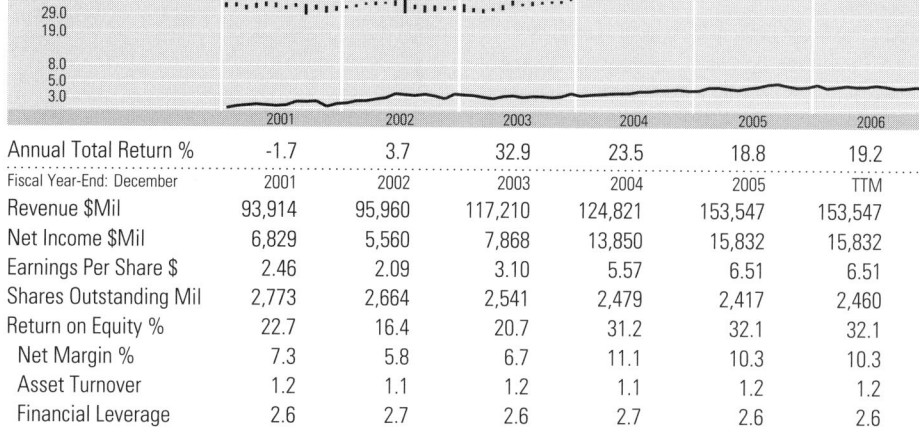

Annual $Price High Low	38.91 29.05	41.62 30.19	46.60 30.48	55.28 43.88	68.98 51.87	73.46 58.06
	2001	2002	2003	2004	2005	2006
Annual Total Return %	-1.7	3.7	32.9	23.5	18.8	19.2

Fiscal Year-End: December	2001	2002	2003	2004	2005	TTM
Revenue $Mil	93,914	95,960	117,210	124,821	153,547	153,547
Net Income $Mil	6,829	5,560	7,868	13,850	15,832	15,832
Earnings Per Share $	2.46	2.09	3.10	5.57	6.51	6.51
Shares Outstanding Mil	2,773	2,664	2,541	2,479	2,417	2,460
Return on Equity %	22.7	16.4	20.7	31.2	32.1	32.1
Net Margin %	7.3	5.8	6.7	11.1	10.3	10.3
Asset Turnover	1.2	1.1	1.2	1.1	1.2	1.2
Financial Leverage	2.6	2.7	2.6	2.7	2.6	2.6

Valuation Ratios	Stock	Rel to Industry	Rel to S&P 500
Price/Earnings	11.1	0.9	0.5
Price/Book	3.6	1.1	0.9
Price/Sales	1.2	0.6	0.4
Price/Cash Flow	9.6	1.1	0.7

Major Fund Holders	% of Fund Assets
ProFunds Europe 30 Svc	5.50
Dreyfus Premier Worldwide Growth A	4.95
MainStay ICAP International I	4.81
Vanguard Energy	4.31

Thesis   By Elizabeth Collins, 12-13-06   Stock Price as of Analysis: $72.13

French oil giant Total's robust upstream portfolio should enable it to increase production for years to come.

Total has invested heavily in its oil and gas exploration and production business. We believe this part of the energy chain--the upstream segment--enjoys an economic moat because OPEC will cut output to ensure high prices. As one of the biggest firms in the oil patch, Total also benefits from economies of scale and geographic diversification. In addition, we think that Total is relatively well positioned to exploit two key advantages. First, the firm has less exposure to mature hydrocarbon basins like those in North America, where production is falling and energy resources are becoming increasingly hard to find. Total has a solid pipeline of new projects in the Middle East and Africa, which should allow the firm to meet its aggressive growth targets. Second, because political factors play such an elemental role in the oil industry, Total's French roots can open some doors. For example, Total has operations in Iran, an area no U.S. company can touch.

Despite these advantages, Total's foray into political hot spots, along with France's stance on international issues, could also result in significant hurdles for growth. In the campaign by international oil companies to access more Middle Eastern oil reserves, Total may be at a disadvantage when it comes to investing in Iraq. When it's time to award production contracts, the new Iraqi government might be more willing to work with U.S. or British firms. And in countries like Venezuela and Bolivia, Total has been stung by changing political and tax regimes. Still, its geographic diversity means that political pitfalls in any one area shouldn't hurt the overall health of the firm too much.

Besides exploration and production, Total has extensive downstream operations--which include refining and marketing--as well as a large chemical segment. It has taken a disciplined approach to investing in these businesses. Despite currently strong refining margins, the firm probably won't significantly expand its European refining capacity anytime soon--it wasn't long ago that the industry suffered from a glut of capacity and resultant weak margins. Instead, Total will focus on expanding downstream activity in Africa and Asia. Also, in May 2006, Total spun off part of its chemical business, whose profitability pales in comparison with Total's other operations.

Total System Services TSS

Data as of 12-29-06

	Rating	Fair Value	Last Close	Consider Buy	Consider Sell	Yield %
	★★★	$24.00	$26.39	$18.50	$30.10	1.02

Industry	Business Risk	Moat Size	Investment Style	Sector
Data Processing	Average	Wide	Mid Growth	Business Services

Company Profile

TSYS provides payment processing services and related products such as credit evaluation and fraud detection to credit card issuers. It also offers merchant card processing services through its Acquiring Solutions subsidiary. Approximately 16% of the company's revenues are generated internationally.

Management Stewardship Grade [C]

Synovus Financial Corporation owns 81% of TSYS' stock, so it controls the direction of the company, and investors are simply along for the ride. This might change, though, as Synovus' CEO has recently stated that he is looking at the possibility of spinning off TSYS. TSYS management would prefer a spin-off, as that would free their hands to pursue a more active acquisition strategy and expand the company's footprint. Given the restraints imposed by Synovus' majority stake, executive and director ownership is acceptable at 3% of outstanding shares. Executive pay is not unreasonable, and the fact that no options were granted in 2003 suggests that pay is tied to company performance. Additionally, the company is not excessive with option grants, which totaled less than 1% of outstanding shares in 2005. TSYS' stewardship could be improved by allowing cumulative voting, which would give outside investors a greater voice.

1600 First Avenue P.O. Box 2567 www.tsys.com
Columbus, GA 31902-2567

Growth [B+]	2002	2003	2004	2005
Revenue %	7.0	10.3	12.7	35.0
Earnings/Share %	20.8	10.9	7.0	30.3
Book Value/Share %	19.0	20.4	18.3	18.1
Dividends/Share %	12.5	14.8	80.6	57.1

Profitability [A+]	2003	2004	2005	TTM
Return on Assets %	14.1	11.7	13.8	13.9
Oper Cash Flow $Mil	266	332	239	343
- Cap Spending $Mil	125	54	41	29
= Free Cash Flow $Mil	141	278	198	314

Financial Health [A+]	2003	2004	2005	09-30-06
Long-term Debt $Mil	30	5	4	2
Total Equity $Mil	733	865	1,013	1,137
Debt/Equity Ratio	0.0	0.0	0.0	0.0

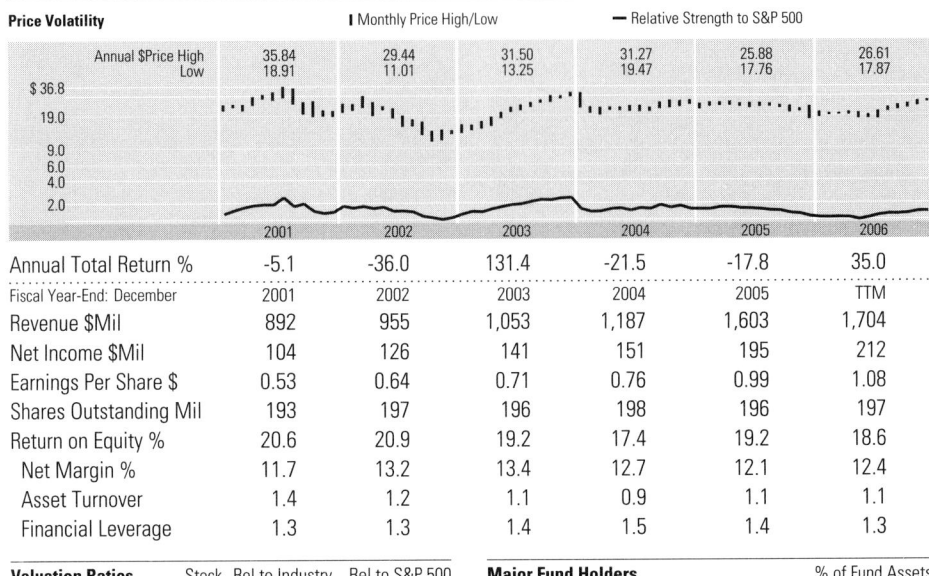

Competition	Market Cap $Mil	12 Mo Trailing Sales $Mil	Price/Cash Flow	Return On Assets%	Debt/Equity	Total Return% 1 Yr	Total Return% 3 Yr
Total System Services	5,197	1,704	15.2	13.9	0.0	35.0	-3.9
First Data	19,543	10,806	8.4	4.4	0.4	9.9	5.6

	2001	2002	2003	2004	2005	2006
Annual $Price High	35.84	29.44	31.50	31.27	25.88	26.61
Low	18.91	11.01	13.25	19.47	17.76	17.87
Annual Total Return %	-5.1	-36.0	131.4	-21.5	-17.8	35.0

Fiscal Year-End: December	2001	2002	2003	2004	2005	TTM
Revenue $Mil	892	955	1,053	1,187	1,603	1,704
Net Income $Mil	104	126	141	151	195	212
Earnings Per Share $	0.53	0.64	0.71	0.76	0.99	1.08
Shares Outstanding Mil	193	197	196	198	196	197
Return on Equity %	20.6	20.9	19.2	17.4	19.2	18.6
Net Margin %	11.7	13.2	13.4	12.7	12.1	12.4
Asset Turnover	1.4	1.2	1.1	0.9	1.1	1.1
Financial Leverage	1.3	1.3	1.4	1.5	1.4	1.3

Valuation Ratios	Stock	Rel to Industry	Rel to S&P 500
Price/Earnings	24.4	1.1	1.2
Price/Book	4.6	0.9	1.1
Price/Sales	3.1	0.9	1.1
Price/Cash Flow	15.2	0.7	1.0

Major Fund Holders	% of Fund Assets
Marco Targeted Return	3.16
Blue Chip Investor	2.86
American Century Technology Inv	1.40

Thesis By Brett Horn, 12-14-06 Stock Price as of Analysis: $26.12

The loss of Bank of America's business will negatively affect Total System Services in the short term, but we think TSYS maintains a wide moat based on its scale advantages, the strength of its TS2 system, and opportunities for international growth.

The credit issuer market has become increasing consolidated, and the top 10 issuers now account for 88% of credit card outstandings in the U.S. The larger size of the leading issuers, specifically Bank of America and J.P. Morgan, has given them the critical mass to make processing in-house economically feasible, potentially decreasing their reliance on third-party processors such as TSYS. The loss of Bank of America, TSYS' largest customer, will have a material impact on the firm's revenue base in 2007.

However, TSYS should continue to achieve returns on invested capital in excess of its cost of capital for some time to come, in our opinion. TSYS is a market leader in credit card processing, handling 85% of Visa and MasterCard credit cards in the U.S. and 39% of all domestic credit cards. Due to the scalability of the company's business, its market position has allowed the company to maintain solid operating margins in the low 20% range, despite pricing pressure from major issuers. Additionally, TSYS has benefited from the significant investments the company has made in its TS2 processing system, which management believes sets the "gold standard" for the industry. The number of new clients TSYS has won in the last few years and the fact that it has generally been winning head-to-head contests with its main rival, First Data, support that claim.

Given the significant market penetration the company has already achieved in the U.S., the firm is looking overseas for further growth. TSYS has achieved some notable successes internationally, signing its first Japanese and continental European clients in 2005. Europe, in particular, offers significant opportunities for TSYS to bring its economies of scale to bear against the smaller, national processors that currently serve these markets.

In 2005, TSYS acquired Visa's 50% stake in Vital Processing Services, its merchant processing arm, and renamed the business TSYS Acquiring Solutions. TSYS Acquiring is now wholly owned by TSYS and accounts for 15% of sales. TSYS is unusual in that it is strictly a processor and doesn't look to control the merchant relationship. This gives it an edge in attracting merchant acquirers as TSYS positions itself as a partner, not a potential rival.

We'd gladly buy TSYS' shares at a reasonable discount to our fair value estimate.

Data as of 12-29-06

Toyota Motor ADR TM

	Rating	Fair Value	Last Close	Consider Buy	Consider Sell	Yield %
	★★	$108.00	$134.31	$83.30	$135.30	0.00

Company Profile

Toyota Motor Corporation designs, manufactures, and finances motor vehicles and related products and services. Total sales are about $173 billion with automotive operations providing more than 90% of all revenues. Japan and North America each provide about one third of sales, Europe accounts for about one tenth, and the rest of the world makes up the remaining fifth. Based in Japan, Toyota trades on the New York Stock Exchange as an American depository receipt.

Management   Stewardship Grade [NA]

As a Japanese company, Toyota's management structure differs from most public U.S. corporations. Toyota is managed by a board consisting of 27 senior managing directors and 44 non-board managing officers. Together, these groups are responsible for running the company. Like many foreign companies, Toyota is exempt from certain rules required of U.S. companies, such as the need for independent directors. To its credit, Toyota has taken steps to comply with the spirit of the U.S. rules including actions such as appointing additional board-level auditors and filing regular U.S. GAAP financial statements.

Industry	Business Risk	Moat Size	Investment Style	Sector
Auto Makers	Average	Narrow	Large Value	Consumer Goods

Competition

	Market Cap $Mil	12 Mo Trailing Sales $Mil	Price/Cash Flow	Return On Assets%	Debt/Equity	Total Return% 1 Yr	3 Yr
Toyota Motor ADR	217,700	186,677	9.8	5.0	0.5	28.4	26.0
Honda Motor ADR	72,206	87,921	14.1	5.9	0.5	39.2	22.1
DaimlerChrysler AG	62,526	187,555	4.0	1.5	—	24.3	14.0

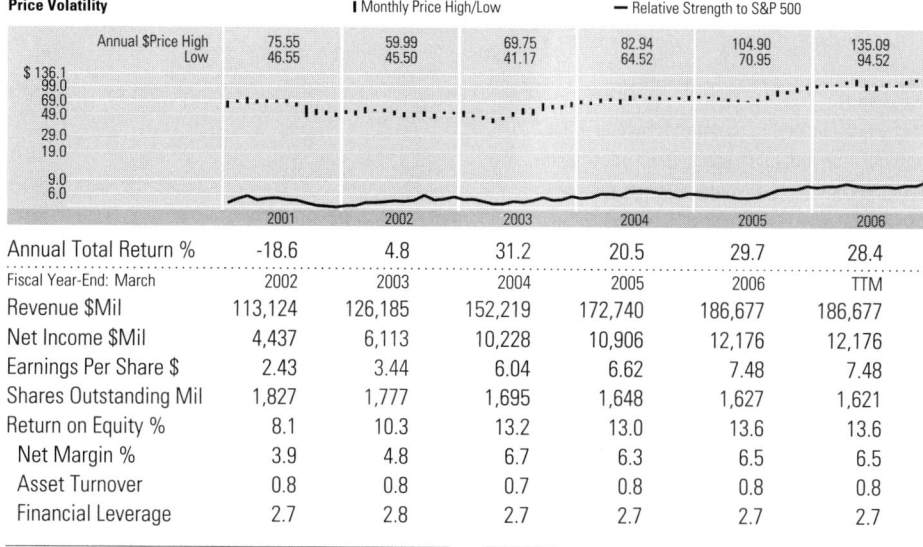

Annual Total Return %	-18.6	4.8	31.2	20.5	29.7	28.4
Fiscal Year-End: March	2002	2003	2004	2005	2006	TTM
Revenue $Mil	113,124	126,185	152,219	172,740	186,677	186,677
Net Income $Mil	4,437	6,113	10,228	10,906	12,176	12,176
Earnings Per Share $	2.43	3.44	6.04	6.62	7.48	7.48
Shares Outstanding Mil	1,827	1,777	1,695	1,648	1,627	1,621
Return on Equity %	8.1	10.3	13.2	13.0	13.6	13.6
Net Margin %	3.9	4.8	6.7	6.3	6.5	6.5
Asset Turnover	0.8	0.8	0.7	0.8	0.8	0.8
Financial Leverage	2.7	2.8	2.7	2.7	2.7	2.7

Valuation Ratios	Stock	Rel to Industry	Rel to S&P 500	Major Fund Holders	% of Fund Assets
Price/Earnings	17.9	1.0	0.9	IXIS CGM Advisor Targeted Equity A	6.07
Price/Book	2.4	1.1	0.6	Ariel Focus	5.92
Price/Sales	1.2	1.5	0.4	Legg Mason Classic Valuation Prim	4.23
Price/Cash Flow	9.8	1.0	0.7	Markman Core Growth	4.04

Thesis   By John Novak, 11-30-06   Stock Price as of Analysis: $120.05

Intense competition, cyclicality, and heavy capital requirements limit returns on capital for all automakers, but we think Toyota's product lineup, manufacturing expertise, and strong balance sheet will enable the firm to continue gaining market share at the expense of global competitors.

Once known primarily for its small cars, Toyota's burgeoning product lineup should allow it to overtake General Motors as the world's largest automaker by 2009. In an industry with long product development cycles, fickle customers, and evolving technologies, Toyota has spread its bets by introducing models across the spectrum of vehicle price points. The strategy appears to be working, as Toyota now has leading positions in markets ranging from sub-$10,000 cars designed for rapidly growing emerging markets to luxury segments once dominated by European manufacturers. In the short term, the balanced product portfolio should allow Toyota to minimize the cyclical volatility inherent in the auto industry. In the long run, the range of offerings should help retain buyers as their needs evolve and they move up the income ladder.

Toyota's vaunted manufacturing capabilities and manageable fixed cost structure should help the company weather the industry's inevitable rough seas more steadily than most. Competitors have narrowed a once-wide manufacturing productivity gap, but we think Toyota's newest initiatives to work closely with suppliers from the earliest stages of R&D through final production will enable the firm to generate operating margins that consistently rank among the industry's best. In addition, Toyota's legacy costs for pension and retiree health care remain manageable, helping boost profitability and freeing additional funds for reinvestment when compared to Detroit. Finally, Toyota is reducing its exposure to fluctuating foreign exchange rates by locating plants in end-user countries.

Although Toyota's prospects appear bright, our enthusiasm is tempered by the tough economics of the auto industry. Demand for vehicles is growing slowly in mature Western economies, and while emerging markets such as China, India, and Eastern Europe offer tremendous opportunities, competition for market share in these regions is already intense and new global competitors are emerging. What's more, the outcome of Detroit's ongoing restructuring efforts is far from certain, and Toyota could face tougher competition if today's beleaguered automakers are able to shed legacy costs and emerge as leaner competitors.

1, Toyota-cho
Toyota City, Japan 471-8571
www.toyota.co.jp

Growth [NA]	2003	2004	2005	2006
Revenue %	9.2	11.6	7.3	13.4
Earnings/Share %	38.8	62.2	3.6	18.7
Book Value/Share %	0.8	20.4	13.7	18.3
Dividends/Share %	28.6	25.0	44.4	38.5

Profitability [NA]	2004	2005	2006	TTM
Return on Assets %	4.9	4.8	5.0	5.0
Oper Cash Flow $Mil	19,246	22,077	22,322	22,322
- Cap Spending $Mil	13,101	17,908	24,591	24,591
= Free Cash Flow $Mil	6,145	4,169	-2,270	-2,270

Financial Health [NA]	2004	2005	2006	03-31-06
Long-term Debt $Mil	—	46,629	47,967	47,967
Total Equity $Mil	77,419	84,100	89,807	89,807
Debt/Equity Ratio	—	0.6	0.5	0.5

Data as of 12-29-06

Transatlantic Holdings TRH

	Rating	Fair Value	Last Close	Consider Buy	Consider Sell	Yield %
	★★★★	$85.00	$62.10	$54.20	$102.50	0.82

Company Profile
Transatlantic Holdings is a New York-based reinsurer that services a global client base. The company offers property and casualty products, including marine, fire, auto liability, medical malpractice, and aviation reinsurance. Transatlantic's clients include insurers and reinsurers; sales are made directly and via brokers. About 50% of sales originate outside the United States. American International Group owns about 60% of the shares and effectively controls the company.

Industry	Business Risk	Moat Size	Investment Style	Sector
Reinsurance	Above Avg	Narrow	Mid Value	Financial Services

Competition

	Market Cap $Mil	12 Mo Trailing Sales $Mil	Price/Cash Flow	Return On Assets%	Debt/ Equity	Total Return% 1 Yr	3 Yr
Transatlantic Holdings	4,097	3,929	—	2.3	—	-6.8	-0.5
XL Capital	12,993	9,748	—	-1.8	—	9.3	0.1
Arch Capital Group	4,999	3,317	—	2.2	—	23.5	18.7

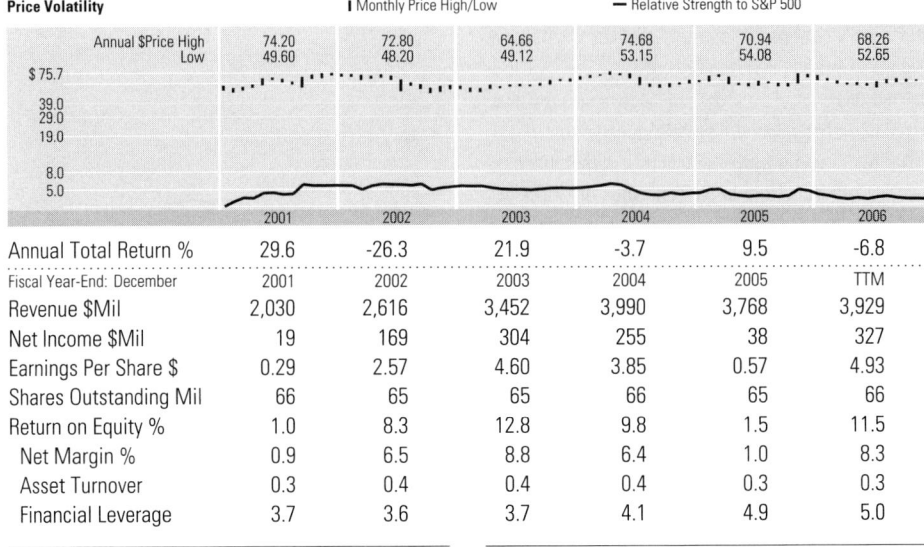

	2001	2002	2003	2004	2005	2006/TTM
Annual Total Return %	29.6	-26.3	21.9	-3.7	9.5	-6.8
Revenue $Mil	2,030	2,616	3,452	3,990	3,768	3,929
Net Income $Mil	19	169	304	255	38	327
Earnings Per Share $	0.29	2.57	4.60	3.85	0.57	4.93
Shares Outstanding Mil	66	65	65	66	65	66
Return on Equity %	1.0	8.3	12.8	9.8	1.5	11.5
Net Margin %	0.9	6.5	8.8	6.4	1.0	8.3
Asset Turnover	0.3	0.4	0.4	0.4	0.3	0.3
Financial Leverage	3.7	3.6	3.7	4.1	4.9	5.0

Management
Stewardship Grade [B]

In our view, leadership constitutes an important source of Transatlantic's competitive advantage. Several recent entrants in the reinsurance market are experiencing turnover in senior positions. In contrast, many Transatlantic managers have been with the firm for many years, which helps the firm amass and retain underwriting insight. Collectively, directors and officers own roughly $50 million in Transatlantic stock, an amount we believe aligns their interest with shareholders'. Return on equity, underwriting profit, and long-term share price performance targets determine compensation, which further lines up management's interest with shareholders'. Robert Orlich remains CEO, but he surrendered the chairman position to AIG CEO Martin Sullivan in May. We welcome the formal split of the chairman and CEO positions, but the move doesn't spark a change to our stewardship grade. With its 60% equity stake, AIG effectively controls Transatlantic, but this doesn't bother us. Transatlantic's results have been good, and the stock price has increased about 1.5 times more than the S&P 500 Index over the past decade.

Valuation Ratios

	Stock	Rel to Industry	Rel to S&P 500
Price/Earnings	12.6	1.0	0.6
Price/Book	1.4	1.0	0.3
Price/Sales	1.0	0.6	0.3
Price/Cash Flow	—	—	—

Major Fund Holders

	% of Fund Assets
Davis Financial A	9.37
Tweedy, Browne American Value	4.84
JHT Financial Services Trust Ser I	3.08
CastleRock	1.96

---

80 Pine Street
New York, NY 10005
www.transre.com

Growth [C-]

	2002	2003	2004	2005
Revenue %	28.8	32.0	15.6	-5.6
Earnings/Share %	791.7	79.1	-16.3	-85.2
Book Value/Share %	9.4	16.9	8.7	-2.2
Dividends/Share %	5.4	7.1	18.5	10.6

Profitability [B]

	2003	2004	2005	TTM
Return on Assets %	3.5	2.4	0.3	2.3
Oper Cash Flow $Mil	921	905	630	—
- Cap Spending $Mil	—	—	—	—
= Free Cash Flow $Mil	—	—	—	—

Financial Health [NA]

	2003	2004	2005	09-30-06
Long-term Debt $Mil	—	—	—	—
Total Equity $Mil	2,377	2,587	2,544	2,833
Debt/Equity Ratio	—	—	—	—

Thesis By Bill Bergman, 12-04-06 Stock Price as of Analysis: $62.07

Transatlantic's strong financial status and respected industry position reinforce the firm's narrow economic moat. Our fair value estimate is $85 per share.

Transatlantic's competitive advantage comes from a strong balance sheet, the product of two decades of successful risk management in specialized casualty reinsurance markets. Casualty losses can take years to be accurately identified, and premiums are invested for several years before paying related claims. The firm's investment portfolio is 3 times larger than equity capital, building a cushion for return on equity and reducing the propensity to take on risky investments to reach for yield. We think underwriting results also benefit from Transatlantic's investment leverage. Because the firm can earn a decent return on equity from its investment income alone, the temptation to boost premium revenue via optimistic underwriting declines.

Transatlantic's solid underwriting and claim-payment history helps produce a virtuous underwriting cycle. A strong balance sheet and the ability to take on large risks help Transatlantic take lead positions when underwriting its reinsurance treaties. This allows the firm to control the price, terms, and conditions of the treaty policies it assumes. Its accumulated casualty reinsurance underwriting expertise would be difficult to replicate, and its expertise improves with each contract. In our opinion, Transatlantic's underwriting record and association with American International Group allow the firm to boost operating leverage without difficulty maintaining its ratings. The firm writes about $1.30 of premium for each $1 of equity, which helps increase return on capital.

New capital flooded the reinsurance market after the 2005 storm losses in the form of startups, recapitalized reinsurers, and an upswing in capital market instruments like catastrophe bonds. However, we don't think these developments impair Transatlantic's narrow moat. In our view, the firm with the smartest capital--not the most capital--holds the best investment prospects. Despite the flow of capital into the reinsurance market, Transatlantic's proven claim-payment ability and solid underwriting will attract business, as the firm's primary insurer clients are concerned with prompt claim payments. Transatlantic is likely to capture new property business, and we think customers will pay premium prices for its security.

Data as of 12-29-06

TransCanada TRP

	Rating	Fair Value	Last Close	Consider Buy	Consider Sell	Yield %
	★★★	$33.00	$34.95	$28.10	$43.30	3.21

Industry	Business Risk	Moat Size	Investment Style	Sector
Pipelines	Below Avg	Narrow	Large Value	Energy

Company Profile
Calgary-based TransCanada is among the largest pipeline operators in North America. It owns about 25,400 miles of natural-gas pipelines, most of which transport gas from Alberta to the eastern United States and Canada. More than half the gas produced in western Canada is brought to market via a TransCanada pipeline. About 32% of TransCanada's sales come from wholesale power generation; the company had over 6,000 megawatts of generating capacity at the end of 2005.

Management   Stewardship Grade [A]
Harold Kvisle was appointed president and CEO in early 2001 after joining TransCanada in 1999. In 2005, Kvisle earned C$2.4 million in cash compensation and received payments from a 2003 long-term incentive plan of C$1.9 million, putting his total compensation slightly above average for his peer group. Overall we think TransCanada's compensation plan provides proper incentives for its managers. Management gets the thumbs-up for starting to expense its stock options in 2002, and stock-option grants in 2005 were flat or slightly lower from the previous year. Management provides excellent disclosure on a number of fronts, from compensation plans to quarterly operational data, earning TransCanada our highest corporate-governance rating. The only mark against the company is the result of its poison-pill shareholder-rights plan.

Competition

	Market Cap $Mil	12 Mo Trailing Sales $Mil	Price/Cash Flow	Return On Assets %	Debt/ Equity	Total Return % 1 Yr	3 Yr
TransCanada	17,029	5,061	10.8	4.8	1.5	15.1	21.4
Duke Energy	41,613	13,318	18.8	1.9	0.7	26.3	23.2
Williams Companies	15,576	12,719	9.3	0.9	1.2	14.4	40.0

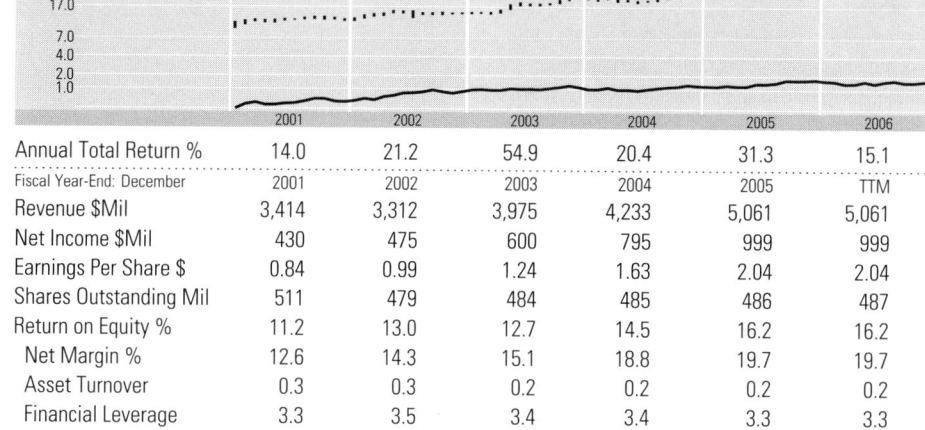

	2001	2002	2003	2004	2005	2006
Annual Total Return %	14.0	21.2	54.9	20.4	31.3	15.1

Fiscal Year-End: December	2001	2002	2003	2004	2005	TTM
Revenue $Mil	3,414	3,312	3,975	4,233	5,061	5,061
Net Income $Mil	430	475	600	795	999	999
Earnings Per Share $	0.84	0.99	1.24	1.63	2.04	2.04
Shares Outstanding Mil	511	479	484	485	486	487
Return on Equity %	11.2	13.0	12.7	14.5	16.2	16.2
Net Margin %	12.6	14.3	15.1	18.8	19.7	19.7
Asset Turnover	0.3	0.3	0.2	0.2	0.2	0.2
Financial Leverage	3.3	3.5	3.4	3.4	3.3	3.3

Valuation Ratios	Stock	Rel to Industry	Rel to S&P 500
Price/Earnings	17.1	0.6	0.8
Price/Book	2.8	1.1	0.7
Price/Sales	3.4	1.5	1.2
Price/Cash Flow	10.8	1.1	0.7

Major Fund Holders	% of Fund Assets
FBR Gas Utility Index	4.93
Fidelity Canada	2.83
Meehan Focus	1.30
ING Global Equity Dividend A	1.24

Thesis By Michael Cumming, CFA, 12-14-06 Stock Price as of Analysis: $34.65

Although natural-gas supplies from western Canada continue to decline, TransCanada continues to develop enough new projects to keep its long-term prospects rosy.

TransCanada's core natural-gas pipeline business has been hampered in recent years by the double whammy of declining gas production in western Canada and cuts in allowed returns by regulators. The company is working to counter this trend by investing in other areas, notably power generation. TransCanada will invest more than C$1 billion over the next five years on the Cartier wind power project and the refurbishment of two nuclear reactors at the Bruce facility in Ontario. Other major projects include proposed liquefied natural gas (LNG) terminals in Quebec and off Long Island and a partial conversion of the Mainline gas pipeline to oil transportation with a new extension to Cushing, Okla. The important advantage these projects will hold for TransCanada compared with its gas pipelines is the ability to negotiate rates directly with customers and improve returns through cost cuts and improved efficiency. Longer term, TransCanada should benefit from the proposed pipelines to run from Alaska and the Mackenzie Delta region of northern Canada. We think that at least one of the northern projects will get done eventually, providing new gas to fill TransCanada's pipelines for many years.

Most of TransCanada's expansion projects face competitive pressure that could prevent one or more of the projects from being completed. Most of this competition comes from Calgary-based rival Enbridge, which wants to expand a crude-oil pipeline from the oil sands, build an LNG terminal in Quebec, and participate in the Alaska and MacKenzie pipeline projects. At this point, we think both companies' oil projects will move forward, but we doubt both Quebec LNG projects will. For now, we think TransCanada holds the edge on the northern projects, but that could change depending on regulatory rulings and the ability to reach an agreement with producers. In addition, increased demand for natural gas for oil sands production in northern Alberta could draw volumes off of TransCanada's system, reducing reinvestment opportunities and thus further hurting the earnings power of the system.

We give many pipeline companies in our coverage universe a wide-moat rating, but TransCanada earns only a narrow-moat rating. Declining gas production in Alberta and lower allowed returns reduce the moats of many of the company's pipelines as their earnings power diminishes.

TransCanada Tower 450 - 1st Street S.W. www.transcanada.com
Calgary, AB T2P 5H1

Growth [NA]	2002	2003	2004	2005
Revenue %	-1.2	8.1	-2.5	11.4
Earnings/Share %	19.2	13.5	20.5	16.5
Book Value/Share %	-0.2	5.6	7.1	9.2
Dividends/Share %	11.1	8.0	8.3	5.1

Profitability [NA]	2003	2004	2005	TTM
Return on Assets %	3.7	4.3	4.8	4.8
Oper Cash Flow $Mil	1,351	1,334	1,572	1,572
- Cap Spending $Mil	279	408	623	623
= Free Cash Flow $Mil	1,072	926	949	949

Financial Health [NA]	2003	2004	2005	12-31-05
Long-term Debt $Mil	7,377	8,798	9,040	9,040
Total Equity $Mil	4,722	5,471	6,159	6,159
Debt/Equity Ratio	1.6	1.6	1.5	1.5

Data as of 12-29-06

Tribune TRB

	Rating	Fair Value	Last Close	Consider Buy	Consider Sell	Yield %
	★★★	$35.00	$30.78	$27.00	$43.90	2.34

Industry	Business Risk	Moat Size	Investment Style	Sector
Media Conglomerates	Average	Narrow	Mid Value	Media

Company Profile

Tribune is one of the country's largest media companies. It reaches more than 80% of U.S. households and is the only media organization with newspapers, TV stations, and Web sites in the nation's top three markets. Tribune's newspapers include the Los Angeles Times, Chicago Tribune, and Newsday. Its broadcasting group operates more than 20 TV stations, superstation WGN on national cable, an AM radio station, and the Chicago Cubs baseball team.

Competition

	Market Cap $Mil	12 Mo Trailing Sales $Mil	Price/Cash Flow	Return On Assets%	Debt/ Equity	Total Return% 1 Yr	3 Yr
Tribune	7,353	5,527	13.2	3.4	0.9	4.2	-14.1
Gannett	14,167	7,880	9.8	6.9	0.7	1.9	-10.5
Washington Post Co	7,167	3,813	13.1	6.9	0.1	-1.5	-1.0

Management

Stewardship Grade [D]

Dennis J. FitzSimons became president of Tribune in 2001 and has since had the roles of CEO and chairman bestowed upon him, too. In 2005, FitzSimons took home annual compensation of $1.3 million, along with 200,000 stock options. We find this pay package to be reasonable, although we would have preferred to see restricted-stock awards instead of options. We're pleased to see that Tribune has only one class of voting stock, a rarity in newspaper publishing. But we do have reservations about Tribune's stewardship. Although FitzSimons has a healthy amount of options, we'd like to see all of the company's directors and executive officers have more skin in the game; as a group, they hold only 2% of Tribune's outstanding shares. We're also critical of the fact that in 2005, Tribune paid its former president of Tribune Publishing and director more than $50,000 per month for consulting services on an as-needed basis. Other knocks include antitakeover provisions such as staggered board elections and golden-parachute pay packages, overly generous stock-option grants in the past, and the fact that FitzSimons has the responsibilities of three individuals.

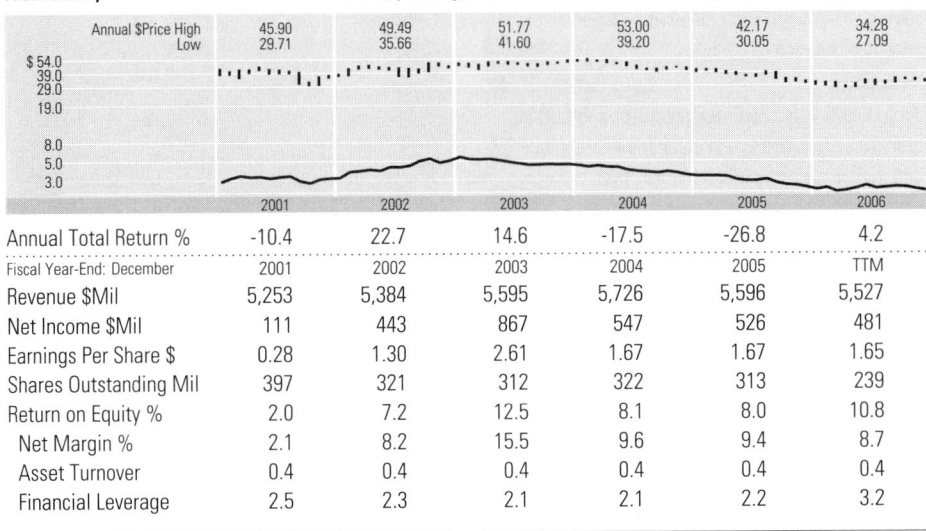

Price Volatility | Monthly Price High/Low — Relative Strength to S&P 500

	2001	2002	2003	2004	2005	2006
Annual $Price High	45.90	49.49	51.77	53.00	42.17	34.28
Low	29.71	35.66	41.60	39.20	30.05	27.09
Annual Total Return %	-10.4	22.7	14.6	-17.5	-26.8	4.2
Fiscal Year-End: December	2001	2002	2003	2004	2005	TTM
Revenue $Mil	5,253	5,384	5,595	5,726	5,596	5,527
Net Income $Mil	111	443	867	547	526	481
Earnings Per Share $	0.28	1.30	2.61	1.67	1.67	1.65
Shares Outstanding Mil	397	321	312	322	313	239
Return on Equity %	2.0	7.2	12.5	8.1	8.0	10.8
Net Margin %	2.1	8.2	15.5	9.6	9.4	8.7
Asset Turnover	0.4	0.4	0.4	0.4	0.4	0.4
Financial Leverage	2.5	2.3	2.1	2.1	2.2	3.2

Valuation Ratios	Stock	Rel to Industry	Rel to S&P 500
Price/Earnings	15.9	0.6	0.8
Price/Book	1.7	0.5	0.4
Price/Sales	1.3	0.4	0.4
Price/Cash Flow	13.2	0.8	0.9

Major Fund Holders	% of Fund Assets
Ariel Appreciation	4.93
Regions Morgan Keegan Sel MidCap Value A	4.03
Primary Income	3.83
Ariel	3.56

435 North Michigan Avenue
Chicago, IL 60611
www.tribune.com

Growth [D]	2002	2003	2004	2005
Revenue %	2.5	3.9	2.3	-2.3
Earnings/Share %	364.3	100.8	-36.0	0.0
Book Value/Share %	26.3	16.0	-1.4	2.3
Dividends/Share %	0.0	0.0	9.1	50.0

Profitability [B]	2003	2004	2005	TTM
Return on Assets %	6.1	3.9	3.6	3.4
Oper Cash Flow $Mil	1,159	1,073	659	557
- Cap Spending $Mil	194	217	206	210
= Free Cash Flow $Mil	965	856	453	347

Financial Health [B-]	2003	2004	2005	09-30-06
Long-term Debt $Mil	2,382	2,318	2,959	4,075
Total Equity $Mil	6,921	6,730	6,619	4,451
Debt/Equity Ratio	0.3	0.3	0.4	0.9

Thesis By James M. Walden, CFA, 12-18-06 Stock Price as of Analysis: $31.67

Traditional-media companies are at a crossroads, and no firm is a better poster child for current conditions than Tribune, in our opinion. Tribune is facing the same industry headwinds caused by changing media-consumption habits and advertising trends as other operators of publishing and broadcasting assets (but exacerbated by Tribune's presence in large cities, in our estimate). Its total revenue slipped 2.3% in 2005 from the year before, and in the first nine months of 2006, each of the company's segments contributed to an additional year-to-date decline of 3.1%. Such difficult conditions, along with a cross-media ownership strategy that hasn't panned out, circulation overstatements, and a damaging tax-court case, have contributed to Tribune's languishing stock price over the past few years.

Despite Tribune's current challenges, we think the company holds attractive cash-generating assets. Tribune's insiders think so, too, but some aren't happy with how they're being run. Frustrated with Tribune's stock-price performance, the Chandlers (the family that became major Tribune shareholders when Tribune acquired Times Mirror in 2000) have pushed for a breakup of the media conglomerate in hopes of unlocking value for shareholders. Tribune's management and board are currently evaluating various strategic alternatives, which include the sale of the entire firm or the sale or spin-off of various assets.

We think there are almost countless potential outcomes to the situation. A sale of the entire company would most likely be the most tax-efficient, given the low cost basis of the individual assets. Here, a buyer would probably sell off any assets it didn't wish to keep, similar to what McClatchy did when it acquired Knight Ridder. A tax-free spin-off of certain assets, such as its collection of TV stations, is another option. If Tribune decides to sell individual assets, we're convinced it would receive top dollar for them. Recent TV station deals, including the sale of nine of Emmis' TV stations, indicate that firms remain hungry for such assets. However, Tribune must be careful about how it proceeds due to potentially high tax bills. Whatever course of action Tribune undertakes, we think that some type of material transaction will occur; it's not likely shareholders would accept the status quo.

Tribune is taking steps to unlock value for its long-suffering shareholders. We applaud management for finally acting and are hopeful that it will do a better job stewarding shareholders' capital in the future than it has in the recent past.

Data as of 12-29-06

Tyco International TYC

	Rating	Fair Value	Last Close	Consider Buy	Consider Sell	Yield %
	★★★★	$36.00	$30.40	$27.80	$45.10	1.32

Company Profile

Tyco is a multi-industry firm with annual sales of $41 billion. Its businesses are currently reported in four operating segments: electronics, fire and security, health care, and engineered products and services. In 2006, the board approved a plan to split the company into three separately traded entities, with health care and electronics each spun off to shareholders as separate companies in tax-free stock dividends. We look for the transaction to be completed around March 2007.

Management   Stewardship Grade [B]

Chairman and CEO Ed Breen, who was named to the posts in 2002, is the only nonindependent member of the 12-member board. He deserves much credit for righting what was a very leaky ship when he came aboard. In his first year, he introduced an entirely new slate of independent directors, replaced the senior management team, and hired two new segment presidents. He also reconfigured the bonus structure to better align management interests with those of shareholders and created an ombudsman network (charged with investigating reported fraud) that reports directly to the audit committee. David FitzPatrick, an integral part of the company's turnaround, handed his CFO duties to Chris Coughlin, most recently of Interpublic, in 2005. Governance seems adequate, as board members are elected annually, and management compensation isn't egregious. That said, we're a bit disappointed that incentive compensation doesn't contain a return on capital tether; it's based solely upon operating profit, earnings per share, and free cash flow generation. Board members are paid a modest salary, along with deferred stock units annually. But because its members are all relatively new, the board as a whole doesn't have much skin in the game. The largest directly owned stake among independent members is less than $1.5 million at current prices.

The Zurich Center, Second Floor 90 Pitts Bay Road www.tyco.com
Pembroke, Bermuda HM 08

Growth [C-]	2003	2004	2005	2006
Revenue %	3.6	12.1	3.5	4.2
Earnings/Share %	NMF	187.0	8.3	25.9
Book Value/Share %	8.9	7.7	8.4	11.5
Dividends/Share %	0.0	0.0	700.0	-25.0

Profitability [C]	2004	2005	2006	TTM
Return on Assets %	4.4	4.8	5.8	5.8
Oper Cash Flow $Mil	5,205	6,154	5,594	5,594
- Cap Spending $Mil	1,127	1,354	1,569	1,569
= Free Cash Flow $Mil	4,078	4,800	4,025	4,025

Financial Health [A+]	2004	2005	2006	09-30-06
Long-term Debt $Mil	14,518	10,599	9,365	9,365
Total Equity $Mil	30,362	32,515	35,419	35,419
Debt/Equity Ratio	0.5	0.3	0.3	0.3

Industry	Business Risk	Moat Size	Investment Style	Sector
Diversified	Average	Narrow	Large Value	Industrial Materials

Competition

	Market Cap $Mil	12 Mo Trailing Sales $Mil	Price/Cash Flow	Return On Assets%	Debt/ Equity	Total Return% 1 Yr	3 Yr
Tyco International	60,461	40,960	10.8	5.8	0.3	6.8	5.1
Johnson & Johnson	191,415	52,252	14.5	18.5	0.0	12.4	10.8
Honeywell International	36,939	30,367	13.2	6.2	0.3	24.1	13.2

Price Volatility | Monthly Price High/Low   — Relative Strength to S&P 500

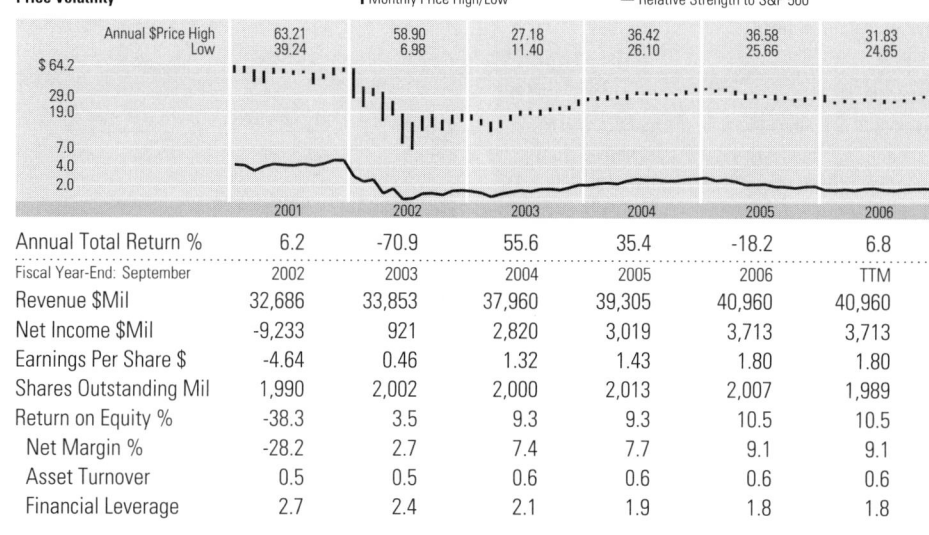

| Annual $Price High | 63.21 | 58.90 | 27.18 | 36.42 | 36.58 | 31.83 |
| Low | 39.24 | 6.98 | 11.40 | 26.10 | 25.66 | 24.65 |

	2001	2002	2003	2004	2005	2006
Annual Total Return %	6.2	-70.9	55.6	35.4	-18.2	6.8

Fiscal Year-End: September	2002	2003	2004	2005	2006	TTM
Revenue $Mil	32,686	33,853	37,960	39,305	40,960	40,960
Net Income $Mil	-9,233	921	2,820	3,019	3,713	3,713
Earnings Per Share $	-4.64	0.46	1.32	1.43	1.80	1.80
Shares Outstanding Mil	1,990	2,002	2,000	2,013	2,007	1,989
Return on Equity %	-38.3	3.5	9.3	9.3	10.5	10.5
Net Margin %	-28.2	2.7	7.4	7.7	9.1	9.1
Asset Turnover	0.5	0.5	0.6	0.6	0.6	0.6
Financial Leverage	2.7	2.4	2.1	1.9	1.8	1.8

Valuation Ratios	Stock	Rel to Industry	Rel to S&P 500	Major Fund Holders	% of Fund Assets
Price/Earnings	15.4	0.8	0.7	Clipper	9.44
Price/Book	1.7	0.5	0.4	Davis Financial A	7.45
Price/Sales	1.5	0.8	0.5	Fidelity Select Industrial Equipment	6.49
Price/Cash Flow	10.8	0.8	0.7	Ariel Focus	6.27

Thesis   By Eric Landry, 11-16-06   Stock Price as of Analysis: $30.33

We think each of Tyco's parts enjoys distinct advantages and that the businesses are collectively worth more as separate entities than together.

Within its four unrelated lines of business, Tyco enjoys competitive advantages unavailable to lesser rivals. In electronics, for instance, Tyco is the world's largest manufacturer of passive components and enjoys scale economies in research and development and its global manufacturing base. In health care, the firm enjoys leading market positions, well-respected brands such as U.S. Surgical, Mallinckrodt, Kendall, and Valleylab, and recurring revenue that makes up about half of the business's top line. In fire and security, Tyco's ADT brand is by far the largest player in a business where the ability to spread revenues over a relatively fixed cost base matters. Its security business is several times the size of the next-largest competitor, and it enjoys the widest national exposure by far. And in engineered products, Tyco is the market share leader in many of its markets.

These advantages notwithstanding, we don't think the current combination of operations increases the firm's advantages. Each business has different sales channels, cost structures, and customer characteristics, limiting the leverage of combining them. And even though Tyco generates a combined $41 billion in annual revenue, pure size doesn't necessarily equate to scale benefits across business lines. All three businesses would enjoy the same degree of scale whether consolidated or separated, as each employs a discrete set of fixed costs.

For these reasons, a breakup makes sense, in our opinion. The one-time $1 billion cost (about $0.50 per share) is substantial, but we believe it's outweighed by the benefits of having three focused companies. For instance, we think current management is right to assume that a stand-alone health-care company will be better able to attract top-tier talent if it doesn't have what is perceived to be a stodgy industrial operation impeding its stock performance. All three companies should also be better able to compete for value-accretive acquisitions once separated. And with each company obligated to meet detailed public-company reporting standards, investors will get much better disclosure.

In the meantime, Tyco's stock buyback program, through which the firm has bought back over 4.4% of its diluted shares in fiscal 2006, is allowing shareholders to participate more fully in any convergence toward the company's fair value.

UAP Holding UAPH

Data as of 12-29-06

	Rating	Fair Value	Last Close	Consider Buy	Consider Sell	Yield %
	★★	$22.00	$25.18	$17.00	$27.60	2.98

Industry	Business Risk	Moat Size	Investment Style	Sector
Chemicals	Average	Narrow	Small Value	Industrial Materials

Company Profile

UAP Holdings' sole subsidiary is UAP Agri Products, the largest independent distributor of crop protection chemicals, fertilizer, seeds, and noncrop inputs in North America. About 55% of the products it acquires are sold directly to growers, while the balance is sold wholesale to retailers. UAP also provides value-added services like crop management, biotechnology advisory, custom blending, and inventory management.

Management   Stewardship Grade [B]

L. Kenneth Cordell came to UAP in 2001 from FMC Agricultural Products Group. He was named chief executive officer upon the acquisition of UAP by Apollo Management in 2003. UAP Holdings completed its initial public offering a year later. As of November 2006, Apollo still controlled 16.6% of the firm. However, it recently announced plans to sell its remaining stake in a secondary offering. Since 2002, Cordell and his management team have led UAP to significant improvements in working-capital levels and earnings before interest, taxes, depreciation, and amortization through lean operating initiatives, restructurings, and rationalizations. For example, UAP has managed to greatly lower its administrative cost structure by reducing its 10 operating companies into five divisions. We think management is fairly compensated for its efforts, but we're not fans of the staggered board of directors, a common antitakeover provision.

7251 West 4th Street
Greeley, CO 80634
www.uap.com

Competition	Market Cap $Mil	12 Mo Trailing Sales $Mil	Price/Cash Flow	Return On Assets%	Debt/ Equity	Total Return% 1 Yr	3 Yr
UAP Holding	1,284	2,779	—	2.7	0.9	27.7	—
Royster-Clark							
Helena Chemical							

Price Volatility — Monthly Price High/Low — Relative Strength to S&P 500

				17.40 13.96	20.64 13.70	25.45 17.72
	2001	2002	2003	2004	2005	2006
Annual Total Return %	—	—	—	—	21.4	27.7

Fiscal Year-End: February	2002	2003	2004	2005	2006	TTM
Revenue $Mil	2,770	2,527	2,452	2,507	2,728	2,779
Net Income $Mil	-37	25	46	29	66	48
Earnings Per Share $	—	—	—	—	1.27	0.91
Shares Outstanding Mil	—	—	—	—	51	51
Return on Equity %	-12.6	4.3	59.8	24.7	41.6	24.0
Net Margin %	-1.3	1.0	1.9	1.1	2.4	1.7
Asset Turnover	2.0	1.9	1.9	1.9	2.0	1.6
Financial Leverage	4.7	2.3	16.5	11.5	8.7	8.8

Valuation Ratios	Stock	Rel to Industry	Rel to S&P 500
Price/Earnings	27.7	1.5	1.3
Price/Book	6.5	2.0	1.6
Price/Sales	0.5	0.3	0.2
Price/Cash Flow	—	—	—

Major Fund Holders	% of Fund Assets
Fidelity Select Chemicals	3.95
First Eagle Fund of America Y	2.87
SunAmerica Focused Small-Cap Value A	2.57
Presidio	2.39

Growth [D]	2003	2004	2005	2006
Revenue %	-8.8	-3.0	2.2	8.8
Earnings/Share %	NMF	NMF	NMF	NMF
Book Value/Share %	—	—	—	NMF
Dividends/Share %	NMF	NMF	NMF	NMF

Profitability [C+]	2004	2005	2006	TTM
Return on Assets %	3.6	2.2	4.8	2.7
Oper Cash Flow $Mil	342	-1	62	-18
- Cap Spending $Mil	15	15	16	20
= Free Cash Flow $Mil	326	-16	46	-38

Financial Health [D+]	2004	2005	2006	08-31-06
Long-term Debt $Mil	309	296	306	175
Total Equity $Mil	77	116	160	199
Debt/Equity Ratio	4.0	2.5	1.9	0.9

Thesis By Ben Butwin, 11-02-06 Stock Price as of Analysis: $23.47

UAP's unmatched size, diverse product base, and extensive geographical network have made the firm the predominant agricultural distributor in North America. We expect the company to leverage its competitive strengths to gain market share and maintain its industry-leading status.

Suppliers like BASF, Bayer, and Monsanto rely on middlemen to access a highly fragmented population of farmers and growers. None are larger than UAP, whose 340 stores, 1,100 sales representatives, and 90,000 customers translate into market share roughly equivalent to its next three largest competitors combined. These size and scale advantages lead to more efficient distribution, superior bargaining power, and better access to capital--all key ingredients that solidify UAP's narrow moat.

These attributes have allowed UAP to steal share from smaller competitors and generate enough cash to participate in the growing industry-consolidation trend. The firm is seeking out tuck-in acquisitions of distributors and retail customers that have no overlap with its existing geographical footprint. These maneuvers are desirable to both parties, in our opinion. UAP will fortify its competitive strengths while providing its new subsidiaries with improved sourcing, pricing, and customer access.

But acquisition growth is just half of the story. Internally, UAP will focus on three product avenues: seeds, fertilizer, and private-label brands. While it claims 20% share in chemical products, growth potential there has been fading. Seeds are being biologically engineered to enhance certain traits, thus eliminating disease, expanding crop yields, and reducing the need for chemical treatment. Yet UAP should be able to boost its incremental returns by aggressively cross-marketing its seed and fertilizer products to existing chemical customers.

Alongside this one-stop-shop philosophy is the firm's growing emphasis on its proprietary brands. These products are often tailored to meet the needs of specific customers and provide higher margins than those sourced from outside suppliers. Private-label revenue as a percentage of chemical and seed sales totals about 14% and is growing at a torrid pace.

Still, no matter how you slice it, agriculture is a slow-growth industry with relatively meager margins. Macroeconomic risks remain, as unfavorable weather threatens to reduce profitability without chance for recovery until the next crop season. But the business favors larger distributors with advantages of scale, and we believe UAP is in prime position to expand at or above industry growth rates for some time.

UBS AG UBS

Data as of 12-29-06

Rating ★★★	Fair Value $60.00	Last Close $60.33	Consider Buy $46.30	Consider Sell $75.20	Yield % 2.09

Industry	Business Risk	Moat Size	Investment Style	Sector
International Banks	Average	Wide	Large Growth	Financial Services

Company Profile
Courtesy of its world-class private banking operations, UBS is the largest asset manager in the world, with about $2.4 trillion in assets. In addition, it has a prestigious investment bank on Wall Street and provides retail and business banking services in Switzerland. All these entities have been accommodated and marketed aggressively under the UBS brand.

Management
Stewardship Grade [NA]

UBS has a top-class management team. Chairman Marcel Ospel is the former CEO of UBS and its predecessor, the Swiss Bank Corporation. Peter Wuffli, former CFO and head of UBS' asset-management division, was appointed group CEO in 2003. Huw Jenkins assumed the CEO role at the investment bank in 2005, replacing John Costas, who now serves as chairman at the investment bank. Marcel Rohner runs the group's private bank. The executive team is young and has been entrenched since the rebranding, which bodes well for shareholders. Compensation, though high in absolute terms, is slightly below average among Wall Street firms and is tied to performance. Total board of director and executive compensation amounted to $182 million in 2005, of which Ospel took home $20 million. To better align management's interest with that of shareholders, senior executives are required to accumulate UBS shares worth 5 times the average cash component of total compensation of the preceding three years over a period of five years.

Bahnhofstrasse 45 www.ubs.com
Zurich, Switzerland CH-8098

Competition

	Market Cap $Mil	12 Mo Trailing Sales $Mil	Price/Cash Flow	Return On Assets %	Debt/ Equity	Total Return % 1 Yr	3 Yr
UBS AG	118,774	7,706	—	0.7	—	29.6	23.6
Citigroup	273,691	86,566	—	1.3	—	19.6	8.4
Morgan Stanley	86,198	32,195	—	0.8	—	45.9	14.8

Price Volatility
Monthly Price High/Low — Relative Strength to S&P 500

Annual $Price High/Low	29.52/19.03	26.32/16.90	34.18/18.63	42.29/32.31	49.30/38.47	63.39/47.58
	2001	2002	2003	2004	2005	2006
Annual Total Return %	-7.6	-1.2	45.6	25.5	15.8	29.6

Fiscal Year-End: December

	2001	2002	2003	2004	2005	TTM
Revenue $Mil	4,608	6,604	10,021	9,598	7,706	7,706
Net Income $Mil	1,911	3,541	4,614	6,497	11,881	11,881
Earnings Per Share $	—	—	2.03	3.00	5.46	5.46
Shares Outstanding Mil	—	—	2,232	2,107	2,111	1,969
Return on Equity %	5.4	8.9	16.2	21.0	25.9	25.9
Net Margin %	41.5	53.6	18.4	19.8	154.2	154.2
Asset Turnover	0.0	0.0	0.0	0.0	0.0	0.0
Financial Leverage	22.2	23.3	43.9	49.6	38.4	38.4

Valuation Ratios

	Stock	Rel to Industry	Rel to S&P 500
Price/Earnings	—	—	—
Price/Book	2.6	1.0	0.6
Price/Sales	15.4	3.7	5.3
Price/Cash Flow	—	—	—

Major Fund Holders

	% of Fund Assets
Hartford Global Financial Svcs HLS IA	6.25
Oppenheimer Quest Value A	5.71
Jennison Financial Services A	5.56
Hartford Global Financial Svcs A	5.45

Growth [NA]

	2002	2003	2004	2005
Revenue %	32.7	51.7	-4.2	-19.1
Earnings/Share %	—	NMF	48.0	82.0
Book Value/Share %	—	NMF	4.2	72.5
Dividends/Share %	—	—	—	—

Profitability [NA]

	2003	2004	2005	TTM
Return on Assets %	0.4	0.4	0.7	0.7
Oper Cash Flow $Mil	2,517	-22,408	-51,121	—
- Cap Spending $Mil	1,018	923	1,530	—
= Free Cash Flow $Mil	—	—	—	—

Financial Health [NA]

	2003	2004	2005	12-31-05
Long-term Debt $Mil	—	—	—	—
Total Equity $Mil	28,476	30,954	45,814	45,814
Debt/Equity Ratio	—	—	—	—

Thesis
By Ganesh Rathnam, 11-20-06 Stock Price as of Analysis: $60.50

Having integrated its businesses under one brand, UBS is heavily promoting it. Its three business divisions--wealth management, investment banking, and Swiss corporate and retail banking--are all solidly run, earning their cost of capital during market downturns and far exceeding it in favorable market conditions. They provide the firm with a wide economic moat. We think UBS is poised to continue its success, and we'd welcome the opportunity to buy shares at bargain prices.

Wealth management is the rock on which UBS' foundation is built. The asset-management business has one of the most attractive business models, and UBS is far and away the biggest asset manager in the world, with about $2.4 trillion in client assets. UBS derives 40% of operating profits from its wealth-management and asset-management businesses. Despite its size, UBS has agilely adapted to rapid developments in the private banking industry. When the European Union called for greater transparency to prevent tax evasion and money laundering, UBS was quick to open an office in Singapore, where secrecy laws were tightened to attract private banks. It invested heavily in promoting its brand and established offices in several wealth-creating regions in Asia to capture business from the rapidly growing ranks of wealthy individuals in those economies. It is developing Dillon Read, a subsidiary, as an alternative investment-management company, to capitalize on the growing trend toward nontraditional asset classes. We're glad to see UBS reinvesting to widen its moat in the private banking business.

UBS' other crown jewel is its investment bank, which accounts for 37% of operating profits. It consistently ranks among the top Wall Street firms, both in prestige as well as profits. The investment bank provides several fee income streams such as debt and equity underwriting fees, merger and acquisition advisory fees, fee income from structured products and derivatives, and profits from market making and proprietary trading. Acquisitions like Banco Pactual in Brazil help UBS leverage its position in the United States to develop a lucrative franchise in developing economies.

The Swiss retail and business banking division continues to be a cash cow for UBS, delivering 16% of its operating profit. In a consolidated market characterized by anemic growth, UBS controls costs tightly, delivering 43% operating margins. We think management is adept at creating shareholder value, and we'd invest in UBS shares at the right price.

Ultra Petroleum UPL

Data as of 12-29-06

Rating ★★★★	Fair Value $63.00	Last Close $47.74	Consider Buy $40.10	Consider Sell $76.00	Yield % 0.00

Industry	Business Risk	Moat Size	Investment Style	Sector
Oil/Gas	Above Avg	Narrow	Mid Growth	Energy

Company Profile
Houston-based Ultra Petroleum engages in the exploration and production of oil and natural gas in the Green River Basin in Wyoming and offshore in Bohai Bay, China. At the end of 2005, Ultra reported proven reserves of 2.022 trillion cubic feet of natural-gas equivalent. Daily production averaged 201 million cubic feet in 2005. Ultra's production is about 85% natural gas, and reserves are about 98% natural gas.

Management
Stewardship Grade [C]

Chairman, president, and CEO Michael Watford is an industry veteran who has been with Ultra since 1999. Before that, Watford gained experience running a high-growth oil and gas company as CEO of Nuevo Energy. Other Ultra executives have substantial exploratory and engineering experience in the Green River Basin and China's Bohai Bay. Until recently, management's cash compensation has been fairly modest. As Ultra's revenue has grown, management's cash compensation has increased and option issuance has declined. In 2005, options granted to employees reflected a little less than 1% of the shares outstanding, with executives claiming just under 50% of the options issued. As of April 11, executives and board members owned about 8% of the firm. We like management's large position in the stock and think executive compensation is fair.

363 North Sam Houston Parkway East Suite 1200
Houston, TX 77060   www.ultrapetroleum.com

Growth [A]	2002	2003	2004	2005
Revenue %	2.8	187.1	113.1	99.4
Earnings/Share %	-58.3	480.0	134.5	107.4
Book Value/Share %	0.6	48.5	74.6	111.3
Dividends/Share %	NMF	NMF	NMF	NMF

Profitability [A+]	2003	2004	2005	TTM
Return on Assets %	13.1	20.3	26.9	22.6
Oper Cash Flow $Mil	90	175	414	464
- Cap Spending $Mil	117	197	284	438
= Free Cash Flow $Mil	-27	-21	130	26

Financial Health [A]	2003	2004	2005	09-30-06
Long-term Debt $Mil	104	112	21	110
Total Equity $Mil	149	268	571	588
Debt/Equity Ratio	0.7	0.4	0.0	0.2

Competition	Market Cap $Mil	12 Mo Trailing Sales $Mil	Price/Cash Flow	Return On Assets%	Debt/ Equity	Total Return% 1 Yr	3 Yr
Ultra Petroleum	7,254	609	15.6	22.6	0.2	-14.4	56.6
EnCana	39,483	14,266	5.3	10.0	0.4	2.6	33.2
Noble Energy	8,529	2,927	5.3	7.8	0.4	22.5	30.2

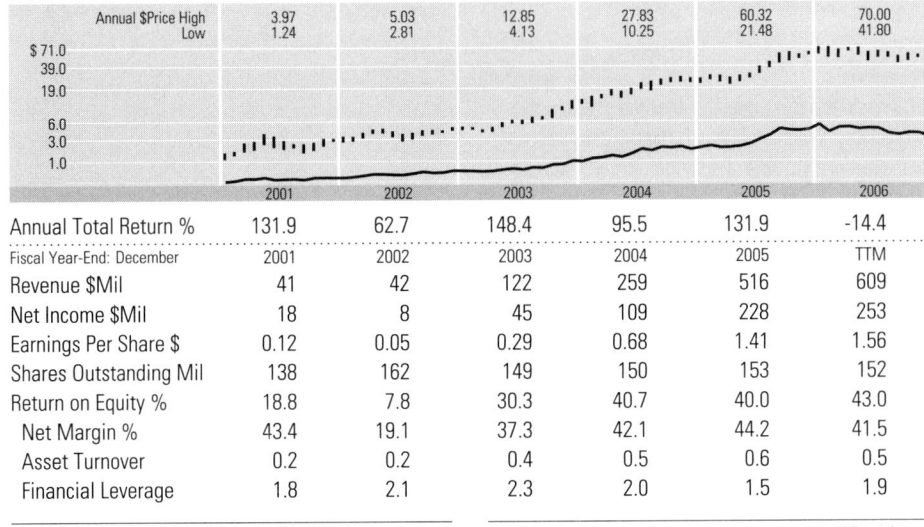

Price Volatility — Monthly Price High/Low — Relative Strength to S&P 500

Annual $Price High/Low	3.97/1.24	5.03/2.81	12.85/4.13	27.83/10.25	60.32/21.48	70.00/41.80
	2001	2002	2003	2004	2005	2006
Annual Total Return %	131.9	62.7	148.4	95.5	131.9	-14.4

Fiscal Year-End: December	2001	2002	2003	2004	2005	TTM
Revenue $Mil	41	42	122	259	516	609
Net Income $Mil	18	8	45	109	228	253
Earnings Per Share $	0.12	0.05	0.29	0.68	1.41	1.56
Shares Outstanding Mil	138	162	149	150	153	152
Return on Equity %	18.8	7.8	30.3	40.7	40.0	43.0
Net Margin %	43.4	19.1	37.3	42.1	44.2	41.5
Asset Turnover	0.2	0.2	0.4	0.5	0.6	0.5
Financial Leverage	1.8	2.1	2.3	2.0	1.5	1.9

Valuation Ratios	Stock	Rel to Industry	Rel to S&P 500
Price/Earnings	30.6	2.4	1.5
Price/Book	12.3	3.8	3.0
Price/Sales	11.9	6.3	4.1
Price/Cash Flow	15.6	1.8	1.1

Major Fund Holders	% of Fund Assets
Morgan Stanley Cap Opportunities B	6.48
Morgan Stanley Inst Focus Equity A	6.13
Morgan Stanley Focus Growth B	5.35
PF Van Kampen Mid-Cap Growth A	5.08

Thesis By Eric Chenoweth, CFA, 12-12-06   Stock Price as of Analysis: $50.90

Ultra Petroleum is an oil and gas company worth keeping an eye on, in our opinion. Valuable natural-gas properties in Wyoming's Green River Basin have made the firm one of the lowest-cost producers of natural gas in North America.

Of the independent North American producers we cover, Ultra Petroleum has posted the lowest cost per unit of natural gas produced over the past five years. More importantly, we think the firm will continue its reign as the lowest-cost producer for at least several more years. Since 2001, Ultra's finding and development costs (what it pays to add new natural-gas reserves), at less than $0.40 per thousand cubic feet on average, have been the lowest among the firms we cover. In a commodity business like oil and gas, being the low-cost producer is a big advantage.

Ultra's low-cost advantage rests in its enviable position in the Green River Basin. The company owns interests in about 135,000 acres in the region, of which a little less than 13,000 are developed. Ultra's acreage covers small portions of the Jonah Field and a large swath of the Pinedale Anticline. Wells already drilled in the region have been quite impressive, costing about $5 million and adding about 8 billion cubic feet of reserves. Ultra's Green River Basin assets should provide the company with an outlet to reinvest capital at a rate well above its cost of capital for some time. We think Ultra can build shareholder value through internal growth for many years.

Ultra's business in the Green River Basin comes with its fair share of risk, however. Like other Rocky Mountain producers, Ultra must contend with environmental obstructions to oil and gas development on its properties. Winter drilling restrictions, though somewhat more relaxed now, still slow the pace of oil and gas development between November and May. Price differentials between the Rocky Mountains and the rest of the United States have been wide at times, translating into weaker average natural-gas selling prices for Rocky Mountains producers relative to those in other regions. It's likely that these pricing differences will continue to haunt producers in the Rockies from time to time until greater pipeline capacity is built in the region.

Ultra's other oil and gas assets sit in Bohai Bay, China. These assets also have tremendous economics. However, the China business is a very small portion of Ultra's revenue and less attractive than its Green River Basin assets, in our opinion.

Data as of 12-29-06

Unilever NV UN

	Rating	Fair Value	Last Close	Consider Buy	Consider Sell	Yield %
	★★★	$27.00	$27.25	$23.00	$35.40	3.14

Company Profile

Netherlands-based Unilever NV, together with U.K.-based Unilever PLC, control Unilever Group. Unilever consists of three main divisions: food (56% of revenue), home care (18%), and personal care (26%). As stand-alone entities, Unilever's divisions would be the world's third-largest food company, second-largest home-care company, and third-largest personal-care firm. Brands include Lipton teas, Hellmann's mayonnaise, Dove soaps, Breyers ice cream, and Knorr soups and sauces.

Management   Stewardship Grade [NA]

Despite several moves by Unilever to restructure its management team and organizational structure, we feel that more changes are needed. By abandoning the dual chairman and CEO positions that had been in place at the Anglo-Dutch company for 75 years, Unilever has taken only minor steps toward dismantling a dual headquarters and management structure that has kept it from being an efficient and responsive competitor in the marketplace. With many of the firm's rivals looking to emerging markets for future growth, Unilever needs to be far more nimble than it has been in the past or else it runs the risk of losing the first-mover advantage it worked so hard for in key markets such as China, India, and Indonesia. The company also has serious work to do in Europe, where slower economic growth and the proliferation of hard discounters have hampered results. We feel that the company would be best served by splitting its operations into two separate companies: one focused on household and personal products and the other one focused on packaged foods. With little real overhang between these two different product categories, each individual company would be far better equipped to react to changes in the marketplace than Unilever is currently capable of doing as a single entity.

Weena 455 P.O. Box 760   www.unilever.com
Rotterdam, Netherlands 3000 DK

Growth [NA]	2002	2003	2004	2005
Revenue %	-6.3	-11.6	-9.7	2.9
Earnings/Share %	25.3	31.7	-0.7	38.1
Book Value/Share %	-44.5	29.5	15.6	17.6
Dividends/Share %	8.5	0.0	9.6	4.8

Profitability [NA]	2003	2004	2005	TTM
Return on Assets %	6.6	7.2	10.6	10.6
Oper Cash Flow $Mil	4,286	6,891	5,451	5,451
- Cap Spending $Mil	1,147	1,215	1,145	1,145
= Free Cash Flow $Mil	3,139	5,676	4,306	4,306

Financial Health [NA]	2003	2004	2005	12-31-05
Long-term Debt $Mil	11,413	9,442	7,687	7,687
Total Equity $Mil	7,400	9,951	9,954	9,954
Debt/Equity Ratio	1.5	0.9	0.8	0.8

Industry	Business Risk	Moat Size	Investment Style	Sector
Food Mfg.	Below Avg	Narrow	Large Value	Consumer Goods

Competition

	Market Cap $Mil	12 Mo Trailing Sales $Mil	Price/Cash Flow	Return On Assets%	Debt/ Equity	Total Return% 1 Yr	3 Yr
Unilever NV	46,726	49,679	8.6	10.6	0.8	25.0	12.4
Procter & Gamble	203,656	72,214	16.8	6.8	0.6	13.4	11.3
Nestle SA ADR	138,417	73,660	16.8	8.8	—	20.9	14.7

Price Volatility

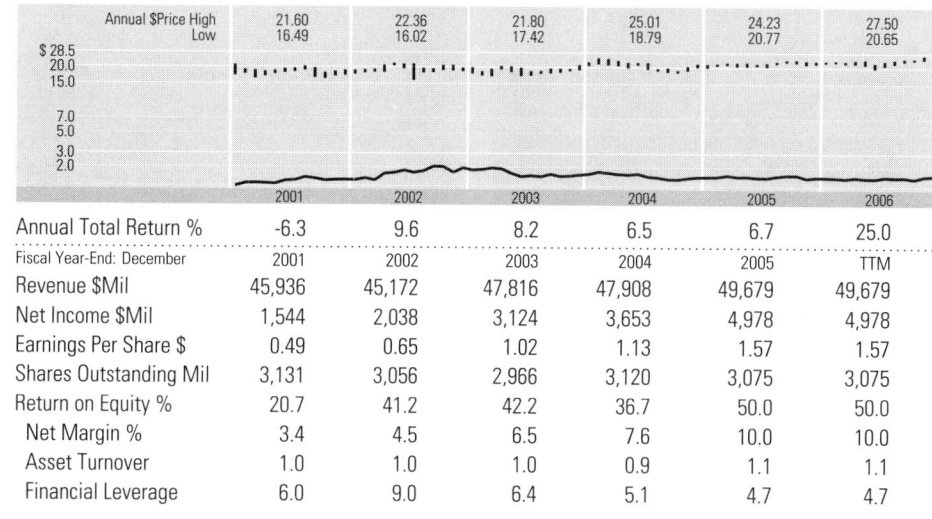

	2001	2002	2003	2004	2005	2006
Annual $Price High	21.60	22.36	21.80	25.01	24.23	27.50
Low	16.49	16.02	17.42	18.79	20.77	20.65
Annual Total Return %	-6.3	9.6	8.2	6.5	6.7	25.0

Fiscal Year-End: December	2001	2002	2003	2004	2005	TTM
Revenue $Mil	45,936	45,172	47,816	47,908	49,679	49,679
Net Income $Mil	1,544	2,038	3,124	3,653	4,978	4,978
Earnings Per Share $	0.49	0.65	1.02	1.13	1.57	1.57
Shares Outstanding Mil	3,131	3,056	2,966	3,120	3,075	3,075
Return on Equity %	20.7	41.2	42.2	36.7	50.0	50.0
Net Margin %	3.4	4.5	6.5	7.6	10.0	10.0
Asset Turnover	1.0	1.0	1.0	0.9	1.1	1.1
Financial Leverage	6.0	9.0	6.4	5.1	4.7	4.7

Valuation Ratios	Stock	Rel to Industry	Rel to S&P 500
Price/Earnings	17.4	0.8	0.8
Price/Book	4.7	1.0	1.1
Price/Sales	0.9	0.5	0.3
Price/Cash Flow	8.6	0.6	0.6

Major Fund Holders	% of Fund Assets
Fidelity Select Consumer Staples	6.29
Brown Advisory Value Equity Instl	3.47
Fidelity Select Consumer Discretionary	3.37
Hartford Focus Y	3.24

Thesis   By Greggory Warren, CFA, 12-05-06   Stock Price as of Analysis: $26.40

Even though Unilever has done a terrific job of trimming down its brand portfolio and cutting unnecessary costs out of its core operations, we feel that its inability to drive consistent top-line growth has led to dramatic market share losses and left management struggling to find a solution. Unfortunately, the company's dual operating structure--with headquarters in both London and The Netherlands--limits its ability to respond quickly to changes in its competitive landscape.

Unilever has significant presence in its categories. The company is one of the largest global producers of packaged foods, focusing mainly on soups and sauces, dressings, tea-based beverages, and ice cream. Unilever is also one of the world's largest manufacturers of household and personal products, selling such basic items as laundry detergents, skin- and hair-care products, and deodorants. Strong brands--such as Knorr, Hellmann's, Lipton, Dove, and Pond's--allow Unilever to acquire favorable shelf space and charge premium prices for its products, justifying a narrow-moat rating for the firm.

While a company with such characteristics might normally earn a wide-moat rating, we have tempered our enthusiasm for Unilever given the maturity of its core markets and the intense competition it faces.

Sales growth has been problematic in Europe, where slower economic growth and the proliferation of hard discounters have hampered results. While Unilever has traditionally overcome weakness in its more mature markets through its leading presence in emerging and developing markets, the company has also recently come under attack from a reinvigorated Procter & Gamble, which gained significant exposure in many of Unilever's emerging and developing markets through its acquisition of Gillette last year.

Even with the improvements Unilever made to its product portfolio, the firm's operating margins continue to come in well below those of its closest competitors. Profitability in packaged foods, which makes up close to 60% of total sales, has been dismal, with household and personal products doing little to pick up the slack. In industries where profit margins ultimately determine how much money a company can spend on marketing and brand support, Unilever's weaker position versus its peers could undermine sales growth and profitability longer term.

With little being done to improve the company's dual operating and management structure, which has kept Unilever from being an efficient and responsive competitor in the marketplace, we see no real catalyst for long-term performance improvement.

Data as of 12-29-06

United Parcel Service B UPS

	Rating	Fair Value	Last Close	Consider Buy	Consider Sell	Yield %
	★★★★★	$88.00	$74.98	$75.00	$115.50	2.03

Industry	Business Risk	Moat Size	Investment Style	Sector
Transportation	Below Avg	Wide	Large Core	Business Services

Company Profile

Based in Atlanta, UPS is one of the world's largest residential and commercial package delivery companies. Its domestic ground delivery network comprises local truck routes and distribution centers linked to a national hub-and-spoke system that uses various modes of transportation to move packages around the country. UPS also has a large international presence, particularly in Europe and Asia, and it provides logistics services for major businesses as well.

Management   Stewardship Grade [B]

Chairman and CEO Mike Eskew has held the top job at UPS since 2002. We think he and his team have done a respectable job, but they need to do more to generate returns for shareholders. Over the past five years, UPS shares have outperformed the S&P 500 Index but underperformed both FedEx and the Dow Jones Transportation Average. This is a bit surprising, given the firm's strong free cash flow and returns on invested capital. However, UPS' operating margin hasn't improved since 1999, the firm has a war chest of cash with no clear plan for deployment, and its capital structure is inefficient (UPS has a credit rating of AAA). From a corporate-governance perspective, we generally like what we see: The full board is elected annually, compensation is reasonable, and employee/founder ownership is unusually high (40%-45% of outstanding shares). On the other hand, we aren't fond of the dual classes of common stock (employee-owned shares have 10 votes per share, while other shareholders get 1 vote per share), nor do we like the firm's charter provisions enabling blank-check preferred stock and limiting shareholders' ability to act by written consent or call a special meeting. We also would prefer that the chairman and CEO positions be held by separate individuals.

55 Glenlake Parkway, NE
Atlanta, GA 30328
www.ups.com

Growth [B]	2002	2003	2004	2005
Revenue %	3.1	7.1	9.2	16.4
Earnings/Share %	33.8	-9.3	14.9	18.4
Book Value/Share %	22.6	18.8	10.2	5.1
Dividends/Share %	0.0	21.1	21.7	17.9

Profitability [A+]	2003	2004	2005	TTM
Return on Assets %	9.7	10.1	11.0	11.4
Oper Cash Flow $Mil	4,576	5,331	5,793	5,318
- Cap Spending $Mil	1,947	2,127	2,187	2,874
= Free Cash Flow $Mil	2,629	3,204	3,606	2,444

Financial Health [A]	2003	2004	2005	09-30-06
Long-term Debt $Mil	3,149	3,261	3,159	3,113
Total Equity $Mil	14,852	16,378	16,884	17,177
Debt/Equity Ratio	0.2	0.2	0.2	0.2

Competition	Market Cap $Mil	12 Mo Trailing Sales $Mil	Price/Cash Flow	Return On Assets%	Debt/Equity	Total Return% 1 Yr	3 Yr
United Parcel Service B	80,494	46,873	15.1	11.4	0.2	1.8	2.4
FedEx	33,307	33,132	9.4	8.1	0.2	5.4	17.4
TNT NV ADR	20,678	12,654	16.8	8.3	0.3	41.0	25.8

Price Volatility

	2001	2002	2003	2004	2005	2006
Annual $Price High	62.50	67.10	74.86	89.11	85.84	83.99
Low	46.15	54.25	53.00	67.22	66.10	65.50
Annual Total Return %	-6.1	17.2	19.9	16.4	-10.5	1.8

Fiscal Year-End: December	2001	2002	2003	2004	2005	TTM
Revenue $Mil	30,321	31,272	33,485	36,582	42,581	46,873
Net Income $Mil	2,399	3,182	2,898	3,333	3,870	4,123
Earnings Per Share $	2.10	2.81	2.55	2.93	3.47	3.77
Shares Outstanding Mil	1,126	1,120	1,128	1,130	1,112	1,074
Return on Equity %	23.4	25.5	19.5	20.4	22.9	24.0
Net Margin %	7.9	10.2	8.7	9.1	9.1	8.8
Asset Turnover	1.2	1.2	1.1	1.1	1.2	1.3
Financial Leverage	2.4	2.2	2.0	2.0	2.1	2.1

Valuation Ratios	Stock	Rel to Industry	Rel to S&P 500
Price/Earnings	19.9	1.0	1.0
Price/Book	4.7	1.1	1.1
Price/Sales	1.7	1.1	0.6
Price/Cash Flow	15.1	1.1	1.0

Major Fund Holders	% of Fund Assets
Rydex Transportation Inv	8.74
Delaware Pooled Large-Cap Growth Eqty	4.62
Delaware Large Cap Growth Instl	4.44
Delaware U.S. Growth A	4.23

Thesis By Peter Smith, 10-19-06 Stock Price as of Analysis: $75.25

United Parcel Service is one of the world's largest package delivery and logistics firms, handling almost 15 million packages daily. Though competition has picked up in its stronghold, domestic ground, we still expect UPS to generate industry-leading returns and free cash flow for years to come.

UPS is one of the four major global integrators, competing with FedEx, DHL, and TNT. Through its surprisingly flexible business model and enormous network, it offers both ground and express (air) services as well as freight and logistics services worldwide. The broader industry has strong growth dynamics, high barriers to entry, and is in the midst of rapid consolidation--all of which work in UPS' favor, in our view.

UPS' traditional strength has been in domestic ground, which accounts for almost half of its total revenue. As FedEx and DHL have built out their domestic networks, however, they have been competing more aggressively with UPS in this business. Though UPS' pricing power is at risk, the firm is well entrenched with many of its customers, and a plenitude of business has kept pricing rational, for the most part.

Internationally, UPS' growth opportunities are more abundant and profitable. The company has invested heavily in Europe and Asia and expects to increase its presence in both areas. It also hopes to increase its share of packages crossing international borders, as UPS' yield per package on those shipments is almost double that of any of its other services. Unlike its domestic strategy of growing at the market rate, its international goal is to grow faster than the global market.

Of the four major integrators, UPS generates the best returns and strongest free cash flow. We attribute this to several factors, including its strategic use of efficiency-enhancing technology and employee-owner culture. We look to these same factors, along with the firm's extensive global infrastructure, to justify our wide moat rating.

Despite UPS' superior returns, its shareholder returns have trailed peers' in recent years. Some of this has to do with its stagnant profitability--UPS' operating margin, while strong, is at the same level as it was six years ago despite increased volume. However, the firm's capital structure is also inefficient (very little leverage), and a large share repurchase or acquisition is becoming increasingly likely. We expect action of some sort to happen soon that, along with continued profitable international growth, should drive shareholder value.

Data as of 12-29-06

United Technologies UTX

	Rating	Fair Value	Last Close	Consider Buy	Consider Sell	Yield %
	★★★	$60.00	$62.52	$51.10	$78.80	1.62

Industry	Business Risk	Moat Size	Investment Style	Sector
Diversified	Below Avg	Wide	Large Core	Industrial Materials

Company Profile

United Technologies is a true conglomerate, operating six distinct businesses serving highly engineered industrial and aerospace markets. The aerospace market represents 36% of sales. Aerospace segments include Pratt & Whitney aircraft engines, Hamilton Sundstrand aerosystems, and Sikorsky helicopters. Otis elevators represents 23% of sales. Carrier heating, ventilation, and air conditioning and refrigeration represents 30%. Fire and security rounds out the firm's businesses.

Management   Stewardship Grade [A]

Management is a strong suit at United Tech. With returns on equity consistently exceeding 20%, we think that management has done an excellent job of maximizing shareholder value. Management has spent $2 billion buying back shares over the last two years. CEO George David has been at the helm since 1994. David deserves credit for assembling the current stable of attractive businesses and crafting the company's international growth strategy. He earned approximately $27 million in total compensation in 2005. That's a substantial package even for a large multi-industrial company like United Tech. However, considering United Tech's excellent financial performance, we think it's within the range of acceptability. On the other hand, we'd like to see fewer board members with backgrounds in politics and more with backgrounds in finance and investing.

United Technologies Building One Financial Plaza   www.utc.com
Hartford, CT 06103

Growth [B]	2002	2003	2004	2005
Revenue %	1.1	10.0	20.7	14.1
Earnings/Share %	15.4	6.1	12.6	14.8
Book Value/Share %	-0.1	40.8	21.2	19.1
Dividends/Share %	8.9	15.8	23.3	25.7

Profitability [A]	2003	2004	2005	TTM
Return on Assets %	6.7	6.6	6.7	7.0
Oper Cash Flow $Mil	2,875	3,596	4,334	4,293
- Cap Spending $Mil	530	795	929	948
= Free Cash Flow $Mil	2,345	2,801	3,405	3,345

Financial Health [A-]	2003	2004	2005	09-30-06
Long-term Debt $Mil	4,257	4,231	5,935	7,067
Total Equity $Mil	11,707	14,266	16,991	18,934
Debt/Equity Ratio	0.4	0.3	0.3	0.4

Competition

	Market Cap $Mil	12 Mo Trailing Sales $Mil	Price/Cash Flow	Return On Assets%	Debt/Equity	Total Return% 1 Yr	3 Yr
United Technologies	62,748	46,303	14.6	7.0	0.4	13.7	11.6
General Electric	383,564	161,022	12.8	2.5	2.2	9.4	9.0
Boeing	70,249	59,114	9.4	2.7	0.8	28.4	30.4

Price Volatility | Monthly Price High/Low — Relative Strength to S&P 500

Annual $Price High/Low	43.70/20.05	38.85/24.42	48.34/26.76	53.14/40.34	58.89/48.43	67.47/54.20
	2001	2002	2003	2004	2005	2006
Annual Total Return %	-16.8	-2.7	55.4	10.7	10.0	13.7

Fiscal Year-End: December	2001	2002	2003	2004	2005	TTM
Revenue $Mil	27,897	28,212	31,034	37,445	42,725	46,303
Net Income $Mil	1,938	2,236	2,361	2,673	3,069	3,493
Earnings Per Share $	1.92	2.21	2.35	2.64	3.03	3.47
Shares Outstanding Mil	955	958	958	994	990	1,004
Return on Equity %	23.2	26.8	20.2	18.7	18.1	18.4
Net Margin %	6.9	7.9	7.6	7.1	7.2	7.5
Asset Turnover	1.0	1.0	0.9	0.9	0.9	0.9
Financial Leverage	3.2	3.5	3.0	2.8	2.7	2.6

Valuation Ratios	Stock	Rel to Industry	Rel to S&P 500
Price/Earnings	17.6	1.0	0.9
Price/Book	3.3	1.0	0.8
Price/Sales	1.4	0.8	0.5
Price/Cash Flow	14.6	1.1	1.0

Major Fund Holders	% of Fund Assets
Fidelity Congress Street	5.40
Oppenheimer Quest Value A	5.39
Oak Value	5.11
MassMutual Premier Value L	5.09

Thesis By Tom D'Amore, CFA, 12-13-06 Stock Price as of Analysis: $64.21

United Technologies offers investors an attractive mix of value-creating properties: powerful market positions in most served markets, robust sales growth fueled by high exposure to expanding international markets, and an effective productivity-improvement program for boosting profit margins.

United Tech generates 60% of sales from markets in which it holds the number-one or -two market share position. Its Carrier unit is the world market leader in heating, ventilation, and air conditioning (HVAC). Its Otis unit is the world leader in elevators. Its Fire & Security unit is number-two in electronic security and fire safety. These markets are highly fragmented, leaving plenty of opportunity for market-share expansion and increased sales growth. United Tech also controls respectable market positions in large aerospace markets including aircraft engines (Pratt & Whitney), helicopters (Sikorsky), and aerospace systems (Hamilton Sundstrand).

While United Tech's end markets are largely industrial, we forecast top-line growth in the high single digits through at least 2007, excluding acquisitions. Driving this growth is United Tech's successful expansion into international markets, which generate approximately 60% of sales. The firm has enviable franchises in emerging markets, including China and India. For example, Otis controls approximately 75% of the Chinese elevator market, which is growing at 15%-20% annually and now represents nearly one third of the world's installed base of elevators.

Compelling sales growth is also being driven by the company's high exposure to the aerospace industry, the firm's largest end market at approximately 36% of sales. Due to strong secular trends driving increased demand for air travel, we think that sales of aerospace products will increase at high single digits at least through 2008.

Finally, we're fans of United Tech's proprietary productivity improvement program, Achieving Competitive Excellence (ACE). Through the ACE program, United Tech focuses on consistently improving manufacturing productivity, enabling the company to methodically increase its market shares and raise profit margins. A case in point is United Tech's Otis division, which has been steadily increasing global market share and raising its profit margins by continuously improving the quality of its product line and simultaneously reducing its cost structure.

Data as of 12-29-06

UnitedHealth Group UNH

	Rating	Fair Value	Last Close	Consider Buy	Consider Sell	Yield %
	★★★	$58.00	$53.73	$44.70	$72.70	0.06

Industry	Business Risk	Moat Size	Investment Style	Sector
Managed Care	Average	Narrow	Large Growth	Healthcare

Company Profile
UnitedHealth Group is a diversified health services provider serving 70 million people. It's a market leader in health insurance products that include both risked-based products where it assumes the risks of related medical costs, and fee-based services to large employers that prefer to self-insure. It also sells dental, vision, group insurance, and other ancillary products.

Competition

	Market Cap $Mil	12 Mo Trailing Sales $Mil	Price/Cash Flow	Return On Assets%	Debt/Equity	Total Return% 1 Yr	3 Yr
UnitedHealth Group	72,374	51,787	11.9	7.7	0.4	-13.5	22.2
WellPoint	48,789	54,285	—	5.7	—	-1.4	27.3
Aetna	22,540	24,654	—	3.7	—	-8.3	36.7

Price Volatility
Monthly Price High/Low — Relative Strength to S&P 500

Annual $Price High/Low	18.20/12.63	25.25/16.96	29.34/19.60	44.38/27.73	64.61/42.63	62.93/41.44
	2001	2002	2003	2004	2005	2006
Annual Total Return %	15.4	18.0	39.4	51.4	41.2	-13.5

Fiscal Year-End: December	2001	2002	2003	2004	2005	TTM
Revenue $Mil	23,454	25,020	28,823	37,218	45,365	51,787
Net Income $Mil	913	1,352	1,825	2,587	3,300	3,456
Earnings Per Share $	0.70	1.07	1.48	1.97	2.48	2.56
Shares Outstanding Mil	1,251	1,213	1,177	1,250	1,264	1,347
Return on Equity %	23.5	30.5	35.6	24.1	18.6	19.6
Net Margin %	3.9	5.4	6.3	7.0	7.3	6.7
Asset Turnover	1.9	1.8	1.6	1.3	1.1	1.1
Financial Leverage	3.2	3.2	3.4	2.6	2.3	2.6

Valuation Ratios	Stock	Rel to Industry	Rel to S&P 500
Price/Earnings	21.0	1.0	1.0
Price/Book	4.1	1.2	1.0
Price/Sales	1.4	1.2	0.5
Price/Cash Flow	11.9	0.8	0.8

Major Fund Holders	% of Fund Assets
Legg Mason Partners Aggressive Growth A	8.02
Fidelity Select Medical Delivery	7.79
Marsico Focus	7.54
Columbia Marsico Focused Eq A	7.40

Management
Stewardship Grade [D]

Corporate governance at UnitedHealth is abysmal, in our view. An independent investigation concluded that former CEO Bill McGuire was likely involved in backdating options, inflating his compensation at the expense of shareholders. The report also detailed significant conflicts of interest between McGuire and former director William Spears who served on the compensation committee and helped negotiate McGuire's 1999 employment contract. The findings of the investigation demonstrate the failure of this entrenched board, where directors were either negligent, corrupt, or both.

The company made several changes in reaction to pressure from shareholders and intense publicity regarding its poor governance. Changes include ending equity awards to executives with well-established equity positions, eliminating severance compensation in connection with a change in control, establishing an annual grant date for stock options, eliminating the staggered board in favor of annual elections, and reducing board compensation. These changes are progress in reforming the company's poor governance, but these practices should have already been adopted. We cannot in good faith give the company credit for improved corporate governance when it has ignored shareholders' best interests for so long.

9900 Bren Road East
Minnetonka, MN 55343
www.unitedhealthgroup.com

Growth [A-]	2002	2003	2004	2005
Revenue %	6.7	15.2	29.1	21.9
Earnings/Share %	52.7	39.0	33.1	25.9
Book Value/Share %	17.3	19.2	96.2	63.3
Dividends/Share %	0.0	0.0	100.0	0.0

Profitability [A]	2003	2004	2005	TTM
Return on Assets %	10.3	9.3	8.0	7.7
Oper Cash Flow $Mil	3,003	4,135	4,326	6,079
- Cap Spending $Mil	352	350	509	567
= Free Cash Flow $Mil	2,651	3,785	3,817	5,512

Financial Health [A-]	2003	2004	2005	03-31-06
Long-term Debt $Mil	1,750	3,350	3,850	6,450
Total Equity $Mil	5,128	10,717	17,733	17,646
Debt/Equity Ratio	0.3	0.3	0.2	0.4

Thesis By Brandon Troegle, 12-11-06 Stock Price as of Analysis: $50.09

UnitedHealth's corporate governance is troubling, but we still think the company itself is well-run and that its large product offering, significant size, and operational performance give it a narrow moat.

We like UnitedHealth's breadth of products and services and expect further market share gains. Its products reach virtually every demographic in its market, and it's the market leader in several of them. The company provides more fee-based administrative services to employers than risk-based coverage, a trend that should continue and provide some margin protection. The company has market leadership positions in Medicare Part D and Medicare Advantage. It is also a leader in consumer-driven health plans. Additionally, we expect robust growth in the small but high-margin specialized health services and Ingenix segments, which should help mitigate rising cost trends that we expect in the traditional risk-based services.

With its bevy of products and national reach, UnitedHealth enjoys the advantages of its scale. Its costs and risks are spread over a larger member base, and the firm has more leverage in negotiating contracts with physicians and hospitals. Additionally, its national platform and comprehensive offerings make it attractive to large corporations. The national footprint also protects it from a regional downturn.

As UnitedHealth has grown both organically and through acquisition, it has demonstrated strong operational performance that we expect to continue. The company has been acquisitive in its growth, which poses risks, but we believe the consistent and strong returns on invested capital during this time are evidence it has made good acquisition choices and integrated them well. The company continues to yield significant free cash flow, giving it ample capital.

UnitedHealth still has significant risks, though, as investor sentiment has waned in reaction to the much publicized option backdating scandal. The delay in filing its second- and third-quarter 10-Qs, investigations by the Securities and Exchange Commission and Department of Justice, and former CEO Bill McGuire's ouster after 15 years at the helm highlight the seriousness of the situation. Stephen Hemsley, who was president and COO, has taken over as CEO. While management transitions can be difficult, our concerns are mitigated by the fact that McGuire was replaced from within by an executive who knows the company well. We think this reduces the risk that the company's strong operational, fundamental, and acquisition success will be jeopardized.

© 2007 Morningstar, Inc. All rights reserved. Intended for United States residents only, this report is for information purposes and should not be considered a solicitation to buy or sell any security. Download your free reports at http://www.morningstar.com/goto/2007Stocks500

Data as of 12-29-06

US Bancorp USB

	Rating	Fair Value	Last Close	Consider Buy	Consider Sell	Yield %
	★★★	$38.00	$36.19	$29.30	$47.60	3.84

Industry	Business Risk	Moat Size	Investment Style	Sector
Super Regional Banks	Average	Wide	Large Value	Financial Services

Company Profile

US Bancorp is one of the 10 largest banks in the United States by asset size. It serves more than 10 million customers in 24 states and has about 2,400 retail locations along with more than 4,600 ATMs. The bank provides typical services like savings, checking, money market, and individual retirement accounts, as well as products such as trust services, asset management, and insurance.

Competition

	Market Cap $Mil	12 Mo Trailing Sales $Mil	Price/Cash Flow	Return On Assets %	Debt/ Equity	Total Return % 1 Yr	3 Yr
US Bancorp	63,617	13,499	—	2.2	—	26.3	11.8
Bank of America	239,758	68,368	—	1.3	—	20.7	15.2
Wells Fargo	120,049	34,770	—	1.7	—	16.8	10.4

Management — Stewardship Grade [A]

We credit management for keeping shareholders' interests at the forefront of its strategy, as the bank's solid operating performance has allowed it to meet its stated goal of returning at least 80% of annual income to shareholders through buybacks or dividends. CEO Jerry Grundhofer is formerly the chief executive of Firstar, which combined with the old US Bancorp in a 2001 merger of equals. He succeeded his older brother, Jack, who had headed the old US Bancorp since 1990. By the end of 2006, Grundhofer will hand the reins to COO Richard Davis, who we think is a ready and able successor. Davis' early public comments lead us to believe that US Bancorp's strategy will remain intact, with perhaps an added emphasis on improving existing operations rather than future acquisitions. Aside from the company's poison pill, we believe US Bancorp's corporate governance is solid, and we think the firm's managers are shareholder-friendly. Jerry Grundhofer has been the driving force behind US Bancorp's increased focus on community banking. US Bancorp's option grants are low, and the company was an early adopter of retroactively expensing stock options.

800 Nicollet Mall
Minneapolis, MN 55402-4302
www.usbank.com

Growth [C-]	2002	2003	2004	2005
Revenue %	2.2	4.0	1.0	3.7
Earnings/Share %	87.5	17.0	13.0	11.0
Book Value/Share %	13.1	4.4	2.0	5.9
Dividends/Share %	4.0	9.6	19.3	20.6

Profitability [A]	2003	2004	2005	TTM
Return on Assets %	2.0	2.1	2.1	2.2
Oper Cash Flow $Mil	8,682	5,225	3,412	—
- Cap Spending $Mil	—	—	—	—
= Free Cash Flow $Mil	—	—	—	—

Financial Health [NA]	2003	2004	2005	09-30-06
Long-term Debt $Mil	—	—	—	—
Total Equity $Mil	19,393	19,539	20,086	19,926
Debt/Equity Ratio	—	—	—	—

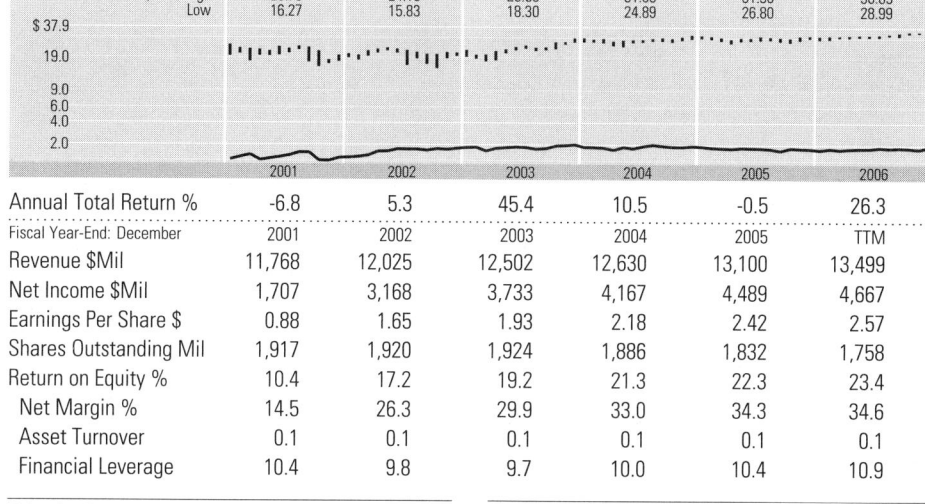

Price Volatility — Monthly Price High/Low — Relative Strength to S&P 500

	2001	2002	2003	2004	2005	2006
Annual $Price High	25.70	24.16	29.59	31.65	31.36	36.85
Low	16.27	15.83	18.30	24.89	26.80	28.99
Annual Total Return %	-6.8	5.3	45.4	10.5	-0.5	26.3
Fiscal Year-End: December	2001	2002	2003	2004	2005	TTM
Revenue $Mil	11,768	12,025	12,502	12,630	13,100	13,499
Net Income $Mil	1,707	3,168	3,733	4,167	4,489	4,667
Earnings Per Share $	0.88	1.65	1.93	2.18	2.42	2.57
Shares Outstanding Mil	1,917	1,920	1,924	1,886	1,832	1,758
Return on Equity %	10.4	17.2	19.2	21.3	22.3	23.4
Net Margin %	14.5	26.3	29.9	33.0	34.3	34.6
Asset Turnover	0.1	0.1	0.1	0.1	0.1	0.1
Financial Leverage	10.4	9.8	9.7	10.0	10.4	10.9

Valuation Ratios	Stock	Rel to Industry	Rel to S&P 500
Price/Earnings	14.1	1.0	0.7
Price/Book	3.2	1.5	0.8
Price/Sales	4.7	1.3	1.6
Price/Cash Flow	—	—	—

Major Fund Holders	% of Fund Assets
Allianz RCM Financial Services Instl	7.57
Senbanc	6.16
T. Rowe Price Financial Services	5.30
Destination Select Equity	4.90

Thesis By Jim Callahan, CFA, 10-17-06   Stock Price as of Analysis: $33.24

US Bancorp's diversity and profitability serve its shareholders well.

Despite its large size, US Bancorp hasn't lost touch with the little guy. The bank's 2,400 branches across 24 states are split between metropolitan and rural markets, while its 500 grocery store locations--which cost one sixth what an average branch costs--help lower total overhead and add convenience. The very core of its retail bank is customer service, and its Five Star Service Guarantee underscores the importance placed on service under the leadership of CEO Jerry Grundhofer. With new retail banking initiatives rolling out, we believe US Bancorp's position in retail banking will remain strong despite much tougher market conditions.

Like many large diversified banks, US Bancorp derives about half of its revenue from fee-based businesses. The key contributors are its wealth-management and payment-processing segments, which combine for most of the fee-based revenue. While wealth management is a natural extension of any bank's product portfolio, US Bancorp has been proactive in expanding this business. Since 2002, the bank has acquired several asset managers that have helped total assets under management reach $143 billion. Now that this unit--like payment processing--enjoys some scale, we expect US Bancorp's industry-leading 2.2% average return on assets and 23% average return on equity to continue to increase.

Through acquisitions in the United States and Europe, the attractive payment-processing unit's fee income now totals 36% of total noninterest income and has grown 18% compounded annually since 2000. We believe transaction volume will continue to rise, driving US Bancorp's transaction processing revenue to nearly 50% of total fee income by 2010.

We've had our concerns about US Bancorp, but we've been proved too cautious. With above-average capital to deploy and strong profitability ratios, US Bancorp competes for commercial loan growth on price: What it sacrifices in net interest margin, it will more than recover in asset growth. Although we're not enamored with this approach, we can't argue with the recent results. US Bancorp's net interest margin has declined, but other profitability metrics have held firm while the loan portfolio expands.

US Bancorp has historically generated value for its investors, returning more than 80% of annual profits to shareholders. We expect this trend to continue, and we'd invest in this company at the right price.

Data as of 12-29-06

UST UST

	Rating	Fair Value	Last Close	Consider Buy	Consider Sell	Yield %
	★	$44.00	$58.20	$33.90	$55.10	3.92

Industry	Business Risk	Moat Size	Investment Style	Sector
Tobacco	Average	Wide	Mid Value	Consumer Goods

Company Profile

UST is a holding company for U.S. Smokeless Tobacco Company and Ste. Michelle Wine Estates. The company manufactures smokeless tobacco products under well-known brand names like Copenhagen and Skoal. Its wine division produces wines from Washington and California sold under the Chateau Ste. Michelle and Columbia Crest labels. The firm's products are sold mainly in the United States, with the wine division contributing 14% of total sales and 5% of operating profit in 2006.

Management Stewardship Grade [C]

While we are encouraged to see UST finally splitting its chairman and CEO roles, this does little to overcome the broader issues facing the company. With outgoing chairman and CEO Vincent Gierer taking the role of nonexecutive chairman, current president and COO Murray Kessler will take the top job at the smokeless tobacco firm. Having served as president of UST's smokeless tobacco division from April 2000 to November 2005, and then as president and COO of the firm over the past year, Kessler is certainly familiar with the business. He has been a driving force behind UST's efforts to increase category growth by attracting adult smokers to smokeless tobacco through one-on-one marketing initiatives and product innovation. We take issue with some of UST's compensation practices, like paying Gierer a $5 million retention bonus if he stayed through to his planned retirement date of Dec. 31, 2006. Given the lost market share, declining profitability, and inconsistent earnings over the past five years, we also find it difficult to accept the hefty increases Gierer saw in annual compensation during 2003, 2004, and 2005. UST does gain some points, though, for clean financial statements and a willingness to share critical industry data, even when it is not flattering to the firm.

100 West Putnam Avenue www.ustinc.com
Greenwich, CT 06830

Growth [D]	2002	2003	2004	2005
Revenue %	3.4	3.4	6.1	0.7
Earnings/Share %	NMF	NMF	67.9	1.3
Book Value/Share %	NMF	NMF	NMF	689.9
Dividends/Share %	4.3	4.2	4.0	5.8

Profitability [A+]	2003	2004	2005	TTM
Return on Assets %	18.5	32.0	39.1	38.2
Oper Cash Flow $Mil	-705	565	561	586
- Cap Spending $Mil	49	70	90	63
= Free Cash Flow $Mil	-754	495	471	523

Financial Health [A]	2003	2004	2005	09-30-06
Long-term Debt $Mil	1,140	840	840	840
Total Equity $Mil	-115	10	75	87
Debt/Equity Ratio	ELB	87.8	11.2	9.6

Competition

	Market Cap $Mil	12 Mo Trailing Sales $Mil	Price/Cash Flow	Return On Assets%	Debt/ Equity	Total Return% 1 Yr	3 Yr
UST	9,364	1,840	16.0	38.2	9.6	49.5	23.8
Reynolds American	19,353	8,488	13.3	7.5	0.6	43.9	38.3
E&J Gallo Winery							

Price Volatility

Monthly Price High/Low — Relative Strength to S&P 500

Annual $Price High Low	36.00 23.38	41.35 25.30	37.79 26.73	48.97 34.00	56.90 37.59	59.49 37.96
	2001	2002	2003	2004	2005	2006
Annual Total Return %	32.2	1.0	13.3	42.2	-10.8	49.5
Fiscal Year-End: December	2001	2002	2003	2004	2005	TTM
Revenue $Mil	1,619	1,674	1,732	1,838	1,852	1,840
Net Income $Mil	492	-271	319	531	534	512
Earnings Per Share $	2.97	-1.61	1.90	3.19	3.23	3.15
Shares Outstanding Mil	164	169	167	165	164	161
Return on Equity %	84.6	NMF	NMF	EUB	EUB	EUB
Net Margin %	30.4	-16.2	18.4	28.9	28.9	27.9
Asset Turnover	0.8	0.6	1.0	1.1	1.4	1.4
Financial Leverage	3.5	NMF	NMF	173.5	18.2	15.4

Valuation Ratios	Stock	Rel to Industry	Rel to S&P 500
Price/Earnings	18.6	1.0	0.9
Price/Book	107.2	5.2	26.1
Price/Sales	5.1	2.8	1.8
Price/Cash Flow	16.0	1.2	1.1

Major Fund Holders	% of Fund Assets
American Heritage	5.46
DWS Dreman Concentrated Value A	4.54
Dreman Contrarian Large Cap Value	4.37
DWS Dreman High Return Eq A	3.45

Thesis By Greggory Warren, CFA, 12-13-06 Stock Price as of Analysis: $56.50

With such recognizable brands as Skoal and Copenhagen, UST controls more than 90% of the domestic market for premium smokeless tobacco products. This dominant position allows the firm to generate industry-leading operating margins and returns on invested capital. The rapid growth of the discount segment, however, has let competitors encroach on UST's dominance, with the company struggling to hold on to market share outside the premium segment. As major cigarette manufacturers Reynolds American and Philip Morris USA (a subsidiary of Altria) enter the category, we believe the future will be rocky for UST.

Until the mid-1990s, the moist smokeless tobacco market in the United States was dominated by a small number of premium brands, the majority of which were produced by UST. With discount brands making up barely one tenth of the category, two of UST's closest competitors, Conwood (recently acquired by Reynolds American) and Swedish Match, introduced "price/value" brands into the market. UST responded by getting more aggressive with its peers in the marketplace, taking actions that ultimately led to the filing of antitrust lawsuits by both of its competitors. The intense scrutiny of UST following the suits, as well as the $1.3 billion cash payment the company had to make to Conwood in 2003, allowed the discount portion of the market to grow from a 12% share in 1998 to more than 40% in 2006.

With the company's premium smokeless products priced nearly twice as much as the average discount brand, it is not difficult to see why the discount segment grew so rapidly. Even though UST has done a good job of stimulating category growth through product innovation and one-on-one marketing events, the firm continues to lose premium customer purchases to the price/value brands. UST's move to lower the average retail price of its products, through promotions targeted at markets in which the company has been losing the greatest amount of share, has also failed to reverse this product mix deterioration.

With Reynolds American acquiring Conwood, which has emerged as the dominant name in the discount segment, and Philip Morris USA test-marketing its own smokeless tobacco product, we believe the road ahead has become all that more difficult for UST. With all of these factors working against the firm, it seems unlikely that UST will be able to maintain its incredibly high profitability and returns on capital over the long term.

Data as of 12-29-06

UTi Worldwide UTIW

	Rating	Fair Value	Last Close	Consider Buy	Consider Sell	Yield %
	★★★★	$38.00	$29.90	$29.30	$47.60	0.20

Company Profile

UTi is a global third-party logistics firm offering a complete suite of supply-chain management services, including freight forwarding, customs brokerage, order management, contract logistics, road distribution, and other solutions. As of June 2006, it had freight forwarding offices in 301 cities in 61 countries and managed 137 logistics centers to support its contract logistics business. It also has offices in 103 cities in 64 countries operated by exclusive agents.

Management
Stewardship Grade [C]

We really can't argue with the exceptional shareholder returns that management has delivered since the company went public in 2000, but we do have some corporate-governance concerns. CEO Roger MacFarlane has 34 years of experience in the industry and has been in the top spot since 2000. Before that, he was CEO of the Americas region within UTi for five years. We like his long-term focus and extensive experience, and we think his lieutenants are also a talented and experienced group. However, we think an otherwise high-quality organization should have better corporate-governance standards. Specifically, UTi's charter contains many antitakeover provisions and squelches shareholders' rights by putting only one third of the board up for election each year (we prefer annual re-election of the full board). Moreover, although most of UTi's shareholders are in the United States, the company's incorporation in the British Virgin Islands and many of its officers' residence in foreign countries make it difficult for shareholders to protect their rights versus the company and its managers. We also frown on certain provisions in the firm's long-term incentive plan, including ambiguous hurdle rates, unspecified vesting provisions, and the ability to reprice options.

19443 Laurel Park Road Suite 107 www.go2uti.com
Rancho Dominguez, CA 90220

Growth [A-]	2003	2004	2005	2006
Revenue %	31.5	28.4	50.4	23.3
Earnings/Share %	48.0	-57.4	50.0	26.8
Book Value/Share %	74.5	-66.8	22.2	19.7
Dividends/Share %	0.0	26.8	20.8	30.5

Profitability [NA]	2004	2005	2006	TTM
Return on Assets %	6.4	6.5	7.0	5.9
Oper Cash Flow $Mil	66	71	131	128
- Cap Spending $Mil	19	21	18	21
= Free Cash Flow $Mil	47	51	113	108

Financial Health [NA]	2004	2005	2006	07-31-06
Long-term Debt $Mil	7	15	30	211
Total Equity $Mil	386	474	587	611
Debt/Equity Ratio	0.0	0.0	0.1	0.3

Industry	Business Risk	Moat Size	Investment Style	Sector
Transportation	Average	Narrow		Business Services

Competition

	Market Cap $Mil	12 Mo Trailing Sales $Mil	Price/Cash Flow	Return On Assets%	Debt/Equity	Total Return% 1 Yr	3 Yr
UTi Worldwide	2,885	3,338	22.5	5.9	0.3	-3.2	32.6
United Parcel Service B	80,494	46,873	15.1	11.4	0.2	1.8	2.4
FedEx	33,307	33,132	9.4	8.1	0.2	5.4	17.4

Price Volatility

Annual $Price High/Low	6.71/3.72	8.82/5.23	12.94/7.33	24.33/12.55	33.57/20.91	36.32/21.35
	2001	2002	2003	2004	2005	2006
Annual Total Return %	-2.3	34.6	44.5	80.4	36.8	-3.2

Fiscal Year-End: January	2002	2003	2004	2005	2006	TTM
Revenue $Mil	890	1,170	1,503	2,260	2,786	3,338
Net Income $Mil	19	29	45	68	88	93
Earnings Per Share $	0.75	1.11	0.47	0.71	0.90	0.94
Shares Outstanding Mil	25	26	91	93	94	96
Return on Equity %	10.7	9.0	11.6	14.2	15.1	15.2
Net Margin %	2.2	2.5	3.0	3.0	3.2	2.8
Asset Turnover	2.2	1.9	2.1	2.2	2.2	2.1
Financial Leverage	2.3	1.9	1.8	2.2	2.1	2.6

Valuation Ratios	Stock	Rel to Industry	Rel to S&P 500
Price/Earnings	31.7	1.5	1.5
Price/Book	4.7	1.1	1.1
Price/Sales	0.9	0.6	0.3
Price/Cash Flow	22.5	1.6	1.5

Major Fund Holders	% of Fund Assets
Roxbury Mid Cap Instl	2.93
TCW Growth Insights N	2.55
JPMorgan Dynamic Small Cap A	2.42
DF Dent Premier Growth	2.40

Thesis By Peter Smith, 12-04-06 Stock Price as of Analysis: $29.27

UTi Worldwide's profitable non-asset-based business model, experienced management team, and growing suite of logistics services should make the firm a valuable partner to global shippers for years to come.

UTi is a third-party logistics company, which means it assists shippers with managing their supply chains. It adds value not just by purchasing cargo capacity in bulk and reselling that capacity to customers that can't get the bulk discount on their own, but also by presenting its customers with ideas on how they can make their supply chains more efficient and less costly. UTi owns no assets pertaining to the movement of freight, freeing up cash for other purposes.

When it went public in 2000, UTi was primarily a freight forwarder. Management soon came to the conclusion, however, that going head-to-head with the likes of Expeditors International, a larger and much more profitable freight forwarder, was not the best path to long-term value creation. Instead, it decided to expand the firm's services so that it could offer a complete outsourced solution to shippers (something Expeditors doesn't do). It is not the only firm to try this approach: Exel (recently purchased by Deutsche Post) has a similar model but has yet to integrate all of the moving parts into a total solutions package.

To build this model, UTi opted for the acquisition route. Management's rationale was that it would take too long for the firm to build the necessary expertise and knowledge, so it would rather acquire smaller, established players with experienced management teams and proven skill sets. Though we're usually skeptical of acquisitive growth strategies, this approach has turned out quite well so far, mostly owing to UTi's strict discipline in targeting solid operators and not overpaying for them.

We see two challenges: First, the firm needs to convince customers both old and new of the value inherent in a total outsourcing approach. We suspect shippers may balk at first to such heavy reliance on one partner, but they could ease up quickly if the cost savings are sufficiently convincing. Second, UTi needs to integrate all the various technology platforms. Though its technology is currently considered topnotch, further integration will be necessary to truly provide the efficiency gains of a total outsourcing approach.

Though this approach is not without risk, and the road may be bumpy at times, we expect UTi's above-market returns to continue for the foreseeable future.

Data as of 12-29-06

Valassis Communications VCI

Rating	Fair Value	Last Close	Consider Buy	Consider Sell	Yield %
★★★	$14.00	$14.50	$10.80	$17.50	0.00

Company Profile

Valassis' business comprises four main product lines. In addition to FSI, the company also does run-of-press advertising, which involves brokering ad space on behalf of newspapers. Its cluster target segment includes product samples packaged with newspapers or delivered separately to the home. The 1 to 1 segment includes direct-mail and direct-marketing operations. Valassis' overall customer list includes 91 of Advertising Age's 100 Leading National Advertisers.

Management   Stewardship Grade [B]

Valassis has adequate corporate-governance policies, but a few areas could be improved, in our opinion. Alan Schultz has been CEO and chairman of the board since 1998. We'd prefer to see these roles split. In 2005, Schultz received total cash compensation of $1.6 million and restricted stock worth $779,000. We believe the company is reasonable with its option grants, which represented around 2% of outstanding shares in each of the past three years. We're not fans of the poison pill that the company has in place, which we believe can hurt shareholder value by making it more difficult for the firm to be acquired.

Industry	Business Risk	Moat Size	Investment Style	Sector
Publishing	Average	Narrow	Small Value	Media

Competition	Market Cap $Mil	12 Mo Trailing Sales $Mil	Price/Cash Flow	Return On Assets%	Debt/ Equity	Total Return% 1 Yr	3 Yr
Valassis Communications	693	1,066	8.1	8.4	1.7	-50.1	-21.2
News Corporation	70,411	25,559	21.6	6.2	0.4	34.8	7.2

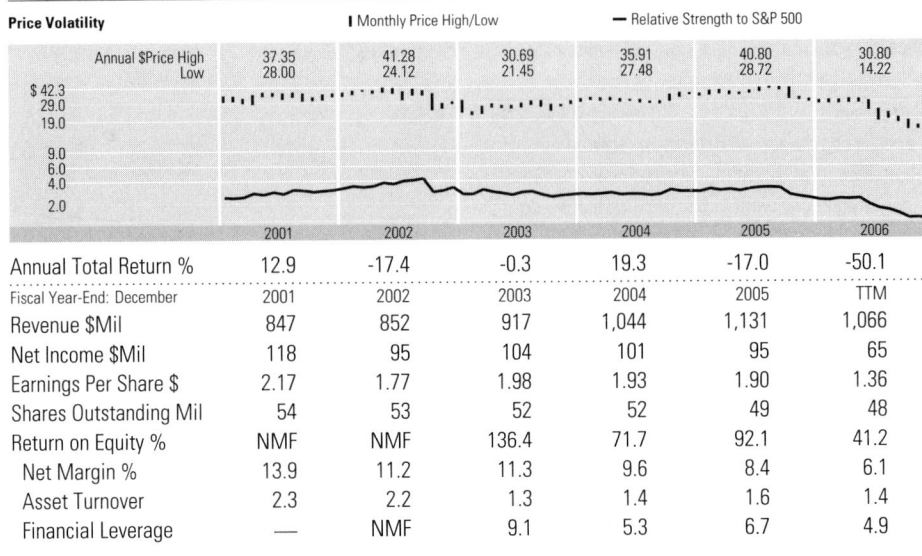

	2001	2002	2003	2004	2005	TTM
Annual Total Return %	12.9	-17.4	-0.3	19.3	-17.0	-50.1
Fiscal Year-End: December	2001	2002	2003	2004	2005	TTM
Revenue $Mil	847	852	917	1,044	1,131	1,066
Net Income $Mil	118	95	104	101	95	65
Earnings Per Share $	2.17	1.77	1.98	1.93	1.90	1.36
Shares Outstanding Mil	54	53	52	52	49	48
Return on Equity %	NMF	NMF	136.4	71.7	92.1	41.2
Net Margin %	13.9	11.2	11.3	9.6	8.4	6.1
Asset Turnover	2.3	2.2	1.3	1.4	1.6	1.4
Financial Leverage	—	NMF	9.1	5.3	6.7	4.9

Valuation Ratios	Stock	Rel to Industry	Rel to S&P 500	Major Fund Holders	% of Fund Assets
Price/Earnings	10.7	0.4	0.5	Hotchkis and Wiley Small Cap Value I	2.15
Price/Book	4.4	0.7	1.1	Fidelity Small Cap Retirement	1.86
Price/Sales	0.7	0.3	0.2	Hotchkis and Wiley All Cap Value A	1.77
Price/Cash Flow	8.1	0.6	0.6	BlackRock Mid Cap Val Opportunties A	1.46

Thesis By Michael Corty, CFA, 11-02-06 Stock Price as of Analysis: $14.86

High barriers to entry have enabled Valassis Communications to carve out an economic moat, in our opinion. Its freestanding inserts (FSIs) are promotional coupon books that are distributed in the Sunday newspaper to about 60 million American households. Valassis serves as an intermediary between advertisers and its national database of more than 500 newspapers.

Both newspapers and advertisers benefit from their relationship with Valassis. The newspapers receive fees from Valassis, while also garnering higher readership because of the value of coupons included in the newspaper. Advertisers willingly pay for promotional space in the coupon books because Valassis offers a wide distribution network that allows its clients to pinpoint the local markets to which its message is delivered.

Thanks to high barriers to entry, Valassis and News America Marketing, a subsidiary of News Corporation, share a duopoly in the FSI business. Attempts by new entrants have been unsuccessful because the two established players guarantee newspapers a certain amount of dollars in coupons, something an upstart cannot do. The only way to obtain the wide distribution required by advertisers is to pay up for it, and newspapers charge the same amount for the right to insert a 6-page book as they would a 30-page book. The beauty of the business model is that as the average book size increases, so do incremental profits.

However, current competitive dynamics lead us to believe that Valassis' economic moat is only narrow. Over the past several years, News America has aggressively reduced pricing in order to take market share from Valassis. As a result, between 2002 and 2005, Valassis' operating margins fell from 19% to 13.5%. Also, consumer packaged goods manufacturers have options other than FSI for reaching consumers, including Catalina Marketing's point-of-sale coupons, which have higher redemption rates than FSI coupons. On an even broader scale, newer media like the Internet are attracting ad dollars for branding and promotions.

Additionally, we have some concerns about Valassis' pending acquisition of Advo, a direct marketing company. Valassis paid a hefty premium (about 50% higher than the stock price the day before the offer) for a business that generates much lower operating margins. We think Valassis' shareholders would be better off having capital returned to them through a dividend or shares repurchases as opposed to this acquisition.

19975 Victor Parkway
Livonia, MI 48152
www.valassis.com

Growth [C-]	2002	2003	2004	2005
Revenue %	0.6	7.5	13.9	8.3
Earnings/Share %	-18.4	11.9	-2.5	-1.6
Book Value/Share %	NMF	NMF	85.4	-23.4
Dividends/Share %	NMF	NMF	NMF	NMF

Profitability [A]	2003	2004	2005	TTM
Return on Assets %	15.0	13.7	13.7	8.4
Oper Cash Flow $Mil	123	77	116	86
- Cap Spending $Mil	18	19	25	11
= Free Cash Flow $Mil	104	58	92	75

Financial Health [A-]	2003	2004	2005	09-30-06
Long-term Debt $Mil	260	274	260	260
Total Equity $Mil	76	141	104	157
Debt/Equity Ratio	3.4	1.9	2.5	1.7

Data as of 12-29-06

Valero GP Holdings VEH

	Rating	Fair Value	Last Close	Consider Buy	Consider Sell	Yield %
	★★★	$26.00	$24.82	$20.00	$32.60	1.04

Company Profile

San Antonio-based Valero GP Holdings owns the general partner interest, incentive distribution rights, and 21.4% of the limited partner units of Valero LP, a master limited partnership that was spun out of refiner Valero Energy in 2001. Valero LP owns most of Valero Energy's pipelines, terminals, and storage facilities. Valero Energy is selling its 59% stake in Valero GP Holdings, though both companies share the same chairman.

Management   Stewardship Grade [NA]

Curtis Anastasio, an able executive retained when Valero purchased Ultramar Diamond Shamrock, serves as president and CEO of Valero GP Holdings. The company's chairman is Bill Greehey, who is also the chairman and former CEO of Valero Energy. Valero Energy has stated its intention to sell its 59% stake in the holding company, and in December began a secondary offering, that, if successful, will leave Valero Energy with a 6% stake, and 0% if underwriters exercise their right to sell additional units. Separately, Greehey will purchase 4.7 million units and will have a 12% stake in Valero GP Holdings. Despite the secondary offering and the departure of two Valero Energy executives from the board of Valero LP, in our view Valero Energy is still very much in control of Valero GP Holdings and will remain so as long as its leadership comes directly from the parent company, though we certainly approve of Valero Energy's decision to reduce its ownership stake, and we appreciate that Greehey will own 12% of the company--that should go a long way toward ensuring management has common unitholders' interests at heart.

1 Valero Way
San Antonio, TX 78249

Growth [NA]	2002	2003	2004	2005
Revenue %	19.9	-55.9	-32.5	6.6
Earnings/Share %	NMF	NMF	NMF	NMF
Book Value/Share %	—	—	—	—
Dividends/Share %	NMF	NMF	NMF	NMF

Profitability [B-]	2003	2004	2005	TTM
Return on Assets %	4.1	4.7	4.9	4.1
Oper Cash Flow $Mil	23	22	17	17
- Cap Spending $Mil	2	0	0	0
= Free Cash Flow $Mil	21	22	17	17

Financial Health [A]	2003	2004	2005	09-30-06
Long-term Debt $Mil	—	271	266	1
Total Equity $Mil	106	114	142	560
Debt/Equity Ratio	—	2.4	1.9	0.0

Industry	Business Risk	Moat Size	Investment Style	Sector
Pipelines	Average	Narrow	Small Core	Energy

Competition

	Market Cap $Mil	12 Mo Trailing Sales $Mil	Price/Cash Flow	Return On Assets %	Debt/ Equity	Total Return% 1 Yr	3 Yr
Valero GP Holdings	1,055	NMF	63.0	4.1	0.0	—	—
TransCanada	17,029	5,061	10.8	4.8	1.5	15.1	21.4
Williams Companies	15,576	12,719	9.3	0.9	1.2	14.4	40.0

Price Volatility

Fiscal Year-End: December	2001	2002	2003	2004	2005	TTM
Revenue $Mil	99	118	52	35	38	NMF
Net Income $Mil	36	27	16	18	20	24
Earnings Per Share $	—	—	—	—	—	—
Shares Outstanding Mil	—	—	—	—	—	43
Return on Equity %	11.8	11.0	15.3	16.2	14.3	4.3
Net Margin %	36.9	22.7	31.1	52.2	53.9	NMF
Asset Turnover	0.1	0.2	0.1	0.1	0.1	0.1
Financial Leverage	2.4	3.1	3.7	3.4	2.9	1.0

Valuation Ratios	Stock	Rel to Industry	Rel to S&P 500
Price/Earnings	—	—	—
Price/Book	1.9	0.8	0.5
Price/Sales	28.0	12.7	9.7
Price/Cash Flow	63.0	6.4	4.3

Major Fund Holders   % of Fund Assets

Thesis By Jason Stevens, Stock Price as of Analysis:

The appeal of Valero GP Holdings stems from two factors--the favorable underlying economics of Valero LP VLI and the upside inherent in publicly traded general partnerships. In our view, partnership units offer investors an opportunity to enjoy the stable cash distributions associated with master limited partnerships (MLPs) while retaining the potential for faster growth, but they come with increased risk when compared with the core business.

Valero GP Holdings owns the general partner and incentive distribution rights of Valero LP, as well as 21.4% of its limited partner units. It has no operations or assets outside of this ownership stake and is entirely dependent on the underlying business. That's not necessarily a bad thing, in our view. Valero LP has an entrenched position in the crude oil and refined products pipeline and storage business, and warrants a narrow moat and a below-average risk rating due to its returns on invested capital, cash flow strength, and asset portfolio.

Because of its ownership stakes, Valero GP Holdings receives nearly 30% of the cash paid out by Valero LP, based on current distribution levels, and as distributions increase, the general partner receives an increasing share of the total payout. The reason for this is the incentive distribution rights the general partner holds, which entitle Valero GP Holdings to receive an increasing share of the total cash payout as the level of quarterly distributions to unitholders increases. As Valero LP raises distributions, its general partner enjoys an increasing share of the total pie, and it also gets the cash received from its ownership of 21% of the LP units.

There are three downsides to this. First, Valero LP's partnership agreement caps the incentive distribution rate at 25%, compared with 50% for most MLPs, which limits upside for the general partner. Second, Valero LP is under no obligation to pay more than a minimum quarterly distribution, and in hard times, this could seriously impact the general partner's cash flow and ability to make its own distributions. And third, the partnership agreement gives limited partner unitholders the right to remove the general partner by a simple majority vote, excluding any units controlled by the general partner. While this is exceedingly unlikely, in such an event, Valero GP Holdings would become nothing more than an investment company holding common units of an MLP. These factors give us pause, and lead us to assign an "average," instead of "below-average," risk rating to Valero GP Holdings.

Varian Medical Systems VAR

Data as of 12-29-06

	Rating	Fair Value	Last Close	Consider Buy	Consider Sell	Yield %
	★★★	$47.00	$47.57	$36.20	$58.90	0.00

Company Profile
Varian Medical Systems is a global provider of radiotherapy systems used in cancer treatment. Its oncology products (82% of sales) include linear accelerators, treatment simulation products, and treatment planning software. Varian also manufactures X-ray and flat-panel imaging technology (13% of sales) for medical and industrial applications. Its California-based Ginzton research center focuses on developing next-generation medical technologies.

Management
Stewardship Grade [B]

Timothy Guertin replaced Richard M. Levy as CEO in February 2006. Guertin joined the firm in 1976; he had run the company's flagship oncology division since 1990 and served as president and COO for a year. Levy, who had led the firm since 1999, stayed on as chairman of the board, and we expect he will continue to play an active role in shaping Varian's strategy. Management and directors own a combined 4.8% of the company, with Levy owning 2.5%. We think compensation and governance are for the most part appropriate. Option compensation is moderate, and performance goals appear clearly linked to shareholder value creation. Our only major objection is Varian's twin takeover defense measures. The company has three classes of directors serving staggered terms. It also employs a change-in-control agreement that protects senior executives in the case of an unsolicited takeover.

3100 Hansen Way
Palo Alto, CA 94304-1030
www.varian.com

Growth [B]	2002	2003	2004	2005
Revenue %	19.3	18.6	11.9	15.6
Earnings/Share %	37.3	28.3	27.1	20.7
Book Value/Share %	18.4	8.5	9.0	23.0
Dividends/Share %	NMF	NMF	NMF	NMF

Profitability [A+]	2003	2004	2005	TTM
Return on Assets %	14.2	15.7	16.2	16.2
Oper Cash Flow $Mil	234	252	202	202
- Cap Spending $Mil	24	44	41	41
= Free Cash Flow $Mil	210	208	160	160

Financial Health [A]	2003	2004	2005	06-30-06
Long-term Debt $Mil	53	57	49	49
Total Equity $Mil	624	659	797	797
Debt/Equity Ratio	0.1	0.1	0.1	0.1

Industry	Business Risk	Moat Size	Investment Style	Sector
Medical Equip.	Average	Narrow	Mid Growth	Healthcare

Competition	Market Cap $Mil	12 Mo Trailing Sales $Mil	Price/Cash Flow	Return On Assets%	Debt/Equity	Total Return% 1 Yr	3 Yr
Varian Medical Systems	6,140	1,598	30.4	16.2	0.1	-5.5	10.9
Siemens AG ADR	87,817	107,241	14.4	3.2	0.5	17.3	8.8
Philips Electronics NV AD	45,147	38,062	17.3	8.9	0.2	22.8	9.8

Price Volatility
| Monthly Price High/Low — Relative Strength to S&P 500

	2001	2002	2003	2004	2005	2006
Annual $Price High	19.31	25.65	35.65	46.49	52.92	61.70
Low	13.50	15.80	23.70	29.63	31.65	41.10
Annual Total Return %	4.9	39.2	39.3	25.2	16.4	-5.5

Fiscal Year-End: September	2002	2003	2004	2005	2006	TTM
Revenue $Mil	873	1,042	1,236	1,383	1,598	1,598
Net Income $Mil	95	130	168	207	245	245
Earnings Per Share $	0.67	0.92	1.18	1.50	1.81	1.81
Shares Outstanding Mil	135	136	136	132	131	129
Return on Equity %	19.6	22.7	26.9	31.3	30.7	30.7
Net Margin %	10.8	12.5	13.6	14.9	15.3	15.3
Asset Turnover	0.9	1.0	1.0	1.0	1.1	1.1
Financial Leverage	1.9	1.9	1.9	2.0	1.9	1.9

Valuation Ratios	Stock	Rel to Industry	Rel to S&P 500
Price/Earnings	26.4	0.9	1.3
Price/Book	7.7	1.4	1.9
Price/Sales	3.8	0.8	1.3
Price/Cash Flow	30.4	1.3	2.1

Major Fund Holders	% of Fund Assets
AXA Enterprise Equity A	3.53
Janus Triton	3.44
Tamarack Mid Cap Growth I	3.38
Janus Adviser Small-Mid Growth C	3.38

Thesis By Mark E. Lanyon, CFA, 12-01-06 Stock Price as of Analysis: $49.71

Varian Medical Systems dominates the global market for radiotherapy, a medical technology niche focusing on radiation-based cancer therapies. We think this firm's outsize market share, customer relationships, and industry-leading technology will deliver a sustainable stream of economic profits.

Varian has 60% global market share in intensity-modulated radiation therapy (IMRT), a groundbreaking approach to cancer treatment developed in the 1990s. Before IMRT, radiation therapy was a labor-intensive process that also destroyed healthy tissue surrounding a tumor. IMRT systems allow for highly accurate dosing, drastically reducing harmful side effects. These systems also bundle Varian's imaging technology and software, allowing for diagnostic imaging, treatment planning, monitoring, and feedback. Varian's technology has automated cancer treatment.

As a majority of oncologists now rely on Varian's proprietary technology for the full spectrum of life-saving services, switching costs are very high. This competitive advantage is fortified by Varian's healthy research and development budget (nearly 3 times that of rivals like Elekta), complex government regulations governing radiation hardware, patent protection, and extensive relationships with leading cancer research centers. These conditions, which deter new market entrants and provide technological lead time, make for a narrow economic moat around Varian's core franchise.

Varian's North American market share is nearing saturation at 70%, but we see several trends that should sustain growth. The firm is moving to its next generation of treatment systems, image-guided radiation therapy (IGRT). The higher list price for IGRT-equipped systems ($3 million versus $1.9 million for IMRT) should provide a sustained boost to revenue. In addition, Varian's increasingly accurate radiation capabilities have attracted the attention of new medical fields. Neurosurgeons are now considering IMRT for certain treatments, opening the door to a $250 million market.

Regulatory concerns are the most obvious risk. A drastic decline in Medicare reimbursement rates related to radiotherapy treatment could hurt customer purchases. Also, the commodity nature of Varian's X-ray product business is a drag on the more profitable oncology group.

We believe, however, that Varian's competitive advantages and growth prospects outweigh these issues. We would gladly invest at the appropriate valuation.

Data as of 12-29-06

VCA Antech WOOF

	Rating	Fair Value	Last Close	Consider Buy	Consider Sell	Yield %
	★★★	$33.00	$32.19	$25.40	$41.30	0.00

Company Profile
Founded in 1986, VCA Antech is the largest operator of freestanding, full-service animal hospitals and veterinary diagnostic labs in the U.S. With about 375 pet hospitals and 1,200 vets, the firm handled 4.9 million patient visits in 2005. It traded publicly from 1991 to 2000. After the company ran up a huge debt load to fund a buying binge in the late 1990s, a private-investment group purchased and recapitalized the firm. VCA Antech came public again in 2001.

Management   Stewardship Grade [C]
We give VCA Antech middling marks for corporate stewardship. Robert Antin has been CEO, president, and chairman since he founded the company in 1986 with his brother, Arthur Antin, who remains COO. Both brothers were previously involved with AlternaCare, a chain of freestanding surgical centers they founded. The five-member board includes three outsiders and one member of Leonard Green & Partners, the lead firm that purchased VCA, which had been a public company, in 2000 and took it public again in 2001. The firm recently revised its stock-option policies, and we like that it aims to hold average option issuance at a reasonable 2% of shares outstanding. Further, CEO Antin's 3.3% equity stake is sizable enough to make us comfortable. However, his compensation remains a bit rich, in our opinion. We'd be willing to overlook that if it weren't for his employment contract, which is renewed annually for a five-year period. If Antin leaves the firm or dies, VCA is obligated to continue paying his salary for the remaining years left on his contract. Additionally, we frown on VCA's $1.1 million payment last year to Internet marketing firm Zoasis, which is owned by the Antin brothers. These types of related-party transactions leave a bad taste in our mouth.

12401 West Olympic Boulevard
Los Angeles, CA 90064-1022

Growth [B+]	2002	2003	2004	2005
Revenue %	10.5	13.3	23.8	24.6
Earnings/Share %	NMF	89.3	43.4	6.6
Book Value/Share %	NMF	133.2	40.8	32.5
Dividends/Share %	NMF	NMF	NMF	NMF

Profitability [B]	2003	2004	2005	TTM
Return on Assets %	7.8	8.6	7.6	11.0
Oper Cash Flow $Mil	76	86	115	115
- Cap Spending $Mil	15	24	29	30
= Free Cash Flow $Mil	61	62	86	84

Financial Health [B+]	2003	2004	2005	09-30-06
Long-term Debt $Mil	315	391	447	385
Total Equity $Mil	162	233	309	409
Debt/Equity Ratio	1.9	1.7	1.4	0.9

Industry	Business Risk	Moat Size	Investment Style	Sector
Medical Goods/Svcs.	Average	Narrow	Mid Growth	Healthcare

Competition	Market Cap $Mil	12 Mo Trailing Sales $Mil	Price/Cash Flow	Return On Assets %	Debt/Equity	Total Return % 1 Yr	3 Yr
VCA Antech	2,688	958	23.4	11.0	0.9	14.2	27.7
Idexx Laboratories	2,482	714	22.3	17.0	0.0	10.2	19.1

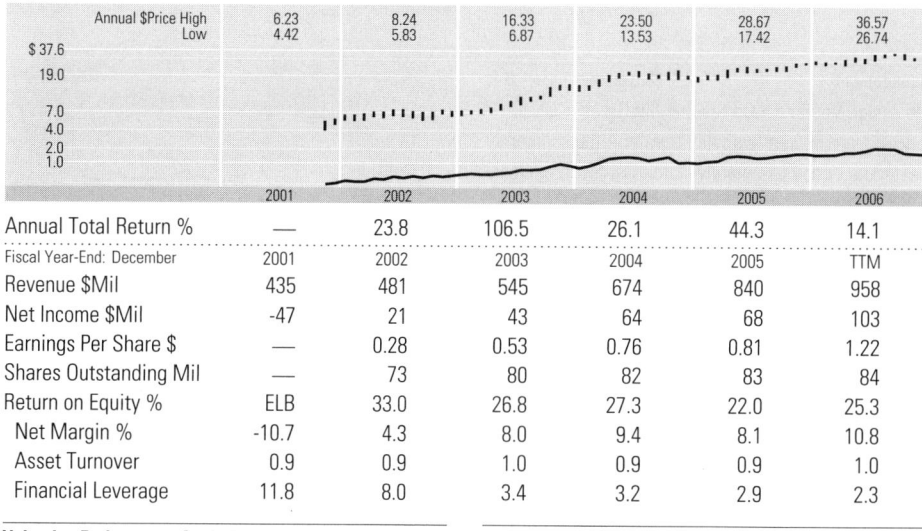

Price Volatility — Monthly Price High/Low — Relative Strength to S&P 500

| Annual $Price High/Low | 6.23/4.42 | 8.24/5.83 | 16.33/6.87 | 23.50/13.53 | 28.67/17.42 | 36.57/26.74 |

	2001	2002	2003	2004	2005	2006
Annual Total Return %	—	23.8	106.5	26.1	44.3	14.1
Fiscal Year-End: December	2001	2002	2003	2004	2005	TTM
Revenue $Mil	435	481	545	674	840	958
Net Income $Mil	-47	21	43	64	68	103
Earnings Per Share $	—	0.28	0.53	0.76	0.81	1.22
Shares Outstanding Mil	—	73	80	82	83	84
Return on Equity %	ELB	33.0	26.8	27.3	22.0	25.3
Net Margin %	-10.7	4.3	8.0	9.4	8.1	10.8
Asset Turnover	0.9	0.9	1.0	0.9	0.9	1.0
Financial Leverage	11.8	8.0	3.4	3.2	2.9	2.3

Valuation Ratios	Stock	Rel to Industry	Rel to S&P 500
Price/Earnings	26.4	1.2	1.3
Price/Book	6.6	2.2	1.6
Price/Sales	2.8	4.7	1.0
Price/Cash Flow	23.4	1.4	1.6

Major Fund Holders	% of Fund Assets
Capital Management Small Cap Instl	3.80
Tamarack Mid Cap Growth I	3.51
UBS U.S. Small Cap Growth Y	3.09
Ashport Small/Mid Cap C	3.03

Thesis By Debbie S. Wang, 12-08-06 Stock Price as of Analysis: $33.90

A "tail"-blazer in its field, VCA Antech makes pet health care a very attractive opportunity for human investors, in our view.

As the nation's largest operator of animal hospitals and veterinary diagnostic labs, VCA Antech is poised to take advantage of the $38 billion market for pet products and services. Spending on pets has seen 8% compound annual growth since the mid-1990s as pets have come to be thought of as valued family members. Animal health care (vet services and medicines) account for 47% of the total spent on pets each year. Like health-care procedures for humans, pet health services and treatment options have expanded substantially in recent years as the result of research and technological advances. Although vets in private practice may find it difficult to afford all the new high-tech equipment, VCA's deeper pockets make it easy to install endoscopes and X-ray and ultrasound machines in its approximately 375 hospitals. This translates into more procedures and higher revenue per patient.

The real gem at VCA is the diagnostic lab business, one of the fastest-growing segments of animal health. The dominant player in this arena, VCA operates a nationwide network of 27 labs that serve more than 15,000 of the 17,000 animal hospitals in the United States. The company has lab services down to a science. An impressively large transportation fleet provides twice-a-day pickup service in metropolitan areas, and most hospitals can receive same-day results. Further, the labs employ about 90 specialists in pathology, endocrinology, and hematology who consult with clinicians on diagnosis and treatment options, providing a level of high-touch customer service. Also, we find the hefty lab operating margins--north of 40%--extremely appealing; they're much better than Quest Diagnostics' human diagnostic operating margins of 17%.

Finally, we like the cash-oriented nature of the pet health business. Unlike human health care, where payment and pricing pressure often manifests itself in the form of third-party payers such as insurance companies, pet health services operate on a cash-and-carry basis. For example, pet owners pay by cash or credit card for more than 95% of VCA's procedures at the time of service. Considering that pet health-care costs are still a relatively small proportion of a household's income, we expect pet owners can shoulder higher pet-care costs in the intermediate term. This leaves plenty of room for VCA Antech to grow.

Ventana Medical Systems VMSI

Data as of 12-29-06

	Rating	Fair Value	Last Close	Consider Buy	Consider Sell	Yield %
	★★★	$47.00	$43.03	$36.20	$58.90	0.00

Company Profile
Ventana Medical designs and manufactures advanced staining instruments and reagents used to detect, diagnose, and monitor infectious diseases. The company distributes its products to histology and cytology laboratories worldwide. Ventana's recently introduced Symphony system has also enabled the firm to enter the primary staining business.

Industry	Business Risk	Moat Size	Investment Style	Sector
Medical Equip.	Average	Narrow	Small Growth	Healthcare

Competition

	Market Cap $Mil	12 Mo Trailing Sales $Mil	Price/Cash Flow	Return On Assets%	Debt/Equity	Total Return% 1 Yr	3 Yr
Ventana Medical Systems	1,593	226	36.5	12.8	0.0	1.6	29.1
Danaher	22,297	9,200	16.1	8.7	0.4	30.0	17.0
Leica Microsystems							

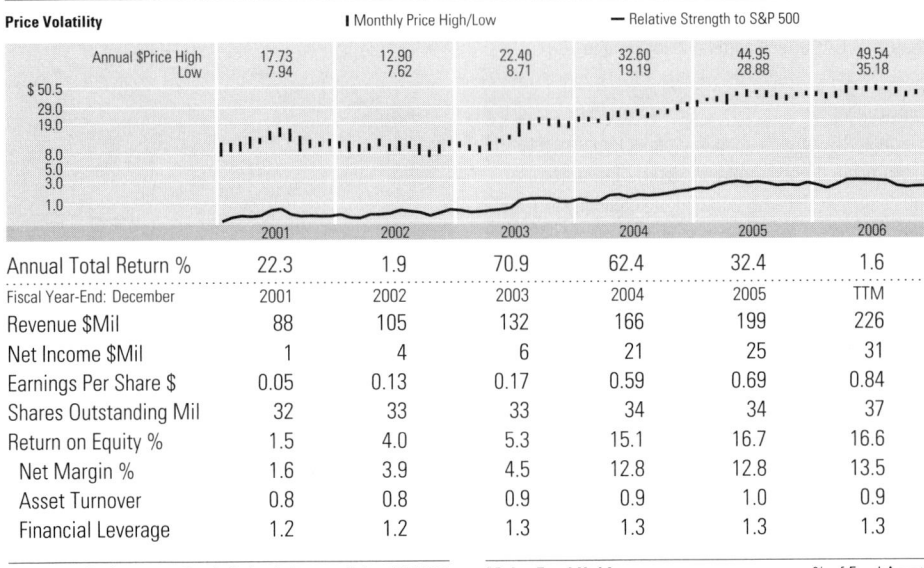

	2001	2002	2003	2004	2005	2006
Annual $Price High	17.73	12.90	22.40	32.60	44.95	49.54
Low	7.94	7.62	8.71	19.19	28.88	35.18
Annual Total Return %	22.3	1.9	70.9	62.4	32.4	1.6

Fiscal Year-End: December	2001	2002	2003	2004	2005	TTM
Revenue $Mil	88	105	132	166	199	226
Net Income $Mil	1	4	6	21	25	31
Earnings Per Share $	0.05	0.13	0.17	0.59	0.69	0.84
Shares Outstanding Mil	32	33	33	34	34	37
Return on Equity %	1.5	4.0	5.3	15.1	16.7	16.6
Net Margin %	1.6	3.9	4.5	12.8	12.8	13.5
Asset Turnover	0.8	0.8	0.9	0.9	1.0	0.9
Financial Leverage	1.2	1.2	1.3	1.3	1.3	1.3

Management Stewardship Grade [B]
We assign Ventana a B Stewardship Grade. Our concerns are limited; we would prefer if the company elected its directors annually instead of for three-year terms, abandoned its antitakeover poison-pill provision, and issued restricted stock in lieu of options. We think the executive compensation packages are rather modest and we approve of the operating metrics, such as capital-allocation efficiency, used in determining annual bonuses. However, the company's executives have profited immensely from the generous option-granting policy; in 2006 alone, insiders took home roughly $12 million in profits from exercising stock options. Despite these sales, the company's executives still hold more than 15% of the company in the form of stock and options, which tells us they are willing to have some skin in the game. We approve of the company's decision to split the chairman and CEO duties.

Valuation Ratios	Stock	Rel to Industry	Rel to S&P 500
Price/Earnings	51.2	1.8	2.5
Price/Book	8.6	1.6	2.1
Price/Sales	7.0	1.5	2.4
Price/Cash Flow	36.5	1.5	2.5

Major Fund Holders	% of Fund Assets
Bender Growth C	3.56
SunAmerica Biotech/Health A	2.46
Fidelity Aggressive Growth	2.32
Fidelity Advisor Aggressive Gr A	2.32

1910 Innovative Park Dr.
Tucson, AZ 85737
www.ventanamed.com

Growth [B]	2002	2003	2004	2005
Revenue %	20.1	25.6	25.5	19.9
Earnings/Share %	177.8	36.0	247.1	16.9
Book Value/Share %	6.6	2.1	22.3	5.4
Dividends/Share %	NMF	NMF	NMF	NMF

Profitability [A-]	2003	2004	2005	TTM
Return on Assets %	4.2	11.8	13.0	12.8
Oper Cash Flow $Mil	24	34	42	44
- Cap Spending $Mil	6	13	18	24
= Free Cash Flow $Mil	17	21	24	20

Financial Health [A]	2003	2004	2005	09-30-06
Long-term Debt $Mil	2	2	2	2
Total Equity $Mil	112	141	152	185
Debt/Equity Ratio	0.0	0.0	0.0	0.0

Thesis By Alex Morozov, CFA, 12-06-06 Stock Price as of Analysis: $41.73

Ventana Medical Systems' dominant position in the advanced cancer screening market bodes well for its attempt to penetrate the larger and potentially more lucrative initial testing business. However, the firm's success in this field may be hindered by a tougher competitive environment and the availability of cheaper alternatives.

Ventana's instruments are used in pathology labs to detect and monitor cancer. The screening process consists of primary staining, where tissue samples are stained to detect abnormalities, and advanced staining, performed when additional testing is required. Ventana controls nearly 60% of the advanced staining market because it introduced the first fully automated platform. The company has installed nearly 2,000 systems since its initial release three years ago, expanding the total unit base to 6,000. We think there is room to grow, as more than half of laboratories worldwide still use semiautomated instruments.

A large unit base provides Ventana with a predictable and highly profitable stream of recurring revenue. Each platform uses twice as many reagents as its semiautomated counterpart and, at a price per kit 6-8 times higher than the competition, generates profit margins on reagents in excess of 80%. Such lucrative returns are likely to attract new entrants to this field, but we think Ventana is well insulated from the competitive pressures. Staining systems are expensive to replace and can't be used in conjunction with competitors' reagents. Frequent system upgrades provide Ventana with an additional defense against its rivals.

Now Ventana is turning its eye toward primary stains. In early 2006, the firm launched the first fully automated primary staining platform and is banking on its expertise and name recognition in advanced stains to support its rollout. However, we are not certain the firm can replicate its success in advanced testing in the primary stain segment. Primary screens are more routine and less expensive than advanced stains, which may preclude some laboratories from purchasing the $125,000 systems and paying on average 8 times the cost of a manually stained slide. The market for primary stains is also more competitive and dominated by privately held Leica, with a 53% share.

Despite uncertainties surrounding the firm's foray into primary staining, we are optimistic about its prospects. We expect Ventana will maintain its grip on the advanced stain market and could capture a sizable share of the primary stain segment by 2010.

Data as of 12-29-06

Verizon Communications VZ

Rating	Fair Value	Last Close	Consider Buy	Consider Sell	Yield %
★★★	$39.00	$37.24	$30.10	$48.90	4.35

Company Profile
Verizon is the incumbent local phone company serving about 30% of the U.S. It also provides Internet access and other data services and television services. Following the acquisition of MCI, the firm provides telecom services to businesses around the globe. Verizon Wireless, the firm's 55%-owned partnership with Vodafone, serves 57 million customers nationwide. Verizon agreed to sell its Latin American assets and spun of its directories unit, Idearc, during 2006.

Management   Stewardship Grade [C]
We think Verizon's stewardship is average on the whole and relative to peers. Our biggest concern is executive compensation, which we think is excessive. CEO Ivan Seidenberg's total compensation routinely tops $10 million per year--including salary, bonuses, and restricted-stock awards--and hit nearly $20 million during 2005. Bonuses have shown little variation over the past few years. We think the language surrounding Verizon's bonus plan is indicative of the firm's compensation practices: The CEO's "target" bonus is 125% of his base salary, but if the firm hits its performance objectives, he gets 150% of this amount. In other words, the real target payout is closer to 200% of base salary. We do like that much of the CEO's 2005 compensation was in the form of performance stock units, which vest based on the performance of Verizon shares and the achievement of certain objectives. Seidenberg, who has been at the head of a regional Bell since the mid-1990s, took the chairman title at the end of 2003 from former co-CEO Charles Lee. We would prefer to see the CEO and chairman roles split. Most of the members of the board have served Verizon or one of its predecessors for a decade or more, a plus for experience but also a sign of entrenchment. We like the level of information the firm provides about the business in its quarterly earnings releases.

1095 Avenue of the Americas
New York, NY 10036   www.verizon.com

Growth [B]	2002	2003	2004	2005
Revenue %	0.8	0.6	5.7	5.4
Earnings/Share %	964.3	-24.8	149.1	-5.0
Book Value/Share %	1.7	2.2	9.9	6.2
Dividends/Share %	0.0	0.0	0.0	3.9

Profitability [B+]	2003	2004	2005	TTM
Return on Assets %	1.9	4.7	4.4	3.7
Oper Cash Flow $Mil	22,467	21,820	22,012	24,988
- Cap Spending $Mil	11,874	13,259	15,324	16,279
= Free Cash Flow $Mil	10,593	8,561	6,688	8,709

Financial Health [B]	2003	2004	2005	09-30-06
Long-term Debt $Mil	39,413	35,674	31,869	30,154
Total Equity $Mil	33,466	37,560	39,680	46,279
Debt/Equity Ratio	1.2	1.0	0.8	0.7

Industry	Business Risk	Moat Size	Investment Style	Sector
Telecom Svcs.	Average	Narrow	Large Value	Telecommunication

Competition

	Market Cap $Mil	12 Mo Trailing Sales $Mil	Price/Cash Flow	Return On Assets%	Debt/ Equity	Total Return% 1 Yr	3 Yr
Verizon Communications	108,723	88,881	4.4	3.7	0.7	34.9	8.0
AT&T	137,384	60,171	9.0	4.9	0.5	51.6	16.3
Comcast A	88,095	24,531	14.4	2.1	0.6	63.3	8.7

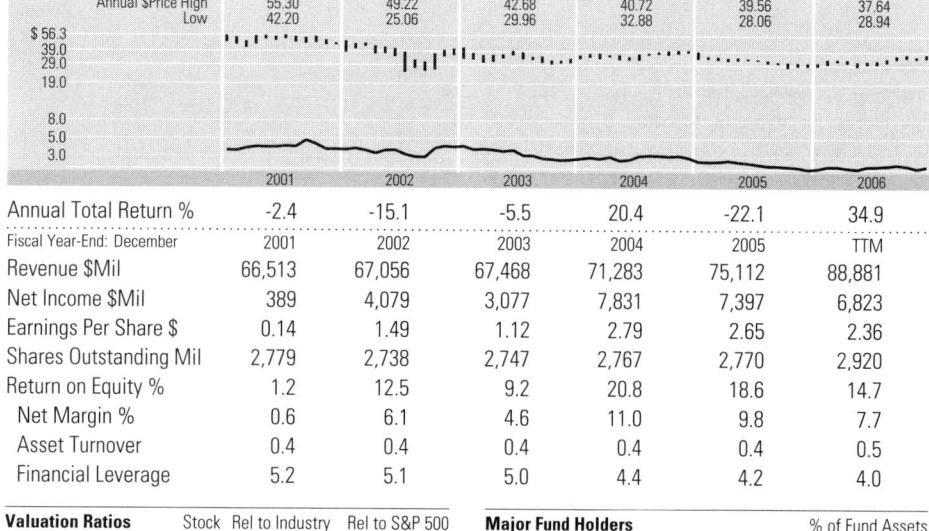

Price Volatility — Monthly Price High/Low — Relative Strength to S&P 500

	2001	2002	2003	2004	2005	2006
Annual $Price High	55.30	49.22	42.68	40.72	39.56	37.64
Low	42.20	25.06	29.96	32.88	28.06	28.94
Annual Total Return %	-2.4	-15.1	-5.5	20.4	-22.1	34.9

Fiscal Year-End: December	2001	2002	2003	2004	2005	TTM
Revenue $Mil	66,513	67,056	67,468	71,283	75,112	88,881
Net Income $Mil	389	4,079	3,077	7,831	7,397	6,823
Earnings Per Share $	0.14	1.49	1.12	2.79	2.65	2.36
Shares Outstanding Mil	2,779	2,738	2,747	2,767	2,770	2,920
Return on Equity %	1.2	12.5	9.2	20.8	18.6	14.7
Net Margin %	0.6	6.1	4.6	11.0	9.8	7.7
Asset Turnover	0.4	0.4	0.4	0.4	0.4	0.5
Financial Leverage	5.2	5.1	5.0	4.4	4.2	4.0

Valuation Ratios	Stock	Rel to Industry	Rel to S&P 500
Price/Earnings	16.1	0.9	0.8
Price/Book	2.3	0.5	0.6
Price/Sales	1.2	0.5	0.4
Price/Cash Flow	4.4	0.5	0.3

Major Fund Holders	% of Fund Assets
ProFunds Telecom UltraSector Inv	18.68
Fidelity Advisor Utilities T	13.44
Fidelity Select Telecommunications	11.68
Fidelity Select Utilities Growth	9.90

Thesis By Michael Hodel, CFA, 12-06-06 Stock Price as of Analysis: $34.95

With the spin-off of the directory publishing business complete and the Latin American asset sales progressing, Verizon Communications is financially strong, with its focus squarely on maintaining a strong telecom business. While increasing competition and technological change make the future of the fixed-line industry uncertain, we think the firm's strategy is the right one. Also, Verizon Wireless, the firm's 55%-owned venture, remains the industry's standout performer.

In recent years, Verizon hasn't been as intent on returning cash to shareholders as many of its peers, and it has been the most aggressive in upgrading networks. Divestitures during 2006, coupled with recent management comments, indicate the firm is going to continue investing heavily in networks for the next several years. This strategy creates uncertainty concerning the ability to generate acceptable returns on investment, highlighting why we think telecom in general isn't a great place to invest absent a very attractive price.

However, we believe Verizon's plans to push fiber optics all the way to consumers' homes (FiOS) offers the best chance to maintain customer relationships. Verizon and its peers have been dealing with the same issue: The core fixed-line business continues to generate good cash flow, but competitive pressure is heightening as customers migrate to wireless and cable companies increasingly vie for customers. We believe Verizon's new network allows the firm to offer services superior to those of cable and gives it a platform to, at a minimum, keep pace with cable over time. Verizon has already made this network available to about 6 million homes, around a third of its planned build.

While the residential business garners a lot of attention, Verizon is also placing a lot of emphasis on the fixed-line business services market, which now constitutes about 40% of the unit's sales. While this business is very competitive, we think Verizon has an advantage, thanks to its local networks throughout the Northeast and the global MCI network.

We continue to think Verizon Wireless is a good business and the best of the U.S. carriers. It continues to capture more than its share of industrywide growth while consistently generating strong margins and improving customer loyalty. Of the industry's remaining big three players, only Verizon Wireless has approached the market with a consistent brand over the past several years and doesn't face ongoing merger-integration issues.

Data as of 12-29-06

Viacom B VIA.B

	Rating	Fair Value	Last Close	Consider Buy	Consider Sell	Yield %
	★★★	$40.00	$41.03	$30.80	$50.10	0.00

Company Profile
Viacom is a global media company with several leading cable network properties, including MTV, VH1, BET, Nickelodeon, Comedy Central, and Spike TV. Viacom's Paramount Pictures produces original motion pictures and owns a library of 2,500 films, including the Godfather series and Titanic. Its Famous Music unit publishes music. Viacom was split off from CBS Corp. at the end of 2005.

Industry	Business Risk	Moat Size	Investment Style	Sector
Media Conglomerates	Average	Narrow	Large Growth	Media

Competition

	Market Cap $Mil	12 Mo Trailing Sales $Mil	Price/Cash Flow	Return On Assets%	Debt/ Equity	Total Return% 1 Yr	3 Yr
Viacom B	28,691	10,598	23.7	5.9	0.1	-0.3	—
Time Warner	86,932	44,532	14.4	4.9	0.5	26.4	6.8
Walt Disney	70,886	34,285	11.7	5.6	0.3	44.3	14.2

Price Volatility
| Monthly Price High/Low — Relative Strength to S&P 500

Annual $Price High/Low: 2005: 44.95/20.50; 2006: 43.90/32.42

Annual Total Return %	—	—	—	—	—	-0.3
Fiscal Year-End: December	2001	2002	2003	2004	2005	TTM
Revenue $Mil	5,498	6,051	7,304	8,132	9,610	10,598
Net Income $Mil	—	—	339	294	1,257	1,241
Earnings Per Share $	—	—	—	—	—	—
Shares Outstanding Mil	—	—	—	—	—	699
Return on Equity %	—	—	2.1	2.2	16.1	17.6
Net Margin %	—	—	4.6	3.6	13.1	11.7
Asset Turnover	0.2	0.3	0.3	0.4	0.5	0.5
Financial Leverage	1.4	1.4	1.4	1.4	2.5	3.0

Management   Stewardship Grade [C]

Chairman Sumner Redstone, 82, controls Viacom through the 46 million-plus A shares--representing more than 70% of the outstanding voting shares--held by his family-owned National Amusements. (The more-liquid B shares don't come with a vote.) By the same means, National Amusements also controls CBS, and Redstone is its chairman, too. Recently, Redstone's daughter Shari has become more active; she's now vice chairman at Viacom and CBS. In 2006, Philippe Dauman--a longtime associate of Redstone's--replaced Tom Freston as CEO. Freston had not been moving into the digital space fast enough for Redstone. Dauman brought along his business partner Tom Dooley, who will slide into the CFO role at the start of 2007. In 2005, Redstone was paid more than $24 million (including restricted shares), while former CEO Freston earned just less. While neither received option grants in 2005, they did each receive more than $4 million in restricted shares, which are supposed to be used to motivate managers; with control of more than 90 million Viacom shares already, we don't think Redstone needs any more motivation. Overall, Redstone hasn't been a great steward of outside shareholders' capital over the years.

Valuation Ratios	Stock	Rel to Industry	Rel to S&P 500
Price/Earnings	—	—	—
Price/Book	4.1	1.2	1.0
Price/Sales	2.7	0.8	0.9
Price/Cash Flow	23.7	1.4	1.6

Major Fund Holders	% of Fund Assets
Fidelity Select Multimedia	6.62
Fidelity Select Leisure	5.70
Thompson Plumb Growth	5.08
BBH Core Select N	4.50

1515 Broadway
New York, NY 10036
http://www.viacom.com

Growth [A]	2002	2003	2004	2005
Revenue %	10.1	20.7	11.3	18.2
Earnings/Share %	NMF	NMF	NMF	NMF
Book Value/Share %	—	—	—	—
Dividends/Share %	NMF	NMF	NMF	NMF

Profitability [B]	2003	2004	2005	TTM
Return on Assets %	1.5	1.6	6.6	5.9
Oper Cash Flow $Mil	1,911	1,990	1,627	1,210
- Cap Spending $Mil	114	141	193	194
= Free Cash Flow $Mil	1,797	1,849	1,434	1,015

Financial Health [B+]	2003	2004	2005	09-30-06
Long-term Debt $Mil	628	292	5,702	458
Total Equity $Mil	15,816	13,465	7,788	7,032
Debt/Equity Ratio	0.0	0.0	0.7	0.1

Thesis By Jonathan Schrader, CFA, 11-17-06 Stock Price as of Analysis: $39.31

The name has been around for many years, but Viacom as it presently exists was created only recently, when the old Viacom (now called CBS CBS) spun off its cable networks, movie studio, and music publishing businesses to its shareholders. While CBS now controls the CBS network, dozens of radio and television stations, and many other valuable media assets, the new Viacom is dominated by its cable networks--including MTV, Nickelodeon, and BET--which contributed about 70% of 2005 sales and an even higher percentage of profits.

What these networks have in common is success in offering appealing programming that attracts hard-to-reach audiences--teens, children, and African-Americans, respectively. Because of their popularity, Viacom has been able to charge above-average rates to cable operators (for the right to carry their networks) and advertisers (for the right to market products to their audiences). This two-prong revenue stream has made Viacom's cable networks extremely profitable. Viacom has traditionally used much of this profit to introduce its cable networks to international markets.

Viacom's other major property is Paramount Pictures, which has struggled over the past several years. The studio improved in 2005, but was still only the seventh-highest-grossing studio in the U.S. market. Now that it's no longer buried inside a much larger firm, Paramount will have to perform relatively well in order not to drag down Viacom's results. To boost results, Viacom brought in Brad Grey of Sopranos fame and purchased Dreamworks SKG, which placed just behind Paramount in 2005 market share. The success of this investment is still to be determined.

Viacom has also invested heavily in its Web properties, including MTV Overdrive and Comedy Central's Motherload. While these offerings have been successful, Viacom has still had trouble maintaining its high historical growth rate in the face of stiff online competition from the likes of Google, Yahoo, and the many other online media firms that can offer advertisers large audiences and the ability to precisely, easily, and immediately quantify the success of their marketing efforts, something that traditional media have been unable to do.

Because of these advantages, online competition will probably only increase in the coming years, making it harder for Viacom's cable networks to increase sales. With this said, we still think Viacom's assets are quite attractive and would be willing to take a position in the shares if given the opportunity.

Vodafone Group PLC ADR VOD

Data as of 12-29-06

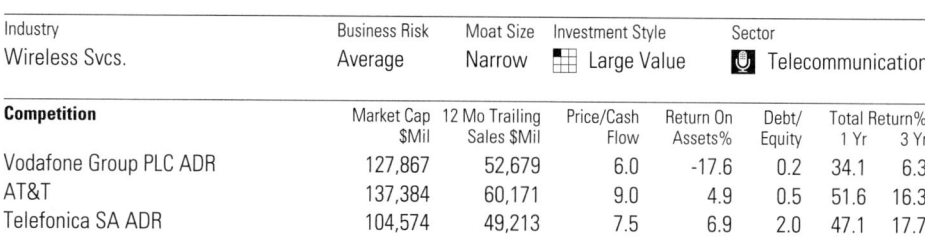

	Rating	Fair Value	Last Close	Consider Buy	Consider Sell	Yield %
	★★★	$30.00	$27.78	$23.10	$37.60	4.51

Industry	Business Risk	Moat Size	Investment Style	Sector
Wireless Svcs.	Average	Narrow	Large Value	Telecommunication

Company Profile

With 191.6 million proportional customers (total customers multiplied by its ownership interest), Vodafone is the second-largest wireless phone company in the world behind China Mobile (in which it owns a 3.27% stake). It is also the largest carrier in terms of the number of countries served and is the most global wireless company in the world. Vodafone has majority control in 17 countries and a minority interest or partnership in 22 others.

Management   Stewardship Grade [B]

Vodafone's management has traditionally been well regarded. Arun Sarin, who was CEO of Airtouch, a U.S. wireless firm that Vodafone acquired, replaced Christopher Gent as CEO in 2003 and continued Gent's acquisition and growth strategy until he sold the Japanese, Swedish and Belgian units. However, in the summer of 2006 Sarin came under increased scrutiny as the stock price was lower than when he took over three years before. At the 2006 shareholders meeting, 15% of the firm's shareholders either voted against him or abstained from voting for him. Most of senior management has come up through the ranks or from firms Vodafone has acquired. This has helped retain key employees and integrate acquisitions into Vodafone. The company has been criticized for excessive pay by European standards, but Sarin's pay package seems reasonable by U.S. standards. We like that many of the firm's option grants are performance options that require a specific return on the stock, some as high as 18% annually before they vest. CFO Andy Halford was previously CFO of Verizon Wireless, which he helped lead to the fastest growth rates in the United States in 2003 and 2004. Vodafone's corporate governance is quite good. We were pleased to see the firm finally take a large write-off of its goodwill, but are concerned that a second one followed so quickly.

Vodafone House The Connection   www.vodafone.com
Newbury, United Kingdom RG14 2FN

Growth [NA]	2003	2004	2005	2006
Revenue %	33.0	10.5	-20.5	10.0
Earnings/Share %	NMF	NMF	NMF	NMF
Book Value/Share %	-1.7	-12.5	-0.3	-18.6
Dividends/Share %	—	—	—	—

Profitability [NA]	2004	2005	2006	TTM
Return on Assets %	-5.7	4.3	-17.6	-17.6
Oper Cash Flow $Mil	21,641	20,251	21,253	21,253
- Cap Spending $Mil	7,567	7,893	8,043	8,043
= Free Cash Flow $Mil	14,074	12,358	13,210	13,210

Financial Health [NA]	2004	2005	2006	03-31-06
Long-term Debt $Mil	23,591	24,887	29,386	29,386
Total Equity $Mil	208,965	214,430	149,670	149,670
Debt/Equity Ratio	0.1	0.1	0.2	0.2

Competition

	Market Cap $Mil	12 Mo Trailing Sales $Mil	Price/Cash Flow	Return On Assets%	Debt/Equity	Total Return% 1 Yr	3 Yr
Vodafone Group PLC ADR	127,867	52,679	6.0	-17.6	0.2	34.1	6.3
AT&T	137,384	60,171	9.0	4.9	0.5	51.6	16.3
Telefonica SA ADR	104,574	49,213	7.5	6.9	2.0	47.1	17.7

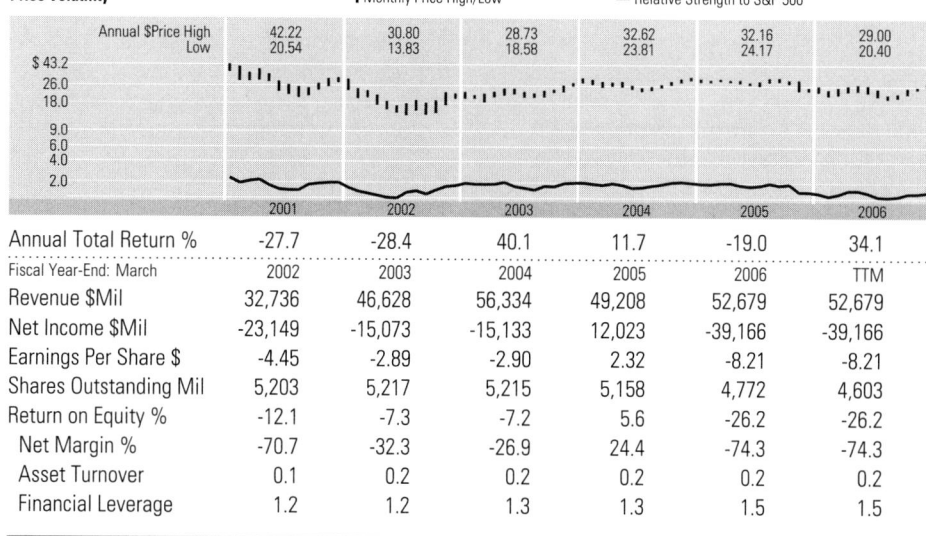

Annual Total Return %	-27.7	-28.4	40.1	11.7	-19.0	34.1
Fiscal Year-End: March	2002	2003	2004	2005	2006	TTM
Revenue $Mil	32,736	46,628	56,334	49,208	52,679	52,679
Net Income $Mil	-23,149	-15,073	-15,133	12,023	-39,166	-39,166
Earnings Per Share $	-4.45	-2.89	-2.90	2.32	-8.21	-8.21
Shares Outstanding Mil	5,203	5,217	5,215	5,158	4,772	4,603
Return on Equity %	-12.1	-7.3	-7.2	5.6	-26.2	-26.2
Net Margin %	-70.7	-32.3	-26.9	24.4	-74.3	-74.3
Asset Turnover	0.1	0.2	0.2	0.2	0.2	0.2
Financial Leverage	1.2	1.2	1.3	1.3	1.5	1.5

Valuation Ratios	Stock	Rel to Industry	Rel to S&P 500
Price/Earnings	NMF	—	—
Price/Book	0.9	0.3	0.2
Price/Sales	2.4	0.6	0.8
Price/Cash Flow	6.0	0.7	0.4

Major Fund Holders	% of Fund Assets
Rydex Telecommunications Inv	6.66
ProFunds Europe 30 Svc	4.05
Artisan International Value	3.85
California Investment Euro Gr & Inc Dir	3.24

Thesis By Allan C. Nichols, CFA, 12-19-06 Stock Price of Analysis: $28.48

Vodafone has added a focus on profitability to its already impressive scale and scope, a combination that we think gives the firm a narrow economic moat.

Vodafone is the world's largest wireless phone company by revenue. It is split into two regions: Western Europe and almost everything else, with Europe accounting for about three fourths of reported revenue and profits. Vodafone's scale in Europe gives it an advantage over competitors, allowing it to source handsets and equipment at lower prices. The firm can also develop a product in one country and roll it out to many others at minimal additional expense. The firm generally has done a great job of using these advantages to enter new markets.

Vodafone has stumbled at times, though, and it has often seemed more interested in its global footprint than profits. We've been very pleased to see the firm finally admit mistakes in 2006 and sell its struggling Japanese business, its Swedish business, and its minority stake in Belgium. We believe that the firm received excellent prices for these assets that would have been difficult to turn around or had minimal growth prospects, and Switzerland could soon join the list. Vodafone took this money and paid a special dividend of 9 billion pounds ($17 billion) and made acquisitions in emerging markets, where it has a better chance of seeing its advantages translated into profits. We like that management now requires acquisitions to generate a return at least 2 percentage points above the risk adjusted cost of equity of a given country. We also think that many potential targets in emerging markets these days would not fit this criterion and that Vodafone's purchases will be reduced in the future.

Vodafone holds several minority positions, one of which--its stake in Verizon Wireless--is hugely important. We believe that Verizon Wireless is the best-run wireless firm in the U.S. Vodafone's profitability, margins, and return on investment also rise significantly by counting its proportional stake in Verizon Wireless' operating profit.

Though emerging markets only account for one fourth of sales, we expect them to drive growth. Western Europe is near saturation, and most growth there will come from selling newer services, such as Internet access and video downloads. With termination rates (fees from other carriers to connect their customers) falling, overall growth will be minimal. Emerging markets, though, are growing more than 20% annually, on average, and many of these countries still have low penetration rates.

Data as of 12-29-06

Vornado Realty Trust VNO

Rating	Fair Value	Last Close	Consider Buy	Consider Sell	Yield %
★★	$103.00	$121.50	$87.80	$135.20	2.68

Company Profile
Vornado Realty Trust is a diversified real estate investment trust that owns or has an interest in more than 85 million square feet of space in several property sectors. Properties are primarily in New York City, Washington, D.C., and Chicago. The office portfolio accounts for nearly two thirds of cash flows. Vornado also owns 33% of Alexander's, 33% of Toys 'R' Us, 20% of GMH Communities Trust, and 16% of Newkirk MLP.

Management
Stewardship Grade [C]

Chairman and CEO Steven Roth is a consummate value investor, willing to take risks with out-of-favor assets. He also writes some of the best shareholder letters, in our opinion. In the past 10 years, Roth has transformed Vornado's assets from largely retail properties into a diverse collection. President Michael Fascitelli is a good complement to Roth, bringing Wall Street savvy to the company. Since coming on board in 1996, the former Goldman Sachs banker has built the company's strong presence in New York and Washington, mostly through large acquisitions. He has been handsomely rewarded for these deals, receiving a $25 million restricted-share bonus in 2002. The remainder of the management team is also tremendously talented, making Vornado one of the best-managed REITs operating today, in our opinion. Although Vornado doesn't hold quarterly conference calls, we think the company's disclosure goes above and beyond in its quarterly financial supplement. Holding the company back from achieving a higher Stewardship Grade are some related-party transactions, staggered director elections, and the relatively high pay packages. But given that insiders own 18% of the company, we are confident management acts with a focus on long-term value creation.

888 Seventh Avenue www.vno.com
New York, NY 10019

Growth [A]	2002	2003	2004	2005
Revenue %	46.2	7.9	14.0	48.7
Earnings/Share %	-22.7	99.0	14.5	-19.5
Book Value/Share %	-14.4	11.1	-1.6	20.1
Dividends/Share %	1.2	9.4	4.8	27.9

Profitability [A-]	2003	2004	2005	TTM
Return on Assets %	4.6	4.9	3.6	3.4
Oper Cash Flow $Mil	536	681	763	—
- Cap Spending $Mil	337	404	958	—
= Free Cash Flow $Mil	—	—	—	—

Financial Health [NA]	2003	2004	2005	09-30-06
Long-term Debt $Mil	—	—	—	—
Total Equity $Mil	3,078	3,435	4,429	4,508
Debt/Equity Ratio	—	—	—	—

Industry	Business Risk	Moat Size	Investment Style	Sector
REITs	Below Avg	Narrow	Large Core	Financial Services

Competition	Market Cap $Mil	12 Mo Trailing Sales $Mil	Price/Cash Flow	Return On Assets %	Debt/Equity	Total Return % 1 Yr	3 Yr
Vornado Realty Trust	17,259	2,696	—	3.4	—	51.1	36.9
Forest City Enterprises A	5,943	1,195	—	1.6	—	54.8	36.3
Colonial Properties Trust	2,159	573	—	2.8	—	18.3	13.1

Price Volatility | Monthly Price High/Low — Relative Strength to S&P 500

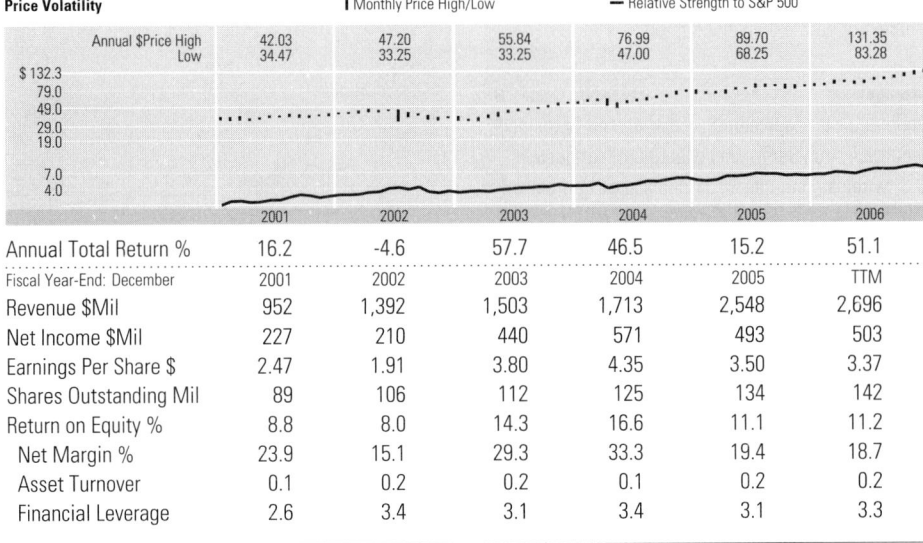

Annual $Price High	42.03	47.20	55.84	76.99	89.70	131.35
Low	34.47	33.25	33.25	47.00	68.25	83.28
	2001	2002	2003	2004	2005	2006
Annual Total Return %	16.2	-4.6	57.7	46.5	15.2	51.1

Fiscal Year-End: December	2001	2002	2003	2004	2005	TTM
Revenue $Mil	952	1,392	1,503	1,713	2,548	2,696
Net Income $Mil	227	210	440	571	493	503
Earnings Per Share $	2.47	1.91	3.80	4.35	3.50	3.37
Shares Outstanding Mil	89	106	112	125	134	142
Return on Equity %	8.8	8.0	14.3	16.6	11.1	11.2
Net Margin %	23.9	15.1	29.3	33.3	19.4	18.7
Asset Turnover	0.1	0.2	0.2	0.1	0.2	0.2
Financial Leverage	2.6	3.4	3.1	3.4	3.1	3.3

Valuation Ratios	Stock	Rel to Industry	Rel to S&P 500
Price/Earnings	38.2	0.8	1.9
Price/Book	3.8	0.9	0.9
Price/Sales	6.4	0.8	2.2
Price/Cash Flow	—	—	—

Major Fund Holders	% of Fund Assets
Adelante U.S. Real Estate Secs Y	7.94
SSgA Tuckerman Active REIT	6.94
JHT Real Estate Sec Trust Series I	6.80
JHFunds2 Real Estate Secs 1	6.68

Thesis By Akash Dave, 11-06-06 Stock Price as of Analysis: $115.61

Vornado Realty Trust's trophy assets are located in some of the best markets in the world and throw off cash that can be profitably redeployed by the company's value-oriented, long-term-focused management team. This combination is worthy of a narrow economic moat, in our opinion.

Unlike many real estate companies that specialize in a particular property type, Vornado's portfolio spans almost the entire range. However, a common theme underlies the whole collection: The properties were acquired at deep discounts to their intrinsic worth, redeveloped, and re-leased at higher rental rates. Vornado does not always limit itself to the conventional real estate arena, often exploiting opportunities overlooked by competitors. We think management's real estate savvy makes it possible to unlock value in both traditional and nontraditional channels, enabling Vornado to produce high returns regardless of the real estate cycle.

Vornado is well positioned for the future, in our view. With debt and preferred equity accounting for about 41% of total capital, the company has a flexible balance sheet for making opportunistic investments. Also, Vornado's eclectic portfolio provides steady cash flow that can be used to fund promising redevelopment opportunities. For instance, Vornado has major repositioning projects in New York City and Washington, D.C., that will allow it to reinvest incremental capital at favorable returns. These developments should also breathe new life into the surrounding areas, and by having other properties strategically positioned nearby, Vornado stands to benefit, since the existing assets will command greater rents.

We think Vornado possesses one other key advantage. With about 80% of cash flows from just New York and Washington, D.C., the company has positioned itself in markets with limited supplies of buildable land and tough building regulations, ensuring high barriers to entry for rivals. Further, Vornado gains an edge over more geographically diversified rivals for the best property deals and tenants. Its portfolio statistics reflect this market dominance; at 94%, Vornado's occupancy rate is nearly 8 percentage points above the national average.

Finally, we like that insiders own 18% of the company, a stake that ought to keep them focused on increasing their net worth alongside that of other shareholders. We wouldn't think twice of investing in Vornado, should the shares trade at a reasonable discount to our fair value estimate.

Data as of 12-29-06

Vulcan Materials VMC

Rating	Fair Value	Last Close	Consider Buy	Consider Sell	Yield %
★★★	$80.00	$89.87	$61.70	$100.20	1.65

Industry	Business Risk	Moat Size	Investment Style	Sector
Mining (Nonmetal)	Average	Narrow	Mid Core	Industrial Materials

Company Profile

Vulcan Materials' main business is aggregate quarries, which produce stone, sand, and gravel for use mostly in concrete and asphalt. Aggregates make up about 70% of total sales while asphalt and ready-mix concrete make up the balance. The public highway and infrastructure end markets consume nearly half of total production while the commercial and residential construction markets constitute the balance.

Management   Stewardship Grade [B]

Donald M. James has been chairman and CEO since May 1997. He leads a seasoned team that has shown skill in carving out a leading low-cost position in a commodity industry. Besides James, the other board members are independent and staff all key committees. Management pay practices are in line with the industry, and bonuses are tied to various metrics including economic profit (return on capital minus cost of capital). We're most impressed by management's ability to sniff out fast-growing markets and establish leading positions there. The company has excelled with acquisitions, which is crucial in an asset-driven business where resources are scarce and dwindling. The best opportunities for synergies involve purchasing struggling operations and bringing them up to Vulcan's standards. Management and board members own just over 3% of the company (including options), helping align their interests with those of outside shareholders.

1200 Urban Center Drive   www.vulcanmaterials.com
Birmingham, AL 35242

Growth [B]	2002	2003	2004	2005
Revenue %	-6.7	6.1	6.3	18.0
Earnings/Share %	-23.5	14.5	45.8	34.7
Book Value/Share %	6.1	6.0	10.5	5.1
Dividends/Share %	4.4	4.3	6.1	11.5

Profitability [A]	2003	2004	2005	TTM
Return on Assets %	5.4	7.8	10.8	13.0
Oper Cash Flow $Mil	519	581	473	563
- Cap Spending $Mil	194	204	216	364
= Free Cash Flow $Mil	325	377	258	199

Financial Health [A+]	2003	2004	2005	09-30-06
Long-term Debt $Mil	608	605	323	322
Total Equity $Mil	1,803	2,014	2,127	1,913
Debt/Equity Ratio	0.3	0.3	0.2	0.2

Competition	Market Cap $Mil	12 Mo Trailing Sales $Mil	Price/Cash Flow	Return On Assets%	Debt/ Equity	Total Return% 1 Yr	3 Yr
Vulcan Materials	8,486	3,281	15.1	13.0	0.2	35.1	26.4
Cemex SAB de CV ADR	26,008	15,094	7.7	7.9	0.8	14.2	40.0
Rinker Group ADR	12,933	5,108	13.7	16.7	0.3	28.6	48.6

Price Volatility   ❙ Monthly Price High/Low   — Relative Strength to S&P 500

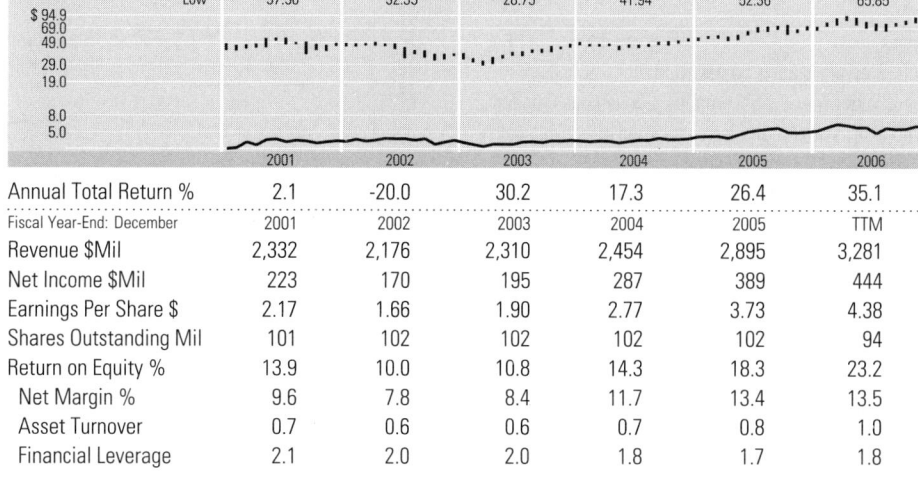

	2001	2002	2003	2004	2005	2006
Annual $Price High	55.30	49.95	48.60	55.53	76.31	93.85
Low	37.50	32.35	28.75	41.94	52.36	65.85
Annual Total Return %	2.1	-20.0	30.2	17.3	26.4	35.1

Fiscal Year-End: December	2001	2002	2003	2004	2005	TTM
Revenue $Mil	2,332	2,176	2,310	2,454	2,895	3,281
Net Income $Mil	223	170	195	287	389	444
Earnings Per Share $	2.17	1.66	1.90	2.77	3.73	4.38
Shares Outstanding Mil	101	102	102	102	102	94
Return on Equity %	13.9	10.0	10.8	14.3	18.3	23.2
Net Margin %	9.6	7.8	8.4	11.7	13.4	13.5
Asset Turnover	0.7	0.6	0.6	0.7	0.8	1.0
Financial Leverage	2.1	2.0	2.0	1.8	1.7	1.8

Valuation Ratios	Stock	Rel to Industry	Rel to S&P 500
Price/Earnings	20.0	1.1	1.0
Price/Book	4.4	1.1	1.1
Price/Sales	2.6	0.8	0.9
Price/Cash Flow	15.1	1.1	1.0

Major Fund Holders	% of Fund Assets
Stratton Multi Cap	3.57
Fidelity Select Construction&Housing	3.55
SunAmerica Focused Value A	2.75
Excelsior Equity Opportunities	2.51

Thesis By Matthew Warren, 11-30-06 Stock Price as of Analysis: $88.72

Competitive advantage in the stone quarry business is based on three factors: location, location, and location. Because Vulcan owns quarries in numerous attractive markets, we think the company is surrounded by a narrow economic moat.

When a contractor buys stone, sand, or gravel, it's motivated to use the nearest quarry. The economics are simple: Stone aggregates cost about $7 per ton at the plant site--a rough average that varies widely based on regional scarcity--but incur an additional $0.10-$0.15 per ton for every mile in the back of a truck. In general, transportation costs reduce a quarry's addressable market to a 50-mile radius (markets lacking quarries are the exception, and they are usually served by rail or water). Vulcan sits in a strong position, as it owns quarries in nine of the ten fastest-growing cities in the nation.

Strategically located sites like these sustain their competitive advantage for a long stretch as new quarry permits are elusive at best. NIMBY--not in my back yard--objections are pervasive, as local governments are loath to allow a quarry's noise, dust, and traffic into their communities. The resulting supply constraint creates a favorable pricing environment and allows Vulcan to protect margins. In fact, aggregate companies have a history of pricing ahead of inflation.

Vulcan's sheer size--it has a 9% share of the highly fragmented aggregate market--has other advantages as well. For instance, management has significant leverage when negotiating with plant and equipment suppliers, a critical edge in this asset-intensive industry. Vulcan can also spread the fixed costs of geologists and engineers over more quarry sites, sealing its position as a low-cost producer in this commodity business.

This enviable market position allows Vulcan to capitalize on steady demand. Aggregates exhibit much lower volatility than many other construction supply businesses because half of total sales are tied to public infrastructure projects. These aggregate-intensive endeavors are politically popular because of the numerous jobs they create and the tangible benefits they provide to constituents. They also receive dedicated federal funding from gasoline taxes, which is matched and supplemented on both the state and local levels. Steady demand, favorable pricing, and huge barriers to entry are a recipe for Vulcan's steady performance over time.

Data as of 12-29-06

W.P. Stewart & Company WPL

	Rating	Fair Value	Last Close	Consider Buy	Consider Sell	Yield %
	★★★★	$18.00	$15.84	$13.90	$22.60	7.13

Industry	Business Risk	Moat Size	Investment Style	Sector
Money Mgmt.	Average	Wide	Small Value	Financial Services

Company Profile

W.P. Stewart is an asset-management firm that provides equity investment services to clients worldwide. Based in Bermuda, it has analysts and portfolio managers in North America, Europe, and Asia. Many of the firm's clients are high-net-worth individuals. Most of the firm's other business comes from trusts, partnerships, or private corporations. About 30% of the firm's managed assets belong to clients outside the United States.

Management — Stewardship Grade [F]

W.P. Stewart is not a poster child for shareholder-friendly governance. Eponymous founder William P. Stewart and his associates effectively call all the shots. Stewart stepped down as CEO in May 2005 but remains chairman. Henry B. Smith, former CEO of Bank of Bermuda, took over as CEO but had to leave after less than a year because of poor health. The board is currently conducting a search for a new chief executive. Management, retired management, and their families recently owned more than 56% of the company's shares. Individual outside shareholders are prohibited from voting more than 5% of the shares regardless of how many they own, and all outside shareholders together are limited to only 20% of the vote. This guarantees complete control by insiders. Executive compensation is not disclosed, and the firm also does large amounts of business with firms owned by friends and family.

Trinity Hall, 43 Cedar Avenue www.wpstewart.com
Hamilton, Bermuda HM LX

Growth [D+]	2002	2003	2004	2005
Revenue %	-14.6	-13.5	28.2	-2.9
Earnings/Share %	-29.2	-21.5	46.3	-37.4
Book Value/Share %	-2.9	7.2	14.4	-8.7
Dividends/Share %	0.0	0.0	0.0	0.0

Profitability [A]	2003	2004	2005	TTM
Return on Assets %	30.5	38.3	26.3	26.3
Oper Cash Flow $Mil	54	67	69	69
- Cap Spending $Mil	0	1	1	1
= Free Cash Flow $Mil	54	66	68	68

Financial Health [NA]	2003	2004	2005	12-31-05
Long-term Debt $Mil	—	—	—	—
Total Equity $Mil	115	131	122	122
Debt/Equity Ratio	—	—	—	—

Competition

	Market Cap $Mil	12 Mo Trailing Sales $Mil	Price/Cash Flow	Return On Assets %	Debt/ Equity	Total Return % 1 Yr	Total Return % 3 Yr
W.P. Stewart & Company	742	148	—	26.3	—	-28.1	-5.1
Goldman Sachs Group	84,890	34,181	—	1.0	—	57.4	28.3
Mellon Financial	17,360	5,092	—	2.0	—	26.0	12.3

Price Volatility

	2001	2002	2003	2004	2005	2006
Annual $Price High	29.63	31.73	25.57	23.74	25.75	24.19
Low	18.01	14.35	14.94	18.70	20.84	9.50
Annual Total Return %	6.0	-27.9	27.3	16.4	4.8	-28.1

Fiscal Year-End: December	2001	2002	2003	2004	2005	TTM
Revenue $Mil	161	137	119	152	148	148
Net Income $Mil	80	55	43	63	40	40
Earnings Per Share $	1.71	1.21	0.95	1.39	0.87	0.87
Shares Outstanding Mil	43	44	44	45	46	47
Return on Equity %	70.4	51.3	37.6	48.0	32.9	32.9
Net Margin %	50.0	40.4	36.3	41.5	27.1	27.1
Asset Turnover	1.1	1.0	0.8	0.9	1.0	1.0
Financial Leverage	1.3	1.2	1.2	1.3	1.3	1.3

Valuation Ratios	Stock	Rel to Industry	Rel to S&P 500
Price/Earnings	18.2	0.6	0.9
Price/Book	6.1	1.4	1.5
Price/Sales	5.0	0.8	1.7
Price/Cash Flow	—		

Major Fund Holders	% of Fund Assets
Phoenix Small-Cap Growth A	2.13

Thesis By Jeffrey Ptak, CPA, CFA, 12-14-06 Stock Price as of Analysis: $15.52

W.P. Stewart & Co.'s niche strategy should continue to buoy profits, if not spur rapid growth.

Unlike its peers in the money management industry that typically offer myriad products geared to various investor types, W.P. Stewart & Co. runs focused portfolios of blue-chip growth stocks exclusively for wealthy individuals and institutions. With virtually all of its assets under management in private accounts, the company has a scant presence in the mutual fund arena. Thus, Stewart lives and dies with its niche.

Yet, focus has its benefits. Stewart's specialized strategy means that it need not support the costly distribution network that's typically necessary to sell mutual funds. Stewart also conserves resources by largely outsourcing business development to unaffiliated third parties that serve as a referral source. Thus, the company claims one of the leanest cost structures around, with a scant 100-person-plus head count supporting roughly $8 billion in AUM.

The upshot has been handsome profitability: Operating margins have consistently exceeded 40%. Moreover, since Stewart is headquartered in tax-haven Bermuda, its tax rate has typically skirted 15% of pretax income. Consequently, free cash flow averaged 45% of revenue from 2001 through 2005.

Until recently, Stewart also boasted a stable AUM base, as the assets of the well-heeled tend to be stickier than mutual fund investors'. Stewart's high-touch client service approach, which often finds portfolio managers doubling as client service reps, also explains Stewart's high client retention rate.

Yet, cracks in this model have appeared. Stewart has been bleeding AUM in recent years amid stylistic headwinds--its forte, blue-chip growth stocks, has remained out of favor--and competitive pressures. Recently, for instance, Stewart lost over $100 million in AUM when clients followed a pair of portfolio managers who bolted to a hedge fund.

This episode underscores the threat that Stewart faces from hedge funds and the demands of an increasingly restive clientele. Whereas in the past many high-net-worth investors sated themselves with traditional long-only strategies like Stewart's, they're now often demanding alternatives. Rivals are also crowding the high-net-worth market.

Against that backdrop, we expect AUM will continue to trickle out in 2007 and stabilize thereafter. However, operating margins are likely to be slightly lower in the future, reflecting the reality that the battle to land and keep customers will be stiffer in the future.

Data as of 12-29-06

W.W. Grainger GWW

Rating	Fair Value	Last Close	Consider Buy	Consider Sell	Yield %
★★★	$67.00	$69.94	$57.10	$88.00	1.59

Company Profile
W.W. Grainger supplies customers with the facility-maintenance products they need to run their operations smoothly. Customers can choose between shopping in one of approximately 600 branch stores or having catalog or Internet purchases shipped directly from a distribution center. Operating segments are split into branch-based distribution (U.S. and Canadian are now reported separately) and lab safety, which houses all direct-marketing sales.

Management
Stewardship Grade [B]

Richard Keyser became CEO of Grainger in 1995 after serving the company in other roles since 1986. The entire board of directors is elected each year, and independent directors staff all key committees. The current CEO and David Grainger--a major shareholder and former chairman and CEO--are the only insiders on the board. Pay and stock-option issuance are in line with industry practices, and directors and executive officers have skin in the game, owning more than 16% of the company, so shareholder interests should be well represented. Also, discretionary cash bonuses are based on a combination of sales and return on invested capital targets, further aligning management's goals with those of shareholders. Management has been methodical in its approach to improving its market position. The company completely revamped its distribution centers and reduced redundant shipments for catalog orders. During this timeframe, management also conducted independent tests in various markets before implementing its market expansion program, to much success.

100 Grainger Parkway www.grainger.com
Lake Forest, IL 60045-5201

Growth [C-]	2002	2003	2004	2005
Revenue %	-2.3	0.5	8.2	9.4
Earnings/Share %	21.7	9.8	27.2	20.8
Book Value/Share %	4.5	13.3	12.8	10.7
Dividends/Share %	2.9	2.8	6.8	17.2

Profitability [A]	2003	2004	2005	TTM
Return on Assets %	8.6	10.2	11.1	12.6
Oper Cash Flow $Mil	394	406	433	462
- Cap Spending $Mil	74	128	112	126
= Free Cash Flow $Mil	320	278	320	336

Financial Health [A+]	2003	2004	2005	09-30-06
Long-term Debt $Mil	5	0	5	5
Total Equity $Mil	1,845	2,068	2,289	2,277
Debt/Equity Ratio	0.0	0.0	0.0	0.0

Industry	Business Risk	Moat Size	Investment Style	Sector
Distributors	Below Avg	Narrow	Mid Core	Business Services

Competition

	Market Cap $Mil	12 Mo Trailing Sales $Mil	Price/Cash Flow	Return On Assets%	Debt/Equity	Total Return% 1 Yr	3 Yr
W.W. Grainger	6,017	5,812	13.0	12.6	0.0	-0.1	15.6
Fastenal	5,416	1,745	43.0	19.3	—	-7.4	13.9
MSC Industrial Direct Co.	2,622	1,318	19.6	13.4	0.3	-1.5	15.4

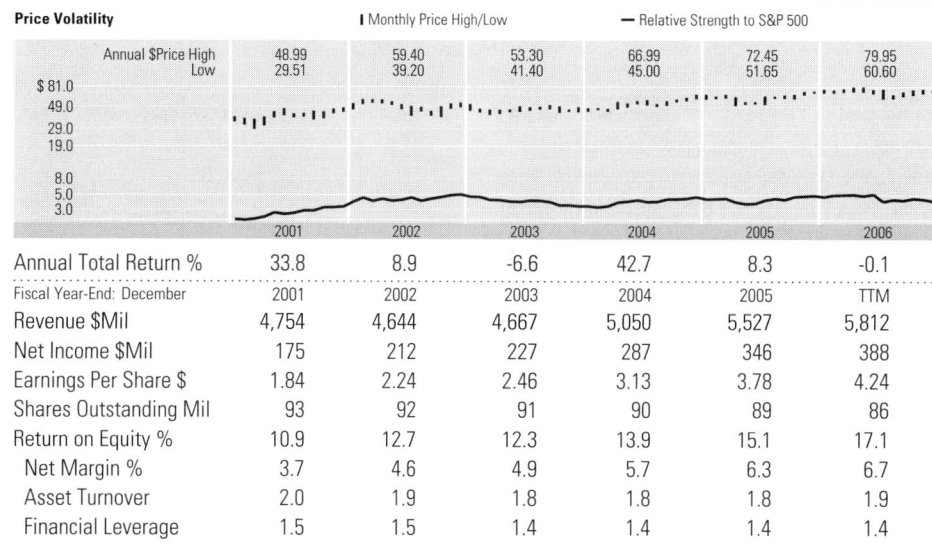

	2001	2002	2003	2004	2005	
Annual Total Return %	33.8	8.9	-6.6	42.7	8.3	-0.1
Fiscal Year-End: December	2001	2002	2003	2004	2005	TTM
Revenue $Mil	4,754	4,644	4,667	5,050	5,527	5,812
Net Income $Mil	175	212	227	287	346	388
Earnings Per Share $	1.84	2.24	2.46	3.13	3.78	4.24
Shares Outstanding Mil	93	92	91	90	89	86
Return on Equity %	10.9	12.7	12.3	13.9	15.1	17.1
Net Margin %	3.7	4.6	4.9	5.7	6.3	6.7
Asset Turnover	2.0	1.9	1.8	1.8	1.8	1.9
Financial Leverage	1.5	1.5	1.4	1.4	1.4	1.4

Valuation Ratios	Stock	Rel to Industry	Rel to S&P 500
Price/Earnings	16.5	0.9	0.8
Price/Book	2.6	0.9	0.6
Price/Sales	1.0	0.8	0.3
Price/Cash Flow	13.0	0.5	0.9

Major Fund Holders	% of Fund Assets
Security Select 25 A	4.51
FMI Focus	3.88
Valley Forge	3.77
Crawford Dividend Growth I	3.26

Thesis By Matthew Warren, 12-15-06 Stock Price as of Analysis: $71.00

W.W. Grainger distributes a broad range of maintenance, repair, and operations (MRO) supplies to facilities managers. While the firm is extending its lead over small regional competitors, Home Depot Supply's aggressive entry into the market could undermine Grainger's size advantage.

With single-digit share in a highly fragmented market, Grainger has been a longtime leader of broad-line MRO distribution. The firm's glossy catalog is backed by roughly 115,000 in-stock items at its distribution centers, including everything from industrial motors to janitorial supplies. For customers with more-pressing needs, Grainger's 600 branches offer immediate solutions (such as sourcing critical parts to restart a production line). Grainger maintains an edge over direct distributors when serving unplanned and time-sensitive demands.

To build on its strategy, Grainger added five distribution centers and expanded four others. The expanded network allowed for catalog orders to ship directly from distribution to the customer. Also, daily restocking allows branches to simultaneously reduce safety stocks and broaden its selection. With an improved supply chain, Grainger launched a multiyear program to improve branch coverage in its top 25 markets. Beginning in 2004, Grainger has been relocating and expanding stores to improve convenience. While Grainger has methodically improved its stores, supply chain, and information systems over recent years, it now seems a shame that the firm wasn't more aggressive in its efforts to consolidate the MRO marketplace.

With the acquisition of Hughes, Home Depot Supply is emerging as the largest, most-diversified distributor in what it labels the "$410 billion professional market." Home Depot's cradle-to-grave strategy involves targeting building expenditures all the way from infrastructure and construction to maintenance and interior upgrades. In 2006, this newly combined entity expects $12 billion in sales from 900 locations, versus roughly $6 billion in sales from 600 locations at Grainger. Initially, only a portion of HD Supply will directly target the $140 billion North American MRO business. However, this should evolve as HD Supply introduces additional products across acquired stores, and begins expanding geographically toward its goal of 1,500 locations and $23-$28 billion in sales by 2010. While integrating disparate acquisitions into a cohesive platform should prove quite challenging, Home Depot brings forth an impressive new-store team, massive buying power, and logistical expertise.

Data as of 12-29-06

Wachovia WB

	Rating	Fair Value	Last Close	Consider Buy	Consider Sell	Yield %
	★★★	$58.00	$56.95	$44.70	$72.70	3.76

Company Profile

Wachovia is the fourth-largest bank in the United States, with more than $555 billion in assets. Based in Charlotte, N.C., Wachovia offers retail and business banking, brokerage, asset-management, and investment banking products. Larger purchases--such as the nearly $40 billion spent on Golden West and SouthTrust--have been pricey but have made a significant positive impact on Wachovia's business model.

Management Stewardship Grade [A]

Although we prefer internal growth to acquired growth, we give Wachovia's management team credit for its solid record. Former First Union head Ken Thompson is the CEO of the combined firm, and shareholders have handsomely outperformed Wachovia's peers. Since the Wachovia-First Union merger, the firm has focused heavily on improving corporate governance, and we believe the bank has been largely successful. Wachovia was one of the first to expense stock options, and it has an annual option-issuance cap of 25 million shares. Wachovia has done a nice job of aligning management's interests with those of long-term shareholders. Senior managers must hold 75% of their stock awards until retirement, and managers are paid based on whether Wachovia produces economic profits for shareholders. Lastly, Wachovia has eliminated its tiered system of electing board members--commencing annual elections for all members by 2008--and has adopted a majority voting provision, essentially giving shareholders more power.

One Wachovia Center www.wachovia.com
Charlotte, NC 28288-0013

Growth [B+]	2002	2003	2004	2005
Revenue %	26.7	12.7	13.2	13.9
Earnings/Share %	79.3	22.3	19.8	10.0
Book Value/Share %	-8.4	3.4	42.8	-13.2
Dividends/Share %	4.2	25.0	32.8	16.9

Profitability [C+]	2003	2004	2005	TTM
Return on Assets %	1.1	1.1	1.3	1.3
Oper Cash Flow $Mil	-5,758	-7,854	5,706	—
- Cap Spending $Mil	1,149	960	2,762	—
= Free Cash Flow $Mil	—	—	—	—

Financial Health [NA]	2003	2004	2005	09-30-06
Long-term Debt $Mil	—	—	—	—
Total Equity $Mil	32,428	47,317	47,561	51,180
Debt/Equity Ratio	—	—	—	—

Industry	Business Risk	Moat Size	Investment Style	Sector
Super Regional Banks	Average	Narrow	Large Value	Financial Services

Competition	Market Cap $Mil	12 Mo Trailing Sales $Mil	Price/Cash Flow	Return On Assets%	Debt/Equity	Total Return% 1 Yr	3 Yr
Wachovia	90,049	27,749	—	1.3	—	12.0	11.3
Bank of America	239,758	68,368	—	1.3	—	20.7	15.2
J.P. Morgan Chase & Co.	167,551	59,650	—	0.9	—	25.6	13.2

Price Volatility | Monthly Price High/Low — Relative Strength to S&P 500

Annual $Price High Low	36.60 25.22	39.88 28.57	46.74 32.12	55.01 43.05	56.28 46.30	60.04 50.85
	2001	2002	2003	2004	2005	2006
Annual Total Return %	16.1	19.5	31.8	16.8	4.3	12.0

Fiscal Year-End: December	2001	2002	2003	2004	2005	TTM
Revenue $Mil	14,071	17,828	20,089	22,740	25,900	27,749
Net Income $Mil	1,613	3,560	4,259	5,214	6,643	7,197
Earnings Per Share $	1.45	2.60	3.18	3.81	4.19	4.52
Shares Outstanding Mil	1,097	1,359	1,327	1,347	1,556	1,581
Return on Equity %	5.7	11.1	13.1	11.0	14.0	14.1
Net Margin %	11.5	20.0	21.2	22.9	25.6	25.9
Asset Turnover	0.0	0.1	0.1	0.0	0.1	0.1
Financial Leverage	11.6	10.7	12.4	10.4	10.9	10.9

Valuation Ratios	Stock	Rel to Industry	Rel to S&P 500
Price/Earnings	13.0	1.0	0.6
Price/Book	1.8	0.8	0.4
Price/Sales	3.2	0.9	1.1
Price/Cash Flow	—	—	—

Major Fund Holders	% of Fund Assets
Senbanc	7.25
Allianz RCM Financial Services Instl	5.94
Fidelity Select Banking	5.93
ProFunds Banks UltraSector Inv	4.81

Thesis By Jim Callahan, CFA, 10-18-06 Stock Price as of Analysis: $55.54

We believe Wachovia's purchase of Golden West Financial shows promise. We initially frowned upon the 11% premium paid over our Golden West fair value estimate, but further analysis showed some attractive potential. Wachovia gained access to the Western markets--a long-desired goal--and offers its broad product portfolio to Golden West's highly successful salesforce. Further, Golden West added some organic growth and credit quality to the firm. Along with Wachovia's relaunched credit card product, we look forward to seeing accelerating product sales and bottom-line growth.

We like the platform Wachovia has built, but we acknowledge the risks in a growth-by-acquisition strategy. Wachovia is working on reducing its own expenses, and the ongoing cost-cutting initiative could remove up to $1 billion annually, although we have not given the bank full credit in our forecast despite its year-to-date success. With the Golden West acquisition on the books, Wachovia will be further pressed to generate operating expense benefits and higher returns. That said, we still believe Wachovia's purchases provide a strong platform for growth going forward. Executed properly, Wachovia's business model is capable of tangible returns on equity of 30%.

Wachovia's largest and most-profitable segment is its retail bank, and this unit has performed well considering the current environment. With arguably one of the best retail operations among the top banks, Wachovia has fared well despite rising interest rates, squeezed net margins, and greater competition for deposits. The 2004 addition of SouthTrust added a low-cost deposit base, allowing Wachovia to hold its own in the face of increased competition. With banks across the industry generating healthy loan growth with minimal losses, we view Wachovia's recent performance as average, but the potential for cross sales with the bank's three additional operating segments gives Wachovia an edge.

Wachovia's market-related businesses generate healthy fee income. We like the strong transition we're seeing from commission-based brokerage accounts into asset management-oriented relationships that provide steady, recurring fee income. Further, other businesses that generate healthy recurring revenue--such as asset management and insurance--continue to grow. We believe Wachovia's noninterest income will grow nearly 10% annually and generate 45% of total revenue.

Data as of 12-29-06

Walgreen WAG

	Rating	Fair Value	Last Close	Consider Buy	Consider Sell	Yield %
	★★★	$51.00	$45.89	$39.30	$63.90	0.62

Company Profile

Walgreen operates about 5,500 drugstores in 47 states and Puerto Rico. Prescription drugs account for 64% of total sales. The remainder of sales include nonprescription drugs, health and beauty items, toiletries, food, beverages, and general merchandise. The firm operates its own pharmacy benefit manager service.

Industry	Business Risk	Moat Size	Investment Style	Sector
Specialty Retail	Average	Wide	Large Growth	Consumer Services

Competition

	Market Cap $Mil	12 Mo Trailing Sales $Mil	Price/Cash Flow	Return On Assets%	Debt/Equity	Total Return% 1 Yr	3 Yr
Walgreen	46,048	47,409	18.9	10.2	—	4.4	9.3
CVS	25,456	41,480	14.5	6.4	0.4	17.6	20.7
Rite Aid	2,895	17,542	12.0	17.4	2.2	56.3	-2.9

Management   Stewardship Grade [B]

Walgreen likes homegrown talent and has had little turnover at the top. Until 2005, just five CEOs had led the company since its founding in 1901. Jeffrey Rein recently became the company's sixth. Like former CEO and current chairman Dave Bernauer, Rein worked his way up the corporate ladder, beginning as an assistant store manager in 1982. Bernauer's ongoing involvement with the company as well as Rein's intimate knowledge of the business should ensure a smooth transition, in our view. We think Bernauer and Rein earned reasonable compensation in fiscal 2006 and beneficially own enough stock to adequately align their interests with those of shareholders. We like that Walgreen issues restricted shares, but we would rather management be offered those shares in lieu of--not in addition to--stock options. We are pleased that incentive compensation for all executives is based on the company achieving return on invested capital benchmarks. Directors stand for election annually and receive more than 50% of their compensation in the form of Walgreen stock.

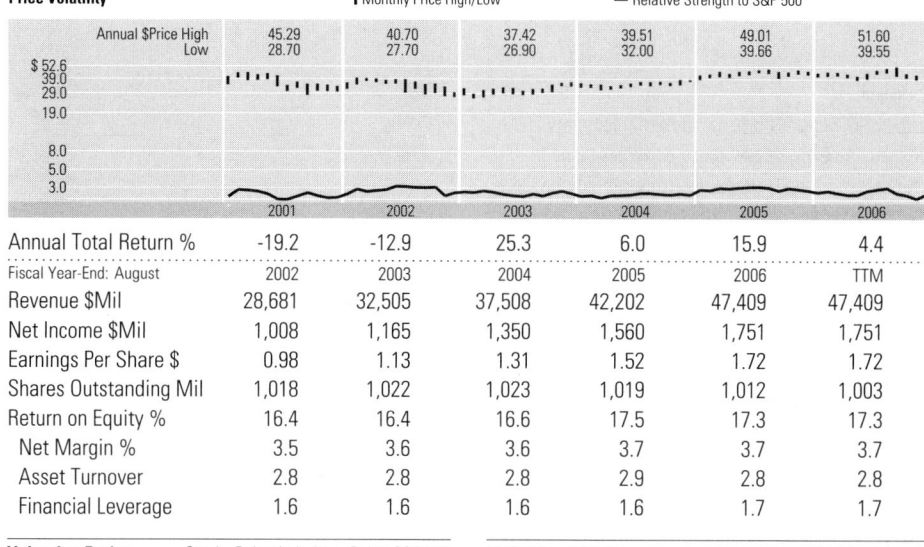

Price Volatility

Annual Total Return %	-19.2	-12.9	25.3	6.0	15.9	4.4
Fiscal Year-End: August	2002	2003	2004	2005	2006	TTM
Revenue $Mil	28,681	32,505	37,508	42,202	47,409	47,409
Net Income $Mil	1,008	1,165	1,350	1,560	1,751	1,751
Earnings Per Share $	0.98	1.13	1.31	1.52	1.72	1.72
Shares Outstanding Mil	1,018	1,022	1,023	1,019	1,012	1,003
Return on Equity %	16.4	16.4	16.6	17.5	17.3	17.3
Net Margin %	3.5	3.6	3.6	3.7	3.7	3.7
Asset Turnover	2.8	2.8	2.8	2.9	2.8	2.8
Financial Leverage	1.6	1.6	1.6	1.6	1.7	1.7

Valuation Ratios

	Stock	Rel to Industry	Rel to S&P 500
Price/Earnings	26.7	1.1	1.3
Price/Book	4.6	1.2	1.1
Price/Sales	1.0	1.0	0.3
Price/Cash Flow	18.9	1.1	1.3

Major Fund Holders

	% of Fund Assets
Sentinel Capital Growth A	5.60
IXIS CGM Advisor Targeted Equity A	4.09
Dreyfus Premier Tax-Managed Growth A	4.02
Delaware Pooled Large-Cap Growth Eqty	3.92

200 Wilmot Road   www.walgreens.com
Deerfield, IL 60015

Growth [B+]	2003	2004	2005	2006
Revenue %	13.3	15.4	12.5	12.3
Earnings/Share %	15.3	15.9	16.0	13.2
Book Value/Share %	15.2	14.4	9.7	14.7
Dividends/Share %	7.2	16.8	22.4	22.5

Profitability [A]	2004	2005	2006	TTM
Return on Assets %	10.1	10.7	10.2	10.2
Oper Cash Flow $Mil	1,644	1,371	2,440	2,440
- Cap Spending $Mil	940	1,238	1,338	1,338
= Free Cash Flow $Mil	705	134	1,102	1,102

Financial Health [A]	2004	2005	2006	08-31-06
Long-term Debt $Mil	—	—	—	—
Total Equity $Mil	8,140	8,890	10,116	10,116
Debt/Equity Ratio	—	—	—	—

Thesis By Mitchell P. Corwin, CFA, CPA, 11-27-06 Stock Price as of Analysis: $40.10

Competitive threats to retail drugstore chains have intensified, with CVS and pharmacy benefit manager Caremark RX agreeing to merge and Wal-Mart heavily discounting more than 300 generic drugs to $4 per prescription. While the Wal-Mart action is a negative, we are more concerned about the CVS-Caremark transaction because of CVS' ability to influence plan design and develop incentives for consumers to choose their stores over Walgreen. After all, the foundation for Walgreen's wide economic moat stems from its head start in finding and developing the best store locations.

Though we do not know how Walgreen will respond, we believe it will do so in a way that mitigates CVS' ability to poach its pharmacy customers. As a result, we are not inclined to change our moat rating for Walgreen. Given the changing industry landscape, however, we view the company's risk as average today instead of below average in prior years, increasing the margin of safety we would require to invest.

No matter how the industry evolves, Walgreen should benefit from the rapid growth of prescription drug spending. An aging baby boomer population, increased use of pharmaceuticals for health-care needs, a new Medicare prescription drug benefit, and more generic drug introductions should all provide strong tailwinds for the industry. Prescription drug spending is key for Walgreen, since it derives 64% of its total sales from dispensing pharmaceuticals.

Since the early 1990s, the company has had a laserlike focus on being the first to build larger, freestanding stores on high-traffic corners, recognizing that convenience is paramount in driving traffic and building consumer loyalty. Walgreen's steady pace of internal growth and high store productivity has led to consistent double-digit earnings growth and the highest returns on invested capital of any drugstore chain.

Despite the numerous options available for consumers looking to fill prescriptions, many still favor the convenience of the corner drugstore, and Walgreen is adept at choosing the best corners. We estimate that a Walgreen store, on average, generates 30% more sales than its nearest competitor, CVS, thanks to an average of 265 prescriptions filled per store per day compared with CVS' average of about 215. This volume advantage is important because, with low incremental margins on prescription drugs, increased customer counts lead to increased sales of higher-margin convenience items.

Wal-Mart Stores WMT

Data as of 12-29-06

Rating	Fair Value	Last Close	Consider Buy	Consider Sell	Yield %
★★★★★	$58.00	$46.18	$49.40	$76.10	1.45

Company Profile
Wal-Mart Stores is the largest retailer in the world, with nearly 7,000 stores around the globe. It operates about 1,100 Wal-Mart discount stores, 110 Neighborhood Markets, 580 Sam's Clubs, and around 2,200 Wal-Mart Supercenters (which combine supermarkets and discount stores) in the United States and Puerto Rico. It runs more than 2,700 stores internationally.

Management — Stewardship Grade [A]
Former COO Lee Scott became CEO in February 2000. He leads an experienced group of senior managers, many of whom have gradually risen through the Wal-Mart ranks. We like the board's good mix of internal and external directors, and we think corporate governance is strong. Management and the board avoid conflicts of interest, directors are elected every year, and the company is open to shareholder proposals. Given the shaky performance of the shares over the past couple of years, we could take issue with management's bonuses over that period, but because we think the company is on the right track, and the firm is still generating returns well above its cost of capital, we're not too concerned. Insiders own just over 40% of Wal-Mart stock, much of which is held by members of late founder Sam Walton's family.

702 S.W. Eighth Street
Bentonville, AR 72716
www.walmartstores.com

Growth [B+]	2003	2004	2005	2006
Revenue %	12.6	11.6	11.3	9.5
Earnings/Share %	21.8	15.6	16.4	11.2
Book Value/Share %	13.1	12.3	16.3	9.4
Dividends/Share %	7.1	20.0	44.4	15.4

Profitability [A-]	2004	2005	2006	TTM
Return on Assets %	8.6	8.5	8.1	7.2
Oper Cash Flow $Mil	15,996	15,044	17,633	19,584
- Cap Spending $Mil	10,308	12,893	14,563	15,600
= Free Cash Flow $Mil	5,688	2,151	3,070	3,984

Financial Health [B]	2004	2005	2006	10-31-06
Long-term Debt $Mil	20,099	23,258	30,171	27,776
Total Equity $Mil	43,623	49,396	53,171	58,763
Debt/Equity Ratio	0.5	0.5	0.6	0.5

Industry	Business Risk	Moat Size	Investment Style	Sector
Discount Stores	Below Avg	Wide	Large Core	Consumer Services

Competition	Market Cap $Mil	12 Mo Trailing Sales $Mil	Price/Cash Flow	Return On Assets%	Debt/ Equity	Total Return% 1 Yr	3 Yr
Wal-Mart Stores	192,479	339,150	9.8	7.2	0.5	0.1	-2.9
Target	49,000	56,727	11.3	6.9	0.6	4.7	15.6
Costco Wholesale	24,229	60,151	13.3	6.3	0.0	7.9	14.3

Price Volatility — Monthly Price High/Low — Relative Strength to S&P 500

	2001	2002	2003	2004	2005	2006
Annual $Price High/Low	—	58.75 / 41.50	63.94 / 43.72	60.20 / 46.27	61.31 / 51.08	54.60 / 42.31	52.15 / 42.31
Annual Total Return %	8.9	-11.8	5.7	0.5	-10.3	0.1

Fiscal Year-End: January	2002	2003	2004	2005	2006	TTM
Revenue $Mil	204,011	229,616	256,329	285,222	312,427	339,150
Net Income $Mil	6,592	7,955	9,054	10,267	11,231	10,936
Earnings Per Share $	1.47	1.79	2.07	2.41	2.68	2.62
Shares Outstanding Mil	—	—	4,353	4,260	4,191	4,168
Return on Equity %	18.7	20.2	20.8	20.8	21.1	18.6
Net Margin %	3.2	3.5	3.5	3.6	3.6	3.2
Asset Turnover	2.5	2.5	2.4	2.4	2.3	2.2
Financial Leverage	2.3	2.4	2.4	2.4	2.6	2.6

Valuation Ratios	Stock	Rel to Industry	Rel to S&P 500
Price/Earnings	16.6	0.8	0.8
Price/Book	3.3	0.9	0.8
Price/Sales	0.6	0.7	0.2
Price/Cash Flow	9.0	0.8	0.7

Major Fund Holders	% of Fund Assets
Clipper	6.89
GMO U.S. Quality Equity IV	6.16
FMI Large Cap	6.13
Rydex Retailing Inv	5.75

Thesis By Joseph Beaulieu, 12-11-06 Stock Price as of Analysis: $46.00

Toward the end of 2005, Wal-Mart--already one of the largest firms in the world--was intently focused on continuing to increase its store base and win additional business from current customers. But after a difficult 2006, when the firm's same-store sales growth ground to a near-halt, Wal-Mart appears to be adjusting its priorities. We're pleased to hear management talking more about balancing growth and returns on investment, and using the attributes that make it a wide-moat firm.

At its most successful, Wal-Mart has used its leverage over suppliers and its operational savvy to drive strong returns on invested capital, so we're glad to see signs that it is returning to those core strategies. In recent quarters, despite the rising percentage of groceries in the company's revenue mix, total gross margins have continued to increase as a result of higher initial markups and fewer markdowns on general merchandise. Inventories are growing much more slowly than revenue, and this trend should continue to boost gross margins while reducing working capital requirements--two things that help drive returns on investment.

Wal-Mart's recent announcement that it's slowing expansion in the U.S. was heartening. Selective placement of new stores in mature markets could help increase the frequency that some consumers shop at the stores without too much cannibalization of existing stores, but now that almost 85% of American households are already shopping at a Wal-Mart every year, we think that U.S. expansion opportunities are somewhat limited. In addition to reducing cannibalization of the existing store base (and thereby improving same-store sales growth), slower store expansion should help increase free cash flows.

Wal-Mart does still have opportunities for incremental growth. Its international business (especially in Central and South America) is growing quickly. Additionally, getting customers that just shop Wal-Mart for food and cleaning supplies to purchase things like housewares or electronics would help drive growth and boost margins.

Over the next few years, we hope to see Wal-Mart manage its business less for growth and more for cash flows. While ongoing expansion in Central and South America and ongoing improvement in U.S. stores will require some investments, we think Wal-Mart is at a developmental stage where it can and should be returning much more value to shareholders through share repurchases and dividends.

Data as of 12-29-06

Walt Disney DIS

	Rating	Fair Value	Last Close	Consider Buy	Consider Sell	Yield %
	★★	$31.00	$34.27	$26.40	$40.70	0.91

Company Profile

Disney owns the rights to some of the most famous characters ever created, including Mickey Mouse, Winnie the Pooh, and the Muppets. These characters and others are featured in several theme parks Disney owns or licenses around the world. Disney makes live-action and animated films under several labels and owns or has a stake in several popular TV networks, including ABC, ESPN, Lifetime, and A&E. Disney also owns and operates dozens of TV and radio stations in the U.S.

Management   Stewardship Grade [B]

In October 2005, Bob Iger replaced Michael Eisner as Disney's CEO. Their styles appear to be very different, and we're favorably impressed by Iger's early efforts. Iger has shown a willingness to experiment with new technology while reinforcing Disney's commitment to high-quality content. He was able to smooth relations with Pixar's Steve Jobs--which had turned sour toward the end of Eisner's tenure--so that Disney wouldn't lose the valuable profit stream that Pixar has provided over the years. Iger is on Disney's board, but not as chairman. That role is filled by former Sen. George Mitchell, who is set to retire from the chairmanship at the end of 2006; he will be replaced by current board member John Pepper, former CEO of Procter & Gamble. Disney's board has made great strides in improving governance recently, but we think further improvements are achievable. Over the past couple of years, shareholders have paid millions for company cars, personal security, personal travel on company planes, and directors' legal bills, and will continue to pay annual bonuses (totaling more than $22 million) to Michael Eisner for nearly three years after his departure.

500 South Buena Vista Street   www.disney.com
Burbank, CA 91521

Growth [B]	2003	2004	2005	2006
Revenue %	6.8	13.6	3.9	7.3
Earnings/Share %	1.6	80.6	8.9	34.4
Book Value/Share %	0.6	7.0	1.3	22.5
Dividends/Share %	0.0	0.0	14.3	12.5

Profitability [B+]	2004	2005	2006	TTM
Return on Assets %	4.4	4.8	5.6	5.6
Oper Cash Flow $Mil	4,370	4,269	6,058	6,058
- Cap Spending $Mil	1,427	1,823	1,299	1,299
= Free Cash Flow $Mil	2,943	2,446	4,759	4,759

Financial Health [A]	2004	2005	2006	09-30-06
Long-term Debt $Mil	9,395	10,157	10,843	10,843
Total Equity $Mil	26,081	26,210	31,820	31,820
Debt/Equity Ratio	0.4	0.4	0.3	0.3

Industry	Business Risk	Moat Size	Investment Style	Sector
Media Conglomerates	Below Avg	Narrow	Large Growth	Media

Competition

	Market Cap $Mil	12 Mo Trailing Sales $Mil	Price/Cash Flow	Return On Assets%	Debt/Equity	Total Return% 1 Yr	3 Yr
Walt Disney	70,886	34,285	11.7	5.6	0.3	44.3	14.2
Time Warner	86,932	44,532	14.4	4.9	0.5	26.4	6.8
Viacom B	28,691	10,598	23.7	5.9	0.1	-0.3	—

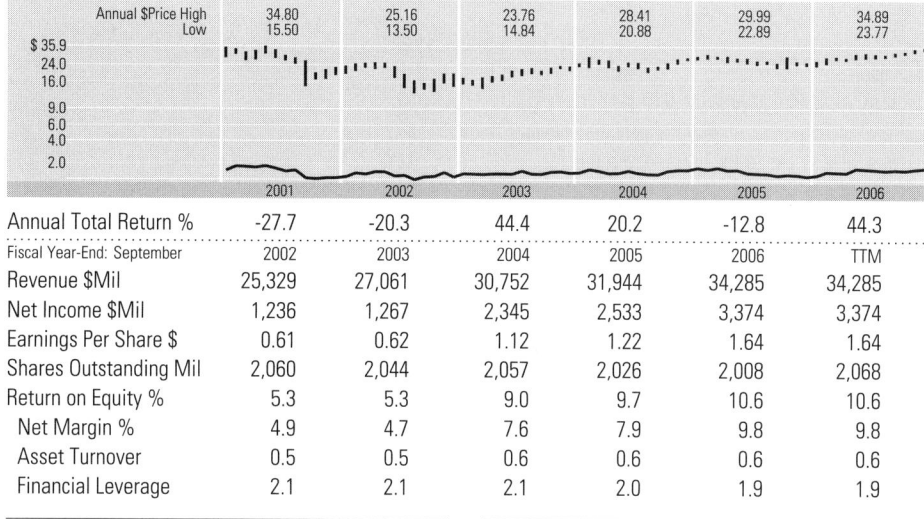

Annual Total Return %	-27.7	-20.3	44.4	20.2	-12.8	44.3
Fiscal Year-End: September	2002	2003	2004	2005	2006	TTM
Revenue $Mil	25,329	27,061	30,752	31,944	34,285	34,285
Net Income $Mil	1,236	1,267	2,345	2,533	3,374	3,374
Earnings Per Share $	0.61	0.62	1.12	1.22	1.64	1.64
Shares Outstanding Mil	2,060	2,044	2,057	2,026	2,008	2,068
Return on Equity %	5.3	5.3	9.0	9.7	10.6	10.6
Net Margin %	4.9	4.7	7.6	7.9	9.8	9.8
Asset Turnover	0.5	0.5	0.6	0.6	0.6	0.6
Financial Leverage	2.1	2.1	2.1	2.0	1.9	1.9

Valuation Ratios	Stock	Rel to Industry	Rel to S&P 500
Price/Earnings	20.9	0.8	1.0
Price/Book	2.2	0.7	0.5
Price/Sales	2.1	0.6	0.7
Price/Cash Flow	11.7	0.7	0.8

Major Fund Holders	% of Fund Assets
W.P. Stewart & Co Growth	8.15
Eagle Growth	6.03
Constellation Pitcairn Select Value II	5.01
Longleaf Partners	4.83

Thesis By Jonathan Schrader, CFA, 11-13-06 Stock Price as of Analysis: $32.26

For years, we've been unenthusiastic about Walt Disney, thanks to its poor corporate governance, poor profitability, and poor investment decisions (to name a few reasons). Disney's growth over the past several years--which occurred only because results in the early part of this decade were so awful--did nothing to change our position. Even after this growth spurt, return on invested capital was still below the company's weighted average cost of capital in 2005.

However, we see changes that bode well for Disney, the most important being the management tone that new CEO Bob Iger has set: It strikes us as collaborative, open-minded, and daring. In a time when all media companies are struggling with the challenges and possibilities presented by the convergence of media and technology, Iger has openly questioned the business practices of his firm and rivals, while also experimenting with new methods of distribution, like distributing hit shows Lost and Desperate Housewives through Apple's iTunes store and ABC's own Web site.

The "new" Disney also made a bold bet to revitalize its animation business, acquiring Pixar in an all-stock deal; Pixar's former shareholders now own a little less than 12% of Disney. While Disney's live-action studio has had some big hits over the past several years, its animation studio has--with only a couple of exceptions--produced duds. (Altogether, Disney's studios are now worth far less than its cable networks, especially sports behemoth ESPN.) Recent animation-related profits have come almost exclusively from Disney's deal to cofinance and distribute Pixar's films, which about to end.

In buying Pixar, Disney got more than just a library of hits and future releases; it also got CEO Steve Jobs and Pixar's very talented team of managers and creators. Many of the creative types at Disney hope that the arrival of Pixar's people takes the company back to the time when Walt was there and the focus was on the product, not the bottom line. We don't think products and profits are exclusive. By making better products--not just better animated pictures, but also better live-action films, better theme park attractions, and so on--profits should follow.

If Disney's creative spark is relit with the addition of the Pixar team, giving away 12% of the company to Pixar's shareholders will have been well worth it. If politics and bureaucracy prevent this renaissance at Disney, then Disney shareholders will wish the deal had never happened.

Warner Music Group WMG

Data as of 12-29-06

Rating	Fair Value	Last Close	Consider Buy	Consider Sell	Yield %
★★★	$26.00	$22.95	$16.60	$31.40	1.70

Industry	Business Risk	Moat Size	Investment Style	Sector
Media Conglomerates	Above Avg	Narrow	Mid Growth	Media

Company Profile

With about $3.5 billion in revenue, Warner Music Group is one of the largest music companies in the world. More than 80% of Warner's revenue comes from recorded music, which has a roster of almost 40,000 artists. The rest of Warner's sales come from music publishing. Warner Music was formerly a subsidiary of Time Warner, was purchased by a consortium of private equity investors in 2004, and is now a public company trading on the NYSE.

Management — Stewardship Grade [C]

Edgar Bronfman Jr. is Warner's chairman and CEO. Bronfman is best known for losing billions of dollars for his family by selling Seagram to Vivendi in an all-stock transaction. Though the Bronfmans made their fortune in liquor, Edgar Jr. has a long association with the entertainment business. He initiated Seagram's purchase of MCA and later acquired PolyGram, making Seagram's recording business the largest in the world. While Bronfman is Warner's public face, he reports to the private-equity investors who own most of Warner, especially Thomas Lee. Bronfman personally owns about 2% of Warner, while an investment group he heads owns another 9%. Thomas Lee owns more than one third of Warner's equity. Bronfman is joined by some of the best-known players in the music business, including Lyor Cohen, who helped build Island Def Jam into one of the most successful labels in the business. All of Warner's execs take home exorbitant paychecks, standard practice in the entertainment industry.

75 Rockefeller Plaza
New York, NY 10019
www.wmg.com

Growth [NA]	2003	2004	2005	2006
Revenue %	—	—	NMF	0.4
Earnings/Share %	NMF	NMF	NMF	NMF
Book Value/Share %	—	—	—	NMF
Dividends/Share %	NMF	NMF	NMF	NMF

Profitability [D]	2004	2005	2006	TTM
Return on Assets %	-27.9	-3.8	1.3	1.3
Oper Cash Flow $Mil	438	205	307	307
- Cap Spending $Mil	39	30	30	30
= Free Cash Flow $Mil	399	175	277	277

Financial Health [D]	2004	2005	2006	09-30-06
Long-term Debt $Mil	—	2,229	2,239	2,239
Total Equity $Mil	280	89	58	58
Debt/Equity Ratio	—	25.0	38.6	38.6

Competition

	Market Cap $Mil	12 Mo Trailing Sales $Mil	Price/Cash Flow	Return On Assets%	Debt/Equity	Total Return% 1 Yr	3 Yr
Warner Music Group	3,423	3,516	11.2	1.3	38.6	21.0	—
Sony BMG							
EMI							

Price Volatility
| Monthly Price High/Low — Relative Strength to S&P 500

Annual $Price High/Low: 2005: 19.55 / 14.70 ; 2006: 31.00 / 19.23

	2002	2003	2004	2005	2006	TTM
Annual Total Return %	—	—	—	—	21.0	
Fiscal Year-End: September						
Revenue $Mil	NMF	NMF	NMF	3,502	3,516	3,516
Net Income $Mil	-6,026	-1,353	-1,422	-169	60	60
Earnings Per Share $	—	—	—	—	0.40	0.40
Shares Outstanding Mil	—	—	—	—	143	149
Return on Equity %	ELB	-85.3	ELB	ELB	103.4	103.4
Net Margin %	NMF	NMF	NMF	-4.8	1.7	1.7
Asset Turnover	—	—	—	0.8	0.8	0.8
Financial Leverage	1.9	2.8	18.2	50.5	77.9	77.9

Valuation Ratios	Stock	Rel to Industry	Rel to S&P 500
Price/Earnings	57.4	2.3	2.8
Price/Book	59.0	17.9	14.4
Price/Sales	1.0	0.3	0.3
Price/Cash Flow	11.2	0.7	0.8

Major Fund Holders	% of Fund Assets
Legg Mason Partners Capital I	2.18
Kinetics Small Cap Opportunities	1.66
Hartford Global Leaders HLS IB	1.44
Seligman Global Growth A	1.40

Thesis By Jonathan Schrader, CFA, 12-06-06 Stock Price as of Analysis: $23.72

Warner Music Group has a long, distinguished history. Its labels, which include Warner Bros., Atlantic, and Elektra, have represented some of the most successful recording artists of the past 50 years, including Led Zeppelin, Madonna, and the Eagles.

Recent history, however, has not been so kind to Warner. Online file sharing and increasing broadband penetration have made it easy for consumers to build music collections without ever paying Warner a dime for one of its CDs. Evidence of this is the 25% drop in industrywide CD shipments from 2000 to 2005. If not for favorable exchange rates, Warner's revenue would have also declined during this period.

Because of this weakness and a need to raise cash, Time Warner opted to sell Warner Music to current chairman and CEO Edgar Bronfman Jr. and several private-equity investors for $2.6 billion in 2004. The new owners made significant cost cuts in the first year and then filed to take Warner Music public. The company began trading in May 2005.

While Warner owns some of the best content in music, we're not sure that the company's existing business model will lead to robust sales in the future. Previous transitions--for example, from vinyl to CD--ultimately resulted in tons of cash for artists and executives, as listeners spent hundreds or thousands of dollars updating their music collections. This time, though, it's different.

In moving from vinyl to cassette to CD, Warner was always in control of its content. In the movement from physical to digital, the consumer--not Warner--has been in control. Warner hopes to regain control via litigation, digital rights management software, and promotion of legal downloading. To date, the firm has had limited success with this strategy, and only time will tell if Warner and its industry peers will be able to put the genie back in the bottle.

Because of this uncertainty, we've assigned Warner only a narrow moat (its huge catalog of hit songs and the oligopolistic nature of its industry would otherwise support a wide-moat rating). Our above-average risk rating results not just from the uncertainty surrounding Warner's business model but also from the heavy debt load the company carries from the private-equity buyout.

Washington Mutual WM

Data as of 12-29-06

	Rating	Fair Value	Last Close	Consider Buy	Consider Sell	Yield %
	★★★★	$52.00	$45.49	$40.10	$65.20	4.53

Industry	Business Risk	Moat Size	Investment Style	Sector
Savings & Loans	Average	Narrow	Large Value	Financial Services

Company Profile

Seattle-based Washington Mutual, soon to be known only as WaMu, began operations in 1889 primarily as a home loan company. It is now the largest U.S. thrift, with about $350 billion in assets. Its main segments include a retail banking operation with more than 2,200 branches, the country's third-largest mortgage bank in terms of originations, a commercial group that originates multifamily and subprime loans, and a credit card division formed by its acquisition of Providian.

Management   Stewardship Grade [B]

Although his credibility was damaged somewhat by difficulties in the mortgage banking unit that led to big earnings misses recently, we think CEO Kerry Killinger has proved to be an adept executive at the helm of WaMu. Killinger also asserts--and we agree--that the current management teams over all the company's various segments are the strongest WaMu's ever had. We applaud management for its discipline in sticking with long-term strategies and focusing on generating adequate returns on capital. For example, WaMu slowed its asset growth in 2006 and plans to slow it more in 2007 because management has determined that using its capital to repurchase its undervalued shares, rather than invest in new assets, will provide a higher expected return. Management has proved that it maintains a similar discipline for all of its capital deployment, including acquisitions, so we rest a little easier knowing that shareholders' money is in good hands. Even though WaMu is a financial powerhouse, compensation at the top still seems relatively high, and option grants have typically been generous. However, the firm was an early adopter of stock-option expensing, and option grants have decreased since. We are also pleased to see that upper management's pay tends to move in tandem with the firm's performance.

1201 Third Avenue www.wamu.com
Seattle, WA 98101

Growth [C]	2002	2003	2004	2005
Revenue %	30.3	7.0	-13.0	16.2
Earnings/Share %	12.3	4.7	-22.6	14.4
Book Value/Share %	29.3	2.4	12.2	24.8
Dividends/Share %	18.2	32.1	24.3	9.2

Profitability [B-]	2003	2004	2005	TTM
Return on Assets %	1.4	0.9	1.0	1.0
Oper Cash Flow $Mil	11,075	-19,715	1,765	—
- Cap Spending $Mil	1,053	585	607	—
= Free Cash Flow $Mil	—	—	—	—

Financial Health [NA]	2003	2004	2005	09-30-06
Long-term Debt $Mil	—	—	—	—
Total Equity $Mil	19,742	21,226	27,616	25,966
Debt/Equity Ratio	—	—	—	—

Competition

	Market Cap $Mil	12 Mo Trailing Sales $Mil	Price/Cash Flow	Return On Assets %	Debt/Equity	Total Return % 1 Yr	3 Yr
Washington Mutual	42,998	14,984	—	1.0	—	9.6	9.6
Bank of America	239,758	68,368	—	1.3	—	20.7	15.2
J.P. Morgan Chase & Co.	167,551	59,650	—	0.9	—	25.6	13.2

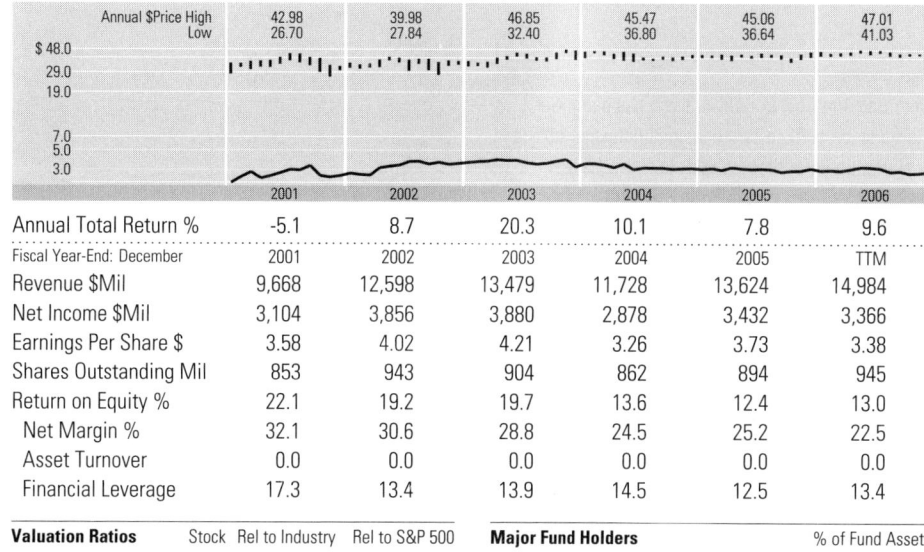

	2001	2002	2003	2004	2005	2006/TTM
Annual Total Return %	-5.1	8.7	20.3	10.1	7.8	9.6
Fiscal Year-End: December	2001	2002	2003	2004	2005	TTM
Revenue $Mil	9,668	12,598	13,479	11,728	13,624	14,984
Net Income $Mil	3,104	3,856	3,880	2,878	3,432	3,366
Earnings Per Share $	3.58	4.02	4.21	3.26	3.73	3.38
Shares Outstanding Mil	853	943	904	862	894	945
Return on Equity %	22.1	19.2	19.7	13.6	12.4	13.0
Net Margin %	32.1	30.6	28.8	24.5	25.2	22.5
Asset Turnover	0.0	0.0	0.0	0.0	0.0	0.0
Financial Leverage	17.3	13.4	13.9	14.5	12.5	13.4

Valuation Ratios	Stock	Rel to Industry	Rel to S&P 500
Price/Earnings	13.5	0.7	0.7
Price/Book	1.7	1.0	0.4
Price/Sales	2.9	0.6	1.0
Price/Cash Flow	—	—	—

Major Fund Holders	% of Fund Assets
Oakmark Select I	14.92
DWS Dreman Concentrated Value A	6.93
Constellation JSAM Large Cap Value	5.84
Touchstone Large Cap Value A	5.81

Thesis By Ryan Batchelor, CPA, 12-04-06 Stock Price as of Analysis: $44.32

We think Washington Mutual has an attractive banking strategy that makes it a compelling long-term investment candidate.

WaMu's retail bank has been very successful, entering several major cities and taking deposit market share from established competitors. As the firm entered new markets in recent years, it opened as many as 250 new stores (WaMu's equivalent of a bank branch) per year. WaMu expects to open fewer stores over the next couple of years as it seeks to expand primarily within its existing markets.

WaMu's approach to banking is simple but very effective: It offers convenient, hassle-free banking in an open, retaillike environment devoid of the stereotypical tellers behind a counter, opting instead for a more personal environment where customers meet tellers at small stations disbursed throughout the store. Customers seem to approve, as evidenced by 19% annual deposit growth over the past five years. Although we think the days of relatively easy sky-high deposit growth have ended for WaMu, the firm has established good customer relationships that allow for future opportunities through cross-selling new products augmented with modest deposit growth.

The bank offers customers traditional retail depositary products, and it focuses its lending primarily on home-equity loans and lines of credit. It now offers credit cards as well, thanks to its purchase of Providian in 2005. We think the Providian deal was smart, as it filled a big hole in the bank's consumer product line and so far has performed better than management's and our expectations.

Management also believes that its mortgage banking group provides a competitive advantage in establishing customer relationships. Once WaMu establishes a mortgage relationship, it attempts to get customers to defect from their existing banks by offering attractive retail banking products. The firm's research shows that customers with more than one product are 30% more likely to stay with the bank.

Despite management's optimism, we're not convinced that WaMu's mortgage bank provides any big advantages; in fact, in many ways, it's been a thorn in the side, struggling with hedging inefficiencies and high expenses during the past two years. We're encouraged by some recent progress and divestitures that we've seen in this unit, and management is still working feverishly to trim expenses. Ultimately, though, we believe WaMu's mortgage bank will become less important to the firm as diversification continues.

Data as of 12-29-06

Washington Post Co WPO

	Rating	Fair Value	Last Close	Consider Buy	Consider Sell	Yield %
	★★★★	$850.00	$745.60	$724.30	$1116.00	1.05

Company Profile

The principal business activities of Washington Post consist of newspaper publishing (principally The Washington Post), television broadcasting (through the ownership and operation of six TV broadcast stations), cable television systems, the provision of educational services (through its Kaplan subsidiary), and magazine publishing (principally Newsweek magazine).

Management

Stewardship Grade [B]

Chairman and CEO Donald Graham has been in charge since 1991, after serving as publisher of The Washington Post for 21 years. He oversees a conservative team that is forthright with investors. Graham's compensation is extremely reasonable; his annual salary has remained $400,000 for the past several years. The company also has a strong board of directors that includes Warren Buffett, Barry Diller, and Ronald Olson (Charlie Munger's law partner). The only knocks we have against Washington Post's governance are the existence of a separate share class with unlimited voting rights, which Graham controls, and the fact that Graham has the roles of both chairman and CEO. Overall, though, we think Washington Post's leadership is among the best around, and its stewardship of shareholder interests should be a model for others.

1150 15th Street N.W. www.washpostco.com
Washington, DC 20071

Growth [B]	2002	2003	2004	2005
Revenue %	7.2	9.9	16.2	7.7
Earnings/Share %	-11.3	17.7	37.7	-5.8
Book Value/Share %	8.9	11.9	16.2	9.4
Dividends/Share %	0.0	3.6	20.7	5.7

Profitability [A]	2003	2004	2005	TTM
Return on Assets %	6.1	7.7	6.8	6.9
Oper Cash Flow $Mil	338	562	523	546
- Cap Spending $Mil	126	205	238	273
= Free Cash Flow $Mil	212	357	284	273

Financial Health [A+]	2003	2004	2005	09-30-06
Long-term Debt $Mil	422	426	404	400
Total Equity $Mil	2,063	2,405	2,638	2,813
Debt/Equity Ratio	0.2	0.2	0.2	0.1

Industry	Business Risk	Moat Size	Investment Style	Sector
Media Conglomerates	Below Avg	Wide	Mid Core	Media

Competition	Market Cap $Mil	12 Mo Trailing Sales $Mil	Price/Cash Flow	Return On Assets %	Debt/Equity	Total Return % 1 Yr	Total Return % 3 Yr
Washington Post Co	7,167	3,813	13.1	6.9	0.1	-1.5	-1.0
Time Warner	86,932	44,532	14.4	4.9	0.5	26.4	6.8
Gannett	14,167	7,880	9.8	6.9	0.7	1.9	-10.5

Price Volatility | Monthly Price High/Low — Relative Strength to S&P 500

Annual $Price High	651.50	743.00	819.50	999.50	982.03	815.00
Low	470.00	516.00	650.03	790.21	716.00	690.00
	2001	2002	2003	2004	2005	2006
Annual Total Return %	-13.2	40.5	8.1	25.2	-21.5	-1.5

Fiscal Year-End: December	2001	2002	2003	2004	2005	TTM
Revenue $Mil	2,411	2,584	2,839	3,300	3,554	3,813
Net Income $Mil	229	203	240	332	313	330
Earnings Per Share $	24.06	21.34	25.12	34.59	32.59	34.37
Shares Outstanding Mil	9	10	10	10	10	10
Return on Equity %	13.6	11.1	11.6	13.8	11.9	11.7
Net Margin %	9.5	7.9	8.5	10.1	8.8	8.7
Asset Turnover	0.7	0.7	0.7	0.8	0.8	0.8
Financial Leverage	2.1	2.0	1.9	1.8	1.7	1.7

Valuation Ratios	Stock	Rel to Industry	Rel to S&P 500
Price/Earnings	21.4	0.8	1.0
Price/Book	2.5	0.8	0.6
Price/Sales	1.9	0.5	0.7
Price/Cash Flow	13.1	0.8	0.9

Major Fund Holders	% of Fund Assets
Kinetics Internet	5.06
Wisdom Inv	4.53
Weitz Value	4.28
Weitz Partners Value	4.25

Thesis By James M. Walden, CFA, 12-18-06 Stock Price as of Analysis: $759.12

The Washington Post Company still bears the corporate name of its storied newspaper, but much of the firm's recent success comes from Kaplan, the company's education segment. Over each of the past three years, Kaplan has experienced average top-line growth of about 32%, and it now accounts for almost half of Washington Post's total revenue. Kaplan's surge has been heady, but we think it will continue to be the company's growth engine.

In our opinion, most of Kaplan's growth opportunity will come from international expansion, where management continues to feed the business with prudent acquisitions. We also see significant opportunity in Kaplan's online educational programs. At the end of 2005, Kaplan University had around 24,000 students in online programs, an increase of 26% from the end of 2004, and Concord Law School, the world's first entirely Internet-based accredited law school, watched its enrollment swell more than ninefold to 15,000 students. Given the increasing acceptance of online education, we expect these enrollment figures to continue to build. As Kaplan University's online and traditional offerings continue to prosper, we anticipate Kaplan's higher-education businesses will overtake its supplemental-education operations in 2006 as Kaplan's largest source of revenue.

While Kaplan has provided the spark lately, we think that the flagship newspaper continues to provide the The Washington Post Company with its wide economic moat. In our opinion, the Post's moat is wider than most newspapers' because of its focus on political content, giving it a tight lock on its readership, which includes the leaders of the federal government. According to recent figures provided by the firm, almost 90% of the executive and legislative branches read the daily edition of the Post. We think the Post's unmatched political journalism will ensure such readership captivity (and double-digit operating margins for the newspaper-publishing segment) for the foreseeable future.

We think very highly of the company's management, but we think it faces some formidable challenges. Higher education is a very cyclical business; as the economy grows, workers are less inclined to leave their jobs for additional schooling. Also, management may be stretched thin as the company sees significant expansion. Still, we'd be very comfortable owning shares in Washington Post, knowing that its solid executive team is investing our capital in a way that creates long-term shareholder value.

Waste Management WMI

Data as of 12-29-06

	Rating	Fair Value	Last Close	Consider Buy	Consider Sell	Yield %
	★★★★	$45.00	$36.77	$34.70	$56.40	2.39

Company Profile
Waste Management is the largest provider of solid waste management in the United States, with a 28% market share. The firm has about 30,000 collection trucks and nearly 300 landfills. It is also the largest recycler in the United States. It markets these services to 27 million commercial, industrial, and residential customers. About 57% of the company's revenue comes from collection; the rest is generated by transfer, disposal, and recycling services.

Management — Stewardship Grade [B]
David Steiner took the helm in March 2004, succeeding turnaround guru Maurice Myers, who had been CEO since 1999. (Myers retired as chairman in November 2004 and was succeeded by John C. Pope.) We expect Steiner, who was promoted from CFO, to execute the same game plan set forth by his predecessor. Accounting scandals and botched mergers plagued Waste Management in the late 1990s, severely tarnishing its image. Myers succeeded in resurrecting the firm, largely through improving information technology, which was almost nonexistent before he arrived. Because waste services firms operate on a local level, information flow is critical. We expect a continued focus on careful, data-driven analysis of local markets, with the goal of leading the industry toward higher tipping fees. Finally, we anticipate the recent change in executive compensation, which now links rewards to improving operating margins and returns on invested capital, to further tie management's goals to those of shareholders.

1001 Fannin Street Suite 4000   www.wmx.com
Houston, TX 77002

Growth [C-]	2002	2003	2004	2005
Revenue %	-1.0	3.9	7.5	4.5
Earnings/Share %	66.3	-20.3	51.9	29.8
Book Value/Share %	0.2	9.7	8.6	5.7
Dividends/Share %	0.0	0.0	7400.0	6.7

Profitability [B+]	2003	2004	2005	TTM
Return on Assets %	3.1	4.5	5.6	5.7
Oper Cash Flow $Mil	1,926	2,218	2,391	2,530
- Cap Spending $Mil	1,200	1,258	1,180	1,239
= Free Cash Flow $Mil	726	960	1,211	1,291

Financial Health [B]	2003	2004	2005	09-30-06
Long-term Debt $Mil	7,997	8,182	8,165	7,780
Total Equity $Mil	5,602	5,971	6,121	6,160
Debt/Equity Ratio	1.4	1.4	1.3	1.3

Industry	Business Risk	Moat Size	Investment Style	Sector
Waste Management	Average	Narrow	Large Core	Business Services

Competition	Market Cap $Mil	12 Mo Trailing Sales $Mil	Price/Cash Flow	Return On Assets%	Debt/Equity	Total Return% 1 Yr	3 Yr
Waste Management	19,672	13,452	7.8	5.7	1.3	24.2	10.1
Republic Services A	5,307	3,043	9.2	6.1	1.2	9.9	17.6
Allied Waste Industries	4,523	6,003	6.4	1.2	2.5	40.6	-4.0

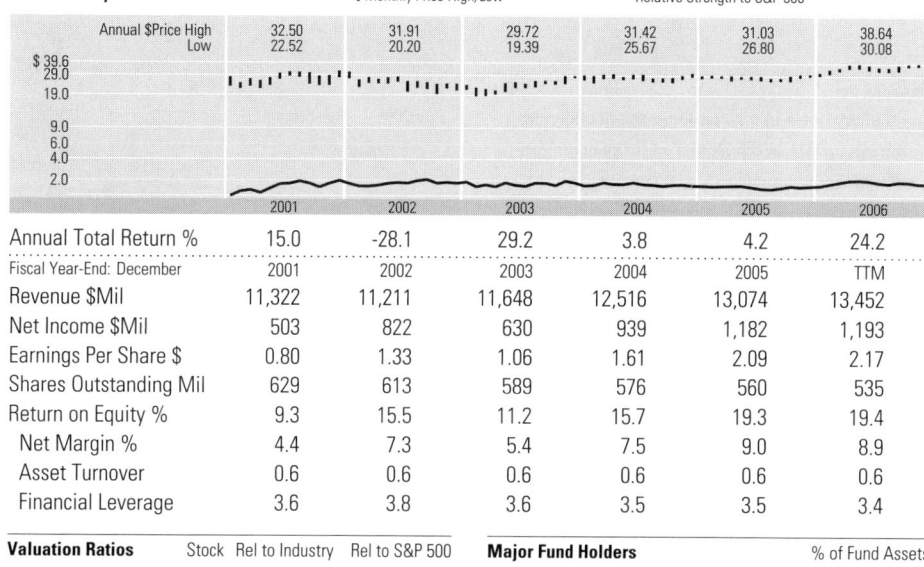

	2001	2002	2003	2004	2005	TTM
Annual Total Return %	15.0	-28.1	29.2	3.8	4.2	24.2
Fiscal Year-End: December	2001	2002	2003	2004	2005	TTM
Revenue $Mil	11,322	11,211	11,648	12,516	13,074	13,452
Net Income $Mil	503	822	630	939	1,182	1,193
Earnings Per Share $	0.80	1.33	1.06	1.61	2.09	2.17
Shares Outstanding Mil	629	613	589	576	560	535
Return on Equity %	9.3	15.5	11.2	15.7	19.3	19.4
Net Margin %	4.4	7.3	5.4	7.5	9.0	8.9
Asset Turnover	0.6	0.6	0.6	0.6	0.6	0.6
Financial Leverage	3.6	3.8	3.6	3.5	3.5	3.4

Valuation Ratios	Stock	Rel to Industry	Rel to S&P 500
Price/Earnings	16.9	0.7	0.8
Price/Book	3.2	0.9	0.8
Price/Sales	1.5	0.8	0.5
Price/Cash Flow	7.8	0.8	0.5

Major Fund Holders	% of Fund Assets
Fidelity Select Environmental	13.02
BBH Core Select N	4.86
Cookson Peirce Core Equity	4.27
Rice Hall James Mid-Cap Inv	4.11

Thesis By Brian Nelson, 11-28-06 Stock Price as of Analysis: $37.12

Waste Management's unrivaled network of landfills and disciplined approach to pricing should drive solid free cash flow generation and increased returns on capital for many years to come.

Because of the extensive permitting efforts required to develop new disposal sites, landfill ownership has become the primary competitive advantage in the solid waste industry. Boasting 277 solid waste landfills, Waste Management owns the most extensive disposal network--greater than Allied Waste (166), Republic Services (59), and Waste Connections (35) combined. Since industry pricing emanates from landfills (all solid trash takers must have access to a disposal facility), Waste Management is a price setter and, in some closed markets, can charge hefty disposal fees (tipping fees) to trash takers lacking viable disposal alternatives.

However, in markets with several competitor-owned landfills, pricing power can be attained only when landfill operators increased prices in unison. This has traditionally been difficult to accomplish because of the industry's roll-up origins, which spawned a growth-at-any-cost managerial approach. But recently, management changes and a shift to asset optimization from market share expansion across the industry have stimulated the adoption of more disciplined pricing. Operating in this improved environment, Waste Management has found great success executing its Pricing Excellence Program, as evidenced by its core yield (excluding fuel surcharges) jumping nearly 3% in 2005, the highest in recent memory. Although higher prices have increased the firm's customer defection rate, we expect ongoing profitability improvements, since most lost volume comes from lower-margin accounts.

A better industry pricing environment is not all that bodes well for Waste Management. The firm's internalization rate (the percentage of company-collected waste that is dumped in company-owned landfills) is poised to steadily increase as a result of asset swaps and planned divestitures, which will send $900 million of lower-margin, poorly integrated operations to the auction block. Higher internalization reduces expensive disposal fees paid to third parties and should boost the firm's margins in coming years. We expect Waste Management's planned divestitures, pricing initiatives, and cost-cutting efforts to boost returns on invested capital to a sustainable 11% by 2008 (from 8.5% in 2005), above our cost of capital assumption of about 8%.

Data as of 12-29-06

Waters WAT

	Rating	Fair Value	Last Close	Consider Buy	Consider Sell	Yield %
	★★★	$50.00	$48.97	$42.60	$65.60	0.00

Company Profile
Waters provides analytical instruments for pharmaceutical, biochemical, and industrial customers. Approximately 70% of sales are attributable to liquid chromatography instruments, consumables, and services. The company also sells and services mass spectrometers and instruments for thermal analysis.

Management   Stewardship Grade [B]
We give Waters and its long-tenured CEO Douglas Berthiaume a "B" Stewardship Grade. We admire companies that align executive compensation packages with business performance, and in our opinion, Waters is one of these companies. We were pleased to see that all executive officers received lower bonuses in 2005, following disappointing performance by the company. We were equally pleased with Berthiaume's decision to decline a board-recommended salary increase and option grant. We like the shareholder-friendly annual director election and approve of the modest retainers paid to independent directors. The executive team as a group controls nearly 6% of the company's stock, which indicates to us that the company's managers are willing to have some skin in the game. We would, however, prefer if Waters abandoned its antitakeover provisions and split the chairman and CEO duties.

34 Maple Street
Milford, MA 01757
www.waters.com

Growth [C]	2002	2003	2004	2005
Revenue %	3.6	7.7	15.3	4.9
Earnings/Share %	31.3	22.9	35.8	-4.4
Book Value/Share %	16.5	-5.7	19.1	-55.7
Dividends/Share %	NMF	NMF	NMF	NMF

Profitability [A+]	2003	2004	2005	TTM
Return on Assets %	15.1	15.3	14.1	14.5
Oper Cash Flow $Mil	157	259	298	265
- Cap Spending $Mil	35	66	51	51
= Free Cash Flow $Mil	122	193	247	214

Financial Health [B]	2003	2004	2005	09-30-06
Long-term Debt $Mil	125	250	500	500
Total Equity $Mil	590	679	284	261
Debt/Equity Ratio	0.2	0.4	1.8	1.9

Industry	Business Risk	Moat Size	Investment Style	Sector
Medical Equip.	Below Avg	Wide	Mid Growth	Healthcare

Competition	Market Cap $Mil	12 Mo Trailing Sales $Mil	Price/Cash Flow	Return On Assets%	Debt/Equity	Total Return% 1 Yr	3 Yr
Waters	4,970	1,226	18.7	14.5	1.9	29.6	13.9
Agilent Technologies	14,242	5,627	21.8	41.2	0.4	11.2	9.0
Thermo Fisher Scientific	7,157	2,864	21.9	4.8	0.2	50.3	21.9

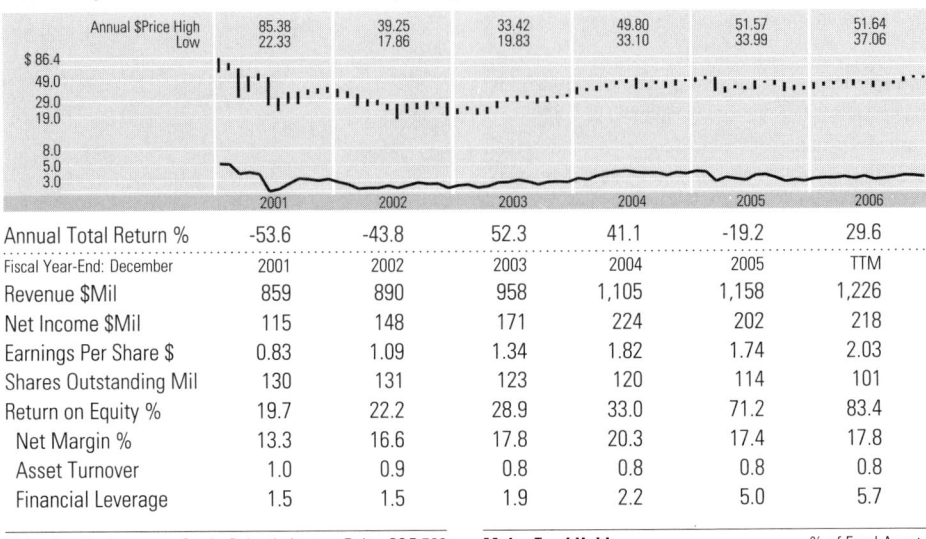

	2001	2002	2003	2004	2005	2006
Annual Total Return %	-53.6	-43.8	52.3	41.1	-19.2	29.6
Fiscal Year-End: December	2001	2002	2003	2004	2005	TTM
Revenue $Mil	859	890	958	1,105	1,158	1,226
Net Income $Mil	115	148	171	224	202	218
Earnings Per Share $	0.83	1.09	1.34	1.82	1.74	2.03
Shares Outstanding Mil	130	131	123	120	114	101
Return on Equity %	19.7	22.2	28.9	33.0	71.2	83.4
Net Margin %	13.3	16.6	17.8	20.3	17.4	17.8
Asset Turnover	1.0	0.9	0.8	0.8	0.8	0.8
Financial Leverage	1.5	1.5	1.9	2.2	5.0	5.7

Valuation Ratios	Stock	Rel to Industry	Rel to S&P 500
Price/Earnings	24.1	0.8	1.2
Price/Book	19.0	3.5	4.6
Price/Sales	4.1	0.9	1.4
Price/Cash Flow	18.7	0.8	1.3

Major Fund Holders	% of Fund Assets
Saratoga Health & Biotechnology B	5.92
Live Oak Health Sciences	5.51
Constellation HI AM Large Cap Quality St	3.89
Calvert Capital Accumulation A	3.30

Thesis By Alex Morozov, CFA, 12-07-06 Stock Price as of Analysis: $50.55

Waters' focus on the chromatography and mass spectrometry markets continues to pay off. The firm is generating results worthy of its wide-moat status, and we remain bullish about its long-term prospects.

Waters makes instruments for a variety of applications, from laboratory research and drug manufacturing to nutritional labeling and plastics production. The company is known for its high-performance liquid chromatography instruments, which separate compounds for purification, quality control, and other research-and-development activities. Waters is also second only to Applied Biosystems in mass spectrometers, which are used to identify a compound's composition and structure.

Waters' bread and butter is its chromatography operations, where the company enjoys a strong 20%-25% market share. The firm's main competitive advantage in this sector is the ability to innovate, as illustrated by the recent introduction of its ACQUITY Ultra Performance Liquid Chromatography system. The new technology separates Waters from the competition by providing the company's clients with a level of technical performance unmatched in the industry. While the new platform is still in its infancy, the company expects ACQUITY to eventually become an industry standard and drive revenue growth for years to come. An increasing adoption rate should also propel sales of high-margin chromatography columns, which are used with the platform and improve the performance of the company's mass-spectrometry business.

The ACQUITY system should inject a much-needed boost into mass spectrometry, as results have been lackluster over the past four to five years. Declining sales to large pharmaceutical clients and a slew of patent challenges that the company lost in 2002 have cast a shadow over its mass spectrometry operations. We think that Waters has finally addressed these issues, and we expect to see a drastic improvement in mass spectrometry performance over the next several years. The firm is offsetting weakness in demand from big pharmaceutical clients by growing sales to smaller biotech firms and contract research organizations. We are starting to see the signs of a recovery in capital-spending trends, and we think Waters is well prepared to capitalize on this turnaround. The company is in the process of releasing several new mass-spectrometry devices, and it should also benefit from an increase in sales of hybrid liquid chromatography-mass spectrometry systems, thanks to the success of its UPLC platform.

Weight Watchers International WTW

Data as of 12-29-06

Rating	Fair Value	Last Close	Consider Buy	Consider Sell	Yield %
★★★	$54.00	$52.53	$41.60	$67.70	1.33

Company Profile
Weight Watchers International is the leading provider of weight-loss services. It operates in 30 countries. At the heart of its weight-loss program are its weekly meetings that provide customers with advice and support. It also sells a range of products including snack bars, books, and point calculators. Additionally, the company receives royalty revenue from its franchisees and licenses its powerful brand, which provides it with new revenue streams.

Management   Stewardship Grade [B]
Linda Huett announced her resignation as the firm's CEO, effective at the beginning of 2007. Huett accomplished much during her tenure, including tripling the company's sales over the last seven years. Huett will be succeeded by David Kirchhoff, who has worked closely with her over the last seven years, giving us some comfort about the transition. Kirchhoff was previously CEO of WeightWatchers.com, and most recently served as the company's COO for Europe and Asia. Weight Watchers is controlled by European private-equity firm Artal Luxembourg, which bought the company from Heinz in 1997. Outsiders have very limited influence, and multiple takeover defenses dilute what little power they have. Top executives are paid reasonably; compensation appears to be variable and well aligned with performance. However, aside from Huett, ownership stakes in Weight Watchers among executives are very small, which may not align their interests very well with those of shareholders. Eliminating its staggered board of directors would also serve to improve its Stewardship Grade.

175 Crossways Park West   www.weightwatchers.com
Woodbury, NY 11797-2055

Growth [C+]	2002	2003	2004	2005
Revenue %	29.8	16.6	8.6	12.3
Earnings/Share %	NMF	0.0	30.5	-2.3
Book Value/Share %	NMF	288.3	11.3	NMF
Dividends/Share %	NMF	NMF	NMF	NMF

Profitability [A+]	2003	2004	2005	TTM
Return on Assets %	18.7	22.4	20.9	21.9
Oper Cash Flow $Mil	233	252	297	275
- Cap Spending $Mil	5	5	15	15
= Free Cash Flow $Mil	228	247	282	260

Financial Health [B-]	2003	2004	2005	09-30-06
Long-term Debt $Mil	454	466	741	802
Total Equity $Mil	181	196	-81	-103
Debt/Equity Ratio	2.5	2.4	ELB	NMF

Industry	Business Risk	Moat Size	Investment Style	Sector
Personal Svcs.	Average	Wide	Mid Growth	Consumer Services

Competition	Market Cap $Mil	12 Mo Trailing Sales $Mil	Price/Cash Flow	Return On Assets %	Debt/ Equity	Total Return % 1 Yr	3 Yr
Weight Watchers International	5,115	1,199	18.6	21.9	NMF	7.9	11.0
H & R Block	7,426	4,757	74.1	5.1	0.3	-4.0	-4.3
Weight Watchers Internati	5,115	1,199	18.6	21.9	NMF	7.9	11.0

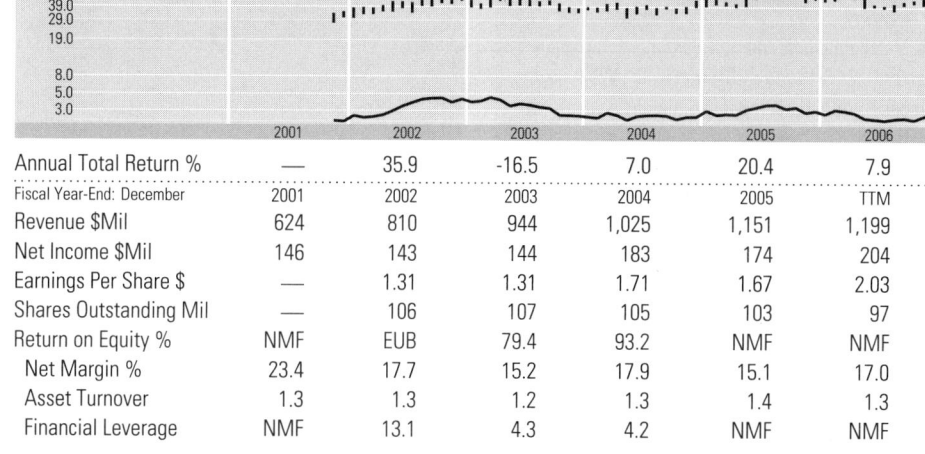

Annual Total Return %	—	35.9	-16.5	7.0	20.4	7.9
Fiscal Year-End: December	2001	2002	2003	2004	2005	TTM
Revenue $Mil	624	810	944	1,025	1,151	1,199
Net Income $Mil	146	143	144	183	174	204
Earnings Per Share $	—	1.31	1.31	1.71	1.67	2.03
Shares Outstanding Mil	—	106	107	105	103	97
Return on Equity %	NMF	EUB	79.4	93.2	NMF	NMF
Net Margin %	23.4	17.7	15.2	17.9	15.1	17.0
Asset Turnover	1.3	1.3	1.2	1.3	1.4	1.3
Financial Leverage	NMF	13.1	4.3	4.2	NMF	NMF

Valuation Ratios	Stock	Rel to Industry	Rel to S&P 500
Price/Earnings	25.9	1.0	1.3
Price/Book	—	—	—
Price/Sales	4.3	2.0	1.5
Price/Cash Flow	18.6	0.6	1.3

Major Fund Holders	% of Fund Assets
Delaware Pooled Focus Smid-Cap Gr Eq	5.34
Delaware Select Growth A	4.63
Delaware Pooled All-Cap Growth Equity	4.63
TrendStar American Endeavor	3.28

Thesis   By Kristan Rowland, 11-06-06   Stock Price as of Analysis: $47.21

Weight Watchers is the worldwide leader of weight-loss services, with a well-respected brand.

According to the Centers for Disease Control and Prevention, 30% of U.S. adults (60 million people) are obese and 65% are overweight, which creates a large market opportunity for Weight Watchers. Over the last 20 years, the percentage of obese Americans has doubled, and there has been about a 50% increase in overweight adults. As this demographic population has swelled, demand for weight-loss solutions has risen, and the weight-loss industry, including Weight Watchers, has prospered.

Other developed nations are encountering this epidemic, as fast food consumption grows and people lead more sedentary lifestyles, creating a larger opportunity for the industry. According to the American Obesity Association, in a majority of the countries in Europe, the rate of obesity has increased by about 10%-40% over the last 10 years. This trend bodes well for Weight Watchers, with its dominant market position and its behavioral approach to weight loss, which can be a sustainable part of a person's lifestyle over the long term.

Weight Watchers is noted for producing desired results, but its programs take time and discipline, which is why fad diets promising quick results can negatively impact its attendance. It faces competition from commercial weight-loss programs such as Nutri/System and Jenny Craig, self-help diets such as Atkins and South Beach, meal-replacement products, dietary supplements, surgical procedures, weight-loss drugs, and nutritionists. However, Weight Watchers has no major peers in group-based educational weight loss. No firm has successfully replicated its model because it is too expensive to create a brand that generates sufficient attendance at regular meetings in disparate locations.

Weight Watchers has struggled to improve its attendance recently, particularly in Europe, but we believe a couple of initiatives will prove successful over the long term. In an effort to attract members, it plans to enact program enhancements across the board in 2007. When changes to its program occur, it tends to boost attendance. Also, a focus on increasing member retention should also help boost attendance. To accomplish this, the firm is offering a different pay scheme, which should also help members stick to the diet. Successful members are the firm's best advertising, because it benefits from referrals. We would take advantage of any short-term weakness to invest in shares of this leading weight-loss company.

WellPoint WLP

Data as of 12-29-06

	Rating	Fair Value	Last Close	Consider Buy	Consider Sell	Yield %
	★★★★	$88.00	$78.69	$67.90	$110.30	0.00

Industry	Business Risk	Moat Size	Investment Style	Sector
Managed Care	Average	Narrow	Large Growth	Healthcare

Company Profile

WellPoint is the largest health insurer in the U.S., with more than 34 million members. It serves 14 states as an independent licensee of the Blue Cross and Blue Shield Association, and also serves members throughout the U.S. as Unicare. Revenue is generated from a broad product suite including risk-based health insurance, administrative-only services, and specialty insurance products including vision, dental, prescription drugs, life and disability, and behavioral health.

Management   Stewardship Grade [C]

We are slightly upgrading WellPoint's corporate Stewardship Grade to a "C" from a "D". We think the company's director compensation policy, which was updated in 2005, appropriately motivates the board with compensation skewed toward equity instead of cash. Additionally, we anticipate that WellPoint will adopt a more measured approach to options issuance going forward. We continue to believe, however, that WellPoint's management compensation practices are overly generous and reduce shareholder value. The board targets executive compensation in the 50th to 75th percentile in an industry that is already egregiously overpaid. While we like the fact that the 14 of 16 board members are independent, we think shareholders would be better served if the chairman and CEO roles were split and if the board was not staggered.

120 Monument Circle
Indianapolis, IN 46204-4903
www.anthem-inc.com

Growth [A+]	2002	2003	2004	2005
Revenue %	27.2	26.3	24.0	116.8
Earnings/Share %	NMF	20.8	11.9	29.2
Book Value/Share %	NMF	-4.1	192.8	-35.3
Dividends/Share %	NMF	NMF	NMF	NMF

Profitability [B+]	2003	2004	2005	TTM
Return on Assets %	5.8	2.4	4.8	5.7
Oper Cash Flow $Mil	1,159	1,303	3,257	—
- Cap Spending $Mil	111	137	162	—
= Free Cash Flow $Mil	—	—	—	—

Financial Health [NA]	2003	2004	2005	09-30-06
Long-term Debt $Mil	—	—	—	—
Total Equity $Mil	6,000	19,459	24,993	24,143
Debt/Equity Ratio	—	—	—	—

Competition

	Market Cap $Mil	12 Mo Trailing Sales $Mil	Price/Cash Flow	Return On Assets %	Debt/Equity	Total Return % 1 Yr	Total Return % 3 Yr
WellPoint	48,789	54,285	—	5.7	—	-1.4	27.3
UnitedHealth Group	72,374	51,787	11.9	7.7	0.4	-13.5	22.2
Aetna	22,540	24,654	—	3.7	—	-8.3	36.7

Price Volatility

Monthly Price High/Low — Relative Strength to S&P 500

	2001	2002	2003	2004	2005	2006
Annual $Price High	25.95	37.75	41.45	58.88	80.40	80.37
Low	20.50	23.20	26.50	36.10	54.58	65.50
Annual Total Return %	—	27.1	19.2	53.3	38.8	-1.4

Fiscal Year-End: December	2001	2002	2003	2004	2005	TTM
Revenue $Mil	10,445	13,282	16,781	20,815	45,136	54,285
Net Income $Mil	342	549	774	960	2,464	2,946
Earnings Per Share $	—	2.26	2.73	3.05	3.94	4.58
Shares Outstanding Mil	—	238	277	305	611	620
Return on Equity %	16.6	10.2	12.9	4.9	9.9	12.2
Net Margin %	3.3	4.1	4.6	4.6	5.5	5.4
Asset Turnover	1.6	1.1	1.3	0.5	0.9	1.1
Financial Leverage	3.1	2.3	2.2	2.0	2.1	2.1

Valuation Ratios	Stock	Rel to Industry	Rel to S&P 500
Price/Earnings	17.2	0.8	0.8
Price/Book	2.0	0.6	0.5
Price/Sales	0.9	0.8	0.3
Price/Cash Flow	—	—	—

Major Fund Holders	% of Fund Assets
AllianceBernstein Global Health Care B	8.71
DWS Value Builder A	8.23
DWS Equity Partners A	7.33
Integrity Health Sciences A	7.30

Thesis By Brandon Troegle, 10-19-06 Stock Price as of Analysis: $76.67

WellPoint's operates in a very competitive industry, but we like its narrow moat. With 34 million members, it is the largest health insurer based upon enrollment, and it has market-leading positions in 13 of its 14 markets. We expect this dominant player to grow even stronger.

WellPoint's competitive position is improving on most fronts. The merger with Anthem at the end of 2004 further strengthened its position as the largest holder of Blue Cross and Blue Shield licenses in the country. The more recent acquisition of WellChoice provided a strong presence in New York and strengthened its national accounts presence. As WellPoint continues to integrate these companies, it should realize further costs savings as a result of its scale. With fixed costs spread over a larger member base, the company's membership size improves its negotiating power with medical providers and should enable WellPoint to obtain the most-favorable terms in the market. This purchasing power will be increasingly important and could help insulate WellPoint from the price competition and margin erosion we expect in the industry.

While the scale benefits are important, the company has other significant advantages as well. Namely, as an independent licensee of Blue Cross and Blue Shield, WellPoint has one of the most recognized brands in the health insurance industry. We think this provides substantial benefits to the company and enhances WellPoint's ability to compete with other insurers for national accounts. WellPoint also has a very broad network, which should continue to help drive all segments, but especially national accounts. Additionally, we think the company is smart in adopting consumer-driven health plans. Its acquisition of Lumenos improves its consumer-driven health plan offering, which should see substantial growth in the coming years.

WellPoint is likely to make more acquisitions, of both Blue Cross and non-Blue Cross plans. The firm has already demonstrated itself to be an effective integrator, and we think this experience will be valuable as the industry consolidates.

We think WellPoint has a sustainable advantage and will continue to perform well, despite the tougher industry conditions that we expect. While we think overall market growth will be minimal, we believe WellPoint can steal customers from smaller providers in the market. Meanwhile, the firm generates significant cash flows that can be used to buy back shares, make acquisitions, or be returned to shareholders via dividends.

Data as of 12-29-06

Wells Fargo WFC

Rating	★★★★
Fair Value	$41.00
Last Close	$35.56
Consider Buy	$31.60
Consider Sell	$51.40
Yield %	3.04

Company Profile

Wells Fargo operates more than 6,000 banking and mortgage lending offices in the United States and abroad. The bank offers a robust line of consumer financial services, including online banking, trust, brokerage, credit cards, and insurance. It also makes real estate, corporate, and consumer loans. After merging with Norwest in 1998, it became one of the nation's top mortgage providers.

Industry	Super Regional Banks
Business Risk	Average
Moat Size	Wide
Investment Style	Large Value
Sector	Financial Services

Competition

	Market Cap $Mil	12 Mo Trailing Sales $Mil	Price/Cash Flow	Return On Assets %	Debt/Equity	Total Return % 1 Yr	3 Yr
Wells Fargo	120,049	34,770	—	1.7	—	16.8	10.4
Citigroup	273,691	86,566	—	1.3	—	19.6	8.4
Bank of America	239,758	68,368	—	1.3	—	20.7	15.2

Price Volatility | Monthly Price High/Low — Relative Strength to S&P 500

	2001	2002	2003	2004	2005	2006
Annual $Price High	27.84	26.72	29.59	32.02	32.35	36.99
Low	19.13	20.75	21.65	27.16	28.81	30.31
Annual Total Return %	-20.3	10.3	29.5	9.0	4.5	16.8

Fiscal Year-End: December

	2001	2002	2003	2004	2005	TTM
Revenue $Mil	20,981	25,249	28,389	30,059	32,949	34,770
Net Income $Mil	3,411	5,710	6,202	7,014	7,671	8,231
Earnings Per Share $	1.97	3.32	1.83	2.05	2.25	2.42
Shares Outstanding Mil	1,714	1,704	3,362	3,380	3,372	3,376
Return on Equity %	12.6	18.8	18.1	18.7	19.0	18.5
Net Margin %	16.3	22.6	21.8	23.3	23.3	23.7
Asset Turnover	0.1	0.1	0.1	0.1	0.1	0.1
Financial Leverage	11.3	11.5	11.3	11.4	11.9	10.9

Management — Stewardship Grade [B]

The most impressive part of Wells Fargo's corporate strategy is that it's not complex, and we credit the management team for its meticulous execution. Consistency of message is critical to a corporate strategy's success, and CEO Dick Kovacevich has been preaching his message since his Norwest days, despite the banking fads (mergers with investment banks, the hype of Internet-only banks, zero-down, no-document mortgages) that have come and gone. A testament to this bank's deep bench of managers is the number of ex-executives who now run other banks. At $8 million annually, Kovacevich's pay is big but warranted, in our opinion. However, we disagree with management's philosophy on stock-option expensing. Were it not for a change in accounting law, Wells Fargo would not have begun expensing options in 2006. The relatively small cost--which we estimate at about $102 million--reflects the bank's minimal use of options, so we don't believe the change is significant to shareholder value. Otherwise, Wells Fargo's corporate governance is above average.

Valuation Ratios

	Stock	Rel to Industry	Rel to S&P 500
Price/Earnings	14.7	1.1	0.7
Price/Book	2.7	1.2	0.7
Price/Sales	3.5	1.0	1.2
Price/Cash Flow	—	—	—

Major Fund Holders

	% of Fund Assets
Fidelity Select Banking	7.74
Wisdom Inv	6.77
ProFunds Banks UltraSector Inv	6.74
Constellation Pitcairn Select Value II	6.37

Thesis By Jim Callahan, CFA, 10-18-06 Stock Price as of Analysis: $36.81

Competitive advantages can arise from several different sources, and we believe Wells Fargo's moat comes from its focus on cross-selling and wallet share. If successful, any bank that cross-sells gains deeper customer relationships, more profit-generating assets, and typically higher retention. But while many banks appear more interested in expanding geographically, Wells Fargo focuses on increasing wallet share, a strategy that dates back to its predecessor bank, Minneapolis-based Norwest. Today, Wells Fargo boasts top-three deposit market share in 15 of its 23 states, and its cheap deposit base provides attractive lending spreads above its peers'.

Wells Fargo has one of the better-run and most consistently profitable business models in banking. Over two thirds of its income derives from retail banking, with wholesale banking accounting for 25% and consumer finance--credit cards, mortgages--adding 8%. We believe Wells Fargo is capable of continuing its 20-year record of double-digit revenue and earnings growth, solidifying its wide moat. Its revenue is 40% fee-driven, but management aims to increase this through higher trust and investment banking income. With the large investments already made in this high-return business, we expect Wells Fargo's 20%-plus returns on equity to continue for years to come.

Although we acknowledge that Wells Fargo's portfolio has risky real estate exposure, we believe the issue is overblown. California, Arizona, and Florida account for 18% of the bank's residential real estate portfolio, but only California exceeds 2%. Further, the bank doesn't originate the potentially dangerous adjustable-rate mortgages or negative-amortizing loans (in which small minimum payments lead to loan balances growing over time). If we were to assume that losses quadruple--a spike similar to the 1990 commercial real estate crisis--for two years, then recover to normalized levels over the next three years, our fair value would drop by $4 per share. We do not expect such a real estate blowup to occur, but we think the exercise supports our current opinion.

Wells Fargo's long-term record is impressive, but we believe its growth story is not over yet. The number of products per retail and commercial customer continues to rise, providing the majority of revenue growth. Although the bank's footprint covers only the West and Midwest, we expect management to continue with its in-territory, wallet-share-focused growth rather than expand eastward.

420 Montgomery Street
San Francisco, CA 94104
www.wellsfargo.com

Growth [B-]

	2002	2003	2004	2005
Revenue %	20.3	12.4	5.9	9.6
Earnings/Share %	68.5	-45.0	12.1	10.0
Book Value/Share %	12.3	-42.8	8.7	7.9
Dividends/Share %	10.0	36.4	24.0	7.5

Profitability [A]

	2003	2004	2005	TTM
Return on Assets %	1.6	1.6	1.6	1.7
Oper Cash Flow $Mil	31,195	6,485	-9,333	—
- Cap Spending $Mil	—	—	—	—
= Free Cash Flow $Mil	—	—	—	—

Financial Health [NA]

	2003	2004	2005	09-30-06
Long-term Debt $Mil	—	—	—	—
Total Equity $Mil	34,255	37,596	40,335	44,397
Debt/Equity Ratio	—	—	—	—

Data as of 12-29-06

Wendy's International WEN

	Rating	Fair Value	Last Close	Consider Buy	Consider Sell	Yield %
	★★★	$33.00	$33.09	$25.40	$41.30	1.80

Company Profile
Wendy's is one of the world's largest restaurant firms, with its flagship chain of 6,741 restaurants (78% franchised) in 50 states and in 18 other countries/territories. The company also owns 70% of the upscale fast casual chain Cafe Express (19 units in Dallas and Houston) and has a 29% stake in casual dining chain Pasta Pomodoro (46 units in California and Arizona).

Industry	Business Risk	Moat Size	Investment Style	Sector
Restaurants	Average	Narrow	Mid Core	Consumer Services

Competition

	Market Cap $Mil	12 Mo Trailing Sales $Mil	Price/Cash Flow	Return On Assets%	Debt/ Equity	Total Return% 1 Yr	3 Yr
Wendy's International	3,905	3,777	9.5	4.2	0.3	30.5	24.9
McDonald's	54,825	21,790	13.3	9.4	0.6	34.6	23.9
Yum Brands	15,586	9,444	12.9	13.7	1.5	26.8	21.6

Management — Stewardship Grade [B]

After more than 30 years with Wendy's, including six as CEO, Jack Schuessler resigned in April 2006, amid heavy pressure from activist shareholders. Kerrii Anderson, who joined the company in 2000 as an executive vice president and CFO, succeeded Schuessler as CEO, while James Pickett, a longtime director, took over as chairman. The company also recruited Dave Near, a successful Wendy's franchisee and son of former chairman, CEO, and president Jim Near, to fulfill the new role of chief operating officer. Given Wendy's past struggles, we believe this shakeup in the leadership team was necessary. The board should also benefit from the addition of three new directors nominated by Nelson Peltz's Trian Partners, which holds a 7% stake in the company. In 2005, Schuessler and Anderson earned reasonable salaries of $1.1 million and $0.5 million, respectively. Neither collected a bonus in the year, as the company did not achieve its earnings per share and return on asset goals. Both, however, received very generous packages of restricted stock. We do believe that management and the board have a decent record of doing right by shareholders, but disapprove of the company's staggered board, poison pill, and other takeover defenses.

Price Volatility

Annual $Price High/Low	14.29/9.37	19.48/12.25	19.30/11.23	20.02/14.87	26.42/17.20	35.95/25.25
	2001	2002	2003	2004	2005	2006
Annual Total Return %	13.3	-5.8	47.5	2.9	44.6	30.5

Fiscal Year-End: December

	2001	2002	2003	2004	2005	TTM
Revenue $Mil	4,316	4,917	3,149	3,635	3,783	3,777
Net Income $Mil	194	219	236	52	224	121
Earnings Per Share $	1.65	1.89	2.05	0.45	1.92	1.03
Shares Outstanding Mil	—	—	114	113	115	118
Return on Equity %	18.8	15.1	13.4	3.0	10.9	6.6
Net Margin %	4.5	4.5	7.5	1.4	5.9	3.2
Asset Turnover	2.1	1.8	1.0	1.1	1.1	1.3
Financial Leverage	2.0	1.9	1.8	1.9	1.7	1.6

Valuation Ratios

	Stock	Rel to Industry	Rel to S&P 500
Price/Earnings	20.3	0.7	1.0
Price/Book	2.1	0.4	0.5
Price/Sales	1.0	0.5	0.3
Price/Cash Flow	9.5	0.6	0.7

Major Fund Holders

	% of Fund Assets
Longleaf Partners Small-Cap	7.68
AIM Trimark Endeavor A	3.46
PF Van Kampen Mid-Cap Growth A	2.43
Homestead Value	1.97

P.O. Box 256 4288 West Dublin-Granville Roa www.wendys.com
Dublin, OH 43017-0256

Growth [D+]

	2002	2003	2004	2005
Revenue %	13.9	-36.0	15.5	4.1
Earnings/Share %	14.5	8.5	-78.0	326.7
Book Value/Share %	42.7	22.2	-2.9	18.9
Dividends/Share %	0.0	0.0	100.0	19.8

Profitability [B]

	2003	2004	2005	TTM
Return on Assets %	7.5	1.6	6.5	4.2
Oper Cash Flow $Mil	430	502	477	411
- Cap Spending $Mil	342	341	371	327
= Free Cash Flow $Mil	88	161	106	83

Financial Health [A+]

	2003	2004	2005	09-30-06
Long-term Debt $Mil	693	594	616	545
Total Equity $Mil	1,759	1,716	2,059	1,845
Debt/Equity Ratio	0.4	0.3	0.3	0.3

Thesis By John Owens, CFA, CPA, 11-27-06 Stock Price as of Analysis: $33.05

After a few difficult years, Wendy's core business looks poised for a turnaround. We now see several reasons to be more optimistic, including a revamped and more focused management team, exciting new menu offerings, significant cuts in corporate overhead, and substantial potential to expand restaurant-level profitability.

Wendy's has struggled in recent years, suffering from the negative impact of hurricanes, all-time-high beef costs, and the infamous chili finger hoax. Adding to its woes were management miscues, including a slip in operating standards, a dearth of new products, a poorly timed price increase on its Junior Bacon Cheeseburger, and a weak ad campaign. Meanwhile, McDonald's and Burger King improved their competitive positioning on all these fronts. As a result, Wendy's limped along in 2003 and 2004, then same-store sales fell more than 3% in 2005. The segment's profitability also took a hit, with the operating margin dropping to 9.4% in 2005 from 13.1% in 2002.

After serious prodding from activist shareholders, the board and management are making changes to reinvigorate the core business. The company spun off Tim Hortons, sold the Baja Fresh chain, and is pursuing strategic alternatives for Cafe Express. The company also reorganized its management team. We believe these changes will bring more focus and new energy to the Wendy's brand.

We're also optimistic about the burger chain's new products, including Frescata Sandwiches, a Vanilla Frosty, and more nutritious kids' meal choices. These additions to the menu should spur higher top-line growth, in our opinion. Wendy's is testing several other promising offerings, including a breakfast menu.

Management has committed to cutting $100 million of general and administrative costs by early 2007, largely driven by reduced staff at corporate and field offices. The company also sees potential to improve restaurant-level operating margins by 500 basis points over the next three years. A new double-sided grill, which will be rolled out to the entire system by the end of 2008, should lead to faster cooking and reduced labor. We think new store systems and supply-chain management initiatives could generate considerable savings as well.

There are still considerable risks. Poor execution of these initiatives could badly damage the business. Even if successful, rivals like McDonald's and Burger King could respond aggressively, or even irrationally, to any market share losses.

Data as of 12-29-06

Wesco Financial WSC

Rating ★★★★	Fair Value $515.00	Last Close $460.00	Consider Buy $438.80	Consider Sell $676.10	Yield % 0.32

Company Profile

Diversified holding company Wesco Financial is 80% owned by Berkshire Hathaway, which controls it. Wesco serves as a conduit for select Berkshire investments, including Coke and P&G. Wesco also owns businesses that provide insurance, rent furniture, and custom-manufacture steel. Wesco offers supercatastrophe reinsurance. Kansas Bankers Surety provides bank insurance. Precision Steel services niche steel markets. CORT leases furniture and offers relocation services.

Management   Stewardship Grade [A]

Wesco's management is the best in the business. Charles Munger, chairman and CEO since 1984, is a self-made billionaire thanks to his exceptional investment talent. Berkshire Hathaway chairman Warren Buffett, who contributes to Wesco's capital-allocation and investment decisions, is widely acknowledged as one of the best investors of all time. The only downside we see is that Munger is 82 and Buffett is 76. Munger draws an annual salary of $100,000, but this is paid by Berkshire, not Wesco. It's not often investors benefit from such talent without footing the bill. Like Buffett, Munger holds an annual shareholders' meeting. Wesco's meeting is held in Pasadena, Calif., each May. We strongly recommend that interested investors attend.

301 East Colorado Boulevard Suite 300 www.wescofinancial.com
Pasadena, CA 91101-1901

Growth [A]	2002	2003	2004	2005
Revenue %	2.6	6.7	-17.1	74.4
Earnings/Share %	0.3	41.8	-36.5	521.2
Book Value/Share %	2.3	6.2	1.9	5.4
Dividends/Share %	3.2	3.1	3.0	2.9

Profitability [A]	2003	2004	2005	TTM
Return on Assets %	2.9	1.8	10.8	10.7
Oper Cash Flow $Mil	55	56	101	—
- Cap Spending $Mil	51	77	97	—
= Free Cash Flow $Mil	—	—	—	—

Financial Health [NA]	2003	2004	2005	09-30-06
Long-term Debt $Mil	—	—	—	—
Total Equity $Mil	2,078	2,117	2,230	2,348
Debt/Equity Ratio	—	—	—	—

Industry	Business Risk	Moat Size	Investment Style	Sector
Insurance (General)	Below Avg	Narrow	Mid Core	Financial Services

Competition

	Market Cap $Mil	12 Mo Trailing Sales $Mil	Price/Cash Flow	Return On Assets %	Debt/ Equity	Total Return % 1 Yr	3 Yr
Wesco Financial	3,275	914	—	10.7	—	19.9	10.4
American International Gr	186,296	110,593	—	1.2	—	6.1	3.2

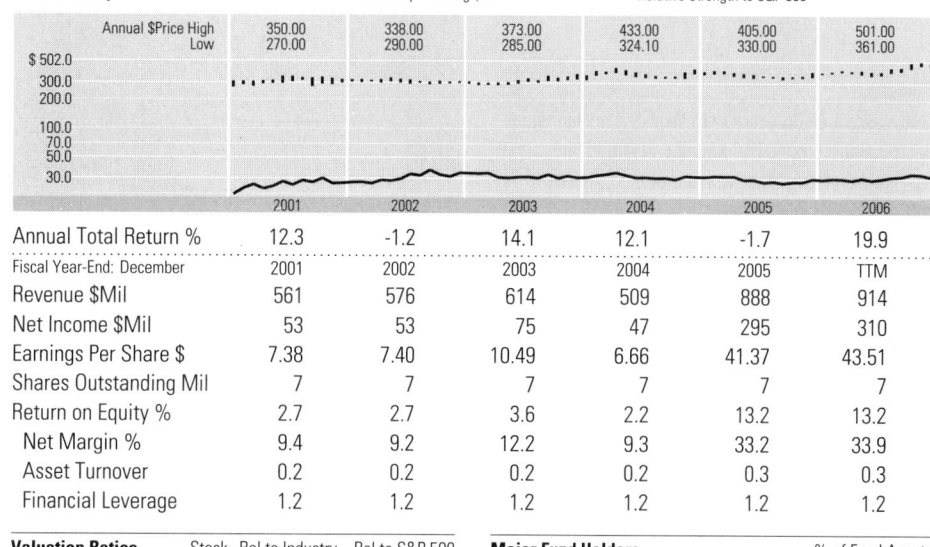

	2001	2002	2003	2004	2005	2006
Annual $Price High	350.00	338.00	373.00	433.00	405.00	501.00
Low	270.00	290.00	285.00	324.10	330.00	361.00
Annual Total Return %	12.3	-1.2	14.1	12.1	-1.7	19.9

Fiscal Year-End: December	2001	2002	2003	2004	2005	TTM
Revenue $Mil	561	576	614	509	888	914
Net Income $Mil	53	53	75	47	295	310
Earnings Per Share $	7.38	7.40	10.49	6.66	41.37	43.51
Shares Outstanding Mil	7	7	7	7	7	7
Return on Equity %	2.7	2.7	3.6	2.2	13.2	13.2
Net Margin %	9.4	9.2	12.2	9.3	33.2	33.9
Asset Turnover	0.2	0.2	0.2	0.2	0.3	0.3
Financial Leverage	1.2	1.2	1.2	1.2	1.2	1.2

Valuation Ratios	Stock	Rel to Industry	Rel to S&P 500
Price/Earnings	10.6	0.7	0.5
Price/Book	1.4	0.7	0.3
Price/Sales	3.6	2.1	1.2
Price/Cash Flow	—	—	—

Major Fund Holders	% of Fund Assets
Meehan Focus	2.47
Robeco Boston Partners All Cap Val Instl	1.03

Thesis By Justin Fuller, CFA, 12-11-06 Stock Price as of Analysis: $490.00

Wesco is an investment vehicle for majority owner Berkshire Hathaway. Wesco's managers, chairman Charles Munger and Berkshire CEO Warren Buffett, are arguably the best investors of our time, and their investments for Wesco earn good returns on capital.

Wesco accumulates funds for investment by reinsuring large catastrophes via agreements with parent Berkshire Hathaway. Wesco accepts premiums to cover "mega" catastrophe risks on similar terms to Berkshire, and then invests these funds for the benefit of shareholders. While the economics of this business can be immensely attractive, few reinsurers have been as successful as Wesco or Berkshire.

We think Wesco's success in reinsurance is due to a couple of moat-widening advantages. Wesco benefits from the financial strength of Berkshire, which yields the firm a AAA credit rating. This financial strength is a powerful advantage in the competitive market for large, long-duration risks, as it helps Wesco attract the "first look" at many profitable contracts. Wesco also benefits from the specialist underwriting skill of Berkshire unit National Indemnity, the industry's most profitable catastrophe reinsurer. In fact, despite industrywide hurricane losses over the last two years, Wesco's underwriting margin still averaged an impressive 23%.

We'd gladly take underwriting results like these, but we continue to believe much of Wesco's future value creation will come from management's ability to deploy its burgeoning capital into attractively priced investments. Munger and Buffett declare no strategic plan other than to opportunistically buy wide-moat firms at discounts to their fair values.

Presently, Wesco's subsidiary investments include insurer Kansas Bankers Surety, which offers a tailored line of specialty bankers insurance products and has established enduring relationships with many Midwestern banks. Precision Steel, which manufactures niche steel products, earns adequate returns in a brutal market, and occasionally larger profits when steel prices are high, as they are now. Furniture rental subsidiary CORT has endured a tough couple of years but has recently seen its results modestly rebound.

These are all decent businesses, but we continue to acknowledge that Wesco's largest investment remains its $1.2 billion--$175 per share--cash hoard. On this front, management's decision to keep Wesco's powder dry and wait for attractive opportunities should eventually reward long-term shareholders.

Westamerica Bancorporation WABC

Rating ★★★	Fair Value $54.00	Last Close $50.63	Consider Buy $46.00	Consider Sell $70.90	Yield % 2.57

Company Profile
Based in San Rafael, Calif., WestAmerica focuses its lending activities on small business and commercial real estate. The bank offers commercial lending, mortgage banking, cash management, and other financial services. WestAmerica has more than $5 billion in assets across more than 80 branches in Northern and Central California.

Industry	Business Risk	Moat Size	Investment Style	Sector
Regional Banks	Below Avg	Narrow	Small Value	Financial Services

Competition

	Market Cap $Mil	12 Mo Trailing Sales $Mil	Price/Cash Flow	Return On Assets%	Debt/ Equity	Total Return% 1 Yr	3 Yr
Westamerica Bancorporation	1,558	244	—	2.1	—	-2.1	3.1
Bank of America	239,758	68,368	—	1.3	—	20.7	15.2
Wells Fargo	120,049	34,770	—	1.7	—	16.8	10.4

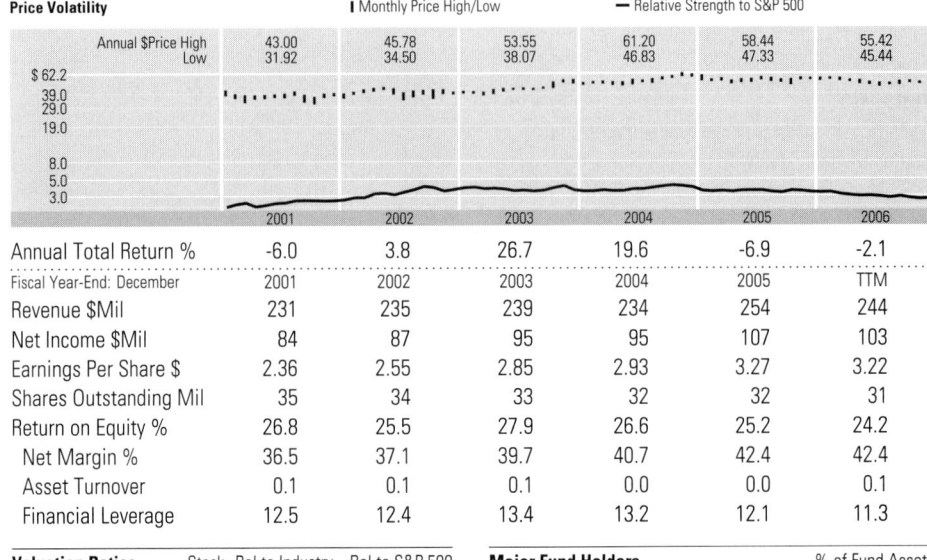

Price Volatility — Monthly Price High/Low — Relative Strength to S&P 500

Annual $Price High Low	43.00 31.92	45.78 34.50	53.55 38.07	61.20 46.83	58.44 47.33	55.42 45.44
	2001	2002	2003	2004	2005	2006
Annual Total Return %	-6.0	3.8	26.7	19.6	-6.9	-2.1
Fiscal Year-End: December	2001	2002	2003	2004	2005	TTM
Revenue $Mil	231	235	239	234	254	244
Net Income $Mil	84	87	95	95	107	103
Earnings Per Share $	2.36	2.55	2.85	2.93	3.27	3.22
Shares Outstanding Mil	35	34	33	32	32	31
Return on Equity %	26.8	25.5	27.9	26.6	25.2	24.2
Net Margin %	36.5	37.1	39.7	40.7	42.4	42.4
Asset Turnover	0.1	0.1	0.1	0.0	0.0	0.1
Financial Leverage	12.5	12.4	13.4	13.2	12.1	11.3

Management — Stewardship Grade [B]
With their explicitly stated strategy and impressive record, chairman and CEO David Payne and his management team deserve most of the credit for WestAmerica's performance. We see consistency in the bank's cost-cutting strategy with regard to management compensation. In fact, Payne's cash compensation has been static for three years, amounting to $842,000, well below the peer average. Cash and stock bonus awards are tied to the achievement of target performance metrics like return on equity, credit quality, and bank efficiency. Payne owns 7.1% of the company--a very significant stake that aligns his interests with those of shareholders, in our opinion. Stock-option grants are typically less than 2% of shares outstanding, although Payne received 45% of all options granted in 2005, 2004, and 2003. We like that the 10-member board is subject to annual elections, but we don't like that director compensation excludes stock grants and the fact that the chairman and the CEO roles aren't separate.

1108 Fifth Avenue www.westamerica.com
San Rafael, CA 94901

Growth [D]	2002	2003	2004	2005
Revenue %	1.8	1.8	-2.3	8.5
Earnings/Share %	8.1	11.8	2.8	11.6
Book Value/Share %	13.5	2.1	8.1	17.7
Dividends/Share %	9.8	11.1	10.0	10.9

Profitability [A+]	2003	2004	2005	TTM
Return on Assets %	2.1	2.0	2.1	2.1
Oper Cash Flow $Mil	115	114	120	—
- Cap Spending $Mil	4	3	2	—
= Free Cash Flow $Mil	—	—	—	—

Financial Health [NA]	2003	2004	2005	09-30-06
Long-term Debt $Mil	—	—	—	—
Total Equity $Mil	340	359	427	427
Debt/Equity Ratio	—	—	—	—

Valuation Ratios	Stock	Rel to Industry	Rel to S&P 500
Price/Earnings	15.7	0.9	0.8
Price/Book	3.6	1.2	0.9
Price/Sales	6.4	1.1	2.2
Price/Cash Flow	—	—	—

Major Fund Holders	% of Fund Assets
FAM Equity-Income Inv	4.39
Dunham Small Cap Value N	1.99
FAM Value Inv	1.92
Westcore Small-Cap Value	1.69

Thesis By Michael Kon, CFA, 12-15-06 Stock Price as of Analysis: $50.65

In the crowded California market, WestAmerica has carved out a very profitable niche. The result: industry-leading returns to owners.

WestAmerica provides commercial and retail banking services through a network of branches in Northern and Central California. The bank differentiates itself by targeting small to midsize businesses and their owners. WestAmerica combines the personal attention of a community bank with the sophisticated products of a large institution to attract high-quality customers. By emphasizing the personal touch, the bank strives to form long-lasting relationships with its clients. In our opinion, these relationships widen the bank's economic moat and reduce its business risk.

WestAmerica also boasts outstanding asset quality. Although a benign credit environment contributed its share, the bank's conservative lending practices also deserve applause. WestAmerica is a shrewd lender that shies away from risky products, like option ARM mortgages. Hence, net charge-offs of average loans over the past five years were a mere 0.12%, compared with about 0.30% for California rivals.

Another quality of the bank is its ability to keep expenses in check. WestAmerica's cost controls generate, on average, an outstanding 43% efficiency ratio--noninterest expenses expressed as a percentage of total revenue. Most of the WestAmerica's rivals, on the other hand, struggle to maintain an efficiency ratio of below 60%. This has also helped the bank to deliver an eye-popping average return on equity of 25% over the past decade.

WestAmerica also enjoys a very solid stream of noninterest income. The main source is charges on deposits, which constantly grew over the past decade. But what's most impressive to us is that WestAmerica earns more in fees on deposits than the interest it pays on those same deposits. This basically means that instead of earning interest, depositors are paying WestAmerica to hold their money for them.

The bank's main challenge is, in our view, top-line revenue growth. This could prove difficult for a bank with a conservative underwriting philosophy and no solid history of internal growth. Still, with an industry-leading return on equity, we wouldn't hesitate to snap up the shares if they traded at an appropriate discount.

Stocks 500

Data as of 12-29-06

White Mountains Insurance Group WTM

Rating	Fair Value	Last Close	Consider Buy	Consider Sell	Yield %
★★★★★	$795.00	$579.43	$613.00	$996.10	1.38

Company Profile

White Mountains is a Bermuda insurance holding company. Subsidiaries include OneBeacon, which offers specialty commercial and property insurance, and Esurance, an online direct-sale auto insurer. WTM Re is a top 20 global reinsurer and offers broad coverage via brokers, while Montpelier Re is a minority-owned property reinsurer. Symetra sells life insurance and annuities. White Mountains Advisors invests the firm's capital and manages more than $20 billion of client assets.

Management   Stewardship Grade [A]

Management is the critical ingredient at White Mountains, as its talent, continued rationality, and supportive incentive structure are the source of the firm's narrow moat. Much of the value at White Mountains originates in managerial talent, be it via investing the firm's capital, insuring the right risks at the right prices, or acquiring successfully. While we think the firm is unusually overweighted with capable executives, we attribute most of the success to an incentive system that fosters value creation. White Mountains' executives are rewarded for long-term growth in intrinsic value per share--a proprietary measure that incorporates economic value, tangible book value, and market value over rolling-three-year performance periods. We applaud this incentive structure, as it not only demands profitable underwriting, but also actively discourages unprofitable underwriting, which can rapidly boost sales and earnings per share, but will eventually obliterate capital. Best of all, managers eat their own cooking--salaries and bonuses reflect value created, and directors and officers collectively own about 7.7% of the firm, a $533 million investment.

80 South Main Street   www.whitemountains.com
Hanover, NH 03755-2053

Growth [D+]	2002	2003	2004	2005
Revenue %	30.1	-9.8	20.0	1.7
Earnings/Share %	—	NMF	68.9	-33.5
Book Value/Share %	—	NMF	21.6	-5.2
Dividends/Share %	0.0	0.0	0.0	700.0

Profitability [B-]	2003	2004	2005	TTM
Return on Assets %	1.5	2.2	1.5	2.2
Oper Cash Flow $Mil	-509	-557	-285	—
- Cap Spending $Mil	—	—	—	—
= Free Cash Flow $Mil	—	—	—	—

Financial Health [NA]	2003	2004	2005	09-30-06
Long-term Debt $Mil	—	—	—	—
Total Equity $Mil	2,979	3,884	3,833	4,119
Debt/Equity Ratio	—	—	—	—

Industry	Business Risk	Moat Size	Investment Style	Sector
Insurance (Property)	Average	Narrow	Mid Value	Financial Services

Competition

	Market Cap $Mil	12 Mo Trailing Sales $Mil	Price/Cash Flow	Return On Assets%	Debt/ Equity	Total Return% 1 Yr	3 Yr
White Mountains Insurance Group	6,246	4,503	—	2.2	—	5.3	9.5
St. Paul Travelers Compan	37,047	24,802	—	2.8	—	22.9	13.7
Swiss Reinsurance ADR	27,461	28,315	—	0.7	—	19.0	9.9

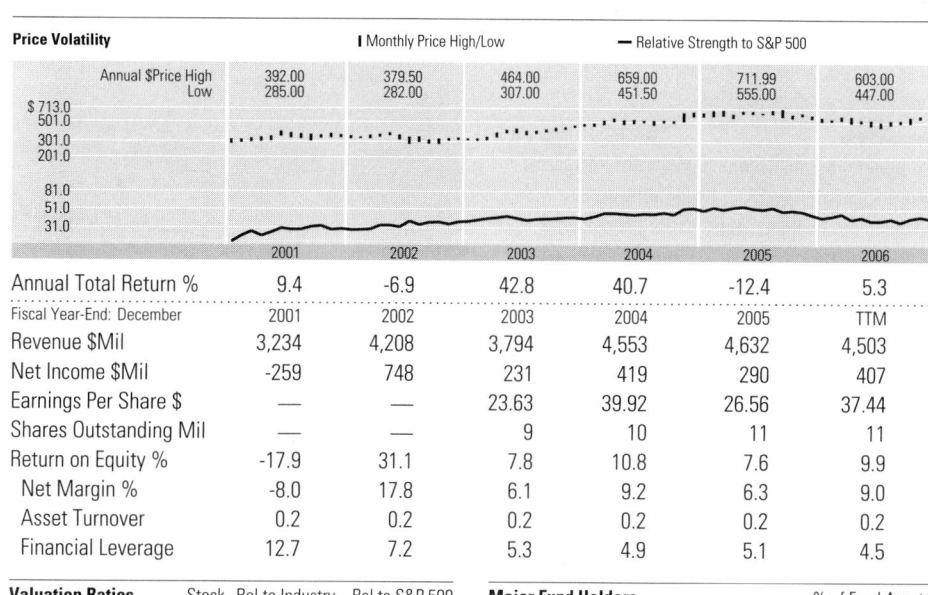

Price Volatility — Monthly Price High/Low — Relative Strength to S&P 500

	2001	2002	2003	2004	2005	2006 TTM
Annual Total Return %	9.4	-6.9	42.8	40.7	-12.4	5.3
Revenue $Mil	3,234	4,208	3,794	4,553	4,632	4,503
Net Income $Mil	-259	748	231	419	290	407
Earnings Per Share $	—	—	23.63	39.92	26.56	37.44
Shares Outstanding Mil	—	—	9	10	11	11
Return on Equity %	-17.9	31.1	7.8	10.8	7.6	9.9
Net Margin %	-8.0	17.8	6.1	9.2	6.3	9.0
Asset Turnover	0.2	0.2	0.2	0.2	0.2	0.2
Financial Leverage	12.7	7.2	5.3	4.9	5.1	4.5

Valuation Ratios	Stock	Rel to Industry	Rel to S&P 500
Price/Earnings	15.5	1.1	0.8
Price/Book	1.5	0.9	0.4
Price/Sales	1.4	1.0	0.5
Price/Cash Flow	—	—	—

Major Fund Holders	% of Fund Assets
Wisdom Inv	5.57
FAM Equity-Income Inv	5.41
FAM Value Inv	5.29
CNI Charter RCB Sm Cap Val R	4.43

Thesis   By Justin Fuller, CFA, 12-13-06 Stock Price as of Analysis: $586.76

Although White Mountains is an insurance holding company, we view it as an investment vehicle--either for the acquisition of insurers or profitable insured risks.

Making acquisitions is a key competency that fulfills a rare dual role at White Mountains: business expansion and wealth creation. Over the past few years, the firm entered life insurance by acquiring Symetra, boosted its casualty portfolio by buying Sierra, and expanded its property reinsurance business by acquiring Sirius and Tryg-Baltica. But wealth creation is key. By patiently and opportunistically seeking motivated sellers, management acquired each firm for less than book value--and arguably below fair value. The firm also scooped up an aviation underwriting team from a distressed reinsurer, adding expertise without exposure to historical claim liabilities. White Mountains also shrewdly mitigates the substantial risk of acquiring another insurer's claim liabilities by requiring adverse development insurance to protect against unforeseeable increases, or by purchasing only the renewal rights, enabling it to sell the insurance on a "go forward" basis.

The insurers White Mountains owns are characterized by very disciplined underwriting, which is doubtless easier when acquisitions generate growth and executive incentives reward only profitability. The firm amplifies this discipline with talent and insight. Most notably, subsidiary OneBeacon has rapidly decommodified many products by zeroing in on niche underwriting markets where it boasts an informational advantage. By customizing insurance protection for unusual risks in less competitive markets like tuition reimbursement with an increasing range of pricing tiers, OneBeacon can exploit its advantages by offering finer pricing that still fosters underwriting profits. This business has also developed more finely segmented policies for small and midsize businesses that allow it to compete in markets where many competitors offer only much broader coverage options.

Patient acquisitions and disciplined underwriting are even easier when management is confident that idle capital will be compounded by one of the better value-investing teams in insurance. Better still, these investments are often made in unregulated tax-free entities in Bermuda, an important bonus for returns that can be capital gain-heavy.

White Mountains profits by awaiting opportunities. We think investors should do likewise with its shares.

Whole Foods Market WFMI

Data as of 12-29-06

	Rating	Fair Value	Last Close	Consider Buy	Consider Sell	Yield %
	★★★★★	$72.00	$46.93	$55.50	$90.20	1.28

Industry	Business Risk	Moat Size	Investment Style	Sector
Groceries	Average	Narrow	Mid Growth	Consumer Services

Company Profile
Whole Foods is the largest U.S. retailer of natural and organic foods. It owns about 190 supermarkets targeting customers interested in health, nutrition, food safety, and the environment. The stores sell high-grade conventional and organically grown produce and grocery products; environmentally safe household items; meat, poultry, and seafood free of growth hormones and antibiotics; bakery goods and takeout meals; and vitamins, homeopathic remedies, and body-care products.

Management — Stewardship Grade [A]
We think corporate governance at Whole Foods is sound. Founder John Mackey earned a very reasonable salary and bonus of $482,000 in 2005, and he has recently announced that he will be dropping his annual pay down to $1. The company has an interesting policy related to management compensation that effectively ties it to 19 times the average salary of its regular employees. In effect, Whole Foods employs a yearly salary cap. Even as a high-growth company, Whole Foods values capital discipline. The extent to which the firm achieves returns in excess of its cost of capital factors heavily in determining incentive compensation, impacting employees all the way down to the store level. Financial disclosure is excellent. Same-store sales are broken out into five groups of stores based on age, and the company is pretty open about costs to open new stores, ongoing costs for remodeling, and long-run goals for sales and operating margins. While we agree with the desire of Whole Foods to better align the interests of its employees with its own through the use of stock options, we think the amount given out annually has been excessive.

601 N. Lamar Suite 300
Austin, TX 78703
www.wholefoods.com

Growth [A]	2003	2004	2005	2006
Revenue %	17.0	22.8	21.6	19.3
Earnings/Share %	19.7	25.3	0.0	42.4
Book Value/Share %	27.5	22.0	36.6	-2.0
Dividends/Share %	NMF	NMF	86.7	513.1

Profitability [A]	2004	2005	2006	TTM
Return on Assets %	8.5	7.2	10.0	10.0
Oper Cash Flow $Mil	330	411	453	453
- Cap Spending $Mil	266	324	340	340
= Free Cash Flow $Mil	64	87	112	112

Financial Health [A+]	2004	2005	2006	09-30-06
Long-term Debt $Mil	—	13	9	9
Total Equity $Mil	950	1,366	1,404	1,404
Debt/Equity Ratio	—	0.0	0.0	0.0

Competition

	Market Cap $Mil	12 Mo Trailing Sales $Mil	Price/Cash Flow	Return On Assets%	Debt/Equity	Total Return% 1 Yr	3 Yr
Whole Foods Market	6,708	5,607	14.8	10.0	0.0	-37.2	14.1
Kroger	16,551	63,293	7.4	4.7	1.3	23.3	8.0
Safeway	15,320	39,728	7.5	4.6	1.0	47.2	17.6

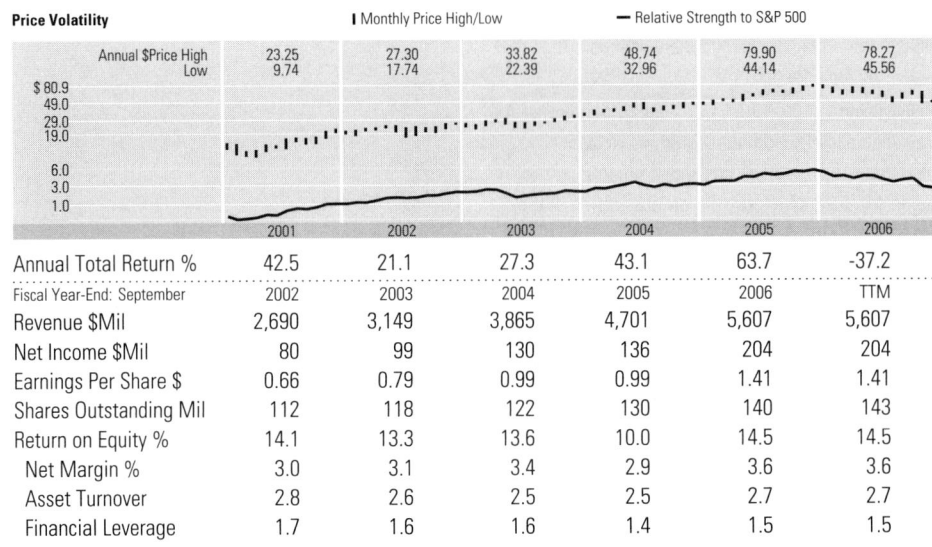

Price Volatility — Monthly Price High/Low — Relative Strength to S&P 500

Annual $Price High/Low	23.25/9.74	27.30/17.74	33.82/22.39	48.74/32.96	79.90/44.14	78.27/45.56
	2001	2002	2003	2004	2005	2006
Annual Total Return %	42.5	21.1	27.3	43.1	63.7	-37.2

Fiscal Year-End: September	2002	2003	2004	2005	2006	TTM
Revenue $Mil	2,690	3,149	3,865	4,701	5,607	5,607
Net Income $Mil	80	99	130	136	204	204
Earnings Per Share $	0.66	0.79	0.99	0.99	1.41	1.41
Shares Outstanding Mil	112	118	122	130	140	143
Return on Equity %	14.1	13.3	13.6	10.0	14.5	14.5
Net Margin %	3.0	3.1	3.4	2.9	3.6	3.6
Asset Turnover	2.8	2.6	2.5	2.5	2.7	2.7
Financial Leverage	1.7	1.6	1.6	1.4	1.5	1.5

Valuation Ratios	Stock	Rel to Industry	Rel to S&P 500
Price/Earnings	33.3	1.5	1.6
Price/Book	4.8	1.6	1.2
Price/Sales	1.2	3.0	0.4
Price/Cash Flow	14.8	1.6	1.0

Major Fund Holders	% of Fund Assets
Hillman Focused Advantage	4.88
Parnassus Workplace	4.73
Parnassus Mid-Cap	4.30
Fidelity Select Environmental	4.18

Thesis By Mitchell P. Corwin, CFA, CPA, 12-01-06 Stock Price as of Analysis: $48.28

In 2007, Whole Foods will be laying the groundwork for a multiyear square-footage expansion that we believe will cement the firm's premium brand in food in a way similar to Starbucks in coffee.

Whole Foods is a unique food retailer that, because of its culture, has no peer, in our view. The company adeptly melds social and profit motives. Its workforce not only feels a commitment to altruistic goals, such as helping the environment, but also has the incentive to consistently raise the bar, thanks to compensation tied to creating economic value. Over 90% of Whole Foods' stock options are doled out to non-executives, from store managers to cashiers.

We believe an empowered culture enables Whole Foods to innovate quickly, ensuring that the company provides one of the most compelling shopping environments and generates the buzz to drive store traffic. In 2006, the average Whole Foods store generated $593,000 per week in sales, compared with around $300,000 for a typical supermarket. Combining this productivity with a sales mix favoring higher-margin perishable products allows the company to turn $8 out of every $100 in sales into operating cash flow, versus $3-$5 for a typical grocer.

Amid decelerating comparable-store sales trends recently, there has been concern that the Whole Foods brand is losing some of its luster and competition is catching up. We acknowledge that the conventional supermarkets have improved their offerings, but none, in our view, is creating stores like the newer Whole Foods that serve not simply as a grocery store, but also as a "third place," or an alternative to the home or office. In our opinion, the conventional grocers simply can't replicate Whole Foods. Discount chains have left them resource constrained, limiting how much they can invest in labor and store ambiance, and their brand identities are fairly cemented in the minds of consumers.

As Whole Foods embarks on a plan to accelerate square footage growth and experiences tough comparisons, near-term financial trends will be weaker than in the recent past. However, we believe the new stores will reignite top-line momentum. Whole Foods' total sales today represent just 1% of the total grocery industry, and its fresh food venues offer alternatives to quick-service restaurants. The company is far from saturation, in our view.

Whole Foods has barely scratched the surface of its potential. We believe the company's favorable multiyear growth prospects and the abundance of operating cash flow thrown off by its stores will drive robust shareholder returns.

Data as of 12-29-06

Williams Companies WMB

	Rating	Fair Value	Last Close	Consider Buy	Consider Sell	Yield %
	★★★	$24.00	$26.12	$18.50	$30.10	1.32

Industry	Business Risk	Moat Size	Investment Style	Sector
Pipelines	Average	Narrow	Large Growth	Energy

Company Profile

Tulsa, Okla.-based Williams is an integrated natural-gas firm with exploration and production, gas midstream, gas pipeline, and power trading businesses. Together, the segments produce, gather, process, and transport natural gas. At the end of 2005, Williams had proved natural-gas reserves of 3.4 trillion cubic feet, 14,700 miles of long-haul pipelines, 8,100 miles of gathering pipes, and over 15 gas processing and treating plants.

Competition

	Market Cap $Mil	12 Mo Trailing Sales $Mil	Price/Cash Flow	Return On Assets %	Debt/ Equity	Total Return % 1 Yr	3 Yr
Williams Companies	15,576	12,719	9.3	0.9	1.2	14.4	40.0
Kinder Morgan	14,177	9,788	9.2	2.5	2.7	19.2	26.3
El Paso	10,778	4,814	4.0	1.6	3.6	27.1	24.0

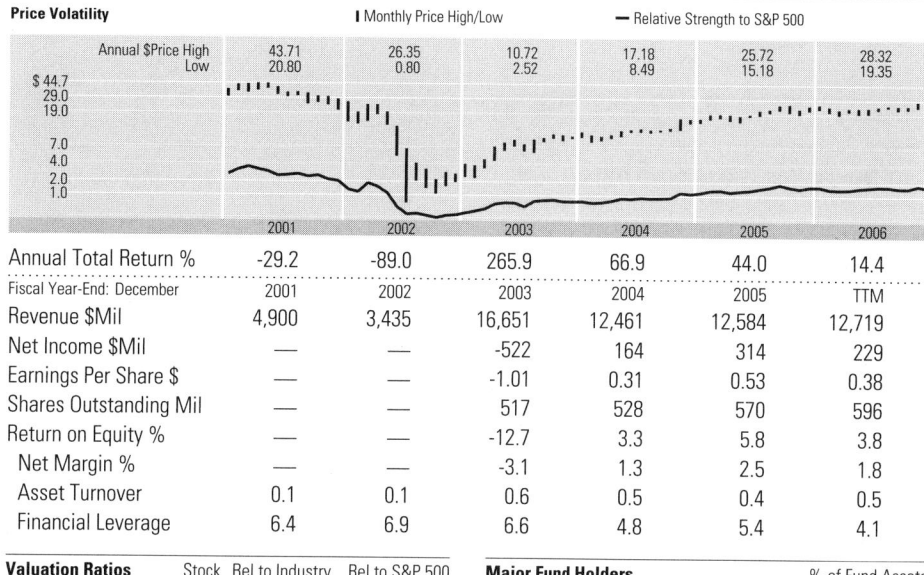

	2001	2002	2003	2004	2005	2006
Annual $Price High	43.71	26.35	10.72	17.18	25.72	28.32
Low	20.80	0.80	2.52	8.49	15.18	19.35
Annual Total Return %	-29.2	-89.0	265.9	66.9	44.0	14.4

Fiscal Year-End: December	2001	2002	2003	2004	2005	TTM
Revenue $Mil	4,900	3,435	16,651	12,461	12,584	12,719
Net Income $Mil	—	—	-522	164	314	229
Earnings Per Share $	—	—	-1.01	0.31	0.53	0.38
Shares Outstanding Mil	—	—	517	528	570	596
Return on Equity %	—	—	-12.7	3.3	5.8	3.8
Net Margin %	—	—	-3.1	1.3	2.5	1.8
Asset Turnover	0.1	0.1	0.6	0.5	0.4	0.5
Financial Leverage	6.4	6.9	6.6	4.8	5.4	4.1

Management   Stewardship Grade [B]

Chairman, president, and CEO Steven Malcolm has remained at the helm throughout Williams' turnaround and can now refocus on Williams' core businesses. Malcolm was promoted to president and CEO in late 2001 and became chairman in early 2002, at the time when the energy trading markets began their post-Enron collapse. Malcolm and the majority of his senior operating team have 15-20 or more years of experience at Williams, including its turnaround years. We give management credit for its turnaround efforts, as Williams was earlier than other power traders in forging settlements for the California power crisis and other litigation and in restoring liquidity and financial health. After forgoing a bonus in 2002, Malcolm received cash bonuses of $1.6 million in 2003, $2.7 million in 2004, and $2.3 million in 2005. Instead of cash bonuses, we think Malcolm's restricted-stock and option awards, which totaled over $3 million in 2004 and 2005, will serve as better long-term incentives. Overall, Malcolm's pay package looks relatively high but justified given the turnaround he helped orchestrate at Williams. We applaud Williams' effort to boost transparency by holding seminars to discuss its trading business and exploration and development efforts. However, we would like to eventually see a separate chairman and CEO at the helm of Williams.

One Williams Center
Tulsa, OK 74172
www.williams.com

Valuation Ratios	Stock	Rel to Industry	Rel to S&P 500
Price/Earnings	65.3	2.3	3.2
Price/Book	2.6	1.0	0.6
Price/Sales	1.2	0.5	0.4
Price/Cash Flow	9.3	0.9	0.6

Major Fund Holders	% of Fund Assets
Jacobs and Company	6.63
Security Select 25 A	6.19
JHancock Large Cap Equity A	5.55
JHancock Large Cap Intrinsic Value A	5.21

Growth [D]	2002	2003	2004	2005
Revenue %	-29.9	384.8	-25.2	1.0
Earnings/Share %	—	NMF	NMF	71.0
Book Value/Share %	—	NMF	18.2	-2.3
Dividends/Share %	-38.2	-90.5	100.0	212.5

Profitability [D]	2003	2004	2005	TTM
Return on Assets %	-1.9	0.7	1.1	0.9
Oper Cash Flow $Mil	770	1,488	1,450	1,682
- Cap Spending $Mil	956	787	1,299	2,172
= Free Cash Flow $Mil	-186	701	151	-490

Financial Health [D]	2003	2004	2005	09-30-06
Long-term Debt $Mil	11,040	7,712	7,591	7,275
Total Equity $Mil	4,102	4,956	5,428	6,071
Debt/Equity Ratio	2.7	1.6	1.4	1.2

Thesis   By Catharina Milostan, 11-21-06 Stock Price as of Analysis: $26.93

Williams' recovery is now fully under way with project-driven growth at its exploration and production (E&P), gas gathering and processing (gas midstream), and pipeline units. We'd still like to see further debt reduction and remain concerned over its smaller but potentially volatile power trading portfolio.

Williams has come a long way from its post-Enron liquidity troubles earlier this decade and can now generate cash flow to fund growth. We like how Williams' integrated natural-gas business is strategically well-positioned in fast-growing basins in the Rockies, Mid-Continent, and Gulf Coast. In contrast to E&P-only companies, Williams can generate earnings by not only selling its natural-gas production, but also by earning fees for gathering, processing, and transporting natural gas.

Williams sold many assets during its restructuring, but managed to keep key E&P, midstream, and pipeline assets tied to major, long-lived Rockies and Mid-Continent producing basins. Williams now plans to invest more than $1.5-$2 billion in each of the next three years to ramp up natural-gas drilling and to expand midstream and pipeline transportation capacity. Williams' E&P unit compares favorably with many E&P peers, as a top-25 U.S. natural-gas producer with above-average drilling success and reserve replacement results. Williams has large positions in highly desirable, lower-risk "resource type" basins including the Powder River Basin in Wyoming and Piceance Basin in Colorado. These resource basins can support several years of developmental drilling without the need for riskier or costly exploratory drilling. Williams' midstream operations are in the heart of new Rockies, Mid-Continent, and deep-water Gulf of Mexico producing basins that require greater gas gathering and processing capacity. Williams is also planning new or expanded pipeline transportation capacity to draw more natural gas eastward to markets in the Midwest and Northeast.

Despite the success of its turnaround to date, Williams still faces some hurdles. We'd like to see further debt reduction and remain concerned over its smaller, but still volatile derivatives portfolio. The company paid down 44% of its debt from 2002 highs and received credit-rating upgrades. However, its debt levels—the firm has a net debt/total capitalization of 47%—are still high compared with peers'. The trading business may be a drag on earnings and a source of earnings volatility for at least a few more years.

Data as of 12-29-06

Williams Partners LP WPZ

Rating	Fair Value	Last Close	Consider Buy	Consider Sell	Yield %
★★★	$43.00	$38.70	$33.20	$53.90	4.15

Company Profile
Williams Partners is a natural-gas pipeline and processing company formed by its parent, The Williams Companies Inc., in 2005. Williams Partners owns 40% of Discovery Producer Services in Louisiana and 100% of the Four Corners natural-gas pipeline and processing system in New Mexico. The company owns another gas-gathering pipeline off the coast of Alabama, and an NGL fractionator and storage facility in Kansas.

Management — Stewardship Grade [C]
Williams Partners has no employees--the executives of Williams Companies Inc. also run Williams Partners. Several other energy companies that have spun off infrastructure assets into public partnerships share management, so the practice is not uncommon. Williams Partners was formed largely for the favorable tax treatment and incentive structure of an MLP, and Williams Companies owns a 21% limited partner interest and all of Williams Partners' 2% general partner interest and incentive distribution rights, so we're not concerned about the lack of direct management. Although conflicts of interest are inevitable, we've seen no evidence that management is not acting in the best interests of the partnership. Overall, the company has average corporate governance, with a Stewardship Grade of C. The most significant factor negatively affecting the units is the lack of unitholder control that is common to MLPs. Williams Partners could improve its corporate governance by separating the chairman and CEO roles and providing management an ownership position.

One Williams Center
Tulsa, OK 74172-0172

Growth [D+]	2002	2003	2004	2005
Revenue %	-11.8	10.0	44.8	26.3
Earnings/Share %	NMF	NMF	NMF	NMF
Book Value/Share %	—	—	—	—
Dividends/Share %	NMF	NMF	NMF	NMF

Profitability [NA]	2003	2004	2005	TTM
Return on Assets %	2.3	-6.1	2.0	4.3
Oper Cash Flow $Mil	7	3	2	23
- Cap Spending $Mil	1	2	4	6
= Free Cash Flow $Mil	5	1	-2	17

Financial Health [D+]	2003	2004	2005	09-30-06
Long-term Debt $Mil	—	—	—	150
Total Equity $Mil	30	17	217	251
Debt/Equity Ratio	—	—	—	0.6

Industry	Business Risk	Moat Size	Investment Style	Sector
Pipelines	Average	Narrow	Small Core	Energy

Competition	Market Cap $Mil	12 Mo Trailing Sales $Mil	Price/Cash Flow	Return On Assets%	Debt/Equity	Total Return% 1 Yr	Total Return% 3 Yr
Williams Partners LP	836	60	36.5	4.3	0.6	30.2	—
Enterprise Products Partn	12,514	14,421	9.8	3.5	0.8	29.2	13.3
Energy Transfer Partners	5,999	7,859	11.0	7.3	1.6	65.5	47.7

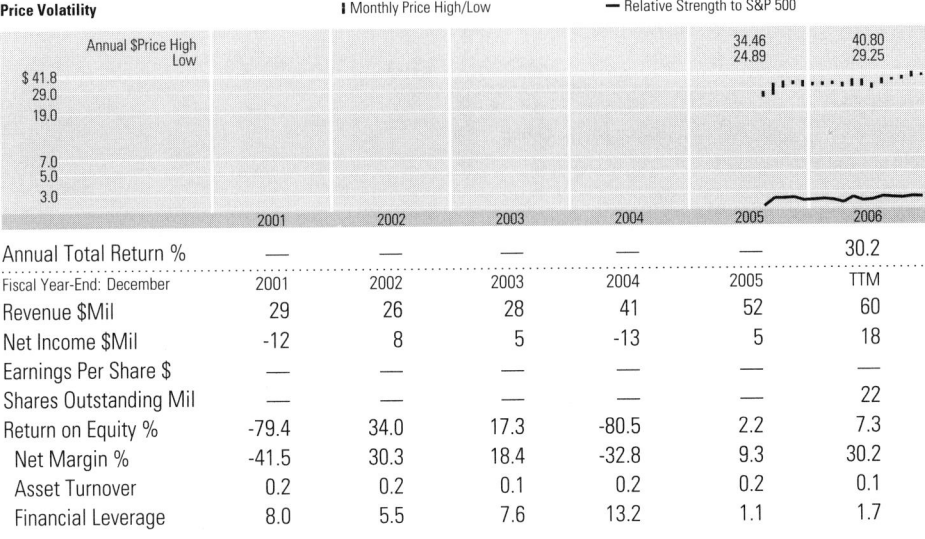

	2001	2002	2003	2004	2005	TTM
Annual Total Return %	—	—	—	—	—	30.2
Fiscal Year-End: December	2001	2002	2003	2004	2005	TTM
Revenue $Mil	29	26	28	41	52	60
Net Income $Mil	-12	8	5	-13	5	18
Earnings Per Share $	—	—	—	—	—	—
Shares Outstanding Mil	—	—	—	—	—	22
Return on Equity %	-79.4	34.0	17.3	-80.5	2.2	7.3
Net Margin %	-41.5	30.3	18.4	-32.8	9.3	30.2
Asset Turnover	0.2	0.2	0.1	0.2	0.2	0.1
Financial Leverage	8.0	5.5	7.6	13.2	1.1	1.7

Valuation Ratios	Stock	Rel to Industry	Rel to S&P 500
Price/Earnings	—	—	—
Price/Book	3.3	1.3	0.8
Price/Sales	13.8	6.3	4.8
Price/Cash Flow	36.5	3.7	2.5

Major Fund Holders	% of Fund Assets
Evergreen Utility & Telecomm A	2.46

Thesis By Catharina Milostan, 12-20-06 Stock Price as of Analysis: $38.10

Williams Partners LP is well positioned for growth thanks to well-placed natural-gas gathering and processing (gas midstream) businesses in growing U.S. producing basins. The desire by its parent, Williams Companies, to shed more assets also helps, giving Williams Partners acquisition opportunities.

Williams Partners was formed in February 2005 when Williams Companies spun off a 40% interest in the Discovery gas midstream system in the Gulf of Mexico, plus all of the offshore-Alabama Carbonate Trend pipeline and Kansas-based natural gas liquids (NGL) storage facilities. Williams Companies sweetened the pot in June 2006 with the sale of a 25.1% interest in the Four Corners gas midstream system in the prolific San Juan basin in New Mexico. Williams Partners stepped up with the $1.223 billion purchase of the remaining 74.9% share of Four Corners in mid-December 2006. Williams Partners' gas gathering pipeline systems and gas processing facilities warrant our narrow moat rating as systems with a reputable operating history get first crack in tying in new fields to drive up gathering and processing volumes.

2007 could be a banner year after the late 2006 purchase of the rest of the Four Corners midstream complex in the heart of the prolific San Juan basin. As with gas midstream peers, Williams Partners must service new wells to offset lower gathering and processing demand from more mature, declining fields. This is where Williams Partners has an edge, as its Discovery system can tie into new deep-water Gulf of Mexico wells. Williams Partners' Four Corners system gathers about 37% of San Juan Basin gas production, giving it an edge to capture rising coalbed methane production.

As its late 2006 Four Corners purchase illustrates, Williams Partners' close relationship to its parent, Williams Companies, puts it in a good position for acquisition growth. The parent owns a 21% limited partner interest and all of Williams Partners' 2% general partner interest, and the same people manage both firms more like a combined entity.

We look for acquisitions plus drilling-driven gas processing volumes to provide ample cash for distributions. Since its IPO, Williams Partners increased its quarterly distribution nearly 30% to $0.450 for an annualized yield of 4.2% at our fair value estimate. This still puts Williams' distribution near the low end of the range of MLP yields under our coverage, but we expect strong growth over time to bring it more in line with peers.

Data as of 12-29-06

Williams-Sonoma WSM

	Rating	Fair Value	Last Close	Consider Buy	Consider Sell	Yield %
	★★★★	$39.00	$31.44	$30.10	$48.90	0.95

Company Profile

Williams-Sonoma offers products for the home through retail stores, catalogs, and the Internet. Its offerings include bath and storage products, bedding, cookware, furniture, and tableware. The company's retail concepts include Williams-Sonoma, Pottery Barn, Pottery Barn Kids, PBteen, West Elm, and Williams-Sonoma Home. The company operates about 580 stores in the United States and Canada, seven catalogs, and six Web sites.

Industry	Business Risk	Moat Size	Investment Style	Sector
Furniture Retail	Average	Narrow	Mid Core	Consumer Services

Competition

	Market Cap $Mil	12 Mo Trailing Sales $Mil	Price/Cash Flow	Return On Assets%	Debt/Equity	Total Return% 1 Yr	3 Yr
Williams-Sonoma	3,526	3,687	11.1	10.7	0.0	-26.5	-2.4
Bed Bath & Beyond	10,770	6,137	16.6	15.6	—	5.4	-3.5
Pier 1 Imports	521	1,710	—	-10.7	0.4	-29.5	-32.5

Management — Stewardship Grade [B]

Howard Lester, who has been chairman since 1986 and was CEO for many years, resumed the CEO position on a temporary basis following the resignation of Ed Mueller in July 2006. While we respect Lester's extensive experience and vision, the high turnover of CEOs at the firm since Lester originally gave up the post concerns us. Most senior managers are fairly new to the company. The board consists of Lester, chief marketing officer Patrick Connolly and seven outside directors. Management compensation appears to be fairly reasonable, although we do not approve of Williams-Sonoma's spending $37 million to buy a corporate jet in 2003. The company's corporate stewardship is above average. In particular, we are big fans of the firm's quarterly earnings releases, which give investors plenty of detail on how the different concepts are performing, as well as on management's expectations for financial results. Executive officers and directors own just under 10% of William-Sonoma's common stock.

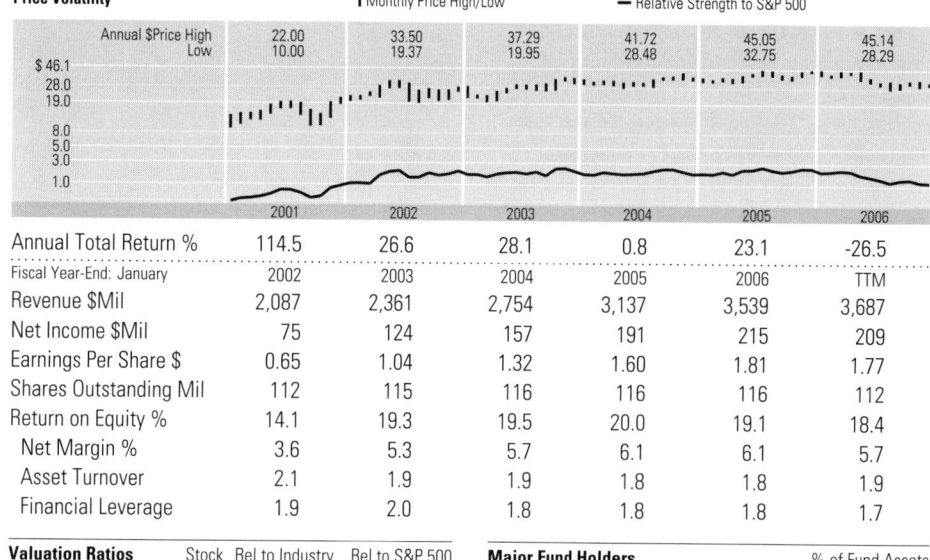

Price Volatility

	2002	2003	2004	2005	2006
Annual Total Return %	114.5	26.6	28.1	0.8	23.1	-26.5

Fiscal Year-End: January	2002	2003	2004	2005	2006	TTM
Revenue $Mil	2,087	2,361	2,754	3,137	3,539	3,687
Net Income $Mil	75	124	157	191	215	209
Earnings Per Share $	0.65	1.04	1.32	1.60	1.81	1.77
Shares Outstanding Mil	112	115	116	116	116	112
Return on Equity %	14.1	19.3	19.5	20.0	19.1	18.4
Net Margin %	3.6	5.3	5.7	6.1	6.1	5.7
Asset Turnover	2.1	1.9	1.9	1.8	1.8	1.9
Financial Leverage	1.9	2.0	1.8	1.8	1.8	1.7

Valuation Ratios	Stock	Rel to Industry	Rel to S&P 500
Price/Earnings	17.8	1.0	0.9
Price/Book	3.1	0.7	0.8
Price/Sales	1.0	0.7	0.3
Price/Cash Flow	11.1	0.8	0.8

Major Fund Holders	% of Fund Assets
W.P. Stewart & Co Growth	3.07
Goldman Sachs Growth Opportunities A	2.49
Permanent Portfolio Aggressive Growth	2.40
Strategic Partners Mid Cap Growth M	2.12

3250 Van Ness Avenue
San Francisco, CA 94109
www.williams-sonoma.com

Growth [B]	2003	2004	2005	2006
Revenue %	13.1	16.7	13.9	12.8
Earnings/Share %	60.0	26.9	21.2	13.1
Book Value/Share %	16.8	25.5	18.6	18.3
Dividends/Share %	NMF	NMF	NMF	NMF

Profitability [A]	2004	2005	2006	TTM
Return on Assets %	10.7	11.0	10.8	10.7
Oper Cash Flow $Mil	209	304	348	316
- Cap Spending $Mil	212	181	152	177
= Free Cash Flow $Mil	-3	123	197	140

Financial Health [A+]	2004	2005	2006	10-31-06
Long-term Debt $Mil	28	19	14	13
Total Equity $Mil	805	958	1,125	1,136
Debt/Equity Ratio	0.0	0.0	0.0	0.0

Thesis By Anthony Chukumba, 11-30-06 Stock Price as of Analysis: $31.72

Williams-Sonoma has practically cornered the market on yuppie trappings for the home. Its core Pottery Barn and Williams-Sonoma brands have become almost synonymous with upscale, mass-market home furniture and furnishings. The success of these concepts has allowed Williams-Sonoma to launch related brands targeting different consumers, including Pottery Barn Kids and PBteen, which offer goods for younger consumers, and Williams-Sonoma Home, which offers higher-end home furnishings than its Pottery Barn brand. West Elm, which sells value-priced home furnishings and furniture, has also been well received by customers.

Successful management of its different concepts has allowed Williams-Sonoma to build strong brand-name recognition and customer loyalty with higher-income, middle-age consumers. We believe the company has a narrow economic moat. Operating multiple concepts also diversifies Williams-Sonoma's revenue stream--if one is struggling, others can pick up the slack. We believe the firm has years of strong growth ahead as it expands its newer concepts, which have little product overlap with its older ones, minimizing cannibalization. Williams-Sonoma has also been one of the leading retailers in selling products across the retail, catalog, and Internet channels. The company tests new concepts through catalogs and the Internet, which allows it to refine the merchandise and marketing strategies before making the larger investment required to open stores.

Williams-Sonoma has been an impressive performer, with annual revenue growth averaging 14% over the past five years. This growth was due to a combination of new store openings, solid single-digit growth in comparable-store sales, or comps (sales at stores open at least a year), and 14% average annual gains in catalog and Internet sales. The company has steadily increased its operating margin every year since 2000, mainly thanks to better product sourcing and improving distribution operations. Despite its rapid expansion, Williams-Sonoma generates decent free cash flow, part of which it has used to repurchase stock.

Our one major concern is that given its higher price points, Williams-Sonoma will probably see sales suffer more than its lower-price peers will in an economic slowdown. Sales growth declined significantly at the start of the last economic downturn. The company also is increasingly relying on its newer concepts for growth, and any major flops would hurt sales growth and profits.

Data as of 12-29-06

Windstream WIN

	Rating	Fair Value	Last Close	Consider Buy	Consider Sell	Yield %
	★★★	$13.00	$14.22	$10.00	$16.30	8.75

Company Profile

Windstream was formed in July 2006 via the merger of Alltel's fixed-line business and Valor Communications. The firm serves about 3.3 million phone lines, 2 million long-distance phone customers, and more than 600,000 high-speed Internet access customers, generating about $3.4 billion in revenue. Windstream's operations are located in 16 states, primarily in the Southeast and southern Midwest. The firm has agreed to sell its directory publishing unit to a shareholder, with an expected close during 2007.

Management   Stewardship Grade [C]

Alltel shareholders control about 85% of Windstream's shares, and Alltel executives have filled the majority of high-level positions at the firm. Alltel's former CFO, Jeff Gardner, has assumed the CEO position. He has 20 years of telecom experience, primarily in financial roles, which should be a strength given the firm's need to focus on cash flow and management of its capital structure. Alltel's former secretary, Francis "Skip" Frantz, is the new firm's chairman. He brings an extensive background in the legal aspects of the telecom business, including regulation and mergers and acquisitions. Most top Valor executives have left, though Grant Raney, who headed operations at Valor, has stayed on as an area manager, running the Valor properties. A representative of Welsh, Carson, Anderson & Stowe, Valor's largest private-equity backer and now a holder of 4% of Windstream's shares, is the lone Valor representative on the new firm's board. Welsh, Carson will be exchanging its stake for ownership of Windstream's directory publishing business during 2007. We think stewardship at Alltel has been average, and we expect the same at Windstream. Our biggest issue with Alltel's stewardship was its compensation practices. Also, Windstream has a poison pill that will make a hostile takeover more difficult.

Las Colinas Tower I 201 East John Carpenter Fwy, S
Irving, TX 75062   www.valortelecom.com

Growth [D+]	2002	2003	2004	2005
Revenue %	12.9	3.6	2.0	-0.3
Earnings/Share %	NMF	NMF	NMF	NMF
Book Value/Share %	—	—	—	—
Dividends/Share %	NMF	NMF	NMF	NMF

Profitability [C+]	2003	2004	2005	TTM
Return on Assets %	2.9	-1.4	1.8	2.1
Oper Cash Flow $Mil	166	144	191	324
- Cap Spending $Mil	70	66	57	64
= Free Cash Flow $Mil	96	78	134	260

Financial Health [C]	2003	2004	2005	09-30-06
Long-term Debt $Mil	1,427	1,599	1,181	5,477
Total Equity $Mil	50	6	572	603
Debt/Equity Ratio	28.6	EUB	2.1	9.1

Industry	Business Risk	Moat Size	Investment Style	Sector
Telecom Svcs.	Average	Narrow	Mid Core	Telecommunication

Competition	Market Cap $Mil	12 Mo Trailing Sales $Mil	Price/Cash Flow	Return On Assets%	Debt/Equity	Total Return% 1 Yr	3 Yr
Windstream	6,780	558	20.9	2.1	9.1	37.4	—
AT&T	137,384	60,171	9.0	4.9	0.5	51.6	16.3
Verizon Communications	108,723	88,881	4.4	3.7	0.7	34.9	8.0

Price Volatility   I Monthly Price High/Low   — Relative Strength to S&P 500

Annual $Price High/Low: 16.17/11.22 (2005), 14.43/11.13 (2006)

	2001	2002	2003	2004	2005	2006
Annual Total Return %	—	—	—	—	—	37.4

Fiscal Year-End: December	2001	2002	2003	2004	2005	TTM
Revenue $Mil	425	480	497	507	506	558
Net Income $Mil	—	16	58	-28	35	173
Earnings Per Share $	—	—	—	—	—	—
Shares Outstanding Mil	—	—	—	—	—	477
Return on Equity %	NMF	NMF	116.8	ELB	6.2	28.7
Net Margin %	—	3.4	11.7	-5.5	7.0	31.1
Asset Turnover	0.2	0.2	0.2	0.3	0.3	0.1
Financial Leverage	NMF	NMF	40.9	304.6	3.4	13.5

Valuation Ratios	Stock	Rel to Industry	Rel to S&P 500
Price/Earnings	—	—	—
Price/Book	11.2	2.6	2.7
Price/Sales	12.2	5.3	4.2
Price/Cash Flow	20.9	2.3	1.4

Major Fund Holders	% of Fund Assets
SunAmerica Focused Value A	2.71
ING MFS Utilities I	2.18
MFS Utilities A	2.12
JHT Utilities Trust Ser I	2.10

Thesis By Michael Hodel, CFA, 12-13-06 Stock Price as of Analysis: $14.22

Windstream offers a more manageable debt load, smaller demands on its cash flow, and much greater scale than most rural phone companies we follow.

Windstream is the combination of Alltel's former fixed-line phone business (85% of the business) and Valor Communications. Alltel has a long history in the telecom industry, and we've long been fans of its ability to manage the fixed-line business. Valor was created in 2000 to buy rural phone exchanges from GTE (now part of Verizon). It worked to improve these assets, upgrading the networks and offering new services. Valor's business has also generated strong margins and cash flow. Both firms were beneficiaries of a competitive environment that is much tamer than that in more-urban markets. Valor's service territory, in particular, is deeply rural, containing an average of 11 phone customers per square mile. Only 45% of these customers have access to cable modem service, and about 12% have been offered cable telephony. Alltel's fixed-line unit has faced stiffer competition; overall, about 75% and 35% of Windstream's customers can get cable modem and telephone services, respectively.

Alltel and Valor each contributed unique strengths to the business. The threat of competition pushed Alltel to improve its networks and add new services faster than Valor. Alltel had signed up a greater proportion of customers for high-speed Internet access (DSL) service, which is important because we believe DSL is a critical tool to generate additional revenue and keep phone customers. Alltel can provide DSL service to about 75% of its customers and has upgraded its network to offer higher speeds to many more than is typical in rural areas. As a stand-alone fixed-line company, Valor's local marketing strategies were more refined, and Windstream has adopted tactics like door-to-door sales.

While Windstream's rural markets have faced relatively modest competition to date, we expect cable companies will eventually expand their offerings to smaller markets. Windstream is better prepared financially to handle this threat than many smaller rural carriers. The firm's debt load, relative to the size of its cash flow, is among the lowest among high-yield telecom firms. The dividend payout, at about 70% of free cash flow, is also reasonable for now. Still, we think competitive threats, including new technologies like WiMax, could hurt the firm if its financial obligations preclude it from investing adequately in its networks. Changing regulation could also hamper subsidies and access payments from other carriers needed to maintain cash flow.

Data as of 12-29-06

Wipro ADR WIT

	Rating	Fair Value	Last Close	Consider Buy	Consider Sell	Yield %
	★★	$14.00	$16.15	$10.80	$17.50	0.66

Company Profile

Founded in 1945 and based in Bangalore, Wipro is one of the world's largest IT services providers. Wipro Technologies provides IT (68% of operating income) and business process outsourcing services (5%) to U.S. and European clients. Wipro Infotech (6% of operating income) provides IT hardware, software, and services to Indian, Asian, and Mideast clients. Consumer care (4% of operating income) manufactures and distributes consumer products within India.

Management   Stewardship Grade [NA]

Azim Premji, chairman and CEO, inherited the company at age 21 after his father's abrupt death. He is now the second-richest person in India due to his 81% stake in Wipro shares, which are valued at around $18 billion. Premji, now in his 60s, received about $97,000 in base salary in fiscal 2006 and another $392,000 in commissions. Premji also receives funding of his pension equivalent to 15% of his annual salary and commission.

Shareholders of Wipro's American Depository Receipts, traded on the New York Stock Exchange, may demand a lack-of-control discount to the firms' fair value estimate, given the limited rights of ADR holders and Premji's significant majority ownership.

Doddakannelli Sarjapur Road
Bangalore, India 560 035
www.wipro.com

Growth [NA]	2003	2004	2005	2006
Revenue %	28.0	36.4	39.2	30.4
Earnings/Share %	0.7	18.0	56.9	26.1
Book Value/Share %	28.9	30.9	21.2	36.8
Dividends/Share %	—	—	—	—

Profitability [NA]	2004	2005	2006	TTM
Return on Assets %	16.5	21.4	20.4	20.4
Oper Cash Flow $Mil	234	423	456	456
- Cap Spending $Mil	90	147	169	169
= Free Cash Flow $Mil	145	276	287	287

Financial Health [NA]	2004	2005	2006	03-31-06
Long-term Debt $Mil	—	—	—	
Total Equity $Mil	1,051	1,295	1,765	1,765
Debt/Equity Ratio	—	—	—	

Industry	Business Risk	Moat Size	Investment Style	Sector
Business Appl.	Average	Narrow	Large Growth	Software

Competition	Market Cap $Mil	12 Mo Trailing Sales $Mil	Price/Cash Flow	Return On Assets %	Debt/Equity	Total Return % 1 Yr	3 Yr
Wipro ADR	23,026	2,397	50.5	20.4	—	36.3	25.6
IBM	146,342	89,593	9.8	8.8	0.4	19.8	3.0
Infosys Technologies ADR	29,525	2,152	49.3	26.9	—	36.8	31.5

Price Volatility — Monthly Price High/Low — Relative Strength to S&P 500

	2001	2002	2003	2004	2005	2006
Annual $Price High	10.96	7.33	8.17	12.85	12.75	16.39
Low	2.83	3.70	3.05	5.81	8.80	10.18
Annual Total Return %	-27.0	-8.4	44.0	59.7	-2.5	36.3

Fiscal Year-End: March	2002	2003	2004	2005	2006	TTM
Revenue $Mil	702	884	1,266	1,809	2,397	2,397
Net Income $Mil	176	175	216	352	458	458
Earnings Per Share $	0.13	0.13	0.16	0.25	0.32	0.32
Shares Outstanding Mil	1,390	1,388	1,388	1,392	1,405	1,426
Return on Equity %	31.4	23.5	20.6	27.2	25.9	25.9
Net Margin %	25.1	19.8	17.1	19.5	19.1	19.1
Asset Turnover	1.0	1.0	1.0	1.1	1.1	1.1
Financial Leverage	1.2	1.2	1.2	1.3	1.3	1.3

Valuation Ratios	Stock	Rel to Industry	Rel to S&P 500
Price/Earnings	50.2	1.7	2.4
Price/Book	13.0	1.5	3.2
Price/Sales	9.6	1.5	3.3
Price/Cash Flow	50.5	2.0	3.5

Major Fund Holders	% of Fund Assets
Chicken Little Growth	1.88

Thesis By Mike Ford-Taggart, CFA, 12-20-06 Stock Price as of Analysis: $15.27

Founded in 1945 as a vegetable oil manufacturer, Wipro has evolved into one of the world's largest information technology services firms. We believe that its strong positioning in offshore IT services and management's commitment to deriving high returns on capital make Wipro a great company to own for the long-term, assuming investors can fetch a fair price.

Wipro's global IT services business--the key to Wipro's growth--will continue to benefit from the strength of the overall market and several offerings, in our opinion. First, the IT offshoring market in India is expected to grow by 24% on average annually for the next five years, according to Nasscom (India's software and service trade group), capitalizing like other Indian IT firms on the global trend toward outsourcing to low-cost regions. Second, Wipro's research and development offering (25% of total revenue) distinguishes the firm: It is considered the world's largest outsourcer for R&D work. For example, Wipro helps Intel design and test chips before global distribution, tests Sun Microsystems' server software, and examines Cisco's routers and switches. Third, Wipro has become one of India's largest acquirers of non-Indian companies, buying niche firms to complement existing, industry-specific capabilities. Lastly, like other Indian IT firms, Wipro has recently implemented an IT consulting group to compete for high-level work from target clients. We believe that all of these factors will lead to revenue growth rates significantly above those of its non-Indian rivals.

Demonstrating management's commitment to maintaining high returns, Wipro's business process outsourcing offerings have recently been restructured. BPO is only 5% of total revenue, but often clients will bundle the service within a larger IT contract. Historically, Wipro focused on voice services BPO (call centers), doing both outbound and inbound work. Management determined that call center pricing was deteriorating due to competition from even-lower-cost regions, and that this jeopardized long-term returns. Therefore, the business was reconfigured: Call center work will be de-emphasized (except for large clients that need customer support lines, like help desks) in favor of transaction processing. Wipro has made a couple of small acquisitions in the transaction processing space, including mPower, which has a joint venture with Mastercard. The transition depressed BPO operating margins temporarily--to as low as 9%--but they have since improved to around 20%.

Data as of 12-29-06

Wisconsin Energy WEC

	Rating	Fair Value	Last Close	Consider Buy	Consider Sell	Yield %
	★★	$43.00	$47.46	$36.60	$56.50	1.94

Industry	Business Risk	Moat Size	Investment Style	Sector
Electric Utilities	Below Avg	Narrow	Mid Value	Utilities

Company Profile

Wisconsin Energy is a holding company principally engaged in the generation, transmission, and distribution of electricity and natural gas. The company's electric and gas utility businesses are the largest respective energy providers in Wisconsin. Electricity operating revenue accounts for two thirds of the firm's total revenue; the remainder comes from the natural-gas business.

Competition

	Market Cap $Mil	12 Mo Trailing Sales $Mil	Price/Cash Flow	Return On Assets%	Debt/ Equity	Total Return% 1 Yr	3 Yr
Wisconsin Energy	5,552	4,036	7.7	3.1	1.1	24.2	15.1
Xcel Energy	9,383	10,259	6.4	2.7	1.2	30.5	15.9
Alliant Energy	4,385	3,425	10.1	0.8	0.6	39.4	19.4

Price Volatility

| Monthly Price High/Low — Relative Strength to S&P 500

Annual $Price High	24.62	26.48	33.68	34.60	40.83	48.70
Low	19.13	20.19	22.56	29.50	33.35	38.16
	2001	2002	2003	2004	2005	2006
Annual Total Return %	3.6	15.5	36.7	3.4	18.7	24.2

Fiscal Year-End: December	2001	2002	2003	2004	2005	TTM
Revenue $Mil	3,343	3,051	3,308	3,406	3,816	4,036
Net Income $Mil	219	167	244	306	309	330
Earnings Per Share $	1.86	1.44	2.06	2.57	2.61	2.79
Shares Outstanding Mil	117	115	117	118	117	117
Return on Equity %	10.5	7.7	10.4	12.3	11.5	11.8
Net Margin %	6.6	5.5	7.4	9.0	8.1	8.2
Asset Turnover	0.4	0.3	0.3	0.4	0.4	0.4
Financial Leverage	4.5	4.4	4.2	3.8	3.9	3.8

Management Stewardship Grade [B]

CEO Gale Klappa and CFO Allen Leverett joined Wisconsin Energy in 2003 after serving at highly respected Southern. They have brought an increased focus on customer satisfaction and financial performance, both of which were lacking under the previous management. The pair has made impressive strides on each of these fronts, and we expect continued improvement. Klappa received $3.3 million in total compensation during 2005, the majority of which was a performance bonus. Despite unclear financial measures for CEO compensation and a rich conditional severance of roughly $9 million, Wisconsin Energy ranks comparatively high in terms of stewardship, shareholder-friendliness, and financial disclosure. While the majority of the board is made up of independent directors, we would prefer to see a separation of the CEO and chairman positions.

Valuation Ratios

	Stock	Rel to Industry	Rel to S&P 500
Price/Earnings	17.3	1.0	0.8
Price/Book	2.0	0.5	0.5
Price/Sales	1.4	0.8	0.5
Price/Cash Flow	7.7	0.7	0.5

Major Fund Holders

	% of Fund Assets
Putnam Utilities Growth & Income A	2.72
Morgan Stanley Utilities B	2.51
Van Kampen Utility A	2.44
Primary Income	2.25

Thesis By Ryan McLean, 12-11-06 Stock Price as of Analysis: $47.99

Wisconsin Energy's outlook may not electrify, but the significant growth prospects ahead of this regulated utility make it a worthwhile opportunity for long-term investors. Income investors seeking strong dividend growth might want to consider looking elsewhere, however, as the company's policy of increasing dividends at only about half the rate of earnings growth will keep a lid on payouts for the foreseeable future.

Underinvestment of electricity infrastructure in the state of Wisconsin has contributed to a favorable growth environment for the company. Consequently, Wisconsin Energy has received approval from regulators to expand its asset base substantially. Capital expenditures have averaged $500 million—or 25% of sales—over the past five years and are projected to double over the next five under the company's Power the Future (PTF) program. The firm will invest $2.9 billion in new investments alone between 2006 and 2010. These include two coal-fired and one natural-gas-based electricity generation facility. Regulators have granted the firm a comparatively robust return on equity of 12.7% on its PTF investments. Although the firm will not realize the full increase in earnings from these plants until they are put into operation, preapproved rate increases provide excellent earnings visibility.

One downside to the aggressive investment program is that Wisconsin Energy is spending more on capital projects than it is generating in operating cash. We anticipate, however, that the firm will turn cash-flow positive by 2010. The firm's reinvestment of funds has resulted in a below-average dividend payout of about 35% over the past three years. We expect this ratio to decline further in the medium term as management's stated dividend policy is to raise payouts at only half the rate of earnings growth in order to fund its expansion. This should help the firm maintain a debt/capital ratio of around 60%, even as it adds to its base. Historically, Wisconsin Energy has earned 8% on invested capital—nearly 1 percentage point above its cost of capital.

Wisconsin Energy's PTF investments will expand the firm's asset base and hence its earnings. Since returns on earnings are preset at relatively attractive levels, we think Wisconsin Energy presents investors an opportunity to capture above-average earnings growth at below-average risk.

---

231 West Michigan Street P.O. Box 2949
Milwaukee, WI 53201   www.wisconsinenergy.com

Growth [C-]

	2002	2003	2004	2005
Revenue %	-8.7	8.4	3.0	12.0
Earnings/Share %	-22.6	43.1	24.8	1.6
Book Value/Share %	5.6	6.3	5.1	8.4
Dividends/Share %	0.0	0.0	3.8	6.0

Profitability [C+]

	2003	2004	2005	TTM
Return on Assets %	2.4	3.2	3.0	3.1
Oper Cash Flow $Mil	530	599	577	721
- Cap Spending $Mil	649	667	795	963
= Free Cash Flow $Mil	-119	-68	-218	-241

Financial Health [C]

	2003	2004	2005	09-30-06
Long-term Debt $Mil	3,571	3,240	3,031	3,035
Total Equity $Mil	2,359	2,492	2,680	2,804
Debt/Equity Ratio	1.5	1.3	1.1	1.1

Wm. Wrigley Jr. WWY

Data as of 12-29-06

	Rating	Fair Value	Last Close	Consider Buy	Consider Sell	Yield %
	★★★★	$59.00	$51.72	$50.30	$77.50	1.92

Industry	Business Risk	Moat Size	Investment Style	Sector
Food Mfg.	Below Avg	Wide	Large Growth	Consumer Goods

Company Profile

Wm. Wrigley Jr.'s chewing gum is sold in more than 180 countries. Its brand names include Wrigley's Spearmint, Doublemint, Juicy Fruit, Freedent, and Extra chewing gum. The Amurol subsidiary makes chewing gum under the Big League Chew and Hubba Bubba brands. The company markets its products in the United States and abroad. Sales outside North America account for more than 60% of the company's total sales.

Competition

	Market Cap $Mil	12 Mo Trailing Sales $Mil	Price/Cash Flow	Return On Assets%	Debt/ Equity	Total Return% 1 Yr	3 Yr
Wm. Wrigley Jr.	14,371	4,568	22.9	10.6	0.4	-0.7	7.2
Nestle SA ADR	138,417	73,660	16.8	8.8	—	20.9	14.7
Cadbury Schweppes PLC ADR	22,367	11,879	11.2	7.5	1.0	14.7	15.2

Management Stewardship Grade [C]

Wrigley recently ended decades of family members running the show, hiring William Perez as its first outsider CEO, replacing Bill Wrigley Jr. Despite Perez's recent unceremonious exit from footwear icon Nike, we think he will be a good fit at Wrigley. Before taking the reins at Nike, Perez spent more than 30 years at SC Johnson, including eight years as CEO. Like Wrigley, SC Johnson is a family-owned business with a strong focus on building brands and competing worldwide. While we view the separation of the CEO and chairman roles as a positive, we still aren't fans of the firm's dual-class share structure, which cements Wrigley Jr.'s voting control over the company. Executive salaries and other compensation appear reasonable to us, though we don't think it's necessary to require the CEO to use the corporate jet for personal as well as corporate travel. We think director compensation is fair, and we like that directors are required to have an ownership stake in the company that amounts to at least 2 times their annual retainer. However, we think directors should be subject to election annually, rather than every three years.

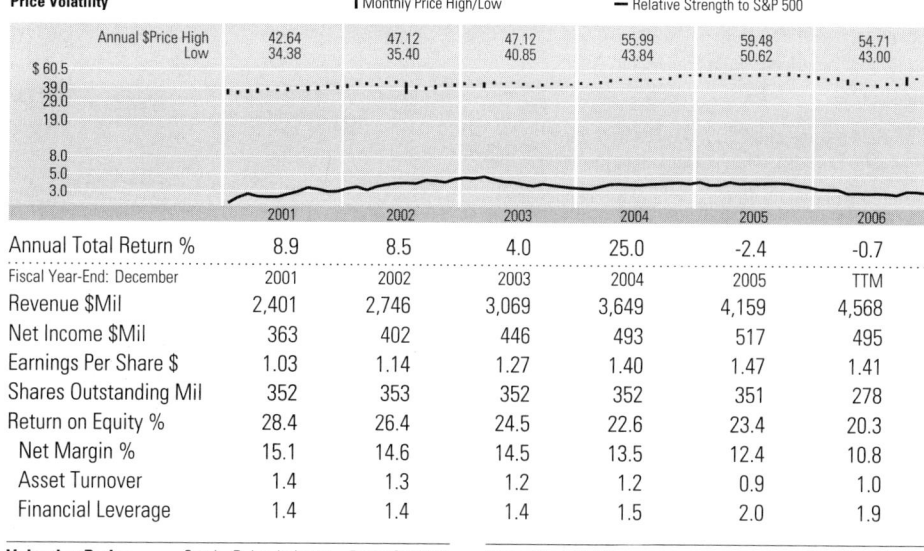

Price Volatility — Monthly Price High/Low — Relative Strength to S&P 500

Annual $Price	High	42.64	47.12	47.12	55.99	59.48	54.71
	Low	34.38	35.40	40.85	43.84	50.62	43.00
		2001	2002	2003	2004	2005	2006
Annual Total Return %		8.9	8.5	4.0	25.0	-2.4	-0.7

Fiscal Year-End: December	2001	2002	2003	2004	2005	TTM
Revenue $Mil	2,401	2,746	3,069	3,649	4,159	4,568
Net Income $Mil	363	402	446	493	517	495
Earnings Per Share $	1.03	1.14	1.27	1.40	1.47	1.41
Shares Outstanding Mil	352	353	352	352	351	278
Return on Equity %	28.4	26.4	24.5	22.6	23.4	20.3
Net Margin %	15.1	14.6	14.5	13.5	12.4	10.8
Asset Turnover	1.4	1.3	1.2	1.2	0.9	1.0
Financial Leverage	1.4	1.4	1.4	1.5	2.0	1.9

Valuation Ratios	Stock	Rel to Industry	Rel to S&P 500
Price/Earnings	36.8	1.7	1.8
Price/Book	5.9	1.3	1.4
Price/Sales	3.1	1.8	1.1
Price/Cash Flow	22.9	1.5	1.6

Major Fund Holders	% of Fund Assets
Destination Select Equity	4.95
McCarthy Multi-Cap Stock Instl	4.29
Marco Targeted Return	3.98
JHancock Large Cap Select A	3.53

Thesis By Mitchell P. Corwin, CFA, CPA, 11-20-06 Stock Price as of Analysis: $51.41

Wm. Wrigley Jr.'s significant miscalculation regarding the strength of acquired confectionery brands from Kraft Foods has caused consternation among investors, but we believe the firm is taking positive steps to revive the purchased brands and cement its U.S. leadership position in chewing gum. A slowly improving domestic business and continued international prosperity paint a bright long-term picture.

While blaming poor timing and some unpleasant discoveries made after acquiring brands including Life Savers and Altoids, Wrigley also underestimated how little Kraft had invested behind the brands, and early sales trends under Wrigley were weak. As a result, the company announced in early 2006 that it would step up marketing spending and earnings would come in lower than previously expected.

Also, we believe integration difficulties along with stepped-up competition, primarily from Cadbury Schweppes, exposed some chinks in Wrigley's domestic armor, where the company lagged its international businesses in supply-chain flexibility, marketing, and innovation capabilities.

A recent shuffling of top management indicates that Wrigley is addressing the domestic competitive issues, and we believe the company's 60% market share in chewing gum is safe. In addition, as Wrigley improves innovation and boosts advertising of the acquired brands, it should be able to harness its distribution capabilities to increase shelf space of those brands at key impulse checkout areas of convenience stores and drug stores.

A stronger U.S. foundation will be beneficial, but the real driver for Wrigley's favorable long-term prospects lies internationally, where the company derives about 60% of its total sales. Early investments in foreign markets have given the firm leading share positions around the globe. In addition to holding dominant gum share in developed markets, such as England and Germany, Wrigley has gained a foothold in emerging markets, such as China and Russia, where it should benefit in the years ahead from growing per capita consumption.

Over the long run, Wrigley is an international story, but we are confident that solving some domestic issues will allay near-term concerns. Wrigley has a history of being able to build brands, so we believe it will be able to revive the acquired brands. In 2001, the company introduced a new chewing gum brand, Orbit, to the United States. Today, it ranks as the second-best-selling gum brand.

---

410 North Michigan Avenue www.wrigley.com
Chicago, IL 60611

Growth [A]	2002	2003	2004	2005
Revenue %	14.4	11.8	18.9	14.0
Earnings/Share %	10.6	11.2	10.6	4.6
Book Value/Share %	19.2	19.8	19.7	1.3
Dividends/Share %	8.1	7.5	6.9	16.2

Profitability [A]	2003	2004	2005	TTM
Return on Assets %	17.6	15.6	11.6	10.6
Oper Cash Flow $Mil	645	725	758	627
- Cap Spending $Mil	220	220	282	329
= Free Cash Flow $Mil	425	504	476	297

Financial Health [A]	2003	2004	2005	09-30-06
Long-term Debt $Mil	—	0	1,000	1,000
Total Equity $Mil	1,821	2,179	2,214	2,441
Debt/Equity Ratio	—	0.0	0.5	0.4

Wyeth WYE

Data as of 12-29-06

Rating	Fair Value	Last Close	Consider Buy	Consider Sell	Yield %
★★★	$45.00	$50.92	$34.70	$56.40	1.98

Company Profile

Wyeth discovers, develops, and manufactures pharmaceuticals, vaccines, biotechnology products, and other medicines. Its pharmaceutical business accounts for about 83% of total revenue. The consumer health-care segment sells over-the-counter products such as Advil, Robitussin, and Centrum vitamins, accounting for about 12% of revenue. The company's animal health segment accounts for the remaining 5% of its revenue. Wyeth changed its name from American Home Products in 2002.

Management
Stewardship Grade [C]

Robert Essner took over the CEO position in 2001 from John Stafford, who had served in the role for the previous 15 years. In 2003, Essner also assumed the role of chairman. Essner has held various other executive positions at Wyeth including president, chief operating officer, and president of Wyeth-Ayerst Laboratories, where he was responsible for the domestic pharmaceutical business. Under Essner's reign, we have seen a continued focus on biotechnology, a common sentiment across the pharmacy industry. In addition, the company has focused on productivity and cost efficiency, cutting its salesforce, and increasing R&D spending and productivity over the past several years, with more projects in the research pipeline and a higher portion devoted to new molecular entities.

We don't have too many qualms with Wyeth's corporate governance. We like that the entire board stands annually for elections. We also like that options aren't hoarded by top executives, but instead appear to be spread across the company. We still prefer to see the CEO and chairman roles split, as this offers more checks and balances among executives.

Five Giralda Farms
Madison, NJ 07940-0874
www.wyeth.com

Growth [C+]	2002	2003	2004	2005
Revenue %	4.3	8.7	9.5	8.1
Earnings/Share %	93.6	-53.8	-40.9	196.7
Book Value/Share %	99.2	14.3	4.1	22.0
Dividends/Share %	0.0	0.0	0.0	2.2

Profitability [A]	2003	2004	2005	TTM
Return on Assets %	6.6	3.7	10.2	11.3
Oper Cash Flow $Mil	2,911	2,879	2,352	2,931
- Cap Spending $Mil	1,909	1,255	1,081	1,167
= Free Cash Flow $Mil	1,002	1,623	1,270	1,763

Financial Health [A-]	2003	2004	2005	09-30-06
Long-term Debt $Mil	8,076	7,792	9,231	9,235
Total Equity $Mil	9,294	9,848	11,994	14,807
Debt/Equity Ratio	0.9	0.8	0.8	0.6

	Industry	Business Risk	Moat Size	Investment Style	Sector
	Drugs	Average	Wide	Large Core	Healthcare

Competition	Market Cap $Mil	12 Mo Trailing Sales $Mil	Price/Cash Flow	Return On Assets%	Debt/Equity	Total Return% 1 Yr	3 Yr
Wyeth	68,574	19,877	23.4	11.3	0.6	12.9	8.2
GlaxoSmithKline PLC ADR	157,300	39,536	14.5	18.7	0.7	8.0	7.6
Novartis AG ADR	134,175	32,526	16.6	10.6	0.0	11.3	9.6

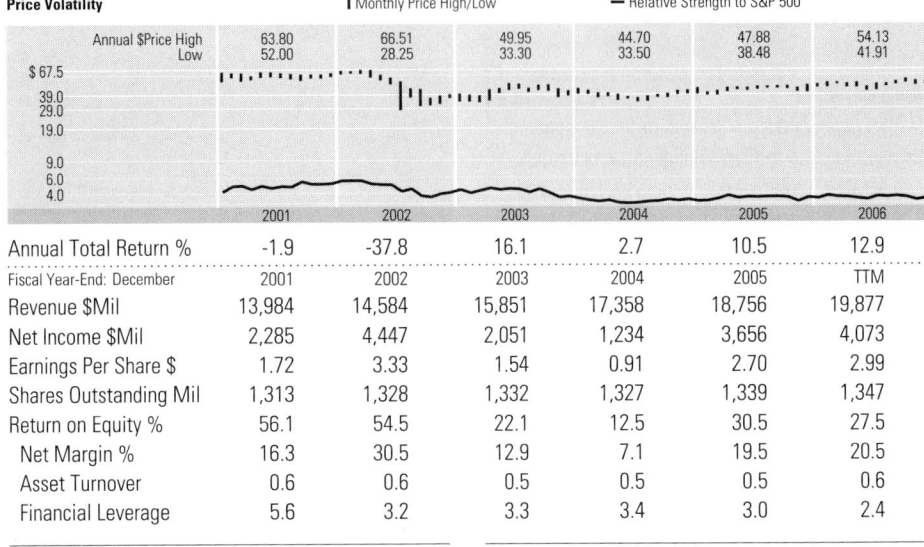

Annual Total Return %	-1.9	-37.8	16.1	2.7	10.5	12.9
Fiscal Year-End: December	2001	2002	2003	2004	2005	TTM
Revenue $Mil	13,984	14,584	15,851	17,358	18,756	19,877
Net Income $Mil	2,285	4,447	2,051	1,234	3,656	4,073
Earnings Per Share $	1.72	3.33	1.54	0.91	2.70	2.99
Shares Outstanding Mil	1,313	1,328	1,332	1,327	1,339	1,347
Return on Equity %	56.1	54.5	22.1	12.5	30.5	27.5
Net Margin %	16.3	30.5	12.9	7.1	19.5	20.5
Asset Turnover	0.6	0.6	0.5	0.5	0.5	0.6
Financial Leverage	5.6	3.2	3.3	3.4	3.0	2.4

Valuation Ratios	Stock	Rel to Industry	Rel to S&P 500
Price/Earnings	17.0	0.7	0.8
Price/Book	4.6	0.9	1.1
Price/Sales	3.5	0.8	1.2
Price/Cash Flow	23.4	1.4	1.6

Major Fund Holders	% of Fund Assets
Kinetics Medical	7.84
DWS Dreman Concentrated Value A	6.32
Gartmore Global Health Sci A	6.27
Munder Healthcare Y	6.21

Thesis
By Brandon Troegle, 12-21-06 Stock Price as of Analysis: $51.00

Wyeth has an impressive portfolio of drugs and has built a decent research pipeline over the last several years. We think it's poised to overcome threats regarding patent expirations and litigation over the next several years.

We like Wyeth's portfolio, which is balanced across various therapeutic classes. Effexor, its top-selling drug and the world's leading anti-depressant, represents 18% of total sales. Other blockbusters include Enbrel for rheumatoid arthritis and psoriasis, Prevnar, which vaccinates against pneumococcal diseases, and proton pump inhibitor Protonix. Wyeth's strategy focuses on three platforms--small molecules, vaccines, and biotechnology products. Like others in the industry, it is investing in biologics. But with almost $5 billion in revenue from biologics and a significant investment in a new development and manufacturing facility, Wyeth seems more committed to this area than some peers.

Wyeth has refocused its research and development efforts over the last several years, and while much of the outcome is yet to be seen, the number of projects in the pipeline and percentage related to new molecular entities versus life cycle management has increased significantly. While we aren't incredibly enthusiastic about any particular drug, the breadth of the pipeline is significant, and we think Viviant and Aprela for osteoporosis, and Pristiq for depression and symptoms of menopause, offer promise.

Enbrel and Prevnar are the most important drugs driving incremental growth over the next five years, and we think these, along with new drugs such as antibiotic Tygacil and others in the pipeline, will help offset the effects of patent expirations on Effexor, Protonix, and Zosyn. Much of Wyeth's future success will be the result of its effectiveness in life cycle management, and we expect Wyeth to continue to employ tactics to protect itself from patent expirations. The firm is launching an improved formulation of Zosyn and attempting to switch over existing Zosyn users, as a way to mitigate generic competition.

Wyeth also faces a patent challenge on Protonix and litigation concerning hormone replacement therapy drugs, and it continues to be the focus of litigation concerning fen-phen. While the fen-phen matter still lingers, and litigation that has hampered cash flows over the past several years could continue to be a drag in the future, the firm has made substantial progress resolving outstanding cases.

Data as of 12-29-06

Wyndham Worldwide WYN

Rating	Fair Value	Last Close	Consider Buy	Consider Sell	Yield %
★★★★	$42.00	$32.02	$32.40	$52.60	0.00

Industry	Business Risk	Moat Size	Investment Style	Sector
Hotels	Average	Narrow	Mid Growth	Consumer Services

Company Profile

Wyndham Worldwide was spun off from Cendant in 2006. The company sells and manages time-share resorts, operates a vacation exchange, and franchises more than 6,300 hotels. Time-shares are sold under the Trendwest and Fairfield brand names and exchanged over the RCI network. Hotel brands include Wyndham, Ramada, Days Inn, Knights Inn, Howard Johnson, Super 8, and Baymont.

Competition

	Market Cap $Mil	12 Mo Trailing Sales $Mil	Price/Cash Flow	Return On Assets %	Debt/ Equity	Total Return % 1 Yr	3 Yr
Wyndham Worldwide	6,344	3,733	11.8	3.1	0.3	—	—
Marriott International A	18,868	11,720	20.9	7.5	0.6	43.4	28.2
Hilton Hotels	13,493	7,013	42.8	2.8	2.4	45.6	27.7

Price Volatility

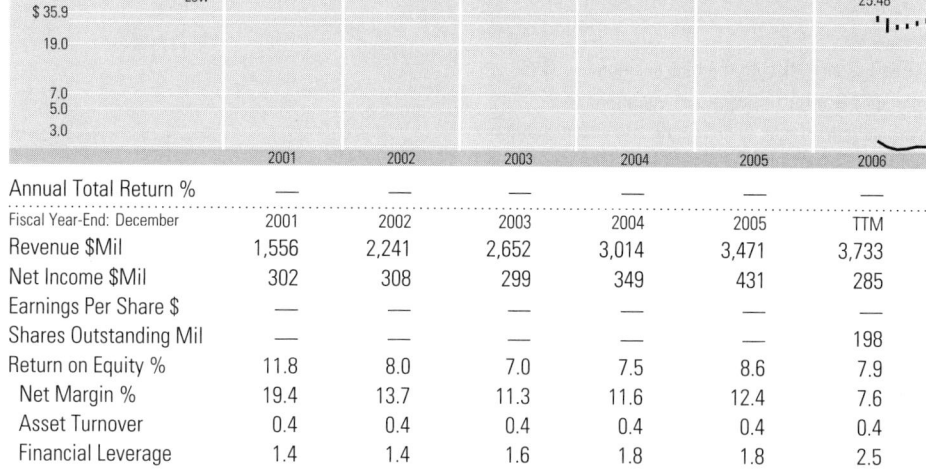

Management Stewardship Grade [C]

Chairman and CEO Stephen Holmes has worked for the company or one of its predecessors for 16 years. He was paid more than $2.2 million in cash in 2005 and awarded nearly $5 million of Cendant stock. This is on the high end of what his peers received, even though he delivered comparable results. We'd prefer Holmes to take a larger equity stake in the firm; he currently holds less than 1% of shares outstanding. The larger stake would help align his interests with those of common stakeholders. We are also disappointed that Wyndham has decided to classify its board of directors in an effort to thwart unwelcome takeovers. We believe the board and managers should be open to strategic alternatives that could be beneficial to stockholders.

Fiscal Year-End: December	2001	2002	2003	2004	2005	TTM
Revenue $Mil	1,556	2,241	2,652	3,014	3,471	3,733
Net Income $Mil	302	308	299	349	431	285
Earnings Per Share $	—	—	—	—	—	—
Shares Outstanding Mil	—	—	—	—	—	198
Return on Equity %	11.8	8.0	7.0	7.5	8.6	7.9
Net Margin %	19.4	13.7	11.3	11.6	12.4	7.6
Asset Turnover	0.4	0.4	0.4	0.4	0.4	0.4
Financial Leverage	1.4	1.4	1.6	1.8	1.8	2.5

Valuation Ratios	Stock	Rel to Industry	Rel to S&P 500
Price/Earnings	—	—	—
Price/Book	1.8	0.3	0.4
Price/Sales	1.7	0.5	0.6
Price/Cash Flow	11.8	0.3	0.8

Major Fund Holders	% of Fund Assets
Thornburg Core Growth A	2.55
Keeley Mid Cap Val	2.02
Bishop Street Strategic Growth Instl	1.86
FBP Value	1.79

Thesis By Jeremy Glaser, 11-20-06 Stock Price as of Analysis: $30.94

After its spin-off from Cendant, Wyndham Worldwide is ready to polish its rusty hotel brands and expand its lucrative time-share businesses. Even with a focused management team, however, the road ahead is hardly a pleasure trip.

More than one third of Wyndham's revenue comes from selling vacation time-shares. The time-share industry, tarnished by a reputation for aggressive sales techniques and other unsavory tactics, is cleaner after the entry of large players like Disney, Marriott, and Starwood. The new entrants have been a double-edge sword for Wyndham, though; their well-known brands have attracted new consumers, but they also represent a considerable threat to Wyndham's lesser-known Trendwest and Fairfield brands. The firm is retiring its older brands and unifying the business under the Wyndham brand. Although Wyndham lacks the cachet of Disney or Marriott, we think this move will enable it to better compete for time-share buyers. Still, we believe Wyndham's recent double-digit growth in the time-share business will slow.

Wyndham caters to more transient travelers through its lodging segment. It sells nearly one fourth of all room nights in the U.S. economy hotel sector through its Days Inn, Howard Johnson, and Knights Inn brands. However, the economy segment hasn't grown as much as the upscale properties since the lows of 2003. Unlike business travelers with generous expense accounts, customers for Wyndham's economy hotels are sensitive to price, and large increases in nightly rates may force them to cancel their trips altogether.

Although Wyndham's hotels have posted less-than-stellar results, the franchise model guarantees a revenue stream even when hotels are half empty. Wyndham does not actually own any of the hotels that bear its brand names. Instead, it charges third-party owners an up-front franchise fee when hotels open and a percentage of annual revenue to cover the cost of advertising, national reservation systems, and corporate overhead. This provides Wyndham with a revenue stream that is less sensitive to the gyrations of the travel market.

Still, in order to grow, Wyndham must increase hotel revenue--and hence its royalty fee--and add new properties to the franchise system. Management needs to work hard to put the shine back on its brands, especially the upscale Wyndham Hotels, to attract new franchisees and command higher rates. Given the intense competitive landscape, we believe growth will be difficult to attain.

Seven Sylvan Way
Parsippany, NJ 07054

Growth [NA]	2002	2003	2004	2005
Revenue %	NMF	NMF	NMF	15.2
Earnings/Share %	NMF	NMF	NMF	NMF
Book Value/Share %	—	—	—	—
Dividends/Share %	NMF	NMF	NMF	NMF

Profitability [NA]	2003	2004	2005	TTM
Return on Assets %	4.2	4.2	4.7	3.1
Oper Cash Flow $Mil	99	142	488	538
- Cap Spending $Mil	102	116	134	174
= Free Cash Flow $Mil	-3	26	354	364

Financial Health [NA]	2003	2004	2005	09-30-06
Long-term Debt $Mil	—	1,478	1,687	1,021
Total Equity $Mil	4,283	4,679	5,033	3,612
Debt/Equity Ratio	—	0.3	0.3	0.3

Xerox XRX

Data as of 12-29-06

Rating	Fair Value	Last Close	Consider Buy	Consider Sell	Yield %
★★★	$18.00	$16.95	$13.90	$22.60	0.00

Industry	Business Risk	Moat Size	Investment Style	Sector
Office Equip.	Average	Narrow	Large Core	Industrial Materials

Company Profile
Xerox manufactures document-production and document-management equipment and software. The firm enjoys leading positions in the majority of its target markets, including high-end digital and color production and office equipment. Xerox now concentrates only on digital and color office printers as well as professional services.

Competition

	Market Cap $Mil	12 Mo Trailing Sales $Mil	Price/Cash Flow	Return On Assets%	Debt/Equity	Total Return% 1 Yr	3 Yr
Xerox	16,361	15,766	10.7	5.5	0.7	15.7	7.6
Hewlett-Packard	112,070	91,658	9.9	7.6	0.1	45.2	22.7
Canon ADR	75,441	34,222	13.7	10.2	0.0	46.7	23.0

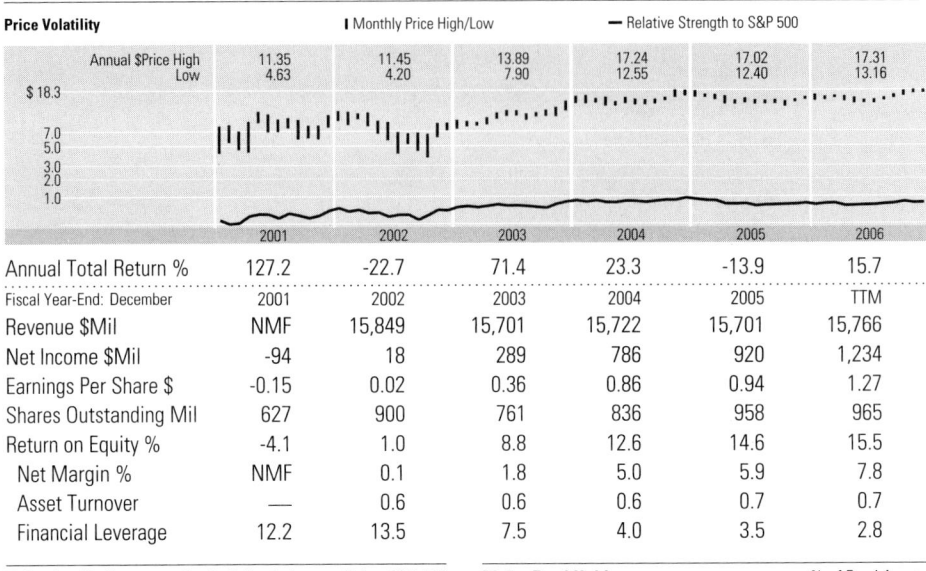

Price Volatility — Monthly Price High/Low — Relative Strength to S&P 500

Annual $Price High/Low	11.35/4.63	11.45/4.20	13.89/7.90	17.24/12.55	17.02/12.40	17.31/13.16
	2001	2002	2003	2004	2005	2006
Annual Total Return %	127.2	-22.7	71.4	23.3	-13.9	15.7

Fiscal Year-End: December	2001	2002	2003	2004	2005	TTM
Revenue $Mil	NMF	15,849	15,701	15,722	15,701	15,766
Net Income $Mil	-94	18	289	786	920	1,234
Earnings Per Share $	-0.15	0.02	0.36	0.86	0.94	1.27
Shares Outstanding Mil	627	900	761	836	958	965
Return on Equity %	-4.1	1.0	8.8	12.6	14.6	15.5
Net Margin %	NMF	0.1	1.8	5.0	5.9	7.8
Asset Turnover	—	0.6	0.6	0.6	0.7	0.7
Financial Leverage	12.2	13.5	7.5	4.0	3.5	2.8

Management — Stewardship Grade [B]
Anne Mulcahy, a 30-year company veteran, took the helm in May 2000 and launched a gut-wrenching turnaround that not only pulled the company from the brink of bankruptcy but has positioned it for growth. In 2005, the board instituted a new Long Term Incentive Program (LTIP) that has done away with options. Under the terms of the plan, executives are to be granted the performance shares based on weighted performance targets--diluted earnings per share (60%) and net cash from operations (40%)--and the shares vest over a three-year period. Although, we would prefer these metrics to skew toward revenue and operating profits, we still want to applaud the board's decision to get rid of option grants. Last year, Mulcahy was awarded $8.1 million worth of performance shares, in addition to her $2.5 million cash compensation, a handsome reward for her efforts. Her sizable stock-option awards, granted before 2005 add up to 5.5 million shares, or 0.5% of Xerox's fiscal 2005 diluted share count. However, the entire management team still has only a 1% stake in the company. Over time, we would like to see an increase in executive ownership to at least 3%. Our remaining complaint is a change of control agreement, which rewards executives in the case of a hostile takeover.

800 Long Ridge Road
Stamford, CT 06904
www.xerox.com

Growth [D]	2002	2003	2004	2005
Revenue %	NMF	-0.9	0.1	-0.1
Earnings/Share %	NMF	EUB	138.9	9.3
Book Value/Share %	-41.9	94.9	66.7	-5.5
Dividends/Share %	NMF	NMF	NMF	NMF

Profitability [C+]	2003	2004	2005	TTM
Return on Assets %	1.2	3.2	4.2	5.5
Oper Cash Flow $Mil	1,879	1,750	1,420	1,528
- Cap Spending $Mil	197	204	181	188
= Free Cash Flow $Mil	1,682	1,546	1,239	1,340

Financial Health [A-]	2003	2004	2005	09-30-06
Long-term Debt $Mil	6,930	7,050	6,139	5,904
Total Equity $Mil	3,291	6,244	6,319	7,961
Debt/Equity Ratio	2.1	1.1	1.0	0.7

Valuation Ratios	Stock	Rel to Industry	Rel to S&P 500
Price/Earnings	13.3	0.7	0.6
Price/Book	2.1	0.5	0.5
Price/Sales	1.0	0.9	0.3
Price/Cash Flow	10.7	0.7	0.7

Major Fund Holders	% of Fund Assets
Integrity Growth & Income A Load Waived	4.69
Oakmark Select I	4.36
SunAmerica Focused Large Cap Value A	3.64
Delaware Pooled Large-Cap Value Eqty	3.11

Thesis
By Irina Logovinsky, CPA, 10-20-06 Stock Price as of Analysis: $16.00

Although some still associate Xerox with copiers, today, the company is better known for its digital presses, multifunctional devices (the ones that can print, copy, and scan) and prowess in document management. As a result of this broad expertise, Xerox boasts a large installed base of office machines that generate a lucrative revenue stream of consumables and services, securing a narrow economic moat for the firm.

The combination of systems and services differentiates Xerox from hardware-only manufacturers. The firm's services arm designs strategies to make document production less costly and more efficient for its large clients. It uses Six Sigma tools and simulation software to identify inefficiencies in printing and automates document production. As part of the process, Xerox replaces outdated and disparate machines with multifunctional devices connected to the network. Given Xerox's extensive knowledge, clients have signed long-term service contracts for Xerox to oversee their document management needs.

At the heart of Xerox's growth strategy are color and digital printing. The firm's color equipment has been rapidly adopted due to an explosion of graphic-rich Web pages, presentations, and marketing brochures. And since color products use more supplies, profits in this segment are 5 times higher than in the black-and-white market. Another source of growth is the firm's digital presses, which are quickly becoming a product of choice for many commercial printers worldwide. This high-revenue opportunity for Xerox brings in $500,000 per machine and an annuitylike stream of supplies and maintenance contracts. These presses can produce limited volume, customized print jobs that would be uneconomical on analog printers. It is no surprise that digital printing's share of commercial revenues is expected to increase from 10% to 20% by 2010.

Nevertheless, things are not getting easy for Xerox. Not long ago, its reign in the digital press niche had been undisputed, but with HP, Kodak, and now Canon's entrance, this subsegment is getting crowded. In the office equipment sector, Xerox's track record with the small and medium-size accounts has not been consistent, in spite of its success with enterprise clients. Despite these difficulties, we still believe that Xerox has a better technology and deeper relationships with its end customers and channel partners than the competition. Its lead in services should lay the foundation for future profits.

Data as of 12-29-06

Xilinx XLNX

	Rating	Fair Value	Last Close	Consider Buy	Consider Sell	Yield %
	★★★★	$28.00	$23.81	$21.60	$35.10	1.43

Industry	Business Risk	Moat Size	Investment Style	Sector
Semiconductor	Average	Narrow	Mid Growth	Hardware

Company Profile
Xilinx is a leading maker of programmable-logic devices and related software products. Its logic chips are designed into electronic devices, primarily in end markets such as communications, storage, industrial, and consumer electronics. Xilinx's global customer base of 7,500 electronics equipment makers uses the firm's software to program the chips to their specifications.

Competition

	Market Cap $Mil	12 Mo Trailing Sales $Mil	Price/Cash Flow	Return On Assets %	Debt/Equity	Total Return % 1 Yr	3 Yr
Xilinx	8,006	1,870	14.6	11.7	—	-4.3	-14.0
Altera	7,121	1,250	15.1	13.1	0.0	6.2	-4.6
Atmel	2,945	1,693	12.3	1.0	0.1	95.8	-0.2

Management
Stewardship Grade [B]

CEO and President Willem Roelandts has headed Xilinx since 1996 and assumed the role of chairman of the board in August 2003. Roelandts serves on the board of the Semiconductor Industrial Association. CFO Jon Olson joined the company in 2005. Management is rich in industry experience, with Roelandts and Olson having held positions at HP and Intel, respectively. Executive compensation is reasonable compared with rival firms, and insiders own about 2% of the company. In fiscal 2005, Xilinx began issuing a quarterly dividend, which we consider a positive sign of its strength and commitment to shareholders.

Price Volatility

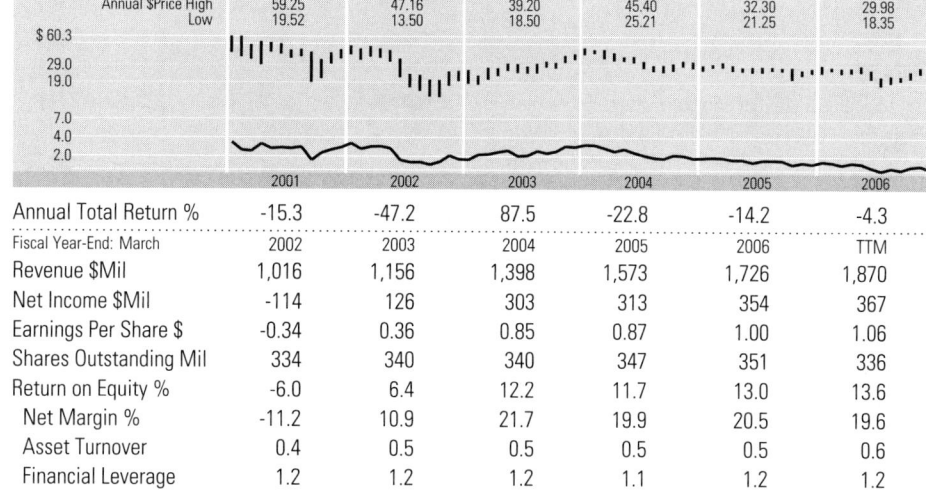

Annual $Price High	59.25	47.16	39.20	45.40	32.30	29.98
Low	19.52	13.50	18.50	25.21	21.25	18.35
	2001	2002	2003	2004	2005	2006
Annual Total Return %	-15.3	-47.2	87.5	-22.8	-14.2	-4.3

Fiscal Year-End: March	2002	2003	2004	2005	2006	TTM
Revenue $Mil	1,016	1,156	1,398	1,573	1,726	1,870
Net Income $Mil	-114	126	303	313	354	367
Earnings Per Share $	-0.34	0.36	0.85	0.87	1.00	1.06
Shares Outstanding Mil	334	340	340	347	351	336
Return on Equity %	-6.0	6.4	12.2	11.7	13.0	13.6
Net Margin %	-11.2	10.9	21.7	19.9	20.5	19.6
Asset Turnover	0.4	0.5	0.5	0.5	0.5	0.6
Financial Leverage	1.2	1.2	1.2	1.1	1.2	1.2

Valuation Ratios

	Stock	Rel to Industry	Rel to S&P 500
Price/Earnings	22.5	0.8	1.1
Price/Book	3.0	0.8	0.7
Price/Sales	4.3	1.0	1.5
Price/Cash Flow	14.6	0.9	1.0

Major Fund Holders

	% of Fund Assets
Pin Oak Aggressive Stock	5.08
Aston/ABN AMRO Mid Cap Growth N	3.97
VALIC I Science & Technology	3.61
Fidelity Advisor Electronics T	3.59

2100 Logic Drive
San Jose, CA 95124
www.xilinx.com

Growth [B]	2003	2004	2005	2006
Revenue %	13.8	20.9	12.5	9.7
Earnings/Share %	NMF	136.1	2.4	14.9
Book Value/Share %	-1.9	24.7	6.8	3.6
Dividends/Share %	NMF	NMF	NMF	40.0

Profitability [A]	2004	2005	2006	TTM
Return on Assets %	10.3	10.3	11.2	11.7
Oper Cash Flow $Mil	433	275	489	547
- Cap Spending $Mil	41	61	67	63
= Free Cash Flow $Mil	391	214	422	483

Financial Health [A+]	2004	2005	2006	09-30-06
Long-term Debt $Mil	—	—	—	
Total Equity $Mil	2,483	2,674	2,729	2,698
Debt/Equity Ratio	—	—	—	

Thesis
By Larry Cao, CFA, 11-16-06 Stock Price as of Analysis: $28.21

For investors who like leaders in a growing industry with an economic moat, Xilinx is worth a serious look.

As the largest producer of programmable logic devices (PLDs), Xilinx has benefited from the rapid growth of this industry, which has outpaced that of the overall semiconductor industry. PLDs are logic blocks that are programmed after production. The design flexibility allows users to reduce their products' time to market and avoid the high up-front cost of developing an application-specific integrated circuit (ASIC). However, the redundant logic and routing make the PLD architecture inherently more costly and, for many years, limited its application to mostly prototyping.

The advance of small-geometry processes, especially moving to 65 nanometers, is tilting the cost/benefit calculations more in favor of PLDs. The cost of PLDs goes down proportionately with ASICs, as wafer consumption is lower at narrower line widths; but in dollar terms, a PLD's price will come down faster as it has a higher starting point. ASIC design engineers, on the other hand, will have to deal with more leakage issues and spend more time on verification as more functions are crammed into smaller spaces on a wafer. These favorable dynamics have driven more widespread adoption of PLDs, often at the expense of ASICs. As the ASIC market is several times the size of PLDs, we believe Xilinx's growth will continue to outpace that of the overall chip industry.

We believe Xilinx has developed its moat by becoming the standard for designers. Xilinx and competitor Altera combined have 80% share of the PLD market. They have a few standard platforms each. It takes time for designers to get comfortable with the proprietary chip architectures and software, and it takes more time to be efficient. Consequently, they tend not to switch unless a competitive product has a clear advantage.

Xilinx overtook Altera in market share in 1998 with the introduction of its much more user-friendly software, steadily expanding its share to 50% at the expense of smaller players. In the following round of competition, Xilinx launched its new generation of products six months behind Altera, causing some concern about potential market share change down the road.

We believe favorable dynamics in the PLD industry will continue to drive adoption and revenue growth, and Xilinx, as the leader of the industry, will be a prime beneficiary.

Data as of 12-29-06

XTO Energy XTO

	Rating	Fair Value	Last Close	Consider Buy	Consider Sell	Yield %
	★★★	$53.00	$47.05	$40.90	$66.40	0.67

Company Profile
Fort Worth, Texas-based XTO Energy engages in the exploration and production of natural gas and oil. Its gathering and processing operation accounts for less than 5% of total revenue. At the end of 2005, XTO reported proven reserves of 7.62 trillion cubic feet of natural-gas equivalent, with average daily production of about 1,330 million cubic feet. Natural gas makes up about 80% of XTO's proven reserves. All of XTO's properties are in the United States.

Management   Stewardship Grade [D]
Bob Simpson is chairman and CEO. Steffen Palko, Simpson's longtime partner and cofounder of XTO, retired from the president's post in 2005 and was replaced by Keith Hutton, who was previously vice president of operations. Hutton also took Palko's spot on the board. All told, board members and management own more than 7% of the company's outstanding shares. We like to see veteran management with such a significant stake, but a number of other factors reduce our enthusiasm for this team. Management compensation has been extraordinarily high, in our view, and is likely to remain so. We do like that XTO's investor and quarterly presentations, available on the company's Web site, provide investors with a wealth of useful and detailed information on the company.

810 Houston Street Suite 2000   www.xtoenergy.com
Fort Worth, TX 76102

Growth [A+]	2002	2003	2004	2005
Revenue %	-3.4	46.8	63.8	80.6
Earnings/Share %	-26.7	8.0	111.9	108.6
Book Value/Share %	8.5	12.5	113.3	49.0
Dividends/Share %	8.0	35.2	278.2	150.0

Profitability [A]	2003	2004	2005	TTM
Return on Assets %	8.0	8.3	11.7	15.5
Oper Cash Flow $Mil	794	1,217	2,094	2,826
- Cap Spending $Mil	675	638	1,518	2,191
= Free Cash Flow $Mil	119	579	576	635

Financial Health [B]	2003	2004	2005	09-30-06
Long-term Debt $Mil	1,252	2,043	3,109	3,370
Total Equity $Mil	1,466	2,599	4,209	5,491
Debt/Equity Ratio	0.9	0.8	0.7	0.6

Industry	Business Risk	Moat Size	Investment Style	Sector
Oil/Gas	Average	Narrow	Large Growth	Energy

Competition	Market Cap $Mil	12 Mo Trailing Sales $Mil	Price/Cash Flow	Return On Assets%	Debt/ Equity	Total Return% 1 Yr	3 Yr
XTO Energy	17,217	4,554	6.1	15.5	0.6	12.2	43.3
Devon Energy	29,649	11,274	4.3	9.4	0.3	8.1	33.7
Apache	21,909	8,424	4.8	12.0	0.2	-2.3	19.0

Price Volatility

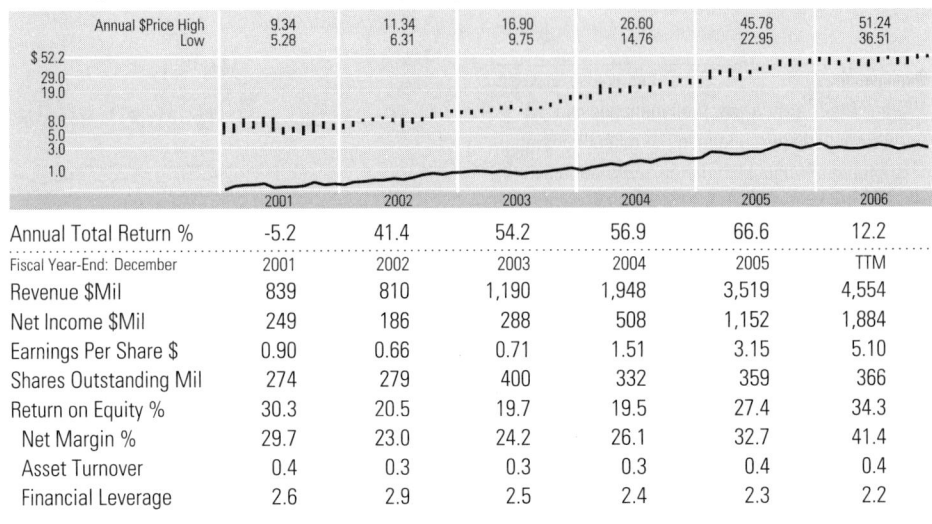

	2001	2002	2003	2004	2005	2006/TTM
Annual Total Return %	-5.2	41.4	54.2	56.9	66.6	12.2
Revenue $Mil	839	810	1,190	1,948	3,519	4,554
Net Income $Mil	249	186	288	508	1,152	1,884
Earnings Per Share $	0.90	0.66	0.71	1.51	3.15	5.10
Shares Outstanding Mil	274	279	400	332	359	366
Return on Equity %	30.3	20.5	19.7	19.5	27.4	34.3
Net Margin %	29.7	23.0	24.2	26.1	32.7	41.4
Asset Turnover	0.4	0.3	0.3	0.3	0.4	0.4
Financial Leverage	2.6	2.9	2.5	2.4	2.3	2.2

Valuation Ratios	Stock	Rel to Industry	Rel to S&P 500
Price/Earnings	9.2	0.7	0.4
Price/Book	3.1	1.0	0.8
Price/Sales	3.8	2.0	1.3
Price/Cash Flow	6.1	0.7	0.4

Major Fund Holders	% of Fund Assets
Oakmark Equity & Income I	4.38
Phoenix Strategic Growth A	3.66
Stratton Multi Cap	3.56
Hallmark Small-Cap Growth R	3.53

Thesis By Eric Chenoweth, CFA, 10-25-06 Stock Price as of Analysis: $47.27

A disciplined strategy has helped XTO Energy assemble a portfolio of high-quality natural-gas producing properties and boost operating margins and returns on invested capital.

XTO's strategy is not unique. Rather, focus and discipline as well as large positions in a number of key natural-gas producing regions in the United States are what sets the company apart. XTO acquires and develops onshore oil and gas properties in the United States, typically in regions with an established production record. XTO boosts investment in these properties, leading to higher production. Much of XTO's strategy hinges on its ability to produce more from these properties than previous owners or other bidders anticipated.

Oil and gas production is risky and capital-intensive. Management's ability to allocate capital effectively is crucial. Over the past five years, XTO has spent about 0.5% of its sales on exploration, much less than the average independent producer. Instead of spending money to find new deposits, XTO funnels nearly all of its capital and effort into acquiring and exploiting established oil and gas reserves. So far, the strategy has worked brilliantly. In each of the past five years, XTO's operating margins and returns on invested capital have been among the best of the independent producers we cover.

Higher natural-gas prices have played a role in XTO's explosive growth and profitability too. Since 1999, natural-gas prices have more than quadrupled, boosting XTO's sales and increasing the value of the firm's reserves. Thus far in 2006, XTO has been reinvesting its record cash flows more heavily in developing its properties as opposed to acquiring new ones. Although the firm continues to do deals, the balance between acquisitions and development spending has shifted from what we saw in past years. In 2004, it spent $1.9 billion acquiring oil and gas properties, eclipsing its previous record of $675 million spent in 2003. In 2005, XTO's acquisitions again topped $1.5 billion. In 2006, XTO plans to spend more than $2 billion on development.

XTO holds several risks. There's no guarantee that its new properties, or those it acquires in the future, will live up to its high expectations. Additionally, given its larger size, the company will have to find more or larger acquisitions to replace depleted reserves. Further, if natural-gas prices fall, returns on invested capital could slip.

Data as of 12-29-06

Yahoo YHOO

	Rating	Fair Value	Last Close	Consider Buy	Consider Sell	Yield %
	★★★★★	$34.00	$25.54	$26.20	$42.60	0.00

Industry	Business Risk	Moat Size	Investment Style	Sector
Media Conglomerates	Average	Narrow	Large Growth	Media

Company Profile

Yahoo is the most popular Internet destination in the world, attracting 500 million users every month. Yahoo operates Web sites in more than 30 countries, including 34% ownership of Yahoo Japan. Yahoo offers its users numerous free services including search, e-mail, instant messenger, financial information, news, video downloads, and a variety of community platforms. Advertising accounts for about 85% of sales. The remaining 15% comes from fees on premium services.

Competition

	Market Cap $Mil	12 Mo Trailing Sales $Mil	Price/Cash Flow	Return On Assets %	Debt/Equity	Total Return % 1 Yr	3 Yr
Yahoo	34,740	6,224	20.6	11.0	0.1	-34.8	4.0
Microsoft	293,538	45,352	20.8	19.8	—	15.8	7.6
Google	140,979	9,319	42.4	15.4	0.0	11.0	—

Management Stewardship Grade [C]

In our opinion, Yahoo was well managed by CEO Terry Semel and his colleagues through the post-Internet-bubble era. The company not only avoided bankruptcy--a fate suffered by many dot-coms--but is now the most popular Internet destination in the world. For its efforts, management has been extremely well rewarded. In the past two years, Semel has unloaded shares worth more than $400 million, accounting for a majority of the $635 million in stock that Yahoo's top five insiders sold in that period. After this, Semel still held more than 18 million shares or options (mostly the latter) worth more than $200 million at the start of 2006. Yahoo's compensation policy seems somewhat excessive to us, although we do recognize that Semel has been at the helm while Yahoo has increased in value by billions of dollars. However, our confidence in Semel is faltering, as Yahoo has been lackluster on the acquisition front and slow in releasing new major products. Founders David Filo and Jerry Yang combined still own about 10% of Yahoo's shares, ensuring that they have continued influence on Yahoo's future direction. Yang remains on Yahoo's board, which is chaired by Semel.

701 First Avenue
Sunnyvale, CA 94089
www.yahoo.com

Growth [A]	2002	2003	2004	2005
Revenue %	32.8	70.5	120.0	47.1
Earnings/Share %	NMF	350.0	222.2	120.7
Book Value/Share %	24.6	56.2	48.6	17.9
Dividends/Share %	NMF	NMF	NMF	NMF

Profitability [B+]	2003	2004	2005	TTM
Return on Assets %	4.0	9.1	17.5	11.0
Oper Cash Flow $Mil	428	1,090	1,711	1,686
- Cap Spending $Mil	117	246	409	709
= Free Cash Flow $Mil	311	844	1,302	976

Financial Health [A+]	2003	2004	2005	09-30-06
Long-term Debt $Mil	750	750	750	750
Total Equity $Mil	4,363	7,101	8,566	8,067
Debt/Equity Ratio	0.2	0.1	0.1	0.1

Price Volatility

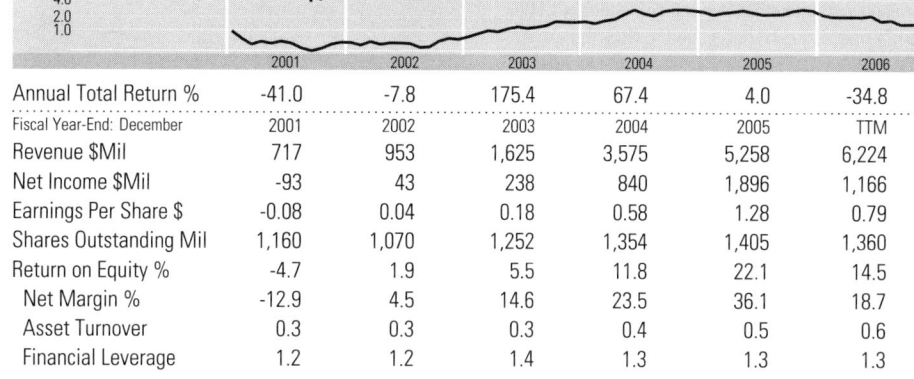

	2001	2002	2003	2004	2005	2006
Annual $Price High	21.69	10.68	22.74	39.79	43.45	43.66
Low	4.01	4.47	8.18	20.57	30.30	22.65
Annual Total Return %	-41.0	-7.8	175.4	67.4	4.0	-34.8

Fiscal Year-End: December	2001	2002	2003	2004	2005	TTM
Revenue $Mil	717	953	1,625	3,575	5,258	6,224
Net Income $Mil	-93	43	238	840	1,896	1,166
Earnings Per Share $	-0.08	0.04	0.18	0.58	1.28	0.79
Shares Outstanding Mil	1,160	1,070	1,252	1,354	1,405	1,360
Return on Equity %	-4.7	1.9	5.5	11.8	22.1	14.5
Net Margin %	-12.9	4.5	14.6	23.5	36.1	18.7
Asset Turnover	0.3	0.3	0.3	0.4	0.5	0.6
Financial Leverage	1.2	1.2	1.4	1.3	1.3	1.3

Valuation Ratios	Stock	Rel to Industry	Rel to S&P 500
Price/Earnings	32.3	1.3	1.6
Price/Book	4.3	1.3	1.0
Price/Sales	5.6	1.6	1.9
Price/Cash Flow	20.6	1.2	1.4

Major Fund Holders	% of Fund Assets
ProFunds Internet UltraSector Inv	6.86
Fidelity Select Leisure	6.73
Fidelity Select Multimedia	6.09
BlackRock Global Technology A	5.33

Thesis By Larry Witt, CFA, 10-30-06 Stock Price as of Analysis: $25.95

As competitors continue to innovate, forge partnerships, and make acquisitions, Yahoo has been seemingly stuck in the mud. Product delays, lackluster earnings, and a lack of headline acquisitions have disappointed advertisers, users, and shareholders alike. Google and community Web sites like MySpace, Facebook, and YouTube continue to capture market share at the expense of Yahoo. Furthermore, Google's advertising platform is superior to Yahoo's, resulting in better results for Google and advertisers. If Yahoo's new advertising platform does not perform as expected, the firm may never recover.

Despite its recent struggles, Yahoo remains the most popular destination on the Web, with 500 million unique users per month. Products with high switching costs--like e-mail and stock portfolios--should help retain a large portion of these users, while newer products like Flickr and Yahoo Answers should help attract new users. The company should also benefit from its operations abroad and recent venture into mobile advertising. A robust portfolio of products, nascent opportunities, and a history of surviving difficult times should allow Yahoo to continue generating economic profits for years to come.

As people spend more time on the Internet and less time on traditional media, advertisers continue to shift more of their dollars online. Boasting the largest online audience in the world, Yahoo has been able to capture a disproportionate share of this advertising, which now accounts for 85% of the company's revenue. Although Yahoo may currently be ceding market share, this could prove temporary as trendier Web sites eventually lose their appeal and fickle consumers move on. In the end, we think consumers will continue to take advantage of Yahoo's unparalleled number of free offerings, including e-mail, search, news, and maps.

Yahoo also makes money by charging fees for premium services, including extra storage and music downloads. As the creation and distribution of online content improve, we think consumers will be increasingly willing to pay for access to good content (akin to the adoption of cable television). Media companies will probably use Yahoo to distribute their content, as the company already has the necessary infrastructure as well as the largest user base on the Web. Besides generating fee revenue, the online distribution of music, videos, and television should provide Yahoo with additional advertising opportunities as well.

Data as of 12-29-06

Yum Brands YUM

	Rating	Fair Value	Last Close	Consider Buy	Consider Sell	Yield %
	★★★	$61.00	$58.80	$47.00	$76.40	0.90

Industry	Business Risk	Moat Size	Investment Style	Sector
Restaurants	Average	Narrow	Large Core	Consumer Services

Company Profile
Yum Brands is the world's largest fast food company, based on number of units. Its portfolio includes more than 34,000 company, franchise, license, and joint-venture restaurants in more than 100 countries. Four of the company's restaurant brands—KFC (14,016 units), Pizza Hut (12,605 units), Taco Bell (5,835 units), and Long John Silver's (1,159 units) -- are the global leaders of the chicken, pizza, Mexican-style food, and quick-service seafood categories, respectively.

Management — Stewardship Grade [C]
David Novak has served as president of Yum since 1997 and was named CEO and chairman in 2000 and 2001, respectively. Under his leadership, the company's shares have more than tripled since the spin-off from PepsiCo in September 1997. In 2005, Novak earned $4.2 million in salary plus bonus and received an option package worth an estimated $3.9 million at the date of grant. He also garnered about $1.0 million in other benefits, which mostly consists of preferential earnings on his deferred compensation plan along with perks, such as personal use of the company aircraft. While Novak's record as CEO has been impressive, we do not believe he warranted $9.1 million in total annual compensation in 2005, which exceeded the combined amount earned by the CEOs of McDonald's and Wendy's. We think Yum has a deep and experienced team of executives, averaging more than 12 years of experience with the company. Overall, management and directors, who as a group beneficially own about 3% of the company, have demonstrated fair stewardship. We were encouraged that the company declassified its board in 2005, but we do not approve of the company's poison pill and other takeover defenses. We'd also prefer for the roles of chairman and CEO to be split.

1441 Gardiner Lane
Louisville, KY 40213
www.yum.com

Competition	Market Cap $Mil	12 Mo Trailing Sales $Mil	Price/Cash Flow	Return On Assets%	Debt/Equity	Total Return% 1 Yr	3 Yr
Yum Brands	15,586	9,444	12.9	13.7	1.5	26.8	21.6
McDonald's	54,825	21,790	13.3	9.4	0.6	34.6	23.9
Wendy's International	3,905	3,777	9.5	4.2	0.3	30.5	24.9

Price Volatility — Monthly Price High/Low — Relative Strength to S&P 500

	2001	2002	2003	2004	2005	2006
Annual $Price High	26.66	33.17	35.40	47.47	53.79	63.68
Low	15.78	20.70	21.55	32.13	44.74	44.21
Annual Total Return %	49.1	-1.5	42.0	37.8	0.2	26.8

Fiscal Year-End: December	2001	2002	2003	2004	2005	TTM
Revenue $Mil	6,953	7,757	8,380	9,011	9,349	9,444
Net Income $Mil	492	583	617	740	762	809
Earnings Per Share $	1.62	1.88	2.02	2.42	2.55	2.85
Shares Outstanding Mil	293	296	294	291	286	265
Return on Equity %	NMF	NMF	NMF	46.4	52.6	60.9
Net Margin %	7.1	7.5	7.4	8.2	8.2	8.6
Asset Turnover	1.6	1.4	1.5	1.6	1.6	1.6
Financial Leverage	—	—	—	3.6	3.9	4.4

Valuation Ratios	Stock	Rel to Industry	Rel to S&P 500
Price/Earnings	20.6	0.7	1.0
Price/Book	11.7	2.0	2.9
Price/Sales	1.7	0.8	0.6
Price/Cash Flow	12.9	0.9	0.9

Major Fund Holders	% of Fund Assets
Oakmark Select I	7.58
Longleaf Partners	4.92
IXIS Harris Associates Focused Value C	4.88
Longleaf Partners International	4.33

Growth [C-]	2002	2003	2004	2005
Revenue %	11.6	8.0	7.5	3.8
Earnings/Share %	16.0	7.4	19.8	5.4
Book Value/Share %	NMF	NMF	NMF	-7.0
Dividends/Share %	NMF	NMF	NMF	115.0

Profitability [A+]	2003	2004	2005	TTM
Return on Assets %	11.0	13.0	13.4	13.7
Oper Cash Flow $Mil	1,099	1,186	1,238	1,204
- Cap Spending $Mil	663	645	609	570
= Free Cash Flow $Mil	436	541	629	634

Financial Health [A-]	2003	2004	2005	06-30-06
Long-term Debt $Mil	—	1,731	1,649	1,932
Total Equity $Mil	—	1,595	1,449	1,328
Debt/Equity Ratio	—	1.1	1.1	1.5

Thesis By John Owens, CFA, CPA, 11-27-06 Stock Price as of Analysis: $60.90

Yum has a collection of very strong brands and tremendous growth potential overseas. We are especially enthusiastic about its long-term prospects in China. Nevertheless, we would recommend a significant discount to our fair value estimate, given strong industry competition and other concerns.

Yum has four leading brands in their respective categories: KFC, Pizza Hut, Taco Bell, and Long John Silver's. These chains, along with A&W, account for more than 20,000 domestic restaurants. In 2005, these restaurants increased system sales 5% and generated $760 million in operating profit (down 2% over the prior year). We believe KFC and Taco Bell are executing well in the United States, with 6% and 7% same-restaurant sales growth in 2005, respectively. Pizza Hut is struggling, however, as key competitors offer a better value to customers, in our view. The chain's domestic same-store sales were flat in 2005, while rivals Papa John's and Domino's were both around 5%.

In China, Yum has established a dominant leadership position, with more than 2,000 KFC units and 300-plus Pizza Hut casual dining restaurants. In 2005, the China division increased its system sales 13% and delivered $211 million in operating profit (up 3% over the prior year), despite the challenges of avian flu and a red dye scare. With China's growing middle class, we see tremendous prospects for further growth. Yum plans to open more than 400 new restaurants in China in 2006.

Outside China, Yum's international division, which consists of nearly 12,000 restaurants in more than 100 countries and territories, is showing impressive growth. In 2005, its system sales increased 9% and operating profit rose 10%, to $372 million. With a strong presence in Japan, Great Britain, Canada, and Australia, the company is expanding further into megamarket opportunities like continental Europe, India, and Russia and plans for at least 770 new units in 2006.

Despite its leading brands and ample opportunities for growth, Yum still has some significant challenges. KFC remains vulnerable to future outbreaks of avian flu. Rivalry in the quick-service restaurant sector is also intense. While McDonald's has increased its focus on the Golden Arches, Yum's top management must oversee its three giant brands as well as Long John Silver's, A&W, and East Dawning. With so much on management's plate, it is not surprising that Pizza Hut has lost ground to its chief rivals.

Data as of 12-29-06

Zebra Technologies ZBRA

	Rating	Fair Value	Last Close	Consider Buy	Consider Sell	Yield %
	★★★★	$45.00	$34.79	$34.70	$56.40	0.00

Company Profile
Zebra Technologies sells bar-code and plastic ID printers and readers in 90 countries. More than 90% of Fortune 500 companies use Zebra printers. The company has sold around 5 million printers; its new product lineup includes radio-frequency identification printer/encoders and wireless mobile solutions. Zebra also offers software, connectivity products, and printing supplies.

Management
Stewardship Grade [C]

Chairman and CEO Edward Kaplan, the business manager since forming Zebra with Gerhard Cless in 1969, will retire as CEO as soon as a replacement is found. Chief engineer Cless has managed the company's successful research and development program since the beginning. Both men are longtime board members and hold sizable ownership positions. Corporate governance is generally fine, but there are a few red flags. The board is staggered, and the two cofounders own a corporation that owns facilities used by Zebra; the lease payments are about $200,000 a month, and the agreement extends to 2014.

333 Corporate Woods Pkwy
Vernon Hills, IL 60061
www.zebra.com

Growth [C+]	2002	2003	2004	2005
Revenue %	5.7	12.8	23.6	5.9
Earnings/Share %	15.3	25.5	29.7	-6.6
Book Value/Share %	19.0	19.6	20.6	7.6
Dividends/Share %	NMF	NMF	NMF	NMF

Profitability [A+]	2003	2004	2005	TTM
Return on Assets %	13.1	14.0	12.2	8.3
Oper Cash Flow $Mil	102	121	93	61
- Cap Spending $Mil	8	16	14	20
= Free Cash Flow $Mil	94	105	78	42

Financial Health [A+]	2003	2004	2005	09-30-06
Long-term Debt $Mil	0	0	0	—
Total Equity $Mil	652	798	851	919
Debt/Equity Ratio	0.0	0.0	0.0	0.0

Industry	Business Risk	Moat Size	Investment Style	Sector
Computer Equip.	Average	Narrow	Mid Growth	Hardware

Competition	Market Cap $Mil	12 Mo Trailing Sales $Mil	Price/Cash Flow	Return On Assets%	Debt/Equity	Total Return% 1 Yr	3 Yr
Zebra Technologies	2,451	729	39.9	8.3	0.0	-18.8	-7.2
Symbol Technologies	3,806	1,795	16.1	5.6	0.0	16.6	-3.8

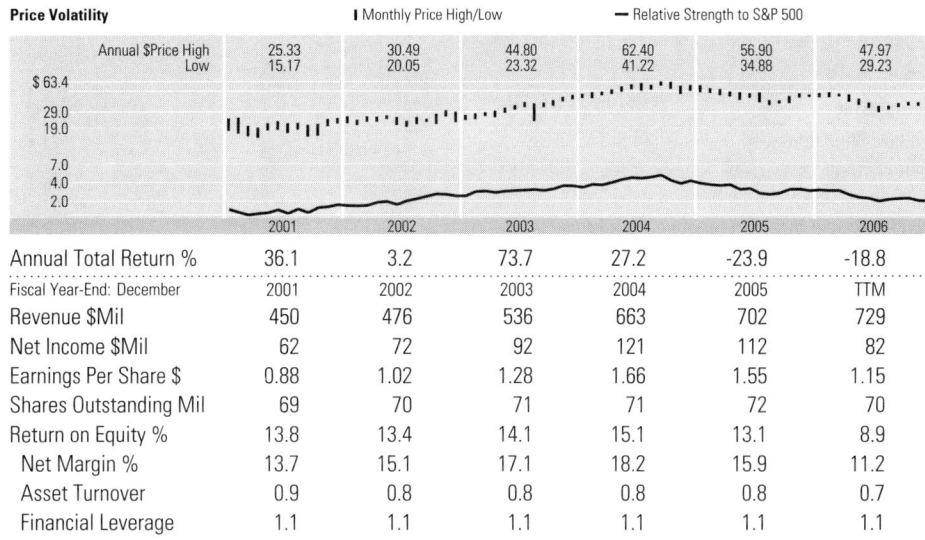

Annual $Price High	25.33	30.49	44.80	62.40	56.90	47.97
Low	15.17	20.05	23.32	41.22	34.88	29.23
	2001	2002	2003	2004	2005	2006
Annual Total Return %	36.1	3.2	73.7	27.2	-23.9	-18.8
Fiscal Year-End: December	2001	2002	2003	2004	2005	TTM
Revenue $Mil	450	476	536	663	702	729
Net Income $Mil	62	72	92	121	112	82
Earnings Per Share $	0.88	1.02	1.28	1.66	1.55	1.15
Shares Outstanding Mil	69	70	71	71	72	70
Return on Equity %	13.8	13.4	14.1	15.1	13.1	8.9
Net Margin %	13.7	15.1	17.1	18.2	15.9	11.2
Asset Turnover	0.9	0.8	0.8	0.8	0.8	0.7
Financial Leverage	1.1	1.1	1.1	1.1	1.1	1.1

Valuation Ratios	Stock	Rel to Industry	Rel to S&P 500
Price/Earnings	30.8	1.1	1.5
Price/Book	2.7	0.5	0.7
Price/Sales	3.4	1.3	1.2
Price/Cash Flow	39.9	2.6	2.7

Major Fund Holders	% of Fund Assets
Schwartz Value	4.03
Ave Maria Opportunity	3.59
FPA Perennial	3.30
SunAmerica Focused Mid-Cap Value A	3.21

Thesis By Rod Bare, 12-01-06 Stock Price as of Analysis: $34.33

Zebra Technologies has many attractive attributes, despite a recent soft patch in sales. It has healthy profit margins, a strong balance sheet, and an excellent management team with an appropriate ownership stake. Building on this strong foundation, Zebra is executing a three-part strategy that we think positions it well for success.

The first part is international expansion. Zebra's core bar-code and plastic ID products have performed so well in the maturing U.S. markets that management is investing heavily to expand the company's presence in Mexico, China, and Eastern Europe. Mobile bar-code and printer systems continue to truly enhance productivity for several large global customers. While their lumpy purchasing behavior sometimes gives the market heartburn, large retail accounts still need this hardware for supply-chain efficiency. Zebra's ongoing investment in international distribution appears to be a strong foundation for growth across several product lines.

Industry-specific offerings are the second area of focus. The Food and Drug Administration recently mandated the use of bar-code technology to augment the safety of patient drug administration in medical facilities. The pharmaceutical industry is also very interested in Zebra's technology to track expensive or highly regulated drugs. Health-care spending on bar-code technology is alive and well in pockets; broader spending should soon emerge, driven by upgraded IT infrastructure in hospitals and attractive safety benefits.

The third component of Zebra's strategy is maintaining its leadership role in the emerging RFID market. A generic RFID device is a small transmitter embedded in a label stuck to the side of a shipping carton. RFID devices use low-power signals to provide supply-chain computers with real-time updates on carton location, contents, and reorder levels. Wal-Mart has a couple of hundred suppliers implementing the technology, and Zebra products are used in several of these initiatives.

Zebra's future looks bright. The international and vertical market strategies alone are significant opportunities. RFID still has some technical and economic challenges, but the opportunity is emerging with new, more robust standards. Our biggest concern remains the impending acquisitions that management assures us are just around the corner. Zebra's acquisition record is okay, but acquisitions are tricky, and it takes only one bad one to derail a firm. The good still outweighs the bad at Zebra, though; we'd invest at the appropriate discount.

Data as of 12-29-06

Zimmer Holdings ZMH

	Rating	Fair Value	Last Close	Consider Buy	Consider Sell	Yield %
	★★★	$79.00	$78.38	$67.30	$103.70	0.00

Industry	Business Risk	Moat Size	Investment Style	Sector
Medical Equip.	Below Avg	Wide	Large Growth	Healthcare

Company Profile
Zimmer is a leading provider of orthopedic medical devices. The firm focuses primarily on joint reconstruction, where it leads key niches including knee and hip implants. Reconstructive implants accounted for 83% of the firm's sales in 2005. The balance was generated from related surgical tools, devices to treat traumatic injuries, and spinal column treatments. Zimmer's core operational activities include device development, manufacturing, and marketing.

Management   Stewardship Grade [B]
We give Zimmer a good Stewardship Grade, but we caution investors about the imminent transition of the firm's top manager. Ray Elliott has announced his plan to retire as Zimmer's president and CEO in the first half of 2007; he will remain the firm's chairman for an interim period. We were surprised by this announcement given Elliott's young age. Also, the firm did not immediately announce a successor, so many questions surround the long-term leadership of Zimmer. We think this transition may prove difficult given Elliott's long tenure at the top of Zimmer; he's led Zimmer as a public company and as a division of Bristol-Myers Squibb since 1997. We hope Zimmer maintains its transparency under its new leader. We especially like its detailed reporting of segment information in each quarterly and annual report. But there is room for improvement. We hope compensation comes down from the stratosphere. Elliott took home $10 million in 2005, which raised our eyebrows. We think the firm's board remains very small--five people serving three-year terms. We also dislike that Zimmer's board rejected the majority vote of shareholders to declassify the board in 2006 and will require 80% to do so in the 2007 vote. Given this board structure and attitude, we think shareholders will find it difficult to make changes.

345 East Main Street
Warsaw, IN 46580
www.zimmer.com

Growth [B]	2002	2003	2004	2005
Revenue %	16.4	38.5	56.8	10.2
Earnings/Share %	NMF	25.2	33.5	33.8
Book Value/Share %	NMF	699.7	7.1	17.5
Dividends/Share %	NMF	NMF	NMF	NMF

Profitability [A]	2003	2004	2005	TTM
Return on Assets %	6.7	9.5	12.8	13.4
Oper Cash Flow $Mil	495	862	878	1,044
- Cap Spending $Mil	45	101	105	124
= Free Cash Flow $Mil	450	761	773	920

Financial Health [A+]	2003	2004	2005	09-30-06
Long-term Debt $Mil	1,008	624	82	101
Total Equity $Mil	3,143	3,943	4,683	4,804
Debt/Equity Ratio	0.3	0.2	0.0	0.0

Competition

	Market Cap $Mil	12 Mo Trailing Sales $Mil	Price/Cash Flow	Return On Assets%	Debt/Equity	Total Return% 1 Yr	3 Yr
Zimmer Holdings	18,705	3,410	17.9	13.4	0.0	16.2	3.8
Johnson & Johnson	191,415	52,252	14.5	18.5	0.0	12.4	10.8
Stryker	22,439	5,221	25.1	14.1	0.0	24.5	9.9

Price Volatility | Monthly Price High/Low   — Relative Strength to S&P 500

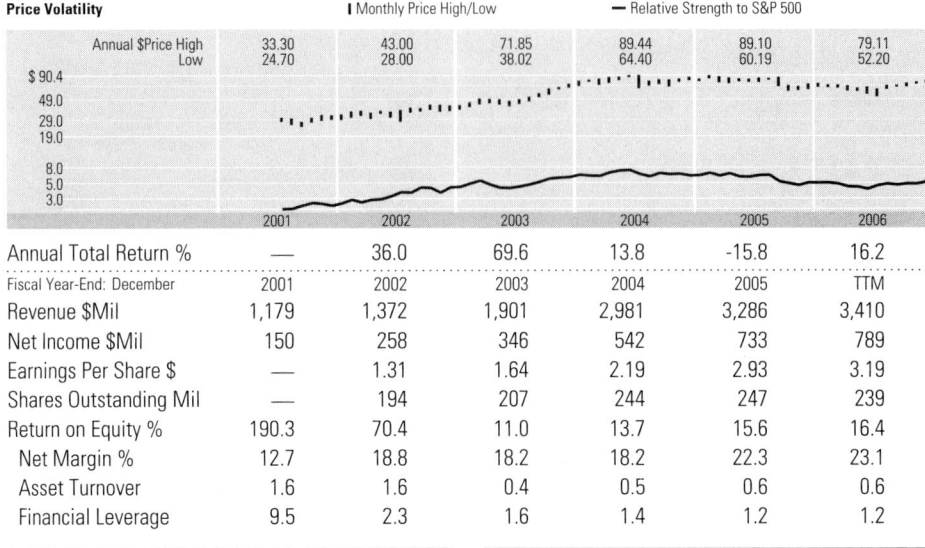

		2001	2002	2003	2004	2005	2006 TTM
Annual $Price High			33.30	43.00	71.85	89.44	89.10	79.11
Low			24.70	28.00	38.02	64.40	60.19	52.20
Annual Total Return %		—	36.0	69.6	13.8	-15.8	16.2
Fiscal Year-End: December	2001	2002	2003	2004	2005	TTM
Revenue $Mil	1,179	1,372	1,901	2,981	3,286	3,410
Net Income $Mil	150	258	346	542	733	789
Earnings Per Share $	—	1.31	1.64	2.19	2.93	3.19
Shares Outstanding Mil	—	194	207	244	247	239
Return on Equity %	190.3	70.4	11.0	13.7	15.6	16.4
Net Margin %	12.7	18.8	18.2	18.2	22.3	23.1
Asset Turnover	1.6	1.6	0.4	0.5	0.6	0.6
Financial Leverage	9.5	2.3	1.6	1.4	1.2	1.2

Valuation Ratios	Stock	Rel to Industry	Rel to S&P 500
Price/Earnings	24.6	0.8	1.2
Price/Book	3.9	0.7	1.0
Price/Sales	5.5	1.2	1.9
Price/Cash Flow	17.9	0.7	1.2

Major Fund Holders	% of Fund Assets
AIM Trimark Endeavor A	5.07
Pacific Advisors Growth A	3.93
Delaware Select Growth A	3.82
Delaware Pooled All-Cap Growth Equity	3.79

Thesis By Julie Stralow, CFA, 11-22-06 Stock Price as of Analysis: $73.50

Zimmer Holdings stands out in a very attractive industry. Zimmer leads several key orthopedic device categories that possess high entry barriers and sticky physician relationships. We think these positive attributes combined with Zimmer's manufacturing and marketing prowess will help the firm generate excellent returns for the long run.

Zimmer claims a leading market position in reconstructive devices, including top spots in knee and hip replacements. This leadership remains very stable because orthopedic surgeons typically display high levels of brand loyalty. With patient outcomes dependent on the skills developed using a particular manufacturer's devices, surgeons have little incentive to switch once comfortable with a supplier's product set. Therefore, as long as Zimmer's innovation cycle doesn't fall dramatically behind competitive cycles, the firm should continue leading and benefiting from growth in these key niches.

Long-term growth trends look promising, too. Joint replacements are typically preceded by years of wear and tear on the body. Aging and osteoarthritis can lead to the painful breakdown of hips and knees. With baby boomers entering their later years, procedure volumes should balloon over the next couple of decades. Two conflicting factors also should lead to healthy procedure growth--more active lifestyles and expanding waistlines. For those active in sports, many expect to pursue higher-intensity activities for a longer period of time than in previous generations. These activities can place additional stress on joints and lead to more, and earlier, replacements. On the other hand, joints are taking a beating under heavier bodies as the obesity epidemic takes its toll. These trends suggest procedure growth will accelerate over the long run.

Worries about society's ability to pay for this volume growth persist, though. The vast majority of industry sales are paid for by government entities, like Medicare. These entities might have to cut reimbursement rates for procedures, which would pressure profits of industry customers (hospitals) and could trickle down to industry participants in the form of lower prices. Price declines could curtail growth and contract margins.

We think Zimmer is in a great position to tackle these challenges, though. Its lean manufacturing operations keep gross margins at the top of the industry. Also, its prowess in physician education helps maintain and cultivate close physician relationships. Zimmer appears to be the cream of this topnotch crop of companies.

Glossary

This section explains how to use the data found in this publication to make better investment decisions.

Glossary

% Annual Change
A company's year-on-year growth in a given measure, such as sales per quarter or earnings/share per quarter.

% of Fund Assets
In the Major Fund Holders table of the Stock Report, the percentage of each fund's assets invested in the particular stock.

12-Month Trailing Sales
A company's sales over the most recent four quarters.

1-Year Total Return %
A stock's total return (including capital gains and dividends) from one year ago to the present.

3-Yr Avg Return %
see Average Return

90-Day Treasury Bill
see U.S. 90-Day Treasury Bill

A

Annual High
The highest price the stock has reached during a calendar-year period. If this price is much higher than the stock's current price, it generally means the stock has run into problems.

Annual Low
The lowest price the stock has reached during a calendar-year period. If this price is much lower than the stock's current price, it means the stock has fared well recently.

Asset Turnover
Equal to total revenue divided by total assets. Asset turnover measures a company's efficiency, or how many dollars of revenue it generates for each dollar of assets. Like most financial ratios, asset turnover can vary greatly across industries, so it's often more useful to compare a company with its peers than to the market as a whole. For example, grocery stores have high asset turnover, because they sell high volumes of low-priced goods.

Assets
All company-owned resources that are expected to provide benefits to that company's business. Total assets, as with other balance-sheet items, are shown in millions of dollars and are current as of the last day of the specified reporting period.

Average Daily Volume
The average number of shares of a stock that have been traded per day over the previous 12 months. Average daily volume is a rough gauge of a stock's popularity in the market.

Average Return
The annualized return of a stock, including both capital gains and dividends, over a multiyear period such as three or five years. This figure represents the annual return an investor would have received if the stock's returns were evenly spread across the time period.

Average Shares Outstanding
see Shares Outstanding

B

Balance Sheet
A statement of a company's financial position at a certain point in time. The balance sheet tells how much a company owns (its assets), how much it owes (its liabilities), and the difference between the two (its equity), which represents the part of the company owned by shareholders. The basic equation underlying a balance sheet is:

Assets - Liabilities = Equity, which can also be expressed as:
Assets = Liabilities + Equity

Bear Market
A period when stock prices fall and investors are pessimistic. Bear markets usually aren't labeled as such until stock prices have slipped by 15%. The opposite of a bear market is a bull market.

Book Value
Equal to a company's total assets minus its total liabilities; also known as equity or net worth.

Book Value/Share
Book value (also known as equity or net worth) divided by shares outstanding. Book value/share is a handy way to see how much equity is represented by each share of stock.

Book Value/Share % Growth
One of the key variables in determining whether a company is increasing shareholder wealth over time. Growth in book value per share (also known as equity per share) typically comes from two sources: retained earnings (earnings the company does not pay out as dividends) and new share issuances. Young, capital-hungry companies typically achieve high equity/share growth through the second method.

Bull Market
A period when stock prices rise and investors are optimistic. The opposite of a bull market is a bear market.

Business Risk
In the Stock Report, a rating describing a company's level of business risk as scored by Morningstar analysts on each of seven different risk factors:

- How cyclical is the company's industry?
- How healthy is the company's balance sheet relative to other companies in its sector?
- How does the company's free cash flow compare with its sales?
- How sustainable is the company's operating cash flow?
- How big are the company's revenues relative to other companies?
- How big is the company's economic moat?
- Is there some nonfinancial issue looming in the future that could materially affect the company's fortunes?

The scores are summed to produce a composite, which is translated into a below average, average, above average, or speculative risk rating.

C

Capital Gains
Investment gains resulting from a rise in a stock's price. (Conversely, capital losses result from a fall in a stock's price.) Capital gains (or losses) and dividend income are the two components of a stock's total return.

Capital Spending
Money invested in the future growth of a business; also known as capital expenditures. Capital spending includes spending on property, plants, and equipment, as well as on intellectual properties such as software, trademarks, and patents.

Cash Flow
The amount of cash a company generates. It's similar to net income (earnings), except that cash flow excludes any noncash items. This can make a big difference in industries such as cable TV, where many companies have heavy depreciation charges that depress earnings but don't affect cash flow.

Cash Flow From Operations
The cash flow a company generates from the day-to-day operation of its business. This figure can be found in a company's cash-flow statement. The other two types of cash flow found on this statement are cash flow from investing activities (such as capital spending) and from financing activities (such as issuing stock).

Company Name
A shortened version of the company's legal name.

Company Profile
A description of the company's main business operations. The company profile for each Stock Report is written using information taken from the firm's annual reports and updated as necessary by the analyst covering the company.

Competition
In each Stock Report, a table listing a company's most important competitors.

Consider Buy
The price below which we think investors should consider purchasing a stock. The Consider Buying price is equivalent to the price at which a stock would earn a 5-star rating. For example, a stock with low risk would have a Consider Buying price 15.5% below our estimate of its fair value. Be sure to take your individual circumstances—including diversification, risk tolerance, and tax considerations—into account before making a final purchase decision.

Consider Sell
The price above which we think investors should consider selling a stock. The Consider Selling price is equivalent to the price at which a stock would earn a 1-star rating. For example, a stock with low risk would have a Consider Selling price 31% above our estimate of its fair value. Be sure to take your individual circumstances—including diversification, risk tolerance, and tax considerations—into account before making a final selling decision.

Consumer Price Index
An index measuring the price of a fixed basket of consumer goods in the United States. Released monthly by the U.S. Department of Labor's Bureau of Labor Statistics, the Consumer Price Index is commonly used to measure inflation.

Credit Suisse First Boston High Yield Index
An index measuring the value of a wide selection of high-yield bonds. It is often used as a benchmark for high-yield bonds and funds.

Current Assets
Cash plus any assets that a company expects to convert to cash within a year, such as short-term investments, accounts receivable, and inventories. The current assets figure doesn't mean much in isolation, but in comparison with current liabilities (*see Current Ratio*), it's a good measure of a company's short-term liquidity.

Current Liabilities
Liabilities that a company expects to pay within a year, such as short-term debt, accounts payable, and interest payable. The current liabilities figure doesn't mean much in isolation, but in comparison with current assets (*see Current Ratio*) it's a good measure of a company's short-term liquidity.

Current Ratio
Equal to current assets divided by current liabilities. The current ratio is a measure of a company's liquidity and ability to meet its short-term obligations. A high current ratio is generally good, because it means that the company has plenty of liquid assets to work with. However, companies with low inventories and reliable cash flow can afford to operate with lower current ratios than riskier companies can.

D

Debt %
The percentage of the company's long-term capital that is composed of long-term debt. For nonfinancial companies, it is derived by dividing the total long-term debt by the sum of total shareholders' equity and total long-term debt and multiplying by 100. For financial companies, the calculation is:

[Total Assets - (Equity + Preferreds)]/Total Assets = Debt %

Debt/Equity Ratio
Equal to long-term debt divided by shareholders' equity (also known as net worth or book value). A company with a high debt/equity ratio is riskier than one with a low debt/equity ratio, because interest on long-term debt is a fixed cost that must be paid regardless of how well the business is doing.

Debt Leverage
see Financial Leverage

Debt/Total Capital
Equal to long-term debt divided by total capitalization (market cap plus long-term debt). Debt/total capital shows how much long-term debt the company uses as a percentage of its total long-term capital; the higher the number, the more a company has leveraged its capital structure with debt.

Depreciation & Amortization
Noncash charges taken against a company's profits for the deterioration of an asset's value over its useful life. Depreciation refers to the reduction in value of a tangible asset (such as a factory), and amortization refers to the reduction in value of an intangible asset (such as goodwill).

Direct Investment
A plan that allows investors to purchase shares directly from a company, without a broker or other intermediary. Such plans are often combined with DRIPs (dividend reinvestment plans).

Dividend
A portion of a company's profit that is paid directly to shareholders, generally expressed in a per-share amount. The raw dollar amount of a company's dividend gen-

erally doesn't mean a lot except in comparison with its stock price (dividend yield) or its earnings per share (payout ratio). Many fast-growing companies pay no dividend, preferring to invest all of their profits back into the company.

Dividend Yield

A stock's dividend per share divided by price per share. Companies with a high dividend yield tend to be profitable but slow-growing, and they tend to be in industries such as tobacco and REITs. Companies that pay no dividend at all, including most technology companies, have a dividend yield of zero.

Dividends/Share % Growth

The percentage change in a company's dividend for a given year (or the annualized change, for periods longer than one year); also known simply as dividend growth. If a company's dividend has been growing steadily, that's generally a sign that the company is healthy and management has confidence in its prospects. Conversely, a falling dividend (indicated by a negative dividend growth rate) is usually a sign that the company is having financial troubles.

Dow Jones Industrial Average

The most widely known stock-market index. The 30 companies in the Dow are selected by the editors of *The Wall Street Journal*. Their prices are added together and divided by a divisor that changes when a new company replaces an old one in the index, or when any company in the index splits its stock. The Dow isn't as accurate a measure of the market as the S&P 500 or the Wilshire 5000, but it's still popular because it's been around so long and the companies in it are so well known.

Dow Jones Transportation Average

An index measuring the value of 20 stocks in the airline, railroad, trucking, and shipping industries. Like the better-known Dow Jones Industrial Average, it is price-weighted, meaning it is based on the prices of the individual stocks, rather than their market capitalizations.

Dow Jones Utility Average

An index measuring the value of 15 gas- and electric-utility stocks. Like the better-known Dow Jones Industrial Average, it is price-weighted, meaning it is based on the prices of the individual stocks, rather than their market capitalizations.

DRIP (Dividend Reinvestment Plan)

A plan that allows stock investors to have their dividends automatically reinvested in shares of a stock. Such plans can be handy for long-term investors who don't care about getting short-term income from dividends. Companies with DRIPs are generally well established and may be good choices for beginning investors who are just starting to buy stocks.

E

Earnings Growth

see Net Income Growth

Earnings Per Share (EPS)

How much profit a company has made per share within a given period. EPS is a fairly arbitrary number by itself, because the company can control the number of shares outstanding through splits and buybacks. But comparing a company's most recent EPS to its EPS in previous years and quarters (adjusted for any splits) is one of the most common ways of telling how fast the company's profits are growing.

Earnings/Share % Growth

see EPS Growth

EBITDA

Short for earnings before interest, taxes, depreciation, and amortization. EBITDA is often used instead of net income by companies with heavy depreciation charges on their income statements. Investors should always look at EBITDA with caution, because it's not officially sanctioned by the nation's accounting rules, and there's no standard way of figuring it. Still, it can be a useful number to know in conjunction with—but not in place of—reported net income.

Economic Moat

see Moat Size

ELB (Exceeds Lower Boundary)

In the Stock Report, an indication that the available data are too low to be meaningful.

EPS (Continuing Operations)

A company's earnings per share from the day-to-day operations of its business, excluding discontinued operations, extraordinary items, and accounting changes.

EPS Growth
The percentage growth in a company's earnings per share (EPS) over a certain period, usually a quarter or a year, compared with the same period a year earlier. EPS growth is more directly relevant for shareholders than net income growth because it expresses this growth on a per-share basis.

Equity
In accounting terms, a firm's total assets minus total liabilities; also known as book value, net worth, or shareholders' equity. This figure tells you what part of a company is owned by its shareholders and represents (very roughly) the break-up value of the company: If the company were to sell off all its assets and use the money to pay off all its liabilities, total equity is the amount of cash that would be left over. (Equity can also mean "stock," as in the term "equity mutual fund.")

Equity %
The percentage of the company's long-term capital that is composed of equity, including retained earnings and total shareholder investment in the company.

Equity/Share % Growth
see Book Value/Share % Growth

EUB (Exceeds Upper Boundary)
In the Stock Report, an indication that the available data are too high to be meaningful.

Exchange
A marketplace where stocks can be traded. The two biggest exchanges are the New York Stock Exchange and the Nasdaq. The American Stock Exchange (AMEX) used to be the main alternative to the NYSE, but now it lists only small- and mid-cap stocks, and gets most of its business from trading options and similar financial instruments. Stocks that are not traded on any exchange are called "over-the-counter" stocks, and they tend to be much riskier and more volatile than listed stocks.

F

Fair Value
An estimate of a company's value per share. Morningstar analysts estimate a stock's fair value using a discounted cash-flow model that takes into account their estimates of the company's growth, profitability, riskiness, and many other factors over the next five years. This fair value is then compared with the stock's market price to figure its Morningstar Rating.

Financial Health Grade
One of the three quantitative grades that Morningstar assigns to each stock as a quick way to get a handle on its fundamentals. To get a good grade in this area, a company should have low financial leverage (assets/equity), high cash-flow coverage (total cash flow/long-term debt), and a high cash position (cash/assets) relative to its sector. Also, companies with improving financial health are rewarded, while those with deteriorating health are punished.

Financial Leverage
Equal to total assets divided by total equity. Financial leverage measures the extent to which a company's assets are financed by debt. A company with high financial leverage is generally risky, but industries vary in their average financial leverage, so it's a good idea to compare a company with its peers rather than the market as a whole. Financial companies, for example, inherently have much higher financial leverage than other companies.

First Boston High Yield Index
see Credit Suisse First Boston High Yield Index

Fiscal Year
A company's yearly accounting period. A firm's fiscal year is often, but not necessarily, the same as the calendar year. Some companies have fiscal years ending in March, June, or September rather than December, and many retailers have fiscal years ending in January, after the holiday season has ended.

Fiscal Year End
The month in which a company's fiscal year ends. This date can differ from Dec. 31.

Float
The percentage of a stock's shares outstanding that are not held by individuals and corporations closely associated with the company. Float can give you a good idea of how volatile a stock is likely to be. If a company's float is small, say 10%-20%, that means there isn't a big supply available for the public to buy. If demand

outstrips this limited supply, the price can shoot up quickly; if that demand dries up, the price can plunge just as fast.

Forward P/E
Equal to a stock's price divided by Wall Street analysts' average EPS estimate for the current fiscal year. A growing company's forward P/E will typically be lower than its trailing P/E, because its forecasted earnings for the current year are generally higher than its earnings for the previous year.

Free Cash Flow
Equal to operating cash flow minus capital spending. Free cash flow represents the cash a company has left over after investing in the growth of its business. Young, aggressive companies often have negative free cash flow, because they're investing heavily in their futures. As companies mature, though, they should start generating free cash flow.

G

Goodwill
The difference between the purchase price and the book value of a company being purchased by another. Goodwill is listed as an asset on the purchasing company's balance sheet. Companies were previously required to subtract, or amortize, goodwill from earnings over a period of years, but that is no longer the case. Instead, companies are now required to write down goodwill only if they determine that the value is impaired.

Growth Grade
One of the three quantitative grades Morningstar assigns to each stock as a quick way to get a handle on its fundamentals. To get a good grade in this area, a company's sales should be growing rapidly and consistently relative to its sector. Erratic or slowing growth detracts from a stock's growth grade.

I

Income
The portion of a stock's total return derived from dividends. Capital gains are the other component of total return.

Industry
A company's primary area of business. Morningstar's industry classifications are more specific than sectors and are useful for honing in on groups of companies that do the same thing. For example, within the hardware sector, there are such industries as optical equipment, wireless equipment, computer equipment, and semiconductors, each with its own idiosyncrasies.

Initial Public Offering (IPO)
An event in which shares of a company are sold to the public on a stock market exchange for the first time. Many IPOs received a lot of attention during the Internet bubble because of their stocks' rapid price appreciation. However, even in a bull market, it's very difficult for ordinary investors to benefit from IPOs, because only well-placed insiders can generally buy shares at the IPO price.

Inventories
Roughly speaking, the value of the goods that a company has manufactured (or bought wholesale) but not yet sold. Inventory growing at a faster rate than a company's assets may indicate the firm is having trouble turning over that inventory.

Investment Style
see Morningstar Style Box

IPO
see Initial Public Offering

J

JSE Gold (U.S. Dollars)
An index measuring the market value of several gold-mining stocks traded on the Johannesburg Stock Exchange. It tends to track gold prices and is commonly used as a benchmark for gold-related stocks and funds.

L

Last Close
The stock's most recent closing price.

Lehman Brothers Aggregate Index
An index measuring the value of a wide variety of investment-grade government and corporate bonds, as well as asset-backed and mortgage-backed securities. It is widely used as a benchmark for the performance of bonds and bond funds.

Lehman Brothers Corporate Index
An index measuring the value of a wide variety of U.S. corporate bonds. It is widely used as a benchmark for the performance of corporate bonds and bond funds.

Liabilities
All of a company's obligations to nonowners for cash, goods, or services in a given year. Total liabilities include current liabilities and long-term debt.

Long-Term Debt
Money that a company has borrowed for a period of time longer than a year. A company's long-term debt has little relevance as a raw number, but when compared with shareholders' equity (see *Debt/Equity Ratio*), it's a good measure of how leveraged the company is. An excessive amount of long-term debt is dangerous, because the interest on that debt must be paid no matter how well the business is doing. Also, rising long-term debt over time is a warning sign.

M

Major Fund Holders
In the Stock Report, a table listing the mutual funds with the greatest percentage of their assets in a particular stock.

Management
In the Stock Report, the section where Morningstar analysts describe the background and experience of the company's top management. The management text also covers topics such as executive compensation and corporate governance.

Market Capitalization
The total value of all the publicly traded stock in a company; equal to price per share times shares outstanding. Market cap is a rough guide to a company's size, but some young companies without a lot of revenue have large market caps because the market expects them to grow rapidly. Market cap is used by Morningstar to classify stocks as small cap, mid-cap, or large cap.

Moat Size
The measure of the competitive barrier, if any, that gives a company an advantage over its rivals and allows it to generate above-average returns on invested capital. Four major types of economic moats are high customer switching costs, economies of scale, intangible assets such as brands or patents, and the network effect. Morningstar divides stocks into three categories according to moat size: wide moat (companies with the strongest competitive advantage), narrow moat (those with some competitive advantage), and no moat (those with no sustainable competitive advantage).

Morningstar Rating for Stocks
The Morningstar Rating for stocks is calculated by comparing a stock's current market price with Morningstar's estimate of the stock's fair value. Our rating system also includes risk adjustment, so that it's more difficult for a company with above-average business risk to earn a 5 star rating.

Each of the five star-rating levels is defined based on expected returns, which assume that the stock's market price and fair value eventually converge. Under our system, 3-star stocks are those that should offer a "fair return," one that adequately compensates for the riskiness of the stock. Three-star stocks should offer investors a return that's roughly comparable to the stock's cost of equity. (The cost of equity is often called a "required return" because it represents the return an investor requires for taking on the risk of owning the stock.)

Five-star stocks should offer an investor a return that's well above the company's cost of equity, and high-risk 5-star stocks should offer a better expected return than low-risk 5-star stocks. On average, we expect 5-star stocks with below-average risk to return at least 15.5% annualized over the next three years. Because the hurdle rate for stocks with above-average risk is higher, we'd expect a 30.5% annualized return for a 5-star stock with above-average risk. Conversely, low-rated stocks have significantly lower expected returns. If a stock drops to 1 star, that means we expect it to lose money for investors over the next three years, based on our assesment of the stock's fair value.

Ratings can change because of a move in the stock's price, a change in the analyst's estimates of the stock's fair value, or a combination of the two.

Morningstar Risk for Stocks
see Business Risk

Morningstar Style Box (Stocks)
A visual tool that summarizes a stock's size and value/growth characteristics; similar to the equity style box found in Morningstar's mutual fund products. The nine-box matrix displays a stock's market capitalization in relation to its price multiples. Along the vertical axis of the box, Morningstar categorizes the stocks by market capitalization. Large-cap stocks make up the top 70% of the U.S. market's total market value, mid-cap stocks make up another 20%, and the rest are small-cap stocks. (Because some large caps are so huge, there are actually many fewer large caps than small caps.) Along the horizontal axis, each stock is categorized as growth, core, or value. A given stock's style assignment depends on two components: a growth score, based partly on projected earnings growth and partly on historical growth in sales, earnings, cash flow, and book value; and a value score, based partly on the stock's P/E ratio and partly on its price/book, price/sales, and price/cash flow ratios and its dividend yield. The value score is subtracted from the growth score to get an overall score, which determines the stock's style assignment.

MSCI EAFE
An index maintained by Morgan Stanley Capital International that measures the combined market value of a selected group of stocks from Europe, Australasia, and the Far East. It is one of the most commonly used benchmarks for international stocks.

MSCI Emerging Markets
An index maintained by Morgan Stanley Capital International that measures the combined market value of a selected group of stocks from 26 emerging markets, including Latin America, Eastern Europe, and most of Asia except for Japan and Australia. It is commonly used as a benchmark for emerging-market funds and stocks.

MSCI Europe
An index maintained by Morgan Stanley Capital International that measures the combined market value of a selected group of stocks from 16 West European countries. It is commonly used as a benchmark for European stocks.

MSCI Latin America
An index maintained by Morgan Stanley Capital International that measures the combined market value of a selected group of stocks from seven Latin American countries. It is commonly used as a benchmark for Latin American stocks.

MSCI Pacific
An index maintained by Morgan Stanley Capital International that measures the combined market value of a selected group of stocks from Pacific Rim countries, including Japan. It is commonly used as a benchmark for Pacific Rim stocks.

MSCI World
An index maintained by Morgan Stanley Capital International that measures the combined market value of the stocks in all of MSCI's international indexes. It is commonly used as a benchmark for non-U.S. stocks.

N

Nasdaq Composite
A composite measuring the cumulative market cap of all the stocks traded on the Nasdaq stock market exchange. Because the Nasdaq exchange is heavily weighted with technology stocks, the Nasdaq Composite is often used as a proxy for the performance of the technology sector.

Net Income
A measure of how much profit a company has earned within a given period; also known as earnings. Declining net income is generally a sign of trouble, while rising net income is a sign of growth. Remember also that net income includes all charges and credits, including noncash charges such as depreciation and merger write-offs. For companies in some industries, such as cable TV, EBITDA and operating income are used more often than net income.

Net Income Growth

The percentage growth in a company's net income over a certain period, usually a quarter or a year, compared with the same period a year earlier. By comparing net income growth with revenue growth, you can see whether a company has been able to translate increased revenues into increased profits.

Net Margin

Equal to net income divided by revenue. Net margin is the most common measure of profitability. Be sure to look at it in context, though; some industries (such as grocery stores) inherently have low net margins, while others (such as software) have the potential for much bigger net margins.

Net Worth

The difference between total assets and total liabilities; also known as shareholders' equity or book value.

NMF (Not Meaningful)

In the Stock Report, an indication that the available data are not meaningful.

Noncurrent Assets

Assets that the company expects to keep for more than one year. They include plants and equipment, long-term investments, goodwill and other intangibles, and deferred costs. Noncurrent assets plus current assets equal total assets.

Noncurrent Liabilities

Money a company owes, but not until one year or more in the future. Although a variety of line items can appear under this heading, the most important one by far is long-term debt. In fact, noncurrent liabilities can be used in a pinch as a proxy for a company's long-term debt.

O

Operating Cash Flow

How much actual cash a company has generated from its day-to-day operations. Operating cash flow adds depreciation and other noncash charges back into net income. It's similar to EBITDA, except that it includes interest and taxes. Like EBITDA, operating cash flow is favored by many companies with heavy depreciation charges, such as cable companies and many entertainment companies. However, cash flow should be used only as a supplement to net income, not as a substitute for it.

Over-the-Counter Stocks

Stocks that aren't traded on an exchange. Usually they are issued by smaller companies, are traded less often, and are riskier than other stocks. Brokers deal directly with other brokers to buy and sell over-the-counter stocks.

P

Payout Ratio %

Dividends per share divided by earnings per share, expressed as a percentage. The higher a company's payout ratio, the more of its earnings it pays out as dividends. Companies with high payout ratios tend to be mature, slow-growing firms without a lot of expansion opportunities, while those with low payout ratios tend to be younger companies with more growth potential.

P/E Ratio

see Price/Earnings Ratio

PEG Payback Period

The number of years it would take for a company's cumulative earnings to equal its stock price, given the company's earnings growth rate and its P/E. The longer the PEG payback period, the more expensive the stock is.

PEG Ratio

A stock's forward P/E divided by its projected five-year EPS growth. The PEG ratio indicates how much investors are paying for a company's growth, and some people use PEG as a way to find growing companies that are undervalued by the market. However, PEG means little in isolation, so it's a good idea to compare a given company's PEG with those of similar companies in its industry.

Preferred Stock

A class of stock that pays a set dividend that is often higher than the dividend of common stock. Preferred-stock shareholders are paid before common-stock share-holders if the company liquidates or declares bankruptcy, but they usually don't get to vote on company business decisions.

Price Range

The highest and lowest prices a stock has achieved during a certain period (such as a month, a year, or five years). A large range means that the stock has been volatile.

Price Volatility

The degree to which a stock's price has risen and fallen over a period of time. A price graph, such as that in the Stock Report, is a good way to get a quick idea of a stock's price volatility.

Price/Book Ratio

A stock's price divided by book value per share (or, alternately, market cap divided by total book value). Price/book used to be one of the most popular valuation measures behind P/E, but it has lost some of that popularity recently. That's because book value measures only tangible assets that show up on a balance sheet, but the value of many technology companies comes primarily from their people and ideas.

Price/Cash Flow Ratio

A stock's price divided by annual operating cash flow per share (or, alternately, market cap divided by total annual operating cash flow). Price/cash flow can be an especially useful valuation measure for comparing stocks in industries that typically have a lot of depreciation charges, such as the cable industry, or for valuing foreign stocks, because cash flow minimizes the effect of accounting differences.

Price/Earnings Ratio

A stock's price divided by earnings per share (or, alternately, market cap divided by net income). P/E is the most common valuation measure for stocks, because it shows how much investors are willing to pay for a dollar of a company's earnings. However, like any valuation measure, P/E should be viewed in the context of a company's industry and the broader market.

Price/Sales Ratio

A stock's price divided by annual sales per share (or, alternately, market cap divided by total annual sales). Price/sales can often be a useful alternative to P/E when a company's earnings are negative or temporarily depressed; thus, it's commonly used to value younger companies with no earnings.

Profitability Grade

One of the three quantitative grades that Morningstar assigns to each stock as a quick way to get a handle on its fundamentals. To get a good grade in this area, a company should have a high return on assets relative to its sector, and its ROA should be consistent and improving.

Projected Five-Year EPS Growth %

The average annualized earnings growth that Wall Street analysts are predicting for the company over the next five years. This number is used to calculate forward P/E.

Q

Quick Ratio

Equal to a company's current assets minus inventory, divided by current liabilities. The quick ratio measures a company's balance-sheet liquidity.

R

Rating

see Morningstar Rating for Stocks

Relative Strength

A measure of the price return of a stock versus that of the S&P 500 Index—the higher the relative-strength figure, the better the stock has performed versus the index. On a price graph, if the stock's line is above the index line, it indicates positive relative strength, while a line below the index line indicates negative relative strength.

Return on Assets %

Equal to net income divided by total assets. ROA shows how much profit a company generates on its asset base. It differs from return on equity (ROE) in that a company can boost its ROE by taking on more debt, but the same strategy will not affect ROA. Another way to calculate ROA is net margin times asset turnover.

Return on Equity %
A financial ratio that measures a firm's return on shareholder investment (the shareholders' equity or the net worth of the company). ROE is a useful gauge for determining how efficiently a company is using the shareholders' investment. Unlike return on assets, it considers the amount and cost of debt.

Revenue
How much money a company has brought in within a given period. Revenue is most useful in the context of revenue figures for previous years and quarters, but total revenue by itself is one common way to measure the size of a company. Remember, though, that just pulling in revenue is not enough for a company; it needs to make a profit in order to survive in the long term.

Revenue % Growth
The percentage growth in a company's revenue over a certain period, usually a quarter or a year, compared with the same period a year earlier. High growth is usually desirable, but if a rapidly growing company is losing lots of money (like many Internet companies), it can grow itself out of business.

Risk Measure
see Business Risk

ROA
see Return on Assets

ROE
see Return on Equity

Russell 2000
The most commonly used benchmark for measuring the performance of small-cap stocks. Updated annually by the Frank Russell Company, the Russell 2000 consists of the 1,001st through 3,000th largest companies in the U.S. in terms of market cap.

Russell 2000 Growth
An index measuring the performance of companies in the Russell 2000 with relatively high price/book ratios and projected growth rates. The Russell 2000 Growth is used as a benchmark for small-cap growth stocks.

Russell 2000 Value
An index measuring the performance of companies in the Russell 2000 with relatively low price/book ratios and projected growth rates. The Russell 2000 Value is used as a benchmark for small-cap value stocks.

Russell Midcap Growth
An index measuring the performance of companies ranked 201st through 1,000th in terms of market cap, with relatively high price/book ratios and forecasted growth rates. The Russell Midcap Growth is used as a benchmark for mid-cap growth stocks.

Russell Midcap Value
An index measuring the performance of companies ranked 201st through 1,000th in terms of market cap, with relatively low price/book ratios and forecasted growth rates. The Russell Midcap Value is used as a benchmark for mid-cap value stocks.

Russell Top 200 Growth
An index measuring the performance of the 200 largest U.S. companies in terms of market cap, with relatively high price/book ratios and forecasted growth rates. The Russell Top 200 Growth is used as a benchmark for large-cap growth stocks.

Russell Top 200 Value
An index measuring the performance of the 200 largest U.S. companies in terms of market cap, with relatively low price/book ratios and forecasted growth rates. The Russell Top 200 Value is used as a benchmark for large-cap value stocks.

S

Sales
All the money a company has taken in from the sale of goods or services; also known as revenue. With the exception of banks and some other financial companies, interest income is not included in sales.

Sector
A company's general area of business. Morningstar divides stocks into 12 sectors according to their primary business, grouped into three larger "super-sectors." The Software, Hardware, Telecom, and Media sectors make up the Information group; Health Care, Consumer Services, Business Services, and Financial Services make up the Service group; and Consumer Goods, Industrial Materials, Energy, and Utilities make up the Manufacturing group. Because sectors can differ greatly

in their characteristics, comparing a stock with its sector rather than the market as a whole is generally a better way of putting it in the proper context.

Sector Risk
The danger that the stocks of many of the companies in one sector (like health care or technology) will fall in price at the same time because of an event that affects the entire industry.

Shareholder's Equity
The difference between a company's total assets and total liabilities; also known as net worth or book value.

Shares Outstanding
The average number of shares a public company had on the market during a certain period of time, usually a quarter or a year. This figure is used to calculate earnings per share and other per-share numbers.

S&P 400 Index (S&P MidCap 400)
One of the most common indexes used to measure the performance of midsize companies, or those with market caps between $1 billion and about $5 billion.

S&P 500 Index
One of the most common indexes used to represent the U.S. stock market. Contrary to popular belief, it doesn't just consist of the 500 biggest U.S. companies; the members of the index are selected by the Standard & Poor's Index Committee and range in size from small caps to large caps. However, because it's a market-cap-weighted index, the largest companies have a heavier influence on its performance. (Also known as the S&P.)

Stewardship Grade for Stocks
Morningstar stock analysts assign a Stewardship Grade to most of the companies in Morningstar's coverage universe. We evaluate the demonstrated commitment to shareholders of each company's board and management team. Our assessment is divided into three general areas:

- Transparency.
- Shareholder Friendliness.
- Incentives, Ownership, and Overall Stewardship.

Morningstar stock analysts base Stewardship Grades on public filings, previous management actions, conversations with company officials, and their own expertise.

We assign the grades on an absolute scale—not on a curve or on an industry-peer basis. Therefore, if a company engages in practices that we think do not reflect good stewardship of investors' capital, it will receive a poor grade regardless of how other firms may have scored.

Our Stewardship Grades can be interpreted as follows:

A means "Excellent"
B means "Good"
C means "Fair"
D means "Poor"
F means "Very Poor"

For a small number of companies we cover, sufficient data to assign a complete grade was unavailable. These firms will receive a designation of "NA," indicating that the rating is not applicable.

Stock
A piece of ownership in a company. You may buy stock hoping the company will pay you a portion of its profits, or a dividend. You also hope the company will increase its earnings so your stock will become more valuable. Some classes of stock let stockholders vote on company matters.

Stock Exchange
see Exchange

Stock Option
The right to buy specific amounts of a company's stock at a fixed price no matter how much the stock is selling for. If you had an option that let you buy at $5 and your company's stock was worth $7, you'd make $2 by exercising your option.

Stock Split
An event in which the number of a company's shares increases, while the price per share decreases in exact proportion. Contrary to popular belief, stock splits actually do nothing to benefit shareholders directly. If you own 100 shares of a stock that costs $50, and it splits 2-for-1, you're left with 200 shares of a stock that costs $25—the total value is still $5,000. Still, some people believe that stock splits are a bullish sign, because they tend to indicate that management believes its share price will continue to rise.

Style Box
see Morningstar Style Box

Sustainable Growth Rate
An indication of how fast a company can theoretically grow without outside financing, given its current profitability, dividend policy, and debt levels. The sustainable growth rate is equal to return on equity (ROE) times (1 - payout ratio). A company whose sustainable growth rate is much lower than its EPS growth rate will have to find external sources of funding, either debt or equity.

T

Technical Analysis
A stock-picking method based on such things as price patterns and the trading volume in a stock. Technical analysis ignores fundamental factors such as the quality of a business or its management; as a result, it's not of much worth to long-term investors.

Thesis
In the Stock Report, our analyst's opinion of a stock, supported with an explanation of the company's strengths and weaknesses.

Ticker
A unique symbol assigned to every publicly traded company for identification. Tickers of stocks trading on the New York Stock Exchange contain one, two, or three letters; those trading on Nasdaq contain four letters; those trading over the counter contain four letters plus a Q at the end; and some foreign stocks contain four letters plus a Y at the end.

Total Cash Flow
All the cash a company generates, including noncash charges and credits. Total cash flow is calculated by adding back depreciation and amortization, deferred taxes, and other sources of cash to net income in each year.

Total Equity
see Equity

Total Return %
Represents shareholders' gains from a stock over a given period of time. Total return includes both capital gains and losses (the increase or decrease in the stock price) and income (in the form of dividend payments). It is calculated by taking the change in the stock's price, assuming the reinvestment of all dividends, then dividing by the initial stock price, and expressing the result as a percentage.

Total Shares Mil
see Shares Outstanding

TTM (Trailing 12 Months)
The most recent four quarters for which a company has reported financial results. Looking at a company's TTM results, rather than those for the most recent fiscal year, generally gives more up-to-date numbers. This is especially important for fast-growing companies.

U

UR (Under Review)
In the Morningstar Rating or Fair Value section of the Stock Report, an indication that the Morningstar analyst has placed the stock under review.

U.S. 90-Day Treasury Bill
Bills issued by the U.S. government that are used as a common measure of short-term interest rates.

V

Valuation Ratios
Ratios that measure how expensive a stock is. Beware, however—no single valuation ratio is perfect, and it's best to look at several different ratios in the appropriate context.

W

Wilshire 4500
An index consisting of all the stocks in the Wilshire 5000 Index minus the 500 stocks in the S&P 500 Index. Like the Wilshire 5000, it measures the combined market value of these stocks and is used as a benchmark for small- and mid-cap stocks.

Wilshire 5000
One of the most common indexes for measuring the performance of the entire U.S. stock market, including companies of all sizes. Although it originally contained 5,000 stocks, the index now measures the combined market value of more than 6,000 stocks.

Wilshire REIT
An index measuring the combined market value of equity real estate investment trusts (as opposed to mortgage REITs) with market caps above $1 billion. It is used as a benchmark for equity REIT performance.

Y

Yield %
Equal to a stock's annual dividend per share divided by its price per share; also known as dividend yield.

YTD
Year-to-date, or since the beginning of the current calendar or fiscal year. A stock's YTD total return is its return since Jan. 1 of the current calendar year.